THE CARIBBEAN
&
RIMLANDS

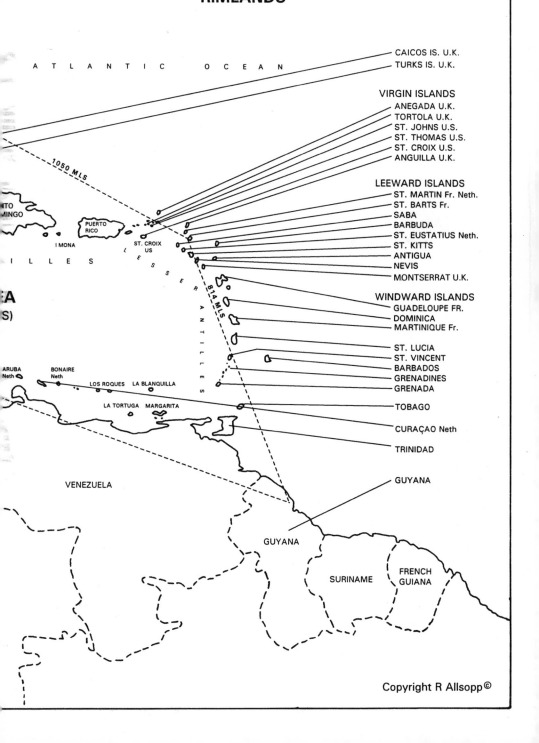

A T L A N T I C   O C E A N

CAICOS IS. U.K.
TURKS IS. U.K.

VIRGIN ISLANDS
ANEGADA U.K.
TORTOLA U.K.
ST. JOHNS U.S.
ST. THOMAS U.S.
ST. CROIX U.S.
ANGUILLA U.K.

LEEWARD ISLANDS
ST. MARTIN Fr. Neth.
ST. BARTS Fr.
SABA
BARBUDA
ST. EUSTATIUS Neth.
ST. KITTS
ANTIGUA
NEVIS
MONTSERRAT U.K.

WINDWARD ISLANDS
GUADELOUPE FR.
DOMINICA
MARTINIQUE Fr.

ST. LUCIA
ST. VINCENT
BARBADOS
GRENADINES
GRENADA

TOBAGO

CURAÇAO Neth

TRINIDAD

GUYANA

1050 MLS

814 MLS

PUERTO RICO

NTO MINGO

I MONA

ST. CROIX US

L E S S E R   A N T I L L E S

I L L E S

EA (S)

ARUBA Neth

BONAIRE Neth

LOS ROQUES   LA BLANQUILLA

LA TORTUGA   MARGARITA

VENEZUELA

GUYANA

SURINAME   FRENCH GUIANA

DICTIONARY OF
CARIBBEAN
ENGLISH USAGE

DICTIONARY OF CARIBBEAN ENGLISH USAGE

EDITED BY

RICHARD ALLSOPP

WITH A

FRENCH AND SPANISH SUPPLEMENT

EDITED BY

JEANNETTE ALLSOPP

OXFORD UNIVERSITY PRESS

Oxford University Press, Walton Street, Oxford OX2 6DP
Oxford New York
Athens Auckland Bangkok Bogota Bombay
Buenos Aires Calcutta Cape Town Dar es Salaam
Delhi Florence Hong Kong Istanbul Karachi
Kuala Lumpur Madras Madrid Melbourne
Mexico City Nairobi Paris Singapore
Taipei Tokyo Toronto
and associated companies in
Berlin Ibadan

Oxford is a trade mark of Oxford University Press

Published in the United States by
Oxford University Press Inc., New York

British Library Cataloguing in Publication Data
Data available

Library of Congress Cataloging in Publication Data
Data available
ISBN 0-19-866152-5

3 5 7 9 10 8 6 4

Typeset by Latimer Trend & Company Ltd.
Printed in Great Britain by
Bookcraft (Bath) Ltd.
Midsomer Norton, Avon

For many neighbours

To harness, by naming, creation around;
To label, unwritten, folk thoughts that abound;
To fight life, with language sole arm of the fighter,
Their tongue is the pen of a ready writer.

S.R.R.A.

How can I dialogue . . .
if I start from the premise
that naming the world is the task of an elite,
and that the presence of the people in history
is a sign of deterioration which is to be avoided?
How can I dialogue . . .
if I am closed to—and even offended by—
the contribution of others?

> Paulo Freire, *Pedagogy Of The Oppressed*
> (tr. Myra B. Ramos). Printed by permission of The Continuum Publishing Company.

The beginning of Wisdom
Is
Knowing who you are.
Draw near and listen.

> Swahili Proverb

CONTENTS

PERSONNEL

Co-ordinator and Editor   S. R. Richard Allsopp

Editorial Adviser   Laurence Urdang

Research Associate (1990–)   Jeannette E. Allsopp

RESEARCH ASSISTANTS

Cave Hill Campus, UWI

Rodina Herbert (1974–5)   Audrey Burrowes (1979–87)

Myrna Martineau (1975–80)   Cecilia Francis (1989–90)

Yvette Keane (1975–8)   Alma Taitt (1990)

Part-time (at various times between 1975 and 1990): L. Alexander; M. Alexander; J. Allsopp; Y. Allsopp; E. Best; A. Burrowes; R. Cole; G. Crichlow-Brathwaite; L. Darmanie; C. Francis; S. Gill; W. Griffith; R. Henry; H. Hyman; I. Inniss; L. Inniss; M. Isaac; D. Jules; A. C. Matthews; M. Moseley; S. Phillips; D. Singh; W. Singh; M. Taitt; H. Taylor; C. Toppin; M. Williams; Fifth Formers of the St Michael's Girls' School (1973–6).

Overseas: Ron Hall (London); John and Kathleen Kaye (Washington); Marjorie Mann and team (Ottawa).

St Augustine Campus, UWI

Judy Antoine (1979–80)   Winford James (1981–3)

Patricia Aquing (1981–3)   (Tobago)

Clive Borely (1981–2)   Betty Joseph (1981–3)

Wendy Sealey (1982–3)

Mona Campus, UWI

Yasmin Stewart (1979–80)

Belize University Centre, UWI

Colville Young (now Sir Colville) (1979–82)

Oswald Sutherland (1979–82)

University of Guyana

Kuntie Ramdat (1976–78)   Claudith Thompson (1976–80)

Part-time (1977–9): N. Barker; S. Griffith; L. Harry; C. John; D. Ramphal; K. Singh.

CONSULTANTS

African Languages

Akan (Twi, Fante, Nzema)	Jack Berry, Northwestern U.
Igbo	Benson Oluikpe, U/Nigeria
Yoruba	Ayo Banjo, U/Ibadan
	Kole Ọmọtọṣọ, U/Ife (1978)

Other Languages

Amerindian Languages (Guyana)	Amerindian Languages Project, U/Guyana (1977–80)
Chinese (Cantonese and Hakka)	John Tjon-A-Yong, Guyana, 1987
Hindi/Bhojpuri	Satesh Rohra, U/New Delhi, U/Guyana; Peggy Mohan, Howard U. (1979–82)
Spanish	Jeannette Allsopp, Erdiston Teachers' College, Barbados (1983–92)

Caribbean Flora

Taxonomic Identification	E. G. B. Gooding

INFORMANTS

African Languages (at various times, 1967 and between 1975 and 1986)

Bini	R. Ezomo
Ci-Nyanja	O. Muzombwe; S. Mchombo
Ẹdo	A. Amayo (U/Ibadan)
Efik	N. Ekanem (SOAS, U/London); N. J. Udoeyop (U/Ibadan Press)
Ewe	E. Adjorlolo (Broadcasting Station, Accra)
Fante	A. B. K. Dadzie (Kumasi U.)
Fulani	C. Hoffman (U/Ghana); I. Mukoshy
Gã-Adangme	O. Appiah, M. Kropp (U/Ghana); Bureau of Ghana Languages (Accra)
Hausa	I. Mukoshy; I. Amadi Ume
Idoma	Robert G. Armstrong (U/Nigeria); S. Amali
Igbo	I. Amadi Ume
Ijọ/Ịzọn	Kay Williamson (U/Port Harcourt)
Isoko	B. Mafeni; O. Obuke

Kikongo & Lingala	Ungina Ndoma (Northwestern U.)
Ki-Yaka	Y. M. A. M'Teba
Krio	Jack Berry (Northwestern U.); M. Broderick
Mende	Richard Spears (Northwestern U.); M. Bangura; J. Sengova
Nupe	J. O. Ndagi; F. A. Umaru
Nzema	I. K. Chinebuah (U/Ghana)
Shona	Hazel Carter (SOAS, U/London); L. I. Ferraz (U/Zimbabwe); W. Qwete (U/Ibadan); J. Chafota
Twi	L. Boadi, B. S. Kwakwa (U/Ghana)
West Afr. Drumming	J. H. Nketia (U/Ghana)
West Afr. Pidgin	I. Amadi Ume
Wolof	M. Cham (U/Wisconsin)
Yoruba	A. Adetugbo, S. A. O. Babalola (U/Yaba); A. Bamgboṣe (U/Ibadan); O. Lamidi; A. O. Obilade; J. Sterk (U/Wisconsin)

Other Languages

Gullah	John Roy (Columbia U.)
Irish English	Loretto Todd (U/Leeds)
Sranan	Christian Eersel (U/Suriname); G. Huttar (Summer Institute of Linguistics)

Computerization

Specialist Adviser	Marvel O'Neal
Assistant (1990–2)	Hazelyn Devonish

Typists and Keyboarders

Leona Darmanie	Camileta Neblett
R. Campbell	J. Gilkes
L. Johnson	A. Taitt
L. Lewis	D. Sandiford

UWI Advisory Committee* 1979–91

Dennis Craig, Professor, School of Education, Mona—Chairman 1979–90

Mervyn Alleyne, Professor, Dept. of Linguistics and Use of English, Mona

Lawrence Carrington, Reader, School of Education, St Augustine

Helen Pyne-Timothy, Senior Lecturer, Dept. of Language and Linguistics, St Augustine—Chairperson 1990–1

(* Campus Deans were formally added to the Committee in 1989)

ACKNOWLEDGEMENTS

A sincere effort has been made to include the name of every person or institution that has helped in the collection of data, but it has not been practical to list the participants in the various territorial workshops who, for example, amounted to 76 in Antigua and over 100 in Guyana and St Vincent (though many others were, of course, quite small). On the other hand I have tried, by writing out their first names in full, to recognize in this small way some persons whose continued or particular extra efforts to help the exercise merit special mention.   R.A.

Funding of the Caribbean Lexicography Project, obtained from the following sources, is gratefully acknowledged:

The Ford Foundation 1971–3, 1974–6
Barclays Bank International 1974–7
American Council of Learned Societies 1974–5
The Government of Guyana 1975–82
The Government of Barbados 1977–87, 1990–1
International Development Research Centre (Ottawa) 1977–8
The Government of Trinidad and Tobago 1981–3
University of the West Indies 1979–92
UNESCO 1980–1, 1988
The Commonwealth Foundation (London) 1985

Special thanks are due to the Government of Guyana and to the University of the West Indies whose funding at critical times prevented the Project from halting altogether.

Accommodation: The Project was based at the Cave Hill Campus of the UWI from its inception. Offices and equipment were also provided for Research Assistants at the University of Guyana (Faculty of Arts), the UWI at St Augustine (ISER), and the UWI Extra-Mural Department in Belize.

Data-collection: Assistance was received from persons and institutions in the collection or verification of data in or in relation to the following territories, at various times between 1973 and 1991. An asterisk (*) against the name of an institution or place indicates that a data-collection workshop was held there with teachers and other interested participants, and usually of about five days' duration:

ANGUILLA: Education Officer; teachers of the Valley Community Centre* and other schools; B. Buchanan; A. Hodge; I. Richardson.

ANTIGUA: UWI Resident Tutor E. Bird; Leeward Islands Teachers Training College*; Chief and other Education Officers; Chief Agricultural Officer; A. Crick; V. Evelyn; B. Farquhar; O. Josiah; R. Prince; I. Richards; H. Roberts; Dorcas White.

BAHAMAS: UWI Representative G. Hamilton; Director of Education; Learning Resource Centre* (Nassau); San Salvador High School*; South Andros Senior High School*; Rock Sound High School* (Eleuthera); Principal and staff, College of the Bahamas; Curator, Botanic Gardens; Chief Agricultural Officer; R. Bain; C. Bethel; K. Bethel; L. Davis; Hon. E. Dupuch; A. Hilton; J. Holm; G. Morley; Fr. K. Sands; A. Shilling.

BARBADOS: Erdiston Teachers' Training College*; Dept. of Archives; Ministry of Agriculture; Fisheries Dept.; Supreme Court Registrar; H. Boxill; J. Callender; E. Deane; H. McD. Forde; E. Greaves; M. Hutt; G. Davis-Isaacs; P. McConney; E. Payne; Erica Pile; Kenneth Pile; R. Quintyne; F. Ramsey; D. Seale; F. Spencer; C. Sylvester; Pat Symmonds; A. Taitt; G. Tutt; V. Weekes; L. Wellington; P. Went; J. Wickham; W. Willock. *Steelband*: G. Cheltenham (National Cultural Foundation); G. P. Mendoza.

UWI Cave Hill campus colleagues in various Faculties, Units, etc.: C. Barrow, B. Callender, Sean Carrington, F. Chandler, N. Duncan, B. Farquhar, I. Gibbs, C. Hollingsworth, L. Jackson, Anthony Lewis, N. Liverpool, E. Moore, Alan Moss, A. Phillips, M. Pidgeon, D. Sardinha, A. Thompson, K. Watson.

BARBUDA: V. Browne (Warden); Holy Trinity School*; C. Beazer; Mam Peg; E. Samuel.

BELIZE: UWI Resident Tutors V. Leslie and J. Palacio; Education Officers E. Gutierrez and R. Cayetano; Belize Teachers' College*; University Centre*; Dangriga*; La Inmaculada RC School* (Orange Walk); Ministry of Agriculture; Dept. of Archaeology; Chief Forest Officer; Govt. Entomologist; S. Coleman; J. Courtenay; A. Forde; D. Humes; G. Stuart.

BERMUDA: M. Bean.

BR. VIRGIN ISLANDS: UWI Representative B. De Castro; Chief Education Officer; Chief Agricultural Officer; Chief Information Officer; BVI High School* (Tortola); Anegada Primary School*; St Mary's Primary School* (Virgin Gorda); R. O'Neal; D. Penn; V. Penn; J. Wheatley.

CAYMAN ISLANDS: Ministry of Education* (Grand Cayman); Senior Information Officer; A. Benjamin; L. Bodden; R. Bodden; A. Ebanks; A. Kohlman.

DOMINICA: University Centre; Ministry of Education; Dominica Teachers' Training College*; Division of Culture; Government Information Service; Konmité Pou Etid Kwéyòl; Chief Agricultural Officer; Chief Fisheries Officer; Director of Forestry and Wildlife; Secretary, WINBAN; Alwyn Bully; R. Burnett; H. Clarendon; Olive Harris; F. Henderson; Verna Liverpool; O. Marie; A. Peter; Douglas Taylor; M. Zamore.

GRENADA: UWI Resident Tutor B. Steele; Grenada Teachers' Training College*; Ministry of Social Affairs; Chief Fisheries Officer; C. Clarendon; J. Copland; J. Finlay; Claude Francis; V. Francis; C. Glean; E. Glean; Alister Hughes; Crofton McGuire; G. Payne; Wilfred Redhead; L. Seon; C. Sylvester; Myrna Taitt.

GUYANA: Ministry of Education; Teachers' Training College*, (Georgetown); New Amsterdam Government Secondary School* (Berbice); Anna Regina School* (Essequibo); Aishalton* (Rupununi); Linden* (Demerara R.); Mabaruma* (NW Region); Ministry of Agriculture; Chief Fisheries Officer; Guyana Forest Commission; Walter Roth Museum; Guyana Rice Board; E. Abrahams; Herbert Allsopp; Philip Allsopp; J. Bennett; B. Carter; I. Cornette; E. Croal; C. Dolphin; L. Dolphin; C. Hollingsworth; E. Hubbard; M. Khan; B. Laud; M. Lowe; I. McDonald; L. Munroe; C. Rodway; S. Sadeek; Arthur Seymour; L. Slater; Sr. A. Tang; John Tjon-A-Yong; Clement Yansen; V. Yong-Kong.

University of Guyana members of various Faculties, Units, etc.: Amerindian Languages Project, Z. Bacchus, Joel Benjamin, V. Bentt, Dean Bynoe (Educ.), Dean Carr (Arts), G. Cave, Walter Edwards, Desiree Fox, Joycelynne Loncke, John Rickford, Ian Robertson, S. Tiwari, B. Tyndall, University Herbarium.

JAMAICA: Ministry of Education; Mico Training College*; Shortwood Teachers' College*; Sam Sharpe Teachers' College*; Ministry of Agriculture; Librarian, Hope Gardens; Jamaica Information Service; Secretariat, International Bauxite Association; Bureau of Standards; J. Carnegie; Jean D'Costa; C. Lewis; E. Miller; Daphne Nicholson; E. O'Callaghan; R. Reid.

UWI Mona campus colleagues of various Depts.: Mervyn Alleyne; Pauline Christie; Dennis Craig; I. Goodbody; D. Hall; Maureen Lewis; V. Mulchansingh.

MONTSERRAT: UWI Resident Tutors G. Irish and H. Fergus; University Centre*; Chief Education Officer; Director of Agriculture; Govt. Information Officer; M. Allen; E. Bellot-Allen; L. Bishop; Ivan Browne; D. Greenaway; Hughon James; Alfreda Meade.

ACKNOWLEDGEMENTS

NETHERLANDS ANTILLES: Linda Richardson-Badejo.

NEVIS: Inspector of Schools; Charleston Secondary School*; Chief Agricultural Officer; O. Dyer; P. Kalski; H. Liburd; Franklyn Manners; P. Williams.

ST KITTS: UWI Resident Tutor V. Josse; Ministry of Education; University Centre*; Teachers' Training College* (Basseterre); M. Archibald; Hon. F. Bryant; Lorna Callender; J. Challenger; H. Ellis; G. Glasford; J. Halliday; O. Hector; L. James; C. Joseph; A. Ribiero; D. Richardson; R. Thomas.

ST LUCIA: UWI Resident Tutor Pat Charles; Ministry of Education; St Lucia Teachers' College*; Vieux Fort*; Ministry of Agriculture, Lands and Fisheries; Folk Research Centre; Mouvman Kwéyòl Sent Lisi; WINBAN; Librarian, OECS; Fr. P. Anthony; Embert Charles; L. Didier; S. Edward; S. French; M. Gill; H. Isaac; Martha Isaac; A. James; Robert Lee; E. Martyr; G. Sarjusingh; J. Sifflet; Kieran St Rose; M. St. Rose; E. Tobias; C. Trezette; R. Yorke.

ST VINCENT AND THE GRENADINES: UWI Resident Tutor H. Williams; Ministry of Education; Memorial Hall* (Kingstown); Chief Education Officer F. Toney; Deputy Chief Information Officer E. Crick; Editor, *The Vincentian*; V. Brereton; A. Da Silva; Marcia Hinds; K. Huggins; E. John; Yvette Keane; A. Keizer; Cameron King; Earle Kirby; E. Providence; B. Richards; C. Richards; J. Sylvester; V. Thomas; Grace Williams; I. Williams.

SURINAME: J. Defares; Christian Eersel; E. Essed; S. Kishna; J. Park.

TOBAGO: Senator Jacob D. Elder; Dept. of Education; Fairfield Complex* (Scarborough); Yvette Arnold; Eugene Blackett; Winford James; V. Wheeler.

TRINIDAD: Ministers of Education Hon. O. Padmore and Hon. C. Joseph; Chief Education Officer; Valsayn Teachers' Training College*; Corinth Teachers' College*; Chief Fisheries Officer H. Wood; Chief Agricultural Officer; Chief Information Officer; Cislyn Baptiste; J. Habib; Anthony Lewis; Earl Timothy.
Steelband: H. Puckerin (UWI); A. McQuilkin (Despers); C. Lindsey.

UWI St Augustine campus colleagues of various Faculties, Depts., etc.: Lawrence Carrington; V. Jones; Jake Kenny; Charles McDavid; Sylvia Moodie; H. Phelps; G. Pollard; Helen Pyne-Timothy; Compton Seaforth.

TURKS AND CAICOS ISLANDS: Chief Minister Hon. J. McCartney; Chief Education Officer E. Ersdaille; Grand Turk High School*; North Caicos Junior High School*; South Caicos Primary School*; I. Buchanan; C. Duncanson; S. Garland; C. Hutchings; H. James Snr.; Hope James; D. Jones; H. Sadler; N. Turner.

US VIRGIN ISLANDS: (St Thomas) Enid Baa; Vincent Cooper; Chief Agricultural Officer, Dept. of Agriculture; Norwell Harrigan; Arona Peterson; Gilbert Sprauve; Edward Towle.
(St Croix) Arnold Highfield; M. Scott.
(St John) Lito Valls.

Use of other Scholars' Works: All dictionaries, grammars, and other works of reference for African, Amerindian, Indic and other foreign languages which have been used in etymological and other researches are acknowledged in the comprehensive list of Citation Codes for Bibliographical References. Each such work is given full bibliographic identification after its listed Citation Code. In the body of the Dictionary, a Citation Code is given in brackets each time the particular work to which it refers is used as authority for any etymological or other data indicated. *Examples*: Cp (*ADMY*) Yoruba *baba* 'father'; Cp (*WIED*) Igbo *anya ukwu* (= eyes big) 'greed'. In such cases *ADMY* and *WIED* are references to Abraham's *Dictionary of Modern Yoruba* and Williamson's *Igbo–English Dictionary* for which full bibliographic identification is given within the list of Citation Codes.

INTRODUCTION

THE CARIBBEAN REALITY

Be one's environment small or large, the need for a reliable inventory of it in order to live intelligently and thence creatively is unquestionable and, accordingly, a sufficient justification, if one were needed, for a lexical record. In western writing cultures, of which the Caribbean is a part, that record must be professionally lexicographical. That is the object of this book.

It is now 500 years since the Caribbean first disclosed itself to Columbus and submitted its indigenous peoples and cultures fatally to European misjudgement. An emptiness of population followed while European adventurers made tentative calls, Englishmen among them. Sir Francis Drake watered his ships at an uninhabited St Christopher (St Kitts) in 1585 (later settled by Thomas Warner, 1624). Sir William Courteen's ship 'found' an empty Barbados in 1625 and his English settlers followed in 1627. So settled the English tongue permanently in the Caribbean, in the company of others. The many-faced generations of replacement peoples who followed through the centuries developed, though unrespected and ill-documented, ways of life—in a new and common historical experience within a unique ecology also new to them—out of which evolved today's Caribbean culture: Caribbean birds, fishes, and crawling things, Caribbean fruit and foods, forest flowers, bush medicines, timber trees, building styles, body wear, mixed folklore, folksongs, festivals, dances, music, religious expression, skin-shade identification, household idiom, colonial terms, etc. All these required new labels, new adaptations and compoundings of European labels, and therefore essentially needed expression of a different life-view from that of Europe, obviously in a home-made Caribbean idiom. As home-made, the Caribbean linguistic product has always been shame-faced, inhibited both by the dour authority of colonial administrators and their written examinations on the one hand, and by the persistence of the stigmatized Creole languages of the labouring populace on the other.

Nevertheless the facts of that open-ended list in the preceding paragraph made Caribbean language a reality, and the emergence of the obligatory self-reliance and nationhood of many English-speaking territories made its organized documentation a necessity. Scholarly attention to Anglophone Caribbean Creole studies began soon after World War II, the present author's MA Thesis (Univ. London, 1958) on Guyanese Creole pronominal forms being probably the first such dissertation on record. However, there followed two decades of independent nationhood and what was called 'statehood' of Caribbean territories with consequent political reinforcement of the need for self-recognition. Although that had already begun to be stated through notable postwar 'West Indian' literature, it is necessary to show, as tabulated below, the geopolitical distribution of the English language that ultimately gives substance to the present work.

Caribbean territory	Area in sq. miles	Population (est. 1987–90)		Remarks
Anguilla	35	7,200	(1987)	
Antigua and Barbuda	108 62	79,000		Independent 1981/11
Bahamas	5,380	253,000		Over 700 islands Independent 1973/7
Barbados	166	256,000		Independent 1966/11
Belize	8,866	179,800	(1988)	Independent 1981/9
Dominica	290	78,030	(1990)	Independent 1978/11
Grenada and Carriacou	120 13	110,000		Independent 1974/2
Guyana	83,000	750,000	(1989)	Independent 1966/5
Jamaica	4,244	2,410,000	(1988)	Independent 1962/8
Montserrat	40	12,250	(1988)	
St Kitts and Nevis	68 36	47,000	(1988)	Independent 1983/9
St Lucia	238	142,000	(1989)	Independent 1979/2
St Vincent and Grenadines	133 17	104,000 9,000		Over 100 islands Independent 1979/10
Trinidad and Tobago	1,864 116	1,190,427	(1988)	Independent 1962/8
Turks and Caicos	193	12,350	(1990)	
Virgin Islands (British)	59	14,786	(1990)	About 40 islands
Virgin Islands (US)	136	103,200	(1988)	(50% St Croix, 46% St Thomas)
TOTAL	105,184	5,758,043		

THE NEED FOR A NORM

Scattered around one million sq. miles of sea, this aggregate population of 5.8 million speakers unevenly distributed over numberless discrete land-masses totalling a mere 105,000 sq. miles appears statistically insignificant in contrast with the massive English-speaking domains of North America, the British Isles, and Australia. Nevertheless, when it is observed that these territories include twelve independent nations in their number, each with a linguistic entitlement to a national standard language, size and statistics cease to be major considerations as other more serious realities come to the fore: What is the right/wrong *national* way to speak? May local or regional usage be *formally* written? By what criteria is *acceptability* to be judged, and acceptability to whom—Britain, North America, the 'international' community, other Caribbean states, teachers? On what ground can any local or folk 'thing-name' be rejected as 'wrong' and what other name is 'right' and why? Who decides? What spelling shall be determined (and by whom) for items nationals never bothered to spell until now that they need to write them? What terms are unparliamentary, libellous, offensive? What *norms*, what *guide* must national examiners and those of the (then emergent) Caribbean Examinations Council observe?

Clearly the answer to these and other pertinent questions could not be found by reference to British or North American English. Their dictionaries (and 90 per cent of those used in the Caribbean are published in England) practically ignored Caribbean items and totally ignored Caribbean usage; their grammars were neither conveniently normative nor related to Caribbean needs.

As for 'grammar' or 'correct English', regionwide and perennial complaints began and continue about the 'poor standard of English' written by Caribbean students, employees and even university graduates; such complaints regularly go in pair with statements (often in newspapers) that 'Standard English' is a clearly defined model which is either being incompetently taught or interfered with by the encouragement of local dialects, or confusingly compromised by university linguists. Such complainants did not trouble to notice that the concept of 'Standard English' was now a widespread and confusing problem both in its original homeland and internationally, but these matters will be more appropriately addressed in the statement following on Caribbean English.

EARLIER LEXICOGRAPHY IN THE CARIBBEAN

As for dictionaries, however, although Caribbean life-style had from time to time prompted a few local glossaries, in no case did any territorial authority, let alone government, take any of them seriously but, remembered only as popular literature though they be, tribute is due here to those I have found and used:

J. A. Van Sertima (1905) *The Creole Tongue* (Georgetown, Guyana), 60 pp.

J. G. Cruikshank (1916) *Black Talk—Notes on Negro Dialect in Br. Guiana* (Georgetown, Guyana), 76 pp.

F. A. Collymore (1955) *Glossary of Barbadian Dialect* (Bridgetown), 120 pp.

C. W. Francis (*c.*1971) *Popular Phrases in Grenada Dialect* (St George's), 36 pp.

C. R. Ottley (1965, 1971) *Creole Talk of Trinidad and Tobago* (Port-of-Spain), 100 pp.

G. A. Seaman (1967) *Virgin Islands Dictionary* (St Croix), 32 pp.

A. J. Seymour (1975) *Dictionary of Guyanese Folklore* (Georgetown), 74 pp.

C. A. Yansen (1975) *Random Remarks on Creolese* (Margate), 58 pp.

L. Valls (1981) *What a Pistarckle* (St John, USVI), 139 pp.

In 1967 the first scholarly regional dictionary appeared, Cassidy and Le-Page's *Dictionary of Jamaican English* [DJE] (CUP), 489 pp. (2nd edn., 1980, 509 pp.). Designed on historical principles it therefore fully documented Jamaican basic Creole lexicon, together with upper-level Jamaican originals in international English. Notwithstanding its scholarly achievement and acclaim, its design was above or outside of the everyday needs to which the foregoing questions on 'national standard language' pointed. It is also naturally seen as limited to Jamaica although its linguistic scholarship is regional in reach and importance. Most unfortunate of all is the fact that neither this nor its smaller cousin, Holm and Shilling's *Dictionary of Bahamian English* (Lexik, 1982, 228 pp.) is in general use by educators in their source territories.

MOVES TOWARDS CARIBBEAN LEXICOGRAPHY

Yet, parallel with these developments, and perhaps inevitably at the material level, the inadequacy of imported British and American dictionaries to answer the legitimate needs of national and territorial examination practice prompted recognizable yet cautious appeals for help. Among the resolutions passed at their Easter 1967 Conference in Trinidad by the Caribbean Association of Headmasters and Headmistresses was the following:

Resolution 6: **Whereas** the general interchange of teachers among the Caribbean territories is increasing, **Be it resolved** that this Association request the appropriate department of the University of the West Indies to compile a list of lexical items in each territory and to circulate these to schools for the guidance of teachers.

Obviously a call for territorial 'lists of lexical items ... for the guidance of teachers' shied far away from the need for a *common authentic Caribbean lexicographical reference*. The school Heads could not be accused of challenging the authority of British and American dictionaries. They wanted *complementary* help, but they were evidently unaware of the actual dimensions of their request.

The Resolution was sent to the University of the West Indies (UWI) Registrar at Mona, Jamaica, who passed it to the present author for information, I being at that time the designer and University Moderator of the *Use of English*, a compulsory undergraduate first-year course. Fortunately the Headteachers' request also lay within my interests as I had begun collecting data for a glossary of Guyanese English well before I had joined the University at Barbados in 1963, my first series of related articles on 'The Language we Speak' appearing in A. J. Seymour's literary journal *Kyk-Over-Al* from 1949. In Barbados contact with local and Eastern Caribbean students, a visit to Belize in 1965 and regular inter-campus business visits to Jamaica and Trinidad provided welcome opportunities to cross-reference and expand my data territorially, so that by the time of the Headmasters' 'request' of 1967 I already had some ten shoe-boxes each of about 1,000 6 × 4 cards and many loose unfiled cuttings, notes and other material, the collection being aimed now at a Glossary of Caribbean English, but not a dictionary. This latter, my private data-collection experience had already shown to be forbidding, and furthermore etymological requirements seemed quite overwhelming. Still, a start with inquiries into African language background had been made in my visits, with the help of W. H. L. Allsopp in 1967, to universities at Legon and Kumasi in Ghana, and Lagos and Ibadan in Nigeria.

About this time an independent suggestion was made that OUP's *Pocket Oxford Dictionary* might be used as a base for producing a 'Caribbean Pocket Oxford Dictionary' for schools by removing a couple of thousand selected entries of theirs to make room for an equal number of Caribbean items. This seemed to me, as I think the present work has sufficiently proved, quite impractical. However, an *Australian Pocket Oxford Dictionary* was done along those lines.

The UWI's Caribbean Language Research Programme funded by the Ford Foundation first in 1969 provided the opportunity for me to introduce and initiate as part of that Programme, in 1971, the Caribbean Lexicography Project with myself, its designer, as Co-ordinator, based at Cave Hill, Barbados. The undertaking which I outlined was agreed on as follows:

A survey of usage in the intermediate and upper ranges of the West Indian speech continuum. This will involve (1) the collecting of speech recordings in different social situations from persons involved in education, commerce and industry, the public services and public life as well as in the lower social strata of society; (2) a study of predominant attitudes towards and the levels of acceptability of the forms and structures discovered in (1); (3) the compilation, arising out of (1) and (2) together with a related and in-depth survey of lexis, of a dictionary of West Indian usage.

CONTENT

That agreement set in train my definitive work on the Dictionary of Caribbean English Usage. I designed it to provide the following:

1. As complete an inventory as practicable of the Caribbean environment and life-style, as known and spoken in each territory but not recorded in the standard British and American desk dictionaries.

2. The cross-referencing of different names for the same item throughout the Anglophone Caribbean. Exs.: —**golden-apple** (*Bdos*) ‖**golden-plum** (*Belz*) ‖**Jew-plum** (*Jmca*) ‖**pomme-cythère** (*Gren, StLu, Trin, ViIs*)

—**susu** (*Dmca, Gren, StLu, StVn, Tbgo, Trin*) ‖**asue** (*Baha*) ‖**box** (*Guyn*) ‖**meeting** (*Bdos*) ‖**pardner** (*Jmca*) ‖**syndicate** (*Belz*)

3. The identifying of different items called by the same name in different territories.
Exs.: —**ackee** (*Jmca*) in contrast with **akee** (*Bdos*)
—**doctor-bird** (*ECar*) in contrast with **doctor-bird** (*Jmca*)
—**pepperpot** (*Bdos, Gren, Guyn*) in contrast with **pepperpot** (*Angu, Antg, Jmca*)

4. Some guidance as to acceptability of certain word-forms and usages frequently encountered in speech and sometimes in writing in various parts of the Caribbean. Exs.: **blam** (vb), **force-ripe** (adj, vb), **pretensive**, **stupidness**, **tinnen** (adj, n) **touchous**, **trouble** (vb), **vexen** (vb)

5. Some account of the status and function of certain dialectal forms particularly such as have become part of the regional vocabulary and/or may be encountered in West Indian literature, proverbs or sayings. Exs.: **all-you, backra, bobol, buse, braata, dem so, jumbie, jook, mamaguy, obeah, pappyshow, plimpler, shak-shak, you-all**.

6. Guidance as to the form and function of French Creole loan-words current in the spoken English of St Lucians, Dominicans and Grenadians. Exs.: they were **malpaléing** people; poor **malèwèz!**; to have **bouch-kabwit**; to look **kabousé**.

[Spellings and usage to be settled in collaboration with relevant academic workers in St Lucia and Dominica, later using the *Handbook For Writing Creole* of the Mouvman Kwéyòl Sent Lisi.]

7. Lexical explanations of a number of Hindu and Muslim terms occurring increasingly in Caribbean culture from Guyana and Trinidad. Exs.: **arti, Bhagwat Jag, daru, Eid, Holi, Hosein, Phagwa, mandir, masjid, Youman-Nabi**.

8. Expansions of an increasing number of regional acronyms— CARIFTA, CARICOM, CAIC, CONCACAF, ECLA, etc. and of National Honours—**C.C.H.** (*Guyn*), **C.H.B.** (*Bdos*), **G.C.S.L.** (*StLu*), **O.N.** (*Antg & Brbu, Jmca*), **T.C.** (*Trin & Tbgo*), etc.

9. A rationalization and/or guide for the authentication of spellings that have remained conjectural or experimental so far. Exs.: **bazodi** (cp **basodee** etc.); **bobol** (cp **buball** etc.); **cou-cou** (cp **cookoo** etc.).

10. The listing of idiomatic expressions derived from or associated with headword entries, explaining their particularities as Caribbean wherever appropriate, giving some guidance as to status if considered necessary, and indicating their origin if possible. Exs.:

to cut your eye at/on/after somebody; to have eye-turn; it's me and you; to make your eyes pass somebody; to put your mouth on somebody/something; to kiss/suck your teeth; to take sick.

11. Etymological information as available.

12. Identification of regional pronunciation where necessary or useful, using the symbols of the International Phonetic Association (IPA) with the convenient modifications used by American linguists; particularly also showing differences of accentuation and pitch that distinguish

(*a*) Caribbean from British and American speech, exs.:

bad-talk /1′2/ (*CarA*) 'slander'
rudeness /1′2/ (*Jmca*) 'fornication'
sweet-man /1′2/ (*ECar*) 'an exploiting male lover'

(*b*) one meaning from another within some Caribbean speech communities, exs.:

one time /1′2/ (*CarA*) 'without the risk of delay'
one time! /3′1/ (*CarA*) 'there and then; instantly'
just now /1′2/ (*Bdos*) 'soon'
just now /2′1/ (*Bdos*) 'a short while ago'

A commitment to this outline (with the exception of item 11) was set out in a printed expository brochure which was circulated to all Ministries of Education, Teacher Training Colleges and academic colleagues in the Caribbean, and to a number of external agencies. The work had hardly begun, however, but three things became clear. First, supportive citations from both spoken and written sources would be necessary to validate senses and usages. How else could one authenticate those in relation to many of the items, especially the idioms given as examples above? A quantity of field notes I already had would supply citations from oral sources, but it was clear that more corroboration would have to be solicited in data-collection workshops and tours. As for citations from written sources, I and eventually all Research Assistants and some volunteers (all included in the list of Acknowledgements) set about reading and excerpting a large selection of West Indian literature, newspapers and printed writings of every kind in the Anglophone Caribbean, committing duly identified excerptions to cards. In these ways accountability was being ensured. Indeed the corpus of written sources expanded enormously and, although some books were excerpted fully while others were only minimally so, the total identification of written sources amounted to over 1,000 West Indian books, journals, etc., as the Citation Codes for Bibliographical References in the following pages will attest.

Second, it was clear that the work would be as much materially weakened by the absence of etymological data as it would be rendered culturally valuable and academically useful by the inclusion of such data. Accordingly I set about the daunting task of etymological researches (adding especially from grammars and dictionaries of African languages to what I had already gleaned in early efforts in visits to universities in Ghana and Nigeria and at Howard and Wisconsin). However, this decision slowed progress down very considerably, notwithstanding the great and indispensable contributions especially of the late Professor Jack Berry and Professor Ayo Banjo who both visited the Project at some length to help with African languages, as also did Dr Satesh Rohra to help with the Hindi/Bhojpuri items (see Acknowledgements).

Third, the techniques of lexicography were not to be assumed. I was therefore fortunate in being able to visit Professor Walter Avis, editor-in-chief of the *Dictionary of Canadian English* (1967) at the Royal Military College (Kingston, Ontario), Dr H. Bosley Woolf, editor of *Webster's (Eighth) New Collegiate*, at Springfield, Massachusetts, and both Dr Robert Burchfield, editor of the *OED Supplement*, and Mr J. B. Sykes, editor of the *Concise Oxford Dictionary* (7th edn.) and other members of the Dictionary team at Walton St. and later St Giles', Oxford, between 1972 and 1974. These visits were warm experiences, very humbling but equally enlightening. Between that time and 1984 I paid three more visits to Oxford (and also contributed a few Caribbean items to the *OEDS*). Much was gathered from discussions both in those visits and with colleagues at biennial conferences of the newly formed Dictionary Society of North America.

Specifically important at this period, however, was a visit to the Project at Cave Hill in 1977 by Prof. F. G. Cassidy, of the well-known *Dictionary of Jamaican English*. His assessment, commissioned by the UWI, was favourable, and more particularly his advice practical and valuable. His recommendation that a Senior Assistant be urgently appointed fell through only for lack of funds, and slow progress became an increasingly serious problem.

In the same context, but some years later when Oxford University Press were chosen as publishers, they and the UWI agreed on the choice of Laurence Urdang Inc. to provide 'supervisory editorial, lexicographic and technical help' in the preparation of the Dictionary. Mr Urdang's expertise in lexicography, perhaps especially because it is well established both in Britain and the United States, was an invaluable advantage as the work proceeded. From about 1987 to early 1992 he reviewed once, and commented on nearly the whole printout (some 4,000–5,000 pages) of the draft manuscript. The few places in the text where his personal information is acknowledged in the notes to entries are only a token reflection of the professional debt the work owes to him, and if there is criticism in any regard, as there may be, it must be assigned to myself as author, possibly in places where I disagreed with a professional convention that obscured Caribbean grass-root realities, or where perhaps the editorial length and time the work called for produced some other weakness.

ACADEMIC QUESTIONS

Although a dictionary on historical principles such as Cassidy and LePage's *DJE* needs to be undertaken on a regionwide scale at some time, the present is not such a work. There is a one-hour time difference and several hours' flying time between Guyana and Belize; within this boundless Caribbean panorama, there is the challenge of a dynamically evolving life, one which is largely without inventory but in which the everyday machinery of literacy controls all national advancement. The immediate 'work' priority is, therefore, not a chronicle of our linguistic past, but a careful account of what is current, at least as an available basis for intra-regional intelligence. Therefore a descriptive work is clearly indicated, i.e. one that reliably itemizes the environmental data and details the current life-style agenda of the English-speaking Caribbean; descriptive, yet not so without important qualification. Words and expressions like **bound-place, company-path, cob, creole, be behind somebody like a slave-driver, giving laugh for peas-soup, gone in Maxwell Pond**, etc. that are in a grey area of currency serve to remind us that even at the surface of today's communication the historical dimension is still with us, although it is far more massive at the etymological roots of Caribbean English. In dealing with those features a chronicling of some of the partnership between historical, social and linguistic developments from the seventeenth century to the present is involved in the work.

Again, words and expressions that are in a grey area of acceptability as 'educated' speech or writing raise another academic question. Consider, for example, **hard-ears** (adj), **cut-tail, suck-teeth, to break stick in your ears, to force-ripe** a fruit, **to pound somebody's name, to wuk up,** etc. In observing both a written form and a working status in each such case, in making unavoidably subjective judgements of that status even when backed up by selected citations, the work has a prescriptive aspect. Again, in omitting the mass of Caribbean basilectal vocabulary and idiom in favour of the mesolectal and acrolectal, and using a hierarchy of form-alness in status-labelling the entries throughout, the work is being pre-scriptive. This is in keeping with expressed needs, and with the mandate agreed and supported by successive regional resolutions (see Endorsements below).

The practical neglecting of basilectal vocabulary cannot, however, mean a linguistic or even operational despising of it. The weight of evidence of the pages of West Indian literature soon settles that question. As examples Guyanese Edgar Mittelholzer writes:

Jannee frowned and sucked his teeth, uttering a deep ominous sound. 'One o' dese days me an' he going come to grip. Yesterday me pass hospital gate an' 'e shout out provoke me. Me na say nutten. Me waitin' good. One o' dese day 'e go provoke me bad an' me go bus' 'e tail' *MCT:38* (1941)

Jamaican Roger Mais writes:

An' de ole knee was a sose-a tribulation . . . / Rheumatism must be, so de doctor-man did say when she went to de doctor-shop . . . an' did tell him 'bout de pain-a-joint. / Scasely can sleep night-time wid de man snorin' widouten a trouble in de world, stretch out side-a her, de bed a-go crips-crips every time him turn. *MHJT:72* (1953)

Trinidadian Samuel Selvon writes:

[And one day] The old man went up to Chaguanas . . . And when he come back he bust the mark. / 'Betah,' he say, 'I think you coming big man now, and is time you get wife.' *SWOS:83* (1957)

Such extracts, which can be paralleled hundreds of times from scores of authors of West Indian literature—from Guyana through the Bahamas to Belize—do much more than answer the academic question of the place of Caribbean Creole dialects in the inventorying of Caribbean culture and environment. They make it obvious that the presence of the folk, represented by their own language, has a dominant place in any genuine account of

xxvi

Caribbean life, and therefore in its literature. From 1940 to the present no worthwhile author's serious work is without it. Creole dialects are a pan-Caribbean reality which no professional lexicography, whatever be its mandate, can simply ignore. Moreover they introduce problems of spelling and presentation on which authors may justly seek guidance, and problems of sense and function of which especially non-creole readers of West Indian literature—and many young native persons now are—may properly seek authentic explanation. Those responsibilities lie squarely in the domain of a regional dictionary, and this book, in anticipation of reasonable inquiry, attempts, from its opening pages, to treat a limited number of basilectal particles, function words, pronominal and a few other traditional Creole forms that occur in Caribbean narrative dialogue as reported in fiction, newspaper columns, and court records. Indeed, as the extracts above demonstrate, the basilectal shades so readily into the mesolectal that treating the one often involves explaining the other. (The terms *basilect*, *mesolect*, and *acrolect*, in the origins of which Caribbean Creole studies played indeed a prominent part, are listed entries in the Dictionary for the reader's benefit.)

ANSWERS EMERGING

A broad, general, but fundamental answer emerges from the foregoing considerations: a pioneer and long overdue work of this nature, required to answer practical needs, must focus pointedly on that objective, not being constrained by the historical/prescriptive/descriptive categorizations of modern linguistics, nor being embarrassed by preference for academic conventions over grass-root Caribbean realities. A good case in point is syntactic classification or 'parts-of-speech', but there turned out to be other cases not so easily identified or determined.

In all lexicography the line separating lexicon from grammar is often fuzzy, because meaning rests heavily upon function and function is basically the domain of grammar, being also determined wholly by context and structure. In Caribbean English (CE) the function of an item can vary tangentially from the set of possibilities in British or American English, so making function more difficult to categorize: the Standard English (SE) item *like* may be adj., prep., adv., conj., noun or verb; but in the complete CE sentence *Like you vex* 'You seem to be annoyed', *like* belongs to none of the SE categories. Again, what is and what not 'idiomatic' in the generally understood sense of that word? Is the phrase *behind me like a slave-driver* inadmissible as 'idiom' because its sense is entirely derivable from the sum of its parts? These and other particularities of Caribbean phrasing and structure are the reasons why a following essay on Caribbean English is considered necessary as part of the front matter of this Dictionary, as also the addition of 'Usage' to its title. For a Caribbean English Dictionary cannot really skip such problems. Even if it may be faulted for attempting too much, it must at least address the facts, although it can only do so briefly.

For these and one other reason, namely that educators have largely abandoned the teaching of grammatical structure, the Dictionary laboriously identifies, for the Caribbean reader's benefit, the grammatical function of all listed phrases (*adj phr*, *n phr*, *vb phr*, etc.) with a consistency not found, perhaps because not thought necessary, in current standard desk dictionaries. However, for practical purposes, the label *vb phr* is used to identify both actual 'verb phrases' and what are properly 'phrasal verbs'.

Of a number of other grammatical features that need particular recognition in a Caribbean lexicon, some were best treated collectively. However, within the practical considerations of this work, only four could be given that focus: Echoic Words (i.e. ideophones), Names of Natives (i.e. adjectival place-name derivatives), Passivity, and Plural Forms. These are four productive areas of open lists of items and functions that could not practically all be itemized in a work of this size. Their case is also treated in the essay on Caribbean English.

BASES OF AUTHORITY

The principal authority on which the foregoing answers and decisions and indeed all else in the work are based is its comprehensive and entirely Caribbean source of material. They are as follows:

- Thirty-eight data-collection Workshops in twenty-two territories from Guyana to Belize. (These are identified in the list of Acknowledgements.)

- Transcriptions of tape-recorded spontaneous speech, and field-notes made in all of those territories.

- Responses to a checklist of 300 idioms of Caribbean English, unidentified as to territorial source, presented one each in four 6 ins. × 4 ins. boxes per sheet. The inquiry in a 'box' was designed to elicit individual identifying, paralleling, or varying of the structure and/or sense of each idiom, the respondent being also invited to indicate in a list of possibilities the frequency, rural/urban placement and social status of each idiom. These checklists were both answered by participants at the Workshops referred to above and distributed by correspondence to others.

● Individual responses to an open list of thirty-two categories of Caribbean life-style, including such as folk medicines, children's games, the idiom of funeral, wedding, and childbirth practices, superstitions, etc.

● Responses to Pictorial Questionnaires (comprising photographs and postcards) on

House-Building Styles	Ornamental Flora
Landscape	Wild Flora
Cartage	Fruit
Industry	Trees
Boats	Birds
Domestic Life	Fishes
Folk Life	Insects
Hair Styles	Religion

These Pictorial Questionnaires were used both at the Workshops and on field-trips.

● Excerpts from several hundred written sources (see Citation Codes for Bibliographical References Used in the Dictionary in following pages). They include the following:

Novels and short stories
Local and regional histories and geographies
Journals and pamphlets
Handbooks and guides
Reports and similar documents
Newspapers throughout the region
Folksong and calypso collections
Handwritten schoolwork, competitive short stories, and plays (all identified as 'Ms' in the illustrative citations)
Magistrate's court records
Parliamentary Hansards (*Bdos, Gren*)
Selected UWI (Faculty of Arts and General Studies) Caribbean Study Papers

(The system of coding ensured acknowledgement of every citation used from any source.)

● Specially commissioned vocabulary collections of:
Guyana rice, sugar, timber, and bauxite industries.
Trinidad cocoa industry.
Loan-words from the Indic cultures in Guyana and Trinidad.
Loan-words from the French Creoles of St Lucia, Dominica, Grenada commonly used in the *current English* of these territories.

In addition the following persons, as the work was publicized, generously put at my disposal their personal collections of territorial vocabulary and expressions:

Herman D. Boxill (Barbados)	Maureen Warner-Lewis (Trinidad)
Leslie W. Slater (Guyana)	Claude W. Francis (Grenada)
Jacob D. Elder (Tobago) [*Folklore*]	

Lastly, as the work progressed, I sent out personally addressed circular letters to Government officers in many Caribbean territories—particularly in Departments of Agriculture, Fisheries, Forestry, and Information Services—and to colleagues at the UWI and the University of Guyana, seeking in each case authentic information on a specific item: the taxonomic identification of many folk-named ecological items, origins and official or alternative names, national honours, etc. Over 200 such circulars were sent and all sources of information received are gratefully listed among the Acknowledgements.

Within this considerable body of accredited sources there is one that must not go unnoticed with mere mention. It is the now considerable body of 'West Indian' literature in English—novels, short stories, poetry, plays—that has shown itself overwhelmingly eligible to demand, and fully adequate to support with pervasive A to Z *illustrative* citations at all sociolinguistic levels, a *Dictionary of Caribbean English Usage (DCEU)*. Admittedly I have taken 'West Indian literature in English' to embrace everything from the English translation of the *Journal of Christopher Columbus,* through early historical accounts (or republished extracts of those accounts wherever lexicologically relevant or useful) to Lady Nugent's Journal, Anthony Trollope's travels, and other nineteenth-century writing; but citations from them have been minimal, the massive bulk of illustrations being drawn from post-1940 West Indian literature; and the newspaper excerptions, though going back as early as 1952, bulk largely in the years after 1970.

The authentication provided by this literary source, however, brings into sharper focus a problem indicated earlier, namely the lexicographer's professional responsibility to identify the 'syntactic class' or 'word-class' or 'part-of-speech' of what appear, in Standard English terms, to be grammatically unique functions of some words and phrases in Caribbean English. In this task I found great help in R. Quirk and S. Greenbaum's *University Grammar of English* (Longman, 1973), and I used that work as my main authority and guide in labelling syntactic particularities in Caribbean English.

THE WORK AS A CULTURAL AGENT

As a cross-referencing exercise in the labelling of the Caribbean ecology and the idioms of the regional life-style, as a record, through the large availability of citations of the sameness-with-differences in the historical and social background to the wide spread of Caribbean literature, Caribbean lexicography is equipped to function as a cultural agent. No different in this regard from other non-British regional dictionaries when they emerged at landmark times in their nations' history—*Webster's in the USA* in 1828, the *Dictionary of Canadian English* in 1967, the *Australian National Dictionary* in 1988—the *DCEU* should be an inward and spiritual operator of regional integration even more powerful as a signal of unity than a national flag would be. The design of the dictionary therefore seeks to answer at least some important needs at the material level of inter-territorial data for schools, at the academic level of areal linguistic information, and at the executive level of mutual neighbourly knowledge of regional states. If this work helps, as it indeed can, to break down insular barriers, set up bridges and link up cultural roadways through the Anglophone Caribbean for a start, it will have served ultimately its highest purpose.

Related to its regional function there is an even stronger call on, and, one hopes, an equally strong response from the work as a cultural agent. The weight of evidence supplied in this work should provide sufficient ground to build Caribbean pride to replace the earlier colonial shame-facedness and inhibitions bedevilling this region. The great value of the etymological investigations recorded is their demonstration that although the dialects of the British Isles (and Wright's *English Dialect Dictionary* has been my major authority) have played a predictable part in the development of Caribbean English, the linguistic and social forces originating particularly in sub-Saharan Africa have also played a striking part in that development; so striking indeed as to raise the question whether their influence has not been much greater. Later and to a much lesser extent forces from the Indic sub-continent and a little from southern China add their share.

With the Chinese input I am wholly unequipped to deal, but the little I have done with help from my friend John Tjon-A-Yong of Guyana, earlier cursory contacts made at Ohio State University in 1970, and later at the SOAS (London) through Hazel Carter, suggests that scholarly rewards await investigations into Chinese loans—only a few nouns have been detected so far—in Guyana, Trinidad and Jamaica.

The expansion of the Indic sub-culture in the mainstream of Caribbean culture is, however, relatively on a much larger scale and wider spread, especially in the Eastern Caribbean, and this is reflected in the Dictionary.

By expository glosses of the names of Hindu and Muslim religious festivals, ceremonies and related items and expressions, customs, foods, domestic items, apparel, etc., that have become or are becoming part of the everyday life of Guyana and Trinidad (and are spreading northward in the region) the work cuts a path, for the first time routinely available, towards a necessary understanding and cultural integration of the East Indian West Indian. In gathering information in this exercise I was much assisted by Kuntie Ramdat in Guyana and Patricia Lalla-Aquing in Trinidad. The Hindu sub-culture is, however, massively Bhojpuri and the etymological explanations of this cousin dialect of Hindi and of Perso-Arabic are owed to Satesh Rohra (University of New Delhi on loan to University of Guyana) and Peggy Mohan (Howard University). Here again there is a huge demand for scholarly investigations into the Indo-Creole cultural and linguistic syncretisms in Guyana and Trinidad. Such work would be both enlightening and fraternally valuable especially in those countries, indeed in many other places.

However, as indicated earlier, above all others it is sub-Saharan African 'talk' that emerges in this work as the sharpest, if so far unacknowledged or even rejected, influence on today's Caribbean English 'talk'. It is wrong to seek, as answer, the number of 'African' loan-words. Given the grim social history of the Caribbean they are both misleadingly few and generally of low status: **bassa-bassa, jook, kokobe, kongkongsa, nyam, obeah, wunna, yabba**, etc. They are utterly swamped by British and American standard words (even if with shifted usage) and dialectal items. Indeed, the fact that even Indic loan-words, after a mere century and a half, are more readily available and in such respectable domains as those listed in the preceding paragraph, itself indicates that a loan-word count is not a valid way to demonstrate the Afro-Caribbean cultural presence.

For a better start let the reader look at items like **cut-eye, hard-ears, suck-teeth**, etc.—Caribbean compounds of English words as labels of Caribbean particularities of behaviour for which the etymological explanations are found in African languages. They are folk-translations, in word and deed, of African cultural 'modes'. Everyday phrases, too, such as **You do well!, let your hand drop, got to call somebody aunt/uncle, pick up your foot/heels and run, run your mouth**, etc. are ways of putting things calqued or 'copy-translated' from one or other, sometimes several sub-Saharan African languages. These idioms reflect an African life-view and there are hundreds of them surviving in Caribbean English, far more than could have been suspected when I first submitted my idiom checklist for comment by African native speakers. (See lists of Consultants and Informants in the Acknowledgements.)

Moreover many aspects of Caribbean life—foods, festivals, ceremonies, beliefs, practices related to births, marriages, cures, burials, etc. have a massive vocabulary which is sometimes suggestively African—

> **dokunu**; **jonkunu**; **queh-queh**; **pukumina**; **saraca**; etc.

sometimes clearly Anglophone—

> **stay-home soup**; **Carnival**; **big-drum dance**; **Nation dance**; **tie-heads**; **bush-bath**; etc.

sometimes a mixture of both—

> **bake bammy for somebody**; **kaisonian**; **comfa-dance**; **Rastafarianism**; **to obeah somebody**; etc.

In most cases there are related idiomatic expressions, and, especially in the case of festivals and beliefs, there is always a whole glossary of terms and idioms only some of which are recorded in this Dictionary. In every case, by unemotive, expository glossing, cautious etymological references and sometimes footnote cross-referencing, the work has tried to sensitize the reader to the reality, nature and dimensions of the Caribbean's African background, and to invite investigative intelligence to dislodge the old programmed contempt for Black African cultures.

I have only scratched the surface and found that scholarly research into the linguistics, particularly the pragmatics of the African background to Caribbean language in general has a boundless domain to explore. For these investigations have given two more, and significant indications, further strengthened when the huge domain of proverbs (of which I have used very few as illustrative citations) is added. First, in regard to Caribbean language in general, it can be demonstrated many times over that the structure and sense of a Caribbean Anglophone basilectal/mesolectal Creole idiom or proverb parallel those of a Francophone Caribbean Creole idiom or proverb. Thus for example—

koupé zié	**[to] cut [your] eye [at somebody]**
lafen ka tjenbé mwen	**hunger holds me**
ou ni djèl-kabwit	**you have goat-mouth**
zié-yo fè kat	**their eyes make four**
zòwèy-li wèd	**his ears [are] hard**
etc.	

The significant point here is that neither are the French Creole structures modelled on Standard French idiomatic or other structures nor are the Anglophone Creole structures modelled on Standard English structures. Nor can they in fact have been modelled on each other. Their *identical* structure can only be accounted for by their having a common ancestor. The etymological data in this Dictionary show all the Anglophone Creole expressions in the right-hand column (and scores of others like them) to be of African linguistic origin, hence the 'common ancestor' must be the same, that is an *African way of putting things* originating in African sub-Saharan languages, the Niger–Congo family of languages.

The consequent and second point is that these pervasive parallels send a strong message of genetic relationship among the sub-Saharan African languages, a message from the Caribbean of a oneness of African cultures from the Akan to the Zulu.

PROBLEMS OF SIZE AND CONTENT

The amount of data and related material accumulated by 1981 led to the belief that a fairly comprehensive coverage of Caribbean lexis was now available for professional inventorying; and in 1982, with fund-seeking as its main objective, a Demonstration Preprint of *Selected Entries of a Dictionary of Caribbean English Usage* was prepared. It contained 97 camera-ready 11 ins. × 8 ins. pages of Entries with illustrative citations, sub-senses, etymological data, usage and orthographic notes. It proved, however, operationally too ambitious as a model, some Entries occupying more than a page.

Practical considerations necessitated selective editing, eliminated items being left hopefully for a larger work at a later time. It emerged that what had to be eliminated (many names of fishes, wild plants, woods, folk-idiom variants, etc.) and areas which man-hours did not suffice to explore (such as the historical vocabulary of multi-territorial slave and plantation life) are an amount of material very likely greater than what is now presented in this book. Comprehensiveness could not therefore be its aim. Rather, focus had to be on thoroughness of investigation and the verifiability of the information given in respect of every Entry. This required a *concise description* of ostensive items such as fruit, bird, fish etc. using additional recognition criteria such as use, habitat etc.; and a *contextual definition* of idioms. Moreover, having regard to the importance of Usage in the title, wider spans of attention than would have been expected had to be given to a large number of small words such as **a, all, go, so, them, to,** etc.

It is hoped that these considerations, taken together, will not only justify themselves upon inspection, but that the eventual content of the book, within its size, will serve to stimulate the needed succession, to take in more of the Anglophone Caribbean ecology in its space and considerable cousinhood of cultures in their depth.

COMPUTERIZATION

Concise and accurate cross-referencing, a main artery of the work, really called for the support of a Computer Unit, but such was not the good fortune of the Lexicography Project. In the circumstances the work of designing an elaborate coding system, solving a number of machine problems, and the inducting of successive keyboarders was taken on as a voluntary responsibility by a campus colleague, Marvel O'Neal of the Mathematics Department at Cave Hill, after paying a visit to Oxford in 1985. For this fundamental work and for being on call for many years, the Project owes a considerable debt to him.

IBM and compatible desk-top computers were finally used, providing a total capacity of 100 megabytes. The software that ultimately proved most serviceable for our needs was ISIS and this was used, with UNESCO's permission. In its use Hazelyn Devonish of the Cave Hill Law Library also gave much valuable voluntary help especially in the last stages of machine preparation of the material for the publishers.

ENDORSEMENTS AND THANKS

It is important to record the endorsements of this Dictionary as a needed regional work, if only to remind the audience it addresses, which includes all educators and professional persons both in the Caribbean and in the West Indian diaspora in Britain, Canada and the United States, that the work here presented was promoted and advanced in large part by those endorsements; and whereas the long passage of time may have caused impatience to become doubt, then abandonment in the minds of some, the work nevertheless now cautiously recommends itself to the attention and use of all, with the awareness that expected yield is the test that all endorsement entails.

The endorsements were as follows:

1973 CARIFTA Ministers of Education (Agenda Item II) (Barbados)
Resolved
> To support the efforts of the University of the West Indies to provide an authentic statement of the lexical usage of the English-speaking Caribbean.

1975 Heads of Government of CARICOM States (St Kitts)
(Agenda Item 22)
> *Noted* the importance of the Caribbean Lexicography Project.
> *Agreed* that Member States should assist (in data-collection)
> (Consideration of funding was deferred)

1976, 1982 Registrars of the Caribbean Examinations Council wrote (and repeated) to the Standing Committee of Ministers of Education:

> The Dictionary of Caribbean English Usage (DCEU) Project currently being undertaken by the UWI, should be one of the most important reference books in respect of any CXC examination. It is hoped that the Dictionary ... will be available in sufficiently large numbers to make source materials written in any Caribbean setting intelligible to persons in other Caribbean areas.

1979 UWI appointed a three-member Advisory Committee to report on the progress and funding needs of the work.

The highest form of endorsement is, of course, personal help and involvement; and in the twenty-one years that this work has been in the making some persons have made unforgettable contributions to its survival and progress which I must record.

First is Aston Preston, late Vice Chancellor of the UWI, who, wishing to rescue the Project after the end of Ford Foundation initial funding in 1973/74, permitted me to hunt for funds on my own, and when I had had encouraging success in this, introduced University funding from all three campuses as of 1979. That principle has been substantially responsible for the Project's survival up to its fulfilment, with the Cave Hill campus taking the responsibility in the last few years.

The late President Forbes Burnham of Guyana independently saw the value of the work as an instrument of integrative regional education, and offered the support of both the Government and the University of Guyana. That Government's unconditional support, totalling over US $100,000 in the five years 1975–80, made possible the bulk of the data-collection on location throughout the region, so giving a solid base to the work.

Mr George Money, Vice-Chairman of Barclays Bank International, and stationed in Barbados, encouraged the Bank's notable help (1974–6) which financed the first Research Assistant at Cave Hill.

The British High Commission in Barbados, in 1989, while the present Project was nearing its end and with progressive updating in prospect, made a practical gift of the newly edited twenty volumes of the 2nd edition of the *Oxford English Dictionary* [OED2]. This proved immediately useful.

Special thanks are also due to my colleagues Dennis Craig and Helen Pyne-Timothy, successive Chairpersons of the UWI's Advisory Committee. Their leadership, tact, and encouragement at all times and Helen's creative optimism and considerable extra effort when she was overwhelmed with other responsibilities as University Dean did much to save the work and ease anxieties at crucial times.

No work, especially of this kind, can proceed effectively without reliable and loyal ground support. In this regard all my Research Assistants deserve warm recognition. The longest serving was Audrey Burrowes who was seconded to the Project from the Barbados Teaching Service for eight years. Indeed, as the list of their names in the Acknowledgements will show, they were, with the exception of two in Belize, all women! Perhaps deserving of special mention among them is Claudith Thompson in Guyana who managed finances, workshops and many aspects of data-collection, largely unsupervised, for many years. In the office at Cave Hill Leona Darmanie typed thousands of excerptions on cards during the first eight years, and Camileta Neblett during the last four years keyboarded most of the manuscript, both with quiet steady production in the most pleasing manner.

Many an author finds it proper to thank a spouse for help in the preparation of a work, but in this case it is a most grateful duty to thank my wife Jeannette. Her designation on an earlier page as my Research Associate gives no indication of how much, in the last six or seven years, the progress and completion of the Dictionary owe to her interest, zeal and energy. Her command of Spanish language and philology provided first some timely aid to my etymological inquiries. As a trainer of foreign-language teachers she grew interested in adding a Caribbean French and Spanish Supplement to the work, and with that in view she took courses in modern linguistics at Cave Hill while acquiring skills in the process of computerization and joining the Project as a part-time assistant. Together we shared in laborious diggings at the libraries at Yale and Gainesville (USA) and in one inquiry visit to Oxford. Erdiston Teachers' College permitted her secondment full-time to the Project in 1990 and, at a critical time, her organizational skills and increasing understanding of the Project's needs in all departments made her contribution a saving boon. She further enhanced her workmanship through an International Lexicography Course at the University of Exeter's Dictionary Research Centre, and now stands in a fair way to expand her own contribution to Caribbean Lexicography.

It remains to thank some libraries, perhaps the earliest being Howard University's Moorland-Spingarn Library where, in 1969, librarian Dr Dorothy Porter helped me find early writings relevant to the Caribbean and American slave life. On my own campus at Cave Hill special thanks are due for generous, long loans of reference works, for the library's useful holdings on African languages though limited, and to librarians Jeniphier Carnegie and Alan Moss for guidance in regard to the West Indian Collection and otherwise. Also at Cave Hill, Messrs Carl Branch and Paul

Gibbs of the Learning Resource Centre proved a great find, ably producing the maps and the Steelband diagram which I had prepared in some doubt, yet hope, as to the practicality of their inclusion in such a book. Other persons whose names, unfortunately, I did not note are also to be thanked for help, and for permission to use 'the stacks', at the Universities of Victoria (Canada), Ibadan (Nigeria), Ohio State, Wisconsin, Florida (Gainesville), and Yale (in the USA), and the School of Oriental and African Studies, London.

Lastly my regret that this work has taken so long is rendered sharper by the passing of three great personal friends who had looked forward to its emergence, Joel Benjamin of the University of Guyana Library, Arthur J. Seymour of Guyana and H. Aubrey Fraser of the Norman Manley Law School in Jamaica. Their persistent, almost impassioned encouragement and Arthur's and Joel's ready response to my inquiries are a living remembrance for me. May this work honour their high expectations. In contrast I can only marvel at the number of times I came near believing the opposite view of others, and one far more often expressed, that the work would never be finished. It is therefore in a spirit of great thanks to God and cautious optimism that I offer this Dictionary to all Caribbeans. However, no dictionary is ever complete; moreover in Caribbean circumstances, not only are omissions inevitable, but the perfectly all-embracing definition is a challenge which I may often not have adequately met. These shortcomings, and others that will inevitably be discovered, may well fuel those who are more prone to condemn such work as interference with the legacy of England's language and literature. But I am cheered by some words of Samuel Johnson, reported in James Boswell's account of his life, in a letter to a friend in 1755, the year he was finishing his great Dictionary: 'I now begin to see land, after having wandered ... in this vast sea of words. What reception I shall meet with on the shore, whether the sound of bells and acclamations of the people ... or a general murmur of disbelief, I know not: whether I shall find upon the coast a Calypso that will court, or a Polypheme that will resist!' He added characteristically that he did not, however, fear Polypheme (J. Boswell, *Life of Johnson*, OUP pb, 1980, p. 197). The irony in my case is that I may well need to fear calypso!

On the other hand, wherever knowledgeable readers detect such shortcomings or error, their justified criticism would be most useful and welcome if it takes the form of corrective or amending information sent for the improvement of any ongoing work.

RICHARD ALLSOPP

Director, Caribbean Lexicography Project
UWI at Cave Hill, Barbados, 1992

CARIBBEAN ENGLISH

Lexicographers of diaspora varieties of English risk being (and usually are) charged with inviting degradation of long-recognized, proper British English, locally used and available to all but the unambitious or wilfully careless. Even the independent-minded Noah Webster was wary of such a possible charge as he embarked on his *American Dictionary of the English Language* (1828), and went to England 'attempting to bring about some agreement or coincidence of opinions in regard to unsettled points in pronunciation and grammatical construction'. A century and a half later Walter Avis was registering a stern complaint against false attitudes to Canadian English, in the introduction to his *Senior Dictionary of Canadian English* (1967); and W. S. Ramson and others, in the introductory material to *The Macquarie Dictionary* (1982, rev. 1985) felt obliged to make their case for the 'emancipation' of Australian English, as having a quality in its own right.

Cultural insecurity is the reason, and if it has so noticeably affected the national soul of those large, independent, politically safe and economically sturdy dominions of English kinship, one can readily understand how much more severely that problem afflicts the disconnected, fledgeling ministates of non-English kinship which make up the Caribbean, most of them with populations about or even much less than that of a small town in any big country of the world. The teaching of English as the exclusive national language of a nation of less than 100,000 people seems at first unquestionably to have to be the teaching of 'World English'. That conclusion will, however, soon be found to be simplistic, against the background of the questions raised in the previous essay. The realities of local national speech and of regionalisms, the conflict by invasion of Americanisms with 'British Standard' (if these can still be distinguished), the status of literate expressions which arise in local law-courts or in the texts of Caribbean literature and find themselves on the tongues of local parliamentarians—all these raise questions of morphological 'legitimacy', of syntactic 'acceptability', ultimately of the linguistic identity of one's local, and of one's neighbour's, i.e. of the *regional* product as an obvious *part of 'World English'*. What that part is it is necessary to show to the nervous Caribbean inquirer.

THE AGE OF ENGLISH IN THE CARIBBEAN

It was the vexed Protestantism and resolve of Henry VIII's and Anne Boleyn's daughter, Queen Elizabeth I, backing the aggressive seamanship of her ocean-going knights Hawkins, Drake, Frobisher, and Ralegh in their anti-Spanish adventures that, within less than a century after Columbus, brought the English tongue to the Caribbean and Caribbean vocabulary into the English language.

John Hawkins, 'being assured', according to Richard Hakluyt, 'that Negros were very good merchandise in *Hispaniola*' began what later became known as 'the triangular trade' in 1562/3 with a voyage between London, *Sierra Leona (sic)* and *Hispaniola*. This led to his wide-ranging voyages to Guinea and the West Indies in one of Elizabeth's own ships, the *Jesus of Lubeck*, between 1564 and 1568, selling slaves all along the Spanish Main, and sometimes leaving a number of his crew too. It is historically true that the English language had begun making substantial thrusts from Plymouth to the West Indies and South America long before it did so to North America. It was seamen's English that brought Protestantism's mailed fist into the rich belly of the 'New World', as the logical forerunner of the religious hands that guided the *Mayflower* to North America some half a century later in 1620. If this sounds exaggerated one need only recall that Sir Francis Drake's great plundering armada of twenty-five ships sailed in 1585 on what is historically known as 'Drake's West Indian Voyage'; and a hazardous channel in the Virgin Islands is still known today as 'Drake's Passage'.

Hakluyt's *Principall Navigations, Voiages and Discoveries of the English Nation* published in 1589 and Ralegh's *Discoverie of the Empyre of Guiana* published in 1596 brought to Oxford University and London's royal Court many new words each telling an exciting story: *tabacco* ('of great vertue'), *cassavi* ('a bread made of roots'), *pines* ('the princess of fruits that grow under the sun especially of Guiana'), *cocos nuts*, *flying fish*, *manati* ('most excellent and wholesome meat'), *egript* (egret) and *flamingo*, the *armadillo* given to Ralegh by a *Guianian Cazique*, *canoa*, *hamaca* ('which we call brasill beds'), the riches and magnificent *overfalls* of Guiana, the dread July *huricanos* of the *West Indies*, etc.

Shakespeare did not fail to pick up the information. He has his Falstaff praising one of the two 'Merry Wives of Windsor' in 1599 in these words: 'She is a region in Guiana, all gold and bounty. I will be cheator to them both, and they shall be exchequers to me. They shall be my East and West Indies and I will trade them both' (*The Merry Wives of Windsor*, I. iii).

English settlements which followed in the region, ranging from the failures (Charles Leigh in Guiana, 1604) to the finally successful (Warner in St Kitts, 1624) make the English language in the Caribbean the oldest exportation of that language from its British homeland in the present fraternity of World English.

With the new King James I Authorized Version of the Bible appearing in 1611 together with all the works of Shakespeare (who died in 1616) giving final shape at the same period to the structure of Modern English, the language was all set to grow in vocabulary, and Caribbean settlement and plantation life were going to be one of its earliest major sources. Within a century Anglophone Creoles were to become its first distinct overseas by-products and joint ancestors of today's Caribbean English.

TERRITORIAL DISTINCTIONS

Whereas Canadian English and Australian English, benefiting from the single land-mass of their respective homelands, can each claim general homogeneity, Caribbean English is a collection of sub-varieties of English distributed, as the list in the previous essay shows, over a large number of non-contiguous territories of which two, Guyana and Belize, are widely distant parts of the South and Central American mainland. Their history, both pre- and post-Columbian, joins with their geography to further complicate the language picture in the territories covered in this work.

Through Guyana came hundreds of nouns, necessary labels of an 'active' ecology, from the languages of its aboriginal indigenes of the nine identified ethnic groups, two Arawakan—Arawak (Lokono) and Wapishana; six Cariban—Akawaio, Arekuna, Makushi, Patamuna, Carib, Wai-Wai; and one Warrau. (*Information from W. Edwards, Amerindian Languages Project, University of Guyana.*) From these sources Guyanese have scores of names of commercial timbers—**mora, crabwood** karapa, **simarupa, tauronira, wamara, wallaba,** etc.; fishes—**arapaima, haimara, paku, yarrow, perai;** birds—**curri-curri, powis, sacki,** etc.; animal life—**abouya, labba, maipuri, yawarri,** etc.; everyday life—**matapee, tacouba, warishi,** etc.; pests and crawling things—**kabaura fly, acoushi ants, labaria snake, camoodi,** etc. This is a vocabulary that amounts to hundreds of everyday words known to Guyanese but *not* to other Caribbeans.

In the same way through Belize come words from the three Mayan languages—Kekchi, Mopan, Yucatecan; and from the Miskito Indian language; and from Garifuna, the Afro-Island-Carib language of Vincentian ancestry. Therefore again much Belizean everyday vocabulary—**craboo, gibnut, waika, wari-tick, wowla, ziricote, dugu ceremony,** and scores of Central American Spanish loan-words—**habanero, panades, relleno, tamales, punta,** etc.—all these are generally unknown to the rest of the Caribbean, yet many can suddenly come to regional attention, for example through literature such as Zee Edgell's *Beka Lamb*.

Taino, Tupi and other Carib and Arawak remainders also survive isolated in some Caribbean islands—**bacha, boutou, colibri, titiri, zandoli,** etc. They are similarly unknown, except by chance, in the wider Caribbean. One of the jobs of this book is to make one package of as many as possible such disparate items of Caribbean English, showing them to be of equal status with those more widely known—**agouti, barbecue, mauby, canoe, manioc,** etc. and scores of fruit—**avocado, guava, papaya, sapodilla,** etc.

In the post-Columbian era the settlement history of St Lucia (which changed political ownership no fewer than fourteen times between the English and French) and to a lesser extent of Dominica, Grenada and Trinidad, has left a powerfully operative vocabulary of Francophone loans, diminishing in presence in the order given, it is true, but 'powerful' because it includes adjectives, verbs and many elements in idioms. Some examples have been given in the list of areas of 'Content' in the previous essay, but the actuality of literature is always more convincing. As example, in Roderick Walcott's play *The Banjo Man* (pub. 1976) he gives his characters typical lines of St Lucian English with free inmixes of French Creole. Thus

ADOLPHUS: Bring some [anisette] let me *goutez*.

You know well Pascal is *mamapoule*, *coquade* that cannot even talk, making 'baa-baa' like *cabritte*.

Now remember as *Magistrat*, anybody who behave bad have to pay a fine of one pound to me. So *gardez cor-ou*.

MA STANIO: So who'll give *mépuis* for us now? Who going to give joke, and beat *tamboo*?

And you too old to get *jalou*, Pappa ... Is old *malfinis* that prefer young chicken.

That story *fini*, Pappa.
etc.

As these samples will show, this aspect of Caribbean English presents a problem in the quantity of French Creole loans in free operation especially in St Lucia, so that a limitation, to a large extent subjective, had to be put on their selection for entry into this Dictionary.

Differences in settlement history have made for differences in the present-day English of the Caribbean territories in another way. St Lucia and Dominica (where the French cultural presence has been kept far more alive by their proximity to Martinique and Guadeloupe respectively) have marked similarities in their English at all levels. Grenada and

Trinidad with only the older 'French Revolution' French connections may also be paired as to their English. For the same reason there are many lexical and other differences between Trinidadian and Tobagonian English, Tobago having had no French influence. Tobago, Guyana and Antigua, on the other hand, have notable linguistic similarities surfacing out of their Anglophone Creoles. For reasons such as these Trinidad and Tobago, Antigua and Barbuda, Grenada and Carriacou, St Vincent and The Grenadines, St Kitts and Nevis, must be treated *in linguistic terms*, as they are in this Dictionary, as *ten* separately identified linguistic areas, notwithstanding and fully respecting the political reality that they are five nations.

Again, Dutch ownership or presence in Guyana for nearly two centuries (1621–1803) has left marked lexical influence on its low-lying Holland-type coastal landscape, and Roman Dutch Law also on the legal vocabulary of plantation land tenure, with terms unknown elsewhere in the Caribbean.

Danish ownership (1672–1917) of today's US Virgin Islands, admittedly with an early and lasting presence of Dutch planters and missionaries, and later of American traders, has left Danish place-names and a few words, together with many traces of Dutch in the present English of those islands.

Irish influence, through the early 'barbadoesing' (a unique place-name verb in the English language) of post-Cromwellian bond-servants and their being quartered next to slaves, played the particular role of distinguishing Barbadian pronunciation of English; and ultimately from that base Irish English played a wider lexical role, especially in idiomatic input, in general Caribbean English.

ALLONYMS

Caribbean regionalisms of another kind, that is, different names or labels established in different states for the same referent, require special linguistic recognition, political independence bestowing on each such item 'standardness' in a national language, and linguistic principle bestowing equality of status in all cases. Hence, for example, the referent taxonomically identified as *Melicoccus bijugatus (Sapindaceae)*, called **guinep** in many territories (whether independent or not), is called **canep, chenep, chennette, kinip, mapo, quennette, skinop, Spanish lime,** or **tjennèt** —and a number of variants of these—in a number of other Caribbean territories, and has been so known for decades in those places, even if spellings have varied (or sometimes not been attempted). There is no linguistic justification for regarding one name as superior or inferior to another (though variant spellings are admittedly a different matter). They are of equal status, each one being *another name* for the same referent. As the term 'synonym' ('alike') has its own established and slightly different connotation in English, the term ALLONYM ('other name') is used in this context in this Dictionary specifically to designate each equivalent. Accordingly there are, cited above, ten CE allonyms of the referent *Melicoccus bijugatus*.

Since, however, a referent is defined only once in the Dictionary, one allonym is chosen (usually the one identified with the most territories) to carry the gloss, and this allonym is, merely for convenience, referred to as the *main* or *primary allonym* to which all others are referred for the statement of meaning. These others are, therefore, more conveniently referred to as *secondary allonyms* for purposes of discussion. Thus, in the examples given above, **guinep** is used as the *primary allonym* and the nine other equivalents are the *secondary allonyms*. (See the following Explanatory Notes.)

GENERAL CHARACTERISTICS

The Sound

There tends to be more lung pressure and mouth pressure behind the articulation of Caribbeans. Caribbean English (CE) generally sounds louder than homeland British English and, in its most uninhibited use, is accompanied by more release of laughter and exclamatory sounds, and much more facial and hand gesture than would characterize spoken British and North American English.

Although general homogeneity cannot be claimed for CE, as has been pointed out, and indeed Jamaican, Barbadian, Trinidadian and Guyanese intonations are noticeably different, there is a general sense in which a 'West Indian accent' is distinguishable as such anywhere in the world. Likely reasons for this are the general quality of CE vowels, the sharp reduction in the number of diphthongal glides and, the most distinguishing feature of all, the phrasal intonation in which the separation of syllabic pitch and stress in CE is a major factor of difference from spoken Standard English (SE). For example:

	SE pattern	CE pattern
teach.er	/2′1/	/1′2/
foun.tain-pen	/3′2 1/	/1′1 2/
ex.er.cise	/3′2 1/	/1′1 2/
e.du.cat.ed	/3′2 2 1/	/1′1 2 2/

where, with numbers representing high-low pitch (or tone) levels and the accent marking the stress, it will be noted that accent and highest pitch systematically coincide in SE but are usually separated in general CE. This is a feature most marked at the folk level, but it is susceptible of shifts. For example *calypso* may be pronounced with the pattern /ı′21/ or /112′/, Jamaica /ı′21/ or /ı′12/ or /12′2/ and so on, stress (i.e. breath force) being usually on the first syllable (as if the word is 'attacked') whether that first syllable carries higher pitch or not. (Many Caribbean readers may disagree with this analysis, but it should be noted, by way of example, that calypsonians and other Caribbean folk-singers automatically exploit this very facility, and also that Caribbean broadcasters in striving to switch from such patterning to what they believe to be that of spoken IAE or SE, enunciate faultily.)

Making no claims of phonetic detail, the author's broad experience of data-collection for this Dictionary nevertheless allows of some generalization of the phonological stock that middle-level or mesolectal or 'standard average Caribbean' uses. Such a generalization of the phonemes follows. (The symbols used are the modified IPA symbols used by American linguists. They are listed with examples on a later page.)

Vowels	i	u
	ɪ	ʊ
	e	o
	(ə)	
	ɛ	ʌ
		ɒ
	a	
Glides	aɪ ɒʊ ɒɪ ɪu/yu	
Consonants	p b t d k g	
	č j	
	m n (ŋ)	
	l r	
	f v (θ) (ð) s z š ž h	
	y w	

Brackets ( ) indicate that, in middle-level speech, the phoneme is commonly replaced by another, thus

(ə) > ʌ (θ) > t, f
(ŋ) > n (ð) > d

These replacements usually all apply to the same speaker, so reducing his/her stock of phonemes to

10 instead of 11 vowels (cp a different 12 in RP*)
4 glides (cp 8 in RP)
21 instead of 24 consonants as in RP

(* Received Pronunciation (RP) as represented in A. C. Gimson's *Introduction to the Pronunciation of English* (Edward Arnold, 1980).)

Some other variations may be noted, as follows:

(i) Vowels of British SE which are absent from the table above [ɜ:] [æ] [ɔ:] [ɒ:] do occur in some varieties of CE. Many Trinidadians and Vincentians, for example, use [ɜ:] in *bird, word, heard*, etc. Also, the vowels of some speakers, especially in Barbados and The Bahamas, have a marked nasality (but of a different quality in those two places). Vowel lengthening too, for emphasis, is a very common mesolectal feature, *the whole year* becoming [ðɪ ho::l ye::r] etc.

(ii) Although the levelling of SE diphthongs is a marked feature of CE at all levels, some of them, especially the centring set [ɪə] [ɛə] [eə] [oə] [ʊə] appear in some acrolectal varieties of CE, and others [ie, uo, ou] occur in near-basilectal varieties. However, it is not normal to make diphthongal distinctions in CE, as it is in SE, between pairs such as *hear* and *hair*, *tore* and *tour*. They are, in CE, homophonous pairs, either, as more usually, with levelled vowels [e] and [o] respectively, or with the same glides [eə] and [oə] respectively.

(iii) All consonants tend to be articulated with more breath force in CE than in SE. In particular the plosives [p, b, t, d, k, g] can, as a result, be accompanied by intense aspiration in emotive contexts. Among many large communities (Guyana, Jamaica, Barbados) palatalization of [k, g] occurs before the vowel [a] producing regular pronunciations like /kyart/, /gyardn/, etc., a feature notably lacking in Trinidadian speech.

(iv) Participial '-ing' is commonly replaced by '-in' [-ɪŋ > -ɪn] at all levels of speech throughout the Caribbean.

(v) Similarly the pronunciation of '-th-' in all positions, whether voiced SE [ð] or unvoiced [θ] is commonly rendered as /d/ or /t/; occasionally (as in Barbados) [θ] is replaced by /f/; and, also in Barbados, the SE sound [ž] (as in *usual, treasure, occasion*, etc.) rendered as [ǰ].

(vi) Pre-consonantal /r/ (as in *hard, word, organ, bird*, etc.) and final /r/ as in *car, hear, fire*, etc. are always pronounced in middle-level and usually in upper-level speech in Guyana, Barbados, Jamaica, Belize and many other territories, but not in Trinidad, St Vincent and most other Eastern Caribbean islands.

(vii) The sound /h/, especially in initial position, is lost noticeably in Jamaica, even in the speech of educated persons, whence *(h)im, (h)ave, (h)ow, (h)ard*, etc.; and it also occurs in nonstandard pronunciations— *(h)argue, (h)ice, (h)oil*, etc.—among the same speakers.

Recognition of these variations has necessarily received limited representation in the Dictionary not simply because of constraints of space but more because the gathering of sufficient and accurate information on their distribution and on many other sociolinguistic phonological variations was not possible in the circumstances of my data-collection. It is a rich field for research in historical linguistics and in phonology.

Word-form

Two features account for most of the word-form developments in CE—the Creole discomfort with consonant clusters, especially final consonant clusters (symbolized in this book as /-cc/) which persists through the mesolectal levels of speech, and a basic Creole economy of expression which maximizes the use of the stock of vocabulary, principally by the device of functional shift or 'conversion'.

Final consonant clusters are often reduced, so affecting the tensed endings of verbs, as will often be noted in the following

- *He beg for one, she say no, and he kill the vine*
- *I ask the man why he skin up the table and he ask me who I talking to;* etc.

The feature also affects pluralization in several ways, principally by the absence of the pluralizing phonemes /-s/ /-z/ in the names of foods, fruits, birds, animals, etc.; hence

- *some* **bake**, *plenty* **plantain** *and* **banana**, *a flock of* **powis**, *two* **manicou**, etc.

See the special article on PLURALS as an entry in the Dictionary.

By the grammatical device known as functional shift, words are converted, at all levels of CE, in part-of-speech and sense. This multiplies considerably the coverage of its vocabulary as will appear much, but by no means fully inventoried, in both entries and citations; many adjectives function as adverbs (**good, bad, safe, funny, careful**, etc. for *well, badly, safely, carefully*, etc.); nouns, adjectives, ideophones function as verbs (to **rice** somebody, to **sweet** somebody, to **vups** past somebody, etc.); and the reverse also occurs, verb or adjective functioning as noun (to like plenty **eat**, a real **stupidy**, etc.), verb or noun as adjective (a big **eat** man, **obeah** people, etc.). This well-known linguistic feature is such a strongly marked characteristic of CE that it has been necessary to represent it distinctively in the Dictionary by superscript marking of separated entries, for example **bad**[1] adj, **bad**[2] adv, **bad**[3] n, **sweet**[1] adj, **sweet**[2] adv, **sweet**[3] vb tr, etc.

Phrasing

The putting together of words in an organized way, the grammatical feature known as syntax, is for most people the core, and for many the whole of what is generally meant by 'grammar'. For these many, English grammar is determined in England, distorted in America and destroyed in Caribbean talk. Leaving that argument on one side and taking 'grammar' to be nothing more or less than the set of principles and conventions by which a language operates, one can consider rationally the grammar of CE. In so doing, one must recall that Caribbean literature, despite its enormous output after World War II, played no part up to 1940 in the organized development of the regional features of CE which are the concern of this Dictionary. Consequently, unsettled structures proliferate today from the basic level of spelling through to word-order and idiomatic phrasing.

A large subject, therefore, the matter of the Grammar of CE has been cut down here to a few notices to facilitate the user's understanding of this Dictionary.

(i) The case forms of pronominal forms are treated as separate entries to allow for treatment of a number of functions and features not relatable to case; hence—

I, me, my, my own, mine(s), meself/myself,
he, him, his, his own, heself/himself,
they, them, their, theyself/themself/theirself/themselves, etc.

are headwords, sometimes with related idiomatic phrases.

(ii) Similarly most parts of 'operator' verbs are made separate entries since they have developed semantic and idiomatic functions independent of their base verbs; hence—

be, am, is, are, ain't, was, were, been, being,
do, does, don't, did, done,
have, has, had,
go, going, gone,
can, can't, could/could-a,
will, would/would-a,
must, must be/mussy

are all headwords, with related idiomatic phrases where appropriate.

(iii) With few exceptions transitive verbs *in their base forms* can signal either the active or the passive voice, according to the semantic context.

So **eat** means 'has/had been eaten' in the CE sentence *All the bread eat already*. See the article on PASSIVITY as an entry in the Dictionary.

(iv) At the mesolectal level questions are always asked without subject–verb inversion, i.e. by imposing a question tone on the declarative word order; hence CE *You going back? You went back?* would mean 'Are you going back? Did you go back?' This inquiry word-order is a Creole economy that reaches through to the acrolect, and will also be found in evidence in the citations in the Dictionary.

(v) Intensity of expression is characteristic of CE and is in evidence in many ways, perhaps principally in reduplicated forms—*big big big*, *stupid stupid*, *fraidy-fraidy*, etc., or by repetition of whole phrases or sentences. This characteristic must be taken for granted, reduplicated forms only being listed in the Dictionary in special cases—**bassa-bassa** (n), **fool-fool** (adj), etc.

(vi) Another common if milder form of intensifying one's expression in Caribbean English is a phrasing device known as fronting, focusing, front-focusing, front-shifting or sometimes predicate-clefting (the number of names indicating the widespread notice that this feature has attracted in the study of many Creoles with African linguistic linkages). By this device the main verb of a short utterance is introduced and stressed at the beginning of a short statement in which it is going to recur in normal position, thus adding impact to its use. Exs.: *Is write that little boy write and tell de fader,* 'That boy, though only a boy, actually wrote and told the father'; *She ain['t] buy no new dress. Is borrow she borrow it,* 'She didn't buy that dress, new though it looked. She actually borrowed it!' This can be done also with nouns: *Is five dollars I hear you say five dollars?* 'Did I really hear you say five dollars or do my ears deceive me?'

(vii) In language study, an idiomatic phrase is generally understood to be a lexical entry in itself such that its meaning is not detectable from the separate meanings of the words that compose it. Exs.: SE *not one's cup of tea, keep one's pecker up*, etc., AmE *get to first base, give someone the runaround* etc. Whereas there are also many culture-specific phrases in CE, its character is not adequately represented by them but by a larger body of expressions which are peculiar to Caribbean talk but not necessarily unanalysable (as idioms are expected to be). Thus, for example, **cut your eye at somebody**, **suck your teeth, be behind somebody like a slave-driver, pick up your foot and run** may all convey their meanings readily enough to an outsider but without yielding the emotive intensity carried by each of them successively—contempt, disgust, annoyance, fright. Even more straight-forward in meaning are expressions like **the rain has held up, to tell you the truth, go along your way, till you can't see** etc. but the last three for example are used in CE in contexts of uncertainty, caution, and violence respectively in a way unlikely in SE. Accordingly a large number of phrases are recorded in this Dictionary, because they distinguish the texture of Caribbean talk from that of British spoken SE, an idiomatic phrase being here regarded as a way of putting things that bears a socio-historical connotation particular or peculiar to the Caribbean without reference to its analysableness.

Further, it will be noticed, in the examples of CE idiom just cited, that they are structured with the pronouns *you, your, somebody*, instead of the lexicographically conventional *one, one's, someone*, which do appear in the British and American examples that precede them. This is because the SE impersonal pronoun *one* is so alien to the texture of CE that its use would immediately be received, whether in speech or writing, as comically hyper-acrolectal. Indeed, in modern linguistic terms, its 'grammaticality' in CE could fairly be questioned. It is a safe prediction that no Caribbean speaker would say or write **to cut one's eye at someone, *to suck one's teeth, *be behind someone like a slave-driver, *pick up one's foot and run, *go along one's way, *till one can't see*, etc. except for sheer entertainment. CE is characteristically direct and personal communication; therefore it is taken as required policy in this book to represent all idiomatic phrases using the pronouns *you, your, somebody* (abbr *sb*) in realizing the texture of the language that is here being catalogued. Similarly the preference in CE for the concrete to the abstract determines that expressions such as *the rain is falling, the rain has held up/stopped, the rain is going to come*, etc. are the norm rather than the abstract or 'dummy' SE phrases *it's raining, it's stopped raining, there's going to be rain* etc. Accordingly *rain*-subject and other like phrases are listed as idiomatic in this Dictionary. Etymological explanations often show such phrasing to be paralleled in African languages or in Irish or English dialectal structures.

Vocabulary

The vocabulary of Caribbean English comprises the whole active *core vocabulary of World English* as may be found in any piece of modern English literature, together with all *Caribbean regionalisms produced by the ecology, history and culture* of the area.

The sources of the regionalisms, with some examples, are as follows:

Amerindian survivals: cashew, guava, manioc, mauby, etc.
African survivals: Anancy, bakra, cut-eye, dokunu, hard-ears, your mouth got no cover, etc.
Archaic English: learn (=teach), proven, stupidness, tinnen, etc.
British dialects: cuffuffle, feg, hard, moffrey, etc.

The Bible and the Book of Common Prayer: [a]noint, beforetime, bounden duty, whosoever, etc.

Creole influence: all-you, massa, oonoo, pickney, etc.

Dutch influence: grabble, koker, mauger, stelling, etc.

French influence: crapaud, diablesse, morne, palette, etc.

French Creole influence: J'ouvert, mauvais-langue, z'affaire, z'herbe-à-femme, etc.

Portuguese influence: bacalao, farine, mustee, mulatto, ole yard, etc.

Spanish influence: avocado, boledo, mamaguy, parang, zapats, etc.

Indic influence: douglah, pelau, roti, sari, sindoor, etc.

Chinese influence: che-fa, whe-whe, washikongs, etc.

American influence: drugstore, guys, kids, truck, etc.

Whereas many of the loans from European languages are obviously settled 'corruptions' (ex.: **ole yard** (Guyn) < Pg *olhado* 'evil eye') the matter of the French Creole loans is problematic. Not only are they often borrowed from the French Creole language that is still fully functioning in its own right in St Lucia and Dominica, but more significantly they are, as spelled in the examples in the list above, morphologically not French. For example, French would be *mauvaise langue* (f.) 'bad language' whereas the Trinidadian term is not only differently pronounced but means **bad-talk**, and is used as noun, adjective and verb. Scholars in St Lucia, Dominica, Trinidad and Martinique, and two related research organizations the *Mouvman Kwéyòl Sent Lisi* (StLu) and the *Konmité Pou Etid Kwéyòl* (Dmca) have therefore together provided a phonemically rationalized orthography for the Creole language of these islands. It is given in *The Handbook for Writing Creole* and is used, as the recommended system, in this Dictionary. However, for the ease of the uninitiated reader, the popularized forms are always listed and the reader there referred to the systematized spellings where the item of vocabulary is fully treated; hence, for example, the seeker of **mauvais-langue** is referred to **mové-lang** for all information on that item.

A further point is that the regionalisms of CE have been diffused in the area by various circumstances and therefore unevenly. A popular Trinidadian calypso can take one or other folk term like **mové-lang**, **mamaguy**, **kongkongsa** to any other territory and there introduce or animate its use. To a lesser extent migration, increased inter-island huckstering, the media etc. have accounted for the unpredictable spread of otherwise island-specific terms. Accordingly, although each entry-item, whether word or phrase, has been labelled with the territory or territories to which it belongs according to the data collected, such labels are not to be taken as restrictive. Contrariwise, an entry-item labelled as *CarA* (Caribbean) is not to be taken as being in use in all, perhaps not even in most Caribbean territories, but rather in too many to list conveniently. In general, whenever an entry-item has been found to be assignable to six or more territories it has been labelled *CarA* or, if it appears to have no occurrence in Jamaica, The Bahamas or Belize, it has been labelled *ECar* (Eastern Caribbean).

Lastly, it is very important to note that *in the same territory* a referent (that is, the actual thing or idea denoted by the entry-item) has more than one 'name' or designation. For example, the bush called **cerasee** in *Bdos* is also there called **miraculous bush** and **sersee(-bush)**. This happens mostly with folk-names of plants, but multi-designation is a fairly widespread feature of CE. David De Camp once mapped twenty-one different names for one type of cutlass and thirty for another (some names overlapping) in Jamaica (see *Creole Language Studies II*, Macmillan, 1961, pp. 70, 75).

Whereas this Dictionary by no means accommodates such enormous variety, it does accommodate small sets, reliably reported, as in the case of **cerasee** cited above. However, the recurrence of multi-designation as a feature in many territories introduces the real hazard that the entry-item chosen as designation in this Dictionary may be 'right' for some but 'wrong' for other nationals of the same territory who know it to be applied to something different. In such cases, for items of flora the safest check for authentication is the taxonomic identification given within the entry. In other cases a careful reading of the descriptive gloss should help. In all cases of unsatisfactory resolution of queries, however, the reader would do a great service to the improvement of Caribbean lexicography by sending useful information, even if only in the nature of the query, to the Director of the Project.

Etymology

The list of sources of the lexicon of CE illustrated in the foregoing section will serve to demonstrate the huge dimensions of the etymological underground of CE. The problem has been referred to in the Introduction, and lists of consultants and informants in foreign languages have been given in the Acknowledgements. The various sources of the rest of the information are cited at the ends of entries.

In regard to British dialects a list, with abbreviations as used in Wright's *English Dialect Dictionary*, is given on a later page. The list is evidence of a considerable spread of possible British dialectal influence but nothing more precise than that. The reference to one, two or several British counties in an etymological note must be taken as evidence of possible linkages, not as proof of direct sources. Perhaps that should be obvious when several counties are named for one etymon.

The same applies a fortiori to references to African languages. The spread of languages referred to, and usually preceded by *Cp* ('Compare'), from Senegambian *Wolof* in the far west to Zimbabwean *Shona* and Mozambican *Tsonga* in the far south, is evidence of great meaning for the human history and culture of both Africa and the Caribbean, and the cases should be seen as pointers—and I hope sound ones—for linguistic as well as historical follow-up, but should not be taken as proof of 'direct line of descent'. There will be, of course, some exceptions where the coincidence of phonic and semantic and historical factors amounts to proof. Examples of such cases are **bakra** from Efik, **kongkongsa** from Twi, **susu** from Yoruba, etc. To help the reader locate the African languages referred to in this book an end-paper map is provided. In preparing it I drew upon information provided in the introductions to many of the grammars and dictionaries of African languages which I consulted, and I was further helped by consulting M. Mann and D. Dalby's *A Thesaurus of African Languages* (Hans Zell, 1987).

'Standard', 'Accepted', 'Formal'

The term 'standard' strongly implies fixed objective measurement, as in relation to weights and measures. It is therefore bound to be problematic in application to a living language, for in such a case (*a*) relatively little can be unquestionably fixed, and (*b*) the determination and judgement of what is to be measured and by what criteria are all ultimately subjective matters. Up to the reign of King George V, however, there was no problem for English, because there was no question as to who or what was 'correct'. H. C. Wyld (*A History of Modern Colloquial English*, Blackwell, 1920, pp. 2, 3) simply records that 'the genuine article' is a *'class dialect'*, set by 'certain social strata' from 'the great [English] public schools', and this he calls Received Standard English, all other homeland British 'offshoots' being of a lesser breed. ('Received' implied 'as received at Court', leading to the term later adopted, *Received Pronunciation* (RP).)

In such a setting North American English, if mentionable, was below the salt, Australian English 'in waiting' at the table, and the native speech of the Caribbean a kitchen variety, if English at all. War and dollars, however, causing a marked rise in social and political fairplay from 1945 onward, élitism was replaced by acceptability, so immediately changing the framework in which Standard English must be defined: language is essentially a social act. Furthermore, whereas social factors had largely limited considerations so far to speech, the previously unnoticed truth, namely that Spoken Standard and Written Standard are not the same, now had to be recognized and accommodated within a definition: Commonwealth literatures, among them notably African, Indian and Caribbean, now asserted themselves finding, even more than acceptance, acclaim in England, and making old pedagogical rigidity regarding 'grammar' untenable.

R. Quirk (*The Use of English*, Longman, 1962, p. 99) defines Standard English as 'that kind of English which draws least attention to itself over the widest area and through the widest range of usage' and he adds (p. 100) 'it is particularly associated with English in a *written* form'. The *Oxford English Dictionary* (2nd edn. 1989) defines Standard English as 'that variety of a spoken or written language of a country or other linguistic area which is generally considered the most correct and acceptable form, as *Standard English, American,* etc.'

Both these definitions completely reject élitism, both are cautiously levelling in social terms and markedly lacking in restrictiveness. They do not harness pronunciation to the speech of any particular group, but rather attempt to harness the structure of what is written. Their emphasis is on *a kind of averageness* including, one may reasonably assume, average elegance in the form of simplicity, clarity and correctness of structure. The problem is that these and similar propositions evidently try but fail to escape value judgements wholly, the only conclusion that unquestionably follows from them being the admission that there are several brands of Standard English in the world—British SE, American SE, Canadian SE, Caribbean SE, Australian SE, etc. from which it must also unquestionably follow that each brand must share a substantial part of a core that is accepted as World English. It is proposed here to call the whole such core *Internationally Accepted English* (IAE) (adopting a label already in use by some Caribbean linguists). That may be further clarified by defining **English** as follows:

> **English** *is the language developed out of Anglo-Saxon by the people of England whence it spread since the early seventeenth century to become the common native or primary language of many nations and races distributed in every continent on earth. It is an analytic language with a morphology strongly characterized by adaptive features, the sense of any continuous utterance being governed by and dependent on a strong traditional word-order (subject + verb + complement) as its international structural base, which can accommodate a number of distinctive national features at all linguistic levels, chiefly in the field of lexicon.*

In this book the abbreviation IAE refers to the core of English clinically defined as above, while the abbreviation SE refers in general to British SE, or, as some British linguists have more carefully identified it, 'the Standard Dialect of English'.

British SE, it must be further understood, while contributing more than any other SE to the core IAE, does not cover the whole of it. For example American SE *drugstore, gas station, billion* ('a thousand million') are IAE while parallel British SE forms *chemist's, petrol pump, billion* ('a million million') hardly belong there. On the other hand British SE extends well beyond the core IAE in the particularities of its idiom and cultural labelling. For example *to have had it, to be quids in, to keep one's pecker up* in spite of *being sent down*, are good British SE but beyond the embrace of IAE.

Within the same framework of reasoning Caribbean SE has also contributed notably, if quantitatively less, to the lexicon of the core IAE while having a very large body of regionalisms which have not entered that core. These regionalisms have the unique status of belonging to a conglomerate of several Standard Englishes, those of the nations and states of the former British West Indian colonies—of Barbadian SE, Jamaican SE, Guyanese SE, Trinidadian SE, etc. That conglomerate is *Caribbean Standard English.*

However, a problem still remains which the Caribbean situation highlights. It is most important to note that the terms used above all refer to national Standard Englishes, not to Standard national Englishes. The latter represents a different notion and presents difficulties. A Standard national English would certainly 'attract less attention to itself' (using Quirk's definition) within its own borders, but is likely to do quite the reverse anywhere else. The Barbadian who says *'Why wunna don[']t go [a]long and behave wunnaself?'* or writes *'Bajans did not expense themselves to go to the test match because they feel Barbados was unfaired by the selectors'* is using general, regular, *accepted* and accordingly *standard* Barbadian structures, but they would not be accepted as Formal even in Barbados. The *Formal Barbadian* (or Barbadian Standard English) equivalents would be *'Why don't you-all go along and behave yourselves?'* and *'Barbadians did not spend their money to go to the test match because they felt Barbados had been cheated by the selectors.'*

The same kind of distinction applies throughout the conglomerate of Englishes of the Caribbean, and it can hardly be denied that that kind of distinction applies everywhere else in World English too. That is, no doubt, why the terms 'Standard' and 'Accepted' (expanding 'Received') still lead to double standards and usually to controversy. As one grasps for what is non-controversial, for a basic certainty, what seems to emerge is this, that no educated persons will doubt or question whether they are hearing or reading *Formal* English, pronunciation being of least importance, and structure (morphological and syntactic) being almost the total indicator.

In this context and against the background of the content of Caribbean English as outlined in this essay, the conglomerate that is Caribbean Standard English may be defined as follows:

The literate English of educated nationals of Caribbean territories and their spoken English such as is considered natural in formal social contexts. There being many such territories, each with its own recognizable 'standard', Caribbean Standard English would be the total body of regional lexicon and usage bound to a common core of syntax and morphology shared with Internationally Accepted English, but aurally distinguished as a discrete type by certain phonological features such as a marked levelling of British English diphthongs and a characteristic disconnection of pitch from stress as compared with British and American sound patterns.

In this book the abbreviation CE, for 'Caribbean English', is used in broad reference to that definition.

Levels of Formalness

Now able to avoid arguments about what is 'standard', 'substandard' or 'nonstandard' in CE, we may also avoid the further subjective problems of assigning the controversial, even nebulous labels of 'slang', 'colloquial' to CE usage by recognizing instead a hierarchy of Formalness. With a view to maintaining objectivity, that hierarchy may be rationalized, using four descending levels—*Formal, Informal, Anti-Formal, Erroneous*. The *Anti-formal* level will be further sub-categorized into *Creole, Jocular, Derogatory, Vulgar*. These, being applied to any word, word-form, usage, phrase or other structure, whether spoken or written, are defined as follows:

Term	Abbreviation	Meaning
Formal	[F]	Accepted as educated; belonging or assignable to IAE; also any regionalism which is not replaceable by any other designation. *No personal familiarity is shown when such items are used.*
Informal	[IF]	Accepted as familiar; chosen as part of usually well-structured, casual, relaxed speech, but sometimes characterized by morphological and syntactic reductions of English structure and by other remainder features of decreolization. *Neither inter-personal tenseness nor intimacy is shown when such items are used, and the speaker is usually capable of switching to the upper level when necessary but more easily to the lower. Such forms constitute the bulk of everyday CE.*

Anti-formal	[*AF*]	Deliberately rejecting Formalness; consciously familiar and intimate; part of a wide range from close and friendly through jocular to coarse and vulgar; any Creolized or Creole form or structure surviving or conveniently borrowed to suit context or situation.

When such items are used an absence or a wilful closing of social distance is signalled.

Such forms survive profusely in folk-proverbs and sayings, and are widely written with conjectural spellings in attempts at realistic representations of folk-speech in Caribbean literature.

Erroneous or *Disapproved*	[*X*]	(1) Not permissible as IAE although evidently considered to be so by the user. (*Sparingly chosen as entry-items; only some of the frequent cases that may be encountered are included in the Dictionary to accommodate the seeker after help in usage.*)

Examples of such error are:

born(-ed, -ing) vb tr; *full* vb tr, 'fill'; *regards to* prep phr, 'regardless of'; *snat* n 'snot'; *strive* vb intr, 'thrive', etc.

(2) Disapproved, on stated grounds. Ex.: **ackee** 3.[*X*] = **akee**, indicating that the spelling 'ackee' should not be used as an alternative to the spelling 'akee' since they represent quite different popular fruits.

The sub-categories of the *Anti-formal* level are as follows:

Creole	[*AF-Cr*]	A Creole or Creolized form or structure.
Jocular	[*AF-Joc*]	An inoffensively jocular item.
Derogatory	[*AF-Derog*]	A derogatory or offensive term or phrase.
Vulgar	[*AF-Vul*]	A vulgar, obscene or indecent expression.

With the exception of F, which must be assumed when no label is given, it has been necessary to assign the foregoing abbreviated labels throughout the Dictionary, based upon the author's own judgement as a native Caribbean, but also backed up as much as feasible by the evidence of citations. Wherever the bogey of value judgement has emerged, introducing error, the justified criticism of any observant reader, preferably supported by useful evidence, would be very welcome.

S.R.R.A.
1992

GLOSSARY OF
LINGUISTIC TERMINOLOGY
USED IN THE DICTIONARY

Acrolect(al) [See as Entry-items in the Dictionary]

Affrication The development of the affricative sounds [č], [ǰ] from other sounds, especially in Fr Cr (loan-words). *Exs.* initial consonants in **tjè-bèf; djè** derived from Fr *cœur* + *bœuf; guerre.*
(See also **Palatalization**)

Allonym 'Other name', i.e. an *equivalent* name or term used in another territory. (Cp. 'synonym', which only means 'similar term'.)
Exs. **guinep** (*Guyn, Jmca, etc.*), **akee** (*Bdos, StVn*), **chenette** (*Dmca, StLu, etc.*), **skinip** (*Gren, StKt*) are four allonyms. (See the essay on Caribbean English for more.)

Aphaeresis The loss of one or more sounds or letters at the beginning of a word. *Exs.* **custom** < *accustom*; **cause** < *because*; etc. Hence **aphaeretic**, adj.

Aphesis The loss of a single unaccented vowel at the beginning of a word. *Exs.* **way** (adv) < *away*; **nuff** (**nough**) < *enough*; etc. Hence **aphetic**, adj.

Apocope The loss of a sound or of letters at the end of a word. *Exs.* **draw** < *drawer*; **less** (vb) < *lessen*; etc. Hence **apocopic**, adj.

Apport A word brought into Caribbean English in or nearly in its original form and function from native or immigrant cultures—Amerindian, African, Indic, or Chinese languages, British dialects, Fr Creole. (These are too many to be identified each time in the Dictionary, but they are not 'loans' or 'borrowings' as, for example, so many of the names of CE flora and fauna, such as *gooseberry, periwinkle, sparrow,* etc. are.)

Aspect The nature or kind of action indicated by the *form* of the verb *in a context*. (Cp. 'tense' which indicates the 'time' of the action.) Thus 'he *talks* (all the time)' HABITUAL aspect, 'he *talk-talk* (till I get weary)' ITERATIVE aspect, 'he *done talk*' COMPLETIVE aspect, etc. (It is a vital feature of syntax in African and Caribbean Creole languages.) Hence **aspectual**, adj.

Assimilation The process by which one sound becomes similar to another that is next or near to it by the influence of its proximity. *Ex.* **plimpler** < **pimpler**. Cp. **Dissimilation**.

Back-formation A new word formed by cutting off what sounds or looks like the suffix of another word. *Ex.* **Portuguee** conceived as the sg form of *Portuguese* (which sounds like a pl form). More often a new part-of-speech is the result: *Ex.* **pork-knocking** as verbal from **pork-knocker**, n., which seems to be based on 'to pork-knock' vb.

Basilect(al) [See as Entry-items in the Dictionary]

Blend The deliberate telescoping or overlapping of two words to form a new one which combines the meanings of the original two. *Exs.* **apartel** < *apart(ment)* + *(ho)tel*; **blam** < *bang* + *slam*.

Calque A copy-translation into another language (in this case into Creole or Creolized English) of a word or phrase from an original language (in this case an African, Indic or European foreign language). *Exs.* CE **foot-bottom** 'sole of the foot', cp Twi *naŋ-ase* (*naŋ* 'foot' + *ase* 'bottom') 'sole of the foot'; CE *How many years you have?* 'How old are you?' (*Dmca, StLu*), cp. Fr *Quel âge avez-vous?* Hence **calquing**, the process of copy translating in this manner in the development of CE.

Catachresis An error in the use of a word or phrase. *Exs.* **censor** (vb) instead of *censure* vb; **on a whole** adv phr ... *on the whole*; **a number of them was** ... *a number of them were*, etc. Hence **catachrestic**, adj.

Consonant Cluster, abbr /cc/. A group of two, three or more consonants initially (/cc-/ as in *strong*), medially (/-cc-/ as in *gentl(e)man*) or finally (/-cc/ as in *first*). (These are often reduced at the lower levels of CE, producing forms like 'trang', 'ge[m]man' 'fus'.)

Decreolization The process of development of people's speech over a period of time from basic Creole (basilectal) structures such as /mi na waan fo tek non/ through *A ain['t] wan[t] take none* towards *I don't want to take any.*

Denasalization The loss of a nasal phoneme or sound in a word, or the replacement of that sound by a non-nasal vowel. *Exs.* (the festival) Hos*ein* > **Hosay**; Fr chard*on* béni > **shadow-benny**.

Dissimilation The process by which two sounds, in the same word, that have some similarity in their articulation, prompt a change in one of them. *Exs.* Feb*r*uary > /febyuweri/; gue*st*s > /gesiz/. Cp. **Assimilation**.

Enclitic (particle)	A shortened form that has its own syntactic function, but is affixed or 'tacked on' to the end of a word. *Ex.* the **-a** in **coulda, couldna, gonna** (could *have*, could *not have*, going *to*). Cp. **Proclitic (particle)**.
Epenthesis	The insertion of a sound in a word to make it easier (for a particular kind of speaker) to pronounce. *Exs.* 'athaletic' < athletic'; **Kittitian** < 'Kittsian'; **tambran** < 'tamarind'; etc. Hence **epenthetic**, adj.
Etymon, pl Etyma	The earliest identifiable origin of a word. *Ex.* The etymon of **backra** is (Efik) *mbakara* (*all* + *master*) 'white men generally'. An account of the development of meaning and function from the etymon to the present form and usage of a word is its **etymology**. Hence **etymological**, adj.
False Refinement	A pronunciation or a form of word or phrase which has been erroneously altered so as to sound refined, in the estimation of a particular speaker or group of speakers. *Exs.* 'laugh', 'aunt' pronounced 'loff', 'ont'; the fish **kurass** (< Arawak *koraso*) spelled *cuirass* to resemble a Br SE word; **molly** (*Guyn*) < Hin *maali*; etc. See also **Overcorrection**.
Homograph	One of two or more words that are identical in spelling but not in meaning and not necessarily in sound. *Exs.* **bass** 'boss', **bass** 'a kind of fish', **bass** (pronunc 'base') 'a boom-pan'; **Dominican** /ɪ'ɪ2ɪ/, a native of Dominica, **Dominican** /ɪ2'2ɪ/, a native of Santo Domingo.
Homonym	One of two or more words that are identical in sound and spelling (whether or not capitalized) but not in meaning or origin. *Exs.* **mash** vb 'to step on', **Mash!** vb (< Fr *marche*) 'Go away!', **Mash** n abbr of **Mashramani**.
Homophone	One of two or more words that are identical in sound but not in meaning or origin and often not in spelling. *Exs.* **ackee** (*Jmca*), **akee** (*Bdos*)—different fruits; **susu** n (*Trin*); **susu** vb (*Jmca*), etc.
Hypocorism	A name, word-form or phrase used to express affection or endearment. Hence **hypocoristic**, adj.
Ideophone	[See the article ECHOIC WORDS as an Entry-item in the Dictionary]
Mesolect(al)	[See as Entry-items in the Dictionary]
Metanalysis or **Misplaced Juncture**	A faulty division of sounds in a word, or between consecutive words, causing a new word to be produced. *Exs.* **Anancy** (< Twi *ananse*) becomes **a Nancy** and thence **Nancy**; from the Fr pl *des avocats* [dezavoka] comes a Fr Cr sg *yon* **zaboca**; etc.
Metathesis	The transposition of the order of sounds in a word. *Exs.* **aks** < *ask*; 'voilin', 'voilence' < 'violin', 'violence'.

lx

Metonymy The (metaphorical) substitution of an item for something greater to which it is related. *Exs.* (SE) the *Crown* for 'the Queen' or 'the State'; CE **rice** for 'support' (i.e. provision of rice as food).

Misascription A wider term than SE *malapropism*, it is the ascribing or application of the wrong sense or use or grammatical function to an SE word through ignorance. *Exs. refuge* 'garbage' (for 'refuse'); *to loose* as a spelling for 'to lose'; *to lay down* for 'to lie down', etc.

Misplaced Juncture See **Metanalysis**

Nasalization The rendering of a sound, a word or a stream of speech audibly 'through the nose'. An utterance so rendered is said to be **nasalized**.

Overcorrection The conscious but erroneous adjustment of the pronunciation or form or choice of a word or phrase in order to avoid what is thought to be wrong but is actually right. *Exs.* Saying 'B*o*rbados isn't l*o*rge' for 'B*a*rbados isn't l*a*rge'; All are welcom*ed*; it couldn't happen at a w*o*rst time; etc. See also **False Refinement**.

Overlap(ping) The blending or telescoping of two correct idiomatic structures or phrases to produce an incorrect one. *Exs. in regard to + as regards >* **in regards to**; *with a view to + in (the) view of >* **with the view of**.

Palatalization The development or introduction of the sound /-y-/ or /-i-/ between any of the consonants /p, t, k, d, g/ and a following vowel. *Exs.* /kyart/ 'cart'; /gyardn/ 'garden'. Also the development of the sounds [č] [ɉ] from other sounds in certain contexts. *Exs.* [ču·n] 'tune'; Fr Cr **djab** [ɉab] < Fr *diable* (see **Affrication**).

Paragoge The addition of a sound or letter to the end of a word for no obvious reason. *Exs.* outlawd*ed*, becaus*en*, Dad*s*, etc. Hence **paragogic**, adj.

Proclitic (particle) A shortened form that has its own syntactic function, but is affixed to the beginning of a word. *Ex.* the **a-** of **a-we, a-yo[u]**; or **a-go, a-see**, etc. for all-we, all-you; (be) go*ing*, (be) see*ing*, etc.

Prop Complement A complement added to a verb to strengthen its meaning or render this obvious. *Exs.* 'to bathe/wash *your skin*'; 'to hold *a mind* that sth is so'.

Prosthesis The addition of a sound or syllable at the beginning of a word to make it easier to pronounce (for a particular kind of speaker). *Exs. nuse, nusual* (Bdos) 'use, usual'; *scrush, spliers* (Belz) 'crush, pliers'; *hice, hoil* (Jmca) 'ice, oil', etc. Hence **prosthetic**, adj.

Reduplication The repetition of a part or (more usually in CE) the whole of a word or phrase to indicate various kinds of emphasis. *Exs. big, big, big* 'very big'; *stupid stupid* 'very stupid'; *sof[t]y-sof[t]y* 'soft in many spots'; *Don[t] bother, don[t] bother, don[t] bother, you hear! Don[t] bother!*

Some CE nouns manifesting reduplication survive from African languages: **bassa-bassa, putta-putta, shack-shack**, etc.

Referent
The actual thing, notion or idea that a word or phrase refers to. Hence the referent of *chair* is the actual piece of furniture one sits on; the referent of the noun **hard-ears** is the actual behaviour one sees manifested by a person having that habit; etc.

Reinforcement
The convergence or near coincidence in both sense and sound of two possible but different sources of a Creole or CE word, such that either source may have reinforced or helped the other in developing the sense and usage of that word in present CE. *Ex.* (16c. Eng) *cuff* vb 'to strike, to buffet' + (Twi) *Kofi*, a common West African male name, whence CE **Cuffy**, symbolic name of a Black man who is not to be trifled with.

Semantic Shift
A change in the sense and/or usage of a word induced by its association with a particular context. *Exs.* **culvert** (a water passage) > 'bridge'; **koker** (a drainage device) > 'sluice'.

Synecdoche
The substitution of a part for the whole (*Ex.* **a wheel** for 'a bicycle') or the whole for a part (*Ex.* **the law** for 'a policeman').

EXPLANATORY NOTES

TERMS IN USE

An **Entry** is the entire set of information about an item; that is to say from the alphabetically listed item itself through all its senses, sub-senses, citations, phrases, etymological and usage notes.

An **Entry-item** is a Headword at the beginning of an Entry, or Phrase (usually numbered) within the Entry.

A **Superscript numeral** is a small raised number at the end of a Headword to distinguish it from its homograph used in another function or sense. Exs. the numbers 1, 2, 3 in **bad¹** adj, **bad²** adv, **bad³** n, or **mash¹** vb tr, **mash²** imper vb, **Mash³** n.

An **Allonym** is 'another name' for the same item (whether fruit, bird, idiom, etc.) used somewhere else (in another or the same territory). All allonyms are exact 'equivalents' and, for convenience, the definition is given only once, at one of them, and this one is referred to as the **Primary Allonym**, and the other(s) as the **Secondary Allonym(s)**. Secondary allonyms are each referred to the Primary for their definition.

KINDS OF ENTRY-ITEM

(1) A **Headword** is at the head of the Entry which deals fully with that item, its position in the items listed in the Dictionary being determined by alphabetical order. As a general rule Headwords which are 'noun + noun' compounds are hyphenated, whereas 'adjective + noun' compounds are in general not hyphenated but treated as noun phrases. Exs. **can-cup, candle-fly, cane-arrow**, etc. are nouns whereas **white cedar, white eddoe, white gaulin**, etc. are noun phrases.

There are, however, exceptions. 'Adjective + noun' compound Headwords are hyphenated in cases where the adjective element is more nearly a bound constituent than a mere qualifier. CE speakers will recognize such cases as usually dominated by the folk-level /1′2/ pitch pattern. Exs. **bad-cow, bad-belly, bad-eye**, etc.; **sweet-eye, sweet-man, sweet-mouth**, etc. The same principle applies when such compounds are qualifiers in a phrasal Headword. Exs. **black-belly sheep, flat-hand dildo, green-back turtle**.

The *listed form of the Headword* is the form morphologically preferred in this Dictionary although the form(s) seen in the citation(s) may differ either as to spelling or hyphenation.

(2) A **Headword with superscript numeral** is one of two or more Headwords with the same spelling, even if differentiated by hyphenation or upper case.

(3) A **Variant Form** is given in brackets immediately after the Headword. Variant Forms are separated by commas.

Exs. **gui.nep (ge.nip, gi.nep)**.

The Headword first given is the preferred form recommended in this Dictionary. Variant Forms are usually listed in alphabetical sequence, no order of preference being indicated.

(4) A **Headword** with one or more letters **in parentheses** is an item for which more than one spelling has been found. It may be spelled with or without the bracketed letter(s). Thus there are two alternative spellings for each of the items

ca(f).fuf.fle and **cat(t).ha**

and actually four possibilities of each of the items

chi(g).ga(h) and **cob(b)-skin(ned)**

In such cases the user may choose to omit the bracketed letters.

When a part of a compound item is bracketed, the indication is, similarly, that the item occurs in two alternative forms, with or without the bracketed element.

Exs. **Cey.lon(-man.go)**
chil.lum(-pipe)
chen.ille (plant)

(5) A Headword or any component of a Phrase with one or more letters **in square brackets** is listed in the same alphabetical position as if the letter(s) were not bracketed. The bracketed letter(s) must, however, be understood to be omitted in pronouncing the Entry-item (as the IPA representation will show).

The bracketed letters are used instead of the conventional raised comma (') to enable instant visual identification of items characterized by well-known Caribbean vernacular phonemic replacements. (See The Sound in the essay on Caribbean English.)

Exs. **stan[d]-home** *n* (Guyn) [*AF*]
t[h]ief.in[g] *adj* (CarA) [*AF-Cr*]
hard-mout[h] *adj* (Bdos)
[h]im *pron* (Belz, Jmca) [*AF-Cr*]

(6) A **Related Form** is a morphologically related form of a Headword which it is found convenient to treat concisely in the same Entry. Related Forms are separated from the Headword by semi-colons, without brackets. Exs. (i) **ab.hor** vb tr; **abhor.ring** vb tr; **ab.hor.rent** adj; (ii) **bad.der**; **bad.dest** adj

(7) A **Phrase** is any sequence of words one of which is the Headword in whose Entry it is listed. Each Phrase is listed within an Entry in alphabetical order and numbered for ready reference. Its syntactic function is also given (adv phr, n phr, vb phr, etc.).

(8) A **French Creole loan-word** is a Headword with a spelling standardized as represented in the *Handbook for Writing Creole* (1983) of the Mouvman Kwéyòl Sent Lisi. Such spelling being new to most readers, the popular form is both entered after it as a Variant and also separately entered in its own right, but cross-referenced to the standardized form where the full Entry is given.

Thus, for example: '**mové-lang (mauvais-langue)**', and another '**mauvais-langue. See mové-lang**'.

(9) An **Acronym** or an **Abbreviation** (in block capitals) refers to a Caribbean institution, or identifies a National Honour. (Such as refer only to local political, union, commercial, or other organizations are omitted.)

(10) A **Special Article** is one dealing with a special feature of CE. There are four such, each in block capitals: ECHOIC WORDS, NAMES OF NATIVES, PASSIVITY, PLURALS.

ORDERING OF AN ENTRY

An Entry is ordered in the following sequence.

1. The **Headword**, with syllabic divisions marked by dots to facilitate pronunciation. The system of syllabication adopted is that used in *Webster's Ninth Collegiate Dictionary* (*WCD9*). Exs. **ba.li.si.er, ta.u.ro.ni.ro**

Related Forms, if any, are listed in sequence after the Headword, without brackets, separated by semi-colons.

2. The **Variant Form(s)** in brackets, immediately after the Headword, and also with syllabic divisions marked. Exs. (**ba.li.zi.er, ba.li.zyé**); (**ta.u.ra.ne.ro**).

3. The **Pronunciation**, in square brackets, given in International Phonetic Association (IPA) symbols as modified by American linguists. (See list.) Variant pronunciations are indicated within the same brackets, each preceded by a swung dash ($\sim$). In some cases **Stress** is marked within such Pronunciation, as main (a high-set mark '), strong (double high-set mark '') or rarely, secondary (a low-set mark ‚).

4. In many cases the **Pitch-contour** or **Tone-pattern** of a Headword is indicated immediately after the Headword or its Pronunciation using a system of digits between slashes. The digits 1, 2, 3, 4 represent gradations from low to high as a matter of convenience (but CE speech can use a much wider range, from lower- to high-pitched in some contexts and these are omitted in this book). **Main Stress** is marked by accenting one digit. (It will be noted that the Main Stress often does not coincide with the highest pitch.) Exs. **alms-house shoes** /2′31/; **ta.u.ro.ni.ro** /1′1121/; **advantageous** /12′21/; **Au.gust-flow-er** /1′122/.

The commonest CE contour or pattern for disyllables is /1′2/ and for trisyllables /1′12/, and accordingly these are usually not indicated. Cases where Pitch-contour differentiates meaning are always indicated, sometimes with an added Usage Note. Exs. CE **bad-eye** /1′2′/ vs IAE *bad eye* /2′1/; CE **one-time** /1′1/ vs /1′2/ vs /3′1/.

5. **Part-of-Speech** or **Syntactic Function**

5.1 This, given in italics, may be a simple standard abbreviation such as *n*, *adj*, *adv*, etc. (noun, adjective, adverb, etc.) for a one-word Entry-item. A hyphenated compound is one word. If it comprises more than one word, the item is labelled *n phr*, *adj phr*, *adv phr*, etc.

Exs. **all**² *pron*
  all and all *pron phr*
  ad.van.tage-tak.er *n*
  af.fou yam *n phr*

5.2 In many cases, however, the **Syntactic Function** needs a descriptive label because of important differences of structure and usage between CE and Br SE, on which the concepts of syntactic function are based. Such labelling is sometimes put in explanatory form in square brackets.

Exs. **a**¹¹ *proclitic vbl particle*
  afòs (ah fuss, first) *excl adv*
  all³ *adv intensifier (passing into this function, in many phrs, from adj* **all**¹*)*
  is¹ **2. (ii)** [Unstressed interrog, introducing an emphatic question].

6. Abbreviated **Territorial Label(s)** identifying the place(s) in which the Entry-item is current. (See list of Abbreviations.)

Exs. (Angu) or (Bdos, Guyn) etc.
When the item may apply to six or more territories of the Caribbean area it is usually given the general label (CarA). When its range does not, according to available data, appear to include *Jmca*, *Baha*, *Belz*, and *CayI*, but includes a number of Eastern Caribbean territories, it is labelled (ECar).

7. The **Status Label** is abbreviated in square brackets immediately after the Territorial label. It indicates the level of Formalness with which the item is associated in the place(s) with which it is identified. (See the section on Formalness in the preceding essay on Caribbean English.) Exs. [*IF*], [*AF-Cr*], [*Vul*], etc. In cases of

flexibility or range of status a double indication is given. Exs. [*IF/AF*], [*AF/IF*], [*AF-Joc/Derog*].

8. The **Allonym(s)** are equivalent 'other name(s) or designation(s)' of the Entry-item as occurring in other territories. Each allonym in a set is preceded by two thin vertical bars and followed by its place(s) of occurrence. Exs. ‖ *asue* (Baha) ‖ *box* (Guyn) ‖ *meeting* (Bdos) ‖ *pardner* (Jmca) ‖ *syndicate* (Belz) are the given Allonyms of **susu** (ECar). For convenience, they are given together as a set only once, at the entry for **susu**, and there printed in bold italic. They are Secondary Allonyms to *susu*. In each, as Entry-items, they are referred to ‖SUSU (so printed) for their Gloss, *susu* being used as Primary Allonym. (See the section on Cross-Referencing at the end of these Notes.)

9. The **Subject Label**, where necessary, is given in square brackets immediately before the Gloss. It identifies the context of the Gloss and may be of many categories—[Hist], [Banana Ind], [Sugar Ind], [Cricket], etc.

10. The **Gloss** is the 'meaning' or 'sense' of the Entry-item. It is descriptive and often includes semi-encyclopedic information in order to ensure identification of the referent (which may have several Allonyms in the Entry). In the cases of an item of flora or fauna, the full **Taxonomic Identification** is usually included last, in italics, to ensure technical identification also.

When there is more than one Gloss to an Entry-item, they are numbered 1, 2, 3, etc., each Gloss being followed by its own related citation(s).

In some cases there is a need for **Sub-senses** to a numbered Gloss, and Roman numerals are used to number such sub-senses. See, for example, **casha 1. (i)** ... **(ii) ... 2.**, where (i), (ii) are Sub-senses of the first Gloss.

11. The **Illustrative Citation** is a brief *quotation* from a written or oral source illustrating the sense of the Entry-item in context. Each such quotation is followed by a dash and an abbreviated reference to its written source with page number, or to its territorial source if oral.

Exs.—CWFYS:29 (referring to page 29 of a book).

—Peo I.ii p.76 (referring to page 76 of Vol. 1 No. 2 of a periodical or journal).

—AdN (76.10.12,p.4) (referring to page 4 of a newspaper dated 12 October 1976).

—Guyn (Ms) (referring to an excerpt from a handwritten text from a territory).

Etc.

All such abbreviations of reference sources are discrete and are listed alphabetically with full bibliographical information in the Citation Codes for Bibliographical References given in later pages.

Oral sources are indicated by a dash followed by the source territory in brackets. Thus

—(StVn)

means that the speaker of the utterance quoted was in or from St Vincent. When the citation is of an exchange between two speakers, that is indicated by the abbreviations *S1* .../*S2* ...

Citations from oral sources are regularly represented with letters in square brackets; for example

While all de rowin[g] was goin[g] on she jus[t] si[t] do[w]ng in de corner and stan[d] easy. —(*Guyn*)

This device, while indicating that the letters are not registered in the speaker's vernacular pronunciation, facilitates the reader's ready recognition of the words being said.

12. Etymology

Wherever available, information on the linguistic, historical and/or sociological origin or semantic association of an Entry-item is given within square brackets after the Citations or, if no Citation, after the Gloss. The same position applies to Phrases. In many cases particular etymological data or references follow separate Glosses or Phrases.

13. (Usage) Notes

These are preceded by the symbol □ and come last in an Entry. This area is freely used not only to advise on some aspect of Usage but also to refer the reader to any other useful information or related item in the Dictionary.

14. Phrases

14.1 Phrases are listed as a general rule under a separate number, next after all the Glosses have been completed. They are then sub-numbered in a sequence determined by the alphabetical position of the first word in each Phrase. So, for example, in the Entry for **go** *vb intr*, after five different Glosses there is 6. *PHRASES*, thereafter sub-numbered thus

6.1 **able to go with (sb)** *adj phr* (Angu, Mrat, etc.) through to

6.36 **to hell and go** *adv phr* (Guyn)

Sub-senses or different Glosses of the same Phrase are also numbered with Roman numerals. Hence, for example,

6.24 **go on** *vb phr* has four Sub-senses:

(i) (CarA) [*AF*] + Gloss, Citations, etc.

(ii) (Jmca) [*IF*] + Gloss, Citation

(iii) (Guyn,Trin) [*IF*] + Gloss, Citation

(iv) (Jmca) [*AF*] + Gloss, Citation

Further, an extension or slight variation of the same Phrase with a separate sense is given next with an extended sub-number. Hence, for example, next after

6.24 (**go on**) there is

6.24.1 **go on with (sth unpleasant)** *vb phr* (CarA) [*IF*] + Gloss, Citation, etc.

Note, similarly, a common use of this device in

6.34 **go with (sb)** *vb phr* (Jmca, Tbgo, etc.)

6.34.1 **go with (sth)** *vb phr* (CarA)

6.34.2 **Go with that!** *imper vb phr* (Nevs, StKt)

14.2 A Phrase with one or more of its components in **parentheses** must be read as occurring in alternative forms, with or without the bracketed element.

Exs. **give (sb) a child** *vb phr*

making (a) child *vb phr*

every day (as) God send *id phr*

14.3 A Phrase with components separated by a slash must be understood to occur in more than one form, as for example,

cut your eye after/ at/ on sb *vb phr*

drink soup off/ over sb's head *vb phr*

or in more than one context, as for example,

catch jail/ the mad-house/ trouble, etc. *vb phr*

14.4 Every Phrase is labelled according to its Syntactic Function (as will be noted in the examples cited above), most often determined by its syntactic head.

When there is no defining head or the Phrase is a mere statement, it is labelled *id phr* (idiomatic phrase).

Exs. **rain builds** *id phr*
rain holds up *id phr*
Is me and you! *id phr*
It have, etc. *id phr*
Etc.

HOW TO USE THE CROSS-REFERENCING FACILITY

Many Headwords and Phrases are cross-referenced to equivalent Headwords and Phrases which have the same meaning (or referent) but which are used elsewhere in the same territory or more often in another territory. Thus

Ex. 1 **akee (ac.kee)** *n* (Bdos, StLu, StVn) **1.** ‖ GUINEP (CarA)

Ex. 2 **ears-hard** *adj* (Belz) ‖ HARD-EARS (CarA)

Ex. 3 **eat** *vb tr* (CarA) **3.** *PHRASES* **3.1 eat bird-seed** *vb phr* (Guyn) ‖ EAT PARROT (CarA)

In Ex. 1 the noun **akee** (with a variant spelling) is, in sense 1, referred to the Entry for **guinep**, because **guinep** is 'the same thing', i.e. has the same meaning or referent. So the Gloss at **guinep** serves for **akee** *and for several other equivalent names in other territories.* **Guinep** is chosen as the *Primary Allonym* and all other allonyms or *Secondary Allonyms* are listed in sequence at the Entry for **guinep**. The Entry for **akee** while carrying no Gloss may, however, have a Citation and Etymological and Usage Notes related to the name **akee**. It will also be noticed that **akee** is used in three territories whereas its Primary Allonym **guinep** has a wider Caribbean coverage.

In Ex. 2, similarly, the adjective **ears-hard** is referred to **hard-ears**, as the Primary Allonym, for its meaning; but a Citation and Etymological Note are given at the Entry **ears-hard** as particular to that item.

In Ex. 3, a Phrase **eat bird-seed** is referred to another Phrase **eat parrot** as its Primary Allonym. (The Primary Allonym, in this case, happens to be another item in the same Entry, but the Primary Allonym of a Phrase may just as easily have been located in another Entry, as in the case of the preceding Exs. 1 and 2.)

Sometimes, as in Ex. 3, no further information (i.e. no Citation, etc.) is considered necessary beyond the reference to the Primary Allonym.

ABBREVIATIONS

CARIBBEAN TERRITORIES

Angu	Anguilla	Jmca	Jamaica
Antg	Antigua	Mart	Martinique
Baha	Bahamas	Mrat	Montserrat
Bdos	Barbados	Neth	Netherlands Antilles
Belz	Belize	Nevs	Nevis
Berm	Bermuda	Panm	Panama
Brbu	Barbuda	PtRi	Puerto Rico
BrVi	British Virgin Islands	Srnm	Suriname
CarA	Caribbean Area/Region	StDo	Santo Domingo
CayI	Cayman Islands	StKt	St Kitts
Crcu	Carriacou	StLu	St Lucia
Dmca	Dominica	StVn	St Vincent
ECar	East Caribbean	Tbgo	Tobago
FrGy	French Guiana	TkCa	Turks and Caicos
Gren	Grenada	Trin	Trinidad
Grns	Grenadines	USVI	US Virgin Islands
Guad	Guadeloupe	Venz	Venezuela
Gull	Gullah	ViIs	Virgin Islands
Guyn	Guyana		(US and Brit.)
Hait	Haiti		

COUNTIES OF THE BRITISH ISLES
(ADAPTED FROM THE *EDD*)

Abd.	Aberdeen	Cum.	Cumberland
Ant.	Antrim	Der.	Derbyshire
Bck.	Buckinghamshire	Dev.	Devonshire
Bdf.	Bedfordshire	Dmf.	Dumfries
Bnff.	Banff	Don.	Donegal
Brks.	Berkshire	Dor.	Dorsetshire
Cai.	Caithness	Dub.	Dublin
Chs.	Cheshire	Dur.	Durham
Cmb.	Cambridgeshire	e.An	East Anglia
Con.	Connaught	Ess.	Essex
Cor.	Cornwall	Glo.	Gloucester
Crk.	Cork	Gmg.	Glamorgan

Hmp.	Hampshire	Per.	Perth
Hnt.	Huntingdonshire	Rut.	Rutland
Hrf.	Herefordshire	Rxb.	Roxburgh
I.Ma.	Isle of Man	Sc.	Scotland
Inv.	Inverness	Shr.	Shropshire
Ir., Irel.	Ireland	Slg.	Stirling
Ken.	Kent	Som.	Somersetshire
Lan.	Lancashire	Stf.	Staffordshire
Lei.	Leicestershire	Sth.	Sutherland
Lin.	Lincolnshire	Suf.	Suffolk
Lnk.	Lanark	Sur.	Surrey
Lns.	Leinster	Sus.	Sussex
Lon.	London	Uls.	Ulster
Mid.	Middlesex	Wal.	Wales
Nhb.	Northumberland	War.	Warwick
Nhp.	Northampton	Wil.	Wiltshire
Not.	Nottingham	Wm.	Westmorland
Nrf.	Norfolk	Wor.	Worcestershire
Oxf.	Oxfordshire	Wxf.	Wexford
Pem.	Pembrokeshire	Yks.	Yorkshire

GENERAL LIST OF ABBREVIATIONS
USED IN THE TEXT

abbr	abbreviated/-tion	/-cc-/	consonant cluster (final, intervocalic, initial)
adj	adjective		
adv	adverb		
AmE	American English	CE	Caribbean English
Amer	America	cit(s)	citation(s)
art	article	cm(s)	centimetre(s)
attrib	attributive/-ly	comb	combination(s)
aux	auxiliary	comp	complement
B	broadcast item	cond	conditional
Bhoj	Bhojpuri	conj	conjunction
bibl	biblical	conn	connective
Br	British	Cp	compare
BrE	British English	Cr	Creole
C	century	def	definite
/-c-/	consonant	derog	derogatory/-ily
Cap	capital letter	dial	dialect/-al
CarA Cr	Caribbean Creole	Du	Dutch

E; Eng	English	Irel	Ireland
Ed	Editorial	Is. Carib	Island Carib
EE	Earlier English	Joc	jocular/-ly
	(c.1625–c.1837	lang	language
	for the purpose of	lb(s)	pound(s)
	this work)	masc	masculine
emph	emphasis; emphatic	metaph	metaphorical/-ly
erron	erroneous/-ly	ModE	Modern English
esp	especially	n	noun
etym	etymology/-ical	N; No	North
evid	evident/-ly	naut	nautical
Ex(s)	example(s)	n.d.	no date
excl	exclamatory;	neg	negative
	exclamation	nom	nominative
exp	expression	obj	object/-ive
fem	feminine	ObS	obsolete/-escent
folk etym	(See pop etym)	OE	Old English
foll	following	orig	originally
fr	from	P/A	Perso-Arabic
Fr	French	pa. part	past participle
Fr Cr	French Creole	pa. t.	past tense
ft	feet	perf	perfect
fut	future	perh	perhaps
gramm	grammar/-tical	pers info	personal information
Gull	Gullah	Pg	Portuguese
H	(newspaper) headline	phr(s)	phrase(s)
Hd	(Parliamentary)	pl	plural
	Hansard	pop etym	popular etymology,
Hin	Hindi		also folk etymology
Hist	historical	poss	possible/-bly
IAE	Internationally	possess	possessive
	Accepted English	prec	preceding
id	idiomatic	pred	predicate
ideoph	ideophone	pref	prefix
imper	imperative	prep	preposition/-al
Ind	Industry	pres. t.	present tense
indef	indefinite	prob	probably
infl	influence(d)	pron	pronoun
ins	inches	pronunc	pronunciation,
interr	interrogative/-ly		pronounced
intr	intransitive	Prov	proverb
IrE	Irish English	redup	reduplicate/-ted/-tion

ref	refer; reference	Sran	Sranan Tongo
refl	reflexive	sth	something
rel	relative	subj	subject
RP	(British) Received	suf	suffix
	Pronuncation	syn	synonym/-ous
S; So	South	tr	transitive
S1/S2	1st speaker/2nd	trans	translation
	speaker	usu	usually
sb	somebody	vb	verb
Sc	Scottish	Vul	vulgar
SE	Standard English	W Afr	West African
sg	singular	WAPE	West African Pidgin
Shak	Shakespeare		English
Skr	Sanskrit	wd	would
Sp	Spanish	wh	which

SYMBOLS

/   *In a Phrase Entry*, separates alternatives in sense or structure:

    when the day/ night comes
    cut your eye after/ at/ on sb

    In a citation, indicates the start of a new line or paragraph in the original text:

      I who in 1951 swallow hook line and sinker / and eat from bramble to timber / when de beast from de east / came forward . . .

‖   Indicates that a Primary Allonym follows.
‖   Indicates that a Secondary Allonym follows.
/ /   Virgules enclose phonemic spelling: /stik brok in yo eez/
[ ]   Square brackets enclose pronunciation given in phonetic symbols.
~   Swung dash indicate that a variant pronunciation follows.
( )   *In a spelling*, indicate that the sound, the letter, the part of a word or of a phrase so bracketed is sometimes included in the pronunciation, spelling or form of the word or phrase: **nyam(p)s, shirtjac(k), red-skin(ned)**
[ ]   *In a spelling*, indicate that the sound which would be represented if the letter(s) so bracketed were 'pronounced' is absent in the speaker's articulation: **lef[t] [u]pon han[d]; you ca[n't] gi[ve] me**; or in the case of '-th-' sounds, is replaced by [-t-]: **t[h]ing, wit[h]out, pat[h]**.
>   Becomes; develops into.
<   Is derived from.
→   Up to (when followed by a year); according to (when followed by a book code).
□   Indicates that a Usage Note follows.

STRUCTURE OF AN ENTRY

Superscript number — **a⁸** (-a) [a ~ ʌ ~ ə] *enclitic vbl aux particle* (Car A) — Word-class / Syntatic function

Status label (Informal) — *[IF]* [After modals *could, should, would, might,* and their negs] Have. **a.** *We ent have no fowl. If we had thief it you, think we woulda stand here cool so?*—RTCS:22 **b.** *She might a went to bed*

Book source of preceding citation — *already. Enough time in the mornin', eh?*—MHBT: — Citation

128 **c.** *'You shouldn't a meddled,' Metro called to father.*—PBDB:35 [Reduced form of aux vb *have* in unstressed positions. An EE dial form. Cp *EDD A* VI. *A* v 3. 'have': Sc.] — Etymological note

Pitch-Contour / Intonation pattern — **bad-hand** /1´2/ *n* **1.** (CarA) An injured or sick — Sense number

hand or arm. *You know he has this bad-hand that forced him to give up the cricket.*—(Antg) **2.** (Dmca) A power to cause evil. **3.** *PHRASE* **3.1** — Phrase numbering

pass bad-hand on (sb/sth) *vb phr* (Dmca) *[IF]* — Status label (Informal phrase)

Primary Allonym — ‖ PUT BAD-EYE ON (STH) (Belz, Guyn) *She won't go by there when she is taking the baby out for a walk because she really believes those people will pass bad-hand on the child.*—(Dmca) □ Distinguish from *bad hand* /2´1/ 'a hand that is bad (as in a game of cards)'. — Usage Note

Variant Form — **ca·beche** (ca·viche) [ˈkabič ~ ˈkavič] *n* (Guyn) — Pronunciation (alternatives)
Primary Allonym — ‖ ESCAVEITCH FISH (Jmca) *Their grandmother was an old Madeira Portuguese and she used to prepare some real sweet cabeche—you know fish and garlic and so—to go with the souse [u]pon a Saturday.*—(Guyn) [Pg *escabeche* 'marinade, pickle used for fish or meat'] — Etymological source

Superscript number (including variants) — **ca(f)·fuf·fle²** (**cuf·fuf·fle², ker·fuf·fle²**); — Variant spellings
Related form — **ca(f)·fuf·fling** *n* (Bdos, Guyn) *[AF—Joc]* Con- — Status label (Anti-Formal, Jocular)
fusion and trouble. **a.** *Since the demise of the 1958–61 West Indian Federation ... there has been much debate over the critical pathway which West Indianism has been following. Such 'caffufling' as has taken place has seemly produced desultory efforts ... in the region.*—NaT (75.10.12, p.9) **b.** — Citation numbering
Oh, how I wish all this kerfuffle would end. Then I could really start to have fun.—AdV (65.12.12, p.16) [By functional shift. See prec] — Newspaper source of preceding citation

Asterisk denoting this item in Fr & Sp Supplement — **ca·la·lu★** (cal·(1)al·(1)oo (ou, u), ka(1)·la·loo) — Variant spellings
Pronunciation (applied to all variants) — [ˈkalalu] *n* **1.** (CarA) ‖ *agouman* (StLu) ‖ *bhaji* (Guyn, Trin) ‖ *calalu-bush, dasheen-bush* — Secondary Allonyms
(Tbgo, Trin) ‖ *spinach* (CarA) ‖ *wild spinach*
Territorial labels — (Antg, Bdos, Mrat, StVn) ‖ *zèbaj* (StLu) ‖ *zép-ina* (Dmca) Any of a number of plants with edible, succulent leaves wh are cooked as green vegetables, esp those of the *Amaranthus spp*, but — Taxanomic information (Botanical species)
also DASHEEN and other leaves. (See as separate entries CATERPILLAR CALALU, CHINESE CALALU, WATER-CALALU). **2.** **(i)** (Dmca, StVn, Tbgo, — Sub-sense numbering
Secondary Allonym — Trin) ‖ *calalu-soup* (Mrat, StVn) ‖ *crab-and-calalu* (Guyn) ‖ *pepperpot* (Angu, Antg) A very thick soup made of CALALU I or DASHEEN leaves — Small capitals denoting items defined in the dictionary
and other ingredients such as okras, root vegetables, dumplings, crabs or crayfish, saltbeef or ham-bone, green peppers, and seasoning, and usu served as a main meal, often on Sundays.
Sub-sense numbering — **(ii)** (Dmca, Gren, Jmca, StVn) ‖ *cook-up* (Bdos

Headword (with Syllabic dots) — **Deep·va·li** (Deep·a·va·li, Dip·va·li) ['di ·pavali] *n* (Guyn, Trin) [Indie] ‖ DIVALI (Guyn, Trin) The original Hindi name of DIVALI. [Hin < *diipak* 'light' + *vali* 'line', hence 'line of light'] □ These forms are less current than the dial Bhoj Usage Note (Information) — *Divali*. — Subject label (Context)

Pronunciation (I.P.A.) — **de·ter·ma** ['dɪtʌrmə] *n* (Guyn) [*Timber Ind*] A tall tapering forest-tree yielding a pinkish timber; it is highly resistant to insects, and is used for building; *Ocotea rubra* (*Lauraceae*). — Subject label / Taxonomic information (Botanical name)

Headword (preferred form first) / Primary Allonym — **dev·il-grass** (dev·il's grass) /ˈɪ 12/ *n* (*phr*) (Bdos, Guyn, Trin) ‖ BAHAMA GRASS (CarA) **a.** *The picture then showed the pipe almost completely surrounded by devil grass most of which was about 3 ft high. At the time, this caused the area to be a* Citation (in italics) — *breeding ground for mosquitoes.*—AdN (74.10.28, p.6) **b.** *Devil's Grass and Zoysia are notoriously* — Pitch-Contour / Intonation pattern

Pronunciation variants — **dho·ti** [dhoti ~ doti] *n* (Guyn, Trin) [*Indic*] ‖ *capra* **1.** (Trin) An EAST INDIAN man's white loin-cloth consisting of a single piece of cloth wrapped around the waist, folded over and passed loosely between the legs. [Hin *dhotii* 'loin cloth'] — Subject label (Context) / Gloss (which includes another item in the Dictionary)

Sense number — **dig·ging** *n* **1.** (Jmca) ‖ LEND-HAND (Tbgo) On *Saturday, dem have digging or Saturday morning crop. Di odder district people dem come in to help. We buy bread and salt beef and mix wash and drink wid it. Di man dem dig di hole and di woman dem plant di corn or yam head or potato* Sense number — *slip.*—SSLG:28 **2.** (Guyn) A site in the interior — Primary Allonym (relating only to one sense)

Variant forms / spellings / Primary Allonym — **djèp** (ġep, jep) [jɛp] *n* (Dmca, StLu, Trin) ‖ JACK-SPANIARD (ECar) [Fr Cr<Fr *guèpe* 'wasp' + palatalization /g > dj/]

Superscript number — **done¹** *vb* (CarA) **1.** *as a base vb* [X] To finish; to bring or come to an end. **a.** *'Well, den, we better start now if we intend to done this evening,' remarked Bo-Bo.*—Har, 1974:20 **b.** *The water in the kitchen was doning.*—Tbgo (Ms) **c.** *You must done dat befo[re] you start dis.*—(Trin) **2.** as Syntactic function (part of speech) — a pa. part. [AF–Cr] (be, have) finished; (be, have been) used up. **a.** *Man, you come now all the whisky done.*—(Bdos) **b.** *I ain't talkin[g] no more. I done.*—(Antg) **c.** *Look how he come and done the work so quick.*—(Guyn) **3.** PHRASES **3.1** done with *vbl adj phr* (Bdos, Guyn) Exhausted; done for; ruined. *Whistler's Note disappointed again. As usual he showed good speed but was done with by the mile post.*—NaT (75.05.18, p.27) Phrase numbering — **3.1.1** done with (sb/sth) *vb phr* (CarA) [AF– Status label (Anti-Formal, Creole) — Cr] To bring, come, put an end to your relationship with (sb or sth). **a.** *And Vera say that my own home troubles now begin and ups with she baby and gone by she mother and say she done with* Citation numbering — *me.*—CISH:131 **b.** *He los[t] so much money and*

— Status label (mark of disapproval) / Citation from a hand-written source / Citation from an oral source / Phrase numbering / Word-class / Syntactic function / Citation numbering

PRONUNCIATION

CARIBBEAN ENGLISH

Vowels

Key word	Phonetic symbol	Phonemic spelling
beat	[i]	/ii/
bit	[ɪ]	/i/
bait	[e]	/ee/
bet	[ɛ]	/e/
but	[ʌ]	/o/
bat	[a]	/a/
bath	[aː] [aˑ]	/aa/
bite	[aɪ]	/ai/
Bob	[ɒ]	/o/
bout	[ɒʊ]	/ow/
boy	[ɒɪ]	/oi/
bo	[o]	/o/
boat	[oː] [oˑ]	/oo/
buff	[ʊ]	/u/
boot	[u]	/uu/

(*Note*: The Phonemic spelling system is adapted from that used by F. G. Cassidy. See *CJT: 433*.)

Nasal Vowels

Nasal Vowels, identified mostly in Etymological Notes, are marked with a tilde [˜] above, thus [ŏ, ĭ, ã, ɔ̃, õ, ŏ, ɛ̃]. The spelling system used to represent the occurrence of three of them in French Creole loan-words is given in a separate list below.

The **voiceless vowel** occurring medially in *eh-heh* is represented as [h].

Consonants

The sounds [p, b, t, d, k, g; m, n; l, r; f, v, s, z, h; y, w] are rendered, generally speaking, in the same way as in Internationally Accepted English, and are represented by the same letters, whether in phonetic or phonemic spelling. Symbols are used to represent other sounds as follows.

Key word	Phonetic symbol	Phonemic spelling
*ch*ur*ch*	[č]	/ch/
*j*u*dg*e	[ʝ]	/j/
si*ng*	[ŋ]	/ng/
*f*m	[Φ]	/f/
*th*ing	[θ]	/th/

lxxvi

*th*is	[ð]	/dh/
*sh*oe	[š]	/sh/
*J*ouvert	[ž]	/zh/
Eh! Eh!	[ʔ]	/ʔ/
mm-mm	[m̃ʔm̃]	(Unreleased [m] interrupted by glottal stop)
mm-hm	[m̃hm̃]	(Unreleased [m] interrupted by devoicing)

AFRICAN LANGUAGES

Original items from African languages which are given in Etymological Notes are spelled as written in their sources of reference (whether dictionary, grammar, or otherwise), *except that tones (pitch-levels) are not marked*. The systems used in those sources differ somewhat, but the source of an item is always cited, and so may be consulted. Specific mention may be made here of the systems used for two languages often cited—Twi and Yoruba—and one or other of those systems is used for writing many of the other African languages.

For Twi, Christaller's dictionary, reference *DAFL*, uses the following symbols of the IPA system to represent the same sounds in Twi:

Vowels a, [ɛ], e, i, [ɔ], o, u (all vowels can be nasalized)

Consonant [ŋ]

However, Christaller uses the following spellings for two palatal consonants:

ky [č]

gy [ɟ]

Illustrative examples:

n'asõ yɛ deŋ 'his ears are hard'

ŋkɔŋkɔnsa 'hypocrisy'

ani-suo 'eye-water'

ŋkaŋkye 'cake'

For Yoruba, Abraham's dictionary, reference *ADHL*, uses the spellings ẹ, ọ, ṣ for the sounds represented by IPA [ɛ], [ɔ], [š] and the spellings an, ẹn, in, ọn, un for IPA [ã, ɛ̃, ĩ, ɔ̃, ũ].

Illustrative examples:

oju wọn ṣe mẹrin 'their eyes make four'

fun m 'for me'

ọmọ 'child'

INDIC LANGUAGES

The principal Indic language from which there are apports is Bhojpuri, a dialectal cousin of Hindi. Etymological notes further include references principally to Hindi, Urdu and Perso-Arabic.

The same phonemic spelling used (and illustrated above) for **Caribbean English** is used for items from Indic sources with the following additions for **consonants**.

The spellings bh, chh, dh, gh, jh, kh, ph, th represent /b, ch, d, g, j, k, p, t/ respectively *with aspiration*. Aspiration is much modified and irregular in Indic apports in CE.

Examples

bhagwat, achha, dhoti, ghee, jhandi, khan, phulourie, katha

The spellings ḍ, ṛ, ṭ represent /d, r, t/ *with retroflection* (i.e. with the tip of the tongue turned backwards). Original retroflection is lost in Caribbean Indic apports.

ALPHABETIZATION OF SOUNDS IN FRANCOPHONE CREOLE LOAN-WORDS

Spelling	Sound	Sample Words	Spelling	Sound	Sample Words
a	[a]	bwa	n	[n]	nèg-jaden
an	[ã]	fanm	ng	[ŋ]	lang
b	[b]	béké	ny	[ɲ]	montany
ch	[š]	bouch	o	[o]	koko-bèf
d	[d]	dité	ò	[ɔ]	kòkòm
dj	[ɟ]	djab	on	[ɔ̃] [õ]	ponm
é	[e]	lahé	ou	[u]	soukouyan
è	[ɛ]	bèf	p	[p]	papiyòt
en	[ɛ̃]	pwayen	r	[r]	géritou
f	[f]	foula	s	[s]	sikyé-fig
g	[g]	gwo-zié	t	[t]	tèt
h	[h]	halé	tj	[č]	tjè-bèf
i	[i]	pwin	v	[v]	vay-ki-vay
j	[ž]	Jouvè	w	[w]	wòb
k	[k]	konmès	y	[y]	dwiyèt
l	[l]	lanmowi	z	[z]	zòfi
m	[m]	mouchwè			

(*Note*: This spelling system has been adopted from *The Handbook for Writing Creole*, St Lucia, 1983.)

A

A¹ [e] (Guyn) [*AF—Derog*] [First letter of the alphabet, used as an abbr for 'ass'] A person who puts on foolish airs; a person who displays his or her social prejudices. **a.** *I don't bother with them nowadays. Since they been to England and come back they behavin[g] like two As.*—(Guyn) **b.** *He is a B.A., widout goin[g] to university, yo[u] know.*—(Guyn) □ Recognised [*Joc/Derog*] ref to a person who is seriously disliked. The abbr in cit b. is widely understood as 'big ass'.

A² (Ah) [a] *pron 1st pers sg* (CarA) [*IF*] ‖ **uh** (Bdos) I (usu in unstressed positions). **a.** *A'm thinking of going to that show too.*—(Guyn) **b.** *Ah didn't want to bawl out because dey daag woulda start barkin' an ah didn't want da nosey neighbour hearin'.*—AaW.I.2, p.25 [Cp *EDD A* IV. pron 'I' in Irel, N Cy and some of the Midl counties. N Irel 'A'm saying …'; Yks 'A wish a'd been theer …' (as well as Dur, Cum, Wm, e Lan, w Wor), also *SND A, Ah, Aw, Aa, A'* 1st pers pron (both emphatic and unstressed): 'I wid a dun it if A could; Aw was up at Allokirk the day', etc. These E dial influences would have coincided with or reinforced a number of W Afr sources. Note Krio *a* 'I'; *KNED* Nembe *a* 'I', ex *a boyo*, 'I am coming'; *SIBC* Igbo 1st pers pron subj *a—m*, ex *a-coro-m-akwa*, 'I want (an) egg'] □ Oral, or in the written representation of *IF* dialogue. Sometimes in the combination *A'm*, 'I am', presented simply as *Am*. Cap A is a sufficient spelling, even if it is sometimes pronounced (Bdos) [ʌ]. See UH.

a³ [a] *indef art* (*replacing 'an' before a vowel or 'h' mute*) (CarA) [*X*] An. **a.** *You is a idiot or what?*—(Bdos) **b.** *It goin[g] tak[e] [a]bout a hour.*—(Guyn) **c.** *If you are in Business you need a Adding Machine you can depend on.*—AdN (Ad, 73.05.19, p.10) [Cp*EDD A* 1. indef art 2. Used in place of *an* before a vowel or h mute (Nhb, nYks); wYks 'a idle, ill-tempered gossip'; Sur 'half a hour agoo'; Wil: The article an is never used. 'Gie I a apple', etc. Also *SND* Sc *A* (indef art) 1. In modern colloq usage *a* occurs before a vowel as well as before a consonant in most of the dials. This tendency dates from an earlier period and occasionally shows itself in earlier literature and local records] □ The *SND* etym comment for Sc dial applies aptly to CE even in the serious speech of educated persons. Elimination of SE morphological discrimination is a notable feature of Cr economy causing many a slip in the written lang, as evidenced in cit c.

a⁴ [a] *indef art* (*followed by mass-noun or count-noun without the link of a quantitative phr*) (CarA) [*X*] **1.** A loaf of (bread), job of (work), shower of (rain), word of (thanks), pair of (shoes), etc. **a.** *You could be hanged for stealing bread at one time and now we are told that somebody, a young man, perhaps, who steals a bread—and there are people who have done that, Sir, —that somebody who steals a bread is going to be disqualified from entering Parliament for ever.*—Bdos (Hd, 74.08.27, p.3943) **b.** *The fellars say 'we only want you to help we to get a place to stay and tell we how to get a work.'*—STLL:67 **c.** *A see a rain coming eh!*—(Gren) **d.** *A went to to[w]ng to buy a new shoes fo[r] the boy.*—(Guyn) **2.** A coin or note to the value of (so much). **a.** *All to make a sixpence for a tin of corned beef.*—WBH:33 **b.** *They would say 'If you give me a two shillings, sir, I buy some fish.'*—SDP:38 **c.** *If de boy work for a five dollars, a twenty dollars even—and she know—she tak[e] it away!*—(Bdos) [1. is prob from the infl of Cr, in wh the economy of this usage is common. 2. is prob from the notion of coin or note as a single item, but E dial infl is also poss. Cp *EDD A* 1. indef art 1. Used redundantly with substantive or adj 'not worth a sixpence' (1800); *SND A* 3. before words of number 'I'll tak a sax or sieven o' them'; etc]

a⁵ (an) [a] *semi-adj* (CarA) [*IF*] **1.** One; a certain (esp of a stated day or named person). **a.** *A day she come all dress up say she was going to court.*—(Guyn) **b.** *An afternoon las[t] week A'm sure A heard her crying in the house.*—(Bdos) **c.** *Mr Adams suggested that W—and L—struggled with a gun which was taken from W—and given to a Anderson R—, who threw it out through a window.*—AdN (74.01.23, p.1) [Prob E dial infl as in *EDD A* VIII. prep 3. *on, in*, with cits from Wm 'Et wes a Monda mornin', Suf 'We'll go a Sunday', etc, where *a* notwithstanding its prep function attracts the sense of *a* (indef art or adj) by its position] □ CE *a* here connotes vagueness, a lack of precise identity although focusing on actuality. Hence, in cit c. 'a Anderson R—' the vague *a* indicates 'somebody I don't know called Anderson R—' SE *one* is a safe replacement in writing. **2.** PHRASES **2.1 on a day** [*IF*]; **[u]pon a day** [*AF*] *adv phrs* (Bdos) In the daytime. **a.** *When it's cool I like to sit outside on a day.*—HDB **b.** *[U]pon a day you don[t] usually see she becau[se] she workin[g] nights.*—(Bdos) **2.2 on a morning** [*IF*]; **[u]pon a morning** [*AF*] *adv phr* (Bdos) ‖ ON MORNINGS (Bdos) See ON Phr 7.4 **a.** *The* *area known as Greaves End was utilised by many of the labouring class who desired a sea-bath early on a morning.*—AdM (77.01.09, p.11) **b.** *When I bathin[g] [u]pon a mornin[g] I do[es] see she hustlin[g] goin[g] to work.*—(Bdos) **2.3 on a side** *adv phr* (Bdos) [IF] On one side; on its side. **a.** *Among other things Jordan said he had found the cash register tilted on a side.*—AdN (73.10.03, p.1) **b.** *The boat in the Careenage was on a side for them to repair it.*—(Bdos) **2.4 on a whole** *adv phr* (Bdos) [X] As a whole; in general; taken or considered altogether or as a unit. **a.** *I think Kerry Packer is opening up the field for cricketers on a whole, and West Indian cricketers in particular.*—Bdos (Ms) **b.** *This is a major breakthrough for the band and Barbadian music on a whole, for in addition to the fame ... which the group will be getting, Barbadian music has now been given a chance to establish itself on the world scene.*—NaT (76.05.16, p.7) **c.** *I maintain that if CBC is going to put on a programme on slavery, then it should show a programme dealing with the topic slavery on a whole and not just one aspect of the subject.*—AdN (76.10.09, p.4) [Overlap of IAE 'on the whole' and 'as a whole']

a⁶ [a ~ ʌ] *prep, unstressed phrasal linking particle.* (CarA) [AF] Of (in all functions, in unstressed positions, of this particle). **a.** *De prettiest speed boat come from board a de man-o-war ship ... De King a Kings wonder wha kind a boy dat.*—WFSFB:47 **b.** *The cop opened the bag and saw 20 cakes of soap. Asked how he came into possession of them, Riley said: 'Possession a wah?'*—WeS (75.07.04, p.20) **c.** *I ent take no notice a she nuh, ah cook a big pot a greasy rice wid plenty a pigtail.*—MN (57.10.30, p.3) **d.** *I couldn't call (cause de wind, you know).*—AaW.I.1, p.8 [By opening and backing of IAE unstressed vowel *o* [ʌ] (< 'of') in all its functions—as possessive or phrasal link or phrasal particle, as in cits. Cp also *EDD A* VIII. in very general sense, + cits from wYks '... could get a bit a naturable rist'; Lin 'Out a work'; etc] □ Widely current in oral contexts even among educated CE speakers, and readily written in folk dialogue as in cits.

a⁷ [a] *prep, pre-nominal particle (occasionally stressed)* (CarA) [AF] In general prep senses: in, into, to, on, at (the). **a.** *Boat gone a-falls.*—Guyn (Prov) **b.** *You mean to say dat a man have to go a mountain go load up 'eself lek one donkey?*—FGSDS:33 **c.** *That woman too like walkabout. As you miss her, she gone catch up a somebody else yard.*—WeG (73.02.07, p.11, Partyline) **d.** *What's wrong with its Montserrat Workers? ... Dem no gat mout too? Dey no ha fo go a supermarket too?*—MtM (76.10.22, p.8) **e.** *In those days your grandmother or old aunt could still manage somehow to feed you and, you know, put clothes a you back, but not today, sir, not in these days.*—(Guyn) [A prob reinforcement of W Afr infl by dial sources. Cp Hausa *ADHL a*, (5) prep 'at', 'in' ... *a Kano* 'at Kano', *adaki* 'in the house', *a wuya* 'on his neck', *a kasa* 'on the ground'; (6) 'to' ... *a gidam* 'to the compound', *a kofa* 'to the doorway') all of wh structures are reflected in

CarA Cr. Cp also *EDD A* VIII. prep. In very general sense. 1. 'at', denoting place, + cit w Wor 'E were a chu'ch o' Sundy ...' 3. 'on', 'in', + cit N Cy 'A this side'; Lan 'He went a-horseback ...' 4. 'to', + cit wSom 'I be gwain in a town'. *A* pref³, perh < OE prep *on*, very common in various dials of Sc, Irel and Eng, ex Dur 'Tek the cows afield'] □ This is a strong basilectal particle in Anglophone Crs. Its treatment here is limited to cases where it is considered irreplaceable even in upper-level speech contexts, or where it seems deliberately used to add a Cr bluntness to a communication. Its strength in such contexts may also account for a development in the function of 'at' in CE. (See AT *prep* 2.) Outside of wholesale Cr contexts this prepositional usage usu signals code-switching among educated speakers with a desired effect in mind (ex cit d.). In pursuing such effects, stress may be added, wh is not poss in the case of a⁶.

a⁸ **(-a)** [a ~ ʌ ~ ə] *enclitic vbl aux particle* (CarA) [IF] [After modals *could, should, would, might,* and their negs] Have. **a.** *We ent have no fowl. If we had thief it you think we woulda stand here cool so?*—RTCS:22 **b.** *She might a went to bed already. Enough time in the mornin', eh?*—MHBT:128 **c.** *'You shouldn't a meddled,' Metro called to father.*—PBDB:35 [Reduced form of aux vb *have* in unstressed positions. An EE dial form. Cp *EDD A* VI. *A* v 3. 'have': Sc. Often used in vul lang as an abbr of *hae*. Cum 'I waddent a hed a cloon', etc; wSom *have*, when followed by a consonant, sometimes written *ha*, but seldom aspirated. This is the commonest of all the forms, and it is occasionally heard even before a vowel. Also *JSD A* is often used in Vul lang as an abbr of *hae* (i.e. *have*), the aspirate being suppressed: 'That he ... should a come'. *VSCT* also notes Shak: 'She might a been a grandam ere she died' (*Love's Labours Lost*, V.2.17); 'So would I a done by yonder sun' (*Hamlet* IV.5, 64)] □ A region-wide oral usage wh authors often find necessary to write in natural dialogue. A standardized **would'a** or **would-a** would solve the problem of representing this dial form in literature. See OF².

a⁹ **(-a)** [a ~ ʌ ~ ə] *enclitic vbl infin particle* (CarA) [AF] To (infinitive particle). **a.** *Dey only gonna tell lies.*—(Baha) **b.** *But A wan[t] [t]a gi[ve] her a good present you know?*—(Trin) **c.** *I got-a eat like anybody too.*—(Bdos) **d.** *But I gwan a travel.*—WFSFB:40 [As *SND A* prep¹ [ə] used instead of *to* before an infinitive + cits *Aa'm gaun a gee yoo sumthing* 'I'm going to give you something'; 'There's gaunna be an unco crap the 'ear'. A worn-down infinitive participle in enclitic attachment mainly to dial 'wan', 'gon', 'got', 'had'] □ Usu written enclitically as **wanna, gonna, gotta,** the occurrence of this AF form in present CE speech is much boosted by dial AmE infl via pop songs and the media.

a¹⁰ **(a-, ah, ar)** [a] *proclitic vbl aspectual particle* (CarA) [AF—Cr] ‖ *de⁴* (Baha, Belz, StKt) [Indicating that the action of the vb wh it precedes is happen*ing*, thus *a-come, a-knock*, etc, mean 'coming', 'knocking', etc] *-ing*. **a.** *Surprisingly, though, employers ... have managed to establish an unholy alliance with shortsighted workers 'Me naa wok wid nobody who a tek out Provident Fun' has been the attitude of these workers.*—MtM (77.05.06, p.4) **b.** *Someone shouted to the defendant 'Police a come; so if you got anything, be careful'. The defendant said that ... he went inside to warn her of the approach of the police.*—Las (75.06.13, p.1) **c.** *Lots of good singers in Jamaica ... but nobody knows about them because they do not have the right people to promote them. Only one man creating and everybody else a follow.*—JdN (75.06.13, p.1) **d.** *No friends, no friends in the country / Poor man a see / Trouble a come in the country.*—VoS (76.04.17, p.7) **e.** *Such a way my people are a-sing, though! You know they will sing all night to night so till east wind brings the morning? Torch-light and long-time hymns, and memory a-knock at my mind.*—RND:169 **f.** *After the death sentence was passed and before he was led from the dock, the youth ... told the trial Judge: '... your time ah go come one day too.'*—WeG **g.** *He said, 'Morning, Country. How time ar treat you?' Frances Ann replied, 'Time no treat me too bad, Country. How it ar treat you?'*—PKKK:86 [An unstressed pre-verbal particle marking durative aspect of the Cr vb it precedes; widely current in CarA Cr in wh it has ‖ forms [da], [də], Fr Cr [ka]; hence prob of W Afr orig. Cp *DAFL* Twi *adow*, 'tilling' < *dow*, 'till'; *adidi* 'eating' < *didi*, 'eat', etc; also *WEBC* Ewe /*a-*/ is future tense indicator placed before the stem and after the subject, ex *woava*, 'they will come'; also *ADMY* Yoruba: *á* I. prefixed to a vb to denote the future, ex *won a lo*, 'they will go'; *á* III. prefixed to a vb to denote agent, doer, ex *abe* (*thing* + /*a*/ + *cut*), 'razor', *akole* (*man* + /*a*/ + *build house*), 'builder', etc. The characteristic W Afr functioning of this particle would have been helped in CarA Cr by the comparable functioning of the phonically similar EE pre-verbal particle of *a-hunting*, etc. See next] □ In strictly Cr contexts (cit a.), this particle is traditionally conceived as separate, though with its increasing use for artistic (cits d., e.) or other (cits b., c.) purposes in de-creolized contexts, a hyphenated a- is preferable. Although it is largely restricted to the oral medium of the stigmatized CarA Cr, it is appearing increasingly in writing throughout the CarA (except in *Bdos*, where it survives only residually in the oral form [də]) for purposes of actual reportage (cits a., b., f.), of introducing a desired 'roots' element (c., h.), or of literary style (d., e.).

a¹¹ (a-) [a] *proclitic vbl intensifier particle* (CarA) [*IF*] [Duplicates the sense of *-ing* in the vb to wh it is attached] In the act of; in the process of. **a.** *Didn't you just hear the man a-slandering me?*—PBDB:33 **b.** *'How yer do, chile?' I aks her, / 'I dere 'pon em' is what she say. / Now yer wan know what she meanin? ... / She meanin she dere a-leaning / upon de mercy er de Lord.*—JBJ:89 **c.** *She went through the ground and finally to a big rock where she straightened up a-stretching and*

a-looking all around her ... and standing next to her was another woman with her hand under her chin and looking over her shoulder and a-pointing.—FDI:58 [A survival of the EE *a* + pres. part. wh *OED* (*A* prep¹, 13.) identifies as arch or dial, being retained mostly in southern dialects and AmE, except in a few phrs ex *to go a begging*. Also *EDD A* prep¹ Sc, Irel not found in Eng counties, + cits from Irel 'I'm a thinking', e Lan 'Gon a-working'. Also *SND A* prep¹, cit 'Wee lark keeps a singing': *A* prep³, cit 'Ye're lang a comin', etc. The particle is only a structural vestige without meaning in ModE] □ A hyphenated *a-* is established spelling. CE writers regionwide make use of this EE (< OE) vestigial particle for stylistic effect since it coincides with the structure and effective function of the Afr-based Cr proclitic A¹⁰.

a¹² [a] [With rising pitch pattern /12/ or /13/] *question tag* (CarA) [*IF*] **1.** ‖ **eh¹** (CarA) Phrase-terminal signal of a yes-no question: Are you?; Is he? etc. *You coming, a?*—(Bdos) **2.** ‖ *m?* (CarA) Requesting that a question be repeated: Beg your pardon? *S1: Yo[u] go[t] de tickets?/ S2: A? / S1: Yo[u] got de tickets? / S2: Yes.*—(Bdos) [Cp *CGAF:142* Twi *a?* interrogative particle at the end of a sentence] □ An oral form. Writers of dialogue prefer to use the ‖ **eh?**. Restricted to persons in familiar relationship within the same age group. Resented if used by children to adults.

a¹³ (aa, a-a) [ˀa ~ ˀa:: ~ aˀa] [With marked high pitch] *excl* (CarA) [*AF*] ‖ **Eh!**¹ **3.** (CarA) ‖ **Eh-eh!**¹ (CarA) Exclamation of surprise, shock, annoyance, etc. **a.** *S1: Yo[u] heard about the accident? / S2: No / S1: Yes, a man get killed. / S2: Aa!*—(Guyn) **b.** *A-A, But wey yuh goin wit dat tape-line, Mary?*—ExP (76.04.19, p.16, Cartoon) **c.** *On seeing the blood, Miss Babylyn halted abruptly. / 'A-a! A-a! The blood plenty, we! You ain't to touch it', she warned seriously.*—PGIP:28 [Cp *CGAF:145* Twi *a, hâ*, 'exclamation of pleasure, displeasure', etc. Also *ADHL* Hausa *a a'a* (Sense A). 'Fancy!' *KNED* Nembe *aá* 'shout of surprise'. Also *FED* Fulani *a'a* (rising tone), 'exclamation of surprise'. Also *KED* Krio *a-a* (high-high), 'expression of mild surprise']

THE FORMS a¹⁴ TO -a²⁰ ARE CarA Cr ITEMS WH, THOUGH WRITTEN IN NARRATIVE DIALOGUE, ARE NOT ADOPTED INTO CE EDUCATED SPEECH BUT THEY MAY AFFECT ITS STRUCTURE.

---

a¹⁴ (ah) [a] *Cr linking vb or copula* (vb 'to be') (CarA) ‖ *da⁴* 1. (Belz, Jmca) Am, is, are. **a.** *... an me a man no mek joke at all.*—WFSFB:43 **b.** *Simon: Lizzy a wan awl oman. / Vie: Awl or young, oman a oman.*—Bav.1, p.4 **c.** *Moutar an guitar a two differen ting.* (= *Mouth-say and guitar-play are two different things*).—Guyn (Prov) **d.** *All de time me ah say dat Dorcas White ah somebody wid colour.*—WoV [Prob of Afr origin. Cp *GLPF* Ki-Yaka (one of 8 prefixal functions of *a-*) copula with determined predicate; ex *Tadji Buka a-dibaba* (= 'Buka's father is the stutterer']

a[15] **(ah)** [a] *Cr focusing vb* (CarA) [*Cr*] ‖ *da*[4] 2. (CarA) [Introducing a complete statement with added emphasis] It is. **a.** *'Officer mek mi tell yu de Gad truth, a hustle mi hustle it'. Witness said that he valued it at about $60.*—WeS (74.01.18, p.6) **b.** *A no tief mek yuh departed / A no lie mek yuh departed / But a Fearful mek we careful.*—FCV2:85 **c.** *Ah nerves tek me wha mek you see me stap dere.*—FGSOS:35 **d.** *A gole mek bakra a dead.* (= *It's gold that kills the white man*).—Guyn (Prov) [The pervasive occurrence of this sentence-initial particle in Anglophone in CarA Creoles suggests W Afr syntactic sources wh have not been identified. However cp etym of ‖ *da*[4] 2., of wh it may be a reduced form]

a[16] **(ah)** [a] *Cr initiating vb, introducing wh-question* [Introducing a wh-question usu with some added emphasis] Who/What/Where/, etc is it that? **a.** *One of the men said: 'A wey this police guy a go?'*—StA(JA) (70.07.11, p.5) **b.** *A wha she a do?*—LMFF:42 **c.** *A huu da nak a mi doo* (= *Who is that knocking at my door?*)—(Guyn) **d.** *... ah who you did mean?*—LaS (76.04.10, p.4) [Prob of Afr orig. Cp *GLPF* Ki-Yaka *a-*, in *a-ni*, personal interrogative 'who', 'which'; only used initially and always followed by the subjective personal pron, ex *A-ni a tsi puga mamba?* 'Who poured the water?']

a[17] [a] [With stress + high pitch] *Cr demonstrative pron* (CarA) [*Cr*] That (SE demonstrative pron). *A baby wa cry a house and a baby wa cry a doe no same ting.* (= *That baby which cries in the house and that baby which cries at the door are not crying for the same reason*).—Guyn (Prov) [Prob by reduction of SE 'that' > /dat/ > /da/ > /a/] □ See *DJE a*[4] A.

a[18] [a] [Unstressed + low pitch] *Cr rel conj* That; who; which (SE relative conj). *Man a cou[r]tenin mus[t] go gay.* (= *The man who is courting must dress gaily*).—Guyn (Prov) [Prob from reduction of SE 'what' in informal function as rel conj in CarA Cr: /wat/ > /wa/ > /a/] □ See *DJE a*[4] B.

a-[19] **(ah-)** [a] *Cr pronominal pref to 1st & 2nd pers pl prons:* A-WE; AYO; AH-YO(U) (CarA) [*AF—Cr*] See A[LL]-WE, ALL-YOU as separate entries.

-a[20] [a ~ ʌ] *Cr intrusive vowel* (*esp after final stop consonants*) (A Cr linking sound). **a.** *Laka Dutch axe cut all two side.*—Guyn (Prov) **b.** *Looka, wuna lef mo!*—(Bdos) [By paragoge, or vowel epenthesis, or possibly as *DJE a*[8] 'due to phonetic analogy with W Afr langs (ex Twi)'] □ *Laka* 'like', *Looka* 'Look!' are evid the most frequent current examples of this feature. Others *Watcha* 'watch!', *ana* 'and' are rare.

A.A. (Guyn) Golden Arrow of Achievement; the third highest national honour of Guyana, awarded for distinguished service to the State; it is an arrow-shaped gold pin; the letters may be written after the recipient's name. **a.** *The A.A*

is the third highest award for service to the nation, after the OE and the CCH.—(Guyn) **b.** *Altogether 16 persons received the Medal of Service* (*M.S.*) *9 persons the Arrow of Achievement* (*A.A.*)—Guyana Today. Issue No.3, p.13

Aaa cha! **(Aaa chach!)** [a::ča(č)] *excl* [*AF*] (Expression of annoyance and disgust.) *Aaa Chach! Gie de 'oman some Conguh Pump.*—RFGW:57

aa·jay [ˈaʲe] *adj* (USVI) [*AF*] Wild with anger· *He mus' be gone aajay to carry on so.*—RDVI:57

aam **(om)** [a:m ~ ɒ:m] *excl* (CarA) [*IF*] [Expression of hesitation or uncertainty] (SE) Er. **a.** *Aam! Wait a minute, let me see.*—(Bdos) **b.** *S1: Well om, you are going to do it or you want me to? / S2: Aam! you do it, no!*—(Guyn) □ May be standardized as *aam*, in wh form it most frequently occurs in speech. Occurs at all levels of *CarA* speech.

Aa·ron's rod *n phr* (Jmca) ‖ GLIRICIDIA (Angu, etc) *In December, 'Aaron's rod' is a fringe in many hedges. See how massed and gay these blooms are now on the Half Way Tree frontage of Sugar Manufacturers' Association's office garden.*—DaG (66.12.18, p.18) [From the fact that the stick catches and grows (i.e. becomes alive, hence name from story of the rod of Aaron, (*Num XVII.8*) when it was stuck in the ground] □ Not the same as the English plant referred to by the same name in *COD, EDD,* etc.

aback[1] *adv* **1.** (Guyn) Behind or to the rear of the planted fields of a sugar plantation; behind any large dwelling house. **a.** *Twenty-six cane cutters from Ogle Estate were reported injured yesterday when a trailer in which they were travelling aback capsized.*—GyC (76.06.01, p.9) **b.** *For sale—Large sound two-storey house. Shop below. Garage. Another sound large house aback. Plenty land. Central part of Georgetown.*—DaC (52.08.03, p.12) **2.** (Baha, Jmca, Trin, USVI) [*IF*] Ago. **a.** *She an er boy friend did have a lickle misunderstandin a few years aback and she did lose de fingers in de wrenglin.*—DaG (66.12.04, p.4) **b.** *I had the girl here and she take all my chairs and wares, about three month aback.*—RLCF:67 **c.** *Man he done sell da house from some time aback.*—RDVI:57 [Cp *EDD* aback adv 4. Of time: 'ago, since' + cit from Abd 'Eight days aback a post came frae himsel' (1758). This usage has not survived in present SE] **3.** PHRASE **3.1 go aback** *vb phr* (Guyn) To go into the cane fields to work; to go into the provision farms beyond the cane fields to work. **a.** *'Oh? I suppose that means we'll have to find another overseer. Two probably. Not all of them will be prepared to work as hard as Jem'. / 'I thought you used to go aback?' Madeleine asked innocently. 'You do ride?' / Joan stared at her. 'I do ride yes. But I do not go aback ...'* —NR:30 **b.** *Police reports from the area state that a group of villagers were going aback to their various points when gunmen ... opened fire on the defenceless people.*—EvP (64.07.03, p.1) [Cp

EDD aback (In Sc and all n. counties to Lin and Chs, Stf, War) adv 2. 'behind, to the rear' + cit from Ayr: 'The third that gaed a wee aback'] □ In present BrE, *OED* says *aback* is now confined chiefly to nautical lang. *W3* says it is 'archaic' or 'nautical' in AmE. The development of this sense (wh seems confined to Guyn plantation life) is reflected in the *OED* cit (1878) 'Aback there is nothing but flood.' It is easily nominalized as in the phr '*to come from aback*'.

aback² *prep* (Bdos, Guyn) Behind; at the back of. **1. a.** *The reports had told of indiscriminate shootings (two small boys claimed they were shot at while picking akees aback a West Coast property).*—NaT (74.09.22, p.3) **b.** *Eighty more families will be provided with homes being erected on a 6.7 acre plot in Greater Georgetown. This project is aback the site for the Textile Factory adjoining South Ruimveldt.*—GyN (Jan.75, p.4) [By functional shift of ABACK¹ 1.] □ Refers only to situation in relation to property. More often replaced by phr ABACK OF. **2.** *PHRASE* **2.1 aback of** *prep (phr)* (Bdos, Guyn) ‖ *back of* (CarA) **(i)** (Situated) immediately behind; in or at a place at the back of; (AmE) back of. **a.** *Work has begun on the demolition of the wall which for years enclosed a molasses tank in the compound aback of the Empire Theatre.*—BdN (64.04.14, p.5) **b.** *Guyana recorded its fourth fire in one week yesterday when the top flat of a two-storey building in a yard aback of the Alberttown Police Station was gutted, leaving four persons homeless.*—GyC (77.12.19, p.1) [Cp *EDD aback* (In Sc and all the N counties to Lin and Chs, Stf, War) prep 1. Of position: 'behind, to the rear (usu with prep *of*' + cits from Nhb 'Howay aback o' the hoose an' aa'll show ye.' Stf, N Lin: 'It's aback o' the beer barril.' Also *SND Aback o'* prep phr 1. 'behind, to the rear of' + cit from Rxb 'It's lying aback o' the door' (1923)] **(ii)** (Bdos) Behind; underlying; at the root of; (AmE) back of. *In fact, so widespread have been the canefield conflagrations since (the) Minister of Agriculture and Consumer Affairs appealed for emphasis to be put on the reaping of green canes that it is hard to believe that some element of spite is not aback of it all.*—AdN (77.03.05)

A·ba·co·ni·an [aba'koniən] *n, adj* (Baha) (Person) belonging to Abaco Island in the Bahamas. **a.** *In fact, many visitors return to Abaco year after year intrigued by its way of life and praising Abaconian hospitality.*—DBH:62 **b.** *Mr Lowe, a native Abaconian, was appointed headmaster of the public school at Cherrkee Sound, Abaco in 1950.*—NaG (78.04.08, p.1)

ab·bay* (**ab·bey**) [abe] *n* (Jmca) ‖ *oil-palm* (Guyn, Trin) A tall palm with bushy fronds or 'branches', wh also bears abundant bunches of reddish date-like fruits the outer covering of wh yields an oil; *Elaeis guineensis (Palmaceae)*; the fruit of this tree. *The Abbay or Oil Palm is an African species which rarely produces its oil-laden fruits in this island.*—HIPJ [*DAFL* Twi *a-bɛ* 'palm, palm tree'; the species of palm from wh

palm-wine and palm-oil are obtained, the most common in Western Africa. In Twi, *a-bɛ*, 'palm' is the general prefix for names of other oil-yielding palms *DAFL abefufu, abetuntum,* etc]

ABC class /1121/ *n* (CarA) The infant class of a primary school. **a.** *Teacher Bessie used to start the youngest ones in Little ABC and the next year they would go on to Miss Bourne in Big ABC.*—(Guyn) **b.** *... until rumour made its way out to us that there was no more room in ABC class.*—HCCM:34 ['ABC' as the beginning of literate learning]

abeer *n* See ABIR

abeng (horn) *n* (Jmca) [Hist] A bull's horn used by the Maroons of *Jmca* as a signal, or as a musical instrument. **a.** *There had been a good deal of talking and laughter going on among the grown-up Maroon people, but now they had become quieter. Suddenly, the abeng sounded. The abeng was the bugle of the Maroons and it was made from the horn of a cow. Its sound was low at first. Then it slowly grew louder and louder and higher. At last, it seemed as if it was racing around the tree-tops. The Maroons used the abeng to call up their people. It could be heard for miles around and was blown in such a way as to tell warriors whether they were being called for a battle, or for a talk in the Council-house.*—RTYW:3 **b.** *Musical instruments ... were almost entirely African. These were flutes ...; the abenghorn; a mouth violin or 'bender', the banjo...* BCSJ:225 [*DAFL* Twi *abɛŋ* 'horn of animals; flute, whistle, wind-instrument, musical instrument'. The form AB-ENG HORN is a characteristic CE redundant compound]

a·ber·deen *n* (Tbgo) ‖ CIGALE (Trin) *The aberdeen makes its piercing whistling sound in the later afternoon.... It flies rather than jumps as other crickets do.... It's what they call 'cigale' in Trinidad.*—Tbgo (Ms) [However cp *OED aberdevine* (unknown etym) wh is a small Br song bird]

ab·hor *vb tr*; **ab.hor.ring** *vb tr*; **ab.hor.rent** *adj*; **ab.horence** *n* (CarA) [X] (vb tr) To cause disgust or loathing; (adj) causing disgust; loathsome; (n) loathsomeness; horridness. **a.** *She was not quite sure why each moment she should catch herself thinking, longing. But the knowledge of what she thought so abhorred her consciousness that she always drove it to oblivion.*—PCOS:93 **b.** *It is the most abhorring piece of literature on birth control to reach the printers. It carried a picture of the Virgin Mary on the cover and bore a wicked caption.*—NaT (74.09.01, p.18) **c.** *This kind gesture was sponsored as a community service by the Trinidad Chamber of Commerce ... But their kind gesture was overshadowed by the abhorrence of the mounds of rubbish piled up on the sidewalk.*—ExP (73.01.05, p.17) [Perh from EE, as *OED abhor* v 3. 'causally'; 'to make one shudder; to horrify; to cause horror or disgust'. Mostly impers *Obs* + cit 1604 from Shak (Oth) 'I cannot say Whore.

It does abhorre me, now I speake the word']
□ This usage is an inversion of the sense accepted
in present IAE in wh the person abhors the
object, act, thought, etc, not the object the person
as in the cits.

abir (abeer) ['abi·r] *n* (Guyn, Trin) ‖ *phagwa*
(Guyn) [*X*] **1.** The red mica powder or red liquid
dye wh participants in the open-air celebration
of the Hindu festival of Holi or Phagwa throw
on each other in fun. *The Phagwah celebrations
in Berbice were the biggest ever. Men, women and
children of all races and religious beliefs took part
in the fun, splashing abeer, water and powder [on
each other] to mark the Hindu festival.*—GyC
(76.03.18, p.15) [Hin < Perso-Arabic *abir* 'mica
powder'; name transferred to the liquid dye
made from it] □ PHAGWA sometimes used (*Guyn*)
to mean *abir* is erron. **2.** PHRASE **2.1 play abir**
vb phr (Guyn) To throw ABIR on each other. *On
Phagwa day relatives and friends visit each other's
homes to exchange greetings with the playing of
Abeer and Powder and [to partake of] the sweetmeats which are being prepared.*—GyC (76.02.16,
p.9) [A prob calque from Hin *rang khelnaa*, 'to
pour coloured water on each other during the
Holi festival', *rang* 'colour' + *khelnaa* 'to play'.
Cp E *play marbles*, etc]

a·bi·zé [abize] /1'12/ *vb tr* (StLu) [*IF*] To use
(sth) or (sb) roughly, without consideration; to
misuse. **a.** *How you like to abizé the man's things
so? The man leave his things there so you can use
them with discretion. You don't have to overuse
them so!*—(StLu) **b.** *You want to abizé me? Why
you don't hire a servant?*—(StLu) [Fr Cr -:Fr
abuser 'to make ill use of']

able *adj* PHRASES **1. able with (sb/sth)** *adj phr*
complement of *'to be'*, often neg (CarA) ‖ *able to
go with (sb)* (Angu, Mrat, StKt, StVn) ‖ *able to
handle, manage (sb/sth)* (Dmca, Jmca) ‖ *good
for (sb)* (Dmca, StLu) ‖ *can handle (sb/sth)*
(Belz) ‖ *can go with (sb)* (Nevs) ‖ *can take on
(sb/sth)* (Gren) Able to cope with (sb/sth). **a.**
*He thought he could take advantage of her because
she was a woman but she showed him she was able
with him.*—(Guyn) **b.** *He was not able with that
kind of work. It needed a much younger man.*—
(Bdos) **c.** *I really tired, you know. I find these
days I ain't able with people.*—LDCD:200 **d.**
*That man is a boxer and when it comes to a fight,
I'm not able with him.*—Belz (Ms) [An equivalent
structure occurs in many Afr langs. Cp Wolof:
ken munul dara či moom, (nobody not able nothing
in him) 'Nobody can manage him'; Mende: *numu
gbi ɛ gu ngi maa,* (no person all not able him on)
'Nobody can control him'; Twi: *me ntumi no* (*I
not able him*) 'I am no match for him'; Idoma: *o
bi ɛ glla ng* (he hold her able not) 'He cannot
manage her' (i.e. his wife); Ki-Yaka: *ka m'kuka
ko* (he him able not) ('He cannot manage him');
etc. Note also *KED* Krio *ebul 4. vb* 'be a match
for', ex *A ebul am* 'I am a match for him'. Cp
also *EDD able adj 3.* able for 'fit to cope with'.
Irel *'Ah, he never be able for the attorneys'* (1848).
Also present rural Uls E: *'She was well able for*

*him. He'll have a more civil tongue in his head
from now on'* (L. Todd, pers info)] □ The neg,
wh is frequent, is sometimes also used jocularly
as in cit d. **2. able to go with sb** *adj phr,*
complement of *'to be'* (Angu, Mrat, StKt, StVn)
‖ ABLE WITH (SB) (CarA) **a.** *The woman was able
to go with him, I tell you—she won the fight!—*
(Mrat) **b.** *The boy needs a man in the house—the
mother ain't able to go with him now, he too
big!*—(StVn) **3. big able** *adj phr* (*intensifying*)
(Bdos, Guyn) [*AF—Joc*] Very big. **a.** *She always
walks about with that big able foolish boy. A don't
know why she can't find nobody else to go [a]long
with.*—(Bdos) **b.** *My dear, he took the money and
bought a big able car for all to see!*—(Guyn) [Cp
SND able adj 3. 'physically fit, strong'. (Gen
Sc; obs in SE) + cit from Uls (1931) 'A big
able fellow (well set-up, hefty')] **4. can (not)
spell able** *vb phr* (Belz) [*AF*] (Not) able to do
what you say you can; (not) dare. **a.** *She thinks
she can control him but she can't even spell able.*—
(Belz) [Cp *EDD able* adj 5. 'to spell able, to
perform a difficult task in fulfilment of a boast'
+ cit from N Irel 'Can you spell able? (Are you
sure you can do what you are bragging about?)']
**5. did able; should/will/would able (to do
sth)** *vb phrs* (Bdos) [*X*] Was able; should/will/
would be able (to do sth). **a.** *Las*[*t*] *year I did
able buy a Christmas dress bu*[*t*] *no*[*t*] *dis year.*—
(Bdos) **b.** *Yo*[*u*] *can*[*t*] *ge*[*t*] *any meat scraps today
bu*[*t*] *yo*[*u*] *would able to get some tomorro*[*w*].
—(Bdos) [Prob due to interference from Cr in
wh *be* is absent before a predicative adj. Hence
the development of tensed and modal phrs from
'*I able*']

Ab·ner, Bab·ner, La·dy's knee *n phr*
(Guyn) ‖ *aka baka* (USVI ‖ *Hobner, Bobner,
Lady's knee* (Bdos) (First line of) a children's
rhyme used to eliminate players, the last one left
being thus chosen as the one to play first in
whatever game is about to begin. *Let's say Abner
Babner and pick who is to play first. Ready? Go!
Abner, Babner, lady's knee, / Ocean, potion, sugar
and tea, / Potato bake (roast) and English cake
(toast) / Out goes he/she/you.*—(Guyn)

a·bo·li·tion pay·ment *n* (Trin) A sum of
money paid to an employee as a legally due
compensation for ending his employment; sev-
erance pay. *Also all of the employees ... will
be allowed to take up appointments with Textel,
although they have received abolition payments—
compensation for losing their jobs—according to a
reliable source.*—ExP (72.10.24, p.28)

abound *vb tr* (Bdos) [Of land as property]
Border on; have a common boundary with (another property). *Harding said that after he had
finished work he came home and found the cow
with its throat cut and lying on a pasture abounding
Mayers' land and Sandford Tenantry.*—AdN
(73.10.13, p.1) [Shift in sense of*OED abound* v
2. Obs 'to set limits to' + cits–1627] □ Rare;
occurs more commonly in the form *bound* in
legal statements about property, in the phr *abut
and bound on.*

about[1] **(bout)** [abaʊt~bʌt] *prep* (CarA) [*X*] [Used as a loose connective after vbs or expressions implying the sense 'talk'. It has, in such contexts, the sense of *to, by* or connective *that*, or may be omitted altogether] **a.** *In one of your previous articles reference was made about the presence of heart worms in dogs.*—TrG (73.02.04, p.11) **b.** *... they were so impressed about it.*—WeS (75.03.07, p.24) **c.** *S1: What did they actually say? S2: They were saying about how they would get gasolene.*—(Guyn) **d.** *Mr B— spoke on some of the plans in the making for the Public Service and mentioned about the five-day working week.*—AdN (73.03.25, p.1) **e.** *So I would like to know that something is done to investigate about the raiding of the Post Office of the Troumaca district.*—ViN (73.10.19, p.5) **f.** *Don[t] tell me* [a]*bout yo*[u] *weary! Come an*[d] *move de chairs.*—(Bdos) [Infl by the implied sense of 'talk' in the vb or phr immediately preceding]

about[2] **(bout)** [abaʊt] *adv* (Bdos, Guyn) In phrs ‖ *[a]bout here* [IF], ‖ *round about, [a]round and about* [X] in this/that place or area. **a.** *When I was practising law about here you were nowhere around; so what do you know about me?*—Bdos (Hd, 73.02.13, p.73) **b.** *Mind your language—you have children round about, you know!*—(Guyn) **c.** *Less yo*[ur] *noise, man! They have decent people round and about!*—(Guyn) [An extension of the usage of *OED about* A. (without obj expressed) adv I. 2. 'in the neighbourhood, without defining the exact direction']

a·bou·ya [a'buya] *n* (Guyn) ‖ *bush-hog* (Guyn) **1.** A small type of wild, forest pig or peccary wh is hunted for its meat. *The collared peccary or, as it is locally named, abouya, is about the size of a small pig, blackish-grey in colour with a lighter band extending from under the neck across the shoulders, collar-wise ... Whilst surveying on the Kaburi River the cook arrived one day in great excitement, he having met a drove of abouya on the trail ... That night I had fried abouya brain for dinner—a most dainty dish.*—RALG:98 [*BAED* Arawak *abuya* 'peccary, a So Amer wild animal related to the pig'] □ The pl is exceptional (see cit); the name is regularly replaced in urban usage by *peccari (-y)* of wh the *abouya* is one variety. **2.** PHRASES **2.1 stink as abouya; stink as a bunya** *adj phr* (Guyn) [*AF*] Having a strong unpleasant body odour. **a.** *I don't know why he don't go an*[d] *bathe—always stink as a bunya!*—(Guyn) [< CE *stink* adj 'stinking' a ref to the bad smell produced by the animal's dorsal scent gland] □ The form ... *a bunya* is erron, by misplaced juncture < *abouya* and from urban ignorance of *Guyn* forest fauna. See BUNYA.

above[1] *adv, prep* (CarA) ‖ *upperside* (StKt, Tbgo) Beyond; (often) to the east (or windward side) of. **a.** *He lives in the house above Mrs Gumbs.*—(Angu) **b.** *I can vividly remember a cane fire in Waterford when I was a boy ... and people were frantic in their effort to put it out. On Tuesday night a fire raged above where I live like an inferno and no one seemed to care.*—SuS (80.05.25, p.4)

c. *Furnished House available above the airport at very reasonable rates.*—NeC (Ad, 77.07.09, p.2) [Cp *OED above* A. adv 3. '... farther from the sea'. In all these ECar islands their windward side is east facing the Atlantic Ocean, and the more populated west coast (including their capital city and port) is on lower lying land and facing the Caribbean Sea. This situation may have infl the development of this usage, wh is not, however, clear cut] □ Cp BELOW.

above[2] *adj* (Bdos) East; further. *Please Use Above Gate* [*East Side*]—Bdos: (Supermarket parking notice)

ab·stract[1] *n* (Belz) Any pendant worn on a necklace. **1.** *That's a beautiful abstract you're wearing on that necklace—where did you get it?* —(Belz) [Prob from designs that remind one of abstract art] **2.** A ridiculous thing; nonsense; an eccentric person. **a.** *Only an abstract like my grandfather would live in a house like that all alone.*—(Belz) **b.** *What you are saying is nothing but abstract, man! What you want to say the carpet flew away or something?*—(Belz)

ab·stract[2] *adj* (Belz) Odd; very unusual; bizarre. *That was a really abstract movie—all about werewolves, vampires and ghosts.*—(Belz) [Probably by functional shift of ABSTRACT[1]]

abuse [abyu·z] *vb tr* (CarA) ‖ *buse* (ECar) [*AF*] ‖ *use up* (Belz) To use loud, dirty and threatening language to sb. *After losing his job he refused to seek another. Whenever she spoke to him about seeking employment he would abuse her. He gave her several beatings.*—StA(JA) (73.02.10, p.5) [*OED abuse* v 7. 'to wrong with words; to speak injuriously of or to; to malign, revile' + cit from Shak (Oth). Also *abuse* sb 7. '... injurious speech; abusive language'] □ This vb rarely occurs in any other sense in general CE. It is most often used at the folk level in the aphetic form BUSE. (See).

a·ca·cia* [a'kešʌ~a'kašʌ] *n* (TkCa, Trin) ‖ *ca-sha(w)* 1. (Jmca, Nevs, StKt, ViIs) ‖ *cassie* (Antg, Jmcaa) ‖ *kasha* (Jmca) ‖ *sweet-briar* (Bdos) ‖ *wild poponax* (Jmca) ‖ *zakacha* (Dmca) A large, spreading shrub or small tree about 10 ft high thriving on waste land, with frail limbs armed throughout with long thorns; it bears short pods and little globose yellow flowers; *Acacia farnesiana,* or *A. tortuosa* (*Leguminosae-Mimosaceae*).

a·ca·ra *n* (Baha) ‖ ACCRA (CarA)

ac·cept *vb intr* PHRASES **1. accept that** (Bdos) [*X*] To assume that; to believe that; to take it for granted that. *The Post Office is a universally recognised institution where ... people have a strong measure of trust. They simply post a letter or package and accept that it will go to its intended destination, and what is more that it will get there unopened.*—AdN (72.06.10, p.4) [A misascription. This is a syntactic shift due to the

IAE sense of *accept* 'to receive, hence, to believe']
2. accept to (Bdos) [*X*] To agree to; to accept
an invitation or offer to. *With an offer from the
No.1 singing group of the day, the Opels, to join
the group as lead singer Clarence accepted to replace
Anthony N—, who was about to leave for Britain.*—AdN (73.06.16, p.6) [Note *SND accept* v
followed by an inf. A Scotticism = consent
(Rare) + cit 'A man who accepts to be deacon
of such an incorporation, has no reason to apprehend danger from public debt' (1799)]

ac·cess dam *n* (Guyn) An earth dam built
to provide access from a main road through
plantation property to farm lands or any other
kind of development wh cannot easily be reached
by other means.

ac·cord·ing *adv* (CarA) [*X*] **1.** Suitably; de-
pendably; in a manner determined by the circumstances. **a.** *When you are out in public like
that you must behave according.*—(Bdos) **b.** *S1:
Does a child love its mother more or father more? /
S2: Well, accordin'; sometimes the mother and
sometimes the father.*—RLCF:227 [Cp *EDD according* adv, cit from wSom 'D'ye think ye'll be
able for come? / Well can't tell ye exactly, 'tis
'cordin whe'er I've a-finish or no'] **2.** PHRASES
2.1 accordin(g) as how *conj phr* [*X*] According
to how (much); in relation to what. ... (*About
how much do you give?) Is accordin' as how I
could make, not a regular amount.*—RLCF:76 **2.2
according to; accordingly to** *prep phrs* [*X*] In
keeping with the requirements of; depending
upon. **a.** *She didn[t] make the dress according to
what the mother want.*—(StVn) **b.** *Her peerents
has to removed from where she is living according
to repair.*—Jmca (Ms) **c.** *It is very common practice
nowadays for political parties to say one thing this
moment and change to something else the next
accordingly to how the party purpose is suited.*—Jfa
(1968, p.2) [Cp *EDD according* adv Wor, Glo,
Som and var dial 'comparatively, in proportion
to, dependent upon' (in general use) + cit from
Glo: 'He's the biggest according (i.e. in proportion) to his age.' Also Obs E as *OED according*
B. adv 'in a manner logically agreeing with the
premises'; = 'accordingly'. Also *AVB* Rom 1.3
'concerning his Son Jesus Christ our Lord,
which was made of the seed of David, according
to the flesh'. Also *EDD accordingly* adv Yks, Lin
+ Note, Yks. This word is hardly ever heard in
the sense of consequently + cit 'Jack's tallest,
but Jim's taller accordingly to his age' (1891)]
2.3 according to Hindu/Muslim rites *prep
phr* (Guyn, Trin) [Esp of weddings] In accordance with Hindu or Muslim religious
requirements. *Mr Sunny M— and his bride, the
former Hafeeza A—, who were married according
to Muslim rites [are] pictured above.*—ExP
(72.10.26, p.6) [See prec note]. **2.4 it is according** [*X*] It depends on the circumstances
or situation. *I do take a drink, but it is according.*—
(Bdos)

ac·cou·ri (a·cou·rie, a·ka·ree, a·ko·ri) *n*
(Guyn) ‖AGOUTI (Baha, etc) [Cariban. Cp

GDAA:199 Arekuna *akuurii* 'agouti', (*FTCC:
137*) Macusi *akuri* 'agouti'. Also *EILCA:45* Arawak (*Guyn*) *hokuuireeruu* 'agouti']

ac·cra (ac·kra, a·cra, ak·wa) *n* (CarA) ‖ *acara*
(Baha) ‖ *akara* (Gren) ‖ *akwa-lanmowi* (StLu)
1. (Tbgo, Trin) A fritter made of shredded
saltfish mixed in a batter of flour and seasoning.
2. (Baha) A small fried cake made by dropping
a pastry mixture of crushed black-eye peas and
other ingredients by the spoonful in hot oil.
[*ADMY* Yoruba *akara* 'an oily cake made from
beans ground and fried'] □ The form *accra* is
the most common, popularized by wide currency
in *Trin*. Usu without pl -s except in distinct
numerative contexts: 'We ordered fifty accras for
the party'.

ac·cra-and-float *n* (Trin) A saltfish fritter
and a small bake both fried in oil, eaten in
combination as a snack. [ACCRA + FLOAT]

ac·cus·tom *vb* PHRASES **1. accustom(ed) (of)**
vb (*phr*) (Bdos, Trin) [*X*] (To be) accustomed to
(doing sth). **a.** *Barbadians are accustomed purchasing foreign canned vegetables at prices far
higher than the fresh product, and they do this
without complaint.*—AdN (75.02.22, p.4) **b.** *She
was not accustom of people treating her like that
in her husband's lifetime.*—(Bdos) [From characteristic CarA Cr absence of vbl pa.t. marker
/-d/ and reduction of 'to' to [ʌ] wh here re-
surfaces as 'of'] **2. accustom with (sth)** *vb phr*
(CarA) [*X*] (To be) accustomed to (sth). **a.** *She
replied, 'They uses to call she Miss Essie before she
married, and they accustom with that, and they
still call her that.'*—RLCF:66 **b.** *Miss Tate, what
do you? You playing you donno how people like
what they accustom wid.*—PPGD:14 [Prob by
overlap of *accustomed to* + *familiar with*, with
characteristic Cr absence of /-d/ in (the former]
3. (not) accustomed to things *id phr* [*IF*]; **not
accustomed to anything/nothing** [*IF*]; **ain[t]
accustom to not[h]ing** [*X*] (CarA) [IF] (Not)
accustomed to good things; (not) accustomed
to a high standard of living. *Those people not
accustomed to anything and if you give them carpet
an[d] all that they will soon have it full of mud.*—
(Guyn) □ Occurs mostly in the neg form.

ace-deuce [e·s-'dyus] *n* (Belz) [*AF*] Bosom
friends; close companions. *If you lay a finger on
Tom, you will have to reckon with Jack as well.
Those two are ace-deuce.*—(Belz) [As close as the
ace (one) and deuce (two) of cards]

achar (achaar, atchar [ača:r] *n* (Guyn, Trin)
[Indic] A mixture of pieces of green mango and
other fruit with peppers, ground massala, vinegar
and salt in mustard oil; it is an E Indian preserved
condiment. [Bhoj *atchaar* < Hin *achaar*,
'pickles']. □ Also in erron forms *amchar, an-
char* by folk etym from Hin *aam* 'mango' +
char 'four' perh in ref to the quartering of the
mango wh is the chief ingredient.

Ach·ha! [ačča] (Guyn, Trin) [Indic] **1.** Good!; Okay! All right!; Fine! [Hin *Achchhaa!*, Good!; Well!; All right!] **2.** PHRASE **2.1 Achha bhaiya!** All right, brother!; Well okay then, brother! [Hin *Achchhaa* + *bhaiya*, 'brother'] □ A leave-taking formula among East Indian males.

a·chi·po·ko *n* (Guyn) See ASIPOKO

acid *n* (Bdos, Guyn) [*AF*] **1.** Plain rum. [Prob due to the sharp effect of undiluted rum on the palate and throat] **2.** PHRASE **2.1 fire the acid** [*AF*] To drink rum. **a.** *The boys were firin*[*g*] *the acid since mornin*[*g*] *so by two o'clock they were loud, loud, yo*[*u*] *know—ready for anything.—* (Bdos) **b.** *Well I would get away from the wife a Saturday night an*[*d*] *meet at one o*[*f*] *the houses, yo*[*u*] *see, to fire the acid wit*[*h*] *the fello*[*w*]*s.—* (Guyn)

ac·kee* (akee) ['aki] *n* (CarA) ‖ *ackee-apple, vegetable-brain* (Jmca) ‖ *Jamaica-ackee* (StVn) **1.** A pendent, scarlet, pear-shaped fruit, splitting in three when ripe and disclosing three shiny black seeds attached to a cream-coloured flesh wh is edible; it is borne in small clusters on a flowering evergreen tree; *Blighia sapida* (*Sapindaceae*). *Ackees must be allowed to burst open on the tree, because if picked and opened by hand, they can cause poisoning, if cooked and eaten.*—AdN (77.09.02, p.8) [*DJE*: Kru *a-kee*, and cp Twi *aŋkye*, 'a kind of wild cashew'] □ **1.** The alternative spelling **akee** is not recommended in ref to this fruit, as that serves to distinguish a different *ECar* fruit. (See.) *Ackee* is officially the 'National Fruit' of *Jmca*. **2.** Without -*s* when referring to a meal, '*a dish of ackee*', '*it's ackee for lunch*', etc. With -*s* when the meaning is 'fruits'—*selling ackees, tree full of ackees,* etc. **2.** PHRASE **2.1 ackee and saltfish** *n phr* (Jmca) A meal made of the boiled and fried flesh of ripe ackees, cooked with oil, onions and salted codfish.—*DJPVP:12. Secondly, he [the new Governor-General of Jamaica] is a man of the people, as Jamaican as 'ackee and saltfish'.*—DeM (62.11.03, p.3) **3.** [*X*] See AKEE

ac·kra *n* (Dmca, Jmca, StLu, Trin, USVI) See ACCRA

a·co·ma *n* (Gren, Trin) ‖ MASTIC (Baha, etc)

a·cou·rie *n* (Guyn) See ACCOURI

a·cou·shi-ant(s) [a'kuši an(t)s] *n* (Guyn) ‖ *bachac* (Trin) ‖ *coushi-ants* (Guyn) ‖ *cush-cush, (cuss-cuss)ant(s), drogher-ant(s), kooshi, kuse, kushay, kushy-ant(s)* (Guyn) ‖ *parasolant(s)* (Trin) ‖ *tactac-ant(s)* (Dmca) ‖ *umbrella-ant(s)* (Belz, Guyn) A half-inch long, black or brown ant wh cuts off pieces of green leaf that it carries underground to rot and grow fungus on wh it feeds; its habit of moving in columns with the piece of green leaf held high gives it the alternative names of PARASOL or UMBRELLA ANT; *Atta sexdens* or *A. cephalotes* or *Acromyrmex octospinosus* (*Formicidae*). *Farmer*

R— said that acoushi ants and hard-back beetles are posing a great problem to him and he was given advice recently on the control by the Agricultural Field Assistant. Since then, some of the acoushi ants' nests have been settled.—GyG (73.04.03, p.5) [An Amerindian name. Cp *EILCA:46* Arawak *kuusee* 'kushy ant'. Also *BAED* Arawak *khose* 'parasol ants wh are fond of eating the leaves of garden plants'] □ This is the official name in Guyn, as a recognized insect pest.

ac·quee·ro *n* (Guyn) See AKUYURU

acre mon·ey *n phr* (Guyn) [Law] A small annual rent per acre due from a person to whom the Government has granted rights to an area of land for purposes of prospecting, or of operating the timber or other industry.

a·cro·lect *n* [Linguistics] The best level of spoken English developed in a (Commonwealth Caribbean) territory; the educated English of a Caribbean territory that may be considered the Standard English of that territory; the best-structured, unaffected speech at wh a dialect-speaking community aims. [< Gk *acros* 'peak, summit' + *lektos* 'speech'. The term was coined by W.A. Stewart, writing on the 'Urban Negro Speech' of Washington, U.S.A.: 'this kind of speech wh is generally considered the 'best' in the Washington Negro community, and it seems to be the model aimed at in formal education.... I will refer to this topmost dialect in the local sociolinguistic hierarchy as acrolect'. (in *Social Dialects and Language Learning*, eds. R. Shuy et al., 1964, p.15). The concept has since then been conveniently applied to Caribbean Anglophone situations]

a·cro·lec·tal *adj* [Linguistics] Related or belonging to the best-structured, unaffected speech that is native to a CarA territory. [*Acrolect* + adj suf -*al*]

across PHRASE **walk across (sb)** *vb phr* (Bdos) [*IF*] To cross the path of (sb). *I remember particularly a certain gentleman in Dover whose horses seemed to like walking across people who are going home early in the morning in their cars, and we have had serious accidents caused along that road.*—Bdos (Hd, 75.05.20, p.5098)

act; act up [ak(t)] *vb intr* (Bdos, Guyn, Jmca) [*IF*] **1.** To behave in the manner of a person who is mentally disturbed; to show signs of madness. **a.** *Since her husband died she has been 'ackin' steadily and the family have tried to watch her.*—(Bdos) **b.** *... and it was decided that my friend should be referred to the Observation Ward. So they went down to the police station and made a complaint that he was of 'unsound mind' and that he was 'acting up'.*—SuC (78.03.19, p.10) [Cp *EDD act* (as used in Irel and many listed counties of England) implying 'action of a reprehensible nature'] □ This folk usage appears to be long established. It occurs in such modified forms as '*act like he*[*'s*] *not* / *ain*[*t*] *right in his* *head', 'not act like his head is too good'*. **2.** To behave; to conduct yourself; to react. **a.** *You['re] just a child but you['re] trying to act like if you're a big woman.*—(Belz) **b.** *You should have told me all those details, so that when he came to me with his nonsense and complaints I would know just how to act.*—(Guyn) [A specific sense of *OED act* v 3. *arch* 'to carry out an action, perform'] **3.** PHRASES **3.1 act up yourself** [ɛkʌp yʌsɛlf] *vb phr* (Belz) [*AF*] To make a fool of yourself. **a.** *He don[t] know what he talkin[g] [a]bout. He only go de[re] an[d] ac[t] up [h]imself an[d] make people laugh at him.*—(Belz) [*EDD act* 6. 'to act oneself; to play the fool' + cit from wCor 'He was tipsy and acting himself fine'] **3.2 act on** *vb phr* (CarA) To take action against (sb); [of medicine] to have a (usu laxative) effect on (sb). **a.** *P.C. Braveboy and J— happened to see 'Spiderman' with a Cassette Radio player identical to the one described by Fr S—. Immediately they acted on the suspect and were able to make him talk.*—ToR (76.03.28, p.3) **b.** *Man, dat medicine act on me an[d] had me goin[g] de whole day.*—(Guyn) [A specific sense of *OED act* 10. b. 'to act on: to exert influence on; affect']

ac·tion¹ *n* (StKt) [*IF*] A bowel movement. *Well I drink some salts and it really give me the action.*—(StKt) [From the sense of ACT ON (Phr 3.2, cit b. of ACT]

ac·tion² *vb tr* (Guyn) [*X*] To take legal action against (sb). *She say she goin[g] to action dem in court—but she always ready to action people—she's too cantankerous.*—(Guyn)

Adam's nee·dle* *n phr* (CarA) ‖ **bridal wreath** (Angu) ‖ **sentinel** (Angu) ‖ **yucca** (CarA) An upright plant, with stiff, green, two-foot long, sharp-pointed leaves radiating densely from its single stem; it bears after many years a large, cone-shaped cluster of pearl-white flowers; *Yucca aloifolia* (*Liliaceae*). (Also called ‖ **Spanish bayonet** in some gardening books) (*VISTP:* 27). [From the thread-like growths hanging from leaves of some varieties (*Yucca filamentosa*), and ref to Gen.111. 7.]

ad·hoc·ism [adhɒkızm] /1'122/ *n* (Bdos) The practice or habit of dealing with a critical matter in some convenient way according to the circumstances or demands of the moment, without relating the particular decision to a policy. *There is so much adhocism in Government whether in health, trade or finance. Everything is static and you deal with a problem as it comes up.*—Bdos (Hd, 74.12.19, p.767) [Lat *ad hoc* 'to/for this thing' + Gk *ism*, noun-making suff with sense 'system or principle', but with the added connotation of disapproval. Cp *McCarthyism, Jingoism,* etc] □ This evidently CarA invention reflects a felt need for a *Derog* n as indicated in *OEDS adhoc* c. (Nonce-words) adhoc(k)ing, adhoc-ery, ad-hoc-ness with cits 1930–61; Also in *BDNE:1·ad'hocery* (-*ccey,* -*ckery*) as AmE from 1968.

ad·hoc·ra·cy [adhɒkrasi] *n* (Trin) [*Derog*] Government of a country or the running of any large organization by means of rulings or decisions wh are convenient to prevailing circumstances, but not related to any established policy. *Perhaps the biggest questions here of all are the matter of public acceptability and the issue of secession from Tobago. What the freewheeling adhocracy has done over the 20 last years has been to develop a level of local administration run from Whitehall and from the Prime Minister's personal St Ann's Estate.*—TaP (77.01.16, p.1) [*Adhoc* (as prec) + Gk -*kratia* 'power', by analogy with demo-cracy, auto-cracy, etc. Adhocracy is noted in *BDNE:1* as AmE from 1970]

ad·hoc·ra·tic *adj* (Guyn) [*Derog*] [Of decisions] Made to suit the convenience or circumstances of the moment with no necessary relation to general policy. *Through geographical circumstances, the Jamaican government has been spared what would have doubtlessly been severe pain for its 'adhocratic' foreign policy were it to have had to decide to allow that island to be used as a staging post for Cuban troops going to Angola. Jamaica is too close to Cuba and too far from the Atlantic to have been helpful.*—SuC (76.01.10, p.13) [From adhocracy on the analogy of democratic]

Ad·min·is·tra·tor (CarA) [Hist] The chief colonial executive officer of an island whose population and resources were too small to warrant the appointment of a resident Governor. *Under the (1956) Constitution the Government of Dominica was administered by an Administrator (as representative of the Governor of the Windward Islands) assisted by an Executive Council which consisted of, apart from the Administrator, the Crown Attorney and Financial Secretary as ex-officio members.*—SDD:16

ad·mi·ral(s) *n* (Bdos, Guyn) ‖ **edger-boy biscuit(s)** (Guyn) ‖ **hard-boys** (Bdos) [*Obs—AF*] A hard salt biscuit about two inches square. *Her job then was to pack biscuits into barrels. The names of the biscuits were applied to sizes as the large ones were called Admirals, the medium were called Middles and the smallest were Crackers or Commodores.*—DAAD:6 [From the commercial name impressed on the biscuit wh was produced in the early 1900s, and still referred to by older folk]

ad·mire *vb tr* (Bdos) [*IF*] To marvel at; to feel or express surprise at. *I had to admire the damage that the fire did.*—HDB:1 [EE sense—1876, also dial E in Irel, etc. See *OED admire* 2. and *EDD*] □ Perh obsolescent.

adobe (house) [ado:b] *n* (*phr*) (Belz) ‖ **ajoupa** (Dmca, etc) ‖ **mud-house** (Guyn) A hut-like dwelling using the earth, rammed and smooth, as floor, with thickly clay-coated walls and a roof of thatched palm leaves. *Adobe houses are mostly used by the Maya Indians, with whom they are traditional. Although the word adobe really means* *flat sun-dried bricks and houses made with them, it is applied in this country to clay-coated houses. The local house is rectangular with a framework of 'bush sticks' (saplings and withes) which follows a centuries old conventional design. With their white walls, painted doors and shutters and neatly trimmed thatch the adobe houses look most attractive.*—ABSBH:91 [Sp *adobe* 'a brick not yet burnt, baked in the sun', perh < Arabic *atob* of same meaning. Sp *adobar* 'to make sth up']

ad·vance *vbl adj* (CarA) [X] Advanced. **a.** *Admitting he, too, was guilty of such actions, the student, who will take advance level GCE in mathematics, chemistry and literature, nevertheless said that he made a point of studying during the term as much as he could.*—ExP (72.02.14, p.3) **b.** *'A different, but a more better, more advance place than where I come from ...' he said.*—CWFYS:17 [By characteristic CarA Cr absence of vbl pa. part. /-d/ in speech, commonly reflected in this written form] □ Also a frequent occurrence in otherwise educated CE speech.

ad·vance back *vb phr* (Tbgo) [X] Move back, move away; retreat. *The conductor told the passengers to advance back to keep clear of the driver.*—(Tbgo)

ad·van·tage[1] *n* (CarA) [IF] **1.** An unfair act; a piece of bullying; an unfair advantage. *If I see advantage taking place, I can't stand by and not do anything.*—(Tbgo) **2.** PHRASES **2.1 take advantage/of/on/over (sb)** *vb phr* (CarA) [X] To bully; to take a mean advantage of (sb); to treat (sb) very unfairly. **a.** *But I find the Prefects don't stop the bigger boys taking advantage of smaller boys.*—(Trin) **b.** *When you are married and you are not working your husband tends to take advantage on you.*—Guyn (Ms) **c.** *When yo[u] de[re] bad dem same man does try fo[r] tak[e] advantage over yo[u].*—(Guyn) □ SE to *take advantage of* generally applies to circumstances, situations. When applied to persons it implies 'cheating, outwitting unfairly', never physical beating as it regularly does in CE. In the physical sense in SE one 'gains an advantage over' or 'has the advantage of' an opponent.

ad·van·tage[2] *adj* (CarA) [X] Grossly unfair; very unjust; bullying. **a.** *Butts: Iron man does get on ignorant eh? Why all you fellas so advantage?*—HPP:10 **b.** *You want to stay in de wicket all afternoon and got us over here sweatin[g]! You advantage, man.*—(Nevs) [By functional n > adj shift of ADVANTAGE[1]]

ad·van·tage[3] *vb tr* (CarA) [X] To bully; to misuse (sb) grossly; to subject (sb) to unfair pressure. **a.** *He met a Mr Leo D— and said to him they were taking the youth to the station 'to advantage him'.*—ToR (77.07.06, p.3) **b.** *I turned to him and tell him 'is because I am not from the village of Tabernacle and because I haven't got even a cousin in the village and because he knows my leg broken twice and I get it burnt up again make three times—that's why you advantaging me*

like that.—DeM (73.07.06) [Prob by functional n > vb shift of ADVANTAGE[1]]

ad·van·ta·geous [ad'vantıȷʌs] /12′21/ *adj* (Belz, Tbgo, Trin) [X] Unfair; unjust; bullying; very inconsiderate. **a.** *Yu want chance me, but yu wouldn't go knock no man like that. (Shrieking) Yu too advantageous!*—HF:49 **b.** *You look for the best piece of the family land and take it for yourself; I didn't say anything. Now you want to claim part of my portion as yours. You too advantageous!*—(Tbgo) [Prob a refinement of the Cr usage preserved in ADVANTAGE[2], but cp also obs and rare E usage as *OED advantageous*[2] 'apt to take advantage']

ad·van·tage-ta·ker *n* (Bdos, Guyn, Jmca, Trin) [IF] One who has the habit of taking a very unfair advantage of others; a barefaced bully. *'You smoking? Not in my house!' And she boxed Maisie right and left about the face until to save herself Maisie ran from the room. / Then he heard Maisie's voice outside raised. 'You old advantage-taker! But I am not going to take this so, though.'*—JMA:153 [ADVANTAGE[1] + *taker*, 'one who takes']

ad·vice [advais] *vb tr* (Trin) [X] Advise. *'All right mister London', Galahad say, 'You been here for a long time, what you would advice me as a newcomer to do?' / 'I would advice you to hustle a passage back home to Trinidad today.'*—STLL:23

ad·vi·ces *n pl* (Bdos) Opinions offered in order to help people out of difficulties; pieces of advice. **a.** *Dear Christine, / I am always reading your advices and I would like a problem solved*—NaT (83.01.01) **b.** *Not long ago the Very Rev Dean Harold Crichlow, in a sermon at St Michael's Cathedral, spoke of the barriers which divide the Barbadian society and offered us the benefit of his advices in breaking down such walls ... / These are advices easily given, and of which both young and old are not unaware.*—CTOY [Perh a survival of 18C E. Cp *OED advice* 8., cit (1710) 'A mail from Holland which brought me several Advices'] □ In current E the pl usu refers to military intelligence or formal 'communications sent from a distance' COD.

ad·vi·so·ry *n* (CarA) Official advice from the meteorological service giving warning, location, intensity, path and precautions needed concerning tropical storms and hurricanes; (SE) a weather advisory. [Hurricane information sheet]. □ OED2 lists as AmE

ad·vo·cate /1′12/ *vb intr* PHRASE **advocate for** (Bdos, Guyn) [X] To propose or advance (an idea, suggestion, plan, etc); to advocate. **a.** *Mr C— started to advocate for this system of voting from the year 1919.*—DaC (53.04.23, p.2) **b.** *... and I sincerely hope that I will be able to make this contribution towards the old age pensioners for which I have been advocating over the years.*—Bdos (Hd, 76.03.19, p.6382) [Obs E usage, as

OED advocate 1. intr 'to plead *for*' (arch) + cit–'1872 'I am not going to advocate for this sense' [of the word]]

aer·at·ed (drink/water) [eiretid] /ı'12'2/ *n (phr)* (CarA) ‖ COOL-DRINK (CarA) □ These terms are giving way to *soft drink, sweet drink*, less often also to *soda*.

ae·ta *n* (Guyn) See ITE

af·ford *vb tr* (Bdos) *PHRASE* **afford (sb) to do (sth)** (Bdos) [*X*] To allow or enable (sb) to do (sth). **a.** *Jamaica established a trade-centre and permanent trade exhibition in Port-of-Spain last October and this affords Mr B— to keep in touch with the CARIFTA market by visiting countries on a regular basis.*—AdN (72.12.15, p.1) **b.** *Early last year I was then told that I was not working for enough money to afford me to pay the rent, although all the time people who work for less than I do make applications ... and got houses.*—NaT (74.03.03, p.4) [A shift in sense of *OED* afford 5. 'to give of what one has, bestow, grant', as in expressions like 'the trees afforded some shade', to mean 'offer', 'allow'] □ IAE *afford* does not take this type of complement.

af·fou yam *n phr* (Jmca, Tbgo, Trin) See AFU YAM

afire *adv PHRASE* **catch afire** *vb phr* (CarA) [*X*] To catch fire; to start to blaze. **a.** *The oil-stove flared up and her dress caught afire.*—(StVn) **b.** *Well yo[u] know Carnival time de whole o[f] Trinidad ketch afire.*—(Trin) **c.** *One building obliquely opposite the service station-restaurant caught afire, and the roof and first storey ... were destroyed.*—AdN (71.06.04, p.1) [/-a-/ interpolated by anaptyxis. (Cp *thataway* 'that way' in BrE) and infl by SE adv *afire* in predicative position as in 'the house is afire']

afòs (a(h) fus(s), fuss¹, first) [a'fʌs] *excl adv* (Dmca, Gren, Trin) [*AF*] **1.** [Introducing an excl] To what an extent!; How! **a.** *I see people running, running / and some cry / and some shout / and some scream; / and some saying 'Praise God' / a fus dose people glad.*—TLTH:18 **b.** *Now they stood around the carcass. 'Look at 'e eye', Joe said. 'It look like 'e dead long time. Ah fuss 'e stink'*—SABS:24 **2.** [Adv intensifier] To such an extent; so much. **a.** *They could eat an ostrich, ah fuss they hungry.*—RLCF:206 **b.** *They hide the judges' name / Ah fuss they shame.*—Cso (Sparrow) [< 17C Fr *à force*, 'violently' as in *prendre à force*, a sense wh the expression has lost in Mod Fr. Sense 2. may refl a modern IF Fr sense 'plentifully', as in *en recevoir à force*. Hait Cr *afos* is only listed *HCEF* as conjunction] □ This is an item of high frequency in *Trin* speech rising to *IF* status. As an indicator of strong feeling it always begins its clause. The form *a fòs* is desirable as indicating the Fr Cr orig of this phr and avoiding confusion with Trin E *fuss* 'first'. See FIRST 1.

afraid (of) *adj* (Gren) [*AF*] [Of the human body] Disagreeably sensitive (to). *If coreilli bush is being used as a contraceptive some salt is added to the drink. Informants maintain that a woman's womb is 'afraid' of salt and bitterness (coreilli bush is very bitter) and so the womb just open up.*—LSFMG:14

Af·ri·ca *n PHRASE* **go(ne) back to Africa** *vb phr* (Guyn) [*AF*—*Joc*] [Of a black man] To marry a black woman or one much darker in complexion than himself. [By contrast with the habit of marrying a woman of lighter skin-colour to produce children less dark-skinned than the father, wh is considered to be moving away from the man's 'African', i.e. slave, origins]

Af·ri·can *n, adj* (CarA) **1.** [Hist] (A slave) born in Africa (as opposed to one born on a W Indian plantation); [post-emancipation] a black person with no physical traits of white mixture. *In 1826 the slave population of Trinidad was 15, 291 Creole and 7, 832 African.*—(Caq 4. 3, 4) **2.** (A custom, game, etc) having features originating in Africa, and usu involving words or phrases of unidentified origins or meaning. □ The earlier pejoration attached to this word is less popular in present CE but has not disappeared except in strictly cultural (usu also rural) connections (sense 2.) As a ref to race it is rare.

Af·ri·can na·tion-dance *n phr* (Gren) See NATION-DANCE

Af·ri·can·ness [afrıkannıs] *n* **1.** The fact of being black or of African descent. **2.** Features, behaviour, or emotions considered characteristic of people of African descent. [Adj *African* + noun-forming suffix *-ness*] □ In recent times the term *Africanity* has also emerged, with a connotation of social dignity.

Af·ri·can tu·lip-tree* *n phr* (CarA) ‖ *tulip tree* (CarA) ‖ *water-spout* (Bdos, StKt) A large, green, bushy, ornamental tree bearing clusters of bright red, tulip-shaped flowers (with central buds containing liquid under pressure) and long narrow pods; *Spathodea campanulata* (*Bignoniaceae*); also known as 'fountain tree', 'flame of the forest', 'bâton de sorcier' *HAT*. [African (because the tree was first botanically recorded on the Gold Coast of Africa, 1787, *FIS*) + *tulip* (because of the brilliance, shape and texture of the flower)] □ This name is sometimes erroneously used as an alternative for the *cordia*.

Af·ro¹ *adj, n* (CarA) **1.** (Of, related to or emphasizing) a person's blackness (Ex: Miss Afro Personality Contest); identifying AFRICANNESS or African heritage (Ex: *Afro Drumming*). **2.** [Usu without capital] A round-headed hairstyle adopted by both male and female persons of African descent in wh the natural quality and thickness of the hair are emphasized. **3.** *PHRASES* **3.1 go afro; go into afro** *vb phr* (CarA) [*IF*] **(i)** [Mostly of women] Adapt the hair to the round-headed style known as AFRO. **(ii)** Dress in African style, esp on formal occasions. **3.2 wear (an) afro** *vb phr* (CarA) To dress the hair in AFRO style or to wear a wig of the same kind. [By analogy with such prefixes as Euro-, Anglo-, Franco-, etc, then by abbr used as adj as a preferred replacement of *African, Negro* in sense 1., thence a noun esp infl in this function by sense 2. In sense 1. it is also used in combinations identifying ethnic orig. See AFRO-³]

af·ro² *vb tr*; **afroed** *adj* (CarA) To style the hair in the round-headed fashion known as AFRO. *A black woman's face takes on a new beauty when her hair is afroed.*—Guyn (Ms) [By functional shift of AFRO¹, sense 2.]

Af·ro³ *pref* (CarA) [The term AFRO replaces the term 'Negro' in general references to person, nationality or racial stock, and in such cases capitalization seems appropriate; hence *Afro ballet, Afro descent, Afro-Guyanese*, etc. Secondly, by extension, it refers to some associated type of article or a style (often in attributive, sometimes vbl function) and in such cases lower case 'afro' seems appropriate; hence *afro beads, afroed, afro-haired, afrojack*, etc where the specific sense 'Negro' becomes secondary or misleading. Hyphenation may be used where *Afro* is properly a prefix rather than an attributive n. Hence *Afro-Guyanese, afro-haired*, etc but *Afro drumming, afro shirt*, etc]

Af·ro-A·me·rin·di·an *adj* Comprising both black and Amerindian people. *Besides there are significant Afro-Amerindian communities in several of the countries mentioned above.*—AdN (73.05.06, p.11) □ Contrast *boviander*

Af·ro bal·let *n phr* (Bdos) Stage-dancing, considered characteristic of African culture, in wh body movements are much more vigorously emphasized than foot movements.

af·ro beads *n phr* (CarA) A set of necklaces made of beads, small seeds and shell worn by both men and women as part of a fashion of dressing considered African.

Af·ro-Ca·rib·be·an [-ka'ribiən] *adj, n* (CarA) ‖ *Afro-West Indian* (CarA) (Of or associated with) any Caribbean person(s) of African descent. *The show moved from folk songs and old calypsoes to dances of Afro-Caribbean and East Indian culture.*—ExP (76.08.02, p.10) □ Similarly *Afro-Bahamian/-Barbadian*, etc in ref to any CarA State, but particularly where there is, in contrast, a notable part of the population that is non-African.

Af·ro·cen·tric *adj* Focusing interest or consideration more on African cultures and items than on any others; principally concerned with African people and things. [By analogy and in contrast with *Eurocentric* (as BNDE:2), and used by *CarA* sociologists from the 1960s]

af·ro chain *n phr* (CarA) A large symbolic chain necklace with a central piece or pendant, usu worn by men as part of a fashion of dressing that is considered African.

af·ro clothes/dress *n phr* (CarA) Brightly coloured formal dress considered more characteristic of African culture, esp (for men) varieties of AFRO-JAC(K) and (for women) loose-fitting flower-patterned dresses with matching headwear.

af·ro comb *n phr* (CarA) ‖ *afro pick* (CarA) A type of comb usu with a handle shaped like a head and neck, and long prongs of metal, wood, or hard material, used for tending the AFRO hairstyle.

Af·ro-Cre·ole *adj* Of basically African origin but having particular characteristics developed in a Caribbean territory. *The French influence is everywhere in our Afro-Creole culture; most noticeable in our patois.*—HTDS:109

Af·ro-French *adj* Of mixed African and French origin. *Carnival, or Masquerade, as it was more popularly called in Dominica, was strongly an Afro-French festival.*—HTDS:94

af·ro hair·do; **af.ro hair-style, af.ro-style hair.do** *n phr* (CarA) The round-headed hairstyle more commonly called the AFRO¹ 2.

af·ro-hair·ed *adj* (Bdos) Having the hair in the round-headed style known as AFRO¹ 2; AFROED. [AFRO¹ 4. adj + *hair* + *ed*, as derivational adj compound. Cp SE formations such as *levelheaded*, etc]

Af·ro-In·di·an *adj* (Guyn, Trin) Combining or representing people of both African and East Indian descent, or the influences of their two cultures.

af·ro·jac(k) (af·ro-jac) /1'12/ *n* (CarA) ‖ *afro shirt* (CarA) A short-sleeved upper garment of light colourful material, without collar or buttons, but with minor embroidery; it is used by men as casual wear replacing the European jacket. *Today tourists can buy afro-jacs ... along the beaches.... The afro-jac has also fitted into the trend towards unisex clothing and is worn with equal pride by both male and female today.*—NaT (75.10.26, p.15) [Abbr of AFRO¹ + *jacket* and by analogy with SHIRT-JAC]

af·ro pick *n phr* (CarA) ‖ AFRO COMB (CarA) [From its use in plucking or pulling apart the close strands of hair]

af·ro puff *n phr* (CarA) [Of a girl's hairstyle] A soft round mass of hair produced by teasing and shaping the tied-off ends.

Af·ro-Sax·on *adj, n* (CarA) [Derog] (Characterizing) a person, esp a man, of black or brown skin who follows modes of behaviour and speech that are considered characteristic of English, or generally of white people. *Even at the United Nations, West Indians reject African for European and American models to such a degree that some Africans regard Jamaica as a reactionary black English outpost in the lap of America and term the West Indians 'Afro-Saxons'*—FCR:325 (D. Lowenthal) [By analogy < SE *Anglo-Saxon*]

af·ro shirt *n phr* (CarA) ‖ AFROJACK (CarA)

Af·ro-West In·di·an *adj, n* (CarA) ‖ AFRO-CARIBBEAN (CarA) *The true culture of the Afro-West Indian ... has been unjustly depraved by the White man; but drumming as an indigenious part of our national heritage can never be nationally ignored*—NeJ (74.11.15, p.2)

af·ter¹ *prep* (CarA) **1.** [As extension of vbs implying pursuit or attack] In pursuit of; at. **a.** *I thirty-four but I look good, pet. Down to young boy whistle after me when I walk the street.*—HF:13 **b.** *The dog jumped after me and I turned back.*—(StVn) **c.** *She threw the stick after the cat.*—Guyn (Ms) [Cp*EDD after* 7. 'to be after, to be in pursuit of, to follow, to aim at', etc + cits from N Cy. Cp also *OED after* 4. b. 'to be, go, send after sb or sth'] **2.** For (in sense of longing, hankering). *Look! You can['t] go out and leave this child like that! This child cry whole day after you.*—(Guyn) [Cp *OED after* 5. e. (with vbs, etc. of desire)] **3.** (Bdos, Guyn) [In telling the time of day] Past. **a.** *It is half after two already.*—(Guyn) **b.** *I'll be there about quarter after three.*—(Bdos) [As *OEDS after* prep 8. b. Past (a certain hour). Now chiefly dial and US *EDD after* 3. 'of time: used instead of 'past' when speaking of the time of day' + cits from Oxf, Suf, Dev] **4.** (Guyn) For more than (a certain length of time); still ... after. *A tell yo[u] she really neglects that child. I ain[t] know how it ain['t] dead. Look, some days you can hear that poor child crying after two hours, you believe me?*—(Guyn) **5.** PHRASES **5.1 be after (sb) to do (sth)** (Dmca, StLu) [*IF*] ‖ BE BEHIND (SB) TO DO (STH) (CarA) See BEHIND¹ 1. *All de time he after me to do m[y] hair in afro an[d] now A do it he don[t] like it.*—(StLu) **5.2 talk after sb** (Guyn) [*IF*] Rely on what sb says; take it from sb. *Listen—and you can talk after me! That old lady gave him all her business to handle and he robbed her! I know that!*—(Guyn) [Cp *OED after* 12. c. 'in accordance with the statements of' Obs or arch]

af·ter² *causal conj* (CarA) [*IF/F*] **1.** Seeing that; since; because. **a.** *After you didn't come I thought the pain must have started bothering you again.*—(Guyn) **b.** *After she walk all here wid it you have to give her some.*—(Gren) **c.** *After you so stupid A must bawl at you!*—MCET]:56 **2.** Inasmuch as; whenever; if it so happens that. **a.** *On the whole, there would be much better standards of health if such hostels are formed. I say so because after some mothers cannot support their families they go into prostitution.*—AdN (72.12.15, p.4) **b.** *My father, after you see him stop talking, you*

look out! It's blows next.—(Guyn) [Cp *OED after* prep 9. 'of temporal and logical sequence: subsequent to and in consequence of' This prep use easily slips into the function of a causal conj i.e. *after* + noun clause > *after* + conditional, temporal, etc clause in CE] **3.** PHRASES **3.1 after all is said and done** (CarA) [*IF*] When the facts are fully faced; when the talking is over and it is time for action. □ A conversational catch phrase. **3.2 after that** *conj phr* (Dmca) [In simple conj sense and function] After. *Miss C— declared: 'We would like the terrorists to know that they must release Mr H— immediately, that they must give up their guns and it is only after that this is done, that the Government will appoint someone to talk to them.'*—AdN (81.02.14, p.1) [Perh a survival from EE. Cp *OED after* c. 1. b. with relative particle only. Arch + cit (1611) 'After that the king had burnt the roule'] **3.3 after when** *conj phr* (Guyn, Jmca, StVn) [*X*] [In both temporal and causal functions] After; seeing that. **a.** *After when she came back, dey went to de beach.*—(StVn) **b.** *After when [h]e hit me, A hit [h]e back.*—(Guyn)

af·ter³ [ˈaːftʌ] *adv, conj* (Belz, Jmca) [*IF*] [Denoting protest] Surely; after all. **a.** *Lawyer: You saw the intruder on the bed with the lady? / Child-witness: Yes, sir. / Lawyer: What did he do to her? (No answer) Lawyer: Come, come. What did he do? Why won't you tell the court? / Witness: After you know, sir.*—Belz (CR) **b.** *You expect me to believe that? After, I wasn't born big [i.e. I wasn't born yesterday]*—(Belz) □ Almost restricted to speech since, in this function, AFTER requires strong stress on and lengthening of the initial vowel.

af·ter-call *n* (Guyn) The second note or sound wh is heard just before the BUCK-TOP stops spinning. (*YRRC:13*). *The aftercall was the musical sound somewhat like the note of a cello heard when the top is to cease spinning.*—DGF:4 [The wailing sound of the top is considered 'calling'. Cp *OEDS after-sound* 'a subsequent sound; an echo']

af·ter-call buck top *n phr* (CarA) A BUCK TOP made with holes appropriately cut to produce an AFTER-CALL.

af·ter-claps *n* (Belz) [*AF*] Consequences; bad effects or results; aftermath. *I hear Tom is messing with drugs. I hope he can stand the after-claps.*—(Belz) [*EDD afterclap* sb (as used in Sc and many listed counties of Eng through to Dev and Cor). 1. 'evil consequences' 2. 'unexpected sequel']

af·ter-crop *adj* (CarA) **1.** ‖ CROP-OVER (CarA) *They listened intently as he told his story. It was about a beautiful woman who came to the After-crop dance and lured one of the young men to the edge of the cliff.*—DMM:39 **2.** Pertaining to the period of unemployment after the harvesting of the sugar-cane crop. *The Union was demandiang that provision be made to finance the* *workers during the long after-crop season.*—Bdos (Ms)

af·ter-cul·ti·va·tion *n* (CarA) [Agric Ind] Any process or method of soil culture (such as loosening, prick-forking, etc) applied between the planting of the crop and its reaping. *Clean-weeding has been condemned in Banana cultivation. Weeds other than grasses should be encouraged. After-cultivation is not necessary unless the soil structure becomes poor and compacted and it becomes necessary to increase aeration and water absorption. Forking frequently damages the banana roots.*—AdM (72.04.16, p.10)

af·ter·noon *n* (Bdos, Guyn) [*AF—Joc*] The buttocks, esp large protruberant female buttocks; steatopygia. [Prob from the general nautical sense of *aft*, 'hinder part of a ship' (women also being sometimes humorously referred to in *AF CE* as 'craft', 'cruiser'), whence *afternoon* as Joc euphemism]

a fus (ah fuss) *excl adv* (Dmca, etc) See AFÒS

afu yam (af·fou yam) *n phr* (CarA) ‖ YELLOW YAM (CarA) **a.** *But we have 'Afu yam' and Congo potato.... 'Congo Afua' is a common nickname which Black Charlotteville mothers give to their children when they are careless about clean clothes and tidiness in appearance.*—EFSLC:36 **b.** *This is what we generally calls the afu yam but I think some people calls it negro yam—you find it have a rough skin and two foot like.*—(Jmca) [Prob < Twi *afũ-afũ*, 'rough, rugged', and reinforced by Twi *afúw*, 'cultivated ground'] □ *Afu*, satisfying both etym and pronunc is preferable.

again[1] *adv* **1.** (Belz, Gren, Trin) [*IF*] More; still; in addition. **a.** *SI: We won't have enough time to eat this dinner ... we're near to landing. / S2: Oh no! I'm sure we have half an hour again on this aircraft.*—(Trin) **b.** *You suck all de plum and A still give you two again.*—(Gren) **c.** *You drank your tea. Now what do you want again?*—(Belz) **2.** (CarA) [*IF*] [Indicating a change of mind or of situation, after 'not'] Any longer; any more. **a.** *'According to the price list given by the JLA at de-control, plain grass-fed animals should not be sold for more than $20 a 100 lbs, but those animals don't seem to exist again', a butcher on May Pen said.*—DaG (71.05.17) **b.** *What has been happening is the complete divorce of the average Trini from the decision-making process ... so much so that he appears not to care again and is leading his own life.*—BoM (72.02.02, p.3) [A probable transfer of concept from Afr langs. Cp DAFL Twi *e-bio*, 'again, futhermore, any more'; in neg sentences 'no more', ex *ɔmma bio*, 'He's not coming any more'; also Efik, Kikongo, etc. Such idiomatic bases could have been reinforced by an extension of the SE sense of (not) *again* '(not) another time' to mean '(not) any other time', as *OED again* adv 4. 'another time' + cit from Shak 'I shall not look upon his like again' (Hamlet I.2, 188)] □ This *IF* usage is clear in speech where, however, sentence intonation

safeguards its meaning. **3.** (CarA) [Indicating a wish to remember something] **a.** *You remember that gal he used to have? What she name again?* —RTCS:10 **b.** *Boy, which school you going to again?*—(Guyn) **c.** *I forget who is the Attorney-General again.*—(Bdos) [As *OEDS again* A. adv 4. a. + cit 1853 from Dickens 'What do you call him again?'] **4.** (CarA) [Adding emphasis to the question or statement it terminates] **a.** *Well of course! If she sees you so with another woman, what you expect her to think again?*—(StVn) **b.** *Child, how you can give away all yo[ur] pencils like that? Yo[u] too stupid again!*—(Guyn) **c.** *Constable: You sure you see him put de fowl down a trap door? / Vio: If I sure again! Just go under de house, he have a bundle of fibre on top de trap-door and some ole chairs. Move dem and you going see.*—RTCS:24

again[2] [age·n] /14'/ *excl* (Antg, StKt) [Indicating spontaneous agreement] Yes, definitely! *SI: You goin[g] to de fete tonight? / S2: Again! That can't pass me, boy.*—(StKt) [Cp IF IAE 'You can say that again', expressing strong approval]

against *prep PHRASES* **1. object against (sth)** (ECar) [X] Object to (sth). *It is especially the Evangelical Fundamental Churches here who object against the ... 'non- Christian' character of the contract.*—CaC (73.02, p.6) **2. obtain a divorce against (sb)** (ECar) [X] Obtain a divorce from (sb). [*He] was charged with the murder of Sylvia G—who in 1974 had obtained a divorce against him.*—GyC (76.04.27) [Overlapping structures such as 'object to' + 'speak against', a 'divorce from' + 'a judgement against', etc]

a·ga·ve* [ˈagavi ~ ˈageːv] *n* (CarA) ‖ *Antigua-Pride* (Antg) ‖ *cactus* (Belz, Dmca, Gren, Jmca) ‖ *careta* (USVI) ‖ *century-plant* (Bdos, Trin, USVI) ‖ *coratoe* (Jmca) ‖ *dagger-plant* (Antg, Dmca, StVn) ‖ *lang-bèf* (Dmca, StLu) ‖ *may-pole* (Bdos) ‖ *rope-bush* (Guyn) ‖ *silk grass* (Bdos) ‖ *sisal* (Baha, CayI, Jmca) One of a family of succulent plants (*Agavaceae*) with long, thick, fibrous, stiff and spine-tipped leaves radiating from the root; they are often used as barrier hedges (esp the types known as CENTURY PLANT (*Agave americana*) and SPANISH NEEDLE (*Agave angustifolia*). [Botanical name from Gk *agave* 'noble', prob in ref to the elegance of the various species or of the central flowering pole of a number of them]

age·a·ble [ˈeʲabl] *adj* (Bdos, Belz, Tbgo) Very old; advanced in years. **a.** *... an ageable woman, walking as if in pain, with head cocked on one side.*—HF:51 **b.** *I saw them take an ageable woman from the back seat.*—Tbgo (CR)

a·gee·dee *n* (Gren) See AGIDI

a·gen·cy shop *n* (CarA) Any workplace or combination of workplaces in wh trade union representatives serve as agents and receive dues from employees who are union members, and obligatory equivalent payments from non-union members, as being within the bargaining unit. **a.** *In reply to the further demand by Mr Freeland that CCL withold its support for an agency shop in Antigua, Mr Benjamin said: 'We support the agency shop. We do not believe in free riders. We will support any union, any government that practices the agency shop.'*—AdN (72.04.29, p.2) **b.** *Mr Morgan said that where the Agency Shop could be implemented departmentally, the union was prepared to give the green light for its implementation until it became operative throughout the public service.*—AdN (73.02.20, p.5) [*Agency* + *shop* 'a workplace in trade union terms'. The term is of American orig]

age-pa·per *n* (Belz, Jmca) [*IF*] [Hist] ‖ **birth-paper** (CarA) ‖ **born-paper, kagaj** 1. (Guyn) Birth certificate. *Well, James Creary has given us a seed, who is Garth on his age-paper, but Son-Son to me.*—RND:232

a·gi·di (a·gee·dee, a·gri·di) [agidi~agridi] *n* (Baha, Gren, Guyn, Jmca) A pudding prepared from very fine-ground cornmeal or fully mashed boiled corn, seasoned and wrapped in pieces of plantain or almond leaf; [by extension] (*Jmca*) A dish of crushed boiled corn or yam variously prepared and served. [A W Afr name for a similar food. Cp *ADMY* Yoruba *agidi* = *ẹkọ* 'a solid food made from maize' *ADHL* Hausa *apidi* 'a type of blancmange made from guineacorn'; *KED* Krio *agidi* 'food made of boiled ground corn'; etc]

a·gist·ment fees [aɟistmɛnt fi:z] *n* (Guyn) [Hist] A fee charged for allowing cattle to graze on communal pastures maintained by the Government. *The Ministry of Agriculture used to charge what were called agistment fees, up to about 30 years ago, for allowing cattle to graze on communal pastures, but these pastures are not very common nowadays.*—(Guyn) [*EDD agistment* sb Yks ... Wil 'the feeding of cattle at a fixed rate; pasturage ...' + cits–'1889. *OED agistment* 3. 'the rate levied or profit made upon the pasturing of another's cattle + cits–'1809]

a·gou·man ['agumã] *n* (StLu) ‖ CALALU 1. (CarA)

a·gou·ti* (a·gu·ti) *n* (CarA) ‖ **accouri** (Guyn) ‖ **Indian rabbit** (Belz) [*AF*] The agouti; a rabbit-like rodent of greenish-brown body, wh is hunted for its meat; *Dasyprocta aguti* or *D. cayanus* (*Dasyproctidae*). [So Amer Amerindian name. Cp *DGEG* Guarani *acuti* 'kind of rabbit'; *Dasyprocta aguti azarae*. Evid the Arawakan equivalent of the Cariban *akuri* (see ACCOURI wh is restricted to Guyn, whereas *agouti* is the form common to Guyn and many CarA islands. Cp *BDFC* (1666) *Agouti*, lièvre du pays (= local hare) 'picouli' i.e. a particular Carib equivalent of a more generally known name in 1666. The name is likely to have been spread northwards into the *CarA* through Arawak migrations, the young animals being easily tamed and reared for

their meat] □ An unchanged pl is sometimes found. Ex: '... *alligators, agouti, deer* ...'.

agree (gree) *vb intr* (CarA) [*IF*] **1.** To be or dwell in harmony; to have no cause for bad feelings for each other. **a.** *But in the country area Indians and blacks used to agree quite well until the politicians came and set them against each other.*—(Guyn) **b.** *The mother and the daughter can't gree at-all—they always quarelling over one thing or another.*—(Belz) **c.** *I say, 'Worrell, me and you don't gree and why you come here and juck me and pull at me?'*—Bdos (CR, 71.05.17) [*OED agree* (Also aphetized as *gree* 11. 'to be in harmony or unison in opinions, feelings conduct, etc; to live or act together harmoniously; ... + cit (1596, Shak: Merchant of Venice) 'How dost thou and thy Master agree?'] **2.** PHRASE **2.1** (**a)gree back** *vb intr* (Bdos, Gren) [*X*] ‖ **make back up, talk back** (CarA) To become friends again; to make up your differences. **a.** *The accused and I have agreed back since the incident.*—Bdos (CR, 70.01.13) **b.** *Two little girls whom I had parted in a fight, told me a week later: 'We gree back now, but she gree back first.'*—HDB:1 [Cp *OED agree* 9. intr 'to come into accord or harmony; make up differences'. Still dialectal 'Kiss and 'gree again'. Note also *AVB* (Matt.5.25) 'Agree with thine adversary quickly']

A·gri·cul·tur·al De·part·ment *n phr* (CarA) [*X*] Agriculture Department; Department of Agriculture; government department responsible for the organization and development of agriculture in the whole or part of a territory. **a.** *Vacancies exist in the Agricultural department for Farm Demonstrators, Grade II, for which applications are invited.*—BeB (65.06.23, p.4) **b.** *Is the Agricultural Department doing nothing about the 'take over' of love vine in town and rural areas?*—ViN (77.08.19, p.11) **c.** *They had always thought the fruit came out of the earth in the night to grow on the branches, until the day the man from the agricultural department explained about pollination.*—SABS:83 □ In almost every such case 'Department' is qualified by the 'activity' noun in attributive function—*Education, Finance, Fire, Highways, Immigration, Information, Lands and Mines, Police, Sanitation, Transport and Harbours, Treasury* (Departments); or by a n phr of wh the first element is the adj—*Cultural Affairs, Foreign Affairs, Geological Surveys, Public Works* (Departments). Alternately '*Department of* + n' is used. The adj *-al* forms usually apply to equipment, operations, and persons: *educational* materials, *Financial* Treasurer, *Cultural* Attaché, etc. Hence, *agricultural* equipment, development, advisers, officers, superintendents, etc, the high frequency of wh terms in the CarA probably accounts for the erroneous extension of the term also to 'Agricultu*ral* Department'.

a·gri·di *n* (Baha) See AGIDI

agro-based *adj* (Bdos) Derived from or obtained through agriculture; dependent on land-cultivation. *Barbados stands to benefit from AGRO-EX 74, the exhibition of agro-based products held in St Vincent recently ... Among the Barbados agro- based products on display were beer, malt, rum, biscuits, instant yam, animal feed, macaroni and PDC.*—NaT (74.09.22, p.2) [Pref *agri* (< agriculture) with preferred combinative /-o-/ (cp Afro- Indo-), pa. part. + *based* in adj function. Also perh infl by Gk *agros* 'land' as in *agronomy*] □ The term *agro-based* (as also others following) is a natural extension of the use of *agro-* wh emerged in IAE in the 1960s together with *agri-* wh it has largely replaced. See *BDNE 2* wh lists many other new *agro-* compounds both with and without hyphen.

a·gro·cli·ma·tic *adj*; **agro.cli.ma.tic.al.ly** *adv* (CarA) Pertaining to climate as it specifically affects agriculture. **a.** *This, Sir, also illustrated my point that there is little climatic variation especially when we are thinking of agroclimatic differences (between Dominica and Barbados).*— AdN (73.09.03, p.4) **b.** *In Barbados we have recently begun to accept that not all of our so-called sugar cane lands are agroclimatically suitable for cane, and that there are many areas in which sugar cane yields will always be well below economic levels.*—AdN (73.09.03, p.4) [See AGRO-BASED]

a·gro-in·dus·tri·al *adj*; **agro-in.dus.try** *n* (Bdos) (Pertaining or related to) industry based on large-scale land-cultivation. **a.** *We ought seriously to consider whether we are not already dangerously neglecting the development of our agro-industrial economy for which these islands are naturally suited, while going for tourism.*—Bdos (Ms, 1978) **b.** *In the main Mr Haydock blames poor transport facilities for the lack of industry in St Vincent. When these improve he foresees a thriving agroindustry.*—StVn (Barclays Newsletter) [See AGRO-]

agua *n* (Guyn, Trin) See AGWA

a·gui·nal·do [agınaldo] *n* (Trin) ‖ *Spanish Christmas Carol* (Trin) One of a number of rural Christmas songs composed in Creolized Spanish on themes of the Nativity and the Resurrection, and sung from house to house in the northern communities of Trinidad as part of the activities of PARANG. *The texts of the aguinaldos are narratives from the Gospels ... in ... short poetic verses sung at the pungent pace of a Spanish carol.*—TPOT:21 [Sp *aguinaldo* 'a Christmas box, a New Year's gift' + probable semantic shift to mean the song soliciting the gift wh, in this case, takes the form of food and drink]

agwa(h) (**agua**) *n* (Guyn, Trin) [Indic] A matchmaker; a person who is requested by the parents of one of the parties to arrange the marriage of a Hindu or a Muslim boy or girl. *The agwah could be a man or a woman, but especially when the parents at first display resentment to the union, the agwah plays a vital part in arranging the wedding and he or she enjoys a prominent place in the actual wedding and is heavily 'feted' in recompense for his services.*—Guyn (Ms, 1980) [Hin *aguaa* 'one who comes forward for the work of others, matchmaker < *age* adv 'in front of' + *-wa* (denominative suffix) 'doer']

ag·wa·sa (**ag·ua·sa, gwa·sa**) *adv* PHRASE **gone agwasa** *vb phr* (Antg) [AF] ‖ *gone (a)cross* (Guyn) (To have been) lost, confiscated; (to have) disappeared. *An elderly lady who lives in my area always giving the little boys horrors. Provided they playing cricket and the ball go over her fence, she simply look out her window and say 'that gorn agwasa', and that's that.*—Antg (Ms)—Antg (Ms) [Perh of W Afr orig. Cp *DAFL* Twi *guaa*, 'to take away']

ah [a] Popularized written form 'A', 'a', 'a-' in many creolized functions. [As 1st pers sing pron; see A[2]. As proclitic vbl particle; see A[10]. As linking vb; see A[14]. As initiating vb; see A[16] As introducing a wh- question; see A[16]. As pron pref to 1st & 2nd pers pl pron; see A[19]] **2.** PHRASES **2.1 Ah good!** [a'gʊd] (StKt) [AF] ‖ GOOD so! (Guyn) It serves you (him, etc) right. *News of Norman Manley's failure in the Jamaica elections was the cause of many comments here. A crisp and meaningful expression, which filled the bill quite accurately, was that made by a labourer. It consisted of barely two words 'ah good'. This in our Kittitian lingo means 'it serves him right'. The words 'ah good' usually give the one who utters them a deep sense of satisfaction when fate dishes out a well deserved punishment to some one.*—DeM(SK) (62.04.14, p.1) [Cr A[15] (AH) as initiating vb + GOOD as excl of approval] **2.2 Ah right!** ['a:rat] (Belz) [AF] ‖ *no mo(re) than true* (Guyn) It's perfectly true! That's exactly the case! ... *the recent action of the Public Service Union shows without doubt that people who have accused them of being anti-government were right. Ah right. Consider the facts.*—BsT (81.03.29, p.2) [Cr A[16] (AH) as inititiating vb + *right* adj 'correct, true'] **2.3. Ah so!**; **Is so!** (CarA) [AF] ['asʌ] [Indicating disappointment or disapproval] So that's how it is!; That's how they are, (things stand, etc)! So that's the position! **a.** *A se[e]! Ah so! So allyo ain[t] comin[g] to de weddin[g] den!*—(Guyn) **b.** *After the death sentence was pronounced and before he was led from the dock, the youth ... told the trial judge: 'Ah so Parnell, you hear? Your time ah go come one day too.'*—WeG (72.12.13, p.35) [Cr A[15] (AH) + *so* adv 'thus']

Ah chot/chut! [a''čʌt] *excl* (Tbgo) [AF] [Expressing mild contempt] Nonsense! Rubbish! *Pastor Grey: I had a long talk with the doctor. Pa Benjy: (aside) Ah chut! Doctah what?*—Tbgo (Ms)

a(h) fus(s) *excl adv* (Trin) See AFÒS

Ah·ma·di [a'ma:di] *n* (Guyn, Trin) [Indic] A member of an unorthodox sect of Muslims who interpret the teachings of the Koran according to their leader Mirza Ahmad. [Hin < Perso-Arabic *ahmadii*, a Muslim sect named after its founder Mirza Ghulam Ahmad]

ah-we-ya *pron, 1st pers pl* (Antg) [*AF—Cr*] See A(LL)-WE

Ai![1]; **Ai man!** *excl* (CarA) [*IF*] [Used in greeting or hailing sb] Hi! Hey! **a.** *Ai Ai! Is you I calling.*—(Trin) **b.** *Ai man! Is so you passing me?* —(Guyn) [Reduction of SE *Hi* by aphaeresis]

Ai![2] (Aie(e)!, Ay(e)!); Ay-ay-ay!; Ah-ya-hai! etc *excl* (CarA) ‖ *Ayuo!* (Mrat) ‖ *Hoy!* (Bdos) *excl* (CarA) [*AF*] **1.** Exclamation of sorrow, pain or distress. **a.** *Jamaicans put a world of meaning into their exclamations, many of which came from Africa. Aie (three syllables), eeem, eh-eh, and the eloquent cho!*—(Globe & Mail, Toronto, 76.01.24, p.41) **b.** *Ay, ay ay / I think is me fate you want to try / I never see / Anybody who is more nasty.*—SCTR:15 [Cp W Afr parallels, ex *DAFL* Twi *ai, aai, aii* 'ah me!, alas!, woe!'] **2.** Excl of surprise or pleasure. **a.** *When dey go in papa, dey meet one big pot. You know wha pot ah talkin' 'bout! Ah ya hai! ... full o' peas an' rice! Dey si down, dey start to eat.*—EMRP:32 **b.** *Ay! A true Mexican beauty / she hair long to she bamsie / ... she end up in me casa, Ay!*—Trin (Cso, Sparrow, 1983) **c.** *Aye, Aye, Joe da was ah good sermon dis morning, ah din noe we did rating so high.*—PGI:45 [Cp W Afr parallels, ex *ADHL* Hausa *ai* 'well! fancy! what!'; Krio *KED ay!*, 'exclamation of acute pain or pleasure']

aid-don·ing *adj, n* (Guyn) The giving of economic assistance (as part of a country's foreign policy) to less developed countries. *Prime Minister Forbes Burham has called on aid-doning countries to provide the type of aid which China has given to Guyana.*—SuC (76.05.30, p.1) [Back formation from *aid-donor* n 'giver of (economic) aid']

ain'(t)[1] [ɛn(t)~ɛ~ɪn] *neg marker* (CarA) [*AF*] **1.** Negation of the vbs *be, do, have* as follows: am not; isn't, aren't; wasn't, weren't, doesn't, don't; didn't; hasn't, haven't; hadn't. **a.** *Well the jury see him cry and they believe him ain[t] guilty.*—(Jmca) **b.** *I aint see the car hit Leslie. I aint know about the car P522 striking another car.*—Bdos (CR) **c.** *I turned to him and tell him, James is three weeks that you ain't give me anything. You don't know how I living.*—Bdos (CR) **d.** *Wha[t] ain[t] pass you ain[t] miss you.*—Guyn (Prov) **e.** *I know dat if by da[t] time I ain[t] finish it A couldn[']t finish it.*—(StVn) [Cr adoption of 17C E *ain't~an't* (as in London dial) during the process of decreolization, to take the place of the universal Cr neg marker *na*. In present AF/IF CE it still maintains its position immediately after the subject and before the vb in both declarative and inquiry sentences] □ This form is universally condemned in serious writing and *Formal* speech. However, its function in CE is much wider than in IAE and , as the cits from Court Records demonstrate, it is indispensable

in the most serious speech of less educated persons. It also gains some currency in the dialogue of an increasing number of *CarA* short stories and plays. **2.** PHRASE **2.1 ain't have time with that** (Trin) [*AF*] (To) have no time to spare for sth; (to) be quite indifferent about sth. *People have to get up four o'clock to draw water! No water! But the Government ain't have time with that; they busy buildin[g] race course!*—(Trin) **2.2 ain't nowhere; ain't deh nowhere** (Guyn) [*AF*] (To) be left with no money; (to) be completely outdone in a transaction, competition, etc. *The poor old lady had all her business in the hands of that damn scamp of a lawyer and, I tell you, when he done with her she found out she ain['t] nowhere!* -(Guyn) [Perh from the idea of being quite 'lost' (not knowing where you are) for lack of funds, etc] **2.3 ain't what you want makes you fat** *catch phr* (TkCa) [*AF*] Don't refuse sth because it is not exactly what you want; make do with what you can get. *You seems as if you are not satisfied with this dress. Ain't what you want makes you fat, tis what you get.*—TkCa (Ms) **2.4 it ain't (got/have)** *introd phr* (CarA) [*AF*] There isn't; there aren't. **a.** *... and you know and I know that it ain't many people round the place what feel that way in these days and times.*—NaG (78.06.01) **b.** *It ain't got all that fuss in it.*—(Guyn) [Cp dial *MTAL:568* AmE *Ain't nobody never been there*, in wh *ain't* functions also in the sense of 'there isn't' in double negation] □ See also ENT

ain'(t)[2] [en(t)~ɛ(t)~an] (Guyn) *Q-word (introducing a yes-question)* (CarA) [*AF*] ‖ *and* 1. Surely; isn't it true that.... **a.** *But ain't is the same thing I say, Tiger? / How is the same thing? You must learn to express yourself good, girl, like me.*—SABS:159 **b.** *How you mean seven fifty? Ain[t] five dollars is what you charge me the last time?*—(Guyn) [Poss a calque from W Afr langs, many of wh signal inquiry with an initial Q-word. Cp Yoruba *ṣe, nje̩~iṣu* all operating in this way. Also note *KED* Krio *ɛnti* indicating expectation of agreement, etc. Also Ghanaian E 'Isn't it he hit you?' (= Didn't he hit you?) This function would be reinforced by the sense of AIN'T[1]] □ See also ENT

air[1] *n* PHRASES **1. give the ball (some) air** *vb phr* (CarA) [Cricket] [Of a bowler] To flight the ball; to use a higher trajectory than usual. *Here he comes—oh, and he gives that one a lot of air and had the batsman a little surprised there—of course he is a bowler who likes to change his pace every now and then.*—Bdos (B) **2. bring/put (sth) over the air** *vb phr* (CarA) To broadcast (sth). **3. come over the air** *vb phr* (CarA) To be broadcast.

air[2] *vb intr* (ECar) **1.** To broadcast by radio or television; to put on the air. *The broadcast time was wrong. The perfectly good instructions and demonstrations were aired when the farmers were either out in their fields or already in bed after a day's work.*—AdN (72.12.31, p.4) □ Usage largely restricted to journalism. **2.** PHRASES **2.1**

air off yourself; air out yourself; air yourself (on sb) *vb phr* (CarA) [*AF/IF*] **(i)** To make an irritating display or use of your higher status or of your authority; to lord it over (sb); to give yourself airs. [*OED air* 5. fig (meaning infl by *airs* 'affected gestures') 'to show off, parade ostentatiously' 5. b. refl and intr. The prep extensions *off, out* are overlaps with *show off, air out* (in the sense 'display')] **(ii)** ‖ *le[t]go your mouth* (Baha, Jmca, Mrat, Nevs) [*IF*] [By extension] To be openly rude to (sb) in the presence of others; to make rude and boisterous fun of an opponent in public. **2.2 air (out) your mouth on (sb)** *vb phr* (CarA) [*AF/IF*] ‖ *beat your mouth (on sb/sth)* (Jmca, StLu) ‖ *cuss (sb) out* (Belz, TkCa) ‖ *fly your mouth* (Guyn) ‖ *give sb mépwi* (Dmca) ‖ *give your mouth air* (Guyn, StLu) ‖ *lay (sb) out* (Baha) ‖ *leggo your mouth/tongue* (Baha, Jmca, Mrat, Nevs) ‖ *let loose* (Baha) ‖ *open (up) your mouth (on sb)* (Gren, Jmca, Mrat) ‖ *wash your mouth /tongue (on sb)* (Dmca, Nevs, TkCa) To speak aggressively or abusively and at length (to sb or about sth). **a.** *Since the son got arrest you should hear how those people air their mouth on that poor woman. I tell you, I am sorry for her.*—(Bdos) **b.** *What happen girl? What you airin[g] out you[r] mout[h] so for? Like you want everybody to know we business.*—(Tbgo) **c.** *When they dismissed their servant she got out on the road and really aired her mouth on them.*—(Guyn) [Cp Yoruba *da ẹnun bo*, ('*pour out mouth upon*') in ref to a number of people abusing one person]

air con·di·tion[1] *n phr* (CarA) [*X*] Air-conditioning material or machine; air conditioner. **a.** *The studio is completely insulated with fibre glass air condition and is very colourful.*—AdN (71.12.11, p.6) **b.** *... when one of the newly housed lowered the volume of his 23 inch TV set ... and put on the air condition.*—BoM (73.04.06, p.27) [By functional and semantic vb > n shift, prob also infl by cases like *airlift, airmail* wh function both ways]

air con·di·tion[2] *adj* (CarA) [*X*] Air-conditioned. **a.** *Come in. We're open. Air condition.*—Bdos (Notice) **b.** *Air condition lounge upstairs.*—Trin (Notice) [By functional vb > adj shift]

air·crafts *n pl* [*X*] See PLURAL FORMS

air·dash[1] *vb* (Guyn) To rush by aeroplane; to fly hurriedly to a destination. *Two Defence Force soldiers were airdashed to the city with burns suffered when their lorry caught afire*—DaC (74.02.16, p.16) [< *IF* 'dash by air'. Cp IAE *airlift*] □ Vb almost restricted to *Guyn* journalese though the n (see next) is in more popular *Guyn* currency. However *BDNE2* cites its occurrence as vb intr stating that 'the term appears to have originated and to be used chiefly in India'.

air·dash[2] *n* (Guyn) **1.** A hurried journey by aeroplane. [By functional shift from vb] **2.**

PHRASE **2.1 do/make an airdash** *vb phr* To make a hurried journey by aeroplane.

air·ish [erɪ̃ʃ] *adj* (Guyn) [*IF/AF*] Given to showing off (usu offensively). *He wouldn't listen to correction because he wanted to be airish with all those people around.*—Guyn (Ms) [Adjectival adaptation of AIR YOURSELF, blended with SE *put on airs*. A different development from *OED airish* (Obs) 'of or belonging to the air']

air-plant *n* (Angu) ‖ LEAF-OF-LIFE (Guyn, Trin) [Perh from the leaf's ability to produce young plants even when cut off and pinned to a wall, as if living 'on air']

air·play *n* (Bdos) The playing of a record on the air; broadcasting, esp of a musical recording. *... the Sandpebbles released their latest album, 'A Visit to Bridgetown, Barbados', and with the new craze it's going great guns and has been given a lot of airplay.*—NaT (76.08.01, p.7) [*Air,* n (as instrumental prefix—cp 'airmail') + *play* vb (as in 'play a record'] □ Journalistic but useful, since it is unambiguous (cp 'broadcasting' as the alternative).

air·y·bank (hair·y bank) ['(h)eribaŋk] *n* (Guyn) A kerosene tin or metal canister used by PORKKNOCKERS to store cups and spoons or to keep valuables.

aja *n* (Guyn, Trin) [Indic] Father's father; paternal grandfather. *'Not necessarily', said Daddy. 'Meh ole aja what come from India, he tell me it have a story dat in we fore-parents' country up in dem Himalaya mountains it does have ah kin' ah creature dem people does call a 'yeti'.*—Peo III.22, p.14 [Bhoj *aaja* < Hin *daadaa* 'paternal grandfather']

aji *n* (Guyn, Trin) [Indic] Father's mother; paternal grandmother. *Bhauji and bhabhi for brother's wife ... aja and aji or dada and dadi (father's father and mother) are some of the linguistic legacies from North India.*—LCTC:14 (C. Jha) [Bhoj *aaji* < Hin *daadii* 'grandmother']

a·jou·pa [a'jupa] *n* (Dmca, StLu, Tbgo, Trin) ‖ *adobe, cabbage-house* (Belz) ‖ *takeda* (Belz) An Amerindian or Amerindian-type hut usu with wattle-and-daub walls and a thatched roof. (See cit a.). **a.** *... they used to be built, these ajoupa houses, with branches or young trees an inch in diameter. These saplings, or round wood as they were called, were about seven feet long, and provided the framework for the dwelling. At the corners or eaves the round wood would be tied by liane vines or string if handy. Further uprights would be put in to reduce the space between them. The next stage is to weave in and out of these, behind and in front of the round wood. The bamboo springs into place, making any other support unnecessary. This horizontal weave is then plastered with clay, which seals the wall and finishes it off. The roof is framed and secured and thatched with bound bundles of grasses, or shingled with carat or timite* *fronds or leaves.*—ACTT:133 **b.** *Every evening we saw the sun go down from the thatched shelter she called the ajoupa, I the summer house.*—RWSS:74 **[** < (*BDFC:14*) Carib *ajouppa* 'appentis' i.e. a shed] □ Cp BENAB.

aka ba·ka *n phr* (USVI) ‖ ABNER BABNER (Guyn) *'Aka baka, aka or akka or tiki-tiki. Nigger bake a batch a cracker'. These are lines used as a sort of casting of lots or choosing a leader in a game to be played. Hardly remembered today.*—USVI (Ms, 1984, A. Peterson) **[** Cp Igbo *aka bụ aka* (pronounced *aka b' aka* 'hand is hand'). As each word is said a player is touched and so eliminated.]

a·ka·ra (a·ka·ro) *n* (Baha, Gren) ‖ *accra* (CarA)

a·ka·ree *n* (Guyn) See ACCOURI

a·ka·ru *n* (Guyn) See AKUYURU

A·ka·wai·o (Ac·ca·way, Ac·cou·ai, Ack··a·woi, Ack·wi·a, Aka·way·i, Aka·woi, etc Wac·ca·wa)** ['akawayo] *n* (Guyn) ‖ *waika* (Belz) An Amerindian 'ethnic group' in Guyn, wh is of Carib stock, closely related in habits and lang to the AREKUNA, and dwelling mostly in the area north of Mount Roraima near the border with Venezuela. □ Of a large number of variant spellings, the form *Akawaio* occurs most frequently in recent writings and research, though *MAGH: 3; 295* uses *Akawoi* as the accepted form.

akee (ac·kee) ['aki] *n* (Bdos, StLu, StVn) **1.** ‖ GUINEP (CarA) *She handed him a bunch of ackees from the tray and, taking one between his teeth to remove the tough skin, he enjoyed sucking the fleshy seed.*—Bdos (Ms, 1978) **[** This tree is a native of South and Central Amer (see etym of GUINEP) whereas ACKEE (*Jmca*) is a native of W Afr. The use of the same name for two quite different fruits by different groupings of African slaves may in some way be related to their belonging to the same botanical family, *Sapindaceae*] □ The alternative spelling *ackee* is not recommended in ref to this fruit as that serves to distinguish the different and widely known National Fruit of *Jmca*. **2.** [*X*] See ACKEE

a·ko·ri[1] *n* (Guyn) See ACCOURI

a·ko·ri[2]**-seed** (o·che·ri/o·ka·ri-seed) [akʌri si:d] *n* (Guyn) The seed of the AWARA palm, used to make a smaller BUCK-TOP. [A *Guyn* word of Amerindian orig] □ *Akori* accords with the commonest pronunc. The 'och-' spelling (*OGEP:2*) is otherwise unaccounted for.

aks (ax) [aks] *vb tr* (CarA) [*X*] Ask. *But, Vera, why you think I ax you where we going if I ain't want to go out with you? Looka, I ax you a simple question. And I axing you again: where we going this bank holiday?*—CISH:98 [Survival of an early E variant pronunc 'ax' wh, *OED* notes, was 'down to nearly 1600 the regular literary

form and still used everywhere in midland and southern dialects' + cit at *ask* 2. b. (1803) 'A true born Londoner, Sir, of either sex, always axes question, axes pardon and at quadrille axes leave'. Also common in Irel: 'Jestice is all I ax' (*JESI:98*)] □ This *X* form occurs as a fixture with some CE speakers, even when educated.

a·ku·yu·ru (ac·quee·ro, a·kwi·ro, a·ka·ru, ku·ru, ku·yu·ru)** *n* (Guyn) A palm whose trunk is ringed at intervals with long, black spines, and wh bears large, heavy, upright clusters of orange-coloured fruit with an edible pulp and large, hard, black seeds; *Astrocaryum tucuma* (*Palmaceae*)—OGEP:26 [The tree is in many ways a larger version of the AWARA] [*BAED* Arawak *akhoyoro* 'a palm tree with spines all over that bears bunches of edible fruit']

ak·wa-lan·mo·wi [akwa lãmowi] *n* (StLu) ‖ ACCRA (CarA) **[** < ACCRA + Fr *lanmowi* < Fr *la morue*, 'codfish' with closed juncture. The compound distinguishes the fritter from *akwa-chou* made with a vegetable]

alarm *vb intr* (CarA) [Of a clock] To make a ringing or other noise to wake sb up. **a.** *Before I went to bed I set the clock to alarm at four.*—(Guyn) **b.** *He got up before the clock alarmed.*—(Bdos) **c.** *You know the peep-ee-peep peep-ee-peep you hear when one of those digital watches is alarming?*—(Trin) [Prob back-formation from *alarm clock* on the analogy of such IAE formations as *guide book, searchlight* etc] □ Not standard BrE or AmE usage.

a·larm·ing; a.larm.ish *adj* (Guyn, Trin) [*X*] Exaggerative; alarmist; ready to excite or alarm others. **a.** *Don't believe what she's telling you. It wasn't as terrible as all that. She's too alarming.*—(Guyn) **b.** *Wha happen, yuh alarmish, eh? Wha yuh ballin out so for, yuh nuff to wake up de neighbours an dem. Come, come quick, look wey here.*—ExP (73.04.29, p.7, 10) [-*ing* by misascription on the analogy of cases like 'charming', 'accommodating', etc; -*ish* with Derog sense by analogy with 'bookish', 'womanish', etc] □ SE *alarming* 'surprising and disturbing' is applied to things or situations.

al·co·hol·i·day *n* (Guyn) [*AF—Joc*] A holiday or festive period that is spent mostly in drinking strong liquor. **a.** *Whatever the explanation, this is no time to have a two-day alcoholiday and becoming as high as a kite.*—SuC (76.04.18, p.7) **b.** *Man! Easter, Phagwa, Eid—wha[t]ever yo[u] call—is big alcoholiday for he—you know how A mean?*—(Guyn) [Blend of 'alcohol' + 'holiday']

al·fa·gats (all·fo·gats, al·pha·gat·ters)** [alfʌgats] *n* (Bdos, Guyn) [*X*] See ALPARGATA(S)

all[1] *adj* (CarA) [*IF*] **1.** [Followed by a noun in the singular] Every (suggesting many and varied).. **a.** *The entire family helped with the building on an evening. They were there already, all man jack with a paint brush, painting hell out* of the front wall.—JPB:125 **b.** *You could do all kind of dirty work for a member of any government and when the time comes, you will get the kick.*— NeJ (73.08.31, p.2) [Cp EE and dial E 'all kind/ manner of' wh may have been preserved in CarA Cr; also perh reinforced by calques from Afr langs. Note Cr provs such as *Guyn* 'Rain no fall a all man door-mouth same time'. Later also poss further reinforcement from Bhoj *sab logo* (all folk) 'everybody', *sab kuchh* (all thing) 'everything'] □ Notwithstanding its EE roots, this structure is unpermitted in ModE and replaced by 'all' + n pl ('all kinds, etc') or 'every' + n sg ('every kind, etc'). **2.** [Adding emphasis to the condition or state described] (see also ALL³ 1., 2.). **a.** *Ah does have pain in all me back and all me belly hurtin.*—OT:30 **b.** *And a little short man in a brown pinstripe suit and a old limeskin hat push through all the circle of men and women and holler: 'No, no, no! Don't fight!'*—CISH:10 [Cp Yoruba *gbogbo inu mi*, 'all belly inside me', in wh *gbogbo* 'all' is used in similar context. Cp also SE usage in 'with all my heart', etc] **3.** PHRASES [Combined with another adj or pron] **3.1 all and singular** *adj phr* (ECar) ‖ **all that** (Bdos, Belz) [Of the sale of land] The whole without excepting any part (of the place identified). **a.** *All and singular those two pieces or parcels of land the First thereof at Fullerton in the Ward of Cedros in the island of Trinidad comprising Two Acres more or less.*—ExP (71.12.16, p.19) [OED *singular* A. 7. c. phr *all and singular* now *arch* + cits–'1875] □ 'It is a comprehensive (legal) term often employed in conveyances, wills and similar documents wherever land is conveyed by Deed as distinct from a conveyance by way of transfer for a certificate of Title' (*pers info, N. Liverpool*). **3.2 all two** /2'1/ *adj phr* (CarA) [AF/IF] ‖ **all two both; both all-two** (Bdos) [AF] Both. **a.** *Well, I know this is going to be a fight to watch, 'cause all two of them is giants at stick-licking.*—CISH:10 **b.** *I'm talking to all two you.*—(CayI) **c.** *... but there was neither penny nor cent in sight. Maybe the penny roll away when he roll back to the stone. But there it was, all two both lost.*—LICMS:49 **d.** *Or will it chance that all two vessels / will blindly pass each other by?*—HAA:10 [Cp OED *all* A. 11. *all both, all two* Obs (Fr *tous les deux*). However, except for the occasional occurrence of *both* in the phr as in *Bdos*, the older E phr may have had less infl on this CE commonplace than calquing from Afr langs. Cp Twi *abien nyinaa* (two + all), Ewe *wo kple eve* (two + the + all) Nupe *guba-ba* (*two-all*), Yoruba *mejeji* (*all-two*), Ci-Nyanja *Bonse BaBili* (*all two*), etc, all of wh are standard phrs meaning 'both'] **3.3 all two both** [X] See ALL TWO (see cit above) **3.4** [combined with a pl pers pron] **all-we, all-you** See as separate entries.

all² *pron* (CarA) [IF] **1.** Whatever. **a.** *All you do / can't get through / I still ain' goin' married to you.*—Cso (Sparrow) **b.** *'Careful all you do!' Uncle Leonard's voice came up to them from the dug-out.*—SJS:132 **2.** Everything; all things, matters, etc. **a.** *I am going to work now, so all to*

you.—(Bdos) **b.** *All for your information. / Yours faithfully, etc.*—Guyn (Ms) [From the collective sense 'all things' as in *all is well*, etc] **3.** PHRASES **3.1 all and all, all in all** *pron phrs* (Bdos, Gren, Guyn, Jmca) [IF] Everything; all without exception. **a.** *Is m[y] only daughter—and she is all and all to me.*—(Gren) **b.** *Dis is all an[d] all that A have an[d] A bring.*—(Guyn) **c.** *Now I stop working, me son is me all in all. He is all I got to depend 'pon.*—EFLBB:12 [OED *all A* adj 8. d. *all in all* (with latest cit–'1878). Cp KED Krio *ɔl-inɔl* n 'person on whom one is entirely dependent'. See also ALL³ Phr 5.1 ALL AND ALL] **3.2 all and everyone** *pron phr* Every single one. *Electricity problems on the other hand affect all and everyone of us.*—ExP (73.05.26, p.4) [Cp OED *all* A. 12. 'distributed to each member or part of the whole' ... *all and each, all and sundry* ... (12. c.) *all and every*] **3.3 all a penny** *id phr* (Bdos) [AF] Cheap because plentiful. **a.** *In the days of my childhood flying fish was considered cheap at ten for the bit. When it reached 'all a penny' often they were not counted.*—NaT (78.05.05, p.5) **b.** *Before the advent of the refrigerator an extra large catch of flying fish would result in they being sold all a penny, i.e. a purchaser might buy as many fish as he could conveniently need for a penny.*—CGBD:10 [= 'All (the fishes) you could carry with you for the payment of two cents' (in the days, up to the 1950's in *Bdos*, when the cent and penny had buying value and fish vendors also had almost unmanageable quantities of flying fish in season to get rid of, and no storage facilities)] □ By extension the phr is also applied to anything going very cheap. **3.4 all fall down** *id phr* (Gren, Trin) [AF] There is (was, will be) great disorder, confusion or trouble. **a.** *Good children perfunctorily go through the motions of worship void of any sense of conviction, but purely out of the wish to be obedient to their parents, or to conform to social norms. It is a case of parents gone and all fall dong.*— Peo.2.19 **b.** *All we can hope for is that our various fruits and vegetables will rescue us from a big depression. Even that we have to handle very carefully or else all fall down.*—GrV (91.12.28, p.6) **3.5 all is one** *id phr* (Bdos, Guyn) [AF] ‖ **all (is) (the) same khaki pants** (ECar) It makes no difference; they're all alike; (SE) it's all one. **a.** *He can come and do it any time. Sunday even, I don[t] min[d]. All is one.*—(Bdos) **b.** *It doesn't matter which one you give me; all is one.*— (Guyn) [Cp OED *all* c. 5. *all one*] **3.6 all like me/you/(etc) (so)** *pron phr* [AF] Persons of my (your, etc) kind or class. **a.** *Bwoy, all like me could never grow things like that.*—WeG (73.06.06) **b.** *All like you so couldn't get a job there years ago—you had to be white, or near-white but now they have jet black girls in there.*—(Bdos) **c.** *Remember, when the airline was launched how nuf a we laugh kyeh-kyeh, say, how all like we fe run air line. Nuff a we did say, it soon mash up.*—WeG (75.04.15, p.15) □ *Derog* or sarcastic. **3.7 all (like) here/there so** *adv phr; n phr* (CarA) [AF] (In) this or that place or part. **a.** *I was in terrible pain all here so.*—(Guyn) **b.** *In dose days Monkey tail was well woollen, you know; papa, all here so* *is wool … padna.*—EMRP:33 **c.** *But you remember how the dust from the St Vincent volcano fell on Barbados? So if Russia let off a atom bomb anywhere there so, all like here so would be destroyed.*—(Bdos) **3.8 all like now (so); all (like) this time (so); all now (so)** *adv phrs* (CarA) [*IF*] ‖ *all like so* (Belz) ‖ *this time so* (Baha) At this time; at that moment; during the time in question; meanwhile (See also ALL³ Phr 5.8). **a.** *The WICBC board and its selectors have acted wrongly, and all like now they are a stumbling block in the way of some of the world's greatest players.*—NaT (78.04.12, p.7) **b.** *Now all she said was, 'St Mary's ain't open today. No shops ain't open today, either. Today is Carnival and all now is Jou Ouvert'.*—AKM:9 **c.** *If he wasn't a doctor you would be laughing the other side of your face all now so.*—JJM:7 **d.** *All this time we have to buy sugar at 50 cents per lb, flour at 58 cents, rice at 62 cents per lb and bony chicken back is 95 cents per lb.*—ViN (76.06.18, p.7) [The sense is 'all (the time) we are talking here/were talking there' in wh the pron function of *all* is lost and it becomes a mere intensifier focusing on the time in ref] □ Often in emotive contexts. Cp next. **3.9 all (is) (the) same khaki pants** *id phr* (Trin) [*AF—Joc*] See KHAKI PANTS Phr 1. **3.10 all (of) that** *pron phr* (CarA) [*IF*] Typically like that; exactly as described. **a.** *S1: But I believe she was lying! / S2: Oh she is all of that.*—(Bdos) **b.** *And don't talk about fetes, bridge and sporting … You know they were all that.*—(Guyn) **3.10.1 (not) have all of that in it** *id phr* (CarA) [*IF*] ‖ *(not) call for all of that* (Bdos, StVn) ‖ *(not) have all that fuss in it* (Guyn) ‖ *(not) need all of that* (ECar) [*IF*] (Not) involve so much bother; (not needing to) cause so much trouble. **a.** *But selling a little piece of land shouldn't have all of that in it. If I had known I would never have started.*—(Bdos) **b.** *Look! You comin[g] or you ain[t] comin[g]? Because I ain[t] able wid so much argument! It ain[t] got all o[f] dat in it.*—(Guyn) [Cp Yoruba *nkan wa nmu e* 'something be inside it', and Igbo *ihe di n'ime ya* 'thing that is inside it', wh are idioms similarly used. Cp also StLu Fr Cr *tut sa an dan-i* 'all that is in it', in the same context]

all³ *adv intensifier (passing into this function, in many phrs, from adj ALL¹)* (CarA) [*IF—Derog*] **1.** Wholly and nothing but; only. **a.** *But look at him, eh? A man that, as he open his mouth, is all church and bible and so forth, and then he would rob that poor woman!*—(Guyn) **b.** *Big splash it was, but all mouth it turned out to be, because once again we are being smothered by the continuous outpouring of oily particles of soot.*—ExP (72.03.11, p.13) **c.** *Now A done give you me money, you turn round and buse me, you all for yourself.*—(Nevs) [Cp OED *All* adv 1–4. Cp also ALL¹ 2.] **2.** esp **all down/up**, etc [*IF/AF*] [Indicating much, in distance, space or time] As much/far away/far out, etc as. **a.** *A copper could be all four feet wide.*—Gren (Ms) **b.** *We would pick up weself and go sea-bathing all down Christ Church where the rich white people live.*—MBGB: 13 **c.** *Today they had people from all in San Juan*

and Laventille, come to look for work.—SABS: 136 **d.** *Most of the times they just lose a new man like you somewhere in the country, all up by Cunaripo and all sorta outa the way places.*—NTMM:24 [Cp OED *all* C. adv 11. 'with prep of extension … gives completeness'. However in CE the prep is sometimes omitted or the prep phr reduced, *all in* < 'all up in', so that *all* develops the function of a mere intensifier, hence 3. next] **3.** [*AF*] Even. **a.** *All in de presence of de Lord he does got eyes for de women.*—(Bdos) **b.** *One of my friends in Papine market says if you want to see how woman batter, check there all four in the a.m. and see the women in the hills struggling with some accessories … to get tidied up to face the day.*—WeG (Partyline) **c.** *All when she studying, she still on the phone.*—(StVn) □ Emotive, often stressed. **4.** [With implied negation] No matter how much; however much. (See also the phr 5.6 ALL THE … below). **a.** *All the vicar explain to the test that it was necessary for the witness to sign the register, the fellar decide that he not putting his name to any paper.*—STLL:41 **b.** *At night when his parents are not at home and I at home by myself he come feeling me up and all I curse him and tell him I am going to tell his mother, he still won't stop.*—NaT (76.02.01, p.18, Dear Christine) **c.** *Sometimes I had broken a glass or saucer just through carelessness, and all I cried afterwards was never enough to mend the broken thing again.*—WCR:22 **5.** PHRASES **5.1 all and all** *adv phr* (Gren) [*X*] All in all; all things considered. *All and all I spend a good day.*—(Gren) [Probably a shift of SE idiom 'all in all' (OED *all* A. 8. d.) through pronunc [al ən al] The phr occurs also in KED Krio *ɔl-ɛn-ɔl~ɔl-ɛn-ɔl*, 'in short', *ɔl-ɪn-ɔl* adv 'everything considered'. Cp also ALL² Phr 3.1 ALL AND ALL] **5.2 all how** *adv phr* (CarA) [*AF*] In all ways; anyhow; no matter how. **a.** *She had three lists with names of my mother and daughter and father written all over the paper, upside down and all how.*—BoM (74.10.11, p.8) **b.** *All how ah telling the bird not to eat the fig my mother would bury me alive for one grain of fig it still eat it.*—STTG:37 **5.3 all on a sudden so** *adv phr* [*AF*] All of a sudden; suddenly. *Then all on a sudden so, Mammy flash cross me mind.*—SNWIC:263 **5.4 all out** *adj phr* (Guyn) [*IF*] Helplessly drunk. *She had drank so excessively, that she had to be taken away in the ambulance. After the prosecutor had related how she was found 'all out' and the ambulance had to be summoned … Nelga gave her explanation.*—DaC (52.08.22, p.3) [Cp IAE *passed out*] **5.5 all round that time; all like that time so** *adv phr* (CarA) [*AF*] About that time. **a.** *Well all round that time he used to be eyeing her off but she didn't know.*—(Guyn) **b.** *A: You comin in nine o'clock? / B: All roun dat time.*—OT3:3 **5.6 all the** (followed by a front-shifted vb) (CarA) [*IF*] [Stressing uselessness of action stated in the vb] No matter how much; however much. (See also 4. above) **a.** *And all the beg she beg the woman to have mercy on her and make her stay and work a little longer so she could have something to mind the baby, the woman say no.*—SNWIC:64 (M. Townshend) **b.** *All de try he try, he couldn[t]* *succeed.*—(StVn) **c.** *All the talk you would talk to the boy, he just wouldn't stay in school and learn.*—(Guyn) **[**A surfacing in CE of 'front-shifting', a characteristic CarA Cr feature in wh the vb is shifted to the head of the utterance as a kind of cognate subject, nominalized and stressed. A similar feature is found in many African languages. Exs Igbo *Obibia ibialu* 'the coming you come'; Twi *Oye a oye (he do that he do)* 'a doing which he does'; Ci-nyanja *ku-thamanga kumene anathamanga* 'run that he ran'; etc**] 5.7 all the same; all-a-same** *adv phr* (CarA) *[AF]* Nevertheless; just the same; however; though. **a.** *He ought to shame. De man in even col' yet. But, all de same, it mus come to light; he did always got he eye pon de gal.*—BGPS: 40 **b.** *Allasame, ah sorry for Lloyd Best but it remind me bout de advice ah did offer NJM, an dat is: Youth Alone Is Not Enough.*—ToR (76.09.19, p.6) **c.** *The girl didn't bother all the same. For all the mother did, she still married the boy.*—(Gren) **[**By functional shift of the SE phr, where it is usu predicative as in 'it's all the same to me'**]** □ Frequently used to indicate a change of mind or condition. Not so used in SE. **5.8 all the time; all this time** *adv phr; conj phr* (CarA) *[IF]* **(i)** While; during the time that. **a.** *The rice could be boilin[g] all the time you seasonin[g] de beef.*—(Guyn) **b.** *All the time he was carryin[g] on with her the wife was hornin[g] him too.*—(Bdos) **(ii)** Meanwhile; in the meantime; at the same time. (See also ALL² Phr 3.8) **a.** *Pap all the time licking she till she bawl because she come home an' forget to buy split pea or green plantain in the market, or something or the other like that...*—MHBT:15 **b.** *I will clear the clothes line just now, but hang your clothes on the line all the time.*—(Tbgo) **[**By positional shift of the phr from connective to initial or terminal position in the sentence**] 5.9 all the while** *adv phr* (Gren, StVn) *[X]* Habitually; regularly. **a.** *Don't vex with her for doing that now, she does not do it all the while.*—(Gren) **b.** *I go to Mustique all the while.*—(StVn) **5.10 all time** *adv phr* (CarA) *[X]* **(i)** Always; at all times. **a.** *'That Conrad, he too wicked. He all time making trouble', they would say to Joel, too afraid of Sybil's anger to mention it to her. 'He always down by de jetty at school time or limin' by the cinema. Las' week he way up at Miss White tiefin' mangoes.'*—FGSOS:53 (D. Pollock) **b.** *He does all time hit de guy.*—(Gren) **(ii)** At any time. *Q: Did you hear Pemberton say anything after the officer took away the things? / A: Yes, he said they could all time go with them because they done wash and they are not able to find any blood on them.*—LaS (74.04.27, p.4) **[**Cp also *GBB* Gullah *alltime*, 'at all times': *KED* Krio *ɔltɛm* 'at all times' + phrs. A likely calque from Afr langs. Cp Yoruba *ni igba gbogbo* (*at-time all*) 'always', Igbo *mgbe dum* (*time all*) 'always', etc**] 5.11 all to** *adv phr; prep phr* (CarA) *[IF]* **(i)** Except for. *She had typed the whole thing all to the last page and a half.*—(Guyn) **[**No connection with *OED all to* in Obs contexts (*All* 1. 12–15). The phr is prob from IrE: 'All to' means 'except': 'I've sold my sheep all to six', i.e. except six. This is merely a translation from

the Irish as in *Do marbhadh na daoine uile go haon triúr*: 'The people were slain all to a single three'] (Keating)—*JESI:210* **(ii)** *adv phr (intensifier) [AF]* Even; unlikely though it may seem. **a.** *All to the boy very parents give up on he.*—(BrVI) **b.** *I tell yo[u] all to the stain-glass window them melt out with the heat.*—(Guyn) **5.12 all up to now** *adv phr* (CarA) *[AF]* Still; even up to the present time. **a.** *'And all up to now I can say it's Challenger's pig', he said in answer to Mrs M— 'whether or not it now had on brown hairs.'*—LaS (76.10.02, p.10) **b.** *You know it was Christmas he had the accident and all up to now he still in hospital?*—(Bdos) **5.13 all where** *adv phr* (CarA) *[X]* Wherever. **a.** *He was assured of support all where he spoke.*—RLCF:227 **b.** *All where they tramped you could see the mess they left.*—(Guyn) **5.14 and all** *adv phr* (CarA) *[IF]* **(i)** [Adding stress or expressing surprise, contempt, etc] Also; too. **a.** *The president and all was against the motion.*—Belz (Ms) **b.** *Everything raising; money hard to get and work harder. Even sweet drink and all going up.*—HFGA:57 (D.S. Joseph) **c.** *And every week God sent I was down to the Labor Office asking them for him. Today and all I went.*—MTCP:27 *[EDD and all adv, conj, and prep phr. Sc, Irel and counties of Eng from Nhb to Dev 1. adv 'And everything else' 2. Expletive and emphatic + cits ex from s.Ir 'Grand company coming to the house and all, and no regular man to wait'* (1862)] **5.14.1 You and all!** *id phr [AF]* ‖ *Youself too! / You too!* (Guyn) [After a pers pron, indicating rebuke] How unreasonable! **a.** *She know he will quarrel if the breakfast is late, and yet she will stay next door talking instead of getting on with the cookin[g]! She and all!*—(Guyn) **b.** *John: An' Ma, what 'bout me pants? De ones I does wear to church too tight. / Mrs Brown: You an all. I jus' here telling de girls dat they have to wait till I hear from you father. I ent got no money.*—Bdos (Ms) [Cp also Krio *You en all* (indicating surprise and rebuke); WAPE *emu all*, (expressing defiance). Similar structures are known in Afr langs. Fulani *an fu!* 'You too/all!' (dismissal of disgust); Igbo *unu ncha!* 'You all!' (in defiance)] □ An independent phrase always said with falling intonation usu terminating an utterance. **5.15 and all the way like that; all the way so** *adv phrs* (CarA) *[AF]* And so on (and so forth). **a.** *Well after I talk to him, you know? and explain, and all the way like that, and then he go and see for himself, well he like he took a different attitude after that.*—(Guyn) **b.** *He don't know how to divide? He share out the thing one here two dere, all the way so till all gone.*—(Bdos) **5.16 at all; at all at all** *adv phrs* (CarA) *[IF]* **(i)** [Strongly emphasizing a wh-question, or neg interr or conditional utterance] Indeed! As a matter of actual fact! **a.** *But who is he at all to be laying down rules for us?*—(Trin) **b.** *If you bother me at all at all today, you go nowhere!*—(Guyn) **c.** *'You ent see 'im at all, at all, at all?' she kept asking. Then she turned away from the Police ... and began to bawl.*—TrG (80.02.03, p.25) [Prob from the early infl of Irish bond servants. Cp *JESI:43* In our Anglo-Irish dialect the expression *at all* is often duplicated for emphasis: 'I'll grow no corn this year at all at all'; 'I have no money at all at all'. So prevalent is this among us that in a very good English grammar recently published (written by an Irishman) speakers and writers are warned against it. This is an importation from Irish. One of the Irish words for 'at all' is *idir* (always used after a negative), old forms *itir* and *etir* > *nir bo to! do Dubthach recc na cumaile stir*, 'Dubthach did not wish to sell the bondmaid at all'. In the following old passage, and others like it, it is duplicated for emphasis *Cid beac, itir itir, ges do obar*: 'However little, it is forbidden to work, at all at all'. ('Prohibitions of beard', O'Looney)—*JESI:43*] **(ii)** (Trin) [*AF*] With all speed; at full speed. *His mout wide open like a mechanical digger. I take off at all. The lion take off behind me.*—OJS: 3 [Poss overlap and reduction of two SE idioms, 'at (full)' + '(with) all (speed)'. However, note *EDD* at prep VI. phr (i) *at all*, used in positive clauses: 'absolutely', 'altogether' + cit from Irel 'It's the greatest fun at all'] **(iii)** [*AF—Rastaf*] No. **a.** *The negative is rendered by 'nah' 'nah way dread' or 'atall-I'.*—SSRB:28 **b.** *S1: De dread want some o[f] dis ital? / S2: At all-I, de one sip earlier.* (= *Does brother want some of this meal? / No, I have already had something.*)—(Bdos) **5.17 for all** (CarA); **still/yet for all** (Gren); **still and all** (Antg) *adv phr; conj phr* Notwithstanding the fact (that); nevertheless; though. **a.** *For all she wearing the big veil in Church, me, I can see that the child is pregnant.*—HF:14 **b.** *Look at all the things that woman did to him and still for all he never left her.*—(Guyn) [Cp *OED all* A. 9. c. + latest cit 1871 from Burns 'A man's a man for a' that'. Also *for* prep 23. **a.** 'in spite of' rare: **b.** in conjunctional phrases ... 'although' ... rare + latest cit 1866. Also *EDD all* phr 11. *for all* 'in spite of, notwithstanding' + cit from eYks 'Ah wadn't gan, for all maisther said Ah was']

all-age school *n phr* (CarA) ‖ *composite school* (Bdos) A school accommodating children of ages 5 to 16. *Most Out-Island (or Family Island) schools are 'all-age' schools. A programme is in progress to replace 'all- age' schools with separate primary and secondary schools where a number of students and distance to the schools are feasible.*—DBH:252

al·la·man·da* *n* (CarA) ‖ *buttercup* (CarA) ‖ *yellow-bell* (Angu, Antg, Tbgo) An ornamental woody climber bearing small clusters of bell-shaped flowers about four inches long, the best known variety being a bright yellow; *Allamanda cathartica (Apocynaceae)*. ['Native of Brazil ... the generic name commemorates Dr Allamand, professor of natural history in Leyden in the last part of the 18C'—HKS:7]

all-com·ers *n* (Guyn) All persons interested in applying, challenging, etc; all and sundry. **a.** *... on two or three occasions rented a batteau from the chairman of the village council at the rate he usually hires the craft to all-comers...*—DaC (53.02.06, p.2) **b.** *He had the boy tuned to concert pitch for that scholarship exam, ready to meet and*

beat *all-comers.*—(Guyn) [Perh an unusual E structure, but note *EDD comers* sb pl Cum, Yks, Lin in phr *comers and goers* 'visitors, callers'] □ Listed in *W2* only (1934) but neither *W1* nor *W3*, this may be an Americanism perh now obs.

all-day *adj, n* (ECar) Lasting for a whole day; [by extension, n] a FETE wh begins in the morning and goes into the night. **a.** *Savary has been in the spotlight of young chicks in this country for years now, because of his mammoth all-day picnic productions.*—SuP (74.12.08, p.7) **b.** *They hav-in[g] a all day in No.45 at Grand Anse! You goin[g]? A hear is music and food fo[r] so.*—(Gren)

al·le·vi·ate *vb tr, intr* (StVn, Trin) [*X*] Improve. **a.** *I beg our government to alleviate our poor suffering villages by giving us our money back as Tobago is clearly not in the least thankful or interested.*—ExP (72.11.16, p.3) **b.** *The letter said members of the league were prepared to volunteer their services, to help alleviate conditions in the district.*—ExP (72.02.04, p.11) **c.** *In that dreadful World Economic Depression that staggered out countries between 1929 and 1933 many went hungry, jobless and hopeless. But it alleviated within half a decade.*—ViN (74.01.04, p.4) [A misacription of sense and function perh by confusion with *ameliorate*] □ SE *alleviate* = 'lighten, lessen (burdens, grief, etc)'.

al·ley [ali] *n* **1.** (Guyn) A long narrow unnamed passage cut through a regular municipal block of houses for the purpose of drainage; it is usu fenced on both sides by high galvanized-iron sheets and carries a shallow concrete water-passage or gutter down its centre connecting the two gutters on opposite sides of the block. [Special application of *OED alley* 3. 'a passage between buildings'] **2.** (USVI) An area for strolling or shopping enclosed by buildings. [Extension of *OED alley* 2. 'a bordered walk or passage' esp in AmE, as *WCD9 alley* 1. 'a garden or park walk bordered by trees' or 3. 'a thoroughfare through the middle of a block...'] □ The BrE sense *OED* 3. of 'a... lane, usu only wide enough for foot passengers', (not applicable in *Guyn*) applies in *Bdos* to a named passage exs 'Dromedary Alley', 'Crichlow Alley', etc, leading off a main business thoroughfare.

al·ley-cat/dog/rat *n* (Guyn) [*AF—Derog*] A person who survives on pickings begged or stolen; a shameless scrounger. [By ref to strays and vermin found in Guyn drainage alleys]

al·ley-gate *n* (Guyn) A gate (made of wood or corrugated zinc sheets) to prevent persons from walking through or dumping garbage in a drainage ALLEY.

al·ley-head box *n phr* (Guyn) ‖ *bin²* (Bdos) An open wooden box about 8ft x 4ft x 4ft for containing public refuse, placed at either end of a drainage ALLEY.

all-fours *n* (Tbgo, Trin) A competitive card game for two pairs of players, wh is won by the pair that first gains fourteen points; points are awarded for the highest card, lowest card, the Jack and each game in the series, the Jack being the key card in each game. *The men, as in English pub life, go down to the 'Snackette' to play 'all fours', to brag and drink.*—ACTT:161

al·li·ga·tor-pear *n* (CarA) ‖ *avocado (pear)* (CarA) A rough-skinned variety of AVOCADO. *The native home of the avocado pear (Persea americana) is on the mainland of tropical America, it being originally indigenous to Mexico, whence it spread to Peru and the Antilles ... It was not until 1696 that it was referred to as the 'avocado, or alligator pear tree' in Sir Hans Sloane's Catalogues of Jamaican plants.*—MTBH:108 [*Alligator* may be a corruption of (Aztec) Nahuatl *ahuacatl* (see *DJE*), the fruit being indigenous to Mexico. Cp also Sp form *aguacate* current in Belz (pers info C. Young); the rough, dark, leathery skin of some varieties may also have infl the name. *Pear* from resemblance in shape to European pear, *Pyrus communis (Rosaceae)*, to wh it is, however, not related] □ The name *alligator pear* is freely interchangeable with *avocado, avocado pear* at folk level in most of the CarA.

all-in-one [ᴅl-ɪn-wᴅ·n] /1'12/ *n* (Guyn) ‖ *ca-lalu* 2.(ii) (Dmca, Gren, Jmca, StVn, Trin) ‖ *cohobblopot* (Bdos) ‖ *cook-up* (Bdos, Guyn) A meal in wh ends of meat, vegetables, peas and rice are boiled together in one pot. [*All* (ingredients) *in one* (pot). Cp Wolof *benacin* 'one pot', Hausa *dafa duka* 'cook-all', Krio *one-pot*, etc, names for a meal made by cooking everything together]

al·li·son tu·na *n phr* (Baha, Berm, USVI) A large deep-sea fish of high food value distinguished by long yellow dorsal and anal fins; *Neothunnus allisoni*—(ADF:64). *Allison tuna; Best months are June, July and August. Best place—all deepwater areas off the Bahamas.*—DBH:263

all-mouth *adj* (Bdos, Guyn) [*AF—Derog*] Talkative and unreliable; unable to do more than boast or threaten. a. *Don't mind all-mouth Liston—he does only talk everything.*—(Bdos) b. *They're just all-mouth people who can't offer you a dollar or won't raise a finger to help you when you get yourself in trouble following what they say.*—(Guyn)

al·lot·ment *n* (CayI) Part of a seaman's wages paid monthly to his family at home by the hiring firm. *When you get your call after a month your wife can go in the bank and get your allotment.*—(CayI)

all-out blast *n phr* (StVn) [*AF*] A big house party in wh there is much hard drinking.

al·low PHRASE **allow (sb) to know** *vb phr* (Bdos, Guyn) [*AF*] ‖ *make (sb) to know* (Guyn)

[*AF*] Inform (sb); state firmly to (sb); let (sb) know (some censure). a. *Well, Phillips tell 'e straight dat he din rude, an' Sir Denis get vex an' allow he to know dat 'e din like how 'e did getting on.*—NaT (80.02.22, p.7, Lickmout Lou) b. *The next time I see him cross my door, I am going to allow him to know that this is a decent home, you understand me? He can't bring advantage in here, dammit!*—(Guyn) [By misascription of the sense '*let* sb do sth' with the force of the SE idiomatic usage in 'let him know who is boss']

A[ll] right[1] [a:raɪt ~ ᴅraɪt]; **Al.right then!** *Greeting form* (CarA) [*IF*] 1. [In friendly meeting or leave- taking] a. *Howdy Miss Meertens, I passin[g]. Aa-right!*—(Guyn) b. *S1: Hi, like you goin[g] sportin[g] today! / S2: Aw-right, aw-right!*—(Bdos) c. *Well all right fellars, till to-morrow then.*—(Trin) d. *Farewell marker: 'alright then'.*—DJPVP:1 2. [Stressed. Indicating a warning or threat] a. *Look I'm not going to say one more warning to you all, you know! All right!*—(Bdos) b. *If you know how I sweat myself to help that man! And now just a little thing he can't do for me! All right.*—(Gren)

all right[2] **(al·right)** [ᴅ(l)raɪt ~ ɔ:raɪ(t)] *adj phr* 1. (Trin) [*AF*] [Of a person] Good to have as a friend; compatible. *'Earline's an all right craft', he told his mother, 'not stickish either'.*—JPB:119 2. (Guyn) [*IF*] ‖ *you do well!* (CarA) [Of a person] Fit to be ignored. a. *Everytime he preach you can bet he goin[g] ask for money. Every Sunday is money! He's all right.*—(Guyn) b. *Elvie laughed. 'Look girl, I can['t] bother wid you, yeh!' she said. 'You all right.'*—Guyn (Ms) □ Said with falling intonation, and often accompanied by sarcastic hand gesture.

all·spice* *n* (CarA) ‖ *Jamaica pepper* (Trin) ‖ *pimento* (CarA) The dried unripe berries of a large tree (*Pimenta dioica* or *P. officinalis* (*Myr-taceae*) wh are used as a flavouring agent. [From *all* + *spice*(s) because the dried berries are said to combine the flavours of clove, cinnamon and nutmeg. The simplified name (without pl -s) may be due to Cr infl, the tree being native to Jmca, introduced throughout the CarA, and the product commercialized with this name]

a[ll]-we; **a(h)we** [a'wi]; **a-we, aw.we (all-a-we, all-o(f)-we)** ['a(la)wi] *pron*, *1st pers pl* (CarA) [*AF—Cr*] ‖ *a-we dis* (Guyn) ‖ *ah-we-ya* (Antg) ‖ *arbee, ar-we* (Nevs, StKt) We; us; our; [except that the fuller form ALL-O'-WE is not usu possessive] a. *Black women who came into the store ... discussed the war. 'Watch how prices going to go up! All-we pore people is de people who is going to suffer.'*—MLDS:153 b. *The Creole would say, 'That's right, massa, get plenty of coolies to grow canes for ah we to grind.'*—LCTC:37 c. *Wen dem Korean spen all dis pesh pon Uncle, look out, nex ting you know dey getting fishing rights in ahwe water yes.*—ToR (76.02.05, p.6) d. *Trinidad carnival epitomises that largely elusive 'all a we is one' Caribbean feeling.*—SuC (77.02.06, p.6) e. *All o' we may be one, but what a dismal* *prospect if all o' we must be the same one, a world of faceless nonentities.*—CTOY:79 **f.** *The third said 'Me ah say so too. Me ah say she ha colour, me didn know she black lek ah we ya.'*—WoV (68.11.17, p.40) **g.** *Arbee goin see who is de better man.*—StKt (Ms) **h.** *This belong to ar-we.*—(Nevs) **i.** *Elbers, now a porkknocker also claimed that the accused 40-year-old R. R— told him 'Awwe go part? ... Na mek Eastman get am.'*—DaC (52.05.01, p.13) **[***All* + pl pron is a known feature of Afr langs wh may account for such structures as these (cp also ALL-YOU, YOU-ALL) ex Isoko: *mai kpobi* (we + all), 'all of us'. The widely current Cr form /awi/ may also have been infl by such a pron form as Yoruba: *awa* 'we' (a stressed nominative form). The form *all-o[ʃ]-we* > *all-a-we* is due to reinforcement *all* + *a(ll)we* in wh *a[ll]* loses its sense; prob also to infl from SE phr 'all of us'] □ Common in *Joc* contexts in writing, being regarded as a symbolic Creolism.

a[ll]-we-self [a wi'sɛlf] *refl pron, 1st pers pl* (Guyn) [*AF—Cr*] ‖ *we-all-self* (Crcu) Our-selves. *A-we poor people have to look after a-we-self.*—(Guyn) **[** < A[LL]-WE (as prec) + SE suff *-self*] □ See also WESELF.

all-you (all·yer, all·yuh, a > yo, all all-yo[u], all o[ʃ] all·yo, all o[ʃ] you-all) *pron (phr) 2nd pers pl* (CarA) [*AF*] ‖ *a[ll]-yo-dis* (Guyn) ‖ *all o[ʃ] wunna* (Bdos) ‖ *among-you* (Crcu, Gren, Guyn) ‖ *you-all* (CarA) You (pl); all of you, [also as possessive] your; belonging to or typical of all of you. **a.** *'Why all you can't live like the people in Belleville?' he said.*—LICMS:113 **b.** *Come on gentlemen, get up off all you knees, and stand on your feet like intelligent and fearless men, and stop men from laughing at you, and telling you to shut up when you get up to speak in that assembly.*—DeM (75.05.27, p.7) **c.** *... it look to me like now o' all-you intend to take een education.*—LDCD: 225 **d.** *God! Why all allyer women so?*—JMRS: 49 **e.** *My brother read more books than all of all-you put together.*—NHMB:462 **f.** *A[ll] yo-dis is too scraven.*—(Guyn) **g.** *Be-Jesus Christ, I could have tell all o' you-all, all o' this would have happen when you make a coloured man the director.*—CPM:126 [The addition of *all* to a pl pron is a known phrasal device in Afr langs, ex Hausa *duka ku* 'all you', Idoma *ɛjɛɛjaa* 'all you', etc. In Yoruba *gbogbo yin* 'all you' is esp emphatic since *yin* (< *eyin*) is already 'you' (pl). (See also etym notes at ALL-WE; YOU-ALL). As the strength of *all-you/you-all* weakened with time, the phr was expanded to *all of all-you/you-all* to stress the collective sense] **2.** *attribute to a n* [*IF*] You (as a type of people, identified by the following noun). **a.** *Ah know how allyuh Indian people like allyuh roti and rum, you know.*—SABS:41 **b.** *Iron man does get on ignorant eh? Why all you fellas so advantage!*—HPP:10 **c.** *I wish I was like allyou Jamaican' Moses say, 'all you could live on two-three pound a week.'*—STLL:10 □ Pron-ounced with closed juncture. The connotation is not complimentary, 'the same as you bunch of—', 'you lot'.

all-you **self∫-selves** [ɒlyʊ-sɛlf/-sɛlvz] (CarA) [*AF*] Yourselves. **a.** *If allyuh know w'at is good foh allyuhself yuh better pull alyuh tail from this coco an' dis silk cotton tree.*—TrG (23.9.79, p.6) **b.** *All you only care about all yuh selves.*—DP:35 **[** < ALL-YOU (as prec) + SE suff *-self/-selves*]

al·mond* ['amʌn(d)] *n* (CarA) ‖ *almonds* (Belz) ‖ *Barbados-almond, Demerara-al-mond, Indian almond, West Indian almond* (variously in ECar—*LNFV*); ‖ *zaman* (StLu) An ornamental shade tree whose branches spread in widely separated horizontal layers, with large oval green leaves that turn reddish brown before falling; it bears a tough-skinned oval-shaped fruit with an edible kernel; *Terminalia catappa* (*Combretaceae*). **a.** *Get some ammons from de ham-mons tree.*—(Belz) **b.** *The almond tree which was plentiful seemed to grow wild. Our almond trees bear a fruit which is about an inch and a half in length, and about an inch across. Generally, it is oval in shape, with a thick skin which covered a seed almost as large as the fruit itself. In this seed is a kernel, which can be extracted by hammering. This kernel looks like the commercial almonds that we now buy, but not as large.*—EBT:12 [From 'almond' shape of fruit, though not related to the commercial sweet and bitter almond wh is botanically identified as *Amygdalus communis* (*Rosaceae*), 'closely related to the genus *Prunus*' *OED*. The plant is of Malayan origin] □ In *Belz*, commonly used as if a standard plural /(h)amanz/, from Cr infl (cp *ants, ears, ashes*, etc). However an intrusive /h-/ occurring in speech is not found in writing. The Sp name *almendra* is also some-times used in *Belz*.

al·most *adv* (Bdos, Jmca) [*X*] [Used loosely as an intensifier] **a.** *Almost no matter where you live these days, the chances are that you are in a district beset by an expanding number of repairable cars by the roadside.*—AdN (73.09.10, p.3) **b.** *She was surprised that he should have been able to fall asleep so soon, so soundly, leaving her on the brink of this new and wonderful revelation of himself. Almost she could have been the tiniest bit resentful of this.*—HFGA:108 (R. Mais) **c.** *But store man-agers, too, know of the almost perfection of the modern-day shoplifter.*—AdN (71.11.27, p.1) **d.** *How to keep beef on the mixed Angus and shorthorn stock in a climate that never had any spring or autumn ... Carl Brandt's herd with its infusion of Indian stock was one of those which had almost nearly solved the problem.*—HSAG:31 [Mis-ascription of the qualifying function of SE adv *almost* 'very nearly', wh is an approximator, not an intensifier. Cit c., though awkward, reflects a rare usage in *OED almost* 2. b. (cit—1875) 'His almost impudence of manner']

alms-house shoes /2'31/ *n phr* (Bdos) [*AF*] Brown, canvas, rubber-soled shoes; brown sneakers (*AmE*). *But you can imagine him wear-in[g] them alms-house shoes to go to classes? He like he doesn't care how he looks!*—(Bdos) [By association. This cheapest of footwear used to be worn by alms-house inmates in *Bdos*]

al·oe(s)* [alo(z)] *n* (*pl*) (CarA) ‖ *bitter aloes* (Jmca, Guyn) ‖ *sempervive* (Jmca) ‖ *siempre vivi* (USVI) ‖ *simper-wivy* (CayI) ‖ *simple/ single/sinkle-bible* (Jmca) ‖ *simpri-vivie* (Angu) ‖ *sink-on-bible* (Belz) ‖ *sinti-biby* (Mrat) **1.** A small cactus-like plant with thick fleshy dagger-shaped leaves about half a metre long rising in a rosette cluster straight from a ground-base; its bitter slimy juice is used for a number of medicinal and cosmetic purposes; *Aloe vera* (also *A. vulgaris, A. barbadensis* (*Liliaceae*))—FFGM. **a.** *Aloe was at one time used to treat a wide variety of ailments in both humans and animals. Most housewives would have a plant growing in the yard and the jelly-like substance in the thick fleshy leaves would be used to treat colds, intestinal disorders, burns, abrasions and a host of mishaps and maladies.*—AdN (82.03.21, p.7) **b.** *There is a section in which cacti and succulents can be seen including the notorious* (ahem) *Aloes. Feast your eyes on these without comment.*—AdN (72.03.05, p.3) [Use of first part of botanical name, usu in pl form perhaps from occurrence of 'myrrh and aloes' in the Bible, (*Ps 45:8, etc*). However, the *aloes* of the Bible, a fragrant spice derived from a wood (*OED aloe* 1.), is unrelated] **2.** ALOES (Guyn) A prostitute. *Prostitutes are also known as lime, aloes, and cabbage, terms which bring the senses into play.*—RFGW:80 [Prob from the medicinal use of aloes juice as a contraceptive]

alone *adv* (CarA) [X] Only; just; exclusively. **a.** *But I am not sure, as he doesn't come to my house alone, although he says he loves me best of all. He also has a girl with two children for him.*—NaT (76.04.04, p.18) **b.** ... *they were putting on the finishing touches when the fire started and spread so rapidly that only one fan alone was saved.*—Cay (75.06.12, p.5) **c.** *You see three mango alone on me table and you take two, how you so bright.*—(Gren) [Shifted use of *OED alone* 11. 8., 9.] □ In ModE this sense of *alone* is reserved for contexts like 'you alone can help me']

a·long·side of *prep phr* (StKt) Together with; in addition to. *At this stage we can do no more than to express our humble duty to the Queen alongside of our sympathy to Her as head of the Royal Family at this time of their sad bereavement.*—LaS (65.03.30, p.1) [Cp *EDD alongside* of *prep phr*—'beside' (Southern counties of Eng). See also etym note at ALONG WITH 1.]

along with *prep phr* **1.** (CarA) [IF] Together with; side by side with. **a.** *His books along with his clothes were all found by the side of the trench where he left them.*—Guyn (Ms) **b.** *The Police received a report from Marjorie Y— of Rivero Street that at about 8.45 p.m. Friday she was along with her three sisters and her children, one in a stroller, in Albert Street West ..., when suddenly a*

truck approach them under a high rate of speed, hitting against the stroller knocking the baby out of the stroller and into the drain.—BeB (65.06.12, p.1) [As *OED along* 3. b., c., esp c., with shift of focus to physical closeness rather than association] **2.** (Jmca) [By extension] [IF] Living together with; cohabiting with; having a steady sexual relationship with. **a.** *I am in love for the past six months with a boy of 19. I am 18. I have a child who is two years old but I am not along with the father.*—DaG (67.03.26, p.10, Magazine) **b.** *In her defence F— said she is along with complainant's brother whom she has a child with.*—StA(JA) (71.07.03, p.5)

aloo (alu) [a·lu] *n* (Guyn, Trin) [Indic] Potato; common root vegetable of the plant *Solanum tuberosum* (*Solanaceae*) used as food. *What had life been for him? Days in the field, evenings playing with other children, roti and aloo in the night.*—SABS:6 [Hin *aaluu* 'potato'] □ Occurs as a loan word mostly in Indic folk-speech of *Guyn, Trin*.

aloo-pie *n* (Guyn, Trin) [Indic] A small pie made with a filling of fried mashed potato and seasoning, popularized as a snack.

al·par·ga·ta(s) ['alpagatʌ(z)] *n* (CarA) ‖ *alfagats* (Bdos, Guyn) ‖ *poor-donkeys, saphats* (Bdos) ‖ *sampats, sapats, zapats* (CarA) ‖ *sh-ampata* (Jmca) A type of sandal of plaited rope, or cut from a piece of motor-car tyre or wood; its toeless upper is a broad instep strap made of canvas, leather, or other suitable material. ... *worn like a sandal.* / *I do not know exactly how the names given to these were spelt but can only do so phonetically and that is 'alphagatta' or 'sepat', and I have not seen these used since World War II.*—AdM (79.06.17, p.15) [Sp name for a type of home-made footwear common in Venezuela and Panama, whence it was introduced by labourers esp to ECar] □ The original Sp spelling is preferable to the many conjectural ones (See ALFAGATS). However the /r/ is not pronounced. See also ZAPATS.

al·read·y [ɒ(l)'rɛdi] *adv* (CarA) [X] [In neg, interr, and conditional structures] Yet. **a.** *I wonder if she finished making the dress already.*—Guyn (Ms) **b.** *A wonder if she come from to[w]ng a[l] ready.*—(Gren) **c.** *Lady the Biabou bus gone a[l] ready?*—(StVn) [A misascription by infl of Cr in wh /di bos gaan aredi/ could be a statement (= has already gone) or, with intonation change, a question (= Has ... gone yet?)]

al·to pans *n phr* (Trin) [Steelband] ‖ DOUBLE-SECONDS (Trin) **a.** *The background or harmony pans are the Alto pans, Tenor pans, Guitar pans, Cellos and Basses.*—ACTT:108 **b.** *Next come the altos, or double-seconds: these too are twin instruments, but with a lower range, like an orchestra's violas, and are therefore taller, about a quarter of a full drum's height.*—Cat.5.1, p.20 [From the contrast of 'alto' with the shriller pitch of the 'soprano' wh name is also used sometimes for the highest-pitch pans] □ Both *alto* and *soprano* are now, however, obsolescent names.

a·lu·mi·na *n* (Guyn, Jmca) The fine white powder (aluminum oxide), wh is extracted from metal grade bauxite by a special process, and smelted to make aluminium.

al·ways *adv* **1.** (Bdos, Guyn) [X] Without exception and without doubt. **a.** *Always when is time to do work you will find she gone home.*—(Guyn) **b.** *He doesn't like me to go anywhere. Always he wants to know where I went and with whom. He likes to know that I am at home always.*—NaT (76.09.12, p.26, Dear Christine) [Prob infl by Cr intonation] □ Carrying no special stress itself in this context, *always* in sentence-initial position nevertheless indicates by higher pitch that what follows is emphasized. In ModE, *always* does not open a sentence. Sentence-initial *always* is 'obs or dial' in *OED always* 3. 'nevertheless, still'. **2.** (Guyn) [IF] *That's typical of* (sb) ... *S1: She promise me de dress fo[r] today, but when I go she say she ain't finish it yet, she sorry. / S2: She always!*—(Guyn) [Perh a development of the emotive force of the preceding with the loss of its orig meaning] □ Said with strong falling intonation expressing the speaker's disgust with the person referred to.

am[1] *part of vb* BE (CarA) **1.** [AF] See BE[1] 2., 4(ii) **2.** [IF] (Reduction of) I am (See A[2] and □ Note)

am[2] *pron* (*3rd pers sg*) (Belz, Guyn) [AF—Cr] ‖ UM (CarA) **1.** *De $5* [*note*] ... *look like um din good. I ask people next to me to look at it, and dem say it good, and so me tek am*—Guyn (CR, 1954)

-am[3] *Cr vb suffix* (Guyn, Trin) [AF] [Empty suffix to a vb, characteristic of the creolized Eng of rural East Indians in *Guyn* and *Trin*] *You doam same thing. You gettam house which side Barataria, gettam land, cow.... You live dat side, plantam garden, live good. In those few words Ramlal summed up things.*—SABS:7 □ Often in *Joc* use as an ethnicity marker to typify uneducated Indic speech in *Guyn* and *Trin*.

a·ma·di·li (Belz) ‖ ARMADILLO (Guyn) □ See HAMADILI.

a·ma·ryl·lis* *n* (CarA) ‖ *crocus*[2] (Bdos, Guyn) ‖ *rain-flower* (Jmca) ‖ *snowdrop* (Bdos) A small lily borne each on a single stalk, 6 to 8 ins high, growing directly out of the ground; it grows wild along grassy roadsides, and is commonly of three varieties—pink, yellow, and white; *Zephyranthes citrina* or *Z. tubispatha* or *Amaryllis t. (Amaryllidaceae). While away in a spot secluded / Tall stalks of amaryllis grew.*—JBJ:103 □ This name is used mostly by learned writers and in gardening literature, nor is its specific application to any particular type clear. Folk-names differ and are common.

A·ma·zon fly *n phr* (Guyn) A parasitic fly introduced into the Caribbean to feed on the insect pest known as the CANE-BORER; *Metagonistylum minense.*

am·ber[1] *n* (Belz, Jmca) ‖ *rasam* (Belz) Hardened resin, esp as used in folk-medicines, OBEAH, etc *They use amber with chicken weed and copaiba as a treatment for venereal disease, which they call 'the runnings'*—(Belz)

am·ber[2] *n* (StLu); ‖ *am.ber.fish* (Berm) ‖ AM-BERJACK (CarA) *Now comprising top grade group to be sold at 45 cents a pound are: Abbacore, amber, barber ...*—VoS (65.03.10, p.3)

am·ber·jack* (**am·ber-jack**) *n* (CarA) ‖ *amber*[2] (StLu) ‖ *amberfish* (Berm) ‖ *ocean jack* (Belz) A popular edible fish that is greenish-red in colour and of average weight 18 lbs; *Seriola dumerili. Bahamian waters teem with virtually every species of salt-water fighter including amberjack, marlin, tuna ...*—DBH:89

am·char (**an·char**) *n* (Guyn, Trin) See ACHAR □ Note

A·mer·i·can silk-cot·ton* *n phr* (BrVi) ‖ *cotton* 3. (CayI) ‖ *duppy-cho cho* (Jmca) ‖ *French cotton* (Bdos) ‖ *milky bush* (TkCa) ‖ *silk bush* (Baha) A seashore shrub growing to about 9 ft high, with large silky oval-shaped leaves wh give a latex when broken; it bears sparse bunches of pinkish flowers and large green 'wind'-pods; *Calotropis procera (Asclepiadaceae).*

A·mer·in·di·an *n, adj* (CarA) ‖ *buck* (Guyn) ‖ *Carib* (Dmca, StVn, Trin) A member of the mongoloid race of people whose many nations or 'tribes' were the original inhabitants of the Caribbean and the Americas; [by extension, *adj*] deriving from or belonging to the lang or culture of these people. **a.** *Anthropologists have grouped the Amerindian tribes of Guyana in the following way: Arawakan (Arawak or Lokono, Wapishana); Cariban (Akawaio, Arekuna, Makushi, Patamuna, Carib, Wai-Wai); and Warrauan (Warrau).*—Guyn (Ms) **b.** *... endangered himself needlessly by hanging far out from the running-board to sing to people on the road, Tunapuna, Naparima ... Guayaguayare, Chacachacare ... and back—the glorious Amerindian names ...*—NHMB:79 [Blend of *Amer(ican)* + *Indian*, these people having been called 'Indians' in error by Columbus] □ The term is in regular *Formal* use in CE mostly with ref to the Amerindian people of *Guyn* and *Srnm*, the term CARIB being generally used with ref to the small indigenous remainders in *Dmca, StVn* and *Trin*.

A·mer·in·di·an Cap·tain *n phr* (Guyn) ‖ *Touchau* (Guyn) The officially recognized leader of an Amerindian village in *Guyn. And Whereas the Amerindian Captains and other Leaders of the several Amerindian Communities by Resolution dated Sunday 8th February, 1970 accepted the said recommendations. / And Whereas* the Government of Guyana, after consultations with the said Amerindian Captains and Leaders also accepted the said recommendations and undertook their implementation...—Guyn (Amerindian Act, 1976)

A·mer·in·di·an pep·per·pot n phr (Guyn) A meal made by boiling pieces of fish and wild meat in the previously boiled juice of the bitter cassava or 'cassava water' with much pepper and seasoning. Amerindian pepperpot is not like what we call pepperpot with casareep. It is a whitish, grayish colour and like a thick, heavy soup, but it is very tasty to eat with cassava bread.—Guyn (Ms)

among prep (Bdos) [X] Belonging to; within the ranks or group of. The dispute over the 'windfall' money from the last sugar crop has given the new Barbados Progressive Union of Workers an opportunity to embarrass the well-established Barbados Workers' Union, and its general secretary, Mr Frank Walcott among the island's sugar workers.—AdN (63.12.29, p.6)

amongst prep (CarA) 1. [With intensifying effect] Within; particularly among. We are equally fed up and disgusted with not seeing that others who commit crimes, and whose crimes are the Big ones, The Big Crimes amongst Big People, are never apprehended.—TrU (70.09.26, p.1) 2. [X] Amidst. 3. PHRASE 3.1 (A)mongst your **sex!** excl (BrVi) [To a junior or inferior person] Be off with you! Go find your playmates! Know your place. Boy, I a big woman to you, you hear? I know when you born. Mongst your sex!—(BrVi) □ A sharp reprimand for precociousness or presumptuousness in a young person.

among-you (Crcu, Gren, Guyn); (amongstyou) (Gren) pron [IF] ‖ all-you, you-all (CarA) You (pl); your (pl); (belonging to) all of you. Wait till among-you fader come! He going to beat every man jack.—(Guyn) [Perh an EE pron phr. Cp Shak, much ado V. 1. 'You have among you killed a sweet and innocent lady']

amount n (CarA) [IF] [Used in ref to countable items, esp people] Number. a. My slip is clearly a Jamaicanism as we here are very fond of saying 'an amount of people' instead of 'a number of people'.—DaG (66.11.30, p.16) b. Check the amount of Bajans leaving this homeland to do their own thing successfully in the USA, Canada, and England.—AdN (73.05.18, p.4) c. Would it not have been better to double the amount of holidays (except for civil servants)...?—ViN (73.11.02, p.2) [Perh a survival of EE. Cp OED amount 1. b. 'sum total ... in number' + cit 1801 'to the amount ... of twelve or fourteen'] □ In present IAE, amount 'quantity, supply' relates to mass nouns (water, mud, rice, etc).

Amy Amy [emi emi] n phr (StVn) A girls' game in wh one, the 'Amy', standing at a distance from a semi-circle formed by the others, advances performing different actions called for in

the song sung by the group, then chooses a partner to 'dance ma-rin-ga' and that partner becomes the next 'Amy'.

a·na·con·da* n (Trin) ‖ camoodi (Guyn) A very large amphibious snake of the boa family that crushes its victims; Eunectes murinus. a. In the water lurk anacondas large enough to swallow whole a six-foot alligator.—ACTT:175 b. All the small rodents, and even the larger game ... are preyed on by snakes. Pre-eminent among these are the boas.... There are four of them, the rainbow boa, Book's tree boa (cascabel), the common boa constrictor or macajuel, and the anaconda. The last named, some twenty-five feet in maximum length, is more at home in water than on land and is more or less confined to swampy areas.—ACTT: 170

a·na·kwa (ha·na·kwa) /1'12/ n (Guyn) A large, brown, bush bird of Guyn, related to the common hen and dwelling mostly on the ground. When the weather is about to change from dry to wet this bird makes the constant sound 'anakwa-anakwa'.—(Guyn) [From the sound it is said to make]

a·na·na n (Dmca) See ZANNANNA

A·nan·cy[1] (A·nan·si, An·nan·cy) n (CarA) ‖ Boro Nancy, Bo Anancy, Brer Anancy (CarA) ‖ Compè Zayen (Dmca, Gren, StLu) 1. The cunning rascal and hero of a countless number of CarA folk-tales (originating in W Afr, esp Ashanti, folklore) in wh he is a mythical spider in human form, usu outwitting opponents of superior strength, or barely escaping being caught, but always amusing in his greed and selfishness. a. Anancy is a spider; / Anancy is a man; / Anancy's a West Indian / And West African.—FCV2:137 b. ... and at dusk, listened with his brothers while the old cook told tales of Anansi the Spider-man, his wife Crooky, his adversary Takoomah.—MGWI:59 [DAFL Twi ananse-sɛm 'a tale of Ananse, being a mythic personage genially called agya Ananse (Hon Ananse), to whom great skill and ingenuity is attributed (but who is usu caught in his own snare), a personification of the spider. His wife is kɔnnɔre, his son ntikuma'] 2. [By extension] A person whose cunning or untrustworthiness is detected or revealed. Look here, boy, don't get me out! If you spen' twenty cents out a dollar, how di change could be fifty cents? You di try play anaansi 'pan me!—Belz (Ms) □ The variant Anansi is nearest to the Twi original.

a·nan·cy[2] (-spi·der) (nan·cy (-spi·der)) n (CarA) A large, brown house-spider, Hetoropoda venatoria; also (in Belz) a small, grey fly-eating spider. a. 'Look at the anancy spinning its web,' she said.—Belz (Ms) b. Now see all the nancy rope on the books.—(Jmca) c. It was a big able nancy spider I was throwing water on because I didn't want to kill it and bring bad luck.—(Guyn) [DAFL Twi ananse, 'spider', Ananse kokuroko 'the great spider'. The form nancy may be due to metanalysis *a* + *nancy* < *ananse*, or to aphesis. The redundant compound *(a)nancy spider* would have developed as the orig meaning of *anancy* was gradually lost]

A·nan·cy horse *n phr* (Belz) [*AF—Joc*] A bicycle. *Drunk man can['t] ride anancy horse, otherwise he going fall.*—(Belz) [= *Anancy's horse*; from the resemblance of the spokes to a spider's web]

a·nan·cy·ism (a·nan·cism) *n* (Jmca) Use of trickery to achieve success; the gaining of one's ends through cunning. **a.** *You know, of course, that Anancy, that beloved spider, is the inventor of the freeness mentality. Nowhere in the vast literature on anancyism is there an instance of Anancy paying for anything. Ananciologists have justified this attitude to life by arguing that Anancy is a small creature who ... has to employ his wits to protect himself against much larger predators and competitors.*—DaG (67.05.07, p.8) **b.** *Lack of trust and confidence kills business. Intensified Anancism holds us back within a vicious circle of declining efficiency, sagging morale and declining production.*—DaG (80.01.12, p.8) [*Anancy* + *ism* = 'system or principle' attributed to Anancy] □ *Anancyism* is the clearer and therefore preferable form of this useful derivative; but capitalization is unnecessary, since it is a kind of behaviour (cp *chauvinism*) not a theory (cp *Marxism*).

A·nan·cy-sto·ry (Anan·si-sto·ry, nan·cy-sto·ry) *n* (CarA) **1.** A folk tale about Anancy. *Animals were given personal, characteristic natures; we have remaining examples of this in the Anancy Stories.*—LMFF:70 **2.** [By extension] An absurd explanation; a silly or unbelievable story. *I know you will come up with a lot of anancy-stories. When you cannot get through with your National Health Scheme, you will tell the people that the middle-class doctors are not supporting it.*—Bdos (Hd, 76.10.12, p.51) [See AN-ANCY[1] 2.]

a·na·to* (a(n)·nat·to, ar·not·to) *n* (CarA) ‖*roucou* (Dmca, Gren, Guyn, StLu, Trin) A small tree bearing clusters of dark-red, spiny, oval-shaped pods wh open when mature to expose numerous, bright-red, waxy seeds from the pulp of wh a cosmetic or vegetable dye is made; the seeds of this tree or the dye made from them; *Bixa orellana* (Bixaceae). **a.** *The Accaways ... are recognised, at first sight, by a large lump of arnotto, stuck upon the hair over the forehead—with which they paint themselves, both to strike terror and as a defence from the bite of insects, by its properties.*—HIN:20 **b.** *A third order for annatto has been placed with the Jamaica Agricultural Society by a firm in the country overseas, bringing up to 300 tons the volume of this colouring matter which the Society has been asked to supply at short order.*—WeG (72.12.20, p.12) [Cariban. Cp *GDAA* Akawaio *anondö*, Arekuna *anontö*, 'fruit used to make red dye with wh Amerindians paint themselves'] □ The spelling *anatto* is common,

but note *OED anatta/o* and *WCD9 annatto*. Other variants *'anonto'*, *'onoto'* also occur.

an·ba·zou·di [ābazudi] *adj* (StLu) ‖BAZOUDI (ECar) [Fr Cr < Fr *abasourdi* with initial nasalization]

an·char *n* (Trin) See ACHAR □ Note

an·cho* *n* (Trin) ‖*blue-fish* (Trin) An edible blue fish with a blunt head, heavy projecting lower jaw, and stout, flattish, oblong body, of average weight about 15 lbs; *Pomatomus saltatrix* (Pomatomidae).. *We might even be paying $20 for a pound of Cro-Cro or Ancho.*—SuP (80.03.16, p.11)

an·cho·a *n* (Gren) ‖ANCHOVY (StLu, Trin)

an·cho·ba (an·cho·va) *n* (Antg) See ANTROVER

an·cho·vy* ['ančAvi] *n* (StLu, Trin) ‖*anchoa* (Gren) ‖*antrovy, windward sprat* (StVn) ‖*pisiette* (StLu) ‖*za(n)chwa* (Trin) A name popularly applied to any of a number of small, sardine-like, edible fishes, of wh one of the commonest is a silvery-skinned variety; *Engraulis eurystole* (Engraulidae); also *Anchoa lyslepsis* or 'dusky' anchovy. *There are two basic groups that occur in the Caribbean—the sardines and the anchovies* [*and*] *there appears to be a great deal of interchange in naming these species amongst the islands in that the terms anchovie, anchoa, z'anchois, herring, sprats are used.*—Trin (Ms) □ The name occurs most frequently as a collective *sg* like most fish-names (cod, herring, etc), but the *pl* form *anchovies* has prob given rise to an erron variant *sg* **anchovie**.

and [an(d)] *conj* **1.** (CarA) [*IF*] ‖*ain't*[2] (CarA) [Introducing a neg question expecting the answer 'Yes'] Isn't/wasn't it that ...?; Don't/didn't ...?; Surely. *The dark girl with a huge-boned face had said off-handedly, 'You asking me? Ask Mrs Patrick. And she is Mrs Fergus' good friend?'*—JJM:92 [A refinement of Cr initial *ain[t]* /en/ introducing a question expecting the answer 'yes' as in /en da iz di waan/ 'Isn't that the one?'] □ In speech it always has low pitch, but often strong stress. **2.** [*conditional*] (CarA) [*IF*] If (implying disapproval, warning or threat). *Afa: Oui! Is better than priest saying bettise about God .... Tell us what you see, garcon, and you put God in it, I cut your throat!*—WSAD:21 [Cp *OED* and C. *conj* conditional = 'if'. Prob from EE *an* as in 'an't please you' (see *OED an, an'* 2.] **3.** [*with prep sense*] (CarA) [*IF*] Against (implying a threat of violence, esp as in foll phr). PHRASE **It's me and you!** *id phr* (CarA) [*AF/IF*] You'll have me to reckon with! *Boy, if you break that lamp, is yo[ur] father an[d] you when he come home!*—(Bdos) [A prob calque from many W Afr langs wh have a similar statement of threat: exs Igbo *Mu na gi* 'Me with you'; Yoruba *Emi kpelu e* 'Me with you'. Cp also Krio *Na mi en yu go do* 'You and I will have it out' (*pers info, M. Broderick, 1975*)] **4.** PHRASES **4.1 and all the way like that** *filler* *phr* (CarA) [*IF*] And so on; as you will understand or can imagine. *Well after she lef[t] me I take up with this one, and we live along. See? And all the way like that. We had two children, grow up, all the way like that.*—(Bdos) □ Occurs in semi-educated conversational narrative. **4.2 and another locust!** *terminal phr* (Guyn) [*IF*] [In calling an end to a tiresome narrative, argument, etc] Enough! No more! *Awright, awright! And another locust! Ow! You all not tired arguing with one another?*—(Guyn) [Ref to a folktale wh repeats 'and another locust came and ate another grain of corn' as often as the listener can bear hearing the repetition] □ Applied to children's talk, mostly by old people. **4.3 and done** *adv intensifier phr* (CarA) [*IF*] Without bungling and delay; properly and finally; at once and have finished with it. *That time I made the tea and the dinner too, you know? One thing and done.*—(StVn) **4.4 and no fun; and no mistake** *adv intensifier phr* (CarA) [*IF*] Without any doubt; as surely as ever. *And no fun, you know, he was a first-class workman once he was off the rum. First class!*—(Guyn) [Prob from Irish infl. Cp *JESI:9* 'A very usual emphatic ending to an assertion ...' 'That horse is a splendid animal and no mistake.' Listed in *PDCP* as early 19C, noting other similar phrs 'and no error, ... flies, ... kidding'] **4.5 and Sam and the duppy; and Sam Duppy** *augmentative phrasal tag in the exp* 'everybody and Sam and the duppy' (Bdos) [*AF—Joc*] Everybody; Tom, Dick, and Harry and his brother; the world and his wife. *Well in those days the fashion parade was the Agricultural Exhibition in Queen's Park where you have everybody and Sam and the duppy.*—(Bdos) [By folk etym prob from *StLu* Fr Cr *tout moun ansam* [tut mun ansam] (< Fr *tout le monde ensemble*) 'everybody together', prob developing into 'everybody and Sam', with the addition of 'the duppy' to include even the unwanted or unseen] **4.6 and so; and such like** *augmentative tag (terminating phr or list)* (CarA) [*AF*] And (the) other things or matters or persons of that kind. **a.** *All I could say was, I call him up, yes, an' I appeal' to him, as a fellow writer, an' so.*—SGJ:43 **b.** *Well of course yo[u] got to make out estimates, know how much paint yo[u] require, an[d] such like.*—(Guyn) **4.7 and them; and they; and those** *collectivizing* (CarA) [*AF/IF*] **(i)** And or with the other persons of his/ her group; and those with whom he/she keeps company. **a.** *Even the businessmen, some of them ... are saying 'but boy, say what you like when Gairy and them in power, money passing'.*—Gren (Hd, 78.02.17, p.41) **b.** *She told him ... if that was the way he treated innocent people, she hoped Guy H— and they would get away.*—TrG (73.08.03, p.3) **c.** *Ingrid, Pedro and those gone to the beach.*—(Bdos) **(ii)** [*AF*] [By extension, indicating kind] And people or things of that sort or type. *But whenever big things happen, I does go out and look all about, at the hills, and the trees, and the sky, and them. And I does get a funny feeling, as if strength coming inside me. That must be God.*—SABS:118 [From the system of

marking pls or collectives in CarA Cr morphosyntax /di gyal-dem/, /di wiil-dem/, /di wayt-piipl-dem/, 'the girls, the wheels, the white people'. Ultimately a calque from some Afr langs wh pluralize nouns by suffixing the 3rd person pl pron, ex *WEBC* Ewe *devi* + *awo* (*child* + *them*) 'children', *ate* + *awo* (*tree* + *them*) 'trees'. Note also that in Twi *CGAF:63* 'The plural pron *nom* (they) is added to names of persons in order to mark in an indefinite way the followers and companions of that person, himself included: *Paulo nom* ... 'Paul and his company ...'.'] □ These are mesolectal refinements of the CarA Cr structure with a linking 'and'. The awkwardness of *AF* '*them/they*' is overcome by '*and those*'. **4.8 and the pin/wire bend** *phr-formula for terminating folk tales* (Gren, Guyn) And that's the end of the story. *They fled in the opposite direction at breakneck speed, while Brer Manicou walked safely home. An' so de story end de wire bend;* / *An' I must go home an' see me nen-nen.*—STTG:45 □ Also *Joc*, applied to any inconclusive or tiresome account given by a child. Cp 4.2 AND ANOTHER LOCUST. **4.9 and thing** [an 'tɪŋ] *augmentative tag* (CarA) [*AF*] And so on; and other things of that sort; and all that is related to such things. **a.** *I have to pay water rates, light bills, and for the children who are at school I have to buy books and thing for them.*—Bdos (CR, 70.10.28) **b.** *Maybe Dr Ram wants to see bands made up only of East Indians, with tassa-drumming and ting.*—BoM (79.06.15, p.19) [A prob calque from W Afr langs, ex 'In Mfantse [Fante] we say something similar: *Oenya kaar na adze*, 'He has acquired a car and thing'—*pers info, G.D. Hagan*] **4.10 and to(o) besides** [an tʊ bɪsaɪdz] /1112/ *double conn phr* (Guyn, Tbgo, Trin) [*X*] And what is more; furthermore. *I am not leaving, put me out; and to besides, you can't put me out.*—Tbgo (CR) □ Usu in strongly emotive contexts. **4.11 come and go (along)** (CarA) [*IF*] Let's go! Look! *Come and go [a]long and don['t] bother with the stupid boy, you hear.*—(Bdos) [By refinement of Cr serial vb 'come go > come we go', wh sequences still occur at AF level] □ In familiar persuasive speech. **4.12 go and come back; go to come back** (CarA) [*AF/IF*] To go out intending to return very shortly. *I goin[g] dong de road and come back.*—(Gren) [See GO Phr 6.29] **4.13 go and do** (CarA) [*IF*] To cause to happen. *'Look what you go and do now!' said his mother pointing to the spilt porridge, but Arnold did not seem too concerned about what he had gone and done.*—Guyn (Ms) [By refinement of Cr *go do* [gʌ dʊ] in wh 'go' is properly an aspect-marker of intention or purpose. The structure may also be infl by similar IF IAE structures as 'go and see', 'try and do', 'come and eat', etc (as *OED and* 10.)] □ In CE *go and do* is always clause-final, requiring no object in this function. Note difference from IAE as in *AVB* Luke 10.37, 'go and do likewise'. **4.14 take and hit/knock (sb)** (Bdos, Guyn) See TAKE Phr 18. **4.15 well and** (+ *vb* or *adj*) *adv intensifier phr* (Baha, Belz, Jmca, Guyn) [*IF*] Very much; greatly; intensely.

You well and dance up with the girls, eh?—(Guyn) [See more at WELL[1] Phr 2.1]

An·dro·sian *n, adj* (Baha) (A person or thing) native to or characteristic of the island of Andros, the largest of the Bahama Islands.

An·e·ga·da Pas·sage *n phr* (CarA) A passage of very deep sea to the east of Anegada separating the Virgin Islands from the Leeward Islands. ... *a group known as the Lesser Antilles stretching across the entrance to the Caribbean Sea. In the shape of an arc bowed out toward the Atlantic Ocean, they extend for 540 miles from the Anegada Passage, near the Virgin Islands, southwards almost to the coast of South America.*—TWDWE: 7

An·e·ga·di·an [anɪ'ga·diən] *n, adj* (CarA) (A person or thing) native to or characteristic of Anegada, one of the Br Virgin Islands. *Rev Isidore Mahony Norman and his sister, Mrs Louis Potter, native Anegadians and long time residents of San Pedro de Marcoris, spent an enjoyable vacation last week with family and friends in their home island.*—IsS (73.05.12, p.3)

an·gel·fish* (**an·gel-fish**) *n* (CarA) Any of a number of varieties of small, flat, roundish fish with brilliantly contrasting colours, noticeable wing-like trailing fins, and fan-shaped tail; *Pomacanthus arcuatus, Holocanthus bermudensis,* etc (*Chaetodontidae*). [These fishes appear to range from *Berm* to *Guyn,* varying greatly in size from about 6 ins to over 20 ins long] *The most striking thing about the reef fishes is the variety of their shapes, markings, and colours. The queen angelfish, trailing gossamer wings above and below its chrome-yellow tailfin, is clothed in a tapestry of light-blue, dark-blue, gold and scarlet.*—TLDVG:17 [Prob from lace-like appearance of wing-like fins of some varieties] □ *Angelfish,* as a single word, occurs more often in the literature.

an·gel·i·ca *n* 1.* (USVI) A herb whose stalk and leaves are used medicinally; *Angelica archangelica* (*Umbelliferae*). *Made into a tea with vinegar added angelica is helpful in preventing severe colds. Also clears the lungs and liver, blockage of the urinary tract, and eases colic.*—PHPVI:10 2. An ornamental shrub with variegated leaves, usu dark green with a white margin, popular as a hedge plant in the *USVI; Polyscias guilfoylei* (*Araliaceae*). *Angelica, one of the easiest and quickest to grow of all hedge plants ... requires both topping and shearing to obtain a thick hedge.*—VISTP:37 3. (Gren) ‖*angelica-tree* (Jmca) A flowering tree of medium height with fern-like leaves and bearing small, fleshy, inedible berries; *Aralia filicifolia* (*Araliaceae*). *The angelica is a decorative flowering tree but the leaves can be used as a purgative.*—Gren (Ms)

an·ge·lin* (**an·ge·leen**) [anɟeli·n] /112/ *n* (CarA) ‖*cabbage-bark tree* (Belz, Jmca) ‖*dog-almond* (ViIs) ‖*wormwood* 2. (Jmca) A hardwood tree with a rounded head, dark green leaves; it bears reddish-pink flowers and a hard, plum-like fruit; *Andira inermis* (*Papilionaceae*). *Angeleen is a valuable timber tree,* [*whose*] *bark is* [*also*] *a powerful narcotic and anthelmintic ... said to cure 'bots' in horses.*—GHC:218 [*OED angelina.* Cp also *NMID* Brazilian Pg *angelim* 'Brazilian hardwood tree'. See also *DJE*]

an·gel's trum·pet* *n phr* (Baha, Jmca, Trin) ‖*trumpet-flower* (Bdos) An erect, ornamental plant whose fairly sturdy but brittle central stock grows to about 15 ft, with branches from the ends of wh hang very attractive, long, white or coloured, trumpet-shaped flowers wh are fragrant at night; the plant's seeds, leaves, and roots have strong narcotic properties; *Datura suaveolens* or *Brugmansia arborea, Datura* (*Solanaceae*). [Prob from fragrance, beauty + trumpet-like shape. Cp DEVIL'S TRUMPET]

an·gi·neel *n* (Tbgo) *The angineel is a poisonous tree with leaves that blister the skin.*—Tbgo (Ms) [Prob erron for MANCHINEAL]

an·gle[1] *n* (Dmca) A meeting point of two streets; a corner. *For Sale: Lot at angle of Hillsborough and Hanover streets with building thereon.*—DoC (Ad, 65.03.20, p.2)

an·gle[2] *n* (Antg) ‖*ketchie* (BrVi) A marble game in wh one player places a number of marbles as his stake in a large triangle drawn on the ground, and another tries, by 'booting' at them with his own, to hit as many out as he can, his own marble becoming 'dead' if it fails to come out of the triangle. *He can['t] try that angle again. I tell you his marble dead!*—(Antg)

An·gos·tu·ra bit·ters *n phr* (CarA) ‖*bitters* 3 (Bdos, Guyn) A brown, bitterish, aromatic liquid made from a blend of gentian root extract and other vegetable spices, and used to flavour drinks and cooking; it is patented and bottled in Trinidad. [From the town of Angostura, Venezuela, where it was first made in the early 19c, now renamed Ciudad Bolivar]

An·guil·li·an (**An·guil·lan**) (CarA) *n, adj* (Angu) (A person or thing) native to or characteristic of Anguilla. *Anguillians must not co-operate with anyone coming from overseas to do the valuation on houses.... Registering his protest against the overseas Valuers and at the same time reflecting the Anguillian situation, Mr Webster told his 500 listeners: 'We must understand that these people from away are accustomed to more sophisticated houses, higher wages and they pay by the square-foot and square-yard.'*—AaT (75.10.10, p.1) □ The form *'Anguillian'* is preferred and used in Anguilla, the form *Anguillan* occurring mostly in other *CarA* newspapers.

ani *n* (Jmca) ‖JUMBIE-BIRD 3. (Guyn) *The ani* (*Crotophaga ani*) ... *more correctly described as the Smooth-billed Ani ... in Jamaica ... widely* known as the Blackbird and sometimes as the Tick-bird ... belongs to the family of the Cuckoos.— TIBJ:11 [Sp variant of Ameriandian name of the bird. Cp *DGEG* Guarani, *anó* 'kind of bird, Crotophaga ani' with variant Sp names *ani*, *anu*, etc]

an·i·mal flo·wer *n phr* (Bdos) A tiny and colourful, sensitive plant-like form found attached to bedrock in still, shallow sea-water, closing up and shrinking as one tries to touch it; the sea-anemone. **a.** *Our Animal Flower Cave in St Lucy is almost worthless as a tourist attraction now because we have allowed all and sundry to go and pull at and kill off nearly all the animal flowers and it is hard to find any nowadays.*—Bdos (Ms) **b.** *In this sea-cave are serpulae or sea-worms, locally known as 'animal flowers', of various tints, chiefly yellow.*—AdM (76.09.05, p.7) [The name 'Animal Flower' was invented by Rev G. Hughes in 1750. He devoted Ch IX of his book (*HNHB: 293–298*) to the subject 'The Animal Flower', wh he had discovered in the Parish of St Lucy, noting 'God's amazing Providence which ... endued the Arms or Feelers of this Animal with a fine yellow Colour, and hath ordained it to differ in this Particular from the several Tribes of fungous Animals, that are always found cleaving to the Rocks in the Sea'. He also referred to 'a great Number of Animal Flowers of the same Species with the yellow large ones'. Note that *OED* lists *animal flower* (*animal* C. 1.) but with earliest cit 1833, and also *sea anemone* (*anenomone* 2.) with earliest cit 1855: 'The extensive group known popularly as Sea-anemones or Animal flowers, from the blossom-like appearance of their expanded disks and tentacles and their gorgeous colours']

an·ise* [ani·z] *n* (Mrat, StKt, ViIs) ‖*aniseed* (Guyn, StVn) ‖*anisud* (BrVi) ‖ *nanni* (Dmca) **1.** A plant, about 1-1/2 ft high, from whose white flowers seeds are formed wh are used as a folk medicine and in cooking; *Pimpinella anisum* (*Umbelliferae*). *Anise makes an excellent tea which expels gas from the stomach and bowels. It is excellent for gas pains, cold, flu, cough, griping and high blood pressure.*—Lal 1.1 [See *COD*, etc, the plant being of European source]

an·i·seed *n* (Guyn, Mrat, StVn) ‖ ANISE (Mrat, etc) *The aniseed leaf is fern-like with a sweet smell like liquorice. The leaves are boiled to relieve gas pains and to flavour beverages. The seeds are also used in this way and can be used for spice.*—StVn (Ms) [< *anise* + *seed* with shift in usage, by synecdoche, in this case displacing the orig]

a·ni·sud *n* (BrVi) [*IF*] ‖ ANISE (Mrat, etc) [Perh by confusion of taxonomic name *anisum* with *aniseed*. Cp also *DJE anisou*, 'a medicinal preparation from aniseed']

An·ju·man *n* (Guyn, Trin) One of the denominations of the Muslim religion in Guyana and Trinidad. **a.** *As is customary during the month of Ramadan (fasting) the Anjuman will visit the*

following *Jamaats: Hague on the 14th, La Jalousie 17th and No.2 Canal Polder 21st.*—GyG (57.04.13, p.9) **b.** *An Imam's refresher course sponsored jointly by regions C and D of the Religious and Social Services Committee of the Anjuman Sunnat ul Jamaat Association will be opened at the ASJA Girls College.*—TrG (67.02.07, p.9) [Urdu *anjuman*, 'association, league, organization']

an·na·fè *adj* (Dmca, StLu) [*AF*] Prone to get into trouble; meddlesome. *How you so annafè? You always finding yourself in trouble.*—(StLu) [Fr Cr < Fr *en affaire(s)*, literally 'in troublesome matters' though this meaning does not apply in Mod Fr]

an·nat·to (an·not·to) *n* (CarA) See ANATO

Anne po·ta·to *n phr* (TkCa) ‖ SWEET-POTATO (CarA) *There are two types of Anne Potato in the country, one with a white skin and the other with a purple to red skin. Both types have a creamish colour inside with white streaks throughout it. A potato with the same description could be found throughout the island under a different name, since potatoes here are named after people who grow them most.*—TkCa (Ms) [Established folk name in *TkCa* from person with whom earliest or most abundant early cultivation is associated—(*Ms*, *D. Jones*)]

an·ni ant *n phr* (Guyn) A large, black, forest ant about an inch long that is said to have a vicious bite; *Paraponera clavata*. *The Anni ant is generally found in coconut plots and when the ants are disturbed, they swarm out of the nest making a stridulating noise common to the species. The sting is excessively painful and will bring on fever in a susceptible individual.*—Guyn (Ms) □ Also referred to *IAIG:147* as the **black manoorie ant**.

a·noint [(ʌ)naɪnt] *vb tr* (CarA) To massage or rub the body or part of the body with a curative oil or ointment. **a.** *My sister twisted her ankle that day and I was going to get old Miss Beaton to [a]noint it.*—(Belz) **b.** *Well they come and [a]noint me down with belladonna and glycerine, my whole body, and I slept well and feel good the next day.*—(Guyn) [As *OED* anoint 1. a. and 4. general senses wh have been largely displaced in ModE by the special sense of a religious ceremonial act. *OED* also notes older aphetized form *noint* up to 17C] □ Current mostly among older or rural folk as [naɪnt].

a·no·le* (a·no·li(s)) ['anoli] *n* (Gren, StLu) ‖ *zandoli* (Dmca, StLu, Trin) The common tree lizard, grey (*Anolis aeneus*) or green (*Anolis richardi*), or yellowish. *The generic name for the tree-lizards Anolis comes from 'anole' an old French creole term for the animals. In St Lucia most tree-lizards are called 'zandoli'.*—LST:10 [< Carib *anooli* 'very large, grey, lizard'. See *BDFC:221*]

an·oth·er *adj PHRASES* **1. another locust** See AND Phr 4.2 **2. another one** *pron phr* (CarA) [*IF*] ‖ *something else* (CarA) One who worsens a bad situation by being unreasonable; one who is an additional nuisance. **a.** *The people upstairs crochety a[l]ready and you['re] [o]blige[d] to mak[e] so much o[f] noise with the records? You're another one!*—(Guyn) **b.** *The child stays up and tries to do her homework as the mother quarrels about her work at school, and then the father—he's another one—grumbles about the light bill.*— (Bdos) [Poss transfer of a W Afr idiom. Cp Yoruba *nkan ni e* ('something it is you') 'you're quite a character', or *da nkan miran* 'become something else', both said in contexts similar to those in the cits above. The possibility of an Afr source is reinforced by the occurrence of *SLFC sé an lòt* 'that's another one', and *Gull* use of the same idiom as in CE, both in the same contexts. Note, however, from IrE 'It's one thing after another and you're another one/thing'—(*pers info, L. Todd*)] □ In contexts of mild rebuke, and said with a fall-rise intonation.

anse *n* (Gren, StLu) A small bay, usu a sheltered one, with a stretch of beach. *There are hundreds of anses round the island's miles of coast line. Anse is a picturesque word deriving from the old French, meaning handle on a pot. Thus it is quite fitting for any small bay or cove.*—EOCT:196 [< 17C Fr *anse* '... also, a nooke, bay, gulfe or arme of the sea' (Cotgrave), a sense superseded in Mod Fr by the orig 'handle of a pot, cup']

an·swer ['ansʌ(r)] /2'1/ *vb tr* (Gren, Guyn) [*IF*] **1.** To affect (a person's body). *Anything that excites me it answer me in me head.*—(Gren) [Semantic extension of SE sense 'to account to' as *OED answer* 7. b. (Obs)] **2.** *PHRASES* **2.1 answer (sb) back** /1'12/ *vb phr* (CarA) [*IF*] To reply; to answer. *I asked him a question but he didn't answer me back.*—(StVn) □ A pleonastic phr, distinct from IAE *answer back* 'make impudent answer, to rebuke, etc' (*COD* colloq), wh sense is, however, also very common in CE with ‖ *back-answer*, etc. **2.2 answer (sb) down in your belly** *vb phr* (Tbgo) [*IF*] To answer inaudibly and sulkily. *I called out to him and asked him how things were. The man hardly want to talk to me; he answer me down in his belly. I started wondering whether I had offended him in some way.*—(Tbgo)

ant-bear* *n* (Belz, Guyn) ‖ *ant-eater* (Belz, Guyn, Trin) Name used in *Belz* and *Guyn* for the ANT-EATER, but usu applied only to the largest species *Myrmecophaga jubata* (*Edentata*); a hairy, bushy-tailed forest animal about 2 ft high with a long snout and sticky tongue that enables it to feed on ants. **a.** *There are three kinds of ant-bear in Belize—the Giant, the Large and the Pigmy. The first is rare, but the second, a tree climber 'Tamandua tetradactyla', represented on the four cent stamp, is commoner.*—Belz (Ms) **b.** *The Great or Giant Ant-Bear ... walks along with a peculiar shuffling gait, owing to the immense claws on its front feet ... used for tearing open the hard clay nests of the ground ants on which he alone feeds.*

He is a terrestrial animal and, unlike his smaller relations, does not climb trees.—RALG:8 ['Bear', from the huge claws with wh it can kill an attacker, the very hairy body and bear-like walk of the largest variety]

ant-eat·er *n* (Belz, Guyn, Trin) ‖ ANT-BEAR (Belz, Guyn) *The Lesser Ant-Eater or Tamandua has a snout shorter than the ant-bear, but still elongated; the tail is prehensile and the animal is arboreal.*—RALG:10 [See *OED*]

an·tee nan·nee *n phr* See AUNTIE NANNEE

an·thu·ri·um* **(li·ly)** *n* (*phr*) (CarA) An ornamental ground or pot plant of many varieties, valued for its bright pink or yellow or white, leathery, heart-shaped spathe with a firm, long, fleshy and knobbly spike sticking out of it; *Anthurium andreanum/barbadosense/crystallinum, etc* (*Araceae*). *The bridal bouquet was a joy to behold resplendent with red and yellow anthuriums surrounded by white geraniums.*—Trin (Ms) [Gk *anthos* 'flower' + *oura* 'tail' + Neo-Latin adj ending -*ium*—*CED*]

an·ti·des·ma (an·ti·des·mon(d)) *n* (Guyn) A small tree growing to about 12 ft high, with large, elliptical leaves, and clusters of berries that are red-black with a purplish pulp when ripe; *Antidesma ghaesambilla* (*Euphorbiaceae*). **a.** *Oh this is what they call antidesmond, is a fruit town-people don['t] really know because it grow mostly in the bush in the country. It bear a berry chil[d]ren like to eat.*—(Guyn) **b.** *The juice pulp of the fruit of the antidesma is eaten fresh or made into a refreshing drink or wine.*—OGEP:2 [Adapted from taxonomic name with alternative form -*desmond* by folk etym]

An·ti·guan [an'ti:gʌn] *adj, n* (A person or thing) belonging to or characteristic of Antigua. *Antiguans realize, like Barbadians, that tourism is the mainstay of the national economy.*—Antg (Ms)

An·ti·gua-bal·sam *n* (Antg) A wild green shrub bearing tiny berries that are purple when ripe. *An infusion of Antigua-balsam is a folk medicine used for 'pain in the belly'.*—Antg (Ms)

An·ti·gua-heath* *n* (Bdos, Gren, Trin) ‖ *Chinese firecracker* (Gren) ‖ *humming-bird trumpet* (Trin) ‖ *sweet-william* (Dmca, Guyn, Jmca) A slender-limbed, bushy, garden shrub with long, drooping green stems, bearing only tiny leaves and small clusters of scarlet, tubular flowers about an inch long; *Russelia equisetiformis* (*Scrophulariaceae*).

An·ti·gua-Pride *n* (Antg) ‖ AGAVE (CarA) *Standing nobly like half-a-dozen sentinels dotting the hillside are the flowering poles of the Antigua Pride each rising out of its base of thick green leaves shooting like tongues out of the ground.*—Antg (Ms)

An·til·le·an [an'tɪliʌn] *adj, n* (A person or thing) belonging to or characteristic of the islands of the West Indies; native to the culture of any part of the islands and territories enclosing the Caribbean Sea. *Curaçao. The People: 150,000 Antilleans of mainly Arawak, African, Spanish, Portuguese and Dutch descent. Dutch element calls itself 'Curaçoens'. Though Dutch is the official language, Antilleans speak Papiamento, lyrical patois of Portuguese, Dutch, Spanish and English.*—Cat.6.1 [< *Antille(s)* + *an*] □ Mostly found in Du or Fr writing or translations in E as identifying non-white or non-metropolitan people and culture of the W Indies, prob infl by the Du (*de Antillen*) and Fr (*les Antilles*) names for these islands. In CE *West Indian* is used with similarly ethnic and hist connotations but usu omitting ref to the mainland territories, while *Caribbean* is non-emotive in general or geographic ref to the whole area, and *Antillean* exceptional, reserved mostly for technical contexts.

An·til·les ['antɪli·z] *n pl* (CarA) Collective name used for all the Caribbean islands except The Bahamas and conceived as falling into two broad groups—the Greater Antilles (Cuba, Jamaica, Hispaniola, Puerto Rico) and the Lesser Antilles comprising all the others to east and south of these four. *Philippe de Poincy ruled over French possessions in the Antilles for twenty-one years until his death on St Christopher in 1660.*—BL (A. Brown) [< Pg *Antilha*, Sp *Antilla*, legendary name of a land mass or group of islands supposed, prior to Columbus's voyage (1492), to lie in the far west Atlantic. After Columbus's discovery the Sp *las Antillas* began to be used to refer to 'the West Indies']

an·ti·man *n* See AUNTIE MAN

an·ti·na·ni *n* See AUNTIE NANNEE

an·ti·state [anti-stet] *adj* (Guyn) Politically subversive; aimed at disrupting existing law and order in a country. *The Prime Minister warned that he would not allow the University of Guyana to be used as a cover for anti-state activities.*—(Guyn) [*Anti* 'against' + (the) *state* in the sense of 'recognized civil government']

an·tro·ver (an·cho·ba, an·cho·va, an·tro·va) *n* (Antg, Brbu) ‖EGGPLANT (CarA) **a.** *I had dukana, saltfish and antrovers for lunch today.*—Antg (Ms) **b.** *Available at the Peasant Development Depot: Cucumbers 25 cents per lb. Antrovas 15 cents per lb.*—WoV (69.01.14, p.2) □ *Antrover* (*LNFV*) appears to be the preferred spelling, but much variation is found, esp as the word occurs in speech mostly as a creolized collective sg *anchoba* or *choba* of wh *antrovers* may be a refinement.

an·tro·vy *n* (StVn) [*IF*] ‖ANCHOVY (StLu, Trin) □ Spelling prob owing to folk pronunc.

ants *n pl* (CarA) [X] Ant. **1.** □ The pl form is widely used in CE at the folk level in place of the SE sg. *Ants* (sg) persists in better educated speech in company with many *X* mass-noun pls, *ashes, furnitures, mails,* etc; it is also the regular form in compounds ANTS- BUSH, ANTS-NEST, etc below, and *DJE* lists **ants-bird, ants-pick, ants-wood** in *Jmca* usage. **2.** (Trin) [By extension] A person who is a parasite. *And also you have to look for work. I not saying you is a ants, but it have enough ants already in London.*—STLL:21

ants-bush* *n* (Guyn) A green weed with slender stem, and finger-length, lance-shaped leaves with tiny white flowers growing in the axil; it grows in bushy clusters, has a pungent, sourish smell, and is used as a folk medicine; *Struchium sparganophora* (*Compositae- Asteraceae*). **a.** *He makes out a list which includes local herbs such as 'ants bush' and 'cow-foot bush' or 'pain killer bush' which in themselves are well known for their believed medical value in curing eczema and ring worm, and reducing swelling.*—COYN:14 [From the fact that it attracts stinging, red ants to nest at its roots]

ants-nest *n* **1.** (CarA) Any nest of (usu red) ants built in the ground with an outlet on the surface. *The groundsmen were using Jeyes fluid to remove the ants nests from the cricket field.*—Bdos (Ms) **2.** (Trin) ‖**comehen** (Belz) ‖**duck-ants nest** (CayI, Jmca) ‖**wood-ants nest** (Bdos, Guyn, TkCa) ‖**wood-lice nest** (Belz) A nest of termites. *This mango tree had a big ants-nest in the fork of the tree and the trail led to the house which the ants were just eating up.*—(Trin)

a·nui·sance [anyusʌns] *n* (Belz) [X] Nuisance. *Playin dem radio loud! Do late da-night. Wan dam anuisance.* [A creolism prob due to metanalysis of 'a nuisance']

an·wa·jé¹ [ãwaže] *adj* (StLu) [AF] **1.** ‖VEX¹ (CarA) *The child behaved so bad she got me really anwajé.*—StLu (Ms) **2.** [AF] So anxious that you can hardly wait. *I know you anwajé to hear what I'm going to say.*—StLu (Ms) **3.** [AF] Rough and aggressive; of unpleasant manners. *He didn['t] grow up a nice boy—I remember him always anwajé.*—(StLu) [Fr Cr < Fr *enragé* 1. 'angry', 2. 'extremely keen' 3. 'wild and unrestrained', this third sense being more associated, however, with madness of dogs]

an·wa·jé² *adv* (StLu) [AF] Madly; discourteously. *He was driving so anwajé that I was scared till we reach home.*—(StLu) [By functional adj > adv shift of ANWAJÉ¹]

anwajé³ *vb tr* (StLu) [AF] To annoy; vex; infuriate. [By functional adj > vb shift of ANWAJÉ¹]

an·y¹ ['ɛni] /33/ *adj* (CarA) [X] **1.** Some. *A frail and dejected figure of a man, V— lives at the scorn of his neighbours, whom he still refers to as* *his friends. However, there is one person who has extended any sympathy to his condition.*—NaT (76.09.05, p.20) **2.** adj [X] All. *The water settles in the springs and when these start moving they take along with them any soil, leaving the stone.* / *Soil erosion in the island is continuing to threaten the safety of many villages.*—AdM (71.05.02, p.1) **3.** adj (CarA) [X] Just any, no matter how imperfect. *If these men want to form an opposition party to oppose their ex-colleagues, let them resign their seats, demand early by-elections and face the electors again under their new banner. We do need an opposition in Parliament but I do feel, strongly, that any opposition is not good enough.*—ExP (72.07.06, p.21) [The high pitch and strong initial stress that characterize these uses of *any* in oral CE cannot be rendered in writing where one or other supportive addition to the sentence structure is necessary] □ The economy of pitch-differentiated CE usage wh is poss only aurally, needs expansion in the written medium. **4.** [X] Either. **a.** *S1: Any of dese two would do you?* / *S2: Yes any one.*—(Bdos) **b.** *Yo[u] could aks any one of de two o[f] dem de[re] to help you.*—(Bdos) [By misascription or characteristic Cr extension of function] **5.** PHRASES **5.1 any and everybody**; **any and everything** *intensifier pron phr* (CarA) [IF] Any person/thing without discrimination; anybody whoever/ anything whatever. *A'm not saying A would have any an[d] everybody fo[r] my friend, but I am sure nobody can call me a unfriendly person.*—(Trin) [Abbr of *anything and everything, anybody and everybody* while keeping the emphatic sense] □ These depreciatory phrs are common in emotive contexts in CE. (Cp SE *each and everyone*).

an·y² *adv* (CarA) [AF] **1.** [Following a neg] In any way; at all. *The fact that Margaret was a married woman did not influence Joseph any. Married or unmarried, he could not see her stranded as she was with no means of transportation to her home.*—GyG (56.08.16) [A reduction of 'in any way' prob brought from AmE. See *OEDS* any 7. b.] **2.** PHRASE **2.1 any at all** *intensifier adv phr* (Jmca) [IF] [An emotive tag intensifying an inquiry or supposition] Indeed!; Anyhow!. *Instead of answering the question directly, Mr Tyson asked himself, 'But what is this country coming to, any at all?'.*—SJT:22 [Perh a blend of *anyhow* and *at all* used as emotive tags in similar contexts]

an·y·bod·y *pron* (CarA) [IF] People, in general; the public; one (pron); we/us; you (impers). **a.** *You can tell that to anybody but not to me because I know better.*—(Guyn) **b.** *It bears a kind of wild apple not good for anybody to eat.*—(BrVi) **c.** *Why must he pick her up every morning? Let her catch a bus. It is for anybody.*—(Bdos) □ This is not the stressed SE use = 'anybody at all'. The pitch is neutral. **2.** PHRASE **2.1 anybody own** *possessive pron phr* (CarA) [X] Anybody's; anyone's. *She don['t] min[d] who weddin[g] it is. Anybody own! She must stan[d] up and see every person who come an[d] go—how they dress is what she lookin[g] at.*—(Trin)

an·y·how *adj* (Guyn, Trin) [X] Indifferent; uncaring; uninvolved; slapdash. *In fact Deborah is convinced that Trinidadians must forget their 'anyhow attitude', for this is no good to us.*—SuP (79.06.24, p.14) [By functional shift of adv *anyhow* 'haphazardly']

an·y part (an·y place) *adv phrs* (CarA) [AF] Anywhere. **a.** *Boy, I search the place upside down but A couldn['t] fin[d] the thing any part, A tell you.*—(Guyn) **b.** *I am sure I didn't leave it any place. If anybody has it they took it from my bag.*—(Bdos) [Prob by Cr infl in response to *which part*, 'where' wh *DJE* lists as *Belz*, *Guyn*, *Trin* besides being *Jmca*. Cp also *KED* Krio ɛnipat 'anywhere'. Cp also *W2*, *W3* AmE *anyplace* adv 'in any place']

an·y·thing *pron* (CarA) [AF] **1.** A person related (to); a relative. *I can['t] laugh, I tell you, beca[use] if the person was anything to me I would really feel it.*—(StVn) □ In cond, interr or neg constructions. See also *nothing* wh is similarly used. **2.** PHRASE **2.1 (If) it's anything** (CarA) [IF] (If) there is any cause (for concern, alarm, action, etc). **a.** *It has a special switch at the side so that if it's anything you can shut down the whole system before any damage happens.*—(Bdos) **b.** *Tell her she mustn['t] mind A didn['t] come. It isn't anything. When I see her I would explain.*—(Trin)

an·y·way (an·y·where) *adv* (CarA) [AF] ‖ **no-way, nowhere** (CarA) [After a neg] At all; in any way. *Dis time [h]e only foolin' de girl. [H]e ain['t] buy no car anywhe[re]. Is de place [h]e workin at car [h]e drivin[g].*—(Guyn) [A refinement of Cr double neg for emphasis *not … no way* < *not … any way*, then a confusion or false refinement of *any way* 'in any way' to 'anyway' 'anywhere', context also sometimes contributing to this confusion as in cit]

an·y·ways *adv, conj* (Jmca, Trin) [AF] In any case; anyhow; however. *Anyways as Tanty Merle uses to say wen yuh livin in de same street wid people yuh cyar preten you aint know bout dem or cut yuh eye wen yuh sees dem.*—TrG (72.10.12, p.12, Letter from Port-of-Spain) [Prob a survival of 19C E. *OED anyways* 2. (with cit from Dickens) is similar but marked 'dial or illit'. *WCD9* notes as *archaic or chiefly dial* in AmE]

an·y·wheres *adv* (Jmca) [X] Anywhere. *A man not safe anywheres at all.*—SNWIC:264 (M. Townshend) [Prob infl by such forms as *anyways* and SE *whereabouts*. Listed in *DSUE:1* as a late 19–20C solecism]

A·pan Jhaat (Aa·pan·jhaat, a·pan·jat) ['a:pʌnja:t] *n phr* (Guyn, Trin) [Indic] One's own kind, caste, community or race. **a.** *Indian racist leaders like Daniel P. Debidin … argued that Indian interests in Guiana would be lost and submerged in an African-dominated Federation. And so originated the slogan 'Apan Jhaat' (literally, own race)—the use of racist emotionalism to frighten the Indians away from the PPP*—JWOT:

114. **b.** *and by the time the British Government had decided to grant new elections ... Jagan was already compaigning with the Hindi slogan 'Apan Jhaat', meaning 'Vote for your own'./The votes were cast strictly along racial lines with Jagan winning 47 per cent of the total votes*—BDTM: xx **c.** *Don't worry! Everybody voting apanjat when election time come round.*—Guyn (Ms) [Bhoj *aapan jaat* < Hin *apnaa* 'one's own' + *jaat* 'caste, community', emotively extended to mean 'race' in such a slogan as (Bhoj) *aapan jaat naa bhulaiba*, 'Don't forget your people', said to be current at election time esp in *Guyn* in the 1950s and 1960s] □ Properly two separate words, commonly capitalized, often conceived as a single form and used in adj or adv function. The aspirated form *jhaat* is prob a false refinement.

a·part·el *n* (Bdos) A hotel consisting entirely of self-contained apartments, each provided with all domestic necessities for occupants to store, cook, and eat their own food. *Heywoods comprises small hotels and apartels with a total of 360 rooms, shops and ancillary tourist oriented facilities on a shared basis. It was expected to provide jobs for 200 in the tourist trade.*—AdN (83.01.06, p.4) [A blend of *apart*(ment + *ho*)*tel* first appearing as hotel industry innovation in *Bdos* in the form *Apartotel* thus '... to be constructed at Chancery Lane, Christ Church. The 10-storey project to be known as Melia Barbados Apartotel ... / Mr Norman Holmes said that the impact of the 'apartotel' with its 350 rooms would be considerable as far as the economy of Barbados was concerned ... it would employ about 500 people in the management and running of the enterprise.'—*AdN* (73.02.13). Cp also AmE *motel*, *boatel* and Japanese-English hybrid *ryotel* < Japanese *ryokan* 'inn' + Eng *hotel*]

apart from *prep phr* (Bdos) [X] So far from; instead of. *Mr Adams said that it was always the intention of the BLP to have one of the series of public meetings in that area. | And furthermore, said Mr Adams, apart from writing off the St John constituency, the BLP has a man of stature who will oppose Mr Barrow in his constituency in the 1976 general elections.*—AdN (74.05.29, p.1) [A misascription of SE *apart from* 'excepting' 'not considering'] □ This usage is occasional.

a·part·ment *n* (Guyn, Jmca) A room rented as a dwelling but not fitted with housekeeping facilities. *No Cooking Allowed In Apartments. By Order of the Proprietor.*—Jmca (Notice) [Cp *COD apartment* 'single room in a house'] □ In CE this modified BrE use of the word ('a rented single room') operates side by side with the AmE use 'a set of rooms completely equipped as a dwelling (or sometimes an office) for rent'. In the tourist islands the AmE sense is displacing the Br.

ap·ple *n* (CarA) **1.** NOTE This fruit-name is (as *OED apple* 2. notes) in general 'used with the greatest latitude' in ref to a number of fruits

in CE. In some territories it applies commonly to one locally grown fruit as in Bdos (= GOLDEN-APPLE), ViIs (= SUGAR-APPLE)—wh is unrelated to the European apple *Pyrus malus* (*Rosaceae*). Otherwise it is a common suffix, naming a fruit also unrelated to *Pyrus malus*. This latter may or may not be distinguished as **English/ice/ imported apple**. Context appears always to prevent any confusion. The suffixed cases BELL-APPLE, CUSTARD-APPLE, etc are separately treated in this book. **2.** PHRASE **2.1 apple and fish** *n phr* (ViIs) A meal of boiled, green SUGAR-APPLES and fish. *Apple and fish is a favourite dish when apples are in season.*—(BrVi) □ This is a set phr, one of the 'food' mass-nouns of wh there are many in CE. One may 'boil, cook, eat, like, serve (etc) apple and fish'. Cp also *ackee and saltfish, blackeye and rice, cou-cou and ochro slush, pudding and souse*, etc.

ap·ple-ba·na·na* *n* **1.** (Belz, CayI, Guyn, Jmca, TkCa) ‖ *bacuba* (USVI) ‖ *Chinee banana* (Jmca) ‖ *dwarf-banana* (Baha) ‖ *fig* (Bdos, StKt, StVn, TkCa) ‖ *finger-rows* (Antg, Brbu) ‖ *lady-finger* 1. (Nevs) ‖ *rock-fig* (Gren) ‖ *sicri* (Mrat) ‖ *silk-banana* (Nevs, StKt) ‖ *silk-fig* (Antg, Nevs, StKt, Tbgo, Trin) ‖ *sugar-banana* (Baha, TkCa) A short, fat, or 'dwarf' variety of banana whose flesh when ripe is firm, smooth, and sweet (but not suitable for cooking when green as most other varieties are); *Musa chinensis* (*NPHT:185*) or *Musa cavendishii* (though *PTT:227* says this distinction is unnecessary and uses the general *Musa sapientum* (*Musaceae*). *Nowadays a good hand of apple-bananas, which is the sweetest kind of banana, you payin[g], well, running into dollars—when I remember they used to be penny a piece when you could get them.*—(Guyn) [Prob because the firmness and sweet smoothness of the flesh remind one of a European apple] **2.** (Baha) ‖ BLACK BANANA (Jmca) [The *Baha* confusion of names may be due to the closer resemblance of the purplish colour of the skin of this variety to that of an apple]

ap·ple-blos·som cas·sia* *n phr* (Bdos, Gren, Trin) ‖ *cassia* (Bdos) ‖ *stinking toe* (Belz) An ornamental tree that comes out about mid-year in large, rich clusters of rosy-pink flowers, wh are succeeded by long, brown, cylindrical pods; *Cassia javanica* (*Leguminosae- Caesalpiniaceae*). *The apple blossom cassia, a native of the Malayan region, grows very rapidly and is well worthy of more extended cultivation in Trinidad.*—PTT:108 [From resemblance of the flower-clusters to large apple blossoms]

ap·ple-bush *n* (Grns) The SUGAR-APPLE tree.

Ap·ple·ton *n* (Jmca) [IF] A popular, light, smooth rum produced by Appleton Estate in *Jmca*; (loosely) rum in general. *Rum, for many Jamaicans and others who have come to favour this liquor, has for a long time worn the label 'Appleton'. It is the name used in requests at home or in bars or clubs for a drink of rum—'An Appleton'.*—Jmca (Ms)

ap·prov·ed pas·ture *n phr* (Jmca) [Agric] A fenced area of high-producing va.ieties of grass such as Pangola, Guinea, coast-cross, etc, specially approved by the Ministry of Agriculture for the rearing of cattle—*(Jmca (Ms, D. McLeod)). Definite and creditable improvement ... by the system of finishing steers and heifers on feedlot, and also by the method of finishing on approved pastures. These were for ... feedlot and approved pastures beef under the price decontrol measure effected by Government yesterday.*—DaG (70.01.31, p.1, Farmer's Weekly)

a·pri·cot ['aprikʌt] (StLu) ‖ MAMMEE (APPLE) (CarA) *There are quite a lot of apricots in the market today.*—(StLu) [An E name imported prob because of resemblance of the flesh, although only in colour and taste, to the temperate-zone fruit of that name. That fruit, *Prunus armeniaca* (*Rosaceae*) is not, however, related] □ [X] Sometimes also pronounced *'abricot'*, but not so commonly used in *StLu* E as the *CarA* alternative MAMMEE APPLE or even the Fr Cr ZAB(W)IKO.

a·que·duct ['akwidʌkt] *n* (Guyn) [Sugar Ind] A short concrete channel built to allow the higher punt canal to cross, at right angles, a lower drainage-irrigation canal on a SUGAR-CANE plantation. *An aqueduct is similar to a bridge except that ... it carries a canal ... when the canal bed level is sufficiently higher than the torrent level of the sideline drainage trench [whose] water runs below it freely or under syphonic pressure.*—Guyn (Ms) [Restricted sense of SE *aqueduct*] □ Restricted to sugar-estate and rural communities in *Guyn* and often pronounced [arkidʌk ~ arčidʌk] etc.

A·ra·da (Ar·ra·dah) *n* (Gren, Crcu) A group identified as one of the African NATIONS of Carriacou who keep the tradition of THE BIG DRUM DANCE. *This is one of three or four Arada items, appropriate to the so-called Arada nation, originally from Dahomey.*—EtF (1956) p.3

a·ra·ma·ta *n* (Guyn) See AROMATA

a·ra·pai·ma *n* (Guyn) A river fish reaching a length of 15 ft and weight of some 400 lbs, found in Guyana; *Arapaima gigas* (*Osteoglossidae*). *The Arapaima is the world's largest fresh water fish, and as such should be preserved carefully, Dr Rankin said.*—DaC (52.09.08, p.1) [First mentioned 1840 by R.H. Schomburgk by this name. 'A mispronunc of Makushi *warapaimö* < *warak* 'yarrow' (a smaller variety of the fish) + *paimö*, a suff meaning 'extra large' '—*Guyn (Ms, D. Fox)*]

a·ra·pe *n* (CarA) See AREPA

A·ra·wak *adj, n* (CarA) ‖ *Lokono* (Guyn) **1.** (Of or belonging to) the unwarlike race of so-called American Indian or Amerindian peoples who were inhabiting the Caribbean islands from the Bahamas to Trinidad, and coastal So America

at the time of Columbus's voyages, and who are believed to have originated in the Guianas. **a.** *The warlike Caribs, unlike the benign Arawaks, resisted the Spanish conquistadors, and therefore survived. The Bahamian Arawaks, however, vanished like a vapour.*—TrI (76.02.07, p.7) **b.** *This fearsome-looking skull once belonged to a proud Arawak Indian whose tribe lived at Chancery Lane, Barbados and fished off the south coast of the island.*—Barclays Newsletter (76.03.01, p.1) **2.** *n* [By extension] The language of the Arawak or LOKONO people; the major language of the ARAWAKAN language family, called LOKONO by the speakers themselves. *... the main reason why Carib men spoke one language (Carib) and the women another (Arawak) is that many of the women were captive Arawaks and their female descendants.*—KMRFBC:11 [*Arawak* is the anglicized version of Sp *Arauca* or *Arahuaco* (M.R. Key, *The Grouping of South American Indian Languages*). HTDS says 'The word 'Arawak' means 'eaters of meal', ... the manioc which they grew', but gives no source for this etym. Arawaks are numerous in *Guyn* and *BAED* (intro p.iv.) states 'The term Arawak is a name coined by non-Lokono, though the people themselves, the Arawaks as they are called, now use that term instead of Lokono.' One theory is that this 'foreign' European label may have developed from one of the So American locations (Araua ?) of Lokono settlement]

A·ra·wak·an *adj* (CarA) Of or belonging to a family of more than eighty Amerindian languages wh were distributed from the southernmost reaches of the Amazon basin north and west through So America and the Caribbean to the Bahamian islands, but currently represented by a small surviving number including Arawak and Wapishana (*Guyn*) and Island Carib (*Dmca*). *There are two Arawakan tribes in Guyana viz the Arawaks (Lokono) and the Wapishanas. At present, the Arawaks inhabit the coastal areas of Guyana. They are regarded by most scholars as the direct descendants of the Arawakan people who migrated to what is now Guyana, from the Orinoco area.*—EILCA:1 [ARAWAK + suff *an*]

a·ra·wa·na *n* (Guyn) A river fish with a moutn set at right angles to the axis of the body and a dorsal fin continuous with the ventral fin round the tip of the tail—*Guyana Cacique Diary, 1977. The arawana, which is found mainly near waterfalls is well- known in Bartica and is very tasty.*—Guyn (Ms) [Prob Amerindian]

ar·bee; ar-we *pron*, 1st *pers pl* (Nevs, StKt) [*AF—Cr*] See A(LL)-WE

ar·bi·tra·ry *adv* (Bdos) [X] Randomly; without order or system; anyhow. **a.** *He picks the dominoes arbitrary.*—Bdos (Ms) **b.** *You can['t] go out there wit[h] drinks in yo[ur] head and drive arbitrary or yo[u] will get in trouble.*—(Bdos) [By both semantic and functional shift from adj *arbitrary* intrepreted narrowly as 'uncontrolled']

ar·chi·pel·a·go *n* (CarA) [*IF*] Any chain of islands forming a rough arc as do the Caribbean islands. *The litany of recurring political disturbances throughout the archipelago—Guyana, Trinidad, Grenada, Anguilla, Jamaica—in this first decade of independence or internal self-government gives witness to the enduring inability of the political institutions of the Westminster model constitutions to come to grips with the fundamental economic and social crises of the people.*—AdN (72.07.09, p.4) [Folk etym, infl by *arch*—interpreted as 'a curve' whereas *archi* + *pelago* < Gk *archein* 'chief' + *pelagos* 'sea' and orig referred to the Aegean Sea and thence to the massive group of islands crowding that sea. There is no question of an 'arc' or 'curve'] □ The term *archipelago* may also properly be applied to such subgroups in the *CarA* as The Bahamas, the Virgin Is and the Grenadines.

are [ar] *pres pl of vb 'to be'* (CarA) [*X*] **1.** [Loosely for another tense, modal or aspectual phr of vb 'to be'] Were; have been; can be; may be, etc. **a.** *It had been explained that there are many reasons why that had been happening.*—Guyn (Ms) **b.** *Within the past ten years the sea-eggs are lessening, he said.*—BdN (64.08.01, p.1) **2.** [After a sum of money as subject] Is. *An estimated one million dollars are needed for general restoration. Already, $300, 000 have been raised by the clergy and congregation.*—Cat.6.1 [From conceiving 'dollars', 'cents', etc as count-nouns instead of the sum of money 'collectively' as a mass-noun] **3.** Am; is. **a.** *Is not I dat are to blame.*—(Mrat) **b.** *Frighten Shirley bus out 'You carn see de man are dead?'*—LMFF:26 [Hypercorrection of Cr /a/ as A[14] (See)]

ar·e·a·wide *adj* (ECar) Covering the whole area (as identified in the context). *The five-man Mark V Combo from Virgin Gorda in the British Virgin Islands, were recently adjudged the outright winners of the LIAT 'Beat the Bands' contest in the areawide Eastern Caribbean competition.*—AdN (71.02.13, p.6) [By analogy from SE *country-wide, nationwide, worldwide*, the use of suff -*wide* developing from the sense of *OED wide adj* 1. b. 'conventional epithet of words denoting an extensive area', and 2. 'extending over ... a large space or region']

A·re baap! *excl* (Trin) [*IF*] [Indic] Oh father! (exclamation of surprise or mild vexation). *Are baap! de win[d] jus[t] blow do[w]ng all de clothes from de line!*—(Trin) [< Hin *are*, excl of surprise + *baap* 'father', the latter word being sometimes omitted in this loan from *Trin Bhoj*, wh shows a change in word order from orig Hin *Baap re!*] □ More likely rural *Trin* and among older Indic speakers.

A·re·ku·na (A·re·cu·na) *n* (Guyn) A Cariban stock of Amerindians, said to be the tallest and darkest of skin, dwelling in the area about the sources of the Orinoco and Mazaruni rivers on the Guyana-Venezuela border. *The Arecunas grow, spin and distribute most of the cotton which*

is used by the Macusis and others for hammocks and other articles. The Arecunas also supply all blow-pipes.—IAIG:272 [Cariban]

a·re·pa (a·rep, a·ra·pe) [a'rep(ʌ)] *n* (Trin) A fried cornmeal pie with a richly seasoned meat or fish filling. *... and filled her basket with all manner of goodies. There was Arape, a cornmeal pancake with spicy meat filling, molasses balls, sugar cakes, black pudding, and many other things besides.*—HLTS:58 [Sp *arepa* 'a griddle-cake made of soaked maize ground into a paste or dough'. In Trin E the final unstressed vowel is vestigial or lost; the form *arape* is a case of metathesis]

arm *n* PHRASES **1. fold your arms** *id phr* (Guyn) ‖ *fold your hands* (Guyn) To remain uninvolved in what is happening; to sit idly while others do the work. *'When you are dealing with events, with people and with thoughts,' Cde Burnham told the gathering, 'you cannot fold your arms and be inspired.'*—GyC (78.06.08, p.1) **2. pull out your arm (and hit sb)** *id phr* (Dmca) [*AF*] ‖ *out hand (and hit sb)* (Guyn) To raise your arm to hit deliberately. *The boy pull out his arm and hit his brother one blow.*—Dmca (Ms) **3. (Oh) me arm! (me arm hole!)** *excl* (StKt) [*AF*] [Expressing surprise or shock] Oh my!; Oh my God! *Oh me arm, I forgot my purse at home.*—(StKt) [Said to be euphemistic for 'My arse']

ar·ma·dil·lo* ['armadɪlʌ] *n* (Guyn) ‖ *armado* (Belz) ‖ *goopie* (Trin) ‖ *(h)amadili* (Belz) ‖ *peba* (Guyn) ‖ *tatu* (Gren, Trin) ‖ *yesi* (Guyn) One of two kinds of burrowing forest animal wh is hunted for its flesh: 'This animal has a sort of overcoat of a hard horn-like substance, jointed in bands in the middle and with large fore-and-aft cowl-shaped plates something after the principle of an ancient knight's armour' (*RALG:13*), a rat-like head and a notable horned tail; *Tatusia peba* or *T. novemcincta* (the small armadillo, about 3 ft in length overall), and *Dasypus novemcinctus giganteus (Dasipodidae)* (the giant armadillo, wh can exceed 5 ft in overall length and is found in Guyana). *Before I knew what was happening an enormous creature like an armoured car rushed out of the hole, planted its feet on my chest, covered me with earth, flung me violently on my back, and was away ... It was an armadillo, clumsy looking in its domed carapace, with pointed nose and pointed tail running so fast that in a minute it was out of sight.*—GWW:94 [Sp 'the little armed one', from the resemblance of its covering to armour, and its habit of rolling itself into a ball to defend itself against blows]

ar·ma·do *n* (Belz) ‖ARMADILLO (Guyn) [Sp 'the armed one']

ar·man *n* (StLu) ‖ALMOND (CarA)

arm·chair *n* (Guyn) ‖BERBICE CHAIR (Guyn) *They found him lying in the arm-chair with his legs up on the folded extensions—his favourite reclining posture—on the verandah.*—Guyn (Ms)

□ A restricted *Guyn* use of IAE *armchair*, applied to a reclining chair of local design.

arm-hole *n* (CarA) [*IF*] Armpit. *Dis time look [h]e marchin[g] [a]bout de place wid de stick in [h]e arm-hole like [h]e t[h]ink [h]e is some blasted general.*—(Guyn)

arm·hole-dress *n* (Bdos, Trin) [*IF*] A sleeveless dress. *Many people think that armhole dresses are not suitable for work.*—MCETJ:64 [As *COD armhole* + *dress*]

ar·my-ant(s) *n* (Trin) ‖ *soldier-ant(s)* (Trin) ‖ *ya(c)kman* (Guyn) A species of forest ant wh, at a certain stage in their reproductive cycle, move off in columns, the main column carrying eggs, larvae and pupae, while other foraging columns attack small fauna; *Eciton burchelli* (*Dorylinae*). *Columns of army ants spread out killing spiders, insects, lizards, snakes, birds, and even small mammals.... Army ants are forest dwelling but occasionally enter dwelling houses in forested areas.*—Trin (Ms, 1984) [From their habits of moving in columns and foraging]

Ar·nold *n* (Bdos, Guyn, Jmca) [*AF*] ‖ *dat²*, **whitey** (Jmca) Pork. [Rastaf] *At another spot, the visitors heard the word 'Arnold' being repeated several times and were subsequently enlightened to the fact that Mr Arnold and Maas Pork alias Mr Whitey come out of the same stable.*—WeG (75.04.15, p.15, Partyline)

ar·not·to *n* (Guyn) See ANAT(T)O

a·ro·ma·ta (a·ra·ma·ta) *n* (Guyn) A Guyana forest tree growing up to 100 ft in height with a flat, rounded crown, and yielding a very tough, straight-grained, brown timber with lighter streaks; its bark is used medicinally; *Clathrotropis brachypetala* (*Papilionaceae*)—FFPG. *Aromata works fairly easily, finishes smoothly with a natural polish and is suitable not only for making furniture, but for house-framing and boat-building.*—Guyn (Ms) [An Amerindian name, perh Arawak (*HLNPG:118*)]

a·ro·po *n* (Trin) A dance of Sp origin performed in some areas of Trinidad. *They do the aropo in places with a strong Spanish influence like Maracas valley. You would hardly find it in Tobago.*—(Trin) [Perh < Sp *arrobo*, 'rapture, ecstasy']

around *prep* (CarA) [*IF*] 1. [In statements of time] About; approximately at, in (a stated time). *Around three days after she started working Mrs Watkins told her that she would be expecting some visitors for tea.*—PCOS:133 2. In the same place as; in the area of. *You will always find him around the girls.*—(Trin) □ OEDS *around* 4. b. notes the use of *around* in regard to statements of time (sense 1.) as AmE.

Ar·ra·dah See ARADA

ar·rang·er *n* (ECar) [Steelband] The musical director of a STEELBAND who orchestrates a piece of music assigning to each player particular parts of it for his pan, pair or set of pans. *Each band contracts an arranger to organise its music; he may write down at least some of the arrangement, or will carry it in his head, inventing and enriching as he goes along ... calling out the notes or demonstrating them himself.*—Suj No.17, 1989, p.19

ar·ra·wah *n* (Guyn) [*X*] See AWARA

ar·ri·e·ro *n* (Belz) A guide who is also in charge of a team of pack horses or mules in extensive bush journeys in Belize. *In the bush areas, where there is no grazing, the animals are fed on the leaves of the breadnut tree ... and the services of an experienced arriero (muleteer) are essential, for preference one with a good knowledge of the route to be transversed.*—ABSBH:30–31 [Sp, 'muleteer']

ar·row¹ *n* (Guyn) Folk name of a plant or tough reed used by Amerindians in Guyana for making arrows. (See also ARROW-CANE, etc.) *Arrow is a special plant mostly planted in the old field. ... Arrow roots are planted in a sandy old field and shoots are used for arrows.*—Guyn (Ms) [Loose semantic shift by assoc with *arrow*, the weapon. Cp *bamboo*, similarly used to refer to the plant or a (bamboo) stick. It may be that the term applies to more than one species of plant so used. *IAIG:303* states without elaboration 'The very long shafts (of the various arrows) are of a peculiar reed', whereas the cit above seems to ref to a hardwood shrub] □ Likely to be restricted to areas of Amerindian settlement in *Guyn*.

ar·row² *n* (CarA) ‖ *cane-arrow* (Bdos, Guyn) ‖ *flag* (Jmca) ‖ *tassel* (Baha) 1. The yellow fibrous shaft about 3 ft long with a silky white, tassel-like flowering that grows from the top of a ripening sugar-cane; (also occasionally applied to) shorter similar growth from the corn (maize) plant. *The arrow of the sugar-cane was showing and the workers knew that the cane was ripe.*—Guyn (Ms) [As *OED arrow* sb 7. b.] 2. PHRASE **2.1 in arrow** *adj phr* (CarA) [Of sugar-canes] Bearing arrows and therefore nearing maturity.

ar·row³ *vb intr* (CarA) [Of sugar-canes] To bear arrows; to put out arrows as indication of maturing. *The presence of pests may sometimes be indicated by the way the canes arrow or fail to arrow.*—Guyn (Ms) [By functional n > vb shift of ARROW²]

ar·row-cane *n* (Guyn) ‖ *arrow-grass, arrowwood* (Guyn) ‖ *wild cane* (Jmca) A tall, toughstemmed, cane-like shrub abundant in swampy ground; *Gynerium sagittatum* (*Gramineae*)—(*AFPJ*). (Poss the same as ARROW¹.) *The stems of the arrow cane form the outer core of blowpipes and are also used for arrows.*—Guyn (Ms) [From use by *Guyn* Amerindians for making arrows] □ See description at cit for ARROW-GRASS.

ar·row-grass *n phr* (Guyn) ‖ARROW-CANE (Guyn) *For the shafts Yuhme had cut down a few inflorescent scapes of arrow grass, straight, slim, pith-centred cylinders, fifteen or twenty feet tall, from among the thick, high clumps that grew around the village. He discarded the flowering apices with their clouds of yellow-silver spikelets, then dried and chopped them into five- or six-foot lengths, the slenderer from nearer the tip for bird, fish, or poison-arrow shafts, the stouter portions for the heavier missiles used against big game.*—GWW: 257

ar·row-head fish trap *n phr* (CarA) A large cage made of wire on a wooden frame, in the shape of a bent rectangle (roughly resembling a large arrowhead, hence the name), with a slightly conical entrance curved downwards into the cage so that a fish may easily enter and be trapped. *The fish traps used presently are the wire arrowhead trap, a rectangular wire trap and the Haitian cane Z trap.*—Baha (Ms, R. Thompson)

ar·row·root* *n* (CarA) ‖ **toloman** (Dmca) **1.** A flowering herb growing up to about 1 m high whose tuberous roots are used to produce a starch; *Maranta arundinacea (Marantaceae)*. *Government intends to rehabilitate the banana industry, encourage an increase in coconut production, double the acreage of arrowroot and increase the overall factory space.*—ViN (76.07.09, p.1) **2.** ‖ **arrowroot starch** (CarA) ‖ **St Vincent arrowroot** (CarA) A fine white starch produced from crushing the dried tubers of the arrowroot plant, used commercially and in cooking. *Arrowroot: The dried roots or tubers are pounded to powder and made into an infusion. The liquid is used internally for diarrhea. Helpful to teething infants.*—PHPVI:12 [The etym explanation offered by *OED* dating from a 1696 quotation may be questioned—'from use made of the fleshy tubers to absorb poison from wounds ... of poisoned arrows'. Corruption of an Amerindian name for this indigenous CarA and So Amer plant is poss. Cp *DGEG* Guarani *arari*, 'kind of dried starch'; *aruru*, 'name of a tree'; *EDWLG* Warau *aru*, 'cassava root', *aramutu*, 'starch'; *BAED* Arawak *haro*, 'starch, a granular substance found in plant cells'. Cp also early Sran *araroetoe* listed in *FNEW* with an alternative form *aroeroe*, 'arrow-root'] □ Properly written as one word, not hyphenated or separated.

ar·row·root pap *n phr* (CarA) A porridge or thick drink made by mixing a paste of AR-ROWROOT STARCH in briefly boiled milk. *Arrowroot pap should not be too thick, almost like a heavy milk drink, is excellent for babies.*—Trin (Ms)

ar·row·root starch *n phr* (CarA) ‖ARROW-ROOT 2. (CarA) *There is a great world demand for arrowroot starch, and all the indications point to further increases in the use of this commodity.*—ViN (76.07.02, p.3)

ar·row-wood *n* (Guyn) ‖ARROW-CANE (Guyn)

arse¹ (**ass¹**) *n* (CarA) [*Vul*] **1.** [Emphatic *Derog* ref to a person in the sense '-self'] *... only paying deir arse to do nothing half o[f] de day.*—(Antg) [Emphatic synecdoche, *arse* being used as a crude ref to the whole person] **2.** PHRASES **2.1 as arse/ass** *adv intensifier* (CarA) [*Vul*] [Adding emphasis to an adv or adj] Very, very. *... and England is cold as arse, I tell you.*—(Trin) **2.2 carry away your arse/ass with blows** *vb phr* (Guyn) [*Vul*] ‖ **cut/tear your arse** (CarA) To flog severely; to whip soundly. *One day they send home to say he stole some other boy pen. Boy! Father want carry [a]way [h]e arse wid blows.*—(Guyn) [Metaphor expressing same idea as IF E 'tear strips off sb'] **2.3 Carry your arse/ass!** *vb phr* (Guyn) [*Vul*] ‖ **Carry your tail!** (Guyn) ‖ **Haul your arse!/backside!** (Bdos) Get out of my sight!; Arse off! *Look boy, carry your arse out o[f] he[re] and don[t bother me!*—(Guyn) **2.4 cut your arse/ass** *vb phr* (CarA) [*Vul*] See Phr 2.2 above. *But nowadays people let their children get away with a whole set of rudeness ... while they themselves know their own parents would have cut their arse in their day.*—(Trin) **2.5 Haul your arse/ass!** *vb phr* (Bdos, Trin) [*Vul*] ‖ **Carry your arse!** (Guyn) See Phr 2.3 above. *Looka, haul your arse! And don[t bother come back neither!*—(Bdos) **2.6 in your arse/ass** *excl tag* (CarA) [*Vul*] [Merely adding emphasis to the prec n] *... by God!; ... dammit! August done, and before yo[u] could turn roun[d] twice Christmas in yo[ur] arse!*—(Trin) **2.7 make yourself an ass** *vb phr* (ECar) See MAKE Phr 5.40 **2.8 no arse/ass** *terminal adv intensifier* (Guyn, Trin) [*AF—Vul*] Intensely; extremely; like hell **a.** *I got to work no ass to upkeep the home and he busy gamblin[g]* —(Guyn) **b.** *Dis time A frighten no ass!*—(Trin)

arse² (**ass²**) *adj* (CarA) [*Vul*] [Expressing frustration] Damned; accursed. *Well look at my arse cross dis mornin[g], before I open me eye police in me door.*—(Gren) [By functional n > adj shift adding *Derog* effect to the sense of the n]

arse-lick·er (**ass-lick·er**) *n* (CarA) [*Vul*] One who acts in a noticeably servile and fawning manner for the purpose of remaining in favour with, or gaining favours from, a superior. *This is the same Gairy that has done away with the intelligent and conscientious Grenadians in the Civil Service and instead has rammed the Service with Ignoramuses and Ass-lickers.*—NeJ (75.07.27, p.2) [Contemptuous comparison esp with dog's habit of licking the backside of a bitch to encourage coition] □ The occurrence in writing is bold, and rare except in the yellow press of *Gren, Trin*. The term is not listed in *DSUE:1, 2* (though *arse-wiper* is, *DSUE:2*), nor *OED*. *OEDS* only notes *arse-licking* (see next).

arse-lick·ing (**ass-lick·ing**) *vbl adj, n* (CarA) [*Vul*] Disgustingly servile or fawning (behaviour). *From the way the old Choko reads the situation, Eric W. has a way of dealing with the arse-licking types who use him as a watershed for their ambitions.*—BoM (79.06.29, p.3) [See prec.

Also *OEDS arse sb* 3. offers cits from 1912, though in CarA Cr and oral CE the term is prob much older] □ See ARSE-LICKER.

arse·ness *n* (Trin, Tbgo) [*Vul*] ‖ *stupidness* (CarA) Irritating folly; provoking nonsense; vexatious stupidity. *Another thing I know about the clan is that they are strong PNMites. Ask Karl. So that probably explains the arseness Tom had to say at the meeting.*—BoM (79.06.29, p.11) [*Arse²* adj + SE *-ness* 'a condition or instance of being ...'] □ See ARSE-LICKER.

ars·nick·er* *n* (Baha) ‖ *kwabyé nwè* (Dmca, Gren, StLu) A blue-grey heron that is about 50 ins tall when fully grown; the Great Blue Heron; *Ardea herodias* (*Ardeidae*) (*MTBH*). *The arsnicker is an enormous water bird frequently met with on the beaches or in the small inland ponds.*—Baha (Ms)

ar·ti (ar·tee) ['a·rti] *n* (Guyn, Trin) **1.** A traditional ceremony performed (by the circular movement of a lamp with a camphor-scented flame) before a deity or any reverend personage in order to obtain his blessing. *Then Gurudeva performed arti—moving a lighted camphor on a brass platter circularly round the images; first round Krishna and Radha, then over the other pictures of Vishnu and Shiva, and last of all over his own drawing of the Monkey God.*—NAGOS: 76 □ The relevant phrases are: **do/perform arti 2.** [By extension] The administering of the blessing itself to individuals by a celebrant. *Besides the ... anointing, the mother formally blesses the boy with water and camphor fire (arti) before he leaves for the bride's home.*—Trin (Ms) □ The relevant phrases are: **pass/receive/serve/share/take arti 3.** [By extension] The ceremonial gift of money or flowers offered by the recipient of the blessing. *... the Jhandi wasn't over yet but just as she throw her aarti so, the son come and call her.*—(Guyn) [Hin < Skr *aartrikaa*. It occurs in Hin phrs *aarti ghumaanaa*, 'to revolve, take round a.'; *–karnaa* 'to do, perform a.'; *–lenaa*, 'to receive a.'; *–utaarnaa*, 'to perform (deliver the blessing of) a.'. This last phr > Bhoj *utaare̩ aarti* is still used in *Guyn* by rural Hindus]

Ar·til·ler·y, The *n phr* (Guyn) [Hist. In colonial Br Guiana] The branch of voluntary, part-time, local troops responsible for firing ceremonial gun-salutes and leading ceremonial parades; [by assoc] young men of upper middle-class and of light skin and hair. *'... and he's an Artillery man. He plays football for the Artillery Club.' / Sylvia remembered that Russell had told her that the Artillery Company—a unit of the local militia—accepted only young men of good coloured families.*—MLDS:104

A·ru·ban *adj, n* (CarA) (A person or thing) belonging to or characteristic of the island of Aruba, (one of the Leeward set of the Netherlands Antilles off the coast of Venezuela. *About 62,000 Arubans, predominantly African; and over 36,000 are descendants of the Arawaks, Dutch,* *and other races. Polite, hospitable people with a flair for languages.*—Cat. 6.1, p 42

a·ru·ma·ha·ni [ə'rumahani] *n* (Belz) A GARIFUNA group dance for men, in wh they join hands and move while they sing solidarity songs recounting their experience.—*E.R. Cayetano. Disappearing are gunjei, / Wanaragua, tira, / Abeimahani, arumahani and hungu-hungu; / Many of our kin have become ashamed / To speak Garifuna.*—CCD:5 [GARIFUNA word, *Belz*]

ar·we ['a·wi] *pron* (Antg, Nevs, StKt, USVI) [Commonly written form of the 1st pers pl pron in the Cr of the Leeward Is] We; us; our. See A[LL]-WE □ Also *'arbe(e)'* in *StKt*.

Ar·ya; **Ar.yan** *n* (Trin) Shortened form of ARYASAMAJIST. *And yet some Aryas in Trinidad read the A.D. sixteenth-century scripture, the Ramayana of Tulsidas, and celebrate the birthday of Rama. However, their main festivals are the birth, death and enlightenment anniversaries of Dayananda.*—LCTC:10

Ar·ya·sa·ma·jist (Ar·ya Sa·ma·ji(st)) ['a·r-yasama:ᴊɪs(t)] *n* (Guyn, Trin) A follower of an unorthodox Hindu religious order, the Arya Samaj, founded by Swami Dayanand in the latter half of the 19C in India, and introduced into *Guyn* and *Trin* by Bhai Parmanand in 1910. *For the Aryasamajists, however, Devali has a special significance since it was on Devali Day, 1883, that [their founder] Swami Dayanand ... passed away.*—GyC (76.10.22, p.24) [Hin *aarya*, 'Aryan', 'noble' + *samaaj*, 'society' + SE suff *-ist* 'an adherent of']

ar·you ['a·yu] *pron* (StKt) [Commonly written form of the 2nd pers pl pron in *StKt* Cr] You; your.

as¹ *conj* **1.** ['a:z] /3'/ (CarA) [*IF*] As soon as; immediately as; from the moment that. **a.** *Me do everyting fi mek she happy and still she no satisfy ... but as she come in she start pon me.*—SSLG:94 **b.** *As she open the door he hit her one lash.*—Dmca (Ms) [Prob a survival of a W Afr tonemic distinction, also helped by borderline senses of SE *as* 'when' as in 'As the judge entered the court room, everybody stood up', or 'because' as in 'As he heard his father's voice, he ran and shut the door'] □ An emotive creolized usage often opening an utterance and differentiated from SE conj *as* by carrying the main stress with lengthened vowel and by characteristically higher pitch wh may spread to some of the foll utterance or drop sharply on the next word. This differentiation cannot be represented in standard orthography, but its semantic significance is maintained in CE speech and is used in written schoolwork. **2.** [az~ᴀz] (CarA) [*IF*] [Subordinator, with ellipsis] As ... as (with first element suppressed); like. *A boy child would change him, they would be happy again as the first time.*—SABS:190 □ This uncoordinated use of unstressed *as*, common in CE, has an occasional parallel in *IF* E. Cp 'He came quick as an arrow', or 'Christian children all must be / Mild, obedient, good as he' (Hymns A.& M., No.329). **3.** (CarA) [*IF*] As much as. *In those days we used to produce so much sugar we could sell as we liked, and still have plenty to use in the colony.*—Guyn (Ms) [Cp ALL[3] adv 2., by wh it may have been phonically infl] **4.** (CarA) [*X*] [In various uses as an unnecessary link-word] *He has certainly made his political future precarious and has placed sufficient dynamite in the hands of rival political parties as to ruin the slender chances of his party recapturing the Government at the next elections.*— BdN (64.03.29, p.8) [A remainder from the co-ordinating conjunctive pair *as ... as* or *so ... as* overlapping with some other adj or adv structure having the same sense] **5.** PHRASES **5.1 as best as** *conj phr* (CarA) [*X*] As best; as well as; howsoever. **a.** *The poorer classes which form the bulk of the population fend for themselves as best as they could.*—ExP (72.03.20, p.15) **b.** *Women and girls ... scrubbed, dusted, polished and cooked in order that they may do as they pleased Saturday night and Sunday afternoon, satisfied that their duty, as best as could be managed with what was available, had been done.*—EBL:26 [By overlap of SE idiom *as best you can/may* and subordinating conj *as well as*] **5.2 as how** *conj phr* (Guyn, Trin) [*IF*] Seeing that; since. *Ah say 'Officer, as how de night so hot we only come up here to cool orf.'*—MN:51 **5.3 as if** *conj phr* (Guyn) [*IF*] (You/they, etc behave) as if; (It is just) as if; Do you/they think that ...? *As if I am beholden to any of them!*—(Guyn) □ Restricted to motive speech, introducing a supposition wh the speaker is rejecting with anger. **5.4 as much (as) to say** *conj phr* [Introducing a statement of sth imagined] (CarA) [*IF*] In a manner that means/meant. *Soon, frustrated St Lucians would shrug their shoulders even in the face of the worst examples of official corruption, as much as to say, 'so what else is new!'.*—WBAM:170 **5.5 as well** *conj phr* (Bdos, Guyn) [*X*] And also; but also. *It also prevented them from establishing any serious links outside the university, so that ... they moved by themselves. As well they suffered from a ... general lack of seriousness*—MaN (73.11.11, p.8) □ *As well* may not initiate a sentence in IAE. **5.6 as you see me (him, etc) here/there** *id phr* (CarA) [*IF*] See SEE Phr 3.1, 3.14.

as² *prep* **1.** (CarA) [*X*] Just like. **a.** *It was so in San Fernando, a thriving town forty miles south of Port of Spain, where Old Man became as one of the community.*—SABS:51 **b.** *He behaved as a fool and paid for it.*—Bdos (Ms) **2.** (CarA) [*X*] [In various uses as an unnecessary prep link] *Though there is agreement that trade unions should participate in political questions it is not clear as just exactly what form and content this participation should take.*—NeC (72.04.08, p.7) [An element intruding from an alternative structure to wh it properly belongs] **3.** PHRASES **3.1 as a don-know-what** *adv phr intensifier* (Gren, Guyn) [*AF—Cr*] In the extreme; as ... as ever (with first element suppressed). *Watch her! She womanish as a don-know-what!*—FPGD:14

[From Cr *as I don't-know-what*, the pron 'I' becoming *A* and thence confused with def art *a*, so making the structure 'don-know-what' become a noun] **3.2 as all (of) that** *adv phr intensifier* (CarA) [*IF*] [Usu after a neg or in inquiry] So very. *He wasn['t] drivin[g] as fas[t] as all o[f] that.*—(Tbgo) **3.3 as cording to** *prep phr* (Jmca) [*AF—Cr*] **(i)** As acknowledged by. *I stopped in the market near me to check out some fruits being as how, as cording to me, I'm on a diet and should eschew the bread and such hard food.*—WeG (75.04.08, p.15) **(ii)** Because of. *As corden ti dat, all dem blue-eye / Wite American, / Wa great granpa was Englishman / Mus go back a Englan!*—FCV:2 (L. Bennett) [A phr perh partly felt to be performing a similar function to that of *OED as* B. 14., introducing a clause used to attest a statement ...' + cit from Shak, Rich II. 'This sweares he, as he is a Prince ...'] **3.4 as far as (sb/sth) is concerned** *prep phr* (CarA) As regards; with reference to; in the matter of; so far as it concerns (sb or sth). *As far as your first question is concerned I could not get any answer on that since all the Merrymen are out of the island.*—AdN (77.06.17, p.8) □ A cliché often misused and often introducing an awkwardly long n phr. **3.5 as regard/regarding/regards to** *prep phr* (CarA) [*X*] As regards; regarding; in regard to. *It can also be seen that personalities are very rife in the House and jealousy as regards to the Premier is very pronounced.*—WoV (68.10.16, p.2) [Overlapping of the three SE forms of this prep (phr) given in the gloss] **3.6 as to** ['a:ztʊ] *prep phr* (CarA) [*IF*] [Expressing strong contempt for or derision of a person] As for ... ! *Dora: 'Don't call me name you know. Is Sarah tell me so!' / Campbell: 'As to she!'*—Tbgo (Ms) □ An emotive creolized usage restricted to speech, always initial, introducing a person's name or a pron, and distinguished from the SE prep phr by the strong stress and long vowel of *as*, and by carrying the meaning of contempt by itself (cp SE *as to* 'with respect to'). Cp also AS¹ 1. **3.7 as towards** *prep phr* (Trin) [*X*] As to; about. *Ignorance as towards the true significance of this occasion seems to have come from the Head of Government down.*—ExP (72.02.28, p.17) [A prob overlapping of *as to* + (attitude, etc) *towards*] **3.8 as versus** *prep phr* (Bdos) [*X*] As compared with; as against. *We want to know:* (*1*) *Did the Government recently subsidise rice to the tune of some EC $1 million?* (*2*) *If so how much of this rice was consumed by animals as versus humans?*—AdN (73.10, 06, p.4) [The sense of *versus*, as in 'one idea versus another', overlaps with the phr *as against*]

as³ *adv* **1.** (Bdos, Guyn) [*X*] [After a neg, with implied comparison] So (qualifying an adj or adv). **a.** *She wanted that kind of basket but not as big.*—(Guyn) **b.** *Although Government was aware of the needs of the poorer people of the island, they could not cater as fully to the needs of these people, and therefore depended on private individuals and organisations to supplement the assistance given to the poor.*—AdN (72.11.07, p.1) **2.** (Guyn) [*IF*] So (qualifying an adj). *And they are as stuck up* *with themselves!*—(Guyn) □ An emotive usage adding intensity to the foll adj (phr) wh receives a rising inquiry-type tone.

a·sa·fi·es·ti·a *n* See ASAFOETIDA □ Note

a·sa·foe·ti·da [asa'fɛita] *n* (CarA) ‖*fedity* (Bdos) A resinous substance of a very unpleasant smell that is rolled into pellets or little balls and used in folk medicine, or sometimes tied in a little bag hung on the body as trusted protection against evil spirits. *Campbell also said that among the miscellaneous drugs used and recommended by obeahmen are commanding oil, confusion powder, asafoetida, musk oil, St John oil, white lavender,* ...—GyC (76.07.11, p.31) □ Also *asafiestia* and other folk forms arising from its popular use.

A·sa·lam-wa·li·kum (**As·sa·laam·u-a·li-·kum**) *Greeting phr* (Guyn, Trin) 'Peace be with you', a Muslim greeting to wh the reply is 'Wa-li-kum-salam'. (See etym). *From Hazrat Amir Sadrudin / Assalaamu-Alikum / As the Islamic world enters the Sacred Month of Ramadan I send greetings and best wishes to all my brethren in Guyana.*—GyC (76.08.27, p.7) [Urdu < Perso-Arabic *al-salaamu* 'greeting', 'peace' + *li kum* 'with you'. The reply is *wa-li-kum* 'and with you'] □ Common among religious Muslims in *Guyn* and *Trin* but occasionally copied by others.

asha *n* (USVI) A pickle made of cut limes preserved in vinegar and salt. *Oh yes, I like asha better than hot pepper with my food.*—(USVI) [Prob < ACHAAR]

asham (**ashum**) *n* (Antg, Brbu, Gren, Jmca) ‖*brown-George* (Jmca) ‖*chili* (StVn) ‖*chilibibi* (StVn, Tbgo, Trin) ‖*coction* (Jmca) ‖*corn-sham* (Belz, Gren) ‖*kaksham* (Jmca) ‖*parch-corn* (Belz) ‖*sansam* (Trin) ‖*sham-sham* (StVn) A confection made by pounding or grinding roasted corn and brown sugar together; in some places grated coconut and other ingredients are added. *There's enough corn to make asham and asham pap.*—(Brbu) [< *DAFL* Twi *o-siám*, 'parched and ground corn'] □ The variant *ashum* is evid restricted to *Antg*. Another variant *hasham* is also characteristically *Jmca*.

ashamed *vbl adj* PHRASE **ashamed for your-self** (Trin) [X] Ashamed of yourself. *Now having met the girl of his dreams he was ashamed for himself for the manner in which he had spoken to her.*—Exp (73.02.11, p.6) □ SE permits *ashamed for* (*sb*) 'ashamed on account of (sb)', but requires 'ashamed *of* oneself'.

A·shan·ti [a'ʃanti] *n, adj* (CarA) [Hist] **1.** Name of the people inhabiting a very large middle area of modern Ghana stretching down to the coast, about two million in number and with Kumasi as their traditional main city. *The Negro brought to the West Indies many elements of the culture of a large number of African peoples, the Shango*

religion of the Yorubas, Vodun, which is the Dahomey term for all deities, the Spider-tales of the Ashanti Akan people, proverbs, words, snatches of music...—SWI:58 **2.** The lang of these people, also called Twi. □ Properly *Asante*, part of the larger *Akan* group of W Afr peoples (see *DAFL: xiii*), but the spelling 'Ashanti' was popularized by 18C and 19C E accounts. Large numbers of slaves having been taken from the Ashanti, this lang accounts for many Africanisms in CarA Crs.

ash·es [aʃɪz ~ asɪj] [X]] *n* (CarA) Ash. *And he was so crude he would drop the ashes from the cigarette on the floor. True! I couldn't believe my eyes when I saw his hand hangin[g] over the side of the chair and this ashes on the floor right there!*—(Bdos) □ A pl form unpermitted as a sg in IAE, though it has survived as such in *IF* CE from Cr in wh a number of items are so treated (*a ants, a teet[h]*, etc). However the pl form was evid common in EE (see *OED ash* 1. a. + latest cit-'1806), and remains in religious contexts 'sackcloth and ashes', 'dust to dust, ashes to ashes'; so these sources may also account for its survival in CE. The form *ashish* is also listed as typical of early Am Black E in *GBB:288*, as also of Krio in *KED ashis* 'ash, ashes'.

ash·es-wa·ter *n* (Guyn, Jmca, Trin) A mixture of ash and water often used as a remedy for plant blight. *She threw ashes-water in the pot which contained the fern.*—Guyn (Ms)

a·shi·shi Pam·pi ['aʃɪʃi pampi] *n* (Belz) [AF] A person who is covered in dust and dirt. *Yo[u] look like ashishi Pampi.*—(Belz) [Perh < *ashes-y*, an adj derivative of *ashish*, as in folk pronunc (cp early Am Black E form noted at *ashes*) + *Pompey*, also with folk pronunc /pampi/ ref to a folk figure now forgotten]

Ash·ram ['a:ʃram] *n* (Guyn, Trin) A building used mainly for Hindu religious meetings and meditation. *On two lots will stand an Ashram, for religious activities and on the other, the first Temple in the West Indies, dedicated to Lakshmimata, the Goddess of Light.*—ExP (72.10.12, p.18) [Hin *aashram* 'hermitage, abode']

a·si·po·ko (**a·chi·po·ko**) ['asipoko ~ 'aʧipoko] *n* (Guyn) **1.** A fruit-bearing Guyana forest-tree growing to about 100 ft in height, and yielding a very tough timber; *Pouteria guianensis* (*Sapotaceae*). *A very tall forest tree, the asipoko yields a tough timber which is very hard to saw or nail, but very good for heavy construction work.*—Guyn (Ms) **2.** The edible, small, round, yellow fruit, borne by the tree of the same name, with a thick skin, many seeds and scanty flesh that is sweet and stainy to taste. *The porkknockers sometimes eat a yellow fruit called asipoko or achipoko, which drops from a tree in the forest and somewhat resembles the sapodilla in taste.*—Guyn (Ms) [< Arawak *asepoko* [asɛpoko], 'a red- barked tree yielding a white latex and edible fruit'—*D. Fox*]

ask *vb tr* **1.** [Note: The pronunc [aks] often occurs throughout the *CarA* sometimes even in the speech of well-educated persons. Far the commonest pronunc, however, is [a:s] with pa.t. [a:st]. All these forms may represent later survival in CE of the EE forms represented in the *OED* note: ' ... *Acsian, Axian* survived in *ax*, down to nearly 1600 the regular literary form, and still used everywhere in midl. and south dialects, though supplanted in standard English by *ask*, originally the northern form. Already in 15C the latter was reduced dialectally to *asse*, pa.t. *ast*, still current dialectally.'] **2.** PHRASES **2.1 ask (sb) (the) question** (Guyn, Jmca) [*IF*] [Of a man] To ask (a woman) to have sexual intercourse. *Dis is a decent home, yo[u] hear? No man ain['t] dare come an[d] ask my daughter question like dem over de[re].*—(Guyn) □ Cp Phr 2.6 below. **2.2 asked out** ['a:st ᴅᴜt] *adj phr* (Bdos, Guyn) [*AF—Joc*] Wearing trousers that are torn in the seat. *Also used facetiously, as 'I see you're asked out', which would imply that the trousers of the boy addressed were torn in the seat.*—CGBD:4 [Pun on 'your arse (is) out' from Cr pronunc of 'ask' /aas/] [In many phrs after a negative] **2.3 can't ask you to trot** *id phr* (Bdos, Guyn) (You are) above reproach. *And when it came to his work, you know, nobody could ask him to trot, believe me. You had to admire how he went about what he had to do.*—(Guyn) **2.4 Don't ask** *vb phr* (CarA) [Adding emphasis to following phr or clause] Of course ...; you may be sure (that). *Man she went to the party with all the expensive clothes and don't ask how the boys were all after her for a dance.*—(Guyn) **2.5 not ask you cran(n)anah** *neg vb phr* (Mrat) [*AF*] ‖ *not ask you how old you are/be* (CarA) [*IF*] ‖ *not ask you who made you* (Guyn) ‖ *not take your height* (Guyn) **(i)** To completely ignore any person or obligation; to take no notice of anyone or anything; to ignore an obligation. **a.** *So Parchy, you stop dere dry so an' nyam off a big old-de- debble tuppence bread an' no even ask me crannanah? Ah hope to God you know whe' to find somebody potato groun' to go an' dig potato an' roas' when hungry start to buss your skin.*—FGSOS:35 (G. Irish). **b.** *Him jus[t] step in de house an[d] tak[e] up de bag an[d] [h]im never even as[k] me how old me was.*—Jmca **(ii)** [Esp of medicine] To have no effect (esp not causing any bowel motion). *De doctor medicine ain['t] no good. I[t] don['t] even ask me how old A be.*—Nevs (Ms) **(iii)** [*AF*] [Of food] To be quite insufficient to satisfy your hunger. *I so hungry that that little plate of food don't even ask me how old I be.*—Antg (Ms) **(iv)** [*AF*] [Of clothes] To fit so well as to cause no discomfort. *Girl A wear dem new shoes today and dey in ask me how old A is.*—(Bdos) **2.6 not ask (you) what you have to sell** (Bdos) [*AF*] [Of a man] To decline to request sexual intercourse. *Christine should I destroy this woman that is breaking up my marriage, or should I move and leave my husband and her in peace? Answer me quick for my nerves are gone so I may do anything at anytime. My husband doesn't ask me what I have to sell. He isn't able when he finish

with this woman.*—NaT (75.02.23, p.18, Dear Christine) □ Cp Phr 2.1 above.

as·pect *n* PHRASE **from the aspect that** *conj phr* (Bdos) [*X*] In view of the fact that; seeing that. **a.** *Such a situation is understandable from the aspect that Barbados was never exposed to the diverse influences as her sister islands. As was stated before, 329 years of British influence could not be easily forgotten.*—AdV (64.04.19, p.17) **b.** *I would disagree with that statement from the aspect that the Indians in Barbados form too small a percentage to pose a threat.*—Bdos (Ms)

ass *n* (CarA) See ARSE

ass-head *n* (Jmca) ‖ *horse-head* (Jmca) A brightly coloured mask in the shape of a horse's or ass's head worn by a male dancer in the JUNKANOO (John Canoe) masquerade. **a.** *But poor Jackass was too ashamed after that. He would never go the John Canoe, so every year somebody dresses up like Ass-head and jump John Canoe. That's how Ass-head get into John Canoe; and that's why Jackass always looks like him sorry for himself. Is Anansi cause it all to happen.*—SWI: 150 [*DJE* lists only *horse-head*, of wh [a·s-hee·d] is a likely *Jmca* folk pronunc; but the confusion of name may also be due to the indistinguishable shape of the mask] □ Cp DONKEY-MAN (Guyn).

ass·e· boo [a:sibu ~ a:sibo] *n* (StVn) [*AF—Joc/ Derog*] [Mild form of rebuke] A stupid person; a person who behaves in a dim-witted or idiotic manner. **a.** *Today I sure Asseboo, when you applied for your teachers job, if Government had told you the school is too small to employ you, would have been a rumpus. Now they give you a job, instead of shutting up and go on drawing wages out of my hard earned taxes that you don't deserve you are trying go think you can embarrass your employers.*—ViN (75.11.14, p.2) **b.** *But he is a real asseboo, takin[g] all he money an[d] gi[v]e she!*—StVn (Ms, 1985) [ASSIE, diminutive of 'ass' + *boo*, reduced form of BOOBOO² 2.]

As·sem·bly Rooms *n phr* (Guyn) [Hist] Popular name of a very large wooden building near the business centre of Georgetown, home of the planters' and businessmen's 'Georgetown Club', famous as a theatre and ball room until its destruction by fire in 1945. **a.** *I have a pleasing recollection of Mr Bridges in the 'pit' of the Assembly Rooms on a night that 'The Shop Girl' was staged.*—POTS:81 **b.** *For Sylvia, after 1937, Hallowe'en held a different significance ... [Russell] had told her that he was going to the Hallowe'en dance that night in the Assembly Rooms.*—MLDS: 113

ass·i·fied *vbl adj* (Bdos, Guyn, USVI) ‖ *poor-great* (Guyn) **1.** [*AF—Joc*] [Usu of persons of humble origin] Pompous; snobbish; foolish. *I don[t] boder wid dem any more. Like since de broder come back a lawyer and dey sen[d]in[g] de li[tt] l[e] sister to Bishop's High School dey get really assified.*—(Guyn) **2.** [*AF—Joc*] Thick-skulled;

unintelligent; stupid. *He can't even follow a simple direction; he really assified.*—(Guyn) [Cp *OED assify* v 'turn into an ass', but also, esp in regard to sense 2., cp SE *ossify* + CE folk pronunc]

ass·ish·ness *n* (Guyn, Tbgo, Trin) [*IF*] ‖ *stupidness* (CarA) Nonsense that causes anger; intolerable folly. **a.** *You wait and see, once they feel they are people they themselves won't put up with the assishness that goes on around here.*—JPB: 90 **b.** *Dr W. M— Tobago West MP, has called the draft Bill (constitution) seeking internal self-government on the island 'assishness'.*—BoM (79.05.04, p.30) **c.** *He likes to talk a lot of assishness.*—(Guyn) □ Strongly emotive. The sense, like that of CE STUPIDNESS (wh is weaker) is distinct from 'stupidity, assinine quality' as given in *OED* (with latest cit–'1623). *Assish, assishness* are not listed in *COD8* or *WCD9*. Cp also ASSNESS.

as·sist *vb tr* PHRASE **assist sb to (do sth)** (Trin) [*X*] To assist in (doing); to help to (do). **a.** *Well East Indian people are like that—you see the wife, the children they all assist to run the shop, and any time o[f] day or night!*—(Trin) **b.** *Mr Foster: 'It is true to say that Malik assisted your son to get out that legal problem?' / Yes, Sir.*—AMAM:37 [By overlap of two vb phrs, *assist* + *in* + gerund (*-ing*) and *help* + *to* + base vb]

ass·ness *n* (Trin) [*AF—Vul*] ‖ *stupidness* (CarA) An act or action that causes great provocation. **a.** *What assness really going on with the Tourist Board? I couldn't believe my eyes last week Wednesday when I saw bold-face, bold face on the front page of the Guardian a picture of a Swiss beauty who came to Trinidad to take pictures that would be used to promote Trinidad abroad.*—BoM (80.03.14, p.13) [A word of lower status formed by reduction of ASSISHNESS, indicating stronger feeling. Also reflects Cr facility of using any noun in adj function]

Ass·o·ci·at·ed State *n phr* (CarA) [Hist] Any one of the East Caribbean island-states of Antigua, Dominica, Grenada, St Kitts-Nevis-Anguilla, St Lucia, St Vincent wh, as former colonies were, in 1967, given a new type of association (whence the term) with Britain, by wh each controlled its internal affairs with power to amend its constitution including the power to declare itself independent, Britain being, in the arrangement, responsible for defence and external affairs. **A**ssociated Statehood ceased with the opting for independence by each state at various times between 1974 (Grenada) and St Kitts-Nevis (1983). **a.** *Grenada is one of the six West Indian Associated States of the Windward Islands which in 1967 got a home-rule constitution, with Britain retaining responsibility for Defence and External Affairs. Each of the Associated States has a built-in option for independence without recourse to the British Parliament if two-thirds of the local legislature and two-thirds of the votes in a referendum approve.*—ExP (72.10.24, p.12) **b.** *The Associated States,*

comprising *Grenada, Antigua, St Kitts, St Lucia, Dominica and St Vincent, have got a population of more than half-million who depend mostly on an agriculture-intensive economy.*—AnS (73.02.28, p.5)

ass-pipe *n* (USVI) [*AF*] ‖ BAHO (Nevs) *To the music of accordion (and perhaps a 'bombadine' or French horn), guiro (a dried gourd scraped for percussion with the rib of an umbrella), triangle, keg-drum, guitars and 'ass pipe' (a length of hollowed-out bamboo) fifty couples wiggled and waggled probably chanting in unison a well-known folk song.*—HVVIS:108 [Joc ref to the fact that the pipe is taken from the 'backside' or 'arse' of the car] □ See BASS-PIPE.

asu(e) ['æsu] *n* (Baha) ‖ SUSU (Dmca, etc) *His 'asue' was his system of financing. These were an unsophisticated people, not far removed from their African ancestry. The 'asue' was a system of saving money, and financing. There were those individuals in a community who having proven themselves trustworthy 'kept' the asue. Small groups of people would place in the hands of these 'asue keepers', an equal sum of money every week; this was called a 'hand'. Each week, one of the participants was given the sum total of all the 'hands', and this was repeated each week, until all 'hands' were drawn; and then the process started all over again. It is sometimes customary for the operator of the asue, to collect a small percentage of the sum, as an operational cost.*—EBT:17 □ The alternative spelling **asu**, pl **asus**, is also used. Note: 'For example, the Bahamian Asu and the Yoruba esusu are essentially the same thing'—MTTBT:23.

at *prep* (CarA) **1.** (+ name of a country) In. **a.** *The only place at which I came across any vestiges of the yellow fever was at Trinidad.*—TWISM: 224 **b.** *In 1847 there arrived at Barbados two men who played a very large part in the formation of the 'Rio Pongas Mission' as it became to be known.*—NaT (75.09.07, p.7) **c.** *Manager of the B.G. Rice Marketing Board, said yesterday he was at a loss to understand the reported shortage of rice at Essequibo. Reports a few days ago stated that the rice shortage at Essequibo was acute over the last two weeks.*—DaC (52.10.29, p.1) [Perh a residue of Br colonial E. Cp cit from *OED* at 2. 'he is at the Indies'] □ ModE uses *at* + a town/port, *in* + a country/state. **2.** [*IF*] (+ an identified place) [After a vb signifying active movement] To. **a.** *They may be carrying some things at the Park; they may be carrying things on which they have worked, to various places.*—Bdos (Hd, 76.06.22, p.6830) **b.** *She's always saying never bring nobody else at her house or she will call the police.*—NaT (76.05.02, p.19) **c.** *I will be going at the 7.45 show.*—(Guyn) [Perh orig due to a false refinement of Cr A[7] 'to, into, etc (+ a place)', and reinforced by misplaced juncture in such cases as /a di paak/ /a di shoo/, etc becoming 'at the park/show', etc, in contexts after the vbs *go, carry, come, reach*, etc where *at* is not permitted in IAE. Hence perh also developing the functions at sense 3.] **3.** (CarA)

[*IF*] (+ personal pron or identified person) At the house or home of (the person specified). **a.** *Coroner: You ever supported her? | Witness: Not at all Sir. It's a rumour. | Coroner: You ever slept at her? | Witness: No; at the family.*—DaC (52.07.13, p.6) **b.** *You must be thinking that you are talking to Barrow or to one of the little children home at you.*—Bdos (Hd, 75.04.22, p.5029) **c.** *That time she went at the cousin to hide from the police.*—Antg (Ms) [This function of AT could be a CE refinement of Cr A⁷. However both EE and IrE also feature this usage. Cp *OED at* 3. *at a person*, 'in the immediate presence or company of', *Obs* + cits–'1500; also *at* 12. **b.** 'into the presence of, near to', *Obs*, + cits–'1678 including Shak. For IrE cp *JESI:26* 'I was at him for half a year' = 'with him'] **4.** [*X*] [In various loose associations with the object of a vb tr, often a personal pron] [An extension of the preceding vb tr emphasizing motive or purpose in its sense] **a.** *I watch at [h]im good and A say, You know dat is a lie.*—(Guyn) **b.** *When I called at him, he looked around and saw us at a store.*—Guyn (Ms, 1975) **c.** ... *the beings whose exemplary aspect it was that shone forth to recommend at you every commodity proposed to your daily preference, from macaroni to the Kingdom of Heaven.*—HCCM: 90 [With 'watch at (h)im', 'call at him' (cits a., b.) cp Cr /mi luk im/ /mi showt im/ wh require no connective /a/ after /luk/ /showt/. The insertion may be due to overcorrection or false refinement; extension to the other verbs such as 'recommend' (cit c.) in emotive contexts would follow] **5.** [In loose replacement of other preps] [*X*] **(i)** Of. **a.** *In recognition at this achievement, Mrs Johnson-Guthrie was honoured by her company, Jamaica Mutual Life, earlier this year.*—WeS (75.07.13, p.1) **b.** *The writer is making fun at the Buddhists.*—StKt (Ms, 1966) **(ii)** On. ... *and the Speaker of the House of Representatives, Mr Arnold Thomas will meet Sir Ellis and Lady Clarke at their arrival at the Red House for the swearing-in.*—ExP (73.01.31, p.1) **(iii)** In. *But I believe the voyage was rough, but today I can enthusiastically say the new era is at sight, from what I saw a few days ago.*—NeJ (75.05.23, p.4) **(iv)** About; etc. ... *and they send to say they sorry at what happen.*—SNWIC:210 **6.** PHRASES **6.1 at all** *adv phr* (CarA) See ALL³ Phr 5.16 **6.2 at length and at last** *adv phr* (CarA) [*IF*] ‖ *length and at last* (Antg) ‖ *length and last* (Bdos) Ultimately; finally; after a long time. **a.** *At length and at last, Papa and Partner set out and Sam and Leni set out behind them.*—Guyn (Ms, 1980) **b.** *A wait an[d] wait an[d] at length an[d] at las[t] he come wid de food.*—(Gren) [*DJE* suggests a blend of two phrs from Sc E *at length and at long* + *at long and at last*] □ Often preceded by (*un*)*til* in Guyn E, this cliché is widely encountered in *IF* CE narrative. **6.3 at the least** *adv phr* (BrVi) [*X*] [Expressing emphasis] Surely; surely not. *You ain mean me, at the least.*—(BrVi) [By emotive misascription] **6.4 at weekend** *adv phr* (Trin) [*IF*] During the weekend. **a.** *The World heavyweight boxing crown, now worn by Joe Frazier is in jeopardy. This view was expounded here at weekend by a Jamaican*

sportsman who passed through on his way to Guyana on business.—EvN (73.01.08) **b.** *It is understood that the party Top-brass will be holding an urgent meeting at weekend amid rumours of his possible expulsion.*—Bdos (B) [Journalistic abbr for the fuller phr. See MONTHEND, YEAREND]

at·char *n* See ACHAAR

a·te·li·er *n* (Dmca) [Hist] A work gang of plantation slaves. ... *apart from a little history, all we really have to rely on, are the stories handed down from the days of slavery. It is from these old tales that we learn that the first non-African dress was the uniform or livrée of the estate, and that uniformed slaves worked together in gangs called 'ateliers'.*—Did, 1972:25 [Fr *atelier* (in secondary sense) 'work gang'. Cp *chef d'atelier*, 'head foreman, overseer']

At·kin·son *n* ['a(t)kınsın] (StLu) [*IF*] ‖ *tilapia* (Guyn) Popular name in St Lucia of the *Tilapia mossambica (Cichlidae)*, a small, edible, dark grey river fish. *The Atkinson is common in our rivers and freshwater ponds. It multiplies rapidly and can weigh over three pounds.*—StLu (Ms, 1978) [From name of Mr Harry Atkinson who introduced the fish into *StLu* in the 1950s—(*pers info, P.A. Murray*)]

atop¹ *adv* (Guyn) Above; [by extension] (at or to a work site) higher up river. **a.** *Judge-Advocate: Do you believe God Almighty a'top? Dose (slave): Yes.*—LMSPJS:53 **b.** *His workmates reported that he had gone atop many days ago and had not been heard from since.*—Guyn (Ms) [Cp *OED atop* A. adv 'at the top, above' + (latest cit–'1877)]

atop² *prep* (Bdos, Guyn, Trin) Above; on top of; on. **a.** ... *and the roof and first storey of the building which housed an insurance office atop the bank office were destroyed.*—AdN (71.06.04, p.1) **b.** *Has anybody in Tobago noticed what happened to the large sign painted atop the roof of this building and which indicates that this is Crown Point Airport?*—ExP (72.10.26, p.23) [Cp *OED atop* B. prep 'on the top of' + latest cit–'1868]

a·tou·ta ['atuta] /1'12/ *n* (Gren) ‖ YELLOW-YAM (Antg, etc) [See YANM ATOUTAN. The unqualified form *atouta* is used mostly by older rural folk]

at·trac·tion-oil *n* (StKt) [Obeah] ‖ *commanding oil* (Guyn) A scented oil given by an OBEAH-MAN/-WOMAN to be used by a client in a prescribed way as a believed means of gaining or regaining the affections of a lover. *Other items on exhibit [in the obeah case] were: Peaceful home Oil, Musk, Compelling Powder, Uncrossing Oil, Commanding Powder, Domination Powder, Flaming Powder, Attraction Powder, Attraction Oil, Uncrossing Powder, a hypodermic syringe, Chinese Oil, Indian Oil, Lucky Planet Oil, Hindu Grass Oil, Zodiac Oil, and Success Dream Book.*—DeM(SK) (63.08.31, p.3) □ See also ATTRACTION POWDER.

at·trac·tion-pow·der *n* (StKt) [Obeah]
‖ *compelling powder* (Guyn) A talcum powder,
coloured by the addition of some other ingredient, and given by an OBEAH-MAN/-WOMAN
to be used by a client as a believed means of
gaining or regaining the affections of a lover.
□ See prec.

au·ber·gine ['obʌ(r)ži·n] *n* (Antg, Gren, StVn,
Trin) ‖ EGGPLANT (CarA) **a.** *Last week Geest
Industries Ltd, shipped to the United Kingdom:
33,534 cartons or 452 tonnes of bananas and 6,283
packages of vegetables, christophenes, aubergines,
limes, sweet potatoes, lime-juice, mace, coconuts,
ginger and peppers...*—ViN (76.02.13, p.3) **b.**
*Jimmy, suddenly energetic, pulled back weeds, look-
ing for what had been planted and showing what
had grown: deformed, pale aubergines, stunted ochroes...*—NG:21 □ This IAE name for the fruit
of the egg-plant tends to be restricted to the
official domain.

aught (ought) [ɒːt] *n* (Belz, Guyn) Nought;
zero. *S1: What played in the boledo tonight? /
S2: Aught eight.*—(Belz) □ Usage current in
Belz, and among older folk in *Guyn*, though rare
in IAE.

Au·gust bank (ho·li·day) *n phr* (CarA) ‖ *Au-
gust-Holiday* (Mrat, Nevs, StKt, StVn) ‖ *Au-
gust-Monday* (BrVi, Dmca) ‖ *Carnival Monday* (Antg, Brbu) ‖ *Emancipation Day* (CarA)
[Hist] A public holiday, on the first day or
often the first Monday in August to mark the
anniversary of the abolition of slavery as from
1st August, 1834. **a.** *During the first year of
the operation of the agreement workers when not
required to work will be paid for the first five public
holidays which occur after the coming into operation
of the agreement—Good Friday, Whit Monday,
August bank holiday—at normal basic rates of pay
provided they have worked the whole working days
immediately preceding and following the public
holiday.*—AdN (73.01.22, p.1) **b.** *The day after
the church excursion, which was the August bank,
he took ill and that was it—he never went back to
work.*—(Bdos) □ The parallel names currently
given to the same holiday in different territories
have, in some cases, ex *Caricom Day, Carnival
Day*, developed different associations as they
have replaced the purpose of the orig name. In
Jmca, StVn, recognition of the day has been
abandoned.

Aug·ust-flow·er* /1'122/ *n* (Guyn) ‖ *fla-
mingo-bill* (Baha) ‖ *Jack-in-the-beanstalk*
(USVI) A slender ornamental soft-wood tree
growing to about 20 ft, with a light foliage of
compound leaves, and bearing large, fleshy, pink
or white flowers and very long, thin, flat, yel-
lowish- brown seed pods, all of wh are often
cooked; *Agati grandiflora* or *Sesbania grandiflora*
(*Papilionaceae*). **a.** *... and she could season curry
really sweet with August flower.*—Guyn (Ms) **b.**
The [August] flower and young leaves are cooked

*and eaten like green vegetables and spinach re-
spectively.*—OGEP:79 [Perh from the time of
annual flowering in Guyn]

Aug·ust-Mon·day /1'122/ *n* (BrVi, Dmca)
‖ AUGUST-BANK HOLIDAY (CarA)

Aug·ust-plum *n* (Belz) ‖ CHILLI-PLUM (Antg,
etc) *You can tell the August plum by it would lose
all the leaves when it full of fruit. Is a sweet plum
though.*—(Belz) [Prob from time of bearing in
Belz. For *Jmca AFPJ:435* notes 'flowers and
fruits later in the year (from Sept–Nov)'. Note
also CHILLI PLUM, cit b.] □ The name *hog-plum*
is, even in *Belz*, sometimes indiscriminately applied to this variety, though the *hog-plum* is a
larger, commoner and less fancied variety of the
same family.

aunt [aːnt] *n* (CarA) [*IF*] **1.** A respected female
friend of any young person's family (often used
as a form of address by the young person). *...
young men who at an early age had found themselves in the streets, without families, knowing only
the older men of some houses as 'aunts'.*—NG:
103 **2.** PHRASES **2.1 got/have to call (sb) aunt**
See CALL Phr 3.10 **2.2 live at your aunt** (Bdos,
Gren, Guyn, Trin) [*IF*] ‖ CATCH HELL (CarA) **a.**
*Things was really bad wid her until she meet and
married wid him. Couldn[t] get anything to do,
she was like livin[g] at she aunt, A tell you, for a
long time.*—(Bdos) **b.** *... but when it is remembered
that the expression to be living at one's aunt is
synonymous with 'living in hell', it is obvious that
there is a sinister aspect to the relationship.*—
CGBD:4 [A prob calque via Fr infl in *Gren,
Trin* < Fr slang *chez ma tante* 'at the pawn-
brokers', hence 'to live at your aunt's' = to live
in dire circumstances.]

aunt·ie (aunt·y) *n* (StKt) [*AF—Joc*] **1.** [Of
young women] The onset of the menstrual
period. **2.** PHRASES **2.1 Auntie coming to town**
id phr (StKt) [*AF—Joc*] The menstrual period
is about to begin. *Me belly hurtin[g] me. Auntie
mus[t] be comin[g] to to[w]ng.*—(StKt) [Prob from
Joc ref either to regular unwelcome visits (see
AUNT Phr 2.2) or to receiving free gifts from a
familiar country aunt] □ Teenage euphemism.

Aunt·ie Flo·ra *n phr* (Antg, StLu) [*AF—Joc*]
‖ *Flora* (Dmca, Gren, Guyn, Tbgo) The floor.
*If you wet this bed again you sleep on Auntie Flora
after now.*—Antg (Parent to child) [Joc name for
'the floor']

aunt·ie-man (an·ti·man, aun·ty-man) ['aː-
ntima·n] *n* [*AF*] (CarA) **1.** ‖ *mama-man* (Jmca)
‖ *manicou-man* (Trin) A man who behaves in
womanish ways; a sissy; general term of abuse for
any male considered to be lacking in masculine
qualities. **a.** *Peter, if you don't stop playing with
dolls you'll end up being a real antiman.*—SGAC
b. *If I were you I would't grieve too much, for in
fact who wants a man who listens to other women
pounding your name. As a child, I used to hear
the old folk refer to such men as 'Auntie Men'. ...*

Do you want an 'Auntie man', or a real loving man who will stand up for you and not let people who do not care for you pour junk into his ear? —NaT (77.04.17, p.22, Dear Christine) **c.** *Mona: Georgie stop behaving like some kind ah anty man.*—Tbgo (Ms, Play) **2.** (CarA) ‖ *bam-bam-man, bamsie-man* (Trin) ‖ *batty-man* (Antg, Guyn, Jmca) ‖ *buller* (Bdos) ‖ *mako*[1] 2, makoumè 3 (Dmca, StLu, Trin) ‖ *pantyman* (Antg, Gren) A male homosexual. **a.** *Well-Well! You mus' be a good auntieman ... refusing a good short time for fifty-cents.*—SNGD:29 **b.** *British Ante-Men*—'*Britain's homosexuals are estimated to total at least 600, 000'. So says a news report from London on Monday which dealt with the decision taken by the House of Lords ... which would legalise the practising in private of the un-natural and disgusting habit by consenting ad-ults.*—LaS (65.05.28) [Perh from assoc of *aunty* with 'intimate companionship' + *man*. However an Afr calque is poss. Cp *DAFL* Twi *ɔ-banim-mere* (> *ɔ-banim* + *ɔ-bere*, man + female) 'an effeminate man'] □ *Auntie-man* is commonest spelling and pronunc.

Aunt·ie Nan·nee (An·tee na·nee, an·ti-·na·ni, aunt·ee non·nee) *n phr* (BrVi) **1.** The dragon-fly. *Mosquito hawks, known locally as 'Auntee Nonnees', flit across the pool constantly. Songs about 'Auntee Nonnees' are sung by children in the Virgin Islands and throughout the West Indies. On St John, children sing: 'Auntee Nonee, come pound guinea corn, Ring-ting-a-ling-a-ling'. From Tortola to Antigua, children sing: 'Antee Nonnee, thread your needle Long, long time Hand on Lucy-Ba-Lucy-Ba-Lucy Long, long time'.*—JNHSJ:38 **2.** The red cotton bug, *Dysdercus spp. The Auntie Nannee is a major pest of cotton and a minor pest of sorghum and all Hibiscus spp.*—BrVi (Ms) □ Cp *RDVI*:57 'any of a variety of unusual insects from a dragonfly to a beetle. Variations depend on small community tra-ditions'.

Auouh·sah (Awou·sah) *n* (Crcu) One of the Nation Dances of Carriacou (see cit). **a.** *The Auouhsah and the Churde (cud) are warlike tribal dances designed to imitate the tribal warfares of the African. The song and drum beat which ac-company the dance have a fearful, weird ap-pearance.*—DCC:17 **b.** *The 'Awouhsah' and the Churde' (pronounced Cud) are war-like tribal dances put on to imitate the tribal warfares of the Africans. The songs and the drumbeat have a weird and fearful sound and the actions of the dancers seem to suggest more of fighting than of dancing. But the Awouhsah and the Churde are now seldom indulged in here in Carriacou.*—PGIP:28 (O. Buxo) [Prob folk pronunc of Hausa, a very large W Afr ethnic group]

auto·claps *n* (Jmca) [*AF*] Trouble that leads to more trouble. **a.** *According to my un-derstanding, this thing called balance of payment lives in every country and if you don't treat it right, it cause a whole heap a autoclaps. Well for some time now, we've been pulling style on B— of*

P— and the result is a thing call austerity.—WeG (72.12.06, p.12, Partyline) **b.** *We have strike down here like oonu have now inna winter. Mam, Right now we have bread strike. That is to say union and bakeries in autoclaps and town baker stop bake bread.*—WeG (72.12.06, p.12, Partyline) [Evid a coinage dating from the early 1970s]

Au·tumn crop *n phr* (Guyn) [Rice Ind, Sugar Ind] ‖ *big crop, second crop* (Guyn) **1.** [Rice Ind] The rice crop wh is sown during the months of May to July to be reaped during the months of September to November the same year. *The rains have come with the rice industry on the verge of beginning harvest of an expected bumper autumn crop. The industry expected 130, 000 tons of rice this autumn to add to 50, 000 tons reported from the earlier spring crop.*—AdN (73.09.15, p.1) **2.** [Sugar Ind] The sugar-cane crop wh is planted during the months of July to November to be reaped in the following year during the months of July to December. [Name due to traditional use of European seasonal labels for times of the year, the harvesting of this crop in both industries coinciding with the season of Autumn in Britain] □ See also SPRING CROP.

av·e·nue *n* (Guyn) **1.** A tree-lined walk (esp in Georgetown) flanked by two one-way roads. **a.** *They should make avenues in Campbellville and Greater Georgetown by filling up those trenches properly and planting them with nice trees with the one-way roads on both sides like Camp and Main Streets.*—Guyn (Ms) **b.** *Sylvia took the avenue in Main Street, walking in the shade of the Sawan trees.*—MLDS:25 **2.** (Bdos) One of a series of parallel streets in a particular (and usu urban) area, in relation to wh they are named, being distinguished only by number. **a.** *We were now in Belleville where the white people lived, and the streets bordered by palm trees were called av-enues.*—LICMS:116 **b.** *She livin[g] up in 2nd Avenue Pine, doin[g] a li[tt]le dress-makin[g].*—(Bdos) □ Orig applied to such a series of avenues in Belleville (Bridgetown) wh were decorated with Royal Palms, the name was later applied to any other series of streets.

av·er·age[1] *n* (Bdos, Guyn, Trin) [*X*] Estimated length of time. **a.** *In 1969, I returned to Trinidad on two occasions, spending an average of three weeks here on each occasion.*—AMGM:22 **b.** *Well, you have to take an average of how long that amount would have to boil before you have to put in sugar.*—(Bdos) **c.** *Well A lie do[w]ng de[re] wid dis average dat de train won[t] pass till five o'clock.*—(Guyn) [By misascription of the use of the word in various senses of approximation]

av·er·age[2] *vb* (CarA) [*X*] **1.** Estimate; assess. **a.** *Mr Kenneth S— secretary of the Elite and Rocklyn bus companies, said yesterday: 'We pro-pose suggesting to the Minister to average a certain amount weekly for each pensioner, add the amount to the pensioner's present pension and let the pen-sioner be free to pay the fare'.*—AdN (73.01.20, p.5) **b.** *The man stop to pick up some goods, the*

three boys average where to begin the scene....—
Guyn (Ms, 1975) **c.** *I had to average how much
sugar to put in when she go [a]way wid de measure.*—(Bdos) **2.** [*X*] Make a judgement regarding
the timing or placing of sth. **a.** *When the rain
came do[w]ng I average you must be only meet
halfway.*—(Bdos) **b.** *In cricket if you can't average
that ball right, well you won[t] las[t] an over.*—
(Guyn) **c.** *She also said Family Planning is not
to stop women from having children but to average
them.*—Antg (Ms, 1973) [By misascription of
sense, as for the n, + shift of function]

a·vo·ca·do (-pear)* *n* (CarA) ‖ *alligator-
pear* (CarA) ‖ *butter-pear* (Belz) ‖ *pear*[1] (CarA)
‖ *zabòka* (Dmca, Gren, StLu, StVn, Trin) A
pear-shaped fruit, 6 to 9 ins long, with a leathery,
green or brown skin wh is easily removed when
ripe; it is prized for its thick, light green, cheese-
like flesh wh encloses a single, loose seed; *Persea
americana* (*Lauraceae*). **a.** *The current avocado
pear season started with small fruit selling at 6
cents to 10 cents, and medium and bigger fruit for
15 cents and perhaps 20 cents.*—WeG (73.07.18,
p.9) **b.** *Avocado. Also zaboca or alligator pear.
Sometimes called midshipman's butter. A pear-
shaped or round fruit usually used for salads.*—
WCFV:9 [Sp corruption, by folk etym, of Aztec
ahuacatl, wh may also be the source (through Sp
renderings *aquacate*, *avigato*) of the E corruption
alligator pear. See etym note at ALLIGATOR PEAR,
also *OED*, *DJE*] □ The names *avocado*, *avocado pear* are of higher status than *alligator
pear*, and are the most widely known and used.

Awa(h)! *excl* (StLu) [*AF*] Neg exp indicating
strong ridicule, despair, disappointment, objection, impossibility, etc. **a.** *There was no peace
in the Mabouya Valley for the Doc when he tried
to hold a meeting at La Ressource. He summoned
all his resources to cope with the hecklers of La
Ressource but awah! If only the people could be
told under what party ticket he proposes to contest
the next elections he might even have found a way
out.*—CrU (75.12.26, p.4, Queek Quak) **b.** *Awa,
man! I don't think I'll get this money after all!*—
(StLu) **c.** *S1: Well the quickest way to get from
Vieux Fort to Castries is by plane! You can manage
that? / S2: Awa!*—(StLu) [Fr Cr, prob < Fr
Horreur!] □ Some older speakers add *wi* as an
intensifer.

await *vb* [*X*] **1.** (Guyn, StVn) [In loose senses
without clearly connoting expectation] Wait for;
hope for. **a.** *The people of Union Island look
forward to seeing him or another Doctor in the
near future. We hope not to await a visit like this
one for another year.*—ViN (73.10.19, p.3) **b.**
*Well in those days you build a vat and await the
rain to fall to fill it.*—(Guyn) **2.** vb intr PHRASE
await to do (sth) (Bdos, Jmca, Trin) [*X*] Wait
(expecting) to do (sth). **a.** *He added: 'It is these
same members of the staff who will be serving
the public in their new building which they are
anxiously awaiting to see completed.'*—AdN
(71.12.13, p.2) **b.** *Every so often we hear that a
forest of parking meters are stored in Jamaica*

and await, for some reason, to be erected.—DaG
(71.07.04, p.2) **c.** *They are awaiting to take away
with them one of those young maidens who visit
the river alone to fetch water.*—ExP (72.06.25,
p.10) [Prob from the obscured infl of Cr pre-
verbal A[10]. Cr /mi a weet fo di reen/ 'I am waiting
(hoping) for the rain', /mi a weet fo go tong/ 'I
am waiting (expecting) to go to town' show that
/a weet fo/ may be a tr or intr vb phr with similar
senses to those illustrated above, refined as 'await
to' in present CE]

a·wak·en *vb pa. part.* (Bdos, Gren, Guyn) [*X*]
Awakened; awaked; awoken. **a.** *Reports reaching
us from relatives and friends of the family said
that Mr and Mrs T— were asleep when they
were awaken by a loud noise on their bedroom
window.*—ToR (75.12.21, p.1) **b.** *The first premise is that no child can learn except his curiosity
has been awaken or unless the interest aroused by
the curiosity is strong enough to satisfy.*—Bdos
(Ms, 1964) **c.** *I slept the whole day and wasn't
awaken until after midday by my wife.*—Guyn
(CR) □ Confusion commonly caused in educated
CE by the past-participial appearance of *awaken*,
wh is properly a normal SE base-verb, duplicate
of *awake*.

a·wa·ra (a·war·ra(w)) ['awara~a'waːrʌ~
'ᴅwʌrʌ] *n* (Guyn) ‖ *arrawah* [*X*], *ocherie*
(Guyn) A red or reddish-yellow ovoid fruit about
1-1/2 in long with tough skin covering a tough,
fibrous layer of pulp, of the same colour, on the
hard black shell of its large seed; it is borne in
very large bunches on a forest-palm that rises to
over 30 ft and is covered along its trunk and
branches with clusters of formidable, black
spines; *Arystocaryum tucumoides* (*Palmaceae*). **a.**
*A stone was .hurled at him. Two awara seeds hit
him in the chest. He did not retreat. Palm seeds.
Think of it. What children!*—RWIN:59 (E. Mittelholzer) **b.** *... and the fruits of palms which were
its favourites and which during times of abundance
it buried in the earth. Awarra fruits were its
favourite and when they were in season John was
away.*—SuC (76.09.19, p.13) [*BAED* Arawak,
awara 'spiney palm ... bearing red edible fruit']
□ The pl *awaras* is normal though in folk usage
a collective Cr pl is common *'plenty of awara in
the market'*, *'teeth yellow from eating awara'*,
etc. The spelling and pronunc *arrawah* are a
corruption by metathesis.

a·wa·ra-drink *n* (Guyn) A drink made from
the softened flesh of the AWARA fruits after burying them for several days (see cit b.). **a.** *The
biggest surprise you are likely to experience at
Orealla, is to see the villagers making awara drink.
You would have heard about all sorts of local and
home made drinks but Awara drink beats them
all.*—GyC (77.04.17, p.21) **b.** *The ripe orange-
coloured fruits of the awara palm are collected and
buried for two weeks. After that period they are
taken out and the flesh is scraped off from the seeds
and formed into balls. The balls are then mixed with
water and sweetened with sugar. Alternatively, the*

balls can be mixed with sugar-cane juice. The drink is now ready for use.—Balp, I.4:6

a·wa·ra-straw;   a.war.ra(w)-straw   *n* (Guyn) A straw made by stripping and drying the young leaves of the AWARA palm; it is much used as handicraft material. **a.** *He straightened himself from the packing of the eggs, and faced the white woman with the pretty awarra-straw basket.*—SBB:38 **b.** *She lifted the broad-rimmed awarra-straw hat from its bed on her forehead, looked up and down the busy street, and shuffled across in her nearly sole-less 'slip-slops'.*—SAGF: 14 **[**Cp *IAIG:259*, 'Instead of a bellows a fan of definite shape, woven of the young leaflets of a palm (*Astrocaryum tucumoides*) is used. *179*, 'The young leaves are ... used to make the fans ... which are an indispensable property of all Indians'**]**

away[1] *adv* (CarA) **1.** Abroad; overseas (esp in Britain or N Amer). **a.** *I bought this away.*—CGBD:4 **b.** *I know that you have a brother who is away studying law.*—DP:35 **[**Developed evid from the SE sense of *away* 'out of the country' as in 'He's gone away to Scotland', 'away over the ocean', etc, this particular sense dominates CE usage, prob for historical and geographical reasons**] 2.** PHRASES **2.1 away from** *prep phr* (Antg, Jmca, Trin) [*IF*] Except for; apart from. **a.** *I was home all last year, away from two weeks I was in St Kitts.*—(Antg) **b.** *It's only the chi[ld]ren, but away from that I would come.*—(Jmca) **c.** *But when you really come to look at it, oui! Away from Carnival we don['t] have a lot to offer the tourist in Trinidad, you know.*—(Trin) **[**By adv > prep shift. Cp similarly SE *apart (from)***] 2.2 from away** *adv phr; adj phr* (ECar) [*IF*] ‖ *from foreign* (Jmca) From abroad; foreign. *This is tantamount to saying that the only time one should bathe is when visitors are at the door! / But then this is a cargo culture where we put on our Sunday best to greet people from 'away'.*—SuP (79.10.07, p.4) **2.3 go away; gone away** *vb phrs* (CarA) [*IF*] To go abroad; to travel out of the island or territory. **a.** *It's a damn pity that some people forget they culture so fast, when they go Away!*—CPM:85 **b.** *EPF: Yer know, Esther. When yer grow up—It would be kind of nice if yer could go away and study—on a Island scholarship or something. Come back—Big! Yer know! Make everybody respect yer.*—JMRS:20 **c.** *I went away for August so I didn't get to go to the wedding.*—(Tbgo) **2.4 over-in-away** *adv*) (Bdos) [*AF*] Abroad (esp in Britain or N Amer). *It is related that ... a Guyanese returned from over-in-away bearing a large number of large packages addressed in large letters to the President of the Cooperative Republic*—NaT (92.10.22, p.6, O. Jackman)

away[2] *n* (CarA) [*IF*] ‖ *foreign* (Jmca) Any foreign land, usu one outside the Caribbean. **a.** *When I first began travelling abroad with a new frequency after adolescence came upon me, I used to be utterly taken by the oceanic dimensions of the outside world—or, 'away', a term we don't seem to hear so often in this day and age.*—Peo, 3.22:52

b. *The inference is that he who says 'breakfast' is a fool because of his Guyaneseness whereas the superiority of those who are more au fait with 'away' is taken for granted.*—GyG (69.12.10, p.11) **c.** *De waiters en gine notice yuh / Onless yuh from 'away'.*—Pel (77.12.09, J. Layne-Clark) **d.** *She prefers to work with people from away because they pay better.*—(StVn) **[**By nominalization of AWAY[1]. Cp AWAY[1] Phr 2.2**]**

away[3] *adj* (Bdos, Guyn, Trin) [*IF*] Foreign; belonging or related to or coming from some place abroad, esp Europe or N Amer. **a.** *This don['t] look like wood from here! It look like away wood.*—(Guyn) **b.** *It also stores relatively well for travel to away markets and maintains its freshness for a fair period when compared with other varieties. The pawpaw tree will grow virtually anywhere in Barbados.*—SuS (83.05.24, p.32) **c.** *Then there is no new work from new and younger playwrights. Playwrights in exile are writing for an alien stage for alien people to play local parts, which at any rate are sentimental and archaic, and best suited for Away stage.*—TrG (73.08.05) **[**By functional shift of AWAY[2] n. Cp similar adj development of SE *away* in relation to competitive sport—*away matches, wins*, etc**]**

a-we (a'we, awee) ['awi] *Cr pron* (Antg, Guyn, Mrat) [*AF—Cr*] See A(LL)-WE. □ The Cr form *a-we-dis*, with the focused sense 'we, not including you/them' (cp *ah-we-ya* (Antg)) survives only among rural, often East Indian, folk in *Guyn*.

A·wou·sah *n* (Crcu) See AUOUSAH

ax *vb tr* (CarA) See AKS

axe-man *n* (Trin) [*IF*] A person in authority who decides on the dismissal of employees. *There have been no recent dismissals although the axe-man is reported to be still wielding his blunt instrument in the search for disloyal, undisciplined subversives of the established order.*—TaP (75.11.16, p.3) **[**Analogical *axe* + *man*, in the sense of a person associated with or having charge of sth, esp common in CE, cp *cartman, dance man, rubbishman*, etc. For the sense cp also BrE *hatchet man*, AmE *hit man***]**

axe·mas·ter* *n* (Belz) ‖ *black ironwood* (Jmca) ‖ *ebony* 5 (Vils) ‖ *ironwood* (CarA) A forest timber of black and extremely dense, heavy texture; *Krugiodendron ferreum (Rhamnaceae)*—NPHT:62. *We have a wood in Belize we call the axemaster which must be one of the hardest woods in the world.*—Belz (Ms, 1978)

Ay-ay-ay! *excl* (CarA) See AI[2]

Ayo[1] *excl* (Trin) [*IF*] Goodbye. *Ayo, see you tomorrow then.*—AFSTE:15 **[**Fr Cr > Fr *adieu*, 'goodbye'**]**

ayo[2] *vb intr* (Trin) [*AF*] [Esp of a kite] To be cut loose and disappear; to fly away; to flee; to get lost. *When one of the threads gave way the* boys would call this 'ayo', after which there would be little possibility of the owner getting his kite back. The 'ayoed' kite would take a windy sail for miles over the Gulf of Paria until it dropped to the water or disappeared from sight.—ExP (76.02.08, p.25) [From Joc fuctional shift of AYO[1]]

a'you pron (CarA) See ALL-YOU

Ayuo! excl (Mrat) ‖ AI[2] (CarA) 1. Ayuo! Look wha[t] happenin[g] do[w]ng de[re]!—(Mrat)

azaan (azan) [a'za:n] (Guyn) The call to prayer for Muslims made five times daily by the muezzin, with both hands raised to his ears, from the left minaret or on the left side of the mosque. **a.** The muezzin said: 'I am sorry, I have to leave, the imam has just arrived and it's time for azaan.'—SDT:27 **b.** I woke early this morning in time to hear the muezzin of the masjid sound the azaan for worshippers.—Guyn (Ms, 1978) [Perso-Arabic adhaan Hin azaan 'call to prayer'] □ The spelling **azan**, occasionally seen, represents the pronunc less well.

B

-b- In Creolized E speech /-b-/ often replaces /-v-/, requiring spellings in dialogue such as *berry, bex, ebba, hab, lib, nebba, sabby, shub,* etc for 'very', 'vex', 'ever', 'have', 'live', 'savvy', 'shove', etc. This surviving Cr pronunc is prob accounted for by the absence of the sound /v/ from a large number of Niger-Congo langs (*WALS:51–52*) particularly W Afr langs wh were the orig langs of the bulk of the slaves.

B' [bə ~ bʌ ~ bʊ] [*AF*] [In folk tales] 'Brother', the title usu given to every male character except the King. *The folk-lore of the Bahamas is mostly concerning animals.... The popular stories deal with such subjects as 'B'baracouti an' b'man', 'B'parakeet and' b'frog' and 'B'loggerhead an' b'conch', etc.*—LISI:8 [By reduction from Bro[th]er > Bro > B']

baa·da (ba·da) *n* (Jmca) [*IF*] Respectful form of address used to a senior male relative, esp an uncle. [*Jmca* Cr, poss from Afr source (*DJE*)] □ Sometimes confused with *Jmca* Cr *bredda,* 'brother'—(*DJPCP:8*).

baa·ji *n* (Guyn, Trin) See BHAJI

baa·na *n* (USVI) [*AF—Vul*] ‖ BAM-BAM[1] (CarA)

baas [ba:s] *n* (Belz, Guyn, Jmca) [*AF*] Boss; master. *The grass ploughed up and fed into mortar of houses / for master for mister for massa for mortal baas.*—BMP:46 [Du *baas*, 'master', 'governor', 'boss'. Cp also such contexts as *hij is de baas van die koe* 'he is the master of this cow'. The word would have come in its orig form through long Du participation in the Slave Trade and reinforced in its use by its suitability to a number of contexts in Cr society. See also BOSS] □ Occasionally used in literary contexts for effect. See cit. Cp MASSA.

Bab *n* (Gren) [*AF—Joc/Derog*] A policeman. *No one can blame the 'Babs' because they are doing their duty. They have to obey commands even if (ironically) they are deranked in the end.*—ToR (76.08.25, p.6) [Joc abbr < BABYLON 2.]

Ba·ba[1] [ba:ba] *n* 1. (Dmca, Jmca) [*IF*] Term of respect used in addressing a father; folk title used before the name of a respected older male. *The Caribs greeted him as an old friend and presented a welcome ceremony of chants and gifts of food. Despite their kindness, Baba Raymond, as the Caribs called him, remained cautious.*—HTDS:20 [The term occurs in many langs of the Niger-Congo group. Cp *ADMY* Yoruba *baba*, 'father', any kinsman of the same generation as one's father'; (said to any senior male) Sir!; also Fulani *baaba*, father; also *ADHL* Hausa *baba*, father; namesake of one's father; also *SSBC* Shona *baba*, father; married man; etc] 2. (Belz) [*AF*] God (esp in the Cr expression /*tengk Baba*/ 'thank God'. *T[h]enk Baba, A reach home safe and sound.*—(Belz) □ A creolism that survives in familiar use at higher levels of *Belz* speech.

ba·ba[2] [ba:ba] (CarA) [*IF*] 1. A baby. *Come and look at the nice baba Auntie Jennie has.*—(Guyn) [Cp *DAFL* Twi [ɔ-ba] 'offspring, child, son', of wh *baba* may be an infantile reduplication popularized in Cr society; also Twi [ɔ-babaa], 'daughter'] □ Widely used in child talk in CE. 2. (Belz) [By extension] [*IF*] A baby's feeding bottle; the baby's feed. *Grace! Go wash de baby baba good an[d] clean.*—(Belz)

ba·ba[3] *vb intr* (Belz) [*AF*] To dribble. *A hate when people baba inna de[ir] sleep.*—(Belz) [By functional n > vb shift < Sp *baba*, 'spittle, slaver, drivel']

ba·bache (ba.bash) *n* (Trin) ‖ BUSH-RUM (Gren, etc) [Prob of Fr Cr orig. Cp *DECG babawaz*, name of a home-made rum-based drink of *Guad*]

ba·ba·deen; ba.ba.din *n* (Dmca, Trin) [*X*] (Erron spellings for) BARBADINE. *... pommes cytheres 6c and 8c ... babadeen 25c.*—TrG

ba·ba·lé (ba·ba·lait) ['babale ~ 'bɒbɒle] *n* (Gren) ‖ SOURSOP DRINK (CarA) *Soursop— Sweet-acid fruit used for ices and cooling drinks 'Babalait'.*—GNHIG:87

ba·ball *n* (Dmca, Gren, Tbgo, Trin) See BOBOL

ba·ba·woo·le (ba·ba·wu·le) *n* (Mrat) ‖ *bamba-wule, lady's yam* (Dmca) A type of yam 'with a lot of hairs on it'. *Babawoole is ready for reaping in September.*—Mrat (Ms)

ba·boo *n* (Guyn, Trin) See BABU

ba·boon *n* (CarA) [*AF—Derog*] Term of personal abuse implying ugliness and rough manners. *An[d] look [h]e face, de dam[n]* *baboon!*—(StVn) [Cp (*KED*) Krio *babu fes* (baboon face) 'very ugly face; person with such']

ba·boon-cap *n* (Belz) A shiny, yellow-skinned fruit about the size and shape of an egg, having a soft clammy, sweetish, highly-scented flesh around a hairy seed; it is borne on a tree of medium height with small leaves; *Couepia dodecandra.* **a.** ... *trees with guava, mayplum, even bananas and one had a patch of sweet potato, sweet-lemon, baboon-cap, breadfruit and wonderful to recall, one had a pomegranate tree.*—ReP (80.05.25, p.10) **b.** *Children love babooncap.*—Belz (Ms)

ba·bre·cut¹ (ba·bra·cot¹, ba·bri·cot, bar·ba·cot) *n* (Guyn) **1.** [Hist] A small framework platform made of dried limbs or sticks, raised several feet above the ground inside the hut, used by Amerindians for storing things or for sleeping on. *Bonny, who was advanced in years, ... and several others that could afford the trouble, always slept on a barbacot about 6 and sometimes 8 feet high above the surface of the earth.*—SJJS: 195 **2.** [By extension] A similar framework of sturdy green limbs about 2 or 3 ft above the ground, out of doors, for smoking or slow-roasting meat or fish; a wooden barbecue rack. **a.** *A babracot is a stage of green sticks, built over a fire, on which the meat is laid and exposed for a long time to the action of the smoke. Meat, fish and even eggs treated in this way become very tasteless, but retain their nutritive powers for a long while, and may either be eaten without further preparation or may be further cooked.*—IAIG:248 **b.** *The fish is cleaned and placed on a babricut over a moderate fire until cooked.*—Balp.I.4, p.3 □ Also attrib, hence **babrecut fish.** See next. **3.** [By extension] Preserved fish or meat smoked on a BABRECUT. ... *and some babrecut I didn't like the taste of.*—Guyn (Ms, 1978) **4.** An Amerindian hunter's platform built around the trunk of a tree to allow a better shot at game; a woodcutter's platform for felling trees. *After the tree was felled, usually from a 'babracot' (a structure of saplings on which he stood, to enable the feller to throw the tree at a point above the buttresses)...*—Tim:36 (1957) [*BAED* Arawak *barabakua* 'a low platform for storing anything in a house, in the yard or in a boat'. Cp also *DWPU* Papiamentu (Bonaire) *barbakoa* (= platform in a tree for chasing birds from a corn-field); also *DWSN* Surinamese Du *barbakot* (= wooden scaffold for a woodcutter). The ending -cot/-cut may be due to Du infl or to folk etym because of the use of the device for sleeping on] □ The spelling **barbacot**, nearest the Arawak original, is now obs (cit 1. is 1796). Guyn E **babrecot** is due to metathesis. ModE **barbecue** is another development of the same word, sense 2.

ba·bre·cut² (ba·bra·cot²) *vb tr* (Guyn) ‖ **cabane¹** 2 (Jmca) To smoke or roast fish or meat slowly on a *babrecot*, so as to preserve it. *As the provisions which he thus gets have to be carried home, often a journey of some days, and as even*

after that they have to last for some time, the meat and most of the fish is smoked and babracoted.—IAIG:248 [By functional n > vb shift of BABRACOT¹ 2.] □ The term, still in use in the *Guyn* hinterland, is not in urban use. The sense 'to preserve' is missing from ModE *barbecue*, vb.

ba·b(r)ee dove *n phr* (Guyn) A woodland bird, about 12 ins long, mostly brown in colour but with a greyish-white forehead, a blue-grey crown, red-circled eyes, and red legs; the grey-fronted dove or *Leptotila refaxilla* (*Columbidae*). *Babee dove eats sweeter than chicken.*—(Guyn) [Prob < *Barbary Dove* though this name is applied to a different dove in *BBWI:108*] □ Prob related to the GROUND-DOVE (*CarA*).

ba·bu (ba·boo); **ba.bu-man** *n* (Belz, Guyn, Jmca, Trin) **1.** [AF—Derog] An old East-Indian man, usu bearded and poor. **a.** *Don't you worry with them baboos you see beggin[g] about the street, yo[u] se[e]! I[t]'s when they dead you hear ho[w] much money they find on them.*—(Guyn) **b.** *Yesterday we see a old babu-man passin[g] he[re] wit[h] a stick in [h]e han[d] an[d] a ol[d] bundle on [h]e back.*—(Trin) **2.** [By extension] [AF—Derog] Any adult male of unsightly appearance. *How you could dress in yellow pants? You want to make yo[ur]self a dam[n] babu?*—(Guyn) **3.** [By extension] [AF—Joc] ‖ **booboo-man** (Belz, Guyn, Tbgo, Trin) An imaginary, ugly old man, referred to in order to frighten young children. **a.** *The mother said, 'If you don't behave yourself I will let the baboo-man come for you tonight.'*—Trin (Ms, 1982) **b.** *I will let baboo take you, too!*—(Belz) **4.** Respectful form of address to an elderly man, usu with a beard. *Salaam Baboo* (= *Good morning, Sir*).—Belz (Ms, 1982) [< Hin *babu*, 'Mr, a respectful form of address; an educated man'. The term evid retains some of that status in *Belz* (sense 4.), though it has suffered pejoration in E (see *OED Baboo*, esp cits from 1866 ff) wh remains in general CE usage]

ba·by¹ *n* ['Newborn child' and extended senses] **1.** (Bdos) [Child talk] A doll. [Cp *OED baby* 2. 'a doll, puppet' (*Obs*)] **2.** (Gren, StVn) [Child talk] A bud or the soft seed of a pod. *The spongy male bud of the breadfruit, or the 'breadfruit baby', is used in play by children.*—Guyn (Ms) **3.** (Gren, Jmca) The silken strands appearing as an ear of Indian corn ripens. **4.** PHRASES **4.1** ‖ **eye-baby** (Guyn, Jmca) The pupil of the eye, often called ‖ **the baby of the eye.** *The baby o[f] she eye grey, like a cat one.*—(Bdos) [A likely Afr calque. Cp Yoruba *omo l'oju* (child in eye) 'pupil of the eye'; also Nupe *egi eye* (child eye) 'pupil of the eye', etc] **4.2 be in the baby's way** *vb phr* (Nevs, StKt) To be pregnant; to be in the family way. *My daughter is in the baby's way for the past six months.*—Nevs (Ms, 1978) **4.3 get/make (a) baby (for sb)** *vb phr* (CarA) [IF] To be visibly pregnant; to be with child by a certain man. **a.** *He told the magistrate that at the time he was not working and his wife was 'getting baby' so he stole the purse with the hope of paying for medical treatment for his wife.*—GyC (75.12.22, p.2) **b.**

You would believe it was the same man she was makin[g] a baby for that turn roun[d] and beat her?—(Tbgo) **4.4 take the baby** *vb phr* [Of a doctor] To perform an abortion.

ba·by[2] *vb* (Trin) [*IF*] **1.** To be visibly pregnant; to be in the family way. *Some news of Jennifer, the last time I saw her she was babying, my dear, but I don't think she has had it yet.*—Trin (Ms, 1983) **2.** (Tbgo, Trin) To nurse (an injury); to treat (an injury) with very noticeable concern. *He sat babying his fractured wrist.*—Trin (Ms, 1980) **3.** [*AF*] (Gren) [Of an ear of corn] To put out the first silken strands as it begins to ripen. *Eh! This corn baby early. Mus[t] be the weather!*—(Gren)

ba·by-bush *n* **1.** (Nevs) ‖ LEAF-OF-LIFE (Bdos, etc) *A bush-tea made from the leaves of baby-bush is used in Nevis for teething troubles.*—Nevs (Ms, 1973) **2.** (StVn) ‖ CHRISTMAS-BUSH (CarA)

ba·by-chill/-cold *n* (Belz, Jmca) ‖ LYING-IN COLD (Antg, etc) *After delivery it is believed that the woman is particularly vulnerable to 'chilling of the blood', a condition known as 'baby-chill'. She must avoid washing her hair and covers her head in a turban.*—Pra No.1278, V.213:850

ba·by-cu·cum·ber *n* (Guyn) ‖ **baby-pump-kin** (Guyn) ‖ **lizard-food** **2.** (Bdos) A soft, oblong fruit about 2 ins long and an inch in diameter, with a thin skin and rich pulp wh are both red when ripe, embedding small brown seeds; it is borne on a wild, massively parasitic, leafy vine with white flowers; *Coccinia indica* (*Cucurbitaceae*). *The paling was covered with the vine of the baby cucumber and what the birds left we children would sometimes eat.*—Guyn (Ms) □ Evid sometimes called WILD CUCUMBER in *Bdos* and 'used to play BABY POT'; a fruit fitting the description found growing wild in *Bdos* is identified as *Coccinia grandis*—GLPFB:413.

ba·by-fath·er (**ba·by's father**) *n* (*phr*) (Jmca) [*IF*] ‖ **child-father** (Bdos, Guyn) A man who is the father of an unmarried mother's child. **a.** *As the baby-father you are expected to support the child whether you live with your baby-mother or not.*—Jmca (CR, 1978) □ Cp also BABY-MOTHER.

ba·by ice-ap·ple *n phr* (Guyn) A small, glossy, red, ovoid berry about one centimetre in diameter with one seed embedded in a sweet, juicy, creamy, white-brown pulp; it is borne on a low shrub with branches of small pink flowers, sometimes used as a hedge plant; *Ixora spp* (*Rubiaceae*)—(*OGEP:2*).

ba·by-lime* *n* (Guyn) ‖ **Chinese lemon** (Jmca) ‖ **lime-berry** (Trin) An oval-shaped berry about half-an-inch long, with a bright red, oily rind with blackish dots, and sticky, greenish-white pulp around one or two greenish seeds; it is borne on a spiky shrub about 6 ft high; *Triphasia trifolia* (*Rutaceae*)—(*OGEP:3*).

Ba·by·lon [ˈbabɪlʌn] *n* (CarA) [*AF*] [Rastaf] **1.** Any Western-style society or government and its supporters, particularly in the Caribbean; the Caribbean Establishment. *The many young people who are frustrated and disillusioned about the so-called 'Babylon' society cannot just be told to be patriotic and show loyalty to our political leaders when there are many unanswered questions about the conduct of public business.*—NeC (75.09.13, p.4) **2.** The police; a policeman; a fireman or any agent employed in the established protective services of any (Caribbean) society. *Those devils only brutalize poor people, when they patrol in strength, you know, gun or no gun. They're a bunch of cowards, most of them. They only have brass face and gun play for poor defenceless people. This same West Kingston can bear plenty witness to that, plenty witness to Babylon brutality, from the time Black man first turn policeman.*—SJT: 80 **3.** Any of the great white Western powers, esp the United States of America. *Our moral disintegration began when we began to adore and lust for Babylon, and many of our so-called leaders encouraged Babylon system, their argument being that they were fighting communism. Babylon, you see, was not to send us her wheat fields, ... or her petroleum deposits. No, Babylon sent us her gangsters, ... her drugs, her filthy, decadent movies, books, magazines, ... and Belize became another garbage heap for Babylon's waste.*—AmA (80.06.13, p.2) **4.** Anyone who approves or seeks after material wealth and security by political, commercial, or dishonest means; anyone who disapproves of, or does not spiritually adopt and support or practise RASTAFARIANISM. *Others say Rasta hates Babylon and society. Babylon represents those who take bribes to do their jobs. Babylon represents the police who brutalise mankind for promotion and fame.... Babylon represents the society that says 'money comes first and humanity second'. Babylon represents the nation that spends money on weapons of war rather than on weapons of peace. Babylon represents the politician who tries to fool the people by making promises knowing full well that he will never fulfil them. I and I say that Babylon must fall.*—ExP (79.12.01, p.5) [Bibl ref to 'Babylon', by members of the RASTAFARIAN cult, as the seat or symbol of wickedness, pride and defiance of God, as described, for ex, in Isaiah Ch 47. Originating in *Jmca*, the term has spread throughout the CarA with the RASTAFARIAN cult] □ The name is also often used attrib, as may be seen in cits. It is also subject to much *Joc* usage by educated persons outside the RASTAFARIAN cult throughout the CarA.

Ba·by·lon-land *n* (Jmca) [*AF*] Jamaica; [by extension] any country or State in wh the RAS-TAFARIANS condemn the national life-style. *That man, that said Dr Buxton, was for us, the poor of Babylon-land. For us, I tell you! He was for us and they had was to take him away from us, I can see that. Babylon government really couldn't sit back and see us grounding with Bredda Buxton. That dangerous...*—SJT:38 [BABYLON (senses 1., 3.) + *land* 'country'. A Cr semantic redup]

ba·by-moth·er (ba·by's moth·er) *n* (*phr*) (Jmca) [*IF*] ‖ *child-mother* (Bdos, Guyn) An unmarried mother, usu with a recognized relationship with her child's father. *Two girls have three children for him. One baby-mother is in America and the other is in the country.*—DaG (66.12.11, p.4, Magazine) □ Cp also BABY-FATHER.

ba·by-pot *n* (Guyn) ‖ *dolly-pot* (Antg) Children's make-believe cooking, played as a game together. *The children were playing baby-pot in the yard with mud cakes and leaves and seeds.*—Guyn (Ms, 1976)

ba·by-pump·kin *n* (Guyn) ‖ BABY-CUCUMBER

ba·ca·lao (bac·ca·low); back.a.yow, ba-.cle.ow [bakalʊ~bakaydʊ] *n* (CarA) [*AF*] 1. Saltfish; salted codfish. 2. [*Vul*] The unwashed female pudenda. [< Pg *bacalhau*, 'codfish' or Sp *bacalao, bacallao*, 'codfish'. Cp also *FNEW* Sran *Bakjau* 'American dried fish. (Port)'. Sran having no notable Sp infl, the term is more prob a Pg loan surviving from slave times and reinforced in later times at the folk level by contact with Portuguese indentured labourers, or labour contacts with Spanish-speaking CarA countries. Cp also *DCHP* Canadian E BACCALAO (< Pg *bacalhao*, 'codfish') (*G.1779*) 'dried codfish'; also BACCALAOS, the Atlantic codfishing grounds from Labrador to Nova Scotia] □ Particularly common in Joc contexts in *Trin*.

ba·ca·no(e) (ba·ca·nole) ['bakano(l)] *n* (Tbgo, Trin) ‖ TRUMPET-BUSH (Bdos, etc) [See BWA-KANO]

bac·cha·nal (bac·ca·nal) [bakana·l] /1'12/ *n* (Tbgo, Trin) [*AF*] 1. Very noisy merry-making; noisy fun (often with strong sexual overtones). **a.** *'We'll have the steelband playing, roti, rum, baccahanal! We going to have a fete big as Carnival,' Miss Cleothilda called out.*—LDCD:203 **b.** *... Ray Burnett had bent over her shoulder to whisper: 'Elizabeth Grant is one bacchanal girl, she could hold people attention like fire man. That is craft!'*—JJM:44 [< Fr *bacchanale* n f. 'uproarious dance, orgy, drunken revel', also *bacchanal* n m. 'uproar, row'. The words (very old in Fr, n f. 1155 m m. 1559 (*LLFL*) would have entered through Trin Fr Cr society esp in relation to pre-lenten carnival revelry] 2. [By extension] A vulgar brawl; a spectacular row or fight. **a.** *'Phyllissia had a fight at school today,' Mother explained. / He looked into my face and bellowed, 'Christ, but it must have been one bacchanal. But don't tell me. I know it's the other girl I have to shed a tear over.'*—GTF:22 **b.** *That is the only solution I can see to the Tobago question after all the bacchanal in Parliament last week when the island's two Members of Lower House clashed.*—BoM (70.06.29. p, 10) 3. [By extension] Chaos; a state of the most noisy and complete confusion. *'Man, I tell you—I there minding me own business. People to the right of me breaking things. People to the left of me breaking*

things. People all around raising all kinds of bacchanal, and they pick me. Me!' He put both hands to his chest...—GTF:66 4. [By extension] A scandal; a cause for great grief; very disreputable conduct; corruption. *Everyone doing what the jackass they like, the country running itself and everything running to the dogs. What this place needs is a strong hand to make all of these jump-me-up people work for their living. To stop the bacchanal short.*—JJM:90

bac·cha·nal·ism *n* (Trin) The desire for or the pursuit of gaiety and rough revelry. *The big tadjahs were on the streets of St James and San Juan—the two focal points for the celebration of 'Hosay'—last night.... The organisation ... condemned what it termed the revelry, the alcoholic splurge and the bacchanalism 'which now surrounds what was once a very solemn and sorrowful occasion'.*—ExP (73.02.14, p.28) [*Bacchanal* + SE suff *ism* 'typical condition of']

bac·coo (bac·cou, bac(k)·oo, bak·(k)oo) *n* (Bdos, Crcu, Gren, Guyn, Trin) ‖ *mons* (Dmca) An active, wicked spirit believed to take the form of some small, living, partly human being, that must be kept in a bottle and may be commanded either to bring its owner great wealth or to do harm to other persons; [by extension] an unknown evil spririt under sb's control, buried or hidden somewhere to do harm to another. **a.** *The hushed rumour is that the deaths were more than a coincidence and the curse of the baccoo is stalking the group. Baccoo is believed to be an Amerindian obeah.*—BoM (75.01.03, p.24) **b.** *'I know a man who had a bakoo,' said Gee. 'All of a sudden this man get a lot of money. He used to buy bananas to feed this bakoo 'pon. And one day the bakoo escape from the bottle he used to keep it in and smash up everything in the man house. From that day he couldn't sleep at night. He start imagining this bakoo come back to kill he. In the end he go mad.'*—HMCH:68 [Cp *FNEW* Sran, *bakroe* 'dwergspook; Kabouterman' (dwarf-ghost; elf) also *WSN* Saramaccan *bakulu*, 'dwerg-geest; kabouter' (dwarf-spirit; elf). The word, evid spreading from *Srnm* through *Guyn* to the ECar, is of Afr orig < Proto Niger-Congo pl prefix *ba* + *ku* (root for) 'death, corpse', etc, whence 'from a generalized Niger-Congo point of view, *baku* has the etymological meaning of 'the dead', 'spirits' or 'ghosts''—(*pers info*, Prof R.G. Armstrong). Cp also (*HMNP:254–258*) an account of *bakru* showing several 'points of resemblance' between Georgia Negro folklore and '... Paramaribo, Dutch Guiana, where the belief in the dwarfs called *bakru* causes mothers to instil in their children much ... fear ... These dwarfs, half wood, half flesh, are 'given' by a practitioner of evil magic to a client who wishes wealth. They 'work' for their owner; should someone try to strike them, they present the wooden side and then kill the one who has tried to harm them' (*pp.254–255*)] 2. [By extension] A poltergeist; a wicked spirit that will molest a house for a long time by causing solid objects to fly about, scaring but not hurting any human beings. ... *but if it is sent for evil purposes it will cause stones to fall on your house, clothes to fall off the line and other unpleasant phenomena. The bacoo is usually associated with children just reaching puberty.*—Gren (Ms, 1976) **3.** [By extension] [*AF—Joc*] Any ugly person, esp a short man.

bac·cra *n, adj* (CarA) See BACKRA

ba·cha *n* (USVI) [*AF*] ‖ BACHIE (Guyn, Trin)

ba·chac(k) (ant) (ba·chak, bat·chac) *n* (Tbgo, Trin) ‖ ACOUSHI ANT(S) (Guyn) *Bachac ants plod by the thousand along their well-kept highways, strip the vegetation of its foliage with neat semicircular incisions and transport the severed bits to their nest, there to chew them into a mulch. On this mulch the ants cultivate the fungus that is their sole food.*—ACTT:173 [Perh from a So Amer Ameridian lang. Cp *DWPU* Papiamentu (Curaçao) *badjaka* 'kind of large ant'; also *TDV* Venz Sp *bachaco* 'a large and voracious ant, reddish and sometimes black in colour, of wh many species are known' + cit-1950 'The bachacos carry pieces of green leaves to their nests to store them to feed on later']. □ The commonest spelling *bachac*, pl *bachacs*, is pref.

ba·che·lor *adj* (Guyn, Trin) [*AF*] PHRASE **live bachelor** *vb phr* ‖ LIVE BACHIE See BACHIE 2. Phr *The son is often eager to leave his parents' home and to set up quarters for himself—to 'take manship on my account' and to 'live bachelor'.*—RLCF:161

ba·che·lor's but·ton* *n phr* (CarA) ‖ *dame-and-cavalier* (Dmca) A small flower with stiff petals in a globular cluster ranging in colour from white to deep purple, and borne profusely on a bushy plant about 2 or 3 ft tall, easily cultivated in gardens or pots; *Gomphrena globosa* (*Amaranthaceae*). *The bright purple of the bachelor's buttons contrasted sharply with the seared yellow of the pumpkin vine which was growing among some rocks.*—SuS (80.10.26, p.29) [A European name for a number of such daisy-like flowers (See *CED*) but evid particularized in the CarA] □ [*IF*] *bachelor button*, sometimes [*F*] *bachelors' buttons*.

bach·ie (bach·y, bat·chie, bat·chy) [bači] (Guyn, Trin) [*AF*] ‖ *bacha* (USVI) ‖ *bachelor* (Guyn, Trin) **1.** *n* A room or other small place where a man lives alone or wh is maintained by a man for private love affairs. *The meetings began to get more and more infrequent ... and she found out that other women were visiting his 'batchie', some of them schoolgirls too ... and they drifted apart.*—BoM (74.06.07, p.9) **2.** *adj* PHRASE **live bachie/bachelor** *vb phr* (Guyn, Trin) [Esp of a man] To live alone in a BACHIE. *The young men nowadays, and the young women too, want to go off, as soon as they get a job and live bachie.*—(Guyn)

back¹ *n* (CarA) **1.** [Referring to the human body] Bodily strength; [by extension] sexual vigour. *Piaba is a bush good for de back, man piaba*

fo[r] de man, an[d] woman piaba fo[r] de woman.—(Guyn) **2.** [Referring to a building] (CarA) The rear section of a home esp the kitchen or lavatory; the yard space behind a front house or building. **a.** *There was a knocking at the door while she was at the back and she pushed off her apron and hurried to see who it was.*—Guyn (Ms, 1977) **b.** *She gone in the back.*—(Bdos) **c.** *He was living in the back of the Cinema.*—Gren (Ms, 1978) [Cp *OEDS back* sb¹ 3. b. 'a room at the back of a house on the first, second or third floor'. Also *OEDS back*—A. 5. exs *back-garden, back-kitchen*, etc] **3.** [Referring to land] (Guyn) ‖ BACK-LANDS (Guyn) *Judge: What place did you see him then? / Witness: The same place, in Success back, half way between the canes and the plantain walk.*—LMSPJS:25 □ This may be common ex-colonial usage. Cp *WDAC* Australian *back block, back country, outback*, referring to areas far from water or settled districts. Also *DSAE:2* So Afr *backveld* 'rural areas remote from city life'. Also *DCHP* Canadian *back clock, back country, backlands, backsettler*, etc with the same connotation. **4.** PHRASES **4.1. be glad to see the back of (sb)** *vb phr* (CarA) [*IF*] ‖ *be glad to get the rid of (sb)* (Bdos) To want very much to see (sb) go away and not return; to be anxious to see (sb) resign or quit a job. *He was a disaster as Principal of the Training College. The Ministry was too glad to see the back of him!*—(Bdos) **4.2 be on (sb's) back** *vb phr* (CarA) [*IF*] To harass, press or persistently worry (sb to do sth). *The children were on my back to go to the drive-in but I was just too tired to move.*—(Guyn) □ Cp *IF* SE *get off my back*, as *OEDS back* sb¹ 23. d. **4.3. behind God's back** *adv phr* See BEHIND¹ Phr 3. **4.4 burst (sb's) back** *vb phr* (Dmca) [*AF*] ‖ POUND (SB'S) NAME (CarA) See POUND Phr 3.2 *Because they are not on good terms with Mrs B—they burst her back.*—Dmca (Ms, 1977) **4.5 keep/put clothes on sb's back** *vb phr* (CarA) [*IF*] See CLOTHES¹ Phr **4.6 on the back of it** *adv phr* (Bdos) In addition; what is worse. **a.** '*And you laughing,' his mother said. 'You kill the neighbour pumpkin vine, and on the back of it you laugh?'*—LICMS:9 [Cp *OED back* sb¹ 23. e. *on, upon the back of* 'close behind'] **4.7 rob (sb) belly and back** *vb phr* See BELLY Phr 3.2

back² *adj* (CarA) **1.** Situated in the rear part or behind. *The last thing he did before he died was to get a carpenter to repair the weather side of the house, the back wall as well as the back fence.*—Guyn (Ms, 1984) [By functional shift of BACK¹ n. Cp also *OED back—in comb* 4.—'more commonly written in two words'] □ See also BACKDAM, BACK-GALLERY, BACK HOUSE, BACKSTEP. **2.** [*IF*] In arrears; owed. *Then the landlord decided he could not accommodate me any longer since I owed him back rent.*—ExP (73.08.12, p.1) [Cp SE *back pay* and see *OEDS back* a. 3.]

back³ *vb tr* **1.** (CarA) To carry (any heavy load) on the head, shoulder, back or by hand. *In the old days the women made some money backing salt in baskets from the salt ponds.*—TkCa (Ms, 1978) [Functional shift of *back¹* 1. esp as the load is mostly carried on the labourer's back. Cp *KWS: 17* 'Back is the accepted verb meaning carry something on one's back in a basket, with the strap handle across the forehead or around crossed wrists. (Caymanians once kept their yards beautiful by 'backing' sand from the beach and spreading it smoothly over the yard'] □ Cp also DROGUE. **2.** (Belz) [By extension] [*IF— Derog*] To carry (news); to bear (tales). *The main thing is these interfering Bessie who back the news.*—HF:14 □ Cp also CARRY-GO-BRING-COME (*Jmca*). **3.** (CarA) To stand with your back to (sb or some place). **a.** *Don't back me when I'm talking to you please.*—(Guyn) **b.** *On 28th April 1970 I was staying up talking with Myrtle and Lucille talking. I was backing Emmerton Lane.*— Bdos (CR, 71.05.25) □ Noted in AmE (*WCD9* 4. back vb 3. 'to have the back in the direction of sth') but not in BrE. **4.** (CarA) ‖ *back-up* (CarA) [Entertainment] To improvise and co-ordinate (a band's) instrumental, and sometimes background vocal, accompaniment for a singer of CALYPSO, REGGAE or similar folk ballad. **a.** *The Blue Rhythm Combo will back calypsonians the Mighty Destroyer, Styler, Grynner, and Dragon while the Checkmates will back Pitch-up and Liar.*—AdN (79.06.27, p.2) **b.** *It features a tune written by Cuthert Browne and titled 'I'm Too Old' and one by Boo Rudder titled 'In My Dreams'. Both are vocals with very solid backing and are in the popular disco beat.*—NaT (76.10.31, Al's Grapevine) [From the sense of 'backing up', 'supporting'] □ See BACKING GROUP. **5.** (ECar) [*IF*] To take off your jacket or shirt intending to labour or to fight. *The Minister for Communications and Works would never back his jacket to cut a cane hole, the leader of the House could never be approached to take off his jacket and cut a cane hole.*—Bdos (Hd, 74.06.21, p.3657) [Cp *OED back* v 15. 'to push back' as in cit from Dickens 'Backing his chair a little'] **6.** *vb intr* (Guyn) To reply tartly. *... and a female voice backed: 'But is who tell him me want a break?'* —SBB:22 **7.** (Grns) To cut open the back of a fish for corning with salt. *... a sharp kitchen knife she used for backing fish.*—Grns (Ms, 1973)

back⁴ *adv* (CarA) **1.** [Often followed by *in, home, there, where*] In or at a place from wh the speaker comes. **a.** *Back in the States, Blacks would fix up a guy like that one time!*—(BrVi) **b.** *All of a sudden ah hear dis big noise poundin on our front door. Man it was dark—dark inside in dey back wey me an meh sista an our crazy brodder was.*—Aaw.1.2, p.23 **2.** *As part of vb phr* [*IF*] **(i)** [Ref to an action] In retaliation; in return; in reciprocation; in reply. **a.** *The accused asked her to leave his yard and when she didn't do so immediately, he chuck her, she chucked him back, ... then he struck her the blow which fractured her jawbone.*—LaS (78.05.20, p.12) **b.** *Tobin told the magistrate that he had lost several things in the Barrack Room so he 'decided to steal back, but was unfortunate.'*—CzN (77.01.24, p.3) **c.** *After the others had gone, Brother C. told me that he had heard back that very afternoon from my 'godfather' and that it was all arranged for me to*

leave Mahaica on the following day.—CBM:28 [In ModE this use of 'back' occurs in bound phrasal vbs *call back, give back, pay back*, etc, whereas in CE it is used freely with a strong retaliatory sense] **(ii)** [Ref to the repeating of an action or the return of a condition] Again; once more. **a.** *Anyway this man's car went to get repair so I could not see him but he would phone me. Now that he has back the car I don't see him and he doesn't call like before.*—PeL (80.03.21, p.12, Dear Christine) **b.** *The calypsonian said that he would sing the song back so we could hear the words properly.*—Trin (Ms, 1978) [Cp *OED back* adv 7. 'in reversal of action or change ... so as to restore former circumstances or relations'] □ *IF* CE uses *back* widely as a free verb-linked suffix. Other exs: **ask back for sth, close back, get up back ~ get back up, go in back, mend back, use back**, etc. See further phrs below. They are not admissible in Formal E. **3.** PHRASES **3.1 [a]gree back** *vb phr* (Bdos, Gren, Guyn) [*X*] See AGREE Phr 2.1 **3.2 beg back (your papers)** *vb phr* (Bdos, Guyn, Tbgo) [*AF*] See BEG Phr 2.1 **3.3 make back** *vb phr* (Bdos, Guyn, Tbgo) [*IF/AF*] See MAKE Phr 5.9 **3.4. talk back** *vb phr* (Bdos, Guyn, Tbgo) [*AF*] See separate entry.

back-a-bush (back-bush) *adj* (Jmca) [*AF*] Of or situated at a place or places in the far-away countryside. *Several conferences with the authorities, who lack sufficient manpower to station constables in remote 'Back-a-Bush' villages, have been held and are continuing.*—WeG (73.10.03, p.19) [BACK⁴ 2. adv (of place) + *Cr* A⁷ ('in, at the') + *bush*. The second alternative may be < BACK², adj + *bush*]

back·a·na·han(d) *adj* (Belz) [*AF*] Tricky; obviously untrustworthy; known to have a catch in it. *Do de t[h]ing right or no do am! No come wid yo[ur] backanahan[d] way!*—(Belz) [< *back + under + hand*, a blend of *backhand* (< SE *backhanded*, 'equivocal') + *underhand*, with creolized under > /anda/ > /ana/]

back-and-bel·ly ['bakanbeli] /1'122/ *n* [*AF*] (Guyn) ‖ *back-and-neck* (StKt) ‖ *mauger-yow* (Guyn) **1.** A very thin, skin-and-bones person, esp a woman. *She is just like if she don't eat good food. She should shame the way the clothes just hang [u]pon she, just back-and-belly.*—(Guyn) **2.** ‖ *panya machete* (Belz, Jmca) 1. ‖ *Spanish bill/ cutlass/machete* (Jmca, USVI) A machete or farmer's cutlass sharpened on both edges (i.e. on the straight back and curved belly, hence the name). **3.** [By extension] ‖ *panya machete* (Belz, Jmca) 2. ‖ *Spanish machete* (Jmca) [*AF*] A very deceitful person; sb who causes harm to both sides by carrying news back and forth. *Considering the fact that they are friends, she should not have said such a terrible thing about her. She is a real 'back-and-belly' rat.*—Jmca (Ms, 1978) [Metaph transfer of sense 2.]

back-and-neck *n* (StKt) [*AF—Derog*] ‖ BACK-AND-BELLY (Guyn) 1. *Hire car went a tuŋg go* *put poor Bum Bum pan ice / Fuh a week—/ Luk say he a back an' neck. / Dem get dead bax ou four hundrid dalla*. (= 'Hire cars went to town to put poor Bum Bum on ice / for a week / Looks as if he was just skin-and-bones / They got a coffin for four hundred dollars')—LMFF:22 ['Back-and-neck' is used to refer to the neck and back portion of chicken usually sold as one piece ... the cheapest part of chicken that one can buy in St Kitts/Nevis' (mostly bone and very little flesh)—*J. Flemming*]

back·an·swer[1] *n* (CarA) [*IF*] ‖ *back-talk*[1] (CarA) ‖ *high-cheeks* (StVn) ‖ *hot-mouth* (Guyn) **1.** A saucy reply; a quick, embarrassing reply from a young person or a subordinate. **a.** *And she would answer, 'Who lookin' at you? Me? Well, an' you must be lookin' at me, too.' And that, Gurudeva would find, was 'too much back-answer'; and he would right away busy himself on her with fist or foot, or with almost anything he could catch hold of.*—NAGOS:29 **b.** *All you woman got too much back-answer in you mouth. Shut up I say!*—RTCS:6 [< BACK[4] 2.(i) + *answer*] **2.** PHRASES **2.1 give/got/have back-answer(s)** *vb phr* (CarA) [*IF*] ‖ *have hot-mouth* (Guyn) [*AF*] To answer impudently; to backchat. **a.** *Oh–ho, you giving back answers too! You getting on preposterous! You getting on a high horse, you playing in-dignant!*—SABS:175 **b.** *Don't worry to give me no back-answers. I ain't taking no rudeness from you.*—ELFBB:7 **c.** *She got so much o[f] back-answer when you talk to her—nobody have back-answer like she have, A tell you.*—(StVn)

back·an·swer[2] *vb* (CarA) [*IF*] ‖ *back-talk*[2] (CarA) ‖ *give (sb) high-cheeks* (StVn) ‖ *give (sb) hot-mouth* (Guyn) To make a ready and rude reply to a superior. **a.** *Child! Before you do what I say you only looking to back-answer me.*—(StVn) **b.** *All she knows to do is to back-answer people—that's why she can'[t] keep work.*— (Guyn) □ By functional shift of BACK-ANSWER[1]. More emotive than current E *answer back* 'make impudent answer'.

back-a-wall *n* (Jmca) [*AF*] See BACK-O'-WALL

back·a-yow *n* (Guyn) [*AF*] See BACALAO

back-back *vb* (CarA) [*X*] ‖ *back-to-back* (Guyn) **1.** To move or cause to move backwards; to step back; to reverse (a vehicle). **a.** *... an de doctor bird back backin quick quick outa de flowers and gone.*—BMP:69 **b.** *He went on: 'The accused was still coming at me and I was backing back when I saw someone grab him from behind by his collar.'*—DeM(SK) (61.08.05, p.4) **c.** *The cab stopped, several yards away from her. And the driver (a big, strapping man) siddown and watch the old lady totter up the road, parcels and all, and wouldn't back-back one inch to help her.*—WeG (75.04.08, p.15) [A Cr redundant compound] **2.** [By extension] [*AF—Joc*] To change your mind; to go back on a decision. **a.** *If the people read this, that you are going to write off their arrears, you can understand they are going to*

back-back; so you had better introduce and write off early and start early.—Bdos (Hd, 76.10.12, p.55) **b.** *But this time only the unpredictable Bishop Webster might be around to bless the statue due to arrive here from China. The Adventists have started backing back, the Anglicans do not worship false idols—animate or inanimate— Chandu's congregation are bound to outvote him again.*—NeJ (74.11.15, p.6)

back·bone PHRASE **get in (sb's)backbone (to do sth)** *vb phr* (Jmca) [*AF*] See BEHIND[1] Phr 1

back-bull *n* (Guyn) A semi-circular piece of brown paper attached to the top end of a SINGING ANGEL kite to produce a buzzing sound as the kite flies high. *I got kind of mixed up with the front bull and the side bull and the back bull. But the two rows of frills I put on did give the kite a rakish cut.*—SuC (76.04.18, p.7)

back-dam (back·dam) *n* (Guyn) [Sugar Ind] **1.** A dam constructed to demarcate the rear boundary of an estate. It becomes a dam because it is usually required to perform the function of protecting the estate from flooding while also providing passage for persons, and sometimes vehicles, at the rear of the estate.—*(pers info, P. Allsopp)*. *Beyond the canefields was the back dam, the limit of the plantation, and beyond the back dam was the bush, just visible as a deep-green smudge.*—NR:10 **2.** [By extension] The area of land beyond the cane-fields of a sugar estate on wh estate labourers do provision farming. *A canecutter, who launched a cutlass attack on a tractor driver because he refused to take him into the back-dam of Leonora Estate will have to serve a two year term of imprisonment.*—GyC (76.07.12, p.3) **3.** [By extension] An area of land far away from a village assigned to the villagers for pro-vision farming. *He listened to other complaints and promised that there would be adequate supplies of foodstuff made available at Kwapau and for those in the backdam and he pledged also to look into improved sanitation and medical and emergency facilities.*—SuC (77.05.15, p.1) □ The *back dam* (two words) is a dam, but the sense of the term is dominated more by its great distance from the front-lands of the plantation than by its function as an engineering device. Hence BACKDAM (properly one word, senses 2., 3.) has developed the general sense of an area far re-moved and is applied to distant farm-land.

back·door *n* (Guyn) [*IF*] A back entrance; [by extension] a back way (out of sth or some difficulty). *The sea ain't got no backdoor,* ((1.) *You must know to swim if you are in a boat;* (2.) *there is no easy way out of certain difficulties).*— Guyn (Prov) □ The wider IAE 'a back way (in to some privilege)' is also current.

back-feed *vb tr* (CarA) [Sugar Ind] To supply the stored BAGASSE, as fuel to the boilers by hand when that wh is automatically supplied from the ground canes has halted. *The contraption was intended to reduce employment at the same time as* *it destroyed the valuable raw material. For its successful performance would have meant a reduction in the number of bagasse house men; doing away with the need for baling bagasse, also the necessity to use men for back-feeding the boilers when grinding operations were suspended for one reason or another.*—LaS (65.04.06, p.1) **[** < SE *back* vb 'support, help' + *feed* vb**]**

back-foot *n* (CarA) **1.** The hind leg (of an animal). **a.** *The horse broke a back-foot and they had to shoot it.*—(Guyn) **b.** *Nancy stan[d] up on [h]e back foot and say, 'Not me!'*—StVn (Folktale) **2.** [Cricket] The batsman's leg placed behind the crease. **3.** *PHRASE* **3.1 off the back-foot** *adv phr* (CarA) [Of a batsman] Standing on the right leg (behind the crease) and hitting the ball very sharply and contemptuously. *It was a short-pitched ball and he played a wonderful shot off the back-foot and hooking it for a straight four.*— Bdos(B) **[** < Cr *foot* 'the whole leg'**]**

back-gal·ler·y *n* (Guyn) The rear section of the first floor of a building running along its length, under its own shed-like roof; it is usu enclosed, with windows and jalousies all around, but is sometimes partly open in the style of a veranda. **a.** *They seldom went away on a Sunday, without coming in to the back gallery to bid us good bye. They were all standing together, and I went into the hall to get a glass of wine.*—LMSPJS (Rev John Smith's Defence Address) **b.** *One ... back gallery 18 ft by ... 7 ft sitting on 5-1/2 ft wooden blocks with concrete base.*—DaC (52.06.29, p.12) [BACK² 1. + *gallery*] □ Cp *DJE back-jamb* (*Jmca*) wh is, however, not in current use, though evid referring to a similar structure.

back-hair *n* (Guyn, StVn) Hair on the back of the head and neck (often softer than the rest of one's hair).

back-house *n* **1.** (Bdos) The rear part of a house (as opposed to the FRONT-HOUSE and usually (in older traditional buildings) comprising the dining room area and kitchen. **a.** *I had tea and a bun in the back house.*—LICMS:7 **b.** *In its path of destruction this huge rock, the same height as that of the back house of the Phillips', smashed into a sty. The boulder went on to flatten banana plants.*—BdN (66.09.04, p.1) **2.** (CayI) An outdoor toilet built several yards behind the house; a latrine.

back·ing group *n phr* (CarA) [Entertainment] A band maintained by a professional singer of CALYPSO, REGGAE, or similar folk ballad, to co-ordinate and improvise instrumental, and sometimes background vocal, accompaniment for his/ her performances. **a.** *With Reggae for days, this side, which is world-famed Johnny Nash's backing group, opened its tour with a tight bandstand at the Esplanade on Monday.*—NaT (75.09.28, p.7) **b.** *Sparrow's 'Troubadours' were his backing-group and sometimes they travelled with him on tour.*— (Bdos) **[** < BACK³ 4.**]**

back·lands *n* (Guyn) ‖ *back¹* 3. The lands of the SECOND and THIRD DEPTHS of a sugar plantation; farm land some distance upland from a coastal village. **a.** *The pump at Golden Grove will drain the backlands of Golden Grove Nabaclis, usually flooded with excess water from the hilly sand and clay belt.*—GyG (75.11.25, p.9) **b.** *The Officer-in-charge came and together we went through the prison compound. Then to the vast backlands where farming is done.*—GWFW:74 □ See also BACKDAM 3., ABACK¹, and Phr GO ABACK.

back of *prep phr* (CarA) [IF] **1.** ‖ *aback of* (Guyn) Behind; at the back of. **a.** *Many traffic sign posts have been placed on the edge of the kerb instead of back of the sidewalk ... [and] have been hit by vehicles rounding bends.*—AdN (72.10.07, p.4) **b.** *Apply to A. Mazaharally, 15 Water St, back of Boodhoo & Sons.*—DaC (Ad, 53.03.01, p.12) **c.** *His home was just back of the shop, the same building.*—SABS:52 □ *OED* AmE *back* adv 14. *back of* 'behind' (In US). The phr is widely used in *IF* CE in ref to place. **2.** *PHRASES* **2.1 back o(f) ba-ho** [bak-ʌ-ba-o] *adv phr* (Gren) [*AF—Joc*] ‖ *behind God's back* (CarA) (In) any place so far in the country as to be out of reach by normal transport; in the farthest backwoods. *She come from back-o[f]-ba-o, is why she can't talk good.*—(Gren) [Perh of Fr Cr origin. Cp *ba-ho* < Fr *bas* + *haut*] **2.2 back of the damp** *adv phr* (TkCa) [IF] (In) the northern suburb of Cockburn Town in Grand Turk. □ Cp BACK-SALINA. **2.3 back o(f) the yard** *n phr* (Baha) [IF] ‖ *backyard* (CarA) The area behind the house used for domestic activities. *Irrespective of the size of 'back o' the yard', there were certain essentials present. There was a well, an oven made of rocks and mortar; a kitchen and an 'out-house'.*—EBT:3

back-out *n* (Bdos) [*AF—Joc*] A woman's dress made to leave much of the back exposed. ... *'half-naked' outburst in their fashion—the minis, the back-outs, the chest-outs and so on.*—Baw (Dec. 77)

back-o'-wall (**back-a-wall**) ['bak-ʌ-wa·l] *n* (Jmca) [*AF*] The slums of Kingston, Jamaica; [by extension] any Jamaican slum. **a.** *And so we rode on fearlessly through the back-o'-wall neighbourhood of West Kingston, across to Parade, up Orange Street, to Torrington Bridge, and then he let go the reins of his 'horse', daring the snipers to shoot him down.*—SR:34 **b.** *Don't speak to me you come from back-a-wall. You a back-a-wall gal.*—Jmca (Ms, 1978) **[** < 'back of (the) wall', a once popular ref to a particular slum area of West Kingston, *Jmca*, on the border of the city, esp in the mid-1960s. There was, however, no actual wall**]**

back-pock·et *n* (CarA) The hip pocket; the pocket at the back of a pair of trousers. *He jus' flick he fingers dem and shove he hand to he backpocket and haul out the two sticks as he walk 'cross to he second pan.*—Kri '78

back·ra (bac·cra, bak·ra, buck·ra) [bakrʌ ~ bʌkrʌ] *n, adj* (CarA) [*AF*] ‖ *backra-man* (Guyn) ‖ *béké* (Dmca, Gren) ‖ *bétjé* (StLu) **1.** A white person, esp a white man. **a.** *When blackman t[h]ief he/him t[h]ief half-a-bit, when backra t[h]ief he/him t[h]ief whole estate.*—CarA (Prov) **b.** *Poor Families Fund. Amount previously acknowledged … $6,091.40 / Bajan Baccra …$9.60.*—AdN (74.09.28, p.1) **c.** *… surrounded by round-shouldered backras on Broad Street.*—BMP:35 **d.** *At the level of servants they knew that there could be much to eat and drink after the 'white folks', the backra people had had their banquet.*—EFOT:63 **e.** *said. 'Backra land. Where Missis Queen live.'*—PCOS: 187 [From *GDEL* Efik *mbakara* (< pl pref, *mba*, 'all, the whole' + vb tr, *kara* 'encompass, master, understand'), 'White men generally … because of their superiority in arts, etc…' (also) 'black men practising the arts and customs of civilized life are sometimes called (*mbakara* >) *makara* or by way of distinction *Obubit Makara*, 'Black Makara'. The Efik, being long established middle-men at the slave-trading centre at Calabar, E. Nigeria, would prob have established the item as a loan-word and spread it among slaves of other language groups who also brought it to the New World] □ In this sense now mostly used in *Joc* CE, rarely with pl -s, and so often attrib that there is little practical distinction between n and adj functions. See separate entries below. **2.** [By extension] A person, whether white or not, who is in a position of great authority; any important person who is feared. **a.** *Le[t] me go and do de backra wo[r]k.*—(Guyn) **b.** *'It is backra duppy, a bad man duppy,' says one.*—SJW: 26 **3.** [By extension] [*Derog*] ‖ BACKRA NIGGER (Tbgo) A person more nearly white than black in physical appearance, esp one who despises black people; a quadroon, octoroon, etc. *Those backra people feel they white but little do they know that 'whiteness' is more than skin-colour!*—Antg (Ms, 1980) **4.** [*Derog*] [(Esp in phr) POOR-BACKRA] [Hist] A white Barbadian indentured plantation servant in the 17C; a present-day white peasant or low-level worker who is a descendant of the 17C indentured servants (See POOR-WHITE). *… dat slack mister merchant wid dat black cattle hat / an e cravat: dat / poor backra rat.*—BMP:14

back·ra fire *n phr* (Guyn) [*AF—Joc*] Electricity. [See *GDEL* Efik *Makara* n; *Mbakara* n. Note stating that the term is used to qualify items introduced by Europeans, whence '*A Makara Cow*' i.e a horse, etc] □ Humorous use by older folk.—*YRRC:34.*

back·ra-john·ny (back·ra john·nie) [bakra-jɒni] /1'21'2/ *n (phr)* [*AF—Derog*] **1.** (Bdos) ‖ POOR WHITE (CarA) *The cultural tradition of Barbados could no more ignore the 'Backra Johnnie' than it could the Negro.*—NaT (74.06.16, p.12) **2.** (Trin) ‖ BACKRA NIGGER (Tbgo) *You use people fer your own selfish ambitions, because you want to get to de top. So go to yuh backrajohnny and dem. We don't want you, and if you remain*

you go be only humbling yourself.—DP:41 □ An emotive term wh is more offensive in some places than in *Bdos.*

back·ra-man (back·ra/buck·ra man) ['b'akrʌ-ma·n] *n (phr)* (CarA) [*AF—Joc*] ‖ BACK-RA (CarA) **a.** *We going pick the backraman canetops!*—SNWIC:248 (S. Sadeek) **b.** *Now that the Backra man has said it maybe those who think otherwise will agree.*—BsT (81.05.10, p.2) **c.** *[The negro] thinks that the mulatto is too near akin to himself to be worthy of any respect. In his passion he calls him a nigger—and protests that he is not, and never will be like buckra man.*—TWISM:84 [Cr redundant expansion of BACKRA n 1.]

back·ra mis·sy *n phr* (CarA) [*AF*] [Hist] The daughter of a sugar planter; [by extension, Derog] any snobbish young lady. *Since de other one married to dis white engineer she now behavin[g] like backra missy, m[y] dear!*—(Guyn) [BACKRA, adj + MISSY]

back·ra-nig·ger *n phr* (Tbgo) [*AF—Derog*] ‖ *backra-johnny* (Trin) ‖ *béké-nèg* (Dmca, Gren) ‖ *blue foot* (StKt) ‖ *red Ibo* (Jmca) ‖ *red nigger* (CarA) A mulatto; a light-skinned person of mixed black and white ancestry who is despised. *That blame backra nigger only tryin[g] to push around people.*—(Tbgo) [BACKRA, adj + nigger]

back·ra pick·ney *n phr* (CarA) [*AF—Joc*] **1.** [Hist] Any White child; [by extension, Derog] any light-skinned child. **2.** PHRASE **2.1 answer for backra pickney** *vb phr* (Guyn) [*AF—Joc*] To explain your way out of a serious plight; to account for bad work or failure of responsibility. *You better don['t] spoil dat wo[r]k, yeh, or you will really have to answer for backra pickney.*—(Guyn) □ Used by older people, and a prob ref to the ritual murder of Molly Schultz, a five-year old White child, about 1917 in *Guyn.*

back-sa·li·na *n* (TkCa) The southern suburb of Cockburn Town, Grand Turk. [= 'Behind the salt lake'; hence also used in adv phr]

back·sheesh (back.sis) *n* (Guyn) See BAKSIS

back·side *n* (CarA) [*AF—Vul*] **1.** Arse. *'Backside Talk and Committee Adjourns In Disorder' / … Mr Edwards took objection to the use of the word 'mullets' and when he saw debate continuing he requested withdrawal thereof, 'otherwise' he said, 'I will get up and tear holes in his backside' (referring to the Opposition Leader).*—TrU (67.03.01, p.1) □ Considered an improper word in CE though admissible in BrE, AmE. **2.** PHRASE **2.1 haul/take your backside** *vb phr* (Tbgo, Trin) [*AF—Vul*] ‖ HAUL YOU[R] ARSE (Bdos) See ARSE Phr 2.3

back-squeeze *vb phr* (Tbgo, Trin) [*IF*] To withhold (a part of sth due, esp money); to give grudgingly. **a.** *You see she back-squeeze the money so much for the materials that that house ain't* *build strong.*—Trin (Ms, 1982) **b.** *Don't back-squeeze on the liquor, man! Bring out the Scotch.*—(Trin)

back·step (back-steps) *n* (Gren, Guyn, Tbgo, Trin) A stairway outside and leading to the back entrance or kitchen-door of a house; backstairs. **a.** *When our parents were out we would enjoy the nancy stories the old cook would tell us on the backstep in the moonlight.*—Guyn (Ms, 1968) **b.** *She had been standing up in the kitchen thinking all these things but now she started to walk down the backsteps. But she was taking her time.*—AKM:24 [BACK² + step] □ The word is more often used in the sg in *Guyn* E.

back·store *n* (CarA) The rear section of the building housing a supermarket, department store, etc wh is shut off from the main store and in wh goods are prepared for display and sale. *Former Guyana Stores employee Shirley Lewis, charged with the larceny of a tray of eggs from the store's supermarket, yesterday claimed that she got the eggs from the 'backstore' and not from the supermarket. She said that on the day of the alleged theft there were no eggs on display in the supermarket.*—GyC (78.03.03, p.8) [BACK² + store. Cp SE *backstage*] □ Written as one word, but cp FRONT STORE.

back-talk¹ *n* (CarA) [IF] ‖BACK-ANSWER¹ (CarA) *When I tell your fader about all de back-talk you give me he goin[g] give you a proper beating.*—(Angu) [BACK⁴ 2 'in reply' + talk] □ Also in vb phrs **give/got/have back-talk**. Cp BACK-ANSWER¹ PHR 2.1.

back-talk² *vb phr* **1.** (CarA) [IF] ‖BACK-ANSWER² (CarA) *She is a girl who takes nothing from anybody—she back-talks even her parents.*—Guyn (Ms, 1975) [By functional shift of BACK-TALK¹] □ Cp BrE *answer back, talk back* with the same sense. **2.** (StKt) To talk behind (sb's) back; to say bad things about (sb) in their absence. *She likes to go and say all kind of bad things about you. She like to back-talk you.*—(StKt) □ Prob infl by CE BAD-TALK².

Back-to-Africa movement *n phr* (Jmca) [Hist] A movement first associated with the name Marcus Garvey, aiming to encourage West Atlantic Caribbean and American people of African descent to treat Africa as motherland and possibly to migrate there; it flourished in the 1920s/30s and was later partially revived with the development of RASTAFARIANISM. *The Jamaican White is trying so hard to disappear for nobody cares very much to be in such an uncomfortable position. They comb their ancestry for that little touch of colour which will enable them to claim that they, too, can take part in the Back-to-Africa movement, or for that matter, the Back-to-St Elizabeth movement.*—DaG (68.04.18, p.8)

back-to-back¹ *n* (Bdos) One of the dances done by slaves as part of general merry-making. *… thus proclaiming the start of their own creative*

dances. Be it the Treadmill, Four Points of the Mill, Chiggoe-Foot Dance, the Hepdo, Back-to-Back and Four-Knee Polka, or the most beautiful of them all, the Joe-and-Johnnie, which defies description.*—AdN (78.06.24, p.4)

back-to-back² *vb* (Guyn) [X] ‖BACK-BACK (CarA) *'All right Freddie, back to back in the garage now,' she said.*—Guyn (Ms, 1978)

back-up¹ *vb phr* (CarA) **1.** ‖BACK³ (CarA) 4. *The Police Band was no exception. After all, they're a band too, and, as though to remind us of this fact, they came out like we never heard them before. After they had contributed their versions of this year's Trinidad calypsonians' tunes, they provided back-up to our local calypsonians.*—VoS (76.03.04, p.8) □ Occasionally also 'back-stop'. **2.** PHRASE **2.1 back (sb) up** *vb phr* (Jmca) [AF—Cr] To pester (sb) (to do sth). (Cp BEHIND Phr 1.) *Imagine all de time you back me up fe go, and now me go you a-quarrel how me catch man.*—Jmca (Ms, dialogue)

back-up² *n* (CarA) [Entertainment] A band hired to BACK-UP¹ a folk singer. □ Cp also BACKING-GROUP.

back·ward answer *n phr* (Gren) [X] Back answer. *The children does give their mother backward answer.*—(Gren) [Prob an overcorrection]

back·wards *adj* (Bdos) [X] Backward. *Be-Jesus Christ, when you see me leff this blasted backwards place call Barbados, that is the last time I eating salt fish. I eating steaks!*—CWFYS:93 [A misascription of SE *backwards* adv]

back·way *adv* (Belz) [IF] **1.** Backwards; in reverse. *'I don't even understand what's going on these days,' confessed John John. 'The world is turning backway.'*—HF:33 **2.** PHRASE **2.1 drive backway** *vb phr* (Belz) [IF] To reverse (a motor vehicle). *Drive the car backway.*—(Belz)

back·yard¹ (back-yard, back yard) *n (phr)* (CarA) **1.** ‖*back of[f] the yard* (Baha) A (usu fenced) area at the back of a house usu used for kitchen-gardening, rearing poultry, etc, or dumping garbage. **a.** *Mr Cole is president of the Home Growers' Club which was founded in 1975 specifically for the purpose of encouraging Bahamian home owners to cultivate their backyards with vegetables.*—NaG (78.04.08, p.1) **b.** *Poultry sounds came up from the back-yard. Duck-quacking and the squawk of a hen, the throaty gurgle of a rooster.*—MLDS:36 **c.** *All over Barbados in people's backyards, around their houses, in the streets, in open places, in dumps and quarries there is evidence of an excess of solid waste accumulating in the country.*—Bdos (Hd, 74.12.03, p.4293) **2.** An area behind a main or front house in wh there is a BACK-HOUSE or a building with separately rented rooms. **a.** *He turned into their long tunnelled gateway on Frederick Street and walked to the far end of the deep back-yard, for theirs was the last barrack-room close to a high wall that*

separated the yard in the next street.—SWNIC:
228 (I. Khan) **b.** *I live in a neighbourhood that
creates a lot of vice. It is a backyard house and
everyone makes good use of it. I like to relax with
a cool drink ever so often. A lot of happenings
escape my eyes except this one.*—SuC (78.08.13,
p.11) □ Best spelt as one word, and often used
attrib, the word connotes lower social status and
more domestic privacy than IAE *backyard*. See
next.

back·yard² *adj* [*IF*] Situated in or belonging
to the area behind a house; [by extension] unsophisticated; of low standard. *The boys ... had
come home with him after school and were quickly
deep in a hilarious game of backyard cricket.*—
Bdos (Ms, 1978) [By functional n > adj shift of
BACKYARD¹]

ba·cu·ba (ba·co·ba, ba·cou·ba, ba·cu.va) *n*
1. (USVI) ‖ APPLE-BANANA (Belz, etc) **2.** (Guyn)
‖ BUCK-BANANA (Guyn) □ Mostly used by older
rural folk. **3.** (Neth) [Loosely] (Alternative name
for) 'banana' or a hand of bananas. *In the Netherlands Antilles the plantain, which is inedible
until cooked, is called banana. The banana usually
associated with corn flakes is called bacoba. To
avoid confusion, bananas are referred to as plantains in these recipes.*—FWWC:6 [Cp *BDFC:
174* Carib *baccoucou* 'figue' (i.e. banana). Perh
influenced also by *DAFL* Twi *bakua* 'stalk of a
plantain or banana tree' + *-ba* (dim. suff) 'small,
little']

bad¹ *adj* (CarA) [*IF*] **1.** [Esp of a part of the
human body] Hurt; injured; sick; diseased. **a.**
She has had a bad ankle for some years now.—
(Guyn) **b.** *He had to give up cricket because of his
bad knee.*—(Bdos) □ Cp SE 'bad teeth' in similar
sense, but CE usage is extensive. See BAD-BELLY,
etc as separate entries. **2.** [*IF*] Terrible; dreadful.
*'Uh-huh' she gasped, on noticing the blood. 'See
everything call me in time. Bad, bad Loupgarou
haunt this place. But after what I do here at twelve
today and again at six, eet no go come back. Cost
only $40. Big job and critical, leetle money.' I
heard her tell my mother.* –PGIP:24 (E. Westman)
3. [*AF—Joc*] [Entertainment, esp of per-
formance] Excellent; of superior quality. *Both
local and foreign observers have predicted, that
this year's celebration will be bright, beautiful and
b-a-d. As a result most business men have planned
a little Christmas pocket during the course of the
season.*—Bet.1:9 [See note at BAD² 3.] **4.** PHRASES
4.1 bad as yaws *adj phr* (Tbgo) [*AF*] [Of
behaviour or conditions] Very unruly; beyond
control. *Those children are as bad as yaws, I don't
know what to do with them again.*—Tbgo (Ms,
1982) **4.2 be bad enough** *vb phr* (CarA) [*IF*]
‖ **be bad off** (Baha) ‖ **be but bad enough** (Angu)
‖ **be looking the other side** (Tbgo) ‖ **be well
bad** (Gren, Jmca) ‖ **be well low** (Nevs) ‖ **take
down low** (StVn) To be extremely ill; to be
almost at death's door. *I hear he's bad enough in
hospital and not expected to live.*—Guyn (Ms,
1968) [A prob calque from Afr langs. Cp Ci-
Nyanja, *wadwala mokwana* (He-is-ill enough) 'He

is very ill'. Also *StLu* Fr Cr *mové asé* 'bad
enough' used with the same sense] **4.3 go bad**
vb phr (CarA) **(i)** [Esp of fruit] To spoil; to
deteriorate. *The court was told that the man,
Clifford, went to a family at Moolchan Trace in
Fyzabad some time on March 13 and told them
that their business was 'going bad' and that he
had come to assist them with some prayers.*—ExP
(73.02.02, p.15) **(ii)** ‖ **turn out bad** (CarA) [Of
persons] To become loose and uncontrollable, a
criminal, a prostitute, etc. **4.4 play bad** *vb phr*
(Bdos, Guyn, Nevs) [*AF*] [Of young persons] To
make a show of being unruly; to look aggressive
while lacking courage. *Is bad she playing or she
only giving bold-talk?*—Nevs (Ms, 1973) **4.5
turn out bad** *vb phr* (CarA) **(i)** [Of a bruise]
To fester; to become infected. **(ii)** [Of persons]
‖ GO BAD (CarA) **(ii)** See GO Phr 6.14

bad² *adv* (CarA) [*AF*] **1.** Badly; terribly; dread-
fully; awkwardly. **a.** *She said, 'Pure madness!
Only Chris' knows if all this is going to get Dr
Buxton back that job of his at the university. I
can't see it. I jus' can't see it.' Gran' Ma Tyson
shook her head despondently. 'It's going to end bad,
bad. I know it.'*—SJT:56 **b.** *That car park bad.
They leave it bad.*—(Guyn) [A mesolectal survival of characteristic Cr adj > adv shift, displacing all adv *-ly* forms in Cr] **2.** [*AF*]
Excellently; splendidly. **a.** *Dis must o' bin one
Elder now / Who stan' an' take each card / Off
erry single wreat' ta read, / An' boy, he could read
bad!*—WIE:41 **b.** *Dear Mr Editor, / Three cheers
for Brother Louisy. Only now I can see the brother
coming out real bad.*—CrU (76.11.06, p.3 [See
note at sense 3.] **3.** [*Post-vbl compliment*] Very
much. *I love this boy very bad indeed, but I don't
know if he loves me as bad as I love him.*—NaT
(75.09.24, p.18, Dear Christine) [A prob calque
from W Afr langs. Cp Wolof, *rafettay am baxul
(beauty her bad)* 'She is very beautiful'; also
Hausa, *yana son Minaari mugun soo, (he loving
of Minaari bad of love)* 'He loves Minaari very
much'; also Yoruba, *O l'owo buruku, (he has
money bad)* 'He has very much money'; also
Nupe, *Tsado maṇ nyaṇnyaṇ nwgyaa, (Tsado able
dance very bad)* 'Tsado can dance very well'; also
WAPE *A sabby am bad bad* 'I know him/it very
well'; etc] **4.** [*Post-adj intensifier*] Very; considerably; intensely. **a.** *She told me that she made
those hats herself and that if the hats sell well then
her income is not bad. But just now, 'things are
slow bad'.*—DaG (67.11.12, p.7) **b.** *The soup
taste nice bad; how did you make it?*—SGAC:37
[Influenced by the position and sense of the
prec] **5.** PHRASES **5.1 behave bad** *vb phr* (CarA)
[*AF*] **(i)** To misbehave; to be unruly. *Behaved
Bad In Court: Fined*—DaC (H, 52.08.07, p.3)
(ii) ‖ GET ON BAD (CarA) See GET Phr 3.18 and
Note *Yo[ur] father goin[g] behave bad when [h]e
fin[d] out you didn[t] go to lessons.*—(Guyn) **5.2
deh bad** [dɛ ba·d] /2'2'/ *vb phr* (Guyn) [*AF—Cr*]
To be in an unsafe position or situation; to be
in a predicament. *And when the police actually
find the marijuana in your house, you can try
blaming the youngsters, but I tell you, you deh bad,
boy!*—(Guyn) [< Cr DEH³ *vb* 'to be placed' +

bad adv 'in a bad way'] □ A Cr phr of high frequency, often used *Joc* in *Guyn* E. **5.3 get on bad** *vb phr* (CarA) [*AF*] ‖ *behave bad* (CarA) To quarrel loudly in objecting to sth; to lose your temper for good reason; (BrE slang) to carry on. **5.4 got/have it bad (for sb)** *vb phr* (Guyn) [*AF*] ‖ *got/have (bad) typee (for sb)* (Guyn) To be deeply infatuated (with sb). *She got it so bad for Ken that even when the man go [a]cross the river, you see her there waitin[g] for the boat to come back.*—(Guyn) **5.5 take in bad** *vb phr* (CarA) See TAKE Phr 9.1 **5.6 too bad / 3′1/** *adv phr* (CarA) [*IF*] Very much; intensely. **a.** *Old woman: I shame too bad, Pa.*—LICMS: 203 **b.** *When the father saw the wales the child had received from the flogging at school he quarrelled too bad, I tell you!*—(Guyn) [A prob calque from Afr langs in wh there is sometimes no distinction between 'too' and 'very'. Cp Kikongo, yela *mbikibeni*, 'very sick', 'too sick'; Mende, *waa*, 'very much', 'too much'] □ Note that there is a marked high pitch on *too* dropping low on *bad* in this phr, wh cannot be represented in writing.

bad³ *n* (CarA) [*AF*] **1.** Evil; evil things; obeah. **a.** *I am not one of those wishing the Government bad.*—WeG (73.07.11, p.22) **b.** *We don't want to say, like the Baptist woman told us, 'you're dealing in bad.' For we don't believe in that kind of business.*—SuP (74.12.08, p.5) **2.** PHRASES **2.1 do (sb) bad** *vb phr* (CarA) [*AF*] ‖ *work obeah on (sb)* (CarA) To cause (sb) to become incurably sick or mentally ill through the use of evil powers. *He ain[t] no good for himself now. They say people do him bad.*—(Guyn) **2.2 make bad between (persons), with (sb)** *vb phr* (CarA) [*AF*] To cause a person or persons to become bad friends. *Well she wouldn[t] pay back de money she borrow and da[t] is wha[t] mak[e] bad wid de sister.*—(Bdos) **2.3 talk bad about (sb)** *vb phr* (CarA) [*AF*] ‖ BAD-TALK (SB) (CarA) *You can't, as a young lady, go out with every man who invites you out or people will begin to talk bad about you.*—(Guyn) [Cp Yoruba *sọrọ ẹni buruku* (*say word about him/ her bad*) 'speak ill of him/her'] □ The phr has a milder connotation than that of some of the equivalents given.

Ba·dam! (Ba·dam·bam!, Bad·dam!) *excl ideoph* (CarA) [*IF*] ‖ *Bradarax!* (Bdos) ECHOIC WORD indicating that the speaker has seen sb/ sth fall heavily or receive a severe blow (and frequently forming part of a statement about the fall). *You know, it was like a sort of lucky punch. Baddam! And everybody fall down.*—ExP (71.12.02, p.20)

Ba·daow! (Ba·ow!, Bo·dow!) *excl ideoph* (CarA) [*AF*] ‖ *Bup!, Budup!* (CarA) ECHOIC WORD representing a blow. *Three Men Waiting In His Home ... Bam!—Bodow! / Innocent, peace-loving citizens are being attacked, mugged ... Sheafe ... told the Bomb the blows from his attackers left him unconscious.*—Bom (74.11.15, p.8)

Ba·dap(s)! (Bra·dap(s)!) *excl ideoph* (CarA) [*AF*] ‖ *Bap(s)!* (CarA) **1.** ECHOIC WORD representing a fall. *Badap! Look how da lady jus[t] fall do[w]ng.*—(Guyn) **2.** ‖ BAM! (CarA)

bad-be·haved /1′12/ (bad-be·hav·ing) / 1′122/ *adj* (CarA) ‖ *bad-mannered* (StLu) ‖ *malkasé* Dmca ‖ *outlawdish* (Belz) ‖ *outlorded* (Bdos, Guyn, Jmca) Unruly; noisily ill-mannered; grossly misconducting yourself. *The Minister of Education is not a bad-behaved person. Sometimes he takes a few drinks out there and gets a little confused.*—Bdos (Hd, 76.08.04, p.7149) [Cp Yoruba *hu iwa buruku* 'behave bad'; also N IrE 'bad-behaved'—*L.Todd*]

bad-be·hav·iour /1′122/ *n* (CarA) Noisy misconduct (esp of young persons). *You never see a police talk too hard to a sailor no matter what bad behaviour he have.*—LICMS:191 □ Distinguish from normal *bad behaviour* /2′111/ 'any behaviour that is unbecoming'.

bad-bel·ly; bad-bow·els /1′22/ *n* (CarA) [*IF*] **1.** ‖ *belly-work(s), belly-working* (Guyn, StVn, Tbgo) ‖ *the belly* (ECar, TkCa) ‖ *the runnings* (Antg, Baha, Tbgo) Diarrhoea; running of the bowels, esp in babies, over a period of several days. **2.** [Of BAD-BELLY only] **(i)** (Tbgo) False pregnancy, believed to be brought about by evil magical influence. **(ii)** (Jmca) Any abdominal disorder in women after pregnancy. **(iii)** /2′11/ (Guyn) [Of a woman] Proneness to produce deformed or physically blighted children.

bad-blood /1′2/ *n* (Guyn, Tbgo, Trin) **1.** A condition, thought to be of the blood, causing itching bumps to appear on the skin (esp of children). **2.** (CarA) A family proneness to any disease that causes skin-disorder, such as eczemna, etc. *They have bad blood in that family— you see how all of them got sores.*—(Guyn) **3.** (Tbgo, Trin) Evil in a person's nature. **a.** *The bad blood in his veins caused him to be in and out prison.*—MWL **b.** *All yoh hear dat now? All you hear what she say? She have bad blood, yes. All you hear she t'reaten meh. I going straight to the station, an' tell dem she want to kill meh. She jealous because my daughter get married an' she ent have nobody.*—MN:2 **4.** (Jmca) Bad relationship; personal conflict; trouble. *You not careful he get us all into bad blood with the people in the yard.*—MHJT:17 □ The pitch pattern distinguishes *bad-blood* /1′2/ above from IAE *bad blood* /2′1/, 'ill feeling' to wh sense 4 is near but different, as the cit illustrates. See also BLOOD Phrs.

bad-bow·els /1′22/ *n* (Bdos, Guyn) [*IF*] See BAD-BELLY *An attack of the 'bad-bowels' may result in much vomiting, as in the case of severe gastric influenza which has been afflicting many people in Barbados over the last weeks.*—AdN (79.03.18, p.11)

bad-boy /1'2/ *n* (Guyn) [*AF*] ‖ *bad-head*[2] (Belz) ‖ *bad-john* (ECar) A male criminal; a potential criminal; a lawless and violent young man. *It is no secret that they do not have enough vehicles and their Divisions are understaffed. But they have still been able to put the crunch on the 'bad boys' and reduce the crime rate for 1975.*—SuC (76.07.15, p.17) □ Pitch differentiation provides important distinction from IAE *bad boy* /2'1/ 'naughty, wicked, etc boy'.

bad-cow *n* (Guyn) ‖ DONKEY-MAN (Bdos) □ Also sometimes MAD-COW.

bad·den [ba·dn] *PHRASE* **badden your head** *vb phr* (Tbgo, Trin) To induce a feeling of delighted crudeness from drinking liquor or from use of narcotic drugs. *In order to compensate for this disorder, he develops a paranoia for manual labour, an arrogance for discipline, a dislike for good manners, an aversion to hygiene, a hatred for clean surroundings, plaits his hair in dread-locks, shoots pool the whole day long, and if he isn't baddening his head with a colombie, is either rolling dice, squeezing cards or guzzling endless grog.*— ExP (79.12.02, p.8) [BAD[1] adj 2. + vb forming suff -*en*. Cp *harden, deepen*, etc. See also BAD-HEAD[2]]

bad·der; **bad.dest** *adj* (CarA) [*AF*—*Joc*] More/most daring or exciting. **a.** *He big just like you, but younger … / He lay-lay like you but badder.*—Cso (Sparrow, 1983) **b.** *This will be coming and getting down strong to highlight the fact that the Equals are possibly the funkiest, grooviest and the baddest, hottest musicians today. The L.P. will be released in time for the tour.*—GyC (76.09, p.15) [Comparative and superlative forms of BAD[1] 3.]

bad-drive[1] /1'2/ *vb* (Tbgo, Trin) [*IF*] To drive recklessly; to scare another motorist by your dangerous driving. *Watch that fellow with the yellow car. I know he will bad-drive you and then drive off smiling.*—(Trin)

bad-drive[2] /1'2/ *n* (Tbgo, Trin) [*IF*] A deliberate act of inconsiderate driving (of a car). *Yesterday Mervin got a terrible bad-drive from a taxi-driver who just swung in front of him and stopped to drop a passenger.*—(Trin) [By functional vb > n shift of BAD-DRIVE[1]]

bad-eye /1'2/ *n* (Belz, Guyn) [*IF*] ‖ *maldjo* (Gren, StVn, Tbgo, Trin) ‖ *ole-yard* (Guyn, StVn) **1.** An evil spell or bad magical infl caused by looking with envy or a false show of goodwill at (sb or sth) (esp a baby or a flourishing plant); the power to cause such evil. *If you have a well kept flower or kitchen garden you must protect it from persons with 'bad eye'. An 'ole poe' (chamber pot) or blue bottle placed upsided down on a stick offers the best protection from the evil eye.*—ExP (72.09.03, p.26) [A prob calque from Afr langs. Cp Yoruba *fi oju buruku si* 'put ugly eye on', *fi oju oro si*, 'put vengeance eye on'; also Igbo *olɛ anya ɔjyɔ*, 'look (sb) ugly eye'; also Kikongo

ntadidi ye disu diambi 'look with bad eye', etc] □ Distinguish from IAE *bad eye* /2'1/, 'an eye with affected vision'. **2.** *PHRASES* **2.1 cut (out) (the) bad-eye** *vb phr* (Belz, Guyn) [*IF*] ‖ *cut maldjo* (Gren, Trin) To cure or prevent the effects of BAD-EYE. *Some people put a silver coin at the bottom of a pot of croton or fern so that 'bad-eye' may be cut out and to help the plant to strive (= thrive).*—COYN:19 **2.3 put bad-eye on (sb/sth)** *vb phr* (Belz, Guyn) [*IF*] ‖ *pass bad-hand on (sth)* (Dmca) ‖ *put jumbie on (sth)* (Mrat) ‖ *put maldjo on (sb/sth)* (Gren, StVn, Trin) ‖ *put mouth on (sth)* (Baha, BrVi, TkCa) ‖ *put spirit on (sth)* (Dmca) To cause (a baby, plant or crop) to sicken continuously by means of some magical influence believed to be in an envious or malicious gaze. *It looks like somebody put bad-eye on my good, good anthurium lily. It's drooping and would neither come nor go.*—(Guyn)

bad-feel·ing(s) /1'22/ *n* **1.** (CarA) ‖ *bad-feels* (Bdos) A feeling of sickness in the stomach, often with a headache; nausea, cold sweat and dizziness. *The next morning he went to the market straight from bed, taking care not to walk on the cook-shop side, where the smell of fried food might give him bad-feelings.*—HMCH:87 **2.** (StLu) A worried mind. □ BAD-FEELINGS pl is preferred in most territories. **(A) bad-feeling** is the commoner term in *Belz, StKt*.

bad-feels *n* (Bdos) [*IF*] ‖ BAD-FEELING(S) 1. (CarA) *The term 'Bad feels' can include anything from the dizzy head, the 'dark eye' or 'dark eyes' to a severe attack of diarrhoea, the 'bad bowels' leading quickly to the 'cuttings and the runnings' sufficiently descriptive of this common affliction.*—AdN (79.03.18, p.11, M. Hutt)

bad-fe·ver /1'22/ *n* **1.** (USVI) [*IF*] Malaria. **2.** (Guyn) [*IF*] Typhoid. *Typhoid which some people call bad fever, is found all over the world, especially where there is poor sanitation (drainage and toilet facilities) and where the water supply is also poor.*—MiR (65.02.28, p.8) □ Distinguish from *bad fever* /2'11/ 'any fever that is intense'.

bad-flesh /1'2/ *n* **1.** (Guyn) [*IF*] ‖ *bad-skin* (Jmca) [Of persons] Skin that is quickly infected by bruises, insect bites, etc. **2.** (Bdos) [*IF*] ‖ *proud-flesh* (Bdos) Dead skin-tissue raised up around a healing sore, wound, etc. □ Distinguish from *bad flesh* /2'1/ 'flesh that is not good' in any other general context, ex of edible meat.

bad-food /1'2/ *n* (Bdos, Tbgo) ‖ *stan[d]-home* (Guyn) ‖ *stay-home sauce/soup/tea* (Bdos, Guyn) [*AF*] Food or beverage that is prepared with ingredients that are believed magically to influence a man to choose a particular woman, or to prevent him from leaving one he has chosen. *If he keep on goin[g] by that girl the mother go give him bad-food. You can bet!*—(Tbgo) □ Distinguish from *bad food* /2'1/, 'food that is spoiling, not good'.

bad-foot /1'2/ *n* **1.** (CarA) [*IF*] A leg that is injured or diseased. *At that time he still had the bad-foot and was walking with a limp.*—(StVn) **2.** PHRASE **2.1 got/have bad-foot** *vb phr* (Guyn) [*IF*] To be a carrier of misfortune wherever you go. *Is since she comin[g] in yo[ur] house dat you have all dis trouble on yo[ur] head! You ain[t] know she got bad-foot?*—(Guyn) □ Distinguish from *bad foot* /2'1/ 'a foot that is bad' in any other general context, ex '*Your sketch is all right except for bad feet.*' A pl of BAD-FOOT /1'2/ is also very unlikely.

bad hair ['ba·d he·r] *n phr* (CarA) ‖ **bad soil** (Tbgo) ‖ **coarse hair** (Angu, Mrat, StKt) ‖ **hard hair** (Belz, Bdos, Guyn) ‖ **knotty hair** (Angu, BrVi) ‖ **knotty/natty head** (Belz, StVn) ‖ **nigger-head** (StVn) A black person's hair, esp a woman's, that is naturally short, thick, close and difficult to comb. **a.** *The Dowdens were dark-complexioned, and the Baynes, though sallow-complexioned, had definitely bad hair; the two Bayne girls had had to use a hot comb to straighten theirs.*—MLDS:89 **b.** ... *my hair was quite hopeful enough ... I han't very bad hair cause it use to comb.*—Aaw.I.1, p.28 □ See also PICKY HAIR, GOOD HAIR.

bad-hand /1'2/ *n* **1.** (CarA) An injured or sick hand or arm. *You know he has this bad-hand that forced him to give up the cricket.*—(Antg) **2.** (Dmca) A power to cause evil. **3.** PHRASE **3.1 pass bad-hand on (sb/sth)** *vb phr* (Dmca) [*IF*] ‖ PUT BAD-EYE ON (STH) (Belz, Guyn) *She won't go by there because she really believes those people will pass bad-hand on the child.*—(Dmca) □ Distinguish from *bad hand* /2'1/ 'a hand that is bad (as in a game of cards)'.

bad head[1] *n phr* /2'1/ **1.** (Guyn) [*IF*] Bad memory. *I have a very bad head for faces—I very often don't recognise people I have met before.*—(Guyn) **2.** (Guyn, Jmca, Mrat, StVn) [*IF*] ‖ **balahoo brains** (StKt) ‖ **blunt head** (Baha) ‖ **hard head** (CarA) Poor brains; lack of intelligence. *Except for that one girl all of them M— children have bad head; they couldn[t] pass a thing at school.*—(Guyn) **3.** (Baha, Bdos, StLu, StVn, TkCa) ‖ **head (is) bad** (StKt) ‖ **head (is) not good** (CarA) The condition of being mentally unstable; a condition of insanity without violence. *'Plaguin' wid nerve trouble,' 'sick in de head', 'bad head', madness and 'going crazy' are the most common terms used to describe the individual that has a mental problem.*—MTTBT: 119 **4.** (Gren, Tbgo) [*IF*] A condition of noticeable drunkenness. *Look how the boy gettin[g] on! So young and all that drinkin[g], now he has a bad head!*—(Gren)

bad-head[2] /1'2/ (Belz) [*AF*] ‖ BAD-BOY (Guyn □ Distinguish pitch from BAD HEAD[1] /2'1/.

bad-john (bad·john, bad john, Bad John) / 1'2/ [ba·jɒn ~ ba·d-jʌn] *n* (ECar) [*AF*] **1.** ‖ BAD-BOY (Guyn) *A revenge calypso of his encourages* the police to step up action against 'hooligans' of the area. The Chief of these is Fisheye, who had always enjoyed his notoriety as a 'bad-john'.*—ExP (79.08.19, p.22) **[**Prob *bad* + *John*, as a loose Derog reference to a man. Cp *DAS* AmE *dumbjohn* 'a stupid person' *Long John* 'a thin, lanky man'**]** **2.** PHRASE **2.1 play bad-john** *vb phr* (ECar) [*AF*] [Of a youngster] To make a show of violent behaviour; to pretend to be a ready ruffian. *The two of them wanted to play bad-John, and the two of them get licked down.*—NG:188

bad·john·ism ['badjɒ·nızəm] /1'122/ *n* (Trin) [*IF*] ‖ **badmannism** (Jmca) Violent and lawless conduct in the open. *I hope Geddes does not want to take us back to the days of bad-johnism when black people in the ghettoes rioted against each other.*—BoM (79.10.19, p.3)

bad-lamp *n* (CarA) A lamp used in praying for evil, in practising OBEAH.

bad-life /1'2/ (**bad-liv·ing**) /1'22/ *n* **1.** (Jmca) Slum life; living conditions involving squalor, quarrels and sexual looseness. **a.** *My parents quarrel night and day and when the bad-life takes them they turn it over on us the children and often times I am chased out of the house.*—StA(JA) (79.08.20, p.14) **b.** *Tomorrow is another rent day ... not even a dime, not even a dime ... so when the rent man comes honey. Tell him that woh hoh, you wont get no money for this bad living tenament flat ... Rent man rent man, the rent man.*—JdN (79.12.02, p.22, Black sounds of Freedom) **2.** BAD-LIVING (Tbgo) Quarrelling; openly bad relationship. *When you married and you and your wife living in your parents' home, it does cause bad-living.*—(Tbgo) □ Distinguish from *bad life* /2'1/, *bad living* /2'11/ 'reprehensible personal life, living'.

bad-luck·ed ['bad-lʌkɪd]; **bad-luck.y** ['bad-lʌki] /1'22/ *adj* (CarA) [*IF*] Unfortunate; ill-starred; usually or always unlucky. **a.** *As a batsman he was very bad-lucked on tour; he missed his century no less than three times after reaching the nineties.*—(Guyn) **b.** *'Mother of eleven' writes: I am 37. Aunt Elsie I am very bad lucky with men. They say they love me but as soon as I get pregnant I don't see them again until the baby is born.*—DaG (67.03.26, p.10) **c.** *He wondered suddenly if there was something bad-lucky in the walk from Tranquility School and through Lapeyrouse cemetery to Woodbrook.*—JJM:138 □ In most territories the terms appear to be free alternatives, though *bad-lucky* has wider currency, except in *Belz* where only *bad-lucked* has been noted.

bad·ly *adv* PHRASE **1. be badly off** *vb phr* [*X*] [Often loosely in IF contexts] **(i)** To be dangerously ill. *'About 6.30 the next morning I got a message asking me to get to the hospital because my wife was 'badly off'. But ... she had died at 4.30 a.m.—two hours after he received the 'badly off' message.*—ExP (72.10.24, p.3) **(ii)** To be feeble-minded; to be senile and given to silly acts. *You can see she badly off, yes! Every day she goin[g] out an[d] buyin[g] castor oil and if you see the house, full o[f] bottles o[f] castor oil.*—(Gren) **(iii)** To be facing a difficulty. *If you have to walk so far tonight, you really badly off.*—(Nevs) □ These are shifts in sense wh conflict with that of IAE *be badly off* 'be in great hardship', that being still, however, a major sense in CE. **2. feel badly** *vb phr* (CarA) [X] To feel bad; to feel sick. *They say she just complained of feeling badly and before they could get a doctor she was dead.*—(Tbgo) **2.1 feel badly about (sth)** *vb phr* (CarA) [X] To feel sorry, regretful or disappointed about (sth). *One of the furniture manufacturers said: 'I feel very badly about the situation and, I do not see why Barbadians are continuing to import furniture that is being manufactured locally.'*—AdN (72.02.22, p.5) □ These phrs, like the next, are due to overcorrection. SE idiom is *feel bad, look bad.* The addition of *-ly* in such phrases in CE is a false refinement by reaction to Cr BAD², adv. **3. look badly** *vb phr* (CarA) [X] To look bad; to look unseemly; to be unsightly or unbecoming. *Anyway I feel to myself it looks very badly to see a very young girl with a woman's husband.*—NaT (77.01.16, p.18, Dear Christine) □ See prec.

bad·man·ism (**bad·man·nism**) /1'122/ *n* (Jmca) [IF] ‖ *bad-johnism* (Trin) Aggressive conduct intended to cause public embarrassment to others. *Government MP Anthony Capleton said this clause protected the tenant from those landlords who wanted to play 'badmannism' and he went on as far as suggesting that the penalty in the law of a fine of $2,000 or 12 months imprisonment should not have an alternative of a fine.*—-JdN (76.06.20, p.7)

bad-man·ner·ed /1'22/ *adj* (StLu) ‖ BAD-BEHAVED (CarA) *That class is too bad-mannered for any teacher to control.*—(StLu)

bad-mind¹ ['ba:d-maɪn] /1'2/ *n* (CarA) [AF] Malice; spite; animosity; the harbouring of active ill will. *Dr William's closest friends should advise him that the politics of bad mind will not do and that he should positively discourage any further attempt on his side to divide this nation.*—ExP (79.12.01, p.4) [A prob calque from Afr langs in many of wh 'mind' is expressed by the same word for 'heart', 'chest', 'inside-body'. Cp Efik *enye enyene idiọk-esit*, (He/she has bad chest) 'He is angry/malevolent/grudgeful etc'. Also Mende *lima-nyamu* (bad heart/chest) 'hatred', etc; also Kikongo *ntim 'ambi kena wamu* (heart bad he is with) 'he is spiteful', also Yoruba *ni inu buruku* (have bad inside) 'be malevolent'] □ Distinction in sense from *bad mind* /2'1/ 'a naturally malicious mind' is not very great, but still operates in some contexts. Cp 'He got a bad mind and he is unreasonable, that is why he sick. God punishing he,' she added.*—CzN (76.11.29, p.6).

bad-mind² ['ba:d-maɪn] /1'2/ *adj* (CarA) [AF] **1.** ‖ BAD-MINDED (CarA) **a.** *Bad Mind Politics Will Not Do.*—ExP (79.12.01, p.4, (H)) **b.** *She*

too bad-mind, that's why she would never prosper.*—MWL [By functional shift of prec n] **2.** PHRASE **2.1 play bad-mind** *vb phr* (Dmca) [AF] To act spitefully; to react maliciously when offended. *He does play bad-mind. If you trouble him he will wait good till he catch you.*—(Dmca)

bad-mind·ed *adj* (CarA) ‖ *bad-mind* (CarA) Spiteful; malevolent; envious; ungenerous. **a.** *They didn't lend us their wheelbarrow so if we wanted to be bad-minded about it we needn't lend them our ladder.*—(Guyn) **b.** *When I come out and see the bad-minded black son-of-a-bitch we call the overseer, I shake my backside (God forgive me) at him, just to let 'im know that I was people too.*—LICMS:29 [BAD-MIND¹ n + *ed* by analogy with such SE structures as *bad-tempered, hard-hearted,* etc]

bad-mind·ed·ness /1'222/ *n* (CarA) Spite; malevolence; malignant attitude. *The bad-mindedness and the roguishness are largely a product of the old-time manipulative Doctor Politics, which simply cannot help but hold us in contempt, confident that we can be brambled over and over by these facile stratagems.*—TaP (75.12.21, p.6) [Prec + *ness* 'state of being']

bad-mouth¹ /1'2/ *n* (CarA) [IF] **1.** A supposed ability or tendency to bring about misfortune by speaking about it. [Cp Yoruba (Ondo dialect) *da ẹnu bo* (concentrate mouth) 'cause evil by speaking of it'—(pers info, K. Ọmọtọsọ). (See also note at Phr 3.2)] **2.** (Guyn) ‖ BAD-TALK¹ 1 (CarA) *When they discovered the baby had that big bung-navel, I tell you the nurse-midwife came in for some real bad-mouth.*—(Guyn) **3.** PHRASES **3.1 have bad-mouth** *vb phr* (CarA) [IF] ‖ *have goat-mouth* (CarA) ‖ *have bouch-kabwit* (Dmca) To have a habit of expressing a presentiment of misfortune that comes true. **3.2 put your bad-mouth on (sb/sth)** *vb phr* (CarA) [AF/IF] ‖ *Jonah (sb); put your Jonah on (sth)* (Guyn) ‖ *give (sb/sth) bouch-kabwit* (Dmca) ‖ *put goat-mouth on (sb/sth)* (CarA) ‖ *put your mouth on (sb)* (CarA) ‖ *put voodoo on (sth)* (TkCa) To bring (sb) bad luck or to blight an event by expressing negative or evil thoughts about the person or thing. *Whoever put bad-mouth on you, an' that I sure, this [reading of prayers] is going to throw off the black spirit that one of your enemies put on you.... You got enemy in this yard*—MBF:55 [A prob calque from W Afr langs. Cp Yoruba *o fi ẹnun buburu baa jẹ fun mi* (he/she use mouth bad spoil it for me) 'he/she spoiled my business'—(pers info, Dayọ Okunlale). Also Igbo *itinyelu mu ya onu ojo* (you-put me it mouth bad) 'you caused sth to go wrong with my thing'—(pers info, Amadi Ume)]

bad-mouth² /1'2/ *vb tr* (Baha) [IF] **1.** ‖ BAD-TALK² (CarA) **a.** *Why you don't mind your own business instead of always bad-mouthin[g] people?*—(Baha) **2.** (USVI) ‖ PUT YOUR BAD-MOUTH ON (SB/STH) (CarA) See BAD-MOUTH¹ Phr 3.2

bad-mouth·er n (Bdos) [IF] ‖BAD-TALKER (CarA) *Barbadians have developed into a nation of 'bad-mouthers'—scathingly condemning and criticising everything and especially everyone they see or experience.*—AdN (82.12.05, p.8) [< BAD-MOUTH² vb tr + (agential suff) -er]

bad-name /1′2/ n (CarA) [IF] A bad reputation that has some serious effect; costly disrepute; disapproval caused by gossip. *Well all the things that people see her getting on with, with the white-men and so, bring bad-name on the rest of the sisters.*—(Guyn) [< SE 'a bad name' without indef art and intensified in connotation by the Cr pitch-contour in folk speech]

ba·doo (ba·du) n (Jmca) ‖DASHEEN (CarA) *They only had boiled badoo in soup for dinner.*—Jmca (Ms) [DJE gives a poss Hausa origin] □ See EDDOE (*CarA*).

bad-pay /1′2/ adj (Gren, Trin, USVI) [AF—Derog] Painfully slow or unwilling to pay money that is expected or due. *The beginning of the campaign today is also expected to bring in increased party revenue as 'bad pay' members rush to make themselves financial and thus eligible for nomination.*—TrG (76.03.21, p.1)

bad-peo·ple /1′22/ n (Guyn) [IF] [Usu of a family] People reputed to dabble or deal in OBEAH; OBEAH-PEOPLE.

bad-play¹ /1′2/ vb tr (Antg, Bdos, Guyn, Tbgo) [IF] To deceive, harm or injure (sb) by foul play. **a.** *Everybody knows she bad-playing she boy friend.*—CGBD:6 **b.** *Quashie bad-played Peterkin and broke his leg.*—Tbgo (Ms) □ Distinguish from PLAY BAD; see PLAY¹ □ Phr 2.

bad-play² n (Bdos) [IF] PHRASE make bad-play vb phr (Bdos) See PLAY² Phr 1. □ Cp PLAY BAD. See BAD¹ Phr 4.4, PLAY¹ Phr 2.

bad-sick /1′2/ n (CarA) [IF] **1.** Any form of venereal disease, but esp gonorrhea. *Gerry W—forget to tell them about all those Crab Lice, he forget to tell them about all those Bad Sick he always pick up from dirty whores.*—Antg (Ms) [Cp Yoruba *arun buruku* (sickness + bad) 'any dangerous disease for wh there is no cure'—(pers info, A. Banjo). Also Shona *kuva rehosha yakaipa* (to be with-sickness bad) 'to have venereal disease'—(pers info, M. Kumbirai/L. Feraz)] **2.** PHRASE **2.1 catch/get/have bad-sick** vb phr (CarA) To catch some form of venereal disease. *When you see a man limpin[g] [a]long like that and wearin[g] dark glasses, you sure he got bad-sick.*—(Guyn)

bad sid·down [ba:d sɪdʌn] n phr (Jmca) [AF—Joc] Public display of bad ways; bad conduct with indifference. *We have plenty good people round this place and we mustn't let the brebreh ones take over and have people outside judge us by their bad siddown.*—WeG (73.07.11, p.13, Stella's Partyline) [< bad + sit down, from association

of roadside sprawling, or the suggestive sitting of prostitutes, with slum life. Cp KED Krio *bad sidɔm* '(of woman) sitting so as to expose genital organs']

bad-skin n (Jmca) [IF] ‖BAD-FLESH 1. (Guyn)

bad soil n phr (Tbgo) [AF—Joc] ‖BAD HAIR (CarA) *Tha[t] girl have bad soil man, don[′t] care how she plaster it with vaseline, tha[t] hair don[′t] comb good—she should try Afro.*—(Tbgo)

bad-talk¹ /1′2/ n **1.** (CarA) [IF] ‖bad-mouth¹ 2. (Guyn) ‖bad-tongue¹ (USVI) ‖mové-lang¹ (StLu, Tbgo, Trin) ‖scasm (Crcu, Nevs) Malicious gossip or injurious half-truths. *We don't mind her friendship but it is the bad-talk we can't take.*—AFSTE:34 [See BAD-TALK²] **2.** (Jmca, StVn) Carelessly spoken English with many Cr features; sub-standard spoken English. *Boy, you goin[g] to a good school! Talk proper English and stop talking that bad-talk.*—(StVn) **3.** (StKt) ‖C-REOLE¹ 3. (CarA) *Joe: Big University man ah go all ober the islands dem fu hear people tark bad and rite one book pan de bad tark an' dem. | Bell: Dat is true? | Joe: Yes, ef you spwoil de people tark, dem wont ansa you. For what sum carl bad tark is dey natural.*—LaS (77.02.19, p.4, Bits & Pieces)

bad-talk² /1′2/ vb tr (CarA) [IF] ‖bad-mouth² (Baha) ‖ill-speak (Tbgo) ‖malpalé (Dmca, StLu) ‖mové-lang³ (StLu, Tbgo, Trin) ‖pass scasm [u]pon (sb) (Nevs) ‖pound (sb's) name (Guyn, Tbgo) ‖talk bad about (sb) (CarA) **1.** To speak maliciously (usu in private conversation about a person, place or thing) intending to cause discredit, disadvantage or harm. **a.** *One time I hear Mam call she a whore an' Pap vex: 'What you want to bad talk the woman for?' he say. So you see already where she stan'.*—MHBT:80 **b.** *It's all right for you and your friends to be always bad-talking the boy because he doesn't join you in your drinking parties.*—JJM:176 **c.** *The woman officers started to jeer at me and told me that I should never come back here after I had bad-talked the place so much.*—BoM (80.03.14, p.15) [A prob calque from Afr langs. Cp Yoruba *soro buruku* 'to say evil word (about sb)'; also Mende *i yepe a ngiee* 'he talk (bad things about) him'; also Ki-Yaka *kughoya kwa mbi* 'to evil-speak (in order to bewitch) (sb)'. Also possibly reinforced by IrE *bad talk* 'malicious gossip or swearing' ex 'It was bad talk in that house from morning till night'—(pers info, L. Todd)] **2.** [By extension] To condemn openly (esp a public figure or a nation or country). *There are too many politicians who have nothing to say and get up on platforms bad-talking one another. We want better speeches and something constructive from people who should know better.*—AdN (71.07.25, p.7)

bad-talk·er n (CarA) [IF] ‖bad-mouther (Bdos) One who indulges in or makes a habit of evil or damaging gossip. *And of course after his party lost the election and he also broke up with* *his wife, you can imagine how the bad-talkers enjoyed a field day.*—(Guyn)

bad-tongue[1] *n* USVI [*IF*] ‖ BAD-TALK[1] 1. (CarA) [See note at next]

bad-tongue[2] *adj* (Tbgo, Trin) [*IF*] ‖ MOVÉ--LANG[2] (StLu, Tbgo, Trin) *You forever smiling with the boy and now you bad-talking him. You too bad-tongue.*—AFSTE:35 [An Anglophone calque of the more common Fr Cr MOVÉ-LANG]

ba·du *n* (Jmca) See BADOO

bad-ways[1] /1´2/ *n* (CarA) Irritating or unbecoming behaviour; a mean disposition; bad personal habits. *I expect to be married next Easter but I am beginning to wonder if I am doing the right thing. After going out with this man for three years I know plenty of his bad ways. I am worried about the way he picks on me over how long I stay out, how I spend my money and several foolish things.*—NaT (75.12.28, p.22, Dear Christine)

bad-ways[2] /1´2/ *adj* (StVn) [*IF*] ‖ *malkasé* (Dmca) Ill-mannered; of a mean disposition. *Yo[u] see how she bad ways? I help she wash yesterday and now she don[t] want to help me.*—Csp (Y.M. Keane, 1973, p.16) [By functional n > adj shift of BAD-WAYS[1]]

bad-wo·man ['ba·d-(w)ʊmʌn] /1´22/ *n* (Guyn, Tbgo, Trin) ‖ *djanmèt*[1], *jagabat* (Gren, StLu, Tbgo, Trin) ‖ *wabine, wajang* (Trin) A well-recognized prostitute, or [by extension] any woman of loose morals, living in a slum area. *The lyrics were imaginative, breaking with cliche to mention our 'bad women' or 'wajangs'.*—Kri '78:59

bag *n* (CarA) ‖ CROCUS BAG (CarA) **1.** *The back of the shop smelt of curry where his wife cooked and minded the children, and the front-shop smelt of bags—bags of rice and sugar piled up in both corners as you entered, with the flies buzzing and parading on them.* –Guyn (Ms) **2.** ‖ *bag-cloth* (Bdos) ‖ *bagging* (Guyn) ‖ *bag-spread* (Trin) The same jute material used in the wholesale marketing of rice and sugar, opened out or cut (hence A PIECE OF BAG), or sewn together, for various domestic uses for poor people. *In those days you would see the cartman with a bag over his head, just like a hood, using it as a raincoat.*—Guyn (Ms) **3.** PHRASES **3.1 bag of paddy** *n phr* (Guyn) A sack of standard weight 140 lbs of PADDY (*MRFWB:8*). **3.2 bag of rice** *n phr* (Guyn) A sack of standard weight 177 lbs of rice (*MRFWB:8*). **3.3 bag of sugar** *n phr* (Guyn) A sack of average weight 270 lbs of brown sugar. □ See also BULK-SUGAR.

ba·ga·bu ['bagabu] *n* (Jmca) [*IF*] [*Nursery word*] Dried mucus from the nose (usu of a child).

ba·gasse (be·gasse) ['bʌga:s] *n* (CarA) [Sugar Ind] ‖ *magas(se), megass(e)* (Bdos, Guyn,

StKt, USVI) The mass of dry pith of sugar-canes, after all the juice has been mechanically extracted; various industrial uses are made of it. *I would like to stress that agricultural workers and people who work in that industry which we consider as being important to the country ...get exposed to bagasse, and bagasse affects the lungs and produces chronic disease which has gone unrecognised.*— Bdos (Hd, 74.03.18, p.3522) [Fr bagasse < Sp *bagazo*, Pg *bagaço* 'dregs', with a double meaning, formerly 'dregs of society', 'prostitute' (this earlier meaning still applying as secondary in Mod Fr *bagasse*, Brazilian Pg *bagaço*) □ In *Guyn* sometimes also confused with PEGASSE. See also TRASH[1] 1. [Hist].

ba·gasse-board *n* (Guyn, StKt, Trin) A hardboard panel manufactured from densely compressed BAGASSE fibre. *Opening of the long awaited multi-million dollar bagasse board plant has now been pushed back by two months because of a series of setbacks, most involving water supply.*—ExP (72.06.05, p.1)

ba·gasse-dust *n* (Bdos, Trin) [Sugar Ind] ‖ *megasse-dust* (Bdos) The mildly damp sweet-smelling dust wh is raised when bagasse is discharged from the sugar-factory's chutes. *Pneumoconiosis is a pulmonary disease (farmer's lung) which is said to be caused, in one way, by inhaling bagasse dust.*—Trin (Ms)

ba·gasse-house *n* (StKt) [Sugar Ind] ‖ *magasse-logie* (Guyn) ‖ *megasse-house* (Bdos) A huge shed where the bagasse is stored for baling or re-use as fuel in a sugar-factory. *The contraption was intended to reduce employment at the same time as it destroyed the valuable raw material. For its successful performance would have meant a reduction in the number of bagasse house men; doing away with the need for baling bagasse.*—LaS (65.04.06, p.1)

bag-blind[1] /1´2/ *n* (Bdos) A CROCUS-BAG or a flour-bag hung up as a window blind in a poor home. [< BAG 1. + (*window*)-*blind*]

bag-blind[2] *adj* (CarA) [*AF—Derog*] Socially contemptible; of very low class; belonging to the slums. *... an' I only hope yuh see de way to get de rid o' dat good-fuh-nutten bag-blin' bastard dat only keepin' you back.*—NaT (79.12.28, p.5, Lickmout Lou) [From association of BAG-BLIND[1] with dire poverty] □ Offensive. Usu a term of personal abuse.

bag-cloth *n* (Bdos) ‖ *bag* 2. (CarA) (A euph for) BAG or BAG-BLIND. *The sweating labourers with their bag-cloth aprons—crocus turned to good use—hoisted the bags of flour up by pulley into the warehouse, the flour on their faces but not on their pants.*—Bdos (Ms)

bag-fuzz *n* (Bdos, Guyn) Loose fibres obtained from CROCUS-BAGS (to be woven together for handicraft or other folk use). *Nowadays children flying kites can afford the fine strong cord or string* *to enable them to fly their long-streamered kites high into the heavens; there is no longer the need to collect 'bag-fuzz', the loose fibres from a 'crocus bag'.*—AdN (79.04.15, p.10)

bag·gie *n* (Jmca) [*IF*] Knickers for a baby or little girl. *Ganzi shirts for small boys sell at 1/- a piece and an ensemble of a dress and matching 'baggie' for a little girl for 6/-. In fact I have now with me one such little dress and a matching 'baggie'.*—DaG (67.11.12, p.7) [Nominalization of SE adj *baggy* esp in ref to pants]

bag·ging ['bagɪn/ŋ] /1'2/ *n* (Guyn) ‖ BAG 2. (CarA) *Poor old soul! She had nothing but a piece of bagging spread over some old newspapers on the floor to sleep on.*—(Guyn)

bag-spread [bag-sprɛd] /1'2/ *n* (Trin) ‖ *bag* 2. (CarA) A CROCUS-BAG spread out and most often used by East Indians as a mat or for drying rice in the open. *He suffered himself to be led to his food, and piloting him upon the bag-spread she pressed him gently. 'Sit down, Man. Sit down and eat. You are not vexed with your food, are you?'*—NAGOS:154

ba·ha *n* (StLu) ‖ BAHO (Nevs) *An old man beats out a Christmas carol on his drum, an old 'Aboit', the good old drinking song. His friends circle around each with his own creole implement; violin, the good old amba gouge, baha, and quatro; rehearsing the masqueraders who are scheduled to attend the city's fete this year.*—VoS (73.12.22, p.14)

Ba·ha·ma grass* *n phr* (CarA) ‖ **Bermuda grass** (Jmca, Trin) ‖ **devil('s) grass** (Bdos, Guyn, Trin) 'A low creeping grass with slender wiry stems rooting at the joints, and leaves about 1-1/2 to 3 ins long by 1/10 inch wide' (*PTT:180*); it is often used for lawns and golf greens; *Cynodon dactylon (Gramineae-Poaceae). A gradual change is taking place in natural plant growth all the time. Even on the coastal pastures from year to year the grasses on them appear to rotate. Where there was a thick carpet of bahama grass a long tufted grass has crept in, and in another place a patch of bahama grass has appeared where there was none before.*—DaC (52.06.01, p.9)

Ba·ha·ma Is·lands *n phr* (CarA) [Hist] ‖ **Ba-hamas, The** (CarA) (Earlier name, still sometimes formally used, of) The Bahamas. *The Spanish were the first Europeans to explore that area and, in communicating with their New World territories, they were the first to use it as a maritime highway. They looked with awe at a sea-bed which often seemed to rise beneath them. Coral growths of fantastic shapes and abundance reached for the surface and threatened their ships and lives at every turn. Appropriately, they called it bajamar, shallow sea. And from this word derives the name Bahama Islands—islands of the shallow sea.*—ASOB:1 [In a Royal Grant to Lords Proprietors of November 1,1670, the Bahamas were consigned to the nobleman in these terms: They were 'given and

granted ... all those islands called Bahama Eleutheria Vcaius Providente Inagua and all other those Islands lyeinge in the degrees of Twenty and two to twenty and seaven North latitude commonly knowne by the name of the Bahama Islands or the Islands of the Lucayos together with all and singular Port harbours bayes rivers and isletts belonging unto the Islands aforesaid .... / The grant continues for a long way, but the point of it in connection with this subject of Lucayan charts is to note the explicit use of the words Bahama Islands, even though qualified by the definition 'or the Islands of the Lucayos'. Nothing in other documents pertaining to the history and growth of the islands can lead one to suppose other than that from the middle of the seventeenth century on they were regarded in England much more often as the Bahama Islands than as Lucayans, until the latter expression was omitted entirely. On the contrary, cartographers of other countries retained Lucayos as a rule, in one form or another, in preference to Bahamas throughout the seventeenth and eighteenth centuries, and even in some cases, during the nineteenth. *CBL:31, 32*]

Ba·ha·mas blue-pea *n phr* (Baha) ‖ BLUE-PEA (Jmca) *The Clitoria Ternatea, the Bahamas blue pea, grows best from seed, to more than 15 feet.*—NaG (75.10.02, p.5)

Ba·ha·mas, The *n phr* (CarA) A chain of about 700 islands and nearly 2000 cays (pronounced 'keys') beginning only 50 miles off the coast of Florida near West Palm Beach and spaced in a 750-mile arc through 100,000 square miles of Atlantic Ocean. Only 29 of the islands are inhabited. Bimini is the closest island to Florida and Inagua is closest to Haiti.—*Sky Travel, 75/7, p.39. No Spanish settlements were established in the Bahamas, as these islands were of no economic value.... Later the islands became hiding-places for British buccaneers.*—BTCI:113–114 [Columbus used the name 'Las Islas de Arena, (The islands of sand (banks?)), on account of the little depth of water which there was to the south of them'. (*JJCC:44*). A more general name *Islas Lucayas* probably also introduced by him was later replaced on Sp maps by *Archipiélago de las Bahamas*. 'Island-group of the shallows' from wh Br mariners would have taken the name. See also cit at BAHAMA ISLANDS]

Ba·ha·mi·an [bʌhe·miən] /1'221/ *n, adj* (CarA) (A person or thing) native or belonging to The Bahamas.

Ba·ha·mi·an·iz·a·tion (-is-) *n* (CarA) The process and operation of BAHAMIANIZING; the replacement of non-BAHAMIAN owners and employees in the Bahamas by BAHAMIANS. *While ... attempting to officially woo foreign and specifically U.S. investment capital to the Bahamas, Government is now taking a ridiculous short cut to ruin with 'Bahamianization', possibly feeling that they* *have stumbled over a new euphemism for nationalization or expropriation.*—TrI (76.01.26, p.3)

Ba·ha·mi·an·ize/-ise ['bʌhemiənaɪz] *vb* (CarA) **1.** To make (sth) BAHAMIAN in character or appearance, esp involving some change. **2.** To make it necessary, by processes of legislation, for businesses and industries operating in The Bahamas to be controlled by and/or to employ BAHAMIANS. *One government spokesman pointed out to me, however, that these measures are part and parcel of the government's policy to 'Bahamianise' ... the process of training Bahamians to take over from foreigners is speeded up 'and that is what we want. It is not that we dislike foreigners'.*—GyC (76.07.14, p.7)

ba·ho *n* (Nevs) ‖ *baha* (StLu) ‖ *ass-pipe, bass pipe* (USVI) ‖ *boom-pipe* (Mrat) A long hollow piece of bamboo or metal tube, blown as a folk musical instrument producing a bass note. [Prob < Sp *bajo, -a* (adj) (Music) 'bass']

bai·a·ra *n* (Guyn) (See cit). *This fish is remarkable for two great teeth in the front lower jaw, which when the mouth is closed, extend through the sockets in the head. It is very much like the salmon in behaviour, shape, size and colour. Found in the upper Essequibo and Rupununi.*—Cacique Diary 1977 [Arawak name listed in *BAED* as 'a freshwater fish, *Hydrolycus scomberiodes*']

bai·gan (bi·gan) ['baɪgan] *n* (Guyn, Trin) ‖ EGGPLANT (CarA) *I hear the East Indians on the Corentyne call this thing baigan—they hardly say balanjay—that is their name for it and you hear them talk about curry baigan.*—(Guyn) [Hindi/Bhoj name of this fruit]

baiss·ez-dong/-down ['bese-dʌŋ] *n, vb* (Tbgo, Trin) See BÉSÉ-DÒNG

bait-bas·ket *n* (Bdos) ‖ *hamper-basket* (Bdos) A tough, covered, wicker-work basket full of rotting fish; it is hung in the water over the side of a fishing boat to attract esp flying fish wh are then caught in gill-nets.

bait up *vb phr* (Baha) To attract fish near the fishing-boat by throwing scraps overboard or by some other device. **a.** *When moving to a new fishing drop, you first of all 'bait up' the area by throwing scraps of bait overboard.*—TrI (75.03.20, p.13) **b.** *... following the age-old custom of Abaco, [he] knocks the gunwale of the dinghy with a piece of wood to 'call' or 'bait up' the fish. When they have enough fish, the sail is again hoisted and they are homeward bound for a meal of boiled fish and potato johnnycake.*—TrI (75.03.08, p.6)

Ba·jan¹ (Ba·dian, Ba·jun) ['beɪʌn] *adj* (CarA) [*IF*] Of or belonging to Barbados (often with special senses). **1.** [Esp of food, speech, festivities, mannerisms] Specially distinctive of Barbadian folk and culture. **a.** *Bajan Buffet This*

Sunday / Come and enjoy / Flying Fish and Cou-Cou / Pudding and Souse / Pepperpot / ... / Wash down with Corn-and-Oil.—AdN (Ad, 73.02.10, p.3) **b.** *He is reported to have told investigators that the unknown killer is a man who speaks with a 'Bajan' accent.*—ReP (79.10.21, p.8) **c.** *Nonetheless, the Indian is being gradually acculturated in the society. Many Indians speak (and even curse) exactly like Bajans, some have acquired Bajan mannerisms.*—SuS (82.09.12, p.10) **2.** [Esp of black Barbadians] Having an obvious reserve or a kind of common-sense born of hard experience. *And we should play it in a Bajan way and don't do or say anything at all until we sure we see how things going.*—(Guyn) **3.** PHRASE **3.1 Bajan spree** *n phr* (Trin) [*AF—Joc*] A modest impromptu party. *We just had a little Bajan spree to celebrate my birthday.*—(Trin) [< [bə'bedyʌn] a variant pronunc of 'Barbadian', with loss of initial unstressed syllable, whence ['bedyʌn > 'beɪʌn] by affrication in popular speech. Cp 'Injun', 'Cajun' < 'Indian', 'Acadian'] □ The spellings **Badian, Bajun** have now almost completely been replaced by **Bajan**. In *Bdos* the adj occurs increasingly in Formal contexts, providing a more emotive sense than *Barbadian*.

Ba·jan² ['beɪʌn] *n* (CarA) [*IF*] ‖ *Baje, Bim* (Bdos) [*AF*] **1.** A person of Barbadian ancestry, birth and culture as distinct from one of naturalized citizenship. *As soon as you mention a hotel in this country, the hon. member becomes an expert, but I have told the others on that side that he has as much regard for Bajans as I have for hell.*—Bdos (Hd, 73.07.11, p.2519) **2.** [Often Formal] Any citizen of Barbados, esp one in some position of prominence or authority overseas. *Young Bajan's first book of poems / A young Barbadian writer whose ancestry is as mixed as the rich blend of blood that flows through the veins of West Indian peoples, has just published his first book of poems called 'Douglah'.*—GyC (76.07.20, p.5) **3.** (Guyn, Trin) [*AF*] A person who is smart or cunning, but who may also be outwitted. *Why them Bajans stick up in this land? / And they looking quiet as a lamb / As if they cannot do you any harm / But they tricky, tricky and smart / And the women would break anybody heart.*—SCTR:2 (Cso, 1960) **4.** The dialect of English spoken by native Barbadians. **a.** *The use of Bajan is being restricted to commercials ... the use of Bajan is as a rule done in a humorous context ... many Bajans believe that their language ... only serves a purpose if people are 'mekking sport'.*—AdN (73.12.15, p.8) **b.** *Here in the West Indies, our mixed cultural heritage has made us proud inheritors and prisoners of two languages (Bajan and English) (Patois and French) (Papiamento and Dutch), etc ... Several generations of determined schooling have failed to erase the roots- language, because it has been and is a part of the life-force of our community.*—AdN (82.07.08, p.4) **5.** (Guyn) [*Obs*] A small sweet bun often sold in cake shops.—DGF:10 **6.** PHRASE **6.1 raw Bajan** *n phr* (Bdos) The extreme form of the Barbadian dialect of English strongly characterized by a continuous running together of reduced words. *Although there remains so marked a phonological divergence between what is known in Barbados as 'Raw Bajan' and English that it amounts to incomprehensibility to a monolingual speaker of English, the simple device of slowing down the 'Raw Bajan' speaker will probably have the effect of making him comprehensible to a speaker of English; and this is because the syntactic structure and also (though to a lesser extent) the morphology of present-day Bajan have, in the historical circumstances of that island, developed further away from the language of the field- slaves than in the other Caribbean colonies.*—CPLC(2):41 (M. Alleyne)

Ba·jan·ize (Ba·jan·ise) *vb tr* [*IF*] To make something show or be distinctive of the folk roots of Barbadian culture. *I think that our culture was English. Nowadays, however, it is being Bajanised. We are developing our own norms ... most of them based on the influences of the past. An example of what we are trying to do is the Cropover Festival.*—NaT (75.05.04, p.3) [*Bajan*[1] + causative *ize* Cp 'Anglicize'] □ Note some distinction from BARBADIANIZE.

Ba·jan yam (Bar·ba·dos-yam) *n phr* (Gren, Mrat) ‖ WHITE-YAM (Baha, etc) *Bajan yam is the local name for the Guinea Yam. It is a nice white yam with a very thin skin. It grows on a thin vine with small prickles. Its leaves are rather small. It is harvested chiefly in the month of October and as such it is nicknamed October yam.*—Gren (Ms)

Baje (Ba·jee, Ba·jie) [beˑj ~ ˈbeˑji] *n* (CarA) [*AF—Joc/Derog*] ‖ *Bajan*[2] (CarA) A familiar ref to a native (and usu black) Barbadian. **a.** *'Barbados has had a nice soft way of life so far,' says Proud Bajan. Well let's keep it so Baje, else we may be like Egyptian President Anwar Sadat who, after welcoming Russia into Egypt, expelled some 20,000 Soviet 'advisers'.*—AdN (73.01.22, p.4) **b.** *Licks like fire had broken down on Parris' well-built body just because he was honest enough to admit he was 'a Bajee'.*—TrU (60.09.03, p.3) [Abbr of Bajan, the form *Bajie* being more often also Derog] □ See also BIM[1] 1.

ba·ka·dé *n* (Trin) ‖ BARCADERE (Belz, etc) [< BARCADERE by characteristic Trin E deletion of post-vocalic /r/]

bake[1] *n* **1.** ‖ *roast-bake* (Grns, Tbgo, Trin) A large roasted piece of round, flattened dough about 8 to 10 ins in diameter, very popular as a substitute for a loaf of bread. *See you at Pelang's creole Brunch session every Saturday between 11 a.m.–3 p.m. and enjoy bake and smoke herring or bake and saltfish, souse or pelau, or cow's heel soup.*—SuP (Ad, 79.05.13, p.24) **2.** [Usu pl, always pl in Gren, StVn] ‖ *fried-cakes* (TkCa) ‖ *fry-bakes* (Trin) ‖ *fry-dumpling* (Antg, Jmca) ‖ *johnny-cake(s)* 1. (Baha, StKt, ViIs) ‖ *salt-bakes* (StLu) ‖ *soda-bakes* (Guyn) A small, round piece of flattened dough (with a touch of baking soda) about 2 to 3 ins in diameter, fried

brown in very hot oil, several being usu served with a meal. *We had bakes and saltfish for breakfast.*—(Guyn) **3.** [Usu pl] (Guyn, StLu) ‖ *muffin* (Bdos) ‖ *sweet-bakes* (StLu) As 2., with sugar and much baking powder added. **4.** (Antg, Dmca) ‖ *johnny-cake(s)* 2. (Angu) As 2., but baked (not fried) and with butter (sometimes also sugar) in the mixture. **5.** *PHRASE* **5.1 have it in bake and cake** or, **cake and bake**) *vb phr* (Guyn) [*IF*] To have or to seek to have advantages in any circumstances; to want to have it both ways. *Generally, however, the main problem seems to be that workers are overly anxious to get all they can out of the project. ... but it ought to be made known to them, in no uncertain terms, that 'they cannot have it in both cake and bake', and that 'they cannot eat their cake and still have it'.*—GyC (76.09.08, p.10)

bake[2] *vb tr* (Guyn) *PHRASE* **bake a field** (Guyn) [Rice Ind] To expose a field of rice seedlings to steady sunshine as the last stage of their cultivation, after draining out the second and final flooding of the field. *In wet seeding, an adequate depth of water in the field must be maintained until the plant reaches the stage when baking of the field is to be carried out.*—GSNRC:14

ba·kee (ba·kie, ba·ky) [beˑki] *n* (Guyn) **1.** A large tub of galvanized iron, with handles, conical in shape and about 3 ft in diameter at the mouth, used for washing clothes. [Du Cr/Sran *beki*, 'basin, tub' (*WSNE:120*) < Du *bekken*, 'basin'] **2.** [By extension] A mixing bowl. **3.** [By extension] General term for a container such as a tray.

ba·ker *n* (Baha) General term for a domestic oven (gas or electric). *You left the macaroni and cheese too long in the baker and it's dried up.*—(Baha) [Cp *W1 baker* n 2. 'a small portable oven in wh baking is performed' *An Americanism*. This 'Americanism', noted as such in early editions of *W1*, may have been equally current in early colonial *Baha* life]

ba·ker-shop *n* /1'12/ (Guyn) A small scale bakery. *The big bakeries like Harlequin's, Tang's and so on, got clean new modern equipment and slowly ran the little baker-shops in South Georgetown out of business.*—Guyn (Ms)

ba·kie *n* (Guyn) See BAKEE

bak·ing-i·ron *n* (Trin) ‖ *baking-stone* (Antg, Tbgo, Trin) ‖ *comal* (Belz) ‖ *platine* (Gren, StVn, Tbgo, Trin) ‖ *tawa* (Guyn, Tbgo, Trin) A flat, circular (sometimes rectangular) piece of iron, roughly a square-foot in area, used for baking (roasting) ROTI or CASSAVA-BREAD. *Sookdeo still turned the hat, like how the women turn a roti round before slapping it on the baking-iron.*—SWOS:26

bak·ing-pot *n* (Belz) ‖ THREE-FOOT POT (Bdos, etc) *People still use those big baking-pots especially at Dangriga at times like weddings and Carib Settlement Day.*—Belz (Ms, 1978)

bak·ing-stone *n* (Antg, Tbgo, Trin) ‖ BAKING-IRON (Trin) *The Indian lady purchased a broad new baking-stone to make roti for the wedding.*— Trin (Ms, 1970) [The term '-stone' prob refers to the older device of a 'cooking-stone', and survives notwithstanding the replacement of the stone by iron]

bak·koo (ba·koo) *n* (Bdos, Guyn) See BACCOO

bak·ra *n* (CarA) See BACKRA

bak·sis (back·sheesh, back·sis) *n* (Guyn) [*IF*] ‖ BRAATA(S) (Antg, etc) *So if A buy the whole five oranges, what yo[u] goin[g] give me for baksis?* —(Guyn) [Bhoj/Hin > Perso-Arabic *bakhshiish* 'gratuity, tip for a task performed'] □ The terms *baksheesh, buckshee* (*COD*) are from the same source. The wide currency of the form in *Guyn* (without affrication in the second syllable) is due to the large number of Indic market gardeners.

ba·ky *n* (Guyn) See BAKEE

ba·la·gé ['balaJe] *n* (Mrat) [*X*] ‖ EGGPLANT (CarA) [< BALANJAY with denasalization]

ba·lai-doux *n* (Dmca, Gren) See BALYÉ-DOU

ba·lance-par·cel *n* (Guyn) Any merchandise (usu items of clothing) on wh part-payment has been made and wh is kept by the store until the remainder, or 'balance', is paid up (hence the name); merchandise laid away.

ba·lan·gen(e) (be·lon·gen) [balanJɛn ~ bɛlʌnJɛn/-Jin] *n* (Dmca, Gren) ‖ EGGPLANT (CarA) [Prob a blend BALANJAY + MELONGENE]

ba·lan·jay (ba·lan·ge(r), be·lan·ger, bo·lon·jay, bo(u)·lan·ger) ['ba-lanJe ~ belanJe ~ bʌlʌnJe] *n* (Bdos, Guyn, Mrat, StVn, USVI) ‖ EGGPLANT (CarA) *She does cook like a dream. Last night she put down a plate of bora beans and bolonjay in front of me. Oh man! The bolonjay roll round me mouth and I didn't want to swallow it.*—HMCH:69 [By /r > l/ shift and Cr opening of vowel. < Sp *berenjena*, Pg *berinjela*, ultimately < Arabic *al be'enjen* (Cp Swahili *bilingani* for the same fruit). Cp also the form *bolangena* once current in *Jmca*—(*DJE*). For an elaborate etym note see *OED* brinjal] □ The variant *-ger* spellings are prob due to false association by pop etym, with Fr *boulanger* 'baker', perh because of the bread-like shape of the fruit.

ba·la·ta* *n* (CarA) 1. ‖ *bullet-wood (tree)* (Guyn, Jmca, Trin) A large, evergreen forest tree with abundant, leathery leaves and small, edible fruit, producing a very heavy, hard and durable timber and a thick, white gum for wh its bark is tapped or 'bled'; *Manilkara bidentata* or *Mimusops albescens* (*Sapotaceae*). *He could fling the cutlass with the accuracy of a knife-thrower.... The handle was made of balata, and in the sixty years he had had it, he had never*

changed it.—SPOC:19 [(*BDFC:24*) Carib *bálata* 'tree bearing a fruit resembling the date'] 2. (Dmca, StLu, Tbgo, Trin) The small, brown-skinned, egg-shaped, edible fruit (about an inch long) of the BALATA tree with a sweet, sticky pulp, enjoyed mostly by children. *How long since you've had balata, sapodilla and chinee tamarind? You can get all that in Beetham Market this week.*—TrG (76.03.20, p.5) □ The pl form *bal-atas* occurs almost exclusively in ref to the fruit, whereas *balata trees* is the pl used for the 'trees'. 3. (Also *ballata*) (Bdos) An old car tyre used to make a bonfire (hence BALATA BONFIRE) on Guy Fawkes Night, 5th November (when this used to be celebrated up to the late 1970s in *Bdos*). [From association of BALATA with GUTTA PERCHA and esp rubber, and hence with rubber tyres] 4. (Guyn) [*IF*] A cricket ball, esp one made of BALATA shaped by hand and used in children's backyard cricket. *When big John Trim hit a six a man in a tree shouted 'Sail balata!'.*—(Guyn)

ba·la·ta-bleed·er *n* (Guyn, Trin) One who is employed to tap the latex from the BALATA tree by cutting spirally around the bark so that the gum courses down this 'track' (a process known as BLEEDING) to be caught in a container attached at the bottom of the track. *My duties were not onerous, consisting of receiving and checking the provisions and stores of the monthly boats from Rockstone and taking over the balata from the foremen of the various gangs of bleeders.*—Xmt (Dec. 1936, p.14)

ba·la·wou *n* (StLu) See BAL(L)AHOO[1]

bald-bush *n* (Bdos, Jmca) See BALL-BUSH

bald·head (ball·head[1]) ['bɔlhɛd] *n* (CarA) [Rastaf] Any male (esp a black male) whose hair is trimmed or combed and low; [by extension] any man who is not a member of the Rastafarian cult. *Indeed, it was a surprise which created chaos and argument among Rastafari brethren as to whether or not they should respond to this call. Some argued that it was just another bluff by a political Ballhead in search of votes.*—CrU (76.10.09, p.5) [Conceived as the opposite of DREADLOCKS the unlimited growth of a black young man's hair as a mark of membership of the Rastafarian cult]

bald plate[1] *n phr* (Bdos, Gren, Guyn, Jmca, StVn) [*AF*] The bald patch or part of a man's head. *The son was quite a young man when he started showing a bald-plate in the same place at the back of the head like the father.*—(StVn) [By folk etym or blend of SE *bald-pate* + *plate* in ref to its roundness, etc] □ SE *bald-pate* refers to the person, *pate* itself being an obsolete E word for 'head'; note the difference of CE *bald-plate*.

bald-plate[2] [*IF*]; **bald-plat·ed** *adj* (Bdos, Gren, Guyn, Jmca, StVn) [*AF*] Being bald on a part or the whole of one's head; (SE) bald-pated. *They were married at the Presbyterian church when*

*that shiny bald-plated Scotsman was the priest,
but I don't remember his name.*—(Guyn)

bal·du *n* (Belz) [*AF*] ‖ BALLY[1] 1. (Belz) *If I ask
[h]e do somet[h]ing fo[r] me I sure [h]e wa do it
[be]cause [h]e da me baldu.*—(Belz) [< BALEDOR
by reduction. See next, also BALLY[1]]

ba·le·dor (ba·li·dor) (Belz) [*AF*] ‖ BALLY[1] 1.
(Belz) *If me balidor goin[g] I will go too.*—(Belz)
[< *SDGA* Mexican Sp *valedor* 'friend, pal' with
/v > b/ shift]

ba·li·si·er (ba·li·zi·er, ba·li·zyé) [balizye~-
balize] *n* (Dmca, Gren, StLu, Tbgo, Trin) 1.
‖ HELICONIA (CarA) ... *and small palms such as
the anari extend their graceful fronds into the
languid shade. Along the streams and ravines ferns
... grow in great luxuriance. Everywhere the balisier
thrusts on the attention its ostentatious Wagnerian
inflorescences.*—ACTT:170 2. The political em-
blem of the PNM Party of Trinidad-
and-Tobago. *Don't forget Sparrow did mention /
Wear you balisier on Election Day / The Doctor
break away / Wear you balisier on Election Day.*—
SCTR:72 (Cso, Sparrow) [Fr Cr < Fr name
for plants of the Canna family] □ Pronounced
[balize] in *Trin, Tbgo* and occurs most widely in
metaph and associative use because of its political
symbolism in that State (sense 2.).

ba·li·si·er-bird [balize-bɔːd] *n* (Trin) A
humming-bird wh nests in BALISIER bushes and
feeds on its flowers (hence name); the Rufous-
breasted Hermit (*Glaucis hirsuta* (*Trochilidae*)).

ball *n* 1. (CarA) A sweet somewhat bigger than
a drop, made of the boiled-down or stewed pulp
of some fruit, rounded by hand and rolled in
sugar, hence *lime ball, pawpaw ball, tamarind
ball,* etc. 2. (Guyn) [*AF*] A meal, esp the midday
meal. *Eleven o'clock now, when time for me go
home for me ball, you know, he come to dun me
at me workplace.*—(Guyn) [Prob by association
with foll phrs] 3. PHRASES 3.1 **ball of corn** *n
phr* (StKt) A dish made of corn-meal cooked
and rounded by rolling it in a container. 3.2 **ball
of cou-cou** *n phr* (Bdos) A meal of COU-COU
made ready to serve in the shape of a ball; [by
extension] a person's main meal or means of
sustenance. *Mr Chairman, the hon member for St
Michael West would advocate that we do away
with the ball of cou-cou that we get in here on
Tuesdays.*—Bdos (Hd, 76.06.22, p.67) 3.3 **ball
of fufu** *n phr* (Guyn) A serving of FUFU shaped
into a ball in a mortar using a wet spoon.

bal·(l)a·hoo[1] (ba·la·wou, bal·la·hoe, bal-
·(l)a·hou[1] bal·lo·hou, bal·ly·hoo) ['bala(h)u] *n*
1. (ECar) A slender, blue and silver bony fish,
about 6 to 12 ins long, its mouth having a short,
upper jaw over a long, spear-like bottom jaw
(wh gives it the name of *halfbeak* or *needlefish*
in some international literature); *Hemiramphus
balao* (*Hemiramphidae*). *Ballahoo is very similar
to the gar except it has many scales and it does not
grow so big but as it has a lot of bones you better*

fry it than boil it.—(Mrat fisherman, 1973)
[*BDFC:13* Carib *balaou* 'needle, sea-fish',
whence the name *balao* (*ADF:35*), prob a Sp
form, + intrusive /-h-/ in CE, but note surviving
form *balawou* (*StLu*)] 2. (Guyn) See BALLAHOO[2]
3. PHRASE 3.1 **ballahoo and all the crew** *n*
(Tbgo, Trin) [*AF—Joc*] ‖ *Habra, Dabra and
the crew* (Bdos) Everybody you can think of;
every Tom, Dick and Harry. 3.2 **bal(l)ahoo
brains** *n phr* (StKt) ‖ BAD HEAD[1] 2 (Guyn, etc)

bal·(l)a·hoo[2] ['balahu] *n* (Guyn) A narrow,
flat-bottomed wooden boat that can be paddled
by one person, used for getting about on a large
river; a square-sided snub-ended river 'canoe'
built of caulked boards. *As Estates' messenger ...
I had to paddle the Estates' weekly cash canister
in a ballahoo across the river from Grove each
Saturday, accompanied by an overseer.*—DaC
(52.06.25, p.7) [Prob Arawakan. Cp (*BDFC:
242*) Island- Carib (f) *bálaoüa,* 'the sea']

bal·(l)a·hoo[3] ['balahu] /1'12/ *n, adj* 1. (Belz)
[*AF—Derog*] ‖ *konmès* 1. (Dmca, Gren, StLu)
‖ *kadooment* (Bdos) 1. A great commotion; a
noisy, vulgar row. *There was one hell of a ballahoo
in the shop between some woman and the shopkeeper
over change.*—(Belz) [Poss < AmE *ballyhoo* 'a
noisy attention-getting demonstration or talk'
(*WCD9*) perh blended with SE *hullabaloo*] 2.
(Belz) [By extension, semi-adj] [*AF—Derog*] [Of
a person] Shameless; boisterous; vulgar. *Lawd!
she ballahoo yes! She just like passion girl.*—(Belz)
3. (Bdos) 'A ghost dog, about the size of a calf,
makes a loud clanking noise' (*HDB*). *As I have
been informed, it ain't nice for nobody to see a
ballahoo.*—CGBD:6 [Perh vaguely related to
sense 1.] □ Cp STEEL-DONKEY.

ball-and-thread *n* (Angu) ‖ BALL-BUSH (Bdos,
Jmca) [Prob from appearance of the branchless
stalk]

ball-bush* (bald-bush) *n* (Bdos, Jmca) ‖ *ball-
and-thread* (Angu) ‖ *ball-head*[2] (*bush*) (Jmca,
StVn, Tbgo) ‖ *ball-head cashie, bird-honey*
(StVn) ‖ *candle-bush* (Dmca) ‖ *chandilyé,
chandelier* (Trin) ‖ *Christmas candlestick*
(Baha, Jmca) ‖ *governor-balls* (Bdos) ‖ *gwo-
ponpon* (StLu) ‖ *gwo tèt* (Dmca) ‖ *hop-bush*
(StVn) ‖ *la-lavinton* (Antg) ‖ *lion-bush* (Guyn)
‖ *lion's tail* (Bdos, ViIs) ‖ *man-piaba* (Bdos,
Guyn) ‖ *pomp-pomp* (StVn) ‖ *rabbit-food*
(StKt) ‖ *reeler-bulb* (TkCa) A wild herb growing to about 4 ft in height erect with a four-sided
stalk but no branches, having leaves almost entirely on the lower stalk and a few ball-like,
spiky, reddish-brown inflorences spaced along
the rest of its length; the weed is used both
for medicinal and ornamental purposes; *Leonotis
nepetifolia* (*Labiatae/Lamiaceae*). *The bitter juice
of ball-bush leaves is a remedy for worms in children.*—(Bdos) [From the conspicuous ball-
shaped inflorescences] □ The spelling **bald-bush**
is prob a false refinement. There appear to be
many other folk names for this herb, often in
the same territory (ex *StVn*) because of the

Caribbean-wide folk uses of the 'bush'. Others gleaned but not treated elsewhere in this volume are: **bird-suck** (*StVn*) **four-o'clock** (*Baha, San Salvador Is*) **hollow-stalk** (*Angu*) **John-Cutliss John-De-Layne** (*StVn*) **jumbie-balsam** (*StVn*) **quinine-(bush)** (*TkCa*) **spike** (*Jmca*), **touch-me-not** (*TkCa*), **wild-hops** (*Bdos*).

ball·er ['bɒːlʌ] *n* **1.** (Guyn) A stout piece of stick or wood about 4 to 6 ins long on wh a length of kite-string is wound or rolled into a ball (hence name) to be unreeled as the kite is let out. **2.** (USVI) The reel or spool on wh a fishing line (or also a kite-string) is wound. **3.** PHRASE **3.1 be out to the baller** *vb phr* (Bdos, Guyn) [*AF—Joc*] To be as fully stretched out as your resources would allow; to be unable to do or undertake anything more than you are doing. **a.** *A tell de chil[d]ren a[l]ready I can['t] buy not[h]ing mo[re] fo[r] Christmas. I out to de baller!*—(Guyn) **b.** *The banker in an urgent appeal to the Prime Minister complained that the banking system could not take the strain of further taxation as they were, as he put it, out to the baller.*—Bdos (B, 1991)

ball·head[1] *n* (CarA) See BALDHEAD

ball-head[2] **(bush)** *n* (*phr*) (Jmca, StVn, Tbgo) ‖ BALL-BUSH (Bdos, Jmca) *The leaves of the ballhead bush are boiled and the brew used to relieve menstrual pains.*—Tbgo (Ms)

ball-head ca·shie *n phr* (StVn) ‖ BALL-BUSH (Bdos, Jmca) *You boil the ball-head cashie leaves for cold—the taste is very bitter.*—(StVn) [Perh a blend of BALL-HEAD (BUSH) + *cachi*, (Carib word for) a worthless weed (*BDFC:24*)]

bal·lis·ter *n* (Guyn) [*X*] [SE] Baluster. *Genuine Second Hand Doors, Windows, and Greenheart Ballisters.*—GyC (Ad, 75.12.10, p.24) □ A common literate error in *Guyn*.

bal·loon-juice *n* (Bdos, Guyn) [*AF—Joc*] Any of a variety of coloured, aerated, sweet drinks sold in bottles. [Fanciful name, as if produced by rubber balloons wh come in many different colours] □ Used mainly by adult males, to make fun of those who would not drink alcohol.

ball-starch *n* (Bdos, Guyn, Trin) Starch made from BITTER CASSAVA and shaped by hand into fist-size balls for sale. *Women passing by with attractive trays of ball starch, ball thread, lacing, edging, pins, polish and spices, calling out in lilting nasal tones: 'Get yuh ball starch, yuh ball thread, Yuh nutten meg, yuh spice'n clove.'*—Baj (Feb 76, p.15)

bal·ly[1] (**ba·li**) *n* (Belz) [*AF*] ‖ **baldu, baledor, balidor** (Belz) **1.** A man who is a very good friend of another man; a boon companion. *John da fo[r]-me bally an[d] A woulda do anyt[h]ing for John.*—(Belz) [Familiar reduced form of BALEDOR] **2.** [By extension] Any adult male (used

as equivalent of 'man', 'men', 'person'), fellow(s). *Dem bally really tink dat pipple eena dis country da some pack ah fools. Well dem gat wahn nadder guess. Ev·vybody wide awake. Dem bally shouldda go da Electricity Board collection office an out da town an yer wheh pipple di seh.*—BeA(BE) (79.10.06, p.2) □ Does not seem to occur in pl form. **3.** *excl* [Used as an expression of surprise] *Bally! Boy you should have seen him take off when that snake put the head out!*—(Belz) [Cp *Man!, Boy!*]

bal·ly[2] *n* (USVI) An iron ball-bearing about 1-1/4 ins in diameter used in playing marbles. [Perh a familiar form of *ball*]

bal·ly·hoo *n* (Gren, StLu) See BAL(L)AHOO[1] 1.

balm *vb tr* (Jmca) To soak and sponge a client's body in a ceremonial herbal bath while certain psalms are recited, as part of the faith-healing process in a BALM-YARD. □ Cp BARK-DOWN, BUSHBATH.

balm·ing *n* (Jmca) The treatment of the sick through faith-healing procedures carried out in a BALM-YARD.

balm-man *n* (Jmca) A recognized healer who has or helps to operate a BALM-YARD.

balm-oil *n* (Jmca) Any of the oils used by a faith-healer or a SHEPHERD as a massage or a component in healing a client in the BALM-YARD (see cit). *She took several of the herbs and oils from the little table—purity powder, oil of Rutibel-go, crystal musk, the essence of alabaster amd compellance powder—stirring them all in the tub of water. Dinah was ... bathed down while Shepherd John read aloud the Twenty-Fourth Psalm.*—PCOS:160

balm-yard *n* (Jmca) An enclosed yard where faith-healing ceremonies are performed (including devotional fasting, sacrifices, BUSH-BATHS, drumming, dancing, speaking in tongues, ritual feasting, etc) supervised by a recognized BALM-MAN or SHEPHERD or sometimes a woman in the same role. *In the balmyard was a big hut for chapel, where Swine Laners worshipped.*—BGSB:25

ba·lon·gen(e) *n* (Tbgo) See BALANGENE

bal·sam (bush)* ['bɒ·lzʌm-buš] *n* (*phr*) (CarA) Any of a number of different small, flowering shrubs, growing with wild, spear-shaped, pleasant-smelling leaves (pinkish, cream, purplish, etc) wh are crushed and the juice used for a number of medicinal purposes or for BUSH-TEA; *Impatiens balsamina* or *I. sultani* (*Balsaminaceae*), *Justicia pectoralis* (*Acanthaceae*), etc. See esp GARDEN-BALSAM, ROCK-BALSAM.

bal·yé-dou (**ba·lai-doux**) [bal(y)e-du] *n* (Dmca, Gren) ‖ SWEET-BROOM (Guyn) *You take*

*the same balyé-dou you see the people make broom
with and boil it and give the baby for thrush.*—
(Dmca) [Fr Cr < Fr *balai doux* 'sweet broom']

Bam! (**Bram**) *excl ideoph* [*AF*] ‖ *Badap(s)!*
(CarA) 2 **1.** ECHOIC WORD representing the shock
of sudden impact. *De car skid off the road and
hit de lante[r]n post one time! Bam!*—(Guyn)
[Cp *DAFL* Twi *bám, bánbam, bánbambam* adv
'expressing the sound of striking, clapping, lashing, falling'] **2.** [Frequently by extension] Representing suddenness, surprise. **a.** *I didn't talk
to him any more about the matter, but when the
crop season was over and I get the bonus, Bam! I
pack up a few things and I out off from the estate
and went to San Fernando.*—SWOS:83 **b.** *The
taxi approaches South Street Canal Bridge, Bam!
The smell hits me. The canal looks bubbly and solid
today. Land of the Gods! I am home again.*—
BeA(BE) (80.03.08, p.5) **c.** *Not night, Joe. I
mean in a few minutes' time. Everything is just
going to go off bam! pure darkness and then whoosh!
thunder and lightning.*—SH:32

bam-bam[1] (**bam·bam**) /1 2/ *n* (CarA) [*AF—
Joc*] ‖ *baana* (USVI) ‖ *bamsie, bamsey* (Bdos,
Tbgo, Trin) ‖ *bat-bat* (Antg, Guyn, Jmca)
‖ *batty* (CarA) ‖ *botsie* (Bdos) ‖ *boungie* (Baha)
[Child lang] The buttocks. *Jump in any steelband,
pick on any young man. Turn your back to him
but remember to be prompt. Hold him off with one
hand, bounce him with your bambam.*—Cat 4.1,
p.21

bam-bam[2] (**bam·bam**) /1 2/ *n* (Crcu, Gren,
StVn) ‖ *cassava-bread* (CarA) (Guyn) A variety
of CASSAVA BREAD, sometimes with grated coconut added to the cassava, about a quarter of
an inch thick and baked in a SÈK to give it a
perfectly round shape. *Every landowner, small
or large, must plant cassava (sweet or bitter), to
substitute for bread, which is farine and bam-bam
(cassava bread).*—ViN (74.01.11, p.4) [Poss a
hypocoristic form of Gã-Adangme *bami* (see note
at BAMMIE) + Igbo infl. Cp Ngwa dial of Igbo,
gbam-gbam 'a plate for eating'—B. Oluikpe, *Ms,
1979*. This name may have come to be used by
association of shape and manner of preparation]
□ See also BAMBULA (Antg), CASSAVA-CAKE.

Bam-bam![3] (**Bam ba·lam!**) /3'1/, /3'11/ *excl
ideoph* (CarA) [*AF*] Child's exclamation indicating that another child is going to be in
trouble.

bam·bam-man *n* (Trin) [*AF-Joc/Derog*]
‖ AUNTIE-MAN (CarA) **2.** [< BAMBAM[1] + MAN]

bam·ba-wu·le *n* (Dmca) ‖ BABAWOOLE (Mrat)

bam·boo* ['bambu] *n* (CarA) **1.** A length of the
stiff, hollow, jointed stem of the plant *Bambusa
vulgaris* (*Gramineae*) used for picking fruit, steering boats, setting up tents, etc. **2.** PHRASES **2.1
burst bamboo** *vb phr* (Trin) To explode a
BAMBOO-CANNON. **2.2. marry under bamboo**
vb phr (Guyn, Trin) [*AF—Derog*] To marry

according to Hindu rites, performed by a pundit,
usu in a ceremonial MAARU, the guests being
accommodated in a temporary BAMBOO-TENT set
up for that purpose at the bride's house. Hence
a BAMBOO-WEDDING. **3.** (Baha) Name loosely
applied to the central flowering pole of some
types of AGAVE. **4.** (Trin) ‖ TAMBOO-BAMBOO
(Trin)

bam·boo-band *n* (Trin) A TAMBOO-BAMBOO
band.

bam·boo-can·non *n* (StLu) A joint of BAM-
BOO stopped up at both ends, containing a mixture of moistened carbide, shaken by hand and
then set alight so that it explodes; it is a boy's
noise-making device esp at Christmas time.

bam·boo-chick·en *n* (Belz) [*IF*] The iguana
(esp the female fully grown) the meat of wh
when cooked is said to taste like chicken. [From
the fact that it is often caught in bamboo clumps
where it likes to lay its eggs] □ Cp GUANA (CarA)

bam·boo-flag *n* (Guyn, Trin) [*IF*] ‖ JHANDI
(Guyn, Trin)

bam·boo·la *n* (Antg) See BAMBULA

bam·boo-tam·boo *n* (Trin) ‖ TAMBOO-
BAMBOO (Trin)

bam·boo-tent *n* (Guyn, Trin) [*IF*] A temporary structure framed with lengths of BAMBOO,
as an extension to the bride's house, for the
accommodation or performance of a Hindu marriage ceremony. □ See MAARU.

bam·boo-wed·ding *n* (Guyn, Trin) [*AF—
Joc/Derog*] A Hindu marriage ceremony performed under a BAMBOO-TENT by a pundit.

bam·bou·la[1] [bambula] /1'21/ *n* (Tbgo, Trin,
USVI) [Hist] A lively, African street-dance accompanied by singing and drumming, the call-
response singing (in the *USVI* version) being
led by a BAMBOULA QUEEN and dealing often with
social scandal, while a large drum, sometimes
carried in a cart, is played on by two men, one
astraddle and beating with his hands and the
other using sticks beating on its side.

bam·bou·la[2] *n* (Antg) See BAMBULA

bam·bou·la queen *n phr* (USVI) The woman
singer who composes songs extemporaneously,
based on local scandal, and leads the BAMBOULA
street-dancers who would repeat the lines in call-
response pattern.—*Trin* (*Ms*). '*Queen Coziah*', *a
bamboula dancer, headed the riots and the whole
town was scared stiff.*—PHSAV:14 □ Cp
CHANTWÈL.

bam·bu·la (**bam·boo·la, bam·bou·la**) *n*
(Antg) ‖ CASSAVA BREAD (CarA) *Bambula is made
from the flour of the bitter cassava root. The root
is peeled and grated. It is wrung in a clean cloth*

to separate the juice from the flour. The flour is put in the sun to dry. When it is quite dry it is placed in iron rings on an iron-baking stone.—Antg (Ms, 1973)

bam·bye¹ (bym-bye) adv (CarA) [AF] (A little) later on. **a.** Me keep Christmas quite merry, and no tink no harm. Bym-bye me hearee say dem burning all about Montego Bay.—DLVIE:60 **b.** When the bride and groom coming out, the bride frock tail does say 'married sweet', and the groom coat tail does say 'bambye you goin[g] see.'—Gren (old saying) [< OED by and by adv phr]

bam·bye² (bym-bye²) [bambaɪ~bʌmbaɪ] n (CarA) [IF] ‖ **makafouchèt** (Trin) A portion of food left over to be eaten later on. [By functional shift of BAMBYE¹ produced from such contexts as leave that for bambye]

bam·mer-boat n (Guyn) [AF] A dinghy or other small boat used for smuggling articles stolen from a wharf or from a docked cargo vessel. [Prob < SE bum-boat 'any small boat plying with provisions etc for ships' (COD8), and infl by popular ideoph Bam!, 'a sudden blow', with shift of sense 'make a quick hit', whence bammer 'thing used to do so']

bam·mer-boy n (Guyn) [AF] One who smuggles from wharves using a BAMMER BOAT. [There was] a splash in the silent murky waters of the Demerara river [and] he knew without thinking that it was another of the 'Bammer Boys' in operation who had taken a desperate gamble to escape—GYC (75.12.14, p.39) [See BAMMER-BOAT]

bam·mie (bam·my) n (Jmca) ‖ **cassava-bread** (CarA) **1.** A variety of CASSAVA BREAD that is about an inch thick and is baked brown, usu in a DUTCHY. She was ... pounding cassava in a wooden mortar. When the cassava was well beaten, she would squeeze it through a coconut strainer until it was dry. Then the cassava meal would be made into bammies, which were flat, circular cakes tasting like bread.—RTYW:24 [< Gã-Adangme bami 'cakes or bread of cassada' (ZAGL:27)] □ Also sometimes called **bammie-bread, bam-mie-cake. 2.** PHRASE **2.1 fry-fish and bammie** n phr (Jmca) Fry fish is available in most coastal towns. Bammie comes from St Elizabeth and 'Fry Fish and Bammie' is a specialty of the south coast fishing towns like Old Harbour.—DaG (82.03.12, Food Supp, p.4)

bam·sie (bam·see, bam·sey) n (Gren, Tbgo, Trin) [AF—Joc] ‖ BAM-BAM¹ (CarA) And she hair long to she bamsie.—Cso (Sparrow, 1983) [Hypocoristic form of BAM-BAM¹] □ Though Joc, not considered polite usage. See next.

bam·sie-fly n (Tbgo, Trin) [AF—Derog/Vul] Sb who is a persistent or shameless nuisance or bother. I don't know why you have to follow the dam boy everywhere so like some blasted bamsie-fly.—(Trin)

bam·sie-man n (Trin) [AF-Joc/Derog] ‖ AUN-TIE-MAN (CarA) 2.

ba·nab n (Guyn) See BENAB

ba·nak n (Belz) ‖ **bastard cedar** 1., **sangre** (Belz) A forest tree with a thick, smooth, red-brown bark that gives a blood-red sap when cut; it reaches a height of 140 ft and yields a soft, straight-grained wood that is easily worked; Virola koschnyi (Myristicaceae).

ba·na·na* n (CarA) The sweet fruit of a tree of the family Musaceae which matures soft and generally with a yellow skin, and of wh there are many varieties. See, as separate entries APPLE B., BOMBSHELL B., BOTTLER B., BUCK B., CAYENNE B., CHINEE B., CHIQUITO B., CLARET FIG, DWARF B., FIG (B.), FINGER ROWS, FROG B., GREEN B., WARKA B., etc. **2.** (Neth) ‖ **plantain** (CarA) [Wolof banana; also occurs in other W Afr langs] **3.** PHRASE **3.1 behind the bananas** adv phr (Dmca) [AF—Joc] See BEHIND Phr 4. □ In StLu banana refers to the ripe eatable fruit, fig to the green fruit cooked as a vegetable. By Fr Cr infl, StLu Fr Cr banane = 'plantain'. See note at FIG.

ba·na·na-bird n (Baha) ‖ BANANAQUIT (CarA)

ba·na·na-boat n (CarA) A cargo-passenger, ocean-going vessel designed for the shipment of bananas in its refrigerated holds.

ba·na·na-bor·er n (CarA) A weevil the larvae of wh bore into and weaken the base of the banana-tree, also destroying its root system; Cosmopolites sordidus (Curculionidae).

ba·na·na box·ing-plant n phr (ECar) A large shed in wh bunches of bananas are sorted, graded and washed, and hands cut off the stem boxed for shipping overseas.

ba·na·na-day n (ECar) Usu a fixed day each week when bananas are brought by truck from banana-plantations to be loaded on to a BANANA-BOAT by labourers. □ No article, ex: Wednesday is banana-day.

ba·na·na-flag n (Antg) ‖ **banana flag-flag** (Tbgo) ‖ **banana-floggins** (StKt) ‖ **banana-shag** (Bdos) The dry, brown leaf of the banana tree, esp as used for padding.

ba·na·na-flour n (Jmca) A powder made by pounding sun-dried strips of green bananas in a mortar; it is used to make porridge or for cooking.

ba·na·na-jock·ey n (Gren) [AF—Joc/Derog] Anybody who hangs on to or sits atop of (i.e. takes a free 'ride' on) a truck wh is transporting bananas from a plantation into town.

ba·na·na-na·vel n (Jmca) [IF] ‖ **banana-tas-sel** (Guyn) ‖ **pòpòt-fig** (StLu) The large, purple bracts wh open into a flower-like shape at the end of the stem of a bunch of young bananas.

ba·na·na-por·ridge n (Jmca) Porridge made from BANANA-FLOUR or grated green bananas.

ba·na·na·quit* ['bʌna·nʌkwɪt] n (CarA) ‖ *banana-bird* (Baha) ‖ *beany bird* (Jmca) ‖ *honeycreeper* (StVn, USVI) ‖ *see-see bird* (Gren) ‖ *sikyé-bird* (Trin) ‖ *sugar-bird* (Bdos, USVI) ‖ *yellow-breast* (Antg, Bdos, USVI) A bird about 3 ins long, dark grey in colour, with a yellow breast, a white streak over the eye, and known for its love of ripe bananas and grains of sugar, and in some places also for its warbling or making a 'cheep-cheep' sound; *Coereba flaveola newtoni* (*Coerebidae*).

ba·na·na-shag n (Bdos) ‖ BANANA-FLAG (Antg)

ba·na·na-tas·sel n (Guyn) ‖ BANANA-NAVEL (Jmca)

ba·na·na-walk n (Jmca) See WALK²

ba·na·na-wa·ter n (Jmca) ‖ *plantain-water* (Guyn) Water in wh green bananas or plantains have been boiled, usu re-used as a base for other cooking.

ba·nane¹ (**ba·nann¹**) n (StLu) ‖ PLANTAIN (CarA) [Fr Cr]

ba·nane² (**ba·nann²**) n (Dmca) A small, tasty, yellow and black fish caught near the shore.

ba·na·vis (**peas**) n (phr) (CarA) See BONAVIST

ban-ca·rai·la (**ban ca·rai·li/ca·rai·lee/ co·rail·lie /co·ri·la/co·ri·la**) [ba·n-kraɪla/-li] n (Guyn, Trin) ‖ CERASEE (Baha, etc) [< Hin *baan* 'wild, forest' *adj* + *karelaa* 'bitter gourd'. See note at CARAILA] □ This term, though properly applying to the uncultivated variety, seems to be used by the Indic communities (*Guyn, Trin*) for both varieties, the larger of wh is cultivated as a vegetable. See CARAILA.

band¹ n **1.** (Trin) [Hist] A group of STICK-FIGHTERS with strong neighbourhood loyalties who would fight it out with rival groups, esp at festive seasons, in order to enjoy supremacy. **2.** (ECar) [By extension] [At CARNIVAL time (*Tbgo, Trin, etc*), or KADOOMENT (*Bdos*)] A group of hundreds of masqueraders in highly ornate costumes illustrating in sections a particular theme (historical, topical or imaginary, such as 'The Glory that was Rome' 'Signs of the Times', 'Jumbie Jamboree', etc); they JUMP UP through the streets to the music of a STEELBAND, eventually parading on a stage to be judged against rival groups for the championship prize as BAND OF THE YEAR. □ See also BANDLEADER, KING/ QUEEN OF THE BAND. **3.** ‖ STEELBAND (Trin)

band² vb tr PHRASE **band your belly/jaw/guts** vb phr (CarA) [IF/AF] ‖ *tie your belly¹* (CarA) To (prepare to) deprive yourself of many needs in difficult times; to tighten your belt for a long time to achieve a family aim.

ban·da·ra [ban'da:ra] n (Guyn, Trin) [Indic] A large ceremonial feast for relatives and friends held thirteen days after the death of a member of the family. [Hin *bhaṇḍaaraa* 'feast for all']

ban·ding PHRASE **in banding** adv phr (Guyn) [Agric] [Of a sugar-cane field] Left to lie fallow and flooded for 3 to 12 months to allow (the field) to regain fertility. [*Banding* < *bandin* 'in a state of abandon(ment)' < BANDON; hence *in banding* (by false refinement)]

ban·dit n (Bdos) A small firework wh explodes with a loud pop when thrown on the ground or against a hard surface. [From the surprise caused as from a sudden gun-shot]

band·lead·er n (ECar) A person who chooses a theme, conceives the designs of costumes and organizes the participants for a Carnival BAND.

Band of the Year n phr (ECar) The champion BAND in the *ECar* CARNIVAL or *Bdos* KADOOMENT competition.

ban·don¹ (**band·an, band·ed, band·in**) ['ban dɒn] adj (Gren, Guyn, Trin) [AF] [Of land] Left unplanted or unused for a very long time. [< *abandoned* by aphesis + apocope]

ban·don² (**ban·dan**) ['bandɒn] n (Gren, Trin) [IF] ‖ *bandon land* (Guyn) ‖ *rab land* (Bdos) Land left uncultivated for many years, or land unfit for cultivation. □ Often referred to in *Trin* as *the bandon*.

bang (**sb**); **bang off/up** (**sb**) vb tr (phr) (Antg, Nevs, StKt) [IF] To flog (sb); to beat up (sb). *Me an[d] [h]e fight an[d] [h]e bang me off, momma.*—(Nevs)

bang·a (**bang·ar**) [baŋa] n (Guyn, Trin) ‖ *grou-grou-bèf* (Trin) **2.** The large, hard dried seed of the AWARA (*Guyn*) or GROU-GROU-BÈF (*Trin*) palm used by boys as a marble. [Perh < SE *banger*, i.e. sth that hits hard]

bang·a·lang·a ideoph (CarA) [AF] ECHOIC WORD usu reduplicated representing the ringing of a bell.

bang·a ma·ry* (**ban·ga-ma·ry**) ['banŋa ˌme·ri] n (Guyn) A river fish about 8 ins long with an upturned lower jaw and silvery scales; it is of good food value though not highly prized perh because of its great abundance when in season, and its soft flesh; *Macrodon ancylodon* (*Sciaenidae*). [Cp KED Krio *bonga* 'a small fish, usu the commonest and least expensive in the Sierra Leone markets'; also *DJE* Jmca *bangga* 'a small fresh-water fish'; also *IMED* Mende *bɔnga* 'a fish'. The suffix *Mary* may be Derog, indicating 'cheap, common'. Cp again KED *Meri* 'a woman with a peculiar characteristic, ex *meri-wakabɔut* 'a woman fond of not staying at home'] □ See SEA-TROUT.

bang-bang *n* **1.** (USVI) ‖CASSAVA-BREAD (CarA) **2.** (Gren) CASSAVA-BREAD made with grated coconut added. [Cp Twi *ɔ-baŋkye*, 'cassava']

bang-bas·ing *n* (Mrat) [*AF*] A severe beating. [Prob a blend < *bang* 'hit, beat' + (lam)bas(t)ing]

bang-bel·ly *n* (Jmca) [*AF-Derog*] ‖RICE-BELLY (Guyn)

ban·ja¹ *n* **1.** (StVn) [*AF*] ‖EGG PLANT (CarA) [Prob < *ba(l)anger* by reduction] **2.** (StLu) A coarse wild yam that is said to make good eating.

ban·ja² *n* (Bdos) A song or tune for dancing that evidently used to be accompanied by the banjo. [< *banjo* pronounced [banJA] in *Bdos*]

ban·ja·man *n* (Guyn) A small, dark brown, spiny, freshwater fish wh secretes a milky-white substance and is disliked by fishermen; *Aspredo tibicen*. [< *banjo* + *man*, from its shape like a banjo (*RFLG:268*)]

bank¹ *n* **1.** (CarA) The long mound of soil, 'banked up' for the planting of potatoes, yams, etc hence POTATO BANK, YAM-BANK, etc. **2.** (StVn) ‖*banking* (Bdos, Jmca) The sloping embankment, esp of country roads. *The car started to roll down the bank before it could be brought back on the road.*—ViN (65.06.05, p.1) **3.** (Guyn) THE BANK Usu the East Bank of the Demerara River leading south from Georgetown, the opposite side being referred to as the WEST BANK. *He owns a bus that goes up the Bank as far as Grove.*—(Guyn) **4.** (Belz) A farm or village with a river frontage i.e. with the river bank as one of its borders. *Three homes were set ablaze in the sleepy little farming village of Isabella Bank in the Belize District.*—ReP (79.11.18, p.1) **5.** (Belz) [*AF*] A large quantity of money. *Get off some of that bank and invest in some industry, greedy man.*—AmA (80.02.08, p.2) **5.** (Bdos) [*IF*] A bank holiday. CHRISTMAS BANK is the Bank holiday following Christmas Day, i.e. 26th December.—(Bdos)

bank² **1.** *vb tr* (StVn) To run (a car) off the road (with damage resulting). *He swerved to avoid an oncoming vehicle and unfortunately banked his own car.*—(StVn) **2.** *vb tr* (Guyn) To DOUBLE-BANK (sb); to gang up and beat or BUSE (sb). **3.** *vb intr* (Bdos) To join in an outing on a Bank holiday. *We're going banking at River bay on Whitmonday.*—(Bdos)

bank·a- (benk·a-, beng·ga-, bunk·a-) foot/hand *n* (Bdos, Guyn, USVI) A twisted foot, leg, hand, or arm; a leg or foot bandaged because of a long-standing sore or injury. [Perh from a W Afr source. Cp *DAFL* Twi *ɔ-beŋkumfo* 'a left-handed person'; also *KED* Krio *gbɛnkɔ* 'paralysed hand'.]

bank·ing /1′2/ *n* (Bdos, Jmca) ‖BANK¹ **2.** (CarA) □ Distinguish from *banking* /2′1/ 'putting money in a commercial bank'.

bank·ra (-bas·ket) *n* (Jmca) A large square basket made with a cover. [Cp *DAFL* Twi *boŋkara* 'travelling basket']

bank up *vb intr phr* (USVI) **1.** [Of clouds] To gather and darken. **2.** PHRASE **2.1 It's banking up** It looks like heavy rain is coming.

ban·na (ban·ner) (Guyn) [*AF—Joc*] A fellow or a young woman; any young person past adolescence. □ Teenage slang.

ban·ner-bean *n* (Jmca) ‖BONAVIST (CarA)

ban·quet *n* (Guyn) A fund-raising event such as an open-air fair ('ice-cream banquet') or indoor entertainment ('banquet-and-dance') at wh people would be expected to dress attractively.

Baow! *excl ideoph* See BADAOW!

bap¹ [ba·p] *n* (Guyn, Trin) [Indic] Father. [Hin] □ Respectful form of ref or address to any elderly EAST INDIAN man.

bap(s)²! [bap(s)] *excl* (CarA) [*AF*] ‖**Badap(s)!**, **Bam!**, **Brap(s)!** (CarA) ECHOIC WORDS expressing suddenness of a fall, an event, etc. **a.** *Not me, every cat and dog living in Diego Martin. As soon as they feeling themselves ... baps, it's Diego Martin.*—JPB:48 **b.** *Everything going quiet, when all of a sudden, baps! Election in the air.*—TaP (75.11.02, p.5)

bar¹ *n* (CarA) **1.** Part of a retail shop separated by a curtain or partial partition in wh alcoholic liquor is sold, with table and seating for drinking it there, hence often such signs as '*Grocery & Bar*', '*Restaurant & Bar*', '*Variety & Bar*', etc. **2.** PHRASE **2.1 Bar Solid; Solid Bar** *n phr* (Bdos) [In advertising dances] Hard liquor will be available on the premises.

bar² *vb* (Bdos) ‖*tow¹* (Gren, Guyn) To give sb a ride on the cross-bar of a bicycle. *He was barring his little sister down the road when the bike hit a coral stone and they fell.*—(Bdos)

ba·ra¹ (ba(r)·ra(h)) *n* (Trin) An EAST INDIAN patty a few inches in diameter, made from a dough of wheaten flour, ground split peas and turmeric, deep-fried in oil; it is usu served with curried CHANNA, and is very popular as a snack. [Hin *baṛaa* 'a small fried cake of ground pulse'] □ Usu no pl, hence '*two bara*', etc. See also DOUBLES.

ba·ra² (**bar·ra, bar·rie**) *n* **1.** (USVI) The fish BARRACUDA. **2.** (USVI) A castrated male pig; a barrow. [< *barrow* with opening of terminal vowel]

ba·raat (**bar·ri·at, bha·rat**) [ba′ra:t ~ barya·t] *n* (Guyn, Trin) [Indic] A procession from the groom's house to that of the bride, followed by feasting (formerly with drumming some days before the actual wedding). *Thus to a professional,* *such as she undoubtedly was, what was presented to her was evidently not that total chaos which, with the arrival of the bharat, would soon be descending on the wedding house, but something milder*—NF:194 [Hin *baraat* 'a wedding procession'. The variants **barriat, bharat** may be Bhoj. There is no aspirated bh in the orig Hin word]

ba·ra·hi ['baˑrahi] *n* (Trin) [Indic] An East Indian celebration of feasting on the twelfth day after the birth of a son. [Hin *baarahii < baarah* 'twelve']

Bar·ba·di·an [*F*] (Buh·baˑjan) [*IF*] [barˈbedyʌn ~ bʌˈbeɪʌn] *n, adj* (CarA) ‖ *Bajan* (CarA) [*IF*] ‖ *Baje* (CarA) [*AF*] (A person or thing) native or belonging to Barbados. **a.** *Barbadians now have their own Rudolph Walker to shout about! Walker, a Trinidadian was the first black to make it big in British comedy. Now comes another black to British TV screens! His name is Charlie Williams, who, although born in Britain, is of Barbadian parentage.*—SuP (74.06.02, p.8) **b.** *It don' mean dat Buhbajans / Never learn to tell de time / But 'pon dis island in de sun / We know wuh it is to lime.*—PeL (78.01.13, p.2, J. Layne-Clark) □ The spelling **Buhbajan** is Joc, representing a common folk pronunc. See also BAJAN.

Bar·ba·di·an·ism [barˈbedyʌnɪzəm] *n* (Bdos) An attitude to life considered characteristic of BARBADIANS. *When making the original appeal, I put my faith in a unique ideology I like to call 'Barbadianism' and that is the living together of a large group of people in a very small area in a harmony that has baffled and will no doubt continue to baffle, anyone who tries to analyse the phenomenon.*—AdN (77.09.23, p.1)

Bar·ba·di·an·iz·a·tion (-is-) [barbed-yʌnaiˈzeʃʌn] The process or act of making (sth) markedly BARBADIAN in character or appearance. *So CBC-TV has announced the production of its first all-Barbadian television play. This is the first solid bit of evidence of Barbadianisation of TV since all those promises about Peyton Place.*—NaT (75.10.26, p.24)

Bar·ba·di·an·ize/-ise [ˈbarbedyʌnaiz] *vb tr* (Bdos) To make (sth such as an institution, festival, etc) markedly BARBADIAN in character or appearance. **a.** *The writers ... all rely heavily on Standard English spelling and any attempts to 'Barbadianize' a word result in a modification or distortion of the English, reinforcing the layman's concept of Bajan as a 'corruption' or 'distortion' of English.*—Csp (D. Johnson, 1985) **b.** *Featuring a parade of costumed bands accompanied by musical groups, this is part of an all-out effort being made by the Crop-Over Festival Committee to 'Barbadianise' the festival ... / Each band would be expected to portray a Barbadian theme, ... He pointed out that the bands were not restricted to the examples listed but could portray any part of Barbadian life they choose.*—AdN (78.03.12, p.1)

[*Barbadian* + causative *-ize*] □ Cp BAJANIZE wh is the emotive equivalent.

Bar·bad·ian·ness *n* (Bdos) **1.** The better qualities considered characteristic of BARBADIANS. *As we come to terms more fully with ourselves, we gain a sense of Barbadianness which provides us with a strong perspective and helps set our priorities in order.*—Bdos (Ms, 1984) **2.** ‖ BARBADIANISM (Bdos)

bar·ba·dine (ba·ba·din, bar·ba·dene) [ˈba(r)bʌdiːn] *n* (Dmca, Gren, Trin) ‖ GRANADILLA (CarA) [Fr, this name being also used in *Mart* and *Guad*]

Bar·ba·dos-al·mond *n* (ECar) ‖ ALMOND (CarA)

Bar·ba·dos-cher·ry* *n* (CarA) ‖ *cerise* (StLu) ‖ *cherise* (Nevs) ‖ *cherry* (CarA) ‖ *garden-cherry* (CayI, Jmca) ‖ *sour cherry* (StVn) ‖ *West-Indian cherry* (CarA) A small ovoid fruit faintly lobed, up to one inch in diameter and bright red when ripe, with three seeds in acid-sweet flesh; it is widely used for making jam or drink; *Malpighia punicifolia* or *M. glabra* (*Malpighiaceae*). □ Widely referred to in *CarA* simply as *cherry*.

Bar·ba·dos-e·bo·ny *n* (Bdos) ‖ WOMAN('S) TONGUE (CarA) [The tree flourishes wild in *Bdos*, and 'the wood is dark and close-grained and polishes well'—GLPFB:187]

Bar·ba·dos-ed·doe *n* (Gren) ‖ DASHEEN (CarA)

Bar·ba·dos green mon·key *n phr* (Bdos) ‖ GREEN MONKEY (Bdos)

Bar·ba·dos Land-Ship *n phr* (Bdos) A group of (usu rural) men and women formed basically as a Friendly Society; it functions exclusively on land, but is organized and best known as a ceremonial copy of the British Navy, each group being identified by a ship's name ('Iron Duke', 'Revenge', etc) and ranking officers (from Lord High Admiral down); the group parades at chosen times with military-styled band, all members in decorated white uniforms (the women as nurses) and at other times they drill, perform co-ordinated dances, and plait the maypole. □ This social feature, uniquely developed in *Bdos*, is said to go back to the 19C.

Bar·ba·dos-leg *n* (CarA) ‖ BIG-FOOT (Guyn) [So-called first in England, where it is said that soldiers who had been stationed last in *Bdos* got the disease, though they were prob earlier stationed in *Guyn* where the disease has always been prevalent, whereas it has always been exceptional in *Bdos*]

Bar·ba·dos-pride* *n* (CarA) ‖ *dwarf-poinciana* (CarA) ‖ *flower-fence* (Baha, Jmca) ‖ *Pride of Barbados* (CarA) An erect but scanty inflorescence of brilliantly orange-red or yellow flowers and five-inch long green pods, borne on a prickly shrub with foot-long compound leaves; it grows wild but is often cultivated esp as a hedge; *Caesalpinia pulcherrima* (*Leguminosae*). [Said to have been first introduced to the *CarA* in *Bdos* in 1657 (*GWTSB:16*)] □ See PRIDE OF BARBADOS

Bar·ba·dos scho·lar *n phr* (Bdos) See SCHOL-AR

Bar·ba·dos-yam *n* (Gren, Mrat) See BAJAN YAM

Bar·bu·dan [barbyudʌn] *n, adj* (CarA) (A person or thing) of or belonging to the island of Barbuda (wh is part of the State of Antigua & Barbuda).

bar·ca·dere (**bar·ca·dare, bar·qua·dier, bar·que·dier**) [barkʌde·r] *n* (Belz, CayI, Jmca) ‖ *bakadé* (Trin) 1. (CayI, Jmca) A pier or wharf. 2. (Belz) A storehouse built on a pier, used in the logging industry. 3. (Jmca) [Hist] A shipping port. [< Sp *embarcadero* 'pier, jetty, loading platform'] □ The Sp origin suggests *barcadere* as the preferable spelling.

bare [be·r] *adj* 1. (Guyn) [In ref to funds] Hardly enough or barely enough (when something more might have been expected). *My hands/pockets are bare.* (= I am short of cash).— (Guyn) 2. (Baha, BrVi) [Of a boat] For rent or charter without crew. 3. (Bdos, Jmca) ‖ *empty* (Antg) ‖ *naked* (Jmca, Tbgo) Nothing but; only; sheer. **a.** *Man, sometimes you dream bare foolishness.*—(Bdos) **b.** *If one hon. member wishes to get up and say you must not have Mr Hinds because he is bad and another hon. member wishes to get up and say you must not have him because he is good, that is bare confusion; we know they are confused.*—Bdos (Hd, 76.10.06, p.6) 4. (Bdos) [AF] [By extension of 3.] Nothing but, and therefore too much of. *Her room is bare clothes, pack up everywhere, and she even sleep with some on the bed.*—(Bdos)

bare·feet *adj* (CarA) [X] Barefoot; barefooted. *Not all the children go to school. Some are sick. Some have no clothes nor books. All are barefeet.*— ExP (70.12.25, p.1) □ An error of overcorrection.

bare·ly *adv* (Bdos, Trin) [X] Merely; only; simply. *It serves some of them right; they believe that by barely joining and having a political card and playing up to politicians is the avenue to success.*—Bdos (Hd, 76.02.10, p.5993)

bare-neck fowl *n phr* (Bdos, Nevs, StKt) ‖ *clean-neck fowl* (Gren, Guyn, StVn, Trin, ViIs) ‖ *kou-nèt, kou-touni* (Dmca) ‖ *koupliché* (StLu) ‖ *peel-neck fowl* (Belz, Guyn, Jmca, StVn) ‖ *pick-neck fowl* (TkCa) A variety of chicken wh has no feathers on the neck,

sometimes also with its body feathers curled backwards. See SENSEH FOWL

bar·gain *n* (Guyn) [IF] 1. Agreement. 2. PHRASES 2.1 **make bargain (to do sth)** *vb phr* (Guyn) [IF] To arrange or agree (often in secrecy) to do something together, with some advantage to both or all the persons involved. 2.2 **bargain make before country take** [...mɛk...tɛk] (Guyn) [Cr Prov] It is certain that there was some conspiracy or collusion before some unexpected event could take place.

barge *n* 1. (CarA) [Hist] A keel-bottomed boat manned by oarsmen used to ferry passengers and cargo from a ship moored in mid-harbour to shore. 2. (Baha) A slatted wooden cage that could float in the water, for storing live crawfish. *Charles had to establish several crawfish buying stations, at various strategic points about Abaco. Each station he equipped with an ice box and a number of slatted wooden cages, called barges which were moored so they could float in the water. These were for storing live crawfish.*—TrI (70.06.20, p.5) 3. PHRASE 3.1 **Barge tu[r]n over!** (Belz) [AF—Joc] There is big trouble; 'the fat is in the fire'.

ba·ri·ca·der ['barɪkedʌ] *n* (Angu, StKt) [One of two kinds of medicinal plant] 1. BLACK BARICADER ‖ BELLY-ACHE BUSH (Bdos, etc) 2. WHITE BARICADER ‖ PHYSIC-NUT (Bdos, etc)

ba·ri·di ['bʌriːdi] *n* (Guyn) 1. A bird of the hawk family, regarded as a determined and gluttonous hunter. 2. [By extension] A person who is shamelessly self-seeking (of money, runs in cricket, etc). [Perh < Arawak, *bariri* 'chicken-hawk'— EILCA:59] 3. PHRASE 3.1 **eat like a baridi** *vb phr* (Guyn) To eat gluttonously and selfishly.

Ba·ri·ma-plan·tain [bʌri·mʌ plantɪn] *n phr* (Guyn) ‖ BLUGGO (Belz, etc) [From its thriving in the Barima River area in the N. W. Region of *Guyn*]

bark; bark-bath, bark.ing (-down) *n* (CarA) ‖ BUSH-BATH (CarA) [From the use of pieces of bark from certain trees in preparing the herbal bath]

bark down (sb); bark out (sb) (Antg) *vb phr* ‖ *balm (sb)* (Jmca) ‖ *bath down, bathe (sb) down* (Jmca, Nevs) ‖ *wash down (sb)* (Mrat, StKt, TkCa) To give a herbal or BARK-BATH (to sb) either as a remedy for some persistent sickness, or in order to drive away or defend the person from evil spirits.

bark-log (pil·low) *n* (*phr*) (Belz) ‖ *polak* (Belz) A raft made of balsawood (because of its lightness) for floating LOGWOOD downstream for export. [Cit at POLAK explains]

bar·ley PHRASES **find out/know/teach you /tell you where barley grows** (Guyn, Trin) To learn by painful experience; to learn, or make sb learn a tough lesson from the book of life. □ See WHERE Phr 6.1 and cit.

barn-owl n (Trin) ‖ JUMBIE-BIRD 1. (Guyn) *The barn-owl's cry has been described as an eerie rasping hiss or snore: 'kschh'.*—HBTT:128 [From the fact that its habitat is mostly dark, old, or disused buildings where it feeds, esp on rodents and lizards]

Bar·on Bliss Day n phr (Belz) March 9th, a public holiday in Belize, marked by regattas and sea-sports, honouring the memory of Baron Henry Bliss, a philanthropic English benefactor of Belize who died March 9th, 1926.

Bar·on·i·an n (Guyn) A native of Beterverwagting Village on the East Coast of Demerara (about 9 miles from Georgetown). [From Baron van Grovestin, a pre-emancipation owner of the estate, who was well-liked, so that the black freedmen who purchased it (1841) kept the fond pseudonym 'Baronian' previously adopted by them]

bar·qua·dier (bar·que·dier) n (Belz) See BAR-CADERE

bar·ra n (Belz, CayI, Jmca) [AF] See BARA¹, BARA²

bar·rack n (Trin) ‖ *range¹, tenement* (Guyn) **1.** A long, low building raised on short, wooden pillars and consisting of several adjacent rooms under one roof, in each of wh is lodged a labourer and his family on a sugar or cocoa plantation. [Cp *OED barracoon* 'a rough barrack, set of sheds, or enclosure, in wh negro-slaves (originally), ... are temporarily detained'] **2.** [By extension, often *barracks* n sg] The same building in urban slums. *The rooms were about twelve feet by twelve feet, and in this particular barrack...all the doors and windows gave onto the yard which was seventy-five feet wide by thirty feet deep; so that the two rows of rooms, extending along the width of the yard, faced each other*—MBF:90

bar·rack-room n (Trin) ‖ *tenement-room* (Guyn) **1.** One of the rooms in a BARRACK in wh a whole family lives. **2.** [By extension, sometimes *barrack-house*]. Any urban slum dwelling.

bar·rack-yard n (Trin) ‖ *nigger-yard, range-yard, tenement-yard* (Guyn) The area allotted to or enclosed by BARRACKS used for communal domestic purposes by labourers' families, and associated with much rough language and behaviour.

ba(r)·ra·cu·da* (ba(r)·ra·cou·da, ba·ra·cou·ta/-ti, ba(r)·ri·cu·ta) n (CarA) ‖ *bétjin* (Dmca) A spotted silvery-grey, deep-sea fish, often 4 to 6 ft in length; it is very savage and, if caught in certain areas, poisonous; *Sphyraena spp.* [Sp, prob from an Amerindian source. Cp Arawak *bara,* 'sea']

bar·rel-cac·tus n USVI ‖ TURK'S CAP CACTUS (CarA)

bar·ri·at n (Guyn) See BARAAT

bar·rie n (Baha) See BARA²

bar-shop n (StKt) A retail shop that sells grocery items as well as alcoholic liquor with a small area provided for drinking.

bar·sle (bar·zle) n (Tbgo) A medicinal herb with a sweet-smelling leaf. [Perh < (sweet) basil]

Bar·ti·can n (Guyn) A resident of Bartica, the principal river-township in the Essequibo county of Guyana.

Bar·ti·ca Triangle, The n (Guyn) A convenient name for a triangular area of several hundred square miles of land, rich in minerals and timber enclosed by the Essequibo and Mazaruni rivers with Bartica at their confluence (or the apex of the triangle) and a third indeterminate side marked by a high southern plateau beyond wh travel is difficult—*(pers info, P. Allsopp).*

Bas·comb mule n phr (TkCa) [AF] PHRASE Bascomb mule out of the stable [AF—*Joc*] Things have got out of hand; there is a hullabaloo.

base n **1.** (Guyn, Trin) The Base: The American air or naval base during World War II, where many local people were employed, hence the phr *to be working at the Base.* **2.** (Belz) [AF] A hang-out or 'pad' (AmE) where young people gather. *Many of the citizens who loiter at places like this which is called a 'base' gamble, smoke marijuana, plan mugging, or wait until each meal is prepared at their homes. These bases are helping to destroy many Belizeans.*—AmA (80.10.24, p.2)

base out; bas.ing out vb phr (Belz) [AF] ‖ LIME; LIMING (ECar) [By functional shift of BASE 2.]

Bash·aow (-au, -ow)! [bašau] *excl ideoph* (CarA) ECHOIC WORD representing the sound of sth falling into water, of a wave hitting rock, etc.

bash·ie ['baši] n (Gren) ‖ WASH-YOUR-FOOT-AND-COME (CarA) [< SE slang *bash*]

bas·ic-school /1'12/ n (Jmca) A preparatory school catering for children under 6-1/2 yrs of age, and usu run by an old retired primary school teacher.

bas·i·lect ['besilɛkt] [Linguistics] ‖ *creole¹* (CarA)(i) That level of spoken E developed in a(Commonwealth CarA) territory wh is socially regarded as the lowest; it is often referred to as 'broken English', 'dialect', 'flat talk', 'patois' 'raw talk' etc, but in linguistic study as 'creole'.. [Term introduced by W.A. Stewart, 1964, from

Gk *basi* 'bottom' + *lect* (< dialect). See note at
ACROLECT]

bas·ket PHRASES **1. give (sb) basket to back/
carry/fetch water** (CarA) ‖ *have a sieve to
carry water* (Baha) **(i)** To give (sb) a difficult
or nearly impossible task; to make life difficult
(for sb). **(ii)** To pass on a very difficult responsibility to somebody else. [From a very
common motif in W Afr folklore, often ex-
emplified in provs, ex Igbo *Ejiro nkata echu nmiri*
'One does not take the basket fetch water'] **2.
give basket; give (sb) a basket to hold** *vb
phrs* (Trin) [*AF—Joc*] [Variant forms of the prec]
To trick, hoax or mislead (sb); [by extension] to
pull (sb's) leg. **3. hang your basket too high**
vb phr (Baha) [*IF—Joc*] See HANG Phr 3. **4. have
a basket/sieve to carry water** *vb phr* (CarA)
[*IF*] To have a very difficult responsibility or
impossible-looking task. **5. have/hold (the)
basket; take basket** *vb phrs* (Trin) [*AF—Joc*]
To allow yourself to be fooled; to allow yourself
to take some difficult responsibility that is not
your due. □ See as separate entries DUNG-BASKET,
ESTATE-BASKET.

ba·so·dee *adj* (Trin) See BAZOUDI

bass[1] [ba:s] *n* (CarA) [*AF—Cr*] Boss. [Cr pronunc surviving < Du *baas* 'master, foreman,
boss']

bass[2] [ba·s] *n* **1.** (Guyn) Name loosely used for
several species of fish of the family *Serranidae*.
2.* (USVI) Name sometimes given to the TAR-
PON, a very large game-fish (*Megalops atlanticus*),
sometimes to a number of kinds of copperish-red
or red fishes with a black spot near the tail, wh
are of 'excellent food value' (*Sciaenops ocellata*)—
(*ADF*:88).

bass[3] (base) [be·s] *n* (ECar) ‖ *bass-pan, boom-
pan* (ECar) One of a set of four to six whole
steel-drums with one end cut out, and the other
hammered and grooved into large sections to
provide three or four bass notes, so that the set
of pans together provide the whole musical range
of bass notes that their player, the BASSMAN,
needs. (See STEELBAND)

bas·sa-bas·sa[1] ['basa-basa] /1'122/ *n* (Angu,
Bdos, Gren, Guyn, Trin) [*AF*] ‖ *kas-kas*[2] (Jmca)
1. Trouble; noisy disagreement and confusion;
(esp *Bdos*) a quarrel wh ends in a fight. *Man,
you managing a big bassa-bassa. Jasper and Saga-boy
going have a stick-fight, becausing Saga-boy take
Germaine to a Old Year dance last night.*—CISH:
9 [Yoruba *basa-basa* 'nonsense'; *ZAGL* Gã *ba-
sabasa*, n and adv, 'hubbub; disorder; disorderly]
2. PHRASE **2.1 make/play bassa-bassa** (Gren,
Guyn, Trin) To make or cause trouble in a
particular matter; to be very difficult and irritating.

bas·sa-bas·sa[2] *adj* (Antg, USVI) [*AF—Cr*]
Just managing to survive; taking things easy; not
complaining. *S1: How you do? / S2: Me jus' a*

bassa-bassa.—(Antg) [Perh < Sp *basta*, 'enough']

bass-gui·tar·ist (bass-gui·tar-man) *n*
(CarA) ‖ BASSMAN 1. (CarA)

bas·si(e) ['basi] *vb intr* (Belz) To stroll idly; to
pass the time away; to idle. [Perh < Sp *vacilar*
(fig) 'to hesitate, hang back, dither']

bass·man ['be·sma·n] *n* **1.** (CarA) ‖ *bass-
guitarist* (CarA) The player of the bass electric
guitar in a combo. **2.** (ECar) The player of the
BASS-PAN in a steelband.

bass-pan [be·s-pan] *n* (ECar) ‖ BASS[3] (ECar)

bass-pipe *n* (USVI) ‖ BAHO (Nevs) □ Also ASS-
PIPE (USVI).

bas·tard ce·dar* *n phr* (Belz) **1.** ‖ BANAK (Belz)
2. (Gren, Jmca) A tall shade tree whose timber is
useful for furniture making; *Guazuma ulmifolia*
(*Sterculiaceae*).

bas·tard plan·tain *n phr* (StVn) ‖ CAYENNE
BANANA (Guyn)

bat[1] *n* **1.** (Angu, Antg, Bdos, Jmca) Any flying
insect esp moths (wh are often associated with
superstitions among older folk). **2.*** (Guyn)
‖ *leather-bat, night bat* (Bdos) ‖ *micy-bat*
(Antg) ‖ *rat-bat* (Belz, Jmca, Mrat, TkCa) The
fruit-eating bat; any of the flying mammals of
the order *Chiroptera*.

bat[2] *vb* **1.** (CarA) [*AF—Joc*] [Of older persons]
To keep alive and look well for your age. **2.**
(Guyn) [*AF*] To drink strong liquor. *And you
know that woman would sit down and bat her rum
and water with the lawyers!*—(Guyn) [Metaph
usage from cricket] **3.** PHRASE **3.1 bat(ting)
well** *vb phr* (CarA) (See 1). *You wouldn't believe
the old man is eighty, you know? Batting well,
man!*—(StKt)

bat-and-ball /1'12/ *n* (CarA) ‖ *bat-and-
ricket* (Belz) ‖ *scrubby* (Guyn) An improvised
game of cricket often played with a bat made
from the upper stalk of a coconut-branch and a
wooden or balata or other home-made ball.

bat-and-rick·et /1'122/ *n* (Belz) ‖ BAT-
AND-BALL (CarA) ['Ricket' < wicket]

bat-bat (bat·bat) *n* (Antg, Guyn, Jmca) [*AF—
Joc*] ‖ *bam-bam*[1] (CarA) [Child talk] The buttocks of an infant. *My little poudounks has to
learn to put that little bat-bat on that little potty,
or Mummy is going to spank that same little
bat-bat.*—(Guyn) [Cr pronunc of *bot*, abbr of
'bottom' + reduplication □ Not considered *Vul*,
as is BATTY.

bat·chac *n* (Trin) See BACHAC

bat·chie (bat·chy) *n* (Guyn, Trin) See BACHIE

ba·teau ['bato·] *n* **1.** (Guyn) ‖ *bateau-boat* (Guyn) A square-ended, wooden boat about 15 to 20 ft long, built usu with a flat bottom but curving upwards at each end; it serves as river transport esp for farmers using paddle and pole. **2.** (Belz) ‖ PITPAN (Belz) **3.** (Bdos) A small flat-bottomed boat for use in calm water. **4.** (USVI) A dinghy. **5.** (Jmca) A raft for use in rivers. **6.** (Guyn) The CABBAGE-BARK used by children as a toy boat. □ Pl *bateaux*. See also BATO¹.

ba·tel (bat·tel) ['batɛl] *n* (Guyn) [Gold-mining] A round metal strainer used by PORK-KNOCKERS in the process of separating gold-bearing gravel from soil. [Cp Fr *battée* 'basin for washing through gold-bearing sands', also *TDV* Venz Sp *batea* 'oval-shaped wooden utensil ... for sifting, etc']

bath [ba·θ ~ ba·t] *n* (CarA) **1.** Any normal manner of washing the body, hence 'river-bath', SEA-BATH, SHOWER-BATH. **2.** ‖ BUSH-BATH (CarA) □ In CE BATH is not normally used as a vb as it is in BrE, AmE. The n pl is also normally pronounced [ba·θs] in educated CE. Cp BrE [baðz] The normal equivalent verb is BATHE [be·ð]. See. **3.** *PHRASE* **3.1 give (sb) a bath** *vb phr* (CarA) To prepare and administer a special herbal bath (to sb) to heal a persistent sickness or to drive away a besetting evil spirit.

bath down¹ (sb) *vb phr* (Jmca, Nevs) ‖ BARK DOWN (SB) (CarA)

bath-down² *n* (Jmca, Nevs) ‖ BUSH-BATH (CarA)

bathe [be·ð ~ be·d] *vb* (CarA) **1.** To wash the body in any normal way, esp under a shower but also in the river or sea; to have a bath. □ In CE *bathe* is used almost exclusively as the vb derived from *bath*, not functioning as a noun as it does in BrE, AmE. See note at BATH. **2.** *PHRASES* **2.1 bathe down (sb)** *vb phr* (Nevs) ‖ BARK-DOWN (SB) (CarA) **2.2 bathe off** *vb phr* (CarA) To wash or cleanse parts of the body with a rag, esp without wetting the head. **2.3 bathe your skin** *vb phr* (CarA) [IF] To bathe; to wash the body under a shower or in any other routine way (in the river, in the sea, etc). □ Not considered *Joc* or offensive. The supportive complement is prob a reflection of W. Afr semantics. Cp *DAFL* Twi *guare*, 'to wash the whole body'; Contrast *horo*, 'to wash single parts of the body'

bath-net·tle *n* (Nevs) ‖ STINGING-NETTLE (Guyn, Trin) [Prob from use of leaves in a decoction as folk- medicine and in preparing herbal baths]

bath-pan *n* (Belz, Gren, Jmca) A large old-fashioned moveable bath-tub still used as a wash tub for laundering.

bath-pants; **bath-trunk(s)**, **bath·ing-trunk(s)** *n* (CarA) A man's or boy's swimming trunks. □ The sg *-trunk* (sg) is erron.

bath-suit *n* (CarA) A swim-suit or bathing costume for a woman or child; a bathing-suit.

ba·ti·manm·zèl (ba·ti·mam·selle, batty-mam·selle) ['batimamzɛl] *n* (Trin) ‖ POND-FLY (Bdos, Guyn) [Fr Cr perh (with denasalization) < *batiman* (boat) + *zèl* (wings) = flying boat; or *ben* (bath) + *ti-mamzèl* (little girl) *i.e.* 'little girl (at) bath' (?). Cp MAWI-SOSÉ (*StLu*)]

ba·ti·man *n* (Antg, Gren, Guyn, Jmca) See BATTY-MAN

ba·to¹ (ba·teau) ['bato] *n* (Tbgo) ‖ *beater* (Baha, Guyn) A flat wooden cudgel for beating dried PIGEON PEAS in a CROCUS BAG to separate the peas from the husks. [Fr Cr < Fr *baton* 'stick, cudgel', with denasalization] □ *Bateau* is a misleading—(hence erron) spelling.

ba·to¹² ['bato ~ ba'to:] *imper vb* (Guyn) Stop now! (Said by the leader, to stop a continuously repetitive verse of a folk-song). [Prob of W Afr origin. Cp *IGED* Grebo *bati o!*, 'expression used by a person to claim audience's attention'; also *ZAGL* Gã *ba* (strong imperative) 'come' + *to* 'cut down']

bat·tel *n* (Guyn) See BATEL

bat·ty (ba·ti) ['bati] *n* (CarA) [AF-Vul] **1.** ‖ BAM-BAM¹ (CarA) [< *bottie* (hypocoristic form) < bottom, with characteristic CarA Cr vowel opening [a] < SE [ɔ]] □ Usage ranges from *Vul* in most territories with the same connotation as SE 'arse', (ex *carry your batty* (Guyn) (= 'Get to hell away from me')) to the merely unsophisticated, as in *'Teacher I have a boil on my batty and I can't sit down'*—(Antg). It is, however, always best avoided even in *IF* contexts. **2.** *PHRASE* **2.1 like batty and bench** *adj phr* (Jmca) [AF—Joc/Vul] [Of friends] Closely intimate, or always seen together. *You see how Joan and Susie now come close like batty and bench?*—(Jmca) [i.e. 'as close as the buttocks on a bench']

bat·ty-hole *n* (CarA) [Vul] Anus.

bat·ty-mam·selle *n* (Tbgo, Trin) See BATIMANMZÈL

bat·ty-man (ba·ti·man) ['batima·n] (Antg, Guyn, Jmca) [AF—Vul] ‖ *auntie-man* (CarA) ‖ *buller* (Bdos) ‖ *hen* (Tbgo) ‖ *pantyman* (Antg, Gren) A male homosexual. *Rude Bwoy*: Come kiss me, General/*Sufferer*: Go way, battyman!—WOB:180

bat·ty-wax *n* (Tbgo) [AF—Vul] A stupid, gullible person; a nincompoop. [i.e. 'wax of the buttocks', a euphemism for 'shit']

bau·gi(e) (bau·ji) *n* (Guyn, Trin) See BHOWJI

bawl *vb intr* (CarA) [AF] **1.** To weep bitterly but quietly. *When the doctor told her she couldn't have children, my dear, she bawled for days.—*

(Guyn) **2.** (Gren, Trin) To speak enthusiastically; to shout with delight. **a.** *You have disease more than the law allow, and yet you bawlin[g] [a]bout you goin[g] oversea.*—PPGD **b.** *You go bawl when you tas[t]e dis soup boy! Sweet for so!*—(Trin) **3.** To complain openly against a serious hardship, esp lack of money. *A new racket is going on at the docks and small customs brokers like myself are bawling because if it isn't stopped soon we would have to go out of business.*—BoM (77.06.17, p.24) **4.** To exclaim from shock, disbelief, or surprise. *Is bawl I want dem bawl. Me dear, when you see I step off so ... and puffing me cigarette so ... as for when you see me wid hat on. Ay-ay oui foot!*—RTCS:12 **5.** PHRASES **5.1 bawl at/behind (sb)** vb phr (Trin) ‖ *bawl in sb's head* (Gren) To shout (at sb) rudely. **a.** *Better make haste before your mooma begin to bawl behind you, boy.*—KJB:66 **b.** *But Boysie, how you bawling in me head so? How you change-up and rough so tonight?*—RTCS:4 **5.2 bawl down a place** vb phr (CarA) To wail very loudly; to shout at the top of your voice. **a.** *Reports claim that he was in such pain that he almost bawled down the place.*—ToR (76.10.06, p.8) **b.** *Then he try to come near me to hold me. But I tell him that if he touch me I will bawl the house down.*—JMA:183 **5.2.1 bawl down/out/up (sb)** vb phr (Trin) To scold (sb) sharply; to reprimand (sb) severely. **a.** *She raised the matter with him and he didn't like it. He bawled her out, told her to stop spying on him.*—BoM (77.01.14, p.11) **b.** *Although we people in the Caribbean ... still use the British system, he always bawls up the students whenever they submit papers to his class without the American symbols to which he is accustomed.*—BoM (79.10.26, p.13) **5.3 bawl (your mouth out)** vb phr (Tbgo) To shriek, cry out loudly from pain or other distress. **a.** *She bawled at her husband's funeral.*—(StVn) **b.** *In some cases you go to the children's ward in the hospital and you would see a child bawling his mouth out.*—Tbgo (Ms, 1982) **5.4 hold your head and bawl** vb phr (CarA) See HOLD[1]

bay-ber·ry tree *n phr* (Gren, Jmca, Trin) ‖ BAY(-LEAF) TREE (CarA)

bay-front (bay·front) *n* (ECar) The waterfront facing the bay in which boats and ships are at anchor (usu, in the ECar, the harbour of the capital city). □ In many smaller islands *the bay*, unqualified, is used to ref to any part of the seaside or coast.

bay-ge·ra·ni·um* **(-ge·re·ni·a)** *n* (Baha) ‖ *bay-tansy* (Jmca, TkCa) ‖ *sea-thyme* (Baha) ‖ *wild geranium* (Bdos) ‖ *wormwood* 1. (Trin) A wide-spreading, mat-like, seaside vine with rough-textured leaves that are strong-smelling when crushed, and very insignificant green flowers; an infusion of the vine is put to various uses as a folk medicine; *Ambrosia hispida* (*Compositae*).

bay-house *n* (Bdos) A seaside house, usu far from town, used or rented by the month as a family resort.

bay (-leaf) tree* *n phr* (CarA) ‖ *bay-berry* (Gren, Jmca, Trin) ‖ *bay-rum tree* (Berm, BrVi, Jmca) ‖ *bwa denn* (Dmca, Gren, StLu, Trin) Either of two varieties of an evergreen tree, one taller with a thin, flaky, whitish bark and bearing berries, the other with a smooth, grey bark and tiny white flowers, but both with abundant, elliptical, leathery, dark-green leaves wh yield BAY-OIL and BAY-RUM; the leaves are also used as a folk-medicine and for flavouring food; *Pimenta racemosa* (and var *Citrifolia* (*Myrtaceae*)).

bay-lot *n* (Baha) Property with a sea frontage.

Bay·men, The *n* (Belz) [Hist] The earliest settlers of Br Honduras, now Belize wh was also called the Bay Settlement in the late 19C. □ The term has been much revived by 'the descendants of the Baymen' since the independence of *Belz* (1981) The sg is rare.

bay mé·pwi [baɪ mepwi] *vb phr* (StLu) ‖ BUSE (ECar) [Fr Cr < 17C Fr *bailler* 'give, deal out' (see Cotgrave) + *mépris* 'contempt, scorn']

bay-oil *n* (Dmca) A sweet-smelling oil distilled by steam-heating quantities of young leaves and buds of the BAY TREE *Pimenta racemosa* and used in the perfumery trade.

bay-plum *n* (Baha) ‖ COCO-PLUM (Antg, etc)

bay-rum *n* (CarA) A cologne distilled from BAY-OIL and esp favoured in soothing headaches.

bay-rum tree *n phr* (Berm, BrVi, Jmca) ‖ BAY (-LEAF) TREE (CarA)

bay·side *n* (Baha, Bdos, Gren, Tbgo, USVI) The seaside; the beach; in Tobago, the part of the capital town of Scarborough wh runs along the coast.

Bay Street Boys, the *n* (Baha) [IF—*Joc*] The long-established economically powerful White businessmen, who own the stores, etc in Bay Street, the principal street of Nassau.

bay-tan·sy ['be-tanzi] *n* (Jmca, TkCa) ‖ BAY-GERANIUM (Baha)

ba·zo(u)·di (ba·so·dee, ba·soo·di, ba·sou·di, bas·si·dy, ba·za·dee, ba·zoo·di, etc) [bazodi ~ basudi ~ bazadi] *n* (Antg, Dmca, Gren, StLu, Tbgo, Trin) [*AF*] ‖ *anbazoudi* (StLu) **1.** Stunned. **a.** *The blow had him bassody.*—(Trin) **b.** *This dazzling beauty ... has plans to make the adjudicators 'bassidy' with her radiance.*—AnS (67.08.02, p.4) **2.** Bewildered; confused; dizzy. *The Goatman was wandering around in a daze, or as it was put in our native way, the poor fellow was completely bazoodie.*—TtR (78/3, p.5) **3.** Light in the head; turned stupid. **a.** *Child, stop*

*behaving like that or people will think you gone
bazadee.*—RDVI **b.** *You bazoudi or what, you
knocking over everything— watch where you
going.*—(StLu) [Fr Cr < Fr *abasourdi* pa. part <
abasourdir (Archaic) vb 1. 'to deafen, stun, daze',
2. 'to dumbfound, bewilder'. DELF records an
older form *bazir* 'to kill' so that 17C dial Fr may
have retained the /-z-/ sound] □ Though many
conjectural spellings occur because of the wide
regional use of this mostly *Trin* folk term, the
most representative is prob **bazodi**.

be[1] *vb* **1.** NOTE: The absence of *to be* as a
linking verb is a widely noticeable feature of
predication in *CarA* middle-level *IF* speech,
(sometimes also in writing). It survives from a
strong *CarA* Cr feature wh is itself most likely
a reflection of the substratum influence of the
predication syntax of many Afr langs (exs Yoruba
o dara (*he/she/ it good*) 'he/she/it is good'; Ewe
ati-la kɔ (*tree-the high*) 'the tree is high'; Kikongo
ki-adi (*it sad*) 'it is sad' etc). Hence *IF* CE 'I/you/
he/it/we/they hot/very wet, etc' (adj predicate);
'everybody/all the things comin[g] just now/
nearly falling down' (verbal predicate)'/there/
under the bed' (adv predicate), in wh the (right
side) predicates are understood as expressing the
conditions or actions of the (left side) subjects.
In false refinement some less educated speakers
in certain situations insert non-changing IS as
link. In this book CE BE and its parts are treated
separately in normal alphabetical listing, i.e.
BEEN, BEING, IS, WAS, etc. **2.** functioning as *link
vb* (CarA) [*AF*] (Often unchanged, but equivalent to) am/is/are (as required by context). **a.**
*Who Kingsale tink he be? When de time come lay
he wait an see if he ain done try.*—ExP (72.03.05,
p.18) **b.** *S— knocked a flashlight from his hand,
picked up a stone and remarked: 'I want to see
how bad the police be.'*—LaS (76.11.10, p.8) **c.**
*We be on top of the 80's and they ain't even
finished the 70's.*—BeA (80.02.09, p.5) □ This
Cr function of unmarked *be* is becoming less
frequent. **3.** *in frequentative function* (CarA); **be's**
(Baha, CayI); **does be** (ECar) [*AF*] To be habitually. **a.** *Wherever you find the nasty Doris
goin[g] be, there yo[u] goin[g] find her too, she so
stupid.*—(Guyn) **b.** *She always be's the last one to
come school.*—CayI (Ms) **c.** *You does be hot and
sweaty in the afternoon in that corner.*—(Bdos)
[Cp IrE: 'My father bees always at home in the
morning', 'At night while I bees reading my
wife bees knitting'—*JESI:86*. Also 'There does
be a meeting of the company every Tuesday'—
JESI:85] □ *Does be*, in quick speech, is often
reduced [dʌz bi > dz bi > zbi] the last reduction
being erron re-analysed by some writers of dial
as *is be*. **4.** *as durative auxiliary* (CarA) [*AF*] **(i)**
To be (doing sth) continuously. *And naturally
she wasn't prepared to be bringing in money in the
house to let him go out and be spending it all the time
on rum.*—(Guyn) **(ii)** [*IF*] [With person-distinct
changes] To have been continuously. **a.** *I am
living in a house with him for six years and we
were living good until he put himself with a married
woman.*—NaT (79.09.12, p.21) **b.** *You should be
in the house since six o'clock.*—(Bdos) [Cp IrE 'I

am sitting here waiting for you for the last
hour'—*JESI:85*] **5.** *as pa. part* (CarA) [*AF—Cr*]
Been. *If you did only go with a good mind to see
Ganesh, you woulda be better and walking about
by now.*—NTMM:17 [Prob by denasalization/
reduction of [bi·n] or of Cr '*bin*'] **6.** PHRASES **6.1
be in** (St Lucy, etc) *vb phr* (Bdos) [*AF—Joc*]
(Your mind) is wandering; (your thoughts) are
elsewhere. *You is in St Lucy or what? Like you
ain[']t listening to me.*—(Bdos) [St Lucy is the
northernmost parish of Bdos and farthest away
from the centre of things. Any parish far from
Bridgetown could serve in the phr] **6.2 be with**
(sb) *vb phr* (Bdos) [*AF—Derog*] ‖ **deh wit[h]**
(sb) (Guyn) To live in sexual relationship with
(sb), to live together unmarried. *He is with her,
but he don[']t take her nowhere.*—(Bdos) □ The
term implies a more or less temporary relationship, without childbearing, that could be
broken at any time.

be[2] [bɪ] *prep prefixed to an oath* (Bdos, Guyn)
[*AF*] By. **a.** *... and a undertaker-man could make
a mistake like nothing and put a person in a coffin
and nail up that coffin and lower him in a grave
be-Christ, before that dead-man is really a dead-man.*—CWFYS:22 **b.** *But be-damn you, don
you know you's flying in the face of God with
this foolishness?*—MBGB:144 [See *EDD be prep*
(Various dials) 2. 'forming the first unemphatic
syllable of oaths' + many cits from Irel and Eng
from Nhb to Dev. Cp also BY[1] Phr 7.3] □ Also
be-jees, be-Jesus-Christ, be-kiss Mary, etc.

beach-boy *n* (Bdos) A sturdy, young, (usu)
black male prostitute who hangs around beaches
in swim-wear to attract white female tourists.

beach-seine [bič-se·n] *n* (Baha) An enclosing
net with floats, one end being held fast on shore
while the other is towed out seawards by dinghy
in a semi-circle around a school of fish and
brought back to shore where it is drawn in by
fishermen, so entrapping the fish in its meshes.
[*Beach* 'shore' + *seine*]

beach-sein·ing [bič-se·nɪŋ] *n* (Baha) The
method of catching fish by BEACH-SEINE.

bead-vine (bush) *n* (*phr*) (Nevs, StKt)
‖ **crab-eye vine** (Guyn, Jmca, StKt) ‖ **double
scuril** (Brbu) ‖ **gwenn-légliz** (StLu) ‖ **jumbie-
bead vine** (Brbu, Gren, StKt, Trin, USVI)
‖ **red-bead vine** (Jmca) ‖ **wild liqourice** (Jmca)
The vine that bears the JUMBIE BEAD 1., esp in
ref to the use of the leaves or 'bush' as a folk
medicine; *Abrus precatorius* (*Papilionaceae*).

beal *n* (USVI) See BEEL

bean *n* See, as separate entries BUTTER-BEAN,
COMMON-BEAN, COW-BEAN, HORSE-BEAN, JACK-
BEAN, KIDNEY-BEAN, LABLAB-BEAN, MUNG-BEAN,
OVERLOOK-BEAN, RED-BEAN, SALAD-BEAN, STRING-
BEAN, SWORD-BEAN

bean·a *n* (Guyn) See BEENA

bean-bag *n* (Angu, Bdos, Gren, StVn, Trin) A competitive children's game in wh a small bag firmly tied and loosely filled with the dried seeds of various fruits (TAMARINDS, SUGAR-APPLE, etc) is flung either over the head or between the legs of each player to be caught by the player next in line about 5 yds behind until the end of the line is reached. [*Bean* in loose usage here for 'beans or any suitable dried fruit seeds']

beans *n sg* (Belz) [*AF*] A dish of rice and beans (esp as served in a restaurant or other eating-place). *I sat down enjoying a beans while all that was going on on the road.*—Belz (Ms)

bean-tree* *n* (Bdos) ‖ *cutlass-bean* 2. (Jmca) ‖ *devil's tree* (Bdos) ‖ *duppy-machete* (Jmca) ‖ *Judas-tree* (Bdos) ‖ *Lent-tree* (Bdos) ‖ *Spanish machete* (Jmca) A tree 20 to 30 ft tall wh bears the JUMBIE-BEAD 2.; *Erythrina corallodendrum* (*Leguminosae/Papilionaceae*).

bean·y bird [bi·ni bərd] *n phr* (Jmca) ‖ BANANAQUIT (CarA)

bear *vb tr* PHRASE **bear your chafe** *vb phr* (Guyn) See CHAFE Phr 2.1

bear·ance [be·rʌns] *n* (Bdos, Guyn) [*X*] PHRASE **be at (a) bearance** *vb phr* (Bdos, Guyn) [*X*] [Of persons] To be going through a period of strained relationship; to be for a time not on speaking terms. [From a misunderstanding of the SE phr 'at variance' + prob infl of 'forbearance']

beard·ed fig-tree* *n phr* (Bdos) 'A much-branched tree, capable of reaching a height of 15 m ... with dense masses of thin aeriel roots hanging from the branches, many of [which] grow down to the ground where they thicken and either fuse with the main trunk (wh thus becomes deeply ribbed) or form woody props some distance from the trunk'—*GLPFP:124*; the tree bears small yellow fig-like berries; *Ficus citrifolia* (*Moraceae*). [*Bearded*, because of the resemblance of the hanging aerial roots to beards + *fig*, the fig-like berry] □ This tree is thought by some to have given Barbados (= the bearded ones) its name, from their being seen lining the seashore in the 17C.

beast¹ *n* (CarA) [*AF*] 1. [Joc, used in a friendly way in addressing sb] (You) character! (You) smart-aleck! (You) trickster! etc. 2. [Used in an intensifier phr] Devil (of a). *A beast of a rain is coming.*—(Gren) 3. (Jmca) [Derog, with sexual connotation] A woman friend. □ Usu sb else's, not your own.

beast² *adj* (CarA) [*AF*] Beastly good; beastly bad. *This time Viv Richards in beast form, you see, blastin[g] away.*—(Antg)

beast·ness *n* (Jmca) [*AF*] [Of men] wantonness; beastliness. *Tell me who you think is responsible for this leggo beastness in Jamaican men.*—StA(JA) (73.02.10, p.14) [< *beast²*]

beat *vb intr* 1. (Tbgo, Trin) [With unstated obj 'pan' understood] To play a PAN or PANS in a STEELBAND. *Starlift, the defending champions did beat well, but the choice of tune was not the best.*—SuP (80.02.10, p.8) [*Beat* is the standard word for 'hit the PAN with the stick' in all phrs relating to playing in a STEELBAND] 2. (CarA) [*IF*] [With unstated obj 'the road' understood] To trudge; to do hard walking. *People residing in St George's District, Gingerland ... have to beat one or two miles in search of water.*—DeM(SK) (63.11.02, p.12) 3. (ECar) [*IF*] [With unstated obj 'books' understood] ‖ BEAT BOOKS (ECar) *It was a period of beating, beating, beating—day and night. Coffee, tea and books were one's constant companions.*—StVn (Ms, 1974) 4. PHRASES 4.1 **beat a djè** [bit a ʤɛ·] *vb phr* (Gren) [*AF*] To pick at sb in a mood to have a row; to start or carry on a battle of words that will last for many days. *Since de oder day A see she beatin[g] a jè wid me! Is not me what make she go in jail!*—PPGD:16 [= 'beat a war' (Fr Cr *djè* < Fr *guerre* 'war')] 4.2 **beat all cock-fight** *vb phr* [*AF—Joc*] (i) (Belz, Gren, Guyn, Tbgo, Trin) To be unbelievable, unheard of; to be more ridiculous or absurd than anything else (in the matter). *First you mother didn[t] give you de money, den last week you los[t] it, and dis week somebody steal it from you? Well dat beat all cock-fight! What you think I am at all?*—(Guyn) (ii) (Gren) To be outstanding; to surpass all competitors. *You didn[t] see dose jockey in de Guyana horse show? Boy dat beat all cock fight.*—PPGD:16 4.3 **beat bamboo** *vb phr* (Trin) (See cit). *The tradition of the band is strong in the Carnival of present-day Trinidad, but it was interrupted by the Second World War. They included men who beat bamboo, that is, pieces of bamboo of different lengths that were used as drums.*—SWI:151 □ See TAMBOO-BAMBOO. 4.4 **beat (the) books (beat book)** *vb phr* (ECar) [*IF/AF*] To study from books for long hours. *No liming at the Union after beating books until 10 p.m.*—TrG (73.07.07) □ UWI campus 'slang'. 4.5 **beat boom** *vb phr* (Trin) [*IF*] To play the bass PAN in a STEELBAND. *And if you want me play, I go play. I go beat boom. My pan shift so I playing bass.*—HPP:20 4.6 **beat clothes** *vb phr* (CarA) To beat dirt out of clothes in washing them by the waterside (using a BEATER or stone). 4.7 **beat iron** *vb phr* (Tbgo, Trin) To hit a piece of iron as part of the music-making in STEELBANDS, etc at CARNIVAL time. *... and he could beat iron, those lengths of steel that rang out above the lower notes of the drums, ringing out a challenging, pulsating rhythm, chiming the battle cry.*—LDCD:54 4.8 **beat (the) liquor** *vb phr* (CarA) [*AF*] To drink a lot of liquor, esp rum. *I went to the country about 8.30 a.m. this morning and I was shocked as I drove to the country to see about ten young men by a street corner beating some liqour and playing cards.*—Bdos (Hd, 74.03.18, p.3399) 4.9 **beat (a) pan** *vb phr* (CarA) ‖ *beat steel/steelband* (Trin) To play on one of the PANS in a STEELBAND. **a.** *... when at nights he used* *to visit the steel-pan yards and watch his elders beat pan.*—DeM(SK) (76.02.14, p.4) **b.** *More girls are turning to beating pan, … children are occupied daily with new calypso tunes and some youngsters are still undecided as to which band to play with.*—EvN (80.02.05, p.3) **4.10 beat pitch** *vb phr* (Trin) To break up hard pieces of pitch or asphalt into pieces with a pickaxe. **4.11 beat rice** *vb phr* (Guyn) To hit the PADDY-laden stalks against a screen or table in order to free the grains from the stalks; to thresh rice by hand. **4.12 beat (sb) hollow** *vb phr* (Bdos, Guyn) To baffle or outdo (sb) completely. [Cp IrE: 'Hollow, used as an adv … 'Jack Cantlon's horse beat the others hollow…' i.e. beat them utterly'—*JESI:274*] □ The exp seems much commoner, esp among older folk in *Bdos, Guyn*, than in BrE or AmE, not appearing in current dictionaries. See *OED hollow* B. adv 2. + latest cit 1859. **4.13 beat (sb) sick** *vb phr* (Angu) [*AF*] ‖ *beat (sb) soft* (Tbgo) To beat (sb) into a state of collapse. **4.14 beat sb('s) skin** *vb phr* (CarA) [*AF*] ‖ *cut sb('s) skin* (Baha) ‖ *drive (the) licks in sb('s) skin* (Antg, Bdos, Trin) ‖ *line (sb) with licks/blows* (Bdos) ‖ *put a wash of blows on (sb)* (Guyn) ‖ *put the licks (of hell) in (sb)* (Bdos) ‖ *wash sb('s) knot* (Guyn) ‖ *wash sb('s) skin with blows* (Guyn) ‖ *wash (out) (sb's) tail* (Nevs) To thrash (sb) thoroughly; to flog, trounce or beat up (sb) severely. [A supportive or prop complement reinforcing the meaning of the vb, something like a cognate object (cp SE *sing a song*) is characteristic of creolized CE] **4.15 beat steel; beat steelband** *vb phr* (Trin) ‖ BEAT PAN (Trin) **4.16 beat tar** *vb phr* (CayI) [*AF*] ‖ *slap tar* (Bdos) To walk the streets idly, being out of work. [Cp *EDD* (Som, Dev) *beat the streets* 'to run about idly'; *tar* = asphalted road] **4.17 beat the priest (and take his gown)** *vb phr* (Gren) [*AF—Joc*] To do something very wrong and be brazen about it. *You tie the goat on the man land and when he tell you to take it out, you want to fight wid him? Man, you want to beat the priest and tak[e] he go[w]ng!*—PPGD:19 **4.18 beat your drum and dance** *vb phr* (Guyn, Tbgo, Trin) [*AF—Joc*] To praise yourself; (SE)to blow your own trumpet. **4.19 beat your mouth (on sb/sth)** *vb phr* (Jmca, StLu) [*AF—Derog*] ‖ AIR (OUT) YOUR MOUTH (ON SB) (CarA) *… nuff people nowadays don't seem to have nutten better to do than beat dem mout on the Gleaner … Anyway, some of us still have friends.*—WeG (72.10.18, p.11, Partyline)

beat·er [ˈbitʌ] *n* (Baha, Guyn) ‖ *bato* (Tbgo) ‖ *clapper* (Baha, Jmca) ‖ *clothes-batter* (Jmca) A stout piece of wood cut into a shape like a miniature cricket bat, or the thick end of a coconut branch similarly cut, and used to beat wet, soapy clothes in the laundering process. □ In *Baha*, **beater** (So. Andros) ‖ *clapper* (Cat Island).

beat·ing (in the head) *n* (Bdos) [*IF*] A throbbing headache.

beat up[1] *vb intr phr* (Gren, Tbgo) **1.** [Of a chicken] To thrash about on the ground after being beheaded in a ritual killing. *But on the third day, a white cock was killed by snapping off its head by a single stroke of the machete. It was allowed to 'beat' up until it died. The position in which it died has significance.*—PGIP:54 **2.** PHRASE **2.1 beat up yourself** *refl vb phr* (CarA) [*AF*] To overwork yourself in sb else's interest; to work breathlessly at sth (often for a purpose that is not yours alone).

beat-up[2] *adj* (CarA) [*AF—Derog*] [Of a person, esp a woman] Looking unhealthy, scrawny and older than you are; [of a thing] looking battered and ill-used. **a.** *Even Christine's beat-up looking sister, who was living with a man twice her age, came to add to the confusion. Neither Bird nor Stephanie recognized her, as she looked even more beat-up than usual.*—HMCH:41 **b.** *I travelled with Higinio, in an old beat-up jeep, with practically no upholstery.*—Peo 1.1, p.42 [< beat(en)-up, with metaph extension]

beau·ty sa·loon *n phr* (Bdos, Guyn) See SALOON.

beb·rege (beb·ridge) [bɛbrɪj] *n* (CayI, Jmca, StKt) See BEVERAGE

be·cause *conj* PHRASES **1. because of certain/many (etc) reasons** *prep phr* (CarA) [*X*] For certain/many (etc) reasons. *I did not reply to that letter because of many reasons.*—Jmca (Ms) **2. the reason … is because** *introducing noun clause* (CarA) [*X*] The reason is that. *The only reason why this bridge has not been repaired is because it is located in St Andrew.*—Bdos (AdN, 72.12.15, p.4) □ Both these tautological phrs are common in CE.

be·caus·en (be·caus·in(g)) [bikɒ·zn ~ bikɒ·zin ~ bikɒ·zin] *conj* (CarA) [*X*] Because. **a.** *I leggo de rope becausen it would-a squeeze me.*—(CayI) **b.** *Well I mean everybody was surprise: first, becausin' is seldom that people in St Victoria does stop a good fight like this, and next becausin' scarce anybody would risk trying to stop a fight between Jasper and Saga-boy.*—CISH:10 [< SE *because* by paragoge (cp WHICHEN, WHICHIN). The form has been noticed also in Black AmE] □ An illiterate form from Cr surviving in semi-literate speech.

bé·chine *n* (Dmca) See BÉTJIN

bed·ding (bed·dings) *n* (CarA) Old clothes or rags spread on a mattress to absorb children's bed-wetting or spread under the mattress to protect it from being torn by the bed-springs.

bed-grass *n* (Baha, CayI, Nevs, Tbgo) **1.*** (Baha, CayI) A grass with a robust flat blade that bears a soft inflorescence; *Andropogon glomeratus (Gramineae).* **2.** (Nevs, Tbgo) ‖ VETIVER (Dmca, etc) [From the use of these dried grasses to stuff mattresses]

bed·mon·ey *n* (Bdos, Trin) A bribe offered to a doctor or other responsible person at a government-run hospital in order to gain admission quickly, by-passing the waiting list. *Now that you have at last decided to crack down on those unscrupulous doctors who have been bleeding this country with their bed-money racket, I hope to God you do not believe that your job is now over.*—BoM (75.01.03, p.5)

bee *n* (Bdos) [*AF—Joc*] A male homosexual. [< *b*, abbr for 'bugger', BULLER]

bee·deems *n pl* (Guyn) See BIDDIMS

beef *n* (Baha, Jmca) [*AF—Derog*] A sexually desirable woman; a sexually competent woman friend. □ Cp also BEAST[1] 3.

beef-wood *n* (CarA) 1. Name evidently given to various timber woods that are beef-coloured when first cut. 2. (Baha) ‖ CASUARINA (CarA) 3. (Bdos) A flowering evergreen tree that grows to over 40 ft, with shiny leather leaves; *Pisonia fragrans (Nyctaginaceae)*. 4. (Guyn) ‖ BULLET-WOOD (Guyn)

beel (**beal**) [bi·l] *n* (USVI) [*AF*] A motor-car. *You're going to walk your shoe soles off/when you have no beal to crank*—Poem, 1976 (A. Peterson). [Danish *'bil'* [bi·l], abbr < *automobil*, 'motor-car']

been[1] *vb* (CarA) [*X*] 1. *pa. part* Has/have/had been. *But instead, you been spending your lifetime down in Barbados, the same way as your forefathers and foremothers been spending it.*—CWFYS:18 [Development of Cr BIN-A wh is prefixed to the unmarked vb as Cr past time marker. See BIN[1] 3.1] 2. Was; were. *At two o'clock I been on Accra beach, a girl and I.*—Bdos (CR, 71.05.05) [Development of Cr copula BIN 'been', pa.t. of 'be'] 3. *pres part* Being. a. *This indicates that she had no intention of been evasive on these delicate issues.*—Trin (Ms, 1970) b. *The reason the fish started to die this time was due to there been a lesser volume than normal of water in the Belize River.*—BsT (80.04.13, p.12) [Erron, a misascription of 'been' = *bein'* < *being*, with characteristic CE [-n] replacing [-ŋ]] 4. Went. *Constable L— came and pass me and been in the yard.*—Guyn (CR) [From Cr directional BIN < SE *have been*] □ In the functions 1, 2, 4, it may be pronounced [bɪn] if unstressed, otherwise [bin] in all cases.

been[2] (**bean**, **be·ing**) *causal conj* (CarA) [*X*] Since; because; seeing that. a. *One lady said most of the courtship was at the window, until mama warmed up to her, bean he was never invited inside even if it started to rain.*—DaN(ST) (79.02.22, p.9) b. *Bein[g] it was the schoolmaster in there I didn't suspec[t] nothing.*—(Guyn) [*OED Be* B. I. 3. arch or dial *Being, Being that* = it being the case that, seeing that, since' + cit–1815]

bee·na (**bean·a**) *n* (Guyn) 1. A charm made up of certain kinds of plants, orig used by Carib Amerindians to bring success in hunting. *Before an Indian sets out to hunt, he goes through one or more strange performances to ensure success. Round his house he has planted various sorts of 'beenas' or plants ... which he supposes to act as charms to make the capture of game certain.*—IAIG:228 [' 'Beenas' (pl) is the Carib word. I do not know the equivalent in the other languages'—*IAIG: 228* footnote] 2. [*AF*] [By extension] Any charm concocted by an OBEAHMAN (Guyn) to bring success to a client in a particular undertaking or field of endeavour. 3. *PHRASE* 3.1 **to have beena (for sth)** *vb phr* (Guyn) [*AF*] To persist and succeed in doing sth (through apparent self-confidence). □ In the [*AF*] contexts there is usu no pl form.

Bee·Wee *n* (CarA) [*AF*] Abbr for B.W.I.A. (Br West Indian Airways), the national airline of Trinidad & Tobago. *They told him our luggage had gone to Trinidad on a Bee Wee flight, which was not true.*—SuP (80.01.06, p.15)

bèf (**beff**) [bɛf] *n* (Dmca, StLu) A very large, fleshy mango but of stringy texture. [Fr Cr < Fr *boeuf* 'cow', in ref to its size]

be·fore[1] *conj PHRASES* 1. **before bird wife wake** *adv phr* (Guyn) [*AF*] ‖ **before fowl-cock put on him pants/his trousers** (Jmca) [*AF—Cr*] ‖ **before the cat (can) lick its ear** (Bdos) As early as possible in the morning; before dawn. a. *Smith was an ardent cricket fan ... Before 'bird wife wake' [he] was at the pavilion gate to ensure that he did not miss a ball.*—GyC (76.04.12, p.15) b. *Sorry to come on you like this before bird put on his trousers but I had to catch you before you left for school.*—(Jmca) c. *Yes ... yes, let him g'long. Watch, he'll be back before the cat lick it ear.*—MBGB:148 [Cp SE catch phrs *before the birds, before bird-song, before cock-crow*] 2. **before the/this spit dry** *adv phr* (Guyn) [*AF—Cr*] [Esp in ref to sending a child on an errand] In the shortest possible time; very quickly. *Look! A sen[d]in[g] yo[u] to de shop! You better come back befo[re] m[y] spit dry!*—(Guyn) [The speaker spits on the ground and as the spit dries in the sun the time runs out] 3. **before you (could) say 'knife'** *adv phr* (Gren, Guyn) [*AF*] More quickly than you can imagine; with surprising promptness. *They played the fool with this excuse and the next, and by damn! The white man only show [h]e face and before you could say knife they had it fix! Perfect!*—(Guyn) [Cp BrE catch phr 'before you could say Jack Robinson' with same sense]

be·fore[2] *conj* (CarA) [*IF*] 1. ‖ **instead** (Guyn) [*X*] (Followed by a main clause, replacing SE *instead of* + gerund, with the same sense.) *Before you go and look for some wo[r]k, you only si[t] do[w]n de[re] talkin[g] people name.* (= (SE) 'instead of your going to look for a job, etc').—(StVn) [Extension of *OED before* prep B. 11. In preference to; rather than] 2. (ECar) Lest; in order to prevent (+ gerundial phr). *You better go and read your book before I have to beat you.*—(Tbgo) □ These usages have earned a firm place in CE as far simpler alternatives to the gerundial structures and the conj *lest* wh they replace and wh are rare even in the speech of well educated persons.

be·fore·time (be·fore-time, be·fore time) *adv* (CarA) [*IF*] In olden days; in the past. *Beforetime the boats used to be always fishing for Haiti.*—Baha (Ms, 1978) [*OED* beforetime 'in former time, formerly' + latest cit 1865] □ The popular survival of this EE adv esp in lower-level CE speech is prob due to its presence in the Psalms and the *AVB*.

beg *vb tr* **1.** (CarA) [*IF*] To ask for; to beg for. *The wounded girl said: 'I went into Mr Andrew's shop, near to Miss Tavenier, to beg some water.'*—AnS (62.07.06, p.6) **2.** PHRASES **2.1 beg back (your papers)** *vb phr* (Bdos, Guyn, Tbgo) [*AF*] [Esp in ref to marriage or living together] To ask to be forgiven; to seek reconciliation after behaving shamefully. *Me an[d] he fall out but if [h]e beg back [h]e papers an[d] promise to behave [h]eself, well—?*—(Guyn) [Cp *EDD* beg back (Yks, Not, Chs) 'ask to be taken back'. However no special context is suggested] **2.2 begging bread** *vbl adj phr* (Jmca) [*AF—Joc*] [Of shoes, socks, seat of the pants] Having a visible hole. **2.3 beg under (sb)** *vb phr* (Antg) [*AF*] To beg to the point of belittling yourself. **2.4 beg sb (sth)** (Jmca) [*AF*] Please give me. *When he told accused it was ganja, accused said 'Officer beg you a chance.' Accused was arrested.*—WeS (74.03.08, p.15)

be·gasse *n* (CarA) See BAGASSE

beg-beg *adj* (Antg, StVn) [*AF—Cr*] ‖ beggar (Belz) [Esp of children] Given to begging. *Move from me girl! You too beg-beg!*—(Antg)

beg·gar (baa·gah) [be:ga] /1'2/ *adj* (Belz) [*AF—Cr*] ‖ BEG-BEG (Antg, StVn) *Now you can say 'You too baagah,' meaning I'm a barefaced beggar, and I'll plead guilty.*—ReP (79.08.19, p.5)

be·grudge·ful *adj* (Baha) Envious; [by extension] very resentful. *Dreaming of pigs indicates jealousy primarily, but it also indicates greed and being 'begrudgeful'. / Bahamian for being envious.*—MTTBT:152 [SE *begrudge* + *ful*. Cp *OED* grudgeful (rare) 'full of resentment and rancour' + latest cit 1893]

be·have *vb intr* PHRASES **1. behave a good/ nice boy/girl/child** *vb phr* (CarA) [*IF*] To be a good/nice boy/girl/child; (SE) to behave like a good boy, etc. **2. behave bad** *vb phr* (CarA) [*AF*] ‖ GET ON (BAD) (CarA) [*AF*] See GET Phr 3.18 *When the father see how the boy skin mark up wid de lashes, the father went to the school and behave real bad!*—(Guyn) **3.1 behave yourself** *vb refl* (CarA) [*IF*] [Esp in ref to sexual conduct]

To cease from being promiscuous; to stop having affairs outside of marriage. *Well he stop going with the woman and like he make up his mind to behave himself as the children growing big now.*—StKt (Ms) **3.2 Behave yourself!** *excl* (CarA) [By extension] [*AF—Joc*] You're pulling my leg!; You must be joking!

be·hav·iour *n* PHRASES **1. have behaviour** *vb phr* (ECar) [Esp of children] To be well-mannered; to be quiet and respectful (hence next). **1.1 have no behaviour** To be ill-mannered; to be noisy and disrespectful.

be·hind[1] *prep* PHRASES **1. be/get behind sb (to do sth)** *vb phr* (CarA) [*IF*] ‖ *be wild behind sb* ... (StKt) ‖ *fight behind sb* ... (Tbgo) ‖ *get in sb's backbone* ... (Jmca) ‖ *get/stand/stay behind (sb)* ... (CarA) ‖ *rush sb up* ... (CayI) To pester, goad, urge sb (to do sth). **a.** *You'll be surprised how many people go to obeah-men when they have cases. In fact, some people spend more money behind the obeah-men than their lawyers' fees.*—BoM (78.06.23, p.20) **b.** *If the wife didn't stay behind him he never would-a repair that house.*—(Baha) [Cp Yoruba *o pọn si mi l'ẹyin* (he fasten to me at the back) 'he urged me oppressively'; also Igbo *ịkwu ya n'azụ* (stand behind him) 'to urge him watchfully'—(pers info, C. Azuonye)] **2. be behind sb like a slave-driver** *vb phr* (CarA) [*IF*] ‖ *be behind sb foot (to) foot* (Tbgo, Trin) ‖ *be (behind sb) like a leech* (Guyn) ‖ *be (behind sb) like a tak-tak* (Dmca) ‖ *be (behind sb) like ticks* (Jmca, Tbgo) ‖ *be (behind sb) worse than wari-tick* (Belz) ‖ *be/ stick in sb('s) skin* (Gren) ‖ *stick on sb like white on rice* (Baha) ‖ *ticks (sb)* (Jmca) [Often of children] To plague or pester sb to the point of irritation, in order to obtain sth; to pursue sb doggedly, to achieve your own ends. **2.1 be behind (sth)** *vb phr* (Tbgo) [*AF*] To try hard to obtain (sth). *Man, A behind a Datsun 280-C, but they real hard to get yes.*—(Tbgo) **3. behind God's back** *adv phr* (CarA) [*AF—Joc*] [Esp in ref to where sb lives] Very far away from town-life or from any important or well-known place. *We are behind God's back in truth: no water, no phone, half a mile of hot sun from the main road.*—TaP (72.12.03, p.2) [Cp IrE *Back of God-speed* 'a place very remote, out of the way; so far off that the virtue of your wish of God-speed to a person will not go with him so far'—*JESI: 212*] **4. behind the bananas** *adv phr* (Dmca) [*AF—Joc*] Far away from town; deep in the plantation countryside. *Every evening a table was set out in each village, and the people put their names to the paper, or their marks; women in their working clothes; men from fishing, or from 'behind their bananas'.*—Wan (1974:17) □ Cp ABACK adv (Guyn). **5. behind the Bridge** *adv phr* (Trin) [*IF—Derog*] In the back streets or slums. *A former diplomat and Governor General, he is never so aloof that the disadvantaged youth from 'Behind the Bridge' or any other place cannot readily identify with him.*—SuP (77.03.20, p.9) [Ref to that area of Port-of-Spain wh is at the back of the East Dry River where there is the poorest

level of living] □ Cp BACK-O'-WALL (*Jmca*). **6.
behind the wall** *adv phr* (StVn) [*IF*] In prison;
(AmE) behind bars. *In St Vincent, the minimum
penalty for rape is five years behind the wall. Is
that enough?*—StA(SV) (75.06.28)

be·hind² *n* (CarA) [*AF*] [= SE 'the buttocks']
PHRASE **belly full and behind drunk** *n phr*
(Bdos, TkCa) [*AF—Vul*] See BELLY Phr 3.5

be·ing (be.ing as, be.ing that) [biin~bi:n]
conj (*phr*) (CarA) [*X*] ‖ **been²** (CarA) ‖ **by²** (Bdos,
Guyn) As; since; inasmuch as; seeing that. *He
tell me is all right, that I could stay on the job as
the caretaker, being as I was here so long already.*—
SWOS:106 [Pres part of *be*, often *bein'*] □ See
also BEEN².

bé·ké [beke~bɛkɛ] *n* **1.** (Dmca, Gren, StLu)
[*AF—Derog*] ‖ BACKRA (CarA) *The people of Martinique are descended from white creoles or 'békés',
Africans, orientals from India, China and Annam,
and Europeans known as 'békés-France'.*—HWII:
88 [Fr Cr, perh from more than one W Afr lang
source, ex *WTIED* Izon (Ijo) *beké* 'European';
also *KNED* Nembe *bękę* adj 'yellow in colour']
2. (Dmca, Gren) [By extension, AF—Derog]
‖ POOR-WHITE (CarA) *I know of 'békés' who are
just as 'sal'. Sometimes, even more 'sal' than 'nè-
gres'.*—DoH (65.09.04, p.6) **3.** (Dmca, Gren)
[By extension, AF—Derog] ‖ **red(-skin) people**
(Guyn, Trin) A fair-skinned person; a mulatto.
*The child come out like a béké and her father is so
black.*—Dmca (Ms)

bé·ké-nèg [beke~bɛkɛ-nɛg] *n phr* **1.** (Dmca,
Gren) [*AF—Derog*] ‖ BACKRA-NIGGER (Trin) [Fr
Cr < BÉKÉ, 'white person' + *nèg*(re) 'black person'] □ Pl unchanged. **2.** (Gren, Trin) [By extension, AF—Derog] An albino. □ Pronunc prob
affected by regressive assimilation < *nèg*

be·known [bino·n] *adj* (Antg, BrVi, Guyn) [Of
a person] Well-known. *He not beknown to you,
but he is beknown in Antigua.*—(Antg) [A survival
of Obs E: *OED* beknown, ppl adj, Arch, 'known,
acquainted, familiar' + latest cit 1865 from
Dickens]

bel·aire *n* (Dmca, Gren, StLu, Tbgo, Trin)
See BÈLÈ

bel·an·gene *n* (Gren) See BÉLANJENN

bé·lan·jenn (ba·la·gé, ba·lan·gene, ba-
·lan·ge(r), ba·lan·jay, ba·lon·gene, be-
·lan·gene, be·lan·ger, bé·lon·gen, bo·lon·jay,
bo(u)·lan·ger) [belãӡe·n~bɛlanӡen~
bʌlʌ(n)ӡe(n)] *n* (CarA) ‖ EGGPLANT (CarA) *You
can get three bélanjènns these days for fifty cents.*—
(StLu) [Prob by homorganic /m > b/ shift <
MELONGENE. Cp also BALANJAY] □ This spelling
represents the preferred form as a Fr Cr loan.

be·lay [bi'le·] *vb tr* (Guyn, Trin) To thrash (sb)
soundly (usu with a stick or leather thong);
belabour (sb). *Man ah belay him wid blows.*—OT:

4 [A survival of obs E usage. See *OED belay* 6.
intr 'to lay about one (sc blows). Obs rare' +
latest cit 1598]

bè·lè (bel·air, bel·aire, bel·lair, bel·laire)
[bɛlɛ~bɛler] *n* (Dmca, Gren, StLu, Tbgo, Trin)
1. (Traditionally) a vigorous, impassioned, outdoor, group dance performed by women, in
wh they show their figures and fine clothes,
signalling to the male drummers the change of
beat they want by their body movements. [Prob
of W Afr origin re-interpreted by folk etym as Fr
bel air 'lovely looking, fashionable'. Cp *KNED*
Nembe *bęlę* adj, 'tasteful, harmonious, melodious, tuneful, musical, interesting'] **2.** (Dmca,
Gren, StLu) [By extension] A carnival folk-
dance led by a woman solo singer or CHANTRELLE
who dances backwards, giving the time to the
drummer. **3.** [By extension] A number of different (indoor) group- dance forms with changes
of rhythm, infl by the QUADRILLE, performed by
couples usu of violin, banjo, and accordion. **4.**
[By extension] A song of satire, praise, or descriptive social comment, resembling the CA-
LYPSO (wh, however, it precedes historically),
developed by the CHANTRELLE (see **2.** above).

Be·lize ['bɛli·z] *n* The name of the English-
speaking territory in Central Amer called Br
Honduras until 1973 (becoming independent
1981). *Britain's Queen Elizabeth has assented to
the restoration of the name 'Belize' to this British
Central American colony, Premier George Price
announced.*—AdN (73.06.04, p.1) [Said to be
from *Belice* [bɛli·s] the Sp pronunc of *Wallace*,
a Scottish buccaneer who operated from the
Belize (< 'Wallace') River, at the mouth of wh
he had founded Wallace (> Belize) City about
1640]

Be·li·ze·an [bɛ'li·ziən] *n, adj* (A person or
thing) native or belonging to BELIZE.

Be·li·ze·an·iz·a·tion [bɛlizɪənar'zeʃʌn] *n* The
act or process of making sth markedly BELIZEAN
in character.

Be·li·ze·an·ize [bɛ'liziənaɪz] *vb tr* (Belz) To
make sth (such as an institution, festival, etc)
markedly BELIZEAN in character or appearance.

bel·laire *n* (Dmca, etc) See BÈLÈ

bell-ap·ple* *n* (Guyn, Nevs, StVn, Trin, ViIs)
‖ **golden-apple** (Jmca) ‖ **ponm-dilyann/di-
lyenn** (Dmca, StLu, Trin) ‖ **semeto** (Guyn)
‖ **water-lemon** (Bdos, Dmca, Gren, Trin) A soft
fruit about 3 ins long and 2 ins in diameter with
a light and dark-green striped, velvety skin that
turns bright yellow or orange when ripe, with the
seeds filled with a sweet, liquid pulp in wh the seeds
float; it is borne on a climbing vine; *Passiflora
laurifolia (Passifloraceae)*. [From the bell-like
appearance of the fruit hanging under a covering
of leaves] □ Not to be confused with PASSION-
FRUIT of the same family.

bell-cast hood; **bell-hood**; **bell-pel.met** *n* (*phr*) (Bdos) A sun-shade made of wood or tin-sheeting built outside and above a window and with a curved skirt-like flare (like the curve of the side of a bell, hence the name).

bel·ly *n* (CarA) [*AF/IF*] **1.** (A general word used for) the inside of the human body from about mid-chest downwards; abdomen; bowels; guts; womb, etc. □ This word is now widely used though it was once socially unpermitted, and its use is still much avoided in polite conversation and writing: 'When my generation was young, we were severely frowned upon by our elders if we used the word 'belly'. ... Before our time, I may add, 'stomach' was verboten, and this part of the anatomy was referred to as the Little Mary'—*AdN* (*72.03.23, p.19, Topic for Today*)] **2.** A pregnant woman's swollen abdomen; [by extension] the condition or state of pregnancy. **3.** PHRASES **3.1 band your belly** *vb phr* ‖ TIE YOUR BELLY (CarA) See Phr **3.26**(i) *Band your belly and send this boy to high school so they will learn him to turn his back on his family...? Eh?* —SNWIC:241 (E. Lovelace) **3.2 belly and back** (Guyn); **belly, back and side** (Gren) *n phrs in adv function* [*AF—Joc*] [Esp in ref to being robbed, flogged or BUSED] Completely; thoroughly; mercilessly. **a.** *She put her business in the hands of a lawyer and by all accounts he robbed her belly and back.*—Guyn (Ms) **b.** *She got out on the road and cussed them out, givin[g] them belly, back, and side.*—Gren (Ms) **3.3 belly asking your throat if it's cut** *id phr* (Bdos, Gren) [*AF—Joc*] (You are) very hungry. *A si[t] do[w]ng a[t] de hospital from mornin[g] whole day! So you know by t[h]ree o'clock, m[y] belly askin[g] m[y] t[h]roat if it cut!*—(Bdos) [i.e The belly thinks the throat must be cut as no food is getting past it. ODEP, p.34 'The belly thinks the throat is cut', an E prov + cits 1540 to 1738, the latter being its use in Swift's *Polite Conversation*] **3.4 belly boil(ing)** *id phr* (Gren) [*AF*] (You are) very much frightened. *When ah hayre fire in town, me belly bile. Ah tun stupidee. First ting is ah say: 'Lawd have mercy.'*—WeN (52.11.17, p.2, Annie & Josephine) **3.5 belly full and behind drunk** *in adj function* (Bdos, TkCa) [*AF—Vul*] Too sluggish to do anything but relax, having eaten and drunken too heavily; (have) NIGGERITIS. [In this exp *behind* = backside, arse] **3.6 belly cutting** *id phr* (Antg, Guyn) [*AF*] ‖ **belly grumbling** (CarA) (Have) gripes; (have) collywobbles. **3.7 belly is a burying-ground** *id phr* (Guyn, TkCa) [*AF—Vul*] (Of a woman who) has had many abortions. **3.8 belly is big/showing** *id phr* (CarA) [*AF*] (Be) noticeably pregnant. **3.9 belly is on you** *id phr* (StKt) [*IF*] ‖ GOT/HAVE THE BELLY (ECar, TkCa) See Phr **3.21**(i) *If you eat barracuda certain times of the year, yo[ur] belly will be on you!*—(StKt) **3.10 belly is operating you** *id phr* (Antg, Gren, Guyn) [*IF*] (As prec) **3.11 belly is well braced** (Bdos) [*AF—Joc*] *id phr* ‖ **belly raised two inches above the table** (Bdos) [*AF—Joc*] (Be) thoroughly full of good food. *But when at least the empty bag is filled with good food, the person*

can sit back at the table and exclaim in the good Bajan fashion: 'Thank God my belly is well braced.' Or to elaborate: 'Praise the Lord my belly be raised two inches above the table!'—AdV (82.01.24, p.14, M. Hutt) **3.12 belly touching your back** *id phr* (Gren) [*AF*] (You are) empty bellied, starving for something to eat. **3.13 belly works you** *id phr* (Dmca, Guyn, Nevs, StLu) [*AF*] ‖ HAVE THE BELLY (ECar, TkCa) See Phr **3.21**(i) *I can't eat pork at all. My belly will work me.*—(StLu) **3.14 bring belly** *vb phr* (Gren, Guyn, Tbgo) [*AF—Derog*] [Of an unmarried young woman] To become pregnant. *I done warn you-all a[l]ready! The day any o[f] you bring belly in dis house, yo[u] takin[g] yo[ur] bundle an[d] go meet yo[ur] man!*—(Tbgo) **3.15 catch/get/have/ take a cold in the belly** *vb phrs* (CarA) To have an ache or pain anywhere in the lower front part of the body related to some complaint or disorder. *If you walk barefoot on a stone floor you might catch a cold in the belly.*—(Guyn) **3.16 come from the same belly** *vb phr* (Dmca) [*AF*] To be born of the same mother. □ This phr occurs more often in the neg: **not come from the same belly. 3.17 ease your belly** *vb phr* (CarA) [*IF*] ‖ MOVE YOUR BOWELS (CarA) See MOVE Phr **1. 3.18 eat your belly full** *vb phr* (CarA) [*AF*] To eat as much as your stomach can hold; (SE) to eat your fill. **3.19 get/have belly/a big-belly** (CarA) [*AF—Vul*] To become noticeably pregnant. □ Sometimes also HAVE A BELLY. In the alternative phr BIG-BELLY /1′22/ is distinguished in tone from *big belly* /2′12/ 'a man's paunch, or a woman's belly that is not big with pregnancy'. **3.20 give (sb) (a/the) belly** *vb phr* (CarA) [*AF—Vul*] ‖ **breed (sb)** (CarA) [*AF*] [Of a man] To make a young woman pregnant. **3.21 got/have the belly** *vb phr* (i) (ECar, TkCa) [*AF/IF*] ‖ **have bad-belly** (Baha, Belz, Dmca, Guyn, StVn) ‖ **have (the) belly-cutting** (Antg) ‖ **got/have belly-work(ing)** (Guyn, StVn, Tbgo) ‖ **have the/your belly on you** (Brbu, StKt) ‖ **have the going-off** (Mrat, Nevs, StKt) ‖ **got/have run(ning)-belly** (Jmca) ‖ **get/have the running(s)** (Antg, Baha, Bdos, Guyn) ‖ **have work-belly** (Belz) To get/have diarrhoea. *I don't know what he ate that disagreed with him but he had the belly and I couldn't send him to school.*—Bdos (Ms) □ Cp Phr **3.25.** (ii) (Belz, Guyn, Jmca, StVn, Tbgo) To be pregnant. □ Often HAVE BELLY [*AF*]. See also Phr **3.19.** **3.22 keep the wind out of your belly** *vb phr* (CarA) ‖ **keep your stomach** (Guyn) See WIND[1] Phr **3.23 le[t]-go you[r] belly** *vb phr* (Crcu, Gren) [*AF—Cr*] ‖ RUN YOUR BELLY (Antg, etc) **3.24 like your belly** *vb phr* (CarA) [*AF*] To love to eat plenty of food. **3.25 run your belly/ bowels** *vb phr* (Antg, Guyn, Jmca) ‖ **work your belly** (Guyn, Nevs) ‖ **le[t]-go you[r] belly** (Crcu, Gren) To cause you to have diarrhoea. □ Cp Phr **3.21. 3.26 tie your belly** *vb phr* (i) (CarA) [*IF*] ‖ **band your belly** (Dmca, Gren, Guyn, Jmca, StVn) ‖ **band your jaw** (Trin) ‖ **tie your guts** (Nevs) ‖ **tie your waist** (StLu) To make great sacrifices in order to achieve an aim; (SE) to tighten your belt. [The firm tying of the belly in preparation for a hard task or privation is a familiar feature of some Afr cultures. Cp Yoruba *gbe ara di (take body tie)* 'to get ready to undertake a task'—*(pers info, K. Ọmọtọsọ)*. Also Shona *kusunga ura (to tie intestines)* i.e. to minimize suffering from not eating—*(pers info, J. Chafota)*] **(ii)** (Gren, Guyn, StVn) To cause constipation. *If you eat too much guava it will tie your belly, you hear?*—(StVn) **3.27 turn your belly** *vb phr* (Guyn, Tbgo, Trin) *[AF]* To cause your stomach to be upset. *I know I can't stand powdered-milk at all. A matter of minutes it will turn m[y] belly.*—(Guyn) **3.28 work your belly** *vb phr* (Guyn, Nevs) *[AF]* ‖ RUN YOUR BELLY (Antg, etc)

bel·ly-ache bush* *n phr* (CarA) ‖ *black baricader* (Angu, StKt) ‖ *wild cassava* (Jmca) ‖ *(wild) physic-nut* (Bdos, ViIs) **1.** A shrub with deeply-lobed, purplish leaves, little, dark red flowers and hairy stems, bearing a small, capsule-like fruit with mottled seeds from wh a medicinal oil is made; *Jatropha gossypifolia* (*Euphorbiaceae*). [Name due to use: 'The leaves are boiled, buttered, and eaten for colic. A warm decoction is good for a woman who has difficulty in expelling the afterbirth. A decoction is also used for colic.'—*Lal.I.1, p.86*] **2.** ‖ PHYSIC-NUT (Belz, etc) [Perh because a decoction of the fruits is a violent purgative]

bell-yam *n* (Guyn) ‖ CUSH-CUSH (YAM) (ECar) ['BELL YAM or CUSH-CUSH ... Tubers small, bell-shaped ...'—*OGEP:113*, re the *Guyn* variety, whence the name there]

bel·ly-band /1'12/ *n* (Guyn, Trin) A broad piece of brown cotton wrapped firmly around the abdomen of a woman after childbirth.

bel·ly-bot·tom /1'122/ *n* (Jmca) *[AF]* **1.** The womb. **2.** The intestines—*DJPVP*.

bel·ly-bus /1'12/ *n* (Guyn) *[AF]* ‖ *belly-lick* (Belz) A swimmer's fall into the water hitting it belly first instead of managing a headlong dive. [< *belly* + *burst* pronounced [bʌs]]

bel·ly-cut·ting /1'122/ *n* (Antg) *[AF/IF]* ‖ BELLY-WORK(ING)S (Antg, etc)

bel·ly·full /1'12/ *n* **1.** (CarA) *[AF]* Sufficient food to eat; a properly satisfying meal. **2.** (Antg, Dmca, Gren, Tbgo) ‖ MANGO-GRAHAM (StLu) **3.** (Trin) *[AF—Joc]* A cheap kind of heavy cake, often with colouring, sold in large slices. **4.** PHRASE **4.1 to your bellyfull** *adv phr* (Guyn) *[AF]* Until stuffed with food/drink. *Dey not only bus open he shop, drink to deh belly full and tek way he tings, but ... deh beat he up.*—CTT:29

bel·ly-lick /1'12/ *n* (Belz) *[AF]* ‖ BELLY-BUS (Guyn)

bel·ly-pump·kin /1'212/ *n* (Bdos) A large round variety of pumpkin, usu sold in cut pieces (as compared with another long-bodied variety

usu sold whole. See GARDEN-PUMPKIN). [Prob from resemblance to a pregnant belly]

bel·ly-run·ning /1'122/ *n* (Jmca, Mrat) *[AF/IF]* ‖ BELLY-WORK(ING)S (Antg, etc)

bel·ly-soup /1'12/ *n* (Bdos) A soup made by boiling the entrails of the sheep or goat, or the tripe and offal of a cow, with split peas and dry pigeon peas.

bel·ly-wash /1'12/ *n* (Jmca) *[AF—Joc]* A quantity of lemonade made with dark sugar and lime-juice with the seeds, and meant to wash down a satisfying meal (hence the name).

bel·ly-wo·man /1'122/ *n* (Antg, Jmca, Mrat, Nevs) *[AF—Derog/Vul]* An unmarried pregnant woman.

bel·ly-work(s) (-work·ing(s)) /1'12(2)/ *n* (Antg, Gren, Guyn, Jmca, StVn, Tbgo) *[AF/IF]* ‖ *bad-belly* (CarA) **1** ‖ *belly-cutting* (Antg) ‖ *belly-running* (Jmca, Mrat) ‖ *going-off* (Mrat, Nevs, StKt ‖ *run(ning)-belly* (Jmca, Guyn) ‖ *runnings* (Antg, Baha, Guyn) ‖ *work-belly* (Belz, Guyn) Diarrhoea; frequent flowing of loose, fluid faeces for some hours. *All dat pepper an[d] curry and ginger-beer must give you belly-workin[g]!*—(Guyn)

Bel·mo·pan·ese /1'112/ *n* (Belz) An inhabitant of Belmopan, the capital of Belize newly created and named in 1970. [*Bel*(ize) + *Mopan* (from the Mopan Maya) + suff *ese* (cp *Guyanese*)]

bel·na ['bɛlna:] (Guyn, Trin) *[Indic]* A wooden rolling pin used for flattening the dough to make ROTI. *Clean, dark, well-used belna and tawa leaned up in a corner of the kitchen near the fire-place for the next meal.*—Guyn (Ms) [Hin *belnaa* 'rolling pin']

be·long *vb intr* (CarA) *[Hist]* To be duly and rightly resident in; to be legally a resident of. *I seein[g] these strange people [a]bout here. They better go back whe[re] they belong!*—(Trin) [From Hist identification of a slave with the particular plantation that owned him] □ The sense is almost emotive, stronger in CE than in SE. See BELONGER.

bé·lon·gen (be·lon·ger) [belɒnjɛ(n)] *n* (Dmca, Gren) See BÉLANJENN

be·long·er [bilɒŋer] *n* (Baha) One who has been a known resident of a place for a long number of years, although not a native of that place or country. *Last night's statement by Prime Minister Lynden Pindling now makes it abundantly clear why only a select number of Belongers has been granted citizenship. 'This government', he said, 'like any other government of the day, will decide who are qualified to be citizens at the time their application comes up for scrutiny.'*—TrI (75.01.11, p.1)

be·long·er·ship *n* (Baha) The status or recognized condition of being a BELONGER. *In his affidavit supporting his application Mr R— claims that he was granted a Certificate of Belongership on February 8, 1966 for which he paid fifty pounds sterling, and on June 20, 1974 applied to be registered as a Citizen of The Bahamas.*—TrI (76.03.09, p.1)

be·low[1] *adv, prep* (Angu, Antg, Bdos, StLu, StVn) Beyond and (often) to the west (of); (often) to the left (of); (often) to the leeward side (of). **a.** *We walked to a place just below the bakery.*— (Angu) **b.** *D'Arcy A. Scott, Realestate Agent, will be located at Constitution Road, St Michael, just below the Baptist Church and Queen's College.*—AdV (86.12.14, p.3) [See and cp ABOVE. Also cp *OED below* 3. 'nearer to the sea'. Also *OEDS* cites more examples (all US) reflecting the CE usage more nearly, ex: (1845) 'There's ne'er a house either above or below for a matter of fifteen miles']

be·low[2] *adj* [AF] That is to the west or to the left. *Entrance closed. Callers please use below gate.*—Bdos (Notice)

bem·be ['bɛmbɛ] *n* (Belz) [AF] A big, strong, self-important person; a bully (male or female). *E always di play big-time an[d] di tell off piple. E da real bembe.* (= She always likes to show off and tell off everybody. She really thinks a lot of herself).—(Belz) [Cp *Bemba*, 'a Central African (Bantu) people'. Also cp Sp *bemba* 'a Negro's thick lips']

bem-bem *n* (Angu, Antg, Guyn) [AF—*Child talk*] Tummy.

ben *vb* (Jmca) [Cr] ‖ BIN[1] (CarA) 2.

be·nab (ba·nab) [bɪ'nab] *n* (Guyn) Name loosely applied in Guyana to an Amerindian forest hut; (properly) a temporary forest shelter for one or more persons (esp hunters). It is made of palm-branches driven into the ground leaning together, or three or four poles standing with a thatched covering of palms, or a mud-walled and thatched structure, depending on the frequency of the dwellers' need to use it. [*BAED* Arawak *banabo* 'a shelter roofed with leaves' < *bana* 'leaf' + *abo* 'with'. Also *IAIG:208* uses *benaboo* as the name of these temporary shelters, citing *benab* only once as a variant] □ Cp AJOUPA.

ben·ay (ben·e(e)) *n* (Gren, etc) See BENNE

bend *vb intr* (CarA) PHRASE [As part of the widely used formula for ending a folk-tale] [AF—*Joc*] **and the bow/pin/nail/wire ben[d], and the story en[d]** ... and that's the end of my tale.

Bend-Down Pla·za *n phr* (Jmca) [AF—*Joc*] A row of roadside HIGGLERS usu peddling necessary items hard to obtain in shops, because of import restrictions. [Joc ref to the fact that buyers have to bend down to buy since the goods are displayed on the ground]

beng·ga-foot/-hand *n* (Bdos, Guyn, USVI) See BANKA-FOOT/-HAND

be·ni·seed *n* (Jmca) ‖ BENNE (Gren, etc) [Prob infl by SE *aniseed*]

ben·na ['bɛna]; **ben·na song** *n* (*phr*) (Antg, Mrat) A type of two or three-line folk-song repeated over and over; in former times it was considered inappropriate for Sundays or for children; there was a dance to it. □ Cp BANJA 3. (Bdos).

ben·ne* (ben·ay, be·ne(e), be·ni, ben·nae, ben·nay, ben·neh, ben·ni, ben·ny) ['bɛnɛ ~'bɛni] *n* (CarA) ‖ *beniseed* (Jmca) ‖ *gigiree*[1] (Gren, Trin) ‖ *tillie* (Guyn) **1.** (Gren, Tbgo, Trin) The tiny oval seeds of a soft-stemmed flowering herb (the sesame), wh can produce a clear cooking or anointing oil; they are mostly used for making sweetmeats; *Sesamum orientale* or *S. indicum* (*Pedaliaceae*). **2.** usu BENNE-BALLS *n* (Tbgo, Trin) A sticky sweet made of BENNE seeds and melted sugar, shaped into mouthful-sized balls. **3.** BENNIE-CAKE(S)/SQUARE(S) ['bɛni-] *n* (*pl*) (Baha) A sweetmeat made of the same mixture as BENNE BALLS, but covered with parched BENNE/BENNIE seeds and cut into small squares. [< Mandingo *bene* 'sesame'; also *KNED* Nembe *beni* 'shrub used in cookery; wild beniseed']

ben·ye ['bɛnyɛ] *n* (USVI) A breakfast fritter made of a mixture of crushed banana and cornmeal or flour fried in oil. [< Fr *beignet* [bɛɲɛ] 'a fritter']

ben·zine ['bɛnzi·n] *n* (Guyn, Trin) [AF—*Joc*] ‖ BUSH-RUM (Guyn)

Be·quia-plum ['bɛkwɛ-plʌm] *n* (StVn) ‖ JAMAICA-PLUM (Bdos, etc) ... *grabbing a Bequia plum from a large dish of fruits on the dining room table as I went past.*—TRIH:158 [Prob by association with the *Grns* island of Bequia, where the tree flourishes more than in *StVn*]

Ber·bice [bʌrbi·s] *n* (Guyn) **1.** The easternmost county of Guyana, near the principal town of wh the country's mental hospital is situated. **2.** PHRASE **2.1 gone to/heading for Berbice** *vb phr* (Guyn) [IF] To have been sent to or behave as if needing to be sent to the mental hospital. [Cp an old Du phr *naar de Berbisjes gaan* (*to go to the Berbice*) 'to go to hell (in health), to die'—(*pers info*, E. Essed). Berbice was once Dutch owned] □ Similar phrases are used re *Bellevue* (*Jmca*), *Jenkins* (Bdos), etc.

Ber·bice-chair [bʌ(r)'bi·s-čer] *n* (Bdos, Dmca, Guyn, Jmca) A chair about 7 ft in overall length for reclining, the back and bottom making a firm body-curve of tacked-down canvas or carpet material, and the arms extending about 2 ft beyond the body of the chair; in some designs the extension folds inwards to provide a leg-rest. [From its design being originally used in plantation GREAT HOUSE furniture in the County of Berbice in *Guyn*]

Ber·bice Dutch A Cr lang 'with a Dutch-based lexicon still actively spoken by a small community (mostly of Amerindians) living in those areas [on the banks of the Berbice river] at which the earliest Dutch settlements were located'—*I. Robertson (Ms)*.

Ber·bi·cian ['bʌrbišən] /1'21/ *adj, n* (A person or thing) native or belonging to the County of Berbice in *Guyn*.

Ber·mu·da grass *n phr* (Jmca, Trin) ‖ BAHAMA GRASS (CarA) *The sun dried out the wet clumps of long Bermuda grass that grew against the retaining wall of the back garden.*—NG:180

Ber·mu·di·an ['bə(r)myu·diən] /1'221/ (**Ber-.mu.dan**) *adj, n* (CarA) (A person or thing) native or belonging to Bermuda. □ This is the form used in Bermuda, not '*Bermudan*'.

Ber·mu·di·an·i·za·tion *n* The process and operation of BERMUDIANIZING.

Ber·mu·di·an·ize (**-ise**) *vb* To make (sth) Bermudian in character or appearance, esp involving some change; [by extension] to make a principle of employing a very high or total percentage of Bermudian nationals in a business or industry. *I am trying to Bermudianise as much as possible but it is difficult in a small hotel. We have a staff of 18 and two thirds are Bermudian.*—BeS (74.08.10, p.4)

ber·ry *n* 1. (Baha) A purple-black fruit about 1 cm in diameter, with hard skin, and tangy,juicy pulp around a tiny seed; it is borne in clusters on the THATCHBERRY palm. 2. (Bdos) [*AF*] A little money; pennies. *A caretaker in the sense that we are talking about in Barbados is purely a man looking for a little 'berry' and looking for a job.*—Bdos (Hd, 75.11.11, p.5622) [By metaph extension of SE sense 'small fruit'] 3. PHRASE 3.1 **the berry tree is growing in a different yard** (Bdos) [*AF—Joc*] The source of benefit (esp favours bringing financial gain) is now under the control of a different person.

bé·sé·dòng[1] (**baisse·ez-dong, baiss·ez-down**) ['bese-dʌŋ] *n* (Trin, Tbgo) ‖ *bessy-dong*[1] (Bdos, Guyn, Gren, Jmca) A girls' ring-game in wh, the leader giving the time from the centre of the circle, they all clap hands and sing (variations of) 'Baissez! Baissez do[w]ng! For the sake o[f] the pumpkin/plantain, baissez do[w]ng!'; the leader then chooses one player who must match her in WINING (wriggling the waist) as they crouch lower and lower while the others keep singing and clapping. *Baissez dung / This game-song is very common in Trinidad and some versions of it have been reported from Jamaica by Beckwith*

who renders '*pumpkin*' as '*pong-pong*'.—ESGTT: 42 [< Fr Cr *bésé* 'bend down', *bési* 'bow' (cp *VDCSL.II:8*) < Fr *baissez*, + E *down*, reduplicating the lost sense of the original Fr Cr. The game is possibly a survival from the post-slavery era of one of many pre-wedding song-games with sexual suggestion, but transferred to children and rendered harmless by substitution of 'pumpkin' in the song for Cr PUMPUM 'vulva' (note the *Jmca* version in the cit, and cp Twi *pumpuy* 'to swell up as if ready to burst'), or 'plantain' in metaph sense for the male genital organ]

bésé·dòng[2] (**baiss·ez-dong/-down**) *vb intr* (Trin) ‖ *bessy-dung*[2] (Guyn, Jmca) ‖ **hold down** (Bdos) 1. To stoop; to bend down. **a.** *You heard it in the tents not too long ago. You heard it in the Carnival fetes. You yourself woman, must have faced the challenge—'wine for me gyul'. And you baissez-down in the warmth of the moment.*—Peo.1.8, p.33 **b.** *Yo[u] got to bessy-down to pass through this door.*—(Guyn) [By functional shift from the name of the game BÉSÉ-DONG[1], BESSY-DONG[1]] 2. (also BESSIE-DOWN) (Guyn) [*AF*] To curtsy. *When she saw he was a white master, look how she bessie-down, A tell you.*—(Guyn)

be·side *prep* (CarA) [*X*] 1. In addition to; apart from; putting aside (some fact or circumstance); besides. *If it is an April Fool's joke, doc, please think that there are others who will be fooled beside the politicians.*—BoM (73.02.02, p.1) 2. PHRASE 2.1 **get beside yourself** *vb refl* (CarA) ‖ **be (getting) forward** (Tbgo) ‖ **be out-of-place with yourself** (StVn, Tbgo) ‖ **be out of your place** (Nevs) ‖ **come out of your cover** (Dmca) ‖ **not know your distance** (Nevs) ‖ **pass your place** (Jmca, StVn) [Of a young person] To be impertinent (esp in giving a saucy answer to an adult); to forget yourself. *Don't you dare answer me like that! Eh? You're well getting beside yourself!*—(StVn) [A semantic shift of SE *be beside oneself (with grief, rage, etc)*]

be·sides *prep* (CarA) [*X*] 1. At the side of; beside. *... when I went to the theatre I saw her sitting besides a guy whom she tells me is her brother.*—NaT (77.03.20, p.26, Dear Christine) 2. Compared with; next to; beside. *The number of these independent states pales besides those which have not yet reached independence.*—ViN (73.02.10, p.11) 3. Except; excluding. *But this seems to be true for every other country besides our own.*—AdN (71.12.11, p.6)

bes·sy-down (**bes·sie-down, bes·sy-dung**) (Bdos, Gren, Guyn, Jmca) *n, vb intr* See BÉSÉ-DÒNG[1]; BÉSÉ-DÒNG[2]

best[1] *adj* (Gren, Trin) [*AF*] [Initiating an affirmative statement] It's best that; the best thing to do is. *Wit: 'Cecil B— say: 'Like she know you'. / Judge: 'Yes?' / Wit: 'B— turn and say 'Best we knock her out.''*—ToR (77.03.23, p.6) [< 's bes' < is bes' < it's best, with connective 'that' omitted]

best² (bes'-ha, best-had(s)) ['bɛsad(z)] /ı´2/ *adv functioning as a modal particle* [*AF—Cr*] ‖ *better* (CarA) ‖ *better-had* (ECar) [Placed only between subj and vb, adding a mood of warning to the vb] Should/must (with good reason); were best advised (to); (SE) had better. **a.** ... *up comes a woman with a little baby in she arms and say 'Looka., Tessa, I tired holding you chile so long; you bessa tek he from me.'*—CISH:106 **b.** *They might have a watchman looking out. We best hads circle slowly, and come round from behind.*—SPOC:91 □ The forms **best-had(s)** are commonest in *Trin*.

best³ *adv* (CarA) PHRASE **as best as** *adv phr* (CarA) [*X*] As best; in whatever way. *A dictionary should try as best as possible to give the spelling and pronunciation of words as common to different places.*—StVn (Ms, 1971)

Best Vil·lage (com·pe·ti·tion) *n phr* (Tbgo, Trin) An annual series of competitions among the villages of Trinidad, instituted from 1963 by Prime Minister Dr Eric Williams, emphasizing handicrafts, local foods, and folk dances, and ending with a QUEEN contest. □ The official name *Best Village Trophy Competition* is seldom used.

be·ta (bay·ta, be·tah) ['be·ta] *n* (Guyn, Trin) [Indic] Son; (affectionate term of address to) any young EAST INDIAN male. *'All-you is not like he, beta,' he would say cajolingly to his younger sons. 'All-you make for work in field, but Guru is different.'*—NAGOS:86 [Hin/Bhoj *beṭa*, 'son'] □ No change in the pl. The spellings *bayta, betah* also used, are conjectural. Cp BETI (fem). See also BHAIYA

bête-rouge (bèt-wouj) ['bɛtru·š ~ 'bɛtruž] *n* (Gren, Guyn, StLu, Trin) A very tiny, red insect that crawls on to humans who are in low bushes or on the grass, and burrows into the skin causing intense itching before it dies; *Eutrombicula alfreddugesi* (*Trombiculidae*). [Fr = red beast] □ Pl *bêtes-rouges*.

be·ti ['be·ti] *n* (Guyn, Trin) [Indic] **1.** Daughter; (affectionate term of address to) any EAST INDIAN young woman. *Romesh met his sisters at home. They greeted him shyly but he held them in his arms and cried, 'Beti, you must not know your own brother?'*—SWOS:66 □ Pl unchanged. **2.** [*AF—Joc/Derog*] [*non-Indic*] Any East Indian girl, esp one from the country. *Some betis from the country dress up and lookin[g] good.*—(Trin) [< Hin/Bhoj *beti*, 'daughter'] □ The term, in wider and often uncomplimentary use, has been popularized esp by its use in *Trin* CALYPSOES.

bé·tiz (bé·tise) ['beti·z] *n* (StLu) ‖ STUPIDNESS (CarA) *She likes to talk too much bétiz, that's why nobody taking her on.*—(StLu) [Fr *bêtise* 'stupidity, nonsense, folly']

bétjé *n* (StLu) ‖ BACKRA (CarA) [By /k > č/ affrication of the alternative Fr Cr form BÉKÉ]

bé·tjin (bé·chine) [bečin] *n* (Dmca) ‖ BARRACUDA (CarA) PHRASE t[h]ief like a bétjin *vb phr* (Dmca) To steal without being caught; to be a really clever thief. [The BARRACUDA is well known for carrying off the bait]

bet·ter¹ *adj* (Guyn) [In ref to length of time] More (than). *S1: How long you had to wait at the Hospital? / S2: My dear, better than three hours, A sure!*—(Guyn) [As OED better A. I. 3. a., latest cit 1823]

bet·ter² *adv functioning as modal particle* (CarA) [*IF*] [Placed between subj and vb adding a mood of warning to the vb] **1.** ‖ **best²** (CarA) *And Dr W—better take note. Unless he has given up and don't care.*—BoM (73.02.02, p.3) [< SE *you'd better*, with loss of unstressed /-d/ + the non-use of the structure '*had* + pa. part' in Cr. OEDS *better* 4. b. (b) notes this usage as 'orig U.S.'. It is, however, well-established CE from CarA Cr, occurring sometimes with pron subj suppressed. Cp BEST² adv similarly used] **2.** PHRASES **2.1 better don't** *neg modal vb phr* (CarA) [*AF—Cr*] Had better not. **a.** *'Listen,' Brackley say, 'you better don't let me and you have contention.'*—RWIN:101 (S. Selvon) **b.** *Better don'[t] mash m[y] foot wid you wil[d]ness, yoh!*—(Bdos) **2.2 better do (sth) and done** *modal vb phr* (CarA) [*AF—Cr*] (It would be) best to have (sth) done and finished with. *She felt tired of being fooled by the men and thought she better just have a child and done.*—Trin (Ms) **2.3 better-had; hads better** /1´22/ *vb phr* (ECar) [*AF*] ‖ BEST² (CarA) *Yuh know is three times dey van get stick up and people take orf wid dey money. Dey better had fine some nex way to get money in de bank yes boy.*—TrG (72.10.22, p.12) **2.4 better-had don't** *neg vb phr* (ECar) [*AF—Cr*] Had better not. *A know they better-had don[t] make they hand fast wid Miss Cummins fowls! She would put the police on them in no time!*—(Guyn) **2.5 for the better** (Guyn) *adv phr* [*X*] All the more/ the worse. *De more [h]e beat she, she holler for de better.*—(Guyn)

bet·ter³ *vb tr* (Antg, Jmca) [*AF*] To cure sb of an illness. *A bring dis bush will better you. Boil it and drink.*—(Antg)

be·tween *adv, prep* (CarA) [*X*] **1.** [Loosely used to express places, position, or time] In between. **a.** *They say he used to hide his money between the organ pipes and when the church burned he lost all.*—(Bdos) **b.** *She is really a baker but she does a little sewing between.*—Gren (Ms, 1976) **2.** [Loosely used to express approximation] About; within; approximately; roughly. *The University ... is interested in obtaining accommodation, preferably between one to five miles from the campus, for students.*—AdN (Ad, 72.07.08, p.5)

bèt-wouj *n* (StLu) See BÊTE-ROUGE

bev·er·age (be·bish, beb·ridge, bre·bich, etc) *n* ['bɛvrıj ~ 'bɛbrıj ~ 'b(r)ɛbič] (Antg, CayI, Jmca, StKt) ‖ *sugar-water* (Angu, BrVi, Guyn,

StLu, StVn) ‖ *swank* (Bdos, Guyn) Usu a drink of sugar and water only, but sometimes in Jamaica with lime-juice also (hence a lemonade); also in Jamaica any non-alcoholic fruit drink— *DJPVP*. [The variant creolized forms are due to CarA Cr /b/ < E /v/, and the form **brebitch** (*Antg*) to metathesis and devoicing [-ʃ] > [-č]]

bhaat (**bhat, bharth**) [bha:t] (Guyn, Trin) [Indic] Plain cooked rice. [Hin *bhaat* 'cooked rice'] □ Used mostly by older EAST INDIAN folk, or in advertisements for Indic restaurants, but only Joc by younger EAST INDIANS.

Bha·ga·vat (**Bha·ga·wad, Bhag·wat, Bag-·wat**); **Bhagwat Jag/Yagya/Yajna** [bha:gəvat(-d)~bagwat yag(ya)/yaɟna] *n* (*phr*) (Guyn, Trin) [Indic] A series of Hindu prayer-meetings lasting up to seven consecutive nights, based on ceremonial readings from the *Bhagwat Gita*, and specially organized as a sacrificial offering. *Pandit Oudit Narine will be officiating on three Bhagwat ceremonies on the Corentyne coast, as follows: .../ From Sunday, January 27 to Sunday February 3, a seven-day Bhagwat Jag at Pln. Skeldon Line Path, sponsored by the people of the Line Path Settlement.*—GyG (57.01.09, p.7) [Shortened form of *Bhagavat-Katha* religious discourse on the *Bhagavat Gita* 'song- sermon of the Seer Bhagavat', one of the most important Hindu gospels, + (Bhoj) *jag* < (Hin) *yagya* 'ceremonial fire marking a sacrifice'. In the course of the ceremonial recitation of the epic, the celebrant pours ghee on the ceremonial fire]

bhai [bhaɪ~baɪ]; (**bhai·ya, by·ah**) ['bhaɪ-ya~'baya] *n* (Guyn, Trin) [Indic] Friendly or respectful form of address to a Hindu male; [by extension] an East Indian male. [Hin *bhai(y)a* 'brother'] □ In *Trin* the term is sometimes used irrespective of the sex of the person addressed. □ Cp BETA

bha·jan ['baʃa·n] *n* (Guyn, Trin) [Indic] Hindu religious singing (sg); [by extension] the ceremonial song itself (wh may be pl). *And after the katha there would be bhajan or singing, and a great feasting.*—NAGOS:55 [Hin *bhajan* 'devotional song']

bha·ji (**baa·ji, etc; bhaa·gee, etc**) [ba:ʃi] *n* (Guyn, Trin) [Indic] **1.** ‖ CALALU 1. (CarA) [Hin *bhaajii* 'vegetable leaves, (green or cooked)'. The aspiration is generally lost in this word in Indic CE] **2.** [By extension] Any dish comprising mostly edible leaves. *'The bharth finish, the dahl finish too; the bhaji cookin'. / 'Bhaji! What bhaji?' roared Gurudeva. 'Pumpkin vine wid sal'fish.' / 'Pumpkin vine! Who tell you to cook pumpkin vine?' / 'But you always eat it. I thought..'*—NAGOS:31 □ A number of conjectural spellings are found combining various elements of *b(bh)a(aa, ar)j(dg, g, gh, jh) i(ie, ee)*. Indic CE speakers also distinguish many types of *bhaji*, sometimes with qualifying Indic names such as '*chowrai bhaji*', etc, sometimes with others such as '*caterpillar bhaji*', etc.

bha·rat *n* (Trin) See BARAAT

Bhoj·pu·ri ['bhoʃpuri] *n* (Guyn, Trin) A preliterate multi-dialectal lang of northern west-central India, related to Hindi-Urdu and to Bengali; it was spoken by the majority of the EAST INDIAN indentured immigrants to Guyana and Trinidad who came via Calcutta. [Orig centred at Bhojpur (hence the name) in Bihar state, the language, spoken by 'over 20 million people' (U.N. Tiwari: *Origin and Development of Bhojpuri*, 1960, p.xxiii), straddles the borders of Bihar, Uttar Pradesh and Nepal spreading south over several thousand square miles to Calcutta]

bhoon·jal (**bhoon·ja[y], bhun·jal**) [bhun-ɟal~/ɟe] *adj* (Guyn, Trin) [Indic] [Of meat, vegetables, or curry] Cooked until dry (with all broth, gravy, and seasoning absorbed). *Customers are guaranteed a wide variety of food daily which will include cook-up rice, fried and bhoonjal chicken, stewed and pepper-pot beef.*—GyC (77.01.04, p.5) [Bhoj < Hin *bhuujaa* 'parched, roasted, broiled']

bhow·ji (**bau·ji, bhou·gie, bow·gie, bow·ji**) ['bhʊʊji~bʊʊɟi] *n* (Guyn, Trin) [Indic] **1.** Elder brother's wife; sister-in-law. **2.** [By extension] Respectful or appreciative form of address to a mother or elderly East-Indian woman. [Bhoj *bhaujii* 'elder brother's wife'. Cp Hin *bhaabii* 'elder brother's wife'] □ [AF—Derog]. Sometimes jocularly used by non-Indic speakers to refer to any elderly EAST-INDIAN woman.

bi·as ['baɪas] *adj* (CarA) [X] Biased. *I have not read a single good thing about the PPP government or perhaps I am reading the bias papers.*—ViN (73.01.20, p.5) [From characteristic CarA Cr loss of pa· part /-t/] □ A common error, whence also occasionally '*biasness*' [X].

bib·by [bɪbi~bibi] *n* (Baha) [IF] ‖ *bubu* (Guyn) ‖ *kaka-djé* (Gren) ‖ *matter*[2] (Jmca) ‖ *yampi*[2] (Antg, etc) Mucus in the corner of the eye (esp after sleeping). *... and if one wants to actually see a sperrid, one has only to remove some 'bibby' from a dog's eye and put it into their eyes and they will have the gift of seeing sperrid.*—MTTBT:95

biche (**bish, buisse**) [biš] *n* (Gren, Trin) PHRASES **break biche** (**bish, buisse**) *vb phr* (Gren, Tbgo, Trin) [IF] ‖ *break/make lékòl-bich* (Trin) ‖ *burn school* (StVn) ‖ *make toubak* (Dmca) ‖ *skulk* 1. (Guyn) ‖ *skull* (Gren, Jmca) To skip school; to play truant. **a.** *In fact, while at school I use to break biche and go to swim near the Aquatic Club, now the Carlton Hotel.*—SuP (77.03.20, p.7) **b.** *He always making l'école biche—10 o'clock Monday morning I see him kicking ball in the savannah.*—WFCT:13 [< *DELF* early Fr *buis, buisse, bouisse,* 'box-tree' from wh *buisson* 'bush, thicket', whence Fr idiom *faire l'école buissonnière* 'to play truant'. Prob dial *buisse* > *biche* 'bush, thicket', entering into similar Fr Cr idiomatic phr. The loan trans 'make' (<

faire), was prob replaced by 'break' infl by the idea of breaking out of or away from school. Cp also IrE *mitch* 'to play truant from school'—*JESI:295*] □ I. The phr ‖ *make lékòl-bich* is more used in rural Trinidad. 2. Cp also BREAK BUSH (Gren).

biche-break·ing *n* (Trin) Skipping school; truancy. *And to him one thing is clear, and that is his biche-breaking from St Mary's Sixth Form in favour of the cinema has paid some dividends. He was to find out about ... the thing called acting.*—Peo I.5, p.19

bick·le (**bit·tle**) [bɪkl~bɪtl] *n* (Bdos, Belz, Guyn, Jmca) [*AF—Cr*] Cooked food; a meal put on the table. *'Better belly bu[r]st dan good bickle/ bittle spail/was[t]e.'* (= *It is better to let your belly be bursting full than to let good food go to waste.*)—Guyn (Prov) [< *victuals* [vɪtlz] with characteristic Cr /v > b/ shift. See letter в]

bick·le/ bit·tle-boil·er [bɪkl/bɪtl-baɪla] /2'212/ *n* (Guyn) [*AF—Cr/Joc*] A glutton. [Prob from Hist ref to the slave(s) who cooked the victuals and ate more of it than the others]

bi·cy·cle-cart /1'221/ *n* (Belz) A small-load three-wheeled delivery cart made by removing the front-wheel of a bicycle and attaching the remainder to a low-slung, 'open-box' metal frame supported on two wheels.

bid·dims (**bee·deems**) [bɪdɪmz~bidimz] *n* (Bdos, Guyn, Tbgo, Trin) [*AF—Joc*] ‖ **biddim-pants** (Trin) ‖ *flood-pants, gun-mouth (pants)* (Gren, Guyn, Trin) A man's (esp a young man's) trousers that are too short and narrow, only reaching about the ankles. [ECHOIC WORD imitating the sound of a gun, wh such trousers are thought to resemble]

bid·dy ['bɪdi] *n* (Baha) [*IF*] A new-born chicken. [*OED biddy* (obs. exc. dial.) 'a chicken, a fowl' + latest cit 1884. Cp also *OED chicka-biddy* < (chick + biddy) nursery word for a young child]

Bi·dim! (**Bim²**, **Bum**, **Budum!**) *excl ideoph* (CarA) [*AF*] ECHOIC WORDS representing esp the sound of a shotgun or canon, or that of some large object falling with a heavy thud.

Bi·dip! (**Bip**, **Bu·duf**, **Bu·dup**, **Buf**, **Bup!**) *excl ideoph* (CarA) [*AF*] ‖ *Buduf, Buff!* (CarA) ECHOIC WORDS representing the impact of a blow with the fist or an impact like that. □ See also BADAOW

big¹ *adj* (CarA) 1. [*IF*] [Ref to a person's age] Adult or adolescent. *I remember him when I was a child as already a big man to me.*—(Bdos) [An extension of SE *big boy/sister*, etc 'adolescent, older'] 2. [*IF*] (Dmca) [Of a river] In flood. *The river was big so we could not cross it.*—Dmca (Ms) 3. (i) [*IF*] The more or most important one of a pair or set. (a.) THE BIG-CHURCH /1'2/ (Antg)

[Hist] The Anglican Cathedral. (b.) THE BIG-HOUSE /1'2/ (CarA) [Hist] ‖ *The Great-House* (Jmca) The plantation owner's residence. (c.) BIG-SCHOOL /1'2/ (CarA) The elementary school for children over 6 years old (as opposed to the infant or nursery school). □ Distinguish all these from *big church* /2'1/, etc wh would mean any big church, house, or school. (ii) [*AF—Derog*] Of showy importance; only looking important or threatening but of no real effect. **a.** *When he got on the platform he used to try to impress the people with a lot of big English and so on, but they only laughed at him.*—(Guyn) **b.** *Dey should hide she away. Big Governor and t'ing coming and she comin' out in she nightgong.*—NM:11 4. [*AF—Joc*] [Ref to time of day, week, or year, with a semi-adverbial quality] Even though it is; important though (sth) is. *'Big Christmas and I carn even buy a frack,' she exclaimed.*—Nevs (Ms) 5. PHRASES **5.1 come/get big** [*AF*]; **grow /turn (a) big man/woman** [*IF*] *vb phrs* (CarA) Grow up; grow into adulthood. *When children grow big and get sense they will judge their parents.*—(StVn) [Cp Igbo (dial) *topụ tara oke mmadụ* (*grow into man big*) 'grow into an adult' (*C. Azuonye*); also Edo *khian agikpa* (*become big man*) and WAPE *wait make you grow big* 'wait until you grow up' (*A. Amayo*)] **5.2 big for (sb)** *adj phr* (Guyn) [*IF*]; **bigger one for (sb)** (Tbgo) [Of adolescents] Older than (the other). *Which of you is bigger? He is big for you or you are big for him?*—(Guyn)

big² *adv* (CarA) [*AF*] 1. In a way intended to make an impression; ostentatiously; loudly. *'She's always talking big,' he said with a short empty laugh, 'but there's not a thing she can do.'*—MBGB:74 2. PHRASE **2.1 open your mouth big** *vb phr* (CarA) [*AF*] To speak out without caring about who would be embarrassed by what you say. *At the PTA meeting he opened his mouth big and accused a teacher of malingering.*—(Bdos)

big³ *vb tr* (Baha) [*AF—Vul*] To make pregnant. *Big—a term commonly used in the Bahamas for a girl who is pregnant. 'I gon' big her' means that 'I am going to make her pregnant'.*—MBS:53

big-able *adj* (Bdos, Guyn, Trin) [*AF*] Very big indeed; massive; [by extension] frightening in size. **a.** *Before he look to see where he going, with that big-able lorry, he gone and knock down the man fence.*—(Bdos) **b.** *Look at a big-able mosquito on the poor baby sleeping.*—(Guyn) □ Applied to any subject, animate, inanimate or abstract and pronounced as if one word.

bi·gan *n* (Guyn) See BAIGAN

big-and-plen·ty *adj* (Gren) [*AF—Derog*] ‖ *big-and-so-so* (Jmca) ‖ *voluptious* (Guyn) Fat, clumsy-looking and of low quality. □ Usu of a person, but also of a fruit or vegetable.

big-and-so-so *adj* (Jmca) [*AF—Derog*] ‖ BIG-AND-PLENTY (Gren)

big-big /1´2/ *adj* (CarA) [*AF*—*Joc*] **1.** Wishing to appear important without reason (esp in foll phr). **2.** PHRASE **2.1 play big-big** *vb phr* (CarA) [*AF*—*Joc*] To be haughty without reason; to make a false show of pride. □ Distinguish from '*big, big* ...' /2´2´.../ (with further poss reduplication), 'very very big'.

big-bot·tle /1´22/ *n* (Guyn) [*IF*] ‖ *biggie* (Guyn) [*AF*] ‖ *largie, pint-and-a-half* (Bdos) A 26 fluid-ounce (or 750 ml) bottle of rum. [*Witness*] *said he agreed to put up a half-bottle if accused agreed to put up a big-bottle.*—Guyn (CR, 78.06.25)

Big crop *n phr* (Guyn) [Rice Ind; Sugar Ind] ‖ AUTUMN CROP (Guyn) [So called as being the larger and later of the two crops, in each industry, in contrast to the earlier 'small crop']

big-drum *n* (Crcu) Any of the family of three drums each made from a small barrel over one end of wh goat-skin is stretched, tightened and tuned so that the centre or 'mother' drum produces a dominant, higher note; each drum carries a 3-inch diameter hole half-way down its height. The drums, whose loud, rhythmic beat can be heard for away, are used for ceremonial dances.

big-drum dance *n phr* (Crcu) A set of dances organized to celebrate a festive occasion or for a special spiritual reason, beginning with the particular NATION DANCE of the celebrant and followed by others; each dance is performed by two couples who dictate the pattern, rhythm, and length of each successive dance, within a circle of people or BIG-DRUM dance ring. □ See NATION DANCE.

big-dubs *n* (Belz) [*AF*] **1.** A large polished marble. **2.** [By extension] (Affectionate term for) a stocky good-humoured man. [< 'dub', an imported Du marble (Obs)]

big-eye[1] /1´2/ *adj* (CarA) [*AF*—*Joc*] **1.** ‖ *craven* (Gren, Jmca) ‖ *cravichous-minded, cravishing* (Bdos) ‖ *gravalicious* (Baha, Belz, Jmca) ‖ *g(w)o-zyé* (Dmca, StLu) ‖ *lickerish* (Bdos, Guyn, StVn) ‖ *long-belly* (Nevs, StKt) ‖ *long-eye*[2] (BrVi, Nevs, StVn) ‖ *long-hearted* (Nevs) ‖ *raven* 1. (Gren, StVn) ‖ *struck* (Angu) Prompt to choose the biggest one or largest share (esp of food); shamelessly greedy. *You too big-eye, that's why yo[u] snatch de biggest mango an[d] fin[d] it spoil.*—(Gren) [A prob calque from W Afr langs. Cp Igbo *invere anya ukwu* (*you have eye big*) 'you are greedy' (B. Oluikpe); also Yoruba *o ni oju kokoro* (*he has eye of insect* i.e. big eyes) 'he is greedy'—(*pers info, A. Banjo*)] □ Very often in the form **your eye is (too) big**. Cp LONG-EYE, STRONG-EYE. **2.** [*AF*] (StLu) Annoyed; showing anger in your eyes (esp in foll phr). **3.** PHRASE **3.1 look (at sb) big-eye** *vb phr* (StLu) To look (at sb) with your eyes wide with anger.

big-eye[2] *n* (CarA) [*AF*—*Joc*] **1.** ‖ *red-eye* 2. (Belz, Jmca, StVn) Prompt greed; avarice. '*Big-eye choke dog*' (= *Unthinking greed can easily*

embarrass you).—Guyn (Prov) **2.** PHRASE **2.1 have (too much) big-eye** *vb phr* (CarA) [*AF*—*Joc*] ‖ *have (too much) gwo zié* (Dmca, StLu) To be (too) greedy, avaricious, etc. [Cp WIED Igbo *anya ukwu* (*eyes big*) 'greed'. See more at BIG-EYE[1]]

big-eye[3] *n* (ECar) **1.** Name given to more than one kind of small fish (some of wh are edible) with big eyes; *Pseudopereus maculatus*, etc. ... *and the west coast teems with timid little creatures, half-fish, half-insect, called Big Eyes.*—FTT:169 **2.*** (ECar) ‖ *big-eye John, big-eye porgie* (Baha) ‖ *mawiyann* (Dmca, StLu) ‖ *popeye-ranty* (TkCa) 'A bright red fish with striking blue on the upper jaw, its fins yellowish tipped, and of average size 12 ins; it is of good food value; *Priacanthus arenatus* (*Priacanthidae*)'—ADF:57. [The fish has a noticeably large eye in relation to its size]

big-eye John; **big-eye por·gie** *n phrs* (Baha) ‖ BIG-EYE[3] 2. (ECar)

big-foot *n* (CarA) [*IF*] ‖ *Barbados-leg* (CarA) ‖ *filaria, swell foot* (Guyn) An extreme swelling of the leg caused by a parasitic worm of the family *Filariidae* wh is carried by a mosquito and wh lodges and multiplies in the lymphatic vessels of the body, esp the legs; elephantiasis; filariasis. [Also in W Afr langs. Cp IGED Grebo *bo hwɛ* (*foot big*) 'elephantiasis']

Big Four *n phr* (CarA) [*IF*] The four CARICOM territories with the largest populations: Jamaica, Trinidad, Guyana, and Barbados. *I believe that the leaders of the so-called 'Big Four' have been very parsimonious in their attitude to Caribbean integration.*—Bdos (Hd, 74.01.29, p.3112)

big·ge(r)·ty (**big·gi·ty**) [bɪgəti] *adj* (Baha) [*AF*] ‖ BIGGITIVE (BrVi, Guyn)

big·gie (**big·gy**) [´bɪgi] *n* (Guyn) [*AF*—*Joc*] ‖ BIG-BOTTLE (Guyn)

big·gi·tive [bɪgɪtɪv] *adj* (BrVi, Guyn) [*AF*—*Derog*] ‖ *bigge(r)ty* (Baha) ‖ *nuff*[1] 3. (Antg, BrVi) ‖ *uppish* (CarA) ‖ *upstarted* (BrVi, Guyn) Uppish; bumptious; wanting to be seen to be respected by others; showing off yourself (often in phr **biggitive with yourself**).

big-jack* *n* (Dmca, Gren, StVn) ‖ *goggle-eye* 2 (TkCa) ‖ *jack* (Baha, CayI) Either of two kinds of small, grayish fish, distinguished by their relatively big eyes; they are of good food value; *Selar crumenopthalmus* (*Crevalle*) (the smaller of the two kinds) or *Caranx latus* (*Crevalle*)—ADF:61 *The festivities planned for Gouyave have been given a big boost because of recent catches of big-jacks in the area.*—ToR (76.06.27, p.1) [Because larger varieties than the normal JACKS]

big man/wo·man; **big-peo.ple** *n phrs* (CarA) [*IF*] **1.** Adult; grown-up man, woman, person(s).

'*Beg pardon' mak[e] lil boy mash big man foot*' (= *Being able to escape blows by begging pardon makes the young less careful of respect for their elders*.)— Guyn (Prov) □ These terms are in common currency in place of *adults* or *grown-ups*. **2.** PHRASES **2.1 come/get/grow/turn a big man/woman** *vb phr* (CarA) [*IF*] See BIG[1] (CarA) Phr 5.1 **2.2 big-people business/story** *n phr* (CarA) [*AF*] Matters wh are the concern of grown-ups (i.e. in wh children should not be involved). *That girl is always behaving like a woman puttin[g] her mouth in big-people business! If I was there I would-a slap her!*—(Guyn) [Cp Yoruba *ǫrǫ agba* 'words or affairs [of] elders' with the same implication i.e. not the business of children]

big-mouth[1] /1'2/ *n* (CarA) [*AF—Derog*] Empty boasting or boastfulness. *After all his big-mouth, when the white-man turned up he hadn't a damn thing to say, so nobody going to listen to him any more.*—(Gren)

big-mouth[2] (**big-mouth·ed**) *adj* (CarA) [*AF—Derog*] **1.** [Usu of a man] Making empty boasts. **2.** [Usu of a woman] ‖ *fast-mouth* (StVn) ‖ *hot-mouth* (ECar) ‖ *labrish, labbermouth* (Jmca) ‖ *long-mouth* (Guyn) ‖ *mouthy(-mouthy)* (Guyn, Jmca, StKt) Dangerously talkative; unlikely to keep a secret or to keep from expressing a damaging opinion. □ See also MOUTH n Phr 4.34.

big-peo·ple /1'22/ *n phr* (CarA) See BIG-MAN

big-plum *n* (CayI) ‖ JAMAICA-PLUM (Bdos, etc)

big-skin·(ned) *adj* (Guyn) [*IF*] [Of a person] Of robust build; full bodied. *The elder sister was slim but the younger sister was big-skinned and she faced up to the sister's husband.*—(Guyn)

big-stone /1'2/ *n* (Dmca) A kind of hide-and-seek, a children's game in wh a big stone is used to mark the 'home' place from wh one player starts, at a whistle's signal, to go in search of the others who have hidden, and who must get back to the stone without being seen or caught.

big-talk (**big talk**) *n* (*phr*) (CarA) **1.** [*IF*] Big empty promises. *Politicians always come with big-talk and nothing behind it.*—(StKt) **2.** [*AF*] ‖ BIG-MOUTH[1] (CarA) ... *he was utterly fed up with the boasting and big talk he has been hearing from these so called karate experts.*—ExP (73.07.08, p.31)

big-time *adj* (CarA) [*AF*] **1.** [Of persons] Important; successful; famous. *I hear she is married to some big time white man, some big time limey in New York, you know anything about it?*—JPB: 54 **2.** [Of things] Important looking; expensive looking; considerable. ... *the vans were used on February 14 in a big time excursion, to Soufriere, organized by the St Lucia Workers Union for its members and some people attending a seminar.*—VoS (65.03.10, p.1)

big-up[1] *adj* (Bdos) [*AF—Joc*] [Of persons] Highly placed; socially important. *A newsman who has been scooping a big-up soldier with a young girl...recently found himself staring down a gun-barrel*—SaS (92.09.05, p.11) [< . SE big + UP[2]]

big-up[2] *n* (Bdos) [*AF—Joc*] An important person; sb in authority. (*You see, one chap leaked a bit of information to the Press, and the big-ups are determined to find out who it is*)—SaS (91.12.21, p.9)

bilg·ed [bɪljd] *adj* (CarA) [Of a metal container] Of no further use because rusted with holes or too dirty and dented.

bi·lim·bi [ˈbɪləmbi] /1'12/ *n* **1.*** (Guyn, Jmca, Trin) ‖ *bimbling, blimbing* (Gren, Jmca) ‖ *(long) jimbelin* (Jmca) ‖ *sourie* (Guyn) A small, pale, green, cucumber-shaped fruit, about 3 ins long when mature, with a thin skin and a very acid pulp; it is borne in small clusters straight from the trunk and older branches of the small tree, so giving it sometimes (*Trin*) the name CUCUMBER TREE; *Averrhoa bilimbi* (*Oxalidaceae*). *Bilimbi is used for making pickles, curries, preserves, etc.*—PTT:77 **2.** (Jmca) ‖ *jimbling* (Jmca) **2.** [The plant is of Asian origin, and the name prob came into CE via Indic culture. *OED* Tamil *bilimbi*. However cp also Swahili *mbilimbi*, name of the same tree] □ See note at BIMBLING.

bil·i·ous [ˈbɪlyʌs] *adj* (CarA) Suffering from BILIOUSNESS.

bil·ious·ness [ˈbɪlyʌsnɪs] *n* (CarA) A feverish and run-down bodily condition accompanied by whiteness of the tongue, and variously by discoloration of the eyes and by stomach or bowel disorder, wh are commonly assumed to be caused by eating too many sweet things over a period of time.

bill[1] *n* (CarA) ‖ *cane-bill* (Bdos) A type of MACHETE specially useful for cutting sugar-canes, having a light, sharp blade about 12 ins long with a broad end carrying a hook on the dull edge, and narrowing towards the round wooden handle. *Then followed the task of weeding and fertilising the ground and, when the crop was ready, the slaves cut the canes with bills in the same way as they cut them today.*—HBIH:111 [*OED* bill sb[1] 4. refers to a similar implement, of wh the CarA design could have been specially infl by sugar plantation needs]

bill[2] *n* (CarA) [*IF*] ‖ BILL-FISH (CarA) *Now comprising top grade group to be sold at 45 cents a pound, are: Albacore, bill, bonito, cavalli, dolphin...*—VoS (65.03.10, p.3)

bill-fish* (**bill**) *n* (CarA) ‖ *ocean-gar* (ECar) Name applied generally to very large spearfishes wh may weigh several hundred pounds at maturity; they are hunted as game fish (marlin, sailfish, swordfish) or caught when smaller for their food value. *We can see a marked difference especially in the months of March, April and May when we were accustomed to have large catches of marlin, which is better known in Barbados as the bill fish.*—Bdos (Hd, 74.03.18, p.3524) [From the long pointed sword or bill that characterizes these fighting fishes] □ *Billfish* is also given as an alternative folk-name for a number of small GAR-FISHES in some professional listings. (See *ADF:35, 113*).

bil·li·gram *n* (Belz) ‖ *snap (of rum)* (Guyn) A measure of rum served for drinking.

bil·ly-boat *n* (Grns, StVn) ‖ MOSES (Antg, etc)

Bil·ly But·ton *n* (StVn, USVI) [*AF—Derog*] A foolish person who labours without first checking whether or by whom he would be paid; a gullible person who is easily cheated. *Billy Button wok for nutten / Never eat a piece o'mutton.*—StVn (Folk rhyme)

bil·ni *n* 1. (Guyn, Trin) [Indic] A small, wasp-like insect that builds little dome-shaped nests on walls inside houses, but does not sting. [Hin *bilnii* 'a kind of black bee'] 2. (Trin) ‖ CAT-BOIL (Guyn)

Bim[1] *n* 1. [*IF*] A native of Barbados. *At length a Barbadian policeman hove in sight, and was hastily beckoned to by the poor ironer, who, by this time, had nearly come to the end of her strength. The uniformed 'Bim' was soon on the spot.*—TF: 98 2. [*By extension, IF*] Barbados. *New Yorker Has Praise For Bim / Barbados has been praised as the true tropical paradise of the Caribbean by a New Yorker, Mr Donald Hunt.*—AdV (86.02.19, p.9) 3. [*By extension, AF—Joc*] The distinctive way of speaking, or 'accent' characteristic of native Barbadians. *You know the Bajans can't hide because, wherever they are, as soon as they open their mouth it's pure Bim.*—(Guyn) [Prob from Igbo *bem* (< *be mu*), 'my house, home, household, folk, fellows, mates, kind'. The Igbo phoneme /e/ being very close to [ɪ] (*WWPAL: 37*) the term would most likely be received as / bim/ in an Anglophone setting. The very common use of the term in the Igbo lang, wh accounts for the loss of the final unstressed vowel, is attested by such everyday Igbo expressions *Ndi bem* 'People (of) my house' (i.e. My household/ family), *Nwanyi ibem* 'Hello, my fellow-woman!', *Nwoke ibem*, 'Hello, my fellow-man!', these last two being standard greeting formulas. That there was a strong presence of Igbo slaves in early Barbados is attested by the survival of the Igbo 2nd pers pl pron *unu* in present-day Bdos folk-speech. The emphatic signalling among these groupings of Igbos would have spread easily to other Afr slaves and might also have been reinforced; for ex Yoruba *ebí mi* (*family/relation my*) 'My folk/relative' is phonetically close. Household contacts through nurses etc would have spread the term effectively to White usage, thus producing the derivative Bimshire,

an IF/AF colonial English name for 'Barbados' as the home of all 'Bims' or 'root' Barbadians, including therefore Whites. Trollope (1859) notes that 'Bim', 'the name in which they themselves delight' was 'slang' (see *OEDS* cit.), a possible indication of its great age by the mid 19C] □ Sense 2. is increasingly favoured in newspaper headlines in *Bdos* esp in favourable emotive contexts. Sense 3. is current only outside of *Bdos*.

Bim![2] *excl ideoph* (CarA) [*AF*] ‖ **Bidim!** (CarA) □ Unlikely to be used in *Bdos*, because of BIM[1].

bim·bling (blim·bing) ['bɪmblɪŋ ~ 'blɪmbɪŋ] *n* (Gren, Jmca) ‖ BILIMBI (Guyn, etc) [< *bilimbi* by metathesis and assimilation. Note also *OED* Malay *bilimbing* as one origin] □ In *Jmca* the names **bimbling (blimbing)** and **jimbling** are often confused by urban speakers through phonic resemblance and because both fruits are similarly acid.

Bim·shire ['bɪmšʌ] *n* (CarA) 1. [*IF*] Friendly name for Barbados. *Russia Recognises Bimshire / The Soviet Union has declared its recognition of Barbados as an independent and sovereign state.*—AdV (66.11.30, p.1) 2. [*AF—Joc*] A native of Barbados (esp in ref to the person's speech). *Whuh? I carry on like a rattlesnake. Carry on like a true Bimshah! Heah I wuz losin' my foot fo' dem wit' dere bleddy canal an' dey come tellin' me dey wuzn't to blame.*—WTD:42 [See BIM] □ Used in sense 2. usu by non-*Bdos* speakers.

bin[1] *vb* (CarA) [*Cr*] 1. (CarA) *pa.t. copula* ‖ **ben** (Jmca) ‖ **min** (Mrat) Was; were. a. *Only people who bin there know wha others miss / De chance of seeing four bobbies nearly kiss.*—DeM (61.10.21, p.9) b. *He went to the man who had given him the job. 'Man, like dah flour las; Man ah bin drunk,' said he.*—DaC (51.08.15, p.3) 2. (CarA) *pa.t. pre-base-verb aux* ‖ **ben** (Jmca) ‖ **min** (Mrat) (Pastmarker); had (+ pa. part.). *Dem bin ketch one* (= *They caught/had caught one*).—(Guyn) 3. *PHRASAL PARTICLES* **3.1 bin-a** (Guyn) [*Imperfect*] Was/were (+ pres. part). *One Crabdack bin a wa'k a dam* (= *A certain Crab-dog was walking on the dam*)—MEFV:23 **3.2 bin-go** (Guyn) [*Future-in-the-past*] Would have (+ pa. part.). *Dem bin-go ketch one* (= *They would have caught/ were going to catch one*).—(Guyn) □ These Cr forms are often found in the accounts of Court proceedings or in the dialogue of present CE literature. The forms 1, 2 are, however, exceptional in current *Bdos* E, and the forms 3 absent. See BEEN

bin[2] *n* (Bdos) ‖ *alley-head box* (Guyn) An open, three-sided, concrete box built at some street-corners in poorer city areas for the public dumping and collection of garbage. □ Cp STUFF-BIN (Bdos)

birch-gum (budge-gum) *n* (Brbu, CayI, Trin) The gum 'bled' from the BIRCH-GUM TREE, used as a folk cure for boils (*Brbu, CayI*) or boiled to produce a resin for furniture work (*Trin*).

birch-gum tree* *n phr* (Bdos, Brbu, Trin) ‖ *budge-gum* (Trin) ‖ *birch-tree* (CayI) ‖ *fence-post tree* (USVI) ‖ *gonmyé* (Dmca, StLu, Trin) ‖ *gonmyé-sang* (Dmca) ‖ *gumbo-limbo* (ViIs) ‖ *gum-elemi* (Baha, TkCa) ‖ *gum-tree* 2. (Angu, Gren, Mrat, Nevs, StKt) ‖ *incense-tree* (Jmca, Trin) ‖ *log-tree* (BrVi) ‖ *naked-Indian* (Gren, USVI) ‖ *red birch* (Jmca) ‖ *turpentine-tree* (Angu, Antg) ‖ *West-Indian birch* (Trin) A large, deciduous tree that is found in dry places and can reach 60 ft in height; it has a smooth and sometimes shiny, reddish-brown trunk scaling off in papery pieces; all parts of the tree yield a resin of turpentine-like odour, and the bark yields the usable BIRCH-GUM; *PTT*:95; *Bursera simaruba* or *B. gummifera* (*Burseraceae*). [*Birch*, because the bark peels like the European 'birch' + *gum* because of the resin yielded]

birch-tree *n phr* (CayI) ‖ BIRCH-GUM TREE (Bdos, etc)

bird *n* 1. (Guyn) A kind of box-kite fitted with stiff wings. 2. (Bdos, Guyn) [*AF*] ‖ *chick* (Baha, StLu, TkCa) An attractive girl. *Groups converge in several different spots, spilling onto the pavement, noisy and troublesome, now to tease the mini-skirted 'birds' that pass, or to shout some remark to an acquaintance across the way.*—AdV (76.02.25, p.11) 3. (Guyn) [*AF—Joc*] Any thing or situation that is a harsh disappointment. (See Phr 4.2). 4. PHRASES 4.1 **before bird wife wake** (Guyn) [*AF—Joc*] See BEFORE[1] Phr 1. *Every morning Lloyd would have the team up before bird wife wake doing their exercises and push-ups to be in trim for the game.*—(Guyn) □ Cp FOWL Phr 2.2. 4.2 **get the bird** *vb phr* (Guyn) To suffer a serious disappointment (usu to the amusement of others). *Crux of Cde R—'s speech was that the PNC had promised the people fish but they 'got the bird' and the Government's record since it took office in 1964 was a series of slogans bordering on the lunatic fringe.*—GyC (78.03.08, p.1) [Ref sense 3.]

bird-hon·ey *n* (StVn) ‖ BALL-BUSH (Bdos, Jmca) [Prob from the popularity of its reddish ball-like inflorescences for nectar, esp with hummingbirds, whence also called BIRD-SUCK (*StVn*)]

bird-of-par·a·dise *n* 1. (Tbgo, Trin) A chocolate to reddish-brown bird with a bright yellow streak from crown to shoulders and a brilliant green throat and beak, the male having also long thin black feathers projecting beyond the tip of the tail; *Paradisea apoda* (*Paradiseidae*)—HBTT:220. □ The bird has a legal sanctuary on Little Tobago, an islet about one mile off Tobago, but is otherwise rare. 2. (Bdos, Jmca) [By extension] ‖ *wild banana* 2. (Bdos, Jmca, Trin, TkCa) A type of HELICONIA with a large, green sheath that sticks out horizontally and from wh bright orange, blade-like petals rise successively,

with a central blue arrow-shaped stamen, so that the whole cluster resembles a large, brightly coloured bird (hence the name) sitting on a banana-like tree; *Strelitzia reginae* (*Strelitziaceae*).

bird-pep·per* *n* (CarA) ‖ *Cayenne-pepper* (Brbu, Jmca) ‖ *chicken-pepper* (StKt) ‖ *chilli* (Gren, Jmca, Trin) ‖ *finger-pepper* (Baha, Bdos) ‖ *guinea-pepper* (Berm) ‖ *hot-pepper* (Baha, Mrat, TkCa, Trin) ‖ *jumbie-pepper* (BrVi) ‖ *nigger-pepper* (Bdos) ‖ *peggy-mouth* (Antg, Brbu, Mrat) ‖ *piman-zwazo* (Dmca) ‖ *spur-pepper* (Bdos) A small, pointed, cylindrical, red pepper about an inch long, that is very hot; it is borne abundantly on a low, bushy plant that grows easily or wild; the pepper is very widely used to flavour cooking and also medicinally; *Capsicum frutescens* (*Solanaceae*). [From the fact that some birds, including hens, eat this pepper and also propagate it in their droppings]

bird-suck *n* (StVn) See BIRD-HONEY

bird-trap *n* (Baha, Guyn, TkCa) ‖ CALABAN (Jmca)

bird-vine *n* (Dmca, Gren, Guyn, Trin) 1.* ‖ *god-bush* (Jmca) ‖ *kakitè-bwa, kapitenn-bwa* (Gren) ‖ *mistletoe* (Gren, Jmca, Trin) ‖ *scorn-the-earth* (Belz, Jmca, TkCa) ‖ *vage* (Trin) One of many varieties of a rambling, parasitic, bushy shrub with leathery leaves and usu red berries; it roots on and gradually smothers its host trees; it is declared a pest by law; *Phthirusa seitzii, etc* (*Loranthaceae*). [From the fact that birds like the berries] 2. ‖ LOVE-VINE (Baha, etc) □ The confusion of the names *bird-vine* and *love-vine* in some places is prob due to their being both outlawed parasitic plants with similar habits.

birth *vb tr* (Bdos, Jmca, StVn) [*IF*] To give birth to (a child). **a.** *Naomi says although Ruthie was sick to death, is a good thing that she has lost the belly, for she would have birthed a bastard.*—RND:198 **b.** *Myra's father wanted to marry me after he came back from Curacao, although I had birthed you by then, but I put him off.*—TRIH:149 [By functional shift < *birth* n, SE lacking a one-word vb and so giving rise also to CE BORN vb]

birth·night par·ty *n phr* (CarA) A house-party with much drinking and dancing held on the evening of a birthday; [by extension] any similar party held to raise money for house-rent, etc. *It was at a birthnight party that George, a contortionist and Rock, the prince of local comedians came together to give a scintillating performance.*—PeL (80.06.13, p.11)

birth-pa·per *n* (CarA) [*IF*] ‖ *age-paper* (Belz, Jmca) ‖ *born-paper* (Guyn) ‖ *kagaj* (Guyn) Birth certificate. *Birthpaper Shortage / New Born Babes are having a hard time getting their names on the rolls of this country, all because of a shortage* *of registration certificates.*—SuP (80.03.23, p.24)

bish [bɪš] (Gren, Trin) See BICHE (Trin)

bi·shun ['bɪšʌn] *n* (Guyn) The smallest marble used in marble games.

bi·si-bi·si *n* (Guyn) See BIZ.ZI-BIZ.ZI

bis·sy-tea (bis·sey-tea) *n* (Jmca) An infusion made from the grated *bissy* (*Cola acuminata*), or cola nut, used medicinally 'to purify the blood'; it is also said to be an antidote for poison. [*DJE* < Twi *bisé*, Ewe *bisi* 'the kola nut and tree bearing it']

bit *n* **1.** (Guyn) [Hist] A silver coin of the value of eight cents (W Indian) or a quarter of a GUILDER, wh was official currency in Guyana up to the 1950's; (later) the equivalent of eight cents in reckoning costs of small items of merchandise (no coin being referred to). **a.** *I am sorry you had your money cut on your first payday. I got fifteen bits, and I shall be only too glad for you to share it.*—SSOS:43 **b.** *'At the request of the Colony, a special coinage of silver fourpences was approved for Br Guiana in 1888. This request originated from the practice of the local population to reckon in 'Bitts'. The old Br Guiana 'Bitt' was the quarter guilder, and when the rate of 1s. 4d per guilder was laid down in 1840, the 'Bitt' became identical with the English silver fourpenny piece. / Supplies of this English fourpenny denomination ... passed to be minted [in 1856] ... and the Royal Mint struck a special issue for Guiana ... .These coins must be regarded as a colonial issue for Br Guiana'.*—PCBWI:33–34 [From the practice, in the 18C & early 19C, of cutting a sterling silver dollar coin into 'bits', spelt *bitts*, or equal segments of one half, one quarter, or one eighth of the coin, the value of the actual silver so obtained being proportionate: 'The cut 1/2 bitt was widely used throughout the West Indian colonies'—PCBWI:124. See also *PCBWI:123–155* for many pictorial W.I. examples] □ See also BIT-NA-HALF, HALF-A- BIT, TUBBITS. **2.** (Bdos) [Hist] The equivalent of ten cents in reckoning costs of small items (there being, however, no coin). *In the days of my childhood flying fish was cheaper for 'the bit', and considered cheap at ten for the bit—in fact 'fish was washing dung the road' at that price.... A six-bit was the name of a half-crown coin—60 cents.*—NaT (78.05.05, p.5) **3.** (BrVi) [Hist] 'Local currency value = 9d' (*PCBWI:124*); (later) the equivalent to 4 pence (or 8 cents, W Indian) in reckoning costs of small items. *Up to the years 1940s the term bit was used in Anguilla. It was equivalent to 4d British coin. One often heard of a bit worth of fish or a bit worth of potatoes.*—Angu (Ms, 1973) **4.** (Belz) [Hist] The Spanish *real* or its equivalent value of half a shilling. □ 'The term is still used by creoles and Mestizos in reckoning'—Belz (Ms).

bite *vb intr* (CarA) [*IF*] **1.** [Of a part of the body] To itch. *I must really wash my hair—my*

head is biting me so.*—(Mrat) **2.** [Of the abdomen] ‖ *cut* (Bdos, Guyn) To have a sharp, stabbing pain from time to time. *When I feel my belly bitin[g] me so I know I must take a wash-out.*—(Jmca)

bit·er [baɪtʌ] (Baha) ‖ GUNDY (CarA)

bit-'n-a-half (bit-na-half) ['bɪtnahaˑf] *n* (Guyn) (The sum of) twelve cents; [hist] a silver sixpence coin. *'How much you sell in one day?' / 'Wan day!' He held up one finger. 'Sometime two bit, s'illin, bit-'n'alf, five cent.'*—CNH:17 [BIT 1. 'eight cents' + 'and a half' (of eight cents)] □ Still in use among older (esp older rural) folk.

bit·ter-a·loes *n* (Guyn, Jmca) ‖ ALOES (CarA)

bit·ter-bush *n* (CarA) **1.** Name applied to a number of different plants wh are used to provide a bitter infusion that is used as a folk medicine. **2.** (BrVi, Antg) Any bush whose leaves are used to make BITTERS-TEA or BUSH-TEA, 'eucalyptus, privy, white head, maiden-blush, cat-mint and many others'—Antg (Ms, 1973). □ In some communities the names BITTERS(-TEA), BUSH-TEA are actually applied to such bushes. **3.** (Baha) ‖ *bitter-wood* (Baha) ‖ *majoe-bitter* (Jmca) ‖ *snake-root* (Baha) One of two similar kinds of shrub bearing small, reddish-brown berries; the leaves are used medicinally; *Picramnia antidesma* or *P. pentandra* (*Simarubaceae*). **4.** (Gren) ‖ *zèb-a-pik* (Gren, Trin) A bushy plant, a simple leaf of wh soaked in rum provides a folk-medicine for fevers, and a few drops of the same liquor in water used as a vermifuge. **5.** (USVI) A bush a few leaves of wh, boiled or added to drinking water, are used as a folk-medicine to help women in confinement; *Rauvolfia lamarckii* (*Apocynaceae*).

bit·ter cas·sa·va *n phr* (CarA) See CASSAVA

bit·ter-cup /1'12/ *n* (Guyn, Jmca) A cup carved out of the wood of the *lignum vitae* tree (*Guyn*) or *Quassia amara* (*Jmca*) in wh water, placed overnight, draws the bitterness of the wood, to be drunk as a medicine against fevers or loss of appetite. □ See BITTER-WOOD, QUASHIE-BITTERS.

bit·ter or·ange *n phr* (Antg, Bdos, BrVi) ‖ SOUR ORANGE (CarA)

bit·ters *n pl* (CarA) **1.** Name applied to a number of bitter folk-medicinal drinks, such as QUASHIE BITTERS (*Guyn*), etc. **2.** (BrVi, Antg) ‖ BITTER-BUSH (CarA) 1. **3.** (Bdos, Guyn) ‖ ANGOSTURA BITTERS (CarA) **4.** (USVI) Liquor.

bit·ters-tea *n* (Antg) A BUSH-TEA made from BITTER-BUSH and used 'to remedy colds, fever, belly-ache, high blood pressure and even for abortions'—Antg (Ms, 1973).

bit·ter-tal·ly* /1'122/ *n* (Bdos, Guyn) One of two or three varieties of a wide-spreading and branching, twining climber with slender stems and greenish-white florets; the bitter juice of the young leaves and stems is used as a folk-medicine to treat sores and ulcers, and also (in Guyana) as an antidote to snake-bite; *Mikania spp* (*Compositae*)—*FBGMFP:48*.

bit·ter-weed *n* **1.** (Jmca) A strong-smelling bushy herb with narrow leaves and clusters of tiny, yellowish flowers, growing wild, and from wh an oil is extracted and 'used to control hookworm and other intestinal parasites' (*APPJ:17*); *Chenopodium ambrosioides* (*Chenopodiaceae*). **2.** [By extension] (Angu, StKt) [*AF*] A person of rough, wicked, and boisterous character. *You betta watch sum a dem frens you gat. Some a dem a bitter weed. Dem grudge, grudge and dem gat de evil yeye.*—LaS (76.05.08, p.9, 'Bits & Pieces')

bit·ter-wood* (bit·ter·wood) *n* **1.** (Baha) ‖ BITTER-BUSH (Baha) **2.** (Jmca) A tree that can grow to 70 ft in height, bearing bluish-black berries, and yielding the wood from wh the BITTER-CUP is carved; *Quassia excelsa* (*Simarubaceae*). *The bitter extract from Bitterwood or Quassia wood, (so called because it was a Negro named Quashie who first discovered its curative properties) was used in tonics, by brewers of hops, and as an insecticide.*—DaG (66.11.08, p.3) **3.** (Belz) A timber tree attaining a height of 130 ft and diameter of 3 ft with a brittle, dark brown bark, and yielding a hard-grain wood wh is yellow when cut but goes dark on exposure and polishes well; *Vatairea lundelli* (*Leguminosae*).

bit·tle; bit.tle-ball.er *n* (Bdos, Belz, Guyn, Jmca) See BICKLE; BICKLE-BOILER

bi·ya *n* (Guyn) [Rice Ind] A set of young rice seedlings raised in a nursery bed. [Bhoj *biyaa* 'seed, seedling' < Hin *birwaa* 'plant, seedling']

biz·zi-biz·zi* (be·si-be·si, bi·si-bisi, bus·y-bus·y) [bɪzɪ-bɪzɪ] *n* (Guyn) ‖ *bizzy-bizzy grass* (Guyn) Any of three or four varieties of a sedge or sturdy, grass-like reed, round or three-cornered or blade-like, and sometimes with stalks bearing clusters of small, brown flowers; the grass favours swampy ground and is therefore a serious pest in rice-harvesting; *Cyperus articulatus, C. ligularis, etc* (*Cyperaceae*).

biz·zy-biz·zy grass *n phr* (Guyn) ‖ BIZZI-BIZZI (Guyn)

black[1] *adj* (CarA) [Of people] A person of African descent with very dark skin and (usu thick) short hair. ▢ Although *black* has been accepted by many CE speakers in more recent times, infl by Black Amer militancy, as having a wider application to all people of Afr descent, whether wholly or partially so, that is not the acceptation of the term by the majority, shades of skin colour being favourably distinguished by such CE terms as BROWN-SKIN, COB(-SKIN), FAIR(-SKIN), LIGHT-SKIN, MUSTEE, etc. On the other hand *black* is often linked in Derog CE

phrs such as *black-and-stupid, black-and-ugly, black-and-worthless*, etc. See next.

black[2] *n* (CarA) **1.** [*AF*—*Derog/Joc*] [Of people] Wickedness, laziness, or any evil characteristics traditionally associated with African slaves. *Well you know de black in me! I only waitin[g] to hear she bawl out that he beatin[g] she up, too!*—(Guyn) **2.** The colour black (esp in foll phr). **3.** PHRASE **3.1 black is white** *adv phr* (ECar) [*AF*] Thoroughly; without control or restraint. **a.** *Denise watched the little girl losing all her marbles; she was getting good licks in the game, the little boys were beating her black is white.*—JPB:128 **b.** ... *these Americans who spend money black is white.*—ViN (73.01.20, p.2) [Perh of EE provenance. Cp *ODEP* Prov (1763) *To prove that black is white*]

black-ant* *n* (CarA) **1.** A common ant about 1/2 cm long wh infests fruit trees, esp mango and citrus, affecting their output; *Cremastogaster brevispinosa* (*Formicidae*). **2.** PHRASE **2.1 as/like black-ants on soursop** *adj phr* (Gren) [*AF—Joc*] [Of a person, esp a woman] Proud looking; acting or walking haughtily. [A ref to the posture of these ants as they move with their hind-parts cocked up—*PPGD:20*]

black ba·ri·ca·der *n phr* (Angu, StKt) See BARICADER

black ba·na·na *n phr* (Jmca) ‖ BUCK BANANA (Guyn) [Said to refer to dark purple colour at the base of the leaf and of the ripening fruit. This name is also said to be used by some in *Guyn*]

black-bel·ly sheep *n phr* (Bdos) A hornless sheep with short brown hair (not wool), a black belly, and no white spots, bred in Barbados and noted for its meat and its fecundity.

black·ber·ry *n* (Belz) ‖ JAMOON (Guyn) ▢ Note that BrE blackberry is the fruit of a thorny bramble, *Rubus fruticosus*, not a tree.

black·bird /ˈ1ˈ2/ *n* (CarA) **1.** A name very often loosely applied, esp by urban speakers, to any bird that is black, blackish, or mostly black, i.e. no distinction being made between a BLACKBIRD /1'2/ and a *black bird* /2'1/, though the latter may be of quite a different species, sometimes in the temporary colouring of the young, the moulting male, etc. The following are the most widely recognized as BLACKBIRDS **1.1*** (CarA) ‖ *boat-tail* (Gren, Trin) ‖ *ching-ching* (CayI) ‖ *corn-bird* (Guyn) ‖ *kling-kling* (Jmca) ‖ *merle* (Gren, Trin) A jet-black bird about 10 ins long from beak to tail, distinguished by a bright yellow eye, a boat-shaped tail, and a noisy 'chuk-chuk-swee-ee' or bell-like 'ching-ling' as it moves in flocks in search of food, eating exposed food, earth-worms, etc, and being a serious pest of fruit and crops; (*Holo*)*quiscalus lugubris luminosus* (*Passeriformes*). ▢ Referred to in international listings as *Carib grackle, Greater/*

Lesser Antillean grackle □ and sometimes as *Barbados blackbird*. **2.** (Baha, Jmca) ‖ JUMBIE-BIRD 3. (Guyn) **3.** (Gren) ‖ *black see-see* (Gren) A variety of the BANANAQUIT (*CarA*).

black-cake *n* (CarA) ‖ *great-cake* (Bdos) A rich, dark, rum-soaked fruit-cake of heavy pudding-like texture, made dark by using burnt brown sugar as an ingredient; it is kept moist by pouring rum or wine over it, and it is served during the Christmas season and at weddings.

Black Car·ib *n phr* (Belz, StVn) [Hist] ‖ *Garifuna* (Belz) A race of black people descended from the mixing of shipwrecked and escaped African slaves (1675) with Carib women of St Vincent and Bequia (up to 1795), and then exiled in bulk (1797) to the island of Ruatan in the Bay of Honduras, whence they spread to the mainland (1802) and are now mainly at Dangriga (Stann Creek) in Belize. □ The term *Black Carib* is rejected in current usage, replaced by CARIB in *StVn* and GARIFUNA in *Belz*.

black cor·al *n phr* (CarA) Coral with concentric rings wh is found at depths more than 200 ft undersea; it is dark, takes a high polish, and is prized as a semi-precious stone.

black·eye-pea* *n* (CarA) ‖ *cow-pea* (CarA) ‖ *gub-gub* (Trin) A white kidney-shaped bean with a significant black hilum; it is carried in long, thin, smooth pods wh are borne on a climber; the dried beans are very widely used, boiled with rice; *Vigna unguiculata* or *V. sinensis* (*Papilionaceae*).

black·fish (black-fish) *n* **1.** (StVn) The large, black *pilot whale* hunted for its oil and blubber esp off *StVn* and *Grns*; *Globicephala melaena* or *G. marcorhyncha*. **2.** (Brbu, TkCa) A flat, black, scaly fish with a curved forehead and powerful jaws, of average weight about 2 lbs and of good food value; *Tautoga onitis* (*Sparidae*).

black girl in the ring *n phr* (Angu, Brbu) ‖ BROWN GIRL IN THE RING (CarA)

black·guard[1] ['blagyard] *adj* (CarA) [*IF*] Loud, abusive, and scurrilous (esp of behaviour in public). *I don't want any blackguard behaviour in this classroom.*—(Guyn) □ Now usu *blackguardly* in SE.

black·guard[2] *vb tr* (Bdos) [*IF*] To abuse (sb) with loud, foul language. *However, another girl plays around this boy and when she sees me she tries to blackguard me ... when she is with her friends ... on the road.*—NaT (77.03.06, p.34, Dear Christine)

black·guard·ing *n* (Bdos) Loud, scurrilous language and aggressive behaviour. *She found the criminal bar, dealing mainly with what we in Barbados call 'blackguarding', to be time-wasting and crude.*—Bdos (Ms)

black i·ron·wood *n phr* (Jmca) ‖ AXEMASTER (Belz)

black-heart man *n phr* (Jmca) A legendary evil man who, by enticement, steals small children. *When night come down me start get fraid. Me hear all different kind of sound sounding like duppy.... Me tink pon Black Heart Man, who give sweety to children and den tek dem way, and a piece a nervousness tek me.*—SSLG:14 [Perh < black art (with prosthetic /h-/) + man. However, cp HEART MAN (Bdos)]

black-lead ['blak-lɛd] *n* (CarA) ‖ *lead* (CarA) [*IF*] A lead pencil. [*OED black lead* 2. 'the ordinary name of the mineral also called plumbago or graphite ... chiefly used (made into pencils) for drawing or writing ... (The name dates back to days before the real composition of the substance was known)' + cits from 1583]

black-man·go *n* (Belz, Jmca) A rather small, tasty mango with a notable groove from the top half-way down, and a skin that is very thin (*Jmca*) or rather thick (*Belz*) but remaining green when ripe.

black-pep·per grains /1'221/ *n phr* (Angu, Guyn, Jmca) [*AF—Derog*] ‖ PICKY HAIR/HEAD (Baha, etc) *Picky head, picky head, black-pepper grains / Not[hi]n[g] [u]pon [h]e head and not[hi]n[g] in [h]e brains!*—Guyn (children's teasing rhyme) [Joc, from the appearance of the tiny, curled rolls of a young black male's hair]

black-pot *n* (Bdos, Guyn) [*IF*] Soot on the face or hands, from cooking.

black-pud·ding *n* (CarA) ‖ *blood-pudding* (Antg, Gren, StLu, Trin) ‖ *rice-pudding* (Antg) ‖ *pudding* (CarA) [*IF*] A meal prepared by stuffing the cleaned, large intestines of the pig with highly seasoned, boiled rice, or grated sweet-potato or FARINE and bread crumbs, adding cow's blood and boiling the intestines so stuffed and tied, to a sausage-like tightness. *Black-pudding is a West Indian weekend and picnic special, especially served with souse.*—Tbgo (Ms)

black-sage ['blak-se·ɪ] *n* (CarA) [Name given to two similar-looking but botanically unrelated aromatic shrubs] **1.*** ‖ *sage-bush* 1. (CarA) A sturdy, dark-stemmed shrub reaching about 5 ft in height with aromatic, rough- surfaced, serrated, spear-shaped leaves, and spikes of small white flowers and edible, tiny, red berries; the leaves are used for BUSH-TEAS and BUSH-BATHS, while the twigs are variously used, esp with one end of a piece crushed, as a tooth-brush; *Cordia curassavica* (*Boraginaceae*). *Gee ... then rubbed his teeth with a black-sage stick, rinsed his mouth and spat out the water through the window into the yard.*—HMCH:53 **2.** ‖ SAGE-BUSH 2. (CarA)

black see-see *n phr* (Gren) ‖ BLACKBIRD 3. (Gren)

black spi·der *n phr* (Trin) ‖ TARANTULA (Guyn, Trin)

black-strap (mo·las·ses) *n* (*phr*) (Bdos) ‖ *vacuum-pan molasses; VP* (Bdos) The residue or grossest form of molasses settled in the VACUUM-PAN in the processing of sugar-cane; it is used both as a mix for farm animals' feed, and in the rum distilling process. *The pot had a hole in its bottom which was invariably plugged for about 48 hours, and when the plug was removed the 'black strap' molasses just poured out into a special earthenware tray called a drip. This black molasses was collected again and again and taken to the distillery for the manufacture of rum, and this process continued for about a month.*—AdM (76.12.12, p.7) [*Black* (from the colour of molasses) + *strap*, perh n < dial vb. Cp *OED strap* v² dial 'to draw the last milk from a cow ... often metaphorically used for draining anything dry'] □ See also SWEET LIQUOR (Bdos)

black su·gar *n phr* (StKt) [*IF*] ‖ MUSCOVADO SUGAR (CarA)

black-top¹ *n* (Baha, Belz) The asphalted surface of a road. *Recent heavy rains have made the black-top soggy and pedestrians by simply walking on the streets have been carrying away the gunk on the soles of their shoes.*—ReP (79.12.09, p.9)

black·top² *vb tr* (Baha, Belz) To surface a road with asphalt. *All development work completed including blacktopping of roads, installation of rustic street signs...*—DBH:205

black-wil·low* *n* (Baha, Bdos, Gren, Jmca) An erect, medium-sized and shapely, tough-wooded tree, with abundant, shiny, dark green leaves, small, purplish flowers and short, slender pods; the tree is slow growing and very popular in churchyards; *Capparis cynophallophora* (*Capparaceae*). [From its dark appearance in the distance due to the mass colour of its leaves, and their pendulous character wh remind one of the European willow, to wh it is not however related]

black-witch *n* (ViIs) ‖ JUMBIE-BIRD 3. (Guyn)

blad·der *n* 1. (Bdos, Guyn) ‖ *water-blister* (Bdos) ‖ *water-plug* (Gren) A blister, esp a raised pustule on the skin from a burn, etc. *Water-bumps and like blotches and pustules had formed on their skins. And the little children, not knowing better, scratched the itching and biting bladders as they call them.*—TrU (67.02.04, p.1) 2. (Bdos, Guyn, Nevs) A child's toy balloon.

blad·der-bush *n* (Nevs) ‖ LEAF-OF-LIFE (Bdos, etc) [From the brownish-green, inflated, 3-cm tube of the flower wh children soften in their hands and blow up. See BLADDER 2.]

bla·djé ['bla·je] *vb intr* (Dmca, StLu) [*AF*] ‖ BLAG² (Trin) *I left her bladjéing with some friends after school and went home.*—(Dmca) [< Fr *blaguer* + palatalization of /-g-/]

blag¹ ['bla·g] *n* (Trin) [*AF—Joc*] 1. Idle chat to while away time; titillating gossip; false talk. [Fr Cr < Fr *blague* 'tall story, joke'] 2. PHRASES 2.1 **get a blag** *vb phr* To hear a piece of gossip. *Last night I get a blag, I nearly die from shock.*—(Trin) 2.2 **shoot a blag** *vb phr* To prompt, share in, or enjoy the exchange of idle gossip; to BLAG².

blag² *vb intr* (Trin) [*AF—Joc*] ‖ *bladjé* (Dmca, StLu) To chat idly and/or gossip for a long time. [< Fr *blaguer* 'to joke, talk through your hat', etc] □ Pres. part. *blaging*.

blam *vb* 1. (Angu, Bdos, Gren, Guyn, StVn) [*X*] [Of a door] To bang noisily; to slam. 2. (USVI) [*X*] [Of any two objects] To crash or slam noisily (one against the other). [Blend of *bang* + *slam*]

bleed *vb tr* (Belz, Guyn) [Of balata, chicle] To cut a groove in the bark of the (balata or other gum-producing) tree spirally around the trunk so as to let the sticky sap flow (downwards into a container).

bleed·er *n* (Belz, Guyn) One employed to bleed trees for BALATA or CHICLE. (Usu BALATA-BLEEDER (*Guyn*)). *My duties ... consisting of... taking over the balata from the foremen of the various gangs of bleeders...*—Xmt (1936, p.14)

bleed·ing-heart* /1'12/ *n* 1. (CarA) ‖ *caladium* (CarA) Popular name of many varieties of an ornamental 'tuberous plant grown for the sake of their highly coloured, heart-shaped [green] leaves wh are blotched and veined with various shades of red, pink and white, and borne on stalks 1 to 2 ft high' (*PTT:99*) *Caladium spp* (*Araceae*). [From the heart shape of the leaves, and the significant veins, some of wh are red] □ The European flowering plants of this popular name are quite different, belonging to the genus *Dicentra* (*Fumaraiaceae*). 2. (Gren, Trin) A climber with oval-shaped, dark green leaves bearing clusters of bright, red and white flowers; *Clerodendron thomsonae* (*Verbenaceae*).

blim·bing *n* (Gren, Jmca) See BIMBLING

blind *n* 1. (CarA) [*IF*] Any cloth material used as a one-piece window-curtain that cannot be seen through. (See BAG-BLIND¹). 2. (StVn) [*IF*] A short wooden swing-door; a HALF-DOOR. (See also BLIND-DOOR. 3. (Jmca) [*IF*] Wooden louvres that can be closed.

blind-cent; blind-pen·ny *n* (Bdos, Guyn, Trin) 1. A copper coin of the lowest value, but defaced or damaged and therefore barely still acceptable as currency (esp in foll phr). 2. PHRASE 2.1 **not a blind cent/penny** *n phr* No money at all.

blind-door *n* 1. (Mrat) A wooden, single-leaf door of only half or three-quarters the height of the door-way, intended to keep people's eyes out while letting in breeze at the top; the top section is separately hinged, sometimes horizontally. **2.** (StKt) A secondary, light, (sometimes double-leaf) wooden door of three-quarters the height of the doorway, kept closed while the outer (normal security) door is kept open during the daytime. **3.** (TkCa) A door the upper half of wh is louvred or jalousied.

blind-eye [blaɪn-aɪ] *n* **1.*** (Mrat) [*AF*] ‖ *Chinese Christmas tree* (Guyn) ‖ *milk-bush, pencil-bush* (USVI) A tall, green shrub, leafless and cactus-like, with branches crowded with succulent, pencil-like twigs wh contain a milky sap that can cause temporary loss of vision (hence the folk name); *Euphorbia tirucalli* (*Euphorbiaceae*). **2.** (Baha, Jmca) Name given to different plants or trees the sap of wh irritate the eyes when the bark is cut.

block *n* (CarA) A house-builder's block, made of concrete or baked clay, usu with large through-holes, and of different sizes and designs.

block-house *n* (Antg) ‖ WALL-HOUSE (Bdos) [Because it is constructed with BLOCKS cemented together]

block·o·ra·ma *n* (Gren, Tbgo, Trin) An open-air (usu fund-raising) FETE with several STEEL-BANDS and disco music, usu held in the daytime, and most popular in the 1970s.

blo·go *n* (Gren, StVn) See BLUGGO

blood *n* **1.** (CarA) [*IF*] [With extension of SE sense] Personal feeling. (See Phrs 3.4, 3.5). **2.** (Belz, Gren) [*IF*] A relative or a person with whom you feel close fellowship. *I said no, blood, I am anti-communist but I am not involved in, or about to join, any anti-communist league.*—AmA (80.10.24, p.10) **3.** PHRASES **3.1 blood is blood** *id phr* (Gren) ‖ *blood is thicker than water prov* (CarA) Family ties will tell. **3.2 run sb's blood to water** *vb phr* (Guyn) [*IF*] To harass and exhaust (sb). *He would come and give you the work late and then he wants to run your blood to water to get it back.*—(Guyn) **3.3 (your) blood crawls** *id phr* (Gren, Tbgo, Trin) [*IF*] ‖ *(your) skin crawls* (Gren, Guyn) (You) get a creepy feeling; (you) get goose-flesh (SE). **3.4 (your) blood takes/does not take (sb)** *id phr* [*IF*] See SPIRIT[1] Phr 4.4 *I don't usually talk to fellars like this, but I take a fancy for you, my blood take you. Tell me, what you used to do before you come?* —STLL:21 **3.5 (your) blood turns (to) water** *id phr* **(i)** (Gren) (You) become mean and selfish. **(ii)** (Guyn) (You) become weak either from fright or tiredness.

blood-cloth ['blʌd-klɒt] *n* (Antg, Jmca) [*Vul*] ‖ *bombo-cloth* **1.** [*AF*] A folded piece of cloth used by a woman as a sanitary pad during menstruation. **2.** [*Vul*] ‖ *clot* (Guyn) ‖ *cloth, klaat* (Antg, Jmca) **(i)** (Abusive term for) a fool (usu a man). **(ii)** *excl* An indecent exclamation of surprise or anger.

blood-pud·ding *n* (Antg, Gren, StLu) ‖ BLACK-PUDDING (CarA)

blood·wood *n* (Guyn) A secondary forest-tree that grows abundantly in riverine or sandy areas, yielding a soft, pale brown wood wh is used for interior work; the bark, when cut or burnt, yields a thick yellow-red liquid (hence the name) wh is used as a folk-cure for skin disorders; *Vismia angusta* or *V. guianensis* (*Hypericaceae*).

blou [blɒʊ] *n* (ECar) [*X*] A blouse. *The girl who was waiting on me called to the one next to her. / 'Elda, this lady want a pink blou. Is all we have white and yellow blouses?'*—Isl 10/73, p.42 (Random Notes) [Back-formation < *blouse*, erron conceived as a pl form]

blouse [blɒʊz] (ECar) A man's jacket (as well as a woman's upper garment). *The following articles have been found in buses of Motor Transport Ltd—A child's black shoe, a rosary ... and a gent's blouse.*—DaC (53.01.12, p.3)

blow *n* (CarA) [*AF*] **1.** A hurricane; a tropical storm. *Another tropical storm came along in 1928, and the next year the capital was ravaged by the severest 'blow' since 1866.*—ASOB:183 [A combined ref to the wind and its effect] **2.** PHRASE **2.1 (be) a word and a blow** *id phr* (Guyn) See WORD Phr 1.

blow-blow *n* (CarA) [Child talk] Any toy whistle or device with a reed to make a sound when air from a balloon or a paper-roll device is released through it.

blue *n* (CarA) Laundry blue (in a small caked block often wrapped in a rag for use both in laundering and in witchcraft).

blue-bell *n* (Guyn) **1.** ‖ DUPPY-GUN (Jmca) **2.** ‖ BLUE-PEA (Jmca)

blue-bot·tle *n* (Guyn, Trin) A blue half-pint bottle turned upside down on a stick (usu placed in a kitchen-garden to ward off 'evil-eye' or prevent theft).

blue chub *n phr* (StLu) ‖ CACA-BARWEE (Dmca, etc)

blue-draws (**blue-draw·ers**) *n* (Jmca) [*IF*] ‖ DUKUNA (Antg, etc) [Prob from bluish appearance of boiled banana leaf + *draws* < *drawers*, the baggy appearance of the boiled product suggesting a woman's undergarment]

blue-fish *n* (Trin) ‖ ANCHO (Trin)

blue foot *n phr* (StKt) ‖ BACKRA NIGGER (Trin)

blue-hole *n* (Baha) The mouth of a tunnel or cave in the sea-floor (wh shows darker blue because of the depth of water in it, hence the name). *Andros' famed 'blue holes' are bubbling* *their way to increasing attention.... The holes puncture the eastern bank of the largest of the Bahama Islands.... Oceanographers have counted at least 60 of the holes, and estimate there could be hundreds. Many of them descend to 200 feet, and some believe that others could plummet to as deep as 600 feet.*—TrI (70.09.17, p.6)

blue mar·lin* *n phr* (Baha, Bdos, ViIs) A very large spearfish, with a smooth, dark-blue back; it can grow to several hundred pounds in weight and is hunted as game; *Makaira nigricans ampla.*

blue-pea* *n* (Jmca) ‖ *Bahamas blue-pea* (Baha) ‖ *blue-bell* 2. (Guyn) ‖ *blue-vine* (Bdos, Guyn) A sturdy, perennial, climbing vine with much foliage and pea-like flowers that are usu a brilliant blue (but other shades occur) developing into longish pods; *Clitoria ternatea* (*Leguminosae*). *'Blue pea' is ideal for a quick-growing screen and can stand full sun.*—GGIT:115

blue-sack·i(e) *n* (Guyn) A restless, silvery-blue bird, about 6 ins from beak to tail at maturity, with large, dark blue wing feathers; it is fond of mangoes and known for its little shriek 'ski-ski' (whence its name); *Tanagra episcopus* (*Thraupidae*). □ Listed as *blue tanager* in professional literature.

blue-soap *n* (Bdos, Gren) ‖ *washing-soap* (Guyn) A very hard, blue, cheap kitchen and laundry soap.

blue vex *adj phr* (CarA) [*IF*] Extremely angry (though the phr often connotes silent anger). *The wife was blue vex all the time, but she ain't say nothing till she got home, and then she let him have it full blast.*—(Guyn) **b.** *Canadian based Barbadian lawn tennis player Lionel E— is blue vex about the treatment he has received from the Barbados Lawn Tennis Association ... /E—, whose name was omitted from the team chosen by the BLTA ... says he has been 'treated like a second class citizen in his own country and he is absolutely fed up.'*—AdV (90.01.28, p.38) **[** < SE *blue* (with rage, in the face, etc) + CE *vex* < *vexed* (adj). A case of semantic reduplication**]**

blue-vine *n* (Bdos, Guyn) ‖ BLUE-PEA (Jmca) *Blue Vine [which] has brilliant blue flowers ... is sometimes cultivated, but is also found wild in bushy places ... and many other species, with blue, pink, mauve or white flowers occur.*—(GTWF:52)

blug·go* (blo·go) [blʌgʌ ~ ʊ] *n* (Belz, Gren, StLu, Tbgo) ‖ *Barima-plantain* (Guyn) ‖ *bottler banana* (CayI) ‖ *buck-buck* (Tbgo) ‖ *buffert* (Bdos) 1. ‖ *bugament* (Antg, Dmca) ‖ *cocoy(e)* (Dmca) ‖ *djouboul* (StLu) ‖ *doko* (Belz) ‖ *flagu, fulagu-plantain* (Belz) ‖ *four-corner plantain* (Guyn) ‖ *hog-banana* (Baha, TkCa) ‖ *horse-banana* (BrVi, Nevs) ‖ *mafobe* (StVn) ‖ *makambou* (Dmca) ‖ *moko banana, moko plantain* (Tbgo, Trin) ‖ *pompoom* (TkCa) ‖ *waika banana* (Belz) A stout, thick-skinned, four-sided variety of plantain that sticks out at

right angles to the stem of the bunch, and is of such tough texture that it is grated or fed to pigs in some places, though it is of good food value; *Musa balbisiana* (*Musaceae*). □ Pl **bluggoes**. There appear to be many other names, more than one occurring in some territories.

blunt head *n phr* (Baha) [*IF*] ‖ BAD HEAD[1] 2. (Guyn, etc)

bo *n* [*IF*] **1.** (CarA) ‖ BORO (CarA) **2.** (Bdos) ‖ BOY (CarA) ... *'cause straight-leg pants is all de rage now, bo!*—PeL (78.01.20, p.2, 'Out of My Head') [Poss a reduction of 'bro' < 'brother', or of 'boy'. However cp *ZAGL* Gã *bo* (independent form of sec. pers pron) 'you', wh could therefore function as a form of address. Also *WTIED* Izon *bǫ* 'person' (and often used terminally, like CE - **man**]

boar- [bor ~ boʌ ~ bo] *n* (CarA) [*IF*] [Term used to mark the male gender of various domestic animals] **1.** BOAR-CAT *n* (Baha, Bdos) A tom-cat. ... *always fighting like some boar-cat.*—MBGB: 78 **2.** BOAR-HOG *n* (Bdos, Guyn, Tbgo, Trin, USVI) [*IF*] **(i)** A male pig; a boar. **(ii)** [*AF—Derog*] A man of piggish behaviour. ... *since this gentleman resigned they sent us a boar-hog as a manager.*—NaT (76.08.22, p.26) **3.** BOAR-PIG *n* (Antg, Bdos, Guyn, Tbgo, Trin) A boar. **4.** BOAR-RAT *n* (Bdos) A male rat. [*OED boar* 2. Comb as *boar-dog, ...-pig, ...-cat* given as chance or *Obs* forms]

board-and-shin·gle house *n phr* (Bdos, Guyn) ‖ *board-house* (StVn, Trin) ‖ *chattel-house* (Bdos) A small, ground-level wooden house (about 20ft x 10ft) with a shingled, gable roof, and sometimes (Guyn) having also shingled walls. ... *a man has managed to buy a 4,000 square feet plot of land and wants to pull down his board and shingle house and put up a wall structure.*—Bdos (Hd, 74.03.18, p.3452) □ This is the usual application of the name, though sometimes such a house is doubled (with two such roofs) or has a SHED added. See CHATTEL-HOUSE, WALL-HOUSE.

board-house *n* (Trin) ‖ BOARD-AND-SHINGLE-HOUSE (Bdos, Guyn)

boat PHRASE **boat gone a-falls** *id phr* (Guyn) There is no turning back; an irreversible and very serious decision has been taken. [A ref to the shooting of very dangerous rapids by PORK-KNOCKERS in TENT-BOATS]

boat-tail *n* (Gren, Trin) ‖ BLACKBIRD (CarA) 1.1 [From its keel-shaped tail, noticeable esp in the male]

Bob·by-plum *n* (Bdos) See BUBBY-PLUM

Bo·bo-John·ny *n* (StKt) [*AF—Derog*] ‖ BOO-BOO[2] 2. (CarA) [KED *bɔbɔ*, W Afr name given to a little boy when his real name is not known; Adangme *bɔbɔ* 'little'. Also *bɔbɔ jɔn* 'boy John', traditional name for a Krio boy. 'People called Bobo [from the hinterland of the Windward Coast] might have been shipped from Gold Coast ports. Even today the term Bobo is subject to a good deal of confusion, and in the 18th century it probably had an even wider meaning'—*CAST:185*]

bo·bol[1] **(bo(b)·bol(l), bo·ball(e), boh·bohl, bub·all/oll/ul)** ['bɒbɒ·l ~ bʌbɒ·l] *n* (ECar) [*AF/IF*] **1.** Fraud and corrupt practices organized, usu on some scale, by well-placed persons in authority in a company or in government administration. [The word, wh is most widely used in *Trin* may be a modification (with CarA Cr / v > b/ consonant shift and characteristic Trin / a > o/ vowel closure) of Fr Cr *Vaval*, an early (1920s) masque king of *StLu* Carnival, ceremonially 'buried' (thrown into the sea) with much jubilation on Ash Wednesday. The term later came to be associated disparagingly in *StLu* with trading 'speculators' to and from Martinique. (See Caq IV.2, p.113 and Caq VI.4, pp.282–5)] □ The term, wh has strong cynical and even *Joc/Derog* associations, is sufficiently well established in *Trin* usage to produce derivatives (see below). Variant conjectural spellings usu occur in *ECar* territories. **2.** PHRASE **2.1 be in bobol; make bobol** *vb phr* (Tbgo, Trin) [Of a company or government official] To be profitably involved in a network of fraud. **2.2 run a bobol** *vb phr* (Tbgo, Trin) To organize a network of fraud.

bo·bol[2] *vb intr* (ECar) [*IF*] ‖ **bobolise** (Tbgo, Trin) [*Joc*] To steal a company's or public funds or property by fraud, in collusion with others; to be in or run a BOBOL[1]. □ Pa.t. **bobolled**, pres. part. **bobolling**.

bo·bo·lee (/-lie) ['bʌbʌli·] *n* (Trin) [*AF—Derog*] ‖ **Good Friday bobolee** (Trin) A scapegoat; an innocent and patient victim of ridicule; a gullible person. *As usual, the target is one of those approved bobolees that the Guardian is ever willing to cuss in the interest of … 'the free enterprise system'.*—MoK (72.04.28, p.2) [From a Good Friday tradition (now ceased) of young men's dragging through the streets an effigy of Judas stuffed with rags and old clothes and beating it until all the stuffing fell out. Prob < BOBOL[1] I + E diminutive suffix /-i/. Cp *whitey*, etc]

bo·bol·ise ['bʌbɒlaɪz] *vb* (Tbgo, Trin) [*AF—Joc*] ‖ BOBOL[2] (ECar) *After they mis-spend and bobolise the money allocated for housing, they have no houses for people.*—MoK (73.06.22, p.15)

bo·bol·ism ['bʌbɒlɪzm] *n* (Tbgo, Trin) [*AF—Joc*] The practice of BOBOL[1].

bo·bol·ist [bʌ'bɒlɪs(t)] *n* (ECar) [*AF—Joc*] One who misappropriates public or a company's funds. *Remove every head of PNM stooges in all the Public Utilities and jail the thieves and bobolists wherever they are found.*—MoK (72.07.21, p.6)

bo·di (bean)* ['bodi-bi·n] *n (phr)* (Gren, StLu, StVn, Trin) ‖ **bora** (Guyn) ‖ **six-weeks** (Antg, Dmca, StKt) ‖ **yard bean** (Gren, Guyn, Trin) One of two varieties of green or light-brown, cylindrical bean about 1 cm long carried in a slender, foot-long or yard-long pod, wh is borne on a climber; both the beans and the green pods are of excellent food value; *Vigna unguiculata*, var *Sesquipedalis* (*Leguminosae*). [Hin/Bhoj] □ *Bodi* is both sg and pl.

Bo·dow! *excl ideoph* See BADAOW!

bo·dy ['bɒdi] *n* (CarA) [*AF/IF*] **1.** [Independent item in a sentence] Person. [See OED *body* 13. '… an individual. Formerly, as still dialectally, and in combinations of Any-, Every-, No-, Some-, etc, exactly equivalent to the current 'person' + cits (1771) '*a good sort of body*', (1883) '… *a more tidy body*'. However, note earlier E usage (1738) in *SPC:158 Don't be mauming … a Body* so, 'Don't paw me!' Note also Sc E usage as *CSD body* 'a person, a human being; someone, one' (referring to the speaker himself or another). Ex 'Could you no leave a body in peace?'] □ Widely used in speech as the exact equivalent of 'person' as in '*a, the, this, that, one, another, the other, the only, the same, the right, the wrong* BODY'; also in questions (esp *Bdos*) '**which body?**' [*AF*] '**who the body is?**' [*X*]. The pl seldom occurs, there being instead [*AF*] '**all body, all kind o[f] body**'. See also PERSON. **2.** [As linked with a neg] [No] body. □ More emotive in speech than SE *nobody, nobody else*. Exs '**not a (single) body**' '**not one body**', '**not another body**'.

bogle [bo·gl] *vb* (Jmca) To dance with a notable backward inclining of the upper body

boil-in ['bɒɪli·n] *n* (StVn) ‖ **fish boil-in** (StVn) **1.** A soup prepared as a one-pot meal by boiling together a number of root vegetables, breadfruit, green bananas, and dumplings with fish, seasonings, and butter; a SANCOCHE without coconut. **2.** A clear, seasoned broth in wh a few whole fishes, such as JACKS are put. □ The dish is mainly a rural one (sense 1.), with an urban variation (sense 2.). See also COCONUT BOIL-IN.

boil-up [bɒɪlʌp ~ bwaɪlʌp] *n* (Belz) ‖ SANCOCHE (Dmca, etc)

bois [bwa] (and compounds) (Dmca, Gren, StLu, Trin) See BWA

bois-bandé *n* (Dmca, Gren, Trin) See BWA-BANDÉ

bois ca·non (bois ca·not) *n* (Dmca, StLu, Tbgo, Trin) See BWA-KANO(N)

bois d'Inde *n* (Gren, StLu, Trin) See BWA-DENN

bold-face ['bo·l·fe·s] *adj* (ECar) [*AF/IF*] ‖ *brass-face* (Bdos, Guyn, Tbgo, Trin) ‖ *dry-eye, facety* (Jmca) **1.** Brazen; impudent; bare-faced; capable of petty crime (esp theft) or open rudeness without hesitation or embarrassment. *... spirited away by a thief and not one that comes in the night but the bold-face variety who pulls up in broad daylight in a van and makes believe that its an auction sale?*—SuG (74.09.29, p.14) [*OED bold-face* n 'an impudent person' also attrib; *bold-faced* adj '... usually impudent'. The reduction [-st] > [-s] is characteristic of creolized CE] □ The term is widely current in this form, occasionally replaced by IAE *bold-faced*. **2.** PHRASE **2.1 play bold-face** *vb phr* (ECar) To pretend to be brazen or bold; to put on a bold face to cover guilt.

bo·le·do ['bolido] /ı′2ı/ *n* (Belz) A daily lottery with low-priced tickets for wh the winning number is drawn every night. *Gambling is an institution almost revered in Belize. Boledo and Sunday lotteries are legal and run by the government.*—AmA (80.06.06, p.2) [< Sp *bolita* 'little ball', in ref to the small numbered balls used to determine the winning number] □ The term 'lottery' in *Belz* refers to the larger weekly drawing, in contrast to the *boledo*.

bo·li(e) (bo·ly, bou·ley, bowl·ie) ['bo·li] *n* **1.** (Dmca, Gren, Trin) ‖ CALABASH (CarA) **2.** (StVn) [By extension] [*AF–Joc*] A person's head. [Poss a diminutive of *bowl*, from its use; but cp *IMED* Mende *boli* 'a basin'] **3.** PHRASE **3.1 not talk in boli** *neg vb phr* (Gren) [*AF–Joc*] Not to hesitate to speak bluntly, roughly (to sb).

bo·llos [bɔyos] *n pl* (Belz) ‖ TAMALES (Belz) [< Sp = bread rolls, here in modified sense] □ This name, applied to smaller TAMALES is commoner in western Belize, bordering on Guatemala, whereas TAMALES is the commoner name in the north bordering on Mexico, and also in Belize City

bo·lon·jay [bʌlʌnʤe] *n* (Bdos, Guyn) See BALANJAY

Bom·bay-Cey·lon (mango) *n* (*phr*) (Gren) ‖ BOMBAY-MANGO (Jmca, Mrat)

Bom·bay-man·go /2′3ı2/ *n* (Jmca, Mrat) ‖ *Bombay-Ceylon* (Gren) ‖ *Ceylon(-mango)* (StVn) ‖ *East-Indian mango* (Jmca) A fist-sized, greenish-yellow mango with a rich, sweet flesh and a seed loose enough to be easily removed when the ripe fruit is cut around the middle.

bom·bo-clot(h) (bom·bo-clate/-klaat) ['bʌmbʌ-klɒ·t/-kla·t] /ı′ı2/ *n* (Jmca) [*AF-Vul*] ‖ BLOOD-CLOT(H) (Antg, Jmca) [< *bombo* 'the female pudenda' (*Jmca, Tbgo*), prob of Afr origin. Cp *GDEL* Efik *mbumbu* adj 'rotten, putrified, decomposed' (i.e. evil smelling)] □ Associated only with obscene lang.

bo·na·vist* (ba·na·bis, ban·na·bees, bo·na·vis, bu·na·bis) *n* (CarA) ‖ *banner-bean* (Jmca) ‖ *butter-bean* ı. (Baha, Dmca, Guyn) ‖ *hyacinth-bean* (Antg, Berm, Trin) ‖ *lablab-bean* (Jmca, Trin) ‖ *saeme* (StLu) ‖ *sem* (Trin) ‖ *white-bean* (Mrat, Trin) An edible bean borne in a broad, flat pod about 3 ins long with a beaked tip; there are many varieties and colours the commonest of wh appears to be a light green pod (also edible) with white seeds; *Dolichos purpureus, Lablab vulgaris, etc* (*Leguminosae/Papilionaceae*). [From Bona Vista, Sp name for Pg island Boa Vista (Cape Verde Is) 'from which the beans were imported into the New World' (*DJE*)] □ Sometimes also *banavis/bonavis(t) bean(s)* or PEAS.

bone·fish *n* **1.*** (Baha, CayI, TkCa) A very fast-moving, shallow-water, silver-sided game-fish of average weight 5 lbs; it is very bony (hence the name) but makes a very tasty native dish; its large scales are also used in making fancy work; *Albula vulpes* (*Albulidae*). **2.** (Bdos) [*AF*] Filleted (i.e. boned) flying fish prepared for sale. □ Usu *bone fish* in sense 2, < SE *boned fish*.

bon·go¹ ['bʌŋgo] *n* **1.** (Dmca, Tbgo, Trin) ‖ *bongo-dance/-dancing* (Tbgo, Trin) A dance performed at wakes in honour of the dead, done by successive pairs of men (principally) competing face to face in erotic movements, to special drumming, and with singing by people in a ring. *It is customary for the bereaved survivors at a wake-house to join in the dancing of the bongo ... during the last night of the ceremony.*—EFOT:24 **2.** (Antg) ‖ *bongo-drum* (Tbgo, Trin) ‖ *congo-drum* (Bdos) A drum about 2-1/2 ft high, with stretched goat-skin at one end, (the other open), held between the knees and played with the bare hands; its use is specially associated with wakes and festive dancing. [*OGA:64* suggests derived by metathesis < Congo *ngoma* or *mgombo* 'drum'. Note, relevantly, the ‖ CONGO-DRUM (Guyn)]

bon·go² *adj* (Jmca) See BUNGO

bon·go-dance; bon·go-drum *n* See BONGO¹

boo·boo¹ *n* (Guyn) See BUBU

boo·boo²; boo.boo-man ['bubu-ma·n] /ı′2ı/ *n* (CarA) [*AF–Joc*] **1.** A bogey; an imaginary evil spirit that children are told would 'carry them away' if they are wicked. **2.** ‖ *Bobo-Johnny* (StKt) ‖ *country-booboo* (BrVi, Guyn, Tbgo, Trin) A stupid, gullible, uninformed person; (sometimes also) an ugly person. [Cp Yoruba *buburu*, 'bad, evil'] □ The spelling BOOBOO will help to distinguish this word from BUBU (BOO-BOO¹). Cp also ASSEBOO, BABU(-MAN). **3**

boof¹ (buff) *n* [*AF*] **1.** (Tbgo, Trin) An insult; a rebuff. **2.** (Tbgo, Trin) A scolding. **3.** (Guyn, StVn) ‖ CUFF (CarA) **4.** *ideoph* (ECar) ECHOIC WORD used to describe a padded blow.

boof² **(up)** **(buff (up))** *vb phr* (Tbgo, Trin) [*AF/IF*] To scold; to censure severely. *The teacher boofed her up in front of the class, and when she couldn't take the boofin[g] she started to cry.*—(Trin)

boo·kut *n* (Belz) See BUKUT

boom *n* (ECar) [*IF*] 1. (Guyn) A big bass drum used by masquerade bands. 2. (Trin) ‖ *bass-pan* (ECar) Also BOOM-PAN. See STEELBAND DIAGRAM

boom-and-chime (*l*-shine) **band** *n phr* (Belz) A small band made up of an accordion, a banjo, a marimba, two smaller drums and a BOOM or bass drum.

boom-pan *n* (Ecar) ‖ BASS³ (ECar)

boom-pipe *n* (Mrat) ‖ BAHO (Nevs)

boops [bʊps] *n* (Jmca) [*AF—Joc*] A woman's lover who keeps her well-provided with money; a 'sugar-daddy'.

boop·sie ['bʊpsi] *n* (Jmca) [*AF—Joc*] A woman who receives and enjoys the support of a BOOPS.

boo·too *n* (Dmca, Gren, StVn, Trin) See BOUTOU

bo·ra ['bo·rʌ] *n* (Guyn) ‖ BODI (Gren, etc) [Hin/Bhoj. A dialectal variant of BODI]

born¹ *vbl adj* PHRASES 1. **be born back o[f] bush** (Belz)/ **behind cattle back** (Mrat) /**behind cow-tail** (Dmca, Guyn) /**behind God's back** (BrVi, Crcu, Gren, Trin) /**behind jack-ass-tail** (TkCa) /**behind your mother's back** (Bdos) /**in the bush** (Belz, Guyn, Nevs) /**under fig-tree** (StKt) /**under plantain-leaf** (Guyn) / **with ring in your nose** (Belz) *vb phrs* [*AF—Derog*] To be a gullible, naive, uninformed person; to be a country bumpkin; to be stupid. 2. **in (all) my born days** *adv phr* (CarA) [*IF*] In my whole life; for as long as I have lived. *'Never in m' born days,' declared the old lady, wrinkling up her long black face 'I ever hear doctor medicine can cure maljoe.'*—PGIP:14

born²; born.ed; born.ing *vb* (CarA) [*X*] 1. *vb intr* To be born. a. *The baby borns with a birth-mark at the place where the mother is touched.*—StKt (Ms, 1973) b. *But anyhow that is something else and one of these days I could tell you about calf and thing borning.*—Cat 2.2, p.16 2. *vb intr* To bear; to give birth to. a. *I born you and I raise you, and I did everything a mother could do for a son.*—Bdos (Ms, 1976) b. *She borned five children before she was a good twenty-three.*—Gren (Ms, 1978) 3. PHRASE 3.1 **from g born** *adv phr* (Jmca) [*X*] ‖ FROM A CHILD See CHILD Phr 4.1

born-pa·per *n* (Guyn) [*X*] ‖ BIRTH-PAPER (CarA)

Bo·ro [bʊrʊ ~ bʌrʌ ~ brʌ] *n* (CarA) [*IF*] ‖ *B', Bo* 1. ‖, *Br'er* (CarA) 'Brother', form of address to a male, or the title often given to male characters in ANANCY folk-tales, as *Boro John, Boro Nancy, Boro Goat*, etc. [< [brʌ(d)r] 'brother' with loss of [d < ð] and epenthetic [ʌ/ʊ] to overcome the resulting awkward consonant cluster [brər], the form often represented by AmE writers as BRER, though *CarA* writers and tellers of folktales use *B', Bo, Boro* representing various reductions of the form (esp in *Guyn, Jmca*)]

bo·ro-bo·ro *n* (Guyn) See BURA-BURA

bo·ro·kit (**bo·ro·quite,** **bour·ri·quite, bur·ro·keet, bur·ro·quite**) ['bʌrʌki·t] *n* (Trin) ‖ DONKEY-MAN (Bdos) *The borokit is a special masquerade figure of Carnival.*—Trin (Ms) [< Sp *burriquito* 'little donkey'. Cp *TDV* Venz Sp *burriquita* 'a masked person with a dress simulating a woman on a donkey, a typical diversion of Carnival']

bor·row¹ ['bɒrʌ ~ 'bɒro] *vb* (Gren, USVI) [*X*] Lend. *Borrow me a five-dollars, A will give you back mont[h]-end.*—(Gren)

bor·row² ['bɒrʌ ~ 'bɒro] *n* (Gren, Guyn, Tbgo, Trin) [*IF*] 1. A loan; a borrowing (of sth). *Yo[u] could give me a borrow of yo[ur] iron, please?* —Guyn (B: Radio Story, 1979) 2. PHRASE 2.1 **knock a borrow** *vb phr* (Guyn) [*AF—Joc*] To borrow (sth) (esp when done with some bullying by the borrower). *A goin[g] nex[t] door an[d] knock a borrow of dey spade and fork to put dong dese plants [be]fore dey dry up.*—(Guyn) [*OED borrow* (Obs) 4. (rare) 'a borrowing' + cit from Shak. Also *EDD borrow* sb Sc. Nhb. 2. 'anything borrowed']

bo·si(e)¹ **(-back)** (**bos·sy -, bo·sy -, bo·si -, bo·zi-**) ['bosi (-bak) ~ bɒsi-] *n* (Gren, Tbgo, Trin) [*IF*] ‖ *bosi* (Dmca) A hunchback; a person with a hunchback. [Fr Cr < Fr *bossu* 'a hunchbacked person']

bo·si(e)² (**bos·sy, bo·sy**) ['bosi] *vb* (Trin) [*AF*] To beat (sb) severely (i.e. enough to make the person bend double). *If you try to make noise the whole gang attack. They beat you soft and bosie you with cough.*—Cso (Sparrow, 1963)

boss *n* (CarA) [*AF*] 1. [Of people] An expert (at some ordinary activity); a first-class performer. *He is a boss at swimmin[g], you hear! A real swim-boss!*—(Guyn) 2. [Of things] The most popular choice; an excellent and attractive thing. *... just like how miniskirts and hot pants used to be boss. Almost everything is what's in style, handy, in the groove.*—AmA (80.07.18, p.3) [< Du *baas* 'master', (fig) 'a first-rate one', the word being used metaph also as in sense 2., ex: *Wat een baas van een koe is dat!* 'What a boss of a cow (i.e. a first-rate cow) is this!'] □ Also used attrib—*'a boss hat', 'a boss fete', 'a boss idea'*, etc.

boss·man ['bɒsma·n] *n* (CarA) [*AF*] The man in charge; the top man; the winner; Sir (used as a flattering or cynical form of address by one man to another). **a.** *On Saturday last whilst the 'Bossman' was recruiting his Ton-Ton Macoutes to victimize and to intimidate peaceful Grenadians, two of his minions were engaged in a cutlass duel at Moyah, St Andrews.*—ToR (73.05.11, p.8) **b.** *... the panman ... climbed onto his pedestal of glory where he will reign as the 'bossman' until midnight, Carnival Tuesday.*—TrG (73.02.25, p.4) [< BOSS + -MAN³]

both all-two *pron phr* (Bdos) [*X*] ‖ ALL TWO (CarA) See ALL¹ Phr 3.2 *As you know he wus livin' with Bots an' Bambina both all two at the same time, for a long, long time. An' they all had children for him.*—LICMS:145 □ Also *all two both*.

both·er·a·tion [bɒdərešʌn] *adj* (CarA) [*AF*] ‖ DISGUSTING (CarA) *Dese boderation children I got he[re] gi[ve] me headache every day.*—(Guyn) [By functional shift < SE [*IF*] *botheration* n 'annoyance, nuisance']

both-side *adj* (Trin) [*AF*] ‖ TWO-MOUTH (Guyn) *You too both-side, smilin[g] up wit[h] me and goin[g] back and tellin[g] dem.*—(Trin) [By functional n > adj shift of 'both sides' with CE absence of pl /-s/]

bot·sie *n* (Bdos) [*AF—Joc*] ‖ BAM-BAM¹ (CarA) [Child talk] [*Bot* (abbr of bottom) + hypocoristic *-sie*]

bot·tle-flam·beau (StVn, Trin); **bot·tle-lamp** (Gren, Guyn, StKt); **bot·tle-light** (Gren); **bot·tle-torch** (Gren, Guyn) ‖ *boul-di-fé* (Trin) ‖ *bouzay* (Dmca) ‖ *flambeau* (Trin) ‖ *jug-light* (Dmca) ‖ *masanto* (Gren) ‖ *slut-lamp, smut-lamp* (Bdos) ‖ *torch* (CayI, Dmca, Gren, Trin, USVI) A bottle half-filled with kerosene and stuffed with a cloth-wick, used as a home-made lamp out-of-doors, also as a device for catching crabs at night. [*Bottle* + *flambeau* (Fr, 'flame'] □ Pl *bottle-flambeaux*.

bot·tler-ba·na·na *n* (CayI) ‖ BLUGGO (Belz, etc)

bot·tom *n* (Angu, Bdos) A low-lying piece of cultivated or cultivable land, sometimes (as in *Angu*) surrounded by sloping ground. [Cp *OED* *bottom* 4. b 'Low-lying land, a valley, a dell'. + cits to 1803. Note also J. Bunyan, *Pilg. Prog.* I (1678): 'I saw then in my dream that he went on thus, even until he came at a bottom, where he saw ... three men fast asleep.'] □ Current in *Angu*, but Hist in *Bdos* where it occurs in place-names 'Prescod's Bottom', 'Sweet Bottom', etc.

bot·tom-house *n* (Guyn) **1.** ‖ *house-bottom* (Belz) The open area under a wooden dwelling-house wh stands on a number of eight- or ten-foot pillars. *One hangs clothes to dry, puts children's swingers, leaves bicycle or car under the bottom-house.*—Guyn (Ms) **2.** [By extension] The ground (often with a concrete surfacing) under the house, used as an area for domestic service or playing. **3.** A lower or ground-floor dwelling, (i.e. additional living space created by walling-up the under-space described at 1., but having a floor of its own raised 2 ft above the damp ground). **4.** PHRASES **4.1 in the bottom-house** *adv phr* On the ground under the house. **4.2 under the bottom-house** *adv phr* (Guyn) ‖ *under(neath) the house-bottom* (Belz) In the space of the BOTTOM-HOUSE.

bou·can (bou·kan) ['buka(n)] *n* **1.** (Dmca, Gren) ‖ *cocoa-house* (Dmca, Trin) A construction for drying cocoa-beans consisting of a tray-like floor and gable shed, one of wh moves on wheels to protect the drying beans from rain. **2.** (Gren) A very large barn or shed on the floor of wh cocoa-beans are spread to dry. **3.** (Tbgo) ‖ *bramble¹* (Bdos, Guyn, Jmca) A heap of dried saplings and bush raked together for burning. [< Fr *boucan* < (*BDFC*) Carib = a wooden cot or a wooden grill]

bouch-kab·wit *n* (Dmca) **1.** ‖ GOAT-MOUTH (CarA) **2.** PHRASES **2.1 have bouch-kabwit** *vb phr* (Dmca) [*IF*] ‖ HAVE BAD-MOUTH (CarA) [*IF*] See BAD-MOUTH¹ Phr 3.1 **2.2 give (sb/sth) bouch-kabwit** *vb phr* (Dmca) [*AF*] ‖ PUT YOUR BAD-MOUTH ON (SB/STH) (CarA) See BAD-MOUTH¹ Phr 3.2 *Eh! The new bike puncture again? Like somebody give it bouch-kabwit!*—(Dmca)

bo(u)·lan·ger ['bɒlɒnje] *n* (Bdos, Guyn, Mrat, StVn) ‖ EGGPLANT (CarA)

boul-di-fé (boul-de-fay, bul-de-fay, bul·lie-fay) *n* (Trin) ‖ BOTTLE-FLAMBEAU (StVn, Trin) [Fr Cr < Fr ? *boule/bou(te)ille de feu*, 'ball/bowl or bottle of fire']

bounce *vb* (Gren, Jmca, Tbgo, Trin) [*IF*] **1.** To hit (sb) hard; to strike hard against (sth). **a.** *The child won[t] hear and the mother bounce him.*—(Tbgo) **b.** *She bounced the car while reversing.*—(Gren) **2.** PHRASES **2.1 bounce down (sb)** *vb phr* [*IF*] To knock down (sb). **2.2 bounce up with (sb)** *vb phr* [*IF*] ‖ *buck up* (Baha, Belz, CayI, Jmca) To meet or run into (sb) by chance.

boun(d)-bel·ly *n* (Guyn) See BUNG-BELLY

bound-place ['bʌn-ples]; **bound-yard** ['bʌn-yard] *n* (Guyn) **1.** The part of a sugar-estate to wh East Indian indentured immigrant labourers were confined on first arrival. [From 'place in wh new immigrant labourers were kept strictly within bounds, awaiting placement', hence often with emotive connotation] **2.** PHRASE **2.1 find/go back to your bound-place/-yard** *vb phr* (Guyn) [*AF—Derog*] To go back where you belong. □ Suggesting that such a person is of mean origins.

boun·gie (boon·gy, bun·gee) [buŋgi] *n* (Baha) [*AF—Vul*] [Child talk] ‖ BAM-BAM[1] (CarA)

bour·ri·quite [bʌrəkit] *n* (Trin) See BOROKIT

bous (bousse) [bu·s] *n* (Dmca, StLu) ‖ OLD-WIFE (CarA)

bou·tou (boo·too, bu·tou, bu·tu) ['butu] *n* **1.** (Dmca, Gren, StVn, Trin) A short, tough stick used as a weapon. **2.** (Gren, Trin) [*AF*] A policeman's truncheon. *Soon Constable Bartholomew ... strode into the yard and looked around with his hand resting on the bootoo at his side./ 'who you got fighting in here?' he boomed.*—MBF: 39 [Fr Cr *boutou* < Island Carib *butu* 'war club'. Cp *BDFC:52* 'une massue de sauvage *boutou* f.'; also *DECG* Guad Fr Cr *boutou* (mo karayib) 'massue']

bou·zay (bou·zaille) [buzai] *n* (Dmca) ‖ BOTTLE-FLAMBEAU (StVn, Trin) [Perh < Fr *bouteilles* with /z/ replacing /t/]

bo·ve·yan·der *n* (Guyn) See BOVIANDER

bo·vi·an·der (bo·ve·yan·der) ['bʌviandʌ] *n* (Guyn) ‖ *caboco, cabukru, cobungru* (Guyn) A person one of whose parents (usu the mother) is an Amerindian, and the other usu a Black, but sometimes a European man. [< Du *bovenlander* 'upcountry man' (i.e. people dwelling upriver)]

bow·els *n pl* (CarA) See BELLY *Phrase* **have the bowels** *vb phr* (Bdos, USVI) [*IF*] A more polite phr for HAVE THE BELLY.

bow·gie (bow·ji) *n* (Guyn, Trin) See BHOWJI

bowl-for-bat (cricket) *n* (*phr*) (Jmca) ‖ OUT-FOR-PLAY (Guyn)

bowl·ie (bowl·y) *n* (StVn, Trin) See BOLI(E) (Dmca, etc)

bow·ser [baʊzʌ(r)] (Antg, Baha, Dmca, Gren, TkCa) A gasolene station. [*OEDS bowser*, orig a Trade Name, evid chiefly used in Australia and NZ]

box *n* (Guyn) ‖ SUSU[1] (Dmca, etc) [*OED box* sb[2] 4. 'a money-box containing either private or public funds ... b. The money contained in such a box ...' Cp *box-club*; ... 24. (Comb) *box-club* 'a society for mutual aid in distress, a friendly or provident society'] **2.** *Phrases* **2.1 belong to/ throw a box** *vb phr* (Guyn) See SUSU[1] Phr 2.1 **2.2 hold/keep/run a box** *vb phr* (Guyn) See SUSU[1] Phr 2.1

box-crook *n* (Dmca) ‖ CROOK (StVn)

box-fish *n* (Baha, TkCa) ‖ COW-FISH[1] (Baha, etc) [From its squarish, angular profile]

box-hand *n* (Guyn) **1.** ‖ SUSU-HAND (Gren, etc) *Well at the time I had two box-hands to draw, so*

I start to get the house painted.—(Guyn) **2.** *Phrases* **2.1 draw your box-hand** *vb phr* (Guyn) **2.2 have/hold a box-hand** *vb phr* (Guyn) **2.3 pay your box-hand** *vb phr* (Guyn) See SUSU-HAND Phrs (Trin)

box·ing-plant *n* (Dmca, Gren, Jmca, StLu, StVn) [Banana Ind] A large shed for the collection and co-operative boxing of hands of bananas in preparation for shipping.

box-ko·ker /1'22/ *n* (Guyn) ‖ *koker* 2. (Guyn) A device for controlling the flow of water in draining and irrigating (esp rice) lands; it consists of a water passage made about one or two feet wide lined with watertight boards, and having at one end a vertical sliding 'door' or 'cover' that is raised or lowered to release or stop the flow of water.

box-mon·ey *n* (Guyn) Money saved in or drawn from a BOX.

box-oven *n* (Guyn) ‖ *Dutch oven* (Bdos) A portable, wooden, cupboard-like structure about 5 ft high, 4 ft wide and about 3 ft deep with a single, closed door, fully lined on the inside with tin or aluminium sheeting as are also its two or three shelves; a lighted COAL-POT on its floor provides the heat for baking. □ Only now used in rural or INTERIOR areas.

boy *n* (CarA) **1.** [Hist] A servant man. [In 'slave time' the words man and woman were not used to slaves, but only boy or girl; I suppose lest even in that way the idea of their manhood should find admission into the mind of a slave— *BHCBG:227*. Note also poss Irish infl added: 'Every Irishman is a 'boy' till he is married and indeed often long after'—*JESI:223*] **2.** [*IF*] A familiar, friendly form of address to a male of any age. *Until one day, somebody notices some little rust marks and says, 'But ay ay! Like your car falling apart boy?'*—ExP (73.05.20, p.17) □ This form of address is much resented by Black Amer men.

boy-child *n* (CarA) [*IF*] A son; a young boy of any age. [A calque from W Afr langs, ex Mandinka *diŋke* (*child-male*) 'boy, son'. See GIRL-CHILD] □ The term connotes affection.

bo·yo [bɔyʌ~-o] *n* (Belz, Jmca) The name used for DOKUNU in some districts. [Prob due to Latin Amer Sp infl. Cp Sp *bollo* 'something baked; a bun']

bo·zi-back *n* (Gren, Tbgo, Trin) See BOSI(E)-BACK

braa·ta(s) (bra·ta, braw·ter, broth·a, brought·a) ['bra·ta~brɔ·tʌ] *n* (Antg, Belz, Jmca, Mrat, Tbgo, USVI) ‖ *baksis, braatas* (Guyn) ‖ *lanyap* (Tbgo, Trin) ‖ *makin(g)-up* (Guyn) [*AF*] ‖ *nyapa* (USVI) ‖ *overs* 1. (Guyn) ‖ *pwayen* (Gren) **1.** An extra bit of something bought or some other small gift added by the seller, esp in the market-place, to encourage the buyer to come again. [< Sp *barata* 'bargain sale'; also Pg *barato* 'concession, favour, benefit'] **2.** [By extension] Any unexpected extra little gain, advantage or welcome feature. □ The pronunc has undergone some false refinement, hence deviant spellings *brawter*, etc. The final -s/ in the form **braatas** □ (pl only, *Guyn*) may be due to infl by association with **baksis**□ .

Brack·er *n* (CayI) A native of Cayman Brac, one of the three Cayman Islands.

brack·ish *adj* (CarA) [Of a drink] Insipid; lacking sufficient sugar. □ In CE the word relates to a degree of sweetness, whereas in IAE it relates to a degree of saltness.

Bra·dam!; **Bra.daps!**, **Bra.da.rax!** *excl ideophs* (Bdos) [*AF*] ECHOIC WORDS representing the noise of a crashing fall.

Bra·dap(s)! *excl ideoph* See BRADAM, BADAP(S)

Bra·da·rax! *excl ideoph* (Bdos) [*AF*] ECHOIC WORD representing the crash of many things falling to the ground at once. *De pile o[f] plates slip out o[f] his hand and just go bradarax! [u]pon de groun[d] all brok[e] up.*—(Bdos) □ See also BADAM

braf [bra·f] (Dmca) ‖ BROTH 2. (Dmca) [< Dial E as in Dor, Dev *brath* < SE *broth* WEDG:73, + characteristic early CE /th > f/ shift. See -TH I (ii). Cp also *Guad* Fr Cr name *blaf(f)*]

Bra·ga·dap! (Bri·gi·dip!) *excl ideoph* (CarA) [*AF*] ECHOIC WORD representing the sound of a galloping horse, mule, etc.

brai·ger (brai·ga) ['braɪgʌ] *adj* (Guyn) [*AF—Cr/Joc*] Proud and fussy; preening yourself. *They are braiga now wid the[ir] new car!*—(Guyn) [< SE *brag* [bræg > braɪg] + CarA Cr -A²⁰] □ Cp BREGGING (*Belz*).

brakes; **brakes.in(g)** *vb* (Trin) See BREAKS; BREAKSIN(G)

bram¹ *n* **1.** (CarA) [*IF*] ‖ *breakdown* 2, ‖ *bruckins* (Jmca) ‖ *brukdown* (Belz) ‖ *wash-foot-and-come* (ECar) **1.** A noisy, and often disorderly party open to everybody. *... things have gone so low that the hotel is now operating like a bram hall and pleading to locals for their survival at ridiculously low prices.*—WoV (71.09.30, p.1) **2.** (Belz) A type of folk-music with communal singing especially related to BRAMS 1. *Their music consists of the Bruk Down, the Bram and the use of a Boom and Shine Band.*—Bet.1, p.9

bram² *vb intr* (Belz) ‖ TRAMP (Trin) *This parade showed real spirit, although a bit disorganized ... bramming through the streets in true patriotic style.*—ReP (79.09.23, p.2)

Bram!³ *excl ideoph* (CarA) [*AF*] See ECHOIC WORDS

bram·ble¹ 1. (Bdos, Guyn, Jmca) ‖ BOUCAN 3. (Tbgo) **2.** (Gren, Trin) [By extension] [*AF—Joc*] Misleading talk; false promises. *The next thing that has been seriously at fault with this Government ... is the failure of the small farmers, —a lot of bramble, a lot of old talk, but when you look at the actual figure of loans provided ... the picture is very clear, Mr Speaker.*—Gren (Hd, 78.02.01, p.24)

bram·ble² *vb* (Gren, Trin) [*AF—Joc*] To make misleading statements; to knowingly make untrustworthy promises. *[This is] largely a product of the oldtime manipulative Doctor Politics, which simply cannot help but hold us in contempt, confident that we can be brambled over and over by these facile stratagems.*—TaP (75.12.21, p.6)

bram·bler *n* (Gren, Trin) [*AF—Joc*] [Esp of a public figure] One who BRAMBLES.

Braps! *excl iedoph* (CarA) [*AF*] ECHOIC WORD representing the sound of a sudden fall or collapse, or a surprising development.

brass-face *adj* (Bdos, Guyn, Trin) ‖ BOLD-FACE (ECar)

bread *n* (CarA) **1.** [*X*] A loaf of bread. *And now we are told that somebody, a young man perhaps, who steals a bread ... that somebody who steals a bread is going to be disqualified from entering Parliament for ever.*—Bdos (Hd, 74.08.27, p.3943) **2.** (CarA) [*AF*] Money. *The kingdom of the Wizards can accommodate about 2,000 people. No wonder then, that Mr William M—was at the gate. At $12 a person, that's a lot of bread to collect in one night.*—TrG (80.02.03, p.7) [By tranfer of sense from the exp 'work for your daily bread']

bread-and-cheese* *n* (CarA) ‖ *cockspur* (TkCa) ‖ *goat-bush* (Brbu) A bushy, thorny shrub widely used as hedge, or a medium-sized tree of the same family; both bear crinkled, spiralling, reddish pods that split open when ripe exposing shiny black seeds each attached to a spongy white substance wh is eaten by children; *Pithecellobium unguiscate* (the shrub) or *P. dulce* (the tree) (*Leguminosae*). [Name suggested by the colour contrast of the seed and its white edible attachment]

bread·fruit* *n* (CarA) ‖ *bwa pen* (StLu) ‖ *penmbwa* (Trin) ‖ *yanm pen* (Dmca) PHRASES **1. have more guts than breadfruit** *vb phr* (Gren) [*IF*] To be bold, facing a risk (esp a physical one). [Ref to the firm solid inside of the fruit] **2. your breadfruit hang low** *id phr* (Bdos) [*AF*] (You are) vulnerable, unable to take risks. [Because the low-hanging breadfruit is easily stolen]

bread·fruit-swop·per *n* (Bdos) [*AF—Derog*] A person of very low social status (i.e. one who can only swop a breadfruit to meet a personal need). □ Used as a term of insult.

bread kind *n phr* (CarA) Any starchy cooked food—breadfruit, plantains, root-vegetables, dumplings, and also bread. *A good Bajan soup will have plenty of breadkind in it.*—Bdos (Ms, 1979) □ Cp FOOD KIND, MEAT KIND.

bread·nut* *n* **1.** (CarA) ‖ *chatayn* (Gren, StLu, Trin) ‖ *gwenn-pen* (Dmca) ‖ *katahar* (Guyn) A seeded variety of the breadfruit distinguished by the close-packed, conical, spinelike projections covering its skin and a large number of close-packed, edible, chestnut-like seeds wh are roasted or boiled; *Artocarpus altilis* (*Moraceae*). **2.** (Belz, Jmca) A small, yellow, plum-like fruit with an edible brown seed wh is often boiled; it is borne on a tall, hardwood-timber tree whose leaves make excellent animal fodder; *Brosimum alicastrum* (*Moraceae*).

break *vb* PHRASES **1. break away** *vb phr* (ECar) [*AF*] To dance with abandon, free of any partner and caught up by the music; to 'do your own thing' as in DANCING CALYPSO. *When you hear that steelband music coming down the street on J'ouvert morning, man, everybody break away!*— (Trin) [Ref to breaking away from your dancing partner] □ Change of the phrasal vb form for tense or number is unusual. **2. break biche/ bish; break lékòl bich** *vb phr* (Gren, Trin) See BICHE **3. break bush** *vb phr* (Gren) [*AF*] To run away; to escape (*PPGD:18*). [By folk etym (i.e. run into the bush) < BREAK BICHE] **4. Break five(s)!** *vb phr* (Bdos, Gren, Nevs) [*AF*] ‖ *shake five* (Guyn) [In happy greeting or congratulation] Shake hands with me!; Give me your hand, brother! □ A male greeting only. [A ref to the emotional opening of the five fingers of the hand before gripping the other person's] **5. break for yourself** *vb phr* (ECar) [*IF/AF*] To fend for yourself; to look out for yourself. **a.** *Well Mitchy boy, keep your eyes and ears open. I know I can trust you to break for yourself, but remember you, being Premier, are likely to be attacked any time in the same way.*—ViN (72.06.10, p.2, Strolling Scribbler). **b.** *Many members of the party have been operating as if panic-striken ... So many of them seem to be 'brekking for demself' as people apparently try to ensure their own individual political survival with the electorate.*—AdN (76.03.28, p.4) □ See also BREAKS Phr 3.1 **6. break stick in your ears** *id phr* (Gren, Guyn, Tbgo) [*AF*] See EARS Phr 2.1

break·away¹ *adj* (ECar) [*AF*] [Of music] Of the beat and rhythm that would incite people dancing to BREAK AWAY. *When the band change and hit a breakaway tune, —if you see people go wild—old people and all.*—(StLu) [< BREAK AWAY, vb phr, by functional vb > adj shift]

break·away² *n* (ECar) [*AF*] Music for dancing with individual abandon. *... and parties, private*

or public, always end with a hot breakaway and a jump-up.—ExP (72.12.29, p.14)

break·down ['brɛkdʌŋ] *n* (Jmca) ‖ *brukdown* (Belz) **1.** A kind of vigorous dance with much bending of the body, hip-swinging and rival displays of WINING. **2.** A noisy, informal, unorganized FETE with plenty of food, drink and loud music. □ *Brokdong* would be a more suitable spelling. See also BASHIE. [Prob from the complete breaking down of all formality + also stooping down in such dancing]

break·er *n* ['brekər] (TkCa) ‖ GABION(-BASKET) (Bdos, Guyn) [From its function as a breakwater device]

break·fast *n* (CarA) [Obs, but still often among rural or older folk] Lunch; the large midday meal. *They had been sitting together ever since the meal which they took at midday and which was called breakfast.*—LICMS:83 [From the habit of starting plantation work very early, before sun-up, with a large drink of 'tea' as a boost, and going steadily until the heat of the day forced a stop for the first meal or breakfast, wh, in the circumstances had to be quite a large meal]

break·fast-cen·tre; break.fast-shed *n* (Guyn, StKt, Trin) A place where needy school children are provided with a midday meal; a shed where plantation or municipal labourers go for their midday meal. [From prec sense of 'breakfast']

breaks; breaks.ed, breaks.in[g] (brakes, brakes·in[g]) *vb intr* (Tbgo, Trin) [*AF*] **1.** To fend off blows. **2.** [By extension] To make excuses; to avoid; to escape. **a.** *Would you believe even the Public Relations people from Whitehall were approached to sign the bill, but they too 'breaksed'.*—BoM (80.03.21, p.6) **b.** *When you ask him about the money, you find he breaksin[g] a lot.*—(Tbgo) **3.** PHRASE **3.1 breaks for yourself** *vb phr* [*AF*] To defend yourself as best you can. *It was planned that they must each be proficient to 'breaks' for himself on Hosey Day, when opposing gatka-men would meet in combat before Lee Tung's rumshop at the three-roads junction.*—NAGOS:42 □ See also BREAK Phr 5.

bre·bich (Antg); **bre.bish** (StKt); **bre.bridge** (Jmca, Nevs) *n* [*X*] See BEVERAGE [< *beverage*, by combinations of metathesis, assimilation, dissimilation, and characteristic Cr /b < v/ replacement]

breed *vb* (CarA) [*AF*] **1.** *vb tr* To make (a young woman) pregnant. **2.** *vb intr* [Of a young woman] To become pregnant. □ A low form of expression. Cp GIVE BELLY; HAVE BELLY (See BELLY Phrs 3.19, 3.20).

breeze off (Belz, Guyn); **breeze out** *vb phrs* (Guyn, Tbgo) [*AF*] ‖ COOL OUT (CarA) [Cp Igbo *na-anara ikuku* (*receiving breeze*) 'relaxing']

breg·gin(g) [brɛgɪn] *adj* (Belz) [*AF*] Showy; spectacular looking. *He sings mahogany camp music in an easy, unapologetic, indeed bregging manner, which celebrates our survival through those rough and ruffian days.*—AmA (79.12.28, p.12) [< SE *bragging* [brɔaegɪn]. Cp note at BRAIGER]

Br'er (Brer) [bʌɾʌ ~ bərə ~ brʌ] *n* (CarA) ‖ *B', Bo, Boro* (CarA) Brother; Mr—; the title commonly attached to folk-tale characters, esp in ANANCY stories. *As you know Brer Rabbie did not have any mind of his own and as a rule he wanted to do whatever his friend Brer Bookie said.*—TOSR:8 [< [brʌ(d)r] < *brother*. See BORO]

Br'er Nan·cy *n* (CarA) [*AF*—*Joc*] ‖ *Anancy*[1] ‖ *Boro Nancy* (CarA) A person who is not to be trusted; a wily character. *In vain attempts to explain away ... misdeeds committed by the more vicious officers of the force ... the Police Commissioner's Brer Anancy story told in his radio talk today, have left the public ... howling with laughter.*—BeA(BE) (87.03.04, p.12) [BRER + (A)NANSE, the folk-tale 'hero' who always gets out of trouble by trickery]

brew *vb tr* (Bdos, Guyn) To pour (a hot drink such as tea, cocoa, etc) from one large cup into another and back again until it cools.

bri·ar *n* (TkCa) ‖ NICKER (Angu, etc) *Boys use briars from the briar tree to play marbles, and they also rub them on a stone to get hot and burn each other.*—(TkCa)

brick *n* (Guyn) A stone of any size that can be pelted; a small ROCKSTONE. [Cp SE *brickbat*: *OED* 'a piece or fragment of brick ... It is the typical ready missile where stones are scarce'. This exactly fits the *Guyn* sense] □ Regarded as standard *Guyn* usage, the SE sense of *brick* as sth made being rare, since the normal building material is wood.

brid·al wreath *n phr* (Angu) ‖ ADAM'S NEEDLE (CarA) [From its luxuriant white efflorescence]

bride *n* PHRASE **ain't no bride** *id phr* (Bdos) [*AF*] To be no model of virtue, no saint, not a person to trifle with. *To hear a 13-yr old boy say calmly and even proudly to some of his companions: 'I ain't no bride', surprised me a little, for I had associated it with adult women, as a derogatory comment by one upon another. How clearly this usage shows that the word* bride *as used in this sense has no reference to wedding bells and white satin.*—AdN (79.04.15, p.10)

Bridge, the *n* (Trin) PHRASE **behind the Bridge** *adv phr* (Trin) [*IF*—*Derog*] See BEHIND[1] Phr 5.

bri·ga·dis·ta [brɪɡaˈdista] *n* (Jmca) A youth trained in Cuba, under an agreement with Jamaica, in building-construction skills. *She said the private sector building contractors could help the brigadistas develop the carpentry, masonry,* plumbing and other skills they learnt during their one-year stay in Cuba, by giving them the chance to put these skills into practice.*—AdN (79.01.22, p.3) [Sp < *brigada* 'a squad or gang of workers']

Bri·gi·dip! *excl ideoph* (CarA) [*AF*] See BRAGADAP!

brim *n* (Bdos, Mrat, Nevs) ‖ RED SNAPPER (CarA) [< *bream*, as name applied (AmE) to the copper-coloured sunfish *Repomis macrochirus* sometimes also called *brim* (*ADF:112*), wh resembles the RED SNAPPER but is much smaller]

bring 1. *vb tr* (CarA) [*IF*] To give birth to (a child). *Fortunately, she had started to 'bring children' at the early age of fourteen, so now she had three strapping men of fourteen, fifteen and sixteen years old working in the estate.*—TRIH:111 2. *vb tr* (CarA) [*IF*] To develop; to make solid, ripe, desirable, etc. **a.** *Put the jello in the fridge to bring it.*—(Guyn) **b.** *Wrap the soursop in a cloth to bring it.*—(StVn) 3. *vb tr* (Dmca, Gren, StLu) [*X*] To take (sb); to carry (sth). A. *I just now come back home after bringin[g] the boy to school.*—(StLu) **b.** *I bring the carpet outside already to sun it and I put it back.*—(Dmca) [By calque from Fr Cr *poté*, 'bring, carry, take' < Fr *porter* 'carry'. Note also IrE *JESI:225* 'Our peculiar use of [bring] for 'take' ... in such phrases as 'he brought the cows to the field', 'he brought me to the theatre'] 4. *vb intr* (Guyn) [*IF*] [Of placing in a race or competition] To be; to place; to come. *I don't understand how he could bring first in two races last year and this year nearly bring last in everything.*—(Guyn) 5. *vb intr* (StVn, Trin) ‖ *brings* (Guyn, StVn) [*AF*] [In playing marbles] To move your hand a little from the due position in order to get closer to the target. *The two boys fought because one accused the other of 'bringing'.*—StVn (Ms) 6. PHRASES **6.1 bring pigs to a fine market** *vb phr* (Bdos) [*IF*—*Joc*] To suffer bad consequences caused by extravagance, indiscretion, etc. *Post-war Socialism with its promise of a fine living which the community owes to all who merely put in an appearance at a place of work has now brought its pigs to a fine market and the chickens have also come home to roost.*—AdN (72.07.07, p.4) [An EE survival. Cp *OED* pig sb [1] 10. e. 'To drive (or bring one's pigs to a fine, pretty etc market*: (usu ironical) 'to be disappointed or unsuccessful in a venture' + cit from 1748. However the exp goes back to 1600, so dated in *ODEP* as 'Hogs (Pigs) to a fair (fine) market] **6.2 bring (sb) up** *vb phr* (CarA) [*IF*] ‖ *have (sb) up* (Bdos) [*AF*] To bring (sb) up before the court; to have (sb) arrested and/or charged. *Touch me and I bring you up. I bring you up and you spend carnival in jail.*—NHMB:179 **6.3 bring (sth) (and) come** *vb phr* (CarA) [*AF/IF*] To bring (sth) (i.e. back to the speaker); get (sth) and bring it. *Bring the guitar and come, you don't see me waitin[g]?* —(Bdos) [A prob calquing of typical 'serial verbs' from W.Afr langs. See notes at phrasal verbs separately listed below] □ Also often [*AF*] *go bring it come.* **6.3.1 bring (sth) (and) give**

(sb) *vb phr* (CarA) [*AF/IF*] To fetch (sth) for (sb). *Awright, I go bring it give you.*—HPP:14 [As for prec]

brin·gal ['brɪŋgal] *n* (Trin) ‖ EGGPLANT (CarA) [Prob adapted from E loan *brinjal*, infl by Hindi loan BAIGAN for the same fruit in Trin]

bring-and-car·ry[1] /1'122/ *vb intr* (StVn) [*AF—Derog*] To carry news; to bear tales. *Don't say nothing in her presence because she could really bring-and-carry.*—(StVn) [A calquing of typical W Afr lang structure with same meaning. Cp IGED Grebo *nu ha sa kpa sa* (*do pick-news-carry-news*) 'to gossip'. See also use as n below] □ Also used as n: *'She is a real bring-and-carry'.* Cp also CARRY-GO-BRING-COME n, and BACK[3] vb.

bring-and-car·ry[2] /1'122/ *n* (StVn) [*AF—Derog*] ‖ *bring-come-and-carry-go* (BrVi) ‖ *bring-go-and-bring-come* (Gren) ‖ *busy-lickum* (Angu, Bdos, StVn) ‖ *carry-come-and-bring-come* (Mrat) ‖ *carry-go-bring-come* (Jmca, StVn) ‖ *lick-mouth* (Bdos) A tale-bearer; a news-carrier; a tittle-tattle. *She is a real bring-and-carry. Don['t] tell her nothing.*—(StVn) [See prec note and cp the n phr in IGED Grebo *ha sa kpa sa* (*pick news carry news*) n 'gossiping, tale-bearing'. Similar structures occur in other W Afr langs]

bring-come-and-car·ry-go *n* (BrVi) [*AF—Derog*] ‖ BRING-AND-CARRY[2] (StVn)

bring down (sth) *vb phr* (CarA) **1.** To import (merchandise, cinema 'pictures'). [By ref to Europe and N Amer as being 'up north'] **2.** [By extension] To introduce (legislation). *The Guyana Government proposes to bring down legislation that will give foreign men who marry Guyanese women the right to Guyanese citizenship.*—AdN (76.01.18, p.4) **3.** [By extension] (Bdos) To cause (a big row, a disgrace, etc). *And I see the Pastor chupse he mouth and shake he head, but not wishing to bring down neither big row, he ain't do nothing.*—CISH:101

bring-go-(and)-bring-come /1'122/ *n* (Gren) [*AF*] ‖ BRING-AND-CARRY[2] (StVn)

bring off; bring off rope *vb phrs* (Trin) [*AF*] To create a noisy scene; to make a loud display of (not necessarily genuine) vexation. **a.** *On Wednesday, I went back to the station but before I opened my mouth to explain my presence, the Sargeant started bringing off. 'What you want here, you are fit to be put in a cell. You drunk,' he told me.*—BoM (79.06.29, p.23) **b.** *She held on to the open car door and started to bring off rope on the couple. Like magic a crowd materialised enjoying the bacchanal.*—BoM (76.11.12, p.15)

brings; (brings·in[g]) *vb intr* (Gren, Guyn, StVn) [*AF*] ‖ BRING 5. (StVn, Trin) *They don't like him because he's a bully and always bringsin[g] when they playin[g] marbles.*—(Guyn) □ The

other players cry *'Brings! Brings!'* when one player cheats in this way.

broad-bean *n* (Jmca, StVn) ‖ LIMA BEAN (CarA)

broad-leaf thyme *n phr* (Bdos, Guyn) ‖ THICK-LEAF THYME (Bdos, etc)

brok·en; brokes *adj* (ECar) [*AF*] Broke; without money. [*Broken* is a false refinement of IAE slang *broke*; *brokes* is a playful form, cp BREAKS, BRINGS, etc]

Brok·en Tri·dent, The *n phr* (Bdos) (Name denoting) the national flag of Barbados. *But it happened last Friday night in the Kingdome in Seattle, Washington where 47,000 pairs of eyes saw the gold, blue and black Barbados flag and thousands of hands cheered as I, a Barbados member of Alcoholics Anonymous (AA) walked up to the stage and placed the flag in its holder. On that the eventful Friday night the Broken Trident held special significance for me. Since it has been flying, I have never taken an alcoholic drink.*—NaT (90.07.13, p.15)

bro·ko; bro.ko-foot *adj, n* (Trin) [*AF*] Lame, crippled, or deformed (person).

Brom·ley/Brum·ley (Band) *n (phr)* (Bdos) A famous, small dance band, consisting of flute, clarinet, guitar, and drum, played by Bromley and his sons in the 1920's in the Nelson St area of Bridgetown; it was particularly associated with holiday train excursions and Saturday night fun. **2.** PHRASE **2.1 go to (school at) Bromley/Brumley** *id phr* (Bdos) [*AF*] To go to no school at all, and therefore to be a gross and uncultivated person. *I only went to Brumley but de logic o' dah approach escape me, faif!*—NaT (91.11.29, p.9A, Lickmout' Lou) [Prob from association of Bromley's name with a life of idle fun]

broom-palm *n* (Trin) ‖ SILVER-THATCH PALM (Baha, Trin) [From use of its dried fronds tied tight for sweeping]

broth *n* **1.** (ECar) See FISH-BROTH **2.** (Dmca) ‖ *braf* (Dmca) A thick vegetable soup in wh the flavouring ingredient is either fish (= FISH-BROTH), or smoked pork, or smoked MANICOU. □ Esp re sense 2., cp the *Guad* Fr Cr name *blaf(f)*.

broth·er (broth·er-man) *n* (CarA) [*IF*] [Rastaf] **1.** A male member of the Rastafarian cult. **2.** [Esp the form **brother-man**] My brother (a familiar form of address borrowed from the RASTAFARIAN cult).

brought·up·sy ['brɒ·tʌpsi] *n* (Antg, Bdos, Gren, Trin) [*AF—Joc*] Good manners; behaviour that shows well-trained upbringing. [< (*well*) *brought up* + *sy* as in 'courtesy']

brown PHRASE **things are brown** id phr (ECar) [AF] There is little money in hand and none coming.

brown cot·ton n phr (Guyn) ‖ BUCK-COTTON (Guyn)

brown-George n (Jmca) ‖ ASHAM (Antg, etc)

brown girl in the ring n phr (CarA) ‖ **black girl/yellow girl in the ring** (Angu, Brbu) A children's ring game in wh they hold hands moving around in a circle, with one girl dancing in the centre, singing (with change of lines in successive verses)—There's a black (brown/yellow) girl in the ring / Tra la la la la / Show me your motion / Tra la la la la / Run to your partner / Tra la la la la / He/she is sweeter than sugar and plum—after which the dancer's place is taken by another girl, each dancer showing off a hip-swinging motion.

brown-jol·ly n (Jmca) ‖ EGGPLANT (CarA) [Prob by pop etym < E loan brinjal, one common variety of the fruit being a shiny, dark brown] □ A rarer name widely replaced in Jmca by GARDEN EGG.

brown-rice n (Guyn) [Rice Ind] Hulled rice; unpolished rice from wh only the husk has been removed; it is more nutritious than polished or white rice. □ Also commercially called **cargo rice**.

brown-skin adj, n (CarA) (A person) of light or dark brown skin; a person whose skin is noticeably less than quite black; a COB. Cockburn was a brown-skin, very little different than me (i.e. nearly as black as I am).—SDP:40

bruck·ins ['brʌkɪnz] (Jmca) ‖ BRAM¹ 1. (CarA)

Bru·dum! (Bru·dung, Brug·ga·dum, Brug·ga·dung, Brug·ga·lung!, etc) excl ideoph (CarA) [AF] ECHOIC WORDS representing a crashing fall or a loud explosive sound. a. Brugga Dum Ban! Get out! / De likes o' you I could do barrout!—WBS:38 b. ... one day suddenly so / this mountain leggo one brugg-a-lung-go / whole bloody back side / o' this hill like it blow / off like they blastin' stones / in the quarry.—BTA:66

Brug·ga·dum! (-·dung, -·lung!, etc) excl ideoph (CarA, esp Baha, Bdos) [AF] ‖ BRUDUM! (CarA)

bruk·down ['brʌkdʌn] n (Belz) ‖ BRAM¹ 2 (Belz) At Christmas time especially, people go from house to house doing brukdowns and singing brukdown songs such as 'Freetown Gal', 'Ping Wing Juk Me', and 'Bud Bank Wedding' and so on.—Belz (Ms, 1978) □ **Brokdong** would be a more suitable spelling, but BREAKDOWN, BRUKDOWN are conventional.

Brum·ley (Band) n (phr) (Bdos) See BROM-LEY (BAND)

bu·ba-broom n (Jmca) ‖ CABBAGE-BROOM (CarA)

bub·all n (Trin) See BOBOL

bub(b) n (Bdos, Guyn, Mrat) A drink made of milk (in former days fresh drawn from the cow) with sugar, essence, grated nutmeg, and sometimes lime-juice or a dash of rum added, the mixture being made foamy with a SWIZZLE-STICK.

bub·by n (CarA) [AF—Vul] A woman's breast or large pair of breasts together. [OED bubby (Obs & dial) 'a woman's breast' + cit (1686). 'The ladies here may without scandal shew face or white bubbies to each ogling beau'. However such admissible EE usage prob deteriorated into slave-trade slang on the W Afr coast and thence to the CarA. Cp WAPE bobi, bubby 'woman's breast; udder']

bub·by-plum (Bob·by-plum) n (Bdos, Tbgo) ‖ JAMAICA-PLUM (Bdos, etc) [From resemblance of nipple at the bottom of the fruit to that of a female breast or BUBBY. The variant 'Bobby' is prob a euphemism]

bub·oll n (Trin) See BOBOL

bu·bu (boo·boo) [bubu] n 1. (Guyn) [IF] ‖ BIBBY (Baha) 2. (Belz) ‖ bugaboo (Bdos, Jmca) Dry mucus from the nose. □ The spelling **bubu** will help to distinguish this word from **booboo²**.

bu·bul n (Gren) See BOBOL

buck¹ n 1. (Guyn) [IF—Derog] An aboriginal Indian native of Guyana; a Guyana Amerindian. □ Also BUCK MAN, BUCK WOMAN. 2. (CarA) [Derog] A black person (esp a male). a. De man ain't wan[t] work—he like to play sweet-skin buck. (i.e. a lazy idler).—(Bdos) b. Buck town a burn down, buck a pleasure (= Your business is in serious trouble and you don't care).—Trin (Prov—OSTT: 8) [Prob < Du bok 'he-goat', reinforced by 'Du bogre 'bugger' both applied derogatorily to native Indians'—(pers info, J. Benjamin, Univ/Guyn). 'In a Dutch document from the Colonies to the Prince of Orange in July 1790, one reads: 'In the Colonies of Essequibo and Demerara there are Indians or Bokken ...'. This bokken became the 'bucks'. The Dutch translation of bok indicates a wild and/or nimble animal. The Dutch obviously saw these attributes personified in the Indians and dubbed them bokken'—MAGH:4. 'The Interior of Guyana is inhabited by various tribes of Indians who are generally termed Buks'—'Remarks ... by Lt. Col. Hislop, Commander of Berbice, Demerara and Essequibo to Lord Hobart... 30 June, 1802' MAGH:30. Cp also OEDS buck sb¹ 2. d. 'Also applied to any male Indian, Negro or Aboriginal ...' + cits from 1800]

buck² vb tr [AF] 1. (Baha, Jmca) [IF] To strike or bounce against. 2. (Belz) [IF] To confront; to defy. *Yet, despite all this good will and generosity, Sister C— was branded as a rebel because she bucked the Ministry.*—ReP (80.01.27, p.2) **[** < SE *balk* + *butt*. Also cp AmE *WCD9 buck* 2. b. 'oppose; resist' 3. 'charge into opponent's line in football'**]** 3. (ViIs) [*IF*] To FORCE-RIPE (fruit). 4. (Guyn) To soak down (clothes) with soap and leave for some time (to allow the soap to work on dirty spots). 5. *PHRASES* **5.1 buck into (sth)** *vb phr* (Baha) [*IF*] To collide with (sth). *My car was written off after I bucked into a concrete wall.*—Baha (Ms, 1978) **5.2 buck (up) (sb)** *vb phr* (Baha, Belz, CayI, Jmca) [*AF/IF*] ‖ BOUNCE UP WITH (SB) (Gren, etc) **a.** *I would hate to buck him anywhere, because we're not on speaking terms.*—(Baha) **b.** ... *all of we who work in places where we and the public buck up every day, try do better this year nuh?*—WeG (73.01.17, p.12) **5.2.1 buck up to (sth)** *vb phr* (Baha) [*IF*] To bounce against (sth); to strike yourself hard against (sth). *She pushed him so hard that he spun around and bucked up to the steps.*—TOSR:36 **5.3 buck your foot/toe** *vb phr* (Baha, Jmca) ‖ STUMP YOUR FOOT/TOE (ECar) **5.4 buck your head** *vb phr* (Baha) **(i)** To hit your head against (sth) by accident. **(ii)** [By extension] *id phr* To run into trouble (through unwise action).

buck³ *adj* (Belz) [*AF*] Wanting; in hardship. *Brother Eck, tings di buck fu true. I fully agree with you that Belize pipple in fu whan rough year fu true.*—BeA(BE) (80.03.08, p.2)

buck·ba·na·na *n* (Guyn) ‖ *black-banana* (Jmca) ‖ *buffer(t)* 2., *claret-fig* (Bdos) ‖ *dog-banana* (CayI) ‖ *fire-banana* (Tbgo) ‖ *maiden-plantain* (Belz) ‖ *mataboro, red fig* (Trin) A purple-skinned variety of banana, the same in shape and size as the APPLE-BANANA, but toughish in texture when ripe, and so not normally cultivated; *Musa spp* (*Sapientiae*). **[** < BUCK¹, attrib. in *Derog* sense**]**

buck-bead *n* (Guyn) ‖ JUMBIE-BEAD 1. (Brbu, etc) *Crabs Eyes or Buck Beads (Abrus precatorius) is a common climbing plant in bushy places on sandy ground all over the tropics.*—GTWF:54 [From the wide use formerly of these seeds as 'beads' or body ornaments by Amerindian or 'Buck' men and women in *Guyn*: 'The men wind long strings of seeds, now more often beads, red, white or blue, evenly round and round their ankles and their wrists'—*IAIG:197*] □ See also BEAD-VINE BUSH (Nevs, StKt).

buck-buck *n* (Tbgo) ‖ BLUGGO (Belz, etc)

buck-cot·ton* *n* (Guyn) ‖ *brown-cotton* (Guyn) The long-fibred, brownish variety of cotton borne on a low shrub; the juice of the leaves and young buds is used as a children's medicine and the lint as pillow-stuffing; *Gossypium spp* (*Malvaceae*). [*Buck*, prob from its wide growth in the wild state in sandy savannah areas associated with BUCKS¹ 1. (*Guyn*); also to distinguish it from the white variety of SILK-COTTON]

buck·et-a-drop *adv* (Gren, Guyn, Tbgo) **1.** [Of rain or tears] In large amounts (hence foll phrs). **2.** *PHRASES* **2.1 cry bucket-a-drop** *vb phr* (Tbgo) [*AF*] ‖ CRY LONG WATER (CarA) **2.2 rain falling bucket-a-drop** *id phr* (Gren, Guyn) [*AF*] It is raining as hard as ever.

buck·et-pan *n* (Jmca) A bucket. [A redundant form]

buck·le-foot *n* (Jmca, Mrat) [*AF*] **1.** Bow legs. **2.** A bow-legged person.

buck-man; buck-wo·man *n* (Guyn) See BUCK¹ 1.

buck-pot *n* (Bdos) ‖ CONAREE 1. (Guyn) *The larger buck-pot goes back to post-slavery days and is now rarely seen.*—Bdos (Ms) [*Buck*¹ 2. + *pot*]

buck·ra *n* (Bdos, Guyn, Jmca, Mrat, USVI) See BACKRA

buck-ripe *adj* (ViIs) ‖ FORCE-RIPE 1., 2. (CarA)

buck-sick¹ *adj* (Guyn) [*AF—Joc*] ‖ *staked out* (Bdos) Tired of a tedious but necessary task. [BUCKS¹ (*Guyn*) are credited with great endurance before getting 'sick' of any task]

buck-sick² *vb tr* (Guyn) [*AF—Joc*] ‖ STAKE-OUT (Bdos) 2.

buck-top *n* (Guyn) A top made of a dry AWARA or AKORI seed scooped out and a stick fixed through it, on wh a piece of string is wound to set it spinning.

buck-up *n* (Baha) [*AF*] *PHRASE* **all buck-up goes** *id phr* [*AF*] **(i)** All obstacles will be made to give way. **(ii)** Good and bad will be acceptable together. *But in war all buck up goes. If Italian hit muh I cud draw razor on 'im an' gie 'im a riffle an' dey won' take much t' de cote house.*—DSJS:65

buck-yam *n* (Guyn) ‖ CUSH-CUSH (YAM) (ECar) [Prob by association with Amerindian cultivation of this variety. See BUCK¹]

budge-gum *n* (Trin) See BIRCH-GUM [Prob by voicing of [č > ɟ]]

Bu·duf! *excl ideoph* (CarA) [*AF*] ‖ BIDIP! (CarA)

Bu·dum! *excl ideoph* (CarA) [*AF*] ‖ BIDIM! (CarA)

Budup! *excl ideoph* (CarA) [*AF*] ‖ BIDIP! (CarA)

buff¹ [bʊf] *vb tr* **1.** (CarA) To hit (with a dull thud). **2.** (Tbgo, Trin) To insult; to rebuff; to embarrass by ignoring. **3.** *PHRASE* **3.1 not buff on (sb)** *neg vb phr* (Angu) [*AF*] See NOT negator Phr 2.3

Buf(f)²! [bʊf] *excl ideoph* (CarA) [*AF*] See BIDIP!

buf·fer(t) (-ba·na·na) [bʌfə~bʌfərt] *n* (Bdos) **1.** ‖ BLUGGO (Belz, etc) **2.** ‖ BUCK-BANANA (Guyn) □ This name, restricted to *Bdos*, is not distinctively applied though evid sense 1 is the commoner.

bu·ga·boo (bu·ga·bu) 1. (Bdos, Guyn, Jmca) ‖ BOOBOO-MAN (CarA) [*OED bugaboo* 'a fancied object of terror'] **2.** (Bdos, Jmca) Dry mucus from the nose.

bu·ga·ment ['bʌgamɛnt] *n* (Antg, Dmca) ‖ BLUGGO (Belz, etc)

bu·gas ['bʊgʌz~az] *n* (Jmca) [*AF*] ‖ CREPESOLES (Guyn, etc) [Cp *DJE bogro* 'coarse, rough, rugged'] □ Rarely sg.

buisse [bis~biš] *n* (Trin) See BICHE

bu·kut (boo·kut) [bʊkʊt] *n* (Belz) ‖ STINKING-TOE 2. (Belz)

bul·jol [bʊljɒl] (Trin) ‖ *bull-jowl* (StVn) A dish of shredded saltfish seasoned with hot peppers, onions, tomatoes and olive oil (often served with roasted breadfruit or other BREADKIND). [Fr Cr < Fr *brule-gueule* 'burn-mouth', because of its peppered flavouring]

bulk-sugar *n* (CarA) Cane-sugar, as transported in truck-loads and stored and shipped in bulk instead of being bagged. □ See BAG Phr 3.3

bull[1] *n* **1.** (Mrat, Nevs, StKt) ‖ DONKEY-MAN (Bdos) **2.** (Gren, Trin) (Short form of) BULL-PISTLE. (*CarA*). *Well, we all scattered like crazy as he started to pelt blows with the bull.*—BoM (74.10.18, p.18) **3.** (Bdos, Guyn) A semi-circular piece of paper attached to a kite to make a humming sound in flight. **4.** (Tbgo) (Short form of) BOUL-DI-FÉ (*Trin*). **5.** (Bdos) [*Vul*] ‖ BULLER[2] (Bdos)

bull[2] *vb* (Bdos) [*Vul*] To bugger; to be a (male) homosexual. *G— said that he heard M— say that C—'bulled his way through the Gold Coast in St James.'* / *G— said that he understood the word 'bull' to mean to be a homosexual.*—AdV (87.02.13, p.1) [Cp *OED bull* v[1] **1. a.** trans 'said of a bull: to gender with the cow' **b.** intr 'to take the bull; to desire the bull'. Also *to go a-bulling* Obs. The *OED* sense refers to normal intercourse between bull and cow, not 'buggery'. However, the word appears to have had a different history in *Bdos*. Sir Denys Williams, Chief Justice of Barbados, stated in a Judgment dd 87.06.17 'that the natural and obvious meaning of those words ['he bulled his way to success'] to a Barbadian audience is that the plaintiff engaged in homosexual activity ... that the plaintiff ... had ... committed the offence of buggery']

bul·la[1]**(r) (bul·lah, bull·er)** *n* (Jmca) **1.** A cheap, round, flat cake made from flour, heavy dark sugar, and soda, about 4 ins in diameter. **2.** A snub.

bul·la[2] *n* (Baha) [*IF*] The eldest boy of a family (often used in addressing such a person).

bull-boy (Tbgo, Trin); **bull-bud** (StKt) *n* ‖ BULL-PISTLE (CarA)

bull-cow *n* (CarA) [*IF*] A bull. *Respect this woman; if not you have got to reckon with her. From now on I am fighting like a bull cow.* (*Cheers*).—Bdos (Hd, 74.08.27, p.3879) [Redundant compound infl by W Afr marking of masc gender by the addition of 'man/male (kind)' to a base word]

bull·er[1] *n* (Jmca) See BULLA[1](R)

bull·er[2] **(-man); bull** *n* (Bdos, Gren, StLu, StVn, Trin) [*AF—Vul*] ‖ AUNTIE-MAN 2. (CarA) A male homosexual; one who commits buggery. [See BULL[2] and note].

bul·let-wood (tree) *n* (*phr*) (Guyn, Jmca, Trin) ‖ BALATA 1. (CarA) *Many know the tales weaved by balata bleeders—tales of trees oozing blood when cut on Good Friday. To this day most bleeders of the bulletwood tree, which yields milk for balata, have a firm belief that they must abstain from touching any of their woodcutting tools on Good Friday lest they might lose a member of their body or their lives.*—GyN (Mar, 1972, p.1) [From the extreme density of the wood which suggests it would resist even bullets] □ Sometimes also BEEF-WOOD (Guyn)

bull-foot soup *n phr* (ViIs) ‖ COW-HEEL SOUP (Gren, etc)

bull-jow(l) [bʊl-jɒu(l)] *n* (StVn) ‖ BULJOL (Trin) [By folk etym < Fr Cr BUL-JOL, of wh fish, not meat, is the pickled ingredient]

bul·lock's heart *n phr* (Jmca, StVn) ‖ CUSTARD-APPLE (CarA) [From resemblance of mature fruit, in shape and sometimes size, to a cow's heart. Cp ‖ *tjè-b\e'f* (Gren)]

bull-pis·tle [bʊl-pɪsl] /1'22/ *n* (CarA) ‖ *bull-boy* (Tbgo, Trin) ‖ *bull-bud* (StKt) ‖ *cow-cod* (Jmca) ‖ *dog-hunter* (Bdos) A tough, long whip made from the penis of a bull. [< *bull's pizzle*, < *OED pizzle* dial or vulg 'the penis of an animal, often a bull, used as a flogging instrument'. 'Pistle' is prob due to folk etym, by association with 'piss']

bull-seed/-stone man·go *n phr* (Jmca) ‖ MANGO-GRAHAM (StLu) [From its size and resemblance in shape to a bull's testicles. Cp ‖ *koko-béf* (Dmca, StLu) with same imagery]

bull-stone man·go *n phr* (Jmca) See BULL-SEED MANGO

bul·ly *n* (Baha) A device for lobster-fishing consisting of a long pole with a hoop about 18 ins in diameter attached at right angles to one end, with a net (the BULLY-NET) attached to the hoop, and a long stiff wire or TICKLER extending from the end of the pole.

bum[1] [bʊm] *vb* (Bdos, Guyn, StVn, Trin) [*IF*] To beg; to sponge on others. *We decided that we had to get out, and 'bummed' a ride to the airport.*—Peo.1.10, p.42 □ Note difference in CE pronunc [bʊm]. Cp IAE [bʌm].

Bum![2] *excl ideoph* (CarA) [*AF*] ‖ BIDIM (CarA)

bum-drum [bʊm~drʌm] *n* (Bdos) A large bass drum (played on both ends with hand and drumstick in a TUK-BAND). [From the booming sound it makes]

bump *vb* [*AF—Joc*] 1. (Tbgo) To walk with a showy step. 2. (Baha) ‖ PICK FARES (Bdos) See PICK Phr 5.6

bun *n* (Jmca) ‖ JAMAICAN BUN (CarA)

bun-bun [bʌn-bʌn] *n* (CarA) ‖ *pot-cake* (Baha, TkCa) Burnt food, esp rice, caked at the bottom of the pot, relished by some people but also saved for domestic poultry. *Such fowls were kept in the yard ... and were fattened with scratch grain and oats ... and the day's bun-bun and other scraps from the family pot.*—SuS (92.03.22, p.9A, Al Gilkes) [< burn-burn, a characteristic Cr reduplication]

bun·da·rie (bun·du·ri) *n* (Guyn) A large blue-shelled crab that lives in deep holes by the seashore.

bung-bel·ly (boun[d]-bel·ly) [bʌn-bɛli] *n* (Guyn) [*AF*] Constipation. [< bound (i.e. the opposite of *looseness of the bowels* + *belly*]

bun·gee (··ie, ··y) [bʊŋgi] *n* (Baha) [*AF—Vul*] See BOUNGIE

bung-na·vel /1'22/ (Bdos, Guyn, Tbgo, Trin) A protruding navel (esp in children) due to a minor hernia at birth. [Perh from resemblance to *bung* 'stopper of a cask' or < *bound* pronounced (CE) [bʌŋ], from old-fashioned midwifery in wh such a navel was strapped down ('bound') with a 'belly-band']

bun·go (bon·go²) [bʌŋgʌ] *adj* (Jmca) [*AF—Derog*] [Of people] ‖ CONGO (Guyn) [Cp *ADHL* Hausa *buŋgu* 'ignorant lout', *buŋga* 'thing or woman of poor appearance or little value'. Also *SRA:57* the *Bongo*, one of the 'tribes' of the Congo-Nile area of short stature, medium-sized heads, and allegedly cannibalistic]

bun·go-talk [bʌŋgʌ-ta·k] /1'12/ *n* (Jmca) [*AF*] A term understood to refer to the extremest form of uncultivated Jamaican speech, below the level of normal Jamaican Creole, and said to include songs with unidentified 'African' words. [See prec]

bun·go-tough·y ['bʌŋgʌ-tʌfi] /1'122/ *n* (Guyn) [*AF—Joc*] A very young child who behaves, eats and/or plays like a little ruffian.

bun·ya *n* (Guyn) ‖ *cacique* 2. (Guyn, Trin) ‖ *yellowtail*[1] (Trin) 1. A black forest-bird with light yellow beak and bright yellow tail, exceeding 12 ins in overall length; it is the larger of the two varieties of CACIQUE birds, and known for its very long hanging nests; *Ostinops decumanus* (*Leteridae*). [*BAED* Arawak *bunya*, 'large black and yellow bird'] 2. PHRASE 2.1 **stink as a bunya** *adj phr* (Guyn) [*AF*] ‖ STINK AS ABOUYA (Guyn) □ An erron though common phr. See ABOUYA. Phr 2.1 and Note.

Bup! *excl ideoph* (CarA) [*AF*] See BIDIP!

bu·ra-bu·ra* (bo·ro-bo·ro) ['bʊrʌ-bʊrʌ] /1'122/ *n* (Guyn) ‖ *gully-bean* (Jmca) ‖ *jumbie-bubby* (Guyn) [*AF*] ‖ *susumber, turkey-berry* 2. (Jmca) ‖ *wild melongene* (Dmca, StLu) An edible berry about 3/4 in in diameter with many seeds and a red or yellow, powdery skin when ripe; it is borne in small clusters on a wild bush about 4 ft high, with large lobed leaves that have spines on their undersides as also along the stems and branches; *Solanum stramonifolium*, esp in Guyana, or *S. torvum* esp in Jamaica or *S. ficifolium* (*Solanaceae*). *The bura-bura is eaten by children in Guyana, but also often rubbed on their hands to soften the flesh and cause the skin to break if lashed, so getting teachers into trouble.*—Guyn (Ms, 1978) [Prob < *bore-bore* (with Cr intrusive A²⁰), in ref to its many sharp spines wh prick the hand when the fruit is being plucked]

burn *vb* PHRASES 1. **burn (a) bad lamp/candle (for sb)** *vb phr* (CarA) To pray for evil to befall (sb); to try to bring about evil by witchcraft. 2. **burn oil** *vb phr* (Antg, Nevs) [*AF—Joc*] To waste time courting a young woman without any success. 3. **burn school** *vb phr* (StVn) [*AF*] ‖ BREAK BICHE (Gren, etc) See BICHE Phr 4. **let (sth) burn your eyes** *vb phr* (Dmca) [*AF*] ‖ EYES CATCH FIRE (FOR STH) (Guyn) See EYE Phr 8.1

bur·ro·keet (bur·ro·quite) *n* (Trin) See BOROKIIT

burst *vb* (CarA) [*AF*] See BUSS

burst-spoil *vb tr* (Guyn) See BUS-SPILE

bus' *vb* (CarA) [*AF*] See BUSS

buse [byu·z] *vb tr* (ECar) [*AF*] ‖ *abuse* (CarA) ‖ *give mépwi* (Dmca) ‖ *not to forget* (CarA) ‖ *trace*² (Jmca) ‖ *use up* (Belz) To attack (sb) personally in loud, abusive, insulting and usu vulgar language, usu at great length and in public. **a.** *When they fired that servant she got out on the road and bused them so bad they had to close* *the windows.*—(Guyn) **b.** *Cap see he can't get out of the situation no how so he start to buse the English girl, calling she all kind of whore and prostitute, saying how she could go with Daniel.*—STLL:38 **c.** *Because men do not buse each other in Guyana, one frequently finds cases where women buse men, ... If a man in such a situation attempts to buse, he opens himself to the insult of being labeled an antiman.*—Jbs.10.1, p.25 (W.F. Edwards) **[** < SE *abuse.* Cp *OED buse* very rare 'aphetic form of *abuse*', + cit 1589. Also *EDD buseful* adj Wil. 'abusive, foul-mouthed'; *busey* adj wSom 'abusive' (1877)**] 2.** PHRASES [Intensifying the sense] **2.1 buse (sb) inside out** *vb phr* (Nevs) [*AF*] *The mother-in-law went to the house and buse her inside out till the son had to put her out.*—(Nevs) **2.2 buse (sb) off/out/up** *vb phr* (ECar) [*AF*] ‖ *trace (sb) off* (Jmca) ‖ *use (sb) up* (Belz) *Unfortunately, there are some consumers who turn around and 'buse off the clerk' telling her where she came from and wither she is going.*—SuC (78.06.25, p.20) **2.3 buse (sb) right and left** *vb phr* (Guyn) [*AF*] *But is not only the Catholics they busing. They busing the parsons right and left who taking money from the Government.*—CTT: 23 **2.4 buse (sb) stink** *vb phr* (Guyn, Trin) [*AF*] *He ain't dare go now and ask anybody do[w]ng in dere for dey vote—the people will buse him stink.*—(Guyn)

bush[1] *n* **1.** (Belz, Guyn) usu THE BUSH ‖ *the Interior* (Guyn) The deep hinterland, particularly the areas associated with gold and diamond seeking (*Guyn*) or timber industry (*Belz*). [Perh a particularization of sense 2] **2.** (CarA) Uncultivated, forested lands far from urban developments. [Perh from Du infl on the W Afr Slave Coast. Cp Du *bos* 'wood, forest'] **3.** Herbs or weeds, often dried, used as folk medicine, to make BUSH-TEA, and BUSH-BATHS. [See prec note, and cp second sense of Du *bos*, 'bundle of grass, straw'] **4.** PHRASES **4.1 born in/come from the bush** *vb phr* (CarA) [*IF*] ‖ BE A COUNTRY-BOOKIE (Crcu, etc) **4.2 break bush** *vb phr* (Gren) See BREAK Phr 3. **4.3 bush have ears** *id phr* (CarA) [*AF*] (SE) 'Walls have ears'; 'be cautious where you are speaking'. **4.4 drink bush for (sb's) fever** *vb phr* (Gren) [*AF*] To take on (sb else's) burden, troubles, or problems. [Ref to sense 3.]

bush[2] *vb* (Guyn) PHRASE **bush it** *vb phr* (Guyn) ‖ *buss dirt* (Tbgo, Trin) ‖ *put foot* (Guyn) To escape by running away as fast as possible. [i.e. like a runaway slave, into the BUSH[1]]

bush-bath *n* (CarA) ‖ *bark, barking-down, bath* (CarA) ‖ *bath-down* (Jmca, Nevs) ‖ *wash-down*[2] (Mrat, StKt) ‖ *washing-down* (TkCa) A herbal bath prepared from an infusion of various medicinal herbs and pieces of the bark of certain trees, intended to heal a persistent sickness or to drive away evil spirits besetting the body. [The practice very likely originates in W Afr. Cp Yoruba *agbo* 'a bath-water containing leaves of medicinal herbs and barks' (K. Ọmọtọsọ); *won fi agbo wẹ ẹ* 'they bathe him with 'bath-water' (A. Banjo)]

bush-bug *n* (Gren) ‖ STINK BUG (Guyn)

bush-cow *n* (Guyn) ‖ TAPIR (Guyn) [From its usefulness as meat for wh it is hunted]

bush dai-dai ['bʊš dai-daɪ] *n phr* (Guyn) **1.** A legendary small and hideous Amerindian jungle spirit (described as rather like a form of BACCOO). [An Amerindian word of obscure orig., perh Wapisiana *dai*—a prefix denoting 'person' (?). However, note: '... they correspond very closely to ... the horned, hoofed, and tailed devils of our own folk-lore. Of this kind, in Guiana, is the *di-di*, or water-mama, a being with a body not well described, who lives under water'—*IAIG: 352.* However Im Thurm is very likely confusing two different legendary menacing spirits] **2.** [By extension, with shift of sense] [*AF—Joc*] A man orig from the coastal area of Guyana who has taken to living in 'the BUSH' as if trapped there. **3.** [By extension of 2.] [*AF—Joc*] A rough, untutored person (usu a man).

bush-fool *n* (Belz) [*AF—Derog*] ‖ COUNTRY-BOOKIE (Crcu, etc)

bush-hog *n* (Guyn ‖ ABOUYA (Guyn) *Pancho had risen early and gone hunting, and while I was preparing breakfast he returned with a bush hog.*—RWIN:196 (J. Carew)

bush·ie (bush·y) ['bʊši] *n* **1.** (Guyn) [*AF—Joc*] ‖ BUSH-RUM (Guyn) **2.** (Belz) [*AF—Derog*] ‖ COUNTRY-BOOKIE (Crcu, etc)

bush·mas·ter *n* (Guyn, Trin) ‖ *mapepire (zanana)* (Trin) A dark-coloured snake that can exceed 25 ft in length, and is said to be the largest poisonous snake in the world; it is also feared for its readiness to attack and vigorously pursue humans (hence its name); *Lachesis muta* (*Crotalidae*).

bush-med·i·cine *n* (CarA) Various kinds of drink or substances from green or dried herbs, seeds or tree-bark, used as folk-cures for various illnesses; such cures are esp associated with the herbal skills of slaves and their descendants.

bush-rope *n* (Guyn) **1.** Any thin forest lianes or aerial roots of forest trees used for various binding purposes in forest life. **2.** ‖ HAIARI (Guyn)

bush-rum *n* (Gren, Guyn, Trin) ‖ *babash* (Trin) ‖ *benzine* (Guyn, Trin) ‖ *bushie* (Guyn) ‖ *hammond* (Nevs, StKt) ‖ *jack-iron* (Gren, Grns, StVn) ‖ *mountain-dew* (Trin) Unlicensed (and very potent) rum distilled clandestinely from a mixture (called a *wash*) of molasses, ammonia, lemons, etc in a home-made still.

bush-stick *n* (Belz) See cit: *The local house is rectangular with a framework of 'bush-sticks' (saplings and withes) which follows a centuries old conventional design. The walls are close vertical* rows (estacada) of thin bush-sticks thickly coated inside and out with a mixture of burnt lime, clay and hair and other binder and white-washed—ABSBH:91

bush-tea n (CarA) Any infusion of (usu dried) herbs or 'weeds' that are considered medicinal, sometimes including their roots and flowers, to be used as a treatment for some bodily ailment or, esp among older folk, as a supposed means of maintaining health. **a.** *She always kept in the kitchen some dried lemon grass, pieces of gumbo-limbo bark, cerosee bush, and vervine wrapped in brown paper, ready to make various bush-teas.*—Belz (Ms, 1978) **b.** *Leaves are important in the Revivalist Cults of Jamaica ... They are used extensively, for medicinal and magical purposes, especially in the 'bush teas' and 'bush baths' pre-scribed for illnesses and other misfortunes.*—Jmca (Ms, 1957) [< BUSH¹ 2 + TEA 2]

bush-wife; **bush-wo·man** n (Guyn) [*Derog*] A woman who lives with PORK-KNOCKERS to provide companionship and domestic needs.

bus·i·ness¹ [bɪznɪs] n (CarA) [*IF*] **1.** Personal matters or concern; personal association (with sb) or responsibility (for sth). **2.** PHRASES **2.1 got/have business /no business (to be/being ...** vb phr (CarA) [*AF*] ‖ **have no call/calling (to be ...)** (BrVi, Guyn, Mrat, StKt) [*AF*] To have (no) right, reason or proper cause (to be in some identified place); ought (not) (to be, etc). **a.** *You have business to be home when is dark.*—(StVn) **b.** *Marbles got no business bein[g] on the dinner table, boy! Take them away!*—(Antg) **2.2 got/have business/no business with (sb/sth)** vb phr (CarA) [*IF*] To have something/nothing to do with (sb/sth). *Counsel (laughing): 'Look lady I have no business with his lie. It is your lie I have business with.' Witness: 'Oh no. You got to have business with all two lies.'*—SuC (63.05.26, p.2) **2.3 like nobody('s) business** adv phr (CarA) [*AF*] As hard as ever. *After wasting time all year she's working now like nobody's business with the exam coming.*—(Guyn) **2.4 take (sb's) business and make it yours** vb phr (CarA) [*IF*] To interfere in (sb else's) affairs; to get yourself into (sb else's) row.

bus·i·ness² ['bɪznɪs] vb (CarA) [*X*] **1.** Ought; be properly or duly (in an identified place). **a.** *You don[t] business to be walkin[g] de streets at dis time! You business to be at school.*—(Bdos) **b.** *That bucket business right where it is, so please leave it.*—(Baha) **2.** (Often in neg phrases prec by ain't, don't) To have concern or association (with) or responsibility (for). **a.** *I business wid dat? I ain't business wid dat one dam!*—(Guyn) **b.** *The children can do what they like, I tell you! She don'[t] business!*—(Gren) [By functional n > vb shift of BUSINESS¹ esp as in Phrs 2.1, 2.2]

bus·ing ['byu·zɪŋ] n (ECar) [*AF*] ‖ **mépwi** (Dmca) ‖ **tracing** (Jmca) ‖ **using-up** (Belz) **1.** Loud (and often prolonged) personal attack in vulgar terms and/or obscene language. **a.** *Next*

thing busing start and you never hear more. Them really get a tearing up.*—LMFF:44 **b.** *The an-tipathy between Millicent and Joan was known to neighbors, and they knew that it was inevitable that there would be a busin out between the two women at some stage.*—Jbs.10.1, p.34 (W.F. Ed-wards) □ Also ‖ n phrs **busing off/out/up. 2.** PHRASES **2.1 give/hand (sb) a good busing** vb phr (ECar) [*AF*] (As BUSE Phrs 2.1 to 2.4). *He went to the neighbour and handed her a good 'busing'. He threatened to beat her up and the lady, afraid of the enraged Dick, ran into another neighbour's home for safety.*—DaC (53.01.05, p.3) **2.2 put a (good) busing on sb/in sb's skin** (Bdos, Guyn) [*AF*] (As BUSE¹ Phrs 2.1 to 2.4). *He went and picked up with some Albuoystown woman, and one day she found herself to his work-place and put such a busing in his skin, I tell you he had to hide!*—(Guyn)

buss (bus', bust, burst) [bʌs ~ bʌ(r)s(t)] **1.** vb tr, intr (CarA) To snap or cause to snap under tension (as of string, rope, wire, etc.) *The dog burst the chain and chased the children that were teasing it.*—StVn (Ms) [Cp *OED* burst 1. 'often of cords, etc snapping under tension'—obs + latest cit 1718] □ Regarded as Obs in ModE; now regularly replaced in IAE by *break, snap*; the sense of *burst* is generally restricted to 'ex-plode' (as a balloon, bomb, etc) as *OED* burst 2. **2.** vb tr (CarA) [*AF*] ‖ **cut** (CarA) [*AF*] To strike or lash (a part of the body) hard enough to wound. (See Phr 10.14). **3.** (Tbgo, Trin, ViIs) [By extension] [*AF*] To deliver (a blow) sud-denly. (See Phr 10.8, and CUT Phr 3.10). **4.** (Tbgo, Trin) [By extension] [*AF*] To shock or cause surprise by means of (see Phrs 10.3, .4, .6, .7, .10, .11, .12, .13). **5.** (CarA) [*AF*] To break up or break down violently; to cause (some kind of) rash separation. (See Phrs 10.2, .5). **6.** (ECar) [By extension, with diluted sense] [*AF*] To do, have a share in (sth). (See Phrs 10.9, .15). **7.** vb intr (CarA) [*IF*] [Of crockery or glassware] To crack, break or split apart. *If the water is too hot the glass will burst.*—(Bdos) **8.** vb intr (CarA) [*AF*] To be unsuccessful or fail (in). **a.** *When you throw a fete and it buss you must feel too bad though.*—(Trin) **b.** *He passed one subject only and burst in four, lucky he didn't burst the whole damn exam.*—(Guyn) **9.** vb intr (CarA) [*AF*] To happen, be exposed, surprisingly. *They been runnin[g] this bobol and they quarrel, so when the story buss now all two o[f] them in big trouble.*—(Trin) **10.** PHRASES **10.1 behave/gone like cow burst/buss rope** vb phr (Guyn) [*AF*] See COW¹ Phr 2.2 **10.2 burst/buss away/loose /off (sth)** vb phrs [*IF*] See sense 5. **a.** *The man burst loose the door with one lash of a piece of iron.*—Guyn (Ms, 1978) **b.** *She burst off the engagement because he was horning.*—(Bdos) **10.3 burst/buss bam-boo/carbide** vb phr (Gren, Trin) To ignite and explode a joint of bamboo, or a small can, stopped at both ends and containing moistened carbide or some kerosene. *At Christmas time the big boys would have fun bursting carbide and bamboo and startling passers-by.*—Trin (Ms, 1981) **10.4 burst/buss the mark/warning** vb phr (Gren,

Trin) To declare a threat; to make a surprising and frightening statement (as one in authority and able to put it into effect). See MARK¹ 2. *One day he bust the mark and told the girl he was arranging for her to be married.*—Trin (Ms, 1981) **10.5 burst peas** *vb phr* (Tbgo, Trin) To boil peas separately to soften them before cooking anything else (such as rice, etc) with them. **10.6 buss a charge/fine/tax in** (sb) *vb phr* (CarA) To impose or inflict a charge/fine/tax on (sb). *People are also talking about the very light discharge that Magistrate P. give some high society people for weed at the same time that he bussing $500 and $1000 fines on the brothers on the block.*—MoK (73.06.22, p.2) **10.7 buss (a) cry/ (a) laugh** *vb phr* (Guyn, Trin) [*AF—Cr*] To burst into tears/laughter. **10.8 buss a lash/ licks/a stick/a wood in** (sb) **buss** (sb) **a lash/ licks/a stick/a wood** *vb phr* (Gren, Mrat, Trin, USVI) To inflict a severe blow with a whip, stick, etc. *If anybody mad touch dem mangoes, I buss a lash in dem.*—(USVI) **10.9 buss a lime** *vb phr* (Trin) [*AF—Joc*] ‖ *lime¹, pick a lime* (Trin) See sense 6 *The boys were just 'bussing a lime' and having a good time ole talking.*—(Trin) **10.10 buss cunu** *vb phr* (Belz) [*AF—Cr/Joc*] To have sexual intercourse. *Miss Simpson and the king mi di buss cunu / Wai! Wai! Buss cunu!*—Belz (Folk-song—Bes.8.2, p.14) **10.11 buss dirt** *vb phr* (Tbgo, Trin) [*AF—Joc*] ‖ BUSH IT (Guyn) **10.12 buss fatigue/picong** *vb phr* (Trin) [*AF— Joc*] ‖ GIVE FATIGUE/PICONG [*IF*] *We must 'buss' racial picong up to a point* [but] *is picong a worthy pastime?*—TrG (73.04.02) **10.13 buss fire** *vb phr* (Jmca) [*AF*] ‖ *buss loose* (CarA) To break out of control; to catch fire; to explode. *... a guy who just came down from Toronto say I should tell you say that if you think inflation bussing fire down here, you should check Canada-land.*—JdN (78.06.24, p.13) **10.14 buss** (sb)**'s arse** [*Vul*] *... /behind/eye/face/head/knot/skin/tail* *vb phr* (CarA) To thrash (sb) soundly; to flog (sb). *I remember this from my schooldays, they 'bust your tail' with licks if you didn't go to church.*—NG: 87 □ Hence derived n **buss-arse** [*Vul*], **buss-tail** □ [*IF*]. **10.15 buss style** *vb phr* (Trin) ‖ CUT STYLES (ECar) See CUT Phr 3.9 **10.16 kite burst/ buss away** *id phr* (CarA) [*IF*] The string has snapped and the wind has carried the kite away; [by extension] you have lost control of a situation. **10.17 the mark burst/buss** *id phr* (Trin) [*AF*] See MARK¹ 2. **10.18 the pit bursts/bus** *vb phr* (Guyn) [Diamond-mining Ind] [Of a digging] To yield after long disappointment. *After ten weeks the pit ran sand-to-clay in some parts and poor gravel in others. The only spot which gave a few diamonds was that which I was directed by a dream to cut. The pit did 'bus' gloriously.*—Guyn (Ms)

bus-spile/-spoil (burst-spoil) [bʌs-spaɪl ~ spɒɪl] *vb tr* (Guyn) [*AF*] To divide up (stolen goods or anything obtained by questionable means). *The boys ran away with the basket of genips and got behind the house to 'buss-spoil' it.*—Guyn (Ms) [< *burst* 'to break open'

(as a bag) + *spoil* 'loot, booty' (in a collective sense)]

buss-up-shot [ˈbʌs-ʌp-ʃʌt] *n* (Trin) [*AF*] ‖ PARATHA-ROTI (Guyn, Trin) [A Joc name suggested by the resemblance of the flaky pieces to torn pieces of an old shirt, pronounced 'shot' in *IF* Trin E.]

busy-lick-um (busy·lick·um) [ˈbɪzɪlɪkʌm] *n* (Angu, Bdos, StVn) [*AF—Derog*] ‖ BRING-AND-CARRY (StVn)

bu·tou *n* (Gren) See BOUTOU

butt [bʊt] *vb* 1. (Antg, Guyn, StKt, StVn) To strike (an opponent in a fight) violently with the head (esp the forehead). *Hyacinth butt Mrs G—on the breast, tore down her dress...*— DeM(SK) (63.10.05, p.10) 2. (StVn, Trin) [*AF—Joc*] ‖ HORN (CarA) *She butting*[g] *de man day and night and I don't know how he ain*[t] *suspect a thing!*—(Trin) [By transfer of the sense of HORN as used for 'butting'. See OED *butt* vb¹ 2. + latest cit 1853.] 3. PHRASES 3.1 **butt about** *vb phr* (Bdos, Guyn) To knock about; to walk about searching uncertainly. *You see these tourists without enough money to spend up in Oistins and all around, walking and butting about, competing with us to buy bananas.*—Bdos (Hd, 74.03.29, p.247) 3.2 **butt down** (sb) *vb phr* (i) (Trin) To knock down (an opponent) by BUTTING (See BUTT 1. (*Antg, etc*). (ii) (Guyn) [*AF*] To approach or by-pass (sb) impolitely, crudely. *... and the school children nowadays would butt you down the whole year and still want you to buy tickets for their school fair.*—Guyn (Ms) 3.3 **butt out** (near, on, etc) *vb phr* (Bdos, Guyn) [*AF*] To emerge; to come out from a passage or obscure place. *If you make a left there and swing down lowside, you goin*[g] *butt out near Waterford.*—(Bdos) [A survival of EE usage. Cp OED *butt* vb² 4 (*Obs*) [of a road] to issue or lead into + latest cit 1720.] 3.4 **butt up** (on, with) (sb/sth) *vb phr* (ECar) To meet (sb) by chance; to come across or discover (sth) suddenly. *You might run away from the jumbie and butt up with the coffin.* (= *You might jump out of the frying pan into the fire*).—Guyn (Prov)

but(t) and bound (on) [bʌt and bʌŋ(d) ɒn] *vb phr* (Bdos, StVn) [Property Law] To have a common boundary with (another piece of land, a road etc); (*SE*) to abut and bound (on). **a.** *I notice that in the Schedule it is mentioned that the playing field buts and bounds on the public road leading to Gun Hill.*—Bdos (Hd, 73.07.19, p.301) **b.** *That certain piece or parcel of land situate at Workmans ... butting and bounding on lands now or late of Wakefield T—... and on lands now or late of Sybil H— or however else the same may butt and bound.*—AdN (71.12.11, p.14, CR, Notice) [OED *butt* vb 2. (... partly aphetic f. *Abut*) 1. 'to fix or mark (out) the limits of (land, etc) lengthwise' ... Chiefly in the passive and esp in the conveyancing phr *'to be butted and bounded'. Obs* + cits to 1727]

but·ter-bean *n* **1.** (Baha, Dmca, Guyn) ‖ BONA-VIST (CarA) **2.** (StKt, StVn) ‖ LIMA BEAN (CarA)

but·ter-cup *n* (CarA) ‖ ALLAMANDA (CarA)

but·ter·fish* *n* (CarA) (A name applied to several types of) small, frying-pan size of fish, bright pink, grey or yellow, easily scaled and fleshy and tasty esp when steamed; *Cephalopholis fulvus* or *Nebris microps* or *Centropristes striatus*, etc.

but·ter-pear *n* (Belz) ‖ AVOCADO (CarA)

bu·tu[1] *n* **1.** (Gren, StLu, Trin) See BOUTOU **2.** (Jmca) A stupid-looking person. **3.** (Belz) A woman of low character.

bu·tu[2] *adj* (StLu) [AF] ‖ HALF-A-FOOT (Guyn) *Long John Silver was a butu-man, yes!*—(StLu) [Fr Cr < Fr *boiteux* 'lame']

Bux·ton·ian /ɪ'221/ *n* Guyn) An inhabitant (esp a black person) of the village of Buxton, (East Coast, Demerara) traditionally credited with readiness to fight if threatened.

bwa (bois) [bwa] *n* (Dmca, Gren, StLu, Tbgo, Trin) **1.** ‖ FIGHTING-STICK, STICK (ECar) *It was usual for the stickfighter to have his bois 'mounted' (i.e. charmed, invested with invincible powers).*—Trin (Ms) **2.** [By extension] STICK-FIGHTING; the practice or the (pre-carnival) season of STICK-FIGHTING. [Fr Cr < Fr *bois* 'wood']

bwa-ban·dé (bois-ban·dé) ['bwa-bande] *n* (Dmca, Gren, StLu, Tbgo, Trin) A medium-sized hillside tree, with leathery leaves and small white inflorescences; it has a reputation for providing an aphrodisiac from an infusion of a small piece of its bark; *Roupala montana (Proteaceae).* □ 'Other species of trees in *Trin & Tbgo* are known as *Bois Bandé* and presumed also to have aphrodisiac properties. In the *Euphorbiaceae* are *Richeria olivieri* and *R. grandis....* The latter is in the Lesser Antilles'—SMPTT:176. [< Fr Cr BWA + *bandé* < FVA 19c Fr *le bander* 'an erection']

bwa-bwa[1] **(bois-bois)** ['bwa-bwa] *n* **1.** (StLu, Tbgo) A scarecrow. [From the use of pieces of stick to make a scarecrow] **2.** (Short for) bwa-bwa dancer *n phr* (Dmca, StVn) ‖ STILT-MAN (ECar) [Prob a ref to the two stilts]

bwa-bwa[2] *adj* (StLu) Stupid. *She so bwa-bwa she let the people fool her and take all her money.*—(StLu) [By functional shift of BWA-BWA[1] 1., the scarecrow being considered a dumb thing]

Bwa chès! ['bwa 'ʃɛs] /33/ *n phr* (Gren, StLu) See TIM TIM [Fr Cr < Fr *bois* + *sèche* (‖f) (= dry wood), the latter element becoming /chès/ by metathesis]

bwa-denn (bois d'Inde) [bwa-dɛn] *n* (Dmca, Gren, StLu, Trin) ‖ BAY(-LEAF) TREE (CarA) [Fr Cr < Fr *bois d'Inde* 'wood/tree of India']

bwa-ka·no (ba·ca·no(e), ba·ca·nole, bois ca·non, bois-ca·not, bwa-ka·non) ['bwa-kano~'bakano/-ol/-ŏ] *n* (Dmca, Gren, Tbgo, Trin) ‖ TRUMPET-BUSH (Bdos, etc) **a.** *They also constructed rafts of Bois Canot and these 'pwi pwi' are still popular among island fishermen today.*—HTDS:12 **b.** *Long ago if the cold giving you trouble / bacanoe, black sage tea or some soft candle, / Vervine, Christmas-bush or shadow-benny / Bound to pass the cold immediately.*—Trin (Cso, 1976—Lord Relator) [Fr Cr < Fr *bois canot* 'canoe wood', the slender hollow trunk of cork-like wood being used by fishermen to make floats] □ The variant *bwa-kanon (bois-canon)* (Dmca, StLu—HCWP:60 also *Guad, Mart—FFGM:965*) may refer to the hollowness and gun-like shape both of the trunk and long leaf-stalks.

bwa kwa·ib [bwa kwaib]; **Ca.rib Wood** *n phr* (Dmca) A small tree about 10 to 15 ft tall with a bole about 6 ins in diameter when mature; it has thin, whip-like branches full of compound leaves wh are all shed in the dry season when the tree blooms massively in scarlet flowers; (*Sabinea Carinalis (Fabaceae).* It is the National Tree and Flower of Dominica. *The Bwa Kwaib is limited in its distribution to the leeward side of Dominica*—GIS Brochure. [Fr Cr < Fr *bois caraïbe*, 'Carib wood'] □ Caps nec when ref is to the national symbol as in cit. The alternative Eng trans **Carib Wood** seems to be rarely used.

bwa-man (bois·man, bois man) ['bwa-man] *n* (*phr*) (Dmca, Gren, StLu, Tbgo, Trin) ‖ STICKFIGHTER (ECar)

bwa pen [bwa pɛ̃] *n* (StLu) ‖ BREADFRUIT (CarA)

B.W.I.A. (Often pronounced [bi·wi·]) *n* (CarA) (Orig) British West Indian Airways. □ Only the abbr is now used as a trade-name for the national airline of Trinidad & Tobago.

by[1] *prep* **1.** (CarA) [AF] At or to the house (place, office, etc) of (a person). **a.** *You will stay over by me for the night.*—ExP (Mag, 72.12.24, p.7) **b.** *I just called to see how you were. You said you would pass by me last Saturday, and you didn't.*—Peo.3.22, p.13 **c.** *Tig, ah bin by de doctor you know, an' he tell me de same ting dat he did tell you.*—PSFC:27 [Cp OED *by* prep *A* I. 3. ... 'at the house of' (*Obs*) + cit 1712 'I have kept [the letter] by me some months'] **2.** [IF] On, at, or near (a place). **a.** *She lives by 9th Avenue.*—(Bdos) **b.** *I caught the bus in Fitts Village by the gas station and I was going to Eagle Hall by Downes funeral place.*—Bdos (CR, 71.04.19) [Cp OED *by* prep *A* I. 9. 'in the region or general direction of; towards'. However this E usage is largely nautical] **3.** (CarA) [IF] Within or in the course of (a certain time). *The police want you for questioning in connection with these crimes Guy, and they say they will get you by the next two months.*—BoM (73.03.02, p.1) [OED *by A* III. 19. 'In the course of, at, in, on (the time or date of an action or event) (*Obs*) +

cit 1697 '... once by the year ...'] **4.** (CayI) [*IF*] In (a part of the body) (See Phr 6.1). **5.** (Bdos, Guyn) [*X*] Because of. **a.** *By seeing the accused's car caused me to stopped...*—Bdos (CR, 72.07.25) **b.** *As a result, some of our roads are almost impassable by the mounds of filth and debris littered everywhere.*—AdN (73.10.03) **6.** PHRASES **6.1 be sick by the foot, hand, knee, shoulder, etc** *vb phr* (CayI) [*IF*] To have an aching foot, hand, etc. **6.2 by spite** *adv phr* (Gren) [*AF*] ‖ FOR SPITE (CarA) See FOR Phr 17.8 *They sayin[g] is a accident, but we know they t[h]row it do[w]ng by spite.*—PPGD:22 **6.3 By St Peter! By St Paul!** *id phr* (Bdos, Gren, Guyn) A magic formula wh is either (a) repeated while holding a key, gold ring and/ or bible in a particular way in the belief that it would move when the right name in a list of suspected thieves is called, or (b) shouted when a centipede or scorpion is seen, in the belief that that would prevent it from escaping. **6.4 by time (be-time)** ['bɪ-taim] [*AF*]; **by the time** [*IF*] **(i)** *conj phr* (Bdos, Guyn, Tbgo, Trin) As quickly as or even before (an occurrence, event, etc). **a.** *By time he get the message and meet back home, the mother was dead a[l]ready.*—(Guyn) **b.** *By the time you come I will have it ready for you, see?*—(Bdos) **(ii)** *adv phr* (Bdos, Guyn, Tbgo, Trin) By or within that time; in the meantime. *You go out and do what you have to do and I will sweep and wash up by the time.*—(Tbgo)

by² *conj* (Bdos, Guyn, Jmca) [*X*] Because; since; due to the fact that. **a.** *By St Thomas don't have a sea, you won't get hotels there.*—(Bdos) **b.** *By you didn't come two days I say you sick.*—(Guyn) □ See also BEING

by·ah *n* (Guyn) [Indic] See BHAIYA

bym-bye *adv, n* (CarA) See BAMBYE¹

byre [baɪr] *n* (Guyn) [Indic] ‖ DUNKS (Bdos, Guyn, Trin) [Bhoj < Hin *ber* 'plum, jujube'] □ This name is restricted to rural Indic people, the tree being of particular religious significance to Muslims.

C

ca·ba-ca·ba (cab·ba-cab·ba) *adj* (CarA) See KABA-KABA

ca·ba·cal·li *n* (Guyn) See KABUKALLI

ca·ban(e)[1] (ca·baan) ['kaba:n] *n* **1.** (Guyn) ‖ *cabin* (Bdos) A roughly made, low, wooden structure used as a bed, often fixed against the wall of a hut or poor dwelling, or supported on boxes. *A few were resting on their jutesack, or on their rice-straw, on grass-filled sacks on their cabans and khattyas.*—SSOS:53 **2.** (Jmca) [Hist] ‖ *babrecot*[2] (Guyn) [? < Pg *cabana* 'hut'; 'cot'] **3.** (Dmca) Old cloth used as bedding, or to wrap and store mature fruit so they will ripen sweet and unscarred. [By association with sense 1.]

cabane[2] ['kaba:n] *vb tr* (Dmca) To put mature fruit (esp mangoes) in a basket or box covered with old cloth (see CABANE[1] 3.) to ripen them. □ See MANGO-KABANN. Cp FORCE-RIPE[2]. [By functional shift of CABANE[1] 3.]

cab·bage *n* (CarA) [IF] ‖ *tjè-palmis* (Dmca, StLu) The edible, tender, white, inner leaf-bud of the CABBAGE-PALM, cabbage-like in appearance, used in salads or as a pickle preserved in vinegar. □ **1.** The use of this part of the tree accounts for the name of the tree. **2.** This folk usage, already restricted to lower urban and rural levels or older folk, is active mostly in the compounds derived from it (CABBAGE-PALM, etc). *Cabbage* in general use otherwise refers to the vegetable of European origin, *Brassica oleracea* (*Cruciferae*).

cab·bage-bark *n* (CarA) ‖ *bateau* 6. (Guyn) **1.** The large, tough, semi-cylindrical base of the dry leaf-stalk of the CABBAGE-PALM. **2.** The 4-ft long, boat-shaped, dry spathe of the inflorescence of the same tree, used for making baskets, hauled by children as 'boats', etc.

cab·bage-bark tree *n phr* (Jmca) ‖ ANGELIN (Dmca, etc) *The bark [of the cabbage bark tree] has been used in folk medicine as a cure for ringworm of the scalp.*—APPJ:10

cab·bage-bas·ket *n* (CarA) A (usu oblong) basket woven from strips of CABBAGE-BARK.

cab·bage-broom *n* (CarA) ‖ *buba-broom* (Jmca) ‖ *cocoyea-broom* 2. (Gren) The stiff, dried branch of the spent inflorescence of the CABBAGE-PALM fallen from the tree, widely used as a yard-broom. *A cabbage-broom is sometimes hung over a door in the belief that it will keep away evil spirits.*—Guyn (Ms)

cab·bage-house *n* (Belz) ‖ AJOUPA (Dmca, etc) [From the use of the dried fronds of the CABBAGE-PALM in its construction]

cab·bage-palm* *n* (CarA) ‖ *cabbage-tree* (CarA) ‖ *mountain-cabbage* (Antg, Jmca, StVn) ‖ *palmiste* (Dmca, Gren, StLu, Trin) ‖ *pond-top* (Baha) A very lofty palm with a perfectly straight almost cylindrical, grey trunk that may rise to a height exceeding 180 ft, with a large crown of fronds that stand out horizontally; *Oreodoxa oleracea* or *Roystonea o.* or *R. altissima* (*Palmaceae*). *Codrington College is approached by an avenue of some two hundred yards flanked by two silent rows of noble sentinels—cabbage palms each standing a perpendicular hundred odd feet in the sunlight.*—Bdos (Ms) [From the cabbage-like texture of the tender leaf-bud. See CABBAGE] □ Though it is a much taller tree, it is often erron called ROYAL PALM, wh it resembles.

cab·bage-tree *n* (CarA) Another name for the CABBAGE-PALM. *He came from the company path towards the Success line, through some cabbage-trees, to Mr Smith's yard.*—LMSPJS:53

ca·beche (ca·viche) ['kabič ~ 'kavič] *n* (Guyn) ‖ ESCAVEITCH FISH (Jmca) *Their grandmother was an old Madeira Portuguese and she used to prepare some real sweet cabeche—you know fish and garlic and so—to go with the souse [u]pon a Saturday.*—(Guyn) [Pg *escabeche* 'marinade, pickle used for fish or meat']

ca·bin *n* (Bdos) [*Obs*] ‖ CABANE[1] 1. (Guyn) *I don't care if the cabin bre[a]k down / So I get some wh[er]e fuh lay down / Two more rounds and the cabin bre[a]kin' down / So we bre[a]k um down.*—(Bdos, old folk song)

ca·bo·co *n* (Guyn) See CABUKRU

ca·boose [ka'bu·s] *n* **1.** (Baha, CayI) A stove or cooking device made by putting sand or dirt in a large box or tin and making a fire in it; sometimes it is used for baking. *Traditional style kitchens have the 'caboose', a wooden-framed, wooden grill in which charcoal was burnt to cook food.*—CayI (Ms, 1978) □ Cp BOX-OVEN (*Guyn*).

2. (TkCa) ‖ *shed-roof* (Bdos) A smaller section attached to a small house. **3.** (Belz) A hut; a very small house. *'O, let me go home to me own caboose.'*—(Belz) **4.** (Belz) A prison cell. *He was drunk and spent the night in the caboose.*—Belz (Ms, 1981) [Perh infl by or a reduction of Sp *calabozo*, 'prison cell']

ca·bou·ra (-fly) *n* (Guyn) See KABAURO

ca·bou·sé *adj* (Gren) See KABOSÉ

ca·brit *n* (Dmca, StLu, USVI) See KABWIT

ca·bu·kru (ca·bo·co, co·bun·gru) *n* (Guyn) ‖ BOVIANDER (Guyn) *On the larger islands and on the banks of these rapids live a good many Indians, chiefly Caribs, and a few half- breeds between Negroes and Indians, called 'Cobungrus'. These latter retain many good qualities of the Indian, and ... the few good qualities, such as physique and strength, of the West Indian negro.*—IAIG:8 [Prob < Pg *caboclo* 'copper-coloured, red-skinned'. Cp *WSNE* Sran *kaboegroe* 'of mixed ancestry'. See more at COB]

ca·ca[1] **(ka·ca**[1]**)** *n* (CarA) [AF—*Vul*] Excrement (esp human); faeces; high-smelling animal manure. [Cp Pg *caca* 'faeces', *cagar* (Vul) 'to defaecate'; also Sp *caca* 'shit, dirt'; also Fr *caca* '(child's) excrement'; all ultimately < Lat *cacare* 'to go to stool'. The word is likely to have gained its widely established currency and very low status in the New World from early Pg dominance of the W Afr Slave Coast. Note also vb, next]

ca·ca[2] **(ka·ka**[2]**)** *vb intr* (CarA) [AF—*Vul*] To defecate. [Pg *cagar* 'to defecate'. See prec] □ Almost restricted to rural areas, and in ref to children.

ca·ca-bar·wee (ka·ka-ba·wi) *n* (Dmca, Gren, StLu) ‖ *blue chub, green chub* (StLu) ‖ *caca-belly* 1. (Gren, StLu, StVn) A blue-green sea fish, reddish around the head, with large slimy scales; it grows up to about one foot in length and is of good food value. *It look as if you tired eating small jacks and ca-ca barwee. Is slice fish you want?*—RTCS:4 [< *caca* 'shit' + Fr Cr *bawi* < Fr *baril* 'barrel'. See CACA-BELLY]

ca·ca-bel·ly *n* [Name given to different kinds of fishes wh, when caught, give out large amounts of messy excrement stored in a usu bulging abdomen] **1.*** (Gren, StLu, StVn) ‖ *caca-barwee* (Dmca, StLu) The wrasse (*Labridae spp*); also the CHUB 3. (*Scaridae spp*). **2.** (Guyn) ‖ *kakabeli* (Guyn) A small edible fish usu found in foul, shallow river or TRENCH waters; *Poecilia vivipara* (?)—RFLG:69.

ca·ca-da(n) (caca-dent, ka·ka-da(n)) ['kakada ~ 'kakadã] *n* (Dmca, Gren, StLu, Trin) [AF—*Joc*] A little food or a small sum of money given or received as an allowance; a token gift used to get rid of a beggar, hanger-on or other nuisance. *Too much emphasis is still being placed on the cake sales, the bourgeois tea-party and the little 'caca-dent' prizes which the big firms donate.*—CrU (77.03.19, p.2) [< *caca* 'dirt' + Fr Cr *dan* < Fr *dents* 'teeth' (the latter element being denasalized in *Trin* > /da/) = food bits, *either* as left between teeth after a meal *or* as being little more than would merely mess the teeth. The vulgar connotation has, however, largely disappeared]

ca·cao-plum *n* (Trin) ‖ COCO-PLUM (CarA). (See PTT:115)

ca·ca-poule *n* (Dmca, StLu) See KAKA-POUL

cache-cache-ma-balle/-belle *n* (Dmca) See KACH-KACH-MA(N)-BAL

ca·chi·man *n* (Dmca, StLu) See KACHIMAN

ca·chou·rie *n* (Guyn, Trin) See KACHOWRI

ca·cique ['kasik] *n* **1.** (CarA) An Arawakan overlord often referred to as 'king' of an island or of a very large area of land. *He came to the ship after the king, and to him the admiral [i.e. Columbus] gave certain things of the articles of barter, and there the admiral learned that in their language they called the king 'cacique'.*—JJCC: 102 [Via Sp < *BAED* Arawak *kashikwali* 'male head of a household'] **2.** (Guyn, Trin) ‖ *bunya* (Guyn) ‖ *corn-bird* 1. (Trin) Either of two varieties of black and golden-yellow bird, wh make bag-like hanging nests, the larger bird, about 12 ins long, producing a brilliant song; *Cacicus cela* (the larger one), or *Icterus nigrogularis* (*Icteridae*). *On some riverside trees were the peculiar long purse-like nests of yellow caciques or bunyas hanging from the trees.*—SMLNL:12 (V Roth)

Ca·cique's Crown of Hon·our *n phr* (Guyn) The second highest civilian award in Guyana, made for public service of exceptionally high quality and entitling the recipient to put the letters C.C.H. after his or her name.

ca·coon (co·coon) ['kaku:n] *n* (Jmca) A very tough, woody, parasitic climber with very big pods that can be 6 ft long, usu found on tall, riverside or wet forest-trees, and used medicinally and in other folk ways; *Entada gigas* or *Mimosa g.* (*Mimosaceae*). [Cp ADMY Yoruba *kàkàun selà* 'a woody climber with tendrils ... used for tying firewood. The leaf is squeezed into wounds to stanch bleeding'. However ADMY identifies the Yoruba plant as different (*Sapindaceae*). Perh similarities in the type and use of the vine would account for transfer of the name to *Jmca*] □ The *cocoon* pronounc is prob a false refinement: See separate entry.

cac·tus ['kaktʌs ~ 'kyaktʌs] *n* (CarA) [Name loosely applied to plants of widely differing types that have in common 'green succulent, often spiny stems but usu no true leaves' (*PTT:96*) and thrive in dry, sandy or rocky ground, but some of wh do not properly belong to the family *Cactaceae*] **1.** Types of AGAVE esp varieties of the CENTURY PLANT, SISAL and SPANISH NEEDLE, that are not true cacti. [Prob from their thick, fleshy leaves, edged or tipped with sharp spines, and their similar habitat to cacti] **2.** See, as separate entries, BLIND-EYE, COCHINEAL, COLUMNAR CACTUS, DILDO, DONKEY-CACTUS, HEDGE-CACTUS, MONKEY-PUZZLE, MOTHER-IN-LAW-TONGUE, NIGHT-BLOOMING CACTUS, PIPE-ORGAN CACTUS, POPE'S HEAD CACTUS, TURK'S CAP CACTUS.

cac·tus (hedge)* (hedge-cac·tus) *n (phr)* (CarA) ‖ *monkey-puzzle* (USVI) One of two varieties of cactus-like tree, one with triangular, the other with five-angled, close-growing, succulent, green stems that secrete a poisonous, milky juice, have white markings, and are edged with rows of little peaks each bearing a pair of sharp spines; the whole tree resembles a huge irregular candelabrum, so providing, in numbers, an impenetrable hedge (hence the names); *Euphorbia lactea* or *E. neviifolia* (*Euphorbiaceae*).

cac·tus (plant); **night-blooming cac.tus** *n (phr)* (CarA) A climbing garden plant with thick and succulent, triangular stems wh have wavy edges with insignificant spines, and wh at their ends bear large, fleshy, yellowish-white flowers that bloom only in the night; *Hylocereus lemairei* (*Cactaceae*).

cad·dy-old-punch /1'212/ *n* (Guyn) A small, cheap, brown-paper make-do kite. □ See KADI.

ca·dence (ka.dans) ['kadãs] *n* (Dmca) **1.** A popular Dominican type of dance music that blends the Guadeloupean French merengue with the beat of the calypso and sometimes that of the Jamaican REGGAE. □ Sometimes also called *cadence-lypso.* **2.** The dance responding to this music, calling for notable hip and body movements but allowing for much individual variations of these. [? < Fr *cadence* 'rhythm'] □ The spelling **kadans** uses the systematized Fr Cr orthography.

ca·doo·ment (ca·douc·ment, cu·doo·ment) *n* (Bdos) See KADOOMENT □ The spelling *ca-doucment* is perh *Obs*.

cadre [kadər] *n* (Guyn) A trained (and usu young) political activist or militant of socialist ideology, esp one belonging to the political party called the People's National Congress. □ Also often *party cadre.* Pl *cadres* [kadərz].

ca·drille; **ca.dri.elle dance** *n (phr)* (TkCa) See QUADRILLE

ca(f)·fuf·fle¹ (cuf·fuf·fle¹, ker·fuf·fle¹) ['kafʌfl ~ 'kʌfʌfl] *vb tr* (Bdos, Guyn) [*AF—Joc*] To confuse (a person); to cause (a person) to be confused. *Is always better to settle these things yourself because these lawyers only there to cuffuffle you.*—(Guyn) [< EDD *carfuffle* (*curfuffle*) vb

and sb Sc 1. vb 'to disarrange, throw into confusion' 2. sb 'fuss excitement, agitation, disorder']

ca(f)·fuf·fle² (cuf·fuf·fle², ker·fuf·fle²); **ca(f).fuf.fling** *n* (Bdos, Guyn) [*AF—Joc*] Confusion and trouble. **a.** *Since the demise of the 1958–61 West Indian Federation ... there has been much debate over the critical pathway which West Indianism has been following. Such 'caffufling' as has taken place has seemingly produced desultory efforts ... in the region.*—NaT (75.10.12, p.9) **b.** *Oh, how I wish all this kerfuffle would end. Then I could really start to have fun.*—AdV (65.12.12, p.16) [By functional shift. See prec]

ca·gaj; **ca.gaz** *n* (Guyn, Trin) [Indic] See KAGAJ

C.A.I.C. *abbr* Caribbean Association of Industry and Commerce (1955–). □ Based in *Bdos*.

cai·mite; **cai.mi.to** (kai.mit) ['kaimi·t(o)] *n* (Dmca, Gren, StLu, Tbgo, Trin) ‖STAR-APPLE (CarA) [Prob of Carib origin, the tree being indigenous to So and Central Amer]

cake *n* PHRASE **have it in cake and bake/bake and cake** *vb tr* (Guyn) [*IF*] See BAKE¹ Phr 5.1

cake-shop *n* (Guyn) ‖ *bub-shop* (Guyn) ‖*first-aid* (Bdos) ‖*parlour* (CarA) 1. ‖ *variety* (Bdos) A small shop often owned and run by one person living on the premises, selling miscellaneous household, food, medicinal, alcoholic, and other items of everyday needs. *The tragedy began in a cake-shop in the community some nine miles from the city, where patrons were drinking and playing at a pools table.*—GyC (76.11.07, p.36) □ Cp also COLD-SUPPER SHOP (*Jmca*).

cake-walk *n* **1.** (Guyn) A fund-raising show in wh cakes are given as prizes to ladies or couples who compete in various ways (originally by walking around the room with a cake balanced on the head, hence the name); stylish dress and bearing were a principal requirement. *The cake-walk was much favoured by middle-class 'coloured' people, especially at church functions, up to the 1930s and 40s but is rarely heard of nowadays.*—Guyn (Ms, 1980) **2.** (StKt) A feature of masquerading, popular at Christmas.

ca·la·ban (cal·ban, co·la·ban) ['kal(a)ban~kolaban] *n* (Jmca) ‖ *bird-trap* (Baha, Guyn, TkCa) ‖*calavan* (CayI) ‖*zatwap* (Dmca) A light trap for catching birds on the ground, made of light sticks bound with wire in a pyramid shape or a box-shape about 10 ins high. [Prob > BrE dial *callyvan*, with Cr /v > b/ shift. Cp *EDD callyvan* (A common word in e.Som but not ... w.Som) 'a pyramidical wicker trap about ... 9 ins in depth, used to catch birds']

ca·la·bash* *n* (CarA) ‖ *boli(e)* 1. (Dmca, Gren, StVn, Trin) The brown, dried, football-sized gourd of the fruit of the calabash tree, (*Crescentia* *cujete* (*Bignoniaceae*)), halved, scraped out and used as a container or dipper.

ca·la·di·um *n* (CarA) ‖ BLEEDING-HEART (CarA) *Caladiums are natives of tropical America and caladium bicolor grows wild in Trinidad ... they are useful as pot plants and for bedding.*—PTT:99

ca·la·lu* (cal·(l)al·(l)oo (ou, u), ka(l)·la·loo) ['kalalu] *n* 1. (CarA) ‖ *agouman* (StLu) ‖ *bhaji* (Guyn, Trin) ‖ *calalu-bush, dasheen-bush* (Tbgo, Trin) ‖ *spinach* (CarA) ‖ *wild spinach* (Antg, Bdos, Mrat, StVn) ‖ *zèbaj* (StLu) ‖ *zép-ina* (Dmca) Any of a number of plants with edible, succulent leaves wh are cooked as green vegetables, esp those of the *Amaranthus spp*, but also DASHEEN and other leaves. (See separate entries CATERPILLAR CALALU, CHINESE CALALU, WATER-CALALU). 2. (i) (Dmca, StVn, Tbgo, Trin) ‖ *calalu-soup* (Mrat, StVn) ‖ *crab-and-calalu* (Guyn) ‖ *pepperpot* (Angu, Antg) A very thick soup made of CALALU 1. or DASHEEN leaves and other ingredients such as OKRAS, root vegetables, dumplings, crabs or crayfish, saltbeef or ham-bone, green peppers, and seasoning, and usu served as a main meal, often on Sundays. (ii) (Dmca, Gren, Jmca, StVn) ‖ *cook-up* (Bdos, Guyn) A dish of solid food prepared by boiling some of the same ingredients as above (2(i)) together with rice and sometimes grated coconut. 3. (i) *n, adj* (Tbgo, Trin) [By extension] A general mixture. a. *And Trinidad and Tobago in particular is rich in mythology since our people come from so many parts of the world. Added to that, the relative smallness of the country makes the blend richer and deeper. The result is a cultural callaloo.*—ExP (72.09.03, p.26) b. *Now he had a good song, but you can't go on a stage on Carnival Sunday night and sing a calypso reeling off a lot of long African names—certainly not in a callaloo society like ours, where the audience is made up of Indians, Chinese, Syrians, as well as Africans.*—Peo.1.10, p.26 (ii) (Trin) A confusion; a bad mix-up. *Look eh! Leave me out o[f] your calaloo, see! Is your mess and is not me to catch!*—(Trin) ['*Calalú* is eaten by Afrocuban saints and gods; and it is well-known that the Lucumi [i.e. Yoruba] idols only eat the cooked and seasoned foods of their 'homeland' this being one of the most respected ritual requirements. This should suffice to remove any doubt that *calalú* is African'—OGA:94 (trans). OGA:94 suggests as sources Malinke *kalalu* 'many things', also Mandingo *colilu* 'an edible herb resembling spinach'. NE-APR:261 notes that 'Père Labat had, since 1694, noted the use of the dish *callarou* by Negros and poor people in the Fr islands' and that also 'in Haiti *calalou des morts*, made with a mixture of different dishes, was served to participants of the Zombi cult (said to be of Igbo or Carabali origin) before the tomb of a dead person whose spirit needed to be appeased' (trans). Cp *ADMY* Yoruba *ko-ra-lu* vb 'mix several bought things together', also *ADHL* Hausa *kararuwa* '(herbaceous) stalks', and *kalu* 'soup', loan word < Kanuri *kalu* 'leaf' (*KPG:102*). *NEAPR:231*-

232 indicates that the word and its variants were widely known in the countries and islands of the Gulf of Guinea, but in the Caribbean, coastal Central America, and Brazil, with varying applications, only where slaves and their descendants were settled. However, Breton (1666) notes (*BDFC:61*) Carib (women's speech), *ca-rarou, -ora* 'leaf or scale of a tortoise'. Also *DGEG* Guarani *ca'aruru* 'medicinal plant' (of many given names including Sp *cururú, calalú*). Also *NMID* Braz Pg *caruru* 2. 'a dish prepared by stewing minced herbs with oils and spices', also different bot types of *caruru*]

ca·la·lu-bush *n* (Tbgo, Trin) ‖ CALALU 1. (CarA)

ca·la·lu-soup *n* (Mrat, StVn) ‖ CALALU 2. (i) (Dmca, etc)

ca·la·van ['kalavan] *n* (CayI) ‖ CALABAN (Jmca)

cal·ban (co·la·ban) *n* (Jmca) See CALABAN

cal·cin·ed baux·ite [kalsi:nd bɒksaɪt] *n phr* (Guyn, Jmca) The highest quality of bauxite produced by heating bauxite ore of a low-iron content at an extremely high temperature through very long sloping rotating kilns. *Guyana produces most of the world's calcined bauxite which ... is not used for the smelting of aluminium but only for specialised industrial purposes such as the lining of refractories, making electrical insulators, etc.*—Guyn (Ms) □ See also METAL-GRADE BAUXITE.

ca·len·da; ca.lin.da *n* (ECar) See KALINDA

ca·li·so ['kaliso] /1'12/ *n* (StLu) [? Obs] (See cit). *The great moment of these dances is the 'break-away' usually signalled by the playing of a local 'caliso' 'Madiana' (a beach and night club in Martinique), 'Lagé mwe' (let me go), or 'Bobot' (a local Don Juan). The song is played in short repetitive phrases like the 'syncopation' of Trinidad carnival music. The dancers 'breakaway' from their partners and each dances an ecstatic solo.*—Caq 4.2, p.109 [See CALYPSO]

call[1] *vb* (CarA) [*AF/IF*] 1. *vb tr* [In identifying sb or sth] (i) [*IF*] Name; (who/which is) named/called. a. *I forget what they call this fruit again.* (i.e. *I forget the name of this fruit*).—(Gren) b. *The second son, the one they call Ezra, he delivered the address.* (i.e. *... whose name is Ezra*).—(Guyn) (ii) [*AF—Derog/Joc*] [Same sense, but usu with *you* as subject] a. *None o[f] them ain[t] know what you call decency.*—(Antg) b. *You call dem few scraps you put [u]pon de table food?*—(Tbgo) [A prob calque from W Afr langs. Cp Twi *Abofra a wɔfrɛ no Kofi* (= child that they-call him Kofi) 'a child whose name is Kofi'] 2. [*In passive sense, without a complement*] (CarA) [*X*] To be called. *Herman, you call! You ain[t] hear? [i.e. You are being called].*—(Guyn) 3. *PHRASES* [In looser general use with a complement in many Phrs, as follows] 3.1 **call down on (sb)** *vb phr* (Bdos)

[IF] To challenge or confront (sb) (usu with embarrassment implied). *He did not even tell me he was marrying this other woman, but when I call down on him he had to say it was true.*—(Bdos) [Prob by extension of SE *call down* 'reprimand'] **3.2 call egg** vb phr (Jmca) [AF] [Of a hen] To cluck after laying an egg. **3.3 call for (sth)** vb phr (Tbgo) [IF] ‖ FEEL FOR (STH) (CarA) *Whenever she pregnant she callin[g] for green mango.*—(Tbgo) **3.4 call it/that George** (Guyn, Tbgo, Trin); **call it Wally** (Bdos, StVn) id phrs [AF] To agree that a matter is ended or settled; (SE) to call it quits. **a.** *The court heard that Edgar S— bought a 'Solo' soft drink at a Morvant cafe on September 21 last year and discovered a black substance in the drink. He then went to the firm and asked for $500 'to call it George'.*—ExP (72.10.25, p.13) **b.** *Let us start early and finish all the interviews today, then we can call it Wally, because we can do the rest by round-robin.*—(Bdos) **3.5 call (sb) everything but a child of God** vb phr (TkCa) [AF] ‖ BUSE (SB) (CarA) **3.6 call (sb) full-mouth** vb phr (Guyn) [AF] ‖ *call (sb) raw* (Angu) To address an elder or senior by the first name or without saying Mr, Mrs, or Miss. **3.7 call (sb) raw** vb phr (Angu) [AF] ‖ CALL (SB) FULL-MOUTH (Guyn) **3.8 call the spirit** vb phr (Baha) (See cit). *'Calling the Spirit' is a ritualistic form of Obeah practice to either obtain knowledge that can be utilised for good or evil. The Obeah practitioner that has the power to manipulate a spirit, can send a spirit to possess a person (e.g. possession) or haunt (hag) a house or property.*—MTTBT:92 **3.9 call to (a child)** vb phr (Nevs) [IF] ‖ SPEAK/TALK TO (CarA) *Mama please call to Jean, she hitting me!*—(Nevs) **3.9.1 call to (sth)** vb phr (Guyn) [AF] [Often in a question with *you* as subj] To have something to say about (sth); to have a concerned comment to make about (sth). *You know when the mother think she gone to Sunday school, is the boy she gone to see? Well what you going call to that? (i.e. ... what can you say about that?)*—(Guyn) **3.10 got/have/is to call (sb) aunt, uncle** vb phr (CarA) [IF] To be niece or nephew to (sb) (by blood relationship as opposed to casual friendly relationship of that person to your parents); to be in such a relationship but more than one generation or otherwise removed. **a.** *The term aunt is rarely employed directly. A woman will not say that such and such a child is her niece, but 'She the child is to call me aunt'; similarly the child will say when referring to her aunt, 'I am to call her aunt.'*—CGBD:4 **b.** *First let me tell you about Buddy. He is to call my father uncle and we grew up together. It was Buddy, Bill and then me.*—NaT (91.11.29, p.9A, 'The Lowdown') [Cp Wolof *Fatou war na ooye Karim nidyiaye* 'Fatou she has to call Karim uncle'; also Kikongo *Fuete kumbokela nguankazi* 'He must call me uncle'; also Ci-Nyanja *Akuyenera kuwatana atsibweni* 'He/she has to call him uncle'; also Mende *Ndopoi ji ɛ kenya-loi yie* ('This child not uncle-call do' i.e. is disrespectful)] **3.11 have just called (sb's) name** vb phr (CarA) [IF] To have been talking about (sb) a few moments before the person (coincidentally) turns up. □ Cp WALK ON YOUR NAME (Guyn).

3.12 play call id phr (Guyn) [X] The game officially begins. *Play didn't call until 2 o'clock because of rain.*—(Guyn) **3.13 school call** id phr (CarA) [X] School begins. *I jumped out of bed but school had already called.*—Guyn (Ms, 1978)

call² n 1. (CarA) [AF] ‖ *calling* (CarA) Right; claim (see Phr 3.2). *What call you have in their mango tree when yo[ur] mother have mango home?* —(StVn) [Also AmE dial as in 'You have no call to be rude to me'—(pers info, L. Urdang). Cp *W3* 2. *call* n 3. b. 'necessity, justification'] **2.** (CayI) An offer of a seaman's job (See Phr 3.1). **3.** PHRASE **3.1 get your call** (CayI) To be called up for a seaman's job (having put your name on a waiting list). See ALLOTMENT **3.2 got/have no call (to do sth, to be in a particular place, etc)** id phr (CarA) [AF/IF] To have no right (to do, to be, etc). *They're only children—they have no call to give you all that trouble.*—(StKt) [Cp *JESI:230* IrE *call* 'claim; right' + ex 'Put down that spade, you have no call to it'. Also *OED call* sb 8. 'duty, need, occasion' right' + latest cit 1858]

call·ing n (CarA) [IF] ‖ CALL² 1. (CarA) *You are a child and you have no calling in other people business nor in other people yard.*—(Guyn) [*OED calling* 9. d. = *call* sb 8. (as prec) + latest cit 1857]

cal·la·lu (cal.la.loo) n (CarA) See CALALU

ca·lyp·so¹ ['kalɪpso] /1ø1/ n (CarA) ‖ *cariso* (Dmca, Gren, Trin) [Hist] ‖ *kaiso* (ECar) **1.** A popular satirical song in rhymed verse, now mostly associated with Trinidad, commenting on any recognized figure(s) or aspect(s) of Caribbean social life, and more often performed by a male singer with much body gesture and some extemporization directed at anybody in the audience. *In the weeks leading to the beginning of Lent, crowds flock to the Tents to enjoy calypsoes.*— Trin (Ms) [Hence, in attrib use *calypso contest, calypso show, calypso singer, calypso talent* etc, and phrs below]. **2.** [By extension] The composition and performance of these topical songs as a competitive professional art. *Calypso is now a recognized part of Caribbean culture.*—Antg (Ms) **3.** The type of tune or music with a beat characteristic of this composition. *Steelbands will be judged on the basis that they play any tune other than a calypso.*—ExP (73.02.20, p.15) [Hence in attrib use *calypso band, calypso beat, calypso group, calypso music, calypso tempo* etc and phrs below. See also ROAD-MARCH] **4.** The individualistic or BREAKAWAY dancing related to this type of music. *The Rontano Movement will present several dance demonstrations: 'Do Your Thing' [Jazz]... 'Black Magic Woman' [Creative], 'Garrot Bounce' (calypso).*—AdN (73.02.17, p.9) [< Efik *ka isu* 'go on!', also KID Ibibio *kaa iso* 'continue, go on', a common phrase used in urging sb on or in backing a contestant. The Efik-Ibibio being the established middlemen in the slave trade (ex at Calabar) the slaves of other ethnic groups would have brought this item (as

they did BAKRA) to the *CarA* as part of the private
vocabulary of slave life. In the context of *CarA*
plantation-life, crowds backed creole teasing-
songs against MASSA shouting '*Ka iso!*' wh gradually lost its original meaning. *Kaiso* is still
the regular *ECar* folk name, not *calypso*. The
phonological development /ka-iso > kariso >
kaliso/ is attested by CARISO (*Dmca*, etc), CARUSO
(*USVI*), and CALISO (StLu) this last recognized
as 'another form 'Calisseaux' ... in use at the
same time as 'Carisseaux''—(Espinet & Pitts,
Land of the Calypso, 1944, p.47). The development > *calypso* is through corruption
(through folk etym) by English writers in the
1930s, influenced by the name (Calypso) of the
amorous island nymph of Greek mythology, plus
an anglicized shift in pitch pattern /ɪ'12/ > /
ɪ'21/] **5.** *PHRASES* **5.1 dance calypso** *vb phr*
(CarA) See BREAK Phr 1. BREAK AWAY (ECar)
*You can't pick up a girl to dance calypso and want
to hold on to her.*—Guyn (Ms) □ The article *a/
the* is usu omitted in this and similar phrs below.
5.2 play calypso *vb phr* (CarA) To play tunes
of this type for dancing. *They asked the band to
stop playing reggae and to play calypso.*—Bdos
(Ms) **5.3 sing calypso** *vb phr* (CarA) To sing
songs of this type (as an art). *They will clap you
off the stage if you enter the competition and
you can't really sing calypso.*—Trin (Ms) □ Pl
calypsoes (preferred to *calypsos*).

ca·lyp·so² *adj* (CarA) [*IF*] Having and showing
carefree merriment, gaiety or exuberance in colour, style, manner, etc. *West Indians were renowned as flamboyant, happy-go-lucky, 'calypso'
cricketers, lacking in the great Victorian virtue of
temperament.*—The   Observer,   (London,
84.08.19, p.7) [By functional shift and extension
of CALYPSO¹ n] □ Hence *calypso colours* [i.e.
bright and varied], *calypso cricket, calypso
girls, calypso people*, etc

ca·lyp·so crown *n phr* (ECar) The crown or
trophy won by the CALYPSO KING/QUEEN.

Ca·lyp·so King/Queen *n phr* (ECar) The
winner or champion singer in the calypso contest
of a national CARNIVAL.

ca·lyp·so·ni·an ['kalɪpsonɪən] /ɪ'1221/ *n*
(ECar) ‖ *kaisoman* (ECar) [*IF*] A competitive
professional singer of calypsoes. [*Calypso* + *ian*
n prob on the analogy of *Tobagonian*, etc.]

ca·lyp·so tent *n phr* (ECar) The building
(though in earlier years a tent and hence the
name) used by or associated with a particular
team of CALYPSONIANS who present CALYPSO
SHOWS there throughout the CARNIVAL season.

ca·lyp·so war *n phr* (Trin) A stage contest
between two or more CALYPSONIANS in wh each
tries to outdo the other(s) in CALYPSO skills and
esp in mutual mockery in extempore rhyming
song, the winner being judged by acclamation.
□ See also PICONG.

cam·bi·o [kambio] *n* (Guyn) A place, either
within the commercial banking system or privately run, where it is permitted to buy or sell
hard currency at a rate set by the operator.
*The official expressed concern about the continuing
decline in the value of the Guyana dollar at the
cambios where, on Thursday, the US dollar was
being traded at a record high of 70 Guyana dollars
compared with one for 55 when the cambios opened
their doors just over sixteen weeks.*—AdV
(90.07.07, p.7) [Adaptation of international
monetary term *cambio* (Sp) 'exchange (rate)',
(Italy) 'money']

ca·moo·di (**ca·mou·die**) ['kamudi] *n* (Guyn)
A very large non-poisonous snake that crushes
its victims; it is of two kinds—the LAND-CAMOODI
‖ MACAJUEL (*Trin*)) and the WATER-CAMOODI or
ANACONDA (*Eunectes gigas*) wh can exceed 30 ft
in length. [*EILCA:57* Arawak *kamudu*, name of
this snake]

camp¹ *n* (Trin) ‖ MAS-CAMP (Trin)

camp² *vb tr* (Mrat) ‖ FORCE-RIPE² (CarA) (esp
in ref to mangoes—*Mrat*)

cam·pan·e·ro ['kampanɛro] *n* (Trin) A common, whitish, forest bird with coffee-brown
head, black wings, the male having stringy
wattles hanging from its throat, and noted for
its bell-like song, hence also known as *anvil bird*
and *bearded bellbird*; *Procnias averano carnobarba*
(*Cotingas*). [Sp = 'bell-ringer' said to be its
Venz name]

cam·pesh* (**cam·peche, kan·pèch**) ['kampeš]
n (Dmca, Gren, Trin) ‖ *logwood* (Belz, BrVi,
Gren, Jmca, Trin) 'A small, spiny, spreading,
slow-growing tree ... chiefly valued for its hard
and heavy heart-wood from wh is extracted a
deep red dye used by dyers and printers' *PTT:
183*; the timber provides a great heat-giving fuel;
*Haematoxylon   campechianum   (Leguminosae-
Caesalpiniceae). Dye was extracted from the roots,
and the bark of the 'campesh' is even boiled for
staining floors prior to polishing.*—PGIP:37 [Fr
campêche 'campeachy wood, logwood']

can *modal aux vb* (CarA) [*X*] [Widely used in
Formal speech and universally used in AF/IF
speech and writing as = *may, might, could*
whence some particular phrasing] **1.** (Implying)
please. *You can sit on the terrace for me, sir, while
I now settin[g] the dining hall.*—StVn (Waiter to
hotel guest) **2.** Might; could; is/was permitted
to. *When I asked the nurse if the doctor attended
to the child's hand, she said the doctor told her
the child can go home.*—NeJ (74.11.15, p.4) **3.**
PHRASES **3.1 can/could as well** *vb phr* (CarA)
[*X*] May/might just as well. **a.** *There seems to be
a lot for discussion this week so we can as well
go right to it.*—ViN (73.01.27, p.2, Strolling
Scribbler) **b.** *Since you are going up there you
could as well take this with you.*—(Bdos) **3.2 can
shake hands** *vb phr* (CarA) [*IF*] See HAND¹ Phr
4.3.

CANA ['ka:na] *abbr* Caribbean News Agency (1976–).

ca·nal *n* (Guyn) A deep, wide and straight waterway dug to supply water to irrigate plantation or other lands under cultivation. □ Should be distinguished in *Guyn* from *drain*, TRENCH, wh properly apply only to drainage, not to irrigation waterways. See also MIDDLE-WALK, POLDER.

ca·nals pol·der *n phr* (Guyn) A large empoldered area of West Demerara irrigated by two long east-west canals, the adjacent cultivated lands and village areas being called Canal No.1 and Canal No.2.

ca·na·ri *n* (ECar) See CONAREE

can·bou·lay (cannes-bru·lées, kann·bou·lé) ['kanbule] /1'12/ *n* (Trin) **1.** [Hist—19C] The firing of the sugar-canes at night to facilitate harvesting the next day; (also) the accidental or deliberate burning of fields of sugar-cane. [In every case there was spectacle and excitement as the slaves were marshalled to control or extinguish the fires, and the burnt canes had to be harvested without delay to prevent 'souring'. The event became associated with pre-harvesting plantation celebration] **2.** The festive carrying of lighted torches and beating of drums through the streets to celebrate [19C] Emancipation Day annually (August 1st), and then transferred to mark the opening of CARNIVAL (recently more often called CANNES-BRULÉ(E)S). [Fr = 'canes burnt' > Fr Cr *kann boulé* 'canes (are) burn(ing)', the form *cannes brulées* a n phr with verbal pa. part. being a false refinement of the Fr Cr sentence] □ The spelling *can-(ne)boulay* appears to have been adopted by Port-of-Spain newspapers esp in relation to the riots resulting from the police suppression of the torch festival in 1881.

can-can (pet·ti·coat) *n (phr)* (ECar) An underskirt of stiff material used to give the outer skirt more body.

can-cup *n* (Antg) ‖TIN-CUP (ECar)

can·dle-bush *n* (Dmca) ‖BALL-BUSH (Bdos, Jmca) [Prob from its erectness. Also called *candle-bush stick* in some parts of *Dmca*; and cp also ‖*Christmas candlestick* (Baha, Jmca)]

can·dle-flower *n* (CayI) ‖CHRISTMAS-CANDLE (Bdos, etc)

can·dle-fly* *n* (Guyn, Trin) ‖*labelle* (Dmca) ‖*lamp-fly* (StKt) ‖*lamp-lighter* (Baha) ‖*larbelle* (StVn) ‖*peeny-wally* (Jmca) A brown insect about 2 cm long with a yellowish-brown luminous abdomen wh 'blinks' like a light each time it raises its wings in flight; a firefly, family *Lampyridae*.

can·dle-grease *n* (Bdos) ‖SOFT-CANDLE (Gren, etc)

can·dle·stick *n* (Jmca) ‖CHRISTMAS-CANDLE (Bdos, etc)

can·dle·wood *n* **1.*** (Bdos) A light-brown, hard wood used in construction and boat-building, yielded by a tree of medium height; *Cupania americana* (*Sapindaceae*). **2.** (Guyn) A heavy and very tough 'yellowish-pinkish' wood useful for salt-water piling, sleepers, bridges, etc, yielded by a forest tree 120 ft or more tall; *Parinari campestris* (*Rosaceae*) (*FBGMFP:48*). **3.** (Jmca) A light, easily split wood that burns readily, yielded by a medium-sized, flowering, woodland tree; *Amyris plumieri* (*Rutaceae*). *Candlewood torches make our road as bright as day. You know how you make candlewood shine? Go into the woodland and find a limb as big as your wrist and a half. Strip the bark partways down, and leave it hanging over your hand to keep off the sparks. Sharpen the point, then light it with a lucifer-match. And then how it will burn bright!*—RND:4 □ There appear to be other woods by the same name in *Baha, CayI, Gren, Guyn, Jmca.*

cane-ar·row *n* (Bdos, Guyn) ‖ARROW² (CarA) *Fields of tall cane arrows towering like ships' masts high above an ocean of greenery*—SuS (79.12.23, p.13)

cane-bill *n* (Bdos) ‖BILL¹ (CarA)

cane-blade *n* (Bdos) The long, slender, blade-shaped and sharp-edged leaf of the sugar-cane.

cane-borer *n* (CarA) [Sugar Ind] The larva of a small, light brown moth, *Diatraea saccharalis*. See MOTH-BORER

cane-fire *n* **1.** (CarA) A controlled fire set to some fields of sugar-cane to facilitate their being harvested the next day. □ See CANBOULAY. **2.** (Antg, Bdos) A fire deliberately set to destroy fields of sugar-cane or to force their immediate harvesting. *However the frequent cane-fires now made accurate prognosis quite impossible and greatly upset government planning.*—AdN (72.03.23, p.1)

cane-hole *n* (CarA) **1.** One of a line of shallow holes each about 4 ft square and dug about 6 ft apart on a cane-field in wh (in earlier times) the sugar-cane was planted. **2.** [By extension] The clump of canes growing from the original hole. *Mr Speaker, some of us would also remember the men digging cane holes at eight and nine cents per hundred, ... and cutting the canes in those days at twelve cents per one hundred holes.*—Bdos (Hd, 74.12.03, p.4267)

cane-li·ly* /1'22/ *n* (Bdos) A type of THATCH wh is a large, bushy shrub with long, blade-like leaves with light-coloured margins, dried and used for basket-work and mat-making; *Pandanus utilis* (*Pandanaceae*). *And the day's work is done. Now these young reapers trudge wearily back home ... their crop of cane-lily on their heads, ... Perhaps*

*when you buy your decorative place mat, or hand-
bag, you might spare a thought for the folk who
gather the lilies, and appreciate them more!*—PeL
(80.11.14, p.1)

cane-meat *n* (Bdos) CANE-TOPS when used as
livestock fodder.

ca·nep (ca·nop) ['kanʌp] *n* (Baha, TkCa)
‖ GUINEP (CarA) *Nearly everybody had a good
Guinep tree. ... In mid-summer they produce myri-
ads of fruits in grape-like clusters or bunches. We
called them ca'neps, but our neighbours in extreme
southern Florida, where they also grew well, call
them Spanish limes. Coloured, and shaped somewhat like a lime, but smaller, they could be as sweet
as sugar or as sour as limes.*—EBT:8 [< Arawakan
guenepa to wh it is a closer form than the more
regular *guinep*] □ The spelling *ca'nep* in the cit
is exceptional.

cane-piece *n* (CarA) A small landowner's
patch of land where sugar-cane is cultivated on
contract to the nearest factory.

cane-punt *n* (Guyn) [Sugar Ind] ‖ PUNT
(Guyn)

cane-row(s)[1] *n* (CarA) ‖ CORN-ROW[1] (CarA)

cane-row[2] *vb* (CarA) ‖ CORN-ROW[2] (CarA) *Joke
on Eddy ... he'd had his Afro cane rowed for fun
and was walking round without his cap...*—WeG
(73.03.21, p.2, Partyline)

cane-syr·up *n* (CarA) ‖ *fancy-molasses,
sweetenin(g)* (Bdos, StKt) A shiny, dark brown,
heavy syrup, refined molasses (in the last stage
before the crystallization of cane-sugar), that is
commercially retailed.

cane-top *n* (CarA) ‖ *cane-meat* (Bdos) The
top end of a stalk of sugar-cane cut off in harvesting and collected for use as livestock fodder.

ca·nip ['kanɪp] *n* (Mrat) ‖ GUINEP (CarA)

Can·je pheas·ant* ['kyanyʌ fɛzʌnt] /2'211/ *n
phr* (Guyn) ‖ *hanna* (Guyn) A bird about 22 ins
long from head to tail with conspicuous, erect
crest features, a shaded brown body flecked with
creamy white feathers, and a creamy white
breast; the young have distinctive minor wing-tip
claws with wh they climb, and they can dive some
distance under water when frightened (*CBGB:
49–50*); *Opisthomocos hoatzin* (*Opisthocomidae*).
The Canje Pheasant (or '*Hanna*' or '*Hoatzin*') *is
the national bird of Guyana.*—Guyn (Ms) [*Canje*,
from the name of the area in Berbice (Guyn)
where it is mostly found + *pheasant* from its
resemblance to a pheasant] □ See WCD9 *hoatzin*.

can·ker-ber·ry* (kan·ka-ber·ry) *n* (CarA)
‖ *corberry* (Angu) ‖ *ka-berry* (Angu, BrVi) A
bright-red berry borne in loose little clusters on
a wild bush with dark green leaves carrying

short little yellow prickles on their underside
and stems; *Solanum bahamense* (*Solanaceae*).

can·kie (can·kee, kaan·ki) ['ka·ŋki] *n* (Guyn)
‖ DUKUNA (Antg, etc) [*DAFL* Twi (Asante)
ŋkaŋkye 'cake' (N.E. Voc), Fante *kãŋkyew* =
dɔkono 'boiled maize bread'] □ The spelling
kaanki best suits the folk pronunciation and
origin of the name. See CONKIE.

Can·na·bal Day *n phr* (Belz) [Hist] Carnival
Day (Ash Wednesday). *Traditionally, some years
ago Ash Wednesday in Belize, was Cannabal
Day—a Creole linguistic corruption of Carnival
Day; but not anymore.*—BeA (BE) (81.03.07,
p.14)

can·na (li·ly)* *n (phr)* (CarA) One of many
varieties (mostly red, pink, yellow, or spotted)
of garden-lily borne in terminal inflorescences
on tall, slender, erect cane-like stalks with broad,
pointed, sheath-like green leaves and prickled
capsules containing a large number of round
black seeds resembling shot; (mostly) *Canna
indica* (*Cannaceace*).

can·nelle *n* (StLu) ‖ CINNAMON (TREE) (CarA)
[Fr = cinnamon (bark)]

cannes-bru·lées *n* (Trin) See CANBOULAY

can·non-ball tree* *n phr* (CarA) ‖ *comb-
and-brush* (Gren, StVn) ‖ *forbidden fruit*
2.(iii) (Guyn) A tall, forest-type, ornamental
tree, the lower part of its trunk producing untidy-
looking, rope-like branches wh bear large, waxy
and very fragrant flowers and inedible, hard-
shelled, round fruit the size of a cannon-ball
(hence the name); *Couroupita guianensis* (*Lecythidaceae*).

ca·noe [kanu·] *n* (CarA) **1.** A slender, wooden
boat with pointed ends, made by digging or
burning out and shaping the cut trunk of a
forest-tree; or one with open ends made by
curing and 'setting' the tough bark or 'wood-
skin' of certain kinds of forest-tree; it is propelled
by paddling. [< *TLWI*:4, 20 Carib *kanawa*,
Arawak *kanoa*, Taino *canoe*, name of the craft
noted by Columbus: '*canoe' is a vessel in which
they navigate, and some of them are large and some
small*—JJCC:112] **2.** PHRASE **2.1** canoe never
bore punt *id phr* (Guyn) [*AF/IF*] That is an
absurd excuse/explanation, etc. [Because a
(wooden) canoe can never punch a hole in (the
hull of) a PUNT.]

ca·nop *n* (Baha, TkCa) = etym note at See
CANEP

cant; cant over *vb (phr)* (Tbgo, Trin) [*IF*] To
overturn; to turn or bend over (in both *tr* and
intr senses). **a.** *Piece of the road break on the left
side; the tractor cant in a deep drain there.*—Tbgo
(CR, 79.04.03) **b.** *The accused fell; he was canting
down on the sand.*—Tbgo (CR, 75.05.05) **c.** *He
cant over a whole bucket of paint on the ground.*—

(Trin) [Cp *OED cant* v² 2. b. 'to turn over completely; turn upside down' (+ latest cit 1855); 5. intr 'to turn over'; often '*to cant over*']

can'[t] [kya:n(t)~ka:n(t)]] /3'1/ *neg vb* (CarA) [*AF/IF*] **1.** [Often contrasts with *can* [kyan] only by vowel length, sometimes with added differentiation of high-falling pitch] Cannot. □ Many guess-variant spellings occur. See CYAN. **2.** PHRASES **2.1 can'[t] done!** *id phr* [*AF*] **(i)** (CarA) What an excess of, a great amount of (whatever the subject is)! **a.** *Man, Carnival time, sport can'[t] done!* (*i.e. ... such a lot of fun!*)—(Trin) **b.** *In those days they were living in Murray Street—and motor car and dress can'[t] done, you know!* (*i.e. ... they lived such a life of cars and dressing!*)—(Guyn) **(ii)** (Jmca) [By extension, as adverbial intensifier after an adj] So very; exceedingly. *Him* [*s*]*tupid can'[t] done!* (*i.e. He's exceedingly stupid!*)—(Jmca) **3. can't have pins with (sb)** *vb phr* (Bdos) Cannot cope with (sb); cannot keep up with (sb). *And the Mighty Gabby who is not only the King of Calypso ... but now as an actor, you can't have pins with him.*—NaT (77.06.19, p.2)

can·ton·nier (can·ton·neer) ['kyantʌne·r] *n* (Bdos) An hourly paid labourer who cleans roadsides and gutters. [Fr *cantonnier* 'road-mender']

ca·pi·tain-bois *n* (Gren) See KAPITENN-BWA

ca·pra [ka'pra:] *n* (Trin) [Indic] **1.** ‖DHOTI (Guyn, Trin) **2.** Any length of cloth used as a garment by EAST INDIANS (such as a man's turban or a woman's loose skirt wrapped through the legs for field labour). [Bhoj < Hin *kapṛaa* 'an unstitched piece of cloth']

Cap·tain *n* (Guyn) ‖ *headman*, *Touchau* (Guyn) The Amerindian who is elected head of his village to serve a four-year term, being, during that period, paid a monthly salary by the Guyana Government to wh he is responsible for maintaining law and order and all community organization; a village headman. □ Specific to Local Government Administration in the INTERIOR of Guyn. Cp TOUCHAU.

ca·rai·la (ca·ril·la, co·re·il·li, ka·rai·la) ['kʌraɪla] *n* (Guyn, StVn, Trin) ‖ *coolie-pawpaw* (Gren) The larger variety of CERASEE cultivated esp in Indic communities for the use of the fruit as a vegetable and also as a folk medicine; *Momordica balsamina* or *M. charantia* (*Cucurbitaceae*). [Bhoj < Hin *karelaa* 'bitter gourd', *karailii*, 'small bitter gourd'] □ A number of other variant spellings are found: *carailla/-li, cari(l)lee, caryla, corei(l)lee.*

ca·ram·bo·la* /1'121/ *n* (Belz, Gren, Guyn, Jmca, StVn, Trin) ‖ *coolie-tamarind* (Gren, Trin) ‖ *five-finger* (Guyn, Mrat, Trin) A 'translucent yellow, five-winged fruit (and so star-shaped when cut across)' (*PTT*:77) about 4 ins long, juicy and very acid, borne in small clusters on a small flowering tree; the fruit is widely used

for making jams and jellies or dried and eaten as a sweet; *Averrhoa carambola* (*Oxalidaceae*).

ca·rat ['kara·t] *n* (Trin) [Indic] A tall palm, with particularly large, fan-shaped leaves, about 8 ft across, and deeply divided (like fingers); the leaves make an excellent thatch; *Sabal glaucescens* (*Palmae*). □ Hence (*Trin*) **carat house, carat hut, carat leaf, carat palm, carat roof.**

card-cut·ter *n* (Guyn) A hired fortune-teller who uses one or two decks of cards to tell the future of and advise sb in trouble [Cp Irish (*JESI:231*) *card-cutter* 'a fortune teller by card tricks ... pretty common in Limerick ... but regarded as disreputable']

CARDI (C·A·R·D·I·) ['kardi] *abbr* (CarA) Caribbean Agricultural Research and Development Institute (1975–). □ Based in *Trin.*

care *vb tr* (CarA) **1.** To take good care of (sth); to look after or tend (a sick person) PHRASE **1.1 care yourself!** *imper refl* (CarA) [Parting formula] Be careful of your own well-being! Be good to yourself. **2.** ‖ *mind*² 1. (CarA) [*IF*] To care for, bring up, raise (children, esp when not your own). *When the mother died, the aunt cared them.*—(Guyn) [*OED care* v 6. tr c. 'to take care of, guard, preserve with care' (dial) + cit 1881 'If you care your things ... it is surprising how long they may be made to serve'] □ *Care* has become standard CE usage fully replacing IAE vb phrs *care for*, *take care of*.

ca·reen·age ['kari·neʒ] /1'21/ *n* (Bdos) ‖ CARENAGE (Gren, etc) *The Careenage is essentially a port for small ships and can only accommodate vessels with a draft of under 20 ft... The Careenage is basically used for schooners and steel-hulled vessels transporting fruit and general cargo from other West Indian ports to Barbados.*—AdN (77.10.05, p.3) [< Fr *carénage* [See next]. *OED careenage* b. 'a careening place' + Note 'In sense b. the Fr *carénage* is much used in the W Indies']

ca·re·nage ['karena·ʒ] /1'12/ *n* (Gren, Trin, USVI) ‖ *careenage* (Bdos) **1.** [Hist] An inner harbour of shallow draft where small vessels, esp schooners, were careened (turned on their sides) for repairs. **2.** The wharf-side of a shallow inner harbour where fish and inter-island GROUND-PROVISIONS are sold. *Police picked up the third alien on the Carenage, St George's, as he was about to board a schooner for the island ward of Carriacou*—AdN (71.12.06, p.10) [< Fr *carénage* 'careening place, docking']

ca·re·ta ['karɛta] *n* (USVI) ‖ AGAVE (CarA) [Perh from a Sp variant of ‖ *coratoe*. See note there]

ca·rey ['keri] *n* (Grns, USVI) ‖ HAWKSBILL (TURTLE) (CarA)

car·goo (car·gou) *adj* (Trin) See KAGOU

Car·ib *adj, n* (CarA) **1.** [Hist] (Of or belonging to) any member of an ethnic group of warlike Amerindian people native to the northwestern regions of South America, including the Guyanas, and the East Caribbean islands esp *Trin, StVn, Dmca*; (also of) their language. [Sp *Caribe* < Arawak *karifidu* 'Carib' (*EILCA:57*) < Carib *karinha* 'person' (*GLDG:37, E.T. Peasgood*). Cp also *BDFC:61 Caraibe* 'calinago'. Cp *JCC:147* 'The admiral [Columbus] says further that in the islands wh he had passed they were in great terror of the Carib; in some islands they call it 'Caniba' but in Española 'Carib'.' See also GARIFUNA] **2.** (Dmca) (Of or belonging to) any of the mixed Creole descendants of ISLAND CARIBS inhabiting the central east coast of Dominica and speaking French Creole. **3.** (Belz) (Of or belonging to) any of the BLACK CARIBS [*Derog*] or GARIFUNA; (also of) their language. *Taylor ... met a Black Carib School teacher who spoke Carib at home, Spanish and Mopan in the village and taught in English and Maya at school*—KMRFBC:59

ca·ri·ba ['kari·ba] *n* (Jmca, Trin) ‖SHIRTJACK-SUIT (Bdos, Guyn)

Ca·ri·ban *adj, n* (Belonging to) the ethnic group of peoples and languages once found in the E Caribbean islands, along the southern mainland perimeter of the Caribbean Sea, and in the northwestern area of South America (but now only residually in the E Caribbean islands), the remaining peoples/languages in Guyana being Akawaio, Arekuna, Makushi, Patamuna, Carib and Wai-wai.

Ca·rib·be·an[1] ['karıbıan] /1'211 ~ 112'1/ *adj* **1.** Of or belonging to the chain of islands from Trinidad to Cuba, but often also taken to include the South and Central American rimlands from Guyana to Belize. **2.** [In broad cultural or economic senses] West Indian (embracing essentially the Anglophone territories of the area, including The Bahamas). **3.** [Loosely in ref to all peoples of the area] ANTILLEAN. [Developed from Sp *Islas de los Caribes* wh came into 16c Eng as 'Isles of the Caribbees' (pronunc /112'/) in ref to the CARIB people inhabiting The Eastern islands of the archipelapo; thence by shift, 'The Caribbees' referred to the islands, then to the whole area. In later Eng the SE adj suff *-ean* replaced *-ees*, on the analogy of *European* with a similar pitch-coutour /112'/ wh is, however, less normal than /12'11/ or /1'211/ as in other SE naming adjs—American, Bahamian, Canadian, etc]

Ca·rib·be·an[2] *n* **1.** The Caribbean; the West Indian islands as a geographical unit. **2.** The Caribbean Sea. **3.** *n pl* The peoples of the area as a cultural entity. *Some twenty members of the staff dressed up in costumes depicting Africans Arabians, Chinese and Caribbeans.*—Zodiac Mag, Dec. 1971 [By functional adj > n shift of CARIBBEAN[1]]

Ca·rib·be·an Com·mon Mar·ket *n phr* (CarA) A trading arrangement among the 12 member-states of CARIFTA, established by the Treaty of Chaguaramas, Trinidad (1973), for complementary industrial programming within the Association and common negotiating positions in external trading.

Ca·rib·be·an Com·mu·ni·ty *n phr* (CarA) ‖*CARICOM* (CarA) A legal international grouping, first established by the GEORGETOWN ACCORD (1973) and later expanded (1974) to include the 12 member-states of the CARIBBEAN COMMON MARKET and The Bahamas, for the purpose of effecting functional cooperation in all essential fields of national economic development and coordination of foreign policies. □ See TREATY OF CHAGUARAMAS.

Ca·rib·be·an·iza·tion (-i.sa-) *n* (CarA) The act or process of CARIBBEANIZING. *Explaining the concept of Caribbeanisation, he said that ... it was a systematic policy of working and planning towards the goal of locally directing and controlling the Caribbean tourism industry.*—AdN (79.06.18, p.3)

Ca·rib·be·an·ize (-ise) *vb* (CarA) To make sth (such as an institution, a festival, etc) markedly CARIBBEAN in staffing, ownership, composition or appearance. *And I would have liked to have seen the Corporation better set up ... having the impetus to acquire banking institutions so as to 'Caribbeanise' them, to acquire Insurance Companies to 'Caribbeanise' them, to acquire the telegraphic media ... in order to 'Caribbeanise' them.*—Bdos (Hd, 74.01.29, p.3114)

Carib Set·tle·ment Day *n phr* (Belz) ‖GARIFUNA SETTLEMENT DAY (Belz)

Ca·rib wood *n phr* (Dmca) See BWA KWAIB.

CARICOM ['karikɒm] /1'12/ *abbr* (CarA) CARIBBEAN COMMUNITY (1974-).

CARIFESTA ['karifɛsta] /1'122/ *abbr* (CarA) Caribbean Festival of Creative Arts (inaugurated in Guyana, 1972).

CARIFTA ['karıfta] /1'21/ *abbr* (CarA) Caribbean Free Trade Association, consisting, by agreement of Heads of Government (1965), of Antigua, Barbados, and Guyana and expanded (1968) to include Dominica, Grenada, Jamaica, Montserrat, St Kitts-Nevis-Anguilla, St Lucia, St Vincent, Trinidad & Tobago, and (1971) Belize, all members being required to reduce the barriers to free trade within the area of the Assioation and to operate a common tariff on goods from outside the area; (hence also often) Caribbean Free Trade Area.

ca·ril·la *n* **1.** (Also **carilli**) (Trin) See CARAILA **2.** (Gren) ‖CERASEE (Baha, etc)

ca·ri·so ['kariso] /1'21/ n (Dmca, Gren, Trin) [*Obs*] ‖ CALYPSO (CarA) *During pre-Carnival peri-ods when the chantwells rehearsed, the people in the tenements joined in the Kalinda songs and sang the chorus. It was in these back-yards that the earliest carisoes were sung*—Jfi.3.3, p.193 [< Efik-Ibibio *ka iso* + intrusive /r/, this word later becoming CALYPSO] □ See also CARUSO.

ca·rite* ['kari·t] n (Trin) ‖ *Spanish mackerel* (Angu, Antg, Bdos, Gren, Guyn) A fish of 4 to 6 lbs, dark blue above with oval orange-yellow spots irregularly marking its back and sides, a silvery belly and very few scales; it is very pop-ular for its high food value; *Scomberomorus mac-ulatus (Scombridae). Carite makes the biggest contribution to the annual production of fish in Trinidad and Tobago.*—Trin (Ms) [*TDV* Venz Sp *carite* 1. 'Sea fish with a long body and wide mouth', etc (trans). *SDGA* identifies *carite* as Carib name of a fierce Venz river fish.]

Car·ni·val [ka(r)nəval] /1'12/ n (ECar) The massive, nationally organized festival of com-petitive, costumed street-dancing, CALYPSO sing-ing, etc held usu in the last four days before Ash Wednesday, but shifted in some territories (ex Antigua, St Kitts, St Vincent) to other festive times of the year. [SE *carnival*, but more likely (*Trin*) < Fr *carnaval* (note th pronunc above), wh is < Ital *carnevale* with metathesis, < Lat *carnem levare* 'remove the meat'. *OED* notes that the derivation from *carne vale* 'farewell to the meat' is erron pop etym] □ 1. Normally used as a proper noun without article (cp 'Christmas') It was *like Carnival, for Carnival, during Car-nival*, etc. Hence also attrib use in phrs such as *Carnival Band, Carnival Day, Carnival Monday, Carnival season, Carnival Sunday Night, Carnival time*, etc See also DIMANCHE GRAS, J'OUVERT, MAS.

Car·ni·val Band n phr (ECar) See BAND[1] 2.

Car·ni·val Mon·day n phr (Antg, Brbu) ‖ AU-GUST BANK HOLDAY (CarA)

Car·ni·val Queen n phr (ECar) ‖ *Queen of the Bands* (Tbgo, Trin) The young lady judged to be in the most outstanding costume as QUEEN of a parading CARNIVAL BAND in the competition organized for that purpose.

car·pen·ter-boss n (Guyn) A house-builder who employs a team to work with him to build a house.

car·pen·ter-grass n (Jmca) ‖ GARDEN-BALSAM (Bdos, etc)

car·pet-dai·sy* n (Bdos) ‖ *churchyard-grass* (Mrat) ‖ *creeping ox-eye* (Jmca) ‖ *daisy* (Guyn) ‖ *honey-bee flower* (Bdos) ‖ *marigold* (Jmca, TkCa) ‖ *Mary-Gold* (Jmca) ‖ *zèb-a-fanm* 2. (Dmca) A creeping, spreading herb that 'roots at each node on the stem' (*HCWP:32*) so cov-ering the ground, thriving in poor roadside or

seaside soil; it has small, light green, lobed leaves and bright yellow flowers about 3/4 inch in diameter borne singly at the end of each stem; *Wedelia trilobata (Compositae-Asteraceae). Car-pet-daisy is dangerous for cattle and stock as it makes the females lose their babies.*—Bdos (Ms) [*Carpet*, from its ground covering habit + *daisy* from resemblance to IAE *daisy*]

Car·ri·a·cou·an ['kariakuən] /1'1121/; **Car-·ri.a.cou.ni.an** ['kariakuniən] /1'11211/ adj, n (A person or thing) native or belonging to Car-riacou, an island North East of Grenada. □ *Car-riacouian, Carriacounian* are occasional al-ternatives, the latter less common.

car·ri·on-crow* /1'112/ n (Guyn, Jmca) ‖ *cor-beau* (Gren, Trin) ‖ *crow* (Baha, Guyn) ‖ *John Crow* (Belz, Jmca) A vulture about 24 ins long, with an almost naked grey (some species red) head and neck and dull black body plumage; it feeds on rotting animal carcasses (hence its name); *Coragyps atratus (Cathartidae).* □ The European *carrion-crow* is quite a different bird, *Corvus corone (Corvidae).*

car·ri·on-crow bush n phr (Guyn) ‖ CHRIST-MAS-CANDLE (Bdos) [Perh by folk etym < *BAED* Arawak *karakararo* 'a slender plant [bearing long ... flowers] that inhabits damp swampy re-gions'—a description that fits this plant. How-ever, this name may also be due to the unpleasant smell of the flower; it is not used for interior decoration, but the juice of the leaves is used as a cure for skin infections. Cp Arawak *kara* 'juicy', *rero* 'broad-leaved grass']

car·ri·on-crow man n phr (Guyn) [*AF—Derog*] ‖ *duppy-agent* (Bdos) A person who can-vasses the business for an undertaker when sb dies.

car·ry vb tr (CarA) 1. To take, guide, escort (sb); to lead, drive (animals). **a.** *On the morning of the last election from 6 o'clock I was out carrying my wife and myself to vote at Oistin, carrying the lady two houses away from me to vote at Little Hopewell, carrying my maid to vote at St Chris-topher.*—Bdos (Hd, 76.02.03, p.5919) **b.** *The neighbours hated them because they had carried two cows and some goats to the police pound.*—Guyn (Ms) 2. To cause to go (esp in phr CARRY TO COURT). **a.** *The argument came to blows and they carried one another to court.*—(Mrat) **b.** *If you eat pawpaw with the seeds it will carry you to the toilet a lot.*—(Tbgo) [Prob from IrE. Cp *JESI:232* IrE *carry* 'to lead or drive': ... 'carry the horse to the forge' ... 'I will carry my family this year to Youghal'. Also *OED carry* v 5. 'to conduct, escort, lead, 'take' (a person) with one, without ref to the mode of conduct.... Now *arch* or *dial*'] □ Cp also BRING 3. **3.** *PHRASES* **3.1 carry away** vb phr (CarA) [*IF*] **(i)** To steal (sth, money, etc). *If you go to the plantation and say that they have to vest this land in the Crown, ... the newspapers will stir up a hornet's nest and say you want to carry away the land from the people.*—

Bdos (Hd, 74.06.21, p.3468) **(ii)** [Esp in ref to evil spirits] To cause (a person) to disappear mysteriously. *Few Caymanians would carry rum with them at night for fear of attracting one of these malicious people, who it seems really have 'carried people away'.*—FDI:22 **3.2 carry down (sb)** *vb phr* **(i)** (CarA) [*IF*] To arrest and take (sb) to the police station; to take (sb) to a mental hospital by force. *He run in the house and hide but the mother call the police to carry him do[w]ng.*—(StVn) **(ii)** (Jmca) [*AF*] To rob, cheat, swindle (sb). *But if he sees me four times for the day, I have to give him money.... I love this guy to the bottom of my heart, but still, not because of love I am going to make a man carry me down.*—WeS (74.08.02, p.8) [*IF*] **(iii)** (Baha) [*IF*] To cause (sb) to contract a crippling sickness or to die by OBEAH. *She would remove the harm from a client if he or she had an 'evil-fix', but although she knew how to harm (or 'carry-down', in Obeah terminology) someone, she never did it.*—MTTBT:83 **3.3 carry (sb/sth) (and) go** *vb phr* (Guyn, StVn) [*AF*] To take (sb) somewhere; to take (sth) away. **a.** *She carry him go country las[t] week.*—(StVn) **b.** *Bertram! You see dis plate you leave here? Come carry it and go!*—(Guyn) [Prob calque from typical W Afr serial vbs] **3.4 carry a (girl/lady) out** *vb phr* (CarA) [*IF*] To take a (girl/lady) out on a social engagement; to 'date' (a girl). *Well he come and see me and like me and he start to carry me out, you see.*—(Guyn—old woman) **3.5 carry the same head** *vb phr* (Mrat) [*IF*] ‖ CAN SHAKE HANDS *vb phr* (CarA See HAND[1] Phr 4.3 **3.6 carry yourself (da[t] side)!** *excl vb phr* (Antg, Guyn) [*AF*] ‖ MOVE YOURSELF! (Bdos, etc) *'Gwan!' she shouted 'Carry yourself an' put grass befo'e the cow!'*—SSOS:119 [Cp Yoruba *ba ara ẹ da sọ hun! (take your body turn yonder)* 'Be off with you!'] **3.7 carry your arse/ tail** *vb phr* (Guyn) [*AF—Vul*] ‖ MOVE YOURSELF (Bdos, etc) *She can carry she tail waay she sleep out las' night.*—SSOS:144

carry-go-bring-come ['kyari-gʌ-briŋ-kʌm] /1'1122/ *n* (Jmca, StVn) [*AF—Derog*] ‖ BRING-AND-CARRY (StVn)

car·toon [kyartu:n ~ kyartʌn] *n* (Bdos, BrVi, Guyn) [*X*] Carton. *For Sale: 14 Cartoons Gestetner Paper, 12 metal Desk Pedestals...*—AdN (Ad, 73.04.25, p.4) □ A catachresis. Spelling affected by pronunc. *Cartoon, carton,* are distinct in IAE.

cart-road *n* (Bdos) ‖ *feeder-road* (Guyn) ‖ *interval* (Bdos, Jmca) ‖ *trace* (Trin) A narrow, unsurfaced roadway leading out from the backlands of a plantation to permit the carting of produce or supplies to or from the highway.

ca·ru·so [kɛɾʌso] /1'12/ *n* (USVI) A teasing song on topical events and its associated music and (formerly) street-dancing, performed during festive seasons, esp Christmas/New Year. [See etym of CALYPSO of wh this is a related form]

car·y·la *n* (Guyn) See CARAILA

ca·sa·reep (cas·reep, cas·sa·reep) ['kazrip /-rip ~ kasrip] *n* (CarA) A thick, dark-brown liquid resembling molasses, produced by boiling down the juice squeezed from grated BITTER-CASSAVA to remove poison, and used to make and preserve PEPPER-POT 1. *Cassareep ... reduces all flesh to one flavour, its own, and ... has antiseptic qualities wh keep meat boiled in it good for a long time. The result is ... the far-famed pepper-pot, which, first made by the Indians, all settlers in the West Indies have now learned to make and like.*—IAIG:260 [Orig not quite clear though the word is credited as *Guyn* Amerindian (the 'Indians' in the cit above). Cp HIN:136 (ref d. 1825) *casiripe* 'a preservative made from the juice of the cassava, boiled and flavoured with red pepper'. Also note *J.P. Bennett (Ms, 1986)*: 'The word casareep derived from the Arawak word *Kashiripo*. It is the juice of the cassava tubers ... boiled to the consistency of molasses.... Arawak people thought it assumed the colour of a potato called *kashiri* so it was referred to as *kashiripo'*]

cas·cade (cas·cate) [kaske·d/t] *vb intr* **1.** (Baha) To vomit. *Please excuse Archibald from school last week he was sick and cascading.*—Baha (Ms, 1978) [Cp *OED cascade* v 1. c. Vul 'to vomit'. *Obs* + cits 1771–1878. Also *W1* (1847) *cascade* v 1. 'to vomit; to puke' (+ Note) *Colloq* or Vul in Amer, Provincial in Eng. Also *W3* (1961) lists as vb 2. dial 'vomit'] □ Evid more often pronounced /-t/ but written 'cascade' in *Baha*. **2.** (Jmca) [Of women] To have a heavy menstrual flow.

cas·ca·du (cas·ca·doo) /1'12/; **cas.ca.du.ra** / 1'121/ ['kaskadu(ra)] *n* **1.*** (Trin) ‖ *hassar, toe-nail fish* (Guyn) A river-fish about 6 ins long with dark, one-inch, curved interlocking scales like armour-plating wh are only removed after boiling; its creamy-white flesh is a highly prized delicacy; *Callichthys littoralis (Callichthyidae)*. *Legend has it that those who eat the cascadura must return to end their days in Trinidad.*—Trin (Ms) [Sp *cascara* 'shell' + *dura* 'hard'] □ The full form *cascadura* is less common. **2.** (StVn) ‖ CORN-ROW(s) (CarA) [Prob from a supposed resemblance to the rows of the fish's scales]

cas·cate *vb intr* (Baha) See CASCADE

ca·sha(w) (ka·sha) ['kaša ~ 'kyašʌ] *n* (Angu, Jmca, Nevs, StKt, ViIs) **1.*** (Name applied to more than one species of) a very thorny, evergreen shrub that can exceed 8 ft in height; it bears fragrant, little, round, yellow flowers and (in some varieties) pods, and grows wild, often abundantly, in arid, uncultivated land; it may be either of the following two: **(i)*** ‖ *acacia* (TkCa, Trin) ‖ *cashi(e), coshi(e)* (StVn) ‖ *cassie, cossy* (Antg, Jmca) ‖ *cusha* (Angu, Mrat) ‖ *pika (tree)* (Gren, Trin) ‖ *sweet-briar* (Bdos) *Acacia farnesiana* or *Vachelha farnesiana (Leguminosae-Mimosaceae)* **(ii)*** ‖ *cashaw* (Angu, Jmca) ‖ *mesquit tree* (Trin) *Prosopis chiliensis* or *P. juliflora (Leguminosae-Mimosaceae)*. [Prob a coincidence or convergence of Carib and Afr terms,

further helped by BrE botanical name *acacia*.
Cp *BDFC:24* Carib *cachi* 'arbres avortés ...
parce que la terre ne vaut rien' (trees stunted ...
because the soil is worthless); also *DAFL* Twi
kasɛ 'thorn'; also *ZAGL* Gã *kose; kuse* 'bush'
(land)**] 2.** [*AF*] ‖*cusha* (Angu, Mrat) ‖*pika*
(Gren, Trin) ‖*pimpler* (Bdos, Guyn) [By ex-
tension] A thorn (on any kind of plant or tree,
though particularly those in sense 1.).

ca·shee (co·shi(e)) *n* (StVn) See CASHI(E)

ca·shew* *n* (CarA) **1.** ‖*cashew-apple* (Jmca,
Mrat) ‖*cashew-cherry* (Mrat) ‖*cashew-nut*
(Antg, Brbu) ‖*cherry* 2. (Angu, BrVi, Mrat,
Nevs, StKt) ‖*cherry-nut* (Angu, BrVi, StKt)
‖*cushew, kushu* (Antg, Bdos, Gren, StVn,
Tbgo) ‖*pomme* (Dmca, StLu) ‖*pomme-noire*
(StLu) A small, pear-shaped, yellow fruit about
2 ins long carrying a brown, crescent- shaped
nut on the outside; the juicy flesh of the fruit is
of a tangy taste; the fruit is borne on a medium-
sized tree, *Anacardium occidentale* (*Anacardiaceae*). *The so-called 'fruit' is the fleshy
flower stalk ... juicy, somewhat astringent.... At
the end of this edible flower-stalk is seated the
curiously shaped true fruit, the kernels of which
are known as Cashew Nuts.*—PTT:66 **[** < Tupi
acaju. Cp also *BDFC:6* Island Carib *iacaicachi*
'acajou rouge, arbre'] **2.** (Guyn) ‖MALACCA-
APPLE/-PEAR (Antg, Guyn)

ca·shew-apple/-cher·ry/-nut *n* See
CASHEW 1. (CarA)

ca·shi(e) (ca·shee, co·shi(e)) [kaši ~ kɒši] *n*
(StVn) ‖CASHA 1. **(i)** (Angu, etc) [This form may
refl more Carib than other infl. See note at
CASHA] □ The form *coshi(e)* is prob owing to
false refinement.

ca·shi·man (ca.shi.ment) *n* (Dmca, StLu)
See KACHIMAN

ca·si·ri (cas·si·ri) ['kasi·ri] /1 2 2/ *n* (Guyn) An
Amerindian drink 'made of boiled cassava meal
with a dash of boiled cassava juice and coloured
with a potato named *kashiri* and left to ferment'—
J.P. Bennett (Ms, *1986*). **[** < *BAED* Arawak
kashiri 'a slender purple potato, edible but
mostly used as a colouring agent'. However,
evidently the *kashiri* potato was originally the
main ingredient and hence the name of the drink.
Cp *IAIG:264*: 'A much pleasanter drink ...
casiri, is made of sweet-potatoes and sugar-cane.
A little cassava is sometimes added. Generally
... it is prepared simply by boiling the ingredients
and allowing them to ferment. It has a pretty
pink colour, due to the sweet- potatoes; and
when well made it tastes not unlike thin claret.'
Cp also *FTCC:142* Carib *kitcire* 'cassava']

cas·sa·da *n* (CarA) [*Obs*] See CASSAVA [Note
ADMY Yoruba *kasada* 'baked, grated cassava'.
However, this pronunc may also be partly due
to the absence of /v/ in some Afr langs, is still
heard among very old rural speakers, and is

found in some early accounts. Ex *'He cassada
ent good ... so waterish'—CNH:9*]

cas·sa·va *n* (CarA) **1.*** ‖*cassada* (CarA) [*Obs*]
‖*cassava-stick* (Guyn) ‖*manioc* (ECar) A long,
hard-fleshed, root-vegetable with a stiff leathery
skin and white inside; it is of two distinct kinds:
SWEET CASSAVA (*Manihot dulcis*), and BITTER CAS-
SAVA (*Manihot esculenta* or *utilissima* (*Euphorbiaceae*). [See cit]. *Two kinds are usually
recognised, Sweet Cassava usually eaten as a vegetable, boiled or roasted, and Bitter Cassava
from which starch is extracted and Cassava Farine prepared. 'The roots contain a glucoside
poison ... but this is dissipated when thoroughly
roasted. The so-called 'sweet cassava' contains
this poison principally in the outer rind, while
in the so-called 'bitter cassava' it is more evenly
distributed through the root' Kew Bull., XII,
1936. From Bitter Cassava the following products are prepared: Cassava farine ...; Cassareep
...; Cassava starch ...; Tapioca ...*—\PTT:217–8
[Perh via Arawakan through Sp and Pg. Cp
Journal of Christopher Columbus: 'Wednesday,
December 26th (*1492*): The king ... gave [the
admiral] a repast ... and some of their bread
which they call 'caçabi'—*JJCC:125*. Cp Sp variants *casabe, cazaba* 'cassava'] **2.** PHRASE **2.1 a
stick of cassava** *n phr* (Guyn) ‖*cassava-stick*
(Guyn) A cassava (in ref to the roughly stick-like
shape and length of the roots of some varieties wh
can weigh several pounds). □ ‖*Manioc* (ECar) is
sometimes used in this particular sense in *Dmca,
Gren*.

cas·sa·va-bake *n* (Bdos) [*Obs*] ‖CASSAVA-
BREAD (CarA) *There were big estate tubs filled with
black strap or sweet liquor; rumbullion or kill-devil
as rum was called in those days; salted pork, bread,
pone and cassava bakes known as 'hats' because of
their shape.*—SCO:4

cas·sa·va-bread *n* (CarA) ‖*bam-bam*[2] (Crcu,
Gren, StVn) ‖*bambula* (Antg) ‖*bammy* (Jmca)
‖*bang-bang* (USVI) ‖*cassava-bake* (Bdos)
‖*choky banjo* (Angu) A dry, flat, round, unleavened, and biscuit- like 'cake' made from the
grated meal or CASSAVA-FLOUR of the BITTER
CASSAVA and prepared in a number of ways: (i)
a thin, brittle, sun-dried mixture from a mild
salt-and-water paste, 12 to 18 ins in diameter
(*Guyn*); (ii) a smaller kind, from a thicker, more
cake-like mixture baked brown over fire (*Jmca*);
(iii) a sweetened kind with grated coconut, sugar,
and raisins and baked in a pan (*Baha*), etc.
*Cassava Bread, a staple food for both Indians
and Africans for centuries, has recently achieved
gourmet status as a Virgin Islands delicacy when
toasted and served with butter, cheese, honey,
caviar, or 'as is'. The 'bread' is actually a large
18 inch, thin, slightly limp sheet 'baked' on an iron
over charcoal. / If toasted or kept dry, Cassava
Bread will outlast hardtack.*—JNHJJ:51 □ See
also CASSAVA-CAKE (*Belz*).

cas·sa·va-cake *n* (Belz, Guyn) ‖ *quinch, sugar-cassava* (Guyn) A sweet variety of CAS-SAVA-BREAD made with sugar, milk, grated co-conut and baked in a pan, *OR* with the sweet layer sandwiched in between dryer layers of cassava. □ See also BAM-BAM².

cas·sa·va-coo-coo *n* (Tbgo) A sticky dish (see COU-COU) made from SWEET CASSAVA boiled and pounded in a mortar. *To provide the adequate attitude in the dead ones 'spirit food' (cassava coo-coo and goat head soup) is served to the spirits.*—EFSLC:32

cas·sa·va-fa·rine *n* (Dmca) ‖ FARINE (Angu, etc) *The only cash products, arrowroot and cassava farine, had to be carried overland to Roseau.*—HTDS:78

cassava-flour *n* (CarA) The dried meal of the grated BITTER CASSAVA from wh the poisonous juice has been extracted by squeezing, used to make CASSAVA-BREAD. *Afterwards Mother will get out the osnaburg wringing-cloths. We will put the grated cassava in these. Then two of us to each cloth, we will wring and squeeze and pulp the juice through the cloth into the bowl. Tomorrow the juice will be on the barbecue to be dried into starch, while the cassava will be dried and pounded in the mortar to make the cassava flour for our bammie cakes.*—RND:87

cas·sa·va-pone *n* (Bdos, Guyn) ‖ *pone* 2. (Bdos, Guyn, Trin) A baked pudding made of a mixture of grated cassava, grated coconut, a few currants, butter, sugar, and spices, served (often sold) in solid slices.

cas·sa·va-squeez·er *n* (CarA) ‖ MATAPEE (Guyn)

cas·sa·va-starch *n* (CarA) A starch obtained by drying in the sun the poisonous juice of the grated BITTER-CASSAVA. □ See cit at CASSAVA-FLOUR.

cas·sa·va-stick *n* (Guyn) ‖ STICK OF CASSAVA (CarA) See CASSAVA Phr 2.1 [< *DAFL* Twi *kɔtɔ baŋkyé* 'stick cassava']

cas·sa·va-wa·ter *n* (Angu, Dmca, Guyn, StLu) A poisonous water left after being used to facilitate the squeezing of juice from grated BITTER-CASSAVA, sometimes used to poison animals.

cass-cass (kas-kas) ['kas-kas] *adj* (Guyn) [*AF-Derog*] [Of things] Disreputable looking; of low grade; [of persons] of untidy appearance suggesting low character or status. **a.** *A don'[t] like dis dress. It lookin[g] too cass-cass.*—(Guyn) **b.** *The woman he married, my dear, can't know no better because she come from a cass-cass family in Albuoystown.*—(Guyn) [Cp *DAFL* Twi *kasãkasã* 'very thin, lean'; *akasakasa* 'dispute, quarrel'; also *ADMY* Yoruba *kaṣa-kaṣa* 'nonsense';

ADHL Hausa *kaskas-* (stem indicating) 'of low status']

cas·si·a *n* (Bdos) ‖ APPLE-BLOSSOM CASSIA (Bdos, etc)

cas·sie (cas·see, cos·sy) ['k(y)asi] *n* (Antg, Jmca) ‖ CASHA 1. (i) (Angu, etc)

cas·si·ri *n* (Guyn) See CASIRI

cast-eye(s) ['kya·s(t)-aɪ(z)] *n* (Belz, Jmca, Mrat, StVn) ‖ *cokey-eye* (Gren, Tbgo, Trin) A squint; a cock-eye or cock-eyes; (SE) cast in the eye. *Dear Doctor, My little son has cast eyes. What can I do? / Dear Mother, Squint, (cast eye), may be organic or functional.*—ReP (80.03.30, p.4, Your Doctor) [Cp *OED* cast sb 33. cast of the eye 'a slight squint' + latest cit 1825. However *COD8* lists cast in the eye]

cast-net ['kya·s-nɛt] *n* (CarA) **1.** ‖ *seine* (Guyn ‖ *sprat-net* (Angu, Belz, CayI, Jmca, Nevs, ViIs) ‖ *throw-net* (StLu) A fisherman's circular net about 12 ft in diameter, carrying lead weights around its circumference and controlled by a long cord at the centre by wh it is thrown over a shoal of fish in shallow water. **2.** (Angu, StVn) (SE) A seine; a large net some 200 yds long and about 9 ft deep on poles at each end, floats along its upper edge and weights on its bottom edge, fixed by one pole near the shore while the other is towed out seawards and around back to the shore to encircle fish. □ Both the terms *cast-net, seine* are loosely used, as above, but they can properly be distinguished as *cast-net* for sense 1., *seine* for sense 2. See also HOOP-SEINE.

cas·tor; **cas.tor-leaf/-nut** *n* (Angu, BrVi, CayI, Mrat) See CASTOR-OIL

cas·tor-oil **(bush/plant/tree)*** *n* (*phr*) (CarA) ‖ *castor* (Angu, CayI) ‖ *castor-leaf bush* (Antg, Nevs) ‖ *castor-nut* (Angu, BrVi, Mrat) ‖ *oil-leaf (tree)* (Bdos) ‖ *oil-nut (tree)* (Belz, Jmca, TkCa) A robust shrub that can reach 8 or 9 ft in height, with big, light-green, star-shaped leaves and bearing upright clusters of big, round, spiny, green pods that split into segments, the seeds yielding a powerful laxative oil (*castor oil*); the leaves are applied to relieve swellings, fevers, and headaches; *Ricinus communis* (*Euphorbiaceae*).

cast up *vb phr* (Bdos, Guyn, StLu) [*IF*] To vomit; to throw up. *But Betty says, 'When she belly hurt, she don' feel eatish,' and 'I cas' up and it make me cool.' She also 'yucks up!'.*—SCYT:113 [Cp *OED* cast v 25. 'to throw up from within; to vomit'.... + note: 'Now only of hawks or other birds (exc *dial*)'; also cast 83. b. *cast up* 'to vomit' (*Obs* or *dial*)]

cas·u·a·ri·na* (cas·u·ri·na) [kažəri·nʌ ~ kazʌri·nʌ] *n* (CarA) ‖ *beef-wood* 2. (Baha) ‖ *mile tree* (Bdos) ‖ *needle-and-thread* (Guyn) ‖ *whistling pine/willow* (Gren, Jmca, StVn,

Trin) ‖ *willow* (Jmca) 'A very quick-growing tree ... assuming a tall, narrow shape resembling a conifer, 18–36 m high, ending in a conical spire wh waves to and fro in the wind' (*GLPFB: 115*); it has abundant, long, needle-like, leafless branches; the tree is widely used as a wind-break, for soil-conservation, etc; *Casuarina equisetifolia* (*Casuarinaceae*). [A Malay loan-word via Australia, the tree being also called *Australian pine* in some botanical literature]

cat *n* PHRASES **1. before (the) cat (can) tick its ear** *adv phr* (Bdos) See BEFORE 1. **2. cat eat your dinner/supper** *id phr* (Gren, Guyn) ‖ CRAPAUD SMOKE YOUR PIPE (ECar)

ca·ta *n* (Gren) See CATTA

ca·ta·co(u) (**ka·ta·ku**) ['katakʊ /-u] *n* **1.** (Angu, Antg, Baha, USVI) ‖ CUTACOO (Jmca) **2.** (Angu) [? *Obs*] ‖ CROOK (StVn) [Prob < *DAFL* Twi *kotokú* 'bag, sack, pouch' + vowel opening /o > a/ or an orig dial variation] □ Cp CUTACOO of wh this may only be a variant pronunc.

cat-and-mouse; **cat-and-rat** *n* (Belz, BrVi, Dmca, Guyn, StLu, StVn) A children's game in wh one or more circles are formed in wh a player (the 'mouse/rat') may take refuge from another chasing him as the 'cat', a new 'mouse/ rat' being dislodged for chasing when the circle is entered.

cat·a·pla (USVI); **cat.a.palm** (Dmca, Gren) A poultice. [< SE *cataplasm* 'a poultice' with reduction of final consonant cluster]

cat-boil *n* (CarA) [*IF*] ‖ *bilni* 2. (Trin) ‖ *cattle-boil* (Antg, Gren, StVn, Tbgo, Trin) ‖ *cub-bitch-boil* (Jmca) ‖ *hog-sty(l)e* (Baha, Jmca) ‖ *pussy-boil* (Brbu) A stye believed to be a penalty for taking back something that was at first freely given. □ The term is almost restricted to styes in children, but also used among grown-ups either jocosely or because 'stye' is an unfamiliar word.

catch (**ketch**) [k(y)ač ~ k(y)ɛč] *vb* (CarA, exc. in cases specified) [Note: In very wide use, this word is often pronounced 'ketch' even in middle-level educated CE speech] **1.** *vb tr* [In general senses] To succeed in getting, apprehending, seizing, taking hold of, etc. *You notice how the disciples didn't catch his meaning and Jesus had to explain these parables to them.*—Bdos (B) **2.** *vb tr* To understand (sth or sb). **a.** *So nobody wants a car around after 5 years. Especially the manufacturers. You ketch the point?*—ExP (Ad, 73.05.20, p.17) **b.** *Well don't pay him all at once if you want him to come back—you catch me?* —(Guyn) **3.** *vb tr* [Of an event, rain, etc] To come upon or surprise (sb in some place or condition). *I remember that year, Tenth Independence catch me without a job.*—(Bdos) **4.** *vb tr* [*IF*] ‖ *catch to* (Belz, Jmca) To reach, arrive at (a place). *By the time we catch Goyave the radiator blow and we have to stop.*—(Gren) [Cp

OED *catch v* 10. 'to reach, attain, arrive at (a goal) (*Obs*)' + cit 1393] **5.** *vb tr* [*IF*] To be taken ill with, (SE) to come down with (sickness). *If those mosquitoes sting you you will catch fever and ague.*—(Guyn) [Cp *OED catch* v 33. 'to take or contract a disease'. However SE requires the article 'to catch *a* fever, *the* disease, etc'] **6.** *vb intr* [Of transferred plants or cuttings] To take root; to show signs of life and growth; [of seeds] to sprout. *I stuck some bougainvillea cuttings in the ground and watered them but they didn't catch.*—(Bdos) **7.** *vb intr* [By extension] [Of liquid substances, such as ice-cream, starch, etc] To jell; to get firm; to harden. [Cp *EDD catch* v 5. (Of water) 'to begin to freeze' (Wil, Som, Dev); 6. (Of wax) 'to congeal, grow thick' (Nhp, Glo, Wil, Som)] **8.** PHRASES **8.1 catch afire** [*X*]; **catch on fire** [*X*] *vb phr* To catch fire. [*OED catch* v 44. cites *catch a fire* as earlier form of *catch fire* + cit 1601. See also AFIRE] □ See also EYE[1] Phr 8 EYE CATCH FIRE FOR SB/STH. **8.2 catch a glad** *vb phr* (Trin) [*AF*] To feel an outburst of joy; to burst into a fit of laughter. **8.3 catch a skid** *vb phr* (StVn) To slide or skid suddenly. *He was racing along the side of the bank on the hill when his vehicle caught a skid and overturned.*—ViN (65.08.07, p.2) **8.4 catch a vaps** *vb phr* (Gren, Tbgo, Trin) [*AF*] To do (sth) upon a sudden urge; to be suddenly inspired (to do sth). *What happen? You ketch a vaps? Four o'clock in the mornin[g] and you get up to bake?* —(Trin) **8.5 catch back yourself** (Tbgo) [*AF/ IF*] See Phr 8.12 *I was standing near to the edge of the road. I don't know what happened. When I catch myself I was in the hospital lying ... I was unconscious for one month ... I catch myself myself the last week in September.*—Tbgo (CR, 77.02.28) **8.6 catch hell** *vb phr* (CarA) [*AF*] ‖ *catch (your) arse* (ECar) [*Vul*] ‖ *catch hell/ France* (Tbgo, Trin) ‖ *catch Old Harry* (Guyn) ‖ *catch your nennen/royal/skin/tail* (Trin and variously ECar) ‖ *live at your aunt/ nennen* (Bdos, Gren, Guyn, Trin) ‖ *meet/see/ smell hell* (Bdos, Guyn, Jmca) ‖ *see your days* (Guyn) To experience great difficulty in making ends meet, or in doing a task; to suffer great hardship. **a.** *In good seasons the crops grew green and flourished, but in droughts we caught hell, 'boiled bush' and drank 'hot water tea'.*—ACTT: 148 **b.** *If the young men are catching arse, young girls are possibly seeing it worse. Many pretend to be employed by doing smocking at a rate of 23 cents a piece ... and it is possible to complete only two at very most three in a day ... 69 cents.*—MaN (73.11.11, p.8) **c.** *And there is only one price—the expensive one—which many Barbadians are catching their royal to pay.*—AdN (73.04.29, p.3) [Cp *OED catch* v 30. 'to get, receive or incur (something injurious or unpleasant)' (*colloq*). See also next] □ The exp and ‖ ‖ are of high frequency, many of those given being mixed, blended or expanded in CE. **8.7 catch jail/the mad-house/trouble, (etc)** *vb phr* (CarA) [*IF*] To find yourself in jail, in the mad-house, in serious trouble, etc. [By extension of 8.7] □ Sometimes the obj becomes subj, ex: *jail, mad-house, (etc) will catch you*. Sometimes the name of the national institution is used instead, ex: *Glendairy catch him* (Bdos) i.e. Glendairy Prison. **8.8 catch the power/spirit** *vb phr* To be possessed by some supernatural force, shivering, falling to the ground, shouting, speaking in tongues, etc. **8.9 catch up** *vb phr* (i) [*IF*] To catch fire; to flare up; to burst into flame. **a.** *The child was playing with matches and the bed catch up and the house burn down.*—(Guyn) **b.** *Somebody threw a cigarette end on the dry grass and it caught up.*— (Bdos) (ii) [*AF*] [Parting formula, sometimes said by itself] (Until we) meet again! (I will) see you later! *Okay, I got to go now, so we'll catch up!*—(Trin) **8.9.1** [By extension] **catch up yourself** (Dmca) To recover from an illness or from any disaster (such as fire, loss of money, etc). (See also Phr 8.12) **8.10 catch your dead** *vb phr* (Guyn) [*X*] To catch your death. **8.11 catch your hand** *vb phr* (Bdos, Guyn, ViIs) [*IF*] ‖ **turn your hand** (Gren, Jmca, Vils) To earn some money to meet a minor personal obligation or desire. *Barbados is poor-poor but sweet enough. That's why I going back.... Soon as I catch my hand here.*—MBGB:14 [Cp *OED* catch v 38. 'to obtain, get (money, etc)...' Perh 'hand' 'hand'] **8.12 catch yourself** *vb phr* (CarA) [*IF*] (i) ‖ **catch back yourself** (Tbgo) ‖ **catch up yourself** (Dmca) To come to your senses; to regain your presence of mind; to become fully aware of what is happening or recover consciousness. (See also Phr 8.9.1). **a.** *And when you ketch yourself, is a whole rotten car you have on your hands.*—ExP (Ad, 73.05.20, p.1) **b.** *She was not quite sure why each moment she should catch herself thinking, longing. But the knowledge of what she thought so abhorred her consciousness that she always drove it to oblivion.*—PCOS:93 (ii) (Antg, Gren, Guyn, Tbgo, Trin) [Esp as a command] To know your place; to be careful of how you speak to a senior, superior, etc. *Catch yourself, boy! You know is your teacher you talkin[g] to?*—(Trin) **8.13 get catch/ketch** *vb phr* [*AF*] [Of an unmarried woman] To become pregnant. [Prob refers to being 'exposed' or 'deceived', but cp *EDD* catch 7. 'to be pregnant' + cits from Stf, War, Wor] **8.14 i[t']s you/we/ me (etc) to catch** *vb phr* (Trin) [*AF*] You/we (etc) are given an immediate or sudden responsibility (often burdensome or unfair). *Don[']t give out the tickets without gettin[g] the money because when time come[s] to pay in, is you to catch!*—(Trin) [By metaph extension from various children's ring games in wh the person to do the chasing or 'catching' of the next 'victim' is unexpectedly called upon to do so]

cat·char [ˈkačaˑr] *n* (Guyn) [*AF*] A person who tries to do harm in another person's love affair; [by extension] anyone who talks out of turn or would not mind his own business. *Claude N—, 32, was alleged to have called beer garden owner George W—, 35, ... a 'catchar' ... because he felt that he was hiding one of his waitresses from him.*—GyC (75.12.12, p.3) [An Indic loan. Bhoj < *khachchar* 'mule—used as term of abuse']

catch·er [ˈk(y)ačər ~ kɛča] *n* (ECar) ‖ **catcher-coop** (Guyn) ‖ **catchers** (Baha) ‖ **coop**[1] (StVn, USVI) ‖ **hoop** (ECar) A children's game of hide-and-seek played in a number of different ways, but in wh the person being chased is 'caught' by being touched and then in turn becomes the chaser.

catch·er-coop *n* (Guyn); **catch.ers** *n* (Baha) See CATCHER

cat-claw *n* (StKt) ‖ FIT-WEED (Bdos, etc) □ See also CAT'S CLAW CREEPER.

cat·er·pil·lar-ca·la·lu *n* (BrVi, Guyn) Either of two similar-looking kinds of tall, erect, bushy herb with smooth, succulent stems wh are reddish-brown to green, with grainy-looking, yellowish flowers clustered along soft spikes; the pale green, spoon-shaped leaves are used as a CALALU; *Amaranthus spinosus* (with some thorns) or *Amaranthus dubius* (without thorns) (*Amaranthaceae*). *The caterpillar calalu need not be cultivated, as it thrives as a weed in rough pastures, gravelly ground, and on roadsides. It is, however, the favourite 'bhaji' used by East Indians, and makes an excellent dish with fine-shrimps.*—Guyn (Ms) [From the resemblance of the limp, three-inch-long, flowered spikes to caterpillars]

cat-eye *adj, n* (Bdos, Guyn, StVn) [*AF*] [Of a non-European, and esp a black person] (Having) grey-green irises of the eyes. *He liked this brown-skin cat-eye girl with good hair.*—(Bdos) [From a supposed resemblance to a cat's eyes]

cat·fish *n* 1. (Belz) ‖ **catto** (Belz) [*AF*] A dark-grey, flat-mouthed, whiskered river-fish that scavenges and is not eaten. 2. (Guyn) ‖ **skin-fish** (Guyn) A bluish, flat-mouthed, whiskered river and coastal fish that grows to about 2 ft long; it has no scales, and so is despised as food by some people. 3.* (StLu) [*IF*] A medium-sized and tasty sea-fish; *Ariidae* spp.

cat·ma·ran [ˈkyatmaran] *n* (Guyn) A device used for collecting fish trapped on the mudflat of the seashore, consisting of a wide piece of lightwood board about 9 ft long with a box fixed on it; it is pushed along by the fisherman using one foot. [Prob a loan-word by Indic infl < Tamil *kaṭṭumaram* 'a kind of ship-to-shore raft' See *OED* catamaran 1.]

cat's claw creep·er *n phr* (Trin) ‖ GOLDEN SHOWER (Bdos) [Ref to the claw-like tendrils by wh the vine climbs]

cat·sprad·dle [k(y)atspradl] *vb* (Bdos, Trin) [*AF*] 1. *vb intr* To fall headlong and sprawl on the ground. 2. *vb tr* ‖ **maulsprig** (Bdos) To beat (sb) flat with punishing blows. [Prob a ref to a cat's falling from a height on its outstretched paws + *OED* spraddle (dial) v intr 'to sprawl'. Perh also infl by SE *spread-eagle*]

cat·ta (ca·ta, ka·ta) ['k(y)ata] *n* (Antg, Gren, Guyn, StVn, Tbgo, USVI) ‖ *cotta* (Angu, Antg, Gren, Jmca, StVn, ViIs) ‖ *cotto* (USVI) A round pad of cloth or dried leaves, placed on the head to ease the carrying of a load. [Cp *CBCD* Congo *nkata* 'a pad for the shoulder or head'. Also *DAFL* Twi *ŋkata* 'a covering']

cat-tail* *n* (CarA) ‖ *chenille (plant)* (Trin) ‖ *red-hot cat('s) tail* (Jmca) A cultivated garden shrub that can grow to 8 ft, bearing bright red, silky, cylindrical, pendent, tail-like flowers 1 to 2 ft long and contrasting sharply with the plant's large, bright green, heart-shaped and serrated leaves; *Acalypha hispida* (*Euphorbiaceae*).

cat(t)·ha *n* (Guyn, Trin) [Indic] See KATHA

cat·tle-boil *n* (Antg, Gren, StVn, Tbgo, Trin) ‖ CAT-BOIL (CarA) [Prob < CAT-BOIL by epenthesis, but the orig of both terms is unknown]

cat·tle-e·gret* *n* (Bdos, Guyn, Trin) ‖ *cowbird* (BrVi, Jmca) ‖ *crane* (Guyn) ‖ *tick-bird* (Trin) ‖ *white egret* (Angu, Bdos, Jmca) ‖ *white gaulin* (Angu, Dmca, Gren, USVI) A white or (sometimes) greyish or buff-coloured bird about 20 ins long with a conspicuous pointed yellow bill, a longish duck-like neck, and yellow legs; it feeds on insects in pastures esp near cattle (hence the name); *Bubulcus ibis* (*Ardeidae*).

cat·tle-tongue* *n* (Antg, Brbu, Mrat, Nevs, StKt) ‖ *Christmas-bush* 2. (Angu) ‖ *cowtongue* (Tbgo) ‖ *crab-bush* (BrVi) ‖ *cure-forall* (Bdos, Guyn) ‖ *géritou* 1. (Trin) ‖ *ram-goat bush* (Nevs, USVI) ‖ *salve bush* (Baha, TkCa) ‖ *tabak-djab* (StLu) ‖ *tabak-zonbi* (Dmca) ‖ *wild-tobacco* (Jmca) A wild herb sometimes more than 6 ft tall with light-green, pleasant-smelling, six-inch-long, spear- shaped leaves that have a rough, sometimes bumpy surface and a soft, woolly underside; the leaves are widely used for curative 'teas', poultices, etc; *Pluchea symphytifolia*, or *P. carolinensis*, also *P. odorata* (*Compositae*). [From the nature of the leaf, recalling the rough surface and soft underside of a cow's tongue]

cat·to ['kyato] *n* (Belz) [*AF*] ‖ CATFISH 1. (Belz)

cat-wire *n* (Bdos) [*IF*] Barbed wire. [Prob < *cat(tle)* + *wire*, with reduction of intervocalic /-CC-/, from its use for fencing in cattle. Cp CHICKEN-WIRE]

caub (cawb) *adj* (Guyn) See COB

cause ('cause) [ka·z] *conj* (CarA) [*AF*] Because. **a.** *I ran ahead to tell my parents to keep the door open, cause they were right behind me. I couldn't call (cause a the wind, you know).*—Aaw.1.1, p.8 **b.** *But I can't stay in this village no more now, 'cause everybody know who I is.*—CISH:19 [< SE *because* by aphaeresis, but *OED* lists as Obs or dial with cits from 16C onwards]

caus·en ['ka:zn]; **caus.in(g)** ['ka:zɪn/ŋ] *conj* (Bdos, CayI, Guyn, Jmca) [*X*] ‖ BECAUSEN (CarA) **a.** *I don't rightly know exactly but it must have been within a fortnight 'causen I don't like to put a knife to it till the fruit's nigh on gone.*—FDI:50 **b.** *Well now, we all three closer together than ever before, causin' we all three got broken foot.*—CISH:27 **c.** *For I hanging on. I take up the Bible. Not causing I is this big-able Christian-minded person. It ain't true.*—HFGA:115 (A. Clarke) [Prob a further development of CE CAUSE (< SE *because*) with paragogic /-n > -en > -in/, then /-in > -ing/ by false refinement]

ca·val·li* (ca·va·li, ca·val·la, ca·val·ly) ['kavali/-la] /1'12/ (CarA) ‖ *coubally* (Belz) ‖ *couva(l)li(e)* (Gren, Trin) ‖ *crevalle* (Gren, Trin) ‖ *jack, toro*[1] (Guyn) A large sea-fish (often 20 to 30 lbs) distinguished by its smooth arch from head to tail, bluish-green back, silvery- brassy sides, very fine scales, and deeply forked tail; it moves in large schools and is said to fight fiercely when hooked; its flesh is tough; *Caranx hippos* (*Carangidae*). [Perh a corruption of *crevalle* wh is the form appearing widely in the marine literature, whereas *cavalla* is listed as a fish of the mackerel family (*Scombridae*)] □ The name recognized everywhere, even where alternatives exist, is *cavalli*. There are also many varieties: *amber cavalli, horse-eye cavalli, roundhead cavalli*, etc.

ca·viche *n* (Guyn) See CABECHE

cawb *adj* (Guyn) See COB

cay; caye [ki:] *n* (CarA) One of a number of tiny, low-level islets, usu uninhabited or privately owned; (AmE) a key. [Sp *cayo* 'islet, reef'] □ The spelling preferred in *Belz* is *caye*, elsewhere *cay*.

Ca·yac(k) (Ka·yak) ['kayak] *n* (Gren) [*AF—Joc/Derog*] A native of the island of Carriacou; a Carriacouan. *Grenada has water spoiling, and as a result of that there is no need to attempt to conserve; and when I raised the question years ago, I was told as a 'Cayack' I would know that. Yes, because we have the good sense to be able to conserve [water], because we in Carriacou, don't have rivers.*—Gren (Hd, 77.04.25, p.207) [Abbr < *Carriac*(ou) by palatalization of /-r-/] **2.** [By extension] [*AF—Derog*] A country bumpkin. □ The sense is offensive. Carriacou is an island to the north of, and part of the state of Grenada.

ca·yan pep·per *n* (Brbu, Jmca) See CAYENNE PEPPER

caye *n* (CarA) See CAY

ca·yenne-ba·na·na* *n phr* (Guyn) ‖ *bastard plantain, short banana, Trinidad banana* (StVn) A banana wh has a blunt end, noticeable 'sides', and is usu smaller and shorter than the regular types of commercially cultivated bananas; it is often cooked unripe as GREEN BANANAS or GREEN FIGS; *Musa spp*.

ca·yenne-pep·per (ca·yan-pep·per, ca·yon-pep·per) ['kayɒn-pɛpʌ] *n* (Brbu, Jmca) ‖ BIRD-PEPPER (CarA) [Prob a corruption of an Amerindian name, this pepper being 'probably a native of tropical America' (*AFPȝ:657*). Cp *DGEG* Guarani *kiỹi* [kənyi] 'pepper'. No association with Cayenne, Fr Guiana, is known. See *OED*]

Cay·man Brac·er ['kemʌn brakər] *n phr* An inhabitant of Cayman Brac, the second largest of the Cayman Islands. □ The /-k/ sound of the place name is kept in the derivative.

Cay·man·i·an ['kemaniən] /1'221/ *adj, n* (A person or thing) of or belonging to the Cayman Islands.

cay·on-pep·per *n* (Brbu, Jmca) See CAYENNE-PEPPER

C.B.U. *abbr* (CarA) Caribbean Broadcasting Union (1970–).

C.C.A. *abbr* (CarA) Caribbean Conservation Association (1967–).

C.C.C. *abbr* (CarA) Caribbean Conference of Churches (1973–).

C.C.H. *abbr* (Guyn) Cacique's Crown of Honour, the third highest Guyanese national award (1970–); the letters are placed after the recipient's name.

C.C.L. *abbr* (CarA) Caribbean Congress of Labour (1960–).

C.D. *abbr* (Jmca) Commander of the Order of Distinction, a national honour awarded for distinction through service to Jamaica; the letters are placed after the recipient's name. □ See also O.D..

C.D.B. *abbr* (CarA) Caribbean Development Bank (1970–); its headquarters are in Barbados.

C'dear! (cuh-dear!) *excl* (Bdos) [*IF*] (An expression of sympathy, regret, pained surprise, etc.) Dear me! O my goodness! etc. *And Hunte come out and watch her walk away and then he sit down in the road and start to cry, all his shoulders shaking. And the people, some saying, 'C'dear, she shouldn't leff him so.'*—CISH:93 [Prob < *Good dear!* as a euphemism for 'Good God!' perh from dial BrE or IrE infl. Cp *OED dear* C. 'Used interjectionally ... *Dear bless, help, save us (you)*: ejaculations ... implying an appeal for higher help (*Obs* or *dial*). *Dear knows!* 'Goodness knows, Heaven knows.' These uses with a vb suggest that *dear* represents ... a fuller *dear Lord!* Thus *dear knows!* is exactly equivalent to *the Lord* or *God knows!*...' + cit 1880 (*Antrim & Down*) *Dear bless you! Dear help you! Dear knows!*, a common rejoinder ... probably meant originally 'God only knows'. (Note that these last *OED* exs are from IrE, wh has strongly influenced *Bdos* E.)]

cei·ba [si·baȷ] *n* (CarA) ‖ SILK-COTTON TREE (CarA) [< *BAED* Arawak *shiba-dañ* 'a large hard-wooded tree', *-dañ* being the standard Arawak suffix for 'tree'] □ Chiefly literary.

ceit·ful *adj* (Guyn, Jmca, StVn) [*AF—Cr*] Carrying news and lying; deceitful. *Ceitful live at handful door-mouth* (= *The deceitful person carries gossip to gain cheap reward.*)—Guyn (Prov) [< SE *deceitful* by aphaeresis]

ce·le·ment *n* (BrVi, Dmca, Gren, StKt) See CILIMENT.

cel·lo-pan(s) ['čɛlʌ-pa·n] *n* (Trin) A joined set of three PANS for one player, each PAN cut to be two-thirds or three-quarters the length of an oil-drum, with the surface sunk to a depth just less than the bass pans but segmented to provide five or six notes (each); they are of a mellower tone than the GUITAR-PANS, with wh they take up a middle position in the traditional arrangement of a STEELBAND. [From the resemblance of the timbre of the note produced to the tone of a cello] □ See diagram of THE STEELBAND in the Appendix.

cen·sor *vb*; **cen.sor.ship** *n* (CarA) [*X*] Censure (SE vb and n). **a.** *He objected to being censored for his absence when he was ill.*—Bdos (Ms) **b.** *She had been amazed at the way in which Mrs Davis took the censorship of her husband. Christ, what a hell of a fight would have broken out had it been her!*—PCOS:73 [A catachresis that may originally be due to non-distinction of [š], [s]]

cen·ti·pede (san·ta·pee) [sɛntipi·(d) ~ santəpi] *n* (CarA) [*AF—Derog*] A woman given to brawling and fighting; a foul-mouthed prostitute. [Perh by ref to the vicious sting of the orig crawling myriapod] □ The refined orig pronunc is less common. See SANTAPEE.

cen·tri·fu·gal /1'121 ~ 12'21/; **cen.tri.fu.gal bas.ket, cen.tri.fuge** /2'21/ *n* (*phr*) (CarA) [Sugar Ind] A machine for separating sugar crystals from molasses, consisting of a large, vertically mounted, cylindrical metal basket, with thousands of tiny perforations through wh, as the basket rotates at extremely high speed, the liquid molasses is expelled, leaving the sugar crystals trapped within. [By adj > n functional shift of SE *centrifugal* for technical use. See SE *centrifuge*]

cen·tu·ri·an; **cen.tu.ri.on** *n* (Bdos, Belz, Guyn) [*IF*] **1.** A person who is 100 years old; a centenarian. **2.** (CENTURION only) (Guyn) [*IF*] A cricketer who scores 100 runs. [< *century* 'one hundred' (instead of *centenary*) + SE adj suff *ian*]

cen·tu·ry-plant (sen·try-plant) *n* (Bdos, Trin, ViIs) ‖ *agave* (CarA) A particular variety of AGAVE, *A. americana* or *A. barbadensis*, wh has small, sharp, marginal prickles on its succulent, 5 ft long, spine-tipped leaves, and grows a central pole-like effloresence after many years, then dies. [Said to be due to a popular belief that the plant flowers after a hundred years. However the fact that the plant is used as a rough rural boundary marker (*Bdos*) and has a sturdy, sentry-like pole may also account for its name]

ce·ra·see* ['sɪɾʌsi ~ 'sʌɾsi ~ 'sʌɾʌsi] *n* (Baha, Bdos, CayI, Jmca, TkCa) || **ban-caraili** (Guyn, Trin) || **carilla, carilli** (Gren) || **circe(e)-bush** (Bdos) || **coolie-pawpaw** (Gren) || **konkonm-kouli** (StLu) || **lizard-food** (Bdos, Nevs, StKt) || **maiden-apple** (Mrat, Nevs, StKt, StVn, ViIs) || **maiden-blush** (Angu, Antg, Mrat, Trin) || **maiden-bush** (Antg, Mrat, StKt) || **mi-raculous bush, miraculous vine** (Bdos) || **pomme-coolie** (Dmca, Mrat) || **popilolo** (Tbgo) || **sersee, sersey** (Bdos) || **sorosse, sorossi** (Baha, Belz) || **sorrow-seed** (Tbgo) || **wash-a-woman bush, washer-woman bush** (Nevs, StKt) || **wild corilla** (Guyn, Trin) A slender, vigorously spreading vine with strong-smelling, five-lobed leaves; it bears a warty, ribbed, yellow-skinned fruit, of two varieties (the larger about 5 ins long) with a pointed tip; the fruit splits open when ripe exposing bright red, sticky seeds wh are sweet, though the skin is bitter; both leaves and fruit are widely used for a number of folk-medicinal purposes; *Momordica charantia* or *M. balsamina* (*Cucurbitaceae*). [Prob of Afr orig. Note number of || in s- that approximates to '*cerasee*'. See || || CARAILA, BAN-CARAILA] □ This name is applied most often to the 'bush', hence sometimes **cerasee-bush**. See also CARAILA.

ce·rise (ce·res) ['sɪɾɪ·z] *n* 1. (Trin) Name variously applied to || GOVERNOR-PLUM (Baha, etc), or || JAMAICA-PLUM (Bdos, etc), or esp in rural areas SOUR CHERRY (Trin). 2. (StLu) [siwiz] || BARBADOS-CHERRY (CarA) [Fr = 'cherry', variously used in Fr Cr]

cer·tain *adj* (CarA) 1. (Often used with sense of) particular. 2. *PHRASE* 2.1 (**in) a certain way** *adj phr* (Bdos) [*IF*] Smart-looking; tidy; in a condition fit to be inspected. *They just happen to be just that much more fortunate that perhaps that particular morning they had their heads tied with a clean headtie and they looked, as we would say, a certain way that the Manager said they would suit to be in his house.*—Bdos (Hd, 1975, p.4976)

Cey·lon (-man·go) *n* (*phr*) (StVn) || BOMBAY-MANGO (Jmca, Mrat)

C.F.N.I. *abbr* Caribbean Food and Nutrition Institute (University of the West Indies at St Augustine, *Trin*) (1971–).

chaa·ti (cha·tee, chha·ti) [čha·ti] *n* (Guyn, Trin) [Indic] || **nine-day** 2(ii) (Guyn, Trin) A festive celebration held (among people of Hindu culture) six days or sometimes nine days after the birth of a child. [Hin *chhaṭhii* 'ceremony performed on the sixth day after child-birth'. The shift of the original custom to the ninth day may be due to cultural creolization]

cha·ben [šabɛ̃ ~ šabã] (Dmca); **cha.bin(e) (sh-a·been)** [šabi·n] (StLu, Trin) *n* [*Derog*] || **raggay** (StVn) 1. A person of mixed African and European descent who has a dull sort of pale brown skin, coarse reddish hair and sometimes freckles and greyish eyes. [Fr Cr < 17C Fr. R. Cotgrave's *Dictionarie* (1611): *Chabins* 'The sheepe of Berry (whose wool is verie thicke, and as long as goats haire)'. In France this type of animal was once thought to be a cross between a sheep and a goat, and the notion of a thick-haired cross-bred animal (cp Fr *mulâtre* < mulet) was transferred to this particular type of Negro 'half-breed'] □ The spelling SHABEEN occurs mostly in *Trin* Though both forms pertain to a colour-type and are usu genderless, the form [šabi·n], reflecting an orig Fr fem, is now used by some speakers, esp in Dmca, to refer to a female of the type.

chac-chac (chak·chak, shack-shack) [šak-šak] *n* (ECar) A small, dried gourd (such as a small calabash) containing pebbles or hard seeds, with a stick fixed through it by wh it is held and rattled, in pairs, as musical instruments; (Sp) maracas. *The music is made by voices, three drums played with the hands and numerous chac-chacs or maracas.*—Efl.1011, p.2 [See SHACK-SHACK] □ The spelling **chac-chac** appears to be widely used in specific ref to this musical instrument, and **shack-shack** for a toy, etc., whereas **chak-chak** occurs in Fr Cr speaking islands.

cha-cha [ča-ča] *n* 1. (Guyn, Trin) [Indic] Uncle; (also loosely used as an affectionate term of respect for any senior male relative). [< Hin *chaachaa* 'uncle'] 2. (USVI) [*AF*] A white Virgin Islander of Fr descent, esp a member of a suburban group in St Thomas.

cha·cha·la·ca *n* (Belz, Grns, Tbgo) || COCRICO (Tbgo, Trin)

cha·chun·dar ['čačʊnda·r] /1'12/ *n* (Guyn, Trin) [*AF—Derog*] [Indic] An EAST INDIAN young woman who is in close friendship with or bears a child by a Black young man. [< Hin *chhachhuudar* 'a mole, a shrew', prob from its burrowing, nocturnal, and rat-like appearance and habits, by pejorative transfer in Indic CE, though the term is not so used in orginal Hindi] □ A term of insult specific to Indic speakers.

cha·co·ni·a* [čakoniaɟ] *n* (Tbgo, Trin) || **Pride of Trinidad & Tobago, Trinidad's Pride, Wild Poinsettia** (Tbgo, Trin) A slender, branched forest-tree wh puts out three to four-foot-long sprays of flaming red flowers, blooming annually about late August (near the anniversary of the Independence of Trinidad & Tobago, and hence its National Flower); *Warszewiczia coccinea* (*Rubiaceae*). [Name honouring Gen. Chacón, last Spanish Governor of the island]

Cha·co·ni·a Med·al *n phr* (Trin & Tbgo) See C.M.T.

cha·do(n)-bé·ni [šadō-ɓeni ~ šado-bɛni] *n* (Dmca, StLu, Trin) See SHADO-BENI

chafe [če·f] *n* (Guyn) 1. A long and painful inconvenience or suffering. 2. PHRASE 2.1 bear your chafe *vb phr* (Guyn) To endure your share of suffering. a. *No bread, I try cassava bread. I'll band my waist and bear my chafe.*—GyC (74.02.03, p.6) b. *My very soul cries out for you, you, you! I've borne my chafe for four months now and I cannot bear to live without you anymore.*—GyC (77.03.13, p.9)

Cha·gua·ra·mas A·gree·ment *n phr* (CarA) [*IF*] The Treaty of Chaguaramas, signed by Heads of (Anglophone) Caribbean Governments on 4th July 1973, establishing the CARIBBEAN COMMUNITY (CARICOM) out of the CARIFTA Agreement. [From the town of Chaguaramas, *Trin*, where the Treaty was signed]

chal·ice *n* (Jmca) [*AF*] [Rastaf] ‖ CHILLUM PIPE (Guyn, etc) *True Rastafarians shun the material world, ... and regard the smoking of marijuana (Jamaican ganja) as a sacrament, (the pipe often referred to as a chalice).*—(Caa.I p.28)

chal·ta* [ˈčalta·] *n* (Guyn, Trin) [Indic] ‖ *elephant-apple* (Guyn) An irregularly shaped, smooth, green, gourd-like fruit, turning yellowish when ripe, with a sour, creamy flesh; it is borne on a spreading, flowering, evergreen, bushy-topped tree with reddish-brown stems, about 25 ft tall; the ripe fruit is popularly used for Indian preserves such as ACHAR; *Dillenia indica (Dilleniaceae)*. [Bhoj/Hin *chaltaa* 'a kind of evergreen tree and its fruit']

cha·mar (cha·maar) [ˈčama·r] *n* (Guyn, Trin) [*Derog*] [Indic] ‖ *low nation* (Guyn) An East Indian person of low social standing. *'I vow,' he told himself, 'to have nothing to say to that boy, he a Brahmin, and I a chamar.' A chamar, a sweeper and worker in leather.*—NAGOS:70 [Hin *chamaar* 1. 'cobbler, shoe-maker' 2. 'a low caste in the traditional Hin caste system'] □ As a term of insult it is specific to Indic speakers.

cham·pagne PHRASE have champagne taste(s) and mauby pocket(s) (ECar) [*AF—Joc*] See MAUBY Phr 2.1

chance PHRASE Gi(ve) me a chance! (Guyn, Tbgo, Trin); Gi(ve) me a fat chance *excl, id phr* (Trin) [*AF*] Stop harrassing me! Be off with you, and leave me to myself (my business, etc)! [Less strongly] Be reasonable (more considerate, etc). *'How you expect me to know?' ... 'Well if you don't know why you don't shut up.' 'Oh gawd, Helen, give me a fat chance, na.'*—JJM:30

chan·dan [ˈčandan] *n* (Guyn, Trin) [Indic] A red mark of sandalwood paste put on the forehead of a Hindu to indicate his high caste. [Hin *chandan* 'sandal-wood']

chan·de·lier (-bush) *n* (Trin) See CHANDILYÉ

chan·dil·yé (chan·de·lier) [ˈšandilye] *n* (Trin) ‖ BALL-BUSH (Bdos, Jmca) [From the resemblance of a stand of the plants to a stand of lights]

chang-chang *vb tr* (Gren) [*AF—Joc*] ‖ ZUG UP (Tbgo, Trin) [Said to be an echoic ref to the sound made by the barber's cheap scissors]

change[1] *n* (ECar) [*AF*] 1. A small sum of money to be lent or earned. 2. [By extension] A small additional portion of money or of time. 3. PHRASES 3.1 and change *n phr* [Extension of sense 2.] a. *Let's say it will cost some $200 and change (i.e. 'a little over $200').*—(Trin) b. *But we don't have to have a snap election, we have three years and change to go, three years and change. We have not yet used up two years, so we have the balance.*—Gren (Hd, 78.12.01, p.68) 3.2. a piece of change *n phr* [Extension of sense 1.] *It is like somebody coming to borrow a piece of change from you. You can duck them some of the time, but you cannot go on ducking.*—Bdos (Hd, 74.08.27, p.3855) [By shift of SE sense of 'coins of small value']

change[2] *vb tr* (CarA) PHRASE change your mouth *vb phr* (CarA) [*AF—Derog*] See MOUTH Phr 4.4

chan·na [ˈčana] *n* (Guyn, Trin) [Indic] 1. Chick pea, fried with salt, or boiled and seasoned, served as an inexpensive snack; (the hard pea of the plant) *Cicer arietinum (Papilionaceae)*, commercial name (Sp) 'garbanzo'. [Hin *chanaa* 'grain, chick pea'] 2. PHRASE 2.1 go(ne) for channa *vb phr* (Guyn) [*AF—Joc*] [Of money or anything valuable] To be as good as lost; to be wasted, seized, or lost through thoughtless dealing. a. *What of the thousands of dollars in pipes which lie below the building? / My information is that around $100,000 will now go for 'channa', because of the dramatic decision to put Telecoms at the old Water Works site.*—DaC (52.09.24, p.4) b. *Close you minds to what women does say ... 'cause when they put the food down in front of you and start talking, you gone for channa ... you finished, done for.*—HMCH:69 [By ref to what was once regarded as the cheapest of E Indian foods]

chant·wèl (chant·relle, chant·well) [šã twɛl ~ šãtrɛl] *n* (Crcu, Dmca, StLu, Trin) 1. [Hist, esp as CHANTRELLE] The woman singer and dancer leading the BELAIR, giving the lead-line to a chorus in wh sharp social satire is introduced. *Up to the early 1900s the chantrelles also sang at stick-fighting competitions while pairs of competitors battled to overpower each other.... As the Carnival developed some chantrelles began singing in the tents now known as 'calypso tents'.*— Trin (Ms, 1982) 2. [*Obs esp as* CHANTWELL] (Name formerly applied to) a male calypsonian. *This attitude has been one of the main reasons why the music has not been considered by a majority of* *people ... of any importance where the message is concerned, even though many Chantwells (name referred to long-time kaisonians) before have tried hard to maintain the true standards.*—Cam.8, p.17 [Fr Cr < *chanterelle*. (R. Cotgrave's *Dictionarie* 1611) 'the treble in singing'; also *chanteresse* 'a woman that sings much', wh may have influenced the early Fr Cr usage. The development /-r- > -w-/ is normal in Fr Cr, and '-well' is due both to false Anglicization and loss of fem sense as male singers took over, sense 2.]

chap *vb tr* (CarA) [*IF*] See CHOP

cha·pat·ti ['čapa·ti] /1'22/ *n* (Guyn, Trin) [Indic] A flat, thin, coarser kind of ROTI. [Hin name *chapaatii* < *chipṭaa* 'flat'] □ Also listed as *chupatty* in COD.

cha·plé (cha·plet) [šaple] (Trin) *n* 1. (Regular word in use for) the string of beads known as the rosary. 2. PHRASE 2.1 **say the chaplet** *vb phr* (Trin) To say the rosary; to count prayers on the string of beads provided for the purpose (RC church). [Fr Cr < Fr *chapelet* 'rosary']

cha·po·ti ['šapoti] /1'12/ *n* (Dmca, StLu) ‖SAPODILLA (CarA) [Fr Cr < Fr *sapotille* (< Sp *sapodilla*, name of fruit) with initial palatalization]

chap·pals [čapalz] *n pl* (Trin) [Indic] Flat leather sandals; light, topless leather slippers. [Hin *chappal* 'slipper']

char·ley-price (char·lie-price) *n* (Belz, Jmca) A very large rat. ... *having fowls or dogs scratching in the litter or the rats and charley prices playing 'ketch' at nights.*—ReP (79.11.25, p.2) [From name of Sir Charles Price, 18C planter and Speaker of the House of Assembly in *Jmca* who is believed to have introduced the rat in *Jmca* to combat cane-rats. See *DJE Charles Price rat* for a full account] □ In *Belz*, by contrast the terms **rat, ratta**, refer to a mouse or small rat.

char·poy ['čarpɒɪ] *n* (Trin) [Indic] A rough cot made of interwoven strings in a wooden frame. [Hin *chaarpaaii* 'bedstead, cot' < *chaar* 'four' + *paayaa* 'foot']

chat¹ *n* (CarA) 1. Persistent familiar talking (esp of young persons) that could lead to trouble. 2. Sauciness; impertinence. 3. PHRASE 3.1 **to give a lot of chat** *vb phr* (CarA) [*IF*] [Of young persons] To have a habit of giving saucy answers.

chat² *vb* (CarA) [*IF*—*Joc/Derog*] PHRASES 1. **chat down (a girl)** *vb phr* (Bdos, USVI) [*AF*—*Joc*] To talk familiarly with (a girl) in order to persuade her to make a date. 2. **chat foolishness/stupidity, etc** *vb phr* (Angu, Antg, Jmca) [*IF*] To talk nonsense. 3. **chat (sb's) name** *vb phr* (Jmca) [*AF*] ‖POUND (SB'S) NAME (CarA) See POUND Phr 3.1 4. **chat up(sb)** *vb*

phr (CarA) [*AF*—*Joc*] To talk familiarly, ingratiatingly; to gossip (with a personal motive). *There were two items in the news this week which were just up my street ... yours, too, if you like chat-up chat-up bout what other people say.*— StA(JA) (73.02.10, p.14, Partyline)

cha·tayn (cha·tany, cha·taigne) ['šataɪn~ šateŋ] *n* (Gren, StLu, Trin) ‖BREADNUT 1. (CarA) [Fr *châtaigne* 'chestnut' from close resemblance of the seed, in taste and use, to European chestnut] □ The Fr Cr spelling of the sound [ŋ] is evid not agreed on in Dmca /ny/, Guad /ngn/, StLu /ni/, hence there are possible differences in the spelling of this item.

chat·tel-house *n* (Bdos) ‖ *board-and-shingle house* (Bdos, Guyn) A single-roofed BOARD-AND-SHINGLE house, or one of about the same size (about 20ft x 10ft x 8ft) with a galvanized-sheet roof, (originally) sitting on a GROUNDSEL of loose stones so that it could be removed wholly by its owner from leased land. [OED *chattel* 4. 'a movable possession; any possession or piece of property other than real estate or a freehold'. However note ibid. 5. *chattel-interest* 'an interest in leasehold property' + cits. Hence legally 'chattel-house' = movable, inheritable house] □ This name now widely applies also to this type of house (Bdos) fixed to its foundations i.e. not movable.

chaw [čɒ:] *vb* (CarA) [*AF*—*Cr*] Chew; chew on (sth for a long time). **a.** *Yo never see dog chaw razor.*—Jmca (Prov) **b.** *Since yuh mother didn't uses to let you chew chewing gum, you chawing 'pon tha' pork skin till just before evensong and service.*—PeL (80.05.02, p.10, A. Clarke) [OED *chaw* v 'a by-form of *chew* ... used in Eng in 16C and now in Sc and some E dialects. *Chaw* was very common in 16–17C (Eng lit) ... It is now esteemed vulgar...'. Cp also IrE *JESI*: 97 *chaw* for *chew*: *chawing the rag* 'continually grumbling, jawing, and giving abuse'. Also current in dial AmE, ex 'Store tobacco is flat black plug, but these fellows mostly chaws the natural leaf twisted'—*Adventures of Huckleberry Finn*]

chaw-stick *n* (Jmca, Trin) ‖CHEW-STICK (CarA)

C.H.B. *abbr* (Bdos) Companion of Honour of Barbados, a national honour awarded for distinguished national achievement and merit; it is the second highest national award, and the letters are placed after the recipient's name.

che-boeuf *n* (Gren) See TJÈ-BÈF

che-che [čiči~čeče] *adj, n* [*AF*—*Derog*] 1. (Nevs, StKt) ‖ *backra-johnny* (Bdos) ‖ *Frenchie, mooshay* (StKt) ‖ *red chenke* (Antg) A POOR-WHITE native of St Kitts-Nevis. 2. ‖RED (-SKIN) MAN/WOMAN (CarA) [*AF*—*Derog*] 3. (Antg) A person of light complexion with freckles. 4. (Antg) A cowardly and unattractive boy. [Perh by reduction and reduplication of *che*(*nke*) < RED CHENKE (*Antg*) or (by the same processes) of (*Fren*)*chie* < FRENCHIE (*StKt*). Both these processes are commonly used in Derog contexts]

check *vb tr* [*AF/IF*] **1.** (CarA) [*IF*] ‖ **check out, check with** (CarA) To visit and inquire of (sb); to go/come and ask (sb). *I don't have any in stock right now, but check me next week and I might have some by then.*—(Bdos) **2.** (Gren, Trin) [*AF*] [Of a young man] To date (a girl) regularly; to be a regular visitor to a home with marriageable daughters. *A notice him checkin[g] Wendy and them every couple days.*—(Trin) **3.** [*Usu imperative*] (CarA) [*AF*] ‖ **check out** (CarA) Listen to (this)! Look at (that)! **a.** *Check this, no! A postman suing some people for a dog-bite!*—(Bdos) **b.** *Check the smiles that girl giving him!*—(Antg) **4.** PHRASES **4.1 check at some place** *vb phr* (CarA) [*IF*] To inquire at some place. **4.2 check back** *vb phr* (CarA) [*IF*] To call or inquire again. *He suggested that I 'check back' in the afternoon. I did as I was requested, only to have the morning's experience—a long wait and a request to 'check-back'—repeated.*—ViN (77.08.19, p.11) **4.3 check out** *vb phr* (CarA) [*IF*] To observe (sb) openly or secretly; to visit (sb) for a purpose; to investigate, examine or verify (sth). **a.** *The thief ... was in the old bus, checking me out and waiting for an opportunity to distress me.*—ReP (80.06.15, p.2) **b.** *Dr Elder felt fairly certain that his shirt jac was acceptable after he had checked it out with Senate President Dr Wahid Ali.*—ExP (72.01.21, p.4) [Prob by infl of AmE 'Pop' talk] **4.4 check with (sb)** *vb phr* (CarA) [*IF*] To put your inquiry to (sb). *Don't ask me, I don't deal with that. Check with the supervisor.*—(Bdos) [As prec]

checks-worth *n* (TkCa) Some sickness of the body (such as the swelling of the leg) believed to be caused by some supernatural evil.

chee·lum *n* (Trin) See CHILLAM

cheese–cut·ter *n* (Bdos) See CUTTER

cheese-on! (Bdos); **cheese-on/and -bread!** (Bdos, ViIs) *excl* [*IF*] Expression of surprise and admiration (esp among young people). [Substitution for *Jesus!*]

che·la·me·la *n* (CayI) ‖ GOOSEBERRY (CarA)

che·mise [šimi·z] *n* **1.** (CarA) [Hist] A long white dress, with low, round neck, long sleeves, and tied at the waist, worn by household slave women, sometimes with a shorter print-skirt over it. □ See CHIMMY¹ (*Trin*). **2.** (USVI) [? *Obs*] A woman's white short-sleeved bodice. **3.** (Antg, Guyn, Trin) ‖ *chimie* (Antg) ‖ *shimmy* (Guyn, StKt) [*IF*] A baby's loose-fitting garment. [Fr *chemise* 'woman's night-gown, smock' (esp in 17C)]

chem·ist [ˈkɛmis(t)] *n* [AF—Joc] **1.** (StKt) A person who distills unlicensed rum (known as

HAMMOND) in hide-outs. *The illicit rum chemists at Brownhill are having a dusty time with the anti-hammond police squad.*—DeM(SK) (62.02.17, p.12) **2.** (Nevs) An abortionist.

che·nep; **che.nip** [ˈčɛnɛp~čɛnɪp] *n* (Gren, Tbgo) ‖ GUINEP (CarA) [Blend of *chenet*(*te*) + *guinep/kinip* (See these)]

che·net(te) (**chen·nette, tjennèt, quenette**) [ˈčɛnɛt] *n* (Dmca, StLu, Tbgo, Trin) ‖ GUINEP (CarA) *Fruit in season are chataigne, 20 cents a pound; chenette, 25 cents a bunch; navel oranges, 10 for $1.*—TrG (74.10.05, p.5) [By initial affrication < Fr *quénette, quenette* (*StLu*) < *quénèpe* (*Hait*) (—'*NPHT:341*) < Arawakan *kenepa* (See GUINEP] □ *Chenet* is a less frequent but satisfactory spelling, also helping to explain the *Gren* and *Tbgo* variant **chenep**.

chen·ille (**plant**) [šɛnil (plant)] *n* (*phr*) (Trin) ‖ CAT-TAIL (CarA)

che·nip *n* (Gren, Tbgo) See CHENEP

chenks *n* (Jmca) ‖ CHINKS¹ (Gren)

chen·nette *n* (Dmca, StLu, Tbgo, Trin) See TJENNÈT

chè·pal·mis *n* (Dmca, StLu) See TJÈ-PALMIS

che·ra·mi·na (**che·re·mi·la, cher·ry·mi·na**, etc) [ˈčɛrəminə~čɛrimilə/-minə] *n* (Jmca) ‖ GOOSEBERRY 1. (CarA) □ Through the phonic resemblance, some urban speakers confuse this name with **cherimoya**, (a fruit wh is less well known).

che·ri·mo·ya* [čɛrimɔyə] *n* (Berm, Jmca) A large egg-shaped fruit with white pulp and black seeds, borne on a large shrub that is cultivated, though not very common; *Annona cherimola* (*Annonaceae*).

cher·ise *n* (Nevs) ‖ BARBADOS-CHERRY (CarA)

cher·ry *n* **1.** (CarA) ‖ BARBADOS-CHERRY (CarA) **2.** (Angu, BrVi, Mrat, Nevs, StKt) ‖ CASHEW 1. (CarA)

cher·ry·mi·na *n* (Jmca) See CHERAMINA

cher·ry-nut *n* (Angu, BrVi, StKt) ‖ CASHEW 1. (CarA)

cher·ry-pep·per *n* (Baha, Trin) ‖ *wiri-wiri pepper* (Guyn) A variety of *Capsicum frutescens* (*Solanaceae*) borne on a pot plant. (See cit foll). *The cherry pepper becomes covered with fruits about the size of peas, at first yellowish and changing to red. There is a more robust variety with smooth roundish fruits about one inch in diameter, having rich variations in colour starting yellow suffused with mauve, later intensifying to bright yellow becoming orange and finally scarlet.*—PTT: 104

chest-cold n (CarA) ‖ COLD² 2. (CarA)

cheups¹ (chupse, chupes) [čʊps] excl, n (Dmca, Gren, Tbgo, Trin) [AF/IF] ‖ SUCK-TEETH (CarA) **a.** That afternoon I dropped in at a friend and casually told him of my little worry. 'Cheups' he said, 'that is something to worry 'bout?' —ExP (72.07.06, p.16, R. Akong) **b.** Teacher: Keep quiet for me please. Just take the work as it is, right? ... (Chorus of Cheupses and 'Alright we go do it, we go do it'.)—Kai '78, p.31 [Imitative word representing the sound of SUCKING THE TEETH, then nominalized as in cit b.] □ This is the most commonly used spelling, esp in (Trin), others being **cheeups(e), chewps, choops, chups(e)**. The pl (cit b.) presents no problem. See also STEUPS, a frequent alternative (ECar) spelling, and cp SUCK-TEETH n.

cheups² (cheup, chupse, chupes) [čʊp (s) ~ čʊp(s)] vb intr (Dmca, Gren, Tbgo, Trin) ‖ SUCK YOUR TEETH (CarA) **a.** Ruby cheupsed because she has enough trouble just finding food for hungry mouths without getting too highfalutin about it all.—TrG (72.09.16, p.5) **b.** ... and about two o'clock in the morning I had to open the back door to let him out because he was cheupsing so much.—BoM (75.01.31, p.24) **c.** Vernon 'cheu-ped' annoyingly: ... Her words always dug sharply in his brain.—ExP (72.03.12, p.20) [By functional shift of n, CHEUPS¹, but perh also infl by Sp chupar 'to suck'. Note variant **cheup**, cit c.]

chew-stick n **1.** (CarA) A short twig (of the BLACK-SAGE bush or other suitable plant), stripped of its bark, chewed at one end and then used to clean the teeth. **2.*** (Gren) ‖ **chaw-stick** (Jmca, Trin) A flowering, woody vine, small lengths of wh are also used to clean the teeth, having a slightly bitter and frothy sap; Gouania lupuloides or G. domingensis (Rhamnaceae).

ch·ha·ti ['čha·ti] n (Guyn, Trin) See CHAATI

chib·bal (chib·ble) [čɪbəl ~ čɪbl] n (ViIs) [IF] An aromatic herb whose root-bulb is used as a folk-medicine and also to season cooking; it is sometimes also called **chervil** [< SE chervil (wh is a different plant in Europe) + infl of Sp cebolla 'onion, bulb']

chib·bly [čɪbli] n (Aneg) Children's name for LOVE-VINE (CarA).

chic·char·nie ['čikča·ni] /1'22/ n (Baha) A legendary, mischievous figure, said to be three-legged, half bird and half human, to live in or near SILK-COTTON TREES on Andros Island, and to be readily harmful to humans esp if laughed at. [? Perh of confused Afr orig. Andros is a very large, heavily forested, swampy and mostly uninhabited Baha island. Cp DARE chickamy chickamy craney crow (name of a Southern US hawk-catching-chickens children's game, also called Old Witch) + cit (1935) 'That ... most African of games', DARE also noting that it is frequently a 'witch' that tries to catch the other players]

chick·en-hawk* n (CarA) ‖ **gri-gri¹ 1.** (Gren) ‖ **malfini** (StLu) A greyish-brown bird of prey, 15 to 20 ins long, with broad wings and broad black-and-white banded tail, its voice a rasping shriek as it swoops mainly on rats, mice and lizards but sometimes also on small birds and young chicks, hence its name; Buteo platypterus antillarum or B. latissimus or a red-tailed variety also B. jamaicensis (Accipitridae).

chick·en-pep·per n (StKt) ‖ BIRD-PEPPER (CarA) [Because it is eaten on the plant by hens]

chick·en-wire n (BrVi) ‖ WIRE-MESH (Guyn) [From its use as an enclosure in poultry-rearing]

chick·i·chong ['čikičɒŋ] n (Trin) **1.** A popular cage-bird about 5 ins long, mostly black with a brown belly and short thick beak, its song 'a fairly long, musical series of clear whistled notes' (FGBTT:435); Oryzoborus angolensis (Fringillidae). **2.** [IF—Joc] ‖ KADI (Guyn)

chic·le; **chic.le-ġum tree, chic.le tree** [čikle-] n (phr) (Belz) (Name commercially used for) the SAPODILLA/SAPADILI tree as the producer of gum the original name of wh is chicle. Our assets have always been wood and the chicle in our forests.—BeT (65.07.22, p.1) [Sp < Nahuatl tzictli, name of the gum]

chi·cle·ro [či'kle:ro] n (Belz) A man employed to tap or 'bleed' the gum or latex of the SAPODILLA tree for export. The Chicleros, who are mostly local Indians, each produce from 500 to 2,000 pounds of gum in a season, depending on their skill.—ABSBH:56 [Sp]

chi(g)·ga(h) (chig·ger) n (CarA) See CHI-GO(E)

chi(g)·goe-foot dance n phr (Bdos) [Hist] A Negro dance performed on the heels, orig developed (and so named) because the toes were infected with CHIGOES.

chi·go(e) (chi(g)·ga(h), chig·ger, chig·goe) [čɪgʌ ~ čɪga] n (CarA) ‖ **jigger** (CarA) A blood-sucking flea that infests sandy ground, the female of wh burrows under the human skin, esp of the foot, lays eggs, and swells up, causing a tickling itch, then intense irritation or even loss of toes, though it can also drop out or be removed with a sterilized needle; Pulex penetrans or Tunga penetrans. [A Cariban word. Cp GDAA:51 Ak-awaio chiigò; Arekuna chiikò 'chigoe, jigger flea, Pulex penetrans'. Also Cp FTCC:233 Apalaii (southern Guianas) tcikò 'sand fly'. However note coincident African forms, ex ADMY Yoruba jiga 'the chigoe-flea (Tunga penetrans)' and many others (TAGD:195 cites six others + Gullah jiga) wh would account for the ‖ **jigger**]

child (chile) [čail(d)] *n* **1.** (CarA) [*IF*] [A common form of intimate greeting between two females of any age] Dear! My dear! **a.** *Christine, child, the coldsweats and the palpitations concerning this ... thing, bother me so much, that I nearly commit fraud.*—PeL (79.12.07, p.2, A.T. Clarke) **b.** *I said to the other lady: 'All these babies to see the doctor or to have their shots?' She said to me, 'Yes, child.'*—TrI (76.03.02, p.3) □ The spelling *chile* is often used in narrative dialogue, representing the commoner pronunc in this context. Cp BOY 2. **2.** (Baha) [*IF*] (Used in familiar ref to) any adult person (male or female). *Wen I gone home las' Tuesday I see Unkle Hezekiah wid he face on d' table an' he tongue stickin' out writin' vun letter. Boy, dat chile cud write bad too.*—DSJS:87 **3.** (CarA) [As a suff] BOY-CHILD, GIRL-CHILD (used to distinguish) 'infant boy', 'infant girl' esp when new-born. [As in many Afr langs. Cp Igbo *nnwa-nwoke* (= child + male) 'boy', *nnwa-nwanyi* (= child + woman) 'girl' etc] **4.** PHRASES **4.1 from a child** [*IF*]; **from (since) I was/ (you were, etc) a child** [*X*] *adv phr* (CarA) ‖ *from I born* (Jmca) From childhood; ever since I was a child. **4.2 get/have/make a child for (sb)** *vb phr* (CarA) [*IF*] [Usu of an unmarried woman] To be pregnant by, or to bear a child whose father is (sb named). **4.3 give (a woman) a child** *vb phr* (CarA) [*IF*] To make (a woman) pregnant. *She goin[g] to go on knockin[g] herself about until some man comes along and give her a child and that will settle her.*—(Antg) **4.4 making (a) child** *vb phr* (CarA) [*AF/IF*] (Be) pregnant. See MAKE Phr 5·3

child-fa·ther /1′22/ *n* (Bdos, Guyn) ‖ *baby-father* (Jmca) The acknowledged father of a child to whose mother he is not married. *My child father separated from his wife over two years ago when he came to live with me.*—NaT (75.05.25, p.18, Dear Christine) [< *child's father*, with characteristic Cr absence of possessive /-z/ and hence mostly written without hyphen] □ A **children-father** is one who so fathers more than one child.

child-mon·ey *n* (Bdos, Guyn) [*IF*] ‖ CHILD-SUPPORT (ECar)

child-mo·ther *n* (Bdos, Guyn) ‖ *baby-mother* (Jmca) An unmarried mother (usu one who is in partnership with an acknowledged CHILD-FATHER).

Child·ren! Child·ren! *n phr* (ECar) A children's chase-and-catch game that starts with a call-response routine beginning with the chaser calling 'Children! Children!' (Response: 'Yes Mama!').

child·ren-pro·per·ty *n* (Guyn) ‖ FAMILY LAND (Bdos, etc)

child-sup·port *n* (ECar) ‖ *child-money* (Bdos, Guyn) A sum of money (sometimes fixed

by a Court Order) paid regularly by a CHILD-FATHER to his CHILD-MOTHER.

chile *n* (CarA) See CHILD

chi·li [čili] *n* (StVn) ‖ ASHAM (Antg, etc) [A reduced form of CHILIBIBI]

chi·li·bi·bi [čilibibi] /1′122/ *n* (StVn, Tbgo, Trin) ‖ ASHAM (Antg, etc) *Ma had a spot in the market on Sunday mornings, and she spent a great part of the week ... making guava-cheese and guava jelly, sugar-cake, nut-cake, bennay-balls, toolum, shaddock-peel candy, chilibibi ... On these days we hung slyly about the kitchen, if only to feed on the smells.*—HCCM:26 [From an older form *chiribibi*, 'a powder of parched maize' (*TTPCG: 20*), d. 1869, but poss still surviving according to some reports. □ This is the widely known name among older speakers, evid replacing ‖ *sansam*.

chil·lam (Guyn); **chil.lum (che(e)·lum)** (Trin); **chil.lum-pipe** (Jmca) *n* A long clay pipe used for smoking ganja (marijuana). [Hin *chilam* 'the bowl of a hugga pipe']

chil·li *n* (Gren, Jmca, Trin) ‖ BIRD-PEPPER (CarA)

chi(l)·li-plum* ['čili-plʌm] *n* (Antg, Bdos, Gren, Tbgo, Trin) ‖ *August-plum* (Belz) ‖ *cerise* 3. (Trin) ‖ *chinee plum* (Gren) ‖ *garden-plum* (Guyn) ‖ *hog-plum* 2. (Baha, Belz, Jmca, TkCa) ‖ *Jamaica-plum* (Gren, StVn) ‖ *plum* 3. (Antg, Mrat, StVn) ‖ *pwinn* (StLu) ‖ *sugar-plum* (Guyn, Jmca) ‖ *yellow plum* (Belz, CayI, Jmca, Trin) A small, yellow, tough-skinned, ovoid fruit, about an inch long, with a hard, ribbed seed surrounded by soft, sweet, amber-coloured pulp, and borne in small bunches on a low, spreading tree; the yellow-skinned variety (forma *lutea*) of the JAMAICA-PLUM, *Spondias purpurea*, (*Anacardiaceae*). Chili Plum: *In season August to October.*—GHG:252 [Cp *WCD chili ~ chilli* < Nahuatl *chilli*, name of a pepper. The resemblance of the small, yellow plum to a small, yellow pepper, of wh there are several varieties, may account for the use of this name to distinguish this variety of plum from the more common *hog-plum* wh is also yellow] □ Spellings *chile, chilly* are evidently conjectural. This plum is often loosely referred to as *hog-plum*, but a clear distinction should be made. *ACPRV:382* also lists *Bequia-plum* among alternative names, but that name properly applies to the purple variety. (See JAMAICA-PLUM).

chil·lum (-pipe) *n* (Jmca) See CHILLAM

chim·ie [šimi] *n* (Antg, Guyn) ‖ CHEMISE 3. (Antg, Guyn, Trin)

chim·my[1] [šimi] *n* (Trin) [*AF—Joc*] A woman's long loose-fitting undergarment. *You mean they can't have an ole mas band without a chimmy or some bizarre representation of a woman's breast?*

We're tired of that. It's no longer funny.—AdN (77.02.23, p.14) [Reduction of CHEMISE 1.]

chim·my² [čɪmi] *n* (Jmca) [*AF*—*Joc*] ‖ UTENSIL (Bdos, Guyn) [Reduction of SE *chamber-pot*]

chi·na·man *n* (CarA) [Cricket] A left-arm bowler's ball spun from the wrist and turning in to the right-handed batsman. [Ref to Ellis 'Puss' Achong, Chinese West Indian test cricketer who first bowled such a ball at Manchester, England 1933, dismissing an English batsman who remarked 'Fancy being bowled by a bloody Chinaman!'—*(pers info from Tony Cozier, from a tape-recorded account by Ellis Achong)*]

chin·cha·ry (chin·che·ree/·ri) ['čɪnčəri] *n* (Angu, USVI) ‖ RAIN-BIRD¹ 1. (CarA)

chi·nee ba·na·na ['čaɪni bʌnɑ·nʌ] *n phr* (Jmca) ‖ APPLE-BANANA (Belz, etc) [The fruit was introduced into Jmca from China in 1846—*DJE*. Note also taxonomic name *Musa chinensis*—*PTT*]

chi·nee-bump¹ ['čaɪni-bʌmp] *n* (Jmca) [*IF*] ‖ CORK-SCREW¹ (Bdos, etc) *She have hair in chinee bump.*—Jmca (Ms)

chi·nee-bump² *vb tr* (Jmca) [*IF*] ‖ CORK-SCREW² (Bdos, etc) *I don't like to chinee-bump my hair when I wash it. I prefer to loose it out and let it dry.*—(Jmca)

chi·nee ca·la·lu* (chi·nese ca·la·lu) ['čaɪni(z) kalalu] *n phr* (Guyn) A green, succulent, climbing vine bearing a small berry that is purple when ripe, and smooth, succulent, roundish leaves (about 2 ins in diameter) wh are edible and used as a CALALU; *Amaranthus* Spp.

chi·nee co·co·nut *n phr* (Tbgo, Trin) ‖ DWARF-COCONUT (Belz, etc)

Chi·nee-cre·ole ['čaɪni-kriol] /1′212/ *n* (Trin) ‖ *Chinee-dougla* (Guyn) ‖ *Chinee-royal* (Jmca) A person one of whose parents is Chinese and the other either African or East Indian. [*Chinee* (< *Chinese*) + *creole* n [Hist] a black or light-complexioned person born in the W Indies]

Chi·nee-doug·la ['čaɪni-dʌgla] /1′212/ *n* (Guyn) [*AF*] ‖ CHINEE-CREOLE (Trin) [*Chinee* (< *Chinese*) + *dougla* (< Hin *dogalaa* 'a cross-breed, mongrel')]

chi·nee ed·doe ['čaɪni ɛdʌ] /1′212/ (Guyn) [*AF*] See CHINESE EDDOE

chi·nee plum ['čaɪni plʌm] *n phr* (Gren) [*AF*] ‖ CHILLI-PLUM (Antg, etc) *It was two school chi[ld]ren had a li[tt]le fight over couple chinee plum.*—(Gren) [Prob < *chilli plum* by folk etym]

chi·nee-roy·al ['čaɪni-rɔyal] /1′122/ *n* (Jmca) [*AF*] ‖ CHINEE-CREOLE (Trin) [*Chinee* (< *Chinese*) + *royal* < Sp *real*, a silver coin worth

one-eighth of a dollar, remaining in circulation after the introduction of Br minted currency up to the early 19C (*PCBWI:92*), but considered a discredited currency next to Br sterling. The notion of discredit was evidently maintained and more widely applied in *Jmca* Cr]

chi·nee yam ['čaɪni ya·m] *n phr* (Guyn, Trin) ‖ POTATO-YAM (Trin) 'This yam differs considerably from the other species ... Instead of making one large tuber, a varying number of smaller ones are formed somewhat resembling the potato. These are cylindrical in shape, mealy, somewhat yellowish in colour and of excellent flavour'—*PTT:151*; *Dioscorea esculenta* (*Dioscoreaceae*). ['Originated in Indo-China' —*OGEP:115*]

chi·nep [čɪnɛp] *n* (Gren) ‖ GUINEP (CarA) [By palatalization /k-/ or /g-/ forms of the original. See note at GUINEP.]

Chi·nese cab·bage* *n phr* (CarA) ‖ *pakchoy* (Guyn, Jmca, Tbgo, Trin) A thick-leaved variety of cabbage plant with a noticeable thick, white stem; it is much used as a vegetable ingredient in fried dishes; *Brassica pekinensis* (*Cruciferae*).

Chi·nese ca·la·lu *n phr* (Guyn) See CHINESE CALALU

Chi·nese Christ·mas-tree *n phr* (Guyn) ‖ BLIND-EYE 1. (Mrat)

Chi·nese ed·doe *n phr* (CarA) ‖ DASHEEN (CarA)

Chi·nese fire·crack·er *n phr* (Gren) ‖ ANTIGUA-HEATH (Bdos, etc)

Chi·nese lem·on *n phr* (Jmca) ‖ BABY-LIME (Guyn)

Chi·ne(se) yam ['čaɪni(z) ya·m] *n phr* (Guyn, Trin) ‖ *potato-yam* (Trin) 'This yam differs considerably from the other species ... Instead of making one large tuber, a varying number of smaller ones are formed somewhat resembling the potato. These are cylindrical in shape, mealy, somewhat yellowish in colour and of excellent flavour'—*PTT:151*; *Dioscorea esculenta* (*Dioscoreaceae*). ['Originated in Indo-China' —*OGEP:115*]

ching-ching *n* (CayI) ‖ BLACKBIRD 1.1 (Antg, etc) [From one of the sounds made by the bird. Cp KLING-KLING (*Jmca*)]

chink¹ *n* (Bdos, Guyn, Jmca) A small, oval, purple, bedbug that smells bad when squashed; *Cimex lectularius* (*Cimicidae*). *There was a time when the children of the poor black masses of this country were to be found with chiggers between the toes; lice in the hair; and chinks in the clothing.*—NaT (78.06.16, p.6) [OED chink, Obs form of *chinch* sb¹ 'bug'. Also *WI chinch* n 2., also called *chink-bug* 'an insect ... resembling a bed-bug in its disgusting odor' However, note also *WIED* lgbo *chinchi* 'bedbug' wh suggests the poss early currency of the term among W. Afr slaves.] □ Usage now generally restricted to older or rural folk.

Chink² *n* (Guyn) [*AF—Derog*] A Chinese person. □ An offensive term.

chinks¹ *n* (Gren) [*AF*] ‖ **chenks** (Jmca) A small, grudged bit of anything, esp food. [Cp *OED* *chinch* adj 'niggardly, sparing, miserly'. CE *chinks* may be an Obs form of this.]

chinks² *vb tr* (Gren, Tbgo, Trin) [*AF—Derog*] **1.** To give sparingly, esp in serving food or drink, out of selfishness. *Don't chinks the food, man! Put some more on my plate!*—(Tbgo) [By functional n > vb shift of CHINKS¹] **2.** [By extension] To stop or slow down a development by meanly withholding or hesitating over your contribution. *We would therefore look with horror at a conception of Caribbean integration which is chinksed at the harmonisation of fiscal incentives, at the establishment of marketing protocols, common tariffs, development banks and investment companies.*—TaP (73.07.01, p.2) **3.** PHRASE **3.1** **chinks on sb/sth** *vb phr* (Trin) [*AF*] To deny unfairly; to cheat by taking a mean advantage. *This is not simply a matter of one governmental department chinksing on another. It is a situation that could endanger the public and … set our social welfare programme back.*—ExP (73.02.18, p.9)

chinks·y (Bdos); **chink.y** (Tbgo, Trin) *adj* [*AF*] ‖ **kanchi** (Guyn) Mean; miserly; small (esp of a piece of something or a contribution). *I think it looks chinksy for Barbados to be going to Antigua, Bermuda, St Vincent, Grenada and the Cayman Islands and not offering hospitality to the representatives of those countries in return.*—Bdos (Hd, 75.03.17, p.4663)

chip¹ *vb intr* **1.** (CarA) To walk with short, sharp steps; [of old people] to walk with a steady, brisk but rather shuffling step. *Every morning you would see her chipping along going to work with her head straight, not minding a soul.*—Guyn (Ms) [*OED* chip v² (chiefly North) b. intr 'to step along nimbly, trip along'. Prob also infl in CE by SE *trip along*] **2.** (Dmca, Tbgo, Trin) [By extension of sense 1.] To shuffle along, JUMPING sedately, esp along the streets, to the beat of STEELBAND music. *… and fans left the tent chipping to the music of C. Bradley's band playing the calypso.*—TrG (80.01.13, p.1)

chip² *n* (CarA) A short, quick step. *The slow bowler took two chips up to the crease and sent down a leg break.*—HDB [By functional shift of CHIP¹ 1.]

chip³ *vb tr* PHRASE **chip your teeth** (Tbgo) ‖ SUCK YOUR TEETH (CarA) *The nurses are so ill-mannered that if patients call them more than two times they begin to chip their teeth at you.*—Tbgo (Ms)

chip-chip *n* (Tbgo, Trin) A tiny shell-fish like a clam, roughly triangular in shape, about one inch long at the base and occurring in many different colours, having sometimes two or more on its grooved shell; the shell is used for making ear-rings, etc, and the flesh is highly prized as food; *Donax striatus* or *D. denticulatus* (*Mollusca*). *Chip-chip are delicious and are used for an occasional meal by many people in Trinidad.*—Trin (Ms) [*TDV:346* Venz Sp *chipechipe, chipichipi* 'molusco bivalvo, pequeño, de sabor muy agradable'. The word is prob of Amerindian orig, the Sp form surviving in Trin] □ Pl unchanged. Note cit.

chip-chip sugar-cake *n phr* (Gren, Trin) ‖ SUGAR-CAKE 2. (Guyn) [From *chip* vb reduplicated, to represent the chipping up of the coconut]

chi·qui·to ba·na·na [čĭkito bʌna·nʌ] *n phr* (Trin) ‖ SIKYÉ (SUCRIER)-FIG (Trin) [Sp *chiquito* 'very small, tiny'. Note that the brand name in the US for the banana imported from Central Amer by United Fruit Co. is *chiquita*. In the late 1930s/early 1940s, their advertizing agency created a character (resembling Carmen Miranda) who was named Chiquita, and sang: I'm Chiquita Banana and I come to say Bananas have to ripen in a certain way. If they're flecked with brown and have a golden hue, Bananas taste the best and are the best for you, etc—(*pers info*, L. Urdang)]

chi·rise *n* (Nevs) See GOVERNOR-PLUM 1.

chis(s) [čɪs] *n* (Guyn, Trin, USVI) A chest or cannister made of iron or wood. [< *chist*, an EE pronunc of *chest* current (*OED*) from the 14C–17C. Cp cits from Chaucer (1386) and later (1601) 'Cloths and apparels bestowed in chists and coffers']

chive(s) [saɪv(z)] *n* (*pl*) (Trin) ‖ ESCHALLOT (Bdos, Guyn) □ Note pronunc in spite of spelling. Also often **cives**.

Cho! [čʊ] *excl* (Belz, Jmca) **1.** Exclamation of mild disgust (with a situation that should be better than it is), hence also of impatience, annoyance, etc. **a.** *Cho' man! Do Better Than That.*—WeG (H, 73.01.17, p.31) **b.** *What about this hurricane business, eh? Noticed anything peculiar? / Like what? / The strong breeze, man. / Cho! / Cho, nuh? You wait until it gathers enough speed and blows you straight up to Blue Mountain Peak, boy. You wait!*—SH:30, 31 [Cp *DAFL* Twi *twô* [čɔ] interj. Surely! Also *ADFEF* Ewe *tsoo* 'excl de surprise'] **2.** [By extension] Exclamation of disbelief. *'Oh,' I replied, 'They just devalued your dollar.' 'Cho!' he said incredulously. 'They wouldn't fool with that!'*—ReP (80.01.06, p.11)

cho·ba ['čʊbʌ] *n* (Antg); (**chu·ber, tru·ba, tu·ber**) (Antg, StKt) [*IF*] ‖ EGGPLANT (CarA)

[Prob < ‖ *anchoba* ~ ‖ *antrover* (*Antg*) by aphaeresis and misplaced infl of E *tuber*, because of its use as a vegetable]

cho·cho [čočo] *n* (Baha, Belz, Jmca, TkCa) ‖ CHRISTOPHENE (CarA) [Cp Sp *chocho* 'lupin, a leguminous herb'. But *SDGA* Lat Am Sp *chocho* 'vulgarism (popular in Mexico, Cuba and Spain) for the female vulva', also the name of 'a fruit of a tree ... about 12 centimetres long ... with a coarse skin that remains green in maturity'. The Sp 'vulgarism' may have been of Afr orig. Cp *DAFL* Twi *twɔtwɔ* (obsc) 'vagina'. However the Sp masc inflexion—*-o* must have influenced a shift in meaning to the male testicle, thence an extension of *chocho* as a vul name for this fruit because of its shape and the sparse hair-like growths on its skin; hence cp *TDV* Venz Sp *chocho* 2. 'male genital' 3. *Lupinus humilis* 'a vegetable with a very hairy skin'] □ Pl **chochoes**.

cho·co·late [čɒ·klɪt] *n* 1. (Guyn) Finger-length sticks (hence CHOCOLATE STICKS) rolled by hand from portions of a heavy mixture of finely ground or pounded cocoa beans and hot water; these STICKS are stored or sold for use in making CHOCOLATE TEA. 2. (CarA) ‖ *chocolate lumps* (TkCa) A breakfast item made by dropping spoonfuls of a dough or thick batter of flour, sugar, eggs, and cream into boiling cocoa, producing lumps wh are cooled and stored to be used to make a sweetened, hot drink; [by extension] any hot drink made from any commercially marketed, cocoa-based powder.

cho·co·late-tea [čɒ·klɪt-ti] /1'21/ *n* (ECar) [*IF*] ‖ *creole cocoa* (Trin) A hot breakfast ‖ *cocoa-tea* (CarA) ‖ *country-chocolate* (Jmca) drink made by boiling a CHOCOLATE STICK, CHOCOLATE LUMP, or the powder from ground cocoa beans, and adding milk and sugar. [A redundant compound < CHOCOLATE (as prec) + TEA 'morning drink' (*CarA*)]

cho·ka [čo·ka ~ čokha] *n* (Guyn, Trin) A method of cooking a side-dish of green vegetables, coconut, potatoes, or (in *Guyn*) shredded saltfish, by frying in hot oil or roasting over an open flame, then seasoning. [Bhoj < Hin *chokhaa* 'purée of boiled or roasted vegetables'. In *Trin*, Indic speakers often retain the aspiration /kh/] □ Sometimes qualified, ex: **aloo-choka, balanjay-choka, saltfish-choka**, etc.

choke-and-rob[1] *vb* (Guyn) ‖ *lock off* (Guyn) [*AF*] To attack a person from behind by hugging the neck violently with one arm (hence 'choke'), while robbing a trouser-pocket or grabbing a handbag with the other.

choke-and-rob[2] *adj, n* (Guyn) (Of or concerned with) the act of choking and robbing (as prec). **a.** *A spate of muggings, similar to the much publicised choke-and-rob incidents in Guyana, has broken out in Barbados.*—NaT (77.03.06, p.1) **b.** *You will find that every case of Choke and Rob before the Court when being taken summarily is*

postponed *for a great length of time.*—GyC (77.02.27, p.8)

choke-and-rob·ber *n* (Guyn) A thief who CHOKES-AND-ROBS. *A release from the Ministry of Information yesterday made it clear that the campaign is aimed at all wrongdoers—from choke-and-robbers to white collar criminals.*—GyC (77.12.11, p.1)

cho·ky ban·jo *n phr* (Angu) [*AF—Joc*] ‖ CASSAVA-BREAD (CarA) *Cassava bread* (*St Kitts and Nevis*) *is also called Choky Banjo, Hard-Time, Hard-Labour, and also Husy in Anguilla.*—Angu (Ms, 1978)

chook [čuk] *n, vb* (Mrat, Nevs, StKt, Tbgo, Trin, USVI) 1. ‖ JOOK *vb, n* (CarA) 2. *vb tr* To plant a seed or seedling. *A goin*[g] *chook some corn dis weekend.*—(Tbgo) [A devoiced form of *jook*]

chook-chook *n* (Dmca) See CHUK-CHUK.

choo·la (chool·ha) *n* (Guyn, Trin) See CHULHA

chop[1] (chap) [čɒp ~ čap] *vb* (CarA) To strike (sb) very hard with the sharp edge of a cutlass or similar weapon so as to maim or kill. *Under further cross-examination, he said he did not encourage M—to chop Joe S—'s neck.*—AMAM: 106 □ Although the word is widely used in this sense, its other IAE senses (*to chop wood, chop down trees*, etc) are also normally current. *Chap* is the regular folk pronunc

chop[2] (chap[2]) *n* (CarA) 1. A sharp blow, or the deep wound caused by the blow, struck with a sharp heavy weapon. *In a family dispute at Fyzabad on Christmas Day, S—, a mechanic, received chops with a cutlass.*—ExP (72.12.28, p.15) 2. PHRASE 2.1 **fire/pelt a chop at (sb)** *vb phr* (Guyn) [*IF*] To strike at (sb) with a sharp heavy weapon. *Mr B— said that the accused pelted a cutlass chop at the neck of B— who put up his hand to ward off the blow and ... his hand was completely severed.*—GyC (75.12.11, p.3)

chos·sel[1] (chos·sle[1]) [čɒsl] *vb* (Bdos) [*AF*] [Of a youngster] To attract a girl's friendship; to begin dating a girl. *When his regular girlfriend's gone away he chossels this other girl, but he's not really serious about her.*—(Bdos) [Poss < SE *jostle*, vb, with devoicing (cp *jook* ~ *chook*) with the sense 'jostle other young people to obtain favours of opposite sex'. Poss also a blend of *choose/ chick* + HUSTLE] □ Usage as vb, though prob the original, is now much rarer than as n (See next).

chos·sel[2] (chos·sle[2]) [čɒsl] *n* (Bdos) [*AF*] 1. A girlfriend or a boyfriend (but more commonly the former). 2. ‖ CRAFT (ECar) *When he could control himself Roy said 'Look I going out here and look for a chossel to dance.'*—Bdos (Ms, 1976) [By functional shift of CHOSSEL[1] vb]

chote[1]; **chote up** [čoˑt (ʌp)] *vb* (*phr*) (Guyn) [*AF*] ‖SWEET-TALK[2] (CarA) *He was leaning on his bicycle by the stand-pipe choting up the girl while she was washing the clothes, and if you see how she was laughing, too.*—(Guyn) [Cp *SDGA* Am Sp *chotear* 'to joke, not to treat a matter seriously']

chote[2] [čoˑt] *n* (Guyn) [*AF*] **1.** ‖SWEET-TALK[1] (CarA) **2.** Impressive talk about your self-importance, in an effort to persuade another person. [By functional vb > n shift of CHOTE[1]] **3.** *PHRASE* **3.1 give (sb) (a lot of) chote** *vb phr* (Guyn) [*AF*] To try to persuade a person by flattery or impressive talk about yourself.

chou ca·ra·ibe [šu karaiˑb] *n phr* (StLu) ‖TANNIA (CarA) [FR = 'Carib cabbage']

chou·val-bon·dyé [šuval bɔ̃dye] /1ʹ212ʹ/ *n* (Dmca, StLu) ‖GOD-HORSE (CarA) [Fr Cr < Fr *cheval* 'horse' + (*bon*) *dieu* '(good) God'. See etym note at GOD-HORSE] □ Either name, *chouval-bondyé* or *god-horse*, is likely to be used in the spoken E of *Dmca* or *StLu*. The former is commoner but less likely to be written.

chow·tal [čɒʊtaˑl] *n* (Guyn, Trin) A special type of song sung during the PHAGWA festival by a group (usu of men) alternating by sections and using drums and small cymbals. [Hin *chautaal* 'a rhythmic cycle of four beats; a song sung with that rhythm']

Christ·mas bank /1ʹ12/; **Christ.mas bank-hol.i.day** *n phr* (Bdos) Boxing Day; 26th December. *I was saying that if these canes aren't cut soon we would be celebrating* [*crop-over*] *ka-doooment day on Christmas bank-holiday.*—AdV (92.03.13, p.9, E. Lewis)

Christ·mas-bush /1ʹ12/ *n* **1.*** (CarA) ‖*baby-bush* 2. (StVn) ‖*jaok-in-the-bush* (Jmca) ‖*Mary-Magdalene* (Gren) A straggling, sometimes erect shrub that can exceed 6 ft in height, with slender stalks, spear-shaped leaves with a sweetish smell, and small, white to light mauve flower-heads that bloom in close-packed bunches about December (hence the name); both leaves and flowers are used medicinally for flu and fever and in poultices; *Eupatorium odoratum* (*Compositae*). **2.** (Angu) ‖CATTLE-TONGUE (Antg, etc) **3.** (StKt) ‖SNOW-ON-THE-MOUNTAIN (Antg, etc) □ The name appears to be applied also to other plants that flourish about December and have some use as folk-medicines.

Christ·mas-can·dle* /1ʹ122/ *n* (Bdos, Dmca, Nevs, StLu) ‖*candle-flower* (CayI) ‖*candlestick* (Jmca) ‖*carrion-crow bush* (Guyn) ‖*king-of-the-forest* (Jmca) ‖*ring-worm-bush* (Bdos, Gren, Jmca, Trin) ‖*sa-sparilla* (VIs) ‖*séné-mawon* (StLu) ‖*t-arantan, wild-senna* (Trin) A sprawling shrub with pale-green compound leaves consisting of pairs of broadly oblong leaflets and very showy,

golden-yellow flowers in almost cylindrical clusters at the ends of erect stalks sticking up well above the foliage (suggestive of upheld candles and hence some of the folk-names); the leaves are used medicinally for skin disorders; though the flowers, in some habitats, are said to be of unpleasant smell; *Cassia alata* (*Leguminosae-Caesalpiniaceae*). [From its seasonal flowering about Christmas]

Christ·mas can·dle·stick *n phr* (Baha, Jmca) ‖BALL-BUSH (Bdos, Jmca) *The Christmas candlestick* [*is a*] *rather common weed of the fields, roadsides and waste ground, ... flourishing all the year but mainly from October to March.*—AFPJ: 643

Christ·mas-flow·er *n* **1.** (Dmca, Jmca, StVn, Tbgo) ‖POINSETTIA (CarA) **2.** (Nevs) ‖LEAF-OF-LIFE (Bdos, etc)

chris·to·phene (**chris·to·phine**)* *n* (ECar) ‖*chocho* (Baha, Belz, Jmca, TkCa) A light-green, pear-shaped vegetable about 4 to 6 ins long with a furrowed and slightly hairy skin (*PTT:280*), flesh of the texture of squash or vegetable marrow, borne on a climbing vine with big, rough, roundish leaves; *Sechium edule* (*Cucurbitaceae*).

chub *n* **1.** (CarA) ‖*parrot-fish* (CarA) Any of a number of varieties, of different colours, of a fish weighing an average of about 2 to 3 lbs, with prominent scales, a usu slimy head, and tough but tasty flesh; *Scaridae spp.* **2.** (Angu, Antg) One of two varieties of a dark-grey fish, with small scales and a tough flesh, that is usu caught in smooth water away from reefs. **3.** (StLu, StVn) ‖CACA-BELLY 1. (Gren, StLu) **4.** *PHRASE* **4.1 have chub guts** *id phr* (StVn) [*AF*] [Of a child] To have distended bowels.

chu·ber *n* (Antg, StKt) See CHOBA

chuk-chuk (**chook-chook**) [čʊk-čʊk] *n* (Dmca) ‖FIT-WEED (Bdos, etc) [Prob < *jook-jook* with devoicing [ʝ > č], referring to the prickly, tough, leaf-like petals of the flowers] □ Name used mostly in the purely Anglophone north-east area of *Dmca*.

chul·ha (**choo·la, chool·ha, chu·la**) [čʊla ~ čʊlha] *n* (Guyn, Trin) [Indic] A rural fireplace, usu on the ground, made of a mixture of mud and cow-dung shaped and plastered by hand and baked hard, to serve as the family cooking-place. [Hin *chuulhaa* 'a fireplace, hearth'. The aspirated form is less frequent among CE Indic speakers]

chu·pid (**chu·pit**) [čʊpɪd /-ɪt] *adj* (CarA) [*AF—Cr*] Stupid; gullible; uninformed; light-headed. *A-A, after all you t'ink Barbados people chupid so nuh? ... You en see how much ah dem in de police now?*—WeN (52.11.03, Annie & Josephine) [< SE *stupid* with characteristic reduction /st- > t-/ (cp /tan/ < stand, etc) with affrication /ty

> ch/, and devoicing of final /-d > -t/] □ This
form is commonly found in the narrative dialogue of *CarA* writings. It is a less intense term
than *stupid* in CE.

chu·pid·ee (chu·pid·ie, chu·pid·(d)y) ['ʧʊ
pɪdi] *n* (CarA) [*AF—Cr/Derog*] ‖ *stupidie*
(CarA) A gullible, uninformed person; an idiot.
[< *chupid* (as prec) + *ie*, familiar diminutive.
Cp IAE *oldie*]

chu·pid·ness (chu·pit·ness) [ʧʊ
pɪdnɪs~ʧʊpɪtnɪs] *n* (CarA) [*AF—Cr*] ‖ STU-
PIDNESS (CarA) *Africa behine we now, man....
Doan mine you see de Minister a Culture talkin'
all dat chupidness. We ent want dis Africa business;
we want American motor car.*—MN:19 □ Common in familiar folk speech, considered less
intense than CE *stupidness*, esp in the exp *talk
chupidness* 'talk silly nonsense'.

chu·pit *adj*; **chu.pit.ness** *n* (CarA) See CHUPID,
CHUPIDNESS

chups(e) (chupes) *n, vb* (Dmca, Trin) See
CHEUPS

church·ward·en *n* (Bdos) [Hist] The administrative officer chosen from the elected
members of the VESTRY as head of the Board of
GUARDIANS, to see to the carrying out of its
responsibilities of local administration in the
PARISH. [From ref to the person's earliest established function, the maintenance of the Parish
Church, to wh were later added all functions
of secular local government] □ The post was
abolished with the end of Local Government in
1958.

church·yard-grass *n* (Mrat) ‖ CARPET-DAISY
(Bdos) [Because its uncultivated growth is encouraged in churchyard cemeteries]

chu·ri ['ʧuri] *n* (Guyn, Trin) [Indic] A thin
bangle of gold, silver, or other material (sometimes glass), or a collection of such bangles worn
on a woman's forearm. [Hin *chuuṛii* 'bangle,
ring'] □ Pl *churia* (Hin) or *churis*.

chur·ki (chur·kee) ['ʧʊrki] *n* (Guyn, Trin)
[Indic] A tuft or a long lock of hair left in the
middle of a Hindu man's head, the rest of the
hair being shaven, during a period of special
religious observances. [Hin *churki* 'a lock of
hair']

chut·ney *n* (Guyn, Trin) [Indic] A secular
Hindu song with a very lively rhythm, used with
instrumental accompaniment for dancing. *The
East-Indian dominated United National Congress,
a splinter of the ruling party, while not relying
heavily on advertisements, has one theme song, in
chutney style, which urges the electorate to 'Vote
UNC'.*—AdV (91.12.11, p.10) [< Hin *chaṭnii*,
'a hot condiment made from a mixture of crushed
green mangoes, pepper, garlic salt and other
spices.' (This condiment, in a much milder form

> SE chutney, commercial chutney). The orig
connotation of spiciness, liveliness, is adapted to
describe the music]

ci·gale ['siga·l] *n* (Trin) ‖ *aberdeen* (Tbgo)
‖ *rain-bird*[2] (Gren, StLu) A large, dark-bodied
insect with compound, membranous wings; it
lives in tall trees and makes a high-pitched,
saw-like sound at dusk; insect of the genus *Que-
sada* (*Cicadidae*). *If you are both nature-lovers
who thrill to the sound of birds at sunrise and the
call of the cigale at eveningtime there are a number
of old-fashioned country houses dotted in various
parts of the island.*—ExP (73.04.29, p.2) [Fr
cigale 'cricket']

ci·li·ment (ce·le·ment) [sɪlimɛnt] *n* (BrVi,
Dmca, Gren, StKt) [*X*] ‖ CINNAMON (TREE)
(CarA) [By /n > l/ shift < CINNEMENT < *cinnamon*] □ An illiterate name, rarely spelled, but
evid occurring in rural usage in many places,
esp for the item used as a spice.

cin·na·mon* (tree) *n* (*phr*) (CarA) ‖ *cannelle*
(StLu) ‖ *ciliment* (BrVi, Dmca, Gren, StKt)
‖ *cinnement* (Gren, Trin) ‖ *spice* (Bdos, Dmca,
Gren, Guyn) The small tree *Cinnamomum zeylanicum* (*Lauraceae*), but more esp its long, leathery green and strongly aromatic leaves, or pieces
of its dried bark, both used for flavouring food
and drink. □ Sometimes confused with *bay leaf*
because of similarity of appearance and use of
both for yielding oil and for flavouring.

cin·ne·bone *n* (Guyn) See SENEBONE

cin·ne·ment [sɪnimɛnt] *n* (Gren, Trin) [*X*]
‖ CINNAMON (CarA) [< SE *cinnamon*]

Cir·cas·sian bead/bean/seed *n phr* (Jmca,
Trin, USVI) ‖ JUMBIE-BEAD 3. (Gren, etc) [A
European name prob imported from the USA,
where it is one of the names used also for the
RED SANDALWOOD tree (*ACPRV:173*)]

cir·ce(e)-bush [sɜrsi-buʃ] *n* (Bdos) ‖ CERASEE
(Baha, etc)

ci·rique *n* (Dmca) See SIWIK

cive(s) [saɪv(z)] *n* (Gren, Trin) ‖ ESCHALLOT
(Bdos, Guyn) [< SE *chives* with loss of initial
affrication, or perh a spelling pronunc of Fr
cives] □ Also written *syve* (Gren).

cive-and-thyme [saiv-an-taim] *n* (Gren) Seasoning made up of chives and thyme-leaves.

claim *n* (Guyn) A large tract of land and water
(in the interior of *Guyn*) the boundaries of wh
are identified on a licence wh permits the holder
to prospect for gold and diamonds within that
area. *A tiger ... was shot dead on Sunday morning,
December 28 by Mr Norbert St Rose close by a
camp on a claim of Apaiqua named 'Britton'
belonging to Mr C.J. Mortley, well-known claim
holder of the district.*—DaC (53.01.12, p.3)

clam·my-cher·ry* (clam-/clam·(m)a-/ clam·man-cher·ry)/ı′ı22/ n (CarA) 1. (CarA) ‖ *clam-and-cherry* (StKt) [X] ‖ *duppy-cherry* (Jmca) ‖ *fig*³ (TkCa) ‖ *gum-tree, kaka-poul* ı. (StLu) ‖ *koko-poul* (Dmca) ‖ *sticky berry* (Antg) ‖ *turkey-berry* (Antg, Mrat) A round, cream-coloured fruit about half an inch in dia-meter, with a sweet, scanty, sticky pulp sur-rounding a single seed; it is borne in large clusters on a small tree with arching branches without flowers; *Cordia obliqua (Boraginaceae). Children use clammy-cherry as paste for their kites and they sometimes eat the sweet stainy pulp.*—Antg (Ms, 1977) 2. (Brbu, Jmca, Mrat, Tbgo) ‖ *duppy-cherry* (Jmca) ‖ *manjack*² (Dmca, Gren, Tbgo, ViIs) ‖ *wild-cherry* (Belz) ‖ *wild clammy-cherry* (Bdos) A round, bright-red fruit about one centimetre in diameter with a sweet, sticky pulp surrounding a single seed, borne in lux-uriant clusters on a large deciduous tree with white flowers; *Cordia collococca (Boraginaceae). The sweet scarlet clammy-cherries are greedily eaten by birds and are fed to chickens and turkeys in Tobago.*—PTT:135 [*Clammy* (for its stick-iness) + *cherry* (for its appearance, esp the red variety)] □ There is some confusion in the use of the same name for the two varieties, the latter of wh is however less widely distributed in the *CarA*. The form '*clammy-*' is the only one justified by the etym.

clap·per n (Baha, Jmca) ‖ BEATER (Baha, Guyn) □ This name is used in Cat Island (Baha), ‖ *bea-ter* in So Andros.

clap·per-bush n (USVI) ‖ LEAF-OF-LIFE (Bdos, etc)

clar·et-fig (Clarke-fig) n phr (Bdos) ‖ BUCK-BANANA (Guyn) [From its purplish-red 'claret' colour. '*Clarke*' by folk etym, 'Clarke' being a widely current *Bdos* family name]

clar·et-nut (Clara-nut n (Guyn) ‖ DWARF-COCONUT (Belz, etc) [From the slightly purplish colour of some *Guyn* varieties. The form *Clara* is prob owing to folk etym]

class adj (CarA) [IF] Of a high quality (esp of a player's performance). *They probably did not expect to hear the class music they heard. By the following night the word had spread far and wide and a sell-out crowd at the Palm Beach gave the message that St Lucia had been turned on.*—AdN (73.09.08, p.8)

clay·ed sug·ar n phr (Bdos) [Hist/Sugar Ind] Sugar dried over a period of several weeks by a drip process in large clay pots with a hole in the bottom through wh the resulting BLACK STRAP MOLASSES was collected.

clay pipe n phr (CarA) A small, cheap tobacco pipe made of white clay and popular long after the post-slavery era, esp among old women.

clean¹ adj (CarA) 1. [In particular ref to a black person's skin] Smooth; unblemished. (Hence adjs *clean-faced*, CLEAN-SKINNED). 2. ‖ *sharp* 3. (Guyn) [Of a non-white person's facial features, esp the profile] Having a straight nose and thin lips considered more typical of a European. *Your great grandmother had clean features and used to stand up proud.*—(Bdos)

clean²; **clean out** vb intr (phr) PHRASE **day clean (out)** id phr (Baha, Bdos, Guyn) [IF/AF] Day dawns, breaks; the sun is about to rise. **a.** *It was still dark outside, although the day was cleaning slowly.*—CBM:88 **b.** *I remember, mus' have been after six o'clock, day done clean.*— (Baha) [Prob calque from W Afr langs. Basically an association of 'bright' with 'clean'] □ See also DAY-CLEAN, n.

clean-neck fowl n phr (Gren, Guyn, StVn, Trin, ViIs) ‖ BARE-NECK FOWL (Bdos, etc)

clean off vb phr (Tbgo, Trin) [IF] ‖ *wash off* (Bdos) To wash the body with a wet wash-cloth, (of a woman) esp the genitals.

clean-out n (CarA) [IF] PHRASE **take a clean-out** vb phr (CarA) [IF] 1. To purge the body by taking a strong laxative. 2. [Of women] To take a dilatation and curettage, known as 'D and C'.

clean-skin(ned) adj (CarA) [IF/AF] 1. Hav-ing a smooth, dark face and unblemished skin. 2. ‖ CLEAR-SKIN(NED) (CarA) *At the time the fairer your skin, the more privileged you were. Blackness was a curse. This ideology persisted until Garvey came into the picture. The bourgeois and the 'clean skin' people opposed the movement (U.N.I.A.) vigorously, but it grew.*—ToR (73.05.27, p.3)

clear adj (CarA) [Of persons] ‖ CLEAR-SKIN(NED) (CarA) *Now we have found our very own at last / No more hot comb to press the hair / No more bleach creams to make us clear ... Because we know that ... black is beautiful.*—Bdos (Cso—Mighty Duke, 1969) [Cp OED clear 4. d. 'of the com-plexion, skin, etc. Bright, fresh and of pure colour ... esp implying ... transparency of the surface skin ...' + cit 1801: 'Persons of delicate fibres, of smooth, lax and clear skin']

clear-skin(ned) adj (CarA) [IF/AF] ‖ *clean-skin(ned), clear* (CarA ‖ *fair*¹ (CarA) ‖ *fair-skin(ned), light-skin(ned)* (CarA) Having a light or very light-brown complexion and soft hair. *A good-looking clear-skin girl from Cane Garden with hair down she back?*—MBGB:62

clear sugar n phr (Bdos) The lightest brown, straw-coloured sugar, with very fine crystals from wh most of the molasses has been extracted, so being less sweet but preferred at table. □ See DARK SUGAR, WHITE-SUGAR, YELLOW-CRYSTAL SUGAR.

clerk·ess (clerk·ist) [klʌ(r)kɛs/-kɪs] n (Bdos, Guyn, Trin) [X] A saleswoman in a store. **a.** ...

*go to town as a clerkess / stannin up all day in she
stockin an pride.*—BMP:43 **b.** *In B.G. Negroes
support all leading commercial centres, stores,
pawnbrokeries, etc., but ... there are few if any
dark-skinned clerkists.*—DaC (52.04.01, p.2)
[*W3 clerkess* (chiefly Scot) 'a female clerk'. Also
OEDS + earliest cit 1923] □ The term is disliked in *Bdos* and used mostly by older folk. The
form **clerkist** is prob due to false analogy (cp
typist etc).

cling-cling *n* (Jmca) See KLING-KLING

cloak *n* (Guyn) A raincoat. [Perh Hist, *cloak*
being the earliest E name for a covering garment
of this kind. *Mackintosh, raincoat* were 19c
words, *rainwear* 20c]

cloak up *vb intr* (Guyn) **1.** To draw your body
together or hug yourself as when feverish or
cold. *At the funeral I saw her cloaking up in the
corner as if she didn't want anybody to talk to
her.*—(Guyn) **2.** [Of chickens] To look sickly and
droopy with the head tucked into the chest and
the eyes closed.

clos·et [klɒzɪt] *n* (CarA) An outside wooden
latrine with a pit. *Of course the toilet there is none
of the modern with water and flushing and all that.
This one has a closet pit and it has not been
cleaned for ten years and now it is full and running
over.*—BoM (75.02.14, p.5) [Cp *OED closet* 7.
'short for ... water-closet'. However there is no
water-flushing in CE *closet*] □ This is almost the
only sense in wh the word occurs in CE, other
SE senses being regarded as literary.

clos·et-man *n* (CarA) [*AF—Derog*] A sanitary
inspector. [Because, esp in former times, CLOSETS
were the main sanitation problem in private
property]

clot [klɒt] (Guyn); **(cloth)** [klɒːt] (Jmca) *n* [*Vul*]
‖ BLOOD-CLOT(H) 2. (Antg, Jmca) [*Vul*]

clothes[1] [kloːz] *n pl* PHRASE **keep/put clothes
on (sb's) back** *vb phr* (CarA) To manage to
provide (sb) with clothing fit to wear in public;
to prevent (sb) from going in rags. *After the
father died the mother had a real battle to keep
the clothes on their backs so they could keep going
to school.*—(Guyn) [Cp IrE *have/keep/put a stitch
(of clothes) on your back*: 'Without the brother
the children wouldn't a had a stitch on their
back'—(*pers info, L. Todd*)]

clothes[2] *vb tr* (Antg, Jmca) [*AF*] To provide
(sb) with clothes; to keep (sb) duly clad. [By
functional n > vb shift of CLOTHES[1]]

clothes-bat·ter *n* (Jmca) ‖ BEATER (Baha,
Guyn) [Prob *DJE batter* vb 'beat severely' +
clothes]

club *n* (USVI) ‖ LEND-HAND (Tbgo) *When they
ready to build, was no problem. They just had club
and everybody build together.*—(USVI)

Cmde *abbr n as title* (Guyn) Comrade—the
official form of addressing a man or woman,
adopted by the Government of Guyana from
about 1964 in pursuance of socialist patterns.

C.M.T. *abbr* (Trin & Tbgo) The Chaconia
Medal of the Order of the Trinity, a gold, silver,
or bronze medal awarded as a national honour
for long and meritorious service in promoting
community spirit and national welfare in Trinidad & Tobago; the letters are placed after the
recipient's name. [From CHACONIA, the National
Flower of Trin & Tbgo]

coag [koˑg] *n* (Guyn) A thick drink made by
beating eggs in milk with sugar and some rum
added. [Poss associated with *EDD cog* sb[3] (Sc,
Irel, etc) 1. 'a hollow wooden vessel for holding
milk, broth etc'] □ Also written **cogue, coag,
cug**

coal-burn·er *n* (CarA) Someone who produces charcoal in bulk by burning wood in a
COAL-PIT.

coal-keel (coal-kiln) [koˑl-kiˑl] *n* (Angu,
USVI) ‖ COAL-PIT (Brbu, etc) [< *coal* + *kiln*.
OED gives pronunc /kil, kiln/ and cits wh indicate [kiˑl] ex 1626 *Bacon* 'The drying of malt
upon the Keele'] □ The same pronunc applies
to both spellings, the form **-keel** being justified
from EE.

coal-pit *n* (Brbu, Dmca, Gren, StVn, ViIs)
‖ *coal-keel* (Angu, USVI) ‖ *coal-kiln* (Angu)
‖ *coals-kill* (Jmca) A pit dug about 6 ft x 10 ft
x 2 ft deep, surrounded by a mound of earth
about 3 ft high, in wh hardwood branches are
laid, and covered with green leaves and earth to
be slowly burnt into charcoal. *It will be remembered that when charcoal-burning was still a
profitable small industry here, cattle would ... stand
closely to leeward of a 'coal-pit' in order to savour
the fumes.*—GNHIG:33 □ In *ViIs* the name also
applies to a surface-burning method without a
dug pit.

coal-pot *n* (CarA) ‖ *coal-stove* (Baha, TkCa)
‖ *iron-pot* (Baha) A small, round, cast-iron,
charcoal-burning, open stove consisting of a container bowl about 15 ins in diameter and about
6 ins deep with a grate in its bottom, supported
on a neck about 6 ins high and with an opening
for air; it is used for roasting and cooking or for
heating flat-irons. [< Du *koolpot* < *kool* 'charcoal'
+ *pot* 'pot, jar, container'. Cp Sran *korpatoe*
'coal-pot'. Originally (and still in some places)
described on invoices for importation as *Dutch
stoves*, these portable field 'cookers' were prob
introduced in 17C by the Dutch, whence the
Eng homophone 'coal pot']

coals *n pl* (CarA) Charcoal sold as fuel for
cooking. [The pl is the regular CE form, prob
in ref to the pieces of charcoal. Cp *OED coal* 4.
(Obs). Used in pl or as a collective sing]

coals-kill n (Jmca) ‖ COAL-PIT (Brbu, etc) **[** < *coals*, as prec + *kill*, prob an EE survival = 'kiln'. See *OED kiln/kil, kiln/* + cits with 'kill' as variant, ex 1611 (Bible) 'bricke kill'—Jer XLIII.9**]**

coal-stove n (Baha, TkCa) ‖ COAL-POT (CarA)

coarse hair n phr (Antg, Mrat, StKt) ‖ BAD HAIR (CarA)

coarse-salt n (Antg, Guyn) ‖ *pond-salt, pan-salt* (Brbu, TkCa) Unrefined salt, in lumps, obtained in some islands by the evaporation of trapped sea-water, and used in pickling pork, preserving fish, etc.

coarse-shrimp(s) n (pl) (Guyn) Any variety of large shrimp including prawns. *In those days when coarse shrimp was washing ashore you would get a basketful for a shilling.*—Guyn (Ms) ['Coarse' by comparison with FINE SHRIMPS] □ Commonly occurs as a collective singular as in cit.

cob (caub, cawb) [kɒb ~ kɒ:b] adj, n (Bdos, Guyn) ‖ *brown-skin* (CarA) ‖ *cob(b)-skin(ned)* (Bdos) ‖ *cobre* (Guyn) (Person) of brown skin; (also loosely applied as n to any person whose skin is not quite black.) **a.** *I went over to Mr Smith's house, and saw a lady named Miss Kitty Stewart, a cob woman.*—LMSPJS:54 **b.** *Brown skin blonde and fair-skin / Smooth black brunette and cob...*—SJEV:18 [Prob < Pg *cobre* 'copper' or *caboclo* 'copper-coloured, red-skinned', both of wh forms may have produced loans. Cp Twi *kɔbere* 'copper' (*DAFL*: Pg loan); Ewe *kɔba* 'copper coin'; Yoruba *kɔbɔ* (< Eng copper). See also note at CABUKRU] □ In some places the term suggests a person who feels he/ she is of better quality because his/her skin is not quite black. (The form pronounced **caub** seems to be esp *Guyn*).

cob-beach n (Nevs) ‖ COWITCH (CarA)

cob-ble (co-ble) [kɒbl] n (ViIs) A small coastal fishing-boat equipped with a sail. *Availing themselves of their owners' boats [slaves] absconded to Puerto Rico until an Act of 1787 effectively curtailed the practice by making it obligatory to keep a white man on board every fishing boat or cobble not hauled out of the water and secured every night.*—DHBVI:82 [*OED coble* 2. 'a sea fishing-boat with a flat bottom ... used chiefly on the N.E. coast of England' + cits to 1845]

cob-bler n **1.** (Bdos) The black sea-urchin whose thin shell bristles with long, black, moving spikes wh, if stepped on, puncture the skin, causing severe pain; *Diadema antillarum (Echinoidea). Mr Bourne noted that Barbadians never ate 'cobblers' but that, like sea-eggs, 'cobblers' were hardly seen between the sea rocks nowadays.*—AdV (87.03.20, p.6) [Perh from resemblance of black spine to a cobbler's needle] **2.** (ECar) The FRIGATE or MAN-O'-WAR bird; *Fregata magnificens*

(Fregatidae). Sitting on the beach overlooking Carlisle Bay ... we watched a male Frigate Bird or Cobbler circling on wide cranked wings well out to sea.—AdN (79.03.21, p.7) [Name said to be due to the shape of its beak] **3.*** (BrVi, Dmca, StVn) ‖ *kawang* (Dmca) A broad, flat-bodied, silvery fish with a round forehead, of the *Pompano* family, growing to about 2 ft in length and of excellent food value; *Trachinotus carolinus (Carangidae).*

cob(b)-skin(ned) adj (Bdos) ‖ COB (Bdos, Guyn)

cob-le n (ViIs) See COBBLE

cob-re n, adj (Guyn) ‖ COB (Bdos, Guyn)

co-bun-gru n (Guyn) See CABUKRU

cob-web vb (Guyn, Tbgo, Trin) To brush away the cobwebs from the ceiling and upper parts of (a room, dwelling, etc). *The campaign which started last weekend involves cob-webbing and dusting of the office, the weeding of the court's compound and the painting of the fence around it.*—GyC (70.05.20, p.11) [By analogy with *dust* vb]

cob-web-broom n (Guyn) A broom with a long, slim handle and slight, sparse bristles, used for COBWEBBING a room; any broom improvised for such a purpose.

co-ca-beh (co-co-bay) n (CarA) See KOKOBE □ Also *cockabeh, kuckabeh*, etc.

co-chi-neal (cac-tus)* ['kɒčɪni-l k(y)aktʌs] / ɪ'ɪ21'2/ n (phr) (Guyn, Jmca, Trin) ‖ *cactus* (Belz, Guyn, Jmca) ‖ *cruchineel* (Guyn) [X] ‖ *flat-hand dildo* (Bdos) ‖ *pear-bush* (TkCa) ‖ *plimpler-pear* (Jmca) ‖ *prickle/prickler/ prickly pear* (Baha, Bdos, CayI, ViIs) ‖ *rachette* (Trin) ‖ *scrushineel* (Bdos) [X] A cactus that looks like a small tree made up of a number of jointed, succulent, pad-like, oblong green stems, the more mature of wh bear a yellowish-red flower and edible red fruit; the younger ones have clusters of sharp spines, and are widely used for the medicinal value of their slimy pulp; *Opuntia spp*, or *Nopalea cochenillifera* or *Cereus spp (Cactaceae).* [< Fr *cochenille* < Sp *cochinilla*, the red bug that feeds on this cactus, also the red dye made both from crushing this insect and from the red fruit of the tree] □ 1. The name is also often applied (ex in *Guyn*) to the sliced stem used as a poultice pad: '*to put some cochineal on a swollen foot*'. 2. The forms *cruchineel, scrushineel* are illiterate variants.

co-cho-nie n (Dmca, StLu) See KOCHONNI

co-chore¹ [kočo·r] vb (Guyn) [AF] **1.** To carry news or tell tales about others in order to gain favours from a superior. **2.** ‖ SWEET-TALK² (CarA) [Prob < SE *cajole* 'to prevail upon by delusive flattery' *OED* + regressive assimilation /a > o/, + devoicing [ʒ > č] + /l > r/ shift]

co·chore[2] [kočo·r] *n* (Guyn) [*AF*] **1.** The practice of COCHORING. **2.** ‖SWEET-TALK[1] (CarA) **3.** A person who COCHORES; a person whose friendly conversation is not to be trusted. [By functional shift of COCHORE[1] vb] □ Cp also MOUTHAMASSY (*Jmca*).

cock[1] *n* (CarA) **1.** (Dmca, StVn, USVI) ‖COCK-AND-HEN (Angu, etc) □ Sometimes pl COCKS. **2.** PHRASES [Ref to either of E senses 'rooster [IF] or penis [Vul]'] **2.1 give (sb) (the) cock** *vb phr* (Guyn) [*AF—Vul*] ‖*cock*[2] 2. (Guyn) To trick or outsmart (sb) by unfair means; to cause (sb) to have unexpected problems or meet obstacles. **a.** *He get a date to meet the Union near to Christmas, you see, so they come under pressure to accept a settlement and he just gave them the cock.*— (Guyn) **b.** *Dis car really giving cock. As you repair one thing something else gone.*—(Guyn) **2.2 hear better cock crow** *vb phr* (Gren, Guyn, Tbgo) [*AF—Cr/Joc*] To have heard a better one than that; to have known more believable assurances (than the one being given) come to nothing. *She says she only lets her boyfriend kiss her and that nothing else could happen, but I've heard better cock crow, boy!*—(Tbgo) **2.3 when cock get/ make teeth** *adv phr* (Gren, Tbgo, Trin) [*AF—Cr/Joc*] ‖WHEN FOWL(-COCK) CUT/GET TEETH (CarA) See FOWL Phr 2.3 *Is years now A hearin[g] how [h]e goin[g] buil[d] dis house! Like he goin[g] buil[d] it when cock make teet[h].*—(Gren)

cock[2] *vb* **1.** (CarA) [*AF*] To stick up awkwardly; to slope or slant noticeably. *If you leave that board cocked like that, it will throw down people.*— (Guyn) [This usage and the many phrases that follow, related to it, seem to stem from *OED cock* v[1] III. 'to stick or turn up.... To stick stiffly up or out [app with ref to the posture of a cock's neck in crowing...]' + cits from 1600–'] **2.** (Guyn) [*AF—Vul*] ‖GIVE (SB) (THE) COCK[1] 2.1 (Guyn) *He made them do a lot of humiliating work and was cocking them all the time with foolish threats, or with promises he never meant to follow up.*—(Guyn) **3.** PHRASES **3.1 cock back** *vb phr* (CarA) [*IF*] **(i)** To slope or slant backwards. **(ii)** [Of a person] To sit leaning back in a haughty manner. *Well Rabbit in de part wid de drivin' of de horse an' he in de back cock' back.*—EMRP:51 **3.2 cock off (yourself)** *vb phr* (CarA) [*AF*] ‖*cock up your foot/feet* (CarA) To sit with an air of importance; to recline, esp with the feet up, in a lordly manner. *Don't bother to sit there and cock off yourself as if somebody bound to feed you! Go and look for work!*—(Guyn) **3.3 cock out** *vb phr* (CarA) [*IF*] To stick out; to jut out. *Do you see that rock that is cocking out there over the sea? We used to sit down there and fish.*— (Tbgo) **3.4 cock ten** *vb phr* (Guyn) [*AF—Joc*] ‖*chop ten, cut ten* (Jmca) ‖*kòkté your leg* (Dmca) ‖*sit down janm-an-kwa* (Dmca) ‖*sit like Miss Priss* (Baha) ‖*sit like Miss Queensie* (Dmca) To sit with your legs crossed, esp when others are working. [Prob the sense of 3.1 and 3.2 blended with the idea of showing ten toes. Note ‖*cut ten* (*Jmca*). However see also Fr Cr KOKTÉ wh may have given Guyn Cr COCK TEN

by folk etym. *Guyn* was Fr controlled territory 1782–84] **3.5 cock up (your foot/feet)** *vb phr* (CarA) **(i)** [*AF—Joc*] ‖*cock off yourself* (CarA) To relax with haughty indifference. *A man like me who should be cock up drinkin' a good rum, ...*—KTT:14 **b.** *I am not criticising the present engineer. I am satisfied that he is doing his best, but if I were retired I would go home and cock up my feet and be satisfied with whatever I got.*—Bdos (Hd, 73.03.20, p.2044) **(ii)** [*AF—Derog*] [Of a woman] To sit with the legs up, in a way that is considered indecent. *Some does got to work to try and get their attention; I know I had was to keep fixing my bodice, opening my legs wide, and cocking up in the chair to get Best attention.*—PeL (78.05.12, p.5)

cock-and-hen *n* (Angu, Antg, Nevs, StKt, Tbgo) ‖*cock-fight* 1. (Bdos, BrVi, Jmca, StVn) ‖*cock(s)* (Dmca, StVn, USVI) ‖*cokyoco* (Gren) A children's game played with two stamens of the flower of the FLAMBOYANT tree or two sections of the pod of a mahogany or LOCUST tree, each player pulling his against the other's to get the anther (of the stamen), or pointed tip of the pod-section held by the other, to break off first.

cock-and-hen tree *n phr* (Angu, Antg, Nevs, StKt) ‖FLAMBOYANT (CarA) [Prec + *tree* (i.e. that bears the flower with wh the game is played)]

cock-bot·tom /1´22/ *n* (Tbgo, Trin) [*AF*] High, protruding buttocks. [*cocked*, Cr pa. part. of COCK[2] vb + *bottom*, prob reinforced by resemblance in shape to a cock's tail.]

cock-chick·en /1´22/ *n* (Guyn) ‖FOWL-COCK (CarA) [A redundant compound = *male chicken*, a prob calque from W Afr langs. Cp Yoruba *akukọ (a)die* (*cock* + *chicken*) 'cock']

cock-fight *n* **1.** (Bdos, BrVi, Jmca, StVn) ‖COCK-AND-HEN (Angu, etc) **2.** (Guyn, Tbgo, Trin) A boys' game in wh one, riding piggy-back on another, fights another one similarly mounted, trying to throw him to the ground. *In fact, she loved to play the rough game that was popular at the time—Cockfight. On the back of one of her brothers, she would kick and attack her sisters on the backs of the others.*—PuN (76.06.20, p.7)

cock·le *n* (Guyn) A shiny, hard-backed beetle about an inch long that flies into houses at nights, attracted by lights during the rainy season; *Scarabaeidae rutelinae* (*Coleoptera*).

cock-liz·ard* *n* (Bdos) The male of the common, grey-green, tree lizard, which is larger than the female and displays a yellow throat-fan; *Anolis aeneus* (*Lacertilia*). [From the resemblance of the throat-fan to a cock's wattles] □ There is no 'hen' lizard.

cock-mac·la·la *n* (Belz) See Note at MACLALA.

cock·roach-grass *n* **1.*** (Gren, StKt, Trin) ‖*French weed* (BrVi) ‖*wandering Jew* (Baha,

Jmca, USVI) A trailing plant rooting at its joints as it spreads in shady places, its two-inch-long spear-shaped leaves, purplish- green with lighter bands above and purplish-red below, making it attractive as an ornament; *Zebrina pendula* (*Commelinaceae*) or *Tradescentia tricolor*. [Perh from vague resemblance of purplish, ground-running leaves to cockroaches] **2.** (Tbgo) ‖ VE-TIVER (CarA)

cock·set *n* (Tbgo, Trin) ‖ MOSQUITO DESTROYER (CarA) *One theory being considered by the Fire Services is that the blaze was started by a lighted piece of mosquito destroyer (cockset).*—TrG (80.01.03, p.1)

cock·spur *n* **1.** (TkCa) ‖ BREAD-AND-CHEESE (CarA) **2.** (CayI) ‖ NICKER (Angu, BrVi) **3.** (Belz) A medium-sized tree with large, recurved thorns, because of wh it is planted as a fence in rural areas; *Acacia costaricensis* (*Mimosaceae*). **4.** (Angu) A wild shrub bearing red berries. **5.*** (Jmca) A straggling, semi-parasitic shrub, armed with recurved spines and growing high among trees; *Pisonia aculeata* (*Nyctaginaceae*). [The re-semblance of the recurved spines or thorns on all these shrubs to cock's spurs prob accounts for the varied application of the name]

cock·tail-fruit *n* (StKt) ‖ PASSION-FRUIT (CarA)

cock·y-eye *n, adj* (Gren, Tbgo, Trin) See COKEY-EYE

co·co¹ (co·co-yam, soft co·co, hard co·co) **1.** *n* (Belz, Jmca) ‖ DASHEEN (CarA) *Other roots introduced from the East or from the Pacific islands—eddos or cocos and the like—were less im-portant than yams, though six distinct varieties were known by Lunan's day.*—Caq II.4:32 **2.** (Jmca) ‖ TANNIA (CarA) *Cocoes—or 'hard cocoes' as it is better known in the island's market places to distinguish it from soft cocoes of the 'Minty' variety—were harvested in sufficient quantities right across the island this week that the AMC obtained a residual 3, 440 lbs to buy.*—DaG (73.02.10, p.9, Farmer's Weekly) [Cp *DAFL* Twi *kooko* 'an edible root of three kinds, one (of wh) came from Jmca'; also *ZAGL* Gã-Dangme *koko* 'a plant with roots like the yam, and eaten like it'; also *IMED* Mende *koko* 'a kind of coco-yam'. See *DJE coco* for an elaborate etym] □ Pl *cocoes* (cp *eddoes*, etc) is preferable to pl *cocos*. **3.** PHRASE **3.1 roast coco for sb** *vb phr* (Jmca) [AF—Joc] See ROAST¹ 2.

co·co² *n* (BrVi, StKt) ‖ FARINE (Angu, etc)

co·co³ *n* (Jmca) [AF] A lump on the head caused by a hard blow. *Looking for signs of the appalling clobbering the man had claimed to receive, all my friend could discern was a small nick on his cheek.... No bump on his head, no coco, so no sign of struggle.*—DaG (67.03.26, p.8) [Perh < *Joc* Sp *coco* 'nut (= head)']

co·coa¹ ['koko] **1.*** (Dmca, Gren, Trin) ‖ *cocoa beans* (CarA) The dark-brown seeds, extracted from the large, warty, ovoid pods of the cocoa tree, *Theobroma cacao* (*Sterculiaceae*), marketed in bulk for commercial processing. [*OED* < Sp *cacao* < (Aztec, Nahuatl) *cacauatl*] **2.** (CarA) (Name loosely applied to) any hot drink made from one or another form of imported, com-mercially processed powder from COCOA I.; (sometimes also loosely called) CHOCOLATE. **3.** PHRASE **3.1 dance (the) cocoa** *vb phr* (Dmca, Gren, Trin) To polish wetted cocoa beans by having barefooted women tread in them, for several hours, as if dancing, in large shallow troughs or 'trays'. *First I noticed the girls who were dancing the cocoa whispering and smiling among themselves, as if at a secret joke.*—SWOS: 16

co·coa² *n* (Mrat) A pale brown fish caught near the shore, said to be easily scaled and of good food value.

co·coa-bas·ket *n* (Dmca, Gren) A large, deep basket about 3 ft in diameter with a hump in the centre, made of plaited WISTS, originally used by women labourers for carrying loads of cocoa-beans (hence the name), but nowadays market-vegetables, etc, on their heads. *... when we stopped women carrying the cocoa basket with wet cocoa on their heads at the agricultural farms ... we were thinking of ... the pregnant mother jumping a drain with a basket of cocoa.*—Gren (Hd, 78.09.08, p.18)

co·coa-bean(s) *n* (CarA) ‖ COCOA¹ 1. (Dmca, etc)

co·coa-house *n* (Dmca, Trin) ‖ BOUCAN 1. (Dmca, Gren)

co·coa-knife *n* (Dmca, Gren, Tbgo, Trin) ‖ *gullet* (Tbgo, Trin) An iron blade with a sharp-edged, thumb-like piece curving outward, or a G-shaped blade with a sharp inside edge, made with a socket to fit on the end of a long pole for picking tree-crops, esp cocoa-pods. *We had long bamboo rods with cocoa-knives at the ends of them and all day long we went from tree to tree reaching for the cocoa-pod stems and stabbing at them or twisting them, letting the pods fall beneath the tree.*—AGDR:104

co·coa pa·gnol; **co.coa pa.yol** [koko-payɒl] *n phr* (Trin) [AF—Derog] A contemptuous term for a PAYOL. [From 'the fact that PAYOLS tra-ditionally worked on cocoa and coffee plantations and lived in the 'bush''—S. Moodie (Ms, *1982*)]

co·coa-pod *n* (CarA) See COCOA¹ 1.

co·coa-shade *n* (Trin) ‖ GLIRICIDIA (Angu, etc) Also recorded as NICARAGUAN COCOA SHADE (*PTT:173*).

co·coa-tea *n* (CarA) [IF] ‖ *chocolate-tea* (CarA) [IF] Hot cocoa or chocolate drink, esp when served as a breakfast drink. *In addition, the Association is preparing a 'real creole' breakfast which will consist of ham, buljol, black pudding and hops with cocoa-tea, coffee-tea or green-tea.*—ExP (73.05.26, p.6) [COCOA¹ + TEA, generic Cr name for any kind of early morning drink] □ See also CHOCOLATE-TEA.

co·co·bay; co.ca.beh, co.co.bé, co.co.bea ko-.ko.be [kʌkʌbɛ] *n* (CarA) **1.** Leprosy. **2.** [*AF—Derog*] [Often *adj* as personal abuse] (Having) a skin that looks diseased or repulsive with sores. [*DAFL* Twi *kokobé* 'leprosy'] □ *Cocobay* appears to be the most widely used spelling. The word survives mostly in sense **2.**, and in some Cr proverbs, ex: *If yo gat cocobay you can't get yaws* ('If you are in the very worst of troubles, a lesser trouble cannot affect you'). **3.** *PHRASE* **3.1 to have cocobay on top of yaws** *Prov and id phr* (Guyn, Trin) [*AF—Joc*] To have much worse trouble added to already bad trouble.

co·co-boeuf *n* (Dmca, StLu) See KOKO-BÈF

co·co-cou·lie *n* (StLu) See KOKO-KOULI

co·co-mac·ca (Jmca); **(co·co-ma·kwak)** (USVI) *n* (Bdos) A seasoned, hardwood stick, about 4 to 5 ft long, usu with a knobbly end, used for self-defence by watchmen, etc, or in professional STICK-LICKING. *A great Baron Aldenburg runs behind me with a coco-macca stick large as the tower on Morant church.*—RND:68 [< Sp *coco* n 'face' or adj 'hard' + *macaco* 'ugly, deformed'] □ Cp HAKYA-STICK

co·co·mar (ko·ko·mar) ['kokomar] *n* (Crcu) ‖ OLD-HIGUE (Guyn) *In Carriacou, the word 'Coco-mar' is used instead of witch- craft. The female is the Sucoyan and the male, the Ligarou. Both male and female suck blood from human beings through their connection with the devil.*—DCC:21 [? Cp Fr *cauchemar* 'nightmare']

co·com-coo·lie *n* (StLu) See KONKONM-KOULI

co·co·nut *n* **1.*** (CarA) The fruit of, and the tree *Cocos nucifera* (*Palmae*). □ (The compounds that follow refer to this sense unless otherwise stated). **2.** [In culinary contexts] The hard, brittle, white kernel of the mature fruit that is usu grated] **3.** (CarA) [*AF—Joc*] The human head. *If you don'[t] stop boderin[g] me A goin[g] bu[r]s[t] yo[u] coconut.*—(Trin) **4.** (Trin) [By extension] **(i)** [*AF—Joc*] A butt with the head (esp using the forehead to give an opponent a hard blow with your head). **(ii)** [*AF*] [In gen senses] Any hard blow. *... and a model young man of this country—young and not scared easily. Young enough to take plenty 'coconuts' on his way through life.*—SuP (79.10.14, p.21) **5.** *PHRASE* **5.1 give (sb) a coconut** *vb phr* (Trin) [*AF—Joc*] To hit (sb) very hard, esp on the head.

co·co·nut-bake *n* (Tbgo, Trin) ROAST-BAKE, the dough of wh was mixed with grated coconut or with COCONUT-MILK.

co·co·nut-bat *n* (CarA) The curved upper end of the branch of a coconut tree, cut off and shaped for use as an improvised cricket-bat.

co·co·nut boil-in [kokonʌt-bɒIl-i:n] *n phr* (StVn) ‖ *oil-down* (Gren) A meal in wh fish or pork, CALALU, breadfruit, and/or GROUND PROVISIONS are boiled to a heavy soup-like mixture in COCONUT-MILK and served as one dish.

co·co·nut-bread *n* (Bdos) ‖ *sweetbread* (CarA) A heavy loaf flavoured with grated coconut, SPICE, and raisins and baked in a pan.

co·co·nut-broom *n* **1.** (Antg, Bdos, Trin) ‖ *cocoyea-broom* (Gren, Tbgo, Trin) ‖ *pointer-broom* (Guyn) A yard-broom home-made from the dried spines of the leaves of the coconut-branch, tied in a tight bundle. **2.** (Jmca) Name also applied sometimes to a BUBA-BROOM.

co·co·nut-cake *n* (Baha) ‖ SUGAR-CAKE **2.** (Bdos, Guyn)

co·co·nut-dig·ger *n* (Guyn) A sharpened, short piece of metal with a handle, or a much shortened CUTLASS sharpened to a keen point, used for opening WATER-COCONUTS or easing out the kernels of DRY-COCONUTS in the copra industry.

co·co·nut-drop *n* (Jmca) ‖ SUGAR-CAKE **2.** (Bdos, Guyn)

co·co·nut-jel·ly *n* (CarA) The soft, immature, jelly-like lining or unformed kernel of the young, or 'water' coconut.

co·co·nut-juice *n* (Gren) ‖ COCONUT-MILK (CarA)

co·co·nut-milk *n* (CarA) ‖ *coconut-juice* (Gren) The sweet, milk-white juice squeezed under pressure from the grated kernel or 'meat' of the dry coconut, used in cooking. □ See CO-CONUT-WATER.

co·co·nut-oil *n* (CarA) An oil for cooking or cosmetic use, produced domestically by boiling COCONUT-MILK in a large pot, or commercially by crushing copra. *The coconut oil expressing and refining plants now utilize all copra produced in St Vincent for the production of edible oil.*—ViN (76.07.09, p.3)

co·co·nut-walk *n* (Guyn) A coconut estate. □ Mostly rural usage. See WALK².

co·co·nut-wa·ter *n* (CarA) The liquid contained inside the young green coconut; it is a refreshing drink. □ Often referred to as *coconut-milk* by non-*CarA* persons.

co·coon *n* **1** (CayI) A dark brown, heart-shaped, flat seed about 2 ins long and 1/2 in thick, wh is put to a number of folk and medicinal uses; it is prob the seed of the CACOON pod, and is washed ashore in numbers in the Cayman Is 2. (Jmca) See CACOON.

co·co-plum *n* 1.* (CarA) ‖ *bay-plum* (Baha) ‖ *cacao-plum* (Trin) ‖ *fat-pork* (ECar) ‖ *pork-fat-apple* (Berm) ‖ *zikak* (Dmca, StLu) A small, round, brownish, sometimes blue-brown fruit about an inch in diameter, having a single seed in scant, white, spongy, sharp-tasting pulp with a thin uneven skin, and borne on a shrub-like tree with round, leathery leaves thriving in dry, windy places; *Chrysobalanus icaco* (*Rosaceae*). 2. (CayI) ‖ DUNK(s) (Bdos, etc) 3. (TkCa) ‖ JAMAICA-PLUM (Bdos, etc) [Cp *BDFC:317 prune rouge* 'icacou' (name used by Carib females), also *TLWI:21* Taino *hicaco*, Is. Carib, Guajiro *kaako* 'coco plum'; all of wh incidentally favour the alternative pronunc 'cacao' (*Trin*)]

co·cor·ite (**co·ker·ite, ko·ker·ite**) [kok ʌrɪt~ko·krɪt] *n* (Guyn, Trin) A brown, egg-shaped fruit with a pointed tip, its tough skin covering a scanty but sweet, creamy pulp around a very hard- shelled black seed; it is borne in giant clusters on a tall palm topped with a dense spread of plume-like branches; *Maximiliana caribaea* or *M. regia* (*Palmaceae*). [*BAED* Arawak *kokoriti*, 'a type of palm-tree wh bears large bunches of small, edible fruit']

co·cotte (kò·kòt) *n* (Dmca, StLu, Trin) [*IF*] 1. A hen. [Fr *cocotte* 1. 'hen' 2. (*Ma cocotte* 'My little ducky/darling'. 3. 'a loose woman'] 2. [By extension, often MY COCOTTE, a term of endearment to a lover or a young child] Darling. □ Note (*Dmca, Guad, Mart, StLu*) Fr Cr *kòkòt* (< Fr *cocotte*) 'a woman's vulva'.

co·coy(e) (**kòkòy**) [kɒkɒɪ] *n* (Dmca) 1. ‖ BLUGGO (Belz, etc) See KÒKÒY 2. (Name sometimes applied to) the English-based Creole introduced into the northeast area of Dominica by immigrant labourers from Antigua and Montserrat. [Indicating 'crude' quality (of language) i.e. like the variety of fruit called COCOY 1.]

co·co-yam *n* (Jmca) See COCO¹ □ Rare in this combination wh is preferred by non-native writers.

co·co·yea (ko·ko·yé) [kokoye~kokiye] /1'12/ *n* (Gren, Tbgo, Trin) 1. Any part of the coconut-branch esp the spines and leaves, used in many folk ways. 2. ‖ POINTER (Guyn) [Perh Fr Cr *kokoyé* < Fr Cr *coco* 'coconut' + (Fr suff) *ier* 'tree'. However, note *BDFC:272* Carib *le palmiste appellé* (= cabbage palm called) *cocoyé*. The word may therefore be of entirely *Trin* Carib origin, perh reinforced by Fr Cr]

co·co·yea-broom /1'121/ *n* 1. (Gren, Tbgo, Trin) ‖ COCONUT-BROOM (Antg, etc) 2. (Gren) ‖ CABBAGE-BROOM (CarA)

co·cri·co* [kokriko] *n* (Tbgo, Trin) ‖ *chachalaca, Tobago pheasant* (Belz, Tbgo, Trin) ‖ *coquericot* (Belz) A brownish game-bird,

about the size of a hen, with a grey head and long, reddish, rounded tail; it moves in small flocks whose quaint, loud calls are heard at dawn and evening; *Ortalis ruficauda* (*Cracidae*). [Imitation of the sound the bird makes] □ The spelling *cocorico* also occurs, but is not official, the COCRICO being one of the two National Birds of *Trin & Tbgo*. It is a native of *Tbgo* and *Venz*, but is not found in *Trin*.

coc·tion [kɒkšɒn] *n* (Jmca) 1. ‖ ASHAM (Antg, etc) [By overcorrection < KAKSHAM] 2. A form of ASHAM made into balls and coloured. [Prob a blending of CORN-SHAM and KAKSHAM]

cof·fee-tea *n* (CarA) A hot drink made with ground coffee or any folk substitute for coffee (esp as a morning drink). [*Coffee* + TEA in general sense 'a hot morning drink'] □ Usage now mainly restricted to older folk.

cog [kɒg ~ kag] *vb tr* (ECar) ‖ *fudge* (Trin) [Esp of school-children] To copy work surreptitiously from another student. *Barbados is doing their own thing and we should try our own too. Barrow's policy works in Barbados and not in Antigua. So Mr Premier please stop cogging.*—WoV (71.03.17, p.2) [IrE *cog* 'to copy surreptitiously; to crib something from the writings of another and pass it off as your own'. One schoolboy will sometimes copy from another: 'You cogged that sum'— *JESI:237*. Cp also *OED cog* vb³ 3. 'to employ fraud or deceit, to cheat' (Obs). Also 6. 'to produce ... cunningly and fraudulently' (Obs)]

co·hob·blo·pot (**co·hob·ble·pot, co·hob·ble-a-pot**) [kʌhɒblʌpɒt] *n* (Bdos) 1. [*Obs*] ‖ ALL-IN-ONE (Guyn) '*Cohobble-a-pot*' *was the all-inclusive meal produced in the mill-yard by putting every imaginable available kind of vegetable into a pot along with chunks of beef from the carcass of a newly killed ox. The pot was a three-legged iron pot, for which, as need arose, because of numbers usually, kerosene tins were often substituted.*—AdN (79.06.01, p.4) 2. [By extension] The variety show on the last night of the CROP-OVER festival (*Bdos*) in wh the best performances from all the singing and dancing competitions of the CROP-OVER season are presented as one programme.

co·hune nut [kʊhu·n nʌt] *n phr* (Belz) A fist-sized, brown nut with a pointed tip, its tough fibre covering a black shell the size of a large egg, but so hard that cracking it to get the valuable oil-yielding kernel is very difficult; the nut comes in massive bunches on a palm of medium height; *Orbignya cohune* (*Palmaceae*).

co·ker·ite *n* (Guyn) See COCORITE

co·key-eye (**co·key/co·qui/co·cea-eye, cock·ey-eye, co·ki-eye, co·qui-eye**) ['koki-aɪ] /1'12/ (Gren, Tbgo, Trin) [*AF—Joc*] ‖ *cast-eye(s)* (Belz, Jmca, Mrat, StVn) 1. *n* A squint; a cock-eye or cock-eyes. *The days when his schoolmates and even relatives called him 'cokey', are* *gone. Kieron now confidently looks the world straight in the eye.*—TrG (80.01.13, p.11) **2.** *adj* Cock-eyed. *The show must have the worst P.A system, the worst technician and most of all a 'cockey-eye' camera which never shows the true Trinidad spirit that happens on these shows.*—ExP (81.06.10, p.5) [Prob < SE *cock-eye(d)* with the latter element characterized by CarA Cr prosthetic /y-/ added to 'eye'. (The form 'yeye', so spelt, is attested in many CarA Crs.) Hence [kɔk-yaɪ] > [koki-aɪ] by misplaced juncture, so accounting for the spellings, and COKEY as a *Joc* abbr] □ The spelling *cokey-eye* is that most commonly used in *Trin*.

co·ky·o·co *n* (Gren) ‖COCK-AND-HEN (Angu, etc)

co·ky·o·co tree *n phr* (Gren) ‖FLAMBOYANT (CarA)

co·la·ban *n* (Jmca) See CALABAN

co·las ['kolas] *n* (CarA) A black emulsion of bitumen in water wh, combined with gravel, is used in the cold state, setting hard, for patching pot-holes in roads. *Where a grass track had been there was now a wide cutting metalled with jagged stones, raw and newly broken, waiting for a roller to crush, for colas to cover.*—Bim (IV:16, E. Napier) ['A shortened version of *Cold Asphalt* ... the bitumen used, about 60 percent by volume (with 40 percent water) being derived either from natural asphalt or as a by-product of oil-refining'—*H.O. Phelps (UWI, Trin)*]

cold¹ *adj* (Guyn, StVn) [Esp of food material that is normally packed airtight, such as biscuits] Soft (as opposed to crisp, fresh) from being left uncovered or exposed for too long).

cold² *n* (CarA) **1.** ‖*fresh-cold* (CarA) (SE) A head-cold (i.e. with sneezing, runny nose, sore-throat, etc). **2.** (SE) A chest-cold; a rattling cough, with the spitting of phlegm (often called simply a *bad cold*). *The prisoner said he had been a patient of the Doctor. In answer to the question why he had been breaking the law, he replied, 'You know, sir, that I am a sick man and cannot do hard work as the cold had settled on my lungs.'*—JAA: 74 **3.** ‖*fwédi* (Dmca, StLu) Any pain, ailment associated with pain or physical disorder of any part of the body, and often with some fever; hence *a cold in the back, belly, bladder, bowels, eye, foot, hand, knee, neck, shoulder, side of the face, stomach,* etc. [Yoruba *otutu* 'coldness, sickness' is similarly used. See etym note after PHRASES] **4.** *PHRASES* **4.1 catch/get/ take (a) cold (in some part of the body)** *vb phr* (CarA) ‖*catch a/the draught* (esp *in the eye*) (Antg, Baha, Gren, Guyn) ‖ *catch/get/take the cold* (Trin) ‖ *get fwédi* (Dmca, StLu) To be sick or ailing, with a noticeable pain (in the part of the body mentioned). [Most prob calques from W Afr langs. Cp Yoruba *otutu mu mi l'owo* 'cold catches me in the hand', the same phrase being used ending ... *l'ęsę* '... in the foot', ...

lęhin '... in the back', etc] □ See also LYING-IN COLD. **4.2 cold in the belly** *n phr* (CarA) ‖*froust and flu* (Baha) See sense 3. **4.3 cold in straw-bed** *n phr* (Baha) ‖LYING-IN COLD (Antg, etc) *If you start to work too soon after the baby come, you will catch cold in straw bed.*—(Baha) [*OED* straw sb¹ 2. b. *In the straw:* 'in childbed, lying-in' + cits 1661–1832] □ See STRAW Phrs for *Baha* variants of this phr.

cold-sup·per shop *n phr* (Jmca) A shop selling prepared food such as fritters, roasted bread-fruit, corn pone, BEVERAGE and other items normally bought by workmen for their midday snack. □ Cp *cake-shop* (Guyn), *snackette* (Bdos, etc).

co·li·bri (cou·li·bri) [kʌlɪbri ~ kʊlɪbri] /1'12/ *n* (Dmca, Gren, Grns) ‖DOCTOR-BIRD 1. (ECar, Guyn) *The Antillean Crested Hummingbird is about 3-1/4 ins. Still generally called Coulibri or Crested Hummer, the male at all events can at once be identified by its crest; not so the female which does not possess one; Orthorynchus cristatus (Trochilidae).*—DBGSV:55 [Said to be Carib name] □ However this name is applied, with some qualification, in many parts of the Lesser Antilles to several varieties of hummingbirds.

col·lec·tive *adj* **1.** (Bdos, Guyn, Nevs) [X] [Of persons] Collected; calm; unruffled. *Although the mother's sudden death shocked everybody she was quite collective and was able to make all arrangements for the funeral.*—Guyn (Ms) [A malapropism for 'collected'] **2.** (Gren, Tbgo, Trin) [IF] Sensible; in full control of your faculties; [of an old person] having a fully active memory and mind in spite of old age.

col·lec·tor·ate *n* (Jmca) Office or building containing offices for the collection of taxes, revenues, and fees payable to the government; office of the Collector of (municipal) taxes. [Prob by analogy with *directorate*. Cp *OED* collectorate b. 'the residence or place of business of a collector' with no precise application. The *Jmca* usage is particular and evid exclusive]

col·lins *n* (Bdos) ‖CUTLASS (CarA) **a.** ... *and even his latest demonstration of going and taking a collins and with his Minister of Agriculture and others going into the fields as if they are labourers themselves has not penetrated the working class people of this country.*—Bdos (Hd, 74.11.26, p.4181) **b.** *I have seen boys 15 yrs old going with collins to plantations to cut canes.*—Bdos (Hd, 76.06.08, p.6619) [From the name of an early 19c American manufacturer Samuel W. Collins of Connecticut. See *MAD Collins ax* Cp GILPIN] □ The pl, wh should properly be *collinses*, evid does not occur, the word remaining unchanged (as in cit b.) by characteristic CE reduction of final /-CC/.

Col·o·ny, the *n* (CarA) (Name generally used locally to refer to) any Br island or territory in the Caribbean. *The following comment on a public* meeting is taken from an issue of the 'Herald' of January 1930 and will illustrate what I mean: 'The election campaign is now well on its way, and the repeated advice in this journal to electors to demand public utterances have borne fruit. Most of the candidates all over the colony have met their electors on the platform and during the next three weeks there will be more meetings.—WCR:30 [OED colony 4. b. 'the territory peopled by such a community' [i.e a body of settlers connected with a parent state]] □ This usage, common before the independence of several territories i.e. up to the 1960s, still survives among older folk, and is generally understood in CE to have only this meaning.

Col·o·ny House /ı'ıı2'/ *n phr* (Guyn) [Hist] 1. The residence of the Governor. (Later replaced by the term GOVERNMENT HOUSE). 2. A special residence in the chief township of a COUNTY for the Governor's use when visiting, or for senior government officers visiting on official duties.

col·our *n* (CarA) 1. A brown or light-brown (instead of a black) skin. *He ain't lookin[g] at black girls at all! Only lookin[g] for somebody wid colour, so let him go [a]long an[d] see what [h]e goin[g] get, too!*—(Guyn) 2. PHRASE 2.1 **have colour** *id phr* (CarA) [IF] To be LIGHT-SKINNED or BROWN- SKINNED. *One of the children draw dark but the other have some colour.*—(Antg)

col·our·ed [kʌlʌ(r)d] *adj* (CarA) [Of persons] Having a brown, light-brown or CLEAR skin, being of mixed black and white races; not East Indian and not dark-skinned; not considered black because racially mixed, as can be seen by the appearance of the person's skin and (usu) hair. **a.** *It is almost unnecessary to explain that by coloured men I mean those who are of a mixed race—of a breed mixed, be it in what proportion it may, between the white European and the black African. Speaking of Jamaica, I might almost say between the Anglo-Saxon and the African; for there remains, I take it, but a small tinge of Spanish blood. Of the old Indian blood there is, I imagine, hardly a vestige. / Both the white men and the black men dislike their coloured neighbours. It is useless to deny that as a rule such is the case.*—TWISM:76 **b.** *In the Town Hall she felt as good as the other coloured people present.... She looked around the hall.... She could not see a Portuguese or a Chinese or an East Indian. A few black people. All the rest coloured people of the respectable middle- class. Good-family people.*—MLDS:89

co·lum·nar cac·tus *n phr* (Bdos) ‖ DILDO 1. (CarA) *Well up the slope I spotted a single four-stemmed plant of the endemic Columnar Cactus, Cephalocereus barbadensis, only about 4 ft high.*—AdN (80.02.20, p.13) □ The distinguishing name COLUMNAR CACTUS is found mostly in formal listings. Otherwise the plant is commonly called *cactus* like all other varieties.

co·mal ['kumal] *n* (Belz) ‖ BAKING-IRON (Trin) *The cassava is peeled, washed and grated. The water is drained from the grated cassava in a wowla and left overnight. The next day the drained cassava is sieved and baked on a comal.*—Belz (Ms, 1978) [< (SDGA central Am sp comal, < Aztec comalli 'thin earthenware disc for baking tortillas', etc]

comb-and-brush (tree) *n (phr)* (Gren, StVn) ‖ CANNON-BALL TREE (CarA) [From the resemblance of the peculiar central portion of the large flower to a brush with stiff spikes]

come *vb intr* 1. (CarA) [IF] [In imperative functions, used to add pressure or persuasion to a foll statement] **a.** *Come, child! Eat up! You keepin[g] me back!*—(StVn) **b.** *Come, ho[w]-much you askin[g] fo[r] dat bunch o[f] plantain?* —(Guyn) **c.** *A[ll]right, come now! Le[t] me hear you answer dis one!*—(Bdos) 2. (CarA) [AF] To perform, do (usu well); to succeed. **a.** *S1: Well how A come? / S2: You comin[g] good! (How am I doing? You're doing fine!).*—(BrVi) **b.** *A like dat dress! You really come!*—-(Guyn) 3. (ECar) [IF] [Culinary arts] to develop to its desired state; to jell; to solidify. *When you makin[g] ice-cream with fruit you should put in some powder[ed] milk to help it to come.*—(Guyn) [Cp OED come 15. 'Butter is said to come when it forms in the churn'] 4. (CarA) [AF] To become; to turn out to be; to develop (into adulthood, etc). **a.** *'You mus' keep yourself clean an nuh come dirty,' Sybil would say as she inspected the khaki pants and crisp white shirt she had so lovingly laundered and ironed.*—FGSOS:53 **b.** *A man must have a friend to talk to, otherwise he come like some of them old people talking to themself!*— -SABS:206 **c.** *Marie left here a little child, but you would be surprise to see how she come big now.*—(Bdos) 5. (CarA) [AF] [Preceding another vb (esp such as talking, telling, saying etc) intensifying its sense] (*Don[']t come tellin[g] me you can[']t mek it! You have to do it!*)—(Guyn) 6. (Guyn) [AF] [Of a game] To end abruptly by some surprise development (See Phr 7.12). 7. PHRASES 7.1 **come and** (foll by a second vb (phr)) *vb phr* (CarA) [Suggesting purpose, intention, etc as in foll phrs.] 7.1.1 **come and get a child** *vb phr* (CarA) To become pregnant (without being married). 7.1.2 **Come and go along!** *vb phr* (CarA) Come let us go (home)! 7.1.3 **come and take five** *vb phr* (Gren) To pay a visit that is intended to be very short. [Development of common Cr structure *come + vb* ex /kom go, get, tek, etc reflecting W/ Afr serial vbs] 7.2 **come behind (sb/sth)** *vb phr* (Gren) [IF] To keep seeking out (sb or sth) from love or covetousness. 7.3 **come clean** *vb phr* (CarA) [IF] To stop being dishonest; to be unexpectedly helpful by telling the truth. 7.4 **come down** *vb phr* (CarA) [Of a river or GHAUT] To flood or overflow its banks with rushing waters. [A ref to water running down from the mountains in times of heavy rains] □ Not used in Bdos, Guyn. 7.5 **Come go!** *vb phr* (CarA) [AF] Come with me! 7.6 **come good** *vb phr* (CarA) [IF]

To be particularly clever or convincing in your performance when it is being tested. *The band will have some 300 members and Khan boasted other bandleaders will have to 'come good to beat me'.*—ExP (72.11.29, p.3) □ Hence also *come better.* **7.7 come on hard/strong** *vb phr* (CarA) [*IF*] To give a performance that is especially pleasing; to respond to a challenge with an effective show of power. **7.8 come out** *vb phr* (CarA) **(i)** [Esp of colonists] To arrive (in the W Indies) from England. **(ii)** [*AF—Cr; Joc/ Derog*] To emerge from or be born in (a slum or unknown place, as often in foll question). *But whe[re] you come out?*—(Guyn) **7.8.1 come out of your cover** *vb phr vb phr* (Dmca) ‖ GET BESIDE YOURSELF (CarA) See BESIDE Phr 2.1 **7.9 come to words** *vb phr* (Guyn, Trin) To fall out and quarrel noisily. [By analogy from SE *come to blows*] **7.10 come wrong** *vb phr* (Guyn) To fall out; to have a serious disagreement. **7.11 coming to come** *vb phr* (CarA) [*AF*] Showing signs of improvement or of a good outcome. **7.12 the game come** *id phr* (Guyn) ‖ *Story done!* (Guyn) The game is up!; It's all over with you!; (SE) Your goose is cooked! *Boy if you don't pass this examination, believe me, the game come! I'm going to take you out of school!*—(Guyn)

come-come-say *adj* (Brbu, Jmca) [*AF—Cr*] See Note at KONGKONGSA

co·me·hen [kʌmɛhɛn] /1'12/ *n* (Belz) ‖ ANTS-NEST. **2.** (Trin) [< Sp *comején* 'termite']

com·fa-dance (**cum·fa-dance**) *n* (Guyn) A dance of vigorous body motion performed by one or two women to the beating of big drums, intended to bring about spirit possession from wh the promoters may draw some benefit. [< Twi *ɔ-kɔmfo* 'a fetish-man, possessed with or prophesying by a fetish ..... 'The *kɔmfo* pretends to be the interpreter and mouthpiece either of the guardian spirit of a nation, town, or family, or of a soothsaying spirit resorted to in sickness or other calamities'—*DAFL*] □ Largely restricted to rural areas.

com·mand·ing oil; **com.mand.ing pow.der** *n phr* (CarA) ‖ *attraction-oil/powder* (Guyn) ‖ *compelling oil/powder* (CarA) A sweet-smelling oil (or powder) made up by an OBEAH-MAN to be used by a person who wishes to win or control a lover, or to control or defeat (i.e 'command', whence the name) an evil spirit. □ See also DOMINATION OIL.

co·m(m)ess [kɔmɛs] *n* (Gren, Tbgo, Trin, USVI) See KONMÈS

co·m(m)ess·ie (**kon·mèsi**) [kʌmɛsi] *adj* (StVn) [*AF*] Meddlesome; causing mischief by interfering and gossiping. [< Fr Cr COMESS + SE adj suff -*ie*, or by blend with *messy*]

com·mon *adj* (CarA) [Of persons] Vulgar; readily given to dirty language and behaviour; basically ill-bred and low-minded. □ This is the dominant sense in CE, other SE senses of the adj occurring in rarer, educated contexts.

com·mon bean *n phr* (Antg) ‖ STRING-BEAN (CarA) [Prob from its easy growth and popularity in kitchen-gardens]

com·mon-breed /1'12/ *adj* (CarA) [Esp of dogs and poultry] Of no particular pedigree; small-bodied and of poor quality in appearance, but hardy.

com·mon en·trance ex·am·in.a.tion *n phr* (CarA) ‖ *eleven-plus examination* (CarA) A competitive examination for children just past the age of eleven for selective entry into Government Secondary Schools.

com·mon·ness *n* (CarA) **1.** [*IF*] Vulgarity; crude behaviour, esp when loud, dirty language is used. **2.** [*AF*] Sexual intercourse between unmarried persons, or the soliciting of sexual intercourse with no discretion. *Never had he talked with a white woman whose words said commonness, though he had heard how straightforwardly suggestive they can be.*—SBB:39

com·pa·dre [kʌmpadrɛ] *n* (Belz) ‖ COMPÈ (CarA) [Sp *compadre* 'godfather, pal']

com·pa·dre·ship [kʌmpadrɛšip] *n* (Belz) Personal friendship as a COMPADRE, considered to be as binding as close kinship. *Accordingly, people require social ties that are stronger than friendship to ensure some stability in the availability of labourers. This is provided through links of compadreship, which is felt to be sufficiently enduring.*—Nas (II.4, p.6) [Blend of Sp COM-PADRE (as prec) + SE (*friend*)*ship*/(*kin*)*ship*]

com·pa·ny *n* (CarA) **1.** [*X*] Friend(s); companion(s); person(s) of the same class. *If she and you is company, well go whe[re] she is, but don'[t] bring her in here.*—(Guyn) **2.** [*X*] Bad company. *You like too much company and company does always bring trouble.*—(Bdos) **3.** [*IF*] Companionship (usu sexual; see Phr 5.1). **4.** Being in the same place (with sb; see phr 5.2). **5.** *PHRASES* **5.1 keep company (with sb)** *vb phr* (CarA) [*IF*] To have an ongoing sexual relationship (with sb) *He and the typist keep company but it isn't generally known.*—Antg (Ms) **5.2 keep my/your, etc company** *vb phr* (CarA) [*IF*] (SE) To keep me/you, etc company. [Prob by overcorrection, *keep me/you/them, etc company* being erroneously assumed to be using Cr possessive /*mi, yo, dem*/, the regular SE idiomatic structure being unrecognized] □ Hence also formal CE phrs like *keep John's company* for SE *keep John company.*

com·pa·ny-path *n* (Guyn) A wide strip of reserved land separating two sugar-estates. [Hist ref to the Dutch West India Company, the original colonizers of Guyana; one of the land-tenure terms kept by the British] □ Cp INTERVAL (Jmca).

com·part·ner *n* (Jmca) ‖ COMPÈ (Belz, ECar) [Blend of Sp COMPADRE + SE *partner*]

com·pè (**com·pere, com·pey, kon·pè**) [kɒmpɛ] *n* (Belz, ECar) [*IF*] ‖ *compadre* (Belz) ‖ *compartner* (Jmca) A close male friend, usu one who is the godfather of your child or of whose child you are the godfather. *That night there were macommès and compès in the house and we were sitting on Tantie's knees while she recounted the triumph.*—HCCM:57 [Fr Cr < Fr *compère* 'godfather', also 'comrade'] □ The variant spellings may be regularized as *konpè*, the original Fr form *compère* being represented sometimes in writing, esp in NANCY STORIES, but never in folk-speech where it is a very significant kinship term.

com·pel·ling oil; **com.pel.ling pow.der** *n phr* (CarA) ‖ COMMANDING OIL/POWDER (CarA)

com·pere [kɒmpɛ] *n* (ECar) ‖ COMPÈ (Belz, ECar) *When John's compere whispered to him that there was to be a raid on his still, John lost no time.*—OTTTT:47 [< Fr *compère*. See COMPÈ]

Com·pere A·nan·cy/Czien/Tig, etc *n* (Dmca, Gren, StLu, StVn) ‖ *Anancy*[1] (CarA) Brother Anancy, etc (the common form of address used in animal folk-tales). *One day Compere Tigre and Compere Czien went to the market and found that the prices were very high and they did not have enough money to buy what they wanted.... Compere Tigre and Compere Czien filled a paper bag with some breadfruit and fish cakes and hid it outside the market gate.*—PGIP:52 [See prec]

com·pey *n* (Belz, ECar) See COMPÈ

Com·pè Za·yen; **Com.pere Czien, Kon.pè Za.yen** [kɒmpɛ zayɛ̃] *n phr* (Dmca, Gren, StLu) ‖ COMPERE ANANCY (Dmca, etc) [Fr Cr COMPÈ + *Zayen* < Fr (*le*)*s araignée*(*s*) 'spider' (by misplaced juncture), 'spider' being a calque of Twi *ananse*]

com·plain[1] *n* (Guyn, StKt) [*X*] Complaint. '*I went to make a complain and while I in there I wanted to explain when the girl hit me what she said,' Williams explained.*—DeM(SK) (63.10.26, p.10)

com·plain[2] (**sb**) (Antg, Guyn, StKt) (**com·plain for** (**sb**)) (Bdos) *vb* (*phr*) [*X*] To lodge a complaint against (sb); to complain about (sb's action or behaviour). **a.** *So the government, nakedly exposed for what it is, ... have complained a citizen for Sedition.*—WoV (72.04.22, p.1) **b.** *Sometimes you find that passengers complain for particular drivers, but if a driver can get them liking him, they will ride with him all the time.*—SuS (87.05.24, p.32)

com·pli·ment [kɒm'plimɛnt] /1'2'1/ *n* (Bdos) A wedding invitation, wh is regarded as a mark of personal family friendship (i.e. as paying the receiver a compliment of kinship). □ Distinguished by its pitch-pattern from the SE abstract n *compliment* /2'11/.

com·po·site school *n phr* (Bdos) ‖ ALL-AGE SCHOOL (CarA)

com·press /1'2/ *n* (Guyn) ‖ SNOW-CONE (CarA) [Because the ice was *compressed*, in former days, in an ice-shaver. See SHAVE-ICE]

con·a·ree (**ca·na·ri, ka·na·ri**) ['kɒnari ~ 'kanari] /1'12/ *n* **1.** (Guyn) ‖ *buck-pot* (Bdos) ‖ *karahi* (Guyn) An open, round-bottomed, iron basin about 15 ins in diameter, with two handles, used by poorer folk for cooking a family meal, or with a wooden cover, for POTTING PORK. **2.** (ECar) [*Obs*] A locally made clay basin (of similar proportions to 1.) used (esp in former times) for cooking food that required long processes (PEPPERPOT, guava jelly, etc). [Perh < *Kanuri*, name of an ethnic group of Northern Nigeria from wh a number of slaves were taken]

CONCACAF *abbr n* (CarA) Confederation of North Central American and Caribbean Football Associations (the continental federal grouping of Federal International Football Associations to wh belong the national Football Associations of *Antg, Baha, Bdos, Belz, Berm, Gren, Guyn, Jmca,* and *Trin/Tbgo*. [< Sp *Confederación Norte Centroamericana y del Caribe de Fútbol*, the headquarters being in Guatemala since its founding in 1961]

con·cern *vb* (CarA) [*X*] **1.** Concerned [often as verbal adj, in pseudonyms in letters to newspapers, as *Concern Citizen/Parent*, etc]. *... and the room hot as hell and full of cigarette smoke but nobody don't concern 'bout this, they only want to fete.*—CISH:90 **2.** To have responsibility for (sth); to be connected with (sth). *A fellow on a bicycle cart accosted me, pointing to a splendid, imposing residence and asking: 'Yu cansarn wid dah?'*—ReP (80.04.27, p.12) [Cp EDD *concern* 7 *vb* 'To associate' + cit from Hrf: *We don't consarn with them*. 8 *vb* 'To worry, trouble + cit from Shr: 'I dunna consarn myself wi' sich nonsense'*] **3.** **(i)** To be the business or property or responsibility of (sb) [often in neg]. **a.** *This bicycle concern you?*—(Guyn) **b.** *That's between your momma and daddy. It don't concern you. Stop worrying about big people's problems.*—MBGB:80 **(ii)** [Usu of a woman] To be the sexual partner of (sb). *That woman you see him always talkin[g] to? Well she concern him.*—(Bdos)

Con·chy Joe (**Con·chie Joe**) [kɒŋki jo] *n phr* (Baha, TkCa) [*Joc/Derog*] **1.** A Bahamian LOCAL WHITE. **2.** A Bahamian POOR-WHITE. **3.** A Bahamian of mixed race, ranging from mulatto to near-white, particularly such a person showing a feeling of social superiority.

con·con·sa (**con·co·sa, con·go·sa**) *adj* (Antg, etc) [*AF*] See KONGKONGSA

con·fine-cold; **con.fine.ment-cold** *n* (Antg, Brbu, Nevs) [*AF*] ‖ LYING-IN COLD (Antg, etc)

con·ga·tay (**con·go·tay, con·kan·tay, con-** ·**quin·tay**) [kʌŋgʌte ~ kʌŋkʌnte] *n* (Belz, Gren, Guyn, Tbgo, Trin) ‖ *gungude* (Belz ‖ *plaintain-porridge* (Jmca) A porridge made from the meal obtained by pounding sun-dried slices of plantains or green bananas; it is used esp for feeding infants. [Cp *ZAGL* Gã-Adanme *kokonté* 'cassada dried in the sun and afterwards made into a flour'] □ See PLAINTAIN-FLOUR.

Con·go[1] [kʌŋgʌ/-ga] *n* (CarA) [*Derog*] A person who is black, whose standard of living is of the lowest, speech uneducated and language rough, and who is also considered basically stupid and ignorant. [From the Hist fact that slaves from the Congo (both the Central Afr country and the basin of the river so named) arrived in the CarA far later than the W Afr masses of slaves, esp after the Br abolition of the Slave Trade (1807). The Congoes were strongly despised by the established creolized slave population, and consequently the stigma of stupidity was attached to the type and passed on to present times]

con·go[2] [kʌŋgʌ/-ga] *adj* (CarA) [*Derog*] [Of a person] Black, of rough-looking features or dress, poor, and generally uninformed. [From prec]

con·go[3] *n* (Dmca) ‖ CORN ROW (CarA)

con·go-drum *n* (Bdos) ‖ BONGO[1] 2. (Antg)

con·go·sa *adj* (Antg, Trin) See KONGKONGSA[1]

con·go peas *n phr* (CayI) ‖ PIGEON-PEAS (CarA)

con·go pump ['kʌŋgʌ-pʌmp] *n phr* (Guyn) ‖ TRUMPET-BUSH (Bdos, etc) *They would get two dry congo-pump leaves and boil them well, let the water cool and drink a cup every day for kidney troubles or high blood pressure.*—Guyn (Ms)

con·go·tay (**con·kan·tay**) *n* (Belz, Gren, Guyn, Tbgo, Trin) See CONGATAY

conk·ie (**can·kie, kaan·ki, kan(g)·ki, kon·kee**) ['kɒŋki] *n* (Angu, Bdos, StKt, Tbgo) ‖ DUKUNA (Antg, etc) [See CANKIE. The vowel closure [a] > [ɒ ~ ɔ] would be due to CE false refinement]

con·quin·tay *n* (Tbgo, Trin) See CONGATAY

con·vert *vb tr PHRASE* **convert a house** *vb phr* (Bdos) To rebuild a (usu small, four-walled) house without the occupants needing to move out during the process: starting at the back, each new wall or section is built outside the old one and the replacement effected, so that in stages all the old walls and lastly the roof are replaced. □ The process is also referred to sometimes as *remodelling*.

coo-coo[1] *n* (Bdos, Crcu, Gren, Guyn, StVn, Trin) See COU-COU

coo-coo[2] *n* (USVI) See KUKU □ Different spellings *cou-cou* (for the food), *kuku* (for a baby's bowel movement) help to distinguish these items, and also an adj (see next), all having the same pronunc.

coo-coo[3] *adj* (Nevs) [Of a person] Ugly. [Perh attrib extension of COO-COO[2]]

cook *vb tr PHRASE* **cook a man's head** *vb phr* (StKt) ‖ *give (sb) bad-food* (Bdos, Tbgo) ‖ *give (sb) stay-home sauce/soup* (Guyn) [Of a woman] To give a man food prepared with ingredients wh she believes would magically make him choose or stay with her as his mate.

coo·ka *n* (Mrat) See KUKA

cook·ing-fig *n* (Trin) ‖ GOVERNOR-FIG (Trin)

cook-shop *n* (Guyn) ‖ EATERY (Bdos, etc)

cook-up *n* (CarA) 1. ‖ *calalu* 2(ii) (Dmca, Gren, Jmca, Stvn) ‖ *seasoned rice* (Antg, Jmca) An ALL-IN-ONE including peas or beans and rice, and often boiled in COCONUT-MILK. 2. An out-of-doors house-party to wh friends are invited and at wh a COOK-UP or other folk-dish is the principal item served; [by extension] a cook-out held by a club. [Cp Hausa *dafa duka* (*cook all*) 'a meal made by cooking everything together'] □ See also CALALU 2(ii)

cool-drink *n* (CarA) ‖ *aerated drink* (CarA) ‖ *soda* (Jmca) ‖ *soft-drink, sweet-drink* (CarA) Any bottled, fizzy beverage sold commercially; (SE) carbonated drink/water; (AmE) soda (pop).

cool·er *n* 1. (Guyn) ‖ DEMERARA-WINDOW (CarA) [From the design wh keeps out the sun while allowing air to enter the house through the closed, wooden, louvred window; also, in earlier times, a block of ice was placed there to cool the intake of air] 2. (StKt, TkCa) A DUTCH-JAR (esp one used (StKt) in the process of distilling illicit rum). [From shift in use of keeping water cool to serving as a 'condenser'] 3. (BrVi) ‖ COOLING (ECar) *The leaves of the love-bush are steeped in boiling water and drunk as a cooler for blood complaints.*—BrVi (Ms)

coo·lie; **coo.lie-man, -woman, -boy, -girl, -people** [kʊli ~ kuli] *n* (CarA) [*Derog*] An EAST-INDIAN person. [Of Indic origin. See *OED coolie* wh notes that a similar word, ex Tamil *kuli* n 'hire' occurs in several Indic langs, but that the term is more likely to have gained currency as the name, *Kuli*, of a numerous Guzerat 'tribe' of labourers. The name was used and spread, esp in the 17C, by Europeans in India (spreading also to China) for 'a native hired labourer or burden-carrier' (*OED coolie* 2.). The name was thus attached to 18C immigrant East Indian indentured labourers in the *CarA*, at first without stigma, ex *'Give me my heart's desire in Coolies, and I will make you a million of hogsheads of sugar'*—*TWISM:170*. It then came to be applied to all East-Indian persons in post- immigration times] □ Though widely used, also attrib (*coolie dress, food, temple*, etc) this term is generally regarded as offensive, and in *Guyn* its use in public is forbidden by law.

coo·lie col·our(s) *n phr* (Gren, Guyn, StVn, Tbgo, Trin) [*Derog*] Bright pink, red, yellow or green or combination of any of these colours, esp of cloth or in dress. [From the association of such colours with materials and items used by Indic peoples in their ceremonies and folk festivals]

coo·lie-doug·la *n* (Guyn) [*Derog*] A usu dark-skinned person one of whose parents is EAST-INDIAN and the other of African descent. [< *coolie* 'E Indian' [Derog] + DOUGLA] □ The term is used mostly of a child of such mixed parentage.

coo·lie-flag *n* (Guyn, Trin) [*Derog*] See JHANDI

coo·lie-paw·paw *n* (Gren) [*AF*] ‖CERASEE (Baha, etc) [*Coolie* [Derog] 'East Indian', suggesting an inferior type of or false pawpaw, or perh a confused ref to the use of the larger variety as a vegetable by East Indians. See CARAILA.]

coo·lie-plum [kuli-plʌm] *n* **1.** (Jmca) ‖DUNK(S) (Bdos, etc) **2.** (Gren) ‖CHILLI PLUM (Antg, etc) □ In *Gren Chinee plum* is an alternative and commoner name.

coo·lie-ta·ma·rind *n* (Gren, Trin) ‖CARAMBOLA (Belz, etc)

cool·ing /1'2/ *n* (ECar) ‖*cooler* 3. (BrVi) **1.** A drink variously made from the crushed or boiled leaves of certain plants or by soaking burnt bread in water, taken as a remedy for skin rash or supposed impurities of the blood. **2.** (Sometimes) a plant whose leaves are so used. [From the belief that skin rash shows the need for cooling of the blood. Cp *OED cooling* ppl adj 1. a. 'of medicines, etc: lowering the temperature of the blood'] □ In sense 1. the term is not usu used with 'a' or 'the'. The affected person *'makes/ takes cooling', 'the leaves are good/taken for cooling'*, etc.

cool out *vb phr* (CarA) [*IF*] ‖ *breeze off* (Belz, Guyn) ‖ *breeze out* (Guyn, Tbgo) To sit and relax; to recline idly (esp if there is work to be done). *The Minister told the House of Assembly yesterday that he paid a surprise visit to a work site ... where four men were on the job, but not one man was at work. He said one man was 'cooling out' under a tree; another man emerged from a house after he arrived and yet another was standing in a drain.*—AdV (86.11.26, p.1) [Originally 'to take a rest, esp in the shade of a tree, from the heat of the sun', from wh a more general sense

developed, associated with laziness. See Note at BREEZE OFF]

coo·noo·moo·noo *n* (CarA) See KUNU-MUNU

coop[1] *n* (StVn, USVI) ‖CATCHER (ECar) [Cp *OED coop* v[1] 2. c. (U.S polit. slang.) 'to nab and confine persons (to make them vote for a party)'. This mid 19C Amer sense may have been part of wider colonial usage, with or by functional shift: See *OED coop* int 2. *coop* or *coop and seek* (U.S) 'the game of 'hide and seek' (1884). See next]

coop[2] (coup) *vb tr* (Nevs, StKt) [*IF*] **1.** To keep a sneaky watch on (sb); to spy on (sb's movements). **2.** To try to get hold of (sb's favours or money) to serve your own ends; [of a man] to try to seduce (a woman). [Perh < COOP[1] by functional shift and some shift of sense]

co-op·er·a·tiv·ism *n* (Guyn) The policy, politically adopted about 1970 by the Government of Guyana (thereafter called The Co-operative Republic of Guyana), by wh people's co-operatives in trading, industries, etc are or- ganized and helped throughout the country to promote self-reliance and national development. [*Co-operative*(s) n + -*ism*, suff denoting political system]

coo·yon *n* (Stlu, Trin) See KOUYON.

cop-cop (ant) *n* (*phr*) (Guyn) See KAP-KAP ANT

cop·per[1] *n* (CarA) [*IF—Hist*] **1.** A one-cent or two-cent bronze coin, with a British monarch's head embossed on one face, in common use in the Caribbean in colonial times. □ Often applied particularly to the two-cent coin, or 'penny'. **2.** *coppers n pl* A small wage; a small sum of money.

cop·per[2] *n* (CarA) [Sugar Ind] **1.** One of a number of large iron basins, varying in size from 4 to 6 ft in diameter and up to 2-1/2 ft deep, in wh cane-syrup was boiled in the process of manufacturing sugar. **2.** The disused basin from the sugar-factory once widely used in rural areas as a water container.

cop·per[3] *n* (Gren, StVn) An iron vessel in wh BAMBAM or CASSAVA BREAD is prepared. See SÈK

coque·li·cot ['kokliko] *n* (USVI) See KOKREKO

co·que·ri·cot [kʌkrikʌ] *n* (Belz) ‖COCRICO (Tbgo, Trin) [This Fr style spelling is used in *Belz*, naming the bird from the sound *cocricó* wh it makes] □ A game-bird hunted as such in *Belz*, protected by law in *Tbgo* as the National Bird.

co·qui (-eye) *n* (Tbgo, Trin) See COKEY-EYE

co·ra·be·ti ant *n phr* (Guyn) See COROBETI ANT

cor·al-bean *n* (Gren) ‖ JUMBIE-BEAD 2. (Bdos, etc) □ See also BEAN-TREE.

co·ra·li·ta* *n* (CarA) ‖ **coral-vine** (Jmca) ‖ **honey-bee bush** (Antg) A rambling, climbing vine with light-green, heart-shaped leaves and tiny, bright pink, heart-shaped flowers borne in lacy, string-like clusters; the vine thrives as a parasite in wild or uncultivated conditions; there is also a rarer white-flowered variety; *Antigonon leptopus (Polygonaceae)*. [Mexican Sp]

cor·al-stone *n* (Bdos) Quarried limestone coral, cut into blocks about 2 ft x 1 ft x 1 ft, used for building the outer walls of houses.

cor·al-vine *n* (Jmca) ‖ CORALITA (CarA)

co·ra·sol (co·ro·(s)sol) [kowosol] *n* (Dmca, StLu) See KÒWÒSÒL

co·ra·toe ['kʌrata ~ 'kyʌrʌtʌ] *n* (Jmca) ‖ AGAVE (CarA) [Cp *TDV* Venz Sp *coroto* (Vul) 'male genitals'; also *corota* 2. 'female genitals' 3. 'plant used for making house roofs'. Note that the phallic symbolism of the plant may also be reflected in the ‖ **male-pole** (Bdos)]

cor·beau (kò·bo) ['kobo] *n* (Gren, Trin) **1.** ‖ CARRION-CROW (Guyn) [Fr *corbeau* 'crow', with Fr Cr pronunc, but see Note at CARRION-CROW] □ 1. Notwithstanding the *ECar* pronunc, the original Fr spelling, with pl CORBEAUX, is widely used, and the alternative COBO(s) found in some writings (ex *MHBT:78*) is not recommended. **2.** Although the bird is not found in *Bdos, Tbgo*, its name is known; *Bdos* pronunc [kʌbʌ]. **2.** PHRASE **2.1 play dead to catch corbeau (alive)** *vb phr* (Mrat, Tbgo, Trin) [IF] To pretend to be ignorant or unaware of sth or to remain silent in order to bait (sb). *The police were able to surprise them because, you know playing dead to catch corbean alive, for a long time they seemed to be doing nothing about the matter, like if they forgot.*—(Trin) [Metaph, i.e. pretend to be a carcass in order to bait the furtive (corbeau)]

cor·ber·ry *n* (Angu) ‖ CANKER-BERRY (CarA)

cor·di·a* (red cor·di·a, scar·let cor·di·a) *n* (*phr*) (Angu, Bdos, CayI, StKt) A medium-sized ornamental tree with dark-green, oval leaves, a good scatter of clusters of red flowers borne throughout the year, and insignificant, whitish, plum-like fruits; *Cordia sebestena (Boraginaceae)*. □ Sometimes confused with the **African tulip**, a much larger ornamental tree wh it roughly resembles.

co·re·il·li *n* (Guyn, StVn, Trin) See CARAILA

co·ri·al ['koria·l] *n* (Guyn) A round-bottomed, Amerindian, river canoe about 15 to 25 ft long, made by burning out or digging out a tree trunk

and shaping to a point at each end. [Carib *kuriiyara*, Arawak *koriara* 'dugout canoe, corial'—*TLWI:4*; *TLWI's* historical evidence, from Island Carib, is corroborated by present-day *Guyn* Arawak *koriara* 'high prowed dugout made for sea travel'—*BAED:27*. Also Macusi *kulial* 'canoe, dugout'—*FTCC:142*]

cork¹ *vb* (Gren, StVn, Trin, USVI) [IF] To cause (sb) to be constipated. *Eating plenty green guavas will cork you.*—(StVn) [< SE *cork* in sense 'to stop up, block']

cork² *n* PHRASE **your cork duck** *id phr* (Guyn) [AF—Joc] You are in hopeless bad luck; you have definitely lost what you were trying to save, win, etc (cp SE lose hook, line and sinker). [Cr vb structure = *your cork has ducked*, i.e. been carried away, gone for good. Metaph from line-fishing]

cork-hat *n* (CarA) **1.** A sun helmet partly or wholly lined with a layer of cork, formerly worn by white colonists (brown ones by overseers, white ones by planters and senior administrators); (SE) a pith-helmet **2.** A white sun helmet with an extended back to shade the neck, worn by policemen.

cork-screw(s)¹ *n* (Bdos, StVn, Tbgo) ‖ **chinee-bump¹** (Jmca) ‖ **nigger-plait¹** (CayI) ‖ **pa-piyòt** (StLu) ‖ **pig-breast** (Nevs) **1.** Name given to a temporary styling of a black woman's hair when it is tied in neat rows of regular clumps to ease drying after being washed, and in preparation for being set later in any finished style. **2.** PHRASE **2.1 have your hair in cork-screw** *vb phr* (Bdos, StVn, Tbgo) [From the spiral turning of the hair in finishing each clump]

cork-screw² *vb tr* (Bdos, StVn, Tbgo) ‖ **chinee-bump²** (Jmca) ‖ **nigger-plait²** (CayI) ‖ **pa-piyòt** (StLu) ‖ **pig-breast²** (Nevs) To style hair in the temporary manner known as CORK-SCREW(s). *Cork-screwing the hair with a little All-Ways grease after washing helps to soften it.*—(Bdos) [By functional shift of CORK-SCREW¹]

corn¹ *n* (CarA) [The only name used for maize or Indian corn; *Zea mays (Gramineae-Poaceae)*] **1.** The hard dried grains of corn (esp as used for poultry feed or ground to make CORNMEAL). **2.** One cob of corn or corn on the cob (hence pl CORNS), esp for boiling or roasting. (See ROAST-CORN). *She said, 'I have a policy of never selling stale corn to my customers and I always buy as many corns as would sell. It is very hard work because when I take the corns home I have to husk them.'*—AdN (78.10.23, p.7) **3** PHRASE **3.1 lose corn and husk** *vb phr* (Guyn) [IF] To gain neither one thing nor the other; to lose all around through misjudgement. □ SE *corn* (cp E Hist The Corn Laws) refers to wheat or oats.

corn² *n* (StKt) **1.** ‖ COU-COU (CarA) **2.** PHRASES **2.1 corn and saltfish** *n phr* (StKt) A meal of COU-COU and SALTFISH wh is very popular. **2.2**

turn corn *vb phr* (StKt) To cook a meal of CORN (wh has to be turned with a wooden spoon as it is shaped into a ball while being boiled). □ A more popular alternative name in *StKt* to ‖ FUN-GEE

corn[3] *n* (Trin) **1.** Rum. *If you exist just for drinking corn, / Or baddening yuh head / Yuh go heavy just like lead.*—Cso (1971) [Prob old colonial usage. Cp *OEDS corn* 5. b. U.S 'corn-whiskey' + cits from 1820] **2.** PHRASE **2.1 corn and oil** *n phr* (Bdos) [*IF*] A mixture of rum and FALERNUM.

corn[4] *vb tr* **1.** (CarA) To pickle, or cure with salt, in order to preserve (esp pork but also fish). [*OED corn* v 3. 'pickle, preserve with salt'] **2.** *vb tr* (CarA) [*AF*] To chastise severely. (See Phr 4.1) **3.** (Bdos) [*AF*] To make plenty of money with apparent ease. *Rapidly growing underground economy in Barbados is corning over $15 million from goods brought into the island illegally, re-labelled and sold.*—NaT (82.05.20, p.20) [Prob a corruption of SE *coin money*, perh reinforced by sense 1: It is an excessive amount of pork that requires *corning* 'pickling' and being kept in a large CORN-JAR] **4.** PHRASE **4.1 corn your backside/behind/tail, etc** *vb phr* (CarA) [*AF*] (Sense 2. intensified) [By metaph extension of the sense 'to pickle']

corn-bag *n* (BrVi) ‖ CROCUS BAG (CarA)

corn-bird *n* **1.** (Trin) ‖ CACIQUE **2.** (Guyn, Trin) 2. (Guyn) ‖ BLACKBIRD 1.1 (CarA)

corn cou-cou/coo-coo *n phr* (BrVi, StVn, Tbgo) ‖ COU-COU (CarA)

corn-dump·ling /1′22/ *n* (StKt) ‖ DUKUNA (Antg, etc)

cor·ner *n* **1.** (Guyn) ‖ *grass-corner, road-cor-ner* (Guyn) [*IF*] The edge of the road. (See Phr 3.1). **2.** (Baha) ‖ *gap* (Bdos) A small, narrow, unimportant looking street. (See Phr 3.2). **3.** PHRASES **3.1 keep to/walk in the corner** *vb phr* (Guyn) [Esp as a warning to children] To keep to the edge of the road. **3.2 through that corner** *prep phr* (Baha) Down that little street.

corn-flour *n* (Bdos, Guyn) ‖ CORNMEAL (CarA) [Cp BrE 'a fine-ground flour used as a thickening agent', vs AmE 'a coarse-ground flour variously used']

corn-jar *n* (Bdos) ‖ *England-jar* (Antg) **1.** A sturdy, earthenware, wide-mouthed jar about 2-1/2 ft high, with bulging shoulder and tapering towards its base, formerly used for importing salt-pork from England for labourers' food. **2** PHRASE **2.1 put your hand in a[n] empty corn-jar** *vb phr* (Bdos) [*AF—Joc*] [Of a man] To marry a girl of no means or of poor means.

corn·meal *n* (CarA) ‖ *corn-flour* (Bdos, Guyn) The fine, milled, yellow meal ground

from grains of CORN[1], often simply called 'corn', and widely used in folk foods. □ Hence *corn/cornmeal* (sometimes *corn-flour*) as qualifiers of COU-COU (*BrVi, etc*), DUMPLING (*Dmca, Jmca, Tbgo*), **pap** (*Guyn*), **porridge** (*Bdos, Guyn, Jmca*), **pone** (*Tbgo*), **pudding** (*Antg, Brbu*).

corn-pep·per *n* (Bdos) BIRD-PEPPERS pre-served in salt and vinegar to be used in seasoning food.

corn-pone *n* **1.** (Bdos, Guyn, Jmca, Tbgo) ‖ *cornmeal pudding* (Antg, Brbu) A heavy, baked, sweet pudding made of CORNMEAL and (often) grated coconut. **2.** (Jmca) (Name some-times used for) DOKUNU.

corn-row[1] *n* (CarA) ‖ *cane-row(s)* (Bdos, Gren, Jmca, StVn, Tbgo, Trin) ‖ *cascadu* (StVn) ‖ *congo*[3] (Dmca) ‖ *guinea* (Nevs, StKt, USVI) ‖ *guinea-row* (Baha, TkCa, Trin) ‖ *plaits* (CayI) A Black woman's hairstyle in wh the hair is braided in thin, tight rows along the scalp, usu straight from the forehead to the back of the head but often also with spiral and other patterns. *Years ago corn-row plaits were ridiculed as 'picky-picky' hair. Today it is the height of fashion.*—GyC (76.06.27, p.6) [Poss a Joc ref to the resemblance between the neat parallel braids and rows of planted corn or (note ‖) of plantation sugar-cane. The original Afr names in each lan-guage were prob lost in time]

corn-row[2] *vb* (CarA) ‖ *cane-row*[2] (CarA) To style the hair in CORN-ROW[1]. *If you change the Afro and corn-row your hair, it will grow back fast.*—(Bdos) [By functional shift of CORN-ROW[1]]

corn-sham *n* (Belz, Gren) ‖ ASHAM (Antg, etc) [A blend of *corn* (the main ingredient) + ASHAM, an original W Afr name]

corn-stick *n* (Dmca, Gren, Tbgo) A dry corn-cob used as a scrubber in washing clothes.

co·ro·be·ti-ant (co·ra·be·ti-, cou·ra·bet-·ty-) *n* (Guyn) A tiny, red ant (about 1mm in length) with a notable sting; it is found in groups in damp places; *Formica micrergates* (Form-icidae). [Cp < Arawak *korebeii* 'small red ant'—EILCA:46]

Co·ro·man·te(e)/ti (Cro·man·ty) *n* [Hist] **1.** (CarA) Name used to identify a particular kind of slaves from the Gold Coast noted both for their sturdiness and fidelity on the one hand and for their fierce vengefulness when ill-treated. [From name of a coastal Fante town, variously spelt Cormantyn, Kormantine, etc, about 80 miles west of Accra, used as a slaving post by the English and Dutch in the early 17C. Sug-gestions of a Coromante 'language' and 'people' prob refer to Fante, a lang closely related to Twi] **2.** (Crcu) Name of a particular NATION DANCE (see cit). *For example, there is the Co-romanti which on any occasion, is the dance per-formed at the opening of the festivity. A certain* *rhythm is played on the drums and the sponsor of the occasion, followed by the dancers and singers, parade around the ring, throwing rum and water as they go.*—PGIP:28

co·ro(s)·sol-di·able *n* (Dmca) See KÒ-WÒSÒL-DJAB

corp·ie *n* (Jmca, StKt) [*AF*] (Familiar form of addressing) a policeman. [Abbr < (police) corporal]

Cor·po·rate Ar·ea *n phr* (Jmca) The municipal district embracing Kingston and St Andrew as one Corporation, (hence the name, as well as the abbr K.S.A.C.) under a mayor.

cor·rupt·ed *adj* (Belz) [*X*] Corrupt. *Perhaps no penalties are prescribed because the bill does not prohibit corrupted behaviour by a Minister. It is just silent on the matter. Thus a corrupted Minister would not be breaking any law or code, so long as he stays short of actual criminal conduct.*—BeA (80.04.12, p.2) [An over-correct form] □ A common but erron *Belz* usage, where the condition of being 'corrupt' (SE adj) is meant, and not suffering the effect of having been 'corrupted' (SE pa. part. as vbl adj).

co·ruck·le [kʌ'rʌkl] (Antg) (**co·rut·tle**) [kʌ'rʌtl] (BrVi) *n* [*AF*] ‖ *couchument* (Tbgo) A muddle or mixture of things belonging to sb; various disparate belongings; paraphernalia. [Cp Sc and N Eng dial *CSD ruckle* 19C 'a heap, pile, collection of objects, esp one loosely or carelessly thrown together'. *Co-*, of CORUCKLE, may be an intensifier suffix (cp commotion, confusion, etc). *Coruttle* is prob a variant form]

co·shi(e) *n* (StVn) See CASHI(E)

cos·kel [kɒskɛl] *adj* (Trin) 1. [Of dress] Being ridiculously mismatched in colours. 2. [Of persons] Dressed in ridiculously clashing colours in an effort to be attractively fashionable. [Prob < Sp *cosquillas* n 'a tickling, a joke' with dial shift > adj in Trin Cr Sp]

cos·sy *n* (Antg, Jmca) See CASSIE

cost *n* PHRASE **at all cost** *adv phr* (CarA) [*X*] At all costs; by any means; without a doubt. ... *the Premier of St Lucia still looked away, avoiding eyeball to eyeball contact with his listeners at all cost—as usual.*—WBAM:186 [Overlap or confusion with SE idiom *at any cost*, + typical CE discomfort with /-sts/ as terminal consonant cluster]

co·ta·coo ['kɒtaku] *n* (USVI) See CUTACOO

co·tay-ci co·tay-la (**co·té-ci co·té-la**) *n phr* (Dmca, Tbgo, Trin) See KOTÉ-SI KOTÉ-LA

cotch¹ *n* (Jmca) [*AF*] ‖ SCOTCH (Bdos) *You just go down to you' work, an' try an' get anoder place to sleep to-night. If y'u caan't, I will give you a*

cotch when you come home.—DJC:129 [< SCOTCH by aphaeresis. See SCOTCH (*Bdos*)]

cotch² *vb* (Jmca) [*AF*] 1. *vb tr* To wedge; to squeeze (sth or sb) into a narrow place. 2. [By extension] *vb intr* To lodge temporarily and inconveniently with sb. 3. *vb intr* [By extension of 2.] To lean or depend lazily on (sb) for support; to shirk work.

cot·ta (**cot·ter**, **cot·to**) ['kɒta/-ʌ] *n* (Antg, Jmca, StVn, USVI) ‖ CATTA (Antg, etc) **a.** *She lifted her basket of vegetables and yams above her head and lowered it gently on to the thick coil of the cotta.*—SJS:5 **b.** *From early dawn the road was coloured with long lines of slaves, most of them with baskets on their heads cushioned by a cotta made of coiled-up, dried plantain leaves.*—PSOS:229 [< CATTA by vowel-closure /a > o/ prob due to false refinement]

cot·ton *n* 1.* (CarA) ‖ *cotton-bush* (ViIs) The shrub, native to the Caribbean, with green or brownish, lobed leaves, large yellow or purplish flowers, and a ball-like capsule that bursts open when ripe disclosing the soft white fibre wh is used commercially, the best known variety being SEA-ISLAND COTTON; *Gossypium hirsutum* or (the sea-island variety) *G. barbadense maritimum* (*Malvaceae*). 2. (CarA) The fibre harvested from the plant. 3. (CayI) ‖ AMERICAN SILK-COTTON (BrVi)

cot·ton-bush *n* (ViIs) ‖ COTTON 1. (CarA)

cot·ton-tree *n* (Baha, Belz, Jmca) ‖ SILK-COTTON TREE *An obeahman would cast an evil spell on a person by driving a nail into a Cotton Tree, calling upon an evil spirit to order a person's shadow to leave their body and dwell in the Cotton Tree.*—Jmca (Ms)

cou·bal·ly ['kubali] *n* (Belz) ‖ CAVALLI (CarA)

couche-couche (**kouch-kouch**) [kuš-kuš] *n* (StLu) ‖ CUSH-CUSH³ (Dmca, etc) [Falsely Fr *StLu* pronunc of CUSH-CUSH] □ There are a white variety and a purplish in *StLu*.

cou·chu·ment [kučumen(t)] *n* (Tbgo) [*AF—Joc*] ‖ CORUCKLE (Antg) [Prob < SE *accoutrement*, esp in its military sense 'the equipments of a soldier other than arms and dress' *OED*]

cou-cou (**coo-coo¹**) [kuku ~ kʌku] *n* (CarA) ‖ *corn(meal)/corn-flour cou-cou* (BrVi, Guyn, StVn, Tbgo) ‖ *fungee* 1. (Angu, Antg, Brbu, Nevs, StKt, StVn, ViIs) ‖ *turn-coo-coo* (Trin) ‖ *turn-corn* (Nevs, StKt) ‖ *turn corn-meal, turn-meal* (Jmca) 1. A mixture of cornmeal, okras (and sometimes peas) and butter, boiled and stirred with a COU-COU STICK until firm enough to be shaped into a ball; it is usu served with steamed fish. [The wide occurrence of this name in the Southern *CarA* strongly suggests a W Afr origin, though sources are uncertain or unconvincing. Cp *DAFL* Twi ŋkuku 'a species of yam', also Twi *kuku* (from Eng) 'a cook'; similarly *ADHL* Hausa *kuku* (from Eng) and *ADMY* Yoruba *kuku* (from Eng) 'a European's cook'. These latter only indicate, however, that the word *kuku* was widely used in colonial W Afr for a professional cook. Twi ŋkuku is a more likely origin] □ 1. The spelling *cou-cou* is now generally established in *Bdos* with which territory the meal is historically most associated, hence its adoption here. Other spellings *coocoo* (esp), *cookoo, cuckoo* occur in many places. See note following COO-COO². □ 2. Variations without cornmeal still bear the name: *breadfruit coucou, cassava coucou, pumpkin and potato coucou*, etc. See FUNGEE 2. 2. PHRASES **2.1 ball of cou-cou** *n phr* (Bdos) See BALL Phr 3.2 **2.2 turn corn cou-cou** *vb phr* (Bdos) See TURN¹ Phr 4.2 **3. 2.3 you and me cou-cou don't boil/soak** *id phr* (Guyn, Tbgo, Trin) [*AF—Cr*] We don't get along well together; we are too different kinds of people to be together.

cou-cou stick *n phr* (Bdos, Tbgo, Trin) ‖ *turn-stick* (Antg, Brbu) A smooth, flat, oblong piece of wood about 12 ins long and 2 ins wide with rounded edges and ends, used for stirring and shaping COU-COU into a ball.

cough *n* (Guyn, StVn, Trin) [*AF*] **1.** Tuberculosis. □ Without articles *a, the,* wh would change the meaning to refer to normal coughing from a chest cold; except that in an expression such as 'the children are suffering from *cold and cough*', the meaning is restricted to coughing from chest colds. **2.** PHRASE **2.1 have cough** *vb phr* (Guyn, StVn) [*AF*] To suffer from tuberculosis.

could *modal aux vb* (CarA) [*X*] [Note: CE speakers tend to use this as an all-purpose aux loosely indicating shades of possibility both past and present] **1.** Can. **a.** *You name it, we could do it.*—ToR (Ad, 76.07.18, p.6) **b.** *Earl, with thirteen children and three grand-children said: 'Is only because we poor they could treat we so.'*—ExP (73.02.04, p.1) **2.** May; might. **a.** *Perhaps it could not be proved that way, but if a survey is conducted it could be determined.*—Jmca (Ms, 1974) **b.** *Jamaica's sugar cane farmers have been urged to reap every stalk of cane for the 1973 harvest so that the country could be able to retain its export quotas.*—AdN (72.12.03, p.5) **3.** [Expressing a neutral request] Would please. *You could use that chair because this one ain['t] safe.*—(StVn) **4.** [With emotive stress and high pitch on foll vb] Be very competent or capable (of action expressed in the foll vb). *Boy, he could eat!* (= *He is capable of eating an enormous amount of food*).—(Trin) **5.** PHRASES **5.1 could as well** (+ vb) (Bdos) May/might just as well (+ vb). *But it was silly to try to enlighten Maffi. It wasn't any use. He could as well have spoken to the tattered torsos the lazy waves puffed up on the shores of Coco Té.*—WTD:72 **5.2 could only** (Bdos) [*AF*] Must certainly. *'You could only want killing'. And the venom in the voice and demeanour*

of the threatener is intense.—-AdV (81.01.18, p.8) [From common Cr use of /ku~kud/ as general aux in affirmative contexts and /kun~ kyaan/ in neg ones]

could-a (could·a) (+vb) *past modal aux vb* (CarA) [*AF—Cr, usu followed by infin vb*] Could have (+ pa. part.). *In the days when you coulda get saltfish and condensed milk and so forth.*—StA(JA) (73.02.10, p.14, Partyline) [*Could* + *have* reduced to enclitic /a/. See A⁸] □ Usu written *coulda, could'a*, in narrative dial, *could-a* offers a standardized way of presenting the enclitic. See also WOULD-A.

could of (+ vb) *past modal aux vb* (CarA) [*X*] ‖ *could-a* (CarA) Could have (+ pa. part.). *He could not of climbed the tree so he decided to take his slingshot and shot down some mangoes.*—Guyn (Ms) [A false refinement of COULD-A through the stage could've [kʊdəv > kʊd ɔv]] □ This widely occurring error also admits a neg infix as in cit.

cou·li·bre *n* (Dmca, Gren, Grns) See COLIBRI

cou-nette *n* (Dmca) See KOU-NÈT

count *vb tr* (Gren) [*AF*] **1.** To talk about other people's affairs in a mean way, calling names; to BAD-TALK others. (Hence foll phrs). **2.** PHRASE **2.1 count (sb's name/people('s) business)** *vb phr* (Gren) [*AF*] To relate bad things about (sb). [By aphaeresis < SE *recount* 'tell in detail']

count·er-flour *n* (Gren, Jmca, Tbgo, Trin) Flour sold by the pound over the counter (hence name) dipped from an open bag; flour that is not packaged.

coun·try-band *n* (StLu) ‖ QUADRILLE BAND (CarA)

coun·try-boo·boo (-bu·bu) /1'122/ *n* (BrVi, Guyn, Mrat, Nevs, StKt, Tbgo) [*AF—Derog*] ‖ COUNTRY-BOOKIE (Crcu, etc)

coun·try-book·ie (-book·ey, -book·y) ['kʌntri-bʊki] /1'122/ *n* (ECar) [*AF—Derog*] ‖ *Bobo-John(ny)* (StKt) ‖ *bush-fool, bushy* 2. (Belz) ‖ *country-booboo* (BrVi, Guyn, Mrat, Nevs, StKt, Tbgo) ‖ *country-buck* (Bdos) ‖ *country-Johnny* (Belz) An uninformed and unrefined person, esp one from the country come to town; a person who is easily fooled. *There he was, standing vacantly with his shoes in his hand, like some country-bookie that didn't know how to wear them.*—Gren (Ms) [*Country* + *bookie*, perh = *buckie*. Cp *OED* buckie Sc 2. 'a perverse or refractory person' perh also infl by BUCK (note *Bdos* ‖)]

coun·try-buck /1'12/ *n* (Bdos) ‖ COUNTRY-BOOKIE (Crcu, etc) [See BUCK]

coun·try-choc·o·late [kʌntri-čɒ·klɪt] *n* (Jmca) ‖ CHOCOLATE-TEA (ECar)

coun·try-John·ny /ɪ'ɪ22/ n (Belz) ‖COUN-TRY-BOOKIE (Crcu, etc)

Coun·ty n (Guyn) [Hist] One of the three orig 'colonies' of Berluce, Demerara, and Essequibo variously owned by the Dutch, English and French until brought together under English ownership (1803) and administered as 'counties' under one Governor (1831), [Cp Br E *county*, a large territorial division of England with its own history] □ The term now survives only in legal and land-ownership documents.

coup-de-main (Dmca, StLu) See KOUDMEN

cou·ple [kʌpl ~ kʌpəl] adj (CarA) [IF] **1.** A few. *What annoyed the woman most was that the couple dollars enclosed in the letter was not to be found when the letter was opened a second time.*—ToR (77.02.06, p.3) [< SE noun *couple* 'a pair', but widely used with omission of 'of' (< SE *a couple of*), hence developing both the function and sense of the SE pronominal adjs *some, few*] □ In careful writing *a couple of* (+n) occurs, but rarely in everyday speech. **2.** PHRASE **2.1 couple mornings** n phr (CarA) [AF] A short, hardly noticeable period of time. *After the complaints the police watched for couple mornings and that was all.*—(Guyn)

cou-plu·ché n (StLu) See KOU-PLICHÉ

cou·ra·bet·ty-ant n phr (Guyn) See COROBETI ANT

cou·ri·da* (cou·ri·da-bush, cou·ri·da tree) ['kʊrɪda] n (phr) (Guyn) A medium-sized tree of the mangrove family, thriving in coastal and riverside waters with thick, blackish, curved but stilt- like intertwining, aerial roots; its wood is used for fuel; the Black Mangrove; *Avicennia nitida (Verbenaceae).* [< *BAED* Arawak *koroda* 'a kind of tree that grows near the sea']

court·en; **court.en.in(g)** vb intr (CarA) [X] ‖**friend; friendin[g]** (Tbgo, Trin) ‖**friendsin(g)** (Guyn) **1.** [Esp of a man] To court, woo a woman. *Man a-courtenin must go gay.*— Guyn (Prov) **2.** [Of both man and woman] (To be) in close friendship, intending to marry; SE (to be) in courtship. *So after a couple years of courtening, there they stan' as man an' wife.*— YFOC:11 [< SE *courting* becoming Cr vb stem [ko(r)tɪn > ko(r)tn], hence also [ko(r)tnɪn]. Cp similarly FISHENIN(G)] □ Now mostly used by older folk, though still *CarA*- wide. See FRIEND-IN[G].

court-shoes n pl (Bdos, Guyn) ‖**pump(s)²** (Nevs, StKt, Tbgo) A pair of lady's high-heeled shoes for formal wear; (BrE) pumps. [*Court* in ref to formal wear]

coush·i ant(s) n phr (Guyn) ‖ACOUSHI ANTS (Guyn) [*BAED* Arawak *khose* 'parasol ants']

cous·in [kʌzn ~ kʌzɪn] n (CarA) **1.** [Among black people] Any distant relative. *In fact cousins are so many that a man might make specific reference to his cousin-family.*—Caq 4.2, p.154 **2.** [Esp in rural areas] (Respectful form of address esp by younger persons to) any mature adult friend of your parents. *Mummy, Cousin Dinah is here.*—(Guyn) **3.** [Only in rural areas, perh obs] (Friendly form of address replying to) a friendly looking black stranger. *S1: Good morning! / S2: Awright, cousin!*—(Guyn)

cou-tou·ni n (Dmca) See KOU-TOUNI

cou·va(l)·li(e) [kʊvali] n (Gren, Trin) ‖CA-VALLI (CarA)

cou·yon n (Trin) See KOUYON

cov·er n PHRASES **1. come out of your cover** vb phr (Dmca) ‖ GET BESIDE YOURSELF (CarA) See BESIDE Phr 2.1. **2. mouth has/ain't got no cover** id phr See MOUTH Phr 4.34

co·ver·ty-po·cham (co·vet·ti po·cham) n (Trin) See KOUVÈTI-PÒTCHANM

cow¹ n (CarA) [IF] **1.** Cattle [Note: Commonly used [IF] in sg only]. **2.** PHRASES **2.1 come to drink milk, not to count cow** vb phr (ECar) [IF] To be there, to be participating in (sth), for expected gain and not to waste time. **2.2 (like when) cow buss rope** adv phr (Guyn) [AF] In an angry or enraged manner. *This time when he hear 'another six months', see how he lookin[g] at the magistrate like cow buss rope.*—(Guyn) **2.3 mind(ing) cow** vb phr (Guyn, Trin) [IF] Rear(ing) cattle. *In those days the Indians would take a boy out of school to mind cow.*—(Guyn)

cow² (cow-work) n (Guyn) [IF] **1.** Work done regularly for private gain using employer's equipment and stealing materials and time; BOBOL on a smaller scale. **2.** PHRASES **2.1 run cow; work cow** vb phrs (Guyn) [IF] To organize work on the side for personal gain using your employer's equipment, materials and time. *Vibart was employed at the Bakery, and ... it seems that he was running his own little 'cow' on the side. Though, as was seen, when he appeared before the Beak on a charge of larceny, there was very little profit in it.*—DaC (52.09.16, p.3)

cow-bean; **cow-bush**; **cow-ta.ma.rind** ['kʊu-tam[b]rɪn] /ɪ'22/ n (Baha) ‖WILD TAM-ARIND **1.** (Belz, etc) *The small Cow Tamarind trees that grow along the roadsides of all tropical areas are a common weed of the Legume family but they have many uses. The seeds ... are strung as jewelry ... Pods and leaves make a high protein fodder for cattle.*—HHTT:63 [From the use of the plant as cattle fodder (see cit) + *tamarind*, from resemblance of dry pods and compound leaves to those of the tamarind tree]

cow-bee n (Bdos) The bumble bee. [From its size]

cow-bird *n* (BrVi, Jmca) ‖ CATTLE-EGRET (Bdos, etc) [From its feeding on insects on the bodies of, or near to, grazing cows]

cow-bush *n* (Baha) See COW-BEAN

cow-cod *n* (Jmca) **1.** ‖ BULL-PISTLE (CarA) **2.** (Also a rural food delicacy, hence) COW-COD SOUP.

cow-fish *n* (Baha, Gren, Mrat, StLu) **1.** ‖ *box-fish* (Baha, Guyn, TkCa) ‖ *shell-fish* (ECar) A yellowish fish often more than 12 ins long, with irregular, bluish spots and stripes, roughly triangular or squarish in shape, with two horns over the eyes and a hard shell covering nearly the whole body; it is often roasted, its food value being good; the horned trunkfish; *Lactophrys quadricornis (Ostraciidae)*. [From the cow-like appearance of its head] **2.** (TkCa) ‖ KABWIT **2.** (StLu) *We call that cow-fish for the horns on the head, but I don't think nobody eat it.*—-(TkCa)

cow-foot (bush)* *n* (*phr*) (Belz, Guyn) ‖ *candle-bush* **2.** (Trin) ‖ *monkey-hand* (Dmca) A shrub that can exceed 5 ft in height, of two or three varieties, all noted for their medicinal value; it has broad, shiny, veined, dark-green leaves, an infusion of wh is a folk-medicine for menstrual pains; the wilted leaves are used for headaches; *Lepianthes peltata* or *Piper tuberculatum* or *Pothomorphe peltata (Piperaceae)*. [Prob from the shape of its leaf (*Guyn*) wh resembles an enlarged imprint of a cow's hoof. The plant is often actually called *cow-foot leaf.*]

cow-foot soup *n phr* (Baha, Belz, Jmca) ‖ COW-HEEL SOUP (Gren, etc)

cow·hage *n* (StKt) See COWITCH.

cow-heel soup *n phr* (Gren, Guyn, StVn, tbgo, Trin) ‖ *bull-foot soup* (ViIs) ‖ *cow-foot soup* (Baha, Belz, Jmca) A thick soup the principal ingredient of wh is the ankle and hoof of the cow boiled to a gelatinous softness, with seasoning, vegetables, and dumplings added.

cow·itch* (**cow·hage**) [kʌwič ~ kʌw(h)eˑj] *n* **1.** (CarA) ‖ *cobbeach* (Nevs) ‖ *monkey-tambran* (Baha) ‖ *pwa-gwaté* (Dmca, Gren, StLu) A pod, brown when ripe, about 4 ins long and over half-inch wide, borne in clusters on a wild, climbing vine (*cow-itch bush/vine*); each pod is densely covered with noticeable hairs that cause extreme irritation on touching the skin, though the vine is used as a folk-medicine to worm children; *Mucuna pruriens (Papilionaceae)*. [*OED cowage, cowhage < Hin Kawach*. The widely occurring form *cowitch* is therefore due, by pop etym, to association with the itching property of the hairs; the spelling *cowhage*, wh still occurs occasionally (ex *StKt*) is nearer the original] □ The name is also loosely applied to other plants with irritant hairs on leaves, or juices in stems, as in foll ex. **2.** (Trin) A vine with hand-sized, lobed leaves and attractive yellowish flowers with irritant hairs and seed-pods; *Dalechampia pruriens (Euphorbiaceae)*.

cow-man *n* (Guyn) ‖ DONKEY-MAN (Bdos)

cow-mouth *n* (Guyn) A box-like, wooden extension, with spaces between the boards and usu covered with a sloping piece of galvanized iron sheeting, built on to a kitchen to take a COAL-POT or mud-stove. [From the rough resemblance in shape to a cow's head]

cow-pea *n* (Baha, Belz, Berm, CayI, Jmca, TkCa) ‖ BLACKEYE-PEA (CarA)

cow-skin *n* (Bdos) A whip (orig for slaves) made of plaited cowhide attached to a stick.

cow-tail *n* PHRASE **born behind cow-tail** *vb phr* (Dmca, Guyn) See BORN[1] Phrs 1.

cow-ta·ma·rind *n* **1.** (Trin) ‖ *saman* (CarA) **2.** (Baha) ‖ *cow-bean* (Baha)

cow-tongue *n* (Tbgo) ‖ CATTLE-TONGUE (Antg, etc) [From the feel of the leaf, recalling the rough upper surface and smooth underside of a cow's tongue]

crab-and-ca·la·lu *n* (Guyn) ‖ CALALU **2.**(i) (Dmca, etc) □ The dish is also referred to by this name 'in a Louisiana Cr cradle song entitled 'Crab dans Calalou''—*NEAPR:261* (trans). Also sometimes *calalu-and-crab* (*Trin*).

crab-back *n* (CarA) The shell of the crab, stuffed with well-seasoned, cooked crab-flesh, then baked and served as a delicacy.

crab-bush *n* (BrVi) ‖ CATTLE-TONGUE (Antg, etc)

crab-dog *n* (Guyn) **1.** A small, stout-bodied, greyish animal of the raccoon family, with short legs, bushy tail, and a face with sharp snout resembling that of a fox; it feeds on crabs and snails and has an unpleasant smell; *Procyon cancrivorus (Procyonidae)*. **2.** [AF—Derog] (An insulting term for) a person who is mean and untrustworthy.

cra·ben (**cra·bin**) [kr(ɪ)eb(ɪ)n] *adj* (Belz, Jmca, Nevs) [X] See Note at CRAVEN

crab-eye (**crab's-eye(s)**) *n* **1.** (Guyn, Jmca, StKt) ‖ JUMBIE BEAD **1.** (Brbu, etc) **2.** (Bdos, Tbgo) ‖ JUMBIE BEAD **2.** (Bdos, etc) [From its resemblance to a crab's eyes. Cp also Sp name *ojos de cangrejo* used in Puerto Rico *APPʃ:9*. A white and red variety, CRAB-EYE **2.**, might have contributed as much or more to this folk-name]

crab-eye vine *n phr* (Guyn, Jmca, StKt) ‖ BEAD-VINE (BUSH) (Nevs, StKt)

crab-foot *n* (Belz, Guyn, StVn) [*AF—Joc*] ‖ *crapaud-foot* (Trin) ‖ *crapaud-going-to-wedding, crapaud-writing* (Gren) ‖ *crapaud-long-toe* (Tbgo) ‖ *spotters-and-skinners* (Bdos) [Elementary School] Ugly, uneven, or undeveloped handwriting (of a child). [Suggesting resemblance to the uneven marks made by a crab's crawling along the sand]

crab-grass* *n* **1.** (Guyn, Trin) A creeping grass of pastures and wasteland, rooting at the nodes and putting up long, slender, hairy stalks and leaves; *Digitaria ascendens* (*Gramineae-Paniceae*)—*ACWWI:23.* **2.** (Bdos, Gren, Jmca, TkCa) Name given to three or more quite different varieties of creeping, sea-coast or pond-side grasses, with plant-like hairy stalks; it is of no particular use except for binding the loose soil; *Paspalum distichum* and *Sporobolus virginicus*—*GLPFB*; *Stenotaphrum secundatum*—*AFPJ:175*, etc.

crab·ier (kwab·yé) [krabie ~ kwabye] *n* (Crcu, Dmca, Gren) ‖ GAULIN (CarA) [< *LLFL* Fr = 'crab-eating heron' (trans)]

crab·ier noir (kwab·yé nwè) *n phr* (Dmca, Gren, StLu) ‖ ARSNICKER (Baha) [Fr = 'black crab-eating heron']

crab-oil *n* (Guyn) A whitish, slightly smelly oil originally made by ARAWAKS by crushing the nuts of the CRABWOOD tree (hence the name) and used as a body-oil against insects; it is now made, esp in rural areas, from palm nuts and used as an ointment. [See CRABWOOD]

cra·boo* *n* (Belz) A yellow-skinned, cherry-like fruit about a half-inch in diameter, with a sweet creamy-brown flesh clinging to its single hard seed; it is borne profusely on a tree about 12 ft tall; *Byrsonima crassifolia* (*Malpighiaceae*).

crab·wood* *n* (Guyn) A light brown, straight-grained wood, some varieties pinkish with (rarely) whitish streaks; it is obtained from a forest-tree that can reach 170 ft in height, and widely used for furniture and house-building; *Carapa guianensis* (*Meliaceae*). [< *BAED* Arawak *karaba* 1. 'lubricatiog oil' 2. 'a crabwood tree'. The name prob developed from the compound 'karaba-wood']

crack-li·quor (crack·ed-li·quor) /1ʹ22/ *n* (Bdos) ‖ *vizou* (Dmca) Cane-juice after the first boiling and clarification process (obtained warm, direct from the sugar-factory). [*Crack*, in the sense of 'break down', 'in contrast with *break* in its full sense' (*OED crack* 15., 17). This sense recognized in *OEDS crack* 23. 'to compose by the application of heat ...', but in ref to oil-refining. Hence *crack* here prob refers to the first breaking down of raw cane-juice] □ *Crack-liquor* is the preferred spoken form. Cp SE *crack-brain* 'a crazy fellow' where also *crack* = *cracked*.

craft [kra·f] *n* **1.** (ECar) [*AF—Joc*] ‖ BIRD **2.** (Bdos, Guyn) *Lord, that is life for you, that is it. To meet a craft there, and take she out some place.*—STLL:69 [Cp *DSUE 1* and *87. craft 2. sweet craft* 'a woman': nautical: 20C. Cp also *DSUE 1* and *51. cruiser* 'a harlot'. So the term may have been brought by sailors] **2.** (Gren) [By extension] ‖ CHOSSEL[2] (Bdos) □ Tends to be old-fashioned.

crane *n* (Guyn) (A name loosely applied to) any bird of the heron family, and often to the CATTLE-EGRET.

cra·paud [krapo] *n* (CarA) [*IF*] **1.** A frog or toad of any kind. [Fr *crapaud* 'toad'; *DELF crapaud* 12C < *crape* 'muck', in ref to the animal's habitat] □ This is the term in widest folk use in CE. *Frog* is used in formal contexts, but *toad* almost never; nor is any biological distinction made between frog and toad. **2.** PHRASE **2.1** **crapaud smoke your pipe** *id phr* (ECar) [*AF—Joc*] ‖ *all the salt in Turks Island couldn't save you* (CayI) ‖ *be in duck's guts* (Bdos) ‖ *cat eat your dinner/supper* (Gren, Guyn) ‖ *go[ne] through the eddoes* (Bdos) ‖ *your cork duck* (Guyn) ‖ *the dog dead with you* (ECar) (To be) done for; (to be) in a hopeless state of disaster; (to have) reached a stage (of trouble, poverty, loss, etc) that is almost beyond rescue. *The cocaine user has to pay no less than $25 for a 'fix', and unlike marijuana, once a person becomes hooked on it then crapaud smoke his pipe!*—BoM (75.03.28, p.11) [Orig uncertain, but there is a suggestion that you are so deep in the mire that your 'pipe' (of leisure) is left for the crapaud (that dwells in the mire) to use at his leisure] □ The phr is most common in *Trin*.

cra·paud-foot *n* (Trin) [*AF—Joc*] ‖ CRAB-FOOT (Belz, Guyn, StVn) [Suggesting the uneven toe-prints of a CRAPAUD hopping in mud]

cra·paud-go·ing-to-wed·ding (cra·paud-writ·ing) *n* (Gren) [*AF—Joc*] ‖ CRAB-FOOT (Belz, etc) [See CRAPAUD-FOOT]

cra·paud-long-toe *n* (Tbgo) [*AF—Joc*] ‖ CRAB-FOOT (Belz, etc) [See CRAPAUD-FOOT. Also a ref to the long central, finger-like toe of the CRAPAUD]

crav·a·cious (crav·e·cious) [kraveŠAs ~ -iŠAs] *adj* (Bdos, Trin) [*AF—Joc*] ‖ LICKERISH 2. (Antg, etc) [Blend < CRAVEN + [vor]acious/[avar]icious]

crav·en [kre·vn ~ krievin] *adj* (Gren, Jmca, Nevs, StVn, Tbgo, Trin) [*AF—Cr*] ‖ LICKERISH 2. (Antg, etc) [< *OED craving* ppl a. 1. 'that asks or begs earnestly' 2. 'hungering'. For the CE reduction -ing > -en [iŋ < n] cp COURTEN, etc] □ A common folk pronunc also occurs with /v > b/ shift as **craben** (Belz, etc).

crav·en·ous [krevnʌs] *adj* (StVn) ‖ LICKERISH 2. (Antg, etc) [Blend > CRAVEN + SE *ravenous*]

crav·i·chous-mind·ed (crav·ish·ing, cra·v·i·cious) [kraˈvɪčʌs- ~ ˈravišɪn] *adj* (Bdos, Trin) [*AF*] ‖ BIG-EYE¹ (CarA) [Blends of SE *craving* + *covetous*, the latter often pronounced [kʌvɪčʌs] in CE]

craw *n* 1. (CarA) [*AF—Derog*] A person's stomach; guts. 2. (Gren, StVn) [*AF—Derog*] A deep feeling of ill-will towards (sb). *You best stop interferin[g] wid me! Tak[e] me out o[f], yo[ur] craw!*—(StVn) 3. (USVI) [*AF—Joc*] Boldness; cheek; audacity; nerve! [Modified sense of AF 'guts'] 4. PHRASES 4.1 **have (sb) in your craw** *vb phr* (Bdos, Gren) [*AF—Derog*] To harbour feelings of vexation or ill-will towards (sb). 4.2 **ram (sth) down (sb's) craw** *vb phr* (Bdos) [*AF—Derog*] To repeat (usu some kind of instruction) insistently to (sb); to force (sb) to accept (sth, or your view) against their resistance. 4.3 **stuff your craw** *vb phr* (CarA) [*AF—Derog*] To eat gluttonously; to overeat.

crawl PHRASE **blood crawls** *id phr* (Tbgo, Trin) [*IF*] ‖ SKIN CRAWLS (Guyn) See SKIN Phrs 4.17

craw·ny [krɒ·ni] *adj* (Antg, Bdos, Jmca) [*AF—Cr*] [Esp of children and fruit] Thin, skinny, and unhealthy- looking; small, with a withered, or poorly developed appearance. [< *OED scrawny* U.S 'lean, scraggy', with Cr loss of /s-/ by aphaeresis, as in COTCH (*Jmca*) < *scotch*]

cra·zow [krezaʊ] *n* (Tbgo, Trin) [*AF—Joc*] 1. A mentally unstable person; sb who behaves irrationally. 2. A clown. [? Infl by SE *crazy*]

cra·zy-ant(s) *n* (Gren, Mrat, StVn) ‖ *madants* (Jmca) A very fast-moving and erratic, harmless black ant.

crea·ture *n* 1. [kričʌ] (Bdos, Gren, Guyn) An old, poor (and usu black) woman. [< *OED creature* 3. 'a human being' b. (b) ('sometimes with a shade of patronage'). Indeed the term in CE is usu applied to a woman who needs or is seeking help] 2. [kri·tɒ] (Baha) Any animal, but more often livestock. [Cp *OED creature* 2. 'an animal' (often as distinct from 'man') b. U.S (rural) esp applied to cattle] 3. [kritɒ ~ krɪtʌ] (Baha) [*AF—Derog*] An ugly person. [As *OEDS critter* (Joc variant < *creature*) ... 'a person (usu disparaging)'] □ In *Baha* written **creeter**, usu in dial phr '*an ugly creeter*'.

cred·it¹ *n* (Bdos, Guyn) 1. Belief or trust that usu turns out to be misplaced. 2. PHRASE 2.1 **give credit that (sth is so)** *vb phr* (Guyn) To feel quite sure that (sth is so). *The way she talked I gave credit that she had already written to tell you about it, and I am surprised to find that she hasn't.*—(Guyn) □ See CREDIT².

cred·it² *vb* (Bdos) 1. Believe (sth that is doubtful). *If ELC is right about this Jamaican book lunacy—and ... I can scarcely credit that he is right—the Jamaican Government really has some out-of-this-world ... pooh pahs!*—AdN (74.03.28,

p.4) 2. Assign (blame, fault or sth discrediting) to sb. *I am not crediting malice to any one, I am simply saying that the various forms of taxation in this country however well meaning, have now crossed the danger line, and that Barbados as an island can only suffer in the long run from what is happening now.*—AdN (75.11.23, p.4) [Shift in connotation of SE *credit* wh has a favourable sense] □ A reversal of the favourable SE connotation of *credit* n, vb.

creech-owl *n* (Belz) [*X*] Screech-owl. [By aphaeretic loss of /s-/, a common feature of Belz folk- speech]

creek *n* (Guyn) A small, inland tributary of a river, usu between 10 and 40 ft wide. □ The same as AmE usage, but cp BrE 'a small sea-coast or river bay'.

creek-wa·ter *n* (Guyn) The dark, wine-coloured water of inland CREEKS. *If you drink creek-water and eat labba you must come back to Guyana.*—Guyn (Prov)

creep·er *n* (Jmca, Nevs) A device for retrieving FISH-POTS, consisting of a piece of iron or a length of heavy piping fitted with a number of iron prongs that hook the wire-netting of the FISH-POT as it is dragged (or 'creeps'—hence the name) along the sea-bed at the end of a cord.

creep·ing ox-eye *n phr* (Jmca) ‖ CARPET-DAISY (Bdos)

cre·ole¹ [krio·l] *n* [Note: The term, in all its senses, connotes New World, esp *CarA*, family stock, breed, and thence quality. Originally (17C) it was evidently used with pride by European colonists (esp the Fr) to refer to themselves as born and bred in the 'New World', and spelt with capital C. (ex Napoleon's wife Joséphine de Beauharnais was a *Créole*). It was then extended to distinguish 'local' from imported breeds esp of horses and livestock, then slaves locally born as different from original African importees. With this sense the status of the word dropped (18–19C) among whites but rose among blacks and COLOUREDS locally born, and freedmen. In many post- emancipation *CarA* societies the term then became (19– 20C) generally a label either of a class embracing non-white persons of 'breeding' or an excluded class of 'ill-bred' blacks. There were, however, some particular senses, usu derogatory. Below, the senses referring to people are listed first] 1. [Referring to people] **(i)** (CarA) [Hist] [*Obs*] ‖ CREOLE WHITE (CarA) *When it was a question ... of defending their own internal structure, the white Jamaicans' ambivalence ... again defeated them ... / After all, all Jamaican creoles were colonials, but it does not follow that all colonials in Jamaica were creolized.*—BCSJ:101 [< Sp *criollo* adapted from Pg *crioulo*. The Sp etymologists Corominas and Pascual (1989), noting that the Pg origin is undisputed (and perh < *criar* 'to create') also indicate that the word may ultimately have been of African origin, citing Garcilaso el Inca (Peru, 1602) as follows (trans J. Allsopp): 'It's a name that the negroes invented.... It means among the negroes 'born in the Indies'; they invented it to distinguish those ... born in Guinea from those born in America, because they consider themselves more honourable and of better status than their children because they are born in the fatherland, while their children are born abroad, and the parents are offended to be called *criollos*. The Spanish, in like manner, have introduced this name into their language to mean those born [in America]' **(ii)** (CarA) [Hist] [*Obs*] A Caribbean black person born a slave, one or both parents being plantation slaves. *He was a young negro, tall and slim, naked except for a loincloth. He was a Creole, born in captivity.*—NR:12 [See prec. This and all following senses and uses relate to the Europeanized development of the term] **(iii)** (CarA) (An inclusive polite term for) a COLOURED *CarA* person of good manners and social standing. **(iv)** (Guyn, Trin) [? Becoming obs] A COLOURED or dark- skinned person, but not an EAST INDIAN. **(v)** (Belz) A COLOURED or black person who is not a GARIFUNA. **(vi)** (CarA) [Loosely applied] Any black Caribbean person; an Afro- Caribbean person. *There are at present few influential creole-owned and/ or managed business places in St Kitts.... The natives should take an example from the Arabs, Indians and Syrians.... It is high time for our creoles to exercise the correct initiative.*—DeM(SK) (62.09.08, p.4) **(vii)** (Dmca, StLu) A non-white person whose first language is Fr Creole or PATWA[1]; [esp of a woman] one who wears a MOUCHWÈ and long dress. **(viii)** (Baha) A person who is an albino. [< *Créole* < Sp *criollo* 'native- born' [in the New World] < Sp/Pg *criar* 'to produce, nurse, raise, breed'] □ Currently the senses referring to people appear to be going slowly out of use. Already in some places (ex *Bdos*) it is no longer so used. **2.** [Referring to animals] (Bdos, Trin) A race-horse bred in the island. *This race brings together the cream of Barbadian-bred creoles and promises to be a keenly contested affair.*—NaT (75.11.02, p.17) **3.** [Usu cap, referring to language] (CarA) **(i)** ‖ *bad-talk* (StKt) ‖ *basilect* (Linguistics) ‖ *creolese* (Guyn) ‖ *patois* (Jmca) ‖ *slangs* (ECar) (Name used, mostly at University level, for) any one of a family of langs developed in the Caribbean territories by African slaves in contact with one or more of the European langs English, French, Spanish, Portuguese or Dutch, becoming a first language for succeeding generations, and surviving in many places today as a lingua- franca among their descendants; any modified (but still not systematically written) present-day form of one of those languages used in the English-speaking Caribbean. *I have always maintained that it is possible for students to learn to speak and write good English in the class-room, while retaining facility in Creole in the streets. If these are two different languages, then let's learn two different languages.*—AmA (80.06.06, p.7) □ See BASILECT. **(ii)** ‖ *French Creole, Kwéyòl* (Dmca, Gren, StLu, Trin) ‖ *Patwa* (CarA) A modified

(and sometimes systematically written) French-based form of such language current in the *CarA*. □ In this sense, pronunc [kweyol] and written form *Kwéyòl* in *Dmca, StLu*.

cre·ole[2] [krio·l] *adj* (CarA) **1.** [Hist/Obs] [Of persons] Born in and [of animals] bred in the Caribbean. **a.** *Few European white men now turn to Jamaica in quest of fortune.... The Creole children of these Europeans of course remain.*—TWISM:83 **b.** *The Nugents were clearly upholders of British culture and tradition. They were critical of creole departures from the 'established' norm then, though they did nothing themselves to upset the local status quo.*—BCSJ:111 [By functional n > adj shift of CREOLE[1]; also for foll senses] **2.** Of, belonging to or typical of the life-style and culture of today's black W Indians; hence many compounds such as *creole bread* (home-made bread perh with coconut milk as an ingredient), *creole cooking/food* (meal made by using ingredients such as coconut, breadfruit, pigeon peas, root vegetables, saltfish, bay-leaf seasoning, etc), *creole Christmas, culture, dance, music*, etc. **3.** [Of agricultural products] Of a variety originally developed or bred in the Caribbean; hence many compounds such as *creole arrowroot, cane, plantain, tomato*, etc.

cre·ole co·coa *n phr* (Trin) ‖ CHOCOLATE-TEA (ECar) [CREOLE[2]. 2 + COCOA]

cre·ole cof·fee *n phr* (Guyn) ‖ WILD COFFEE (Guyn, etc) See WILD COFFEE 1. (Guyn, Jmca, Trin) [*Creole*, as a native bush + *coffee*, because the seed pods are used as a coffee substitute]

Cre·ole Day *n phr* (Dmca) The last Friday in October, designated annually by this name as of 1980, to promote recognition of all aspects of Dominican Fr Creole culture (see CREOLE[1] 3(ii)); all business and broadcasts are conducted on that day in KWÉYÒL, national creole dress is worn, and Creole dishes are served.

cre·ole gang *n phr* (Guyn) [Sugar Ind/Hist] ‖ *third gang* (Bdos) ‖ *weeding-gang* (Guyn, Jmca) A work gang of boys and girls, the children of sugar plantation labourers, employed to do lighter tasks such as weeding, cleaning of drains, manuring, etc. □ The practice ceased in the early 1900s but is still remembered and referred to by old folk.

cre·ol·ese [kriʌli·z] *n* (Guyn) ‖ CREOLE[1] 3.(i) (CarA) *Gregory took the opportunity to tell them a story about two black girls just come to town from the East Coast. He lapsed into creolese for greater effect.*—MLDS:115 [CREOLE[1] 3.(i) + *ese* 'style of language' as in SE *officialese, journalese*, etc. However the term, now only *Guyn*, might have originated with shift of sense from *Bdos* where it appears (1825) in ref to Barbadian White people]

cre·ole white *n phr* (CarA) ‖ *creole*[1] 1.(i) (CarA) ‖ *local white* (Guyn) A Caribbean person of strongly marked European stock, with no obvious signs of African mixture. *The manager was creole white; he probably had a great-great-grandfather or grandmother who was pure black but whose blood had become invisible amid the bucketfuls of white blood supplied by succeeding forebears.*—MLDS:142

cre·ol·ism *n* (CarA) [Ling] A word, phrase, or usage borrowed from the particular CREOLE (language) of a territory but used for convenience or in error in the formal spoken or written English of that territory. *Exs:* 'She was *bad-talking* the neighbours'; 'the house caught *afire*'.

cre·ol·ist *n* (CarA) [Ling] A scholar who makes a special study of CREOLE languages. [By analogy < SE *linguist*]

cre·ol·ist·ics *n* (CarA) [Ling] The special study of CREOLE languages. [By analogy < SE *linguistics*]

cre·ol·i·za·tion (-i·sa·tion) *n* (CarA) The process or stages of being CREOLIZED. □ The term, applied earlier esp to architecture, is now most often applied to lang.

cre·ol·ize (-ise) (CarA) 1. *vb intr* (i) To develop marked Caribbean characteristics. (ii) *vb tr* To cause (sth that was originally foreign) to become Caribbean in character. *The temples and mosques of the first half of the twentieth century (in contrast to those of the last two decades of the nineteenth century) exhibit a marked discontinuity with ancestral India in their architectural features, while displaying many of the indigenous features of colonial architecture. Thus these temples and mosques can be said to have been creolised.*—-STAMG:17 [OED creolize 2. tr 'to naturalize in the W Indies or adjacent regions'] 2. [Esp of European langs] To undergo or cause to undergo marked changes in linguistic structure as used particularly by black CREOLES in the Caribbean.

cre·ol·ized Eng·lish *n phr* (CarA) [Ling] Spoken English that has retained some obvious structural characteristics of CREOLE (language) while it develops more of the features of internationally accepted spoken English. □ 1. In the following gradation, stages (c) (d) (e) are creolized English (= *I told him*) (a) / *mi tel am* / (b) / *mi tel im* / (c) / *a tel im* / (d) / *a tol im* / (e) / *a told im* / (f) / *ai told [h]im* / (g) / *ai tould [h]im* /. □ 2. Some linguists prefer the term DECREOLIZED (English, etc) to describe the same development.

crepes [krɛ·ps] *n* (Jmca) [IF] Popular abbr of CREPESOLES *Jmca*.

crepe·soles [krɛpsolz] *n pl* (Guyn, Jmca, Tbgo, Trin) ‖ *bugas* [AF] ‖ *crepes* [IF] (Jmca) ‖ *half-cuts* (Bdos) ‖ *hoppers* (Antg, Mrat) ‖ *pumps* (Bdos) ‖ *punkasal* (Crcu, Gren) ‖ *puss (-boots)* (Jmca) [AF] ‖ *rubbers* (BrVi, StKt) ‖ *soft-mash* (StVn) ‖ *soft-shoes* (Bdos, Gren, StLu) ‖ *soft-walkers* (Angu, Mrat) ‖ *washicongs* (Tbgo,

Trin) [IF] ‖ *yachtings, yachting-shoes* (Guyn, Jmca) Rubber-soled, canvas shoes usu with laces; (BrE) plimsolls; (AmE) sneakers. [By extension of *OEDS* crêpe 2. 'in full *crêpe rubber*: India rubber ... with a corrugated surface'. 4. *Comb* ... *crêpe sole* 'the underside of a shoe covered with crepe rubber'] □ Sometimes, in some territories, it becomes fashionable to apply trade names to these shoes.

cre·valle ['krəval] *n* (Gren, Trin) (The less frequently used name of) the CAVALLI. □ Given in marine literature as the name of a large family of 'murderous' sea-fish of low food value. See *ADE*: 60–62; also note at CAVALLI

cri·bo [kribo] *n* (Gren, Trin) A non-venomous blackish snake that can grow to 7 ft in length, looking like an enormous eel as its pointed head has no neck; it lives in wet places feeding on rats and other snakes, esp the venomous FER-DE-LANCE; *Clelia clelia groomei.*

Crick-crack! *excl* (ECar) Formula used to introduce a NANCY STORY or folktale, and also (usu with an accompanying rhyme) to end it. □ In some cases the story-teller first cries out *Crick*! and the audience response is *Crack*! i.e. Go ahead!

cris·to·fine (-phene) *n* (Nevs, StVn) See CHRISTOPHENE

croak·er¹* *n* (Bdos) ‖ *crocro* (StVn) A silvery, sea-shore fish weighing one to two pounds and of excellent food value; *Micropogon undulatus* or *M. furnieri* (*Sciaenidae*). [From the croaking sound it makes]

croak·er² (croak·er-liz·ard) *n* (Jmca) An unpleasant-looking house lizard of the gecko family with sucker-pads on its feet enabling it to walk on ceilings; it makes a croaking sound (hence the name).

crock *n* (Dmca) ‖ CROOK (StVn) [Prob < CROOK + vowel-opening [ʊ > ɒ]]

cro·cro [krokro] *n* (StVn) ‖ CROAKER¹ (Bdos) [Prob < CROAKER by assimilation]

cro·cus¹ ['krʌkʌs] *n* (CarA) [IF] See CROCUS-BAG

cro·cus²* ['kro·kʌs] *n* (Guyn, Jmca, Trin) ‖ AMARYLLIS (CarA) □ This name is also used in Bdos for the yellow variety.

cro·cus-bag/sack (cro·cus, cruck·cuss, kro·kos-bag, ku·kus-bag) [krʌkʌs-bag] /1´21/ *n* (CarA) ‖ *bag* (CarA) ‖ *corn-bag, cruder bag* (ViIs) ‖ *sugar-bag* (CarA) 1. A sack about 2 ft wide and 4 ft deep, made of brown, coarse-woven jute, used as the standard container for the wholesale selling of PADDY, rice, or sugar. ... *stench of flour and stale cod-fish and sugar in crocus bags...*—PCOS:18 [< *Corchorus capsularis* or *C.*

olitorius (*Tiliaceae*) the botanical name for the plant that yields the fibre *jute*. It must be assumed that the shortened form *corchorus* must have been regularly used in the plantation era in ordering this merchandise from India before the Hindi word *jute* replaced it in Eng about 1746, *OED*. Then, by metathesis and dissimilation [kɔrkrʌs > krɔkrʌs > krʌkʌs], the form 'crocus', so spelt, came into regular currency. *Jute* or *jute bag* is rarely heard in CE] □ Of the many conjectural spellings found, *crocus*, although pronounced [krʌkʌs], is by far the most widely used. 2. PHRASE 2.1 **Empty crocus bag can'[t] stan[d] up, full crocus bag can['t] ben[d]** (Belz (Prov)) ‖ *Empty bag can['t] stan[d] up*... (CarA) A hungry man can't work, and a well-satisfied man will not yield. *We chocho farmers of Pull Trousers Creek Village are true blue communists, Comrade Visitor, but empty crocus bag can't stand up so we want a little advance, and we want more holidays.*—BsT (79.10.14, p.12) 3. (Occasionally) a sack of similar size but of any coarse material used to contain merchandise of any kind. **a.** *Under command of Mr Owen S—, Assistant Commissioner, the raiders destroyed 161 acres of fully grown ganja trees, eight acres with nurseries, 160 crocus bags of cured ganja, and nine crocus bags of ganja seeds.*—StA(JA) (73.02.10, p.16) **b.** *During the rainy season, ... the crabs begin running on the Northern Highway and hundreds of Belizeans leave the city to capture them in crocus sacks.*—AmA (80.06.27, p.1) 4. ‖ BAG 2. *n* (CarA) ‖ *crocus sacking* (Baha) **a.** *The vast canefields stood silvery in the early light. A mild norther was blowing, chilly enough for people out- doors to put on the crocus-bag cloaks over their clothes.*—RPME:91 **b.** *... a sheet made of several crocus bags sewn together. She took up the crocus-bag sheet.*—PCOS:35

cro·cus sack·ing *n phr* (Baha) ‖ BAG 2. *n* (CarA) *During this period, women sat around (as they did in the older sponge clipping and packing days), sewing bottles into sacks after the wooden cases had been opened. Crocus sacking, as it was called, made packages which were easier to handle and to stack on board ship.*—JBJ:18

Cro·man·ty *n* (Crcu, Jmca) See COROMANTEE

crook *n* (StVn) ‖ *box-crook* (Dmca) ‖ *catacou* 2. (Angu) ‖ *crock* (Dmca) ‖ *donkey-box* (Antg) A double carrier consisting of two side-baskets, or made of light, curved, iron bars or wood (BOX-CROOK) slung across the back of a donkey, for transporting GROUND-PROVISIONS, etc. [*OED crook* 9. 'a support or frame of wood ... slung in pairs panier-wise across the saddle of a pack-horse for carrying loads' (*Somerset and Devon*) + earliest cit 1657 f. Ligon *Barbadoes*]

crook-stick *n* 1. (Tbgo, Trin) ‖ HOOK-STICK (Belz, etc) 2. (Guyn) A wooden staff with a curved head (like a shepherd's crook) used by the leader of a folk sect; a crosier. [A redundant compound *crook* 'staff' + *stick*]

crop *n* (CarA) □ See, as separate entries AUTUMN-CROP, BIG-CROP, FIRST- CROP, SECOND-CROP, SMALL-CROP, SPRING-CROP.

crop-o·ver (crop·o·ver) *n, adj* [Sugar Ind] ‖ *after-crop* (CarA) 1. (CarA) The end of the sugar-cane harvest and activities immediately following, related to this period. *The sugar-plantation periods 'dead season', 'croptime', 'high season', and 'cropover' were the traditional seasons of the year.*—FCR:326 (Lowenthal) [From characteristic Cr sentence *de crop over* 'the crop is over', this becoming a noun *the crop-over*] 2. *Crop-Over n* (CarA) [Hist] **(i)** The days of great festive merry-making observed on each sugar-plantation particularly by the labourers, starting with the delivery of the last harvested canes in decorated carts; the crop-over festival. **(ii)** (Bdos) National festivities (officially promoted since the 1970s) during July to mark the end of the sugar-cane harvest, ending with a national holiday for KADOOMENT. 3. (Crcu) A MAROON held to prepare land for farming—*DFOC:28*.

crop-sea·son (crop-time) *n* (CarA) [Sugar Ind] The period of the reaping of the sugar-cane harvest. □ Usu the early months of the year in the ECar, hence the idea of a *season*. However in some places, ex *Guyn*, there were two crops per year, hence two *crop-times*.

cross[1] *n* (CarA) [IF] 1. Some trouble, misfortune, or burden that is not easily got rid of; a detestable and unfair problem. [Metaph ref to the cross of Christ + infl of SE *curse*, with metathesis of /r/] 2. A young person or a husband whose persistently embarrassing behaviour is a test of Christian patience. 3. One who always seems to cause frustrating trouble. 4. PHRASE 4.1 **Look at my cross/crosses!** *excl phr* (CarA) [IF] See what a great problem I now face! *But look at my crosses! Curls and all now. And take trolley this time of night by sheself. Oh God, a force-ripe woman!*—MBGB:86

cross[2] *adj* 1. (CarA) [Of a dog] Fierce; vicious; that bites people. [A specific use of *OED cross* a. 5. b. 'ill- tempered, etc'—but applied in SE only to persons] 2. (Guyn) [X] [Of a person or a house] Cursed; blighted; bedevilled.

cross[3] *vb tr* 1. (CarA) [IF] ‖ *cross up* (CarA) [IF] To challenge and thwart or succeed in frustrating (sb) for a time; to come into daring conflict with (sb). *You wait and see. I planning something for you, you hear me? I going show you nobody don't cross Pa John like that!*—CISH:120 [Cp SE *cross swords with* (sb), *cross* (sb's) *path*] 2. (Bdos, Guyn) [IF] To occur to the mind of (sb); (SE) to cross the mind of (sb). *You mean it didn'[t] cross you that yo[ur] mother would be waitin[g] on you?*—(Bdos) 3. (Baha, Guyn) To put a curse on (sb). *If a young girl gets pregnant for a married man and his wife threatens to 'cross' the baby and so either stop its birth or cause the baby to become deformed.*—MTTBT:155 4.

(CayI) To go past; to overtake. *He crossed me going at about 50.*—(CayI) **5.** PHRASE **5.1 not cross foot** *neg vb phr* (Bdos) [*IF*] ‖NOT PUT A FOOT. See FOOT Phr 2.11.

cross[4] *prep, adv* (CarA) [*X*] Across. **a.** *Trumper said, 'then we goin' to creep right cross the bush, you followin' me an' takin' the time from me. We got to get over yonder by the trees.'* –LICMS:188 **b.** *'Not me I ain't going cross', was the cry of a woman declining to be driven across the damaged structure.*—AdV (88.10.08, p.1) [From characteristic Cr loss of /a-/ by aphesis. But the same in *OED cross* prep = Across *'poetic* or *dial.'*]

cross-eye *n* (Dmca, Gren) [*AF*] ‖CUT-EYE (CarA) See CUT Phr 3.11.1 PHRASE **watch (sb) cross-eye** *vb phr* (Dmca) [*AF—Cr*] ‖GIVE (SB) A CUT-EYE (CarA) See CUT Phr 3.11.1.

cross (your) foot *vb phr* (Bdos) ‖PUT FOOT 2. (Guyn) *I go to my Bank in New York, but I do not cross foot at F.N.C.B. in Broad Street.*—Bdos (Hd, 73.06.19, p.2394)

cross up *vb tr phr* (CarA) [*IF*] ‖CROSS[3] 1. (CarA)

crow *n* (Baha, Guyn) ‖CARRION-CROW (Guyn, Jmca) □ The European *crow* is quite a different and a smaller bird of the family *Corvidae* wh includes the rook, raven, and jackdaw.

crown-and-an·chor *n* (Jmca) An illegal gambling game played with dice on a board.

crown land *n phr* (CarA) [Hist] All land in a (Br Caribbean) territory that is not privately or commercially owned, including foreshore, riverbeds, forest-lands, and mountains. [As owned by the Br Crown]

cru·chi·neel (**crutch·i·neel**) *n* (CayI, Guyn) [*X*] See COCHINEAL [Erron, sometimes also *crushineel* (cp SCRUSHINEEL) perh by pop etym since the succulent stem is often crushed to release the pulp for medicinal use]

Cru·cian [krušʌn] *n, adj* (ViIs) See CRUZAN

cruck·(c)uss ['krʌkʌs][*n* (Bdos) [*IF*] See CROCUS BAG

cru·der bag *n phr* (ViIs) ‖CROCUS BAG (CarA) [By pop etym < Lat Am Sp *crudo* 'sackcloth', + infl of SE adj *cruder*]

crutch *n* (Guyn) [*IF*] **1** The backside or seat of a pair of trousers; (hence phr foll). *The police held him by the crutch and carried him down.*—(Guyn) **2.** PHRASE **2.1 patch in the crutch** *n phr* (Guyn) A seat-patch on a pair of trousers (regarded as a mark of poverty, esp of boys). [< BrE *crutch* = *crotch* 'the fork of the human body'. However the BrE sense always refers to the front of the trousers associated with the male genitals, not the seat, although such a sense was

evid once possible: note *OED crutch* 8. a. + cit (1771) 'I clapped my hand under his crutch, and … pitched him head foremost into the river']

crutch·i·neel *n* (CayI) [*X*] See COCHINEAL

Cru·zan (**Cru·cian, Cruz·i·an**) [kružən ~ krušən] *n, adj* (ViIs) (Person or thing) of or belonging to St Croix, *USVI. And afterwards it is pleasant to sit in one of the cafes in the old Danish colonial town, Christiansted, capital of St Croix, sipping a glass of what they call Cruzan (pronounced Crooshan) rum.*—Cat IV.2, p.12 [< Santa Cruz, the name first given to the island by Columbus in 1493 being *Isla de la Santa Cruz*. The name was changed to *St Croix* by the Fr on seizure in 1650. The pronunc [sɪnt krɒɪ] and [krušʌn] may have begun with Br ownership in 1801 or U.S. infl from the 1860s] □ Of the three alternating spellings *Cruzan* seems to be preferred.

cry *vb* PHRASES **1. cry long water (out of your eye)** *vb phr* (CarA) [*AF/IF*] ‖*cry big water* (StLu) ‖*cry bucket-a-drop* (Tbgo) ‖*cry burying cry* (Belz) ‖*cry living eye-water* (Trin) ‖*cry long cry-water* (Antg) ‖*cry long eye-water* (Antg, Belz, BrVi, Guyn, Tbgo) ‖*pléwé gwo/go glo* (Dmca, StLu) ‖*cry water to boil yams* (Angu) [Esp of children] To shed copious tears over a matter of no great importance; to weep insincerely; to shed crocodile tears. **a.** *Many de day I cry long water out o' me eye when I see I din have nothing to give me children.*—EFLBB:20 **b.** *The girl cried long water out her eyes just to fool me off.*—StVn (Ms) [A prob calque from Afr langs. Cp Yoruba *da /se/ yo omi l'oju (pour /make/ produce water from eye)* 'Shed insincere tears'] **2. cry bucket-a-drop** *vb phr* (Tbgo) [*AF*] ‖CRY LONG WATER (CarA) **3. cry burying-cry** [kraɪ bɛrɪŋ-kraɪ] *vb phr* (Belz) [*AF*] ‖CRY LONG WATER (OUT OF YOUR EYE) (CarA) *Don[t] bother cry no burying-cry [u]pon me, you wi[ll] stay home.*—(Belz)

cry-cry *adj* (ECar) [*AF*] [Of a child] Fretful and given to much noisy crying. *This child so cry-cry. If you just talk too loud, she'll start to cry. Worse if you touch her.*—(Trin) [By characteristic Cr reduplication to indicate intensity + functional vb > adj shift]

cry-wa·ter *n* (Antg, Bdos) **1.** [*IF*] ‖EYE-WATER (CarA) *I see the glisters of the sunshine on the crywater on her face, and then I feel crywater running down my face too.*—Com (1974:38, T. Callendar) **2.** PHRASE **2.1 cry long cry-water** *vb phr* (Antg) [*AF*] ‖CRY LONG WATER (OUT OF YOUR EYE) (CarA) *All the long cry-water you cry you ain[t] goin[g] le[t] me change my mind.*—(Antg)

C.T.O. *abbr* (CarA) Caribbean Tourism Organization (combining, as from 1989, the former C.T.R.C. and the former Caribbean Tourism Association in New York City) with headquarters in Bridgetown, *Bdos.*

C.T.R.C. *abbr* (CarA) Caribbean Tourism Research (and Development) Centre, an or- ganization representing 28 English-, French-, Spanish-, and Dutch-speaking *CarA* territories, in operation 1974–1988, based in Bridgetown, Barbados. □ *Development* was added to the title in 1978 without changing the abbr. See C.T.O..

cua·tro (qua·tro) [kwatro] *n* (Gren, StLu, StVn, Trin) A small, four-stringed folk-guitar, producing high-pitched notes; it is an indispensable instrument in accompanying PARANG songs or other festival folk-music. [Sp *cuatro* 'four' in ref to the strings, the instrument being of Latin Am Sp origin] □ See note at QUATRO.

cua·trist [kwatrıst] *n* (ECar) A skilled or professional player of the CUATRO. *Venezuelan composer and cuatrist Hernán Gamboa will meet with Barbadian folklorists at the Venezuelan Institute for Culture on Friday.*—Bdos (Ms, 1986) [CUATR[o] + *ist* as in *pianist*, etc]

cu·ban fly *n phr* (CarA) [Sugar Ind] A blackish fly about two-thirds the size of a house-fly; it is a parasite introduced for the biological control of the insect pest known as the MOTH-BORER; *Lixophaga diatraeae* (pers info, an *Gibbs*)

cub·bitch (cub·bidge) [kʌbǐč~kʌbɪǰ] *adj* (Jmca) [AF—Cr] Both stingy and greedy. *They judged men quickly and without error, by whether 'their spirit take to them' or not, discerning in a moment that the new overseer on the property was 'bad minded', the shopkeeper covetous or 'cubbitch', the new teacher conceited or 'consequential'.*—SWI:153 [< SE *covetous*, pronunc [kʌvíčəs] with loss of final unstressed syllable. The pronunc [kʌvǐčʌs] prevails in many parts of the *CarA*]

cub·bitch-boil *n* (Jmca) [AF] ‖CAT-BOIL (CarA)

cuck·oo *n* (CarA) [X] See COU-COU □ An unneccesary homograph in ref to a food, when this spelling is best reserved for the bird so known.

cuck·oo-ma·ni·oc [kʊku mayɒk] *n* (Dmca, Gren) ‖RAIN-BIRD[1] 2. (CarA)

cu·cu [kuku] *n* (ViIs) See KUKU

cu·cum·ber-tree *n* (Trin) The tree bearing the BILIMBI fruit. See BILIMBI

Cud·joe *n* (CarA) See KOJO □ This looser spelling is widely used.

cud·joe-bush/-root *n* (Brbu, etc) See KOJO-BUSH/-ROOT

cuff[1] *n* (CarA) 1. A blow with the clenched fist; (SE) a punch (to the face or body). [OED *cuff* sb[2] 1. 'a blow with the fist, or with the open hand; a buffet cp *fisticuff*. The wide CE use of *cuff* exclusively in the sense of SE 'a punch' is

prob a survival from EE, reinforced by Afr sources (directly) as ex Yaka *kufi* 'the closed fist', *kafu* 'impact', or indirectly through the popular Twi name *Kofi/Cuffy* applied to a rugged type of person] □ Only the sense 'blow with the open hand' (COD) appears to survive in ModE, *fisticuffs* (pl only) being the proper SE equivalent of CE **cuff(s)**. In CE 'a blow with the open hand' is differentiated as a **slap**. (See cits and etym note at CUFF[2] vb). 2. *PHRASES* 2.1 **fire/ throw a cuff at (sb)** *vb phr* (CarA) To hit out at (sb) with the closed fist; to punch at (sb). 2.2 **down/pelt/put (a) cuff/(the) cuffs (in/on (sb)** *vb phr* (Guyn) [AF] To punch (sb) viciously.

cuff[2] *vb tr* (CarA) To hit (sb) with the clenched fist; to punch (sb). **a.** *It seems to me that I am cuffing against a wall with a naked fist.*—Bdos (Hd, 76.03.19, p.6382) **b.** *The policeman then started 'roughing up' the man, cuffing and slapping him, and then held him by the back of his pants and literally 'jerked' him down to the police station.*—ExP (73.02.07, p.17) [By functional n > vb shift of CUFF[1]. However 19c E usage can have reinforced this use as vb. Cp Dickens, *Great Expectations* (1860): 'Whether suborned boys ... might be engaged to fall upon me in the brewery, and cuff me until I was no more' (Longmans edition p. 103)]

Cuf·fie (Cuf·fy) *n* 1. (CarA) See KOFI 2. (Guyn) [Spelt as CUFFY] National hero of Guyana as accredited leader of the 1763 Slave Rebellion.

cuf·fin *n* (Bdos) See CUFFUM[2]

cuf·fuf·fle *vb tr, n* (Bdos, Guyn) [AF—Joc] See CAFUFFLE □ The form **cuffuffle** is commoner in *Guyn*.

cuf·fum *n* (Bdos, Guyn) 1. The tarpon (*Megalops atlanticus*), a large brilliantly silvery, sea and river fish with big scales; it can exceed 150 lb in rivers (*Guyn*) and 350 lb in open sea, and (esp the young) has the habit of leaping several feet out of the water and diving back in. *The cuffum, as the Tarpon is best known in this colony [may] rise close to the boat in the river, their action very much resembling that of porpoises. The leaping habit of the cuffum can ... prove very embarrassing.*—RFLG:145 2. (Guyn) ‖*cuf.fin* (Bdos) ‖*poopalick* (Belz, Jmca) ‖*skin-(the)-cat* (Baha, USVI) A somersault, esp one in the sea while swimming. 3. *PHRASE* 3.1 **skin cuffins** *vb phr* [IF] (Bdos) ‖*skin (the) cat* (Baha, USVI) ‖*throw cuffum* (Guyn) ‖*turn corn coo-coo* (StVn) To perform a somersault esp while swimming or river-bathing. [''Turning cuffums' i.e. summersets, from cuffums, a species of fish, seems to be of local origin'—TF:66. The ref is to Bdos, 1889, but the name seems to be lost today. However the idiom refers to the fish's habit, sense 1]

cuir·ass *n* (Guyn) [X] See KURASS □ Not to be confused with the properly named *cuirass- fish* 'mailed catfish' *Loricaria cataphracta RFLG:24.* As a spelling representing KURASS it is false.

cul·bert *n* (Guyn, Trin) [X] See etym of CULVERT

cul·vert [kʌlvʌ(r)t ~ kʌlbʌ·t] *n* (Guyn, Trin) The thick concrete walls of the opposite edges of a covered channel that allows water to pass under a road or railway, but, esp in Trinidad, the part of each wall that stands 2 ft above the level of the road. *The men ... sit expatiating and putting the world to rights on the culverts under the street lamps.*—AGTT:161 [By shift of sense of SE *culvert*, wh is properly the whole constructed passage. However, these drainage devices having been widely turned to folk-use as seats (note cit) and also because of popular /v > b/ pronunc (whence sometimes CULBERT), the shifted sense has become commoner, while the original sense survives in Public Works Dept reports. In addition there seems to be a natural confusion, as noted in *OED*: 'In connexion with railways and highways, it is sometimes disputed whether a particular structure is a 'culvert' or a 'bridge'']

cum·fa *n* (Guyn) See COMFA

cu·nu-mu·nu *n* (CarA) See KUNU-MUNU

cu·ra·çao·le·ni·an [kyurasole·nɪən] *n, adj* (CarA) (A person or thing) native or belonging to curaçao, in the Leeward Neth. Antilles

cu·ra·re [kyurarɪ] *n* (Guyn) A paralyzing poison made by Amerindians from the bark and juice of a creeping plant called wourali or urari (*Strychnos toxifera*) (*IAIG:313*), thrown into a stream to catch fish or smeared on arrow-heads for hunting. [Prob orig Macusi, as 'the Macusis were noted as the famous wourali makers'—HIN:137]

cure-for-all /1′12/ *n* (Bdos, Guyn) ‖ CATTLE-TONGUE (Antg, etc) [From its many folk-medicinal uses]

cu·ri·os·i·ty-leaf *n* (CayI) ‖ LEAF-OF-LIFE (Bdos, etc)

cur·ri-cur·ri (cur·ry-cur·ry) *n* (Guyn) ‖ SCARLET IBIS (Trin) [*BAED* Arawak *kore* 'red', the colour of the bird + reduplication]

cur·ry *adj* (CarA) [As in compound names of many popular dishes—*curry-beef, curry-chicken, curry-goat*, etc] Curried, i.e. of any meat or fish dish prepared with saffron-coloured 'curry-powder' or 'massala' as the dominating ingredient. □ The stricter forms *curried-beef*, etc are widely superseded in CE by these *curry*-forms wh can be justified by the comparable pattern of SE 'fruit-cake', 'pepper-steak', etc (See *AMEWF:82*).

curse *vb* (CarA) **1.** To use indecent language loudly and angrily (about or directed at sb). **a.** *The Beak fined him $10.00 for beating his wife; $5.00 for cursing, and reprimanded and discharged him for threatening the constable.*—DaC (53.08.17, p.3) **b.** *They stood up in the main road and curse me loud and nasty.*—Bdos (CR, 1970) □ This is the dominant usage in CE, always associated with violent behaviour (cp SE 'curse and swear and carry on'), the vb being rarely used in CE in its orig SE sense 'to put a curse on'. Note Phrs and see also CUSS. **2.** PHRASES **2.1** **curse (sb) bad** *vb phr* (CarA) [*AF*] ‖ **curse hell out of (sb); curse (sb) to hell** (CarA) [*IF*] ‖ **curse (sb) past their burying place** (Bdos) [*AF—Joc*] ‖ **curse (sb) stink; curse (sb) up-side[d] down** (CarA) [*AF*] To CURSE (sb) intensely, without restraint, in public, etc. □ Many other intensifying adv phrs occur in the same context. See also Phrs at CUSS.

cus-cus (grass) *n* (*phr*) (Gren) See KHUS-KHUS (GRASS)

cu·sha [′kuša/-ʌ] *n* (Angu, Mrat) ‖ CASHA 1.(i), 2. (Nevs, etc) (i.e. the tree or the thorn)

cush-cush[1] (**cuss-cuss, kus(s)-kus(s)**) [kuš-kuš ~ kus-kus] *n* (Angu, Guyn, USVI) **1.** (Angu, Guyn) Meal made from grated cassava or the grated white kernel of the coconut, or (often) the latter in dry form (after the milky juice has been squeezed and washed out of it), used with sugar added, as a sweetmeat. *While it was baking he husked a coconut, broke the nut in halves and with his knife scraped the kernel into cush-cush which he washed and squeezed, catching the milk in the saucepan.*—SBB:92 **2.** (USVI) The fine leavings of BAGASSE. *Some of the molasses was used in making mash for rum. One mash was made of one part molassess, five parts water, and sometimes cush-cush (fine pieces of cane stocks).*—JNHSJ:26 **3.** (USVI) Any fine dusty leavings, such as remain in a sack of charcoal—SVID. [Sense 1. < Bhoj *kuch-kucha* < Hin *kuuchnaa* 'to crush, pound'. From this sense, associated with 'leavings' of grated coconut, the other senses prob developed]

cush-cush[2] **ant(s)** (**cuss-cuss ants**) [′kuš-kuš ~ kus-kus ant(s)] *n phr* (Guyn) ‖ ACOUSHI ANTS (Guyn) *The mourners were attacked by a herd of cuss-cuss ants, whose nest they had disturbed as they stood round the grave.*—SNWIC:224 (R. Heath) [A reduplicated variant of (*EILCA:46*). Arawak *kuusee* 'kushy ant'] □ Sometimes simply '(the) *cush-cush*'.

cush-cush[3] (**yam**)* [′kuš-kuš (ya·m)] *n* (*phr*) (ECar) ‖ **bell-yam, buck yam** (Guyn) ‖ **couche-couche** (StLu) ‖ **Indian yam** (Jmca) ‖ **yampie** (Belz, CayI, Jmca) A distinctly smaller variety of yam, generally oval and growing in clusters, slightly pink and sweetish when cooked, and 'there are several varieties [of cush-cush yam] varying considerably in shape and colour. It is generally considered to be the most palatable of the yams grown in the W Indies.... [The tubers] form a rosette of more or less fleshy structure above the main tuber at the ends of wh smaller tubers are formed—*PTT:151; Dioscorea trifida,* (a small variety of *Dioscoreaceae*). [From the floury nature of the boiled yam. Cp *ADHL* Hausa *kush-kush; kus-kus* (Arabic) 'a wheaten food']

cu·shew *n* (Antg, Bdos, Gren, StVn, Tbgo) See KUSHU

cuss[1] [kʌs ~ kɒs] *n* [*AF*] **1.** (CarA) Dirty words; abusive language; (AmE) cusswords. [< SE as *OED curse* sb 2. 'a profane oath', but developed as in 19C AmE *cussword*. See *OED cuss* sb, esp sense 3.] **2.** (Gren) (Plenty of) unnatural bad luck. (See Phr 4.2) **3.** (Gren) Behaviour or an act that deliberately causes sb else much trouble. *Imagine, people hoping to have their passports to travel last week are still being told 1988 May and June. What but cuss could cause such madness?* —InF (87.08.21, p.28) [< SE, as *OED curse* sb 4. 'evil inflicted by divine or supernatural power' (with pronunc developed as in prec sense)] □ Used in both senses 2., 3. as a collective, without pl form. **4.** PHRASES **4.1 drop/throw (some) cuss in (sb); fire (some) cuss at (sb); give (sb) some good cuss** *vb phrs* (CarA) To attack (sb) with dirty, abusive words. *Although he was Prime Minister he wouldn't hesitate to drop some stinking cuss in anybody who didn't deliver what he wanted.*—(Guyn) [< *drop*, etc, adding intensive force + CUSS 1.] **4.2 have cuss** *vb phr* (Gren) To be prone to bad luck (as if under a curse). *Well, wha[t] happen to we never happen to nobody else—boy! Like Grenadians really have cuss.*—(Gren) [< *have* + CUSS 2.]

cuss[2] (**cuss off, cuss out**[1], **cuss up**) *vb* (*phr*) (CarA) [*AF*] **1.** To speak loudly, roughly and in great anger to (sb) in an open row; to CURSE (sb) intensely. [< CE *curse* [IF] 'to swear at'] **2.** To say harsh or unpleasant things to hurt (sb) (without shouting); to scold (sb) roughly. *'I cussed out my secretary this morning,' Tony said. 'She was late and then she spent half an hour in the toilet.'*—JPB:99 □ See also *air out your mouth,* AIR[2] Phr 2.2.

cuss-cuss ant(s) *n phr* (Guyn) See CUSH-CUSH ANTS

cuss-out[2] (**cussing, cuss·in[g]-off/-out /-up**) [ˈkʌs(ɪn) /(ɪŋ)] *n* (CarA) Loud, rough, angry swearing between two or more persons in an open row. *There was an incident where a Constable of this unit cursed the Commissioner and there was a 'cuss-out' between them.*—Trin (Scott Drug Report, AdV, 87.02.17, p.6) [By functional shift of vb phr]

cus·tard-ap·ple* *n* (CarA) ‖ *bullock's heart* (Jmca, StVn) ‖ *cachiman* (Dmca, StLu) ‖ *Jamaica-apple* (Baha) ‖ *snat-apple* (Gren) ‖ *tjè-bèf* (Gren) A heart-shaped fruit (about the size of an adult's fist) that has a pinkish-cream or brownish skin marked with a noticeable network of lines, and a grainy, yellowish, sweet pulp resembling 'custard' (hence its name); *Annona reticulata* (*Annonaceae*).

cus·tom *vb* (Bdos, Gren, Guyn, StVn) [*X*] **1.** Accustom. *You shouldn'[t] custom yourself to so much salt.*—(Guyn) **2.** Accustomed (to). *She custom doing that since she was small.*—(Bdos) [< SE *accustom* by aphesis]

cus·tos *n* (Jmca) The chief magistrate of, and also the Governor-General's representative in, a parish in Jamaica. [Latin, 'a guardian'] □ Pl is *custodes.*

cut 1. *vb intr* (Bdos, Guyn) [*IF*] ‖ *bite* (CarA) **2.** [Of the bowels] To have griping pains. (Cp Phr 3.13). *vb tr* (CarA) To speak (a language) well. (See Phr 3.3). **3.** PHRASES [With many varying senses] **3.1 cut a bet** *vb phr* (Guyn, Tbgo, Trin) [Of children] To seal a bet made between two young persons by linking the little finger of the right hand each in the other, and then having a third person, as witness, part them sharply, saying 'Cut!' **3.2 cut card(s)** *vb phr* (Bdos, Guyn, USVI) To foretell (as a professional CARD-CUTTER) or find the reason for sb's personal problems, using a deck of playing cards. *After cutting the cards the whole matter unfolded. She has an enemy that she believes is her friend. This is a tall dark woman that has children and combs her hair with two plaits in the back and one in front.*—PKKK:46 **3.2.1 cut your cards straight/upright** *vb phr* (Guyn, Tbgo, Trin) [*IF*] To be honest but careful in your own interest; to be cautious in your dealings with sb so as to gain your ends without offending. [Prob a metaph from card playing] **3.3 cut language (English, French, Spanish, etc) good** *vb phr* (CarA) [*AF*] To speak (a particular language) fluently, impressively. *And since she come back from England, if you hear how she cuttin[g] de English!*—(StVn) **3.4 Cut it out!** *excl* (ECar) [A sharp reprimand] Stop it right now! **3.5 cut Lent** *vb phr* (Tbgo, Trin) [Of school children] To agree with each other to observe Lent by some playful requirement, with some agreed and playful penalty. *'Cutting Lent' was then as much part of school life as exercise books and tambran sauce, and we lived through the forty days of Lent receiving clouts from disapproving adults and cuffs from schoolmates with whom we had 'cut Lent'.*— ExP (73.04.23, p.9) [A ref to the 'cutting' or parting of the hooked fingers of the two persons in agreement. See Phr 3.1] **3.6 cut loose** *vb phr* (ECar) [*IF*] To behave or act with sudden vigour or violence (as if you have broken out of or abandoned all restraint). *After painstakingly reaching his century he cut loose and actually went on nearly reaching a second.*—(Bdos) **3.7 cut maldjo** *vb phr* (Gren, Trin) See MALDJO Phr 2.1 **3.8 cut out** *vb phr* (CarA) [*AF*] To get away (from a party, a crowd, etc); to make an escape. **3.8.1 cut (out) bad-eye** *vb phr* (Belz, Guyn) See MALDJO Phr 2.1 **3.9 cut styles (cut old style)** *vb phr* (ECar) [*AF—Joc*] ‖ *buss style*

(Trin) To behave in a showy manner to catch attention. **3.10 cut (sb's) arse** [*AF—Vul*]; **cut sb's backside/behind/skin/tail** [*IF*] *vb phrs* (CarA) To flog or beat up (sb) severely. [A ref to the cow-hide whip used on slaves, wh would cut the flesh] **3.11 cut the eye of (sb)** *vb phr* (Guyn, Tbgo) [*IF*] To ward off (sb's) BAD-EYE; to prevent the evil, magical influence of (sb's) envious or malicious gaze from harming a garden crop. *There is a local superstition also met with in West Africa, that if planted around a plantation the maljoe (jack bean) 'cuts the eye' and so prevents petty theft.*—PTT:103 **3.11.1 cut your eye after (sb)** (*Jmca, Mrat*) **/at, on (sb)** *vb phr* (CarA) ‖ *give (sb a) cut-eye* (CarA) ‖ *watch (sb) cross-eye/cut-eye* (Dmca, Gren) [Of a woman] To look rudely or angrily at (sb), deliberately close the eyes while turning the head sharply away, as a gesture meaning 'I detest you'. [Of Afr origin, the same gesture being widely known in West and Central Afr. Cp Igbo *a wa la anya* 'Don't cut eyes!' (= Don't be rude!)] **3.11.2 cut your eye at (sth)** *vb phr* (Guyn) To decide to deprive yourself of sth you want but cannot afford. [Prob a lesser extension of 3.11.1 with a more generally applicable sense] **3.12 cut the mustard** *vb phr* (Bdos) [*AF—Vul*] [Of a man] To satisfy a woman in sexual intercourse. [By shift of sense of AmE slang *cut the mustard*, 'to reach a satisfactory standard', wh, by pop etym, < orig AmE idiom *cut the muster*, 'to pass muster, i.e. to pass the critical examination of a formal military inspection' (See W3 *cut* vb, Phr *cut the muster/mustard*.)] **3.13 cut your belly** *vb phr* (CarA) [*IF*] To cause sharp pains, gripes, in the bowels. *The senna pods cut me belly for true.*—(Guyn)

C.U.T. [si-yu-ti] *abbr n* (CarA) The Caribbean Union of Teachers, embracing teachers' unions in 14 English-speaking Caribbean territories with Bermuda included, and formed in the 1970s out of the older Caribbean Confederation of Teachers, its secretariat being sited in whichever territory its elected secretary is. □ Often written CUT with same pronunc.

cut·a·coo [ˈkʌtaku] *n* (Jmca) **1.** ‖ *catacou* (Antg, Baha, USVI) ‖ *cotacoo* (USVI) One of various types of pouch or basket, a small closed type used by fishermen or hunters (*Antg, Jmca*), a large open one carried on the head (*USVI*), etc. **2.** (Jmca) ‖ MATAPEE (Guyn) [< *DAFL* Twi *kotoku* 'bag, sack, pouch']

cut-arse *n* (Bdos, Guyn, Trin) [*AF—Vul*] See CUT-TAIL (CarA)

cut-down *n* (Bdos, Guyn) **1.** ‖ *cuttie* (Guyn) A beer-bottle of rum containing 10 ozs, or just less than three gills, officially called 'a reputed half-pint'. [Ref to the amount as being cut down by the capacity of the beer-bottle wh was less than that of the regular HIP- FLASK] **2.** [*AF—Joc*] A noticeably short man.

cut-eye *n* (CarA) ‖ *cross-eye* (Dmca, Gren) **1.** A woman's gesture of contempt for sb, shown by her looking at the person and closing her eyes while turning her face sharply away. **2.** PHRASE **2.1 give cut-eye; give (sb) a cut-eye** *vb phr* (CarA) [*AF—Cr*] ‖ CUT YOUR EYE AT (SB) (CarA) See CUT Phr 3.11.1

cut·lass (**cut.lash**) [kʌtlʌs ~ kʌtlɪs ~ kʌtlaš] *n* (CarA) ‖ *collins, sword* (Bdos) ‖ *gilpin* (Tbgo, Trin) ‖ *ponia* (Tbgo) A labourer's tool for cutting canes, bush, etc, consisting of a wooden handle on a heavy metal blade of varying length and shape, but usu 12 to 18 ins long with an upturned tip; a machete. [< *OED cutlass* 'a short sword with a flat wide slightly curved blade ... now esp the sword with wh sailors are armed'. This sense has shifted in CE, but the use of the *cutlass* as a weapon is still common] □ *Cutlash*, regarded as illiterate in CE, is an 18C E form noted in *OED*.

cut·lass-bean *n* (Jmca) **1.** ‖ JUMBIE-BEAD **2.** (Bdos, etc) [The stamens of the flower resemble a cutlass] **2.** ‖ BEAN-TREE (Bdos)

cut-skin *n* (Baha) [*AF*] ‖ CUT-TAIL (CarA)

cut-tail *n* (CarA) [*AF*] ‖ *cut-arse* (Bdos, Guyn, Trin) ‖ *cut-skin* (Baha) A whipping; a flogging. *A regular whipping was given out like medicine, three times a day ... I am not speaking about brutality, but merely a good cut tail. / If you pushed and shoved in the milk and biscuit line it was a cut tail ... / If you told a lie it was a cut tail, if you were late for school it was a cut tail.*—AdV (92.03.27, p.9, E. Lewis) [See CUT Phr 3.10]

cut·ter; cheese-cutter *n* **1.** (Bdos) ‖ *hops* (Trin) A sandwich made of a sliced small loaf of bread with a piece of ham, cheese or fish in between (used as a snack to cut hunger and hence the name). *I know what people eat for lunch today. Until we gave children hot meals they were eating cutters too.*—Bdos (Hd, 73.07.11, p.2472) **2.** (Gren, Guyn) [Often in pl: CUTTERS] Any of a number of small salty or pickled items served at drinking parties (to cut the effect of alcohol and hence the name).

cut·tie *n* (Guyn) [*AF*] ‖ CUT-DOWN (Bdos, Guyn)

cut·ting *n* (Antg, Guyn) [*IF*] A gripe or pain in the lower abdomen. *Some people come to see me for what they call a cutting in the belly, which could be anything from indigestion to serious appendicitis.*—(Guyn—A doctor) □ See CUT **1.** and Phr 3.13.

CXC [si-ɛks-si] *abbr n* (CarA) Caribbean Examinations Council, the official body responsible for organizing secondary school-leavers' examinations for most of the English-speaking Caribbean territories, its headquarters being in Barbados. [X used as convenient abbr for *examinations*] □ Always written without stops.

cya(h)n (cyant, cyar, cyah) [kya·n(t) ~ kya:] *neg modal vb* (CarA) [*AF—Cr*] Can't; cannot. **a.** *Well boys, in Grenada we use to stay on the sidewalk and hustle a dollar but we cyan do that here.*—PGIP:49 **b.** *He cyar remember buying shrimps but he glad for it because shrimps scarce dese days.*—ExP (72.08.27, p.20) [< SE *can't* by palatalization of initial [k-] and also esp in *Trin*, by denasalization and reduction of final consonant cluster /-nt/] □ These other spellings **(cyaan, kyaan**, etc) are frequently used by *CarA* writers of dialogue in attempts to represent the pronunc. See CAN'T.

cyp* [sɪp] *n* (Tbgo, Trin) Any of several varieties of a medium-weight wood, varying in colour from white to yellowish-brown, with a wavy grain; it is durable and much favoured for furniture and construction, some varieties also for boat-building; the wood of a tree of the *Nectandra* spp or *Ocotea* spp (*Lauraceae*). [Fr Cr < Fr *cypre*, by apocope] □ Sometimes erron spelled *sip*.

Czien [zayɛ̃] *n* (Gren) See COMPÈ ZAYEN

D

-d- □ In Creolized E speech [-d-] often replaces [ð] 'th', requiring spellings in dialogue such as *de, dis, dat, dere, mudda, faada, bade*, etc for 'the', 'this', 'that', 'there', 'mother', 'father', 'bathe', etc. This is surviving Cr pronunc due to the absence of the sound [ð] from Niger-Congo langs in general (*WALS:51–52*), and hence from the orig speech of the slaves. See also -T-.

da¹ (dᴧh); dat *pron, adj* (CarA) [*AF—Cr*] **1.** That. *Da is de man da[t] buy da house.*—(Guyn) [Reduction of SE 'that' by [ð > d] shift and loss or light articulation of final consonant] □ This form is esp preserved in *CarA* provs. **2.** *PHRASE* **2.1 Da fo[r] lick you/them! (etc)** *id phr* (Bdos, Trin) [*AF*] That's your/their (etc) affair! That serves you/them (etc) right! *'If you' don't like it, dar-foo-lick-you, girl.... My mouth is mine to do what the hell I like with it*—MBF:139

da² *def art* (ViIs) [*AF—Cr*] The. *Da fuss ting dat a hear was a lil squeaking from somebody shakin a bed or sometin.*—Aaw.I.2, p.23 □ This form occurs as a loose variant of *de* 'the' (also in provs) elsewhere in the *CarA*, though it is less often written. Cp next.

da³ (CayI) [*AF—Cr*] **1.** *pers pron* They. **2.** *adv* There. □ A loose variant pronunc, usu [de] in both cases in most of the *CarA*.

da⁴ *vb* (Belz, Jmca) [*AF—Cr*] **1.** *copulative* ‖ *a¹⁴* (CarA) [*Cr*] Am, is, are. *Now dis boy, yuh know what is de boy name? Codan Colorado—dat da de boy name.*—WFSFB:46 **2.** *focusing* ‖ *a¹⁵* (CarA) [*Cr*] It is (introducing a statement with emphasis). *Da one poor fowl coob when di hen crow louder dan di fowl cock.*—Belz (Prov) [Cp functions of Ewe *dɔ* and of Igbo *de* 'to be' as set out in *TAGD:214*. Cp also *DAFL* Twi *da* 2. 'to be situated'. Also *ADMY* Yoruba *dà ʙ.* 'become'] □ 1. These coincident forms are esp preserved in provs, and still occur in deliberate folk usage in the speech of educated persons in *Belz*. 2. Cp DE³

da⁵ (dah) [da~dᴧ] *pre-vbl aspectual particle* (Jmca) [*AF—Cr*] ‖ *a¹⁰* (CarA) ‖ *do²* 1. (Bdos) -*ing* (indicating that the action of the verb it precedes is happening). *Back to Africa Miss Matty? Yuh no know wa yuh dah sey?*—FCV2:166 (L. Bennett) [See DE⁴ (Baha, etc)] □ Occurs in Cr speech, and preserved in dial literature.

da⁶ (dah) *prep* (Baha, Belz, Jmca) [*AF—Cr*] ‖ *a⁷* (CarA) At, in, into, on, to (the). *Wen e get da de place de fust somebody e see deh (is) e wife whe e jus done kiss.*—WFSFB:37 [Cp Ewe *ɖe* 'towards, to, on'. See *TAGD:210*] □ Occurs widely in *Belz* Cr speech, and also preserved elsewhere in dial literature.

D.A. *abbr* (Bdos) Dame of St Andrew of the Order of Barbados; it is a national honour awarded for extraordinary and outstanding achievement and merit in service to Barbados or to humanity at large; the recipient is entitled to be addressed as Dame and to have the letters written after her name. □ See also K.A..

daa·da (da·da) ['da·da] *n* **1.** (Dmca, Guyn) [*IF*] (Respectful name for) an old black woman (usu poor and often also a child's guardian or nurse). [Cp *ADFEF* Ewe *dada* 'mother'; also *DAFL* Fante *dadaa* 'old'; also *IGED* Grebo *daadaa* 'very old'] **2.** (Guyn, Trin) [Indic] Paternal grandfather; (also used as a term of respect for) the eldest brother in the family. [Hin *daadaa* 'paternal grandfather']

daal (dahl, dal, dhal, dholl) [da:l~dɒ:l] *n* (Guyn, Trin) [Indic] A paste or powder made from yellow split peas to be put into a type of ROTI or used to make a very thick seasoned soup. [Bhoj < Hin *daal* 'pulse'] □ Spellings with /h/ suggest aspiration, wh is not represented either in present CarA or original Hindi pronunc. The spelling *dholl* is due to false refinement.

daal pu·ri [da:l puri] *n phr* (Guyn, Trin) [Indic] A type of ROTI with a filling of DAAL, often fried in ghee; it is a standard part of the meal at Hindu weddings. [Hin DAAL + PURI □ Often loosely called *puri.*

Dab·ra *n* See HABRA, DABRA AND THE CREW

da·chine *n* (CarA) See DASHEEN

dad·dy! (daa·dy!) ['da:di] *excl* (Antg, Tbgo) [*AF*] ‖ PAPA! (Antg, etc) [Prob a folk transfer < PAPA! because of an apparent equivalence in meaning]

dag·ger-log *n* (Antg, Dmca, StVn) The central stalk or 'dagger' of the CENTURY-PLANT, dried and used by fishermen as a float or for making rafts.

dag·ger-plant *n* (Antg, Dmca, StVn) ‖ *agave* (CarA) The variety of AGAVE also known as the CENTURY- PLANT (*Agave americana*) its tough central pole-like stalk being called a 'dagger'.

D.A.H. *abbr* (Dmca) The Dominica Award of Honour, the highest national award of the Commonwealth of Dominica; the letters may be written after the recipient's name.

dai·sy *n* (Guyn) ‖ CARPET-DAISY (Bdos)

da·ka·ma [daka:mʌ] /1′21/ *n* (Guyn) [Timber Ind] A large forest-tree, yielding a tough, reddish-brown wood wh is mostly used for building, and the bark for medicinal purposes; *Dimorphandra conjugata* (*Caesalpiniaceae*)—FFPG:22. [*BAED* Arawak *dakama* 'a tall tree mostly found growing on white sand']

dal·li *n* (Guyn) [Timber Ind] A tall forest-tree yielding wood used for carpentry and making coffins; *Virola surinamensis* (*Myristicaceae*)—FFPG:23. [*BAED* Arawak *dali* 'a large tree with light whitish wood commonly found in swamps']

dam *n* (Guyn) 1. Any of the embankments of packed mud built to contain a cane-field or rice-field and control their irrigation, being also used as a footpath by labourers. □ See BACKDAM, MIDDLE-WALK DAM, SIDE-LINE DAM. 2. [*IF*] [By extension] Any mud-surfaced country road or public path.

dam·age¹ *n* (Belz) [*X*] [Used with indef art as in cit] Result of damage such as a breakage, crack, dent, etc. *E's tractor hit against the other tractor causing a damage to a new radiator.*—BsT (79.08.29, p.10) □ IAE would usu require 'some damage' or 'damage' in such contexts.

dam·age² *vb tr* 1. (Guyn, Tbgo, Trin) [*X*] To injure (the body). **a.** *I did not run in and collar him by the throat. I first got damaged and chucked down the step.*—Tbgo (CR) **b.** *A man whose right hand was damaged several places by the propeller of a launch was admitted to the Georgetown Hospital yesterday.*—GyC (76.03.26, p.13) 2. (Antg) [*X*] To break (a glass, etc). □ IAE *damage* vb is used with some kind of property, not a person, as object; and it always entails possible re-use.

dame-and-cava·lier *n* (Dmca) ‖ BACHELOR'S BUTTON (CarA)

Dame Lor·raine [da·m lɔre·n] *n phr* (Trin) A traditional CARNIVAL figure, a man dressed in grotesque woman's costume with oversized breasts and buttocks, elaborate hat and dress and dancing with sexual suggestiveness.

dam·sel ['damsl] *n* (Gren, StVn, Trin) ‖ GOOSE-BERRY 1. (CarA)

dam·son ['damsn] *n* (Belz) ‖ JAMOON (Guyn)

dance *vb* PHRASES 1. **dance belair/calypso/ reggae/spouge, etc** (CarA) *vb phr They were tired of dancing calypso and wanted to dance reggae.*—(Bdos) □ Regularly used without following def art and often also with sg n as object, hence id phrs. Cp IAE *dance a/the waltz, rhumba,* etc or *dance waltzes, rhumbas,* etc. 2. **dance (the) cocoa** *vb phr* (Dmca, Gren, Trin) To polish cocoa with the bare feet. See COCOA¹ Phr 3.1 *When the beans are ready for polishing women are employed to dance the cocoa, and every crop they make some money dancing cocoa.*—Trin (Ms) 3. **make (sb) dance** *vb phr* [*IF*—*Joc*] **(i)** To flog (a child) all over the body (hence causing dance-like movements in fending off the blows). *When your father come home, he goin[g] make you dance with blows for breakin[g] that window.*—(Guyn) **(ii)** [By extension] To subject (sb) to a lot of hostility and spite. *Now she has found out about this outside child, she making him dance.*—(Bdos)

dance-hall *n* (Jmca) A type of REGGAE music marked by electronically produced bass rhythms, but without the message-carrying lyrics characteristic of REGGAE; it is heavily influenced by pop-music themes but maintains the popularity of the REGGAE beat in dance-halls, hence the name. □ The term is now much used in the ECar.

dandan *n* (CarA) [*AF—Joc*] 1. A child's pretty dress. 2. [By extension] New and pretty clothes of a woman. *'An' you must make a nice dandan to go down 'pon de wharf to meet him',* put in Ethelrida—MBF:48

dan·de·li·on *n* (Jmca) ‖ WILD COFFEE (Guyn, etc) □ This plant, *Cassia occidentalis* (*Leguminosae*), resembles the European dandelion *Taraxacum officinale* (*Compositae*) in being also a weed that bears yellow flowers and is also used as a folk-medicine for kidney complaints.

dan·dy-horse *n* (Belz) A merry-go-round. [Cp *OED* dandy-horse '… an early form of the bicycle'; however note *OED* cit 1892 '… a patent for this dandy or hobby-horse', so the sense *hobby-horse* i.e. 'horse on a merry-go-round' may also have been current in late 19C E for *dandy-horse*]

dark *adj* (CarA) [As qualifying 'eyes'] Growing dim-sighted. *She was getting too old to read as her eyes were getting dark.*—Bdos (Ms) [Cp *OED dark* a. 9. 'not able to see; partially or totally blind' *Obs* exc. *dial*]

dark-crys·tal sugar *n phr* (Guyn) [Sugar Ind] ‖ DARK SUGAR (CarA) □ Also called *d.c. sugar* by older folk.

dark eyes *n phr* 1. (CarA) Dimness of sight. 2. (Bdos, Guyn) Dizziness associated with BAD-FEELINGS.

dark sug·ar *n phr* (CarA) [Sugar Ind] ‖ *dark-crystal sugar* (Guyn) A dark brown sugar wh is sweeter than CLEAR SUGAR because its crystals contain more molasses. *You burn dark sugar to a liquid state to use in making Christmas cake.*—(Bdos)

da·ru ['da·ru] *n* (CarA) [*AF—Joc*] Rum, or any strong liquor associated with drunkenness. [Bhoj < Hin *daaruu* 'liquor'] □ The term, originating in Indic communities esp in *Guyn, Trin*, is in wider *Joc* use in the *CarA*.

dash *vb tr* (CarA) [*IF*] 1. To toss, throw or pitch (not necessarily with violence). *Both of them are untidy! They dash their clothes all over the floor.*—(Jmca) 2. PHRASE 2.1 dash a lash in (sb/sth) *vb phr* [*AF*] To strike (sb/sth) violently with a whip, stick, etc. ... *so he took the club, dash one lash in the old front door, and it fly open.*—Bdos (Ms, 1977) □ Cp SE *drop a lash on sb* in wh the sense *drop* is also intensified.

da·sheen* (da·chine) ['dašin ∼ 'dašin] *n* (CarA) ‖ *badoo* (Jmca) ‖ *Barbados eddoe* (Gren) ‖ *Chinese eddoe* (Gren, Guyn, Trin) ‖ *(soft) coco* (Jmca) ‖ *eddoe* 2. (Berm) ‖ *eddoe-head* (Bdos) A large round tuber, about 5 ins in diameter, of a toughish texture, producing a number of smaller corms or SUCKERS of smoother texture (these SUCKERS being called EDDOES in some territories); the plant is distinguished by its big heart-shaped, purple-tinged leaves (wh are edible), on tall leaf-stalks growing straight from the tuber; *Colocasia esculenta globulifera* (*Araceae*). ... *while the starchy rootcrops dasheen and tannia are four pounds for 25 cents and 25 cents a pound respectively.*—ExP (73.06.01, p.3) [Prob < Fr (*chou*) *de chine*, creolized in Fr CarA islands. Cp ‖ *Chinese eddoe* and also the name *taro de chine* for same plant *TVIT:52*] □ This vegetable is sometimes called **cocoyam**, or **taro** in botanical literature; see also EDDOE, TANNIA.

da·sheen-bush *n* (Tbgo, Trin) ‖ CALALU 1. (CarA)

da·shi·ki ['daši·ki] *n* (Trin) A man's short-sleeved upper garment that is fairly loose-fitting, without collar or buttons, V-necked, and usu of plain material brightly embroidered around the neck and borders. [Black Amer loan < *ADMY* Yoruba *da-n-ṣiki* (< Hausa *dan ciki*) 'gown wh has wide armpits and wh reaches to the knees']

dat¹ *pron, adj* (CarA) [*AF*] See DA¹

dat² *n* (Jmca) [Rastaf] Pork. [Jmca Cr pronunc of 'that (thing)', a euphemism for 'pork' wh is despised by the RASTAFARIAN cult] □ See ARNOLD

date-palm* *n* (CarA) 1. A palm averaging in height about 18 ft with a notably rough trunk crowned by long branches curving out and down, so making it a popular decorative tree; it bears no dates in the W Indies; *Phoenix dactylifera* (*Arecaceae*). 2. Name loosely applied to other

varieties of short-trunked decorative palms that bear clusters of inedible little fruit.

daugh·ter [dɒ·ta] /1'2/ *n* [Rastaf] 1. A female member of the RASTAFARIAN cult, and usu one of the acknowledged sexual partners of a BROTHER. 2. Any young black woman, esp one sympathetic to the RASTAFARIAN cult.

day *n* PHRASE 1. for days *adj or adv intensifier phr* (ECar) [*AF—Joc*] Very (good); extremely (good). a. *Fete for days, boy!* (i.e. *A very good party*).—(Trin) b. *Maestro's LP for '77 ... is bad for days!*—SuP (77.01.09, p.6) 2. in all my born days *adv phr* (CarA) [*IF*] In all my life; for as long as I have lived. *In all my born days I never hear anything like this. Well! look what we come to!*—BeA (80.02.16, p.5) □ This phr also occurs in AmE. 3. see your days *vb phr* (Guyn) [*AF*] ‖ CATCH HELL (CarA) 4. when the day come(s) *adv phr* (Bdos, Guyn) [*AF/IF*] See WHEN Phr 3.6 *His sickness keep me up so much every night dat A can[t] face the job when the day come.*—(Guyn)

day-boat *n* (Bdos) [Fishing Ind] A small engine-powered fishing boat with a covered cabin but no refrigeration facility, wh means it can only make one-day fishing trips.

day-clean *n* (CarA) Dawn; the brightness of daybreak just about sunrise. a. *Every morning he had to get up before day clean, saddle up his horse, and go up to Cannaree village to catch the people home before they wake up.*—Tbgo (Ms, 1966) b. *We prepared to continue our journey at day-clean, rolling up the tow-lines and re-loading the cargo.*—RWIN:186 (J. Carew) [Prob a calque from W Afr langs] □ See also CLEAN² vb. Cp FORE-DAY MORNING.

D.C. *abbr* (Belz, Guyn) See DISTRICT COM-MISSIONER

d.c. sug·ar *n phr* (Guyn) Abbr = dark-crystal sugar (*Guyn*). □ Used mostly by older folk.

de¹ (dey²) [di ∼ dɪ ∼ də ∼ de] *def art* (CarA) [*Cr*] The. *E tek de one a de pigs an e gone to dis fella house an e sell uh.*—WFSFB:39 [< SE *the* by [ð > d] shift] □ A spelling commonly used in folk narrative dialogue, *dey* being a rare variant. See DEY².

de² (deh², dey³) [de ∼ dɛ] *adv* (CarA) [*Cr*] There. a. *Look over de*[h]! *Look it de*[h] (*Look over there. There it is*).—(ECar) b. *Dis hand pick up two hundred dolla' / Lying dey in open street.*—KTT:11 [< SE *there* by [ð > d] shift and leveling of diphthong in [ðɛə]] □ Spellings used in folk narrative dialogue.

de³ (deh³, dey⁴) [dɛ ∼ de] *stative vb* (CarA) [*Cr*] 1. Am; is; are (Pres t. of vb 'to be' with locative complement stated or implied). a. *Yo would find she husband and children de home and she de nex*[t] *door.*—(Guyn) b. *One Sunday when ah dey home* _an' ah have time, ah mus' try it out._—WeN (53.03.09, p.2) **c.** _S1: How you do? S2: Me dear, I deh_ (= I am here/there, just as you see me)—(Guyn). [Prob a structural infl from more than one Afr lang. Cp _DAFL_ Twi _de 4._ 'to contain, to be'; exs _ne din de_ (His name is what?) _ɔde Kofi_ (It is Kofi). Also _WIED_ Igbo _dị_ 'to be (in a state of)'] □ Also used in writing folk dialogue. The coincidence of these forms does not cause ambiguity even in the hearing of educated CE speakers, pitch and context serving to differentiate function in such a case as _De de de_ /121/ (They are there!) or _De de de?_ /123/ (Are they there?). Cp also DA⁴ **2.** _PHRASES_ **2.1 deh bad** _vb phr_ (Guyn) See BAD² Phr. 5.2 **2.2 de(h) together** _vb phr_ (CarA) [_AF—Cr_] [Of a man and a woman] To be living openly together. **2.3 de(h) with (sb)** _vb phr_ (CarA) [_AF—Cr_] [Usu of a woman] To be kept or supported as a sexual partner. **2.4 the two of them de(h)** _id phr_ (Guyn) [_AF—Cr_] [Of a man and a woman] They have a secret sexual relationship. _I hear that he and the secretary de._—(Guyn) □ Cp Phr 2.2 above.

de⁴ (dey⁵) [dʌ ~ dɛ] _pre-vbl particle_ (Baha, Belz, StKt) [_Cr_] ‖ A¹⁰ (CarA) **a.** _Mary A neva far from faintin', / To see how A de use plenty seasonin'._—LMFF:36 **b.** _Bell: You know, Joe, a dey tink sum ting? Joe: Wha' dat?_—LaS (76.06.19, p.4, Bits & Pieces) [Prob a structural infl from W Afr langs. Cp note at DE³, and also (_TAGD:214_, note 5.) 'Igbo _de_ is placed before the verb root ... to make the present progressive form of the verb. This form in Igbo expresses the continuance of an action rather than the actual time of it'. DA⁵ (_Jmca_) is prob a variant of this form]

dead¹ _used as vbl adj_ (CarA) [_X_] Be/was/were dead; has/had died; has/had been dead. **a.** _'Lord! and when they come and tell me that my father dead, I cry and I cry till I couldn't find water to cry with no more.'_—CWFYS:20 **b.** _My husband dead now ten years._—(Tbgo) [Prob reinforced by W Afr Lang structure, in wh the verbal adj is a common feature, but see next] □ This is common folk usage and often written. It easily shades into the full vbl use of DEAD².

dead² _vb intr_ (CarA) [_X_] **1.** To die; died. [Filling all the positions of these verbs, combining with all modals (can/could/could-a, etc), and taking an _-ing_ form] **a.** _To dead; what is to dead? Not dead I fraid._—WSAD:17 **b.** _An old woman who look like she would dead any minute come out of a carriage, carrying a cardboard box and a paperbag._—STLL:13 **c.** _It look to me like Matilda going soon dead._—CISH:116 **d.** _Vibert boy yu could ah dead._—KTT:14 **e.** _I come to tell you dat ole man Gussie Smith deading._—GR:27 (F. Squires) [Cp _OED dead_ v _Obs_ exc. in local or nonce-use. I. intr 1. 'to become dead; to die'. However _OED_ gives evidence of intr use in BrE only up to 17C, except that _to dead_ intr survived with a different sense in AmE slang in 19C and evid still does (cp _DAS dead_ v 1. 'to loaf or sponge'). (_To dead_ vb tr 'to kill' survived longer

in BrE. See _OED_.) The wide folk use of _dead, deadin(g)_, vb intr in CE is prob due to reinforcement by the usage of DEAD¹] **2.** _PHRASE_ **2.1 nearly dead/want dead with/from laugh** _vb phr_ (CarA) [_AF—Cr_] To laugh yourself limp; to laugh uncontrollably. **a.** _And she father sing back 'Yu better put yu backside inside.' Boy I want dead with laugh. Ask Fergie!_—Jbs.X.1:30 (W. Edwards) **b.** _A hearty laugh is followed by a description of how 'I dead from laugh.'_—SJW:72

dead³ _n_ **1.** (CarA) [_IF_] A corpse. **a.** _Nathan look nice as a dead._—CWFYS:20 **b.** _Deads are mostly buried in white, ghosts are usually dressed in white. The colour of the dead's skin is referred to as white._—Antg (Ms, 1973) [By shift from the SE general sense as in 'the burial of the dead' to specific ref to a person, as in cits] **2.** (Bdos, Guyn) [_AF—Joc_] [By extension] Trouble or some problem that is entirely yours. _I am sorry for him. If he did not go that is his dead. I am nothing to do with that._—Bdos (Hd, 74.08.27, p.3838) **3.** (CarA) [_AF_] Death. _He had to stand up too much in the rain in the police job and that is how he get his dead._—(Guyn) [Cp _OED dead_ sb² 'the northern form of the word _death_, formerly in regular use with Northern writers (dede) and still dialectal in Scotch (deid) pronounced [did] esp in certain locutions, ex _tired to dead_ (deid), _to be the dead_ (deid) _of any one_']

dead-house _n_ (Bdos, Belz, Guyn, Tbgo) The house where a deceased person lived. [Prob < dead³ 3. i.e. 'death-house'] □ The term applies to such a house only in ref to the holding of the wake, the burial, and the acts associated with expressing sympathy, such as drinking and eating after the burial.

dead-peo·ple bird _n phr_ (Baha) [_IF_] ‖ JUMBIE-BIRD 3. (Guyn) [From the bird's entirely black colour and its habit of congregating in cemeteries, among other open grassy places, in hunting insects] □ Distinguish from **death-bird** (Baha).

dead-wa·ter _n_ (CarA) The water with wh a corpse has been washed and wh is believed by some to have supernatural properties.

deal _vb intr_ (Belz, Dmca, Gren, Guyn, Tbgo, Trin) To practise witchcraft of the kind that involves trading living souls or 'dealing' with the devil. _We don't want to say, like the Baptist woman told us, 'you're dealing in bad.' / For, we don't believe in that kind of business._—PuN (74.12.08, p.5)

deal·er _n_ (Belz, Dmca, Gren, Guyn, Tbgo, Trin) A person (usu a man) who DEALS.

dear-aunt /1'2/ _n_ (Bdos, Guyn) (Term of address for) a great-aunt or an aunt much older than your parents, esp when such a person is the only aunt alive.

death-bird *n* (Baha) ‖JUMBIE-BIRD 1. (Guyn) [From the superstition that its eerie shriek over a house at night is an omen of death] □ Distinguish from *dead-people bird* (Baha) [*IF*].

de·cre·ol·i·za·tion ['di:kriolaɪzešən] *n* (CarA) [Ling] The process of gradual but unorganized changing from the established structures of a CREOLE language towards those of a European lang.

Deed-and-fait[h]! ['di·dənfet]; **Deed, no!** [di·d-nʌ] *excl* (Bdos) [*AF—Cr*] That's the truth, I'd swear!; I/you must agree! [< Indeed and in faith!]

Deep·va·li (**Deep·a·va·li, Dip·va·li**) ['di·pavali] *n* (Guyn, Trin) [Indic] ‖DIVALI (Guyn, Trin) The original Hindi name of DIVALI. [Hin < *diipak* 'light' + *vali* 'line', hence 'line of light'] □ These forms are less current than the dial Bhoj *Divali*.

deh¹ *pron* See DEY¹

deh² *adv* See DE²

deh³ *stative vb* See DE³

dem¹ *pron, adj* (CarA) [*Cr*] **1.** *obj pron* Them. *Dey say don't come wid dat by dem.*—TrG (72.08.06, p.10, Letter From Port-of-Spain) **2.** *subj pron* They. *Dem ha so much fat chat and dem can't do widout de help.*—MtM (63.01.26, p.3, Chit Chat) **3.** *possessive pron* Their. *De Rastas got a right to get dem religion featurin' dey, too.*—NaT (86.09.19, p.7, Lickmout' Lou) **4.** *demonstr adj* ‖*them²* (CarA) Those. *De Fire Station is one ah de first place dem touriss does see, wot you tink dey saying bout us?*—ToR (77.10.13, p.5, Cotay Si Cotay La) **5.** *in sg function* [*AF*] Him/her *Whoever t[h]ink dey can beat me, let dem try.*— (Bdos) [< SE *them* by [ð > d] shift, but its multi- functional pronominal use prob reflects similar features in pron functions in several W Afr langs. Such features could have been reinforced by some EE usage. Note *OED* them B. 3. 'used for nominative *they*.... Now only *dial* or *illiterate'* + cits–'1901 Them wasn't our only troubles. Also B. 5. 'As demonstr adj = Those. Now only *dial or illiterate'* + cits–'19C ... *them chaps*, etc] □ This form, in all these functions, is widely written in narrative dialogue. Cp DEY¹

dem² *post-nominal pl marker* (CarA) [*Cr*] ‖*them³* (CarA) **1.** The group or set of (whatever noun it follows). *Ah warnt see wha' de dog dem a bark for.* (= *I want to see what the dogs are barking for*).—LaS (77.10.29, p.3, Bits & Pieces) [A likely structural transfer from W Afr langs, some of wh form the pl of nouns by adding the 3rd pers pl pron form for 'them/they' (ex Ewe) or a word meaning 'people' (ex Gã-Adangme) to the noun. See *TAGD:223*] **2.** PHRASE **2.1** **an[d] dem** *post-nominal collectivizing phr* (CarA) [*Cr*] ‖*and them* (CarA) [*IF*] And others of the same group or set. *He ready to shoot down workers to please de capitalist employers and dem.*—CrU (74.10.12, Cocky & Stocky) [By addition of *and* to DEM² in the process of DECREOLIZATION]

De·me·ra·ra [dɛmʌra·ra∼dɛmɪra·ra] /1'122/ *n* (CarA) [Hist] Br Guiana (now Guyana). [Name of the principal COUNTY of Br Guiana in wh the capital, Georgetown, is situated] □ The name was once commonly used as a ref to the whole country and is still so used by many older people throughout the *CarA*.

De·me·ra·ra-al·mond *n* (ECar) ‖ALMOND (CarA)

De·me·ra·ra-shut·ter/-win·dow *n* (CarA) ‖*cooler* 1. (Guyn) A wooden close-louvred window, usu about 2 ft wide and 4 ft long, hinged at its top and held open by a stick attached to its base. [From DEMERARA as being the original place of its design, to keep out both sun-heat and rain]

De·me·ra·ra-sug·ar iso}n (British name for) YELLOW-CRYSTAL SUGAR (*Guyn*). [< *Demerara* as place of origin]

De·me·ra·ri·an [dɛmʌra·rɪən∼-re·rɪən] *n* A native of Br Guiana (now Guyana). □ This name is still used by older folk in the *CarA* for a *Guyanese*.

dem·self; **de(s).self, dey.self, duh.self** [dɛsɛlf ∼ desɛlf ∼ dʌsɛlf] *refl pron* (CarA) ‖*themself* (CarA) [*Cr*] **1.** *pl* Themselves. **a.** *You ain't saying at all dat is de Police officers demself dat playing a power-game dere.*—CrU (74.07.13, Cocky & Stocky) **b.** *De people can really enjoy desself.*—CrU (72.07.01, p.8, Cocky & Stocky) **c.** *Bahamians dese tinkin' 'bout rulin' deyself, / Dey wan' know what it is ta be free.*—WBS:14 [Prob < EE *themself, theirself.* See *OED* themselves, etym note: 'in standard E *themself* was the normal form to c 1540, but disappeared c 1570'. (Further note) III. '*their*—substituted for *them*—prevalent dialectally'. However *OEDS*, for themselves, cites 20C form *theirself*. Hence the forms *themself, theirself* prob survived in dial E beyond the 16C, and from those forms CE derived *demself, desself*] **2.** *sg* Himself/herself. *Anybody who t[h]ink desself too great-up to come in my house can stay [u]pon de road an[d] wait for me to vote for dem*—Guyn □ See also THEMSELF, THEIRSELF, THEYSELF.

de·pot [dɪpo·] *n* **1.** (Bdos, Guyn) A (usu small) shop selling one kind of item at retail; hence FURNITURE DEPOT, MEAT DEPOT, etc. [By shift in sense of 'store-house' to 'selling place'. See *OED* depot 4.] **2.** (Guyn) ‖POLICE DEPOT (Guyn)

de·ter·ma ['dɪtʌrmə] *n* (Guyn) [Timber Ind] A tall tapering forest-tree yielding a pinkish timber; it is highly resistant to insects, and is used for building; *Ocotea rubra* (*Lauraceae*).

Dev·il *n* (CarA) A CARNIVAL, JUNKANOO or MASQUERADE figure, a man wearing a grotesque mask, frightening costume (or in some cases all-over black) with a tail, and carrying a fork as he dances with frightening gestures at the head of a BAND.

dev·il-fish* *n* 1. (Guyn) The giant Atlantic ray, an enormous black bat-like creature that can weigh over 1000 lbs; it can leap several feet out of the water; *Manta birostris* (*Ceratoptera vampyrus*). [From its double snout resembling devil's horns, and from its frightening appearance and behaviour] □ Also called *sea-bat* in some fishing literature. 2. (Baha) An octopus.

dev·il-grass (dev·il's grass) /1'12/ *n* (*phr*) (Bdos, Guyn, Trin) ‖ BAHAMA GRASS (CarA) **a.** *The picture then showed the pipe almost completely surrounded by devil grass most of which was about 3 ft high. At the time, this caused the area to be a breeding ground for mosquitoes.*—AdN (74.10.28, p.6) **b.** *Devil's Grass and Zoysia are notoriously intrusive and where they are nearby great care will be needed to keep them at bay.*—AdN (76.02.08, p.5)

dev·il('s) horse·whip *n phr* (Jmca) ‖ MAN-BETTER-MAN (Dmca, etc)

dev·il's tree *n phr* (Bdos) ‖ BEAN-TREE (Bdos) [Prob from association of blood-red 'beads' or 'beans' shed at Lent. See ‖ *Lent-tree*]

dev·il's trum·pet *n phr* (Jmca) ‖ THORN-APPLE (Bdos, etc) [From the claw-like appearance of petals that open at night, the pungent smell and ugly leaves]

dev·il-whip *n* (Guyn) ‖ MAN-BETTER-MAN (Dmca, etc)

dew-fish *n* (Guyn) See JEW-FISH

dew-plum *n* (CayI) See JEW-PLUM

dey¹ (deh¹) [de~dɛ] *pron* (CarA) [*Cr*] ‖ *duh* (Bdos) 1. They. *De government giving dem good road and cutting all de grass dey can' find to keep de place tidy.*—CrU (74.03.09, Cocky & Stocky) 2. Their. *... wastin' dey time an' dey car gas each week.*—WBS:9 3. *in sg function* [*AF*] He/she *The last body dat been in dere, is dey t[h]ief it*—(Guyn) [< SE *they, their* by [ð > d] shift and levelling of diphthong] □ A spelling commonly used in folk narrative dialogue. Cp DEM¹

dey² *def art* (USVI) [*Cr*] See DE¹ *Wake up! ... meh son it have somebody outside in dey yard. I hear dem walkin aroun outside shufflin in dey bush.*—Aaw.I.2, p.23 □ This spelling represents a rarer *CarA* folk pronunc.

dey³ *adv* (CarA) See DE²

dey⁴ *stative vb* (CarA) See DE³

dey⁵ *pre-vbl particle* (StKt) See DE⁴ □ This spelling represents a rarer CarA folk pronunc.

de·ya *n* (Guyn, Trin) See DIYA

dey·self *refl pron* (CarA) [*Cr*] See DEMSELF; THEIRSELF

dhal (dhol(l)) *n* (Guyn, Trin) [Indic] See DAAL

dhan [da·n] *n* (Guyn, Trin) [Indic] ‖ *paddy* (Guyn) Unmilled rice still in the brown husk, used as poultry feed. [Bhoj < Hin *dhaan* 'unhusked rice'] □ This is the normal name in *Trin*. See PADDY.

dho·ti [dhoti~doti] *n* (Guyn, Trin) [Indic] ‖ *capra* 1. (Trin) An EAST INDIAN man's white loin-cloth consisting of a single piece of cloth wrapped around the waist, folded over and passed loosely between the legs. [Hin *dhotii* 'loin cloth']

diab·lesse (Dmca, etc) See DJABLÈS

dick·ie *n* (Gren, StVn) The boot or trunk of a car. [By shift of sense of *OED dicky* sb 9. b. 'a seat at the back of a carriage for servants, etc'. In present BrE one sense (*COD*) 8 is an 'extra folding seat at the back of a vehicle']

dicks *n pl* (StVn) [*AF—Joc*] PHRASES cut/talk **dicks** *vb phr* To speak with such careful pronunc as to sound affected; [Derog] to speak with a noticeably English accent in order to impress people. [Prob < *dig*, as joc abbr of 'dignified' + devoicing of final /g > k/ + *Joc* /-s/ as in CUT STYLES]

dick·ty (dic·ty) [dɪkti] *adj* (Antg, Baha) [*IF*] [Usu of women] Elegantly dressed; [Derog] proud and haughty looking; [of a hairstyle] glamorous and showy. [Prob < (SE) *dignity* with reduction and devoicing of intervocalic consonant cluster [dɪgnəti > dɪgnti > dɪkti]]

did¹ *aux vb, unstressed pa.t. marker* (CarA) [*AF—Cr*] 1. [Indicating simple pa.t. of the immediately following base vb] **a.** *Sophie did need some work doing round the house, and to tell the truth she was kinda tired axing Junior.* (= needed).—NaG (78.06.01, Satirically Speaking) **b.** *'Lawd God, Mr Lattimer, sah,' he said, 'I t'ink I did know it was your car. What you doin[g] down here to-day, sah?'* (= knew).—HVUW:14 **c.** *Dat is de girl mother did really want him to marry.* (= wanted).—(Guyn) 2. [Indicating pa.t. but incorporating imperfective aspect in the immediately following base vb] *Dat time he did work at Sprostons.* (= used to work; was working).—(Guyn) [Part of a later stage of Anglophone DECREOLIZATION, prob infl by liturgical usage as in 'The serpent beguiled me and I did eat'. This usage also persisted in SW E dialects into the 19C (see *OED do* 25. a.) and such sources perh provided added and more powerful infl in developing CE. The structure at sense 2., older and now rarer, developed into that of DID². See next] □ Not to be confused with stressed SE *did* pa.t. of emphatic *do*, as in '*You did eat one, didn't you!*'

did² *aux vb, unstressed imperf t. marker* (CarA) [*AF—Cr*] [Followed by *-ing* form of vb] **1.** [SE aux] Was; were. **a.** *The corpse sat up and chuckled maliciously. 'I know I did going catch wunnah,' it croaked.*—GR:30 (F. Squires) **b.** *Dey did try to dismiss her but dey didn['t] know who dey did playin[g] wid.*—(Guyn) **2.** [SE perf progressive aux] Has/have been. *Nancy an' me did saving them up a long time now.*—BaW:34 [See prec]

did³ *linking vb* (Bdos, Gren) [*Cr*] **1.** [In all functions of pa.t. of vb *to be*] Was; were. **a.** *Me dear, it look like jus' yesterday did Chrismus an' now is March a'ready.*—WeN (53.03.09, Annie & Josephine) **b.** *Sgt Holder said that the accused told him: 'Officer, I did drunk ... give me a chance.'*—AdN (74.10.22, p.1) **c.** *Well, Ness, I en got to tell you how de people dat did at de hearin' start whisperin'.*—NaT (80.02.22, p.7, Lickmout' Lou) [Perh from an early stage in DECREOLIZATION, but this function of *did* persists widely in *Bdos* folk speech, perh influencing DID⁴. See next] **2.** *PHRASE* **2.1 had did to (do sth)** *vb phr* (Bdos) [*Cr*] ‖ HAD WAS TO (DO STH) (CarA) *I couldn't fin' no meat fuh de goat, an' I had did to go all de way down Jack-me-Box Gully to look fuh some.*—Bdos (Ms, Play, 1976)

did⁴ *aux vb, pa. perf. tense marker* (CarA) [*X*] [Indicating that the action of the immediately following vb has or had taken place at some time in the past. Frequently in the neg *didn't*] **1.** Has/ have (+ pa. part. of vb). **a.** *Your face seems familiar. Did we meet before?* (= Have we met?). —(Antg) **b.** *'I also used to get a woman who goes away to bring in the shoes for me but she didn't go away recently,' the watchman said.* (= Hasn't gone).—AdV (88.03.26, p.1) **2.** Had (+ pa. part. of vb). **a.** *After he had admitted that he did go into her yard at that time, the case collapsed.* (= Had gone).—Guyn (Ms) **b.** *Quinby said that he did not know the teacher's name. He did not see him before that day.* (= Had not seen).—AdN (74.06.13, p.1) □ These uses of *did* may be permitted in AmE but not in BrE.

did·dle·doo ['dɪdldu] *n* (ECar) [*X*] See DILDO 2. [< DILDO, with insertion of /-d-/ by epenthesis]

die *vb intr PHRASES* **1. almost die laughing; nearly die laughing** *vb phrs* (CarA) *When I saw how she was dressed, carrying a rolled umbrella too, man I almost died laughing.*—(Guyn) See LAUGH Phrs; also DEAD² **2. die bad** *vb phr* (CarA) [*IF*] To die displaying great fear of death.

dif·fer·ent to *prep phr* (Bdos) [*X*] Except for. *The children are well, thanks, different to the cold.*—(Bdos)

dig *vb tr PHRASES* **1. dig horrors** *vb phr* (ECar) [*AF—Joc*] To be very troubled and uneasy in mind; to live in unhappy or unsatisfactory conditions. *To quote the Mighty Sparrow, 'We digging horrors'. The fact of the matter is that mass 'Starvation ain't far'. As a people we just 'can't take it no more'.*—NeJ (75.02.14, p.5) **2. dig out sb's eye** *vb phr* (Tbgo, Trin) [*AF*] ‖ JOOK OUT SB'S EYE (CarA) *Playing to many rounds of applause from his home crowd, he showed how the big oil corporations were 'diggin' out we eye.*—TaP (75.11.02, p.10)

dig·ging *n* **1.** (Jmca) ‖ LEND-HAND (Tbgo) *On Saturday, dem have digging or Saturday morning crop. Di odder district people dem come in to help. We buy bread and salt beef and mix wash and drink wid it. Di man dem dig di hole and di woman dem plant di corn or yam head or potato slip.*—SSLG:28 **2.** (Guyn) A site in the interior of Guyana where a prospector is digging for gold or diamonds. [Often in pl **diggings**]. *I have known the balata-bleeders, and woodcutters as well as coal-burners adopting the same methods of safeguarding and preserving their ration of pork—but many of these also worked in the 'diggings', gold and diamond fields.*—BGPS:43

dil·do ['dɪldo] *n* **1.** (CarA) ‖ *(columnar) cactus* (Bdos) ‖ *pipe-organ cactus* (ViIs) 'An erect leafless, rather stout cactus, sometimes 30 ft with columnar stem', and similar branches well spaced, all pointing upwards, each 'about 2 to 4 ins in diameter with seven to ten blunt ribs' lined with sharp, inch-long spines and occasionally bearing purple flowers and fruit—*PTT*:96; *Cephalocereus moritzianus* or *C. royenii* or *C. swartzii* (*Cactaceae*). **2.** (ECar) ‖ *diddledoo n* (ECar)) [*X*] Name loosely applied to varieties of cacti. [*OED dildo²* *Obs* 'a tree or shrub of the genus *Cereus*' + cits from 1696; therefore the name prob survives from EE use in the CarA]

dil·ly (dil·lie) *n* (Baha, TkCa) ‖ SAPODILLA (CarA) [A diminutive of *sapodilla*] □ Now the normal usage.

Di·manche Gras [dimãʃ gra·] *n phr* (Tbgo, Trin) The great festivities promoted to climax the CARNIVAL season on the last Sunday night before the beginning of Lent, including the CALYPSO KING competition, the King and Queen of Carnival costume competitions, etc. [Fr (= 'Meat Sunday') the last Sunday on wh orthodox Christians are permitted to eat meat before the restrictions of Lent, and hence the climax to a week-end of unrestricted enjoyment]

din·ner *n* **1.** (CarA) The third and (usu) largest meal of the day (in former times and still in some rural areas, not necessarily a night meal). **2.** *PHRASES* **2.1 cat eat your dinner** *id phr* (Guyn) [*AF—Joc*] See CAT Phr **2.2 (expect) tea, breakfast and dinner** *id phr* (Guyn) (To expect to have) all your needs provided as sb else's responsibility; (to BUM) food and shelter.

dip *vb* (CarA) [*AF/IF—Derog*] **1.** To enter (into a conversation, argument or quarrel) without being expected or invited to do so. *He was the first to ask, 'Goin' to hitch up an' dip into big-man talk when you get to Kingston, too?'*—SD:11 [Cp *OED dip* 7. *fig* 'to immerse, involve, implicate (in any affair esp of an undesirable kind)'. However *OED* notes this usage is 'chiefly in passive' and *Obs* + cits–'1798] **2.** PHRASE **2.1 dip your mouth/nose in (sb's) business** *vb phr* (CarA) [*AF—Derog*] To interfere presumptuously in a dispute. *According to Thompson, Vassell replied: 'How you so presumptious and bright? Imagine, me talking to me baby mother and you dip you mouth in it.'*—DaG (70.03.24, p.4)

dip-and-fall-back; **dip-and-run-down** *n* (Jmca) ‖ *run-down* (CayI, Jmca) A meal of mackerel or SALTFISH boiled down in COCONUT-MILK until this is of an oily, grey, custard-like consistency, into wh are dipped separately boiled root-vegetables, dumplings, or roasted bread-fruit. [From the dripping back or running down (the hand) of the oily sauce when it is dipped into] □ See *DJE* for many other *Jmca* folk names of this meal. Cp also SANCOCHE (*Trin*).

Dip·vali *n* (Guyn, Trin) See DIVALI

di·rect [dairɛk(t)] (CarA) [*X*] **1.** *adj* [Used in several contexts as a general indicator of definiteness] Definite; exact; identical; certain; specific, etc. **a.** *Bwoy, I must be a direct boogs, but I seem to think that kind of setting could excite more people's imagination than what I saw the other night.*—StA(JA) (72.11.18, p.10, Partyline) **b.** *This is the direct cutlass I saw him with.*—Tbgo (CR, 76.04.22) **c.** *I know a direct place where you can buy rum on Sundays.*—(Guyn) [By shift of sense. Cp *OED direct* a. 5. 'straightforward' (also *Obs*) 'positive, absolute'] **2.** *adv* [Similarly used] Definitely; exactly; etc. *It wasn['t] direc[t] a party, only a few friends to dance a little.*—(Bdos)

di·rect·ly [dairɛkli] *adv* (Antg) [*X*] Obviously; definitely. *You look direc[t]ly different with that hairstyle.*—(Antg)

dirt-box *n* (Belz) A wooden garbage box, with a lid and door, often built on to the fence of a dwelling-house. *... but no provision is made in the plan for a dirt box to suit the size of the family which will use the building. Result: There are hundreds and hundreds of houses being built and perhaps many thousands now built which have no planned place for garbage.*—ReP (79.11.25, p.2) □ Cp STUFF-BIN (*Bdos*).

dirt-pan *n* (Jmca) ‖ STUFF-BIN (Bdos) [*Dirt* 'garbage' + PAN *Jmca*]

dirt-truck *n* (Belz) A garbage-collecting truck. [Cp *DAE dirt cart* 'a rubbish cart']

dirt·y¹ [dʌrti] *n* (Guyn) [*AF/IF*] Human or animal filth; faeces. *The place smell like somebody step in dog dirty and bring it in the house.*—(Guyn)

[By functional adj > n shift of SE *dirty*, and often used as the only acceptable euphemism for E *shit*. Prob also infl by false refinement of DUTTY¹ 3.]

dirt·y² [dʌrti] *vb* (Guyn) [*AF/IF*] To ease the bowels; to defecate. [By functional n > vb shift of DIRTY¹; also prob a false refinement of DUTTY³] □ This is the only euphemism available to many *Guyn* for *shit* vb.

dis [dɪs] *pron, demonstr adj* (CarA) [*IF*] This. [By regular CarA Cr [ð > d] shift] □ A pronunc widely heard throughout the *CarA* even among educated speakers and commonly so represented in written narrative dialogue.

dis·course¹ [dɪsˈkoːs] *n* (Belz, Guyn) An informative discussion or an enlightening exchange of gossip. *The village standpipe, though a focal point for community discourse, was invariably used to fill open utensils which collected impurities during transportation or during storage in the home.*—Guyn (Ms) [Cp *OED discourse* sb 3. 'talk, conversation'—*arch*] □ More likely among rural and prob older speakers. ModE *discourse* is largely restricted to literary contexts.

dis·course² **1.** *vb intr* (Belz, Guyn, Mrat) To converse intelligently; to speak carefully on a serious subject. *This is not an indication that very few people can discourse in English, for many people can when they consider the occasion warrants it.*—Mrat (Ms, 1966) [As *OED discourse* v 3., though this usage is hardly current in ModE. Also *EDD discourse* 3. v 'to talk to, hold conversation with' + cit from IrE, 1848. See sense 2.] **2.** *vb tr* (StVn) To present for appreciative listening (including music). *Refreshments were then served, during which the Royal St Vincent Police Band discoursed some lively airs.*—ViN (73.02.10, p.1)

Dis·cov·er·y Day *n phr* (CarA) The day (recognized as a national holiday in some islands) commemorating the date of Christopher Columbus's first sighting of that island. □ In some islands the name **Discovery Day** has been replaced by another, marking some other kind of national observance on the same date (ex *Dmca, StLu, StVn*). See INDEPENDENCE DAY, NATIONAL DAY.

dis·gust; **dis.gus.ted** [ˈdɪsgʌs] *adj* [*X*] Fed up with or tired of a situation; feeling frustrated. **a.** *I read so much till I get disgus'.*—(BrVi) **b.** *He was disgusted after failing twice so he didn't sit again.*—Bdos (Ms) [< SE *disgusted* with characteristic Cr use of base vb as pa.t. form, and functional vb > adj shift. For the sense here cp *OED disgust* v 4. 'to cause such aversion as to deter a person from a proposed purpose']

dis·gus·ting *adj* (CarA) [*IF*] ‖ *botheration* (CarA) [*AF*] [Esp of children] Troublesome; restless and irritating in be-haviour; [of things or situations] generally annoying or frustrating.

a. *You know you disgusting! Why you don't sit down and behave?*—(Bdos) **b.** *That car is too disgusting! This is the fourth time it's left me on the road.*—(Trin)

dis·tance *n* PHRASE **not know your distance** *vb phr* (Nevs) [*IF*] ‖ GET BESIDE YOURSELF (CarA) See BESIDE Phr 2.1 [Cp SE *not know your place* + *keep your distance*]

Dis·trict Com·mis·sion·er *n phr* (Belz, Guyn) [Hist] The chief government executive and administrative officer responsible for an area remote from the capital and formally identified as a 'District'. (See cit). *Each of the other District Commissioners is, in addition to his administrative duties, District Magistrate, Justice of the Peace, District Coroner, Sub-Treasurer, Sub-Collector of Customs, Registering Officer (franchise), District Postmaster, District Registrar, and Film Censor. He also supervises the work of the Police (for which purpose he ranks as a Commissionered Officer), Prison, Public Works, Telephone and Telegraph and other departments in his District. He has the power to perform civil marriages. Until 1956 he was also Chairman of the Town Boards in his District.*—ABSBH:13 □ Often abbr as *D.C.*. Cp also CUSTOS (*Jmca*).

di·té·pé·yi* (**di·tay-pay·ee**) *n* [dite-pei] (Dmca, Gren, StLu, Tbgo, Trin) ‖ *goatweed* (Jmca) ‖ *wild-tea* (Guyn) An erect, roadside bush growing to about 4 ft in height with longish, toothed leaves and little, pinkish-white flowers; the bush is widely used to make BUSH-TEA for colds and for 'cleaning the blood and the skin'; *Capraria biflora* (*Scrophulariaceae*). [Fr Cr < Fr *du thé* (*du*) *pays* 'country tea']

Di·va·li (**De·va·li, Dip·va·li, Di·wa·li**) [di 'va·li] *n* (Guyn, Trin) [Indic] ‖ *Deepavali* (Guyn, Trin) The annual Hindu festival of lights beginning with the appearance of the October/November new moon, and honouring Lakshmi, the Hindu goddess of light, by the lighting of DIYAS lining driveways, fences, stairways, windows, etc, symbolizing the triumph of light over darkness, Good over Evil. [Bhoj shortened form of Hin DEEPAVALI. See etym note there]

dix·ie (**dix·y**) *adv* (Bdos) [*AF*] PHRASES **1. behave/get on dixie** *vb phr* (Bdos) [*AF*] To quarrel noisily with (sb); to 'raise hell'. *When she find out the daughter was already four months pregnant, I tell you she get on real dixie.*—(Bdos) **2. do dixie** *vb phr* (Bdos) [*AF*—*Joc*] To make an exciting and successful show (of whatever is being done); to make things go the way you want them to. *The business must be doing well because I see they got car and lawn-mower and doing dixie where they live.*—(Bdos) [A ref, with shift of sense, to Amer Dixieland jazz music wh inspired excesses in ballroom dancing in the 1930s]

di·ya (**de·ya**) [di·ya] *n* (Guyn, Trin) A lamp in the form of a small deep clay saucer filled with oil or ghee and having a cotton wick; hundreds

of them are lit for the display of light in the Hindu festival of DIVALI. [Hin *diyaa* 'lamp'] □ Pl *diyas/deyas*, the latter being a spelling commonly used.

djab-djab (**jab-jab**) [Jab-Jab] *n* **1.** (Dmca, Gren, StLu, Tbgo, Trin) A traditional costumed figure of CARNIVAL, portraying the devil. (See cit). *And there were the jab-jabs, men in jester costumes, their caps and shoes filled with tinkling bells, cracking long whips in the streets, with which they lashed each other with full force, proclaiming in this display that they could receive the hardest blow without flinching at its coming, while feeling what, at its landing, must have been burning pain.*—LDCD:121 [Fr Cr < Fr *diable* 'devil' by affrication of /dy-/ and with Cr reduplication] **2.** PHRASE **2.1 play djab-djab** *vb phr* (Gren, Trin) To be one of a costumed group of CARNIVAL devils whipping each other. *One year we had all four played mas'—Toddan and Mikey played djab'djab' and Mikey carried Toddan on his shoulders, letting him down when they stopped to do their accosting act.*—HCCM:124

djab·lès (**diab·lesse, jab·lesse**) [JablƐs] *n* (Dmca, StKt, StLu, Tbgo, Trin) ‖ *adjablès* (Dmca) ‖ *ladjablès* (Creu, Gren, StLu, Tbgo, Trin) A legendary evil creature, appearing usu on a lonely road in moonlight, assuming at first the form of a very pretty young woman, finely dressed, in order to lure a man into a wooded or bushy place before revealing herself as an old crone with cloven hoofs, who will cause the man to go mad or die. [Fr Cr < Fr *diablesse* 'she-devil']

djab-mo·la·si (**jab-mo·las·si**) [Jab-molasi] *n* (Trin) A traditional CARNIVAL figure portraying the devil, his costume comprising short pants, tail, horns, chains, pitch-fork, and skin greased with molasses or dirty motor-oil wh he threatens to rub on spectators unless they give him money. [Fr Cr < Fr *diable* 'devil' + E *molasses*]

dja(n)·mèt¹ (**ja·met(te)**) ['JamƐt ~ 'JãmƐt] *n* (Dmca, StLu, Tbgo, Trin) [*AF*—*Derog*] ‖ *BAD-WOMAN* (ECar) *'Oh God, Elaine,' he told her holding his hands over his ears, 'me head too hot tonight to take you on.' / 'Eh, is I have it hot?' she asked him, 'or is the jamette 'oman you friending with? The whabeen cow whose husband yer horning?'*—JJM:171 [Fr Cr, said to be < Fr *diamètre*, 'diameter', in the sense of a line dividing the upper from the lower half of the social circle. Note cit at adj use next, but the term is strongly reparded as ref to a woman, and may instead perh be a Fr Cr corruption of *FVA* 19C Fr *jeannette* 'a double-barrelled harlot'] **2.** [By extension] ‖ YARD-WOMAN (Guyn) □ The spelling *jamette* is the one commonly found.

dja(n)·mèt² (**jam·ette**) ['JamƐt] *adj* (Dmca, StLu, Tbgo, Trin) [Of people in general] Of a low and disreputable class; belonging to the slums. *The members of this group rejected the norms of the society in their way of life. They were the reverse of the upper-class elite and the ethos of*

this jamette sub-culture reflected the social con-
ditions under which they lived. They had a burning
desire to move towards respectability as it was
defined way up above their social level.—Jfi: III.2,
p.193 [By functional n > adj shift of DJA(N)MÈT¹]

djè [Jɛ] *n* (Gren) [*AF*] **1.** A row; cantankerous
behaviour. [Fr Cr < Fr guerre 'war' by affrication
of /g-/] **2.** PHRASE **2.1 beat a djè** See BEAT Phr
4.1

djèp (gep, jep) [Jɛp] *n* (Dmca, StLu, Trin)
‖ JACK-SPANIARD (ECar) [Fr Cr < Fr *guèpe* 'wasp'
+ palatalization /g > dj/]

djou·boul (ju.boule) [ˈjuˑbuˑl] *n* (StLu) ‖ BLU-
GGO (Belz, etc) [Fr Cr name, mostly rural in
StLu]

djou·kou·too *pron, adj* (Gren) See JOUKOUTOO

do¹ *vb* [Note: DID, DOES, DON'T are treated as
separate entries] **1.** *vb tr* (CarA) [*AF/IF*] [A
convenient function-word in loose general use]
To be engaged in or be responsible for (some
kind of activity). **a.** *Some nite back, the polis doing*
patrol (an yet some people say dey no doing nuttin)
wen dey see a vehicle stop by a banana field.—ToR
(75.02.07, p.3) **b.** *Who is doing the funeral?* (*i.e.*
which undertaker, etc).—(Bdos) **2.** *vb tr* (CarA)
[*IF/AF*] **(i)** To cheat or trick (sb); to harm or
hurt (sb). **(ii)** [*IF*] To hurt sb's feelings (by
doing sth deliberately against the person's interest); (SE) to do (sth hurtful) to (sb). *I really*
love this man and would try anything to turn his
mind from this girl in spite of all the things he did
me.—NaT (77.06.26, p.30, Dear Christine) **(iii)**
[*AF*] ‖ PUT (SB) SO (CarA) See PUT Phr 18 To
cause permanent harm to sb's mind by witchcraft. **a.** *She do the man so he would marry*
her.—(Guyn) **b.** *You see how he walkin[g] about*
crazy singin[g] to heself? Dey do him so because
he put dey fader in jail.—(Gren) □ Only the
unchanged base form *do* seems to occur in this
usage, but other forms of the vb occur in many
related Phrs. **3.** PHRASES **3.1 do sb (like) this/**
that *vb phr* (ECar) [*AF/IF*] To mistreat (sb); to
be unfair to (sb). **a.** *She said 'Boy you mean you*
would really do me this? I am your mother!'—Mrat
(Ms) **b.** *My brother ... got between us and he said,*
'Why you doing my sister like that?'—Tbgo (CR,
77.11.22) **3.1.1 do (sb) so/something** *vb phr*
(ECar) [*AF/IF*] **(i)** ‖ PUT (SB) SO (CarA) See PUT
Phr 18 **(ii)** To interfere with (sb); to bother (sb).
Teacher I don't know if somebody do him something,
but I didn't do him anything.—(Bdos) **(iii)** To be
unfair to (sb); to cheat (sb). *I'm not going to let*
them do me so this time!—(Mrat) [Prob a calque
from W Afr langs. Cp Yoruba *ẹnikan ni o ṣe ẹ*
bẹẹ (*somebody did you like that*) 'somebody
made you sick by means of witchcraft' (*pers*
info, K. Ọmọtọṣọ)] **3.1.2 Wha[t] do you/him,**
(etc)? *id phr* (CarA) [*AF—Cr*] **(i)** What is wrong
with you/him, (etc)? Why are you behaving like
this? **(ii)** What is your sickness/ailment/trouble,
etc? **4.** [*Aux to imperative vb tr, as initial or*
terminal intensifier tag] (CarA) [*IF*] Please, I beg

you! **a.** *The song 'Do Mr Charlie do, don't beat*
me Mr Charlie, do!' was sung. This portrayed
victims of the Treadmill pleading with the overseer
not to beat them.—SCO:6 **b.** *Do, Massah God,*
make him keep his promise.—PCOS:28 [As *OED*
do 30. **b.** 'For emphasis, do is also added to the
main imperative'. However the CE usage is more
intensely emotive. This may have an EE positional source. Cp Iago's cynical usage in (*Shak*)
Othello II.1.1.167: *Ay, smile upon her, do*] **5.** *vb*
tr/intr (CarA) [*IF*] [Accompanied by a demonstrating gesture, hence phrs with or without
obj of vb.] PHRASES **5.1 do** (some part of the body)
so/like this/like that To make a particular kind
of movement (as demonstrated). **a.** *Since I fell*
down I cannot do my right arm so.—(StVn) **b.**
Demonstrating as he spoke Atkins said he did like
'this' with the knife.—AdN (72.11.01, p.1) **6.** [*In*
passive function] (CarA) [*AF*] Is/was/has been,
etc done. *She make the dress all pucker up at the*
wais[t] and I ain[t] like how it do—(Guyn) **7.** *vb*
intr (Bdos, Guyn) [*IF*] To behave (usu in some
unpleasant way). *I know how she can do, you*
know, when the craziness gets in her head.—(Bdos)
8. PHRASES **8.1 all you do** *id phr* (CarA) [*AF/*
IF] [Cautioning] Whatever you (may) have in
mind. *All you do, remember the kind of man*
you dealing with, yeh!—(Gren) **8.2 and do not**
(+**vb**) *dummy neg element* (Bdos) [*X*] And not
See DON'T 2. *I would like to see the Prime Minister*
go to bed and do not wake up from sleeping.—Bdos
(Hd, 75.03.17, p.4684) **8.3 do a business for**
(sb) *vb phr* (Guyn) To manage to bring serious
trouble upon (sb); to do spiteful and great harm
to (sb). **8.4 do and do (until sth happens)** *vb*
phr (Bdos, Guyn, Trin) [*IF*] To persist in or
keep repeating some stupid spiteful act (until
some unhappy result occurs). *Child, put down*
that mug! You will do and do until you break
it.—(Trin) **8.5 do back (sth to sb); do (sth)**
back to (sb) *vb phr* (CarA) [*AF*] To do a spiteful
act (to sb) in retaliation for the same offence
done to you. *Teacher she mess up my dress and I*
only do it back to her.—(Guyn) See BACK⁴ 2(i)
8.6 do bad *vb phr* (CarA) [*IF*] ‖ *do dixie* (Bdos)
(i) To behave (whether in quarrelling or dancing)
in a completely unrestrained manner. **a.** ...
people's vouchers have been held up for more than
a year in some cases. People threatened to shoot
and do bad if they did not get their money. —Bdos
(Hd, 75.02.04, p.4525) **b.** *Photographer Theo*
Greaves caught this traditional Barbadian tuck
band, complete with dancer (at right) 'doing bad'
along Eagle Hall, St Michael.—AdN (77.10.04,
p.1) **(ii)** ‖ *do bad things* (Guyn) [*IF*] [Esp of a
woman] To indulge yourself in many different
sexual relationships. **8.7 do cold with (sb)** *vb*
phr (Gren) [*AF*] To be not on speaking terms
with (sb). *Wha[t] happen you and Anita have*
noise? A fin[d] all you doing col[d] wid one another
dese days.—(Gren) **8.8 do dixie** *vb phr* (Bdos)
[*AF—Joc*] See DIXIE Phr 2. **8.9 do for (sb)** *vb*
phr **(i)** (CarA) [*AF*] To bring personal harm to
(sb); to make much trouble for (sb). *When they*
fell out as neighbours she threatened to do for
them, so they have always been suspicious of her

movements—(Gren) [< do (a bad business, sometimes involving witchcraft) for (sb)] □ Usu distinguished from sense (ii) by strong stress and higher pitch on *do*. **(ii)** (Bdos, Guyn) [*IF*] [Of a woman] To perform needed domestic services for (a bachelor, widower or old person). *He didn't marry again after the wife died, but just got this lady to do for him and the child every day*)—(Bdos) □ The tenses of this usage are almost limited to the pres, the continuous, and the habituative (*is/was doing, used to do*). **8.10 do for more** *vb phr* (Baha, Guyn) [*IF*] To be quite unreasonable (in expectations, demands or treatment of sb). *Brer Rabbie said to Brer Bookie's cousin, 'Man, I tired a Brer Bookie making a fool outa me! Jes wait till I ketch him, I goin' put an en' ta him once an fer all! Das ya cuz fer true but he does do fer more!'*—TSOR:10 [A prob calque from W Afr langs. Cp Yoruba *O ṣe aṣeju* (*you do over-do*) 'you have exceeded your limit'—(K. Ọmọtọṣọ). Cp also next; also DO³ Phr 3.2] **8.10.1 do for the more** *vb phr* (Bdos) [*AF/IF*] To behave worse than before. *Man, when the police come, she do for the more.*—(Bdos) [See prec] **8.11 do quick** *vb phr* (Tbgo, Trin) [*IF*] To make haste; to hurry up, be quick about it. *'Do quick, nuh' she said. 'Look the bus coming, I don't want to miss it.'*—Tbgo (Ms) **8.12 do rudeness** *vb phr* (Baha, etc) [*AF*] See RUDENESS Phr 2.1 **8.13 do (sb) so; do (sb) something** *vb phr* (CarA) [*AF/IF*] See at 3.1.1 above **8.14 do a thing; do their thing** *vb phr* (Jmca) [*AF—Joc*] To get married. *Mr Mystic ... that is Richard Thelwell, and Hope Robb, the teevee announcer with those big glasses and the velvety voice, did a thing the other day, to become Mr and Mrs team.*—WeG (73.07.18, p.11, Partyline) □ Usu said of popular entertainers, and prob a reflection of Am pop lang. **8.15 do things up brown** *vb phr* (Baha) [*AF*] To do things thoroughly; to make a great success of what you do. *Man he cum back here wid wun paper reach from here t' Barbados full o' cruise ship an' hotel 'greemun an' ting. He does do tings up brown. Man dat feller do more fer d' Bahamas an' talk less 'bout it dan enybuddy else in dis town.*—DSJS:86 [Prob a metaph from the baking of bread] **8.16 do to your mind** *vb phr* (Guyn) [*AF*] ‖FOLLOW YOUR MIND (CarA) *I can't tell you whether to go or not. Do to your mind.*—(Guyn) **8.17 do up** *vb phr* **(i)** (Bdos, Gren, Guyn) [*IF*] To repair and renovate (a house); to refurbish and decorate (a place, a piece of furniture, etc). **(ii)** (Bdos, Guyn, USVI) [*AF*] To launder (clothes). **8.18 do well** *vb phr* (CarA) [*AF/IF*] To be inconsiderate (of others), thoughtless (of your own well being). (Usu in foll phr). **8.18.1 You do well!** *excl* (CarA) See ALL RIGHT² 2. **a.** *Your father can barely afford to pay for your books and clothes and you want to be vex because he can't send you to Trinidad with the school-team? I tell you! You do well!* —(Guyn) **b.** *You do well to let John cuss you like that and get away with it.* —(Belz) [Prob a calque or notional transfer from W Afr langs. Cp Yoruba *O dara bẹ̀* ('It is good that way') often used sarcastically to mean 'You are being very unfair'— (pers info, K. Ọmọtọṣọ)] **8.19 do with**

(sb) *vb phr* (Gren) To get on well with (sb); to be on good terms with (sb). *Since she say me son t[h]ief she fowl, A ain[t] doin[g] wid her again.*— (Gren) **8.20 do without** *vb phr* (Guyn, Nevs) [*IF*] ‖LEAVE YOURSELF UNDONE (Guyn) *You know how many days I do without, so these children would have enough to eat?*—(Nevs) **8.21 do your own thing** *vb phr* (CarA) [*AF/IF*] **(i)** [*AF*] ‖**break away** (ECar) ‖*do your thing* (CarA) ‖*knock your own thing* (Belz) To enjoy yourself (esp in dancing) in a completely uninhibited manner. **(ii)** [*IF*] To refuse to consider or consult others; to be deliberately uncooperative. *Dr Williams advised ... that the territories could not possibly hope to achieve their declared national goals and objectives on the basis of each one doing his own thing.* —TrG (73.08.29, p.3) **(iii)** To make carefully considered personal decisions (usu with good results). *He wandered through a series of careers (amateur photography, salesmanship and gardening) before deciding to 'do his own thing' and become an itinerant wayside vendor.* —NaT (78.08.11, p.2) [This phr and the next, though their currency has much increased in CE in the 1970s prob from AmE infl, have *CarA* roots perh through a common notional transfer from W Afr langs. Cp Sran phr *Wie egi sani* 'we own thing'; also the ‖**break away** of sense 1.] **8.22 do your thing** *vb phr* (CarA) [*AF*] **(i)** ‖DO YOUR OWN THING (CarA) See PHR 8.21 (I) above *After the parade through Roadtown to the music of many bands, the procession reached the carnival village where judging took place on each troupe as they, in turn, 'did their thing' in the form of a dance.* —Zodiac (Dec:71) **(ii)** To do what is your proper duty. *In our area, the need 'to do our thing' is essential to the evolution of our society to meet the aspirations of our people. Circumstances and conditions in the countries which did our thing for us are forcing us into maturity.* —AdN (73.01.12, p.1)

do² *pre-vbl aspectual particle* [*Cr*] [dʌ~dū] **1.** (Bdos) ‖DA⁵ (Jmca) **a.** *Dat chair foot do come off* (*i.e. that chair-foot is coming off*).—(Bdos, 1979) **b.** *But customs change. Not so many years had elapsed before we were all singing 'Mammy, Me Belly Do Hurt Me,' and using a good many other words not previously permissible.*—AdN (72.03.23, p.19, Topic For Today) **2.** (StKt) [Expressing habituative aspect] ‖DOES (CarA) **a.** *A do be sick* (*i.e. I am often sick*).—(StKt) **b.** *He do be dere late* (*i.e. He is usually there until late*).—(StKt)

do³ [du] *n* **1.** (CarA) [*AF—Joc*] ‖*fete* (ECar) Any party, dance, or JUMP-UP (but usu of a private nature). *By 6 p.m. everybody jumping in de steelban to get de last do.*—Vip.1.1 [Cp *OED do* n sb¹ 2. b. 'something done in a set or formal manner; a performance' *dial* or *vulgar*] **2.** (CarA) [*AF/IF*] Any act or thing done. [Cp *OED do* n sb¹ 2. a. 'the action of doing or that wh is done' ... *rare* or *arch*.] □ Usage in this sense is rare except in foll phrs. **3.** PHRASE **3.1 do for do** *n phr* (CarA) [*AF*] Tit for tat; a bad act done in retaliation (esp in prov exp). *Do for do is not* *obeah.* 'Tit for tat is natural, not supernatural.'—Prov **3.2 overdo the do** *vb phr* (Guyn) [*AF/ IF*] To carry matters, demands or expectations beyond a reasonable point. *There's a standing rule that people not in the queue should not be sold. But this is Guyana, and nobody seems to mind much if there is an occasional breach of the rule, once they don't overdo the do.*—GyC (76.01.18, p.7) [See note at DO¹ Phr 8.10]

doc·tor-bird *n* **1.*** (ECar, Guyn) ‖ *colibri* (Dmca, Gren, Grns) ‖ *doctor-booby* (Bdos) Any of several varieties of (usu greenish) humming birds; *Trochilidae spp.* [Folk name, from its habit of visiting from flower to flower probing with its long (in some varieties also curved) beak, like a doctor calling on patients] **2.** (Jmca) ‖ *long-tail doctor-bird, streamer-tail* (Jmca) A hummingbird, of wh the male has a small brilliant metallic green body, black crested head, bright red bill, and two black trailing tail feathers about 6 ins long; *Trochilus polytmus* (*Trochilidae*), the National Bird of Jamaica; also STREAMER-TAIL or LONG-TAIL DOCTOR-BIRD. [As for sense 1, but said to be due also to the long tail feathers suggesting a doctor's stethoscope]

doc·tor-boo·by *n* (Bdos) ‖ DOCTOR-BIRD 1. (ECar, Guyn)

Doc·tor-Dy·ett [dɒktʌ dayɪt ~ daɪt] *n* (Mrat, StKt) ‖ OLD-MAID (BUSH) (CarA)

doc·tor-fish* *n* (CarA) One of three varieties (purplish-brown, dark grey, or blue) of a flat, roughly oval-shaped fish about 10 ins long, with a small mouth, very prominent gills, and two sharp, scalpel-like spikes on each side near its tail; it is of good food value; *Acanthurus chirurgus* or *A. bahianus* or *A. coeruleus.* [Prob because of the two lancet-like spikes near its tail. *ADF:33* gives alternative names as *surgeon fish, lancet-fish, medicos*]

doc·tor-fly *n* (Belz) A fruit-season insect resembling a large house-fly, with bright-green eyes, and a yellowish body with black patches; its sharp blood-sucking sting ('like an injection', hence the name) causes an infected swelling; *Tabanus spp.*

doc·tor-shop *n* (CarA) [*IF*] A pharmacy; a chemist's shop; a drug-store. *You still sick? The boy became aware of his mood. You been taking the medicine I get from the doctor-shop for you?* —SPOC:88 [Cp *EDD* Doctor 1. sb comb (2) *doctor's shop* 'a surgery'. The term must have first been spread by E people, being in wide early *CarA* currency] □ Still used by older folk mostly in rural areas, but generally replaced by *drug-store.*

dod·der ['dɒdʌ] *n* (Antg, BrVi, Jmca, Mrat, Trin) ‖ LOVE-VINE (CarA) [*OED dodder* 'common name of the genus *Cuscuta* (*Convolvulaceae*) comprising slender leafless plants like masses of twining threads, parasitic on many plants']

does [dʌz ~ dəz] *low-pitch aux vb marking habitual aspect* **1.** (CarA) [*X*] ‖ *is²* (Bdos, Guyn) [Indicating that the action or state indicated by the immediately following vb is regular, usual, or habitual] **a.** *The Cooks does not cover the food they leave it expose so flies can rest upon them. We does not get a balanced meal.*—TaP (75.11.30, p.11) **b.** *17-year old Joseph of Basseterre, who claimed 'I does work on sea' Tuesday this week ended up with twelve months in jail.*—LaS (78.05.20, p.12) **c.** *When the white man have he business, all of them does get together. But when we black people do something, the other set does get against them!*—SCP:41 (C. Sealy) [CarA Cr infl /doz/ ~ /-z/ functions in *ECar* Cr as a habituative aspect marker, though this feature is notably absent from *Jmca* Cr] □ Some speakers use a cliticized form /-z/ as in 'He's eat late on Saturdays' and this may be re-analysed (sometimes in writing) as 'He is eat late, etc'. See IS² **2.** PHRASES **2.1 does be** (+ **adj or vb-ing**) (ECar) [*X*] ‖ *be¹* 3 (CarA) [Intensifying a statement of habitual state or action] *Even at time o[f] the year when it does be dark early, he does still be gardenin[g] long after six o'clock.*—(Bdos) **2.2 does can't** (+ **vb**) (Bdos) [*X*] [Adding habituative intensity to a neg aux] *Dey does have so much bad behaviour dat some of the people dat pay does can['t] get in.*—(Bdos) **2.3 does don't** (+ **vb**) (Bdos) [*X*] [Cp prec] *And now I done writin' in dialect because dey does doan teach dat in school.*—NaT (73.12.30, p.4, Letter)

do-flick·y (doo·flick·y) [duflɪki] *n* (Bdos) **1.** (Loose name for) any gadget, tool, etc. **2.** [By extension] Any organized event during a folk-festival season such as CROP-OVER. [Sense 2. prob infl by BrE slang]

dog¹ *n* [Used in oaths and many *Derog* phrs expressing anger or symbolizing cheapness, low worth, misfortune, etc, the animal being held in contempt at the folk-level] PHRASES **1. Dog better than you!/dem!** *id phr* (Gren) [*AF—Joc*] You/they are worth nothing; you/they have become socially contemptible. *And now they don['t] have the money, look how they livin[g]! Dog better than dem!*—(Gren) **2. Dog bite me!/you!/dem!** *excl* (Bdos) [*AF—Derog*] Dammit! Damn you/them! etc. **3. Dog blind me!** *excl* (Bdos, Jmca) [*AF—Derog*] (May) God blind me! (I swear by) God! [Cp *OED* Dog 'deformation of the word *God,* used in profane oaths' *Obs*] **4. dog dead (the dog dead at your door/with you); your dog(s) dead** *id phrs* (ECar) [*AF—Joc*] ‖ CRAPAUD SMOKE YOUR PIPE (Ecar) See CRAPAUD Phr *The car burn up with the house, and they find out the insurance wasn't paid up, so now the dog really dead with them.*—(StKt) **5. knocking dog** *vbl adj phr* (Guyn) [*AF—Joc*] [Esp of seasonal foodstuff] Available in great abundance; be in such quantities as to make sellers beg for buyers. **6. not fit for dog to hear** *id phr* (Gren) [*AF—Derog*] [Of language] Terribly foul; disgracefully indecent.

dog[2] *adv* (*in attrib function*) (Tbgo, Trin) [*AF*] PHRASE **dog cheap** *adj phr* (For sale) at an unbelievably low price. [Prob infl by SE *dirt cheap* used in same sense]

dog[3] *vb intr* PHRASES **1. dog back** *vb phr* (Gren, StVn, Tbgo, Trin) [*AF—Derog*] To beg your way back into sb's friendship; to swallow your pride in begging for help from sb who has grossly insulted you. **2. dog behind (sb)** *vb phr* (Tbgo, Trin) [*AF—Derog*] To be servile to (sb) expecting to gain (sth); to seek favours from (sb) without self-respect.

dog-al·mond *n* (ViIs) ‖ ANGELIN (CarA)

dog-and-bone *n* (Gren, Guyn, Nevs) A children's game in wh two lines of players are drawn up facing each other at a distance (each player numbered to pair with one diagonally opposite) with some object in the middle, wh must be grabbed by a player, whose number is called, before his pair-number can get it, and without being touched by the latter before he gets back to his place in line.

dog-ba·na·na *n* (CayI) ‖ BUCK-BANANA (Guyn)

dog-hunt·er *n* (Bdos) ‖ BULL-PISTLE (CarA) □ Cp HUNTER (Mrat, etc)

dog·wood* *n* (Baha, Jmca, USVI) A tree growing 30 to 50 ft in height when mature, bearing clusters of small white flowers and winged pods; its hard timber is used for making cart-wheels and boat-frames, its crushed bark to stun fish or, decocted, as a cure for mange in dogs (possibly hence its name); *Piscidia piscipula* or *Erythrina p.* (*Papilionaceae*).

doh [do] *neg vb* (Dmca, Gren, Trin) [*AF—Cr*] See DON'T

do·ko *n* (Belz) ‖ BLUGGO (Belz, etc.) □ This name is current in urban *Belz*. See also ‖ *flagu plantain, waika banana*.

do·ku·nu (doo.koo.noo, duc.koo.noo) ['dɒkʊnʊ -u] /1'12/ *n* (Belz, Jmca) ‖ DUKUNA (Antg, etc) [< Twi *ɔ-dɔkono* 'boiled maizebread' *DAFL*, but see also DUKUNA] □ This name appears to be more widely used than other equivalents in *Jmca*. Variant spellings **duckono, dookoono** are also used.

dol·ly-pot *n* (Antg) ‖ BABY-POT (Guyn)

do·losse u·nit *n phr* (Bdos) A device weighing about 3 tons, cast in concrete in the shape of six massive arms joined at right angles to each other; the devices are heaped together and ranged to provide a breakwater in sea-shore conservation.

dom·in·a·tion-oil/-pow·der *n* (StKt) A similar oil/powder to COMMANDING-OIL/-POWDER offered by an obeahman to enable his client to control a spouse, a lover or a desired partner.

Do·min·i·can [dɒmɪn'ikən] /112'1/ *adj, n* (CarA) (A person or thing) native or belonging to (the WINDWARD ISLAND State of) Dominica in the Lesser Antilles. □ Note the difference in pitch and stress wh distinguishes this meaning from that of **Dominican** [dʌ'mɪnɪkən] /12'21/ wh refers to the Republic of Santo Domingo, part of the island of Hispaniola in the Greater Antilles.

Do·min·i·can rug *n phr* (CarA) A floor-mat of differing shapes, sizes and designs made from the light brown, dried fibre of the VETIVER grass, first popularized in and exported from Dominica (hence the name).

Do·min·i·ca-yam *n* (StVn) ‖ YELLOW-YAM (Antg, etc)

Do·min·ic fowl [dɒmənik fʊl] *n phr* (CarA) A domestic fowl with barred black and light-grey feathers, rose-coloured comb and yellow legs, resembling the Plymouth Rock fowl but of a smaller breed.

done[1] *vb* (CarA) **1.** *as a base vb* [X] To finish; to bring or come to an end. **a.** *'Well, den, we better start now if we intend to done this evening,'* remarked Bo-Bo.—Har, 1974:20 **b.** *The water in the kitchen was doning.*—Tbgo (Ms) **c.** *You must done dat befo[re] you start dis.*—(Trin) **2.** *as a pa. part.* [*AF—Cr*] (Be, have) finished; (be, have been) used up. **a.** *Man, you come now all the whisky done.*—(Bdos) **b.** *I ain't talkin[g] no more. I done.*—(Antg) **c.** *Look how he come and done the work so quick.*—(Guyn) **3.** PHRASES **3.1 done with** *vbl adj phr* (Bdos, Guyn) Exhausted; done for; ruined. *Whistler's Note disappointed again. As usual he showed good speed but was done with by the mile post.*—NaT (75.05.18, p.27) **3.1.1 done with (sb/sth)** *vb phr* (CarA) [*AF—Cr*] To bring, come, put an end to your relationship with (sb or sth). **a.** *And Vera say that my own home troubles now begin and ups with she baby and gone by she mother and say she done with me.*—CISH:131 **b.** *He los[t] so much money and still he can't done with gambling.*—(Guyn) **3.1.2 Done with that!** *id phr* (Bdos, Gren) [*IF*] ‖ *finish with that* (CarA) [Emotive expression of finality] That's that!; That's the end of the matter (so far as sb is concerned)! *He decided he would sleep in a tree here, cool breeze anywhere, decided he was not working for any man, God nor the devil; finished with that. Done. He made up his mind. Done with that.*—Bdos (Hd, 75.07.15, p.5240) **4.** *imper vb* (CarA) [X] Stop! **a.** *Ow! Done now, no! Don't beat me no more!*—(Guyn) **b.** *Well, me en want to talk no dead talk now nuh, oho! done dat an' tell me wha happenin' in town.*—WeN (52.12.22, p.6, Annie & Josephine) **5.** *aspectual marker of completion of an action* (+ *vb*) (CarA) [*AF—Cr*] Have/had finished + (*vb*) -ing. *Calvin mother do a real good job, and when she done pack the things, and she inspect the clothes* *that Calvin carrying way, she tie-up the two valises with a strong piece o' string.*—CWFYS:93 **6.** *in post-vbl position, emphasizing completion* (CarA) [*AF—Cr*] *Completely. He will wait until everything wash up done and then ask if he could help.*—(Bdos) **7.** *aspectual marker of an established state or condition* (CarA) [*AF—Cr*] [Indicating that the matter or condition stated by the verb or complement is unquestionable, unchangeable, etc] *Well you know how he done love his rum already, so Saturday afternoon is rum-shop time.*—(Guyn) **8.** PHRASES **8.1 can't done** *id phr* (CarA) [*AF/IF*] See CAN'T Phr 2.1 **8.2 done dead** *vbl adj phr* (*post-posed*) (CarA) [*AF—Cr*] (Be) quite dead. *Before they could start to think* [*a*]*bout callin*[*g*] *doctor, the man done dead.* —(Gren) **8.3 done gone** *vbl adj phr* (*post-posed*) (CarA) [*AF—Cr*] (Be/have) gone beyond recall. *Although it is a case of trying to lock the barn when the cow done gone, they (meaning 'the authorities') will have to hire two watchmen.* —AmA (80.02.22, p.9)

done² *n* (Antg) [*AF—Joc*] PHRASES [Esp of teenagers] **1. get the done** *vb phr* (Antg) [*AF—Joc*] To be dropped by a boyfriend or girlfriend; to lose your boyfriend/girlfriend. **2. give sb the done** *vb phr* (BrVi) [*AF—Joc*] To drop a boyfriend/girlfriend; to end a known love affair. [By AF functional vb > n shift, with the sense 'finish, end']

don·key-box *n* (Antg) ‖ *dum-box* (BrVi) ‖ *dung-box* (Mrat) ‖ *hamper* (Jmca) A BOX-CROOK that may also be used for transporting manure to PROVISION grounds.

don·key-cac·tus *n* (USVI) ‖ SPANISH NEEDLE **1.** (Bdos)

don·key-danc·er /1'212/ *n* (Bdos) ‖ DONKEY-MAN (Bdos)

don·key-eye *n* (Gren, Tbgo, Trin) ‖ NICKER (Angu, etc)

don·key-man /1'21/ *n* (Bdos) ‖ *bad-cow* (Guyn) ‖ *borokit* (Trin) ‖ *bull* 1. (Nevs, StKt) ‖ *cow-man* (Guyn) ‖ *donkey-dancer* (Bdos) ‖ *giddy-horse* (Bdos) ‖ *mad-bull (dancer)* (Guyn) A traditional masquerade figure, being a man masked and dressed as a woman, dancing in a gaily coloured, decorated framework in the shape of a donkey (or horse or cow), and usu the main figure of a trio or foursome of dancers accompanied by a TUK-BAND. □ Cp *DJE* cow-head, horse-head as JOHN CANOE figures (*Jmca*).

don·key-spi·der *n* (StKt) ‖ *matoutou* (StLu) A big black spider (said by some to be the tarantula).

don't (doan) [do·n(t)] *vb neg* (CarA) [*AF—Cr*] ‖ *doh* [do] (denasalized form esp in *Gren, Trin*) **1.** (CarA) [*AF—Cr*] *fixed neg operator* [In DE-CREOLIZED speech] *Doesn't; don't. Whenever I*

ask him for something for the child he says that he *don't have money even though he works for a good salary.*—NaT (79.10.10, p.25, Dear Christine) **2.** (CarA) [*X*] *simple pre-vbl neg marker Not.* **a.** *He says to me 'You going leave and don't give me the drink?'*—DeM(SK) (63.07.27, p.4) **b.** *You can steal and don't even know it.*—AdN (H, 88.09.11, p.11) **c.** *It could be that the amount of money they have causes them to don't care who they offend.*—Bdos (Exam Ms, 1974) **3.** (CarA) [*AF—Cr*] *replacing all functions of Cr negator* / *na/, /en/* [*In* DECREOLIZED *speech*] *Ain't; isn't; haven't, etc.* **a.** *Is a long time some of you don't write Stella.*—StA(JA) (73.02.10, p.14, Party-line) **b.** *Tiefin doan bad like crucifyin!*—MOHW: 20 **c.** *If we get dat money de world belongs to we. Dat time I doh studying if I is fisherman again.*—RTCS:5 **4.** PHRASES **4.1 don't ask** *introductory (intensifier) tag* (CarA) [*IF*] [Emphasizing that what follows in the clause (wh it begins) is/was a certainty] **a.** *Don't ask how she scream when she heard what happen to the husband!*—(Bdos) **b.** *I used to spend school holidays in the country and don't ask if I and others from town were not regarded with respect.*—StA(JA) (73.02.10, p.14, Partyline) **4.2 don't be + vb-ing** *neg imperative* (CarA) [*IF*] Do not + vb. *Don't be saying things like that about your sister!*— (Bdos) **4.2.1 don't be + adj** (usu in a subordinate clause) (CarA) [*IF*] Am/is/are not. Said Magistrate L—, 'If you don't be careful, he may get into further trouble and you are going to regret it.'*—AdN (76.02.11, p.1) **4.3 Don't care¹!** /2'1/ ~/2'2/ *neg vb phr* (CarA) [*AF/IF*] ‖ **Don't mind!** (CarA) **(i)** [As simple imperative] Let it not worry you; it doesn't matter. *You ain't got a ticket? Don't care, you can get one at the door.*— (StVn) **(ii)** [As a truncated main clause, introducing a supposition] I don't care (if, when, how, etc); never mind (if, when, how, etc). *She is a baby to me. Don't care how big she get she is still my baby.*—PCOS:44 □ Note differentiation in pitch from adj function. See DON'T-CARE². **4.4 Don't mind!** *neg vb phr* (CarA) See Phr 4.3 ‖ DON'T CARE¹ (CarA) **a.** *'He say he ain' coming to the fête tonight,' Rita said sadly. 'Don't mind, we can go without him you know,' her friend replied.*—Antg (Ms) **b.** *Don't mind what you do, the weeds will spring up again quick time.*—(Guyn)

don'·t-care² [dõ-ke(r)] /1'2/ *adj* (CarA) [*AF*] [Esp of a person's attitude] Indifferent; unfeeling; irresponsible. *Mr Editor, I would like to know if there is a fault in the telephone system or is it due to negligence of some of the 'don't care' telephone operators?*—AnS (62.04.27, p.2) [By functional shift of DON'T CARE¹ *vb phr.* See DON'T Phr 4.3] □ Adj compounds from a neg vb are rare in IAE except in commercial or journalistic short-cuts—*no-claim bonus, no-go situation.* However *OED* does list *don't care* 'used as adj = careless, reckless'.

don't-care-damn ['dʌŋkeda·m] /1'12/ *adj* (Gren, Guyn) [*AF*] Utterly indifferent, unfeeling and irresponsible. *This don't-care-damn policy at the General Hospital must stop. I am of* *the candid opinion that had Peters seen a doctor immediately after his accident the leg could have been saved.*—ToR (76.09.27, p.8)

don't·car·ish (don't·car·ish) /1'22/ *adj* (Bdos, Guyn, StLu) [*AF/IF*] Showing little or no concern; unresponsive; generally indifferent. *One must admit that after working an entire day she would be tired, but for customers to get this 'don't-carish treatment' is rather disgusting.*—AdV (73.12.21, p.4) [DON'T-CARE² adj (prec) + *ish*, SE suff with sense 'somewhat less']

doo·koo·noo *n* (Belz, Jmca) See DOKUNU

door-mouth *n* (CarA) [*AF—Joc*] **1.** The entrance to a dwelling or building; door, doorway or threshold. [A prob calque from W Afr langs. Cp Nupe *eko misun* (*door* + *mouth*) 'door'; Igbo *onu uzo* (*mouth* + *door*) 'door', etc] □ Often used in Derog contexts. Note foll phr. **2.** PHRASE **2.1** **sit down at (sb's) door-mouth** *vb phr* (Guyn) To beg (sb's) favours without pride.

do·rey (do·ry) *n* (Belz, CayI) **1.** A small dug-out canoe used on rivers and for coastal transportation. *Hunting is done at night with shot-guns, headlights and small dugout doreys.*—ABSBH:62 **2.** A small round-bottomed paddle-boat built for coastal fishing, or fitted with a sail (a 'sailing dorey') and used for pleasure, esp racing. *These Sailing Dories require the greatest of sailing skills not only to win but to survive the distance of the racing course without capsizing.*—BsT (80.02.24, p.5) [*DMEI* Miskito *dori, duri* 'canoe'; *duri wakaya* (< *wakaya* 'sail') 'to canoe'. Cp also *BAED* Arawak *duru* 'a large tree with very light softwood' (from wh possibly a dug-out canoe can be made)] □ Both pls **doreys, dories** occur, the former being commoner. *W3* lists '*dory*, also *dorey*' described as a deeper V-shaped vessel for riding waves.

Dor·set·shire-Hill Ba·jan [dɒ̃ʃtʌ-hɪl be-jan] *n phr* (StVn) [*AF—Derog*] ‖POOR-WHITE (CarA) [Ref to the place near Kingstown, *StVn* where a number of POOR-WHITE immigrants from Bdos chose to live together from the 1860s. See *SROB:97ff*] □ Note particular pronunc.

dot·ish [dotɪʃ] *adj* (CarA) **1.** [Esp of old people] Senile; unable to reason. **2.** [*IF*] [Of young people] Stupid (as if born so); mentally deficient. *I told them they can't play the game. Maureen S— come telling me why I ain't shut my dotish mouth.*—Tbgo (CR, 80.01.03) [Cp *OED dotish, doatish* arch. 'silly, imbecile'. The term has, however, added emphasis and is very active in CE]

dou·ble-bank *vb tr* **1.** (Guyn, USVI) To gang up against and beat a person. **2.** (Guyn) To join together to tackle a hard task and get it done quickly. *Acting Crown Counsel said that the accused was among those who attended a 'kiap' at the instance of Anastatia. At these gatherings,* *residents would get together and 'double-bank' work.*—DaC (n.d)

dou·ble-firsts *n* (Trin) ‖*double-tenors* (Trin) A set of four joined pairs of PANS, each pair for one player and each pan less sunk than, but with the same rim-depth as the LEAD-PANS, providing a range of 32 high-pitched notes per pair; the set flanks the LEAD-PANS in the front line of a STEELBAND to provide the melody. [*Double* from the 'pairing' + *first*, as being in the front line + *s* from the number of pairs] □ See STEELBAND diagram in Appendix.

dou·bles *n* (Trin) A type of sandwich made of two BARA with a filling of curried CHANNA, popularly sold as a snack.

dou·ble scu·ril *n* (Brbu) ‖BEAD-VINE (BUSH) (Nevs, StKt)

dou·ble-se·conds *n* (Trin) ‖*alto-pans* (Jmca) ‖*second-pans* (Trin) A row of (usu) four pairs of joined PANS, each pair manned by one player, and each pan cut to be about one quarter the depth of an oil-drum, with the surface less sunk than that of the TENOR PANS and segmented to provide about ten notes each wh are of the tone of the lower treble notes of a piano; this row forms the second line in the arrangement of a STEELBAND. [*Double*, from the 'pairing' + *second* from their position + *s* pl, from the number of pairs] □ See STEELBAND diagram in Appendix.

dou·ble-te·nors *n* (Trin) ‖DOUBLE-FIRSTS (Trin) [By ref to the high pitch of the PANS]

dou-dou (doo·doo) [dudu] *n* (Dmca, Gren, StLu, Tbgo, Trin) [*IF*] [A term of warm endearment] Darling; my sweet (little one). '*Put you' trust in God, doodoo', Ma Christine kept saying. 'Put you' trust in God' ...| 'Don't cry, doodoo-darlin'', said Ma Christine, gently patting her on the shoulder.*—MBF:101 [Fr Cr < Fr *doux* 'sweet' + emotive reduplication] □ Most common in *Trin* folk speech, but copied through calypsoes, etc by many in ECar.

dough-boy [do-bɒɪ] *n* **1.** (Baha, Jmca, TkCa) A kind of (usu tough) dumpling boiled in soup. **2.** (Guyn, StVn) ‖*dough-bread* (Jmca) A kind of small, hard, home-made sweetbread, from pieces or ends of dough kneaded, sometimes with COCONUT-MILK and a little baking powder but not allowed to rise much. **3.** (Guyn) [*Joc*] A poorly mixed or baked cake that fails to rise.

dough-bread *n* (Jmca) ‖DOUGH-BOY 2. (Guyn, StVn)

doug·la(h) [dʌgla] *n* (Gren, Guyn, StVn, Tbgo, Trin) ‖*royal* 1. (Jmca) A Caribbean person of mixed African and Indian (or sometimes Chinese) parentage. *Her mother was light-brown, with hair wavy and heavy like the hair of a douglah.*—MLDS:35 [< Hin *dogalaa* 'hybrid, mongrel' i.e. esp in ref to animals] □ The term retains its original pejorative connotation in Indic communities, but not in wider usage. The spelling *dougla* is the more frequent, though the pl may then be confused with SE name Douglas Hence *douglah* may be preferred.

dou·ill·ette (dou·i·ette) *n* (Dmca, StLu) See DWIYÈT

dove [do·v] *vb tr* (ECar) **1.** (Guyn, StKt) To boil down slowly and let simmer (esp meat with pigeon peas). **2.** (Tbgo) To half-cook (meat to help preserve it). **3.** (USVI) To pot-roast (esp pork)—*SVID*.

down¹ [dɒʊn ~ dʌŋ] *adv* (CarA) **1.** [As often in SE and followed by preps *at, by, to*] (Indicating direction or situation) towards, near, inside (the sea, river or waterside), hence foll phrs. **2.** *PHRASES* **2.1 down at/by** the carenage, Customs, Bathsheba (seaside resort), etc *adv phr* (CarA) [*IF*] **3.** [Loosely used alternatively with *up*, sometimes followed by prep *in*] Away (from the city or some central spot), hence foll phrs. **4.** *PHRASES* **4.1 down here/there** *adv phr* (CarA) ‖ **out here/there** (CarA) In this/that Colony (i.e. away from Britain). **4.2 down/up** in the country (or in some rural area named) *adv phr* (CarA) [*IF*] Far away (from town).

down² [dɒʊn ~ dʌŋ] *prep* (CarA) [*AF*] [Loosely used alternatively with *up*. Cp DOWN¹ 2.] In, at (some place away from town or some central point); some way along. **a.** *I'm going down Essequibo for the holidays.*—(Guyn) **b.** *And this man has children up street, he has children down street.*—PKKK:20 **2.** *PHRASES* **2.1 down by** *prep phr* (CarA) ‖ **up by** (CarA) **(i)** [*IF*] At, near (some well-known place). *A shoemaker at the corner down by where there was the fire last month.*—(Guyn) **(ii)** [*AF*] At the home of (sb). *I was spending time down by my aunt at the time.*—(StVn) **2.2 down the islands** *adv phr* (Bdos) In one of the smaller islands of the Eastern Caribbean. *Mr Chairman, I once did a case down the Islands for a political party, and this is what happened.*—Bdos (Hd, 75.03.26, p.871) **2.3 down to** *prep phr in adv function* (CarA) [*AF—Derog*] [Adding emotive emphasis to a following statement] Even (including sb or sth you would not expect). *Down to the daughter who calls herself a Christian curses people.*—(Guyn)

down³ [dɒʊn ~ dʌŋ] *adj* (Jmca) **1.** [Of a river] Swollen; overflowing its banks and flooding. [Ref to water running down from the mountains after heavy rains] □ Often in vb phr (*the river (has)*) COME DOWN. **2.** *PHRASE* **2.1 be/get down on (sb) to do (sth)** *vb phr* (Tbgo) [*IF*] To press, try to force (sb) to do (sth).

down⁴ [dɒʊn ~ dʌŋ] *vb tr* **1.** (CarA) [*AF*] To drop or let go of sth sharply. *Look, boy, do[w]ng me bike an[d] use you own!*—(Guyn) **2.** *PHRASES* **2.1. down blows/a cuff/a lash, etc, in (sb)** *vb phr* (Guyn) [*AF*] To hit sb severely; to beat (up)

(sb). **2.2 down hand on/upon (sb) or (sth)** *vb phr* (CarA) [*AF—Joc*] To seize (sb/sth) firmly.

down·fall *n* (Bdos) ‖ CALABAN (Jmca) [Because the trap falls down on the bird]

down·house *vb tr* (Antg) To belittle; to treat as of no account. *Though you always downhouse my opinion I usually turn out to be right in the end.*—(Antg)

down-is·land *adj* (USVI) [*IF*] Of or belonging to one of the (usu less developed) islands to the south and east of the US Virgin Islands. *When it is considered that the population is largely 'down island' only a few generations removed, there is little justification for the attitude of superiority and snobbishness which citizens display towards 'aliens'.*—DHVUS:ii □ The term is somewhat derogatory, with a derivative **down-islander**.

down·stairs *prep*; **down.stairs of,** *prep phr* (ECar) [*IF*] Below (a person's dwelling); on the lowest floor of (a named building). **a.** *Anyone desirous of protecting his investment should check the list of Registered Insurance Companies at our Office downstairs Olives Hotel.*—ViN (Ad, 73.10.19, p.13 **b.** *Twenty-seven volumes of a newspaper which was published in St Kitts through slavery and emancipation, were discovered by Mr Charles Gumbs, Assistant to Archivist Mr E.C. Baker, downstairs of the Public Library.*—DeM(SK) (63.03.30, p.9)

drag *n* (CarA) [*AF*] **1.** The action of drawing hard on a cigarette or 'joint' of marijuana. Hence foll phrases **2.** *PHRASES* **2.1 give a drag** *vb phr* (CarA) [*AF*] To pass a 'joint' of marijuana (to a companion smoker) **2.2 have/take a drag** *vb phr* (CarA) [*AF*] To suck or draw temporarily on a 'joint' of marijuana

Drag brother(s) *n phr* (Trin) (One of) a group of young men who make a living by selling domestic hand-crafted items esp in leather and wood in street- side booths or in the open in downtown Port-of-Spain. [< AmE *drag* as in *main drag* 'main street; road'; but association with CE *drag* n (see prec) may have also infl this term]

drag·gers *n pl* (Nevs, StKt) **1.** Old shoes worn around the house. **2.** (Nevs, StLu) ‖ *rubber-slippers* (CarA) Casual rubber sandals held on the foot by a V-shaped thong fitting between the toes.

draught *n* (Antg, Baha, Gren, Guyn) [Esp in foll phr] *PHRASE* **catch a/the draught** *vb phr* To catch a cold (esp in the eye); to have a redness in or discharge from the eye.

draw¹ **1.** *vb tr/intr* (CarA) [Of a swelling] To subside; to cause (a swelling) to go down (esp as a result of application of poultice or plaster or medicine). *Making up a poultice using cochineel and cornmeal, she positioned it in the area so that* *the inflammation would 'draw' at the correct place, and secured it with a bandage of clean cloth.*—Her II:24 **2.** *vb tr* (CarA) [Of sickness] To cause a person to lose weight (Hence esp foll phr). **3.** PHRASE **3.1 be/look drawn** *vb phr* (CarA) To show loss of weight through illness or grief, esp in the lines of the face. **4.** *vb tr* (CarA) To take away as something duly received; to withdraw. *Police state that on August 28 last, Mr Chin gave a man certain documents to draw sugar from a city wharf.*—WeS (74.09.06, p.32) [Prob infl by SE sense as in *to draw money from a bank*, but CE usage is much wider esp in *Jmca*] **5.** PHRASE **5.1 draw your hand** *vb phr* (CarA) [In ref to SUSU] See SUSU-HAND Phr **3.1 6.** *vb tr* (CarA) [X] [Replacing IAE vb phrs that normally require adv extension] To draw, pull up (a chair); to draw, move, pull aside/away/out, etc (sth). **a.** *Draw the chair nearer to me.*—(Bdos) **b.** *Draw your foot and let me fix the carpet.*—(Guyn) **c.** *Draw that piece of wood let me see if it's the right length.*—(Jmca) **7.** PHRASE **7.1 draw your brakes** *vb phr* (Guyn) To press, put (your foot) on the brakes. [From the habit of pulling up the brake-levers on a bicycle] **8.** *vb intr* (CarA) [AF] [Of a person's complexion] To be born with a skin-colour noticeably different from that of the family. *The youngest one draw dark and with a chinee-eye like.*—(Guyn) **9.** PHRASES **9.1 draw a fine** *vb phr* (Guyn, StKt) [Of an offender or an offence] To incur or entail a fine in a court of law. *He was as soon apprehended by Police, ... released on bail after being charged with breaking into enclosed premises. In Court some days later he drew a 30-dollar fine.*—LaS (76.06.16, p.3) **9.2 draw your photo** *vb phr* (Gren, Guyn) [AF] To have your photograph taken. *I got to go town to draw me photo for a passport.*—(Guyn)

draw² *n* (Antg, Baha, Bdos, Guyn) [X] Drawer. *... and $700 cash was stolen from a desk draw at the Alpha Hotel between 8.30 p.m. Wednesday and 1 p.m. Thursday.*—TrI (76.02.06, p.1) [< [drɒər] prob by characteristic CarA Cr dropping of final post-vocalic /-r/. Cp cases of *there*, *where*, etc. However note also AmE *DAE* and *MDA draw* 'a drawer as in a chest or cabinet' + cits from 1692]

draw-back *n* (Bdos, Guyn) [AF] A modest bribe; money paid as a personal inducement to sb in getting sth done. [Prob a surviving colonial usage. Cp AmE *W3 drawback* 1. c. 'money refunded ... as a special often secret favor or inducement—cp *kickback*']

draw-buck·et *n* (Baha) ‖ SKILLET¹ (Bdos)

dray; dray-cart *n* **1.** (Antg) A flat, open-sided, two-wheeled cart, with short shafts, pulled by a man; it was used in former times for transporting goods, or fire-wood, but is not much seen nowadays. **2.** (Bdos) A four-wheeled, V-shaped cart about 10 to 15 ft long, high-sided, and drawn by a mule, used esp in former times for transporting cut canes from field to factory. **3.** (Guyn) A flat, open-sided, four-wheeled cart about 16

ft long, usu drawn by two donkeys, and used esp in former times for transporting domestic goods over long distances. *The youths in groups of 30, 50 or more would walk through a village singing carols, while others would use a dray cart or truck.*—GyG (74.12.05, p.9)

dread¹ *n*; **dread broth.er, dread.locks-man** *n phrs* (CarA) [Often pl] **1.** A (usu black) male member of the RASTAFARIAN movement who wears his hair uncut and falling in long, plaited or matted locks about his shoulders. [A ref to God-given power, extending the usage in the *AVB* Old Testament, from the reading of wh the RASTAFARIAN movement generally justifies itself. Cp for ex *Ex XV, 16* 'fear and dread shall fall upon them; by the greatness of thine arm'] **2.** Any person who adopts a similar hair-style and appearance. *Also the word 'dread' is sometimes used negatively ... to refer to a person with dreadlocks who is not necessarily practising the other teachings of Rastafari so that it is not unusual to hear one remark: 'He in a Rastaman, he is a dread' where 'dread' and 'he' are derogatory terms. In Jamaica, a Dread is a true Rastafarian.*—SSRB: 32 **3.** The beliefs, practice, and/or expression of RASTAFARIANISM in any form such as hair-style, choice of food, smokes, music, etc. *He said: 'The cult of dread' has many causes, some dreads are good and well meaning people merely seeking their identity.'*—SuS (81.02.22, p.1) **4.** (Baha) [AF—Joc] A youngster, esp a teen-age boy, who takes risks to show off.

dread² *adj* (CarA) **1.** [IF] RASTAFARIAN; belonging to or associated with the DREADS. *Dread music (Rastafarian) is gradually exercising a powerful influence on Belize, and we think this is good, not only in terms of dread's black conscious content, but also because dread love is not the wishy-washy, sentimental promotions of the West's excessive emotional indulgence.*—AmA (80.03.14, p.2) **2.** [AF] [Of a person] Difficult to get along with (usu because aggressive and self-opinionated); generally unacceptable. *But to add to the horrors you had some dread commentators saying all sorts of funny things as they feel it is their duty to add to the torture.*—ToR (77.06.19, p.12) **3.** [AF] [Of a situation] Full of hardships and difficulties. *The scene is really dread here without regular water and electricity.*—Guyn (Ms)

dread³ *excl* (CarA) [AF—Tag] **1.** [Rastaf] Term indicating brotherhood among Rastafarian brethren. *You no sight, dread. Sight how dem ballheads make de I an' dem walk down to dey office an put a sign to say No Visitors. Is pure jesterin, ah tell you!*—CrU (76.10.09, p.5) **2.** ‖ *Man!* (CarA) A semi-exclamatory term of familiarity among teenagers. *That's looking good, dread!*—(Bdos)

Dread Act; **Dread Law** *n phr* (Dmca) [IF] An act of law passed in Dominica as *The Prohibited and Unlawful Societies and Association Act*, in 1976, to control the activities of DREADS.

dread·lock·ed *adj* (CarA) [Of a man or boy] Having your hair in DREADLOCKS. *Almost daily, incidents involving dreadlocked, frowsy hooligans surface in Barbados. Whether they are perpetrated by real Rastafarians or by disgruntled social dropouts masquerading under the cover of the movement, is not always clear.*—AdN (80.10.26, p.24) [DREAD[2] adj + (SE) *lock* n + SE vbl adj suff *-ed*]

dread·locks (dread-locks, dread locks) *n* (phr) *pl* (CarA) ‖ **locks** (CarA) [AF—*Joc*] The hairstyle of a black person, adopted as characteristic of a RASTAFARIAN, the hair remaining uncut and falling in plaited or matted locks about the shoulders. [DREAD[2] adj + (SE) *locks* n]

dread·ness *n* (CarA) A state of restive frustration; a condition of anguish but not without hope. *Caribbean Youth from Jmca to Guyn are today in a perpetual state of dreadness. Filled with vitality and yearning and love of life, aware, most of them, to some extent (and by all kinds of names ex Black Power, Caribbean Power, etc) of the dread, of the 'I-Power' within them, they stand trembling at the gates of promise and possibility.*— CaC (75/1, p.13) [DREAD[2] adj (senses 2., 3.) + SE suff *-ness*]

dread-talk *n* (CarA) ‖ **Rasta talk** (CarA) [IF] The RASTAFARIAN cult dialect of E in wh the vocabulary of creolized E is imaginatively adapted and the personal pronoun system adjusted to represent the believer's view of the world. [DREAD[2] adj + SE *talk* 'speech'] □ An ex is: *Babylon can't higherstand. De chalice upfull for I-man i-ditate. You sight up?* = The police/establishment cannot understand [that] the smoking of ganja is the right way for me/us/you/them who are believers [to be helped] to meditate deeply. Do you understand? (See V. Pollard in *Caq XXVIII:4, pp.17 ff*).

dream *vb tr* (CarA) **1.** [IF] To have a significant dream about sb (often in ref to a dead person). *I've dreamt my mother / What do you want, mother? / Please speak to me.*—Bes.V.2, p.25 **2.** To have a prophetic dream in wh a dead person brings or signals a message to you. *'Your dead mother dream me and tell me the gods are angry.' Beaunash almost convinced her with these arguments.*—FGSOS:66 **3.** PHRASE **3.1 dream bad/good** *vb phr* [AF] To have a bad/good dream. *... and if you dream good and you lucky people might get something, maybe Miss World might win in truth, but if you dream bad and you unlucky well is licks down the line.*—Gren (Hd, 77.04.06, p.83)

dress[1] *vb* PHRASE [Re clothing] **dress down**[1] *vb phr* (ECar) [IF] To dress up in the finest clothes. [Most often as vbl adj phr] DRESSED DOWN. *Dressed down in his glad rags, the cat was there from 3 p.m. planning his moves during the show, obviously anticipating breaking off some love after cinema.*—NaT (75.11.16, p.7, Al's Grapevine) [Prob indicating 'dressed down to the toes'

or 'down to the last detail'] □ See also DRESS[2] vb Phr 3. DRESS DOWN[2].

dress[2] *vb* PHRASES [Re movement] **1. dress [a]cross** *vb phr* (Antg) [AF/IF] To move a little aside or over. **2. dress back** *vb phr* (Antg, StKt) To move backwards a little. *I waved the knife in front of me to keep him off. The more I dressed back the more he came to me. / I dressed back into the chair.*—DeM(SK) (62.11.10, p.9) **3. dress down**[2] *vb phr* (CarA) ‖ **dress round** (Gren, Tbgo, Trin) ‖ **dress up** (Antg, Gren, Jmca, StKt, StVn) ‖ **size round/up** (Bdos) To move over a little (usu to make room for one or two more persons to sit). [Prob by transfer from military usage]

dress·er *n* **1.** (Bdos, Jmca) ‖ **bedroom-dresser, dressing-case/-table, vanity** (Guyn) A lady's dressing-table, as a piece of bedroom furniture with mirror, and drawers in wh clothes are kept. [Cp AmE *DAE dresser*[1] 2. 'a bureau or dressing table'] **2.** (Dmca, Guyn, StLu) ‖ **press** (Angu, Bdos, Jmca, Trin, USVI) **(i)** A wardrobe; a clothes closet. **(ii)** A cupboard. [Prob by shift of sense 1., with ref to storage of clothes] **3.** (Bdos, CayI, Guyn) **(i)** ‖ **kitchen-dresser** (Guyn) A kitchen counter or table, on wh food is prepared (meat dressed, etc) and (sometimes) washed WARES put to drain. **(ii)** (Bdos, Guyn) [In loose usage] ‖ **wagon** (Bdos) [Cp *EDD dresser* sb[1]. In gen dial use in Sc Irel and Eng 1. 'a long kitchen sideboard, sometimes fixed to the wall, on wh crockery, etc is placed'. Also IrE: *Dresser* 'a set of shelves and drawers in a frame in a kitchen for holding plates, knives, &c.'—*JESI: 251*]

dress·ing-case/-ta·ble *n* (Guyn) ‖ DRESSER 1. (Bdos, Jmca)

drink *vb* PHRASES **1. drink bush for (sb's) fever** *vb phr* (Gren) [AF] See BUSH[1] Phr 4.4 **2. drink milk not (to) count cow** *vb phr* (CarA) [AF—*Joc*] See cow[1] Phr **3. drink soup/water off/over (sb's head)** *vb phr* (Belz, Dmca, ECar) [AF—*Joc*] To be much taller than (sb). *The men don[']t like to dance wid she, [be]cause she could drink soup off mos[t] of them head.*—(Gren)

dri·vay (dri·vé) *vb* (Dmca, StLu, Trin) See DWIVÉ

drive *vb tr* [Used in many phrases to indicate crude, vigorous action] PHRASES **1. drive a hand in (sb)** *vb phr* (Bdos, Guyn) To punch (sb) violently with your fist; to CUFF (sb) very hard. **2. drive a lash in (sb)** *vb phr* (Bdos, Guyn) To lash (sb) violently with a whip or stick. **3. drive (the) licks in (sb's) skin/tail** *vb phr* (Antg, Bdos, Trin) [AF] ‖ BEAT (SB'S) SKIN (CarA) See BEAT Phr 4.14 *... back then, nothing sweet a white man more than drive licks under a black man's tail.*—SSHL:50 □ A more interesting phr than BEAT SB's SKIN. **4. drive a (hard) spoon** *vb phr* (Guyn) To be a great eater; to eat vigorously. **5. not to drive a stroke (of work)** *vb phr, neg* *only* (Bdos, Guyn) To be persistently idle; not to do any gainful or helpful work at all. *I hear that he hadn't driven a stroke for years, not since the birth of his fifth child more than thirty years ago. Apparently he then decided that the situation was hopeless and that no effort of his could improve it.... Sometimes I see ... [him] in the street but he is never doing anything more strenuous than clutching a loaf of bread.*—WCR:83 [Cp *OED drive* 19. 'to carry on vigorously ... a trade, etc'; also 25. b. 'to work hard']

dri·vé *vb intr* (Dmca, Gren, Trin) See DWIVÉ.

driv·er *n* (CarA) [Sugar Ind] **1.** [Hist] ‖ *slave-driver* (CarA) A trusted male slave in charge of a labour gang of slaves whom he controlled with a whip. **2.** [In post-slavery times] **(i)** An overseer's male assistant in control of a small work- force. **(ii)** (Bdos) A woman in charge of the THIRD GANG. *During the time that these children were employed, if they stopped for five minutes to relax, the women who were drivers would punish them by giving them lashes with what was called in those days a 'cow-skin'.*—Bdos (Hd, 74.12.03, p.4267)

dro·gher *n* (Guyn) See DROGUER

dro·gher (dro·guer)-ant [dro·gər ant] *n* (Guyn) ‖ ACOUSHI-ANT (Guyn) [Fromn its habit of carrying its food, bits of leaves, lifted above its head, like a DROGUER]

drogue (droag, drog, drogh, drough, drug) [dro·g ~ drɒg] *vb tr* (CarA) To haul, carry or transport (some heavy load) by strenuous human labour. *Pancho and Woody were droughing the bales and boxes we had unloaded over to the camp site at the other end of the portage.*—RWIN:184 (J. Carew) [Cp *EDD droog* vb[1] 'to pull forcibly, to tug, to drag at'; vb[2] 'to do dirty, heavy work'. However the wide occurrence of the term (esp in rural areas) in the *CarA* may be due to some reinforcement as a back-formation from *drogher* (see next). Note *OED drog* v 'to carry in a drogher'. Note also *OED* and *COD drogue* n with senses clearly relating to strain and dragging] □ The spelling *drogue* (also used in *COD* as n) is the least ambiguous for the commonest pronunc [dro·g].

dro·guer (dro·gher, drou·gher) [drogər] *n* (Guyn) One of a small group of labourers employed to carry the heavy packs of supplies and equipment of a surveying, prospecting or exploring team in the INTERIOR of *Guyn*. [Prob > DROGUE + SE suff -er, with reinforcement from *OED* 16. c. Du. *drogher* 'a [clumsy] W Indian coasting vessel' wh engaged (*OED*) *drogher-men* (Comb sense b.)]

drop[1] **1.** *vb tr* (Bdos, Guyn) To deliver something (at a place). *D— was given six pieces of zinc sheets by Rickford B— to drop in his hand-cart to B—'s home. The sheets were not delivered and when arrested, D— could not say what had become of*

them.—DaC (53.02.06, p.3) **2.** *vb tr* (CarA) To give sb a lift (in a car or any vehicle) (Hence foll Phr 3.1). **3.** *PHRASES* **3.1 drop sb by/down/to/up (some place)** *vb phr* [IF] *And I begged him to drop me up home, that's how I come in so early.*—(Bdos) [From the idea of depositing a thing or person, but much commoner than in SE; as *OED* v tr 19. 'to deposit from a ship or vehicle; to sit down; also to leave (a packet) at a person's home'] □ In the remaining phrs the underlying sense of 'depositing' remains, with some variations. **3.2 drop (some) cuss in (sb)** *vb phr* (CarA) [AF] See CUSS[1] Phr 4.1 **3.3 drop flesh** *vb phr* (Bdos, Guyn) [IF] ‖ *fall away, fall off* (Bdos, etc) [Of a person] To lose weight (from illness or grief). **3.4 drop foot** *vb phr* (Jmca) [AF—*Joc*] To dance without restraint, with stamping, jumping up, etc. *Acting Mayor Algon Samuels went on to Curphey Place after the Mayor's cocktail party to drop foot to Byron Lee in the welcome fete.*—WeG (72.10.11, p.13, Partyline) **3.5 drop (a) hand in (sb)** *vb phr* (CarA) [AF] To hit (sb) with the closed fist; to CUFF (sb). **3.6 drop hand on (sb)** *vb phr* (Guyn) [AF—*Joc*] [Of the police] To arrest, seize hold of (sb). **3.7 drop a/the lash(es) on (sb)** *vb phr* (CarA) [IF/AF] **(i)** To flog (sb). *You could not drop the folk titles of respect or some body might drop a lash across your back.*—ACTT:149 (E.M. Roach) **(ii)** [AF—*Joc*] [By extension] To make a decision that shocks (sb). *The Prime Minister is only waiting till the next budget to drop the lash on the car dealers.*—(Bdos) **3.8 drop/throw remarks** *vb phr* (Bdos, Guyn) ‖ *pass remarks* (Bdos, Guyn) To make a comment intended to irritate or offend sb while not speaking directly to that person. *You know the tone and the voice level—just low enough to seem to be in private conversation, just loud enough that those nearby can hear clearly. Something like dropping remarks to upset someone to whom you are not speaking.*—AdN (82.12.05, p.8) [Cp SE *let fall a remark* with similar, though less intense implication] **4.** *vb intr* (CarA) To fall. **5.** *PHRASES* **5.1 drop down**[1] *vb phr* (CarA) [Of a person] To fall to the ground sick or dead (usu in some public place). **5.2 drop to sleep** *vb phr* (CarA) [X] To drop asleep; to fall asleep. [By misplaced juncture < SE pa.t. *dropped asleep*] **5.3 let sb's word drop** *vb phr* (Gren) [IF] **(i)** To let sb finish speaking, giving due attention to what has been said (i.e. without rushing in or interrupting). **(ii)** To let an offending word pass without comment. **5.4 let your hand drop** *vb phr* (Guyn) To be inactive, or expect sb else to solve your problem, when you should be doing sth about it yourself.

drop[2]; **drop-down**[2] [IF]; **drop-up** [IF] *n* (CarA) A lift in a car. *He said that he was a taxi driver, and was the person who had stopped at Eagle Hall on the night of January 5, and offered W—'s wife a drop home in his car.*—AdN (80.04.15, p.1) [By functional vb > n shift of DROP[1] 3.1]

drop³ n (CarA) **1.** Any of several kinds of small cake made by dropping a spoonful of sweet batter (often mixed with grated coconut) on to a baking pan. (Hence also often COCONUT-DROP). **2.** A small dumpling made by dropping a piece of dough or thick batter into boiling soup.

drop-car n (Guyn) A taxi that is hired from a garage. *We ordered a drop-car from Cheong's garage to go to the funeral.*—(Guyn)

drop-cord n (CarA) ‖ *expansion-cord* (CayI) An extension electric cord (esp when fitted with a bulb at one end); an extension cord for any electrical power tool.

drop-pan (drop-hand (?)) [drɒpan] n (Jmca) A folk lottery game, resembling WHE-WHE, played by using numbers aligned with symbols, one of wh is drawn making all holders of that number winners. *When told that Drop Pan lottery tickets were not sold there he asked for direction. A man came out of the house to accompany him and during their search for the lottery house Quashie told of his dream and coming good fortune.*—BGSB:7 [Orig uncertain, as the pronunc leads many speakers to conceive the name as in the alternative spelling, though only the first has been seen in print]

drop·pers n pl (Antg, Jmca, Nevs, StKt, ViIs) Dumplings made of pieces of dough shaped with a spoon and dropped into boiling soup.

drop-roof n (Bdos) A split-level roof looking as if one wing of a gable-ended roof has dropped (hence the name).

drop-shed n (Antg, Nevs, StKt) **1.** ‖ *shed-roof* (Bdos, Mrat) A flat sloping roof of a section added to extend the dwelling space of a small gable-ended house, such as a CHATTEL- HOUSE. **2.** ‖ *lean-to* (Mrat, Nevs) [IF] The dwelling space so added.

drough vb tr (CarA) See DROGUE

drou·gher n (Guyn) See DROGUER

drown·ded [drʌndɪd] adj (Belz, Guyn, Jmca) [X] Drown; drowned. **a.** *Itanami goin[g] drownded me.*—Guyn Folk song **b.** *E seh, 'Couldn't yuh know me nearly drownded?'*—WFSB:41 [An over-correct or surviving E dial form, listed in OED as Vul variant of *drowned*. (However, Jonathan Swift (SPC: Dialogue I) records its use in London's 'Polite Conversation' (1738): '*Don't throw water on a drounded Rat*') Also in AmE dial (*MTAL:527*) as pa.t. and pa. part. of *drown*]

drug vb tr (CarA) See DROGUE

drug-store n (CarA) ‖ DOCTOR-SHOP (CarA) [IF] □ This is the normal CE term, *pharmacy* being considered very formal, *chemist's* almost *Joc* BrE.

drunk·ie; **drunk-man** [drʌnk-ma·n] /1′2/ n (CarA) [AF/IF] A drunkard; a drunk.

drunk·in[g] [drʌnkɪn] /1′2/ adj (CarA) [AF] **1.** Very drunk (hence often in noun DRUNKIN[G] -MAN). [From folk pronunc of SE *drunken*] **2.** Caused by drunkenness. *Also coming towards the end / One or two drunking conversations / Develop into drunking argument / And nearly slide into drunking fight.*—YFOC:32

dry¹ adj **1.** (CarA) [IF] [Esp of women] Thin; skinny; noticeably lacking in attractive roundness of limbs. **2.** (Bdos, Gren, Guyn, StVn) [IF] Left without money or needed resources; [in a card game] having a bad hand. *He doubled his bets and took bets all round, but that didn't help. They cleaned him out dry; bone dry and tonight, nobody would lend and Zittie was not there.*—Isl 73/6, p.21 (W. Redhead) **3.** (Guyn) [Of a black person's hair] Short or lacking smoothness or care. **4.** (Bdos, Guyn) [Of bowel pains] Griping without known cause or evident result. (Hence foll phr). **5.** PHRASE **5.1 get/have a dry bel-lyache/cutting/gripe** vb phr To suffer unaccountable gripes.

dry² adv PHRASES **dry so; dry dry so** adv phr (CarA) [AF] **(i)** Without due ceremony. *You can't go and marry the man dry so! What wrong with you at all? You must have a little thing even for your friends even if you lef[t] out your family.*—(Gren) **(ii)** Without apparent provocation, cause or warning; unexpectedly. **a.** *He come and lick her one kick! With his foot, I tell you! Dry dry so!*—(Tbgo) **b.** *Nowadays the thieves are walking in your house and taking up your things dry so, and walking out.*—(Bdos)

dry-co·co·nut(s) /1′222/ n (pl) (Guyn, Trin) [Coconut Ind] Coconuts that have been allowed to ripen and dry up on the tree, so that the hard kernels and brown fibrous husks may be traded.

dry-eye adj (Jmca) ‖ BOLD-FACE (Ecar)

dry food n phr **1.** (Bdos, Trin) A meal mainly of GROUND PROVISIONS served without gravy. □ Cp STEW-FOOD Bdos. **2.** (Guyn, Tbgo) ‖ *food; food-kind* (Bdos, Jmca) A meal mainly of root vegetables, with very little meat or fish.

dry-goods store /1′21/ n phr (CarA) A store that sells only cloths, linens, sewing items, and articles of ladies' and men's dress. [As W3 *dry goods* 'textiles, ready-to-wear clothing ... as distinguished from hardware, jewellery, groceries, and wet goods']

dry·ing-shed n (Gren) [Cocoa Ind] A shed shaped like a roof-top to protect cocoa beans from rain during the drying process, either fixed on low walls or mounted on wheels to be rolled on rails to cover the DRYING- TRAY.

dry·ing-tray n (Gren) [Cocoa Ind] A large, wide, wooden platform with raised edges, wheeled on rails into and out of the DRYING-SHED to permit the sun-drying of cocoa-beans spread out on it.

dry-peas *n pl* (CarA) Dried pigeon peas (*Cajanus cajan-Papilionaceae*), the normal ingredient of PEAS AND RICE.

dry-stone wall *n phr* (USVI) ‖ DRY-WALL 1. (Baha, etc)

dry-wall *n* Baha, Mrat, Nevs, StKt, TkCa) **1.** ‖ *dry-stone wall* (USVI) A wall about 4 ft high made by the careful stacking of large pieces of loose stone, without mortar (hence 'dry') and used as a fence or for terracing. **2.** ‖ GROUNDSEL (Bdos)

dry-well *n* (Bdos) ‖ *suck(-well)* (Bdos) [Sugar Ind] A hole some 6 to 8 ft across dug perpendicularly in the ground (at its lowest spot if the ground is uneven) and as deep as necessary to reach a layer of sand that would cause flood-waters to be drained and 'sucked' away, the edge of the hole being built round in coral stone. *As was usual there were many dry-wells or sucks located at the Hope, and one morning one of the other labourers came and advised the owner that Sammy was sitting at the side of one of these wells which was about 150 ft deep.*—AdM (76.02.22, p.7) [DRY, from the dryness of the hole most of the year round + *well* 'a hole in the ground']

dub *n* **1.** (CarA) ‖ *dub-music* (CarA) A two-beat rhythm given principally by bass and drums without a dominating tune but originally derived from REGGAE (and so largely associated with Black folk-culture in the Caribbean), recorded on the flip-side of a record originally intended to provide for a singer's improvization but later used purely for dancing. **2.** (CarA) **(i)** The type of amorous dancing done to DUB-MUSIC in wh partners keep their bodies in close contact from head to foot. **(ii)** A public dance, esp at a disco, at wh only DUB-MUSIC is played. *A neighbour said the incident was probably connected with 'dubs' kept at a disco in the area, noting that since the closure of Paul's Disco at Lands End, St Michael, many 'dubs' were held up there.*—AdV (89.02.26, p.1) **3.** [By extension] ‖ *dub-poetry* (CarA) [By CE functional vb > n shift and with extended sense < SE *double* vb in sense *OEDS dub* v⁵ 'to impose (additional sounds) on to an existing recording; to transfer (recorded sound) on to a new record']

dub-music *n* (CarA) ‖ DUB 1. (CarA)

dub-po·et·ry *n* Lines meant to be spoken, generally to a two-beat rhythm, and dealing mostly with the life experience and/or point of view of Black people in or from the Caribbean.

duck¹ *n* PHRASE **be in duck's guts** *vb phr* (Bdos) [AF—*Joc*] ‖ CRAPAUD SMOKE YOUR PIPE (Dmca, etc)

duck² *vb* PHRASE **your cork duck** *vb phr* (Guyn) See CORK²

duck-ant(s) *n* (*pl*) (CayI, Jmca) ‖ WOOD-LICE (Angu, etc) [Perh related to *DAFL* Twi *dúkuu*, *adj* 'reduced to small particles; eaten up' wh is the condition of wood caused by the ants] □ See also ANTS-NEST 2.

duck·et(s) *n* (*pl*) (Angu, Antg, Mrat) Tough leather boots, esp a tall type useful for going into high bush. [Perh from name of a Br manufacturer]

duc·koo·noo *n* (Belz, Jmca) See DOKUNU

duck-weed *n* **1.** (Guyn) ‖ WATER-HYACINTH 1. (Bdos, etc) **2.*** (Bdos) A flat, green, floating pond-plant with small flowers; *Lemna perpusilla (Lemnaceae).* **3.*** (Bdos) A mat-like weed with fleshy leaves and little yellow flowers, flourishing densely on seashore land or damp ground; *Pectis humifusa (Compositae).*

du·enne [dwɛn] *n* (*often pl duennes*) (Trin) See DWENN

duff *n* (Guyn) A tough dumpling made of corn-flour and usu put in METAGEE. [Cp *OED duff* sb¹ < a northern pronunc of *dough* (cp SE *enough*) 'a flour dumpling boiled in a bag'. Also *EDD duff* 'a pudding made of flour and water, sometimes with suet also' (Sc, Irel, Cum, Yks, etc)]

du·gu [dugu] *n* (Belz) A Garifuna rite presided over by a priestess, with women playing a prominent role; it is an earth-related ceremony held at the home of a dead parent or grandparent to propitiate or placate that person's soul, and it involves feasting, drumming, and ritual dancing over a few days during wh persons of the particular family are obliged to be participants. [Garifuna, abbr of *adugurahani* 'thanksgiving']

duh [dʌ] *pron*; **duh.self** [dʌsɛlf] *refl pron* (Bdos) [*Cr*] See DEY¹; DEMSELF (CarA) *Duh walkin' 'bout playin' duh great but en a t'ing mo' dan prostitutes duhself*—NaT (79.06.01 p.5, Lickmout' Lou)

du·hen·de [duɛndɛ] *n* (Belz) ‖ TATADUHENDE (Belz) □ A shortened form. Cp DWENN (*Trin*).

du·ku·na ['dukunabɛ ~ 'dukana] /1'12/ *n* (Antg, BrVi, Mrat, StVn) ‖ *blue-draw(er)s* (Jmca) ‖ *boyo* (Belz, Jmca) ‖ *cankie* (Guyn) ‖ *conchi* (Nevs) ‖ *conkie* (Angu, Bdos, StKt) ‖ *corn-dumpling* (StKt) ‖ *dokunu* (Belz, Jmca) ‖ *pémi* (Tbgo, Trin) ‖ *pone* 3 (Jmca) ‖ *stew-dumpling* (Bdos, StVn) A small pudding made of varying mixtures of grated SWEET-POTATOES, grated coconut, CORNMEAL, PLANTAIN-FLOUR, raisins, spices, sugar, and essence, wrapped in a (SEA-) GRAPE leaf or piece of banana or plantain leaf and steamed. [Akan, Cp Gã-Adangme *doko na* 'sweeten (vb) mouth', *doko nõ* 'sweet (adj) thing' *ZAGL*; also Twi *ɔ-dɔkono* 'boiled maize-bread' *DAFL*] □ The Gã-Adangme source seems to have infl the form in *ECar* territories, attested also by variant spellings *doucouna, ducana, dukona*, while the Twi word appears to have affected the form used in *Belz, Jmca*. Pl is unchanged: *to like, to eat*, etc *dukuna* refers to a meal of two or three of the puddings.

dull sea·son *n phr* (Antg, StKt) ‖ OUT-OF-CROP SEASON (Bdos, Guyn) *Now that the sugar crop is grinding to a halt all of us rightly begin to turn our attention to the period we traditionally call the Dull Season.*—LaS (75.07.09, p.2) [*Dull* in ref to the absence of money to spend and hence of commercial activity]

dumb-bread *n* (USVI) A heavy bread baked without using yeast and sometimes made with cornmeal.

dumb-fruit; **dumbs** [dʌmz] *n* (*pl*) (Antg, StKt) ‖ DUNKS (Bdos, etc) [See notes at DUNKS]

dum-box *n* (BrVi) ‖ DONKEY-BOX (Antg) [Perh erron for DUNG-BOX]

dumps *n pl* (Antg) ‖ DUNKS (Bdos, etc) [See notes at DUNKS]

dun·cy *adj* (CarA) [IF] [Of a schoolchild] Very slow to learn and considered stupid; *SE* dunderheaded. [< *OED dunce* sb 5. 'a dullard' + adj suff -*y*]

dun·dus (dun·does) [dʌndʌs] *n* (Guyn, Jmca) An albino, or the condition of being an albino. (See cit). *Blondes, with golden hair falling to their waists, have been heard to attribute their shortage of pigmentation to a family weakness for the production of dundus.*—DaG (68.04.11, p.8) [Cp *CBCD* Congo *ndundu* 'an albino'] □ The term seems to remain unchanged in the pl. However it also occurs as a family name in some places, with the orig sense evid lost. Cp RAGGAY (*StVn*).

dung-bas·ket *n* (Bdos, Jmca, Nevs, StKt) **1.** A light, tough, panlike basket of WIST or tamarind twigs, about 2-1/2 ft in diameter, used for distributing manure or dung on plantations, and carried on the head by women labourers. **2.** (Nevs) ‖ *estate-basket* (Nevs) A deeper kind of the same basket that is also used for carrying GROUND PROVISIONS. **3.** PHRASE **3.1** give sb **dung-basket to carry water** *vb phr* (Bdos, StKt) See BASKET Phr 1.

dung-box *n* (Mrat) ‖ DONKEY-BOX (Antg)

dungs [dʌŋz] *n pl* (Guyn) ‖ DUNKS (Bdos, etc)

dunk(s)* [dʌŋk(s)~dʌŋs] *n* (*pl*) (Bdos, Guyn, StKt, StVn) ‖ *byre* (Guyn) ‖ *coco-plum* (CayI) ‖ *coolie-plum* 1. (Jmca) ‖ *dum(b)-fruit* (StKt) ‖ *dumps* (Antg) ‖ *dungs* (Guyn) ‖ *governor-plum* 2. (Belz) ‖ *Jew-plum* (CayI) ‖ *juju(be)* (Baha, Jmca) ‖ *koko-kouli, ponm siwèt* (StLu) ‖ *pomme-surette* (Angu, Nevs, StKt) A small,

apple-shaped plum, yellow shading into light-brown when ripe, with a white, brittle, sweetish-sour flesh around a single, stone-hard seed; it is borne on a medium-sized, spreading, and very prickly tree many varieties of wh stink when in blossom; *Ziziphus mauritania* or *Z. jujuba* (*Rhamnaceae*). [Orig *dung-tree* from the distinctly dung-like smell of the young blossoms in the wind. However, the objectionable naming of the fruit *dung* by back-formation led to several euphemisms, principally *dunk*, but also *dumb*, *dump*] □ Since the word occurs mostly in the pl in ref to the fruit, the form *dungs* pronunc [dʌŋs~dʌŋz] (also spelt *dounce* by E. Mittelholzer) is used in *Guyn*. Other variant spellings abound: *donce, dongs, donks, down(e)s, dums, duncks*, etc.

dup·py[1] (**dup·pie**) *n* (Baha, Bdos, Belz, CayI, Jmca) ‖ *jumbie* (Baha, ECar) **1.** A harmful, invisible, supernatural presence believed to be raised from the dead; an evil spirit that sometimes talks. *Girls working night shift at the Intel plant are now scared out of their pants because of what they feel is a presence of a duppy on the premises. It all started two weeks ago when one of the girls was slapped in her face by something which nobody could see.*—NaT (87.05.08, p.9) [Perh from more than one African source, associated with a fearsome creature. Note *DAFL* Fante *adɔpe* 'a species of ape (= *aboatia*)...said to be so fierce as to kill 20 men at once'. In *Guyn* CBT (p.62) cites '*People 'fraid Adopi too much...a-bush a-night*', *Adopi* being 'a little hairy creature, human in shape but...with knees that cannot bend...said to live in the bush', 'Prob (p.8) a blood relation of the *Duppy* of the Jamaican Negro'. However, Cp also phonic resemblance of *LDKF* Kikongo *ndoki* 'sorcerer, bewitcher who takes sb's life by witchcraft'] **2.** PHRASES **2.1 set duppy on sb/sth** *vb phr* (Jmca) [IF] To cause someone or some place to be haunted by an evil spirit. *Is the truth, Parson. You don't know, but many of your church members believe in and practise necromancy. They formed a committee and pay an obeahman to set duppy on 'im!*—BGSB: 54 **2.2 take duppy off sb/sth** *vb phr* (Jmca) [IF] To have an evil spirit removed; to be exorcised. **2.3 the duppy and the dog** *n phr* (Bdos) [AF—Joc] ‖ HABRA, DABRA AND THE CREW (Bdos) [AF—Joc] *In those days you had the Exhibition in Queen's Park every December and you would see the higher ups and better-offs, the rich, the poor, the duppy and the dog.*—(Bdos) **3.** ‖ *duppy-ghost* (Jmca) An apparition associated esp with dark roads and the silk- cotton tree; the unhappy and sometimes headless ghost of sb; a walking dead person, met at night, that is said to have all the appearance of a living person except for one feature such as the hands or feet turned the wrong way. **a.** *He told her how when people died their souls went up to heaven to be judged, but that their duppy still remained on earth and could be used for both good and evil.*—PCOS:162 **b.** *In my past amateurish study of spirits, I have divided them into three precise groups, wraiths, visitors at death and ghosts. Caymanians call all three* *duppies.*—FDI:11 c. ... *like say when you dream at night that duppy-ghost is a-chase you and you cry out and Mother hugs you and you wake up.*—RND:18 **4.** (Bdos) [*AF—Joc*] A corpse. *Duppies $5.00 Apiece./There is some complaint that before the Death Card leaves the ward for posting at the Gate an orderly who is the boss of the show sells the dead to the undertakers by telephoning them, and is paid a commission. The duppy vendor keeps all the money he receives and does not share it with the men who have got to lift the said duppy about.*—TrU (63.10.09, p.5) **5.** (Bdos, CayI, Jmca) ‖ **baccoo** Guyn) A malevolent spirit that may be kept in a bottle, to be released to do harm to sb; a malevolent spirit that may take some frightening animal form or other form. **a.** *Obeahmen can 'catch them in bottles' in Jamaica. If someone wants to harm a neighbour he may get an Obeahman to do this and then to bury the bottle beneath the threshold of the neighbour's house. When the unfortunate man enters or leaves his home, the duppy comes out of the bottle.*—Pra 1278/213:848 **b.** *There had been the stories about duppies who appeared as calves with machine-parts tied to their tails and legs and with flashing eyes and bellowing utterances.*—SD:11 **c.** *Duppy can be in the form of a bright light, an animal and can change into something else or disappear.*—FDI:65 **6.** (Bdos) [Rastaf] Any meat, esp pork. *We were eating some food and arguing about funky music. He told us he was not eating yet and to leave his 'duppy' (pork) until he got back.*—NaT (77.08.04, p.3) [Most likely of W Afr orig. Senses 1–5 are associated with fear of the dead, sense 6. with dead meat, wh is despised in Rastaf philosophy] □ The term *duppy* is widely known in the *CarA* even where *jumbie* is the normal term. In *Bdos* both terms are used, but *duppy* is commoner. In *Baha* both terms appear to be equally current.

dup·py² *adj* (Baha, Bdos, Belz, CayI, Jmca) [*AF—Derog/Joc*] ‖ **jumbie²** (ECar) False; misleading; comical; of low status; spurious. *Walking slowly back together, the sergeant said, 'It's been almost what you might call a duppy raid, eh?'*—SJS:162 □ Loose usage, but often as first element in folk names. See separate entries, and many others (*Jmca*) in *DJE*. Cp also JUMBIE² in similar usage.

dup·py-a·gent *n* (Bdos} [*AF—Joc*] **1.** An undertaker. **2.** ‖ CARRION-CROW MAN (Guyn)

dup·py-ba·sil* *n* (Bdos) [*IF*] ‖ **mosquito-bush** (CarA) ‖ **wild basil/barsley** (Jmca) A small shrubby herb with strongly aromatic leaves and insignificant, greenish flowers, growing commonly in waste places (*GTWF:114*); *Ocimum micranthum, O. sanctum*, (*Labiatae*). *Mosquito Bush is an alternative name for the Duppy Basil, itself a delightful name for the branched herb growing commonly on roadsides and waste places and bearing whorls of small, pale violet tubular flowers. The same name is used for another shrubby herb also called the White Hopweed, both names being used by Hughes.*—AdN (79.05.06,

p.14, M. Hutt) □ See also notes at JUMBIE BALSAM (*Guyn*), JUMBIE BASIL (*Guyn*).

dup·py-cap (dup·py-cup) *n* (Jmca) [*AF—Joc*] ‖ DUPPY-PARASOL (Bdos) [See DUPPY-PARASOL. The variant CAP is prob due to the shape of the cap-like variety, and the rarer CUP a folk variant]

dup·py-cher·ry *n* (Jmca) ‖ CLAMMY-CHERRY (CarA)

dup·py-cho·cho *n* (Jmca) ‖ AMERICAN SILK-COTTON (BrVi) [< DUPPY² 'false' + CHOCHO, from resemblance of 'wind' pods to the vegetable]

dup·py-crab* *n* (Bdos) A large; white, land crab that lives in swamp-holes and emerges at nights (hence the name); *Cardisoma guanhumi* (*Cecarcinidae*). □ Cp JUMBIE-CRAB (*USVI*), GHOST-CRAB (*Jmca*) wh are different.

dup·py-dust *n* (Bdos) ‖ **grave-dust, jumbie powder** (Guyn) Dust taken from inside a grave or obtained from the bones of the dead for use in the practice of OBEAH. [For a comparable W Afr practice note the foll: Another substitute that was reported was using some soil from the grave of an accused witch. An example of one such case was reported from Mafi when one of their number had been buried in the Northern Region of Ghana, and it was subsequently indicated that he started killing people in Mafi. Since it was impossible to observe a traditional homtodzoe ceremony, or even obtain nail parings or hair clippings, messengers were sent to obtain soil from the grave, returning it to Mafi. Here a prayer was offered and the soil burned, and the deaths reportedly ceased, attesting to the acceptability of this substitute ritual as far as the lineage was concerned—*Iai XLVII4, p.367*]

dup·py-ghost *n* (Jmca) See DUPPY, cit c.

dup·py-gun *n* (Jmca) ‖ **blue-bell** (Guyn) **1.** ‖ **many-root(s), minnie-root** (CarA) ‖ **menow-weed**‖ (JMCA) ‖ **monkey gun** (Bdos) A sturdy wayside herb growing to about 2 ft high, with attractive blue-violet (rarely white) trumpet-shaped flowers and thin inch-long seed-pods wh explode when damp (hence the name); *Ruellia tuberosa* (*Acanthaceae*). *Take for instance our 'duppy-gun' which may be a popping toy for children—they rub it with spit—but is more important to grown-ups who know to use its thick roots for female complaints.*—Jmca (Ms) [From the explosion of the ripe pod in rain or when handled] □ See more at MINNIE-ROOT.

dup·py-ma·chete [dʌpi-mašɛt] *n* (Jmca) ‖ BEAN-TREE (Bdos)

dup·py-nee·dle* *n* (Bdos) ‖ **monkey-needle(s)** (Bdos) ‖ **needle-grass** (Bdos, Trin) ‖ **railway-daisy** (Trin) ‖ **Spanish needle, Spanish nettle** (Jmca) An erect weed growing

2 to 3 ft high, with square stems, divided leaves and bearing daisy-like florets wh are really clusters of tiny barbed spines that catch on to clothing or skin, hence the name; *Bidens pilosa* (*Compositae*).

dup·py-para·sol* *n* (Bdos) [*AF—Joc*] ‖*duppy-cap* (Jmca) ‖*duppy-umbrella* (Bdos, Jmca) ‖*jumbie-parasol* (Gren, Tbgo, TkCa, Trin) ‖*jumbie-umbrella* (CarA) ‖*sperrit-umbrella* (Baka) An inedible mushroom, usu of the type having a smooth, round, soft and cap-like top on a short stem, or a tougher frilly-edged semi-circular outgrowth from rotting wood; both are found in damp shady ground or animal manure. *When the Federal Government could function admirably with three Ministers—a Prime Minister, a Minister for Foreign Affairs, and a Minister for Home Affairs, what are we to think of the multiplicity of ministers who have sprung up like 'duppy parasols' all over these ideal holiday resort islands?*—AdN (61.02.12, p.4) [DUPPY, from association with night and shadowy places + *parasol*, in particular ref to the variety that resembles an 'umbrella' or 'parasol']

dup·py-pick·ney *n* (Jmca) [*AF—Joc*] [Of a child; used as a teasing name in children's games] A booby; the fool of the crowd. *'The last one roun' to the launch,' Iris challenged, 'is a duppy pickney!'*—SJS:134 [< DUPPY[2] + PICKNEY]

dup·py-pinch *n* (Bdos) [*AF—Joc*] Any discoloration or blemish of the skin of unknown cause. [< DUPPY[2] + SE *pinch*]

dup·py-rid·in(g)-horse [ˈdʌpi-raidin-hars] /1'2112/ *n* (Jmca) [*AF*] ‖GOD-HORSE (CarA) [DUPPY[1], from the fact that this insect is difficult to detect because of its stick-like appearance, motionless stand and ability to assume the colour of its background; + *riding-horse* 'horse for riding' from its resemblance to a 'match-stick' toy horse]

dup·py-tucks (**duppy-lucks**) *n pl* (Bdos) [*AF*] Creases in badly ironed clothes. [< DUPPY[2] + SE *tucks*]

dup·py-um·brel·la *n* (Bdos, Jmca) [*AF—Joc*] ‖DUPPY-PARASOL (Bdos) *At Sam Lord's Castle we observed with interest a fine collection of fungus bracts, a species of what we call 'Duppy Umbrellas', growing on the dead trunk of a cordia tree. There were layers of these beige-yellow semi-circular outgrowths from the gnarled bark, horizontal, soft, finely ribbed on the under- sides. Most people will not touch them on the grounds that they are poisonous.*—AdN (78.12.13, p.7, M. Hutt) [See DUPPY-PARASOL] □ The term is also loosely applied by some speakers to any kind of mushroom.

Dutch jar *n phr* (Guyn) ‖*corn-jar* (Bdos) ‖*England-jar* (Antg) A large wide-mouthed earthenware jar of varying depths up to 4 or 5 ft (prob used in earlier times for importing pickled meat from Europe), used mostly for keeping drinking water cool in rural areas.

Dutch ov·en *n phr* 1. (Bdos) ‖BOX-OVEN (Guyn) 2. (Baha) A round metal pan about 12 to 15 ins in diameter and about 6 ins deep, with a lid and a semi-circular handle, used as a portable oven for baking bread or JOHNNY-CAKES over a coal-fire.

Dutch pot *n phr* 1. (Baha, CayI) ‖THREE-FOOT POT (Bdos, etc) *The coconut oil was made in large pots such as the one in the museum. They were called 'Dutch Pots', and were used by housewives in the 700 Bahama Islands to process coconut oil.*—TrI (76.02.02, p.4) 2. (Jmca) ‖*dutchy* (Jmca) A heavy, deep pot (of cast iron or thick aluminium) with a rounded bottom, handles and lid, used for roasting or baking.

dutch·y *n* (Jmca) [*IF*] ‖DUTCH POT 2. (Jmca)

dut·ty[1] [dʌti] *n* (CarA) [*AF*] 1. Mud; earth; soil (i.e. in any quantity or form). *One-one dutty build dam* (A little bit of earth at a time will build a complete dam).—Guyn (Prov) [Prob < *DAFL* Akan *dote* 'soil, earth, clay, mud'. Prob also infl by DIRTY[1]] 2. The ground. *Me no eat bread wa fall da dutty* (= I won't eat bread that fell on the ground).—Belz (Ms of dialogue) 3. Dirt or mess of any kind (including human or animal faeces). *Fowl-dutty is good manure.*—(Bdos) [Prob by semantic shift of sense 1. + infl of SE *dirt*. See DIRTY[1] n]

dut·ty[2] [dʌti] *adj* (CarA) [*AF*] Dirty. [By functional n > adj shift of DUTTY[1]]

dut·ty[3] [dʌti] *vb* (CarA) [*AF—Vul*] ‖DIRTY[2] (Guyn)

dwarf-ba·na·na *n* 1. (Baha, Trin) ‖APPLE-BANANA (Belz, etc) 2. (Trin) A banana borne on a short tree (4 to 6 ft high) and better known as GOVERNOR-FIG.

dwarf-co·co·nut* *n* (Belz, Dmca, Gren, StKt) ‖*chinee coconut* (Tbgo, Trin) ‖*claret-nut* (Guyn) ‖*yellow-boy* (Bdos) ‖*yellow-dwarf (coconut)* (Belz, Jmca, StLu) A yellow-skinned variety of coconut that is noticeably smaller than the normal green- skinned ones but borne in fuller clusters on a short trunk; it is preferred for its sweeter water. [*Dwarf* in ref to the short trunk, but perh also to the smallness of the nut]

dwarf-poin·ci·a·na *n* (CarA) ‖BARBADOS-PRIDE (CarA) [From strong resemblance of both the flowers and compound leaves of this shrub to those of the tree *Poinciana regia* of the same family]

dwell·ing-house *n* (CarA) A building erected for people to live in (usu a small and simple kind); (SE) a dwelling. *More than 3300 new dwelling houses were erected in the rural areas* *of Br Guiana last year.*—Br Guiana Bulletin (56.08.08) [Prob a part of sugar-plantation vocab (cp CHATTEL-HOUSE), but also a typical CE redundant compound (cp BOY-CHILD, etc)]. □ The term *dwelling* by itself is exceptional in CE, and the term *dwelling-house* almost restricted to real estate and legal contexts.

dwenn (du·enne) *n* (Trin) A legendary little creature, the spirit of an infant who died before it was baptized and now wanders in the forest, its feet turned backwards, its big head covered with a large mushroom-shaped hat so that its face is not seen, joining with others of its kind in bands to lure children or hunters into the forest until they are led astray. [Fr Cr < Sp *duende* 'goblin, mischievous child', but perh infl also by Fr form *duègne*, implying 'nuisance'] □ Cp DUHENDE (*Belz*).

dwi·vé (dree·vay dri·vé, dri·vay) [dwive~ drive] *vb intr* (Dmca, Gren, Trin) [*AF—Joc*] To walk about in the streets without a fixed purpose; to be out and about for the fun of it. *The end of my own story—and an enjoyable one at that was provided on the BWIA flight where the smiling faces of my kind of people clearly said: 'All you finish dreevaying? Well come go home!'*—TrG (74.09.29, p.14) [Fr Cr < Fr (nautical) *dériver* 'to drift'] □ The pronunc [dwive] is commoner in *Dmca*. The systematized and preferrable spelling is *drivé*.

dwi·yèt (dou·ill·ette, dou·i·ette) [dwiyɛt] *n* (Dmca, StLu) A traditional costume consisting principally of a full-length dress of brightly printed cotton over a lace or embroidered pet-ticoat, a shawl or 'foulard' around the shoulders and an elaborately tied, coloured headkerchief. [Fr Cr < Fr *douillette* adj 'dainty, delicate' in 17C sense (see Cotgrave)] □ The *dwiyèt*, more fully *wòb dwiyèt*, is the official national costume of *Dmca*.

dye[1] *adj* (Guyn) [Indic] Yellow. *The Sadhu man wears a dye gown*—Guyn (Ms) [< Hin *dai* 'yellow, gold-coloured', hence homophonic with SE *dye*]

dye[2] *n* (Guyn) [Indic] Powdered turmeric, esp as used ceremonially in Hindu marriages.

dye-yam *n* ['dai-ya·m] (Guyn) ‖ YELLOW-YAM (Antg, etc) □ This name is used mostly by rural Indic folk in *Guyn*. See DYE[1].

E

'e (e, ee) [i] *pron, 3rd pers sg* (CarA) [*AF—Cr*] ‖ *him, im* (Jmca) **1.** (masc) He; him; his (i.e. serving in nom, obj, and possessive functions). *'E keep 'e wife workin' for 'e* (*He keeps his wife working for him*).—(Guyn) **2.** (fem) She; her (in nom, obj, possessive functions). *De stomach 'e gat now / Da no fi Jan teng Gawd / Da fe 'e husband.* (*The* [*pregnant*] *stomach she has now is not for John, thank God; it's for her husband*).—Bes:4:6, p.26 **3.** It; its. *Dog foot brok' 'e fin' 'e massa doormout* ([*When the*] *dog's foot is broken it finds its master's door*).—Guyn (Prov) [< SE *he*, in Creolized use, by calquing from Afr langs, in many of wh one 3rd pers sg pron form serves for all genders, ex Yoruba *o*, Igbo *ya* (also all cases), Efik *enye*, etc] □ So used in speech only, but frequently written in narrative dialectal dialogue, except in *Jmca*.

ear·hole *n* (Bdos, Guyn) [*AF—Joc*] Ear. *You could hear the church bells from St Barnabas Church, miles and miles of sugar canes away, over the fields, coming right up to your two earholes.*—CWFYS:29

ear·ly *adv* PHRASE **1. early o'clock** *adv phr* (Bdos, Jmca, Tbgo, Trin) [*IF*] Very early. ... *with the powerful display of batting provided by Vivian Richards getting in among the runs early o'clock, making the first 100 of the tour.*—Peo. 1. 11, p.76 **2. in the early/earlies** *adv phr* (Bdos, Guyn) [*IF*] At an early stage; early enough. *If you had put a stop to his bossiness in the earlies, he wouldn't have been so domineering now.*—Guyn (Ms)

earn·est [ʌː(r)nɪs] *adj* (Belz) [*X*] Honest. *He was not earnest, only telling lies.*—Belz (Ms) [A misspelling caused by overlapping pronunc of *honest, earnest*. Also poss confusion in sense with SE *in earnest*]

ears [erz~eəz~eˑz] *n pl* (CarA) **1.** [*X*] [Often used as the only form, the sg *ear* not occurring in uneducated speech] Ear. *A mosquito was singing in my ears whole night.*—(Guyn) □ Cp similar usage of *teeth, ants,* etc. **2.** PHRASES **2.1 break stick in yo(ur) ears** *vb phr* (Gren, Guyn, StKt) [*IF*] To make yourself deaf to the pleas, advice or warnings of others. [< Cr /stik brok in yo eez/ with same sense, apparently from the accident of deafness caused by puncturing the eardrum while cleaning the ear with a dry twig] **2.2 your ears (are) hard** *vb phr* (CarA) [*IF/F*] ‖ *your head (is) hard* (Nevs, etc) ‖ *you have (a) hard*

head (Baha, etc) You are stubbornly disobedient. [A likely calque from W Afr langs. Cp Twi *n'aso yɛ de!* (*His ear(s) be hard*) 'He is stubborn'; also Yoruba *eti ẹ di* (*ear(s) his blocked*) 'He is stubbornly disobedient'] □ See also HARD-EARS.

ears-hard [eˑz-haˑ(r)d] *adj* (Belz) [*AF*] ‖ HARD-EARS² (CarA) *Ears-hard pikni will have to feel* (= *The stubbornly disobedient child will have to be flogged*).—Belz (Prov) [See HARD-EARS]

earth-burn·er *n* (Guyn) One who produces hard, red clay or 'burnt earth' in bulk, for road surfacing, by a process of slow burning of prepared mounds of mud.

ease up¹ *vb phr* (ECar) [*AF/IF*] **1.** To stop teasing or harassing (sb). *Garcon, leave me I say—ease me up! Go somewhere else and blow your top!*—TLTH:23 **2.** To help (sb) out of a difficult situation (usu without questioning the worthiness of the case). *The friend beg him for a meal, and Bart do without eating himself and ease up the friend.*—STLL:45

ease-up² *n* (ECar) [*AF*] **1.** Help given to or received by sb in a difficult situation. (Hence foll phrs). **2.** PHRASES **2.1 get a[n] ease-up** *vb phr* (ECar) [*AF*] *Everybody hard-up, and you can't get a ease-up from your best friend.*—SWOS: 156 **2.2 give (sb) a[n] ease-up** *vb phr* (ECar) [*AF*] *Man A not wo[r]king since t[h]ree months now, you ca[n't] gi[ve] me a little ease up Sir?* —(Gren) [Cp *EDD* ease 1. sb (2) (Sc, Yks, etc) *to give an ease up*, 'to give a helping hand']

eas·i·ly *adv* (Guyn) [*X*] Cautiously; quietly. *The dog was barking so I got out of bed as easily as I could and then pulled the blind easily to peep outside.*—Guyn (Ms)

East Bank, the *n phr* (Guyn) ‖ *bank¹* 3. (Guyn) The heavily populated farming and plantation area along the east bank of the Demerara River stretching some 30 miles south from Georgetown, Guyana; (commonly abbr as *E.B.D.* in postal addresses).

East Coast, the *n phr* **1.** (ECar) ‖ *windward (coast)* (Dmca, Gren, StVn) The Atlantic or eastern coast of most *ECar* islands, considered rural (as opposed to the urbanized western or Caribbean coast). **2.** (Guyn) The heavily populated farming and plantation area along the

Atlantic coast of Guyana stretching eastwards from Georgetown to the Abary Creek (commonly abbr as *E.C.D.* in postal addresses).

East·er-flow·er *n* (Bdos, Trin) A climbing shrub that bears abundant, hanging clusters of small, mauve flowers about Easter (hence the name); *Securidaca diversifolia* (*Polygalaceae*).

East·er-li·ly* *n* 1. (Berm, Trin) A white or pinkish-white, trumpet-shaped lily about 6 ins long, borne in horizontal clusters on a strong, fleshy stalk about 3 ft tall; *Lilium longiflorum* (*Liliaceae*). 2. (Bdos, Dmca, Guyn) A bright red lily borne two or three together on short stalks; *Hippeastrum puniceum* (*Amaryllidaceae*).

East-Ind·i·an *adj, n* (CarA) ‖ *coolie* (ECar) [*Derog*] ‖ *Indian* 1. (CarA) [*IF*] 1. (Of or belonging to) a West-Indian person or such a descendant of a person who was originally from that part of the Asian sub-continent loosely called India, embracing a number of different linguistic, cultural and national groups, with the same physical appearance of light or dark brown skins and long, shiny black hair 2. [Hist] (Of or belonging to) an original immigrant, IN-DENTURED labourer from India or his/her descendant who is a West-Indian by naturalization or by birth. [By contradistinction to *West-Indian*, as of the mid 19C with the beginning of post-emancipation immigration of INDENTURED *Indian* labourers from the *East*] □ Also in contradistinction to the ‖ *Indian* [*IF*] wh, in earlier literature, referred to the Aboriginal American Indian who is now distinguished by term AMERINDIAN].□ The ‖ *coolie* adj, n [*Derog*] is offensive.

East-Ind·i·an man·go *n phr* (Jmca) ‖ BOM-BAY-MANGO (Jmca)

eas·y[1] *adj* (CarA) [*IF*] 1. [Replying to an inquiry made as a greeting] Having no problems; in good health, etc, thank you. *S1: How you doin[g]? / S2: Easy, man. Easy.* 2. Indifferent; not worried about a particular situation or circumstance. *If the Government agrees to this I am easy; if the Government had decided they would not give it, I would be easy too, because I feel the same way.*—Bdos (Hd, 74.07.09, p.3690) 3. [With special sense after neg] (Not) co-operative; (not) unwilling to be aggressive. *You have to be careful with that sergeant! He's not easy, boy!*—(Jmca)

eas·y[2] *adv* (CarA) [*X*] 1. Cautiously; quietly. *... because the police never work so easy as when they come around Trade Union strikes, because all they do is to come around and see what is going on.*—Bdos (Hd, 74.09.10, p.3997) 2. Easily; readily. *You're big and strong and handsome and the juice of life still run like a stream through you; you can find another mate easy-easy.*—PCOS:48 3. PHRASES 3.1 **stan[d] easy** [sta:n izi] *vb phr* (Guyn) [*AF—Cr*] To be quiet; to make no sound. *While all de rowin[g] was goin[g] on she jus[t] si[t] do[w]ng in de corner and stan[d] easy.*—(Guyn)

3.2 take it easy *vb phr* (CarA) [*IF*] (i) To be or to remain calm. (ii) To move or proceed with care and caution. *They had a lot of school children on the road so you had to take it easy, if not you knock them do[w]ng.*—(Trin)

eas·y-chair *n* (Angu) A rocking chair·

eat *vb tr* (CarA) 1. [In playing chess, draughts] To take an opponent's piece. 2. (Tbgo, Trin) [*AF—Vul*] [Usu of a man] To have sexual intercourse (usu outside of marriage). [Prob by infl of W Afr langs. Cp *ADHL* Hausa *či* 1. 'eat' 11. 'win, conquer' 16. 'sleep with a woman'. Also Nupe *gi* 'eat; (Vul) have sexual intercourse with a woman'] 3. PHRASES 3.1 **eat bird-seed** *vb phr* [*AF—Joc*] ‖ EAT PARROT (CarA) 3.2 **eat from bramble to timber** *vb phr* (Gren) [*IF*] To believe a foolish explanation or an unlikely story; to be easily deceived; to be gullible. *I who in 1951 swallow hook line and sinker / and eat from bramble to timber / when de beast from de east / ... came forward after making marse in Aruba / proclaiming dat he was the Messiah.*—Gren (Ms, 1981) 3.3 **eat nice** *vb phr* (CarA) [*IF*] ‖ *eat sweet* (CarA) [Of food only] To be enjoyable and pleasant to the taste. *This rice and peas eat nice, you see!*—(Jmca) 3.4 **(not) eat nice** *vb phr* (StVn, Tbgo, Trin) [*AF*] [Of people; neg use only] (Not) to be trifled with; (not) to restrain violent anger. *She couldn't offer her house for the fete because her parents don't eat nice and would turn everybody out at midnight.*—Trin (Ms) [By analogy with food that is not pleasant to the taste. See prec] 3.5 **eat parrot; eat parrot backside/bambam/bottom/ head/soup** *vb phr* (CarA) [*AF—Joc*] ‖ *eat bird-seed* (Guyn) To be overbearingly talkative. *Oh boy shut up! You ain[t] weary talkin[g]? You eat parrot bottom or what?*—(StVn) 3.6 **eat sweet** *vb phr* (CarA) [*IF*] ‖ EAT NICE (CarA) (See Phr 3.3 above)

eat·er·y *n* (Bdos, Guyn, StVn) [*AF*] ‖ *cook-shop* (Guyn) An inexpensive eating-place, usu with its door open to the street, selling cooked food. *The cleanup was dramatic, with many awfully drab, rundown, hole-in-the-wall 'eateries' and cook shops being transformed into clean attractive restaurants.*—AdN (76.10.12, p.4)

eat·ing so·da *n phr* (Guyn) Bicarbonate of soda.

eat-man *n* (ECar) [*AF—Joc*] A gluttonous man; an insatiable eater.

e·bo·ny *n* 1.* (Bdos) ‖ WOMAN-TONGUE TREE (CarA) 2.* (Baha, CayI, Jmca) ‖ *ketto* (Jmca) ‖ *red-wood* (Baha) A slender tree about 30 ft tall with a tough wood; *Hypelate trifoliata* (*Sapindaceae*). 3.* (Guyn) [Timber Ind] A forest-tree about 100 ft tall, with a deeply fluted, erect trunk, producing a deep purple, very hard wood that is used for inlays, walking sticks, etc; *Swartzia bannia* (*Caesalpineaceae*). 4. (CarA) [Name given to a number of trees whose wood is very hard, heavy, and usu difficult to work with] **5.** (ViIs) ‖ AXEMASTER (Belz)

ebo·ny-ber·ry [ɛbni-bɛri] *n* (Angu) ‖ JAMOON (Guyn)

E.C. *abbr* [i·si·] Eastern Caribbean (esp used in ref to currency expressed in *EC dollars*).

E.C.C.M. *abbr* (CarA) Eastern Caribbean Common Market, an establishment set up in 1968 for the development of closer union and concerted action among its seven *ECar* member states in all economic and social matters; now administered by the Economic Affairs Secretariat of the OECS in Castries, St Lucia. □ The seven member states are *Antg/Brbu, Dmca, Gren, Mrat, StKt/Nevs, StLu, StVn/Grns.*

ECHOIC WORD (*marked excl ideoph*) (CarA) A descriptive vocable used to convey an impression adding vividness to the meaning of any utterance, phrase, or sentence that describes a noise, action, movement, or the nature of an incident or a combination of these. The form is spontaneous in character and may occur by itself as a mere imitative sound representing an action observed or sensed, or it may form part of a descriptive phrase at its beginning, middle, or end. In many instances it is reduplicated; or different ones may be strung together for greater effect. An *Echoic word* generally has two functions in CE: 1. Representing the actual sound, action or incident, and in this case frequently behaving like an SE interjection, occurring immediately at the beginning or end of, though sometimes separated from, its related phrase— Ex: *Badap!* See that woman fall! 2. With metaphorical shift, indicating the suddenness, surprise or impact of an event, and in this case usu occurring as part of a phrase or sentence, functioning in the same way as and so replacing a structured SE adverbial or n phr. Exs: *It fell bradarax* ('It fell hard and loudly'); *Me heart dis go buff-bim—BJL:30* ('My heart beat madly'); *She give him bups* ('She gave him a hard blow'); *After the bambalula bambulai / he was a slave again—BTA:262* ('After the drumming and dancing/ ...') Most Echoic words begin with / b-/ and this suggests a set of patterns in general use (See separate entries for many of these): **(i)** [Indicating a fall] *badam, badap(s), bam, bap(s), bradam bradap(s), bram, brap(s);* **(ii)** [Indicating a noisy crash] *bradarax, braggalunga, brudum brudung, bruggadumbam, bruggadung, bruggalung-dung;* **(iii)** [Indicating a heavy blow] *bidim, bidip, bim, bip, buduf, budup, buf, bup;* **(iv)** [Indicating a noisy blow or collision] *brudum, brudung, budum, budung, bum.* Some are rather specific in form and ref: *bangalanga* for the sound of a bell; *bashaow, bluzhung* for falling, plunging into water; *brag-a-dap, brigidip* for a galloping horse, mule, etc; *fm* for a bad smell; *plai, (s)plax* for a lash, slap, etc; *prax* for something snapping; *wap* for a lash Others are the subject of spontaneous invention or mixtures, of wh the foll are

exs. **a.** ... *and I see Big Joe tekking up rocks and throwing at the house and the glass-windows and I hearing changalang changalang all the time, and a voice inside the house screaming, and a baby crying.—CISH:127* **b.** *Eric coun't stand it no more. He step back and run up and ... daddaie ...! he give the pig one kick right in its ribs. And the pig collapse and dead, easy so.—CISH:96* **c.** *Next thing I hear a pix-pax, bradax and then brug-a-down. Well then I started to look round, and I thought I see some shadow, and I say, if you ent a ghost, you is a tief.—Bdos (NIFCA Ms, 1977)* **d.** *The whole morning he deh 'scung-young-young' and the piece-a car won't even start.—(Guyn)* [*Echoic words* is a convenient label used here for 'ideophones', the linguistic term for a feature that is widely characteristic of sub-Saharan Afr langs, of wh they are clearly a limited remainder in CE. WALS (p.461) cites C.M.Doke's definition of the term in ref to Bantu langs as 'a vivid representation of an idea in sound ... [describing] manner, colour, smell, action state or intensity'. They proliferate in Niger-Congo langs (see WALS (459–474) for a full discussion), but the linguistic phenomenon, evid uniquely African, is transferred conceptually rather than as actual etyma into CarA crcoles and via DECREOLIZATION, seem limited in present CE to contexts of action, sound and intensity]

eck·y-beck·y [ɛki-bɛki] *n* (Bdos) [*AF—Derog*] ‖ POOR-WHITE (CarA) [Perh a Derog reduplicated compound of Ijo *beke* 'European'; or a mocking combination of *WIED* Igbo *Ekee* 'God' + Ijo *beke* 'European'] □ This is the most *Derog* of a number of ‖ terms used in *Bdos.*

ECLAC [ɛklak] *abbr* Economic Commission for Latin America and the Caribbean, an intergovernmental organization founded in 1948 by United Nations Economic and Social Council for the purpose of developing and strengthening co-operative, regional economic growth and external trade in ways that would benefit each of its forty member states, wh include all CARICOM member states. □ *eclac's CarA* subregional headquarters are in *Trin.*

é·cole-biche ['ekol-'biš] *n* See LÉKÒL-BICH

ec·ze·ma [ɛgzima] *n* (ECar) One of several scabby, pustular boils appearing on the skin, esp the legs of children. □ SE *eczema* (sg) is the name of the disorder, but in CE the sg refers to each boil, hence *an eczema* sg, and more commonly *eczemas* pl.

ed·do(e) *n* (CarA) **1.*** (Guyn) ‖ *pulp(ing)-eddoe, white eddoe* (Bdos) A root-vegetable about the size of a potato, borne in sets of side-tubers or SUCKERS on a central corm; it has a fibrous skin, is slightly slimy when peeled, but is smooth-textured and much favoured in making soup; *Colocasia esculenta* var. *Antiquorum* (*Araceae*). □ The EDDOE is generally distinguished from the DASHEEN by its much smaller size, unused central corm and inedible leaves. **2.** (Berm) ‖DASHEEN (CarA) [*DAFL* Fante ɛdwo 'yam'; cp also *KID* Ibibio *edomo* 'potato yam'] □ See BADOO, COCO (*Jmca*). **3.** PHRASE **3.1 (go) through the eddoes** *vb phr* (Bdos) [*AF—Joc*] ‖ *crapaud smoke your pipe* (Dmca, etc) To be done for, ruined, finished; to have become decrepit. *Today in our country, many standards have been allowed by sheer neglect, irresponsibility or bad example to 'go through the eddoes'.*—AdN (89.01.15, p.6A) □ Most often in the form *gone through the eddoes.*

ed·doe-head *n* (Bdos) ‖DASHEEN (CarA) *The eddoe-head is generally not much favoured in Barbados but is sometimes used by poor people for making soup; but we use the suckers, the white eddoe.*—(Bdos)

ed·do(e)-top *n* (Antg) ‖ *dasheen-bush* (Tbgo, Trin) The leaves and stalks (esp the young ones) of the DASHEEN or EDDOE plant used in cooking PEPPER-POT, CALALU, etc.

edge up[1] **(to sb)** *vb phr* (Antg, Guyn, StVn) [*IF*] To try slily to gain attention and acquaintance (of sb who is considered important); to try to win (sb's) favour. *You could see him doing all he could to edge up to her all the time but she won't pay him no mind.*—(Antg)

edge-up[2] *adj* (StVn) [*AF*] [Of a person] Trying obviously to become friends (with sb). *But why she so edge-up? Millie don't like her and she still steady goin' by her.*—StVn (Ms)

edg·er-boy bis·cuit(s) *n phr* (Guyn) A later name for ADMIRAL(S).

ed·i·ble oil *n phr* (Guyn) (Formal name for) any vegetable oil used for frying food; cooking oil.

ed·u·ca·tion PHRASE **take education** [*IF*]; **take in (your) education** *vb phr* (CarA) To get yourself educated by going to school; to learn as much as you can from text-books and schooling; to be successful at school.

een·a [i·na] *prep* (Jmca, Mrat) [*AF—Cr*] ‖ *ina* (Antg, Belz, Jmca, Mrat) In; inside of. *Soon time me see people queue up / Me look pon dem an say 'lawd! / De whole queue load a dem look like / Dem live eena one yard.'*—FCV:103 (L. Bennett) □ A dial spelling often found in narrative dialogue. See INA

ef (**ef·fen, ef·fin**) [ɛf~ɛfin] *conj* (CarA) [*AF—Cr*] ‖ *iffing* (Bdos) If. **a.** *... an' one wite woman come 'long in er car an' aks 'er ef she get any lime an' lemon or tomater.*—JBJ:80 **b.** *You seein' the doctor in the mornin' honey effen I have to carry you.*—MHJT:66 **c.** *Effin I did embezzle public funds or caffuffle de authorities like dey appear to be doin' nowadays, I know dey goan quick enuf tek me to court.*—AdN (73.04.07, 'Off The Cuff') [Note *MCPP:19* 'The most prevalent [London]

Cockneyism [of the sixteenth and seventeenth centuries] was the use of the short *e* in words wh were more correctly pronounced with short *i*. Machyn and the churchwardens frequently use such spellings as ... *tell* (till), *ef* (if), etc.' Also cp *Amer Speech* (1931) VI p.230 'Such old forms of English as ... 'effin' for 'if' may be heard in the ordinary speech of the natives [of Oregon]'] □ Dial forms and pronunc often so represented in narrative dialogue.

ef·fect [ɛfɛkt] *vb tr* CarA [*X*] To affect; to have an effect on. *The rain did not effect the wicket enough to stop play.*—Bdos (Ms) □ A common confusion of *affect* and *effect* prob due to pronunc.

Egas! (**Igas!**) [i·gasŋ] *excl* (Dmca, StLu) [*AF*] See cit. *'Egas!'* is perhaps the most characteristic St Lucian expression. It derives from 'ish' (son) and 'garce' (prostitute), but this meaning has been lost. The word now signifies any sharp contact, a blow, a gunshot, an automobile crash, a fall, or even a kiss. Action movies are called 'Egas pictures' and the cry rising from the theatre can be heard a mile from Castries on a Saturday night.—Caq 4: 2, p.105, D.J. Crowley

egg-fruit *n* **1.** (CarA) (A name occasionally found for) the EGGPLANT. **2.** (Baha) A kind of fruit resembling or related to the PASSION-FRUIT. □ This fruit does not appear to be well-known in Nassau and this name prob belongs to the FAMILY ISLANDS.

egg·plant* (**egg-plant**) *n* (CarA) ‖ *antrover* (Antg, Brbu) ‖ *aubergine* (Antg, Gren, StVn, Trin) ‖ *baigan* (Guyn, Trin) ‖ *balagé* (Mrat) ‖ *balangene* (Dmca, Gren) ‖ *balanger* (StVn) ‖ *balanjay* (Bdos, Guyn, StVn) ‖ *banja* (Mrat, StVn) ‖ *bélanjenn, bélanjin* (Dmca, Gren, StLu) ‖ *bo(u)langer* (Bdos, Guyn, Mrat, StVn, USVI) ‖ *bringal* (Trin) ‖ *brown-jolly* (Jmca) ‖ *chuber* (Antg, StKt) ‖ *egg-fruit* (CarA) ‖ *garden-egg* (CayI, Jmca, TkCa) ‖ *melongene* (Dmca, StLu, Trin) ‖ *melonger* (BrVi, StKt) ‖ *truba* (Nevs, StKt) ‖ *volanjay* (Bdos) A smooth-skinned, usu ovoid and also usu purple-skinned fruit with soft, corky flesh, about 4 ins long; it grows on a low, bushy shrub (also called the *egg-plant*), and is widely used as a vegetable, boiled, stuffed, etc; *Solanum melongena* (*Solanaceae*). **a.** *Eggplant, Eleuthera style / ... 1 large eggplant, peeled ... Cube eggplant, add to mixture ... cook gently ... until eggplant is tender. Serve with fish or meat.*—SCCW:64 **b.** *There are many varieties of egg-plant some with paler skins turning yellow, some big and round and weighing up to two pounds, but the best eating ones are dark purple.*—Guyn (Ms) [*Egg* (from the usu ovoid shape of the fruit) + *plant*, though the name is more commonly applied to the fruit than to the plant] □ The spelling as one word (or a hyphenated alternative) recommends itself to distinguish the fruit from the *plant* and to facilitate usage ex *'slice two large eggplants'*. Note cits.

eh¹ [ɛ] /2 ∼ 23/ *excl with pitch distinctions* (CarA) [*IF*] **1.** *Phrase-terminal signal of a yes-no question* ‖ A¹² (CarA) *you ever see white people do that, eh?*—(Trin) **2.** (*Question signal*) [In responding to a question] What did you say? (i.e. Please repeat your question). *S1: You been out and come back? / S2: Eh? / S1: I ask if you been out a[l]ready and come back.*—(Guyn) **3.** *excl* (*High rising pitch*) ‖ A¹³ (CarA) [Expressing great surprise] Did I hear you correctly? *S1: You hear Arnold dead? / S2: Eh? S1: Yes, Arnold dead.*—(Guyn) [Cp Yoruba ɛ '? 'I beg your pardon!' (i.e. I can't believe my ears)] □ In both cases (2., 3.) only acceptable between peers; considered rude from younger to older persons. **4.** *excl (with lower, sometimes falling pitch)* (CarA) [*IF*—*tag*] **(i)** [Suggesting the answer 'Surely!'] *Wouldn't you agree? Bwoy, when you're in the public eye, your triumphs as well as tragedies cannot be hidden eh?*—StA(JA) (73.02.10, p.14, Partyline) **(ii)** [Suggesting caution or threat] *Take note! Beware! Look mister, if you know what good for youself you better leave de fowl alone eh.*—RTCS:19 [The sounds [ɛ], [ɛ̃] (i.e. both without and with nasalization) or lengthened as in *WTIED* ĩ̜zọn *éee* 'That's it!' or reduplicated as in *WIED* Igbo èe ẹ 'Yes', *IGED* Grebo *ẽhẽẽ* 'expression of pleasure', etc, and with various pitches superimposed, occur widely in W Afr langs to express agreement, disagreement, surprise, sorrow, warning, answering a call, or adding emphasis to a statement. Its W Afr use, wh can signal opposite meanings tonally, is quite definitive within a given context in a particular lang; and its wide occurrence in CE folk-speech, demonstrated in the above and following entries, shows noticeably similar phonological features correlated with both plain and emotive responses between peers] □ In both cases (2(i), 2(ii)) *eh* is attached to the last word without a break.

eh² [ɛ] *neg vb* (Gren, Trin) [*Af*—*Cr*] Ain't. *Is it also true that she went on the road and found people who eh have union cards working and she say she go tell Dr Cross?*—NeJ (74.11.15, p.8) [By reduction and denasalization of *ain't* [ɛnt > ɛn > ɛ̃ > ɛ]] □ Dial form often so written in narrative dialogue, esp of *Trin*.

Eh! Eh!¹; **Eh-eh!¹** [ɛˀɛ∼ɛːˀɛ∼ɛˀɛː] /33/ *excl* (CarA) [*AF*—*Cr*] ‖ *Mm-mm* 3. (CarA) [Expressing some degree of surprise, introducing or ending a statement]. **a.** *'Eh-eh! You ain't know?'* *he say. 'Man, you missing a big bassa-bassa. Jasper and Saga-boy going have a stick-fight.'*—CISH: 9 **b.** *At 76 years of age she appears to be in wonderful condition and good health. When asked how she accomplished this she replied forcefully, 'Bush Medicine, wha Doctor? Eh Eh!'*—Aaw 1: 1, p.18 [See etym note after EH¹] □ A much higher pitch (sometimes with one element lengthened) may be used to express greater surprise, often in such cases with some degree of vexation; less often, a much lower pitch may be used to express surprise with disappointment or disapproval. Many emotive variations in pitch also occur in folk situations.

Eh-eh!² [ɛˀɛ∼ɛ̃ˀɛ̃] /21 ∼ 31/ *neg excl* (CarA) [*AF*—*Cr*] ‖ *Mm-mm* 1. (CarA) **1.** No! [Cp *WIED* Igbo *ee e* /121/ 'No!'] □ Common in folk speech; sometimes nasalized, as in *Dmca*. **2.** Expressing an expectation of bad news or some bad happening. In such cases the second element may be lengthened [ɛˀɛː:] /21/). *Eh-ehh! A feel da was goin[g] happen!*—(Guyn) [See etym note after EH¹]

Eh-heh! [ɛhɛ] *excl* (CarA) [*AF*—*Cr*] ‖ *Mm-hm* (CarA) **1.** /11' ∼∼12'/ Yes. *The tone of her 'yes' was unusually formal. As a matter of fact, 'yes' was the wrong reply. Sonia's reply should have been 'mm-hm' or 'eh-heh' or 'yeh, man', or some such friendly, homespun vocable. Not 'yes'. 'Yes' was when you vex, or when replying to a stranger.*—TRIH:118 [Cp *WIED* Igbo *ee e* /112/ 'Yes!'; *eeye* /112/ 'Yes! Certainly', also Yoruba ɛhɛ 'Yes', etc] □ Very common in folk speech, sometimes with one or both elements nasalized [ɛ̃ɛ̃], or the second element may be lengthened and stressed to express greater approval [ɛ'hɛ::]. **2.** (*With emotive variations of high level or high rising pitch, and with the second element sometimes lengthened*) [Expressing surprise, delight, or dismay] Is that so?; Now we know!; etc. *Eh-heh! So that is why she married so hush-hush!*—(Antg)

Eid [iˑd] *n* (Guyn, Trin) [Indic] **1.** (Shortened ref to) a Muslim religious festival. (See next). *The Muslim community turned out to mosques to begin the celebrations of Eid.*—GyC (76.09.26, p.20) [Perso-Arabic *eid* 'festival'] **2.** PHRASE **2.1.** **Eid Mubarak** *adj phr* (Guyn, Trin) [Indic] Happy or Blessed Festival (to you). [Perso-Arabic *mubarak* 'happy, blessed']

Eid-ul-A·zah (**Eid-ul-Adha**) [iˑd-ʊl-aza ∼ -adha] *n* (Guyn, Trin) [Indic] The Muslim religious festival in the twelfth month (Zilhajj) of the Muslim calendar; it falls 2 lunar months and 10 days after EID-UL-FITR, celebrating Ibrahim's (Abraham's) obedience to God in his readiness to sacrifice his son Ishmael (Isaac), the celebration being marked by the ceremonial killing of an unblemished sheep, goat, or cow to provide feasting for the family and for the poor. [Perso-Arabic *eid ul azha* 'festival of the covenant'] □ The festival is observed as a public holiday in *Guyn*.

Eid-ul-Fitr [iˑd-ʊl-fɪtər] *n* (Bdos, Guyn, Trin) [Indic] The Muslim religious festival observed on the first day after the end of Ramadan, the month of religious fasting and ninth month of the Muslim calendar; it falls 12 days earlier every year of the Gregorian (i.e. Western) calendar, and the celebration is marked by joyous feasting and acts of charity. [Perso-Arabic *eid ul fitr* 'festival of the release']

eight·pen·ny-nail *n* (Bdos, Jmca) See SIX PENNY-NAIL

eights (of rum) *n* (*phr*) *sg* (Gren) A quantity of rum amounting to about one eighth of a 26 oz bottle (i.e 3-1/2 ozs), wh is the smallest retailed. *On the same night four policemen were seated around a table at Georgie's bar drinking an eights of rum and a coke.*—ToR (77.07.03, p.1) [< SE *eighth* by folk pronunc, whence 'an eights' as a sg form. Notecit]

ei·ther [iˑðə~iˑdʌ] *adj functioning as determiner* (Bdos) [X] [With emotive emphasis] Any. **a.** *Wha[t]! Don[t] keep eider woman?*—(Bdos) **b.** *I bet I could move you with this stick doe, and pick you out from either other passenger.*—Bdos (Ms, Play) □ See also NEITHER² wh is sometimes similarly used.

el·der* (**el·der·ber·ry**) *n* (Belz, Bdos, Brbu, Jmca, USVI) A large shrub with clusters of little white flowers and (in some varieties) also berries; its leaves are generally used as a folk-medicine; *Sambucus simpsonii* (*Caprifoliaceae*). [From resemblance to European *elderberry*]

el·der·bush* *n* (Bdos, Guyn) A shrub bearing clusters of bell-shaped yellow flowers and pods; its leaves are used, boiled or squeezed, as a folk-medicine; *Tecoma stans* (*Bignoniaceae*). *This common wayside shrub belongs to the family Bignoniaceae and its numerous bright yellow flowers account for another local name, buttercup. But why it should be called elderbush it is difficult to understand, for it has no resemblance to the European elder bush with its cluster of dark blue berries from which the strong and tasty elderberry wine is still made in Britain.*—AdN (70.01.17, M. Hutt)

e·lec·tric eel *n phr* (Guyn) ‖ *numb-fish* (Guyn) A dark, scaleless, eel-like fish, 4 to 5 ft in length, that lives in the rivers of Guyana and is said to be capable of delivering a shock of over 300 volts, if touched; *Gymnotus electricus* (*Electrophoridae*).

el·e·phant-ap·ple *n* (Guyn) ‖ CHALTA (Guyn, Trin) [Prob from its gourd-like size and appearance]

el·e·phant-grass* *n phr* (CarA) ‖ *Napier grass* (Jmca) A coarse grass growing to some eight or more feet in height, with nodes and flowering spikes resembling miniature sugarcane; it was once widely grown as cattle fodder; *Pennisetum purpureum* (*Gramineae*).

el·e·phant's ear* (**el·e·phant-ear(s)**) *n phr* (Baha, Bdos) An ornamental variety of the DASHEEN and EDDOE family with inedible bulbs; it bears two-foot-long, spear-shaped, shiny green leaves with a wavy surface and flourishes in damp soil; *Xanthosoma spp.* [From the size and pointed shape of the leaf]

E·leu·the·ran [ɛˈlyuəərʌn] *n, adj* (A person or thing) native or belonging to the island of Eleuthera in The Bahamas.

e·lev·en-plus (**ex·am·i·na·tion**) *n* (*phr*) (CarA) [IF] ‖ COMMON ENTRANCE (EXAMINATION) (CarA) □ Also written *11 +*

El·lick *n* (Bdos) PHRASE **as late as Ellick** *adj phr* (Bdos) [AF] Very late, but still hurrying. [= Alec? Said to refer to the bell-ringer of a church who was frequently late for his job.— (*pers info, Mrs Erica Pile*)]

else *conj* (CarA) [X] Or; or else. **a.** *When he ain't fightin' de other children, else choppin' dem, else stonin' dem, he drownin' dem.*—TRIH:141 **b.** *But some felt that the festival was not as Barbadian as it should have been and parts of it should be omitted, else it would be in danger of losing its Bajan quality.*—AdN (76.05.16, p.7) [Prob by loss of unstressed *or* in phr *or else*]

E·man·ci·pa·tion Day *n phr* (CarA) ‖ *August bank holiday* (CarA) [Hist] 1st August (still celebrated as a public holiday on the first Monday in August in some Caribbean territories). [Commemoration of 1st August 1834, official date of the end of slavery in Br colonies). □ The original date is sometimes referred to as *Freedom Morning*.

em·bar·rass·ed [ɛmbarast] *adj* **1.** (Jmca) [IF] Pregnant. **2.** (StLu) [X] Busy; burdened with work. [Calque in E of Fr Cr *anbawasé* 'busy' < Fr *embarrassé*]

em·bar·rass·ing *adj* (StLu) [X] Tedious (esp of work being done); burdensome. [See prec]

em·pa·na·das (**em·pa·na·des, em·pe·na·da**) *n* (Belz) ‖ *panades* (Belz) A kind of large patty made of a tortilla fried soft and folded over with fish inside, regularly served with onion and vinegar. [Sp *empañada* (< *pan* bread) the name for this food. The pl form has come to be used as sg in *Belz*, with some variants as shown, but these forms occur mostly in writing, while the form PANADES (by aphaeresis) prevails in speech]

Em·pire Day *n phr* (CarA) [Hist] A colonial holiday (see cit) that ceased to be recognized as territories became independent. *On May 24, Empire Day is celebrated as a public holiday. The Administrator addresses the crowd from a kiosk in Columbus Square, on which sit the Administrator's family, members of the Legislative and Executive Councils, their families, and heads of departments. Boy Scouts, Girl Guides, Brownies, Cubs, and other organisations perform a march-past and school children sing patriotic songs. Later the children toast the Queen in aerated drinks or lime squash, and eat buns of sweet bread, cakes, and sweets provided by the government.*—Caq 4:2, p.ll6 [May 24, Queen Victoria's birthday, was chosen as the symbolic date to honour the Br Empire]

em·pol·der¹ *vb tr* (Guyn) ‖ *empole* (Guyn) [X] To enclose a great area of low-lying and swampy land by connected dams so as to allow the area to be drained for cultivation or land development. *These include plans to empolder lands so that farm lands could be reclaimed, the construction of a koker for the proper drainage of the area and the establishment of a sawmill.*—GyC

(76.04.27, p.2) [SE em- < en- (as in *enclose*) + Du *polder* 'reclaimed bog-land'] □ This is the only form used in *Guyn*. Cp *OEDS impolder* (1898–').

em·pol·der[2] *n* (Guyn) ‖ *polder* (Guyn) **1.** The area of land that has been EMPOLDERED. *Drainage for Canals Empolder and East Demerara is associated with the term inundation which means 12 ins or more water covering the roots of vegetable crops and fruit trees.*—DaC (52.08.03, p.2) **2.** One or all of the connected dams empoldering an area of land. *Deo Sestrie has survived more than eight floods in the Pomeroon district on his thirty-five-acre farm thanks to his solid empolders.*—Guyn (Ms, 1977) [By vb > n functional shift] □ Also used attrib, ex '*an empolder scheme*'.

em·pol·der·ment *n* (Guyn) The system of enclosing low-lying land by dams to prepare it for drainage and development; empoldering.

em·pole [ɛmpo·l] *vb* (Guyn) [X] ‖ EMPOLDER (Guyn) *Sir / We are farmers struggling at Ithaca asking you please to empole the lands we trying to farm here.*—Guyn (Ms, 1972) [< EMPOLDER by apocope and reduction of final /-CC/]

emp·ty [ɛmti] *adj* (Antg) [AF] **1.** ‖ BARE **3.** (Bdos, Jmca) *I don['t] have any figs dis time. Is empty mango I have.*—(Antg: Fruitseller) **2.** PHRASE **2.1** **Empty (crocus) bag can'[t] stan[d] up**... CarA (Prov) See CROCUS BAG Phr 2.1

en [ɛn] (CarA) [AF—Cr] See EN(T)

end·ing (of the month/week/year) *n (phr)* (Bdos, Guyn) [IF] End (of the month, etc). *And one time, when I was a little boy, coming on towards the ending of the year, there on the road that leads to Waterford out of Station Hill, I had to run real desperate to escape three men in a black car.*—SuS (79.09.23, p.l7, T. Callender) [Cp *OED ending* vbl sb 2. 'the concluding part of a piece of work, etc; formerly also, of a space of time'] □ Occurs esp in prep phrs after *about/at/ before/by/ towards the .....*

end·less *adj* (StLu, Tbgo, Trin) [AF/IF] A great number or amount of; in great abundance. *Last weekend we went to a party in Arima. So much people was there—we could hardly move around. Man, endless people in the place.*—(Trin) [A semantic shift in application from non-material things (ex 'endless difficulties') to material things. Prob also infl by SE *numberless*]

Eng·land-jar /1'12/ *n* (Antg) ‖ CORN-JAR (Bdos)

Eng·lish ap·ple* /1'122/ *n phr* (Bdos, BrVi) The imported European apple (*Pyrus malus* (*Rosaceae*)) of the red or yellowish-green variety (i.e. as distinguished from a number of *CarA*

fruits of different genus and family though called APPLES).

Eng·lish Church /1'12/ *n phr* (CarA) [IF] The Anglican Church or Church of England. □ Often used without determining article in contexts contrasting it with ROMAN CHURCH.

Eng·lish·fied (**Eng·lish·i·fied**) [ɪŋglɪš(i)faɪd] [IF]; **Eng.lish.fy** [ɪŋglɪšfaɪ] [AF] *adj* **1.** (CarA) [Esp of sb returned from England] Having a noticeable English accent and generally regarded as having a more refined presence. **2.** (Guyn) [Esp of EAST INDIANS] Urbanized and/or westernized in dress, habits, and speech.

Eng·lish plum *n phr* (Nevs) ‖ GOVERNOR-PLUM **1.** (CarA)

Eng·lish po·ta·to* /1'1122/ *n phr* (CarA) ‖ *a-loo* (Guyn) ‖ *Irish potato* (CarA) ‖ *potato* (CarA) ‖ *white potato* (Antg, Bdos, Guyn, Mrat, StVn) The (internationally known) potato orig imported from England (hence the name); *Solanum tuberosum* (*Solanaceae*). *Government's cut-back on the importation of English potatoes, has forced some of the island's hotels and public eating places to find substitutes in locally grown 'ground provisions'—sweet potatoes, yams and breadfruit.*—AdN (74.02.28, p.1) □ So called also to distinguish it from the locally grown *sweet potato* wh is included in the term *ground-provisions*. (See cit).

enough[1] [(i)nʌf ~ (a)nʌf] *pron* (CarA) [X] ‖ *nuff* (CarA) [Cr] [Without special emphasis] Plenty; a great amount; a lot (in number). **a.** [E]*nough o[f] dem a[t] de Port does t[h]ief (= A lot of them at the Port steal).*—(Bdos) **b.** *Their house always had sugar, rice, milk and enough more that the shops didn't have.*—Guyn (Ms) [< SE *enough* adj 'sufficient' by functional shift, and infl by such SE structures as '*Enough of that!*' '*Enough of the canes were burnt to ruin the crop*', etc in wh the sense implied is 'too much, too many'] □ In this CE function *(e)nough* usu precedes the n phr it qualifies, and is often written *nuff* in narrative dialogue, but tends to appear as 'enough' in handwritten work.

e·nough[2] [i'nʌf ~ a'nʌf] *adj* (CarA) [IF] [With special emphasis] Very much; a great many. **a.** *We had rain enough last week and the whole of Georgetown was flooded at one time.*—Guyn (Ms) **b.** *Fellows enough lost toenails kicking football in the road.*—NaT (78.01.25, p.14) [As *OED enough* adj 1. a. 'sufficient in quantity and number (with sb in sg wh it usu follows)'. However the SE usage lacks the special stress that accompanies the CE usage] □ In this CE function *enough* always follows the n (phr) it qualifies.

enough[3] [inʌf ~ anʌf] *adv intensifier* (CarA) [IF] **1.** So very. **a.** *She admitted that there was a time she used to sell outdoors. Said she: 'I am glad enough to come out of the sun.'*—AdV (84.03.31, p.1) **b.** *Silla sucked her teeth cynically. 'I tell yuh,* *you best be swift, if not somebody come and trample you quick enough.'*—MBGB:186 [Adaptation of SE postposition usage as in *long enough* 'sufficiently long', but with emotive intensity added] □ In this function ENOUGH follows the adj or adv it qualifies. **2.** [By ellipsis of an understood adj, keeping its intensifying effect] Sufficiently bad/ overwhelming, oppressive, etc. (Hence foll phrs). **3.** *PHRASES* **3.1 enough to make a dog sick** *adj or adv phr* (BrVi) [*AF*] [Esp of a dwelling place] In an extremely filthy condition. **3.2 enough to pelt dog with** *adj phr* (Guyn) [*AF— Joc*] [Of fruit or food] More than can be eaten; in too great abundance.

en(t) [ɛ̃ ~ ɛn ~ ɛnt] *neg marker and Q-word* (CarA) [*AF—Cr*] **1.** (Dial spellings of) AIN'T. **a.** *It had one time somebody get kill an' all. Me dear, dat en no enjoyment, dat is war an' I en dey in dat.*—WeN (53.02.16, p.2) **b.** *Puzzled, he said—'Ent is here ah leave me bag of fish and dat nice big fat rabbit? Must be ah little higher up!'*—PSFC:36 [From the folk pronunc, with variants due to lessening of stress □ See AIN'T¹, AIN'T² for full range of occurrences. The spellings above occur freely as loose alternatives in narrative dialogue. Cp also EH² (Gren, Trin). **2.** *Tag question* (Bdos) Ain't it?; Isn't that so? *A porter at a airport (yuh does call dem Red-Caps, ent?*—Nat (92.09.04, P.9, Lickmout Lou)

es·ca·be·che [ɛskabiče] *n* (Belz) A dish prepared by adding a substantial quantity of sliced onions that have been soaked in vinegar, together with red pepper, oregano leaves, and other seasoning to a well-boiled chicken broth, with the boiled chicken removed, cut up, and browned for serving. [Sp *escabeche* 1. 'pickle, brine' 2. 'soused fish'. The first meaning appears to have infl the *Belz* usage and the second the *Jmca* ESCAVEITCH(ED)]

es·cal·li·on (es·kel·li·on) *n* (Jmca) ‖E-SCHALLOT (Bdos, Guyn) ... *popularly called skellion in Jamaica and used as an onion substitute or with onions for seasoning meats, fish, chicken, and mutton, escallion thrives as a companion plant for roses.*—RJH:19 [< SE *scallion* perh by false refinement (note cit) or prosthesis, or infl by *eschallot*. OED notes the form as *Jmca* 1847]

es·ca·veitch(·ed) fish [ɛskavič(t)fiš] *n phr* (Jmca) ‖*cabeche* (Guyn) ‖*scaveeched fish* (Jmca) A dish of fish that has been deep fried, drained, and then pickled (hot or cold) in a mixture of vinegar and oil, red pepper, spices, sliced CHOCHO, etc. *Escaveitched fish and bammy is a delightful Sunday morning Jamaican dish.*—Jmca (Ms) [See ESCABECHE (*Belz*)] □ The added vbl *-ed* in **escaveitched** is a false refinement. See etym, and cp SALT-FISH vs *salted- fish*.

es·chal·lot* [(ɛ)šalɒt] *n* (Bdos, Guyn) ‖*cives, chives* (Gren, Trin) ‖*escallion* (Jmca) ‖*seasoning* (Bdos, Guyn) [*IF*] ‖*shelote* (Guyn) [*X*] ‖*skellion* (Jmca) Shallot or scallion, a plant whose small onion-like bulb and slender, green,

hollow leaves are esp favoured as seasoning; *Allium ascalonicum* or *A. fistulosum* (*Liliaceae*). [< Fr *échalote* 'shallot, scallion']

Ess·e·quib·i·an [ˈɛsɪkwɪbiən] /1'1221/ *n, adj* (Guyn) (Person or thing) native or belonging to Essequibo, the largest COUNTY of *Guyn*.

es·tate *n* (CarA) [*IF*] A plantation (sugar-, cocoa-, coconut-, etc) including the fields, factory, and all living quarters. *Recently I was on hand to see a fire which was started in an estate around 12 o'clock. By 4 o'clock this fire was still raging and had completely gone out of the estate's field and into the surrounding fields. These fields are owned by peasant farmers.*—AdM (74.03.10, p.5) □ The formal SE sense of 'property' occurs only in legal documents in CE.

es·tate-bas·ket *n* (Nevs, StKt) ‖ DUNG-BASKET 2. (Bdos, etc)

e·ta; ete, etia *n* (Guyn) See ITE

et·na *n* (Belz) A small, portable oil-stove. *'So ah pour kerosene in Paisano etna, light it, put the frying pan on de fire wid coconut ile coverin' de bottom.'*—YPF:19 [From a commercial brandname]

eu·phor·bi·a [yu'fɔrbiʌ] *n* (Gren) ‖SNOW-ON-THE-MOUNTAIN (Antg, etc) [Botanical name of the genus]

e·vap·o·ra·tor *n* (CarA) [Sugar Ind] One of a series of very large, cylindrical, closed vessels, connected by pipes; sugar-cane syrup is boiled under pressure in a succession of these vessels, becoming more concentrated as it passes from one to the next. [Ref to the steam wh is trapped in the boiling process and piped from the top into the next vessel]

even *PHRASES* **1. even although** *conj phr* (Bdos) [*X*] Even though. *I do not care what anybody says, I am for Shadow Ministers. Even although they call me Mr Know All.*—Bdos (Hd, 73.02.13, p.1802) [Overlapping of *even though* + *although*] **2. even self** *adv phr* **(i)** (ECar) [*X*] [Emphasizing a neg context] (Not) even; (not) at all. **a.** *The simplest job he even self can't start.*—Tbgo (Ms) **b.** *I even self offer him the money to go, but he say no.*—(Guyn) **(ii)** (Tbgo, Trin) [*X*] [Introducing a suggestive supposition] Even if; even supposing. *An' ah feel dat what dey could try to do now is to leh she come for carnival, nuh, even self she only look orn.*—NM:21 **3. not even ... far less** (Bdos, etc) See FAR Phr 1.(i)

eve·ning(-time) *n* (Baha, Bdos, CayI, Gren, Jmca, StVn) Any time between noon and sunset, but esp the period between about 2 and 5 p.m. [Cp *W3* AmE *evening* 1. b. (chiefly South and Midland) 'the time extending roughly from noon to twilight']

ev·er *adv* (Bdos) [*IF*] Always. *She soon called her grandmother to support her. Said granny: 'We ever call it Pennyhole. They change it to Gemwick so we write Gemwick, but we ever call it Pennyhole.'*—NaT (77.02.27, p.35) [Survival of archaic E. See *OED ever* 1. 'Always, at all times; ...' (Now arch or literary) + cit 1831 *'Ever must the Sovereign ... be fitly entitled King'*]

ever·green *n* 1. (CarA) Name loosely applied to a number of bushy shrubs and/or large shade trees that are green and keep their leaves all the year round. 2. (Bdos, Jmca) Different varieties of very large, bushy, green shade trees bearing inedible pea-sized fruit and putting down aerial roots; *Ficus nitida*, also *F. benjamina* (*Moraceae*).

ev·er since[1] *prep phr and subordinating conj* (CarA) [*IF*] ‖ *every since* (Bdos) [*X*] 1. *prep phr* From the time of; because of. *Ever since the fire, the family scattered.*—Guyn (Ms) 2. *subordinating conj* From the time that; since the day that. *Ever since the boy won the scholarship and went to England they start to be pretensive.*—(Bdos) □ In both functions SE *since* is adequate, *ever* being an intensifier, often stressed, implying cause.

ev·er since[2] *adv phr* (CarA) [*IF*] ‖ *every since* (Bdos) [*X*] 1. Since then; from that time to now. *My former boy friend and I disagreed in 1973 and ever since I was without one as I did not want a repeat occurrence.*—NaT (76.08.29, p.22, Dear Christine) [By ellipsis, from the prep and conj senses of EVER SINCE[1]] 2. A long time ago. *It is an unfair, stupid and ignorant tax because you are taxing production.... It ought to have been removed ever since, but nobody on that side has any interest in these matters.*—Bdos (Hd, 75.03.26, p.869)

eve·ry since [ɛvri sɛns]; **eve.ry long time since/sense** /2′2121/ *prep, conj, adv phrs* (Bdos) [*X*] ‖ EVER SINCE[1], EVER SINCE[2] (CarA) **a.** *Every since the change over of the festivities nine years ago from November 5, Guy Fawkes Day to November 30, Independence Day, the crowds that flocked to the mill-yard have gradually dwindled, Mr Hill said.*—AdN (75.11.13, p.8) **b.** *Every long-time sense you went down the road and now get back?*—(Bdos) [Folk pronunc of EVER SINCE with epenthetic vowel /-i-/ between consonants]

eve·ry·time *adv* (Gren) [*X*] (Almost) always; most times. *She does sell groun[d] nut everytime, but she do[n't] ha[ve] today.*—PPGD:30 □ Usu also written as one word, like SE *'everywhere'*.

ex·cept[1] *prep* (CarA) [*IF*] 1. Excepting; except for; apart from. *I find the prices are pretty good and except the food shortages and the fuel crisis, many things I find easy to buy.*—NaT (75.12.23, p.3) □ In the best Mod IAE *except* is not used as a free alternative to *excepting, except for* as it tends to be used in CE (see cit). 2. PHRASE 2.1 **except from** *prep phr* (Gren) [*X*] Excepting; apart from. *We have no others except from that.*—(Gren) [By overlap: except (for) + (apart) from]

ex·cept[2] *conj* (CarA) [*X*] Unless; if ... not. *But all this would not have been possible except the Government was disposed to spend large sums of money to make Antigua not look inferior to other cricketing centres in the Caribbean.*—AnS (73.02.28, p.1) [This is archaic E usage, but kept alive in CE by many instances in the *AVB* exs 'except the Lord build the house' *Ps 127:1* 'except a man be born again' (John 3.3), etc. *W3* also lists *except* conj as acceptable AmE]

ex·cuse *n* (CarA) [*IF*] 1. Permission (obtained after explanation or apology). 2. PHRASES 2.1 **ask for an excuse** *vb phr* (CarA) [*IF*] To ask to be excused; to ask to be permitted (to leave, cross sb's path, etc). 2.2 **get an excuse** *vb phr* (CarA) [*IF*] To get permission (from sb in authority, for leave of absence, etc). [By shift in sense of *excuse* 'apology' to 'acceptance' hence to 'permission'] 2.3 **have me for an excuse!** *id phr* (Belz) [*X*] Please excuse me! Please forgive my error! *I laughed and said: 'Do I look like a millionaire?' and we both laughed and he replied: 'Have me for an excuse,' and we parted, both enjoying the exchange.*—ReP (80.04.27, p.12) [A hypercorrection due to false refinement, or an overlap of SE *have me excused* + CE *I ask for an excuse.*]

Ex·ec·u·tive Coun·cil (**Ex Co**) *n phr* (CarA) [*Hist*] A small body of persons presided over by the Governor of a Br colony and including the Colonial Secretary, the Attorney General, some Governor's nominees and a minority of elected members all drawn from the LEGISLATIVE COUNCIL; it was the equivalent of a Cabinet of Ministers. See also LEGISLATIVE COUNCIL.

ex·pan·sion-cord *n* (CayI) ‖ DROP-CORD (CarA)

ex·pat [ɛkspat] [*AF—Joc*]; **ex.pa.tri.ate** [ɛkspetriɛt] *n* (CarA) An immigrant, esp a white foreigner, and one often employed in a local job. *So many of us moan when expats appear to take over. But isn't it our own fault?*—BeS (74.08.24, p.4) [Particular shift in sense from 'out of his own country' to 'not belonging to this country', and hence with a strong emotive connotation attached. 'Expatriot' was also written, by one informant, for EXPAT]

ex·pense your·self *vb refl phr* (Bdos, Guyn, Tbgo, Trin) Put yourself to undue expense. *Part of the discrimination against women is in the area of Family Law where a woman has no custody of her child at law unless she goes to court and expenses herself in a contest and the judge eventually gives her custody.*—Bdos (Hd, 76.03.14, p.3316) [By functional n > vb shift. This usage does not occur in IAE, but cp similar functional shift in IAE *inconvenience*]

ex·pens·ious [ɛkspɛnšʌs] *adj* (Gren) [*X*] Expensive. [Prob by analogy with similar derivatives in IAE (exs *vicious, contentious*, etc) wh have unpleasant connotations]

ex·plain (sb) *vb tr* (Trin) [*X*] Explain to (sb). *I explained him the facts but he wouldn't believe me.*—Trin (Ms) [By deletion of prep extension, and prob also infl by such vbs as *give, offer, tell,* in similar sense]

ex·po·li·ca·ted [ɛkspɒlɪketɪd] *adj* (Antg) Excused; forgiven. [Prob a product of false refinement, or corruption of EE *expolite* 'polished', or a combination of both] □ Evid almost restricted to the phr *Have me expolicated* 'Please forgive/excuse me' (i.e. for some indiscretion). Now tends to be in *Joc* use.

ex·pres·sion(s) *n* (*pl*) (Bdos, Guyn, Tbgo, Trin) Dirty words; obscene language; foul swearing. *The young people nowadays, when you talk to them, ready to give you back expressions.*—(Guyn) [A euphemism, but often qualified by 'dirty', 'vulgar', 'nasty', etc]

ex·tra-strong /1'12/ *n* (Bdos, Guyn) A small, round, white, imported peppermint sweet. □ Often used by older folk to mean any mint sweet.

eye¹ *n* PHRASES **1. (Not) bless your eye(s) on (sb/sth) again** (*neg*) *vb phr* (ECar) [*IF*] (Not) be fortunate enough to see (sb/sth) again. *... but for all I know I may never ever bless my eyes on you again, so I take this opportunity to remind you o' one or two things.*—LICMS:304 **2. cut your eye after/at/on/upon (sb)** *vb phr* (CarA) See CUT Phr 3.11.1, also CUT-EYE phrs **2.1 cut your eye at (sth)** *vb phr* (Guyn) See CUT Phr 3.11.2 **3. eye is (too) big** *id phr* (CarA) [*AF*] *His eyes so big, he takes the biggest piece of meat.*—(StLu) See BIG-EYE¹ **4. eyes bounce** *id phr* (Gren) [*AF*] ‖ EYES MAKE FOUR (CarA) See Phr 14. *Only when we eyes bounce she does tell me howdy.*—(Gren) **5. eyes burn you** *vb phr* (Dmca) ‖ EYES CATCH FIRE (FOR STH) (Gren, etc) See Phr 8.1 **6. eyes bursting with sleep** *id phr* (CarA) [*AF/IF*] Eyes (are) heavy with sleep. **7. eyes butt up** *id phr* (Angu, Nevs) [*AF*] ‖ EYES MAKE FOUR (CarA) See Phr 14. **8.1 eye(s) catch fire (for sth)** *id phr* (Gren, Guyn, StVn, Tbgo) [*AF*] ‖ *eyes burn you (for sth)* (Dmca) ‖ *eye(s) get red (for sth)* (Belz) ‖ *have red-eye (for sth)* (CayI) ‖ *let sth burn your eyes* (Dmca) ‖ *look with red-eye (at sth)* (Jmca) ‖ *put your eye (on sth)* (Bdos, Guyn, StVn) ‖ *red your eye (after sth)* (Belz) ‖ *skin catch fire (for sth)* (Jmca) To develop a burning desire to have sth, immediately on seeing it. *It is all well and good skipper. The white man eye catch fire for gold long time.*—CBM:175 [A prob calque from more than one Afr lang. Cp Yoruba *oju gba ina jẹ* (*eye take eat fire*) 'to crave sth seen for the first time'. Also Shona *kutsu ukisa ma ziso* (*make red both eye*) 'eyes redden to get sth'] **8.2 eyes catch fire (for sb)** *id phr* (Guyn) To feel an immediate physical attraction (to sb of the opposite sex). [Cp Yoruba *oju ẹ gbana* (*eye his catch-fire*) 'he became very jealous'] **9. eye(s) (get) dark** *id phr* (Bdos, Guyn, Nevs) [*IF*] (i) (Your) sight is failing (from old age). *And sir, me eyes lil dark, and ah could not see to*

read the summons so ah carry it to the barman fu leh he read it fu me.*—DaC (53.02.04, p.1) **(ii)** (You) feel ill, as if about to faint. *But comrade now I can hardly write at all, / My legs are paining, my eyes are getting dark / It is the fourth day of a hunger strike.*—CPS:48 **10. eyes don't meet** *id phr* (Guyn) [*AF—Joc*] (To be) estranged; (to be) avoiding each other. *Since they had the row over the fair their eyes don't meet.*—(Guyn) [See note at Phr 14] **11. eye(s) (come) full** *id phr* (Gren, Tbgo, Trin) [*AF*] To be near tears; (your eyes) fill with tears. *When I see the funeral passing, I tell you, me eye full.*—(Tbgo) **12. eye (is)/eyes (are) long** *id phr* (ECar) [*AF—Derog*] To be characteristically covetous. *Every dress you see you want. Your eyes too long.*—(Angu) **13. eyes make fire (for sb)** *id phr* (Gren) [*AF—Joc*] To be looking out anxiously for sb's arrival. *Well me chil[d]ren eyes mus[t] be makin[g] fire for me by now, since dis mornin[g] A leave home and A now gettin[g] back.*—(Gren) **14. eyes make four** *id phr* (CarA) [*IF*] ‖ *eyes bounce* (Gren) ‖ *eyes butt up* (Angu, Mrat, Nevs, StVn) ‖ *fall in each other's eyes* (Dmca, StLu) ‖ *meet under four eyes* (StVn) (Your) eyes look straight into the other person's eyes as you face each other; (two persons) look at each other face to face. *All this time Father's and Aaron Docre's eyes were making four with each other, and they do no' look away from one another.*—RND:33 [A prob calque from more than one Afr lang. Cp Yoruba *oju wa di mẹrin* (*eye our make four*) 'our eyes met'] **15. eye(s) pass (sb)** *id phr* (Guyn) [*AF/IF*] (You are) rude to (sb) (usu senior in years or status). *But you didn't hear how that child answer her mother? Her dam eyes pass her own mother—who else they won't pass?*—(Guyn) □ In this form the pa.t. is rare. More often in the form *make your eyes pass (sb)* (See Phr 23., also EYE-PASS). **16. eye (is) raw** *id phr* (Nevs, StKt) [*AF*] (You are) covetous and bare-faced; (you are) shamelessly greedy. **17. eye (is) strong** *id phr* (Guyn) [*AF—Derog*] (To be) to STRONG-EYE. **18. eye(s) turn** (Antg, Guyn, Jmca, StKt, StVn); **eye(s) turn up** (Angu, Nevs) *id phrs* [*IF*] Get/have a feeling of dizziness, faintness (usu associated with hunger or weakness); get EYE-TURN. [Cp Yoruba *ebi ko mi l'oju* (*hunger takes me in the eye*) 'I am dizzy, faint from hunger'] **19. fill your eye** [*IF*]; **full your eye** [*AF—Cr*] (CarA) Be very satisfying in appearance, quantity, quality, etc. *Just as Bussa, it is claimed, did not 'full the eyes' of many of his contemporaries, the heroes of our times have not always found favour with theirs. So we find that Bussa's image is said to have suffered because too little is known about him.*—AdV (88.05.28, p.6) [A prob calque from more than one Afr lang. Cp Yoruba *wọ l'oju* (*penetrate in eye*) '(sth) strongly attracts you'; also Shona *kugutsa ma ziso* (*fill up both eyes*) 'to satisfy' (*pers info, J. Chafota*)] **20. jook out sb's eye** *vb phr* (ECar) [*AF*] See JOOK¹ Phr 7.3.2 **21. long (out) your eye (on sth)** *vb phr* (Antg, Mrat) [*AF*] To look with shameless covetousness (on sth you have just seen). See also LONG-EYE **22. make eye(s) after (sb)** *vb phr* (Jmca) [*AF*] [Esp of a man] To look at (sb) with sexual desire. **23.**

make your eye(s) pass (sb) *vb phr* (Guyn) [*AF/IF*] ‖ **take your eyes and pass (sb)** (Guyn) To treat or speak with noticeable disrespect or boldness to sb (who ought to be respected). *She was a poor but decent black girl and one day ... the messenger in the office made his eyes pass her and she put him in his place in quick time.*—(Guyn) [A prob calque from W Afr langs. Cp Yoruba *fi oju fo* (*make eye(s) jump over* (*sb*)) 'to ignore sb as being of no importance'. (*K. Ọmọtọsọ*)] □ See also Phr 15. and EYE-PASS. **24. put your eye on (sth)** *vb phr* (Bdos, Guyn, StVn) To crave something almost immediately upon seeing it. *Don[t] bother put your eye on dis cassava pone. It going to the cake-sale.*—(Bdos) □ See also LONG EYE, RED-EYE 2. **25. shut your eye at (sth)** *vb phr* (CarA) To connive at (sth); to deliberately ignore (some kind of misconduct). *The police, by shutting their eyes at street-corner gambling, are encouraging our young people in a dangerous habit.*—Belz (Ms) [Perh infl by SE idiom *close your eyes to (an incident)*] **26. take your eyes and pass (me/sb)** *vb phr* (Guyn) [*AF*] (A more intense form of) MAKE YOUR EYE(S) PASS (ME/SB). *I ask him why he calling me and he shouted again: 'Thomas Thomas.' I tell him 'Meself and you no friends; don't tek you eyes and pass me.'*—DaC (53.04.ll, p.5) [A prob calque of a common W Afr serial vb structure '*take sth + do sth*']

eye² *vb tr* (CarA) PHRASES **eye off/up (sb)** *vb phr* (CarA) [*AF*] [Esp of a man] To look steadily or frequently at (sb), with amorous or sexual desire. [An intensified form of SE *to eye* (*sb*) with similar sense] □ Also, but less often, *eye down (sb)*.

eye-ba·by *n* (Guyn, Jmca) ‖ BABY OF THE EYE (CarA) See BABY¹ Phr 4.1

eye·ball *n* (Belz, Guyn) [*AF/IF*] The most precious child of a family. *Of all the children she was the father's eyeball.*—Belz (Ms)

eye-cor·ner *n* (Guyn, Jmca) [*IF*] The corner of the eye. *Somehow, even when I was cooking in the kitchen which was behind the living room my eye-corner would constantly be aware of the desk.*—CWT:3

eye off (sb) *vb tr* (CarA) See EYE²

eye-pass *n* (Guyn) ‖ **pass-eye** (Guyn) Deliberate and brazen insulting behaviour to a person who is older, or socially equal or superior; challenging presumptuousness. *Loose me, man. She kyaan come up me step and call me whore. That is eye-pass. This is eye-pass, man. What she think she is at all? But I going settle she.*—Jbs.10.1, p.33 (W.F. Edwards) [See EYE¹ Phr 23.] □ See also EYE¹ Phr 15. The term is very frequently used in *Guyn* but appears to be unknown elsewhere in CE.

eye-turn *n* (Guyn, StVn) [*AF*] Dizziness or faintness (usu associated with hunger); vertigo. *She added that she was lying on a box, following on a seizure with 'eye-turn' when the kicking incident occurred. She denied that she was sleeping.*—DaC (53.05.20, p.1) [See note at EYE¹ PHR 18]

eye-wa·ter *n* (CarA) [*AF*] **1.** ‖ **cry-water** (Antg, Bdos) Tears. *Crying-time is finished now. You never see people with eye-water like Mother and Ruthie and Zekiel and Naomi.*—RND:142 [A calque from many Afr langs, exs Yoruba *omi l'oju* (*water from eye(s)*) 'tears', also Igbo *anya mmili* (*eye water*) 'tears', etc; cp also Sran *watr'ai* 'tears', Fr Cr (*Dmca*) *glo-zyé* (*water eye*) 'tears', etc] □ In present CE the word suggests 'tears that are not genuine' (note foll phrs), though it evid had no such connotation in earlier times (note cit). **2.** PHRASES **2.1. cry living eye-water** (Trin); **cry long eye-water** (Antg, Belz, BrVi, Guyn, Tbgo) *vb phr* [*AF/IF*] ‖ CRY LONG WATER (OUT OF YOUR EYES) (CarA) *She cried long eye-water at the man's funeral and now she wouldn't even pay to weed around the man's grave.*—(Guyn) [Cp Yoruba *da omi l'oju* (*pour water from eye(s)*); also *KED* Krio *kray wata na yay* 'shed tears profusely'; also *DECG* Fr Cr *pléwé go dlo* (*cry big water*) 'weep bitterly'] **2.2 pour/put down eye-water** (Antg, Brbu, Guyn); **put water in your eye** (Nevs, StKt) *vb phr* [Occasional variants of Phr 2.1]

F

f [f] □ Occurs in some *ECar* folk speech as a replacement of '*th*' [θ] and so represented in narrative dialogue. Exs: *fing* (*StLu*) 'thing', *Braffit* (*Guyn*) 'Brathwaite', *braf* (*Dmca*) 'broth', *faif* (*Bdos*) 'faith', *teef* (*Bdos*) 'teeth'

fa [fa] (*CarA*) *prep* [*AF—Cr*] (Dial spelling of) *for* (often used in narrative dialogue wherever ‖*fo[r]* functions in Cr speech). *E seh, 'Now is yuh chance fa go ax fa me.'*—WFSFB:46 (P. Gillett) **[** < SE 'for' [fɔ·] by vowel opening] □ See also FE, FER, FI, FO, FU.

fa·çade [fasa·d] *n* (*Guyn*) A large, vertical, square-shaped or quadrangular front built to give a picture-frame effect to the face of a modern dwelling-house facing the street. **[** < SE use of Fr façade 'front']

fa·çade-trench [fasa·d-trɛnč] *n* (*Guyn*) [Rice and Sugar Ind] A large drainage canal running along the frontage of a rice or sugar plantation to collect water from a number of shallower subsidiary drains on the plantation and channel the water to a sluice or larger drainage canal. **[** < SE *façade* 'front' + TRENCH (*Guyn*) 'canal']

face *n* (*CarA*) □ See BOLD-FACE, BRASS-FACE, as separate entries. PHRASES **1. face favour (sth)** *id phr* (*Guyn, Jmca*) [*IF*] See FAVOUR **2. face looks knowing** *id phr* (*Guyn, Tbgo*) [*IF*] (Sb's) face looks familiar. **3. in your face** *adv phr* (*Gren*) [*IF*] ‖TO YOUR FACE (*Bdos, Guyn*) **4. make up your face** *vb phr* (*CarA*) [*IF*] ‖*puff up* (*Gren*), ‖*pull up* (*Dmca*), ‖*push up* (*Nevs, StKt*), ‖*put up* (*Angu, Nevs*), ‖*swell up* (*Gren*), ‖*turn up* (*Guyn, StLu*), ‖*your face* (i) [Esp of children] To grimace disapprovingly (at food, chores, etc); (SE) to pull a long face; to look unwilling. **(ii)** [Mostly of children] To look annoyed (in response to sth said). [Prob infl by SE *make a face* + Afr idiomatic calques. Note number of ‖ ‖, and cp Yoruba *ba oju je* (spoil/ruin face) 'to pull a long face'] □ Cp SE sense relating to cosmetic treatment wh does not apply to this CE phr. See also next. **5. screw up** (*Dmca, Gren*), **skin up** (*ECar*), **twist up** (*Gren, Guyn*), **your face** *vb phr* (A more intense form of) MAKE UP YOUR FACE (*CarA*). See prec phr. [Cp note to Phr 4., and also Yoruba *o fa oju ro* (*he pull/stretch face bitter*) 'he pulled a long face'] **6. set (up) your face** *vb phr* (*Antg, Bdos, Nevs, Trin*) [*IF*] ‖*puff up your face* (*Gren*) To assume a threatening look; to look set for a quarrel. **7. show (sb) a bad face** *vb phr* (*Jmca, Tbgo,*

Trin) [*AF/IF*] To treat sb (esp a boyfriend or girlfriend) with obvious vexation, coldness or disapproval. **8. to your face** *adv phr* (*Bdos, Guyn*) [*IF*] ‖*in your face* (*Gren*) [*IF*] (Of sth said) brazenly, boldly and/or insultingly in your presence. □ More emotive than SE *face to face*.

face-ba·sin *n* (*Jmca*) **1.** An enamel wash-basin (used esp in rural areas for washing the face and hands)—*DJPVP*. **2.** (*Baha, Jmca*) [By extension] [*IF*] A bathroom sink.

face-man *n* (*Baha, Jmca*) A personable and well-dressed young man who is a criminal in disguise; a con man.

face·ti·ness; fa.cey.ness *n* (*Jmca*) [*AF/IF*] Uppitiness; bumptiousness; impudence; barefacedness. **a.** *One Jamaican 'lady' coming from foreign the other day even reach a new low in up-in-the-air facetiness. When she couldn't haul and pull the stewardess any more, she call her 'Sky maid'.*—WeG (75.04.15, p.15, Partyline) **b.** *She held the baby closer to her and prepared herself to ward him off if he ever brought up any of his faceyness to her.*—DaG (66.12.18, p.4) **[** < FACETY, but cp AmE *feistiness*]

face·ty [fıesti] *adj* (*Jmca*) [*AF*] ‖*bold-face* (*ECar*) Bold and bare-faced; brazen; impudent. *Matty say it mean we facety / Stan up pon we dignity / An we don't allow nobody / Fe teck libarty wid we.*—FCV2:158 (L. Bennett) [Perh a corruption or blend of Obs SE *facy* + infl of *hasty, fisty, nasty*. See next. However note W3—chiefly Southern AmE 'quarrelsome', also 'inclined to put on airs' < (*Obs*) *feist* 'a person of little worth', also 'of bad temper']

fa·cey [fesi ~ fıesi] *adj* (*Belz, Jmca*) [*IF*] ‖BOLD-FACE (*ECar*) *Old and wrinkled-up as he was, he was as fresh and facey like any young-boy.*—DaG (66.12.18, p.4) **[** < OED *facy* (*Obs exc dial*) characterized by 'face'; insolent, impudent + cit from 1605 'These … facy, nasty … rogues'. However DSUE 1. lists *facy* 'impudent' as current 17C–20C, becoming dial from 19C] □ Though *facey, facety* appear to be in free variation in *Jmca*, the former appears to be the older form with the latter tending to be commoner in folk speech.

fa·da; fad·der [fa·da ~ fadʌ] *n* (*CarA*) [*Cr*] **1.** ‖*father*[2] (*CarA*) (Dial spellings often found in narrative dialogue for) father. **2.** [As a kind of intensifier after a prec n] *Boy! He bring home a big, big American Buick! That is car fadder!—* (Guyn) [See FATHER²]

faint·ish; **fain.ty, fain.ty-fain.ty** /1'122/ *adj* (CarA) [*IF*] **1.** Feeling dizzy or faint. **2.** [Of smells] Nauseating; sickening. *Our school was a slum school in the heart of the dirty back streets littered with fruit skins, reeking with the 'fainty-fainty' smell of rotten and rotting fruit.*—WCR: 41 [Adj form < SE *faint* wh occurs in CE mainly as a vb]

fair¹ *adj* (CarA) ‖ CLEAR-SKIN(NED) (CarA) *I never wondered how my mother had come by her skin. She was what they called a very fair mulatto. I was brown.*—LICMS:310

fair² *adv* **1.** (CarA) [*IF*] Exactly; directly; on the right spot. *I do not know what was thrown. It did not hit me. It did not catch me fair. It hit the partition.*—Gren (CR, 1972) **2.** PHRASE **2.1 catch (sb) fair** *vb phr* (CarA) **(i)** [Of sth thrown] To hit (sb) with full force. **(ii)** To catch (sb) red-handed, flagrantly. *He went in and caught them fair, all two o[f] dem naked!*—(Bdos) **3.** (Baha) Certainly *Den I get outer mer seat as fas as I cudda squeeze out an make fer de steps dem, an man, I fair slide down to de bottom, I so terrify.*—JBJ:83 [Cp *OED fair* adv 9. c. 'completely, fully, quite'. (*Obs* exc *dial*) + cits–'1868]

fair·maid *n* (Guyn) ‖ *fairy-maid* (Tbgo) ‖ *mama-glo* (Dmca, Gren, StLu, Trin) ‖ *river-muma* (Jmca) ‖ *water-mama* (Guyn) A legendary mermaid-like creature with a beautiful face who is said to be seen combing her long hair (and sometimes singing) at the waterside on moonlight nights, using a bright comb; the comb, if obtained, is a lure that may lead to great fortune, to death, or to sb's disappearance (esp that of a young man). [Name owing to belief that the creature is white-skinned, young and also lovely, though some beliefs make her face unseen or ugly]

fair-skin(ned) *adj* (CarA) ‖ CLEAR-SKIN(NED) (CarA) *I am glad to see that nowadays they are no longer looking to see whether you are fair skinned or black skinned, but at one time if you were black skinned you went to Empire, if you were fair skinned you went to Spartan and if you were white skinned you went to Pickwick and that was the test in years gone by.*—Bdos (Hd, 74.07.09, p.3690)

fair·y-maid *n* (Tbgo) ‖ FAIRMAID (Guyn) *I myself saw a fairy-maid one day. I have not invented her. We were in the coconut field, my father and I, and there she was, suddenly out of nowhere, a clay brown woman gliding to the water hole from which our cattle drank. I called to my father and pointed her out, but he replied with muted warning, 'Leave her alone. Mind your business, boy.' Taciturn and spare of speech, he never afterwards told me who or what she was.*—ACTT:

156 (E.M. Roach) [Combination of notions in SE *fairy* + *maid*]

Faith! **(faif)** [feˑt ~ feˑf] (Bdos); **Fait[h]-o-God!** *excl* (Mrat) **1.** [Sometimes accompanied by kissing the palm of the right hand] 'Truly! I'd swear (to the truth of what I've said).' **2.** PHRASES **2.1 Deed-and-faith!** *n excl* (Bdos) [Another form of FAITH! with some added disgust] **[** < SE *Indeed and in faith*] **2.2 True to faith!** *adv excl* (Guyn) [A milder form of FAITH!]

fa·ji·na [fahiˑna] *n* (Belz) ‖ LEND-HAND (Tbgo) *On Friday October 3, 1980 the teachers of Belize Teachers College held a fajina to clean and beautify the college compound.*—Belz (Ms) **[** < So Am Sp. Cp *TDV* Venezuelan *fajina* 'work done by a group of persons']

fa·ler·num *n* (Bdos) A light alcoholic syrup, the main ingredients of wh are said to be rum and lime juice, used as a liqueur or as a base for rum-mixed drinks. [Believed by some to be derived from the reply of the black inventor of the drink 'Yo gat fa learn um' (= You have to learn it) when asked by his plantation masters what was the secret recipe. (The recipe is still not widely known). Also possibly 'from sentimental association with Falernian' *CGBD*5:39, the famous wine of Falernus in ancient Campania]

fall *vb* **1.** *vb intr* (Tbgo) [Of an unmarried young woman] To become pregnant. [Cp *OED fall* v 22. a. 'In moral sense, ... esp of a woman: To surrender her chastity'] □ Largely limited to folk speech and hardly occurring in pa.t. **2.** *vb tr* (Jmca, Mrat, Nevs) [*AF*] To seduce (a young woman, esp a virgin). *'Me poor gal pickney only sixteen. Know nothing 'bout life. What we must do? Only to take up man.... 'Auntie, please, you don't have to tell me all this, please.' 'Him was old enough to be me father ... and him take advantage o' me. Him fall me, Tom.'*—GI:147 (O. Patterson) **3.** *vb tr* (Guyn) [*AF*] To bring down, knock down (a bird or animal) by hitting or shooting; to fell (a bird or animal). *Me not been know me fall the fellah till me hear 'quack- quack-quack ... quack!'*—SSOS:74 [Cp *OED fall* v 51. (*Obs*) 'to bring or throw to the ground'. The resemblance to the learned SE correlate *fell* is prob accidental] **4.** PHRASES (General) **4.1 fall in each other's eyes** *vb phr* (Dmca, StLu) [*IF*] ‖ (THEIR) EYES MAKE FOUR (CarA) See EYE¹ Phr 14. **4.2. fall to sleep** *vb phr* (Guyn) [*X*] To fall asleep. [By overlap with SE *put to sleep*] **4.3 make (sb's) hand fall** *vb phr* (Antg, Guyn) [*IF*] See HAND Phr 4.20

fall away¹ *vb phr* (Bdos, CayI, Guyn, Trin) [*IF*] ‖ DROP FLESH (Bdos, Guyn) See DROP¹ Phr 3.3 *... after all this time he's been away? Who sent for him? And where did he get the fancy suit and hat he's wearing and those long toe shoes? Oh, God, look how this boy has fallen away in his skin!*—MTCP:27 [Cp *EDD fall* v II. 15 Comb (5) -*away* 'to grow thin, weak, waste away, pine'

+ cits from Sc, Yks, Mid, w.Som] □ Often in folk speech in the form *fall way* [AF].

fall-away² *n* (Jmca) A falling off; a drop (in quantity); a decrease. *A fall-away of 36 head of cattle took place this week in deliveries passing through the Livestock Clearing House in Kingston. Deliveries this week amounted to 288 head altogether, while last week the total was 324.*—DaG (Farmer's Weekly, 70.01.31, p.1) [By functional + semantic shift of FALL AWAY¹]

fall off *vb phr* (Bdos) [*IF*] ‖ DROP FLESH (Bdos, Guyn) See DROP¹ Phr 3.3

falls *n pl* (*but may be sg in context*) (Guyn) **1.** A waterfall. *Kaieteur is a magnificent falls; our Kaieteur falls is a wonderful sight.*—(Guyn) **2.** PHRASE **2.1 boat gone a-falls** *id phr* (Guyn) [*IF*] See BOAT Phr

false mam·mee *n phr* (USVI) ‖ PITCH-APPLE (ViIs) [From its resemblance to a small MAMEE-APPLE, belonging also to the same family, but inedible, hence 'false']

false name *n phr* (Guyn) A nickname (usu of a provocative kind). *At school the boys called him 'Lipticus', a false name which referred to his thick lips and always annoyed him.*—Guyn (Ms)

fam·i·ly *adj, n* (CarA) [*IF*] **1.** (Sg or pl implied) A relative; relatives. **a.** *I said to him 'You don't have to do that you know, and he is your family.'*—AMAM:148 **b.** *Like many Barbadians, and other Caribbean peoples I, too, have family in Trinidad and Tobago.*—AdV (88.03.24, p.6) **2.** [By extension] *adj* Related to. (See foll phr). *The word 'family' is used not only as a noun but also almost in the sense of an adjective meaning 'related to'. 'Me and him is family' means simply that we are relatives. In order to show that bananas and plantains belong to the same species, a farmer may say, 'banana is family to plantain'.*—SWI:121 **3.** PHRASE **3.1 be family to (sb)** *vb phr* (CarA) [*IF*] Be related (even by distant ties of blood) to (sb). [A prob calque from more than one Afr lang. Cp Yoruba *jẹ ara ile* (*be family house*) 'be related to'; also Edo *ẹgbẹẹ ọkpa iran khin* (*family one they be*) 'they are related to each other'; etc]

Fam·i·ly Is·land(s) *n phr* (Baha) ‖ *Out Islands* (Baha) [*Obs*] Any of the 700 islands that make up The Commonwealth of The Bahamas, except New Providence (the seat of Government), particularly any of the sixteen main island groups around New Providence that the archipelago comprises. [Official replacement (for its emotive value) of the former term OUT IS-LANDS after political independence of The Commonwealth of The Bahamas in 1973]

fam·i·ly-land *n* (Bdos, Jmca, Mrat) ‖ *children-property* (Guyn) ‖ *generation-property* (Baha) Land that cannot be sold because it is recognized as belonging to all succeeding generations of the identified members of a particular family. □ See also SEED, phr FROM SEED TO SEED (*Bdos*).

fa·mous *adj* (CarA) [*Often X*] Notorious; well-known (for sth mean, unpleasant, etc). **a.** *She ain[t] got no class—she's a famous yard-woman from Lombard Street.*—(Guyn) **b.** *Dis Montserrat is famous for rain you know! Oh Yes! We does get rain and rain here.*—(Mrat) [Cp OED *famous* 3. (*Obs*) 'in a bad or neutral sense: notorious' + cits to 1837]

fan·cy¹ /1´2/ *adj* (Trin) [Of a Carnival BAND's costumes] Showing sufficient elaborateness to be distinguished from the traditional type (hence, for ex, *Fancy Indians, Fancy Sailors*, etc are different from *Indians, Sailor Bands*, etc). □ Note pitch differentiation from FANCY².

fan·cy² /2´1/ *vb tr* **1.** (Guyn, Trin) [*IF*] To approve of (sth); to like (the idea of doing sth). *'Well, having told Joe something, did he then go on to ask Joe anything?'—'Yes.' 'What?'—'He asked Joe if he fancied what he had told him.'*—AMAM:61 **2.** (StVn) [*AF/IF*] To be inclined to resemble (sb). *When she was young she more fancied the mother, but now she like she got her own features.*—(StVn) [By semantic shift of SE *fancy* 'to take a fancy to; to like'. Possibly also infl by CE FAVOUR] □ Note pitch differentiation from FANCY¹ *adj*.

fan·cy-mo·las·ses /1´2122/ *n* (Bdos, StKt) ‖ CANE SYRUP (CarA) *In 1903 a trial shipment of fancy molasses, manufactured at Rugby Plantation in St Thomas, was sent to Canada. This type of molasses was made by using the entire cane juice without removing any of the sugar content. Happily, this experiment was well received in Canada and from it was born an industry that has brought a great deal of money to the island.*—HBIH: 146 [From its shiny and syrupy appearance, in contrast with the dark boiled-down and viscous molasses]

fa·ne·ga *n* (Trin) A commercial unit of weight measure (for cocoa and coffee beans) amounting to 110 lbs. [Sp *fanega* 'grain measure = 1.58 bushels' (a quantity measure in Spain wh seems to have been greater in Latin Amer)]

fan-leaf palm *n phr* (Bdos) ‖ SILVER-THATCH PALM (Baha, Trin) [Because of the resemblance of the leaf, as a pot plant, to a lady's fan] □ Also loosely called **garden-palm, palm plant, pot-palm** in Bdos where it is popular as a pot plant.

fan·ner *n* (Baha, TkCa) A shallow, oval, straw-work sieve used for winnowing corn grits, rice, etc, but often also as a carrier on the head. *They packed large fanners full of fruits and vegetables which they carried on their heads, and also some baskets in their hands.*—TOSR:31 [Adaptation of SE *fanner* 'a winnow', but still commonly used in rural areas]

far *adv* PHRASES **1. far less** *adv phr* **(i)** (CarA) [*IF*] [Often following a clause introduced by *'even'*, *'not even'*, or having such a sense indicated] Worse still; the more so. **a.** *Even these white people could see that far less me but we all know Barbados is Little England.*—Bdos (Ms, 1976) **b.** *The public roadway is no place to store this kind of thing. Obstruction of normal traffic is by itself an abuse, far less having it pose a threat to schoolchildren.*—ExP (72.06.01, p.23) □ Note that this phr is sometimes confused with SE *far more.* **(ii)** (Bdos, Dmca, StLu, StVn, Trin) [*IF*] ‖ **much less** (Belz, CayI, Guyn, Nevs) [Ending a statement to reject an idea that has been proposed] So unlikely is it!; [elliptically] let alone—. *How can they expect the man to buy a car? Why he can hardly afford a good bicycle, far less!*—(Bdos) [By ellipsis, i.e. 'far less is it likely that what you say can be so'] **2. far more** *adv phr* (Guyn, Tbgo, Trin) [*X*] [Often confused with SE *far less* and used interchangeably with Phr 1.] And so all the more unlikely. **a.** *She not going on a plane far more on a boat.*—(Trin) **b.** *He wan[t] buy a fridge and he can't afford a prappa bed far more.*—(Guyn)

fare *n* PHRASE **pick fares** *vb phr* (Bdos) [*AF*] To be a prostitute. *She also admitted in court that she was a prostitute. 'I have no other job, but picking fares and I do not pick pockets.'*—NaT (83.03.17, p.3) [Euphemistic analogy from taxi-driver's phr *pick up a fare* 'to take an unknown passenger on board']

fa·rine (**fa·win**) [fari·n~fawi·n] *n* (Angu, Dmca, Gren, Guyn, StLu, StVn, Tbgo) ‖ *cassava farine* (Dmca) ‖ *coco²* (BrVi, StKt) ‖ *manioc-farine* (StLu) A coarse-grained meal made by stirring the grated residue of bitter cassava (after squeezing out the poisonous juice) in a large open iron pot over fire. *Farine is used in a number of ways, as a cereal, thickening gravy, making dumplings, or eaten raw with zaboca, 'Farine and Pear'.*—StLu (Ms) [< Fr *farine* 'flour' or (esp in *Guyn*) Pg *farinha* 'flour, meal' from Amerindian contact with Brazil. Note also SE *farina* 'flour or meal of corn, nuts or starchy roots']

farse *adj*; **farse.ness** *n* (Gren, Tbgo, Trin) [*AF—Cr*] Dial spellings widely used for CE FAST; FASTNESS.

fast (**farse, fas', fass**) *adj* (CarA) [*AF/IF*] **1.** ‖ *gypsy* (Bdos) ‖ *jeps* (Nevs, StKt) ‖ *malicious* (Bdos) Too inquisitive; meddlesome; interfering in other people's business. *'You might think I fast,' Seeta said, 'but I have a purpose in asking.'*—SPOC:80 [Prob a semantic extension or shift of SE *OED fast* adj 10. b. 'disregardful of propriety or decorum'. Cp also *CSD* Sc *fest, fast* 2. 'busy, occupied'] □ The dial alternative spellings are often used in narrative dialogue in representing this sense. **2.** Impertinent; bold and rude; presumptuous. *'Is I who pinch him, that is why he cry,' Urmilla's mother said. 'Nigger boy put he black hand in my betah baby face! He too fast*

again!'—SABS:47 **3.** PHRASES (Intensifying senses of the above) **3.1 fast and forward** (Gren); **fast and out of place** (Tbgo, Trin) *adj phr* [*IF*] Intolerably impertinent. **a.** *As great as that visiting Chinese Cultural Group may have been, I still find them fast and out of place to attempt to dictate to the audience just when, where and why they must be applauded.*—BoM (75.05.16, p.24) **b.** *Imagine the British Government questioning Grenada's purchase of arms from Chile! Callahan and Judy Hart really fast and forward with themselves.*—ToR (78.02.09, p.5) **3.2 fast with yourself/himself, etc** *adj phr* (CarA) [*AF*] Rather personally impertinent. *An' she real farse wid she self, you know. She say she want mih to sleep een, den she go turn rong and say she ent want mih to bring mih husband in de yard. Ah tell she, 'Madam, it ent only you one could have husband, nuh, an' I ent business wid your own, so you bes' had lef mine wey he dey.'*—MN:33 **4.** Quick moving in gaining the interest of sb of the opposite sex; sexually aggressive. *But he wouldn't get anything from me, Mr Haynes. I know these young men well. They very fast, you know, but I can see after myself.*—JMA:97 [Cp *OED fast* adj 10. a. 'Of persons: Living too fast ... dissipated ...'] **5.** PHRASES **5.1 be/get fast with (sb)** *vb phr* (CarA) [*IF*] [Of a man] To become sexually aggressive towards (sb). **5.2 make your hands fast with (a girl)** *vb phr* (CarA) [*IF*] [Of a man] To seduce or almost succeed in seducing (a girl). **5.3 make your hands fast with (sth)** *vb phr* (CarA) [*IF*] [Of a child] To interfere with, try to take or steal (sth) (esp food, or anything that might be damaged). **5.4 play fast with (sth)** *vb phr* (Guyn, StKt) [*IF*] To use or attempt to use (sth) (esp money) without permission, but intending to replace it. **5.5 pull (or try) a fast one** *vb phr* (Guyn) [*AF*] To succeed (or try to succeed) in doing sth that is deceptive or artful. [From English slang with some shift in CE] **5.6 your hand is (too) fast** *id phr* (CarA) [Of a child] You are interfering with some item that belongs to a grown-up person.

fast·en¹ *vb intr* (CarA) [*X*] To stick or get stuck (in mud, etc); to get caught in a position so that shifting without damage is not possible. **a.** *The tractor fastened in the wet field.*—Guyn (Ms) **b.** *She began to feel irritable and swore as her dress fastened halfway down and refused to budge further.*—PCOS:126 [CarA Cr use of SE vb tr with passive sense]

fast·en² *adj* (Guyn) [*AF—Cr*] [Of a coin] Singly equal in value to two or more smaller units, (hence a ‖ *fasten two shilling* 'a two-shilling piece', a ‖ *fasten twenty-five cents* 'a twenty-five cent coin/piece', etc). [< SE *fastened* 'secured together']

fast-fast *adv* (CarA) [*AF*] As quickly as you can imagine. *The news got round fast-fast that she'd returned.*—PCOS:180

fast-mouth adj, n (ECar) [AF] ∥BIG-MOUTH² (CarA) Straightway Jenny went to Rosie's door step and called her a news carrier, a mischiefmaker, a fastmouth and all that she could think of.—PKKK:46

fast·ness n (CarA) [IF] 1. Inquisitiveness; meddlesomeness; interference in other people's business. [FAST adj 1. + -ness] 2. Impertinence; boldness; presumptuousness. [FAST adj 2. + -ness] 3. Sexual aggressiveness. [FAST adj 4. + -ness] 4. PHRASES 4.1 bring/come/go with/take your fastness to (sb) vb phrs (CarA) [IF] [According to context, in senses 1., 2., 3. above] To pry; to be openly rude to (sb); to make clear sexual advances to (sb).

Fa·ther¹ /1'2/ n (CarA) (Form of address or ref to) your priest, or (sometimes) your male parent. □ Distinguish from father /2'1/ the routine ref to anybody's male parent.

fa·ther² (fad·der, fa(r)·da, fa(r)·tha) / 2'1∼2'2/ n (CarA) [AF/IF] ∥papa, puppa (Tbgo, Trin) [Used as an intensifier of another n wh it often follows] A tremendous, terrific, or most impressive one (of sth). **a.** He looked for Jimmie, the father of cussers, only twelve years' old.—OJS:21 **b.** 'It's another trumpet ... ' Selina said uncertainly. 'How yuh mean, girl—another trumpet? This is the trumpet of trumpet. This is trumpet fatha! The best yuh could buy from the best store out there on Fifth Avenuh in New York. Is the only one in the world like it.'—MBGB:109 **c.** When she walk down a street so, every man turning around to look at her. You can't miss her at all. That girl have personality father.—JJM:48 [A prob calque of DAFL Twi papa, papaapa adv 'very good, very well, very much' and used in similar position: wahwe no papa 'he beat him very much' cp CE 'he got a father of a licking']

fa·ther-in-law n (Bdos, Guyn, Jmca) [X] (Sometimes loosely used to mean) a step-father.

fa·thom n (Baha, BrVi, CayI) The length of the outstretched arms or about 6 ft (used as a measure of rope or any distance on land. See cit). Because the sea is so much a part of the life of Grand Caymanians, nautical terms are common. Land distance is measured in fathoms much of the time—'for about fifteen fathoms from the gate', 'twenty fathoms down the road' and 'up the beach about five hundred fathoms.'—KWS:20

fa·tigue¹ vb (CarA) [IF] [Esp of children] To bother, pester, or worry (a parent or grown-up). Child don't fatigue me! Go outside and play!—(Guyn) [By semantic extension of SE fatigue 'to wear (sb) out']

fa·tigue² (fa·teeg) ['fa·tig] n (Tbgo, Trin) [AF] ∥picong (Trin) 1. Continuous teasing, banter, or joking at sb's expense. Much of the fun came, not only from the calypsoes, but from the exchange of 'fatigue' between M.C. Lord Melody and the Mighty Sparrow. Judging from the audience's response, Melody got the better of the exchanges. In fact, he brought the house down with his 'Belmont Jackass'—a reply to Sparrow's 'Madame Dracula'.—TrG (61.01.07, p.2) 2. PHRASES 2.1 give (sb) fatigue vb phr (Tbgo, Trin) [AF] To tease (sb) continuously; to test (sb's) patience by teasing. 2.2 take fatigue vb phr (Tbgo, Trin) [AF] To withstand steady teasing. [By semantic extension of SE fatigue 'strain']

fat-pork n 1. (ECar) ∥COCO-PLUM 1. (Antg, etc) One of the common trees of the palm marsh which rejoices in the imaginative local name of fatpork; is also a common and characteristic species of the sea shore in association with the sea-side grape.—ACTT:177 2. (Belz) A chunk of (pickled) salt-beef.

fat·ty bum-bum n phr (Gren, Tbgo, Trin) [AF—Joc] A very fat person, esp a woman with large buttocks.

fa·vour vb 1. (CarA) [IF] ∥feature (Bdos) [Esp of persons, but also of inanimate things] To resemble. **a.** You ain favour yer pa fer nuttin! Yer jes like yer no good pa.—TOSR:38 **b.** Dat dress favour one dat ah have.—OT3:9 2. (Jmca) [By extension, used in similes] To look like; to look as if. (See FACE Phr 1.) But nobody ever said it as well as this Jamaican girl I was once trying to put a serious move on. 'Man, go from here,' she said in disgust, 'wid your face favour when thunder clap puss in a banana walk!' In other words, my face reminded her of what a cat's face would look like if the cat were walking through a banana plantation when all of a sudden a loud boom of thunder scared the hell out of the cat.—NaT (85.11.19, p.10) [A survival and extension of EE. Cp OED favour v 8. 'to resemble in features; (rarely) to have the look of' + cits 1609–1867] □ Cp also FANCY² 2.

fa·win [fawi·n] n (Dmca, StLu) See FARINE [By regular /r > w/ shift in CarA Fr Cr]

fe; fi [fi∼fi] prep (Jmca) [AF—Cr] For. (A dial form widely used in narrative dialogue wherever 'for' functions in Jmca Cr speech.) Another phrase often used to describe relationship is 'fe we', that is 'for we, for us, of our family or kin'. 'Anybody fe we' means 'anyone who is of our family'.—SWI:121 □ See also FA, FER, FO, FU.

fea·ture vb tr (Bdos) [IF] ∥FAVOUR 1. (CarA) 'C'dear, I never see girl-children so features their father as these two, Silla.'—MBGB:58 [A survival of EE. Cp OED feature vb 1. trans. 'to resemble in features, esp in ref to family likeness (Now chiefly dial.)' + cits 1755–1881]

Fed·er·a·tion, The 1. n phr (CarA) The political union of ten Anglophone Caribbean island-states, Antigua-Barbuda, Barbados, Dominica, Grenada, Jamaica, Montserrat, St Kitts-Nevis-Anguilla, St Lucia, St Vincent & the Grenadines, Trinidad & Tobago, wh was formed in January 1958 and dissolved in February 1962. **2.** *n* (Bdos) [Not cap] A big noisy brawl; many people rowing and fighting. *Somebody must of said something to old Mr Gay Lisle about Birdie looks and he up hand and give the man one! And soon the whole place was like federation. The rum bottles flying. The women and children screeching like bombs was falling—*MBGB:118 [A Hist ref to the violent disorder, known as the Federation Riots, in *Bdos* in 1876, wh were related to planters' rejection of a proposed federation of Barbados and the WINDWARD IS.]

fed·i·ty *n* (Bdos) [*AF*] ‖ASAFOETIDA (CarA) [A corrupted form of *asafoetida*]

feed·er-road *n* (Guyn) [Rice & Sugar Inds] ‖CART-ROAD (Bdos, Guyn)

feed·er(-ta·ble) *n* (CarA) [Sugar Ind] A long sloping metal trough on to wh sugar cane is pushed by a conveyor belt to be cut up by rotating knives before being fed into the grinders.

feed·er(-trench) *n* (Guyn) [Rice & Sugar Inds] One of a system of shallower drainage canals that channel flood waters into a deeper FAÇADE-TRENCH or main drainage canal.

feed·ing *n* (Gren) [*AF—Vul*] **1.** Sexual intercourse. *Patrice, he claims at this stage approached one of the girls for 'feeding' and she told him off.*—ToR (77.03.27, p.1) **2.** [By extension] A young woman with whom a man desires to have sexual intercourse.

feed-lot *n* Jmca A fenced area of approved pasture land in wh cattle are fed for about three months on special fodder to produce the best quality of beef.

feel *vb* PHRASES **1. can't hear will feel** *id phr* (CarA) [*IF*] [Said to children in varying forms]. See HEAR Phr 4.11 **2. feel a fool** *vb phr* (CarA) [*AF*] To feel foolish; to feel like a fool. *Tiger feel a fool. Him sit on the horse with him head all confuse.*—TM:15 **3. feel for fish** *vb phr* (Guyn) To seek out fresh-water fishes by hand in the soft mud of a shallow or drained TRENCH, trapping the fish in a part of the trench by closing in from opposite ends while shying soft mud in the water to frighten them. **4. feel for (sb)** *vb phr* (CarA) [*IF*] To feel sympathy or concern for (sb's misfortune or disadvantage). **a.** *We would also like to extend our thanks to those who have felt for our safety, and to those who conducted unceasing searches for us until we were safe.*—IsS (75.06.16, p.9) **b.** *... it gave him a lot of sympathy from the people. They felt for him because it was obvious to them that his platform had been denied the big guns.*—NaT (76.09.05, p.13 [Cp *OED feel v* 14. *feel with, for sb* (a person, his sufferings) but evid a 19C usage] **4.1 feel for (sth)** *vb phr* (CarA) [*IF*] ‖**call for (sth)** (Tbgo) To have a (sudden) craving for (sth); to feel like having (sth). *I felt for some soursop ice-cream only to find you-all*

children had eaten all.—(Guyn) **5. feel like** *vb phr* (CarA) [*IF*] (Ellipsis for) feel like doing (sth that is an obligation); feel ready, able (to undertake sth). *Now, in the Sanitation and Cemeteries Board some people will sit down and sign cheques when they feel like. Some people are afraid to say: 'You are not doing your job properly, and I will have to revoke your appointment.'*—Bdos (Hd, 73.12.18, p.3023) □ Usu in sentence terminal position in this sense. **6. feel shame** *vb phr* (CarA) [*X*] To feel ashamed; to feel embarrassed by your or sb's misconduct or guilt. *The boy made the mother feel so shame she wouldn't even open her windows when the day come.*—(Bdos) [SHAME adj < SE *ashamed* by characteristic Cr aphesis and apcope] □ SE *shame* n usu requires a determiner in such a phr: *feel some/any/no/the shame.* **7. feel small** *vb phr* (CarA) [*IF*] ‖**look small** (CarA) To feel or be humiliated; to be embarrassed by an insult. **8. feel sweet** *vb phr* (CarA) [*IF*] **(i)** To experience a pleasing sensation; to feel sensual pleasure, bodily happiness. *The children felt so sweet on the merry-go-round they didn't want to stop.*—(Bdos) **(ii)** To begin to feel merry from (alcoholic) drink. *He came in feeling sweet and huggin[g] and kissin[g] up all the women.*—(Guyn) **9. feel to do (sth)** *vb phr* (CarA) [*IF*] To feel inclined or disposed to do (sth); to feel (strongly) prompted or driven to do (sth) (usu violent); (SE) to feel like doing (sth). **a.** *So read on, right on and laugh when you feel to laugh, and smile when you feel to smile.*—OJS:ii **b.** *That boy does make me so mad, sometimes I feel to lick him in his head.*—(StVn) [A poss calque from W Afr langs. Cp Yoruba *o fẹ bi* 'he feels/wants to throw up'] **10. feel to yourself** *vb phr* (CarA) [*IF*] To feel in your heart of hearts; to have a purely personal feeling. *I feel to myself that no member of a family has the authority to make their sons or daughters choice.*—NaT (79.06.27, p.27, Dear Christine) [SE *feel* + an emotive prop-complement] **11. make (sb) feel your hand** *vb phr* (ECar) [*AF*] See HAND phr 4.19

feel up *vb phr* (CarA) **1.** [*IF*] [Ref to fruit] To test the firmness by squeezing. *Secondly don't 'feel-up' things like mangoes, tomatoes and naseberries. The seller doesn't take too kindly to people who 'feel-up, feel-up' the merchandise.*—Foc. xv. 2, p.59 **2.** [*AF—Vul*] [Of a man] To squeeze and caress the body (of a woman) in order to arouse sexually. *And a man came in, and started to feel-me-up, and I thought it was you, so at first I didn't put up a fight.*—CPM:169

feg *n* (Angu, BrVi, Guyn, USVI) ‖**fig²** (Bdos) ‖**peg¹** (Gren, Jmca, StVn, Trin) ‖**plug** (Baha, Belz ‖**slice** (StLu) ‖**sprig** (Antg) A segment or section of fruit, esp of a peeled orange or of garlic, but also (esp in *BrVi*) a section of a SUGAR-APPLE or SOURSOP containing a seed. [A Sc and northern BrE pronunc of *fig* with dial sense as given in *EDD*: *fig* sb 1. Various dial uses in Irel, Eng, and Colon. Also in forms *fag* ...; *feg* Nhb, Dur, Wm Glo, Wil, Som, ... 5. A division of an orange + cit NhB, Dur. 'These used to be called figs ... some fifty years ago' (1877). Also *JSD: feg* sb 1. 'a fig'. This is the common pronunc in Scotland]

fel·la(r) [fɛla] *n* (CarA) [*AF—Joc*] (Dial spellings often used for) fellow. (Cp similar nonstandard (eye-dialect) *feller*). *Jim boy tru but ya kno who a larnatics dem fellars in de concil dey went to London and dey tal we at da park we are free.*—TiM (75.12.19, p.5)

fence-post tree *n phr* (USVI) ‖ BIRCH-GUM TREE (Bdos) [From its frequent use in demarcating large tracts of property because of its sturdiness, long life, and distinctive trunk]

fen·ky-fen·ky [fɛŋkɪ-fɛŋkɪ] *adj* (Jmca) [*AF—Cr/Derog*] 1. Weak in body or spirit; sluggish; slow to act or react. 2. Stupid; irritatingly helpless. □ Often used by parents in criticising children.

fer [fʌ] *prep* (CarA) [*AF—Cr*] (Dial spelling often used esp in the Bahamas for) for. *Da man Duvalier mussy fool fer true ef he ain pick up he money wen it fall down.*—JBJ:81 See also FA, FE, FI, FO, FU

fer-de-lance ['fɔrdɪlans] *n* (Dmca, StLu, Trin) ‖ *mapepire (balsin)* (Trin) ‖ *serpent* (StLu) ‖ *tomagoff* (Belz) A poisonous brownish snake that can grow to 7 ft in length; it has triangular head and slightly upturned snout; *Bothrops caribbaeus (Crotalidae)*. [Fr = lance-iron i.e. lance's head, from the triangular shape (and deadly strike) of its head] □ Cp LABARIA.

fer·ry-stel·ling *n* (Guyn) A STELLING, or wharf, for the mooring and boarding of a river ferry.

fetch *vb tr* (Gren) To reach (a place). *But what about mid-day, when it is necessary to fetch home, have lunch and return to school within the time allowed?*—ToR (64.10.23, p.2) [By semantic shift of nautical E. Cp *OED fetch* 10. *Naut.* 'to arrive at, come to, reach']

fetch away *vb phr* (Guyn, StVn) ‖ *get away* (Bdos, Tbgo) Trin) [Of friends] To fall out and quarrel; to disagree violently; to come to blows. *The tale-bearing continued until one day the two of them fetched away and had an awful brawl in the yard*—StVn (Ms) [Evid by semantic shift of *OED Fetch* 13. *Fetch away* 'To move or shift from its proper place; to get loose', with a connotation of violence. Cp cit 1805 'we fetch away and are tossed to the farthest side of the cabin'. Also poss extension of nautical sense as at FETCH.]

fete[1] **(fèt)** [fɛ·t] *n* (CarA) 1. A (usu open) houseparty or a public dance or JUMP-UP, usu with much food, rum-drinking, and spreeing. 2. [By extension] A picnic, excursion, or other form of organized group entertainment with plenty of dancing, food, and drink. (See compounds below). 3. [*AF—Joc*] [Often without determiner]

Merrymaking (esp of a wasteful, aimless kind). *Further, we must ensure that the additional time we gain from a five- day week is not totally lost to fete and cocktails.*—ExP (72.03.05, p.7) [Fr Cr < Fr FÊTE 'festival, festival-holiday'; but the accent is not used in CE] 4. PHRASES 4.1 **fete for so** *n phr* (ECar) [*AF*] Great merrymaking; a big FETE. *Well you know, is Carnival week-end coming up, and is fete for so all over the place.*—(Trin) 4.2 **planning fete** *vb phr* (Trin) [*AF*] Preparing to enjoy yourself with a big party or through much partying. 4.3 **throw (a) fete** *vb phr* (CarA) [*AF/IF*] To have a free house-party to wh your friends may also invite their friends. *Birthday, holiday any kin[d] o[f] day he is a man like to throw fete.*—(Trin)

fete[2] [fɛ·t] *vb intr* (ECar) 1. To make merry by dancing, JUMPING UP, eating, and drinking; to party and spree generously. a. *'I am convinced,' he said, 'that no other people in the world can fete like Trinidadians.'*—MtM (77.03.04, p.6) b. *They had moved in imagination from one parang to the other, from one house to the other, dancing and singing and feteing.*—JJM:16 [By functional n > vb shift of FETE[1]] □ Both the forms FETEING, FETING occur. 2. PHRASES 2.1 **fete down (the place)** *vb phr* (intensified) (Trin) [*AF*] To do much feteing. *But between you and me I feted down the place so much this Christmas, that even my wife wished me Merry Christmas on New Year's morning.*—SuP (75.01.19, p.12) 2.2 **fete up (sb)** *vb phr* (intensified) (Trin) [*AF*] To make (sb) do much free partying (usu to flatter or persuade); (*SE*) to fête (sb). *And G.C. will arrange a free helicopter ride for the Press boys and fete them up.*—MoK (72.06.23, p.4)

Fête La Mar·guerite (Fèt La Ma·gwit) *n phr* (StLu) See LA MARGUERITE

Fête La Rose (Fèt La Woz, Fèt La Wòz) [fɛt la wɔz] *n phr* (Dmca, StLu) See LA ROSE

fete-match [fɛ·t-mač] *n* (Gren, Tbgo, Trin) A friendly, non-competitive (usu cricket) match accompanied by much music, eating, and drinking by the players, their families and friends.

fet·er [fɛ·tər] *n* (CarA) 1. Anybody participating in a FETE. 2. A person fond of attending or of THROWING FETES.

fete-time *n* (Tbgo, Trin) Any season such as Christmas, Carnival, or the end of examinations when FETES are expected to be numerous. *Fetetime will always be pan-time for very many Trinidadians. And not surprisingly, despite the fact that it is against the law for steelbands to parade on the streets without special permission the Christmas holidays brought out several steelbands on the road in various parts of the country.*—ExP (72.12.28, p.13)

fe·ver *n* PHRASES 1. **drink bush for (sb's) fever** *vb phr* (Gren, Trin) [*AF*] ‖ TAKE UP (SB'S) FIRE-RAGE (Antg, etc) See FIRE-RAGE Phr 2.1 2.

sweat fever for (sb); sweat for (sb's) fever
vb phrs (Belz) ‖ TAKE UP (SB'S) FIRE-RAGE (Antg,
etc) See FIRE-RAGE Phr 2.1

fe·ver-grass* *n* (CarA) ‖ *lemon-grass* (Bdos,
Dmca, Gren, Guyn, TkCa, Trin) ‖ *tea-grass*
(TkCa) A bushy grass growing in dense clumps
sometimes exceeding 3 ft in height, with long,
thin, sharp-edged leaves and a longer nodding
stalk in the centre carrying a sparse, brownish,
flower-like cluster; the leaves are strongly lemon-
scented when picked or crushed and widely used
in TEAS or BUSH-BATHS as a folk-medicinal cure
for fevers, colds, etc; *Cymbopogon citratus* (*Gramineae*).

few *adj* 1. (CarA) [X] (Often used in sense of)
quite a few; a fairly high number of (esp in Phr
2.1). 2. PHRASES 2.1 few very well *adj phr*
(CarA) [X] *They had few very well in church this
morning though the weather was so bad* (*i.e. There
were many people in church, etc*).—(Bdos) 2.2 fire
a few *vb phr* (CarA) [X] See FIRE² Phr 6.1 3.
adv (Guyn) [AF] Skimpy; unsatisfactory in size
or quantity. *I don't buy from her. She want too
much and even the pumpkin look so few.*—(Guyn)

fi [fɪ ~ fi] *prep* (Belz, Jmca) [AF—Cr] For; to
*The cop took up the parcel, opened it and saw one
tape deck. Asked where he got it the accused said:
'A mi father gi mi fi sell.'*—WeS (74.01.18, p.6)
See FE

fid·dle-wood* *n* (CarA) A tough, pale-
coloured timber yielded by three or four varieties
of trees some 60 ft tall, 'with papery, peeling bark
and 4-angled branches' *PTT:117*, and bearing
hanging clusters of small flowers and inedible
berries; *Citharexylum spp* (*Verbenaceae*). [Name
said to be from use of wood for making fiddles
and guitars. However, Carl Linnaeus ... translated the W Indian name Fiddle- wood into two
Greek words, latinised as cithara and exylon:
fiddle and wood. But ... Charles Sprague
Sargent, director of ... Arnold Arboretum of
Harvard University, stated that the name Fiddle
Wood is a corruption of the French colonial
name Bois Fidele, literally 'trusty wood,' an
allusion to the strength and toughness of the
wood from trees of this genus—AdN (79.05.27,
p.18, M. Hutt)]

field-ne·gro/-man/-slave *n* (CarA) [Hist]
‖ *field-nigger* (CarA) [AF—Derog] An African
slave who worked in cane or cotton fields (and
therefore considered much less favoured than
and socially inferior to the HOUSE-NEGRO).

field-nig·ger *n* (CarA) [AF—Derog] (A term
of abuse used among black people for) a black
person who shows shameless deference to whites.
See FIELD-NEGRO □ Cp also HOUSE-NIGGER. The
(revived) currency of these terms in present CE
seems to be infl by black AmE usage.

fields, the *n pl* (Guyn) Diamond-fields or
gold-fields i.e. places in the INTERIOR of Guyn

where there are temporary settlements of prospecting PORK- KNOCKERS. □ To be distinguished
from pl of 'rice-field', 'cane-field', 'cotton-field'
wh are never referred to in *Guyn* as THE FIELDS.

fi·esta *n* (Belz) The feasting and rituals related
to DUGU.

fife-man (Guyn); **fif.er** (Mrat) *n* A man who
plays the fife in a MASQUERADE BAND.

fig¹ *n* 1. (CarA) Word in more general use
for BANANA *CarA*. Hence FIG-LEAF, FIG-SKIN,
FIG-TREE, RIPE FIG = banana-leaf, -skin, etc.
□ See also GREEN FIG. 2. PHRASES 2.1 fig and
bluggo (Gren) A cooked vegetable meal in wh
GREEN FIGS and BLUGGOES are the main ingredients. 2.2 fig and saltfish (ECar) A cooked
meal of GREEN FIGS, SALTFISH, onions and tomatoes. 3. (Bdos, StKt, StVn, TkCa, USVI)
‖ APPLE-BANANA (Belz, etc) 4. (Guyn) Usu FIG-
BANANAS of wh there are different types, SOUR-
FIG (a very small thickly bunched banana of
sourish sweetness), SWEET-FIG (a very small
loosely bunched sweet banana), etc. See also
CLARET FIG, SILK FIG [Note *OED* FIG¹ sb 1. c.
'in the East and West Indies popularly applied
(like the corresponding words in Fr, Sp, and
Pg) to the Banana ...' + cits from 1582. Also
HNHB:176 'And as the Fruit of the Banana-tree
is often by the most ancient Authors called a
Fig, I may, I hope without Presumption ... look
upon the Fig-tree in Paradise to be no other
than the Banana-tree' (1750). To this is added,
in modern times, the infl of CarA Fr Cr *figue*
'banana' vs *banane* 'plantain'. See note at BA-
NANA]

fig² *n* (Bdos) ‖ FEG (Angu, etc)

fig³ *n* (TkCa) ‖ CLAMMY-CHERRY (CarA) 1. [Prob
erron from resemblance of fruit to a number of
ficus varieties of the family *Moraceae* also called
'fig', 'wild fig', etc. See *ACPRV:68–75*]

fight¹ *vb tr* (CarA) 1. [IF] To cause much
difficulty or trouble (to do sth); to make (sb)
struggle (to do or finish sth). *Without a father
you know the children are fighting me to feed and
clothe and keep tidy.*—(Guyn) 2. PHRASE 2.1 fight
behind (sb) to do (sth) *vb phr* (Tbgo) [AF]
‖ BE BEHIND (SB) TO DO (STH) (CarA) See BEHIND¹
Phr 1. *Some parents fight behind their children
trying to give them a good education only to see
them turn ungrateful.*—(Tbgo) See BEHIND¹ Phr
1. 2.2 fight sleep; sleep fights you *id phrs*
(CarA) To struggle or try hard to stay awake. 3.
[AF] ‖ *fight with (sth)* (Antg, Guyn) *vb phr* To
struggle, try hard (to do sth). *The whole day he
been fighting to finish that gate.*—(Bdos)

fight² *n* (CarA) [IF] A tremendous effort; a
struggle against odds and hardships. **a.** *He had
a fight to chop down that tree.*—(StKt) **b.** *She
had a real fight to keep those children going to
school.*—(Tbgo)

fight at/with (sth) *vb phr* (Antg, Guyn) [*AF*] ‖ FIGHT[1] 3. (CarA) *S1: The poor child there fighting with the work. / S2: Well if she fight at it she will succeed.*—(Antg)

fight down (sth) *vb phr* (Jmca) [*IF*] To struggle against (sth); to try to prevent (sth). *Fathers and some mothers in the Employers Federation do not need maternity leave for their wives and children so they are fighting down the passing of this law.*—DaN(JA) (79.11.29, p.7)

fight-for-in·nings /1'122/ *n* (Trin) ‖ OUT-FOR-PLAY (Guyn)

fight·ing-stick *n* (ECar) ‖ **bwa** (Dmca, Gren, StLu, Tbgo, Trin) ‖ ***stick***[1] 1. (ECar) [*IF*] A STICK-FIGHTER'S weapon, a stick of very tough wood, sometimes ringed with metal at each end. (See cit). *The fighting stick ranges from 5 to 6 ft in length and is usually about seven-eighths of an inch in diameter. It is most frequently made from the cog-wood or yellow poui tree although some informants have given a long list which includes the gasparee, anaree, and even the sour- guava. There are secret formulas for cutting the wood and preparing a stick.*—Jfi, III.2, p.194

fight off (with) (sb); **fight up (sb)** *vb phrs* (CarA) [*AF*] To attack (sb) with bumptious or unexpected aggressiveness. **a.** *Now the boy grow big he ready to fight off the father when the father talk to him.*—(Guyn) **b.** *From a little girl she learn to fight up with the brothers for the food.*—(Jmca)

fight up with (sth); **fight up yourself (to do sth)** *vb phrs* (CarA) [*AF*] ‖ **kill out/up yourself** (CarA) To hustle and strive diligently (to make or do sth). *The Trinidadian placed in this same situation might either be found doing the robot dance in front of a juke-box; or in some derelict back-yard fighting up with a massive head-piece intent on killing them next year carnival.*—ExP (Supplement) (79.12.02, p.8) **b.** *Don't fight up yourself to fork this garden, I'll help you to do it next week.*—(Guyn)

fi·la·ri·a ['faɪlerɪʌ] /1'221/ *n* (Guyn) ‖ BIG-FOOT (Guyn) □ Properly the disease *filariasis*, 'filaria' being the biological name of the worm that causes the disease.

file-fish *n* (Bdos, StLu) ‖ KABWIT (StLu)

fill *vb tr* (CarA) PHRASES 1. **filled of** *vbl adj phr* (BrVi) [*X*] Full of; filled with. *His argument is filled of emotionally toned words.*—BrVi (Ms, 1973) [By overcorrection or misascription of adj function of SE *filled*] 2. **fill your eye** [*IF*]; **full your eye** [*X*] *vb phr* (CarA) See EYE[1] Phr 19.

fi·lo·to [filoto] /1'12/ *n* (Gren) A home-made gun, usu made from a piece of galvanized piping. [Perh related to Fr *filou* 'a rogue'] □ Cp PIPE-GUN.

fin *n* (Baha) The leg of a crab·

fi·nan·cial [faɪnanšəl] /1'22/ *adj* (CarA) **1.** Fully paid up with your membership fees or subscription and so in good standing (in an organization). *Only financial members are allowed to vote.*—(Regular clause in the Constitutions of clubs, etc) **2.** [*AF/IF*] Having money necessary for sth. *Christmas came and found her not too financial.*—Bdos (Ms)

find 1. *vb tr* (CarA) [*AF—Derog*] Seek out (and go back to); be off, betake yourself to. [Esp in foll phrs]. **2.** PHRASES **2.1 find where you live** *vb phr* (USVI) [*AF—Derog*] ‖ ***find your place*** (Trin) ‖ ***find your yard*** (Jmca) To go home; to go back to wherever your sort can have come from. **2.2 Find your hole!** *imper vb phr* (Trin) [*AF—Derog*] 'Be off with you and mind your own dirty business!' *Zandoli find your hole. (i.e. Lizards should go where lizards live?)*—Trin (Prov) **2.3 Find yourself (in here!—outside! etc)** *imper vb phr* (CarA) [*AF*] 'Get back (into the house/outside, etc) at once!' □ A rough order, usu said to a child. **3.** *vb tr* (Bdos, Guyn) To provide (a servant, subordinate or child) with food and/or clothing; to support. *We had a noise over it, and so we broke up. He still finds the children though. He wanted us to make back; but my mother says no and I agree.*—PeL (78.03.17, p.11) [*OED find v* 19. 'to support, maintain or provide for (a person)'] **4.** *vb intr* (Tbgo, Trin) [*IF*] **(i)** To think, consider (sth to be so). **(ii)** [In general use] To be of the opinion that. *'That commercial so sickening, eh! Ah doh know why they doh take it out nah?' Ishmael agreed with her, and said so. 'Ah really find they should make ah new one,' he said.*—ExP (72.03.12, p.20) **(iii)** [Often terminal] To agree (with an opinion expressed). *He resemble his father a lot, you don't find?*—(Trin)

find-fault ['faɪn-fɒ·lt] *adj* (Antg, Guyn, StVn, Tbgo) [*AF*] ‖ **find-faultin(g)** (Bdos) Ready to pick out little faults; irritatingly prone to criticise. *Don't bother with her, girl! She too find-fault! The dress fit you good and look nice!*—(Antg) [By functional vb phr > adj shift of SE *to find fault with sth*]

fine *adj* (CarA) **1.** [*IF*] [General use] Thin; slender; inadequately small. **a.** *Elsie's legs are too fine for her body.*—(Guyn) **b.** *This writing is too fine for me to read.*—(Bdos) [Cp *OED fine adj* II. 7. d. 'extremely thin or slender'] □ This sense is unambiguous in CE in the contexts in wh it occurs. The SE sense 'excellent' is, however, also current but more likely in educated speech and also easily identified by context. **2.** (Guyn) [Of a person's facial features] Of delicate lines, particularly having a straight nose, small nostrils, thin lips, and not too big a face. [Cp *OED fine adj* II. 9. (Obs) 'of bodily constitution: delicate, sensitive, tender' + cits–'1661'] □ Whereas *fine features* also occurs as a term in SE, the term in CE strongly connotes 'nearer European than African in facial lines'.

fine-fine /1'2/ adv (Guyn) [AF] In minute and tiresome detail. *Well A telling[g] you to be careful who yo[u] go out wid and whe[re] dey carryin[g] you, and A don't have to tell yo[u] everyt[h]ing fine-fine!*—(Guyn)

fine-salt n (Guyn, Jmca) Table salt [By contrast with COARSE-SALT]

fine-shrimp(s) n (Guyn) ‖ **white-belly shrimp(s)** (Guyn) A variety of small, whitish shrimp seasonally caught in great abundance and often dried in small quantities, shelled or unshelled; *Penaiedae spp.* [By contrast with COARSE SHRIMP(S)]

fin·ger n 1. (StVn) ‖ **grain** (Gren, StVn, Tbgo) A single banana or plantain as part of a bunch. *Banana bunches should be sleeved as soon as fingers start turning upwards.*—ViN (73.02.07, p.12) 2. (CayI) ‖ **tengaleh** (Guyn) The claw or claws of a crab.

fin·ger-board n (Bdos, Jmca) A narrow horizontal piece of board, pointing a direction or signalling a street-name, mounted on a sign-post or lamp-post. □ SE *finger-post* is a special 'guide-post' wh would carry CE FINGER-BOARDS. The association prob accounts for the CE word.

fin·ger-man n (Bdos, Belz) [AF—Derog] A Judas; a person who betrays the whereabouts of sb in hiding. [As OED *finger* v 1. (Obs) 'to point at with the finger' 2. c. 'to apprehend ... person' + CE suff -MAN']

fin·ger-pep·per n Baha, Bdos ‖ BIRD-PEPPER (CarA) [From its shape]

fin·ger-rows (**fin·ger-rose**) n (Antg, Brbu) ‖ APPLE-BANANA (Belz, etc) [Perh from resemblance of the hands on a bunch of this small variety to several rows of fingers. Note FINGER 1. The alternative spelling—ROSE—is prob a phonic conjecture] □ Sometimes also *finger-rolls*.

fin·gle [fɪŋgl] vb [Derog] 1. (Bdos) To pass the fingers idly on, along or around some object as if feeling its shape absent-mindedly. *And the 'trained by experience' managers, who could have been spotted miles away in all-over white, fingling pocket watches from chains attached to their waists, have gone into retirement, leaving their inheritance to dynamic young men.*—NaT (75.11.16, p.9) 2. (CarA) (i) To handle, touch or squeeze (sth) officiously; to examine (sth) by feeling it over and over with the fingers. *Child, do not fingle my expensive jewellery! Leave it alone.*—(Guyn) (ii) [Of fruit on display for sale] To touch or press with the fingers in order to test firmness. *Lady, if you goin[g] buy, buy! But don['t] go fingling my tomatoes.*—(Belz) (iii) [AF—Vul] [Of a man] To handle and caress (a woman's body) in order to arouse her sexually. *He must have tried to fingle the girl and that's why she slapped him.*—(Nevs) [Prob < Obs E *fangle* [fæŋgl] wh would become 'fengle' > 'fingle' in CE. Cp OED *fangle* v¹ (Obs)

'to trifle'; also CSD *fangle* 'to trap, ensnare, tangle'; also OED *fingle-fangle* n (Obs), but with vbl use = 'to trifle with'. The infl of SE *finger* vb 'to explore with the fingers' prob only reinforced the dial survival of FINGLE in CE with much the same sense, though this form is so widespread in CE as to call in question its actual development from SE *finger* by /r > l/ shift (lambdacism) in so many different territories. Normally SE [fɪŋgə(r)] > CE [fɪŋgʌ] □ CE maintains a working distinction between *finger* n, vb and *fingle* vb.

fin·ish vb (CarA) 1. vb tr [IF] To put a stop to (sth). *Mr Rayside added that he had painted some of the houses of the residents after they had complained to him ... 'but I had to finish that since they wanted me to do it every year.'*—AdV (88.01.28, p.1) 2. PHRASE 2.1 **finish with that** id phr [IF] ‖ DONE WITH THAT (Bdos, Gren) *If Mr Freddie Miller said something, he has said it and we are finished with that.*—Bdos (Hd, 75.02.04, p.4536) □ A common phr in *Bdos* wh, like the ‖, indicates finality and anger. 3. vb intr [AF] To come or to have come to an end. *They used to give us a ten-minute coffee break on mornings, and that finish, as now only management are allowed tea or cokes and they order it at their desks.*—NaT (76.08.22, p.26, Dear Christine) 4. *indicating completive aspect* [AF—Cr] To have completed (the doing of sth stated in the next vb). *I finish hand in the broom at the Public Works Office since yesterday morning before I dress for the wedding.*—OTTTT:52 5. PHRASE 5.1 **be finished (doing sth)** vb phr (CarA) [X] To have finished (doing sth). *You can clean mine for me too when you're finished.*—WBH:88 [This is a 'false' passive due to erron re-analysis of Cr *you finish* (= you have finished) as a case of a missing aux *be* (see 6. below) instead of the actual missing aux *have*] □ SE *I'm/you're*, (etc) *finished* = 'I'm/ you're', (etc) *done for*. This 'false' CE passive is in common use, with the meaning above, but is misleading in IAE. However in AmE *I am finished* is acceptable = 'I have finished'. This is hardly so in BrE. 6. vb intr, as a full passive (CarA) [X] [A development of 3.] To have been brought to an end, used up, sold out, etc; to have been completed. a. *People had to leave their work and run quick and get a few pounds before the flour finished.*—Guyn (Ms) b. *'Sit down,' he said, 'the shoes will finish just now.'* (= *Work on the shoes will soon have been completed*).—Cat VI.1 (E. Lovelace) [Development from characteristic Cr semantic transformation of vb tr to passive sense without using 'be']

fin·ny (**fi·ni**) [fɪni] adj (Bdos, Gren, Guyn, Mrat, StVn) [Esp of the hand or foot] Sick; twisted; crippled. (Hence often in compounds FINNY-FOOT, FINNY-HAND). a. *Well he got to be careful crossing the road with that finny-foot he got.*—(Gren) b. *You holding that pen like if you finny. You know how to write at all?*—(Bdos) [Prob < Fante *mfina* 'stunted'. Cp also DAFL Akyem Twi *bafáne* 'a child who did not learn to walk in the first two to seven years']

fip *n* (Jmca) [*AF*] **1.** The smallest imaginable amount of money; a worthless sum. [*OED fip, fipenny* = five pence, once evid current in US. See also *DJE fip*] **2.** PHRASE **2.1 ain'[t]/not worth a fip** *adj phr* (Jmca) [*AF/IF*] Worthless; valueless. □ *Fippence* is still known to old folk in *Bdos*.

fire¹ *n* (CarA) PHRASES **1. eye(s) catch fire for (sth/sb)** *id phr* (Gren, etc) [*AF*] See EYE¹ Phrs 8., 8.1. **2. eyes make fire for (sb)** *id phr* (Gren) [*AF—Joc*] See EYE¹ Phr 13. **3. Fire, fire, bu[r]n me hand!** *id phr* (Guyn) [*AF—Cr*] ‖ *Fire bun!* (Baha) [Phrase used by a third party to indicate that a spectacular fight or row between two others is immediately about to take place] **4. licks like fire** *n phr* (ECar) [*AF*] ‖ *licks like peas* (ECar) [*AF*] A trouncing. □ Often used figuratively in ref to a beating in some competitive game. **5. push fire** *vb phr* (CarA) [*AF/IF*] To provoke a big row (esp one in wh others will be the major participants).

fire² *vb tr* (CarA) [*AF/IF*] [Used in many general senses as analogous to 'fire a shot'.] **1.** To deliver (a severe blow) (hence foll phrs). **2.** PHRASES **2.1 fire a blow/lash** *vb phr* (CarA) ‖ *pelt/throw a blow* (Guyn) To hit out at or strike (sb) severely (with the hand or using any object). *Alloo gave him a blow with the cutlass at Singh's head and he ducked.*—GyC (76.05.06, p.7) □ Hence similarly *fire a box/chop/cuff/ hand/kick/lash/lick/some licks* **3.** To pelt, hurl, or pitch (sth) hard (at sb) (hence foll phrs). **4.** PHRASES **4.1 fire bottles/rocks/stones, (etc) at (sb)** (CarA) [*IF*] To hurl (any of these objects) with the intention of injuring or damaging. *He fired a lick at me with his hand. I went down the step into the yard and took a pan and fired it at him. It struck him in his head.*—Dem(SK) (62.08.18, p.2) Hence also in relation to quarrelsome speech: **4.2 fire back** *vb phr* (Trin) [*IF*] To answer loudly and sharply. **4.3 fire curses/ (some) cuss** *vb phr* (CarA) [*AF/IF*] To swear vehemently (at sb) using dirty language. *Enrique sit up and pelt the crutch after them, and he begin to fire some curse in Spanish.*—SWOS:45 **4.4 fire yourself!** *imper vb phr* (Antg, Guyn, Nevs, Tbgo) [*AF*] ‖ *fire your skin* (Tbgo) ‖ *fire your tail* (Guyn) ‖ MOVE YOURSELF (CarA) *Look! Fire yourself inside and change your clothes and do your homework.*—(Guyn) □ Used in strong emotive contexts. **5.** (CarA) [*AF—Joc*] To drink (hard liquor). *So, let's join the ladies over there by the oleanders, and fire some more liquor before you go to eat.*—CPM:30 **6.** PHRASE **6.1 fire one** *vb phr* (CarA) [*AF—Joc*] [Of a man] To have a drink (of usu undiluted rum) in company with others; [by extension, often] to share in a session of hard drinking with others. Hence similarly: *fire a booze/a drink/a few/the grog/a rum*, etc. **6.2 fire (sb) a drink** *vb phr* (Guyn) [*AF—Joc*] To get liquor for (sb) to drink. *Fire me a stiff rum-an-ginger.*—SBB:27

fire-ba·na·na *n* (Tbgo) ‖ BUCK-BANANA (Guyn)

fire-bu[r]n [faya-bʌn] *n* [*AF*] **1.** (Belz, Guyn, Jmca) The burnt-out ruins of a building. **2.** (Guyn) Fire-damaged goods salvaged and sold cheap. **3.** (USVI) A rowdy, riotous person (such as would start a fire or a riot). **4.** (Jmca) [Rastaf] A swear word used to dismiss BABYLON. □ See also FIRE¹ *n* Phr 3.

fire-hag [faya-haɛg] *n* (Bdos) ‖ SOUKOUYAN (Ecar) □ Mostly rural and evid not as widely known in *Bdos* (as its CarA ‖ ‖).

fire-rage *n* **1.** (Antg, Bdos, Guyn, Tbgo, Trin) [*AF*] Intense, uncontrolled, noisy anger. *One time I was always getting in fire-rage and fighting like wunna too.*—CISH:11 **2.** PHRASE **2.1 pick up/take up (sb's) fire rage** *vb phr* (Antg, Bdos, Guyn) [*AF*] ‖ *drink bush for (sb's) fever* (Gren, Trin) ‖ *sweat fever for (sb)* (Belz) To take up (sb else's) quarrel or contention and pursue it vigorously as if it were your own. *But it was he who took offence at the mild reprimand. Although it was not addressed to him, he immediately appointed himself the offender's defence counsel and took up his fire-rage.*—NaT (89.07.05, p.6A) **3.** (Guyn) [*AF—Derog*] ‖ *fire-tail* (Bdos) A person given to loud-mouthed, undisciplined anger; a firebrand.

fire-stick *n* (Belz, Guyn, Jmca, StVn, Tbgo, Trin) **1.** A burning stick borrowed from a neighbour to start your own wood-fire, or a charred stick from a previous wood-fire that would catch fire easily (hence foll prov). *Old fire-stick don't take long to catch* i.e. A former love affair is often not difficult to re-kindle.—Guyn (Prov) **2.** [Usu pl] A thin dry twig collected for starting a fire to cook on. □ Both senses now mostly rural, but see STICK¹ 2.

fire-tail *n* (Bdos) ‖ FIRE-RAGE 3 (Guyn) □ Usu applied to a woman.

firms *n* (Bdos) [*IF*] [Cricket] ‖ OUT-FOR-PLAY (Guyn) [< *firm* (sg) indicating that each group (of about three boys) in the competitive cricket game is like a 'firm' or 'company', each bringing benefit to the other]

first *adv* **1.** (Trin) [*X*] ‖ AFÒS 1. (Trin) *First I vex, eh!* i.e. I'm extremely annoyed!—(Trin) [By folk etym and false refinement of Trin Fr Cr A FOS 'strongly, greatly' with loss of unstressed initial vowel /-a-/] **2.** (Guyn, Jmca) **(i)** [*IF*] At first; formerly. *First, they used to live in Berbice; it's only a few years now they've been living in town.*—(Guyn) **(ii)** [*AF*] First time (that sth happened). *Him hear a lot about it, but now dis was de first him see it.*—(Jmca) **3.** PHRASES **3.1 first time** *adv phr* (CarA) [*IF*] At one time in the past. *First time they used to give away mangoes there.*—(StVn) □ Similar to 2.(i) above. **3.2 first to begin (with)** *adv phr* (CarA) [*IF*] In the first place. *First to begin with, I was not properly invited, and I don't care much for her anyway so I'm not going.*—(Tbgo)

first-aid n (Bdos) ‖ *cake-shop* (Guyn) A small shop, usu a part of, or attached to, the house of its owner, making available minor domestic items and lesser patent medicines up to late hours in the night. [By extension of the sense 'emergency help', including the supply of simple medicines]

first-crop n (Guyn) [Rice Ind; Sugar Ind] ‖ *small crop, Spring crop* (Guyn) **1.** [Rice Ind] The rice-crop sown during the end-of-year rainy season and reaped in March-April of the following year. *Caterpillar damage is usually more serious in the first crop [Spring] than in the second crop [Autumn].*—Guyn (Ms) **2.** [Sugar Ind] The sugar-cane crop reaped in April-May after a year's maturing. [So called as being the earlier of the two crops, in each industry in *Guyn*] □ See also SECOND CROP.

first-depth n (Guyn) [Sugar Ind; Hist] The amount of land originally granted to a planter for sugar-plantation development, uniform in width and measured inland from the coast to whatever distance or 'depth' was necessary to contain 250 roods (62-1/2 acres) of land, two-thirds of wh had to be developed before a second 'depth' further inland would be granted—*RLLG:136.* □ The term is now usu applied officially to the inland boundary of such an orig first grant.

first gang n phr (Bdos) See GANG (cit and * Note)

fish n PHRASES **1. feel for fish** vb phr (Guyn) See FEEL Phr 3. **2. fish-and-bammy** n (Jmca) A popular folk meal. See BAMMY **3. fish-and-float** n (Bdos) A once popular folk snack. See FLOAT *At special places on the Garrison there could be nut sellers, and above all the 'fish and float' vendor. These women were part of our past history and frequented the streets of Bridgetown especially on a Saturday night when each had her coal-pot going with the fry-pan on it with the 'lard oil' boiling hot, and in this they used to place their wares so that the customers always purchased hot food.*—AdN (76.04.18, p.12) **4. fish-and-fungee** n (USVI) A popular folk meal. See FUNGEE **5. fish boil-in** n phr (StVn) ‖ BOIL-IN (StVn)

fish-broth [fiš-brɒ-f-brɒ-ə] n **1.** (Dmca, Gren, StLu, Tbgo, Trin) ‖ *braf, broth* (Dmca, StLu) ‖ *fish-tea* (Belz, Jmca, StVn, Tbgo, TkCa, Trin) ‖ *man-soup* (Antg) A (usu thick) grey, seasoned, vegetable soup, the main flavouring ingredient being fish; or a thinner more broth- like variety using fish-head or whole JACKS. **2.** (Gren) A similar fish-soup using red-snapper and further reddened with ketchup or tomatoes.

fish·en vb intr; **fish.en.in(g) (fish(i)nin(g)** pres part (CarA) [X] (Folk-speech vb forms for) fish, fishing (the participle occurring more often). *I sez ter mersef, 'Well Antie Nana yer dun had yer gud times all yer life fishenin' an ting.'*—JBJ: 87 [Perh < *fishing* pronunc [fiš(ɪ)n]n and, being

more frequently heard, mistaken as the base form of the vb; or by epenthetic insertion of / -n-/. Cp similarly COURTENIN] □ Often used in narrative dialogue.

Fish·er·man's Birth·day n phr (Gren) June 29, the (Christian) feast of St Peter (the 'big fisherman') and St Paul, celebrated, esp in Gouyave and fishing towns in Grenada, with the blessing of fishing-boats and a day of merry-making.

fish-kind n (Guyn, Jmca, StVn) Any kind of fish cooked as part of a meal (as opposed to MEAT-KIND). □ Cp similarly BREAD-KIND.

fish-pot n (CarA) A cage lowered to the sea-bed for trapping fish; it is about 6 or 7 ft in overall length, made of wire-netting on a wooden frame and of various shapes, with a funnel-shaped entrance through wh fish can enter but not escape. See POT-FISH

fish-tea n (Belz, Jmca, StVn, Tbgo, TkCa, Trin) A FISH-BROTH, esp when served very hot in a cup.

fit¹ adj **1.** (Guyn, Jmca, StVn) [IF] [Of a person, or (sth) made; occurring mostly after a neg] Worthy; able; pleasing to see or taste. **a.** *Carpenter what? Look how he make de step! He ain't fit.*—(StVn) **b.** *This jelly you make ain't fit. Is so lumpy, I can['t] spread it.*—(Guyn) [Cp OED *fit* a. 4. 'properly qualified, competent'] **2.** (CayI, Gren, Jmca) [Of fruit] Ripe and ready to be eaten. *The guineps aren't fit yet—they will be sour and sticky.*—(CayI) [Cp OED *fit* a. 5. 'prepared, ready']

fit² vb (Guyn, Jmca) To be fitting (for a particular purpose); to suit. *You can't wear this hat with that dress—the other one fits it better.*—(Guyn)

fit-bush n (Jmca, StKt) ‖ FIT-WEED (Bdos, etc)

fit-weed* n (Bdos, Gren, Guyn, Jmca, Tbgo, Trin) ‖ *cat-claw* (StKt) ‖ *chadon-béni* (Trin) ‖ *chuk-chuk* (Dmca) ‖ *fit-bush* (Jmca, StKt) ‖ *shado-beni* (Gren, StLu, StVn, Tbgo, Trin) ‖ *shadow-vinnie bush* (StVn) ‖ *shallow benay* (Trin) A pungent smelling, folk-medicinal, wild herb; it has foot-long, narrow, serrated leaves growing in rosette form from its base, and one or more central stalks bearing green flowers with stiff, sharp-pointed petals; *Eryngium foetidum (Umbelliferae)*. [From its wide use as a BUSH-TEA to treat fevers, colds and esp fits in children]

five num adj PHRASES **1. break five(s)!** (Guyn); **give me five!** (Dmca, Nevs) vb phrs [AF] Shake hands with me! (i.e. in warm, brotherly friendship). **2. give the high five** vb phr (CarA) [AF-*Joc*] [In cricket or other competitive team games] To slap the open palm of your raised hand against that of another member of your team in clamorous jubilation over a success. [Ref to five fingers of the hand]

five-fin·ger *n* (Guyn, Mrat, Trin) **1.** ‖ CA-RAMBOLA (Belz, etc) [From the five-winged shape of the fruit] **2.*** (Angu, StKt, USVI) ‖ *ink-berry (tree)* (Jmca) An ornamental shrub with hard, stiff stems and shiny green leaves; it bears blue berries; in some places the plant is used as a Christmas tree and in others the leaves are used as a folk-medicine; *Randia aculeata* (*Rubiaceae*). **3.** (Baha, TkCa) Name applied to more than one slender shrub with five-lobed leaves that are used as folk medicines.

fix[1] *vb tr* **1.** (CarA) [*IF*] ‖ *fix up* (CarA) **(i)** To serve or attend to (sb in a place of business). *Anybody fixing you, sir?*—(Guyn) **(ii)** To repay a debt. *I went by the garage the following day. I told him, 'I came to fix you up now—to pay you your money.'*—Tbgo (CR, 73.12.05) **(iii)** [*AF*] [By extension of prec] To settle accounts with, take revenge on, or deal very severely with (sb). *The follow-up was a very important part of Mrs Parkinson's advice: 'After you fix him, make sure you broadcas' the joke to everybody in the school. That way you really do the dirt on him for good an' all.'*—SJS:19 **2.** (CarA) ‖ *hag* (Baha) **(i)** To use OBEAH to put a spell on (sb) to harm the health or control the will (esp in connection with marriage) of that person. *... and the women who come for them, especially married women say they want to fix their husband's outside women who became pregnant.*—BoM (77.01.07, p.16) **(ii)** To put a charm or a defensive spell on (sb) or (more often) on (sth) by some supernatural means (usu OBEAH.) **a.** *One of the nurses approached the ailing lady and whispered that she could 'do something' to fix the lady so she could have the operation safely ... and the poor lady was only too willing to get cleared from the evil spirit so she could have the operation.*—BoM (74.06.07, p.4) **b.** *If a hog plum tree were not 'fixed', it was a sure target for raiding.*—EBT:11

fix[2] *n* (CarA) [*IF*] A supernatural device for causing, or for warding off evil. *We used to be told that certain 'obeah' experts from Fox Hill were employed to do the special jobs. This made a 'fix' particularly potent, and not to be messed with under any circumstances.*—EBT:9 [By functional vb > n shift of FIX[1] 2.(i), 2.(ii)]

fix up[1] *vb tr* **1.** (CarA) [*AF/IF*] ‖ FIX[1] (CarA) **2.** (Guyn) [Indic] To arrange a marriage (as the go-between for the parents of one of the prospective spouses). □ This is the official function of an *agwa* 'matchmaker'.

flag *n* (Jmca) ‖ ARROW[2] (CarA)

fla·gu plan·tain; **fu.la.gu plan.tain** *n phr* (Belz) ‖ BLUGGO (Belz, etc) □ Name used in Stann Creek area, so prob Garifuna. See also DOKO, WAIKA BANANA.

flam·beau [flambo] *n* (Trin) ‖ BOTTLE-FLAMBEAU (StVn, Trin)

flam·boy·ant (tree)* [flamboyant (tri)] *n (phr)* (CarA) ‖ *cock-and-hen tree* (Angu, Antg, Nevs, StKt) ‖ *cokyoco tree* (Gren) ‖ *flame tree* (Trin) ‖ *flame-of-the-forest* (Trin) ‖ *po-inciana, royal poinciana* (ECar) ‖ *shack-shack tree* (Antg, BrVi, StLu, StVn) A tree of medium height often with a short buttressed trunk, supporting a massive, umbrella-shaped crown that sheds its feathery leaves to burst into a mass of densely clustered, flaming red flowers for about two months, after wh it becomes bare with long, dark hanging pods; there are also orange and yellow-flowered varieties; *Delonix poinciana regia* (*Leguminosae-Caesalpinoideae*). [Fr = 'flaming' (< *flamboyer* vb to flame) the name being applied late 19C to describe the striking redness of this tree in flower] □ The spelling *flamboyante*, used by some botanists, does not appear to be justified. Fr *arbre flamboyant* would be masc.

flame-of-the-for·est *n* (Trin) ‖ FLAMBOYANT (CarA)

flame-tree *n phr* (Trin) ‖ FLAMBOYANT (CarA)

fla·min·go-bill *n* (Baha) ‖ AUGUST-FLOWER (Guyn)

flap *vb* PHRASE **flap your mouth** *vb phr* (Bdos, Guyn) [*AF—Derog*] ‖ *run your mouth* (CarA) To chat away, saying more than you should; (SE) to blab.

flap·pers *n pl* (Nevs) ‖ RUBBER-SLIPPERS (CarA)

flash[1] *n* (CarA) [*IF*] Showiness; bravado. *I am being stunned and shocked eye-witnessing how these lawless reckless drivers overdo it with 'flash' up to 70 m.p.h. passing through our village.*—DoH (65.05.15, p.2)

flash[2] *vb* (CarA) [*AF—Joc*] **1.** *vb intr* To dress showily. *She flashing since she come back from New York.*—(StVn) **2.** *vb tr* To show off (clothes, an engagement ring, or any fine new possession such as a car, boyfriend, etc). **3.** *vb tr* [*IF*] [By extension] To give (sb) a quick glance (of anger, approval, friendliness, etc).

flash·y *adj* (CarA) [*IF*] [Esp of dress] Showy; smart-looking in appearance.

flask *n* (Bdos) ‖ HALF-BOTTLE (Bdos)

flat[1] *adj* (ECar) **1.** ‖ *raw* (Bdos) [Of speech] Unrefined; strongly characterized by open vowels and other marked features of local folk speech. *All in all, Sir, when you hear us speak you get a flat Bajan accent, but even the Reporters find it difficult to report him because they cannot determine what he is saying.*—Bdos (Hd, 77.03.19, p.6352) [Prob a ref to the noticeable difference in, or near absence of stress contrasts compared with SE. Also cp *OED flat* 12. (*Obs*) 'of an accent: unstressed'] **2.** PHRASE **2.1 talk flat** *vb phr* (ECar) [*AF/IF*] To speak the kind of local dialect more typical of less educated or rural people.

flat² *n* **1.** (Angu) [Salt Ind] A shallow wooden flat-bottomed barge about 10 ft x 6 ft x 1 ft deep used for harvesting salt on salt ponds. **2.** (Baha) A small flat-bottomed harbour vessel used for ferrying cargo. *The 'John B' was a flat not a sloop. This was the type of vessel used at Governor's Harbour. Flats carry centre-boards.*—TrI (70.05.26, p.3)

flat-form *n* (Bdos, Belz, Guyn) [*X*] Platform. *A minister get up on a flatform two Friday nights ago, and say that he doesn't know anything about Pond.*—CPM:59 [Folk etym (prob infl by flat boards), also + regressive assimilation infl by 'form'] □ A commonly heard form.

flat-hand dil·do *n phr* (Bdos) ‖COCHINEAL (CACTUS) (Guyn, etc) [From the resemblance of the pad-like stem, short in the *Bdos* variety, to the hand placed flat, + DILDO]

flat-o-the-earth* [flat-ʌ-dɪ-ʌrt] *n* (Guyn) A weed that is prostrate or low-growing (hence the name), with thin limbs, small, smooth, oval leaves and terminal spikes of little white flowers; the whole plant is used as a folk-medicine; *Microtea debilis* (*Phytolaccaceae*).

flat·tie *n* (Guyn) ‖HALF-BOTTLE (CarA)

fla·vour·some *adj* (Jmca) [*IF*] **1.** [Of food] Tasty. **2.** [Of a restaurant] Serving tasty or exotic dishes. *This Italian restaurant is well on its way to becoming one of the more 'flavoursome' eating places in Kingston-town.*—DaG (Supplement, 70.07.05, p.15) [By analogy. Cp SE quarrelsome, etc]

fleet *n* PHRASE **fleet of blows/licks** *n phr* (Guyn, Tbgo, Trin) [*AF—Joc*] A severe thrashing; a thorough beating. [By metaph transfer. Cp *OED fleet* sb¹ 2. 'a number of persons, birds or other objects moving or employed in company. Now *rare* exc. *dial.*']

fleet·y *adj* (Guyn) [Esp of footballers] Swift; nimble; (SE) fleet-footed. [An EE survival] Cp *OED fleety* adj *rare* = fleet adj i.e. 'swift, nimble']

flesh *n* **1.** (Bdos, StVn) ‖*flesh-kind* (Gren, Guyn) ‖*relish* (Angu, Baha, StKt, USVI) Any kind of meat or fish that is cooked as part of a main meal. **2.** (CarA) [*AF*] The human hand (i.e. as offered in a handshake). **3.** PHRASE **3.1 give me some flesh** *vb phr* (CarA) [*AF—Joc*] ‖*give me some skin* (CarA) ‖*touch the flesh* (Guyn) Shake my hand (i.e. in hearty, often congratulatory greeting). **4.** (CarA) [*AF—Derog*] ‖*piece of flesh/skin* (CarA) An attractively shaped girl or any woman thought of sexually. *Is some flesh we got line up for tonight. One*

of them from Martinique.—HMCH:58 [Cp Bibl lang 'sinful lusts of the flesh', etc]

flesh-kind *n* (Gren, Guyn, Jmca, StVn) ‖FLESH 1. (Bdos, StVn) *How dey en see jacks for a long time, an' how dey mout waterin' to eat dis jacks, an how dey in have no flesh kind to go wid de two t'ree bluggoe dey have.*—WeN (Annie & Josephine, 53.03.09) [Analogical with BREAD-KIND, MEAT-KIND]

flex *n* (Gren) ‖POINTER (Guyn) *Flex is used in making kite-frames.*—(Gren)

flick-blade knife *n phr* (Bdos, Guyn, StKt) ‖*ratchet-knife* (Jmca) A large pocket-knife with a long, pointed, spring-operated blade that flicks open when the back or side of the knife is pressed; (SE) flick-knife; (AmE) switch-blade knife.

fli·ers *n pl* (Antg, Trin) **1.** Old-fashioned baggy trousers made of a cheap light material (that flaps in the wind, hence the name). **2.** The cheap light cloth of wh such trousers are made.

flip-flops *n pl* (Baha, TkCa) [*IF*] ‖RUBBER-SLIPPERS (CarA)

flit *vb tr* (Baha, Bdos, Belz, Guyn) To spray with an insecticide (esp to keep away mosquitoes and bed-bugs). [From a commercial insecticide of this name that became popular in the 1930s, sold with a pump spray or *flit-can*]

flit·ter *n* (CarA) [*X*] Fritter; a small cake fried in deep fat; the ingredients are usu crushed soft fruit (banana, pumpkin, etc) but sometimes also shrimp or other sea-food. [By /r > l/ shift < SE *fritter*]

float *n* (Bdos, Guyn, Tbgo, Trin) A piece of dough mixed with baking powder or yeast and salt, fried in hot oil until it puffs, browns, and floats; a BAKE 2. with yeast. □ Hence the names of popular roadside snacks: ACCRA-AND-FLOAT *Trin*, FISH-AND-FLOAT *Bdos*.

flock-bull *n* (USVI) A stud bull·

flood-pants *n pl* (Guyn, Trin) [*AF—Joc*] ‖B-IDDIMS (Bdos, etc) [Joc ref suggesting that the trousers are so short that the ends would not get wet in walking through a flood] □ Other Joc phrs such as *pants expecting flood*, etc also occur.

floor-bed *m* (Jmca) [*AF*] ‖FLORA (Dmca, etc)

floor·ing /1'2/ *n* (CarA) Floor. *As the house had a wooden flooring, water would leak through on the tenants below.*—Guyn (Ms) □ Commonly used in some territories, esp in rural areas, instead of IAE *floor*.

Flo·ra (**floor·a**) *n* (Dmca, Gren, Guyn, Tbgo) [*AF—Joc*] ‖*Auntie Flora* (Antg) ‖*floor-bed* (Jmca) **1.** The floor (whether bare or covered with BAGGING) used for sleeping. (Hence foll phrs.) **2.** *PHRASES* **2.1 knock/take/sleep on** or **with/use Flora/Auntie Flora** *vb phr* (Dmca, Gren, Guyn, Tbgo) [*AF—Joc*] To sleep on the floor.

flounce [flʌŋs] *vb intr* (Guyn) To dance (as in a MASQUERADE-BAND) with vigorous body and swift movements barefoot, to the music of a flute-and- drum band. *Each band averages about eight persons, sometimes going as high as 12. They include two drummers, a flutist and several 'flouncers' or dancers. 'When you see a real masquerader dancing or flouncing, you know straight away this is the real flounce,' Mr Pilgrim says.—*(Guyn, AdN 79.12.25, p.10) [Note *OED flounce* v 2. 'to throw the body about' + phr *to flounce it* 'said of a woman dancing'**]**

flounc·er *n* (Guyn) **1.** A practised dancer in a MASQUERADE-BAND. **2.** [Esp of a woman] One who can dance like a practised masquerader.

flour·y *adj* (Angu, Mrat, USVI) [Of fruit] Grainy or lumpy in texture because immature; not as sweet as it should be.

flow·er-fence *n* (Baha, Jmca) ‖BARBADOS-PRIDE (CarA) [From the wide use made of the trimmed prickly flowering shrub as a hedge or fence**]**

flup(s)! [flʊp(s)] *ideoph* (CarA) (ECHOIC WORD representing) a swift, sudden (and often unexpected) action. *The inside of the ball-point pen just flew out, flups! And I couldn't get it back in.*—(Tbgo)

flux·y *adj* (Belz, Jmca, StVn) [*IF*] [Of fruit, esp mangoes] Immature; blemished; FORCE- RIPE. Cp TOUCHED.

fly¹ *vb* (CarA) [*AF/IF*] **1.** *vb intr* To move, act or rush, usu with force or with violent intention. (Hence many phrs.) **2.** *vb tr* To let fly (i.e. like a trap). **3.** *PHRASES* **3.1 fly down (sb's) throat** *vb phr* (Guyn) [*AF*] To reply rashly, in a rage. *Ah can't open me mouth to say a word about David but you want to fly down me throat.*—MLDS:154 **3.2 fly off** *vb phr* (CarA) [*AF*] To fly into a temper; to become suddenly enraged. [Cp *OED fly* v¹ 9. c. *fly off* '(of cannon) to be fired'] **3.3 fly out of your skin** *vb phr* (Bdos) [*AF—Joc*] ‖*jump out of your skin* (CarA) To get violently excited (at the approach of some person or event). *You don't exactly fly outa your skin every time you wife does have a belly ache.*—SNWIC:208 (A.N. Forde) **3.4 fly (up) at/to (sb)** *vb phr* (CarA) [*AF*] To rush aggressively at (sb); (SE) to fly at (sb). **3.5 fly (up) in (sb's) face** *vb phr* (CarA) [*AF*] To burst into angry words with (sb). □ Physical and emotive rather than the cynical SE *fly in the face of God/the truth* (to openly disregard ...). **3.6 fly (up) in sb's head** *vb phr* (CarA) [*AF—Joc*] [Of alcoholic liquor] To go to (sb's) head; to make (sb) dangerously drunk. *His Worship in passing sentence told the accused that shop-keepers encouraged customers to*

come to their shops to drink and enjoy themselves and 'when the liquor fly up in their heads' they are badly treated.—ToR (75.10.08, p.3) **3.7 fly your mouth** *vb phr* (Guyn) [*AF—Derog*] ‖ AIR YOUR MOUTH (CarA) See AIR² Phr 2.2 See also RUN Phr 6.11 RUN YOUR MOUTH

fly² *n* (Guyn) A fermented sweet drink made by 'setting' peeled white potatoes, crushed eggshells, mace, lime-juice and much water for a few days before sweetening and pouring into tightly-corked bottles, the corks of wh 'fly' when the drink is 'ripe' (and hence the name).

fly·ing ant(s) *n phr* (*pl*) (Bdos, Jmca) ‖RAIN-FLY (CarA)

fly·ing fish* *n phr* (CarA) A tropical Atlantic fish of good food value, averaging about 9 ins in length; there are several varieties of this family of fishes (*Exocoetidae*) with large pectoral fins wh enable them to rise out of the water and skim above it for some distance; the *fourwing* flying-fish (*Hirundichthys affinis*) is the variety most widely marketed in the ECar. *There be also of sea-fishes, which we saw coming along the coast, flying, which are of the bigness of a smelt, the biggest sort whereof have four wings, but the others have but too. ... There is an unnumerable young fry of these flying-fishes, which commonly keep about the ship. ... Of the bigger sort of these fishes we took many, which both night and day flew into the sails of our ship*—PVES:65-66 (John Sparke's narrative of John Hawkins's Second Voyage to the coast of Guinea and the Indies, 1565)

fm! [Φm̄] /4/ *ideoph* (Guyn) ECHOIC WORD representing the sensing of a bad smell. [Cp *ZAGL* Gã *fũ* n 'bad smell, stink']

FOCUSING; FRONTING: See Introduction: CARIBBEAN ENGLISH, General characteristics.

fo(h) [fʊ~fʌ] *prep* [*AF—Cr*] (CarA) **1.** (Dial spelling often used for) For. *Everybody ... waiting patiently fo dey ting to come in.*—Aaw.I.2, p.24 [Perh infl by Yoruba *fun* 'give' wh frequently functions in that lang with the sense of 'for'] **2.** (Also dial, infinitive marker) To. *She said, slowly, 'Ah shame fo walk down de street.'*—MBM:17 [Prob infl by *for* so used in some BrE dialects. Note *WEDG:298* 'In s.Chs n.Stf w.Som *for* is used as the sign of the infinitive of purpose, as 'hast gotten a bit for mend it with?'] □ Both these senses occur often in narrative dialogue. See also FA, FE, FER, FI, FU.

fo·fi-eye [fɒ·fi-aɪ] /1'12/ *n* (Bdos, Guyn) [*AF—Derog*] An eye with a discoloured, whitish eyeball.

folks *n pl* (CarA) [*IF*] **1.** People. *Premier Barrow told the 1600 folks that Frank Walcott is a servant of the Union.*—TrU (64.02.01, p.1) □ Often used as a free alternative where SE would require *people* or the collective *folk.* (See phrs.) **2.**

PHRASES **2.1 country/town/older/younger, etc folks** *n phr* (Guyn) [*X*] Older/younger folk. *The country folks can still dance the kwe-kwe.*— Guyn (Ms) **2.2 I/we, (etc) is folks too** *id phr* (Trin) [*AF*] I am/we are people (worthy of consideration) too.

fol·low *vb tr* **1.** (Antg, Guyn, Tbgo) [*IF*] To accompany (sb). *I don[']t feel like going alone. Follow me do[w]ng the road, no!*—(Antg) [As *OED follow* v 3. a. 'to go along with (a person) as a companion'] **2.** *PHRASES* **2.1 follow (bad) company** *vb phr* (CarA) To mix with young people of bad reputation. *He is in jail today, just a young man, from following company.*—(Guyn) **2.2 follow friends** *vb phr* (CarA) [*IF—Derog*] [Of girls] To mix with those who seem to be seeking sexual fun. **2.3 follow your mind** *vb phr* (CarA) ‖ **do/work to your mind** (Guyn) [*AF*] ‖ **go with your mind** (Bdos) To be guided by your own feelings or thinking; to make your own decision; to do as you see or think fit. *You see if I had followed my mind, I would have stayed home and so stayed out of trouble.*—(Bdos) **3.** (CarA) [*IF*] [Of evil spirits] To haunt (sb). *When 'jumbies follow a person' he gets sick—he cannot do his work. His family suffers, his children starve.*—EFOT:19 [Cp *OED follow* 5. b. (*Obs*) 'to visit (a person) with (affliction, etc)']

fol·low-fash·ion /1'122/ *n, adj* (CarA) [*IF*] ‖ *follow-foot* (Belz) ‖ *follow-pattern* (Bdos, Guyn) (One who is) ready to imitate what sb else is doing. *'You know what's happening to you, Joey?' Colin said. 'You 'follow-fashion' too much, man. You spend your time imitating your father and all the politics you hear him talking about.'*— SJT:18

fol·low-foot (mon·key) *n (phr); vb (phr)* (Belz) [*AF/Joc*] ‖ FOLLOW-FASHION (CarA) *As a people, we do tend to 'follow-foot monkey', and young people esp tend to mimic the well-known.*—AmA (80.02.08, p.2a)

fol·low-me /1'12/ *n* (Guyn) A vicious, half-inch long wasp with a black-and-yellow striped abdomen, that builds its nest in trees and will implacably pursue anyone who interferes with the nest (hence the name).

fol·low-pat·tern /1'122/ *adj* (Bdos, Guyn) ‖ FOLLOW-FASHION (CarA) *Furthermore, to imply that there is some follow pattern action in our decision to take steps to legalise abortion because this has been done by Britain, denies Barbadians the ability to tackle their problems as they see fit, and attributes to us a mere 'Little England' mentality.*—AdN (80.03.08, p.4)

fol·ly *n* (TkCa) A broad vehicular way separating salt ponds.

fond-name *n* (Bdos, Guyn) Pet-name; a name used from childhood by one's close associates.

food *n* **1.** (CarA) (General ref to) the solid meal of the later part of the day. *The whole day gone and I ain't even had my food yet (i.e. nothing after an early morning 'tea' or breakfast).*—(StKt) **2.** *PHRASE* **2.1 our food don't/ain't/no(t) cook(ed) in the same pot** *id phr* (CarA) [*AF—Derog*] ‖ *rice don't (etc) cook in the same pot* (Guyn) (Said of persons who are) not of the same social type (in spite of appearances); not acceptable as associates. **3.** (Jmca) ‖ **hard-food** (Bdos, Jmca, Trin) ‖ DRY FOOD 2. (Guyn)

food-car·ri·er *n* (Guyn) ‖ **shut-pan** (Jmca) A set of close-fitting enamel containers, tiered in a rack with a handle, and used for sending a hot lunch to sb at work.

food·in /1'2/ *n* (Guyn) [*AF—Joc*] A growing child who eats heartily.

food·ist /2'1/ *n* (Bdos, Guyn) [*AF—Derog*] An adult glutton. □ Cp FOODIN.

food·kind *n* (Bdos, Jmca) ‖ DRY FOOD 2. (Guyn) *The cured and cleansed yams, dasheen, tomatoes and nuff more things, so pretty they seemed unreal. I have never seen such well groomed 'food kind' in my life.*—WeG (73.06.06, Partyline) □ Cp also BREADKIND (CarA)

foo-foo¹ *n* **1.** See FUFU **2.** (Antg, Tbgo) ‖ FUNGEE (Angu, etc) [An occasional alternative name] **3.** (Bdos, Jmca) [*AF—Derog*] A naive, silly person. [Prob a reduplicated form with loss of final /-l/ Cp FOOL-FOOL] **4.** (CayI, Mrat, StVn, USVI) A form of witchcraft used to befuddle sb. *You foo-foo aint gwine work.*—StVn (Ms) [Prob related to 3.] **5.** (Dmca) ‖ FOU-FOU (Dmca) □ See FUFU wh evid occurs as an alternative spelling to some of these senses besides 1. However the spellings may usefully serve to differentiate. See □ Note at FUFU 3.

foo-foo² *adj* (Belz, Gren, Jmca) [Of a person or situation] Stupid; foolish; silly. [Related to FOO-FOO¹ 3. by functional shift]

fool¹ *adj* (Baha, Belz, CayI, Jmca) [*AF—Cr*] Foolish; stupid. *Da man Duvalier mussy fool fer true ef he ain pick up he money wen it fall down.*—JBJ:81

fool² *n* **1.** (CarA) [*AF*] [SE sense, but often without determiner **a.** *Fool talkin but na fool listenin* i.e. A fool is talking but it's not a fool who is listening—CarA (Prov) **b.** *Since she get money, like she turn fool*—(Guyn) **2.** (Baha, Belz) [*AF—Cr*] Foolishness; stupidity. *Stop your fool, Johnny. Before you met Elizabeth, when we used to go to Riverside, you were not dusty then like you are making yourself now. Shake off dust, man.*—HF:44 **3.** *PHRASES* **3.1 form (the) fool** *vb phr* (Angu, Antg, BrVi, Dmca, Gren, StLu) To play the fool (with or in a serious matter); to treat a serious matter without seriousness. *'Those who elect a government must look to it for proper leadership; and, if it is not given, at some time*

they will say these fellows are forming the fool,'
said Mr Mason.—VoS (65.03.10, p.1) **3.2 make
yourself a fool** vb phr (Bdos, Guyn) [AF/IF]
To embarrass yourself in public; (SE) to make
a fool of yourself.

fool-fool adj (Belz, Gren, Jmca, StKt, StVn)
[AF—Cr] **1.** Simple-minded; unenlightened. De
marnin' she reach, Pampo ask Millie to press he
bes' suit. Tell de fool-fool 'oman, he get invitation to
go institute.—LMFF:21 **2.** Provokingly stupid;
foolish. You know, Mr Engineer, you creating a
hell of a problem! Look, maybe best thing is forget
this whole fool-fool matter.—YFOC:16

fool off/up (sb) vb tr phr (CarA) [AF/IF] To
fool, deceive or get the better of (sb) by means
of promises and blandishments. 'I hope you don't
fool off too many Jamaican women,' she said mock-
ingly. 'Peggy is telling everyone how sly you are.'—
TLTH:64

fool·y adj (Antg, USVI) [AF—Joc] Foolish;
stupid; stupefied. One of the customers got very
impatient and told the shopkeeper that 'women goin
mek an ass of him. It look like when Baily see
women he does tun fooly'.—Vip.1.1

fool·y-(the)-fifth [fuli-(dɪ)-fɪf] n (Bdos, Guyn,
StVn) [AF—Joc] An idiot; a person who has just
done sth idiotic or stupidly thoughtless. I found
myself at the door like a real fooly-the-fifth without
the tickets.—(Guyn) [Perh a joc ref = the king
of fools]

foon·gee n (ECar) See FUNGEE

foot [fʊt] n (CarA) [IF] **1.** The whole or any
part of the leg from the thigh down to the toes.
Her foot up to her waist was in the water in
the drain.—ToR (77.03.23, p.6) [Likely due to
calquing from Afr langs. Cp KPG wh cites the
same word for leg as for foot in 15 Afr langs,
and words differing only morphologically in over
100 langs, pp.40–43] □ This CE non-distinction
is very widespread in and above the folk-level.
Hence many phrs in wh the senses are mixed,
but more in wh the sense leg is meant. **2.** PHRASES
2.1 foot ain't/don't deceive you id phr (Guyn)
[AF—Joc] (You) escape, running as fast as your
legs can carry you. **2.2. foot and foot** (Jmca,
StKt); **foot by foot** (Guyn); **foot to foot** (Tbgo,
Trin) adv phrs [IF] As closely as possible next
to or behind (sb); watchfully, step for step; doggedly. See BEHIND¹ Phr 2.P— then related that
he was in Mac's shop and when he left, 'Papa' L—
who was there 'foot and foot behind him, follow
him until he butt up on his knife' and he was sure
he was dead 'by now.'—DeM(SK) (63.07.27, p.4)
□ Cp IAE neck and neck wh, however, implies
racing whereas the CE phr does not. **2.3 foot
(is) hot** id phr (Tbgo, Trin) [AF—Joc] [Esp of
a woman] (You) like to walk about much, or to
travel restlessly. **2.4 foot (is) long** id phr (Guyn)
[AF—Joc] (You) can walk/have walked a great
distance (in a relatively short time). **2.5 foot
(is) tied** id phr (Guyn, Trin) [AF—Joc] [Usu

metaph] (You are) trapped, caught, caged. Lloyd
Best is quoted as saying the electorate is 'bazodie',
and that the Tobago House of Assembly Chairman's
'foot is tied' in Tobago.—BeA(TO) (11/81)
□ More emotive than IAE hands are tied 'prevented by circumstances'. **2.6 foot (is) too short**
id phr (Guyn) [AF—Joc] (You have) arrived too
late (esp for a good meal); (you have) missed
your rightful chance. **2.7 foot [u]pon ground**
id phr (Bdos) [AF—Joc] (By) hard, steady walking or running. The car ain['t] workin[g] so i[t']s
foot [u]pon groun[d] to get to work today.—(Bdos)
2.8 Foot, wha[t] you make for! (Belz); **Foot,
whe[re] you deh!** (Guyn) id phrs [AF—Joc]
[Imaginary question by sb in fright calling on
his legs to carry him away fast] [It] was only a
dog in the dark, but he get frighten like hell!
Foot whe[re] you deh! De man take off like a
bullet!—(Guyn) **2.9 lap your foot** vb phr (Nevs)
[AF/IF] To sit with your legs crossed (instead
of helping with work being done); to fold your
legs and relax. [Prob a survival of an EE sense.
Cp OED lap v² 2. (Obs) 'to fold (together)' +
cits—'1790] □ Cp COCK TEN (Guyn). **2.10
make foot** vb phr (Tbgo) [AF] ‖PUT FOOT
(Angu, etc) See below PHR 2.13. **2.11
not put a/your foot** neg id phr (Guyn, StKt)
‖ **not cross foot** (Bdos) Not to go, enter, visit
(some place); (SE) not to darken the doors (of
sb). I don't care where she live, even if is next door
to me. I would never put foot there.—(Guyn)
□ Used in contexts of intense feeling. **2.12 put
foot** vb phr (Angu, Brbu, Gren, Guyn, Nevs,
StVn, Trin) [AF] ‖ **make foot** (Tbgo) ‖ **pick up
your foot/heels** (Bdos, Guyn, Jmca) ‖ **pull foot**
(Jmca) ‖ **put foot and run; put foot [u]pon
ground** (Bdos) ‖ **put your foot in your hand**
(Jmca) ‖ **take foot** (Belz, CayI, Jmca, Nevs)
‖ **take up your foot and run** (Bdos, Jmca) To
run away in panic; to flee as fast as your legs can
carry you. **2.13 see foot** vb phr (Guyn) [AF] To
see how fast sb runs away. They put one to watch
for the police and as soon as he whistle, then you
see foot!—(Guyn) [Cp SE idiom to show a clean
pair of heels] **2.14 stretch your foot** vb phr
(CarA) [IF] To stretch your legs; to take a casual
stroll. **2.15 take foot** vb phr (Belz, CayI, Jmca,
Nevs) **take up your foot and run** (Bdos, Jmca)
[AF] ‖ PUT FOOT (Angu, etc) See above PHR 2.12

foot-bot·tom n (Bdos, Guyn, Jmca) [AF—Cr]
The sole of the foot. Duh ready to treat Bajans
like duhself like dirt, but duh would lick de tourisses
foot-bottom.—NaT (87.02.13, p.6, Lickmout
Lou) [A prob calque from W Afr langs. Cp Twi
naʒ-ase (foot-bottom) 'sole of the foot.']

foo·tey (**foo·tee, foo·ti(e), foo·ty**) [fʊti ~ futi]
semi-excl adv intensifier (Trin) [AF] **1.** (Often as
a casual qualifier in a sentence) I swear it! You
may be damned sure! white people ... make divorce
law ... but they ain't footie use it, because their
best friend going to say they wutless—MBF:136
2. PHRASE **2.1 footey well** adv phr (Trin) [AF—
Joc] As sure as hell! [Fr Cr < Fr foutu 'fucked,
fucking, etc' still an obscene oath in Mod Fr,
but surviving in present Trin Cr with its original

sense all but completely lost] □ The anglicised spelling may be conceded here marking the difference in connotation from the Fr Cr orig. The forms given are the only ones found.

for *prep (and also functioning as a general connective focusing on some person, action, situation, etc)* (CarA) [*IF*] □ Note: The following are only some illustrations, listed alphabetically, of the wide convenience made of this particle throughout CE. Cp similarly WITH. **1.** (CarA) [*IF*] Allowing. *Christine, I cannot talk to her for the child to hear, and this has caused a big confusion between us.*—PeL (80.03.21, p.12) **2.** (CarA) [*X*] As. *They are also required to pay $20 per week for service charge.*—AdN (72.03.10, p.4) **3.** PHRASE **3.1 for (a) joke** (CarA) [*AF/IF*] Just in fun; as a prank. □ Cp Phr 17.4 FOR NO JOKE. **4.** (StLu) [*X*] At. *The child sucked his teeth for the teacher.*—(StLu) **5.** PHRASE **5.1 come/go for (sb)** *vb phrs* (Bdos, Guyn) [*IF*] To come/go at (sb) (in verbal attack). *As soon as he opened the door, she went for him before he could say anything.*—(Guyn) **6.** (CarA) [*AF*] Because of. *... and then he curses me for this woman, whom he just knew about two years ago.*—NaT (76.07.04, p.30) **7.** (Antg, BrVi, CayI) [*AF*] Belonging to (mostly referring to children). *Which Jean you mean? Jean for Mina or Jean for Ruth?*—(Antg) **8.** (CarA) [Of child-bearing] By (a man as the father). *From sixteen I had this man. Now I am 24 and have two kids for him.*—PeL (79.04.12, p.8, Dear Christine) **9.** (CarA) [*AF*] Complaining against (sb); about (sb). *She went to my mother for me because I cuffed her.*—(Guyn) **10.** (CarA) [*X*] Of. **a.** *W— and R— were found guilty for the larceny of a valise.*—AdN (72.01.08, p.1) **b.** *It is also said that after a midday meal, which is the purpose for the luncheon hour, both teachers and students tend to be sleepy and listless.*—ViN (73.02.10, p.4) **c.** *Fogarty, regular purchasers for the mats over several years, put in the order just days before the mats were made up.*—DaC (72.04.08, p.1) **11.** (CarA) [*X*] In (doing sth). **a.** *He was rude for saying that to her.*—(Bdos) **b.** *This must be a balm for these weary souls and its value is enhanced by the efforts the Ladies of Charity make for administering to spiritual welfare.*—GyG (52.06.22, p.6) **12.** (CarA) [*X*] On (esp in foll phr). **13.** PHRASE **13.1 for purpose** *adv phr* [*X*] ‖ *for spite* (CarA) On purpose; spitefully. *I don't want to hear how you sorry, cause I know you do it for purpose.*—(Bdos) □ Usu said in accusing (sb) of malice. Cp FOR SPITE. See Phr 17.8 **14.** (CarA) [*X*] To. **a.** *He will sell the apples for anybody who will buy.*—StLu (Ms) **b.** *We shall look forward for a very satisfactory agreement with the employers.*—ExP (72.01.02, p.11) **15.** (CarA) [*X*] With (esp in foll phr). **16.** PHRASE **16.1 charged for** *vb phr* [*X*] Charged with (i.e. a criminal offence). *Persons who were not on the scene of the demonstration were charged for taking part.*—DoH (72.04.08, p.1) [These many non-IAE uses of *for* are prob infl by the similarity in sound and function of Yoruba *fun* [fũ]: note *ADMY* Yoruba *fun* B. '(verb used as a preposition < *fun* A. 'give'), with senses (+ cits)

'for; on; to; against; on account of; during'. The phrs below refl a similar infl, prob reinforced by Twi *fa* 'take' also in prepositional function: note *DAFL* Twi *fa* 27. 'serves to express the E preps 'though, by, etc'. Similarities in the usage of Gullah *fuh* [fʊ] suggest a still wider range of Afr infl] **17.** PHRASES **17.1 big for (sb)** *adj phr* (Guyn) [*AF—Cr*] Older than (sb); the elder (of the two). *You big for he or he big for you?* 'Are you older than he, or is he older than you?' —(Guyn) **17.2 feel for (sb/sth)** *vb phr* (CarA) [*IF*] See FEEL Phrs 4., 4.1 **17.3 for days** *adv or adj intensifier phr* (CarA) [*AF*] Very much; very good or very well indeed. **a.** *The wife was surprised to find that the more she boiled the pumpkin, the more water appeared in the pot. It was springing water for days.*—NaT (78.06.23, p.6) **b.** *The outfit was dramatic for days and when she came down King's house steps, you could hear the gasps of appreciation.*—WeG (73.07.11, p.13) **c.** *Boy! That girl could sing for days!*—(Trin) **17.4 for no joke; not for a joke** *adv phr* (Bdos) [*AF—Joc*] See JOKE¹ Phr 2.2 **17.5 for now** *adv phr* (Bdos) [*IF*] For the time being; at present (but with uncertainty as to the future). *Haymans: No canes for now.*—AdV (82.05.05, p.1 (H)) **17.6 for purpose** *adv phr* (CarA) [*X*] See PHR 13.1 above **17.7 for so** *adv intensifier phr* (ECar) [*AF—Joc*] **(i)** Abundantly; with excellence; in a most surprising or startling way; (hence many common phrs in wh it is semi-adj, semi-adv, such as *fete for so, rain for so, vexed for so*, etc.) **(ii)** (Sometimes by itself as a complimentary response) Most certainly! No doubt about it! *S1: You coming back for Carnival, then? / S2: For so!*—(Trin) □ Cp FOR DAYS Phr 17.3., wh often occurs in the same contexts. **17.8 for spite** (CarA); **for the same spite** (Guyn) *adv phr* [*X*] ‖ *by spite* (Gren) Spitefully, in retaliation with malice. *For the same spite, I won't give you none.*—(Guyn) □ Usu said by the person doing the spiteful act. Cp FOR PURPOSE. **17.9 for sport** *adv phr* (CarA) [*IF*] For the fun of it. *I can't stand people who can't play a game for sport. They always must win!*—(Jmca) **17.10 for true** [futru] /1'2/; **for truth** *adv phrs* (CarA) [*AF/IF*] [Often with higher pitches, /1'3/ etc, as an inquiry in response to a piece of news] Really; truly; for a certainty; (SE) in truth. **a.** *Hendrickson got up, holding his side then said 'You mean you stab me for true' before he fell again.*—LaS (78.05.17, p.1) **b.** *But you know I didn't think of that! I could get a job with them for truth!*—SABS:108 [**For truth** is prob a false refinement of Cr [futru], blended with IAE *in truth*] □ An emotive phr, often reduplicated at the folk level: **Fo[r] true, fo[r] true!** /1'212/. **17.11 Something for yourself** *pron phr* (CarA) [*AF*] See SOMETHING Phr 1. **17.12 what ... for (?)** *direct/indirect inquiry phr* (CarA) [*IF*] Why. **a.** *What are you laughing for?*—(Guyn) **b.** *I don't know what he wasted his time going there for?*—(Bdos) [Cp *ADMY* Yoruba *fun* B. 6. 'in emphatic relative sentences, *fun* stands at the end' ex *kin lo dara fun (What is it good for)* 'Of what use is it?'] □ **1.** Distinguish 17.12 from IAE structures like *What are you waiting for?* in wh *for* is part of the phrasal vb 'to wait for', and *what* means 'what thing'. **2.** FOR also occurs in CE (as sometimes in dial AmE) as a connective extension to some vbs wh require no such extension or require connective *that* in such structures. Exs *expect for*, *like for*, *want for*, etc (*you to be on time*).

for·bid·den fruit *n phr* **1. (i)** (Name given in various territories to) an edible fruit believed to be the one, or symbolic of the one that Eve gave Adam to eat (*Gen 3:3–6*). **(ii)** (Belz) The grapefruit. **(iii)** (Gren, Guyn, Trin) ‖ SHADDOCK (CarA) [Prob, in 1.(ii), 1.(iii), from the resemblance of many mature pear-shaped varieties, to a large woman's breast, and so symbolic of 'lust'. Cp similar notion in 1.(iv)] **(iv)** (Guyn) ‖ PASSION FRUIT (CarA) **2. (i)** (Name given in some territories to) an attractive looking fruit that is, however, poisonous or inedible (hence 'forbidden'). **(ii)** (Bdos) ‖ JUMBIE SOURSOP (Antg, etc) **(iii)** (Guyn) Fruit of the CANNON-BALL TREE.

force-ripe¹ (forced-ripe) [fo[r]s[t]-raip] *adj* (CarA) ‖ *buck-ripe* (ViIs) **1.** [*IF*] [Of fruit] Picked when fully mature and ripened under cloth or other covering; prematurely ripened and so less sweet. **2.** [*AF*—*Joc*] [By extension, of a youngster] Precocious and therefore offensive in behaviour; too advanced in dress or conduct for his/her age. *This twelve-year-old forced ripe woman, as she can't be called anything else, told me that if I bring a child in here she is going to kill it.*—NaT (76.06.20, p.26, Dear Christine) [*Force* n + *ripe* adj. A prob calque from W Afr langs. Cp *IGED* Grebo *kpemle* (< '*kpe* 'force', n + *mle* 'squeeze', vb) n 'forced growth, prematurity'. Also Grebo *gbodɔ* 'be forced ripe'. Also (re sense 2.) cp *SGE:89* Ghanaian E *small boy danger* with same sense] □ For similar though rare word-formation (n + adj = adj) in IAE cp *farm-ripe*, *oven-brown*, *war-weary*, etc.

force-ripe² (force-rip·en) *vb tr* (CarA) **1.** ‖ *buck²* 3. (ViIs) ‖ *camp²* (Mrat) To make (picked fruit) ripen quickly by wrapping in cloth or keeping under cover. *Bishop Granville Williams of the Spiritual Baptist Apostolic Church feels that the action is like 'force-riping' the fruit. He says for Barbados it seems too fast, although he expected it to happen/Williams argues putting condom dispensers in the hands of anybody could be dangerous, since we have people who abuse everything.*—SuS (88.06.26, p.40) **2.** [Esp of mangoes] To squeeze (mature fruit) between both hands until soft enough to suck. [By functional shift of FORCE-RIPE¹ adj] □ *To force-ripe* vb IF is an exceptional word-formation pattern in IAE, but cp a similar formation *to oven-brown*. Cp Note at FORCE-RIPE¹

fore-day morn·ing *n phr* (*often functioning as adv phr*) (CarA) [*IF*] Before dawn; the time between darkness and sunrise. *But there is no mercy in these things, esp when you are poor, so early one morning, like the police do with search warrants, early morning, fore-day morning before*

you get your senses, they come and swoop down like a raven.—Bdos (Hd, 87.02.11, p.214)

for·eign *adv* (Jmca) PHRASE **from foreign** *adv phr* [X] ‖ *from away* (ECar) From abroad; from overseas. *Man, she inna one hysterics for Government say that through austerity, dem not allowing importation of any more apples and grapes and pears from foreign.*—WeG (72.12.06, p.12, Partyline)

for·eign·er [fɑrɪnə] /1′22/; **for.eign.er-fel.low/-peo.ple, etc** *n* (Bdos) A person from one of the other *ECar* islands, esp one whose native language is PATWA, or Fr Creole. *The area is famed for the peddling of fruit, mostly by foreigners who have adopted Barbados as their home and very often by day and by night there is the nauseating smell of rotting fruit and other refuse.*—AdN (74.02.24, p.17) □ In Bdos the term tends to be used only with this pitch and only with this ref, white visitors being generally called 'tourists, Canadian, English, etc'; whereas in general CE such persons wd be referred to as *foreigners* / 2′11/, with noticeable pitch-differentiation.

for·get *vb* PHRASES **1. ain't/didn't forget (sb)** *neg vb phr* (CarA) [*AF*] ‖ BUSE (CarA) *They annoyed the woman downstairs and she went out on the road and didn't forget them.*—(Guyn) **2. ain't/ didn't forget to (do sth)** *neg vb phr* (CarA) [*AF*] To do (sth) with wilful or spiteful thoroughness. *The poor wife raised her voice one day about the women he keeps, and he took off his belt and didn't forget to beat her skin.*—(Belz)

form *vb* (Jmca) [*AF*] **1.** To behave (as if); to appear; to seem. *'Hi, no!' replied Jane. 'I wouldn't be so ungrateful. Don't I born in de country too? It would be foolish of me to form like I did born in Kingston.'*—DJC:18 [Perh infl by military sense in relation to troops, i.e. to arrange, fix oneself in a particular order or way. Cp *OED form* v¹ 8. b.] **2.** PHRASE **2.1 form (the) fool** *vb phr* (Angu, Antg, BrVi, Dmca, Gren, StLu) [*AF/ IF*] See FOOL² Phr 3.1

fort·y-e·lev·en [fɔrti-lɛvn] *num adj* (Bdos, Guyn) [*AF*—*Joc*] So many as to be too many; an unnecessary number of (times, things, persons). *One day a police jeep come through the village, swing up the tracks towards the house where Wingrove live, stop; and about forty-eleven policemen jump out, swinging club and thing and pulling out handcuff like they come to prevent a riot.*—CISH: 113

for·ward¹ [fawʌ(r)d ~ farad] *adj* (CarA) [Of a young person] Presumptuous; saucy; not knowing your place as a child or youth. □ This usage, though also current in IAE, is of much higher frequency in CE, overriding all other IAE adj uses of the word, and commonly occurring in *AF* contexts when a child is being sharply reprimanded, ex as '*too dam/blasted forward*'. Note common pronunc [farad] esp in *Belz*.

for·ward[2] [fawʌ(r)d] (CarA) [Rastaf] **1.** *vb intr* To come/go/move forward; to get on/out; to move out/away. *Brother Spaulding yu mean to tell I man, that I will have to pack up I belongings and forward? But, I thought that I and I was suffering brothers!*—WeS (73.02.09, p.21) **2.** PHRASE **2.1 forward up** *vb phr* (Jmca) [*AF—Joc*] To advance noticeably; to improve much in your performance; to become prominent. *The Jaycees forward up in town this week with the big West Indies Jaycees convention in session.*—WeG (72.10.11, p.13, Partyline) **3.** *vb tr* To receive or accept (sth) as good. *Let the parents feel that you are clean-cut, so if you get a cut, at least you'll cut them cleaner than these Rasta-boys who incidentally forward no un-clean.*—CrU (77.03.19, p.7) [By functional shift (sense 1.) and thence semantic shift (sense 2.) of FORWARD[1] adj]

for·ward·ness *n* (ECar) Boldness; impertinence. [FORWARD[1] + SE suff -*ness*]

fou [fu] *adj* (Gren) [*AF—Joc*] Mad; crazy; (have) taken leave of your senses. *Ay-ay, but look dis man nuh! Two dollars? Man you fou! If you doh want me put a lawyer in you skin for me wares, pay me eh. Ay-ay. I ent no small-change woman nuh!*—RTCS:25 [Fr Cr < Fr *fou* 'mad; stupid']

fou-fou (foo-foo) [fufu∼fwufwu] *n* (Dmca) Any of three very small varieties of green and blue hummingbird, the males crested, the females uncrested; *Orthorhyncus cristatus* (*Trochilidae*)—BBWI:97, 137. [Fr Cr < *fwou-fwou* < Fr *frou-frou* 'fluffy little thing' or 'rustle' in ref to the sound of its wings] □ The recognition of the /r/ in *frou-frou* as spelled in the literature seems to have disappeared in general writing.

fou·lard (fou·la) [fula·[d]∼fuya:d] *n* (Dmca, StLu) A shawl or large neckerchief of decorative material partly covering the bodice of a dress so that its ends tuck into the belt; it is worn as part of the national costume. [Fr *foulard* 'silk neckerchief']

four *numeral adj* PHRASES **1. eyes make four** *vb phr* (CarA) [*IF*] See EYES Phr 14. **2. meet under four eyes** *vb phr* (StVn) [*IF*] ‖ EYES MAKE FOUR (CarA)

four-and-a-half *adv* (Guyn, Tbgo) Thoroughly; fully; extensively; all around. **a.** *A man quarrels with his unruly son and threatens to beat him 'four and a half'.*—Caq IV. 2, p.155 (H.B. Meikle) **b.** *Boy don'[t] open me door four-and-a-half and expose me house like dat.*—(Guyn) [< SE (nautical) *fore-and-aft*, by folk etym]

four-cor·ner (plan·tain) *n* (phr) (Guyn) ‖ BLUGGO (Belz, etc) [From its noticeably angular four-sided shape]

four-eye (fish) *n* (phr) (Guyn) A surface fish common in shoals at river-mouths, with very prominent eyes divided externally each into an upper and lower part (so making four and hence the name), enabling it to see both above and below the surface of the water; *Anableps tetrophthalmus*.

four-o'clock (bush)* *n* (phr) (Angu, Baha, Bdos, Gren, Jmca, Trin) A wild plant that grows 3 to 4 ft high in shaded places, and of many varieties, bearing bell-shaped pink, yellow, white, or red flowers that open about 4 o'clock (hence the name) and last through the night; the leaves are widely used, crushed, in a poultice for sprains, or boiled as a folk-medicine; the black seeds are said to be poisonous; *Mirabilis jalapa* (*Nyctaginaceae*).

four·pen·ny-nail *n* (Bdos, Jmca) See SIX PENNY-NAIL

fowl *n* (CarA) **1.** (General name used for) poultry, but more often a hen. *There is a noise inside the house of clinking china, then a crash, followed by a fowl crowing.*—RTCS:18 □ 1. IAE particularises *domestic fowl, hen, cock, rooster, chicken* in such contexts. See FOWL-COCK. **2.** From this sense many common CE compounds follow: Exs *fowl-coop, -curry, -dung, -egg, -farm, -pen, -run*, etc may be mentioned here, IAE substituting *chicken-* as the first element in all such cases. **2.** PHRASES **2.1 put fowl to mind corn** *vb phr* (BrVi) [*AF—Joc*] To make a very foolish decision of trust. **2.2 rise with the fowls** *vb phr* (Bdos) [*IF*] To be up before dawn; to get out of bed as early as possible. □ Cp BIRD[1] Phr 4.1. **2.3 when fowl (-cock) cut/get teeth** *adv phr* (CarA) [*AF—Cr/Joc*] ‖ **when chicken get teeth** (Baha) ‖ **when cock get/make teeth** (Gren, Tbgo, Trin) Never ever. [A calque from W Afr langs. Cp Yoruba *nigbati adię hu ehin* 'when fowl grow tooth', with same meaning]

fowl-cock *n* (CarA) **1.** ‖ *cock-chicken* (Guyn) A domestic cock; a rooster. [A redundant compound < *fowl* + *male*, a prob calque from W Afr langs. Cp Gâ *wuo nu* 'cock' (< *wuo* 'chicken' + *nu* man, male)] **2.** PHRASE **2.1 before fowl-cock put on him pants** *adv phr* (Jmca) [*AF*] See BEFORE[1] PHR 1.

fowl-foot grass* *n phr* (CarA) ‖ *pyé-poul* (Dmca, StLu, Trin) A weedy grass with fairly stiff, smooth, noded leaves growing from the base, and a central stem about a foot high, topped by a small spray of hairy-looking spikelets spread like a hen's foot; *Eleusine indica* (*Gramineae*).

Fox Hill dia·lect *n phr* (Baha) A dialect of Bahamian E, spoken by a community just outside Nassau (Fox Hill, hence the name), in wh it is believed there are more traces of African retentions than anywhere else in the Bahamas. *They were talking the Fox Hill dialect, a combination of fragments of African and English Languages, local Bahamian dialect, accented deeper than in some other parts of the island. To these children from a more urban part of the Western*

District it was just like a foreign language.—
TOSR:30

fraid [fre·d ~ frıed] *adj often used as vb* (CarA)
[AF—Cr] (To be) frightened; (to be) afraid of
(sb/sth). *'Well Joe man, tell de Constable de whole
thing nuh man, you fraid? After all you is a big man,
man.' 'Fraid who? I ent fraid nobody.'*—RTCS:22
[< SE *afraid* by aphesis, but prob much infl by
IrE and various E dialects in wh *fraid* often
occurs. See EDD *afraid*]

fraid·y [fre·di ~ frıedi] *adj* (Antg, CayI, Jmca,
StVn, Tbgo, Trin) [AF] Timid; fearful; afraid
or very unwilling to speak up for yourself. [FRAID
(as prec) + Cr diminitive suff -Y. Cp STUPIDY,
etc] □ Cp AmE [child talk] *fraidy-cat* n 'coward',
perh infl by Black AmE.

France n (CarA) [IF] (A euphemism for) hell
(often as an oath). *Boy, woman is France, yes!
Dey tell you dey love you, but dey doesn't mean it,
nuh, true.*—MN:7 [A ref to France as the scene
of doom and horror where many West Indians
died in World War I] (Hence foll phrs in wh
informal IAE would use *hell*) PHRASES **Get to
France out of here/there!; give (sb) France;
Go to France!; have/put (sb) in France; How/
what/when/where/who/why the France ...?;
Oh France!; play France with (sb); put
France on (sb); To France with that/them,
(etc)!**

franc·o·men (frank·o·men(t)) [fraŋkomɛn]
adv (Gren, Tbgo, Trin) [AF] **1.** [Of speaking]
Bluntly; without hesitation or restraint. *You have
to come out francomen and tell him damn-well no,
eh!*—(Trin) **2.** [Of an act] Brazenly; [Of theft]
red-handed. *A ketch him frankomen so with the
coconuts under me tree.*—(Tbgo) [< Sp *franca-
mente* 'frankly, openly; definitely'. The spelling
with *-k-* sometimes used is infl by SE *frank*, and
the /a > o/ shift is prob due to false refinement]

fran·gi·pa·ni* ['franɪpani] n (CarA) ‖ *jasmine*
2. (CayI) A small, multi-branching tree with
sprays of long, spear-shaped, waxy green leaves
wh are shed before clusters of rosette-like red
or white flowers burst out covering the tree; the
flowers are sweet-smelling at night, but the latex
of the limbs and leaves is poisonous; *Plumeria
acutifolia* or *P. rubra* (red variety) or *P. alba*
(white variety), (*Apocynaceae*). [Said to be
named after Muzio Frangipani, a 16C Italian
Marquis who used the perfume made from these
Central American flowers to scent his gloves.
However, 'the plant was [at first?] named after
the Frenchman Plumier, a pioneer in West Indian botany, and as such its name was *Plumieria*,
but in course of time it has become corrupted
to *Plumeria*'—GWTSB:43] □ The tree, 'a native
of The West Indies and Central America'
GWTSB:42, is of many flowering varieties ranging through orange, pink, yellow, and cream.

fraud *vb* (Antg) [X] To cheat; to defraud; to
rig (an election). [< SE *defraud* by aphaeresis,
and widened sense]

fray [fre·] n (Bdos) A small, silvery fish that
moves in large shoals, often used as bait or
cooked to make FRAY-CAKES. [Poss a survival
from EE, —cp OED *fray* v⁴ (Obs) 'to fry' +
cits-1568; or from a dial pronunc of SE *fry*
'small fish']

fraz·zle *vb* (Guyn, Trin) To fray or ravel out;
to become or make ragged at the edge(s). *He ...
cut a toothbrush from the hibiscus fence. He chewed
at the end of the stem and scrubbed his teeth with
it when it frazzled out.*—SABS:12 [OED *frazzle*
v. *dial*. and US 'to fray, tear to rags or ribbons'
+ cits-1895] □ This function and sense are evid
not still current in SE, largely replaced by *fray*.

freck n (Guyn) A small amount of money
(begged for or) given in charity. [Perh related to
EDD Sc *fraik, freck* 2 sb 'flattery, coaxing']

fré·di (fre·di) n (Dmca, StLu) See FWÉDI

freebs *n sg or pl* (Antg, USVI) [AF—Joc] ‖ FREE-
NESS (CarA)

free-col·oured n (CarA) [Hist] A person of
mixed race (black and white) who had been a
slave, or one of whose parents had been a slave,
and had his freedom bought or granted before
the abolition of slavery. *It was cynically observed
by the white planter class that the free coloureds
were predisposed to make common cause with them
against the mass of blacks.*—IHB:27

free ma·son *n phr* (Jmca) ‖ MASON-MARABUNTA
(Guyn)

free·ness n (CarA) [IF—Joc] ‖ *freebs* (Antg,
USVI) **1.** Something for nothing; a free hand-out
of money or goods (as something expected by
the receiver). *In its first term of office, the Government's Attorney General, Mr Henry Forde,
declared that Barbados was more socialist than
Cuba and proceeded to support his contention with
illustrations. Many preferred to disbelieve him,
being made uncomfortable when required to look
facts in the face. Some applauded, deluded by the
prospect of freenesses.*—NaT (84.04.13, p.6) **2.** A
party or picnic at wh there is plenty of food and
drink and to wh you go uninvited or unknown
expecting to share in everything. *There will be
dances in every open space, pool, nook and crannie
by the Brass and steelbands. There's always something to do and some place to go with a little
freeness in between.*—LaS (77.12.24, p.1) [Cp
OED *freeness* 'Now *rare*' 2. 'readiness; generosity, liberality' + cits-1709] □ This obs SE
abstract noun is given a concrete sense in CE.
Note pl *freenesses* in cit 1.

free-pa·per n (CarA) [IF] **1.** [Hist] A document signed by a slave-owner acknowledging
the slave's bought or granted freedom. [< SE

free[dom] + paper] **2.** PHRASE **2.1 your free-paper bu[r]n** *id phr* (CarA) [*AF—Joc*] Your holiday is over; it is necessary to stop joking and turn to serious hard work. *'You'd better make the best of the free time, son,' he told Jonah. 'In a few weeks, the ol' free paper burn, eh?' He chuckled hoarsely.*—SJS:8 [*Burn* is here used with CarA Cr passive sense 'has been burnt' i.e. is no more]

free-sheet *adv* (Tbgo, Trin) [*AF*] Freely and thoughtlessly; without consideration or restraint. *... and all dem people renting free sheet and not paying a penny in tax, bold face, bold face.*—JJM: 29

freeze *n* (Baha, Dmca, Gren, StLu) A children's game in wh any member of the group is required to stay frozen in one position if caught at any time breaking the agreement for that game; [such an agreement is usu a simple one such as agreeing to keep your fingers crossed continuously]

freight-cart *n* (Bdos) **1.** ‖ *cane-rack* (Bdos) A V-shaped cart, usu long and four-wheeled (but there were shorter, two-wheeled ones) drawn by two or more donkeys or mules and hired as sugar-plantation transportation of canes in CROP-TIME, or of goods between factory and town. **2.** ‖ *freighter* (Bdos) A two-wheeled BOX-CART, with a tray some 10 or 12 ft long built on its top for transporting loads of timber (hence the name), or for displaying quantities of fruit for sale; it is pushed by hand.

French ca·shew *n phr* **1.** (Guyn) ‖ CASHEW 1. (CarA) **2.** (Gren) ‖ MALACCA-APPLE (Antg, Guyn)

French cot·ton *n phr* (Bdos) ‖ AMERICAN SILK-COTTON (BrVi)

French Cre·ole *n phr* **1.** (CarA) ‖ PATWA (Dmca, etc) **2.** (Trin) A near-white person with Caucasian type hair, often with a French family name originating from the late 18C immigrants to Trinidad from Martinique and Guadeloupe.

French·ie *n* **1.** (StKt) [*AF—Derog*] ‖ POOR-WHITE (CarA) [Prob a Hist ref to descendants of settlers in the orig Fr sections of St. Kitts who would have lost status, as disfranchised Roman Catholics, when the English took over the whole island in 1690. Cp ‖ *mooshay* (StKt)] **2.** (USVI) [*AF*] A descendant of an 18C French immigrant community, mostly of farmers and fishermen, still living as a group in St Thomas.

French thyme *n phr* (StVn) ‖ THICK-LEAF-THYME (Bdos, Guyn)

French weed *n phr* **1.** (BrVi) ‖ COCKROACH-GRASS Gren, etc) **2.** (Antg) ‖ WATER-GRASS (Bdos, etc)

fres·co (fres·ko) *n* (Belz) ‖ SNO-CONE (Bdos) [Sp *fresco* 'cool, fresh']

fresh¹ *adj* [Note: This word seems to have assumed rather particular dominant applications in some places while still keeping all its broader general SE senses among educated speakers] **1.** (CarA) [*IF—Derog*] ‖ **fresh-up** (CarA) **2.** [Esp of young persons and old men] Sexually cheeky; making suggestive advances to sb of the opposite sex. **a.** *What daughter is safe from the fresh and rude men who are cruising these streets looking for their own pleasure?*—TrI (70.09.15, p.3) **b.** *At Port Station, the court heard D. B— allegedly admit having raped the women and stolen their jewellery because they were 'too fresh'.*—VoS (76.10.09, p.1) **2.** PHRASES **2.1 (be) fresh and fast** (Gren); **(be) fresh and forward** (BrVi); **(be/play) fresh (up) with yourself** (CarA) [*AF/IF—Derog*] To be bold and impertinent; to be sexually presumptuous or promiscuous. **3.** (Guyn, StVn) [Of meat, esp chicken] Raw-smelling; unseasoned (but not stale). **4.** (Bdos, Tbgo, Trin) [Of fish] Rank and unpleasant smelling (i.e. needing lime-juice to 'cut' the smell); stale-smelling. □ In *Bdos* this sense is found among older or rural folk in the expression **This fish smells fresh**; but see FRESH-FISH 5. (Bdos) [Of teenage pop music] The latest and most popular. *The kind of music blaring from a minibus has a lot to do with its popularity on the road. For a driver and his conductor to maintain 'ratings' among these 'jetsetting' teenagers, the music must be 'fresh' and his stereo quality top notch.*—SuS (87.05.24, p.32)

fresh² *adv* (CarA) [*X*] **1.** Afresh; again. *As soon as I go and get the phone message the row start fresh.*—Bdos (CR, 70.01.14) **2.** Recently; newly. *We were informed 'A woman fresh dead in the village'.*—Isl (10/73, p.42)

fresh-cold *n* (CarA) ‖ COLD² 1. (CarA)

fresh-cut *n* (Jmca) ‖ GARDEN-BALSAM (Bdos, etc) [From the use of its leaves, sometimes steeped in white rum, as a plaster for a fresh wound]

fresh-fish *n* (Bdos) ‖ POT-FISH (CarA) [Because sold 'fresh' upon landing (with a string through their gills)] □ In *Bdos* the term is used to distinguish such fish from FLYING-FISH esp when the latter are in seasonal abundance.

fresh·ness *n* (CarA) Impertinence (esp such as is sexually suggestive). *Poor as she was, she decided if he ever tried any of his freshness on her she would tear up the ticket right there before him and throw the pieces in his old face. Yes, she would!*—DaG (66.12.18, p.4) [< FRESH¹ 1. + *ness*]

fresh-up *adj* (CarA) [*AF—Derog*] **1.** Precocious; uppish. *Tobago definitely cannot make the grade without Trinidad. These 'fresh-up' islanders have the gumption within recent times to be calling for self-rule and all that.*—EvN (80.03.27, p.4) **2.** ‖ FRESH¹ 1. (CarA)

fresh-wa·ter Yan·kee *n phr* (Trin) [*AF—Derog/Joc*] A native West Indian person who picks up a North American accent after a short visit to the US or Canada.

fres·ko *n* (Belz) See FRESCO

fret with (sb) *vb phr* (CarA) To quarrel quietly or show your annoyance with (sb). [An extension of the SE vb intr sense *fret* 'to be fretful, irritated'. Cp *OEDS fret* v[1] 9. '*fret about, at, over*, etc']

fried(-bakes, -dump·lings, etc) See FRY-

fried-cakes *n pl* (TkCa) ‖ BAKE(s)[1] 2. (Bdos, etc)

friend[1] [frɛn[d]] *n* (CarA) [*IF*] A lover; a sexual mate. □ Commonly so used in funeral announcements of older folk.

friend[2] *vb* (CarA) [*IF*] **1.** To form a sexual relationship. **2.** PHRASE **2.1 friend/friends with (sb)** *vb phr* (CarA) [*AF/IF*] ‖ **be friends/friendly with (sb)** (CarA) [*IF*] To have an understood sexual relationship with (sb) without marriage. (See FRIENDING). '*If I don't love a woman, I could friend with she for donkey's years. But when it comes to married. Not meself*'.—STTG:59 **2.2 friend up with (sb)** *vb phr* (CarA) [*AF/IF*] To have a close (prob living-in) sexual relationship with (sb); [E slang] to shack up with (sb).

friend·in(g) [frɛn(d)ɪn/ŋ] *vb-ing intr* (Tbgo, Trin) [*AF/IF*] ‖ COURTENIN[G] (CarA) *A man could be friending with one woman, living with a second, and married to a third; and he may also be married to a woman with whom he was formerly living and friending. The friending relationship is one in which a man visits or meets a woman at intervals for sexual intercourse, and in which he has certain obligations to the woman and to any children of his that she may bear.*—RLCF:48 [By functional shift (n > vb) of SE *friend* n] □ This (and *friendsing*, Guyn) are present-day CE social terms, replacements of the older *courtenin[g]*, though there is a difference in that *friendin[g]* may not necessarily culminate in marriage whereas *courtenin[g]* had to.

Friend·ly Bur·i·al So·ci·e·ty *n phr* (Guyn) An association of old people who contribute a small sum monthly to ensure that the expenses of a decent funeral will be met.

friend·ly (with/to (sb)) *adj phr* (CarA) [*IF*] ‖ FRIEND WITH SB (CarA) *I have never refused to give him bed service, but he is friendly with a pondfly for a woman just a little way from our house.*—NaT (75.02.23, p.18)

friends *n pl* PHRASES **1. be friends with (sb)** *vb phr* (CarA) [*IF*] ‖ FRIEND WITH SB (CarA) [*AF/IF*] *I am nineteen years of age and am 'friends' with a man of twenty-three. My mother does not*

approve of our friendship. She thinks that he is fooling me.—NaT (76.09.12, p.26, Dear Christine) **2. follow friends** *vb phr* (CarA) [*IF*] See FOLLOW Phr 2.2

friends·in(g) [frɛnzɪn(g)] [*vb*]-*ing intr* (Guyn) [*AF—Joc*] ‖ COURTENIN(G) (Guyn) [By functional shift /n > vb/ of *friends* n] □ See also FRIENDING and note.

frig·ate-bird* *n* (CarA) ‖ *cobbler* 2 (Bdos) ‖ *man-o-war bird* (CarA) A tropical Atlantic sea-bird with a 7 ft wing-span, a long, down-turned beak and forked tail, the male being all black, the female white-breasted and brown-backed; this bird is noted both for its high long-distance soaring and for seizing fish from other sea-birds; *Fregata magnificens* (*Fregatidae/Pelicaniformes*).

fright *n* PHRASE **fright got/have/hold you** *id phr* (Bdos, Guyn) [*AF*] (You are) gripped/stiff with fright. *The bag uh pumpkins fall down off she head, and I hear that fright had she so, that the pants waist leh go, and it drop down by she ankle.*—Bdos (Ms Play, 1977) [A prob calque from W Afr langs. Cp similar CE exps with *hunger, cold,* etc]

fright·en[1] [fraɪkn] *vb tr* (CarA) [*X*] **1.** To fear (sb/sth); to be terrified by (sb/sth). **a.** *The boy frighten his father too bad.*—(Guyn) **b.** *Children always frighten the dark.*—(Bdos) **2.** PHRASES **2.1 frightened for (sb)** *vb phr* (CarA) [*X*] To fear, be afraid of (sb). *They send a lot of people down here and have a lot of cocktail parties and find out what the Government is thinking. I am not frightened for them, Sir. They cannot execute on me or levy on me.*—Bdos (Hd, 75.10.09, p.975) [Prob from IrE. Note: 'I am afraid of her', 'I am frightened at her', are both correct English, meaning 'She has frightened me': and both are expressed in Donegal 'I am afeard for her', 'I am frightened for her', where in both cases *for* is used in the sense of 'on account of'—JESI: 30. The spelling-pronunc *friken* is also noted as Irish as a variant of *frecken* 'to frighten' (*EDD*)] □ See also FRIGHTEN[2] Phr 2.2 **2.2 make sb frighten(ed)** *vb phr* (CarA) [*X*] **a.** *It made us frighten the way he laughed.*—LICMS:165 **b.** *It was the police and their presence made me frightened.*—Antg (Ms, 1973)

fright·en[2] [fraɪtn ~ fraɪkn] *adj* (CarA) [*AF—Cr*] **1.** (Be) afraid; (become) afraid or frightened. *If a man frighten to die, he frighten to die, an' there's no gettin' away from that.*—LICMS:138 [By shift (pa. part. > adj) of FRIGHTEN(ED)[1] with characteristic CarA Cr reduction and loss of *be*, resulting in a possible ambiguity] □ Whether CE *I frighten him* has an *AF* sense 'I am afraid of him', or a Formal sense 'I frightened him' is resolved largely by context, partly by pitch. **2.** PHRASES **2.1 Don't frighten!** [do·n fraɪkn] *neg imperative* (CarA) [*AF—Cr*] Don't be afraid! Don't let yourself be worried! **2.2 frighten for (sb/sth)** *adj phr* (CarA) [*AF—Cr*] ‖ *frightened* *for* (*sb*/*sth*) (CarA) (Be) afraid to face (sb/ sth). *And since de people not so frighten for the Constables they seeing everywhere Military with gun.*—CTT:34 □ See FRIGHTEN[1] Phr 2.1 **2.3 get frighten** [gɛ(t) fraɪkn] *vb phr* (CarA) [*AF—Cr*] To be scared; to panic. *Trumper said 'Sometimes I get frighten when I see my mother baby starin''.* —LICMS:129

Fright·en·Fri·day /1′21′2/ *n* **1.** (Bdos, Guyn, StVn) [*AF—Joc*] A timorous person; sb who is painfully lacking in self-confidence. **2.** (StVn) [*AF—Derog*] An ignorant person whose silly behaviour gives him away. [Perh a characteristic redundant compound < CarA Cr FRIGHTEN[1] (adj) + FRAIDY, and influenced by Daniel Defoe's timid character 'Friday' in ROBINSON CRUSOE]

friz·zle-fowl (Bdos, Gren, Guyn, Tbgo, Trin); **friz.zly fowl** (Angu, BrVi) *n* (*phr*) ‖ SENSEH-FOWL (CarA) [< SE *frizzle* vb [Of hair, etc] 'to curl up in small crisp curls'. But cp also 'Friesland hens, with their feathers all turned the wrong way'—George Eliot: The Mill on the Floss, Ch IX]

frog-ba·na·na (**frog-plan·tain**) *n* (CayI, Jmca) ‖ BLUGGO (Belz, etc)

frog-hop·per *n* (Guyn, Trin) [Sugar Ind] A bug wh is a pest that lays its eggs at the base of sugar-cane stalks where they hatch into forms that live in masses of spittle-like froth; these forms feed on the roots and grow into adult insects wh feed on the leaves, blighting growth; *Aneneolamia spp.*

from[1] *prep* (*and also functioning as a connective before adjs and adv phrs of time, so developing into a conj as next listed*) (CarA) [*IF*] [Note: The foll list presents illustrations of its prep senses listed alphabetically for convenience] **1.** (CarA) [*IF*] Among; from among. *And from those who can read, there are some who cannot understand the real implications of scientific language.*—Bdos (Ms, 73.12.12) **2.** (CarA) [*IF*] Because of; owing to. *We record the sad passing of Miss Henrietta Phippa at the Cunningham Hospital on Saturday 30th ultimo where she was confined from a stroke.*—LaS (62.01.05, p.1) **3.** (CarA) (**i**) [*IF*] By. *Yesterday there were no lads diving coins thrown from tourists in the Careenage.*—AdN (74.02.16, p.5) (**ii**) (Bdos, Guyn) [Of child-bearing] By (a woman as the mother). *But there is a boy who says he loves me. He has a child from a girl and he says he loves this girl too.*—NaT (76.08.15, p.18 Dear Christine) □ Cp FOR 8. (**iii**) (CarA) [*IF*] By means of; by operating. *Since the door couldn't be opened from the lock, I guessed it had to open from a bolt.*—(StKt) **4.** (CarA) [*IF*] For (a period of time). *He has been absent from Grenada from the past four months and is expected to return over the week-end.*—VaN (63.20.12, p.1) **5.** PHRASE **5.1 from** [**a**] **long time** *adv phr* (CarA) [*IF*/ *AF*] For some time now; since some time ago. *Please say you mean it, Caldo. I love you from a long time.*—HF:23 **6.** (CarA) [*IF*] Of. *When it*

struck the pole a part from the car flew off and struck the guard-wall.*—(Bdos) **7.** (CarA) [*IF*] Since/in (the month of). *He left here from May.—* (CayI) **8.** PHRASES **8.1 from a child** [*IF*] *adv phr* (CarA) See CHILD Phr 4.1 **8.2 from early** *adv phr* (CarA) [*IF*]; **from early o'clock** (Bdos) [*AF*] From an early hour, day, time, year; from early childhood; long ago. **a.** *A keen sportsman from early, he represented his school at country inter-school sports in 1966.*—AdN (77.01.03, p.2) **b.** *Said Permanent Secretary Cornelius Lubin: 'Cabinet from early laid down the conditions under which the university would operate'.*—AdV (84.07.01) **8.3 from ever since** *adv phr* (CarA) [*IF*] For some time now; from a time long ago. **8.4 from hell freeze/froze** *adv phr* (Baha) [*AF*] For an unbelievably long time. □ Usu referring to waiting or expectation. **8.5 from hinder** [**you**] [fram henda] *conj phr* (Antg) [*AF—Cr*] So that you may not. *Come out o[f] de rain from henda you ketch col[d].*—(Antg) [Evid a corruption of 'to hinder you from'] **8.6 from in front** *adv phr* (Tbgo, Trin) [*AF*] See FRONT Phr 3.2 **8.7 from morning** *adv phr* (Gren, Tbgo, Trin) [*AF*] From the outset; for as long ago as I can remember. *From morning I don't like fish especially rock-fish. Give me chicken or pork any day.*—(Tbgo) **8.8 get/have change from (a dollar coin, or a money bill)** *vb phr* (Baha, Bdos) [*IF*] To be able to change (a coin or note in the act of buying or selling). *If you don't have change from five dollars you can keep it and I will come back.*—(Bdos, buyer to seller) □ FROM also occurs redundantly in CE in such expressions as *from off/off from, from out of*, etc from wh it may, in most cases properly be omitted. Similar prep phrs occur in *AF* or dial AmE.

from[2] *conj* (CarA) [*X*] From the time that. **1.** [Before a n or adj with ellipsis of *he/she was, we/ you/they were*, esp in foll phrs]. **2.** PHRASES **2.1 from a baby; from a child/boy/girl; from, jg born; from small; from young** (CarA) *adv phrs* [*X*] From babyhood, childhood, birth, youth, etc. **a.** *I know the Police Officer, Dennis Leacock from a baby. I helped to mind him.*—Bdos (CR, 71.05.25) **b.** *He was there from Evangaline Phillips raised him from small.*—Tbgo (CR, 76.11.03) [Prob a calque from W Afr langs. Cp Igbo *site na nwata* (*from at child*) 'from childhood'] **3.** (Jmca, StVn, Tbgo, Trin) From the moment that; from when. [*X*] *When Lodge woke me the room was in darkness. From we went to bed until I got the shot, I never turned the light on.*—DaG (66.12.06, p.4) **4.** PHRASE **4.1 from God make/send morning** *adv phr* (BrVi) [*AF—Cr*] From early morning.

front *n* **1.** (Guyn) The area of a sugar-estate facing the sea or the river, also called the FRONT-LANDS. (Cp ABACK, BACK-DAM). **2.** (Guyn) The main or public road through such an area, sometimes called the FRONT-ROAD. **3.** (CarA) PHRASES **3.1 in front** *adv phr* (Bdos) [*AF*] Before; previously. *I had come to the University the year in front.*—Bdos (Ms) **3.2. from in front** *adv phr*

(Tbgo, Trin) [*AF*] Beforehand; with due warning. *A tellin[g] all-you from in front don't touch my car.*—(Trin)

front-house *n* 1. (Bdos) ‖ *front-room* (Baha, Bdos, Jmca, Nevs, StKt) The living-room area of a dwelling, esp such as the gable-ended CHATTEL-HOUSE part, often including the bedroom (to wh an extension or SHED-ROOF has been added at the back for general domestic purposes). 2. (Guyn) The house that faces the road, being the foremost of two or three buildings on a single property-lot. □ Cp BACK-HOUSE

front·ing[1] (Bdos, StLu, StVn, Trin); **front·ish** (Tbgo, Trin) [*AF*] Pushy; presumptuous; rude and indiscreet. *'We go get jail anyhow, that frontin' policeman wha' on George Street beat, he tell me he only waiting for carnival to shove all o' we in jail.'*—JPB:126

FRONTING[2]: See introduction: CARIBBEAN ENGLISH, General characteristics.

front·lands *n pl* (Guyn) See FRONT 1. (*Guyn*)

front-road *n* 1. (Guyn) See FRONT 2. (Guyn) 2. (Bdos) Any main traffic road to wh poorer residential roads lead.

front-room *n* (Baha, Bdos, Jmca, Nevs, StKt) ‖ *front-house* (Bdos) The parlour or living- or drawing-room area of a dwelling, with windows looking out onto the road.

frowst and flu *n phr* (Baha) ‖ COLD IN THE BELLY (CarA) See COLD[2] 3.

frupse [frʌps] *n* (Bdos, Guyn) [*AF—Derog*] A mean, worthless little person or thing; (sb) or (sth) of no account.

frups·y *adj* (Bdos, Guyn, Trin) [*AF—Derog*] Very worthless-looking; tawdry (thing); bedraggled (person).

fry-bake(s) *n* (Trin) ‖ BAKE(S)[1] 2. (Bdos, etc)

fry-dump·lin(g) *n* (Antg, Jmca,) ‖ BAKE(S)[1] 2. (Bdos, etc) *Fry dumplin or fried flour dumplings [are] also popular as breakfast and supper dish.*—DJPVP:12

fu (fuh) [fʊ ~ fʌ] *prep* (CarA) [*AF—Cr*] 1. (i) (Dial spelling often used for) For (in narrative dialogue wherever this item functions in Cr speech). ... *'Then wan man come and bring wan $5 note', the witness continued. 'He call fuh wan shilling banana.'*—DaA (52.09.13, p.4) (ii) As part of Cr poss phr before a *n* (Belz, Jmca) **fu he/him, me, she/her, we/you, etc** His, my, her, our, your, etc. *Fu we National Camp.*—AmA (H, 80.07.18, p.9) 2. As *infin* marker (CarA) [*AF—Cr*] a. *Da fu lick yo!* (= *That's to beat you, i.e. make you think*).—Bdos (popular phr) b. *None live a country and none come roun' de village dem fu encourage you fu do some ting.*—LaS

(77.02.19, p.4, Bits & Pieces) □ Commonly found in combinations **ga fu, ha fu** 'have to, must' in Cr narrative dialogue.

fudge *vb* (Trin) ‖ COG (Guyn) [< SE *fudge* vb 'to fit together in a makeshift or dishonest way' (but with this sense particularized in ref to cheating at school)]

fu·fu (foo-foo) *n* 1. Baha, Belz, Guyn, Jmca, Tbgo) ‖ *hudut* (Belz) ‖ *pound-plantain* (Trin) A food made by pounding boiled, green plantains (in some places ripe plantains, yams, or cassava) into a dough-like mass in a wooden MORTAR, shaping the same into a ball with a wet spoon, to be served with soup. [DAFL Twi *fufuu* 'foofoo' with same meaning; also ZAGL Gã-Adangme *fufu* 'a favorite food of the natives, a dough of mashed yams, cassava, or plantains, eaten to soup'; also several other W Afr sources, ex ADMY Yoruba *fufu* 'grated cassava', etc] 2. PHRASE 2.1 ball of fufu *n phr* (Guyn) See BALL 3.3 [Cp DAFL Twi *fufuu-tow* 'a ball of foofoo'] 3. (Belz) (Name also applied to) ripe plantains cut up and fried together—(Rep, 80.05.11, p.6). □ It is preferable to use the spelling FUFU for this as a food item to distinguish it from other items carrying the same name. See FOU-FOU and foll senses. 3. See FOO-FOO 2. (Antg, Tbgo) 4. ‖ FOO-FOO[1] 4. (CayI, etc)

fu·fu-man·go /1'212/ *n* (Guyn) ‖ MANGO-GRAHAM (StLu)

fuh [fʊ ~ fʌ] *prep* (CarA) [*AF—Cr*] See FU

full[1] *adj* 1. (CarA) [Of fruit] Quite mature; ready to be picked and left to ripen off the tree, or ready to be cooked. *Peel and core one medium-size full breadfruit.*—ExP (Mag, 73.04.15, p.16, Recipes) 2. (CarA) [*IF*] [Of a person] In mature adulthood; able-bodied and responsible. *Part-time General Domestic Servant (full woman) with working experience. Apply in person.*—AdN (78.02.22, p.12, Wanted Ad) 3. (CarA) [*IF*] Fully qualified, recognized; complete. a. *I used to drive buses and do inspector work in between then. I am a full inspector now.*—Bdos (CR) b. *When the accused was under the tree I could not see his full face.*—Bdos (CR, 71.05.05) 4. (Mrat, Tbgo, Trin) [*AF—Derog*] ‖ FULL-UP[2] 1. (Antg, Mrat) *Every year he only know to have the poor girl full.*—(Trin) □ See further adj uses in established combinations listed separately below. 5. PHRASES 5.1 full of mouth; full of [a lot of] talk/tongue (CarA) [*AF—Derog*] (i) Emptily boastful; bragging without being able to do what you are bragging about. (ii) [Esp of young people] Saucy; ready with a rude answer.

full[2]; **full up**[1] *vb* (*phr*) (CarA) [*X*] 1. To fill; to fill in, out, or up. a. *'But I couldn't sip drinks like a social drinker would. I had to full my glass with the alcohol beverage, and very seldom I would want the chaser. I had to feel my drink.'*—AdV (89.02.24, p.7) b. *Parmassar spoke to me and* *asked me if it was deep enough, and I told him you can see where the soil change; to go a little bit deeper before fulling up and just as you go down—on some steps going deeper, to clear out the loose dirt.*—AMGM:34 **c.** *'Big City' always confuse when he have forms to full up, and in the old Brit'n it have bags of that to do.*—STLL:79 [Prob survival in CE of EE usage. Cp *OED full* v² (*Obs*) 'to make full, to become full' + cits–1647; but also present AmE *W3 full*⁴ vb intr (of the moon) 'to become full' + vb tr (of sewing) 'to make full'. Cp also present ScE, *CSD full* vb tr 'to fill, load'] □ Notwithstanding present limited AmE and ScE usage the vbl function is not regularized in present educated IAE. **2.** PHRASE **2.1 full your eye** *vb phr* (CarA) [X] See EYE¹ 19. *If that pine full you[r] eye yo[u] can tak[e] it for a dollar.*—(Guyn)

full³ *adv* (Guyn, StVn) [X] Fully; completely; [of a look] squarely in the face. **a.** *Our houseboy came down the valley, a dead rat dangling from one hand. 'I meet it half dead, mistress, so I full dead it,' he explained gravely as he held it out to me.*—SCYT:117 **b.** *As I notice he wouldn['t] watch me full I know something wrong.*—(Guyn) [Cp *OED full* C. adv 2. 'completely, entirely, fully' + cits–early 19C]

Ful·la (-man/-peo·ple) *n* (*phr*) (Guyn) Muslim(s). □ The term is more often used derogatively. [Perh surviving from *Fula[ni]*, the W Afr ethnic group who were mostly Muslims]

full butt [fʊl bʊt] *adv phr* (Guyn) [AF] [Of sb on the move] (Rushing) without hesitation or a second thought; (coming at you) head-on. [Ref to a bull charging with its head down]

full-mouth(ed) *adv* (Angu, Guyn, USVI) **1.** [Of a child addressing a grown-up] Disrespectfully (i.e. using the person's first name, or without adding 'Mr', 'Mrs', or 'Miss'). **2.** PHRASE **2.1 call sb full-mouth** *vb phr* (Guyn) See CALL¹ Phr 3.6

full time *adv phr* (CarA) [IF] (SE) High time; so late as to be immediately necessary. *It is full time Government stop watching crime and violence and do something positive to eradicate this cancer from within our society.*—JdN (76.06.20, p.7)

full-up² *adj* **1.** (Antg, Mrat) [AF—Vul] [Of an unmarried woman] Pregnant. **2.** PHRASE **2.1 full-up (with sth)** (CarA) [X] Full (of sth). *She take up four sheets o' paper, the fountain-pen full-up with ink, and she sit down, meantime the headache pounding like hell.*—CWFYS:44

fum-fum /1'2/ *n* (Belz) [AF] A thorough beating (esp of a man by a woman).

fun¹ *n* PHRASES **1. Ain't/don't/not make fun to (do sth)** *vb phr* (Gren, Guyn) [AF] To do (some significant act) thoroughly. **a.** *And I didn't make fun to step give dem too you know. Watch nuh! I take me time, dear.*—RTCS:18 **b.** *He*

don'[t] make fun to beat [h]is wife skin.—(Guyn) **2. Carry/make/take your fun (to sb or some place)** (CarA) [IF] To show, display precocious or inappropriate behaviour (with sb or in some place). **3. Fun can't done!** *id phr* (CarA) [AF] There is/was/will be endless fun!

fun² *vb intr* (CarA) [IF] To have fun; to enjoy yourself (esp in public, playing pranks, etc). *The colourful day cannot easily be forgotten by anyone as he spectates or participates marching shouting, dancing, 'funning', and just doing almost anything.*—Bet.1, p.9 □ Still so used in AmE. See WCD.

fun (-and) -take *n* (Baha, Tbgo, Trin) A game of marbles with some variations (either taking or giving back all the opponent's marbles).

fun·gee (foon·gee, fun·gi, fun·ji) [fʊnji] *n* **1.** (Angu, Antg, Brbu, Jmca, Nevs, StKt, ViIs) ‖ COU-COU (Bdos, etc) **2.** (StVn) A spicy variety of COU-COU prepared with arrowroot starch, hence jelly-like and semi-transparent. **3.** ‖ FOO-FOO¹. 2 (Antg, Tbgo) [Cp *DAFL* Twi *fugyee* (adj) soft, mealy (of boiled yam). Cp also *TAGD:89* Kimbundu *funzi* 'cassava mush'; also *CBCD* Congo *fundi* 'flour, porridge'; also *ADMY* Yoruba *funjẹ* '(sth) given to eat', wh may have influenced the *CarA* pronunc] □ The spelling *fungi*, commonly occurring, is undesirable since it suggests a pronunc /g/ as in the pl of SE *fungus*. Other spellings are *foongie, fungy,* etc but the most suitable is *funji*, and the commonest *fungee*.

funk¹ *n* (CarA) [AF] ‖ *funky¹* (USVI) **1.** Both the matter and the bad smell of the secretion under the foreskin of a male penis or an unwashed female vulva (also said to be related to the stimulation of sexual intimacy); smegma. [Prob related to FM wh is prob < Gã *fũ* 'bad smell, stink; scent'] □ The word is almost unused in this sense in present CE, being remembered only by some older men; but it helps to explain later sense developments. **2.** ‖ *funky¹* (CarA) [By extension] Sexually stimulating dancing or the music related to that. *Our repertoire now includes a cross section of today's music and ranged from funk to soul to folk, to calypso, much of which is our own original material.*—ADN (73.04.20, p.6) □ This sense was developed in Black AmE but readily adopted in the *CarA*.

funk² *vb* (Antg) **1.** *vb tr* To prepare a fruit (esp a mango) for eating by squeezing it all over. **2.** (Nevs) *vb intr* To stop growing or developing (esp of fruit); to be put off in some unexplained way. [Perh vaguely related to FUNK¹]

funk·y¹ (funk·i) *n* (USVI) **1.** ‖ FUNK¹ 1. (CarA) **2.** (CarA) ‖ FUNK¹ 2. (CarA) *Spouge is to my ears a mixture of Reggae, Calypso and Funky, delivered at a hard driving pace which not even the most bruckdown could resist. It did sweet.*—WeG (75.05.20, p.15, Partyline)

funk·y² *adj* (CarA) **1.** Smelly (esp of the human body); [by extension] sexually attractive. *'Swamp dogs and funky women' are invited to Tyson's jungle pad, 19 Don Miguel Road, San Juan, tomorrow night. Music by the Fantabulous Herbie Mann.*—ExP (72.02.04, p.7) **2.** [Of young people's dancing and music for that dancing] Erotic; passionate; exciting. ... *Since then the groove at the 'Whiskers' has been very funky with sound-off by people like the Sandpebbles and the Troubadours.*—AdN (72.07.08, p.6, Al's Grapevine) □ **1.** Also note *funkier, funkiest*. **2.** The AmE synonymous term *groovy* returns euphemistically to the idea of the female pudenda (see FUNK¹ 1). Note cit at 2.

fups [fŭps] *ideoph* (CarA) [*AF*] **1.** [An ECHOIC WORD denoting some swift, sudden, or speedy action]. **2.** *vb intr* [By extension] To do sth quickly, suddenly (hence many ready-made vb phrs: *fups by/in/off/out/past*, etc. To move swiftly by, in etc. □ This is a spoken form for wh no written cits have been found.

fur·ni·tures *n pl* (CarA) [*X*] Furniture; furnishings. *For sale / Living Room Furnitures, Freezer and Stove. Reasonable offer accepted.*—BeT (Ad, 79.09.05, p.6) □ A commonly found form, prob infl by IAE (pl) *furnishings*. See PLURAL FORMS 1.

fus(s)¹ [fʌs] *adv* (Tbgo, Trin) [*AF*] ‖AFòS (Tbgo, Trin) *Explainer is making such a stirring plea for Caribbean unity and solidarity ('fuss ah does vex to hear a Trinidadian bad-talking a Jamaican').*—ExP (77.02.11, p.17) □ See also FIRST. This term always comes first in a clause or sentence to intensify what follows.

fuss² *n* (Jmca) A big noisy quarrel or fight. **a.** *During the period they had their child and they had several fusses over the care of the child, as his wife seldomly fed the child.*—StA(JA) (71.07.3, p.5) *The police state that Mr Lee was stabbed in his left breast with a ratchet knife during a fuss with a woman.*—WeG (75.04.03, p.27) [Intensified sense of IAE *fuss*]

fuss³ **(with sb)** *vb phr* (Jmca) To quarrel violently or fight (with sb). *Norma C— told Mr Justice Wilkie (acting) in the Divorce Court yesterday, that her husband fussed with her and beat her on several occasions. Once, when she was four months pregnant, he again fussed with her and beat her all over her body and on the head with a piece of car tyre.*—StA(JA) (70.07.11, p.5)

fwé·di (fre·di, fré·di) ['fwedi] *n* (Dmca, StLu) **1.** ‖COLD² 3. (CarA) *While warm from exertion one must never drink water, particularly cold water. This 'apwidas' (imprudence) results in 'fwédi' (cold) which describes anything from a head cold to syphilis.*—CaQ IV.2, p.114 [Fr Cr < Fr (?) *froidure* 'coldness', or perh dial survival of *froidi*, pa. part. of *froidir*, 'to become cold', though this Old Fr vb is last recorded (*DELF*) in 12C] **2.** PHRASE **2.1** **ġet fwédi** *vb phr* (Dmca, StLu) ‖CATCH A COLD (CarA) See COLD² phr 4.1

G

g [ji·] *PHRASE* **get/got the 'g'** *vb phr* (Guyn)
[*AF—Joc*] To understand and manage (to do
sth); to acquire the know-how; to get the hang
(of sth) *It goin[g] take yo[u] some time before yo[u]
get the 'g' to work dis machine*—Guyn [Perh from
initial letter of *get, got*]

ga[1] *vb* (CarA) [*AF—Cr*] See GAT

ga[2] *aux vb* (Baha) [*AF—Cr*] Going to. *In fact
he was so interesting that he was trying to get all
the young people in the neighbourhood to go with
him but they tell him that them people wasn't ga tell
them nothing what they didn't know before.*—NaG
(75.03.06, p.2) [< Cr GO in its aux function as
a future modal, + opening of vowel /o > a/.
See GO 2(ii)] □ Commonly found in *Baha* Cr
narrative dialogue.

ga·bi·on(-bas·ket) [ge·biɒn-] *n* (Bdos, Guyn)
‖ **breaker** (TkCa) A cage (about 2-1/2 ft x 1-1/
2 ft x 1-1/2 ft) made of tarred wire mesh, packed
tight with rocks, and stacked closely one against
the next to defend soft seaside land against erosion. [< Italian *gabbione*. See *COD, WCD*, etc]
□ BrE and AmE *gabion* may be earth-filled and
is associated with [Hist] fortifications or foundation works.

ga·da·ha (gad·da·ha) *n* (Guyn, Trin) [*AF—
Derog*] [Indic] A fool; an idiot; a jackass. *Then
there was the scene in the principal's office: ... the
English principal patient, then firm, and finally
exasperated; the old man enraged, muttering,
'Gaddaha! Gaddaha!'*—NTMM:16 [Bhoj < Hin
gadha 'donkey'. Cp *DJE godahaw* 'donkey' wh
is prob a phonic shift of the same Indic loan]
□ A common term of abuse among or by East
Indians, the more offensive feminine **gadahee/-
hi** being less often used, applied to women.

gaff[1] [gya·f] *vb intr* (Guyn) [*AF—Joc*] ‖ OLD-
TALK[2] (Tbgo, Trin) *Members complained that
they were not being attended to by public servants
who were always reading newspapers or 'gaffing'
at their offices.*—GyC (76.08.13, p.17) [< CSD
So Sc *gaff vb* 2. 'babble, chatter']

gaff[2] [gya·f] *n* (Guyn) [*AF—Joc*] ‖ OLD-TALK[1]
(Tbgo, Trin) *Minister of Sport, Cde. Shirley
Field-Ridley was host to the members of the basketball team from the People's Republic of China
yesterday at a luncheon at the Umana Yana. In
this picture the Chinese and local players are caught*

in a 'gaff' just before eats.—GyG (75.11.25, p.22)
[By functional *vb > n* shift of GAFF[1]]

Gair·y·ite [geriaɪt] *n* (Gren) [*Derog*] An open
supporter of the much disputed political policies
of (Sir) Eric Gairy, who was Chief, then Prime
Minister of Grenada from 1967 to 1979. □ The
term *Gairyism* [*Derog*], referring to such policies also occurs esp in newspapers.

gajé [gaže] *n* (StLu) 1. A person who is believed
to have used witchcraft or made a pact with
the devil in order to increase his wealth and
well-being. 2. ‖ LOUGAWOU (Dmca, etc) 1. [Fr
Cr < Fr *gager* 'to lay a bet; to hire (servant)';
or by aphaeresis < *engager* 'to pledge, commit
(yourself); to engage (sb) in your service', the
ref in Fr Cr always involving the devil]

ga·la·ba *n* (StVn) ‖ GALBA (Dmca, etc)

ga·la·vant ['g(y)alavant] *vb intr* (CarA) [*Derog*]
SE gallivant. □ The spelling *galavant* is also
found in AmE, but the word, with this spelling
and pronunc, is widely used in CE.

ga·lay[1] *adj* (Gren) See GALÉ

ga·lay[2] *vb intr* (Trin) [*AF—Joc*] To hesitate; to
dilly-dally; to speak or act indecisively. *It has
been the oldest trick in the political book—galaying
and galaying and galaying, refusing resolutely to
break the pack for fear that the people would finally
perceive the Benevolent Dictatorship that the Government was holding in its hand.*—TaP (76.03.28,
p.8) [< Fr Cr *galeux* 'itchy, having the scabies',
hence prob shifting in sense to 'continually
scratching your head']

gal·ba* *n* (Dmca, Gren, StVn) ‖ *galaba* (StVn)
A tall shade tree used as a wind-break, bearing
inedible fruit but yielding a very tough timber
that is used to make wheels and boats; *Calophyllum antillanum (Guttiferae).*

gal·deen *n* (Gren, Grns) See GAULIN

ga·lé (ga·lay) [gale] *adj* (Gren) [*AF—Derog*]
Having a skin full of sores, scabs, eczema, etc.
[Fr Cr < Fr *galeux* 'mangy, scurfy']

gal·ler·y[1] [galəri ~ gyalʌri] *n* 1. (StKt, USVI)
An open railed veranda, usu with a roof supported on a few slender pillars, added to the

front of a modest dwelling. **2.** (Bdos, Guyn, Trin) An addition to the ground floor of the main body of a house, in front, or on all four sides, with many windows, jalousies and louvres, as an area for entertaining visitors. **3.** (USVI) A covered sidewalk for public use. [Evid tropical adaptations of EE senses of *gallery* (cp *OED gallery* 1, 2, 5.), but the architectural meanings in the *CarA* are not properly met by any ModE sense of the word] □ Re 2., a first-floor gallery on all four sides, typical of large two-storeyed houses, is called a *fore-and-aft* or *four-and-a-half gallery*.

gal·ler·y² *vb intr* (Gren, Trin) To show off; to make an attractive display of yourself. *Who in this world can pose and gallery and make more style than a Trinidad woman.*—BoM (80.03.14, p.13) [By functional n > vb shift of GALLERY¹ 2.]

gal·lon-pan/-tin *n* (Tbgo, Trin) A small (one-gallon) or large (four-gallon) rectangular metal can turned to household use.

gal·van·ize¹ (**gal·van·ise**) *n* (CarA) ‖ *zinc(-sheet)* (Guyn) A corrugated metal sheet (or a set of these) coated with zinc against corrosion and used as roofing or fencing material. *Sheets of galvanise went up around the Roodals Drive-in Cinema yesterday as the management moved to meet the stipulations drawn up for the public showing of the controversial film 'The Exorcist' by the Cinematograph Film Censorship Board.*—AdV (75.02.25, p.1) [< *galvanized iron*, in ref to the 'galvanizing' process of electro-chemical coating with zinc. Cp *OED galvanized* ppl. a. 2. 'coated with metal by galvanism. Also incorrectly *galvanized iron* the trade name of iron coated with zinc']

gal·van·ize² (**gal·van·ise**) *adj* (CarA) [X] [Of piping, a bucket or other container] Made of galvanized metal; galvanized. *You had was to buy one of them big galvanise basin and boil the water and full it up, or else go to the public bath.*—STLL: 57

ga·ma·la·me/-mi *n* (Baha, TkCa) See GUM-ELEMI

game *n* PHRASE **the game come** *id phr* (Guyn) [AF] See COME Phr 7.12

gang [gaŋ~gyaŋ] *n* (CarA) [Hist, Sugar Ind] See cit. *The labourers on each plantation were divided up into three 'gangs'. Those who were skilled and well trained, both male and female, formed the first class gang and those who had a certain amount of skill but were not yet fully trained were referred to as the second class gang. The children from about 8 to 14 years formed the third class gang, and each gang had an individual over them who was referred to as the 'driver'.*—AdM (79.06.17, p.15, E. Stoute) [Adapted < 17C E, as *OED gang* sb¹ 9. 'a company of workmen; (b) a company of slaves or prisoners'] □ In some

islands other qualifying names were used for the three categories. Exs: For the first *big gang* (Antg) ‖ *first gang* (Bdos) ‖ *great gang* (Dmca); for the second *small gang* (Antg) ‖ *second gang* (Bdos); for the children *creole gang* (Guyn) ‖ *third gang* (Bdos) ‖ *weeding gang* Jmca.

gang-gang [gaŋgaŋ] *n* (Guyn, Jmca, StVn, Tbgo, Trin) [AF/IF] (Familiar form of addressing) an old woman; granny. [Cp *GDEL* Efik *Ñ-kam* 1. 'grandmother' 2. 'a common title by wh any old woman is addressed'; also *KID* Ibibio *ŋkam* 'my grandmother', perh reduplicated for affectionate address with resulting voicing and assimilation < *ŋkamŋkaŋ*]

gan·sey (**garn·sey**, **gan·zi(e)**) ['ga·nzi] *n* (Bdos, Jmca) ‖ *guernsey* (Belz) A jersey or T-shirt, esp a coloured one; a pullover. [*OED Guernsey* 2. a. 'a thick, knitted, closely-fitting vest or shirt, generally made of blue wool, worn by seamen'. Guernsey and Jersey are Br Channel Islands from wh the names are derived] □ Term more likely to be used by older or rural folk.

gap [gap~gyap] *n* **1.** (ECar) The short breach in the kerb or roadside providing entrance to a property; a short path leading to a house. *Don't park in my gap—you will block my entrance.*—(Tbgo) **2.** (Bdos) A narrow roadway leading off a main road, and usu a cul-de-sac. *The people living there are forced to bring their garbage to a point where it will be collected by the trucks. In most cases, it is brought to the top of the gap or road at the point where it adjoins the main highway.*—AdN (74.08.26, p.4) □ Cp CORNER 2. (Baha)

gap·i·a-mouth *n* (USVI) [Derog] ‖ WHITE-CORNER (Guyn) [Ref to a mouth that 'gapes', stays open'. Pronunc perh via Vils Du Cr < Du *gapen* [gapə] one meaning of wh is 'to yawn from hunger', poss in ref to malnourishedd slaves. Cp also *OED gape* sb 3 *The gapes* + variant *gaps*, 'a disease in poultry causing opening of the mouth'. Also *DARE gape* B. 2 ex 1899 *Gearpy* [gyaapee] 'inclined to [yawn]'. Cp also WAPIA]

gar·bage-pan *n* (StVn) ‖ STUFF-BIN (Bdos)

gar·bar ['gaba·r] *n* **1.** (Guyn, Trin) [AF] Nonsense; foolish confusion; trouble (esp in foll phrs). [Bhoj < Hin *garbar* 'confusion, disorder, chaos'] **2.** PHRASES **2.1 make garbar** *vb phr* (Guyn, Trin) [AF] To cause trouble. *'Put the boy down!' Doorne insisted, blocking Tengar's path. 'Move out the way, old man, and stop making gar-bar,' Tengar said, still good-natured.*—GI:159 (Jan Carew) **2.2 play garbar** *vb phr* (Guyn, Trin) [AF] To play the fool; to be irritatingly troublesome.

gar·den-bal·sam* *n* (Bdos, Jmca, Trin, USVI) ‖ *carpenter-grass* (Trin) ‖ *fresh-cut* (Jmca) ‖ *toyo* (Guyn) A flowering herb of different varieties, about 2 ft high, often specially grown (hence name) for its pleasant-smelling leaves wh are used for a BUSH-TEA; *Justicia pectoralis* (*Acanthaceae*). *Although called 'garden balsam' it is not related to the true Balsams* (*Impatiens*).—PTT:199 □ In *Jmca* the name seems to apply both to this bush (also called FRESH-CUT) and to an actual balsam (*Impatiens balsamina*)—*AFPJ:378, cp p.691.*

gar·den-cher·ry *n* (CayI, Jmca) ‖ BARBADOS CHERRY (CarA)

gar·den-egg *n* (CayI, Gren, Jmca, TkCa) ‖ EGGPLANT (CarA) ... *but women are the traders, selling yams and sweet potatoes, calalu and escallion, thyme and peppers, okra and aubergines or garden-eggs as Jamaicans call them, pumpkins and a smaller kind of squash known as chocho.*—SJW:33

gar·den-grapes *n pl* (Nevs, StKt) European green or purple grapes locally grown on garden arbours.

gar·den-ma·roon *n* (Crcu) ‖ LEND-HAND (Tbgo) [< (preparing ground for a market-) garden + MAROON¹ 2.]

gar·den-peas *n pl* (Trin) A small variety of green peas borne abundantly in short pods on a flowering climber, and much valued as food, esp in making DAAL; *Pisum sativum* (*Leguminosae-Papilionaceae*).

gar·den-plum *n* (Guyn) ‖ CHILLI-PLUM (Antg, etc) [Prob distinguishing this plum as cultivated and rarer in *Guyn* than the common HOG-PLUM wh grows wild]

gar·den-pump·kin *n* (Bdos) A long but smallish pumpkin with a bulging end, having few seeds and a finer texture, when cooked, than the larger round BELLY-PUMPKIN.

Ga·ri·fu·na [garifuna] ɪ′211 *n* (Belz) ‖ *Carib* 3. (Belz) 1. A dark-skinned race of people permanently settled in southern Belize and now centrally based in the township of Dangriga, the descendants of a warlike mixed race of escaped Africans and Caribs in St Vincent who were forcibly transported to Ruatan Island off the Honduran coast in 1797; (formerly called) Black Caribs (a name now rejected) or (less often) Caribs. 2. The Africanized Island-Carib language spoken by these people. [Note: On the following days, or in November 1493, Columbus and his crew made contact with some of the inhabitants—the second group of 'American Indians' to become known to history. Those encountered on the first voyage, the Taino of Haiti, had already told Columbus about these warring 'Cariphúna' (from which our words Carib and cannibal have been derived) who by advancing through the Lesser Antilles had at the time occupied the most easterly part of their island.— *TADH:1* (*D. Taylor*)] □ The pl form in their lang is *Garinagu*, and this may have contributed to

other confused spellings wh are found in print: *Kalinaku, Careepfouna, Calleenago*, etc.

Ga·ri·fu·na Set·tle·ment Day *n phr* (Belz) ‖ *Carib Settlement Day* (Belz) November 19, observed as a national holiday in *Belz* to commemorate the agreement in 1823 made between the Br administration and the GARIFUNA (called 'Caribs' at that time) permitting them permanent settlement with property in the area around Stann Creek.

gar·lic-pork *n* (Guyn, Trin) Cubed pork marinated in vinegar, garlic and herbs, boiled in the marinade until dry, then fried in its own fat; it is traditional Christmas fare originating with the Portuguese in the population.

garn·s(e)y* *n* (Bdos) See GANSEY

gar(r)* (**gar-fish**) [ga·(r)~gya] *n* (CarA) 1. ‖ *zòfi* (Dmca, StLu) Any of several varieties of the needle-fish family, generally small, slim-bodied, with typically long, spear-like jaws, some varieties being seasonally plentiful and edible; they are bony, the bones being distinctively blue-green; *Strongylura spp.* 2. Any of a few varieties of the bill-fish family, large and tough-skinned, with an elongated body and long, spear-like jaws, but of poor food value; *Lepisosteus spp.* [Survival of EE *gare* < OE *gar* 'a spear, javelin'. See *OED* *garfish*]

gar·rot *n* [*AF—Derog*] 1. (ViIs) A West Indian who is not a native of the *ViIs*; an outsider; a non-belonger. 2. (StKt) An Antiguan. *Yet we must learn as a Federation to look upon a 'Garrot' or a 'Bajan', to say nothing of a Nevisian, as if they belonged to St Kitts, just as Kittitians would belong to Dominica or Grenada.*—DeM(SK) (62.08.11, p.1)

ga(t) *vb* (CarA) [*AF—Cr*] 1. To have; to possess. *Dey only gat money but dey ain[t] gat no culture.*—(Guyn) 2. modal aux **ga[t] to/fo (do sth)** ‖ *ha fu (do sth)* (CarA) Has/have to must (do sth) *All he study is how she pretty / An' he mus' married—Even if he gat to tief de money.*— LMFF:20 [< SE *got*, pa.t. of *get*, used as CarA Cr base vb. Cp *brok[e], left[t], los[t]*] □ This spoken form is written only in Cr narrative dialogue. See GOT

gat·ka *n* (Trin) [Indic] A form of traditional East Indian stick-fighting esp displayed during the Muslim HOSEIN festival. ... *Gurudeva beamed. First he would see to getting his sticks mounted, then he would see about practising the gatka.*—NAGOS:38 [< Hin *gadka, gatka* 'a cudgel, a blunt wooden sword']

gau·lin (**gal·deen, ga·lin, gar·ling, gaul-(d)in(g)**) [gɒːlɪn~gɒ·ldɪŋ] *n* (CarA) ‖ *crabier* (Crcu, Dmca) (Name loosely applied to) any of a number of varieties of coastal swamp birds, often also found in open country, that may be types of egrets, herons, or cranes, usu with long beaks and slender necks, slim bodies and notably long, thin legs; they sometimes stand on one leg as they hunt for aquatic life or field insects. They range in colour from white through blue-green to dark brown, and in varieties from 12 to 30 ins tall. [Evid orig a Sc name for a kind of water-bird. See *OED gawlin* (1703). *OED* also lists *gaulin* (1705) for *Jmca* only. However *BBWI* (pp.30-38) describes seven varieties of *gaulin* ranging throughout the W. Indies and into tropical America. The name may have been spread by Sc sailors and settlers] □ The variant spellings are prob due to overcorrection.

ga·yap (ga·i·appe) [gayap] *n* (Trin) ‖ LEND-HAND (Tbgo) *Residents of Tabaquite will hold a 'gayap' on Sunday from 7 a.m to clear six acres of land, first phase in a bid to build a school in the area.*—TrG (74.09.13, p.9) [< *TDV* Venz Sp *cayapa* 'group of persons who, together, carry out a task without payment' (trans). The word, wh appears to be from a coastal So Am Amerindian lang, appears in *Trin* Fr Cr, with voiced initial consonant /k > g/ as *gaiappe*. See KAYAP. Cp also *ADHL* Hausa *gayya* 'communal work' (farming, etc), though the Venz Sp seems a more likely source]

ga·yelle (ga·yal) [gayɛl ~ gayal] *n* (Trin) **1.** An arena for cock-fighting. **2.** A ring or square for stick-fighting. [Fr Cr < Am Sp *gallera* 'coop for game-cocks', *galleria* 'pit for cockfighting' with /r > l/ shift of the third consonant] □ It seems that at one time *gayal* was reserved for sense 2., but currently *gayelle* has displaced it, covering both senses.

ga·zette-pa·per *n* (Trin) Old newspaper (used for wrapping, spreading on the ground, etc). *... cheap shoddy toilet paper that is just impossible to use. And as the quality goes down ... if it goes any lower, we shall all have to resort to gazette paper.*—BoM (79.09.07, p.9) [Ref to the first newspaper printed in *Trin* and called the 'Trinidad Gazette']

G.C.M. *abbr* (Bdos) Gold Crown of Merit of the Order of Barbados, a national honour awarded for highly meritorious service or achievement in science, the arts, literature, sport, civic duties or other endeavour worthy of national recognition; the letters are placed after the recipient's name.

G.C.S.L. *abbr* (StLu) Grand Cross of the Order of St Lucia; it is the highest rank of the Order, and is awarded only to a person appointed as Governor-General of St Lucia, empowering that person to use the title 'His/Her Excellency' for life.

gear (down/up) for *vb phr* (Bdos, Guyn, Trin) [*AF/IF*] To prepare for; to make yourself ready for (sth), by dressing up, taking a position, etc. **a.** *Queen's College gearing for big day of sports.*—GyC (76.11.10, p.15 (H)) **b.** *Long before the argument began he done gear up for a row.*—

(Trin) [A prob EE survival. Cp *OED gear* v 1. (*Obs*) 'to adorn, array, dress' (+ cits up to 1833) 3. + *up* 'to harness (a draught animal)'. See next] □ The phr *gear down* 'dress elaborately' is listed in *CGBD* for *Bdos*.

gears *n pl* (Guyn) [*AF/IF*] Fine clothing. *... not much is made from stealing but what is made is spent as fast as possible on drinks, women and 'gears'.*—GyC (77.02.13, p.12) [Cp prec and *OED gear* sb 1. (*Obs* as pl) 'apparel, attire, dress, vestments' + cit (1792) 'Dressed in holiday geers']

gee·ra [jira] *n* (Guyn, Trin) [Indic] Cumin seed, a small greyish grain wh is ground as an ingredient of curry powder or for seasoning DAAL. [Bhoj < Hin *jiiraa* 'cumin seed']

Gem of the Antil·les *n phr* (CarA) (A popular touristic name for) St Vincent.

Gen·er·al No·tice *n phr* (Jmca) ‖ SEPARATION NOTICE (Gren, StKt)

gen·er·a·tion-pro·per·ty *n* (Baha) ‖ FAMILY-LAND (Bdos, etc)

ge·nip *n* (CarA) See GUINEP

gen·tle·man *n* PHRASE **My gentleman!** *n phr* (Bdos) [Respectful form of address to a man] Sir! □ Commonly used by older folk.

gen·tle·man's *n phr* (Baha, Jmca) (Euphemism for) any form of venereal disease.

George PHRASE **call it/that George** *id phr* (Guyn, StLu, Tbgo, Trin) See CALL[1] Phr 3.4 *If up to now you can['t] fin[d] it, better call it George and come le[t] we go [a]long!*—(Bdos)

George·town Ac·cord, The *n phr* (CarA) The agreement signed in Georgetown *Guyn* at the conclusion of the Eighth Conference of Commonwealth Caribbean Heads of Government in April, 1973, by wh the Caribbean Community or CARICOM was established.

geor·gie-bun·dle (**geor·gy-bun·dle**) *n* (CarA) [*AF—Joc/Derog*] **1.** A small bundle of all your scanty possessions packed up for you to be off with. *But if he thought he was just going to walk out like that he had another thing coming. For just as he was about to step out the door with his georgy bundle the girl and her family grabbed him and pitched endless blows in his tail.*—NaT (76.07.18, p.7) **2.** [By extension] A collection of odds and ends belonging to sb.

gep *n* (Trin, StKt) See DJÈP

ger [gʌ] *vb* (Baha) [*AF—Cr*] (A spelling commonly used in Baha dial writing for) GO 2 (ii). *I ger give yer a good lickin', hear?*—JBJ:80

gé·ri·tou (ge·ri·tou, **guér·ir-tout**, **guér·it-tout**) ['geritu] *n* **1.** (Trin) ‖ CATTLE-TONGUE (Antg, etc) **2.** (Gren) ‖ LEAF-OF-LIFE (Bdos, etc) **3.** (USVI) ‖ JACK-IN-THE-BUSH (Jmca) **[Fr Cr < Fr *guérit tout* 'cures everything'. Cp ‖ *cure-for-all* (Bdos, Guyn), for sense 1. and other ‖ indicating its wide folk-medicinal use]**

get *vb* [Note: The forms GA(T), GOT are treated as separate entries] **A.** As vb tr/intr **1.** (CarA) [*IF/AF*] To have; to own; to possess; to acquire specially. **a.** *Before they look to get a lil house they lookin[g] to get motor-car.*—(Bdos) **b.** *'De lady dere sellin' her punkin an' ting on de dock an' one white woman come 'long in er car an' aks 'er ef she get any lime an' lemon or tomater'.*—JBJ: 80 **c.** *These children ain[t] get no manners at all.*—(Guyn) **2.** (CarA) [*AF—Cr*] *giving passive sense to a* foll vb *in its base form, as in* **get beat, get bite, get call, get ketch, get kill,** *etc* To be/have been beaten, bitten, called, caught, killed, etc. *He used threats about killing me. He'd better think twice. I didn't know I was going to get beat up when I took him on or he would have ended up in the mortuary-*NaT (Mag 90.04.27, p.15) □ Such phrs occur commonly in narrative dialogue. **B.** In various idiomatic phrases, sometimes bordering on or combining the above senses. **3.** PHRASES **3.1 get a child (for sb)** *vb phr* (CarA) [*IF*] ‖ **get baby (for sb), make baby/a child (for sb)** (CarA) [Usu of an unmarried mother] To have/bear a child (by sb). Cp Phr 3.7. **3.2 get and talk** *vb phr* (Bdos, Guyn) [*IF—Derog*] To chat irresponsibly; to gossip. *It is no use getting and talking about 'we represent the people' because the very people that belong to the Union are the very people who live in St Lucy, St Joseph and Bridgetown, and when disease starts and the tourist industry has come to nought, all of us are going to suffer*—Union members and all.—Bdos (Hd, 73.10.23, p.2694) **3.3 get a phone-message** *vb phr* (Bdos) [*IF*] To make a call on sb else's telephone. (See PHONE-MESSAGE Phr 2.1). **3.4 get a pick/a play** *vb phr* (CarA) [*AF/IF*] To be chosen, selected to play (usu in a game of cricket). **3.5 get a time with (a woman)** *vb phr* (Guyn, Trin) [*AF—Vul*] To seduce (a woman); to have casual sexual intercourse with (a woman). **3.6 get away** *vb phr* (Bdos, Tbgo, Trin) [*AF*] ‖ FETCH AWAY (Guyn, StVn) *Don't tie your sheep on my land or me and you going to get away.*—(Tbgo) **3.7 get baby** *vb phr* (CarA) [*AF—Cr*] To give birth; to bear a child. □ This phr is neutral (i.e without the connotation of 3.1 unless followed by *for (sb)*). **3.8 get back (subjects from an examination)** *vb phr* (Bdos) To gain passes in (the subjects named). *She had got back ... ten subjects at O Level at one sitting.*—NaT (89.09.01, p.8) **3.9 get behind (sb) (to do sth)** *vb phr* (CarA) [*IF*] ‖ BE BEHIND (SB) (TO DO STH) (CarA) See BEHIND[1] Phr 1. □ See also KEEP Phr 3.2. **3.10 get beside yourself** *vb phr* (CarA) See BESIDE Phr 2.1 **3.11 get big** *vb phr* (CarA) [*IF*] [Of a child] To grow up into your teens; to reach the age of responsibility. *'Beta,' his father said, 'you getting big, you looking strong.'*—HFGA:149 (S. Selvon)

□ Also GET A BIG MAN/WOMAN [*AF*] 'to become an adult'. **3.12 get down** [gɛt dʌn] *vb phr* (CarA) [*AF*] [Of dancing] To dance individually and animatedly in a crouching or semi-crouching position. *We find that the tourists come to have a good time, the older folks come to listen and the young people come to get down.*—TrI (76.01.03, p.5) **3.12.1 getting down** *vb phr* Bdos, Guyn [*IF*] [Of an old person] Becoming decrepit; needing to be cared for. *Mother is getting down now, you know, so we have to leave somebody in the house with her*—(Guyn) □ Usu restricted to the *-ing* form **3.13 get fast with (sb)** *vb phr* (CarA) [*IF*] See FAST Phr 5.1 **3.14 get horrors** *vb phr* (ECar) [*AF*] See HORRORS Phr 2.1 **3.15 get ignorant** *vb phr* (CarA) [*AF*] To become angry and behave or speak very roughly. *... for God know I am not a liard, an' I wouldn't like anybody to call me one, for I might get ignorant, and be rude to dem.*—DJC:53 **3.15.1 get sb ignorant** *vb phr* (CarA) [*AF*] To enrage sb; to cause sb to behave in a rough and embarrassing manner. **3.16 get in the ropes with (sb)** *vb phr* (Antg, Bdos) [*AF*] To start a noisy quarrel with (sb). [Prob a metaph from boxing] **3.17 get in with (sb)** *vb phr* (CarA) [*IF*] **(i)** To form an intimate (and often sexual) friendship with (sb). **(ii)** To be in collusion with (sb); to join with (sb) to do sth that must not be exposed. **3.18 get on** *vb phr* (CarA) [*AF*] ‖ **behave bad** (CarA) ‖ **go on** (CarA) To quarrel loudly and without restraint so as to embarrass or frighten sb. **a.** *Child, don't be so vulgar, that is not the way to get on when walking on the streets!*—DoH (65.06.19, p.9) **b.** *If the 'hog' wants a staff-member, he sits at his desk and growls your name. I wouldn't tell you about when he drinks two rums how he gets on.*—NaT (76.08.22, p.26, Dear Christine) □ Also **get on bad/common/funny/ignorant**, etc, with the predicative complements emphasizing or qualifying the same sense. **3.19 get sense** *vb phr* (CarA) [*IF*] **(i)** [Of a child] To become aware of the world; to grow into maturity. □ Often in the Phr **grow and get sense. (ii)** [Of an adult] To discover you have been fooled; to become wiser to the truth. *This is a different time now. The people get sense and you can't tell them the Treasury dry and that kind o[f] rubbish.*—(Bdos) **3.20 get small** *vb phr* (Tbgo, Trin) [*IF*] To lose weight; to grow slim or look thin. **3.21 get the rid of (sth)** *vb phr* (Bdos) [*X*] To get rid of (sth). *I had this pain in my knee so long and all I do I can't get the rid of it.*—(Bdos) **3.22 get the spirit** *vb phr* (CarA) To be so seized with religious emotion that the eyes close or become glazed, while the body shakes, pitches, or dances as the person sings or speaks 'in strange tongues'. *A typical prayer meeting would last from 6 p.m to 6 a.m. Those attending would sing 'Sankeys', give testimony, and 'get the spirit'.*—HVVIS:108 **3.23 get up and get** *vb phr* (Bdos, Guyn) [*IF*] To stop idling and make a move forward; to make a prompt and resolute effort in your own interest. *It is for this reason that for the Nth time in this House, I call on Government to get up and get, and do something positive in this sphere of our laws.*—Bdos (Hd, 75.05.20, p.5083) **3.24 get**

vex(ed) *vb phr* (CarA) [*AF/IF*] To become angry; to be vexed (by sth). **a.** *So I get vex and tell them a few words, and they get vex and tell me some too, and then I get vexer and had to put my hand 'pon them.*—CISH:125 **b.** *You are the Minister and you are the one who gets vexed when I say you are not doing anything but you brag that you spend $38 million a year in the Ministry.*—Bdos (Hd, 75.01.28, p.4496) □ The phr occurs most commonly in the *AF* form **get vex**, *vex* being widely sensed as adj in CE, as in cit (a), though it is a vb tr in SE. **3.24.1 get (sb) vex(ed)** *vb phr* (CarA) [*AF/IF*] To make (sb) noticeably angry. *Elaine had better watch her steps and not get me mad vex this hour of the night.*—JJM:192

G-G *abbr* (CarA) [*IF*] Governor-General (the titular head of state, as representative of the Queen of Great Britain, in all independent ex-British Caribbean territories that have not chosen to become Republics).

ghaut (**ghut, gut**) [gʌt] *n* (Mrat, StKt, ViIs) **1.** A valley or cleft in a mountain- or hill-side, esp one down wh water runs to the sea after rains. *The Police and Preventive Officers are now carrying the fight to the ghauts, hills and mountains where illicit distilleries of 'hammond' operate.*—DeM(SK) (62.02.03, p.2) **2.** [By extension] Any stream of water running into the sea, but esp one coming down the hill-side. *If you drink the water of Runaway Ghaut, you're bound to come back to Montserrat.*—(Mrat saying) [Prob a colonial transfer of Anglo-Indian *ghaut* < Hin *ghat* 'a landing stage at a river, and the path of descent to it' (N.B. This name is still used for a riverside washing platform by East Indians in *Guyn*). Cp *OED ghaut* 2. 'a mountain pass' (of Anglo-Indian origin); however, see Note at GUT]

ghaut (**gut**)**-ap·ple** [gʌt-apl] *n* (Antg) ‖ MONKEY-APPLE 2. (Bdos, Guyn)

ghaut (**ghut**)**-plum** [gʌt-plʌm] *n* (Angu, Antg, BrVi, Nevs) ‖ HOG-PLUM 1. (CarA)

ghin·gie (**ghin·gee, gin·gee**) *n* (Guyn, Trin) See JHINGIE

ghost-crab *n* (Jmca) A small, flat-bodied, whitish crab that seeks its food on the seashore at nights (hence the name); *Ocypoda albicans* (*Brachyura*). □ Cp DUPPY-CRAB *Bdos*, JUMBIE CRAB *Gren*, *USVI* wh are not the same.

Gi·ant Des·pair *n phr* (Nevs, StKt) A big-bodied, costumed, CARNIVAL figure with a head-dress intended to frighten onlookers, reciting passages from the Bible while he dances. [A 'copy' of the character so named in Bunyan's *Pilgrim's Progress*] □ Evid restricted to *StKt* and *Nevs*.

gi·ant fig *n phr* (Gren) ‖ LACATAN BANANA (CarA)

gib·nut [gɪbnʌt] *n* (Baha, Belz, Jmca) ‖ *labba* (Guyn) ‖ *lappe* (Trin) ‖ *paca* (Belz, Guyn) A robust, brownish, coarse-haired rodent resembling an enlarged guinea-pig, sometimes 2 ft in length and a foot in height, with rows of white spots on its sides; this forest animal is hunted for its much prized delicate meat; *Coelogenys paca* (*Rodentia*). *The main course at the dinner was rice and red kidney beans with gibnut, a local rodent which is a delicacy.*—SuS (85.10.13, p.12) [Perh < *give* + *nut* (with Cr /v > b/ shift), this vegetarian animal being readily attracted by nuts. See *RALG:62*] □ The pl appears to be unchanged.

gid·dy-head *n* (Bdos) See HEAD[1] Phr 4.18 *And nobody has told me he has cancer or sugar, which is how the average Barbadian refers to diabetes. But I am amazed at the number of people who have told me they have the 'giddy-head' and cold sweats.* (*Aside—Senator Tull*) *'The swing head'.*—Bdos (Hd, 87.07.13, p.537)

gid·dy-horse *n* (Bdos) ‖ DONKEY-MAN (Bdos) □ An alternative and perh more recent name in *Bdos*.

gi(e) [gɪ ~ gi] *vb tr* (CarA) [*AF—Cr*] **1.** Give. *The cop took up the parcel, opened it and saw one tape deck. Asked where he got it the accused said: 'A mi father gi mi fi sell'.*—WeS (74.01.18, p.6) [Prob *CSD* Sc *gie* 'give' (late 18C), perh reinforced by characteristic CarA Cr loss of final consonant, by infl from W Afr langs] □ This form occurs commonly in narrative dialogue. **2.** (Trin) [*AF—Vul*] [Of a man] To copulate with. *She mus[t] remember me! / I gie she a[l]ready.*—Trin (Cso)

gi·gi·ree[1] (**gi·gi·ri**) [ɟɪɟɪri] *n* (Gren, Trin) ‖ BENNE 1. (Gren, etc)

gi·gi·ree[2] (**gi·gi·ri**) [ɟɪɟɪri] *adj* (Trin) [*AF*] Jumpy; nervous; uneasy and frightened. *Well she see this man lookin[g] like a plain-clothes police an[d] askin[g] a lot o[f] questions, and she get well gigiree.*—(Trin) [Prob by association with the popping of GIGIREE (BENNE) seeds) when being fried; also perh infl by SE *jittery*]

gil·back·er* [gɪlbakʌ] *n* (Guyn) A large, yellow and grey, scaleless fish with notably wide mouth, often exceeding 80 lbs in weight, and highly prized for its tasty flesh; it is mostly caught at river mouths; *Sciadeichthys flavescens* or *S. emphysetus* (*Siluridae-Ariidae*). [< Du *geel* 'yellow' + Cr *baka* 'back'. Cp Sran *geribaka*, name of the same fish]

gill (**jill**) [ɟɪl] *n* (Guyn) [*Obs*] A penny; a British copper coin about 1-1/4 ins in diameter and worth two cents (i.e. one fiftieth part of a dollar). [Prob < SE *gill* 'a quarter of a pint', from wh such combined forms as *gill-cup*, *gill-glass* could have caused a shift in sense from the measure to the cost of some liquids, and thence to the value of the coin, up to the early 1900s] □ The term is now known only to older folk. The production of the coin was discontinued after Independence (1966).

gil·pin [gɪlpɪn] n (Tbgo, Trin) ‖ CUTLASS (CarA) *Would you describe this cutlass to us please?/It is one, am, estimate it to be about two feet ... It is what we call locally a gilpin ... [but] the bent end of the blade was cut off.*—AMAM:66 [From the name and trademark of the Br manufacturer W. Gilpin & Co, makers of 'edge tools and steel,' at Cannock, Staffordshire, 1763-1938. (Info fr The Tool & Trades Hist. Soc., Kent). They were wholesale suppliers to W. Indian sugar plantations of 'matchets and cutlasses' of blade length 18 in to 26 in usu with a curved tip] □ This name is now more often associated with its use as a weapon than as a tool. Cp COLLINS

gin·al¹ (jin·al) [ʃɪnal] n (Jmca) [AF—ʃoc/Derog] A trickster (usu a man); a person who is so cunning as to be dangerous. [< (Cr pronunc) ginarl < SE *General*, in mocking ref to cunning and resourcefulness]

gi·nal² adj (Belz, Jmca) [AF—ʃoc/Derog] Able to find a quick, smart solution of a difficulty; cunning; devious. *A group ... called on the local radio stations to stop playing the song 'Woman Ah Ginal Fuh True' because it is insulting and disrespectful to women*—AdN (81.07.25)

gi·nal·ism n (Jmca) See cit. *He said that in Jamaica the rampant philosophy ... could be called 'ginalism'. This meant, he added, 'getting whatever I want by fair means if possible or foul means if necessary'*—WeG (75.08.29)

gine [gaɪn] vb (Bdos) [AF—Cr] ‖ GOIN (CarA) *'I don't like snakes,' I replied angrily, 'and if you bring that thing nearer me, I gine pelt you and dah overboard'.*—Com '74:21 (R. Branch) [By vowel opening [< gʌin < goɪn < goɪn]] □ This form, so spelt in narrative dialogue, occurs widely in folk speech in *Bdos*.

gi·nep n (CayI, Dmca, Mrat) See GUINEP

gin·gee n (Guyn) See JHINGEE

gin·ger-beer n (CarA) A sharp-tasting, non-alcoholic drink made by either fermenting or boiling grated ginger root with sugar and a variety of spicy ingredients.

gin·ger-li·ly n 1*. (Bdos) ‖ **red ginger-lily** (Bdos) A bright crimson, cone-shaped spike of closely clustered lily-like bracts, borne at the end of an erect stalk about 4 or 5 ft tall, with blade-shaped leaves; the plant grows densely; *Alpinia purpurata (Zingiberaceae)*. **2.** (Guyn, Jmca, Trin) A fragrant lily of many varieties (white, yellow, pink, cream, etc) with conspicuous lobes; a small cluster of three or four

flowers on noticeable stems stands at the head of a firm, fleshy stalk; *Hydechium spp (Zingiberaceae)*.

gin·ger-tea n (CarA) An infusion of ginger root widely used as a folk medicine, esp for stomach aches.

Gin·ger Tho·mas n phr (USVI) A small, funnel-shaped, yellow flower borne in small clusters on a dense, spreading, bushy shrub wh can reach 20 ft in height and wh also bears long, thin, pointed, yellow pods; *Tecoma stans* or *Stenolobium s. (Bignoniaceae)*. □ The **Ginger Thomas** is the national flower of the *USVI*.

gi(n)·nip n (Mrat) See GUINEP

girl-child n (CarA) [IF] A daughter; a young girl of any age. *But there are a minority of parents who would consider it their righteous duty to expel from their homes girl children who committed the unpardonable sin of getting pregnant out of wedlock.*—AdN (72.11.13, p.4) [Perh a calque from W Afr langs, ex Mandinka *dinmuso (child female)* 'girl, daughter'. Note also Hin *beti* 'girl' contrasting with *beta* 'boy'] □ The term normally occurs in emotive contexts, not always, however, indicating affection as is the case with BOY-CHILD.

G.I.S abbr (CarA) Government Information Service.

give¹ vb A. vb tr 1. In many IF phrases (see foll) with a loose general sense of doing sth to sb, or permitting or causing sth by some action or by behaving in some (usu unpleasant) way. **2.** PHRASES **2.1 give a holler** vb phr (CarA) [AF] To shout (in alarm); to bawl (for help, etc); to cry out loudly. **2.2 give (a lot of) mouth** vb phr (CarA) [AF—Derog] [Esp of a young person] To be saucy without restraint; to be ready with disrespectful talk. **2.3 give a man everything/ sex** vb phr (CarA) [IF] ‖ **go all the way** See GO Phr 6.6 (CarA) [Of an unmarried young woman, esp a virgin] To allow a man to have sexual intercourse with you. *Don[t] be a fool now and give him everything, or you will see him soon done wit[h] you.*—(Gren) **2.4 give a suck-teeth** vb phr (CarA) [AF/IF] See SUCK Phr 3. **2.5 give (a woman) a baby/child** vb phr (CarA) [AF] To make an unmarried woman pregnant. □ The phr usu refers to a young woman's first pregnancy. **2.6 give back-answer(s)/back-chat** vb phr (CarA) [AF/IF] [Esp of children] To answer (grown-ups) saucily. **2.7 give credit (that sth is so)** vb phr (Bdos, Guyn, Tbgo) [IF] To feel sure (that sth is so); to confidently assume (that sth is happening as expected). *The way she talked I gave credit that she had already written you about it, and I'm surprised to find she hasn't.*— (Guyn) **2.8 give fatigue** vb phr (Tbgo, Trin) See FATIGUE Phr 2.1 **2.9 give Jack his jacket** vb phr (Bdos) [IF—ʃoc] To give credit or honour where it is due. *The achievements of this Government over the past 14 years—let us give Jack* *his jacket—cannot be anything else but mi-raculous.*—Bdos (Hd, 75.10.09, p.977) □ Cp Phr 2.16. **2.10 give laugh for peas-soup** *vb phr* (Jmca) [*AF—Joc*] **(i)** [Of a visitor] To keep up a lively conversation long enough to oblige your hosts to invite you to join in the family meal (i.e. peas-soup). **(ii)** [By extension] To chat and gossip instead of sharing in work to be done; to turn attention away from your laziness by talking continuously. **2.11 Give me five(s)/some flesh/some skin!** *imper vb phr* (CarA) [*AF—Joc*] [In congratulation or elated greeting] Shake hands with me! ['Five' in ref to the fingers] **2.12 give picong** *vb phr* (Tbgo, Trin) **(i)** [Of calypso contestants] To engage in a CALYPSO-WAR. **(ii)** [By extension] To tease (sb) mercilessly. [See PICONG] **2.13 give (sb) a basket to carry water** *vb phr* (CarA) See BASKET Phrs 1, 2. **2.14 give (sb) a bath** *vb phr* (CarA) To administer a herbal bath, sometimes for spiritual reasons, to a sick person. **2.15 give (sb) a break/a chance** *vb phr* (CarA) [*AF—Joc*] To stop making unfair fun of (sb); to stop pulling (sb's) leg (often in foll phr). *PHRASE* **2.15.1 Gi(v)e me a break!** (CarA) [*AF—Joc*] You must be pulling my leg! **2.16 give (sb) a jacket** *vb phr* (Jmca) [*AF—Joc*] [Of a married woman] To bear a child by another man and pass it off as your husband's. □ Cp Phr 2.9 **2.17 give (sb) a phone-message** *vb phr* (Bdos) [*IF*] To allow (sb) to use your telephone to make a personal call. *Run over quick an[d] ask Miss Boyce to give you a phone-message and call yo[ur] father home quick*—(Bdos) **2.18 give (sb) a piece** *vb phr* (CarA) [*AF—Joc*] [Of a woman] To allow a man to have casual sexual intercourse with you. **2.19 give (sb) a search** *vb phr* (Jmca) [*AF*] To make or carry out a search (of a place); to search (sb). *Someone said, 'Boy, police give us a search'. He said that they did not find any parcel on him.*—WeS (74.07.12, p.10) **2.20 give (sb) bed-service** *vb phr* (Bdos) [*AF—Joc*] [Esp of a mature woman kept by a man] To have an agreed sexual relationship in return for satisfactory maintenance. **2.21 give (sb) big rocks to hold** *vb phr* (Bdos) [*AF—Joc*] [Of a woman] To accept a date or make a social appointment with a man wh you do not (intend to) keep; to hoax your suitor. **2.22 give (sb) a cut-eye** *vb phr* (CarA) See CUT Phr 3.11.1 **2.23 give (sb) France** *vb* (ECar) [*IF*] To give or cause (sb) a lot of trouble or pain; to quarrel implacably with (sb). **a.** *The gate gave him France to put up.*—(Bdos) **b.** *The wife used to give him so much France over the money that he would deliberately come home drunk every Friday.*—(Guyn) [See FRANCE] **2.24 give (sb) good** *vb phr* (CarA) [*AF*] To give (sb) a severe tongue-lashing or a beating; to lambaste (sb). *Mr Haynes, I give him good and he ain't say a word. He hang his head like a dog.*—JMA:183 □ Cp also Phrs 2.23, 2.26, 2.32. **2.25 give (sb) horrors** *vb phr* (CarA) [*AF—Joc*] To make (sb) become frustrated, angry or disgusted; to provoke (sb) (sometimes in fun). **2.26 give (sb) Old Harry** *vb phr* (CarA) [*AF—Joc*] **(i)** To berate or lambaste (sb). **(ii)** To tease (sb) relentlessly. [< SE *Old Harry*, a Joc name for the devil] **2.27 give (sb/sth) one-eye** *vb phr* (Bdos,

Guyn) [*IF*] **(i)** To eye (sb/sth) furtively. **(ii)** To keep a watchful neighbourly eye on (sb/sth). **2.28 give (sb) right** *vb phr* (CarA) [*IF/AF*] To side with or decide in favour of (sb); to support (sb's) contention. *And if the husband beat her I would give him right, too! Believe me to God she deserve it!*—(Tbgo) [Prob a calque from W Afr langs. Cp Yoruba *da are fun ẹnikan* (*judge right give somebody*) with same sense; similarly *da ebi fun ẹnikan* (*judge wrong give somebody*)—(K. Ọmọtọsọ)] **2.29 give (sb) rounders** *vb phr* (Trin) [*AF—Joc*] To give (sb) the run-around; to be evasive, deceptive or irritating in dealing with (sb). [Metaph from the game of rounders] **2.30 give (sb) the done** *vb phr* (BrVi) [*AF*] To end a romantic relationship with (sb); to drop (a boyfriend or girl-friend). **2.31 give (sb) the go-by** *vb phr* (Guyn) [*AF/IF*] To snub or slight (sb); to deliberately avoid associating with (sb who may lower your social standing). **2.32 give (sb) the licks of Lisbon** *vb phr* (Guyn) [*AF—Joc*] ‖ GIVE (SB) GOOD (CarA) Phr 2.24.; See also LICK[2] Phr 3.5. **2.33 give (sb) wrong** *vb phr* (CarA) [*AF/IF*] To take sides against (sb); to judge (sb) to be in the wrong. *America can't just go in and bomb people like dat! A mus[t] gi[ve] dem wrong.*—(StKt) [Prob a calque from W Afr langs. See note at Phr 2.28] **2.34 give skin-teet[h]** *vb phr* (CarA) [*AF—Derog*] To grin while concealing ill-feeling; to grimace or laugh cynically. *She will talk wit[h] you an[d] give a lot o[f] skin-teet[h] just to fin[d] out yo[ur] business and den carry it all over de place.*—(Guyn) **2.35 (your) mind gives you (that sth is so/to do sth)** *id phr* (CarA) [*IF*] (You) feel almost certain, have a foreboding (that sth is/will be so, or ought to be done). **a.** *My mind gave me that that marriage was not going to last you know.*—(Guyn) **b.** *When my mind give me to do something I always follow my mind, an[d] I fin[d] I never wrong.*—(Guyn) □ See MIND[1] Phr 9. **B. phrasal 2.36 give away** *vb phr* (CarA) [*X*] To give way; to collapse or break down. *Sgt Austin, chauffeur to the Governor-General, explained yesterday that the 'clutch gave away'. The President and Governor General were transferred to a security car and taken to the University.*—TrG (74.09.11, p.1) [A hypercorrection or false refinement of SE *give way*, infl by educated correction of such CarA Cr expressions as *go [a]way*, etc] **2.37 gi[ve] on/[u]pon a man** *vb phr* (Tbgo, Trin) [*AF—Joc/Vul*] [Of a woman] To invite a man, in some obvious way, to return your affection; to be ready to give yourself to a man you like.

give[2] *prep* (CarA) [*AF—Cr*] **1.** For. *Well you ent want me comb you hair give you?*—RTCS:11 **2.** [By extension, with other prep senses relating to context] At; on; to; etc. **a.** *Don't push up you[r] mout[h] gi[ve] me! I am a full woman!*—(Antg) **b.** *When dey go to get an' dey en get, dey comin' back an' cry gie you.*—WeN (53.03.09, p.1, Annie & Josephine) [A prob calque from W Afr langs. Cp Yoruba *fun* 'give', which, 'as a second verb … is generally translated by a preposition [to, for] …. Bilingual Yorubas tend to use *fun* rather indiscriminately to translate 'for'—*RTYY:83, 84*]

gi(z)·za·da [giza:da] /ɪ'2ɪ/ *n* (Jmca) A small round open tart baked with a filling of grated and sugared coconut. [< Sp *guisado* 'prepared, cooked, stewed', pa. part. of *guisar*] □ Often spelled with -*zz*-, though -*z*- is recommended by the etym.

glass-bot·tle *n* (ECar) [*IF*] ‖ *grass-bottle* (ECar) A piece or pieces of broken bottle (esp when lying about where people may walk). *When she went in to the hot water stream the sole of her feet got cut with glass bottle and I had to take her to the Hospital that same morning in my car.*—LaS (74.04.27, p.6) [Survival of a characteristic CarA Cr redundancy *glass + bottle*]

glas·sie (**glas·sy**[1]) *n* (Bdos) ‖ NUT-CAKE (Guyn) [Said to be from its hard, shiny almost translucent surface; but this may be a folk-etym reinforcement of the original *glacé* (a Fr loan-word in SE) 'candied or crystallized' in ref to sweets]

glas·sy[2] *n* (Belz, Guyn) A (usu small) glass marble.

gli·ri·ci·di·a* (**gli·ri·ci·da**) *n* (Angu, Bdos, StLu, StVn) ‖ *Aaron's rod* (Jmca) ‖ *cocoashade* (Trin) ‖ *glory-cedar* (Angu, Dmca, Gren) ‖ *growing stake, quick-stick* (Jmca) ‖ *rainbush* (Mrat, StVn) ‖ *raindrops, windbreak* (StKt) A tree growing up to about 20 ft, whose sparse branches shed their leaves in the dry season and come out in an abundance of lilac flower clusters along their lengths; the plant is commonly used for fences or shading paths; *Gliricidia sepium (Leguminosae-Papilionatae). ... and just up the road, the tall slender Gliricidia trees are putting out their pale pink inflorescences. The tree belongs to the Pea Family, Leguminosae. It grows very quickly and will make an effective fence. In the island of St Lucia, along the south-east coast between Troumasse and Vieux Fort, these hedges are frequent, the shrubs growing less than a foot apart, the slim stems about 2 ins across.*—AdN (78.01.11, p.6, M. Hutt) [From botanical name *Gliricidia sepium*]

Glo·ri·a-Sat·ur·day *n* (Trin) The Saturday between Good Friday and Easter Sunday; Holy Saturday.

glo·ry-ce·dar (**glo·ri·i·ci·da, glo·ri·si·di·a**) *n* (Angu, Dmca, Gren) ‖ GLIRICIDIA (Angu, etc) **a.** ... *but they told her to use some glory-cedar leaves from the fencing and make some tea.*—Gren (Ms) **b.** *The clean-limbed glorisidia/Is in her heliotrope*—'February' (E. M. Roach, 1950) [By pop etym from first element of botanical name *Gliricidia sepium*] □ The plant is not of the cedar family.

glu-glu *n* (Dmca) The edible part or the edible seeds of any ornamental palm-tree. [See cit]. *We*

just say glu-glu for the tree because you eat the heart, which is really the fruit. All fruit of any palm that is eaten is called glu-glu.—(Dmca, 1977) [Prob < GRU-GRU by /r > l/ shift]

G.M.O. *abbr* (CarA) Government Medical Officer, a qualified doctor employed by a Government and assigned to a particular post or district.

go *vb intr* [Note that GOING, GONE are also treated as separate entries] **1.** (Bdos) [*IF*] [In taking leave of sb] To be leaving, departing. *I go.*—(Bdos) [A prob calque of leave-taking form from W Afr langs. Cp *SIBC:89* Igbo *a lawala m* (*I go my home*) 'Goodbye'] □ Also I GONE (CarA) See GONE[1] **2. (i)** [gʌ~go] (CarA) [*AF—Cr*] [Immediately followed by a non-stative vb] Go and. *Why you don['t] go as[k] him you[r]self?*—(Guyn) □ In this function [gʌ] is the more usu pronunc. **(ii)** [go~gʌ] *fut aux vb* (CarA) [*AF—Cr*] Will; would. **a.** *'Is all right,' she told him, displaying the will that to this day, sweeps aside tasks that would fell most men. 'I go work and help. The children go work and help.'*—Peo I.1. p.19 (K. Roxburgh) **b.** *I told them to leave her there, when she get up she go go.*—ToR (77.03.27, p.1) [Survival of the basic CarA Cr future marker *go* [gʌ], with neg form AIN['t] GO] □ In this function *go* still occurs widely in uneducated speech (or narrative dialogue) or is used for comic effect, but is not otherwise written. **3.** *second element in a dynamic serial vb* (CarA) [*AF—Cr*] **(i)** And (i.e. connecting the action of two vbs). **a** *Yo[u] breed de woman chil[d]—yo[u] bes[t] go go look fo[r] wo[r]k* (= you've made the woman's daughter pregnant—you'd better *go and* look for work).—(BrVi) **b** *So he run quick go tell de mother*—(Guyn) **(ii)** And go/ went to; to go to (adding urgency to the action of the preceding vb). *The night when she start to holler I tell you [h]e walk go to[w]ng quick for a doctor.*—(StVn) [A prob calque from W Afr langs in many of wh the vb meaning 'go' is similarly used. See *TAGD:210, 211* for exs from Ewe, Fante, etc] **4.** *semi-transitive (followed by a place-name)* (CarA) [*AF/IF—Cr*] Go to (a place). *We having a by-election in our district, because the Parliament representative resigning to go America.*—SPOC:81 [Cp the use of 'go' in Twi: *mɛkɔ Kumase* (*I go Kumasi*) 'I am going/will go to Kumasi'] **5.** (Tbgo) [*IF*] [Often neg] To get along well together; to see eye to eye. *The two of them can't go at all.*—(Tbgo) **6.** *PHRASES* **6.1 able to go with (sb)** *adj phr* (Angu, Mrat, StKt, StVn) ‖ ABLE WITH SB (CarA) See ABLE Phr 1. **6.2 As it go, it go** *id phr* (Dmca) [*AF/IF*] Whatever happens, let it happen! I really don't care. **6.3 can go with sb** *vb phr* (Nevs) ‖ ABLE WITH SB (CarA) See ABLE Phr 1. **6.4 go aback** *vb phr* (Guyn) See ABACK[1] Phr 3.1 **6.5 go after (a young woman)** *vb phr* (Gren) [*IF*] To desire to marry. *They say was the big daughter he was goin[g] after, but she di[d]n['t] like him.*—(Gren) **6.6 go all the way** *vb phr* (CarA) [*IF*] ‖ GIVE A MAN EVERYTHING (CarA) See GIVE[1] Phr 2.3 **6.7 go along straight and do (sth)** *vb phr* (Nevs)

[IF] See GO STRAIGHT (ALONG), ETC Phr 6.26
6.7.1 go [a]long (your way) vb phr (CarA)
[AF/IF] To be off and away (and usu out of
trouble). Look, I better go [a]long m[y] way befo[re] I get in trouble, yes!—(Trin) **6.8 go and
come** vb phr (Guyn, Tbgo) [AF/IF] To be
unstable, esp mentally; to be too unreliable to
be trusted with any responsibility. That girl
crazy, you know. Take it from me: she does go and
come. A know what A telling you.—(Tbgo) □ But
cp GO TO COME (BACK) Phr 6.29. **6.9 go and (do
sth)** aspectual aux vb phr (CarA) [IF] [Indicating
the speaker's objection to or displeasure with
the action stated in the following vb] **a.** Girl, I
in big trouble. Big, big trouble. If you know what
Tiger go and do! He go and invite two Americans
he does work with to come for Indian food tonight!—SABS:161 **b.** People are sort of saying
something like this in their heads ... 'why did
he have to go and die. That wasn't supposed to
happen.'—SuS (85.03.31, p.31) [Cp sense 3.
and etym note thereto. Go and + vb is a CE
refinement, with the same sense, developed from
CarA Cr go go + vb] **6.10 go and see** id phr
(Gren) [AF] But the truth is; whereas in fact.
He playin[g] boss, go and see, dey don[t] even
want him on de estate.—PPGD:33 (adapted) **6.11
go around** vb phr (Bdos, Guyn) [IF] ‖ go on
(Jmca) See PHR 6.24 (II) [Of a young man and
woman] To be dating each other steadily. Now
let us look at sex within the relationship where two
teenagers are going around.—PeL (78.05.19, p.4)
6.12 go [a]way vb phr (CarA) [IF] **(i)** To go
abroad (esp to Britain, Canada, or the USA to
study or to live). **(ii)** Go [a]way! imper vb phr
(Bdos) [AF] See PHR 6.34.2 ‖ GO WITH THAT!
(Nevs, StKt) How you mean you ain[t] know Mr
Stevens? Girl go [a]way, do!—(Bdos) **6.12.1 go
away with Southwell** vb phr (CayI) [IF] To
join the hired crew of an international cargo
shipping line. He got his call an[d] he gone away
wit[h] Southwell.—(CayI) [From the name of a
firm that hired crew for international bulk-
carriers, many CayI men earning a living by this
means] **6.13 go back (doing sth)** vb phr (CarA)
[IF] To begin doing sth again (esp after being
warned against doing so). The doctor tol[d] [h]
im if he go back smokin[g] an[d] drinkin[g] don[t]
bother come back to him.—(Guyn) **6.14 go bad**
vb phr (CarA) [IF] **(i)** [Of a machine, etc] To
break down; [of food or fruit] to spoil. **(ii)** [Of
a young woman] To become a prostitute; (SE)
to turn out bad, go to the bad. **6.15 go by** vb
phr (Bdos) [IF] To keep (sb) going; to drink (esp
rum) or eat. Auntie, you have anything to go by?
I hungry enough!—(Bdos) **6.16 go down** [go
dʌn] vb phr (Bdos) [AF] **(i)** To go into the mental
hospital. **(ii)** [Cricket, of a batsman] To score
steadily and with energy. Man, hear the runs!
Like both o[f] them gone down, man!—(Bdos)
[Perh an extension of (i) i.e. 'scoring like mad',
or a metaph from 'going down the wicket' (=
going at the bowling). But cp also PUT YOUR
HEAD DOWN] **6.16.1 go down in (food)** vb phr
(Bdos) [AF] To eat (the food) ravenously. Look
how he goin[g] do[w]ng in de peas an[d] rice!—
(Bdos) [Perh related to prec senses i.e. 'to eat

like mad', or referring to the eater bending the
head down without lifting it while eating] **6.17
go for channa** vb phr (Guyn) [AF—Joc] See
CHANNA Phr My information is that around
$100,000 will now go for 'channa', because of the
dramatic decision to put Telecoms at the old Water
Works site.—DaC (52.09.24, p.4, 'Down in
Demerara') **6.18 go for yourself** vb phr (Baha)
[AF] **(i)** ‖ BREAK FOR YOURSELF (ECar) See BREAK
Phr. 5. An' jus' wen he wuz gon tell muh more de
meetin broke up or broke down or sump'n an'
evrybuddy gone fer deyself—DSJS:92 **(ii)** To
dance with much display Man, wen da' p'leece
ban' hit wun li'l note dere dat time dem fellers gon
step off. Lookout, son, dey goin' fer deyself.—
DSJS:90 □ Cp also BREAK Phr 1 Break away
(ECar) **6.19 go here** vb phr (Bdos, Mrat) [AF]
To go just a short distance away. I goin[g] here
an[d] come back. See that the pot don[t] boil
over.—(Bdos) **6.20 go home** vb phr (Gren) [AF/
IF] To speak in gross, defamatory terms to
or about a member/members of your own or
another's family. ... the two female nurses, began
cursing each other in the Maternity Ward. When
one of them decided to 'go home' with her remarks,
a fight broke out which almost ended with one
getting her head broiled in a nearby sterilizer.—
ToR (78.05.14, p.1) **6.20.1 go home for sb** vb
phr (Bdos) [IF] To ask a young woman's parents'
permission to marry her. It is about six months
we have been seeing each other and he wants to go
home for me, but my parents say no man isn't coming
home for me, not before I am in my twenties.—NaT
(75.09.14, p.18, Dear Christine) **6.21 go jam-
ming/jumping** vb phr (CarA) [Carnival, etc] To
join in noisy, festive, day-time street dancing
6.22 go light vb phr (Jmca) [AF] To run as fast
as you can; to speed off like a bird. Tell Deacon
they have caged us in the lock-up and that we will
go before Custos in the morning. 'Put foot in hand
and go light, Bro' John,' Davie tells me.—RND:
54 [Cp SE light-footed] **6.23 go off** vb phr **(i)**
(CarA) [AF/IF] To go off your head; to be
insane. **(ii)** (Nevs, StKt) [IF] [Esp of a child]
To ease your bowels freely (esp after taking a
purgative). **6.24 go on** vb phr **(i)** (CarA) [AF]
‖ GET ON (CarA) See GET Phr 3.18 **a.** Christine,
do you think it is fair for a man to get on the way
he go on after I am trying to help him?—NaT
(77.04.17, p.22, Dear Christine) **b.** She knew
she could trust the old bitch, no matter how stupid
she might go on at times.—PCOS:37 □ Often also
go on bad, (cp also GET ON BAD) though, as in
cit b, other adj complements may follow with
the same general sense—**go on foolish, funny,
ridiculous**, etc or commonly a phr or clause
introduced by LIKE, prep or conj: go on like a
jackass; go on like he mad, etc. **(ii)** (Jmca) [IF]
‖ GO AROUND (Bdos, etc) See PHR 6.11 Dear Janet,
I am 17 and my boyfriend is 18. We have been
going on for the past four years, and during that
time he met another girl.—WeS (74.05.17, p.8)
(iii) (Guyn, Trin) [IF] To carry on with, or
persist in sth displeasing or dangerous. He's
goin[g] to go on and go on until he catch jail.—
(Guyn) **(iv)** (Jmca) [AF] To happen or take
place through some arrangement. W- ran to the

*small gate and said, 'No V-, no V-, no knife play
naw go on in here today.'*—DaG (70.03.24, p.4)
6.24.1 go on with (sth unpleasant) *vb phr*
(CarA) [*IF*] To do or say (sth objectionable as
expressed by a following abstract noun). See cit.
*What your parents are going on with is foolishness.
I did not know you still had people in Jamaica
thinking like this.*—StA(JA) (82.03.24, p.12)
□ An *IF* variant of GO ON + adj (see prec Phr
(i)). Hence *go on foolish, stupid*, etc [*AF*] > *go
on with (a lot of) foolishness, stupidness*,
etc [*IF*]. **6.25 go one-side** *vb phr* (Bdos, Guyn)
[*AF*] **(i)** To move out of the way. **(ii)** Go one-
side! *imper vb phr* (Guyn) [*AF*] ‖ GO WITH THAT!
(Nevs, etc) See PHR 6.34.2 *You mean after all
dat food you eat, you still hungry for chocolate?
Child go one-side!*—(Guyn) **6.26 go straight
(along) and do (sth)** *aspectual vb phr* (Bdos,
Guyn, Nevs) [Adding strong intention to the
action stated in the latter vb] To do sth with
malice. *My child ain['t] do you nothing an[d]
how you could go straight along an[d] strike her?*
—(Guyn) **6.27 Go that side!** [gʌ da[t] said]
imper vb phr (Guyn) [*AF—Cr*] ‖ GO WITH THAT!
See PHR 6.34.2 (Nevs, StKt) □ Note the Cr pronunc wh prevails with this phr. **6.28 go through
the eddoes** *vb phr* (Bdos) See EDDOE Phr 3.1
6.29 go to come (back) *vb phr* (CarA) [*IF*] To
go away expecting, or being expected, to return
shortly. *I wish to say finally, Mr Speaker, that
the Minister should, to use a slogan, the Minister
should go to come. The Minister should go back
home and come back with a serious Budget to
tackle the problems of this country.*—Gren (Hd,
77.04.26, p.324) [Cp Twi *mekɔ maba* 'I go [with
the intention] to come [again]'—*CGAF:73*]
□ Also often *go and come back* (CarA) in the
same context. (Cp Phr 6.8). **6.30 go to do (sth)**
aspectual vb phr (CarA) [*IF*] [Indicating the
action stated in the latter vb was incomplete or
unsuccessful] To attempt to do sth. *W— said
that after the tyre was stuck, V— came out and
went to 'juck' the accused with a knife and she
blocked his hand from 'jucking' H—.*—AdN
(73.05.03, p.1) [Prob from infl of W Afr vb
structures. Cp Igbo *ọ gara ịfụnyụ ọkụ* (He/she
went to blow out lamp/fire) 'He/she attempted to
blow out the fire/fire'—(C. Azuonye)] □ Cp
neg phr next. **6.30.1 not go to do (sth)** *neg
aspectual vb phr* (CarA) Not mean to do (sth
that you have done); to do (sth) accidentally
or unintentionally. *Don['t] cry, darlin[g]! Yo[ur]
brother di[d]n['t] go to hit yo[u] so hard. He was
only playin[g].*—(Guyn) □ Cp prec phrs 6.26,
6.30. **6.31 go to France** *vb phr* (CarA) [*IF*] To
go to hell. *Who din like it could go to France!*—
NaT (78.06.30, p.14, J. Layne-Clark) [See
FRANCE] □ Often imperative. **6.32 go to town
on (sb/sth)** *vb phr* (ECar) [*AF/IF—Joc*] To give
(sb) a thorough tongue-lashing; to eat up (food);
to exhaust (a matter, etc). *We can't go into the
length and breadth of this affair. If the Baptists
had written to us direct we would have gone to
town on the affair. But remembering we read it
from another paper, we just have to say we are
sorry.*—ViN (73.05.05, p.2, Scribbler) **6.33 go
up the road for (sb)** *vb phr* (Guyn) [*AF—Joc*]

To start and carry on a brawling row with (sb).
6.34 go with (sb) *vb phr* (i) (Jmca, Tbgo, Trin)
[*IF*] To be the sexual friend of (sb). *I am 23
years old and was going with a man for eight years
and during that time I bore him four children.*—
WeS (74.06.28, p.8, Dear Janett) **(ii)** (Angu,
Mrat, Nevs, StKt) [*IF*] To fight ably with (sb).
(See PHRS 6.1., 6.3) *He did not interfere with him
but F- held on to him and he couldn't 'go with
him' so he had to defend himself.*—DeM(SK)
(61.01.04, p.7) **6.34.1 go with (sth)** *vb phr*
(CarA) [*IF*] To go off with (sth); to steal (sth).
*He left his bicycle outside the store and somebody
went with it.*—(Bdos) **6.34.2 Go with that!** *imper
vb phr* (Nevs, StKt) [*AF*] ‖ **Go [a]way!** (Bdos)
‖ **Go one-side! Go that side! Go yo[ur] way!**
(Guyn) [An expression of contemptuous disbelief or dismissal] Be off with you! *Big Carnival
and dey expect people mus[t] come an[d] do half-
day wo[r]k? Le[t] dem go wid that!*—(StKt) **6.34.3
go with your fastness (to sb)** *vb phr* (CarA)
[*IF*] See FASTNESS Phr 4.1 **6.34.4 go with your
mind** *vb phr* (Bdos) [*IF*] ‖ FOLLOW YOUR MIND
(CarA) See FOLLOW Phr 2.3 *If I did go with my
mind I would not be here to blame for all this
foolish nonsense, I would have keep my mouth
shut.*—Bdos (Ms, Play, 1976) **6.35 Go yo[ur]
way!** [gʌ yu we] *imper vb phr* (Guyn, Tbgo,
Trin) [*AF*] ‖ GO WITH THAT (Nevs, StKt) See
prec PHR 6.34.2 *Don['t] come to me wid no cock-
and-bull story! Go yo[ur] way!*—(Guyn) [Cp
OED go 7. b. '... In present literary use *to go,
wend one's way* survive as archaisms; mod dialects
have only the imperatives *go, come your (thy)
way (or ways)*] **6.36 to hell and go** *adv phr*
(Guyn) [*AF*] [Adding intensity to the meaning
of the prec vb] **a.** *If she comes to me with that
nonsense, I would chase her to hell and go!*—
(Guyn) **b.** *An[d] yo[u] should see how she dress
off to hell and go for dis weddin[g].*—(Guyn)

goad·ie/-y *n* (Bdos, Guyn, Tbgo, Trin) See
GODY

go·an *vb* (Bdos) [*AF—Cr*] See GOIN[G] 2. and
Note

goat *n* PHRASES **1. goat bite you/your foot** *id
phr* (Bdos, Gren, Guyn) [*AF—Cr/Joc*] ‖ **goat-
mouth bite you** (StVn) **(i)** You seem to be
bewitched, or always unlucky; you never seem
to know what you are about. [Perh a calque.
Cp Yoruba *ewurẹ bu u jẹ* (*goat bite him*) 'he
is impotent'] **(ii)** [By extension] [Of a young
woman] You seem unable to get married. **2.
in goat-heaven and kiddie-kingdom** *adj phr*
(Bdos) [*AF—Joc*] See HEAVEN Phr 1.

goat-bush *n* (Brbu) ‖ BREAD-AND-CHEESE
(CarA)

goat-fish* *n* (CarA) Any of a few varieties
(pink, yellowish, spotted, etc) of a fish of the
mullet family, about a foot long when fully
grown, with two long, spiny feelers under its
mouth; it is valued for its firm, tasty flesh;

Mullidae spp. [From the resemblance of its 'feelers' (i.e. barbels) to a goat's 'beard']

goat-head soup *n phr* (Jmca, Tbgo, Trin) ‖ *mannish-water* (Jmca) A highly seasoned (often peppery) soup in wh the head and offal of the goat are boiled; the meal is a popular one served or sold on festive occasions, and associated (in *Jmca*) with virility, and (in *Tbgo*) with propitiating the spirits of the dead. □ Cp GOAT-WATER (*Antg, etc*).

goat-heav·en *n* (Bdos, Gren) PHRASE **be in goat-heaven** *vb phr* (Bdos, Gren) [*AF—Joc*] To be in a state of bliss; to feel great inward joy. □ The phr *and kiddie-kingdom*, expanding the same meaning, is often added in *Bdos*.

goat-mouth *n* (CarA) [*AF—Joc*] ‖ *bouch-kabwit* 1. (Dmca) A believed ability, possessed by some individuals, to deliberately frustrate sb's effort or cause some minor misfortune by predicting failure. *Lawd, Rachael, don' set yu goat mouth 'pon de people them; yu always preachin' crosses.*—PCOS:181 [From the belief or experience that certain plants are blighted or die after having their leaves partly eaten by goats] 2. PHRASES 2.1 **goat-mouth bite you** *vb phr* (StVn) [*AF—Joc*] ‖ GOAT BITE YOU (Bdos, Gren, Guyn) [*AF—Joc*] See GOAT Phr 1. (ii) *If she can get a man, why you can['t] get one too? Wha[t] happen to you, goat-mouth bite you?*—(StVn) 2.2 **have goat-mouth** *vb phr* (CarA) [*AF—Joc*] ‖ HAVE BAD-MOUTH (CarA) See BAD-MOUTH Phr 3.1 *Don't bother tell me anything about how I doin[g] this cake because you have goat-mouth and you just goin[g] to make it fall.*—(Tbgo) 2.3 **put goat-mouth on (sb/sth)** *vb phr* (CarA) [*AF—Joc*] ‖ PUT YOUR BAD-MOUTH ON (SB/STH) (CarA) See BAD-MOUTH Phr 3.2 *And who knows the price we in the Eastern Caribbean may be called upon to pay, one of these not too distant days, to deal with our own Haitian AIDS/refugee/drug/prostitution problem? I am not putting goat mouth on anybody. But history inexorably proves, alas, that what goes around comes around.*—SuS (87.12.13, p.6)

goat-rose *n* (Trin) ‖ OLD-MAID(BUSH) (CarA)

goat's foot creeper *n phr* (Guyn) ‖ IPOMEA (CarA)

goat-wa·ter *n* (Antg, Mrat, Nevs, StKt) A heavy, tasty soup made by boiling chunks of goat's meat or mutton (sometimes including bones and parts of the entrails) with spices, peppers, vegetables, burnt flour or sugar and sometimes liquor added; the meal is the most popular item served at weddings and parties. □ Cp GOAT-HEAD SOUP (*Jmca, etc*).

goat·weed *n* (Jmca) ‖ DITÉ-PÉYI (Dmca, etc)

go·bi(e) (goo·bi(e), gu·bi) [gʊbi] *n* 1*. (Angu, Nevs, USVI) The calabash (fruit or tree); *Crescentia cujete* (*Bignoniaceae*). 2. (Angu) A CALABASH bowl used as a dipper. 3. (Guyn) (i) The dried, empty shell of a CALABASH with a small hole at the top, used to store water or as a fisherman's float in still water. (ii) (Guyn) [*AF—Joc*] [By extension] The human head.

gob·let [gʌblɪt] *n* 1. (Bdos, Guyn) ‖ *monkey* (Bdos, Gren) A covered pitcher shaped like a large kettle, made of porous brown clay, in wh water is kept cool by evaporation. 2. (Antg, Dmca, Nevs) ‖ *monkey* (Gren) A long-necked open clay jug for keeping and serving cool water. 3. (Jmca) A large water jug used for toilet purposes. [Prob a confusion of SE *goblet* 'a metal or glass drinking vessel' and SE (Anglo-Indian) *goglet* 'a long-necked vessel for holding water'. See both in *OED*]

go-by *n* PHRASE **give (sb) the go-by** *vb phr* (Guyn) See GIVE¹ Phr 2.31

God¹ *n* PHRASES 1. **behind God('s) back** *adv phr* (CarA) [*AF—Joc*] See BEHIND¹ Phr 3. *The whole family gone dead, you see? The house burn up while they all sleeping. They so far behind God back, nobody could know when it happen.*—GI:212 2. **every day/night/week as God send(s)** *adv phr* (Bdos, Guyn) [*IF*] Every single day/night/week. □ Used in emotive contexts mostly by older folk. 3. **God spare life** *id phr* (CarA) [*IF*] ‖ *(If) Life spare* (CarA) [A leave-taking formula] If God spares my (and your) life! (i.e. I will see you again). □ Used by older and rural folk.

God² *intensifier adj* (CarA) [*AF*] [Adding stress to the meaning of *every* or *one*] (Every) single; one only **a.** *Every God minute you bringing home all kinda nonsense from that place.*—SNWIC:258 (M. Townshend) **b.** *The one God shoe I have, I can['t] mash it up wid no marchin[g].*—(StVn)

god-bird* *n* 1. (Gren, Guyn, StVn) ‖ *house-wren* (Gren, Guyn) A small, brown, noisy warbler that usu builds its nest in the eaves or ceilings of houses; *Troglodytidae spp*. 2. (Baha, TkCa) Any of three or four varieties of green-backed hummingbird; *Trochilidae spp*.

god·broth·er; god·sis·ter *n* 1. (CarA) The son/daughter of your godfather. 2. Anyone who has the same godfather as yourself. 3. [Indic] (Guyn, Trin) A person who has ceremonially taken the same spiritual leader as yourself.

god-bush *n* (Jmca) ‖ BIRD-VINE 1. (Dmca, etc) [From the unusual feature of this parasitic shrub flourishing without rooting in the ground, but directly on the bark of the host tree]

god·fa·ther *n* (CarA) [*IF*] See cit. *The word 'godfather' has entered the Trinidad vocabulary meaning someone in a position to help you, a sponsor or patron who comes to your aid when necessary. Its original meaning, of course, referred to the sponsors who were Godfathers at a child's baptism.*—TrG (76.04.11, p.7) □ The cit for *Trin* holds good for all the *CarA*.

god·fa·ther·ism *n* (Guyn, Trin) The practice of employing or promoting persons not by merit but through personal relationship, or by favour; nepotism.

god-horse* *n* (CarA) ‖ *chouval-bondyé* (Dmca, StLu) ‖ *duppy-riding-horse* (Jmca) ‖ *guava-lobster* (Gren) The green praying mantis or the brown, wingless stick-insect (the latter growing up to 8 ins in length) of the family *Phasmidae*. *In my childhood I was once said to be as thin as a god-horse and, since this insect was said to be a messenger of misfortune, I hated the idea.*—Bdos (Ms, 1976) [A prob calque from W Afr langs. Cp the Fr Cr parallel, also *ADHL* Hausa *dokiŋ Alla* (*horse of God*), children's name for the mantis. See also etym note at DUPPY RIDING-HORSE]

god·sis·ter *n* See GODBROTHER

go·dy (**goad·ie/-y**) [go·di] *n* (Bdos, Guyn, Tbgo, Trin) [*AF—Vul*] Abnormally swollen testicles due to a rupture; hydrocele. [Perh from *OED* (*Obs*) 16C SE *gourdy* adj 'swollen ..., stuffed out']

go-for·wards *n pl* (Bdos, Trin) [*AF—Joc*] ‖ RUBBER-SLIPPERS (CarA) [From the fact that the footwear can stay on the feet only if one walks forward]

gog·gle-eye *n* (Baha, Bdos, Guyn, Jmca) 1. (CarA) A fish with prominent (ringed or bulging) eyes that may be a variety of JACK, sunfish, or snapper. 2. (TkCa) A small, slender, silvery JACK moving in schools and popularly eaten fried dry, with bread; *Carangidae spp.*

go·in(g) *vb* (CarA) 1. ['go·ɪn] pres. part. of GO (in its general functions as vb intr in CE). [*IF*] [Used in pres. t. contexts without prec vb 'to be'] *How de sive an' thyme an' de tomato goin'? (smiling) Ee goin' good oui, dare as ee dare ah sell ah good bit a'ready, eh heh ...*—PGIP:43 2. [gʊɪn~gʊ(ʌ)n~gã~gwa(ɪ)n] GINE, GOAN (Bdos), GON, GUN (*CarA*), GWAN (*Belz, Jmca*) GWINE (Guyn, Jmca) fut aux vb [*AF—Cr*] a. *... and he used to say he going give me ten children?*—RTCS:10 b. *But in trut' I wonder whether dey goan punish dose wutless fellas? Nuttin' bout dat in de papers.*—AdV (73.04.07, p.4, 'Off The Cuff') c. *'We goin' need a boat mechanic,' Mrs Parkinson said.*—SJS:141 d. *Open dey door, an when dey ting come in, we gon jus' gang up on it.*—Aaw.I.2, p.24 e. *I told him that I gun stand up and see a lot of wonna so get beat and I gun watch.*—Bdos (CR, 70.01.09) [A mesolectal development of CarA Cr fut aux GO (See GO 2 (ii)). Its neg form is *ain['t] goin(g)* = SE '*will not*'. See the forms GWAN, GWINE as separate entries.] □ Distinguished in function 2. by weak stress and reduced articulation, the form occurs only in speech and is represented by a number of notional spellings in narrative dialogue. Notice that cit e. is from a Magistrate's Court Record.

go·ing-off /1'12/ *n* (Mrat, Nevs, StKt) [*AF/IF*] ‖ BELLY-WORK[ING]s (Antg, etc)

gold·en-ap·ple /1'122/ *n* 1*. (CarA) ‖ *golden-plum* (Belz) ‖ *Jew-plum* (Jmca) ‖ *ponm-sitè* (Gren, StLu, Trin, ViIs) A solid, roundish fruit 3 to 4 ins long and about 2-1/2 ins in diameter with a tough, slightly veined skin wh is gold-yellow when ripe; it has a firm, acid-sweet, yellow flesh surrounding its spiny seed; this fruit is borne in clusters on a medium-sized tree; *Spondias cytherea* or *S. dulcis* (*Anacardiaceae*). [The name is prob derived from its colour and size wh make it easily associated with the 'golden apple' of Greek myth, awarded by Paris to Venus. See note at POMME CYTHERE] 2. (Jmca) ‖ BELL-APPLE (Guyn, etc) 3. (Baha) A kind of orange.

Gold·en Ar·row·head, The *n phr* (Guyn) (Official name of) the national flag of *Guyn*. *The populace might have been poised to start dropping terms like 'colony' and 'BG' the instant the Golden Arrowhead was raised.*—GyG (69.10.12, p.11) [From its design]

gold·en-plum /1'12/ *n* (Belz) ‖ GOLDEN-APPLE (CarA)

gold·en-show·er* /1'122/ *n* (Bdos) ‖ *cat's claw creeper* (Trin) A massive, parasitic climber, with clawed tendrils, wh covers the whole of a tree or wall, when it blooms, in festoons of yellow, funnel-shaped flowers (hence the name); *Macfadyena unguis-cati*, or *Bignonia u.-c.* (*Bignoniaceae*).

gom·bay (Jmca); **gom·bey** (Berm); **goom·bay** (Baha); **gum·bay** (Belz) 1. (Baha, Jmca) A round or square-topped, goat-skin drum played with the hands; several of them are used as central to the rhythm of a particular festive dance of the same name (see 3.). [More than one Bantu lang source seems possible. Cp Kikongo *ngoma* 'drum', and see next] 2. (Baha) A notched stick with a sturdy string attached, serving as a musical instrument. [Cp *SHDNL* Ci-Nyanja *gumbu* 'musical bowstring and cord attached; struck by a reed, the cord being fingered ... with the other hand'] 3. (Baha, Belz, Berm) (i) The festive music with the special beat and rhythm provided by GOOMBAY drums, with cow-bells and whistles added. a. *One thing is certain: If you can sit still when a group of Bahamian musicians break into Goombay, it's time to take your pulse.*—DBH:84 b. *Borrow gumbay no tey till daylight* (= *Free musicians will not play till dawn*).—Belz (Prov) (ii) The vigorous, hip-wiggling, costumed dancing and songs using the rhythm of the festive music. (iii) [By extension] A mid-year festival or season of such music and dancing, esp in *Baha*. *While the goombay bells are ringing / Groups promote Bahamian scene, / Staging folklore, singing, dancing, / Ne'er so active they had been.*—WIE:51 [Cp Bantu langs, Ci-Luba, Kituba, Lingala *ngombe* 'a cow'. Sometimes a framed paper cow or a horned cow-head forms part of the costuming in some places]

gom·mier (gonm·yé) ['gɒmie·] *n* (Dmca, StLu, Trin) ‖ BIRCH-GUM TREE (Bdos, etc) [Fr = 'gum tree' (by wh name the tree is called in some islands)] □ Also **gommier-sang (gonmyé-sang)** (Dmca) because of the red bark of some varieties < Fr *sang* 'blood']

gon [gʌn] *vb* (CarA) [*AF—Cr*] See GOIN[G] 2. and □ Note

gone[1] [gɒ:n] *vb* A. In independent function. **1.** *pa. part. of vb intr* GO in perfective contexts (CarA) [*AF/IF*] [Used without preceding *be* or *have* aux] *S1: I thought they gone to England! / S2: No, they ain['t] gone to England, the whole family gone to Canada.*—(Trin) □ The neg is expressed by preceding *ain['t]* [*AF*] as in cit, *haven['t]*, or *di[d]n['t]* [*AF—Cr*]. **2.** *In vbl adj function* (Bdos, Guyn, StVn) [*AF*] ‖ **gone [a]cross** (Bdos, Guyn) ‖ **gone overboard** (Nevs, StKt) ‖ **gone up** (Jmca) (Be) pregnant. *A woman said, bringing her head close to the neighbour's ear, 'Cutsie makin' child for Boysie ... she three months gone.'*—LICMS:97 □ The term suggests an unwanted pregnancy. **3.** (CarA) [*AF*] [In taking leave of sb] Be leaving, be on your way (as in Phr 4.1). **4.** PHRASES **4.1 I gone** *id phr* (CarA) [*AF*] ‖ **I go** (Bdos) See GO 1 I'm off!; See you later! **a.** *I have never experimented with drugs. ... If I am in a group of fellows and someone decides to roll a spliff, I gone.*—AdV (92.10.16, p.9). **b.** *Ah coming back later and tell you more. Ah gone.*—WeN (54.04.27, p.2, Annie & Josephine) **B.** In many phrases, often developed from those given at GO 6, but others are independent. The following are representative. **4.2 as part of a serial vb** (CarA) [*AF—Cr*] **a.** *... and I tell him tell 'Ess' when she come I gone going look some hog-meat for the pig.*—LaS (75.01.25, p.2) **b.** *Well, so de man run gone, an in two shakes of a duck tail e write de letter.*—WFSFB:34 See GO 3. **4.3 gone [a]cross** *vb phr* (Guyn) [*AF—Joc*] **(i)** To die; (to be) dead [Notionally, to cross the River Jordan, symbolic in folk belief of the river of death]. **(ii)** [By extension] (To be) lost, stolen, gone for good. *When I come back outside de store I fin[d] m[y] bicycle gone [a]cross.*—(Guyn) **(iii)** [Of a woman] (To become) pregnant against her wishes or efforts to prevent that. **4.4 gone agwasa** *vb phr* (Antg, USVI) (To be) lost, stolen, gone for good. **4.5 gone and (do/done sth)** *aspectual aux vb phr* (CarA) [*AF—Cr*] [Indicating objection to the action stated in the latter verb] *You mother gone and dead and lef' me with you, and looka how you wanta mek she memory shame after I try so hard with you.*—CISH:28 [See GO Phr 6.9] **4.6 gone clear** *vb phr* (CarA) [*AF*] **(i)** (To have) broken free and (be) running away. [Metaph ref to a horse gaining a clear lead in a race].] **(ii)** [By extension] (To have) cleared out and disappeared. **4.7 gone for channa** *adj phr* (Guyn) [*AF—Joc*] As good as lost; given away or sold for next to nothing; wasted; stolen. [See GO Phr 6.17] **4.8 gone overboard** *adj phr* (Nevs, StKt) [*AF—Joc*] ‖ GONE 2. (Bdos, etc) **4.9 gone through the eddoes** *adj phr* (Bdos) Done for; ruined; lost,

damaged, or decrepit beyond hope of recovery. [See EDDOE Phr 3.1., GO Phr 6.28] □ The phr occurs most often in this form. **4.10 gone to come** *vb phr* (CarA) [*AF*] (To be) absent for a short while. [See GO Phr 6.29] **4.11 gone up** *adj phr* (Jmca) [*AF*] ‖ GONE 2. (Bdos, etc)

gone[2] *vbl adj* (CarA) [In ref to day, week, month, year] **1.** That has just passed; last; the most recent. *New Year's Day gone, the morning I was sitting on my doorstep as I like to do when I got something to think about.*—CISH:9 **2.** (Bdos, CayI) [Indicating the same day the week before] *Wednesday gone [a] week.*—KWS:9

gonm·yé *n* (Dmca, StLu, Trin) See GOMMIER

goo·bie *n* (Angu, Nevs, USVI) See GOBI

good[1] *adj* (CarA) [*AF/IF*] **1.** [Expressing intensity according to context] Heavy; intense; plentiful; severe, etc. **a.** *She got a good fall from the step.*—(Guyn) **b.** *But let one good rain fall in the next few minutes, and that rain will explain better than I can why the very best thing people can do with a pond like this is to leave it like it is!*—JJHAI:91 **c.** *... then a callalloo soup is prepared with good salt, and sold together with the corn meal.*—FNOD (Ms) [Perh a CE extension of SE *good* in special use as *OED good* A. 20. 'qualifying a ... statement of quantity ... and usu greater than what is stated', also *COD* 6. *good* 10. 'thorough, ample, considerable'. Prob reinforced by CarA Cr use of SE *good* and *bad* in reversed senses] **2.** PHRASES **2.1 be good for sb** *vb phr* (Dmca, StLu) [*AF*] ‖ BE ABLE WITH SB (CarA) See ABLE Phr 1. **2.2 be good for yourself** *vb phr* (CarA) [*AF*] To be sb to be reckoned with; to be always ready with a startling or aggressive answer or defence. *Neither of them could hit the other. Then they stopped. They walked to each other, smiled and shook hands. 'You good for yourself,' the challenger told Dinnoo.*—NAGOS:49 **2.3 head is not good** *id phr* (CarA) [*IF*] See PHR 2.5 below **2.4 Good for you!/all-you/he/she/them!; Good so!; Is/it good so!;** *excl id phrs* (CarA) [*AF*] [Expressing malice] It serves you/all of you/him, etc, right!; I am glad to hear what happened to you/him, etc! **a.** *... ready ears strain to drink it all in, punctuating the telling with expressions ranging from shock and disbelief—'Oh Gawd! No!' to sadistic glee—'Good for she!' 'Dat nice!'*—ExP (73.02.25, p.21) **b.** *I tell you not to play over de[re] an[d] if de dog bite you, good so!*—(Guyn) [A prob calque from W Afr langs. Cp Yoruba *odara bẹ*, Igbo *ọ dọ mma otu ahu*, (both = *It is good like that*) used in same context as CE **good so!**] □ Used mostly by children and young persons, with very strong stress on *good*. **2.5 not good in the head** *adj phr* (CarA) [*IF*] ‖ **head is not good** (CarA) Not right in the head; mentally unstable. [Cp Yoruba *ori rẹ ko dara* (*head is not good*) 'he is mentally unsound']

good[2] *n* (Bdos, Guyn) [*IF*] Good news. *So where've you been all these years? Tell me, what's all the good?*—(Bdos)

good³ *adv* (CarA) [*X*] **1.** Well; (and equivalent senses according to context) carefully, exactly, properly, quite, thoroughly, etc. [Hence its common use in this sense as complement to many verbs in CE: *behave/eat/go/learn/study/walk*, etc *good*] **a.** *'Cry good, child,' Vera Brownford said. 'Cry good. If you don't cry you will get sick. Oh, Lawd, it hard to lose a man. Cry good, child. It much easier.'*—HFGA:36 (J. Hearne) **b.** *'Just the odder day he marrid. Now it eh make a month good an she leave he tail',* Big Joe said.—ExP (72.08.27, p.20) **c.** *I remember it good, good, good.*—LICMS:80 [Perh reinforced by W Afr semantic infl (cp GOOD¹ Phrs 2.4, 2.5) or a survival of EE usage, as *OED good* B. adv 'well' + cit–'1887 'I'll fix them good ...'] □ In this function GOOD is frequently reduplicated for emphasis in CE (cp cit c.). **2.** *qualifying an adj or a vb* (Bdos, Trin) [*X*] Very; certainly; thoroughly. **a.** *These people in Trinidad good wutless, you know.*—HFGA:57 (D. Samaroo) **b.** *He take his time an[d] make her wait till [h]e good finish the work.*—(Trin) **3.** PHRASES **3.1 come good** *vb phr* (CarA) [*AF*] See COME Phr 7.6 *The girl, Jeannette B—19, was said to have told the policeman as she drew a knife from her waist: 'If you coming to me, come good. I ain't afraid of any policeman.'*—AdN (69.10.03, p.7) **3.2 get on good** *vb phr* (CarA) [*AF*] ‖ **live good** (CarA) To live amicably; to be on good terms with each other. **3.3 give (sb) good** *vb phr* (CarA) [*IF*] See GIVE¹ Phr 2.24 **3.4 good and proper** *adv phr* (CarA) [*X*] Thoroughly; soundly. *'We must do it good an' proper this time, eh,' Uncle Leonard said, 'which means more than an 'our an' a 'half, by my reckonin'.*—SJS:140 **3.5 going good** *greeting phr* (CarA) [*IF*] (To be) fine! *How you? Going good?* (= *How are you? Are you fine?*).—(Bdos) **3.6 live good** *vb phr* (CarA) [*AF*] ‖ GET ON GOOD (CarA) See Phr 2.2 **3.7 look (at) me good!** *vb phr* (Guyn) [*AF/IF*] ‖ **Watch me good!** (Guyn) Look at me squarely in the eye! (i.e. either as a test that you are telling the truth, or to make sure that I am most serious about what I say). **3.8 Stan[d] good!** [sta·n gʊd]; **Stay good!** *leave-taking phrs* (Guyn, Jmca) [*AF/IF*] Keep fit and fine until we meet again. **3.9 take sth good** *vb phr* (CarA) [*AF*] To face [a tragedy], receive [bad news] bravely, cheerfully. *But she really bore up at the husband's funeral. She took it good.*—(Baha) **3.10 Walk good!** *sending off phr* (CarA) [*AF*] Get home safely. **3.11 Watch me good!** *vb phr* (Guyn) [*AF*] ‖ LOOK (AT) ME GOOD! (Guyn) See Phr 3.7

good-be·hav·ed *adj* (CarA) [*X*] Well behaved; well mannered. *She spoke of the accused being a good-behaved person, god-fearing, respectful and non-violent.*—AdN (76.11.16, p.1) [< GOOD³ adv 'well' + SE *behaved*]

Good Fri·day bo·bo·lee *n phr* (Trin) ‖ BOBOLEE (Trin)

good hair *n phr* (CarA) [Of a black person] Hair that is wavy and/or soft; long hair; any hair showing strong evidence of European mixture.

The drive in the family came from Ma who was proudly aware that it was from her that Sal inherited the good hair and the brown skin.—FDA:20 □ See also BAD HAIR, PICKY HAIR.

good hand *n phr* (CarA) [*IF*] PHRASE **have a good hand** *vb phr* (CarA) [*IF*] To be lucky in planting and growing things; (SE) to have green fingers. [A prob calque from W Afr langs. Cp *KED* Krio *gud an* 'good hand' (= 'Natural expertise at cooking or other work involving expert use of the fingers')]

good head *n phr* (CarA) [*IF*] Intelligence; good memory; special aptitude (for sth). PHRASE **have a good head for sth** *vb phr* (CarA) [*IF*] To be especially good at doing or remembering (sth). *I must say the old lady has a good head for faces. I didn't think she would remember me.*— (Guyn) [A prob calque from Afr langs, the same phr occurring in CarA Fr Cr (Cp *SLFC bon tèt* 'intelligence') and Gullah. However it could have been reinforced by IrE. Cp N. Irel *He has a good head on him, that lad* (= He is bright—*L. Todd.* Note also SE 'a good head for figures')]

Good night! *greeting or leave-taking phr* (CarA) [Used both on arrival as a mark of courtesy and at departure] Good evening! Goodbye! *'Yes,' agreed Mr Cordai, seizing my hand and wringing it fervently. 'Good night Chief, good night.' I had learned, by trial and error in Georgetown, that 'good night' was used as a greeting any time after the sun had gone down, and it was a trifle confusing until you got used to it.*—GTSA:22 □ SE *Good night!* is limited to leave-taking. In CE it is a standard arrival greeting.

goods *n pl* (CarA) Groceries; foodstuff (esp when in commercial bulk). *Mr Duff said: 'It has become a habit of a lot of drivers of goods vehicles to convey persons in their trucks without having a permit for this.'*—ExP (73.03.22, p.3) [A specialized use of *OED goods* C. 8. 'saleable commodities, merchandise, wares (now chiefly applied to manufactured articles)'. The latter in CE = DRY GOODS]

gool [gu·l] *n* (Guyn) [In children's games] Home; place agreed as 'sanctuary reached' in any catching game. [Perh a development from IrE *cool.* Cp *JESI:239* 'Cool: hurlers and football players always put one of their best players to mind cool or stand cool, i.e. to stand at their own goal or gap, to intercept the ball if the opponents should attempt to drive it through. Universal in Munster. Irish *cul* (cool), the back']

goom·bay *n* (Baha) See GOMBAY

goo·pie ['gupi] *n* (Trin) [Rare] ‖ ARMADILLO (Guyn)

goose·ber·ry* ['guzbɛri ~ 'gʊz(ʌ)bɛri] /1′22/ *n* (CarA) ‖ **chelamela** (CayI) ‖ **cheramina** (Jmca) ‖ **damsel** (Gren, StVn, Trin) ‖ **jimbling, (short) jimbelin** (Jmca) ‖ **Otaheite gooseberry** (Jmca,

Trin) ‖ *raspberry* (Antg) ‖ *sour barge* (Jmca) A small, round, cream-coloured fruit about 3/4 inch in diameter, with a ribbed surface, a hard and very acid flesh and one hard seed; the fruit is borne in small clusters straight from the trunk and limbs of the tree; *Phyllanthus acidus*, or *P. distichus* (*Euphorbiaceae*). [Prob from partial resemblance to BrE *gooseberry* (*Grossulariaceae*) in colour, size and acidity]

goose(-iron) *n* (CarA) A tailor's iron wh is filled with hot charcoal. [< SE *goose* with same sense, but the pl *gooses* being awkward, GOOSE-IRONS gained currency in CE, reinforced by characteristic CarA Cr redundant compounding]

gòs·po (gos·po) [gɒspo] *n* (Dmca, Gren, Trin) ‖ SOUR ORANGE (CarA) *He had decided that the gospo, a mixture of the orange and the lemon and the shadduck, which one ate, had extraordinary virtues. There was one gospo tree on the estate, and the fruit had been used by the children to play cricket.*—NHMB:421 [Fr Cr [g(w)os-po] < Fr *grosse peau* 'rough skin', the rind of this fruit being rough enough to be used for scrubbing]

got (gat) [gɒt~gat] *vb* (CarA) [*AF*] **1.** *vb tr* [*AF—Cr*] **(i)** [In loose general use replacing SE *have*] Have; has; had; have/has got. **a.** *'I got a sick leg, gran'ma. I got a sick leg,' he exclaimed.*—AHR:3 **b.** *Got manners, nuh child!*—(Guyn) **c.** *Anancy got plenty family, yuh know!*—WFSFB:30 **d.** *When I told him he still got six cents for me he get vex.*—Bdos (CR, 71.04.19) **(ii)** [Often used absolutely, with 'some', 'none', 'it' being understood as unstated obj] **a.** *Who got, got, an[d] who ain['t] got ain['t] got!* (= *Those who have some have some, and those who have none have none*).—(StVn) **b.** *Mr Retailer! /If You Want Potatoes, R. L. Seale Got! /If You Want Onions, R. L. Seale Got! etc.*—SuS (86.08.24, p.31 (Ad)) **2.** *modal aux* **got to (do sth)** [*AF*] To have to (do sth). *Man, today you got to hit dem, an even then they tell me 'if you spank me I will bring my fadda!'*—Aaw I.1, p.14 [A refinement of CarA Cr GA[T]] □ The widely current use of *got* in these functions prompts many educated CE speakers to use AmE *gotten* in place of *got* as the pa.t. of *get*, and this is now much seen in writing.

got·ten *vb pa. part.* (CarA) Got (pa. part. of get). *If the Draytons had ever gotten a fair break, spouse would have been more popular.*—NaT (80.03.07, p.10) □ This form, normal in AmE, is occurring increasingly in written educated CE. See note at GOT.

gouge [gu·ž] *n* (StLu, Trin) See GOURD

gourd [gu·d] (**gou(r)ge**) [gu·ž] *n* (BrVi, StKt, StLu, Trin) **1.** ‖ *lauki* (Guyn) ‖ *marrow* (CarA) ‖ *squash* (CarA) ‖ *vegetable marrow* (Bdos, Jmca) Any of a few varieties of a green, smooth-skinned vegetable, sometimes club-shaped about 3 ft long, or shorter and bottle-shaped, bulging much at the end, borne on a sturdy trailing climber with hand-sized, heart-shaped leaves; it is peeled and its firm white flesh cooked when young, or (some varieties) used when dry, scooped out, as a water container; *Lagenaria vulgaris*, or *L. siceraria*, or *Cucurbita pepo* (*Cucurbitaceae*). **2.** (Jmca) ‖ CALABASH (CarA) □ Sense 2. (*Jmca*) applies only to **gourd**.

Gov·ern·ment-House *n* (CarA) ‖ *King's House* (Jmca) The official residence of the Governor or Governor-General of a *CarA* territory.

gov·er·nor-balls *n* (Bdos) ‖ BALL-BUSH (Bdos, Jmca) *... but by reading that the 'man piabba' ... is the same plant familiar to me as 'Governor balls' (Barbadians know it better as 'lion's tail') and that it is a febrifuge as well as the base of a bath for prickly heat?*—SuS (80.06.15, p.7, J. Wickham)

gov·er·nor-fig *n* (Trin) ‖ *cooking-fig, dwarf banana* 2. (Trin) A stout variety of banana borne on a short tree and widely used as a vegetable (GREEN FIG) cooked with fish, etc.

gov·er·nor-plum *n* **1*.** (CarA) ‖ *cerise* 1. (Trin) ‖ *chirise, English plum* (Nevs) ‖ *miwiz* (StLu) ‖ *psidium* (Guyn) A purple, marble-sized fruit, with many seeds in a firm, sour-sweet, brown pulp (that has to be softened by squeezing or rubbing before being eaten); it is borne on a small tree covered in spines and with brown-green leaves; *Flacourtia indica* (*Flacourtiaceae*). □ In *Trin* GOVERNOR-PLUM and CERISE are variant regional names for this fruit. **2.** (Belz) ‖ DUNK(S) (Bdos, etc) **3.** (Tbgo, Trin) ‖ JAMAICA-PLUM (Bdos, etc) □ In *Trin* **governor-plum** seems to be the commoner rural name for this fruit.

grab·ble [grabl] *vb tr* **1.** (Bdos, Gren, Guyn, Tbgo) To grab (sb) roughly (usu with both hands); to seize or snatch up (sth) hurriedly or rashly. **a.** *The accused came right in front of me by the Hospital. He grabbled me by my neck and take off my chain.*—Bdos (CR, 71.05.21) **b.** *One of them, herself the wife of a fireman, grabbled a bucket with the intention of helping to put out the fire but realised that by then it was too big a fire.*—CzN (76.12.23, p.2) [Evid a survival of EE as *OED grabble* 4. (*Obs*) 'to handle rudely or roughly' + cits 1684–1790; also *EDD grabble* v 1. (Brks) 'to grasp, seize, grab'. Perh also reinforced, esp in *Guyn* and *Tbgo* by Du *grabbelen* 'to scramble (for a thing)'] **2.** PHRASES (*variously intensifying sense 1*.) **2.1 grabble hold of (sb) 2.2 grabble on to (sb/sth), -upon (sb) 2.3 grabble up (sth)** To seize hold of (sb/sth) violently. **3.** (Jmca, USVI) To dig or scratch (the earth); to dig (sth) out of the earth. [Cp *OED grabble* 1. 'to feel or search with the hands' + cit 1869 'to grabble for trout (i.e. to grope in holes for them)'. Note also GRABBLER, next]

grab·bler *n* (Bdos) A long, pointed, iron implement used for digging up potatoes and yams. [See GRABBLE 3.]

grab·i·li·cious/-shus *adj* (Baha, Belz) See GRAVALICIOUS

graft·ed (man·go) *n* (*phr*) (CarA) ‖ *Julie-mango* (Angu, Bdos, Gren, Guyn, Jmca) A variety of mango with a noticeable 'chin', often purplish at the top when mature, and having a notably flat seed and a sweet, juicy flesh for wh it is highly prized; *Mangifera spp.* [From the fact that the seed seldom grows 'true' and most successful trees are grafted] □ Many other good varieties of mango are cultivated by grafting, and why the label is widely understood to apply to this one is not clear. The ‖ *Julie* is a more distinctive name.

grage [graj] *n* (Antg, Dmca, Mrat) A device used for making a rasping, scraping or dry rattling sound, as a folk musical instrument in a masqueraders' street-band; it is sometimes a hard, dry, fibrous gourd with its seeds inside, sometimes a grater or perforated piece of tin wh is scraped with a piece of wood. □ See RAKE-AND-SCRAPE BAND, SHAK-SHAK.

Gra·ham(-man·go) [gream(-maŋgo] *n phr* 1. (StLu) ‖ MANGO-GRAHAM (StLu) 2. (Dmca, Gren) A medium-sized mango, the seed of wh is easily removed, and wh is highly prized for its quality. □ Cp BOMBAY-MANGO (Jmca)

grain¹ [gre·n] *n* 1. (Gren, StVn, Tbgo) ‖ FINGER 1. (StVn) *When I take up back the bunch of fig he wrung out a grain* (= *When I picked up the bunch of bananas again, he wrung one banana off the bunch*).—Tbgo (CR, 82.05.25) 2. (i) (Gren) [Of fish sold in numbers] A single fish. *It is only fish that most people can afford these days. In many areas you should see the people rush out to buy flyers ten grains for a dollar.*—Gren (Ms, 76.07.20) (ii) (Bdos, BrVi, StVn) [By extension] A single unit of anything in mass such as peas, hair (of the head), etc. (iii) (BrVi, Guyn) [Often after a neg and sometimes in an abstract sense] The smallest bit. **a.** *Not a grain o[f] rain ain['t] fall.*—(BrVi) **b.** *Bu[t] he ain['t] got a grain o[f] shame to do a t[h]ing like dat.*—(Guyn) [Cp *OED grain* 5. b. (*Obs*) 'one of the parts of a collective fruit' + cit 1660: 'Excellent grapes wh they ... unload without hurting the least grain'. Also *EDD grain* sb² 5. 'a particle, a small quantity of anything' + cits 'grain o' shame .../ o' hay .../ o' sense, etc]

grain² *adj* (Guyn) [AF] Single. *Well I been to to[w]ng one grain time, one grain time!*—(Guyn, a rural farmer) [Prob by functional n > adj shift of GRAIN¹ n, in a general sense; but note also *KED gren* 3. after cardinal numbers (indication of a limit) ex *wan gren* 'one grain' = one only, etc. So this *Guyn* usage may reflect some calquing from an Afr source]

grain³ *n* [Often *pl*] (Antg, Baha, Bdos, Mrat, StKt) An iron bar about 4 ft long and about one inch in diameter with a curved, sharp-pointed end or with a curved, barbed fork at its end, used to spear fish or eels, or hook conchs in holes at low tide. *He liked to sit and watch him make pairs of grains, which when attached to the end of a long pole, were used to spear fish from a dinghy or the shore.*—TrI (75.03.05, p.10) [Cp *OED grain* sb² 5. *Obs exc dial.* b. (pl, commonly construed as *sing*; formerly also spelt *grainse*) 'a fish-spear or harpoon with two or more 'grains' or prongs'. Also *EDD grain* sb 8. 'a peculiar fish-spear or harpoon, gen. with four barbed points'] □ The sg form seems to be preferred in most places, replacing the more careful phr as in cit.

grain⁴ *vb* (Antg, Bdos) To spear fish, eels, etc with GRAINS³. *Sometimes we went diving for mussels and conchs, or graining sea cats (really small octopuses) fishing for eels and so on.*—AnS (74.01.26, p.5) [By functional n > vb shift of GRAIN³]

graine-en-bas-feuille *n* (Dmca, Gren, Trin) See GWENN-ANBA-FÈY

gran·a·dil·la* (gren·a·dil·la) *n* (CarA) ‖ *bar-badine* (Dmca, StLu, Trin) A heavy, yellowish-green, melon-shaped fruit wh is borne on a vine and has a nearly liquid pulp inside in wh the seeds seem to float; the fruit is popular in making iced drinks and punches; *Passiflora quad-rangularis* (*Passifloraceae*). [Sp (*little grenade or cannon-shot*) 'passion-fruit'; the fruit is said to be native to Central America]

gra·na·dit·ta *n* (Jmca) A type of PASSION FRUIT (also called 'sweet granadilla') about the size of a hen's egg, with a hard skin that ripens purple; *Passiflora lingularis* (*Passifloraceae*).

grand *adj* (Gren) [AF—*Joc*] ‖ POOR-GREAT (Guyn) *They so grand wit[h] deyself although they so poor.*—(Gren) [Cp *OED grand* B. sb 1. b. *To do the grand* 'to put on airs']

grand-charge¹ [gran-ča·j] *n* (StLu, Tbgo, Trin) [AF—*Joc*] 1. A big bluff; a loud but empty boast, promise or threat. [Fr Cr < Fr *grand[e]* 'great' + *charge* 'exaggeration, overacting, ca-ricature' (a literary/artistic sense of Fr *charge*)] 2. PHRASE 2.1 **make (your) grand-charge** *vb phr* (StLu, Tbgo, Trin) [AF—*Joc*] ‖ *grand-charge²* (Tbgo, Trin) To make a showy bluff of serious action; to make a pretence of doing or of intention to do some public act only to attract attention. *I must say I had a good laugh watching N— keep a poker face while making this big national grand charge of Opposition unity. I have been watching these politicians for so long that I know unity is the last thing in their petty minds.*—BoM (80.01.04, p.8)

grand-charge² (grand·charge) *vb intr* (Tbgo, Trin) 1. ‖ MAKE (YOUR) GRAND-CHARGE (StLu, etc) See GRAND-CHARGE¹ Phr 2. [By extension] To give a false, superior, image of yourself. *All we can now do is to watch and pray, and look at our newly-appointed chancellor to see if he* *is only grand-charging or whether he has the guts to put his spine where his mouth is. Time alone will tell!*—ExP (72.02.13, p.4) **[**By functional n > vb shift of GRAND-CHARGE[1]**]**

grand·fa·ther *n* (Gren, Guyn) [*AF—Joc*] [Added as an intensifier of sense before or after a noun, hence semi-adjectival] ‖ *grandmother* (Bdos) A very big, nice, attractive, etc one (of whatever item it applies to) **a.** *The costume had a grandfather of a head-piece.*—(Gren) **b.** *Man, look at car gran[d] fada!*—(Guyn) □ See also GRANDMOTHER.

Grand-Man *n* (Srnm) See GRANMAN

grand·moth·er *n* (Bdos) [*AF—Joc*] ‖ G-RANDFATHER (Gren, Guyn) *Well, I know this is going to be fight grandmother, a fight to watch, 'cause all two of them is giants at stick-licking.*—CISH:10

grand·stand [granstan[d]] *vb intr* (Bdos, Tbgo, Trin) [*IF—Joc*] To make a public show or argument or threat or risky-looking action intended purely to impress onlookers while sth is being disputed. *Dr Haynes also declared his view that members of the Barbados Union of Teachers (BUT) were not 'grandstanding' when they marched in support of their position.*—AdV (89.02.09, p.5) **[**By functional n > vb shift of SE *grandstand*, and its association with excitement. Cp also SE idiom *play to the gallery* with the same notion**]** □ Cp GRAND-CHARGE[2] vb 1. with closely similar meaning. No pa.t. form appears to be used, except perh **made a grandstand**, though *is/was grandstanding* is common esp in *Trin.*

Gran·man; Grand-Man *n* (Srnm) The chieftain or Head Man of a Bush-Negro village or ethnic group in *Srnm.* **[**Sran < Sp/Pg *grande* 'great' + Du *man* 'man'. The term was orig applied to the Governor of *Srnm***]** □ '*The Granman*' is an officially recognized title, with certain rights, in *Srnm.* The form *Grand-Man*, sometimes found, is anglicized and unnecessary.

gran·ny *n* (Baha, TkCa) A folk midwife·

gran·ny-back·bone *n* **1.** (Guyn) A flat-stemmed and slightly twisting, woody, forest climber used as a folk-medicine for pains, but esp, together with other BUSHES, in a decoction as an aphrodisiac; *Chododendron candicans (Menispermaceae)*—FFPG:II, p.45. **[** < *BAED* Arawak *tete-ahabo* 'a flat liana' < *tete* 'grandmother' + *ahabo* 'backbone'. GRANNY-BACKBONE is a trans of this, because of its medicinal fame. See next**] 2.** (CarA) A climbing plant, also used for its aphrodisiac properties; *Lygodium spp*—HLNPG:217. **[**Prob by association through the 'Weed Song' of Guyn wh became famous in the *CarA* in the 1930s. The song, (wh included a list of folk-medicinal weeds such as, '*minni-root, gully-root, granny-backbone, etc*' many of wh were associated with sexual uses) was adopted

in many *CarA* territories as their own. The names of many *Guyn* BUSHES may have been adapted to local items through this medium**]**

gran·ny-sug·ar *n* (Guyn) [*IF—Joc*] Very tiny, brown grains of wood residue that pour out in little runnings from termite-infested furniture or walls. *The Courts in Guyana are generally in dire need of repairs. There are Courts where the granny sugar falls on the desk as lawyers do their work.*—GyG (75.11.04, p.6) **[***Granny*, suggesting age + *sugar*, from resemblance to fine brown sugar**]**

grant *n* (Guyn) [Timber Ind] ‖ *timber-grant, wood-grant* (Guyn) A government concession of many hundred acres of forest-land to a person or company, for industrial logging. *The evidence was given yesterday by Rookhan, grant labourer, who said he saw Baksh approach Harricharran at the Timber landing at Canals.*—DaC (53.02.07, p.5)

grap *n* (Dmca, Gren, StLu, Tbgo, Trin) A bunch or cluster (esp of coconuts, less often of other fruits). **[**Fr Cr < Fr *grappe* 'cluster, bunch' (esp of grapes)**]**

grape *n* (Bdos, CayI, Guyn, Jmca) ‖ SEASIDE-GRAPE (CarA) □ The name, however, increasingly indicates the commercially imported (and very different) European grape (*Vitaceae spp*).

grape-tree *n phr* (Bdos, CayI, Guyn, Jmca) The tree bearing the SEASIDE-GRAPE.

grass *n PHRASE* **pass for grass** *id phr* (Guyn) [*IF*] To be treated with disrespect or contempt because you are or have become poor or have lost your social position; to be considered safe to snub.

grass-bot·tle *n* (ECar) [*X*] ‖ GLASS-BOTTLE (ECar) **[** < GLASS-BOTTLE by /l > r/ shift, prob reinforced by folk etym, since the pieces of bottle often lie in uncut grass**]**

grass-cor·ner *n* (Guyn) [*AF*] ‖ *corner, parapet* (Guyn) *PHRASE* **in the grass-corner** *adv phr* (Guyn) At/to the side of the road. *Child, walk in the grass-corner befo[re] yo[u] get knock do[w]ng.*—(Guyn) **[**Ref to the grassing of the PARAPETS**]**

grass-gang *n* (Trin) [Sugar Ind] ‖ CREOLE-GANG (Guyn) *... the children of the grass-gang, walking briskly along the road single file, their heads practically hidden by tall, wide bundles of wet grass, hardly able to see, and, because of the weight on their heads and the grass over their faces, unable to make more than slurred, brief replies to taunts, were easy objects of ridicule.*—NHMB:23

grass-knife *n* (CarA) A sickle. *Grass knives in their hands they thrashed away at the rice which reached up about their thighs.*—Kai. 8, p.52

[From its most regular use for cutting long grass, though it serves for harvesting rice, picking coconuts, etc]

grass-piece n (CarA) A pasture. *Today nobody gives you land for playing fields except very rarely, and even although we have done with the mules and the horses, the grass-pieces are not given over.*— Bdos (Hd, 76.07.27, p.7055)

grass-quit* (**grass·quit**) n (CarA) Any of a few varieties of sparrow (generally grey, brown, dark-green, some varieties having white or yellow patches on neck or head); *Fringillidae spp.*

grass-snake n (CarA) Any of a few varieties of small (often shiny brown or dull green) non-poisonous snakes that do not live in trees.

grat·er vb tr (Bdos, Belz, Jmca, Tbgo, Trin) To grate (esp coconut kernels) using a grater. [By functional n > vb shift < SE *grater* or perh from a mispronunc of *grate up* vb tr phr with characteristic Cr loss of final consonant]

grat·er-cake n (Jmca) ‖ SUGAR-CAKE 1. (Bdos, etc) [< *grater* + *cake* = cake made by using a grater (to grate the coconut). Cp *AMEWF*:74 SE compounds like *finger-print*]

grat·er-wood n (Trin) ‖ BLACK-SAGE 2. (CarA) [Perh from the roughness of the stems and leaf-surface]

gra·va·li·cious (**grab·i·li·cious**) [ˈgra valɪšʌs ~ grabɪlɪšʌs] adj (Baha, Belz, Jmca) [*AF— Joc*] ‖ BIG-EYE¹ (CarA) *He frowned at the derogatory remarks that are made by some competitors of other funeral directors in order that they (the former) could get the service.... The association's president also felt that 'the chaps in this area are so gravalicious they would live and see you die'.*—NaG (75.10.1, p.1) [Blend of *greedy* or *grab* and *avaricious* with /r > l/ change]

grave-dust n (Guyn) ‖ DUPPY-DUST (Bdos)

grease-hand/-palm n (Gren, Tbgo, Trin) [*AF*] A bribe. [< SE idiom *to grease one's palm* 'to bribe']

greas·y-bush* n **1.** (Baha, Jmca) ‖ WOMAN-PIABA (Bdos, Guyn) *Greasy-bush or honey-weed has a pinkish-mauve flower that attracts birds and bees for its nectar.*—Jmca (Ms) [Prob from velvety and perh also soapy character of its leaves. Note *HCWP*:50 Fr Cr *herbe savon* (= soap bush)] **2.** (Tbgo, Trin) A weedy shrub growing into a robust climber with hairy stems and leaves, wh are broadly elliptical, and white, curved inflorescences wh develop into little dry nuts; the plant is used to make an infusion for 'cooling the blood' or for BATHS for the sick; *Tournefortia hirsutissima (Boraginaceae).*

great adj (Bdos) [*AF—Joc*] ‖ POOR-GREAT (Guyn) *And to fall from favour, ... meant the*

return to the standpipe by the corner, and subjection to the verbal hostility of the proper standpipe crowd! / The humiliation was sore. 'How come you wearing shoes and stockings at the standpipe! You great?'—SuS (80.04.06, p.10) [Perh a survival of EE usage. Cp *OED great* A. 12. 'of high social or official position; of eminent rank', etc. In Bdos cp *CGBD5. great-kind* 'applied to pure bred stock and ... fruit and vegetables of best quality' + cit showing Joc application also to persons]

great-cake n (Bdos) ‖ BLACK-CAKE (Guyn, etc)

great gang n (Dmca) ‖ FIRST GANG (Bdos) See GANG (cit and Note) *The land was cleared of trees and bush and burnt by 'great gangs' composed of the strongest men and women under a driver.*—HTDS:42

Great House (**Great·house**) n (phr) (CarA) [Hist] ‖ THE BIG HOUSE (CarA) See BIG¹ 3. (i) (b) *Rung by the village bell-ringer, it reminded the workers that estate owner Matt Brown, who lived in the Great House on the hill, expected all his people to be indoors.*—RPME:13

gree [griː] vb intr (CarA) [*AF—Cr*] Agree. *She was a beautiful woman, and lovely. (But when she and me ain't greeing, man, Boysie, you don't know I have never see a more uglier bitch in the world!)*—CWFYS:71 [< SE *agree* by aphesis] **2.** PHRASE **2.1 gree back** vb phr (CarA) [*AF—Cr*] To resume a friendly relationship after a serious row. □ The dial forms are commonly written, usu as *'gree*, in CE narrative dialogue.

greed·y n (CarA) [*AF—Cr*] Greed; avariciousness (esp in relation to food). *Greedy will kill you.*—WSAD:13 [By characteristic CarA Cr adj > n shift. Cp similarly HUNGRY]

gree-gree n (Gren) See GRI-GRI

green-back (**tur·tle**) n (CarA) See GREEN TURTLE

green ba·na·na (**green fig**) n phr (CarA) The young, immature banana cooked as a vegetable, often with SALTFISH. □ Exceptional in *Guyn*.

green canes n phr pl (Bdos) [Sugar Ind] Mature or ripe sugar-canes with green tops or fronds (i.e. as opposed to canes that have been burnt to facilitate quick reaping). *Common sense should tell you, Mr President, that the differential between cutting burnt canes and cutting green canes is much too small in this country.*—Bdos (Hd, 74.03.28, p.465)

green chub n phr (StLu) ‖ CACA-BAWI (Dmca, etc)

green fig n phr (CarA) See GREEN BANANA

green gold n phr (ECar) [*AF—Joc*] (A euphemism for) flourishing banana crops or sugar-cane crops.

green·heart* *n* (Guyn) [Timber Ind] A forest-tree that can reach over 120 ft in height with an erect trunk rising some 80 ft before branching, yielding a heavy, hard, straight-grained brown to yellowish-green wood; it is extremely durable and resistant both to termites and river-water, and hence it is prime construction material; *Ocotea rodiaei* (*Lauraceae*).

green leaf *n phr* (Antg, Dmca, Gren, Trin) A children's game in wh each participant must have a green leaf to show at any time when called upon, or accept a punishment if caught without it.

green mon·key *n phr* (Bdos, Gren, StKt) ‖ *Barbados green monkey* (Bdos) A long-tailed monkey of about 12 lbs at maturity, with a brownish-grey coat and many greenish-yellow hairs that give it a greenish appearance (hence the name); the species (now a pest) is thought to have developed special physical features in the *ECar* though orig introduced from W Afr; *Cercopithecus aethiops sabaeus* or *C. mona*.

green peas *n phr pl* (Bdos, Gren, Guyn, Trin) ‖ PIGEON-PEAS (CarA)

greens *n pl* (CarA) **1.** Fresh lettuce, watercress, parsley, etc, eaten uncooked with a meal (hence also sometimes loosely called SALAD). **2.** ‖ *herbs* (Baha, USVI) Green, leafy vegetables, including young beans in the pod, wh are boiled or steamed as part of a meal.

green tea *n phr* (CarA) Ordinary tea as made from steeped (imported) tea-leaves. □ SE *green tea* (see *OED*, *W3*) refers to tea made with unprocessed leaves, but the CE term, now largely restricted to rural or older folk, served esp to distinguish commercially sold 'tea' from *CarA* BUSH-TEA and other kinds of hot drink wh were called *cocoa-tea*, *coffee-tea*, etc. See also TEA.

green tur·tle* *n phr* (CarA) A sea-turtle with a smooth, oval, olive-brown shell up to 4 ft long; its weight can exceed 500 lbs and its light green flesh is most valued for making turtle soup; *Chelonia mydas* (*Chelonidae*). [From the colour of its meat] □ The alternative name GREEN-BACK TURTLE is misleading.

green verbs *n pl* (Guyn, Trin) [*AF—Joc*] Incorrect English, esp as spoken by sb who is trying or expected to speak correct English, and esp marked by incorrect agreements or tense-forms of SE verbs. *You does talk a lot o' green verbs, brother: what is dat? My children suppose' to be listenin' to yuh, an' they supposes to have a better standard of English, an' I uses to t'ink you shouldn't be on dat ting at all. Betaudier, yuh cyah fin' a way to speak better language?*—Peo.I 1, p.24 [Green in Joc sense of 'unripe, immature' + *verbs* as the main test of correctness in CE]

Gren·a·da dove *n phr* (Gren) A dove about 12 ins long with a dark-brown back, cinnamon to mauve breast, white forehead and belly; it is a unique species of ground-dwelling, forest-bird with a mournful coo, though it is rarely seen; *Leptotila wellsi* (*Columbidae*). □ It is the National Bird of Grenada.

Gren·a·di·an *n, adj* (CarA) (A person or thing) native or belonging to the island-state of Grenada.

Gren·a·di·an·i·za·tion (-is-) *n* (CarA) The process or act of making (sth) markedly GRENADIAN in character or appearance.

gren·a·dil·la *n* (CarA) See GRANADILLA

Gren·a·dines, The *n pl* (CarA) A large group or archipelago of small islands and rocks (many of wh are unnamed) stretching some 60 miles south from St Vincent to Grenada, of wh the following, known as *The St Vincent Grenadines*, form part of the State of St Vincent: (order from North) Bequia [bɛkwɛ], Petit Nevis, Quatre Is, Battowia, Baliceaux, Mustique, Petit Mustique, Savan Is, Petit Cannouan, Cannouan, Mayreau [maɪro], Tobago Keys, Sail Rock, Union, Prune Is, Petit St Vincent. (The largest is Union). The following, *The Grenada Grenadines*, form part of the State of Grenada: (order from North following Petit St Vincent)—Petit Martinique, Carriacou, Saline Is, Frigate Is, Large Is, Kick 'em Jenny, Les Tantes, Ronde Is, Caille Is.

greng-greng *n* (Trin) [*AF—Joc*] A black person's hair that is very short and coarse in texture, esp at the back of the head. [Cp *DAFL* Twi-Fante [kraŋŋ] 'rough, rugged, coarse' + perh Derog reduplication, common in CarA Cr, and /k > g/ voicing] □ Sometimes also used as adj (note etym): GRENG-GRENG HAIR.

gri·chi-gri·chi   (**grit·chee-grit·chee,** **gush·ee-gush·ee**)   [grɪči-grɪči ~ gʌši-gʌši]   *n* (USVI) ‖ SENSITIVE PLANT (Bdos, etc) *Gushee-gushee is a small plant, native of tropical America, with thorny stems that creep through the grass. The leaves are sensitive to the touch and close up at once. Children on St John, St Thomas, and St Croix sing a song, 'Gushee-gushee, shut your do' / Ole man comin' to bite your toe'. The Sensitive Plant bears a small lavender dandelion-type bloom.*—JNHSJ:54 [A folk name, prob < Du *Grietje* [gri·čə] 'Peggy'; the shy behaviour of the plant attracts female names in other places (see main ‖) and the reduplication is prob Joc. *HPVI*: *32* cites the children's rhyme as 'Gritchee-Gritchee shut up yo' do'. Two gendarmes is coming fo' yo'. The form GUSHEE-GUSHEE may be due to folk etym or a children's corruption]

gri-gri¹ (**gree-gree**) *n* (Gren) **1.** ‖ CHICKEN-HAWK (CarA) **2.** ‖ SPARROW-HAWK (CarA)

gri-gri² (palm) *n(phr)* (Trin) ‖ *pimpler-palm* (Guyn) One of two closely similar varieties of a slender, curving, pale-barked palm, its trunk ringed and its compound leaves armed with sharp black spines; it grows to about 20 ft and bears clusters of small edible fruit with a hard seed and scanty pulp, one variety scarlet and pea-sized; *Martinezia caryotaefolia* and *M. corallina* (*Palmae*). □ The name seems to be applied to other varieties of spiny palm by popular confusion. See *FFGM:396-7* for variant classifications of *Aiphanes spp.* See also GROU-GROU.

grind[1] *vb* **1.** *vb tr* (CarA) [Sugar Ind] [Of a sugar-factory] To crush sugar-cane between a system of rollers in the first stages of making sugar. *Guyana Sugar Corporation Chairman Harold Davis said that only Rose Hall, Blairmont, Enmore, La Bonne Intention, Wales and Leonora factories were grinding during the week.*—GyC (78.01.15, p.1) □ The vb is semi-intr in this function, the understood object *sugar-cane* being unstated (as in cit). In this function the forms *to grind, grinding* are common, but the pa.t. *ground* is rare in speech. Cp SE *grind* vb tr 'to reduce to small particles', usu with a stated obj 'coffee, grain', etc. **2.** *vb tr* (StLu, Trin) [IF] To anger (sb); to cause (sb) frequent or recurring vexation. *Her blasted lateness nearly every day just grinds me, you hear?*—(StLu) **3.** [By extension] *vb intr* (StKt, Tbgo, Trin) [AF] To get into or be in a state of inactive anger or fury. *The party supporters now grindin[g] [be]cause they los[t] the election.*—(Trin) **4.** *vb intr* (CarA) [AF—Vul] **(i)** To have uninhibited sexual intercourse with impassioned movements of the hip. *Eh! Madam has found a nice young planterman! Come to bed, nice blond boy! Madam will grind with you herself!*—RND:226 **(ii)** [By extension] To dance usu on one spot while rotating the hips to imitate a passionate sex act. *Jumping, jamming, wining and grinding; gyrating hips in skimpy costumes—the women of Carnival all came to play.*—Pic: 31 [The senses 2, 3, 4 may have developed metaphorically from 1. Sense 4 also occurs in AmE]

grind[2] *n* **1.** (Tbgo, Trin) ‖ *grindings* (StKt) Anger from frustration; problems of life; troubles; stinging grief, etc. [By functional vb > n shift of GRIND[1] 2, 3.] **2.** (CarA) A manner of dancing with marked sexual gyrations of the hips. [By functional vb > n shift of GRIND[1] 4.] **3.** PHRASE **3.1 bear/stand/stick your grind** *vb phr* (Tbgo, Trin) [AF] To withstand the blows, shocks or general troubles of life (esp in relation to some particular misfortune or situation).

grind·ing *n* (CarA) [Sugar Ind] The period of continuous crushing of harvested sugar-cane and processing of the juice, during wh a sugar-factory works non-stop. *To visit Marjorie tomorrow would be difficult; leave would have to be obtained, and it was now the grinding, and therefore the busiest season of the year.*—WTTBB:189 [Vbl n < GRIND[1] 1] □ Perh more likely to be used attrib: the grinding season.

grind·ings *n pl* (StKt) ‖ GRIND[2] 1. (Tbgo, Trin) *I have supported PAM at my fullest. I have lost*

many friends; I have gained many enemies, lost patronage in business and also have been robbed of many opportunities. However, I still hold on, bear my grindings and hope that we shall overcome some day.—DeM(SK) (76.06.05, p.8)

grip *n* (Bdos, Guyn) A cheaper kind of large VALISE, usu made of rein forced cardboard. *Now me, when an goin' on plane, /Ah doesn't like to carry nothin' in me hand, /Ah does put every thing in de grip/An' have me two hand swingin' free*—KTT:21 [Cp COD8 *grip* n.6 'a travelling bag']

grits·y *adj* (Baha) [IF] [Of teeth] With yellow-scum; dirty with food particles between; un-scrubbed. [Metaph ref to the yellowish mealy appearance of (U.S.) (*hominy*) *grits*, wh is popular in *Baha*]

grit·ty hair *n phr* (Angu) ‖ PICKY HAIR/HEAD (Baha, etc)

grog·ist *n* (Gren, Tbgo, Trin) [AF—*Joc*] A heavy drinker (esp of rum). [SE *grog* + SE -*ist* by Joc analogy with such words as *druggist*, or a blend of *grog* + *specialist*. Cp FOODIST]

groove-and-tongue *n, adj* (Guyn) ‖ *grooving-tongue* (Bdos) (Builder's board) having a groove along one edge and a matching ridge or tongue along the other so that such boards can be made to fit tightly together for the construction of floors, walls or roofs; (IAE) tongue-and-groove. □ Br and AmE *match[ed]-board* for the same item appears to be unknown in CE.

groov·ing-tongue *n, adj* (Bdos) ‖ GROOVE-AND-TONGUE (Guyn)

gros bourg(e) *n phr* (Dmca) See GWO BOUG

Gros Mi·chel (ba·na·na) (Gwo Mi·chèl) [ˈgro-mišɛl ~ gwo-mišɛl ~ gros-mičɛl ˈbʌnanʌ] *n (phr)* (CarA) The largest and most prized of all cultivated varieties of banana, borne on a very large bunch; it is also said to be the best suited for export; *Musa Pisang raja* (*Musaceae*). [Fr = 'Big Michael', in ref to size of the tree, the fruit, and the bunch wh can exceed 5ft in length. The Fr name, perh originating in Cameroun, was introduced via *Mart* in the 19c to *Jmca*.]

gros-pom·pom; gros-tête *n* (StLu) See GWO PON PON; GWO-TÈT

gros-zié *n, adj* (Dmca, StLu, Trin) See G(w)O ZYÉ 1, 2.

grou-grou (gru-gru, gwou-gwou, gwu-gwu) [grugru ~ gwugwu] *n* (Gren, StVn, Tbgo, Trin) ‖ *macaw* 2. (Antg, Bdos, StKt) ‖ *macaw-palm* (Bdos) ‖ *macca*[2](-*palm*) (Belz, Jmca) **1***. An erect palm reaching a height of about 30 ft, its tough trunk and its fronds covered at intervals in long, stout black spines; it bears abundant clusters of reddish fruit with an edible but scanty pulp on a hard seed; *Acrocomia aculeata (Palmae). Gru-Gru kernels yield a valuable oil.... Gru-Gru kernels in good condition would find a ready market in the United Kingdom at prices approximating to those of palm kernels...if offered in commercial quantities.*—PTT:59 **2.** A shorter variety of the *Acrocomia spp* bearing a smaller green-skinned fruit, with a sticky, scanty pulp. **3.** [By extension] The fruit of either variety, the sticky pulp of wh children eat. **4.** PHRASE **4.1 be hard like gru-gru/banga seed** *vb phr* (Trin) [Of a person] To be very stubborn.

grou-grou bèf (**gru-gru bèf, gwou-gwou bèf, gwu-gwu bèf**) *n phr* (Trin) ‖ *macca-fat* (Jmca) **1.** A tougher variety of the GROU-GROU, though the term is mostly understood to refer to its much bigger fruit with an extremely hard nut (hence sense **2.**). [*Bèf* is Fr Cr (< Fr *boeuf*) 'bull, cow', regularly used to indicate a large-sized fruit, ex *mango-bèf*] **2.** ‖ *banga(r)* (Guyn, Trin) The dried hard seed of the same used by boys as a marble. **3.** PHRASE **3.1 be hard like banga (seed)** *vb phr* (Trin) See GROU-GROU Phr 4.1

ground[1] [grʌŋ(d)] *n* (CarA) **1.** (The surface of the earth, and hence, by extension) the floor of any dwelling (wh in the slave era was often the surface of the earth). *The glass fell on the ground but the carpet saved it from breaking.*—(Bdos) **2.** PHRASE **2.1 foot [u]pon ground** *id phr* (Bdos) [AF—*Joc*] See FOOT Phr 2.7 □ See GROUNDS as separate entry.

ground[2] [grʌŋ(d)] *n* (CarA) **1.** [Hist] ‖ *niggerground* (Guyn, Tbgo, ViIs) An area of land at the rear of a sugar-plantation assigned to slaves to grow their own food. *Most estates had some flat land for sugar, some swampy land for grass in times of drought, and some mountain land for fuel and 'grounds' where the slaves grew their food.*—SJW:25 **2.** [By extension] A personal vegetable garden behind a house or far away in the back-lands of a sugar plantation.... *within hailing distance of the man with the machete and hoe sweating beneath the gaudy sun, planting his steeply tilted 'ground' with corn and cassava*—SJW:1 [Cp EDD ground sb 5. 'a farm, esp an outlying one'] **3.** PHRASE **3.1 go (out) to ground** *vb phr* (Jmca) To go to your farm to work. *'Mi going to ground go dig some sweet potato',* he said, and turned to go.—DaG (67.11.12, p.4. Short Story) **3.2 work (the) ground** *vb phr* (CarA) [AF/IF] To till a piece of land for planting root vegetables.

ground[3] *vb intr* (CarA) To sit and talk with or among poor, socially deprived people in gatherings in their own neighbourhood in order to help them develop a sense of their social and political rights. [A ref to sitting on the ground, with functional n > vb shift] □ See GROUNDING, GROUNDS, GROUNDSING.

ground·a·tion(s) *n (pl)* (CarA) See GROUNDING(S)

ground-ball *n* (CarA) [Cricket] ‖ *groundeater* (Guyn) ‖ *grounder* (Bdos) **1.** ‖ *underhand (ball)* (Dmca, Guyn) A ball that is bowled underhand along the ground all the way. **2.** A ball that keeps very low after hitting the ground when bowled; a shooter.

ground-bas·ket *n* (CarA) A large, round, deep basket without handles or cover, made of interwoven bamboo strips or sturdy WIST; it is used to bring provision from the GROUND to market or sometimes to catch fish by hauling it through the water.

ground-dove* *n* (CarA) **1.** ‖ *tobacco-dove* (Baha) ‖ *toutwèl* (Dmca, Gren) A greyish-brown bird about 9 ins long, with scaly-looking breast feathers and cinnamon-coloured wings; it nests on the ground or in low places and hardly flies, moving rather in short, jerky bursts, dwelling abundantly in wide open ground and often feeding in pairs; it makes a much repeated cooing sound and is the subject of superstitions in some places; *Columbigallina passerina* or *Columbina p.* (*Columbidae*). **2.** ‖ *mountain-dove* (ViIs) ‖ *peadove* (Jmca) ‖ *seaside-dove* (Gren) ‖ *wood-dove* (Bdos) A pinkish-brown bird about 10 to 12 ins long with darker brown wings; it makes a mournful, resonant cooing, nesting in low trees but spending much of its life on the ground in open places or yards; *Zenaida aurita,* also *Z. auriculata* (*Columbidae*). □ The name seems also to be applied to a few other varieties of both of the types described above.

ground-eat·er *n* (Guyn) [Cricket] ‖ GROUNDBALL (CarA)

ground·er *n* (Bdos) [Cricket] ‖ GROUND-BALL (CarA)

ground-foods *n pl* (Belz, USVI) ‖ GROUNDPROVISIONS (CarA)

ground·ing(s) [grʌndɪŋ(z)] *n (pl)* (CarA) ‖ *groundation(s)* (CarA) ‖ *groundsing* (Bdos) The act of talking together, sincerely and for as long as is necessary, with or among socially deprived people in their own neighbourhood or dwelling-places, many sitting relaxed on the ground (hence the term). *In the island itself, the St Lucia Forum (a loosely unstructured group of graduates) had begun conducting 'groundings'—as Walter Rodney had earlier done elsewhere.*—CaC (8/77, p.11) [< *ground*[3] vb intr]

ground-itch [grʌŋ-ič] *n* (CarA) **1.** An itching skin sore or sores caused by hookworm larvae entering the skin through the soles of the feet (hence the name). *The children here are poor and many of them come to school barefooted and would you believe that these children are suffering from what we used to know as ground itch. Imagine that, in this day and age.*—BoM (75.02.14, p.5) **2.** [In animals] Foot rot. *Foot rot (ground itch) is caused by a bacterial organism (Sphaerophorus necrophorus) penetrating through surface injuries....*

The disease is most common in areas that are rough and/or wet and swampy. Thus our coastland region affords near ideal conditions for foot rot.—Guyn (Ms, 1976)

ground·liz·ard* *n* (CarA) ‖ *zagada* 1. (Gren) A lizard that grows to more than 12 ins in length, has a beak-like snout and wriggles rapidly along the ground, not climbing trees (hence its name); it is scaly and some small varieties are bronze coloured; *Ameiva dorsalis* or *A. exsul* (*Lacertidae*). □ In a number of islands this lizard is wrongly thought to be an exclusively indigenous species.

ground-pro·vi·sions *n* (*pl*) (CarA) ‖ *provisions* (CarA) ‖ *ground-foods* (Belz, USVI) (Collective name for) all varieties of starchy vegetables wh are locally grown on lands (or GROUND, hence the name), once set aside on or near sugar plantations for slaves and (later) labourers to provide their daily food; any or all of the foll: breadfruit, cassava, dasheen, eggplant, green figs, plantains, sweet potatoes, yams, etc.

grounds *adj* (CarA) [*AF/IF*] [Of a person] Belonging to or identified with the grass-roots of society and known by your fellows as straightforward and ready to talk. *I'm sure there are some grounds guys up in England there who would like to have words with a sister from home.*—WeG (73.07.11, p.13 Partyline) [By functional n > adj shift of *ground* 'earth' (hence perh a development or shift of the sense 'earthy') + characteristic IF CE paragogic '-s'. Cp BROKES adj] □ Cp also GROUNDSING

ground·sel (**ground·sill**) *n* (Bdos) ‖ *dry-wall* 2. (Baha, etc) ‖ *rubble-stone foundation* (Angu) The foundation for a small, wooden house, such as a CHATTEL HOUSE, made up by closely stacking large pieces of stone so that they stay together without mortar. *Another woman, who rents a house in the tenantry, said that on Wednesday water had risen to the height of her groundsel which is about 2 ft and she was unable to get in or out of her home.*—AdV (66.08.21, p.9) [By shift of meaning < SE *groundsel* 'a timber serving as a foundation to carry a superstructure, esp of a wooden building' *OED* + prob blending with *OED ground-wall* (*Obs*) 'a foundation'; also infl by SE *sill* 'bottom slab of a door or window']

grounds·ing [grʌnzɪŋ] *n* (Bdos, Guyn) [*AF/IF*] ‖ GROUNDING (CarA) *The little real change that has come, has come only when the leaders involved themselves. Now Yoruba and others like it also run that risk unless they start 'groundsing'—getting out of their niche and making contact outside.*—MaN (73.11.11, p.8) [< GROUND³ vb intr + paragogic '-s'. Cp FRIENDSING, similarly patterned]

grow *vb* 1. *vb intr* (CarA) [*IF*] [Of a human being] To be raised, reared or brought up (in sb's care); to develop from childhood to adulthood (in

some particular place, condition or context). *S1: Where you grow? / S2: I grow with my aunt in Essequebo.*—(Guyn) □ More than the normal SE sense of physical bodily development, CE *grow* focuses on circumstances of survival, esp on being fed and cared for, (hence the foll sample of many phrs). 2. PHRASES (CarA) [*AF/IF*] 2.1 **grow a big man/woman; grow big** To approach or reach adulthood. 2.2 **grow at/with (sb)** To be brought up, cared for, by (sb) (ex an aunt, godmother, etc). 2.3 **grow bad** To grow up undisciplined and crude. 2.4 **grow poor** To grow up in poverty, etc. □ Note that in such Phrs as 2.3, 2.4, SE *grow* 'to become' would be so understood only in Formal (educated) CE. 2.5 **If I plant you, you goin(g)/will grow?** *id phr* (CarA) [*IF*] See PLANT Phr 3. *vb tr* (Gren, Tbgo, Trin) [*AF*] ‖ **grow up** (Gren, Tbgo, Trin) [Esp of a foster-parent] To bring up or raise (a child). **a.** *My aunt is the one that grow me.*—(Trin) **b.** *So why she can[']t sweep de place? Is so we growin[g] she up?*—(Gren) [Perh by semantic shift of SE *grow* vb tr wh is applied only to plant life] 4. *vb tr* [With the general sense 'to develop'] PHRASES 4.1 **grow a bab** *vb phr* (StLu) To show anger in your face; to make plain your annoyance. *Ou meme too! If you had was to sign for de grocery bills of de business you wouldn't grow a bab and daccord dat a skeleton haunting de damn place.*—CrU (74.03.09, Cocky & Stocky) [E + Fr Cr *bab* < Fr *barbe* 'beard'; hence grow a beard (*Joc*) = pull a long face or bristle with anger] 4.2 **grow a daughter** *vb phr* (Jmca) [Rastaf] [Of a BROTHER] To court and train a young girl in the ways of the Rastafarian cult so that she leaves home and joins the cult as one of his acknowledged sexual partners.

grow·ing-stake/-stick *n* (Jmca) ‖ GLIRICIDIA (Angu, etc) *Him get pikni quick, quick, quick / Six in a row laka growin' stick.*—Jmca (Ms, Student's verse, 1978) [From the fact that a large stake of the tree stuck in the ground will grow, hence its use for fences]

grub·bing *n* (Bdos, Jmca, Trin) [*AF*— University] The practice of subjecting new University students to organized, rough, and often unpleasant pranks as supposedly traditional rites of initiation; AmE hazing. [< SE *grub* n 'larva' i.e. earliest stage of (insect) life + functional n > vb shift *to grub*, 'to make a grub of or consider to be a grub', whence *grubbing*]

grub·by hair *n phr* (StVn) ‖ *picky hair/head* (Baha, etc)

grudge *vb tr* (CarA) [*X*] To be envious of (sb) (for sth not necessarily stated); to begrudge (sb). *When they realized that the boss was calling on her for everything the others in the office grudged her.*—StKt (Ms) [< SE *begrudge* 'to envy (sb) the possession of (sth)' by aphaeresis, or < *grudge* vb tr by confusion of sense]

grudge·ful *adj* (CarA) [*IF*] Maliciously envious. *Mr Nurse is a quiet man and anybody who*

says these things about him must be grudgeful.—
ViN (73.04.28, p.4) [< SE *grudge* 'resentment'
+ CE *grudge* 'to envy' + '-ful' by analogy with
such SE items as *deceitful, painful,* etc]

grudge-pea* *n* (Gren) ‖ *horse-bean* (Bdos,
Jmca, Trin) ‖ *jack-bean* (Jmca, Trin) ‖ *maldjo²*
(Gren, Trin) ‖ *overlook-bean* (Bdos, Jmca)
‖ *sword-bean* (Bdos) A green, bushy plant whose
stems sometimes grow long and begin to climb,
bearing purple flowers with a few white lines,
and stiff, green pods about an inch wide and a
foot long that can be used as a vegetable; *Canavalia ensiformis (Leguminosae-Papilionaceae). If
planted round a garden, grudge pea is thought
to 'cut the eye' of envy, and so prevent petty
thefts.*—GNHIG:78 [Name may be due to the
fact that the vegetable pod is poisonous unless
boiled in two waters, or to the belief that the
plant wards off 'evil eyes' i.e. of persons with a
grudge against the owner. Note other names
MALDJO², OVERLOOK with similar association]

gru-gru [grugru] *n* (Gren, StVn, Tbgo, Trin)
See GROU-GROU

gru-gru bèf (gwou-gwou bèf, gwu-gwu
bèf) *n phr* (Trin) See GROU-GROU BÈF

grum·ble *vb intr* (CarA) [*AF*] **1.** [Of the bow-
els] to gripe; to make a rumbling sound. [Prob
< SE *rumble*] **2.** PHRASE 2.1 **belly grumbling**
id phr (CarA) See BELLY Phr 3.6.

grunt* *n* (CarA) Any of a great many varieties
of medium-sized fish of high food value, having
in common red lips or inner mouth and making
a grunting sound when taken out of the water;
Haemulidae spp or *Pomasyidae spp. The huge
family of grunts contains many species, the most
common being the yellow and white lateral-shaped
variety that hang in schools beneath the coral trees,
in shallow waters. After dark the Grunts disperse
to feed individually about the reef.*—Chg (1978),
p.117

gua·bin(e) [(g)wabi·n] *n* (Trin) A small, edible
fresh-water fish with large scales; it lives in
unpleasant swamps and is easily caught; *Hoplias
malabaricus (Characinidae).* [< *TDV* Venz Sp
guabina 'a voracious river and lake fish'] □ See
also WABEEN (*Trin*).

Gua·de·lou·pe·an *n, adj* (CarA) (A person or
thing) native or belonging to the Fr Caribbean
island of Guadeloupe.

gua·na [gwa·na] *n* (CarA) [*IF*] ‖ *bamboo-
chicken* (Belz) The iguana, a giant edible lizard
that can grow to 5 ft in length. *Salted 'guanas'
are still sold by the hundreds in market at Cockburn
Town (Turks and Caicos Islands).*—NaG
(75.10.15, p.2) [< *TLWI:21* Taino *iguana* <
Arawakan *ioana,* with loss of /i-/ by aphesis]

gu·an·go [gwaŋgo] *n* (Jmca) ‖ SAMAN (TREE)
(CarA) *He was also very hungry so he sat on a*

*guango stump near the trough and ate from his
journey-bag.*—RPME:74 [Latin Am Sp. See
DJE]

guard [ga(r)d] *n* (CarA) **1.** Some object or
objects put in a small packet, or a piece of garlic
or washing blue in a piece of cloth, hung around
the neck or on the underwear to keep off evil
spirits. *A letter to H- from Camella of Anguilla
dated June 13, 1963, states: 'My head is bothering
me a lot. I am sending you a measure of my finger
... I want you to send me a guard and something
to bathe myself, clear up the house. You will find
the piece of thread.'*—DeM(SK) (63.08.31, p.3)
□ Cp GUZU 2. **2.** A charmed object, such as a
bottle spotted with white paint and turned upside
down on a stick, or an animal's skull similarly
placed, in a vegetable garden or GROUND, to
prevent harm from evil eyes.

guard·i·an *n* (Bdos) [Hist] A member of a
Board (of Guardians) appointed by a VESTRY
from among its own elected number of property-
owners, to administer poor relief in the PARISH.

guard-wall *n* (Bdos) A thick, concrete or coral-
stone wall about 6 to 8 ft high around private
property, guarding the grounds against being
seen esp from the road (hence the name).

Guat [gwat] *n* (Belz) [*AF—Derog*] A native of
Guatemala. **a.** *Speaking about its own stand the
Amandala declared: 'We say that the Guats never
did own Belize'*—AdN (76.11.03, p.7) **b.** *About
a month ago one such Guat had a fuss with a
Creole woman, her neighbour. The Guat threatened
the Creole and pulled a knife on her*—ReP
(80.01.13, p.15) [By *Derog* reduction < GU-
ATEMAL(TEC)AN, a native of Guatemala, the territory bordering on *Belz.* Cp IAE *Derog* Jap <
Japanese]

Gua·te·mal·te·can *n, adj* (Belz) (A person or
thing) native to Guatemala. [< Sp *guatemalteco/
-a* adj 'Guatemalan', there being many natives
of neighbouring Guatemala in *Belz* who use the
Sp adj form to refer to themselves]

gua·va [gwavʌ]* *n* (CarA) A tough-limbed tree
bearing one of many varieties of roundish, yellow-skinned fruit with sweet or sour, pink or
white flesh in wh many hard, tiny seeds are
embedded; *Psidium guajava (Myrtaceae).* [Gen-
erally considered as < Sp *guayaba* 'guava', the
fruit being native to the CarA, and prob 'discovered' by Columbus. However, an illustration
from Benzoni's *Historio del Mondo Nuovo,* 1563
(see *JJCC:31*) clearly labels the tree *guaiaua* the
Taino/Arawakan form wh is nearer the surviving
CE (and IAE) *guava*]

gua·va·ber·ry* *n* (ViIs) A purple, smooth-
skinned, juicy berry borne on a small tree that
resembles the GUAVA tree but has a thicker foliage
with smaller leaves; the fruit or a syrup made
from it is added to rum to make a popular

Christmas drink; *Eugenia floribunda* or *E. disticha* (*Myrtaceae*).

gua·va-cheese *n* (CarA) A confectionery made by squeezing the boiled pulp of ripe GUAVAS through a sifter and boiling again with an equal amount of brown sugar to so firm a consistency that, when cooled, it can be cut into small cheese-like chunks (hence the name).

gua·va-days *n* (Gren, Guyn) ‖ HARD-GUAVA DAYS (Guyn)

gua·va-lob·ster /1'212/ *n phr* (Gren) ‖ GOD-HORSE (CarA) *One of the longest insects in the world, 8 ins without the antennae, is the Guava Lobster, God-horse, Diapherodes gigantea; it is one of the walking stick-insects occurring in Grenada and St Vincent. Its vestigial wings give it the appearance of a Chinese dragon; it feeds on the leaves of Mangoes, Guavas, etc.*—GNHIG:22

gua·va-time *n* (Mrat) ‖ HARD-GUAVA DAYS Guyn

gua·ya·be·ra *n* (Belz) A man's shirt made of light material and worn outside the trousers, typically having four pockets, a variety of decorative pleats and buttons, and long sleeves; it is popular semi-formal wear. [Am Sp *guayabera* 'light blouse'] □ 1. Sometimes spelled *-rr-* in *Belz.* 2. Cp SHIRTJAC (*Guyn*) wh is short-sleeved and usu plain.

gub·by-face *n* (Nevs, StKt) 1. A mask used in Christmas masquerading. 2. [By extension] An ugly person.

gub-gub [gʌb-gʌb∼gᴜb-gᴜb] *n* (Trin) A pale variety of small pea belonging to the BLACK-EYE PEA family but with a white spot instead; it is esp popular as a soup base; *Vigna spp.* [Prob < Congo *nguba* 1. 'kidney' 2. 'peanut', with characteristic CE reduplication. Cp *DJE* (*Jmca*) *gubgub peas* (wh does not seem current) and AmE *goober peas*, both suggested as being from the same Afr source]

gu·bi(e) *n* (Angu, Nevs, USVI) See GOBI

guen·sey [gɛnsi] *n* (Belz) ‖ GANSEY (Bdos, Jmca) □ Used mostly by older or rural folk.

guér·ir-tout (**guér·it-tout**) *n* (Trin, Gren, USVI) See GÉRITOU

guh [gʌ] *vb* (CarA) [*AF—Cr*] Go. □ A representative dial spelling sometimes used in narrative dialogue. See esp GO 2.(i), (ii).

Gui·an·an (**Gui·an·i·an, Guy·an·an**) [gay an(i)an] *n, adj* [*Obs*] [X] (Replaced in pres CE by) Guyanese. *... but it pleased God that the Canoa was carried downe the streame, and that certain of the Guianians met it the same evening, and having not at any time seen any Christian, nor any man of that colour, they carried Martynes*

into the land to be wondred at.—Sir W. Ralegh 'The Discoverie of Guiana' 1596 ed. V.T. Harlow, 1928, Argonaut Pr., Lond p.20 □ These terms, based on such SE analogies as *American, Canadian* (cp also CE JAMAICAN, GRENADIAN) have disappeared from CE. They either occur in early historical records (as in cit) or in the writings of uninformed non-*CarA* writers.

Gui·a·na scholar (**Guya·na-**) *n phr* (Guyn) See SCHOLAR

guil·der [gɪldə(r)] *n* 1. (Neth, Srnm) The standard monetary unit of *Neth* and *Srnm* (sometimes also called the Surinam Florin) divided into 100 cents. 2. (Guyn) [Hist] (i) A silver coin, originally the basic unit of Dutch currency, that continued to be used in Br Guiana up to 1839, valued at twenty Br pence at that period. (ii) A conventional unit of value equivalent to sixteen Br pence, but in the form of four Guyana BIT[T]S (or 'eight-cent pieces'), there being no actual guilder coin; this remained in effect from 1840 until Guyana's Independence (1966), when this system of monetary counting was abandoned. □ Many old, and esp rural folk still count in bits and guilders.

gui·nea [gɪni] *n* (Nevs, StKt, USVI) ‖ CORN-CANE-ROW (CarA) *... sickness cause ma hair to drop and so I tell dem to plat it in guinea for me. Yo call dis guinea because it make it grow!*—AawI.1, p.28 [< *Guinea*, as a general ref to Afr or things African, the *CarA* slaves having come first from the W Afr coast known as the Guinea Coast] □ Hence also **guinea-plait, -row, -style** as variant names of the same hairstyle in the *CarA.*

gui·nea-bird* /1'12/ *n* (Bdos, Guyn, Jmca) A guinea-fowl or guinea-hen; *Numida meleagris* (*Numididiae*) [From its native origin in Africa. See prec]

gui·nea-corn* *n* (CarA) One of a number of varieties of small-grained corn of different colours (black, white, red, yellow) borne in compact, elongated brush-like bundles, sometimes branched, at the end of tall, sturdy stalks that resemble maize, with long curving leaves at intervals; most varieties are ground into GUINEA-CORN flour, for various food uses; *Sorghum vulgare* or *S. durra* (*Gramineae*). [*Guinea*, prob because it is 'largely cultivated in Africa'—*PTT: 284*] □ Also called **sorghum** or **millet** in some agricultural literature.

gui·nea-grass* *n* (CarA) A coarse grass exceeding 3 ft in height with long blades at the nodes and a soft brush-like efflouresence high above the leaves; it grows in persistent clumps and is much prized as cattle fodder; *Panicum maximum* (*Gramineae-Poaceae*). [*Guinea* because the grass is 'a native of Tropical Africa'—*MTPG:426*]

gui·nea-hen-bring-ram-goat (story) n (phr) (Mrat, Tbgo) [AF—Joc] A cock-and-bull story; a rigmarole. 'Bwoy, stop you nanci story an' tell me wha' mek you don't bring no wood. No come to me wid no guinea-hen bring ram goat you know-'—Monno interrupt he story.—FGSOS:40

gui·nea-hen weed n phr (Baha, Bdos, Jmca) ‖ GULLY-ROOT (CarA)

gui·nea-pep·per ['gɪni-pɛpʌ] /1′122/ n (Berm) ‖ BIRD-PEPPER (CarA)

gui·nea-row [gɪni-ro]/1′12/ n (Baha, TkCa, Trin) ‖ CORN-ROW 1. (CarA)

gui·nea-shark* n (ECar) An enormous shark with a marble-grey body that can exceed 50 ft in length, and a tail-fin with a very wide span; its mouth is at the tip of the snout and its head and body are covered in round, whitish spots; it is said to be harmless to man; (SE) the whale shark; Rhincodon typus (Rhincodontidae) And I was told by my uncle that in sailboat days the guinea shark would come under the boat and rub against the hull, as if scratching its back—SaS (93.09.11, p.5) [From the resemblance of its spotted skin' to the African guinea-fowl]

gui·nea-yam* ['gɪni-yam] n (Dmca, Gren, Jmca, Tbgo, Trin) ‖ white-yam¹ (Baha, etc) A yam of wh there appear to be two closely resembling varieties Dioscorea cayennensis (the YELLOW GUINEA) and D. rotundata (the WHITE GUINEA) (PTT:150) though considered the same by some authorities (FFGM:249) Guinea is a long yam, sweet, white.—Gren (Ms) [Said to be native to W Afr, hence this name. 'Today W Afr produces two-thirds of the world's supply of yam with Nigeria alone producing one-half of this supply. Eboe (Dioscorea rotundata) is the most important species grown in this area.'—Cta.8.4, p.2]

gui·nep* (ge·nip, gi·nep) ['gɪnɪp ~ 'gɛnɪp] n (CarA) ‖ akee (Bdos, StLu, StVn) ‖ canep, canop (Baha, TkCa) ‖ canip (Mrat) ‖ chenep, chenip (Gren, Tbgo) ‖ chennette (Dmca, StLu, Tbgo, Trin) ‖ chinep (Gren) ‖ kenip, ki·nip, kinnup, kinop (Baha, Belz, BrVi, Dmca, Guyn, StKt) ‖ mapo (Trin) ‖ skinip, skinop (Gren, Guyn, StKt) ‖ Spanish lime (Trin) ‖ tjennèt (Dmca, StLu) A marble-sized fruit with a tough, green skin covering a scant but pleasant-tasting, salmon-coloured pulp on a hard seed; it is borne in large grape-like bunches on a big, deciduous, green tree that usu has a thick trunk; Melicoccus bijugatus (Sapindaceae). While the lad was sucking a guinep the seed slipped down his throat and he died from suffocation.—WeS (74.07.26, p.32) [< 'Am Sp quenepo, Melicocca spp, and quenepa, its fruit < Arawakan' (DJE) pronunc kenepa; also Guyn Arawakan genipa (Balp.4.3, p.2) or Genipa americana (IAIG:317) from the seeds of wh Guyn Amerindians produce a well-known blue-black body dye. These two variants will account for many of the forms

listed above] □ The spelling **genip** appears to be frequently used, though **guinep** better represents the regularly used pronunc. Also note cit.

gui·ro [(g)wi·ro] n (Nevs, ViIs) A musical instrument made from the dried shell of a hard-skinned variety of gourd (about a foot long) on wh lines are cut crosswise, and scraped with any sharp-pointed metal to provide a rhythmic rasping sound. [Sp guiro 1. 'bottle gourd' 2. '(Mexico, Venz) musical instrument made from it'] □ The pronunc [wi·ro] is preferred, notwithstanding the spelling. The instrument is noted in TDV Venz Sp as guiro or huire.

gui·tar-pan(s) [gita-pan(z)] /1′12/ n (Trin) A joined pair of PANS for one player, each PAN cut to be half the length of an oil-drum, with the surface sunk to about the same depth as the DOUBLE-SECONDS but segmented to provide about seven or eight notes (each) wh are of a lower pitch than the DOUBLE-SECONDS but higher than the CELLO-PANS, with wh they form the third line in the arrangement of a STEELBAND. [From the resemblance of the timbre of the note to the sharp tone of a guitar]

gu·lab-ja·moon/-ja·mun n (Guyn, Trin) [Indic] A sweetmeat made by frying balls of a flour-and-milk dough in deep oil and cooling them in thick syrup. [Bhoj < Hin gulab 'rose' (from its smell) + JAMOON from its resemblance to this fruit]

gul·let (gò·lèt) n (Tbgo, Trin) ‖ COCOA-KNIFE (Dmca, etc) [DECG Fr Cr gòlèt 'a pole' < Fr gaule 'a pole' + -ette (diminutive), a ref to the necessary mount, hence prob orig gullet-knife, then abbreviated. Also possibly infl by the throat-like (gullet) shape of the cutting projection]

gul·ly¹ n 1. (Bdos, Jmca) A narrow, sloping, deep drop in the land surface wh becomes a seasonal water-course; it is frequently considered a garbage-dump and place of scavenging. ... the 'mounts of these Bajan that come from down some gully or up some hill behind God back and ain use to nothing.—MBGBS:13 2. (Baha) [By extension] Hungry scavenging; a state of disaster. I guess dat between dem an' d' Chamber of Commas dey make arrangement fer winter wedder t' cum early so dese Nassau peepul wont dead wid d' gully.—DSJS:31 [The Baha association with scavenging may also be affected by GULLY²] 3. PHRASES 3.1 **gully got you** id phr (Baha) You are very hungry. Befo' we cut off d' engine we had a whole contingent rite on board tellin' us say gully got um an' say dey wan' sum corn beef.—DSJS:15 [See GULLY².] 3.2 **the gully is out** id phr (Bdos) Water is rushing through the gully after heavy rains. □ Cp [river] COME DOWN (Jmca). See COME phr 7.4.

gul·ly² (gul·lie-bird) n (Baha, Brbu) The sea gull, esp a black-headed kind, wh dives to catch fish. □ The Phr **gully got you** (Baha) (see

GULLY[1] Phr 3.1) may also in some contexts be associated with this bird meaning 'you are caught'.

gul·ly-bean n (Jmca) ‖ BURA-BURA (Guyn) [GULLY[1] in Derog sense + *bean*]

gul·ly-plum n (Bdos) [*IF*] ‖ HOG-PLUM (CarA) *From the unrelated Cashew family, Anacardiaceae with about sixty genera including the delectable Mango, comes our Golden Apple, Spondias cytherea and the Hog Plum or Gully Plum, S. mombin.*—AdN (79.6.3, p.16, M. Hutt) [Prob because the tree thrives in uncultivated environments such as GULLIES. See etym note at HOG PLUM]

gul·ly-root* n (CarA) ‖ *guinea-hen weed* (Baha, Bdos, Jmca) ‖ *kojo-bush* (Brbu) ‖ *kojo-root* (Dmca, Gren, StVn) ‖ *strong-man weed* (Jmca) An erect weed about 3 ft tall with tough stems ending in one or two nodding spikes of tiny, white flowers and having long, elliptical, pointed leaves; the whole plant when crushed smells strongly like garlic; it is widely used as a folk-medicine for fevers, aches, and skin disorders; *Petiveria alliacea (Phytolaccaceae)*. [Perh because the weed thrives in rough, stony ground and has a tough, deep root, wh is specially credited with its medicinal properties]

gul·ly-watch·man n (Tbgo) ‖ POND-FLY (Bdos, Guyn) [GULLY[1] IN *Derog* ref to its likely habitat]

gum-bark n (Mrat) The bark of the GUM-TREE 2. wh is used as an after-birth folk medicine. [Cp LOG-BUSH (BrVi)]

gum·bay [gʊmbe] n (Belz) See GOMBAY (Jmca)

gum·bo-lim·bo n (ViIs) ‖ BIRCH-GUM TREE (Bdos, etc) [Perh another form of GUM-ELEMI (Baha), the same tree]

gum-e·le·mi (ga·ma·la·mi) [ˈgʌm-ɛl ɛmi ~ ˈgamalami] n (Baha, TkCa) ‖ BIRCH-GUM (TREE) (Bdos, etc) [Perh a corruption, by folk etym, of SE *gum arabic*, wh is pronounced as one word [gʌmarabɪk] by older persons in many *CarA* territories. Prob then *gum-arabic* > GAM-ALAMI, GUM-ELEMI, GUMBO-LIMBO, etc by recognizable phonological shifts. The use of the resinous product of the bark as a *gum* would account for the borrowing of the name *gum arabic*]

gum-tree n 1. (StLu) ‖ CLAMMY-CHERRY 1. (CarA) [Popular name, from stickiness of the pulp, used as gum by children] 2. (Angu, Gren, Mrat, Nevs, StKt) ‖ BIRCH-GUM (TREE) (Bdos, etc) [From the gum-resin formed from the juice after evaporation]

gun vb (CarA) [*AF—Cr*] See GOIN[G] 2. and □ Note. *I ain' gun sen yer in de ambulans an on de stretcher if yer promise ter walk to de car real slow.*—JBJ:87

gun·dy [gʊndi] n (CarA) ‖ *biter* (Baha) ‖ *mòdan* (Gren, Trin) ‖ *pincher* (Baha) ‖ *tengaleh* (Guyn) The large pincer claw of a crab or lobster.

gun·go(-peas) [gʊŋgʌ (-pi·z)] n (Belz, CayI, Jmca) ‖ PIGEON PEAS (CarA) [Cp *LDKF* (Vili, i.e. a coastal, dialect of) Kikongo *ngungu* 'peas']

gun·gu·de n (Belz) ‖ CONGATAY (Belz, etc) [< CONGATAY by voicing of /k-/and /t-/]

gun-mout(h) (pants) n (*phr*) (Bdos, Belz, Dmca, Gren, Guyn, Trin) [*AF—Joc*] ‖ BIDDIMS (Bdos, etc) ... *who only minutes before had been teasing him about the old-fashioned 'gun mouth pants' he wore.*—ToR (77.07.03, p.3) [From the markedly tapering (hence gun-barrel-like) shape of long trousers, esp as worn by youngsters, when wide-bottomed or baggy trousers were/are regarded as the proper fashion]

gup·py n (CarA) ‖ MILLIONS(-FISH) (CarA) [See cit at MILLIONS(-FISH)]

gush·ee-gush·ee [gʌši-gʌši] n (USVI) See GRICHI-GRICHI [Prob a children's corruption or variant]

gut n See GHAUT ... *and when my mother went to the gut to wash clothes, I would run down to the hill to Mr Christian's home, which was about two city blocks away.*—AawI.2, p.57 □ This appears to be the preferred spelling in the USVI.

gut-apple n (Antg) See GHAUT-APPLE

guts n pl (CarA) [*AF—Derog*] 1. The abdomen; (hence, by extension) the belly, the stomach. 2. PHRASE 2.1. be in guts gully vb phr (Bdos) [*AF*] To be in serious difficulties. 2.2 tie your guts vb phr (Nevs) [*AF*] ‖ BAND YOUR BELLY (Dmca, etc)

gut·ta·perc (gutta-perch) [gʌtapʌrk ~ gʌta pərč] n (Bdos) A boy's catapult or slingshot made of a short forked stick with a piece of rubber or strong elastic attached to its two ends. *Boys he know does behave real bad, and throw rock-stones at dogs and cats, and lick-down sparrow-birds and wooddoves with guttapercs.*—AdN (80.12.25, p.10, T. Callender) [< *gutta percha*, a whitish rubber made from the latex of the gutta-percha tree (see *OED*) and used commercially. In CE the term was first associated in the 1930s with the brand name of a popular canvas, rubber-soled shoe. From the tongue of such an old shoe, it appears, in *Bdos*, a piece was used for the central piece of the catapult, but the name *gutta-percha* was also used as another name for 'rubber', wh is the essential part of a catapult] □ The spellings **guttaperk, gutterperk** have emerged in the 1980s, mainly due to the use of the name to identify a call-in radio programme in wh questions are 'slung' at the moderator.

gut·ter·smith n (Guyn) A man who makes any part of the guttering system for the outside of a house using galvanized sheeting.

gutter·smith·ing n (Guyn) The trade or work of a GUTTERSMITH. *For reasonable charges in guttersmithing, consult Farley's Cycle, Tinsmith and Repair Shop.*—DaC (Ad, 52.06.01, p.12)

Guy·an·an n, adj See GUIAN[I]AN

Guy·an·ese n, adj (CarA) (A person or thing) native to Guyana (formerly Br Guiana). [The suff -ese, wh is unique in ref to CarA territories (cp also earlier GUYAN[I]AN) is prob due to Du adjs, Guianese, Guyanees, the Du having owned the territory before the British and left several surviving place names. Cp similarly Fr Guyanais; however the infl of Romance suff -ese, as in SE Lebanese, Genoese, etc is less likely than the Du source] □ The n is unchanged in the pl: 'Two Trinidadians and two Guyanese'.

Guy·an·i·za·tion (-is-) n (CarA) The process or act of making (sth) markedly Guyanese in character or appearance.

gu·zu(m) (gu·zung) [guzu(m) ~ guzuŋ] n (Belz, Jmca) **1.** An act or wish by wh some supernatural bad influence is believed to affect sb or sb's effort. **2.** [By extension] A charm or amulet prepared in order to protect sb against evil. *She became so anxious over me that she did have consultations ... with Papa Dias and made me wear again, as I did as a small child, a red string with a guzu round my neck, this time to protect me against those who were jealous of my success*—SASW:24. **3.** PHRASE **3.1 put/set guzu on (sb)** vb phr (Belz, Jmca) [AF] To aim to cause (sb) harm by ill-wishing or by some act guided by superstitious belief. [Prob of Bantu orig. See DJE]

gwan [gwan] vb (CarA) [AF—Cr] **1.** (Belz) Goin(g) [In finite senses. See GOIN(G) 1.] *Well, de boy happen to git into one big lagoon, yuh know, travel, gwan long, an wen e look e into one lee village, yuh know, an e see one big smoke.*—WFSB: 42 **2.** (Belz) Going [As Cr future marker. See GOIN(G) 2.] *Ha! Mountain Pigeon, bawl top yonder: Brudda Cra—ne! Brudda Crane! Fa true, all yuh money gwan done. John Anancy gwan carry yuh money.*—WFSB:31 **3.** (Jmca) ‖ **go on** vb phr [In both neutral and emotive senses] To behave, perform. See GO Phr 6.24 (i) *Bwoy, Mayor Brown, we call yuh name fe nuff things and yuh gwan good fe true.*—WeG (75.04.08, p.15, Partyline) **4.** PHRASE **4.1 gwan with** vb phr (i) (Jmca) ‖ GO ON WITH vb phr (CarA) See GO Phr 6.24.1 *Bwoy, dem is fighting words, Me never know say parson gwan with that kind of thing too.*—StA(JA) (73.02.10, p.14, Partyline) (ii) (Guyn, Jmca) [In excl contexts] Go away; be off; get out. *If you stay there and think that cops only good to be styled Babylon, you can gwan. When them motorcycle bwoys decide to drop hand and foot pon stunt riding, them was very boss.*—Sta(JA)

(72.11.18, p.10, Partyline) (iii) (Guyn, StVn) [In emotive contexts] Go and (do sth). *Look! Yo[u] better gwan read yo[ur] book!*—(StVn) [From the fusing of *go + on*, or (4 (iii)) *go + and* with intrusive /w/ by labialization. Cp OEDS Irish dial E pronunc *gwan* 'go on'. However, EDD go 3 cites the pres. part. forms *gwain, gwan, gwine* for several Eng counties throughout the 19C, exs: where be'st thee gwain? (Stf, 1823); I were gwine up street (Dev, 1896). Together these may well be the early source of the CarA Cr form and its many functions] □ This representative dial spelling commonly occurs in narrative dialogue.

gwen·less [gwɛnlɛs] adj (StLu) Weak; spineless; unable to do what you are expected to do. [Fr Cr *gwenn* 'seeds, testicles' + SE suff -less 'without', from the Fr Cr phr *nonm-san-gwenn* 'man without testicles' (i.e. man without respectable manliness)]

gwenn-an·ba-fèy (graine-en-bas-feuille) [gwɛn-ãba-fɛi] n (Dmca, Gren, Trin) ‖ *seed-under-leaf* (StVn, Tbgo, Trin) One of two or three varieties of a short, erect, green weed with a single stem, branching at intervals, the branches resembling compound leaves; the seeds are green or reddish and borne on the underside of each leaf-stalk (hence the name); an infusion of the plant is used for BATHS, fevers and, it is believed, producing abortions; *Phyllanthus amarus* or *P. urinaria* or *P. tenellus* (Euphorbiaceae). [Fr Cr < Fr = seed below leaf]

gwenn-lé·gliz n (StLu) ‖ BEAD-VINE (BUSH) (Nevs, StKt) [Fr Cr < Fr *graine* 'seed' (bead) + *l'église* 'church', prob from its use]

gwenn-pen [gwɛn-pɛ̃] n ‖ BREADNUT 1. (CarA)

gwine [gwaɪn] fut aux vb (CarA) [AF—Cr] See GOIN[G] 2. and □ Note. *'Den tell me, Mr Eliot,' one of the men said; he looked like a cane worker or a small farmer, in for the day. 'How we gwine do when election come? Who gwine win dis time?'* —HFGA:45 (J. Hearne) [See etym note at GWAN 4.]

gwo boug (gros bourge, gros bouge) [gwo-bu·g] n (Dmca) [AF—Joc] A very well-to-do upper-class property-owner or one from such a family; a white, colonial, government top-official or other local resident V.I.P.; (SE slang) a big shot. *The transition from a 'little man's government' to a 'gros boug' elitist regime will not be smooth.*—DoH (72.01.15, p.5) [Fr Cr < Fr *gros bourge* 'big chap/bloke' with characteristic Cr reduction of /-CC/. The term *bougre* appears always to have been Derog in Fr, and prob appealed to the Cr speakers as suitable ref to their white masters] □ The alternative spellings -BOURG[E], -BOUGE are false refinements infl by BOURGEOIS. The pl, usu written *gros bougs*, is usu pronounced like the sg.

Gwo Michèl *n phr* (Dmca, StLn). See GROS
MICHEL

gwo pon pon *n phr* (StLu) ‖ BALL-BUSH (Bdos,
Jmca) [Fr Cr. < Fr *gros pompon* 'big pompom'.
Cp *Mart* name *pompom-soldat* 'soldier's tuft']

gwo tèt [gwo tɛ·t] *n* (Dmca) ‖ BALL-BUSH (Bdos,
Jmca) [Fr Cr < Fr *gros tête* 'big head']

gwou-gwou (**grou-grou, gwu-gwu**) [gwu-
gwu] *n* (Dmca, StLu) See GROU-GROU

gwou-gwou bèf (**grou-grou bèf, gwu-gwu
bèf**) [gwu-gwu bɛf] *n* (Trin) See GRUO-GROU BÈF

g(w)o-zyé (**gros-zié**) [gwo-zye~go-zye] *n*,
adj **1.** (Dmca, StLu) [*AF*] ‖ BIG-EYE¹ (CarA) **2.**
(Trin) A type of small fish with bulging eyes
that lives near the shore. [Fr Cr < Fr *gros yeux*
'big eyes'] **3.** PHRASES **3.1 be (too) g(w)o-zyé
3.2 have (too much) g(w)o zyé** *vb phrs* (Dmca,
StLu) ‖ BE/HAVE (TOO MUCH) BIG-EYE (CarA) See
BIG-EYE¹, ²

gwu-gwu (**gwou-gwou, grou-grou, gru-
gru**) [gwugwu] *n* (StLu) See GROU-GROU

gwu-gwu bèf [gwu gwu bɛf] *n phr* (Trin) See
GROU-GROU BÈF

gyap [gya·p] *vb intr* **1.** (Belz, Mrat) [*AF*] To
yawn. **2.** (Nevs) [*AF—Vul*] [Of a woman] To sit

with your legs wide apart in a manner that looks
indecent. [< SE *gap* n 'an opening' by functional
and semantic shift]

gym-boots *n pl* (Trin) ‖ *jim-boots* (Trin) [*X*]
‖ *yachting-boots* (Guyn) Ankle-high, rubber-
soled, canvas boots (sometimes with a rubber-
patch ankle-guard) favoured for outdoor or
gymnasium games. □ Included within the broad
meaning of 'sneakers'. See CREPESOLES.

gyp·sy [ʃɪpsi] *adj* (Bdos) [*AF—Derog*] ‖ *fast* ɪ.
(CarA) ‖ *malicious* (Bdos) **2.** Irritatingly inquisitive and likely to repeat what you have
found out. *Marriage is the single instance left for
human people to work out their own destiny—or
go their separate ways without interference from a
benevolent but gypsy political authority.*—AdN
(79.02.12, p.7, Topic For Today) [Prob by infl
and functional n > adj shift of *OED gipsy* 2. b.
'a contemptuous term for a woman, as being
cunning, deceitful, fickle or the like'] □ Usu
applied to a woman or child, and not as offensive
a term as MALICIOUS (*Bdos*) 2.

gyp·sy-in-the-moon·light *n* (StVn) A children's ring game, using the rhyme 'Gypsy in the
moonlight, gypsy in the dew / Gypsy never come
home till after two'.

gyp·sy-mouth *n* (BrVi) [*AF—Derog*] A talkative person who often talks nonsense.

H

h [h] □ The sound /h-/, esp in word-initial position, comes and goes in uneducated speech in many parts of the *CarA*, without there being any apparent system in its appearance or absence. The feature persists in the speech of some educated persons. On the whole it occurs most noticeably in *Jmca*, as in the following cits: /wi av som hopm pan di tri/ *'We have some [that] open on the tree.'*—(Jmca) /di legz iz nat haati. Hartraitis in di fut/ *'The legs is not hearty. Arthritis [is] in the foot.'*—(Jmca) /fishamaan niid ais an hoil far im boot/ [A] *fisherman need[s] ice and oil for him [i.e. his] boat.'*—(Jmca) See also -TH-.

ha; **hab** *vb tr* (CarA) [AF—Cr] **1.** Have (in all its functions both as main and aux vbs). **a.** *We ha to wait till mama come, because e en have nothing here.*—PSFC:24 **b.** *You tink de Queen hab one Bible?*—LaS (76.06.19, p.4, Bits & Pieces) [< SE *have* by characteristic loss of /-c/, or /hab/ with characteristic /v > b/ shift (see -B-)] □ This spelling is often used in narrative dialogue. **2.** PHRASE **2.1 ha fu (do sth)** *modal aux vb phr* (CarA) [AF—Cr] ‖ GA(T) FO (CarA) See GA(T) **2.** *Yo[u] ha fu eat wha[t] yo[u] can get.*—(Antg)

ha·ba·ne·ro [abanɛ·ro] *n* (Belz) A very hot red, yellow, or green pepper, much used in cooking. [Sp n, adj = '(person or thing) from Havana (Cuba)'. The connection with hotness is obscure, possibly *Joc*]

Hab·ra, Dab·ra, and the crew *n phr* (Bdos) [AF—Joc] ‖ *he, she and t[h]ingamerry* (Bdos) [AF—Joc] ‖ *Haiah and Kaiah and Buddy-born-drunk* (Bdos) [AF—Joc] ‖ *Nepsha and Kaiah* (Bdos) [AF—Joc] ‖ *the duppy and the dog* (Bdos) [AF] ‖ *tout moun bakaila* (Bdos, StLu) A large indiscriminate crowd including everybody you can think of; 'the world and his mother'; 'Tom, Dick, Harry, and the rabble'. *The poet Robert Southey in 1837 asked pertinently 'Who was Jack Robinson, the one whose name is in every body's mouth, because it is so easily and so soon said?' As well ask who were Tom, Dick, and Harry, or in Barbadian terms, Nepsha, and Kiah, or Habra, Dabra, and the crew, or the duppy and the dog.*—AdN (80.07.13, p.6, M. Hutt) [Prob < SE *abracadabra* sometimes used as a loose ref to what is unworthy or worthless] □ The phr and its parallels now tend to be used by older and rural folk. The phrs tend to express a stronger mixture of derisive contempt than IAE *Tom, Dick and Harry*, though they generally represent the same idea.

hack·i·a-stick *n* (Guyn) See HAKYA-STICK

hack·le *vb* **1.** *vb intr* (Jmca) To exert yourself; to work very hard or too hard. **2.** *vb tr* (Jmca) To harass (sb); to cause (sb) much trouble. [Cp *EDD hackle* vb[8] (Mid Som) 'to undertake with energy'] **3.** PHRASE **3.1 hackle up**[1] *vb phr* (Baha) [AF] To beat up (sb) in a fight; to maul. *Brer Rabbie thought quickly an' replied to Brer Bookie in a friendly tone, 'Man, what we squabblin' fer? If we hackle up one anudder udder people could come an' take we sweet surup, ya know.'*—TOSR:15

hack·le-up[2] *adj* (Baha) [AF] **1.** [Of persons] Physically deformed (esp when so from birth); disabled or seriously injured. **2.** [Of things] Untidy looking; damaged. *Yo[u] can[']t go out with them hackle-up trousers.*—(Baha) [By functional vb > adj shift of HACKLE UP[1]]

had *vb* (CarA) [X] **1.** Have/has had; had had. *'I had this bicycle three years now.'* / *'Yesterday you said you were not sure how long you had the bicycle.'*—Bdos (CR, 1976) □ The absence of the SE perf. and past-perf. t. structures of *have* is common in such time-situation contexts in the speech and writing of educated persons throughout the *CarA*. Cp WAS. **2.** PHRASES **2.1 it had (sth)** *existential introductory phr, pa.t.* (Dmca, Gren, StLu, Tbgo, Trin) [AF—Cr] There was/were. *It had rain, oui and it had some people shelterin[g] in the shop an[d] they see it.*—(Trin) [See HAVE Phr **3.15** IT HAVE] **2.2 had not** *id phr* (Bdos) [X] Had it not been for. *I did never trust them. Had not for you, I wouldn'ta have nothing to do with Wig.*—Bdos (Ms 1976, T. Callender) **2.3 had was to** *modal vb phr* (i) (CarA) [X] ‖ *had did to* (Bdos) Had to; was/were obliged to. **a.** *An' ol'-timers will remember / In them days we had was to dodge / From old Mr Matthews, the truant-officer.*—YFOC:9 **b.** *Well, Christine, by the time I reach-back here in my humble home, I was feeling poorly. And I had was to call another person and ask about my rights.*—PeL (79.12.07, p.10, Dear Christine) [The widespread *CarA* occurrence of this structure suggests that it may be a calque of an aspectual feature in some W Afr langs. Note Nigerian Pidgin E *I was to go to market*, 'I had to go to the market'— (*pers info, I. Amadi Ume, 1977*); also cp Yoruba *mo ni lati lọ lana* (I have + 'obligation-marker' go yesterday) 'I had to go yesterday'— (*pers info, A.O. Obilade, 1975*)] □ This structure, well established in folk speech, sometimes occurs also

in the serious writing of literate persons. **(ii)**
(Bdos, Gren) Had intended to; was/were due or
expecting to. *This is something I had was to do,
donkey-years now. Write a little thing in appreciation of a certain body.*—PeL (80.03.28, p.6,
Austin Clarke)

hads *vbl particle* (ECar) [*AF—Cr*] PHRASES **1.
best hads** *modal vb phr* (Guyn, Tbgo, Trin) See
BEST² *'You best hads get it for me,'* Moses say, *'or
I set the police after you. I ain't fooling, man.'*—
STLL:39 **2. hads better** *modal vb phr* (Bdos)
See BETTER² Phr 2.3 BETTER-HAD (ECar) *You
hads better not make me screel-out and call a
police, for you, yuh.*—PeL (80.08.01, p.2, Austin
Clarke) □ These dial speech forms are often
written in narrative dialogue.

hag¹ (heg, higue) [hɛg ~ haɪg] *n* **1.** (Baha, Belz,
StVn) ‖SOUKOUYAN (Dmca, etc) **2.** (Bdos, Belz,
StVn) [By extension] A person who is a wretched
nuisance. *Ah meet yo night an marning yo like a
heg pan me.*—StVn (Ms, 1974) [A development
from Obs E. See *OED hag* sb¹ 1., 2., 3.]

hag² (heg) [hag ~ hɛg] *vb tr* **1.** (Baha) ‖*fix*
(Baha) To set a bewitching SPERRIT on a (person
or a house); to cast an evil spell on (sb or sth).
'Dat house haunted' and *'don go dere Doc—you'll
get hagged,'* greeted me as I paid a visit there one
afternoon to *'case the joint'.*—MTTBT:179 **2.**
(Bdos, Belz) [By extension] To pester; to harass.
[A development from Obs E. See *OED hag* v²
'to torment, trouble as the nightmare', etc]

hag·gi·di [hagɪdi] *n* (Belz) A porridge made of
cornmeal boiled and soured, then seasoned and
sweetened. [Prob a variant of AGIDI (*Baha*, etc)
with prosthetic /h-/]

**Hai·ah and Kai·ah and Bud·dy-
born-drunk** *n phr* (Bdos) [*AF—Joc*] ‖HABRA,
DABRA, AND THE CREW (Bdos)

ha·i·a·ri* (ha·i·ar·ry) [haya·ri] *n* ‖*bush-rope*
2. (Guyn) A very sturdy, parasitic forest vine,
the roots of wh are pounded and thrown into
the river as a means of drugging fish, wh are
thus easily caught over a wide area; it is sometimes loosely called 'fish-poison'; *Lonchocarpus
densiflorus* (*Papilionaceae*). [< *BAED* Arawak
name of this vine]

hail [(h)e·l] (CarA) **1.** *vb tr* To greet (sb) in
passing. *I hail her up there by Mr Adderley.*—
(Baha) **2.** *imper vb* [Rastaf] (A greeting associated
with members of the Rastafarian cult) Hello
brother/sister! *Mary im full a confusion, / Instead
a 'Me' im does sey I man. / An instead a sayin'
'Good Morning', / Is hail he goin bout shoutin'.*—
LMFF:37 **3.** PHRASES **3.1 hail for sb/sth** *vb
phr* (Bdos, Gren) **1.** To call for (sb/sth) in praise
or expressing loud admiration; to back (a side
in a match, etc). *Well all o[f] dem hailin[g] fo[r]
Independence because Worl[d] Bank go len[d] dem
millions!*—PPGD:35 **3.2 Hail I!** *id phr* (CarA)

[Rastaf] Greetings to you! [In the phr *I = I-man*
i.e. brother/sister]

ha·i·ma·ra* [haɪma·ra] *n* (Guyn) A large,
fresh-water fish with dark scales and weighing
over 30 pounds when mature; it is much prized
for its flesh, lives in forest creeks, and is very
ferocious; *Macrodon trahira* or *Hoplias ma-
crophthalmus* (*RFLG:81*). [*GDAA:264* Arekuna
aimara (name of this fish) + prosthetic /h-/]

hair [he·r ~ heə ~ hɛ] *n* (CarA) [Usu qualified in
CE, not as to its colour as in SE, but as to its
texture. See cit] *As a member of the West Indian
coloured middle-class, she conceived of human hair
in terms of 'good' and 'bad'—sometimes 'good' and
'hard'; 'good' hair is hair that is European in
appearance; 'bad' or 'hard' hair is hair of the
kinky, Negroid type.*—MMAO:59 □ See BAD
HAIR, GOOD HAIR, HARD HAIR, PICKY HAIR.

hair-braid·ing *n* (Bdos) The styling of (a
black woman's) hair in CORN-ROW. □ The vb *to
corn-row* is used but rarely 'corn-rowing', hence
hair-braiding (recently copied from AmE) is
used to refer to the process.

Hai·roun [haɪru·n] *n* (StVn) (Said to be) the
original Carib name of the island of St Vincent.
*At the time of discovery, the island was inhabited
by Caribs who called the island Hairoun 'Land of
the Blessed' in whose hands it remained until 1627
when a grant of the island was made to Lord
Carlisle by Charles I.*—Svi (79/8, p.4) [The
source of this etym is not given. *BDFC:352* gives
the Carib name of St Vincent as *Iouloumain*]

hair·y man·go *n phr* (Belz, Gren, Jmca, Mrat,
Nevs, StVn) ‖*long mango* (Guyn, Tbgo, Trin)
‖*mango-bab* (Dmca) ‖*mango-fil* (StLu)
‖*mango-long* (Bdos) A common variety of
mango that is about 4 ins long and ripens with
a greenish skin; it is very juicy but its texture is
stringy and its fibres stick between the teeth
when it is sucked (hence the name 'hairy').

hair·y worm *n phr* (Guyn) A fleshy, yellowish
green, slug-like caterpillar, one or two inches
long, wh is the larva of a butterfly; it is armed,
at intervals along its body, with hairs wh sting
severely, causing painful, itching bumps on your
skin; (*Sibine*) spp ((*Limacodidae*), of the order
(*Lepidoptera*)). □ The name is also applied (in a
general way of warning to tree-climbers) to the
dense, brownish cocoons of the pupae wh also
sting.

Hai·tian [he·ʃən] *n, adj* (A person or thing) of
or belonging to the State of Haiti.

hai·ti-hai·ti (tree) [heti-heti] *n (phr)* (USVI)
‖SEASIDE-MAHOE (Bdos, etc) *The shade of the
Haiti-haiti tree is welcome along Cruz Bay Beach
and Reef Bay Beach. Tea from the blossoms is good
for colds. If you need a rope in a hurry, the bark
can be stripped. Amerindians in the Amazon still
do this.*—JNHSJ:55

hak·ya-stick (hack·i·a-stick) *n* (Guyn) ‖ *ockya-stick* (Bdos) A very hard stick, usu about 4 or 5 ft long and usu with a gnarled end, cured from a limb cut from a hakya tree; it is prized as a ready defensive weapon. [< *BAD* Arawak *hakuya* 'a large tree with hard wood'] □ Cp COCO-MACCA.

ha·la·ri /1'12/ *n* (Belz) [*AF—Joc*] A woman of low character who is given to brawling. [Said to be a metaph ref to a noisy brown bird of that name wh also moves in flocks]

ha·lé (ha(l)·lay (-sweet)) *n* (Dmca, Trin) A soft, sticky sweet that stretches when pulled. [Fr Cr < Fr *haler* 'to pull']

half-a- [hafa-] *adj prefix* (ECar) [*AF—Derog*] Of poor quality; old and misshapen; almost worthless, etc; hence *half-a-car/-man/-shoes*, etc. [< SE (being only) half of a (sth)]

half-a-bit /1'22/ *n* (Guyn) [Hist] **1.** A tiny silver coin with the value of one eighth of a GUILDER or four cents (W Indian) (wh went out of circulation about the early 1900s). *Two sense man can['t] share one silver half-a-bit.* (= *Two tricksters cannot share one small coin.*)—Guyn (Prov) ['The last local coinage of the guilder system was authorised [in] 1836, and consisted of a guilder, quarter guilder, and eighth guilder. On this issue the [new] colonies' name was correctly inscribed Br Guiana'—*PCBWI:33*] **2.** The sum of four cents (Guyn) in reckoning the cost of small items in the market. *'Oh, me Gaad ...' says the girl, almost in tears. 'Ef a did want de plantains couldn' a did pay fo' dem! A got de half-a-bit in me pocket.'*—CNH:24 □ Used mostly by older folk, or otherwise Joc.

half-a-foot (half-foot) /1'12/ *adj* (Bdos, Dmca, Guyn, Jmca, Tbgo, StVn) [*IF—Derog*] Having lost part or the whole of one leg (whether using a crutch or having a wooden leg). *In the street near the inn many miserable objects present themselves, such as old Negroes passed service, with half a foot or without toes.*—Jbm XXXV. 1, p.22 [< CE *foot* 'the whole leg'; hence 'half-a-leg' + a shift from an adj phr, as in cit, to a more usual pre-nominal adj]

half-a-hand [hafaha·n] /1'12/ *adj* (Guyn, StVn) [*IF—Derog*] Having lost part or the whole of one arm. [< CE *hand* 'the whole arm'; hence 'half-an-arm'. Cp HALF-A-FOOT]

half-a-i·di·ot (half-i·di·ot) /1'1222/ *n* (Bdos) [*AF—Derog*] A person who is too foolish to be worth taking notice of; a contemptible fool. *Surely, Mr Morris, any half-idiot should know that a reduction in the quantum of a tax only benefits those paying the particular tax.*—NaT (90.03.18, p.6)

half-and-half *adj* (Guyn, Tbgo, Trin) [*IF*] ‖ *half-hearty* (Bdos, Guyn) Feeling just passably well; so-so; not in high spirits.

half-bag *n* (Guyn, Trin, ViIs) A unit of measure for rice, pods, sugar, etc equivalent to about a hundredweight (112 lbs); a bag made to contain this amount. [From the fact that a regular-sized or normal commercial bag of grain, etc, weighs about two hundred weight]

half-bot·tle *n* (CarA) ‖ *flask* (Bdos) ‖ *flattie*, *hippie* (Guyn) ‖ *hip-flask* (Bdos) A small round-shouldered and flat-sided bottle containing three gills (12 oz) of rum; it is made with a slightly curved body to fit conveniently into a man's hip-pocket (hence other names). *... just finished a 'big bottle' the accused came, said that they were sporting on an empty bottle and offered to put up a 'big' if McPherson bought a half-bottle.*—DaC (52.05.01, p.13) □ The term by itself is generally understood to imply 'of rum'; otherwise its contents would be stated.

half-cuts *n pl* (Bdos) ‖ *low-cuts* (Bdos) Canvas shoes (or CREPESOLES) made with a toe-piece and sole of tough rubber, and a longer tongue and laced-up area than PUMPS. *Back in the tenantry some 'half-cuts' were hanging by their tongues from a clothes line, put out to dry.*—SuS (80.10.26, p.29) [i.e. like canvas boots cut 'half-way' or below the ankle] □ Cp HI(GH)-CUTS (Bdos).

half-door *n* (CarA) A wooden door whose single panel is cut horizontally across the middle, so allowing the lower half to be kept closed for privacy, while the upper half stays open for ventilation and communication; (AmE) Dutch door. *I was frightened. I looked over the half-door to see what was happening outside.*—LICMS:15

half-heart·y *adj* (Bdos, Guyn) ‖ HALF-AND-HALF (Guyn, etc) [Prob a blend of CE HALF-AND-HALF + SE *hail-and-hearty*; perh also infl by SE *half-hearted* 'not very energetic'] □ Used mostly by older folk.

half-i·di·ot (Bdos) [*AF—Derog*] See HALF-A-IDIOT

half-scald [ha·f-ska·l] *adj* (Guyn) [*AF—Derog*] **1.** Having an unattractive or unhealthy-looking, light-coloured skin; being of marked European mixture; a mulatto with reddish skin. □ Often used *Derog* of Portuguese in *Guyn.* **2.** [By extension, in more general use] Cheap-looking; of low quality. [< SE *half-scalded* with characteristic CarA Cr apocope or pa.t. /-ed/ deleted]

hall *n* (CarA) **1.** The drawing-room or sitting-room of a house (as distinct from its gallery or galleries) in wh guests are entertained. *The evening fell silent and sombre. I sat down in the sitting room—wh we called the hall—and my mother was in the bedroom and there was not a sound.*—AGDR:60 [A modification of *OED* hall 2. 'the large public room in a mansion ... etc', used for receptions, banquets, etc' + cits 13C to 19C. The later SE sense, *OED* hall 8. 'the lobby or entrance passage [of a house]' + cits

17C to 19C, does not apply in the *CarA*] **2.** The proprietor's residence or GREAT HOUSE on a sugar-estate, usu with a name (exs *Eagle Hall, Rose Hall*, etc) wh was often transferred to the whole estate and in many cases has now become a place-name. [Cp *OED* hall 3. 'the residence of a territorial proprietor; a baronial ... hall']

Hal·le·lu·jah [halıluya] *n* (Guyn) An AM-ERINDIAN religion, or a member of that religion, the main known feature of wh is a slow ce-remonial dance in wh members hold on to each other chanting, as they move in a circle, or form a chain; it was developed under Christian missionary influence. *Mama Josephine resides at Amopopokai, the headquarters of the Hallelujahs. At least once per year all votaries of this religion who cross international borders, gather at Am-opopokai for their special celebrations.*—Guyn (Ms, 1976)

hal·wa(h) *n* (Guyn, Trin) [Indic] A sweet pudding made of parched flour, ghee, and eggs, but sometimes sharply spiced with curry powder and black pepper; it is served on ceremonial occasions and esp in the ninth-day celebration after the birth of a child. [Hin *halvaa* (*haluaa*), original name of this sweetmeat]

(h)a·ma·di·li *n* (Belz) [X] ‖ ARMADILLO (Guyn) [Prosthetic /h/ + AMADILI, folk pronunc of AR-MADILLO]

ha·mans [hamanz] *n* (Belz) [X] Almond. *After eating this hamans I will plant the seed.*—(Belz) [< SE *almond* + prosthetic /h-/ and vowel opening, with development of a pl as a sg form]

ham·bug *vb* (CarA) [X] See HUMBUG[1]

ham-cut·ter *n* (Bdos) ‖ *hops-and-ham* (Trin) A roll or small loaf sliced horizontally, with a slice of ham and a piece of dressed lettuce placed in between; it is regularly sold as a canteen snack.

ham·mond *n* (Nevs, StKt) [IF—*Joc*] ‖ BUSH-RUM (Gren, etc) *The prosecution's case was that Menelva R— smashed a bottle of hammond when Policemen were conducting a search in Joseph Q—'s yard.*—DeM(SK) (63.09.07, p.10) [Popular shortened form of *Hammond Report*, the whole name being at first jocosely applied to this liquor, as 'sth publicly rejected as unacceptable', be-cause the Civil Servants Commission's 'Ham-mond Report', of the late 1950s, was condemned in those terms; the Joc transfer is now becoming standardized]

ham·per *n* **1.** (Jmca) ‖ DONKEY-BOX (Antg) **2.** (StKt) A tall, covered, wicker-work, clothes bas-ket.

ham·per-basket *n* (Bdos) ‖ BAIT-BASKET (Bdos)

ha·na·kwa (ha(n)·na·qua(h)) *n* (Guyn) See ANAKWA [Prosthetic /h/ + ANAKWA]

hand[1] *n* (CarA) **1.** The whole arm, from the shoulder to the fingers, of the human body; any part of the whole limb (upper arm, forearm or hand). *The man moved closer to the bent figure in the doorway, with the now silent infant cradled comfortably in his hands.*—DaG (67.11.12, p.4, J. Pattinson) [Prob a calque from W Afr langs in many of wh there is no lexical distinction between SE *hand* and *arm*. Exs Igbo *aka* 'hand; arm'; Twi *nsa* 'hand; arm'; etc] □ Cp FOOT, used with similar non-distinction in CE. Hence common CE expressions such as *he broke his hand/foot*, '(SE) he broke his arm/leg', *She got her hand squeezed in the door*, '(SE) she got her fingers squeezed', etc. **2.** [Of bananas, plantains] Each cluster of four to twelve or more fruits pressed tightly together, and borne in tiers around the thick stalk of a bunch; each mature cluster is cut close from the stalk to be marketed, or (in the case of bananas) to be boxed for shipping. *The usual difference in fruit filling be-tween the upper and lower hands of uncovered bunches is considerably reduced, as is the variation between the front and back fingers.*—Win I.3, p.10) **3.** (Baha, Gren, Guyn, Jmca) ‖ SUSU-HAND (Gren, etc) *Each week, one of the participants was given the sum total of all the 'hands', and this was repeated each week, until all 'hands' were drawn; and then the process started all over again.*—EBT: 17 **4.** PHRASES **4.1 be hand and foot to sb** *vb phr* (Tbgo) [IF] [Of a person or thing] To be indispensable to (sb); to be of vital service to (sb). **4.2 be sick/die on your hand** *vb phr* (CarA) [IF] To be a burden to you as a sick (usu bedridden) person, or (as a corpe) requiring burial procedures. [Cp Yoruba *o şaisan si mi l'owo* (*he fall-sick to me on the hand*) 'he fell sick in my hands'—(pers info *A. Banjo*)] □ Cp SE (*to have a responsibility*) *on your hands*. The CE idiom particularizes this usage, perh influenced by calquing from some W Afr langs. Cp also IrE *on me* 'to my detriment'—*JESI:27*. **4.3 (two persons) can shake hands** *id phr* (CarA) [IF] ‖ *(two persons) can live in the same house* (Nevs, Tbgo) ‖ *carry the same head* (Mrat) **(i)** Share the same view, attitude, likes, or dislikes (more often in a particular matter). *When I heard him express those particular views in committee I knew we could shake hands.*—(Guyn) **(ii)** Have the same unusual disposition or tastes. [Cp Yor-uba *Gba l' owo* (*Take by the hand*) 'shake hands (for that)' i.e. as a sign of agreement in a par-ticular issue—(pers info *K. Omotoso*)] **4.4 catch your hand** *id phr* (Guyn) [AF] ‖ *turn your hand* (Jmca) To work to earn some urgently needed money; to do an extra or outside job to make up for meagre wages. *The gyms had said that they wanted a postponement because most of their members were 'catching their hand' during the Christmas season.*—GyC (75.12.10, p.26) **4.5 deh/lef[t] [u]pon han[d]** [dɛ/lɛf pʌn ha·n] *vb phr* (Guyn) [AF—Cr] [Usu of a marriageable young woman] To be left unmarried; to be on hand in your parents' home hoping for a suitor. *The son go out and marry a light-skin girl but the two sisters lef[t] [u]pon han[d].*—(Guyn) **4.6 down hand in/on (sb)** [dʌŋ ha·n ın/ɒn] *vb phr*

(CarA) [*AF*] (i) To deal (sb) a pounding blow. (ii) To grab sb very roughly. **4.7 drive a hand in sb** *vb phr* (Bdos, Guyn) See DRIVE Phr 1. **4.8 drop (a) hand in (sb)/on (sb)** *vb phrs* See DROP[1] Phr 3.5 **4.9 Fire, fire, bu[r]n me hand!** *id phr* (Guyn) [*AF—Cr*] See FIRE[1] Phr 3 **4.10 hand is fast** *id phr* (CarA) [*IF*] (i) [Of a child] (You) are mischievous, interfering. (ii) (You) have a tendency to steal. [Cp Hausa *da saurin hannu* (*with fastness of hand*) 'thieving'] □ Cp MAKE YOUR HANDS FAST. See FAST Phr 5.3. **4.11 hand [is] long; hand (is) longer than your foot** *id phrs* (Gren) [*AF*] You have a known tendency to steal; you have been caught stealing before. □ Restricted to petty theft esp of domestic items. **4.12 hand is short** *id phr* (Guyn) [*IF*] (You) are temporarily short of money. *Well I couldn't pay them off right away as my hand was a little short that month, so I asked them to give me some time.*—(Guyn) **4.13 hand is tight** *id phr* (CarA) [*IF*] (You) are tight-fisted; (you) are mean and ungenerous. **4.14 hands are light** *id phr* (Baha) [*IF—Joc*] (You) are light-fingered, thieving. **4.15 haul in your hand** *vb phr* (Guyn) [*AF/IF*] (i) To cut down your spending. *Next year you goin[g] on pension, you have to begin haulin[g] in yo[ur] hand from now.*—(Guyn) (ii) [Of a vendor] To offer less than the usual quantity for sale for the same price. *It look like you haul in yo[ur] han[d] wit[h] dis bora! Last week yo[u] had such nice big parcels.*—(Guyn) **4.16 have a good hand** *vb phr* (CarA) [*IF*] To be successful in (home or kitchen) gardening **4.17 let your hand drop** *vb phr* (Belz, Guyn) [*IF*] To make no serious effort to help yourself; to give up or be idle when there is serious work to be done. *She didn't just let her hand drop. She bestirred herself and made cakes to sell for a living.*—Guyn (Ms) [Cp *DAFL* Twi *n' aba apa* (*his arm slack*) 'he is despondent'; *n' aba mu abu* (*his arm drops*) 'he is disheartened'] **4.18 los[t] [u]pon your hand** *vb phr* (Guyn) [*AF—Cr*] See LOSS[1] Phr 2.2 **4.19 make sb feel (the weight of) your hand** *vb phr* (ECar) [*AF*] To clout, thump, lash, or severely strike sb. **4.20 make sb's hand fall** *vb phr* (Antg, Guyn) [*IF*] To disappoint or cause shame to (sb) by failing to achieve sth; to belie your promise. *Yo[u] mean dat wid all da[t] mout[h] you got yo[u] cou[ld]n[t] even mak[e] a li[tt]l[e] bir[th]day speech?—Aw man yo[u] make me han[d] fall!*—(Guyn) **4.21 make your hands fast** *vb phr* (CarA) [*IF*] [In different contexts] See FAST Phrs 5.2., 5.3., 5.6. **4.22 out/up (your) hand and hit (sb)** *vb phr* (CarA) [*IF*] [Esp of young persons] To deal (sb) a sudden and severe blow with the fist. **a.** *The first time he tried to handle her, she just out hand and hit him such a box in his face—he never touch[ed] her again!*—(Trin) **b.** *But yo[u] mus[t] control him! Not let him up [h]is hand an[d] hit [h] is big brother any time like that! Eh-eh!*—(Guyn) [Prob a calque from W Afr langs. Cp Yoruba *fa owọ yọ na* 'put out hand [and] beat (sb)'; also *gb' owo s' oke na* 'take hand up [and] beat (sb)'— (pers info *K. Omọtọsọ and A. Banjo*)] **4.24 pass through/under sb's hands** *vb phr* (Bdos, Guyn) [*IF*] To be taught or trained by sb who

is a celebrated teacher. [A transfer of the metaph ref to good teaching as the 'moulding' or 'forming' of character, etc] □ This phrase tends to be used mostly by older folk. **4.25 put in hand / ı'2ı/; put your hand in sth** *vb phrs* (Guyn) [*AF/IF*] To give much needed assistance (esp to sb in a fight). **a.** *Fight start and when Rajesh see Sonny gettin[g] beat up, he put in han[d].*—(Guyn) **b.** *If America di[d]n[t] put in de[ir] han[d] for Englan[d], Englan[d] was goin[g] lose de war.*—(Guyn) □ Distinguish from IAE *put in hand* /2ı2'/ 'to have (sth) undertaken'. **4.26 put your hand on (sb)** *vb phr* (CarA) [*AF*] To flog sb severely; to clout or clobber (sb). [Cp IrE *to lift your hand to sb* 'to beat or flog sb'—*L. Todd*] **4.27 stan[d] yo[ur] han[d]** *vb phr* (Guyn, Trin) [*AF*] To pay for a round of drinks or solid food and drinks (as an act expected of you). [Perh a blend of SE *stand sb a drink* + *show your hand* (i.e. show what you're worth)] **4.28 turn your hand** *vb phr* (Gren, Jmca, ViIs) [*AF*] ‖ CATCH YOUR HAND (Bdos, etc) See CATCH Phr 8.11 '*... the last test tube blew up the other day when I was trying to tun me han mek chemical ... never work at all.*'—DaG (Mag, 79.09.02, p.6) **4.29 with (your) two long hands** *adj phr* (ECar) [*AF—Joc*] (i) Empty-handed; having no belongings or possessions to your name. *You can[t] get married jus[t] sudden so wit[h] yo[ur] two long hands! Whe[re] yo[u] put yo[ur] wife to live?*—(Gren) (ii) Bringing nothing to help with work to be done. *You can[t] come wid yo[u] two long hands and say yo[u] come to help! You come to eat!*—(Guyn)

hand[2] *vb tr* (CarA) [*IF*] To give (sth hurtful such as a blow, insult, etc). *He went to the neighbour and handed her a good 'busing'. He threatened to beat her up and the lady, afraid of the enraged Dick, ran into another neighbour's home for safety.*—DaC (53.01.05, p.3)

han[d][3] [ha·n] *vb tr* (ViIs) [*AF*] ‖ HORN[1] (Baha, etc) *I sure dey goin[g] ge[t] divorce[d] because she always lookin[g] to han[d] he.*—(BrVi) [< *OED* horn v 2. (*Obs*) 'to cuckold' + characteristic CarA Cr—[ɔ > a] vowel opening, whence /harn/ > /haan/, the latter form coinciding with /haan/ 'hand' and prob being so interpreted by folk etym, influenced by HAND[2]]

hand-bas·ket *n* (CarA) A small (often round) sturdy, open basket with a handle, used for shopping or for carrying a labourer's food into the fields. [Because carried in the hand (cp SE *handbag*) as opposed to the common large open basket that is to be carried on the head]

han·dle (sb) *vb tr* (CarA) **1.** To cope with and overcome (an opponent in a dispute). **2.** PHRASES **2.1 be able to handle (sb)** *vb phr* (Dmca, Jmca); **can handle (sb)** *vb phr* (Bdos, Belz) ‖ (BE) ABLE WITH SB (CarA) See ABLE Phr 1. *The people givin[g] him hell in de papers but he can handle all o[f] them, mo[re] than one at a time too!*—(Bdos)

han·dle your·self (well) *vb refl phr* (CarA) [*IF*] To show competence or skill in an open argument, competitive sport, or struggle. *The female spectators throw themselves into the boxing with a frenzy that is almost unmatched by the males around them, seeming to become more personally involved, on an emotional level, with the way the boxers handle themselves.*—AdN (74.01.12, p.8)

hand-mid·dle *n* (Belz, Guyn, Jmca) [*AF*] **1.** The palm of the hand. *Whenever m[y] han[d]-middle itch I know I goin[g] get money.*—(Guyn) [Cp Twi *nsa-yam* (*hand-inside*) 'palm of the hand'] **2.** (Belz) Emptiness of the hand, (hence foll phr). **3.** PHRASE **3.1 on hand-middle** *id phr* (Belz) [*AF—Joc*] Without pay; for nothing.

han·dy·man *n* (StLu) ‖ MAN-O[F]-BUSINESS (Bdos) **1.**

hang *vb* PHRASES **1. hang kin[g]dola** [hɛŋ kɪndola] *vb phr* (Belz) [Sailing] To lean outboard while pulling on or harnessed by a rope attached to the mast of a sailing DOREY to counter-balance the opposite pull of the wind in the sail; (SE) hike out. *These races are run with unballasted 16-foot sailing dories with outsize sails and a crew of three, one of whom has to 'hang kingdola' all the time from a harness to keep the boat upright.*—ReP (79.10.07, p.8) **2. hang the jack** *vb phr* (Tbgo, Trin) [Card-playing] To capture the jack of trumps from the opposing pair in a game of ALL-FOURS by playing a higher face-card and so gaining three points. **3. hang your basket/hat too high** *vb phr* (Baha, Guyn, StLu) [*IF—Joc*] To plan or begin an undertaking that will cost more than you can afford; to be too ambitious for your ability. **4. hang your mouth where the soup drips** *vb phr* (Guyn) [*AF—Derog*] See MOUTH Phr 4.11 **5. hang with fruit** *vb phr* (Baha) [Of a tree] To be laden with or bend under the weight of fruit. *'De tree fair hang wid mangrer (mango), or dilly (sapodillo), or orange, or coconut.'* Plural is never used. *'Hang wid or wit' means that the tree is laden with a good crop, 'it fair hang' being an emphasis on the quantity.*—JBJ:80

hang·ing; so.cial hang.ing *n (phr)* (StVn) The mock execution on a makeshift gallows of the effigy or effigies of a person or persons known to be guilty of incest or shameful adultery; it is a ceremonial, rural, folk punishment carried out with much noise in midnight moonlight.

hang·ing-press *n* (Jmca) A wardrobe; (BrE) a clothes-press. [For the hanging of clothes, the unqualified name PRESS usu applying in *Jmca* to a 'chest of drawers']

hang·man *n* **1.** (Bdos) [*IF*] A man that is to be executed by hanging. *One of the customs of this village and others nearby was that on the morning a 'hangman' would be put to death, everyone would congregate on the hill a few yards away from the gallows window and listen to the fall of the trap.*—Com, 1974, p.34 [< a man to hang

(with CE passive force 'to be hanged'). Cp similar SE word-formation in *flashlight*] **2.** [hɛŋmʌn] (Bdos, Gren, Guyn, Jmca) [*AF—Derog*] A ruffian; a brutish reprobate. *Mus[t] be dat hengman next[t] door dat pick up m[y] fowl-cock an[d] sell it.*—(Gren) [Perh by extension of sense 1., but cp OED *hangman* 1. b. 'a term of reprobation' + cits–'1645]

han·na *n* (Guyn) ‖ CANJE PHEASANT (Guyn)

hap·haz·ard [haphazɪd] *adv* (Baha, Bdos) [*X*] ‖ *happosite* (Gren) Suddenly; unexpectedly; without due consideration. *'I may be guilty because I didn't know where I was,' Earl W— told Chief Magistrate Kermit Ireland. / 'I pick up haphazard,' he said, 'and my head was swinging and I didn't know where I was.'*—TrI (70.10.06, p.1) [By functional and semantic shift < SE *haphazardly*, in its lesser sense 'by chance']

hap·pos·ite [hapozɪt] *adv* (Gren) [*X*] ‖ HAPHAZARD (Baha, Bdos) *Boy, A wasn['t] prepare[d] for anyt[h]ing so, it catch me happosite.*—(Gren) [Prob a combination of folk etym, influenced by 'opposite' (i.e. to expectation), and HAPHAZARD (*Bdos*)]

har·bour *n* (Guyn) [*X*] A light, raised wooden frame of trellis-work, wire-netting, or dried coconut branches on wh a fruit-bearing vine is trained. [Cp OED *harbour* sb² (*Obs*) 'a frequent spelling of *arbour* from the 16C'. The *Guyn* usage may be a survival of this; or the /h-/ may be prosthetic by infl of folk etym SE *harbour*] □ It seems preferable to use SE *arbour* with some shift in sense, than IAE *harbour* in a likely misleading sense.

har·bour·ing-house *n* (Belz) A brothel run by a madam in wh young girls are offered living accommodation.

hard¹ *adj* [Many further senses of this word are given below in separate entries of compound forms] **1.** (CarA) [Of fruit] **(i)** Not mature; quite unripe; that will not ripen if picked. □ In ref to fruit such as guavas, mangoes, bananas, that yield somewhat to hand-pressure when mature enough to be picked. **(ii)** Past maturity; tough or dry in texture. □ In ref esp to coconuts and to the condition of some vegetables such as cassava and yams. **2.** (Jmca) [Of a person] Fully adult; mature and getting on in years (esp in relation to marriageability). *I remember her as hard already when I was a little girl.*—(Jmca) [Cp EDD *hard* 4. 'big, strong, robust, growing' + cit (Som. 1825) 'hard people, adults'] **3.** (CarA) [Of a black person's hair] Thick, short and resistant to combing. **4.** PHRASE **4.1 hard as/like banga/gru-gru seed** *id phr* (Trin) See GROU-GROU Phr 4.1 and GROU-GROU BÈF Phr 3.1

hard² *adv* (CarA) [*IF*] **1.** With intensity (but often used idiomatically different from SE, hence foll phrs). **2.** PHRASES **2.1 drink hard** *vb phr* (CarA) [*IF*] To be a hard drinker. **2.2 holler/**

talk hard *vb phr* (CarA) [*IF*] To shout; to speak loudly. **2.3 play a radio, etc (too) hard** *vb phr* (CarA) [*IF*] To play a radio, etc (too) loudly. **2.4 sleep hard** *vb phr* (CarA) [*AF*] To be a heavy sleeper; to sleep deeply. *Ah coulda hardly open meh sleepy, nampy eyes when ah hear dis cause ah was sleepin so hard when meh brodder come runnin in meh room.*—Aaw.I.2, p.23 [Cp *EDD hard* 2. Phr 7. (wYks) *hard on* 'fast asleep']

hard-back[1] *n* (Bdos, Guyn) A small, black, oval beetle about one inch long; they swarm seasonally in the early night; *Ligyrus tumulosus* (*Coleoptera*). [From the hard wing-casing wh is crushed between the fingers to kill the beetle when it becomes a nuisance in the home]

hard-back[2] *adj* (CarA) [*AF—Derog*] [Of a person] Approaching middle-age or older; old enough to know or do better. *Would you believe that they have got so caught up in the thing that big, hard-back men are singing 'Brown Girl In The Ring' on television now.*—BoM (73.01.12) **hard-boys** *n* (Bdos) [*AF*] ‖ ADMIRALS (Bdos) [From the hardness of these biscuits] □ Only remembered by older folk.

hard-boys *n* (Bdos) [*AF*] ‖ ADMIRALS (Bdos) [From the hardness of these biscuits] □ Only remembered by older folk.

hard co·co *n phr* (Jmca) ‖ TANNIA (CarA) *Cocoes—or 'hard cocoes' as it is better known in the island's market places to distinguish it from soft cocoes of the 'Minty' variety—were harvested in sufficient quantities right across the island this week that the AMC obtained a residual 3, 440 lbs to buy.*—DaG (Farmers Weekly, 73.02.10, p.9)

hard-dough bread *n phr* (Jmca) A fine-grained, dense white loaf, popular with rural folk and labourers (*DJPVP:11*).

hard-ears[1] [ha(r)d-e(r)z] *n* (CarA) [*IF*] Stubborn or persistent disobedience. *It's your hard-ears that made you break your hand although I told you don't play on the road.*—(Guyn) [Noun made from the calque (*your*) *ears are hard* from W Afr langs (see EARS Phr 2.2)] □ Used only in ref to children.

hard-ears[2] [ha(r)d-e(r)z] *adj* (CarA) [*IF/F*] ‖ *ears-hard* (Belz) ‖ *harden[ed]* (ECar) ‖ *hard-head[ed]* 3. (Baha, Belz, Dmca, Gren, Guyn, Nevs, Trin) **1.** Stubbornly disobedient. *And I felt the sting of the belt tight on my leg, and she cried again louder than ever. 'Hard ears you won't hear, hard ears you must feel.' The laughter burst through my tears, for she had called up with those words the image of the class room and the pot-bellied teacher Mr Bruce, whom we mocked with the same words: 'Hard ears you won't hear, hard ears you must feel.'*—LICMS:121 [By functional shift of HARD-EARS[1] n and a refinement of Cr/*yu tuu haad eez*/ 'you're too stubborn and disobedient'] □ Used only in ref to children, its strong connotation not replaceable by any single SE word.

2. *PHRASE* **2.1 hard-ears you can't hear, own-way you will feel** *id phr* (CarA) See HEAR Phr 4.11

hard·en[ed] [ha·(r)dn] *adj* (ECar) [*AF*] ‖ HARD-EARS[2] (CarA) *On being questioned on behalf of the police, she agreed that she had to move from Belle Eau Road and leave her son, ... because 'he used to give some trouble: he was 'harden'; when I spoke to him he did not listen to me. I could not handle him.'*—ExP (73.02.15, p.3) [A refinement influenced by ‖ *hard-ears*; but also perh by *EDD harden* vb and adj (Sc, Irel, NhB, Yks, etc) 'to be obdurate, incorrigible' used in pass + cit (sStf, 1895) 'Yo ca' talk him o'et, he's tu hardened']

hard-face[d] *adj* (Bdos, Guyn) [*AF—Derog*] [Of a woman] Having a harsh, disillusioned look; looking now too old to be marriageable.

hard-food *n* (Bdos, Jmca, StVn) ‖ *food* 3 (Jmca) Cooked GROUND PROVISIONS as the substantial part of a meal. *... and below that were the 'hard' food, yams and sweet potatoes, a few more stems of green bananas, plantains, a large green breadfruit.*—PCOS:66

hard-gua·va days *n phr* (Guyn) ‖ *guava-days* (Gren, Guyn) ‖ *guava-time* (Mrat) ‖ *t-amarind season* (Jmca) Hard times (i.e. when it may be necessary to eat even hard green guavas, or tamarinds, etc as the only easily available food).

hard hair *n phr* (Belz, Bdos, Guyn) ‖ BAD HAIR (CarA) *The Afro really suits people with hard hair, even the men, because you see the hard hair keeps the shape really well.*—(Guyn) [Cp Twi *tiri ŋhwi deŋ* (head-hair hard) 'tough hair']

hard head[1] *n phr* (CarA) [*IF*] ‖ BAD HEAD[1] 2. (Guyn, etc) [*IF*] *The boy has a hard head—you have got to teach him the same thing over and over again. Can't learn—head is too hard.*—Nevs [Cp Yoruba *ori ti o d'ota* (head which (*it has*) turned to rock) 'head of a dullard']

hard-head[2]·**(ed)** *adj* [*IF*] **1.** (Guyn, Tbgo, Trin) ‖ HARD[1] 3. (CarA) **2.** (CarA) ‖ BAD-HEAD[2] 2. (Guyn, etc) *The boy really hard-head you know, he cyan understan[d] a t[h]ing dey tell [h]im at school.*—(Guyn) [Cp Yoruba *ori ti o d'ota* (head which has turned to rock) 'head of a dullard'] **3.** (Baha, Dmca, Gren, Mrat, StLu, StVn, TkCa) ‖ HARD-EARS[2] (CarA) *Child didn't I tell you to move your shoes? Why you so hard head?*—(Baha) [Cp Igbo *ọ bụ onye isi-ike* (he/she be somebody head hard) 'he/she is obstinate']

hard·head·ed·ness *n* (CarA) The state of being both obstinate and stupid. *When we face you and you say you will pass your Bill, we know you will pass your Bill, but then the country will suffer for the foolhardiness and the hardheadedness of people who will not look further than their* noses.—Gren (Hd, 68.09.04, p.35) [From senses 2., 3. of HARD-HEAD[ED]]

Hard·ing, Mr *n phr* **1.** (Guyn) [*AF—Joc*] (A name symbolizing) a hard task-master, usu sb in secondary authority. *The girls didn't like him as a store-walker, because he was a real Mr Harding, you know!*—(Guyn) **2.** (Bdos) [Hist] An effigy of a man, stuffed with straw and wearing a hat, wh was ceremonially burnt on the last night of the CROP-OVER festival, supposedly to symbolize the driving away of hard times that threatened ahead. *A feature being re-introduced to the Festival this year, is the burning of the effigy of 'Mr Harding' wh in the past symbolised hard times and represented all cruel gang-drivers.*—NaT (75.05.18, p.1)

hard-mout[h] *adj* (Bdos) [*AF—Derog*] Arguing and/or resisting when it is time to pay up for work done or to pay back a loan. [Cp *OED* hard-mouthed 2. 'self-willed; obstinate']

hard-seed *n* (Bdos) [*AF*] **1.** A person admired for his professional competence and skill in some public activity. **2.** [By extension] A young man who has his way with women.

hard-up *adj* (CarA) [*AF—Joc*] Unable or failing to attract a steady boyfriend or girlfriend. *Wingrove, where it is you now come from? You think that I so hard-up that you can just walk 'way and lef' me, and then stroll back here whenever you please?*—CISH:110 □ A particular use of SE hard-up 'out of currency' or 'desperate'.

hard-yam *n* (Guyn) ‖ YELLOW-YAM (Antg, etc) □ Prob one hard Guyn variety, since the *yellow-yam* is also used in Guyn.

hars·let (**hars·lick, hars·lit, has·let**) [ha·(r)zlɪt ~ ha·(r)zlɪk] *n* (Baha, Bdos) Part of the offal (esp the liver) of a pig; it is used as part of a meal. *Then there would be cook-shops preparing harslit, belly-soup, or rice and stew.*—NaT (74.08.04, p.5) [*OED* haslet, harslet ... (The spelling *harslet* appears to arise from the long [a·]) 'a piece of meat to be roasted, esp part of the entrails of a hog' + cits-'1872]

ha·si·ka·ra [hasikara] /1'122/ *n* (Gren, Trin) [*AF*] **1.** Noisy trouble; fuss. **2.** PHRASE **2.1 make hasikara** *vb phr* (Gren, Trin) [*AF—Joc*] (i) To cause stupid trouble that will lead to a row. (ii) To make an excessive, noisy, row. □ Cp BASSA-BASSA (*Gren*, etc) wh, however, appears to have a wider spread of meaning. [Perh < Hin *hāsiikar* adj 'ludicrous, ridiculous']

has·let *n* (Baha, Bdos) See HARSLET

has·sar ['hasa] *n* (Guyn) ‖ CASCADU(RA) (Trin) [< *BAED* Arawak *asa* 'a small highly-prized, edible fish' + prosthetic /h-/]

haul *vb tr* **1.** (CarA) [*IF*] To pull (in wide general senses where IAE *pull* may also be so used in informal contexts. See cits). **a.** *Haul in the door/window.*—(USVI) **b.** *Haul open the door and let in the breeze.*—(Gren) **c.** *Haul off/on a dress/your trousers* (to undress/dress hurriedly).—(Guyn) **d.** *Haul out some money from a purse.*—(Bdos) □ Cp (c) with Phr 4.4 below. **2.** (CarA) [*IF*] To carry (a heavy load by hand). *Perhaps one of your readers can enlighten me as to why the residents of Tyrrel Street ... have water only for a few hours each morning, and must haul buckets and go without baths for the rest of the day, while other parts of the town have running water all day.*—ToR (73.06.10, p.6) **3.** (Tbgo) [*IF*] To reap (esp peas, i.e. by pulling the pods off the shrub or vine). **4.** PHRASES **4.1 haul and pull** *vb phr* (Belz, Jmca) [*AF*] To upset; to confuse; to make a thorough mess of (sth). *So the Miss Jamaica contest is being scrapped by the Festival Commission. So far, the stone has fallen into the pool without a ripple, but since beauty contests is a regular topic for haul and pull, wait little bit and we'll soon have the discussion.*—WeG (75.05.20, p.15, Partyline) □ The phr may be used as a noun (it borders on that in cit = 'to haul and pull' or 'for hauling and pulling') or adj. In such cases it would be better to hyphenate it: 'a room in **haul-and-pull** condition'. **4.2 haul for (fish, etc)** *vb phr* (Baha, Gren Guyn) To catch fish/shrimp by driving them into a widely extended net weighted along its bottom edge and held on poles at each end by two members of the team who haul it in to the shore or river-bank. **4.3 haul in your hand** *vb phr* (Guyn) [*AF/IF*] See HAND[1] Phr 4.15 **4.4 haul off (and hit sb)** *vb phr* (CayI) [*IF*] To draw back (in order to hit out with more force). [Cp *DAE* haul vb 2. b. *haul off* 'to draw back one's fist, arm, etc, preparatory to delivering a blow'] □ Cp the vb tr use in sense 1.(c) above. **4.5 haul (sb's) nara** *vb phr* (Guyn, Trin) See NARA Phr 2.1 **4.6 haul up** *vb phr* (Guyn) [*IF*] (i) To stop (on the street, having arrived at a particular house). *So when [h]e haul up at the gate now all dress up, man, the girl mo[th]er jus[t] put she head out the window and say she ain['t] home.*—(Guyn) [By metaph transfer from 'pulling up' with horse and buggy or vehicle, although the person may be on foot] (ii) [By extension] To stop work. *Trying to finish an order she would work until late before she would haul up.*—(Guyn) **4.7 haul yourself** *vb phr* (Bdos, Guyn, Mrat, StVn) [*AF*] ‖ **haul your skin** (Gren) ‖ **haul your tail** (StKt, Trin) ‖ **Move yourself!** (CarA) To get out and be damned; to take yourself to hell out of here. □ Often used imperatively, sometimes without complement—*Haul!*—and often in such contexts with Vul complements other than those given. However the phr is also used in milder contexts. See ‖ **move yourself**.

haul-and-run ban·dit *n phr* (StVn) A purse-snatcher; a street-thief who grabs anything valuable from a person and flees.

haul-up *adj* (USVI) [*AF*] Sick-looking, with your shoulders drawn in and your arms together as if feverish.

Hau·sa *n* See AUOUHSAH

ha·van (ha·wan) [hawan] *n* (Guyn, Trin) [Indic] A ritual burning of an offering as part of a religious Hindu celebration. [Hin *havan* 'offering']

have *vb tr* **1.** (CarA) [X] Has; had. **a.** *All this have been the principal bones of contention in a clear cut UDP campaign.*—BeA(BE) (79.11.16, p.11) **b.** *Water for the heifers at Vernamfield also have to be trucked as no water is there.*—DaG (70.01.30, p.1, Farmer's Weekly) **c.** *I ask him if he have any girl friend and he said no. I said 'How much children do you have?' and he said one.*—NaT (76.09.05, p.18, Dear Christine) [Perh mostly because of infl of CarA Cr in wh the base verb functions as an item of lexical content without SE changes for number or tense. However this case may also be reinforced by the infl of IrE, in wh a similar use of *have* is noted: In Waterford and South Wexford the people often use such verbal forms as is seen in the following: 'Does your father grow wheat still?' 'He do.' 'Has he the old white horse now?' 'He have.' As to '*has*', Mr MacCall states that it is unknown in the barony of Forth: there you always hear 'that man have plenty of money'—he '*have*'—she have, &c. The Rev. William Burke tells us that 'have' is found as above (a third person singular) all through the old Waterford Bye-Laws; which would render it pretty certain that both 'have' and 'do' in these applications are survivals from the old English colony in Waterford and Wexford—*JESI:81*] **2.** (Dmca, StLu, Tbgo, Trin) [X] [In asking or telling age] To be. **a.** *'But what age you?' he asked. 'I have twenty-two,' she was smiling. 'And you?' 'I have twenty-five.'*—SROH: 111 **b.** *How many months your child have now?* (How old is your child?).—(Tbgo) [By calquing, through Fr Cr, from Fr 'Quel âge avez-vous? J'ai vingt-deux', literally 'What age have you?' I have twenty-two'] **3.** PHRASES **3.1 have a baby/ child for (sb)** *vb phr* (CarA) [IF] See FOR 8. **3.2 have again** *vb phr* (Gren) [AF] To have all you can want (of sth); to have plenty of money. *They pay plenty nutmeg bonus this year, so we have again!*—(Gren) **3.3 have a man/woman** *vb phr* (CarA) [IF] To have a companion for sexual reasons. **3.4 have a mind** *vb phr* (Gren, Tbgo, Trin) [IF] See MIND¹ Phr 5. *I knew he was going to refuse your offer; I had a mind so.*—(Tbgo) **3.5 have a right to (be somewhere, do sth)** *vb phr* (CarA) [IF/AF] See RIGHT¹ Phr 2. *You shouldn['t]-[h]a[ve] been on the street that time o[f] night! You had a right to be at home.*—(Guyn) **3.5.1 have no business/ right to (be somewhere, do sth)** *vb phr* (CarA) [IF/AF] See RIGHT¹ Phr 2.1 **3.6 have baby** *vb phr* (CarA) [AF] To give birth to a child. *I heard I was pregnant in May of this year and the doctor said I was to have baby in January of next year.*—JdN (79.11.29, p.7) **3.7 have colour** *vb phr* (CarA) [AF] [Of a person] To be brown or not quite black of skin. *I have more colour dan you, and I know I black, because I know me place.*—DP: 41 **3.8 have in (sth)** *vb phr* (CarA) [AF/IF] To

contain. **a.** *The customs will insist on knowing what each box has in.*—(Trin) **b.** *In his address, Dr Richard Cheltenham who represented the accused, said that the Prosecution's case had in major fundamental weaknesses.*—AdN (75.01.25, p.1) □ Pronounced as if one word ['havin ~ 'havi·n] and widely used with the sense above, this CE phrasal vb uses a prepositional extension *in* like an adverbial adjunct (= *inside*). SE would require *have in it* or *have sth in it.* **3.8.1 have in some liquor/rum, etc** *vb phr* (ECar) [AF—Joc] To be obviously drunk. *A man might have in some alcohol and may use abusive language to a policeman and he may put up a little fight.*—Bdos (Hd, 75.10.09, p.987) [By Joc extension of sense of 3.8 = to be full (of liquor)] **3.9 have it bad for (sb)** *vb phr* (Guyn) [AF] To be passionately in love with (sb) (who is being less passionate). **3.10 have it to say** *vb phr* (CarA) [IF] See SAY¹ Phr 3. **3.11 have (sb's) name all over the place** *vb phr* (Bdos, Guyn, Tbgo) [IF] See NAME¹ Phr 2. **3.12 have (sb) to know (sth)** *vb phr* (Bdos, Guyn) See KNOW Phr 1. **3.13 have sb/ sth to do sth for/with** *vb phr* (CarA) [IF] To have an obligation (wh is stated) in respect of sb/sth. **a.** *On mornings I have the children to take to school.*—(Bdos) **b.** *I[t']s true I have the little money to work for but then I have all the clothes and the books to buy.*—(Trin) □ SE would require a different word order, or a distinctive (not neutral) stress pattern or a passive construction after *have* in such contexts i.e. *I have to take the children to school* or *I have children to be taken to school.* **3.14 have (sb) up** *vb phr* (i) (Bdos) [AF] To bring (sb) before the court; to have (sb) summonsed. *A goin[g] ha[ve] you up if dat dam[ned] dog bite me, yeh!*—(Bdos) (ii) (Jmca) ‖ HOLD (SB) IN YOUR MIND (CarA) See HOLD Phr 5.10 *Well I was on the board that didn't give her the job, so she probably has me up, yo[u] see.*—(Jmca) **3.15 it have** *existential introductory phr* (Dmca, Gren, StLu, Tbgo, Trin) [AF—Cr] ‖ THEY HAVE (CarA) **a.** *You remember when it didn't have no school?*—SPOC:87 **b.** *Poopa, da' was a fete! I mean it had free rum free whisky and some fellars beating Pan from one of them band in Trinidad.*—FCV2:208 (D. Walcott) [By calquing through Fr Cr < Fr *il y a* (*it has there*) 'there is/are'] □ This phrase with pa.t. *it had*, is normal at the folk level in all the CE territories where there is Fr Cr in use or in the historical background, and seems to occur through imitation in other territories as well. **3.16 they have** *existential introductory phr* (CarA) [AF] ‖ *it have* (Dmca, Gren, StLu, Tbgo, Trin) There is/are. **a.** *I hear they have a holiday next Monday. I[t']s true?*—(Bdos) **b.** *They have some people in this place that you can't trust at all.*—(Guyn) **3.16.1 they have (sb) to bury/to hang/to jail** *id phr* (Bdos, Guyn) [IF/AF] Some (identified) person is going to be buried/hanged/jailed. **a.** *If she go [a]long livin[g] like dat they will soon have her to bury, the way t[h]ings happenin[g] these days.*—(Bdos) **b.** *She would never, never control the boy; that's why now they have him to hang.*—(Guyn) □ This phr usu indicates the speaker's endorsement of the burial, etc as a final, deserved penalty. **3.17 You have me there!** *id phr* (Bdos, Guyn) *[IF/AF]* I cannot think of an answer to your inquiry; You've got me stumped! *S1: How much would you say the house would sell for? / S2: Well, you have me there!*—(Guyn)

ha·wan *n* (Guyn, Trin) See HAVAN

hawk·er *n* (Bdos) ‖ *higgler* (Jmca) A person who sells fruit, vegetables, and small items of non-perishable food by the roadside, or under licence in an open market-place. *If the Hon. Member gets headlines for what he has just said he will be the darling of all the hawkers in the Fairchild Street market if he goes there.*—Bdos (Hd, 74.12.03, p.4299) □ Cp SE *hawker*, mainly a person who walks about selling goods, a sense now obsolete in *Bdos*. Cp HUCKSTER, TRADER, VENDOR.

hawks·bill (tur·tle)* *n* (*phr*) (CarA) ‖ *carey* (Grns, USVI) A sea-turtle that has a small head with a hawk-like beak (hence its name), and overlapping multi-coloured plates on its oval back wh is about 3 ft long; it was commercially valuable for producing turtle-shell and making turtle-soup and is protected by law; *Eretmochelys imbricata* (*Chelonidae*). □ In CE accounts **hawksbill** as one word is the standard form, replacing IAE *hawk's-bill*.

H.B.M. *abbr* (Trin & Tbgo) The Humming Bird Medal of the Order of the Trinity, a gold, silver, or bronze medal awarded as a national honour for loyal and devoted service wh has brought benefit or prestige to Trin & Tbgo in the person's field of endeavour; the letters are placed after the recipient's name. [From the popular name of Trinidad as 'The land of the humming bird']

(h)e [(h)i] *pron 3rd pers sg* (CarA) *[AF—Cr]* [Used or occurring frequently in speech in other functions than as subj of a vb or as nominative case] **1.** [*X*] Him. **a.** *Most unpopular was David S—, of whom it was said 'He couldn't even get a black chauffeur; had to get a white one to drive he.'*—Baw (76/12, p.9) **b.** *Two young men came up behind them and grabbed he and the Australian man.*—BeA(BE) (80.01.19, p.7) **2.** [*X*] His. *S— told the Court, 'I never bleed as much as he for he teeth not as good as mine.'*—DeM(SK) (62.09.22, p.10) **3.** *[AF—Cr]* It; its. *Dog foot brok, he find he massa door-mouth* (When the dog's leg is broken, it will find its master's door).—Guyn (Prov) **4.** [*Cr*] ‖ *him* (Jmca) She; her. *The village women whispered "E gettin' 'e pain. 'E go ge' baby today'* (She's getting her pains. She's going to give birth today).—Guyn (Ms, short story) [These functions are all survivals of basilectal CarA Cr /i/ 'he' wh, except in *Jmca*, functions unchanged for case and gender] □ See also 'E, and HE OWN at OWN 1.(ii).

H.E. [e·či] *abbr* (CarA) His Excellency the Governor. *If we're going to invite H.E. we will have*

to start on time and all o[f] that, so you better don't bother.—(Guyn)

head¹ *n* **1.** (The human head but often used with special ref to) the mind, the memory, thoughtfulness, etc (as reflected in many of the phrases at **4.**). □ Although *head* is often similarly used informally in IAE, the word for *head* occurs widely in more formal idiom in a number of Afr langs. Cp for ex Twi *ti-pa* (good head) 'intelligence', *ti-bone* (bad head) 'bad character, poor intellect', etc. Likely calques from other Afr langs are given in etym notes of some phrs below. **2.** [Of root vegetables] The central corm (of yam, eddoe, etc) on wh smaller tubers grow; a whole bulb (of garlic, etc). *Mornin' neighbour. Marmee say to send an onion, ah tomato, two heads ah garlic an' ah cup ah rice for she.*—Peo.II.18, p.74 **3.** [Banana Ind] The cut-down base of the central stem of the banana tree on wh suckers have grown; this base is re-planted. **4.** *PHRASES* **4.1 carry the same head** *vb phr* (Mrat) ‖ CAN SHAKE HANDS (CarA) See HAND¹ Phr 4.3 **4.2 confuse your head** *vb phr* (CarA) *[IF]* To confuse your thinking; to upset your concentration and cause mistakes. *The children make so much noise that they confuse my head and make me stitch the dress wrong.*—(Guyn) [Cp Yoruba *o da a l'ori ru* (he make him in-head mix-up) 'he got him confused; he made him mad'] **4.3 drink soup off/over sb's head** *vb phr* (ECar) *[AF—Joc]* See DRINK Phr 2. **4.4 fly (up) in sb's head** *vb phr* (CarA) *[AF—Joc]* See FLY Phr 4.6. **4.5 go out of your head** *vb phr* (CarA) *[IF]* (SE) To go off your head; to become insane. **4.6 have a bad head** *vb phr* (CarA) *[IF]* See BAD HEAD¹ 2. **4.7 have a good head for (sth)** *vb phr* (CarA) See GOOD HEAD Phr **4.8 have a long head** *vb phr* (Guyn) *[IF]* See LONG¹ Phr 2.4 **4.9 have a straight head** *vb phr* (CarA) *[IF]* See STRAIGHT¹ Phr 4.1 **4.10 head is hard** *id phr* (CarA) *[IF]* See HARD-HEAD¹[ED] 2. **4.11 head is not good** *id phr* (CarA) See GOOD¹ Phrs 2.3., 2.5. **4.12 head is not sweet** *id phr* (ECar) *[AF]* See SWEET Phr 5.2 **4.13 hold a/one head** *vb phr* (CarA) *[IF]* See HOLD Phr 5.3 **4.14 hold your head and bawl** *vb phr* (CarA) *[AF]* See HOLD Phr 5.13 **4.15 put your head down** *vb phr* (CarA) *[IF]* **(i)** To get down to, concentrate resolutely on, a piece of work. *She was always a child like that. When she put her head down to study, not even her mother couldn['t] move her.*—(Guyn) **(ii)** [Cricket, of a batsman] To bat with determined concentration; to stay in the wicket and keep the side from collapsing. **4.16 steady your head** *vb phr* (CarA) *[AF]* See STEADY Phr **4.17 study your head** *vb phr* (CarA) *[AF]* See STUDY Phr 3.3 **4.18 swinging in the head** *n phr* (Baha, Belz, Guyn, Mrat, TkCa) ‖ *giddy-head* (Bdos) ‖ *mazeness in the head* (Angu, Nevs) ‖ *reeling in the head* (BrVi, Mrat, Nevs) ‖ *spinning in the head* (Jmca, Mrat, Nevs, StKt, StVn) ‖ *swing-head* (Bdos) A feeling of dizziness believed to be associated with blood pressure complaints. [Cp Kikongo *ntu ame zieta-uta zieta* (head of-me turning turns) 'I feel dizzy'. Also Ci-Nyanja *ndi namva chizunguzungu* (I felt *motion-turn-turn*) 'I had a spell of dizziness'] **4.19 turn your head** *vb phr* (CarA) [*IF*] See TURN Phr 4.8 **4.20 trouble on your head** *n phr* (CarA) [*IF*] See TROUBLE Phr 4.2 **4.21 worry your head** *vb phr* (CarA) [*IF*] See WORRY Phr 3.

head² *vb tr* (Bdos, Dmca, Guyn) To carry a heavy load (esp of bananas, sugar-canes) on the head. **a.** ... *women heading bananas to the lighters from the buying shed a few feet away from the Jetty.*—SDD:33 **b.** *Their necks have become stiff heading water from long distances and storing it in water barrels.*—Bdos (Hd, 74.05.21, p.3649) □ The reference is more commonly to acts of paid labour. Cp BACK³ 1. (*CarA*) DROGUE (Gren, Guyn) the senses of wh are not so restricted.

head·ache-bush* *n* (Angu, Baha, Jmca) A weed whose branches and pods, or a shrub whose leaves, when crushed, produce a sharp (and in some kinds slightly unpleasant) smell wh is said to ease headaches; *Hedyosmum spp* (and other families).

head-ker·chief *n* (CarA) ‖ HEADTIE (CarA)

head·ly *adj* (Mrat) Obstinate; headstrong. [Perh a development > *heady* as in *EDD heady adj* (Sc, Cum, Yks, etc) 'headstrong, impetuous, self-willed, etc']

head·man [hɛdma·n] *n* **1.** (CarA) [Sugar Ind] The man who is in charge of a large gang of labourers on a sugar-estate and responsible to an overseer. **2.** (Jmca) The foreman on a large market-garden farm. **3.** (Guyn, Trin) ‖ *Captain* (Guyn) The recognized leader or spokesman of a village.

head·tie *n* (CarA) ‖ *head-kerchief* (CarA) A cloth of either pure white or ornately coloured cotton, worn by a woman, tied around the head, covering the forehead, and knotted at the back or side with two ends sticking out in one of a number of significant ways; in former times each way carried a message to male peers; in *Dmca, StLu,* used as a part of the National Costume. *The house is brightly lit with festive candles. Old women dressed in white gowns and carefully knotted headties sit around the table on which ceremonial food offerings have been placed: rice, farine, popcorn, sago leaves.*—Isl (73/2, p.13)

health PHRASE **see your health** *vb phr* (Gren, Guyn, Jmca, StVn, Trin) [*IF*] See SEE Phr 3.10

heap *n* **1.** (Guyn, StLu, Trin) ‖ *parcel* (Guyn) A small pile of fruit or vegetables set out for retail sale. *Mangoes continue to be 20 and 25 cents a heap of five.*—ExP (73.05.22, p.3) [From commercial sense of SE *heap* 'a large pile of goods for sale'] **2.** (CarA) [*AF—Joc*] ‖ *heaping set* (Gren, Grns) A large number (of people); a large amount (of anything); (SE, loosely) heaps. *He know quite well that a whole heap of them figger that once they Bahamian and have some*

kinda certificate, ... irregardless of whether they coulda produce or not they was entitle to the best jobs available.—NaG (75.03.06, p.2) [Cp *EDD heap* 7. (Var dial and colloq uses in Sc, Irel, Eng and Amer) 'a large number or quantity; a great deal', etc + cit from Suf 'A hape of nonsense'] □ Often in phr *a whole heap of,* in CE.

heap away *vb phr* (Bdos) [*AF*] **1.** To discard; to throw out. *These papers here is fo[r] heap away.*—(Bdos) **2.** To spill. *Mind what yo[u] doin[g] before you heap away all that milk.*—(Bdos)

heap·ing set *n phr* (Gren, Grns) [*AF*] ‖ HEAP 2. (CarA) *It was around 5.30 whilst we were in there we heard a heaping set of noise down the road.*—Gren (CR, 1974)

hear *vb* **1.** (ECar) ‖ *hear to sb* (Bdos, Guyn) To listen obediently; to accept advice. *Not that she is rude. No, but she would not hear when I talk to her and if I repeat myself she will look at me with a wicked smile.*—PeL (80.03.21, p.12, Dear Christine) **2.** *vb imper* (CarA) [*IF*] Listen to what (sb) replied or said! *'Sally, do you have anything to eat in the house, we are famished?' Hear Sally: 'No Mam, is only a little peas soup ah have in the pot, but ah know you and the Master doan eat coconut and it cook with coconut.'*—OJS: 7 □ See also HEAR ME! Phr 4.4 below. **3.** (CarA) [*IF—Tag Q*] [As a terminal adjunct to a short statement inviting agreement, acceptance, or serious notice of the statement] Do you understand? Take note! **a.** *There were the moments of fantastic rapport, too. Like the Caribbean Night party at Jamaica House. That was groundation, yu hear.*—WeG (75.05.20, p.15) **b.** *'Don't make me and you fall out, hear.'*—HF:28 **c.** *'I ger give yer a good lickin', hear?'*—JBJ:80 **4.** PHRASES **4.1 hear better cock crow** *vb phr* (Gren, Tbgo, Trin) [*AF—Joc*] To have heard/seen highly placed persons go back on their word, abandon a firm promise, etc; to refuse to take sb seriously. *He only sayin[g] he won[']t sell de land to any Indian, but I hear better cock crow.*—(Gren) **4.2 hear between me and you** *vb phr* (Tbgo) [*AF*] To cause us to quarrel or fight. *If you interfere with my guitar, you will hear between me and you.*—(Tbgo) **4.3 hear duppy/jumbie** *vb phr* (CarA) [*AF*] To hear or to believe you hear supernatural or unexplained sounds. [< DUPPY¹ and JUMBIE¹] **4.4 Hear me!** *vb imper* (Jmca, StVn) [*AF—Tag*] [Terminal adjunct to a stated threat] Believe me! *If you only touch me, A would lick in yo[ur] face, hear me!*—(Jmca) □ Related to sense 3. above. **4.5 Hear my trial!** *vb imper* (CarA) [*AF/IF*] See TRIAL Phr 2.1 **4.6 hear say (that)** *vb phr* (CarA) [*AF—Cr*] To hear (that). **a.** *I hear say the Maroons have promised to join him, but I do no' believe they will.'*—RND:92 **b.** *I hear say that an anti-communist league has been formed, but I'd like to share with the public that trying to fight communism without Christ is a waste of time.*—BeA(BE) (80.11.15, p.5) [A survival of *AF—Cr* SAY [SE] 'that', as a connective, but with SAY losing its Cr sense prob influenced by

SE *hearsay* (n), or E dial *hear tell* (vb phr) with neither of wh it is not really connected] **4.7 hear sb's mouth** *vb phr* (CarA) [*AF*] See MOUTH Phr 4.12 **4.8 hear to (sb)** *vb phr* (Bdos, Guyn) [*AF*] [Often neg] ‖ HEAR 1. (ECar) **a.** *These children don't hear to nobody. They too own-way.*—(Bdos) **b.** *'If only pa did hear to me an' cut plantain las' mont' , he had said to his mother, 'we wouldda been rollin' up t'ree crop in one.'*—SBB:10 [Cp Yoruba *gbọrọ si mi lẹnu* (*hear word to my mouth*) 'listen to my words'] □ Sometimes also **hear by/ from sb** (StKt). **4.9 hear your ears** *vb phr* (Guyn, Tbgo, Trin) [Often neg] To hear what is being said; to hear yourself talk. *Shut up! Shut up, all of you! My God, I can't hear my ears!*—(Guyn) **4.10 hear your name with sb's name** *vb phr* (Tbgo) [*IF*] See NAME[1] Phr 3. **4.11 (If you/Who) can't hear (you) will feel** *id phr* (CarA) [*IF*] ‖ *Hard-ears you can't hear, own-way you will feel!* (Bdos) [Said to children] If you cannot obey, you will be beaten to make you obey. [See note at WHO Phr 4.3, and cp the same in *StLu* Fr Cr *si u pa sa tan u kai senti*] **4.12 when you hear the shout** *id phr* (CarA) [*IF/ AF*] When the truth is exposed; when an (unexpected) event takes place. *Now I am very worried about my sister who has just lost her boyfriend. He just started acting strange and when you heard the shout he got engaged to another girl.*—NaT (79.10.10, p.25, Dear Christine) [Referring to a loud outcry from shock or surprise, wh is a common event in *CarA* oral cultures] **4.13 You never hear more!** *id phr* (Bdos) [*IF/AF*] Can you imagine such a thing! *Well, yo[u] never hear more! Yo[u] know I see that boy hit [h]is father?*—(Bdos) □ Sometimes put as a question: *You ever hear more?*.

hear-so *n* (Brbu, Jmca) [*AF*] ‖ **say-say** (Antg) ‖ **shu-shu**[1] 1. (Belz, Gren, StKt, Trin) ‖ **susu**[2] (Guyn, Jmca, StVn) Gossip; idle, mischievous chatter. [A reduction of CE *I hear so*, (SE) 'I've heard so', and prob influenced by SE *hearsay*]

heart [ha(r)t] *n* PHRASES **1. have/hold your heart in your hand** *vb phr* (ECar) To be in a state of intense anxiety. *And oft-times when the black colour come to take light from the eye we hold heart in the hand and wait and wonder when the sun would sail daylight into the eye again.*— LICMS:232 **1.1 heart is in your hand** *id phr* (CarA) (Variant of 1.) *'The passengers did not panic but my heart was in my hand,' the pilot said.*—ExP (75.02.09, p.2) □ Cp SE *heart is in one's boots*, with similar sense. **2. heart is long** *id phr* (Nevs) [*IF*] (You are) always ready to grab the biggest share ahead of others. **3. keep (good) heart** *vb phr* (Guyn, Tbgo, Trin) [*IF*] To keep up your courage; to maintain your hope. *Never mind, darlin[g], you must keep heart. He can['t] go on for ever.*—(Tbgo) **4. long your heart on sth** *vb phr* (Guyn) [*AF/IF*] See LONG[3] Phr 3.; cp also Phr 2. above. **5. make your heart turn; turn your heart** *vb phrs* (Gren) [*IF*] To sicken you; to make you feel very upset. *The way the son treat her makin[g] people heart turn.*—(Gren) [Cp *EDD* turn vb 3. Phr (12) *turn one's heart* 'to

cause one to feel sick; to create a feeling of nausea'] **6. send your heart through your mouth** *vb phr* (Guyn) [*IF*] To startle and terrify you; to drive sudden fear into you. [Cp *JESI: 126* IrE *My heart jumped into my mouth* 'You gave me a great start'] **7. trouble with your heart** *vb phr* (CarA) [*IF*] To suffer from heart-disease.

heart-af·fec·tion *n* (Bdos) ‖ HEART-TROUBLE (CarA)

heart·man *n* (Bdos) A legendary being who is believed to collect the hearts of young boys for devil-worship; however cp BLACK-HEART MAN (Jmca)

heart-sunk *adj* (Baha) Deeply distressed; anguished. *A heart-sunk four-year-old, brought suddenly to face the problem of death, wants today to know: 'Are they still going to hang my daddy?'* —TrI (76.01.29, p.1)

heart-trou·ble *n* (CarA) ‖ **heart-affection** (Bdos) Heart disease; any faulty condition of the heart. □ See also HEART Phr 7.

heart·y *adj* (CarA) [*IF*] [Esp in response to an inquiry made as a greeting] In very good health. *S1: How the children? / S2: They all hearty, thanks.*—(Belz) □ Cp also HALF-HEARTY (Bdos).

heat-cloud *n* (Bdos, Guyn) A dark, low-hanging cloud accompanied by still air and uncomfortable heat, sometimes followed by rain.

heats *n pl* (Antg, Guyn, Tbgo) Any kind of small bumps on the skin (sometimes including facial acne and not necessarily accompanied by any irritation). □ Cp SE *prickly heat* wh is associated with irritation of the skin.

heav·en *n* PHRASES **1. in goat-heaven and kiddie-kingdom** *adj phr* (Bdos) [*AF—Joc*] ‖ *in hog-heaven and John-Crow paradise* (Belz) In a state of great (if perhaps temporary) happiness; in seventh heaven. **2. in hog-heaven and John Crow paradise** *adj phr* (Belz) As Phr 1.

heav·y *adj* (CarA) **1.** [*IF*] [Of a woman or animal] Nearing the time to give birth. *Now that cow is so heavy you should stop tying it.*—(Guyn) **2.** [*AF*] [Entertainment Ind] Original and excellent; very pleasing. *... and the Community Centre was hot as Fatman Bopeep with Brass start to jam a heavy kaiso that could very well make the Road March.*—TaP (77.02.13, p.6) □ Prob infl by AmE slang, as also following senses. Cp also *solid* sometimes similarly used in IAE. **3.1** [*AF—Joc; by extension*] [Of personal appearance] Very attractive (in dress or features). *'Boy Jenny McIntosh have a heavy boy friend, when he dresses he looks cool.'*—ToR (73.12.09, p.5) **3.2** Keen; able; knowledgeable. *Rosalind says she loves music by so many people it is hard to tell whom she enjoys most. She is heavy on the late Otis Redding,*

Jim Reeves, Jackie Opel and Sam Cooke.—AdN
(71.12.24, p.6)

heav·y man·ners *n phr pl* (Jmca) *[IF-Joc]* **1.**
Rigid discipline (of a young person); strict control (of a crowd, opponent, etc). *Disturbances,
riots, revolts, call them what you will, now being
experienced in Jamaica, are the inevitable result of
a long period and process of IMF 'heavy manners'.*—AdN (85.01.19, p.4) **2.** PHRASE **2.1 be/
have (sb) under heavy manners** *id phr* (Jmca)
To find yourself/to have (sb) very firmly under
control.

hedge-cac·tus (**cac·tus hedge**) *n* (CarA) See
CACTUS HEDGE (CarA)

hedge·hog fish* *n phr* (CarA) A porcupine
fish of wh there are several varieties, but esp one
that is about 12 ins long and round-bodied,
capable of puffing itself out with air or water to
make its spines more defensive; it is of poor food
value and is often preserved as an ornament;
Diodontidae spp.

heel-and-toe (**dance/pol·ka**) *n* (*phr*)
(CarA) A dance in wh the two partners pair their
feet, stepping first on heel then on toe together;
it was popular in earlier times.

hef(f) *vb tr [X]* **1.** (CarA) (SE) To heft; to judge
the weight of sth such as a vegetable or a piece
of goods by lifting it in one hand. *Hef this parcel
see if yo[u] think is two pounds.*—(CayI) **2.** (Gren,
Guyn) Lift (up); take up. *You done say de word
awready an' you can't gie dem no small jacks, so
you heff up you biggest jacks an' gie dem an' when
dey turn dey back now, you feel you could kill
youself.*—WeN (53.03.09, p.2, Annie and Josephine) [< SE *heft* with characteristic CE
/-CC/ reduction]

heg [hæg ~ hɛg] *n, vb* (Belz, StVn) See HAG¹,
HAG²

heh! [hɛ] *adv* (Antg, Guyn, Tbgo, USVI)
[AF—Cr] **1.** [In giving sth to sb] Here! Take
this! **2.** [With verbal function, followed by an
obj] Here is; take. *Heh de book!*—(Guyn) [< SE
here, with linking vb *be* understood] □ A Cr form
that is considered very crude.

height *n* PHRASES **1. make height** *vb phr* (Bdos)
[AF] To run as quickly as possible (through fear
or anxiety). *After I see the big commotion, girl, I
mak[e] height for home.*—(Bdos) **2. not take sb's
height** *vb phr* (CarA) *[IF]* ‖ **not pick sb's height**
(StVn, Tbgo) To rudely ignore sb; to deny sb
the courtesy of listening. *His mother can't control
him and I tried to talk to him too but he never
took my height.*—(StKt) [Cp Yoruba *o ka mii si
yɛpɛrɛ* (he measure me be nothing) 'he treated me
as of no account'. Also similar phr in *Dmca* Fr
Cr *i pa pwen hotè mwen* (he not take height my)
with same sense]

heist *vb tr* (Baha) See HICE

he·li·co·ni·a* [hɛlikoniʌ] *n* (CarA) ‖ *balisier,
balizyé* (Dmca, Gren, StLu, Tbgo, Trin) ‖ *lobster-claw* (Bdos) ‖ *waha* (Belz) ‖ *wild-plantain*
(Guyn, Trin) A brilliant inflorescence of large,
red or yellow, or red and yellow, boat-shaped
sheaths containing little flowers, and alternating
left and right on a central stem, erect in some
varieties (ex BALISIER) and hanging in others; it
is borne on a wild plant of the banana family;
Heliconia behai or *H. caribaea* or *H. humilis*
(*Musaceae*). [Prob < Gk *Helicon*, the legendary
home of the Muses]

hell *n* PHRASES **1. be hell and scissors** *vb phr*
(Guyn) *[AF—Joc]* To be a fierce, violent row/
time/task/experience, etc. *And yo[u] know her
a[l]ready! She goin[g] quarrel to pay yo[u], you
got to take a part, quarrel for de rest! It will be
hell and scissors!*—(Guyn) [Perh a false refinement, by folk etym, of 'hell and Caesar' (i.e.
a double terror to face) from biblical influence]
2. catch hell *vb phr* (CarA) *[AF]* ‖ *see/smell
hell* (Bdos, Guyn) To suffer; to find yourself in
a lot of trouble. *Boy! Wid all dis double and treble
devaluation de pensioners an[d] ol[d] people are
catching hell, eh!*—(Trin) **2.1 catch hell to (do
sth)** *vb phr* (CarA) *[AF]* ‖ *see/smell hell to
(do sth)* (Bdos, Guyn, USVI) To have severe
difficulty in (doing sth); to experience much
suffering in (getting sth done). **a.** *'We are catching
hell to get the actual cash from the bank. And I have
told them in strong terms,' Mr Gairy said.*—ToR
(76.04.07, p.4) **b.** *The mother was alone an[d]
catch hell to feed them children and gi[ve] them
shoes to go to school with.*—(StVn) **3. lend (sb)
hell** *vb phr* (Tbgo, Trin) *[IF]* To give (sb) hell;
to provoke or quarrel violently with sb. *'It was
all a joke. Let's see how red we could make Mother
Bridget. So we lent her hell!'*—JJM:52 **4. see/
smell hell** *vb phr* (Bdos, Guyn) *[AF]* ‖ CATCH
HELL (CarA) See HELL Phr 2. *He urged the
electorate to rid themselves of political re-
crimination and oppression, charging that never in
the history of the country have so many people
been 'smelling so much hell'.*—NaT (78.07.07,
p.18) **5. to hell and go** *adv phr* (Guyn) *[AF]*
See GO Phr 6.36

hel·lo *excl* **1.** Hello? /1 3′/ (Bdos) *[IF]* I beg
your pardon?; Please repeat what you have just
said! **2.** /3′1/ (Bdos, Guyn) [Sharp warning to a
junior] Mind your manners!; You forget yourself!

help-out *n* (Gren, Trin) *[IF]* Any little assistance (esp a small sum of money). *He comes
around on Fridays and I usually give him a little
help-out, because I'm sorry to see how he is now.*—
(Trin)

help (sb) down/up (with sth) *vb phr* (CarA)
To help (sb) to lift sth down (from the head) or
up. *She could carry an enormous heavy basket of
vegetables but to start two men would help her up
and on arrival two again would help her down with
the huge load.*—StVn (Ms)

hen *n* (Tbgo) *[Derog]* ‖ BATTY-MAN (Antg, etc)

herb *n* 1. (CarA) [Rastaf] [Often sg and without article] Marijuana; *Cannabis sativa* (*Cannabaceae*). **a.** *The only thing that we the people learn when a Marijuana case arises is: the police arrested a brother in possession of Marijuana, Ganja, Eyrie, Weed, Herb, Grass or whatever name they may call it.*—ToR (76.07.08, p.7) **b.** *He told us that dropping out of school, liming in the street and smoking herb was the way to ruin ourselves.*—Bdos (Ms) [Name used in the RASTAFARIAN cult to indicate sacredness of *Cannabis* as the 'herb of meditation', prob a term borrowed from the Bible. Cp AVB *Ps 104:14* 'He causeth the grass to grow for the cattle, and herb for the service of man'] □ See HOLY HERB. **2.1** (Baha) *usu pl* ‖ GREENS (CarA) *I tink I gon buy sum 'erbs an' watermelon an' ting t' open up wun shop on Bay Street an' be wun big bizness man.*—DSJS:50 **2.2** (Baha, USVI) *usu pl* GREENS and vegetables. □ Sometimes called MIXED HERBS (Baha). **3.** (Nevs, StKt) *pl* Chives and scallion. *As would be expected during the mid-week there would not be an abundance of leafy green vegetables, but there were a few heads of lettuce chive and thyme (herbs and thyme), carrots, sweet potatoes, dry coconuts and peanuts.*—LaS (76.06.26, p.8)

herb-tea *n* (Jmca) An infusion of senna pods; it is a laxative often given to children—(*DJPVP*:24).

here[1] *adv* (CarA) In this place. PHRASES **1. Look/See her (it, etc) here!** *id phr* (CarA) [*IF*] See LOOK Phr 4.5 **2. You see me here** *id phr* (CarA) [*IF/AF*] That's how I am although I may not look it. *I am not goin[g] out to beg nobody for not[h]ing! I very proud, you see me here.*—(StKt) □ Sometimes *as/where you see me here.* Similarly used is *you see her/him/them there.*

here[2] *n* (CarA) [*X*] **1.** This place. **a.** *I told him 'Here don't belong to me I have to pay rent for here'.*—Bdos (CR, 1971) **b.** *When Rossetta go out an see how Babylon live, when she meet new friends, what you think going to happen? Here will satisfy her no more.*—PCOS:108 [Prob chiefly infl by calquing from Niger-Congo Afr langs in many of wh the word for locative adv 'here' derives from or coincides with the noun for 'place'. Cp *DAFL* Twi *Me ha yɛ me yaw sɛ* (*My here makes me hurt much*) 'It's here that I feel much pain'. However SE infl is also possible. See note foll] □ In SE *here* (n) occurs in restricted contexts as obj of trans vb or prep (exs *leave here, from here,* etc) but not as subj as in CE cits above. See also THERE, WHERE[2]. **2.** PHRASES **2.1 down here; down in here** *n phrs* (CarA) [*X*] The area/place down here. *Down in here floods badly in rainy weather.*—(Guyn) □ IAE wd require *It floods ... down here.* **2.2 in here** *n phr* (CarA) [*X*] This room/house, etc. *'I once had plans for in here,' Clive told Senina.*—MBGB:199 **2.3 out here** *n phr* (CarA) [*X*] This place/part/area that is outside/exposed, etc. *Out here is too hot. Let's go inside.*—(BrVi) □ IAE would require *It is too hot out here.*

he·ri·do·ri [heri-dori] *n* (Guyn) A children's game played by using a stick about 18 ins long to toss or hit a smaller stick (about 4 ins long) away from a fixed point, and then measuring the distance achieved, using the long stick as the counter; the counting is called using the special terms 'heri, dori, tilya, chowri, zompa, zeg, zutal'. [From the first two counting terms. Perh Indic]

hers·own *poss pron* (USVI) [*X*] Hers; her own. *That hair on her head ain hersown at all.*—DaN(ST) (78.04.06, p.11, A. Petersen)

[h]e·self [isɛlf] *refl pron* (CarA) [*AF—Cr*] Himself; herself. *A know mi old lady only di strain 'eself fu send me da college right now. 'E no di seh notin but I know.*—HF:50 □ A form occurring only in CarA Cr speech, but often written as in cit in narrative dialogue.

hib *vb tr* **1.** (Belz, Jmca, Tbgo) [*AF—Cr*] To heave; to toss or throw (sth heavy). *Boy hib da ol[d] iron over de fence.*—(Belz) **2.** (Antg) [*AF—Cr*] To shove hard against (sb/sth). *Min[d] me no hib yo[u] do[w]ng! ('Mind, or I'll push you down!').*—(Antg) [Evid < SE *heave* with shortened vowel [i > ɪ] and common CarA Cr / v > b/ shift]

hic·ca·tee (hi·ki·ti) [hɪkɪti ~ hɪgati] *n* (Belz, CayI) A small tortoise with three ridges along its back; it dwells on land or in shallow fresh water and its meat is considered a delicacy.

hice (**heist, hyst**) [haɪs] *vb tr* (Baha, Bdos, Guyn) [*AF—Cr*] **1.** To lift up; to raise. **a.** *Help me hice dis bag o[f] rice.*—(Guyn) **b.** *He was helpin[g] his little brother to hice his kite.*—(Bdos) [< *CSD* Scots *hoise* 'raise, lift up' < SE *hoist* prob helped by nautical infl. Cp also *EDD* *hoist* 'var dial forms: heist, highst, hyste' etc] □ Cp AmE *heist* 'to rob' wh is a variant form and usage. See also HOIST. **2.** PHRASE **2.1 hice yourself** *refl vb* (Guyn, Tbgo, Trin) [*AF—Derog*] ‖ **pick up yourself** (Guyn) To get up; to rise and go. *Look! Hice yo[ur]self and go and do de people wo[r]k.*—(Tbgo)

hid·dy-bid·dy (**hit·ty-bit·ty**) [hɪdi-bɪdi ~ hɪti-bɪti] *n* (Bdos) The same as the game KACH-KACH-MA-BÈL (*Dmca*) except that the player says to each girl seated in the ring 'Hiddy-biddy, hold fast! Shut up your lap tight, tight!'.

hig·gler *n* (Jmca) ‖ **hawker** (Bdos) See cit. *Jamaicans call them 'higglers'. In other islands and Guyana they are known variously as pedlars and hucksters. They travel from country to town with foodstuffs to sell. In town they buy factory-made articles to resell in the country. They make a living from both transactions even after taking account of the bus fares going up and down.*—WoV (71.07.06, p.2) [*EDD* *higgler* 'an itinerant dealer' < *higgle* vb (In gen. dial use in Sc, Irel and Eng) 3. 'to go about with small wares for sale'] □ A *higgler* (perh infl by SE *haggler*) is expected to bargain over prices; a *hawker* is not. Cp HUCKSTER.

high[1] *adj* (Guyn, Jmca, StVn) [*IF*] **1.** Snobbish; haughty. **2.** Having or displaying a better quality of education (esp in speech).

high[2] *adv* PHRASES **jump high, jump low** *id phr* (Bdos, Guyn) [*AF/IF*] See JUMP Phr 5.3

high-bridge /1'2/ *n* (Guyn) A raised bridge over a trench or canal to permit mule-drawn punts to pass under.

high-brown /1'2/ *n, adj* (CarA) [*IF/AF*] (A person who is) of light brown complexion. *And after Emancipation, in islands like Grenada and St Vincent, 'high-browns' the principal property owners, became the new Massas, more privileged than the black masses of 'the people'.*—VoS (77.02.12, p.5)

high-cheeks *n* (StVn) ‖ BACK-ANSWER[1] (CarA) PHRASE **give high-cheeks** (StVn) ‖ BACK-ANSWER[2]

high-col·our /1'22/ *n, adj* (CarA) [*IF/AF*] ‖ *high-yellow* (Baha, Bdos) (A person who is) very LIGHT-SKINNED; (a person) of complexion and features that are much more European than African. *Her straight nose, high colour, thin and even lips which conferred on her claims to distant whiteness, and gave her favour with Maass Harney, the black buckra estate owner, is now considered an aberration, a taint of native blood.*—FDA:20

hi(gh)-cuts *n pl* (Bdos) ‖ *uppers* (Nevs, StKt) Rubber-soled, ankle-high gym-boots.

high-dam *n* (Guyn) ‖ MIDDLE-WALK **1.** (Guyn)

high Eng·lish *n phr* (Guyn, Jmca, StVn, Tbgo) [*Joc*] Carefully spoken educated English (as distinguished from CREOLIZED ENGLISH); spoken English that pointedly displays a higher level of education or shows British English influence. □ Sometimes Derog.

high·fall *vb tr* (ECar) To trip (sb) and cause a headlong fall.

high five *n phr* (CarA) PHRASE **give the high five (to sb)** *id phr* (CarA) [Sport] To slap the open palm of a team-mate's hand with yours, both arms raised high (hence the phrase) as a gesture of success or triumph.

high-wine *n* (Guyn) [Rum Ind] A colourless liquor, about 70% alcohol, wh is a strong dilute form of the first product in the distillation of RUM; it is bottled and sold, being preferred for making punches and for SETTING fruit for making BLACK CAKE, though it is taken by some heavy drinkers. [*high*, in ref to its acoholic content + *wine*, as a euphemism.]

high-yel·low ['haɪ-yɛlʌ] *n, adj* (Baha, Bdos) [*AF/IF*] ‖ HIGH-COLOUR (CarA) *At the bottom of the pile were coloured people with a lot of ridiculous shadings based on degree of colour ... such as the near white, the hard red, the high yellow, the pumpkin yellow, the chocolate brown, the off-black and the black.*—TrI (72.03.08, p.3)

higue [haɪg] *n* (Baha, Guyn) See HAG[1], OLD-HIGUE

hi·ki·ti *n* (Belz, CayI) See HICCATEE

[h]im [(h)ɪm] *pron 3rd pers sg* (Belz, Jmca) [*AF—Cr*] ‖ (H)E (CarA) **1.** [Masc] He; him; his. *And I hear another story about another man who invest about $3,000 of him money in buying up Scotch. What I want to know now is; where him keep it? ... Under him bed?*—WeG (72.12.06, p.12, Partyline) **2.** [Fem] She; her. *The old lady tell de fella, 'She can't gi yuh no answer, but if yuh can come to him, den you can fix'.*—WFSFB: 35 **3.** It; its. *Lizard no plant corn, but him hab plenty.*—Jmca (Prov) [A survival of basilectal Jmca Cr pron function wh has spread to Belz where, however, it is less frequently used in these functions] □ The form, in these functions, is found in narrative dialogue. See also 'E.

hind* [haɪnd] *n* (CarA) One of two or three species of edible fish with a spotted reddish-brown body but varying much in size; ‖ *red hind, rock-hind*, etc; *Epinephelus spp* (see cit). *The Hind is a very common and very handsome fish, and sometimes attains a length of 18 ins. It is of a brownish or rosy-white color, and is marked with numerous deep rose-red spots. Being very voracious, it is easily caught. Its flesh is finely flavored, and is seldom, if ever, poisonous.*—IIOS: 231

hin·ting [hɪntɪŋ] *n* (Nevs) [*AF—Cr*] Thing; something. *Boy look de hinting de[re] right in front of you!*—(Nevs) [< sinting < something. A *Nevs* Cr development]

hip *n* (Baha) **1.** The buttocks; a person's backside. □ A euphemism widely used in both polite and impolite contexts. See foll phrs. Cp BOUNGIE. **2.** PHRASES **2.1 Carry your hip!** *imper vb phr* (Baha) [*AF—Vul*] Get out of here! **2.2 Watch your hip!** *imper vb phr* (Baha) [*AF—Vul*] Mind your manners! □ Cp Vul E 'Watch your arse!']

hip-and-drop *adj* (sometimes in adv function) (Antg, Tbgo) [*IF*] ‖ *hip-shodded* (Bdos, Guyn, Jmca) ‖ *hip-shorted* (Bdos, StVn) ‖ *hop-and-a-drop* (ECar) **1.** Having a deformity of your leg or foot that causes you to limp; having one leg distinctly shorter than the other. **2.** PHRASE **2.1 walk hip-and-drop** *vb phr* (Antg, Tbgo) [*AF*] To walk with your body leaning to one side as if or because you are deformed; to walk with a distinct limp.

hip-flask *n* (Bdos) ‖ HALF-BOTTLE (CarA) □ Cp CUT-DOWN, NIP.

hip·pie n (Guyn) [AF—Joc] ‖HALF-BOTTLE (CarA)

hip-shod·ded adj [AF] **1.** (Bdos, Guyn, Jmca) ‖HIP-AND-DROP (Antg, Tbgo) [Prob an over-correction + /t > d/ voicing of OED hip-shot 'having a dislocated hip-joint'; but cp sense 2. and ‖*hip-shorted*] **2.** [By extension] Clumsy; slipshod; (adv) in a slipshod manner. *You put down everything so hip-shodded.*—(Bdos)

hip-short·ed adj (Bdos, StVn) ‖HIP-AND-DROP (Antg, Tbgo) *The trouble with Ishmael he was hipshorted and could hardly walk a mile in a month.*—Isl II. 1, p.55 [Perh by folk etym, influenced both by OED hip-shot and actual shortening of the leg as a deformity]

hire-car n **1.** (Guyn, StVn) A taxi. **2.** (Guyn) ‖ROUTE-TAXI (Trin) *People who travel by hire-car between Georgetown and Rosignol are very concerned about the high fare that is being charged by drivers. / Many travellers feel that Government should control hire-car fares, as most of the drivers are squeezing the small man.*—GyC (76.09.15, p.13) **3.** (Bdos) A rented car (with a number-plate marked H).

hiss vb PHRASE **hiss your teeth** vb phr (Jmca, Tbgo) ‖SUCK YOUR TEETH (CarA) *The old man looked away and did not answer. Sam hissed his teeth in a fit of desperation and left him alone.*—SWIS:167 (R. Henry) [See KISS YOUR TEETH]

hit vb tr (CarA) **1.** [AF—Joc/Vul] To copulate with (a woman). *'But is no use talking to fellars like you. You hit two-three white women and like you gone mad.'*—STLL:117 **2.** [AF] To eat up or drink up; to consume greedily. *When Bart go round by Moses Moses would say: 'Take a plate from the cupboard and hit a pigfoot and rice,' though the way he say it is no invitation.*—STLL: 48 **3.** PHRASES **3.1 hit (sb/sth) full** vb phr (Bdos, Guyn) [AF] To strike or hit (sb/sth) squarely in the middle (with sth thrown); to land a hard blow. *I do not know if the bottle hit the ground and then cut the accused or if it hit her full.*—Bdos (CR, 1971) **3.2 hit the scene** vb phr (CarA) [AF] To appear; to be recognized and liked. *Ideal for casual wear, the body-fit is the most appealing shirt to hit the scene.*—NaT (Ad, 75.10.06, p.2) □ Cp BrE/AmE Pop slang 'make the scene', similarly used. **3.3 out/up hand and hit sb** vb phr (CarA) [IF] See HAND¹ Phr 4.22

hit·ty-bit·ty n (Bdos) See HIDDY-BIDDY

hm excl (CarA) [IF/AF] [Unreleased /m/ preceded by voiceless breath with variations of pitch] **1.** [Low pitch, sharply stressed] Expressing a threat to a child, that an understood warning is not going to be repeated. **2.** [Unstressed, lengthened] Expressing sympathy or empathy. **3.** [Higher pitches] Expressing (usu mild) surprise. □ See also M, MM-HM.

Hob·ner, Bob·ner, La·dy's n phr (Bdos) ‖ABNER, BABNER, LADY'S KNEE (Guyn) □ The Bdos version of the rhyme used in the game is 'Hobner Bobner baby sneeze / Host, toast, sugar and tea / Potato Roast and English toast / Out goes you'.

hoe-toe-toe adj (Gren) See HOTOTO

hog n PHRASES **1. in hog heaven and John-Crow paradise** adj phr (Belz) [AF—Joc] See HEAVEN Phr **2. 2. have the whole hog in your hands** vb phr (Bdos) To have everything for yourself alone. *The sugar producers have never in my opinion produced the necessary facilities to uplift the industry; and it is the big magnates who know that when they squeeze out the small man they will have the whole hog in their hands.*—Bdos (Hd, 75.10.14, p.5499) **3. like hog under saddle** adj phr (Belz) [AF—Joc] Ridiculous looking.

hog-apple n (Jmca) [IF] ‖JUMBIE SOURSOP (Antg, etc) *Some people call this hog-apple or pig-apple but is really jumbie chocho as you can see it look more like chocho than apple, but only pig can eat that in trut[h].*—(Jmca) [Because eaten by pigs]

hog at (sb) vb phr (Tbgo) [IF] ‖HOG UP 1. (ECar)

hog-ba·na·na n (Baha, TkCa) ‖BLUGGO (Belz, etc)

hog-fea·tures n pl (Bdos, Gren) ‖*pig-face* (Guyn) Those parts of the head of a pig (the jowl, jaws, ears, etc) that are used in making SOUSE.

hog-fish* n (CarA) A reddish fish of mixed colours, with prominent dorsal spines and an elongated snout (hence the name); it grows to about 18 ins and is of good food value; *Lachnolaimus maximus* (*Labridae*).

hog-heaven n (Belz) See HEAVEN Phr 2

hog-meat n **1.** (Jmca, Nevs, StKt, USVI) Some kinds of succulent vine and plant material used for feeding pigs. **2.** (Tbgo, Trin) Pork.

hog-plum* n (CarA) **1.** ‖*ghaut-plum* (Angu, Antg, BrVi, Nevs) ‖*gully-plum* (Bdos) ‖*plum* (Guyn, Trin) ‖*yellow-coat (plum)* (Jmca) ‖*y-ellow plum* (Belz, CayI) A bright yellow, sharply acid fruit about 1-1/4 ins long, mostly taken up by a tough fibrous seed wh is covered by a scant juicy pulp with thin skin, both edible; it is borne in bunches on a tree growing to over 40 ft with a bark covered in sharp bumps, and it has prominent roots; *Spondias mombin* (*Anacardiaceae*). **2.** (Baha, Belz, Jmca, TkCa) ‖CHILLI-PLUM (Antg, etc) *Upon Mr Charles Burnside's grounds we saw a 'hog plum' tree with a plentiful supply of small, green fruit in clusters upon the branches—but not a leaf in sight.*—IIOS:

107 □ In some places, there may be a loose rural/ urban distinction in the use of the name *hog- plum* for these two kinds of yellow-skinned plum. In some cases (TkCa ?) it may also apply to the *Jamaica-plum, Spondias purpurea* [Cp *BAED:14* Arawak *hobo,* 'hog-plum', *DFCB: 317 prune jaune* 'oubou' (name used by Carib males), 'mombem' (name used by Carib fe- males). With *hobo, oubou,* cp Sp *jobo,* the widely current name of the *hog-plum* in Latin America (see *ACPRV:382*). With *mombem* cp the bo- tanical name *mombin,* also *WSNE:172* Sran *mope,* 'hog plum'. The tree, widely indigenous in the *CarA* area, thrives in rough and wild environments, and since its sometimes worm- eaten fruits, dropping profusely when in season, are eaten by cattle, pigs, turtles, etc, this may account for the name 'hog' perh also infl by folk etym < Arawak *hobo.*]

hog's *n* (Baha, Jmca) See HOG-STYE

hog-stye (**hog-style, hog's-eye**) *n* (Baha, Jmca) [*IF*] ‖ CAT-BOIL (CarA) [By folk etym and confusion of sense of SE *stye, hog* also suggesting 'meanness']

hog·styl·ish [hɒgstaɪlɪš] *adj* (Bdos, Guyn, StVn) [*AF*] See HOSTILISH

hog-Thom·as *n* (Bdos, Guyn) [*IF/AF— Derog*] A person who readily shows his crude- ness; a loud and unapproachable person. □ Cp HOG UP 1.

hog up *vb tr phr* 1. (ECar) [*IF*] ‖ *hog at* (Tbgo) To speak roughly to (sb) so as to humiliate. *He was an awful teacher who used to hog up the children so much that every class was afraid of him.*—StVn (Ms) 2. (Baha, Guyn) [*AF*] To eat (food) ravenously. *When the boy finally gave the go-ahead she hogged-up the food.*—SBB:34

hoist *vb* 1. *vb tr* (Guyn) To steal; to carry off. *Deokinanan lit a cigarette and inhaled deeply. He continued his plan to hoist the money from Motie Singh.*—CFMG:32 □ Now perh only so used by older folk, but cp AmE *heist.* 2. *vb intr* (Bdos) [*AF*] To rise up. *Rocks big as you cow pen hois' in the air as if they was one set o' shingles.*—BTA: 66 □ Cp HICE. 3. PHRASES **3.1 hoist your flag** *vb phr* (Crcu) To announce a girl's engagement. [From the custom of putting up a flag at the girl's home when her marriage has been agreed on] **3.2 hoist yourself (up)** *refl vb* (Guyn) ‖ HICE YOURSELF (Guyn, etc)

hold *vb* 1. *vb tr* (CarA) [In general senses] To seize. (i) To lay violent hands on (sb). *Boy if you make me hold you today, I would give you one hell of a licking!*—(Guyn) (ii) To arrest. *When the Police held him the loot was not found on him.*—GyC (76.05.13, p.13) [Cp *EDD* hold vb II. 13. (Irel) 'to arrest'] (iii) [Of hunger, sick- ness] To overwhelm; to take hold of (your body); to attack (your strength, health). **a.** *Eat somet[h] ing before you go! Don[']t le[t] hungry hol[d] you*

[u]pon de dam.—(Guyn) **b.** *They were very stylish people until the sickness came and held the father and they had to struggle to make two ends meet.*— Tbgo (Ms) [‘For ‘I am hungry’ the equivalent expression in many West African languages would be ‘hunger holds me’.’ In West African pidgin or creole English the phrase is ... exactly that: ‘hungry catch me.’ *J. Berry, 1970.* Ex: Yoruba *aisan/iba mu ẹ,* 'sickness/fever holds you'] **2.** *vb tr* (CarA) [*AF—Joc*] [Of evil spirits, bogeys, etc, esp in frightening children] To catch or corner (sb); to confront and strike fear into (sb). *You goin[g] out de[re] playin[g] so late? You ain[']t frighten de duppy hol[d] you?*—(Jmca) **3.** *vb intr* (CarA) [Of an amount or quantity] To fit or be contained (in sth); to be accommodated (in a place). **a.** *I will take it for you once it's not too long or too big to hold in my suitcase.*—(Trin) **b.** *All the people could not hold in the house at the funeral. They were many outside.*—Bdos (Ms) □ This common and accepted CE intr conversion of the IAE trans function of *hold* 'have capacity for' is likely to be considered a fault in SE usage. See also Phr 5.8 below. **4.** *vb intr* (Bdos) To bend or lean the body (across, away, down, over, through). **a.** *A space was cleared and the toastmaster made the small sad bride dance with her groom. She held away from him, a fragile shape against his big frame.*—MBGB:119 **b.** *'Don't talk so loud, the man in front list'ning ... You been going church lately?' | 'Hold over. Lemme tell you something. I get saved.'*—HFGA:110 (A. Clarke) **c.** *The witness said that his car approached the cars and the members of the group, one of whom was a woman in shorts holding through the right front window of G-29.*—SuS (80.02.24, p.12) □ See also Phr 5.12 (iii) below. **5.** PHRASES **5.1 be holding (big)** *vb phr* (Bdos, Tbgo, Trin) [*AF*] To have (a lot of) money. *'If yuh have money yuh stand ah chance; Ah know some black people who will get in because dey holding big. But if tomorrow come and yuh see dey aint have money, case, boy. Dey never to go back.'*—SABS:95 **5.2 hold a (box-/susu-, etc) hand** *vb phr* (CarA) To be a participating contributor in a cooperative BOX, SUSU, etc. **5.3 hold a head** *vb phr* (Guyn) [*IF*] ‖ *hold one head* (Nevs, Trin) ‖ *hold the same head* (BrVi, Trin) ‖ *keep one head* (Antg, StVn) (i) To maintain an opinion firmly. *It didn't matter how much the parents protested. That man held a head against them and eventually his ruling was accepted.*—(Guyn) (ii) To conspire or to stick together in confronting a difficulty. *Those boys must have held one head to raid Rosado's mango tree.*—Belz (Ms) [Perh a blend of IAE *hold one's ground* + *be strong-headed*; or perh a calque from an Afr source] **5.4 hold a mind** *vb phr* (Gren) [*AF*] To suspect strongly. *A hol[d] a min[d] i[t']s he t[h]ief m[y] book.*—(Gren) [Cp *EDD* hold vb II. 16. (nYks) 'to consider, main- tain, think'] **5.5 hold back your head and laugh** *vb phr* (CarA) [*IF*] To throw your head back and laugh heartily. *The man called Juliet was holding back his white bearded head, and was laughing.*—CPM:26 **5.6 hold big rocks** *vb phr* (Bdos) [*AF—Joc*] To be left waiting for sb who is not going to turn up. □ Cp also GIVE SB BIG

ROCKS TO HOLD. See GIVE Phr 2.21. **5.7 hold down a/your man** *vb phr* (CarA) [*AF*] To hold on to your man; to keep a man from taking another woman as his sexual companion. *While the other section, the common low-class counterparts, acquire knowledge that the way to hold down the man of the moment for a little longer is to 'make baby' for him.*—AdV (73.09.12) **5.7.1 hold down a woman** *vb phr* (CarA) [*AF*] To assault a woman sexually. *At night she would always take the long way home because she was afraid some man might hold her down if she crossed the pasture.*—(Guyn) **5.8 hold in** *vb phr* (CarA) ‖ HOLD 3. (CarA) To be able to fit inside (sth). *I've packed my bag and I have to leave these books. They can't hold in.*—(Guyn) □ See note to sense 3. above. **5.9 hold on** *vb phr* (CarA) [*IF*] **(i)** To pause; to wait for a while. **(ii)** [By extension] To avoid a rash conclusion. *Hold on! I am not saying that he was not playing the calypsoes I wanted to hear. Oh no, not at all!*—BoM (75.01.31, p.11) □ A milder exp than HOLD STRAIN Phr 5.11 below. **5.9.1 hold on on/[u]pon sb/one another** *vb phr* (CarA) [*X*] To seize hold of and fight violently with sb/each other. *A tell yo[u] she hol[d] on [u]pon de woman outside a store and give [h]er a good beatin[g]!*—(Bdos) **5.9.2 hold on on/[u]pon (sth)** *vb phr* (CarA) [*X*] To take a firm hold of (sth). *The child held on on the mother's leg, dress and all, because she was afraid of the dog.*—(Tbgo) **5.10 hold sb in your mind** *vb phr* (CarA) [*IF*] ‖ **have (sb) up (ii)** (Jmca) To bear anger in your mind against (sb) for not being helpful; to bear malice or a grudge. **5.11 hold strain** *vb phr* (CarA) [*AF*] **(i)** To be patient; to persevere; to accept delay. *... and what we say is we do not think that they should just strike—have a dispute today and strike tomorrow, and put the community at ransom. Negotiate, and you have within 28 days, and we are saying you hold strain for 28 days, so that the matter could be resolved.*—Gren (Hd, 78.07.14, p.117) **(ii)** [*AF—Joc*] [Of a dancing couple] To cling to each other without moving much. **5.12 hold up** *vb phr* **(i)** (CarA) [Of rain or a vehicle] To stop; to come to a halt. **a.** *The rain that, driven by the wind all day, had soaked the deck thoroughly ... now held up and the clouds turned a lovely pink colour.*—SSMLN:10 **b.** *The lady sitting beside the driver asked him to hold up at the next corner.*—(Trin) □ Cp the following uses of *hold* in ref to *rain, weather*: The statement *The weather has held up* in CE = 'The bad weather has stopped', in Present BrE = 'The promising weather has continued'. The statement *The rain has held up* in CE = 'The rain has stopped', but in Present BrE is unfamiliar. The statement *The rain has held* in Present BrE = 'It has stopped raining for some time now', but is unfamiliar in CE. **(ii)** Not to break down under pressure; not to fall apart. *Sarah noted that Lias' suit was in very poor shape. She wondered if it would hold up for this occasion.*—PKKK:26 **(iii)** (Bdos) [*IF*] To rise after bending down. *'Afterwards blood started coming from both of us, and he ran down Prescod's Bottom to a man who was holding down washing his car. When the man held up and saw him the*

man ran from him. He ran back to me and said 'help me'.*—AdN (76.07.23, p.1) □ See sense 4. above. **5.12.1 hold up (sth)** *vb phr* (CarA) [*IF*] To stop or cause to stop (a car, work, etc) by some signal or call. **a.** *The mother fainted on the road and the child was sensible enough to hold up a car passing and ask for help.*—(StVn) **b.** *'No increase ... cooking gas price controlled!' / 'Dat's nice! A hope dem stop hold up deliveries now den!'*—WeG (75.06.03, p.1, Cartoon) **5.12.2 hold up your clothes/dress at sb** *vb phr* (CarA) [*AF—Vul*] [Of a woman] To expose or make a gesture of exposing your backside to sb as a gesture of contempt or defiance. **5.13 hold your belly/head and bawl/holler** *vb phr* (CarA) [*AF*] ‖ **put your hands on your head and bawl** (Angu, Jmca, Nevs, USVI) [Usu of a woman] To wail and shriek loud and long in grief or shock (occasionally also in laughter). **a.** *She put her hands on her head and bawled. She held her belly and bawled some more. She sat down and buried her head in her lap with grief.*—PKKK:28 **b.** *They say this kind of behaviour will only lead to an invasion of cemetery rapists. And it's only when something happens that everybody go hold their heads and bawl.*—SuP (79.10.21, p.5) [Ref to a prob cultural transfer: W Afr women tie their waists tight in preparation for wailing. Also Cp Yoruba, *o kawọ s'ori sunkun* (*he/she put-hand on-head weep*) 'he/she shrieked with grief'; also Shona *mukadzi wakachema akabata shaya* 'the woman mourned holding cheeks'] **5.14 hold your heart in your hand** *vb phr* (ECar) [*IF*] See HEART Phr 1.

hole[1] *n* (CarA) [Agriculture] **1.** One of a row of shallow excavations prepared for the commercial planting of sugar-cane (hence CANE-HOLE) or root vegetables (hence **cassava-, potato-, yam-hole**, etc). *... organised by the East St George Lisbon Yam Growers Association for the largest yam grown in a single hole. He ran away with the prize for reaping an aggregate of 495 lbs in three holes.*—ExP (73.02.15, p.1) **2.** The amount of produce obtained from the plant in a HOLE 1. *The Agricultural Development Corporation has cassava for sale at 60 cents a hole at Wildey Plantation, Christ Church. / Prospective purchasers are invited to dig the cassava.*—AdN (74.01.27, p.5)

hole[2] *vb* (CarA) [Agriculture] To dig rows of holes in farm or plantation land in preparation for planting. See HOLING

Ho·li *n* (Guyn, Trin) [Indic] ‖ **Phagwa** (Guyn, Trin) The principal Hindu religious festival, celebrated annually about March or April, symbolizing the triumph of good over evil; it is the strictly sacred aspect of the festival in contrast with the folk aspect called PHAGWA. [Hin < *Holika*, name of the evil princess that was burnt to death in her failure to suppress moral good]

hol·ing *n* (CarA) (See cit.) *Lands were prepared by a process known as 'holing' whereby slaves equipped with heavy digging hoes dug out holes* *into which manure was deposited and cane cuttings planted.*—DHBVI:79

hol·ler[1] **(hol·la)** [hɒlʌ] *vb intr* (CarA) [*AF*] **1.** To shout; to cry out in loud alarm (for help, in pain, etc). *'I am the champion,' the former local lightweight champion hollered back to me. 'I am going to beat him (Guyana's Lennox Beckles). I am sure about that.'*—NaT (74.01.06, p.15) [< *OED hollo, hollow, holla* 'to cry out loud, to shout, vociferate'. Note *W3 holler* with same sense.] □ This spelling also permits -*ed* and -*ing* forms without problem **2.** PHRASES **2.1 holler on/at (sb)** *vb phr* (CarA) [*AF*] To shout roughly at (sb) intending to stop, correct or prevent some action. *The watchman saw the boys and holler on them and one of them run away with the bag and the others pelt him.*—Guyn (CR) **2.2 holler/ shout for murder** *vb phr* (CarA) [*AF/IF*] **(i)** To cry 'Murder!' *The witness said he saw a woman bleeding and running hollering for murder.*—Bdos (CR) **(ii)** [By extension] To raise a great noise; to shout aloud so as to attract attention. *If anybody else but the Government did that you would hear the Unions start to holler for murder.*—Antg (Ms)

hol·ler[2] [hɒla] *n* **1.** A shout; a scream. **2.** PHRASE **2.1 give a holler** *vb phr* (CarA) See GIVE[1] Phr 2.1

hol·ly·hock *n* (Bdos, Gren) ‖THISTLE (StKt, VIs)

ho·ly herb/weed *n phr* (Jmca) [Rastaf] Cannabis; ganja; marijuana. *We do not beg, we do not steal, we depend upon the grace of Rastafari for livelihood, we know that he will look after His own, and, most of all, that the holy weed which we smoke guards us from all sickness and gives us wisdom, love and understanding.*—PCOS:52 [See note at HERB]

home PHRASES **1. go home** *vb phr* (Gren) See GO Phr 6.20 **1.1 come/go home for sb** *vb phr* (Bdos) See GO Phr 6.20.1

hom·i·ny-corn *n* (Jmca) A spiced, fragrant porridge made from corn grains, either grated or softened and pulped with the outer skin removed.

Hon·dur·a·ni·an *n, adj* (Belz) (A person or thing) belonging to Honduras. □ This is the term used in Belz, rather than *Honduran.*

hon·ey-ba·na·na *n* (Jmca) ‖APPLE-BANANA (Guyn)

hon·ey-bee bush *n phr* (Antg) ‖CORALITA (CarA) [Because honey-bees are constantly attracted to the flowers]

hon·ey-bee flower /ɪ'1212/ *n phr* (Bdos) ‖CARPET-DAISY (Bdos) [As prec]

ho·ney-cree·per *n* (StVn, USVI) ‖BANANA-QUIT (CarA)

hood; window-hood *n* **1.** (Bdos) ‖*pelmet* (Bdos) A sun-shade made of wood or of tin-sheeting on a wooden frame built outside and above a window. □ See also BELL-CAST HOOD. **2.** (Jmca) [*AF*] The penis.

hook-stick *n* **1.** (Belz, Guyn, Tbgo, Trin) ‖*crook-stick* (Tbgo, Trin) A strong, light stick about 2-1/2 ft long, cut from the forked limb of a tree (so that it resembles the figure 7), used with the left hand to hook and lift grass or low bush, so as to make it easier to chop the base with a machete; it is also used (*Belz*) for catching crabs in holes. **2.** (Bdos) A heavy walking-stick with a curved head as used by old people. [The same device as at sense 1. is used in W Afr. Cp *ADMY* Yoruba *gogo* 'hooked stick for pulling fruit off a tree'; also *WIED* Igbo *ngu* 'long stick with hooked end for plucking fruits']

hoop *n* (ECar) ‖CATCHER (ECar) *He remembered once, playing a game of 'hoop', he had got lost in the cane. Right in the middle of the field he went to hide, and when he wanted to come out he didn't know in which direction to turn*—SABS:81 [From the cry 'Hoo-oop' made by the hiding players as the signal that they are ready to be hunted. Cp *hoop and hide* as *OED hoop* v[2] 1. b. *Hoop and hide* 'the game of hide-and-seek' + cit from 1710]

hoop-seine *n* (Guyn) A shallow fish-net attached to a home-made, wooden hoop about 2-1/ 2 ft in diameter, used to catch fish by hand in shallow water. *Some were catching fish in the abandoned, swamped fields, and shallow weedy canals, with their castnets and hoop-seines.*—SSOS:53

hoo·ri (hou·ri) [huri] *n* (Guyn) A small river-fish of good food value, though somewhat bony; *Hoplias malabaricus (Erythrinidae).* [*BAED* Arawak *huri* 'a moderate-sized fish related to the Aiomora']

hop-and-a-drop [hɒp-an-a-drɒp] *adj* (ECar) [*AF*] ‖HIP-AND-DROP (Antg, Jmca, Tbgo) *For days I had my foot bandaged and walked about hop-and-a-drop like some cripple.*—(Guyn)

hop-bush *n* (StVn) ‖BALL-BUSH (Bdos, Jmca) [? But cp ‖*wild hops* (Bdos) in * Note at BALL-BUSH]

hop·per *n* **1.** [Bauxite Ind] A large, wooden, funnel-shaped chute serving to direct screened bauxite ore on to the conveyor system.

hop·pers *n pl* (Antg, Mrat) ‖CREPESOLES (Guyn, etc.)

hops-and-ham *n* (Trin) ‖HAM-CUTTER (Bdos)

hops(-bread) *n pl* (Trin) A crisp light roll of white bread about 3 to 4 ins in diameter. [From the use, in earlier times, of hops in powdered form as a mild flavouring in the dough of this bread] □ See CUTTER (Bdos)

horn[1] *vb tr* (Baha, Bdos, Dmca, Tbgo, Trin) [*AF/IF*] **1.** ‖ **hand**[3] (ViIs) ‖ **put roach on sb's bread** (Baha) To be unfaithful to (a husband or wife, boy-friend or girl-friend) by having sexual intercourse with or by dating sb else. *Or how many wives cannot understand why their husbands are horning them when they feel they give him everything he wants.*—BoM (77.01.14, p.11) **2.** PHRASES **2.1 horn (sb) with another** *vb phr* (Bdos, Tbgo, Trin) **(i)** To deceive (your spouse or lover) by having a love affair with another. *I know he loves me but he is shy because all the boys in the band told him that I'm going to horn him with one of the boys in the band.*—NaT (74.05.26, p.21, Dear Christine) **ii)** [Of a man] To make a cuckold of (another man); to openly or secretly defeat (a rival) in a love affair. *Even the thought that he could horn a young man must have put some fire in his veins.*—BoM (77.01.14, p.11) [A survival of EE *horn*, as *OED horn* v 2. (*Obs*) 'to cuckold', + cits 1550–1823. Note *OED horn* sb 7. (*Obs*) 'Cuckolds were fancifully said to wear horns on the brow'] □ The vb occurs in CE most commonly in sense 1., and then more often used with a woman as subj. Cp also GIVE (SB) A JACKET (*Jmca*).

horn[2]; **horn·ing** *n* (Tbgo, Trin) [*AF*] **1.** Adultery; infidelity of a lover. **a.** *Well-to-do wives in this country have revealed that their cool, suave husbands are deathly afraid of horn. And, these husbands will go to any length to make sure that their wives are faithful.*—SuP (79.07.01, p.5) **b.** *Well you better change your mind about his name because you going to get horning in his name.*— Tbgo (Ms Play, 1982) **2.** PHRASE **2.1 take a horn** *vb phr* (Tbgo, Trin) To accept the adultery of your spouse without making a public issue of it. *Some women can take a horn with dignity and others can't. And often I have found that those who can't, are themselves playing footloose and fast, running around with men but they never would like their husbands to do the same.*—BoM (76.11.12, p.15)

horn-child *n* (Tbgo, Trin) [*AF-Joc*] A child borne by a married woman through adultery.

horn·er-man *n* (Tbgo, Trin) [*AF*] A man with a reputation for committing adultery.

hor·rors *n pl* (CarA) [*AF*] **1.** Any trying or terrible experience, esp one involving frustration and anger. *Waiting to die and not knowing if you will die or when you will die is real 'horrors'. The authorities should just sentence him to life in jail.*—ToR (75.05.18, p.8) [Cp IAE slang *horrors* 'extreme depression associated with alcoholism or withdrawal symptoms'] **2.** PHRASES **2.1 dig/get horrors** *vb phr* (CarA) [*AF*] To have a dreadful time of it. *Boy, that time I di[d]n['t]*

have money and I was diggin[g] real horrors.— (Trin) **2.2 give (sb) horrors** *vb phr* (CarA) [*AF*] To cause (sb) much trouble, suffering, etc. *I am living in a house with him for six years and we were living good until he put himself with a married woman but she and her husband are not together, and now this man giving me horrors.*— NaT (79.09.12, p.21, Dear Christine)

horse-ba·na·na *n* (BrVi, Nevs) ‖ BLUGGO (Belz, etc)

horse-bean *n* (Bdos, Jmca, Trin) ‖ GRUDGE-PEA (Gren) [This name prob due to the large size of the edible pod, < Cr, *horse* adj applied to larger, coarser varieties ex *horse-banana, -plantain*, etc. Cp EE attrib use as *OED horse* sb. 26.h. 'horse-like, hence coarse, unrefined']

horse-head *n* (Jmca) ‖ ASS-HEAD (Jmca)

horse-man·go *n* (Belz) ‖ MANGO-GRAHAM (StLu) [< CE AF *horse* 'big, large']

horse-nick·er *n* (Bdos) ‖ NICKER (Angu, etc)

horse-plan·tain; **horn-plan.tain** *n* (Guyn, Jmca, Trin) The largest variety of plantain, often exceeding 12 ins in length and borne on a bunch that 'has no pendent axis below the bunch' *PTT: 228.* [See note at HORSE-BEAN. The variant *horn-* is prob owing to resemblance in shape and size to a cow's horn.]

hor·sti·lish [hɒrstaılıš] *adj* (Bdos) [*X*] See HO-STILISH

Ho·sein; **Ho.say** [hose] *n* (Trin) **1.** A Muslim religious festival held annually to commemorate the martyrdom of Hassan and Hosein, grandsons of the Prophet Mohammed; it is celebrated in late February or early March and, at the folk level, with colourful processions and much drumming and dancing. *History has it that the majority of Indians who settled in St James were the Madras Indians and that Hosay is, in fact, ... a feast-day peculiar to and revered by the community in India from which they came. It certainly explains why, over the years, St James has been the centre of Hosay celebrations, even [though], ... on Hosay nights there were only three hosays on display.*—Peo, I.8 (1976) p.42 [< *Hosein*, name of one of the martyrs. The form and spelling HOSAY is due to characteristic Trin Cr de-nasalization] □ *Hosay* is the commonest of many variant spellings, others being *Hoosay, Hoosein, Hosey, Husain, Hussay.* **2.** [By extension] ‖ TADJAH (Guyn, Trin) *Apart from carnival costumes, another traditional product of folk craftsmanship is the tadjah or hosay, which is built and paraded on the streets twice a year—according to the Muslim calendar. It is a sort of paper temple, some twenty-odd feet high.*—ACTT:143 **3.** [By extension] A participant in the stick-fighting display forming part of the HOSEIN celebrations. *On Hosey Day, when all the competing hoseys met at the junction before Lee Tung's long provision* *shop, he would throw his stick into the ring and bravely give out his challenge.*—NAGOS:35

hos·ti·lish (hog-sty·lish, hor·sti·lish) [hɒs taɪlɪš ~ hɒgstaɪlɪš ~ hɒrstaɪlɪš] *adj* (Bdos, Guyn, StVn) [*AF*] Very crude in manners and behaviour; given to rough answers. *... the truck actually coming at her she jumped up and ran. The driver came out of the truck and looked at the door of the shop, wrenched off [sic], and coolly said he didn't do that. He was very hostilish to the lady, then got in the truck and drove off.*—ViN (73.04.28, p.2) [< *hostile* + (SE suff) *ish*, but with an intensifying effect prob due to the infl, by folk etym, of the variant forms wh are linked to *hog, horse*]

hot[1] *adj* (CarA) [*AF*] **1.** [Of colours, dance music etc] Very bright and lively. *Prince is wearing a 'hot' shirt, gold-rimmed sun-glasses, American Air Force fatigue cap, shorts and loafers.*—JMRS:35 **2.** [Of a person] [*AF*—Derog*] Full of and/or displaying sexual desire; [esp of a woman] sexually appealing and also willing. *... and if is hot you hot me can let one of the boys cool you off!*—SNWIC:248 (S. Sadeek) **3.** Visibly busy; taken up with anxious activities. *The inspector was due to come and the headteacher had everybody hot preparing for the visit.*—(Guyn) **4.** PHRASES **4.1 foot is hot** *id phr* (Tbgo, Trin) [*AF—Joc*] See FOOT Phr 2.3. **4.2 hot needle burn(ing) thread** *id phr* (BrVi, Gren) [*AF—Joc*] Sth done hurriedly. *That wedding got to be hot needle burning thread for the lady looks quite 'fat'.*—BrVi (Ms) **4.3 mouth is hot** *id phr* (Guyn) [*AF*] See MOUTH Phr 4.36

hot[2] *adv* (CarA) [*X*] Sharply; severely. *Nothing bite so hot like a scorpion! Oh God!*—(Guyn)

hot[3] *vb tr* (CarA) [*X*] To heat (sth) on a fire. *She didn't have enough coals to hot the iron.*—Jmca (Ms) [By functional adj > vb shift as in CarA Cr from wh it survives]

hot-mouth[1] *n* (Guyn) ‖ BACK-ANSWER[1] (CarA) PHRASES **give/have hot-mouth** See BACK-ANSWER[1, 2]

hot-mouth[2] *adj* (BrVi) [*AF—Derog*] ‖ BIG-MOUTH[2] (CarA)

ho·to·to (hoe-toe-toe) *adj* (*Sometimes in adv function*) (Gren, Trin) [*AF*] **1.** Very much; very many; very great. *She give me a hototo plate o[f] rice and peas.*—(Trin) **2.** In abundance; plentifully. *Man they had mangoes hoe-toe-toe in the market that week.*—Gren (Ms) [Fr Cr, prob *ho* 'great (amount of)' + *to to* (reduplicated) < / two two/ < Fr *trop trop* 'too much, too much', indicating 'far too much', whence its semi-adj, semi-adv function]

hot-pep·per *n* (Baha, Mrat, TkCa, Trin) ‖ BIRD-PEPPER (CarA)

hot-sauce *n* (CarA) ‖ PEPPER-SAUCE (CarA) [*hot* 'piquant' + *sauce*]

hot-shirt *n* (CarA) A man's shirt made of material with brightly contrasting colours and usu worn outside the pants; it is considered suitable festive wear.

hound [hʌn] *n* (Gren, Guyn) [*AF—Derog*] An ill-mannered glutton. □ Rarely written in this sense. Note pronunc. See next.

hound·ish [hʌnɪš] *adj* (Guyn) [*AF—Derog*] Shamelessly gluttonous. *De two o[f] dem so houng[d]ish dat yo[u] can['t] put out all de food one time yo[u] know!*—(Guyn) □ See prec.

hou·ri *n* (Guyn) See HOORI

house *n* PHRASES **1. catch/go house** *vb phr* [*AF*] (Guyn) To get home; to go home directly. *The rain look like it comin[g], so A better catch house.*—(Guyn) **2. (two persons) can live in the same house** *id phr* (Nevs, Tbgo) [*IF*] ‖ (TWO PERSONS) CAN SHAKE HANDS (CarA) See HAND[1] Phr 4.3

house-bot·tom *n* (Belz) ‖ BOTTOM-HOUSE (Guyn) *Suppose when her dad found out he said she couldn't go back to school. It would be the washing bowl underneath the house bottom for her then and no mistake.*—EBL:21 **2.** PHRASE **2.1 under(neath) the house-bottom** *adv phr* (Belz) ‖ UNDER THE BOTTOM-HOUSE (Guyn) *As she walked sleepily down the stairs ... the wake was just livening up. The crowd under the house bottom were clapping and shouting.*—EBL:78

house-ne·gro/-slave *n* (CarA) [Hist] ‖ *house-nigger* (CarA) [*AF—Derog*] A black slave who worked in the white master's house (and so was considered much more favoured than and socially superior to the FIELD-NEGRO).

house-nig·ger *n* (CarA) [*AF—Derog*] (A term of abuse used among black people for) a black person who openly takes sides with whites against other blacks. *The wild racist talk in the recent years, mainly for political reasons, is undermining the Society, and in our Senate discussion is reduced to calling Senators 'House Niggers'.*—AdV (88.09.12, p.6) □ See note at FIELD-NIGGER.

House of As·sem·bly *n phr* (CarA) The legislative body of persons, or the 'lower house', for wh members are chosen by political elections; it is the colonial equivalent of the British House of Commons.

house-rais·ing song *n phr* (CarA) A repetitive group-song with a few two-line verses, sung by a team of men who use the downbeat of the second line as the signal to pull, push, or lift together in building, lifting, or shifting a house.

house-wren *n* (Gren, Guyn) ‖ GOD-BIRD 1.
(Gren, etc)

hous·ing-scheme *n* (Bdos, Guyn) ‖ *scheme¹*
(Guyn) A government housing development
providing homes for low- and middle-income
citizens.

how¹ *interrog adv* (CarA) *[AF]* **1.** [An abbr
greeting] How are (things with) you? *'So how
and thing. Come in from the rain, man. Don't get
wet.'*—SNWIC:180 (M. Anthony) **2.** Why? How
is it that? *'How that woman look so big?'* asked a
security guard and the female in question took to
her heels.*—WeG (73.06.06, p.30) □ Note also
Phr 3.1 foll. **3.** *PHRASES* **3.1 How come?** *interrog
or connective phr* (CarA) *[AF/IF]* How is it that?;
Why?; how it is that **a.** *'How come people have
to go to school to learn a trade, or to learn doctor
or lawyer or engineer or even office secretary work
or cooking, but anybody at all can just get up an'
run a country widdout studying a single thing about
Gover'ment'.*—TRIH:225 **b.** *I miss the weekly
'Gripe' column. Could we have it back please, and
could we begin it please by our supermarkets telling
us how come our bread tastes more and more every
week of soft sugared wool and what happened
to the thin sandwich thickness.*—NaG (75.09.29,
p.2) [Cp Nupe *Ki be*—'How come'—similarly
used; also Yoruba *Ki l'o de ti*—(*What it is come
that*—) 'How is it that—?'] □ Often pronounced
[hʌkʌm] and sometimes written **huccum** in folk
dialogue. Cp SE 'How has/does it come about
that...?' **3.2 How late you got?** *id phr* (Bdos)
[X] What time is it?; How late is it? **3.3 How
you mean?** *id phr* (CarA) *[IF]* [Expressing mild
surprise] What! *She blinked. 'I don't see what you
could do that's better than the movies.' / 'How you
mean? You think people din make sport before there
was movie?'*—MBGB:13

how² *conj* (CarA) [X] [Connecting two main
clauses] That. **a.** *The children then hush all of a
sudden when the accident nearly happen, they
get so frighten how them laughing nearly turn to
sadness.*—LMFF:43 **b.** *We began to quarrel an[d]
she tell my sister how I does t[h]ief money, and
how I go in school an[d] tell endless lie say how we
get big house.*—(Tbgo) [Prob by shift in function
of SE relative *adv how*, 'in what way' in some
contexts such as *The court heard how it all started
one morning.* See *OED how adv* 10. 'with
weakened meaning, introducing an indirect
statement after verbs of saying, etc' = That]
□ This use of *how* often occurs in writing.

how·so·ever; how.som.ever *sentence con-
nector* (Baha, Jmca) [X] However. **a.** *Howsoever,
this Sunday morning, breakfast is finished and we
are on the shady track going to Morant Bay.*—
RND:30 **b.** *Howsomever, lemmer tell yer dis.*—
JBJ:88

hu·bu·bal·li [hububali] *n* (Guyn) [Timber Ind]
The wood of a very tall forest-tree (*Lax-
opterygium sagotii*, *Anacardiaceae*); it is reddish-
brown and fine-grained, and valued in furniture

making for its fine polished finish. [< *BAED*
Arawak *hobobali* 'a tree for furniture wood, so-
called because it closely resembles the hog-plum
tree'. Arawak *hobo* 'hog-plum' + *bali* 'a tree that
looks like another tree']

huck·ster [hʌkstʌ ~ hʌskʌ] *n* (CarA) ‖ *hawker*
(Bdos) ‖ *higgler* (Jmca) ‖ *trader* (Guyn) A person (often a woman) who trades in fruit, vegetables, non-perishable food-items, and small
domestic items, at some fixed place in the open,
usually shared with many other such persons.
□ This is the more general term current in CE,
but there are differences from the other ‖ wh
should be noted, and more esp the difference
from the Derog connotation possible in AmE
and BrE. Cp also TRADER, TRAFFICKER.

huck·ster-bas·ket *n* A sturdy, coverless, oval-
shaped basket about 2-1/2 ft long, with a handle,
and usu made of bamboo, orig used by HUCK-
STERS for peddling their goods (hence the name).

hu·dut [hʊdʊt] *n* (Belz) ‖ FUFU 1. (Baha, etc)

hug-me-close *n* (Bdos) ‖ MAN-BETTER-MAN
(Dmca, etc) [From the clinging characteristic of
the weed. There is also said to be a belief that a
decoction of the weed used in a bath will help a
young woman retain her lover]

hul·ly-gul·ly *n* (Baha) *[AF]* **1.** A young man
who displays a preference for roughness in dress
and appearance as a matter of style. *'Most of the
people were bank and other office employees and a
lot of youths who were dressed hully-gully fashion,'
local freelance photographer Mr Franklyn Fer-
guson said.*—TrI (75.03.19, p.8) **2.** A playboy.

hu·man cry *n phr* (Bdos, Nevs) [X] Hue and
cry. [A corruption through folk etym]

hum·bug¹ (ham.bug) [hʌm'bʌg ~ ham'bʌg] /
1 2'/ *vb tr* (CarA) *[IF]* **1.** To cause annoyance,
bother, or trouble to (sb). **a.** *Why is it that some
parents allow their children to be public menaces?
e.g. the boys who have squeaker type horns on
their bicycles and who delight in humbugging their
neighbours.*—AdN (73.03.31, p.4) **b.** *She would
just say to them, 'Ef yo don axe me no question,
ar won't tell yo no lie, so don hambug me up.'*—
PKKK:100 **2.** To prevent (sb) from doing (sth)
by some trick or wicked act; to thwart; to foil.
*'You are in charge of the CID. Use your men.
Don't let anybody humbug you.'*—TRIH:204 [Cp
OED humbug v 1. *trans* 'to trick, ... hoax, delude'.
However there is a definite shift in sense in CE]
□ The word is much more widely used in CE as
vb than as *n* (*humbug²*), and strongly connotes
'irritation' rather than 'delusion' as in SE. Note
also special CE pitch-distinction from *hum-
bug²*, also observed in SE in the *OED* head-note.

hum·bug² ['hʌmbʌg] /2'1/ *n* (CarA) A person
or thing that is a nuisance. *He added: 'We want
the Ministry to see us not as a humbug but as part
of the educational set-up.'*—ExP (73.06.23, p.24)

[< SE *humbug* sb, wh *OED* notes as 18C slang of unknown origin, with several senses. However it has developed a clear and sharply restricted sense in CE]

hum·grum·shious [hʌmgrʌmšʌs] *adj* (Dmca, Mrat) [*AF*] [Of a person] Rough; coarse; crude in conduct. [Cp *OED humgruffin* '(a made-up word) a terrible or repulsive person'. Also *OEDS humgruffian* + cits 1842, 1825] □ The word is common in *Mrat*.

Humming Bird Medal *n phr* (Trin & Tbgo) See H.B.M.

hum·ming-bird trum·pet *n* (*phr*) (Trin) ‖ANTIGUA-HEATH (Bdos, etc) [From the shape of the floweret and its attraction for humming birds]

hunch *vb tr* (Tbgo) To strike (sb) with the elbow or the knee.

hun·ger *n* (CarA) *PHRASES* 1. **hunger holds you** *vb phr* (CarA) [*IF*] See HOLD 1.(iii) 2. **hunger is killing/wants to kill you** (CarA) [*IF/AF*] (To be) ravenously hungry. *I hadn't eaten the whole day so you can understand how the hunger want to kill me by four o'clock.*—(Guyn) [This is the normal way to say 'I am very hungry' in many Afr langs. Ex Igbo *agụụ chọrọ igugbu m* 'hunger wanted to kill me']

hun·gry *n* (CarA) [*AF—Cr*] 1. Hunger. '*... but when hungry bite you you still have to come back down ... pride and ambition alone can't full gut-ch.*'—FGSOS:34 (G. Irish) 2. *PHRASES* **2.1 hungry hold you; hungry killing you, etc** *vb phr* (CarA) [*AF—Cr*] ‖HUNGER HOLDS YOU, ETC (CarA) See HUNGER Phr 1.

hun·gry-bel·ly *adj* (CarA) [*AF—Derog*] [Esp of children] Ill-nourished; half-starved.

hun·gu-hun·gu [huŋu-huŋu] *n* (Belz) A ceremonial GARIFUNA dance in wh the feet are shuffled backwards and forwards as the body is swayed from side to side.

hunt·er *n* (Mrat, StKt, Trin) A long horse-whip sometimes used by masqueraders who crack it on the ground to clear a path before them. □ Cp DOG-HUNTER.

hur·ri·cane *n* (CarA) A massive moving storm with winds exceeding 74 m.p.h. [< Sp *huracán*, said to be from a Carib lang]

hur·ri·cane-sea·son *n* (CarA) Officially the months from June to October.

hur·ri·cane-warn·ing *n* (CarA) The last public announcement repeated when a hurricane is expected to strike land within 24 hours.

hur·ri·cane-watch *n* (CarA) A public announcement made following a number of Advisory Bulletins, that an approaching hurricane is now likely to strike land.

hur·ry-come-up[1] *n* (CarA) [*AF—Derog/Joc*] A person who has rapidly achieved some social importance after having none at all. *Crown government is the only government for these irresponsible fools who want to change God's order of things. Those hurry-come-ups who forget their origin!*—RND:200

hur·ry-come-up[2] *adj* (CarA) [*AF—Derog/Joc*] Hurriedly put together; shoddy in appearance; not properly prepared. *We were treated, Mr Speaker, to another of those 1976 hurry-come-up, rough-shod measures.*—Bdos (Hd, 76.08.04, p.7113)

hus·band-no·tice *n* (Antg, StLu) A paid notice inserted by a wife in the public press announcing her separation from her husband or disclaiming responsibility for his debts. □ Cp WIFE-NOTICE.

hush *vb tr PHRASE* **Hush your mouth!** *vb phr* (CarA) [*AF*] Shut up!; Be quiet! *Woman, hush yuh mouth and leave me alone. You don't know what it is to lose one of de boys who was close to you.*—DP:19 [A typical CarA Cr use of a prop complement. Cp Fr Cr *pé la bouch* similarly structured with same meaning]

hus·ker [hʌskʌ] *n* (Bdos) [*X*] A HUCKSTER. *He said that he had a valid work permit, and produced documents stating that he was authorised to carry on a trade as a 'husker'.*—NaT (83.03.08, p.1) [< [hʌkstər] by reduction of intervocalic consonant cluster /-kst-/ and metathesis /ks > sk/]

hus·tle *vb tr* (CarA) 1. [*AF*] To strive to obtain sth (esp money) by fair means or foul or by slick begging. **a.** *He done make up his mind that he going work at two car-wash places, and if the Lord hear his prayers, and treat he nice, he going hustle a next job on top o' them two, too.*—CWFYS:91 **b.** *Listen, it is more than high time some minister, while travelling abroad, try to hustle Belize two sets of traffic lights for the Central American Blvd.*—AmA (80.11.21, p.4) 2. [*AF—Vul*] [Of a man] To solicit the sexual friendship of a woman (with the expectation of succeeding). *He told me that you coloured boys coming down here hustling all the white women and would not allow a man like me to get through.*—AdN (77.01.23) [Cp AmE sense *hustle* 'engage in prostitution', this sense being applied in CE, but with lessened force, to the man's approach]

hus·tler *n* (CarA) 1. [*AF*] [Of a man] A slick, fairly well-dressed beggar; a con man. 2. [*IF*] [Of a woman, often used in a good sense] A tireless worker (often one doing more than one job).

hutch *n* (Bdos) A tall, ornamental, French-polished china-cabinet with glass doors, and often with drawers in its lower section. [Extension of *OED hutch* 1. 'a chest or coffer in which things are stored' + cits 1303–1872, the modern SE sense of 'a pen', as for rabbits, being a later 17C development] □ Still current AmE 'an open-front cabinet usu of a rustic style'— (*pers info, L. Urdang*).

hut·ment *n* (Belz) A line of small wooden apartments built end-to-end, provided by the government authorities as low-cost housing for poor families.

hy·a·cinth-bean *n* (Antg, Berm, Trin) ‖ BONA-VIST (CarA)

hy·mer·al·li *n* (Guyn) A very colourful water-snake growing to about 5 or 6 ft in length; it is said to attack only in self-defence and its bite deadly; *Micrurus surinamensis.*

hyst *vb tr* (Baha, etc) See HICE

I

I[1]; **I-and-I, I-man** [aɪ] *pron* (CarA) [Rastaf] Alternative cultist pron forms, replacing all SE personal pron forms, indicating the spiritually bound human self shared by all believers, hence 'I, you, he/she, we, they; me, him/her, us, them; my, your, his/her, our, their'. **a.** *'Oh I see,' Brother Salamanca say, shaking his head smart-like. 'You come to study I.'* / *'Well, not just you, all of you, that is, if you don't mind.'* / *'But all of we is only one of I, for it is only through I that there is the other of we and is only through the other of we that I can know I.'*—PCOS:192 **b.** *Right now, I an' I greatest problem is that dem don't want I an' I in de Concrete, but when I an' I move up country, dem send police to hunt I an' I down and bring I an' I back to the Concrete.*—CrU (76.10.09, p.5) **c.** *I an I scattered and shattered black nation,* / *shall never be restored* / *until I an I return with humble heart,* / *unto I an I God and King.*—Lal I. 1, p.31 (Eli X) **d.** *He said, 'when I man will have to make a move, no one, not even I man brethrens can help I now.'*—ToR (76.04.26, p.6) □ The use of any forms of SE pron in the same utterance as these cultist forms is usu in ref to outsiders. See YOU-MAN.

i-[2] [aɪ-] *stressed prefix* (CarA) [Rastaf] Element (replacing the initial syllable or sound of a word) indicating approval of a name, item, quality or action by RASTAFARIANS, hence for ex ***inana*** *'banana'*, ***Irator*** *'Creator'*, ***itiful*** *'beautiful'*, ***itrol*** *'control'*. [Evid infl both by reflection of the spiritual bond expressed in I[1], and by the pronunc of the last syllable of Ras Tafari, the original name of Haile Selassie, who is the revered head of the cult] □ Many words are similarly transformed in the cultist lang though the principle of selection does not appear to be consistent and some speakers appear to use the device more than others.

i·aut·er [aɪɒ·ɑtʌ] *n* (CarA) [Rastaf] A woman who is an active, participating member of the RASTAFARIAN cult. [< i[2] + (d)aughter. See I-[2]]

Ibo drums (I·bu drums) [ibu drʌmz] *n phr pl* (Guyn) A set of three goat-skin drums of differing sizes, beaten with the open palms of the hands and used for ceremonial dances. (See *DGF:35*).

Ibo (Na·tion)-dance (I·bu (Na·tion)-dance) [ibu nešʌn-da·ns] *n (phr)* (Crcu, Guyn) A ritual dance performed to the beat of drums by a group of persons who maintain they are Igbo ethnic descendants; it is ceremonial and usu related to atonement within their belief system. [< *Igbo*, a large ethnic group of S.E. Nigeria] □ *Nation* is included in the name only in *Crcu*.

Ibo wood [ibu wʊd] *n phr* (Tbgo) A hard, white wood used for building or making seats.

Ibo yam [ibu ya·m] *n phr* (Mrat) ‖ YELLOW YAM (Antg, etc)

ice-block *n* (Dmca, Gren, Guyn) A frozen block of milk-and-egg custard, shaped in the ice-tray of a refrigerator; it is a cooling sweet popular with school-children in some places.

ice-boat *n* (Bdos) A long-range, engine-powered fishing boat about 30 to 40 ft long, equipped in its aft section with a large ice-box for refrigerating fish (hence the name); it is used for fishing trips lasting several days. □ Cp DAY-BOAT.

ice-box *n* **1.** (CarA) [In former times] A wooden box lined with galvanized iron and insulated with saw-dust, for keeping ice; (it is now widely replaced, except in remote places, by the refrigerator). **2.** (Bdos) The large box with lumps of ice, in the aft section of an ICE-BOAT, for keeping the catch of fish refrigerated. **3.** (Tbgo, Trin) [IF] [In former times] An undertaker's temporary container, lined with tin, for removing a corpse packed with ice to a funeral parlour.

ice·ning [aɪsnɪŋ] *n* (Guyn, Jmca) [X] Icing (on a cake). [< *icing* by intrusion of epenthetic /-n-/. Cp FISHENING, etc]

ice-wa·ter *n* (CarA) Water for drinking, made cold with pieces of ice or by being refrigerated. [< *iced water* with characteristic CE loss of / -d/]

ICTA [ɪkta] *abbr* (CarA) Imperial College of Tropical Agriculture; it was founded at St Augustine, *Trin*, in 1921, and absorbed into the University of the W Indies in 1963.

icy-hot *n* (Bdos, Trin) [IF] A thermos flask. □ This term is now used only by older folk.

Idle Hall (Es·tate) *n phr* (Bdos, Dmca, Gren) [AF—*Joc*] ‖ ***Kickstone Co*** (TkCa) ‖ ***Walkers & Co*** (Gren, Guyn) **1.** A state of unemployment

and indifference. [< *idle* adj + HALL 2.] **2.**
PHRASE **2.1 work at Idle Hall** *vb phr* (Bdos,
Dmca, Gren) ‖ *kick stones* (TkCa) To be unemployed (and not too concerned about finding
a job).

i·dle·some *adj* (Bdos, Gren, Guyn) Given to
idling; not diligent; slack. *He used to be a bright
boy but all that malaria seemed to have sapped
him, he became idlesome and his work fell off so
badly that he failed the exam.*—Guyn [Prob by
analogy with such SE forms as *fulsome, gladsome,
wholesome*, i.e. adj + *-some* 'charaterized by
being', though *idlesome* is not recorded in *OED,
EDD*]

idread; **i.drin** *n* (Jmca) [Rastaf] Friend;
brother. [< I-² + DREAD¹ 1.; or + *drin* <
[(brɛ)drɪn] '(bre)thren']

if¹ [ɪf∼ɛf] *conj PHRASES* **1. If I tell you!** *id phr*
(Bdos, Gren, Guyn) [*IF*] Believe me!; You can
take my word for it! *If I tell you, ol[d] retire[d]
people catchin[g] hell to feed deyself on de[ir]
lil pension-money.*—(Gren) **2. if push come to
shove** *id phr* (CarA) [*AF/IF*] If the situation
becomes desperate; if things reach a stage of
crisis. *I also get by, as you bloody-well know, with
the odd bit of law coaching I pick up at the Centre.
And there's the Labour Exchange, if push come' to
shove.*—SCHMH:112 [= If the need to push
(i.e. with a reasonable amount of energy) becomes a need to shove hard (i.e. with all possible
force), as for ex, in moving forward a mud-bound
loaded cart] □ The phr *if push comes to shove* is
used in IAE, a likely loan from CE. **3. if wasn['t]
for sb/sth** *id phr* (CarA) [*AF*] If it wasn't/
weren't for sb/sth; but for sb/sth. **a.** *If wasn['t]
for your aunt, yo[u] would-a starve when yo[u]
mother dead.*—(Gren) **b.** *You see, the family respectable and the lawyer beg for him, but if wasn['t]
for that, they would-a sen[d] him straight to jail.*—
(Bdos) □ The phr *if it wasn't for* is now accepted
in BrE as standard. AmE still requires *if it weren't
for*, retaining the subjunctive—*pers info*, (L. Urdang). **4. if you bad** *id phr* (Guyn, Jmca, StVn,
Tbgo) [*AF—Cr*] [Said as a challenge] If you
think you can't be beaten; if you're looking for
a trial of strength. *If you bad, you come out he[re]
[u]pon de road an[d] say dat again!*—(StVn) **5.
If you hear!**; **If you see!** *id phrs* (CarA) [*AF*]
[Introducing surprising information] You should
have heard (sth said, played, etc)!; You should
have seen (sth, or sth done, happen, etc)! **a.** *If
you hear the dirty words that little child use in
front of all those big people!*—(Guyn) **b.** *If you
see jacks in the market this morning!*—(StVn) □ In
this sense, IF is said with notably contrasting
high pitch. The pattern for *If you hear..., If
you see...* is /4′12/.

If²! *excl* (sometimes introducing a statement)
(CarA) [*AF*] [Expressing certainty or strong
agreement] '*Hah!' Daphne laughed. 'You ain't
put he in he place ...?' 'If?' Claire exclaimed. 'Who
you think I is? I had to ask he if he think he
did talking to one o' he pissy li'l friends!*'—PeL

(78.05.12, p.5) [A truncation of 'If I did? I most
certainly did!; If it was so? It most certainly
was!' etc] □ Uttered with high rising pitch, and
strongly stressed, sometimes lengthened, vowel.

if·fing [ɪfɪŋ] *conj* (Bdos) [*AF*] ‖ EFFEN (CarA)
*What I was asking you, sir, is iffing any of them
four missing files is the one with my personal file
in it.*—CPM:144 [A dial variant of EFFEN, poss
with false refinement]

Igas! (Hi·gas!) [i·gas] *excl* (Dmca) [*AF*] See
EGAS!

ig·no·rance; **ig.no.ran.cy**, **ig.no.rant.ness** *n*
(CarA) [*AF*] Proneness to, or an act of stupid
anger or violence. **a.** *Mr Chairman, I rose slowly.
I was thinking all along how best to answer the Hon.
Member without being rude or unparliamentary,
because ignorance is a curse. The late senior Member for St Andrew once made a statement in this
House about 'ignorancy'.*—Bdos (Hd, 75.03.17,
p.4695) **b.** *Asked why he took up a machete
instead of locking his door in he replied: 'Just
ignorantness.'*—SdB (65.04.13, p.1)

ig·no·rant *adj* (CarA) **1.** [*AF*] Quick-tempered
and rough; given to sudden anger, rough speech
and behaviour. **2.** *PHRASES* **2.1 get ignorant** *vb
phr* (CarA) See GET Phr 3.15 *If anybody only
make me get ignorant an' effect an arrest, I will
take them to the station an' tell such a lie upon
them that them will be sure to punish.*—DJC:107
2.2 get (sb) ignorant *vb phr* (CarA) See GET
Phr 3.15.1 **2.3 get on ignorant** *vb phr* (CarA)
See GET Phr 3.18 * Note. *She didn't let the father
know because he could get on very ignorant at a
thing like that.*—CISH:21

i·la·loo [aɪlalu] *n* (Jmca) [Rastaf] Calalu. [I-²
+ (ca)laloo]

ill-speak *vb tr* (Tbgo) ‖ BAD-TALK² (CarA)
*Those who pretend to be your friends are the same
ones who ill-speak you.*—Tbgo (Ms) □ A false
refinement of *bad-talk* as vb, though it does not
occur as n.

I-lost-my-glove-on-a-Saturday-night *n*
(Angu, Antg, Brbu, Guyn, StVn) A children's
ring game in wh one player, running outside the
ring while the others sing, drops a whip behind
another player during the repetition of a certain
line; that player then has to pick it up and try
to catch the first player by chasing him/her
around the ring.

im *pron, 3rd pers sg* (Belz, Jmca) [*AF—Cr*] See
(H)IM

I-man *pron* (CarA) See I¹ [Rastaf] *Their 'dread'
sounds are hypnotically sweeping across an un-
witting society, as we find more and more people
appreciating the 'I man' dialect in word and song
heard over every radio station in the Caribbean.*—
LaS (76.04.14, p.3) □ Cp also YOU-MAN.

im·mor·tel(le)* *n* (CarA) ‖ *mortel* (Gren, Trin) A tall tree with a thorny trunk and spreading branches that blooms massively in flame-coloured flowers; it thrives on hill-slopes and is widely used in Trinidad as a shade tree for cocoa-plants; *Erythrina micropteryx (Papilionaceae).* [Fr 'immortal', prob from its long life—it is a recognized boundary mark in some territories—or from the retention of colour of the flowers when dried] □ The name is sometimes erron applied to the *flamboyant* wh has a similarly coloured and massive bloom.

im·pa·tion·ate (im·pa·tien·ate) [ɪmpešʌne·t] *adj* (Guyn, Tbgo, Trin) [X] Impatient. *'But, Tiger, dat is all de manners yuh have!' Deen's wife exclaimed. 'You so impatienate yuh can't wait little bit?'*—SABS:134 [< *impatient* with epenthetic breakdown of final consonant cluster]

im·pe·ri·al *n* (StVn) A very large, cultivated mango, resembling the KOKO-BÈF *(StLu).*

im·prove·ment *n* (Bdos, Mrat) The offspring of livestock given to a reliable neighbour to rear on the owner's behalf, with the understanding that half their number will be given back to the original owner. [A prob survival of EE. Cp *OED improvement* 4. e. *(Obs)* 'increase, produce' + cit 1705 'The greatest part of the Wealth and Improvement there consisted in Sheep']

in¹ *prep* (CarA) [Loosely used in many prep functions] **1.** (Bdos, Guyn) [X] [Of a person's age] Approaching (the age of so many years, as stated). *My little girl is in six now* (= *in her sixth year*).—(Bdos) **2.** (CarA) [X] At. **a.** *See you in Carnival!*—Int 8/73, p.30 (Ad) **b.** *The parent concerned ... only sat in her window and quarrelled until her heart was satisfied.*—DoC (65.05.12, p.2) **3.** (CarA) [X] On. **a.** *When you['re] coming home you can buy some bread in the way.*—(Antg) **b.** *He couldn't stand it any longer. He would report the matter, or box the boy in his ear.*—LICMS:61 **4.** (CarA) [X] Into; to. **a.** *But he had not gone in the country, only in town.*—StLu (Ms) **b.** *I enjoy reading it and look forward in reading some more.*—TiM (75.09.19, p.5) **5.** PHRASES **5.1 in (all) my born days** *adv phr* (CarA) [IF] See BORN¹ Phr 2. **5.2 in back of** *prep phr* (Baha, CayI) Behind. [Perh by infl of AmE] **5.3 in here** *n phr* (CarA) [X] This room; this place where we are. *In here is too hot. Let's open all the windows.*—(Bdos) **5.4 in regards to** *prep phr* (CarA) [X] See REGARDS Phr 2.1 **5.5 in respect to** *prep phr* (CarA) [X] See RESPECT Phr 2.1 **5.6 in sb's blood** *id phr* (Gren) [AF] In vexed pursuit of sb; harassing sb. *Although the poor man out o[f] jail, as anyt[h]ing happen, the police in he blood!*—(Gren) **5.7 in the early** *adv phr* (Bdos) [IF] At an early hour or date; in good time. *Contacted yesterday, a senior police official from the Bridgetown Division claimed that Mrs J—had been told 'in the early' that ... if this was not possible, she would receive a refund.*—AdN (73.12.28, p.5) **5.8 in there** *n phr* (CarA) [X] That room; that place where they are. *In there can't hold more than forty people or so.*—(Guyn)

□ Cp Phr 5.3 above. **5.9 in your face** *adv phr* (Gren) See FACE Phr 8 TO YOUR FACE

in² *conj* (Guyn) [AF—Cr] As soon as. *In [h]e hit de road, de police hol[d] [h]im.*—(Guyn) □ Usu with strong stress and high pitch on *in*.

in³ [ɪn] *neg marker* (CarA) [AF—Cr] Ain't. *The policeman got a van. I got in the van and I went to the C.I.D. Nothing else in happen.*—Bdos (CR, 70.01.12) □ A dial spelling often used in narrative dialogue.

in·a (in·na) [ɪna ~ ɪna] *prep* (Antg, Belz, Jmca, Mrat) [AF—Cr] ‖ *eena* (Jmca, Mrat) In; inside; into. **a.** *Dear Departed Federation / Referendum murderation / Bounce you ina outa space / Hope you fine a restin place.*—FCV2:85 (L. Bennett) **b.** *Obeahman bring six red-ants wrap up ina one pretty, pretty paper.*—FGSOS:43 **c.** *Inna the church holy santum / Where the holy bread and wine dah ...*—StVn (Ms, poem) [Prob by characteristic CarA Cr epenthesis > SE *in*, reinforced by W Afr forms, for ex Igbo *na* 'at, in, to'] □ A dial form often so written in narrative dialogue. (Also an eye-dialect spelling found in AmE writing—(pers info, *L. Urdang*))

i·na·na [aɪnana] *n* (Jmca) [Rastaf] Banana. [< I-² + (ba)nana]

in·cense-tree *n* (Jmca, Trin) ‖ BIRCH-GUM TREE (Bdos, etc)

in·crease-peas *n* (Bdos) ‖ *rounceval* (Bdos) Small bean-shaped peas in pods about 8 ins long that are borne on a wild straggling vine; they are cooked green or when dried pale brown; *Vigna spp.* □ Cp BORA, GUB-GUB, YARD-BEAN wh are closely related.

in-crop *adj* (Bdos, Guyn) [Sugar Ind] Employed specifically for the reaping of the sugar-crop. [= During the crop-reaping season] □ Cp OUT-OF-CROP SEASON.

in·den·tured la·bour *n phr* (CarA) [Hist] The working arrangement by wh labourers were imported, esp from the Indian sub-continent, under agreement or 'indenture', to replace slave-labour in the W Indies after Emancipation; the arrangement ceased in 1917.

in·den·ture·ship *n* (CarA) [Hist] The hiring, esp of EAST INDIANS, under the system of IN-DENTURED LABOUR, for a fixed period. *At the end of their indentureship, the labourers were repatriated, if they so chose, and the cost of the repatriation was met from the [Indian Immigration] Fund.*—ExP (72.01.21, p.13)

In·de·pen·dence Day *n phr* (CarA) The day commemorating annually the date on wh a territory ceased to be a British colony and became an independent state and nation; it is usu a public holiday. □ The different annual dates of *Independence Day* are: Antg/Brbu 1st Nov;

Baha 10th July; *Bdos* 30th Nov; *Belz* 21st Sept; *Dmca* 3rd Nov; *Gren* 7th Feb; *Guyn* 26th May; *Jmca* 6th Aug; *StKt/Nevs* 19th Sept; *StLu* 22nd Feb; *StVn/Grns* 27th Oct; *Trin/Tbgo* 31st Aug.

In·di·an *adj, n* **1.** (CarA) ‖ EAST INDIAN (CarA) *The responsible politician must appeal to and encourage the Indians—whether Hindu, Muslim or otherwise—to see themselves as Guyanese first.*— Guyn (Ms) □ The term is used in CE without ref to the present day politically independent nations of the Indian sub-continent. **2.** *pl* (Trin) [Carnival] Member(s) of a band or group dressed in imaginative variations of costumes, including feathered headpieces, beads, etc, representing various 'tribes' of orig AMERINDIANS.

In·di·an al·mond *n* (ECar) ‖ ALMOND (CarA) [Prob ref to the tree's oriental origin]

In·di·an ar·row [ɪnjən ara] *n phr* (Antg, Brbu) Arrowroot (the rhizome, or the starch made from it).

In·di·an rab·bit *n phr* (Belz) ‖ AGOUTI (CarA) [< (Maya) *Indian* + *rabbit*, in ref to the animal's habitat, appearance and use]

In·di·an yam *n phr* (Jmca) ‖ CUSH-CUSH (YAM) (Dmca, etc) [Prob ref to or associated with Amerindian cultivation. Cp ‖ *buck yam* (Guyn)]

In·di·a-rub·ber plant/tree* (In·di·an rub·ber tree) *n phr* (CarA) ‖ *rubber-plant/tree* (CarA) A decorative pot-plant or an ornamental tree with large, leathery, spear-shaped, brownish-green leaves and aerial roots that help it to spread extensively; *Ficus elastica (Moraceae).*

In·di·a-rub·ber vine* *n phr* (CarA) A woody vine with shiny, dark green, oblong leaves; it yields a latex (hence the name) and bears large, mauve, funnel-shaped flowers and ribbed pods wh are poisonous; *Cryptostegia grandiflora (Asclepiadaceae).* □ Often, but erroneously, called *purple allamanda*—PTT:140.

In·dic *adj* Relating to any or all of the langs and cultures of the Indian sub-continent. □ It is particularly important to note, in the context of the *CarA* that this term is used as one free of political, religious or social connotation.

in·di·go blue *n phr* (Guyn) ‖ *maldjo blue* **1.** (Trin) Laundry blue, sold in solid cubes and widely used in superstitious practices. *It was a common practice for parlour proprietors in the early forties to keep a plate or bowl with lime juice and indigo blue under the counter and, for a matter of purification, coins received from customers were deposited therein.*—COYN:19

in·dis·ci·plin·ed *adj* (CarA) [X] Undisciplined; uncontrolled; unruly. *Dr Jacobs... added, 'the West Indian male is a rather indisciplined lot particularly in sex.'*—AdN

(76.02.02, p.1) [By infl of SE *disciplined* (adj), derived from SE *indiscipline* n]

In·do-Guy·an·ese; **In.do-Trin.i.da.di.an, In.do-West-In.di.an** *n* (CarA) An EAST INDIAN person who is a citizen by birth of Guyana/Trinidad/any West Indian territory.

in·dus·tri·al school *n phr* (CarA) A state-run school for boys (and another for girls) who have committed legally punishable offences; in it they are put through a basic curriculum, including some industrial arts, in strictly controlled continuous residence. *'The security measures in these institutions are not safe enough. I know one juvenile,'* he said, *'who has been in the Boys Industrial School since he was ten years old. He is 15 now but he is always escaping from the school.'*—TrI (75.05.01, p.7)

in·flam·ma·tion-bush* *n* (CarA) ‖ *information-bush* (Guyn, Mrat, StKt) Any of two or more herbs, an infusion of wh is taken as a treatment for coughs, colds etc, esp when these cause pains that are believed to be due to an inflamed internal condition.

in·form·a·tion [ɪnfʌ(r)meʃən] *n* (CarA) [X] Inflammation. *Tie it on dey wound and it will draw out all da information.*—Aaw I.1, p.25 [A corruption prob due to reduction of /-CC-/, hence /infla-/ > /infa-/ > /info-/. However, note also *EDD information*, (Lin, Sus, etc) (also in form *infamation*) 'inflammation']

in·form·a·tion-bush *n* (Guyn, Mrat, StKt) ‖ INFLAMMATION-BUSH (CarA) [See INFORMATION prec]

in front[1] *adv phr* (Tbgo, Trin) [AF] In advance; at the outset; in good time. *All right, but I warning you in front, the first time you make a mistake, I not going to take you anywhere where I go.*—SWOS:51 □ Sometimes also *from in front*.

in front[2] *prep phr* (CarA) [X] In front of; before (a place, people). *... and the change jingling in your pocket to make like a big sports in front the children?*—MBGB:146

in·grease·ments *n pl* (Bdos, Guyn) [AF—Joc] Savoury ingredients in cooking or in a prepared meal. *When you pass the big house pon yuh right hand, and tek three-four more steps, all kinds and brands and variations o' roast pork, fryfish, steam potfish, a bake chicken here, and a piece o' sheep foot there, all these various ingreasements hitting yuh belly.*—PeL (80.05.02, p.10, A. Clarke) [Blend of *ingredients* + *grease* 'fatty gravy']

ink-ber·ry (tree) *n (phr)* (Jmca) ‖ FIVE-FINGER **2.** (Angu, etc)

in·na *prep* (Antg, etc) [AF—Cr] See INA

in·side (of) *prep (phr)* (CarA) [X] In. **a.** *Old woman, you making dust fly outside there. You* want to catch sick when that dust fly inside your nose or what?—(Tbgo) **b.** *Anytime that my name appeared inside of a newspaper, was when I said very, very little.*—AMGM:22

in·stead *conj* (Guyn) [*X*] ‖ BEFORE[2] (CarA) *Instead they come home after school the children walk all over the place*—(Guyn)

in·sult·ive *adj* (Guyn, Jmca, StVn, Tbgo, Trin) [*X*] Insulting; offensive. *The phrase 'make your hands fast' is sometimes jovial but sometimes it is rather insultive.*—StVn (Ms, 1973) [By blend of *insulting* + *offensive*]

in·ter·fere *vb intr* (CarA) **1.** To cause annoyance or hurt. □ This sense is dominant in CE, and occurs most commonly in the foll phrs. **2.** PHRASES **2.1 interfere with sb** *vb phr* (CarA) ‖ *trouble*[2] (CarA) To cause vexation to (sb) by provoking, teasing; to attack perversely. *You are a man who is always saying do not interfere with you. Leave me alone, please. You know my tongue is like a razor. Leave me alone!*—Bdos (Hd, 87.11.24, p. 1679) **2.1.1 interfere with sth** *vb phr* (CarA) ‖ *trouble*[2] (CarA) To damage or cause harm to sth by meddling, handling etc. *And there are adults who are making sure that they interfere with the minds of these children by putting drugs in their candy, or in their ice cream or lollipop.*—Bdos (Hd, 87.03.23, p.311)

In·te·ri·or, The *n phr* (Guyn) ‖ *the bush* (Guyn) The hinterland of Guyana; the remote up-river, forest, and/or savannah lands of Guyana.

in·ter·val *n* (Bdos, Jmca) [Sugar Ind] ‖ CART-ROAD (Bdos) *Mr Jonas went down the hill between the canes to the main interval or road leading to the village.*—RPME:29 [Prob a survival of EE. Cp *OED interval* 3. 'a gap, opening' + cits 1489–'1837; also *intervale* 4. (N. Amer) 'a low level tract of land …']

in·to *prep* (CarA) [*X*] **1.** In. **a.** *These are expressions which stick into the ears of a people who now know that their money is withheld against their will.*—TrU (64.02.01, p.8) **b.** *I said I thought it best to discharge it into the sand where it would not harm anyone.*—DaM (65.11.10, p.9) **2.** To. **a.** *He had walked long hours through the dark village roads, but by dawn he began to see the street lights and was almost into town.*—Guyn (Ms) □ In IAE *into town* wd mean 'into the centre of the town'—L.U. **b.** *More and more radio stations are turning into music and longer full time hours (24 hours).*—AmA (80.01.25, p.2)

in·var·i·a·bly *adv* (Gren, Guyn) [*IF*] Usually; often; almost always. *Our roads in Grenada are invariably narrow and bad, but when certain motorists are uncivilised … this makes driving on the road a torture.*—ToR (76.09.26, p.7) □ This common weakening of the force of SE *invariably* may be due to its being used as = 'constantly, always', the senses of wh are also weakened.

i·po·me·a* [ɪpoˈmia ~ aɪpoˈmia] *n* (CarA) ‖ *goat's-foot creeper* (Guyn) ‖ *morning-glory* (Jmca) ‖ *seaside-yam* (Bdos) A showy, creeping vine with ribbed, fleshy, green leaves and crimson-purple flowers; it thrives on sandy beaches covering the ground massively; *Ipomoea pes-caprae* (*Convolvulaceae*). *Looking out through the tangles of stephanotis, ipomea and many other creepers, to watch the breakers in lines of silver light chase each other to the shore, the roar of the surf reduced to a murmur by distance … is enough to make one imagine that he has realised his childhood dream of fairy land.*—HWII:46 □ There are many species of *ipomea*, but the botanical name appears to be commonly applied to this one in popular literature.

i·ra·tion [aɪreˈšən] *n* (CarA) [Rastaf] Creation; nature; whatever is naturally good as created by God. [I-[2] + (c)r(e)ation]

i·rie (**i·rey**) [aɪri] (CarA) [Rastaf] **1.** *adj* Nice; happy; lovely; giving pleasure to the senses (i.e. good to see, hear, taste, smell, feel). [The word may be the current form of a 19C Jmca slave term *eerie*. Note: [M.G. Lewis] records a song entitled 'We very well off', sung by the Negroes in praise of his kindness to them … 'Hey-ho day! neger now quite eerie (i.e. hearty) / For once me see massa—hey-ho day!'—PSS:255. The text of the song referred to includes the interpretation 'hearty'; it was given in Lewis's account (1834) of a visit to Jmca in 1818. See PSS] **2.** [By extension] A signal of approval, happiness or brotherhood, used in greeting or parting. *S1: See you later, dread! S2: Irie!*—(Jmca) □ The term appears still to be most widely used among *Jmca* RASTAFARIANS.

Irish moss *n phr* (Jmca) ‖ SEA-MOSS (CarA) *A popular drink with health food enthusiasts, Irish Moss is believed to aid sexual prowess.*—DaG (82.03.12, p.12)

Irish po·ta·to *n phr* (CarA) ‖ ENGLISH POTATO (CarA) □ The name is a free alternative to *English potato* and *potato*, though more commonly so among older folk. Cp also AmE usage.

iron *vb tr* (Tbgo, Trin, USVI) [Of hair] ‖ PRESS[1] (CarA) *She was always going to iron her hair, to make it straight like white people or Indian people.*—SABS:54

iron-band *n* (Antg) A folk-band comprising a long drum carried under the arm and hand-beaten, a SHAK-SHAK, and a small piece of iron knocked by a longer piece (hence the name); it accompanies the street-dancing of masqueraders. □ Cp TUK-BAND.

iron man [aɪərn maˑn] *n phr* (CarA) [*IF—Joc*] A weightlifter. [A ref both to the lifting of iron weights and to the display of muscular hardness] □ Term commonly used by journalists.

iron-pot [aiərn-pɒt] *n* (Baha) ‖COAL-POT (CarA)

iron-root [aiərn-rut] *n* (ViIs) ‖MINNIE-ROOT (Bdos, etc)

iron·shore [aiərnšor] *n* (CayI) A blackened, jagged coral-stone strip of land that edges and, in some places, overhangs the sea.

iron-weed [aiərn-wid] *n* **1.** (Guyn) ‖SWEET-HEART BUSH (Dmca, Guyn) **2.** (CarA) Any of several weeds used as a folk-medicine to make an infusion that is believed to strengthen the body, esp the back.

iron·wood* [aiərn wʊd] *n* (CarA) ‖ *axemaster* (Belz) Any of several heavy, dense woods, obtained from certain hard forest-timbers, wh are used for uprights and frames of buildings and boats. Exs are *Dalium guianense* and *Swartzia leiocalycina* (*Caesalpiniaceae*) in *Guyn*, *Exostema caribaeum* (*Rubiaceae*) in *Antg*, *Krugiodendrum ferreum* (*Rhamnaceae*) in *USVI*.

ir·re·gard·less *adj*, *adv* (CarA) [X] **1.** *adj* Regardless. *I think that irregardless of whichever party is there, the knife gets wielded where 'other charges' are concerned, so we did not have that sort of money for capital expenditure.*—Bdos (Hd, 87.03.23, p.279) **2.** *adv* [By extension] Notwithstanding; without compromise. *... she would have made her son happy in his grave to insist that the inquiry go on. They wanted the inquiry— irregardless!*—ExP (72.02.13, p.4) [A blend of *irrespective* + *regardless*] □ Though generally condemned as a grammatically unacceptable form, this term occurs commonly in educated contexts in CE.

is¹ *linking vb* (CarA) **1.** [X] [All-purpose pres. t. form of *'be'*] **a.** *Anyhow, people does ask me how I looking so good when I is a 52-year-old woman, and I had 12 children.*—Peo I.1, p.19 **b.** *'Youall and we is really cousin, you know,' he said, 'you is family to us.'*—StVn (Ms) [A development from the CarA Cr principle of an unchanging base verb A, DA, DE *'be'*] □ This occurs mostly in speech, but is often found also in writing. **2.** [AF—Cr] **(i)** [Unstressed, introducing n phr or clause with added emphasis] It is. **a.** *Imagine, all these years, and is the first Mammy ever call Daisy 'Daughter'.*—SNWIC:264 (M. Townshend) **b.** *'Rajo ... Rajo,' I heard my aunt calling, 'time to get up. Is Saturday, you know.'*—HFGA: 62 (I. Khan) **(ii)** [Unstressed interrog, introducing an emphatic question] *'Is what wrong to he?' one woman said to her neighbour ... 'Is where dey bring he from at all?'*—SNWIC:222 (R. Heath) [Perh by elision with loss of intervocalic consonant < *i[t]* is. However this may have been helped by the coincidence of IrE, in wh an initiating *Tis* (< Erse *Is*) functions similarly, as in *Tis to rob me you want*. *Is it reading you are?* (*JESI:51*)] **(iii)** [Unstressed, introducing a front-focused phr or question] It is a fact that. Is it a fact that? **a.** *Is fall he fall down from the*

falaise by rocks by Point Side, his face mash up; I wasn't fraid, he fall and the sea take him.— WSAD:21 **b.** *But is vex he vex, or is joke [h]e jokin[g]?* (= *Is he, in fact, angry or is he merely joking?*)—(Guyn) □ The front-focused idiomatic structure does not seem to be current in *Bdos*. **3.** PHRASES **3.1 Is me and you!**; **Is you and (sb)!** *id phr* (CarA) [AF] [Issuing a warning threat] You will have me/(sb) to reckon with! [A prob calque from several W Afr langs. See AND 3. Phr] **3.2 Is so!** *id phr* (CarA) [AF] Exactly!; That's how it is! *Is so with them! Is so!* (= *That's exactly how they behave!*)—(Bdos) **4.** [By extension] [AF—Cr] There is; there will be. **a.** *... every time I step out with one is a big quarrel for days after.*—SNWIC:211 (A.N. Forde) **b.** *Now I could tell you that if is one thing Sophie believe in that is that if she promise to do something she was ga do it, come hell or high water.*—NaG (78.06.01, J. Thompson)

is² [ɪz ~ əz] *aux vb* (Bdos, Guyn) [AF—Cr] ‖ DOES **1.** (CarA) *... but why you is want to stretch me strait out pun de wrack o de mornin so early for, man?*—BMP:26 [A cliticised form of DOES [(d)əz], sometimes further reduced to [z]]

i·sa·va [aisa·va] *n* (CarA) [Rastaf] Cassava. [< 1-² + (*cas*)*sava*]

I.S.E.R. *abbr* (CarA) The Institute of Social and Economic Research (of the University of the W Indies).

Is·land-Car·ib *n* (ECar) [Hist] **1.** An Amerindian of mixed ethnic stock, the mother Arawak and the father either Carib or already mixed; an early post-Columbian indigenous inhabitant of the *ECar* islands. **2.** The lang of such people, Arawakan in structure and heavily Carib in vocabulary, in wh most words had one form permitted for use by women and another form exclusively for use by men. *The last native speakers of Island-Carib died about 1920.*—TLWI:24

is·land schol·ar *n phr* (CarA) See SCHOLAR

is·land·wide (is·land-wide) *adj*, *adv* (CarA) (Spread) throughout the whole island. *Most important is the participation which was island-wide, also our 'country cousins' showed that they have talent quite equal to those in the Corporate Area.*— StA(JA) (70.07.11, p.10) [By analogy < *nation-wide*]

it *3rd pers sg pron* PHRASES **1. it got** *id phr* (StVn, USVI) [AF] ‖ IT HAVE (Dmca, etc) See HAVE Phr 3.15 *It got more workin' people than white people an' civil servants in Kingsland.*—TRIH:125 **2. it had** *existential introductory phr, pa.t.* (Dmca, Gren, StLu, Tbgo, Trin) [AF—Cr] See HAD Phr 2.1 *You said, 'It had Policemen around and if them policemen don't want to say who do it I ent saying too.' You remember saying that?*—ToR (78.06.25, p.1) **3. it have** *existential introductory phr* (Dmca, Gren, StLu, Tbgo, Trin) [AF—Cr] See HAVE Phr 3.15 *He meet me last night and he* *tell me it have plenty money bury in me land under de silk cotton tree.*—RTCS:4 **4. it make cold/ hot** *id phr* (Gren) [*AF*] [Ref to the weather] It is cold/hot. [A calque via Fr Cr < Fr *Il fait froid/chaud* 'it is cold/hot']

i·ta·bo [itabo] *n* (Guyn) A small meandering stream or a man-made canal connecting two rivers or large creeks; it is used for convenience in avoiding dangers ahead in one waterway by transferring to another. [*BAED* Arawak *itabo* 'a small stream or channel used to avoid dangers in a bigger body of water e.g... waterfalls in a river'.]

ital[1] [aɪtal] *adj* (CarA) [Rastaf] **1.** *adj* [In ref to food] Good to eat as produced by nature, not by killing animals or birds; vegetable. *Brown: 'I have one mouth looking to me for food you know, sah. Is ital food I cook and sell and earn $20 to $30 a week.'*—WeS (74.02.15, p.6) **2.** [By extension, in general contexts] Natural; sensible; God-given. *I believe that if the House of Parliament does not wake up quickly and serious up itself, an ital sound is going to wake them ... to instant reality.*—DaG (78.06.21, p.10) [1-[2] + (vi)tal]

i·tal[2] [aɪtal] *n* (CarA) [Rastaf] Any vegetable, fruit or naturally produced food as distinct from fish or animal flesh; such food cooked without salt. **a.** *'Ital' is the new menu—no salt, no flesh.*—ToR (77.07.27, p.4) **b.** *They will justify Dreadlocks being poisoned for stealing itals, but they will not ask themselves why those in Society like themselves are not caught for deflection of funds and embezzlement.*—CrU (76.10.09, p.7) [By extension of ITAL[1]]

i·ta·to [aɪteto] *n* (CarA) [Rastaf] Potato. [< 1[2]- + (po)tato]

ite (ae·ta, eta, ete, e·ti·a); **ite-palm** [ite~ita-pa·m] *n* (Guyn) A sturdy palm tree growing to a height of about 40 ft with fan-shaped leaves, bearing edible fruit and flourishing in swampy land in Guyana, where it is regarded as the 'tree of life' by Amerindians; *Mauritia flexuosa* (*Palmae*). [*BAED* Arawak *ite* 'a large palm tree that bears huge bunches of edible fruit. All parts of the tree are used to provide food, drink and shelter.']

ix·o·ra*[ɪkzora~ɪgzora] *n* (CarA) A flowering, bushy shrub with leathery, green leaves; its bright red flowers bunch in round, dome-shaped trusses, borne abundantly throughout the year; *Ixora coccinea* (*Rubiaceae*); there is also a white variety.

J

jab-jab *n* (Dmca, Gren, StLu, Tbgo, Trin)
See DJAB-DJAB

jab·less(e) *n* (Dmca, StKt, StLu, Tbgo, Trin)
See DJABLÈS

jab-mo·las·si *n* (Trin) See DJAB MOLASSI

Jack¹ *n* **1.** [Male name used in loose ref to any
person] **2.** PHRASE **2.1 give Jack his jacket** *id
phr* (Bdos, Guyn, Trin) See GIVE¹ Phr 2.9 *The
present deafening silence on the Dean's statement
could, I suppose, spring from the shortness of memory for which the general public is notorious, but
it could also spring from an ungenerous refusal to
give Jack his jacket.*—SuS (80.02.03, p.8) **3.**
(Antg, Bdos, CayI, Tbgo, USVI) [*AF*] [Used
as a familiar introduction to a statement, often
showing surprise or irritation] **a.** *Jack, yo shoudda see me squeezin' in my small self on da
shelf.*—Aaw.I.2:25 **b.** *This is what he said, 'O'
God jack I can't go along with this plan, I would
not be able to sleep at night.'*—Antg (Ms, 1972)

jack² *n* (Gren) [*AF—Joc*] ‖BUSH-RUM (ECar)
*... a high price to pay for being in possession of a
quantity of uncustomed goods, —to wit—two gallons (approx) of 'Jack' and a bottle of Black and
White Whisky.*—ToR (73.09.02, p.2) [Joc abbr
of JACK-IRON]

jack³; jack.fish *n* (*usu pl*) **1.*** (CarA) A small
silvery-grey fish that looks like a herring; bony
but very tasty, it is seasonally caught in great
quantities (hence often pl); *Harengula humeralis*
(*Clupeidae*). **2.** (Short name for) any of a number
of large edible fish of the *Carangidae spp*. See
CAVALLI

jack·ass-cart *n* (Bdos, Guyn) [*AF—Joc*] A
donkey-cart.

jack·ass-rope *n* (Jmca) Black tobacco, locally
grown and cured, twisted into rope-like lengths
(hence the name) wh are coiled for easy marketing and sold by the foot or yard. *She consulted
him often and in public too. Occasionally she
brought him gifts of 'jackass-rope' tobacco for his
ancient clay pipe.*—SD:20

jack-bean *n* (Jmca, Trin) ‖GRUDGE PEA (Gren)
[This name (cp the fairy-tale 'Jack and the Bean-
stalk') may be due to the semi-climbing habit
developed by the plant's elongated stems in
shady places. See *PTT:102*]

jack·et¹ *n* PHRASE **give Jack his jacket** *id phr*
(Bdos, Guyn, Trin) See GIVE¹ Phr 2.9 □ Cp
JACKET² PHR 3.1

jack·et² *n* (Belz, Jmca) [*AF—Joc/Derog*] **1.** The
child of a married woman and a man who is not
her husband. **2.** Any child whose paternity is
denied. [Prob by *Joc* transfer of the notion 'to
put sth on a man (the husband)', 'to give sth
respectable-looking to wear'] **3.** PHRASES **3.1
give (a man) a jacket** *vb phr* (Belz, Jmca)
[*AF—Derog*] See GIVE¹ Phr 2.16 *I heard later
on that the girl was pregnant for him. I asked him
about it and he said it was a lie, the girl wanted
to give him a 'jacket'.*—WeS (75.03.07, p.8) □ Cp
JACKET¹ Phr **3.2 wear a jacket for sb** *vb phr*
(Belz, Jmca) [*AF—Derog*] [Of a man] To accept,
unknowingly, another man's child as your own.
*'Talkin' about Shag,' said Flitters ... 'if he don't
look out sharp he'll be wearin' a jacket for somebody
one of these days' / 'You mean about Euphemia
and Bajun Man?' / 'That's who I'm talkin' about.
Ain't you seen it you'self?'*—MHJT:23

jack·fruit* *n* (CarA) A massive, green fruit
that can weigh over 40 lbs; it has a close-pimpled
skin, grows direct from the trunk of its huge
tree, and is of an irregular oval shape, resembling
a giant misshapen breadfruit; it is cooked unripe,
or the pleasant-tasting gelatinous flesh of its
many seeds eaten when ripe, or the nuts roasted;
Artocarpus heterophyllus or *A. integer* (*Moraceae*).

Jack-in-the-bean·stalk *n* (USVI) ‖AUGUST-
FLOWER (Guyn)

jack-in-the-box* *n* (Bdos, Guyn) A tall,
tapering forest tree, yielding timber often used
for boat-building and flooring; *Hernandia sonora*
(*Hernandiaceae*).

jack-in-the-bush* *n* (Jmca) ‖*christmas-
bush* (CarA) ‖*géritou* 3. (USVI) A straggling
shrub with clusters of small, whitish flowers
and slightly sweet-smelling leaves that have a
smoothly hairy underside; the leaves are widely
used either crushed, wilted, or boiled, for a
number of complaints, esp skin disorders and
coughs; *Eupatorium odoratum* (*Compositae*).
□ The name *Christmas-bush* applies in some
parts of *Jmca*.

Jack-iron (rum) *n* (*phr*) (Gren, Grns, StVn)
[*AF*] ‖BUSH-RUM (Gren, etc) *Right now you have*

a fine of $460.00 for people who sell mountain dew or jack iron or uncustomed liquor and you say that's not enough and you make it $5,000.00.—Gren (Hd, 73.08.24, p.49)

Jack Man·do·ra *n phr* (Jmca) Name used in the traditional statement ending an ANANCY STORY, (in foll phr). PHRASE **Jack Mandora, me no choose none!** *id phr* (Jmca) [*AF—Joc*] I have said and not said!; Let no one accuse me of having said it was he/she!

Jack-me-lan·tern; Jack-o-lan.tern *n* (Baha, StKt, TkCa, Trin) A legendary spirit in the form of a small ball of fire or a strange-looking light moving among trees at night and luring a person to follow it into the distance; the person is said to disappear mysteriously.

Jack-Span·i·ard* *n* (ECar) ‖ *djèp* (Dmca, StLu) ‖ *marabunta* (Guyn) ‖ *maribone* (Gren, Trin) A reddish-brown wasp just over an inch long; it makes a papery brown nest in eaves and trees and its sting is very vicious; *Polistes spp.*

jack up (sb) *vb phr* (Tbgo, Trin) [*AF/IF*] To call (sb) sharply to account for misconduct; to rebuke (sb) sharply. *The mother jacked him up when she caught him pinching the fried chicken.*—(Tbgo)

Ja·cob's *n phr* (Bdos, Guyn) ‖ JOSEPH'S COAT (Bdos, etc) [Prob a confused ref to Jacob's false 'raiment', of *Gen 27:15, 16*, wh was used to mislead; but it was not many-coloured. See JO-SEPH'S COAT]

Jag *n* (Guyn) [Indic] See BHAGAVAT

ja·ga·bat ['jagabat] *n* (Gren, Tbgo, Trin) [*AF—Derog*] ‖ BAD-WOMAN (Guyn, etc) *She try to mamamguy he, dis jagabat / Well not a foreigner at all can['t] interpret that / Dat mean she try to make he a kunumunu / Meanin[g] she want him mind she and she sweetman too / So he beat de wahbeen till she bazodi.*—Trin (Cso—Mighty Conqueror, 1974 (?)) [Prob Bhoj < Hin]

Jah¹ [ja·] *n* (CarA) [Rastaf] **a.** God. *So we use our insight / To carry on with the fight / With Jah— Jah on our side / We know we cannot backslide / Babylon have to let us go.*—VoS (Supplement, 77.12.11, p.29) **b.** (SUFFERER: And that crooked man who Babylon bend/Jah shall make straight)—WOB:167 [From the Hebrew form *Yahweh*] □ The term replaces 'God', and is widely used, in the Rastaf cult.

Jah² [ja·] *adj* (CarA) [*IF*] Belonging to the RASTAFARIAN cult, as a brother. □ Sometimes in *Derog* use by non-Rastafarians.

ja·ko (par·rot)* [žako] *n* (*phr*) **1.** (Dmca) A small parrot wh is mostly green, with a red neck-patch; it is native to Dominica; *Amazonia*

arausica (Psittacidae). **2.** (StLu) ‖ ST LUCIA PAR-ROT (StLu) [Fr *jacquot*, equivalent of SE 'Polly' as pet name for a parrot]

jam¹ *vb* **1.** *vb tr* (CarA) To touch or hit with the body. *Put that table with the glasses more to the side so nobody will jam it in passing.*—(Bdos) **2.** *vb tr* (CarA) [*IF*] To deliberately bounce, shove, or thrust against (sb/sth) with the body (esp with the backside). *... but worst of all the sidewalks were blocked too much by people (mostly from the country districts). Having to hustle from Rose Place to Long Wall is a burdensome task, pushing and jamming through bunches of people who congregate in the centre of the pavement, in threes, sixes and eights.*—ViN (76.05.21, p.5) **3.** *vb tr* (Guyn, Trin) [*AF*] To strike hard and suddenly. **a.** *The last man! He jus[t] go out the[re] and jam them two sixes and match done!*—(Trin) **b.** *She was running across the road and a car jam her down.*—Guyn (Ms) **4.** *vb intr* (CarA) To dance vigorously with abandon (usu in a crowd). *Two women jamming, man hold you own, don't let we down. Jam! Jam! Jam! Them women come to jam and all ah we jamming to sweet pan. Action was yesterday at the Queen's Park Savannah in the North and East Panorama preliminaries.*—SuP (80.02.04, p.1) [By extension of sense 2., the dancing partners often allowing their bodies to bounce against each other] **5.** *vb tr, intr* (CarA) [*AF*] [Of dance music] To play or to be played loudly in order to excite vigorous dancing. **a.** *... and the Community Centre was hot as Fatman Bopeep with Brass start to jam a heavy Kaiso that could very well make the Road March.*—TaP (77.02.13, p.6) **b.** *While dances are due to begin at eight o'clock, the music starts to jam from as early as 6.30. This is a warm-up period during which passersby can hear a sample of what's in store for the night.*—VoS (76.05.08, p.5) [By shift of sense 4.]

jam² *n* **1.** (Bdos, Guyn) An unintended or accidental blow. *The ferry gave the wharf a good jam and broke some planks.*—Guyn (Ms) [By functional vb > n shift of JAM¹ 1.] **2.** (CarA) A crowded, jolly dance-party with plenty of loud, vigorous music. *As part of its continuing community outreach programme, the Holy Innocents Old Scholars Association is holding a 'jam' this evening at the St Thomas-based school.*—AdV (87.11.21, p.8) [By functional vb > n shift of JAM¹ 4.]

ja·maat [jama·t] *n* (Guyn, Trin) [Indic] A congregation of Muslim religious believers identified with a particular mosque, and having responsibility for their own operation within Muslim religious rules; [by extension] a Muslim movement organized through such a congregation. *The annual general meeting of the Kitty Jamaat which will be held on October 30, will consider two motions of far reaching importance to the general membership of the organisation.*—GyC (77.10.18, p.2) [Urdu < Perso-arabic *jama'at* 'meeting; assembly; congregation']

Ja·mai·ca-ac·kee *n* (StVn) ‖ACKEE (CarA)

Ja·mai·ca-ap·ple *n* (Baha) ‖CUSTARD-APPLE (CarA)

Ja·mai·can *n, adj* (CarA) 1. (A person or thing) native to, belonging to, or typical of Jamaica. 2. ‖JAMAICANESE *n* (Jmca) Jamaican is a highly melodic language. Rhetorical negatives appear for the music's sake. *'The proof of the pudding is in the eating' might become 'De proof of the pudding nat ina da eating, den?'. So, in trying to seek a combination of the authentic and the universally comprehensible, I found found myself at the center of a language poised between defiance and translation, for pure Jamaican is comprehensible only to Jamaicans*— WOB:155.

Ja·mai·can bun *n phr* (CarA) ‖ *bun* (Jmca) A dark heavy sweet pan-loaf made with raisins, citron, and spices.

Ja·mai·can·ese *n* (Jmca) ‖ *Jamaican* (Jmca) The CREOLIZED ENGLISH of Jamaica; the whole range of English developed in and characteristic of Jamaica. *In Jamaicanese the word 'rude' often refers to anyone who is openly defiant of constituted authority*—NMM:95.

Ja·mai·can·i·za·tion *n* (CarA) The process or policy of JAMAICANIZING. *A leading Jamaican businessman, Mr Leslie Ashenheim, has said the concept of Jamaicanization can be applied to some sectors of the country's economy, but in other areas it is neither practical nor possible.*—AdN (72.04.12, p.3)

Ja·mai·can·ize *vb tr* (CarA) To make (sth, such as institution, festival, etc) markedly Jamaican in character, appearance, and/or function.

Ja·mai·can pa·tois [Jəmekən patwa] *n phr* (CarA) Jamaican CREOLE. *She said it was unbelievable to hear what some of the waiters were saying about the tourists, in Jamaican patois, of course.*—WeG (73.02.28, p.3) □ This traditional and generally *Derog* term is properly replaced by **Jamaican Creole**. See CREOLE¹ 3(i)

Ja·mai·can pat·ty *n phr* (CarA) ‖ *patty* (Jmca) A light brown, semi-circular pastry, about 6 ins in diameter, with a filling of seasoned, minced meat folded in it; it is commonly used as a snack.

Ja·mai·ca-pep·per /1'2211/ *n* (Trin) ‖ALL-SPICE (CarA)

Ja·mai·ca-plum* *n* (Bdos, BrVi, Gren, Tbgo, Trin) ‖ *Bequia-plum* (StVn) ‖ *big-plum* (CayI) ‖ *bubby-plum* (Bdos, Tbgo) ‖ *cerise, governor-plum* (Tbgo, Trin) ‖ *chilli-plum* (Antg, Bdos, Gren, Tbgo, Trin) ‖ *coco-plum* 3. (TkCa) ‖ *hog-plum* (Baha, TkCa) ‖ *leather-coat plum* (CayI, Jmca) ‖ *May plum* (Belz) ‖ *plum* (Dmca, Gren, Nevs) ‖ *pwinn Mowis, pwinn tété* (StLu) ‖ *red-coat plum* (Jmca) ‖ *red-plum* (CayI) ‖ *scarlet-plum* (Baha, TkCa) ‖ *sweet-plum* (Baha) A red or purple fruit about 1-1/4 ins long, rounded, constricted at the lower end, with a large seed covered by a scant, sweet pulp with slightly leathery but edible skin; it is borne on a low, spreading tree wh sheds all its leaves in the dry season; *Spondias purpurea (Anacardiaceae).* [Prob introduced to the ECar, where it is known by this name, from *Jmca* where, however, it appears to be known rather as **red-coat plum**] □ The similarity in the appearance of the trees (though not of the fruits) of this and the related **chilli plum**, and possibly also the similar taste of their pulp, sometimes causes confusion in the vernacular names.

ja·mette (ja·met) *n* (Dmca, Gren, StLu, Tbgo, Trin) [*AF—Derog*] See DJA(N)MÈT

jam·ming¹ *n* (CarA) 1. Dancing with abandon in a crowd excited by loud vigorous music. *To me Las Lap is the real get-down time. Women and their men (or their men-for-season as the case might be) just grind against each other in the jamming.*—Peo I. 8, p.33 2. A type of loud popular music with a vigorous beat intended to excite a dancing crowd. *Indeed, the majority of masqueraders claim that the jamming of brass provides for a sweeter jump up than the sound of steel.*—TrG (Souvenir, 1977, p.22) [Vbl nouns < JAM¹ 4. and 5.]

jam·ming² *n* (Tbgo, Trin) [*AF/IF*] Severe criticism and/or aggressive pursuit; verbal or active attack. **a.** *Black boys in this country who have married white women are in for some heavy jamming, as a controversy over black-white love shakes the pages of Sunday Punch.*—SuP (74.07.14, p.11) **b.** *Because of the heavy jamming the local pushers and cultivators have been getting from the cops, they have now taken to importing the stuff.*—BoM (79.11.02, p.19) [Extension as vbl n of JAM¹ 2.]

ja·moon* ['Jamu·n] *n* (Guyn) ‖ *black-berry* (Belz) ‖ *damson* (Belz) ‖ *ebony-berry* (Angu) ‖ *jamur* (Bdos) ‖ *Java-plum* (Antg, Jmca) A dark-purple, shiny, and very thin-skinned plum, ovoid and about an inch long, with a rich, juicy, sweet-sour, purple pulp around its single oval seed; it is borne in small clusters on a tall tree with foot-long, lance-shaped leaves; *Syzygium cumini (Myrtaceae).* [Hin *jaamun* 'black plum']

jam-ses·sion *n* (CarA) [*AF*] Any event in wh there is a large, noisy crowd. *Well Tanty used to shop in this grocery every Saturday morning. It does be jam a jam-session there when all the spade housewives go to buy, and Tanty in the lead.*—STLL:62 [A borrowing from AmE *jam session*, (cp also JAM² n 2.) but extended in sense, much infl by JAM¹ vb 2.]

ja·mur ['Jamu·r] *n* (Bdos) ‖JAMOON (Guyn)

jan·dhi *n* (Guyn, Trin) See JHANDI

Jane-and-Lou·i·sa *n* (CarA) A children's ring-game in wh each player or pair of players, successively chosen, mime or act as ordered according to the lines of a song; their part ends with 'Jane and Louisa will now come home' sung to the same tune.

Jan·ku·nu ['jaŋkunu] *n* (Belz) See JUNKANOO

jap·pa-jap·pa *adv* (Gren, StLu) [*AF*] [Of work, personal appearance, etc] In a rough, indifferent manner; crudely. *The man cut the grass so jappa-jappa dat A had to get somebody to do it again.*—(Gren) [Cp Yoruba *ADMY jaba-jaba* 'higgledy-piggledy'; also *jagba-jagba* 'waywardness'; also *KED* Krio *jagbajagba* 'worthless stuff']

jas·mine *n* 1.* (CarA) A climbing or straggling shrub of several varieties, sometimes growing wild but usu cultivated, bearing fragrant, starshaped flowers (white, yellow, purplish, or red); *Jasminum spp* (*Oleaceae*). 2. (CayI) ‖ FRANGIPANI (CarA) [The *CayI* name may be due to some resemblances in the appearance, fragrance and use of the flowers of the two plants. Cp also *CED jasmine* 2., *red jasmine* 'frangipani'; also *CGBD jessamine* (*Bdos*) 'sometimes used to refer to the frangipani tree or blossom']

Ja·va-plum *n* 1. (Antg, Jmca) ‖ JAMOON (Guyn) 2. (Dmca, Mrat, StVn) ‖ ROSE-APPLE (CarA)

jaw *PHRASE* **band your jaw** *vb phr* (Trin) [*AF*] ‖ BAND YOUR BELLY (Bdos, etc) See BAND² *Phr*

jeal·ous *vb tr* (Tbgo, Trin) [*X*] To be jealous of (sb). *Tell me, Suruj Poopa, what cause I have to jealous a thin little woman who can't even make a baby?*—NTMM:136

jeal·ous·y (**jeal·ous·ie**) [jɛlʌsi ~ jɒlʌsi] *n* (CarA) [*X*] A jalousie. *I had looked through the jealousies of the always closed windows at white men leaning over their green-topped billiard table.*—SBBAM:41 [By misascription of spelling, or folk etym (a ref to peeping). Cp *OED jealousy* 6. = jalousie + cit 1834] □ It is more convenient to keep this item distinct from the SE abstract n *jealousy*.

jeal·ous·y-door/-win·dow *n* (Bdos, StVn) A door or window, the two leaves of wh are slatted like a jalousie.

Jees!; **Jeez[e]-an[d]-ages!** [ji·z-an-e]ız] *excl* (Tbgo, Trin) (Euphemism for) Jesus! as expressing astonishment, disgust, etc. *Jeese n' ages, boy, I could be a sailorman every dam' time I see the sea!*—MHBT:99

jel·ly-co·co·nut; **jel.ly-nut** *n* (CarA) A young but fully developed coconut sold for the sweetish liquid or 'water' and white jelly that lines the inside.

jeng-jeng¹ *n* (Belz, Jmca) [*AF—Derog*] **1.** Any worthless or disorderly collection of things. *They put the woman's few jeng-jeng outside and moved the house on rollers. The woman had to sleep on the piazza where she caught a bad, bad cold.*—BGSB:6 **2.** A state of confusion or disorderliness (including personal appearance).

jeng-jeng² *adj* (Belz) [*AF—Derog*] Disreputable in appearance; unpleasant to see or hear. *Heavens, as soon as the morning devotions are over, jeng-jeng music starts spewing forth from this radio station.*—BeA (81.03.14, p.8)

jep *n* (Dmca, StLu) See DJÈP

jeps [jɛps] *adj* (Nevs, StKt) [*AF*] ‖ FAST 1. (CarA) *She too jeps—she always want to know everybody business.*—(StKt) [Perh < GYPSY (*Bdos*) with same sense, or < JEP (*Dmca, StLu*) by functional n > adj shift (+ paragogic /s/) referring to waspish behaviour]

jerk-pork *n* (Jmca) Strips of pork or wild-hog, highly seasoned and peppered, then barbecued or smoke-cured over a wood-fire, the wood, esp ALLSPICE, being chosen to add the special flavour. [< *jerked pork* via Jmca Cr. The vb *jerk* < So Am Sp *charquear* 'to cut up and dry-cure meat'. *OED jerk* vb² gives the source as Peruvian Quechua, but the term must have had other Amerindian cognates (cp *DGEG* Guarani *chiriri* 'to be fried') as it seems to have been adopted early by the Jmca Maroons, prob from Sp contact. The term is almost limited to *Jmca* in CE]

jer·sey ['jə·(r)si] *n* (StVn) ‖ **gansey, vest-shirt** (Bdos) A T-shirt, esp a coloured one.

Jew *n* *PHRASE* **a Jew and a crown** *n phr* (Guyn) [*X*] See JOE *Phr*

Jew-fish (**dew-fish**) *n* 1.* (CarA) A very large brownish fish with a broad, bull-dog-like mouth; it can grow up to 6 ft in length, 500 lbs in weight, and is said to be so lazy that it can be taken without moving while lying on the sea-bed among reefs; it is of very good food value; *Epinephelus* (*Promicrops*) *itaiara* (*Serranidae*). **2.** (Guyn) A very large river fish wh can attain a weight of over 300 lbs and is of good food value; *Plectropoma chlorurum*—RFLG:68. □ The spelling *dew-fish* occurs as a free alternative in *Guyn*. The preference for *Jew-fish* prob relates to the use of this spelling in fishing literature for other very large edible ocean fishes, such as that in sense 1. Neither spelling is etymologically accounted for.

Jew-plum (**dew-plum, June-plum**) [ju(n)-plʌm] *n* 1. (Jmca) ‖ GOLDEN-APPLE (Bdos, etc) 2. (CayI) ‖ DUNKS (Bdos, etc)

jhan·di (**jan.dhi**) ['jhandi] *n* (Guyn, Trin) [Indic] **1.** ‖ *coolie-flag* [*Derog*], ‖ *prayer-flag* (Guyn, Trin) A small, triangular, red or saffroncoloured flag mounted on a tall bamboo pole to show that a ceremony of thanksgiving (usu to the Hindu deity Hanuman) has been held at that home; in some cases a yellow and/or a white flag is also used in ref to other deities. [Hin *jhaṇḍi* 'a small flag'] **2.** [By extension, often cap Jhandi] The religious ceremony of thanksgiving to Hanuman, performed by a pandit; it is held on a Tuesday or a Saturday. **a.** *Belated birthday greetings go out to Mother Dora Latchmie of Better Hope.... Heard she celebrated the occasion with a 'jhandi' at the Kalli Church, Better Hope.*—GyC (77.11.20, p.18) **b.** *He looked toward Gurudeva's kuti, and added: 'He have a spite for me, too; think I ain't go to he jhandi for sake of malice.'*—NAGOS:80

jhin·gie* (ǥhin·gee, ǥhin·gie, gin·gee) [ʒɪŋgi] *n* (Guyn) A type of green squash about 12 ins in length with a tough, ridged skin, borne on a sturdy climbing vine; the green fruit is commonly used in curry and the dried fruit, stripped of its skin, is used as a fibrous scrubber; *Luffa acutangula (Cucurbitaceae)*. [Bhoj < Hin *jhinggii*, name of this fruit vegetable]

jig·ger [ʒɪɡʌ ~ ʒɪɡa] *n* (CarA) See CHIGO(E), a form with wh it appears to alternate freely in some territories. *The father told me that about two weeks previously she had a jigger in her foot. It had burrowed in very deep, and he had cut it out with his knife.*—TrI (70.05.09, p.3) [Prob of W Afr orig. See note at CHIGO]

jill *n* (Guyn) See GILL

jim·be·lin *n* (Jmca) See JIMBLING

jim·bling (jim·be·lin) ['ʒɪmblɪŋ ~ ʒɪmbəlɪn] *n* (Jmca) **1.** ‖ GOOSEBERRY (Bdos, etc) (Also called SHORT JIMBELIN in this sense in *Jmca*) **2.** ‖ BIMBLING (BLIMBING) (Gren, Jmca) (Also called LONG JIMBELIN in this sense in *Jmca*) □ See note at BIMBLING.

jim-boots *n* (Trin) [X] See GYM-BOOTS [By pop etym < *gym*(nasium) + boots]

Jim·my-jar; Jim.my-John *n* (Bdos, Belz, Guyn, StVn) [X] A demijohn; a large bulging bottle, able to contain several gallons of rum and often encased in wicker-work for protection. *There was always a big, round bottle of rum known as the Jimmy John, usually the grand prize.*—Bdos (Ms, 1975) [By folk etym + regressive assimilation < IAE *demijohn* (itself evid a corruption. See long note in *OED*)]

jin·al *n, vb* (Belz, Jmca) See GINAL

jing-ping *n* (Dmca) A folk band consisting of goat-skin drums, a GRAGE, an accordion, and sometimes a banjo or a guitar; it accompanies the street-dancing of masqueraders.

jip [ʒip] *n* (Dmca, StLu A simpler version of the WÒB DWIYÈT, with a lace-necked, white cotton blouse, and bright-coloured, usu knee-length skirt and longer, white petticoat; it is traditional dress and now one form of the national costume. [< Fr *jupe* 'skirt']

jip·pi-jap·pa [ʒɪpi-ʒapa] *n* **1.*** (Belz, Jmca) A beige, fine-textured straw, the fibre of the long, palm-like leaf-blades of a flowering tropical American shrub; it is used for delicate straw-work, esp patterned hats; *Carludovica palmata* or *C. jamaicensis, etc (Cyclanthaceae)*. [A spelling pronunc < SDGA Am Sp *Jipijapa*, a town in Ecuador; the town prob owes its name to the straw wh is widely indigenous in Central Amer] **2.** A panama hat. [By extension of sense 1.]

jit·ney *n* **1.** (Baha) ‖ MINI-BUS (Bdos, Jmca) *A jitney service takes shoppers to and from town to get the things not available in the area.*—TrI (70.05.19, p.6) □ Also *IF* AmE. See *WCD9*. **2.** (Trin) A van or a small truck used for general transportation of goods and materials; it is now considered an old-fashioned vehicle. □ Re sense 2., see PICK-UP² **3.** (Baha) [AF—Derog] A young woman of loose morals. [By metaph extension of sense 1.]

jive¹ [ʒaɪv] *n* (CarA) [AF] Slangy, shallow talk; glib chat; deceitful nonsense. *Don't think I don't try, but they all say, 'yes, but who else are you giving that jive to?'*—JPB:113 [Prob a loan from Black AmE, an extended sense of *jive* 'dance characterized by much individualistic release, improvization, etc'. Cp also AmE/BrE slang *all that jazz* with similar sense]

jive² [ʒaɪv] *vb intr* (CarA) [AF] **1.** ‖ OLD-TALK² (Tbgo, Trin) *But I and Winston were talking, just jiving a little bit to break the monotony somehow, about this lawyer who looked so 'nice' and so on, and we remained where we were.*—Peo I. 6 p.113 **2.** [By extension] To talk nonsense deliberately; to deceive by foolish talk. *Another witness said he was told by one of the robbers: 'We're not jiving, man. This is for real.'*—BeS (74.11.16, p.8) [By functional n > vb shift of JIVE¹]

Jo-and-John·nie *n* (Bdos) [Hist] A dance in wh the partners face each other and develop a back-and-forth, foot to foot movement with the man ultimately straddling the woman's open legs; it was popular in former times among labourers at CROP-OVER celebrations, and is said to be the survival of an African fertility dance.

job·ber(-man) *n* (Guyn) A man who makes a living by carrying loads for people, esp to or from the public market. [From SE vb intr *job* 'to do jobs', with restricted sense]

job·bie¹ (job·by¹) *n* (Bdos) [AF—Joc] ‖ kuka (Mrat) ‖ kuku (ViIs) ‖ kungse (Guyn) ‖ pupu (Antg, Dmca) ‖ tutu (ECar) An infant's bowel movement (esp if on the floor).

job·bie² (job·by²) *vb* (jobbied; jobbying) (Bdos) [AF—Joc] ‖ kungse (Guyn) ‖ pupu

(Antg, Dmca) ‖ *tutu* (ECar) [Of an infant] To defecate.

job-print·er·y *n* (CarA) A small printer's shop that undertakes small printing jobs. □ Also AmE, but not BrE.

Job's tears* *n phr pl* (Bdos, Guyn, Jmca, Trin) ‖ *buck-bead* 4. (Guyn) ‖ *jumbie-bead* 5. (Guyn) The hard, grey, glossy, oval and bead-like fruit of a sturdy, waxy grass wh flourishes in wet places; *Coix lachryma-jobi* (*Gramineae*). [The biblical ref to Job may be due to the tear-drop shape and mournful colour]

joe *n* (Guyn) [Hist] 1. A gold coin, later a note, the value of wh was 22 GUILDERS; it was a Dutch unit of currency used in Guyana up to the late 19C. [< *Johannes*, name of a Pg gold coin—*PCBC:31*] 2. PHRASE 2.1 **cost a joe and a crown** *vb phr* (Guyn) To cost an exceedingly high price. [JOE (as above) + *crown*, the eighth part of a Br pound sterling] □ This phr is still used, sometimes in a corrupted form, *a Jew and a crown*, by older folk.

Joe Heath's (Joe Heap mare) *n phr* (Bdos) [*AF—Joc*] 1. A (proverbial) work-horse. 2. PHRASE 2.1 **like Joe Heath's (Joe Heap) mare** *adj phr* (Bdos) [*AF—Joc*] Exerting yourself noticeably; behaving in an excited, over-busy manner.

John-Bull [Jambʊl] *n* (Antg) A male masquerader who wears a CROCUS-BAG costume stuffed, esp below the waist, with cane-trash and rags; he is accompanied by a drummer who also cracks a long whip at him as he clowns, frightens onlookers, and gets money from them; he appears at Carnival and Christmas time. [Prob a caricature of the white English planter]

John Ca·noe (John Con·nu) *n phr* (Belz, Jmca) See JUNKANOO

John-Ca·noe sticks *n phr* (Belz) Stilts. [From the regular use of stilts by the John Canoe (JUNKANOO) dancers in *Belz*]

John-Charles *n* (Belz, Jmca) One of two or three wild, bushy shrubs from wh an infusion or 'tea' is made as a folk-remedy for colds or 'cleaning the system'; *Hyptis verticillata* (*Labiatae*) or *Cordia globosa* (*Boraginaceae*).

John Crow *n phr* (Belz, Jmca) 1. ‖ CARRION-CROW (Guyn, Jmca) *The birds are a constant joy, even the John Crow, so ugly on the ground with his burial ground plumage and red bald head, but so magnificent in the air. He is not a crow at all, but a vulture of the kind known in North America as Turkey Buzzard or Turkey Vulture.*—SJW:86 [By folk etym < [čaŋkro < kyaŋkro < kyarɪnkro] by palatalization followed by affrication] □ It is sometimes used [AF—Derog] of a person. 2. PHRASE 2.1 **in hog heaven and John Crow**

paradise *adj phr* (Belz) [*AF—Joc*] See HEAVEN Phr 2.

John-Crow bead *n phr* (Belz, Jmca) ‖ JUMBIE-BEAD 1. (Brbu, etc) [Prob from association by some people with misfortune or death, as is also the bird JOHN CROW. Cp ‖ JUMBIE BEAD] □ See also BEAD-VINE BUSH (Nevs, StKt) and ‖.

john·ny-bake *n* (Trin) ‖ BAKE¹ (CarA)

john·ny-cake(s) *n* (*usu pl*) 1. (CarA) ‖ BAKE(s)¹ 2. (Bdos, etc) *Breakfast was all that it should be on Christmas Day. Sprat and his father laid the table and made toast and tea, while Mrs Morrison got ready the fried fish and johnny-cakes which was Mr Morrison's favourite dish.*—DISM:155 2. (Angu) ‖ BAKE(s)¹ 4. (Antg, Dmca) *Bake johnny-cakes in an oven or a pot with fire coals covering the top and serve with butter and eggs, etc (as bread).*—Angu (Ms, 1973) [Perh a corruption of *journey-cake* (see *DAE*), but just as likely from a popular use of *Johnny* as a casual universal name for sb or sth not precisely identified but generally well-known] □ The variety of preparations of the same basic ingredients—flour, sugar, salt, water—whether fried or baked, makes it difficult to define this item rigidly; the one common feature is the popular use of the preparation as a special addition to breakfast. Usu written without capital 'J'.

John·ny-just-come /2'312/ *n* (Guyn) [*AF—Joc*] ‖ JUST-COME (Antg, etc)

John Pub·lic *n phr* (CarA) (A collective term for) the ordinary citizen; (SE) John Citizen. *The Premier would be very well advised to make a thorough investigation into this Ministry of Health.... John Public does not seem to think that all is well in this Ministry.*—ViN (76.06.11, p.4)

joke¹ *n* (CarA) 1. A jest; [often applied to situations] an amusing case, event, etc. 2. PHRASES 2.1 **best of the joke** *n phr* (CarA) [*IF*] The funniest part of an incident being described. *But I ain[′t] gi[ve] yo[u] de bes[t] o[f] de joke yet! Was when the wife open the door, my dear!*—(Bdos) 2.2 **for no joke; not for a joke** *adv phr* (Bdos) [*AF—Joc*] By no means; certainly not. *Christine, I wouldn't do anything at all to hurt her for a joke. Christine, I love this girl very very bad.*—NaT (76.09.12, p.18, Dear Christine) □ But cp FOR Phr 3.1 FOR (A) JOKE. 2.3 **give joke(s)** *vb phr* (CarA) [*AF*] To tell jokes; to entertain by telling amusing tales. *They were just sitting by the bridge liming and giving joke and so.*—(Tbgo) 2.3.1 **give sb the joke** *vb phr* (CarA) [*IF—Joc*] To tell sb a scandalous or interesting (not necessarily amusing) piece of news. *Well hear the joke now! Let me give you the joke! He go in the room smilin[g] expectin[g] to get the job, cock sure! The people tell him, Sir, —that he not qualified! Buff!*—(Trin) 2.4 **Joke is joke!** *id phr* (Guyn, Tbgo, Trin) [*AF*] Enough is enough!; Let there be an end to this nonsense! *Look, joke is joke, y[ou] hear! If I hit yo[u] don[′t] say I ain[′t] tell* *yo[u]!*—(Guyn) **2.5 Joke you making!** *id phr* (Gren, Trin) [*AF*] You can't be serious!; Don't be ridiculous! *The Minister of Finance could only state with regard to planning, that a working document is now in the hands of the Ministers ... Exactly; you never had a document at all ... joke you making! Mr Minister of Finance knows better than that; he knows, he knows.*—Gren (Hd, 78.04.28, p.146) **2.6 like joke** *adv phr* (Tbgo, Trin) [*AF*] In great abundance; plentifully. *Them days the Government spendin[g] money like joke! Now we getting licks like joke!*—(Trin) **2.7 No joke!** *id phr* (ECar) [*AF/IF*] Seriously!; I do mean it! *So let we see if we could find the problems that are involved / Decide how we will get them solved / No joke, I beg you to help make Caricom work.*—Bdos (Cso—Sir Don, 1975) □ Also occurs in *IF* AmE. **2.8 (not) make joke /fun/ sport with (sb/sth)** *vb phr* (ECar) [*AF*] (Not) to be hesitant, indecisive, or casual in dealing with (sb/sth). *Boysie, watch dis late-comin[g] yo[u] goin[g] on with, yeh! This man don['t] make joke to fire people, yo[u] know!*—(Gren)

joke² *adj* (CarA) [*AF*] Ridiculous; nonsensical; phoney. **a.** *We could have more than gotten forty or fifty million US from OPEC; but we get three hundred and fifty thousand joke dollars because they recognise what Grenada, sadly, Mr Speaker, has now become ... one of the recognised latrine countries of the world, with international fascist connections.*—Gren (Hd, 77.07.20, p.21) **b.** *We have found ourselves in this serious situation which makes the whole Chamber look like nonsense, and if we keep on eroding the rules and regulations of the House we will soon become a joke Parliament.*—Bdos (Hd, 73.03.16, p.1942) [By functional n > adj shift of JOKE¹ n]

joke³ (at) (sb) *vb (phr)* (Jmca, Tbgo, Trin) [*AF/IF*] To make fun of (sb); to tease (sb) without malice. **a.** *'Missa Mark,' Lyn joked him from the stool where she sat, looking up from the bowl of rice. 'Missa Mark, you don't know, no, dat it's out of season fe' shootin' bird? Suppose de police catch you shootin' bird dis time of year. Dem lock you up, you know.' 'Cho,' said Mark, 'they wouldn't trouble me.' ... joking her back. 'They don't trouble white people.'*—HVUW:35 **b.** *Those who were not directly affected by the notice joked at the others, telling them they would have to take in washing and keep livestock.*—SABS:107 [By functional n > vb shift of JOKE¹ n]

jok·er *n* (CarA) [*AF—Derog*] A person in authority who is doing his job with annoying incompetence; a person who is considered a disgrace to his post or profession.

jok·ey¹ [Joki] *adj* (ECar) [*AF—Joc*] Ridiculous; amusing; absurd. *The Honourable Leader of the House, whose job and duty it is to move the Motion calling for the setting up of that Committee, keeps promising, in that usual jokey way, 'Yes, we go do it soon, yes it coming soon, yes, next time.'*—Gren (Hd, 78.12.01, p.52) [< joke + y by analogy with SE *funny, messy,* etc]

jok·ey² [Joki] *vb tr* (Belz) [*AF/IF*] To make a fool of. *I write not with intention to criticize or jokey anybody, but to tell it like it is.*—ReP (80.01.13, p.2) □ Often occurs in the phr **to jokey yourself** 'to make a fool of yourself'.

jok·i·fy (jok·i·fie(d)) [Jokifai(d)] *adj* (Gren, Jmca, StVn, Tbgo, Trin) [*AF—Joc*] [Of a person] Jolly; amusing in conversation and behaviour. **a.** *A fos [h]e jokify, eh? When he aroun[d] yo[u] boun[d] to laugh.*—(Gren) **b.** *And slim little Ella was spreading at the hips.... Taylor had teased her and said 'All them who was laughing soon want touch, for seeing is believing but touching is the naked truth', and he would sing the last part. Taylor was like that, so jokify.*—BM:49. [< joke + suff *ify,* by *Joc* analogy from such a form as IAE *Frenchify;* thence its functioning as Cr universal vbl form including pa. part. adj.]

jo·la¹ *n* (Gren) **1.** A large jute bag. **2.** [*AF—Joc*] A handbag that is unbecomingly large.

jo·la² *n* (Nevs) A flat-bottomed little boat, propelled by oars and used for coastal fishing.

jol·li·fi·ca·tion *n* (Angu) ‖ LEND-HAND (Tbgo) *Since they had no money with which to hire labour, they pooled their strength and worked for each other in an exchange labour system; the 'combite' of Haiti, the 'lift system' of the Leeward Islands, or a 'jollification' in which a man who wanted some work done invited his friends and neighbours and provided a hot meal and rum, but made no other payment.*—SWI:152

jom·bi(e) (jom·bay) *n* (ECar) See JUMBIE

Jo·nah¹ *n* (Guyn) [*AF—Joc*] PHRASE **bring/ put (your) Jonah on (sb/sth)** *vb phr* (Guyn) [*AF—Joc*] ‖ PUT YOUR BAD-MOUTH ON (SB/STH) (CarA) See BAD-MOUTH¹ Phr 3.2 *'Everything was going all right until you come and bring your Jonah on the place',* she said as she looked at the mess of spilt milk and sugar. *'Why you don't go away?'* —Guyn (Ms) [From bibl association of the name Jonah with misfortune]

Jo·nah² *vb tr* (Guyn) [*AF—Joc*] ‖ PUT YOUR BAD-MOUTH ON (SB/STH) (CarA) *Somebody like they Jonah this wo[r]k, because all the try you try wit[h] it you can['t] get nowhe[re].*—(Guyn) [By functional n > vb shift of JONAH¹]

jon·jo *n* (Belz) See JUNJO

Jon·ka·noo (Jon·kon·nu) *n* (Baha, Belz) See JUNKANOO

jook¹ (juck¹, juick, juk¹) [Jʊk ~ Jʌk] *vb* (CarA) [*AF/IF*] ‖ **chook** (ECar) **1.** *vb tr* To poke, stab, or wound (sb). **a.** *He start jooking me under me arm with his hands and asking if I know him.*—Tbgo (CR, 1978) **b.** *Brer Bookie pulled Brer Rabbie's hand away from the barrel saying, 'Boy, stop juicking yer finger in dat crack!'*—TOSR:14 **c.** *W— said that after the tyre was* *stuck, V— came out and went to 'juck' the accused with a knife and she blocked his hand from 'jucking'* H—.—AdN (73.05.03, p.1) **2.** *vb tr* [Esp of thorns, etc] To prick or pierce (the skin). **a.** *Where the ground was soft, where hard; where the grass jooked the bare undertoes, where it was welcoming and soft as a feather.*—SCE:51 **b.** *Don['t] climb picka tree why Picka go juk you.*— Gren (Song) **3.** *vb tr* [Of a doctor] To give an injection. **a.** *I did not dare to risk toothache in a foreign land, where the simple English of, 'Oh gorm, man, yuh jookin the wrong tooth!' might have been taken for approval and encouragement.*—TrG (73.07.11, p.6) **b.** *He eeze rite up ter mer, quiet-like, an he jook mer quick in mer arm heavy.*—JBJ: 88 **4.** *vb intr, tr* [Vul] [Of a man] To have crude sexual intercourse (with). *On reaching home Rufus asked for sex but Molly refused to comply and said she will make him see some trouble. He then replied 'If you do not give me, I will juke it.'*—ToR (77.10.26, p.3) **5.** *vb tr* (Baha) To dig meat out of a conch. *Twenty-five conchs were broken, jooked and slopped in an incredible six minutes and fifty seconds by John Reckley of Rocky Creek.*—NaG (75.10.01, p.7) **6.** *vb intr* [Cricket] To bat defensively, keeping a straight bat, stealing the occasional run. *De 'Holy Ghost' stretch down de wicket an 'e jook an 'e poke like tings tight.*— SNWIC:108 (B. St John) [The word has phonic correlates in a number of Afr langs. Cp Mende *jɔkɔ* 'to enter, go in'; Fulani *jukka* 'to poke, knock down (as fruit)'; Hausa *duka* (in coarse talk) 'to have intercourse with a woman'; Tsonga *jukula* 'to dig up grass when clearing land'; Nembe *joku* 'to jut out, protrude'; etc. However, the coincidence of European sources through sailor contact may have reinforced use and spread of the item. Cp Du *deuken* 'to dent' *SND* Sc dial *jouk, jook, juck* 'to duck, dodge, cheat'—this last being of special note re Phr 7.3.2 below. In regard to sense 4. above, note also the development of Black AmE *juke-house* 'a brothel'. Re sense 5. and Phr 7.3.1. cp also AmE *shuck* 'to remove (oysters) from the shell' wh is listed as of unknown origin in *W3 shuck* vb³ 2.] □ The spelling *jook* is the most frequent, taking CE as a whole; *juck* is common in *Bdos*, *juick* in Baha. Only the form JOOK is used in the head-phrases listed below. **7.** *PHRASES* **7.1 jook at (sb/sth)** *vb phr* (CarA) [AF/IF] To stab or make a thrust at (sb/sth) with a sharp-pointed instrument. *Said the accused: 'I began to juck at him. He dropped the bottle, say ah and started to back off. I looked at the knife and saw blood.'*—AdN (76.04.22, p.1) **7.2 jook down (fruit)** *vb phr* To pick fruit (esp coconuts) by poking at the cluster or truss with a long pole. [Cp Fulani *jukka* in etym above] **7.3 jook out** *vb phr* (CarA) [AF] To stick out; to show up as being out of line. *Some say one mountain did sink in de sea an' leave all 'ee peaks jookin' out.*—WBS:13 **7.3.1 jook out (sth)** *vb phr* **(i)** (CarA) [IF] To poke or prise (sth) out (such as an animal or crab out of a hole, the hard kernel out of a coconut, etc). **(ii)** (Bdos, Tbgo, Trin) [AF] [Of clothes] To scrub (clothes on a scrubbing-board). [A ref to the action + getting out the dirt] **7.3.2 jook out sb's eye(s)** *vb phr*

(CarA) [AF—*Joc*] To cheat (sb) in a business deal. *How you could only put in three dollars in gas in de man car, when you know he hand you five dollars? But just because you know he didn't looking at de pump you juck out his eyes.*—Bdos (Ms Play, 1979) [Cp Sc dial *jouk* in etym note above] **7.4 jook your mouth in (sth)** *vb phr* (CarA) [AF] To rush to offer an unsolicited opinion; to embarrass by speaking out of turn. *Not me I ain't juking me mouth in Politics / I would sing about anything but Politics.*—Bdos (Cso—Sir Don, 1975)

jook² (**juick²**, **juk²**) *n* (CarA) [AF/IF] ‖ **chook** (ECar) **1.** A jab or a poke; a wound caused by sth sharp. **a.** *She gave the husband a good jook in the ribs with her elbow to stop him saying too much.*—(Antg) **b.** *One night about 10:00 p.m. I had to call him to take me to the hospital as I was suffering from a nail jook in my feet. He willingly came and took me to the Hospital.*—BeB (65.08.14, p.2) **2.** An injection. *Nurse gave me a jook on this hand yesterday already.*—(Jmca)

jook·ing-board (**juck·ing-board**) *n* (Bdos, Gren, Guyn, Tbgo, Trin) ‖ SCRUBBING BOARD (CarA) [From JOOK¹ Phr 7.3.1 (ii)]

joo·koo·too *adj* (Gren) See JOUKOUTOO

joom [jʊm] *vb intr* (Guyn) [Marbles] To lunge and toss your marble, aiming it at one set on the ground.

Jor·dan·ite *n* (Guyn) A Black, Christian sect whose religious dress is a white turban or head-tie with a long, white robe tied at the waist; they are noted for their open-air, Saturday night meetings, loud Old Testament readings, and fundamentalist interpretations. [From their founder Nathaniel Jordan of Agricola Village, near Georgetown (1921)]

Jo·seph('s) coat* *n phr* (Bdos, Brbu, Jmca) ‖ **Jacob's coat** (Bdos, Guyn) A bushy plant with variegated and usu spear-shaped leaves, ranging in colour from deep purple and red, to green and yellow; it is a popular hedge plant for garden-beds and there are many hybrids; *Coleus blumei* (Labiatae). [A ref to *Gen 38:23* '[Joseph's] coat of many colours'] □ Often referred to as *Coleus* in gardening literature.

jou·kou·too (**djou·kou·too, jusqu'à vous**) [Jukutu] *pron, adj* (Gren) [AF—*Joc/Derog*] **1.** *pron* Even you; insignificant you. *Eh eh! But you dam[ned] rude! Joukoutoo want to wash yo[ur] mout[h] [u]pon me?* (= *Eh! But you're damned rude! Even you want to say rude things about me?*)—(Gren) **2.** *adj* [Of a person] Insignificant; unschooled; of no account. *But look no! Even joukoutoo Margaret gettin[g] invitation to Government House nowadays.*—(Gren) [Fr Cr *jouk* + *ou* < Fr *jusqu'à vous* 'as low down as you' + E 'too', hence = 'even you too', the E adv reinforcing the lost force or sense of the Fr phr]

J'ou·vert (Jour ou·vert) *n phr* (Tbgo, Trin)
See JOUVÉ

jou·vé (jou·vay, jou·vè, jou·vert, j'ou·vert, jour ou·vert) [žuve~žuvɛ(r)] *n* (Dmca, StLu, Tbgo, Trin) **1.** The beginning of the CARNIVAL celebrations before dawn on the Monday morning of the week in wh the Christian observance of Lent will begin; it is set going officially at 5 a.m. with street-dancing to STEEL-BAND music and people playing OLE MAS individually or in BANDS. **2.** [By extension] The first day of Carnival (taken to include the whole day's celebrations, parades and competitions). [Fr Cr *jou-ouvè* (< Fr jour ouvert) 'day start, open' i.e. 'daybreak'] □ **1.** The frequent journalistic reverting to *Jour Ouvert* (Fr = 'Open Day') is a misleading refinement, wh represents neither the pronunc nor the proper sense (See etym). Ideally *jouvé* is the desirable spelling, though *j'ouvert, jouvert* are commonest. **2.** Related terms with obvious meanings are *jouvert-band, jouvert-morning, King (of) Jouvert, Queen (of) Jouvert.*

jub·jub [jʊbjʊb] *n* (Gren, Guyn, Trin) A soft gelatinous looking, coloured sweet that can be chewed or sucked. □ Cp *OED jujube* 2. for a similar sweet, nowadays often medicated.

ju·boule *n* (StLu) See DJOUBOUL

juck *vb, n* (Bdos) See JOOK

juck·ing-board *n* (Bdos, etc) See JOOKING-BOARD

Ju·das-tree *n* (Bdos) ‖ BEAN-TREE (Bdos) [Prob from association of blood-red flowers and 'beads' with Lent. See ‖ *Lent-tree*]

jug; jug-jug [jʌg-jʌg] *n* (Bdos) A well-seasoned, heavy, paste-like mixture made by mincing meat and several cupfuls of PIGEON-PEAS that have been boiled together, with butter and guinea-corn flour added; it is a popular Christmas dish. [Perh of W Afr origin. Cp Igbo *nju* 'full measure' + *ghu* 'boil, cook']

jug-light *n* (Dmca) ‖ BOTTLE-FLAMBEAU (StVn, Trin)

ju·ju *n* (Baha) ‖ DUNKS (Bdos, etc)

ju·jube *n* (Baha, Jmca) ‖ DUNKS (Bdos, etc) [Cp *OED jujube* 1. 'an edible berry-like drupe, *Zuzyphus spp*'. This is not the same fruit but the taxonomic relationship prob gave rise to the CE name]

juk *vb & n* (CarA) See JOOK

Ju·lie-man·go *n* (Angu, Bdos, Gren, Guyn, Jmca) ‖ GRAFTED MANGO (CarA) [Said to have been named after the wife of an agricultural officer at the time of the first successful graft]

jum·bie¹ (jom·bay, jom·bi(e), jum·bee, jum·bey, jum·bi, jum·by¹) *n* (ECar) **1.** ‖ DUPPY¹ **1** (Baha, etc) *Toolwa lived in a lonely wooden cottage three miles away, and the wind and the rain, and perhaps the jumbies, were tearing it down shingle by shingle.*—SWIS:23 (E. Mittelholzer) [Perh of Bantu origin. Note esp the *Kongo-ŋgola* group, of wh *KPG:75* lists eleven languages and dialects in wh there is *nzambi~ndṣambe~ntsambi* 'God', including one, Kansandṣ (= Mbangala by M. Guthrie's Revised Classification) in wh there is *nsambi* 'God', *nsumbi* 'Devil'; also Undaza (= Kota, per M. Guthrie) *inṣambi* 'God', *ndṣumbi* 'Devil'. The linking of good and evil with the same cosmic power is also reflected in some of the original practices with wh the CE word *jumbie* is associated] **2.** PHRASES **2.1 hear jumbie** *vb phr* (ECar) [AF] ‖ HEAR DUPPY (CarA) See HEAR Phr 4.3 **2.2 jumbie (will) blow on you** *id phr* (ECar) [AF] An evil spirit will affect/has affected your health while you sleep at night. *Yet you does fine some people whey have to stop up every little crease wid ole clot' an' paper because dey 'fraid jumbie goin' blow on dem or dey goin' ketch cold or somet'ing so.*—WeN (53.3.2, p.2, Annie & Josephine) **2.3 put/set jumbie on (sb)** *vb phr* (CarA) [IF] ‖ SET DUPPY¹ ON (SB) (Jmca) *As the orchestra of drums played the famous 'Tobago Reel' dance songs, the spirits 'flew into the heads of' (possessed) the dancers and gave them 'messages' about who had 'put the jumbies on the sick' and what medicines were to be used to cure them.*—EFSLC:31 **2.4 beat/shake the jumbie out of (sb); take the jumbie off (sb)** *vb phrs* (CarA) ‖ *take duppy off (sb)* (Jmca) To drive the evil spirit out of (sb) by beating or some form of exorcism. **3.** ‖ DUPPY¹ **3** (Baha, etc) **a.** *'Well, in the first place, if you go to Christ Church cemetery, you will see the vault where the duppies—or jumbies, as you call them in Hiroona—used to fight one another.'*—TRIH:94 **b.** *We had to pass the burial plot, and make a right turn at the corner. 'No wonder they believe in jumbies,' Sandy whispered. 'Look at those funny white things.'*—FGSOS:49 **4.** ‖ DUPPY¹ **5.** (Bdos, CayI) *It's about rockstones falling mysteriously on houses ... called Jumbie. It is about people disappearing, and the sighting of rolling calves and three-legged horses.*—JdN (79.11.29, p.18) □ Cp also BACCOO (*Guyn*). **5.** (Dmca, Guyn) Imaginary bogey man called on to frighten children. *If you don't go to bed I will call the jumbie for you, too!*—(Parent to child) **6.** (USVI) An evil spirit of the dead that assumes human form but sheds its skin at night in order to raid the abode or steal the voice of a living person, an operation wh it must complete before daybreak, when it must hide. *To make sure that the jumbies stay outside your house, put 99 grains of corn, rice or sand either on your roof or near the doorstep. The jumbies will count them all night and be forced to look for the 100th grain. When dawn breaks, they will be forced to leave, and will be foiled in their purpose.... If you hear a voice in the night calling your name, don't answer until you have heard the third call. It could be a* ghost or a jumbie coming to take your voice away from you for his own use.—Aaw.I.2:65 □ Cp OLD HIGUE (Guyn). **7.** (USVI) ‖ MOKO-JUMBIE (USVI) What a strange way to picture a Jumbie, a spirit! da man on stilts no less than eight feet tall, wearing a long pointed hat, dressed in women's clothing and carrying a whip made of raw hyde. That is exactly how Mr Richardson used to carry himself around during carnival time.—Aaw.I.2:13

jum·bie² adj (ECar) [AF—Derog/Joc] ‖ DUPPY² (Baha, etc) [Often used to indicate a spurious, comical, or dangerous quality of an object]

jum·bie-bal·sam* [ˈjʌmbi-ˌbɒlzəm] n (Guyn) ‖ jumbie-basil (Guyn) ‖ toonsie (Trin) ‖ tulsi(e) (Guyn) An erect aromatic herb, growing to about 1-1/2 ft, with small leaves, hairy stems, little brownish flowers and fruit consisting of four nutlets; Ocimum canum (Labiatae). □ The plant, also called jumbie-basil (Guyn), is not used to produce oil or ointment, but rather for its aromatic properties.

jum·bie-ba·na·na n (StVn) ‖ upside-down banana (Bdos) ‖ wild banana **1.** (Dmca, Jmca, StLu, TkCa) A species of purple, inedible, stubby banana that grows in small bouquet-like bunches pointed upwards (instead of hanging like normal bananas); it is borne on a relatively short plant in uncultivated land. Jumbie-banana palm leaves are used to line a grave before the coffin is put down.—(StVn) [JUMBIE² + banana]

jum·bie-ba·sil [jʌmbi-bazɪl] n (Guyn) ‖ J-UMBIE-BALSAM (Guyn) [Prob a more accurate name than JUMBIE-BALSAM. Cp DUPPY-BASIL wh is closely related (note taxonomic name), if not the same]

jum·bie-bead* n **1.** (Brbu, Gren, StKt, Trin, USVI) ‖ buck-bead 1. (Guyn) ‖ crab-eye, crab's-eye(s) 1. (Guyn, StKt) ‖ John-Crow bead (Belz, Jmca) ‖ jumbie-bead seed (Nevs) The hard, glossy, red seed with a black spot, several in each splitting pod, borne on a slender, twining vine with pale pink flowers and compound leaves; the seed is widely used in handicraft and jewellery-making; it is also used as a folk-medicine; Abrus precatorius (Leguminosae-Papilionaceae). **a.** Many of us recall the pretty hand-bags, purses, bed slippers and belts made from the jumbee beads and tantan seeds.—PHPVI:3 **b.** Jumbie bead seeds are boiled in water to form an excellent tea for colds, cough, flu and fevers.—Lal.I.1, p.83 [JUMBIE, prob because these seeds or 'beads' are believed by some to bring misfortune if kept in the home. They are also poisonous if not boiled or parched (APPJ:9) □ See also BEAD-VINE BUSH (Nevs, StKt). This jumbie-bead is borne on a vine, all others on erect plants or trees. **2.** (Bdos, Gren, Tbgo, Trin) ‖ buck-bead 2. (Guyn) ‖ coral bean (Gren) ‖ crab-eye 2. (Bdos, Tbgo) ‖ cutlass-bean (Jmca) The

glossy, half-inch-long, scarlet bean (some varieties with a black spot), several in a six-inch-long pod wh is constricted between seeds; it is borne on a medium-sized tree with thick half-inch prickles, producing blood-red flowers in the early part of the year; Erythrina corallodendron or E. pallida (Leguminosae-Papilionaceae). Jumbie beads, the small red and black seeds of this tree, are used to fill bean-bags and shack-shacks.—Trin (Ms) □ See also BEAN-TREE. **3.** (Gren, Trin, USVI) ‖ buck-bead 3. (Guyn) ‖ Circassian bean/seed (Jmca, Trin, USVI) ‖ coquelicot, kokreko (USVI) ‖ red-bead (Jmca) ‖ red sandalwood (Gren, Jmca, Trin) The hard, glossy red seed, carried nine or ten in a spiral pod about 8 ins long, and borne on a tall, hard-wood, shade-tree with hanging spikes of orange-yellow flowers; Adenanthera pavonina (Leguminosae-Mimosaceae). **4.** (Guyn, Trin) The hard, glossy, scarlet and black seed, about half an inch in diameter, carried one or two in a short, oblong, hairy pod with a short beak; it is borne on a very tall (100-ft) lightwood forest-tree whose younger branches and leaves also have rust-brown hairs; Ormosia coarctata, or O. coccinea, or O. paraensis (Leguminosae-Papilionaceae). The jumbie-bead tree, Ormosia coccinea, known to the Amerindians as barakaro, gives, unlike the 'red sandalwood' variety, a very poor wood to work, having a coarse irregular grain.—Guyn (Ms) **5.** (Guyn) ‖ JOB'S TEARS (Bdos, etc) The plant, called jumbie beads or Job's tears, originated in India but is commonly found on the coastlands of Guyana.... The immature fruit is used like a cereal grain.—OGEP: 96

jum·bie-bead seed n phr (Nevs) ‖ JUMBIE-BEAD 1. (Brbu, etc)

jum·bie-bead vine n phr (Brbu, Gren, StKt, Trin, USVI) ‖ BEAD-VINE (BUSH) (Nevs, StKt) Jumbee Bead Vine, when mature, is covered with open seed pods.... The vine is used in cough syrup.—PHPVI:36

jum·bie-bean n (Baha, Berm) ‖ WILD TAMARIND 1. (Belz, etc) [JUMBIE² adj 'of low status' + bean]

jum·bie-bird n **1.*** (Guyn) ‖ barn-owl (Trin) ‖ death-bird (Baha) ‖ white-owl (Jmca) A white owl, about 15 ins long, that utters an eerie shriek as it flies low, hunting at night, so giving rise to a strong superstition that it is a messenger of death; Tyto alba hellmayri (Tytonidae). Dew fell noiseless and the night wind grew chill. A piper owl sang to the new moon. 'They say them owl is jumbie bird, and nobody never see one,' Tonic said hugging his knees tightly.—GI:163 (J. Carew) [From its nocturnal habits, appearance, and the fact that it is often heard and very rarely seen] **2.** (Trin) ‖ pygmy-owl (Trin) A very small (6 in) brown owl with white underparts that makes a rapidly repeated whistling sound at night, and is seldom seen; Glaucidium brasilianum phaloenoides (Strigidae). [From the fact that it is a commonly heard night bird but rarely seen] **3.***

(Guyn) ‖ *ani, blackbird* 2. (Baha, Jmca) ‖ *black-witch* (ViIs) ‖ *dead-people bird* (Baha) ‖ *merle-corbeau* (Gren, Trin) ‖ *old-witch* (Guyn, Trin) ‖ *rain-crow* (Baha) ‖ *tick-bird* (Jmca, Trin) A jet-black bird, about 14 ins long with a parrot-like beak and a tail half its length; it gives a shrill plaintive 'ooo-eek' as it flies, and usu makes an unbalanced landing; it is often seen in groups in open places such as savannahs and cemeteries, where it feeds on insects and cattle parasites; *Crotophaga ani* (*Cuculidae*). [From its colour, cry, and association with cemeteries, and prob also from its nesting habits. See OLD-WITCH (Guyn)]

jum·bie-bub·by /1'212/ *n* (Guyn) [*AF*] ‖ B-URA-BURA (Guyn) [*Jumbie*, perh from the belief that its juice could soften the skin of the hand to cause harm (see cit at BURA-BURA) + *bubby*, prob from its globose shape]

jumbie-cho·cho *n phr* (Jmca) ‖ JUMBIE SOUR-SOP (Antg, etc) *You find jumbie chocho growing wild. Fruit no good, but the leaf you soften over a fire and they have nothing better for pain, you see!*—(Jmca) [< JUMBIE² adj + *chocho*]

jum·bie-cof·fee *n* (StKt, Trin, USVI) [*IF*] ‖ WILD COFFEE 1. (Guyn, etc) *Jumbie coffee leaves, you boil them too and get out de stink, good for fever and cold.*—(StKt) [JUMBIE² adj 'of low status' + *coffee*, the parched seeds being used as a bitter coffee substitute and also medicinally; also perhaps because animals would eat all other bushes around it, leaving it untouched]

jum·bie-dance *n* (Mrat, Tbgo) Religious dancing organized to induce spirit-possession and divination; it is accompanied by a folk-band such as the WOO-WOO BAND, is impassioned, and can last throughout the night.

jum·bie-para·sol *n* (Gren, Tbgo, Trin, TkCa) [*AF—Joc*] ‖ DUPPY-PARASOL (Bdos) *In moist tropical conditions Fungi and Mycetozoa abound. Of the saprophytes, the harmless 'Jumbie Parasols' occur in pastures.*—GNHIG:64

jum·bie-pep·per *n* (BrVi) ‖ BIRD-PEPPER (CarA)

jum·bie-pow·der *n* (Guyn) ‖ DUPPY-DUST (Bdos) *Cotton Tree Maraj ... became rich and famous for getting rid of people with a potion known as 'jumbie powder'. 'Put it in her salt and mix it well', he wrote ... 'I will work with my air spirit and she will dwindle away into nothingness.' The victim would have dwindled and died if the packet of jumbie powder and talisman had not been intercepted by the Postal Department.... The jumbie powder turned out to be ... arsenic.*—COYN:11

jum·bie-sour·sop* /1'2112/ *n* (Antg, Nevs, StVn) ‖ *Cain-fruit, forbidden fruit¹* (Bdos) ‖ *hog-apple, jumbie-chocho* (Jmca) ‖ *kò-wòsòl-djab* (Dmca) ‖ *monkey-apple* 1. (Bdos,

Nevs) ‖ *monkey-berry* (Jmca) ‖ *mulberry* (CayI) ‖ *pain-cure* (Bdos) ‖ *pain-killer fruit* (Guyn) ‖ *pig-apple* (Jmca) ‖ *pomme-killer* (Dmca) ‖ *yaws(-bush) fruit* (Guyn) The soft greenish-yellow fruit about 3 to 4 ins long and resembling a small pineapple, but having an unpleasant smell when crushed; it is borne sparsely on a small, bushy tree with large, glossy, dark-green leaves; the tree is *Morinda citrifolia* (*Rubiaceae*). *It name jumbie soursop because it ain['t] a fruit you could eat, and it stink, but some people uses it crush to kill bugs, you know, in bed-frame. Jamaica, they calls it jumbie chocho because it shape something so, and sometimes we calls it monkey apple too—all sorts o[f] name—and the people know it because the leaf very, very good for pain, you see.*—(Nevs) [< JUMBIE² adj + *soursop*]

jum·bie-um·brel·la *n* (Gren, Guyn, Mrat, StKt, StVn, Tbgo, USVI) [*AF—Joc*] ‖ DUPPY-PARASOL (Bdos) *Every time I see jumbie umbrella A does wap off their head with a stick.*—(Tbgo)

jum·by² *n* (Guyn) [Sugar Ind] A bamboo or other pole driven into the ground to show the depth required to be reached when a new drain or canal is to be dug by hand-labour. [From jocose association with JUMBIE ∼ JUMBY¹ as a hidden inanimate 'watchman' that can cause a penalty if the work is scamped or if it is interfered with]

jump¹ 1. *vb tr* (Bdos, Tbgo, Trin) [*AF*] To startle (sb); to cause (sb) a sudden fright. *He go up quiet behind Candia and clap his hands, and that jump her and she get vex right away.*—(Tbgo) [Cp AmE *to jump on* (sb) 'to leap upon, attack'. The word is also current in this sense in regard to mugging among some CE speakers] 2. *vb intr* (CarA) [*IF*] To be startled; to shudder sharply from sudden fright. *The loud bang made everybody jump.*—(Guyn) □ Also, in some places, '*the noise jumped everybody*'. Cp sense 1. 3. *vb intr* (CarA) [*IF*] [Of the eye] To twitch repeatedly. *If the left eye 'jumps', it is bad luck, good luck if the right 'jumps'.*—NaT (77.10.07, p.16) 4. *vb intr* (CarA) [*IF*] ‖ *jump up* (CarA) To dance as one of a crowd, jigging or jumping up and down, often with hands in the air, to the beat of loud popular music, esp of the CALYPSO. *After the election results were announced, fun-loving Grenadians took to the streets in carnival fashion and jumped to steelband music until the wee hours of this morning.*—AdN (72.03.02, p.2) □ See also TRAMP 5. PHRASES 5.1 **jump and (do sth)** *vb phr* (Bdos, Gren, Guyn) [*AF*] To set about doing something without due understanding, forethought, or preparation. *Yo[u] have to know wha[t] yo[u] doin[g]! You can['t] jump and say yo[u] makin[g] sponge cake jus[t] like that or it bound to fall!*—(Guyn) 5.2 **jump from your skin** *vb phr* (Jmca) [*AF—Joc*] ‖ JUMP OUT OF YOUR CLOTHES/SKIN (CarA) See Phr 5.5 *After that jump I nearly jump from my skin. For a little cry has come from her, and there she is in my bro's

arms kissing him 'fore all our eyes.—RND:199
5.3 jump high (or) jump low *id phr* (Bdos,
Gren, Guyn, Tbgo, Trin) [*AF/IF*] No matter
how you try to get away (i.e. you are/will be
caught); inevitably. *Of course, you could argue
back that the high octane licking up their mufflers,
and the roads eating up the tyres. But whatever it
is, jump high or jump low, your car is heading for
that junk yard at a faster rate than before.*—ExP
(Ad, 73.05.20, p.17) **5.4 jump on (sb/sth)** *vb
phr* (Gren, Guyn) [*AF*] To suddenly accost (sb);
to set about (sth) rashly. **a.** *You can['t] jump on
me like dat for cricket money! A do[n't] have
money like dat!*—(Gren) **b.** *The man want a quiet
weddin[g] and you now jumpin[g] on big weddin[g]!*—(Guyn) **5.5 jump out of your clothes/
your skin** *vb phr* (CarA) [*AF—Joc*] ‖*fly out of
your skin* (Bdos) ‖*jump from your skin* (Jmca)
(i) To be startled out of your wits; to be scared
suddenly. *The boy threw the little dead snake
on his sister and she nearly jumped out of her
skin.*—Angu (Ms) **(ii)** To rush hurriedly (to get
sth done). *At the clothes factory the women hated
her because whenever she called she wanted people
to jump out of their skin to do whatever it was.*—
Guyn (Ms) □ Note difference from SE *jump out
of one's skin* (*OED skin* sb 5. f.) wh may denote
'extreme delight, high spirits, or surprise'. **5.6
jump up**[1] *vb phr* (CarA) [*IF*] ‖JUMP 4. (CarA)
*Ronnie used to jump-up with Invaders steelband.
Many may well remember being tremendously
thrilled at jumping-up with Invaders in their ren-
dition of Handel's Messiah arranged in calypso
tempo.*—ExP (72.02.18, p.15) **5.7 make (sb)
jump** *vb phr* (CarA) [*AF—Joc*] To keep (sb), or
cause (sb) to be in a state of fear or great anxiety.
*He give that poor girl a child and he won['t] marry
her, but he go and marry a hot-ass Miss Lady that
make him jump, till [h]e had to divorce her before
she sen[d] him to the mad-house.*—(Guyn)

jump[2] *n* (Trin) ‖JUMP-UP[2] (CarA) *Some of the
spectators, as usual, ventured on to the stage for a
jump with the bands.*—ExP (73.03.19, p.13)

jump-in dance (**jump·ing dance**) *n phr*
(Baha) An adult ring-dance around a fire at
night, in wh anyone moved by the rhythm of
the music jumps into the middle of the ring
and dances (see cit). *It is my belief that a
'jump-in' dance is a Bahamian creation, born
out of the vestiges of African culture.... In the
middle of the yard, there was kindled a massive
fire, which provided illumination as well as a
spirit of warmth and jollity, to the event. It also
served to tune the goat-skin drums, which they
used to provide the rhythm for the dance. The
adults formed a ring, and to the rhythm of
drums, augmented by folk songs, akin to calypsos,
they danced the night away. From the ring,
anyone—moved by the rhythm and music—could
jump into the ring, and dance to his soul's delight.
His movements were always lascivious and directed
to one of the opposite sex whom he favoured to
take over from him. He then moved to this
person, who caused her movements to rhyme with
his in perfect co-ordination, until she took his*

*place in the ring.... A 'jump-in' dance was fun
out in the open, under a hunter's moon.*—EBT:
20 [Evid the form *jumping* is a false refinement
for *jump in* from wh the dance clearly derives
its name]

jump·ing; jump.ing-up *n* (ECar) Open-air
JUMP-UP dancing by a crowd, usu to calypso
music. **a.** *'Mas in Queen's Park' will be staged on
Tuesday of next week, starting at 6 p.m. and
featuring road marching, calypso singing, costume
parades, a queen's parade and regular non-stop
jumping to six top steel bands and groups.*—AdN
(72.02.09, p.5) **b.** *She had been washing up the
dishes after supper but at this moment the music
had gone to her head, and she was doing her own
little jumping-up in the kitchen.*—AKM:46 [Cp
JUMP[2], JUMP-UP[2]]

jump-up[2] *n* (CarA) [*AF*] ‖*jump*[2] (Trin) A
dance, whether organized and indoors or unorganized and in the street, in wh people dance
merrily in a crowd but with each individual
jigging or jumping up and down, esp to the
loud rhythm of calypso music, in the manner
characteristic of CARNIVAL.

jump-up-and-kiss-me* *n* (CarA) ‖*kiss-
me-quick* (Dmca, Jmca) ‖*purslane, pussley*
(Bdos, Jmca, StKt, Trin, USVI) Any of three or
four varieties of a low-growing, fleshy-stemmed
herb with a spreading habit; it has small, thick,
silky, oval-shaped leaves and attractive little
flowers wh may be reddish-purple, yellow, or
white; it is eaten in some places and, in others,
boiled as a folk-medicine for worms, or used for
making poultices; *Portulaca oleracea*, or *P. pilosa*,
or *P. grandiflora*, etc (*Portulacaceae*).

June-plum *n* (Jmca) See JEW-PLUM ... *lifted
her small basket of June plums and tangerines,
lowered it, and walked away in the opposite direction from her irritable acquaintance.*—SJS:5
□ As both forms occur, it is not clear wh is
rationally justified or wh has popular preference,
though *Jew-plum* is the only form given in
AFPJ.

jun·jo[1] (**jon·jo, jun·ju**) [JUnJʌ~JUnJU] *n* **1.**
(Belz, Jmca) Any kind of mould (as on stale
bread), moss (as on rocks), fungus (as on old
wood), or mildew. [Cp *KED* Krio *jonjo* 'a mushroom'] **2.** (Guyn) A layer of dirt on furniture or
scurfiness on the skin owing to lack of care;
(sometimes also) visible dirt on the teeth. **3.**
(Guyn) [By extension] A diseased skin, esp with
sores on the legs. [Cp *WIED* Igbo *jọ-njọ* 'to be
bad, wicked, evil'. Note JUNJO[2]]

jun·jo[2] [JUnJʌ] *adj* (StVn) [*AF*] [Of a person]
Stunted or deformed. [See prec]

Jun·ka·noo (**Jan·ku·nu, John Ca·noe,
John Con·nu, Jon·ka·noo, Jon·kon·nu**)
[JɒnkʌnU~JʌŋkanU] *n* (*phr*) (Baha, Belz, CayI,
Jmca) **1.** The leading, male street-masquerader
of a troupe; his costume comprises mainly an

elaborate head-dress (horse-head, cow-head with horns, model house, or tall hat with an ugly mask) and a tinselled or jingling, multi-coloured outfit; he dances to the beat of goat-skin drums, cow-bells, whistles, and other folk-instruments while rushing at or 'frightening' onlookers and receiving money (nowadays organized prizes). *The John Canoe dancers and the Set Girls were seen every Christmas on estates and in towns and villages all over the island. The male dancers were called John Canoes. They wore all kinds of gay and strange costumes, with masks covering their faces. The masks were of many shapes.*—RPME:26 [Most likely of Yoruba origin. See Iai *XLVII.3* (1977) *pp.253–275, Qyǫ* 'Yoruba Masquerades' in wh many features of the costumes and conduct of the annual Egungun (Masquerades) festival correlate with features of *Junkanoo*. Note also (p.259) 'maskers [who] run after those they wish to flog [are] a violent sub-class called *janduku* 'hooligans'. Cp also *ADMY* Yoruba *jo* 'dance' *n-n-kǫn* (general word for) 'things, spells, feats'; also *jankǫn-jankǫn* 'noteworthy' (i.e. person). Note also *KED* Krio *jankoniko* 'to shame publicly' (< Yoruba *Jan-koliko* 'one elevated as a figure of fun or disgrace'. In this latter connection it is to be noted that in *Belz, John Canoes* use stilts. See **John-Canoe sticks**] □ The spelling **Junkanoo**, now well established via official promotion of the festival (sense 2.) in *Baha*, would seem nearest the likely original form of the word. **John Canoe** is commoner in *Jmca* but evid a corruption via folk etym, as are also the other conjectural variants. **2.** (Baha, Jmca) The merry festival of street-dancing and parading led by JUNKANOO (sense 1.) with a troupe of traditional, costumed characters such as Devil, KOO-KOO (*Jmca*) or, in recent times (esp in *Baha*), related to some popular topic; the festival is now largely restricted to the Christmas season. **a.** *Another visitor was standing watching Junkanoo when his wallet was lifted from his pocket around 4.30 a.m.*—TrI (76.01.02, p.1) **b.** *John Canoe dancers from rural Jamaica and city girls from the National School of Drama, got together in the grand Caribbean Night jump-up which ended the Commonwealth Conference celebration at Jamaica House Tuesday night.*—WeS (75.05.09, p.30) **3.** The type of JUMPING-UP or 'rushing' dance characteristic of the JUNKANOO festival (sense 2.) *Kumina, Bruckin party, Quadrille, Jonkanoo; dances that vibrate with the richness of our varied heritage. Somebody should keep them alive.*—DaG (73.02.04, p.30) **4.** [By extension—*Derog*] An idiot; a foolish-looking, foolishly dressed, or a very ugly person.

junk (up) *vb tr (phr)* (Gren, Guyn, Jmca, StVn) [*IF*] To chop or cut up roughly (esp meat); to cut large unshapely pieces off (esp cooked meat). *If you see how she junked pieces off the ham to put on her plate! It looked too bad!*—(Guyn) [Cp *OED junk* vb (b) 'to cut or divide into junks or chunks' + cits mainly from *Jmca*]

ju·pa (ju·per) [jʊpʌ] *n* (Gren) [*AF/IF*] A small, old, broken down, rural dwelling; a poor country-side hut. [Prob < (*Carib*) AJOUPA by aphetic loss of /a-/]

jusqu'à vous *pron, adj* (Gren) See JOUKOU TOO

just *adv* [Loosely used as a palliative or persuasive modifier in many phrs] PHRASES **1. just as** *conj phr* (CarA) [*X*] Like; just like; as; in the same way as. **a.** *It was a bluish dress, just as yours that you had on yesterday.*—(Guyn) **b.** *Khaki pants and white merino, just as most of the shopkeepers in the island wore, were enough for him.*—SABS:62 **2. just for so** *adv phr* (Bdos, Guyn, Tbgo, Trin) [*IF/AF*] Casually; without obvious cause or particular reason. *'Sure,' replied Jairam. 'I know how I spelling. I ain't reach t'ird standard just for so. I know.'*—NAGOS:89 **3. just now** *adv phr* [*IF*] **(i)** (CarA) In a little while; very soon; shortly. **a.** *I am just going down the road. I'm coming back just now.*—(StVn) **b.** *Watch out folks! Just now we're going to have damn few edible animals on this island. The simple reason being that with the present high price of feed, farmers can't afford to produce pigs, etc at saleable prices.*—AdN (74.03.09, p.4, Off The Cuff) □ 1. This usage does not apply to *Belz.* 2. The phr is commonly used to palliate impatience, the speaker not expecting it to be taken seriously. 3. In Bdos the pitch /1′2/ must be used to indicate future sense: *Just give me a minute and I will deal with you just now.*—(Bdos) **(ii)** (CarA) Only a short while ago; a few minutes ago. **a.** *I saw her just now there by the corner.*—(Guyn) **b.** *She only stepped out just now so she can't have gone too far.*—(Bdos) □ 1. Only this sense (i.e. with ref to the immediate past) applies in *Belz.* 2. In Bdos this sense requires the contrastive pitch / 2′1/. **4. just so** *adv phr* (CarA) [*IF*] Without due consideration; without warning. **a.** *But the polyclinic system started overnight, just so, just so out of the bag. A hot flush, you know, came to the head and just so it started. There was no consultation with doctors or anybody, so no guidelines were set.*—Bdos (Hd, 87.03.23, p.309) **b.** *Boss, you fire me? Just so without even asking a question?* —PGIP:49

just-come *n* (Antg, Jmca, Trin) [*AF*] ‖ *Johnny-just-come* (Guyn) A Johnny-come-lately; a newcomer (usu one that irritates). *'Must you be such a J.C.?' one of them chided laughingly. 'The joke was on me: I didn't even know that 'J.C.' among Trinidadians in Toronto means 'Just-come', a know-nothing greenhorn, just arrived from hick country.'*—TaP (75.12.21, p.10)

just·ly *adv* (Bdos, Guyn) [*IF*] Exactly; rightly. *I do remember seeing it, but I can't justly tell you where or when.*—(Guyn) [Prob an EE survival. Cp *OED justly* 5. 'exactly, precisely, accurately' (*Obs exc. dial*) + cits-'1737]

ju·ta [Juta] *n* (Belz, Guyn, Jmca) [*AF—Joc*] **1.** Shoes; footwear. [Bhoj < Hin *juutaa* 'a shoe', hence a *Joc* loan word orig applied to East Indian immigrants] **2** PHRASE **2.1 Big juta, li[tt]l[e] juta, all same price** *id phr or prov* (Belz, Guyn, Jmca) [*AF—Joc*] Anything will do; size or quality doesn't matter. □ Said of an unlearned person or country bumpkin who doesn't know how to choose correctly (orig, the right footwear).

K

K.A. *abbr* (Bdos) Knight of St Andrew of the Order of Barbados, a national honour awarded for extraordinary and outstanding achievement and merit in service to Barbados or to humanity at large; the letters are placed after the recipient's name. □ See also D.A..

kaa·ko·le [ka:kʌle] *n* (Guyn) The merriment, erotic dancing and song-singing organized for a night or two before a country wedding. **[** < Yoruba *kaakile* < *kaakiri ile* 'around-the-house ceremony', held before a wedding, certain items, prepared by the father of the bride or an elderly woman of the family, being placed around the house in a procession'—(*pers info from Ademola Onibon-Okuta, at Ibadan*). Cp *HHTV:90* for a comparable ceremony in *Trin*] □ The original ceremony has evid lost its significance, but one very old, rural informant (1960s) remembered a laying of white sheets and the casting of money on them, in Essequibo (*Guyn*).

kaan·ki (kang·ki, kon·kee) ['ka·ŋki] *n* (Guyn) See CONKIE □ A more suitable spelling than the widely current CANKIE.

ka·ba-ka·ba[1] (ca·ba-ca·ba, kab·ba-kab·ba) ['kaba-kaba ~ 'kɛbʌ-kɛbʌ] /1'122/ *adj* (CarA) [*AF*] **1.** (CarA) [Esp of person or dress] Slovenly looking; ill-fitting, ill-matched, or boorish-looking. **2.** Cheap; worthless; [esp of poultry and livestock] of poor quality. *Kaba-kaba fowl does nyam good corn* (= *The worthless chicken often gets good feed*).—Guyn (Prov) **[**Cp Yoruba *kaba-kaba* (adv used esp in the context of speaking) 'haltingly, unreliably'; but also widely used as adj, adv, = 'below standard', 'of inferior quality', so loaned in Igbo *kobo-kobo* n 'a worthless person', also Ewe *kaba-kaba* 'quick and shabby' (applied to work done)**]**

ka·ba-ka·ba[2] *n* (Guyn, Jmca) [*AF—Derog*] A rough, low, worthless person. *You won['t] see him aɪɔund. He left home years ago and just knocked avout like a kaba-kaba till I hear now he is in the bush.*—(Guyn)

ka·ba·ka·li *n* (Guyn) See KABUKALLI

ka·bau·ro(-fly) (ca·bor·row, ca·bou·ra, ka·boo·ra, ka·boo·ri) ['kabauɾʌ ~ kabʌɾʌ ~ kabura/-i] *n* (Guyn) A grey fly whose bite causes a painful infection of the skin; it is very common in the Guyana hinterland in the wet season;

Simulium spp (*Simuliidae*). *These times of waiting were rendered almost unendurable by the great abundance of the small black kaboori fly, called in the Brazils pium.* From the Atlantic to the mouth of the Roopoonooni the country is quite free from these terrible little blood-suckers; but on this river they abound.... *Wherever they settle on the flesh a small round patch of raised skin, distended by blood, is formed, and is very sore and troublesome.*—IAIG:27 [*BAED* Arawak *kabauro* 'a small grey fly . . . which . . . stings']

ka·ber·ry *n* (Angu, BrVi) ‖CANKER-BERRY (CarA)

ka·bo·sé (ca·bou·sé, kal·bo·sé) ['kabuse ~ 'kalbose] *adj* [*AF*] **1.** (Dmca, Gren, StLu) ‖*kalbosé* (Dmca) Dented; battered; smashed. *If you see how the car cabousé after the accident.*—(Dmca) **2.** (Gren, StLu) Out of shape; unserviceable; [of bodily feelings] aching; limping. *After jumpin[g] up whole day at de Carnival yo[u] mus[t] feel kabosé and you walkin[g] kabosé too.*—(StLu) **3.** (Antg) [kabʌše] [Of a person] Clumsy; crude-looking. *You can['t] expec[t] him to do that neat. He too kaboshay.*—(Antg) [Fr Cr < Fr *cabosser* 'to dent, batter, bash in'] □ Commonest occurrence in *Gren, StLu*.

ka·bu·kal·li (ca·ba·cal·li, ka·ba·ka·li) [kabʌkali] /1'122/ *n* (Guyn) [Timber Ind] A forest-tree exceeding 100 ft in height, with high, buttressed roots; it is evil-smelling when freshly cut; it yields a heavy, dark, reddish-brown, straight-grained wood wh is excellent for furniture and is most highly valued for construction framework and railway sleepers; *Goupia glabra* (*Celastraceae*). [*BAED* Arawak *kabukhali* 'a timber tree that smells like stale urine']

ka·bwit (ca·brit) ['kabwit ~ 'kabrit] *n* **1.** (Dmca, StLu, USVI [*JF*] ‖*cabrita* (USVI) A goat. [Fr Cr < prob dial Fr *cabrite* (f) < *cabri* 'young goat'. Cp also Sp *cabrito* 'kid' wh prob > USVI *cabrita* via *PtRi*] □ Only the form *cabrit* applies to USVI where also ‖*cabrita* is perh commoner. **2.** (StLu) ‖*cowfish* 2. (TkCa) ‖*file-fish* (Bdos, StLu) Any of a number of small, rough-skinned, bony fish of low food value, noted for having one or two little horns above the eyes; filefish; *Balistidae spp*. **[** < KABWIT 'goat' in ref to the fish's horns]

ka·chi·man (ca.chi.man, ca.shi.ment) [ka šimã] *n* (Dmca, StLu) ‖CUSTARD-APPLE (CarA)

[*BAED* Arawak *kashima* 'sugar-apple', a name usu applied to *Annona squamosa* (*Annonaceae*), a closely related fruit but notably different in appearance. See SUGAR-APPLE.] □ The variant spellings are owing to Anglophone interference and Fr Cr nasalization of the original Arawakan name wh was also noted by *BDFC* (p.57) as *gros cahimas rouge* for wh the Carib name *allacallioua* is given.

kach-kach (cache-cache) [kaš-kaš] *n* (Dmca) ‖ NICKER (Angu, etc) *Children use the kach-kach seeds to play a game called kach-kach-man-bal.*—(Dmca)

kach-kach-ma(n)-bal /-ma-bèl (cache-cache-ma-belle) [kaš-kaš-mã-bal/-ma-bɛl] *n* (Dmca) ‖ *hiddy-biddy* (Bdos) A girls' moonlight game in wh they sit in a circle with knees near-closed, while a player, holding a seed or small marble in her clenched fist, goes from person to person saying 'cache-cache, ma balle' and, surreptitiously leaving the seed/marble in one girl's lap, then calls on another to say whose lap it was after the round has been completed. If the chosen player correctly identifies the lap, the first player is 'out'; if wrong, the chosen player is 'out'. [Fr *cache-cache* 'hide-and-seek' + *ma belle* 'pretty girl' or '*ma(n) balle*' in ref to the round object hidden]

ka·chow·ri (ca·chou·rie) [kačᴅʊri] *n* (Guyn, Trin) [Indic] A small fried cake, shaped like a patty, made of ground split peas mixed with flour, ghee, seasoning (and sometimes a little sugar); it is a prized East Indian delicacy.

ka·dans *n* (Dmca) See CADENCE·

ka·di *n* (Guyn) **1.** ‖ *chickichong* **2.** (Trin) A makeshift paper kite with a POINTER frame, usu held on a short string. **2.** [By extension] KADI (OLD PUNCH) *n* (*phr*) A battered old kite. [Yoruba *kadi* 'a small paper with a piece of broom sewn into it and used as a kite, a toy flown by small boys. Originally a leaf was used, and the name is derived from that of a woman whose husband used this device as a fetish to bring her safe delivery in childbirth'—(*pers info* (*1967*) *from Ademola Onibon-Okuta*)]

ka·doo·ment (ca·doo·ment, cu·doo·ment) [kadumɛnt] *n* (Bdos) [*AF*] ‖ *ballahoo*[3] ɪ (Belz) ‖ *konmès* ɪ (Dmca, etc) ‖ *to-do-ment* (Bdos) **1.** Much noise and confusion. *Said Mrs B: 'When I was finishing my bath, I heard a big cadooment, and the boy break into my bathroom with me naked.'*—NaT (77.06.05, p.8) [< *EDD*, various E dials, *k', ka* 'an abbreviation of 'look' in comb with var adv to form exclamatory phr' + *EDD*, many E dials, *doment, dooment* 'a commotion, disturbance; entertainment, merry-making'. Hence the likely phr in *Barbados ka doment* 'Look commotion!' 'Look fun!', in wh contexts it prob developed into a noun. The E dial forms *k', ka* survive in *Jmca* as *Ku!* See *DJE*] **2.** [By extension] Serious trouble; a dilemma. *The*

monkey, whose name is Dianne, has been a pet of Mr Gill for the past two years. The young animal landed itself in a kadooment last bank holiday, when it climbed the utility pole ... and the chain around its waist became entangled in the wires.— NaT (85.08.09, p.20) **3.** [By extension] (*Kadooment*) [F] Open-air fun and excitement, often of a salty kind, esp (in recent times) the annual CARNIVAL-style, one-day festival, with a parade of competing, costumed BANDS, organized as the culmination of the CROP-OVER celebrations. □ Cap *K* required for the festival, sense 3.

ka·gaj; ka.gaz (ca·gaj, ca·gaz) ['ka·gaʤ/-gaz] *n* (Guyn, Trin) [Indic] [*AF*] **1.** Any important paper or personal document such as a birth certificate (BIRTH-PAPER), and esp (*Trin*) a certificate that would qualify its owner for a job. **2.** [By extension] Paper money; money (in general). **3.** [By extension] A newspaper. [Bhoj < Hin *kaagaj/kaagaz* 'paper, document'] □ Sometimes in Joc use by non-Indic speakers.

ka·gou (car·goo, car·gou) ['ka·gu] *adv* (Trin) [*AF*] Looking sad, crestfallen, sickly, or sorry for yourself; lacking in enthusiasm. [Fr Cr < Fr *cagot* 'sanctimonious', *cagoule* 'penitent's hood'. *DCF* Guad *kagou* 'ramolli' (= softened, weakened in courage)] □ The conjectural spellings *cargoo*, etc attempt to represent the [a·] in *Trin* pronunc.

ka·i·mit *n* (StLu, Tbgo) See CAIMITE

ka·i·so ['kaɪso] *n* (ECar) ‖ *caliso, cariso, kaipso* (ECar) (Original and more regular folk-name of) the CALYPSO (*CarA*). **a.** *From 1903 onwards till about 1921, the kaiso followed the oratorical pattern; that is to say, the kaiso was in the nature of a rhetorical recitative in song, sung in the minor key, with eight lines to the stanza.*—Trin (Ms) **b.** *Extempo king, Lord Pretender, in characteristic action, is one of the old kaiso masters who will be featured tonight at the NUGFW Hall, Frederick Street, Port-of-Spain in a show entitled Calypso Extempore. Preddie will engage other oldtimers, Lion, Viking and Beginner in a kaiso war, reminiscent of the early days of the tents.*—TrG (79.07.28, p.7) [See etym at CALYPSO] □ Pl *kaisoes, kaisos.*

ka·i·so·man ['kaɪsoma·n] /ɪ'21/ *n* (ECar) [*IF*] ‖ CALYPSONIAN (CarA)

ka·ka *n, vb* (CarA) See CACA

ka·ka-ba·wi *n* (Dmca, Gren, StLu) See CACA-BAWI

ka·ka-be·li *n* (Guyn) See CACA-BELLY

ka·ka-da(n) *n* (Gren, StLu, Trin) See CACA-DA(N)

ka·ka-djé (ca·ca·jay) ['kaka-ʤe] *n* (Gren) [*AF*] ‖ YAMPI[2] (Antg, etc)

ka·ka-poul (ca·ca·poule, ko·ko·poul) ['kak apul] *n* **1.** (Dmca, StLu) ‖ CLAMMY-CHERRY (CarA) *There was one big kakapoul tree in the schoolyard, the ripe fruit of which contained a transparent gummy substance which only children find edible and which can be used in place of gum.*—StLu (Ms) **2.** (Dmca, StLu) ‖ *old-maid* (CarA) A blue variety of the flower OLD-MAID. *Kakapoul is also used of a little blue flower which we sometimes call periwinkle.*—StLu (Ms) **3.** (Gren) A hardwood tree that bears clusters of small fragrant flowers; *Erythroxylum oxycarpum* (*Erythroxylaceae*). [Cr *kaka* 'excrement, dung' + Fr Cr *poul* 'hen' = Anglophone Cr 'fowl dung'. The connection is obscure]

ka·ki·tè-bwa *n* (Gren) ‖ BIRD-VINE (BUSH) (Dmca, etc) 1. [Perh a corruption of Fr Cr *kakatwé*, 'place for defecating, in the countryside', ref to the plant's habitat + *bwa* 'tree, plant']

ka(k)·sham ['ka(k)šam] *n* (Jmca) ‖ ASHAM (Antg, etc) [*Kaksham* (by progressive assimilation) < *kasham* < *kaan-sham* 'corn-sham', a blend of 'corn' (the main ingredient) + ASHAM, this original Twi name still being found in *Jmca*. The form CORN-SHAM survives in *Belz*] □ This name is also falsely refined as COCTION.

kal·bo·sé *adj* (Dmca) See KABOSÉ

ka·len·da *n* (ECar) See KALINDA

Ka·li Mai Pu·ja/Poo·jay [kali-mai-pu ·ja~pu·je] *n phr* (Guyn) [Indic] A three-day religious celebration held (Friday to Sunday) in honour of the Hindu goddess Kali, to propitiate and defeat the forces of evil; it is particularly a Madrasi cult activity and involves the sacrifice of a goat and ritual flogging of devotees. [Bhoj < Hin *Kali Mai* 'Black Mother' (goddess of destruction) + *puujaa* 'worship']

ka·lin·da (ca·len·da, ca·lin·da, ka·len·da) *n* (ECar) **1.** (Dmca, Gren) A group dance, surviving from slavery and now on the decline, originally considered to be very lascivious. **2.** (Trin) A stick-fight dance event consisting of drumming to a special rhythm and call-and-response singing accompanying the stick-fight. **3.** (Dmca, Trin) [Also KALINDA MUSIC, KALINDA SONG] The call-and-response narrative song and music accompanying the stick-fight (but also as separate entertainment, hence CA-LINDA TENT (*Dmca* [Obs]). [Cp *OGA:107 caringa, calinda, calenda,* giving Père Labat's description (1742) of this as a dance of Afr plantation slaves, '(their) commonest diversion ... originating in the Guinea coast and ... from the kingdom of *Ardá*' (prob Dahomey) with 'gestures and movements ... of the most lewd'. The connection with stick-fighting is not clear, but a link may be provided by the *Jmca* word *calembe* (*DJE*) 'a dance of Afr orig ...' (+ cit 1924) 'two men holding a couple of sticks parallel while a third dances upon them to the strains of the song'. Also *OGA:95* lists *calembé* as poss < *cucalambe* 'an Afr dance'. Cp also *VBHUS:106* Tshiluba *kalanda* 'fame, notoriety']

ka·lin·da band *n phr* (Trin) [Hist ?] A competitive band of stick-fighters representing a particular area; hence **kalinda fighting** (‖ *bwa*), **kalinda-man** (‖ *bwa-man*), **kalinda king** (champion leader of the band).

ka(l)·la·loo (ka·la·lu) *n* (CarA) See CALALU

ka·nai·ma (ke·nai·ma) [kʌnaɪma~kɛnaɪma] *n* (Guyn) [Amerindian] A slayer or evil one, who may be a real man or a spirit that is either invisible or embodied in a bird, reptile, or forest animal, and who is believed to be responsible for the sickness or death of somebody as an act of vengeance. *Indians believe that each individual man has a body and a spirit within that body; and they think that kenaimas use their power of separating spirits and bodies and of sending these spirits to obey their orders, to whatever place they please, and of directing the actions of these spirits. It is, therefore, in the imaginary cases, not the kenaima in the body, but his spirit, which kills or injures.*—IAIG:332 [From Cariban langs. Cp *TWD* Wapishana, *kanaima* 'evil spirit'; also *FTCC:142* Macusi, *kenaima* 'spirit, evil'] See also PEAIMAN

ka·na·ri *n* (ECar) See CONAREE

kan·chi [ka·nči] *adj* (Guyn) [AF] ‖ CHINKSY (Bdos) [Cp *IMED* Mende *kanji* 'bony, skinny'. However, also possibly Indic, as dial form of Hin *kani* 'a particle, a drop'] □ Almost always used in phr *lil kanchi bit* (Guyn). Cp also KENCH (*Jmca*).

kan·ga·lang[1] [kaŋgalaŋ] *n* (Guyn) [AF— *Derog*] A rough, good-for-nothing person; a ne'er-do-well. [Perh notionally associated with KANGALANG[2]]

Kan·ga·lang[2]! [kaŋgalaŋ] *ideoph* (Antg, Bdos, Guyn) [Representing the sound of sth falling with a metallic clatter]

kan(g)·ki *n* (Guyn) See CONKIE

kangse[1] [kaŋs] *vb tr* (Guyn) [AF—*Joc*] ‖ *koks* (Gren) ‖ *konks* (StVn) To hit (sb, usu on the head) with sth light; to tap (a young person) sharply on the head by way of correction. *Jus[t] kangse dat boy an[d] make him shut up fo[r] me!*—(Guyn) [Prob < dial E *EDD conk* 4. vb 'to strike on the nose' + characteristic *Guyn* Cr [ɔ > a] vowel opening + paragogic /-s/] □ The pa.t. form is unchanged.

kangse[2] [kaŋs] *n* (Guyn) [AF—*Joc*] A light corrective blow (usu on the head). *Bet you I gi[ve] yo[u] two kangse if yo[u] don[t] stop playin[g] de fool!*—(Guyn) [Cp *EDD conk* sb 3. 'a blow on the nose'; see also prec] □ There is no pl form.

kan·ka-ber·ry *n* (ECar) See CANKER-BERRY

kann·bou·lé ['kanbule] *n* (Trin) See CAN-BOULAY □ The traditional spelling CANBOULAY is perh institutionalized largely by association with the pre-Carnival riots (*Trin, Feb. 1881*).

kan·pèch [kăpeɛš] *n* (Dmca, etc) See CAMPESH

kan·ya-daan [kanya-da·n] *n* (Guyn, Trin) [Indic] The ceremonial act of the bride's father's giving her, seated on his lap as a virgin, as a gift to the groom. [Hin *kanya* 'a maiden' + *daan* 'a gift']

ka·pi·tenn-bwa (ca·pi·taine-bois) ['kapitɛn-bwa] *n* (Gren) ‖ BIRD-VINE 1. (Dmca, etc) [Perh a corruption. See note at ‖ *kakité-bwa*]

kap-kap (ant) (cop-cop (ant)) [kap-kap~kɒp-kɒp] *n* (*phr*) (Guyn, Jmca) A black or dark brown ant about 1 cm long, its powerful mandibles making a sound wh gives it its name; in numbers they eat the wood of houses at night, making a disturbing sound and driving away or attacking lizards and insects.

ka·pok [kepɒk] *n* (Gren, Guyn, ViIs) ‖ SILK-COTTON (CarA) [Imported name, orig Malay. See *OED*]

ka·pok(-tree) *n* (Gren, ViIs) ‖ SILK-COTTON (TREE) (CarA) *Kapok or Silk Cotton seeds float through the air, though after 50 years, a Kapok is not likely to produce seeds.*—JNHSJ:35 [< Malay *kapoq*, name of the wool surrounding the seeds]

ka·ra·hi ['kara·hi] *n* (Guyn) [Indic] ‖ CONAREE (Guyn) *The karahi is especially used in making bhunjal curry.*—Guyn (Ms) [Bhoj *karahi* 'a heavy stew-pot' of varying sizes; Hin *kaṛaahii* 'frying pan'] □ Also sometimes *kahari* by metathesis.

ka·rai·la(-li) *n* (Guyn, StVn, Trin) See CA-RAILA

ka·re·ba (ka·ri·ba) [kari·ba] *n* (Jmca) ‖ SHIRTJAC SUIT (Bdos, Guyn) *Mr Michael Manley, has led the new trend to informal dress in the island since taking office. He has popularised the 'Kareba', a combination of shirt-jac and matching trousers, which has been accepted for formal wear.* [< *Carib*, suggesting 'typically Caribbean']

ka·sha *n* (Jmca) See CASHA

kas-kas¹ (kass-kass¹) [kas-kas] *adj* (Guyn) [AF—Derog] See CASS-CASS

kas-kas² [kas-kas] *n* (Jmca) [AF—Joc] ‖ BASSA-BASSA¹ (Angu, etc) *The communist scare, as much as other matters, kept the Jamaican society in a state of kas-kas for most of the year.... The kas-kas rose to new heights in October when the unthinkable happened ... Fidel Castro visited Jamaica.*—CaC (2/78, p.15) [< *DAFL* Twi *akasakasa* 'dispute, wrangling, quarrel']

ka·ta *n* (Antg, Guyn, Jmca, Tbgo) See CATTA

ka·ta·har ['katahar] *n* (Guyn, Trin) [Indic] ‖ BREADNUT 1. (CarA) [Bhoj < Hin *kaṭhal* 'jack fruit']

ka·ta·ku *n* (Angu, Antg) See CUTACOO

kat·ha (cat(t)·ha) ['katha:] *n* (Guyn, Trin) [Indic] A Hindu prayer meeting organized at a person's home for some special purpose such as thanksgiving; verses from Hindu scriptures are read and discussed and the offering of a dinner follows. *The cattha began. It went on for a long time. The pundit, his voice quickly settling into a drone, read from the book. At intervals conch horns were blown and bells rung; ... and incense fumes wandered through the tent, a sweet and suffocating presence.*—NF:90 [Hin *kathaa* 'story; religious tale']

ka·wang ['kawaŋ] *n* (Dmca) ‖ COBBLER 3. (BrVi, Dmca, StVn) [Fr Cr < Fr *carangue* 'horse-mackerel; cavally' (though this is a different fish)]

ka·wé [kawe·] *vb intr* (Dmca, Gren, StLu) ‖ W-INE (CarA) *If you see how Mary was kawéin[g] at the dance las[t] night!*—(Gren) [Fr Cr < Fr *carré* 'loin', also *carrer* 'to square up, square off', both perh as argot]

Ka·yak *n* (Gren) See CAYACK

ka·ya·kiit (ka·ya·keet) ['kayaki·t] *n* (Trin) ‖ S-AGE-BUSH 2. (CarA) [< Venez Sp *cariaquito*, name of this medicinal shrub (*NHPT:97*), prob of Carib orig. Cp *BDFC:203* Carib *acaranincati* 'herbalist']

ka·yap (ki·ap, ky·ap) [kayap~kiap] *n* (Guyn) ‖ LEND-HAND (Tbgo) [This term has spread beyond its use among coastal *Guyn* Amerindians. Cp *TDV* Venez Sp *cayapa* (see GAYAP); also *EDWLG:63* Warrau *kazaba* 'co-op work followed by spree', with variants *karaaba, kayaaba*, according to an informant]

keel off/out *vb intr phr* (Guyn, Tbgo, Trin) [AF] 1. To slip away without being noticed. 2. [By extension] [AF—Joc] To pass away; to die. *Look how people does dead and nobody don't know nothing until the milk bottles start to pile up in front the door. Supposing one day I keel off here in this room—I don't take milk regular—I would stay here until one of the boys drop round!*—STLL:115 [Perh orig a nautical term. Cp SE *keel over* 1. 'capsize' 2. (slang) 'die']

keep *vb tr* (CarA) 1. [IF] To organize and run (any group event such as a dance, a wake, a wedding, etc). *They keep dances regularly to make money to pay their rent.*—(Guyn) 2. To be principally responsible for (collecting and keeping the money of) a SUSU. *If you goin[g] keep susu yo[u] better pay when i[t]'s time or yo[u] get beat!*—(Trin) [Extensions of *OED* keep v 12. 'to observe with due formality' and 34. 'to carry on, conduct'] **3.** PHRASES [Including some intr senses] **3.1 keep a fuss** *vb phr* (Bdos, Jmca) [*AF/IF*] ‖ KEEP NOISE (CarA) See PHR 3.8 *After the Co-operatives and the taximen started to keep a fuss about these coaches coming in which obviously would deprive them of revenue, a suggestion was made to the Co-operative that they would run the coaches on behalf of this company.*—Bdos (Hd, 74.11.26, p.4218) **3.2 keep behind (sb)** *vb phr* (CarA) [*IF*] To persist in goading, urging, or driving (sb) (to get sth done). *And she had leave to have the baby, but she had to keep behind the child's father until he 'did the right thing' by her.*—DaC (52.09.21, p.9) □ See also GET BEHIND (SB) (GET Phr 3.9). **3.3 keep by yourself** *vb phr* (CarA) [*IF*] To keep to yourself; to stay away from the company of others. **3.4 keep clothes on your back** *vb phr* (CarA) [*IF*] See CLOTHES[1] Phr. **3.5 keep (good) heart** *vb phr* (Guyn, Tbgo, Trin) [*IF*] See HEART Phr 4. **3.6 keep in/good with (sb)** *vb phr* (CarA) [*AF*] To be careful to maintain good relationship with (sb). *Now dis same Germany wan' keep in good wid Englan' cuz Englan' does let 'er buil' boat an' den same time she go roun' d' corner make 'greemun' wid Italy who don' like Englan'.*—DSJS:26 □ Variants are *keep in* /12'/ *with, keep good* /22'/ *with, keep in good* /12'1/ *with.* **3.7 keep my/your company** *vb phr* (CarA) See COMPANY Phr 5.2 *Helen brightened, 'I am looking forward to this Sunday with my children and my grandchildren around me to keep my company.'*—JJM:150 [*OED keep* 23. notes *keep company* (among many similar structures) as using a specialized sense of *keep*] **3.8 keep noise** *vb phr* (CarA) [*AF*] ‖ *keep a fuss* (Bdos, Jmca) (i) To make a disturbing noise (esp in ref to noisy behaviour). **a.** *If you had to build a house today you would have to look for a geyser, a bath tub, a bidet for the wife, and the toilet is supposed to be one that hardly keeps noise.*—Bdos (Hd, 76.08.04, p.7146) (ii) To quarrel without restraint (with sb); to object loudly and embarrassingly. **b.** *After that Carmen came out of the house and he said to her: 'Ain't I tell you not to let the boy come there? Don't let him come there. I don't want him there.' She then turned to him and said: 'What noise you keeping?'*—AnS (63.10.23, p.4) [Cp *EDD keep* (var. dial. uses in Sc, Irel, Eng, Amer) II. 5. *keep a noise* 'to keep a hollering, to make a noise'] **3.9 keep one head** *vb phr* (Antg, StVn) [*IF*] ‖ HOLD A HEAD (Guyn) See HOLD Phr 5.3 **3.10 keep the wind out of your belly/stomach** *vb phr* (CarA) [*AF/IF*] ‖ *keep your stomach* (CarA) See WIND[1] Phr 2.1 **3.11 keep up (a birthday, wedding, etc)** *vb phr* (CarA) [*AF/IF*] To celebrate (an event) with festivity. *Several hundred pounds of flour, sugar and rice, a dozen or so barrels of vegetables, demi-johns of rum, about twenty goats, and a pig or two represent only a part of the cost of 'keeping up the wedding'.*—HVVIS:107 **3.12 keep with (sb)** *vb phr* (CarA) [*AF*] [Of a man or woman] To live with (sb), or to maintain or be maintained by (sb) in return for sexual favours. **a.** *How you t[h]ink she would mek out if she ain[']t] keep with some man?*—(Guyn) **b.** *'You ain't know all dis time*

when I say dey was friends, people know he was well keeping with her,' she said.—Gren (Ms) [Cp *OED keep* v 20. b. 'to keep a woman as mistress' and 37. 'to reside, dwell, lodge', the two senses being combined in the CE phr] **3.13 keep your cool; keep your head** *vb phrs* (CarA) [*AF*] To control yourself; not to lose your temper or balanced judgment. *I wish some superior officer would tell WPC Marjorie B— to keep her cool. Perhaps they should place her on a leash like the doc says he has his ministers.*—BoM (80.02.29, p.11) **3.14 keep yourself to yourself** *vb refl phr* (CarA) [*AF/IF*] To keep out; to stay away (as an unwanted person). *Not that these two gentlemen kept themselves to themselves. They liked Mrs Feathery very much, but she did not like them.*—AFTF:15 **3.15 keep your stomach** *vb phr* (CarA) See PHR 3.10 *Breakfast will be late, so take a banana to keep your stomach until it's ready.*—(Dmca) **3.16 keep your tail quiet** *vb phr* (CarA) [*AF*] See TAIL Phr 2.4

keep·er *n* (ECar) A sexual companion (whether man or woman) with whom one lives; a common-law spouse. □ The term *keeper* does not necessarily indicate a stable relationship as *common-law husband/wife* usu does.

keep-miss [kipmɪs] *n* (Bdos, Guyn, Tbgo) [*AF—Derog*] ‖ *kep(t)-miss* (Gren, Guyn) ‖ *kip-miss* (Bdos) ‖ *keep-woman* (Antg, Tbgo) A mistress who is sheltered and maintained, together with any children of the association, usu by a married man. *He may be married and have a 'keep miss', and in England if the House of Lords passes the Bill this week the 'keep miss' will have to get something out of the estate too as well as the children.*—Bdos (Hd, 75.07.15, p.5227) [< (SE) *keep* (a woman) + *miss* 'an unmarried woman'. See also KEEP Phr 3.12 KEEP WITH (SB)]

keep-wom·an [kip-wʊmʌn ~ kɪp-ʊman] *n* (Antg, Tbgo) ‖ KEEP-MISS (Bdos, etc)

Kek·chi [kɛ(k)či] *n* (Belz) **1.** An ethnic and linguistic sub-group of Mayan people inhabiting the southernmost inland area of Belize. **2.** The language spoken by these people. □ Pl unchanged. Sometimes *Kekchi-Maya(s)*. See also MOPAN.

kel·lick (kil·lick) [kɛlɪk ~ kɪlɪk] *n* (Belz, CayI, Tbgo) **1.** (Belz, Tbgo) [Fishing Ind] A small anchor. **2.** (CayI) [By extension] A heavy stone used as an anchor. [Cp *CSD* Sc *killick* 1. 'the mouth of a pickaxe'. (The resemblance to the fluke of anchor will account for sense 1.). Cp also *OED* Naut *killick, killock* 'a heavy stone used on small vessels as a substitute for an anchor' (hence sense 2.)] □ The form *killick* is an alternative in *Belz.*

ke·nai·ma *n* (Guyn) See KANAIMA

kench *n* (Jmca) [*IF*] **1.** A very small quantity (of sth named or understood); a very small one (of sth stated in foll phr). **2.** PHRASE **2.1 a kench**

of a (sth) n phr (Jmca) A very little or too little (sth). *But the trouble we had getting [the desk] through the narrow kench of a door in these modern town-houses soon made me forget my sorrow.*—CTW:1 [Cp *EDD* kinch sb 4. 'a small portion or quantity' (Lin.). But cp also KANCHI BIT (*Guyn*)]

ke·nep (ke·nip, ki·nip, kin·nup, ki·nop) ['kɛnɪp ~ kɪnɪp ~ kɪnʌp] n (Baha, Dmca, Gren, Guyn, StKt, StLu) ‖ GUINEP (CarA) [< Arawakan *kenepa/genipa*, name of the fruit, the seed of wh was used for making a blue-black body dye (Balp 4.3, p.2); the variant *kenep* is therefore etymologically the closest, although *kenip*, *kinnup* are more popular spellings. Cp also *NPHT:341 quénèpe* (Hait)] □ This variant, Formal in some territories, is regarded as *AF* in *Guyn* and perh also elsewhere where *guinep* is preferred.

kè·nèt (ken·ette, que·nette, tjenn·èt) ['kɛnɛt] n (StLu) ‖ GUINEP (CarA) [Fr Cr. Cp *NPHT: 341 kenette, quinette* (Guad, Mart)]

ke·nip n (Baha, etc) See KENEP

kenz (kens) [kɛnz] adj (USVI) [*AF—Joc*] Stupid; easily fooled; simple-minded. [Cp *CSD* Sc *kensy* n 'term of abuse for a man' 16C]

keow (kyow) [kiaʊ] n (Tbgo, Trin) A medium-sized, speckled marble that is much prized in playing marbles. *The little fellow, kneeling in the dust, his rump high in the air, his eyes screwed up intently, pitched his mottled keow and hit the steel-bearing plumb.*—MHBT:72 □ Pl usu unchanged.

kep(t)-miss [kɛp(t)-mɪs] n (Gren, Guyn) [*IF—Derog*] ‖ KEEP-MISS (Bdos, etc) *As he sat in the shade of the spreading mango tree, he heard the gentle cry of the infant and without his wanting, his conscience moved him to thoughts of its mother. She was not his wife, but a 'kept miss' who feared his ill temper and cringed from his all too frequent blows.*—PGIP:17 [A refined form of the commoner KEEP-MISS]

ker·ful·fle vb tr, n (Bdos, Guyn) (A rarer spelling of) CAFFUFFLE

ker·nel [kʌrnɛl] n (Bdos, Guyn) A swollen and somewhat painful gland in the groin, usu associated with an untended wound in the leg or foot. [As *OED* kernel sb 4.; but there noted as *chiefly dial.*]

ker·o·sene-pan n (Belz, BrVi) A square-bodied, tin can about 18 ins deep, in wh some commercial product (kerosene, margarine, etc) was imported and wh is now turned to domestic uses. [See PAN¹ 1. etym]

Ke·ru·bee [kerobi] /1'12/ n (Belz) [*AF—Derog*] A GARIFUNA. *There is one thing I can't understand, especially here in Belize City. People refer to men and women of our race as 'Kerubee'. Why? It seems to me that there is not a single Creole person who can resist the temptation of putting us down by referring to us as 'Kerubee'. The Caribs are a well known race of people. We have not forsaken our language for another.*—ReP (79.10.14, p.13) [A corrupt pronunc of *Carib*]

kes·ki·dee n (Tbgo, Trin) See KISKADEE

ketch vb (CarA) [*AF*] See CATCH [*EDD* gives this spelling representing E dial pronunc in Hrf, Brks, Ess]

ketch·ie n (BrVi) ‖ ANGLE² (Antg) □ Noted in Anegada.

ket·tle(-drum) (kit·tle(-drum)) n 1. ‖ *rattle-drum, tittle drum* (Jmca) (ECar) A European snare drum, i.e. a small double-headed drum about 15 ins in diameter, producing a metallic rattling sound; it is slung at the player's side, played with two sticks, and is a key instrument in Caribbean masquerade and street bands. *The kittle drum is a small goat-skin drum played with two sticks to give a syncopated rhythm.*—FMEI:53 [Perh from an early misascription or folk-etym shift of Sc *kittle* (*up*) vb as *CSD kittle*¹ 4. 'to strike up (a tune)'. Some CE speakers still pronounce it *kittle-drum*, and it is often used to start the street music. SE *kettle drum* is a large hemispherical orchestral drum, tuned to a single note, and often one of a standing group of three drums] 2. (Trin) [By extension, referred to only as *kettle/kittle*] A GUITAR-PAN in a STEELBAND. *You tink it easy to tune a pan and beat notes. We making ping pong, kettle and boom. The ping pong is to be played wid one stick, de kettle two sticks, and boom one stick.*—DP:9

ket·to n (Jmca) ‖ EBONY 2 (Baha, etc)

kha·ki-pants PHRASES 1. **all (is) same khaki-pants** id phr (Bdos, Gren, StLu, Trin) [*AF—Joc*] ‖ ALL IS ONE (Bdos, Guyn) See ALL² Phr 3.5 2. **the same old khaki-pants** n phr (Bdos, StLu, Trin) [*AF—Joc*] The same thing as before; a repetition of the same (undesirable, stupid, etc) action(s). *All in all, St Lucia's politics is the same old khaki pants. Pappyshow and more pappyshow. Where do we go from here?*—VoS (77.11.24, p.2) [Perh a derisive ref to the khaki shorts wh were the standard field garb of the former white colonial officers]

khus-khus (grass) (cus-cus, kuss-kuss) [kʊs-kʊs (gra·s)] n (phr) ‖ VETIVER (Dmca, etc) *In Barbados khus-khus is cultivated as a border plant to prevent erosion ... the roots [also] possessing an aromatic substance which is imparted to clothes when the roots are washed and placed between them.*—GLPF:70 [< Hin *cuscus* < *kush* 'a sort of sacrificial grass'. *OED* lists both CUSCUS² ('Hence *cuscus-grass*') and *khus-khus*, with variant spellings, as main entries of the same origin for this item. The commoner occurrence of the latter spelling is due to the commercial use of the roots for making a perfume]

ki·ap *n* (Guyn) See KAYAP

kick *vb tr* PHRASES **1. kick brass** *vb phr* (Gren, Tbgo, Trin) [*AF*] ‖ KICK DUST (CarA) *I had got this report that L— had issued a memo to ... Six Ten banning the voice of Raffique S— over the government station and the boys were kicking brass.*—BoM (75.03.07, p.11) [Prob a euphemism for *kick* RASS/ass, 'kick violently' (i.e. against sb or sth)] **2. kick dust** *vb phr* (CarA) [*AF/IF*] ‖ *kick brass* (Gren, Tbgo, Trin) ‖ *kick hell* (Bdos, Guyn) ‖ *kick sands* (TkCa) To quarrel and carry on; to create a great fuss; to raise hell. **a.** *He was afraid to say he had lost the hammer and saw because he knew his father was going to kick dust.*—(StVn) **b.** *I want to say that that man had kicked hell in his cell before he would receive a meal ... five minutes to twelve when ... it should have been served to him since eleven o'clock.*—TrU (60.12.03, p.1) □ Cp SE (informal) *kick up dust, raise a/the dust.* **3. kick out** *vb phr* (Tbgo, Trin) [*AF—Joc*] To die. *A villager was passing and joined in the conversation: 'She dead early dis marning and dey go bury she tomorrow, please de lard. She kick out when they least expect her to.'*—DMMGT:37 [Cp IF AmE *kick off* 'to die'] **4. kick stones** *vb phr* (TkCa) [*AF—Joc*] ‖ WORK AT IDLE HALL (Bdos, etc) See IDLE HALL [Ref to the action of one who has nothing to do but kick stones about in bored idleness]

kicks·in(g) [*vb*]-*ing participle* (Tbgo, Trin) [*AF—Joc*] Making fun; not being serious; fooling around. *The Parliamentarians were kicksin' on the cricket grounds in Balandra last Sunday. They challenged the Lawrence Woods XI and were soundly beaten.*—BoM (79.05.04, p.25) [< IF E *kicks* 'stimulated pleasure', by characteristic CE functional n > vb shift, + ing [ɪn] with CE pronunc] □ Also widely used as n in *Trin* E.

kick·ster [kɪkstə] *n* (Tbgo, Trin) [*AF—Joc/Derog*] A jester or sb who deserves to be so considered; an amusing person; an irresponsible person. [< IF E *kicks*, as in prec, + *ster* by analogy with *trickster, gangster*, etc]

Kick·stone Com·pa·ny *n phr* (TkCa) [*AF—Joc*] ‖ IDLE HALL (Bdos, etc) See KICK Phr 4. PHRASE **working for Kickstone Company** *adj phr* (TkCa) [*AF—Joc*] Unemployed.

kicks·y [kɪksi] *adj* (Tbgo, Trin) [*AF—Joc/Derog*] [Of a place or event] Full of amusement; [of a person] keenly lively without being too cautious. *The 21-year-old St James beauty says that you Trini guys are a bit too fast for her. And if you'll like to be her speed, you'll just have to cool down on your kicksy way of life.*—SuP (75.02.09, p.1) [< IF E *kicks*, as in prec, + *y* 'full of' as in *icy, thorny*, etc]

kid·die-king·dom (kid·dy-king·dom) *n* (Bdos) [*AF—Joc*] **1.** A temporary state or condition of sheer delight; a fool's paradise. **2.**

PHRASE **2.1 in goat-heaven and kiddie-kingdom** *adj phr* (Bdos) [*AF—Joc*] See HEAVEN Phr 1.

kid·die ram-goat *n phr* (Tbgo, Trin) [*AF*] A male kid; a young male goat.

Kid·dies Car·ni·val *n phr* (ECar) A semicompetitive show in wh children wear elaborate costumes, and some of the regular features of CARNIVAL are imitated; it is usu held on the Saturday afternoon of the week before the usu CARNIVAL weekend.

kid·ney-bean *n* (Baha, Jmca, Trin) ‖ STRINGBEAN (CarA) [From its distinctive shape]

kid·ney-man·go *n* (Antg, Belz, Jmca, ViIs) A sweet variety of mango that is kidney-shaped and usu small.

kill *vb tr* (CarA) **1.** (CarA) [*AF*] [In absolute sense] To make (sb) laugh too much or ache with laughter. *When A hear them cacklin away I know she was killin[g] them wit[h] the story about the police runnin[g] from the dog.*—(Guyn) □ Cp DIE/DEAD WITH LAUGH. See DEAD[2] Phr. **2.** (CarA) [*IF*] [With inanimate subj] To cause great difficulty to do, manage, finish. *That gate killed me to build and hang—took me a whole week.*—(StVn) **3.** PHRASES **3.1** (CarA) [*AF*] [Used in many contexts to give intensive force to an inferred action, state, behaviour, etc] **fever/hunger/ sleep is killing you** *id phr* [*IF/AF*] You are intensely feverish/hungry/sleepy. *BWIA never came till 2 o'clock next morning, so you know how sleep and hunger killing everybody.*—(Antg) [See HUNGER Phr 2.] **3.1.1 kill a laugh, a sleep, etc** *vb phr* To laugh heartily, sleep soundly, etc. ... *he would reply with a sage shake of his fuzzy head, —'Reading is the Key to Knowledge, comrade.' The 'comrade' would go away feeling impressed whilst Samuel killing a laugh.*—Kai. X. p.41 (N. Kissoon) **3.1.2 kill (any food, liquor, etc)** *vb phr* To eat or drink (sth) voraciously, completely. *This time the fellas killing the roti and the Fernandes [rum] so much they couldn't even notice the rain.*—Tbgo (Ms) **3.2 kill (sb/sth) dead** *vb phr* [X] To kill (sb) instantly (by striking or shooting); to destroy (sth) finally. *He jook the knife in the sheep and kill it dead one time.*—CISH: 88 **3.3 kill (sb) with blows** *vb phr* To beat (sb) severely; to trounce or flog (sb) mercilessly. *If her mother hears how she is getting on with the boys she would kill her with blows, you see!*—(Jmca) **3.3.1 kill (sb) with the laugh/with work, etc** *vb phr* To make (sb) laugh intensely, work intensely, etc. *For dey li[tt]l[e] bit o[f] money [u] pon a Friday dey does want kill you wid work.*— (Bdos) **3.3.2 nearly/want to kill yourself laughing** *vb refl phr* (CarA) [*AF*] ‖ ALMOST DIE LAUGHING (CarA) *While all this confusion happening Moses was killing himself with laugh.*— STLL:16 **3.4 kill out yourself; kill up yourself** *vb phrs* (CarA) [*AF*] ‖ *fight up yourself* (CarA) To exhaust yourself. *I kill out myself for thirty odd dollars a week, out in bad weather* *doing special duty to try and make up and these brutes dress up all the time more than office man.*—HF:27 **b.** *Is only me alone and I ain[t] goin[g] kill up meself over dey work, dear!*—(Jmca) □ This phr is more intensive than ‖ *fight up yourself*, is often used in neg contexts and also often *Joc.* **3.5 kill priest** *vb phr* (Gren, Tbgo, Trin) [*AF*—*Joc*] To have done sth that has evidently brought upon you the wrath of God. *Boy I ca[n't] tell how things goin[g] so from bad to worse wid me. Is like if I kill priest, no!*—(Trin)

kill·dev·il *n* (CarA) [Hist] Pure alcohol, later called 'rum'. *Here is where Kill-Devil Rum dripped after going through the 'worm' cistern ... that cooled the alcohol vapors.*—JNHSJ:40 [The name evid originated in *Bdos* as a Joc metaphor, and spread to the rest of the *CarA* as the liquor became popular. See *OED kill-devil* 2. (cit from *Bdos* 1651) 'Rumbullion, alias Kill-Devill ... made of suggar canes distilled, a hott, hellish and terrible liquor'] □ The name is occasionally revived in *Joc* usage. Note cit. See also HIGH-WINE.

kil·lick *n* (Belz) See KELLICK

kil·li-kil·li; **kil.ly-hawk** *n* (Angu, Mrat, USVI) ‖ SPARROW-HAWK (CarA) [Name imitative of its shrill cry when alarmed or attacking]

kim·bo *n* (Bdos, Guyn, Jmca) **1.** The hip. **2.** *PHRASES* **2.1 hand(s) at/in/on your kimbo(es)** *adv phr* (Bdos, Guyn, Jmca) [*IF*] (With) your arm(s) akimbo. *Don't put your hand on your kimbo when you're talking to me.*—(Guyn) **2.2 take your hand(s) out your kimbo(es)** *vb phr* (Bdos) [*IF*] To remove your hands from your hips. *Boy tek yo[ur] hands out yo[ur] kimboes! What[t] you t[h]ink you is a man or what?*—(Bdos) [Possibly an EE survival in CE. Note *OED kimbo* 'in phr *on kimbo*' (= a-kimbo). Possibly, however, an independent CE development by misplaced juncture < SE *hand(s) akimbo* combined with folk etym by wh *akimbo* is interpreted as Cr A⁷ 'on, at the' + a noun KIMBO. This would account both for the pl form and the distinct sense]

kind *n* (CarA) [In ref to categories of food] See BREAD-KIND, FOOD-KIND, MEAT-KIND

ki·nep; **ki.nip** *n* (Belz, StKt) See KENEP

king[1] *n* (CarA) **1.** The man who is the established champion in any traditional folk competition. *About a week before Carnival, the kings were chosen from each village. Ability to lead a group to battle was determined by the strength of an individual as shown in wrestling and in the quality and quantity of literature he could recite. On Shrove Tuesday, they met each other at different villages. This was done separately in the north and the south. The Heroes competed against themselves by moving from village to village, where the kings competed against each other. The same thing happened in the south and finally the King*

of the North led his men to Hillsborough to fight against ... the King of the South and his supporters.—DCC:37 [Perh orig applied (as in above cit from *Crcu*) to the champion stick-fighter who was also in earlier times leader of a band of stick-fighters that did battle with one or more similarly led bands of stick-fighters. See KALINDA BAND, KING STICK-FIGHTER] □ See also QUEEN. **2.** *PHRASES* **2.1 Calypso King** *n phr* (ECar) See separate entry. **2.2 Road-march King** *n phr* (Trin) See ROAD-MARCH

king[2] *n* (CarA) ‖ KINGFISH (CarA) □ This shortened form frequently occurs in lists of marketed fishes.

kin(g)·do·la *n in adv function* (Belz) See HANG Phr 1.

king-fish* (**king·fish**) *n* (CarA) ‖ **king-mackerel** (Trin) A long, round-bodied fish weighing up to 80 lbs with a sleek, dark-grey back and silvery sides and belly; its rich meat is highly prized; *Scomberomorus cavalla (Cybiidae)*. □ See WAHOO.

King J'Ouvert; **King Jour Ouvert** [kɪŋžuvɛ] *n phr* (Tbgo, Trin) The leading male masquerader of a competing OLE MAS BAND displaying the wittiest costumes and placards interpreting a popular topic; he is judged winner and crowned on J'OUVERT morning.

king-macke·rel *n* (Trin) ‖ KING-FISH (CarA) [From its size and its resemblance by body-colouring to the mackerel]

King of Carnival *n phr* (ECar) ‖ KING OF THE BANDS (ECar)

King of the Band *n phr* (ECar) The leading male masquerader of a costumed CARNIVAL BAND; he is the most elaborately costumed man of the BAND, usu also wearing a huge, ornate headpiece. *This year Dhanraj, a bachelor, was bringing out a band entitled 'Gala Africa' in which he was to play the King of the Band. He had decorated a mammoth headpiece.*—ExP (72.03.28, p.1) □ In a BAND of several thousand there are sometimes two KINGS.

King of the Bands *n phr* (ECar) ‖ *King of Carnival* (ECar) The leading male masquerader (or KING) whose costume is judged the most outstanding of all in the CARNIVAL competition; in *Trin* he is chosen on the night of DIMANCHE GRAS. *Mas' Lovers were stunned at the untimely death of Albert Moore yesterday—the man who has won 'King of the Bands' title more times than anyone else.*—ExP (72.01.16, p.1)

king-of-the-for·est *n* (Jmca) ‖ CHRISTMAS-CANDLE (Bdos, etc)

king-or·ange* *n* (Jmca, StKt, Trin) A large sweet variety of TANGERINE; *Citrus sinensis* or *C. reticulata (Rutaceae)*.

King-Sailor *n* (Trin) **1.** The KING of the SAILOR-BAND who wears a big, comically decorative headpiece, sometimes with a mask, and a sparkling, comically-decorated costume modelled on a sailor's uniform. **2.** *PHRASE* **2.1 King-Sailor dance** *n phr* **(i)** (Tbgo, Trin) The CARNIVAL street-dance of the KING-SAILOR in wh the rolling, drunken-looking walk of a sailor is exaggerated, with hopping and many imaginative exhibitionist features added. **(ii)** (ECar) A house-party dance-step characterized by shuffling sideways while wiggling the hips; it was once popular with teenagers.

King's House *n phr* (Jmca) ‖ GOVERNMENT-HOUSE (CarA)

King stick-fighter *n phr* (ECar) The champion STICK-FIGHTER of a region or a territory. *Bois men from all over the country will journey to Enterprise Village in Chaguanas where King stickfighter Gerald Pierre of Arouca will be defending his crown.*—ExP (73.01.31, p.7)

ki·nip *n* (Baha, etc) See KENEP

kin·na [kɪna] *n* (Guyn) **1.** A food or anything edible to wh you are allergic. *Pumpkin is despised and dreaded by many who say it is their kinna.*—SuC (77.06.19, p.20) **2.** [By extension] Anything, place, situation, etc that always vexes you. [Cp *TAGD:108* Mende *kena* 'white spots in the skin caused by destruction of the coloured pigment'. The connection is by no means firm but the allergy (sense 1.) sometimes takes the form of a skin rash]

kin·nup (Guyn); **ki.nop** *n* (Baha, Dmca, Gren, Guyn, StKt, StLu) See KENEP

kip-miss [kɪpmɪs] *n* (Bdos) [*AF—Derog*] ‖ KEEP-MISS (Bdos, etc)

kir·wal [kɪrwal] *n* (Guyn, Trin) [*Derog*] [Indic] A black person. [Bhoj < Hin]

kis·ka·dee* (kes·ki·dee) [kɪskadi· ~ kɛskɪdi·] *n* (Guyn, Tbgo, Trin) ‖ *kis-kas* (Guyn) A bird that is about 9 ins long, with a black head marked by a prominent white stripe around it above the eye; its back is brownish and its throat white, and breast and belly bright yellow; it is widely known for its clear, insistent call from wh its name is derived; *Pitangus sulphuratus* (*Tyrannidae*). [It is widely claimed in the professional literature that the name KISKADEE ~ KESKIDEE derives from a Fr interpretation (*Qu'est-ce qu'il dit?* 'What is it saying?') of the bird's call. However, it is by no means clear why this should be so, as the species makes 'varied, boisterous cries' (*FGBTT:319*; see also p.317) and the onomatopoeic name needs no French □ The alternative spelling *keskidee* (prob infl by the association claimed with Fr) is used only in *Trin & Tbgo*.

kiss *PHRASE* **kiss your teeth (at sb)** *vb phr* (Baha, Jmca) ‖ SUCK YOUR TEETH (AT/ON SB) (CarA) *When she asked and was told the price of the plantains, she kissed her teeth and told the vendor that she could keep them.*—WeG (75.04.08, p.15) [*Kiss* prob suggested by resemblance of the sound. Also HISS YOUR TEETH]

kiss-me-quick *n* (Dmca, Jmca) ‖ JUMP-UP-AND-KISS-ME (CayI, etc) *There is a plant that some call 'Kiss me Quick' or 'Jump Up and Kiss Me' ... sometimes called Coral plant or Fountain plant because the branches from an upright position fall over like a fountain.*—NeC (76.04.03, p.12)

kiss-teeth *n* (Jmca) ‖ SUCK-TEETH (CarA) [From vb phr KISS YOUR TEETH]

kitch·en-bitch *n* (Jmca) A home-made torch consisting of a condensed-milk tin with kerosene oil and a cloth wick stuck through its top; it is fitted with a handle and held to light the way on dark roads in rural areas. [Cp *OED2 bitch* sb¹ 2. c. 'a primitive form of lamp used in ... Canada' + cits indicating the use of a rag wick stuck in a tin of grease]

kitch·en-dress·er *n* (Guyn) ‖ DRESSER 3. (i) (Bdos, etc)

Kit·ti·fo·ni·an [kɪtifo·niʌn] /112′21/ *n* (Guyn) **1.** [*IF-Joc*] A person born in or a long-time resident of Kitty, a suburb of Georgetown, Guyana. **2.** [Perh by extension] ‖ *Kittitian* (CarA) □ The term is commoner among older folk.

Kit·ti·tian [kɪtiʃʌn/-ən] *n, adj* (CarA) (A person or thing) of or belonging to St Kitts (the name always used for St Christopher). *However, since the eighteenth century the island has been popularly known as St Kitts. Its inhabitants are called 'Kittitians'. Curiously, up to early in the twentieth century they were referred to as 'Kittifonians'.*—IHB:2 [Prob < *Kittsian* (cp HAITIAN, VINCENTIAN) + insertion [-tiš-] by dissimilation or epenthesis]

kit·tle(-drum) *n* (ECar) See KETTLE(-DRUM)

Klaat! [kla::t] *excl* (Jmca) [*Vul*] An indecent exclamation of surprise or anger. [Shortened form of BLOOD-CLOTH + Cr vowel opening and lengthening /o > aa/]

kling-kling (cling-cling) *n* **1.** (Jmca) ‖ BLACK-BIRD 1.1 (CarA) **2.** (Guyn) A small, green, forest parrot. [From the bird's cry. Cp CHING-CHING (CayI)]

knock *vb tr* (CarA) [*AF/IF*] **1.** (CarA) [*IF*] To hit or strike; to give (sb) a blow. *She said, 'I had my child in my hand and if you did knock me child I would have have call the police for you.'*—LaS (74.04.27, p.2) [Prob a survival from EE. Cp *OED knock* v trans. 2. 'to give a hard blow; to hit, strike, beat, hammer' + cits from Middle E to Shak] □ This very common CE usage is not acceptable in ModE. **2.** (CarA) [*IF*] **(i)** [By metaph extension] To charge (a high price). *Yes it's true I asked you to make the table but I never expected you would knock me so hard.*—(Bdos) **(ii)** (CarA) [*IF*] To sentence (sb) to serve a long prison term. *When the judge knock him four years the wife screamed!*—(Guyn) **3.** (Guyn) [*AF—Joc*] To eat and/or drink without restraint. *I never see a woman like that who could knock the food and the rum even with men and don[t] get fat!*—(Guyn) [Cp IF ModE *knock back* 'to eat or drink quickly'] **4.** PHRASES **4.1 knock a borrow** *vb phr* (Guyn) [*AF*] To resort easily to borrowing; to casually decide to borrow. *And if she needed an ice-cream can or a couple of chairs or whatever she wouldn't hesitate to run across to the Morrisons and knock a borrow.*—(Guyn) **4.2 Knock board!/ wood!** *imper id phr* (SE) Touch wood! (i.e. for good luck). **4.3 knock dog** *vb phr* (ECar) [*AF—Joc*] [Of an adult] To knock about in boredom; to stay in one place with nothing worthwhile to do. *I don't have money to go to the University so I might as well stay and knock dog here.*—(StKt) **4.3.1 knocking dog** *adj phr* (CarA) [*AF—Joc*] ‖ **licking, washing ashore** (Guyn) [Usu of market-place items] In great abundance; available cheap because so plentiful. *More often than not processors can, or will only, complete [their operations] when there is a glut, when products are knocking dog, so to speak.*—Jmca (Ms, 1974) **4.4 knock Flora** *vb phr* (Dmca, Gren, Guyn, Tbgo) [*AF—Joc*] See FLORA Phr 2.1 **4.5 knock drum/ pan** *vb phr* (CarA) [*AF*] To beat a drum or (in a STEELBAND) a PAN. *In the old days ... the people played anything they liked; one only needed to get a pass to knock drum on the road. Today in St Kitts the Government want to take over everything.*—DeM(SK) (77.12.31, p.3) **4.6 knock your own thing** *vb phr* (Belz) ‖ DO YOUR OWN THING (CarA) See DO[1] Phrs 8.21 (ii), 8.22 *And the day the PUP does anything to threaten the national security and freedom of Belize, then the world will know as usual that here we knock our own thing.*—AmA (80.05.30, p.4) **4.7 knock you down** *vb phr* (Guyn) [*AF*] ‖ LICK YOU DOWN (Guyn) See LICK Phr 4.7.1 **4.8 (smell) knocks you down** *id phr* (Guyn, Tbgo, Trin) [*AF— Derog*] [Of a smell] To be strongly unpleasant. *All the time you're sittin[g] in the gallery the scent of the pig pen is knockin[g] you do[w]ng.*—(Tbgo) **4.9 take and knock (sb)** *vb phr* (Bdos, Guyn) [*X*] See TAKE Phr 18.

knock·a·bout (wom·an) *n (phr)* (CarA) A prostitute of the lowest order.

knot·ty dread *n phr* (CarA) [Rastaf] (A refined form of) NATTY DREAD.

knot·ty hair; **nat·ty hair** [ˈnɒti heˑr] *n phr* (Angu, BrVi) [*IF*] ‖ BAD HAIR (CarA)

knot·ty head; **nat·ty head** [ˈnɒti hɛd] *n phr* (Belz, StVn) [*AF—Derog*] ‖ BAD HAIR (CarA)

know *vb* (CarA) PHRASES **1. have (sb) to know (sth)** *vb phr* (Bdos, Guyn) To say (sth) clearly

and firmly to (sb). *When he came to me with his nonsense, I just had him to know that I am a decent woman.*—(Guyn) **2. know sense** *vb phr* (CarA) [*X*] To be intelligent, sensible. *S1: 'I don't think the full moon have anything to do with it.' S2: 'A-ha! Yuh don't know sense, dat's why. Ah tell yuh, if yuh plant tings wen de moon full, it bound to grow quick.'*—SABS:115 [By overlap: *know* + *have sense*] **3. know what o'clock** *vb phr* **(i)** (Jmca) [*AF*] To be aware of a situation; to know what's what. [Cp *EDD know* II. 1. v (Nrf) *know what o'clock* 'know what is going on'] **(ii)** (Gren) [*AF*] [Often used in threatening a child] To suffer the consequences. *Break that chimney wid your stupidness and you will know what o'clock!*— PPGD:46 **4. know where barley grows** *vb phr* (Guyn, Trin) [*AF—Joc*] [Used in warning or threatening senses] To be brought to your senses; to be forced to behave correctly. *What they want is someone at the helm and a goal around the corner. When I am P.M. they will know where the hell barley growing.*—JJM:91 **5. not know A from bull-foot** *vb phr* (CarA) [*AF—Joc*] Not know what you're about; (to) be blundering and fumbling. *Look who they put as Minister of Health, in charge of doctors and people like that! They will twist him around their little finger because everybody knows he don't know A from bull-foot.*— (Gren) **6. not know not[hi]n[g] [a]bout not[hi]n[g]** *vb phr* (CarA) [*AF—Joc*] To claim or appear to be totally ignorant of the facts; to refuse or be unable to give any helpful information. *Me? I will see and ain[t] see! I won[t] know not[hi]n[g] [a]bout not[hi]n[g]!*—(Bdos) [A Joc survival from basilectal Cr [doˑn noˑ nʌtn bʊut nʌtn] used in situations of self-defence] **7. You know the thing!** *id phr* (CarA) [*AF*] (I see that) you understand (my embarrassment) perfectly! **7.1 You know that way?** *id phr* (Bdos, Guyn) [*AF/IF*] Do you understand the sort of thing, situation, (etc) that I am talking about? *And then although I know about the weddin[g] she ain[t] tell me, so I didn[t] start fixin[g] up and so—yo[u] know da way?*—(Bdos) **7.2 You know you!/me!/them!, etc** /1 3ʹ 1/ *id excl phr* (CarA) [Strongly sarcastic warning] You are well aware of how you (I, they, etc) are capable of behaving!

knuck·le-seed *n* (Nevs) ‖ NICKER (Angu, etc)

kò·bo *n* (Gren, Trin) See CORBEAU

ko·chonn·i (**co·cho·nie**) [ˈkoʃɔni] *n* (Dmca, StLu) [*AF—Derog*] A worthless nothing; a piece of trash or junk. *'Cause he was too damn rude. You come take his place? Piece of cochonie like you?*—SNWIC:282 (R. Walcott) [Fr Cr < Fr *cochonnerie* 'filthiness; obscenity; rubbish'] □ Also used of persons, as an insult, as in cit.

Ko·fi (**Cuf·fie, Cuf·fy**) [kʌfi] *n* (CarA) [*AF— Joc*] (A name loosely applied to) any black man, usu from a rural area, who is considered uneducated but shrewd; a black man who is neither easily fooled nor trifled with. [< *DAFL* Twi *Kofi* name for a boy born on a Friday. The CE associations are now obscure. For Jmca, *DJE* cites 'hot-tempered' for *Cuffee* 1., but also glosses 3. 'easily fooled', wh is the opposite of the usu sense. The association with 'temper' may be infl by CE CUFF] □ The spelling CUFFIE is commonly found.

Ko·jo (Cud·joe) *n* (Guyn) [*AF—Joc*] (A name loosely applied to) any black man, usu from a rural area, who has a reputation for rough-and-ready force, crude strength, or stubborn resistance. [< Fante *Kodwo*, *KED* Ghanaian *Kodzo* '(name of) a male born on a Monday'. The association with roughness is obscure, but possibly infl by SE *cudgel*]

ko·jo-bush/-root   (cud·joe-bush/-root) ['kʌjʌ-buš/-rut] *n* (Brbu, Gren, StVn) ‖ GULLY-ROOT (CarA) [< KOJO + *bush* or *root* (that gives him strength). See STRONG-MAN-WEED]

ko·ker [ko·kʌ] *n* (Guyn) **1.** A large sluice mechanism standing high at the coastal or river-end of a canal or TRENCH; it consists of a heavy, tarred, watertight, wooden floodgate up to 15 ft wide and as deep as necessary, held in closely slotted, concrete fixtures on either side; it is raised and lowered by the chains of a system of pulleys operated by huge spoked wheels on either side wh are turned by hand by two men; it is a vital device in controlling drainage and irrigation and preventing flooding at high tide. *If the koker is not closed in time, the sea water will come in and flood the fields.*—Guyn (Ms, 1973) **2.** ‖ BOX-KOKER (Guyn) [< (18C) Du *koker* 'an underground pipe or culvert for the draining or intake of water'. This is still the only meaning applicable in *Srnm* today, and it obviously applies in *Guyn* to the BOX-KOKER. However, the vital use of the principle in the history of drainage and irrigation in *Guyn* has generated a widening of the meaning to include the large overhead mechanism wh has become common today]

ko·ker·ite *n* (Guyn, Trin) See COCORITE

ko·ko·be *n* (CarA) See COCOBAY

ko·ko-bèf (co·co-boeuf) [koko-bɛf] *n* (Dmca, StLu) ‖ *imperial* (StVn) One of the biggest and most fleshy of cultivated mangoes in the Caribbean [< Fr Cr *koko* < Fr *couilles* 'testicles' + *bèf* (*boeuf*) 'cow, bull, ox'. Cp ‖ *bull-seed mango* (Jmca)]

ko·ko-kou·li (co·co-cou·lie) ['koko-kuli] *n* (StLu) ‖ DUNK(S) (Bdos, etc)

ko·ko·mar *n* (Crcu) See COCOMAR

ko·ko-poul ['kokopu·l] *n* (Dmca) ‖ CLAMMY-CHERRY 1. (CarA)

kòkòt *n* (Dmca, StLu, Trin) See COCOTTE

kò·kòy (cocoye) *n* (Dmca) ‖ BLUGGO (Belz, etc) [Perh orig Fr Cr < *FVA* 19c Fr slang *coquille* 'penis' in ref to its shape and size. Note *DECG*

Guad Fr Cr *kòkòy* 'grosse banane'] □ Spelling may usefully, serve to distinguish the vegetable KÒKÒY from the language COCOY(E)

kokoyé *n* (Gren, Tbgo, Trin) See COCOYEA

ko·kre·ko ['kokriko] *n* (USVI) ‖ JUMBIE-BEAD 3. (Gren, Trin, USVI) □ This name, used in St Croix (*JNHSJ:56*), is prob < Fr *coquelicot* 'red poppy', one of the alternatives cited in *ACPRV: 173*.

koks *vb* (Gren) [*AF*] ‖ KANGSE (Guyn) [See KONKS of wh this is prob a denasalized form]

kòk·té your leg *vb phr* (Dmca) [*AF—Joc*] ‖ COCK TEN (Guyn) *He only want to sit do[w]ng and kòkté his leg while everybody workin[g].*—(Dmca) [Fr Cr < ? Fr *coqueter* 'to be stylish']

kong·kong·sa¹ (con·con·sa, con·go·sa) ['kʌŋkʌ(ŋ)sa] *adj* [*AF*] **1.** (Jmca, Tbgo, Trin) Deceitful; hypocritical; likely to betray your trust. *You can't trust these politicians; they too 'concosa'.*—Tbgo (Ms) **2.** (Antg, Brbu) So biased as to be very untrustworthy; always ready to favour sb of a better class or colour. *You see how she conconsa! She could fin[d] seat for de doctor children, but she can['t] fin[d] none for we.*—(Antg) [By functional shift < Twi *ŋkɔŋkɔnsa* n 'falsehood, duplicity, double-dealing, dissimulation, hypocrisy'—*DAFL*] □ Other forms COME-COME-SAY, CONGO-SAY, etc are the result of folk etym.

kong·kong·sa²; **kon.go.seh** (con·go·say) [kʌŋkʌŋsa ~ kɔŋgʌsɛ/-e] *vb* [*AF*] **1.** (Antg, Brbu) To take sides; to take a biased view. *Well you know a lawyer got to congosay for whoever pay them.*—Antg (Ms) **2.** (Guyn) To gossip about (sb); to encourage and share in BAD-TALK about (sb). *Deh prapaly conguseh me name.*—RFGW: 191 [By second functional shift of prec. Cp also Sran *gongosa* n 'slander' vb 'to slander'—*WSNE*]

kon·kee *n* (Tbgo) See CONKIE

kon·konm-kou·li (co·com-coo·lie) ['kǒ kom-kuli] *n* (StLu) ‖ CERASEE (Baha, etc) [Fr Cr *kokom* < Fr *concombre* 'cucumber' + *coolie* [*Derog*] 'coolie', i.e. suggesting an inferior type of, or false cucumber. The fruit is also a prized vegetable in Indic cooking]

konks *vb* (StVn) [*AF*] ‖ KANGSE (Guyn) [This form is prob from the orig E dial *conk* + paragogic /-s/. See note at KANGSE. Cp also KOKS.]

kon·mès (com·(m)ess) [kǒmɛs] *n* [*AF*] **1.** (Dmca, Gren, StLu, Tbgo, Trin, USVI) ‖ *ballahoo³* 1 (Belz) Noisy disorder; a disturbance; a confused and unsettling situation. *In spite of all de comess / Prospect still ain't make no fuss / The woman was just a pest / But not dangerous.*—Trin (Cso) [Fr Cr < Fr *commerce* 'business', with a strong suggestion of illicit business, whence shift to sense 2.] **2.** (StVn) Scandal; gossip (esp about a scandal). *The people are so malicious and full of commess that they accuse the girl of having an abortion when she was the only in hospital for appendicitis.*—(StVn) **3.** PHRASE **3.1 make konmès (comess)** *vb phr* (Tbgo, Trin) [*AF*] To cause confusion; to create a disturbance. *If you go bring race in this matter, you only mean to make commess.*—(Trin)

kon·mè·si *n* (StVn) See COMESSIE

kon·pè *n* (Belz, ECar, StLu) See COMPÈ

Kon·pe Chyen *n phr* (Dmca) See COMPÈ ZAY-EN

Kon·pè Za·yen *n phr* (Dmca, Gren, StLu) See COMPÈ ZAYEN

koo-koo [kuku] *n* (Jmca) [Hist] ‖ *Actor-Boy* (Jmca) An elaborately costumed, young, male dancer in woman's dress, with a tall ornate headdress, a wig, a fan, and a small eye-mask, and carrying a whip; he is one of the standard, original characters of the JUNKANOO (JOHN-CANOE) parade. [Cp *ADMY* Yoruba *Kuku* a male name; also a vb 'to actually do sth'] □ This spelling is useful for distinguishing the item from COU-COU (Bdos, etc) KUKU (ViIs).

koor·tah *n* (Guyn, Trin) See KURTA

ko·té-si ko·té-la (co·tay-ci co·tay-la, co·té-ci co·té-la) ['kote-si kote-la] /1'23121/ *n phr* (Dmca, Gren, StLu, Trin) [*AF*] **1.** Gossip (usu of the amusing kind). *Look I ain'[t] wan[t] to be in dis coté-si coté-la, yo[u] see! All dis dem sa[y], he sa[y], she sa[y] ain'[t] fo[r] me.*—(Trin) **2.** [Used as an adjunct] And so on and so forth; etcetera. **3.** PHRASE **3.1 and (a) koté-si and (a) koté-la** (Gren, Trin) [*AF*] And much more; and so on and so on. *She screamed she was no fool and she knew what was going on behind her back and she intended to put a stop to it and cote-ci and cote-la.*—BoM (79.02.02, p.9) [Perh a survival in Fr Cr from 17C Fr (Cotgrave) *coter* 'to quote', a cognate phr still existing in Mod Fr argot *être à la cote* (Of a person) 'to be in the news'. If 17C Fr *coter* is seen in the sense 'to repeat (news)' i.e. 'to gossip', then the Fr Cr phr becomes 'gossip (from) here, gossip (from) there'. The rooted existence of this phr as a loan in *Gren, Trin* suggests an old Fr provincial source whose usage may not have been precisely recorded. A less likely alternative is < Fr (ce) *côté-ci* 'this side', + (ce) *côté-là* 'that side', indicating 'news from this place/side and that place/side' or perh 'two sides of a story'] □ Other variant spellings of this widely used phr are COTE-CI COTE-LA (without accents) and COTAY-SI COTAY-LA (esp in *Gren*).

kouch-kouch *n* (StLu) See COUCHE-COUCHE

koud·men (**coup-de-main**) [kudmɛ̃] *n* (Dmca, StLu) ‖ LEND-HAND (Tbgo) *With its self-help programme, the Ministry of Community Development has simply borrowed the idea of the 'coude mein' and worked on it so that it resulted in a more organised effort which benefited the community as a whole rather than a single individual.*—NaT (81.04.13, p.15) [Fr Cr < Fr *donner un coup de main à qn* 'to lend a helping hand to sb'] □ Many uninformed spellings occur besides that in the cit: *cou de main, coup du main,* etc.

kou·lèv [kulɛv] *n* (Dmca) ‖ MATAPEE (Guyn) [From the resemblance of the wicker-work to the skin of a snake. Fr Cr *koulèv* > Fr *couleuvre* 'snake']

kou-nèt *n* (Dmca) ‖ BARE-NECK FOWL (Bdos, etc) [Fr Cr < Fr *cou*, 'neck' + *nette*, (adj f) 'clean']

kou-pli·ché (**cou-plu·ché**) *n* (StLu) ‖ BARE-NECK FOWL (Bdos, etc) [Fr Cr + Fr *cou*, 'neck' + [é]*pluché*, 'plucked']

kou-tou·ni (**cou-tou·ni**) *n* (Dmca) ‖ BARE-NECK FOWL (Bdos, etc) [Fr Cr < Fr *cou*, 'neck' + *tourné* 'turned, shaped (as on a lathe)']

kou·vè·ti pòt·chanm (**co·ver·ty-po·cham, kou·vèti pot·janm**) [kŭvɛti-pɔšãm ~ kŭvɛti pɔžãm] *n* (Dmca, Trin) A crisp, almost wafer-thin, sweet, ginger-flavoured biscuit about 6 ins in diameter, baked light-brown, and most popular with older folk at Easter. [Fr Cr < Fr *couvert de pot-de-chambre* 'chamber-pot cover', from Joc ref to its resemblance to an item so used in earlier times]

kou·wès (**snake**) (**cou·ess**) [kuwɛs] *n* (phr) (Dmca, StLu) A thin, greenish grass-snake with black and white markings on its back; it is about 3 ft long and non-poisonous; *Dromicus juliae*.

kou·yon (**coo·yon, cou·yon**) [ku·yɔ ~ ku·yɔ̃] *n* (StLu, Trin) [*AF—Derog*] A fool; a very stupid person; [sometimes more strongly] a damned ass. *Senator dese fellars not cooyon you know. You tink de fellars go grab a now-for-now knowing dat just now everyting crash!*—CrU (74.08.10, Cocky & Stocky) [Fr Cr < Fr *couillon* 'stupid, silly (person)']

kò·wò·sòl (**co·ra·sol, co·ro(s)·sol**) *n* (Dmca, StLu) ‖ SOURSOP (CarA)

kò·wò·sòl-djab (**co·ro(s)·sol-di·able**) ['kɒ wɒsɒl-ja·b] *n* (Dmca) ‖ JUMBIE SOURSOP (Antg, etc)

kre·ke·teh-hawk* [krɛkɛtɛ-hɒ·k] *n* (Guyn) A dark-feathered hawk about 16 ins long and with a deeply hooked beak; it hunts in swamps, feeding on snails; *Rostrhamus sociabilis (Accipitridae)*.

kro·kos bag ['krʌkʌs bag] *n phr* (CarA) See
CROCUS BAG

Kru·man ['krumʌn] *n* (Guyn) A ruffian; a hoo-
ligan. [Prob owing to a misplaced connection
with 'crude' + man. The Kru languages are a
group spoken in the coastal areas of today's
Liberia and Ivory Coast. It is possible that the
post-Emancipation, voluntary Kru immigrants
to Guyana in the 1840's and 1850's came under
the same contempt from fellow Blacks as the
CONGO people]

ku·ka *n* (Mrat) [*AF—Joc/Vul ?*] ‖ JOBBIE (Bdos)

ku·koo *n* (Bdos) See COU-COU □ This spelling
is used by E. Brathwaite (*Mother Poem*) as perh
more suggestive of the pronunc.

ku·ku (cu·cu) *n, vb* (ViIs) [*AF—Joc*] ‖ JOBBIE
(Bdos) □ This spelling prevents confusion with
COO-COO/COU-COU (*Bdos*), KOO-KOO (*Jmca*).

ku·kus bag ['kʌkʌs bag] *n phr* (Gren) See
CROCUS BAG (CarA)

ku·mi·na ['kʊmi·na] *n* (Jmca) A ritual ceremony of singing, drumming, dancing, and
spirit-possession; it is held to pay necessary respect to the spirits of ancestors at deaths, births,
and other occasions considered critical in the
life of a family; it is now nationally recognised
beyond its original cultist confines. [It seems
generally agreed that the practice is of Kongo
origin. Alleyne (*ARJC:93*) citing Roger Bastide,
notes: 'In Brazil ... the Macumba religion of
the former (Kongo) Cambinda nation recognises
both a supreme deity Ganja Zumba (paralleling
Kumina's King Sombi) and ancestral spirits
called *zumbi*.... The word *Cambinda* provides a
very plausible etymology for *Kumina*. Phon-
ologically, there is support for a development /
mb > m/ and /nd > n/ in African words brought
to the New World'. Again, Brathwaite states:
'In her *Nkuyu* (n.11) Maureen Warner-Lewis
suggests ... that the word *kumina* comes from
UMmbundu *kumona* 'to see; possession', though
Bunseki prefers *kumunu* 'rhythm, the spirit of
rhythm'; though he later said ... that in the
eastern part of Kongo/Zaire (Miss Queenie's
[ancestral] area) *kumina* would translate as
'lion''—E.K. Brathwaite: '*Kumina*' in *Jaj* Vol
42. (Sept. 1978) p.61 f. n. 5]

kungse *n, vb* (Guyn) [*AF—Joc*] ‖ JOBBIE (Bdos)

ku·nu-mu·nu (coo·noo-moo·noo, cu·nu-
mu·nu) *n* (CarA) [*AF—Derog*] A stupid man,
esp one easily fooled and controlled by a woman;
an imbecile. [Cp Yoruba *kunun* 'bashful, lacking
self-confidence'. Also *KED* Krio *munɔ* 'fool,
stupid person'. The two forms may have been
joined in *CarA* Cr as other redundant compounds were]

ku·rass (cuir·ass) ['kʊra·s] *n* (Guyn) A
medium-sized catfish, growing up to 2 ft in
length, with poisonous spines on its fins, 'in fair
demand by the poorer classes owing rather to
its cheapness than delicacy of taste' (*RFLG:73*);
Arius milberti or *A. surinamensis* (*Siluridae*). [<
BAED Arawak *koraso* 'a type of skin fish' (i.e. of
catfish). The spelling *cuirass* is a false refinement]

kur·ta (koor·tah) [kʊrta] *n* (Guyn, Trin)
[Indic] A loose, light-fitting upper garment, usu
high-necked, long-sleeved, and reaching below
the waist; it is traditionally a man's formal garment, made of plain white cotton and worn with
a DHOTI, but embroidered variations are now also
fashionable women's wear. [Hin *kurtaa* name of
this garment]

ku·sha (cu·sha, ka·sha) [kʌša] *n* (Angu, Antg,
Brbu, Mrat) See CASHA

ku·shu (cu·shew) ['kʊšu] *n* (Antg, Bdos, Gren,
StVn, Tbgo) ‖ CASHEW 1. (CarA)

ku·shy (koo·shi)-ant(s) *n* (Guyn) ‖ ACOUSHI
ANT (Guyn) [Perh < ACOUSHI by aphesis, but
note (*EILCA:46*) Arawak *kuusee* 'kushy ant']

kuss-kuss (grass) *n* (*phr*) (Bdos, etc) See
KHUS-KHUS (GRASS)

kwab·yé (crab·i·er) [kwabye ~ krabie] *n* (Crcu,
Dmca, Gren) ‖ GAULIN (CarA) [Fr Cr < Fr *crabier*
'type of crab-eating heron' (trans, *LLFL*)]

kwab·yé nwè (crab·i·er noir) [kwabye nwɛ]
n phr (Dmca, Gren, StLu) ‖ ARSNICKER (Baha)
[Fr Cr < *crabier noir*, 'black crab-eating heron']

kwé·yòl [kweyɔl] *n* (Dmca, StLu) See CREOLE[1]
3(ii)

ky·ap *n* (Guyn) See KAYAP

kyow *n* (Tbgo, Trin) See KEOW

L

lab *n* (Belz) Porridge (made of any of a number of ingredients); hence CASSAVA-LAB, FLOUR-LAB, PLANTAIN-LAB, SEA-WEED-LAB, etc. [Cp *EDD lob* sb¹ 4. 'a thick stew or hash' + cit from w.Yks; also *loblolly* 5. 'any thick spoon-meat; esp thick porridge made of flour or oatmeal'. The *Belz* pronunc has characteristic CarA Cr [ɔ > a] vowel-opening]

la·ba·ri·a *n* (Guyn) A poisonous, dark-coloured, spotted snake often less than 2 ft long, with a flat head and a tapering tail; it strikes speedily and its bite is often fatal; *Bothrops atrox.* [BAED Arawak *labaria* 'labba-spotted snake, fer-de-lance'] □ Cp FER-DE-LANCE.

la-basse (labas(se)) [labas] *n* (Gren, Trin) A spreading, open-air, city dump. **a.** *I suppose we must now sit back patiently and wait for another form of epidemic before something is done about the La Basse.*—ExP (72.01.10, p.15) **b.** *The once clean town of St George's is now the most unclean in the country although we continue to have printed on our garbage trucks 'keep St George's clean'. Here and there are the makings of a 'labasse'*—*Melville Street near to the Sendall tunnel is one such area. There is a lack of public conveniences and those that remain are not fit for use. Because of this neglect there is stench everywhere and the population of flies and rats is on the increase.*—ToR (76.05.19, p.4) [Fr *la basse* 'the shoal, flat, sand-bank', a ref to the swamp-land on the seaward side of the Beetham Highway leading to Port-of-Spain, where city garbage is habitually dumped. The term developed a general usage, with fusion by metanalysis, spreading also to *Tbgo, Gren*] □ Spellings with caps are still common as in '*a/the/this La Basse*'.

lab·ba [laba] *n* (Guyn) ‖ GIBNUT (Baha, etc) *The flesh of the labba is firm, succulent and white, and is esteemed above that of all other local animals to the extent that it has passed into the Colonial legend that 'if one eat labba and drink creek water, one must return to the colony' ... / Labba often come at night ... [and] do not seem to fear dogs.*—RALG:62, 64 [BAED Arawak *laba* 'a spotted medium-sized rodent'] □ The pl is usu unchanged (as in cit).

lab·ber-mouth *adj* (Jmca) [AF—Derog] ‖ BIG-MOUTH² (CarA) [Prob < *blabber*. Cp *OED* BLAB-BER vb 2. 'to chatter', etc. Also E slang *blabber-mouth* 'one who talks too much, indiscreetly, etc']

la·belle (la·bèl) [labɛl] *n* (Dmca) A large species of firefly. *The fireflies ... have a light under their tail, and the larger species, called the Labelle, has two headlights. When together, they are capable of lighting up the area around them, and one Labelle can illuminate a whole section of a darkened room.*—HDNPW:6 [Fr Cr < Fr *la belle* 'beautiful one' but perh from an id phr. The same name is used in *Guad* (see *DECG*] □ See also LARBELLE.

lab·lab-(bean) *n* (CarA) ‖ BONAVIST (CarA)

lab·rish¹ *adj* (Jmca) [AF—Derog] ‖ BIG-MOUTH² (CarA) [< *labberish*. See LABBER-MOUTH]

lab·rish² *n* (Jmca) [AF] Idle chatter; wicked gossip. [By functional shift of LABRISH¹]

La·ca·tan ba·na·na *n phr* (CarA) [Banana Ind] ‖ *giant fig* (Gren) A large, blunt-tipped banana that remains greenish when ripe; its bunch is huge, borne on a tree 12 to 15 ft tall wh is resistant to disease, but the fruit wastes easily and is unsuitable for export. [From the name of the place in the Philippines whence it was introduced to the W.Indies, though the variety (known as *Pisang masak hijau*) originated in Malaysia]

lac·ing(s) *n (pl)* (Guyn, Trin) Shoe-lace(s). *Tie up your lacing before it trip you.*—(Trin)

la·djab·lès (la-diab·lesse) *n* (Crcu, Gren, StLu, Tbgo, Trin) ‖ DJABLÈS (Dmca, etc) *Was all this involved in obeah? Was Lucienne a sou-couyant, or maybe a la-diablesse? Somehow, I couldn't think that she was.*—SDD:63 [< Fr *la diablesse* 'the she-devil' with fusion of the article and noun by metanalysis]

la·dy *n* (CarA) (SE) A woman; any adult female; hence such terms as FISH-LADY—A woman who carries fish about for sale; SHOP-LADY—A woman shopkeeper, etc. ... *and then the Beak took over. 'You ladies are a pack of nuisances,' he declared, as he proceeded, to fix his fines on Phyllis who had used a basin on Doris.*—DaC (51.05.07, p.5) [The term was perh first applied to female slaves, as it was to animals in 19C E. Cp *OED* lady 14. b. 'used jocularly for 'female' with names of animals' (+ cits 1820–1894). (See Note at CRE-OLE¹ for a comparable development.) It may then have been raised in status by female house-slaves:

Cp *OED lady* 14. c. '... usually associated with inferiority of social rank to denote that the person is or claims to be regarded as a lady. [As in] *lady-help*'. In support, note the foll ref to a house-slave in Br Guiana in 1824: 'I went over to Mr Smith's house and saw a lady named Miss Kitty Stewart, a cob woman'—*LMSPJS:54*] □ In present CE LADY is the generally accepted term for a 'woman', while CE WOMAN tends to be offensive.

la·dy-fin·ger *n* 1. (Nevs) ‖ APPLE-BANANA (Belz, etc) 2. (Guyn) A variety of pointed yellow pepper about 2 ins long. 3. (Antg, Guyn, Trin) A slender variety of OKRA.

lady's yam *n phr* (Dmca) ‖ BABAWOOLE (Mrat)

la·ga·hoo (la·ga·hou) [lagahu] *n* (Tbgo, Trin) ‖ LOUGAWOU (Dmca, etc) *Lagahoo? Lagahoo is a man that does turn to animal. Lagahoo is a thing that does pull chain. You never see a Lagahoo?* —*AFTF:61* [A variant Fr Cr development < Fr *loup-garou* with vowel-assimilation /luga- > laga-/ and Fr intervolic /-r-/ displaced by aspiration. See LOUGAWOU for related variants] □ This pronunc/spelling is much used in folk writing in *Trin*.

la·gli (la·glee, la·gley, la·glie) [lagli] *n* (Dmca, StLu, Tbgo, Trin) A gum made from the sticky sap or latex of certain trees (breadfruit, balata, etc) and used to trap birds. *Often even if a bird was not quite caught it could do no more than fly feebly along, its wings sticky with the laglie, its feet catching in any bush it settled on.*—*MHBT: 11* [Fr Cr < Fr *la glu* 'bird lime' by metanalysis. Note loss of force of the orig Fr article demonstrated in cit]

la·gniappe *n* (Tbgo, Trin) See LANYAP

la·hé¹ (la·hay¹) [lahe] *vb intr* (Gren, Tbgo, Trin) [*AF/IF*] To laze; to loaf about; to be idle and shiftless. *If a person just sits and lahay for the whole day, then they will have the energy to work overtime.*—Tbgo (Ms, 1981) [Fr Cr perh < Fr *faire la haie* 'to stand in line'] □ Sometimes also *lahé yourself* (Gren) with same sense.

la·hé² (la·hay²) [lahe] *n* (Gren, Trin) [*AF/IF*] Laziness; idleness; shiftlessness. *... without fuss and bother, without shove and cuss, without employing a lot of Constables bent on la-hay.*—MoK (72.06.16, p.5) [By functional vb > n shift of LAHÉ¹]

la-la·vin·ton (law-la·ving·ton, Lord-La·v·ing·ton) [la:lavɪntʌn ~ lɔ:lavɪŋtʌn] *n* (Antg) ‖ BALL-BUSH (Bdos, Jmca) *To clean the blood you would take and boil white-head broom and law-lavington bush together with bitter mint and inflammation bush.*—SSHL:64 [< Lord Lavington, Governor of the Leeward Is 1771–1776. 'Lavington's Estate' retains his name and prob gave rise to the local name of this prolific bush by association]

La·ma·gwit (La Mar·gue·rite) [lama·gwit] *n* (StLu) ‖ *Marguerite Festival* (StLu) A flower festival focused on the BACHELOR'S BUTTON, 'la marguerite', as its symbol; it is held annually on October 17 in honour of its patron, St Margaret Mary Alacoque. □ See also LAWOZ and Note.

lam·bie (lan·bi) [lambi] *n* (Dmca, Gren, StLu) The meat of the conch; it is a prized delicacy; *Strombus gigas* (Strombidae). [Fr *lambi* 'mollusque marin'—*DECG:172*]

la·mo·wi (lan·mo·wi) *n* (Dmca, StLu) ‖ ACCRA (Dmca, etc)

lamp-fly *n* (StKt) ‖ CANDLE-FLY (Guyn, Trin) [See next]

lamp-light·er *n* (Baha) ‖ CANDLE-FLY (Guyn, Trin) *The eyes of his friends lit up like lamplighters in the dark of night.*—TOSR:27 [From the 'blinking' of the insect's phosphorescent abdomen as the wings are raised in flight]

lamp·shade-bush *n* (Nevs) ‖ LEAF-OF-LIFE (Bdos, etc) [From resemblance of the drooping clusters of small, reddish corollas and open flowers to lampshades]

lan·cers *n pl* (*as sg*) (Dmca, Gren, Tbgo, Trin) A set of five dances in wh pairs make 'figures' rather like N. American square-dancing; it is preserved as part of the rural tradition in some islands. *Drummers and fiddlers entered to make the music for the wedding dance. The older women held up their long skirts to trip the unshod toe in the dust in bélé, reel, jig, lancers and quadrille.*—ACTT:153

land-ca·moo·di *n* (Guyn) ‖ MACAJUEL (Trin)

Land-Ship (Landship) /1'2/ *n* (Bdos) See BARBADOS LAND-SHIP

lang-bèf (langue-boeuf) ['laŋbɛf] *n* (Dmca, Gren, StLu, Trin) ‖ AGAVE (CarA) [Fr Cr < Fr *langue de boeuf* 'ox's tongue' with loss of *de* by syncope]

lang-fanm (langue-femme) ['laŋfam] *n* (StLu) ‖ WOMAN'S-TONGUE TREE (CarA) [Fr Cr: 'tongue (of) woman']

langue-boeuf *n* (Dmca) See LANG-BÈF

langue-femme *n* (StLu) See LANG-FANM

lan·tern-post ['lantʌn-po·s] *n* (Guyn) ‖ WAL-LABA-POLE (Guyn)

lan·yap (la·gniappe, la·yap) ['lanyap ~ 'layʌp] *n* (Tbgo, Trin) ‖ BRAATA (Antg, etc) *The pavement has been blocked off while the new building goes up [as] if, when they purchased the property the owners thought the pavement came as lagniappe.*—ExP (73.06.06, p.21) [< Latin Am Sp *la ñapa* 'extra, bonus', with loss of final /-a/ by apocope, and sometimes with medial denasalization > [layap]] □ The spelling *lanyap* is justified by the etym. The Amer variant spelling *lagniappe* is a Louisiana Fr Cr adaptation of Sp *la ñapa*.

lap *vb tr* (CarA) [*IF*] **1.** To fold or fix (solid material) one part over another. **2.** PHRASE **2.1 lap your foot** *vb phr* (Nevs) [*AF/IF*] See FOOT Phr 2.10

lap-edge *n, adj* (Guyn) ‖ **rabbet-and-spring** (Bdos) ‖ **spring-and-rabbet (board)** (Guyn) (Builder's board) having the edges machined so that each board can fit horizontally on the next, overlapping it slightly (hence the name); it is used in building exterior walls to prevent wind and rain from getting through. **[** < *lapped-edge* or *lap-edged* perh characteristically infl by CarA Cr absence of pa.t. /-d/] □ The pattern is acceptable in SE. Cp *call-girl, flash-light, match-board*, etc.

la·po·ka·bwit (**la-peau cab·rit, la·peau-kab·wit**) [la po-kabwit~kabrit] *n* (Dmca) A goat-skin drum played with the flat of the hand and the fingers; it is the major instrument used in festive street-dancing. *Various groups, wearing colourful costumes, participated in the two-day jump-up to the la peau cabrit beat, steel band and brass band music.*—DoC (65.03.06, p.7) [Fr Cr < Fr *la peau de cabrit(e)* 'goat-skin'; *cabrite* 'she-goat' is earlier provincial/informal Fr < dial Latin *caprita*. The provincial Fr form is widespread in CarA Fr Cr]

lappe [lap] *n* (Trin) ‖ GIBNUT (Belz) *And Britto's wife brought out the portion of lappe that she had been cooking on a wood fire in the yard and they ate and drank and with the music the whole thing was real sweet.*—CaT.VI.1, p.27 (E. Lovelace) [Perh < Arawak *laba* (see LABBA); with devoicing /b > p/; perh also infl by Fr *lapin* 'rabbit', with loss of '*in*' by apocope]

lar·belle [la·bɛl] *n* (StVn) ‖ CANDLE-FLY (Guyn, Trin) [Cp LABELLE (*Dmca*) of wh it is perh a variant form with lengthened vowel in the first syllable]

lard·er *n* (Bdos) ‖ SAFE (CarA) [By shift in sense of SE *larder* 'store room or cupboard for food']

lard-oil *n* (Bdos, Gren, Guyn) Oil made from melted and processed pig-fat and once widely used for cooking. *The old lard oil is passé. Barbadians do not want to deal with any lard oil any more, they have moved on to vegetable oil.*—Bdos (Hd, 87.07.13, p.543)

larg·ie ['larʃi] *n* (Bdos) [*AF*] ‖ BIG-BOTTLE (Guyn)

La Rose *n phr* (StLu) See LAWÒZ·

lash[1] *vb tr* (CarA) **1.** [*IF*] To strike (esp another person) violently with any stiff or heavy object (i.e. not necessarily a whip or thong). **a.** *Barnes*

also said that he was 'lashed' over his eye with a piece of chairback, and after the blood was wiped from over his eye, he was taken to Dr B—.*—AdN (79.04.25, p.2) **b.** *As I left to go and leave the Terminal he lashed me with a bottle on my right breast.*—Tbgo (CR, 77.11.22) **2.** [*IF*] [Cricket, Football] To hit or kick (the ball) with great force. *'Lash, Ken, lash!'—they shouted as the centre-half raced after the ball.*—Guyn (Ms) [Cp EDD *lash* vb 15. 'to work at anything with great vigour. *Cum.* A common expression of encouragement applied indifferently to work or play'] **3.** [*AF—Vul*] [Of a man] to have very vigorous sexual intercourse with (a woman). *Car on a moonlight beach / Man lashing luscious beast.*—Jmca (Ms) [Cp EDD *lash* vb 10. 'to throw or dash anything down with violence; to do anything violently' + cits from *Cor*] □ In IAE *to lash* implies the use of sth flexible. Cp also LICK[1] 1., 2.

lash[2] *n* (CarA) [*IF*] **1.** A violent blow (with any heavy object). *My ear began to bleed a lot as a result of the lash the accused gave me in my left ear with the piece of pine.*—Bdos (CR, 70.01.14) **b.** *The work of the Government over the last five years was like a lash of big stone in we back, and we crawlin' now. We want to stand up again—* Agricultural worker, St Patrick's East.—ToR (76.12.01, p.1) **2.** PHRASES **2.1 fire a lash** *vb phr* (CarA) [*IF*] See FIRE[2] Phr 2.1 **2.2 le[t] go/ leggo a lash** [lɛgo a laš] *vb phr* (CarA) [*AF*] To let fly, hit out violently (with some weapon in your hand). **2.3 pelt/put/throw a lash/(the) lashes/licks** *vb phrs* (CarA) [*IF*] To flog, strike, trounce without restraint. **a.** *She came on to his land and threw a lash at him with the 'collins'. He said that he caught it on his right wrist.*—AdV (73.05.16, p.4) **b.** *'Today,' says an eyewitness to a friend, 'two igrunt men did arguing politics in the bus stand. Next thing you know, the two of them pelting lashes in one another. In two-twos the police had them cross the bridge.'*—NaT (79.02.02, p.23) **2.4 share lashes/licks** *vb phr* (Bdos) [*AF—Joc*] (i) To beat up, flog a number of people together (esp children in a house or class-room). (ii) [By extension] [Politics] To clobber (political opponents). *But lemme remind you, we have to keep the lid on all this, if not, there's going to be a lotta lashes sharing 'bout, a lotta arses are going to be hotted-up, if any of this leak-out.*—CPM:163

last-lap (jump-up) *n* **1.** (Trin) The vigorous revelling and JUMPING-UP in the streets in the final hours before midnight on Shrove Tuesday ending the Carnival celebrations. **2.** (CarA) [By extension] The energetic dancing in the final hour or so of any public festivities or private dance. [Metaph ref to the extra energy put into the last lap of a long-distance race in a stadium]

last-lick *n* (CarA) A children's leave-taking game in wh each tries to be the last to hit or touch the other before parting. **[**SE *last* + CE LICK[2]**]**

las·tro *n* (Trin) See LATRO

la·tan·yé (la·tan·ier) [latanye] *n* (ECar) ‖S-ILVER-THATCH PALM (Baha, Trin) *There were ... brooms made from the dried leaves of the latanier palm lined up for sale along the railing.*—StVn (Ms)

late PHRASE **How late you got?** *id phr* (Bdos) [*X*] See HOW[1] Phr 3.2

lat·ed [letɪd] *adj* (CarA) [*X*] **1.** Too late; belated. *'I would like to see a Jumbie Dance.' 'Well you now lated sir, [be]cause we jus[t] had one.'*—(Mrat) [Perh an EE or dial E survival. *OED* lists with cits 1592–1898 including Shak 1606 *Ant & Cleo* III.xi.3 'I am so lated in the world, that I/ Have lost my way for ever'. Also Cp *EDD lated* pa part (nYks) 'Belated'] **2.** [By extension] Behind the times; slow in acquiring information. *Only now? The man dead last week! But you lated!*—(StVn)

Later! (ECar) **1.** [Said as a friendly form of leave-taking] [Abbr of 'I'll see you later!', the equivalent of Fr *Au revoir*] **2.** PHRASE **2.1 Later for you!** *id phr* (Trin) Be off with you! (i.e. I don't care about seeing you again!)

la·tro(w) (las·tro) *n* (Trin) Abandoned fields; uncultivated land; low, bushy forest. *If you picking coffee or cocoa / Loading boulders or cutting latrow / You still got to learn.*—Cso (1971, Lady Divine) [< Sp *rastrojo* 'stubble, waste-land' with initial /r > l/ shift and loss of final unstressed syllable by apocope]

la(t)·ta *n* (Bdos, Guyn, StVn, USVI) ‖*lota* (Bdos, Trin) A skin disorder causing unhealthy looking, whitish blotches; a form of leucoderma or of vitiligo. [Perh a commoner variant of LOTA[2] with vowel-opening]

laugh[1] **1.** *vb intr* (CarA) **2.** PHRASES **2.1 almost die laughing; nearly die laughing; nearly kill yourself laughing** *vb phrs* (CarA) [*AF—Joc*] To laugh long and loudly until you are near prostration; to guffaw without control. *When I hear how he los[t] his deposit after all that fanfare [h]e make in the election, an[d] everybody t[h] ought he had a good chance—man, I almost die laughin[g].*—(Guyn, 1953) **2.2 hold back your head and laugh** *id phr* (CarA) [*IF*] See HOLD Phr 5.5 **2.3 laugh after (sb)** *vb phr* (Tbgo) [*IF*] To laugh at (sb). *I am not dancing because you will laugh after me, man.*—(Tbgo) **2.4 laugh your belly full** *vb phr* (CarA) [*AF/IF*] (SE) To have your fill of laughter; to laugh as much as you can. *Do you know what is the most amusing thing? Even the people for whom you are doing it, they understand and they are laughing their bellies full. I have witnessed all of this.*—Bdos (Hd, 76.07.27, p.7048) **3.** *vb tr* (Guyn) [*X*] To laugh at (sb). *Yo[u] mus[t]n['t] laugh ol[d] people.*—(Guyn) [Cp *OED laugh* 5. *trans* [*Obs*] 'to mock at, deride' with cit from Spenser, 16C] □ ModE only allows *laugh* vb tr + obj + adv phr comp,

as in *laugh sb out of court.* **4.** PHRASE **4.1 laugh (sb) up** *vb phr* (Grns) [*X*] To mock, deride (sb) together with others. *He had twenty 'outside children'—that is, not by his lawful wife—and that is 'picketing' on a grand scale, one might say. So, they were all 'laughin' he up', but someone warned his detractors that he might 'do they a mischief' if he 'fin' dey faultin' he.'*—Isl 10/73 p.46

laugh[2] *n* (CarA) [*IF*] **1.** Laughter (in a general sense). *When he told them the story if you hear laugh!*—(Trin) **2.** PHRASES **2.1 bus a laugh** *vb phr* (Guyn, Tbgo, Trin) [*AF*] To burst out laughing. *When she start talkin[g] [a]bout takin[g] legal action for a stupid t[h]ing like dat, I jus[t] bus a laugh.*—(Trin) **2.2 give laugh for peas-soup** *vb phr* (Jmca) [*AF—Joc*] See GIVE[1] Phr 2.10. **2.3 kill a laugh** *vb phr* (CarA) [*AF*] See KILL Phr 3.1.1 **2.4 kill (sb) with the laugh** *vb phr* (CarA) [*AF*] See KILL Phr 3.3.1 **2.5 kill yourself with laugh** *vb phr* (CarA) [*AF*] To laugh uncontrollably. *But Ivan and Keith were enjoying themselves, killing themselves with the laugh. Both boys now were pretending to sprinkle sand on the girls' sandwiches.*—JJHAI:79 **2.6 nearly dead/want to dead with (the) laugh** *vb phr* (CarA) [*AF—Cr*] See DEAD[2] Phr 2.1

lau·ki [lɒuki] *n* (Guyn, Trin) [Indic] ‖GOURD (BrVi, etc) [Bhoj *laukii* 'bottle-squash']

lau·ri·er *n* (Trin) See LÒWYÉ (Dmca, Gren)

la·ven·der-grass *n* (Guyn, StVn) ‖VETIVER (Dmca, etc) *The handicraft included blinds and mats made of moocroo and lavender grass, fibre mats, ...*—DaC (51.12.24, p.4) [From the fragrance (said to be highest at full moon) of the dried roots wh are used in wardrobes]

lav·wé (lav·wa, lav·way) [lavwe] *n* **1.** (Dmca, Trin) [In former times] The satirical chorus sung by the crowd (formerly of women) in the street-singing led by the CHANTWÈL. *The loud-speaker echoed across the field through the hot afternoon dust, the people were dancing bele, the drums beat, beat, beat; the women whined a lavway, there was dust, heat and sweat. In it all there was great beauty, power and strength.*—LDSS:19 **2.** (StLu, Trin) [*AF*] [By extension] Spicy gossip. *I went liming with my friend and she gave me the whole lavway about what happened.*—AFSTE:24 [Fr Cr > Fr *la voix* 'voice' in a looser sense = 'loud mouth']

law *n* PHRASE **1. more than the law allow(s)** *id phr* (BrVi, Gren, Guyn, Mrat, Tbgo) [*IF*] (It is) a very unreasonable expectation. *After all they can't expect the poor man, after all his sacrifices for them, to go and mortgage the house at his age! Wha[t] da's more than the law allow!*—(Guyn) **2. put the law out of your favour** *vb phr* (Bdos) To put yourself in the wrong; to do sth indefensible by acting rashly.

la·wa [la:wA] *n* (Guyn, Trin) [Indic] Parched rice, particularly as used in a women's ritual of bringing good fortune to the bride, at a Hindu wedding. [Hin *laawa* 'parched rice']

law·la·ving·ton *n* (Antg) See LA-LAVINTON

law·less [lɒ·lɪs] *adj* (CarA) [*AF*] **1.** Irresponsible and troublesome. *What you chop do[w]ng all the hedge for? You too lawless you know! Why you don['t] go an[d] look fo[r] wo[r]k?* —(Bdos) **2.** [Of a woman] Loose; unashamedly vulgar. *She ain['t] want not[hi]n[g] name[d] 'married'. She too lawless!*—(Guyn) **3.** [Of conversation] Loose; full of dirty jokes and chat about sex. **4.** [Of a manner of sitting] Sprawling, with the legs wide apart. □ **1.** The SE general sense 'spurning the law' is secondary, that of 'being personally indecent' is dominant in CE. **2.** Hence also frequently **lawlessness** n.

law·less·ly *adv* (CarA) [*IF*] Idly; foolishly; improperly; noisily; without caring about correctness or consequence. *Our friendship first started when my eldest brother took up the telephone and dialled a number lawlessly.*—NaT (77.01.30, p.30, Dear Christine)

La·wòz (La·Rose) [la wɔz] *n* (StLu) A flower festival focused on the rose, (Fr) 'la rose', as its symbol; it is held annually on August 31, in honour of its patron St Rose of Lima. *The La Rose Festival, the feast day dedicated to St Rose of the Lima, ... is one of the Flower Festivals which together with its counterpart La Marguerite (October 17th), has played an important part in the political history of the island. The conflict between these two bears strange resemblance to England's Wars of the Roses where rivalry for a flower meant so much. The Rose, loud, colourful and expansive finds expression in its followers' music, noise and love of colour; while the Marguerite (Bachelor's button) with its delicate blues and whites bespeaks a milder set of followers.*—CrU (72.07.01, p.1). □ The Fr Cr form of the name, LAWÒZ, reflecting the pronunc, is increasingly being chosen as the spelling.

lay¹ *vb tr PHRASE* **lay (sb) out** *vb phr* (Baha) [*AF/F*] ‖ AIR YOUR MOUTH ON (SB) (CarA) See AIR² Phr 2.2

lay²; lay down *vb intr (phr)* (CarA) [*X*] To lie; to lie down. **a.** *Harris said he ran down in the yard and ... and the deceased who had run down in the yard was laying on his back.*—AdV (81.02.14, p.1) **b.** *The hoodlum felt reassured as Maria laid on the ground and began undoing her garments. He thanked his lucky stars that he had met such a co-operative customer.*—ExP (73.02.25, p.6) **c.** *'Lay down, bro',' Davie said. Down I am on my belly, and he is packing mud all over me and making mask with reeds for my face.*—RND:165 [Cp OED *lay* 43. 'In intransitive uses, coinciding with or resembling those of *lie* v¹.... Now (except in Naut. lang) only dialectal or an illiterate substitute for *lie*, its identity of form with the pa.t. of the latter no doubt accounting largely for the confusion. In the 17 and 18C ... apparently not

regarded as a solecism' + cits–'1900 'They're all layin' down on the road opposite our door'] □ This widespread CE usage may have E dial roots but is not IAE. *Lay* is firmly trans in ModE.

la·yap [layap-ʌp] *n* (Tbgo, Trin) See LANYAP

lay-wait *vb tr* (Belz, Jmca) To waylay; to lie in wait for (sb). *'You have some undesirables—I don't know where they come from, suddenly infiltrating the area and making the place miserable',* said a resident who prefers to remain anonymous. *'For I don't want a soul to lay-wait me'.*—DaN (80.01.27, p.40) [A survival of EE. See OED *lay* 18. 'to set (an ambush)'; (*obs*) 'to set (watch)' *To lay wait*]

la·zi·o·sis; la·zy.i.tis *n* (Belz, Guyn) [*IF—Joc*] Laziness, regarded jocularly as a disease or affliction; a feeling of sheer indolence; a willingness to shrink from work.

LDCs *abbr* (CarA) Less Developed Countries, a term used to denote those members of CARICOM wh are less economically developed, viz Anguilla, Antigua & Barbuda, Belize, Dominica, Grenada, Montserrat, St Kitts & Nevis, St Lucia, St Vincent & the Grenadines. □ Often so written. See also MDCs

le' (leh) [lɛ] *vb* (CarA) [*AF—Cr*] See LET *Leh we go nuh, I don't feel like going to fete tonight man.*—ExP (72.01.05, p.12, Short Story) [< SE *let* by apocope] □ These dial spellings are frequently used in narrative dialogue.

lead [lɛd] *n* (Bdos, Gren, Guyn, Trin) [*IF*] ‖ *black-lead* (CarA) A lead pencil; any pencil. *'Lemme jes' get dat dong,' Mr Ashley said briskly. 'Like ah go an' forget mih pencil, yes. Miss Marie, pass mih dat coloured lead.'*—MN:76

lead·er-boy ['li·dʌ-bɒɪ] *n* **1.** (Bdos, Guyn) [Sugar Ind/Hist] A lad who led the mule or mules drawing a DRAY (*Bdos*) or PUNT (*Guyn*) loaded with sugar-cane from field to factory. **2.** (Bdos) Such a lad leading a similar cart used for transporting goods between the sugar-factory and Bridgetown; it was drawn by several mules, and the lad sometimes rode the foremost mule and often wore a distinctive pair of trousers cut just below the knee; hence foll phr. **3.** *PHRASE* **3.1 you look like a leader-boy** *id phr* (Bdos) Your trousers are too short for you.

lead-pan [li·d-pan] *n* (Trin) ‖ *ping-pong, tenor-pan* (Trin) [Steelband] One of the set of six leading PANS, each cut about 6 ins deep, from an oil-drum; its surface is sunk deepest of all the PANS, and segmented to provide up to 32 notes of the highest pitch; the set takes the centre of the front line, flanked by the DOUBLE-FIRSTS, with wh they provide the melody. [*Lead* = leading or leader] □ Once also called *soprano pan, violin-pan* though these names seem to be rarely used now.

lead-pipe [lɛd-paɪp] *n* (Bdos) A small, oblong sweetbread made of tough, heavy dough and about 6 ins long; it is popular with schoolboys and workmen. [From its heaviness (i.e. like lead) and resemblance to a piece of piping]

lead-tree [lɛd-tri] *n* (Jmca) ‖ WILD-TAMARIND 1. (Belz, etc)

leaf-of-life* /ı′ı2/ *n* (Bdos, Dmca, Guyn, Jmca, Trin) ‖ *air-plant* (Angu) ‖ *baby-bush, bladder-bush, Christmas-flower* (Nevs) ‖ *clapper-bush* (USVI) ‖ *curiosity-leaf* (CayI) ‖ *géritou* 2. (Gren) ‖ *lampshade-bush* (Nevs) ‖ *love-bush* 2. (Angu, Antg, Bdos, StKt, StVn) ‖ *love-leaf* (Bdos, Gren) ‖ *luck-bush* (Angu, StKt, StVn) ‖ *never-dead* (Nevs, StKt, Trin) ‖ *pla-pla* (Brbu) ‖ *round-the-world* (Bdos) ‖ *wonder-of-the-world* (Bdos, Gren, Tbgo, Trin) ‖ *wonder-world* (Bdos) A succulent plant about 3 to 4 ft high, whose fleshy leaves have lobed margins from wh young plants spring even when the leaves are cut off and left without water or moisture; *Bryophyllum pinnatum* (*Crassulaceae*). [From the leaf's ability to survive and grow, detached and without water]

leaf-scald dis·ease *n phr* (Guyn) [Sugar Ind] A bacterial disease that attacks sugar-cane plants, stunting the stems and causing the leaves to develop white stripes and, as they age, to wither from the tips back, giving them a scalded appearance, the plants ultimately wilting and dying; *Xanthomonas albilineans*.

leaf-spot dis·ease *n phr* (CarA) [Banana Ind] The discoloration of banana leaves in spots attacked by the spores of a fungus (*Corcospora musae*); the disease greatly reduces the plant's food-producing capacity and the quality of its fruit; it is also known as *Sigatoga* (from the place of its first discovery in Fiji).

lean-to *n* 1. (Mrat, Nevs) [IF] ‖ DROP-SHED 2. (Antg, etc)

learn¹ (sth) *vb tr* (CarA) [AF/IF] PHRASES 1. **learn doctor/etc work** *vb phr* (CarA) [AF] See WORK¹ 2. 2. **Learn manners!** *imper vb phr* (CarA) [IF] [To a young person] Where are your manners? 3. **learn sense** *vb phr* (CarA) [IF] (i) To get sense into your head; to grow into maturity. *How could you pick up chewing-gum from the ground to eat? When will you learn sense, child?* —(Tbgo) (ii) To become suddenly aware; to have a rude awakening. *Not me and a lawyer again! I learn sense from two o[f] dem.*—(Guyn)

learn² **(sb)** [lə·(r)n ~ lʌrn ~ la·n] *vb tr* (CarA) [X] To teach; to cause to learn. a. *My bro' says it is four miles, but he and me talk plenty on our way and he learns me to whistle while we walk.*—RND:23 b. *De man is a real traitor. You don't see how he would destroy we for dem people. I sure every day, dey must be learning him to eat wid knife and fork.*—DP:40 c. *... because throughout his years of science, he or she was learnt*

to think scientifically.—Bdos (Ms, 1973) [Prob due to infl of IrE. Note: Learn is used for teach all over Ireland, but more in Ulster than elsewhere. Don't forget to 'larn the little girl her catechiz.' (Seumas Mac Manus.)—(*JESI:283*). However note also *OED learn* II. 'to impart knowledge'. Now *Vul*, sense 4. trans sub-senses a., b., c., d. with many cits—1893 Stevenson 'My father learned it to me']

learn·ing [lʌ(r)nɪn/ŋ] *n* (CarA) [IF] Schooling; book-study. a. *Now you have no education/ While I was taking my learning / You was catching crab and fish in ravine.*—RCWC:3 b. *Never been to school or anything. But don't think I was foolish. I uses to borrow books and magazines from the overseer and study learning.*—SWOS:82

lease-wa·ter *n* (Guyn) [X] See LEES-WATER

leath·er-bat *n* (Bdos) ‖ BAT¹ 2. (Guyn) □ Also NIGHT-BAT (Bdos—in rural areas).

leath·er-coat plum *n phr* (CayI, Jmca) ‖ JA-MAICA-PLUM (Bdos, etc) [Ref to its reddish-brown leathery skin. Also called *red-coat plum* (*Jmca*)]

leave *vb tr* [Note: LEFT is treated separately] PHRASES 1. **leave alone (sth)** *id phr* (Guyn, Trin) [IF] (SE) let alone; not to mention. *The woman said, sweeping out of the shop: 'Life hard enough with you one, leave alone your three worthless children.'*—NTMM:65 2. **leave off** *vb phr* (Belz, USVI) [AF/IF] To quit; to come or to bring to an end. a. *If you're not going to do your job, leave it off.*—WFSFB:18 b. *... and it is hard to distinguish just where folk tales left off (if they ever did) ... and folk music took up.*—Aaw.I.2, p.48 □ In IAE usage *sb leaves a job/leaves it* (not 'off'), also *sb leaves (off) doing sth*; but *sth leaves off* is not IAE. 3. **leave (sb/sth) out** *vb phr* (Bdos) [IF] ‖ *lef[t] out* (Bdos) [AF] To neglect or abandon (esp a spouse or a lover) in favour of another; to exclude (sth) from consideration. a. *I am in love with a married man. He says he loves me very much. He also does things for me to show how much he loves me. He leaves out his wife for me.*—PeL (79.01.05, p.6) b. *... but my last boyfriend who I had before him calls me and he tells me to leave out this boy and let the two of us get together.*—NaT (79.09.12, p.21, Dear Christine) □ A particularized or misascribed sense of SE *leave out* 'to omit' > 'to exclude', common in this context in Bdos. 4. **leave/lef[t] (sb) shap-in[g]** *vb phr* (Guyn) [AF—*Joc*] To outsmart (sb); to disappoint or play (sb) false. *He would tell her to wait at the factory gate or some place for the money, and he would jus[t] go out the back and leave her shapin[g].*—(Guyn) [Metaphor from cricket: the batsman is bowled while shaping up to play a ball wh he never manages to touch] 5. **leave the dead at (sb)** *vb phr* (Guyn, Trin) [AF] To leave (sb) in an unfair plight; (SE id) to leave (sb) 'holding the baby'. *Stand bail for he? Not me, sah! Wha[t] he would just hide and leave the dead at me!*—(Guyn) 6. **leave/**

lef[t] yourself behind/undone *refl vb phr* (ECar) [*AF/IF*] ‖ *do without* (Guyn, Nevs) ‖ *sacrifice yourself* (Guyn, Nevs) To do or go without some necessity so as to enable some close member(s) of the family to be provided for; to leave yourself unprovided in favour of a loved relative. [Cp Yoruba *o se ara re* (*he/she deprives/deprived his/her body*) 'he/she deprived himself/herself', in similar context]

leave-over *adj* (CarA) [*X*] Left-over; unused. *The children used to come to collect pieces of leave-over wood for the mother to cook.*—(Guyn)

leave-over(s) *n* (*pl*) (CarA) [*X*] Left-overs. *Them is the leave-overs, the dregs that go get leave out when Judgement time come.*—KJB:112

leave-pas·sage *n* (CarA) A paid return passage (usu from a Caribbean territory to Britain) given periodically to a senior civil servant or company official as allowed by his service contract. *Mr Walcott said ... leave passages was an old colonial concept dating back to the days Englishmen worked in Africa and ... preferred to return home [to spend their holidays].*—BdN (66.01.19, p.1)

leech *n* (CarA) PHRASE **be behind (sb) like a leech** *vb phr* (CarA) [*IF*] To plague (sb) (usu a senior person) in order to obtain sth or permission to do sth. [Prob a ref to the former medical use of leeches placed on a person's back to suck the person's blood. Cp SE id phr *cling like a leech*] □ See ‖ phrases at BEHIND¹ 2.

lee·pay (**lee·pey**) [lipe] *vb tr* (Guyn, Trin) [Indic] To daub (walls or a cooking place) with a thin, white mixture of water and cow-dung to give a smooth, firm finish that will not crack. *He ignored her remark and said: 'Now go and leepey'—he meant daub—'the whole chulha back again. Leepey it, or I won't eat the food you cook on it.'*—NAGOS:67 [Bhoj *liipee* < Hin *liipnaa* 'to daub']

lees-wa·ter *n* (Guyn) [Sugar Ind] The foul-smelling water bearing the dregs or 'lees' from a sugar factory through a drainage TRENCH out to the river or sea. [< SE *lees* 'dregs'] □ Hence also **lees-water trench** erron spelled **lease-water** by folk etym.

lee·ward *adj, n* (CarA) West; the west (side or area of an island). *The Island itself is 18 miles long and 11 miles wide with a central ridge or backbone running north to south dividing the island almost equally into a Leeward and Windward side.*—Svi:4 □ The term is not so used in *Belz, Guyn.* See also WINDWARD.

Lee·ward Is·lands; Lee.wards, The *n phr pl* (CarA) **1.** [British] The group of islands: Anguilla, Antigua & Barbuda, Montserrat, Redonda, St Kitts & Nevis, the Br Virgin Is. [So referred to as being to leeward of Barbados, wh

was the original Br administrative base] □ Dominica was also included in this group up to 1940. See also WINDWARD ISLANDS 1. **2.** [Dutch] Aruba, Curaçao and Bonaire, a group of small islands off the coast of Venezuela. [So referred to by the Dutch as being to leeward of the main CarA chain of islands] □ See also WINDWARD ISLANDS 2.

left¹; leff¹ [lɛf] *vb tr* (CarA) [*AF—Cr*] **1.** (SE) Left. *Yes, ma, is true we lef a long time now but we never did forget you.*—SNWIC:61 (E. Clarke) [< SE pa.t. *left* with characteristic CarA Cr reduced /-CC/. This pa.t. form then became, as seen at 2. below, the CarA Cr, then AF CE base vb, perh because it was more frequently used by EE speakers in the CarA than the SE base *leave*. Cp as similar cases, /brok, got, los[t], marid/] **2.** Leave [Replacing this SE vb in all its functions and phrs i.e. with infin *to*, all modals (and their negs) *can, could, will, would, should, going to, must,* and pres. part. *-ing*]. **a.** *One weekend it capsize him in bed, Sundee and right into Mondee morning half hour before he is to leff for work.*—CWFYS:99 **b.** *Lef the man dey. Ef we pick he up he gwine lef us in the mess and go.*—ToR (73.02.07, p.3) **c.** *If you don't hurry the bus will left you.*—CayI (Ms, 1978) **d.** *And the people, some saying, 'C'dear, she shouldn't leff him so,' and others saying, 'Serve he right'.*—CISH:93 **e.** *When Tolroy did left Jamaica he bring a guitar with him to Brit'n, and he always have this guitar with him.*—STLL:11 **f.** *Right that very second Calvin swear blind to God that he leffing Barbados.*—CWFYS:90 **3.** [Of a spouse] To abandon, walk out on (your partner). *And Hunte start to ask, 'What happen? Wha' the matter, Joyce? Tell me what I do, but don' leff me so.'*—CISH:93 **4.** PHRASES **4.1 lef[t]/leff out (sb/sth)** *vb phr* (Bdos, Jmca) [*AF—Cr*] ‖ LEAVE (SB/STH) OUT (Bdos) See LEAVE Phr 3. *You know say him was the best law-man in this island? For years. Till him left that out and go join politics.*—SNWIC: 259 (M. Townshend) **4.2 lef[t] [u]pon hand** *vb phr* (Bdos, Guyn) [*AF—Cr*] See HAND¹ Phr 4.5

lef[t]²; leff² [lɛf] *vb tr* (Angu) [*X*] To allow; permit. *He won['t] lef[t] us go to our aunt.*—(Angu) [Perh a survival from Sc. Cp *CSD leave²*, *lefe* 'permit, allow']

Leg Co [lɛ̀ ko] *n phr* (CarA) See LEGISLATIVE COUNCIL

leg·gings *n pl* (Jmca) [*AF/IF*] Soup-vegetables i.e. greens and root-vegetables collected for boiling with beef for a meal of heavy soup. *Here too she purchased not only general vegetables, but also supplies of 'leggings' for the traditional Saturday 'beef soup' dinner.*—DaG (72.02.22, p.3) [By false refinement < Jmca Cr *leggins* < HCEF Hait Cr *legim* < Fr *légumes* 'vegetables'... From Haitian market vendors in Kingston]

leg·go¹ (**le'go**) [lɛgo] *vb tr, intr* (CarA) [*AF*] **1.** See LET GO **a.** *Lord, I never see man could le'go them mouth so like taxi driver. They put them* *mouth on everything.*—LMFF:44 **b.** *Anancy leggo: 'O, cut in a row, Brudda ...'*—WFSFB:31 [< *let go* by apocopic loss of /-t/ and fusion of the two vbs due to frequency of the vb phr] **2.** PHRASES **2.1 leggo a lash** *vb phr* (CarA) [*AF*] See LASH² Phr 2.2 **2.2 leggo your belly** *vb phr* (Crcu, Gren) [*AF*] See BELLY Phrs 3.23, 3.25 **2.3 leggo your mouth** *vb phr* (Baha, Jmca, Mrat, Nevs) [*AF*] ‖ AIR YOUR MOUTH (CarA) See AIR² Phr 2.2

leg·go² [lɛgo] *n* **1.** (Gren, Trin) A JUMP-UP and the wildly exciting dance tune for it. **a.** *The big 'jump-out' on Tuesday afternoon will probably take place around the Carenage. The reason: two television teams will be filming the show and have asked that the Carenage be used for the 'leggo' since it gives a longer and better 'sweep' for the TV cameras.*—ToR (78.05.14, p.6) **b.** *And those who would be coming in a band would get together to rehearse the leggo which they would be singing on both Carnival days.*—ExP (73.02.18, p.11) [< LET GO (LEGGO) 1. by functional vb > n shift] □ Pl LEGGOES (cp CALYPSOES). **2.** (Jmca) [*AF—Derog*] A flirtatious young woman. □ Cp next.

leg·go-beast *n* (Gren, Jmca, StLu) [*AF—Derog*] A young woman of loose morals; a prostitute. *Me sey fe / Play de music / Play de music / Jump like leggo beast / Sip you waters.*—Jmca (Song, 1974) [Orig *Jmca* < LEGGO² in attrib function + *beast* 'animal']

Le·gis·la·tive Council (Leg Co) [lɛ ko] *n phr* (CarA) [Hist] A council for the making and enactment of laws in a Br colony, subject to ratification by the Br Parliament; it comprised the Governor, the Colonial Secretary, the Attorney General, a number of members nominated by the Governor and a (usu lesser) number elected by voters qualified by property-ownership, with the Governor having overriding powers if necessary; the size and proportioned representation in the Council varied in different territories of the Br Caribbean where the system operated widely until the advent of self-government and independence in the 1960s. □ See also EXECUTIVE COUNCIL.

leh *vb* (CarA) [*AF—Cr*] See LE'

lé·kòl-bich (l'é·cole-biche) [leko·l-biš] *n* PHRASE **break/make lékòl-bich** *vb phr* (Trin) ‖ BREAK BICHE (Gren, etc) See BICHE and Note. [Fr Cr < Fr *l'école-buisse* prob abbr of *(faire) l'école buissonière* 'to play truant'. Thence Fr *buisse* > Fr Cr *bis* (as in *DECG:180* Guad Cr *lékòl-bis*) and *bis* > /bich/ by palatalization in *Trin* Fr Cr]

lé·lé-stick [lele-stɪk] *n* (Trin) A swizzle-stick made from a dried, firm, twig cut so that two or three forks at one end serve to agitate the drink when the other end is rubbed back and forth between the palms of the hands. [Fr Cr *lélé*. Cp

DECG Guad Fr Cr *lélé (baton lélé)* with same sense]

lem·on-grass *n* (Bdos, Dmca, Gren, Guyn, TkCa, Trin) ‖ FEVER-GRASS (CarA) *Early ingestions of 'cure-for-all' (Pluchea symphytifolia) and 'lemon grass' (Cymbopogon citratus) teas had convinced me of the efficacy of these potions but how, I asked myself, could my grandmas know?* —SuS (80.06.15, p.7) [From the lemon scent of the crushed leaves]

lend [lɛn(d)] *vb tr* **1.** (Guyn, StVn) [*IF*] To allow the use of; to let have; to give. **a.** *Lend me your phone please (= May I use your phone?)* —(StVn) **b.** *You could len[d] me some sugar?* —(Guyn) **2.** PHRASE **2.1 lend (sb) France/hell** *vb phr* (Bdos, Tbgo, Trin) [*AF/IF*] See HELL Phr 3. **3.** (ViIs) To borrow. *Len[d] a knife and fork from the next table.*—(StTh)

lend-hand [lɛn-han] *n* (Tbgo) ‖ **club** (USVI) ‖ **digging** (Jmca) ‖ **fajina** (Belz) ‖ **garden-maroon** (Crcu) ‖ **gayap** (Trin) ‖ **jollification** (Angu) ‖ **kayap, kiap** (Guyn) ‖ **koudmen** (Dmca, StLu) ‖ **maroon¹ 2.** (Gren, Grns, Mrat) ‖ **morning-work, pardner, partnership** (Jmca) An operation of group labour provided by a person's neighbours and friends in some large, private undertaking such as preparing land for farming or building a house, in return for wh the person provides food and drink and a reciprocal commitment of his/her own labour to others in the group. *When under other conditions men team up to work the lands of each other in rotation this is called len' han' and the work is termed len' han'-work; no wages are involved and payment is really in kind since there is an exchange of labour between members of the group.*—EFSLC:39 [Cp SE vb phr 'lend a hand'. Also poss a calque from W.Afr langs. Cp Igbo vb phr *du aka (accompany + hand)* 'to help'; also Yoruba *ọwẹ* 'reciprocal help in farming'.]

length *n* PHRASES **1. catch/ketch your length** *vb phr* (Trin) [*AF—Joc*] To become settled; to begin to understand what to do. *The wife travels a lot in her job but she manages to come back every few days before he can ketch his length with all them women about the place.*—(Trin) [Metaph transfer of (cricket) phr 'find his length', of a bowler's first efforts to control the pitch of the ball] **2. length and (at) last** *adv phr* (Antg, Bdos) [*AF*] ‖ AT LENGTH AND AT LAST (CarA) *A was thinkin[g] A would have to walk when length and last A see the bus comin[g].*—(Antg)

lens *n* (TkCa) See cit. *Over the past twenty years various attempts have been made to find wells which will yield good amounts of potable (drinking) water. This underground potable water occurs in collections called lenses; the fresher water floats on top of the more saline underground water because fresh water is less dense than salt water. These lenses of fresh water are recharged by rainfall and, in their natural state, are discharged by seepage through the ground to the coastline or mangrove* *swamps. But since in the Turks and Caicos Islands rainfall is low, and, in any case, much of the rainfall is lost by evaporation, it is to be expected that any lenses of potable water will be thin and of poor quality.*—PTCI:28 [Perh related to *OED2 lens* 3. (*Geol.*)]

Lent-tree *n* (Bdos) ‖BEAN-TREE (Bdos) [The tree produces its blood-red flowers and 'beads' or 'beans' in the early or Lenten part of the year]

less[1] *adj* (CarA) [X] Fewer; a lesser number of. **a.** *Barbadians and visitors are buying less books from bookstores, according to a number of bookstore proprietors who report a drop in sales last year.*— AdN (85.04.22, p.6) **b.** *Less tourists came to our island last year than the year before.*—StA(DA) (72.04.07, p.6) [By syntactic misascription or extension of SE *less* adj + mass-noun (ex *butter*) or abstract noun (ex *difficulty*)] □ This use of *less* is found in other Englishes besides CE.

less[2] *adv* PHRASE **far less** *adv phr* (Bdos, Dmca, Gren, Guyn, Tbgo) [IF] [Usu balancing a prec neg 'not even'] Much less (is such a thing likely to be). *Get that job? What, he wouldn't even make the short-list, far less!*—(Bdos)

less[3] *conj* (Bdos, Guyn) [X] Unless. *'Out o' the way, 'less you want a maulsprigging too,' Jasper say.*—CISH:11 [By aphaeresis < SE *unless*]

less[4] *vb tr* (Bdos, Guyn, Tbgo) [X] To lessen, reduce, ease (noise, trouble, etc). **a.** *I say to less the noise in there, you-all hear me?*—(Guyn) **b.** *To less all contention, let every man bring his own soap.*—(Tbgo) [By apocope < SE *lessen*]

Less De·vel·op·ed Coun·tries *n phr pl* (CarA) See LDCs

Less·er An·til·les, The *n phr pl* (CarA) The eastern chain of Caribbean islands stretching from the Virgin Is southwards to Trinidad, including the LEEWARD and WINDWARD ISLANDS and Barbados. [By contrast, as smaller or 'lesser' islands than the GREATER ANTILLES]

let (**le'**, **leh**) [lɛ(t)] *vb tr* (CarA) [AF] **1.** [As SE 'permit, allow to', also used, esp in imperative, implying persuasion or threat. Hence often fused with a Cr pron form esp in speech, sometimes written: **leh allyou, leddem, le' he, let 'e, lemme, le' she, lewwe**] **a.** *Eric, yo' got two dallars yo' can len' me let me tek dis bet?*—TRIH: 125 **b.** *My brother quarrel and tell her no don't send me to school, let her send me to work.*—Mrat (Ms) **c.** *That is police work. So I tell him lewwe go to the police station and report the whole thing.*— HFGA:60 (D.S. Joseph) **2.** PHRASES **2.1 Le[t] me [a]lone!** [lɛ mi ɔloˑn ~ lɛmɪloˑn] *imper vb phr* (CarA) [IF/AF] Stop bothering me!; Go away! **2.2 let (sth) burn your eyes** *vb phr* (Dmca) [AF] ‖EYE(S) CATCH FIRE (FOR STH) (Gren, etc) **2.3 let your hand drop** *vb phr* (Belz, Guyn) [IF] See HAND[1] Phr 2.17

let go (**leg·go, le' go**) [lɛ(t)go] *vb phr* (CarA) [AF/IF] **1.** *vb intr* To cease to restrain yourself; to dance with carefree abandon; to let fly a stream of abuse. **a.** *No festival in Grenada would be complete without Carnival style dancing in the streets and ... Grenadians and their friends from abroad really 'Let Go' in a Grand Easter Jump-up in the streets of St George's.*—Baj 77/5 p.18 **b.** *But what a big man like dat could want wid a girl her age? No wonder de mother leggo!*—(Trin) **2.** *vb tr* (**i**) To release, let loose (sth that has been restrained). **a.** *And seasoned hands keep up their measured beat. | And redeemed crowds let go their lively feet.*—SUB:17 **b.** *One day suddenly so | this mountain leggo one brugg-a-lung-go | Whole bloody back side | o' this hill like it blow off.*—BTA: 66 (**ii**) [AF—Joc] [By extension] To speak (surprising or shocking words, as if triggered). **a.** *Brother Salkey let go twenty Anancy stories together one time so, baps!* TM:101 **a.** *At which point the vendor got into a rage and open her mouth and leggo wud (= word) pon the lady.*—WeG (75.04.08, p.15) **3.** *vb tr* To hit, strike viciously (with). **a.** *According to the witness, the accused was standing and he had a collins in his hand. 'I jumped up out of bed. He let go the collins and I got a lash on my left shoulder,' she told the court.*—AdN (79.01.06, p.2) **b.** *Look man, move out ah me sight yu hear? Before ah leggo de hand on yu.*—KTT:11 **c.** *In his evidence in chief, G— said he saw a fight go on between F— and the accused, and he saw J— with a bottle letting go lashes.*—AdN (72.11.07, p.1) **4.** PHRASES **4.1 le[t] go your mouth** *vb phr* (Baha, Jmca, Mrat, Nevs) [AF]; **let loose** *vb phr* (Baha) ‖AIR YOUR MOUTH (ON SB) (CarA) See AIR[2] Phr 2.2. See also LEGGO[1].

lev·el [lɛvl ~ lɛvɪl] *vb* (Bdos, Guyn) [X] To levy (on). **a.** *The ability of the local authorities to level and collect tolls in respect of the use of village roads, dams, etc, should contribute much in solving the problem of the destruction of village dams, etc, by cattle and vehicles as the local authorities would be in a position to get revenue to compensate them to some extent for wear and tear on roads, dams, etc.*—DaC (53.05.02, p.2 (E)) **b.** *The bailiff been and level on their furniture.*—(Bdos) [A misascription prob infl by the idea of 'making things even' or 'levelling with the ground by taking everything away' i.e. SE '*levying on*']

li·ard[1] [laya(r)d ~ layʌd] *n* (CarA) A liar. *If y'u doubts me y'u can ask Jane, for God know I am not a liard, an' I wouldn't like anybody to call me one.*—DJC:53 [An E dial survival. Cp *EDD liard* sb (Som, Dev, Cor) 'a liar']

li·ard[2] *adj* (CarA) Untruthful; (given to) lying. *... and snapped at me gruffly: 'Who tell yu that?' 'Ma tell mih!' 'Well Ma is a liard ol'-fool.'*—HCCM:32 [By functional n > adj shift] □ A rational replacement for SE *lying* or *mendacious*. See also next.

li·ard·ness *n* (CarA) A lying tongue; the habit of telling lies. *Don't come to me with your liardness* *about how they keep you in at school! I know whe[re] you been! I know what happenin[g]!—*(StVn)

LIAT [li·at] *abbr* (ECar) Leeward Islands Air Transport, *ECar* airline. **[An acronym]**

lick[1] *vb tr* (CarA) *[IF]* **1.** To flog severely; to beat up. **a.** *And some of them get licked, then he tells them, well I cannot help that, but it is not right for your master to lick you and prevent you from coming to chapel.*—LMSPJS:23 **b.** *Whenever you lick the children your husband does lick you with same belt you lick the children with.*—Bdos (CR, 70.05.22) **c.** *But how come you bleeding? Who been licking you?*—RND:53 **[Cp** *OED lick* 6. *slang.* 'to beat, thrash'. This slang term must, however, have been common CE from the slave era: The date of cit (a) is 1824] □ Following from the above, the connotation of 'violent force' dominates CE usage of this word, in contrast with SE 'moistening with the tongue'. The sense 'to defeat ('beat') a problem, or an opponent in competition', esp common in AmE, also occurs in CE. Cp also LASH[1] 1., 2. **2.** To strike hard (with, on sth). **a.** *Banza push heself right up front, / An' dat same fire-hose lick him, / An' yu know how dem ting powerful.*—KTT:52 **b.** *Other news of the Breddarin and Sistarin in New York is that dem licking cricket bat and ball all over the place.*—WeG (75.06.75, p.13, Round Town) **3.** *[AF]* [By extension] To be striking, impressive; to be vigorously in progress. **a.** *Wen dey step off dere dey look like dey wuz heading fer d' Ascot races—stripe pants an' ting lickin', man.*—DSJS:77 **b.** *This time wedding and dance lickin[g] up-stairs and they downstairs having one hell of a row.*—(Guyn) **4.** PHRASES **4.1 Da fo[r] lick yo[u]** [da·fʊlɪkyʊ] *id phr* (Bdos, Trin) *[AF—Cr]* ‖ *Take da[t]!* (Guyn) See how you like that!; Let that be a lesson to you!; Beat that if you can! *'Maybe she does go to church', another had suggested. / 'Church! Dar-fo-lick-you! It got church twelve o'clock in the night? I ask you!'*—MBF:23. □ This clear survival from early Cr is commonly used in *Joc* contexts by educated persons in *Bdos* **4.2 lick about (yourself); lick around** *vb phrs* (CarA) *[AF]* To live loosely; to knock around. *After she lick about so, she expect a decent man to marry she.*—(Bdos) **4.3 lick ashore** *vb phr* (Guyn) *[AF—Joc]* [Of fish, fruit] To be very plentiful. *Mangoes lickin[g] ashore in the market today.*—(Guyn) □ Cp KNOCK Phr 4.3.1 KNOCK-ING DOG **4.4 lick at (sth)** *vb phr* (CarA) *[AF/IF]* To hit (sth) hard; to give a good blow to (sth). *He lick at de door-knob with the blunt end of the axe and it burs[t] open.*—(StVn) **4.5 lick away (sth)** *vb phr* (CarA) To knock (sth) away (esp in breaking open). *The hurricane licked everything away—the house, all the trees and crops—everything!*—(Mrat) **4.6 lick back (sth)** *vb phr* (CarA) To knock away; to knock out; to knock down. *The ball kept low and licked back his off-stump.*—(Guyn) **4.7 lick down (sb/sth)** *vb phr* (CarA) **(i)** *[AF/IF]* To knock down (sb/sth); to bring down (fruit, birds) by pelting stones. **a.** *The bicycle-rider came speeding over*

the minor road into the major road just as the tramcar was coming and nearly get lick down.—OJS:10 **b.** *Boys he know does behave real bad, and throw rockstones at dogs and cats, and thief people fruits off the trees, and lick-down sparrow-birds and wooddoves with guttapercs.*—AdN (80.12.25, p.10, Short Story) **(ii)** To mug and knock out (sb). *People got us classed up as thieves, as crooks; that we does lick down people. But we don't go in fuh that.*—NaT (76.01.18, p.14) **4.7.1 lick you down** *vb phr* (Guyn) *[AF—Joc]* ‖ **knock you down** (Guyn) [Of a smell] Be very strong. *In a tight fitting dress and with the smell of some cheap perfume licking you down, Elaine was ready for anything.*—Guyn (Ms) **4.8 lick in (sth)** *vb phr* (CarA) *[IF]* To bash in; to smash. *If a enemy hit you in your face, on the right hand side, you must then turn round and present him with the other side o' your fisiogomy, and let him lick-in that too.*—CWFYS:24 **4.9 lick loose (sth)** *vb phr* (CarA) *[AF/IF]* To break apart; to detach by a violent blow. *They couldn't find the key, so they used a hammer to lick loose the padlock to open the door.*—(Jmca) **4.10 lick off (sth)** *vb phr* (CarA) *[AF/IF]* [Often used figuratively] To detach violently; to get rid of (esp work) rapidly. **a.** *He told my sister that he would like to come and look for me but he is afraid he gets his head lick off.*—NaT (78.08.04, p.6, Dear Christine) **b.** *No more scrubbing of clothes these days. A washing machine licks that off in no time.*—(Trin) **4.11 lick out** *vb phr* (CarA) *[AF/IF]* **(i)** To knock out of place; to knock away; to dislodge with a violent blow. *The third stone struck the window of my house and licked out five of the flaps of the jalousie window.*—Bdos (CR, 1969) **(ii)** To waste, squander, use out wantonly (money, food, resources, clothing). *The Government was licking out our taxpayers' money over there and our Party had to stop that.*—(Nevs) **(iii)** (Guyn) To stick out (your tongue) derisively. *Nowadays little children lick out their tongue at big people who dare to tell them they're doing something wrong.*—(Guyn) **4.12 lick pap together** *vb phr* (BrVi) *[AF—Joc]* To be of the same (usu humble) social origin. **4.13 lick past** *vb phr* (CarA) *[IF]* To go past at high speed; to speed by. *When you hear all this siren and noise and you think you goin[g] see the fire engine lickin[g] past, the damn thing only movin[g] slow, slow!*—(Trin) **[Cp** *OED lick vb* 7. *slang intr* 'to ride at full speed'**] 4.14 lick through** *vb phr* (CarA) *[AF/IF]* To move on decisively; to make speedy progress with (a task); to get on with it. *It was Guyana's second fire for the year and it had already consumed four of the buildings and was licking through a fifth when the Brigade arrived on the scene.*—GyC (78.01.21, p.8) **4.15 lick up (sth)** *vb phr* (CarA) *[AF]* To damage (sth) beyond repair. *I know the way he does drive cars. Lick them up in no time at all.*—NHMB:515 **4.16 lick your mouth** *vb phr* (Bdos, Trin) *[AF—Derog]* To carry about or join in wicked gossip. *Do you know how bad those malicious brutes would lick their mouth on me if I went back the same way I left?*—MBGB:172

lick² *n* (CarA) **1.** [*AF*] Any sharp blow (with the hand or using any object). *I put my hands to my face and I received another lick in my head.*—DeM(SK) (63.11.2, p.10) **2.** *n pl* [*IF*] Blows; lashes; a flogging, thrashing, beating. □ See also LASH². **3.** PHRASE **3.1 dig (the) licks in (sb)** *vb phr* (CarA) [*AF*] [Boxing] To punch, beat up viciously. *The home crowd had backed their man so much and when Blackmoore started digging licks in him, fellas at ringside begged Dele: 'Don't go down, just stay up.'*—GyC (77.10.09, p.17) **3.2 fire a lick; fire (the) licks** *vb phrs* (CarA) [*AF/IF*] To hit at or to hit (sb) one or several sharp blows or lashes. *He said I must carry the child back inside. I refused. He fired a lick at me with his hand.*—DeM(SK) (62.08.18, p.2) □ See also LASH² Phr 1. **3.3 fleet of licks** *n phr* (Guyn, Tbgo, Trin) See FLEET **3.4 get/take licks** *vb phr* (CarA) [*IF*] **(i)** To be beaten, flogged. **(ii)** [Figuratively, esp in ref to politics] To be decisively rejected, defeated; to suffer losses. *And I hope that the day will never arise when I cannot be a man who can share licks and take licks, and that is what I intend to do in this House of Assembly.*—Bdos (Hd, 75.03.17, p.4661) **3.5 licks of Lisbon** *n phr* (Bdos, Guyn) [*AF—Joc*] A beating up; a severe tongue-lashing. **3.6 licks like fire/peas** *id phr* (ECar) [*AF*] A trouncing. **3.7 line (sb) in/with licks** *vb phr* (Bdos) [*AF*] To chastise (a child) severely; to beat up (sb) thoroughly. *So he is punished in the old fashioned way, his firm parent, unaffected by so much modern bogus psychology. So it is a case of 'line him with licks', bringing the cane down vigorously on his 'afternoon'.*—AdN (79.04.15, p.16) [The phr originally meant 'to cover the body (i.e. like a lining) with lashes'] **3.8 pelt/put/throw (some) lashes/licks in (sb)/(sb's skin/tail)** *vb phr* (Bdos) [*AF*] To thrash (sb) mercilessly. *I would like ... to say that I enjoyed the debate, even Senator Miller and Senator Tull, although they would like to throw some licks in us, and they went off quite a lot, but everyone spoke well.*—Bdos (Hd, 87.03.23, p.335) **3.9 share licks/lashes** *vb phr* (Bdos) [*AF—Joc*] See LASH² Phr 2.4 *I was always promising myself to be able to cut these young boys' tails one day, and when I come out Father Oliver, is licks I go share like water.*—JPB:62 **3.10 take licks** *vb phr* See PHR 3.4 **3.11 throw licks** *vb phr* See PHR 3.8

lick³ *n* (USVI) [*AF*] A little bit (of work grudgingly done). *He don't do a lick of work all day long.*—PKKK:75

lick·er·ish (lic·o·rish, lick·rish, lik·(k)rish) ['lıkrıš] [*AF—Joc*] *adj* **1.** (Bdos, Guyn, StVn) ‖ BIG-EYE¹ (CarA) **2.** (Antg, Bdos, Guyn, StVn, Tbgo, Trin, USVI) [*AF—Derog*] ‖ *cravicious* (Bdos, Trin) ‖ *craven* (Gren, Jmca, Nevs, StVn, Tbgo, Trin)· ‖ *cravenous* (StVn) ‖ *licky-licky* (Jmca) ‖ *raven* (Gren, StVn) ‖ *scraven* (Guyn) Gluttonous; unashamedly and aggressively greedy esp over food; ready to eat left-overs. [*OED lickerish* 2. [Of persons] b. *gen.* and *fig.* 'eagerly desirous, longing, greedy'. Also 4. *Comb.*

lickerish-lipped (+ cits from 16C onward). However the wide CE usage, concentrated only on this sense (see others *OED*) is prob infl by 'licking' of plate/fingers, etc to get the last scrap] □ The alternative spellings appear to be experimental.

lick·ing *n* (CarA) A flogging; a thrashing; a beating. *One of them had jumped up on her dress. She grabbed a stick and gave one of the animals a 'licking'.*—CaY (75.5.15, p.8)

lick-mout[h] [lıkmʊut] *n, adj* (Bdos) [*AF—Derog*] **1.** *n* Cheap gossip; the sharing in or enjoyment of cheap gossip. *He noted that despite the prevalence of the lick-mouth syndrome, 'God our Father does expect those persons who claim the name Christians, not to speak disapprovingly with deliberate intention to injure or hurt a person's character or reputation'.*—AdN (80.03.03, p.1) **2.** *n* ‖ *busy-lick-um* (Angu, Bdos, StVn) A person (esp a woman) who indulges in cheap or wicked gossip. **3.** *adj* [Usu of a woman] Irresponsibly talkative; gossip-loving.

lick·y-lick·y *adj* (Jmca) [*AF—Cr*] ‖ LICKERISH 2. (Antg, etc)

lic·o·rish *adj* (Bdos, etc) See LICKERISH

lie¹ *vb intr* (CarA) [*AF—Joc*] [Only with 1st pers sg pron as subj] **1.** To be mistaken. *I said I been there yesterday? No, A lie! Was the day before!*—(Guyn) **2.** PHRASES **2.1 If I lie, I die!** *id phr* (Guyn, Trin) [*AF*] [Stressing an assurance] I swear upon my life that what I say is so! *You sure? / If me lie me die, skipper.*—CBM:138 **2.2 You lie!** *id phr* (CarA) [*AF—Joc*] You've got to be joking!; Don't tell me that's true! □ Restricted to persons in familiar relationship.

lie²; **li.est** *adj* (CarA) [*X*] **1.** Lying; (most/very) untruthful. **a.** *She too lie! You can['t] believe a word she say!*—(StKt) **b.** *Ugly vibes from Barbados ... and a newspaper editor over there.... 'Your Editor Patrick C— is the liest writer I have ever known.*—PuN (74.12.22, p.17) □ Cp LIARD and Note. **2.** PHRASE **2.1 call sb lie** *vb phr* (StKt) [*AF*] To call sb a liar.

life *n* (CarA) PHRASES **1. (If) God spare life** *id phr* (Bdos, Guyn) [*IF*] God willing; all being well (i.e. if my life is spared). *Next week, God spare life, I will send you some of my cassava when my son come to see me.*—(Guyn) **2.** PHRASE **2.1 (If) Life spare** *id phr* (Belz, Guyn, Jmca, Trin) [*IF*] [As prec]

life-sore *n* (CarA) [*IF*] An incurable (usu diabetic) sore on the lower leg.

life-wa·ter *n* (Bdos, Trin) [Hospital] [*IF*] Saline. □ Esp common among older folk.

li·ga·ru (li.ga.wu) *n* (Dmca, Gren, StLu, Trin) See LOUGAWOU

light[1] *adj* **1.** (CarA) [*IF*] Mentally unreliable. *His head was always a little light, so the rest of the family have to look after him.*—(Guyn) [Cp IrE *light* 'a little touched in the head, a little crazed'—*JESI:286*] **2.** (Baha) *PHRASE* **2.1 hands are light** *id phr* (Baha) [*AF*—*Joc*] See HAND[1] Phr 4.14

light[2] *n* (Dmca, Gren, Trin) [*AF*] **1.** Craziness. **2.** *PHRASE* **2.1 have (a) light** *vb phr* (Gren, Trin) To be crazy. *You ain't leave no meat for your father? Child you have light?*—(Gren)

light[3] *adv PHRASE* **go light** *vb phr* (Jmca) See GO Phr 6.22

light·en *vb tr* (Belz) *PHRASE* **lighten the tongue** *vb phr* (Belz) To use less Cr and more SE structure in speaking. *He is sometimes told 'not to talk so bad' and even develops an instinct for certain social situations where it is 'desirable to lighten the tongue' as the local euphemism puts it.*—Nas, II.4, p.33

light·er; a lit.tle light *adj phr, n* (CarA) [Of a person's skin] Less black; not quite black; brown.

light-skin(ned) *adj* (CarA) [*AF/IF*] ‖ CLE-AR-SKIN(NED) (CarA) **a.** *In Toronto he would have called her 'mixed'. But at home, here, she would be regarded as one of the sought-after light-skinned women.*—CPM:32 **b.** *In such a milieu the light skin guy with 'good' hair (e.g. what was called curly hair or good weeds) was an Adonis.*—AdN (77.03.26, p.4) [See LIGHTER]

lig·num-vi·tae* [lɪgnʌmvaɪti ~ lɪŋʌmvaɪti] *n* (CarA) A medium-sized, evergreen tree with a scaly, brown bark on its slender trunk; its small clusters of deep-blue flowers and bright orange pods make it ornamental, and it yields an extremely hard, resinous wood wh is used for furniture and many other commercial purposes; its leaves and sap also have a number of folk-medicinal uses; *Guaiacum officinale* (*Zyg-ophyllaccae*). [Lat *OED lignum vitae*; the pronunc of the second element is similar to that in CE. (*OED* does not state the reason for the use of a Lat designation, wh is not the botanical name, for this type of tree). Other variant pronunc of the whole name exist in CE—[lɪŋiwaɪti ~ lɪŋliwaɪti], etc—attesting to the wide folk-use of the item] □ LIGNUM-VITAE is the National Flower of Jamaica and the National Tree of The Bahamas.

like[1] *vb tr* **1.** (CarA) [*AF*] [In catenative function with immediately foll base vb] To love to; to like to. *She is not a girl to settle down. She like walk about too much.*—(Gren) **2.** (Bdos) [*IF*] To set up, establish a sexual relationship with (sb). **a.** *But the longface girl is liking some boy from down South, and they almost had to tie 'Gatha down with wet sheets when she found out.*—MBGB: 63 **b.** *The problem is, now, another boy is trying to like me. He is 22. He calls me every night on the phone. I went out with him twice and he kissed*

me once.—NaT (77.03.27, p.30, Dear Christine) **3.** *PHRASE* **3.1 like for (sb) to (do sth)** *vb phr* (Baha, Belz, Trin) [*IF*] To like/wish for/want (sb) to do (sth). *Some of the older folk drove them away, but Tiger would have like for them to come.*—SABS:6 □ This structure is common in AmE but is not BrE. **3.2 like off (sb)** *vb phr* (CarA) [*AF*—*Joc*] To show noticeable affection for (sb).

like[2] *prep* (CarA) *PHRASES* **1. all like now; all like this time so** *adv phrs* (Bdos) [*IF*] At about this time; at a moment like this (i.e. either present or some time ago). *You cannot put people's houses on a pasture in a village and think they will stay there for long. All like now I would imagine the house has disappeared, so the woman has lost everything.*—Bdos (Hd, 87.02.11, p.214) **2. like bush; like fire; like peas; like sand** *adj phrs, semi-adv* (CarA) [*AF*—*Joc*] In great abundance. **a.** *The Trinidad Police who captured the brother came and gave evidence; they told lies like bush to the Magistrate.*—NeJ (75.06.27, p.7) **b.** *There is an urgent need for a Public Enquiry into what is going on in a certain Government-Department. A big, big pappy getting car loans like fire!*—MoK (72.07.14, p.12) **c.** *For the past few weeks, advice about morality and mobility flowed like peas through well dressed audiences at graduation ceremonies.*—ExP (79.07.15, p.4) **3. Like France! adv phr** (ECar) [*AF*] Like hell; ferociously. **4. picture like a picture** *n phr* (Guyn) [*IF*] See PICTURE Phr

like[3] *conj* **1.** (CarA) [*X*] As. **a.** *He said St Vincent's limited resources, being a small state like it was, constantly called in question the viability in isolation of a state that size.*—AnS (73.02.17, p.5) **b.** *Like in previous years, this year's National Agricultural and Trade Show was a success.*—BsT (80.05.11, p.11) □ *Like* occurs very widely in this sense as it does in other Englishes, but is not considered pedagogically acceptable. The same may apply to other senses below. **2.** (CarA) [*AF*] As if; as though. **a.** *There was a little boy who loved to ride the pumpkins in the neighbor's yard—like he was on a horse—by making them rock.*—WFSFB:25 **b.** *As I was about to get upstairs I heard like someone squealed.*—Tbgo (CR, 80.03.04) **c.** *The dog rushed and barked like he saw somebody there.*—Bdos (CR, 1979) **3.** (CarA) [*AF/IF*] [Elliptical subordinator, introducing a statement that is uncertain or suggestive] **(i)** It seems as if; it looks as though; I think. **a.** *Nowadays, like my husband money can't reach me soon enough from the States; I have to credit at the grocery man.*—HF:15 **b.** *As it is, however, all we can say is we are expected to be fooled once again by loud, empty roars in Woodford Square. Like they testing we faith, or what?*—TaP (75.09.28, p.10) **c.** *Like you don't care nothing about [h]our [h]inner man. You don't want to take something more from the shop?*—CTT:25 [Cp similar Yoruba structure as in *Abi ara rẹ ko da 'oni* (= [Question] *Like his body not whole today*) 'It-seems-as-if he is sick today'] **(ii)** (CarA) [*AF/IF*] [Modifier separating two repeated subject elements] It seems. **a.** *'Funny thing,' she held her collar to her chin, 'half past seven ain't strike yet and you in your house. Good times like they slowing down. Things like they goin' bad, love like it running out, heat like it coolin' off. Since when?'*—JJM:112 **b.** *And since they like they ain' want we nowhere in this Christ's world, we have to stick it out wherever the Lord say we going get a little break.*—HFGA:114 (A. Clarke) **c.** *'Yo like yo does feel glad to see yo fadder tun beast,' she screeched back angrily.*—ExP (72.05.26, p.20, Short Story) □ In this very common CE structure the stress may be repeated on the subj element, bringing focus on that subj (cits a., b.); or on *like* (cit c.) in wh case an aspect of intensity is added to the foll vb phr. **4.** (CarA) *[IF]* [Elliptical, indicating that the foll phr or clause is a suggestion] For example, let's say; say something/somebody like. **a.** *Like an Indian or Chinese would take that over and make so much money you would be surprised.*—(Trin) **b.** *They should do those repairs like on a Saturday afternoon or a Sunday when the road is not busy.*—(Bdos) **c.** *He had like a spirit inside he that come talk in he ears and that make what happen to he.*—KJB:211 **5.** *PHRASES* **5.1 like if; like how; like when; like where** *conj phrs* (CarA) *[AF/IF]* [Introducing an opinion, suggestion] I think/would say/would suggest that if, (how, when, where). **a.** *Like if he was a different sort of boy I would try and help him, but not like how he is so rude!* (= *I think that if he were ... but seeing that he is so rude I would not ... help him*).—(Gren) **b.** *Not now, but like when you come back you can do that.*—(Jmca) **c.** *Like where they have all that bush they should clear it and build houses.*—(Guyn) [Cp similar Yoruba structure as in *Bi mo ṣe nṣọrọ* 'Like I am talking' = CE 'Like how I am talking to you here!'—(*A. Banjo and K. Ọmọtọsọ, pers info*)] □ CE *like* in this function can be identified by its omissibility, i.e. the basic meaning of the statement that it introduces would not be altered if *like* were omitted.

like⁴ *adjunct suffixed to a n, adj, vb or adv* (CarA) *[IF]* As it were; all but completely; almost; you might say. **a.** *He used his hand and then he had a piece of stick like.*—Tbgo (CR, 77.11.22) **b.** *When the place is too quiet, even that can make you nervous and timid like.*—CTT:34 **c.** *Jack Barrow was coming to me and my mother took up a chair and blocked him like.*—Bdos (CR, 71.04.29) **d.** *... but he walked Chuck home with me. Yes Sir, Mr Fuller, he did for a fact and we was a-talking to each other quite often like.*—FDI:50

lil¹; mo[re] lil, lil.lest [lɪlɪs] *adj* (CarA) *[AF—Cr]* Little; littler; littlest. **a.** *You're in the store and your mother is saying to the clerk 'I want a pair of Sunday School shoes for the lil girl.' The clerk looked at the 'lil girl' as if trying on shoes on lil girls was the worst part of his job.*—DaN(ST) (78.08.17, p.9, Short Story) **b.** *Dis cucumber mo[re] lil yes, but is no[t] de lilles[t] out o[f] all.*—(Guyn) [< SE *little* by syncopic loss of medial /-t-/] □ These dial forms (esp **lil**, so

spelled) are widely used in CE narrative dialogue.

lil² *adv* (CarA) *[AF—Cr]* ‖ *little* (CarA) 1. A little; somewhat; slightly. *A remanded prisoner who was further remanded for another week, said to the magistrate, 'Sir, I bin in jail 'lil long' you know.'*—EvP (73.04.24, p.4)

Li·ma bean* [li·ma-bi·n] *n phr* (CarA) ‖ *butter-bean* 2. (StKt, StVn) ‖ *broad-bean* (Jmca, StVn) ‖ *white bean* (CarA) ‖ *white pea* (Dmca) A popular, kidney-shaped (usu) whitish bean borne in a compressed, crescent-shaped pod about 2 or 3 ins long; *Phaseolus lunatus* (*Leguminosae/Papilionaceae*).

lim·ber [lɪmbʌ] *adj* *[AF/IF]* (Gren, Guyn, Jmca, StVn) 1. [Of a limb, pole, etc] Slender; bending or too easily bent. 2. (Bdos) [Of a person's body] Limp; supple. *She did stretch out limber, limber. An' I thought she did dead.*—EFLBB:13

lim·bo [lɪmbo·] *n* (CarA) A solo exhibition dance in wh the dancer must display the great suppleness of his/her body from the neck to the ankles, finally bending backwards and, moving forward in this position, pass under a stick set horizontally very near the ground (sometimes as low as 10 ins). [Perh orig by functional adj > vb shift of CE LIMBER. This would be apt in the line of the song *'Nobody could limbo like me'* wh goes with the drum-beat accompanying the dance] □ The vb *to limbo* (as cited in etym) is now mostly replaced by phr *to do the limbo* or *to limbo-dance*.

lime¹ *vb intr* (ECar) *[AF]* 1. ‖ *base out* (Belz) ‖ *buss a lime* (Trin) ‖ *make a lime* (Trin) ‖ *pick a lime* (ECar) To sit, loaf or hang about with others, usu on the sidewalk or other open place, chatting aimlessly, watching passers-by and sometimes making unsolicited remarks to them. **a.** *It is difficult not to be critical when it is found that some of our young people have to stay at home or 'lime' on the street and get into trouble.*—TiM (76.01.16, p.4) **b.** *It all started last Thursday evening, when a group of young men liming outside the Pebbles Restaurant at Shot Hall, allegedly used 'dirty' remarks to a Canadian tourist.*—NaT (74.09.22, p.3) **2.** (ECar) To idle (alone or in work-gang); to chat and relax on the job. *It is only the dedicated farm worker who is prepared these days to stand all day in the hot sun and in the rain to work for a pittance on the farm while his brother limes most of the day on a project for considerably more money.*—ExP (80.03.15, p.4) **3.** (ECar) To pay a casual visit. **4.** *vb tr* (Trin) To look on idly at (some event, usu in company with others); hence phrs. *lime a funeral; lime a wedding*, etc [The term seems to have originated in *Trin* during World War II, evid applied to white American sailors from the naval base who hung around bawdy-house areas in groups. The vb *to lime* seems to have been a popular (shifted) back-formation from 'limey', as a Derog term for a white person of low class]

lime[2] *n* (Trin) [*AF*] **1.** An unorganized social gathering (usu of young people) to pass the time away in chat and banter. *Strange to say, though, when the lime breaks up, and the limers each go their several ways, they still will greet one another next day with a cool 'What going on, Bredder-man?'* —ExP (73.02.25, p.21) □ In this sense *lime* is sometimes qualified by the name of the place or the purpose of the lime hence *a beach lime* 'a gathering on the beach', *a roti lime* 'a gathering to eat roti', etc. **2.** Any identifiable group of idlers. *At the junction it have a small lime of men on benches checking things out.*—TrG (74.07.28, p.12) **3.** The place where such people agree to meet, or do so regularly. *They changed the lime, left him out, but he soon found out the new lime.*— Trin (Ms) [By functional vb > n shift of LIME[1]] **4.** PHRASES **4.1 buss a lime; pick a lime** *vb phrs* (Trin) [*AF—Joc*] ‖ LIME[1] **4.2 make a lime** *vb phr* (Trin) [*IF*] ‖ LIME[1] *As a result several students decided to make a Macqueripe lime. It is while returning that the fatal accident took place.*—BoM (74.06.07, p.5)

lime ball *n phr* (Tbgo) See BALL 1ˑ

lime-ber·ry *n* (Trin) ‖ BABY-LIME (Guyn)

lim·er [laɪmər ~ laɪma] *n* (ECar) [*AF*] An idler; a time-waster; one (usu a man) who stands around with others on the sidewalk or in some public place watching people go by, and sometimes being mischievous. *Maurice M—, a 17-year old limer from Hindsbury Road was wrong to pick his lime on September 5 on Broad Street and as a result he was fined $10 which must be paid in one month or one month imprisonment. M— was found guilty of failing to 'Move and keep moving' when ordered to do so by a member of the Police Force.*— BdN (64.10.01, p.3) □ Cp *OED2* **kerb-crawler,** wh has similar connotation.

lime-skin *n* (Bdos, Guyn) [*AF—Joc*] An old felt hat that has lost its shape, being too small for its user's head; the brim is pulled down to help it fit. *You mean to say that you come / in here wid dat lime-skin cone / that you callin' a hat / pun you head, ...*—BTA:199 [From its resemblance to the skin of half a squeezed lime]

lim·ing [laɪmɪŋ] *n* (ECar) The habit or action of intentional idling in a public place or wasting time on a job. *As one ex-limer, now in his mid-thirties puts it, 'Liming was only looked down upon and regarded as a social problem after it was given a name'. And he pointed out that before the early 1960s—when liming became a fad in Barbados— few people paid any attention to the groups of youngsters who lined the streets and congregated in the bus stand.*—AdM (77.03.27, p.4) [Abstract noun derived from LIME[1] vb]

line[1] *n* (Bdos, Guyn) Any foot-path developed through or alongside a cane-field, farm, or large acreage of commercially used land to facilitate haulage; [by extension] a rugged track across fields. *After a quarrel over the legality of H—'s*

pulling timber over a certain area to which B—took objection ... the men told R—that they would continue to use the 'line'.—DaC (53.02.06, p.3) [Cp *EDD* **line** 4. 'a road'. N.Irel 'The new roads are so called'] □ Sometimes occurs in *Guyn* place naming exs: *Skeldon Line-Path, the side-line trench,* etc.

line[2] *vb tr* (Bdos, Trin) **1.** To lambaste; to berate; to flog [esp in foll phr]. **2.** PHRASE **2.1 line (sb) in/with blows/licks** *vb phr* (Bdos, Trin) [*AF—Joc*] ‖ **beat sb's skin** (CarA) To thrash (sb) (esp a child) without pity. *The word 'lambaste' is commonly used for beating a child: 'Child, if you don't behave yourself, I goin' lambaste you.' This is an alternative to the very much used 'line you with licks'.*—AdN (79.01.14, p.14) [Prob a dial shift of sense. Cp *OED* **line** v[1] 4. 'to cover the outside of; to drape' + cits to 1796. Cp also *CSD* Sc **line**[2] vb tr 2. 'beat, thrash'] □ See also LICKS Phr 3.7.

line-mark *n* (Bdos) A surveyor's landmark in the form of an 'X' cut in the coral, or a piece of iron driven into the ground; it is a legally recognized boundary mark.

ling *n* (Baha, Bdos) **1.** [Children's games] A ring or circle drawn on the ground, marking out the area of play (esp in games of marbles). [< SE *ring* by /r > l/ shift. Cp also *CSD* Sc **ling**[1] n 'a line'] **2.** PHRASES **2.1 get/jump in(to) the ling** *vb phr* (Bdos) [*AF—Joc*] To (be allowed to) join in the game; [figuratively] to take part in what is going on. *When they want you they use you; when they do not want you they kick you, and that is why I am not going to jump into the ling. They did not ask the Bar as a professional organisation to look at this thing and reason it out together.*—Bdos (Hd, 74.08.27, p.671)

lin·ing-cold [laɪnɪŋ-koˑl(d)] *n* (Antg, etc) [*X*] See LYING-IN COLD

lin·ing-house cold [laɪnɪŋ/-ɪn-hʊs koˑl(d)] *n phr* (Guyn) [*X*] ‖ LYING-IN COLD (Antg, etc)

li·on-bush *n* (Guyn) ‖ BALL-BUSH (Bdos, Jmca) □ A lesser known name in *Guyn* than (the widely used) ‖ **man-piaba.** Cp however the *Bdos* ‖ **lions's tail.**

lion-fish *n* (Bdos, Brbu, Mrat) ‖ SCORPION-FISH (CarA) [Perh from its very dangerous sting]

li·on's tail *n phr* (Bdos, ViIs) ‖ BALL-BUSH (Bdos, Jmca) **a.** *At this time the tall way-side plant we call the Lion's Tail is seeding.... some of the stems more than 4 ft high. There are two-inch spherical clusters every 3 or 4 ins up the vertical stem. It is a weed yes. But a weed, can be attractive or even beautiful.*—AdN (78.01.04, p.6—M. Hutt) **b.** *In years gone by people would take this bush they call lion's tail when it's dry and kind-o[f] spray it with gold paint and make a very nice artificial decoration.*—(Bdos) [From the re-semblance of the ball-like inflorescence spaced along the bare upper stalk to the significant tuft of hair at the end of a lion's tail]

li·quor PHRASES **1. under liquors; under your liquor** *adj phrs* (StKt) [*IF*] See UNDER Phr 2.2 **2. have in your liquor** *vb phr* (ECar) [*AF—Joc*] See HAVE Phr 3.8.1

Lis·bon *n* PHRASE **the licks of Lisbon** *n phr* (Bdos, Guyn) [*AF—Joc*] See LICKS Phr 3.5

Lis·bon yam* *n phr* (Bdos, Gren, Nevs, StLu, Tbgo, Trin) ‖ **water-yam** (Belz, Guyn, Jmca, StVn) ‖ **white yam** 2. (Dmca) A very large yam (often having three or four 'fingers'), that is widely cultivated; it has a floury flesh that may be white, cream or pink; *Dioscorea alata*, *(Dioscoreaceae)*. **a.** *Lisbon yams from Barbados were available at 25 cents a pound.... A provision vendor explained that Lisbon yam needs more labour and planning in cultivation.*—ExP (72.03.07, p.8 'Your Food Basket') **b.** *His legs were long and his arms hefty as ripe Lisbon-yams.*—Bim.IV.16, p.279 (K.P. Newton)

lit·ti(e) *n* (Guyn) ‖ PICK-UPS (Bdos, etc)

lit·tle *adv* (CarA) [X] **1.** ‖ *lil²* (CarA) A little; somewhat; slightly. *Well she pressed her hair and stop wearing glasses, so she look little different.*— (StVn) □ SE *little* so used is neg 'hardly'. **2.** For a short while; for a few minutes, days, etc. *Now that the son marry that white girl from England, you jus[t] wait little and see how they goin[g] change.*—(Guyn) [A prob calque from W Afr langs. Cp Twi *twen kakra* (*wait little*) 'wait for a while']

Lit·tle Eight, The *n phr* (CarA) The remaining eight island-states—Antigua & Barbuda, Barbados, Dominica, Grenada, Montserrat, St Kitts-Nevis-Anguilla, St Lucia, St Vincent & the Grenadines—after the withdrawal of Jamaica and Trinidad & Tobago from the W Indian Federation in 1962. ['Little' in relation to the population size and economic power of *Jmca* and *Trin & Tbgo*, wh were the two largest of the ten Federated states]

Lit·tle Eng·land *n phr* (CarA) [*IF—Joc*] Barbados. *It look as if they like Barbadians, because they didn't go to any other islands: they just get some of the boys from Little England—that is what they call Barbados down there—and bring them up to work the transport.*—SWOS:132 [Said to be partly from the notable topographical resemblance of some of the landscape to the English countryside, and partly to the historical legacy of an unbroken settlement by the English since 1627. Collymore *CGBD5:63* cites a note indicating that the Barbadians themselves were using this cognomen before 1835] □ There is some sarcasm implied in the use of the name today.

Lit·tle Four, The *n phr* (CarA) The set of Windward Islands—Dominica, Grenada, St Lucia, St Vincent & the Grenadines—regarded as a possible political grouping after the breakdown of the West Indian Federation in 1962. ['Little' in relation to the size of the population of each]

Lit·tle Sev·en, The *n phr* (CarA) The remaining seven island-states after the withdrawal of Barbados in 1965 from the LITTLE EIGHT. *Chief Minister E.O. Le Blanc stated at Friday's public meeting at the Dawbiney Market that he would not go to London if the other territories (St Vincent and St Kitts excluded) maintain their present attitude towards a proposed 'Little Seven' Federation.*—DoC (65.05.12, p.1)

live¹ *vb intr* PHRASES **1. live good** *vb phr* (CarA) See GOOD³ Phr 3.2 **2. (two persons) can live in the same house** *id phr* (Nevs, Tbgo) [*IF*] ‖ (TWO PERSONS) CAN SHAKE HANDS (CarA) See HAND¹ Phr 4.3

live² *vb intr* (CarA) [*IF*] **1.** [Of a man and a woman] To live together without being married. **a.** *He told his friends that the children didn't belong to him and so I left him. When we used to live he hated the children so much that I couldn't even fix food for them. Now, he isn't supporting them at all.*—WeS (74.06.28, p.8) **b.** *Asked what he had to say, the accused N— explained: 'The female accused knows nothing about them. Both of us live but I did not tell her where I got them'.*—DeM(SK) (74.09.21, p.3) **2.** PHRASES **2.1 live at Easy Hall** *vb phr* (Bdos) [*AF—Joc*] To live in unexpected or unearned comfort. [Cp AmE 'to live on Easy Street'. See also HALL 2.] **2.2 live at your aunt/ nennen** *vb phr* (Bdos, Gren, Guyn, Trin) [*AF*] To experience dire hardships; to suffer privations; to be living unhappily. (See AUNT Phr 2.2) **2.3 live at yourself** *vb phr* (Bdos) [*IF*] [Esp of a young woman] To live on your own; to support yourself; to have no one to depend on. *Now, some weeks the girls get as little as $6. Do you think it is fair for these girls some of whom have children or live at themselves?*—NaT (77.02.27, p.7, Al's Grapevine) **2.4 live bachelor/bachie** *vb phr* (CarA) [*AF*] [Of a man] To live alone; to live as a bachelor. *But Agnes never reply to Lewis letter, and in the end she left him and he never see she again. Lewis went by Moses to learn how to live bachelor.*—STLL:55 □ The phr does not usu connote (SE) 'to live a merry bachelor's life' but rather 'to be one who does without companionship or domestic help'. **2.5 live bad** *vb phr* (Bdos, Guyn) [*AF*] **(i)** [Of a couple, married or living together] To quarrel and fight much of the time; to disturb the neighbourhood regularly with open rows. **(ii)** [Of a young person] To live an unsavoury, wanton, or criminal life. **2.6 live good/well** *vb phr* (ECar) [*AF/IF*] To be on good terms with each other (as a couple, as neighbours etc); to get on well together. *From the time I know meself, them two families never had no quarrel, always live good.*— (Gren) **2.7 live home** *vb phr* (Guyn) [*AF/IF*] [Of a couple] To live together unmarried. *For years they live home, as we say. Never married till* *the children grow up and tell them they mus[t] married.*—(Guyn) **2.8 live like family** *vb phr* (Guyn) [*AF*] To live as good neighbours; to be always ready, helpful friends with each other. **2.9 live till they sun you** *vb phr* (Guyn, Nevs) [*AF—Joc*] To live to a great old age. [A prob ref to the habit of putting decrepit old people out-of-doors to sit in the sunshine] □ *'You will live till they sun you'* is usu said to a person who arrives unexpectedly while he is being spoken of; that is considered a good omen for long life.

live·ly up (sb/sth) *vb phr* (CarA) [*AF*] **1.** To cheer up (a downcast or saddened person); to make or get lively. *He smiled into her face, 'Cho, don't say dem t'ings, honey. Mek us lively-up ourselves. You want to dance?'*—MBM:79 **2.** To brighten up (a place); to make (an event) lively.

liv·er *n* (Tbgo) ‖ BELLY 2· (CarA)

liv·er-string *n* (Guyn) [*AF—Joc*] **1.** The (imagined) vital source of human energy. **2.** PHRASE **2.1 work out your liver-string** *vb phr* (Guyn) [*AF—Joc*] To exhaust yourself with hard work.

liv·ing *adj* (CarA) [*IF*] [Of a man and a woman] Living together [Hence sometimes treated as noun]. *Better a good living than a bad marriage.*—ECar (Catch phrase) □ Similarly **live-with** *n* (*Guyn*), used in same catch phr.

liz·ard-food *n* **1.** (Bdos, Nevs, StKt) ‖ CERASEE (Baha, etc) **2.** (Bdos) ‖ BABY-CUCUMBER (Guyn) *I was rather interested to see the common white-flowered vine Coccinia grandis referred to in your issue of January 11, as 'Wild Cucumber'—for all my life, here in Barbados, I have heard this called 'Lizard Food'.*—AdN (78.01.23, p.4, H.G. Jones) □ See note at BABY-CUCUMBER.

lob·lob *n* (Nevs) ‖ LOVE-VINE (CarA)

lob·lol·ly *n* (Angu, ViIs) A big, uncultivated, shady tree with a very light-grey bark and round, green, leathery leaves; it bears small, sticky fruit wh animals eat, and a parasitic vine thrives on its limbs; *Pisonia subcordata* (*Nyctaginaceae*).

lob·ster-claw *n* (Bdos) ‖ HELICONIA (CarA) *Lobster-claw, or the famous Trinidadian balisier, may be specially cultivated for the exotic brilliance it adds to any floral arrangement, but it takes a lot of watering.*—Bdos (Ms) [From the resemblance of the bract, esp of the red variety, to the fixed part of a lobster's claw]

lob·ster-pot *n* (CarA) A trap made of wire netting, designed for catching lobsters on the sea-bed. □ Cp FISH-POT.

lo·cal[1] *adj* (CarA) **1.** [Of persons] Native to a territory (in sharp contrast to 'expatriate' or 'foreign'). *Such men are not local; they are at heart foreign. They are not nationals; they are denationalised.*—MoK (73.02.02, p.3) **2.** [Of animals and products] Bred or made in the territory

(in sharp contrast to 'imported'). *What weary gift shopper has not been astounded by 'local' craft shops filled to the hilt with gimmicks and trivia made in Hong Kong.*—Isl 72/10, p.4 **3.** [*IF—Derog*] Rough in character; of inferior quality. *And of course she always dresses in the latest fabrics, my dear! Nothing local for her!*—(Trin) **4.** PHRASES **4.1 behave local** *vb phr* (Antg, Bdos, Guyn) [*AF—Derog*] To behave without dignity; to be unnecessarily crude. *But if you see how dem people did gettin' on—pushing and shovin' to get first in line! Man, dey was behavin' real local, doh! Ah tell yuh.*—NaT, n.d. [Extension of sense 3. above] **4.2 buy local** *vb phr* (CarA) To support national industry; to purchase items made within the country. *When Barbadians buy local they help themselves by contributing to our economy, and in my opinion we are getting good quality for our money.*—AdN (72.08.27, p.18)

lo·cal[2] *n* (CarA) A native inhabitant (in particular contrast to a settler, outsider, foreigner). **a.** *Bridgetown yesterday was its usual colourful and busy self, with visitors and locals alike congregating in the commercial banks to get money changed, to deposit or to withdraw.*—AdN (74.02.16, p.5) **b.** *In the basketball match it was a disappointing performance by the locals who were outplayed in every department by the Cubans.*—GyC (77.10.20, p.16)

lo·cal white *adj phr, n phr* (CarA) [*Derog*] ‖ CREOLE WHITE (CarA) **a.** *Again in 1940, Lady Young the Governor's wife wrote privately to Secretary of State Malcolm McDonald that: Local white creoles have no conception of manners, loyalty or any other civilized virtue. They simply do not live in the same box as ordinary human beings, one cannot calculate what any of their reactions are; they are as strange and remote morally as the Africans and low-caste Indians who have, as everything tends to sink, much influenced the whole trend of life in these islands.*—GTMC:XI **b.** *In Jamaica most of the plantation owners were absentee landlords—men who lived in England—but in Barbados a considerable number of estates were owned by local whites.*—HBIH:123 [LOCAL[1] 1. + white (person)]

lock off[1] (sb); **lock (off) the neck/throat of** (sb) *vb tr phr* (Bdos, Guyn, Trin) [*IF*] ‖ **choke-and-rob** (Guyn) To attack (sb) from behind by choking the person's neck in the crook of your arm while disabling or robbing him with your other arm. *He added that while everyone was running, Torrence H—, now deceased, grabbed him around the neck, but H— was accustomed to locking off people's neck when he drank alcoholic beverages. B—said that Ivan H—(T—'s nephew) came close to them and told I—: 'Leggo de man. Whuh you holding de man fuh?'*—AdV (90.07.05, p.5) ['lock off' in ref to locking off the person's breathing and resistance]

lock-off[2] *n* (Guyn) [*AF*] The seizure of sb from behind by choking the neck in the crook of your arm. [By functional vb > n shift of LOCK OFF[1]]

locks *n pl* (CarA) [*AF—Joc*] [Rastaf] ‖ DREAD-LOCKS (CarA) *It is no longer a secret, for example, that when young men of the Rastafari faith are arrested by police the first thing is that their locks are chopped off.*—CrU (76.10.02, p.2)

locks·man (locks-man) *n* (CarA) [*AF—Joc*] [Rastaf] A male Rastafarian.

lo·cust [lokʌs(t)] *n* **1***. (CarA) ‖ STINKING-TOE 1. (Guyn, etc) □ Ref to the pod. **2.** (Guyn) The wood of the timber tree *Hymenea courbaril* (*Caesalpiniaceae*) wh bears the fruit at sense 1.; a very hard, light-brown, straight-grained wood much favoured in furniture-making and boat-building and for pilings.

log-bush *n* (BrVi) The leaves of the LOG-TREE wh are used esp in the island of Anegada for sheep and goats after giving birth to their young. □ Cp GUM-BARK (*Mrat*).

log·ger·head[1]* *n* (CarA) A sea-turtle about 4 ft in length, with a reddish-brown, heart-shaped shell; it has a strikingly large head and weighs about 500 lbs, but its meat is not prized; *Caretta caretta* (*Chelonidae*).

log·ger·head[2]* *n* (Angu) An aggressive member of the kingbird family, about 8 ins long; it is said to attack anyone approaching its nest; *Tyrannus caudifasciatus* (*Tyrannidae*).

lo·gie [loˑʃi] *n* (Guyn) **1.** A long tenement building constructed flat on the ground, comprising ten to twenty rooms; originally designed to house slave families and, later, indentured labour on sugar estates, each room housing one family. *Permission has been granted for the Hague C. M. School to be housed temporarily in the logies offered for use by residents of the district, until other arrangements can be made in respect to a new building.*—DaC (52.02.26, p.3) **2.** [By extension] Any small one-room dwelling built flat on the ground. *So, alone on the damp mud floor of a darkened logie, a woman and her two children, locked in a desperate embrace had slept until morning.*—Kai VIII. 71/12, p.45 [Prob < Fr *logis* 'dwelling', originating in the Fr period of ownership of *Guyn* 1782–84]

log-tree *n* (BrVi) ‖ BIRCH-GUM TREE (Bdos, etc) [Perh because the large bole of the tree provides a log wh is both easily worked for furniture-making and easily carved for making canoes]

log·wood *n* (Belz, BrVi, Gren, Jmca, Trin) ‖ CAMPESH (Dmca, Gren, Trin) *Logwood ... [is] now prized because the honey made from the log-wood blossom is of excellent quality.*—SJW:93

Lo·ko·no *n* (Guyn) The name by wh the Arawak peoples call themselves and their lang. [BAED Arawak *Loko* n 'People known to other

people as Arawak. The lang of the Arawaks'; also *Lokono* n 'People']

lone *adj* **1.** [*X*] (CarA) [Only in phrs] Alone. **2.** PHRASES **2.1 lef me (etc) lone; le[t] me (etc) lone** *id phrs* (CarA) [*AF—Cr*] Leave me (etc) alone!; Go away! □ These phrs are often used in narrative dialogue. **3.** (Belz) [*AF—Cr*] Only. *A mere wind-bag; as the saying goes, 'lone bark and no bite'.*—BeT (81.05.31, p.9) [Prob by aphesis < SE *alone*, but also infl by IrE usage: Cp *JESI: 25 I am in my lone*, etc 'I am alone', etc]

long[1] *adj* (CarA) [*AF/IF*] **1.** [Of a person] Notably tall; of ungainly height and bearing. **a.** *Humphrey Eglantine Pembroke was not quite as long as his name, but like most West Indian boys he was long for his age.*—AHR:1 **b.** *An' yu ain' shame you reach a big long young man an' she still dey ketchin she tail with the lil ol'-house falling-down on she head?*—HCCM:12 **2.** [In many uses, it denotes size or intensity rather than length; so it is often uncomplimentary or Derog; note foll phrs, and separate entries below] PHRASES **2.1 cry long water** *vb phr* (CarA) See CRY Phr 1. **2.2 foot [is] long** *id phr* (Guyn) [*AF—Joc*] See FOOT Phr 2.4. **2.3 hand [is] long; hand [is] longer than your foot** *id phrs* (Gren) [*AF*] See HAND[1] Phr 4.11 **2.4 have a long head** *vb phr* (Guyn) [*IF*] To be far-sighted. *When he bought that land nobody was interested in it and he got it for a song. Now look at the value! But he always had a long head.*—(Guyn) [Cp IrE *You have a quare long head on you, son* 'You've got brains, can plan for the future'—L. Todd] **2.5 heart is long** *id phr* (Nevs) [*IF*] See HEART Phr 2. **2.6 with (your) two long hands** *adj phr* (ECar) [*AF—Joc*] See HAND[1] Phr 4.29

long[2] *adv* (CarA) [*AF*] **1.** For a long time. *I di[d]n[']t know yo[u] lef[t] them after all those years! You been there long!*—(Bdos) **2.** A long time ago; long ago. *Now he want to put up his own statue of the patient Lady—anybody else would have licked him down long.*—NeJ (74.11.15, p.6)

long[3] *vb tr* **1.** (CarA) [*AF—Cr*] To make long. **2.** PHRASES **2.1 long (out) your eye on (sth)** *vb phr* (Antg, Mrat) [*AF*] See EYE Phr 21. **2.2 long out your tongue on (sb)** *vb phr* (Guyn) [*AF*] **(i)** To stick out your tongue at (sb). **(ii)** Talk happily (about sb's misfortune); let your tongue wag. **3. long your heart on (sth)** *vb phr* (Guyn) [*AF/IF*] As 1. **4. long up your face** *vb phr* (Bdos) [*AF*] [Esp of a child] To pull a long face; to pout and look annoyed.

long[4] *adv* (CarA) [*X*] **1.** Along. *I was just walking long the road. I wasn't troubling nobody.*—Bdos (CR, 1971) [< SE *along* by aphesis] **2.** PHRASES **2.1 come long** *vb phr* (CarA) [*AF—Cr*] To come along. **2.2 go long** *vb phr* (CarA) [*AF—Cr*] To go along; to be on your way. □ Often written *'long* in narrative dialogue.

long-belly/-guts adj (CarA) [AF—Derog] [Esp of a man or children] Gluttonous; greedy and voracious. □ Cp BIG-EYE¹

long-bench n (Belz) [AF-Joc] ‖ LONG-METER (ECar)

long-broom n (Guyn) (Usu imported) broom with a broom-stick handle, used indoors (in contrast to a POINTER-BROOM or other folk-type broom).

long eye¹ n phr 1. (CarA) [AF—Derog] Prompt and irritating covetousness; keen desire. *But Tinto was a true Trinidadian with a long eye and the next thing he wanted from the Yankee woman was an estate somewhere in the country—a country house as it were.*—BoM (77.06.17, p.9, Short Story) 2. PHRASE 2.1 **put your long eye on (sth)** vb phr (Angu, Guyn, Nevs) [AF—Derog] ‖ PUT YOUR EYE ON STH (Bdos, etc) See EYE¹ Phr 24 2.2 **throw long eye on (sth)** vb phr (Trin) As prec. 3. (Jmca) [Of a woman] A keen eye for men.

long-eye² adj [AF—Derog] 1. (BrVi, Nevs, StVn) ‖ BIG-EYE¹ (CarA) 2. (Angu, Guyn, Nevs) Irritatingly covetous; having a prompt longing for something just seen. 3. (Jmca) [Of a woman] Having a keen eye for men.

long-foot adj (CarA) [AF] [Of a person] Long-legged. *According to local superstition, delivery is more difficult for long foot women than for short foot women, and, if a long foot woman passes over the legs of a short foot woman, she transmits the difficulties. Short foot women are said to become pregnant very often whereas long foot women take a longer time to conceive.*—DCC:23 [SE long + IF CE FOOT 'leg', with characteristic CE functional n phr > adj shift]

long-guts adj, n (Guyn, Mrat, StVn) [AF—Vul] ‖ LONG-BELLY (CarA)

long-head adj (CarA) [AF/IF] Brainy; clever; far-sighted. [See LONG¹ Phr 2.4]

long-heart(ed) adj (Nevs, USVI) [IF] ‖ BIG-EYE¹ (CarA)

long·heart·ed·ness n (Nevs, USVI) [IF] Greed; great covetousness. *Longheartedness make you tief.*—DaN(ST) (78.04.06, p.11—A. Petersen)

long-man·go /1´22/ n (Guyn, Tbgo, Trin) ‖ HAIRY MANGO (Belz, etc)

long-me·ter n (ECar) [AF-Joc] ‖ *long-bench* (Belz) A person who is long-winded or tiresome in speech or conversation. *She was a real long-meter who would come to visit you from early on a Sunday afternoon and stay till church time.*—(Guyn) [Usu so spelled, though rarely written, perh infl by IAE meter/metre. However prob orig

is *long* + *meet* + *er* 'one who meets for a long time']

long-mouth adj 1. (Guyn) [AF—Derog] ‖ BIG-MOUTH² (CarA) 2. (Jmca) Always ready to eat; ever hungry. *'Long-mouth Clara', too weak with consumption to enter the scramble, looked hungrily at the luscious piece of disinfected mackerel.*—PCOS:25

long out vb phr (CarA) [AF] To stick out (your tongue, hand); to push out (your lips, esp the lower lip) rudely. a. *They only know to long out they hand to people and beg instead o[f] look for work.*—(Bdos) b. *She long out her mouth at her mother, and the mother slap her!*—(Tbgo) [See LONG³]

long-side prep, adv (CarA) [AF] Beside; alongside (of). a. *And come into the swamp water / Right here long-side me / Where this pipe gone and bu's.*—YFOC:13 b. *When the people see him on de boat dey start to point and shout and clap before de boat could well come longside.*—(Trin) [From SE alongside by aphetic loss of unstressed /a-/]

long-tail doc·tor-bird n phr (Jmca) ‖ DOCTOR-BIRD 2. (Jmca) □ One of the names of the National Bird of *Jmca*.

long time¹ /2´1/ adv phr (CarA) [AF/IF] 1. A long time ago; some time ago now. *'Don't go yet', shrieked Charlotte. 'Ah want to tell you dis: you owe me two dollars fo' muffin an' salt fish cake you truss from me long time.*—TRIH:68 2. /1´2/ In the past; in days/years gone by. *I am a Farmer, and I must state I am fed up with Government about the way they pay us for our Bananas. Long time when we sell such fruit, within four days we got pay. Today Government has taken that Industry and three weeks we can't get pay.*—NaT (75.05.23, p.8) 3. /3´1/ [With strong stress-and-pitch differentiation] With hardly any delay; as promptly as ever. *You think in them South American countries people could be runnin[g] out o[f] jail and police catchin[g] them to bring them back to court? No sir! Police shoot them long time!*—(Bdos) □ Note the importance of pitch differentiation in distinguishing these three senses. In sense 3. the vowel of *long* is also often notably lengthened.

long-time² /1´2/ adj (CarA) [AF—Cr] Of days gone by; old-fashioned. a. *Me dear, chil'ren now have plenty more privilege dan long-time chil'ren, because dey showin' dem dese t'ings in pictures.*—WeN (53.03.02, p.2) b. *It's a joke, man, this business of being bad, a bad John. That is a old long time thing. That gone out with the biscuit drum and the three note boom.*—LDCD:190 [By functional adv > adj shift of LONG-TIME¹ 1.]

long-tongue adj (ECar) [AF—Derog] Being a blabber-mouth; indiscreetly talkative. *I know that for some reason he is trying to make a good* *impression on the PM, but doesn't he think that he is overdoing this long-tongue business?*—BoM (75.04.18, p.3)

loo·fah* [lufa] *n* (Gren, Jmca, Trin) ‖ **nenwah** (Guyn) ‖ **torchon** (Trin) A green cylindrical fruit about a foot long, resembling a cucumber with noticeable ridges along its length; its soft, cream flesh carries plenty of seeds, and it is peeled and cooked when young esp by EAST INDIANS; it is better known in its dry, massively fibrous state as a useful scrubber; *Luffa cylindrica* (*Cucurbitaceae*). [From the first element of its botanical name wh comes from the Arabic name of the plant. See also *COD*, etc *loofah*]

look *vb* (CarA) [*AF/IF*] [Often used as if *vb tr*, without supporting preps *at, for*] **1.** To seek, look for (esp with 'work' as obj). **a.** *I cannot for the world understand what is the Governor's role in Antigua. Is he looking a job and if he speaks out he loses it?*—WoV (71.12.01, p.4) **b.** *I lookin' money now. Anywhere I can get it, I goin' to take it.*—SCHMH:189 [Cp *EDD* look 8. 'to look for, search for' + cits from Shr, LnK, etc] **2.** To visit (a friend). *When you live so far in the country yo[ur] family don['t] come and look you.*—(StKt) **3.** (Guyn, Tbgo) To tend, look after (livestock). *Indians bring up the[ir] children to look the cows every mornin[g] [be]fore they go to school.*—(Guyn) **4.** PHRASES **4.1 look about (sth)** *vb phr* (Antg, Dmca, Jmca) To see after, take care of, do some business for (sb). **a.** *The mother took a job and took the eldest girl out of school to look about the younger children.*—(Antg) **b.** *Just a little after, Parson had gone to Kingston to look about the new church bell.*—PCOS:62 **4.2 Look (at) me good!** *vb phr* (Guyn) [*AF/IF*] See GOOD[3] Phr 2.7 **4.3 Look (at) my crosses!/my trouble!** *excl vb phr* (CarA) [*AF/IF*] [Expressing angry surprise] Who would believe what's happening/happened to me! '*Eh, eh,' my mother continued, 'look at my crosses one day. I see the boy coming home limping.*'—NTMM:14 □ Cp Phr 4.14. **4.4 look for (sb)** *vb phr* [*IF*] (CarA) To visit (esp as a concerned friend or relative). **a.** *He phoned two people, his mother and I, 'cause I had to leave him at the hospital because I was home working. I went and looked for him the Wednesday. Myself and the mother used to conversate about his condition.*—NaT (76.08.01, p.13) **b.** *'I live Minnie Street, he live Okra Hill. I don't look for him. I went to the Formatery School (Boys Industrial School). I was taking up my BJCs but I escaped', S—rambled on.*—NaG (76.08.18, p.1) **(ii)** (Trin) To look out for; to perform some needed service for. *As one informant said, 'I myself have plenty of family, but I don' look for them, everybody more look for theirself these days'.*—RLCF:160 **4.4.1 look for what you ain['t]/didn['t] put down** *id phr* (Bdos) [*AF—Joc*] To go about stealing; to be a regular thief. **4.5 Look her (him/it/them, etc) here/there!** *id phr* (CarA) [*IF*] ‖ *See her (etc) here/there!* (CarA) Here/there she (he/it/they, etc) is/are! [A likely calque from a number of Afr langs. Cp Hausa *gaa shi/ta nan* (*Behold thing*

(masc)/thing (fem) here) 'Here it is!'; also Yoruba *wo o mbi yii* (*Look-at it here this*) 'Here it is!] **4.6 look like people** *vb phr* (ECar) [*IF—Joc*] To look presentable; to look as if you are somebody; to improve your personal appearance (from being poor or shabby looking). **4.7 look-look** /1'2/ *vb intr redupl* (CarA) [*AF*] To peep about; to eye furtively; to keep searching, watching, etc. *The whole mornin[g] I notice the two o[f] them lookin[g] -lookin[g], so I know for sure they los[t] somet[h]ing important.*—(Guyn) **4.8 Look [u]pon (sb)!** *excl vb phr* (Guyn, Jmca, StVn, Trin) [*AF—Cr*] [Expressing contempt] But just look at—!; See how contemptible (sb) is! *Look 'pon Mr Solomon him, yu see 'ow funny-funny 'im gwan. Them say dat 'im was big-big Anglican parson, 'im try fe study more dan wha' 'im teacher dem could teach 'im.*—PCOS:89 **4.9 look shame** *vb phr* (CarA) See SHAME Phr 2.2. **4.10 look sharp** *vb phr* (CarA) **(i)** /1'2/ To watch your interest closely; to be keenly defensive. *Who owns the land owns the country and if we don't look sharp we will sell out our heritage and birthright to immigrants.*—Guyn (Ms) **(ii)** /3'1/ [Issuing a threat or warning, esp to children] Beware!; You are risking punishment! *Boy you sucked your teeth at me? / No, mother!! / Look sharp!*—(Gren) [A semantic shift of SE *look sharp* 'be alert', wh is less common a sense in CE] **(iii)** /2'2/ [Of dress] To appear attractive, fashionable or sexy. *She look real sharp, and when he was coming up he notice the trim legs, and the straight lines of the nylons, and the highheel shoes.*—STLL:75 **4.11 look small** *vb phr* (Guyn) [*IF*] ‖ FEEL SMALL (CarA) **4.12 Look story!** *excl vb phr* (Guyn) [*AF*] How absurd!; What a ridiculous thing! *You know in America if you beat yo[ur] own chil[d] you can get lock up? Well, look story!*—(Guyn) **4.13 look the other side; be looking the other side** *vb phrs* (Tbgo) [*IF*] To be slowly dying [From the observation that a dying person often looks away fixedly] □ Cp BAD[1] PHR 4.2. BE BAD ENOUGH **4.14 Look trouble!** *excl vb phr* (Bdos, Guyn) [*AF*] [Expressing sudden distress, alarm at sth about to happen] There's grave trouble ahead now! □ Cp Phr 4.3. **4.15 look with red-eye (at sth)** *vb phr* (Jmca) [*AF*] See RED-EYE 2. **4.16 Look you!** /2'1/ *vb phr* (CarA) [*AF*] [Expressing sharp rebuke] Just look at you! Well I never! *But look you!—Yer too fast with yer ugly self.*—JMRS:49

look·a (**look·er, look·o, luk·u**) [lʊkʊ] *vb intr* (CarA) [*AF—Cr*] Look [in all vbl functions]. **a.** *Hey! Looka that sore foot Peter Laws.... One time he fall down right in the middle of the street and looka my calamity!*—LMFF:43 **b.** *Some behaviour would surface on the cricket field when a youngster, conditioned in his home environment, to say 'may I have ... please?' would shout to his skipper or team mate: 'Looker gimme the ball do!' Such is the 'by-talk' that expresses the other side of a Barbadian behaviour that completes his or her native personality.*—AdV (87.07.25, p.4) [SE *look* + Cr -a[21]] □ These and similar notional spellings are used to represent this common survival from Cr speech in narrative dialogue.

loose[1] *adj* (CarA) PHRASE **lick loose (sth)** *vb phr* (CarA) [*AF/IF*] See LICK[1] Phr 4.9

loose[2] *vb tr* (CarA) [*X*] To lose. *I wonder if the shopkeepers of Barbados have any idea of the amount of business they loose by having to close their doors at 4 p.m?*—AdN (73.02.20, p.4) □ A common misascription (or misspelling?) in written CE.

loose down *vb tr phr* (CarA) To dismantle or take apart (an engine, machine, box, etc).

Lord-La·ving·ton *n* (Antg) See LA-LAVINTON

loss[1] [lɒs] *vb intr, tr* **1.** (CarA) [*X*] ‖ **lost**[1] (CarA) To be lost; to have lost; to lose. **a.** *Nine o'clock in the hands of a police who says that Trevour was loss. Trevour, my only grand-child loss in Barbados?*—CWFYS:36 **b.** *So he get he foot tie up, he loss everything: club, woman, tout bagaye.*—ExP (Mag) (72.12.24, Short Story) **c.** *And, funnily enough the majority of these disgruntled women pointed to the fact that Trinidad men do have big stomachs, and that the men should be the ones to loss weight, not the women.*—SuP (74.10.06, p.9) [< SE pa.t. *lost* with characteristic CarA Cr reduction of /-CC/. Its extended use as a base vb 'to lose' patterns with other CarA Cr base vbs /BROK, LEF, DON/] □ The form *lossin* 'losing' also occurs. **2.** PHRASES **2.1 loss away** *vb phr* (Bdos, Guyn) [*AF—Cr*] To faint; [of a sick person] to lapse into unconsciousness. **2.1.1 loss (sb) away in jail, the bush, (etc)** *vb phr* (CarA) [*AF—Cr*] To be or have been sent to jail/into the bush (etc) for so long a time as to be considered abandoned. *Is not the same Butler that they loss away in jail that they trying their best to honour now?*—MoK (73.06.22, p.15) **2.2 loss [u]pon your hand** *vb phr* (Guyn) [*AF—Cr*] To take/ have taken a risk that proves/has proved costly to you; to become the unexpected loser in some money deal. *Yo[u] better sell off them mangoes cheap before they get rotten and yo[u] loss [u]pon yo[ur] han[d].*—(Guyn)

loss[2] *excl* (Bdos, Guyn) [*IF*] [Euphemism] Lord!; O Lord!

lost[1] [lɒs] *vb* (CarA) [*X*] ‖ LOSS[1] (CarA) *I asked my friend, Kenny / To lend me a penny / But time I reach Tantie it lost.*—TRFSS:15 □ This written form merely represents the dial form LOSS in all its functions. See next.

lost[2] [lɒs] *n* (CarA) [*X*] Loss. *This lost the Company contended was mainly due to Government not honouring its full obligations of import quantitative restrictions imposed on foreign beer and malt in 1971.*—ToR (73.10.19, p.1) [< SE *loss* by overcorrection]

lo·ta[1] (lo·tah) *n* (Guyn, Trin) [Indic] A small brass drinking jug, now mostly used on ceremonial religious occasions. [Hin *loṭaa*, name of this drinking vessel]

lo·ta[2] *n* (Bdos, Dmca, StLu, Trin) ‖ LA(T)TA (Bdos, etc) [cp *DECG* Fr Cr *lota*, name of the same skin-disorder]

lou·ga·wou (la·ga·hoo, la·ga·hou, li·ga·ru, li·ga·wu, lu·ga(r)·hoo) [lʊgawu ~ lugawu ~ lɪgaru ~ luga(r)hu] *n* (Dmca, Gren, Grns, StLu, Trin) **1.** A legendary, evil, male figure that can change his shape wholly or partly into that of a vicious beast or, shedding and hiding his skin, into a moving ball of fire; in another form he sucks the blood of his sleeping victims; he is the male counterpart of the SOU-KOUYAN. **2.** A legendary animal-like apparition that can be heard passing by night with the clank of chains, going on some evil mission. **3.** [By extension] A suspicious-looking old man living alone and feared for his capacity to lay curses or charms on people, while also being able to effect cures with folk-medicine. [Fr Cr < Fr *loup-garou* 1. 'werewolf' 2. 'a recluse'. For some of the characteristics in senses 1. and 3. above see etym note at SOUKOUYAN] □ [lʊgawu] is the common pronunc in *Dmca* and *StLu*, [lugaru] in *Gren*, [lɪgahu] in *Trin*. See also LAGAHOO.

love-ap·ple *n* (StLu) ‖ MALACCA-APPLE (Antg, Guyn)

love-bush *n* (Jmca) **1.** ‖ LOVE-VINE (CarA) □ See note at LOVE-VINE. **2.** (Angu, Antg, Bdos, StKt, StVn) ‖ LEAF-OF-LIFE (Bdos, etc) [From the young people's folk practice of writing a loved person's name on a leaf picked and stuck on the wall. If the leaf survives (wh it usu does), so too, it is believed, will the love]

love-leaf *n* (Bdos, Gren) ‖ LEAF-OF-LIFE (Bdos, etc) [As for LOVE-BUSH 2.]

love off (sb); **love (sb) off** *vb phr* (Jmca) [*AF—Joc*] To make very affectionate and rather obvious advances to (sb). *When my baby was four months old my boyfriend said to me one day: 'Pastor daughter love me off.' I said to him, 'All you have to do is love her back.' Well I didn't take him seriously. However, it happened that he started a relationship with this girl.*—WeS (74.11.22, p.8, Advice to The Lovelorn)

love-vine* *n* (CarA) ‖ *chibbly* (BrVi) ‖ *dodder* (Antg, BrVi, Jmca, Mrat, Trin) ‖ *lob-lob* (Nevs) ‖ *love-bush* (Jmca) ‖ *lub-lub* (StKt) ‖ *macaroni* (BrVi, StKt) ‖ *yellow-dad/-dod* (Angu) ‖ *yellow-dodder* (Nevs) ‖ *yellow-love* (ViIs) A yellow, twining, leafless parasitic vine whose thread-like stems slowly enmesh and smother any bushes or plants that it climbs on; it then leaves its own ground-root to die and lives off the sap of its host as a total parasite; it is declared a pest by law, though it is also used as a folk-medicine; *Cuscuta americana* or *C. indecora* (*Convolvulaceae*). [Perh because of its total embrace of its host, but there is also in some places a belief that if a piece of it thrives on a plant on wh a person's name is carved, then that person's love will be captured] □ Often confused in some places with BIRD-VINE, another outlawed parasitic plant with similar habits, but bushy.

low[1] *adj* (CarA) **1.** ‖ *low-down* (Bdos, Guyn) [Of a person] Low-minded; cheap-minded; of debased thinking and behaviour. **2.** [Of a sick person] Looking unlikely to recover; probably slowly dying.

low[2] *adv* PHRASE **jump high, jump low** *id phr* (Bdos, Guyn) [*AF/IF*] See JUMP[1] Phr 5.3.

low-cuts *n* (Bdos) ‖ HALF-CUTS (Bdos) [By analogy < HIGH-CUTS]

low-down *adj* (Bdos, Guyn) ‖ LOW 1. (CarA) *Low-down nigger people was a special phrase the overseers had coined. The villagers were low-down nigger people since they couldn't bear to see one of their kind get along without feeling envy and hate.*—LICMS:20

low·er·side; low-side *adj, adv* **1.** (Bdos, StKt, Tbgo) Leeward; (to the) west. [Because the leeward (i.e. west or Caribbean) side of most islands tends to be lower, the Atlantic (east or UPPERSIDE) being generally higher and craggy] □ Cp also BELOW, ABOVE. **2.** (Guyn) [In the interior] North; towards the mouth or confluence area of a river. **3.** (Guyn) [Interior] Towards or near the riverbank.

Low is·lands, the /11ʹ22/ *n phr* (Bdos) [*IF*] (Folk name for) the other islands of the Eastern Caribbean, esp those where PATWA (Fr Creole) is spoken [Prob as being to leeward or the LOW-ERSIDE of *Bdos*]

low nation *n phr* (Guyn) ‖ CHAMAR (Guyn, Trin) See also NATION Phr 6.2.

low-rate (low·er·ate) [lo(ə)reˑt] *vb tr* (Bdos, CayI, Guyn, Trin) [*IF*] To belittle; to cause (sb or yourself) to look inferior; to lower (sb or yourself) in public esteem. *Another way we low-rate ourselves, is when our nationals go abroad, they come back speaking in a 'foreign' accent.* SuP (75.03.23, p.9) [Vb formed by reversing vb phr 'to rate low']

lòw·yé (lau·ri·er) [lowye] *n* (Dmca, Gren) One of several varieties of a forest-tree, some bearing flowers and/or berries, and yielding a timber noted for a distinctive smell (one variety fragrant, another unpleasant); the woods are used variously for light cabinet work or house-building; *Nectandra spp* or *Ocotea spp* (*Lauraceae*). [Fr Cr < Fr *laurier* 'laurel']

L.S.M. *abbr* (Dmca) The Long Service Medal, a national award of the Commonwealth of Dominica to be earned in the Disciplined Forces.

lub-lub *n* (StKt) ‖ LOVE-VINE (CarA) [< *love-love* by reduplication and reduction < LOVE-VINE, then with Cr /v > b/ shift]

Lu·ca·yan [lukayan] /1ʹ21/ *n, adj* (Baha) (Of or belonging to) the earliest known indigenous inhabitants of the Bahamas. *The stately and gentle inhabitants of the Bahamas at the time of Columbus called themselves 'Lukkucairi', meaning 'island people', a word which was Anglicized to 'Lucayans'... However, despite their charm and generosity (or perhaps because of it) the Lucayans were mercilessly exterminated in the mere span of a generation.*—TrI (76.02.07, p.4)

Lu·cea-yam [ʹlu·si yam] *n* (Jmca) ‖ WHITE YAM 1. (Baha, etc) *The roar and rattle o' lumber wains and two-wheeled buggies, the cries o' street sellers: Buy your white yam! ... Buy your Lucea yam! ... Yellow-heart breadfruit! ... Hard boiling sweet potatoes!*—RND:19 [< Lucea, a Jmca country town. See also WHITE YAM, cit (a)]

luck-bush *n* (Angu, StKt, StVn) ‖ LEAF-OF-LIFE (Bdos, etc) [As for LOVE-BUSH 2., from wh this may be derived by shift]

luck·y-seed /1ʹ12/ *n* (Guyn, Mrat) A smooth, hard, reddish-brown seed about an inch and a half long and roughly triangular in shape; it is borne on a tall tree and is believed, mostly by children, to bring good luck.

lu·ga(r)·hoo *n* (Gren, Grns, Trin) See LOU-GAWOU.

lu·ka·na·ni* (lu·ku·na·ni) *n* (Guyn) A freshwater fish about 18 ins long when mature; it has a prominent mouth and fine, yellowish scales with dark spots on its sides; it is prized for its tasty flesh; *Cichla ocellaris RFLG:78*. [Cp *BAED* Arawak *lokonañ* 'fresh-water scale fish, yellow-coloured on the breast']

luk·u *vb intr* (CarA) See LOOKA·

lunch *n* (CarA) [In former times] The mid-afternoon tea or snack. *She sat at table with him while he had his tea (called lunch in Guiana).*—MLDS:33 [A remainder from the era of plantation field-work when BREAKFAST was the large midday meal and 'lunch' the meal following later]

lye-wa·ter *n* (Baha, Belz) [In former times] Water to wh ashes from a wood-stove have been added so that it becomes ready for washing dishes and clothes. [< SE *lye* + *water*. A redundancy]

ly·ing-cold *n* (Antg) [*X*] ‖ LYING-IN COLD (Antg, etc) [< *lying-in cold*, by assimilation]

ly·ing-in cold (lin·ing cold) [layın-ın-koˑl(d) ~ lamın-koˑl(d)] *n phr* (Antg, Baha, Bdos, Guyn, Trin) ‖ *baby-chill/-cold* (Belz, Jmca) ‖ *cold in straw bed* (Baha) ‖ *confine(ment)-cold* (Antg,

Brbu, Nevs) ‖ *lining-house cold* (Guyn) ‖ *lying-cold* (Antg) ‖ *swit-kouch* (Dmca, StLu) A sickness with fever caught by a mother soon after childbirth, believed to be caused by her getting up and about too soon after giving birth, and also believed by some to be incurable or fatal. [< SE *lying-in* 'confinement' + COLD² 3. (CarA). *Lying-in* pronounced [layɪn-ɪn] > [laɪnɪn] by assimilation or *lying-in* > *lyin-ing* by metathesis]

M

m [m̃] *excl* (CarA) [*IF/AF*] ‖ A¹² 2. (CarA) [Unreleased /m/ with high, high rising or low rising pitch] 1. [Requesting a re-statement] What did you say?; I didn't quite catch what you said. □ Often written *Hm?* or *Mm?*. Its use, in this and foll senses, is only permitted between peers. 2. [Replacing a tag-question and usu inviting assent] *You like that one, mm?*—(Bdos) 3. ‖ *Eh-eh!*¹, *Eh-heh* (CarA) In various combinations—lengthened [m̃::], reduplicated with glottal stop [m̃ʔm̃] or devoicing [m̃hm̃], or in combinations of these, including reduplication, with a number of pitch variations—to express degrees of approval, denial, pleasure, vexation or surprise; meaning depends upon context of situation and is usu unambiguous. [These same features are variously but widely found in a large number of W Afr langs. See for ex *KED* Krio *m-m* in 3 pitch-differentiated entries expressing 'No!', 'surprise', and 'understanding'] □ See also MM, HM, MM-HM, MM-MM, etc. as separate entries.

Ma; **Ma(a).ma¹**; **Ma(a).mi(e)**; **Mum.my** [ma· ~ ma·mʌ ~ ma·ma ~ mami ~ mʌmi] *n* (CarA) [*IF*] [Affectionate form of address] Mother; an old woman. **a.** *Renouka pleaded. 'All these people looking at we, Ma. Don't shame me, please'* / ... *'Ma, please, please. Be reasonable. What get into you so suddenly?'*—NF:78 **b.** *Old Man: It don't sound good, Ma. It don't sound good at all.* / *Old woman: There ain't much we can do but pray, Pa. Pray.*—LICMS:208 [Prob Eng reinforced by W Afr sources. Cp *DAFL* Twi *mma, mmaa* 'woman', also *WAPE mami* 'mother', both forms perh reinforcing IAE *mama* (with differing pitch superfixes), and Fr *maman*] □ The form *mummy*, (with vowel closure prob by false refinement) occurs mostly in middle-class speech.

maa.ga *adj* (CarA) See MAUGER

maai *n* (Guyn, Trin) See MAI

maa.li [ma·li] *n* (Guyn) [*Indic*] ‖ MAULY (Guyn) [< Hin *maalii* 'a small garland'; also Bhoj name given to this hairstyle]

maa.ma (ma(a)·mie) *n* (CarA) [*IF*] See MAMMY

ma(a).ma man [ma:ma man] *n phr* (Jmca) [*AF-Joc/Derog*] A man who likes to do housework and who often quarrels with his wife for his food. *'You just keep quarreling about the way*

I spend my house-money as if you is a maama man,' said his wife.—Jmca (Ms) [< MAAMA + *man*]

maa.mi [ma:mi] *n* (Guyn, Jmca, StVn) [*AF/IF*] Mother; also an intimate form of address to one's own mother used more frequently by children when they are complaining or seeking attention. **a.** *Maami, look Trevi pinching meh.*—(Jmca) **b.** *Yo[u] maami gwine beat yo[u].*—(StVn) [By vowel lengthening of /a/ in dial usage] □ See also ma

maa.ru (maa.ro(o), ma.ru) [ma:ru] *n* (Guyn, Trin) [*Indic*] A decorated canopy supported by five tall bamboo poles, under wh an orthodox Hindu bride and groom say their marriage vows, usu seated on the ground. [Hin *maaruu*, name of this canopy]

ma.bou.ya [mabuya] *n* (Dmca, StLu) ‖ WOOD-SLAVE (ECar) *Strange looking but harmless is the Woodslave or gecko of the reptile family. It is called the Mabouya locally. It has large eyes and a fat, pink or brown body, a stubby tail, and feet with little pads or suckers. They prey on insects and have a hoarse crackling call.*—HDNPW:13 [*BDFC:158* Carib *esprit malin* (= evil spirit) 'mapoya'; also *BDFC:221 laizard appellé maboya qui a un cris effroyable* 'lizard called 'maboya' wh has a frightful cry']

ma.ca.fou.chette *n* (Trin) See MAKAFOUCHÈT

ma.ca.juel* ['makawɛl] *n* (Trin) ‖ **land-ca-moodi** (Guyn) The boa constrictor or anaconda, a snake sometimes exceeding 20 ft in length; *Constrictor constrictor (Boidae). Boy when ah tell you, when ah was halfway across the river, when ah look so ah see a twenty-foot macajuel snake with he mout wide open waiting fuh me.*—OJS:10 [Prob Sp < a Cariban lang]

ma.cam.bou *n* (Dmca, StLu) See MAKAMBOU

ma.ca.pal (me.ca.pal) *n* (Belz) ‖ WARISHI (Guyn) □ The *Belz* version, used by Maya Indians, is sometimes made of tree-rope.

ma.ca.ro.ni *n* (BrVi, StKt) [*IF*] ‖ LOVE-VINE (CarA) [Prob *Joc*, from resemblance of the yellow thread-like vine to the commercially sold *macaroni.*]

ma.caw¹* [makɒ] *n* (CarA) Any of a number of varieties of a large bird of the parrot family;

it is distinguished by its long tail wh can exceed
half its overall length of some 33 ins, and each
variety is differentiated by its pattern of sharply
contrasting red, blue, yellow, and green colours;
it is indigenous to So Amer with varieties in
many islands; *Ara spp* (*Psittacidae*).

ma·caw²* [makɒ] *n* (Antg, Bdos, StKt) ‖ **grou-
grou** 1. (Gren, etc.) A round fruit with a hard
outer covering, soft, sticky flesh, and a hard seed
wh when cracked open has a white kernel inside
called 'coconut' by children; *Acrocomia aculeata*
(*Palmae*).

ma·caw (-chub) *n* (Antg) A variety of PAR-
ROT-FISH with large, bright blue scales; it is
prized for its tasty flesh; *Scarus caeruleus* (*Scaridae*).

ma·caw-palm *n* (Bdos) ‖ GRU-GRU 1. (Gren)
*The endemic Macaw Palm Aiphanes erosa, the
slender trunks covered with sharp 3 inch spines,
growing commonly in the Gully and in Turner's
Hall Wood and elsewhere.*—AdN (79.01.17, p.8,
M. Hutt) [This form is prob < MACCA by folk
etym or false refinement] □ See also MACCA-
PALM.

mac·ca *n* (Belz, Jmca) 1. The long black thorn
of the MACCA-PALM; [by extension] any thorn.
*Lingering where woodsy smells / Sweep through
the rushes; / Pricked by some sharp macca / Or
briar bushes.*—GA, 1:57 2. The fruit of the MAC-
CA-PALM.

mac·ca-fat *n* (Jmca) ‖ GRU-GRU BÈF (Trin) *You
don't know say nuff people in this here Jamaica
gwan like dem never hear 'bout Stinking-Toe and-
Macca-Fat and such delight? To hear them talk,
is only American apple is fruits.*—WeG (72.12.06,
p.12, Partyline) [< MACCA + *fat* 'big' (?) or a
ref to the oil yielded by the kernel]

mac·ca(-palm); **ma.ca-fat (palm)** *n* (*phr*)
(Belz, Jmca, Mrat) ‖ GROU-GROU (Gren, etc)
*Along the banks were thick rows of fertile-looking
trees and the grey-green, horny, long-thorned
macca.* [*DJE* notes Arawak (Guiana) *macaya*,
macoya 'the macaw palm'. However this name
seems not to be currently known in Guyn. See
PIMPLER-PALM]

mac·co (mac·ko, ma·co) *n, adj, vb* (Dmca,
Gren, StLu, Trin) See MAKO

ma(c)·co·cious [makošʌs] *adj* (Gren, Trin)
[*Joc*] Indulging in petty gossip, news-carrying,
etc; scandalmongering. **a.** *So they began driving
off to lonely out-of-the-way spots and did their
thing and naturally in a macocious country like
Trinidad it was an open secret.*—BoM (79.03.16,
p.9) **b.** *But to the maccocious males, things national
and international are no big thing. They are strictly
concerned with the personal, and even then, with
that which embarrasses, such as who wid who; who
leff who; … -ad nauseam!*—ExP (73.02.25, p.21)
[< MA(C)CO *n* + SE suff *-cious* 'full of']

ma·chete [mašɛt] *vb* (Belz) To chop (esp a
human being) with a machete or CUTLASS. *The
report continues that A— may now lose one of his
hands as a result of the macheting he received from
W—/ Later reports indicate that A— only received
a dose of his own medicine. It is said that sometime
in the not too distant past A— had macheted his
brother-in-law.*—AmA (80.01.02, p.4)

mac·la·la [maklala] *n* (Belz) Any of a number
of different types of lizards of varying sizes and
colours ranging from a small black one about 5
ins long to a large brown one about 10 ins long.
[< *DMEI* Miskito *maklala* 'name of a small
lizard'] □ This is the name generally used in
Belz, the male being called the COCK-MACLALA.
The term 'lizard' is usu only applied to the tiny
green reptile.

ma·com·mère (mac·mere) *n* (CarA) See
MAKOMÈ

ma·cu *n* (Belz) See MAKU

ma·cu·elle *n* (StLu) See MAKWÈL

Ma·cu·s(h)i [makusi~makuši] *n* (Guyn) An
Amerindian ethnic group of Cariban stock,
dwelling in part in the north and central area
of the Rupununi savannah in the INTERIOR of
Guyana. *The Macusis are even darker than the
True Caribs and Ackawoi in colour, but taller,
slighter and better made.*—IAIG:168 [< *GDAA*
Akawaio *maguujii*, Arekuna *makwuchii*, name of
this group]

mad [ma·d] *vb* 1. *vb intr* (CarA) [*AF*] [In semi
modal function before a vb tr] To feel strongly
urged to (do sth); [by extension] to be angry
enough to (do sth). **a.** *Up here was worse than
San Fernando with business and bustling and hustling, and I feel like a fish out of water and I mad
to catch the next train back for South.*—SWOS:
84 **b.** *Look! Get out o[f] my yard, yo[u] hear? I
mad t[h]row dis water [u]pon yo[u].*—(Guyn) [Cp
OED *mad* adj 4. b. 'wildly desirous to do something. (Now rare) + cit 1814 'Mad to wreak his
vengeance …'] 2. *vb tr* (Jmca) [*AF*] To enrage,
infuriate; to make very angry; to madden. *And
another thing, how you decide when to drink the
precious stock? You put yourself on ration? And
which one of your friends good enough to get little?
You see the trauma, cousin? That would-a mad
anybody.*—WeG (72.12.06, p.12, Partyline) [See
OED2 *mad* v 1. trans 'to make mad in various
senses of the adj, to madden, make insane; … to
infuriate, enrage'. Now rare exc. US colloq. Also
DAE *mad* v tr 'to anger, exasperate colloq' +
cit 1893]

ma·dam(e) [madʌm] *n* (CarA) 1. The mistress
of a household. *She insists that this is a common
hazard. She says, 'there are domestic employees
throughout Trinidad and Tobago who have a child,
sometimes more than one, the result of sexual assault
by their employer or one of his drunken friends.' /
'When the 'madam' finds out about the affair, you*

can bet who gets the blame.'—TrG (80.01.07, p.5) **2.** Wife. *The madame giving you worries or what? I ask you for half pound saltfish and, look, you giving me five pounds of onion!*—LDCD:207 [< SE usage as polite form of address to a lady, with shift in CE to the person herself. Cp *OED* madam 1. **b.** (Obs) Substituted for the name of a lady entitled to be addressed as 'madam'; also **3. b.** 'the mistress of a house' (US)] □ CE usage is purely respectful and also prec by **the**.

mad-ant(s) *n* (Jmca) ‖CRAZY-ANT(S) (Gren, etc) *The ant which we call the Mad Ant (Iridomyrmex inquus) is common in the Corporate area, even in downtown Kingston. This is a medium-sized, brownish, ordinary-looking ant, most easily recognizable by its erratic 'this-way-and-that-way' movements as it forages for food, always seemingly in a hurry but never quite making up its mind where it wants to go.*—Jaj 72/3, p.26

mad blood [ma·d blʌd] *n phr* (ECar) **1.** A skin irritation wh causes itching. *When A was small A used to have mad blood and me skin used to raise!*—(Gren) **2.** (Trin) (SE) goose pimples. *Whenever I am feeling cold I get mad-blood.*—(Trin) **3.** (Bdos) A proneness to mental illness. *Don't bother wid she; she can't behave no better. You know very well that she family got in mad blood.*—(Bdos)

mad bull *n phr* **1.** (Bdos, Trin) [Kite-flying] ‖BULL¹ 3. (Guyn) (See cit) *The brightly coloured paper kite must have a 'mad bull' attached, the paper slip which will produce the humming and even roaring sound as the owner makes it loop and loop in intricate gyrations. / Even better, there must be a 'singing angel', an octagon of bulls fixed around the framework.*—AdN (79.04.15, p.10) **2.** See MAD-BULL DANCER

mad-bull (danc·er) *n (phr)* (Guyn) ‖DONKEY-MAN (Bdos) *The best fife man, kittler and drummer will each receive $100, while the best mad bull dancer, flouncer, mother sally dancer and stilt dancer will receive $75 each.*—SuC (77.02.06, p.16) □ Also **mad-cow** (Guyn).

mad·dy ['ma·di] *adj* (CarA) [AF—ʒoc/Derog] Mentally unreliable; somewhat unsettled in behaviour. *But look at dis maddy maddy girl, nuh. She don[']t play to tell dem jus' wha she t[h]ink [a]bout dem plain plain so.*—(StLu) [< SE mad + CE Derog suffix -y. Cp STUPIDY] □ Often reduplicated as in cit.

Ma·dra·si *n* (Guyn, Trin) An East Indian person whose forebears were originally immigrant indentured labourers from Madras State in south India; such a person is characteristically dark-skinned. *'I could tell you what she father is, Darling,' Shantee said. 'A low-caste Madrasi cane-cutter.'*—NF:197

ma·dwas (ma·dras) [madwas~madra·s] *n* (Dmca, Guad, StLu) **1.** Brightly coloured, printed plaid or floral material used to make headties,

handkerchiefs, or skirts for the national costume. **2.** [By extension] Either the headtie or the skirt made from this material; the headtie is fixed in different ways for different occasions. **a.** *A freed female slave ... understandably disdained the slave outfit and altered it into the ghip. This was and remains an ankle length, full and brightly coloured madras or print skirt, worn over a white chemise.*—SDD:45 **b.** *There have been several styles of tying the madras and the imite, and the most popular were the 'tete cassee' the week day head-tie of the douillette wearer—the 'tete jamette' for Carnival wear.*—SDD:27 [< Madras 'city and province in India' where the material was manufactured and exported esp in the slave era. See *DAE*]

ma·fo·be (ma·fo(om)·bay, ma·fu·be) [ma·fʊ bɛ ~ mafumbɛ] *n* (StVn, Tbgo) ‖BLUGGO (Belz, etc) [Prob of Bantu orig; Cp *LDKF* Kikongo *fuba*, pl *ma-* 'green fruit', also *mfuba* 'kind of brown banana']

ma·gas(se); **me·gass(e)** [mʌga:s ~ mɛga:s] *n* (Bdos, Guyn, StKt, USVI) [Sugar Ind] ‖BAGASSE (CarA) **a.** *The crushed cane stalk is called Magas or Bagasse. It is collected and dried in an open shed.*—JNHSJ:28 **b.** *Now that the Racing Season is coming to an end, it would be a good chance to cover the whole race track with megasse and then roll it smoothly. This would fill in all the dangerous holes and make a nice, springy, smooth surface for racing.*—AdN (84.05.17, p.4) ['magas' ~ 'megasse' is due to a dialectal shift /b-/ > /m-/ in the pronunc of the orig word BAGASSE]

ma·gasse-lo·gie [mʌga:s-loji] *n* (Guyn) [Sugar Ind] ‖BAGASSE-HOUSE (StKt)

ma·guf·fy (Mc·Guf·fy) *n* (Bdos) [AF—ʒoc] **1.** A person who is seen as or who sees himself as much more important or knowledgeable than he truly is. *The Barbados Government has told the Bank that it has to be built in Delamere Land—after months and months of expert after expert, of Maguffy after Maguffy from the Bank telling the Government of Barbados where they must put an institution.*—Bdos (Hd, 75.03.17, p.4805) **2.** [By extension and often attrib] Anything that is large and pretentious. *... and if the Government was really interested ... instead of witch hunting to have a big Maguffy enquiry at the Housing ... what they should do then is to look around the country ... and find areas in which they could employ people to let them earn their daily bread and maintain their self-respect.*—Bdos (Hd, 76.10.12, p.60)

ma·ham·bhog *n* (Guyn, Trin) See MOHANBHOG

ma·ha·ra·jin [maharaji·n] *n* (Guyn, Trin) [Indic] (Respectful form of address for) an EAST INDIAN lady. *Ganesh said, 'Don't cry, maharajin. You is a good woman.'*—NTMM:87 [Bhoj, *mahṛajin* 'Brahmin woman']

Ma·ha Sab·ha [maha: sabha: ~ maha: sɑax bha:] *n phr* (Guyn, Trin) The controlling council of orthodox Hindus. *This is why the succession to leadership of the Maha Subha is so important. Contenders believe that they might yet recover lost ground by the capture of a cultural organisation to which it is assumed the majority of Hindus owe allegiance. But the hold of the Maha Sabha on the Hindus is precarious and slowly slipping away.*—LCTC:105 [Hin *maha* 'great' + *sabha* 'assembly', shortened from *Sanatan Dharma Maha Sabha* 'Great Assembly (of) Eternal Duty']

ma·ho(e) *n* 1. (CarA) ‖ SEASIDE-MAHOE (Bdos, etc) a. *The tree under which I was sitting was a wide-spreading Mahoe, with almost circular leaves and a gnarled, twisted trunk and deeply creviced bark. The salmon-pink flowers, strongly veined like a butterfly's wing, are tightly furled as they fall from the tree in numbers dotting the sand.*—AdN (77.11.23, p.6, M. Hutt) b. *The complete equipment of the early Carib canoe included paddles ..., a long pole ..., rope made of 'maho' bark, and a stone anchor.*—HTDS:12 [< *BAED* Arawak *maho* 'a tree whose strong pliable bark is used for cordage'] 2. (Guyn, Trin) [Timber Ind] A tall flowering and fruit-bearing forest tree with large leaves; it yields a tough, light, coarse-grained, greenish-brown wood wh is of a somewhat unpleasant smell when cut, but is used to make cricket bats or for light indoor work; *Sterculia caribaea* or *S. pruriens (Sterculiaceae).*

mai (maai) [ma·ɪ] *n* (Guyn, Trin) [Indic] 1. [Often a form of address] Mother. *'But, mai, these people good to us; we is friends,' ... said Urmilla to her mother.... Her mai had given her much advice on how to keep the child.*—SABS:47 2. [*IF*] Any elderly East Indian woman. [Hin *mai* 'mother; mother-in-law']

maid·en-ap·ple *n* (Mrat, Nevs, StKt, ViIs) ‖ CERASEE (Baha, etc) *Maiden apple goes by different names—washer woman, maiden bush, lizard food to name only a few.*—LaS (75.07.19, p.4) [See MAIDEN'S BUSH/BLUSH]

maid·en-plan·tain *n* (Belz) ‖ BUCK-BANANA (Guyn)

maid·en's blush; maid.ens' bush *n phr* (Angu, Antg, Mrat, Stkt, Trin) ‖ CERASEE (Baha, etc) [From its use in a decoction for relieving young girls' menstrual pains]

mail (boat) *n (phr)* (Baha, Gren, Grns, Guyn, StVn) A boat, either belonging to or commissioned by the government, used as a mail-carrying ferry. *The main link between St Vincent and the Grenadine dependencies is by the 'mail boat' which transports passengers, food supplies, building materials and the 'mail' from the mainland.*—FHB:11 [*OED2* 4. b. (sense 2.) simple attrib; ex. in the names of vehicles employed to carry the mail, as *mail boat*] □ In the CarA the **mail boat** is restricted to use in island-states

with dependencies, or in large countries like *Guyn* with many rivers wh form a communications network; it is however a general passenger and cargo boat as well.

mails *n pl* (CarA) [*X*] (SE) Mail; the collection of letters and parcels (to be) delivered by the Post Office. a. *The numbering of the houses will greatly assist this delivery of the mails.*—AdN (72.12.03, p.2) b. *Mails from London are now despatched five days per week direct to Cayman via New York and Miami and are reaching the islands in two days.*—Nor I. 1. p.24 c. *Closing of Mails—The mails: for London and Gt Britain per 'Ascania' (direct) will be closed at 2.00 p.m. on Tuesday, 22nd instant.*—SkN (63.01.21, p.3) [Overcorrection pluralization. See PLURAL FORMS 1.] □ In consequence *a mail* [*X*] 'a letter' sometimes occurs.

Main Guard [me·n gyard] *n phr* (Bdos) The Central Police Station in Bridgetown. [Cp *OED* main-guard 1. Fortif. 'the keep of a castle; also, the building within a fortress in wh the *'mainguard'* (of a garrison) is lodged' + cits–'1902] □ In *Bdos* this term is used instead of 'Central Police Station'.

mai·pu·ri ['maɪpuri] *n* (Guyn) ‖ TAPIR (Guyn) [*EIAA:54* Akawaio *maibuurii* 'tapir'; *GLOG:37* Carib *majhpuri* 'Tapirus terrestris']

ma·joe-bit·ter *n* (Jmca) ‖ BITTER-BUSH 3. (CarA) [Prob of W Afr orig. Cp *ZAGL* Gã *ɲmãtšu* 'herb used by fetish-priest', also *TAGD* Mende *madzo* 'the leading woman of the Sande, a female society into wh nearly all the girls are initiated']

ma·ka·fou·chèt (ma·ca·fou·chette) ['mak afušet] *n* (Trin) [*AF*] ‖ BAMBYE² (CarA) *In the olden days macafouchette was a perquisite of the cook and butler but now is preserved fridgewise.*—OCTTT:47 [Cp *HCEE* Fr Cr *mak*³, 'portion' + *à*, 'for' + Fr *fourchette* 'fork', hence a collocation = 'a scrap']

ma·kam·bou *n* (Dmca, StLu) ‖ BLUGGO (Belz, etc) [Perh of Bantu origin. Cp. Kikongo *ma-nkondo n pl* 'plantains, a generic term, there being a specific term for each variety'—(pers info, U. Ndoma)]

make [mek ~ mɛk] *vb* [Note: The common folk pronunc throughout CE is [mɛk], wh reflects northern Br dial pronunc (*EDD*)] 1. *vb tr* (CarA) [*IF*] (i) Let; allow; [by extension] cause to. a. *Child, don't make those plates fall down and break.*—(Guyn) b. *Don't make de clothes get wet.*—(StVn) [Cp *OED* make vb¹ 52., 53. Causative senses (as in 'make one's hair stand on end') with shift in CE > 'allow, let'] (ii) [mek] *in imper function* (Jmca) [*AF—Cr*] Let. a. *See de rain. Mak[e] we tak[e] in de clothes.*—(Jmca) b. *Look here boy, make I pass, you hear. Just move.* (*M. Townshend: 'Swinging Door').*—SNWIC: 266 2. [mɛk] *vb intr* (Belz, Guyn, Jmca) [*AF*—

Cr] Be the cause; be the reason. *Yo[u] too lazy. Da mak[e] yo[u] ain['t] pass de exam.*—(Guyn) □ Sometimes *da mek* 'That's why', stands alone in answer to a question beginning *wa mek?* 'Why?'. See WHAT[1] Phr 2.8 **3.** [mek ~ mɛk] *vb intr* (Gren, StLu, Tbgo, Trin) [*AF*] To succeed; to achieve sth; to make it. *When you see a child tells himself that he cannot make, it is the beginning of the end. There was a boy in my school who never wanted to come in the class. I kept asking him why he refused to attend class.... Sir, we ent come to school because we can't make. The teacher putting something on the board and is German she writing dey.*—ExP (79.07.15, p.14) [Cp IF IAE *make it, make the grade* 'to succeed, to manage, achieve sth'] **4.** [mek] *vb intr* (Gren, Trin) [*AF*] To be pregnant. *She makin[g] for Boysie* (= *She is pregnant by Boysie*).—(Gren) **5.1 make four** *id phr* (CarA) [*IF*] See EYE[1] Phr 14. **5.2 it make cold/hot** *id phr* (Gren, Trin) [*AF*] See IT Phr 4. **5.3 make (a) baby/child (for sb)** *vb phr* (CarA) ‖ GET A CHILD (FOR SB) (CarA) See GET Phr 3.1 **a.** *Well, if Renouka come home to me one day and say she making a baby, she not going to leave my house alive.*—NF:77 **b.** *However, 'on the job', pregnant, unmarried girls today get all the conditions of married women.... As a result it is easy for them to prove that 'they is folks too. Dey could make chile'.*—SuP (75.04.13, p.20) [Cp *OED make* vb 17. (Obs), of a mother: 'to give birth to (young) + cits–'1500] **5.4 make a message** *vb phr* (ECar) [*IF*] See MESSAGE Phr 3.2 *When we reach by Virgie's store my mother said 'Look at Iris inside here. She is making some message, let's wait for her.'*—Gren (CR, 77/8) **5.5 make a pappyshow (of sb/yourself)** *vb phr* (CarA) [*AF—Joc*] See PAPPYSHOW[1] Phr 2.1 **5.6 make (a) payass** *vb phr* (BrVi) [*AF*] See PAYASS[1] Phr 3.1 **5.7 make a pistarckle (at/out of sb)** *vb phr* (USVI) See PISTARCKLE 2. **5.8 make as if to (do sth)** *vb phr* (CarA) To make a move as (doing sth); to pretend to be about to (do sth); to feint (an action). *He made as if to pay and suddenly pulled out a knife.*—(Jmca) [Cp *EDD make* vb 14. 'to pretend, feign' + cit (from Sc, Wm) 'We meade as if we were asleep'; also 17. 'to attempt, try' + cit (from N.I.) 'He made to strike me'] □ Cp Phr 5.20. **5.9 make back (up)** [mɛk-bak] [*IF/AF*]; **make up back** [X] *vb phrs* (Bdos, Guyn, Tbgo) ‖ *(a)gree back* (Bdos, Gren) **(i)** To live together again as husband and wife or as bed-companions; to be reconciled (in general terms of friendly relationship); (SE) to make it up. **a.** *She and her husband make back after a year of separation.*—Guyn (Ms, 1979) **b.** *When I asked him why he did not write he said since he had not written for a long time because of this girl, he did not know how to begin. He had also hoped to return home to make back up in person.*—NaT (77.04.10, p.25, Dear Christine) **c.** *The father make back up with his son.*—Tbgo (Ms, 1982) [< *OED make* 96. *make up* 1. (b) (c) (*make it up*) 'be reconciled after a dispute' + CE BACK[4] 2(ii) 'once again'] □ Cp AGREE BACK, TAKE BACK (SB), TALK BACK. **(ii)** [mɛk bak] *vb phr* (Bdos, Guyn) [*IF*] [Dressmaking] Make (a new dress) in the same style as an old one. *I like this*

dress. I'm going to make it back in Paisley.—(Guyn) [< *OED make* 96. *make up* f. (b) 'make (a garment, etc) by fitting and sewing pieces of material cut out for the purpose' + CE BACK[4] 2(ii).] **5.10 make bad between (two persons)** *vb phr* (CarA) [*AF*] See BAD[3] Phr 2.2 **5.11 make bad-play** *vb phr* (Bdos) [*AF*] See PLAY[2] Phr 1. **5.12 make bassa-bassa** *vb phr* (Gren, Guyn, Trin) [*AF*] See BASSA-BASSA[1] Phr 2.1 *Well I tell her to come back nex[t] week, but she started to make bassa-bassa so I had to give her part o[f] the money before she would go away.*—(Guyn) **5.13 make bobol/bubol** [mek ~ mɛk bɒbɒl ~ bʌbɒl] *vb phr* (Trin) [*AF*] See BOBOL[1] Phr 2.1 **5.14 make foot** *vb phr* (Tbgo) [*AF*] See FOOT Phr 11. **5.15 make/making fun/joke/sport** *vb phr* (ECar) [*AF*] **(i)** To say or do sth in fun; to indulge in good-humoured teasing. *But de girl didn['t] mean she would go out wid him, she was only makin[g] joke*—(Guyn) **(ii)** [By extension, esp in arguments] To say or do sth that arouses strong protest. *What! Put vendors on the careenage? But the Government making sport!*—(Bdos). See also JOKE[1] Phrs 2.5, 2.8. **5.16 not make fun to (do sth)** *neg vb phr* (Guyn) [*AF/IF*] To do (sth) with spiteful vigour. *When he heard about how she been dancin[g] up with this fella, I tell you, the husband didn['t] make fun to beat her skin.*—(Guyn) **5.16.1 not make fun with (sb)** *neg vb phr* (Guyn) [*AF/IF*] To tolerate no nonsense from, be aggressive with (sb). *When it come to the homework, the mother didn['t] make fun with him! She won['t] let him play till he done it.*—(Guyn) **5.17 make haste (and do sth)** *vb phr* (CarA) To hurry up; to be quick about (doing) sth. *Mek haste come back from de shop.*—BrVi (Ms) **5.18 make height** *vb phr* (Bdos) [*AF*] See HEIGHT Phr 1. **5.19 make lékol-bich** *vb phr* (Trin) ‖ BREAK BICHE (Gren, etc) See BICHE and * Note. **5.20 make like (doing sth)** *vb phr* (CarA) [*AF/IF*] To seem to be (doing sth); to give the impression of (doing sth). *Bedosa ... took him by the sleeve, and all the time he kept talking and talking, with Shag making like he was trying to shake him off.*—MHJJ:99 □ Cp Phr 5.8. **5.21 make noise** [mɛk nɒIz] *vb phr* (CarA) [*IF*] ‖ *keep noise* (CarA) [*AF*] **(i)** To be noisy. *The teacher used to put me to stand up in front to see that the class didn't make noise while he was away.*—(Guyn) **(ii)** To quarrel; [by extension] to object noisily. *Well you know how yo[ur] fader goin[g] make noise when he hear you loss the bike!*—(Bdos) □ Commonly used in CE where IF SE would use *make a noise, make a row,* though the CE sense is usu more intensive. Note next phr. **5.21.1 make noise in your head** *vb phr* (CarA) [*AF*] [Esp of children] To disturb you with their din; to be noisily troublesome. *Auntie would call out to us 'You-all mother sick! Don't make so much noise in her head.'*—(USVI) **5.22 make sb feel/look small** *vb phr* (Guyn) [*IF*] See SMALL Phr 3.2 **5.23 make sb feel (the weight of) your hand** *vb phr* (Guyn) [*IF*] See HAND Phr 4.19 **5.24 make (sb/sth) go round** (Bdos, Guyn) [*AF*]; **make (sb) snort** *vb phrs* (Bdos) [*AF*] To treat (sb or sth) harshly; to give (sb) a hard time; to devour [food]. **a.** *You see that shirt* *you tear? When yo[ur] father come he go[i]n[g] mak[e] you go round.*—(Bdos) **b.** *The children make the cake go round.*—(Guyn) **5.25 make (sb) jump** *vb phr* (CarA) [*AF—Joc*] See JUMP[1] Phr 5.7 **5.26 make (sb) shame** *vb phr* (CarA) [*AF*] See SHAME[1] Phr 2.3 **5.27 make (sb's) hand fall** *vb phr* (Antg, Guyn) [*IF*] See HAND[1] Phr 4.20 **5.28 make (sb) to know/understand** *vb phr* (Guyn) [*AF*] ‖ ALLOW (SB) TO KNOW (Bdos, Guyn) *And I had to make them to understand that my husband is a magistrate where I come from and they couldn't treat me as they like.*—(Trin) **5.29 (sb/sth) make so** *vb phr* (CarA) [*AF*] See SO[3] Phr 2.1 *This cake getting mouldy. I[t']s the hot weather make so.*—(Bdos) **5.30 make sport** *vb phr* (CarA) [*IF*] See SPORT[1] Phr 3.2 **5.31 make style(s)** *vb phr* (ECar) [*AF*] See STYLE[1] Phr 2.3 *I know she can['t] stay out late. She only makin[g] style. You see when she get home the mother goin[g] give her a good dressin[g] do[w]ng.* —(StVn) **5.32 make toubak** *vb phr* (Dmca) ‖ BREAK BICHE (Gren, etc) See BICHE Phr **5.33 make up (sth purchased with sth extra)** *vb phr* (Guyn) [Of a vendor] To add some item voluntarily to a quantity of sth purchased, when satisfied with the amount sold. See MAKING-UP **5.33.1 make up your face** *vb phr* (CarA) [*IF*] See FACE Phr 4. **5.34 make you mal** *vb phr* (Dmca) [*AF*] ‖ *(sb) do/did you so* (Dmca) To harm (sb) by supernatural means. [< Fr *mal*, 'bad'. This phr is a calque < *faire du mal (à qn)* 'to do sb harm', although the word *mal* is retained in its orig Fr form] **5.35 make your eyes pass (sb)** *vb phr* (Guyn) [*IF*] See EYE[1] Phr 23. **5.36 make your hands fast (with sb/sth)** (CarA) [*IF*] See FAST Phr 5.2, 5.3 **5.37 make your heart turn** *vb phr* (Gren) [*IF*] See HEART Phr 5. **5.38 make your move/play** *vb phr* (ECar) [Of a man] To accost (a woman), with sexual friendship in mind. *Crude fellow, you know! Would go in a dance hall and make his move on the first woman he dance with, boy!*—(Trin) [Metaph from draughts or chess] **5.39 make yourself a fool** *vb phr* (ECar) [*AF/IF*] See FOOL Phr 3.2. **5.40 make yourself an ass** *vb phr* (ECar) [*AF-Vul*] [Often neg] To act very stupidly and/or impudently *Don['t] mak[e] yourself an ass an[d] splash any paint on m[y] clothes, yeh!*—(Guyn) **5.41 make zamie** *vb phr* (Dmca, Gren, StLu, Trin) See ZAMIE[1] Phr. **5.42 Wha[t] make?** *id phr* (CarA) See WHAT[1] Phr 2.8

mak·in(g)-up ['mɛkɪn-ʌp] /1'12/ *n* (Guyn) [*AF*] ‖ BRAATA (Antg, etc) *But yo[u] could gi[ve] me de salad fo[r] makin[g]-up, nuh? A don['t] go[t] to buy dat too!*—(Guyn)

ma·ko¹ (ma·co, mac·co, mac·ko) *n* (Dmca, Gren, StLu, Trin) [*AF—Derog*] **1.** A person that is too inquisitive; a gossip and busybody. **a.** *So Tantie had to take me down to Mrs Hinds, a horrible capitulation, for she'd always sworn she'd never send a dog of hers there, that woman was a mauvais' langue horse-face maco.*—HCCM:36 **b.** *'Who you giving that to?' Louis asked. 'In my day the priests were the best macos you could find, always knowing somebody's business.'*—JPB:87 **c.**

What distinguishes them from the ordinary inquisitive person is the fact that the makoes are malicious gossip spreaders and you can bet that in every conversation they would slip in little sneaky questions ... about you or your friends.—ExP (72.10.12, p.16) [Abbr from Fr Cr MAKOMÈ < Fr *macommère* 'my child's godmother', hence 'my very close friend', this relationship resulting in an intimacy leading to gossip, etc. The term has developed a general sense esp to include men] **2.** [By extension] ‖ *maku³* (Belz) An effeminate man; a peeping Tom. *But a pimp an procurer is worser dan de whore. An de Macko is worserer dan dem all.*—ToR (77.01.16) [Prob also coinciding with /makwo/ > Fr *maquereau* 'a pimp'] **3.** [By extension] A fool; an idiot. *Jookootoo I who went to fight and die for King and Country / Dat was in World War two / Singing Rule Britannia Rule / and growing like a big macco under de Union Jack / Ah remember coming back vex like arse.*—Gren (Ms poem, 1981) □ Preferred pl is with *-es* as in *mangoes* (Cp note at CALYPSO). The spelling most commonly used is MACO. Cp also MACOCIOUS.

ma·ko² (ma·co, mac·co, mac·ko) *adj* (Dmca, Gren, StLu, Trin) [*AF—Derog*] Too inquisitive; meddlesome. *Yes chile, Doris husband throw she out ah window / Ah was dey ah tell yu, / Ah see de whole ting with me own two eye. / How yu mean ah too maco?*—KTT:33 [By functional n > adj shift of MAKO[1]] □ Hence often *mako-man/-woman* instead of MAKO[1].

ma·ko³ (ma·co, mac·co(h), mac·ko) [mak o~makʌ] *adj* (Gren, Tbgo, Trin) [*AF—Joc*] Huge; too big; unreasonably large. **a.** *Yesterday Doreen had a big, mako umbrella—about three of us could fit under it.*—(Tbgo) **b.** *But for some time now the Carenage road has been in a mess and getting worse daily with huge macco potholes like abysses right in the centre of de road.*—BoM (79.09.28, p.3) **c.** *The number of houses, built at public expense, for his hangers-on and supporters, the 'Maccoh' salaries paid to Gairy, other Ministers, Parliamentary Secretaries.*—NeJ (74.12.20, p.1) [Evid of different source from prec. Perh Fr Cr, as HCEF Hait Fr Cr *makòn* 'many, a bundle of' wh is prob > Fr *marquant adj* 'notable, considerable', whence Trin Fr Cr *makò* with characteristic Trin Cr denasalization. This may also account for variant pronunc and spellings]

ma·ko⁴ (ma·co) *vb* (Dmca, Gren, StLu, Tbgo, Trin) [*AF—Derog*] To mind other people's business; to pry into the affairs of others; to spy on (esp sb's sexual intimacy); [by extension] to indulge in gossip (esp of the scandalous sort). **a.** *He makoing everybody business; and his business dirtier than everybody own.*—(StLu) **b.** *I am not makoing Hector. Where I live, I can see straight in her house.*—Tbgo (CR, 80.09.06) **c.** *When he reach dey, he hide in de bush / An' he start to maco all wha' goin' on.*—KTT:90 [By functional n > vb shift of MAKO[1]]

ma·ko·ké-glo n (Dmca) ‖POND-FLY (Bdos, Guyn) [< Fr Cr *koké* 'to copulate' + *glo* 'water'; prob a folk ref to the posture of the insect as it sits on still water. The name is, however, not regarded as Vul] □ See also SOUSÉ-GLO.

ma·ko·mè (**ma·com·mè(re), mac·me(re, ma·cu·meh, ma·kou·mè**) [makɔmɛ(r)~ makmɛ~makumɛ] n (CarA) [IF/AF] **1.** A usu elderly, female friend who is your child's godmother. [Fr Cr < Fr *macommère* 'fellow-sponsor at baptism; partner at a wedding', developing into 'gossip'. See next] **2.** [Also as a form of friendly address] A woman's confidante, good neighbour, dependable friend. **3.** (Dmca, StLu) [By extension, and esp in the form MAKOUMÈ] [Vul] ‖AUNTIE-MAN (CarA) 2. *He's a real makoumè, look at how he acting like a woman. He think he's a woman.*—(StLu) □ The term occurs, esp in territories with no Fr Cr background, with a number of variant spellings such as *macmay, macoomeh,* etc.

ma·ku (**ma·cu**) n (Belz) [AF] **1.** A woman who is a very close friend. **2.** A midwife. **3.** [By extension] An effeminate male. [Abbr < MAKOUMÈ]

mak·wèl (**ma·cu·elle**) [makwɛl] n (StLu) [AF—Derog] A woman who is a malicious gossip; the female counterpart of MAKO[1] I. [Fr Cr < Fr *maquerelle* 'a madam']

Ma·lac·ca-ap·ple/-pear* n (Antg, Guyn) ‖*cashew* 2. (Guyn) ‖*French cashew* 2. (Gren, Guyn) ‖*love-apple* (StLu) ‖*Malay-apple* (Belz, Berm) ‖*otaheite-apple* (CayI, Jmca) ‖*plum-rose* (StVn, Trin) ‖*pomme-malac* (Trin) ‖*pommerac* (Bdos, Dmca, Trin) ‖*pomme-rose, ponm-wòz* 2. (Dmca, StLu) A shiny, red, pear-shaped fruit, 2 to 3 ins long, with white, fluffy, juicy flesh around a single, loose seed; the fruit is borne on a tall, bushy, abundantly flowering tree with long, leathery green leaves; *Syzygium malaccense* or *Eugenia malaccensis* (*Myrtaceae*). [Prob from The Moluccas, islands of the E Indies, from wh the fruit was introduced to the CarA. Cp orig of ‖*otaheite-apple* (*Jmca*)]

Ma·lay-ap·ple n (Belz, Berm) ‖MALACCA-APPLE (Antg, Guyn)

mal·ca·di (**mal·ca·dy**) n (Gren, StLu, Tbgo, Trin) See MALKADI

mal·cas·sé adj (Dmca) See MALKASÉ

mal·djo[1] (**mal·jo, mal·joe, mal·ju, mal·yeux**) [maljo] n (Gren, StVn, Tbgo, Trin) **1.** ‖BAD-EYE (CarA) **a.** *With leaves and plants one could deal with fever, boils, dysentery, cuts, and even 'maljo', the strange fever a child gets when a person with a 'bad eye' looks at him.*—SWI:154 **b.** *The neighbour complained that her baby was getting skinny because it had maljoe.*—(Trin) **c.** *It's nice to have someone in the background wringing*

their hands for you, averting the evil eye—what we call over here mal-yeux.—NG:21 [Perh < Fr *mal* 'evil' + *d'yeux* 'from the eyes' or Sp *mal de ojo* 'evil of the eye'; note also SDGA *mal de ojos* 'name of various folk-medicinal plants used to cure eye-sickness'. Cp also Pg *mau* 'bad' + *olhado* 'look'] **2.** (Belz) [By extension] Evil thoughts; calumny. *The Electricity Board has become the whipping boy, the object of malediction, of most people's 'mal ojo', rightly or not, and the dispute between the Board and employees is further cause for dismay.*—ReP (79.10.07, p.4) **3.** PHRASES **3.1 cut maldjo** vb phr (Gren, Trin) ‖**cut (out) (the) bad-eye** (Belz, Guyn) To cure or prevent the effects of MALJO. **a.** *To cut maljoo give child a strong drink of sweetbroom tea and bathe him with holy-water mixed with salt and asifiesta* (*Asafoetida*).—ExP (72.09.03, p.28) **b.** *... up came Ma Xelia with her own preparation in a teacup. 'I give the baby this to drink first thing—good, you hear, good, good for the maljoe—cut it quick quick.'*—PGIP:14 (E. Westman) **3.2 put maldjo on** (**sb/sth**) vb phr (Gren, StVn, Tbgo, Trin) [IF] ‖PUT BAD-EYE ON (SB/STH) (Belz, etc)

mal·djo[2] (**mal.jo(e)**) [maljo] n (Gren, Trin) ‖GRUDGE-PEA (Gren) [By association with MALDJO[1] from its use: *'If planted round a garden, it is thought to "cut the eye" of envy, and so prevent petty thefts'*—GNHIG:78]

mal·djo blue (**mal·jo blue**) n phr **1.** (Trin) [AF—Joc] ‖INDIGO BLUE (Guyn) **2.** ‖MALDJO COLOUR (Trin)

mal·djo co·lour (**mal·jo co·lour**) n phr (Trin) [AF—Joc/Derog] ‖*maldjo blue* 2. (Trin) The blue violet colour associated with laundry blue. *I ain[']t like that maldjo-colour dress to go out wit[h]. It look really obsocky.*—(Trin) [From association of cubes of laundry blue tied in a small bag and hung on the wrist or around the neck of a baby to prevent MALDJO]

male-pole n (Bdos) See MAYPOLE

mal·é·wé (**mal·heur·eux**) /1'12/ [malewe] n (Dmca, StLu) [AF] A wretched person; a wretch. *Yet, Sundays in and out, he collects fees from us poor malheureux as union members.*—DoH (65.09.11, p.7) [Fr Cr pronunc of Fr *malheureux* 'unhappy one(s)'. The orig Fr spelling, as in cit, is a learned but unrepresentative form. See next]

mal·è·wèz (**ma·li·wez**) /1'12/ [malɛwɛz] n (Dmca, Gren, StLu, Trin) **1.** [AF] [Sympathising with sb] Poor thing. *Pov malèwèz! They should never have done that to her.*—(StLu) [Fr Cr > Fr *malheureuse* 'wretched person', often prec by /pov/ 'pauvre' 'poor', as in cit] **2.** [By extension] [AF—Derog] Wretch! *De maliwez! They should hang him.*—(Dmca)

mal·fi·ni /1'12/ n (StLu) ‖CHICKEN-HAWK (CarA) [< DECG Fr *mansfenil* 'aigle des Antilles', called *malfini* (Guad, Mart) though evid not the same bird]

ma·li·cious *adj* (Bdos) [AF—Derog] 1. ‖*fast* (CarA) Tiresomely inquisitive. 2. [By extension] Deliberately and offensively meddlesome; inquiring about sb else's business in order to cause the person harm.

mal·i·wez *n* (Dmca, Gren, StLu, Trin) See MALÈWÈZ

mal·jo(e) (**mal·ju**) *n* (Gren, StVn, Tbgo, Trin) See MALDJO

mal·ka·di (**mal·ca·di, mal·ca·dy**) ['malkadi] *n* (Gren, StLu, Tbgo, Trin) An epileptic fit; epilepsy (in general); convulsions. *The lady fell to the floor and started ketching malcadi so she was taken to the doctor.*—AFSTE:20 [Fr Cr < Fr IF *mal caduc* 'falling sickness; epilepsy']

mal·ka·sé (**mal·ca·sé, mal·cas·sé**) ['malkase] *adj* (Dmca) ‖BAD-BEHAVED (CarA) *The boy so malkasé he don't even say good morning.*—(Dmca) [Fr Cr < Fr *mal* 'badly' + *cassé* 'broken in' (? from savagery, perh a ref to the breaking of the will of a new slave). Cp in similar context (Cotgrave, 1611) *casse-moeurs* 'rude, savage, uncivil'] □ See also BAD-WAYS²

mal·pa·lan ['malpa·lã] *adj* (Dmca, StLu) ‖MOVÉ-LANG² (StLu, Tbgo, Trin) *Stop talking people name—yo[u] too mal-palan. You will always get in trouble.*—(StLu) [Fr Cr < Fr *mal parlant* 'evil-speaking' a non-Fr collocation; see next]

mal·pa·lé (**mal·par·ler**) /1′12/ *vb tr* (Dmca, StLu) ‖BAD-TALK² (CarA) **a.** *You will find that the tendency to malparler is perpetual and recurrent, and not confined to any special circles.*—StA(DA) (65.08.07, p.1) **b.** *They outside de(re) the whole afternoon malpaléing people.*—(StLu) [Fr Cr < Fr *mal* 'evil' + *parler* 'to speak' a calque the same as BAD-TALK. See etym note there] □ The term enters (note cits) into Eng morphology as a loan word. Cp also MOVÉ-LANG (wh can function as n and vb), POUND SB'S NAME.

Ma·ma¹! *n* (CarA) see MA

Ma·ma²! /13′/; **Ma.ma-o!, Ma.ma.yo!** /113′/ [mama~mamayo] *excl* (ECar) Expresion of astonishment, fascination, anger, rejection, etc. **a.** *Wind I got on my stomach, Mama, is on account I don't get my grub regular, I reckon.*—MHJJ:32 **b.** *And when de two bands clash / Mamayo, if you see cutlash / Never me again / To jump-up in a steelband in Port of Spain.*—ACTT:105 [Perh orig a Joc reflection of PAPA! PAPAYO!, now a generalized alternative excl] □ Cp MAMA¹ as variant of MA.

ma·ma-do-good *n* (Gren) [AF] ‖OBEAH-WOMAN (CarA) □ See also PAPA-DO-GOOD.

ma·ma-glo (**ma·ma-dlo**) [mama-glo/~dlo] *n* (Dmca, Gren, StLu, Trin) ‖FAIRMAID (Guyn) *It was the belief among the Semans dancers that*

'Mama Glo' a Goddess of the river, came at midnight to the emboucherie to wash her feet. Any sacrifice placed there a short while before midnight would be accepted and the request indicated by means of the type of sacrifice would be granted. However, if the person offering the sacrifice should loiter around after laying down the sacrifice in order to see 'Mama Glo' that person would meet with sudden death within five days of that midnight.*—PGIP:18 (T. Philip) [< *maman de l'eau* 'water mother', a prob calque from W Afr langs. See note at WATER-MAMA, and cp ‖ ‖ at FAIRMAID. The form /glo/ < /dlo/ 'de l'eau', by /dl > gl/ is common in CarA Fr Cr] □ 1. There are some variations in the appearance and behaviour, but the basic characteristics of this legendary mermaid-figure—now young and lovely, now old and ugly, always bountiful but deadly—are the same. 2. An anglicized folk etym spelling *mama-glow* sometimes occurs.

ma·ma·guism (**ma·ma·gi·sam, ma·ma·guy·ism**) [mamagızəm~mamagızm] *n* (Gren, Trin) Skilful flattery, teasing or deception, often in a lighthearted manner; the practice or art of such. *In advertising we get carried away by our rhetoric, our erudition, our semanticism. We forget that people who read advertisements are just like you, me, and Bhandat. Ugly and stupid. We want to hear plain talk. We want to hear the truth. And no mamaguism.*—ExP (73.02.13, p.2) [< MAMAGUY + *-ism* by analogy]

ma·ma·guy¹ (**ma·ma·gai, ma·ma·guey, ma·ma·guile**) [mamagaı] *vb intr* (Gren, Tbgo, Trin) To fool; to trick or deceive (esp by flattery); to mislead by blandishments. **a.** *No darling that child aint mine … / Why you brought me up for bastardy / After you mamaguy me and take my money / And still sleeping in William bachy.*—RLCF:219 (Cso) **b.** *An' if yu hear him, talkin' loud and carryin' on, / 'Nice of yu to come, thanks for de lovely gift'. / Now ah feel he was mamaguying me, / Because me didn't have no gift in me hand.*—KTT:71 **c.** *This is a blatant, yet subtle, attempt to mamaguy our people and to set them against the teachers. It is apparent that through these subtle ways that the Voice is trying to mislead the people of this country.*—CrU (77.01.22, p.7) [< Trin Sp, *mamar gallo* 'to suck (the) cock' (a metaph taken from cockfighting in Venz, etc in ref to a fighting cock that only pretends without really fighting. See K. Laurence's explanation in *Caq XVII 2, p.37*)] □ The guess-variant spellings are rare, the form *mamaguile* being prob due to folk etym.

ma·ma·guy² [mamagaı] *n* (Gren, Tbgo, Trin) Deception by flattery; [by extension] lighthearted banter, teasing. *Lena got the new job and he took her to a candlelight dinner and showered her with praise … 'can't keep a woman down … it couldn't happen to a nicer girl', and all that jazz … and she swallowed. / 'Mamaguy and wine is a true smartman's combination.'*—BoM (76.06.11, p.8) [By functional vb > n shift of MAMAGUY¹]

ma·ma-ma·la·die [mama-maladi] *n* (Gren) [Folklore] The restless ghost and/or crying of a woman who has died in childbirth and has been buried with the unborn baby still inside her; her cries are said to be heard for nine nights after her death as her spirit moves between the grave-yard and the house in wh she died. [Fr Cr > Fr *maman* 'mother' + *maladie* 'sickness' prob in ref to the cause of death]

ma·ma-man *n* (Jmca) [*AF-Derog*] ‖ AUNTIE-MAN (CarA) 1.

ma·ma·pool (ma.ma.poule) *n* (Gren, StLu, Ibgo, Trin) See MANMAN POULE

Ma·ma·(y)o! [mama(y)o] *excl* (ECar) See MAMA²!

mam·mee(-ap·ple)* (ma·mey/mam·my-(-ap·ple)) [mami apl ~ ma:mi apl] *n* (CarA) ‖ *ap-ricot* (StLu) ‖ *zabwiko* (Dmca, StLu) A large, spherical fruit that can be 4 to 9 ins in diameter, with a thick, reddish-brown skin, and firm, sweetish, orange-yellow flesh in wh one or more large, hard seeds are embedded; it is borne on a large, tall tree with sweet-scented flowers and dark green, leathery leaves; the timber is used for indoor work; *Mammea americana* (*Guttiferae*). [< *mami*, orig Amerindian name of the fruit + SE *apple* typically used to identify edible fruit in CE]

mam·mee-sa·pote* (ma·mie-sup·port-(er), man·si·port) [mami-sapo·t/sʌpotə ~ mansipo(r)t] *n* (CarA) A brown, rough-skinned, breast-shaped fruit about 3 or 4 ins long, with a fragrant flesh and seed; the flesh is used for making preserves, the seed for scent; it is borne on a medium-sized tree; *Calocarpum mammosum* or *Pouteria sapota* (*Sapotaceae*). [MAMMEE, from its resemblance in skin and texture to the MAMEE-APPLE + *sapote* < Sp *zapote* < Aztec *tzapotl* 'SAPODILLA' from its shape and size] □ Several forms of the name exist through folk etym; the fruit itself is less widely known than MAMMEE-APPLE and the names are confused by some.

Mam·my *n* (CarA) See MA

ma·moo [ma·mu] *n* (Guyn, Trin) [Indic] A maternal uncle; your mother's brother. '*Say pranam to your Mamoo, Children.' Mr Khoja inclined his head to one side and waited for the magic word. The boys mumbled their pran-ams.*—NF:70 [Bhoj *maamuu* < Hin *maamaa* 'mother's brother']

mam·pa(r) la(-man) *n* (Jmca) [*AF—Derog/Vul*] A worthless, effeminate or impotent man; [by extension] a homosexual male playing the female role. '*Him!' exclaimed Sarah con-temptuously; 'him is a real mamparla (effeminate) man! Him 'fraid for him aunt, an' yet him want to 'speak up' female.'*—DJC:38 [< Am Sp *mampolón* 'a common cock, not a fighting cock'. See *DJE2* p.290]

man¹ *n* (CarA) [*IF/AF*] **1.** An adult male whose character and/or personality are to be reckoned with; a strong, able, and usu aggressive male. **a.** *The man Edward Massay!* (= *appreciative greeting from a friend as Edward M—arrives*).—(Guyn) **b.** *If you're on strike you must be man and say so. Don*['t] *say you*['re] *sick.*—(Bdos) **c.** *When last you ever give me even a penny fuh buy food? You an't no man. You is man when man scarce.*—TRIH:22 [Cp *OED man* 6., 7. for the idea of superiority 'an adult male eminently endowed with manly qualities', etc] **2.** [By extension, focusing attention] Any person, as seen in a particular context. **a.** *Dat is how she stop. An den she, fus' man, turn rong an' tell mih de cushion fade* (= *That is how she is. And then she's the first person to turn and tell me the cushion has faded*).—MN:33 **b.** *You think Miss Coombs and dem party will get in? You wait and see, not a man will get a seat.*—(Bdos) **3.** *quasi-indefinite pers. pron.* I; me; someone; we; us; people. **a.** *Pusher, the village loafer, ... watched the blob as it whizzed past his head by inches. /* ... '*You nearly spit on a man, Balgobin,' he said, but he spoke as if he were saying, 'A miss is as good as a mile.'*—SPOC:15 **b.** *I told her about this guy, but she is saying that she doesn't want any 'gunman come shoot her down' and that I am too young and that in two years time I 'will see man drive big car come to her gate, come ask for me.*—WeS (74.06.28, p.8) **c.** *No T.V. is here right now, but sometimes we ask permission to leave in the night. We sleep on cotton mattresses, most of the time without anything like a sheet. Man jus ah suffer. This place really dread man. Ah tell you.*—Antg (Ms, 1975) [Cp *OED man* 4. g. used quasi-pronominally = 'one, any one', but implying ref to the male sex only + cit from Shak (*Tempest*) 'Misery acquaints a man with strange bed-fellows'] □ See also MANKIND. **4.** *sex-free pers. quasi-pron.* Form of address between peers of either sex, in familiarity, persuasion or palliation. **a.** ... *he would say: 'Man, Dalvar, man, got to think of my health, man. At my age I can't run up those stairs like the young chaps.*—SDD:25 **b.** *Man, let me play the thing for today then, and enjoy it, and then see what happen, man!*—CWFYS:83 **c.** '*Aaye, gul, yuh mad or wat, talking to yuhself?' Rita had asked. Urmilla saw her and blushed. 'I only talking to Chandra, man,' she said.*—SABS:131 [Cp *OED man* 4. e. '... dialectally it is in common use as a meaningless expletive, being used in addressing both males and females'. Also *EDD man* 8. 'a familiar term of address to a person of either sex or of any age; often used at the end of a sentence to give it special emphasis; sometimes used as a meaningless expletive' + cits from Sc and most Br dials. Cp also poss phonic infl in the slave era from Du as in *Doe dat niet, man* 'Don't do that, man', *Ach man, dat is mooi* 'Man, that is lovely', in wh the contexts of usage are notably similar] □ In this use CE **man** may occur phrase-initially or terminally, before or after a person's name, or quasi-pronominally without a name (as in cit b.), and is subject to much variation of stress, pitch, and vowel-length determined by emotive context. **5.**

PHRASES **5.1 as man** *adv phr* (Bdos, Gren, Tbgo, Trin) [AF] Decidedly; certainly; to be sure; without doubt. **a.** *If he didn['t] have a knife, as man A would-a lick him do[w]ng.*—(Gren) **b.** *B—T— is a man we have all looked up to for a long time. As man, many of us were disappointed to find he could not handle the chicks last week. He should be made to farm out an apology to us.*—SuS (89.03.12, p.9) **5.2 be a man to sb** *vb phr* (CarA) [IF/AF] To be much older than sb and therefore due to be respected by or responsible for that person. *Mammie, I's a man ta Jimmie? I mus' care for he?*—WBS:26 **5.3 be/ grow a big man** *vb phr* (CarA) [IF] To be/ become a mature adult (male), a grown-up man. *Look! You're still a boy! When you grow a big man you can talk like that.*—(Guyn) **5.4 be man enough to (do sth)** *vb phr* (CarA) [IF] To be bold, courageous enough to (do sth). *I am not like your grandmother, you know, so, Junior, careful. If you want to go to your auntie Elizabeth and you are man enough to go, go!*—JJM:47 **5.5 be more man than sb** *vb phr* (CarA) [IF] To be more able in a show of virility or courage than another man. *That occurred one day with a prisoner who showed that he was more man in the jail than he could have been in his own home (if he has one) outside of the jail.*—TrU (60.12.31, p.1) **5.6 if you name man** *id phr* (Gren, Guyn, Tbgo, Trin) [AF] [Usu in scolding a youngster] If you dare; if you are bold enough. **5.7 sth is a man** *id phr* (Guyn) [AF—Joc] Sth is very costly, selling at a high price. *'House rent,' says one of the tenants 'is a man'. May we ask the question, Lord how long?*—DaC (52.04.09, p.2) **5.8 small man** *n phr* (CarA) [IF] A person (or collectively, persons) of low income; a citizen/citizens who is/are poor; (SE) the little man. *He said that what the enemies of the Government were bothered about was the fact that 'we want to make the small man a real man.'*—GyC (76.03.26, p.3) **5.9 man better man** *id phr* (Mrat, Trin) [AF] [A term of defiant challenge] We/they must fight it out right now; Let them fight it out between them. *This task completed, he stretched out in his bed and thought to himself: 'Now ley D. G— get wey from dat. One t'ing sure, none o' dem getting close to me, and ah know from commonsense now, dat all dis obeah business is pure nonsense. Only wah' touch a man wheder inside o'outside could harm he. When he step out o' he door dis morning he mus' understand dat is man better man.*—FDA:9 [Perh taken from face-to-face challenging at the start of a STICK-FIGHT] □ See MAN-BETTER-MAN.

man²- *masc gender pref* (CarA) [IF] Male; hence many compounds identifying male of species (persons, animals) or varieties (flora): **man-child/-rat/-coconut/-pawpaw/-piaba**, etc. **a.** *If it was in slavery days, Boltin would ha' paid a bigger fine for making a woman lose a man-child—God strike him!*—RND:22 **b.** *Two man-crab can't live in one hole.*—CarA (Prov) [A prob calque from W Afr langs many of wh have such gender-marking compounds. Exs (TAGD:230) Mandinka *diŋ-ke* (*child male*) 'man-child', Igbo *nwanne-nwoke* (*relative man*) 'brother', etc]

-man³ *agential suff* (CarA) [IF] The man who is identified by the function, act, or thing named in the prefix; hence many ready-made compounds: **eat-man, obeah-man, t[h]ief-man, bush-bath-man**, etc. **a.** *And the people in the neighbourhood come and look in at the oval hole in the top o' the mahogany coffin when the undertaker-man had bring him home.*—CWFYS:20 **b.** *Don't enter that race as long as Clyde is taking part. He's a run-man.*—FGW:18 [SE suffixal pattern as in *fireman, repairman*, etc is prob reinforced by calquing from the very common W Afr word-forming device of adding a suff 'equivalent to -*man*' to determine a person as doer.' Ex *DAFL* Akan *-fo* 'person; ... a noun that is now almost exclusively used as a suffix in names of persons']

man·a·ger-bel·ly [ˈmanɪnʤʌ-bɛli] /1ˈ22I2/ *n* (Bdos, Guyn) A (man's) paunch. [From association with the characteristic paunchiness of managers of sugar-plantations]

man·a·koo *n* (Dmca, Gren, StVn, Trin) See MANICOU.

ma·na·tee* (ma·na·ti) [manati] *n* (Antg, Belz, Guyn, Jmca) ‖*sea-cow* (Guyn, Jmca) ‖*water-cow* (Guyn) A large, sluggish, harmless, herbivorous, aquatic mammal, greyish-black in colour; it has flappers and a broad, flat, round tail, can exceed 12 ft in length and weigh several hundred pounds; it dwells in coastal waters and the estuaries of rivers; *Manatus americanus* (Trichechidae). [OED *manatee* < Sp *manati* (Oviedo 1535), < Carib *manattouï* (Raymond Breton, *Dictionnaire Caraïbe* 1665) ...]

man-bet·ter-man* *n* (Dmca, StLu, Trin) ‖*devil('s) horsewhip* (Jmca, StLu) ‖*devil-whip* (Guyn) ‖*hug-me-close* (Bdos) ‖*soldier-rod* (Guyn) An erect, green weed about 2 to 3 ft tall, with thin, tough branches bearing long, thin, greenish spikes of spiny bracts that cling to the clothing or skin of passers-by or animals; an infusion of it is used medicinally for colic, colds, and fever; children use the spikes to tease each other; *Achyranthes indica* (*Amaranthaceae*). [Perh from the use of the spike by children in playful teasing. Cp MAN Phr 5.9]

man·bhogue *n* (Guyn, Trin) See MOHANBHOG·

man·chi·neel* (man·chi·neal) [man čini·l ~ mansini·l] *n* (CarA) An evergreen tree wh can exceed 30 ft in height, usu found near the sea or swampy ground; its fissured bark, shiny green leaves and small apple-like fruit all contain a highly poisonous, skin-blistering latex; its wood is used to a limited extent in furniture making; *Hippomane mancinella* (*Euphorbiaceae*). [OED < Fr *mancenille* a. Sp *manzanilla*, dim. of *manzana* 'apple' in ref to its fruit]

man·da·rin(-o·range)* *n* (*phr*) (Dmca, Gren, StLu, Trin) ‖TANGERINE (CarA) [< Fr *mandarine*. See OED *mandarin²*]

man·dir [mandɪr] *n* (Guyn, Trin) A Hindu temple. **a.** *A seven-day Veda Upadesh or Exposition of the Vedic Religion, organised by the Georgetown Arya Samaj to be held at the Central Vedic Mandir, D'Urban Street, Georgetown, commences as announced previously.*—SuC (76.05.23, p.3) **b.** *And moreover the faithful at the Mandir do assemble for corporate worship and prayers with the Hindu equivalent of Sunday evening service.*— ExP (73.03.25, p.11) [< Hin *māndir* 'temple'] □ Sometimes preceded by **Shiv** in wh case the *mandir* is a temple dedicated to the worship of Shiv, one of the divine Hindu Trinity.

man·ger·ine* [manjərin] *n* (Belz, Guyn, Jmca) A citrus fruit very similar in appearance to the tangerine but larger and lighter in colour; *Citrus spp* (*Rutaceae*). [A blend of *mandarin* + *tangerine*]

man·gle [maŋgl] *n* (Dmca, USVI) ‖ MANGROVE (CarA) [Perh < Fr *manglier* 'mangrove tree']

man·go-bab (**man·go-barbe**) [maŋgo-bab] / ı′21/ *n* (Dmca) ‖ HAIRY MANGO (Belz, etc) [Fr Cr -*bab* < Fr *barbe*, in ref to the long, hairy fibres that cling to the seed when the mango is sucked]

man·go-bèf ['maŋgo-bɛf] *n* (Dmca, Gren, StLu) Name generally given to two or three varieties of very large mango. [Fr Cr *bèf* < Fr *boeuf* 'cow', in ref to its size]

man·go-ca·bane *n* (Dmca) See MANGO-KABANN

man·go-Cey·lon *n* (Dmca) ‖ BOMBAY-MANGO (Jmca, Mrat)

man·go-fil [maŋgo-fil] /ı′21/ *n* (StLu) ‖ HAIRY MANGO (Belz, etc)

man·go-Gra·ham [maŋgo-gream]; **Gra·.ham** (**-man·go**) *n* (StLu) ‖ *bellyfull* (Antg, Belz, Dmca, Gren, Tbgo) ‖ *bull-seed/stone mango* (Jmca) ‖ *fufu-mango* (Guyn) ‖ *horse-mango* (Belz) ‖ *mango-koko-bèf* (Dmca, StLu) A very large mango, one of the kind generally also called MANGO-BÈF.

man·go-ka·bann (**man·go-ca·bane**) *n* (Dmca) A mango that has been ripened under cloth in a basket or box. *Mango-kabann is sweeter than when you let it stay on the tree and ripen there, because when you pick it it is already matwitè, if not it would be force-ripe, not sweet.*—(Dmca) [*Mango* + Fr Cr *kabann* < Fr CABANE[1] 3. used as adj, postposed as in Fr]

man·go-long /ı′12/ *n* (Bdos) ‖ HAIRY MANGO (Belz, etc)

man·go-mou·chach/(-mou·chasse) [maŋ go mušaš ~ mušas] *n* (Dmca, StLu) ‖ STARCH-MANGO (Gren) [Fr Cr *mouchach* 'starch']

man·go-par·lui/pal·wi/pel·o·wie; [maŋgo parlʊwi ~ palwi ~ pɛlowi] *n* (*phr*) (Dmca, Gren, StLu, StVn) ‖ *palwi/parwi-mango* (Bdos) ‖ *Pierre-Louis* (Dmca) A very sweet mango wh is yellow to yellowish-red when ripe, may be small or large and sometimes fibrous in texture; it is roundish in shape, tapering to a point; *Mangifera spp* (*Anacardiaceae*). [< Fr *Pierre Louis* or *Père Louis* prob after the person who produced this variety]

man·go-rose *n* (Dmca, Gren, StLu, Tbgo, Trin) See MANGO-WÒZ

man·go·steen (**man·go·stain**) [maŋgosti:n] *n* (CarA) A round, dark-purple fruit about the size of an orange with sweet, white, pulpy flesh divided into segments with four seeds; it is borne on a flowering tree with thick, leathery leaves, and both fruit and leaves yield a yellow, sticky latex; *Garcinia mangostana* (*Guttiferae*). [< Malay *mangustan*, name of the fruit; the plant was imported to the CarA]

man·go·teen (**man·go·tine**) [maŋgoti:n] *n* (ECar) A small, very tasty mango; *Mangifera spp* (*Anacardiaceae*).

man·go-tété [maŋgo-tete] *n* (Dmca) A mango shaped like a breast, having a point at the end wh is usu softened and the juice sucked out; *Mangifera spp* (*Anacardiaceae*). [Fr Cr < E *mango* + Fr *tété* < Fr *téter* 'to suck at the breast']

man·go-wòz (**man·go-rose, rose man·go**) *n* (*phr*) (Dmca, Gren, StLu, Tbgo, Trin) A small, sweet, juicy mango wh grows to about 2 to 2-3/4 ins in length and has a rosy look when ripe, hence the name; *Mangifera spp* (*Anacardiaceae*). □ The pronunc **-wòz** applies to Dmca, StLu, **-rose** to Gren, Tbgo, Trin.

man·grove* (**man·gró, man·grow**) [maŋ grov ~ maŋgro] *n* (CarA) ‖ *mangle* (Dmca, USVI) Generic term applied to a family of tropical hydrophytic plants with either stilt or breathing roots wh grow in muddy coastal swamps and are covered at high tide by sea water; they are used for tanning or as firewood; *Avicennia spp* (*Verbenaceae*), *Laguncularia racemosa* (*Combretaceae*), *Conocarpus erectus* (*Combretaceae*) and *Rhizophora spp* (*Rhizophoraceae*). *The character of the river-side vegetation within reach of the tide differs somewhat from that which prevails in the higher parts. Generally in the former parts the true forest does not extend to the open river, but between the two a belt of mangrove trees (Rhizophora mangle) stands, raised high above the mud flat on aerial roots, except where in one or two places a projecting spur of the higher real bank runs out above the mud, through the mangroves, into the river.*—IAIG:100 □ There are a number of *CarA* varieties called *red, black, white*, etc *mangrove/mangle*. See also COURIDA.

man·grove-cuck·oo *n* (CarA) ‖ RAIN-BIRD[1] 2. (CarA) [From its habit of nesting in mangrove trees]

man·i·cole-palm n (Guyn) A clumped palm of four to sixteen slender, spineless stems that can exceed 50 ft in height, each with a crown of dense arching fronds; the stems and hard, reddish bark are used in building huts, and the dried branches make good brooms; the young shoots are cooked as a 'cabbage', but the little red fruit are inedible; *Euterpe edulis* (*Palmae*). [Cp *BAED* Arawak *manaka* 'palm tree with tall narrow trunk']

man·i·cou* (**man·a·koo**) n (Dmca, Gren, StVn, Trin) ‖ *yawa(r)ri(e)* (Guyn) A nocturnal, foul-smelling, marsupial rodent the size of a cat with a conical head, a pig-like snout, big ears and eyes, a brown, loosely coarse-haired body, and a long prehensile tail; it eats chickens, and is hunted for its flesh, considered a delicacy by some; *Didelphys opossum* or *D. marsupialis insularis* (*Didelphyidae*). ... *or how the manicou carries its young ones upon its back with all their tails looped round the parent-tail to prevent them from sliding off.*—FTT:82 [Prob a Carib name] □ Closely related to the American tree-living opossum.

man·i·cou-man n (Trin) [*AF-Derog*] ‖ AUN-TIE-MAN (CarA) 1. [Prob ref to the habit of the young animals hanging on to their mother. See cit at MANICOU.]

man·i·oc [manɪɒk] n (ECar) ‖ CASSAVA (CarA) [Of Amerindian orig. Cp *DGEG* Guarani *mandio* 'mandioca, plant and root'. Note also: One of their major gods was Yocahu, the Arawak male god and giver of manioc. If we say 'manioc' carefully we will notice that the last part of the word is the same as the name of the god; Yocahu the god; Maniocca the plant.—HTDS:10. See also *OED* etym note] □ For most speakers MA-NIOC is the exact equivalent of CASSAVA (BITTER- or SWEET-), this latter being universal in CE; for some, however, MANIOC refers to the bitter variety.

man·i·oc-fa·rine n (StLu) ‖ FARINE (Angu, etc)

man jack (**man·jack¹**) n (Bdos, Gren, Trin) [*AF*] 1. Person; individual; (any/every)-body. *Says there ain't nothing to prevent you or me or any man jack once he got the money, there ain't nothin' to stop him ownin' this lan'.*—LICMS:91 [By re-analysis or extension of IF SE *every man jack* (as *OED* man sb¹ 4. m) in the sense *everybody*, whence *man jack* = -body, individual, etc] 2. (Baha) [*AF*] [Friendly form of address, usu between men] *Manjack, come go wit me home.*—(Baha) 3. PHRASES 3.1 **all man jack** n phr (ECar) [*AF*] Everybody together. a. *Gairy took the matter to Cabinet and of course everybody kept quiet, nodding their heads in agreement. But when they got outside all man jack went to have a private drink to voice their opinions.*—NeJ (75.06.06, p.8) b. *They were there already, all man jack with a paint brush, painting hell out of the front wall.*—JPB:125 3.2 **manjack and his**

brother; manjack and sally n phrs (Trin) ‖ TOUT MOUN AND SAM (ECar) See TOUT MOUNE Phr 2.1 a. *But nowadays manjack and his brother brushed shoulders with the whites, and though perhaps there were few scenes like a downtown bar or club, the proprietors sweated in the presence of unknown clientele.*—SPOC:76 b. *He must have been watching the newspaper report of the fine furnishings in homes at the Beetham Estate. / Every manjack and Sally down there has their television, their stereo, sewing machine, fridge and I am sure many have washing machines too.*—TrG (73.04.01, p.12)

man·ja(c)k² n (Dmca, Gren, Tbgo, USVI) ‖ CLAMMY CHERRY² (Brbu, etc) *The tall, white manjack can be seen on the Reef Bay Trail, right side.... It is easier to find the tree by finding the small, green fruits, half-inch or less on the ground most of the year. The fruits are extremely sticky and the mucilage is used for children's kites here and in the West Indies and Guyana.*—JNHST:60 [Prob Amerindian. Cp *DGEG* Guarani *mangaisi*, 'gummy sap extracted from the *mangavi* tree and other resinous trees']

man·jak n (ECar) A black, bituminous substance once mined and still found in bits on the Atlantic coasts of some ECar islands; in Bdos it was once used as fuel for sugar factories or exported as a base for varnish. [See *OED*, cits re Bdos (also re Tbgo) < *mountjack*]

man·kin[d] [mankaɪn] *quasi-pron* (Guyn) [*AF*] [Usu used by males] I; me; people in general. *Mankin[d] seein[g] hell to live and dey only busy harassin[g] you to buy poppy for Poppy Day.*—(Guyn) [Perh infl by MAN¹ 3., wh is used similarly with wider coverage]

man·man·poul(e) (**ma·ma·pool**) [mã mãpu·l ~ mamapu·l] n (Gren, StLu, Tbgo, Trin) [*AF—Derog*] 1. A person who fusses like a mother hen; a very irritating fusspot. [Fr Cr < Fr *maman* 'mother' + *poule* 'hen'] 2. [By extension] A foolish, gullible person. *Six dollars, woman you think I is a mamapool? Look take dat. You get too much and dat is me last five dollars.*—RTCS:25 3. [By extension] ‖ AUNTIE-MAN (CarA) □ Cp MAMPA(R)LA-MAN.

man·ners n pl PHRASES 1. **Learn manners!** *imper vb phr* (CarA) [*IF*] See LEARN¹ PHR 2. 2. **under manners; under heavy manners** [*IF*] *adj phr* (Bdos, Gren, Guyn, Jmca) See UNDER Phr 2.3

man·ners·a·ble *adj* (Antg, Jmca) [*IF/AF*] ‖ *mannersly* (Tbgo) Mannerly; well-behaved; [by extension] polite and co-operative; considerate. *The other day couple of us were under the big tree at Devon House when we started to talk of days that used to be. Bout we grandmother and grandfather and how in the days when we knew them people were mannersable and never cubbitch and bad behaviour like today.*—WeG (73.09.26, p.1, Partyline) [Cp *EDD* mannerable (wSom) 'well-behaved, polite', also *mannersome*. The form ‖ *mannerly* is similarly analogical, with *manners* as base]

ma(n)·ni·ba(l)·li* *n* (Guyn) A large, canopy tree growing to a height of about 100 ft and found mostly in the central rain-forest areas of Guyana; it yields a tough, coarse wood of irregular grain, yellow-brown in colour with white pencil-striping, and is much used in heavy construction work; *Moronobea coccinea* (*Guttiferae*). [*BAED* Arawak *mani* 'a tree that frequents riverbanks', *manibali* 'a large tree that resembles *mani*']

man·nish /2′2/ *adj* 1. (CarA) [Of boys] Impertinent and aggressive; manifesting a tendency towards adult behaviour. a. *You gettin' too mannish when you start callin' yo' betters liars.*—Vip.I.1.p (J. Collins) b. *Mary little brother mannish! He's only nine years and he want to wear long pants.*—(Trin) 2.) (Angu, Baha, Dmca, Jmca, StVn) [Of either sex] Unpleasantly precocious. *In fact, any question about babies, intercourse, boyfriends or girlfriends cause 'worry' in the minds of parents. 'My Lord, what she want to know 'bout dat for,' 'Go away gal—you too fresh!' or 'You better shut your mouth, you too mannish'* …—MBS:4 3. (Antg, Tbgo) [Of children] Pleasantly precocious. *It's a joy to be with her—she's a mannish little girl.*—(Antg) 4. (Tbgo, Trin) [Of a male] Assertive; self-reliant. *I am a mannish Tobagonian. I don't want no outsider to tell me how to run my affairs.*—(Tbgo) [Cp *EDD* mannish adj … also written mannish e.Yks; 'of a youth: aping manhood; overbearing; blustering'. Cp also sense of MAN Phr 5.3]

man·nish-wa·ter *n* (Jmca) [*AF—Joc*] ‖ GOAT-HEAD SOUP (Jmca) [*Mannish*, from association with virility + *water* [*Joc*] 'soup']

man-o[f]-busi·ness [ma-n-ʌ-bɪznɪs] /1′122/ *n* (Bdos) 1. ‖ *handyman* (StLu) A man who serves a particular household by doing all kinds of necessary, minor work such as maintenance, running errands, etc. 2. [*Joc*] A woman's lover on whom she relies for minor, personal favours.

man-o-war bird *n phr* (CarA) ‖ FRIGATE-BIRD (CarA) [Prob from its size and the fact that it attacks other fish-eating birds for food]

man-pi·a·ba *n* (Bdos, Guyn) ‖ BALL-BUSH (Bdos, Jmca) *This same man-piaba you take the leaves, green or dry, and you can do a lot of things with it—boil it, you see—and mix with other bushes sometimes, but nowadays I see the young people take the top and paint it and make ornament—they don['t] know [a]bout it.*—(Guyn) [*Man*, prob because of supposed aphrodisiac properties attributed to this 'bush' when used as an ingredient in a particular decoction, + *PIABA*] □ Cp WOMAN-PIABA.

man-soup *n* (Antg) ‖ FISH-BROTH 1. (Dmca, etc) [Perh from the belief that the fish-head

ingredient is a source of virility] □ The *Antg* variety is usu grey, from the use of green bananas.

many-roots *n* (CarA) See MINNIE-ROOT (CarA)

ma·pe·pire (ma·pi·pire) [mapepiɪ ~ mapɪpɪə] *n* (Trin) Any of a number of very venomous snakes (esp the foll.) 1. **mapepire-balsain** [-balsã] ‖ FER-DE-LANCE (ECar) 2. **mapepire zanana** (Trin) ‖ BUSHMASTER (Guyn, Trin) *The only type of snake I respect however, is the mapepire. He coils himself up and waits for his prey. His poison is deadly.*—OTTTT:48 [? Fr Cr < Fr *mal* + *pis* + *pire* 'bad, worse, worst', + *balsain* < Fr *malsain* (?) 'dangerous'; also + *zanana* 'pineapple' from the diamond-shaped markings of the body]

ma(p)·po *n* (Trin) ‖ GUINEP (CarA)

ma·ra·bun·ta *n* (Guyn) 1. ‖ JACK-SPANIARD (ECar) [Poss from a warning, orig in Yoruba. Cp Yoruba *munra agbọn ta* 'take-care wasp stings'] 2. [By extension] Any wasp. 3. [By extension] A viperish woman.

ma·ran *n* 1. (USVI) One of several varieties of aromatic, bushy shrub growing to about 9 ft, and abundant on uncultivated, rocky ground; it has a number of folk uses, esp as pot-scrubber, insecticide, etc; *Croton spp* (*Euphorbiaceae*). *The white maran was used for medicine. The yellow for washing dishes and scrubbing floors, also as an insecticide for fleas and fowl lice. The wild maran or soja whip for making yard brooms.*—HPVI:3 2. (Guyn) [Timber Ind] A canopy, forest tree growing to over 100 ft in height, with a cylindrical bole of some 60 ft; it yields a tough, reddish-brown wood used for general construction and interior work; *Copaifera guianensis* (*Caesalpiniaceae*).

ma·ras·ma (me·ras·mi, mi·ras·me(e)) *n* (Jmca, StVn, Trin, USVI) 1. An emaciated condition or a wasting away of the body, esp in infants, thought to be due largely to malnutrition; (SE) marasmus; kwashiorkor. 2. [By extension] Any persistent, debilitating sickness. *What ailed him was not positively known: the people in the yard said he had marasma, a generic term which they applied to all forms of disease which they were unable to determine more particularly.*—DJC:150 3. [By association with tuberculosis] A bad cold. *The other evening, I found myself trying to explain to a young lady what is mirasmie. It was the night of the sudden, heavy rains and I warned her to cover her mole lest she get mirasmie. To my surprise, she asked what was that? Me and my fool-fool self, thought that there are still Jamaicans growing up on folk-traditions.*—JdN (79.11.17, p.7) [< SE *marasmus*]

march *vb intr* (CarA) [*IF*] 1. To go with resolve, purpose (down, out, etc to sb or some place). *Look Alfred! Just stop using those words I hearing*

before I march out there to you.—(Gren) **2.** PHRASE
2.1 march yourself *vb refl* [*IF*] To go resolutely
(about sth); to act officiously. **a.** *Just tell that boy
to march himself inside and change his clothes before
he starts playing.*—(Guyn) **b.** *She march she-self
go do it an*[*d*] *nobody ask um.*—(Nevs) [Cp Yoruba
ko ara ṛẹ kuro 'collect and take away yourself,
similarly used—*pers info, K.Ọmọtọsọ*]

ma·ren·ga *n* (Guyn) See MERENGUE·

mar·gate **(fish)*** **(mar·ga·ret/mar·get/**
mar·gret (fish) [mar·gɛt~ma(r)grɪt (fiʃ)] *n*
(*phr*) (Angu, Baha, BrVi, Mrat, TkCa) A white
fish of the grunt family, wh grows to a length of
1-1/2 ft; it is prized for its flavour; *Haemulon
album* (*Pomadasyidae*).

Mar·gue·rite(-Fes·ti·val) *n* (StLu) ‖ LA-
MAGWIT (StLu) *The Marguerite Festival got confused this year, what with Mama Wadleau trying
desperately to promote herself and the Bluffer
trying to edge in his daughter as Mamai Wadleau.
Somehow the Marguerite folk themselves got edged
out.*—CrU (76.10.23, p.4) [See LA-MAGWIT]

ma·ri·anne *n* (Dmca, StLu) See MAWIYANN

ma·ri·bone [maribo·n] *n* (Gren, Trin) [*IF*] A
small variety of JACK-SPANIARD that builds a
paper-like nest. [< MARABUNTA]

Ma·rie-su·cer *n* (StLu) See MAWISOSÉ

ma·ri·gold *n* (Jmca, TkCa) ‖ CARPET-DAISY
(Bdos) □ Often MARY-GOLD (*Jmca*) in folk
speech. Not one of the IAE garden varieties of
marigold; *Calendula officinalis* or *Tagetes spp.*

ma·ri·na (**ma·ri·ner**) [mari·nʌ] *n* (Belz, Dmca,
StVn) ‖ MERINO (CarA) [Perh a folk pronunc of
MERINO]

ma·rin·ga (**ma·ren·ga**) [marɪŋga~marɛŋga]
n (Guyn) □ See MERENGUE.

mar·ish and the par·ish *n phr* (Bdos, Guyn,
Trin) [*AF—Joc*] ‖ TOUT MOUN AND SAM (ECar)
See TOUT MOUNE Phr 2.1 *Winken: Why you want
to get me in trouble, for? ... To cause people to
don't trust me? To cause the marrish and the parrish
to talk a lotta dam clap-trap 'bout me?*—PeL
(81.01.30, p.3, Tom Clarke) [Orig obscure. Prob
from an E dial phr. Note *OED marish* 1. =
marsh + cit 1726, Swift: 'Like a Bridge that
joins a Marish To Moorlands of a diff'rent Parish'. In *Bdos* PARISH could indicate the whole
population of a government administrative dis-
trict] □ The spelling in the cit is particular to
the writer.

mark¹ *n* (Trin) **1.** [Gambling] In WHE-WHE,
any of 36 random symbols (centipede, old lady,
carriage, hog, etc) each identified by a number
(1 to 36); players buy these as chances, and the
winning symbol, kept secret by the 'banker', is
revealed at the given time of play. (See WHE-WHE,

also *MCCL:160* for a full list of symbols). **2.**
PHRASE **2.1 when de mark buss/bu[r]st** *id phr*
(Gren, Tbgo, Trin) [*AF*] When the truth is out;
when the day of reckoning comes; [by extension]
when things come to a head; when confusion
breaks out. **a.** *In the meantime, the big boys here
are busy grabbing all the money they can, and
stashing it away in investments abroad. When the
mark buss they'll just follow their money and leave
us here in the mess.*—BoM (79.08.03, p.28) **b.**
*Go on giving she all yuh money! Yuh go find out
one day wen de mark bust she go leave yuh and go
whoring all over de place—every girl who born in
George Street does turn whore!*—SABS:29 [A ref
to the banker's revealing or 'bursting out' the
secret or winning symbol. See BUSS Phr 10.4]

mark² *vb tr* (CarA) **1.** [Of a pregnant woman]
To cause a mark to appear on the body of her
unborn child, it is believed, by scratching or
touching her body while expressing a yearning
for some item of food; the resulting birthmark
would resemble that item (ex: a fruit). [See *OED
mark* sb¹ 18, note referring to 17C use of phr
'God bless the mark' by midwives at the birth
of a child bearing a mark] **2.** To cause a mark
to appear on your own body, it is believed, by
touching yourself to show the site of an injury;
hence foll phr. **3.** PHRASE **3.1 not marking
myself** *formulaic adjunct* (Bdos, Guyn) [Said
while describing sb else's scar or injury to avoid
receiving the same. See sense 2.] *The thief stabbed
him right here to his throat—not marking myself.*—
(Guyn) [See *OED* note referred to at sense 1.,
also the use several times by Shak of the phr
'God save the mark' in this context, ex: 'I saw
the wound, I saw it with mine eyes, God save
the mark, here on his manly breast—*Rom & Jul
III.2.153*]

marl-hole *n* (Angu, Bdos, Jmca) A limestone
quarry.

ma·ro(o) (**ma·ru**) *n* (Guyn, Trin) See MAARU

ma·roon¹ *n* **1.** (CarA) Any of the descendants
of those slaves who freed themselves by escape
and guerrilla fighting, establishing isolated communities wh have survived in mountain or forest
country (esp in *Jmca*). *Even before the European
occupation of the Island, Negro slaves had escaped
to Dominica or been captured by the Caribs from
settlements on other islands. When the French
arrived, there were already a few Maroons living
in Carib villages or in their own settlements in the
forest.*—HTDS:53 [< Am Sp *cimarrón* 'a wild
savage' < dial Sp *cimarra* 'wild place' < Sp *cima*
'mountain top, tree top'. Note that Castilian
Sp pronunc [θima'ro·n] easily becomes SE 'the
maroon' by folk etym. This term was first applied
to the *Jmca* slaves left to themselves by their
Spanish masters who fled to Cuba after their
defeat by the English in 1655. Its connotation
of 'resistance to recapture' made it applicable
also to Surinam's *bush-negroes* and to all similar cases in the *CarA*] **2.** [By extension] (Gren,
Grns, Mrat) ‖ LEND-HAND (Tbgo) *His older son*

John had begged him to call a maroon but Joey always refused. 'Leh me do me work meself,' he would say, 'next thing you know de whole village asking me for a day's work.'—FGSOS:59 **[**By shift of sense 1, of 'brotherhood for survival', to that of 'co-operative self-help'. The accompanying work-songs, and subsequent feasting and spreeing gave rise to other associated senses. See foll**]** **3.** [By extension] (Crcu, Grns) An annual communal village feast with religious purpose. **4.** [By extension] (Bdos) [*Obs*] An outing and picnic with friends. **[**Noted in *CGBD5*: 66. See also *OED* 'a pleasure party', for wh *OEDS* adds cits –19C**]**

ma·roon[2] *vb* (Baha, TkCa) [Hist] **1.** To go hunting for whatever might be obtained over a wide area (including other islands) for several days. **[**By functional n > vb shift of MAROON[1] n 1.**]** **2.** To have an all-day spree. *They swam in the sparkling sea several times a day, rode horseback for hours on end, drank copious quantities of wine and brandy, went on all day 'marooning' parties to nearby islands and danced till dawn.*—ASOB: 221 **[**By functional n > vb shift of senses of MAROON[1] n 2., 3., 4.**]**

mar·riage [marıʤ] *n* (CarA) [*IF*] [Market huckstering] The pairing of two items being sold by retail, in order to help sell one of them. (See MARRY 1.). *Take a quick peep over the shoulders of people in a crowd and you might hear of the 'marriage' of mangoes ... with sweet potatoes or carrots whose sale might then be slow.*—LaS (75.06.28, p.4) **[**See MARRY **1.]**

mar·ried[1] [marıd] *vb tr* (CarA) [*X*] To marry; to be married (to). **a.** *But I wonder what make him want to married you quick so?*—RTCS:10 **b.** *I tell her to married with him but she say she cannot married with a man she doesn't love.*—TLTH:17 **c.** *This rich-rich Jewish girl I hear is marrieding some Bajan man or other.*—CWFYS:87 **[** < SE pa. part. *married*, functioning as CarA Cr base vb prob because of greater frequency of occurrence in this form than *marry* (cp similarly CarA Cr *done, los[t], etc*); thence adopting *-ing* from SE morphology (note cit c.**]** □ Often also in vb phrs *to married to/up/with (sb)*. See also MARRY Phr **3.2**.

mar·ried[2] *n* (Gren) [*AF*] Marriage. *Something mus[t] wrong wit[h] married if priest ha[ve] to bless it.*—(Gren) **[**By functional vb > n shift of MARRIED[1]**]**

mar·ried-man pork* /1'121/ *n phr* (Guyn) An erect aromatic herb about 2 ft high, with tiny leaves wh are widely used in Guyana for flavouring and seasoning foods; *Ocimum basilicum* or *O. micranthum* (*Labiatae*). [Prob infl by SE *marjoram* by folk etym]

mar·row *n* (CarA) ‖ GOURD (BrVi, etc)

mar·ry *vb tr* (CarA) [*IF*] **1.** [Market huckstering] To sell by retail two items together, one

of wh is in short supply, the other in over-abundance, in order to facilitate the seller's disposal of the latter. (See cit). *For instance a woman is said to 'marry' her peas and carrots, because if she has a plentiful supply of peas and a limited supply of carrots which happens to be scarce and everyone is trying to get—she insists that in order to get a pound of carrots one has to buy a pound of peas. This is referred to as the 'marrying' of goods.*—Mrat (Ms, 1973) **2.** [Rum Ind] To blend professionally for a certain period rums that have been separately matured. *Rum is normally aged for a number of years in oak casks and when this process is completed the contents of each cask are tested by experienced blenders and then mixed in oak vats where the process of 'marrying' the blends takes place. The blended rums are then reduced in strength by the addition of purified water and, after filtering and polishing, they are bottled.*—Cat (IV.2, p.24) **3.** PHRASES **3.1 marry to (sb)** *vb phr* (CarA) [*AF/IF*] To marry (sb); to be married to (sb). **a.** *East Indian people always arrange for their son or daughter to marry to somebody in their own race.*—(Guyn) **b.** *Well tell me the latest since I been away, who marry to who and so on.*—(Jmca) **3.2 marry under bamboo** *vb phr* (Guyn, Trin) [*AF—Derog*] See BAMBOO Phr **2.2**

Marse[1] **(Mass')** [ma·(r)s] *n* (CarA) [*AF—Cr*] Mister, as respectful title of a white male, esp one of the planter class, used by a servant or a black person of the labouring class. *'Listen to him, Mass' Carl,' John Graham said. 'Him know what him say.' He had turned his mule across the little trail.*—SCP:85 **[** < SE *master* with characteristic CarA Cr loss of final /-CC/. The form *mister* similarly reduced would have given the unacceptable 'Miss', hence the use of *master***]** **2.** [By extension] [*AF—Joc*] (In modern times, used as title of) any man who has or displays authority over others. *The world-wide depression of the 1930's left Montserrat truly depressed. All sorts of labour strifes in the Caribbean struck Montserrat also. This brought Marse B. Griffith right into the lime-light > –Labour Union president political aspirant.*—MtM (76.08.13, p.4) □ See also MASSA, and cp *OED* Mas 1., 2.

marse[2] **(mass)** *n* (ECar) See MAS.

Mar·ti·ni·quan (Mar·ti·ni·can) [martınıkʌn] *n, adj* (CarA) (A person or thing) belonging to or characteristic of the Fr island of Martinique. **a.** *Stern Warning For Martiniquan./Misbehaviour in a nightclub landed a young Martiniquan into a District 'A' Criminal Court last Thursday on two charges.*—Adv (93.04.11, p.5). **b.** *The overwhelming majority of Martinicans are descended from both slaves and slave-owners.*—FTT:52.

ma·ru *n* (Guyn, Trin) See MAARU·

ma·ru·di *n* (Guyn) A black-feathered, forest bird the size of a hen, with a red, featherless neck, red legs, and a brown beak; it eats fruit, lives much on the ground and is hunted for its flesh. **[** < *BAED* Arawak *marudi* 'large edible bush bird'**]**

Mar·y-Gold ['mıerı-guol] /ı'ı2/ *n* (Jmca) [*AF*] ‖ CARPET-DAISY (Bdos) □ See MARIGOLD.

Mar·y-Mag·da·lene *n* (Gren) ‖ CHRISTMAS-BUSH (CarA)

mas (mas', mask, masque, marse, mass) [ma·s] *n* (ECar) **1.** The festive merrymaking and street-parading of BANDS at CARNIVAL time, usu beginning with JOUVÉ. **a.** *We cannot get away from the fact that 'mas is mas' and a masquerader is usually identified by his disguise, etc.*—ToR (77.03.09, p.4) **b.** *When we look at mas' over the last few years in St Vincent, we will admit that there have been the inevitable army bands, sailor bands, Indians and cowboys, space men, hippies and 'funk' children, as well as historical portraits and fairy tale fantasies. / But there is a growing emphasis on the projection of distinctively Vinc-entian and West Indian elements.*—Isl 73/4, p.37 **c.** *Do you imagine just any idiot could have con-ceived the idea of confining mask to four streets so that when the inevitable fight broke, American tourists, ... would be within striking distance?*—MN (59.02.17, p.66) **[** < Early Fr *masque* 'masquerader', with loss of final /CC/ and shift of sense to 'masquerading,' thence extension to 'merrymaking'**]** □ The variant spellings *mas', mask, masque* attempt to recognize the etym, while *marse, mass* refl the widely developed folk pronunc. Note cits foll. However, *mas* is the form now most widely accepted and used. **2.** [By extension] The designed costumes of a participating group or BAND, or that of any single participant. **a.** *Carnival's basic structural unit is the Masque band. The word masque (mas') indicates that the bands wear costumes based on some theme in history, current events, films, books, imagination or a combination of these.*—Isl 73/4, p.5 **b.** *John had dressed in his usual Monday morning mas': stuffed brassieres, straw hat, bone holes of spectacles tied around his head, a red pair of cotton short pants, old shoes with stockings held up with fancy garters.*—JJM:44 **3.** (Trin) [By extension] A Car-nival BAND itself or any single player or par-ticipant. **a.** *And then, of course, a couple of sections with the sailors—men—in equally flamboyant at-tire. Plus a head-dress section. / With such a mas', Saldenah believes he has it made.*—ExP (73.01.06) **b.** *Just imagine a man who always playing so dignified and big-shot behaving like this in a Carnival grand-stand! and just because a mas threw his arms around the Madam. Then let the brute see who the mas is!*—AKM:72 **4.** [By ex-tension] ‖ *ole-mas* (ECar) Confusion; trouble; noisy disorder. **a.** *Next ting ah hear is 'pow' like ah hand pass, / An' is den de marse start, / Doris start to bawl like she see de devil.*—KTT:36 **b.** *The attempt by Babylon to sling I was a very desperate one and it was the signed affidavit of Camella that put the scare on them. They feared that should they play, 'mass' would follow. Only continued pressure on a world-wide basis ... shall force them to free I.*—CaC 76/5, p.1 **5.** PHRASES

5.1 make mas with (sb/sth) *vb phr* (Trin) To make (sb/sth) look stupid, silly, contemptible; [by extension] to play havoc with; to damage. **a.** *Dr Ram virtually 'make mas' with Stalin's 'Caribbean Man'. 'Sexist! Racist!' he shouted. Somehow I wondered why so much was read into the calypso.*—BoM (79.06.15, p.19) **b.** *Boy, A make mas wit[h] dat exam paper—everyt[h]ing A study was there.*—(Trin) **5.2 play mas** *vb phr* (ECar) ‖ *run mas* (Dmca) See PLAY Phr 9. **5.3 play mas and 'fraid powder** *vb phr* (Trin) See PLAY Phr 9.1

ma·sa(al)·la *n* (Guyn, Trin) See MASSALA

ma·sa·ku·ru·man (ma(s)·sa·cur·ra·man) *n* (Guyn) A legendary river monster resembling a giant, hairy male, reputed to be active at nights when it destroys boats and devours travellers esp near rapids. *The most widely known lore figures are Bakoo, Old Higue and Masacurraman. The last, a snake-haired, monstrous giant rises out of the water to devour his beholder. An Amerindian lore figure, he is also prominent in the Amerindian lore of French Guiana, where his victims are in-variably women who go down to the water alone.*—Kai.VIII, p.19 [Passed from Amerindian folklore into popular belief, prob helped by the number of boat disasters in the *Guyn* rapids, esp by night]

ma·san·to ['masanto] *n* (Gren) ‖ BOTTLE-FLAMBEAU (Trin, StVn) *We used to take a masanto to go hunting in the forest at night.*—SDP:42 [? From a family name]

mas camp *n phr* (Trin) ‖ *camp¹* (Trin) The temporary headquarters of a CARNIVAL BAND where costumes are designed and made. *To walk into his mas' camp is to walk into an example of the kind of organization required before a Carnival band hits the road. Work sheets are stuck up, files are in evidence, hats and standards hang overhead, and a shoemaker sits hunched among pairs of boots that threaten any minute to push him outside.*—TrC(U) 1974

mash¹ *vb tr* **1.** [X] [Of a vehicle, esp a car] To injure or destroy (sb/sth) by running over. **a.** *If they just miss mashing a pedestrian their first attitude is to curse hell out of that guy for having to walk on the same street that he is passing in his motor car.*—ViN (76.12.23, p.2) **b.** *'I gone, Rachael,' she said, almost with compassion. 'Walk good,' the old woman replied vacantly, 'don' mek cart mash yu.'*—PCOS:41 **c.** *Many mornings you see cats or dogs dead on the road that cars mashed.*—Bdos (Ms) **[** < SE *mash* 'crush'**] 2.** (CarA) [X] [Of a person] To step or tread on (sth, sb's foot, etc) accidentally. **a.** *Be careful! Don't mash the pieces of glass on the floor.*—(Trin) **b.** *About 2.40 p.m. the assaulted man was in a firm's security office, when Rodney went in front of him and mashed his toe. The assaulted man rebuked Rodney, and Rodney cuffed him on his lip.*—EvP (73.03.24, p.4) **3.** (Guyn) [F] [Rice Ind] To thresh (rice) by having bulls tread on the PADDY to separate the grain from the husks, hence the phr *mash rice.* **4.** PHRASES **4.1 like (sb) can't mash ants** *id phr* (CarA) As if too saintly or too cowardly to do anything harmful; having a false appearance of innocence. *See she goin[g] [a] long like she can['t] mash ants and she got two children from two men, you know.*—(Bdos) **4.2** [Motoring] **mash the brakes/clutch** *vb phr* (CarA) [*AF*] To step on the brakes/clutch of a car. **4.3** [Motoring] **mash the gas** *vb phr* (CarA) [*AF*] To accelerate; to step on the gas. **4.4 mash down (sth)** *vb phr* (CarA) [*IF*] [Esp of animals] To smash, bring to the ground, crush (sth). **a.** *The cows walk through my yard and mash down my crops.*—Bdos (B, Call-in programme) **b.** *If you see how Tarzan make de elephants mash down de trash huts and make de natives run.*—(Guyn) **4.5 mash up** *vb phr* (CarA) [*IF*] To destroy; to bring (sth such as an event or proceedings) to an abrupt, noisy end; to break up (sth) by dealing smashing blows. **a.** *There are some holes I know for years on certain roads in Trinidad, that if you don't drive slowly you will mash up your car. So keep up the good works.*—MoK (72.05.12, p.10) **b.** *You jump in me window / Mash up all me china / Man-o-war sailor.*—HVVIS:106 **c.** *Is that not the same Government whose Prime Minister is President for life of that union, who was only a few weeks ago trying to mash up other unions by poaching?*—Gren (Hd, 78/26, p.59)

mash² *imper vb* **1.** (Dmca, Gren, Trin) [Said to a dog] Go! *'Rover! Rover! come quick,' and he looked around more anxiously than ever, and was beginning to move to a position under where Jim was now standing. 'Mash! Mash!' cried Jim as he hopped to the ground and ran off. 'Hole him Rover! hole him!' he cried in vain.*—SDD:43 [< Fr *Marche!* 'Go! Walk!' via Fr Cr and, with /r/ -less Trin, pronunc, coinciding with CE MASH 'step', hence next phr] **2.** PHRASE **2.1 Mash dog!** *imper vb phr* (Gren, Trin) [*AF*—*Derog*] Out of my way!; Get out! *I ent take no notice of she, nuh. I know she ent have no refinement at all, an' I ent even tell she 'mash dorg.' Ah sittin' dong quiet and a singing meh hymns and straight so she take up a big stone an' shy it at meh.*—MN (57.10.26, p.2) □ A marked insult if addressed to a person instead of to a dog.

Mash³ *abbr n* (Guyn) [*IF*] MASHRAMANI celebrations. *Because Mash is a national event, efforts are being made to involve the public and private enterprises as much as possible.*—SuC (81.11.22, p.1)

mash⁴ *vb intr* (Guyn) [*IF*] To celebrate the national festival of MASHRAMANI esp by costumed parades, street-dancing, etc. *Perhaps it was the spirit of 1763 in the air last week, but I could not help but noting that in the midst of the feting and mashing, I found myself drawn more often than usual into the sound and fury of discussions on Socialism.*—GyC (77.03.27) [By functional n > vb shift of MASH³, and also infl by the sense of MASH¹ 2. i.e. 'to tread the streets']

mash(ed)-up *adj* (CarA) [*AF*] **1.** [Of things] Smashed; bent-up and/or damaged beyond use or repair; destroyed. **a.** *There was a crowd assembled around his covered body, a car in the drain and his mashed-up bicycle in the corner.*—Tbgo (Ms) **b.** *... but there is another 10 per cent composed of 'mentally-retarded, emotionally disturbed children. A lot of them in my school come from not simply broken-homes, but mash-up homes.*—ExP (79.07.15, p.14) **2.** [Of persons] Looking and feeling physically ill; having a prematurely aged body; worn out with age and cares. **a.** *Mr Ballantyne, who lives at 36 Hermitage Road, Belmont, said the flu attacked him on December 23, and his body felt 'mashed up' as though he had been battered by a karate expert.*—TrG (73.01.05) **b.** *Please run a photo of mash-up Mr Lawrence and let the people decide who is the leader and who is the nincompoop.*—AmA (81.01.23, p.2) [Pa. part. of vb phr MASH UP in adj function] □ Almost regularized by some speakers, as in cits, in the form MASH-UP.

mash·i·a·ted [mašietɪd] *adj* (Bdos, Guyn, StVn) [*AF*] Smashed; badly damaged; [by extension] sickly looking; poorly. **a.** *What happen to this hat? But it too mashiated to wear.*—(Guyn) **b.** *How in heavens must the thousands of poor people exist? Think of it, a common jack fish or mashiated doggers is for 50 cents and 30 cents per lb.*—ViN (73.08.10, p.4) [Blend of SE *emaciated* + CE MASHED(-UP)]

mash-mout[h] *adj, n* (CarA) [*AF*—*Derog*] (Having) a sunken mouth, with the front teeth missing.

mash-po·ta·to *n* (CarA) A dance in wh both feet are moved in a sideways manner, suggestive of crushing or mashing potatoes. *You did de twis' or de mash potata / At de big ball a Guvment House / On Prince Charles birt-night?*—DeM(SK) (62.11.17, p.9) □ The dance was most popular in the 1960s.

Mash·ra·ma·ni ['mašramani ~ 'mašrəmani] *n* (Guyn) A week of annual national festivities and celebrations surrounding Republic Day, February 23. [An adaptation of Arawak *masaramani* or *BAED mashiri-mehi* 'voluntary work done co-operatively' + *matriman* 'co-operative work followed by a spree' *EILCA:62.* The word was borrowed as an appropriate indigenous label for the National Day celebrations of the newly designated Co-operative Republic of Guyana in 1970]

mas·jid [masjɪd] *n* (Bdos, Guyn, Trin) A mosque; a place of Muslim congregational worship. *Haji Khan said that about 12 prominent Muslims from various parts of Guyana ... will be travelling to Essequibo for the important meeting, at the Anna Regina Masjid Compound. / Afterwards they will go on a tour of the district, visiting other Masjids with the aim of trying to improve the religious and social standards of the people.*—GyC (78.03.10, p.2) [Arabic *masjid* 'place of prayer']

mask *n* (ECar) See MASS

masman [ma·sma·n] *n* (Gren, StLu, StVn, Tbgo, Trin) **1.** A CARNIVAL masquerader. *Two masmen coming down the road, one in blue, one in green—who win? Comanche in red, Apache in blue—you could judge 'Indian'?—that is two different tribes. So who first and who second?* —Peo.I.10, p.29 **2.** [By extension] A leading person as creator, designer, and/or organizer of a BAND. *During the years 1950–1960 'Bottom Town' was at the top of the Carnival Chart—Thanks to names of Samo, Roy Austin, Zorro, Bertie Bramble and also skilful Individual Designers such as Vibert De Shong, Dogie Pitt and a few others. These Masmen have left the scene and with them their talents. Some have gone away, others have cleared the way for the Youths.*—ViN (73.02.03, p.2) □ Also occurs as two words, now often written as one.

ma·son-ma·ra·bun·ta [mesn marabʌnta] *n* (Guyn) ‖ *mud-dauber* (Guyn) ‖ *free mason* (Jmca) An inch-long wasp, yellow in colour with brown wings, wh builds separate little mud nests usu inside houses. [SE *mason* referring to its use of mud + MARABUNTA]

mas·que·rade ['maskʌre·d] /1'12/ *n* (Guyn) [*IF*] One of a small group of dancing street-masqueraders, either STILT-MAN, DONKEY-MAN or DEVIL. [*masquerader* poss by shift of sense from 'action' to 'actor', but more likely by characteristic CE loss of /-r/ in such words; cp DRAW(ER), RULE(R)]

mas·que·rade-band /1'121/ *n* (CarA) ‖ *san-tapee-band* (Guyn) ‖ *tuk-band* (Bdos) A folk band, consisting variously of one bass-drum, one KITTLE, flute, fife, iron-triangle, and rasp or rattle, going through the streets in festive seasons playing music with a rhythm dominated by drum beat; it is usu accompanied by one or more dancing masqueraders.

mass *n* (ECar) See MAS

mas·sa [ma·sa] *n* (CarA) **1.** [Hist] [*AF—Cr*] (In the slave era, required form of address by a slave or labourer to) a white planter or any white man of the ruling class; sir. *Is he your uncle or your cousin? / No, massa. / What then? / He and my father were shipmates, massa.*—RWIN:13 (M. Lewis) **2.** [By extension, in modern times] [*AF—Derog*] Any man who makes a show of his authority. **a.** *Massa day done! Yes, the day of the Massa of the slave whip and absentee plantation owner is done, but the day of our own power-hungry Massas still afflicts Westindians. / The struggle is not over. Massa gone, but Massa dey!*—ToR (77.02.13, p.4) **b.** *You cursed the white massa / You taught us to boo him—he fled / And now you black massa are trying to woo him / But you treat us much worse than he did.*—DeM(SK) (75.09.06, p.6) [< SE *master* by reduction of final /-CC/ and addition of epenthetic /-a/] □ See also MARSE (MASS).

mas·sa day *n phr* (CarA) [*AF—Derog*] The era of slavery; [by extension] the post-emancipation period of black subservience to white rule up to the beginning of the independence of Westindian states in the 1970s. **a.** *Massa day done. Sixteen years ago when Dr Eric Williams coined this phrase, he electrified Westindians.*—ToR (77.02.13, p.4) **b.** *Massa is not a racial term. Massa is the symbol of a bygone age. Massa Day is a social phenomenon. Massa Day Done connotes a political awakening and a social revolution.*—SCE:119 (E. Williams)

ma(s)·sa·cur·ra·man *n* (Guyn) See MASAKURUMAN.

ma(s)·sa·la (ma·sa(al)·la) [masa·la] *n* (Guyn, Trin) A mixture of spices (cumin, turmeric, parched coriander seeds, etc) wh are ground into a powder with or on a flat, round stone (called a *massala stone*) to make a very spicy curry base. *You have to cook like you never cook in you life before. The best things. Grind the massala yourself, don't buy curry powder from Tall Boy. Get achar, get dhal, and make dhal pourri.*—SABS:160 [Bhoj > Hin *masaalaa* 'spice']

mass·e·cuite [masɪkwit] *n* (Bdos, Guyn, Jmca, StKt) [Sugar Ind] A half-solid mixture of heavy molasses and developing sugar crystals obtained after three processes of evaporation or steam-boiling of cane-juice; it is fed into CENTRIFUGES to be separated, by high-speed rotation, into 'pure' sugar and molasses. *The molasses from the early high grade massecuites is recycled to maximise recovery of sugar until finally no further sugar can be economically crystalised from it.*—AdM (74.05.26, p.7) [< Fr *masse cuite* 'cooked mass', but note anglicized pronunc in CE]

mas·tic* *n* (Baha, Bdos, Belz, Gren, Trin) ‖ *acoma* (Gren, Trin) A tall, native forest tree about 50 to 80 ft high and 2 to 3 ft in diameter with small, yellow flowers growing in clusters, and bearing a pale-yellow, plum-like fruit; it yields a hard, heavy, durable yellow-brown timber wh is much prized for building and carved indoor work; infusion made from its bark is said to be a cure for syphilis; *Sideroxylon quadriloculare (Sapotaceae).* □ Sometimes confused with trees of the different *Mastichodendron spp* (See *PTT:282*). However *GLPFB:323* identifies this latter as the *Bdos* variety, though it is now extinct there.

ma·ta·bo·ro (ma·ta·boo·ro, ma·ta·bur·ro) [matabʌro ~ matabu**ro] *n* (Tbgo, Trin) ‖ BUCK-BANANA (Guyn) [Perh Sp *mata* 'plant' + *burro* 'donkey', a ref to the coarseness of the fruit]

ma·ta·pee (ma·ta·pi(e)) ['matapi] /1'12/ *n* (Guyn) ‖ *cassava-squeezer* (CarA) ‖ *cutacoo* 2. (Jmca) ‖ *sebucan* (Trin) ‖ *koulèv* (Dmca) ‖ *wowla* (Belz) An elongated, basket-work cylinder used for squeezing the juice from grated cassava thereby expelling the poison. *The cassava, which slips as pulp from the scraper into the* *trough, is collected and put into a long wicker-woven matapie, which hangs from the roof. The matapie or cassava-squeezer ... is a cylinder, seven or eight feet long and five or six inches in diameter, made of closely woven strips of pliant bark. The upper end is open, and has a loop by which the matapie may be suspended from one of the beams of the house; the lower end is closed, but it also has a loop.*—IAIG:260–261. [< *BDFC* Carib *matabi* (female word for) 'presse à farine' or cassava squeezer. See *IAIG:260, 261* for a description of the use of the *matapie* by women of the 'True Caribs']

match·wood* *n* (Gren, Guyn, Trin) A large native tree wh can grow over 100 ft high, and wh bears numerous small flowers; it produces off-white, soft, non-durable wood wh splits easily and is used mainly for making match-sticks (hence the name); it is also suitable for making drums, canoes and plywood; *Didymopanax morototoni* (*Araliaceae*).

mat-grass *n* (Nevs) ‖ VETIVER (Dmca, etc)

ma·tou·tou [matutu] *n* (StLu) ‖ DONKEY-SPIDER (StKt)

mat·tee (ma(t)·ti(e), mat·ty) [mati] *n* (Guyn) [*AF*] **1.** A close friend; [by extension] another person of the same race, or nation. **a.** *'After all we is mattie' he said 'we must help mattie, so I goin' bring you some sugar and flour.'*—Guyn (Ms) **b.** *I know they got people in this country, in this yard, who live by sucking other people blood, who never put their hand in their pocket except to pull a knife or a gun 'pon their own mattee Guyanese.*—HMCH:117 [< Du *maatje* 'mate'. Note: 'Items such as /mati/ 'a close friend' have been assumed to be phonetic variants of English *mate*. The form, however, follows a regular sound change evidenced in Berbice Dutch in which the Standard Dutch suffix–*tje* becomes /ti/. The Guyanese item is therefore more likely to have been of Dutch origin, *maatje* being the etymon'—(*Carib No.3, 1983, p.13, I.E. Robertson*)] □ In this usage there is no pl form. **2.** (Bdos) [By extension; of females only] Very close friends, perh lesbians. *De two o' dem is matties. Wherever one go you can look for de next one.*—EFLBB:2 □ In this sense the pl form is normal. It is poss the usage came orig from *Guyn*.

mat·ter¹ [mata] *n* PHRASE **matter fix(ed)** *id phr* (Gren, Guyn, StLu, Trin) The problem is solved; that is that. *I would suggest for example that the Ministry of Finance can simply hand over the Ministry to his Excellency the Governor, as we had it in the past, and matter fixed!*—VoS (73.04.07, p.2)

matter² *n* (Jmca) [*IF*] ‖ YAMPI² (Antg, etc)

ma·twi·té (ma·tu·i·té, ma·tu·ri·té) ['matwite] *adj* (Dmca, StLu) [Of fruit] Mature; full. *If the fruit are matwité (full) they will be sweet, so*

mango-cabane (or mango-fèné) is sweeter than when ripened on the tree.—Dmca (Ms)

mau·by (mau·bie) [mɒ·bi] *n* (CarA) **1. (i)** The bitter-tasting bark of the tree *Colubrina arborescens* (*Rhamnaceae*) usu called **mauby-bark. (ii)** A refreshing bitter-sweet, non-alcholic, folk drink made by fermenting or boiling the bark of the **mauby tree**; when unsweetened it is used medicinally to treat diabetes and stomach ailments. [Cp *BDFC:281* Carib *mabi* 'potato whose root is good to eat' + a juice called *mabi-miti*. HNHB (1750) p. 34 notes 'a strong punch' named *mobby*, fermented from 'pounded potatoes, sugar and molasses'. The transfer of the name to a drink made from a fermented bark and thence to the tree itself could have been a later folk adaptation in the slave era] **2.** PHRASE **2.1 have (a) champagne taste with/on (a) mauby pocket** *id phr* (CarA) [*AF—Joc*] To live or attempt to live in grand, showy style while having means that are far too humble to maintain such a style. *For among the unspoken reasons for the failure of many black businessmen are a reluctance to engage in honest hard work and insistence on a lifestyle that illustrates the folly of having a 'champagne taste on a mauby pocket'.*—NaT (76.06.27, p.12) [Both champagne and mauby are gold-coloured liquids with bubbles. The phr contrasts the costliness of the former with the folk economy of the latter]

mau·ger¹ (ma(a)·ga, mau·ga, mau·gre, maw·gre) [mɒ·gʌ~ma·ga] *adj* (CarA) [*AF—Joc*] [Of persons or animals] Thin; skinny; bony and hungry-looking. **a.** *Never mind it lookin' maga. / Dis hand could pelt cutlass / Like Sampson pelt de ass jaw.*—KTT:9 **b.** *Mauger dog never pass ole bone.*—Jmca (Prov) [< Du *mager* 'meagre, lean', with [a > ɒ] vowel closure by false refinement] □ The spelling *mauger* seems to be preferred in non-dial contexts.

mau·ger² (maa·ga, etc)² your·self *vb refl* (Belz) [*AF*] To become thin; to make yourself look sickly. *If some young girl want to make a fool of herself with my husband, why I should panic and mauga myself with worries?*—HF:14 [By functional n > vb shift of MAUGER¹]

mau·ger-yow [mɒ·gʌ-yɒu] *n* (Guyn) [*AF—Joc*] ‖ BACK-AND-BELLY (Guyn)

maul·sprig ['mɒ·lsprig] *vb tr* (Bdos) ‖ CAT-SPRADDLE **2.** (Bdos, Trin) *'What happen? You want to mash up a good fight?' Doris ask from out of the crowd. / 'Out o' the way,'less you want a maulsprigging too,' Jasper say.*—CISH:11

mau·ly (mol·ly) [mɒ·li~mɒli] *n* (Bdos, Guyn) ‖ MAALI (Guyn) A woman's hair rolled and coiled in the shape of a bun at the back of the head. [A false refinement, with [a· > ɒ] vowel closure of the orig Indic MAALI, wh must have spread from Guyn and, in Bdos, been changed by folk etym]

mau·vais-langue [move laŋ] *n, adj, vb* (StLu, Trin) See MOVÉ LANG

ma·vi·sou *n* (Dmca) ‖SAGE-BUSH (CarA) 2.

maw·gre *adj, vb* (CarA) See MAUGER[1].

ma·wi-so·sé (Marie-su.cer) ['mawisose] *n* (StLu) ‖POND-FLY (Bdos, Guyn) [Fr Cr *mawi* + *sosé* (< Fr *Marie* + *sucer*) 'Mary sucks' from the insect's sucking posture when it alights on still water. Cp also ‖*susé-glo* (Dmca)]

ma·wi·yann (ma·ri·anne) *n* (Dmca, StLu) ‖BIG-EYE[3] 2. (ECar)

max·i-tax·i *n* (Bdos, Trin) ‖*pick-up* 1. (Bdos) A small passenger-carrier that can seat about 20 persons; it is privately owned and used as a bus plying a fixed route for a fixed fare. [A blend < *maxi(mum)* + *taxi*] □ Cp MINI-BUS.

Max·well pond *n phr* (Bdos) *PHRASE* **labour/ money gone in Maxwell Pond** *id phr* (Bdos) [*AF—Joc*] Effort or money has been lost, wasted in some unfortunate investment. *I bring you up in the fear o' God and the love o' your fellow-men. An' if after all that you come to tell me that you goin' to Trinidad to jump all 'bout the road like a lunatic, well I tell you I now see where all my time an' money gone, in Maxwell pond.*—LICMS:303 [The phr is historically associated with the former Maxwell (Sugar) Estate in the PARISH of Christ Church in So. Bdos, though no pond or incident has been identified]

Ma·ya (In·di·an); **Ma.yan** *adj, n* (Belz) (Of or belonging to) a Central American ethnic group, survivors of a highly developed pre-Columbian civilization of wh monumental remainders are extant partly in Belize, where three ethnic subgroups still exist—KEKCHI, MOPAN(ERO), YUCATECAN—in southern, middle and northern Belize. *Apart from milpa cultivation the Maya practised other means of agriculture. One was the cultivation of tree crops such as cocoa, breadnut, and avocado.*—PAIB:6

ma·yal; **ma.yal.ism** *n* (Jmca) See MYAL, MAYALISM

May cow *n phr* (CayI) ‖ROLLING CALF (Belz, etc)

may-may-lip·py [memelɪpi ~ mɛmɛlɪpi] / ı'ı22/ *adj* (Antg) [*AF—Derog*] Offensively inquisitive and given to gossip.

May-plum *n* (Belz) ‖JAMAICA-PLUM (Bdos, etc) [Prob due to season wh is usu April to June]

may·pole (male-pole) *n* (Bdos) ‖AGAVE (CarA) [From the resemblance of the tall, sturdy efflorescence to a maypole. The phallic symbolism of the same may account for the erron alternative name by folk etym]

maze·ness [meznɪs] *n* (Angu, Nevs) [*IF*] ‖SWINGING IN THE HEAD (Baha, etc) See HEAD Phr 4.18 *When A stoop do[w]ng A get a mazeness in me head.*—(Angu) [*EDD mazed* (var dials of Sc & Eng) 2. 'dizzy, giddy, confused in the head'. Hence *mazedness*]

MDCs [ɛmdisi·z] *abbr* (CarA) ‖*Big Four* (CarA) More Developed Countries, i.e. that group of orig CARICOM member-states comprising Barbados, Guyana, Jamaica, and Trinidad-and-Tobago, wh have greater populations and economic development than the other eight of the original twelve. □ Cp LDCs.

me [mi ~ mı] *pron*, 1st *pers sg* (CarA) [*AF—Cr*] [Used or occurring frequently in speech in other functions than as obj of a vb or prep] 1. [*X*] [As nominative, esp before *ain't, don't*; also often first item in a subj phr in both speech and writing; sometimes freely varying with folk form A or SE *I* in the same utterance] I. **a.** *Well, me ain't believe in all this do-good foolishness. It don't work out.*—HFGA:58 (D.S. Joseph) **b.** *You never hear that story yet? Well, me don't know where you been.*—StA(JA) (73.02.10, p.14) **c.** *The defendant, 25-year-old Bertram P. ... pleaded not guilty to the battery charge. / ... 'Me and she is friends,' he said.*—DeM(SK) (63.11.09, p.10) **d.** *Christine, me and my boyfriend are to move in a house with his three children but I am afraid.*—PeL (78.08.04, p.6, Dear Christine) **e.** *Well, to tell you the truth, for all the noise ah does make, me don't like that kinder talk. Searching passenger! That is police work. So I tell him lewwe go to the police station and report the whole thing.*—HFGA: 60 (D.S. Joseph) [< SE *me*, prob reinforced by phonic and functional coincidence of 1st pers sg forms of a number of W Afr langs. Exs Twi *me* 'I, me, my', Gã-Adangme *mi* 'I, me, my', Igbo *m'* 'I, me, my', Efik *ami, mi* 'I, me, my', etc. The same would affect sense 2. foll] 2. [*X*] Also **meh, muh** [As possessive] My. **a.** *Me father dead with a spirit, and a sookooyant used to suck me sister till she come thin like a matchstick.*—HFGA:58 (D.S. Joseph) **b.** *Ah coulda hardly open meh sleepy, nampy eyes when ah hear dis cause ah was sleepin so hard when meh brodder come runnin in meh room.*—Aaw.I.2, p.23 3. *PHRASES* **3.1 me and you/he, etc** *id phr* (CarA) [*AF*] [Issuing a threat] You/he (etc) and I will have it out; there will be a serious row between us. **a.** *Incidentally, if you give Sir Garfield Sobers any more cheek, it will be me and you, understand?* —BoM (76.01.01, p.24) **b.** *Mum say, 'Me and her today. Mek she come out yah today come lick yuh.' She start shout again.... 'St James whoring gal. Come out yah!'*—SSLG:34 [A prob calque from W Afr langs. Cp Yoruba *emi pelu ẹ l'oni* 'I and you today', a threat] **3.2 (Oh) Me arm!** *excl* (StKt) See ARM Phr 3 **3.3 me one and God** *pron phr* (Guyn) [*AF*] Just me, utterly alone. *For two whole days and a night I lie down in dis house sick, sick wit[h] not a soul to call. Me one and God.*—(Guyn)

mean vb PHRASES **1. How you mean?** id phr
(ECar) [IF] (i) See HOW¹ Phr 3. *She blinked. 'I
don't see what you could do that's better than the
movies.' / 'How you mean? You think people din
make sport before there was movie?'*—MBGB:13
(ii) excl (ECar) [IF] [With sharp falling pitch,
answering a question that is considered su-
perfluous] *But of course (not)!; Certainly (not)!*
a. *S1: So you enjoyed the wedding, then? / S2:
How you mean?*—(Bdos) **b.** *S1: He actually asked
to borrow fifty dollars? You didn't lend him, did
you? / S2: How you mean?*—(Tbgo) **2. I/you
mean to say** id phr (CarA) [IF] [Introducing
or tagging a statement of disgust or surprise] **a.**
You mean to say you haven't left yet?—(Trin) **b.**
*But child look at the state of this room. I mean to
say!*—(Bdos) [Reduced fr SE 'Do you mean to
say ... ' though this prob occurs much less
frequently than the CE form]

meat n (Bdos) **1.** Fodder (grass, vines, cane
stocks, etc) for livestock or horses. [A prob
survival of dial E. Cp EDD *meat* sb 2. 'food for
animals or birds, provender for horses or cattle;
chaff, hay'] **2.** PHRASE **2.1 pick meat for dead
goats** vb phr (Bdos) [AF—*Joc*] To waste time
pursuing a lost cause. *Michael buyin[g] presents
for Sandra and carryin[g] she to theatre, but she
got a steady man a[l]ready, so Michael only pick-
in[g] meat for dead goats.*—(Bdos)

meat·kind n (CarA) Any meat as opposed to
vegetables or fish. Cp BREADKIND, SALT·KIND. **a.**
*Much of the meatkind was exposed to dust and
flies. / The drive, which is continuing, will be spread
out throughout the Corporate Area and will include
other food vendors whom the inspectors consider
unfit sellers.*—WeS (74.04.19, p.1) **b.** *When it
is lunch time we get a couple pancakes or some
'fry-dumpling' and nothing to drink. Then later in
the afternoon we get oats pap or cornmeal pap
again and nothing to drink. That is all until next
morning. No vegetables, no good meatkind.*—Antg
(Ms, 1975)

mee·rese n (StLu) See MIWIZ

meet vb (CarA) [IF] **1.** To come upon (a situation, a thing, or person in a certain state or
condition). **a.** *Having dug out the earth, I met a
body which was that of a brown-skinned person,
wearing green trousers.*—AMAM:52 **b.** *When we
finally got in our house, we met a lot of neighbours
in the house. They had come to stay with my
mother.*—AawI.1, p.8 **c.** *I born and meet the track
there.*—Tbgo (CR, 1976) [A prob calque from
W Afr langs reinforced by shift in usage of SE
meet. Cp for ex ADMY Yoruba *ba* 'to meet, to
find', the two senses coinciding in the same
word in certain contexts hence producing such
sentences as *mo baa ni leere* 'I met/found him to
be at home', *mo ba omonge naa ni le* 'I found/
met this girl to be virgin', etc. Note also dial E
EDD *meet* vb 3. 'to meet with, light upon, find'
+ cit from Pem 'I met a scissors underneath
the table'; also OED *meet* 5. (rare or poetic)
'to encounter, experience (a certain fortune ...

treatment of a certain kind', now superseded by
meet with. However note New Eng Bible (1961)
Luke VII.12, 'As he approached the gate of the
town he met a funeral', a usage shifted from
OED *meet* 5. and much like CE] **2.** [AF] To
reach; to arrive (at). **a.** *When he meet where I
suppose to drop off, he kept on driving.*—Tbgo
(CR, 1982) **b.** *When I meet home, my mother
asked me where were you so long girl.*—Bdos (Ms)
c. *The car came to sudden stop shattering Boysie's
dreams. 'We meet' the driver said.*—Guyn (Ms,
1971) [A shift of sense 1. Cp EDD *meet* vb 3.,
cit from Yks 'Shall I meet a village before I get
to Aireton?'] □ Similarly Phr 5.2. **3.** (CarA) [AF]
To happen to (sb); to befall (sb). **a.** *I did not tell
her she is a wicked woman. What meet her is she
look for that.*—Tbgo (CR, 1975) **b.** *Me seh wa
dis meet me boy tonight.*—AGM:94 [The same
function as senses 1., 2., but with an abstract
subj, and reversal of animateness to obj of the
vb] **4.** (Guyn) [AF] [Of money] To be sufficient
(for a particular need); to amount to what is
required. *He always drunk an[d] she always dress
up, that's why wid all de big pay, the money
can't meet.*—(Guyn) **5.** PHRASES **5.1 eye(s) don't
meet** id phr (Guyn) [AF] (Be) not on speaking
terms; (be) estranged. *Well since they had the
court case their eyes don['t] meet, so she moved out
from next door.*—(Guyn) □ Cp Phr 5.5. **5.2 meet
at (a place); meet (down) to (a place)** vb phr
(CarA) [AF] To get to, reach, arrive at (a place).
a. *When I meet at Dukwari the next day I started
to make baskets at Oliver's shop. I always make
baskets when I am out at Dukwari landing.*—DaC
(52.05.07, p.5) **b.** *A tell yo[u] de fader meet do[w]
ng to de police station in quick time.*—(Guyn) [=
sense 2., with adv extension by infl of SE phrs
arrive at, get down to (a place)] **5.3 meet bad/
good** vb phr (CarA) [AF] To meet with due
retribution/reward. **a.** *But she mus[t] meet bad
yes, after she take all the man money and then
treat him so awful till he dead.*—(Bdos) **b.** *Thank
you, me boy. God bless you for all you do for me.
You goin[g] to meet good, I know.*—(Guyn) **5.4
meet it hard** vb phr (Bdos, Tbgo, Trin) To find
things difficult; to suffer difficulties, misfortune
(in life). *When you black, you born to meet it hard,
mi baby boy, but you daddy always saying that
you strong.*—Tbgo (Ms, Play) **5.5 meet under
four eyes** vb phr (StVn) [IF] ‖ EYES MAKE FOUR
(CarA) See EYE Phr 14. **5.6 meet up** vb phr
(CarA) [AF] (i) To meet face to face. *When
we meet up I'll tell her just what I think about
her.*—Guyn (Ms, 1980) (ii) To catch up. *I
stopped the car and waited for them to meet up
with me.*—(Tbgo) (iii) To come up to standard;
to meet requirements. *You are not practisin[g]
and if you don['t] meet up I am no[t] lettin[g] you
enter for the Music Festival.*—(Guyn) **5.7 mouth
meet** vb phr (Tbgo) [AF] To have a vulgar row.
*When the two them fall out and their mouth meet
the whole neighbourhood does look to see if they
goin[g] fight.*—(Tbgo) **5.8 your time meet** id
phr (Guyn) [AF] You are getting your just deserts; the time for retribution has come. *I[t']s
good so. Their time now meet for all the bad things
they been doing.*—(Guyn)

meet·ing n (Bdos) ‖SUSU (ECar) *The woman was raising a great outcry, telling the whole street that her neighbour had stolen all the money she had received from the meeting that Saturday.*— (Bdos) **2.** PHRASE **2.1 belong to ...; keep a meeting** vb phrs (Bdos) To participate in ...; to organize a SUSU savings scheme.

meet·ing-turn n (Bdos) ‖SUSU-HAND (ECar) *The other reason is that black people in Barbados and Barbadians in general are not used to stocks and shares and investments. If you bring it down to a meeting-turn and a man can draw every twelfth week, then that is our level.*—Bdos (Hd, 79.07.22, p.5253)

me·gasse n (Bdos, Guyn, StKt, USVI) [Sugar Ind] See MAGAS(SE), BAGASSE

me·gasse-dust n (Bdos) [Sugar Ind] ‖B-AGASSE-DUST (CarA) *We have to look carefully not only at the health of workers exposed to these hazards, but also sometimes at workers in the sugar cane industry who may be exposed to megasse dust giving rise to lesions in their lungs.*—Bdos (Hd, 73.03.20, p.2103)

me·gasse-house n (Bdos) [Sugar Ind] ‖B-AGASSE-HOUSE (StKt) *It is really good for nothing in a wet crop season: therefore, I strongly recommend a megasse-house to be built capable of containing fuel sufficient for five hogsheads of sugar; a precaution absolutely necessary in Barbados.*—RHBP:135

meh [mɛ] pron (CarA) [AF-Cr] See ME. 2 □ A dial spelling.

mek (meck) vb (CarA) [AF—Cr] Make. (See □ Note). **a.** *Everything what scarce back a town plentiful dis side so when I go home I mek sure I ker for my little ones.*—HF:15 **b.** *Blackpudding and souse was filling the atmosphere with the scent, hot and sweet, and mekking everybody belly growl.*—CISH:16 **c.** *From de start a yuh duration / Meck we frighten an frustrate / A no tief meck yuh departed / A no lie meck yuh departed / But a Fearful meck we Careful.*—FCV2:85 (L. Bennett: 'Federation') [A prob survival in CE of E dial pronunc and spelling. Cp EDD make vb¹ (Sc, Irel, Eng and Colon) 1. Present Tense (13) meck (N.I., Cum) (16) mek (Cum, Not, War, Shr) 'Mek 'er a coop o' tay', etc] □ 1. A dial spelling much used in narrative dialogue. See MAKE and cp similarly KETCH, TEK. 2. For Phrs **da mek, wa mek**, wh occur commonly in these forms in some territories, see MAKE vb 2.

mè·lé (mê·lée, me·lee) [mɛle·] n (Antg, Nevs, Trin, ViIs) Gossip; rumour; scandal. **a.** *Come le[t] me gi[ve] you dis hot piece o[f] melee / I jus[t] get [a]bout Dora.*—(Nevs) **b.** *An we talk, talk, talk, / Like ah was gone a whole week / Bout de melee on de street / And ah relate bout de hard life in town.*—ViP.1.1 [Fr Cr < Fr mêlée 'battle, fray'] **2.** PHRASE **2.1 pound mèlé** vb phr (Antg, BrVi, StVn) [AF] See POUND Phr 3.2

me·lon cac·tus n phr (Trin) ‖TURK'S CAP CACTUS (CarA)

me·lon·gene ['mɛlʌnjɛn] (Dmca, StLu, Trin) **(me·lon·gae, me·lon·ger)** ['mɛlʌnjɛ] n (BrVi, StKt) ‖EGGPLANT (CarA) **a.** *The main vegetable in a ratatouille is what we call melongene and the Europeans, aubergine or egg-plant.*—Peo 3.22, p.57 **b.** *Melongene is now probably at a record price for the year—6 cents on average, and even so, they are very fresh looking and shining.*—ExP (71.12.31, p.3) **c.** *Melongenes, plentiful in supply and most reasonable in price, will be the base for all this week's recipes. This vegetable is as old as history itself. I understand that the 'Ancients' called it mad apple because they thought it was poisonous.*—ExP (72.11.30, p.10) [Adaptation from botanical name (Solanum) melongena, wh < Ital melanzana < Lat mela insana 'mad apple', this being one alternative name listed as Antillean in APPJ:33 but not found in current CE. See also BALANJAY, and an elaborate etym note at OED brinjal] □ Often used as a collectivized sg, esp in speech. Note cit b.

me·now-weed n (Jmca) ‖MINNIE-ROOT (CarA) [See etym note at MINNIE-ROOT]

men·to n (Jmca) A type of rural folk-music with a marked rhythm that stimulates hip-swinging dancing; it is accompanied by a song in wh one or two short, spicy verses related to some event are continually repeated; its music is now kept alive mostly by organized competitions. *Thus, too, the Jamaican Mento held the popular scene for over 300 years although I suspect that it was originally an adaptation of the Cuban rumba. As Mapletoft Poulle of Jamaica points out, the Mento has words which portray a story typical to the location, people or events that occur in the country. This music pattern is so physiologically Jamaican that I am yet to hear a genuine Mento beat outside of Jamaica or without a Jamaican drummer on the skins.*—Her I.5 (1976) p.39 [Prob of Afr orig via Cuban Sp. The dance is believed to have been brought to Jmca from Cuba] □ Hence compounds **mento-band/-beat/-music**, etc. Cp CALYPSO.

mé·pwi (mé·pris, mé·puis) ['mepwi ~ 'mepri] n [AF] **1.** (Dmca, StLu, Tbgo, Trin) ‖BUSING (ECar) **2.** (StLu) Aggressive and slanderous gossip; BAD-TALK that is openly meant to cause (sb) harm. *With a fast tongue and a loose waist Laurence Laurent commanded the stage switching her tone from teasing 'picong' to aggressive 'mepris'.*—VoS (68.07.27, p.2) [Fr Cr < Fr mépris, 'contempt', esp as in the phr des termes de mépris 'insults'] **3.** PHRASE **3.1 give (sb) mépwi** vb phr (Dmca) To be verbally abusive or insulting to (sb). *For the amount of mépwi the servant gave them, everybody knew their business.*—Dmca (Ms) □ See also **air your mouth**, AIR² Phr 2.2, BUSE.

me·ras·me/-mi n (Trin) See MARASMA

me·ras·mic *adj* (Trin) [*IF*] Thin; looking emaciated or sickly. *Really taken aback I enquired if that was the way to speak to anyone and the next thing I knew was that this merasmic fellow let fly a chook at my chest sending me reeling out of the doorway.*—BoM (74.08.23, p.24) [< MERASME + SE adj suff -*ic*, or variant of SE *marasmic*]

me·ren·gue (ma·ren·ga, ma·rin·ga) [mɛr ɛŋgɛ ~ marɛŋga ~ mariŋga] *n* (CarA) A dance with lively, rhythmic, body movements. **a.** *I was with a group, then started my own—Johnney's Dance Group. We performed limbo, shango, merengue and the African 'nation dance' at hotels. I always designed the costumes myself.*—IsL 73.10, p.15 **b.** *A truckload of Haitians pulls up. It is bringing off tangy merengue music enjoyed by the most spirited supporters I've seen in a Carnival band.*—TrG (74.09.17, p.4) [PtRi Sp name of a popular dance. See *SDGA*] □ The forms **ma-renga / maringa** occur in *Guyn* perh via dial Pg or *Venz* Sp. **2.** PHRASE **2.1 dance merengue/ marenga** *vb phr* (Guyn) [*AF—Joc*] To writhe in pain. *Mammy took up old higue skin / and pound it in the mortar / with pepper and vinegar / ... / she danced merengue when the pepper / burn up her skin.*—CSP:7

me·ri·no [mɛrino] /12′1/ *n* (CarA) ‖ *marina, merina* (Angu, Belz, Dmca, StVn) ‖ *mariner* (CayI) ‖ *singlet* (Guyn) ‖ *vest* (Antg, Bdos, Guyn) A man's white, low-necked, sleeveless, undershirt (formerly made of merino wool and cotton, hence orig name). *You know the fellow, sir: always in old canvas shoes, black pants and merino. Never wears a shirt.*—TRIH:174 [Prob a survival from the colonial era. Note *OED merino* 3. 'a fine woollen yarn used in the manufacture of hosiery' + cit 1888 (Indian Outfits) '... gauze-merino vests are principally worn']

merle [mɛ·l] *n* (Gren, Trin) ‖ BLACKBIRD 1.1 (CarA) [Fr *merle* 'blackbird']

merle-cor·beau [′mɛ·l-kobo] *n* (Trin) ‖ J-UMBIE-BIRD 3. (Guyn) [Fr *merle* 'blackbird' + *corbeau* 'crow', a characteristic Cr descriptive reduplication, with Fr Cr pronunc]

mer·mos·si *n* (Bdos) See MIAMOSSI

me·self (mer·self, muh·self) [mɪsɛlf ~ mʌsɛlf] *refl pron, 1st pers sg* (CarA) [*AF—Cr*] Myself. **a.** *'But look how Ah take up meself and leave Sweet-man life in town ...' [said J. Martin].*—SABS:18 **b.** *I say ter mersef, 'Man you dus skylark, but ef I bus yer up, yer ger fall heavy.'*—JBJ:81 [Cp *EDD myself* pron ... Also in form *meself* (Irel)] □ A dial spelling much used in narrative dialogue.

Mè·sè Ma·rie *n phr* (Dmca) See MÈZÈ MAWI

mesh-wire *n* (Bdos) ‖ WIRE-MESH (Guyn) *Government has deemed recent complaints over the position of a mesh-wire fence at the Hilton Hotel car park as being 'reasonable' and decided that the*

situation should be remedied as soon as possible.—AdV (88.03.30, p.1)

mes·ple (mes·pel) [′mɛspl] *n* (ViIs) ‖ s-APODILLA (CarA) [< Du *mispel* 'medlar' (*Mespilus germanica*), a Eurasian fruit resembling the SAPODILLA in appearance and use]

mes·quit tree [′mɛskɪt tri] *n phr* (Trin) ‖ CASHA 1.(ii) (Nevs, etc) [AmE loan, *mesquite* < Mexican Sp *mezquite*, name of same tree (*NPHT:39*)]

mes·sage *n* **1.** (Bdos) A telephone call (as made to sb). (See Phrs 3.1, 3.2). **2.** (ECar) Groceries. **a.** *Hurry up, man. Look other people in the shop who want message.*—SABS:163 **b.** *Yesterday grandma asked us to collect the message from the shop for her. But the box was so big and heavy we had to use the car.*—(Trin) **3.** PHRASES **3.1 ask for /ask to get a phone message** *vb phr* (Bdos) [*IF*] (To /ask) to be allowed to use a (neighbour's) telephone. *I only had the phone number, but I couldn't find the place and I had to stop at a house and ask for a phone message. I was a little embarrassed because I was a perfect stranger asking to get a phone message.*—(Bdos) **3.2 give a phone message** *vb phr* (Bdos) [*IF*] To give permission to use a telephone. *Old Woman: 'Mistress, could you give me a phone message? I have to call the doctor.'*—Bdos (Ms Play, 1979) **3.3 make (a) message** *vb phr* (Gren, Mrat, StKt, StVn, Trin) To buy sth at a shop. *Take this list and when you go to town make this message for me.*—(Mrat) [See *COD8 message* n 4. (in pl) Sc, N. Eng 'things bought; shopping'. See also *CSD message* 2. ... *mak or ma(a) message* 'carry out an errand']

me·ta·gee [′mɛtaji]; **me·te(m)** [′mɛtɛ(m)]; **me.tem.gee** [′mɛtɛmji] *n* (Guyn) ‖ SANCOCHE (Trin) *Metagee used to be a favourite Guyanese poor-man's weekend meal.*—Guyn (Ms, 1978) [Cp *DAFL* Twi *metem* 'plantains' or 'bananas' + *gye* (*DAFL*, sense 41.) 'to delight' (be a pleasure). Thus ‖ *metemgee*, the oldest Guyn form of the word would have been = 'the plantains make it good'. In fact the grey colouring of the boiled plantain ingredient is essential to *me-tagee/mete(mgee)*] □ *Mete(m)* is a popular abbr form.

met·al-grade baux·ite *n phr* (Guyn, Jmca) Bauxite of a lower quality (than CALCINED BAUX-ITE), produced by heating ore with a high iron content in shorter rotating kilns to provide the material from wh commercial aluminium is smelted.

me·te (me·tay); **me.tay-me.tay** [mɛte(-mɛte)] *adj* (ViIS) [*AF*] Meddlesome; over-inquisitive; interfering. *'Why you so metay-metay', she said 'mind your own business, no!'*—BrVi (Ms) [< Sp *meterse en* 'to meddle, interfere in'. Prob a loan from PtRi]

me·thai *n* (Guyn, Trin) See MITHAI.

Mex·i·can pop·py *n phr* (Jmca, Trin) ‖ THIS-TLE (StKt, ViIs)

mè·zè-ma·wi (Mè·sè Ma·rie) [mɛzɛ mawi] *n* (Dmca) ‖ SENSITIVE PLANT (Bdos, etc) [Fr Cr < manzè mawi (*Mademoiselle Marie*) 'Respected Miss Mary', prob being a *Joc* ref to its 'properness', recoiling when touched. Cp ‖ *timawi*, ‖ *shame-lady* wh are similarly suggestive]

mi·a·mol ['mayamɒl] *n* (Guyn, Trin) ‖ WILD COFFEE 1. (Guyn) *Miamol seed you roast it and grind it like coffee—is a kin[d] o[f] coffee really—and you can drink it fo[r] yo[ur] kidneys, and miamol leaf you boil for sores too.—*(Guyn)

mi·a·mos·si [maɪamɒsi] (mer·mos·si, mis-·si·mos·si) *n* (Bdos) ‖ WILD-TAMARIND 1. (Belz, etc) [Prob a corruption of the botanical name of the family *Mimosae*, to wh it belongs]

mice; **mi.cey** [maɪs(i)] *n* (Bdos, Guyn, Jmca) [X] A mouse. [Prob from greater frequency of pl form in development of CE. Cp TEETH, ASHES, etc]

mi·cy-bat /1′12/ [maɪsi bat] *n* (Antg) ‖ BAT[1] 2. (Guyn)

mid·dle-walk *n* (Guyn) **1.** ‖ *high-dam*, *middlewalk dam* (Guyn) The wide roadway or DAM built down the middle of a sugar-estate (hence the name) connecting its front lands and the PUBLIC ROAD with its back lands and BACK-DAM, hence often called *middlewalk dam*, *middlewalk road*. **2.** ‖ *middlewalk canal /trench* (Guyn) The central irrigation CANAL of a sugar-plantation, dug down its middle, the excavated soil from wh is thrown up to build the adjacent MIDDLEWALK DAM. *A delegation from the Nos.57–66 Village District is to meet the Minister of Works and Hydraulics, Mr Mohamed Kasim, with a view to expedite the granting of a $10,000 loan for the digging of a side-line and a middle-walk at No.66 Village.*—Berbice Times (65.06.20, p.5) □ *Middle-walk* is loosely used to refer either to the waterway or the roadway according to context. Cp SIDELINE.

mid·night-rob·ber *n* (Trin) ‖ *robber* (Trin) A CARNIVAL masquerader whose costume is an ornate, broad-brimmed hat, a masked face and a whistle, a tunic marked with a skull and cross-bones, long, baggy, cowboy-like trousers, and a cape; he carries a mock-gun and dagger and sometimes a bag into wh his trapped listener is cautioned to put money while he recites ROBBER-TALK.

mile-tree *n* (Bdos) ‖ CASUARINA (CarA) *They cut off a few branches of the trees, and on two subsequent occasions, the last being less than a month ago, these mile trees have fallen again and caused extensive damage to people's property.*—Bdos (Hd, 74.08.20, p.5342) [Perh a folk-name derived from use of this tree in rows for various land-marking and soil-conservation purposes]

milk *n* PHRASE **to drink milk, not to count cow** *vb phr* (CarA) [*AF—Joc*] See COW[1] Phr 2.1

milk-bush *n* (USVI) ‖ BLIND-EYE 1 (Mrat) □ Cp MILKY BUSH.

milk-weed *n* (Bdos, Gren, Tbgo, Trin, USVI) A spreading, erect weed about 1 to 2 ft high with a milky sap and reddish-green, serrated, thinly hairy leaves; the milky sap is used to treat ringworm and a decoction of its leaves to treat asthma; *Euphorbia hirta*, or *E. heterophylla* (*Euphorbiaceae*).

milk·y bush *n phr* (TkCa) ‖ AMERICAN SILK-COTTON (BrVi)

mill *n* (CarA) **1.** [Rice or Sugar Ind] A rice-mill or a sugar-mill. (See MILLWALL.) **2.** [Sugar Ind] Any of the huge rollers used to crush the cane in a sugar-factory. *In most estates, there are four mills through which the cane would pass.*—Guyn (Ms, 1978)

mil·lions (-fish) *n pl* (CarA) ‖ *guppy* (CarA) A species of small freshwater fish. (See cit). *Trinidad is, too, the home of the guppy. Known to the average Trinidadian as 'millions' and now known scientifically as Lebistes reticulatus, the first specimens from Trinidad were named Giradinus guppyi in honour of Mr Lechmere Guppy, our most notable ichthyologist of a hundred years ago and, as guppies, they are now bred in countless aquaria throughout the world. Since they will thrive in heavily polluted streams and drains and feed voraciously on mosquito larvae, guppies in their native land are important allies of man in his incessant war against mosquito-borne diseases.*—ACTT:173 (V.C. Quesnel) [From their massive swarming]

mill·wall *n* (Bdos) The conical stone tower of the wind mill or water mill once used to grind sugar cane. *The Barbados countryside, however, remains much the same—flat gently rolling land-scape with millwall and clump of casuarina marking the plantation great house.*—SuS (84.10.07, p.6) [< SE *mill* + WALL wh in Bdos always refers to a stone structure. Cp WALL-BUILDING]

mi·mo·sa (mer·mos·si, mi·a·mos·si, mis·si·mos·si, etc) *n* (Bdos) ‖ WILD-TAMARIND 1. (Belz, etc) *The Ministry of Agriculture's experimental project in leucaena (commonly known as mimosa or river tamarind) as a livestock feed has extremely attractive potential in many other areas as well.*—AdN (79.06.03, p.5) [From the botanical name of the sub-family of plants to wh this shrub belongs—*Mimosae*, whence, prob pronounced [maɪmɔsi] by a British agricultural officer, come the variations in folk speech illustrated above]

mi(n) *vb* (CarA) [*Cr*] ‖ BIN[1] (CarA) **1.** [As copula] Was; were. *Bell: Ah tink de Irish peeple min bad peeple so dem sen dem out a Ialan.*—LaS (76.07.03, p.4, Bits & Pieces) **2.** [As past aux] Did. **a.** *Larse week e min look as if de Secondary*

School min gat e own hurd. De place min jus full of cattle.—MtM (72.11.24, p.11) **b.** *Yes, Carl, many are now saying that 'di Beacon mi right, dem mi tell we di ting lang time.'*—BeA(BE) (80.03.01, p.2) [< BIN with initial nasalization] □ Spelling forms used in (mostly *Joc*) narrative dialogue. The forms occur mostly in *The Leeward Is, Jmca, Belz*.

mind[1] [maɪn(d)] *n* (CarA) PHRASES **1. do/work to your mind** *vb phr* (Guyn) [*AF*] ‖ FOLLOW YOUR MIND (CarA) **2. follow your mind** *vb phr* (CarA) See FOLLOW Phr 2.3 **3. go with your mind** *id phr* (Bdos) See GO Phr 6.34.4 **4. got/ have mind** *vb phr* (Guyn) [*AF*] To have courage; to be bold; [by extension] to have great ambition. **a.** *Pardner, you got mind. I couldn't face that river to save me mother.*—CBM:62 **b.** *She is a girl don't go out with any and everybody. She has mind, you see her there.*—(Guyn) **4.1 got/have five minds to (do sth)** *vb phr* (Bdos) [*AF*] To feel or be strongly inclined to (do sth, usu rash). **a.** *I got five minds to tek he on and throw some lashes in he myself, you know. Hit he, Sage! Hit he!*—CISH:12 **b.** *Where you now come from? I had five minds was to beat you now.*—Bdos (Ms Play, 1976) □ Cp SE *to have a (good/great/half a) mind to,* similarly used. **5. have a mind** *vb phr* (Gren, Guyn, Tbgo, Trin) [*IF*] To have a particular feeling or premonition (that); [SE] to be of a mind (that). *When I felt the cold breeze last night, I had a mind it would rain today.*—(Trin) □ The connective *that* is often omitted. **6. hold a mind** *vb phr* (Gren) [*AF*] See HOLD Phr 5.4 **7. hold sb in your mind** *vb phr* (CarA) [*IF*] See HOLD Phr 5.10 **8. pay (sb) no mind** (CarA) [*IF*] ‖ **not pay (sb) any/no mind** (CarA) [*IF/AF*] To ignore (sb); to flout a warning; to fail to answer a request, remark, etc. **a.** *We do use the curt saying, conveying disgust that a person ignored some request: 'She didn't tek dog's notice of me' an amusing change from the common 'She 'en pay me no mind.'*—AdN (79.07.15, p.11, M. Hutt) **b.** *My instructions are that you then told Emil: 'Hurry up man! Hurry up! Do what you have to do. Nobody pay any mind to him. Nobody and he round ya gree. Man like that, if even he get kill, nobody was going to give evidence for him!'*—AnS (63.10.23, p.4) □ Also dial AmE *not pay heed/ any mind,* similarly used—(*pers info, L. Urdang*). **9. your mind gives/tells you to (do sth); your mind gives/tells you that (sth is so)** *id phrs* (CarA) [*IF*] You are strongly inclined to do sth, or to a certain view, for no clear reason. **a.** *I couldn't leave him there. I couldn't do it. All my mind is to bring him back here. So what you say? You don't think I better do what my mind give me to do?*—JMA:235 **b.** *She said that when she got over the hill 'a mind told me to look back,' which she did, and saw the accused walking up the hill behind her. She walked faster with the children, the court heard.*—AdV (90.07.25, p.4) [A prob calque from W Afr langs. Cp Yoruba *nkankan so fun mi pé ..: (something tell give me that ...)* 'Something tells me that ...'; also Yoruba *o so si mi l'okan pe ... '*My heart/mind tells me that ...'] □ See also GIVE[1] Phrs 2.35. **10. your mind**

turns from sb/sth *id phr* (CarA) [*IF*] You develop a dislike for sb/sth. **a.** *I had liked him but since he told that lie about me my mind turn from him.*—(Guyn) **b.** *After he got the Brown Belt it look like his mind turned from Karate.*—(Bdos)

mind[2] *vb* (CarA) **1.** [Esp of a woman] To be mother to, rear and bring up (a child). **a.** *'Boy, I not worrying my head,' Tolroy say. 'The old lady get a work at Lyons washing dish, and Tanty staying home to mind the children and cook the food.'*—STLL:52 **b.** *'Brown-skin gal, stay home and mind baby.'*—(Opening lines of a popular *CarA* song) [An extension of *OED mind* 11. vb tr 'to take care of, look after, etc'. However the cits (1694–1884) do not apply specifically] □ Still permissible in SE to some extent, though COD8 restricts current usage to *have charge of temporarily* as in 'mind the house while I'm away'. **2.** [By extension, of a man] To maintain, to provide responsible support for (a child he has fathered, or a wife or a mother). **a.** *After all, with these men in irregularly-paying jobs or earning $40 per week and with possibly two children already to 'mind' how can he possibly take on her too and be able to buy even a underpant once a month?*—DaG (79.11.25, p.23) **b.** *'But I ain't living with no man who ain't want to work and mind his wife. I ain't any woman you must find, and you have to mind me.' And with an air of dramatic finality, she added 'If you ain't want to mind me, I go do it myself.'*—SCP:44 (C. Sealy) **c.** *It is the custom for mothers to insist that their sons should spend time at home 'working and minding' them—spending some money they earn on repaying parents for the care and attention they received when they were too young to work.*—EFOT:10 **3.** [By extension] To keep, rear (animals) for as a private occupation or as a business. **a.** *Do the negroes keep many fowls? / Some of them have a great many, and some not; some of them don't mind any at all.*—LMSPJS:27 **b.** *To add to the problem, some of the residents 'mind' cattle, pigs and goats. One or two are even now toying with the idea of abandoning the area if no help can be sent.*—GyC (76.10.24, p.25) **4.** [By extension] To beware of (sth); to guard against (sth). *Hill had a knife in his hand and he made a swipe at Sylvia's stomach, but she drew away from him, and turned off. I said: 'Hill, mind trouble.'*—AnS (62.10.19, p.5) □ See also Phrs 6.2, 6.3 below. **5.** [By extension] *imper vb* ‖ **Take care** (CarA) [Introducing a warning or threat *against* what is declared in the immediately following statement] Take very good care that (sth stated does not happen); (literary SE) Beware lest. **a.** *'Rupe, you mind you break your neck!' Noreen cried in alarm.*—GR:20 (V. Reid) **b.** *The pint-size dictator was tempted to 'break the ties that bind,' that is, the official secrets act, to prove that he was a hero. But when the crowd shouted, 'Mind you go to jail,' he backed down!*—BeT (65.07.31, p.8) **c.** *'Look! Stamp up de daam place all you like,' he threatened, 'but mind you mash me foot!'*—Guyn (Ms, Story) [A prob calque from Afr lang structures. Cp Kikongo *Keba siwabua* 'Mind/Be careful you (will) fall; also Ki-yaka *Keba wu bwa (Mind/Be* *careful you fall*) 'Beware lest you fall'; also Nupe *Tswa egi yami* (*Be careful my child*) 'Be careful (not to wake) my baby'] □ An emotive pitch-pattern and sustained stress play a significant part in conveying this meaning. The same speakers may say less emotively (SE) 'Mind you come home early' (i.e. without neg sense) or 'Mind you don['t] fall' (i.e. with neg inserted). **6.** PHRASES **6.1 Don't mind!** *neg vb phr* (CarA) [*IF/AF*] ‖ DON'T CARE¹ (CarA) **(i)** [As simple imperative] *The dress got a little stain, but don't mind, you can still wear it for today.*—(Guyn) **(ii)** [As truncated main clause, introducing a supposition] *Don't mind who it is, you mustn't open the door—talk through the window.*—(Bdos) **6.2 mind your mouth** *vb phr* (CarA) [*IF*] See MOUTH Phr 4.17. **6.3 mind your stops** *imper vb phr* (Guyn, Tbgo, Trin) [Esp in addressing young persons] Know your place!; Be careful not to be rude!. *'Yet when you finish you say I am common' said Maisie. 'Who have no respect for Mr Haynes, now? Look here, young woman, mind your stops with me.'*—JMA:193 **6.4 put fowl to mind corn** *vb phr* (BrVi) [*AF—Joc*] See FOWL Phr 2.1.

mines [maɪnz] *possessive pron* (CarA) [*X*] **1.** Mine. **a.** *He reportedly went on to say 'I know you have your gun and I have mines; is who pull first tonight.'*—ToR (77.03.09, p.8) **b.** *Den a girlfriend of mines shout: 'Ruupoorrrt! Dey ketch Tumba!'*—TLTH:18 [Cp *EDD* Sc and Ork *mine's* pron 'mine'; prob reinforced in mesolectal CE by analogy with *SE ours, yours*, etc] **2.** PHRASE **2.1 mines own** *pron phr* (BrVi) [*X*] Mine; my own. *Dem bucket wha' you usin' is mines own.*—BrVi (Ms, 1978) [Cp *CSD* Sc *mine²*, *mines*, + phrs *mines ain, own*, etc 'my own' (from Sh, NE)]

mi·ni-bus *n* (Bdos, Guyn, Jmca) ‖ *jitney* 1. (Baha) One of a fleet of small buses registered as such, stopping at any passenger's convenience; they are privately owned, usu identified by being painted the same colour, and some are individually named. *S—was charged for operating a mini-bus without a road licence and fined $70 or 30 days.*—WeS (74.08.02, p.13) [Particular sense of SE *minibus*, 'a small bus' (*COD8*)] □ See also MAXI-TAXI, PICK-UP.

min·nie-root* **(many-root(s), min·ny-root)** *n* (CarA) ‖ *duppy-gun* (Jmca) ‖ *iron-root* (ViIs) ‖ *menow-weed* (Jmca) ‖ *monkey-gun* (Bdos) An erect weed that grows to about 2 ft in height, with light green, noticeably veined, rough-edged leaves; it bears blue, funnel-shaped flowers and small, elongated pods that explode in rain or when handled; its thick, bundled roots are crushed to make bitter medicinal drinks for various complaints; *Ruellia tuberosa* (*Acanthaceae*). [Prob < *DAFL* Twi *meném* 'to swell, ex of the virile member', in ref to the swollen penis-like shape of cluster of roots at the base of the plant (*Ruellia tuberosa*), also its association with relief for female complaints. '*Minnie*' [mɪni] is phonically close to Twi *meném*, and *AFPJ*:

695 notes that the plant is common in Ghana as well as in the W Indies. The alternative name MANY-R. is prob erron, resulting from folk-etym]

mir·a·cu·lous bush; **mir.a.cu.lous vine** *n phr* (Bdos) ‖ CERASEE (Baha, etc) [From its universal folk use as a treatment for a wide number of skin, blood, and bodily disorders including cancer. See *SMPTT:132*]

mi·ras·me *n* (Jmca, StVn, Trin, USVI) See MARASMA.

mis·er·a·ble *adj* (CarA) [*IF*] [Esp of children] Troublesome; continually mischievous; tiresomely demanding or difficult to control; [of adults] difficult to live or work with; uncompanionable. [By shift and extension of sense of SE *miserable* 'wretched'] □ Cp also DISGUSTING.

miss¹ *n* (CarA) **1.** [Respectful form of address to any woman, followed by her first name, used esp by rural folk] *Miss Ursie is di one who always keep di community going. If she in anyting, it will come out good. But now her pickney dem a leave her ... gone America or Canada.*—SSLG:21 **2.** [*IF*] Mrs. *He told them, 'I saw two lady name Miss Caleb, one was the daughter-in-law, and her husband Mr Caleb, talking in a neighbour yard.'*—Guyn (Ms, Short Story) [By characteristic CE reduction of final /-CC/ < SE / misiz/]

miss² *vb* (Dmca, Guyn) [*X*] **1.** To barely avoid (a mishap). **a.** *Boy, tell your mother you miss a fall, and di carrier go down a precipice.*—SDD:44 (E. Andre) **b.** *I stump my foot and I miss drop the plates, if I didn['t] brace meself [a]gains[t] the door.*—(Guyn) **2.** PHRASE **2.1 miss and do sth** *vb phr* (Bdos, Gren, Tbgo, Trin) [*AF*] To make the mistake of doing sth; to do sth injudiciously. *They like to take advantage of people but I'm setting for them. If they miss and hit any of my brothers or sisters, they are going to find out their mistake.*—(Tbgo) [Cp *EDD* miss vb 6. Reflex 'to make a mistake'; also *OED* miss vb¹ 17. 'to go wrong, make a mistake, err']

mis·si·mos·si *n* (Bdos) See MIAMOSSI

mis·sy [mɪsi] *n* (CarA) [Hist] (Respectful form of address to) a white girl or white unmarried woman. (See BACKRA MISSY). [< SE *miss* + paragogic vowel /i/]

mis·tle·toe ['mɪslto] *n* (Gren, Jmca, Trin) ‖ BIRD-VINE 1. (Dmca) [From the resemblance of the red berries and leathery green leaves to the European *mistletoe*]

mis·tress [mɪstrɪs] *n* (CarA) [Respectful form of address to a woman (usu the mistress of the house, lady in authority or sb perceived to be of higher social status)] *'I'm sorry, mistress,' he said, 'but this afternoon I have to go to watch tennis.'*—AdV (64.05.24, p.8) [Cp *OED* mistress 13. a.

'used vocatively as a term of respect or politeness; = Madam, Ma'am. Obs exc. arch. in general use.' This usage survives in CE] □ Note sharp contrast with SE/IAE in wh it is offensive so to address a lady.

mi·thai (me·thai) [mɪtai] *n* (Guyn, Trin) A finger-like EAST INDIAN sweetmeat made with flour and water, coated with sugar and fried crisp; it is used in religious ceremonies and also sold commercially. [Bhoj < Hin *miṭhaaii* 'sweetness, sweetmeat'.]

mi·wiz (mee·rese) [miwi·z] *n* (StLu) ‖ GOVERNOR-PLUM 1. (CarA) [Fr Cr < Fr *merise* 'wild cherry']

Mm! [m:] *excl* (CarA) [*IF/AF*] [Unreleased, lengthened /m/ used as a response in a number of contexts, excepting negation, with varying pitch superfixes determined by context] □ The use of this communicative device involves a much wider range of pitches and covers a far wider number of contexts than the similar device in IAE. It is, however, not a permitted response from juniors or social inferiors.

Mm-hm! [m̄hm̄] *excl* (CarA) [*IF/AF*] ‖ *Eh-heh!* (CarA) 1. /11'/ or /12/ Yes. *The tone of her 'yes' was unusually formal. As a matter of fact, 'yes' was the wrong reply. Sonia's reply should have been 'mm-hmm' or 'Eh-heh' or 'yeah, man', or some such friendly, homespun vocable. Not 'yes'. 'Yes' was when you vex, or when replying to a stranger.*—TRIH:118 2. /13'/ or /14'/ Is that so? 3. [m̄hm̄:] /25'/ [With sharp rising pitch and variously lengthened second element] How shocking! [See [M] 3., and etym note] □ Normally only acceptable between peers.

Mm-mm! [m̄ʔm̄] *excl* (CarA) [*IF/AF*] 1. /2'1/ ‖ *Eh-eh²* (CarA) No. 2. [m̄ʔm:] /3'1/ [With falling pitch and variously lengthened second element] That's bad news! 3. [m̄ʔm̄::] /55'/ ‖ *Eh-eh¹* (CarA) [With high pitch and lengthened second element] How very surprising! [See M 3., and etym note] □ Normally only acceptable between peers.

mob-o-ton (mob·a·ton) [mɒbʌtɒn] *n* [*AF—Joc*] (Bdos) A large amount; a lot. **a.** *The other day, I get a nail jook in my foot and my wife say I must go to the clinic up at Warrens 'cause it free. So I went up dere and see a mob-o-ton of people; I had to wait for a good hour before the nurse tek muh name.*—NaT (76.07.25, p.5) **b.** *'E' en went to no big school but can spell like the best o we, use big words ... and a mob o ton of vocabulary.*—TM:93 (S. Reid) [Perh a blend of *mob* + (*mar*)*athon*, with characteristic CE [ə > t] shift, so fusing two notions of quantity; a variant spelling *mobaton* also occurs. A fusing of *mob-a*(*nd*)-*ton*, with similar notions, is also a possible explanation]

mo·cha-mo·cha (moc·ca-moc·ca, mo·co-mo·co) *n* (Guyn) See MOKA-MOKA

mock·a·jum·bie; mock-jum.bie, mo.co-jum.bie *n* (Gren, StKt, StLu, Trin, ViIs) See MOKO-JUMBIE

mock-sport; mock-stick *n* (Bdos) [*IF—Joc*] A laughing-stock; usu a person [also by extension] a thing, event, or situation viewed as ridiculous. **a.** *He and his mother seem to take sides against me whenever he and I have a misunderstanding ... and even though I love my boyfriend I am very unhappy living there as I am treated with insults and criticisms all the time. I feel as if I am their mock sport.*—NaT (80.11.12, p.34, Dear Christine) **b.** *It is all very well to award certificates for merely having reached so far as to have sat the exam, but this fools nobody—except, perhaps, a doting parent ... merely cheapens the whole process, and makes a mock stick out of the system which permits—nay, encourages—such folly.*—AdN (84.10.30, p.7) [< SE *mock* n, as in '*make mock of*' in characteristic CE redundant comb with CE SPORT, 'fun' as in *make sport/fun of*. The var *-stick* is a similarly redundant comb perh retaining an EE sense, as in *OED stick* sb¹ 12. (a) 'applied, with qualifying adj, to a person [as in] tough stick, crooked stick'; (b) 'a person lacking in capacity for his work']

mo·co *n* (ECar) See MOKO

mò·da(n) [mɒ·dã] *n* (Dmca, Gren, StLu, Trin) ‖ GUNDY (Antg, etc) [Fr Cr < Fr *mordant* n 'bite, grip'] □ Sometimes denasalized (*mòda*) in Gren, Trin.

mof·fr(e)y [mɒ·fri] *n* (Bdos) [*AF—Derog*] 1. A man or animal that is half male, half female; a hermaphrodite. 2. [By extension] A weak male (person or animal); an effeminate man; a man who is apparently lacking in masculinity. [Cp EDD *morfreydite* (Yks, Lin); *morfery, morfrey, morphrey* (e.An, Nrf, Suf, Lin) 'a hermaphrodite; also used *fig*' + cits (Nrf) 'a malformed sheep'; (suf) 'of a human being, not of a beast. Used by the old only'] □ F. Collymore (*CGBD5*) notes the form as *morphy*.

mo·han·bhog (ma·ham·bhog, man·bhogue) [mohanbhog] *n* (Guyn, Trin) [Indic] A sweetmeat made from a mixture of flour, syrup, and dried fruit, fried dry in ghee; it is blessed by a pundit and served at the end of a festivity. [Hin, name of this sweetmeat]

mo·ka *n* (Tbgo, Trin) See MOKO-BANANA·

mo·ka-mo·ka* (moc·ca-moc·ca, mo·cha-mo·cha, mo·co-mo·co) [mʌka-mʌka ~ mʌkʌ-mʌkʌ] *n* (Guyn) A shrub with flat, heart-shaped leaves and a prickly stalk with a spongy flesh wh, crushed and mixed with salt or urine, is used as a folk treatment for cuts; it grows very profusely in swampy land or at riversides; *Montrichardia arborescens* (*Araceae*). [< *BAED* Arawak *mokomoko* 'spiny plant with pithy insides found on river banks']

mo·ko (mo·co) *n* **1.** An ugly, bedevilled, or frightening person or thing. [Cp *ADHL* Hausa *mugu* 'bad, evil, ugly (person or thing); also *DJE moco* 1. 'an African tribal name of doubtful identity ...' 2. now used as symbolic of ugliness or backwardness.] **2.** [By extension] A born idiot (esp a man). **3.** [By extension] Any rustic thing or person. **4.** (Crcu) One of the NATION DANCES that may be associated with impotence (see *Ethnic folkways*, 1011, (1956) p.3, A.C. Pearse). □ The term is used in *Derog* attrib senses or in compounds. See separate entries.

mo·ko-ba·na·na; mo.ko-fig, mo.ko-plan-.tain *n* (Tbgo, Trin) ‖ BLUGGO (Belz, etc) [See note at MOKO-JUMBIE] □ Sometimes loosely referred to as **moka**.

mo·ko dis·ease *n phr* (ECar) An incurable bacterial disease that attacks esp banana and plantain trees, damaging their fruit and causing the trees to wilt and die. [From the MOKO-BANANA (*Trin*) to wh the disease takes most readily and in wh it was first observed in the early 1900s—P. Hunt (*StLu*)]

mo·ko-jum·bie (mock·a·jum·bie, mock-jum·bie, mo·co-jum·bie) *n* (Gren, StKt, StLu, Trin, ViIs) ‖ STILT-MAN (ECar) *The earliest Moco-Jumbies were simply spirits made up as women, at first on quite short stilts. The Moco-Jumbie teased, frightened and mocked women and children. The reason that stilts were used was because tradition had it that the images of spirits—Jumbies—can float on the air, and so elevation was part of the 'costume'.*—Aaw.I.2, p.5 [< MOKO 1. + JUMBIE, a reinforced compound] □ In *StKt*, and *BrVi* the MOKO-JUMBIE is not in woman's dress. (Cp STILT-MAN, etc).

mole *n* (Bdos) See MOULD

mol·ly *n* (Bdos) ‖ MAULY (Guyn)

monce *n* (Dmca) See MONS

mon·ey-bush *n* (Bdos, Gren, Guyn, Tbgo, Trin) A bushy shrub with little, round, flat leaves, yellow flowers and pods, wh grows wild, esp in swampy ground; the juice or a decoction of its leaves is much used as a folk-medicine for skin infections; *Cassia bicapsularis* (*Caesalpiniaceae*). [Name said to refer to resemblance of its leaves to coins and/or to the belief that it brings good luck if grown in yards]

mong-mong [mʌŋ-mʌŋ] *n* (Gren) [*AF—Joc/Derog*] ‖ POOR-WHITE (CarA) [*Joc* abbr of MOUNT-MORITZ BAJAN (*Gren*)]

mon·goose-gang *n* (ECar) [*AF—Derog*] A hand-picked group of henchmen forming an unofficial secret-police force that carries out acts of brutality or small-scale terrorism at the orders of a political leader or party in power. [Orig *Gren* where, in the 1950s the Ministry of Health in a campaign to eradicate the mongoose as a pest, paid people who brought in mongoose tails as proof of killing. The men so employed were popularly named the 'mongoose-gang'. This name shifted to refer to gangs of political thugs that developed in the later political life of the island, attracting the attention also of other *CarA* territories]

mongst [mʌŋs(t)] *prep* (BrVi, Guyn, Jmca) [*AF*] **1.** Among; amongst. *Him never believe pickney should have free speech. Him used to hinder me from go mongst people.*—SSLG:70 [A prob survival of an EE aphetic form of *amongst*. OED lists 'mongst as a poetic, aphetic form of *amongst* + cits 1590–1871] **2.** *PHRASE* **2.1 Mongst your sex!** *id phr, excl* (BrVi) Know your place!; Be off with you!; Go find your little equals! *Look boy, I am a big woman to you, you hear? I know when you born. Mongst your sex!*—(BrVi) [Mongst + *your sex* 'your kind']

mon·key *n* (CarA) One of two types of earthenware water-jug. See GOBLET 1. and 2. **a.** *The pottery industry of Barbados has fallen upon hard times since refrigerators did away with the need for 'monkeys' to keep water cool.*—IsL 73/10, p.58 **b.** *We would sit in the doorway fronting the garden with a bottle of 'Sun Glow' and the monkey of orange or grapefruit juice on the step between our feet, glasses in our hands.*—Gren (Ms) [Cp OED monkey sb 7. c. 'a globular earthenware water-vessel with a straight upright neck' + cits 1834–1883; also *monkey-pot* 2. 'a vessel used in tropical countries for cooking drinking water' + cit 1897]

mon·key-ap·ple *n* **1.** (Nevs) ‖ JUMBIE-SOURSOP (Antg, etc) *It name jumbie soursop ... and sometimes we calls it monkey apple too—all sorts o[f] name.*—(Nevs) □ Cp alternative folk-names *pomme macaque, pomme de singe* for the same fruit in *Guad, Mart* (FFGM:1188). This fruit is inedible so the pref MONKEY- is prob Joc. Cp MONKEY-TAMBRAN. **2.** (Bdos, Guyn) ‖ *ghaut-apple* (Antg) ‖ *pond-apple* (Jmca) An edible yellowish-brown fruit, about three inches long and nearly round, with pink, dryish, sharp-tasting flesh and brown seeds; it is borne on a small tree in swampy land; fruit of the tree *Annona glabra* (*Annonaceae*). *Monkey apple doesn't have so much juice but children eat it and you make a drink with it—only you don't see it in town.*—(Guyn) [Prob from swampy habitat of the tree wh makes it accessible mostly to monkeys]

mon·key-ber·ry *n* (Jmca) ‖ JUMBIE-SOUR SOP (Antg, etc)

mon·key-fart/-shit *n* (Guyn) [*AF-Vul*] Absolute nonsense; a totally unacceptable statement or claim. □ Cp note at OBSOCKY.

mon·key-fid·dle *n* (TkCa) ‖ WOMAN('S) TONGUE (CarA)

mon·key-gun n (Bdos) ‖ MINNIE-ROOT (CarA) *It belongs to the family Acanthaceae, which includes such well known plants as the Black-eyed Susan, and the Ruellias, one of which is the blue-flowered Monkey Gun or Minnie Roots, which has a narrow woody seed pod which opens explosively a few seconds after the tip is moistened with a finger.*—AdN (78.06.07, p.6, M. Hutt) [From the pods that explode in rain or when handled]

mon·key-mo·tion n PHRASE **make monkey-motion** vb phr (Guyn, StVn) [AF—Joc] To pull funny faces; to perform funny antics. *He can't even control a class. The children are noisy and some even make monkey-motion while he's talking to them.*—(Guyn)

mon·key-nee·dle(s) n (Bdos) ‖ DUPPY-NEEDLE (Bdos) [A variation of DUPPY N. prob by jocose association with the kind of bushy terrain wh also shelters the Barbadian monkey]

mon·key-pis·tol (tree) n (phr) (USVI) ‖ S-ANDBOX-TREE (CarA) [From the explosive pop of the pod, scattering the seeds, when ripe]

mon·key-puz·zle n (USVI) ‖ CACTUS HEDGE (CarA)

mon·key's dinner-bell n phr (Guyn) ‖ SANDBOX TREE Gren, etc) [From the round grooved pods wh resemble an ornamental dinner-bell. Cp also note at MONKEY-PISTOL]

mon·key-sha(c)k-sha(c)k n (Guyn) ‖ WOM-AN('s) TONGUE (CarA) [From the rattling of the pods in the wind, like a child's SHACK-SHACK]

mon·key-tam·bran/-tam·a·rind n (Baha) ‖ COWITCH (CarA) [Monkey in sense of 'idiot' + tambran < 'tamarind' because of resemblance of ripe brown pods to tamarind pods. Whereas one eats the tamarind, only an (uninformed) idiot wd touch this pod the hairs on wh secrete the same venom a wasp uses in its sting]

mons (monce) [mŏ·s] n A little creature in the form of a man supposed to be hatched from an egg wh was laid on Good Friday and kept under the arm of a person who then becomes its master to command it to do good or evil. [Prob Fr Cr < Fr monstre 'monster, evil being' with typical Cr reduction of final syllable cluster /-str/ > /-s/] □ Cp BACCOO (Guyn).

month-end (month·end) n (CarA) [IF] (At/ of the) end of the month. **a.** *So we there fixing up and making we plan to leave month-end, same time that Dennis friend going leave to go back to him home in Guyana.*—SNWIC:265 (M. Townshend) **b.** *Big Month-End Banana Shipment—The April 28–30 shipment of bananas to the United Kingdom was 147 tons (12,688 stems) more than that of April 23.*—DoC (65.05.05, p.8) **c.** *What about the National Festival Song Contest which we hear closes this month-end ... what's the prize list like ... is it still on Mr Nash?*—WeS (75.04.18,

p.17) **d.** *Many months in the making, the Militia was said to have 5,000 members, a figure which it is believed would be doubled by monthend.*—MtM (76.12.03, p.6) [By structural analogy with SE weekend, though different in sense. Cp similarly YEAR-END]

Mont·ser·ra·tian [mɒnsrašən ~ mɒnsəratiən] /1'1221/ n, adj (CarA) (Person or thing) belonging to or characteristic of the LEEWARD ISLAND of Montserrat. [< Montserrat + SE adj suff -ian] □ Sometimes also **Monstratian** [mɒn strešʌn] /12'1/.

Mont·ser·rat o·ri·ole n phr (Mrat) A bird about 8 ins long, mostly black with splashes of gold, and a yellow breast and rump; its voice is a loud, melodious whistle, and it is found only in the mountain forests of Montserrat; it is that island's National Bird; Icterus oberi (Icteridae).

moo·jin n (Bdos) [AF—Joc/Derog] A fool; a stupid person; a worthless idiot. [Perh from EDD dial moch vb² (Sc, Eng) 1. 'to idle, loaf about' 2. 'to play truant from school'; whence phr on the mooch 'gone off loafing; shuffling'. Hence poss mooching (with voicing) > MOOJIN(G) '(being) worthless']

mook (mouk) [muk ~ mʊk] n (Guyn, Tbgo, Trin) A gullible person (esp a man); one who is easily fooled. *You take me for a mook man / But darling try to understand / You could only stick me one time.*—SCTR:28 [Perh a variant of MOKO]

moo·ma(h) [mʊma] [Child talk] Mother. *'Boy, where you does go whole evening instead of stop home here and help your moomah?' his father asked.*—SNWIC:228 (I. Khan)

moo·moo (moo-moo) (CarA) [AF—Derog] A person who is afraid or too shy to speak; [by extension] a silently stupid person; a fool. **a.** *You must tell the teacher when you don't understand. Don't sit at the back of the class like a moomoo when everybody getting on.*—(Nevs) **b.** *Ladies and honoured gentlemen, I move that we declare today that we ain't no damn moo-moos, that we ain't no blasted jackasses, that we arm we selves good and proper to protect our legitimate interests.*—JPB:125 [Cp DAFL Twi e-mumu 'a person who is deaf and dumb'. DJE notes also Ewe, Mende, etc sources]

moon gaz·er (moon·gaz·er) n (phr) (Guyn) A legendary figure, tall with formless legs, who is said to stand at crossroads or to straddle a railway line while gazing steadily at the moon; any human contact with him is said to cause bodily harm.

moo·shay [muše] n (StKt) [AF—Derog] ‖ POOR-WHITE (CarA) [< Fr monsieur by folk pronunc. See ‖ Frenchie (StKt)]

Mo·pan; **Mo.pan.e.ro** adj, n Belz) 1. (Of or belonging to) an ethnic and linguistic sub-group of the MAYAN people inhabiting the middle inland area of Belize; they are said to be the smallest of three such sub-groups. **2.** The language spoken by these people. □ Pl MOPAN unchanged. Sometimes MOPAN-MAYA(s). See also KEKCHI, YUCATECAN.

mo·ra (tree) *n (phr)* (Guyn, Tbgo, Trin) A huge forest-tree that can grow to 200 ft; it has dark green leaves and yields a hard, heavy timber of smooth, brown grain mottled with lighter and darker streaks; it is used for shipbuilding and railway sleepers; *Mora excelsa (Caesalpiniaceae). The mora may well be called the king of the forest; it towers above every other tree and reaches frequently a height over 120 ft.*—R. Schomburgk [*BAED* Arawak *mora*, name of this tree]

more[1] *indef pron, adj* (CarA) PHRASES **1. be more than sb** *vb phr* (ECar) [*IF/AF*] To be more than sb can bear, manage, etc. **a.** *When the pain was more than him, then you see he hustle to a dentist.*—(Tbgo) **b.** *Buy car is more than you, but you still want to buy car.*—(USVI) **2. I never see more!** *id phr* (Trin) [*AF/IF*] See NEVER Phr 2.1 **3. more than the law allow(s)** *id phr* (BrVi, Gren, Guyn, Mrat, Tbgo) See LAW Phr 1. **4. more than (what) John read [a]bout** *id phr* (Bdos) [*AF—Joc*] A great amount of (sth). **a.** *And as doh wuh gine-on at de cinemas en 'nough, / Television does show mo' crime / Dan John read 'bout.*—PeL (77.12.02, p.6, J. Layne-Clark) **b.** *I catching more cold than what John read 'bout.*—HFGA:110 (A. Clarke) **5. to do for more** *id phr* (Guyn, StVn) [*IF/AF*] [Expressing rebuke with disgust] To be very unreasonable. *Although your father has promised you a bicycle for your birthday, you want a birthday party too? Where is he to find the money? O, child you do for more.*—(Guyn) **6. You (n)ever hear more!** *id phr* (Bdos) [*AF/IF*] See HEAR Phr 4.13

more[2] *adv* PHRASE **more so** *adv phr* (Bdos, Dmca) [*X*] Especially; rather; all the more. **a.** *Surely, there can be no discrimination against them, because the cost of living has gone up and it affects low wager earners more so.*—AdN (72.07.15, p.4) **b.** *If we want a good future for Dominica, more so with Independence just next door, we must be fair and just.*—NeC (77.07.09, p.5) [By misascription of SE adj phr *more so* 'of the same kind to a greater degree']

morne [mɔ(r)n] *n* (StLu) A small round hill. *Out of it grows the sun / and the fat valleys of Haiti, / deep mourning waters under the mornes.*—BTA:232 [Cp *LLFL* 3. morne Cr word from (17C) Sp *morro* 'hillock'. Though the word is widely current in Fr Cr in place-names and as a loan, it does not appear as a noun in orig Fr]

morn·ing *n* PHRASES **1. from morning** *id phr* (Bdos, Gren, StVn) From the beginning; from a time far back in the past. *From mornin[g] she was a bright chile, so when she pass de exam ah didn[']t surprise.*—(Gren) **2. on a morning** [*AF*]; **on mornings** [*IF*] *adv phrs* (Bdos) See ON Phr

7.4 **3. [u]pon a morning** *adv phr* (Guyn) [*AF*] ‖ ON A MORNING (Bdos)

morn·ing-crop/-sport/-work *n* (Jmca) ‖ LEND-HAND (Tbgo) *Free work by a large group on another's farm is known as 'morning sport' or 'digging'. Both sexes attend a 'digging', the women being responsible for planting the yam or potato hills, and for preparation of the food.*—LCWFL: 72 □ The commoner term in *Jmca* is prob **digging**.

morn·ing-glo·ry *n* (Jmca) ‖ IPOMEA (CarA)

mo·ro·cot [mʌrʌkʌt] *n* (Guyn) A freshwater fish with a flat body, averaging 2-1/2 ft in length and sometimes growing to weigh 30 lbs; it is much prized for its firm salmon-like flesh and is often salted and dried; *Colossoma spp.* [< *BAED* Arawak *morokoto* 'a tasty freshwater fish the size of salmon']

mo·ro·coy [mɒrɒkɔɪ] *n* (Dmca, Gren, Trin) A land turtle that is particularly prized for its flesh; *Testudo graeca* or *T. tabulata (Testudinidae).* [< *CSED* So Am Sp *morrocoyo* 'turtle']

mor·tar *n* (CarA) A heavy vessel made by hollowing out a bowl-like receptacle in a solid block of cured wood; in it boiled plantains or root vegetables are pounded with a MORTAR-PESTLE to make FUFU, etc. [Specific sense of SE *mortar*, usu a small, lighter vessel used esp in pharmacy]

mor·tar-pes·tle/-stick *n* (CarA) A heavy, wooden pestle about 4 or 5 ft long and about 2 to 3 ins in diameter, used for pounding cooked food in a MORTAR; it is also commonly used as a weapon. *An employee of Guyana National Newspapers died at the Georgetown Hospital yesterday morning following a mortar stick attack. / ... According to reports W— on Friday was involved in an argument with another man during which he was struck on the head and about the body with a mortar stick.*—GyC (77.11.27, p.19)

mor·tel(le) [mɒ·(r)tɛl] *n* (Gren, Trin) [*IF*] ‖ IMMORTELLE (CarA) *Immortelle trees for example, are common enough in Grenada, being used largely for marking boundaries; but their assumption of immortality for the shape and colour of their leaves or flowers when dried, or whatever it may be, is never for a moment allowed in the Colony where they are always and everywhere called 'mortelles.*—DUDG:43 [< IMMORTELLE by aphaeresis]

mo·ses (-boat) *n* (Antg, Bdos, BrVi) ‖ **billy-boat** (Grns, StVn) An open wooden boat, 10 to 20 ft long, often with thwarts for sitting; rowed or sculled, it was orig used to transfer goods and passengers between ship and shore; it is now used by fishermen for various purposes. **a.** *Apropos of that moses boat, old prints of the period show slaves rolling hogsheads down a beach toward a tiny dinghy sort of boat, tipped up on its side by other men, ready to cradle the huge barrel on its thwarts as the reeds did Moses.*—LTTBV:35 **b.** *As a* matter of fact, so successful has this whole operation been that we are actively considering constructing a similar pier for the fishermen so that the fishing boats at Oistins will be able to come right alongside without having to resort to the moses to bring their catches ashore.—Bdos (Hd, 74.03.18, p.3352) [*CGBD5* cites from I. Gale: The Moses was a type of boat used on the Thames for lighterage around the 17th century. The New Englanders, who traded a great deal with the W Indies, saw the need for boats in the islands for carrying sugar to the ships so they built Moses boats and sold them in the Caribbean. The Moses was usu about 18 ft long and usu of shallow draft and could be shipped easily on top of the lumber the brigs usu carried to the W Indies. I. Gale's source is not given, but it would explain the joint occurrence of the name in the CarA and in Massachusetts, listed by *OED moses* 2. as being of separate orig]

Mo·ses-in-the-bul·rush·es *n* (Jmca, USVI) ‖ OYSTER-PLANT (ECar)

mos·qui·to-bush *n* (Guyn, Trin) ‖ *duppy-basil* (Bdos) An aromatic herb, of more than one kind, that is either hung up indoors or burnt outside on a slow fire to keep away mosquitoes, e.g.in *Trin* the herb *Ocimum micranthum* (*Labiatae*). □ See more at DUPPY-BASIL.

mos·qui·to-coil/-des·troy·er *n* (CarA) ‖ *cock-set* (Gren, Tbgo, Trin) A type of manufactured coil of brittle, green material of wh the insecticide pyrethrin is a component; it is set on a thin metal holder and lit at the tip, its very slow burning producing a smoke that drives away mosquitoes.

most[1] [mos(t)] *adj* 1. (Bdos) [X] Greater; better. *Vehicular traffic was forced to 'inch along' through the streets of Bridgetown for the most part of yesterday as motorists tried to acquaint themselves with the new traffic measures.*—AdN (72.12.14, p.1) [By misascription of sense of SE idiom *for the most part* 'generally'] 2. (CarA) [X] Best; greatest; most striking. **a.** *The most day I enjoy was Xmas day.*—Bdos (Ms, 1985) **b.** *The most thing you could just see from the way things going on and from what Mildred had already tell me, it's the parents make the wedding.*—HF:14 3. PHRASE 3.1 **most many** *adj phr* (Bdos) [X] Many; most. *Most many people like to take some time off at Christmas to dress up their houses.*—(Bdos) [By redundancy for emphasis, a common CarA Cr feature prob producing this phr]

most[2] [mos(t)] *adv* (CarA) 1. [AF/IF] Almost. **a.** *In George Street most anything lies in the drains—coconut shells, tattered clothing, broken bottles ..., empty tin cans, dead dogs.*—SABS:20 **b.** *Most all the neighbors would ask Bim's ... opinion on most any subject.... / Bim was well liked by most everyone.*—PKKK:90 **c.** *He slam on he brakes dem an I mos pitch through de winder glass an bus open mer head.*—JBJ:85 [By aphaeresis < SE *almost*] □ A common development also in

AmE. 2. [AF] Mostly. **a.** *Most you find he will come on Tuesdays.*—(Trin) **b.** *Most Oils on Show at Pelican—The first group show for 1974 at the Barbados Arts Council's Pelican Art Gallery comprises 38 pieces. Oils predominate.*—AdN (74.01.27, p.2) [< SE *mostly* by apocope]

most·ly [mosli] *adv* (ECar) [X] Usually; generally; [by shift] almost. **a.** *She find the boss mostly don['t] quarrel if you come late, but now she overdo it an[d] he vex.*—(Guyn) **b.** *From the street, one is attracted to these places by the dimly lit atmosphere and music, mostly always too loud.*—AdN (74.02.24, p.17) [By misascription of SE sense of *mostly*]

moth-bor·er *n* (CarA) [Sugar Ind] The larva of numerous species of insects (esp the small *Diatraea saccharalis* (CANE-BORER) and the large *Castria licoides*), wh bores into the stems of sugar-canes in numbers, making tunnels wh destroy the plant; it is said to be the most destructive of plant insect pests.

moth·er [mʌðʌ ~ mada] *n* 1. (CarA) [Respectful form of address, esp among rural folk, to an old woman, followed by her first or second name] Exs: Mother Sarah; Mother Brathwaite. 2. (CarA) [By extension] (Title added to the name of) an old female herbalist, folk-healer, or spiritual leader. *The 'Psychic or Mother' as some of the females are called, are gifted people who guide their clients on health and general matters, which include herbs for healing.*—RJH:3 3. (Jmca) A female Elder in a religious revivalist group who tends the converts and has other senior responsibilities in a BALM-YARD or other place of African-based folk religion; a similar female assistant to a SHEPHERD. **a.** *A little later the same woman returned with another, older, woman. The latter was dressed in a black silk dress, longer than the rest, and around her waist was a purple cord towards the end of which was tied a pair of scissors and a long steel whistle. Her turban was tall and imposing and made of red, blue and purple cloth. / "Evening, I is de Elder Mother. You come to join de service, Sister?' she asked Dinah.*—PCOS:149 **b.** *After dat [she] get di job to bathe di people dat come to Mass Sam wid problem or sickness. She was di madda fi di yard. She pick di bush and boil dem in Kerosene pan wid whatever come from doctor shop fi bathe dem. When dem come Mass Sam read dem up and recommend dem fi a bath. Sometimes dem get better. Sometime dem don't.*—SSLG:67

moth·er-in-law-tongue *n* (Guyn) ‖ S-ANSEVERIA (ViIs) [Prob a derogatory ref to the colouring and stiffish sword-like shape of the leaf] □ Erron called a *cactus* by some speakers. See note at CACTUS.

Moth·er-Sal·ly /1′112/ *n* (Guyn) ‖ STILT-MAN (ECar) *The white faced 'long-lady' or 'Mother Sallies' with their loose swinging shapeless arms, which are a common feature of Guyana's masquerade bands might in fact have been caricatures* *of the bossman's wife. They would be brought out on special occasions to cavort for the amusement of the bossman and his friends, but the slaves were having a double laugh at his expense.*—Kaie XIV. p.26 (F. Pilgrim)

mot·mot [mɒtmɒt] *n* (Gren, Tbgo, Trin) A bird some 15 to 18 ins long with a significant, blue, double-shafted tail about half its length, the shafts being bare near the end of the tail; it has a blue crown, green back, and cinnamon-coloured breast and underparts; it is a forest bird with many other names, '***King/Queen-of-the-woods***', '***Bouhoutou***' (from its low call), etc; *Momotus momota bahamensis* (*Momotidae*). [< *SDGA* Lat Am Sp *mot-mot*, Peruvian name of this family of birds]

mouch·wè (mouch·oir) [mušwɛ ~ mušwa] *n* (Dmca, StLu) A coloured head-cloth worn by women, specially tied about the crown of the head, often with one end sticking up; this headwear is now a recognized item of the National Costume. [Fr Cr < Fr *mouchoir* 'handkerchief']

mouk (muk) *n* (Guyn, Trin) See MOOK

mould; **mole** [mo·l(d)] *n* (CarA) **1.** A soft, unclosed gap in the skull of a young baby; the fontanelle. *No shake up de baby because yo[u] goin[g] mek e mole drop.*—(Belz) **2.** [By extension] the top of the head (believed to be a very sensitive area through wh illnesses can enter the body). *But if the clouds gather and the rain starts to fall, she must run for shelter immediately, holding up her handbag to protect the 'mould' of the head from the falling rain.*—AdN (79.03.11, p.12) [Cp *OED mould* sb² 'the top or dome of the head; also the fontanelle of an infant's head'. Also *EDD mole* sb² 2. pl (Bdf) 'the space at the top of a child's head before the skull has entirely formed']

Moul·vi [mʊlvi ~ mɒlvi] *n* (Guyn, Trin) [Indic] (Title added to the name of) a Muslim priest. **a.** *So declared Ahmadiyya Missionary Moulvi M. Rasheed in his opening address to the Islamic Youth Seminar last Sunday at the Louisa Row Mosque Georgetown.*—GyC (76.06.25, p.7) **b.** *Prayers were said by a number of Moulvis from various districts and there was reading from the Holy Quran.*—GyC (76.06.30, p.13) [Perso-Arabic > Hin *maulvii*. Cp *OED Moolvee* 'a Mohammedan doctor of the law; applied in India as a complimentary designation for a teacher of Arabic, or a learned man generally'. This complimentary title was evid transferred to and became formal in CE via EAST INDIAN immigration]

mount [mʌŋt] *vb tr* (Gren, StVn, Trin) To invest (an object) with some supernatural power or charm in order to best an opponent or enemy. **a.** *This criminal aspect of obeah has been brought out in the Courts frequently. And it is a well known obeah belief ... that the spirit of a man killed with a 'mounted stick' remains the slave of the murderer forever.*—ViN (73.11.16, p.5) **b.** *The ring had*

been mounted. Imbued with incantations and spells, a spiritual electrified fence aganst malju—the bad eye of envy, spite, and all too human wickedness.—RSMCD:69 [Cp *EDD* mount vb¹ 4. 'to arrange, fix; to equip, furnish; to trim, dress up...' Hence 1. 'mounted', ppl adj: 'equipped, furnished'. Cp also *OED* mount vb 13. (Obs) b. 'to elevate spiritually ...; to excite to a higher degree of activity or emotion'] □ Although the term is best known as applied to the stick-fighter's BWA, it is often also applied to a place such as a 'protected' kitchen-garden or to some animal behaving strangely.

moun·tain-cab·bage *n* (Antg, Jmca, StVn) ‖ CABBAGE-PALM (CarA) [From its height, and also often its habitat in the *CarA* islands]

moun·tain-chick·en *n* (Dmca, Mrat) A large, brown, smooth-skinned, edible frog some 6 to 10 ins long, found largely on mountain slopes; its meat is prized as a local delicacy; frog's legs; *Leptodactylus pentadactylus. The mountain chicken, found only in Dominica and Montserrat, is regarded in both islands as a dining delicacy. This terrestrial frog can grow to a length of ten inches; it is hunted at nights on mountain slopes, its natural habitat. It is a threatened species which could soon disappear unless speedy conservation measures are taken.*—FMEI:40 [< *mountain* (from its habitat) + *chicken* (from the texture and taste of its meat)]

moun·tain-dew *n* (Dmca, Gren, StLu, Trin) [AF—Joc] ‖ BUSH-RUM (Gren, etc) *Right now you have a fine of $460.00 for people who sell mountain dew or jack iron or uncustomed liquor and you say that's not enough and you make it $5,000.00.*—Gren (Hd, 73.08.24, p.49) [Every Irishman understands well the terms cruiskeen and mountain dew, some indeed a little too well; but for the benefit of the rest of the world, I think it better to state that a cruiskeen is a small jar, and that mountain dew is pottheen or illicit whiskey—*JESI:285*]

moun·tain-dove *n* (Vils) ‖ GROUND-DOVE 2. (CarA) *The 'mountain' (mourning) dove (Zenaida aurita) after which Tortola is reputed to have been named because of the large numbers in which it was formerly found.*—HVVIS:XVI

moun·tain-ground/-land *n* (Gren, Mrat, StKt, StVn) Cultivable land on the slopes of the mountains. *If the landowners would take our hint, ... at the same time reserving the Mountain-Lands for sale to the hundreds of peasants who for generations have eked a living from these locations, ... even if none of these hundreds will ever command areas as large as the Mattingleys ... they can ... experience ... status in Owning A Piece Of Mountain-Ground.*—DeM(SK) (77.12.10, p.1)

moun·tain sweet-cup *n phr* (Jmca) ‖ PASSION-FRUIT (CarA)

Mount-Mor·itz Ba·jan [mʌŋ-mɒrɪs beɪʌn] *n phr* (Gren) [*AF—Derog*] ‖ POOR WHITE [Ref to the estate in *Gren* where POOR WHITE immigrants from Bdos chose to settle as market-gardeners from the late 1870s. See *SROB:98*] □ Note pronunc, from wh the more strongly *Derog* MONG-MONG is derived.

mourn·ing dove *n phr* (Baha, BrVi) ‖ MOUNTAIN DOVE (BrVi, etc) [From its plaintive cooing]

mourn·ing ground *n phr* (ECar) [Religion] A dedicated part of an enclosed ground associated with or in the precincts of a Spiritual Baptist church, on wh converts are initiated, by prostration, fasting, prayer, etc, into membership of the sect. *'Degrees are granted through both dreams and visions. Dreams and visions are given mainly after spending time on the mourning ground. During mourning one hopes to receive a 'gift', that is, to find out what his 'work' is ... if everything has gone well the Child is greeted with 'the hand of fellowship' by all the members of the church,* states sociologist, George Simpson in his book *Religious Cults of the Caribbean.*—SuS (82.05.23, p.11)

Mou·sie [mɒusi] *n* (Guyn, Trin) [Indic] (Title used in addressing) a maternal aunt. *'Renouka! But you getting big, girl. I wouldn't know you if I was to see you on the street.' Renouka smiled awkwardly.... 'How are you Mousie?' Renouka came up and kissed her.*—NF:66 [< Hin *mausii* 'mother's sister']

mousse [mus] *n* (Guyn, StLu) [*AF—Derog*] A person, usu a boy or young man, who is at sb's beck and call; a general factotum. [Perh naut infl via Fr. Cp Fr *mousse* 'a ship's boy']

mouth *n n* (CarA) [*AF/IF*] **1.** A person's voice, tongue, or mind. **a.** *... but it so happen, my dear, the landlord must have heard me mouth from outside, and ... he sent word to the overseer to say let me come in to see him.*—LICMS:28 **b.** *If Misses Julia didn't go for police and not people mouth I would keep him. The poor mother must be catching she nennen. She must be poor and out of work. No doubt is what cause her to do that.*—ExP (73.04.29, p.10) **c.** *All that came to her mouth she told them.*—PKKK:102 **2.** [By extension, usu *Derog* and particularly in some of the phrs below] Sth that speaks as if by itself, independent of the person. *Keep your mouth out of their business. Mouth does get people in trouble.*—(Antg) **3.** [By extension] Anything said that is irresponsible or unpleasant; braggadocio. *Don't worry with him sayin[g] he goin[g] put you in court. That's only mouth.*—(Guyn) **4.** PHRASES **4.1 air your mouth** *vb phr* (CarA) [*AF*] See AIR² Phr 2.2 **4.2. be full of (a lot of) mouth** *vb phr* (CarA) [*AF*] To speak irresponsibly, boastfully or rudely. *They were so full of mouth that when they eventually lost the match everybody howled at them.*—(Bdos). **4.2.1 be/got/have two-mouth** *vb phr* (CarA) [*AF*] To be deceitful, hypocritical, unreliable.

Davie sasys Bro' Haze only stopped breeding Ma Lucy because he could find no more names for the pickneys. / But Davie was two-mouthed that time, for I afterwards heard him tell young men at Morant Bay market that Ma Lucy keeps flat 'cause she turns her back at nights.—RND:46 [Perh a calque from W Afr langs. Cp Yoruba ṣe ẹnun meji (*do/have mouth two*) 'to be self-contradicting, unreliable'—*pers info, A. Banjo*)] **4.3 be left/listen with your mouth open** *vb phr* (CarA) [*IF*] To be left aghast. *Straightway Jenny went to Rosie's door step and called her a mischiefmaker, a news carrier, a fastmouth and all that she could think of. Rosie stood and listened with wide open mouth ... not knowing what it was all about.*—PKKK:46 **4.4 change your mouth** *vb phr* (CarA) [*AF—Derog*] ‖ **turn your tongue** (StVn) To say sth quite different from what you said before in the same context; (SE) 'to change your tune (in a disloyal way)'. *Somebody must have bribed him because, when he got into court he changed his mouth, my dear Sir! And the whole case collapsed!*—(Tbgo) **4.5 cover/kibber your mouth** *vb phr* (Jmca) [*AF*] To be tight-lipped about sth. **4.6 dip/push your mouth in sb's business** *vb phr* (CarA) [*AF—Derog*] See DIP Phr 2.1 **4.7 flap/flop your mouth** *vb phr* (TkCa) [*AF—Derog*] ‖ RUN YOUR MOUTH (CarA) See FLAP Phr, also Phr 28 below. [Flop < *flap* with [ɔ] < [a] by false refinement] □ This and Phr 4.8 are more strongly emotive than RUN YOUR MOUTH **4.8 fly your mouth** *vb phr* (Guyn) [*AF—Derog*] ‖ RUN YOUR MOUTH (CarA) *You should hear her flyin[g] her mouth about the father outside children and tellin[g] her mother to chase him out the house*—(Guyn) **4.9 give/got/have (a lot of) mouth** *vb phr* (CarA) [*AF*] [Esp of young persons] To speak audaciously to your elders; to give back-answers. *I couldn't give my father any mouth when he scolded me, but nowadays childern have a lot of mouth and parents take it from them.*—(StVn) [Cp Yoruba *o yanu sorọ* (he quick-mouth speak) 'He speaks too boldly (to an elderly person)'. Also *ẹnun ẹ pọ ju* (mouth his too much) 'to brag; to speak disrespectfully (to an older person)'] **4.10 got/have sweet-mouth** *vb phr* (CarA) [*AF*] To be an able flatterer. **4.11 hang your mouth where the soup drips** *vb phr* (Guyn) [*AF—Derog*] To seek the favour of whatever political party is in power, without shame or principle, in order to safeguard your own livelihood. [A ref to the post-emancipation era, some catching even the drippings of soup] **4.12 hear sb's mouth** *vb phr* (CarA) [*AF*] To hear the loud voice of sb boasting, or challenging, or quarrelling. **a.** *When the papers announced that the boy win a scholarship, if you hear the father's mouth!*—(Trin) **b.** *The two of them met in the street, and hear their mouth quarrelling over the man!*—(Guyn) **4.13 Hush your mouth!** *vb phr* (CarA) [*AF*] See HUSH Phr *'I wish people didn't have to work so hard.' / 'Hush you' mouth, child, you don't know what you talkin' bout'.*—MHJT: 17 **4.14 le[t] go your mouth** *vb phr* (Baha, Jmca, Mrat, Nevs) [*AF*] ‖ AIR YOUR MOUTH (CarA) See AIR² Phr 2.2 **4.15 lick your mouth** *vb phr* (Bdos, Trin) [*AF—Derog*] See LICK Phr

4.16 4.16 make your mouth fast; make your mouth fly *vb phrs* (CarA) [*AF—Derog*] To carry news; to tell tales; to be a blabber-mouth. **4.17 mind/watch your mouth** *vb phr* (CarA) [*IF*] To be careful about what you say. *'Mine you mout' dey, Mr Fitz,' a new voice shrieked. 'My parents born dong de Main. An' if you was to see my children you would t'ink dey was pure Spanish. All a wee is de same t'ing, eh? English people right. Dey should chop up all you. All you does be too farse wid all you self.'*—MN (59.06.03, p.75) [Cp Yoruba ṣọ ẹnun ẹ (watch mouth you) 'mind what you say'—(pers info, A. Banjo)] **4.18 mouth open story jump out** *id phr* (CarA) [*AF—Joc*] ‖ **mouth le[t]-go and story pop out** (Jmca) ‖ **open your mouth and story fly** (Belz) Much that is embarrassing is or will be revealed. *The authorities connived at getting her out of the country quickly, because they knew that if charges were brought against her, mouth open story jump out and a certain Minister would be charged too.*— (Guyn) **4.19 open your mouth (on sb)** *vb phr* (Dmca) [*AF*] ‖ RUN YOUR MOUTH (CarA) See Phr 4.28 below. **4.20 pass your mouth on (sb)** *vb phr* (Dmca, Tbgo, Trin) [*AF—Derog*] See PASS[1] Phr 3.11 **4.21 pay for your mouth** *vb phr* (CarA) [*AF*] See PAY Phr 1. **4.22 not pick your mouth** *neg vb phr* (Angu, Bdos, Guyn, Tbgo) [*AF*] See PICK Phr 5.2 **4.22.1 pick sb's mouth** *vb phr* (CarA) [*AF*] See PICK Phr 5.7 **4.22.2 unpick your mouth** *vb phr* (Trin) [*AF—Derog*] See UNPICK Phr **4.23 prove your mouth** *vb phr* (Trin) [*AF*] See PROVE Phr 3.1 **4.24 push/put your mouth in (sb's) business/story** *vb phr* (CarA) [*AF/IF*] To interfere aggressively in sb else's quarrel; to take sides officiously. *Not me I ain't pushing me mouth in Politics / Nobody can't get me to sing 'bout politics / Don't tell me what Waldo Ramsey should do wid he big alsation dog now / Is he business.*—Cso (Sir Don, 1975) [Perh a calque. Cp Yoruba o ki ẹnun bọ ọrọ ọlọrọ (he put mouth enter word somebody else's work) 'He meddled in another's affairs'] **4.25 not put water in your mouth (to say sth)** *neg vb phr* (Trin) [*AF—Joc*] See PUT Phr 1. **4.26 put mouth on (sth)** *vb phr* (Baha, BrVi, TkCa) [*AF*] ‖ PUT BAD-EYE ON (STH) (Belz, Guyn) **4.26.1 put your mouth on (sb/sth)** *vb phr* (CarA) [*AF/IF*] See BAD-MOUTH[1] Phr 3.2; also PUT Phr 26.1 **4.26.2 put your mouth in your pocket** *vb phr* (Bdos) [*AF—Joc*] To have to pay heavy damages in a libel suit brought against you. **4.27 rest your mouth** *vb phr* (CarA) [*AF*] To stop continuous talking. *Stella has gone off to rest her mouth (among other things) in foreign lands! I am glad for the chile for she works hard and needs the little break.*—StA(JA) (70.07.11, p.10) **4.28 run your mouth** *vb phr* (CarA) [*AF—Derog*] ‖ *fly your mouth* (Guyn) ‖ *open your mouth (on sb)* (Dmca) To say mean, untrustworthy things about sb or some situation. **a.** *As far as they was concern experience didn't count for that much, and once they had their certificates, what didn't mean that they could produce, they was running their mouth.*—NaG (75.03.06, p.2) **b.** *They saying Miss James is his woman. You should hear how Urmilla running she mouth all over the place and*

the kind of lies she telling about how they planning to run away.—NF:276 [See RUN Phr 6.11, also Phr 4.38 below] **4.29 send your heart through your mouth** *vb phr* (Guyn) [*IF*] See HEART Phr 6. **4.30 turn sb's mouth behind his/her back** *vb phr* (Guyn, USVI) [*AF*] To slap, box, strike sb with full force in the face; [by extension] to beat up sb severely. *She said to Jenny 'If you go to Miss Ada ... it will be the last time you talk because I'll take night make day to turn your mouth behind your back.*—PKKK:47 **4.31 wash your mouth on (sb/sth)** *vb phr* (Angu, Antg, Mrat, Nevs, Tbgo) [*AF—Derog*] **(i)** ‖ PUT YOUR BAD-MOUTH ON (SB/STH) (CarA) *From the time they hear he was buildin[g] a house they only busy washin[g] thei[r] mout[h] on him and the whole thing, till up to now the house can['t] build.*—(Nevs) **(ii)** (CarA) [*AF—Derog*] To speak in openly, insulting, or strongly derogatory terms about (sb or some event); to make a display of exposing disgraceful home-truths about (sb or some event) so as to cause grave embarrassment. **a.** *In this statement, Prime Minister Bishop reacted to Prime Minister Adams' call for immediate general elections in Grenada by describing his Barbadian counterpart as a 'yardfowl' who still feels he has not got enough problems in his own backyard that he could find time to wash his mouth in Grenada's business.*—AdN (80.11.09, p.1) **b.** *What Mr Barrow is saying in essence is that the President of the United States has coined a fraudulent phrase. He, Mr Reagan, is using the term Caribbean Basin not to 'launder his clothes', but to 'wash his mouth', on the region.*—AdV (82.04.28, p.4) □ Cp also BAD-MOUTH, GOAT-MOUTH. **4.32 you can't keep your mouth** *id phr* (Jmca, TkCa) [*AF—Derog*] ‖ YOUR MOUTH HAS/AIN'T GOT NO COVER (Angu, etc) **4.33 your mouth got ra-ra** *id phr* (StVn) [*AF—Derog*] See RA-RA Phr **4.34 your mouth has/ain't got no cover** *id phr* (Angu, Bdos, BrVi, Guyn, Mrat, StVn) [*AF—Derog*] ‖ *mouth has no backdoor (Nevs, StKt)* [Also with several other complements as follows] / ‖ *no boundary* (Gren) / ‖ *no bridle* (BrVi) / ‖ *no deep-freeze* (Baha) / ‖ *no hemming* (Nevs) / ‖ *no licence* (Gren) / ‖ *no lining* (Nevs) / ‖ *no padlock* (Dmca) / ‖ *no stopper* (StVn) ‖ *mouth goes like parch benny* (Baha) / ‖ *is like a river* (StVn) / ‖ *mouth runs* (Angu, Antg, Gren, StVn) / ‖ *sleep a-door* (StKt) / ‖ *run your mouth* (Baha, Mrat, TkCa) ‖ *you can't keep your mouth* (Jmca, TkCa) Your tongue wags freely; you cannot be trusted not to repeat whatever you hear. *I will talk out all de things that I know / De different women that got Romeo / He shouldn't mess wid me / He know me mout in have no cover already.*—Cso (Sir Don, 1975) [Cp Yoruba enu ẹ ko ni kọkọrọ ‖ Nupe emi wun de egi yoko-a ‖ Lingala monoko na ye ezanga fungola 'his/her mouth has no key/lock'] **4.35 your mouth is going to/will pay** *id phr* (Bdos) [*AF*] You will pay the costs of libel. *But den dey got others who does like de mudslingin' an' I hear nuff mud sling 'bout in Sin John and Deacons Farm. Somebody mout' gine soon pay all de Dems election expenses!*—NaT (90.10.19, p.11, Lickmout' Lou) **4.36 your mouth is hot** *id phr* (Guyn)

[*AF*] [Esp of young persons] (To be) quick with a rude, cutting answer. **4.37 your mouth is like a river** *id phr* ‖ YOUR MOUTH HAS/AIN'T GOT NO COVER (Angu, Bdos, BrVi, Guyn, Mrat, StVn) [*AF—Derog*] **4.38 your mouth runs like parch(ing) benny/like sick nigger take salts/etc** *id phrs* (CarA) [*AF—Joc/Derog*] You are an endless, nauseating talker; [by extension] you are a blabber-mouth, a ready and dangerous gossip; (SE) 'you run off at the mouth'. **a.** *Henley: 'Please, Matilda, don't let's go over all this again. Your mouth was running the whole night last night just because I came in a little late.*—WBH:13 **b.** *Is no wanda de people does call you 'Pudding Mouth Juliet', you mouth dont take long to start runnin.*—Kai VIII. p.63 [A prob calque from W Afr langs. Cp Igbo *onye onu na-agba kpori-kpori* (*person whose mouth runs 'prattle-prattle'*) 'person who talks too much'—(*pers info, C. Azuonye*); also Yoruba *ẹnu araye nda* (*continuously (at the) mouth people dripping/gushing out*) 'people's mouths are always running' i.e 'It is best not to trust people with confidences'—(*pers info, K. Ọmọtọsọ*)] □ See also RUN Phr 6.11 RUN YOUR MOUTH. **4.39 your mouth sleep a-door** *vb phr* (StKt) ‖ YOUR MOUTH HAS/AIN'T GOT NO COVER (Angu, etc)

mouth·a·mas·sy (Li·za) ['mɒʊt-a-masi laɪza] *n (phr)* (Jmca) ‖ MOUTHAR (Bdos, etc) [Mouth + ? < Twi *mmasa-mmasa* 'confused (words)' + Liza < 'lies' + er (?)] □ Cp also COCHORE² (*Guyn*).

mouth·ar ['mɒʊtar ~ 'mɒʊtə] *n* (Bdos, Gren, Guyn, Tbgo, Trin) [*AF—Derog*] ‖ **mou-thamassy** (Jmca) A dangerously talkative person; sb who cannot be trusted with a secret; a blabbermouth. *Moutar an guitar a two differen ting ('A chattering mouth and a thrumming guitar are quite different things').*—Guyn (Cr Prov) (AGM:24) See also BIG-MOUTH² 2.

mouth-wa·ter [maʊt wɒtə] *n phr* (Guyn, Jmca, StVn, Tbgo) Dribble; saliva. **a.** *He dribbles in his sleep; every morning you could see fresh mouth-water stains on his pillow.*—(Tbgo) [A prob calque. Cp Mandinka *da-ji* (mouth-water) 'saliva'; also *WIED* Igbo *ọnụ mili* (mouth water) 'spittle']

mouth·y (-mouth·y) ['mɒʊti-mɒʊti] *adj* (Guyn, Jmca, StKt) ‖ BIG-MOUTH² 2. (CarA)

move PHRASES **1. move your bowels** *vb phr* (CarA) ‖ *ease your belly* (CarA) [*IF*] To ease your bowels; to have a bowel movement. **2. Move yourself!** [*IF*]; **Move your tail!** [*AF—Vul*] *imper vb phr* (CarA) ‖ *Carry yourself/your tail!* (Antg, Guyn) ‖ *fire yourself* (Antg, Guyn, Nevs, Tbgo) ‖ *fire your skin* (Tbgo)/ *your tail* (Guyn) ‖ *Haul yourself/your tail!* (Bdos, Mrat, StVn) ‖ *Pass yourself!* (Tbgo) ‖ *Pelt your skin!* (StVn) ‖ *Pull yourself!* (StVn, Trin) ‖ *Take a side!* (Tbgo) ‖ *Take yourself!* (Belz, Gren, StKt) ‖ *Take up yourself!* (Jmca, Mrat, StKt) Be off with you!; Take yourself out of my sight!

Go away! **a.** *You expect me to believe that? Move yourself!*—(Bdos) **b.** *Wha[t] da[t]? Kanhai is de greates[t] cricketer? Boy move yo[ur] tail!*—(Guyn) [See notes at HAUL YOURSELF, TAKE YOURSELF] □ Always in strong emotive contexts, sometimes with Vul variants, but sometimes also Joc, with the sense 'Don't tell me that! You must be joking!'

mo·vé-lang¹ (mau·vais-langue¹) [movelãŋ/-laŋ] *n* (StLu, Tbgo, Trin) [*AF—Derog*] ‖ *bad-talk¹* (CarA) Malicious gossip; injurious half-truths; malignant rumours; (SE) 'smear campaign'. **a.** *Some of them exult greatly in their grand role of Dispenser of 'Dem Say' and Minister of Mauvais Langue as they bring and carry bits of salacious information, most of it fabricated or distorted.*—ExP (73.02.25, p.21) **b.** *Mr. Manley has further muddied relations with Trinidad and Tobago. His mauvais langue, before a party convention is not so much wounding or offensive as it is revelatory of hostility, perhaps of envy and to many, of rank canine ingratitude.*—TrG (80.01.31, p.12) **c.** *And he left no doubt in anyone's mind that he had done his homework well. That he had graduated a long time before from the mauvais langue politics of the St Lucia Labour Party and the UWP.*—WBAM:230 [Fr Cr < Fr *mauvais* 'bad' + '*langue*' 'tongue'; evid a Fr Cr calque from W Afr langs parallel to the Anglophone Cr calque BAD-TALK¹. See etym note there. Note that grammatical Fr *mauvaise langue* does not represent, either in pronunc or meaning, the Fr Cr expression] □ 1. The term implies more wit and subtlety than BAD-TALK, this latter being always done 'behind' sb's back' whereas MOVÉ-LANG need not be. 2. The standardized spelling is recommended. However writers regularly (as in cits) use *mauvais langue* with erron variants such as *mauvaise langue* (a false refinement levelling with Standard Fr), *mauvais' langue*, etc.

mo·vé-lang² (mau·vais-langue²) [mo·velãŋ/-laŋ] *adj* (StLu, Tbgo, Trin) [*AF—Derog*] ‖ *bad-tongue²* (Tbgo, Trin) ‖ *malpalan* (Dmca, StLu) Given to malicious gossiping; malignant; deceitful. **a.** *So Tantie had to take me down to Mrs Hinds, a horrible capitulation, for she'd always sworn she'd never send a dog of hers there, that woman was a mauvais' langue horse-face maco.*—HCCM:36 **b.** *Would you believe this must mean there are mauvais-langue blabber-mouths representing the PNM in Parliament because Bertie would never make such a joke with any opposition man.*—BoM (79.04.13, p.6) [By functional n > vb shift of MOVÉ-LANG¹]

mo·vé-lang³ (mau·vais-langue³) [movelãŋ/-laŋ] *vb* (StLu, Tbgo, Trin) [*AF—Derog*] ‖ BAD-TALK² (CarA) **a.** *The way things go in the House these days, it is always hard to distinguish between serious debate and the amount of gun-talk, mauvaise languing and smoke-screening going on.*—BoM (79.07.27, p.10) **b.** *You should 'ave hear the talk round Perenong, skipper; all the pork-knockers say that you make deal with Bullah and he buy* the queen off you. You know how black people tongue can mauvais langue them who they think flourishing too much.—RWIN:192 (J. Carew) [By functional n > vb shift of MOVÉ-LANG[1]] □ Cit b., from a Guyn writer, indicates spreading of the loan to other (non-Fr Cr) territories. See also MALPALÉ.

mox·ie [mɒksi] adj (Trin) [AF] Untidy looking; unkempt; [by extension, of a young woman] unattractive.

Mr Hard·ing n phr (Bdos) **1.** [Hist, Sugar Ind] An effigy stuffed with sugar-cane trash and burnt as part of the CROP-OVER folk festivities. Canes on some of the carts were tied by gay-coloured bandanas which danced in the wind like flags, while one cart carried an effigy of 'Mr Harding'. Mr Harding who symbolised hard times and represented all cruel gang-drivers was made from sugar-cane trash and dressed in an old black coat, a top hat and wore a mask.—SCO:3 [Believed to be a pun on hard referring both to hard-hearted planters and DRIVERS whose tyranny was now suspended, and to hard times ahead (i.e. with no wages) before the next crop when that tyranny would recommence. The burning of **Mr Harding** was said to provide a release for field-labourers' repressed emotions] **2.** [By extension] A person who appears to be suffering great hardship.

M.S.A. abbr (Dmca) The Meritorious Service Award, the third highest national honour of the Commonwealth of Dominica.

much[1] adv (CarA) [X] [Before a pl noun esp after how, so, too] Many. **a.** She didn't get much customers the night before.—PCOS:29 **b.** I said 'How much children do you have' and he said one.—NaT (76.09.05, p.18, Dear Christine) **c.** He prolonged his suffering, appealing so much times and failing.—ToR (75.05.18, p.8) **d.** Too much coconut shells on parapets.—SuC (H, 78.08.20, p.3) [Prob from characteristic CarA Cr and mesolectal economy of word-choice esp where sense is not affected (cp a for an). Prob also helped by similar EE uses of much (see OED much A. 2. b. c. d.) as found for ex in AVB 'much people' or in IF ModE 'much thanks']

much[2] adv (CarA) PHRASES **1. much less; much more** adv phrs (CarA) [X] [Used after a neg statement these phrs are often confused or functionally misascribed in CE] **a.** The needle alone does have me frighten, much less the drilling, O Lord! [i.e. 'and the drilling frightens me much more' or 'much less can I stand the drilling'] —(Bdos) **b.** How I goin[g] go to weddin[g]? Wha[t] I ain[']t even got good clothes to wear [u]pon a Sunday, much less! [i.e. 'much less would my clothes do for a wedding']—(Guyn) **c.** From a child my father never hit me in my own home, much more you the man I married. [i.e. 'so much the more should you not' or 'so much the less have you a right to']—(StVn) □ Cp FAR LESS, FAR MORE. See FAR Phrs.

much up vb phr (CarA) To make much of; to be affectionate to. **a.** ... he start to make much of Brother Bannister daughter, Jen. He was muching up Jen plenty, but nobody say anything, ...— LICMS:132 **b.** 'I not losing my temper,' Bhaskar said quietly. He poured himself some more tea. 'What you want me to do? Love and much them up?'—NF:350 [See EDD much vb[1] (Lin, Hrf, etc) 1. 'to make much of; to pet, fondle, caress; to appease by making much of']

mud-daub·er (Guyn) ‖ MASON-MARABUNTA. □ The commoner folk-name.

mud-head n (CarA) [AF—Joc] (Nickname for) a native of Guyana. **a.** We Guianese were always known as 'mudheads'. If we federate it would just prove we are mud-heads indeed. Trinidad is brewing beer from our rice, and all we Guianese know is to boil and eat it.—GyG (55.03.29) **b.** 'De Bajan man him say,' Ella smiled, 'plantain an' salt fish me don't want 'um, an' de Mud-head man him say, me wish me had 'um, me wish me had 'um.'—WTD:34 [A ref to the muddy coastland area of Guyana on wh most of its population live]

Mud·land; Mud·land·er n (CarA) [IF—Joc] Guyana; Guyanese. **a.** Aussies in 'Mudland'— Georgetown (Reuter) Australia and West Indies teams arrived in Guyana yesterday to a West Indian-style steelband welcome following their thrilling third Test in Trinidad.—ExP (73.03.30, p.26) **b.** The winners of the Trinidad versus Windward Islands tie will meet Bahamas, while the survivors of the 'battle' between the 'Mudlanders' and the Bajans will toss-up with the mighty Jamaicans.—ExP (72.03.09, p.21) [See MUD-HEAD]

Mud, The n phr (Baha) **1.** (See cit) The Great Bahama Bank, an enormous shoal on the west side of Andros nicknamed The Mud, and one of the great sponge beds of the world, was the most popular sponge fishing bed.—MTTBT:39 **2.** PHRASE **2.1 go on the mud** vb phr (Baha) To go sponge-fishing. Of course, sponging lacked much of the excitement and the thrill of adventure which was attached to wrecking. But even so old timers, who as young men went 'on the mud', look back on their voyaging years with deep nostalgia.—ASOB:159

muf·fin n (Bdos) ‖ BAKE(s)[1] 3. (Guyn, StLu) Some say bake and some people say muffin, but is the same thing. Round by us in St George, they usually say muffin.—(Bdos)

muh [mʌ] pron (CarA) [AF-Cr] See ME 2 □ A dial spelling.

muh·self refl pron (CarA) See MESELF·

mu·kro (muck·ra, mu·ku·ru) [mʊkrʌ~ mʌkrʊ] n (Guyn) A tough reed wh grows to a height of 12 ft in swampy ground; after the pith is removed the reed is dried for thatching roofs, weaving baskets, etc. [Amerindian (perh Arawak) name of the reed]

mu·lat·to [myulato ~ malata] n (CarA) [Derog]
A person of mixed white and black parentage;
[by extension] any LIGHT-SKINNED person. **a.**
*But then comes the question, whether the mulatto
is more capable of being educated than the negro,
and more able to work under the hot sun than
the Englishman.*—LMSPJS:78 **b.** *But what a
fool-fool mulatto-man, that! Then dry-time is not
on our land? Then people are not starving?*—RND:
84 **c.** *'I ain want no white man cause I ain
able wid no mulatta chile!' she said.*—Guyn (Ms)
□ The term, wh was historically meant to be
Derog (< Sp *mulato* 'young mule') barely passes
as acceptable in writing in the *CarA* today as a
recognized description of a person of mixed
(white-black) race; but its offensive connotation,
esp with the pronunc /malata/, easily surfaces as
in cits.

mul·ber·ry n (CayI) ‖ JUMBIE-SOURSOP (Antg,
etc) [From its make-up wh prob reminded early
settlers of the European *mulberry*. See *OED's*
note at *mulberry* 1. ... 'the 'berry', of roundish
oval shape, is an aggregate of a multitude of
true fruits covered by succulent calyces'. This
description applies superficially also to the *CarA*
item so called]

mule n (Belz, Guyn, Jmca, Trin) [AF—Derog]
A barren woman. **a.** *In contemporary Jamaica,
barren women are called 'mules' and their child-
lessness is regarded as some form of divine punishment for their transgressions. Jamaica women
are simply expected to have children.*—Jmca (Ms)
b. *Women who are infertile need worry no more.
Booded Mille bush tea taken for seven days will
cure you of 'mule-belly'.*—ExP (72.09.03, p.28)

mule boy n phr (Guyn) A youngster employed
to guide a mule along the side of TRENCHES as it
pulls a number of CANE-PUNTS between field and
factory. *Balli had grown up on a sugar estate, ...
He began as a mule-boy, was hard-working, thrifty
and industrious, had gone through all the vagaries
of estate life and had risen to the position of field
foreman when he retired.*—GyC (77.01.16, p.12)

mul·let* n (CarA) A herbivorous, silver-
coloured fish wh grows up to one foot in length;
it is caught in a seine and can be found in fresh
water (usu near estuaries) and shallow salt water;
Mugil spp, Mugil curema and *M. cephalus* (*Mugilidae*).

mung (-bean)* n (Belz, Guyn, Trin) **1.** ‖ **urdi**
(Guyn, Trin) ‖ **woolly pyrol** (Trin) An ovoid,
yellowish-green bean borne in a short, stout,
hairy pod on a bushy 3-ft-high plant; the beans
are used mostly by EAST INDIANS, crushed for
making DAAL; *Phaseolus mungo* (*Leguminosae-
Papilionatae*). **2.** (Guyn, Trin) A bean varying in
colour from greenish-yellow to blackish-brown,
borne in a narrower pod than the prec on an
erect plant with hairy leaves; the beans are
cooked green or used for making DAAL; *Phaseolus
aureus* (*Leguminosae-Papilionatae*). [Bhoj/Hin
name of this bean]

mur·der·a·tion n (CarA) [AF] **1.** A severe
beating up (esp of a woman or child); [by ex-
tension] a very violent row (usu between two
persons). **a.** *My faada no believe inna no discipline
at all, but murderation. Just pure beating. When
him beat, him beat deadly.*—SSLG:5 **b.** *When she
told the woman she was dismissin[g] her, the woman
turn on her and she fire back jus[t] as hot. Was
murderation break loose in the place.*—(Guyn)
[*Murder* + SE suff *-ation*, by analogy with
botheration, etc] **2.** [By extension] Any calamity,
upheaval or overwhelming trouble. **a.** *Dear Departed Federation / Referendum murderation /
Bounce you ina outa space / Hope you fine a
restin place.*—FCV2:85 (L. Bennett) **b.** *With the
Guyana dollar dropping to a hundred to one US,
you can understand prices are 'murderation'.*—
Guyn (Ms)

mus·co·va·do (su·gar) n (phr) (CarA)
‖ **black-sugar** (StKt) A wet, almost caked dark
sugar, being the first unrefined stage after the
crystallization of molasses, (recently re-
commercialized for use with coffee). *As boys we
used to suck lumps of muscovado which we begged
for at the factory.*—(Bdos) [< Pg *mascavado*
'unrefined, impure' < *mascavar* 'to adulterate'.
(N.B: *OED's* source Sp *mascabado* has not been
found)]

mu·si·cal saw n phr (Baha, Guyn) A 3-ft-long
carpenter's saw used as a musical instrument,
the handle being anchored while the player bends
the blade striking the arc with a piece of wood or
metal, the different arching of the blade yielding
different notes; the serrated edge of the blade is
also scraped for another effect.

mu·sick·er·man n (Mrat) A musican (esp one
of a group hired for a night festivity). *Well you
have to cook plenty with extra for the musicker-men
when you have jumbie-dance.*—(Mrat) [Cp *OED*
musicker (Obs + rare) 'musican' + cits 1425–
1781]

must modal (CarA) [IF] PHRASES **1. must be**;
mus.see, mus.sy [mʌsbi ~ mʌsi] modal vb phrs
[IF/AF] [Note: Occurring at the folk level most
widely in the form spelled MUSSEE/MUSSY] **(i)**
[Functioning as in SE] Must be. **a.** *Wuh dah?
de man mussee mad, bo!*—BMP:43 **b.** *I sez to
mersef 'Jees, My Lord, dis mussy de one dat dus
kill yer orf in de new style.'*—JBJ:88 [Evid SE
must be > /mos-i/ by characteristic CarA Cr
reduction of /CC/, whence /st-b > s/. The fused
form then passes into distinct CarA Cr functions
wh are evid re-interpreted at the mesolectal level,
by false refinement, into CE *must be* with non-
standard functions as in foll cases. The cits
illustrate both forms] **(ii)** [Followed by a pres.
part.] **a.** *All this time she mussy bakin[g].*—Guyn
(Ms) **b.** *'But he does drive a Honda, he mussee
driving the Citroen today for more style, but he
ain't handling so pretty,' my friend responded,
laughing.*—SuS (89.02.12, p.3) **b.** *Dinah said to
Winkie, 'Boy, ya see how ya put we in trouble now!
Ya mussy going take ma licks fer me.'*—TOSR:32

(iii) [Followed by a vb, hence developing an adverbial sense and function] Ought to; (must) probably; (must) likely. **a.** 'Well, is you children, same as mine,' Mabel say. 'You must be know what is best for them.'—CISH:40 **b.** Wuh yuh en know my jaw does still drop evah time I study dah t'ing? De ole people mussee does mo' dan turn in duh grave, faif.—NaT (78.10.27, p.5, Lickmout Lou) **c.** Dey mussie plan ta kill my dog.—WBS:44 **(iv)** [Passing into purely adverbial function] Probably; likely. **a.** You t'ink I must be pick up money. Wha' you expect mah to get it from, wit' butter an' lard so dear, an' sugar four cents a pound. Yo' must be be expect me to steal.—WTD:27 **b.** Sophie say she didn't agree with that because the fella was dead reliable and she was sure that he was ga come. She figger that he must be was in a accident or something.—NaG (78.06.01, Satirically Speaking) **c.** Maureen Small and di odder fair skin pickney mussy used to laugh after me. Deep down, she mussy know me used to tek di one sixpence me have and buy snowcone and give her because mi want her fi me friend.—SSLG:99 **2. must can; must could** modal vb phrs (Guyn, Jmca) [X] Should/must be able to. **a.** You mus[t] can min[d] a wife befo[re] yo[u] tek one.—(Guyn) **b.** I say well she have so much breadfruit she must could give me two.—(Jmca) □ These forms occur sometimes in written schoolwork. Replaced in speech in most other territories by **must be can/could**.

mus·tee [mʌsti] n (Bdos, Guyn) The offspring of a white and a MULATTO parent. [A corruption of Sp mestizo, Pg mestiço, 'half-caste, half-breed', evid so borrowed from EE and surviving in the speech of older and rural folk. See OED mustee + cits 1699–1829]

my possessive pron (CarA) PHRASES **1. My gentleman** n phr (Bdos) [IF] Sir. **a.** The attendant and another man were there, and as he got out of the car he told one of the men 'My gentleman, sell me some gas, please.'—AdN (80.04.15, p.1) **b.** My gentleman, I ent talking to you, you say you is a blindman, walking with a stick and still you pushing yah mouth in everyting yah hear from the time the bus left the stand you ent stop talk yet.—Bdos (Ms Play, 1977) [Prob by analogy with My lady as SE form of address] **2. my one** pers pron phr (Bdos) [X] See ONE² 2.; also ME Phr 3.3.

my·al (ma·yal) [maɪal] adj, n (Jmca) (Of or belonging to) a folk religion in wh the power of spirits of the dead is enlisted in order to cure ills or counteract evil (esp that of OBEAH); it involves the use of herbal medicines and baths, drumming and dancing to induce spirit-possession, ritual sacrifice of fowls, and other ceremonial rites, some of wh are performed under a silk-cotton tree; it is now largely restricted to some rural pockets of Jmca. [Cp ADHL Hausa maye (m.), mayya (f.) 'a sorceress'; also maye vb 'to relieve'. Perh /mayal/ is a connected dial form] □ MYAL does not seem to occur with any determiner such as a, some, the, their, etc. It is usu attrib, hence **myal-dance, -duppy, -ground, -healer**, etc.

my·al·ism (ma·yal·ism) n (Jmca) The practice or performance of MYAL beliefs and rites. [MYAL + SE -ism 'organized belief system' as in Methodism, Hinduism, etc] □ This term is the noun preferred to MYAL by sociologists and observers, esp in writing.

my·al·ist (ma·yal·ist, ma·yal-man/-wo·man, my·al-man/-wo·man) n (Jmca) The man/woman who organizes and leads MYAL healing procedures and ceremonies.

myr·tle-lime n (Antg, Mrat) ‖SWEET-LIME (ECar)

N

n- [n-] (Bdos) [X] [The addition of the sound /
n-/ to words beginning with a vowel, esp 'u-', is
heard in folk speech esp in *Bdos*, but occasionally
also elsewhere. The case below is an example]
*De 'Pampalam' tickets sellin' like peas, as nusual,
anyhow, so CBC or nuh CBC, Combermere gine
be pack fuh de show.*—NaT (90.07.20, p.9A,
Lickmout Lou) [Prob a haphazard folk prosthesis. Cp /h-/] □ See also NUSE.

na¹ [nɒ ~ na:] *negator* [*AF—Cr*] **1.** (CarA) (SE)
No! [Esp at the folk level in answering a question]
S1: You goin[g] to de fair? S2: Na!—(Guyn) **2.**
neg particle (Antg, Guyn) ‖ *nah; nar* (Nevs,
StKt) ‖ *no* (CarA) Not [In all its functions in
SE] **a.** *Bysie bway, me nar tell you no lie, you
know, but me no like to go cut no wood like dis
every Satiday.*—FGSOS:33 (G. Irish) **b.** *Cockroach nah mus walk a fowl-house.* (= *The cockroach must not walk in the fowl's house.*)—Guyn
(Prov) □ In this function NA(H), etc goes, as in
CarA Cr, immediately after the subject. Cp Cr
/i na doz wok satidee/ 'He does not work Saturdays'. See also *DJE naa* + cits. **3.** *neg auxiliary
(with ellipsis)* (Guyn, Nevs, StKt) Isn't, aren't,
etc; doesn't, don't, didn't. **a.** *Na all ass wa start
race does end am.* (= *It isn't every ass that starts
a race that ends it.*)—AGM:33 (Guyn Prov) **b.**
Me see grass, me nar study ants-nest. (= *I saw there
was grass, I didn't think of an ant-nest.*)—MtM
(62.08.25, p.5, Chit Chat) **4.** *neg imper* (Antg,
Guyn) Don't. *Na mek you aze pass you head.* (=
*Don't make your ears pass your head, i.e. Don't be
like an ass!*)—AGM:24 (Guyn Prov) **5.** *introducing an assertion (with ellipsis)* (Guyn) ‖ NO
6. (Guyn, Jmca) [< SE *not* by apocope and with
[ɔ > a] vowel opening. The form also occurs in
many E (esp northern) and Sc dialects = *not*,
but hardly in the positions it takes in AF CE,
wh strongly reflect the position and function of
CarA Cr neg marker *na*] □ These forms, usu
pronounced as shown, though conventionally
spelled 'NO' by writers, are more generally preserved in *CarA* provs; but they may also occur
in *Joc* use in familiar conversation, and so appear
in dial columns in newspapers, varying irregularly with NO, often in the same column.
See NO.

na² [na ~ nʌ] *prep* (Antg, Jmca, Mrat, Nevs,
StKt) ‖ *in(n)a* (Antg, etc) At; in; into; on. **a.** *Ah
hope to God you know whe' to find somebody potato
groun' to an dig potato an' roas' when hungry
start to buss you skin up na Brodericks Mountain
today.*—FGSOS:35 (G. Irish) **b.** *No wanda de
dargs ah bark, dem nevva see pooleece na uniform
yet.* (= *No wonder the dogs are barking; they've
never seen policemen in uniform yet.*)—LaS
(77.10.29, Bits & Pieces) [Perh a direct survival
of Igbo *na* 'at; in; to; from' wh is widely used
in many collocations. See *WIED:295, 296*. See
also note at INA]

naa·ni(e) (nan.ny) *n.* (Guyn, Trin) [Indic]
See NANI.

naa·ra(a) *n* (Guyn, Trin) See NARA

nag *n* (Nevs, StKt) [X] ‖ NOG (Nevs, StKt)
[Pronunc infl by Cr [ɔ > a] vowel opening]

nah(nar) *neg particle* (Nevs, StKt) ‖ NA¹ 2
(Antg, Guyn)

nail PHRASE **pick up a nail** *vb phr* (Antg, Guyn)
[*AF—Joc*] [Of a man] To contract venereal disease. *S1: Bushy is the only fast way to raise cash
for Doc Ling. S2: Why cash for the Doc? S1: Me
pick-up a nail.*—SBB:70 [A Joc ref to the limp
(as if suffering from having stepped on a nail)
characteristic of a man in an advanced state of
the disease]

nail-chook/-jook/-stick *n* (CarA) [*AF/IF*]
A puncture of the skin or any wound caused by
a nail, esp one on the sole of the foot caused by
stepping on a nail. *'Neighb,' he said with a look
of concern, 'gi me some salt, please. One of the
workers get a nail-chook.'*—BeA(TO) (81/11)
[See CHOOK, JOOK]

n(a)int [naint] *vb tr* (CarA) [*AF—Cr*] See NO-
INT

na·jar (na·zar) [naja·r ~ naza·r] *n* (Guyn, Trin)
[Indic] ‖ BAD-EYE (CarA) *... and stringed black
beads to go round his little wrists and neck, to keep
off nazar, otherwise the evil eye, for he was so
pretty.*—NAGOS:130 [Bhoj *najar* < Hin <
Perso-Arabic *nazar* 'glance, look, inspection'.
Also phr *nazar lagaanaa* 'to be under the infl of
the 'evil-eye']

na·ked [nekid] *adj* **1.** (Gren, Guyn, Jmca, Tbgo,
Trin) [*AF*] Bare; mere; just; nothing but; only.
a. *Janice, i[t']s naked calypso you have on the
tape?*—(Tbgo) **b.** *Is only naked man living in de
police station.*—(Gren) **c.** *While de neaga-man
t'ink say 'e got de ants dem lock 'way ... ina de*

*paper fo' hold dem ... an' de mister-man look fo'
de ants dem,'e meet naked paper.*—FGSOS:44 **2.**
(Trin) [By extension] [*AF—Joc*] Plenty of; a
great amount of. *Our good players gone on tour,
yo[u] know, but next time we goin[g] put naked
licks in thei[r] skin!*—(Trin) [An extension of the
sense 'nothing but']

na·ked-In·di·an *n* (Gren, Trin, USVI)
‖ BIRCH-GUM TREE (Bdos, etc) [Perh a Joc ref to
'Red Indian', from the reddish-brown colour of
the bark of this tree]

na·ked-skin *adj* (CarA) [*AF*] Naked; having
little or no clothes on (i.e. from sheer poverty,
not by choice). *I remember him as a naked-skin
little boy running around in the back streets there,
but now politics have made him boss over people who
never were naked-skin like him.*—(Guyn) [Prob a
refl from W Afr langs in many of wh there is
the same word for 'skin' 'body' exs Twi *ho* 'body;
skin', Yoruba *ara* 'body, skin', etc]

na·ked-wood* *n* (Baha) A small tree with a
slender or moderately thick trunk whose smooth,
skin-coloured bark prob accounts for its name;
it bears white flowers and small, red, inedible
fruit, and its aromatic leaves provide a very bitter
infusion used as a medicine for coughs; it is also
prized for its hard wood; *Myrcianthes fragrans*
(*Myrtaceae*).

nak·p·hul [nakphʊl] *n* (Guyn, Trin) [Indic] A
small gold decoration usu in the form of a little
flower, or a tiny ring, worn on one side of the
nose by Indian women. [Hin < *nak* 'nose' +
phuul 'flower']

name[1] *n* (CarA) PHRASES **1. have just called
(sb's) name** *id phr* (CarA) [*IF*] See CALL[1] Phr
3.12 **2. have (sb's) name all over the place**
vb phr (Bdos, Guyn, Tbgo) [*IF*] To spread or
cause scandalous gossip about (sb). **3. hear your
name with sb's name** *vb phr* (Tbgo) [*IF*] To
have your name associated with sb else's, by
rumour, in some improper dealing or sexual
relationship. **4. (or) (you can) change my
name** *id phr* (Guyn) [*IF*] I am as certain of what
I say as I am of my own name; as surely as my
name is—. *I tell you it was Christina I saw in
there with him, or change my name!*—(Guyn) **5.
pound sb's name** *vb phr* (CarA) [*AF*] See
POUND Phr 3.2 **6. walk on your name** *id phr*
(Guyn) [*IF*] To turn up (enter a room, etc) by
coincidence just when or soon after your name
has been mentioned. [Cp Edo *u wa khian fii
ẹvbẹn ruẹn* (*you have (just) walked-into word/
matter your*) 'You have come in upon a discussion
about you' (*A. Amayo*). Yoruba also uses a similar exp to mean 'that the person is not a bastard
and will live long' (*K. Ọmọtọsọ*)]

name[2] *vb* (CarA) [*AF*] **1.** Named; called; by
the name of; whose name is/was. **a.** *My name is
B. N— and I am in love with a girl name H—
but now she has leave me out and gone back to
her former lover.*—NaT (77.06.05, p.26, Dear

Christine) **b.** *They know ... a fellar name Harrison
working in the Red House.*—STLL:10 [< SE
pa.t. vb *named* with characteristic CarA Cr absence of /-d/, and becoming the regular form in
AF CE] **2.** Be called; am/is/are called **a.** *They
wanted the child to name Varicilla and the priest
tell them no.*—(Guyn) **b.** *S1: You name Moses?
S2: Yes, you know I name Moses.*—Com, 1974,
p.46 [By characteristic CarA Cr contextual conversion of tr vbs into passive sense. See PAS-
SIVITY in this dictionary] **3.** *PHRASES* **3.1 What
name so?** *id phr* (CarA) [*AF*] What is that?;
What are you talking about? *If you go tellin[g]
dem you doin[g] lexicography dey goin[g] only as[k]
yo[u] wha[t] name so!*—(Baha) **3.2 Who name
so?** *id phr* (CarA) [*AF*] Who is such a person?;
Who would that be? *S1: She should see a gynae-
cologist. S2:A wha[t]? Who name so?*—(Guyn) **4.**
To be in fact (such a person, thing, condition
as); deserve to be called or duly recognized as.
a. *Some of them think they have to beat up the[ir]
wife to show they name man!*—(StVn) **b.** *All four
daughters got children and not one o[f] dem ain[']t
know wha[t] name 'married'.*—(Tbgo)

NAMES OF NATIVES, & adjs derived
(National Names) (CarA) [The following list
is provided in order to permit the reader to
answer readily the question 'What do you call a
person from—?' The list will show that in many
cases the answer is not obvious and in other
cases there is more than one answer. The items
are generally treated separately in the body of the
dictionary. In cases of alternatives, the preferred
form is always given first. It should further be
noted that some of these are written rather than
spoken forms. One is more likely to hear '*Bequia
people*' than *Bequians*, '*Essequebo people*'
than *Essequibians*, etc. There may be disagreement about the placing of the main stress,
in a number of cases, on the first syllable, but it
is in keeping with the common pitch-contour of
CE wh regularly separates high-pitch from main
stress, ex *Guyanese* /1'12/. (See note on stress in
Introductory pages.) This causes doubt in some
cases, ex *Jamaican* /2'12/ or /12'1/, the former
being more likely at folk-level and also more
emotional, the latter belonging to more neutral
or educated contexts] **Abaco Is** (Baha) A.B-
A.CO.NI.AN [abʌ'ko·niʌn] /11221/ *adj, n* **Andros
Is** (Baha) AN.DRO.VI.AN [an'dro·viʌn] /1221/ *adj,
n* **Anegada** (BrVi) A.NE.GA.DI.AN [ani'ga·diʌn] /
11221/ *adj, n* **Anguilla** AN.GUIL.LI.AN (AN-
.GUIL.LAN) *adj, n* **Antigua** AN.TI.GUAN
[an'ti·gʌn] /121/ *adj, n* **Antilles** ['antıli·z] /1'12/
AN.TIL.LE.AN [an'tılıʌn] /1221/ *adj, n* **Aruba** A.RU.B-
I.AN (A.RU.BAN) *adj, n* **Bahamas, The** BA-
.HA.MI.AN [bʌ'he·miʌn] *adj, n* **Barbados**
BAR.BA.DI.AN ['barbe·diʌn ~ bʌ'be·jʌn] /121/ *adj,
n*; BA.JAN, BA.JUN ['be·jʌn] /12/ *adj, n* [*IF*]; BAJE
[be·j] *n* [*AF*]; BA.JEE ['be·ji] *n* [*AF—Joc*] BIM
n) **Barbuda** BAR.BU.DAN /1'21/ *adj, n* **Belize**
BE.LI.ZE.AN [bɛ'liziʌn] *adj, n* **Bequia** [bɛkwe]
BE.QUI.AN [be'kwiʌn] /121/ *adj, n* **Berbice**
(Guyn) BER.BI.CIAN ['bʌrbišʌn] /121/ *adj, n* **Ber-
muda** BER.MU.DI.AN (BER.MU.DAN) [bʌ(r)
'myudiʌn] *adj, n* **Bonaire** (Neth) BO.NAI.RE.AN

[bɒ'neriʌn] *adj, n* **Carriacou** (Grns) CAR-
.RI.A.COU.AN /ı'ı121/ *adj, n* (KA.YAK) [*AF—
Derog*] /2'ı/ *adj, n* **Cayman Brac** CAY.MAN
BRAC.ER [ke'man-brakər] /ı211/ *n* **Cayman Is,
The** CAY.MA.NI.AN [ke'ma·niʌn] /ı221/ *adj, n*
Cuba CU.BAN /2'ı/ *adj, n* **Curaçao** CU.RA.-
ÇAO.LE.NI.AN [kyurasoleniən] (CU.RAÇAO.AN)
[kyurasoən] *adj, n* **Demerara** (Guyn)
DE.ME.RA.RI.AN ['dɛməra·riʌn ~ dɛməre·riʌn] *adj,
n* **Dominica** DO.MI.NI.CAN [dɒmı'nikʌn] /ı12'ı/
Eleuthera (Baha) E.LEU.THE.RAN [ɛ'lyueərʌn]
adj, n **Essequibo** (Guyn) ES.SE.QUI.BI.AN
['ɛsɛ'kwıbiʌn] /ı1221/ *adj, n* **Grenada** GRE.N-
A.DI.AN [grɛ'ne·diʌn] *adj, n* **Guadeloupe** GUA.
.DE.LOU.PE.AN ['gwadılupiʌn] /ı1221/ *adj, n*
Guyana GUY.AN.ESE ['gayani·z] /ı12/ *adj, n*
Haiti [he·ti] HAI.TIAN ['he·ʃʌn] /21/ *adj, n* **Hon-
duras** HON.DU.RA.NI.AN [hɒnjure·niʌn] *adj, n*
Jamaica JA.MAI.CAN /2'ı12 ~" /ı2'ı/ *adj, n* **Low
Is., The** /ıı'22 (Bdos) [*IF*] FO.REIGN.ER /'ı21/
n **Martinique** MAR.TI.NI.QUAN (MAR.TI.NI.CAN)
/ı'ı21/ *adj, n* **Montserrat** MONT.SER.RA.TI.AN
[mɒn(t)sʌ'ratiʌn ~ mɒn(t)srašʌn] *adj, n* (MON-
.STRA.TIAN) [*IF*] [mɒn'stre·šʌn] *adj, n* **Nassau**
(Baha) NAS.SAU.VI.AN [na'su·viən] /ı221/ *adj, n*
Nevis NE.VI.SIAN [ni'višʌn] /ı21/ *adj, n* **Puerto
Rico** PUER.TO RI.CAN /ı'ı21/ *adj, n* **Saba** [se·bʌ]
SA.BI.AN /2'ı1/ *adj, n* **Santo Domingo** DO-
.MI.NI.CAN [dɒ'mınıkən] /ı2'21/ *adj, n* **St Croix**
['sınt-krɒı] (USVI) CRU.ZAN [kružan] CRU.ZIAN,
CRU.CIAN [krušʌn] *adj, n* **St Eustatius** ['sınt-
yuste·šʌs] (Neth) STA.TIAN ['ste·šʌn] *adj, n* **St
John** (USVI) ST JOHN.I.AN [sın(t)-'joniʌn] /
ı221/ *adj, n* **St Kitts** KIT.TI.TIAN [kı'tıšʌn] *adj,
n* **St Lucia** ST LU.CIAN [sın(t)-'lušʌn] *adj, n* **St
Maarten** (Neth) ST MAAR.TIAN [sınt-'maršʌn]
adj, ST. MARTINER *n* **St Thomas** (USVI) ST
THO.MI.AN (THO.MA.NI.AN) [sın-'tomiʌn ~
to'meniən] *adj, n* **St Vincent** VIN.CEN.-
TIAN [vın'sɛnšʌn] /ı21/ *adj, n* VIN.CIE ['vınsi]
/ı2/ *n* [*AF*] (+ *very intimate*)] **Suriname** SU.
.RI.NA.MESE [surinə'mi·z] /ı112/ *adj, n* **Tobago**
TO.BA.GO.NI.AN [tubʌ'go·niʌn] /ı1221/ *adj, n*
Tortola (BrVi) TOR.TO.LI.AN (TOR.TO.LAN) /
ı221/ *adj, n* **Trinidad** TRI.NI.DA.DI.AN [trını
'dadıʌn ~ -'de·diʌn] *adj, n* (TRI.NI) ['trıni] /ı2/
n [*AF*] (TRIN.TO) ['trınto] *n* [*AF*] (Jmca) **Turks
& Caicos Is** TURKS ISL.AND.ER /2'ı21/ *n* **Virgin
Gorda** (BrVi) VIR.GIN GOR.DI.AN /ı1221/ *adj,
n* **Virgin Is, The** VIR.GIN ISL.AND.ER /2'2ı21/
n (Amer resident of USVI) STATE.SI.DER /'211/
n

nam·py [nampi] *n* (USVI) ‖ YAMPI(E)² (Antg,
etc) *Ah coulda hardly open meh sleepy, nampy
eyes when ah hear dis, cause ah was sleepin so hard
when meh brodder come runnin in meh room.*—AaW
I.2, p.23 □ Also used attrib as in cit. It is perh
an aberrant form. Cp NYAMPI (*StVn*). The form
YAMPI(E) also occurs in *USVI*.

na·na¹ [na:na] *n* **1.** (Antg, Jmca) [*IF*] Grandmother. *When Mammy and Daddy got married
they had to live with Nana until they got a house.*—
(Antg) **[**Cp *DAFL* Twi *nana bea* (*grandparent
woman*) 'grandmother', the word *nana* alone
being applied to either gender. However in some

Akan langs, it appears *nana* was used for the
fem alone. Note Nzema *nana* 'grandmother'
(Bureau of Ghana Languages: Nzema Language
Guide, p.16). Also in CarA Cr slave society the
more significant role of the fem grandparent is
likely to have focused use of the term on her,
gradually excluding the male sense, as is entirely
the case today. Note senses 2., 3.**]** □ Often with
cap, as a form of address. (Although the term is
also widely used in SE in this sense, the two
sources will prob have reinforced each other in
CE. Note further uses foll). **2.** [By extension]
(Guyn, Jmca, USVI) A term of respect for an
old woman, esp one who lives among or looks
after children. □ Should be distinguished from
SE *nanny* who is usu a hired and younger woman,
a nursemaid. **3.** [By extension] (Jmca) A village
midwife.

na·na² [na:nA] *n* (Guyn, Trin) [Indic] A maternal grandfather; your mother's father; [by
extension] your great great grandfather or great
uncle on your mother's side. *He could only say—
and, indeed, he was anxious to say it—that he was
proud of his being Pundit Gurudeva's nana, and
still more proud of his being Pundit Gurudeva's
teacher.*—NAGOS:100 **[**Bhoj < Hin *naanaa* 'maternal grandfather'**]**

nancy-rope *n* (Jmca) Spider's web; cobweb.
Now see all the nancy rope on the books.—(Jmca)
[See ANANCY¹ + *rope* = support on wh he
climbs**]**

nan·cy-(spi·der) [nansi-spaıdʌ] /ı'ı22/ *n*
(Belz, Guyn, Jmca) ‖ ANANCY(-SPIDER) (CarA)
*Many Guyanese, especially old people, believe that
a big, brown nancy spider crawling up the wall is
a sign of money coming to you and they would
never kill it.*—(Guyn) □ The form NANCY-SPIDER
is prob commoner. In some places, ex *Guyn*, it
is prob the only form current in ref to the
particular spider.

nan·cy-sto·ry /ı'ı22/ *n* (CarA) **1.** ‖ ANANCY-
STORY (CarA) *The Nancy stories of Trinidad are
among the few remaining traces of African culture
in the island. These stories tell of the Spider God
'Anansi' of West Africa who was a deity of great
resources especially in getting the better of his
opponents, usually by unfair means.*—OTTTT:
81 **2.** [By extension] [*AF—Joc*] Nonsense. *There
was a time when you couldn't even get inside here.
That is when people believed in the Minister and
his budgetary nonsense. Now the nancy story they
tell us about budget is so expected that people don't
want to come and the Minister should see.*—Gren
(Hd, 73.02.09, p.36) **3.** [By extension and eu-
phemism] [*AF—Joc/Derog*] A lie. **a.** '*I hope you
really like me and you ain't giving me no 'nancy
story,' Germaine say, "cause I love you real bad
too.' And she kiss him.*—CISH:18 **b.** *The nancy
story that 88 percent of the money in the Sugar
Price Stabilization Fund belongs to the growers
and manufacturers of sugar in this island is sheer
nonsense. It is a fallacy created out of the wishful
thinking and the type of delusion which sends people

stumbling after mirages; it simply is untrue and does not—and cannot—square with facts.—LaS (65.03.24, p.1) [See ANANCY STORY] □ This is the form most widely used in CE speech, (rather than ANANCY STORY).

na·ni (**naa·ni(e), nan·ny**) [na:ni] *n* (Guyn, Trin) [Indic] **1.** A maternal grandmother; your mother's mother (or grandmother); your father's maternal grandmother; [by extension] your great aunt on your mother's side. **2.** [By extension] A respected old EAST INDIAN woman who, esp in a village, helps at childbirth and in curing ailments. **[** < Hin *naanii* 'maternal grandmother'] □ Cp NANA¹, NANA². Distinguish from SE *nanny* 'a nursemaid'.

nan·ni [nãni] *n* (Dmca) ‖ANISE (Mrat, etc) [Fr Cr < Fr *anis* 'aniseed' + prosthetic /n-/. Cp similarly Fr Cr *nanné* < Fr *année*]

nan·nie¹ (**nan·nee, nan·ny**) *vb intr* (Baha) [Usu child lang] To defecate. *Brer Bookie was so scared that he turned stiff as a board. He 'nannee' up himself, and in a whimpering voice said, 'Lord, doon take ma now, gimme anudder chance!'*—TOSR:18 [Cp *DAFL* Twi *ne* vb (redup *nene*) 'to ease the body by stool'. DJE lists *nene* as oral Jmca Cr with same sense]

nan·nie² (**nan·nee, nan·ny**) *n* (Baha) Any kind of faeces, whether human or animal. *Before Brer Bookie had gone very far Brer Rabbie who was not dead, started to have 'the glubba, glubba' or 'the ups and downs'. In other words he puked all over the place and at the same time the 'nannie' was pouring from his other end.*—TOSR:16 [By functional vb > n shift of NANNIE¹] □ Cp JOBBY *Bdos*.

Na·pi·er grass [nepiʌ-gras] *n phr* (Jmca) ‖E-LEPHANT GRASS (CarA)

nap·py hair/head *n phr* (Baha) ‖PICKY HAIR/HEAD (Baha, etc) [Cp *OED nappy* adj¹ Now *rare* 'downy, shaggy' < Du *noppig*. (The sense relates esp to coarse cloth and was also spelt *knappy*, occurring mostly up to 18C). Cp also *nap* sb³ b. 'the woolly substance removed from cloth by the process of shearing']

nar [na:] *negator* (Nevs, StKt) See NA¹, NO

na·ra (**naa·ra, na·raa(h)**) [nara~na·ra~nara·] *n* (Guyn, Trin) [Indic] **1.** A disorder of the stomach and intestines believed to be caused by strain or dislocation after lifting sth too heavy or having a bad fall. *And the time came when he himself began to doubt his own powers. He could cure a nara, a simple stomach dislocation, as well as any masseur, and he could cure stiff joints. But he could never bring himself to risk bigger operations.*—NTMM:68 [Bhoj < Hin *naaraa uk harnaa* 'small intestines displacement'. The phr was prob abbr or reduced through lessening linguistic cognizance over a century, leaving only the first item to identify this common complaint

among EAST INDIAN labourers] **2.** *PHRASES* **2.1 haul/pull/rub (sb's) nara** *vb phr* (Guyn, Trin) To anoint the abdomen of (sb) (suffering from NARA) with a kind of pulling action (sometimes using a downturned drinking glass to produce some suction) in order to effect relief. □ Cp the medical process of SE *cupping*.

nase·ber·ry ['ni·sbɛri] *n* (Jmca) ‖SAPODILLA (CarA) **[** < Sp *nespera~nispera* 'medlar', a Eurasian fruit (*Mespilus germanica*) whose name was given to the Central American fruit, from its resemblance. Cp MESPLE. The E suffix *-berry* is perh due to false Anglicization of Sp *-pera*]

nash *adj* (Antg, CayI, Nevs, USVI) [*IF*] Lacking sturdiness of either body or mind; frail and weak; soft-mannered. [Cp *EDD nesh* adj (Many dials. cited) 4. 'delicate in health, weakly, sickly, effeminate'. Also written *nash* (Sc). Cp next]

nash·y *adj* (Tbgo) [*AF*] Thin; skinny; small-bodied. *When I hear 'Doctor' I was looking for a big fellow, not that nashy li[tt]l[e] man.*—(Tbgo) [Prob a familiar development of the prec]

Nas·sau·vi·an [nasuviən] *n, adj* (A person or thing) native or belonging to Nassau, (the capital city of the Bahamas). **[** < Nassau + (epenthetic) /v/ + adj suff *-ian*]

nas·ti·ness *n* **1.** (CarA) [*IF*] Moral cheating; dangerously deceitful behaviour. *If you let them know your business they make you bawl! They full of nastiness, you see them there!*—(Bdos) **2.** (Guyn) [*AF*] Any kind of filthy matter, esp as related to OBEAH, used, esp in food, to gain power over an opponent. **3.** (Gren, StKt, Trin) [*AF—Derog*] [Of a person] A good-for-nothing; a person of cheap, worthless character. **4.** (Guyn, Jmca) Anal sex with a human or an animal.

nas·ty-mouth(ed) *adj* (CarA) [*AF—Derog*] Filthy-tongued; readily given to using very dirty language.

nas·ty (up) *vb tr (phr)* (CarA) [*AF*] To make (sth) very dirty; to mess up, befoul (sth or some place). *Nex' ting Veda an Mildred reach back from church, an' Veda want to know what all dese people doing in she house, sayin' how dey boots nastyin' up she clean floor.*—KTT:82 [By functional adj > vb shift of SE adj *nasty*. Cp also *EDD nasty* adj and vb 4. 'to defile, soil']

na·tion *n* **1.** (Crcu, Guyn, Jmca, Trin) [In ref to people of Afr descent] Any group of Black people who identify themselves as descendants of a particular ethnic group (loosely called 'tribe' by E writers) or regional sub-groups of the Afr (esp W Afr) population before enslavement. *In the mountain villages of Montserrat in Central Trinidad, groups of Negro people who are direct descendants of African slaves have lived since slavery times. These people are grouped into 'nations', i.e., tribal collectivities distinguished partly by residence, partly by the African dialects used* in their rituals and by the body of religious beliefs which guide their secular life. The idea that they are all 'Africans' unites them and gives them a kind of community harmony not commonly encountered in other rural villages in Trinidad. Chief among these 'nations' is the Yoruba people who live mostly in the village of Mayo.—EMRP:23 □ The term is prob so used in many other parts of the (CarA) than those identified above. **2.** (Guyn, Trin) [AF/IF] [By extension] A whole race (except the Europeans) within the total population of a state; (hence foll phrs). **3.** PHRASES **3.1 African nation; Black (people) nation** n phrs (Guyn, Trin) [AF/IF] Black people (taken as a whole in the world). **3.2 Buck nation** n phr (Guyn) [AF] The Amerindian people of Guyana. **3.3 Chinee nation** n phr (Guyn, Trin) [AF] Chinese people (esp those living in the CarA). **3.4 coolie nation** [Derog] **East Indian nation** n phrs (Guyn, Trin) || EAST INDIANS (CarA) **3.5 no-nation** /1'22/ n (Guyn) [AF—Derog] A person (esp a dark-skinned person) of more than two racial mixtures or one whose racial mixture is not readily determinable. **3.6 Potogee nation** n phr (Guyn) [AF—Derog] See POTOGEE **4.** [By extension] (Gren, Guyn) [AF—Derog] A type of person or people; an unpleasant sort of person or people. **a.** I ain['t] know how he get heself mix up wit[h] da[t] family. Dem is a warish nation.—(Guyn) **b.** I is accustom to female behaviour. Dey is a nation a man got to expect anything from.—RTCS:7 **5.** (Guyn, Trin) [AF/IF] [Indic] Caste; (hence foll phrs). **6.** PHRASES **6.1 high nation** n phr (Guyn, Trin) [AF/IF] High caste; an EAST INDIAN who is considered to be of a better class. The name alone can tell you dem is high nation people. All them Chowbay, Doubay and Panday is Brahman people.—(Guyn) **6.2 low nation** n phr (Guyn, Trin) [AF/IF] Low caste; an EAST INDIAN who is considered to be of a low class. 'Chamar' and 'Pariah' are used synonymously for 'Low Nation'. 'Nation' is the 'translation' of 'Jat' or 'Jati', which refers to subgroups or 'castes'.—Guyn (Ms, 1977) [Prob a translation of Hin jaat 'kind; class; race']

na·tion·al n (CarA) A native or a citizen (of a particular State). We believe that the question of the status of non-nationals married to Barbadian women can be easily got around by according these the same status as nationals during the subsistence of the marriage.—AdN (72.03.19, p.4, Ed) □ The term tends to be emotively used by some in recently independent CarA States, to distinguish the native-born from the naturalized citizen, but this is not an officially recognized distinction.

Na·tion·al Bird n phr (CarA) A bird that is indigenous or peculiar to a particular State, and is officially selected as one of the distinctive national symbols of that State; it is protected by law. The Scarlet Ibis is the National Bird of Trinidad, and the Canje Pheasant is the National Bird of Guyana.—Guyn (Ms)

Na·tion·al Cos·tume n phr (CarA) A colourful woman's outfit designed to reflect features

of the cultural heritage in elegant dress-wear; it is officially selected as one of the distinctive national symbols of State. The dwiyèt is part of the National Costume of Dominica.—Dmca (Ms)

Na·tion·al Day n phr (CarA) **1.** || INDEPENDENCE DAY (CarA) □ Sometimes called **National Independence Day. 2.** Any day so designated to commemorate an important event in the history of a Nation or State. **3.** (StLu) An annual public holiday replacing the former DISCOVERY DAY, celebrated on 13 December.

Na·tion·al dress n phr (CarA) **1.** || NATIONAL COSTUME (CarA) **2.** (Guyn) A man's outfit consisting of the short-sleeved SHIRTJAC as the upper garment for casual wear, and the long-sleeved jacket with Nehru-collar (and no tie) as that for official occasions.

Na·tion·al Flow·er; Na.tion.al Tree n phrs (CarA) A flower or tree that is indigenous or peculiar to a particular State and is officially selected as one of the distinctive national symbols of that State. The flower of the Soufrière Tree is the National Flower of St Vincent.—StVn (Ms)

Na·tion·al Fruit n phr (CarA) A fruit that is indigenous to or specially significant in the cultural life of a particular State, and is officially selected as one of the distinctive national symbols of that State. The ackee is the National Fruit of Jamaica.—Jmca (Ms)

Na·tion·al Names (CarA) See NAMES OF NATIVES.

Na·tion·al Tree n phr (CarA) See NATIONAL FLOWER

na·tion-dance /1'12/ n (Crcu) || **African nation-dance** (Gren) || **big-drum dance** (Crcu) One of a number of dances identified with the heritage or culture of a particular 'tribe' or 'nation' (hence the name) of Afr slaves preserved in Carriacou, each distinguished by its own rhythm and body-movement, and performed often by a single dancer or two women and one man to the beat of three BIG-DRUMS. Those described as 'nation dances' are Cromanti, Arada, Chamba, Manding, Congo, Banda, Ibo, Jig-Ibo and Scotch Ibo, Temne, Moko Yegeyege and Moko Bange.—Efl. 1011, p.2 (A.C. Pearse).

na·tion-lan·guage n (CarA) **1.** [A term introduced by E.K. Brathwaite in 1984. See cits] **a.** Nation language is the language which is influenced very strongly by the African model, the African aspect of our New World/Caribbean heritage. English it may be in terms of some of its lexical features. But in its contours, its rhythm and timbre, its sound explosions, it is not English, even though the words, as you hear them, might be English to a greater or lesser degree.—BHOV:13 **b.** It is what I call ... nation language. I use the term in contrast to dialect. The word 'dialect' has been bandied about for a long time, and it carries very pejorative *overtones. Dialect is thought of as 'bad English'. Dialect is 'inferior English'. Dialect is the language used when you want to make fun of someone.*—BHOV:13 **2.** [By extension] The distinctive native dialect of an Afro-Caribbean country either as spoken or as represented in written form. *I refer to what we know as Bajan dialect. How we use language in our own peculiar style. One writer who has mastered this is Bruce St John, who is considered Barbados' foremost 'nation language' poet.*—AdV(Mag) (87.11.21, p.1) [The term appears to have originated from sense 1. of NATION n, there being many isolated pockets of Afr descendants throughout the *CarA* that have preserved ritualistic phrases and sentences used at ceremonies or festivities, the meanings of wh are now lost or much blurred. The users of these phrases, when asked for their meaning, could only affirm that it was the language of their NATION (sense 1.); and hence the term 'nation language' wh Brathwaite endorsed and popularized] □ Sense 2. above tends to deviate from sense 1. partly because of an emotive zeal on the part of some to raise the status of national dialects, but also perh partly because E.K. Brathwaite himself first stated: 'We have also what is called *nation language*, wh is the kind of English spoken by the people who were brought to the Caribbean, not the official English now, but the language of slaves and labourers, the servants who were brought in by the conquistadors'—BHOV:5. This seems to refer strongly to *CarA* Cr BASILECT, while sense 1. focuses on the developed idiomatic structure of CE. Furthermore, although the definition in sense 1 focuses on the Anglophone *CarA* Creoles, the principle underlying it properly embraces also SRANAN TONGO (*Srnm*), PAPIAMENTU (*Neth*); and the CarA FRENCH CREOLES.

nat·ty dread (**knot·ty dread**) *n phr* (Jmca) [Rastaf] A RASTAFARIAN man. [From the matted, uncombed (i.e. knotty) condition of the hair, characteristic of the male members of the cult. The name NATTY DREAD was popularized by an album of REGGAE music so entitled by Bob Marley, released in 1975]

nat·ty hair *n phr* (Angu, BrVi) [*AF*] ‖ BAD HAIR (CarA)

nat·ty head *n phr* (Belz, StVn) ‖ BAD HAIR (CarA) *I never know little Anita so saucy! / She just tell them she love Brads / An' love the natty head an' flat nose.*—YFOC:11

na·vel-string *n* (CarA) PHRASE **your navel-string bury/is buried (somewhere)** *id phr* (CarA) [*AF/IF*] **1.** You are spiritually bound (to some place); your loyalty or attachment (to some land or institution) is or seems predestined. *But why you can['t] leave Buxton at all? What happen, you navel-string bury de[re]?*—(Guyn) **2.** You seem to have a skill, aptitude or the secret of some success in association with some work, institution, etc, wh is inexplicable. *By virtue of the knowledge of fishing he had, Ffolkes grinned*

his mean amusement at us. His navel-string was buried under a rock in Great Pedro Bay of St Elizabeth Parish.—HFGA:83 (V.S. Reid) [A ref to the folk habit of burying an infant's umbilical cord in its parents' home ground, esp under a flourishing fruit-tree (for prosperity), a SILK-COTTON tree (for spiritual protection), or in some place of symbolic significance]

nay·ga (**na·ger, nay·gue, nay·gur**) *n* (CarA) See NIGGER

nay-nay (**ne-ne**) [nene] *adj* (Bdos) [*AF—Joc/ Derog*] Trifling; of little consequence; small and insignificant. *Provided we receive the co-operation of the Opposition, 2 o'clock would be an appropriate time and we would be able to work. It is not a nay-nay meeting as the hon. member thinks, but a regular meeting which is taking place tomorrow.*—Bdos (Hd, 74.03.18, p.3423) [Cp *EDD* nig-nay Sc and Irel 1. sb 'a trifle; a knick-knack; a plaything' 2. vb 'to do what is useless'. Cp also*WIED* Igbo nenị vb 'to disregard; to despise'; also nneni n 'contempt; disregard'. Both Irish and Igbo influences being in evid in Bdos, reinforcement and semantic shift are possible arguments for this form] □ See also NE-NE 2. (*StVn*).

near *adv* (Bdos, BrVi, Guyn, StKt) [*X*] Nearly; almost. *And then the wuthless father had to take him out in a piece of old car and shake up his insides so it near kill him.*—MBGB:30 [A prob survival of EE. Cp *OED near* adv² 5. 'all but; almost.... Now usu expressed by *nearly*' + cits 1200–1891. However, none of the cits illustrates *near* qualifying a finite vb]

nea(r)·ga (**nei·ger**) *n* (CarA) See NIGGER

ne·ar·ga-bid·nis *n* (Nevs, Stkt) See NIGGER-BUSINESS.

neat·en your·self *refl vb phr* (Tbgo, Trin) To make yourself look tidy. *Zeela neatens herself and leaves.*—Tbgo (Ms, Stage direction) [Cp *OED neaten* 'to make neat'. *OED2* adds later cits, but all apply to places, not persons]

Neb·(r)u·a·ry morn·ing; nev.a.wa.ry, ne·v.u.a.ry [nɛb(r)ʊwɛri ~ nɛvawɛri] *adv* (*phr*) (Bdos, Belz, Guyn) [*AF—Joc*] ‖ **never-ready morning** (Guyn) Never. *Lend him money if you['re] stupid, but you can expec[t] it back Nebuary mornin[g].*—(Bdos) [A blend of SE *never* + *February* wh is often pronounc [fɛbyuwɛri]]

neck-back *n* (Guyn, Jmca) [*AF—Cr*] The nape of the neck. *A crowd rushed to the scene of a loud bawling on a Jamaica street.... A woman rushed from the back of the bus and began to beat the man on his 'neck back' with her fist. He, turning round, began to batter her.*—AdN (87.09.12, p.4) [Prob a calque from W Afr langs. Cp *foot-bottom*]

need *vb tr* PHRASE **(not) need all of that** (ECar) [*IF*] ‖ (NOT) HAVE ALL OF THAT IN IT (CarA) See ALL² *Phr* 3.10.1

nee·dle *n* PHRASES **1. hot needle burn(ing) thread** *id phr* (BrVi, Gren) [*AF—Joc*] See HOT[1] Phr 4.2 **2. patch needle and burn thread** *id phr* (Belz) [*AF—Joc*] To be irritatingly idle; to waste time in some senseless way. **3. pick a needle without eye** *id phr* (Baha) [*AF—Joc/Derog*] [Of a young girl] To finally choose to marry a man who is useless to her (i.e. as is a needle that has no eye) after rejecting better suitors.

nee·dle-and-thread *n* (Guyn) ‖ CASUARINA (TREE) (CarA) [From its abundant, long, needle-like, leafless branches]

nee·dle·case ['nidlke·s] *n* (Belz, Jmca) ‖ POND-FLY (Bdos, Guyn) [From the insect's shape, resembling a needle-case] □ Pl often unchanged in speech.

nee·dle-fish *n* (Baha, Dmca) ‖ GAR-FISH (CarA) □ Both the terms NEEDLE-FISH and GAR-FISH occur in fishing literature, though it appears that NEEDLE-FISH is less used by *CarA* fishermen, some applying that name only to small inedible varieties.

nee·dle-grass *n* (Bdos, Trin) ‖ DUPPY-NEEDLE (Bdos, etc)

nee·dle-stitch·es *n pl* (Jmca) [*IF*] A tingling sensation in the arm or elbow; (SE) pins and needles.

nee·dle-work·er *n* (Bdos) ‖ *worker* (Guyn) A dress-maker; a woman employed to sew. *When one of the garment factories opened on the Harbour a few years ago, a lady came to me … [and] told me that she had been a needle worker for about ten years and had gone to this factory on probation for which she was paid $9 a week.*—Bdos (Hd, 73.03.20, p.2164)

neem* (**nim(e)**) [ni·m] *n* (Guyn, Jmca, Mrat, Trin) A large shade tree with small leaves wh produce a bitter juice that is much used by EAST INDIANS for medicinal purposes; the leaves themselves are much used also, esp by MADRASIS, in religious ceremonies; *Azadirachta indica (Meliaceae)*. [Hin *niim*, name of this tree] □ Other spellings *neam, nim* are sometimes used, though NEEM is the one found in botanical literature.

nèg-ja·dan (**nèg ja·den, nègre-jar·din**) [nɛ·g-žadã] *n (phr)* (Dmca, StLu, Trin) **1.** [Hist] A black field slave (usu a male); [Derog] a field nigger. [Fr Cr < Fr *nègre* 'negro' + *jardin* 'garden', the latter term indicating 'working out of doors' in contrast to the house-slave or Derog 'house-nigger', often a female, who worked indoors] **2.** [Carnival] A male masquerader's costume usu comprising a tattered straw hat, colourful shirt tied with a bright big waistband, and knee-long trousers, either rolled up or tattered at the ends; it represents an imitation of the costume of the historical figure (sense 1.).

nèg-ma·won (**nègre-mar·ron**) [nɛ·g-mawɔ̃] *n (phr)* **1.** (Dmca, StLu) [Hist] ‖ MAROON 1. (CarA) [Fr Cr < Fr *nègre* 'negro' + *marron* 'maroon'. See more at MAROON] **2.** (StLu) [By extension] [*AF—Derog*] An unkempt, unruly, and crude-looking person (usu a man).

ne·gro cof·fee /2'212/ *n phr* (Guyn, Trin) ‖ WILD COFFEE 1. (Guyn, etc) [From the folk use by Black people of the seeds of this native weed as a bitter coffee]

ne·gro·man·cy *n* (Angu, Tbgo) [*X*] Necromancy; obeah. [By folk etym, infl by *negro*, < SE *necromancy*. *OED* and *OED2* list *nigromancy* with same sense]

ne·gro-pot; nig.ger-pot /1'12/ *n* (Bdos, Belz, Guyn, Jmca) [*Derog*] **1.** ‖ THREE-FOOT POT (Bdos, etc) □ Usu this referred to one of two or three smaller sizes of the THREE-FOOT POT. **2.** (Guyn, Jmca) A rich one-pot meal (of vegetables, meats, and spices) cooked for a folk celebration.

Ne·gro-yam /1'12/ *n* (Jmca, Trin) ‖ WHITE-YAM 1. (Baha, etc) *Good quantities of Negro yams were taken off by farmers in the Christiana and May Pen areas this week as the heaviest reaping since the start of this crop was recorded.*—DaG (Farmer's Weekly, 71.07.03) [See ‖ *Guinea-yam*, the yam being also the favourite choice in W Afr for pounded *fufu*, whence its prob association with slaves' cooking, and the name] □ This name appears to be in general use mostly in *Jmca*, where *white-yam* is (a rare) equivalent according to some authorities (*AFPJ*:67), but of a distinguishable variety according to others (see *DJE*:NEGRO YAM). In folk use there is also some confusion with AFU YAM (*Jmca, Trin*) and YELLOW YAM (*Guyn*).

ne·gro-yard /1'12/ *n* (CarA) [Hist] The area of a sugar-plantation in wh the slave-dwellings were situated. *Handler points out that no known maps show the locations but that a few sources suggest an area close to the mill yard or Negro yard where the slave village was situated, usually close to the manager's house.*—AdN (78.11.05, p.13) □ The term developed, esp in post-emancipation times, into NIGGER-YARD.

neh (**ner**) [nɛ-nə] *terminal tag* (Bdos, Trin) [*AF*] See NO 7. **a.** *I notice one o' de guv'ment MPs over dey get blow up by a bomb dat did plant in 'e car. Ent duh got some wicked people in dis worl' neh! To t'ink people does set bombs fuh ethers jes' so!*—NaT (90.08.03, p.9) **b.** *'Would you like to meet them?' / 'Meet who?' / 'Stephen, ner. An Gloria, an Rutherford.'*—RSMCD:51

neigh·bour [naɪbə(r)] *n* (Bdos) [*X*] [This X folk pronunc may be a survival of 16C/17C London Cockney. Cp *MCPP:20* 'In a fair number of (cockney) spellings, long *a* and *ai* are replaced by *i* and *y*: … *strynge, nighbower*, etc']

nei·ther[1] [niðə ~ nidʌ ~ naɪðə ~ naɪdʌ] *elliptical co-ordinator* (Guyn, Jmca, StVn, Trin) [X] Nor; or. *She don't talk to me, neither the children.* (= *She doesn't talk either to me or the children; she talks neither to me nor to the children.*)—(StVn) [The ellipsis in the second phr, 'neither (does she talk to) the children', would contrast a standard structure with a non-standard first phr]

nei·ther[2] [niðə ~ nidʌ] *adj, as determiner* (Bdos) [X] 1. ‖ *either* (Bdos) [X] (Not) any [usu preceded by *ain't* or other negator, hence second part of a double neg]. a. *Nineteen fourteen again. Thank God I ain got neither one to send to die in another white-man war.*—MBGB:57 b. *Yo[u] don['t] need neider economis[t] to tell dat prices does go up easy bu[t] dey don['t] come do[w]ng so easy.*—(Bdos) [Cp *EDD nowther* Sc, Eng, Amer, 1. adj 'no, not any'. Also *DNE neither* shows the identical usage in Newfoundland ex cit (1902) 'There's neither maid in Green Bay ... I'd trade that old craft for'] 2. [With loss of negative sense] Any. *If you phone de lumber yard, neider one o[f] de guys dere would call me* (= ... *any one of the guys there would call me*).—(Bdos)

nei·ther-no·ther [niðə-nɒðə] *adj* (Bdos) [AF] [Usu preceded by *ain't* or other negator, hence second part of a double neg] (Not) any other; no other. *I mean, the girl gone back must be a whole year now and Courcey still saying how much he love she and he never going look at neithernother girl again, and wouldn't even tek a night off to carry a girl to a dance though a lot o' them liking he bad bad.*—CISH:99 [A survival from EE. See *OED nother*[2] pron, adj B. adj 'neither' usu *neither nother* + cits–'1640: 'No sir we come with no zick intendment on neither nother zide']

ne-ne [nene ~ nɛnɛ] *adj* 1. (Bdos) See NAY-NAY 2. (StVn) Feeble; foolish; stupid. *Why you let them do that to you? You too ne-ne!*—(StVn) [Perh from a related or the same source as NAY-NAY]

ne(n)·nen[1] (nen, nen·nie) [nɛnɛn ~ nɛn(i)] *n* (CarA) [IF] 1. A godmother. 2. (Term of affectionate address for) a woman, young or old but elderly in relation to a young child, to whom she may be, or plays the role of, an aunt or guardian. *Mr Speaker, there are people in this country, some in this very Hall today who depend on living in this country on the few dollars they get from outside of Grenada from tantie or nenen living in America.*—Gren (Hd, 77.04.06, p.84) [Cp *KID* Efik-Ibibio *nne* 1. 'mother, grand-mother, old woman (address or referent)', (*nne nne* 'grandmother'). 2. 'a term of endearment for a young woman.' The term may have gained wider emotive currency in the slave factories in Efik country, the same as *mbakara* evid did, before enslaved children came to the *CarA*] □ The term does not seem to be used in *Belz*.

nen·nen[2] [nɛnɛn] *n* 1. (Gren, Trin) [AF] [Used as part of an oath] Arse; backside. *Yu leave all dem stores down town, / Yu leave all dem vendors up-town, / To come to my gas station to ask for chock-ice. / Well lord have mercy on me royal nen-nen, / Yu eh know it have crisis? gas-crisis?*—KTT:62 [Cp *DAFL* Twi *nẽ* vb (redup *nẽnẽ*) 'to go to stool; to ease the body; prob + functional shift in CarA Cr. However cp also NAY-NAY adj] □ Any *Vul* connotation the term may orig have had is now covered by wide euphemistic use in TrinE. 2. PHRASES 2.1 **catch/see your nennen** *vb phr* (Gren, Trin) ‖ CATCH HELL (CarA) See CATCH Phr 8.6 *And to boot that was the month John was going abroad. Talk about scholarship! Helen always going on about this scholarship bilge. And is nen-nen they catch to put the boy there! Real salt, they suck salt that month.*—JJM:29 [Cp a euphemism for CATCH YOUR ARSE (see CATCH Phr 8.6) a similar structure wh is *Vul*]

nen·wah (nin·wa(h)) [nɪnwa] *n* (Guyn) ‖ LOOFAH (Trin) [Bhoj *nenuaa*, name of this vegetable]

Nep·sha and Ki·ah [nɛpša-an-kaɪa] *n phr* (Bdos) [AF—*Joc/Derog*] ‖ HABRA, DABRA AND THE CREW (Bdos) *And when you have a quarrel wid she? Look out! She bringin[g] out Nepsha, Kiah, Ampuma an[d] Benny Gaskin to hear she buse you!!*—(Bdos)

ner [nə] *terminal tas* (Bdos, Trin) See NEH

ne·roo yam *n phr* (Guyn) ‖ YELLOW-YAM (Antg, etc)

Neth·er·lands An·til·les *n phr* (CarA) A collective name for several *CarA* islands historically ruled from Holland but now having varying degrees of Dutch political connection; they consist of a northern or WINDWARD group comprising mainly St Maarten, St Eustatius and Saba, and a southern or LEEWARD group comprising mainly Aruba, Curaçao and Bonaire.

nev·a·wa·ry; **nevua.ry** *adv* See NEBRUARY MORNING

nev·er [nɛvʌ] *adv* (CarA) [IF] 1. [Regularly used to stress past negation] Certainly (did) not. a. *The Mt Moritz of today is never as it was in the past, because so many have left that village.*—ToR (76.01.21, p.4) b. *When this new Afro style first come in, I never used to like it.*—HF:13 c. *But at the hospital she never saw a doctor for almost six hours [and] was subsequently taken back home.*—AdN (72.09.30, p.1) □ SE tends to use *never* as a stressed negator only in expressing surprise or strong emotive denial. CE usage is almost unrestrictive. 2. PHRASES 2.1 **I never see more!** *id phr* (Trin) [AF/IF] I never would have imagined/believed such a thing!; (SE) Well I never! 2.2 **You never hear more!** *id phr* (Bdos) [AF/IF] See HEAR Phr 4.13

nev·er-dead /1'12/ *n* (Nevs, StKt, Trin) ‖ LEAF-OF-LIFE (Bdos, etc) [From the leaf's ability to survive and give growth by itself]

nev·er-read·y morn·ing *n phr* (Guyn) [*AF—Joc*] ‖ NEBRUARY MORNING (Bdos, etc) *Me can tell you 'bout accident 'pon this river from now 'till never ready morning. Yes sir, jus' like how you know 'bout doctor work, me know 'bout river.*—CBM:64

nev·er-see-come-(fo[r])-see /1'121(1)2/ *n* (Gren, Guyn, StVn, Tbgo, Trin) [*AF—Derog*] ‖ *new-common* (StVn) ‖ *new nigger* (Bdos) **1.** A person whose amusingly unsophisticated behaviour discloses that he/she is seeing the better things of life for the first time. **2.** A person who fussily shows off new things recently acquired or who makes a bumptious show of new authority or status. *You think I wait for Paris to drink wine? I accustomed to good wines, not like you all never-see-come-sees. Come, Elaine bring the Swiss wine out, cold.*—JJM:39 □ The forms *never-see-come-fo[r]-see[-come-to-see* are Guyn.

Ne·vi·sian [nivišən] *n, adj* (A person or thing) belonging to or characteristic of Nevis. □ Nevis, wh lies to the south of St Kitts, is part of the twin-island State of St Kitts and Nevis.

new brand *adj phr* (ECar) Brand new. *Mr Wong, a priest at the Sacred Heart parish here and editor of the 'Catholic Standard', said yesterday: 'It was a new brand bicycle which was recently presented to me after the last one had been stolen.'*—AdN (73.05.14, p.5) □ This phr is so widely used as to be considered 'standard'. The reversal of *brand new* may have some Br dial root yet undiscovered. However cp *KED* Krio *nyu fresh*, a similar structure.

new-com·mon /1'22/ *adj* (StVn) [*IF—Derog*] ‖ NEVER-SEE-COME-SEE (Gren, etc) *Yo[u] could see she ai[n't] [ac]custom to shoes. She ca[n't] even lif[t] up she foot. She really new-common.*—(StVn) [Perh a blend of SE *new-comer* + CE COMMON]

new-nig·ger /1'22/ *n* (Bdos) [*AF—Derog*] ‖ N-EVER-SEE-COME-SEE (Gren, etc) *You did bound to use dat new bag an[d] shoes so soon? Wha[t] you gettin[g] on like a real new-nigger!*—(Bdos)

news-bee *n* (Bdos) The large black bumble-bee. *The flowers are very attractive to the large Bees which we call News Bees, with their shiny black wing cases, Bees well over an inch long.*—AdN (82.05.05, p.10) [From the folk belief that the appearance of such a bee in the house is a portent of important news]

next *adj* (CarA) [*X*] **1.** Other. **a.** *'The wheels are too narrow to ride in the gravel with ... my next bike had wider tyres.' 'What happened to your other bike?' 'It was stolen!'*—AmA (80.04.03, p.1) **b.** *Once we were not seeing each other for a few months and she met a new boy. Now we are friends once more and she says she loves me and yet she keeps seeing the next boy.*—NaT (76.10.10, p.26, Dear Christine) **2.** PHRASES **2.1 a next** *determiner* (CarA) [*X*] Another. **a.** *But he ain't call it by that name all the time. He christened it by a next*

name.—LICMS:90 **b.** *Your father was never a fool, but, and it's a very, very big but, even he can have a fool for a son, and a next fool for a grandson.*—SJT:60 □ These uses of NEXT are often found in written schoolwork and occur in the speech of educated persons. **2.2 next (s)kin to nothing** *id phr* (Bdos) [*AF—Joc*] Very little; almost nothing. *People having to work for next skin to nothing. The white people treating we like slaves still and we taking it.*—MBGB:60

ni·a·ga (ni·e·ga) *n* (CarA) See NIGGER

nib·bi (nib·by) [nɪbi] *n* (Guyn) The dried strip(s) of a tough, woody, forest liana, pliant enough to be woven to make light furniture; it is esp so used by Amerindians. [Cp *BDFC:226* Carib 'la lienne appellée mibi' f. *mibi*]

nice[1] *adj* (CarA) [*AF*] **1.** [Of a person; in neg and interrog contexts only] Compliant; unwilling to make a fuss. *The mother might be alright, but if you think the father nice, you jus[t] le[t] him see you hol[d] his daughter han[d]! Then you will find out.*—(Bdos) **2.** PHRASES **2.1 ain't/not nice; don't eat nice** *id phrs* (ECar) [*AF—Joc*] [Of a person] Readily aggressive; characteristically quarrelsome. **2.2 eat nice** *vb phr* (CarA) [*AF/ IF*] See EAT Phrs 3.3, 3.4.

nice[2] *adv* (CarA) [*X*] Nicely; well. **a.** *My boyfriend treats me very nice but we couldn't get on and that was why we had to separate.*—WeS (74.04.19, p.8) **b.** *Squandering money feteing, living nice.*—SCTR:5 (Cso line)

nice-up (with) (sb) *vb phr* (Guyn, Jmca, StVn) [*AF*] To make over-friendly advances (to sb) with your own interests in mind; to ingratiate yourself (with sb).

nick *vb* (Bdos, Guyn, Jmca) To throw dice; to gamble. **a.** *On street corners or in shops you find a crowd slamming dominoes, playing a card game, 'nicking' dice or casually passing the time with some lighthearted debate on a variety of topics.*—NaT (77.11.09, p.20) **b.** *It was Friday afternoon and he had lost his entire pay-packet. It had not fallen out of his pocket or been stolen from him; he had lost it 'nicking' with the boys. Of course, George, in his gambling career must have won at some time or the other. But on this afternoon his luck was not in.*—DaC (53.01.06, p.3)

nick·al; nick·le [nɪkəl] *n* (Baha, Jmca, Mrat, Nevs) ‖ NICKER (Angu, etc) [By /r > l/ shift < NICKER]

nick·er* [nɪkər] *n* (Angu, BrVi, Jmca) ‖ *briar* (TkCa) ‖ *chuckle-rock* (Mrat) ‖ *cockspur* **2.** (CayI) ‖ *donkey-eye* (Gren, Tbgo, Trin) ‖ *horse-nicker* (Bdos, Gren) ‖ *kach-kach* (Dmca) ‖ *knuckle-seed* (Nevs) ‖ *nickal, nickle* (Baha, Jmca, Mrat, Nevs) A hard, roundish, dark-grey (or brown, or yellow) seed about 3/4 of an inch in diameter, borne one or two in a very prickly pod on a straggling, prickly bush;

these seeds are commonly used as marbles, but also in some places in preparing folk medicines; the bush bearing these pods, *Caesalpinia bonduc* or *C. bonducella* (*Caesalpiniaceae*). [OED *nicker* sb³ (+ cits from 1675–') = *knicker*¹ 1. 'a boy's 'marble' of baked clay'. The name was prob applied from early times to the seed in the *CarA* because of its usefulness as a marble, and thence to the bush itself]

nig·ger (na·ger, nay·ga, nay·gue, nay·gur, nea(r)·ga, nei·ger, ni·a·ga, ni·e·ga) *adj, n* (CarA) [*AF—Derog/Joc*] (Of or concerning) a Black person or Black people in general. **a.** *They write Dear Don, we didn't think it would be like dis … Dear Don, the way they write and plea a blind man could see I'm boss. Boy they love this nigger, of course.*—Bdos (Cso—Sir Don, 1975) **b.** *You is a poor naygur wid no schooling, five pickney and a sick woman. Dat is trouble enough for you.* —SWIS:52 (J. Hearne) **c.** *So what if they wanted India to win. If it was a Chinee team, all dem Chinee Doctor and shop-keeper woulda feel the same way. An if the team was Syrian, pardner, the Syrians in town woulda cry and close up their store if Syria did lose! Is only nigger does want everybody but deyself!*—RSMCD:24 [Though ultimately from Sp *negro* 'black', the form **nigger** is prob directly from Du *neger* 'black', developing in popular use (as evid by the multiple forms of *CarA*-wide pronunc) during the period of early Du domination of the slave trade in the 17C] □ Though distinctly *Derog*, the term **nigger** is often in *Joc* or 'familiar' use among Black people themselves (see the cits above). However, Black people consider it highly offensive when used by anyone of another race.

nig·ger-bus·i·ness (near·ga-bid·nis) [nɪəgʌ-bɪznɪs ~ bɪdnɪs] *n* (Nevs, StKt) A street masquerade show in wh men (some dressed as women) satirize some public scandal (esp if of a domestic nature involving upper-class families), to the accompaniment of SCRATCH-BAND music; it was once a standard form of Christmas-time open-air entertainment.

nig·ger-gram *n* (Gren, StLu, Trin) [*AF—Joc/Derog*] A piece of unworthy, mean, or silly gossip; a stupid rumour. *Ganesh prospered. He … put up a mansion. Fuente Grove had never seen anything like it…. The Niggergram said that it had more than a hundred windows and that if the Governor got to hear, there was going to be trouble because only Government House could have a hundred windows.*—NTMM:149 [A blend of Derog adj NIGGER + SE (*tele*)*gram*, or (*cable*)*gram*, with analogical inference of 'news'] □ See also NIGGER-MOUTH.

nig·ger-ground *n* (Guyn, Tbgo, ViIs) [Hist] ‖ GROUND² (CarA)

nig·ger-head *n* (StVn) [*AF—Derog*] ‖ BAD-HAIR (CarA) *You see, a lot o[f] people remember him as a li[tt]l[e] nigger-head boy runnin[g] [a] bout—hair never comb, couldn['t] comb!—but now*

politics change all that!—(StVn) □ Cp *COD7* ModE *nigger-head* ~ *negro-head* used with a different sense (but prob becoming rare because considered offensive).

nig·ger·i·tis [ˈnɪgəraɪtɪs] /1ˊ122/ *n* (CarA) [*AF—Joc/Vul*] The strong urge to lie down and sleep after much eating. *Niggeritis is de sickness / Dat does got yuh in it charms / De onlies' disease in dis worl' / Dat yuh's welcome wid open arms!*—PeL (79.09.14, p.11: J. Layne-Clark) [< NIGGER [*Derog*] 'black people('s)' + -*itis* (Gk. suff) 'disease'] □ See also Phr BELLY FULL AND BEHIND DRUNK.

nig·ger-knots *n* (Bdos, Guyn) [*AF—Derog*] The natural hair of a Black person (esp a woman) wh is thick and tough, and has to be pulled hard when being combed. □ The term is one of insult among Black people. Contrast the note at NIGGER.

nig·ger-man/-wo·man *n* (CarA) [*AF—Derog/Joc*] A Black man/woman. *Eh-eh! Not so fast, niggerman. You want to spoil me make-up and ramfle me dress? Eh-eh! I spend too much time on dis thing for yu to spoil it now.*—RTCS:13 □ See the note at NIGGER wh applies to these nouns too. However there is a strong tendency, esp in middle-level CE speech, to use these compounds as familiar or *Joc* references to known individuals.

nig·ger-mout[h] *n* (Guyn, StVn) [*AF—Derog*] The most untrustworthy kind of rumour; a malicious piece of gossip. □ Cp NIGGERGRAM.

nig·ger-pep·per /1ˊ122/ *n* (Bdos) ‖ BIRD-PEPPER (CarA)

nig·ger-plait¹ (nig·ger-plait·ing) [ˈnɪgʌ-plat(ɪn)] /1ˊ12(2)/ *n* (CayI) [*AF—Derog*] ‖ CORK-SCREW(s)¹ *n* (Bdos, etc)

nig·ger-plait² /1ˊ12/ *vb tr* (CayI) [*AF—Derog*] ‖ CORK-SCREW² (Bdos, etc) *In the ol[d]-time days a woman would nigger-plait the hair and keep it so for days, but now i[t']s only if they goin[g] to dress for a weddin[g] or somet[h]ing that they nigger-plait it while they workin[g] durin[g] the day, and then do it up nice to go out wit[h].*—(CayI)

nig·ger-pot *n* (Guyn, Jmca) [*Derog*] See NEGRO-POT *A large 'nigger' pot stood near to an open calabash half-filled with fried fish.*—Kai, No.12 p.33

nig·ger-ten *n* (Bdos) [*AF/IF—Derog*] **1.** ‖ X¹ (Bdos) **2.** The mark X made by any illiterate person and accepted as his or her signature (see cit). *It must be stressed that during the early settlement of Barbados most of the people here could neither read nor write, and it is surprising to see that merchants who were well established in this Island could be included among these; for some of them who were Members of the Vestry of St Michael placed their mark, commonly referred to as 'a nigger ten' on the bottom of the Minutes, and this* *was witnessed either by the Clerk or some other Member of the Vestry who was in a more fortunate position, and had learned the art of reading and writing.*—The Barbados Churchman—Vol.1 No.1 March 1973, p.6 (Edward A. Stoute) [From the use of X as a legally recognized mark of receipt or signature by illiterates, and hence a *Derog* association with Black people in the post-slavery era]

nig·ger-wom·an *n* See NIGGER-MAN

nig·ger-yard /1'12/ *n* (Guyn) [*AF—Derog*] ‖ *barrack-yard* (Trin) **1.** The yard-space allotted to or enclosed by TENEMENT-ROOMS. **2.** [By extension] Any yard in a slum area that is associated with rough language and behaviour. *From the nigger yard of yesterday I come with my burden. To the world of to-morrow I turn with my strength.*—CPR:41 [A Derog development, esp in post-emancipation times, from NEGRO-YARD] □ The term is often used attrib: *nigger-yard behaviour/people*, etc.

nigh *adv* (Bdos, CayI, Guyn) **1.** Near. *I live nigh to her so give me and I will take it for her.*—(Bdos) [As early SE. See *OED nigh* I adv 4. With *to, unto* as 'denoting proximity in place, time' + cits to 19C] □ This use is however listed as 'archaic, literary, or dial' in *COD8*. It would be considered odd or comical in ModE, but cp Phr 3.1. below. **2.** [By extension] [*X*] Nearly. **a.** *The itching this causes is nigh unbearable.*—NaT (81.03.20, p.32) **b.** *She too nigh lost her sight in the bomb blast.*—(Guyn) [See *OED nigh* IV adv 12. 'nearly, almost, all but' + cits 19C] □ This use wd be considered archaic or dial in ModE. It is largely restricted currently to older folk. **3.** PHRASES **3.1 nigh on; nigh to; nigh unto** *adv phrs* (Bdos, CayI, Guyn, Trin) [*IF*] [In non-locative contexts] Almost; near to. **a.** *Gay was a keen musician, and was organist at Holy Innocents Church for nigh on 50 years.*—SuS (82.02.28, p.32) **b.** *You see I've been an undertaker for nigh onto forty years and have had lots to do with the dead and the dying.*—FDI:26 **c.** *I have 53 years and I reach nigh unto deat' five times awready home by me, but ah never feel so bad as ah feeling now.*—MN:38 [Cp *OED nigh* IV adv 12. C. *nigh about, on, upon* + cits-'1887] □ The survival of these phrs in CE is prob much due to Church infl. Some also occur in dial AmE.

night PHRASES **1. Good night!** *greeting phr* (CarA) [Said either on entering or leaving, also as a greeting *en passant*] *The children were so unmannerly! They would come in and see big people there, visitors! And they wouldn't even say 'Good night!', just pass right in.*—Jmca (Ms) **2. when the night come(s)** *adv phr* (Bdos, Guyn) [*AF/IF*] See WHEN Phr 3.6

night-bat *n* (Bdos) ‖ BAT¹ 2. (Guyn) □ In rural areas. Otherwise LEATHER-BAT Bdos.

night-bloom·ing cac·tus *n phr* (CarA) See CACTUS PLANT (CarA)

night-glass *n* (Jmca) ‖ UTENSIL (Bdos, Guyn) *She told me that she got up to use the 'night-glass'.*—StA(JA) (73.05.04, p.1)

night-liz·ard *n* (USVI) ‖ WOOD-SLAVE 1. (ECar)

night·shade *n* (Bdos) ‖ THORN-APPLE (Bdos, etc) [The plant belongs to the poisonous and narcotic *OED nightshade* family. The flowers also open in the night]

nim·bles *n pl* (Bdos, Guyn, USVI) Fowl lice; tiny insect pests living on the bodies of domestic chickens and affecting their health.

nine-day *n* **1.** (Gren, Guyn, Jmca, StVn) The period of mourning after the death of a person, during wh wakes, the burial, and other recognized traditional activities take place. □ Mostly a rural and in many places an outdated practice, though the term is still well-known. See NINE-NIGHT. **2.** (Guyn, Trin) [Indic] **(i)** The period of confinement of the mother after the birth of her child. **(ii)** ‖ *chaati* (Guyn, Trin) The (ninth-day) celebration held to mark the birth of a baby. **3.** PHRASE **3.1 keep up the nine-day** *vb phr* (Guyn, Trin) [Indic] To celebrate the birth of a child with festivities on the ninth day after its birth.

Nine Morn·ings *n phr* (StVn) A period of pre-dawn street festivities and celebrations for the last nine mornings before Christmas Eve. (See cit). *We used to start our celebrations from December 15 and it was called 'Nine Mornings'. We would collect our school friends and go on hikes or any other outing and go to church every morning at 5 o'clock. The service was usually for half an hour, and then when it was finished, there would be steelband in the streets. People would then go to work at 8 a.m.*—AdV (85.12.25, p.3)

nine-night *n* (CarA) **1.** The organized festive singing, dancing, speech-making, eating, and drinking repeated for nine nights after the burial of a dead person; certain rituals of various types are also supposed to be performed during these festivities to ensure the resting of the spirit of the deceased. *Well, one day the old man died. 'Nine-night' was well celebrated and the neighbours within hearing who didn't attend, couldn't sleep for days and nights.*—WeS (74.03.08, p.6) [< SE *nine nights*, the pl form being sometimes used] **2.** The vigorous festive celebrations organized either on the ninth night only, or as the climax of nine nights of festivities after a person's death. *The gathering remained talking about the recent death and about the arrangements for the funeral the next day, and about the possibility of merging both 'Nine-Night' wakes on a convenient date, instead of observing two separate nights of remembrance.*—SD:55 [< SE *ninth night*] □ These terms though well known in most *CarA* territories represent today almost exclusively rural practices. Much of the original religious association is lost, and in some places the terms have become unknown esp among younger people.

ning-ning[1] [nıŋ-nıŋ] **1.** (Guyn) Dizziness; a dazed or giddy feeling; spots before the eyes owing to hunger or a feeling of faintness. **2.** PHRASES **2.1 see ning-ning** vb phr (Guyn) [AF] To be or feel dazed; [by extension] to reel from shock. *If one of those centipedes bite you, I tell you, you will see ning-ning.*—(Guyn) **3.** (Bdos) [Sometimes pl] A numbness or tingling feeling in some part of the body; (SE) pins and needles. *Every nerve in my skin feel like electric wire playing ning-nings in my flesh.*—SNWIC:207

ning-ning[2] n (Bdos) A small bony fish.

nin·wa(h) n (Guyn) See NENWAH

ni·nyam [nınyam] n (Antg, Brbu, Jmca, USVI) [AF—Cr/Derog] Any kind of food prepared for eating; a meal. [Poss a redup form of NYAM, the Cr vb, though it is not clear why the same redup form should have developed as a distinctive noun in separate islands, while the orig W Afr distinctive noun NYAM became a Cr vb]

nip(-bot·tle) n (Bdos, Gren, StLu, Trin) A small, long-necked bottle of liquor containing 1-1/2 gills; the smallest bottle of rum sold, containing what is considered enough for one satisfying drink. *His father left the sentence incompleted as he put the nip to his mouth and gargled the rum as though he were rinsing out his mouth then swallowed it.*—SNWIC:229 (I. Khan) [Cp OED nip sb[2] b. 'a small quantity of spirits, usu less than a glass', + cits-'1890]

nix n (Guyn) [AF—Joc] Absolutely nothing. *If you don[t] gi[ve] me some fat-pork the next time I get guenip I ain[t] givin[g] you nix.*—(Guyn) [Prob a survival of Du niets 'nothing'. Cp OED nix[1] slang 'nothing; nobody', but it is the Du rather than a German orig that would have given the *Guyn* usage] □ Once very common among urban school children. Still used as n and vb in BrE and AmE. See COD8, WCD9.

no[1] **(na(h), nar, neh, nuh)** [no~na~nε~nʌ] negator (CarA) [IF/AF—Cr] [These forms are not in free variation. Their distribution as variants is partly indicated according to the senses listed below.] **1.** (CarA) ‖ *na*[1] (Guyn, Trin) (SE) No! **2.** (CarA) ‖ *na*[1] 2. (Antg, Guyn, StKt) (SE) Not. **a.** *We mus[t] try hard to no le[t] da[t] happen.*—(StKt) **b.** *An[d] who you expec[t] goin[g] to pay fo[r] dat? No me, yo[u] hear?*—(Guyn) **3.** second element of a double neg (CarA) ‖ NUH (CarA) *Dey would make seven lines an when de bands press forward de girls and boys press forward; an when de band press backward, dey all press backward. It wasn't no mashing; it wasn't no chucking. It wasn't no 'you mash me man!'—nothing like dat. Dey wasn't no bottle breaking, an nobody chucking nobody—dere wasn't no killing.*—Aaw I.2, p.8 **4.** neg auxiliary (with ellipsis) (CarA) ‖ *na*[1] 3. (Guyn, Nevs, StKt, StVn) Isn't, aren't, etc; doesn't, don't, didn't. **a.** *'No You, No Me, But We'* (= It isn't you; it isn't me; it's all of us)—UWI (Cave Hill Students' Union) Motto, 1971 **b.** *Me? I ain[t] goin[g]. No give a dam!* (= Me? I'm not going. I don't give a damn!)—(Jmca) **5.** neg imper (CarA) ‖ *na*[1] 4. ‖ *nar* (Antg, Guyn, StKt) ‖ *nuh* (Jmca) Don't. *No hang you clothes all pon one nail.*—DaG (71.07.08, p.12, Jmca Prov) **6.** introducing an assertion (with ellipsis) (Guyn, Jmca) ‖ *na*[1] 5. (Guyn) [Focusing the following phr as fact. The phr is marked by a rising pitch like an inquiry] It is ... isn't it!; Surely it is .... **a.** *No the same thing I tell you?* (= Isn't it exactly what I told you [that happened]?)—(Guyn) **b.** *Which part him goin[g] work? No lie the boy lie?* (= Where would he be working? Surely he's just lying!)—(Jmca) [Prob from a W Afr source. Dr P. Christie (Assertive 'No' in Jamaican Creole—Society for Caribbean Linguistics' Occasional Paper No.10, 1979) points to similar functions of Akan na and Yoruba ni] □ This introductory 'No-' develops into 'NOT-' among some middle-level speakers in (Guyn). **7.** terminal tag (CarA) ‖ *neh* (Bdos) ‖ *ner* (Trin) ‖ *non* (Dmca, StLu) ‖ *nuh* (CarA) [Adding friendly persuasion to a statement or request] Isn't it so?; Don't/Won't you (agree with me)? **a.** *And when he said, 'You like the place, no?', she could reply quickly, 'Yes, ah don' mind it.'* —PCOS:55 **b.** *I don't want to go alone. Come we go, no?* (= ... Come with me, won't you?)—(Trin) [Cp Twi phrase-terminal no 'that, the', wh 'as it points out a thing as already mentioned or known, so it may likewise point out a fact expressed in a sentence' (DAFL: 346). Also Twi sentence-terminal interrogative particle ana? wh turns a statement into an inquiry. Similarly Isoko has a sentence-final emphatic marker na. Such W Afr influences would account better for the pervasive occurrence of this terminal persuasion tag NO ~ NA ~ NUH in CE than the supposition, often advanced, that Sp no, Fr non, wh are often in those langs similarly used, may be its orig in CE. Fr and Sp had slight or no contact infl in many Anglophone CarA Cr communities] □ See the note at NA[1], and also the variant forms as separate entries. PHRASES **8.1 No min[d]!** [nʌ maın] neg adv phr (CarA) [AF] Never mind! It doesn't matter. **a.** *They envy you, no mind, girl!*—(Bdos) **b.** *It could be red, blue, any colour, no mind!*—(Guyn) **8.2 no more than true** adv phr (Baha, Guyn, Mrat, TkCa) Indeed; (and) you may take it as fact; (and it is) quite believable. *He didn't want to lend them the new spade he had just bought because—no more than true—they are a careless lot over there and next thing you know they can't find it!*—(Guyn) **8.3 no must** /2'1/ assertive modal aux (sometimes with ellipsis) (Guyn, Jmca, StVn) [AF] [Focusing the following phrase as obvious or obligatory; marked by inquiry pitch] Must it not ...?; surely must. **a.** *If you have third a something, no must have first and second?*—SNWIC:258 (M. Townshend) **b.** *Yo[u] lef[t] dem on de fire too long! Dem no mus[t] mash up?* (= ... Mustn't they surely be overcooked, uneatable?)—(StVn)

no² *prep, conj* (Belz, Guyn, Trino [*AF*] [With intensifying force] **1.** Like; as much/vigorously/ intensely, etc as. (See Phrs]. **a.** *Dress up no puss back-foot* (= *Dressed up like the cat's hind-leg i.e. much overdressed*).—YCPB (Prov.51) **b.** *Child I'm fightin[g] no fury to finish dis dress A promise de lady for tonight.*—(Guyn) [Perh a W Afr structural survival. Cp Igbo prep *na* 'like, as', wh occurs as a conn particle in that lang. The form, surviving in Cr as /na/ in this function, may have been refined as NO [nʌ~no] by vowel closure at the mesolectal level] **2.** *PHRASES* **2.1 no ass!** [*AF*—Vul]; **no hell** [*AF*] *adv intensifiers* (Belz, Guyn, Trin) Abundantly; intensely; vigorously, etc. **a.** *I tell you he run no ass, like if he see a jumbie.*—(Trin) **b.** *Little as it is, don't let it sting you! It hurts no hell, you hear?*—(Guyn)

nog [nɒɡ] *n* (Mrat, Nevs, StKt) ‖ **nag** (Nevs, StKt) [*X*] A short wooden pillar on several of wh a small house stands, just high enough to be raised off the ground. [*OED nog* sb¹ '… a small block of wood serving for various purposes']

noint (n(a)int) [nɒɪnt~naɪnt] *vb tr* (CarA) [*IF/ AF*] To massage (the body) with some kind of oil, ointment, grease, or herbal infusion for either medicinal or folk-religious purposes; to rub down (sb). *Well they nointed her down with coconut oil and soft-grease after the bush-bath and she felt much better.*—(StVn) [< SE *anoint* by aphesis, though the highly religious, ceremonial association of SE *anoint* is largely lost in CE. Cp also *EDD noint*, used in very many E counties, with differing spellings and pronuncs including *naint*]

noise [nɒɪz~naˑɪz] *n* (CarA) [*IF/AF*] **1.** A commotion; a public disturbance. **a.** *Sometimes you get a load a* [*of*] *noise is a case what create interest or what have scandal inside it.*—LMFF: 45 **b.** *Of course at that time they had a lot o*[*f*] *noise as you know, 1937, so I didn*[*'t*] *want to get mix up in anyt*[*h*]*ing. Use*[*d*] *to stay in the house.*—(Bdos) **2.** [By extension] A quarrel. *I was working with a couple and after we had the first noise about one phone call I told him not to call back there.*—PeL (78.03.10, p.6, Dear Christine) [Cp *EDD* wh lists *noise* 'a quarrel, disturbance, row' for some 14 E counties from Yks to Cor + many cits. This may account for the wide similar usage in CE. See Phrs] **3.** *PHRASES* **3.1 be/get in noise** *vb phr* (Gren, Tbgo, Trin) [*AF*] **(i)** To be in an open row; to find yourself in a lot of trouble. *I know that, with all the promises he is making, the Mayor is going to be in noise if he does not fix the roads after the election.*—Trin (Ms, 1972) **(ii)** ‖ **HAVE NOISE** *vb phr* (Bdos, Gren, Trin) *What happen? Like you an*[*d*] *Mary in noise or what? She do*[*n*]*'t call you when she passin*[*g*]*!*—(Gren) **3.2 have noise** *vb phr* (Bdos, Gren, Trin) To be at loggerheads; to have a running vexed disagreement. *We had 'noise' for six weeks straight and I never knew why until she started to come home at 11 and 12 o'clock at nights after work which ended at 4.*—NaT (89.02.15, p.22) □ Note the difference between this phr 3.2 and **HAVE A NOISE** (sense 2. prec). **3.3 keep noise** [*AF*]; **make noise** [*IF*] *vb phrs* (CarA) See **KEEP** Phr 3.8; **MAKE** Phr 5.21

non [nõ~nʌ] *terminal tag* (Dmca, StLu) ‖ NO 7. (CarA) *But Jim did not move. 'Sir, I diden pick your mango non.' 'I don say you pick,' the man broke in, 'all I say is come down.'*—SDD:43 □ See note at NO. This spelling and pronunc are most likely infl superficially by the Fr Cr medium of the speech of *Dmca, StLu* though the pervasive Anglophone parallel use of NO belie a deep Fr orig.

no-na·tion /1'22/ *n* (Guyn) [*AF—Derog*] See **NATION** 3.5

non-na·tion·al /1'222/ *n* (CarA) A person who is legally resident in but not a native of a particular *CarA* State. *We believe that the question of the status of non-nationals married to Barbadian women can be easily got around by according these the same status as nationals during the subsistence of the marriage.*—AdN (Ed, 72.03.19, p.4)

noo·noo-bal·sam *n* (Antg, Brbu) See **NUNU-BALSAM/BUSH**

nose-hole [noˑzoˑl~noˑzhol] *n* (Bdos, Gren, Guyn, Jmca, Trin) [*AF—Derog*] The nostril; the nose. *Some payin' t'rough duh noseholes / Fuh some house in Gol' Dus' Heights / Wid bar an' den an' TV room / An' multi-colour lights.*—PeL (77.11.18, p.8, J. Layne-Clark) [As *OED nose-hole* 1. (Now dial). Note SE *nostril* < OE *nose-thirl* 'nose-hole']

not *negator in semi-assertive function* **1.** (CarA) [*IF*] [Focusing the following phrase as fact or prompting the answer 'Yes'; there is a rising inquiry-like pitch] Isn't it, surely …? **a.** *Not the same thing I told you?* (= *Isn't it exactly as I told you it would happen?*)—(Guyn) **b.** *Not a police van I see over there?* (= *Isn't that a police van that I see over there?*)—(Gren) □ See NO (*CarA*) 6. and note. **2.** *PHRASES* [Certain CE phrases operate, or have a special meaning only in the negative] **2.1 not (be) able with (sb/sth)** *neg vb phr* (CarA) See **ABLE** Phr 1. **2.2 not ask you how old you be** *neg vb phr* (CarA) See **ASK** Phr 2.5 **2.3 not buff on (sb)** [bʊf] *neg vb phr* (Angu) [*AF*] To snub (sb) pointedly; to ignore (sb) insultingly. *When she come back from the States, for the short while she was here she wouldn*[*'t*] *buff on me, but I hear she married good up there.*—(Angu) [Cp **BUFF** 2. (*Tbgo, Trin*) 'to insult, rebuff'. The notion in this Phr may be 'not even take the trouble to rebuff me'] **2.4 not (doing sth) again** *neg phr* (CarA) See **AGAIN**¹ Phr 2. **2.5 not eat nice** *vb phr* (StVn, Tbgo, Trin) [*AF—Joc*] See **EAT** Phr 3.4 **2.6 not even … far less** *adv phr* (CarA) See **FAR** Phr 1.(i) **2.7 not forget (sb)** *neg vb phr* (CarA) [*AF*] See **FORGET** Phr 1. **2.7.1 not forget to (do sth)** *neg vb phr* (CarA) [*AF*] See **FORGET** Phr 2. **2.8 not go to (do sth)** *neg vb phr* (CarA) See **GO** Phr 6.30.1 **2.9 not make fun to (do sth)** *neg vb phr* (Guyn)

[*AF/IF*] See MAKE Phr 5.16 **2.10 not pay (sb) any/no mind** *neg vb phr* (CarA) [*IF/AF*] ‖ PAY (SB) NO MIND (CarA) See MIND Phr 8. **2.11 not pick/unpick your teeth** *neg vb phr* (Angu, Bdos, Guyn, Tbgo) [*AF*] See PICK Phr 5.2; UNPICK **2.12 not put water in your mouth to (say sth)** *neg vb phr* (Trin) [*AF—Joc*] See PUT Phr 1. **2.13 not (be) sex and size with (sb)** *id phr* (ECar) [*AF*] See SEX¹ Phr 2. **2.14 not so?** *elliptical tag* (CarA) *Isn't that so? Don't force her now, but after a time Jennie will come to church with us. Not so, Jennie?*—Tbgo (Ms) □ A more refined form of NO (*CarA*) 6. Cp Fr tag *n'est-ce pas?* wh is similarly used. **2.15 not take your height** *id phr* (CarA) [*IF*] See HEIGHT Phr 2. **2.16 not talk in boli** *neg vb phr* (Gren) [*AF—Joc*] See BOLI Phr 3.1 ‖ NOT PUT WATER IN YOUR MOUTH TO (SAY STH) (Trin) **2.17 not today/yesterday** *neg adv phr* (Bdos, Guyn) [*IF*] A long time ago; for some time now. **a.** *It isn't today I've been warning her about that habit she has, and I knew it would get her in trouble.*—(Guyn) **b.** *We ain['t] come here yesterday yo[u] know. We know Bajan people, but you only t[h]ink you know them.*—(Bdos) [The same phr occurs in IrE: '"tisn't to-day or yesterday it happened him'—meaning that it is a fault of long standing'—*JESI:18*]

noth·er [nDðʌ ~ nʌdʌ] *adj* (Bdos, BrVi, StVn) [*X*] Other. *Peter and your nother brother were here today.*—(BrVi) [A survival with shift of EE *nother*. See *OED nother*¹ *pron* and *adj* + cits—'1782 'a nother mending' this form giving way in 18C Eng to *an other*, thence to *another*. EE *nother* functioned syntactically more widely] □ See also NEITHER-NOTHER *Bdos*.

noth·ing (**nut·ten**) [nʌtɪŋ ~ nʌtɪn ~ nʌtn] *pron* (CarA) **1.** [*IF/AF*] [Of persons] Of no relationship; not of the same family. *Yes, all two name Brathwaite but are nothing to one another.*—(Bdos) □ Also *IF* AmE usage. Cp also ANYTHING¹ wh is similarly used. **2.** *second element in a double neg* [*X*] Anything. *He leave without telling her nothing and your mother start to love your father. When dis man come back you mother and father did just married and he was vexed.*—TLTH:17 □ Also dial BrE usage. **3.** *PHRASE* **3.1 nothing so** *pron phr* (Bdos) [*IF/AF*] Nothing of the kind. *He told her he was takin[g] her to a fete, but when they got there, was nothin[g] so. Just two other men drinkin[g] rum with some woman or nother.*—(Bdos) □ Other dial pronuncs occur, ex *neffin* [nɛfin] *Bdos*. However [nʌtn] is the commonest in the *CarA* at the folk level.

No·tice *n* (CarA) See GENERAL NOTICE (*Jmca*), WIFE NOTICE *Guyn*

'nough [nʌf] (CarA) [*AF*] See NUFF

now *adv* (CarA) [*AF/IF*] **1.** Just a short while ago. **a.** *You been here long or you now come?* —(Tbgo) **b.** *The bus now gone, you just miss it.*—(StVn) □ In this function NOW precedes the vb, is stressed, and, depending on the context, is marked by a distinctly higher or lower pitch

than the vb. **2.** *PHRASES* **2.1 for now** *adv phr* (Bdos) [*IF*] See FOR Phr 13.5 **2.2 just now** *adv phr* (CarA) [*IF*] See JUST Phr 3. **2.3 (like) now so** *adv phr* (CarA) [*AF*] (At) about this time. *Like now so last week I was getting ready to leave New York.*—(Gren) **2.4 now for now (i)** *adv phr* (CarA) ‖ NOW NOW (CarA) *When I tell you go, I mean now for now. I'm not waiting.*—(Gren) **(ii)** [By extension] *adj, n* (StLu, Tbgo, Trin) [*AF*] Makeshift. **a.** *That had produced 'Speedy Gonzales' politics in which people sought power on a now-for-now basis. If they won, they carried on as usual because they had not taken the time to win genuine popular support. If they lost, they 'faded away'.*—ExP (72.02.20, p.28) **b.** *Senator dese fellars not cooyon you know. You tink de fellers go grab a now-for-now knowing dat just now everything crash?*—CrU (74.08.10, Cocky & Stocky) **2.5 now now (now)!** *adv phr* **(i)** (CarA) [*AF*] ‖ *now for now* **(i)** (CarA) Immediately; right away; with no delay. *... but he want me married him now-now. But nuh, after all, is not so people does get married.*—RTCS:10 □ Sometimes repeated as often as four or five times in emotive contexts in CE.

no·way; no·where [nʌwe(r)] *adv* (CarA) [*AF*] [As double neg] ‖ ANYWAY (CarA) *She didn[']t tell [h]im so noway. Is he make it up.*—(Guyn)

no·wher·i·an *n* (Gren, Guyn, Jmca, Tbgo, Trin) **1.** A person who is not connected with any church or who professes no religious faith. **2.** [By extension] Sb who is not respectable; sb of no consequence. **3.** [By further extension] [*Derog*] An unkempt looking knockabout; a person of no fixed abode. [< nowhere + suff *-ian* by analogy with such forms as Christian (religion), Canadian (place of origin), etc]

N.S.C. *abbr* (StLu) The National Service Cross, a national honour awarded to a senior Police, Fire, or Prison Officer for loyal and devoted service beneficial to St Lucia; the letters may be placed after the recipient's name.

nuff¹ (**'nough**¹) [nʌf] *adj* [*AF—Cr/Joc*] **1.** (CarA) Much; many; a great amount/number of. **a.** *But let there be no question about it, nuff respect is due Serenader. He has seen justice done to his music at last, and it was a well deserved victory, over a field that included four former monarchs.*—SuS (90.08.05, p.33) **b.** *Montego Bay Y's Men's Club Ball is next Saturday night ... and bread raised will be in aid of the North Gully Infant Centre. Like man, the proceeds will pay the staff and run the school, and you know nuff pickney around who need educating.*—StA(JA) (72.11.18, p.10, Partyline) **c.** *Each territory has a particular position to play / But 'nough talk and lil action is what we get / We haven't learned how to come together as yet.*—Cso (Sir Don, 1975) [< SE *enough* by aphesis] □ See ENOUGH¹, ENOUGH², NUFF². The spelling *nuff* is listed in *OED2* as 'orig US', with many cits (1840–') but the form, even if not recorded in writing, is at least simultaneously *CarA Cr*, and with wider usage. See foll entries. **2.** As much as (to); enough, sufficient (to). *I wonder why the Transports bus seat slippery so, flinging yah all bout the bus, and dese fast moving drivers nuff to throw yah outside.*—Bdos (Ms Play, 1977) **3.** [By extension] (Antg, BrVi, Jmca, Mrat, StVn) ‖ BIGGITIVE (BrVi, Guyn) [Mostly applying to children and young women] Officious; precocious; full of a feeling of self-importance; cocky and disrespectful. **a.** *Since when Billy get so nough—cu[r]sin[g] the teacher an[d] all?*—(StVn) **b.** *You can believe she is nuff enough to introduce herself to the Governor wife at the fair?*—(Antg)

nuff² (**'nough**²) [nʌf] *pron* (CarA) [*AF—Cr*] ‖ ENOUGH¹ (CarA) *They announced that nuff of the autoclaps which result when bwoy and gal meet up, comes from the fact, they say, that nuff of our daughters too dumb.*—WeG (73.02.28, p.3, Partyline) [See NUFF¹ 1.]

nuff³ (**'nough**³) *adv* (CarA) [*AF—Cr*] [Often redup] Plentifully; profusely; very much. **a.** *My dear, when your brother held that catch, the crowd rushed on the field and kissed him up 'nough-nough', I must say.*—Trin (Ms) **b.** *And next morning when she went outside she find a bottle with feathers in it, and she frighten 'nuff, 'nuff.*—CISH:119 [< SE *enough*, adv 'sufficiently', with extended sense]

nuff·ness [nʌfnɪs] *n* (Antg, Jmca) [*AF—Joc*] Precocity; offensive showiness; display of false sophistication. *Not only that, she was more than a little visible and nuff, to boot, and you know that Royalty not supposed to be associated with that kind of nuffness. Ah so mi hear.*—WeG (73.07.18, p.21, Partyline) [< CarA Cr NUFF¹ adj 3. + SE suff -*ness* 'state or condition of being']

nuh (**ner**) [nʌ] (CarA) [*AF—Cr*] ‖ *non* (Dmca, StLu) **1.** *second part of a double neg, unstressed* ‖ NO 3. (CarA) *We don['t] want nuh noise bringin[g] nuh police here, you see!*—(Jmca) **2.** *neg imper, unstressed* (CarA) ‖ NO 5. (CarA) *'You mus' keep yourself clean an nuh come dirty,' Sybil would say as she inspected the khaki pants and crisp white shirt she had so lovingly laundered and ironed. 'Where de books, Boy? Nuh forget to eat you lunch, eh.'*—FGSOS:53 (D. Pollock) **3.** *terminal tag* (CarA) ‖ NO 6. (CarA) **a.** *I'm just going to bring a few things so that I can change when we come back here, ner.* -RSMCD:48 **b.** *Sometimes I would say to her I want to hold her in my arms and she would reply 'hold nuh'. I don't know if she does be testing me or not.*—NaT (76.09.12, p.26, Dear Christine) **c.** *But tell me nuh, Vio, what make some people have to powder dey face so thick and put on all dis rouge and lipstick?*—RTCS:18

num·ber *n* (CarA) [*AF—Joc*] A young woman (regarded as one of a number of one man's sexual objectives). **a.** *And now, the first date, in the heart of London, dressed to kill, ready to escort the number around the town, anywhere she want to go, any place at all.*—STLL:74 **b.** *So now he didn['t] wan[t] dis steady number to meet dis new number,*

bu[t] de joke is dat de ol[d] number tell [h]er.—(Guyn)

num·ber-one; **do num.ber-one** *vb* (*phr*) (ECar) [*IF*] [Schoolchildren's lang] To urinate. *Mum, why are Kaiser and Jaillin so vulgar? You know I saw Kaiser do number one behind a tree even when Jaillin was there once.*—MHBT:98

num·ber-two; **do num.ber-two** *vb* (*phr*) (ECar) [*IF*] [Schoolchildren's lang] To defecate.

numb-fish *n* **1.** (Guyn) The electric eel. **2.** (CayI) ‖ SCORPION-FISH (CarA)

nu·nu-bal·sam/-bush (noo-noo-) (Antg, Brbu, Jmca) *n* A low-growing, sweet-smelling herb bearing a little mauve flower; it is used for making BUSH-TEAS and, by some (esp in *Jmca*), in folk-healing practices; *Ocimum spp* (*Labiatae*). [Cp *DAFL* Twi *o-nunum* 'an aromatic plant used like ɛmɛ̃ ('mint, an aromatic herb used as a medicine')]

nuse¹; **nuses** (**to**) [nyu·z; nyu·zɪz(tʌ)] *vb* (*phr*) (Bdos) [*X*] To use; used (to). **a.** *De chil[d] ain['t] learn to nuse a fork yet*—(Bdos) **b.** *I en braggin, but I nuses to be good, good at football*—NaT (80.03.12, p.16, Austin 'Tom' Clarke) [A prosthetic folk form < SE *use* vb; the form NUSES is owing to overcorrection. See N—; see also next]

nuse²; **nuseful** [nyu·s nyu·sfʊl] *n*; *adj* (Bdos) [*X*] Use *n*; useful *adj*. *De car ain['t] no nuse; de bicycle is more nuseful*—(Bdos). [See note at prec.]

nut-cake *n* (Bdos, Guyn, Trin) ‖ *glassie* (Bdos) ‖ *pindar-cake* (Jmca) A flat, brittle sweet made of thickly candied peanuts; (AmE) peanut brittle.

nut-grass* *n* (CarA) A rapidly spreading, pestilent grass with three-angled stems usu a few inches high, bearing short flower spikes; its roots bear many small, nut-like tubers (hence the name), wh make the grass difficult to root out; *Cyperus rotundus* (*Cyperaceae*).

nut·ten [nʌtn] *pron* (CarA) [*X*] See NOTHING

nut·ten-chops [nʌtn-čɒps] *n pl* (ECar) [*AF—Joc*] Nothing to eat. [Joc rhyme with SE *mutton-chops*] □ See also WIND-PIES.

nyam [nyam] *vb* (CarA) [*AF—Cr/Derog*] To eat (voraciously); to eat (sth) as crudely as an animal would. **a.** *Hard time mek dag nyam roas' carn.* (= *Hard times make a dog eat roast-corn.*)—AGM:46 (Guyn Prov) **b.** *He nyam up the bread so fast you would t[h]ink it was runnin[g] away.*—(Dmca) **c.** *Was spending couple days on the Northcoast getting nyamed by mosquitoes in the name of hometown tourism but that is another story.*—WeG (73.11.14, p.13, Partyline) [From a number of overlapping Afr lang sources. (See *DJE nyaams, nyam* for a full treatment.) However, it must be noted that, in the vocabulary of 200 Afr langs checked, *KPG:80—81* lists 47 phonically similar forms (*nama, nyam, nyiama, inam*, etc) as the word for 'meat, flesh' (n) but only 3 (*p.177*) as the word for 'eat' (vb). It is also notable that E *yam*, Fr *igname* (naming the vegetable commonly used as slaves' food) are derived, as nouns, from the same source. The apparent n > vb shift wh occurred everywhere in CarA Cr, from *Guyn* through the islands to *Belz*, is difficult to account for on such a scale. See also NINYAM] □ The form is widely preserved in many CarA Cr provs (note cit (a), less often in *AF—Joc* use as in cit (c). Like other widely recognized Afr survivals in CE, the word is of generally low social status, but somewhat higher in *Joc* contexts, esp in *Jmca* where a Kingston eating place at one time sold a *nyamburger*.

nyam·pi [nyampi] *n* (StVn) ‖ YAMPI(E)² (Antg, etc) [Cp *AFID* Igbo (Ukwaali) *ẹnyampi* 'blind'. See also YAMPI(E)²]

nyam(p)s [nyam(p)s] *n* (Jmca) [*AF—Derog/Joc*] A person (esp a man) who is a weakling; an undependable half-wit. *The word for a man who is utterly worthless and incapable is 'nyamps' the 'ny' sound reflecting a lip curled upwards in contempt.*—SWI:139 [Cp *DAFL* Twi *nyãmma* 'small'. (Only used after proper names); also *nyãmoo* 'lean, feeble'. Perh also infl by Jmca Cr *nyam*, as orig noun 'yam', so implying 'a mere vegetable'. The homorganic /-p-/ is occasionally intrusive; and the prosthetic /-s-/ is prob a

marker of familiar speech, as found in other CE exs *Bruds* 'Brother', *Dads* 'Daddy' (as forms of address). Cp also AmE *gramps* 'grandpa']

nyan·ga; **yan.ga** [(n)yaŋga] *n* (Guyn, Jmca) [*AF—Joc*] **1.** ‖ *yanga*¹ **2.** (Guyn) Pride; putting on airs; showiness (esp in your attire). [Cp *IMED* Mende *nyanga* (esp of women) 'ostentation, style, giving oneself airs'. However note also a poss Bantu connection in *SHDNL* Nyanja *nyang'anyang'a* 'walking softly on tiptoe'] **2.** A person (esp a young man) who dresses showily. *The old man was a real nyanga in his day you know. He tell me he used to wear felt hat, gold tie-pin, carry walking-stick and so on.*—(Guyn) □ Sometimes used attrib in sense 2: *yanga girl, yanga boy*.

nya·pa [nyapʌ] *n* (USVI) ‖ BRAATA (Antg, etc) [Cp LANYAP (*Tbgo, Trin*) of wh NYAPA wd be a related form nearer the Sp orig *ñapa*, 'extra', prob due to the Sp infl of *PtRi*]

ny·lon road *n phr* (Bdos, Guyn, Jmca, StLu) [*AF—Joc*] A road that has been smoothly surfaced with an asphalt mixture laid on by a road-surfacing machine. *We were told that we would be improving these with nylon roads, and if we wanted to run on them we will have to pay additional taxation.*—Bdos (Hd, 75.05.20, p.4889) [A Joc attrib use of SE *nylon* n, as a silky smooth yet tough fabric]

O

o·be·ah¹ (o·be·a¹, o·bi·a(h)¹) [obia] / 1´21 ~ 1´22/ *n* (CarA) ‖ *wanga* (Tbgo, USVI) **1.** A set or system of secret beliefs in the use of supernatural forces to attain or defend against evil ends; it is Afr in origin and varies greatly in kind, requirements, and practice, ranging from the simple, such as the use of items like oils, herbs, bones, grave-dirt and fresh animal blood, to the criminal (though rare), such as the sacrifice of a child's life; it is carried on or WORKED by hidden practitioners in order to gain for their clients success, protection, or cures for mysterious illnesses, as well as cause trouble for, or the death of an enemy. *A Police party last Saturday raided a house on Old Street and seized a number of instruments believed to be those used in the practice of Obeah.*—NeC (77.02.12, p.2) **2.** [By transfer or extension] **(i)** The evil spell believed to be cast upon a person by means of witchcraft. **(ii)** Any out-of-the-way item whatever (such as a corked bottle, tiny blue tied sack, small black doll, etc) the presence of wh cannot be reasonably accounted for but wh is felt to be the carrier of such a spell. **(iii)** The misfortune or illness believed to be caused by the spell. *The villagers died from sheer inability to understand how a germ and not someone's obeah was the cause of the fever.*—EFSLC:31 [No precise origin has been determined, but some items esp in W Afr langs, suggest a connection. Cp *DAFL* Twi ɔ-bayi-fo (*witchcraft man*) 'sorcerer' < *bayi* 'witchcraft'; also *KNED* Nembe *obi* 'sickness, disease'; also Igbo *obi a* 'this (particular) mind, will; also *KID* Ibibio *abia* 'practitioner, herbalist'. *DJE* also notes Efik *ubio* 'a charm put in the ground to cause sickness', a practice known in *Guyn*] **3.** PHRASES **3.1 cut/take off (the) obeah from (sb)** *vb phr* (CarA) To undo, remove the spell or effect of OBEAH by a counter-spell. **3.2 put/set obeah on (sb)** *vb phr* (CarA) To put or to get a practitioner to put the evil spell of OBEAH on (sb) so as to cause the person's failure in some venture or in health. **3.3 work obeah against/for/on (sb)** *vb phr* (CarA) [Of a practitioner] To prepare in secret the charms, say the incantations, etc, wh are meant to bring evil into the life or actions of (sb). *I grew up in a drug store and I know people would come in and purchase five cents in 'Quick-silver' mercury, and they would take this because some friend had advised them to do so, and once they had taken it no one could do them any harm by working obeah for them.*—AdM (74.01.06, p.4, Glimpses of old Barbados) □ See also BAD³ PHR 2.1, MYAL, VOODOO.

o·be·ah² (o·be·a², o·bi·a(h)²) [obia] /1´22/ *adj* (CarA) Related to, carrying on or practising OBEAH¹. **a.** *These are not Christian but obeah beliefs, one might almost say the obeatic practices of obeahism—mentioned on the list are also special drugs for the use in obeah baths, including white lavender and indigo blue.*—Guyn (Ms) **b.** *It is significant that a flag shaped like the Roman numeral ten, painted red on a black background is the Obeah flag. This flag is flown or placed either at a house where Obeah is practised or signifies protection from 'sperrids' or living beings.*—MTTBT:6 □ As in cit (a) there is a *Joc* tendency to use *'obeatic'* as the adj form, though this function is most commonly filled by the noun in attrib position.

o·be·ah³ [obia] /1´22/ *vb tr* (Baha, Belz, Guyn, Jmca) To make (sb) suffer unexplained failure in health or continual misfortune through the effects of OBEAH¹. *Bahamians are increasingly seeking medical help to break what they believe to be evil spells, according to a medical doctor who treated several cases and wrote a book about obeah. 'In the past six months, more people are coming to see me about being 'obeahed',' said Dr T. McCartney, 'and many colleagues have said they are getting a resurgence of people whose behaviour is influenced by this belief system.'*—AdV (85.06.14, p.3) [By functional n > vb shift of OBEAH¹]

o·be·ah·ism [obiaɪzm] *n* OBEAH¹; the practice and/or belief in or the use of OBEAH¹. *Obeahism! It was evident that the cause for Barney's degradation was the result of some evil spell cast upon him by one of those who envied him; such practices of iniquity were commonplace.*—LDSS:28 [OBEAH + SE -*ism* 'condition, practice of a system'. Cp *barbarism, communism*] □ A refinement of OBEAH¹ used by some writers, as also OBEAHIST, next.

o·be·ah·ist *n* (Guyn) One who practices or habitually resorts to the help of OBEAH¹. [OBEAH + SE -*ist* 'supporter of, believer in, perpetrator'. Cp SE forms *racist, arsonist*]

o·be·ah-man/-wo·man *n* (CarA) ‖ *mama-do-good; papa-do-good* (Gren) ‖ *scientist* (Guyn, Gren, Jmca, Nevs) A man or woman who learns and carries out the practices of OBEAH¹ as a secret profession and has paying clients. [Cp

Twi ɔ-bayi-fo, Ibibio *abia* in the etym note at
OBEAH¹]

ob·li·gat·ed *vbl adj* (Bdos) [*X*] Obliged; forced
by circumstances; compelled. *Sir, the children
were sent in those days to work in the fields at the
age of 10 and 12 and some were not even given
the opportunity to go to school. Those who were
given the opportunity to go to school were in most
cases obligated to leave the schools in first and
second standard and to go and work in a gang which
in those days was called the third gang.*—Bdos (Hd,
74.12.03, p.4267) [A misascription of the sense
of SE *obligated* 'legally or morally bound'] □ This
usage tends to appear also outside of CE.

ob·sock·y (ob·zock·ie, ob·zok·ey, etc) [ɒb
sɒki ~ ɒbzɒki] *adj* (CarA) [*AF—Derog/Joc*] 1.
[Of furniture, clothes, colours, etc] Misshapen;
ill-fitting; very odd-looking; clumsily put together. 2. [Of persons] Ungainly and badly
dressed; (esp of women) fat and wearing conspicuously ill-chosen colours or clothing. 3. [Of
situations] Ridiculous; hopelessly unorganized.
[Perh a corruption of a sentence, now lost, from
a W Afr lang. Cp Yoruba *ọbọ* 'monkey' + *sọ* 'to
break wind' + *ki* 'to greet'. Cp MONKEY-FART]

o·cean-gar* *n* (ECar) ‖ *bill-fish* (CarA) Name
applied esp to the swordfish (*Xiphias gladius*),
feared for its aggressive habits when hooked.
[*Ocean*, from its habitat + CE GAR(fish)]

o·cean-jack *n* (Belz) ‖ AMBERJACK (CarA)

o·che·ri-seed *n* (Guyn) See AKORI-SEED

o·chro [okro·] *n* (CarA) See OKRA

ock·ya-stick [ɒkya-stɪk] *n* (Bdos) ‖ HAKYA-
STICK (Guyn) [Prob orig HAKYA-STICK as in
Guyn, with /h-/ loss by aphaeresis and [a > ɒ]
overcorrection] □ Cp COCO-MACCA

O.D. *abbr* 1. (Antg, Brbu) The Order of Distinction, of the Order of Antigua and Barbuda,
a national honour awarded to any person who
has rendered distinguished and outstanding service to the State; the letters O.D. may be placed
after the recipient's name. 2. (Jmca) Officer of
the Order of Distinction, a national honour awarded for distinction through service to Jamaica;
the letters O.D. may be placed after the recipient's name. □ See also C.D.

O.E. *abbr* (Guyn) The Order of Excellence of
Guyana, a national honour awarded to a citizen
of distinction and eminence in the field of human
endeavour of either national or international significance and importance; it is the highest national award, and the letters O.E. may be placed
after the recipient's name.

O.E.C.S. *abbr*(CarA) Organisation of (Anglo-
lophone) Eastern Caribbean States, an international organisation set up in 1981,
encompassing the seven member States of the

E.C.C.M. with the Br Virgin Is as an added
Associate Member, for the promotion of co-
operation, collective defence of territorial integrity and the harmonisation of their foreign
policies.

of¹ *prep* PHRASES 1. **of a certain kind** *adj phr*
(Bdos) [*IF*] [Of a person] Obviously decent;
above the ordinary in class, quality. *Well the
father was a man of a certain kind, you know what
I mean? And he won['t] le[t] the children play
wid any an[d] everybody.*—(Bdos) 2. **of myself/
himself, etc** *prep phr* (CarA) [*IF*] For my/his,
etc part; left to myself/himself, etc. *'I had a
couple of drinks, sir, and the woman was teasing
me,'* said Cyril. *'I of myself don't like bad words,
sir,'* he added.—DeM(SK) (62.03.10, p.10)
□ Also dial AmE. 3. **of a Sunday/weekday, etc**
prep phr (CarA) [*IF*] On Sundays/weekdays, etc.
*Of a day like today, Tuesday, I couldn't tell you
where to find him but of a Sunday he looks after
opening and closing the church so you will find him
there.*—(Guyn) 4. **with a/the view of** *prep phr*
(CarA) [*X*] With a view to; with the intention
or expectation of. *I wonder how long these am-
ateurs will be denied the opportunity to expose their
skill to the general public with a view of gaining
selection to our national team in the future.*—AdN
(72.10.06, p.4) □ In CE, OF is commonly misused where another prep is required in SE idiom.

of² *enclitic vbl particle* (CarA) [*X*] [After modals
could, should, would, might, must] Have [in auxiliary function] *I could of help you fight them, and
you wouldn't of had to mash up the cutlass so
much.*—SPOC:122 [By faulty re-analysis of the
unstressed clitic *'ve* in *could've* [kʊdəv], etc, often
reduced to [-a -ʌ] in CarA Cr (see A⁸); THESE
ARE FALSELY REFINED AS E 'OF', HENCE *could of*,
ETC] □ A common occurrence in written schoolwork.

off¹ *prep* PHRASES 1. **off o[f] (sth)** *prep phr*
(CarA) [*X*] **a.** *He fell off of a ladder.*—Guyn
(Ms) **b.** *He ain['t] mek mo[re] runs off o[f] me
bowlin[g] dan off o[f] yours.*—(Bdos) [Prob a
survival from EE. See *OED off* 7. b.: *off of* as
EE, now dial phr + cit from Shak (1593) 'A
fall off of a tree'. The CE use may be reinforced
by IrE, ex 'To sweep the cobwebs off o' the
sky'—*JESI:44*. Also note AmE *offa* in *OED2*]
2. **off the island** *prep phr* (CarA) Out of the
island; gone away (usu for a short period).

off² *adv* (CarA) [*AF/IF*] [As an intensifier of
action in a vb phr, where *up, away*, or some
turn of phr would be used in SE] Very much;
noticeably, etc; hence such phrs as foll: PHRASES
1. **chat off (sb)** *vb phr* [*AF—Joc*] To chat away
with (sb) carrying most of the conversation. 2.
cuss off (sb) *vb phr* [*AF*] To swear at, loudly
abuse (sb). 3. **eat off (food)** *vb phr* [*IF*] To eat
up or eat out (all the food). 4. **fight off (with)
(sb)** *vb phr* (CarA) [*AF*] See separate entry. 5.
like off, love off (sb) *vb phr* [*AF—Joc*] To show
noticeable affection for (sb). 6. **pose off; style
off, etc** *vb phrs* [*AF—Joc*] See separate entries.

O'Gra·dy-say(s) *n phr* (CarA) A children's game so called because this is the introductory phr wh dictates that a following order is to be obeyed by the playing group; if the leader gives some order such as 'Bend your knees!' without prefacing it by 'O'Grady says—', then all those who obey are eliminated; the winner becomes the next leader. □ There is a similar Eng game called *Simon Says*.

O.H. *abbr* (Antg, Brbu) The Order of Honour, of the Order of Antigua and Barbuda, a national honour awarded to any person who has rendered devoted and loyal beneficial service to the State in any field of human endeavour or for gallantry or other humane action; the letters may be placed after the recipient's name.

oil *n* (CarA) **1.** Cooking oil. **2.** *usu pl* [In the context of OBEAH] Any of several liquid mixtures, sometimes perfumed, given by an OBEAH-MAN/-WOMAN to a client for rubbing on the body in order to gain some infl over or desired effect upon sb; hence **commanding-oil, oil-of-stay-home, St John's oil**, etc.

oil-down [ɒɪl-dʌŋ] *n* (Gren, Tbgo, Trin) ‖ COCONUT-BOIL-IN (StVn) *She had cut up the bread-fruit and was grating the coconut in preparation for a great Saturday 'oil-down' for which she had already bought the salt-beef and pork.*—Gren (Ms) [Prob a ref to the process of boiling down the vegetable and meat ingredients and the oiliness resulting from the use of COCONUT MILK and pork]

oil-leaf (bush/tree) *n (phr)* (Bdos) ‖ CASTOR-OIL (BUSH) (CarA)

oil-nut (tree) *n (phr)* (Belz, Jmca, TkCa) ‖ CASTOR-OIL (BUSH) (CarA)

oil-of-stay-home *n* (CarA) See OIL 2.

oil-palm *n* (Guyn, Trin) ‖ ABBAY (Jmca) *The fruit of the oil palm (African oil palm, abbey palm) is a glossy black becoming reddish-brown when ripe.... The pulp and kernel are used to make oil.*—OGEP:59.

O.J. *abbr* (Jmca) The Order of Jamaica, a national honour awarded to a person of outstanding distinction; the recipient is styled 'Honourable' and the letters may be placed after his name.

o·ka·ri-seed *n* (Guyn) See AKORI-SEED [Prob < AKORI by metathesis]

o·kra* (**o·chro**) [okra (okro)] *n* (CarA) A young, green pod about 4 to 6 ins long, noticeably ridged and pointed, with slimy seeds and flesh, widely used as a vegetable ingredient and in soups; it is borne on a sturdy, low, green flowering shrub branching close to the ground, with lobed, hand-size leaves; *Hibiscus esculentus* (*Malvaceae*). [Cp *AFID* dial forms of Igbo *okworo, ọkwụrụ* 'okra'] □ AmE *gumbo*. Pl **okras, ochroes**,

the latter form being commoner in *Guyn* and occasional in some territories.

old *adj* PHRASE **not ask you how old you be** *id phr* **1.** (Angu, Guyn, Mrat, Nevs, StKt) [AF—*Joc*] [Of medicine] To be of no effect (esp to cause no bowel motion). *A took two Beecham's pills last night and up to now they ain['t] even ask me how old I be. I goin[g] have to take a good dose o[f] senna.*—(Guyn) **2.** (Antg) [AF—*Joc*] [Of a meal] To be so inadequate as to leave you feeling you have not eaten. *Dis li[tt]l[e] soup wid couple yam? Da[t] won['t] even as[k] me how old I be.*—(Antg)

old-fowl *n* **1.** (Guyn) [AF—*Derog*] A mature, unmarried, unattractive, and usu over-dressed woman. **2.** (Gren) [AF—*Derog*] An old prostitute.

Old Harry *n phr* **1.** (CarA) [IF—*Joc*] The Devil; hell (usu only in foll phrs). **2.** PHRASES **2.1 give (sb) Old Harry** *id phr* (CarA) See GIVE[1] Phr 2.26 **2.2 have Old Harry (in doing sth)** *id phr* (CarA) To have much frustration and difficulty (in doing sth). □ Used mostly by older speakers.

old heg; old higue (ole higue) [oˑl-hɛg] (StVn) [(ʊ)oˑl-haɪg] (Guyn, Jmca) *n phr* **1.** ‖ SOUKOUYAN (Dmca, etc) *In the country-side various fetishes are still used to keep Old Higue away. Guards might be fitted round the children's necks, a cube of blue hung over a doorway or chalk marks made on the stairs. The belief in Old Higue is often so deeply-rooted that old women who hardly venture out into the village are sometimes the object of suspicion and hostility.*—Kai 8, p.20 (R. Heath) **2.** (Jmca, StVn) ‖ HEG[1] 2. (Belz, StVn) *Yo[u] ai[nt] tired quarrel? Yo[u] just like a ole heg.*—(StVn) [Evid a combination of the senses of OED hag 1. (obs) 'an evil spirit in female form' 2. 'a witch' 3. 'an ugly repulsive old woman'; these senses flourished in the 16C and 17C and prob suited a translation of the W Afr mythological figure here represented, the addition of 'old' being typical of CarA Cr redundant compounding. Note also that the pronunc [haɪg ~ hɛg] is a natural development from BrE [hæg]]

old-maid (bush)* *n (phr)* (CarA) ‖ *Doctor-Dyett* (Mrat, StKt) ‖ *goat-rose* (Trin) ‖ *kakapoul* 2. (Dmca, StLu) ‖ *periwinkle* (CarA) ‖ *ram-goat rose* (Jmca) A common garden plant growing to about 2 ft in height, bearing small five- or six-petalled flowers of a number of colours, mainly white, purplish, and light-blue; it thrives throughout the year even in dry ground; *Catharanthus roseus* or *Vinca rosea* or *Lochnera r.* (*Apocynaceae*).

Old Poke *n* (Brbu) An effigy of a man fully dressed with bow-tie and hat, wh is paraded and then burnt, with much singing and dancing, on the night of 9th November. □ Cp MR HARDING (Bdos).

old-suck n (Jmca) ‖SOUKOUYAN (Dmca, etc) [*Old* referring to the old woman + *suck*, referring to 'blood-sucking'] □ Mostly rural. See OLD HIGUE

old-talk¹ (ole-talk¹); **old/ole-talk.ing** n (Bdos, Dmca, Gren, StVn, Tbgo, Trin) [*AF—Joc*] ‖*gaff*² (Guyn) **1.** Idle chatter; gossip; social chit-chat. **a.** *On Saturday nights and Sunday mornings, the men from the area still gather at the many shops surrounding the area to 'fire one' and indulge in old talk as well as to discuss the issues and topics of the day.*—NaT(78.06.28, p.15) **b.** *And after his day's work he would go across to the Savannah and play a game of football with the boys, and afterwards go and have an ole talk with fellars who remembered him from schooldays.*—LDCD:182 **2.** Empty talk; fine promises without fulfilment; mere rhetoric. **a.** *With all the old talk about the small man to which we have been treated in recent times, with all the garbage about local this and local that, it is not the small man or even the local man who has been the recipient of the many favours that the IDC has bestowed.*—MoK (72.06.09, p.3) [Perh abbr from 'old people's talk'] □ The term evid originated in and is commonest in *Trin*.

old-talk² (ole-talk²) vb intr (Bdos, Dmca, Gren, StVn, Tbgo, Trin) [*AF—Joc*] ‖*gaff*¹ (Guyn) To indulge in idle chatter; to gossip; to talk irresponsibly for the sake of talking; to make empty promises. **a.** *Have a happy New Year. I hope we won't have to ole talk at the end of next year on all these topics. You want to laugh ... didn't I tell you I was just 'ole-talking'?*—ExP (71.12.29, p.13) **b.** *Go down to San Fernando bus station and you'll see men gambling and sleeping and old-talking and doing all kinds of things, except driving buses.*—BoM (77.07.01, p.29) **c.** *Others just ole talked in little groups, too busy gossiping to bother to jump up.*—NaT (77.02.27, p.6) [By functional n > vb shift of OLD-TALK¹]

old-time adj (CarA) [*AF/IF*] Belonging to the past; of days gone by; old-fashioned. **a.** *We have, and we've been lucky to have good friends of All Ah Wee around to give us some ideas; people like Mrs Christiana Wade, and some of the great old time musicians who started our playing in Scratch bands.*—Aaw.I.2, p.48 **b.** *Whether it be ackee and saltfish, mackerel and bananas, tripe and beans or some good 'old time' red peas soup and pig's tail, enough has to be cooked for several helpings.*—WeG (75.04.01, p.2) **c.** *According to Traffic Chief, Cde. Philbert Clement, all motor cyclists, 'except those who ride the old-time Velo Solex', must wear helmets.*—GyC (77.01.22, p.20) [By functional n > adj shift of n phr 'past time(s)']

old-wife* n (CarA) ‖ *bous(se)* (Dmca, StLu) ‖*(queen-) triggerfish* (StLu) ‖*turbot* (Baha, Jmca, TkCa) A roughly oval, pinkish fish with bluish fins, blue stripes from the nose, and the eye set far back from the mouth; it is of average weight 1 to 2 lb, and its flesh is tasty; it has a very rough but easily removed skin wh is, in

some places, dried and used for scrubbing; *Balistes vetula* (*Balistidae*). [Joc, from the roughness of the skin] □ Not to be confused with *alewife* (*Alosa pseudoharengus*), a small fish.

old-witch n (Guyn, Trin) ‖JUMBIE BIRD 3. (Guyn) *One of the best known birds of Br Guiana is the Old Witch, or Jumbie bird as it is sometimes called, for it occurs commonly about the countryside.... The Old Witch has several different notes and the one principally heard is a plaintive ... ooo-eek!—ooo-eek!!—ooo-eek!!!*—CBGB:29, 31 [Prob from its awkward perching, unattractive dull black colour (the Guyn variety), squeezed beak, and its habit of nesting high up in tall trees, esp the silk-cotton, with wh much superstition is associated]

Old-Year's; **Old Year** n (CarA) [*AF*] (SE) New Year's Eve. **a.** *The taps were dry. Unreasonably dry. I swore. I prayed to high heavens—after all, who could afford to turn up unwashed at an Old Year's fête?*—ExP (73.02.04, p.3) **b.** *... and of course the fancy dress ball or as we Bajans say Old-Year's Night, but known nearly the world over as New-Year's Eve.*—AdN (77.03.20, p.7) **c.** *I will come to see you before Old Year.*—(Guyn) □ OED *old* 12. cites *Old-Year's Day* 'the last day of the year'. However, this is not ModE usage and it is not clear how the phr became the exclusive one used in CE to denote the last day of the year and the festivities associated with it.

ole higue n phr (Guyn) See OLD HEG.

Ole-Mas (Old-Mas') [o·l-ma·s] n **1.** (Dmca, Gren, StLu, Tbgo, Trin) [Carnival] The masquerading festival opening the CARNIVAL celebrations early on JOUVERT morning, characterized by several features: the wearing of last year's (i.e. the old) masquerade costumes, the lampooning of public figures or issues by caricature costumes and witty placards, individual costumes illustrating some well-known phrases or slogans by comic representation, etc. *From there, the streets of Roseau will be jampacked with ole mas' like bush, spreading joy, and carrying on the spirit and gaiety of the jump-up, because mama, dis is mas, and de road mek to walk on carnival day.*—DoC (65.02.27, p.8) [< *old masque* 'last year's masque' (*masque* being Fr, 'mask') with characteristic reduction of /-CC/] □ The form **ole mas** (with lower case in phrs) predominates in current usage. Hence **Ole-Mas Band, Ole-Mas King/Queen. 2.** (ECar) [By extension] Confusion; shambles; a disorganized state of affairs in wh anything unexpected can happen. **a.** *To many people the most astounding fact about this Christmas season was the wild abandon with which people seemed to spend their money. It was like ole mas in town.*—TaP (75.01.04, p.4) **b.** *Ole Mas—shambles in the Tax Department, and nobody responsible for that but the very Government that has started it.*—Gren (Hd, 78.04.26, p.145) **c.** *Dis is a lawless place now, / But we mus' do somet'ing fas' / Or not life in Buhbayduss / Gine soon be bare ole mas'!*—PeL

(79.02.09, p.7, 'Out of My Head') **3.** PHRASES **3.1 play ole-mas** *vb phr* (Dmca, Gren, StLu, Tbgo, Trin) To join in the celebrations of JOU-VERT morning as a costumed participant; to be in an OLE-MAS BAND. **3.2 turn ole-mas** *vb phr* (ECar) [*AF—Joc*] [Of a situation] To become confused, chaotic; to become very confusing and unsettling; to break down into noisy rows. **a.** *Believe me when I say that 'Everything' turn ole mas' in dis country'. Mind you I am no pessimist, but look around you. What do you find, eh? —Chaos! / People are totally confused. They don't know whether they're coming or going.*—ExP (76.03.26, p.27) **b.** *The shaky alliance between the ten islands lasted only about four years and four months.... After two dropouts—Jamaica, then Trinidad—everything 'turn ole-mas'.*—TRIH: 219 **c.** *Dis was ah real high-class place, / But from de time Doris an' she crowd move in / Well, everything turn ole marse. / de man nearly kill she.*—KTT:33 [TURN¹ 2. + OLE-MAS] □ *Everything turn ole-mas* is now a CE catchphrase.

ole-yard [olyard] *n* (Guyn, StVn) ‖ BAD-EYE (Belz, Guyn) *Don't let her see your baby, she might give it oleyard.*—(Guyn) [< Pg *olhado* [olya·do] 'evil eye', with Cr development > 'ole yard' due to folk etym]

O.M. *abbr* **1.** (Antg, Brbu) The Order of Merit, of the Order of Antigua and Barbuda, a national honour awarded to any person who has rendered meritorious service to the State; the letters O.M. may be placed after the recipient's name. **2.** (Jmca) The Order of Merit, a national honour awarded to a person who has achieved eminent international distinction in the fields of Science, Art, Literature or other fields; the recipient is styled 'Honourable' and the letters O.M. may be placed after the recipient's name. □ Note: O.M. (*Antg, Jmca*).

on *prep* (CarA) [Widely used in CE instead of several different preps in SE idiom. The following are some common instances and phrases] **1.** About; against. *I had never complained on any of the kids with whom I grew up.*—ASG:12 **2.** At. *She told him not to trouble her daughter on her work place.*—PKKK:3 **3.** By. *On an arrangement between the manager of the school, and the secretary of the Parent Teachers Association, they were to have a look at the reportedly dangerous roof.*—ExP (72.10.26, p.19) **4.** For. *I was waiting on you to come home before I went out.*—(Bdos) □ This usage also occurs commonly in AmE. **5.** In. **a.** *If all the bananas were on one field we could suggest irrigation but now it would be too costly.*—VoS (73.04.07, p.4) **b.** *Teacher Albena, I wish you God's protection on the remaining years.*—TiM (75.11.28, p.8) **c.** *When he first heard of the 'man living on the mango tree' he thought it was a guerilla and nearly called the police.*—ExP (73.08.12, p.1) **6.** Of. **a.** *The one-time south calypso king sang on the advantage that is still being taken on Black people. The tune entitled—'From here to Eternity' was well

received.*—MoK (73.02.02, p.2) **b.** *If you are short on hardware at home you can also find things like brooms, buckets, spoons, plates and so on.*—AdM (73.02.11, p.8) **c.** *The men refused and walked out on the meeting.*—DaC (53.04.24, p.1) □ Cp SE '*walk out on a person*', but not 'a place'. **7.** PHRASES **7.1 be on dying** *vb phr* (Bdos, Belz, Guyn, StVn, Tbgo) [*IF*] To seem to be slowly dying. **7.2 on a sudden** *adv phr* (CarA) [*IF*] Of a sudden; on a sudden impulse. **7.3 on a whole** *adv phr* (Bdos) [*X*] On the whole; taken as a whole. **7.4 on evenings/mornings** *adv phr* (Bdos) Regularly in the evening/morning; every evening/morning; during the evening/morning. **7.5 on the island** *adv phr* (CarA) [Of a person] Not abroad; in the island (still). **7.6 sick on my/your, (etc) hand** *id phr* (CarA) [*IF*] [Esp of a relative] Sick to my/your personal disadvantage (i.e. being a burden). [Perh from IrE. Cp (Irish) *on me* 'to my detriment' in *JESI:27*]

O.N. *abbr* **1.** (Antg, Brbu) The Order of the Nation, a national honour awarded to any person who has rendered heroic service to the State; it is the highest of the State's national honours; the letters O.N. may be placed after the recipient's name. **2.** (Jmca) The Order of the Nation, a national honour conferred upon a person appointed to the office of Governor-General; the recipient is styled 'The Most Honourable' and the letters O.N. may be placed after the recipient's name. □ Note: O.N. (*Antg, Jmca*).

one¹ *pron* PHRASES **1. All-o[f]-we is one!** *catch phr* (CarA) [*AF—Cr/Joc*] All of us are the same (class of people)!; There is no real social difference between us!; We are all black people together! [A ref to the common CarA historical background of Negro slavery] □ Usu in sarcastic or cynical contexts. **2. fire one** *vb phr* (CarA) [*AF—Joc*] See FIRE² Phr 6.1. **3. One from ten leaves nought!** *catch phr* (CarA) [*IF—Joc*] There must either be togetherness or nothing!; If one (important) participant withdraws from a collective agreement, then the whole agreement is dissolved! [= The figure 1. removed from the number 10., leaves the figure 0. The statement is attributed to Dr Eric Williams, Prime Minister of Trin & Tbgo, as a summary justification for ending the West Indies Federation of 10 island States when *Jmca* withdrew in 1962]

one² *pers pron complement, emphasizing exclusiveness* **1.** *as adv complement to a pers pron* **he/me/she/you one** (CarA) [*AF*] Just he/him/ I/me, (etc) alone. **a.** *Our trouble here is poverty. You stranger, my friend, but I tell you; poverty. Only trouble, poverty. Him one we must lick good.*—SJW:55 **b.** *You mean you one sit down an[d] eat all de food?*—(Gren, 1975) **2.** PHRASE **2.1 me one and God** *n phr* (Gren, Guyn) [*AF—Cr*] Just myself and God. *Hours I walk dat road in de dark, me one and God. I never meet a soul.*—(Gren) **3.** *as refl after a possessive pers pron* **her/his/my/your one** (Bdos) [*X*] Just herself/himself/myself/yourself alone. *The children gettin' big and them hard like wood.... It is only my one and I tryin' my best. I tell the oldest one that I aint buyin' she no presents this year.—AdV (89.12.24, p.15) [Perh from IrE. Cp EDD all 5. all my lone 'alone + cits from N Irel ... 'all my lone', ... 'all his lone'. Also note: 'The same mode ... is found in the Ulster and Scotch phr for to be alone ... always bringing in the personal pronoun: 'I am in my lone', 'he is in his lone', 'they are in their lone'—JESI:25]

one³ ['wɒ:n] adj 1. (CarA) [AF] [Emphasizing size, intensity, violence, etc of the following noun] Such a big, terrific, notorious, over-whelming, etc. **a.** He step back and run up and daddaie ...! he give the pig one kick right in its ribs. And the pig collapse and dead, easy so.—CISH:96 **b.** It was alleged that Georgina suffered a fractured jaw after Liddie admitted he had hit her one box to get out of his yard.—LaS (78.05.20, p.12) **c.** De udder day, jes' as ah was comin' rong by de transfer station, ah slip on de soap an ah get one fall!—MN:26 See also SET2 Phr 6.1 ONE SET OF [A prob calque from W Afr langs. Exs: Yoruba does not use a determiner, so when kan 'one, a certain' is used, a special emphasis is intended, as in o puro kan fun mi (he tell lie one give me) 'he told such a lie on me!'—(A. Banjo); similarly Igbo otu ụgha (one lie) 'such a (big) lie!'] **2.** semi-adverbial (CarA) [AF/IF] [By extension of prec, intensifying sense of a following adj] Such a very; (such) an immensely. **a.** De dress wha e bring fa dat young lady e gwan marry to—de king never see one like uh from the day e was bawn, I mean, one pretty dress!—WFSFB:47 **b.** When she came to, she was whimpering, 'Ira you is one duncy fool!'—TOSR:36 **c.** The Gendarme followed Rob-ert down in the yard and found one big confusion.—PKKK:11 □ In these functions there is considerable stress on **one**, and some vowel lengthening.

one⁴ [wan~wʌn] indef art (CarA) [Cr] A. **a.** When I plague with de heart trouble, I gwan to one doctor to see bout it.—JBJ:86 **b.** 'Well,' e seh, 'I will have fa go cause I done buy one boat an everyting.'—WFSFB:40 □ Usu unstressed and with low pitch the same as SE indef art 'a'; pronunc as shown. The form occurs in writing, as indicated, only in presenting narrative dialogue.

one-eye n (CarA) [IF] **1.** A furtive glance. **2.** A watchful look now and then. She ran to the shop when she heard the news, asking the neighbour to give the baby one-eye until she got back.—Guyn (Ms) **3.** PHRASE **3.1 give (sb/sth) one-eye** vb phr (Bdos, Guyn) See GIVE Phr 2.27

one-one¹ [wa·n-wa·n] /1'2/ adj, pron (CarA) [AF—Cr] A few. **a.** I only see one-one guava on de tree.—(Gren) **b.** The men in the village, and one-one woman too, yo[u] will fin[d] drinkin[g] there.—(Trin)

one-one² [wa·n-wa·n] /1'2/ adv (CarA) [AF/IF] Little by little; one by one; gradually. **a.** One-one dutty build dam (= Slowly the dirt builds up the dam).—Guyn (Prov) **b.** He borrowed a lot

of my books, but I'm getting them back one-one.—(Antg)

one-place /1'2/ adv passing into adj function (Guyn, Trin) [AF/IF] In one place; on one spot; (esp of children) without running about or fidgeting; stable; steady. **a.** As soon as yo[u] turn roun[d] the boy gone—he wouldn['t] stay one-place.—(Guyn) **b.** The tray they give you on the plane, it have a hole like to keep the cup o[f] tea one-place.—(Trin)

one-pot /1'2/ n (Gren, StKt, Trin) ‖ALL-IN-ONE (Guyn) The one-pot dish comes into its own during the middle of the week. This can be in the form of a 'cook-up' rice dish, or the delicious Caribbean soup commonly called 'sancoche.'—ExP (76.03.25, p.6) [Cp Wolof benačin (one pot) 'a meal made by cooking everything together']

one-side¹ /1'2/ adj (CarA) [AF—Cr] Twisted; lopsided; (leaning or fallen) to or on one side. When they finish buil[d]in[g] de house, the whole t[h]ing look one-side.—(StVn)

one-side² /1'2/ adv (CarA) [AF—Cr] **1.** Aside; out of the way. Good man. Put the books one-side and sit down.—KJB:64 **2.** PHRASE **2.1 Go/Move one-side!** vb phr (Bdos, Guyn) See GO Phr 6.25.

one-thing¹ /1'2/~/2'2/ adv (Bdos, Guyn) [AF] [Introducing a statement of self-satisfaction or consolation] Anyway; in any case; at least; nevertheless. Now let these bad-minded Bajan [sic] here talk my name 'cause I only leasing this house while they buying theirs. One thing I got good land home!—MBGB:15 □ Note the sharp contrast in pitch pattern with next.

one thing² /3'1/ n phr (CarA) [IF] [After a neg] [Not] anything at all; [not] a single thing. She took the children and went to England and never said one thing to the husband.—(Guyn) □ Note strong stress and high pitch on **one**. Sometimes the vowel is also lengthened in emotive contexts.

one-time¹ adv (CarA) [IF] [A compound with distinct senses differentiated by pitch contrasts wh must be noted] **1.** /1'1'/ [with even low stress] Once in the past. **a.** One time you used to pay $2 a pound for ham. Now, it is $3.75 some places.—NaT (75.12.23, p.3) **b.** You remember one time people did want to cut down nutmeg to plant banana, t'ings was so bad.—WeN (52.12.22, p.6, Annie & Josephine) **2.** /2'2/ At one and the same time; in full and at once. **a.** We could have had the afternoon shift at the Weigh Office work overtime weighing cane so as to be able to grind off all the cane one time.—DeM(SK) (62.07.07, p.1) **b.** Let us be reasonable once more and let the transport workers have their 20 percent increase one time.—NaT (77.05.22, p.5) **2.** PHRASES **2.1 one time and done** adv phr [AF/IF] At once and have done with it; completely while you are about it; once and for all. Safeguard Your Home One Time And Done.—ToR (Ad, 73.09.21, p.3)

2.2 one time so! *adv phr* [*AF*] Fully and without hesitation. *Brother Salkey let go twenty Anancy stories together one time so, baps!*—TM:101 **3.** /ʒ'ı/ [In story telling] Once upon a time. *One time a king got a daughter, an after e daughter get to perfection, e tek e photo an send it all over de country.*—WFSB:33 (S. Scott) **4.** /ʒ'ı'/~/ʒ'ʒ'/ [with notable stress] [In emotive contexts] There and then; instantly; without a moment's hesitation or a second thought. *Right that very second Calvin swear blind to God that he leffing Barbados. One time. For good. First chance.*—CWFYS:90 **5.** /ı'2/ [In non-emotive contexts] Right away, so as to avoid delay or risk. *I think I better go and get my money from here one-time before she goes out.*—(Guyn)

one-time² /ı'2/ *adj* (CarA) [*IF*] **1.** Of some time in the past. *Is it also true that he is always seen driving around with Ministers of Government and is always with his one time secretary?*—NeJ (76.05.08, p.6) **2.** Rare; exceptional. *Girls who get themselves so deeply involved at 14 must, unless they are raped, [and this is a one-time thing] be prepared to take what follows.*—NaT (77.08.21, p.26)

on·li·est (on·ly·est) [o·nliıs] *adj* (CarA) [*X*] Only and exceptional. **a.** *It's the onliest parish where you can see from St James to St Philip, brag the young folks about their Shop Hill/Grand View home.*—SuS (89.10.15, p.28) **b.** *And Romesh made him study his lessons and do all his homework. If anything, Romesh was the onlyest one who was a friend.*—SPOC:56 [An E dial survival in CE. Cp *EDD* onliest superl adj (Chs, Hmp, Som, Cor, Amer) 1. 'only' 2. 'best, most approved' 3. 'most extraordinary, oddest' + many cits]

on·ly *adv* (CarA) [*AF/IF*] [Regularly used as an intensifier] **1.** (CarA) Decidedly; certainly; definitely. *He's only a thief, that boy. You got to watch him when you see him around.*—(Guyn) **2.** PHRASE **2.1 Is only so** ... *introductory phr* (Gren, Guyn) [*IF*] [Emphasizing a description of intense state or action] ‖ *what a way* ... (Jmca) See how definitely, vigorously, deeply, etc. *Is only so she love that man, yo[u] hear, for all that he does treat her bad.*—(Gren) **3.** (CarA) Continually (often also annoyingly). *Teacher, this boy only hitting me all the time underneath the desk.*—(Bdos) **4.** (Belz) So very; to such a high degree; uniquely. *He's a very good boy, only smart in class and only good at cricket and football too!*—(Belz) **5.** (Jmca) [In calling sth to sb's attention] Just; I tell you! **a.** *Since she married, only see her now!*—(Jmca) **b.** *Only hear this ... would you believe the other night, right amidst the whole heapa little pickney and dem parents dem, you could smell the smell of the smoking herb?*—WeG (75. 04.15, p.15, Round Town)

o·no·to *n* (Guyn) See ANATO

oog·li [uglı] *n* (StVn) ‖ UGLI (Jmca)

oo·na; oo.noo, oo.nu [unu] *pron pl* (Belz, Jmca) See UNU

o·pen *vb tr* PHRASE **open your mouth** *vb phr* **1.** (CarA) [*IF*] To talk out; to reveal (sth). **2.** (CarA) [*AF*] To raise your voice in anger (at sb); to abuse (sb) at length. □ See OPIT IN; also MOUTH Phrs 4.19, 4.28.

op·er·ate *vb* PHRASE **operate you** *vb phr* (CarA) [*IF*] ‖ *work your belly* (Guyn) [Of medicine] To cause (sb) to have a copious bowel movement; [of food] to cause (sb) to have diarrhoea. *If you drink too much ginger beer after eating curry or pepper-pot it will operate you.*—(Trin)

o·pin·a·ted; o.pin.i.a.ted *vbl adj* (Bdos, Guyn) [*X*] Opinionated; stubborn in your views. [< SE *opinionated*, reduced by syncope. *EDD* notes the same in Not, Lei, Nhp, War] □ Often preceded by *self-*.

o·pit in; ope-it-in [opıtın] *vb phr* (Bdos) [*X*] Open it. *The man smiled and told her: 'Opit in.' When the girl did 'opit in' (Bajan for 'open it'), to her surprise there lying between the two slices of salt bread was a crispy $20 bill.*—NaT (76.05.30, p.7) [< *Open it* by metathesis] □ Occurs frequently at the folk level.

op·pos·ite *adj* **1.** (Bdos, Tbgo, Trin) Perverse; contrary; resisting what is reasonable. *I believe that Elizabeth thought there was something mischievous in my argument for that was one of the times when she accused me of being opposite.*—WCR:10 **2.** PHRASE **2.1 catch/take (sb) opposite** *vb phr* (Tbgo, Trin) [*AF/IF*] To approach (sb) at the wrong time; to find (sb) unprepared or in an embarrassing situation. *I feel so shame my godson come to see me this big Christmas time and catch me opposite. I didn[']t have a dollar to give him.*—(Tbgo) [< Cr /hapazit/ 'haphazard', wh by misascription of sense > 'unprepared'; then pronunc > 'opposite' by false refinement.]

O.R. *abbr* (Guyn) The Order of Roraima of Guyana, a national honour awarded to a person who has rendered outstanding service to Guyana; it is the second highest award of the State; the letters may be placed after the recipient's name.

or·di·nar·y *adj* (Bdos, Guyn) [*IF*] [Of a person] Unrefined in behaviour; carelessly crude. [Cp *OED* ordinary 6. (*Obs*) 'pertaining to the common people; common, vulgar; unrefined, low, coarse' + cits–'1741]

orh·ni (or·ha·ni, ohr·ni) [o·rni] *n* (Guyn, Trin) [Indic] A head-covering of thin material worn by EAST INDIAN women; it hangs down to the shoulders and, esp on religious occasions, may be used as a veil. [Hin *orhnii* 'a veil']

or·tan·ique [ɒrtanik] *n* (CarA) A yellow citrus fruit that is a hybrid of the orange and tangerine; its firm skin is not so easily removed as a tangerine's, but its sweet and juicy pulp makes it much prized commercially; *Citrus 'putative X'* (*Rutaceae*). [A blend of *or*(ange) + *tan*(gerine) + (un)*ique*. The fruit was developed and named by Jamaican agronomists]

os·na·burg *n* (CarA) [Hist] **1.** A tough, coarse, dark-grey material, that was used esp for the clothing of slaves. **2.** The clothing made from this material, usu a long, loose-fitting garment. *Wickedness? You call it so? Wickedness to want even rice and flour and osnaburg while buckra Englishman eats bacon and wears Shantung silk?* —RND:15 [*OED* (*Obs*) *Osnaburg* 'a kind of coarse linen, orig made in Osnabrück, North Germany']

O·ta·hei·te-ap·ple ['o·ta·hi·ti-apl] *n* (CayI, Jmca, USVI) ‖ MALACCA-APPLE (Antg, Guyn) [Said to be so named from the island Otaheite or Tahiti, in the So. Pacific, from wh it was introduced to *Jmca*. Cp origin of ‖ *Malacca-apple*]

O·ta·hei·te-goose·ber·ry ['o·ta·hi·ti-guz bɛri] /1'122122/ *n* (Jmca, Trin) ‖ GOOSEBERRY 1. (Baha, etc)

oth·er rest, the *pron phr* (Guyn, StVn, Tbgo, Trin) [X] The others; the rest; the remainder. □ A redundancy frequently occurring in written schoolwork.

oth·er·wise[1] *pron* (CarA) [X] [Loosely used] Other things, persons, etc. **a.** *They sell dry goods, stationery and otherwise too.*—Bdos (Ms) **b.** *We do not accept that any Jamaican newspapermen or otherwise, should be bullied and pushed around by United States security and other personnel on Jamaican soil.*—DaG (71.05.08)

oth·er·wise[2] *adv* (CarA) PHRASES **1. other-(wise) from this/that** *adv phr* (CarA) [IF] Apart from this/that; in other cases. *Only when me mother run out of lil sugar she does send me to buy there, otherwise from that I don't go in there.*—(Guyn) **2. otherwise to this/that** *adv phr* (CarA) [X] Even in addition to this/that; more than this/that. *He does not speak much but always remains most observant. This is the only man who can solve every problem of the prisons. Otherwise to this, men like Dr Eric Williams have to learn from him in politics.*—BoM (74.05.24, p.4)

oui! (**we!, wi!**) [wi] *excl tag* (Dmca, Gren, StLu, Tbgo, Trin) **1.** ‖ **yes** 1. (CarA) [Adding emotive emphasis or intensity to the statement it terminates] Yes indeed!; let me emphasize! **a.** *You believe you are the woman the most beautiful in all this room? / Is you saying that, oui. But she was pleased.*—SROH:110 **b.** *Choonoo bridled. 'Listen,' he said, 'I is me own man, oui; I do wat I want!'*—Bim v.16, p.281 (K.P. Newton) **c.** *On seeing the blood, Miss Babylyn halted abruptly. 'A-a! A-a! The blood plenty we! You ain't to touch it, you know,' she warned, seriously.*—PGIP:

23 [Fr *oui* 'yes', used as characteristic CE sentence tag] □ This form, often spelled WE (occassionally WEE), is used, as indicated above, in islands with a Fr Cr cultural background. **2.** PHRASES **2.1 Oui foute! (Oui foot!, We foot!, Wi·fout!)** [wi fut] /2'2'/ *excl* (Dmca, Gren, StLu, Tbgo, Trin) [AF—*Joc*] [Expressing surprise, wonder] What a thing!; How remarkable!; Would you believe it! **a.** *Oui Foot! But, Annie, you dress-up yes?*—WeN (53.05.18, p.2, Annie & Josephine) **b.** *San Fernando Arts Council will have a second show—'Oui Foute'—in their bid to create a 'Folk Theatre' at the Palms Club on Thursday.*—TrG (73.03.28, p.13) **c.** *We foot! But look at trouble here today!*—Trin (Ms, Short Story) [Fr Cr < Fr *oui foutre* 'Yes, fuck (it)!' orig an obscenity, the sense of wh is completely lost in current informal usage] **2.2 Oui papa!, Wi papa!** [wi papa] /2'1'3'/ *excl* (Dmca, Tbgo, Trin) [Expression of amused surprise, of delight] *If you see the huggin[g] and the kissin[g] when she bu[r]s[t] t[h]rough the door at the airport! Oui papa!*—(Trin) [OUI 1. + PAPA!]

ou·menm too! (**ou-même too!, ou-menm tou**) [u-mɛ·m tu] *id phr* (Dmca, StLu) [AF] ‖ YOU SELF TOO! (CarA) See TOO Phr *But ou-menm too! You mean you sendin[g] dat chil[d] to school at dat hour?*—(StLu) [Fr Cr < Fr *vous-même* 'yourself' + SE *too*]

out[1] *adv* (CarA) **1.** From Britain (to an appointment in the W Indies). **a.** *King George I appointed Mr Ward Rogers Governor, and sent him with a force of one hundred men and an ample supply of all necessary stores to fortify New Providence. He arrived out in 1717.*—IIOS:320 **b.** *A Yorkshireman by birth he had come out first as an engineer and later held the post of Deputy Director of Public Works.*—Guyn (Ms) [As *OED* *out* 2., though this sense became a particularity in the *CarA*] **2.** PHRASES **2.1 out here/there** *adv phr* (CarA) ‖ DOWN HERE/THERE (CarA) **3.** (CarA) [AF] [Used as a phrasal extension to add intensive or frequentative sense to a vb in more cases than in IAE] Exs **3.1 sing out your guts/your inside** *vb phr* (CarA) [AF] To sing so much as to feel physical strain. **3.2 teach out your liver** *vb phr* (Tbgo) [AF] To do too much hard teaching. **3.3 walk out your shoe-sole(s)** *vb phr* (CarA) [IF] To do much hard walking. **3.4 work out your soul-case** *vb phr* (Bdos, Guyn, Tbgo) [AF] See SOUL-CASE Phr 2.1

out[2] *prep* (CarA) **1.** [X] Out of. **a.** *Move out de way! Come out de road A tell you, child!*—(Bdos) **b.** *He pulled the nail out the wall.*—Guyn (Ms) [A prob survival of EE. See *OED* *out prep* 1. 'from within, away from' + cit from Shak, 1607] **2.** [X] Through (a door, window, etc). **a.** *She looked out the window and didn't say a word.*—SABS:86 **b.** *A man is to go out the door to work for the money for the food.*—PKKK:21 □ *OED* lists *out prep* 'out of' as *Obs. arch.* or *dial*; but *OED2* deletes these labels, adding that the usage is 'not Received Standard', though common in US, Austral, N.Z. **3.** PHRASES **3.1 go out (of)**

your head *vb phr* (CarA) [*IF*] To go off your head; to become insane. **3.2 out of (one thing or another)** *prep phr* (Bdos, Guyn, StVn) [*X*] [Indicating comparison, choice] Choosing between; of. *Which you prefer out of these two dresses?*—(StVn) **3.2.1 out of (sb)** *prep phr* (Bdos) [*AF*] At the expense of (sb). *I was with him for nearly a year and I ain't wear a dress out of him yet, I would like to know what kind of man he is.*—NaT (76.07.18, p.30, Dear Christine)

out³ *vb tr* (CarA) **1.** [Cricket] To get (a batsman) out (by any of the rules of the game). *He shied the ball sharply at the wicket but missed, and that's the second time they didn't manage to out him.*—StVn (B) **2.** [*IF*] **(i)** To put out (a light, fire, etc). **a.** *'Could you now out the lights for us please?' asked the lady with the polished accent.*—StLu (Ms, 1975) **b.** *So if I have an aeroplane to go and out fires there is nothing wrong in lighting a fire so that you can see the Prime Minister outing the fire. That will be a real evening show. Light a field of canes and you know he is coming to out the fire in an aeroplane.*—Bdos (Hd, 74.12.10, p.4330) **c.** *A policeman said, 'Will you out your cigarette please?' I outed it.*—NMP:41 **(ii)** [Cricket] To dismiss (a batsman) *That pitch was so damned slow that fast bowling could hardly out anybody*—(Antg) □ Though pedagogically disallowed and regarded as comical, this usage goes back to OE and ME and still survives, though rare, in Mod Br E. See *OED out* vb with cits from 1008 onward including many from 17C and 18C, with tr senses **a.** To put out, expel('sb) [with ppl. adj. *outed*] **b.** To extinguish (a light). Although *OED* labels sense **b.** *Obs exc dial, OED 2.* cites exs well into the 20C. In present CE educated speakers avoid *out/outed/outing a light/ a batsman*, prob through ignorance of the legitimate history of the usage wh has survived at the folk level. Note, however, *COD7, COD8* list *out* vb tr 'to put out'. **PHRASES 2.1 out off (sth)** *vb phr* (Bdos, Jmca, StVn) [*X*] To erase; to rub off. **2.1.1 out off** *vb phr* (Tbgo, Trin) [*AF*] To be off; to go away. *Watch yourself, and if you see fight run like hell, because if things open up hot I outing off fast.*—STLL:103 **2.2 out out** *vb phr* (CarA) [*X*] To put out, extinguish (a light, etc); to abandon (sb) completely. *I out-out man outta my life, honey!*—HFGA:112 (A. Clarke) **2.3 out sb's light** *vb phr* (Bdos, StKt, Tbgo, Trin) [*AF*] To cripple or maim (sb); to put (sb) out of action. **3.** To thrust out your hand [Only in foll phr]. **3.1 out hand and hit (sb)** *vb phr* (CarA) [*IF*] See HAND¹ Phr 4.22

out-a-man (-for-bat) *n* (Gren, Tbgo) ‖ OUT-FOR-PLAY (Guyn)

out-for-play /ɪ'12/ *n* (Guyn) [*IF*] [Cricket] ‖ *bowl-for-bat (cricket)* (Jmca) ‖ *fight-for-in-nings* (Trin) ‖ *firms* (Bdos) ‖ *out-a-man* (Gren, Tbgo) A quickly improvised game of schoolboy cricket in wh any player or member of his small group (called a FIRM in *Bdos*) earns the right to bat by catching or bowling out the batting player; there are no runs in the game.

Out Is·lands *n phr* (Baha) ‖ FAMILY ISLANDS (Baha) *The Out Islands are officially 'the Family Islands' called 'out' because they're geographically removed from Nassau and Freeport, but for those who are seeking sun, sea and a simple semi-tropical way of life, the Out Islands offer a different world of adventure.*—Baha (Ms, 1975) □ This term is officially replaced by FAMILY ISLANDS, though it still occurs in the speech of some.

out·lawd·ed (out·lord·ed) [ʊʊtlɒd·dɪd] *adj* (Bdos, Guyn, Jmca) [*X*] ‖ *outlawdish* (Belz) Openly crude or rude in behaviour; aggressive and rough-tongued. *A child may be so 'dont-carish' as to become 'out-lorded', the equivalent of rude, boorish, intractable, and generally bad-behaved.*—AdN (79.04.15, p.10) [< SE *outlawed* (orig a ref to the ruffian hiding from punishment in the slave era) + *-ed* by overcorrection or paragoge. Cp DROWNDED, LATED. The form *out-lorded*, common in *Bdos*, suggests a further loss of the sense 'outlaw', and the poss infl of folk etym < 'to lord it over sb']

out-of-crop sea·son *n phr* (Bdos, Guyn) ‖ *dull season* (Antg, StKt) The period between the end of one season of cane-harvesting and the beginning of the next. □ Cp IN-CROP.

out-of-place *adj* (CarA) **1.** [Of words used] Embarrassing; [of behaviour, conduct] unbecoming, unworthy of the occasion. *As great as that visiting Chinese Cultural Group may have been, I still find them fast and out of place to attempt to dictate to the audience just when, where and why they must be applauded.*—BoM (75.05.16, p.24) **2.** PHRASES **2.1 be out-of-place with yourself** (StVn, Tbgo); **be out of your place** (Nevs) *vb phrs* ‖ GET BESIDE YOURSELF (CarA) See BESIDE Phr 2.1

out-par·ish *n* (Bdos, Gren) any of the PARISHES well away from the capital; the country districts. *Information reaching our newsdesk yesterday morning stated that teachers and policemen in the out-parishes are still unpaid for the month of February.*—ToR (76.03.17, p.3)

out·port *n* (Jmca) Any of the ports of *Jmca* other than Kingston.

out-room *n* (Jmca) An outside room or shed, formerly or sometimes used as a servant's room.

out·side¹ *n* (CarA) [*AF/IF*] A community or country that is unfamiliar; another island; a foreign land. **a.** *And in addition to island-wide custom she fills orders for 'outside'.*—IsL II.1, p.35 **b.** *Most fellas like to marry a girl of outside, don' mind not knowing the character of a girl outside.*—RLCF:125

out·side² *adj* (CarA) Not belonging to the legally recognized home and household. [Hence many common compounds as foll]. **1. outside-child** *n* A child of an unmarried woman fathered by a married man; a married man's illegitimate child. **2. outside-daughter/son** *n* An illegitimate daughter/son. **3. outside-man** *n* A married woman's lover. **4. outside-woman** *n* A married man's mistress.

o·ver[1] *prep* (CarA) **1.** [*AF*] Over to; over in (another place). **a.** *They've gone over St Kitts to live.*—(Nevs) **b.** *She has a husband over the States, don['t] look like he comin[g] back.*—(Guyn) **2.** [*AF/IF*] Throughout; all over (a place). *But it is still my impression that over Barbados people who rent lands from private landlords would prefer to rent from the government.*—Bdos (Hd, 76.08.04, p.7162)

o·ver[2] /2'2/ *adv intensifier* (Gren, StVn, Tbgo, Trin) [*AF*] So very … indeed; by far (too). **a.** *All-yo[u] show las[t] night was over nice, I really enjoy it.*—(Tbgo) **b.** *I observed that the dresses of the pupils of the Girls' High School are over too short. Why wear mini to such recognised institutions?*—ViN (73.05.19, p.8) [Cp *EDD* over 20. (w.Yks, Not, Lei, etc) 'extremely, particularly']

o·ver[3] *vb intr* (CarA) [*X*] To end; to cease; to finish. **a.** *School overs at three and I have to be home by half past four.*—NMIM:110 **b.** *And especially like now so with the Jour Ouvert just overring, you have so much funny mass, devils coming home and thing.*—AKM:16 [Cp *EDD* over 27. wh shows this usage esp common in Yks]

o·ver a·way; **o.ver and a.way**, **o.ver in a.way** *adv phrs* (Bdos) [*AF*] Abroad; overseas. *Local does not mean inferior or unqualified you know! Do we still believe that anything from over and away is better?*—AdV (90.02.07, p.8)

o·ver·look *vb tr* **1.** (Bdos, StVn) [*X*] To look at (sth) carefully; to examine (work done). *The youngster overlooked my friend's expensive American car with admiration and asked 'How many yards to the gallon?'*—NaT (76.06.20, p.7, Al's Grapevine) □ This sense conflicts with IAE *overlook* 1. 'to fail to observe' 2. 'to superintend'. **2.** (Belz) To bewitch by looking at with an evil eye.

o·ver·look-bean *n* (Bdos, Jmca) ‖ GRUDGE-PEA (Gren) [This name prob due to belief that the plant, distributed around a planted-up area will protect (oversee, 'overlook') the area against evil eyes or prevent petty thefts. Note alternative name MALDJO[2] with same association. Cp OVER-LOOK 2.]

o·vers ['ovʌ(r)z] *n pl* **1.** (Guyn) [*IF*] ‖ BRAATA (Antg, etc) *Bu[t] wait, I ain[t] gettin[g] any overs after I buy so much? Wha[t] [a]bout a couple bananas?*—(Guyn) **2.** (Dmca, Gren) Things, items (esp of food) left over; left-overs.

o·ver·seer [ovə(r)se·r] *n* (CarA) [Sugar Ind] A man who superintends several gangs of field labourers on a sugar-plantation; in earlier times he was usu a young white man on mule or horse-back.

o·ver·stand *vb* (CarA) [Rastaf] To understand. *'I understand,' I say. 'No! You don't understand. That's the trouble with us. Always thinking negative. Never positive. You don't understand. Under means below. That's negative. You overstand!'*—VaN (75.03.29, p.8)

o·ver the hill; **o.ver-the-hill** *adv phr* (Baha) In or belonging to the poor area of Nassau. *The native clubs have blamed their difficulties on the cruise directors of ships putting into port here. They claim the cruise leaders have been deliberately steering visitors away from the over-the-hill establishments.*—TrI (75.01.02, p.9) [A ref to the area in the southern district of Nassau where the poor Black people live; it is separated from the sea-ward area of the city by a ridge or 'hill'. The term is in common currency]

Ow! [ɒʊ] *excl* (Antg, Bdos, Dmca, Guyn, StVn) [Indicating pleading from pain, grief or other emotion] **a.** *Bup! Godmother's fist landed in Charlotte's chest again. 'Ow, Godma!'*—MLDS:15 **b.** *Her manner was simpering and ingratiating. She's such a sweet lil' chile. Ow!*—MLDS:28 [Cp *CGAF:*94 Twi *Ao!* excl of displeasure, regret; also of surprise, astonishment]

own *possessive pron particle* (CarA) **1.** [*IF*] [Adding emphasis to a possessive pers pron] *My own* 'mine'; *your own* 'yours'; *his/her/their own* 'his/hers/theirs'. **1.1** [*AF—Cr*] [As prec] *Me own; you own; he/she own; dey/dem own.* **2.** [*AF*] [As possessive marker after a noun, replacing SE *'s*] Of, belonging to (the prec noun). *The accused said 'all that money is that woman own'.*—Bdos (CR, 69.09.08) □ In these collocations the prec pron or n receives strong stress contrasting with low stress on **own**.

own own /2'2/ *adj phr* (CarA) [*AF*] [Adding emotive emphasis] Very own. **a.** *'Your own,' Mr Foster emphasized. 'Your own own house.'*—LICMS:267 **b.** *I didn't pick you up nor get you by chance. I am your own own mother! And you treat me like that!*—(Guyn)

own-way[1] /1'2/ *n* (CarA) [*AF/IF*] **1.** [Usu of children] Stubborn disobedience; quiet resistance to persuasion or instruction. *Nowadays people allow their children too much own-way and then find they can't control them at all.*—(Trin) **2.** PHRASE **2.1 Hard-ears you can't hear, own-way you will feel** *prov phr* (Bdos) See HEAR Phr 4.11

own-way[2]; **own-way.ish** *adj* (CarA) [*AF/IF*] [Usu of children] Self-willed; obstinate; headstrong. *I have told you to practise your piano as soon as you have had something to eat after you come home from school, but you so own-way that you always run out to play and forget all about it.*—(Jmca) [A prob calque from W Afr langs. Cp Yoruba *ọmọ temi ni maa ṣe* (child 'my own I will do') 'a self-willed child'.]

oys·ter-plant* *n* (Ecar) ‖ *Moses-in-the-bul-rushes* (Jmca, USVI) ‖ *sangria* (USVI) A low, decorative plant with stiff, sword-shaped leaves, dark-green inside and purple outside, about 10 ins long and rising in rosette form straight from the ground; it bears small, white, enclosed blooms that look like a baby in a boat or an oyster in a half-open shell; it is resistant to drought and is much favoured for borders of garden-beds; *Rhoeo discolor* or *R. spathacea* (*Commelinaceae*). [Metaph name from its appearance]

P

pa(a)d·na *n* (CarA) See PARDNER.

paal[1] [pa·l] *n* (Guyn) [Land Surveying] A stake driven into the ground to mark a land boundary. [Du *paal* 'pile driven into the ground; stake']

paal[2] [pa·l] *n* (Trin) [Rice Ind] A rough sheet, made of bags, spread out on the ground for the drying of threshed rice. [Hin]

paal off[1] [pa·l ɒ·f] *vb phr* (Guyn) To provide mud-land or a drainage TRENCH with retaining walls made by driving water-resistant wooden planks or piles side by side into the soil to prevent erosion or slippage; [Engineering] a sheet-pile wall of wood. *When work on the $4,500 project is finished, ... people will need have no fear of floods in the area. However construction work on the koker, and paaling off of the canal can only be done at low tide.*—GyC (77.08.18, p.12) [By functional shift of PAAL *n* + *off* as in SE 'cut off', 'part off', etc]

paal-off[2] *n* (Guyn) 1. A wooden wall built to PAAL OFF land. *Construction of the new paal-off in Sussex Street Canal which was started on November 22, 1975 was held up because of emergency works on bridges.*—GyC (76.01.28, p.3) 2. A temporary narrow dam made by packing mud between two parallel wooden retaining walls to retain water on one side while leaving the other side dry for foundation or other land-preservation work.

pa·ca ['paka ~ pa·'ka] *n* (Belz, Guyn) ‖GIBNUT (Baha, etc) [Sp and Pg *paca* 'timid, shy', also a name for this animal] □ The pronunc [pa·'ka] occurs in *Belz*.

pa(c)·cu (pa·coo, pa·koo, pa·ku) [paku] *n* (Guyn) 1.* An oval, thick-bodied, river fish ranging in colour from reddish-brown to black, about 2 ft long when mature and weighing up to 12 lbs; it feeds in large numbers on a water-grass that thrives in rapids and near waterfalls and is easily caught when the water is low; it is much prized for its food value; *Pacu myletes*, or *Myletes setiger*, or *Colossoma nigripinnis* (*Characidae*). [A So Amer Amerindian name] □ Taxonomically identified by *OED, IAIG:235* and *RFLG:94* with the first two names and by *OED2* with the last. 2. [By extension] [*AF—Derog*] A simpleton, esp a man easily deceived (maritally or otherwise); [cricket] a batsman who

is easily got out. [A ref to the ease with wh the fish is caught while feeding]

pace·man; **pac·er** *n* (CarA) [Cricket] A fast bowler; (SE) a pace-bowler. *Twenty-seven year old Barbados Cricket League pacer Colin Payne, one of the pacemen vying for a place on the local Shell Shield side, yesterday strengthened his claims for inclusion when he bagged five wickets for 67 runs on the second day of the trial match at Kensington Oval*—AdN (72.12.15, p.10)

pack-all *n* (Bdos, Guyn) A large, rectangular covered basket 1-1/2 ft deep, made of WIST or other sturdy material; it has handles and is used like a suitcase for packing all your belongings. □ Although the name seems self-explanatory, see PEGALL.

pa·co·ti *n* (Trin) PHRASE **make pacoti** *vb phr* (Trin) 1. [Of a woman] To be a prostitute. 2. [Of a man] To visit a prostitute. [The supposed ref to Fr Cr pronunc of Fr *pacotille* 'cheap goods' is not clear. More likely is a ref to PACRO-TEA, a sexual stimulant wh may be pronounced [pak(w)o-ti], whence ‖**to make pacro-tea/pacoti** (of a woman) 'to offer' or (of a man) 'to seek sexual stimulation or satisfaction'. The connection with Fr Cr 'pacoti' would then be a folk etym error]

pa·cro (pa·chro [pakro] *n* (Tbgo, Trin) A type of shellfish about 2 to 3 ins long, greenish-black and prominently segmented; it is found on rocks and is used as a folk-medicine but is more prized for its alleged aphrodisiac properties; *Chiton spp.*

pa·cro-tea/-wa·ter [pak(r)oti/-wɒ·tə] *n* (Tbgo, Trin) A drink made by boiling the shellfish PACRO to be drunk as an aphrodisiac. See PACOTI.

pad·der-ten·nis (pad·dle-ten·nis) *n* (Bdos) ‖ROAD-TENNIS (Bdos) *The Barbados Padder (Road) Tennis Association got a tremendous boost yesterday following a donation of much greatly appreciated equipment by Banks Breweries.*—AdV (76.11.05, p.14) [Ref to the use of a round wooden pad as racket by the players] □ These earlier alternative names are mostly replaced by ROAD-TENNIS.

pad·dy[1] (pa·di) *n* (Guyn, Trin) [Rice Ind] ‖DHAN (Guyn, Trin) *The hall [was] used as a* *storeroom for paddy, which sent its musty smell and warm tickling dust everywhere.*—NHMB:530 [As *OED paddy* sb¹ < Malay *padi* 'rice in the straw'] □ Only this name is common in *Guyn*, where also PADDY is the commoner alternative spelling.

Pad·dy² *n* PHRASE **what Paddy gave/gi[ve] the drum** *id phr* (Gren, USVI) [*AF—Joc*] A good beating; a thorough flogging. *Along with the money, free food, housing and all the luxuries shiftless skunks would like to enjoy without having to earn. What they really need is what Paddy gave the drum.*—DaN(ST) (79.02.15, p.9, A. Peterson) [Prob < *EDD paddywhack* IrE 'a severe thrashing', derived from BrE *Paddy* 'a fit of temper' (associated with an Irishman)]

pad·dy-bug *n* (Guyn) [Rice Ind] An insect pest that feeds on the sap of the developing rice grain, causing damage and discoloration of the ripe product; *Oebalus poecilus (Heteroptera)*.

pa·di *n* (Guyn) See PADDY¹.

pad·na(h) *n* (Guyn, etc) See PARDNER

pag·gie (pag·gy) *n* (Belz, Guyn, StVn) ‖ PARGY (ECar)

pai(lle)-ba·nan(e) *n* (StLu) See PAY-BANNANN

pai·me(e)/-mi *n* (Tbgo, Trin) See PÉMI

pain-bush *n* (Tbgo) ‖ PAIN-KILLER (BUSH) (Guyn)

pain-kill·er (bush)* *n* (*phr*) (BrVi, Guyn, Mrat, Nevs, USVI) ‖ *pain-bush* (Tbgo) ‖ *pain-cure*, *wild pine* (Bdos) A small, bushy tree about 6 ft tall, with large, glossy, dark-green leaves wh are commonly used, often wilted over a flame and applied to the body, as a relief for pain; it bears the JUMBIE-SOURSOP; *Morinda citrifolia (Rubiaceae)*. □ See JUMBIE-SOURSOP for other names of the fruit, by wh names the tree is also sometimes called.

pain-killer fruit *n phr* (Guyn) ‖ JUMBIE-SOURSOP (Antg, etc)

paip·sey [pe·psi] *adj* (Bdos, StVn) [*AF—Joc*] Insipid; pale; weak; unattractive. [Perh an extension of an E dial item. Cp *EDD papes* sb (Lan, Chs) Also written *paeps* [peps] 'I...A sort of flour and water gruel...2. *Fig* A foolish youth'.]

pai·sa [paisa] *n* (Guyn, Jmca, Trin) [*AF—Joc*] ‖ PESH (Gren, etc) [Bhoj < Hin *paisaa* 'money; coins'] □ The word has spread from the poor among the Indic community, the whole phr *paisa na ba* 'I have no money' being sometimes popularly used in jest.

pai·wa·ri (pai·wa·ree, pi·war·ri) [paɪwari] *n* (Guyn) A mildly intoxicating drink made by fermenting burnt cassava with grated SWEET PO-TATOES, sometimes with sugar-cane juice added; in Amerindian communities it is drunk in quantity at social gatherings. [Cp *GDAA* Akawaio *pawaruu*, name of an alcoholic drink so made]

pak·choy (pat·choi) [pakčoi] *n* (Guyn, Jmca, Tbgo, Trin) ‖ CHINESE CABBAGE (CarA) *The greens section has patchoi at 25 cents a bundle and watercress at 12 and 25 cents.*—ExP (75.10.30, p.6) [< Cantonese and Hakka Chinese *pakchoy* 'white vegetable']

pa·ku *n* (Guyn) See PA(C)CU

pa·lam-pam *n* (Jmca) [*AF—Joc*] ‖ PAM-PALAM¹ (Bdos, Guyn) *Wat a debil of a bump-an-bore, / Rig-jug an palam-pam!* (= *What a devil of a jostling, fuss and confusion!*)—FCV2:167 (L. Bennett)

pa·lang-a-lang (pa·lang-pa·lang, pang-a-lang, etc) *ideoph* (Bdos, Guyn) [*AF/IF*] ECHOIC representation of any repeated metallic sound (often of a bell). *Anyhow, the Wednesday night she gone 'round behind L. Holder house and pelt the three big rock-stones 'pon top o' the house—palang-a-lang-lang—'causing it did a galvanize roof.*—CISH:117

pal·ette [palɛt] *n* (Trin) ‖ *paleta* (Belz) A small, frozen block of a coloured milky and/or sugary mixture held on a small stick; it is a children's daytime sweet, often on sale in the street. *I think it is easier for you to sell palette and have a nice push-cart, and stroll around all the streets than to buss out your brain to become a big-shot, oui.*—JJM:121 [*Trin* Fr formation by false refinement < So Am Sp *paleta* 'a lollipop'. The Sp form is used in *Belz*]

pal·ing [pelɪŋ/-ɪn] *n* (Bdos, Guyn) A property fence made of wooden staves or of galvanized sheeting. **a.** *He could barely see the figure of a woman through the divisions in the wooden paling of a backyard.*—CPM:38 **b.** *The 75-year-old woman has been suffering at the hands of people who twice pulled down the galvanise paling she put up around her house.*—WeI (91.02.08, p.40) [Extension of SE *paling* 'a fence of pales'] □ In wide use, and often erron spelt 'pailing'.

pal·met·to *n* (Baha, Berm, TkCa) ‖ SILVER-THATCH PALM (Baha, Trin) **a.** *Palmetto thatch served as an effective roofing.*—PTCI:21 **b.** *My bedroom was partitioned off from my sitting room with palmetto sticks.*—Bes IV.5, p.14 □ It seems difficult to identify the exclusive use of this name for a precise variety of palm anywhere. The name seems to be confused with PIMENTO 2. (*Belz*), POND-TOP (*Baha*), and evid sometimes called *primenta* (*Belz*). It is applied loosely to the *Thrinax spp* and *Sabal spp*, two closely related varieties of palm; the dried materials of both are used domestically.

pal·met·to-broom *n* (Baha, Belz, TkCa) The dried fan-leaf of a mature PALMETTO tree tied to make a yard-broom, the stout stalk serving as handle.

palm-fly *n* (Guyn) [X] ‖ POND-FLY (Bdos, Guyn) [From Cr vowel-opening in pronunc of [pɒn(d)-flaɪ > pa·m-flaɪ] and prob also helped by folk-etym, through vague resemblance of the insect's always stiffly outstretched wings, even when at rest, to palm leaves]

pal·mist(e) ['palmis(t)] *n* (Dmca, Gren, StLu, StVn, Trin) ‖ CABBAGE-PALM (CarA) **a.** *The wind cool, the sky ablaze in the west with red, tinted clouds, and against this swiftly passing splendour the tall palmistes ... were black, but with a suggestion of deeper, warmer tints.*—NMIM:208 **b.** *The rafters reached the ground on either side and the smallest inside supporting post was 9 ft high. It was thatched with palmiste leaves supported by lathes of roseau (thick reeds), one end open the other end closed by a wall of roseau and palmiste.*—SDD:38 (R. Allfrey)

pa·lo(w)·ri (-balls) *n* (Guyn, Trin) See PHU-LOURIE.

pal·wi-man·go *n* (Bdos) ‖ MANGO-PARLUI (Dmca, etc)

pam-pa·lam[1] *n* (Bdos, Guyn) [AF—ℐoc] ‖ *pam-pam, palam-pam* (Jmca) Fuss and confusion; any bothersome, noisy row or disorderly proceeding. *Well, after all de pampalam, evaht'ing done, neh! I had a min' from everysence, doh, dat we wunta fin' out who um is dat kill 'Pele'.*—NaT (80.03.14, p.7, Lickmout' Lou) [Reduplicative form, prob < DAFL Twi *pam* 'the report of a gun'; also *pam pam* 'to drive, chase away'; also (Fante) 'to persecute']

Pam-pa·lam![2] *ideoph* (Bdos, Guyn) [AF—ℐoc] ‖ *Pampa-lele!* (Antg) ‖ *Pam-pam!* (Jmca) ‖ *Pampi-luti!* (StVn) [Children's echoic expression showing cynical delight at another child's plight, a flogging, etc; it is often accompanied by the gesture of wringing the hands. Below is a well-known folk-rhyme, usu sung] *Aye, Budda Neffie lock up and he ain do nothing, Pam-palam. / He get nine years for he own grand-daughter, Pam-palam. / He swear by Christ he ain done nothing, Pam-palam.*—MBGB:124 [A prob ideophonic extension of PAM-PALAM[1]]

pam·per [pampʌ] *vb intr* (Bdos) [AF] To feel the sting of lashes, blows. *So he is punished in the old fashioned way, his firm parent ... bringing the cane down vigorously on his 'afternoon' making him 'pamper' with the repeated blows.*—AdN (79.04.15, p.10) [Prob related to PAM-PAM (see prec). Note also that *pam-pam* occurs in USVI as vb tr 'to spank' (SVID)]

pan[1] *n* **1.** (Belz, BrVi, Jmca) [Often applied to a deep container of some sort] A can; a bin; a large empty metal container turned to domestic use; a box. [Cp EDD *pan* sb[1] 3. (Yks) 'a vessel for containing water ... not necessarily or usu shallow; for instance the ordinary garden water-pot is always called 'water-pan'] □ See for ex DIRT-PAN, KEROSENE-PAN. **2.** (CarA) [Sugar Ind] An open, bowl-shaped, iron vessel, 4 ft or more in diameter, three or more of wh were used in former times for the crystallization of sugar through the successive boiling and evaporation of cane-syrup. *You will also be invited to taste ... the freshly made warm sugar straight from the centrifugals, or in the case of a syrup factory—warm from the pan. It's a treat that should not be missed.*—Bdos (Ms, 1973) □ See VACUUM-PAN. **3.** (Guyn) [Gold and diamond-mining Ind] A device used in sifting river deposits for gold or diamonds. **4.** (TkCa) ‖ SALT-PAN (TkCa) *Some of the 'pans' for making salt are square in shape, and vary in size from half an acre to about one or two acres in area.*—PTCI:33

pan[2] *n* (CarA) **1.** ‖ *steelpan* (CarA) A metal, percussion instrument made from the bottom end of a steel oil-drum that is hammered into sections which are tuned to produce different notes; the end is cut off to varying depths to provide different pitches, whence a range from 'soprano-pan' to 'bass-pan'; the full range of groups of pans make up a STEELBAND. *For the past ten years the boys have been playing on pans tuned by their Trinidad-based tuner, Lloyd Gay.*—ToR (77.05.01, p.10) [From the resemblance to a shallow pan of the resulting instrument wh has to be heated and beaten into a concave shape before being sectioned. Both the folk-name and invention are of *Trin* origin] **2.** [By extension] [IF] The music of the STEELBAND. *Sweet pan will again ring out at QRC because of 15 pans donated by the Sylvania East Side Symphony.*—ExP (73.04.19, p.17) **3.** [By extension] [IF] The STEELBAND movement in general. *The history of the steelband as it is officially called, and the pan as it is more familiarly known, is to a point parallel to the history of social struggle in the islands of Trinidad and Tobago. This historic and social evolution is in content a story of pan and people.*—JWSSS:7 **4.** PHRASES **4.1 beat/play pan** *vb phr* (CarA) To play music on a PAN; to play in a STEELBAND. *A coolie man with a paper cup in he hand take a stiff one, a tall dougla called out, 'Soft-grease, you playing pan or drinking?'*—Kri '78, p.16 □ The pl form *pans* occurs only in sense 1; otherwise PAN functions as a collective sg.

pan[3] *adj* (Tbgo, Trin) Of or pertaining to the PAN or STEELBAND. [Hence many compounds and n phrs, some of wh are given in separate entries] [< PAN[2] in attrib function]

pa·na·des (pe·na·da) [pana·dɛz~pɛna·da] *n* (Belz) (Forms used in speech for) EMPANADAS. *On a placid Saturday afternoon at the Garden, fans storm Steve Bent's panades' bucket for a snack.*—AmA (80.01.11, p.1) [See EMPANADAS]

Pa·na·ma dis·ease *n phr* (CarA) [Banana Ind] A disease causing banana trees to wilt, affecting the fruit; it is carried by a fungus in the soil.

Pa·na·ma mo·ney *n phr* (Bdos) Money sent or brought back home by Barbadian emigrant labourers helping to build the Panama Canal; it was widely used by poor Blacks to buy land and educate children.

pan-beat·er; pan.man/.wom.an *n* (CarA) A person who plays a PAN in a STEELBAND. **a.** *His fellow pan-beaters respected him for his disciplined and dedicated approach to pan beating.*—Trin (Ms, 1976) **b.** *Now there are Chinese, Indian, White panmen; middle-class panmen; even pan-women.*—Cat V.1, p.19

pan-boil·er *n* (Bdos, Guyn, StKt) [Sugar Ind] ‖ *sugar- boiler* (Bdos) A professional supervisor of the boiling and evaporation process, in VA-CUUM PANS, in the crystallization of sugar. [< PAN¹ 2. + *boiler* 'one who boils']

pan-cart *n* (Bdos) A wheelbarrow. [From its shape and use] □ This name is commonly used by older folk.

pan-cup *n* (Gren, Mrat) **1.** ‖ TOT 1. (Bdos) [< PAN¹ 1. + SE *cup*; a characteristic CE redundant compound] **2.** [By extension] An enamel cup.

pang·a·lang *ideoph* (Bdos, Guyn) See PALANG-A-LANG.

pan·go·la-grass* *n* (CarA) [Cattle Ind] A low bushy pasture grass specially cultivated as nutritious for cattle; *Digitaria decumbens* (*Gra-mineae*). *He paid no attention to the cattle grazing in the lush, verdant pastures of pangola grass*—RHJSS:11 [< R. Pongola, So Afr, where its value was first noted]

pan·i·a (pan·ya) [panya] *n* (Belz) [*AF*—*Derog*] A Belizean of Spanish descent or originally from one of the neighbouring Spanish-speaking ter-ritories, and usu of lighter complexion. *Pre-rogative my backside! It's since Tama came back from Honduras Republic that she start acting like pania. Every time I did something to help her in the house this afternoon, she said, / 'Gracias Ivy, my corazón!'*—EBL:62 [< *Spaniard* by char-acteristic CarA Cr aphaeresis and apocope] □ The term is esp used by *Belz* Cr blacks de-noting dislike for the separatist social and cul-tural behaviour of such persons. Cp PAYOL (*Trin*).

pan·man·ship *n* (Tbgo, Trin) Skill in playing a PAN. *In those days steelband impact, like that of the tamboo-bamboo, depended not so much on panmanship (which was still rather elementary) as on the strong-arm squad among its exponents.*—ACTT:105 [< PANMAN (see PAN-BEATER) + SE suff -*ship* as in 'seamanship', etc]

pan-mu·sic [panmyusɪk] *n* (CarA) The music made by or played by a STEELBAND. *Without Panorama the big losers are panmen and lovers of sweet pan music.*—SuP (80.01.06, p.8) [< PAN + *music*]

pan·nist *n* (Trin) A highly accomplished STEEL-PAN player who gives solo professional per-formances. [By analogy < (instrument) + *ist* as in IAE *organist, pianist*, etc]

pan·o·lo·gy *n* (Tbgo, Trin) The study and art of STEELBAND music and playing. *'We believe that in the evolution of panology, steel-bands have reached the stage where we can celebrate our coming of age annually with a Steelband Week,' Mr Holder told newsmen.*—TrG (73.03.31, p.3) [< PAN² 2. + SE analogous -*ology* 'study of' as in 'musicology', etc]

Pan·o·ra·ma *n* (Gren, StLu, StVn, Trin) A STEELBAND competition held annually, usu as part of the CARNIVAL celebrations. *Panorama champions in Grenada for 1975 were the Guinness City Symphony of Williamson Road St George's, which won from a field of seven bands with ar-rangements of the Mighty Sparrow's 'ah Diggin Horrors' and Lord Kitchener's 'Tribute To Spree Simon'.*—AdN (75.02.20, p.6) [Pun on the SE *panorama* (< Gk) 'view in all directions'. Cp other borrowed word-formations, often for ad-vertisement, such as 'colorama', 'cyclorama', etc]

pan-salt *n* (Brbu, TkCa) ‖ COARSE-SALT (Antg, Guyn) [From its production in a SALT-PAN. Prob also infl by POND-SALT with characteristic CarA Cr /o > a/ vowel opening]

pan-side *n* (ECar) [*IF*] A usu small, un-sponsored STEELBAND. *It was a day for Pan—strictly Pan—and brass. I had to hear all the pan-sides, so I moved from band to band, and as a result of this, I would like to sound a note of warning to Diamond Steel. Look out!*—VoS (76.03.04, p.8) [PAN¹ 2. + SIDE 'group']

pan-stick *n* (CarA) One of a pair of rubber-tipped sticks about 10 ins long, used for playing the PAN in a STEELBAND.

pant *n* (CarA) [*IF*] A pair of trousers; pants. **a.** *The prosecution's case was that Emile Wigley of Godwin Ghaut awoke on the morning of January 20 to find that a cream pant of his was missing. In the pocket of the pant was a wallet containing $5.*—DeM(SK) (63.08.03, p.10) **b.** *... and Al-bert shave, and dress so-till; same Albert who scorn soap, and wear pant till they have more patch than pant foot.*—TM:45 [A convenient back-formation < SE *pants* n pl. *OED2* lists *pant* sb³ 1. = pants (chiefly US). See PANTS; cp SCISSORS]

pant-foot; pants-foot *n* (CarA) [*X*] One leg of a pair of trousers.

pants *n pl construed as sg* (CarA) [*IF*] **1.** [Often preceded by *a, one*] (A pair of) trousers. *I had* *three pants at my workshop—one was a black terylene and wool, one pants was a black serge and one pants was a light-grey terylene wool.*—Bdos (CR, 70.01.09) **2.** PHRASE **2.1 have on your sitting pants** vb phr (Bdos) [AF—Joc] To make your visit embarrassingly long; to overstay your welcome. *I have referred previously to the delightful surviving custom of getting rid of a visitor who 'has on she sittin' pants' by putting a little salt on the head of the upturned broom in the kitchen.*—AdN (79.03.25, p.18)

pan·tu·ner n (Tbgo, Trin) A man skilled in creating the note-sections and obtaining the accurate pitch of a STEELBAND PAN by heating and hammering. *But the pan-tuners are somehow convinced that he is taking too much of the bread; that he is virtually exploiting them since he sells a tuned pan for approximately three times what he pays the tuner.*—BoM (78.01.06, p.22) □ See also TUNER.

pan·ty·man ['pantima·n] n (Antg, Gren) [AF—Vul] ‖ BATTY-MAN (Antg, etc)

pan-wag·on n (Tbgo, Trin) A mobile, covered platform or frame mounted on wheels, carrying part of a STEELBAND; it is pulled or pushed through the streets in the CARNIVAL celebrations, usu leading a related BAND of masqueraders. *She had seen them go down the hill in their pan-wagons pulled by little boys. And after that she had watched the wildness of the revellers.*—AKM:44 [Pun on or analogous form from SE band-wagon, with similar sense]

pan·ya n (Belz) See PANIA

pan·ya ma·chete [panya-mašɛt/mačɛt] n phr (Belz, Jmca) ‖ *Spanish knife* (TkCa) **1.** A CUTLASS or machete with both edges sharp. **2.** [By extension] A deceitful person; a hypocrite. [PANYA (see PANIA) + *machete*. Metaph ref to the fact that the tool can go/cut either way] □ See BACK-AND-BELLY 2, 3.

pan-yard n (ECar) A fenced, open space, often in a backyard, where a STEELBAND practises and where their PANS are stored.

pap n PHRASE **lick pap together** vb phr (BrVi) [AF—Joc] See LICK Phr 4.12

Pa·pa! (Poo·pa!, Pu·pa!) [papa ~ pupa] excl (Antg, Tbgo, Trin) [AF—Joc] ‖ *Daddy!* (Antg, Tbgo) **1.** (Expression of surprise, usu with amusement or approval). **a.** *Well Papa! Suddenly, he buss out ah laugh. W'en he start to laugh so, he couldn't ah stop.*—TrG (Sunday Mag, 79.05.20, p.2) **b.** *Poopa, da' was a fête! I mean it had / Free rum free whisky and some fellars beating / Pan from one of them band in Trinidad.*—(FCV2:208, D. Walcott) [Cp Twi papa, papaapa adv 'very well, very much, too much' (DAFL)—also used exclamatorily] **2.** [As emphatic tag, esp at end of a neg exp] Cp SE Sir, as in 'No sir!' *A taxi driver ... said, 'Who me? My car on dem*

macadam and big stone? Not me, papa!'*—SABS:8 [By shift of sense 1.] □ Cp MAMA!, PAPAYO!. See also FATHER[2]

Pa·pa Bois (Pa·pa-bwa) [papa bwa] n (phr) (StLu, Trin) A legendary creature in the form of a very sturdy, ragged, old man with beard, very hairy body and cloven hoofs; he is the father protector of the trees and animals of the forests and can take the form of an animal at will, leading a hunter to get lost; he is considered by some to be the male counterpart of LADJABLÈS. *I told Johnson such tales of local superstition as I knew. About Papa Bois, a spirit who lurked in the forests and lured evil hunters away from beaten tracks so that they were lost for days in the jungle.*—SWOS:14 [Fr Cr < Fr papa 'father' + bois 'wood']

pa·pa-do-good n (Gren) [AF] ‖ OBEAH-MAN (CarA) *Because of this Obeah, some of us are mentally ill, some are invalids, some have lost a fortune.... These Zah garda (papa-do-good or mama-do-good) who can see for us because we cannot see for ourselves, have grown fat both in body and in purse, at the expense of their victims.*—ToR (78.03.08, p.9) □ Cp also MAMA-DO-GOOD.

pa·paw* (**pa·pa·ya, paw·paw**) [pa'pɒ: ~ pa'pa·ya ~ pɒ:pɒ: ~ pʌpɒ] n (CarA) A round or oblong fruit that can grow to 12 ins in length and 4 or 5 ins across, yellow when ripe, with a thin skin, thick, sweet flesh, and numerous small black seeds grouped in its hollow inside; it is prized as a dessert and its leaves are used as a meat tenderizer as well as medicinally; *Carica papaya (Caricaceae). And don't talk about puhpaws. (Don't talk to me about 'pawpaws' or 'papaya': that is half the problem right there.) When last you ate a good puhpaw? ... / Of course we have to find resistant strains of the fruit, but not of some pretty-pretty foreign fruit—papaya or pawpaw or whatever—that tastes like reconstituted sawdust, please! Bring back the puhpaw!*—SuS (87.11.15, p.6) [Via Sp > Taino papaya, Arawak papaia, name of the fruit. See TLWI:21] □ Of several variant spellings, including others not listed here, the forms *papaw, pawpaw* are commonest in CE.

pa·pa·yo! [papayo] excl (Gren, Dmca, Tbgo, Trin) [Expression of happy surprise] *Papayo! Yo[u] do[n't] hear you[r] neighbour daughter gettin[g] married!*—(Gren) [Prob > PAPA + suff -o in excl function, with intrusive palatal /-y-/]

Pa·pi·a·men·tu; Pa.pi.a.men.to n (Neth) The Spanish-and-Portuguese-based creole lang, with a dominant Dutch vocabulary, spoken and written in the Neth Antillean islands of Aruba, Curaçao and Bonaire. [< Pg papear 'to chatter, jabber' + Pg noun-forming suff -mento. Hence an originally Derog formation papeamento = 'jabberings'. From this Pg form, pronounced [papiamɛnču] developed the two current forms, one being PAPIAMENTU preferred in Curaçao, the other PAPIAMENTO preferred in Aruba]

pa·pi·yòt[1] [papiyʌt] *n* **1.** (Gren) [*AF—Joc*] A weakling; a frail person; a worthless opponent (in a game). [Fr Cr < 17C Fr *papillot* 'butterfly' (see Cotgrave, 1611)] **2.** (Trin) A twisted bit of brown paper, used as a curler in setting a woman's hair. [From resemblance to a butterfly, origin of sense 1. Note also SE (anglicized Fr) *papillote*, 'a paper frill used by chefs', of similar origin] **3.** (StLu) [By extension] ‖ CORK-SCREW[1]

pa·pi·yòt[2] [papiyʌt] *vb tr* (Dmca, StLu) To put (a woman's hair) in rollers. *She was going to papiyòt her hair as she was going to a party that night.*—(Dmca) [By functional n > vb shift of PAPIYÒT[1] 2.] □ *StLu* speakers may use *papiyon*, esp in Fr Cr sentences. Cp also CORK-SCREW[2]

pap·py *n* (Bdos, Dmca, Trin) [*IF*] **1.** ‖ POOPA **1.** (CarA) *Pappy, as his father was commonly called, would excuse himself from the ceremony and stroll across to Ma Doss for his usual night cap.*—SDD:42 (C. Browne) **2.** [*AF*] A grandfather; [*Joc*] any old man. **3.** PHRASES **3.1 big pappy** *n phr* (Trin) [*AF—Joc*] A man of great influence. *Look you remember Sir Learie Constantine—Baron of Maraval. A big big pappy and a real giant in this country. Well he wasn't too big to cut down to size.*—BoM (74.08.23, p.10) **3.2 old man pappy** *n phr* (Guyn) [*AF—Joc*] An old geezer.

pap·py·show[1] (**pap·py-show, pop·py-show, pup·py-show**) [papišo ~ pʌpišo] *n* (CarA) [*AF—Joc*] **1.** A thing, situation, proceeding or event that is ridiculous or embarrassingly foolish; a nonsensical state of affairs. **a.** *Friends, you know and I know that all this is a lot of pappyshow. None of that nonsense is going to change the price of rice or the price of hops bread.*—TaP (76.02.15, p.11) **b.** *All in all, St Lucia's politics is the same old khaki pants. Pappyshow and more pappyshow. Where do we go from here?*—VoS (Ed, 77.11.24, p.2) **c.** *Uncle Caleb replied that if she wanted to show off her wedding gown, he wouldn't—indeed, he couldn't—stop her. But he wasn't leaving the house to walk in the mud and make himself a poppy-show.*—GR:145 (L. Marrott) [Cp *EDD poppy* sb[2] (Sc, Yks, etc) 1. *poppy-show* 'a peepshow, puppet-show', a device made by children for wh each pays a pin for a 'peep'. Also *puppy* sb[1] 2. *puppy-show* = the same. Cp also *CSD* (ScE) *puppie/poppy show* 'a Punch and Judy show' etc < Fr *poupée* 'a doll'. See also T.E. Murray: 'Poppy Show' (*Amer Speech LXIX No.2, pp 99–122*) wh attests the once wide currency of the originally Eng term with a 'multidimensional life' in the US in late 19C–early 20C. It may then or earlier have reached the *CarA*, where it flourished and survives with shifted sense] **2.** [By extension] [*AF—Joc/Derog*] A person fit to be ridiculed; a perfect fool. *'A magistrate must not be a laughing stock or pappyshow in the State'. The blistering advice came from Defence Lawyer Kenrick R— on Thursday morning last in the St George's Magistrate's Court when he accused Magistrate L— of not 'excercising the authority vested in him'.*—ToR (76.08.29,

p.3) PHRASE **2.1 make a pappyshow of (sb/yourself)** *vb phr* (CarA) [*AF—Joc*] To make a fool of (sb/yourself); to expose (sb/yourself) to great ridicule. **a.** *You making yourself a pappyshow Melda / You making yourself a bloody clown.*—Trin (Cso 'Obeah Wedding'—Sparrow, 1966) **b.** *In the first place, whatever our internal differences, it is clear that we cannot make a pappyshow of foreign governments and/or organisations by wishing to change our nominees, ... at the last moment. No one benefits from that.*—AdN (72.06.06, p.2)

pap·py·show[2] *adj* (ECar) [*AF—Derog*] Ridiculous; absurd; disgraceful. **a.** *Those are the ways, Mr Speaker, that we have achieved fame [as] a pappyshow country.... In North America, when people are on TV and something on Grenada comes up, the way in which it is put, Mr Speaker, is in the context of banana Prime Minister of banana country goes bonkers and bananas over UFO's...*—Gren (Hd, 77.07.20, p.19) **b.** *For example, right now there is a lot of pappyshow politics being played by some of the Government Ministers. All of them running about the place like chicken with they head cut off.*—TaP (76.02.15, p.11) [By intensified attrib use of PAPPYSHOW[1]]

pap·py·show[3] *vb tr* (Gren, StLu, Trin) To mock, make fun of, ridicule (sb). *Why should Bhootra want to come back to this country where he was treated so rudely? Why should he come back here to be abused and pappyshowed?*—BoM (79.08.10, p.3)

Pa·rade Of The Bands *n phr* (ECar) [Carnival] The festive procession along an identified route, of all the BANDS of CARNIVAL (or, in Bdos, KADOOMENT) climaxing in each case with a competitive display before a panel of judges and a large seated audience.

par·a·dise-plum *n* (Trin) A hard, sugar-coated, almond-shaped, pink and white, boiled, sweet plum, usu sold by roadside vendors.

pa·ra-grass* /1'12/ *n* (CarA) A coarse, prostrate grass, with quarter-inch-thick stems rooting at the joints and tall, slightly hairy leaves; it is prized as cut fodder for cattle, but easily spreads out of control on plantations; *Panicum barbinode* or *P. purpurascens* or *Prachiaria mutica* (*Gramineae-Poaceae*). [From Pará the province of Brazil wh is its supposed place of origin]

pa·ra·ka·ri *n* (Guyn) A mildly alcoholic Amerindian drink made by fermenting soaked CASSAVA-BREAD with banana leaves for a few days; it is used esp on Amerindian festive occasions. *But, as an opener to a friendly exchange ... a bowl of parakari was passed to me first and then it went the rounds. A second round would normally come up to be rotated in the same order to enliven the proceedings.*—AGMCI:28 [< *TWD* Wapishana *parakari* 'a drink'] □ The item is best known in the Rupununi District of *Guyn*, though referred to in urban writing.

par·al·lel mar·ket *n phr* (Guyn) The recognized trading in household goods and conveniences, on sidewalks or at any suitable place, by unregistered retailers who travel to obtain such items from neighbouring territories. *The inflation rates after 1975, however, were underestimated because items included in the Consumer Price Index could not be obtained at their official prices due to the growing importance of the parallel market as a source of supply.*—Social and Economic Studies 39.3, p.3 (G.N. Ganga) [*Parallel* 'running side by side with' + *market* 'legitimate trade']

pa·ran·de·ro [paran'dɛ:ro] *n* (Trin) One of a group of PARANG serenaders, led by a skilful improviser. *The true parandero sings in adulation of the Christ story and he sings to share his joy of the facts of that story.*—Peo.I.6/7 (1976), p.54) [Sp *parranda* (see below) + agential suff *-ero*]

pa·rang[1] ['paraŋ] *n* (Tbgo, Trin) ‖ *séwénal* (Dmca) **1.** The practice of house-to-house serenading by groups singing religious songs (AGUINALDOS) in Trinidad Spanish dialect, esp at Christmas, in rural areas also at Easter, accompanied by CUATROS, mandolins, and improvised music-making implements, and often followed by traditional Spanish folk dancing; the traditional art and skill of performance required by this practice; the actual presentation of such a performance in a home. **a.** *Parang is a distinct part of Trinidad culture which dominates our Christmas celebrations. Today foreign Christmas carols have lost their prominence, giving way to parang.*—Trin (Ms, 1986) **b.** *Scores of young people go to Lopinot for the genuine parang.*—Trin (Ms, 1974) **c.** *At the end of a parang, before leaving the home that they visit, the paranderos request the best improvisor among them to sing in praise of their host.*—TPOT:19 **2.** The festival of competitions organized nationally to recognize the custom of PARANG including the crowning of a QUEEN. *The second in the warm-up series of the 1974 parang competition staged by the Trinidad and Tobago Parang Association (TTPA) takes place tomorrow night at the Gasparillo Community Centre.*—TrG (74.11.29, p.13) **3.** The particular type of Hispanic folk music for dancing associated with a PARANG. **a.** *Sebucan and joropo tunes are distinctly parang, not calypsos.*—Trin (Ms, 1973) **b.** *Two are parang records ... by the reigning parang champions.*—ExP (71.12.05, p.22) [< Sp *parranda* (with loss of unstressed final syllable) 'a spree, a binge', also (S. Moodie) 'revelry, a noisy outdoor celebration with music']

pa·rang[2] *vb intr* (Tbgo, Trin) To go from house to house singing traditional and improvised PARANG songs at Christmas. *Let's parang and sing.*—ExP (Mag) (72.12.24, p.11)

pa·rang-band/-group/-side *n* (Trin) A small, sometimes professional, group of PARANDEROS. *Two singles by a then unknown parang band, the Los Alcaran Parang Group.*—Kri '78,

p.62 □ *Parang-side* [IF] is an impromptu or short-lived grouping.

pa·ran·gles [paraŋglz] *n* (Jmca) [*AF—Joc*] Bustle and confusion; trouble and worry; a bothersome situation. *Check out the scene tomorrow at 10.00 a.m. for the contest looks interesting this year. According to Henrietta Daley, the lady in charge of the beauty contest parangles at the Festival Office, the rural beauties are saying a whole lot, baby!*—StA(JA) (70.07.11, p.10, Partyline) [Prob < IrE *paramble*∽EDD *peramble* 2. 'a rigmarole']

Pa·rang Queen *n phr* (Trin) The female lead-singer who is chosen and crowned as the most creative in the PARANG festival competitions (see PARANG[1] 2.).

par·a·pet *n* (Guyn) ‖ *grass-corner* (Guyn) **1.** Either of the banks, 4 to 6 ft wide, lining the sides of urban roads and planted with grass to retain the road against erosion. **2.** A retaining verge planted with grass, lining the sides of a TRENCH or around any maintained ground. *The crowd filled the ground except for muddy patches and overspilled to the parapets on the perimeter of the spacious compound.*—GyC (76.06.17, p.1) [Cp *OED parapet* 3. 'locally, the side-walk, footpath or pavement of a street or road'—a usage noted esp for Liverpool and the West of Eng]

par·a·pet-roof *n* (Bdos, Mrat, StKt) A roof that is protected all around at the lower end of its slopes by a low concrete wall in order to prevent hurricane winds from getting under the roofing.

par·a·sol [parasɒl] *n* (ECar) An umbrella. *It began to rain.... It struck the streets, at first like heavy footfalls of huge drops, then as a deluge. Parasols went up here and there.*—TRIH:65 [< Fr *parasol* 'sunshade, beach umbrella'] □ This is the regular word used by many, esp older, speakers (note cit). SE *parasol* is still a light, lady's sunshade, not usable for coverage from rain.

par·a·sol-ant(s) *n* (Trin) ‖ ACOUSHI ANT (Guyn) [From the habit of carrying a cut piece of green leaf held above its head (i.e. like a parasol) as it makes its way with it to go underground]

pa·ra·t(h)a-ro·ti [pa'ra:tha-ro·ti] *n* (Guyn, Trin) [Indic] ‖ *buss-up shirt* (Trin) A light, white, flaky, pastry-like ROTI wh is much prized for its delicate texture. [Hin *paraaṭha* 'a pancake-like roti fried in ghee']

par·boil·ed rice *n phr* (Guyn) [Rice Ind] Rice produced from PADDY that has been soaked, steamed, and dried before milling to improve its quality and market value.

par·cel *n* (Guyn) ‖ HEAP (Guyn, etc) *What a parcel fo[r] yo[ur] calalu?*—(Guyn) □ PARCEL indicates a bundle, HEAP, a set or small pile.

parch-corn [pa·(r)č-kɒ·(r)n] n (Belz) ‖ASHAM (Antg, etc) □ Sometimes also abbr as /pach/ in *Belz*. [A translation of the orig Twi name (see ASHAM), or a ref to the making of the confection]

pard·ner (part·ner, pa(a)d·na) [pa(r)dnʌ~pa·dna] n **1. (i)** (CarA) [*AF*] [Often as a neutral form of address] (My) friend, companion. **a.** *'But personally,' he said, 'all I love Carnival you can't get me to do a stroke of work around Christmas. Pardner, I prefer Christmas, oui.'*—ExP (72.01.16, p.15) **b.** *The Bajan was so angry he said, 'Watch Partner, if you mash one more potato I will lick you down.' After that his Partner never visited him again because he saw that he was too greedy.*—STTG:74 [PARDNER < SE *partner* with /t > d/ voicing] □ The variants alternate in middle-level speech but the form PARDNER is commoner esp at the folk-level. **(ii)** (Guyn) *often pl* PADNA(S) ‖PORK-KNOCKER(S) (Guyn) *He is eager to speak to all Pork-knockers. When crews are in town he would like to have their group photographs. Many thanks. Looking out for you padnas.*—Guyn (Ms) **2.** (Jmca) **(i)** *often pl* A participant in a PARTNER-WORK arrangement. *Partners are normally male, but in certain areas women too may exchange labour on a time limited and strictly reciprocal basis for certain farming operations such as harvesting, planting and the like.*—LCWFL:73 **(ii)** [By extension] ‖LEND-HAND (Tbgo) **3.** (Jmca) ‖SUSU (Gren, etc) *One case a few months back involved a nurse who came here from the parish of Portland, and started a weekly 'partner'. These Jamaicans who knew that she kept the money in her apartment went there and robbed her of all the cash totalling over $1000.00.*—WeS (74.11.01, p.21) PHRASES **3.1 belong to/throw a pardner/partner** *vb phr* (Jmca) To be a contributor to a saving scheme (called by that name). *He used to throw a 10 s. a-week 'partner' with Wynter, he said, and sometimes she would send Wright for the money. On one occasion when he did not have the 10 s.—Wright paid it for him.*—DaG (66.12.16, p.5) **3.2 draw your pardner/partner** *vb phr* (Jmca) To receive your weekly or monthly lump sum in the savings scheme (called by that name).

par·gy (par·gie) [pa(r)gi] n (ECar) ‖*paggie* (Belz, Guyn, StVn) One of several varieties of small (usu) silvery fish of the porgy family wh swim in shoals near the shore and are easily caught by line and bait; it is bony but of good food value; *Calamus spp.* [Perh < AmE *porgy*, itself from Pg *pargo* wh is nearer the CE pronunc]

par·ish n **1.** (CarA) One of several divisions of an island mapped for the convenience both of administering Local Government and of political representation. *Worthy of consideration perhaps by the Little Theatre Movement and other groups is the possibility of taking small revue groups around the parishes. A minimum of props and a handful of versatile people who double as actors and stagehands could combine to make an economical travelling unit.*—DaG (71.07.04, p.4) [The use of such divisions by the Church of England for apportioning the authority of the Church was transferred to the apportioning of responsibility for Local Government. See *OED parish* 1. a. (Note)] □ See VESTRY. **2.** PHRASE **2.1 marish and the parish** *n phr* (Bdos, Guyn, Trin) [*AF—Joc*] See separate entry, MARISH.

parl·our [pa·rlʌ] n (CarA) **1.** ‖*cake-shop* (Guyn) A small shop selling small, cooked food items, sometimes with accommodation for eating on the premises; a snack-bar. *We have a lot of our meals at parlours. She likes things like hamburgers, roti and hotdogs and would have a cool drink from a bottle anytime rather than something that calls for lighting a stove.*—NaT (75.01.26, p.22, Dear Christine) **2.** An undertaker's accommodation for funerals; (AmE) 'a funeral parlor' or funeral home. *Most funerals take place from parlours these days, not from homes like when I was a child.*—(Bdos) **3.** A ladies' hairdresser's workplace; a beauty parlour. *She runs a parlour that only does braiding.*—(StVn) **4.** (Baha) The living room of a house. *On the average a house would contain: a bedroom for the parents, one or two more for the children, a dining room, and a living room, which we called the 'parlour' or 'the front room'.*—EBT:6

par·lui (par·wi)-man·go n (Bdos) ‖MANGO-PARLUI (Dmca, etc)

par·rot n PHRASE **eat parrot backside/bam-bam** *vb phr* (ECar) [*AF—Derog*] To talk far too much; to be offensively talkative. **a.** *Aw child shut yo[ur] mout[h]! Everything you see you mus[t] say? You eat parrot backside or what?*—(Tbgo) **b.** *Bwana S—the man is so disgustingly patronising ... one must conclude that he is the victim of chronic parrot bambam.*—AdN (77.07.21, p.4) [A combined ref to the tiresome chattering of a parrot and 'verbal diarrhoea']

par·rot-fish n (CarA) ‖CHUB 1. (CarA) [From the shape of the mouth, the upper jaw resembling a parrot's beak, and from the brilliant colouring of several varieties]

par·rot-toed [parʌto·d] /1'12/ *adj* (CarA) Having the toes turned inwards (like a parrot); (SE) pigeon-toed. □ The term, though listed among *parrot* compounds in *OED*, is absent from current desk dictionaries wh however list *pigeon-toed*, a term not used in CE.

part¹ n PHRASE **which part** *conj phr* (CarA) [*AF*] Where. **a.** *He and the girl went to Earls Court, which part Cap had a room at the time.*—STLL:38 **b.** *Beka sat cross-legged on the floor. | 'Gran, when I graduate, I am going away' | 'Going away to which part?'*—EBL:146

part² *vb tr* (Guyn, Trin) [*AF*] To cut (sb, esp sb's face) with something sharp (razor, cutlass, etc). *Totoy: I hear de Dove in hospital. Somebody part he face.*—HPP:3

part·ly adv (Bdos, Gren, Guyn, Tbgo, Trin) [IF] Almost; nearly. **a.** He ate partly all the food.—(Tbgo) **b.** When he get home de moder partly kill him wid blows.—(Bdos) [Cp EDD partly adv (Many E dials) 2. 'almost, nearly']

part·ner; **part.ners** n (pl) (CarA) See PARDNER

part·ner·ship; **part.ner-work** n (Jmca) ‖ LEND-HAND (Tbgo) Partnership is free and voluntary co-work. When A works on B's place, B feeds A and the two start and stop work together. B expects similar treatment in his turn.—LCWFL: 73 □ PARTNERSHIP is the more recent sociologist's term, and is mostly applied to groups, whereas PARTNER-WORK usu pronounced [pardnʌ-wak] is the folk-name and often used to refer to an agreement between only two persons or families.

part-off n (CarA) A rough curtain, folding-screen, or other movable or temporary fixture separating a section of a room or the eating place in a PARLOUR. When we talk of the 'part-off' in our homes, others may not know we mean the wall, or even curtaining, parting off an area; sometimes instead of part-off we may say the 'partition'.—ReP (80.01.20, p.4)

part·y-song n (Trin) A type of song wh, while using a characteristic calypso tune and beat, does not deal with any topical, social, or national issue in its lyrics but with some universal theme of love, dancing, etc; it is popular at dance parties (hence the name) but not in TENTS.

par·wah n (Guyn) See ANNATO

par·wi-man·go n ‖ MANGO-PARLUI (Dmca, etc)

pas·ca·lam n (USVI) Rowdiness; foolish noisiness; fuss and confusion. [< Danish Faste-lavn 'Shrove Tuesday caprice', a historical pre-lenten festival celebrated when St Thomas was a Danish colony. The name became corrupted and the orig sense lost with the disappearance of the celebration]

pa·se·al[1] (**pas·si·al**) [paziya·l~ pasia·l] vb intr (Angu, ViIs) [AF—Joc] **1.** (ViIs) To stroll; to walk about idly (esp when there is work to be done). [In]stead o[f] goin[g] paseallin[g] the whole mornin[g] he should go and look for work.—(BrVi) [< Sp pasear vb tr 'to take (a child, etc) for a walk'] **2.** (Angu) [By extension] To waste time; to idle. □ Cp LIME[1] (ECar)

pa·se·al[2] [paziya·l] n (ViIs) A stroll; a casual walk. I see dem takin[g] a paseal t[h]rough de park a lot o[f] times.—(USVI) [By functional vb > n shift of PASEAL[1]]

pa·shu·ma; **pa·shu·ba** adj (Guyn, USVI) [AF] [Of a child] Undernourished; thin and sickly looking; [of fruit] uninviting; looking undeveloped. [Cp BAED Arawak pashima 'stunted'. However, VWP also lists pachima as a USVI alternative; and FNEW lists Sran pansoema/passoema, 'slow to develop; wizened of fruit and (metaph) of people and children'. The Sran word is said to have been identified as of Loango (i.e. Congo) origin. If so it may be a loan-word, in Guyn Arawak.] □ In Guyn pashuma is often applied to a child who is underfed because fatherless, and sometimes occurs also as n, 'a fatherless child'.

pass[1] vb **1.** vb tr (CarA) To ignore (sb) on the street as socially inferior or as a deliberate insult. After Kathleen won that scholarship and went to Queen's College she would pass her old friends on the road, believe me.—(Bdos) **2.** vb intr (CarA) [Usu followed by for, in ref to skin-colour] To be considered as. See Phrs 3.5, 3.6 below. □ This is a case in wh the characteristic CarA Cr use of the base vb in past-time contexts combines with another Cr characteristic i.e. the reduction of final consonant clusters, such as /-st > -s/, to produce a confused or incorrect use of pass/past in contexts requiring passed or past. Both the senses above and all the phrs following below may be rendered in IF/X CE in past-time contexts using **pass ~ past** = SE passed. See PAST and also the Note after PASS[3] 2. **3.** PHRASES **3.1 eye(s) pass (sb)** id phr (Guyn) [AF/IF] See EYE[1] Phr 15. **3.2 make your eyes pass (sb)** vb phr (Guyn) [AF/IF] See EYE[1] Phr 23. **3.3 pass bad-hand on (sb/sth)** vb phr (Dmca) [IF] See BAD-HAND Phr 3.1 **3.4 pass by (sb)** /2'1'/ vb phr To visit (sb); to stop by (sb's home). Ques: You pass by Mr Warner every day? Ans: No. Ques: How often? Ans: Sometimes two times a week, sometimes once a week, sometimes I don't go.—StKt (CR, 74.04.27) **3.5 pass for grass** vb phr (Guyn) [AF—Joc/Derog] To be or to have become a person of no consequence; to be sb who is treated without respect. **3.6 pass for white** vb phr (CarA) [Of non-white persons] To be considered or treated as white (because of skin-colour and hair-texture). □ Cp SE pass as white (less formally also 'for white') 'be accepted as white', a sense wh is not accurate for the CE Phr. **3.7 pass out** vb phr (Angu, Antg, Mrat) [IF] To pass away; to die. □ Cp SE pass out 'become unconscious'. **3.7.1 pass out (a vehicle)** vb phr (Bdos) [IF] [Of a car, etc] To overtake (another vehicle) on the road. I blew when I was about 30 yards from the car and I proceeded to pass the car out. Just as I got alongside of the car, I heard it strike my car.—NaT (84.05.30, p.2) **3.8 pass remarks** vb phr (Bdos, Guyn) ‖ DROP REMARKS See DROP[1] Phr 3.8 **3.9 pass (the) transport** vb phr (Guyn) [Property Law] See TRANSPORT[1] **3.10 pass through/under sb's hands** vb phr (Bdos, Guyn) [IF] See HAND[1] Phr 4.24 **3.11 pass your hand** vb phr (Bdos, Guyn) [IF] To manage to bribe; to grease sb's palm. With the shortage of cement and everything now you got to pass your hand with the contractors who got a few things piled up, so you can get them to repair your house.—(Guyn) [< metaph abbr of 'pass (your hand with) money under the table'] **3.12 pass (your mouth) on (sb)** vb phr (Dmca, Tbgo, Trin) [AF—Derog]

To say something bad about, malign (sb). **a.** *'Well, Sheila is something all by herself,' Mervyn muttered, 'little more and she would be showing off her bloomer.' | Helen said angrily, 'Not a second and you're not passing your mouth on your children.'*—JJM:103 **b.** *You like to pass on people too much.*—OT2:20 **3.13 pass your place** *vb phr* (Jmca, StVn) [*AF/IF*] ‖GET BESIDE YOURSELF (CarA) See BESIDE Phr 2.1 [Cp SE *not know your place*, with same connotation] **3.14 Pass yourself!** *imper vb phr* (Guyn) [*IF*] [To a child] Get inside/outside!; get away from here! **3.15 take your eyes and pass (me/sb)** *vb phr* (Guyn) [*AF*] See EYE¹ Phr 26.

pass² *n* **1.** (CarA) Permission to pass (between persons who are near or talking to each other). [Perh a reflection of Hist pass laws of the Slave era] **2.** PHRASES **2.1 ask/beg for a pass** *vb phr* (CarA) To ask (a person or persons) to let you get past or get through. *But really, at that time of the night there is not too much pedestrian traffic along the pavement. At times, though, one may have to ask for a pass because some over-enthusiastic customers (and hangers-on) would be involved in some deep debates over topics ranging from life to death.*—SuC (78.02.12, p.12) **2.2 give (sb) a pass** *vb phr* (CarA) To let (sb) get past. **2.3 Please for a pass** *interr vb phr* (CarA) [*IF*] May I pass, please. □ This is the regular form of polite request to pass.

pass³ *adv, prep* (CarA) [*X*] Past. **1.** *prep* [Esp as prep extension in vb phrs, or in stating the time] **a.** *Please, if even you are shortstaffed, still send a young recruit to walk pass the buses; it's amazing how straight and narrow the queues suddenly become.*—AdN (72.07.22, p.4) **b.** *If another flood should hit the area, it would be very difficult for the waters to get pass his empolders.*—Guyn (Ms, 77.02.21) **c.** *Glancing at my watch, which ticks competed with my heart for loudness—it read 17 minutes pass 1 a.m.*—ExP (72.03.19, p.22) **2.** *adv* **(i)** [of place] Past; passing by. *When you were there, did you see anyone go pass?*—Tbgo (CR, 1980) **(ii)** [of time] Past; ago. *Your mother—I will have something to say about her—make me a silk shirt two months pass.*—CWFYS: 42 [From characteristic CE (< CarA Cr) reduction of final /-CC/, whence /paast > paas/. This faulty functional shift is reinforced by the closeness in meaning of SE *pass, past, passed*. See Note after PASS¹ 2.]

pass⁴ *comparative marker* (Belz, Guyn, Jmca) [*AF—Cr*] More than, (hence) very. *Don['t] boder advice he no mo[re]. He pass stupid.*—(Guyn) [A prob calque from a number of W Afr langs wh use the vb meaning 'to surpass, pass' to express strong comparatives, ex (*BSCEGE:45*) Twi ɛyi so sen ɛno (*this big pass that; this is big more than that*) 'This is bigger than that'] □ This usage is now almost wholly restricted to rural folk.

pass-eye *n* (Guyn) [*AF*] ‖EYE-PASS (Guyn) *According to Thomas, who is employed as a watchman in Kingston, youths who gather at the cakeshop always tease him.... 'It's all pass-eye,' he complained to the Beak.*—DaC (53.04.11, p.5)

pas·sion-fruit* ['pašʌn-frut] /1'12/ *n* (CarA) ‖**cocktail-fruit** (StKt) ‖**forbidden fruit** (Guyn) ‖**mountain sweet-cup** (Jmca) A smooth, ball-round fruit about 2 ins in diameter, its thick, green skin turning yellowish when ripe and enclosing an acid-sweet, yellowish, gelatinous pulp with dark-brown seeds; the fruit is borne on a high-climbing vine with shiny green leaves, noted also for its passion-flower type blossoms; *Passiflora edulis (Passifloraceae)*. [From its blossoms the design of wh resembles the more famous 'Passion Flower' (of the same genus) on a smaller scale]

PASSIVITY (CarA) [Grammar] The nature and sense of the SE 'Passive Voice'. Most transitive vbs can convey PASSIVITY in their base or -ing form, in IF CE, by the operation of a principle surviving from CarA Cr: When the subject of a sentence governs a trans vb that expresses an action of wh that subject, by common sense, cannot be the agent, then that vb is analysed as passive, and the subject of the sentence as the object of the action. Hence *the food eat*, 'the food is/has been eaten'; *the baby name already*, 'the baby has been named'; *the ticket pay for*, 'the ticket is/has been paid for'; *the car park bad*, 'the car is badly parked'; *this table put wrong*, 'this table has been put in a wrong place'; *the bicycle riding*, 'the bicycle is being ridden'; *the piano was playing*, 'the piano was being played'; etc. This means firstly that in IF CE PASSIVITY may be determined wholly by the nature of the subject and context, secondly that lexically most CE transitive vbs can carry either an active or a passive sense, depending on the context of the sentence. See also GET 2 for the rendering of PASSIVITY in cases that would otherwise be ambiguous.

pass-out *n* (Tbgo, Trin) An informal game of school-yard cricket in wh there is no wicket and the batsman is out if the ball passes him; the bowler then takes his place as the next batsman. (*Constantine) came to my father's school in St Ann's, Port of Spain, for a short while. A mob of boys used to play 'pass out' in the school-yard.... What I distinctly recall is that in the scramble for the ball he rather stood aside and watched ... this rough and tumble probably did not appeal to him.*—JBAB:107

pass-over *n* **1.** (Bdos) A sudden loss of consciousness; a mild apoplexy or stroke. **2.** (Belz) A shower of rain that passes quickly, driven by a high wind.

past *vb* (CarA) [*X*] Pass **a.** *Just past me a towel, please*—(Bdos) **b.** *As a Portuguese, in America he will past for white*—(Guyn) [By overcorrection < SE *pass*. See □ Note after PASS¹ 2.]

past·elle [pastɛl] n (Tbgo, Trin) A small, boiled, pie-textured pudding made of a seasoned mixture of tiny pieces of beef and pork, raisins, and stuffed olives in a thin layer of cornmeal dough, wrapped and tied in a piece of blanched banana-leaf; it is most popular at Christmas time. [Sp *pastel* 'cake, pie'. The spelling—*elle* is prob due to false Fr infl in *Trin* (where the item is most popular), or to its suggestion of delicacy (cp *demoiselle*), or to distinguish it from E *pastel*]

pa·ta·ki (pa·ta·kee) n (Belz) A large, rectangular basket with bulging sides; it is lined with canvas as water-proofing, and a covered type is used like a large knapsack by forest workers and fishermen. [*DMEI:184* Miskito Indian *pataki* 'basket']

Pa·ta·mo·na(s) (Pa·ta·mu·na(s)) n (Guyn) A Cariban ethnic group of Amerindian people inhabiting the middle western area of the interior of Guyana bordering on the Brazil-Venezuela boundary. (See cit). *Patamunas are at present found in the Northern Pakaraima mountains from the Ireng river in the west to the Kaieteur escarpment in the east (Report 1969:115). Their main villages are at Paramakatoi and Kurukubaru. Oral tradition has it that the Patamunas once lived in lowland forest areas before moving into the mountainous Pakaraima region. This would give informal support to the suggestion that the Patamuna and the Akawaio were once one tribal group.*—Guyn (Ms 1978, W.F. Edwards)

patch vb tr PHRASE **patch needle and burn thread** id phr (Belz) [*AF—Joc*] See NEEDLE Phr 2.

pat·choi n (Guyn, etc) See PAKCHOI.

pat·ois [patwa~patwɒ] n 1. (CarA) ‖PATWA[1] (Dmca, etc) [Fr *patois*, 'provincial dialect'] 2. (Jmca) [*IF*] (A term used by many for) Jamaican CREOLE (see CREOLE 3.(i). □ Sometimes loosely applied to Anglophone *CarA* CREOLES in general. See also note at PATWA[1].

pa·too [patu] n (Jmca) A screech-owl. *He was sometimes called Patoo, which is the countryman's name for the night-owl.*—SD:8 [< DAFL Twi *patu*, 'owl']

pat·ty n 1. (Jmca) ‖JAMAICAN PATTY (CarA) *When Mr John Pringle and a few friends started their patty factory, they were amazed by the demand—and now, incidentally, they produce a much better patty than any to be found in Jamaica.*—Jmca (Ms, 1973) 2. (Guyn) A small, round, meat-filled pastry with crimped edge; it is often used as a cocktail appetizer.

Pat·wa[1] n (Dmca, Gren, StLu, Trin, Trin) The French CREOLE esp of *Dmca, StLu* and its remainders in *Trin* and *Gren*. □ This spelling, using the system of the *StLu* National Research and Development Foundation (NRDF), enables the identification of French-based dialects of a language in its own right i.e. PATWA, as distinct from PATOIS 2., a loan-word via Eng for 'dialect', esp including Anglophone types, but always in a derogatory sense. However the name *Kwéyòl* is preferred to *Patwa* by the NRDF.

pat·wa[2] (pat·ua, pot·wa) [patwʌ] n (Guyn) A fish varying in size from 4 to 8 ins with an olive-green skin covered with pearly spots; it lives in swamps and canals and, though bony, is very tasty; *Cichlasoma bimaculatum (Cichlidae)*. [An Amerindian name]

paw·paw n (CarA) See PAPAW.

pay vb tr PHRASES 1. **pay for your mouth** vb phr (CarA) [*AF*] To suffer some punishment for rudeness, malicious gossip, or slander. *There are scores of men in this country who go around spreading false rumours and telling all kinds of shocking lies about women. Recently one feller was made to pay for his mouth, after he alleged that a schoolgirl was pregnant.*—SuP (74.06.02, p.9) 2. **pay (sb) no mind** vb phr (CarA) ‖NOT PAY (SB) ANY/NO MIND (CarA) [*IF/AF*] See MIND Phr 8.

pa·ya·so /1'21/ n 1. (Belz) [*AF—Joc*] A fool; a buffoon; sb who cannot be taken seriously. [< Sp *payaso* 'a clown'] 2. PHRASE 2.1 **play the payaso** vb phr (Belz) [*AF—Joc*] ‖ MAKE A PAYASS (BrVi)

pa·yass[1] (pi·ass(e)) [paya·s] n 1. (BrVi) [*AF—Joc*] Buffoonery; fooling around. 2. (Guyn) [*AF*] Showing off; making a display of your good fortune. 3. PHRASE 3.1 **make (a) payass** vb phr (BrVi) ‖ *play the payaso* (Belz) To play the fool; to fool around. [(*BrVi*) prob < Sp *payaso* 'clown'; (*Guyn*) prob < Pg *palhaço* 'jester, buffoon']

pa·yass[2] (pi·ass(e)) [paya·s] vb intr 1. (BrVi) To play the fool; to clown around. *He ain['t] doin[g] no work, only payassin[g] [wh]ole day.*—(BrVi) 2. (Guyn) ‖ *perlix, pompasset* (Bdos) To display your good fortune with obvious delight; to show off provocatively. *Well since the daughter gone away wit[h] dis white man, an[d] she say dey goin[g] get married, you know how she payassin[g] [u]pon de neighbours.*—(Guyn) [(*BrVi*) < Sp *payasear* 'to clown around' or (*Guyn*) by functional n > vb shift of PAYASS[1] 2.]

pay-bann·ann (paille-ba·nane) [paɪ-banan] /2'12/; ‖ *pay-fig* [paɪ-fig] n (StLu) A folk festival costume made of banana leaves, used by masqueraders, often those dancing on stilts. *'Kwapo' firecrackers are popularly attached to the 'pai banan' (banana trash) costumes of the Bwa-Bwa dancers, for the fun of seeing the masquerader tear off his costume to keep from being burned in it.*—Caq IV.2, p.107 (D.J. Crowley) [Fr Cr < Fr *paille (de) banane* 'banana straw'] □ See also SENSAY-COSTUME.

pa·yol (pan·yol) ['paybl~panybl] n 1. (Trin) [*AF—Derog*] A person of mixed race (white,

Amerindian and black) usu a member of one or other of the scattered, poor, peasant communities in northern Trinidad that retain remainders of Hispanic culture, such as PARANG and varying degrees of a dialectal Spanish. **2.** (Gren) Any So Am Spanish-speaking person esp a Venezuelan. [< Sp *español* by aphaeresis and denasalization] □ 'Some regard the word *payol* to be as derogatory as 'nigger' or 'coolie'. It is interesting to note that the *payols* refer to themselves in E as 'Spanish' and in Spanish as 'venenzolanos' or 'venezolanos'—*S. Moodie (Ms, 1982).* See also COCOA PAYOL.

peach* *n* (Guyn) A reddish, round fruit about 3 ins in diameter, with brown hairs; it has a sticky pulp with a peculiar flavour for wh it is not very popular; fruit of the tree *Diospyros discolor (Ebenaceae).* [From its resemblance in shape and colour to the European *peach*']

pea-chink [pi-čıŋk] *n* (Bdos) **1.** ‖STINK BUG (Guyn) [*Pea*, because found mainly on pigeon-pea trees, + SE *chink*, a bed-bug. Cp cit *HNHB: 84* 'The Buonavista Chink ... is a small green fly ... and smells when killed like a bug] **2.** A green, lace-winged, smelly insect that feeds on caterpillar larvae; *Chrysopa spp.*

pea-dove *n* (Jmca) ‖GROUND-DOVE 2. (CarA) *The Pea Dove (Zenaida aurita) is referred to in bird books as the Zenaida dove and has a very wide distribution in the Caribbean area.*—TIBJ: 92

pe·ai·man (pi·ai·man, pi·aye) [piaıma·n] / ı'2ı/ *n* (Guyn) [Amerindian] A medicine man who relieves or removes sickness, evil, or fear (esp of the KANAIMA) in members of his tribal community by ritual methods. [Note *FTCC: 145* Macusi *piai* 'medicine man'. However, the word appears to be of general Cariban origin. *IAIG:328 (f.n)* considers it 'an Anglicised form of ... *puyai* ... and occurring in several ... langs of South America'. Perh orig *piaima* (cp *kanaima* from same sources) whence a false suffixation '-man' in its anglicization]

peak·a-pe·ow [pika-pyɒu] *n* (Jmca) A Chinese gambling game played by guessing eight of thirty secretly selected numbers; it is a privately run, unlicensed lottery, the buyer's chosen numbers being marked on a piece of paper. *Going past the next lane he hesitated between buying himself a half-pack of cigarettes with the sixpence he had in his pocket, or investing it in a peaka-peow mark. He decided he would buy the peaka-peow mark, might win a good piece of money, you never could tell.*—MBM:42 [Haka dial of Chinese, the name of this game]

pear[1] *n* (CarA) ‖AVOCADO (-PEAR) (CarA) *To most Barbadians a Pear is an Avocado Pear. The true Pear is Pyrus communis, a member of the Rose family Rosaceae.*—AdN (79.06.17, p.16, M.B. Hutt) [From its resemblance, only in shape, to the European *pear*]

pear[2] *vb tr* (Baha) [*AF—ʒoc*] ‖ROACH[2] (Baha)

pear-bush *n* **1.** (TkCa) ‖COCHINEAL (CACTUS) (Guyn, etc) [Perh from the pear-shape of the pad-like stem. Cp other names PLIMPLER PEAR, PRICKLY PEAR, etc] □ In *TkCa* the succulent buds of this plant are used to make a *pear-bush soup*, cooked with rice as a meal, *pear-bush and rice*, or fermented to make *pear-wine.* **2.** (ViIs) The green leaves of the AVOCADO, wh are used as a folk-medicine after pregnancy. [< PEAR[1] (*CarA*)]

peas *n pl PHRASES* **1. like peas** *adj phr, adv phr* (CarA) [*AF—ʒoc*] Plenty of; in great abundance. **a.** *For the past few weeks, advice about morality and mobility flowed like peas through well-dressed audiences at graduation ceremonies.*—ExP (79.07.15, p.4) **b.** *He added that such malice is usually the product of bad-mindedness, which prevents us from seeing the other as a real person and encourages us to dissect others or 'share licks like peas'.*—AdN (80.03.03, p.1) □ See also LICKS[2] Phr 3.6 LICKS LIKE PEAS. **2. peas and rice; rice and peas** *n phrs* (CarA) A dish of rice boiled with a large proportion of PIGEON-PEAS; it is the regular main dish of *CarA* meals. **a.** *A typical Cruzan picnic at Gentle Winds. Stewed goat, roast pig, souse, peas and rice, potato stuffing, all cooked by local volunteers.*—Vgi I.3, p.9 **b.** *Peas 'n' rice could be described as the staple item in Bahamian cuisine, being as popular here as blackeye peas are in the south of the U.S.*—DBH: 48 **c.** *Sunday special buffet for local residents, Wednesdays for overseas visitors. Come and try out turtle stew, conch and rice and peas, cassava, rundown, etc.*—Cay (75.06.12, p.B4) □ The two forms alternate in many territories, but there is a definite preference for one or the other in certain places.

peas-soup *n* **1.** (CarA) A thick soup made with a large amount of crushed peas, esp PIGEON-PEAS; it is, in many places, a regular week-end meal. **2.** *PHRASE* **2.1 give laugh for peas-soup** *vb phr* (Jmca) [*AF—ʒoc*] See GIVE[1] Phr 2.10

peas·y hair *n phr* (Baha) [*AF—ʒoc*] ‖PICKY HAIR/HEAD (Baha, etc)

pe·ba ['pɛba] *n* (Guyn) ‖ARMADILLO (Guyn) □ Rare. Usage prob restricted to forest-dwellers (See *RALG:12*).

pec·ca·ry* **(-ri)** *n* (Belz, Guyn) ‖*abouya, bush-hog, wild hog* (Guyn) ‖*quenk* (Trin) ‖*wari* (Belz) A species of wild pig with tusks in its lower jaw; it also possesses a dorsal scent gland wh produces a very disagreeable odour; it is hunted for its meat; *Dicotyles torquatus* or *Tayassu pecari, etc (Tayassuidae). Country life 'gree wid anybody, son. Yu eat yu rice, yu beans, yu get yu deer meat, yu peccary, yu gibnut, yu ground food, yu riba fish, everyting fresh.*—HF: 53 [Cp *BDFC:76* Carib *bakira* 'inland pig wh has a vent on its back'. The name underwent several spelling changes in travel accounts]

peck *n* (Bdos) ‖ *peck-hawk* (Bdos) A pickaxe. *I have seen people in St James with pecks and hoes digging away some of the earth and the water will go into the sea.*—Bdos (Hd, 74.11.19, p.4153) [Prob < *EDD pick* sb[1] Sc, Irel, Eng 1. 'a pickaxe']

peck-hawk [pɛk-hɒ·k] *n* (Bdos) [*IF*] ‖ PECK (Bdos) [Perh by overcorrection < *peck* + *axe*, or a blend of PECK + *tomahawk*, from AmE] □ The term is used by older labourers.

peel-neck fowl *n phr* (Belz, Guyn, Jmca, StVn) ‖ BARE-NECK FOWL (Bdos, etc)

pee·ny-wal·ly [piniwali] /1'122/ *n* (Jmca) [*IF*] ‖ CANDLE-FLY (CarA) ... *and then night would fall, literally like a black curtain.... The peeny wally winked around, the frogs came out hop-hopping ... and the whistling toads and crickets made background music.*—BM:13 [Perh Joc < CE PEENY + blend with *CSD* Sc *peelie-wali* 'feeble, thin, sickly'; or + Eng nCy dial *wally* 'a toy, gewgaw'] □ Pl often unchanged as in cit. See also PEERUM.

pee·ny(-wee·ny) (**pin·ny(-win·ny)**) [piniwini ~ pini-wini] *adj* (Bdos, Gren, Guyn, Jmca, StVn) [*AF*] [Children's talk] Very small; tiny. **a.** *She offer me a peeny piece o[f] cake like if she couldn['t] even spare it.*—(Guyn) **b.** *De glass break an[d] a pinny-winny piece o[f] splinter get in me hand but it hurt bad.*—(Gren) [Cp *EDD peeny* adj wYks 'small, puny'; also *weeny* adj in gen dial use, Irel, Eng, Amer 'very small; tiny'] □ In *Guyn* the form PINNY often occurs in the redup form *little pinny*.

pee·rum [pirʌm] *n* (Belz) A large variety of firefly, sometimes also called PEENY-WALLY.

pe(e)·wa(h)* [piwa] *n* (Trin) A round, red fruit, about 1-1/2 ins in diameter, with a tough, fibrous, juicy flesh on a hard kernel; it is borne in large clusters on a tree about 30 ft tall, its trunk covered in rings of long black spines; the fruit is often roasted or boiled for eating, or fermented for a beverage; *Guilielma speciosa* (*Palmaceae*).

pee-whi(s)t·ler* *n* (Bdos) An olive-grey bird with yellowish underparts; it is about 7 ins long, has a harsh 'cheee-se' whistle, and feeds on berries; *Elaenia spp.*

peg[1] [pɛg] *n* (CarA) ‖ FEG (Angu, etc) *The shaddock is a citrus the edible part of which is divided into pegs like oranges.*—Gren (Ms) [Cp *EDD pig* sb[1] var dial uses in Sc, Irel and Eng. Also in form *peg* Brks[1], Der[1] (pig, wCy, peg) 7. 'a segment of an apple or orange']

peg[2] [pɛg] *vb* (Gren, Jmca, StVn, Tbgo, Trin) To separate the sections of a citrus fruit into individual segments. *Peel my orange, but don't peg it. Just cut it in two and I will suck it.*—(Tbgo) [By functional n > vb shift of PEG[1]]

peg·all (**pa·gale**) [pɛgɒ·l ~ paga·l] *n* (Guyn) **1.** ‖ PACK-ALL (Bdos, Guyn) **2.** A small, rectangular, basket-work container about 6 to 8 ins deep, neatly finished and often decoratively patterned, with a close-fitting cover; it is used (generally by older folk) for keeping needlework. [Note *IAIG:278* 'The so-called pegalls are made to contain all loose arrow-heads, a ball of cotton for binding, some wax, such beads and ornaments as are not in use, and all the other smaller properties of the Indian. The pegalls of the Arawaks, Ackawoi and Warraus are generally square in shape. The basket and its lid are of exactly the same shape, ... the latter ... slips over the former and entirely covers it ...' (Also footnote: 'The word *pegalla* is possibly a genuine Carib word; but the form *pack-all* wh is used by the colonists is ... suspicious'). It seems from this evidence that **pegall** is an original Amerindian name and the item now urbanized]

pe·gasse ['pɛga·s] *n* (Guyn) A dark, loose, spongy, peat-like surface layer of soil, sometimes several feet deep, formed from decomposed flora and behind the coastal front-land clays of Guyana. *Fires in the pegasse lands were so prevalent during the dry season due to the combustible nature of pegasse when dry that a Canals Polder Fire Commission had to be instituted in 1940 to study the cause.*—GyC (76.08.22, p.25) [< Pg or Sp *pegajoso* 'sticky, viscous'] □ The word sometimes occurs in error, in *Guyn* urban speech, for **begasse**, the variant of BAGASSE.

pe·gass·y ['pɛgasi] *adj* (Guyn) [Of soil] Composed or consisting of PEGASSE; spongy. *Crop Development Officer Abdul Wahab ... conducted the party over the experimental area of pegasse and pegassy clay soils, aback of Enmore Estate. Dr Wahab told the visitors that although these very acid soils are considered unfavourable for economic cane cultivation, there appeared to be a respectable potential for soya and for cassava.*—GyC (76.11.28, p.5)

peg·gy-mouth /1'12/ *n* (Antg, Brbu, Mrat) ‖ BIRD-PEPPER (CarA)

pe·lau (**pe·leau, pi·lao, pi·lau**) [pilou ~ pɛlou] *n* (CarA) ‖ *rice-below* (Baha) A one-pot meal of rice boiled with pieces of various meats to wh pigeon-peas and chipped vegetables are often added; it is sometimes cooked in COCONUT MILK. **a.** *I recall the year 1969 when members of a youth group posed over huge pots like famous Saraca cooks turning the huge masses of pelau.... Pounds of meat were cooked to feed the seafaring seamen after their adventures in the races.*—Crcu (Ms, C. David, 1972) **b.** *Today she had chipped a red bird pepper or two into the pilao and the flavouring it gave to the chicken and rice was a joyful new pleasure.*—MHBT:35 [Indic, via Urdu *pilao*: An internationally known dish, wh *OED* lists as *pilau, pilaw* + many variant spellings and full etym note] □ Of several conjectured spellings in CE, PELAU is the most frequent. The type of dish is also often qualified as 'chicken (-and beef) pelau', etc.

pel·met n (Bdos) ‖ HOOD (Bdos) [Shift in application of sense of BrE pelmet wh is an inside covering above a window] □ See also BELL-PELMET.

pelt vb tr **1.** (CarA) To throw (sth away, at sb, etc). **a.** People started pelting bottles and cans at the players in protest.—Trin (Ms) **b.** Obviously there are those who will persist in throwing rubbish anywhere except in a bin precisely because no doubt when they were children some unthinking adult said, 'Pelt it 'pun de ground'.—AdN (74.08.13, p.2) □ Cp SE pelt sb with sth with CE **pelt sth at sb**. See many consequent phrs below. **2.** (ECar) To hit; to strike with force. **a.** Somebody pelted the house and the stone rattled down the zinc sheet.—(StKt) **b.** ... and all the time St Hill out there in the forest, crawling on his belly in dirt and stone ... the sun and rain pelting his skin.—WMHC:25 □ Cp SE pelt 'to strike repeatedly (with many small missiles)'. CE usage generally focuses on one blow. **3.** (Bdos, Gren, Guyn) To walk hurriedly; to dash. Every morning you see her pelting down to catch the bus.—(Bdos) □ Cp SE pelt 'to run fast' or '[of rain] to come down hard'. **4.** (ECar) [Cricket, of a bowler] To throw; to bowl in an unpermitted way, by pitching the ball with a stiff arm. **5.** PHRASES **5.1 pelt a cuff** vb phr (Guyn) See CUFF[1] Phr 2.2 **5.2 pelt a lash/(the) lashes** vb phr (CarA) [IF] See LASH[2] Phr 2.3 **5.3 pelt blows** vb phr (ECar) [IF] To hit out, lash wildly. Well, we all scattered like crazy, as he started to pelt blows with the bull, I got one on the arm and I took off like a fish.—BoM (74.10.18, p.18) **5.4 pelt (down) (fruit from a tree)** vb phr (CarA) To throw stones, etc at (fruit in a tree) to bring down fruit. **5.5 pelt (some) licks (in sb's skin/tail)** vb phr (Bdos) [AF] See LICK[2] Phr 3.8 **5.6 Pelt your skin!** excl vb phr (StVn) [AF] ‖ MOVE YOURSELF (Baha, etc) [Skin in the sense 'body']

pé·mi (pai·me/·mie) ['pemi] n (Trin) ‖ DUKUNA (Antg, etc) We have been travelling for more than two hours, so snacks are passed around. Sweetbread and sandwiches. Pone and paime.—(Peo I.5, p.31) [Fr Cr [pɛ̃ mi] < Fr pain de mie 'a bread made from crumbs', a bread with little crust ('qui a peu de croûte'—LLFL)] □ The Fr origin has been 'lost', and replaced by folk etym or notional spellings of wh **paim(i)e** seems to be the commonest.

pen n (Jmca) [Hist] A large country estate of earlier times; the term survives today mainly in place names (May Pen, Slipe Pen Road, etc). ['The use of the word penn, or pen, in Jamaica to mean a farm or property with livestock dates from the seventeenth century, when the first British settlers found the cattle left by the Spaniards running wild'—Editor's f.n., p.12, to Lady Nugent's Journal, 1966] □ The term is restricted to Jmca (though OED lists as 'in the W Indies').

pen·cil-bush n (USVI) ‖ BLIND-EYE 1. (Mrat) □ Also called pencil-cactus in horticultural literature.

penm·bwa [pɛ̃mbwa] n (Trin) ‖ BREADFRUIT (CarA)

pe·ong n (Tbgo, Trin) See PIONG

peo·ple n pl (CarA) [IF] **1.** Person(s) (esp in ref to those of a particular set or origin). **a.** Well my grandmother told me that her parents were Montserrat people.—(StKt) **b.** Carter was peanuts people, but Reagan is cowboy people, so that's why Iran stop playin[g] the ass an[d] le[t] go the American hostages.—(Bdos) **2.** [IF/AF] [Functioning as an indefinite pron more loosely than in SE] Others. **a.** I wouldn't even worry to ask her. She doesn't care about people.—(StVn) **b.** He is a big hulkin[g] brute only lookin[g] to interfere wit[h] people girl children.—(Guyn) **3.** [AF] [Functioning as 1st pers sg pron] I; me; my. **a.** You-all makin[g] so much noise in my head, people can['t] even res[t].—(Guyn) **b.** You-all work people till people foot sore. Well, I done now. I sittin[g] do[w]ng.—(BrVi) **4.** [AF—Joc] [Functioning as a casual indef pron, in contexts signalling contempt] Somebody worth noticing **a.** De daughter ain['t] even know who she child fader is. Dem is people?—(Guyn) **b.** Those are the underlying evils of Trinidad society. Each man thinks he is people. Is time to stop all that.—JJM:91. **5.** PHRASES **5.1 big people** n phr (CarA) [IF] See BIG MAN **5.2 look like people** vb phr (ECar) [IF—Joc] See LOOK Phr 4.6

pep·per·pot (pep·per-pot) ['pɛpʌpɒt] /1'12/ n **1.** (Bdos, Gren, Guyn) A dark-brown stew prepared by boiling together pieces of any kind of wild or regular meat (except fish) with red peppers and other seasoning, sugar, and CASAREEP for several hours, usu in a large earthenware pot; it is kept on the fire-place, with meat, CASAREEP and seasoning being added from time to time, so that the same pot may actually be served from (in Guyn) for weeks, months, or even years. **2.** (Angu, Antg, Jmca) ‖ CALALU 2.(i) (Dmca, etc) □ Note that the two senses apply to meals of very different appearance and taste.

pep·per-sauce n (CarA) ‖ hot-sauce (CarA) A very piquant condiment made from the juice and seeds of ground, red or yellow peppers (Capsicum spp) with mustard, vinegar, and chipped onions added.

pe·rai [piraɪ] n (Guyn) A bluish-black, oval, freshwater fish over 12 ins long, with bright red eyes and a protruding, iron-hard, sharp-edged lower jaw; it is an extremely voracious, flesh-eating fish that swarms to devour living things at the scent of blood; (better known internationally by its Sp name) the piranha; Serrasalmo niger (Serrasalmidae). [Tupi-Guarani pirãi, name of this fish]

per·i·win·kle *n* (CarA) ‖ OLD-MAID (BUSH) (CarA)

per·lix /ɪ'2/ *vb intr* (Bdos) [*AF—Joc*] ‖ PAYASS² 2. (Guyn) □ Often compounded with POMPASSET (*Bdos*).

per·son ['pʌrsʌn] *n* (Bdos) [*IF*] **1.** [Used in speech instead of SE 'body' esp in foll phrs] PHRASES **1.1 no person** /ɪ'22/ [*X*] Nobody. *No person is there, at the door.*—(Bdos) **1.2 some person** /ɪ'22/ [*X*] Somebody. *Some person is there at the door.*—(Bdos) **2.** [In spoken inquiries] ‖ BODY (CarA) ɪ. Used in phrasal equivalents [*IF*] of 'Who?' as in foll phrs. **2.1 Which person?** *pron phr* [*IF*] Who? *Which person goin[g] pay all dat money?* (= *Who is going to, etc*).— (Bdos) **2.2 Who the person is?** *id phr* (Bdos) [*X*] Who is it? □ See also BODY

per·son·al *adj* (Guyn) [*IF*] Presumptuously inquisitive, asking embarrassingly personal questions. *During the conversation with the sentry, another 'personal' soldier became inquisitive about the young lady's whereabouts, after she asked him for the officer. Later, after she 'got through' with the job she was again met by the soldier who proposed a possible relationship.*—GyC (76.10.19, p.7) [By semantic extension of SE *get personal*]

Per·son·al No·tice *n phr* (Bdos) ‖ SE-PARATION-NOTICE (Gren, StKt)

pesh *n* (Gren, Guyn, Tbgo, Trin) [*AF—Joc*] ‖ *paisa* (Guyn, Jmca, Trin) Coins; cash; money. *Wen dem Korean spen all dis pesh pon Uncle, look out, nex ting you know dey gettin fishin rights in ahwe water yes. An is Shrimp dey like.*—ToR (76.05.02, p.6, Cotay Si, Cotay La) [Perh < So Am Sp *peso*, unit of currency; also Fr *pièce* 'coin'; perh also infl by (Hin) PAISA]

pes·ter·ous *adj* (Belz) [Of a person] Trouble-some; being always a nuisance; bothersome; an-noying. [A survival of EE. Cp *OED pesterous* 'having the quality of pestering' + cits 1548–1825]

pe·tit ca·reme [pɪti karɛ·m] *n phr* (Trin) A dry spell lasting for a few weeks in the wet season of September–October. *Things begin, time moves on, the seasons move from dry to wet, to Petit Careme (Indian summer), to wet and back again.*— GTTLA:6 [Fr *petit carême* 'little Lent' = fast-ing, lay-off?]

pe·tit-quart *n* (Trin) See PITIKWÒT

Phag·wa(h) [phagwa] *n* (Guyn, Trin) [Indic] **1.** ‖ *Holi* (Guyn, Trin) The public festive aspect of the Hindu religious celebration of HOLI, marked by sharing in much open-air fun, esp the symbolic splashing of the blood of atonement (*abir*) among participants. **2.** [By extension] [*X*] ‖ ABIR (Guyn, Trin) *He said the people were throw-ing phagwah and he got his shirt all stained up.*— Guyn (CR) [Bhoj < Hin *phaalgun*, the last month

of the Hindu calendar (roughly corresponding to March) in wh the HOLI festival falls, + *wa* masc sg suffix. PHAGWA is the name of the festival prevailing in the Bhojpuri area of India from wh the majority of the East Indian immigrants were drawn]

phone-mes·sage *n* **1.** (Bdos) [*IF*] A telephone call made by you. (Hence foll phrs). □ *Message* is here conceived as communication sent rather than received, and parallel, for ex, with a *tele-graph-message* for wh there is a *message-form*. **2.** PHRASES **2.1 get a phone-message** *vb phr* (Bdos) [*IF*] To borrow and use sb else's tele-phone; to make a call on sb else's telephone. *The captain got out and asked where he could get a phone-message, indicating that he could not speak much English.*—NaT (77.10.07, p.18) **2.2 give (sb) a phone-message** *vb phr* (Bdos) See GIVE¹ Phr 2.17

phu·lou·ri(e)-/pa·lo(w)ri(-balls) [phʊ-lʊuri ~ pʌlʊuri] *n* (*pl*) (Guyn, Trin) Small, round balls made of a highly seasoned mixture of ground split-peas and flour, deep fried. [Bhoj *palauri* < Hin *phulauri* 'gram flour'] □ Other spellings *polorie, poulowri, phoulorie*, etc are found.

phys·ic-nut [fɪzɪk-nʌt] *n* **1.*** (CarA) ‖ *white barricader* (Angu, StKt) A large shrub with large, heart-shaped, slightly lobed leaves; the succulent stems have a reddish, milky sap and bear roundish, green, capsule-like fruit the seeds of wh are purgative; the plant and fruit are put to many medicinal uses; *Jatropha curcas* (*Euphorbiaceae*). □ Also referred to as *Barbados nut* in some writings. **2.** ‖ BELLY-ACHE BUSH (Bdos, etc)

pi·a(b)·ba(h) [piaba ~ pyabʌ] *n* (Bdos, Gren, Guyn, Jmca) One of two kinds of single-stemmed, erect herb that bear a resemblance to each other in their general appearance and are both used medicinally, sometimes being boiled together. See MAN-PIABA, WOMAN-PIABA [*DJE* notes (from Rattray) Ashanti *piaa* 'the plant *Hyptis brevipes* + *-ba* 'small (of plants)'. This, however, refers to 'a mint-like herb' wh is used as a similar folk medicine in *Jmca*. The types referred to as **man-** and **woman-piaba** are quite different plants from the *Hyptis spp*; the adoption of an Afr name for plants with nearly identical medicinal uses may account for the *CarA* re-currence of the name]

pi·ai·man (pi·aye) *n* (Guyn) See PEAIMAN

pi·ass(e) *vb intr* (Guyn) See PAYASS

pib·lan *n* (Belz) A mosquito net; any large netting used to keep off insects. [< Sp *pabellón* 'bell tent, canopy']

pick *vb* **1.** (Guyn, Tbgo) [*IF*] [Of a child's reading] To read haltingly. *You mean you been going to school two years now and you still picking* *so when you read?*—(Tbgo) □ Sometimes also **pick(ing) corn** [AF]. **2.** (CarA) [With 'rice' as obj] To cleanse (rice) by picking out bad grains, dirt, etc with the fingers before cooking. *Lyn was squatted on a stool with a big earthenware bowl on her lap, picking rice, her skirt drawn up over the glossy black knees and tucked primly down.*—RWIN:166 (J. Hearne) [Cp *OED pick* vb¹ 3., wh includes cleansing 'anything'. The phr with *rice* as obj is however the commonest *CarA* use in this sense] □ The phr **picking rice** does not apply to harvesting or reaping rice by hand. In contrast cp SE *picking cotton.* **3.** (USVI) [With 'salt' as obj] To break up and gather (salt) from an evaporated SALT-POND. *But dry weather is the best weather for a salt pond to make salt! After many weeks of little rain, Ivan, Alvin, and Calvin decided to go to the salt pond and 'pick' salt.*—JJHAI:117 [Cp *EDD pick* vb¹ 14. Salt making term: 'to break up and take away the scale that forms on the bottom of a pan during evaporation'] **4.** (Bdos) [With 'sea-eggs' as obj] See SEA-EGG Phr. *Is it illegal to pick sea-eggs before the months ending with the letter 'r'? Is this perhaps merely a recommendation to give the sea-eggs a chance to reproduce?*—AdN (78.08.19, p.4) [Cp *EDD pick* vb¹ 13. 'to detach limpets from a rock'] **5.** PHRASES **5.1 not pick sb's height** *neg vb phr* (StVn, Tbgo) [IF/AF] ‖ NOT TAKE SB'S HEIGHT (CarA) See HEIGHT Phr 2. **5.2 not pick your mouth/teeth** *neg vb phr* (Angu, Bdos, Guyn, Tbgo) [AF] ‖ *not unpick your teeth* (Trin) To say absolutely nothing; to give no reply; [by extension] to make no comment that can be used as information. *You see how people could stand where they are, and humbug you, and confuse you, and make you get yourself in trouble, and you don't even have to pick your teeth to them?*—PeL (79.12.07, p.2, Dear Christine) **5.3 pick a lime** *vb phr* (Trin) [AF—Joc] See LIME² Phr 4.1 [Prob a Joc pun on *lime,* the citrus fruit and LIME² 'loafing'] **5.4 pick a needle without eye** *vb phr* (Baha) [AF—Joc/Derog] See NEEDLE Phr 3. **5.5 pick at (sb)** *vb phr* (Bdos, Guyn) [IF] To continually find fault with (sb); to nag (sb). **5.6 pick fares** *vb phr* (Bdos) [AF—Joc] ‖ *bump* 2 (Baha) [Of a woman] To be a prostitute; to solicit men. *The witness said that he asked her what she was doing there at that time of the night, and she replied that she was looking for money. P— said that he understood her to mean that she was 'hustling or picking fares'.*—AdV (89.10.17, p.5) **5.7 pick sb's mouth** *vb phr* (CarA) [AF] ‖ *pull sb's tongue* (Jmca) ‖ *take sb's tongue* (Dmca, StLu) To encourage a person, by means of tempting conversation or gossip, to reveal private, personal, or secret information. *They only want you to drink with them so they can pick your mouth about what's going on in the office upstairs.*—(Trin) [Cp *EDD pick* vb⁴ 10. (wCy) 'to worm out a secret'. Also, as base of a possible calque, Twi *ti n'ano* 'to scratch open/pick open his/her mouth'] □ See also PICK YOUR TEETH Phr 5.14 **5.8 pick up a nail** *vb phr* (Antg, Gren, Guyn) [AF—Joc] See NAIL Phr **5.9 pick up for (sb)** *vb phr* (CarA) [IF] ‖ TAKE UP FOR (SB) (CarA) *You see the Arabs*

feel that Anwar Sadat was picking up for Israel and that's why they kill him.—(Tbgo) **5.10 pick up sb's fire-rage** *vb phr* (Antg, Bdos, Guyn) [AF] See FIRE-RAGE Phr 2.1 **5.11 pick up with (sb)** *vb phr* (CarA) [IF] To begin a close association with (sb) usu in an unexpected way; to begin a sexual affair with (sb); (SE) to take up with (sb). *From last Christmas up to recently, my husband and I were having awful rows over a woman he picked up with then. He even struck me one night for her.*—NaT (76.06.13, p.18, Dear Christine) **5.12 pick up your foot/heels** *vb phr* (Bdos, Guyn, Jmca) [AF] ‖ PUT FOOT (Angu, etc) See FOOT Phr 2.12 *The white gentl'man didn't know what to do and pick up his heels and run like a ball of fire all the way home.*—LICMS:14 [Cp *DAFL* Twi *ma vb* 8. (Fante) *ma wo naŋ so* 'lift your feet, i.e make haste'. Cp also many CE ‖ phrs with FOOT Phr 2.12; also SE *take to your heels*] **5.13 pick up yourself; pick yourself up** *refl vb phr* (ECar) [AF/IF—Derog] ‖ HICE YOURSELF (Guyn, etc) *Do you mean to tell me if I reside in Silver Sands and I want to make representation to a registering officer I have to pick up myself and go all the way down to Sargeants Village? This is what you call civil service sense.*—Bdos (Hd, 73.03.29, p.242) [A prob calque from W Afr langs. Cp Yoruba *gbe ara rę (to pick up body your)* 'to pick up yourself (with connotation of offensive deliberateness)'—(pers info, K. Ọmọ-tọṣọ)] □ The phr is more often used to imply that the speaker is denouncing the act that he/she is reporting. **5.14 pick your teeth to/with (sb)** *vb phr* (Bdos) [AF—Joc] To indulge in petty gossip with (sb). *Days come and go, and not a friend to pick my teet' with, or swap two ideas.*—HFGA:114 (Austin Clarke)

pick·er (pick·a) *n* (Trin) See PIKA

pick-neck fowl *n phr* (TkCa) ‖ BARE-NECK FOWL (Bdos, etc)

pick·ney (pi(c)k·ni(e), pic·nee) [pɪkni] *n* (CarA) [AF] A young child of Black (or E Indian) parentage; [by extension] any young child (esp a poor one). **a.** *Grandmothers 'took in' disgraced grand-daughters, runaway grandsons, parentless picknees; thousands of Barbadian children were and are raised by their grandmothers.*—AdV (88.11.15, p.17) **b.** *And a good word too, for the Odeon cinema for showing children's films over the past two weeks. My small fry had a great time with 'Bambi' last week and 'Gnomemobile' this week. In a time when nobody seems to remember that pickney need entertainment too.... It was a treat.*—WeG (75.04.15, p.15) **c.** *As soon as the name was known people nodded their heads in gloom. 'Rampas' they said, 'some thiefing coolieman picnie! Ah-we go ha fu watch any ting ah-we have from de time da boy can toddle.'*—LDSS:1 **d.** *The uppity young woman / Who have two bastard pikni / For two different man / And have a belly for a third.*—YFOC:7 [< Pg *pequenino* 'little boy, little one' with reduction by apocope. The term would have been particularly current in the early Pg control of slaving on the Slave Coast, and brought to the *CarA* by the slaves themselves; hence its pervasive occurrence, survival, and variants] □ Many variations are found throughout older and current writings: *pi-caninny, pickinigger, piki-niega, pig-nigger, pickneh, pickinny*, etc. (See DJE *pickney* for a historical list). Note, as in cits b, d, that the term is often used as a collective pl, reflecting CarA Cr folk influence.

pick-up *n* **1.** (Bdos) (Loose name for a) MAXI-TAXI or MINI-BUS. **2.** (Bdos, Trin) A small delivery truck, sometimes mounted with an iron frame to facilitate the transportation of lumber. [Cp *W3 pickup* n 7. *pickup truck* 'a light truck having an open body with low sides and tailboard mounted usu on a passenger car chassis'] □ Though evid IAE, the term is loosely used with variant senses in CE.

pick-ups *n* (Bdos, Dmca, Mrat, Nevs, StLu, Trin) ‖ *litti* (Guyn) ‖ *stones* (Gren) ‖ *tikitok* (StLu) ‖ *trié* (Trin) A children's game similar to the game called (IAE) 'jacks', played with pebbles, seeds, or small marbles. [*Pick-up*, by functional vb > n shift (from the need for skill in picking up the scattered items) + /s/ by analogy, as in *rounders*, etc]

pick·y hair/head; **pick.y-pick.y hair/head** /ı'ı2'2ı/ *n phr* (Baha, BrVi, Gren, Guyn, Jmca, Nevs) [*AF—Joc*] ‖ *black-pepper grains* (Angu, Guyn, Jmca) ‖ *gritty hair* (Angu) ‖ *grubby hair* (StVn) ‖ *nappy hair/head; peasy hair* (Baha) **1.** A Black person's hair (often a boy's) that is naturally sparse and tightly curled in tiny balls, allowing much of the skull to be seen. *He got picky-picky hair. Nothing can[t] make it grow more than that.*—(Guyn) **2.** A Black person's hair that is short, tough, and untidy looking. □ See also BAD HAIR

pi·cong [pikɒŋ] *n* (ECar) **1.** (Trin) [Carnival] A spontaneous, verbal battle in rhymed song between two or more contending CALYPSONIANS, in wh the wit and humorous impact of a contender's improvization determines his supremacy; it is a major item of CALYPSO WAR staged in TENTS. *He described the picong era: 'In those days you did'nt have to be an invited guest to go and perform in a calypso tent. You just went in and declared war. You had to extemporise right there and then. Once I was sandwiched between two men whom I consider two of the greatest calypsonians ever—Lord Executor and Senior Inventor.'*—ExP (72.02.04, p.13) [< *CSESD* CarA Sp *picón* adj 'mocking' < Sp *picar* 'to prick, peck at'. Prob also infl, esp in pronunc, by Fr *piquant* 'spicy'] **2.** (Gren, StLu, Tbgo, Trin) [By extension] [*AF*] ‖ FATIGUE (Trin) *When daddy Holder bought a piano for his family, Geoffrey recalled, some of his friends were ready with their picong: 'But Mr Holder you buying piano and you can't even pay your rent.'*—TrG (73.06.21) **3.** PHRASES **3.1 give (sb) picong; throw picong** *vb phrs* (Tbgo, Trin) [*AF—Joc*] *Boy, every time some delegate gave them a picong, they retorted by*

saying 'Yes, go and tell Moko that', or 'Moko would like to hear such things.'—MoK (72.08.30, p.10) **3.2 take picong** *vb phr* (Tbgo, Trin) [*AF—Joc*] To withstand continued teasing. *If you ca[n't] take picong yo[u] mustn[t] go in politics in this country.*—(Trin)

pic·ture *n* PHRASES **Picture for/to picture!** *n phr* (TkCa) ‖ *Picture like a picture!* (Guyn) ‖ *Picture or no picture!* (Bdos, Jmca, StLu) ‖ *Picture picture!* (Gren) A children's game played with a book in wh pictures appear on some pages, the opponent being asked to guess, by saying 'Yes picture!' or 'No picture!' whether or not a picture will be there when the book is opened haphazardly.

piece¹ *n* (ECar) [*IF*] [Usu as second element of a compound] A small plot of ground or a field in wh something useful grows or is grown; hence *bamboo-, cane-, cocoa-, grass-, yam-* (etc) *piece*. [Cp *EDD piece* sb 9. (Sc, Irel, Eng, Amer) 'a field or close of land, esp arable land']

piece² (CarA) [*AF—Joc*] **1.** A woman (as an object of sexual desire). **2.** Casual sexual intercourse with a woman. **3.** PHRASES **3.1 beg/chase/get/look for a piece** *vb phrs* (CarA) [*AF—Joc/Vul*] [Of a man] To seek (or obtain) casual sexual satisfaction. **3.2 give (sb) a piece** *vb phr* (CarA) See GIVE¹ Phr 18. **3.3 piece of flesh/skin/tail** *n phrs* (CarA) [*AF—Joc/Vul*] A sexually desirable woman. *I meeting that piece of skin tonight, you know. And then, as if it not very important, 'she waiting for me by Charing Cross Station'.*—STLL:68

Pi·erre-Lou·is *n* (Dmca) See MANGO-PARLUI

Pi·er·rot Gre·nade [piɛro grɒna·d ~ pɛwo gri nad] *n phr* (Trin) [Carnival] A male masquerader dressed in one or other distinctive type of clownish costume (variously made up of rags and bells, pieces of jute bags, priest-like cape, wire mask, etc) and always carrying a whip; such masqueraders engage each other in verbal battles, formerly in French Creole, but now by recitations from literature, the use of long words, and PICONG. [< Fr *pierrot* 'clown' + *Grenade* 'Grenada'; this type of masquerading is so labelled in *Trin* as having been introduced there from *Gren* where, however, the prototype 'Pierrot' has disappeared] □ Cp SHORT-KNEE (Gren).

pig *n* PHRASE **bring (your) pigs to a fine market** *vb phr* (Bdos) [*IF—Joc*] See BRING Phr 6.1

pig-ap·ple *n* (Jmca) ‖ JUMBIE-SOURSOP (Antg, etc)

pig-breast¹ *n* (Nevs) [*IF*] ‖ CORK-SCREW¹ (Bdos, etc) *Even men now put their hair in pig-breast style when preparing to set it in an afro.*—Nevs (Ms) [From resemblance of each tied clump to the size and shape of a pig's breast]

pig-breast[2] *vb tr* (Nevs) [*IF*] ‖ CORK-SCREW[2] (Bdos, etc) *She had her hair all pig-breast up from morning, to set it for the dance that night.*—Nevs (Ms)

pi·geon-pea(s)* *n* (*pl*) (CarA) ‖ *congo peas* (CayI) ‖ *green peas* (Bdos, Gren, Guyn, Trin) ‖ *gungo-peas* (Belz, CayI, Jmca) Tender, yellowish-green peas borne five or six together in short, sticky, green segmented pods wh hang in small clusters on a bushy, green shrub about 6 ft tall; the peas, wh grow abundantly, are the most widely used in *CarA* cooking; *Cajanus cajan* (*Papilionaceae*). □ Commonly referred to in many places simply as *peas*, for ex in such *CarA* dishes as *dove peas, peas and rice, stew peas*, etc.

pig-face *n* (Guyn) ‖ HOG-FEATURES (Bdos, Gren)

pig-foot; **pig-knuck.le(s)** *n* (CarA) Pig's trotters, used in a number of dishes in CarA cooking, esp SOUSE. *Well Brackley in fact settle down nicely ... in Ladbroke Grove, with ... the old Portobello road near by to buy rations like saltfish and red beans and pig foot and pig tail.*—SWOS:139 □ Cp note at PIG-TAIL.

pig-tail *n* (CarA) The pickled tail of the pig, a regular ingredient in CarA cooking. **a.** *The super-markets sell you well packaged pig-tail nowadays.*—(StVn) **b.** *It's chowmein, pork-and-beef pepperpot, oxtail soup, cookup with salt-beef and pigtail.*—SBB:30 □ Normally there is no pl -s, as it is conceived as a mass-noun like other foods (note cit (b)).

pi·ka (**pick·a, pick·er**) *n* (Gren, Tbgo, Trin) ‖ CASHA 2. (Nevs, etc) **a.** *Don['t] climb pika tree why / Pika go juk you.*—Trin (Folk song) **b.** *... and never like these rose trees with pickers all over them.*—JJM:67 [Fr Cr < Fr *piquant* 'sharp' (in ref to the thorns) + loss of nasalization, whence the folk etym spelling PICKER]

pi·ka tree *n phr* (Gren, Tbgo, Trin) ‖ CASHA 1(i) (Nevs, etc)

pi·ké (**pi·que**) [pike] (Crcu, Gren, StLu, Tbgo, Trin) A drum dance involving vigorous pelvic thrusts towards each other by a male and female pair of dancers in a ring of others who accompany the drum rhythm with call and refrain in French Creole; it is a traditional folk dance of some rural communities maintaining African roots. *Mention must be made of two of the members over 60 years old who travelled with the group—vivacious pique dancer Nelly Po and drummer Joseph Legir.*—TrG (72.10.22, p.1) [Fr Cr < Fr *piquer* 'to prick, stick, insert']

pi·lau (**pilao**) *n* (CarA) See PELAU.

pi·lot-fish *n* (Jmca) ‖ SERGEANT-MAJOR (Baha, etc)

pi·man-zwa·zo (**pi·ment-(z')oi·seau**) ['p imã-zwazo] *n* (Dmca) ‖ BIRD-PEPPER (CarA) [Fr Cr < Fr *piment* 'pepper' + /z/ (by misplaced juncture) + *oiseau* 'bird']

pi·men·to *n* **1.** (CarA) ‖ ALLSPICE (CarA) *One of the world's most famous tree species is Jamaica's own native pimento or allspice, so named because its flavour and aroma suggest a combination of cloves, nutmeg, cinnamon and pepper. Although it has been introduced widely throughout the tropics, it is said to do best at home in Jamaica.*—Jan 82/ 9, p.28 **2.** (Belz) ‖ SILVER-THATCH PALM (Baha, Trin)

pi·ment-(z')oi·seau *n* (Dmca) See PIMAN-ZWAZO

pim·pler (**plim·pler**) ['pɪmplʌ ~ 'plɪmplʌ] *n* (Bdos, Guyn) ‖ CASHA 2. (Nevs, etc) [< *OED pinpillow* 2. 'The Prickly Pear: so called from its thick stems beset with spines' + earliest cit from 1750 Hughes *Barbadoes* 'The prickly Pimploe hedge ...'. Then by assimilation > *plimplo* + shift of sense noted (*CGBD, 5:80*) 'But the word has now come to mean a thorn or prickle, and is usually pronounced *plimploe* or *plimpler*']

pim·pler-palm *n* (Guyn) ‖ GRI-GRI[2] (PALM) (Trin) □ See also GROU-GROU (Gren, *etc*).

pin *n* PHRASES **1. can't have pins with (sb)** *neg vb phr* (Bdos) [*AF/IF*] To be no match for (sb); to be unable to cope with or outsmart (sb). **2. not raise (a) pin** *neg vb phr* (Gren) [*AF/IF*] See RAISE[1] Phr 6.1.

pinch·er *n* (Baha) ‖ GUNDY (CarA) [Blend of *pinch* + *pincer(s)*, the SE name for these claws]

pin·da[1] (**pin·dar, pin·der**) [pɪnda] *n* (Belz, Jmca, USVI) Peanut(s). [*DJE* cites Kongo (Angola) *mpinda* 'ground-nut']

pin·da[2] [pɪnda] *n* (Guyn, Trin) [Indic] A cooked lump of rice powder, honey, and milk, used in ceremonial offerings, esp by MADRASIS, after a burial. [Hin *pindaa* 'lump of cooked rice' used in this way]

pin·dar-cake *n* (Jmca) ‖ NUT-CAKE (Bdos, etc) *For there were many Free Church people at the market, some selling ..., coconut drop, banana fritters, ginger nut and pindar cakes and suchlike titbits that they had fixed up out of the raw stuff the country people had brought down and were selling back to them.*—RWIN:41 (C. McKay) [< PINDA[1] + cake]

pine·(ap·ple)* *n* (CarA) ‖ *zanana* (Dmca, StKt) The large edible fruit of the ground-plant *Ananas comosus* (*Bromeliaceae*), wh is a native of So America. *Also [the Indians] brought to us hens, sweet potatoes, and pines, which we bought for beads ... and other trifles. / ... Their pines be of the bigness of two fists, the outside whereof is of the making of a pine-apple, but it is soft like the* *rind of a cucumber, and the inside eateth like an apple; but it is more delicious than any sweet apple sugared.*—PVES:29 (John Sparke's 'Narrative of Master John Hawkins' Second Voyage ... begun in A.D. 1564'. The cit refers to Hawkins's landing at Cumana, on the Spanish Main.) [*Pineapple*, as in the cit, refers to the orig item of that name, a pine-cone or (inedible) 'fruit' of the European pine tree (see *OED Pine-apple* 1.) It is this resemblance helped, no doubt, by the firm apple-like texture of the So American fruit, that gave it its name] □ Commonly referred to as *pine(s)* in CE, whence there are many compounds *pine-drink, pine-jam, pine-tart*, etc.

pine-drink *n* (CarA) A very sweet drink made from the juice of the ripe pineapple or from an infusion of its skin peelings.

pine-tart *n* (CarA) A pastry with a filling of grated or jellied pineapple.

ping-pong[1] *n* (Trin) [*IF*] ‖ LEAD-PAN (Trin) *There are many different kinds of pan now in use. The leading pans which supply the melody are the Ping Pong or soprano pans, with twenty-eight to thirty-two notes, embracing both the diatonic and chromatic scales.*—ACTT:108 [Echoic name, from the high-pitched note made on the PAN] □ The name tends to be replaced currently by the formal LEAD-PAN.

ping-pong[2] (Bdos) [*AF/IF*] A snapshot or passport size photograph of a person's face.

ping·wing* (pin·guin) [pɪŋwɪŋ ~ pɪŋgwɪn] *n* (Belz, Jmca, USVI) A shrub about 6 ft high, looking like a wild variety of pineapple plant; its blade-like leaves are edged with stout prickles and form a stiff open rosette protecting its clusters of yellowish, ovoid fruit that are edible when cooked; the plant is used to provide fences, and the leaves are dried for use in thatching and handicraft; *Bromelia pinguin (Bromeliaceae).* [Cp *SDGA piñuela*, name of this plant in Cuba and Central Amer; also poss Sp *piña* 'pineapple' + *SDGA guin*, Carib name in Cuba of a type of reed. The compound 'piña-guin' may describe a 'reed(-like)' pine']

pink-eye *n* (Jmca) ‖ RED-EYE 1. (Bdos)

pink-sage *n* (Baha) ‖ BLACK-SAGE 2. (CarA)

pin·ny(-win·ny) *adj* (Bdos, etc) See PEENY-WEENY

pin-seine *n* (Guyn) A fishing net with a very fine mesh; it is set vertically on sticks and weighted at the bottom, and stands in running water to trap FINE SHRIMPS. [Folk-name for *penaid-net*, one for catching *Penaiedae spp.* See FINE-SHRIMP]

pint-and-a-half *n* (Bdos) [*IF*] ‖ BIG-BOTTLE (Guyn)

pi·ong (pe·ong, py·ong) [piɒŋ ~ pyɒŋ] *n* (Tbgo, Trin) [*AF*] A person who has a keen interest in sth, such as a particular food, game, etc; an enthusiast. [Prob via Fr Cr < 17C Fr *pion* 'excessive drinking' (see Cotgrave), wh comes into mod Fr slang = 'hard drinker']

P.I.P. *abbr* (CarA) [*AF—Joc*] A sycophant; a person who supports the 'party in power' (hence the abbr) for his/her own well-being. [By Joc analogy with many abbr names of CarA political parties, exs P.N.P, P.P.P, P.U.P etc]

pipe[1] *n* (CarA) [*IF*] 1. Any source of piped domestic water, whether a public standpipe or a tap in a house. *'But please tell the people when the pipe is going off so that we could at least store up water to tide us through the time when the pipe is off,' he explained. / The area is serviced by a water vehicle from the Barbados Water Authority during the disruption of service.*—AdV (84.04.01, p.1) 2. [By extension] A tap. *You can't turn off that pipe properly, it needs a washer or something.*—(Jmca)

pipe[2] PHRASE **crapaud smoke your pipe** *id phr* (Dmca, etc) [*AF—Joc*] See CRAPAUD Phr.

pipe-gun *n* (Bdos) A home-made shotgun the barrel of wh is a piece of galvanized piping. □ Cp FILOTO

pipe-or·gan cac·tus *n phr* (ViIs) ‖ DILDO 1. (CarA)

pipe-wa·ter *n* (CarA) Any water drawn from a domestic tap (in a house or yard) or from a standpipe; piped water. □ The term connotes water of an inferior quality in some territories.

pi·pi·ri (pi·pi·ree); **pi.pi.rite** [pipiri(t)] *n* (Dmca, Gren, StVn) One of a few varieties of flycatcher birds, the commonest being a yellow-chested and a grey with whitish underparts; they grow to about 9 ins and make a cry of wh the name is imitative; some are said to be playful, others aggressive; *Tyrannus spp.*

pi·que *n* (Crcu, etc) See PIKÉ

pis·i·ette [pisiɛt] *n* (StLu) ‖ ANCHOVY (StLu, Trin) [Perh Fr root *pisci* + *ette*, 'little fish']

piss-a-bed *n* 1. (Guyn, Jmca) [*AF*] ‖ WILD COFFEE 1. (Guyn, etc) [From the use of an infusion of the seeds of this plant as a folk-medicine to cure bed-wetting in children or for kidney complaints in adults] 2. (Antg) ‖ CARPET-DAISY (Bdos)

piss·(in(g))-tail; **piss.y(-tail)** *adj* (Baha, BrVi, Gren, Guyn, Jmca, Trin) [*AF—Derog/Vul*] 1. [Esp of a young person] Disrespectful or bumptious. 2. [By extension] Officious and of little financial worth or social standing. [A metaph ref to the quality of a mere toddler who is still wetting himself]

piss·pa·rade [pɪspareˑd] *vb* (Bdos) [*AF—Joc*] To delight in showing contempt for or causing the embarrassment of others; to vent anger (verbally). *Christine, I can't even talk to a boy to let them know, for they will just piss-parade on me.*—NaT (76.02.22, p.22, Dear Christine) [Blend of SE *vbs piss up* (Vul) + *parade*]

pis·sy-bush *n phr* (USVI) [*AF*] ‖ WILD COFFEE 1. (Guyn, etc) [As for PISS-A-BED 1.]

pis·ta·cle (pis·tar(c)·kle) [pɪstaˑkl] *n* (ViIs) [*AF—Joc*] 1. A foolish confusion; an uproarious muddle. *But like they can['t] agree over nothing, and everybody shouting—what a pistarckle!*— (USVI) 2. [By extension] A confused idiot; sb who makes a fool of himself or is made a fool of. *That's why everybody was watching me so. They know I didn't have on my own clothes. Through you they make pistakle out of me.*—PKKK:32 [Perh a Joc blend of *piss* + *spectacle*, (as in SE 'make a spectacle of yourself'). Cp PISS-PARADE]

pit *n* (CarA) The area of cheapest seating, on benches immediately in front of the screen, in a cinema. *The pit made so much noise in the love scenes that you couldn't hear the words.*—(Guyn) □ BrE *the pit* is either where the orchestra sit or a respectable seating area behind the stalls. The connotation is quite the contrary in CE.

pitch-ap·ple* *n* (ViIs) ‖ *false mammee* (USVI) A tough-skinned, yellowish-green fruit the size of a child's fist wh, when ripe, yields a yellow latex that hardens and blackens and can be used like pitch (hence the name) to caulk boats; this fruit is borne on a tough, parasitic, spreading plant with aerial roots that may strangle the host tree or trap large boulders (whence another name *strangler fig*); *Clusia rosea (Guttiferae)*.

pitch-oil *n* (Gren, Tbgo, Trin) Kerosene oil. *The children ran to the kitchen and seized the pitch-oil Shama had bought for the lamps.*— NHMB:428 ['The name derives from the era when oil was in fact extracted from the pitch of the Trinidad Pitch Lake'—*OT3:16*] □ Hence compounds *pitch-oil drum, lamp, pan/tin*, 'kerosene drum, kerosene lamp', etc.

pitch·y-patch·y¹ [pɪči-pači] *adj* (Guyn, Jmca) [Of clothes or sb's appearance] Ragged; patched up in several places. [Cp *EDD pitch* sb³ (Cth) 'a dilapidated or badly mended dress; only used in connexion with patch' ... Hence (compounds) (3) *pitchy-patchy* 'untidy, clumsily mended']

Pitch·y Patch·y² *n phr* (Jmca) A JUNKANOO figure. (See cit). *The most flamboyant and athletic of the performers is 'Pitchy Patchy', who dances with rapid, small jumps, forming large circular patterns. The shoulder movement, in combination with sweeping arm extensions, is accentuated by Pitchy Patchy's costume which is made of layered strips of brightly coloured fabric. Although this character appears in the Savanna-la-Mar troupe in pairs Pitchy Patchy dances alone, sometimes running in and out of the crowd of onlookers. Some research has shown that contemporary oral tradition claims that Pitchy Patchy's costume is based on the leafy costumes employed as camouflage by the Maroons during guerilla warfare.*—Jan 82/ 9, p.5 [Prob by functional adj > n shift of PITCHY-PATCHY¹, but note last para of cit]

pi·ti·kwòt (pe·tit-quart) [pɪtikwɒt] *n* (Trin) A half-pint bottle (of liquor, esp of rum). *Ah man like me who does go in de Oval / With me money in me side-pocket, / Ah petit-quart in me back pocket, / An' me two hand swingin' free.*— KTT:27 [Fr Cr < Fr *petit quart* 'little quarter (of measure)']

Pi·ton [pitɔ̃] *n* (StLu) 1. One of two cone-shaped mountains rising some 2500 ft out of the sea, dominating the approaches to Castries and regarded as symbolic of St Lucia. [Fr *piton* 'mountain peak'] 2. PHRASE 2.1 (have to) carry the Piton on your back *vb phr* (StLu) To have an impossible(-looking) task to perform.

pi·war·ri *n* (Guyn) See PAIWARRI.

pit·pan *n* (Belz) ‖ *bateau* 2. (Belz) A square-ended, flat-bottomed river-boat, used as the sole river transport in early days (Belz) but now mostly for amusement in regattas. *Pitpans are punt-like craft hollowed out of a single log and carry up to thirty paddlers; when a pitpan is sawn in half lengthways and a wide plank inserted it becomes a batteau with up to forty paddlers. Both craft are fast disappearing.*—ABSBH:16

place *n* PHRASES 1. be out of your place *vb phr* (Nevs) [*IF*] ‖ GET BESIDE YOURSELF (CarA) 2. find your place *vb phr* (Trin) [*AF—Derog*] See FIND Phr 2.1 3. out-of-place *adj* (CarA) (See separate entry) 4. pass your place *vb phr* (Jmca, StVn) [*IF*] ‖ GET BESIDE YOURSELF (CarA)

plague with (a sick·ness) *vb phr* (Baha) [*IF*] ‖ TROUBLE WITH (A SICKNESS) (CarA) *I's now bout to tell yinna how wen I plague with de heart trouble, I gawn to one doctor to see bout it.*—JBJ:86 [< SE *be plagued by/with* 'be pestered by/with'. See CE PASSIVITY in this Dictionary]

Plai(e)! (plax) [plaɪ] *excl ideoph* (CarA, esp Bdos) [*AF*] See PRAX

plaits *n pl* (CayI) ‖ CORN-ROW¹ (CarA)

pla·nass¹ (pla·narse¹) [planaˑs] *n* (Gren, StKt, Tbgo, Trin) A blow with the flat of the blade of a CUTLASS or machete. *'You see these young people today?' Balgobin raged. 'I should of given him a good planarse,' and he swept his cutlass around, indicating how he should have beaten Pusher with the flat of the blade.*—SPOC:21 [< Sp *planazo* 'a blow with the flat of a sword']

pla·nass² (pla·narse²) [planaˑs] *vb* (BrVi, Gren, Jmca, StKt, Tbgo, Trin) To strike with the flat of the blade of a CUTLASS or machete. *The evidence continued that he raised the cutlass as if to chop her, and, instinctively the wife held on resulting in a cut on her hand, and, as she released the blade, proceeded to 'planass' the wife about the body. She is alleged to have fled to a nearby house and hid under the bed.*—ToR (76.08.22, p.3) [By functional n > vb shift of PLANASS[1]]

plant *vb tr PHRASE* **If I plant you, you goin(g)/ will grow?** *id phr* (CarA) [*IF*] If I ask you a personal favour, will you do it for me? *'Tiger, I want you to promise me one thing. If I plant you, you will grow?' / 'Well, it depends. What is it?'* —SABS:191 [Translation of a Nupe prov: *Mi ga dzo we wa nyiṇ?* (= *I if plant you you-will grow?*)]

plan·tain* *n* (CarA) ‖ *banana* 2. (Neth) ‖ *banane*[1] (StLu) The fruit of a tree of the family *Musaceae* wh matures hard and with a green skin; it is much larger than a banana, and is cooked as a vegetable. See, as separate entries BLUGGO, HORN/HORSE P., MOKO P., WAIKA P., YELLOW P.. [Prob via a Sp corruption of a *CarA* or So Amer native name. Cp *BDFC* Carib 'grosses bananes' (= big bananas) *ballatanna*. The commonly supposed source Sp *plátano*, 'plane tree' is unreliable] □ In *Neth* and some places some people use the name BANANA for this vegetable. (See Notes at BANANA, FIG.) In *Bdos* PLANTAIN = overripe or YELLOW PLANTAIN, the only form marketed.

plan·tain-flour *n* (Guyn) Meal obtained by pounding sun-dried slices of green plantains, used esp for making a nutritious porridge for infants. □ See CONGATAY.

plan·tain-por·ridge *n* (Jmca) ‖ CONGATAY (Belz, etc)

plan·tain-water *n* (Guyn) ‖ BANANA-WATER (Jmca)

plan·ta·tion [plantešʌn] *n* (CarA) *PHRASE* **have a plantation mentality** *vb phr* (CarA) [*Derog*] [Esp of a Black person] To be ready to accept or rationalize a White person's wish or point of view as correct; [by extension] to consider persons of lighter complexion as better or more important people. [A ref to the White supremacy and mulatto hierarchy of the colonial Sugar Plantation era]

plant·er-class *n* (CarA) 1. [Hist] ‖ *plantocracy* (CarA) The totality of European families owning colonial sugar plantations (esp in the era of slavery) and sharing common interests in their social supremacy and political dominance. 2. [By extension] Persons of mainly European descent, regarded as a group with understood loyalties, who have inherited property or other ancestral legacies and currently maintain attitudes of social superiority.

plant-hop·per *n* (Guyn) [Rice Ind] A small insect wh damages the rice plant by sucking the plant juices and laying eggs in the leaves, discolouring them and retarding plant growth; *Sogatodes orizicola.* □ Hence **plant-hopper disease**.

plant·o·cra·cy *n* (CarA) [Hist] ‖ PLANTER-CLASS 1. (CarA) *If you look at the matter carefully, you will see how many of the plantocracy and how many of the others were in Parliament at the time. I went to one of the old members of the plantocracy and he had a complete set of the Laws of Barbados bound in a beautiful green colour.*—Bdos (Hd, 75.01.28, p.4482) [An analogical blend < *plant-(ers)* + *(arist)ocracy*] □ Hence also **plantocrat**, a member of such a class.

pla-pla *n* (Brbu) ‖ LEAF-OF-LIFE (Bdos, etc)

plas·ter *n PHRASE* **have a plaster for every sore** *vb phr* [*AF/IF*] To have an excuse for every problem; to have an explanation for every fault, flaw, accusation, etc.

pla·tin(e) [platin~platɪn] *n* 1. (Gren, StVn, Tbgo, Trin) ‖ BAKING-IRON (Trin) **a.** *Cassava bread is made from grated cassava and baked on a platin or baking sheet or in a pot.*—Tbgo (Ms, W. James) **b.** *Heat a baking iron, the kind known locally as a platine or a heavy fry pan.*—ViN (73.12.29, p.10) [Fr. Cp *DECG* Guad Cr *platin* 'Grande plaque de fonte circulaire sur laquelle on fait cuire la farine de manioc'] 2. (Gren) A large iron basin or COPPER, used in former times for boiling sugar but now used for making CASSAVA-BREAD or FARINE.

play[1] *vb intr* (ECar) [In many phrs referring to some form of personal behaviour] *PHRASE* 1. **play (a) (big) man/woman** *vb phr* (CarA) [*AF*] [Of a child or young person] To behave with the boldness or liberty of an adult; to resist or reject control by your parent or guardian. **a.** *Parents also use the phrase ... sarcastically about a son who is still living with them but who is 'behavin' disorderly, disobedient to parents, playin' big man'.*—RICF:88 **b.** *When I sat down and tried to tell my mother about this she said that I was playing too much woman and so I am afraid to say any more.*—ExP (73.04.29, p.12, Dear Diana) 2. **play bad; play you bad** *vb phr* (CarA) [*AF*] [Often of children's behaviour] Make a show of aggressiveness and rudeness; [of grown-ups] make a mere show of defiance. **a.** *He asked her why she followed him, she took up a stone, she advanced, he stepped backwards, she said, 'All you playing bad' and she struck him twice on his head.*—DeM(SK) (65.03.13, p.10) **b.** *He playin[g] he bad, he going get one beating one o[f] these days, you go see.*—(Gren) □ (Cp MAKE BAD PLAY. See PLAY[2] Phr 1. 3. **play big (big)** *vb phr* (CarA) [*AF—Joc*] To pretend to be more worthy, able, bold, etc than you really are. *When the police was there she frighten like hell, but playin[g] big big, she tell them to come in and start tellin[g] one of them how she know his mother.*—(Guyn) 4.

play Carnival vb phr (Gren, Trin) ‖ PLAY MAS (ECar) *'Oh God, Master Alan, is you really?'* / *'Of course it's me. Who else you think it is?'* / *'Well, you frighten me so bad. I didn't know you does play Carnival.'*—AKM:16 **5. play fast with sth** vb phr (Guyn, StKt) [IF] See FAST Phr 5.4 **6. play fobler** vb phr (TkCa) [AF—Joc] To pretend ignorance or innocence of sth. [Perh related to OED fob vb[1] 'to delude, trick, take in'. Cp OED fobbery nonce-wd 'something of the nature of a pretence'] **7. play France (with sb)** vb phr (Gren, Guyn) [AF/IF] To quarrel violently (with sb); to give (sb) hell. **8. play great** vb phr (CarA) [IF] ‖ **play social** (Trin) To put on airs; to be snobbish without being of any notable social standing. *I know you didn't change. I keep telling Foster that. But he say you playing great and don't have no time for nobody else ... Christine stopped before she said too much.*— HMCH:124 **9. play mas** [ple ma·s] vb phr (ECar) **(i)** ‖ **play Carnival** (Gren, Trin) ‖ **run mas** (Dmca) To participate in CARNIVAL, formerly as one of a group and in disguise, now in costume and usu as a member of a BAND, joining freely in street revelry. **a.** *Although you hear me talking like this don't think I could go and jump up in a band, you know. Or play any mas. Oh no, I won't play the fool like that. But I mean I could enjoy looking on.*—AKM:50 **b.** *But if the costumes are made with quarter-inch iron bars and Number Ten galvanised wire, then those costumes must be too heavy to be worn for any length of time, much less to dance and play mas' in.*—ViN (73.02.03, p.4) [< play 'masque' 'be a masquerader' < Fr masque, 1. 'mask', and formerly also, 2. 'masquerader'] □ See MAS. The forms **play mas'** (with raised comma to recognise its origin) and (rarely) **play masque** also occur. The form **play mass**, occasionally found, is regarded as false. **(ii)** (ECar) [By extension] To behave riotously and/or irresponsibly. **a.** *Early on Monday morning last a band of hooligans playing mas', completely smashed the glass panes on two ... display windows ... / It is understood that the stone-throwing marauders who demolished a bowser owned by the businessman ... also stoned him while at the wheel of his motorcar.*—WeI (65.03.07, p.6) **b.** *Industrial disputes in the Telephone Company and the Postal Services are reportedly 'playing mas' with the local business community. / Bills, cheques and other documents are being held up in the mail and this is further aggravated with a breakdown in telephone communication.*—TrG (74.08.07, p.18) **9.1 play mas and fraid/be afraid of powder** vb phr (Gren, Trin) [AF/ IF—Joc] To look for pleasure, benefits, etc, without accepting risks; to play with fire and be afraid of being burned. *Listen here now. You cannot play 'mas' and be afraid of powder. If you love the man that much, then go after him. Women have been doing that for thousands of years now, and there's nothing to be ashamed of.*—SuP (74.12.08, p.14) [From the old practice at Carnival in wh certain types of masqueraders used to throw flour or talcum powder on other masqueraders and spectators] **10. play ole mas** vb phr (Dmca, Gren, StLu, Tbgo, Trin) See OLE MAS Phr 3.1

11. play social vb phr (Trin) [IF] ‖ PLAY GREAT (CarA) **12. play the payass** vb phr (Belz) [AF] See PAYASS[1] Phr **13. play with yourself** vb phr (CarA) [AF—Vul] To masturbate. □ Also used as imper to dismiss sb insultingly.

play[2] n PHRASE **1. make bad-play** vb phr (Bdos) [AF] To make a show of boldness intended to impress an opponent. *When cross-examined by defence counsel, S— said that while she was dancing, M— had told S— that he would beat him if he made 'bad play'. She said further that when they were downstairs, M—... kept 'going up to him wanting to fight.'*—AdN (72.01.11, p.1) [Prob a ref to the stance taken by a contestant in STICK-FIGHTING. Cp sense 2.] **2. make your play** vb phr (CarA) [IF] **(i)** To make the first move in a contest. [Orig a stick-fighter's first move, often a feint, to draw his opponent into battle] **(ii)** [By extension, of a man] To make a decisive show of desire for close friendship (with a particular woman).

play-play[1] n (CarA) [AF—Joc] [Child-talk] Fun; make-believe; a pretence made in jest. *A didn['t] mean to hit yo[u] hard. It was only play-play.*—(Gren)

play-play[2] vb intr (CarA) [AF—Joc] [Child-talk in games] To pretend (as an act of fun); to make believe. *Play-play you are the doctor and I bring dis child to you.*—(Belz)

play-play[3] adj (CarA) [AF—Joc] Not real; make-believe; imitation. **a.** *And I thought of all the Saturday mornings, the visits, the uneasy nonsenses, the play-play realities and, after all the thinking, I said, 'Yes, Elizabeth, I believe I love you.'*—WCR:16 **b.** *Those unimpressed were influenced less by the symbolism than by the general appearance. The paper is thinner; it feels like play-play money.... Others criticized the window space below the serial number.*—ReP (80.07.05, p.8) [By functional shift of PLAY-PLAY[2]]

please 1. formulaic adjunct vb (Bdos) [IF] [Used as a courtesy tag after Yes, No without expressing wish or option] **a.** *S1: 'Did you go to town today?'* / *S2: 'Yes please.'*—(Bdos) **b.** *S1: 'Can you type?'* / *S2: 'No please.'*—(Bdos) □ Used by speakers who feel the need to show respect in answering sb to whom respect seems due. Cp SE No, thank you vs Yes, please, expressing refusal or acceptance of an offer with contrasting courtesy tags. **2.** PHRASES **2.1 Please for (sth named)!** id phr (CarA) Please may I have (sth, as named). *Please for a drink of water.*—(CarA) **2.1.1 Please for a pass!** inter vb phr (CarA) Please let me pass! May I pass please? See PASS[2] Phr 2.3 **2.2 please God!** formulaic adjunct (Bdos, Gren, Guyn, Tbgo, Trin) God willing! *And is a nice little story too, I think.... All right, Bertyboy. I'll be reading the paper tomorrow please God ... 'Please God'? Yes, man, these days we all start talking like the old people.*—NG:190 □ In much more everyday currency in CE, esp among older folk, than in SE.

plen·ty[1] *adj* (CarA) [*IF*] Much; many; (SE) plenty of; a lot of. **a.** *He had a large estate, servants and plenty money.*—PKKK:92 **b.** *Plenty fools say that, but only poor people so fool.*—WBH:51 [Cp *EDD* plenty (Sc, Irel, Yks, etc) 2. adj 'plentiful', + many cits, but none indicating its use in attrib position, wh is the commonest use of CE PLENTY] □ Note that SE *plenty* also implies sufficiency or over-sufficiency, whereas CE PLENTY is a general term for 'a large number/amount of'.

plen·ty[2] *adv* (CarA) [*AF/IF*] **1.** Very much. **a.** *This type does not flourish in sophisticated communities like Britain.... But you've heard about them plenty in the West Indies and elsewhere.*—TRIH:99 **b.** *'Yes', replied the skin in a tone of deep resignation and despair. 'I am as salt as a cod fish. Plenty plenty.'.*—OTTTT:29 **2.** [By extension, as intensifier] Very. **a.** *That country pepper is plenty hot, I warn you.*—MHJT:32 **b.** *'You think,' I asked, 'that this cache of his is big?' 'Plenty big,' he retorted emphatically.*—FDI:33 [Cp *EDD* plenty (as prec) 3. adv 'sufficiently' + cits 'plenty sweet ...' etc]

plim·pler ['plɪmplʌ] *n* (Guyn, Jmca) See PIMPLER

plim·pler-pear *n* (Jmca) ‖ COCHINEAL (CACTUS) (Guyn, etc) [< PLIMPLER + *pear* perh from shape of stem. Cp ‖ ‖ PEAR-BUSH, PRICKLE PEAR, etc]

plug *n* **1.** (Baha, Belz) ‖ FEG (Angu, etc) **2.** (USVI) The heart or long conical portion attached to the stem and removable from a ripe soursop; it is used in folk-medicine.

plum *n* **1.** (Guyn, Trin) ‖ HOG-PLUM (CarA) *That acridness is the real tropical savour, hidden in sapodillas, plums, pommes cythères and pommes aracs.*—ACTT:14 **2.** (Dmca, Gren, Nevs) ‖ JAMAICA-PLUM (Bdos, etc) *When corn and mango, golden apple, plum an ting riping people can never get hungry.*—PSFC:24 **3.** (Antg, Mrat, StVn) ‖ CHILLI-PLUM (Antg, etc) □ As these cases indicate, in CE PLUM is applied to the commonest type specific to a territory, other less common types in that territory being then distinguished by their qualifying names. In addition to the above see BEQUIA-PLUM, COCO-PLUM, GHAUT-PLUM, GOVERNOR-PLUM, JEW-PLUM, etc.

plum-rose *n* **1.** (Gren, Mrat, StVn, Trin) ‖ MALACCA-APPLE (Antg, Guyn) **2.** (Dmca, Guyn) ‖ ROSE-APPLE (CarA)

PLURAL FORMS [Grammar] **1.** Many times pl forms occur in CE to indicate a grouping or collection of items where only the sg form, as a collective noun, wd be required in IAE. **a.** *We would also like to hear from the Minister something about the mails that never reach the people to whom they are addressed.*—Bdos (Hd, 75.01.28, p.4478) **b.** *She told us of many starvations in other parts of the world.*—Antg (Ms,

1973) **c.** *Trying to avoid the situation H— tried to leave but was stopped by the [two] accuseds.*—ToR (76.06.16, p.3) [These are prob due to over-correction prompted by the normal absence of the pl /-s/ form in CarA Cr and in creolized E] □ Other exs are *advices, aircrafts, beddings, foodstuffs, furnitures, livestocks, machineries, offsprings, sceneries*, etc. **2.** A few pl forms develop a shifted meaning in CE. Exs SLANGS, WORRIES, etc. (Treated as separate entries). **3.** A few nouns tend to be used by many CE speakers only in the pl, where a sg form would occur in IAE. Exs *ants, ashes, shoes teeth*, etc. **4.** A few nouns with difficult final / -CC/ in SE, such as *breakfasts, desks, guests, tourists*, etc are re-analyzed by many CE speakers and presented in the [X] forms /brekfasiz, desiz, gesiz, torisiz/ etc.

po·ca·te·ry (puc(k)·a·ter·y, pur·ka·to·ry) [pʌkateri] *n* (Antg, CayI, Guyn) [*AF*] Trouble; mischief; worry. **a.** *He is a bad type, always got the mother in pocatery.*—(Antg) **b.** *The whole place was in a confusion and purkatory.*—CayI (Ms) [By religious infl < SE *purgatory* 'place of cleansing punishment' with extended sense = a state of trouble, confusion] □ A pronunc nearly like that of 'purgatory' still occurs.

pock·et(s) *n* (*pl*) PHRASE **pull your pocket(s)** *vb phr* (Bdos) [*AF/IF*] See PULL Phr 2.12

Po·co·ma·ni·a [pokomenia ~ pʌkʌmenia] *n* (Jmca) A form of religious group-behaviour expressed in singing, spiritual dancing, spirit-possession, speaking in tongues, and acts for healing; its operative system combines both African and Christian beliefs, and it is particular to Black people esp in urban areas of Jamaica. *At nights, she left Panty alone in the unlighted shack.... She went in search of Drop Pan discussions or attended meetings of the Pocomania group, a pseudo-religious, superstitious cult who worshipped at nightly saturnalias with revelries of praying and dancing to drums.*—BGSB:14 [Prob a Hispano-Anglicized corruption 'poco + mania' of an Afr term. Alleyne (*ARJC:169*) notes: 'Pocomania' seems to be a spelling and conceptual aberration of Europeans. In their general demeaning of African culture, Europeans associated the religion of the slaves with 'a little madness'. As is usual in colonial systems, the colonised have largely accepted the colonisers' pejorative evaluation of them.' Alleyne (*ARJC:96 ff*), accounting creditably for its place within the broad framework of West and Central African religious survivals in *Jmca*, prefers and uses the spelling **Pukumina**, so suggesting etym relation to KUMINA, for wh a Kikongo origin seems likely. Note also (*LDKF*) Kikongo *pukumana* 'to shake, to cause to shiver or tremble' wh may hint at some association with spirit-possession] □ Although *pocomania* remains current (sometimes familiarly reduced to POCO) scholarly sources (*ARJC*, as above, and *SAZJ:127*) prefer PUKUMINA.

po·co-po·co¹ (poc-a-poc¹, po·ka·pok) [po kopoko~pokapo·k] *adv* (Belz, Gren, Jmca, Trin) [*AF—Joc*] **1.** Bit by bit; gradually; in convenient, easy stages. **a.** *I will keep knitting this bedspread poc-a-poc when I get time.*—(Trin) **b.** *When yo[u] will finish if yo[u] handlin[g] this grass-cuttin[g] so poco-poco?*—(Belz) **2.** [By extension] Just a little; not too much. *I like rice and beans just poc-a-poc, not my favourite.*—(Trin) [< Sp *poco a poco* 'little by little']

po·co-po·co² (poc-a-poc²) *adj* (Trin) [*AF— Joc/Derog*] Quiet; unobtrusive, timorous. *He ended his address—on behalf of his constituents—by saying that if other members of Parliament were 'poco-poco' (afraid to talk out) 'I want everybody to know that the representative for St Joseph is a macho man.'*—TrG (80.01.13, p.1) [By functional *adv* > *adj* shift of POCO-POCO¹]

poin·ci·a·na ['pɔɪnsiana] *n* (CarA) ‖FLAM-BOYANT (CarA) *At the end of the dry season and also immediately before it rains the Flamboyant or Poinciana with its scarlet flowers bursts into bloom.*—NeC (76.06.19, p.9) [Named in honour of the Marquis de Poincy, 17C Fr Governor based in St Kitts] ▢ It is the National Flower of St Kitts and Nevis.

poin·set·ti·a* ['pɔɪnsɛtya] *n* (CarA) ‖*Christmas-flower* 1. (Dmca, Jmca, StVn, Tbgo) A garden shrub that can exceed 8 ft in height, cultivated for its luxuriant, large, scarlet, flower-like bunches of bracts that flourish in the Christmas season; *Euphorbia pulcherrima (Euphorbiaceae)*. [From J. Poinsett, who introduced it to the U.S.A. from Mexico in the 19C, though it is now very widely popular in the *CarA*]

point·er /1'2/ *n* (Guyn) ‖*cocoyea* 2. (Trin) ‖*flex* (Gren) The dried spine of the leaf of a coconut-branch. [Because of its use in schools for pointing on blackboards, etc in former times] ▢ Distinguish from SE *pointer* /2'1/ 'any indicator' in concrete or abstract senses.

point·er-broom /1'21/ *n* (Guyn) ‖COCONUT-BROOM (Antg, etc) *You can brok pointer but you can'[t] brok pointer-broom* (= *Unity is strength*).—Guyn (Prov)

po·ke·no·boy, pok.no.boy, pork-and-dough-boy [pʌkʌnʌbwdɪ~pokandobbɪ] *n*(Belz) **1.** ‖*pokeno-palm* (Belz) A slender, many-stemmed palm exceeding 20 ft in height, with fronds some 6 ft long, both stems and stalks being armed with long, sharp, black spines; it bears clusters of hard-skinned, red nuts with a sour, sticky pulp and edible kernel; the stems of the palm provide tough, long sticks made famous as weapons used by slaves in the Battle of St George's Cay but now used as a building material; *Bactris spp (Palmae)*. *Its vibrations cause paddles and pork-and-dough-boy sticks, poised symbolically toward the noon-day sun, to quiver expectantly. It was the nation's first characteristic*

shout: Freedom!—BeT (80.08.10, p.6) [Prob a native name of African or Mayan source corrupted by confusion with a folk-name wh was evid first applied to English woodcutter settlers. See sense 2.] ▢ Poss the same as that called PIMPLER-PALM (*Guyn*) but there are several varieties of palm notably armed with spikes along trunk and fronds in the rimlands of the *CarA*. **2.** [Hist] Forest labourers. See cit. *The forest labourers used to be called the Poke'n'no Boys (Pork and Dough Boys) because under law they received (and still receive) four pounds of fat (cask) pork and seven quarts of flour weekly. This ration is thought to be very ancient. As there were insufficient muskets available many of the slaves who fought in the Battle were armed with fire-hardened lances made from a thin, tough palm; consequently this palm is called today the Pokeno Palm.*—ABSBH: 38 [Note: 'The logwood-cutters' (Dampier 1675) writes 'were then about 250 men, most English, that had settled themselves in several places hereabouts ... I made two or three trips to their huts, where we were always very kindly entertained by them with pork and pease, or beef and doughboys' + f.n. For years afterwards the British cutters all over the Caribbean were known as the 'Pork and Dough Boys'—Caiger S. L. (1951) *Br Honduras Past and Present* p.38]

po·key [poki] *n* (ECar) [*AF—Vul*] The vagina. ▢ Used sometimes by children, often in child molestation cases in court, for want of any other word.

po·lak *n* (Belz) ‖*bark-log* (Belz) A light wood used for making rafts; balsawood; *Ochroma limonensis. Some export interest is being taken in the local Balsawood. This quick growing and extremely light wood, locally called Polak, is marketable from six to ten years from planting. In the early days Logwood, which sinks like a stone in water, used to be freighted from the camps to the out-carrying vessels on rafts made of Polak, hence its other name of Bark Log.*—ABSBH:57

pol·der [po·ldʌ(r)] *n* (Guyn) ‖*empolder²* (Guyn) **1.** A (sometimes vast) low-lying area of marshy or PEGASSY land made fit for cultivation by being enclosed by dams, and drained and irrigated by a system of waterways (hence foll phr). **2.** PHRASE **2.1 canal(s) polder** *n phr* (Guyn) A POLDER irrigated by large canal(s). *Canal No.1 and Canal No.2 give their names to villages in the West Bank Demarara canals polder.*—Guyn (Ms) [Du *polder* 'reclaimed bogland']

po·li·an [poliʌn] *n* (Bdos) [*AF*] A sheet or piece of tarpaulin. [Cp *EDD* pauling Lin 'a tarpaulin; a covering for a cart or wagon'; related to SE *pall* 'a covering (for a coffin) or *pall* (of smoke)']

po·lice *n* (CarA) [*AF/IF*] A policeman. **a.** *I go into a bar, I see one come in for a drink, I leave right away ... Every police is a police, I don't mess with them.* MHJT:26 **b.** *Vincent Spooner, a Police*

Constable, told the Magistrate, that the 26-year-old woman used indecent expressions. / Said Muriel in Court, 'I never insult him. I wouldn't ah tell him so for he is a Police.'—DeM(SK) (63.08.03, p.10) c. Yesterday, the police—a big, stout dark fellow—came down and made us to move at 11 a.m.—TrI (76.01.08, p.1) □ This is the commonest use of the term in CE folk speech, the SE collective or institutional sense being largely inoperative except in careful educated speech.

Po·lice De·pot, the n phr (Guyn) The police headquarters in Georgetown. [By shift in sense from 'the regimental and police armoury and store-house', orig in north Georgetown. See OED depot 3. Mil]

pom·e·lo n (Trin) The lesser, rounder variety of SHADDOCK. [Said to be the orig East Indian name (See PTT:122); but cp CED's suggestion of a Du and Pg origin] □ AmE pomelo appears to apply mostly to 'grapefruit', and loosely also to 'SHADDOCK'.

pomme (ponm) n (Dmca, StLu) ‖CASHEW 1. (CarA)

pomme-can·nelle (ponm-ka·nèl) [pɔm-kanɛl] n (Dmca, StLu) ‖SUGAR-APPLE (CarA) [< Fr pomme 'apple' + cannelle < cannelé 'grooved', in ref to the fruit's surface]

pomme-cool·ie (ponm-kou·li) n (Dmca, Mrat, StKt) ‖CERASEE (Baha, etc) [Perh a loan from Mart, Guad where the same folk-name is used, < Fr pomme 'apple' + CE COOLIE. (Note the ‖coolie-pawpaw (Gren)). The fruit is cooked by East Indians]

pomme-cy·there (ponm-si·tè) [pɔm-sitɛ·(r)] n (Gren, StLu, Trin, ViIs) ‖GOLDEN-APPLE (Bdos, etc) Pommes cytheres are plentiful and selling at $2.50 a hundred.—TrG (72.09.16, p.5) [Fr pomme 'apple' (+ de 'of') + cythère Cythera, a Peloponnesian island sacred to Venus, whence her name Venus Cytherea. Note the botanical name Spondias cytherea. The ref is to the 'golden apple' of Greek myth wh Paris awarded to Venus whom he adjudged 'the most beautiful' of the goddesses, thereby incurring the wrath of Juno and Minerva and leading to the Trojan war] □ It is spelled mostly without the orig Fr accent, and sometimes as one word. The pl is usu **pommes-cytheres** [pɔm-sitɛ(r)z].

pomme-(de)-li·ane (ponm-di·ly·ann) [pɔm(də)lia·n] n (Dmca, StLu, Trin) ‖BELL-APPLE (Guyn, etc)

pomme-kill·er n (Dmca) ‖JUMBIE-SOURSOP (Antg, etc) [Perh a blend of Fr pomme + PAIN-KILLER wh is the name of the bush/tree wh bears the fruit]

pomme-ma·lac ['pɔm-malak] /2'12/ n (Trin) ‖MALACCA-APPLE (Antg, Guyn) [Fr < pomme (de) Malacca, in ref to Malaysian origin of the plant]

pomme-noire (ponm-nwè) [pɔm-nwɒ ~ pɔm-nwɛ] n (StLu) ‖CASHEW 1. (CarA)

pom·(m)e·rac ['pɒmərak] /1'12/ n (Bdos, Dmca, Trin) ‖MALACCA-APPLE (Guyn) In the tangle of branches above the banana trees were clusters of the red, pear-shaped fruit we called pomerac, and finding the tree now, I climbed and picked a good deal.—AGDR:28 [By /l > r/ shift from POMME-MALAC]

pomme-rose (ponm-wòz) [pɔm-roz ~ pɔm-wɔz] n 1. (Dmca) ‖ROSE-APPLE (CarA) 2. (Dmca, StLu) ‖MALACCA-APPLE (Antg, Guyn)

pomme-ser·ette; **ponm-siwèt**, **ponm.-se(r).ret** [pʌmsərɛt ~ pɔmsiwɛt] n (Angu, Nevs, StKt) ‖DUNKS (Bdos, etc) [< Fr pomme 'apple' + surette 'sourish', in ref to its taste. This name prob borrowed from Guad, Mart where it is often abbr as surette]

pom·pa(s)·set(t) (pom·po·zet) [pɔmpɒsɛt /-zɛt] /1'12/ vb intr (Bdos) [AF—Joc] 1. ‖PAYASS² 2. (Guyn) Dah is wuh yuh calls winnin' wif class. I en mekin' nuh sport, doh, Reagan really put Carter to shame, faif. 'E pompasett an' perlix 'pon 'e.—NaT (80.11.07, p.5, Lickmout' Lou) [Cp EDD posset vb² (Yks, etc) 'to dance; to change positions for the next figure (in dancing)'. The latter sense esp implies the showiness wh POM-PASSET connotes. The Bdos term may be re-duplicative or perh a blend of PAM(PALAM) (expressing delight) + posset. EDD also comments that 'the accent is on the last syllable of posset', wh is in keeping with the Bdos pitch-pattern and suggested by some spellings ending -ETT] 2. PHRASE 2.1 pompasset and perlix; perlix and pompasset vb phrs (Bdos) [AF—Joc] To show off very much; to make a long display of your delight. □ This is a commonly used emotive phr. See PERLIX, and note cit above.

pom·poom n (TkCa) ‖BLUGGO (Belz, etc)

pomp-pomp n (StVn) ‖BALL-BUSH (Bdos, Jmca) [Prob < POMPOM, cp (StLu) ‖gwo pompom]

pon prep (CarA) [Cr] 1. On; upon. a. De boy seh, 'But I don wan a go pon sea at all, young lady.'—WFSFB:41 (P. Gillet) b. He saw the jeep 'swerve' into the 'old man' and felled him. He said the impact sounded as though the jeep had struck 'pon a post'.—Dem(SK) (62.08.18, p.2) [< SE upon by aphesis] □ Often so written in narrative dialogue, or as 'pon. 2. PHRASES 2.1 pon a morning adv phr (Bdos, Guyn) [AF] ‖ON MORN-INGS (Bdos) See ON Phr 7.4 Every night I thinking 'bout you and crying so much I does have to put out my pillowcase 'pon a morning to dry in the sun. And Courcey now set up another big lot o' crying.—CISH:105 2.2 pon top adv/prep phr (CarA) [AF—Cr] On top (of). a. She would carry a full basket on her head and a bunch of plantains [u]pon top.—(Guyn) **b.** You lef[t] it [u]pon top of the fridge.—(Bdos) **2.3 pon top the bargain** id phr (Guyn) [AF—Cr] Into the bargain; [loosely] in addition. They would quarrel wid you and still beat yo[u] [u]pon top de bargain.—(Guyn)

pon·che de creme (pon·cha cream, punch au creme, punch de creme) [pŏšdəkrɛ·m ~ pʌnč-(d)ə-krɛm] /1′12/ n (ECar) A viscous, alcoholic drink made of eggs, rum, and spices beaten up in milk; it is a traditional Christmas drink in some places. **a.** Well home is home—you know what a Trinidad Christmas is like, and here there has always been Earline, making punch de creme, entertaining the boys ...—JPB:74 **b.** The argument, no doubt, is that if the natives want to eat ham, drink rum and poncha cream at this time, and feel they are in the laps of euphoria, then let the sods do that and don't rock the boat.—BoM (77.01.14, p.5) [Fr pronunc of punch + Fr crème, 'milk punch'] □ Ponche de creme (without accent) is the name used in recipe books, and also commercialized sometimes with the alternative name of Egg Nog.

pond-ap·ple n (Jmca) ‖MONKEY-APPLE 2. (Bdos, Guyn)

pond-fly* n (Bdos, Guyn) ‖Auntie Nannee (BrVi) ‖batimanmzèl (Tbgo, Trin) ‖gully-watchman (Tbgo) ‖makoké-glo (Dmca) ‖mawi-sosé (StLu) ‖needlecase (Jmca) ‖palm-fly (Guyn) ‖sousé-glo (Dmca) 1. The dragon fly; Anisoptera spp. [From its habit of alighting on still water]

pond-salt [pɒn-salt] n (Brbu) ‖COARSE-SALT (CarA) [The salt is produced by the evaporation of sea-water trapped in sea-side ponds, hence this name. See also PAN-SALT]

pond-thatch*; **pond-top**[1] n (Baha) A variety of low-growing palm with fan-shaped leaves wh are widely used when dried and stripped for straw-work or for thatch-work; Sabal palmetto bahamensis (Palmae).

pond-top[2] n (Baha) ‖CABBAGE-PALM (CarA) See TOP, also PALMETTO

pone n **1.** (Bdos, Jmca, USVI) ‖corn-pone (Bdos, Guyn, Jmca) ‖(potato-)pound (Belz) A baked pudding made chiefly of grated sweet-potato (with currants and sometimes spice), but also of CORNMEAL. **2.** (Bdos, Guyn, Trin) ‖CASSAVA-PONE (Bdos, Guyn) [Of Amerindian origin. W3 Algonquian/Delaware apan 'baked' ... 3. 'a pudding of grated sweet potato, milk, sugar, butter, and spices ... served as a dessert'] **3.** (Jmca) A name used in some districts for DOKUNU.

po·ni·a (pu·nya) [pʊnya] n (Tbgo) ‖po(o)ya (Trin) ‖punyal (USVI) ‖punya(r)k (Jmca) **1.** A short CUTLASS. **2.** A long (usu sheathed) knife. [Prob < SE poniard with characteristic CarA Cr

loss of final /-CC/, but cp also Sp puñal 'dagger, knife']

ponm (Dmca, etc) [Fr Cr] and all PONM- compounds, see POMME and POMME- compounds.

po·ny-glass n (Guyn) A small drinking glass with a capacity of about 2 fluid oz; it is widely used to serve drinks at large functions and sometimes called an **on-the-rocks-glass**. [AmE: W2 pony adj 'of a size smaller than usual', as a pony ... glass ...]

poo·ja n (Guyn, Trin) See PUJA.

pool n (Gren) [Nutmeg Ind] A nutmeg processing station where the nuts are prepared and bagged for export. [From the 'pooling' or collection of nutmegs at one place]

poo·pa(h) (pu·pa, pup·pa) ['pʊpa] n (CarA) [AF] **1.** ‖pappy (Bdos, Dmca) A father; (also as affectionate form of address) Daddy. **a.** No-way No-way ... You beginning to play big shot! You could talk better than your moomah and poopah. Boy! You don't know how lucky you is to be goin' to school.—GI:104 (I. Khan) **b.** Boysie doh have no family. He is de one chile of he parents and both he mooma and poopa dead already.—RTCS:7 **2.** ‖pappy (Bdos, Dmca, Trin) A grandfather; any old man. □ Sometimes Joc. **3.** used as excl (Belz, Guyn, Jmca, StLu) ‖papa! (Trin) O God!; Goodness me!, etc. Poopa, da' was a fête! I mean it had / Free rum free whisky and some fellars beating / Pan from one of them band in Trinidad.—FCV2:208 (D. Walcott) [See note at PAPA!] **4.** (Guyn) (Term of affectionate address to) a small boy. Run pupa. Go bring da[t] bench le[t] you granny si[t] do[w]ng.—(Guyn)

poo·pa·lick (pu(p)·pa·lick) n (Belz, Jmca) [AF—Joc] **1.** ‖CUFFIN (Bdos) **2.** PHRASE **2.1 turn poopalicks** (Belz) ‖SKIN CUFFINS (Bdos)

poor-back·ra n (Bdos) ‖POOR-WHITE (CarA)

poor djab (poor jab) n phr (Gren, StLu) [AF] Poor fellow; poor thing. Poor djab Marguerite. I feel so sorry for her. She so sick and she los[t] the job.—(StLu) [< Fr Cr < Fr pau(vre) diab(le), 'poor devil']

poor-don·keys /1′22/ n (Bdos) [AF—Joc] ‖ALPARGATAS (CarA)

poor-great adj (Bdos, Gren, Guyn, StVn) [AF—Joc] ‖assified **1.** (Bdos, Guyn, USVI) ‖grand (Gren) ‖great (Bdos) ‖poor-show-great (Jmca) Poor but haughty in appearance or conduct; too proud to be seen or known to accept charity or help that is really needed; poor and snobbish. Sometimes a girl of the village, holding herself slightly aloof from the surrounding bawdiness and urged on by her parents and by her own 'poor great' ambition, would become a student nurse and in time would graduate into the self-respect of a profession.—WCR:49

poor-man shop /1'21/ *n phr* (Guyn) A small shop wh deals in the buying and selling of old or used household items, tools, bicycle parts, etc.

poor-me-one[1] *n* (Gren, Tbgo, Trin) [*AF*] **1.** A person who is begging for sympathy; sb with a sorry, dejected look. *How you stan[d] up in a corner like a poor-me-one as if yo[u] don['t] know people?*—(Gren) **2.*** [By extension] A greyish-brown, mottled night-hawk with a distressing cry; *Nyctibius griseus (Nyctibiidae)*. *... and if you stay near the forest or swamp you may hear the melancholy notes of the potoo ... or poor-me-one. During the day this strange night-bird sits upright and motionless on a stump, perfectly camouflaged as it merges with the dead wood.*—ACTT:188

poor-me-one[2] *adj* (Gren, Tbgo, Trin) [*AF*] ‖ **poorthingfied** (Belz) Lonely; sorry-looking. **a.** *Fellars stand up in little groups here and there, all of them looking destitute and poor-me-one.*—STLL:30 **b.** *There will just be one poor-me-one standpipe in the valley. Another case of small mercies.*—TaP (75.05.04, p.1) [By functional n > adj shift of POOR-ME-ONE[1]]

poor-show-great *adj* (Jmca) [*AF—Joc*] ‖ POOR-GREAT (Bdos, etc)

poor·thing·fied [porəɪnfaɪd] *adj* (Belz) ‖ POOR-ME-ONE[2] (Gren, etc) *Toycie gazed fixedly at a clump of grass near her feet. Beka poked her arm. / ... 'Toycie! Don't act so poorthingfied. People will wonder and begin to watch.'*—EBL:102

poor-white *n* (CarA) [*IF—Derog*] ‖ **backra-johnny** (Bdos) ‖ **béké** 2. (Dmca, Gren) ‖ **che-che** (Nevs, StKt) ‖ **Conchy-Joe** (Baha, TkCa) ‖ **Dorsetshire-Hill Bajan** (StVn) ‖ **ecky-becky** (Bdos) ‖ **Frenchie, mooshay** (StKt) ‖ **mong-mong, Mount-Moritz Bajan** (Gren) ‖ **poor-backra** (Bdos) ‖ **red-chenke** (Antg) ‖ **red-leg, red-shank** (Bdos) Any descendant, in a particular Caribbean territory, of the earliest generations of 17C White plantation labourers from the Br Isles, who have stayed socially isolated, generally poor and despised, and sometimes showing effects of inbreeding. (See BACKRA 4.) **a.** *I know that some of these people will not believe me but I have seen what is commonly referred to as 'poor whites, red shanks, poor backra, red legs or backra johnnies' working in the fields at Foster Hall (Bath) and Colleton (St John) and several other plantations.*—AdM (79.06.17, p.15, E. Stoute) **b.** *He ask whether I'd ever know any Poor Whites,'cause their own be a hard lot... They get separate somehow from the other whites an' nobody notice them, black or white... An' he says he didn't think there was any people like them any other part o' the world. They get cut off from their own somehow, an' they had to go on livin' in the same land but as if their skin ain't make no difference. Tis why they call them Poor Whites.*—LICMS:204

pop *vb* **1.** (CarA) [*IF/AF*] [Esp of string, thread, wire, etc] To break, burst, come apart. **a.** *The kite string popped and the kite gone.*—(Bdos) **b.** *This bobbin is popping the thread.*—(Guyn) □ SE *pop* always implies bursting with a sound. **2.** *vb intr* (Jmca) [*AF*] To trick, catch out, outsmart (sb); to outplay (an opponent in a game). *They tried to pop me in the argument by getting me to agree to certain things before I knew what they were going to argue.*—(Jmca) **3.** PHRASES **3.1 pop loose** *vb phr* (CarA) [*AF*] To break away; to break out. *'Lawd God, Mr Lattimer, sah,' he said.... 'All hell pop loose up de town, dem is burnin' everyt'ing dat will burn and dem is gwine kill before long. Riot start, sah, I tell you, bad riot start today.'*—HVUW:14 **3.2 pop (sb's) neck** *vb phr* (CarA) [*AF*] To hang (sb). *Malik? they should have done with him long ago. The 'Mally Wes' (she spits) going and killing all them people—let the brute go. They should pop he neck long time, the old criminal.*—ToR (75.05.18, p.8) **3.3 pop style** *vb phr* (Jmca) [*AF—Joc*] To put on airs; to show off (esp in manner of dress and walking). **3.4 pop your water** *vb phr* (Baha) [*AF*] [Of a boy or young man] To have sexual intercourse (as an early experience in life). *Boys who 'pop their water'—especially with an older female, are not chastised, or even looked down upon, because he is expected to 'sow his wild oats' and 'be a man'.*—MBS:36

pope *vb* (Guyn, Tbgo, Trin) [*AF*] To gain entrance to a show, party, etc without paying; [by extension] to get into something without intending to pay your way. [Perh a survival of EE, as *OED poop* vb[2] (Obs and of obscure origin, with spelling variant POWPE) 'to deceive, cheat' + cits–17C]

pope's *n phr* (USVI) ‖ TURK'S CAP CACTUS (CarA)

pop·eye-ran·ty *n* (TkCa) ‖ BIG-EYE[3] 2. (ECar)

po·pi·lo·lo (po·pa·lo·lo, po·po·lo·la) *n* (Tbgo) ‖ CERASEE (Baha, etc)

po·po *n* (Gren, Tbgo, Trin) [*IF/AF*] (A term of affection for) a baby; [by extension] (a term of endearment for) a woman. *An chilleren, 'Big Brudder' put Maurice Bishop head in he lap, an sing for him, as if was he own Popo.*—ToR (76.11.21, p.6, Cotay si Cotay la)

pò·pòt-fig *n* (StLu) ‖ BANANA-NAVEL (Jmca)

pop·pet (**pop·pit**) *n* (Bdos) A fool; an idiot; a laughing stock. *'When a poor man loose control of the best in himself,' Mr Foster said, 'it ain't his fault at all, it is the fault of you people who go round making poppits of other poor people'.*—LICMS:272 [Cp EDD *poppet* (Yks, etc) 1. 'a puppet; *fig* a silly, vapid female'] □ Cp BrE *poppet* wh is, quite the contrary, a term of endearment for a beloved person, usu a woman.

pop·py-show *n* (CarA) See PAPPY-SHOW

porch *n* (Baha) An outside open gallery; a verandah. *Each house had a verandah—or as we called it—a porch. If the ground was large enough, this went on two sides of the house, and I have known some that had porches on three sides. Sitting on the porch to watch the world go by was the favourite pastime of many families.*—EBT:6 □ Some CE speakers occasionally use the term loosely to refer to the jalousied front gallery of a house. SE *porch* refers to the sheltered entrance to a building such as a church.

pork-and-dough-boy *n* (Belz) See PO-KENOBOY

pork·fat-ap·ple *n* (Baha, Berm) ‖ COCO-PLUM 1. (Antg, etc)

pork-knock·er *n* (Guyn) An independent prospector for gold or diamonds in the rivers and alluvial soil of the INTERIOR of Guyana, using domestic or home-made devices. *Gold has been mined in Guyana for over 100 years and total production has exceeded 3.5 million ounces, most of it brought out of the interior by a peculiarly rugged breed of freelance miners known locally as 'Pork-knockers'. Similarly, of the approximately four million carats of diamonds produced in the past 80 years, more than 95 per cent of them have been discovered by 'pork-knockers' working remote streams in the interior with pick, shovel and sieve.*—Guyn (Ms, 1975) [< (pickled) *pork* + *knocker* '(prompt) eater' i.e. 'a hungry eater of pickled pork'. Cp *EDD knock* (Var dial and colloq uses in Sc, Irel and Eng) 1. (5) *knock in* 'to eat, consume, dispose of food'. See also KNOCK vb 3. (*Guyn*). Pickled pork of wild pig was the regular diet of such prospectors, eaten at the end of a day's work. (Cp also etym note at POKENOBOY 2.) The orig Joc sense has given way to a neutral one denoting a type of worker]

pork-knock·ing *vbl n* (Guyn) The prospecting for and mining of gold and diamonds on an individual basis; the livelihood of a PORK-KNOCKER. [By vbl back-formation < PORK-KNOCKER with the sense of labour dominant]

por·tu·gal [po·čugʌl ~ pɪtigal] *n* (Trin) ‖ T-ANGERINE (CarA) □ The names *portugals, mandarins* are loosely interchangeable in *Trin*, the former being commoner, however, and, for those who make a difference, a larger type than *mandarins*.

Por·tu·guee (Por·ta·gie, Po·to·gee, Po·ta·gi(e), Put·ta·gee) [porčugi· ~ pʌr(d)ʌgi· ~ pʊtagi·] *n, adj* (CarA) [AF—*Derog*] Portuguese. **a.** *In the future amalgamation of races, which will take place here as elsewhere in the tropics, the Portuguee—Madeira element will not be the least efficient.*—TWISM:189 **b.** *'Is these Potogees who cause the trouble, you know,' he said. 'They have their hands in the stinking salt-fish barrel and they are still the first to talk of nigger this and coolie that.'*—NMP:16 **c.** *'Riego?' / 'Yes, Ah t'ink dat was de name he call. It was a Puttagee name.*—

MLDS:240 [A back-formation from SE *Portuguese*, conceived as pl. (Cp *Chinee*). However the form /potagi/ may have come with slaves from W Afr. Cp the Krio items *poto, Potogi* in KED]

pose off *vb intr phr* (CarA) [AF—*Joc*] To strike a pose; to stand or sit with visible pride (usu to be photographed for the press). *I see you posin[g] off with the Prime Minister in the newspaper at the Old Year Dance! Hi!*—(Bdos) [See OFF² adv]

po·sie (po·sey) [pozi] *n* (Guyn, Trin) [AF—*Joc*] ‖ UTENSIL (Bdos, Guyn)

pot¹ *n* (CarA) [As a symbol of family or social relationship] PHRASES **1. eat rice from the same pot** *vb phr* (ECar) [AF—*Derog*] [Of persons] To be of the same sort; to be equally rough having grown up together; to be low social equals. **2. food/rice don't/aint/no(t) cook(ed) in the same pot** *id phr* (CarA) [AF—*Derog*] See FOOD Phr 2.1 **3. (not) make (sb's) pot bubble** (*neg*) *vb phr* (Guyn) [AF—*Derog*] ‖ *(not) put on pot for (sb)* (Nevs) (Not) to provide help and support for (sb); (not) to earn (sb's) subservience. *He can[']t as[k] me not[h]ing. I don[']t got to give him no satisfaction, cau[se] he don[']t mak[e] me pot bubble.*—(Guyn) □ These phrs are more often in neg form. Cp next. **4. put on your own pot** *vb phr* (Nevs) [AF] To manage for yourself; to fend, provide for yourself. **5. the pot burst** *id phr* (Angu) [AF—*Joc*] The friendship/partnership/relationship has ended. *Well since de pot bu[r]s[t] dey don[']t talk to one anoder.*—(Angu)

pot² *vb tr* (Bdos) **1.** To bake (sth) in a pot (esp pork or chicken). **2.** PHRASE **2.1 pot pork for sb** *id phr* (Bdos) [AF—*Joc*] [Of a woman] To cook food for a young man with special ingredients that are believed to help win his love; [by extension] to set out to gain a husband by design.

pot³ *n* (CarA) [Fishing Ind] A FISH-POT. *These vessels would fish on the banks for crawfish and scale fish, using pots and handlines.*—WAAF:40 [*OED pot* sb¹ 5b 'a wicker basket used as a trap for fish or crustaceans' + cits from 1669]

po·ta·to* *n* (CarA) ‖ ENGLISH POTATO (CarA) □ In most places POTATO or ENGLISH or IRISH POTATO is used for the imported product, definitely distinct from SWEET POTATO wh is regarded as a GROUND PROVISION.

po·ta·to-bank *n* (CarA) ‖ BANK¹ 1. (CarA)

(po·ta·to-) pound [pʊtetʌ-pʌŋ] *n* (Belz) ‖ PONE 1. (Bdos, etc) *'Some lemonade and a piece of potato pound?' / 'Yes, please!' Beka said... Miss Ivy lifted a heavy brown pudding from a side table, cutting a generous slice for Beka.*—EBL:72 [< (SWEET-)POTATO, the chief ingredient + *pound* pronounced [pʌŋ], and prob a spelling over-correction < PONE] □ The form *pound* is evid used by itself without ambiguity: '*A little coconut water with some rum to wash down the pound*'—EBL:75.

po·ta·to-yam [ˈpʌte·tʌ-ya·m] *n* (Trin) ‖ CH-INESE YAM (Guyn, Trin) [From resemblance of the multiple tubers to large IRISH potatoes and (in *Trin*) the slight yellowness of its flesh]

pot-cake *n* (Baha, TkCa) ‖ BUN-BUN (CarA)

pot·cake(-dog) *n* (Baha) A mongrel that is fed on remainders from cooking. *That morning Miss May's fowls did not crow as usual and her potcake-dog remained silent on the clap-board step*.—MTTBT:55 [By extension of POT-CAKE¹, the pot scrapings after the cooking of rice and grits providing most of the food of such a dog] □ Cp RICE-DOG (*Guyn*).

pot-fish *n* (ECar) ‖ *fresh-fish* (Bdos) Any kind of edible fish of a lesser quality wh are caught indiscriminately in a FISH-POT.

pot-fish wire *n phr* (BrVi) ‖ WIRE-MESH (Guyn)

pot-foot *n* (Bdos) ‖ PUFF-BELLY-AND-FINE-FOOT (Tbgo)

pot-lick·er *n* (Belz) [*AF—Joc*] ‖ SALMON-TOT RETRIEVER (Bdos) *But she looking quite consumptive/Maaga as a starving pot-licker/Which all Belizeans know to be/The worset kind of dog you could find*.—YFOC:39.

po·to-po·to *n* (Belz, Jmca) See PUTTA-PUTTA

pot·wa *n* (Guyn) See PATWA²

pou·i [pu·i] *n* (CarA) A large, decorative, shade tree wh annually sheds its leaves and comes out massively in flower, a pink variety and a yellow variety; its very hard wood is also favoured by STICK-FIGHTERS; the pink, *Tabebuia pentaphylla*, the yellow *Tecoma serratifolia* (*Bignoniaceae*). [Perh of Carib origin via Fr Cr. The tree is best known in Trin]

pound¹ [pʌŋ(d)] *vb tr* **1.** (CarA) [*AF/IF*] To beat up (sb); batter, pummel (sb). *Australia's attack, however, took a pounding immediately after play resumed with Richardson engineering the assault…. He hammered 114 for a new record …*—AdV (91.03.25, p.28) [Cp *EDD pound* vb³ (Var dial uses in Eng) 1. 'to knock, to beat, pummel; to kick, stamp'] □ See also Phr 3.3 below. **2.** (Trin) [By extension] To criticize (sb) severely; to berate (sb) unmercifully. *I can clearly remember how together we used to pound Trinidadians who returned to this country after a short while in the U.S. of A. with heavy Yankee accents.*—BoM (75.01.17, p.20) □ The pronunc [pɒʊnd] occurs only in careful educated speech, [pʌŋd] is commonest, [pʌŋ] regular at the folk level. **3.** *PHRASES* **3.1 pound mèlé (-melee)** [pʌŋ mele·] *vb phr* (Angu, StKt, StVn, ViIs) [*AF*] ‖ POUND (SB'S) NAME (CarA) See Phr 3.2 below. *Dey other one*

on the end pound melee all day long. Dat time her daughter running round with a married man.—Vip I. 1 (Market Square) **3.2 pound (sb's) name** *vb phr* (CarA) [*AF*] ‖ *bad-mouth (sb)* (Baha) ‖ *bad-talk (sb)* (StLu) ‖ *burst (sb's) back* (Dmca) ‖ *chat (sb's) name, su-su*³ *(sb)* (Jmca) ‖ *ill-speak* (Tbgo) ‖ *mal-palé (sb)* (Dmca, StLu) ‖ *mové-lang (sb)* (StLu, Tbgo, Trin) ‖ *pound mèlé* (Antg, BrVi, StVn) ‖ *pound story* (Dmca, Mrat, StKt) ‖ *su-su*³ *([u]pon sb)* (Guyn, Jmca, StVn) ‖ *trash benny* (TkCa) To join in exchanging bad sentiments or scandalous gossip about (an absent person). *If I were you I wouldn't grieve too much, for in fact who wants a man who listens to other women pounding your name. As a child, I used to hear the old folk refer to such men as 'Auntie Men'. Do you want … a man who will … let people who do not care for you pour junk into his ear?*—NaT (77.04.17, p.22, Dear Christine) [Perh a calque of a metaph from W Afr langs. In W Afr it is customary for two women to pound fu-fu alternating strokes of their pestles in the same mortar] **3.3 pound sb's skin** *vb phr* (Guyn) [*AF*] To beat up (sb) thoroughly. *De husband chase the man and didn[ʼt] forget to poun[d] she skin.*—(Guyn) **3.4 pound story** *vb phr* (Dmca, Mrat, StKt) [*AF*] ‖ POUND (SB'S) NAME (CarA) See Phr 3.2 above. *So some of them who talk 'bout other people case, after a while have some of the same people they talk the news with pounding story on them.*—LMFF:46

pound² *n* (Belz) See (POTATO-)POUND.

pound an[d] a crown [pʌŋ-an-a-krʌŋ] *n phr* (Gren, Guyn, Tbgo, Trin) [*IF—Joc*] A lot of money; too high a price. *These days a new car will cost you a pound and a crown, so I have to nurse this old thing.*—(Tbgo) [< SE *pound* sterling + *crown* (formerly) one eighth of a pound sterling] □ Usage largely restricted to older folk.

pound-plan·tain [pʌŋ-pla·ntɪn] /1ʼ22/ *n* (Trin) ‖ FUFU **1.** (Baha, etc) [< SE *pound[ed]* + *plantain* with characteristic CarA Cr > CE loss of pa. part /-ed/ suffix]

pound-sale *n* (Guyn) A bring-and-buy sale at wh mainly articles of foodstuff weighing about a pound are contributed for sale.

pou·pou (pu·pu) *n, vb* (Antg, Dmca) ‖ JOBBIE (Bdos)

pow [pɒʊ] *n* (Trin) A soft, white, dough-like roll with lightly seasoned minced meat inside. (It is different from a hamburger in that the meat is entirely enclosed in the roll, wh has no crust). [A Chinese name]

pow·er *n* (Gren, Guyn, Tbgo) **1.** A spiritual deity or a spirit that is worshipped through several media, including ritual feasting and dancing, in the context of a particular belief-system or a cult. *Here we have an example of a ritual custom which Shango devotees all over Trinidad observe. But if you were to ask them why do they* feed Ogun before any of the other 'powers', they will reply that it is because he is more powerful than the others.—EMRP:24 **2.** (CarA) [*IF*] The state of spirit-possession. *Arms swung sideways, overhead and in all fashions. They started to jump up with the beat of the drums, moving their waists and shoulders in time with the tune. They were hot and sweating. One fell from exhaustion. But they said 'she was in power'. They meant the spirit had taken possession of her.*—PGIP:54

pow·er·ful *adj* (CarA) [*AF—Joc*] Attractive; beautiful. **a.** *Look at dat pow'ful coat, man. I hear he just land straight from America. Look at 'e walk, I tell you. Mek you mout' water, eh?* —SNWIC:221 (R. Heath) **b.** *I see the piece o[f] flesh does pass he[re], face ain['t] too powerful but the body perfec[t].*—(Tbgo)

pow·er·ful-fool·ish *adj* (Bdos) [*IF*] Making a ridiculous show or use of new or temporary authority; arrogant and overbearing but of no substance.

pow·is [pɒuis] *n* (Guyn) A forest bird about the size of a turkey; it is mostly black, with a white belly, and the head bears a crest wh extends down the back of its neck; it lives mostly on the ground but can fly into trees, it is hunted for its meat and may be aggressive; *Cracidae spp.* [Cariban. (*FTCC:146*) Macusi *powis* 'curassow'] □ It is called the **crested curassow** in professional literature, and is evid related to the *paui* (*Trin*) (See *HBTT:70*).

po·ya [poya~pʋya] *n* (Trin) [*AF*] A type of CUTLASS. *He said, 'Hari, I bet I could cut more canes than you.' Hari laughed. 'Even though I work the whole morning already is a good bet. You must be forget to use poya, your hands so soft and white now.'*—SWOS:68 [Cp PONIA (*Tbgo*) < SE *poniard*. The *Tbgo* form is prob denasalized in *Trin*]

prag¹ (**prog**) [prag~prɒg] *vb* **1.** (Baha, USVI) [*AF*] To beg for (sth); to forage. *Well dey run out of food and start to prag in de area and come back with some mangoes.*—(USVI) [Cp *EDD prog* (In gen dial use in Sc, Eng, Amer) **2.** 'to poke about for, esp with a view to pilfering; to search for; to forage; to beg. The /o > a/ vowel opening is characteristic of CE < CarA Cr] **2.** (BrVi, Mrat) [By extension] To dig (root vegetables) out of the ground. *Christmas foods are prepared; cassava bread made; yams and other root vegetables reaped, or pragged, to use the local patois; the sorrel, which fruits for Christmas, picked.*—FMEI: 47 □ See PROGGING STICK. **3.** (Belz, Jmca) [*AF*] To go hunting. *We gone praggin[g] las[t] night. We ketch wan turtle and we shoot wan deer.*—(Belz) **4.** (Tbgo) [*AF*] To grab; to snatch. [Senses 3., 4., appear to be variants or extensions of the original in *EDD*] □ The spelling **prog** is also used occasionally.

prag² *n* **1.** (Tbgo) [*AF*] A grab; a snatch. *R—just grabble his neck ... and he spin around three times*

and he make a prag again behind the boy with one hand.—Tbgo (CR, 80.09.04) [By functional vb > n shift of PRAG¹ 3.] **2.** (Guyn) [*AF*] [*Usu in pl* **prags, progs**] Any few items of little worth collected by or given to some poor person. *As soon as de mudder come home from de[ir] aunt in to[w]ng, see how dey rushin[g] at de bag to see what prags she bring.*—(Guyn) [By functional vb > n shift of the *EDD* original of PRAG¹ 1.]

pra-pra¹ *vb* **1.** (Gren, Jmca) [*AF*] To steal by snatching, grabbing; to carry off. *Praise God I ent have nothing for him to thief. Come see he must be pra-pra somebody fowl and it get way.*—RTCS: 17 [Cp *DAFL* Twi *pra, prapra* 1. 'to sweep up; to gather' 2. 'to carry off, destroy'. These senses evid extended in foll CE uses] **2.** (Baha) To attack and throw (sb) as in wrestling. *Short of money, he took a room in a cheap lodging house and, as he later jocularly told the story, that night bed bugs prapraed him and threw him out of the bed on to the floor.*—TrI (Ed, 76.09.04, p.3) **3.** (Belz) To sweep up, gather up (things) to make (a place) clean. *I burnt my plantation / My wife and I praprad it with great expectation / We bent and sowed different kinds of seeds everyday until backaches we could no longer stand.*—AmA (81.05.15, p.10)

pra-pra² *adj* (Baha, Gren) [*AF*] Unfair; mixed up; cheating. **a.** *Y'll have Englan' an France fightin' wid Germany gainst Italy an' den d' same time y'll have Englan' an' France fightin' neck and neck wid Italy tryin' t' mop up Germany. Now dat gon be a real pra-pra war, hey, Englan' an' France fightin' on bote sides an' dunno who t' hit firs'.*—DSJS:35 **b.** *Now, you have the problem of changing the method of tax assessment on land, apart from foreign owned and locally owned divided into basic categories of cultivated land and un-cultivated land—now that is trouble. That is look-ing for a lot of trouble. That is looking for unnecessary confusion. That is playing 'pra-pra' marbles when you shouldn't. Who go decide which land is cultivated and how?*—Gren (Hd, 78.04.28, p.145) [By functional vb > adj shift of PRA-PRA¹]

Prax! (**Plai!, Plax!, Splax!,** etc) *excl ideoph* (CarA) ECHOIC WORDS representing the sharp-ness of a lash or slap, or a sudden snap as something breaks. **a.** *In my days, boy! You suck your teet[h] at yo[ur] mother and it was plaie! plax! Yo[ur] head would spin wit[h] de blows!*—(Bdos) **b.** *This time look how Boro Nancy backin[g] [a]way backin[g] [a]way [u]pon de tree limb till so, prax! De limb done break and plashaow! Boro Nancy drop in de river.*—(Guyn)

pray·er-flag *n* (Guyn, Trin) See JHANDI 1.

prec·ke(h) [prɛkɛ] *n* (Jmca) [*AF—Joc*] Trouble; confusion; controversy. *You and me well know from long time that nuff of us going on like we're not supposed to talk to our young people about such things, then when the preckeh come, hear the weeping and wailing and sermon bout how youth nuh good etc etc et very cetera.*—WeG

(73.02.28, p.3, Partyline) [Cp *CSESD* So Am Sp *pereque* 'a nuisance; a bore']

press¹ *n* **1.** (Angu, Antg, Bdos, Jmca, Trin, USVI) ‖ *dresser* (Dmca, Guyn, StLu) A wardrobe. *Where did he keep his clothes at your house? —He had his own bedroom. He had a press.—* AMAM:35 **2.** (Bdos, Guyn) A movable cupboard in wh items (esp in a school-room) are locked away; a kitchen-cupboard. *Even in cases, Mr Chairman, where you find the library system is in operation at some of these schools, a key is kept in the cupboard—the press or whatever it is called.*—Bdos (Hd, 75.03.17, p.4739) □ Cp SE *press*, usu a shelved cupboard fixed to or recessed in a wall. However re sense 1. cp occasional BrE *clothes-press*.

press² *n* (Gren, Trin) ‖ SNO(W)-CONE (CarA) *And there was a huge ice-box with an ice shaver on top of it, where Freddie probably made press, and snowballs, and maybe even ice-cream.*—AGDR:70 [By functional vb > n shift, ref to pressing shaved ice]

press³ *vb tr* (CarA) ‖ *iron* (Tbgo, Trin, USVI) To straighten (the hair of a Black person) by the use of a heated iron comb. *Now we have found our very own at last / No more hot comb to press the hair / No more bleach creams to make us clear.*—Trin (Cso, 1969, Mighty Duke)

pre·ten·sive *adj* **1.** (StVn, Tbgo, Trin) Lacking in confidence; of unsteady character. *Why he should be treated as a freak he cannot understand. / He says: 'I know many men like myself. They are shy, pretensive and afraid to come out in the open. They play only in the dark.... Many women too ... prefer the company of other women but they too are ashamed to come out in the open.'*— ExP (72.10.27, p.16) **2.** (Bdos, Guyn) Snobbish although poor; putting on airs. *You too pretensive. Ah suppose you feel Henry ain' good enough company for you, na? His skin too dark. Only dem high-colour children you want to talk to.*—MLDS:37 [A survival of EE. See *OED pretensive* (rare) 1. 'professed; feigned' 2. 'full of pretence; pretentious, ostentatious' + cits 1640–1907] □ Cp sense 1. often overlaps among CE speakers with SE *pretentious* 'claiming unwarranted importance; showy'. Note that in SE *pretentious* has displaced *pretensive* both in literary and general use.

PRG [pi-ar-Ji] *abbr* (Gren) People's Revolutionary Government, the Government, organized along Marxist lines, wh ruled *Gren* 1979–1983, led by Maurice Bishop. [The popularized abbr ref is used throughout the *CarA*; 'Revolutionary' because the Government came to power by coup d'état March 13, 1979]

prick·le-/prick·ler-/prick·ly pear *n* (*phr*) (Baha, Bdos, CayI, ViIs) ‖ COCHINEAL (CACTUS) (Guyn, etc) *Many uses the prickly pear has, a few of which are for washing the hair, for inflamed eyes, drink as a cooling draught for high blood*

pressure; *a leaf split in half and heated over the coal pot and placed on the sole of the feet with a cold cloth on the head will immediately ease tension.*—HBMV (1976) [From clusters of prickles borne on pear-shaped stems] □ *Prickly pear* is also IAE.

prick·le-yam /1'12/ *n* (Tbgo, Trin) ‖ YELLOW-YAM (Antg, etc) [From the prickly nature of its stems, more noticeable in some varieties than in others]

Pride of Bar·ba·dos *n phr* (CarA) See BARBADOS-PRIDE □ Official form of the name as the National Flower of Barbados

Pride of Tri·ni·dad & To·ba·go (Tri·ni·dad's Pride) *n phr* (Tbgo, Trin) ‖ CHACONIA (Tbgo, Trin) [Name promoted since it became the country's National Flower]

priest *n* PHRASE **kill priest** *id phr* (Gren, Tbgo, Trin) [AF—*Joc*] See KILL Phr 3.5

print *n* PHRASE **be/look like (sb) in print** *vb phr* (Gren, Tbgo, Trin) [AF—*Joc*] To be the spitting image of (sb). *You is a Davidson. Bound to be. You is you[r] father self in print.*—(Gren)

print·er·y *n* (CarA) A printer's shop or works; a commercial printing house. *I just want to say that the Government Printery has worked overtime in order to get these Estimates ready.*—Bdos (Hd, 73.03.13, p.1881) [An EE form always current in CE though unlisted in most Br desk dictionaries. *OED* lists as 'Chiefly US' with cits from 1638; *OED2* adds '*Austral* and *Afr*' with cits–1979]

prog *vb, n* (Baha, etc) See PRAG

prog·ging-stick *n* (BrVi, Mrat) A tough stick used for digging potatoes or other root vegetables out of the ground. [See etym note at PRAG]

prop *vb* **1.** (Bdos) [IF] To lean (on, against sth). *... and she turned to Mrs Bham and asked her what had happened. She added that Mrs Bham was 'propping' on a table and was crying.*—AdN (73.01.16, p.1) **2.** PHRASE **2.1 prop sorrow** *vb phr* (ECar) [IF] To sit looking sad, with your chin cupped in your hands and elbows propped on your knees. *A-A, you t'ink because time not so bright dis time ah goin' stay in ah corner an' prop sorrow.*—WeN (52.12.22, p.6, Annie & Josephine)

pro·per¹ *adj* (Tbgo) [AF/IF] In your right mind; sensible. *Where you dressing to go out in all this rain? You proper?*—(Tbgo)

pro·per² [prɒpp ~ prapa] *adv intensifier* (Guyn) [AF] ‖ PROPERLY (Antg, etc) **a.** *De woman put do[w]ng some proper nasty cuss.*—(Guyn) **b.** *That sounds good, chief. C.S.C.—Crown's special care. / Gosh you can proper twist words.*—CTT:31 [*OED* *proper* B. adv properly 'excellently, finely, hand-somely; genuinely, thoroughly'. Now dial., vulgar or slang + cit 1835, 'I am proper glad you agree with me, Squire', said he] **2.** PHRASE **2.1 good and proper** *adv phr* (CarA) See GOOD[3] Phr 2.4

pro·per·ly *adv intensifier* (Antg, Guyn, StLu, Tbgo, Trin) [IF] ‖*proper* (Guyn) Thoroughly; extremely; very (much). **a.** *They properly hate the Catholics and preach terribly against us, words that I won't repeat.*—CTT:22 **b.** *I hope is for that, because I hear that he properly bold, me ent trusting he.*—(Tbgo) [Cp OED *properly* adv 5. Of degree: 'thoroughly, quite; exceedingly, very'. (Now slang or colloq) + cit 1664, Pepys Diary, '... such variety of pictures, and other things of value and rarity, that I was properly con-founded']

pro·per·ty-a·gent *n* (Guyn) (BrE) An estate agent; (AmE) a real-estate agent.

pros·pect·ing-knife *n* (Guyn) A long, heavy knife serving many purposes and used esp by PORK-KNOCKERS and workers in the INTERIOR of Guyana. [< *prospecting* 'work of a prospector for gold, etc' + *knife*]

proud-flesh *n* (Bdos) [AF] ‖BAD-FLESH 2. (Bdos)

prove *vb* **1.** (Bdos) [Of an animal] To be successfully impregnated; to be with young. [Cp OED *prove* B. 10. (Obs) 'to turn out well; to prosper; to succeed' + cit-'1698 'All the eggs laid under one hen do not always prove'. Also EDD *prove* vb 'of cattle: to turn out to be with young'] **2.** (Bdos, Tbgo) [By extension] [AF/IF] To be successful. **a.** *She bring up three nephews and every one o[f] them prove.*—(Bdos) **b.** *I made a bet of three dollars, but it didn[']t prove.*—(Tbgo) **3.** PHRASE **3.1 prove your mouth** *vb phr* (Trin) [AF] To show or prove that what you have said is true (against a charge of slander). *Tomorrow mornin'! So help me God! I goin' down by the Court house an' take out a summons fer yer. I will make yer prove yer mouth before the doors of Court. What the hell you know 'bout me?*—JMRS:47

pro·vi·sion-grounds/-land *n* (CarA) **1.** [Hist] An area of plantation land set aside for slaves to cultivate their own food. **2.** Rural farm land often far away from its owner's dwelling, cultivated for market gardening.

pro·vi·sion(s) *n* (*pl*) (CarA) [IF] ‖G-ROUND-PROVISIONS (CarA) **a.** *Men crowded into the camp ... carrying sacks or baskets containing a week's food. One said to me: 'Look how a lorry mash up my tin.... Now I have nothing left in which to cook my little provision.'*—Wan (1974, p.15) **b.** *Remove from heat, add water to cover, simmer for 45 minutes. Serve hot with provisions and vegetables.*—ViN (75.06.27, p.10) [< *provision* of food for self-sustenance] □ Pl also so

used in AmE, perh also survival from the colonial era.

prune [pwi·n] *n* (StLu) See PWIN

psi·di·um ['sɪdɪʌm] *n* (Guyn) ‖GOVERNOR-PLUM (CarA) [Perh orig an error as the botanical *Psidium spp* is different from the *Flacourtia spp* to wh this fruit belongs. See the ‖]

Pub·lic Build·ings /ɪ'122/ *n pl* (Bdos, Guyn) The historic buildings wh house the country's Parliament and some associated offices.

puck·a *n* (Gren) A long piece of firm wire bent into a hook at its end; it is poked into crab holes to hook and pull out crabs [Prob < SE *poker*, though it is also said to be a Carib word. However, *BDFC* (p.96) gives the Carib name *yamala* for the same implement.] Cp GRAIN[3]

puc(k)·a·ter·y *n* (Antg, CayI, Guyn) See PO-CATERY

Puer·to Ri·can *adj phr, n phr* (CarA) (A person or thing) native or belonging to Puerto Rico.

pud·ding *n* (Bdos) **1.** Any kind of cake (except the traditional Christmas GREAT-CAKE). **2.** ‖B-LACK-PUDDING (CarA) **3.** PHRASE **3.1 pudding and souse** [pʊdɪŋ an sɒʊs ~ pʊdnən sɒʊs] *n phr* (CarA) A combination dish of slices of BLACK-PUDDING and SOUSE; it is a favoured weekend folk-dish and buffet item.

puff *vb* **1.** (Gren) To get a belly ache, gripe, or colic (from overeating, etc). **2.** PHRASE **2.1 puff up your face** *vb phr* (Gren) [AF] ‖MAKE UP YOUR FACE (CarA) See FACE Phrs 4., 6.

puff-bel·ly-and-fine-foot *n* (Tbgo) [IF] ‖*pot-foot* (Bdos) A kind of plait (esp of Black girls' hair) with the middle-section slack or 'puffed' and the root and end tight.

pu·ja (poo·ja) [pu·ja] *n* (Guyn, Trin) [Indic] An act of prayer and worship of a Hindu deity, either by an individual or collectively in a ritual ceremony. *I make a clarion call to all Hindus to go to your temples and join in the Puja, chant the glory of the Almighty God and pray for His benign Grace.*—GyC (76.10.22, p.25) [Bhoj < Hin *puujaa* 'worship, adoration'] **2.** PHRASES **2.1 do (a) puja** *vb phr* (Guyn, Trin) To perform a private, individual act of (Hindu) worship. *Laughing at me when I do puja. I know the good I doing myself when I do puja, you hear.*—NHMB:135 **2.2 hold/offer a puja** *vb phr* (Guyn, Trin) To hold a ritual PUJA to wh others are invited. **a.** *He stated that, in his opinion, Trinidadians were stauncher Hindus than their counterparts in India. / He said he intended to hold a five-day Puja to celebrate his safe return.*—ExP (72.10.26, p.12) **b.** *Once in six months or so the old man would offer a puja or worship to Hanuman, the Monkey God. But this was not much. It was not a prayer-service really. It was simply a propitiatory* *ceremony to win the favour of Hanuman.—* NAGOS:55

pu·ku·mi·na *n* (Jmca) See POCOMANIA, though the form **pukumina** seems more rational

pull *vb* 1. *vb intr* (Guyn, Tbgo, Trin) [*IF*] [Of persons] To get along well together; to work in harmony. *That Party goin[g] lose because three important people there don['t] pull, and everybody know that.*—(Trin) 2. *PHRASES* **2.1 pull a boat** *vb phr* (CayI, Grns, Guyn, USVI) To paddle, or row a boat. [From pulling on the oar] **2.2 pull a joke (on sb)** *vb phr* (Angu, Jmca, StKt) [*IF*] To make fun (of/with sb); to tease, jest (with sb). *'While thus engaged,' said Francis, 'he pulled a joke on me and in a joke I made a 'bob and weave' move.*—Dem(SK) (63.09.28, p.10) **2.3 pull a note/tune** *vb phr* (ECar) [*IF*] To reach or produce the correct pitch/tune. *But don't be startled by this, since according to the expert himself, the saw cannot hold the 'uptempo notes' one would need to pull a calypso or jazz tune. And added to this is the fact that not every saw will play; according to Leacock only a frown saw will play, for it meets the necessary requirements.*—NaT (78.03.08, p.2) [Combining senses of *pulling* 'exerting effort to reach' + pulling a guitar, etc string] **2.4 pull a skull** *vb phr* (Trin) [*AF*] See SKULL² Phr **2.5 pull brakes** *vb phr* (Guyn) [*IF*] To brake; to step on/apply the brake. *The dower pulled brakes but the car skidded.*—Guyn (Ms) [By transfer from 'pulling up' the brake handles of a bicycle] **2.6 pull bull** *vb phr* (Trin) [*AF—Joc*] To use your private car illegally as a taxi; to run an illegal taxi service with a private car not licensed for such service. *Sometimes I don't get home to Belmont at night unless I can find some off-duty policeman or fireman or even a High Court Marshal 'pulling bull' in their private cars. / And Hector can bet his life I am one man who will not 'snitch' on these people who are my friends.*—BoM (80.01.04, p.16) **2.7 pull foot** *vb phr* (Jmca) [*AF*] ‖ PUT FOOT (Angu, etc) *O Peter, Peter was a black boy / Peter him pull foot one day / ... Oh! Peter was a bad boy; / Peter was a runaway.*—DLVIE:31 **2.8 pull out your arm (and hit sb)** *vb phr* (Dmca) See ARM Phr 2. **2.9 pull (sb's) nara** *vb phr* (Guyn, Trin) See NARA Phr **2.10 pull sb's tongue** *vb phr* (Jmca) [*AF*] ‖ PICK SB'S MOUTH (CarA) See PICK Phr 5.7 **2.11 pull up your face** *vb phr* (Dmca) [*AF*] ‖ MAKE UP YOUR FACE (CarA) [*IF*] See FACE Phr 4. **2.12 pull your pocket(s)** *vb phr* (Bdos) [*AF/IF*] To pay out money with hardship; (SE) put your hand deep into your pocket. *All Barbadians, not only the politicians, have had to 'pull their pockets' and 'fork out' the money to pay for these very same goods and services and have had to absorb the very same rises.*—(AdN (73.04.29, p.4) **2.13 Pull yourself!** *excl vb phr* (StVn, Trin) [*AF*] ‖ MOVE YOURSELF! (Baha, etc) *S1: Mother how you dolling up so? Like yo[u] have yo[ur] eyes on somebody! / S2: Look boy, pull yourself and mind your business.*—(Trin) [Cp usage with ‖ **haul yourself** (Bdos, etc)]

pull·(ed)-down *adj* (Bdos, Gren, Guyn, Trin) [*IF/AF*] Sickly or sickly looking; weak in body (esp after an illness); dejected. *Recovery may be prompt or slow, but the general result is to leave the sufferer very much 'pulled down' or physically weakened.*—AdN (79.03.18, p.11)

pulp(·ing)-ed·doe *n* (Bdos) ‖ EDDOE 1. (Guyn) [In *Bdos* the eddoe is boiled in its skin; then, with the top cut off, it is squeezed by hand or 'pulped' i.e. the edible, slightly slimy flesh slips free out of the skin]

pump¹ *vb* (Tbgo) [*AF*] To beg for and get (esp a free lift in a vehicle); to cadge, hitch (a ride). □ The term is also listed in *CGBD5* for *Bdos* but appears to be no longer current.

pump(s)² *n* (*pl*) 1. (Bdos) (Originally) the cheaper kind of CREPESOLE(S), usu black or brown. *It is wicked to pick up a man who has spent five years in prison and give him a suit of dungaree, a pair of pumps and a $20 bill and send him through the gate.*—Bdos (Hd, n.d) 2. (Bdos) [By extension] Rubber-soled or plastic shoes of many colours and styles (often fashionably known by temporary commercial names). *About 200 children of the Garrison Secondary School were sent home after they had turned up for school on Monday ... wearing pumps and sneakers to school.*—Nat (76.05.02, p.1) [*OED* pump sb² 'a kind of light shoe ... kept on the foot by its close fit ... esp (17C–18C) one worn where freedom of movement was required ...' + cit 1688. 'Pumps are shoes with single soles and no heels.' However this sense (with 'no heels') does not seem to have survived in ModE] □ See notes at CREPESOLES, GYM-BOOTS (= 'sneakers'). The sg is avoided. 3. (Nevs, StKt, Tbgo) ‖ COURT SHOES (Bdos, Guyn) *Not only is the bridal dress ... one of the criteria for judgement, but she [the bride] must be able to 'step' well in her high-heeled white 'pumps'.*—EFOT (Ms) [*OED* pump sb² is restricted in sense to 'a light, low-heeled shoe usually of patent leather' but adds 'worn with evening dress for dancing'. In the W Indies men's dancing pumps, as they were called, would have prob been matched by ladies' high-heeled evening shoes for dancing, and hence a poss shift of the name 'pumps' to these shoes. Note also an *OED* cit 1763: 'The flat-heel'd drudges now are thrown aside for the high pumps with toes of peaked pride'—which suggests a type not accounted for in the *OED* gloss. Note also that *Nevs* (esp) and *Tbgo* flourished with high colonial Eng society in the 18C]

pum·pum [pʌmpʌm] *n* (CarA) [*AF—Vul*] The female genitals. [Prob of W Afr orig. Cp *KED* Krio *pombɔ* 'the female vulva', also *pumpumpum* 'a foolish/stupid person, one who is easily duped', a poss association like BrE (Vul) *cunt*]

punch au creme (**punch de creme**) *n phr* (ECar) See PONCHE DE CREME.

pun·ish *vb* 1. *vb tr* (Belz, Guyn) [*IF/AF*] To try the endurance of (sb); to strain and cause suffering to (sb). **a.** *That gate proper punished him to finish.*—(Belz) **b.** *The cold punish the child so, I had to keep him home for the week.*—(Guyn) [Cp *EDD punish vb* (Sc, Yks, etc and Amer) 1. 'to cause pain or suffering to; to hurt, try, injure; to suffer pain'] 2. *vb intr* (CarA) [By extension] To suffer; to experience much hardship. **a.** *I went to the hospital without a thing in my stomach and I just stayed there and punished till afternoon before the doctor saw me.*—(Mrat) **b.** *De next t'ing you know he will put you out de house and bring one of his high-colour lady friends to live wid him. And den you will punish.*—MLDS:15 [Note last sense of *EDD punish* in prec note + cit from Amer 1896 'I punished so in my new shoes'. Note also, however, that in some W Afr langs the same word serves the two senses *punish, suffer.* Ex Igbo *taa-afufu* 'to suffer; to punish.' (*pers info, Dr C. Azuonye*)]

punk [pʌŋk~puŋk] *n* [*AF—Derog*] 1. (Bdos, Guyn) A stupid person. 2. (USVI) A male homosexual.

pun·ka·sal [puŋkasal] *n* (Crcu, Gren) [*AF*] ‖ CREPESOLES (Guyn, etc) *We don't really say 'pun-kasals'—old people would say 'Pass me that pun-kasal' when they mean one or both shoes, but young people would just ask for a pair of keds in a store.*—(Gren) [Cp Macusi (a Cariban lang) *pukung* 'hunting dog' + *pucaza* 'sandal' (*FTCC: 124, 133*). Poss a mainland Cariban loan word via Island Carib]

punt *n* (Guyn) [Sugar Ind] ‖ *cane-punt, sugar-punt* (Guyn) A flat-bottomed iron barge about 20 ft long, about 8 ft wide, and 3 or 4 ft deep with perpendicular, sides rounded at both ends, for transporting harvested canes along the system of canals or TRENCHES from field to factory, drawn by a mule led along the PUNT-TRENCH DAM. *I remember many years ago seeing punts laden with sugarcane being towed by mules along the trench leading to 'Diamond Estate'. / This trench known up to this day as punt-trench, and the adjoining road as punt trench dam, where sturdy mules walking on the dam would pull these punts which were attached by long chains.*—GyC (77.01.16, p.12)

pun·ta[1] *n* (Belz) A vigorous, erotic group dance accompanied by drumming and singing; it is esp associated with the GARIFUNA. *In Belize the call-and-response song is also found in Carib culture, both in the punta (which adds a refrain to the call and response) and in the wanaragua, or John Canoe, music.*—Bes VIII. 2, p.11) [Prob < Garifuna via Sp. Cp *CSESD punta* 1. '(j) (Carib) taunt; (k) (LAm) group'. The term *punta* also occurs in connection with dancing in other new world Sp cultures. See *SDGA*] □ The dance has been compared by informants with KUMINA (*Jmca*) and PIKÉ (*Crcu, etc*). See next cit.

pun·ta[2] *vb intr* (Belz) To dance the PUNTA. *'The drumming was hotter too', Miss Winny piped up*

... *'sometimes it was only the box we had to beat on but everybody sing and dance and punta till we all fall down. We got the spirit'.*—EBL:76 [By functional n > vb shift of PUNTA[1]]

punt-trench *n* (Guyn) A sugar-plantation canal used for drainage and for the transportation of harvested canes by PUNT.

punt-trench dam *n phr* (Guyn) The waterside footpath on either side of the PUNT-TRENCH, made of banked mud.

pu·nya *n* (Tbgo) See PONIA

pu·nyal *n* (USVI) ‖ PONIA (Tbgo)

pu·nya(r)k *n* (Jmca) ‖ PONIA (Tbgo)

pu·pa (**pup·pa**) *n* (CarA) See POOPA(H)

pu(p)·pa·lick *n* (Belz, Jmca) See POOPALICK

pup·py-show [pʌpišo] *n* (Belz, TkCa) [*AF—Joc*] ‖ PAPPYSHOW (CarA) *After stopping on the side of the street, I observed that over one hundred students, teachers and college students were making a total puppy-show and mockery of the unscrupulous losers of the election.*—BeT (79.12.09, p.7)

pu·pu *n, vb* (Antg, Dmca) [*AF*] See POU POU

pu·ri [puri] *n* (Guyn, Trin) [Indic] ‖ DAAL PURI (Guyn, etc) *Three dozen puri were prepared for the little ceremony.*—(Guyn) [Bhoj < Hin *puurii* 'fried dough'] □ This shortened form, without pl, is common in *Guyn.*

pur·ka·to·ry *n* (Antg, CayI, Guyn) See PO-CATERY

pur·ple·heart *n* (Guyn, Trin) [Timber Ind] A heavy, dark-purple, straight-grained wood yielded by a forest tree exceeding 100 ft in height (in Guyana), most of it a straight bole moderately buttressed; the tough and durable wood is used as building material but is more favoured for furniture, taking a high polish and resisting insects; *Peltogyne porphyrocardia* or *P. pubescens* (*Caesalpiniaceae*). [From the colour of its tough heartwood, though the outer sapwood is white]

pur·pose *n* (CarA) [*IF*] 1. Spite. [Often in foll phr] 2. PHRASE 2.1 **for purpose** *adv phr* (CarA) [*X*] On purpose; spitefully; with malicious intent. *'And she don't hit me for purpose,' Bob said. 'She don't do it for purpose. She does it 'cause she's God-fearing. She always say the Bible say 'Spare not the rod and spoil the child'. And 'tis only that she don't want to spoil me.'*—LICMS:15

purs·lane (**purs·ley**) [pʌrzlen~pʌrzli] *n* (Bdos, Jmca, Trin) ‖ JUMP-UP-AND-KISS-ME (CayI, etc)

push *vb tr* PHRASES **1. if/when push come(s) to shove** *id phr* (CarA) [*AF/IF*] See IF Phr 2. *They* [*the Carnival headpieces*] *might have been light and beautiful, but when push come to shove I am sure they were cumbersome.*—TrG (76.03.26, p.5) [*OED2* lists this Phr (*push vb* 1. n) as N Amer, with earliest cit 1958. However it is likely to have had a longer history in CE, where COME 'become' is also current] **2. push fire** *vb phr* (CarA) [*AF/IF*] See FIRE¹ Phr 4.3 *The husband and wife could have settled their dispute long ago but his mother only pushing fire.*—(Tbgo) **3. push up your face** *vb phr* (Bdos, Nevs, StKt, StVn) [*AF*] ‖ MAKE UP YOUR FACE (CarA) See FACE Phr 4. *Sometimes both young and old men would call me and I make them know their place. Sometimes when I am on the street walking I have to 'push up' my face so no one can call at me.*—PeL (87.12.31, p.7) **4. push your mouth in (sb's business)** *vb phr* (Bdos, Guyn, Trin) [*AF*] To interfere in (a dispute, quarrel); to offer an uninvited opinion in a matter that does not concern you. *My gentleman, I ent talking to you, you say you is a blindman, walking with a stick and still you pushing yah mouth in everything yah hear from the time the bus left the stand you ent stop talk yet.*—Bdos (Ms Play, 1977)

puss [pʊs] *n* (Belz, Jmca) [*IF*] A cat. *She shout from the windo[w] to stop de bwoys stoning de puss.*—(Belz) [Cp similarly *KED* Krio *pusi* < Eng *pussy* 'a cat'; *IMED* Mende *pusi* 'cat'. The familiar English term must have been more widely current, in early colonial times, than 'cat'] □ This is the conventional term used in *Belz, Jmca* for 'cat' even above the folk-level, though *cat* occurs in Formal contexts.

puss-boots *n pl* (Jmca) [*AF—Joc*] ‖ CREPESOLES (Guyn, etc) [Prob humorous folk ref to soft treading in such shoes. Cp sense of AmE 'sneakers']

puss·in [pʊsɪn] *n* (Trin) [*AF*] **1.** A cat or a kitten. **2.** [By extension] [*AF—Joc/Derog*] A young woman.

puss·ley [pʌsli] *n* (Bdos, Jmca, StKt, Trin, USVI) ‖ JUMP-UP-AND-KISS-ME (CayI, etc)

puss·y-boil *n* (Brbu) [*IF*] ‖ CAT-BOIL (CarA)

put *vb* PHRASES **1. not put water in your mouth to (say sth)** *neg vb phr* (Trin) [*AF—Joc*] ‖ NOT TALK IN BOLI (Gren) See BOLI Phr 3.1 *And you know me! When I know I'm right I don[']t put water in me mout[h] to tell whoever it is whe[re] the stops are!*—(Trin) **2. put (a) cuff/(the) cuffs in (sb)** *vb phr* (Guyn) [*AF*] See CUFF¹ Phrs **3. put a lash/(the) lashes** *vb phr* (CarA) [*IF*] See LASH Phr 2.3 **4. put a wash of blows on (sb)** *vb phr* (Guyn) [*AF*] ‖ BEAT SB('S) SKIN (CarA) See BEAT Phr 4.14 □ A more intensive phr than BEAT SB'S SKIN. **5. put away** *vb phr* (ECar) (i) To tidy up (a room), refurbish (a house) (usu for a special occasion). *Did you notice this Christmas how many housewives 'put away house' in red*

and white? It was almost as though ESP was present, so frequently did it happen. And yet this was a decision usually made by each housewife herself.—TrG (73.01.07, p.7) (ii) To prepare (a corpse) for viewing. *You can now express your love and affection for your departed ones by putting them away in a big city way at no extra cost.*—LaS (Ad, 64.12.18, p.2) **6. put bad-eye on (sb/sth)** *vb phr* (Belz, Guyn) [*IF*] See BAD-EYE Phr 2.3 **7. put bad in sb's way** *vb phr* (Guyn, Tbgo) To cause sb to run into trouble or difficulty (often in retaliation for a wrong done). *We hired him and had to fire him for stealing, but we didn[']t put bad in his way, when we knew where he was applying for another job.*—(Tbgo) **8. put down** *vb phr* (CarA) [*IF*] (i) To shed (tears); to utter (bad words). **a.** *Well the woman is dead and he better stop puttin[g] down eye-water and get somebody to look after those children.*—(Belz) **b.** *I would not repeat those bad words Brear Rabbie said; but I can tell you that he put down one piece of cursing.*—TOSR:9 (ii) [Of a vehicle] To garage (it). *The island's entire public transport system was brought to a halt when the workers put down the buses, calling for the resignation of Transport Board chairman.*—SuS (80.06.29, p.2) **9. put foot** *vb phr* (i) (Angu, Brbu, Gren, Guyn, Nevs, StKt, Trin) See FOOT Phr 2.12 *When the estate ranger came along we would scramble up our clothes and put foot through the canefields.*—Guyn (Ms) (ii) [Always neg] (Gren, Guyn, StKt, Trin) ‖ *not cross foot* (Bdos) See FOOT Phr 2.11 *But Tanti Merle livin' in Curepe fifteen years / An' she never put foot in de Oval, / So why today, eh? why today? tell me dat.*—KTT:27 **10. put fowl to mind corn** *id vb phr* (BrVi) [*AF—Joc*] See FOWL Phr 2.1 **11. put France/hell, etc on (sb)** *vb phr* (CarA) To berate severely; to give (sb) a tongue-lashing, lambasting, etc. *I know how to behave ... when I come out and put hell on somebody it is because I feel it is my duty to do so.*—Dem(SK) (61.09.30, p.2) **12. put goat-mouth on (sb/sth)** *vb phr* (CarA) [*AF—Joc*] See GOAT-MOUTH Phr 2.3 **13. put guzu on (sb)** *vb phr* (Belz, Jmca) [*AF*] See GUZU Phr **14. put in hand /** 1'21/; **put your hand in sth** *vb phr* See HAND¹ Phr 4.25 **15. put maldjo on (sb/sth)** *vb phr* (Gren, StVn, Tbgo, Trin) See MALDJO Phr 2.2 **16. put obeah on (sb)** *vb phr* (CarA) See OBEAH¹ Phr 3.2 **17. put roach on sb's bread** *vb phr* (Baha) [*AF—Joc*] ‖ HORN¹ (Baha, etc) **18. put (sb) so** *vb phr* (CarA) [*AF/IF*] ‖ *do(sb)so* (ECar) ‖ *make (sb) mal* Dmca ‖ *turn (sb) so* (Bdos, Guyn) To bewitch, put a spell on (sb) so as to cause mental unbalance or some unexplained sickness. **a.** *'But who put you so that you must sit up in a church morning noon and night, nuh?' the mother would rave.*—MBGB:158 **b.** *Me never faget uncle Pampo / He dead decidin' people put 'im so.*—LMFF:20 **19. put (some) lashes/licks (in sb's skin/tail)** *vb phr* (Bdos) [*AF*] See LICKS Phr 3.8 **20. put the law out of your favour** *id phr* (Bdos) See LAW Phr 2. **21. put (the) licks (of hell) in sb** *vb phr* (Bdos) [*AF*] ‖ BEAT SB('S) SKIN (CarA) See BEAT Phr 4.14 □ A more intensive phr than BEAT SB'S SKIN. **22. put up your face** *vb phr* (Angu, Nevs) [*AF*] ‖ MAKE UP YOUR

FACE (CarA) [*IF*] See FACE Phr 4. **23. put (your) bad-eye, big-eye, eye, long-eye, red-eye on (sth)/(sb)** (See the nouns for those phrs) **24. put your hand on sb** *vb phr* (CarA) [*AF*] See HAND[1] Phr 4.26 *If you don't behave yourself, I am going to put my hand on you.*—(Tbgo) **25. put your head down** *vb phr* (CarA) [*IF*] See HEAD Phr 4.15 **26. put your mouth in sb's business/story** *vb phr* (CarA) [*AF/IF*] See MOUTH Phr 4.24 *When good friends fall out it is best not to put your mouth in their story because you may end up bad friends with both sides.*— (Mrat) **26.1 put (your) mouth on (sb)** *vb phr* (CarA) [*AF/IF*] ‖ PUT YOUR BAD-MOUTH ON (SB/ STH) (CarA) See BAD-MOUTH[1] Phr 3.2, MOUTH Phr 4.26.1 *Also, 'putting mouth on ya' is a type of curse, but does not necessarily have to originate from any Biblical implication.*—MTTBT:86

Put·ta·gee [pʌtagi] *n, adj* See PORTUGUEE.

put·ta-put·ta (po·to-po·to) [pʌtʌ-pʌtʌ] / 1'122/ *n* (Guyn, Jmca) [*AF*] Very soft mud, esp in a pathway or a yard. *After the heavy rainfall the dam was putta-putta all over and our shoes were covered with mud.*—SuC (66.05.06, p.6) [Cp *DAFL* Twi pɔtɔpɔtɔ 'slimy sediment of any thing', also *WIED* Igbo pɔtɔpɔtɔ 'wet, muddy soil'. The form potopoto occurs similarly used in Krio]

puz·zling-box/-tin *n* (Bdos, Guyn) A child's penny-bank box, sealed except for the slot through wh the coin is slipped; a piggy-bank box or tin. [Because getting the coins out is a puzzle to a child]

pwa-g(w)até [pwa-g(w)ate] *n* (Dmca, Gren, StLu) ‖ COWITCH (CarA) [Fr Cr < Fr *pois* 'pea(-pod)' + *gratter* 'scratch' in *CarA* sense = 'itch'. Pronunc /gwaté/ 'gratter' with characteristic Fr Cr /r > w/ shift, but this disappears altogether in *Gren* pronunc **pwa-gaté**]

pwa·yen [pu-ayɛ̃ ~ pwayɛ̃] *n* (Gren) ‖ BRAATA (Antg, etc) *After I buy all these mangoes you can[t] give me no pwayen on them?*—(Gren) [Fr Cr *pou-ayen* < Fr *pour rien* 'for nothing']

pwin (prune) [pwi·n] *n* (StLu) ‖ CHILLI-PLUM (Antg, etc)

pwin-Mo·wis; **pwin-té·té** [pwi·n-mowis/-tete] *n* (StLu) ‖ JAMAICA-PLUM (Bdos, etc) [Fr Cr < Fr *prune* 'plum' + *Morris*, a name; or + Fr Cr *tété* 'female breast' < Fr *téter* 'to suckle (of an infant)'. Cp ‖ *bubby-plum* (Bdos)]

pwin-té·té *n* (StLu) See PWIN-MOWIS

pya(w)-pya(w) [pya·-pya· ~ pyɒ·-pyɒ·] *adj* (Jmca) [*AF—Joc*] [Of a thing] Inferior; of poor quality; [of an animal] skinny; weak; [of a person] insignificant; of no account. *Dem is pya-pya people, but dem have big weddin[g], no pya-pya.*—(Jmca) [Prob of Afr orig. Cp *DAFL* Fante *piapia* 'to constrain'. However see *DJE pyaa-pyaa* for other (non-Afr) suggestions) □ The term is widely used by educated speakers, and appears in *Joc* writing spelled **pyaw-pyaw**.

pyé-poul [pye-pu·l] *n* (Dmca) ‖ FOWL-FOOT GRASS (CarA) [Fr Cr < Fr *pied* 'foot' + *poule* 'fowl, chicken']

pyg·my-owl *n* (Trin) ‖ JUMBIE-BIRD 2. (Trin) *The pygmy-owl or jumbie-bird is.... the commonest local owl ... the call ... is easy to imitate by whistling.*—HBTT:130 [The owl is only '6-1/2 ins' long (*HBTT:129*), hence name]

pyo·ko [pyʌkʌ] *adj* (Gren) [Of fruit, vegetables] Immature; unripe; unready for sale or use, though on sale. [Cp *DJE* Jmca Cr *pyaka-pyaka* var *pyoko-pyoko* 'untidy, messed up' also *pyaa-pyaa* 'weak; poor, inferior', neither form being of clear origin]

pyong *n* (Tbgo, Trin) See PIONG

Q

qua(c)·coo (qua(c)·koo¹) [kwaku] *n* (Guyn, Jmca) [*AF—Derog*] A rough, gullible Black man; [by extension] any Black person who accepts contemptuous treatment. [Prob infl by a combination of SE *quack* + DAFL Twi *Kwaku*, day-name for a boy born on Wednesday; in the latter case cp other Twi day-names (*Kofi, Kwasi* > QUASHIE) wh are also used derogatorily. However, note also DAFL Twi *ɔ-kwaku* 'a monkey']

qua(c)·koo² (qua(k)·ko) [kwakʊ ~ kwaku] *n* (Guyn) An aggressive blue-black wasp; it attacks in numbers and is much dreaded. [Perh an Amerindian name]

qua(c)·koo-ad·ja [kwaku-aja] *n* (Guyn, Trin) A ridiculously overdressed or foolishly dressed person. [Perh related to QUA(C)KOO¹ or other W Afr source. However, CGBD:5 notes *quakahadja* (*Bdos*) 'a puppet of wood or cardboard' and refers to DSUE 1. *quocker-wodger* 'a puppet politician' (19C). The *Bdos* term is not current]

qua·drille¹ (ca·drille) ['kwadrɪl ~ 'kadrɪl] *n* (CarA) **1.** An old-fashioned, now rural, dance for groups of couples, consisting of (usu) five set sequences called 'figures' wh are called out by a leader, the rhythm and movements of each getting quicker; the 'finale' is sometimes also called the *'hot piece'*. [Adaptation of European *quadrille*, wh is a square dance] □ Revival performances of this dance by older folk are popular on festive occasions or at cultural shows in some islands. **2.** (StLu) A village dance at wh a QUADRILLE BAND supplies the music. **3.** PHRASE **3.1 hold a quadrille** *vb phr* To put on such a dance (usu to raise funds).

qua·drille² *vb intr* To dance the known sequences of the QUADRILLE¹.

qua·drille band *n phr* (CarA) ‖ *country-band* (StLu) A band of five or six players with violins, tambourine or SHAC-SHAC, drum, and triangle, providing music for old-fashioned dances, esp the QUADRILLE.

quad·ro·phon·ics [kwadrʊfʌnɪks] *n* (Trin) A set of four linked PANS in a STEELBAND two of wh stand vertically; the rim of each is about 3/8 of a drum in depth and the surface is sunk the same as a DOUBLE-SECOND PAN; the set together carries a full range of notes to allow doubling or harmonizing with any other PAN(s) in the band,

and they are, with the FIRSTS and the SECOND PANS, third in complementing the melody section of a STEELBAND; there are usu two or more such sets. □ The term functions as sg or pl.

quail *vb* **1.** *vb intr* (Bdos, Guyn, Tbgo, USVI) **(i)** [Of leaves] To shrivel up, wither, wilt, or fade. *You must allow the bush to quail before you boil it to make bush-tea.*—Guyn (Ms) **(ii)** (Guyn) [Of certain kinds of fruit] To become soft in an advanced stage of ripeness (as do plantains). **(iii)** (Grns, StVn) [Of a tree] To sicken, lose its leaves and probably die. [Evid a dial or EE survival. Cp *OED quail* v¹ 1. (*Obs* or *dial*) 'of persons, plants, etc: to fade, wither' + cits-1880] **2.** *vb tr* (Bdos, Guyn, Tbgo, USVI) **(i)** To cause (leaves) to wilt by heating. *You have to quail pieces of banana leaf to wrap the conkie in before boiling.*—(Bdos) **(ii)** (Bdos) To braise (meat). **(iii)** (BrVi) To put (wood) to dry before burning (as in making charcoal). *The wood is cut into approximately two-foot strips and then stacked where it remains for two days to quail. Quailing is the drying of wood to a stage in which the colour is between green and ochre.*—Vgi I.3, p.19

quake [kwe·k] *n* (Guyn) A deep wicker-work (usu covered) basket used by fishermen to keep their catch of crabs or fish. [BAED Arawak *kuake* [kʊa·kɛ] 'container for crabs'. The current pronunc prob developed from the spelling]

qua(k)·ko *n* (Guyn) See QUA(C)KOO²

quart *n* (Bdos) A twenty-five-cent piece, being a quarter of one dollar. [< AmE *quarter* with loss of final unstressed syllable by apocope]

quar·ter (-bot·tle) *n* (Gren) A small bottle containing about 6-1/2 fl ozs of rum. *After offering the accused a quarter of strong rum and buying an eighth for himself he said that he left the shop.*—ToR (76.03.14, p.3)

qua·shie ['kwaši] *n* (Antg, Guyn, Jmca) A Black man who is considered to be gullible or stupid, esp such a person who is not familiar with city-life; [by extension] any Black person who is considered to be of no importance. [< Twi *Kwàsí*, name of a male person born on a Sunday. See also DJE *Day-Name*] □ This connotation may have grown out of the surviving use of such orig Afr names by later arrivals, or SALT-WATER slaves, who were despised by CREOLE slaves. (Cp also CUFFY.) The connotation is not, however, universal (currently at least) since *Cuffy, Quashie* are well-known family names in some territories, *StVn*, etc).

qua·shie-bit·ters /1′222/ *n* (Guyn) A medicinal drink made either by using a BITTER-CUP or by soaking a piece of LIGNUM VITAE in a cup of water overnight. [From the use of the wood of the tree *Quassia amara* or *Q. excelsa* for carving the BITTER-CUP, the name *quassia* being said to be derived from 'Kwasi', the name of the Afr slave who revealed the properties of the wood. (See BITTERWOOD 2.). The wide use of this medicine by Black rural folk may, however, have given rise to this term independently]

qua·tro *n* (StLu, Trin) See CUATRO □ This spelling, used by some writers, is prob infl by Fr *quatre* 'four'. However, the Sp origin and name of the instrument renders *cuatro* the preferable spelling.

quat·tie (**quar·tie**) [kwati] *n* (Belz, Jmca) **1.** A small silver coin of the value of a quarter of sixpence (hence the name) or 'penny-ha'penny', evid used up to the early 20C; that cash value (without ref to a coin). *Sir: I have been reading the Gleaner from I was a little girl when it was selling for a quattie, and straight through the years (I am now 65) I have been reading the Gleaner.*— DaG (79.12.03, p.10) **2.** [By extension] A worthless amount of money. *We say a thing 'isn't worth a quartie', but they were only words to me.*—ReP (80.05.18, p.12) □ As the cit at sense 2. (*Belz*) indicates, the word is used (and with diminished meaning) mostly by older folk, but it is preserved in provs and folk-songs.

queen *n* (CarA) **1.** A woman chosen in a competition for skill, competence, beauty, costume, or a combination of these. (See CARNIVAL QUEEN, PARANG QUEEN, and separate entries below). **2.** [Rastaf] A RASTAFARIAN woman who is a sexual companion of a RASTAFARIAN man, and usu also a mother. **3.** PHRASES **3.1 Queen J'Ouvert** *n phr* (Tbgo, Trin) The young woman judged to be wearing the most wittily conceived OLE MAS costume and placard at J'OUVERT, during wh she is crowned. **3.2 Queen of the Band** *n phr* (ECar) The leading female masquerader of a costumed CARNIVAL BAND; she is most elaborately costumed, as the counterpart of the KING OF THE BAND. **3.2.1 Queen of the Bands** *n phr* (Tbgo, Trin) ‖ CARNIVAL QUEEN (ECar) **3.3 Queen of the Bay** *n phr* (Belz) The young lady who is winner of the beauty contest held to celebrate ST GEORGE'S CAYE DAY. [The Bay refers to the Baymen who won the battle in the Bay Islands off Belize] **3.4 Queen of Carnival** *n phr* (ECar) ‖ CARNIVAL QUEEN (ECar)

queen-of-flow·ers* *n* **1.** (ECar) A bushy garden shrub with slender, erect branches bearing showy spikes of flowerets that are sometimes 10

ins long and 3 ins across; there are several varieties including pink, purple, and white; *Lagerstroemia indica* (*Lythraceae*). **2.** (Trin) ‖ **queen's flower tree** (Jmca) A large shade tree about 60 ft tall with plentiful pendent clusters of mauve flowers *Lagerstroemia flos-reginae* or *L. speciosa* (*Lythraceae*).

queen-trig·ger·fish *n* (StLu) ‖ OLD-WIFE (CarA) □ Also called TRIGGERFISH, name of a sub-family of fishes.

queh-queh [kwɛ-kwɛ] *n* (Guyn) A traditional set of celebrations by rural Black families preceding a wedding; it involves the ritual 'buying' of the bride and of the groom, processions from their homes, invitations to ancestral spirits by ritual, and to the living by ceremonial songs, much erotic singing and dancing in wh women play a central role, and drumming and feasting, all of wh reach a climax on the night before the wedding. [Of hardly disputable Afr origin though difficult to trace exactly. In Srnm, *VLCD* (p.17) speaks of 'dances ... accompanied on a small wooden bench ... called *kwakwabangi* [wh is] played with sticks [and] beats out the main rhythm ... the player is specially honoured and referred to as *kwakwa mayoro* 'the kwakwa major'. There is, however, no clear relationship with *Guyn* [kwɛ-kwɛ] A suggested Kikongo source is not clearer. *LDKF* lists Kikongo *kwe-kwe* as evid ideoph representing 1. laughter 2 sounds such as a footstep, but also *kwe-* as evid root of a few verbs such as *kwela* meaning 'to marry; to copulate; to couple'.]

quel·be [kwɛlbɛ] *n* (StVn, Tbgo) A set of songs, drum-rhythms and dances performed by females, and thought to be of Congo origin. (See cit). *The Old Congo drum music was looked down upon by the church members as pagan and the dances which accompanied them were said to be obscene and savage. . . . The chief instrument of percussion . . . was played by females . . . mainly for private domestic family entertainment and really never got transmitted to the younger folk in the village. The quelbè, as the accompanying dance was known among skeptical villagers, never spread from the Clarke family, although Gabriel their son would often sing songs and beat some of the drum rhythms for curious age-peers.*—EFSLC: 21

que·nette (**tjenn·èt**) *n* (StLu) See KÈNÈT

quenk [kwɛŋk] *n* (Trin) ‖ PECCARY (Guyn) [Perh from an Amerindian source. Cp *BDFC:303* Carib 'porc-sanglier' (wild pig) *boinkê*]

quer·i·man* [kwɛrimʌn] *n* (Guyn) A large grey fish said to be exactly like a large mullet; it is much prized for the richness of its flesh; *Mugil braziliensis* (*Mugilidae*). [< *BAED* Arawak *kereme*, given as their name of this fish]

quick sharp *adv phr* (Tbgo, Trin) [IF] ‖ QUICK TIME (Bdos, Guyn, Jmca) *You all getting me vex* *now with the car, car, car. Stop the rot, quick sharp!*—JJM:30

quick-stick *n* (Jmca) ‖ GLIRICIDIA (Angu, etc) *They put up a quick-stick fence on the roadside of their large spreading yard and had, in just over a year's time, a flowering fence out of it.*—Jmca (Ms) [*Quick* in arch. SE sense of 'alive', or ModE 'prompt, speedy' in ref to its ready growth when stuck in ground. See also ‖ **growing-stake**]

quick time *adv phr* (Bdos, Guyn, Jmca) [*IF*] Very promptly; right away; in great hurry. *Well she telephoned her father and he got there quick time and took her home.*—(Jmca)

quiet *adv* (CarA) [*X*] Quietly; sneakily; without attracting attention. **a.** *Well she was big pregnant,* you see, so they just went quiet and get married.*— (Bdos) **b.** *'Is Leela self who write that,'* Ramlogan said. *'I didn't ask she to write it, mind you. She just sit down quiet quiet one morning after tea and write it off.'*—NTMM:39

quinch [kwinč] *n* (Guyn) ‖ CASSAVA-CAKE (Belz, Guyn)

quite *adv* (ECar) [*AF/IF*] [In absolute use, indicating a notable distance] All the way (to, from, in, etc); as far as. **a.** *How you mean brass-face? Where you come from? You living quite up de road and you fowl-cock stray quite down here?*—RTLS:20 **b.** *Mr Minister while you have left Port-of-Spain and have gone quite to Tunapuna, we here, right here in St James are the ones forgotten.*—ExP (72.05.08, p.13)

R

r [ar] (CarA) [*IF—Vul*] (A euphemism for) RASS. □ The letter, instead of the taboo word, is often used in newspaper accounts or Court Records of cases of obscene language.

raa·ted *adj* (Belz, Jmca) See RAHTID

raa·zy *adj* (Trin) See RAZZY

rab *n* (Gren, Trin) [*AF*] **1.** The rowdy, lawless class of people. *Now, ah stand up just by de kitchen door / to make sure I fus gettin' when de food comin' out, / because de amount ah rab I see in dat man wedding / ah tell yu, if you play gentleman, yu starve.*—KTT:70 [< SE *rabble* with /-CC/ reduced] **2.** [By extension] Any rowdy or lawless person (esp a young one); a scallywag. *When I was a child I was not allowed to play with 'rabs' on the street corner.*—Trin (Ms)

rab·bet-and-spring board *n phr* (Bdos) ‖LAP-EDGE (BOARD) (Guyn) [SE *rabbet* 'the grooved or channelled edge of builder's board' + *spring* for the 'sloped edge', prob related to *OED spring* sb¹ 20. (Arch), 'a kind of slope'] □ RABBET is sometimes erron spelled 'rabbit'.

rab·bit-food *n* (StKt) ‖BALL-BUSH (Bdos, Jmca)

rab·bit-meat* *n* (Gren, Trin) A rambling shrub that grows to about 2 ft in height, rooting at the joints; it has hairy stems and bears white flowers, flourishing in moist, shady places; it is commonly fed to rabbits and goats, but is also used as a folk-medicine; *Alternanthera ficoidea* (*Amaranthaceae*).

ra·ben; **ra.ben.ous** [re·bən(ʌs)] *adj* (Antg, StKt, USVI) [*AF*] Greedy; gluttonous. [By /v > b/ shift from SE *raven*, *ravenous*. Cp *OED raven* vb 3. intr or absol a. 'to eat voraciously' b. 'to have a ravenous appetite'. Functional vb > adj shift can have occurred from SE structures such as 'they raven' being interpreted via CarA Cr as 'they are raven'] □ Cp RAVEN (*StVn, etc*).

rab land *n phr* (Bdos) ‖*the bandon* (Gren, Trin) Land with little or no topsoil and unfit for agricultural cultivation. *The Minister is the man concerned with land use policy and he will never get the rab lands and the building lands that he needs if the developers are allowed to run riot with them.*—Bdos (Hd, 75.05.20, p.4982) [Cp *OED2*

*rab*³ Chiefly Cornish (dial) 'rough and stony subsoil; rubble, gravel'. This may be the origin. However note that in *Bdos* E 'rubble-land' would be pronounced, 'rab(ble)-land' esp at the folk level] □ The term is recognized in law in *Bdos*. Note cit.

race *vb* (Baha, Bdos, Guyn, Jmca) **1.** *vb intr* To chase, run hard (after, behind sb). *The parson had forgotten his umbrella and she sent little Boysie racing down the road after him with it.*—Guyn (Ms) **2.** *vb tr* [*IF*] To chase away (sb, an animal). *Da[t] ain[ʔ] no young boy! He been to jail a[l] ready, and if you see him [a]roun[d] here, jus[t] race him out o[f] the yard!*—(Bdos) [Cp *OED race* vb¹ 4. 'to cause to move swiftly']

ra·chette (**wa·chèt, wa·tjèt** (cactus)) ['račɛt ~ 'wačɛt] *n* (Dmca, Trin, StLu) ‖C-OCHINEAL (CACTUS) (Guyn, etc) [< Fr *raquette* 'prickly pear' from racket-shaped stem, with Fr /k/ regularly > Fr Cr [č]. Cp also *DECG* Fr Cr *rakèt, rakyèt* (*Guad*), name of the same cactus]

rack·le [rakl] *vb* (Guyn) **1.** *vb intr* [*AF*] [Of a bird] To warble sweetly. *Towa-towa is a bird does rackle sweet sweet.*—(Guyn) **2.** *vb tr* [*AF—Joc*] To fool, playfully mislead (sb); [by extension] to deceive (a gullible person). *That is true? Or yo[u] jus[t] racklin[g] me?*—(Guyn) [Cp *EDD rackle* (Sc, Lan, Stf, Shr) sb¹ 2. 'noisy, senseless talk'; 5. vb¹ 'to make a clattering noise'. The *Guyn* usage may be accounted for by semantic shift of the E dial word, and then by functional n > vb shift locally]

raff *vb* (Trin) [*IF*] **1.** *vb intr* To rush madly (to get sth). *People were raffing for tickets for the show.*—Trin (Ms) **2.** *vb tr* To snatch up, grab (sth). *The power fly up in the old man head / Raff a belt and nearly killed the poor children dead.*—RLCF:223 [*OED2 raff* 'obs. exc. dial.' refers to a possible Obs Fr origin, *rafer* 'to catch, snatch' listed by Cotgrave. Such dial usage may have survived in *Trin* via Fr Cr]

rag·gay (**rag·get(te)**) ['rage·] *n* (StVn) **1.** An albino. **2.** [By extension] ‖CHABEN, CHABIN (StLu) [Said to have originated from a family associated with the occurrence of albinism. Only one pronunc, as given, is attested although the family name is said to be Fr and spelled *Raggette*] □ Cp DUNDUS (*Guyn, Jmca*).

rag·ged school *n phr* (Bdos) [Hist] A charity school for the children between the ages of five and twelve whose parents were paupers or unknown. The last was closed in 1930. *In 1844 the first Ragged School was opened in Barbados. A Sunday school it was started in Church Village, then a populous slum district of Bridgetown, by James Young Edghill.*—Jbm, 37.4, p.343 ['Ragged Schools were so called because the children who attended them were very poor, and consequently were usually dressed in ragged clothes' (*p.343*) [but] 'even then they shall not be admitted 'if their clothes are so much torn that the children are thereby rendered indecent'' —*Jbm, 37.4, p.346*]

rah·tid¹ (**raa·ted**¹, **wrought·ed**) ['ra:tɪd ~ rɒ·tɪd] *adj* (Belz, Jmca, StKt) 1. [AF] Extremely annoyed; roused to anger. *Him get real rahtid an[d] start brok up everyt[h]ing, you see!*—(Jmca) 2. [By extension, as a qualifier] Damned; blasted. *We playin' dis patient game / So rahtid long.*—LMFF:60 [Generally considered a euphemism for RASS² 4. and its compounds (see RAHTID²). However see note at WROUGHTED of wh **raated** may simply be the Cr pronunc; otherwise an '-ed' formation wd hardly be generated in Cr grammar. Note also *OEDS* rasted 'a substitute for *blasted* 3.' + cit 1919]

rah·tid² (**raa·ted**²) ['ra:tɪd] *excl* (Jmca) [AF] [Expressing surprise, anger, or delight] **a.** *Raated! What yo[u] bring dat in here for? You want de police [u]pon we?*—(Jmca) **b.** *One night, mi dear sir, filled with Christmas spirit, our little family decide to go for a treat to a well-known Chinese restaurant. The pickney dem glad so till and we all went off boasie together. At the restaurant, we were greeted by a gracious hostess who welcomed us to her establishment and made us welcome. Rahtid, we say, business tune. Welcome and all.*—WeG (73.01.17, p.12, Partyline) [Prob much infl by RASS for wh it serves as a euphemism at upper levels] □ The vowel of the first syllable may be much lengthened and the pitch much heightened in this function.

rail¹ [re·l] (Gren, StVn) [X] *vb tr* To bring up (a child), to rear (children). *She godmother rail her from since she small.*—(StVn) [Prob < SE *rear* 'to bring up and educate (a child)' with final /r > l/ shift] 2. PHRASE **2.1 rail (up)**¹ **(with)** *vb intr* [X] To be brought up (by). *But who this chil[d] rail up wit[h]. She ain[t] got manners?* —(Gren) [By characteristic CE passive conversion of a vb tr] □ Now mostly rural usage, but occurring sometimes in written schoolwork.

rail up² **(with sb)** *vb intr phr* (Belz) To complain bitterly and noisily; to be noisily angry. *I was pleased when one person told me that instead of losing his 'cool' when his phone played dumb, he would think of my column and laugh instead. What's the use of fussin' and railing-up! It's bad for the digestion and for one's blood pressure.*—ReP (79.12.23, p.7) [< SE *rail* vb intr 'to utter abusive language (at, against sb)' + *up*, as intensifier]

rail·way dai·sy *n phr* (Trin) ‖ DUPPY-NEEDLE (Bdos) [The dry terrain along wh the former railway track ran eastward out of Port-of-Spain was a habitat of this weed, whose florets resemble daisies]

rain *n* (CarA) PHRASES **1. rain builds** *id phr* (Bdos, Dmca) [IF] ‖ RAIN SETS UP (Bdos, etc) See Phr 6. below *Don[t] open so many windows child. You don[t] see the rain building?*—(Bdos) **2. rain bursts (down)** [bʌrs(ts) ~ bʌsdʌŋ] *id phr* (Guyn) [IF/AF] There is a sudden, heavy downpour of rain. **3. rain comes** *id phr* (CarA) It rains; it is going to rain. **a.** *If the rain comes whole day today like yesterday, we can't have cricket tomorrow, for sure.*—(Gren) **b.** *The rain is coming so le[t] me take in these clothes quick, quick.*—(Guyn) **4. rain falls** *id phr* (CarA) It rains. **a.** *But the trainers need not fear, for the TTC secretary Ray D'Abadie said yesterday, that there are plans for the watering of the track, if the rain doesn't fall.*—ExP (73.01.05, p.20) **b.** *Outside, the rain still falling, he felt that he would come back another time.*— LDCD:239 **5. rain holds up** *id phr* (Bdos, Guyn) ‖ RAIN STOPS FALLING (CarA) *If this rain doesn't hold up soon, it will be too late for me to go out.*—(Bdos) □ See also HOLD Phr 5.12. **6. rain sets up** *id phr* (Bdos, Guyn, StVn) ‖ **rain builds** (Bdos, Dmca) It is threatening to rain; it looks like rain. *Every time I see rain set up I remember I ain[t] buy that umbrella yet.*—(StVn) **7. rain stops falling** *id phr* (CarA) ‖ **rain holds up** (Bdos, Guyn) It stops raining. [These phrs are likely calques from any of a number of Afr langs in wh equivalences to SE idioms beginning 'It—' in regard to rain are in the form of a concrete event i.e. 'Rain (does sth)'. Cp Twi *reto* (*rain falling*) 'It is raining'; also Mende *njei lɔ wama* (*rain much coming*); also Efik *edim etre ndidep* (*rain stop past-fall*) 'It has stopped raining'; also Kikongo *mvula sujanoka* (*rain will rain*) 'It is going to rain'; etc]

rain-bird¹ *n* (CarA) [Any of a number of birds whose presence is associated with the coming or the ending of rain; they include varieties of cuckoo, flycatcher, swallow, and swift (see *BBWI* passim). The following are evid the two best known] **1.*** ‖ **chinchary** (Baha) ‖ **thrush** (Guyn) A bird about 9 ins long with a grey coat and dull white belly, known for its loud, repeated 'pi-pi-reee' and its swift catching of insects in flight; it is a common, wide-ranging bird wh nests in high places and fights other birds; the grey kingbird; *Tyrannus dominicensis (Tyrannidae). … while weather watchers pay close heed to the rainbird who perches on the highest bough so that all may know that bad weather approaches.*— HWII:47 □ It is called both RAIN-BIRD and THRUSH in *Guyn.* **2.*** ‖ **cuckoo-manioc** (Dmca, Gren) ‖ **mangrove-cuckoo** (CarA) ‖ **rain-crow** (Dmca) A bird about 12 ins long with a brownish-grey back and yellowish underparts; its call is a throaty repeated 'ga-ga-gan …'; it nests in mangrove swamps and woodlands; *Coccyzus minor* (*Cuculidae*). □ Not known in *Bdos*, but common in most of *CarA*.

rain-bird² n (Gren, StLu) ‖ CIGALE (Trin) [From the association of the sound made by this insect with rainy weather]

rain-bush (rain·fall-bush) n (Mrat, StVn) ‖ GLIRICIDIA (Angu, etc) *We use the leaves of that same rain-bush you see them use as posts or poles, well the leaves are good for tea.*—(Mrat) [Poss because the tree only puts out leaves in wet weather and sheds them in dry weather]

rain-crow n (Dmca) ‖ RAIN-BIRD¹ 2. (CarA)

rain·drops n (StKt) ‖ GLIRICIDIA (Angu, etc)

rain-flow·er n (Jmca) ‖ AMARYLLIS (CarA) [So named because these flowers spring up immediately after the first heavy rains]

rain-fly n (CarA) ‖ *flying ant* (Bdos, Jmca) A brownish, soft-bodied termite about 1/4 inch long; in its temporary winged stage, it swarms in wet weather, esp at dusk.

rain-tree n (CarA) ‖ SAMAN (CarA) [From the steady dripping of water ('like a drizzle') during the night, caused by transpiration from its massive foliage; this feature may be intensified as the leaves fold up in the night]

raise¹ vb 1. vb tr (CarA) To rear, bring up (a child, family). □ Now commonly IAE (see *COD8 raise* vb 8.), though *OED* lists as chiefly US. The common CE usage accounts for the development of sense 2. 2. vb intr (CarA) [X] To grow up (with sb); to be brought up, taken care of (as a child, by sb). **a.** *She raise with her aunt from small.*—(Mrat) **b.** *J— said the only reason he could think of why S— would try to 'frame' him was because 'we raise together and our spirits don't pull at all. We were always in trouble with each other.'*—VoS (76.05.08, p.10) [By characteristic CE transfer of vb tr into passive sense. See special entry PASSIVITY] **3.** vb intr (CarA) [X] To rise. **a.** *Mr Williams stressed however that the liabilities for benefits under the fund would raise to a higher point.*—AdN (72.07.08, p.1) **b.** *Again Mr Editor you know that when things start to raise and your pay stay one place this is what create bad thing in the country.*—AmA (80.03.21, p.2) **4.** vb intr (Gren, Guyn) [IF] [Of the skin] To come up in bumps. *When A was small A used to have mad blood and me skin used to raise!*—(Gren) **5.** vb tr (Guyn) To lift (a wooden house) off its pillars by a system of blocks and jacks, high enough to build a ground-level flat underneath it. **6.** PHRASES **6.1 not raise (a) pin/straw** neg vb phr (Gren) [AF/IF] To do nothing to help; (SE) not to raise a finger (to help). **6.2 raise ants nest** vb phr (CarA) [AF—Joc] To make trouble; to cause rowing and confusion; (SE) stir up a hornet's nest. *Yes, you go and tell him what they say and raise ants nest.*—(Gren) [Ref to bringing

biting ants to the surface by poking at their nest in the ground] **6.3 raise the colour** vb phr (CarA) (See cit) *We had no doubt whatever that my mother expected us to choose a husband who was at least the same colouring as ourselves, if not lighter. To marry and produce children of lighter colour than oneself was to 'raise' the colour of the family. To raise the colour of the family was to raise its social status.*—GBFBM:24

raise² n (CarA) [AF] A small sum of money asked for and not likely to be repaid. *One of them said he was 'scrunting' and asked her for a 'raise'... As she opened her purse to give him a dollar, the man snatched her bag, threw it to his accomplice and they both ran off.*—ExP (75.12.08, p.4) [By functional vb > n shift of SE *raise* vb as in *raise some money, a loan*]

rake¹ n 1. (Gren, Trin) [AF] A piece of gossip; a spicy bit of news; a malicious rumour. *There are scores of men in this country like Steve, who on the mere evidence of a rake or some ole talk story, accuse their wives of being unfaithful.*—SuP (75.04.06, p.7) [Cp *EDD rake* sb³ 3. Chs 'a gossiping meeting'] **2.** (Belz, Jmca) [IF] A hunch, clue, or some indication by dream, superstition, or hint about the number to play to win in a folk lottery. *After a long silence, GB spoke as if arising from a dream: 'You know what! This might be a good 'rake' in the Drop Pan game. Me is going to buy number three. It is the number for dead rogue.'*—BGSB:67 [Perh from a deviant development of the orig of sense 1.]

rake² vb tr (Guyn) [Kite-flying] To cut the string of another person's kite in the air, by a device on the tail of your own kite, so that the other kite gets lost.

rake-and-scrape¹ vb intr (Bdos, Gren, Guyn) [IF] To save money painfully, bit by bit, for a particular purpose; to gather together every last small resource in order to meet an obligation. *We, as legislators, have to be concerned with this matter because these poor people have to make a supreme sacrifice to rake-and-scrape to deposit money at the Waterworks Department in order to get the service connected to their homes.*—Bdos (Hd, 74.07.30, p.3730) [Metaph from agriculture, trying to prepare infertile land to yield by raking and scraping it]

rake-and-scrape² band n phr (Baha) A rural folk-band comprising a goat-skin or an improvised drum, an accordion, a MUSICAL SAW, a rasp or rattle, and a bottle or piece of iron to add a tinkling effect to the rhythm. □ Cp SCRATCH-BAND.

rak·er [rekər] n (Guyn) ‖ ZWILL (Gren, etc)

ral·ly n (Guyn, Jmca) A group, fund-raising activity sponsored by a church, involving individual effort of its members. (See next). [By functional vb > n shift (and some extension) of SE vb *rally* 'to make a big concentrated effort'.

Note also *OED2 rally* 3. b. (US) 'a mass meeting of the supporters of any specified cause']

ral·ly-card/-tick·et *n* (Guyn, Jmca) A card with dots to be punched for each sum collected; it is used as one means of soliciting funds by formally authorized members of a church for a RALLY.

ram- *n used attrib* (CarA) **1.** The male of a domestic animal; hence compounds—*ram-cat* (*StVn, USVI*) ‖ *ram-puss* (Belz, Jmca) A tom-cat; *ram-goat* (*CarA*) A he-goat; *ram-sheep* (*Bdos*) A male sheep. [Cp *EDD ram* sb¹ 1.(2) *ram-cat* 'a tom-cat' (+ cit from Irel); (a) *ram-lamb* 'a male lamb' (+ cit from Sc)] **2.** PHRASE **2.1 smell like a ram-goat** *vb phr* (Bdos, Guyn, Trin) [*AF—Derog*] To have a high body odour (esp when drunk and wet with your own urine). [Ref to a long-haired type of male goat that harbours ticks and develops a bad smell]

ra·ma·jé (ra.ma.jay) [ramaže] *vb intr* (Trin) [Steelband] To improvise on a given tune (often in competition with other players) on one or a small group of PANS; to play an impromptu composition on a STEELPAN. [Fr Cr < early Fr *ramager* '[of birds] to chirp, warble' (See *LLFL* wh dates it 1585), whence by extension 'to improvise freely'] □ Hence tensed forms **ramajéd**, **ramajéing** (on SE model of *appliqué* vb) or **ramajayed, ramajaying**, if folk spelling is preferred.

ram·fle (ram·ple) *vb tr* (Bdos, Gren, Guyn, StKt, Trin) See [*X*] RUMFLE

ram-goat bush *n phr* **1.*** (StKt) ‖ *ram-goat dashalong* (Jmca) A strong-smelling, bushy shrub bearing yellow flowers and growing to about 5 ft; its coarse, spear-shaped leaves are boiled as a remedy for colds, and the plant is also said to have aphrodisiac properties; *Turnera ulmifolia* (*Turneraceae*). **2.** (Nevs, USVI) ‖ CAT-TLE-TONGUE (Antg, etc) [In both senses, from its strong smell. See prec RAM-GOAT Phr] □ In some places the name is also applied to FIT-WEED, because of its strong smell.

ram-goat rose *n phr* (Jmca) ‖ OLD-MAID (BUSH) (CarA) [Apart from its 'rose' shape, reason for name unknown]

ram·i·er(-pi·geon) [ramie(-pɪʌn)] *n* (ECar) Any of two or three varieties of common pigeon, esp the RED-NECKED PIGEON; also applied to doves; *Columbiformes spp.* [Fr *ramier* 'pigeon', spread from the Fr Cr territories. The form 'r.-pigeon', used sometimes in *Bdos* and elsewhere is a typical redundant compound, the meaning of 'ramier' being unrecognized]

Ram·lee·la (Ra·ma Lee·la) *n* (*phr*) (Trin) [Indic] A Hindu religious festival celebrated over a period of ten days, about early November, during wh there is much entertainment, esp in the form of brightly costumed dramatic presentations of scenes from the Hindu religious epic, the Ramayana. [Hin *Ram* 'Lord Rama' + *liilaa* 'play(s)', i.e. 'plays (in honour of) Lord Rama']

Ram Nau·mi [ram naumi] *n phr* (Guyn) [Indic] A Hindu religious celebration, held to mark the birthday of Lord Rama; the day decreed for it is usu one in early April and is marked by fasting and prayers. [Hin *Ram* 'Lord Rama' + *naumii* 'ninth day of light' (his birthday)]

ram-puss [rampʊs] *n* (Belz, Jmca) See RAM-

ram·sack *vb tr* (ECar) [*X*] To ransack. *According to the Police the fifty year old woman left her home around 6 a.m. on Saturday but when she returned she found her home ramsacked and money and articles missing.*—WeI (68.07.21, p.6) [By / n > m/ assimilation < SE *ransack*] □ A common error in ECar writing.

ram-sheep *n* (Bdos) See RAM-

rang·a·tang [raŋgataŋ] *n* (Gren, Guyn, Jmca) [*AF—Derog*] ‖ *rango* (Trin) [*AF—Joc/Derog*] A coarse, undisciplined man or woman; a rough, belligerent person. [< *orang-outang*, from wh also comes the Joc abbr *rango* in Trin] □ Cp also KANGALANG (*Guyn*). Perh the two forms infl each other.

range¹ [re·ŋ] *n* (Guyn) **1.** ‖ BARRACK(s) (Trin) *No provision seems as yet to have been thought of for the really poor Old Age Pensioners, washers, scrubbers, etc, living alone, who have hitherto eked out a tolerable existence by living in a single room in a range at a rental of from $3.00 to $4.00 per month.*—GyG (55.03.15) □ The term, borrowed from plantation life, is also applied to the same kind of building in the poorest urban areas. **2.** (USVI) A track dividing fields of sugar-cane.

range² *vb tr* **1.** (Gren, Guyn) [*IF*] To arrange (things in a row, etc). [As *OED range* vb¹ 1. though listed there as chiefly in passive use] **2.** (Tbgo) To protect (sth owned) from evil by a magical charm, usu evoked by OBEAH or other supernatural means. **3.** (Gren) To bring some evil (such as mental disturbance, deformity, etc) on (sb), usu by OBEAH. [In senses 2., 3. prob < arrange by aphesis or via Fr Cr *ranger* < Fr *arranger* 'to fix'. Cp FIX¹ 2.(i), 2.(ii)]

range-yard *n* (Guyn) ‖ BARRACK-YARD (Trin)

ran·go *n* (Trin) [*AF-Joc/Derog*] ‖ RANGATANG (Gren, etc)

rank [raŋk~rɛŋk] *adj* **1.** (CarA) ‖ *renkin(g)* (Belz, Jmca, StLu, USVI) Having a strong, esp a fishy, smell. [Cp *OED rank* adj 12. 'having an offensively strong smell'] □ RANK is almost exclusively a pejorative adj in CE. SE connotations such as 'firm', 'luxuriant', 'fertile', etc as in *OED* senses 1–11 are not current in CE.

See foll. **2.** (Jmca) Very harmful; [of a person] very impertinent. [Cp *OED rank* adj 14. 'gross, loathsome'] □ Usu pronounced [rɛŋk] in this sense in *Jmca*.

ra-ra *n* (Gren, StVn, Trin, USVI) **1.** A child's rattle. **2.** PHRASE **2.1 your mouth got ra-ra** *id phr* (StVn) [*AF—Derog*] You can't stop talking; your mouth goes like a rattle.

rare-mouth *n* (Bdos) See RAY-MOUTH

Ras *n* (CarA) A title assumed and used by a male follower of the RASTAFARIAN cult; it is usu followed by the person's cultist name. *Ras Judah turned to face the police. 'The days of Babylon have come', he called, '... to denounce God and make a mockery of I laws.'*—RHJSS:38 [By transfer of the Ethiopian title *Ras* 'Chief, Duke'. See RASTAFARI]

ra·sam [razam] *n* (Belz) [X] ‖ AMBER[1] (Belz, Jmca) [Erron, < *resin*]

rasp·ber·ry ['rasbɛri] *n* (Antg, Brbu) ‖ GOOSE-BERRY **1.** (Baha, etc)

Rass![1] [ra:s] *excl* (CarA) [*AF—Cr/Vul*] **1.** [An obscene expression of anger or astonishment. Uttered with strong stress and with the vowel much lengthened] □ Considered perh the most vulgar of all *CarA* expressions, its use aloud in public is punishable by law in most territories. See R. **2.** [*As post-modifying intensifier of a pron or n phr, in expressing anger*] *I ain[']t done wid [h]e rass yet! I goin[g] make he an[d] all o[f] dem rass pay!*—(Guyn) [A likely development of Du *raas*, root of vb *razen* 'to rage, rave'. In his account of 18C Du Cr *OHMC:256* notes: 'They [the Negroes] express an impatient, painful longing by means of the word *raas*, 'to rage': *em raas goe voor em* (*Him rave go for him*) 'He has a great longing to see him'. From such collocations, i.e. subj + *raas*, to express intensity, *raas* prob became a general loan word, in its own right, as an intensifier on the slave coast, thence spreading and developing a bad connotation in the *CarA*]

rass[2] [ra:s] *n* (CarA) [*AF—Cr/Vul*] **1.** Arse; backside; behind. *'Forty dollars more for these two fours, in your rass, sah! I raise!'*—CWFYS:98 [It slips into this sense and function from its position in the utterance in RASS[1] **2.**, being also strongly influenced by E *arse/ass* esp in such E collocations as *your arse/ass*, wh appears to coincide, by misplaced juncture, with CarA Cr /yu raas/] □ In this sense the word is used in CE in the same compounds, phrases, and contexts as E *arse/ass*, but as a more intensely vulgar alternative. See foll. **2.** [By extension] Nonsense; foolishness; rubbish. *And you open your big mouth to say you give a white woman a child? Don't talk rass, man. And she swung away from him in apparent disgust.*—BPS:40 **3.** [By extension, of a person] A big fool; a most stupid idiot. *Man you're the biggest dumbest rass in this town!*—SNWIC:198 (J. Carew) **4.** [Used attrib in any

context expressing speaker's rage] **a.** *Damn an' blas' yu stinkin' soul to hell! Don' mek me wring yu rass neck, tell me whe' me woman!*—PCOS:44 **b.** *Parboo said, 'Listen, ol' man, stop all this rass business, one time, nuh!' He clapped his hands mock-imperiously. 'You can't keep the Prime Minister o' Big G., an' the Minister o' Information an' Culture waitin', Mr Rass!'*—SGJ:101 **5.** PHRASE **not care a rass** *neg vb phr* (CarA) [*AF—Vul*] [Used only in obscene contexts] Not to give a shit.

rass-clate [ra:s-kla:t] *n* (Jmca) [*AF—Cr/Vul*] [Used only as an obscene expletive] A used sanitary napkin; a piece of cloth so used. *'Big White Chief!' she exclaimed. 'Is what de rass-clate yu doin' frightenin' people fo? Is wha' 'appen to yu now'?*—PCOS:86 [RASS + *cloth*, the latter with Cr pronunc] □ In *Jmca* the term is used in the same contexts as RASS[1] and RASS[2], with equally strong social prohibition.

Ras·ta *n, adj* (CarA) [*AF/IF*] ‖ *Rastafarian* (CarA) **1.** *n* [An abbr in popular use] Pl *Rastas*. **2.** *adj, or in attrib function in several compounds* **Rasta breddren/brethren** *n phr* Members of the R. cult. **Rasta hairstyle/locks** *n phr* DREADLOCKS (CarA). **Rasta man** *n phr* A male RASTAFARIAN. **Rasta queen** *n phr* A female RAS-TAFARIAN; the common-law wife of a RASTA MAN. **Rasta talk** *n phr* The jargon peculiar to members of the R. cult. (See I-); etc. **3.** PHRASES **3.1 go/ turn Rasta** *vb phr* (CarA) [*AF/IF*] [Esp of a young man] To adopt the RASTAFARIAN life style or to join a group of Rastafarians.

Ras·ta·far·i [rastafarai] *n, adj* (CarA) **1.** *n* ‖ R-ASTAFARIANISM (CarA) *Crimes and other misdeeds may be committed by impostors who seek not only to denigrate the character of the movement but also to use Rastafari as a vehicle for their illegal designs.*—AdN (77.10.22, p.4) **2.** *n* A member or (collectively) members of the RASTAFARIAN cult. **a.** *High fines and long prison sentences will not stop Rastafari from smoking herb as can be seen at present.*—CrU (76.10.09, p.7) **b.** *The Press and radio made reports of Okpara's call for discipline among the Rastafari which he indeed forced to repeat throughout his much interrupted speech.*—NMM:62 **3.** *adj, or attrib* ‖ RAS-TAFARIAN (CarA) **a.** *Perhaps even their confused understanding of the Rastafari Movement, which developed out of socio-economic alienation and deprivation has some degree of relevance.*—LaS (76.06.14, p.2) **b.** *There were many occasions when a peaceful Rastafari gathering would be surprised by a police raid.*—CrU (76.12.25, p.23) [< the *Ras Tafari* (< Amharic *ras* 'chief', the title of an Ethiopian feudal lord or prince + *Tafari*, family name of the future Emperor Haile Selassie of Ethiopia). The cult, developed in *Jmca*, believed Ethiopia to be the ultimate home of all Black people, and its Emperor, by his original name, divine. The fusing of the title and name as one, *Rastafari* (note the pronunc) developed as it became a cultist label]

Ras·ta·far·i·an [rastafariən~rastaferiʌn] *n,
adj* (CarA) (A member) of the cult believing in
the divinity of the Emperor Haile Selassi (Ras
Tafari), and the wickedness of established Western-style society wh they characterize as the
survival of Babylon; they follow certain Old
Testament tenets closely, including refusal to
cut the hair, and a belief system wh includes
vegetarianism, ganja-smoking, rejection of private property, etc. **a.** *Repatriation, the Rastafarians were to discover was a more complex
affair than they had anticipated…. The Rastafari
brethren, however, persisted in the belief that all
Africa, and particularly Ethiopia, was ready to
receive them.*—NMM:69 **b.** *Rastafarian anti-
Jamaicanism was less intractable than their critics
would admit.*—NMM:64 [< RASTAFARI + SE
n and adj forming suff *-an*] □ See BABYLON,
DREAD, DREADLOCKS.

Ras·ta·far·i·an·ism;   **Ras.ta.far.ism**   *n*
(CarA) The belief system and life-style of RAS-
TAFARIANS. **a.** *Though the political motivation of
the culprits is unclear, their cultural and/or religious
affinity to Rastafarianism has been discerned by
reports that armed attackers have, in several cases,
been wearing the dreadlocks.*—CaC 77/8, p.1) **b.**
*Rastafarism is a life-style which originated in
Jamaica. A life-style which surfaced from the economic and social failures of the aforesaid society!
Why are 'our younger generation leaving their
homes, or … good schools to join this cult?' Because
they have found that Rastafarism has shown them
a way to escape the doom of an unjust society in
particular, and world in general.*—AdN
(79.06.16, p.4) □ The first is the more frequent
form. For the doctrines of RASTAFARIANISM see
NMM:239.

rat[1] **1.** (Bdos, Guyn, Trin) [*AF—Derog*] A prostitute of the lowest kind. *Kenneth yelled through
the fight, 'My mother says you is a bastard, and
your mother is a rat.'*—JPB:27 [A metaph ref to
SE *rat*] **2.** (Bdos) ‖ RATTA 2. (Bdos, etc) **3.** PHRASE
3.1 make rat to (go/get into a place) *vb phr*
(StLu) [*AF—Joc*] ‖ RAT IN (Bdos) *The two o[f]
them make rat to go in the cinema.*—(StLu) [A
calque < Fr Cr *fè wa* < Fr 'faire (le) rat' 'to act
like a rat']

rat[2] *vb* **1.** (CarA) [*AF*] To behave like a rat.
(See Phrs). **2.** (Trin) [Of a woman] To live as a
prostitute. [By functional n > vb shift of RAT[1]
1.] □ Esp used in the form **ratting. 3.** PHRASES
3.1 rat in *vb phr* (Bdos) [*AF—Joc*] ‖ **make rat
to get into** (StLu) To enter (a place of entertainment) without paying; to gatecrash. **3.2
rat out** *vb phr* (Jmca) [*AF*] To run away (from
friends, responsibilities, etc).

rat-bat *n* (Belz, Jmca, Mrat, TkCa) [*IF*] ‖ *bat*[1]
2. (Guyn) The common fruit bat. [From its
resemblance to a mouse] □ The term 'bat' is, in
these territories as sometimes also in AmE, usu
applied to any moth or flying insect, hence a
distinctive name is used for the mammal.

ratch[1] *n* (Tbgo, Trin) [*IF*] A bad piece of work
done by slipshod or short-cut methods. [Cp Sc
dial *CSD ratch*[3] n 'a scratch'; also *wratch* =
wretch; also *EDD* Sc *ratch* adj 'loose in morals'.
However the vb form, next, may just as well
have infl this function] □ Also used attrib, a
ratch job, ratch work.

ratch[2] *vb* (Tbgo) **1.** *vb tr* To do (a job) hurriedly
or without principle. *They are ratching the road
to finish it quickly.*—(Tbgo) **2.** *vb intr* To act
corruptly. [Perh by functional n > vb shift of
RATCH[1]. However cp Sc dial *CSD ratch*[3] 'to
damage by rough usage; to scratch'; also *wratch*
'to cheat, stint']

rat·chet-knife (Jmca) ‖ FLICK-BLADE KNIFE
(Bdos, etc) *He had an open ratchet-knife in his
hand and he said to her: 'Do you realize I going
to cut out your … belly because you stay long?'*
—DaG (73.02.09, p.26) [Because of a ratchet
in the mechanism to prevent the blade from
closing, once open]

ra·ther [raðə] *vb* (CarA) [*X*] **1.** *vb tr* To prefer;
to choose. **a.** *I rather a girl child than a boy
child.*—RLCF:234 **b.** *As for me and my house,
being caught between the devil and the deep blue
sea …, we would rather inflation than gas.*—AdN
(73.12.24, p.4) [The adv > vb functional shift
may have been transferred from EE into CE via
such cases as *OED2 rather* adv III. 9. d. *would/
have rather* 'to choose or prefer … rather' + cit
1633 'I would rather never to have light than
not to have it always'. However the greater
likelihood is that the /d/ of SE *'I'd/we'd/you'd/
they'd rather + vb'* was lost in developing CE,
so transferring full vb function to RATHER] **2.** *vb
intr* To prefer to; to prefer that. **a.** *He added
'your counsel wittingly or unwittingly in this regard
was not playing cricket. I rather say no more on
this unless pressed.'*—WeG (73.02.28, p.25) **b.**
*'There are two sides to every picture', Mr Leacock
concluded, 'and we should rather presentation of
the two sides come from representative organisations.'*—AdN (75.08.04, p.1) □ This usage
occurs at all levels of CE in all territories.

ra·toon[1] *n* (CarA) [Sugar Ind] **1.** A new shoot
from the base of the sugar-cane, or the old stump
that will grow again after the sugar-cane has
been cut. **2.** ‖ *ratoon-crop* (CarA) The second
crop raised from the new shoots. *The loan made
to him should be more than if he is doing second
ratoons, because he would not have to plough and
do as much weeding…. The cultivation loan for
ratoon canes should be less than on first crop
canes.*—Bdos (Hd, 76.04.27, p.654) [< Sp *retoño*
young shoot]

ratoon[2] *vb* (CarA) [Sugar Ind] [Of a field of
harvested sugar-canes] To grow or cause to grow
into another crop from the previous crop's
shoots. *Once planted a cane field renewed or 'ra-
tooned' itself with new growth after each crop for
about five years depending on the soil and its
care.*—LTTBV:29

rat·pas·sage n PHRASE **take/travel rat-passage** vb phr (Gren, Guyn, Trin) [AF—Joc] To stow away. 'In Grenada, I asked the captain for a passage.' B— testified, 'but he tell me the vessel done clear and he couldn't take me. So I decided to take rat-passage.'—BoM (75.03.07, p.16)

rat·ta n 1. (Belz) [AF—Cr] A mouse or small rat. □ See CHARLEY-PRICE 2. (Antg, Jmca) [AF—Cr] A rat, [usu a large one]. [Perh a loan < Sp rata 'rat'] 3. (Guyn) An imaginary being supposed to 'bring back' a good tooth for a bad one thrown on the roof-top (with the incantation 'Ratta! Ratta! Give me back me teet[h]!'). [Rat + (Cr) -a²⁰] 4. (Bdos, Guyn, Jmca, StVn, USVI) ‖ rat 2. (Bdos, Guyn) [Esp among boys] A moving lump induced in a vein of the biceps of the folded arm by striking the upper arm hard with side of the open hand or by giving the muscle a vigorous pull. 5. (Jmca) ‖ ratta coffee (Jmca) Coffee berries fallen from the tree before (commercial) reaping time and gathered for home use. Elizabeth was all excitement for Christmas. She had been strictly saving the profits from ratta coffee; ratta is the name given to the coffee berries which fall from the shrub before reaping time.— RPME:45 [Because they are said to be cut down by rats, hence also called **rat-cut**. (See DJE]

rat-teeth n (Dmca, Trin) Small, widely spaced teeth.

rat·tle-drum n (Jmca) ‖ KETTLE-DRUM (ECar)

ra·ven ['re·vn] adj 1. (StVn) [AF] ‖ BIG-EYE¹ (CarA) 2. (Gren, StVn, USVI) [AF/IF] ‖ L-ICKERISH 2. (Antg, etc) Ivan did not cook his turtle. He was so raven he ate it raw, even the liver.—JJAIE:16 [Prob by functional shift of SE raven (n), but cp also ‖ craven (Gren, etc), and RABEN (Antg, etc)]

raw adj 1. (Bdos) [IF] [Of speech] ‖ FLAT¹ (ECar) Yet, the Bajan who rejects all this with: 'I is a raw Bajan' is subconsciously admitting that whereas he claims to be proud of his accent and dialect, he nevertheless regards it as being less than polished.— NaT (79.02.02, p.23) □ See also BAJAN² Phr 6.1 RAW BAJAN. 2. PHRASES 2.1 call (sb) raw vb phr (Angu) [AF] See CALL¹ Phr 3.7 2.2 eye (is) raw id phr (Nevs, StKt) [AF] See EYE¹ Phr 16.

raw-eye adj (Nevs, StKt) [AF—Cr] Shamelessly greedy; brazenly covetous.

ray-mouth (rare-mouth) n (Bdos) [Derog] ‖ WHITE-CORNER (Guyn) Is the rare-mouth wun that tief piece of Mr Mottley land.—TM:93 (S. Reid) [Cp EDD ray sb² 'a corner, nook' (Wm). Hence poss a dial ref to the unhealthy corners of the mouth. The form RARE-MOUTH may be by folk etym]

ra·zor-grass* n (CarA) Any of several varieties of erect, tufted grasses or sedges growing about 3 ft tall, their strongly keeled blades having very finely saw-toothed edges that can cut the skin if rubbed against; most bear spikelets of close, tiny, insignificant flowers, and some also bear purplish fruit; Scleria spp (Cyperaceae) or Paspalum spp (Paniceae).

ra(z)·zy (raa·zy) [razi ~ ra:zi] adj (Bdos, Gren, Tbgo, Trin) [AF/IF] 1. Shabby; shoddy; clumsy. I heard a joke today, that someone went into the Town and Country Planning office in a very razzy way, and wanted to know, who was the man you had to give the money to, when you wanted something done.—Bdos (Hd, 73.12.18, p.3034) 2. [Of a person] Unkempt; down-at-heel; untidy. I can't go to the people's function with my hair raazy like this; I have to spruce it up.—Tbgo (Ms) 3. [Of an animal] Skinny; hungry or unhealthy looking. [Perh largely infl by US razzle, loosely referring to 'confuse, confusion'. However cp EDD razzor, razzer vb 'to exhaust, wear out'; also OED Naut razee vb 'to cut down (a ship) in size'; also by extended usage of OED razzia (Arabic) 'a raid for the capture of slaves']

reach vb 1. vb tr (Tbgo, Trin) [AF] To accompany, take (sb). S1: A will reach you by the shop. / S2: Only there? Reach me home, no? —(Trin) □ The SE vb tr uses are also common, but see Phrs below. 2. vb intr (CarA) [AF] To arrive; to turn up. a. The goats escaped before we reached.—(Angu) b. I hear they reach the same time. How come when one was in America and the other in St Vincent? All two reach the said time.—SBHM:2 c. People was always supposed to come and fix something and they never reach and they aint never had the courtesy to make a phone call and explain.—NaG (78.06.01, Satirically Speaking) [Cp EDD reach 5. 'to arrive' + cits from Sc, Yks, etc] □ This vb intr use is widespread in CE. Note its extension in Phrs below. 3. PHRASES 3.1 reach around vb phr (CarA) [IF] [Of news, rumour, etc] To get around. 3.2 reach back vb phr (CarA) [IF] (i) To return. When I reached back home she still wasn't there.—Tbgo (Ms) (ii) [AF] To be in stock again. Shopping one day over on the mainland, I asked for a special kind of material. 'We had, madam, but it finish. I will introduce it to you when it reach back'.—Isl 73/10, p.42 3.3 reach by/to (a place, position, etc) vb phr (CarA) [AF/IF] To arrive at (a place). a. Boy, when ah tell you was confusion fuh so when we reach by Scarborough.—OJS:16 b. Many persons were beaten in the town of Grenville, and many others were assaulted and provoked. Mr Editor, it has reached to a stage where people are in a state of Fear.—ToR (73.06.01, p.4) 3.4 reach out of (a place) vb phr (CarA) [AF/IF] To manage to get out of (a place). a. I heard this noise in the yard but by the time I haul on somet[h]ing an[d] reach out of the house, there wasn['t] nobody.—(Guyn) b. Whilst scrambling out of the hole, I heard Malik say he wanted blood. I reached out of the hole; I stood there and watched Malik chop Joe across the neck with the cutlass.—AMGM:54 3.5 reach up (with sb) vb phr (Guyn) [AF/IF] To meet, encounter (sb); to catch up (with sb). a. Guess who I reach up at the cinema las night—Mavis and she husband. They just come back last week from abroad.—(Guyn) **b.** I walked faster but he started running to reach up with me.—(Guyn) **3.6 reach you to your shoulder/waist** vb phr (Bdos, Guyn) [AF/IF] [Of a growing child] To be shoulder/waist height with you. But the children getting big enough. One reach me to my shoulder and the other almost to my waist already.—(Bdos)

reaches n pl (Guyn) [X] Arrival (of a letter in the hands of its addressee). I hope the reaches of these few lines find you in good health as it leaves me.—Guyn (Ms) □ This is a frequent beginning of domestic letters.

read (sb) (up) vb tr phr **1.** (Belz, Guyn, Jmca, StVn) To interpret the future of and forewarn (sb); to interpret signs, dreams, etc for (sb). She 'read me up'. This is the first thing an 'obeah' doctor does. According to her, reading a spell to cause my death on the day before I took my exam had been set in motion by one of our envious neighbours, whom she later described.—WeS (73.12.07, p.18) **2.** PHRASE **2.1 read and spell for (sb)** vb phr (Guyn, Tbgo, Trin) [IF] To be obliged to explain in detail what should be obvious to (sb).

real [re·l] adv (CarA) [IF] Really; very. **a.** This food is good enough for anybody. You can cook real good.—TRIH:112 **b.** A lovely piece of man; real sweet.—MOHW:18 **c.** Christine, I have a lot of problems, but this one is real big.—NaT (76.06.27, p.18, Dear Christine) [OED2 notes this usage as 'orig Sc and US. Not common in Southern Eng'] □ Occurs widely esp in spoken CE.

re·cei·ver n (Guyn) A kitchen sink. [Cp OED receiver 4. b. 'a tank or reservoir; a vessel to hold anything'. The term may have been popularized in Guyn through the use of vessels called 're-ceivers' in the distillation process in making rum]

red¹ adj (CarA) **1.** [Of colours in general, esp of fruit, flowers, insects, fish, etc] Being of any colour from orange to purple. **2.** [Of a person's skin-colour] [Derog] ‖ **red-skin(ned)** (CarA) Being of any colour from brown to near white, showing varying mixtures of Black and White races. **a.** The High Yellow Bahamian is sometimes classified as 'red' or a Conchy Joe except that he is more 'coloured'. These Bahamians are the direct result of mixed marriages or sexual intercourse of black and white.—MBS:19 **b.** Barbadians often speak about 'red people' alluding to persons of fair skin complexion. Even though the word red is used here to denote a certain colour, it carries with it strong connotations namely that the persons in-volved are the end products of cross breeding between Caucasians and Negroes.—Bdos (Ms) [In many W Afr lang (exs Yoruba pupa, Twi kɔkɔɔ, etc) the same word indicates 'red, brown, yellow' and may also be used in ref to skin colour distinguishing from 'black'. Ex DAFL Twi ɔ-kɔkɔɔ 'a red person whose skin is not of a glossy

black (tuntum) but of a brownish hue'. Cp o-tuntum 'a black person'. Though orig in W Afr evid not derogatory, the transfer of this sense of 'red' prob accounts for earliest CarA usage. See note] □ In CE the term is used insultingly usu by darker-skinned Black people. Cp BROWN-SKIN, CLEAR-SKIN, LIGHT-SKIN, RED-NIGGER. See also BÉKÉ, CHE-CHE. **3.** (Belz) [Of the eye] Envious; covetous. PHRASE **3.1 eye(s) (get) red (for sth)** vb phr (Belz) ‖ EYE(S) CATCH FIRE (FOR STH) (Gren, etc) See EYE Phr 8.1

red² vb tr (Belz) [AF—Cr] PHRASE **red your eye (after sth)** vb phr (Belz) [AF—Cr] ‖ EYE[S] CATCH FIRE (FOR STH) (Gren, etc) See EYE Phr 8.1 [Cp Shona Kutsu ukisa ma ziso (make red both eye) 'eyes redden to get sth' (i.e. immediately coveted)]

red-ant* n (CarA) A reddish-brown ant vary-ing in size from an eighth to a quarter of an inch; its bite stings severely and, though of several varieties in different territories, it is the most common stinging Caribbean ground-ant, its nest being usu marked by a tiny black mound with a hole in the middle; Solenopsis spp.

red-bead n phr (Jmca) ‖ JUMBIE-BEAD 3. (Gren, etc)

red-bead vine n phr (Jmca) ‖ BEAD-VINE (BUSH) (Nevs, StKt)

red-bean n (BrVi, Dmca, TkCa) ‖ STRING-BEAN (CarA) [The reddish brown is the commonest of the many varieties]

red birch n phr (Jmca) ‖ BIRCH-GUM TREE (Bdos, etc)

red ce·dar* n phr (Bdos, Dmca, Gren, Guyn, Nevs) A forest tree that can exceed 100 ft in height, with a spreading crown and large branches; it yields pinkish-brown timber wh is highly prized for its fragrance, smoothness, durability, and resistance to termites; Cedrela odorata or C. mexicana (Meliaceae). [From its pinkish colour in contrast to a white cedar] □ Commonly called CEDAR in many places, being the commonly used type in contrast with the less popular 'white cedar'. The European cedar (as in the Bibl cedars of Lebanon) is a different tree, of the family Pinaceae.

red-chen·ke [rɛd-čɛŋki] n (Antg) [AF—Derog] ‖ POOR-WHITE (CarA) [Prob < red-shankie < RED-SHANKS (Bdos)]

red-coat plum n phr (Jmca) ‖ JAMAICA PLUM (Bdos, etc) [From its reddish-brown or purple skin]

red cor·di·a n phr (Angu, Bdos, CayI, StKt) See CORDIA

red-eye n **1.** (Bdos) ‖ pink-eye (Jmca, etc) Infectious inflammation of the (human) eye caus-ing redness of the white of the eye; haemorrhagic conjunctivitis. □ *Pink-eye* is also SE. **2.** (Belz, Jmca, StVn) [*AF*] ‖ BIG-EYE² (CarA) PHRASES **2.1 have red-eye (for sth)** *vb phr* (CayI) [*AF*]; **look with red-eye (at sth)** *vb phr* (Jmca) [*AF*] ‖ EYE(S) CATCH FIRE (FOR STH) (Gren, etc) See EYE Phr 8.1 **2.2 put your red-eye (on sth)** *vb phr* (Belz, Jmca) [*AF*] To look covetously, enviously (at sth)

red-fig *n* (Trin) ‖ BUCK-BANANA (Guyn)

red-fish *n* (Bdos, Mrat, StVn) ‖ RED-SNAPPER (CarA)

red gin·ger-li·ly *n phr* (Bdos) ‖ GINGER-LILY 1. (Bdos)

red-hind* *n* (Dmca, Gren, Jmca, USVI) A reddish-brown fish spotted all over with scarlet dots, and of average weight 2 lbs; it abounds in Atlantic waters and is of excellent food value; *Epinephelus guttatus* (*Serranidae*).

red-hot cat('s *n phr* (Jmca) ‖ CAT-TAIL (CarA)

Red House, The *n phr* (Trin) [*IF*] The building in Port-of-Spain wh is the seat of Parliament and also houses many government administrative offices. *These buildings must have been still brand-new when Cazabon painted them, for they were opened in 1848. On being finished they were given a coat of red paint and so came to be called 'The Red House'. Today the term 'Red House' is synonymous with 'Government Buildings'. These were the buildings which, with various additions and modifications, were burned down in the historic Water Riots of 1903. The present Red House was opened in 1907.*—AGTT:7

red Ibo [rɛd ibʊ] *n phr* (Jmca) [*AF—Derog*] ‖ BACKRA NIGGER (Tbgo) [< RED¹ 2. [Derog] + *Ibo* [Hist] a W Afr ethnic group from eastern Nigeria]

red-leg (**red·leg**) *n* (Bdos) [*AF—Derog*] ‖ POOR-WHITE (CarA) [Said to be because of the high pink colour of their exposed legs from working in the sun]

red mud *n phr* (Guyn) [Bauxite Ind] The reddish-brown slurry or waste wh is left in quantity after the processed extraction of alumina from bauxite clay; it is further processed for brick-making.

red-necked pi·geon* *n phr* (Jmca) ‖ *ramier(-pigeon)* (ECar) A slate-grey pigeon with a dull, wine-coloured head, neck and upper chest; it makes a purring sound followed by a 'croo-crooo'; there are many sub-varieties, that in Grenada being hunted for its tasty meat; *Columba squamosa* (*Columbidae*).

red-nig·ger *n* (CarA) [*AF—Derog*] A person of African descent with a yellowish skin and very tough hair, often one whose parents are both the immediate offspring of black and white parents.

And what make her precious so? That fading yellow red-nigger skin? Cause she ain't no spring chicken again.—LDCD:21 □ The term is used as a strong insult, usu by dark-skinned Black people. See RED¹ 2., also BACKRA NIGGER.

red-plum *n* (CayI, Trin) ‖ JAMAICA-PLUM (Bdos, etc) [From its colour when ripening]

red-sage* *n* (Bdos) The *Lantana camara* variety of BLACK-SAGE 2. (*CarA*).

red san·dal·wood* *n phr* (Gren, Jmca, Trin) ‖ *jumbie-bead* 3. (Gren, Trin, USVI) Wood of the tall shade tree that bears the JUMBIE BEAD 3, *Adenanthera pavonina*, useful for cabinet-making. *The Red Sandalwood is a shade tree; seeds used in beadwork; wood of cabinet quality; leaves astringent; boils treated with powdered seeds.*—GNHIG:80

red-shanks *n* (Bdos) [*AF—Derog*] (Evid an earlier form of) RED-LEG (*Bdos*). □ Cp RED-CHENKE.

red-skin(ned) *adj* (CarA) [*AF—Derog*] ‖ RED¹ 2. (CarA) **a.** *Red-skin / Skin colour of a blistered pawpaw.*—SJEV:19 **b.** *A few days ago the minister of C. and W. visit the airport. When dey come out of de car, dem workers betting dat de Black skin one is de minister, some of dem say es de Red Skin one ... an wen he leave dem people saying de man tarking as third standard chile.*—ToR (73.02.11, p.3, Letter To Couzen Loftus) □ See CHE-CHE.

red-snap·per* *n* (CarA) ‖ *brim* (Bdos, Mrat, Nevs) ‖ *red-fish* (Bdos) A full-fleshed, big-eyed red fish, paler red on its belly; it can grow to over 20 lbs and is caught in schools in very deep water; it is prized for its excellent food value; *Lutjanus campechanus* (*Lutjanidae*).

red-wood *n* (Baha) ‖ EBONY 2. (Baha, etc) *Growing through the West Indies is the tree we call the Red Grape, Cocoloba swartzii, with additional popular names of Red-wood and Barka Locust, / The tree grows in Turner's Hall Wood and in former days was a desirable timber tree.*—AdN (79.06.10, p.10, M.B. Hutt) □ There is another species of *red-wood* known in *Guyn, Centrolobium paraense* (*Papilionaceae*).

red-yam* *n* (Baha, Gren, Jmca, Nevs, StKt) A yam with a red inner skin when peeled; some varieties have a pinkish and others a white flesh; *Dioscorea spp.*

reel·er-bulb *n* (TkCa) ‖ BALL-BUSH (Bdos, Jmca)

reel·ing PHRASE **reeling in the head** *n phr* (BrVi, Mrat, Nevs) ‖ SWINGING IN THE HEAD (Baha, etc) See HEAD Phr 4.18

re·gard·less (to) *prep* (*phr*) (CarA) [*X*] ‖ *regards to* (Bdos) Regardless of; without considering; no matter. **a.** *... who were notorious* *for voting party—regardless who the candidates happened to be.*—WBAM:219 *b. 'Regardless to whether we get permission or not, we will go ahead with the rally, even if we have to use Independence Square', said Clarke.*—NaT (74.05.12, p.1)

re·gards *n pl* (CarA) [X] **1.** Regard (see cits). *He says: 'a prison should be a community within a community, with a disciplined approach to work and living* [*and*] *with regards for good work.'*—MtM (73.04.13, p.2) [Prob an overcorrection for SE *regard* esp in idiomatic contexts] **2.** PHRASES **2.1 in regards to** *prep phr* (CarA) [X] In regard to; with regard to; as regards; in connection with; in the matter of. **a.** *He spoke on certain matters relating to the position of the Commonwealth in regards to cane sugar production.*—SdB (65.02.27, p.1) **b.** *I read your column all the time and I am writing this letter in regards to a boy who reads it.*—NaT (77.07.31, p.22, Dear Christine) **c.** *The language in passage A is most objective and clear in regards to time and length.*—Mrat (Ms, 1973) [By overlap of SE prep phr structures *in regard to* + *as regards*] **2.2 regards to (sb/sth)** *prep phr* (Bdos) [X] ‖ REGARDLESS (CarA) **a.** *When de show start, you shut dis door and don*[*'t*] *open it regards to who it is.*—(Bdos) **b.** *Everybody still interested in the report regards to how long it take to come out.*— (Bdos) **2.3 with regards to (sb/sth)** *prep phr* (CarA) [X] In/with regard to; (etc as for IN REGARDS TO). **a.** *With regards to the change in behaviour and performance of males, it is my view that it will continue unless our males accept that women now see themselves in completely different roles.*—AdV (90.09.13, p.13) **b.** *With regards to the Prime Minister's statement I can only express my delight.*—(Guyn) [By overlap of SE prep phr structures *with regard to* + *as regards* and prob morphologically influenced by the SE idiom *with (my) kind regards to* (sb) as letter-terminal formula]

reg·gae (reg·gay) [rɛgɛ] *n* (CarA) **1.** A kind of dance-music with a steady heartbeat type of rhythm usu marked on an electric bass-guitar and a RATTLE-DRUM supporting one or two tune-carrying brass instruments; it is accompanied by usu mournful lyrics relating to Jamaican folk-life, and became closely associated with the RASTAFARIAN cult. [The word may have had a wider coverage in other areas of folk-life, not only in *Jmca*, but became particularly focused there on the theme of hardship and protest expressed by the RASTAFARIAN cult, then spread through that medium and esp the folk-level dancing developed from it, through the *CarA* and elsewhere. Cp Yoruba *rege-rege* 'rough; in a rough manner'; also *ADHL* Hausa *rega* (*pa.t. rege*) *vb tr* 'to shake'; also *DJE* Jmca *rege-rege* 1. 'ragged clothing' 2. 'a row'; also Tbgo *rege-rege*, *adj*, 'rough, uncultured' (*pers info*, *J.D.* Elder); also *rege-rege rege-rege* (Guyn, occasional and rural) said by a person playing a rattle for, or an older person participating in, an open-air dance] **2.** The individualistic dancing to the music involving much shoulder and body movement,

with the arms down, fists closed, and the knees bent. □ *Reggae* is now the accepted standard spelling. A pl form is unlikely or rare. (Cp CE CALYPSOES, SE *waltzes*, etc). The term is often used without article and also attrib; hence *to like reggae, reggae beat/music/piece/record*, etc. **3.** PHRASES **3.1 dance reggae** *vb phr* (CarA) To dance to REGGAE music. **3.2 play reggae** *vb phr* (CarA) To play REGGAE music.

re·lish *n* (Angu, Baha, StKt, USVI) ‖ FLESH 1. (Bdos, StVn) *I was given one shilling and sixpence (about twenty cents in today's value) to buy the 'relish' for a family, plus enough for any extras that might drop in at meal time.*—EBT:37 [Perh a survival of an EE sub-sense or dial shift. This is strongly suggested by the cits given at *OED relish* sb[1] 3. b., wh support the CE usage better than *OED's* 'savoury addition to a meal']

re·lle·no [riyɛno ~ riɛno] *n* (Belz) A dish comprising a chicken stuffed with highly seasoned, fried, ground pork, boiled eggs and mixed fruit and peppers, the whole being then boiled in a deep broth darkened with a herb seasoning called 'black ricardo'; it is the celebrated festive dish of Belize. [Sp *relleno* 'stuffed'] □ Sometimes called **relleno soup** in ref to the dark broth served with pieces of the chicken.

re·mo·del·ling *vbl n* (Bdos) See CONVERT

ren·ge [rɛŋgɛ] *adj* (Tbgo, Trin) [*AF—Cr*] [Of a person or animal] Thin; skinny. *He lookin*[*g*] *renge but do*[*n't*] *underestimate him, yo*[*u*] *know. He dam*[*n*] *strong whe*[*re*] *you see him the*[*re*].—(Tbgo)

renk; renk·in(g) [rɛŋkɪn /-ɪŋ] *adj* **1.** (Belz, Jmca, StLu, USVI) [*IF*] ‖ RANK[1] (CarA) *You drive past the Abbatoir, then Wham! A putrid renking odour as you have never smelled before.*—CrU (77.03.26, p.4) **2.** (Jmca) [Of a person] Very impertinent; crude. [From a variant pronunc of RANK < SE *ræŋk*. Cp also *KED* Krio *rɛnk* 'strong, offensive smell (esp of decaying fish)']

Re·pub·lic Day *n phr* (Guyn) February 23rd, the date of the Berbice Slave Rebellion in 1763, the first in the colony that became Br Guiana, observed annually, as of 1970, as Guyana's official Independence Day.

re·spect *n* PHRASE **in respect to** *prep phr* (CarA) [X] In respect of; with respect to; in regard to. **a.** *In respect to that matter I have contacted the Water Authority.*—(Bdos) **b.** *The Government was justified in bringing into play its quasi judicial powers in respect to alien land holding licences.*—MtM (73.06.05, p.4)

rest[1] *vb* **1.** *vb tr* (CarA) ‖ **rest down** (CarA) [*AF*] To place, put down (sth). *Then he see the letter that the postman bring right there on the ledge in the kitchen, where I rest it.*—SNWIC: 240 (E. Lovelace) □ This CE usage is wider in sense that SE *rest* (*sth on a foundation, support, etc*). **2.** *vb tr* (CarA) **(i)** To allow to remain unused. **(ii)** [Of a cane- or rice-field] To let lie uncultivated for some time before being ploughed again. [Cp *EDD* rest sb¹ 1. *rest-piece* 'a piece of land that has not been ploughed for a long time' (Sc and Eng)] **(iii)** [Of a cricketer or footballer] To lay off (a player on tour or during a season) temporarily in the expectation of better performance. □ Cp AmE *rest up*, with similar sense, esp of a player. **3.** *vb tr* (Belz) To put (sb/sth) out of your mind; (SE) to have done with (sb/sth). *'I just do my duty. I don't bother to quarrel with anybody.' | 'Only with John John', she grinned. | He had finished dressing. 'Look here, rest John John.'*—HF:28 **4.** PHRASES **4.1 rest down (sth)/your head** *vb phr* (CarA) [*AF*] To put down, lay (sth)/your head. [A redundancy from sense 1.] **4.2 rest [u]pon your stomach** *vb phr* (CarA) [*AF/IF*] [Of sth eaten] To feel undigested. *I shouldn't-a eat dat big mango so late; it restin[g] [u]pon me stomach now I want to go an[d] sleep.*—(Guyn) **4.3 Rest yourself!** *imper phr* (CarA) [*AF*] Go away!; Be gone with you! **4.4 rest your hand on (sb/sth)** *vb phr* (Tbgo, Trin) [*AF*] To lay hold of (sb); [by extension] to grab or steal (sth). **a.** *Some wayward boys does raid me orange trees but the day I rest me hand on them, is trouble.*—(Tbgo) **b.** *Somebody res[t] the[ir] han[d] on my bicycle outside the lib[ra]ry an[d] I ai[n't] see it again.*—(Trin)

rest² *n* (CarA) [*IF*] **1.** [Often of people, esp members of a family] Others. *S1: Cilla, how you? | S2: I a(ll)right. | S1: And how the rest?* —(Tbgo) **2** PHRASE **2.1 the other rest** *pron phr* (Guyn) [*X*] The others. □ A tautology. Also *other rest of them.*

Rest House *n phr* (Belz, Guyn) A fully furnished and serviced residence in a 'District' (see DISTRICT COMMISSIONER); it is provided for temporary use by travelling Government officials. (See cit) *Government has a Rest House in each administrative centre for the use of officials and other persons travelling on official business. Other visitors are sometimes allowed to stay in a Rest House for a night or two on application to the District Commissioner concerned.*—ABSBH: 92

re·verse back *vb phr*)ECar) [*X*] To reverse (a vehicle); to back (an animal harnessed to a cart). *He asked the driver to reverse back a little more to let him pass.*—(StVn) [SE *reverse* vb + *back* adv] □ One of the commonest redundant phrasal vbs in CE.

Rhyn·land foot *n phr* (Guyn) A length, equivalent to 1.03 ft (Br), originally Dutch and still used officially in Government land-survey and legal documents in Guyana. □ Hence also **Rhynland rod/rood**, equivalent to 12 ft 4 ins.

rice¹ *n* (CarA) PHRASES **1. be sb's rice** *vb phr* (CarA) [*AF-Derog*] To be the only reliable supporter of a person or family; to be sb's provider (from sexual or other motives) [By metonymy, rice being the basic element of food in many CarA territories] **2. cook your own rice** *vb phr* (StVn) [*AF*] To fend for yourself. □ Cp next. **3. rice don't/ain't/no(t) cook(ed) in the same pot** *id phr* (Guyn) [*AF-Derog*] ‖ *food don't (etc) cook in the same pot* (CarA) [Of two persons] Not to be of the same kind or social class; not subject to the same controls; not be partners in the same venture. *She can afford to ignore anyt[h]ing he says, [be]cause the two o[f] them rice don['t] cook in the same pot, you see.*— (Guyn) □ The phr is less often used in the affirmative (also *Derog*) to refer to 'sameness of manners', etc.

rice² *vb tr* (Bdos, Gren, Guyn) [*AF-Derog*] **1.** To maintain financially, feed, support (a servile person, a mistress, etc). *[H]e wan rule me life, like if [h]e does rice me.* (= *He wants to rule my life, as if he maintains me*).—(Guyn) [By functional n > vb shift of RICE¹, and metonymic sense of *rice* (=maintenance)] **2.** PHRASE **2.1 rice at (sb)** *vb phr* (Bdos, Gren, Guyn) [*AF-Derog*] To be maintained, supported as lackey, mistress, etc, by (sb). *Well, whoever en like Lou doin' dah, dah is a matter fuh dem 'cause Lou don' rice at nobody, an' wuh she got to say she gine say.*—NaT (79.12.28, p.5, Lickmout Lou)

rice and peas *n phr* (CarA) See PEAS AND RICE

rice-belly *n* (Guyn) [*AF-Derog*] ‖ **bang-belly** (Jmca) **1.** A swollen abdomen owing to malnutrition **2.** [By extension] A child with such an abdomen.

rice-bil·low/-be·low *n* (Baha) ‖ PELAU(-RICE) (ECar) [< *rice* + PELAU by folk etym]

rice-dog; rice-eater *n* (Guyn) [*AF-Joc/Derog*] A mongrel wh is fed on food remainders, esp rice, and worthless as a watchdog. [By transfer of the connotation of RICE² vb] □ Cp SALMON-TOT RETRIEVER (*Bdos*).

rice-pud·ding *n* (Antg, Brbu, StKt) ‖ BLACK-PUDDING (Guyn) □ Cp SE *rice-pudding*, a sweet dessert.

rick·a·ticks *n pl* (Guyn) [*AF-Joc*] **1.** Bad temper. **2.** PHRASE **2.1 get in your rickaticks** *vb phr* (Guyn) [*AF-Joc*] To become very bad-tempered; to behave angrily for some time. [Cp *EDD rickmatick* (Sc and Irel) 'concern, affair; collection' + cits suggesting rowdiness]

rick-chick-chick con·ga·tay *n phr* (Guyn) A children's game in wh players are set to catch one of their number identified by name during the chanting of a rhyme introduced by this formula.

rid *n* (Bdos, Guyn) [*X*] Riddance (in the particular phr following). PHRASE **get the rid of (sb/sth)** *vb phr* (Bdos, Guyn) [*X*] To get rid of. (See GET Phr 3.21) *My husband does not want me any more. I know that he is anxious to get the rid of me. He seldom sleeps at home.*—GyC

(76.11.14) [Cp *EDD rid* vb[1] and sb[1] 13. pl phr (Cor, Dev) *to get* (*the*) *rids of* 'to get rid of']

rid·dle *n, vb* (CarA) [A formula used in the presentation of a riddle, occurring in various forms, as in foll exs] ‖ *A riddle, a riddle, aree* (Bdos) ‖ *Me[r]-riddle, me[r]-riddle, me[r]-ree* (Guyn, StVn) ‖ *Mer-riddle, mer-riddle, mer ranny-o* (Baha) ‖ *Riddle me riddle, riddle me ree* (Jmca) ‖ *Riddle-O, riddle-O, ree* (Gren), etc. [Prob variants of Br formula as in *OED riddle* vb[1] 2. imper phr *riddle me a* (or *my*) *riddle*, of wh there are also dial variants as in *EDD*, *riddle* vb[3] 'to explain, solve' + cit from Sc *Riddle me, riddle me, rot-tot-tot*. The proliferation of these phrases is prob infl by the early transfer of the wide use of riddles in W Afr folklore to the *CarA*]

ride *vb tr* 1. (Bdos, Gren, Tbgo, Trin) [*AF/IF*] To cause (sb) indigestion. *If you eat cucumber in de night, it go ride you.*—(Gren) [Cp *EDD ride* vb 13. 'to rise upon the stomach' + cits from Sur 'If I eats cold pork it rides so'] 2. (Tbgo) [Of a spirit] To possess (sb) as a medium during ritual dancing. [Cp *OED ride* vb B. 17. a (Of a nightmare, witches, etc), 'to sit upon (a person); to use (one) as a horse'] 3. PHRASE 3.1 **ride (on) your chest/stomach** *vb phr* (CarA) [*IF*] [Of sth eaten] **(i)** [As sense 1.] To cause indigestion. **(ii)** To cause nightmares. [Evid a combination of sense 1. and 2.]

ridge *n* (Belz) Any strip or stretch of land with natural vegetation (i.e. no rise in the ground is implied). [Prob an extension of Br dial usage. Cp *EDD ridge* sb 'a strip of land ... left between furrows' + many cits indicating some space] □ The Belz cemetery is called 'Lord's Ridge'.

right[1] *n* (CarA) [In general sense of duty, correctness] PHRASES 1. **give (sb) right** *vb phr* (CarA) [*AF/IF*] See GIVE[1] Phr 2.28 2. **have a right (to be/being somewhere), to do/doing sth)** *vb phr* (CarA) [*IF/AF*] Ought. *When you see all that fighting start you had a right to get out o[f] there.*—(Bdos) [Prob from IrE. Note: A member at an Urban Council meeting makes an offensive remark and refuses to withdraw it: when another retorts > –'You have a right to withdraw it'—i.e. 'it is your duty.' So > –'You have a right to pay your debts.'—*JESI:21*] □ A common CE idiom at the folk level, stressing a limited sense of *right* 'good cause, good reason'. Note the difference from the legal sense in SE *have the right to be, do*, etc. See next. 2.1 **have no business/right (to be/being somewhere, to do/doing sth)** *vb phr* (CarA) [*IF/AF*] Ought not; be wrong. *But the car had no right being on the grass portion, so what is he claiming?*—(Tbgo)

right[2]? *excl tag Q* (CarA) [*IF*] [Empty intrusive word, with rising pitch, inviting the hearer's approval or encouragement of what is being said] *Well the present Government—right?—is showing that they are determined—right?—to make people feel and believe—right?—that the present financial problems is the previous Government fault, right?' —But a lot of us don[′t] buy that—right?*—(Bdos) □ Perh an orig abbr of the SE tag Q *Am I* (*not*) *right?*, this item, developing as a habit in CE speech from about the 1950s or 1960s, has gradually become a meaningless pause-filler serving as a prop to the hearer's attention while the speaker strives to order the course of his utterance. Accordingly it does not occur in writing.

ring-ding *n* (Belz, Guyn, Jmca) [*AF*] 1. Any kind of noisy excitement, a rousing dance, an open-air row, etc). [A reduplicative form perh referring to the festive folk habit of ringing cowbells, knocking iron, etc. However, cp AmE slang, *DAS wing-ding* 3. 'a ruckus; any noisy or exciting incident; a noisy celebration or argument'] 2. *excl and attrib* [Expression of amused excitement] **a.** *Ring-ding! De row bu[r]s[t] now!*—Guyn) **b.** *The wedding was a ring-ding affair, and now they like they can[′t] pay for it.*—(Belz)

ring-neck *n* (Guyn) [*AF—Derog*] A rough, brawling type of person, esp a woman; a virago. '*You're an old ring-neck,' the Beak addressed Lucy*, as he told her that she will have to pay $3.00 (costs $1.50), while Kulsum who defended the innocence of her 'lil' girl' paid only $2.50.—DaC (53.04.09, p.3) [An erron, but regular spelling for *wring-neck* n, SE *vb phr wring* (*a chicken's*) *neck*]

ring out *vb phr* (Guyn) [Of a telephone] To ring continuously without being answered. [Prob by overlapping: 'telephone rings' + '(person is) out']

ring·worm-bush *n* (Bdos, Gren, Jmca, Trin) ‖ CHRISTMAS-CANDLE (Bdos, etc) [From the common folk-medicinal use of its leaves—either by squeezing the juice or boiling in water—to cure ringworm and other skin disorders]

ripe *adj* (Baha) [*IF*] 1. (Tbgo, Trin) [*AF—Joc*] Ready to burst forth, erupt (as a quarrel, etc). *And even if she did believe, the situation had gone too far, and the whole neighbourhood knew that Miranda was having an affair with the boy next door and bacchanal ripe, as they say.*—BoM (79.02.02, p.9) 2. (Jmca) [*AF—Joc*] [Of a young woman] Precocious; ready for or inviting sexual enjoyment. [Cp *OED ripe* 2. b. '[of persons] Fully developed in body; mature, (obs) marriageable'] 3. (Baha) [*IF*] [Of the moon] Full. *There was a delightful softness to the nights, especially when the moon was ripe; it is at such times that the moonlight could be enjoyed.*—EBT:19

ripe-plan·tain *n* (Baha, Dmca, Gren, StLu) ‖ YELLOW PLANTAIN (Guyn)

rise *vb intr* PHRASE **rise with the fowls** *vb phr* (Bdos) [*IF*] See FOWL Phr 2.2

ri·ver *n* PHRASES 1. **over the river** *adv phr* (Guyn) Across, on the other side of the river. *S1: Well every afternoon I have to go home over* *the river.* / *S2: Oh I didn't know you lived over the river.*—(Guyn) **2. river comes down** *id phr* (ECar, Jmca) The river floods, bursts its banks. [A ref to floodwaters rushing down from the mountain-side]

ri·ver·ain *adj* (Guyn) Of or on terrain bordering or near to a river or CREEK. [As *OED riverain* A 1, 2 + latest cit 1883] □ Listed in *COD7* (1982) but not in *COD8* (1990) as current, though *riverine* and (Law) *riparian* (with same senses as *riverain*) are both retained. In *Guyn* the older Eng *riverain* remains the normal term for all usage.

ri·ver-bot·tom *n* (Belz, Guyn) [AF—Cr] A river bed. *Rockstone a river-bottom no know sun hot* (= *The stone on the river bed does not know the heat of the sun*).—Guyn (Prov)

ri·ver-mu·ma /ı'121/ *n* (Jmca) ‖ FAIRMAID (Guyn)

ri·ver-ta·ma·rind ['rɪvʌ-tam(b)rɪn] /1112/ *n* (Bdos) ‖ WILD TAMARIND 1. (Belz, etc) *The River-Tamarind has been growing wild in Barbados for some years and some farmers are already aware of its potential as an animal feed supplement.*—NaT (79.01.19, p.2) [From the shrub's ability to thrive in rocky coral-stone in dry watercourses and the resemblance of its leaves and dry pods to the tamarind]

r-month(s) *n* (*pl*) (Bdos) The months from September to April, during wh the catching of SEA-EGGS was formerly permitted by law in Barbados; the [former] legal open season for catching sea-eggs. [From the occurrence of the letter 'r' in the names of those months, hence a natural mnemonic for fishermen] □ As of 1989 the legal open season is from September to December.

roach¹ *n* (CarA) **1.** A cockroach. [As *OED, OED2 roach* sb⁴ 'chiefly US'. However this is the standard name for the insect in CE, polite Creole society being said to have had an aversion to the first syllable of SE *cockroach*] □ Note that *roach* in commonest SE usage refers to an edible fish. **2.** PHRASES **2.1 roach on sb's bread** *id phr* (Baha) [AF—Joc] A person who has a sexual relationship with another's spouse or lover. [A metaph ref to such a person as vermin crawling mostly at night] **2.2 eat/get roach on your bread** *vb phr* (Baha) [AF—Joc] To keep/have an unfaithful spouse or lover. **2.3 put roach on sb's bread** *vb phr* (Baha) [AF—Joc] ‖ HORN¹ (Baha, etc) *If a man dreams of a wedding ring, then his wife has a sweetheart 'putting roach on his bread' or 'horning' him.*—MTTBT:153

roach² *vb tr* (Baha) [AF—Joc] ‖ *pear²* (Baha) **1.** To betray a spouse or lover by having an outside affair. *Read the 'Friday Morning's Mail' for incidents of this e.g. the female with three boyfriends with a Mercedes, a Jaguar and a Volkswagen! and her 'roaching' or ('pearing') all of*

them!—MBS:28 **2.** To sleep with the spouse or lover of (sb); to cuckold. *That is the fellow that roaching him all the time.*—(Baha)

road *n* PHRASE **go up the road for (sb)** *vb phr* (Guyn) See GO Phr 6.33

road·cor·ner *n* (Guyn) ‖ CORNER 1. (Guyn)

road-march *n* (ECar) **1.** The street-parading of a fully costumed CARNIVAL BAND once accompanied by a STEELBAND, more recently by a TRAILER playing selected CALYPSO tunes of the season, with a TRAMPING crowd following. (See PARADE OF THE BANDS) **2.** ‖ *tune-of-the-Crop* (Bdos) The calypso tune accounted as the most popular choice of BANDS in such parades. *The road-march of 1955, another institution borrowed from Trinidad, was Kitchener's 'Trouble in Arima'.*—Caq IV.2, p.113

Road-march King *n phr* (Tbgo, Trin) The CALYPSONIAN one of whose tunes wins the competition by being the most popular selection of the BANDS parading in the ROAD-MARCH.

road-ten·nis /12'2/ *n* (Bdos) ‖ *padder tennis, paddle tennis* (Bdos) A game like table-tennis, but played on a smooth road-surface with a court 20 ft × 10 ft marked out, and an 8-in wide piece of board standing on its edge as a 'net'; oval wooden 'bats' serve as rackets. *Young people need jobs. You only have to go along the streets at 11 o'clock in the day and see the boys playing dominoes and road-tennis.*—Bdos (Hd, 73.11.13, p.2849) [< road + (table-)tennis]

roar·ing calf *n phr* (Belz, CayI, Jmca) See ROLLING CALF.

roast¹ *n* (Jmca) [AF] A second job on the side (often kept secret). *One must not forget the taxi-drivers who are always in search of a 'roast'.*—JdN (80.01.08, p.12) [An implied ref to 'roast-plantain' as in ROAST² Phr 2.]

roast² *vb tr* PHRASES **1. roast a time** *vb phr* (StKt, USVI) [AF—Joc] To enjoy yourself thoroughly; to have a very good time. *The Heyliger report went on to comment: Crucians accept the fact that they are pretty conservative about 'roasting a time' during festival. The St Thomian is considered the gayest of Virgin Islanders when it comes to merrymaking.*—DoC (65.03.24, p.6) **2. roast coco/plantain for sb** *vb phr* (Jmca) [AF—Joc] To prepare in secret for the chance of exploiting or tricking sb; to stand by, unsuspected, to take advantage of sb's misfortune. *Dem won[t] help him so him force to sell de house dem ready fe buy. Dem only roastin[g] plantain for him.*—(Jmca) [Symbolizing expectation of sth desirable, a ref to the habit of preparing roasted coco(yam) or plantain to complete a main meal]

roast-bake *n* (Tbgo, Trin) ‖ BAKE¹ 1. (Tbgo, Trin) *Consider the cheaper kinds of fish, like shark.* / *For most people, this is just a popular* *snackfood when teamed with roast-bake (or hops bread) with some spicy, hot sauce.*—ExP (73.05.01, p.3) □ See also COCONUT-BAKE

roast-corn *n* (Bdos, Gren, Guyn, Mrat) Fully ripe corn on the cob roasted usu on a COAL-POT in the open. *A number of people selling roast-corn, a favourite with many Bajans, have decided to set up their corn-roasting coalpots along the new highways at points where they believe motorists will be able to slow down and buy their corn.*—AdN (88.10.05, p.7)

roast-pork (cac·tus)* *n* (*phr*) (Jmca) [*AF—Joc*] A type of cactus with fleshy, flat leaves wh look like bits of meat (hence the name); *Opuntia antillana* (*Cactaceae*). *The only plants remaining to break Sprat's long slide were some unpleasant roastpork cacti. Sprat knew by experience that rolling into a clump of roastpork would only make a bad day worse.*—DSM:8

rob·ber *n* (Trin) ‖ MIDNIGHT-ROBBER (Trin)

rob·ber-talk *n* (Trin) **1.** A practised speech by a CARNIVAL masquerader costumed as a MID-NIGHT-ROBBER bragging of personal, satanic powers, and characterized by meaningless strings of words interspersed with unreal threats to persuade the listener to throw money in a bag. *These [robber-talk] delusions of grandeur and great villainy seem to have a form and delivery all their own. .../ 'Stop! Drop your keys and bow your knees, and call me the Prince of Darkness, criminal Master. For if I gather my teeth and stamp my feet, it will cause disaster. ...'*—Caq IV, 3–4, 1956 (D. Crowley) **[**A ref to the costume of the masquerader. See MIDNIGHT-ROBBER. However, the practice of bragging talk for money or reward in competition wh has notable parallels and a long history in many Black *CarA* communities (see TEA-MEETING) has evid only been incorporated into CARNIVAL festivities in this particular attire**]** □ The actual practice appears to be waning, usage surviving however in sense 2. **2.** [By extension] Excessive language, esp bullying threats from persons in authority. *The joy which suffused the entire gathering could not have been engendered by any scathing attacks on the government nor by any bombastic robber-talk of licks like fire. / It came only because, from the start, the accent was placed on those things which lifted the spirit.*—TaP (75.12.07, p.1)

robe dou·ill·ette (dou·ill·ette, wòb-dwi·yèt) [wob duyɛt] *n phr* (Dmca) See DWIYÈT

rob·in¹* *n* (Angu, Gren, Grns, Nevs, StVn) An edible fish about 6 to 8 ins long, with a silvery blue, roundish body and pointed mouth; it is usu caught in shoals; *Prionotus scutulus* (*Triglidae*). [From the contrasting reddish colour of its fins]

rob·in² *n* (CarA) Any of a number of varieties of colourful, small, chirping birds, having in common only a marked redness of some parts

of the body, i.e. red throat and under-bill (to-dies), or red bill and legs (thrushes), or red throat and under-tail (finches), or reddish-brown bellies (tanagers). □ None of these is evid related to the European robin redbreast *Erithacus rubecula* (*Musicapidae*) although some are called by that folk-name. Note also further difference of No Amer robin *Turdus migratorius* (*Turdidae*). See *BBWI*, index, for *CarA* details.

ro·bot *n, adj* (Jmca) [*AF—Joc*] A privately owned vehicle used illegally to provide public transportation, esp during bus strikes. [Joc ref to the unlicensed, hence unidentified, driver]

rock *n* (Bdos, Guyn) **1.** A stone; a piece of stone. *And he pelt up a big rock and catch Joe right in he head. Sudden so is like if the sky come down, because Joe seeing a lot of bright stars twinkling in front of his eyes.*—CISH:24 □ In *Bdos, Guyn* the difference between *a rock* and *a stone* is commonly blurred. Cp the compound ROCK-STONE (*CarA*). *A stone* is the rarer 'n phr'. In *Guyn* BRICK adds to the confusion. However, note paralleled sense in AmE *W3* 4. *rock* n 2. c. (3) 'an often jagged fragment of rock ranging in size from a boulder to a pebble'. **2.** PHRASE **2.1 give (sb) a big rock/big rocks to hold** *vb phr* (Bdos) [*AF—Joc*] See GIVE¹ Phr 2.21.

rock-bal·sam* [ˈɒk-bɒlzʌm] /1ˈ22/ *n* (Bdos, Guyn, Mrat, USVI) Any of a number of robust types of BALSAM-BUSH that grow in damp, rocky places (hence the name); it is used for making BUSH-TEA, and/or the juice of the crushed leaves is used as a folk-remedy for chest-colds; *Clusia plukenetii* (*Guttiferae*), *Peperomia magnoliifolia* (*Piperaceae*), *Justicia pectoralis* (*Acanthaceae*), etc.

rock-fig *n* (Gren, StVn) ‖ APPLE-BANANA (Belz, etc)

rock-fish* *n* (Baha, Berm, CayI) A large, edible, deep-sea fish of the grouper family; its greenish body is blotched throughout with brownish spots, and its fins edged with yellow; *Mycteroperca venenosa* (*Serranidae*). □ Sometimes confused with the ROCK-HIND. Many fishes identified as 'rockfish' in fishing literature are of a different family, *Sebastodes spp*.

rock-hind* *n* (CarA) A black-spotted species of HIND that lives in reefs; its average weight is about 4 lbs and it is of good food value; *Epinephelus adscensionis* (*Serranidae*).

rock stead·y /1ˈ22/ *n phr* (CarA) **1.** A type of dance-music with a steady, slowed rhythm and a noticeable off-beat; it was developed in Jamaica after the SKA and before REGGAE and shows characteristics of both. **2.** The individualistic dance to this music involving the rocking of the body to and fro, with the elbows bent and the fists closed. [*Rock*, copied from AmE use of the term re pop music + *steady* in ref to the maintaining of the beat]

rock·stone n (CarA) [*IF*] **1.** ‖ *brick* (Guyn) ‖ *rock* (Bdos, Guyn) Any small or large stone. *She could run fairly fast too, but Mr Straker pelt a rockstone at she and it hit she 'pon the ankle.*—CISH:118 **2.** Bedrock or stone as solid, mineral material. *Never let a politician grant you a favour, he will always control you forever and cold ground was my bed last night; rockstone was my pillow too.*—JdN (76.06.20, p.4, Bob Marley) [A redundant compound word of a type common in CE] **3.** PHRASE **3.1 hard as rockstone** *adj phr* [*AF*] (SE) Hard as stone; [of a person's brains] impenetrable; unteachable.

rod n (Guyn) [Land measurement] See RHYN-LAND FOOT

rogue[1] n (Guyn) [Rice Ind] Any type of plant or weed growing within the crop being cultivated. [Cp *OED* *rogue* sb 4. *Hort* 'an inferior plant among seedlings'. The *Guyn* Ind usage particularizes this sense]

rogue[2] *vb* (Guyn) **1.** [Rice Ind] To clear a rice-field of weeds and plants other than the crop before harvesting. **2.** [Sugar Ind] To dig up and burn or bury diseased cane in order to prevent the spread of infection to other plants. [Cp *OED* *rogue* vb 4. 'to free from inferior plants or seedlings. Also, to take out (inferior plants) from a crop']

roll·er ['rola] n (StVn) ‖ SÈK (Dmca, Gren)

rol·ling calf (**roar·ing calf**) *n phr* (Belz, CayI, Jmca) ‖ *May cow* (CayI) A legendary, supernatural creature in the shape of a calf with fiery eyes that roams the streets at night making a sound like the clanking or dragging of many chains and causing panic when it is reported to be about; it is believed by some to represent the punished spirit of a wicked, deceased person. ... *or one will tell a story of how once when he was a child he really saw 're-ally, sah', the Rolling-Calf, with its great red eyes like flaming moons and its hooves of iron and its pied white skin trailing as it ran by an echoing iron chain.*—PWOW:33 [Perh by /r > l/ shift from ROARING CALF, a variant name, though the legend does not refer to a roar] □ Cp STEEL-DONKEY (Bdos).

Ro·man Church /1'12/ *n phr* (CarA) [*IF*] The Roman Catholic Church or Church of Rome. *They go to Roman Church. They are Roman Church people.*—(Guyn) □ Often used without determining article in contexts contrasting it with ENGLISH CHURCH.

roof-horse n (Bdos, Guyn) [Carpentry] A ladder-like device made of pieces of wood nailed crosswise to a long, wooden plank, temporarily fixed on the slope of a roof to give workmen a sure footing. [Because it is said to ride the roof]

roo·go·doo [rʊgʊdu] n (USVI) [*AF—Joc*] A commotion; a noisy uproar. *Tina and Nita joined in so Gustus hit her a few more times swearing he going to kill her. The neighbors on hearing this big roogodoo in the home of the respectful, respectable Bannerfields were more than shocked.*—PKKK: 11 [A characteristic reduplicative word, perh orig ECHOIC, prob also infl by other forms, ex AmE *ruckus*, BrE *ruction*, *EDD* Sc and IrE *rug* 'to tug, tear' + *to-do*, etc. Note also 18C BrE *rigadoon* 'a lively dance'. Cp next]

roo·go·dung [rugʊdʌŋ] *adj* (Antg) [*AF—Joc*] See RUK-A-DUNG

root-bor·er n (CarA) [Sugar Ind] ‖ *white grub* (CarA) The larva of a beetle; it hatches in numbers from eggs laid in the soil and feeds on the roots of sugar-canes and of other crops; *Clemora smithi* or *Cnemarachis portoricensis* (*Melolonthidae*). □ Hence **root-borer disease** (*CarA*), caused by the action of the insects.

roots n *in attrib function* (CarA) [*Rastaf*] **1.** Belonging to or demonstrating your own (and esp African) cultural origins or heritage; showing acknowledgement or consciousness of common folk origins (esp of Black people). **a.** *I did 'Pick-A-Dub' for certain Roots fans. I had made certain rhythms which ... became popular to the Jamaican because it is the virgin rhythm to voice.*—WiW (75.12.18, p.27) **b.** *'Survival' is harsh, 'roots' reggae with political overtones ... which refuses to be influenced by North American culture.*—DaG (79.11.01, p.6) [Orig used in Jmca prob late 1960s evid as n pl in attrib function as abbr for 'African/Ethiopian roots', and spread largely via **roots-reggae** music to AmE and other CE] □ Hence many compounds **roots-brother, -man, -music, -people, -reggae**, etc. **2.** [In excl function as a familiar form of address to an approved person] Good (friend)! *Hail roots! What de I tink bout socialism? Right now I man dig de social, but I no dig de ism.*—WeS (75.02.21, p.22)

roots·y *adj* (CarA) [*IF*] Displaying or favouring the display of (esp African) folk cultural heritage in any aspect of social behaviour. **a.** *But another brother, not so rootsy, for many years has been arguing that people who encourage black youth in Creole are ruining them because it is the Queen's English which is necessary for job advancement.*—AmA (80.06.06, p.7) **b.** *He has been increasingly cast aside in favour of rootsier, more disgruntled artistes now available due to the immense interest in Jamaican reggae.*—Kri,'78, p.61 [< *roots* as orig n pl + SE -*y*, familiarizing adj suffix] □ This form is preferred as adj in absolute function, ROOTS being felt as lower in status, perh more like attrib in function and more particularly Rastaf.

rope-bush n (Guyn) ‖ AGAVE (CarA) [From the use of fibres of the dried leaves to make rough ropes]

ropes n *pl* PHRASE **get in the ropes with sb** *vb phr* (Antg, Bdos) [*AF*] See GET Phr 3.16

ro·ro (row-row) [roro·] *n* **1.** (StLu) [*AF*] Scandalous gossip; (news of) a scandalous event; trouble. **a.** *Much of the script dealt with the rumour (ro-ro) syndrome and the different 'versions' of gossip that get around.*—VoS (76.08.07, p.9) **b.** *When our people attend meetings of that nature, they get carried away by the 'row-rows', while the more pertinent issues just slip by.... For too long have our politicians been capitalizing on this 'row-row' mentality of our people to keep the facts away from them.*—CrU (76.07.10, p.6) **2.** PHRASE **2.1 put sb in roro** *vb phr* (StLu) [*AF—Joc*] To besmirch sb's name; to spread damaging gossip about sb. *Santa, they feeling so bad about the whole situation that they even starting to put you in roro. They say that you always coming when the Daddies are not there and the Mummies are alone.*—CrU (76.12.25, p.14) [Fr Cr perh > Fr *ronron* 'a whirring, buzzing' with denasalization of '*on*']

rose *n* (Guyn, USVI) [*AF—Derog*] A disease that causes serious discoloration and/or disfigurement of the skin, such as erysipelas (*USVI*), elephantiasis (*Guyn*). [From the appearance of some of the disfigurement]

rose-ap·ple* *n* (CarA) ‖ *Java-plum* (Dmca, Mrat, StVn) ‖ *plum rose* (Guyn) ‖ *pomme rose* (Dmca) A rounded fruit the size of an egg, with a marble-sized seed; it is yellow when ripe with sweetish flesh, and is borne on a small flowering tree; *Syzygium jambos* or *Eugenia j.* (*Myrtaceae*). [*Rose* from the smell of its edible flesh]

ro·seau* (**wo·zo**) *n* (Dmca, Gren, Tbgo, Trin) A bamboo-like reed that grows in tall separate stalks; it is used for thatching roofs and making baskets; *Gynerium sagittatum, G. saccharoides, Saccharum sagittatum* (*Poaceae*). *Their houses were of roughly sawn timber with thatched roofs of roseaux and palm branches and one or two rooms.*—HTDS:25 [Fr *roseau* 'a reed'] □ Pl *roseaux*.

rose man·go *n phr* (Dmca, Gren, Tbgo, Trin) See MANGO-WÒZ.

rose·ma·ry(-weed)* *n* (Bdos, Brbu, CayI, Jmca, USVI) A sturdy, evergreen, flowering shrub whose leaves and twigs have a pleasant, aromatic smell; it is used to flavour cooking, to condition the skin, and to yield a perfumed oil; its twigs are burnt to provide ritual incense; *Rosemarinus officinalis* (*Labiatae*).

ro·ti ['roti ~ ruti] *n* (CarA) A kind of unleavened bread made of flour, salt, and water, the dough being rolled flat into thin discs, each baked separately on a baking-iron; it is then used to wrap a serving of CURRY. *Roti is an Indian food which today forms part of the normal diet of the entire population. It is eaten with great relish by everyone.*—ACTT:31 [Hin *rotii* 'bread'] □ Pl *roties* or collectively ROTI. Each baked disc is called *a roti*, but in some places the term *roti-skin* or *roti-shell* is used to distinguish the

single disc from 'several' understood as a meal, whence *curry and roti*, as a dish; also *cook/eat/like roti*, etc.

rot·ten (off) *vb* (*phr*) (CarA) [*X*] To rot. **a.** *If you leave those bananas too long they will rotten.*—(Trin) **b.** *Your finger will rotten off if you point at people's graves.*—(Guyn) [Prob an overcorrection in CE due to its verb-like SE form. Cp SE *fatten, heighten*, etc. However, note as EE form OED *rotten* vb rare 'to rot' + cit from 1611]

rou·cou [ruku] *n* (Dmca, Gren, Guyn, StLu, Trin) ‖ ANATTO (CarA) [*DGEG* (Tupi-)Guarani *urucú*, 'una planta tintorea', *Bixa orellana*. See also OED]

roun·ci·val (**roun·ce·val, run·ci·ful**) [rʌnsiful]/1'12/ *n* (Bdos) ‖ INCREASE PEAS (Bdos) *I have a further 20 acres in food production, i.e. corn, carrots, melons, squash, cucumbers, potatoes, beans, runcifuls, etc.*—AdV (90.10.14, p.12) [OED *rouncival* 1. a. '... specific designation of a large variety of garden or field pea' b. (pl) 'peas of this variety' + cits from 1573 with a variety of spellings] □ This name appears to survive only among rural or farming folk in *Bdos*, using the pronunc shown, but written in different ways. The spelling preferred here, in view of its history, defers to OED.

round[1] *n* (Bdos) The rung of a ladder. *For some time now the Dean ... has had some very touching sermons ... which concerned the whole Barbadian community beginning at the top round of the ladder.*—AdN (75.10.29, p.4) [As OED *round* sb[1] 3. 'a ring or rundle of a ladder' + cits 1573–1875, also COD8 *round* 12. However the form is also considered dial. Cp EDD *round* 12. 'a rung of a ladder' ex Nhp 'The common mode of describing the length of a ladder is to call it 'a ladder of so many rounds'] □ This CE usage may also have been reinforced by overcorrection. Cp CE [grʌŋ] as pronunc of SE *ground*]

round[2] *prep, adv* (CarA) **1.** Around; about. [Often as SE but also often with shift, esp in phrs] *When a man got a good woman he don't know what to do with she. He want somebody to give he a good lash round he head to bring he to he senses.*—HMCH:103 **2.** PHRASES **2.1 round about** *prep phr* (CarA) [*AF/IF*] About; in the area of. **a.** *Round about that time the captain trousers start to give way under the stress and strain of the seasons, and it was Moses who give him a old pair of pants.*—STLL:39 **b.** *They have decent people living round about there, though.*—(Guyn) □ Also dial AmE. **2.2 round here/there** *adv phr* (CarA) [*AF/IF*] In this/that area; in these/those parts; in this/that house. *'What we want round here is some respect' Harrilal said. 'They don't teach you that in school?'*—SPOC:142 [< SE *around here* by aphesis] □ Also dial AmE. **2.3 round and about** *adv phr* (Bdos, Guyn) [*AF/IF*] In many different places. *It is a* *plant you will find round and about. You only have to look.*—(Bdos)

roun·ders *n pl* (Trin) [*AF—Joc*] **1.** Confusion; to-do; mixed up trouble. *Where else you could find all de rounders dat goin[g] on in dis country from January to December.*—(Trin) [Perh a pun on and extension of sense of the game of *rounders* + infl of *rounds, the run-around*, etc] **2.** PHRASE **2.1 give (sb) the rounders** *vb phr* (Trin) [*AF*] See GIVE¹ Phr 2.29.

round-house *n* (Bdos) [Hist; Sugar Ind] The house-shaped structure at the top of a sugar-plantation windmill protecting the mill's hub and turned round on its wheel-bearings to make the blades face the wind from any direction.

round rob·in* /1'22/ *n phr* (Gren, StLu) A slender, edible, scaled, round-bodied fish, greenish-blue above and silvery below, with a narrow bronze stripe on each side from tip to tail; it is of prized food value; *Decapterus punctatus* (*Carangidae*). *Then you have the large round robin which would be retailed at 50 cents per pound, the small round robin 40 cents, that is the new price; the sprats will be retailed at 25 cents per pound.*—Gren (Hd, 74.02.18, p.3)

round-the-world /1'12/ *n* (Bdos) ‖ LEAF-OF-LIFE (Bdos, etc) [Prob a corruption of WONDER-OF-THE-WORLD, the commoner name in *Bdos*, etc]

route-tax·i *n* (Trin) ‖ *hire-car* **2.** (Guyn) A privately owned car that is used as a bus, plying a fixed route; its fares are higher than bus-fares. *... and the route-taxis, the drivers from time to time putting out an arm and making an involved gesture, like a dancer's gesture, to indicate their route.*—NG:197 □ Cp MAXI-TAXI, ROBOT.

roy·al [rɒ·ʌl ~ ra·yal] *n* **1.** (Jmca) [*AF—Derog*] ‖ *douglah* (ECar) A person of mixed Black and other parentage, the other being usu Chinese or EAST INDIAN. *Two little girls from the settlement. Coolie royals.*—HSAG:270 [Prob a metaph extension of Sp *real* [re'al] (Hist) A coin of the lowest value (one quarter of a peseta), people so called in *Jmca* being considered by some as socially very low in status. See note at CHINEE-ROYAL. Cp also sense **2.** next] **2.** (Trin) [*AF—Joc/ Vul*] The arse (as symbolizing the extreme of necessity) [Esp in Phr **4.2** below]. [Perh from the notion of 'being at/of the lowest', relating, also through the Sp hist of *Trin*, to the low worth of the Sp *real*] **3.** (Baha, Guyn) An extreme of emotion such as anger, drunken merriness, etc. **4.** PHRASES **4.1 be in your royal** *vb phr* (Guyn) **(i)** To be heartily drunk. **(ii)** To be abusively angry. **4.2 catch/see your royal** *vb phr* (ECar) [*AF*] ‖ CATCH HELL (CarA) See CATCH Phr 8.6 *What it is that would keep men although by and large, in truth and in fact, they catching their royal to make a living.*—STLL:121

roy·al palm* *n phr* (CarA) ‖ *Victoria-palm* (Baha) A sturdy erect palm similar to the CABBAGE PALM but noticeably shorter, rarely exceeding 50 ft in height, and identified by a definite bulge, usu at the base of the smooth trunk, and by the plume-like drooping fronds that sometimes form a round head; *Oreodoxa regia* or *Roystonea princeps* (*Palmaceae*). *And the Royal Palm, majestic / stands on guard, a tree of pride / Waving high its feathery branches / Over town and countryside.*—JBJ:29 □ See Note at CABBAGE-PALM.

roy·al poin·ci·a·na *n phr* (ECar) ‖ FLAM-BOYANT (CarA) [Trans of part of botanical name (*Delonix*) *poinciana regia*, descriptive of its massive red crown when in flower] □ More commonly called POINCIANA or FLAMBOYANT.

rub *vb* (CarA) PHRASES **1. rub clothes** *vb phr* (Guyn) [*IF*] ‖ *rub out clothes* (Bdos) To scrub clothes (usu on a SCRUBBING BOARD); to hand-wash clothes in a tub. **2. rub down (sb)** *vb phr* (ECar) **(i)** To anoint the body of a sick person. **(ii)** To massage (an athlete) with embrocation. **3. rub out clothes** *vb phr* (Bdos) [*IF*] ‖ RUB CLOTHES (Guyn) See PHR 1. **4. rub (sb's) nara** *vb phr* (Guyn, Trin) See NARA Phrs **5. rub up (sb)** *vb phr* (Guyn) To rub briskly with some medication (a sick person's body). **6. rub up on/ with sb** *vb phr* (CarA) To rub against another's body. **a.** *I was really annoyed. I did not want my clothes rumpled ... I had tried hard to look nice today, and to smell sweet, and I did not want Lennard to rub up on me.*—AGDR:41 **b.** *Middle class people in Barbados pay more for medical services ... and prefer to pay to go to the appointment room because they would not be rubbing up with people who are sweaty.*—Bdos (Hd, 73.06.19, p.2399)

rub·ber-plant/tree *n phr* (CarA) ‖ INDIA-RUBBER TREE (CarA)

rub·bers *n pl* (BrVi, StKt) ‖ CREPESOLES (Guyn) *The poor little children longing for some nice clothes and rubbers on their poor little feet from the hot sun.*—DeM(SK) (77.01.15, p.10) [From their rubber soles]

rub·ber-slip·pers *n pl* (CarA) ‖ *draggers* **2.** (Nevs, StKt, StLu) ‖ *flappers* (Nevs) ‖ *flip-flops* (Baha, TkCa) ‖ *go-forwards* (Bdos, Trin) Casual rubber sandals held on the foot by a v-shaped thong fitting between the toes; (AmE) thongs.

rub·bish *n* (ECar) Garbage; refuse. □ This is the word in general use; hence many compounds: *rubbish-bin; rubbish-cart/truck; rubbish-heap/-hole*, etc. In the same compounds *garbage* sometimes occurs instead of *rubbish-*.

rub·ble-stone/-work found·a·tion *n phr* (Angu) ‖ GROUNDSEL (Bdos) [From the use of loose stones collected from or as rubble] □ Also AmE pronounced ['rubəl-] (*pers info*, L. Urdang).

ruc·tion[1] (ruck·tion) *n* (CarA) [*AF*] **1.** Noise; trouble; disturbance. *No pass the glass and pray hard that Buzz no bother to go start up any rucktion now.*—SNWIC:262 (M. Townshend) [*OED* lists the word, as 'of obscure origin', with extended meaning including 'riot'. The CE sense is limited to individual conduct. Prob IrE. Note: Ruction, ructions; fighting, squabbling, a fight, a row. It is a memory of the Insurrection of 1798, wh was commonly called the 'Ruction'] **2.** PHRASE **2.1 make ruction** *vb phr* (Tbgo, Trin) [*AF*] To cause a commotion. **a.** *Tell me, you call that music? Going down the road, making ruction beating old tins and drums—that is music?* —AKM:39 **b.** *Come on man, give we some glasses. The first speaker went to the bar. 'You want we to make ruction in the place? We does drink rum here every day.'*—SPOC:49

ruc·tion[2] *adj* (Guyn, StVn) [*AF*] ‖ **truction** (StVn) [Esp of children] Aggressive; quarrelsome; cantankerous. *Don['t] let her bring her ruction li[tt]l[e] boy wid her nex[t] time. He always startin[g] fights wid dese children.*—(Guyn) [By functional n > adj shift of RUCTION[1]]

rude *adj* **1.** (CarA) [Esp of a child] Unruly; given to answering back. **a.** *No one could tolerate a 'rude' child (a term which included almost anything 'wrong' that a normal child might do).*—HVVIS: 110 **b.** *The term 'rude', however, is a word of multiple meanings in Jamaican dialect, and is also often used to describe badly behaved children.*—Pra 74/12, p.844 □ CE RUDE is less intense in the connotation of personal offensiveness than SE rude, and the other SE senses (ex crudely made, etc) are almost unknown in general in CE. However the sense of 'coarse, vulgar' is particularized in CE senses 2., 3. **2.** (Jmca, Tbgo, Trin) [Esp of men, boys] Sexually aggressive, esp by means of coarse talk and/or action. **a.** *By the way, that same bit about 'errant parsons' ... a lady came up to me at a spot this week and said 'Hmm. I see where you write about rude parsons. Girl, I could tell you some things, you see'.*—WeG (73.02.28, Partyline) **b.** *I am not travelling in that man's car; he too rude; he always talking about woman and sex and about how he want me and he to spend a weekend together.*—(Tbgo) □ This and sense 3 are spreading via *Jmca* pop culture in the *CarA*. **3.** [By extension, of young people] Making a display of rough, disorderly or sexy behaviour. (See RUDE-BOY). *In Jamaicanese, the word 'rude' often refers to anyone who is openly defiant of constituted authority.*—NMM:95 **4.** PHRASE **4.1 behave/get on rude** (CarA) [Esp in street festivals] To dance vigorously in a sexy manner. *Observed Mr Walrond: 'It is a notion rooted in the belief that ordinary folk cannot be trusted to separate fiction from reality; and might therefore take out of context the advice contained in some calypsos to 'mash up de place' or 'get on rude'.—* SuS (89.10.29, p.10A)

rude-boy (rud·ie boy) *n* (*phr*) (Jmca) [*AF—Derog*] **1.** A young, Black, Jamaican male who is an aggressive social drop-out; he may be a ghetto type, a gang type, or one who adopts some Rastafarian cultist habits. **a.** *In an interview a rude boy ... had this to say: 'There are thousands of them (i.e. rude boys) out there with ambitions, looking work and get none. Some of the places they go, they turn them away. They feel as if they are not part of the society and nobody wants them around.'*—NMM:95 **b.** *Even when provoked, however the police constable confided that he tries to ignore 'rude boys' when they smoke ganja but that they continue to insult him by blowing the smoke into his face.*—DaG (72.07.01, p.3) □ This usage is spreading in *CarA* folk-life. **2.** [By extension] (**rudie, rudy**) Any young male or female who behaves like a social drop-out. *The sooner most Jamaican women stop being 'rudies' and become decent law-abiding citizens, the more men they'll have to stick out their necks for them.*—DaG (66.10.25, p.12) [< RUDE adj 2., 3. + *boy*, or + familiarizing SE suff *-ie*]

rude·ness /1'2/ *n* (CarA) [*AF*] **1.** Sexual intercourse (esp among teenagers). *The vagabonds try to force rudeness on the landlord's daughter ... they nearly outlaw the landlord's daughter.*— LICMS:207 **2.** PHRASE **2.1 do rudeness** *vb phr* [*AF*] [Of young unmarried people] To engage in sexual intercourse; to fornicate. **a.** *Ques. (37) How can I be sure of avoiding pregnancy without using birth control? Ans. Don't do rudeness!*— MBS:65 **b.** *She said, 'Well, just you be careful. You know these New York boys. They don't care who they pick up as long as they think they can do rudeness.'*—GTF:101 [< RUDE 2. + SE *-ness*] □ Note the pitch pattern /1'2/ wh distinguishes this sense in some places, esp *Jmca*, from SE rudeness /2'1/. The rising currency of the specialized sense of CE RUDENESS is however blurring distinction in many cases.

ru·die/dy *n* (Jmca) [*AF—Derog*] See RUDE-BOY 2.

ruk-a-dung (roo·go·dung, ruk-a-tung, ru·ku·dang) [rʌkʌdʌŋ ~ rugʊdʌŋ rukutʌŋ] *adj, n* [Of a dwelling] Dilapidated; tumbledown. [Prob of ECHOIC origin. Cp BRUGGADUNG (Bdos). See ROOGODOO *n* (*USVI*)]

rule *n* (Bdos, Guyn) [*X*] [School] A ruler; a straight, graduated, twelve-inch strip of wood or plastic material wh is used to draw straight lines [< SE *ruler*, by characteristic CarA Cr loss of final /-r/. Cp DRAW (ER)]

Rules of Or·i·gin *n pl phr* (CarA) The rules of trade, agreed within CARICOM, determining the minimum percentage of Caribbean raw material or local labour or processing that must be put into an item manufactured in a CARICOM Member State for it to be considered a rightful product of that State, entitled to duty-free entry into any other CARICOM State.

rum *n* (CarA) **1.** An alcoholic drink industrially distilled from the juice of the sugar-cane, blended and cured in barrels. (See WHITE RUM). [Orig

< (Bdos) *rum bullion*, replacing the ominous *kill-devil* 17C. Note *OED* cit for *rumbullion*: 'the chiefe fudling they make in the Island is Rumbullion, alias Kill-devil, and this is made of suggar canes distilled, a hott, hellish liquor'— *N.D. Davis, 1651 Cavaliers and Roundheads of Barbados*. EE *rum* was adj in 16C–17C cant for 'good, fine, excellent' (see *OED rum* adj[1] 1., 2.) as in *rum booze*, 'good liquor'; the latter element *bullion* < Fr *bouillon* 'a boiled drink' was dropped by the late 17C as the popularity of the drink (see *LHOB:84*) grew, and the common drinkers' abbreviation became RUM. (Cp similarly *grog* < *grogram*, *port* < *Oporto*] **2.** [*IF*] A glass or drink of (usu undiluted) rum. **a.** *At last they called Kaiser's father. He was in Ramlal's rumshop where he had gone for a rum. He was slightly drunk.*— MHBT:59 **b.** *If the 'hog' wants a staff-member, he sits at his desk and growls your name. I wouldn't tell you about when he drinks two rums how he gets on.*—NaT (76.08.22, p.26, Dear Christine) **3.** PHRASES **3.1 have in your rum** *vb phr* (ECar) [*AF—Joc*] See HAVE Phr 3.8.1 **3.2 rum fly to/ get in your head** *id phr* (CarA) [*AF*] (Be) unable to hold your liquor; (let, make) rum go to your head; (become) dangerously drunk. *Well mus[t] be de rum fly to [h]is head an[d] [h]e hit de woman an[d] nearly kill her.*—(Guyn) **3.3 rum talking** *id phr* (CarA) [*AF—Joc*] Something nonsensical or irresponsible is being said in a state of drunkenness. *It was a Friday night and the men, high in their drinks, were shouting about politics at each other. Making little sense. Rum talking, that was it.*—Guyn (Ms) □ The name of the brand or maker of the rum is often substituted, in this phr, for 'rum'; hence *Fernandez talking* (Trin), *Appleton talking Jmca*), etc. **3.4 under your rum** *adj phr* (StKt) [*IF*] See UNDER Phr 2.2.

rum-and-corn(ed)-beef po·li·tics *n phr* (Bdos, Gren, Guyn) ‖*rum-and-roti politics* (Tbgo, Trin) The practice of soliciting political votes from poor or undiscriminating voters by bribing them with food, drink, and merry--making events. **a.** *The only thing I can't assist this Honourable House with accurately is the current price for a pint of strong rum, and I can't assist this Honourable House because it is the members on the other side of the House who engaged in rum-and-corned-beef politics.*—Gren (Hd, 77.04.26, p.297) **b.** *The 'rum-and-corn-beef' politics comes from those politicians who suffer the messiah complex. These are some who go around promising people heaven on earth, a carry over, I believe from colonial days.*—NaT (76.06.13, p.14)

rum-bib·ber; **rum.bo, rum-guz.zler, rum-.mer, rum.mie, rum sou.la, rum-suck.er** *n* (CarA) [*AF—Derog*] ‖*soula* (Dmca, Gren, StLu) A person (usu a man) who is a heavy or habitual drinker of strong rum. **a.** *While not teetotalers, none of the ganja smokers is a serious 'rummer' almost all prefer milder beverages such as beer or stout.*—DaG (72.07.01, p.3) **b.** *He is such a dam[ned] rum-sucker dat I don['t] know*

ho[w] much blood he got lef[t] in [h]is rum-stream.—(Gren)

rum·bler *n* (CayI) The trunk of a car. [Cp *OED rumbler* sb 2. Obs = *rumble* sb 4. 'the hind part of a carriage when so arranged as to provide sitting accommodation (... for servants ...) or to carry luggage' + cits 1808–18; also *OED2 rumble* 4. 'also in a motor vehicle'. The older form *rumbler* has evid survived in the CayI]

rum·fle; **ram.fle, ram.ple** [rʌmfl ~ ram fl ~ rampl] *vb tr* (Bdos, Gren, Guyn, StKt, Trin) [*X*] To rumple (clothing, a bed, etc); to crease, crush, or cause to wrinkle (a part of your dress, a garment). **a.** *She said. 'You can see for yourself what an' what clothes you got ... An' there ain't no need to rumfle them if you take them out as they stand.*—LICMS:309 **b.** *She want somebody to rub she down / And when he finish rub with his / Soft candle you whole bed rample.*—RLCF:221 [Cp *EDD rumfle* (Ken) 'to ruffle, rumple'; also *OED rumfle* variant of *rumple*] □ Of the variant forms *rumfle* is the commonest.

rum-punch *n* (CarA) An iced drink made by mixing rum with diluted fruit juices or syrup, lime juice, and sometimes sugar. *The best known Caribbean drink nowadays is rum-punch, and no matter where it is drunk, whether it be in the private home of the public bar, no two taste alike.*—IsL 73/ 2, p.16

rum-shop /1'1/ *n* (*phr*) (CarA) [*IF*] A liquor-shop where rum is the principal item retailed, usu with an area partitioned off to provide for (usu workmen's) drinking on the premises. *A rum shop, ... does more than sell liquor. The rum-shop is primarily a meeting place where individuals gather to eat, drink, gossip and play games. In this sense it may be described as an informal community centre, catering to the social and leisure needs of the immediate area in which it is located.*—NaT (79.06.20, p.14)

rum-snap *n* (Bdos) ‖SNAP (Bdos, Guyn) *I have to look through the bottom of an upturned glass which once contained a rum-snap.*—AdN (73.02.13, p.4)

run *vb* (CarA) **1.** *vb intr* (CarA) [Of the belly] To be troubled with diarrhoea. *All that mixture of food and drink he had between Christmas and Boxing Day had his belly running.*—(Mrat) [Cp *EDD run* II. 1. 9.(f) *run out* 'to be afflicted with diarrhoea' + cit from Som] □ See also Phr 6.9 below. **2.** *vb intr* (Guyn, Jmca, Trin) [Of crabs, fish] To be in season; to be abundant. **a.** *One of the activities that draw people to the Cocal takes place when crabs are 'running'—the name given to the breeding season of the crabs, when they leave the mangroves and 'run' to the sea to wash off their eggs.*—AGTT:69 **b.** *Sam was the only man who could explain why 'the fish ent runnin'.*—Guyn (Ms, 1976) [Cp *OED run* vb B. I. 8. b. [of fish] To pass to or from the sea; to spawn] **3.** *vb intr* (CarA) [*IF*] [Of a man] To leave a woman in pregnancy; to disclaim fatherhood of a child. *I became aware of yet another ugly aspect of the girl-boy, man-woman relationship. This involved ducking the responsibility of fatherhood, or 'running' as it was commonly referred to by the boys.*—Baw 76/77, p.23 **4.** *vb intr* (CarA) [*AF*] [Of the mouth] To have the habit of blabbing; to blab, be too talkative. **a.** *Don't tell her anything that I just told you, you know. She is one, her mouth runs.*—(Guyn) **b.** *Black people eh. Mouths can run faster than nigger behinds after Epsom salt.*—JJM:60 (See MOUTH Phr 4.38) **5.** *vb tr* (CarA) [*AF/IF*] [With a person or animal as obj] **(i)** To chase or drive away. **a.** *I mean, I don't mind the police running limers, but we were just waiting on transport. They didn't even wait for any answer. Just like that I get a lash to head.*—ExP (72.11.30, p.20) **b.** *When asked about the confrontation the young men ... denied using any form of violence. 'We only run the men from cutting the tree,' they said.*—NaT (90.07.18, p.40A) **(ii)** To chase after; to pursue (with hostility). **a.** *David, 23, however admitted to committing a break-in at Bayland, St Michael. / He said that while committing that offence, 'the whole of the Bayland run me', and that the police charged him for other offences in that area.*—AdV (90.07.25, p.24) **b.** *My sheep had gone to the main road when the dogs started running it.*—Tbgo (CR, 79.09.05) **(iii)** To befriend and pursue (a woman) with physical love in mind. *She left him 'running women' in San Juan.*—ExP (72.01.16, p.18) [Cp *OED run* vb B. II. 42. 'to pursue, hunt (game, etc)'] **6.** PHRASES **6.1 run a joke (at sb)** *vb phr* (Belz, BrVi) [*IF*] To make a joke, fun (of sb). **6.2 run breaking your neck (to do sth)** *vb phr* (Guyn, Tbgo, Trin) [*AF*] To run headlong (to do sth); to hurry at a break-neck pace (on an errand, etc). *When they had a white bishop you see them runnin[g] breakin[g] de[ir] neck to do whatever he want, and wit[h] a black man dey won['t] hardly turn de[ir] head.*—(Trin) □ Also AmE slang (*pers info, L. Urdang*). **6.3 run behind (sb)** *vb phr* (CarA) **(i)** To run after (sb). *He also has some other women that he runs behind.*—NaT (77.03.20, p.26, Dear Christine) **(ii)** To be obsequious, servile towards (sb). *For the whole month you in the man's office trying to get him to give you the job. You do well. I am not running behind anybody like that.*—(Tbgo) **6.4 run bobol** *vb phr* (StVn, Tbgo, Trin) To be part of a team indulging in money-earning fraud; to engage in BOBOL. *Since Gordon bought the new hi-fi set and fixed up the back of the house everybody who meet me going out of their way to ask me what bobol he running.*—JJM:92 **6.5 run cattle** *vb phr* (Mrat) [Of a farmer] To keep, rear cattle; [of land] to be a cattle-pasture, a cattle-run. *A re-distribution of land based on land use. Can you imagine Trants, one of our best cotton-producing estates—running cattle?*—MtM (76.08.13, p.4) **6.6 run come/ go** *vb phrs* (CarA) [*AF*] To come/go quickly, hurriedly; to come/go running. **a.** *'Jesuweb!' she shrieked. 'Children run an' get Mr Ashley that was in de police force. Tell he run come'.*—MN: 76 **b.** *As de boy see de police he run gone.*—(BrVi) [Likely calques via CarA Cr from W Afr serial

vbs] **6.7 run down (a) man/woman** *vb phr* (ECar) [*AF/IF*] To entice a man/woman to be your lover. **a.** *Speedy told Mr Stone if his wife wanted to run down man it was not his fault.*—BoM (79.07.20, p.9) **b.** *He can't sell much insurance because he spends half his time running down the women, le[t] me tell yo[u].*—(Bdos) [Cp *OED run* vb B. II. 73. *run down* h. 'to pursue (game) until caught'] □ Cp also sense 5(iii) above. **6.8 run mas** *vb phr* (Dmca) ‖ PLAY MAS (Trin) **6.9 run your belly** *vb phr* (CarA) [*AF*] [Of food] To cause diarrhoea. See sense 1. above **6.10 run sb's/your blood to water** *vb phr* (Angu, Guyn, Tbgo, Trin) [*AF/IF*] To put sb/yourself to much sacrifice (to get sth done). *His children ran his blood to water to educate them and then they left him. I am not running my blood to water like him.*—(Tbgo) **6.11 run your mouth** *vb phr* (CarA) [*AF*—*Derog*] ‖*flap/flop/fly your mouth* (Bdos, Guyn) To be talkative and untrustworthy; to talk too much and get into trouble. **a.** *To tell the truth, I think he goofed in some of his observations ... but then man free to run him own mouth, except that you have to be on spot sometimes to know how sun hot.*—WeG (73.02.21, p.13) **b.** *Instead of running she mouth for nothing, inquisitive just for the fun / She could make it a money-making business one time and done.*—Cso (Sir Don, 1975) [A transitive restructuring of YOUR MOUTH RUNS. See MOUTH phr 4.38 **6.12 your mouth runs** *id phr* (CarA) [*AF*—*Derog*] See MOUTH Phr 4.38.

Run·away Ghaut *n phr* (Mrat) PHRASE **drink water at/from Runaway Ghaut** *id phr* (Mrat) [Of a visitor] To intend to return to Monserrrat. [A legendary notion associated with *Mrat* pride in that place, a valley with a stream running down to the sea, on the middle west coast of the island, where a heroic stand was made by a British army captain against the invading French in 1712]

run-bel·ly [*AF*]; **run.ning-bel.ly** [*IF*] *n* (Jmca, Guyn) ‖ BELLY-WORK(ING)S (Antg, etc)

run·ci·val (**run·ci·ful**) *n* (Bdos) See ROUNCIVAL

run-down (**run·dung**) [rʌndʌŋ] *n* (CayI, Jmca) ‖ DIP-AND-FALL-BACK (Jmca) **a.** *Breakfast favourites like Ackee and codfish with roast breadfruit, Escoveith fish, ... Jamaican run-down with bammy or bananas etc.*—WeS (Ad, 74.06.07, p.19) **b.** *Sunday special buffet for local residents, Wednesdays for overseas visitors. Come and try our turtle stew, conch and rice and peas, cassava, rundown, etc.*—Cay (Ad, 75.06.12, p.B4) [Creolized pronunc of *run-down*, from the running down of the oily sauce on the eater's hand]

run-mout[h] *n* (Gren) [*AF*—*Derog*] A gossip; a rumour-monger. [See RUN Phr 6.11]

run·ning ant* *n phr* (Bdos, Guyn, Jmca) ‖*sugar-ant(s)* (Bdos, Guyn) [usu pl] A blackish, reddish ant about 1/16 in long that does not sting but infests anything sweet, esp sugar, in quantities, numbers of them often moving swiftly in different directions.

run·nings *n pl* [*AF*] **1.** (Antg, Baha, Tbgo) ‖ BELLY-WORK(ING)S (Antg, etc) *I ... turned to the mother. 'What is the matter with the baby?' I inquired. 'She plagues wit' de runnin's.' Diarrhoea! Now what would Dr Gottlieb do for that?*—TrI (70.09.12, p.10) □ See also RUN-BELLY. **2.** (Belz, Nevs, StKt, Trin) Veneral disease, esp gonor-rhoea. *According to the doctor, the man told him that he had caught 'runnings' and wanted some treatment to that effect.*—SuP (79.04.08, p.1)

rush[1] *vb* **1.** (CarA) [*AF—Joc*] [Esp of a young person] To become over-attentive to (a girl/boy) in order to win her/his affections. **a.** *He began rushing his own cousin and the family cussed him out.*—(CayI) **b.** *The woman also pointed out that because of her son's good looks, many women are 'rushing' him, but he hasn't yet decided to get married.*—DaC (77.01.30, p.4) □ Also AmE slang (*pers info, L. Urdang*). **2.** *vb intr* (Baha) To dance in the street using a particular kind of shuffling, forward-then-backward step as a par-ticipant in the JUNKANOO parade. *Junkanoo ... gets off to a rousing start around 4 a.m and con-tinues until daybreak. Paraders in Nassau 'rush' west along Bay Street, turn south into Frederick St, then east along Shirley St, to Parliament St headed north, back to Bay St again. Cow bells, trumpets and drums accompany the rhythmic Jun-kanoo dancers.*—DBH:290 [Prob from the ap-pearance of 'rushing' or 'hastening slowly' given by the steady movement of the crowd] □ Cp JUMP *vb* (*ECar*) in relation to CARNIVAL. **3.** PHRASES **3.1 rush (sb) up to do (sth)** *vb phr* (CayI) [*AF*] ‖ BE BEHIND SB TO DO (STH) (CarA) See BEHIND[1] Phr 1.

rush[2] *n* [*AF*] **1.** (CarA) [Esp of a young person] Excessive affectionate attention or pursuit. [By functional *vb* > *n* shift of RUSH[1] 1.] PHRASE **1.1 get/give the rush** *vb phrs* (CarA) To get or give obvious, affectionate attention (from or to

another). □ Also AmE slang. **2.** (Tbgo) [*AF/IF*] Abundance; plenty [esp in foll phr] PHRASE **2.1 in a rush** *adv phr* (Tbgo) Plentifully; in abundance. *The market has fish and mangoes in a rush this week.*—(Tbgo)

rush-band *n* (Baha) A BAND of JUNKANOO masqueraders using last year's or other discarded costumes; such a band is often unorganized. [< RUSH[1] 2. + BAND] □ Cp OLE-MAS BAND (*Trin*).

rush·ing *n* (Baha) The manner of dancing in the street of those who RUSH in the JUNKANOO festival.

rush·ing-meet·ing *n* (Baha) A parading, to clapping and music through the aisles of a church (esp the Baptist), in the manner of JUNKANOO RUSHING as part of a joyous, religious festival celebration.

rust *n* (Dmca, Gren, Jmca, StLu) [Banana and Sugar Inds] A reddish-brown discoloration on the skins of maturing bananas or sugar-canes, caused by the feeding of clusters of RUST-THRIPS. *Puerto Rico, Dominican Republic, Panama and more recently Jamaica have all felt the lash of rust, which leaves the canes in a red-brown colour.*—AdN (79.01.25, p.4) [From the resemblance of the blemished areas of skin to rust] □ Also referred to as *rust-thrip disease*.

rust-thrip [rʌst-θrɪp] *n* (Dmca, Gren, StLu) [Banana Ind] A tiny, winged insect ranging in size from half of 1 mm to over 10 mm; it looks like a dark, shiny speck, except when in clusters on the skins of maturing bananas wh it damages; *Chaetanothrips signipennis* (*Thysanoptera*). *There is fortunately an easy way for banana growers to protect their fruit bunches against rust-thrip at-tack; [that is, by] good sleeving.*—NeC (76.09.18, p.10) [RUST, in ref to the discoloration caused + *thrip*, by metanalysis < *thrips* (Gk) 'woodlouse'] □ The sg used in technical literature is *a thrips*, but in CE this form is conceived as pl. Note cit.

S

sa·ba·ku (sa·ba·cou) *n* (Guyn) A bird about 11 ins long with a black body, red back, and white beak; it builds long hanging nests in colonies, and dwells in coastal forests but is not usually caught or caged; and it makes a cackling sound. [An Amerindian name, prob Carib]

Sa·bi·an [se·biən] /2'11/ *n, adj* (A person or thing) belonging or native to Saba, a WINDWARD island of the Netherlands Antilles.

sa·bha [sa'bha ~ 'sa·ba] *n* (Guyn, Trin) [Indic] An assembly; a religious society. [Hin, with variant local pronunc]

sack·i(e) [saki] *n* (Guyn) One of several varieties (blue, reddish-brown, grey-green, etc) of a bird wh grows to about 6 ins in length; it is a lively, playful bird, squeaking repeatedly and, as its common habitat is in coastal, settled areas, it is a popular cage-bird; *Thraupidae spp.* [*BAED* Arawak *sakui* 'a type of small bird']

sack·i·win·kie *n* (Guyn, Trin) See SAKIWINKI.

sa·cri·fice your·self (for sb) *refl vb phr* (CarA) [*IF*] ‖ LEAVE YOURSELF UNDONE (Angu, etc) See LEAVE Phr 6. *I used to sacrifice myself for him.... He wanted to build a house but now all the money is gone, and I still have to live in a rented house from these eight years.*—PeL (79.04.12, p.8, Dear Christine) [Perh infl by idiom of W Afr langs. Cp Yoruba *o se ara rẹ* (*he/she deprive his/her body*) with same connotation] □ CE SACRIFICE YOURSELF is used absolutely, i.e. with complement as in cit. Cp SE *sacrifice oneself to sth* as *OED sacrifice* vb 3. b.

sad·dle *n* PHRASE **like hog under saddle** (Belz) [*AF—Joc*] See HOG Phr 3.

sad·dle-i·ron *n* (Antg, BrVi) A device made of iron and wood, to be mounted on the padded back of a donkey in order to enable it to carry a load in a large box hooked on each flank.

sad·dle-patch/-piece *n* (Bdos, Guyn) A heart-shaped piece of tweed or other strong cloth that is sewn on to the seat of a bicycle-rider's pair of trousers to prolong its life.

sa·dhu (sa·dhoo) [sa:dhu] *n* (Guyn, Trin) [Indic] An ascetic, holy man who has renounced the material world to reflect on the spiritual life

after death; he usu wears the traditional KURTA and DHOTI, has a sacred mark in the centre of the forehead and a sacred necklace, and he officiates at religious functions. [Hin *saadhu* 'good, honest']

saeme [se·m] *n* **1.*** (Guyn) ‖ *yam-bean* (Jmca) An edible, green bean borne in a roundish, green pod about 3 ins long with a pointed tip; *Dolichos erosus* or *Pachyrizus tuberosus* (*Papilionaceae/Fabaceae*). **2.** (StLu) ‖ BONAVIST (CarA) □ Some in Guyn evid also use this name for the BONAVIST.

safe *n* (CarA) ‖ *larder* (Bdos) A wooden-framed, movable cupboard, usu standing on legs, with fine-meshed doors and sides; it is used to provide ventilated storage for food items, safeguarding them from insects. *They had acquired a kitchen safe of white wood and netting.... They must never lean on the safe or handle it with violence.*—NHMB:187 [As *OED safe* sb 1. a. + cits—'1881. However this sense is still widely current in CE, esp in rural life]

sa·ga (sag·ger) *adj* **1.** (ECar) [*AF—Joc*] [Of dress, esp men's] Very fashionable and showy; over-stylish; garish. **a.** *... and saga boys dressed in sheath-like saga pants, 'peg top trousers' and saga coats called Bim-Bams, with wasp waist and a vent in the back.*—SWI:143 **b.** *He developed an absorbing interest in the most bizarre clothing: bright ties and saga cut trousers.*—JJM:83 [Perh < SE *swagger* n and vb, by /CC-/ reduction and functional shift. Note *KED* Krio *swag* 'walk with shoulders moving from side to side'; also *CSD* Sc *swag* 'sway from side to side' (18C–20C); so the term may have spread by diffusion in colonial Eng] **2.** (Trin) [*AF—Derog*] [By extension, of young people] Foppish and unworthy; smart; scampish. **a.** *That boy is Ramlal nephew. Everyone know he is a wotless chile. All he ever going grow up to be is a Port o' Spain saga boy.*—MHBT:27 **b.** *Now what the hell yer say yer have on here? Allyer sagger girls always on-dressing allyerself. Who is you? Rita Hayworth?*—JMRS:37

sage *n* (Bdos, TkCa) See SAGE-BUSH

sage(-bush) *n* (CarA) **1.** ‖ BLACK-SAGE 1. (CarA) **2.*** ‖ *black-sage* 2. (CarA) ‖ *grater-wood, kayakit* (Trin) ‖ *mavisou* (Dmca) ‖ *pink, red, white or wild sage* (Baha, Bdos, Jmca, Trin) ‖ *sweet-sage* (Guyn) ‖ *wild mint* (Jmca) A loosely erect shrub reaching about 6 ft in height, with rough, angular, sometimes prickly stems, and rough-surfaced, serrated leaves with a minty smell, slightly unpleasant when crushed; it bears flat heads of small verbena-like flowers (yellow, orange, red, or white according to variety) and small clusters of tiny, red, inedible berries; the leaves and flowers are used as remedies for chest-colds and dysentery; *Lantana camara*, and other *Lantana spp* (*Verbenaceae*). [From an aromatic resemblance to the European *sage* (*Salvia spp*), of culinary use and a different species]

sag·ger *adj* (ECar) See SAGA

S.A.H. *abbr* (Dmca) The Sisserou Award of Honour, the second highest national award of the Commonwealth of Dominica. [From the SISSEROU parrot, the National Bird of *Dmca*]

Sa·ha·ra-dust *n* (ECar) A very slightly grey-brown haze caused by the spreading of wind-blown dust particles from the Sahara Desert across the Atlantic and covering the whole Eastern Caribbean. *Observers this weekend noted that the setting sun, obscured by the haze, could be looked at directly. / Whipped up by desert winds red Sahara-dust routinely swirls across the Atlantic between June and September, annually. It begins as a dust storm, experts say.*—SuS (85.08.25, p.1)

said *adj* (CarA) [*IF*] **1.** Same. **a.** *The day she got married, on the said day her father died in New York.*—(Gren) **b.** *The gift of a wheel chair was made to the Red Cross through the kindness of some old friends of the Nevis Red Cross. / The said chair was presented by Mr Mompetit at the February general meeting of the Red Cross, at which words of appreciation and thanks were expressed by the Director and other members present, for the chair.*—LaS (76.06.19, p.6) [Infl by legal use of *said* esp in phr 'the said day'] **2.** PHRASES **2.1 said same** *adj phr* (Bdos) [*X*] Very same; selfsame. *Day in day out I unbutton these said same underwear in the said same manner.*—LICMS:87 **2.2 very said** *adj phr* (ECar) [*X*] Exactly the same; selfsame. *I was not surprised to hear because the very said thing happened to me.*—(Guyn)

sa·i·jan* [saɪjan] *n* (Guyn, Trin) [Indic] A long, stiff, slender, green-brown pod wh is borne on a small tree of the same name; it is commonly used as a vegetable, cut up, in curries etc; (the tree) *Moringa oleifera* (*Moringaceae*). [Bhoj *sah-ijan* 'drumstick']

sail *n* (Bdos) [Hist] [Sugar Ind] The rectangular blade of a sugar-plantation windmill, about 20 ft long and made of part board, part lattice-work, and part canvas, the canvas being adjustable according to the wind (hence the name). □ This apparatus, though known by the same name in SE differed somewhat in structure in the CarA from that described at *OED sail* sb¹ 5.

sail·or-band *n* (Tbgo, Trin) A CARNIVAL BAND in wh the costumes are modelled on the American sailor's uniform with glittering items and comical decorative patches added; they carry sticks (orig symbolic of stokers' rods) and may wear face-masks with large noses.

Saint (George, etc) See ST in all cases, listed in alph position.

sa·ki·win·ki* (sack·i-win·kie) [sakiwɪŋki] *n* (Guyn, Trin) A small-bodied monkey (hence sometimes referred to as a 'squirrel-monkey' by Europeans) with golden-olive fur, a human-like head, long, slender arms, and a prehensile tail; it blinks noticeably and gives a bird-like scream when frightened; it is highly prized as an affectionate pet that will stay on its owner's shoulder in public; *Chrysothrix sciureus* (*Cebidae*). [*OED* lists *sakawinki* < Du *sagwijntje*, dim of *sagwijn* 'sagoin' = 'a small So Amer monkey'. Also *OED* separately *saki* 'a So Amer monkey'. The two forms may account for *sakiwinki*, the only form current in *Guyn* for many decades; *IAIG:110* used the form *sakawinki* in 1883. The Du origin, in the context of *Guyn*, is the most likely. Note also Sran-Tongo *sagoewenke* (*WSNE*) 'red-handed tamarin'] □ Pl SAK-IWINKI(E)S.

sa·lac·ca *n* (Gren) See SARACA [By /r > l/ shift of the more current form SARACA]

sal·ad *n* **1.** (Bdos, Guyn) [*IF*] Lettuce. □ This sense is common among older folk, esp in the phr 'cucumber and salad'. **2.** (Jmca) Large tomatoes suitable for a salad dish.

sal·ad-bean *n* (Trin) ‖ STRING-BEAN (CarA) [The boiled green pod is a common item in mixed cold salads]

sa·li·na *n* (TkCa) ‖ *salt pan* (Baha) ‖ *salt pond* (USVI) A shallow catchment of sea-water in wh salt is produced in industrial quantity by solar evaporation. [Sp *salina* 'salt-pan'. See *OED*]

sa·li·pen·ta* (sa·lam·pen·ta, sa·lem-·pen·ter, sa·li·pain·ter) [salɪpɛntʌ ~ salʌpɛnta] *n* (Guyn, Tbgo, Trin) A yellowish-brown reptile of the lizard family, about 2 ft long, with rugged, black bands spaced along its whole body and dark spots on the legs; it feeds on chickens, young birds, and eggs; its flesh is eaten by some people; *Tupinambis nigropunctatus* (*Tejidae*). *Around the pen three large salampentas were figuring an attack.... He pointed to the big, golden-freckled lizards with their lolling tongues.*—SBB: 51 □ Widely called *salipenta* (Guyn, Tbgo). The spelling variants *salampenta*, etc are possibly attempts at learned forms infl by SE *salamander*, wh is however unrelated.

Sal·ly-Sal·ly-wa·ter *n* (Guyn, Jmca, StVn, USVI) A girls' ring-game of wh these are the opening words of a short rhyming song; as it is sung the ring moves clockwise ('to the east') while one player moves anti-clockwise ('to the west') choosing the one 'Sally likes the best' to take her place.

sal·mon-tot re·triev·er *n phr* (Bdos) [*AF—Joc*] ‖ *pot-licker* (Belz) A dog of no known pedigree, loosely kept as a watch-dog, but allowed to forage for some of its food. *... and I think that Barbados is the country which bred the 'Salmon Tot Retriever' as a special breed of animal. Those are the ones who go into the dust bins and turn them over looking for the empty corned beef tins and the empty salmon tot tins. With the Golden Retrievers, the Labradors, etc. we have bred a new dog in Barbados known as the Salmon Tot Retriever.*—Bdos (Hd, 75.05.20, p.5096) [< salmon-tot (= salmon tin) + SE *retriever* 'pedigree dog bred for retrieving game'] □ See also RICE-DOG

sa·loon *n* (Bdos, Guyn) A barber's shop or a ladies' hairdresser's shop. □ The term tends to be used exclusively in these senses, the term BEAUTY SALOON being sometimes used to distinguish the ladies' shop. See next.

sa·loon bar *n phr* (CarA) A shop or part of a shop where drinkers buy and use alcoholic liquor; a drinking parlour or den; a rum-shop. □ An elevated name for an often seedy-looking place.

sa·lop *n* (Gren, StLu, Trin) [*AF—Derog*] **1.** A dirty-looking, unwashed person (esp a woman or a child). **2.** [By extension] A foul streetwoman. [Fr *salop(e)* 'bastard, bitch, prostitute'] □ Often used attrib in sense 1.

salt[1] *n* PHRASES **1. all the salt in Turks Island couldn't save you** *id phr* (CayI) [*IF—Joc*] ‖ C-RAPAUD SMOKE YOUR PIPE (Dmca, etc) *He is so deep in trouble that all the salt in Turks Island couldn't save him.*—(CayI) **2. suck salt** *vb phr* (Dmca, Guyn, Tbgo, Trin) [*AF*] To suffer much hardship; to have a rough time of it. *You're right boy, we have good luck or we would have been sucking salt by now, like this bunch of paupers.*—SDT:5

salt[2] *adj* **1.** (Antg, Jmca, USVI) [*AF*] [Of things] In an unfortunate or very bad state; [of persons] unlucky; ill-starred; in a fix. **a.** *T'ings did salt bad. I start to get wort'less an' don't care, drinkin' the li'l money I scuffle, now an' then, an' goin' from bad to worser, nuh.*—SCHMH:189 **b.** *If I don't get that question on Molière in the exam, well I goin[g] be salt, because that is all I prepare.*—(Antg) **2.** (Bdos) [*AF—Joc*] Noticeably drunk. *He came in so salt that he couldn't risk to climb the stairs and he slept on the couch in the drawing-room.*—(Bdos) [Prob reduced from pa. part *salted* = BrE slang 'pickled']

salt-bake(s) *n* [*usu pl*] (StLu) ‖ BAKE(S)[1] **2.** (Bdos, etc)

salt-bread *n* (Bdos, Guyn) A white roll of bread used at breakfast (as opposed to the smaller dinner roll or to sliced bread). [By contrast with SWEETBREAD, COCONUT-BREAD, etc]

salt-fish[1] (**salt·fish**[1]) *n* (CarA) ‖ *bacalao* (Trin) Salted, dried cod, imported from Canada, historically as standard food for slaves, but currently a valued element in many Caribbean dishes, ex ACKEE-AND-SALTFISH (*Jmca*). *Mr President, I feel that since road workers are not allowed to cook their food as before on the roads, they would need more money to buy perhaps corned beef or perhaps sardines which would be perhaps dearer than if they were allowed to cook their salt fish and bluggoes on the roads.*—Gren (Hd, 58.11.19, p.62)

salt-fish[2] (**salt·fish**[2]) *adj* (CarA) [*AF—Derog*] [By extension of prec, with ref to historical use of the item] Cheap; of low quality, class, or character. *When the Hon Member made the remark about the Union I had to get up and challenge it because it imputes that the Union is a salt-fish organisation.*—Bdos (Hd, 74.08.27, p.3856)

salt food *n phr* (Gren, Guyn) [*IF*] ‖ *salting* (Jmca, USVI) A cooked meal of meat or fish with vegetables (as opposed to a meal of sweet fruit). *You can't fill your belly with mango, banana and soursop every day so. You must eat salt food or you will get sick.*—(Guyn) □ Cp FOOD, DRY FOOD, HARD-FOOD.

salt-goods shop *n phr* (Guyn) A small one-man shop selling groceries and everyday food-stuff.

salt·ing *n* (Jmca, USVI) ‖ SALT FOOD (Gren, Guyn) *Sir: The people cannot obtain the basic meat kind or 'salting' as it is popularly known, so as to balance their diet.*—DaN(JA) (80.01.29, p.7)

salt-kind *n* **1.** (Gren) Salt-beef or saltfish. **2.** (Trin) Any kind of salted meat. **3.** (Baha) Salt-beef, esp as used to flavour the cooking of peas and rice or soups.

salt-meat *n* (CarA) Pieces of salt-beef or SALT-PORK, (esp in relation to their use in flavouring the cooking of rice or other folk meals).

salt pan (Baha, TkCa); **salt pond** (USVI) *n phr* ‖ SALINA (TkCa) *When an area along the margin of one of these ponds is diked off it is called a 'salt pan'. The water in this pan is continuously evaporated by wind and sun. If the rate of evaporation exceeds that of rain fall, salt crystals result.*—ASOB:79

salt-phys·ic(s) [salt-fızık(s)] *n* (Belz, Jmca) Epsom salts or other strong laxative salts. *Ah guess Ah could be all kinds of a fool about dat man, but what it get you, honey, in de end? You want I tell you, what you get in de end it was better you' mother did tek aloes an' salt-physics an' you never was born.*—MBM:141 [< salts + EE *physic* 'medicine']

salt pond *n phr* (USVI) See SALT PAN.

salt-pork n (Guyn) **1.** The pickled meat of the domestic or wild pig (esp in relation to its use by PORK-KNOCKERS). **2.** Pieces of pickled pork on the bone, esp PIG-TAIL, as used in flavouring domestic cooking. *Tanta Moore cooked a big pot of rice and salt pork and peas and vegetables and we sat under the mango tree talking late into the night.*—CBM:28

salt-soap n (Guyn, Trin) Domestic washing soap; kitchen soap. [By contrast with sweet-smelling bathroom soap] □ Cp SWEET-SOAP.

salve-bush n (Baha, TkCa) ‖ CATTLE-TONGUE (Antg, etc) [< SE *salve*, from its medicinal use in relieving aches and pains]

sa·ma·ji; sa.ma.jist [sama:ji/jɪst] n (Guyn, Trin) [Indic] A member of a reformist Hindu religious order, called the Arya Samaj ('Noble Society'). [Hin < *samaaj* 'society, assembly' + *i* 'adherent, member', or + E suff -*ist* 'supporter, believer']

sa·man* (sa·maan) [sama·n] n (CarA) ‖ *cow-tamarind* (Trin) ‖ *guango* (Jmca) ‖ *rain-tree* (CarA) A very large shade-tree wh often exceeds 100 ft in height, has a relatively short, very thick trunk with long, horizontal branches that can exceed 80 ft; it bears masses of showy, pale pink flowers and dark, 6-inch-long, tamarind-like pods wh ripen with a sweet, clammy pulp around the seeds; children and cattle eat the pods; the wood makes good furniture; *Pithecellobium saman* or *Samanea saman* (*Mimosaceae*). [Prob from an Amerindian source via Amer Sp, the tree being native to So Amer]

same adj (CarA) [Often used in elliptical phrs as the foll] PHRASES **1. same (old) khaki pants** id phr (Bdos, Gren, StLu, Trin) [AF—*Joc*] See KHAKI-PANTS Phr 2. *Marxism led to Stalinism and to the same sterile plan of massive industrialization, economic imperialism and guns, guns, guns—just like the United States. Same khaki pants.*—TaP (75.09.28, p.4) **2. same thing (I said)** id phr (CarA) [IF] It's just as I thought; that's just what I told you would happen. **3. same time** adv phr (CarA) [AF] **(i)** At the same time; just at the time; when. *So we there fixing up and making we plan them to leave month-end, same time that Dennis friend going leave to go back to him home in Guyana.*—SNWIC:265 (M. Townshend) **(ii)** Immediately; right there and then. *Jean got vex and cuff Janet / Same time Miss turn around / Miss didn't ask no question / She just start beating Jean.*—TRFSS:29 **4. same way** adv phr (CarA) [AF] In the same way; just so, too. **a.** '*Ambition, over-ambition,' she announced, 'is all one basket o' fruit. Put it 'pon you' 'ead careless, an' you neck feel the pain, same way.'*—SJS:58 **b.** *Them is the sort of people you got to use and exploit. Same way how they exploiting the common working man, ... same way you got to take advantage of them.*—SPOC:35

sam·fie ((sam·fai, sam·fy)-man) [samfai-ma·n] n (Jmca) A confidence trickster; a swindler. *The song commemorated the feat of a City samfie man who sold a tramcar to an unsuspicious countryman.*—DaG (69.05.11, p.30) [Prob of W Afr origin. Note *DAFL* Twi *asama!fo* 'goblin, apparition', *asumanfo* 'sorcerer, magician'. In Twi, -*fo* is agential suffix like '-man' in CE OBEAHMAN] □ The spelling *samfie* is the one generally used, sometimes as an attrib to other nouns ex *samfie government*. The term **samfie-man**, commonly regarded as a *Jmca* term, is sometimes used in other *CarA* territories.

sam·fie·ism (sam·fy·ism) [samfaiɪzəm] n (Jmca) Trickery; ridiculous deception; dishonest dealing. *All that really matters is that a building called a school, a community centre, a house or a hospital physically exists and can be invoked to garner votes at election time. / As things are today however, fewer and fewer Jamaicans continue to be politically mesmerized by this sort of samfyism.*—DaN(JA) (79.09.21, p.7) [SAMFIE (see prec) + SE suff -*ism* 'practice of']

sa(m)·pat(s) (sap·pat, za·pat(s)) [sapat(s) ~ sampat(s) ~ zapat(s)] n (pl) (CarA) **1.** ‖ AL-PARGATA(S) (CarA) *Loaf Soo did this job from a little wooden box before the parlour door, where he perched, one foot on the box, the other foot hanging down; the foot on the bench was bare, the other in a sappat.*—JPB:124 [< Sp *zapato* 'shoe' by diffusion via labourers returning from *Venz, Panm, StDo*. (Note similarly ALPARGATA.) Insertion of homorganic /m/ in some places (*Jmca, Trin*) by epenthesis] **2.** (Belz, Jmca, Mrat) [By extension] [AF] Any old, shabby pair of shoes. **3.** (StLu, Tbgo, Trin) [By extension] [AF—*Joc*] A bashing; a thorough beating. *After winning the third set, they clinched the match by inflicting a Sapat (6–0) on Palmer and Butcher.*—VoS (77.11.29, p.10) [Cp Sp *zapatazo* 'bump, bang, pounding (with the foot)', also *zapatear* 'to treat roughly'. Both < *zapato* 'shoe']

san·coche [saŋkoč ~ saŋkoš ~ saŋkoči] n (Dmca, Gren, Jmca, Trin) ‖ *boil-up* (Belz) ‖ *metagee* (Guyn) A heavy, soup-like, one-pot meal prepared by boiling together a number of root-vegetables, breadfruit, green bananas, cornflour dumplings, SALTFISH, and pickled meat (esp PIG-TAIL) in COCONUT-MILK until the latter becomes a thick grey sauce. [< So Amer Sp *sancocho* 'stew (of meat, yucca, etc)'] □ *Jmca* pronunc [saŋkoči], hence also spelling **sangkochie**. See also DIP-AND-FALL-BACK.

sand PHRASES **1. kick sands** vb phr (TkCa) [AF] ‖ KICK DUST (CarA) *He believe his wife gone out wid a fella an[d] he kickin[g] sands!*—(TkCa) **2. like sand** adj phr (Belz) [AF] ‖ LIKE PEAS (ECar) See LIKE[2] Phr 2. *Tools Like Sand.*—ReP (Ad, 80.01.06, p.4)

sand·box(-tree)* n (CarA) ‖ *monkey-pistol tree* (USVI) ‖ *monkey's dinner-bell* (Guyn) A large forest-tree that can exceed 120 ft in height;

its trunk and limbs are covered with hard, sharp, conical spines, and it bears round, deeply grooved, segmented pods wh explode with a noise when ripe, scattering the seeds; the seeds are used as a purgative and the wood is usable for interior construction; the fresh sap is poisonous; *Hura crepitans* (*Euphorbiaceae*). [From the use, in former times, of the dried shell of its pod as a container for sand to dry ink, before the days of blotting paper]

sand-fly *n* (ECar) Any of several families of tiny, biting midges whose sting leaves blotches on the skin; they swarm seasonally on beaches and in other wet, sandy places; *Culicoides spp; Ceratopogonidae; Psychodidae*, etc.

san·gre *n* (Belz) ‖BANAK (Belz) [Sp = ‘blood’, from its blood-red sap]

san·gri·a [saŋgria] *n* (USVI) ‖OYSTER-PLANT (ECar) [Sp = ‘bleeding thing’, perh from colour of leaves]

San·key [saŋki] *n* One of the emotional, religious songs with inviting melodies, taken from a book of Gospel Songs published by the evangelist composer, I.D. Sankey (1840–1908) and widely popularized by Nonconformist religious missionaries. *A typical prayer meeting would last from 6 p.m. to 6 a.m. Those attending would sing ‘Sankeys’, give testimony, and ‘get the spirit’.*—HVVIS:108 □ The pl **sankies**, sometimes found, is erron.

Sans   hu·ma·ni·té!   [sanzimanite~santimanite] *excl phr* (Trin) [Carnival] No mercy!; No quarter given! [A refrain given by the challenging calypso singer and taken up simultaneously by the audience at the end of each eight-line stanza in wh he boasts of his superior might and word-power, while mercilessly deriding his opponent's lack of the same] [Fr = ‘without human pity’, a phr said to have originated from stick-fighting] □ This phr, though frequently used attrib in hist accounts of the development of the CALYPSO, has now partly faded away. Cp PICONG.

san·sam [sãsam] *n* (Trin) [*Obs ?*] ‖ASHAM (Antg, etc) [Reported *HHTV:289* as the name used in Toco, extreme north-east tip of *Trin*, and identified as ‘African real food’. Perh nearer original Twi *o-siãm* with regressive assimilation. Cp ‖*sham-sham (StVn)*] □ Now widely replaced in *Trin* by CHILIBIBI.

san·se·vi·e·ri·a* ['sansɛvⁱɛrɪʌ] *n* (ViIs) ‖*mother-in-law-tongue, snake-bush* (Guyn) Any of several varieties of an ornamental plant, comprising a cluster of mottled green or variegated, erect and stiffish, sword-shaped leaves (some varieties with a yellow margin) about 2 ft long; they yield a fibre when beaten and dried; *Sansevieria metallica*, etc (*Liliaceae*). □ Wrongly called a **cactus** in some places, perh because it thrives in poor, dry soil.

san·tan·tone [santanto·n] *n* (Guyn) A person of mixed African and Portuguese parentage. [< Pg *santantoninho* ‘a petted, pampered person’ < Santo Antonio ‘St Anthony’]

san·ta·pee [santapi] /1'12/ *n* (CarA) [*AF*] 1. A centipede; *Chilopoda spp.* 2. [By extension] [*AF—Derog*] A contemptible and dangerous, rowdy woman. [Note *NMID* Pg *centopeia* '1. The centipede. 2. (fig) A horrible woman' Perh the CE pronunc and parallel metaph usage are hist dial loans owing to Slave Coast contact with Pg slave-traders.]

san·ta·pee-band /1'121/n (Guyn) [*AF*] ‖M-ASQUERADE-BAND (CarA) *Williams recalls that, as a young boy, he was once punished for running out of the house to watch the parade of Santapee Bands. During the Christmas season these bands played their way through the streets of Georgetown, the musicians and dancers dressed in African costume. The name Santapee was a corruption of the word ‘centipede’, for as the bands threaded their way through the town the onlookers were reminded of the movements of this many-legged little creature.*—MGWI:86 [See cit. However, the name prob also owes much to the association of the wriggling of persons in such bands, esp in former times, with rowdy social elements]

sap *vb* (CarA) [*IF*] To soak or sop (an aching part of the body) by patting it gently with a pad soaked in a cooling lotion or in warm water. *I had no idea they were asking me to run for money. I would have sapped my hip with bay rum, rubbed my knees with fast spittle, tied on painkiller bush and been right in the thick and thin of it.*—DaN(ST) (79.02.22, p.9) [< SE *sop* ‘to wet thoroughly’, by vowel opening] □ Note conflict with SE *sap* ‘to drain or dry (of juice, energy, etc)’, almost the opposite in sense. However **sap** vb is widely established in CE.

sa·pa·di·li *n* (Belz) ‖SAPODILLA (CarA)

sa·pat *n* (StLu, Tbgo, Trin) [*AF—Joc*] See SA(M)PAT. 3

sa·phats *n pl* (Bdos) [*X*] ‖ALPARGATAS (CarA) [A blend from Sp *zapato* ‘shoe’ with infl of ALFAGATS]

sa·pi·dil·la *n* (Berm) ‖SAPODILLA (CarA)

sa·po·dil·la* /1'121/ *n* (CarA) ‖*chapoti* (Dmca, StLu) ‖*dilly* (Baha, TkCa) ‖*mesple* (ViIs) ‖*naseberry* (Jmca) ‖*sapadili* (Belz) ‖*sapidilla* (Berm) ‖*sapotie, shapotie* (Dmca, StLu) A russet-brown, thin-skinned, roundish fruit about 3 ins long, with a sweet, yellowish-brown, succulent pulp around a few shiny, black seeds; it is borne on a tall, bushy tree with leathery leaves; the trunk yields the latex known as *chicle gum*; *Achras zapota*, or *Manilkara z.* (*Sapotaceae*). [Anglicized pronunc of Sp name < Aztec *tzapotl*, name of the fruit]

sa·po·tie n (StLu, Trin) ‖SAPODILLA (CarA)
[Fr Cr < Fr *sapotille* 'sapodilla']

sap·py adj (Bdos, Guyn) [IF] [Of fruit] Too
soft; overripe; [of ground] soppy; soggy. [< SE
soppy by vowel-opening; cp SAP with extended
sense]

sa·ra·ca (sa·rac·ca, sa·ra·ka) n (Crcu, Gren)
A ritual feast on some scale wh is sometimes
accompanied by singing and dancing, and wh
may also last for more than one day; it is offered
as a sacrifice of thanksgiving, for honouring the
dead, or for propitiating evil spirits. [< Hausa
sadaka 'charity, alms (esp associated with honouring the dead)'. See *ADHL*] □ Also sometimes
called SALACCA in *Gren*, though the practice is
less current there than in *Crcu*.

sa·ri (sa·ree) [sa:ri] n (Guyn, Trin) [Indic] A
female garment consisting of a single length of
light, colourful cloth wh is wrapped about the
body so that the whole body is elegantly covered,
with one end draped over the shoulder; it is
traditional wear, used on formal occasions. [Hin
saarii, name of this garment]

sas·pa·ril·la n (ViIs) ‖CHRISTMAS-CANDLE
(Bdos, etc) [Prob < SE *sarsaparilla*, the dried
roots of wh were also once used to treat skin
disorders as the leaves of this tree are in *CarA*]
□ Also referred to as **West Indian sasparilla**
(*PHPVI:62*), perh by way of distinction from
sarsaparilla wh is pronounced similarly.

sat·is·fy vb (CarA) [X] **1.** To be fully satisfied,
surfeited. *No matter ho[w] much food yo[u] put
before him, he never satisfy.*—(StVn) **2.** To be
content; to satisfy yourself; to have your desire
or wish. *I satisfy that I do all I could for him
when he was sick before he died.*—(Gren) [In both
cases by characteristic CE passivization of vb tr,
satisfy] □ See PASSIVITY.

sauced [sɒst] adj (Guyn) [IF] Showing some
(little or great) degree of drunkenness. *When he
gets sauced he gets very quarrelsome like that, so
don't bother with him too much.*—(Guyn) [Cp
DAS AmE slang *on the sauce* 'addicted to heavy
drinking'. Perh also infl by E slang *soused*
'drunk']

sauce·pan [sɒ·spʌn] n **1.** (Antg, Brbu, Guyn)
‖SKILLET I. (Bdos) *She was proud of the new half
gallon bucket and the shiny tin saucepan with the
rice and currie in it.*—SSOS:68 **2.** (Bdos) An
aluminium or enamel pot with a cover and a
long handle.

sa·van·na(h)-grass n **1.** (Guyn, Tbgo) A
coarse grass that grows in low, scattered clumps
(hence also sometimes called '**bunch**' grass); it
flourishes in poor sandy soil of inland savannas
(hence the name); it is cattle fodder of a poor
quality. **2.*** (Bdos, Gren, Jmca, Trin) A low
grass with a creeping habit, rooting at the joints
so that it spreads naturally over pastures or
lawns; it bears flowering spikes and has slender,
fairly smooth leaves (whence also called '**carpet
grass**' if mowed flat); *Axonopus compressus* (*Gramineae*).

sav·ing conj (Bdos) [IF] Unless. *And I know
that a good time can't happen to any and every
man, saving that man stand in possession of
money.*—CWFYS:17 [Cp *EDD saving* 3. Obs
conj (link) 'except']

sa·wa·ri (sa·wa·ree, sou·a·ri) n (Guyn) A
palm tree that bears clusters of hard-shelled nuts
of a rusty brown colour, with a soft, sweet kernel;
Caryocar nuciferum (*Caryocaraceae*) or *Pekea
tuberculosa*. [Prob Arawak, cp *BAED sawarama*
'cabbage palm'] □ Not to be confused with SOU-
RIE (*Guyn*).

say¹ [sɛ ~ sɛ] vb PHRASES **1. Have nothing to
say!** imper vb phr (Guyn) [IF] Say nothing!;
Beware of giving any useful answer! *Don['t] let
anybody draw you into their story! If she ask you
what you think, just tell her you don['t] know.
Have nothing to say!*—(Guyn) **2. it isn't to say
(that ...)** id phr (Bdos, Guyn) [IF] It's not as
if; it is not that. *And Wendy, it isn't to say that
I have lost my sex appeal, because there are other
men I know who find me attractive enough to
hint that they would like to fool around with
me.*—AdV(Mag) (87.08.08, Dear Wendy) **3.
people/they have it to say** id phr (CarA) [IF]
It is being said; the rumour is. *In the political
arena, people are having it to say that the recent
resignation of Mr DaC. E— from the post of
Minister of Agriculture, Science and Technology
was not only due to 'personal reasons' as has been
stated.*—AdN (73.10.14, p.4) **4. say a true
word** vb phr (Guyn) To say something that is
wise, worth thinking about. *Mari has said a true
word there. If all the people here, Chinese, Black
man, Portuguese, Coolie, White man, Buck man,
can laugh at themselves and laugh together—half
the law story would not be there.*—CTT:13 [Af-
firmative adaptation of SE (*sb*) *never said a truer
word*] **5. Say wha[t]?** [sɛ wa(t)] /1'4'/ excl (Belz,
Guyn, Jmca) [AF] What? Surely, you're not
being serious!; Can I believe my ears? *Say
wha[t]? They sen[d] you to borro[w] more money
from me?*—(Jmca) □ (Now also E slang—(*pers
info, L. Urdang*). **6. Who tell you to say so/
that?** id phr (Bdos, Guyn, Trin) [AF—Joc] What
a highly provocative or inadvisable thing to have
said! *When I suggested she might be partly to blame
she went off like a rocket! Who tell me to say so?*
—(Guyn) **7. you won't say?** tag question (Tbgo,
Trin) [IF] Wouldn't you agree?; Don't you think
so? *One day he would buy a house like that. Don't
mind he was Indian.... He could be a big shot too,
you won't say?*—SABS:96

say² [sɛ] n (Bdos) [AF] A disagreement; a row.
*I told him that how could he expect the money he
used to give to serve myself and them two old people.
We never had any more say than that.*—Bdos (CR,
70.09.14)

say³ [sɛ] *conn particle* (CarA) ‖ *seh*² (CarA) **1.** [*AF/IF*] [As simple conj between two main clauses] That. **a.** *Mr Garfield here figures say the strike will come to all of us too.*—RND:318 **b.** *I hear the big men make law say police can't make case on them in the Queen's court.*—ViN (72.11.11, p.8) **c.** *Jus' because dem choose 'e fo' monitor, e' jus' believe say 'e got de bigges' brain in a de class.*—FGSOS:44 **2.** [*AF*] [Introducing direct or indirect speech] **a.** *He tell mer say 'good mornin', smilin' broad.*—JBJ:88 **b.** *Maas Tom ask her say if the old dawg can't eat turn cornmeal. Mam, Putus nearly have heart attack.*—WeG (72.12.06, p.12, Partyline) **3.** [*AF*] [Becoming a semi-disjunct introducing another conj] Actually (that); indeed (that). **a.** *Well, this time Sophie decide say that he was coming bout 8 and he woulda finish in bout a hour.*—NaG (78.06.01, Satirically Speaking) **b.** *You know I never thought that before. I feeling say that we is natives like.*—CTT:38 **4.** [*AF*] [Passing into purposive function] With the belief, thought, or intention that. **a.** *One evening, Miss Telfor take me say she going to Windward for provision.*—STTG:14 **b.** *... but yet found the energy to escort a girl younger than his daughter to Buccoo last week Sunday and make a fool of heself say he dancing disco.*—BeA(TO) (81/10, p.3) **c.** *Only when night come you hear him making a whole lot of stupid noise say he knocking drum.*—PKKK:75 [A near phonic survival in sense 1. of *DAFL* Twi *sɛ* 'that (introducing a noun-sentence that supplies the ... object or other complement of a preceding verb)'; it reflects other senses of the same Twi form in *CarA* Cr, so passing into CE infl by SE *say*. The Twi homophone *sɛ* also functions adverbially 'thus, so; for instance' and this may be reflected in sense 3. Related Twi form *se* vb 'to say within oneself, to purpose, to intend' is prob reflected in sense 4; and its homophone *se* ' = saying (but) often not to be translated, serving as a mere quotation mark' prob also influences senses 1., 2. above. The nearness in sense and function to SE *say* in many *CarA* Cr contexts, ex 'Me hear say Willie dead', will also have reinforced general *CarA* usage passing into AF/IF CE. See *DJE se* 2. for an additional use in *Jmca*, not treated here] □ Note the distinct (creolized) difference in pronunc between conn SAY³ and SAY¹, SAY² n. However in *IF* contexts the forms may merge in some people's speech.

say·bu·can ['se·bukan] *n* (Trin) See SEBUCAN

say-say *n* (Antg, Jmca) [*AF*] ‖ HEAR-SO (Brbu, Jmca) **a.** *Me ain['t] like dis say-say [a]t all! If yo[u] have some[thi]n[g] to say, tell her to her face.*—(Antg) **b.** *Don't involve rasta in your say-say / Rasta no work for no C.I.A.*—Rastaman Vibrations—Bob Marley

say-so¹ *n* (Jmca, StLu, Trin) [*IF*] Assent; approval; agreement. [*This*] *seems to be Compton's main device for jockeying Britain into approving his coveted absolute power of independence without the say-so of the St Lucia electorate.*—CrU (75.12.25, p.2)

say-so² *adj* (Jmca) [*IF*] [Of talk] Unreliable; loosely said. *After the police officers left, Gran' Pa Tyson was the first to speak; he said, 'Funny li'l scrap of say-so evidence they picking up?'*—SJT:72

sca·ji·neal [skaɟini·l] *n* (Belz) [*X*] See COCHINEAL [Prosthetic /s-/, characteristic of *Belz* folk pronunc]

scamp¹ *n* (Guyn) [*IF*—*Joc*] A likeable young male flirt; a young man-about-town. *I never thought that scamp woulda get serious wid anybody, but Maria got him under manners, I tell you!! Weddin[g] bells soon!*—(Guyn) [By Joc modification of SE *scamp* 'a ne'er-do-well; a rascal'] □ Cp VAGABOND *Guyn* sometimes similarly used. Both terms commonly occur in contexts of amusement.

scamp² *adj* (Trin) [*X*] Scampish. *Do[n't] trus[t] him. He too scamp when he ready.*—(Trin) [By functional n > adj shift of SCAMP¹, but retaining more of the offensive sense]

scamp³ *vb tr* (Guyn, Trin) [*AF*] To trick; to fool; to catch by craft or guile. *'Jube!!' he shouted, 'Bobby scamp we! The son of a gutta-rat scamp we! This f-ing thing isn't molasses!'*—SBB:85 [By functional n > vb shift of SCAMP¹, but with more of the offensive sense retained]

scan·dal (**scan·dle**) [skyandʌl ~ skyandl] *vb* (Guyn) [*IF*] **1.** ‖ SCANDALIZE (Trin) [Both *scandal, scandle* occur in EE as nouns, *scandal* as vb *OED* 'to disgrace; to spread scandal about (a person)', but only as Obs or dial. *EDD* notes same usage in W Cor] **2.** PHRASE **2.1 scandal (sb's) name** *vb phr* (Guyn) [*IF*] To bring disgrace on (sb); to defame (sb). *His wife happens to know about our relationship. She is scandling my name all over town.*—GyC (71.11.14, p.29)

scan·dal·ize [sk(y)andʌlaɪz] *vb tr* (Trin) ‖ *scandal* (Guyn) To bring (sb) into disrepute; to bring discredit, shame or disgrace upon (sb). *Said the* [*Law*] *Society of the article in the writ: 'It is calculated and tends to bring the said judges of the court into contempt and to lower their dignity and authority and to bring the administration of justice in Trinidad and Tobago into disrepute and disregard, and to scandalize the said court and judges.'*—ExP (72.06.13, p.1) [As *OED scandalize* 4. 'to bring shame or discredit upon', but marked Obs or poet. *EDD* notes same usage in Yks] □ In ModE this vb tr always means 'to shock (sb) by an impropriety'.

scank *vb* (CarA) See SKANK

scar·let cor·di·a *n phr* (Angu, Bdos, BrVi, Jmca, StKt) See CORDIA

scar·let i·bis* [ska·lɛt-aɪbɪs] *n phr* (Trin) ‖ *curri-curri* (Guyn) A bird of brilliant scarlet plumage when mature, except for black tips to the wings and a long, black curved bill; shaped like an egret, it is a swamp and mudflat bird and feeds on fishes; *Eudocimus ruber* (*Thres-kiornithidae*). □ The **Scarlet Ibis** is the National Bird of Trinidad.

scar·let plum *n phr* (Baha, TkCa) ‖ JAMAICA-PLUM (Bdos, etc) [From its colour when ripe]

scasm [skazəm ~ skyazım] *n* (Crcu, Nevs) [*AF*] **1.** ‖ BAD-TALK (CarA) *The Opposition, buoyed up by the fact, and its confidence in the fact that it is discharging the duties of the people who have elected it, will stand any 'scasm', will stand any scorn, will stand any attack of verbose expressions directed at it.*—Gren (Hd, 68.01.31, p.32, Speaker from Crcu) [< SE *sarcasm* by syncope and with shift of meaning] **2.** PHRASE **2.1 pass scasm [u]pon (sb)** *vb phr* (Nevs) ‖ BAD-TALK² (sb) (CarA)

scat·ter·a·tion [skyatare·šan] *n* (CarA) [*AF-Joc*] The scattering (of a crowd) in a mad scramble for safety. *Da is only big talk from all o[f] dem! If de police fire one shot! I[t']s scatteration!*—(Guyn) [Cp OED *scatteration* 'act of scattering' + OED2 'fact of being scattered'. However CE sense is Joc and particular to its context]

sca·veech·ed fish *n phr* (Jmca) ‖ E-SCAVEITCHED FISH (Jmca)

scene *n* (CarA) [*AF/IF*] **1.** Place or sphere of personal activity. **a.** *In '67 and '68 the band settled down to a steady Antigua scene with limited touring because Arnold could not travel—his mother objected.*—Int (10/73, p.7) **b.** *The 24-year-old Jah Mike said that he has been penetrating the recording scene for a long time but that he was too young and never had much experience. The break which he so badly needs remains elusive.*—DaN(JA) (80.02.07, p.14) **c.** *It is believed in some circles that this is a move to attract the unemployed, the so-called rastas and drug traffickers. We say this is not their scene.*—VoS (76.05.01, p.2) [A loan from Am show business and pop culture, with extended and perh looser uses in CE. See below] **2.** A type of activity or set of beliefs to wh you give your loyalty. **a.** *We are not on any black power scene this time. We are a pressure group out to find jobs at any cost. Our people want jobs.*—BoM (74.04.13, p.1) **b.** *Jehovah Witnesses have come out on a love scene! Love was the message at the Witnesses big circuit assembly at the Himalaya Club, Barataria, last weekend.*—SuP (75.01.19, p.7) **c.** *We have to get off that scene; we have to get rid of the heritage of the previous class biases where 'beauty' is concerned.*—NeJ (75.02.14, p.5) [Cp OED2 *scene* 8. d. wh has similar ModE but less emotive sense than CE] **3.** [Rastaf] [An excl greeting or parting word of brotherly approval] **a.** *Let de brother come! Scene I!* (= *He is/you are welcome.*)—Bdos (Ms) **b.** *So you sight up, youtman! Scene! Forward I.* [= *So you're all right, my young brother! Goodbye! I'm going.*]—Jmca (Ms, poem) □ In *Rastaf* contexts, also used as an interjection of approval (hence also sometimes spelled '*Seen*') encouraging the speaker to carry

on. **4.** PHRASES **4.1 be on a [stated] scene** *id phr* (Gren, StVn, Tbgo, Trin) [*AF*] To be up to something (in connection with sth stated) for personal benefit. **a.** *The Prime Minister, Dr Eric Williams, who is also Minister of Finance, who prepared the Budget, was on 'an energy scene' Sen. Laughlin said. Previous to this, he had been on a 'Meet the People' scene and then on a 'Better Village' scene.*—ExP (75.12.23, p.26) **b.** *They received a wary welcome as everyone was wondering what scene they were on.*—ToR (76.08.25, p.6) **4.2 hit/make the scene** *vb phr* (CarA) [*AF*] **(i)** [Entertainment Ind] To make a dramatically successful first or opening set of performances. *It is now definite that the Merrymen will be headlining the big show there over the Easter weekend. It's an all-Barbadian gig and the most recent addition to the side that will be making the scene is Carolyn Leacock.*—NaT (75.02.23, p.9) **(ii)** [By extension, of style, fashion, etc] To be much liked. (See HIT Phr 3.2) [In AmE slang = 'appear'. Cp OED2 *scene* 8. e. (orig US slang) ... *make the scene* 'to participate in an event or activity', wh is less emotive than the CE phr]

scent [sɛnt] *vb intr* (Guyn, Jmca, StVn) [*X*] To smell; to give off a bad scent. *They had to try to raise the money to save her burying by the poor [law], but it take a couple days, till the body was beginning to scent.*—(Guyn) [A survival of EE as OED *scent* 3. (Obs) 'to exhale an odour; to smell' + cits–'1843]

scheme¹ *n* (Guyn) ‖ HOUSING-SCHEME (Bdos, Guyn) *All the people of the scheme came out to greet their hero, the hat-trick bowler and winner of the match.*—Guyn (Ms) [A survival of EE as OED *scheme* sb¹ 3. (Obs) 'a map or plan of a town'] □ A commonly understood abbr with only this sense in *Guyn*.

scheme² *n* (Trin) [*AF/IF*] Planned fraud; dishonest dealing. *Ah know plenty people who does do all kind of scheme, but because dey have money de police don't do dem nutting.*—SABS:89 [As OED *scheme* sb¹ 5. b. 'a self-seeking or underhand project, a plot'; also AmE WCD9 *scheme¹* n. 3. 'a plan or program of action esp a crafty or secret one'] □ This is the dominant sense in *Trin* E. (Also dominant in AmE).

scheme³ *vb intr* (CarA) To contrive by fraudulent means. *... for the good / God's sake, if you scheme- / in' now to relieve / me now, to sweet / talk me now, to support / me now, just forget / it now, please forsake / me now.*—BTA:31 [As OED *scheme* v. 2, 'to devise plans, esp underhand or with sinister motives' + cits–'1866; also AmE WCD9 *scheme²* vb 'to plot, to intrigue']

schnapp; schnapp-glass *n* (Guyn) See SNAP; SNAP-GLASS

schol·ar *n* In PHRASES **Barbados scholar, Guiana scholar, Island scholar, etc** A young man or woman adjudged winner of the academic competition based on the Advanced Level or other British secondary school examination and given a sholarship to pursue a university degree.

school *n* PHRASES **1. go to school at Brumley** *id phr* (Bdos) [*AF—Joc*] ‖ GO TO SCHOOL IN AUG-UST (CarA) [See BRUMLEY] **2. go to school in August** *id phr* (CarA) [*AF—Joc*] To have (had) no schooling; to show your ignorance. *Don't let him fool you with that. What, you been to school in August or what?*—(StVn)

sci·ence[1] *n* **1.** (CarA) [*AF/IF*] Technique; a required skill in doing. *Let me show you; there's a science in it: You have to catch the lock with the key, pull it out a bit and then turn.*—(Tbgo) **2.** (Guyn, Jmca, Trin) [*IF*] Occult science; OBEAH or practices related to it. *She was using all the science she knew to win back Benoit. But Benoit was a man of science too. 'Science versus Science,' said Maisie and derided Mrs Rouse and Benoit and their traffic with the occult.*—JMA:101

sci·ence[2] *adj* (Antg) [*AF*] [Esp of women] Putting on superior airs; affected in manner (esp of dress and walk); standoffish. *But how you expec[t] her to jump up in a Carnival Band? Eh! She too science for dat, man.*—(Antg)

sci·ence off *vb phr* (Antg) [*AF*] [Esp of a young woman] To be showy; to set out to impress. *She sciencin[g] off with the gold watch she get from America.*—(Antg) [By functional adj > vb shift of SCIENCE[2]]

sci·en·tist *n* (Gren, Guyn, Jmca, Nevs) [*IF—Joc*] ‖ OBEAH-MAN/-WOMAN (CarA) *Everybody knew that Bra' Ambo was a powerful obeahman. Bra' Ambo himself had given it out that he was 'a higher scientist than Bra' Man, for'—and he washed his hands before him, and smiled smugly— 'Bra' Man study de science of de stars, astrology, an' I study de science of de stars too, but I study higher than dat, for I study de science of de De-ad.'*—MBM:84 [SCIENCE[1] 2. + SE suff -ist 'practitioner of'] □ This term, a Joc euphemism, is however used more seriously by some speak-ers.

scis·sors *n pl construed as sg* (CarA) [*IF*] **1.** A pair of scissors. **a.** *... but it appears that Ram's finger nails are just as tough, and no scissors could have done the job. Or maybe there just wasn't a scissors handy.*—DaC (52.06.05, p.3) **b.** *A police report states that at about 5.40 p.m. yesterday, while on duty at the market, Allen had a fuss with McGaw, who allegedly pulled a scissors on him.*—WeG (73.07.11, p.3) [Cp OED scissors 1. **c.** (marked as catachrestic) 'in pl form construed as sg. *rare*' + cits 1832–1906. This period being that of the strong early development of CE, the wide, almost regularized use of the sg def art 'a' is explainable. Its convenience also recommends it. OED2 adds a 1976 US ex. Cp similarly *pants, trousers*] **2.** PHRASE **2.1 be hell and scissors** *id phr* (Guyn) [*AF—Joc*] See HELL Phr 1.

S.C.M. *abbr* (Bdos) Silver Crown of Merit of the Order of Barbados, a national honour awar-ded for meritorious service or achievement in science, the arts, literature, sport, civic duties, or other endeavour worthy of national re-cognition; the letters are placed after the re-cipient's name.

scorch out *vb phr* (Baha, CayI) To erase or wipe out (sth); to scratch out or delete (sth). [Perh < SE *scratch* by metathesis and /a > o/ vowel closure] □ Well established in school talk.

scorn[1] *n* (Tbgo, Trin) [*X*] Revulsion; horror. *When she was well enough to go to school the other children looked with scorn at her badly burnt face.*—Tbgo (Ms) [By semantic shift < SE *scorn* n 'disdain, contempt'] □ SE *scorn* is strongly associated with 'filth, unwholesomeness, evil'.

scorn[2] *vb tr* (Bdos, Tbgo, Trin) [*X*] To spurn or despise (sb); to find (sth) revulsive. **a.** *If, as a writer said, children are now scorned for speaking a standard form of English, those who scorn them are grossly ignorant.*—AdV (86, 02.05, p.4) **b.** *I couldn't be a nurse. I scorn blood and sores and all them things.*—(Trin) [By characteristic CE functional n > vb shift of SCORN[1], reinforced by semantic shift of SE *scorn* vb 'to reject as contemptible'] □ See prec note.

scorn·ful *adj* (Antg, Tbgo, Trin) [*X*] Dis-dainful; fastidious; choosy. *The children went to live in America from small, and now they come back they too scornful. They don[']t want lemonade and peas-and-rice and such like. They only want Pepsi and pizza and a lot o[f] things you got to go out and buy.*—(Antg) [< CE SCORN[2] vb + SE suff -ful. Cp also AmE WCD9 scornful 'con-temptuous']

scorn-the-earth/-ground [ˈskɔrn-dɪ-(h)ʌrt/-grʌŋ] *n* (Belz, Jmca, TkCa) ‖ BIRD-VINE 1. (Dmca, etc) [From the fact that this parasitic bush roots on the host tree and not in the ground]

scor·pi·on-fish* *n* (CarA) ‖ *lion-fish* (Bdos, Brbu, Mrat) ‖ *numb-fish* 2. (CayI) ‖ *stone-fish* (CarA) ‖ *twenty-four hour(s)* 2. (Gren, StKt) One of a number of varieties of fish about 12 ins long with big eyes almost atop its head, gills like jawbones, and many spines sticking out of its head and dorsal fins; the spines are highly poisonous and can paralyse or ultimately kill if stepped upon as the fish lies motionless and camouflaged on the sea-bed among coral rocks; it may be stone-coloured or many-coloured; its flesh is edible; *Scorpaenidae* (esp *Scorpaena plu-mieri*). [From its poisonous injection]

scor·pi·on-tail/-weed *n* (CayI, Jmca) ‖ WILD-CLARY (Guyn, Jmca) [From the shape and curve of the spike of flowerets]

scotch[1] *n* (Bdos) ‖ *cotch*[1] (Jmca) A little room made at the end of a bench on wh others are seated to barely permit one more person to sit;

[by extension] any temporary make-do accommodation provided to help sb out. **a.** *We want to get back there, not as big-time consumers, but as controllers of capital. We do not want a little scotch on the side, as in Rocker's Alley, to enable us to sell David Seale's apples.*—SuS (89.06.04, p.28) **b.** *I didn't mind overnighting in Barbados because I have quite a few friends there and I knew I could always find a scotch with one of them, as they say.*—(Trin) [Perh < *OED* scotch sb² 1., with some shift in sense to 'something wedged in'. The *Jmca* form COTCH may be by early diffusion from *Bdos* with characteristic aphaeresis esp of /s-/ in *Jmca* Cr]

scotch² *vb* (Bdos) ‖ **cotch²** (Jmca) **1.** To squeeze, wedge or be wedged (in); [by extension] to find or be given temporary make-do accommodation. **a.** *She returned to the room carrying a jug filled with water and two glasses. She balanced the jug in the palm of one hand while the glasses scotched between the fingers of the other hand. It was like a circus stunt.*—LICMS:292 **b.** *I jus[t] back here for a li[tt]l[e] business, scotchin[g] by m[y] sister, but she don['t] have a phone.*—(Bdos) **c.** *... and there are a couple of half-baked white girls, prostitutes for that matter, who come down here, scotch on at some of the hotels, and the beach boys marry them and they have a right to bring their bodies in here and sell them and then leave the country.*—Bdos (Hd, 74.08.27, p.3929) **2.** [By extension] To make an opening (by wedging sth in between). *I will just put this chair to scotch the door so as to let in a little breeze.*—(Bdos) **3.** [Esp in ref to shoes] To limp from discomfort; to tread painfully or cautiously. *Girlie, I scotchin[g] [be]cause dese new shoes tight. Don['t] laugh! Good t[h]ing de church ain['t] far!*—(Bdos) [By functional and semantic shifts of SCOTCH¹. Re senses 1., 2. cp also *EDD* scotch vb¹ 3. 'to wedge firmly'. Cp all senses of COTCH² vb (*Jmca*)]

scrab·ble¹ *n* (Tbgo, Trin) [*IF*] A tussle; a scuffle. [Perh < SE *scramble* by homorganic assimilation, or by functional shift or infl of SCRABBLE²]

scrab·ble²; **scrab.ble up**; **scrab up** *vb phr* (Tbgo, USVI) [*IF*] **1.** *vb intr* To struggle. *Instead o[f] scrabblin[g] for a livin[g] here, dey go to the States and get a job.*—(USVI) [< *OED* scrabble vb 3. [of a person] 'to stumble or struggle along' + cits–1900; also 'to struggle or scramble (for sth)' + cits–1861] **2.** *vb tr* [By extension] To grab (up) (sth). *The rain came and spoil the fair because everybody had to scrabble up everything.*—(USVI) **3.** *vb tr* [By extension] To scrape, scratch, dig (esp the skin or the ground). **a.** *He tried to dodge her but this time her hand came away with ... some skin off the side of his belly where her big blunt nails had scrabbed him.*—MHJJ:35 **b.** *The child had a long scratch up to his elbow where the bamboo basket scrab up his hand.*—(Tbgo) **c.** *Cat scrabble (up) ground say he cover coo-coo, then raise he head say he decent.* (= *The cat scratches up the ground superficially to cover its faeces, then raises its head pretending that that is real*

decency.)—USVI (Prov) [Cp *OED* scrabble vb 4. trans 'to scratch about hurriedly with claws or paws' + cits–'1900. However, *scrab* vb (Obs and dial) 1. 'to scratch, claw' + cits–'1880; cp also GRABBLE¹ (*Bdos*, etc) 2. (*Jmca, USVI*) with comparable senses and uses]

scram·ble¹ *vb tr* (Gren, Guyn, Trin) **1.** To grab (sb) roughly; to seize (sb). *It wasn't worth while to spend much time fooling around in the back hills of Willis and New Hampshire for fear that the Police may scramble them.*—Gren (Hd, 68.12.30, p.33) [Cp *OED* scramble vb 2. b '...hence, to seize rapaciously' + cits –'1656. However this sense applies to things, not persons] **2.** [By extension] [*IF*] To scuffle with (sb) (usu having the upper hand). *She scramble him right there and tear off he shirt! See man run from woman that mornin[g]!*—(Trin)

scram·ble² *n* (Gren, Guyn, Trin) A scuffle; a minor fight. *The defendant told the magistrate that when he was leaving the dock he was 'chucked' by Noble and when he returned the chuck a 'scramble' ensued. He also said that several policemen tried to restrain him but he did not see the inspector nor did he cuff the inspector.*—DaC (n.d.) [By functional vb > n shift of SCRAMBLE¹ 2, and / or semantic shift of *OED* scramble n '...hence, an indecorous struggle' + cits–'1907]

scrap gang *n phr* (Baha) An informal group of players in a JUNKANOO parade, their costumes being made up of odds and ends, or scraps of paper and cloth; they parade for fun, not in competition. *Yesterday's parade suffered from poor organization. Far too many scrap gangs were allowed to enter Bay Street and although they made good music, they often got in the way of organized groups, and made their performances difficult.*—TrI (76.01.02, p.1) [The term GANG (rarely replaced by BAND in this context) may refer to the disorganized character or perh, from their shabby appearance, to plantation work gangs] □ SCRAP GANG, out of the above context, wd be quite differently interpreted in the sugar territories. Cp SCRAPPER.

scrap·per *n* (Bdos) [Sugar Ind] A field labourer employed both to complete the reaping of stumps of sugar-cane missed by the chopper of the mechanical harvester and to pick up and pile sticks of cane that fall out from the mechanical loader.

scrap·ping *n* (Bdos) [Sugar Ind] The job or labour of a SCRAPPER.

scratch *vb* (Guyn, StVn, Trin) [*X*] **1.** *vb intr* [Of the skin] To itch. *If you feel the palm of your right hand scratchin[g] it mean you goin[g] get money.*—(Guyn) **2.** *vb tr* [Of food, plants, etc] To cause (your mouth or skin) to itch. *I[t']s a kin[d] o[f] eddoe dat if yo[u] don['t] boil it good, it does scratch yo[ur] mout[h].*—(StVn) [Cp *EDD* scratch sb 6. (Chr, Shr) 'the itch']

scratch-band n (Nevs, StKt, USVI) A rural folk-band in wh a rasp or SHAK-SHAK is used for rhythmic effect, together with bottle, triangle, flute, guitar, etc. [From the scratching sound of the rasp] □ Cp RAKE-AND-SCRAPE BAND, MAS-QUERADE BAND, TUK BAND all with general sim-ilarities in make-up and use.

scratch-bush n (Tbgo) ‖STINGING-NETTLE (Guyn, Trin)

scratch·er n (Trin) A grater-like, folk musical instrument consisting of an elongated piece of thin metal punched with holes, its rough side being scraped with a piece of wood or metal to give an element to the rhythm section of a CARNIVAL band. □ Cp SCRATCH-BAND.

scratch·y adj (Jmca) [IF] Itchy. 'Grass?' asked Mrs Anthony. 'In your shirt?' She was smiling. 'Yes, ma'am. Guinea grass and very scratchy too. My skin itches.'—PCCB:22 [From sense of SCRATCH + SE suff -y. Hence cp COD8 scratchy 2 '(esp of a garment) tending to cause itchiness']

scrav·en [skre·vn ~ skre·bn] adj (Guyn) [AF—Cr/Derog] ‖ LICKERISH 2. (Antg, etc) [Prob < CRAVEN with prosthetic /s-/. Cp SKINOP. How-ever the Guyn term, specially Derog, is prob also affected by association with 'scraping (the plate)' 'eating scraps', etc]

scrawl·y [skrɒ·li] adj (Guyn) [Of a person or animal] Lean and sickly looking, esp (of a person) with a blotchy skin. [< Du schraal 'thin, gaunt' + infl of SE scrawny 'lean']

screel[1] vb intr (Bdos, Guyn, Tbgo, Trin) To shriek in pain, terror, anguish, etc; to scream. **a.** My mother unhooked her belt from a nail and lashed me thoroughly. Bob heard the screeling, and came down to our house listening.—LICMS:120 **b.** When a puppy screels in pain almost immediately one hears the big dogs in the area start to bark.—Bdos (Ms, 1971) [EDD screel vb (from several counties) 'to shriek, squeal'. Also CSD Sc screel 'scream, screech', late 19C]

screel[2] n (Bdos, Guyn) A shriek; a piercing, high-pitched sound. The screel of the whistle of the train / As the engine bounced through the rain.—Guyn (Ms) [By functional vb > n shift of SCREEL[1]. Also EDD screel sb (Nhb, Yks, Sus) 'a shriek, scream']

screw-pine* n (Bdos, Dmca, Nevs, Tbgo, Trin) ‖ thatch (Baha, CayI, Jmca, StKt) ‖ wild pine 2. (Gren) A larger variety of CANE-LILY with 'lanceolate, pineapple-like leaves arranged in spiral form whence the name screw-pine' (PTT:245); it has numerous stilt roots, wh make it useful as a seaside windbreak, though the leaves provide a 'straw' for handcrafted mats, hats, etc; Pandanus utilis (Pandanaceae).

scrid n (Bdos, Guyn) [IF] A little bit of any-thing; a scrap of food, etc. I wrote it on jus[t] a li[tt]l[e] scrid o[f] paper and I los[t] it.—(Bdos) [Cp EDD screed (also scred) (Sc, Irel, Eng, Nfld) sb 1. 'a shred, fragment, crumb; a long thin strip of material, paper, land, etc']

scrip n (Bdos, Guyn) [IF] A brief, folded note (usu sent without an envelope). She sent the headmaster a scrip to tell him that she was ill and he became annoyed.—Guyn (Ms) [EDD scrip sb[2] Obs (Ken) 'a written document; a letter; a bill']

scrub vb tr (Trin) [IF] **1.** To despise (sb) socially; to remove (sb) from your list of re-spected friends. The people who work the land are the angels of our country, but they are scrubbed socially and looked down at as second class citizens. Working the land seems a retrogressive step for the modern young people.—ExP (73.04.25, p.23) [Prob developed from SE scrub out, scrub away 'to erase, remove permanently'] **2.** PHRASE **2.1 scrub (sb's) back** vb phr (Belz) [IF] To speak disparagingly of (sb). You see her smiling with me? Don['t] mind that. When she gets with her crowd them only scrub me back, eh!—(Belz)

scrub·ber n (Bdos) [Obs ?] A member of a group of men who, accompanied by home-made instruments and guitar and KETTLE-DRUM, wd go from house to house at Christmas time soliciting gifts of food, drink, or money, putting their own words to carol tunes, such as the following: 'Hark the herald angels sing / Open the larder and give me something / Peas and rice and Mount Gay mild / Two rums for a man and one for a child', etc. [Perh from 'scrubbing' a folk-instrument. Cp SCRATCHER. Cp also Black Am use of a wash-board (= CE SCRUBBING-BOARD) as a folk per-cussion instrument] □ Mostly in the pl, scrubbers. Better-known to older folk, but still current seasonally in writing.

scrub·bing-board n (CarA) ‖jooking-board (ECar) A wooden washboard with its end cut to form legs, allowing it to be held firmly in a tub of soaked clothes.

scrub·by [skrʌbi] n (Guyn) [AF] ‖ bat-and-ball CarA [School lang] An impromptu game of cricket or football played among boys who are too few in number to form two teams; such a game played on any convenient piece of ground with any suitable material. [Cp OED scrub sb[2] 5. a. scrub-grass b. U.S. scrub-race, -game 'an impromptu race or game between competitors who have not been trained beforehand']

scrunch·ie-need·le (scrunch·i·neel) n (Bdos) [X] ‖COCHINEAL (CACTUS) (Guyn, etc) [By folk etym, (and/or blend) because of the needle-like spines and spongy flesh < SCRU-SHINEEL < cochineal] □ A familiar error in the examination scripts of rural candidates. See also SCRUSHINEEL.

scrunt[1] vb intr (ECar) [AF] To experience very hard times; to barely eke out a living; to have to beg (for sth). **a.** She saw the world of the unmarried *mother ... having to scrunt for money and being fated with the tragedy of reality ... being forced into demi-prostitution.*—BaW 76/12 **b.** *Dear Santa / Don't get vex but our people really scrunting this year so please Santa don't excite them too much or give them any false hope.*—CrU (75.12.25, p.14) [Cp *EDD* scrunt (Sc, Yks) 2. 'to scratch, scrub. Perh also infl by SE *scrounge*]

scrunt² *n* (ECar) [*AF*] Hard times; a meagre, difficult existence. *Trinidad Students On A Scrunt.*—Bom (H, 74.10.25, p.13) [By functional vb > n shift of SCRUNT¹; but cp also *EDD* scrunt sb¹ 1. 'anything stunted in growth or worn down; a stump']

scrunt·er *n* (ECar) [*AF—Derog*] A down-and-out person; a victim of hard times; sb who is forced into begging. *In other words, Mr Speaker, it is like a scrunter down in the Market Square drawing up his Budget; the scrunter knows that he does not have a cent in his pocket, but he draws up his budget for 1978!*—Gren (Hd, 78.04.28, p.196)

scrush·i·neel ['skrʌʃini·l] *n* (Bdos) [*X*] ‖ C-OCHINEAL (CACTUS) (Guyn, etc) [Erron, prob from folk etym (see note at CRUCHINEEL) + prosthetic /s-/ (cp SKINOP)] □ See also SCRUNCH-IE-NEEDLE.

scud *vb tr* (Antg) [*IF*] PHRASE **scud school** *vb phr* (Antg) [*IF*] ‖ **break biche** (Tbgo, Trin) ‖ **skull school** (Gren, Jmca) To absent yourself from school. [Cp *OED* scud vb¹ 1. 'to dart nimbly from place to place']

scut·tle *n* (USVI) A trap-door for gaining access to a basement or cellar in case of a HURRICANE. [*OED* scuttle sb² 2. 'an opening in a roof, floor, wall etc ... closed with a shutter or lid. Now only US']

sea-bat *n* (Guyn) ‖ DEVIL-FISH (Guyn) [From its resemblance to a giant bat, and the fact that it suddenly leaps some distance out of the water]

sea-bath [si·ba·θ] *n* (CarA) A dip in the sea within your depth (i.e. not a swim); (BrE) a bathe in the sea. *I wonder if the appropriate Minister likes taking a sea bath? 'Cause it's really getting increasingly difficult to find a beach minus the stench of rotting sea-eggs.*—AdN (72.10.14, p.4 'Off The Cuff') □ Cp next.

sea-bath·ing [si·beðɪŋ] *vbl n* (CarA) The act or habit of taking a SEA-BATH. *For Sale / One lot land at Morton Bay, Nevis, few miles from Charlestown. Excellent seabathing.*—DeM(SK) (63.05.18, p.9) □ Both the forms SEA-BATH, SEA-BATHING are listed in *OED* (with cits–'1878), though not in standard desk dictionaries. They are very current in CE, SEA-BATHE vb intr being however rare, usu replaced by **take a sea-bath**. Cp BATH, BATHE in this dictionary.

sea-beef *n* (Bdos, Brbu) The meat of the whale, turtle, a kind of sea-snail, etc. □ The term wd have a specific reference according to what form of sea life it is most often obtained from, in a particular island community.

sea-cat *n* (ECar) ‖ *sea-puss* (Jmca) A small, edible variety of octopus.

sea-cow *n* (CarA) ‖ MANATEE (CarA) [A ref to its bulky body]

sea-dam *n* (Guyn) A wide dam built on the bank of a river or at the seashore to prevent flooding. *The children were playing on the sea-dam and went home all muddy.*—Guyn (Ms) □ This item is in common use esp in the rural, coastal areas of *Guyn* wh are below sea-level.

sea-de·fence /1′12/ *n* (Guyn) The system of dams, water-locks, KOKERS, etc wh is devised to prevent the flooding or destruction by the sea of the agricultural coastland of Guyana, much of which is below sea-level.

sea-egg *n* (Bdos, Gren) **1.*** The white SEA-URCHIN, the roe of wh is a prized delicacy, esp in Barbados; *Tripneustes sphoera* or *Echinus s.* (*Echinoidea*). [*Sea*, fr its marine origin + *egg*, in ref to 'roe'] □ See COBBLER, R-MONTHS. In some places (ex *Belz*) the name SEA-EGG is applied to the COBBLER as well. **2.** PHRASE **2.1 pick sea-eggs** *vb phr* (Bdos) [Fishing Ind] **(i)** To collect SEA-EGGS commercially by detaching them from the sea-bed or coral reef. *Government might be forced to curtail the picking of sea-eggs for two years beginning from next year. / This action is being taken to save the industry in light of the declining stock of sea-eggs, experienced during the last six to eight years.*—AdV (86.09.03, p.1) **(ii)** To separate the roe from the shells for sale.

sea-grape *n* (CarA) ‖ SEASIDE-GRAPE (CarA)

seam [si·m] *vb* (Trin) To mark off the discrete note areas in making a PAN for a STEELBAND, by using a hammer and cold chisel to dent or score the lines in the surface radiating from the centre to the rim; the PAN is then said to be *seamed*. *Rubber-tipped sticks and the 'seamed pan' were introduced by pioneer panman, Ellie Manette, and by 1950 the first island-wide steelband competition was held.*—CaC (77/7, p.9)

sea-moss *n* (CarA) ‖ *Irish moss* (Jmca) ‖ *sea-weed* (Belz) A variety of seaweed wh, when cleaned, dried, and boiled, yields a gelatinous cream-coloured liquid wh is sweetened and flavoured as a health drink, esp for children; the drink, called by the same name, is also believed to increase male virility.

sea-puss *n* (Jmca) ‖ SEA-CAT (ECar) [Note that PUSS is more commonly used than *cat* in *Jmca* folk speech. The last syllable of *octopus* wd have reinforced this compound]

sea·side-dove *n* (Gren) ‖ GROUND-DOVE 2. (CarA)

sea·side-grape* *n* (CarA) ‖ *grape* (Bdos, CayI, Guyn, Jmca) ‖ *sea-grape* (CarA) A small, round fruit wh is purple when ripe, with scant, acid-sweet flesh on a hard seed; it is borne in hanging clusters on a sturdy, shady seaside tree with round, leathery leaves; *Coccoloba uvifera* (*Polygonaceae*). [From the resemblance of the hanging clusters to those of the European grape]

sea·side-hi·bis·cus *n* (USVI) ‖ SEASIDE-MAHOE (Bdos, etc)

sea·side-ma·hoe* *n* (Bdos, Guyn, Jmca) ‖ *haiti-haiti* (USVI) ‖ *maho(e)* (CarA) ‖ *sea-side-hibiscus* (USVI One of two varieties of a bushy, spreading tree, often over 30 ft tall, with a small trunk, large, heart-shaped leaves and yellow bell-shaped flowers strongly resembling the hibiscus; it has a tough, fibrous bark and grows well on sea-coasts; it is popular in some places as a decorative, shade tree wh is trimmed to shape; *Thespesia populnea* or *Hibiscus tiliaceus* (*Malvaceae*). □ In botanical literature the tree is found by several other names: *anodyne, beach maho, portia tree, sea hibiscus, Spanish cork, tulip tree*, etc.

sea·side-yam *n* (Bdos) ‖ *ipomea* (CarA) [Prob from resemblance of the purple flower to that of the yam plant]

sea·son·ed rice /1′12/ *n phr* (Antg, Jmca) ‖ COOK-UP 1. (CarA)

sea·son·ing ['si·znɪŋ] /1′2/ *n* (Bdos, Guyn) [*IF*] ‖ ESCHALLOT (Bdos, Guyn) ... *with a little bed of seasoning planted on the shady side of the house.*— Bdos (Ms) □ Distinguish from pres. part. vb *seasoning* /2′1/.

sea-thyme *n* (Baha) ‖ BAY-GERANIUM (Baha) □ This name used on Eleuthera Is. (*Baha*), *bay-geranium* in Nassau.

sea-trout *n* (Guyn) A larger variety of, and sometimes a commercially used name for the BANGA-MARY; *Cynoscion virescenes.*

sea-ur·chin *n* (CarA) One of two varieties of a type of reef-dwelling shell-fish with a round body about 3 ins in diameter, covered in needle-like toxic spines that can exceed 10 ins in length; the white variety, also called SEA-EGG, is semi-spherical and the flesh edible; the black sea-urchin, also called the COBBLER, is flattish and inedible; *Echinoidea spp.*

sea-wall *n* (Guyn) A wall, from 10 to 20 ft thick and 5 or 6 ft high, made of mortar-bound boulders or reinforced concrete, to protect a low-lying coast from the sea at high tides; [by extension] that part of it used as a promenade esp in Georgetown. *The military march 'Pomp and Circumstance' by Elgar will open the Police Band concert on the Sea Wall this afternoon.*— GyG (70.01.10, p.10)

sea-wap *n* (StVn) A large species of porpoise whose fatty flesh yields oil.

sea-weed *n* (Belz) ‖ SEA-MOSS (CarA) *You are what you eat—or for that matter what you drink, and so daily, hundreds of Belizeans, especially men folk, include a pint of sea-weed in their diet.*— BeA(BE) (80.03.15, p.11)

sea-win·dow *n* (Bdos) An area of seashore kept free from construction or building of any kind in order to permit good, public views of the sea. *Wilkinson's body was discovered on an open spot of ground on the land side of the sea window of Welches Road.*—SuS (85.12.22, p.1)

se·bu·can (say·bu·can) [sebu'kan] /112′/ *n* (Trin) 1. ‖ MATAPEE (Guyn) *Cassava bread ... is made by grating fresh cassava which is afterwards strained through a 'sebucan', an Amerindian strainer of basket work.*—TPOT:38 2. An Amerindian maypole dance wh has been preserved at the folk level in the Carib-Hispanic communities of Trinidad. *There are no traditional masques such as found in the Trinidad Carnival, but a group of female fishvendors danced the 'plait-the-ribbon' or maypole dance (in Trinidad called sebucan) for the Coronation Carnival.*—Caq 4.2, p.113 (D.J. Crowley) [Perh a Carib word. The ref in both senses is to weaving or a woven pattern]

seck (sèk) *n* (Gren) See SÈK

sec·ond crop *n phr* (Guyn) [Sugar Ind; Rice Ind] ‖ AUTUMN-CROP (Guyn) [So called as being the later of the two crops, in each industry in Guyana, the earlier being the 'first crop']

sec·ond depth *n phr* (Guyn) [Sugar Ind] See cit. *Plantations were limited to 500 acres in area, 250 acres being granted in the first instance with an extension of another 250 acres out of the second depth when two-thirds of the former had been cultivated. / Second depth was the description given to the additional lands having a common boundary with the original grant and extending further inwards.*—RLLG:196

sec·ond gang *n phr* (Bdos) See GANG (cit and Note)

sec·ond-pan(s) *n* (*pl*) (Trin) ‖ DOUBLE-SECONDS (Trin) *Often we went down with him to the steelband shed where Santa Clara Syncos practised, and sometimes he beat a second-pan.*—HCCM:14

se·cret-fig *n* (Gren) ‖ SIKYÉ-FIG (Trin) [From the Fr *sucrier* 'sugar' adj, by folk etym]

see *vb* (CarA) 1. *vb intr* To be able, by supernatural gift or ritualistic practices, to discover or foretell the cause of sb's troubles and give remedial advice. *What about Mrs Clive, the sugar lady who they say can 'see'? ... She say she could 'see' so much and she coulden see death coming?* □ See SEE-FAR MAN. **2.** *vb tr* [In a market or shop] To look at and buy (sth); to receive, obtain (sth) in your hand intending to buy (it). **a.** *Seller: See dese nice limes he*[re]*!*—(Guyn) **b.** *Le*[t] *me see a packet o*[f] *cigarette de*[re].—(Trin) **3.** PHRASES *vb phrs* **3.1 (as/where) you see me/her (etc), here/there** *id phr* (CarA) [*IF/AF*] [Esp of the emotions or bodily condition] Although I/she (etc) may not look it; though my/her (etc) appearance may not show it. **a.** *My dear, I can*[*t*] *make it today. I'm in a lot o*[f] *pain, as you see me here.*—(Antg) **b.** *She's a wicked something you see her there.*—MTCP:32 [A prob calque from W Afr langs. The type of phr *as you de see am there* is common in similar contexts in WAPE. Cp also Edo *Ẹ i rin ubian ọuban rhọkpa; ọ hio gbe, ubene u mie ọrẹn nii* 'He will not beg anyone; he [is] very proud, as you see him there'. (Dr A. Amayo—U/Ibadan)] **3.2 (can) see with (sb)** *vb phr* (CarA) [*IF*] To (be able to) accept sb's point of view; to (find yourself to) be in agreement with (sb). *He doesn't like Ignatius as a husband for me, but when I told him that I'm aware how weak Ignatius is and that my idea in marrying him is to keep the blood intact and to carry on the name in Berbice, he said that he could see with me.*—MCK:158 [Attested also in Gullah (J. Roy) and IrE (L. Todd)] **3.3 go and see** *id phr* (Gren) [*AF*] See GO Phr 6.11 **3.4 see about (sb/sth)** *vb phr* (CarA) [*IF*] To take care of; to look after; to provide support for. *Lefthander wasn't working nowhere and had this woman making a child for him to see about.*—LDCD:49 **3.5 see foot** *vb phr* (Guyn) [*AF*] See FOOT Phr 2.13 **3.6 see for yourself** *vb phr* (Bdos, Trin) **(i)** To look after your own interests instead of depending on others to do so. **(ii)** [By extension] [*Derog*] To help yourself to other people's property, esp materials belonging to the Government or State. *Moreover, Barbadians have become hardened to the thieving that has been euphemistically termed 'seeing for yourself' and the tales of materials transported from Government projects to build private structures are legion.*— AdN (83.01.06, p.4) **3.7 see France/hell/your days/your nennen/your skin/your tail** *vb phrs* (CarA) [*AF—Joc*] To experience great hardship; to suffer greatly while striving to succeed. **a.** *If you in the poor-ward in this hospital, I tell you, you see France!*—(StVn) **b.** *Where you going? Town? Dollar! ... you know is after eleven already? Dollar or you see your tail till morning.*—HFGA:57 (D. Samaroo) See similar phrs headed CATCH Phr 8.6; also HELL Phrs 2.1, 4. **3.8 See it/me/sb/sth here/there!** *id phrs* (CarA) [*IF*] ‖ *Look it/(etc) here!* (CarA) See LOOK Phr 4.5 Here/there it is!; Here/there am I!; etc. *Here is where we began. I even wrote down the date. See it here. Second of August.*—TRIH:73 **b.** *I am of the opinion that the duppy on this occasion was a 'he', since one afternoon my mother and I were together with my grandfather in his room, when he started pointing to the China cabinet glass. 'See him there,' he kept saying. 'You don't see a man with a little*

beard and him clear?'—WeS (73.12.07, p.18) [A prob calque from W Afr langs. Cp Mampruli (a Gur lang) *n-nya ma (Behold me)* 'Here I am'—*DLOG:24.* See also etym note at LOOK Phr 4.5. In Fr Cr speaking territories substratum infl of Fr *Me/le,* etc *voici!/voilà!* may have helped reinforce this particular structure] **3.9 see ning-ning** *vb phr* (Guyn) [*AF*] See NING-NING[1] Phr 2.1 **3.10 see your health** *vb phr* (Gren, Guyn, Jmca, StKt, Trin) To menstruate. *The worry began when Ella started to see her health. ... It worried her that some little boy's curiosity would one day get the better of him and ... that Ella would come home with ... something in her belly.*—BM:48 **3.11 see your royal** *vb phr* (ECar) [*AF*] See ROYAL Phr 4.2 **3.12 see your way** *vb phr* (Bdos, Gren, Guyn) [*IF*] To be successful; to prosper. *'This world is like hell,' repeated Mr Reggie, standing and holding his forehands in his hands behind his back. 'I labour so hard, yet I can't see my way. It's just as cheap I leave the land abandoned.'*— STTG:55 [< SE *see the way clear* 'to feel able', with some shift in sense] **3.12.1 see your way to (do sth)** *vb phr* (Bdos, Gren, Guyn) [*IF*] To manage to (do sth); to find the means, be in a position to (do sth). *Now, you have a big-able piece of land out there and all I asking is that you keep the pig for me till I can see me way to get a house and build a pen for it.*—CISH:95 [By extension of the prec] **3.13 when you see so** *id phr* (Gren, Guyn, Tbgo) [*IF*] It must be assumed in such circumstances. *These last few days have been cloudy and still and hot—we're in for a long spell of dry weather when you see so.*—(Guyn) [Cp Yoruba *bi o se ri yen* 'as you see that', used in similar contexts—(pers info, A. Banjo)] **3.14 where you see me/him (etc) here/there** *id phr* (CarA) [*IF/AF*] See Phr 3.1 above. **3.15 You see you?** *id phr* (ECar) [*AF/IF*] See YOU[1] Phr 7.

seed *n* PHRASE **from seed to seed** *adv phr* (Bdos) [Of land holding] (That is to be passed on unsold and undivided) from generation to generation. *The owner ... may be somebody in New York, an eighteenth cousin or something like that, and as the people in the country say, the land was left from seed to seed, but it does not really belong to the fellow who has the chattel house and he does not want to put up anything too elaborate because the cousin may come back from America and give him notice.*—Bdos (Hd, 73.03.20, p.1999) [< *seed* (in biblical sense) 'descendants'] □ The phr is used by older folk and the practice is now obsolete. See FAMILY-LAND (*Bdos*, etc).

seed-un·der-leaf *n* (StVn, Tbgo, Trin) ‖ GWENN-ANBA-FÈY (Dmca, etc)

see-far man/wom·an *n phr* (Guyn) ‖ *seer-man/woman* (BrVi, Gren, Trin) **1.** A person who is believed to be able to see into sb's troubles or future and give remedial advice. □ Cp SEE 1. *vb intr.* Cp also similar idea in SE (< Fr) *clairvoyant.* **2.** [By extension] ‖ OBEAH-MAN/-WOMAN (CarA)

Seen! *excl* (CarA) [Expressing approval] *The outfit was dramatic for days and when she came down King's House steps, you could hear the gasps of appreciation. Seen!*—WeG (73.07.11, p.13, Partyline) [Prob an erron rendering of Rastaf SCENE!] See SCENE 3.

seer-man/-wom·an [siɒ(r)-ma·n/wumən] *n* (BrVi, Gren, Trin) ‖ SEE-FAR MAN (Guyn) **a.** *Some of the area's older residents, however, have claimed that since then unknown persons have dug up the treasure with the aid of a 'seer man', a man from Haiti who practises Voodoo.*—Vgi I.3 (1975), p.29 **b.** *In fact, it is alleged that a 'Seer Woman' was contacted in an effort to locate the lost child. The woman is reported to have said that the child is under a bridge and that a tall dark man is responsible.*—ToR (76.06.02, p.3) □ Sometimes *seer*, without suffix. Note similar extended sense of SE *seer*, though the CE pronunc, emphasizing rather the agent suff -ER, is hardly diphthongized as in SE.

see-see bird *n phr* (Gren) ‖ BANANAQUIT (CarA) *Bananaquit's eyes were as keen as her name, 'See-See Bird'. She missed nothing and saw all the happenings of the afternoon in one glance. She was mostly black with a yellowish colour on her chest. Her small black eyes shone with excitement.*—STTG:11 [Prob from the sound it makes]

seh[1] [sɛ] *vb tr* (CarA) [AF—Cr] Say. *'Cho!' Brudda Crane seh. 'I tink I heard me name.'*—WFSFB:31 (P. Gillet) □ This spelling is often used in narrative writing to represent the folk pronunc, perh influenced by next.

seh[2] [sɛ] *conn particle* (CarA) [AF—Cr] ‖ SAY[3] (CarA) *But you and me know seh time so hard we don't have no inclination fe strum nuh guitar and flash the pretty white teeth.*—WeG (75.04.15, p.15) □ This spelling is much used in narrative writing to distinguish the function of this particle in folk usage.

seine *n* (CarA) See CAST-NET (CarA)

sèk (seck) *n* (Dmca, Gren) ‖ *roller* (StVn) A metal ring, made from a barrel-hoop, about 6 ins to 12 ins in diameter and about an inch deep wh, placed in a COPPER, is used to give BAMBAM or CASSAVA-BREAD its round shape. [Fr Cr < Fr *cercle*, 'circle']

self [sɛ(l)f] *emphasizer* (CarA) [AF—Cr] **A.** (Post-posed) [In this function partly influenced by SE co-referential pron -*self* forms, although the orig CE source is prob IrE. See etym note below] **1.** [Emphasizing identity of preceding pron or n (phr)] Myself, etc ..., themselves. **a.** *I self didn't know if I was to clap or not.*—CrU (76.11.10, p.7) **b.** *He self must be ga the pig shut up in he yard.*—PKKK:67 **c.** *If ah din' have dis heavy load of fish on me back tonight ah woulda' pick it up self, self!*—PSFC:35 **d.** *And water was coming outta Enid eyes like Niagara Falls*

self.—CWFYS:30 **e.** *'You all didn't know,' she said. 'It was the stories self you were saying that made me stay.'*—SBBAM:88 **2.** [Emphasizing quality of a prec adj (phr)] Absolutely. **a.** *Dis time, look how de jumbie eye red, red self.*—(Guyn) **b.** *The Jamaican ladies had never approved of my mother, 'because she pretty like pretty self'* *Christophine said.*—RWSS:15 **3.** [Intensifying a prec adv (phr)] Indeed; for a certainty; definitely. **a.** *'And who's your Daddy?' / 'You!' / He smiled. 'Me? I'm not your Daddy!' / 'Yes! You self!'*—SDD:11 **b.** *'I'll get the house despite you!' she cried against his loud laugh. 'I'll buy it yet.' / 'Why not?' He shrugged. 'You can buy it to-morrow-self.'*—MBGB:111 **c.** *Ah, sahib. Why I should make joke with you, eh? You want me call Leela here self, and you could ask she?*—NTMM:30 **d.** *In fact self who know is you fowl? How we know is not some skew you putting on?*—RTCS:19 **4.** [Passing into adv function, often in neg contexts] (Not) ... even; even ... ;(not) at all. **a.** *He'n giving people chance to say no self. Brap! brap! he write me and say he want to married me.*—RTCS:9 **b.** *He can't even fight self.*—(Trin) **c.** *Beating her self wouldn't make her behave better.*—(Guyn) [Prob spread in the early development of CE (17C) through the infl of Irish bond-servants. Note the following: The word 'itself' is used in a curious way in Ireland ... it is not in fact a pronoun at all, but a substitute for the word 'even'. This has arisen from the fact that in the common colloquial Irish language the usual word to express both 'even' and 'itself', is *féin*; and in translating a sentence containing this word *féin*, the people rather avoided 'even', a word not very familiar to them in this sense, and substituted the better known 'itself', in cases where 'even' would be the correct word, and 'itself' would be incorrect. Thus *da mbeith an meud sin féin agum* is correctly rendered 'if I had even that much': but the people don't like 'even', and don't well understand it (as applied here), so they make it 'if I had that much itself.' This explains all such Anglo-Irish sayings as 'If I got it itself it would be of no use to me' i.e. 'even if I got it'; 'If she were there itself I wouldn't know her'; 'She wouldn't go to bed till you'd come home, and if she did itself she couldn't sleep.' (Knocknagow)—*JESI:37*] □ These usages wh proliferate mostly in uneducated speech, occur sometimes in written schoolwork and personal letters. In sense 4 it is sometimes redundant occurring in phrs such as *even self if, self self*. **B.** (Pre-posed) [In attrib function, carrying the sense of A. 1. above] **1.** *adj* (Guyn, Jmca, Trin) [Prec by 'the'] Selfsame; very. **a.** *Is the self minister gave me that form.*—Guyn (Ms, 1978) **b.** *Butts: Man lend de cap'n your knife and stop grumbling. Is dat self pan what go win de competition tonight oui.*—HPP:6 [Cp *OED self* A. 1. b. Preceding the sb *arch, rare* + 18C, 19C cits 'the self deed', 'the self act'] **C.** PHRASES **1. the self said (ones, etc)** *pron phr; adj phr* (Bdos, Guyn) [Absolute or in attrib function] The very same. *And he explain how on Judgement Day the self said spirits that these evil people calling to work obeah 'pon they own brethren going ketch* *them all up and drag them to the lake that burneth with fire and brimstone.*—CISH:119 **[**A redundant form of B. 1., for greater emphasis**] 2. You/he/she/they self (too)!** /ʒˈ21/ *id phr* (CarA) [*AF*] See TOO Phr 7.4 *But Muriel yo[u] can['t] expec[t] de chil[d] to do all dose t[h]ings an[d] still go to school in time! I[t']s only a li[tt]l[e] chil[d] after all. Ow! You self too!*—(Guyn) □ Often reduced to **You/(etc) self!** or **You/ (etc) too!** with same emotive pitch contrast.

self·op·in·i·a·ted [sɛlf-opiniétid] *adj* (Guyn, Trin) [*X*] Self-opinionated. **[**Prob a syncopic reduction of SE original**]**

sem *n* (Trin) ‖ BONAVIST (CarA) **[**Cp SAEME 2. prob pronounced in *Trin* with a shorter vowel /sem/**]**

sem·i-con·tract* [se·men·con·tra bush] *n (phr)* (Gren, Jmca) ‖ **simé-kontwa** (Dmca) ‖ **worm-bush/-weed** (Dmca, Gren, Jmca) A strong-smelling, bushy weed about 2 ft tall, bearing spikes of greenish or (in some varieties) yellowish flowers; it flourishes in open, waste ground and is widely used as a folk-remedy for worms and some intestinal troubles in young children, overdoses sometimes causing death; *Chenopodium ambrosioides* (*Chenopodiaceae*). **[** < *semen contra*, identified in *SDGA* as the name of a folk med herb of another type, widely known in Central Am. It is perh orig a Latin taxonomic label (= seed + antidote) rather than Sp, spreading in this form, infl by folk etym, in the *CarA* because of its medicinal use (cp SEMPERVIVE)**]** □ The folk form SEMI-CONTRACT appears to have replaced the learned form SEMENCONTRA (BUSH) esp in *Jmca* writings on medicinal herbs.

se·mi·tu (si·mi·too) [sɛmitʊ ~ simitʊ] *n* (Guyn) ‖ BELL-APPLE (Guyn, etc) **[***BAED* Arawak *semetho* 'a vine that bears ... a type of granadilla'**]**

semp* [sɛmp] *n* (Trin) A bird about 4-1/2 ins long, the male having a violet-blue back with golden-yellow belly and the female generally greenish; it is a popular cage-bird, most prized for its variety of musical notes; *Euphonia violacea* or *E. musica* (*Thraupidae*). **[**Fr Cr < Fr *simple* 'simple', prob because it is easily trapped**]**

sem·per·vi·ve (si·em·pre·vi·vi, sim- ·pre·vi·vy) [sɛmpʌvaivi ~ simpərvaivi] *n* (Angu, Jmca, USVI) ‖ ALOES (CarA) **[** < *sempervive* (also *semper-vivens*, *sempervivum*) 'ever-living', Obs. Latin SE names (listed in these three forms in *OED* + cits covering 1625–1882) < *Sempervivum tectorum*, botanical name of a genus of rock-garden plant with fleshy, succulent leaves (esp the 'houseleek') used also as a purgative. The name was prob transferred to the ALOES in the *CarA* because of the many resemblances in characteristics, and wide folk use**]** □ Many changes in pronunc occur in different territories, by folk etym. See SIMPAWIRIE, SIMPLE-BIBLE, SINGLE-BIBLE, SINKAWIVY and variants given for

each of them. The form SEMPERVIVE is perh the most commonly found in educated writing.

send *vb tr* **1.** (Bdos, Dmca, Tbgo, Trin) [*IF*] To pass or throw (sth to sb); to drop (sth down to sb). **a.** *If you did send de ball instead o[f] keepin[g] it dribblin[g] we might [h]a[ve] scored a goal.*—(Bdos) **b.** *His teeth sank into the pulpy fruit ... on the ground his two friends were looking up and feeling already the water coming into their mouths. 'Send one for me,' said Tom.*—SDD: 43 **2. PHRASES 2.1 every day/night (as) God send[s]** *id phr* (Bdos, Guyn) See GOD[1] PHR 2. *And every week God sent I was down to the Labor Office asking them for him. Today and all I went.*—MTCP:27 **2.2 send (sb) off** *vb phr* (CarA) [*IF*] To cause (sb) to go mad, become insane. *The way the young people behave nowadays is enough to send you off.*—(Bdos) **2.3 send sth for (sb)** *vb phr* (Gren) [*AF*] To set an evil spell on (sb). *She head ain['t] good. Like somebody sen[d] a spirit for her.*—(Gren) **2.4 send the daylight out of (sb/an animal)** *vb phr* (Trin) [*AF*] To beat (sb) severely; to hit (an animal) hard enough to kill. *I just nearly send the daylight out of that dam chicken. Don't leh me see another chicken in here. I want no fowl and nobody in this kitchen. Remember!*—NAGOS:67 **2.5 send your heart through your mouth** *vb phr* (Guyn) [*IF*] See HEART Phr 6.

se·ne·bone (cin·ne·bone) [ˈsɛnɛboˑn ~ sinɛboˑn] *n* (Guyn) ‖ STRING-BEAN (CarA)

sé·né·ma·won [ˈsene-mawɔ̃] *n* (StLu) ‖ CH-RISTMAS-CANDLE (Bdos, etc)

sen·say(-cos·tume) *n* (Dmca) A CARNIVAL costume worn by men, and consisting of frayed rope cascading from head to foot with a bull-horned mask on the head. *Many of the costumes were altered from those used in tribal festivals of Central African kingdoms. The sensay outfits with cow horns were the most obvious. Rope sensay, pai fig, cloth and paper sensay were worn by the notorious bande mauvais who clashed in great street battles either with each other or with the police.*—HTDS:95 **[**From resemblance to SENSEH(-fowl)**]** □ See also PAY-BANNANN

sense *n* (CarA) **1.** Common sense; mature awareness. **2. PHRASES 2.1 get sense** *vb phr* (CarA) [*IF*] See GET Phr 3.19 **2.2 learn sense** *vb phr* (CarA) [*IF*] See LEARN[1] Phr 3.

sen·seh fowl (sen·sa(y)-fowl) [sɛnsɛ fʊl] *n phr* (CarA) ‖ **frizzle-fowl** (Bdos, Gren, Guyn, Tbgo, Trin) ‖ **frizzly fowl** (Angu, BrVi) ‖ **sh-enshay fowl** (Nevs) A variety of chicken that has its feathers curled backwards, and sometimes also has no feathers on its neck (= BARE-NECK FOWL), this latter kind being often associated with OBEAH. **[***DAFL* Twi *asɛnsɛ* 'a hen without a tail' (a fowl with curled ruffled feathers) + cit 'If somebody is taken ill, this misfortune is 'removed' by sacrificing a tailless hen'**]**

sen·si·ble weed *n phr* (Belz) ‖ SENSITIVE PLANT (Bdos, etc)

sen·si·tive plant* *n phr* (Bdos, Gren, Guyn, Tbgo, Trin, USVI) ‖ *grichi-grichi* (USVI) ‖ *mézé-mawi* (Dmca, Trin) ‖ *sensible weed* (Belz) ‖ *shame-baby* (Guyn) ‖ *shame-bush* (Guyn, Trin) ‖ *shame-lady/-weed* (Jmca) ‖ *ti-marie* (Trin) A sprawling weed with strong and slightly prickly, greenish-mauve stems and little, round-headed, pink flowers, esp noted for the closing up of its compound leaves at the slightest touch (hence its name); it is a persistent herb but is used in some places as a folk-medicine for stomach disorders; *Mimosa pudica* (*Mimosaceae*).

sen·ti·ment *n* (Gren) [*IF*] (Dmca, Gren, StLu) [*IF*] Self-respect; pride. *But Cut'bert youself stu-pid oui! You ent have sentiment. You'n hear de woman say she ent want you?*—RTCS:15 [A sur-facing, with E pronunc, of a loan via Fr Cr < Fr *sentiment* 'feeling; sensibility' (basically), but with a strong notion of 'respect for sb' wh is still dominant in Mod Fr letter-ending formulae '(l'expression de) mes sentiments distingués' (= ... yours faithfully), etc] □ The term occurs mostly in neg contexts '*have no sentiment*', etc.

sen·ti·nel *n* (Angu) ‖ ADAM'S NEEDLE (CarA) [From this plant's erectness]

sen·try-plant *n* (Bdos) See CENTURY-PLANT (CarA)

Sep·a·ra·tion-No·tice *n phr* (Gren, StKt) ‖ *General Notice* (Jmca) ‖ *Personal Notice* (Bdos) ‖ *Wife Notice* (Guyn) A short notice published in the newspaper by a husband or wife declaring that the spouse has left the legal household, disclaiming responsibility for that spouse's outside debts, and sometimes claiming that his/her financial accountability to the house-hold still stands.

Ser·a·phi·na *n* (StLu) ‖ STILT-MAN (ECar) *And Seraphina of St Lucia and Mother Sally of Guy-ana, who wear 10-foot stilts during the Christmas Day parade through the streets, have a definite 'share-the-wealth' function by taking up collections from the second-floor balconies, since traditionally only the well-to-do could afford second stories on their homes.*—AdN (72.12.24, A. Hughes)

ser·geant-ma·jor *n* (Baha, Jmca, StLu) ‖ *pi-lot-fish* (Jmca) A fish about 4 to 6 ins in length, with five vertical black bars on its yellow body (hence the name); it swarms around docks and in coral reefs and is of good food value; *Abudefdul saxatilis*.

ser·pent *n* 1. [sarpɪnt ~ ˈsᴀpᴧnt] (Gren) ‖ TREE BOA (Gren) 2. (StLu) ‖ FER-DE-LANCE (StLu) *Serpents are reported to grow as long as seven feet but the average snake is about three to four feet long. (In St Lucia, the term 'serpent' refers only to the fer-de-lance).*—LST:28 □ The term in CE is almost restricted to the serpent of the Book of Genesis; otherwise 'snake' is almost exclusively used whether referring to a reptile or meta-phorically. However the exceptions are *Gren* and *StLu* where the term is synonymous, in each case, with a particular snake.

ser·see (ser·sey) *n* (Bdos) See CIRCE(E) BUSH

service of song(s) *n phr* (Bdos) A concert of sacred music and recitations held at sb's home or a small community centre, usu with a sequence of food and drink and sometimes a dance; it was formerly popular during festive periods as a means of raising funds.

set[1] *vb* 1. *intr* (Tbgo) [*IF*] [Of persons] [Usu neg] To get along well together; to see eye to eye with another. *If you intend to behave so funny, you and I won't set.*—(Tbgo) [Perh infl by SE idiom *can(not) set horses* 'can(not) work har-moniously together'] 2. PHRASES 2.1 **set down** *vb phr* (Baha) [*AF*—*Cr*] To sit down. *Den er-rybuddy set down an de big bizness begin, yeah man.*—JBJ:82 [Cp *OED set* 143. *set down*, I., *dial* (b) 'to be seated' + cits–'1815; (c) 'to sit down' + cits–'1809] 2.2 **set foot for (a place)** *vb phr* (Trin) To set out for (a destination). *A devout Hindu, Ramphal a vegetarian began mak-ing his fortune almost immediately he set foot for Trinidad. He worked as a cook in the kitchen of the steam boat 'Ganges' that brought him in 1906.*—ExP (72.11.05) 2.3 **set for sb** *vb phr* (Guyn, Tbgo, Trin) [*IF*] To be or get ready to attack or quarrel violently with sb. *Let him come in here late with another cock-and-bull story. I am setting for him.*—(Guyn) 2.3.1 **set (sth) for sb** *vb phr* (CarA) [*IF*] [Of OBEAH] To put (sth) evil in the path or way of sb. See Phrs 2.5, 2.7 below. 2.4 **set fruit/a cake** *vb phr* (CarA) To soak currants, raisins, seeded prunes and other cut or crushed dried fruit in a mixture of strong rum and wine over a period of many days, so pre-paring the major ingredient in making BLACK CAKE. 2.5 **set guzu on sb** *vb phr* (Belz, Jmca) See GUZU Phr 2.6 **set jumbie on (sb)** *vb phr* (CarA). See JUMBIE Phr 2.3. 2.7 **set obeah on/ for sb** *vb phr* (CarA) See OBEAH[1] Phr 3.2 2.8 **set up**[1] *vb phr* (i) (CarA) [Of rain] To threaten; to be surely about to come down. *See the rain how it set up, run quick and take in the clothes.*—(Jmca) (ii) (Baha, Jmca) [*AF*—*Cr*] To sit up till late in the night. [Cp SET DOWN Phr 2.1] (iii) (Jmca) [By extension] To keep an all-night vigil on the first and ninth nights after sb's death. 2.8.1 **set (up) your face** *vb phr* (Antg, Bdos, Nevs, Trin) [*AF/IF*] See FACE Phr 6. **a.** *They t'ink is a shame to eat wid their hand, and they settin' up their face when they see Indian food.*—KJB:110 **b.** *I remember I heckled the Bank Man-ager. The Bank Manager was a little afraid; the Prime Minister set up his face and so on, and I gather that that Bank backed off the Government a little bit.*—Bdos (Hd, 73.06.19, p.2394) [An extension of sense 2.8(i) above. Some speakers add *like rain* to this Phr]

set² *n* **1.** (CarA) [*AF/IF*] A great amount (of) *The husband died and left her in a set of trouble*—(Guyn) **2.** (CarA) [*AF/IF*] [By extension, of persons] A pack; a gang; a big group. **a.** *They are a set of drug-ridden rascals in that area.*—(Bdos) **b.** *We uses to live on a sugar-cane estate name La Romain, and this crop season we was cutting the cane and carting it to the sugar factory. Was a set of Indians living on the estate, and all of we was labourers.*—SWOS:82 [Cp IrE '*Set*: used in a bad sense, like gang and crew—They're a dirty set'—*JESI:319*] **3.** (Guyn, Trin) A number of dances in sequence with one partner. *This time, all they want is to make a pass at the girl an make you look stupid. Before you even order a drink they asking her for a set! An man, if they only get her on the dance-floor, you perish!*—RSMCD:46 [Perh by semantic shift from *OED* set sb² 14. 'the series of movements or figures that make up ... a quadrille; the music to this + cits-'1894; also *set* ppl, adj 8. ... set dance a quadrille, ...] **4.** (Jmca) See SET-GIRLS **5.** (Baha) An item or arrangement of items made up by an OBEAH-MAN/-WOMAN to affect sb's health, behaviour, or fortune. *For example, a common method of 'fixing' one's enemy is to collect grave dirt at midnight, get the Obeah man or woman to place a set, add the grave dirt and bury all this in front of the victim's house. When the victim steps over the 'set', he gets fixed, and either a physical or mental symptom (or both) will occur.*—MTTBT:118 **6.** PHRASES **6.1 one/a whole/a damned set (of)** *n phrs* (CarA) [*AF/IF(Derog)*] [Emotive extension of sense 1] An awful lot/pack (of) '*Ma,' she call out, 'you had me in one set of confusion this morning. You left with the key to the cupboard.*'—STLL:66

Set-Girls *n pl* (Jmca) A group of dancing girls identically dressed in elegant costumes, now forming part of the JUNKANOO parade; the practice dates back to the slave era (see cit). **a.** *Each 'set' consisted of a group of girls who would be dressed identically and elaborately in the same colour. Thus, each set would be known as the 'Yellow Set', 'Blue Set', etc. The girls apparently also grouped themselves according to 'shade' of skin. In their lavish clothing, they would parade the streets singing and dancing and trying generally to outdo each other. These sets have been cited as early as 1776.*—SAZJ:144 **b.** *In time, the Set Girls became part of the elaborate Christmas carnival subsumed under Jonkonnu.*—SAZJ:145

set·ting-hen /1'12/ *n* (Gren, Guyn) **1.** A hen that has been set on eggs to hatch them. **2.** [By extension] A fretful, touchy or unsettled person. [Cp *OED* setting ppl a. 3. 'of a hen: sitting. Now dial' + cits-'1879]

set·ting-up *n* (Baha) ‖SET-UP² (Jmca)

set·tle *vb tr* (CarA) To reduce to silence or obedience (by punishment). *Wait till I come, nuh? I go[i]n[g] settle you good. (= Just wait until I come. I will teach you to obey).*—(Guyn) [Cp *EDD* settle v¹ 1. 'to determine a quarrel; to

reduce to silence, esp by severe treatment; to kill' + cits from Sc, Yks] □ Also common US colloq idiom: *settle (sb's) hash* 'straighten (sb) out once and for all'—(pers info, L. Urdang).

set·tle·ment *n* (Baha, Gren, TkCa) A small, isolated community provided with basic communication and medical facilities serviced by the Government. *These are four settlements; Bottle Creek, Kew, Witby and Sandy Point. The first three are connected by a spine road which continues to Bellfield Landing. Bottle Creek is the largest settlement with a very loose structure. The houses are strung out along three miles of road but there are the beginnings of a centre containing churches, a school and government buildings. Kew is a much smaller settlement laid out fairly compactly on a gridiron pattern. There is a school and two churches. Sandy Point and Whitby consist of a few houses mainly occupied by fishermen and have few community facilities.*—PTCI:12 [Cp *DAE* AmE settlement 2.(2) 'a place where a settler or settlers have established themselves; a village or town']

Set·tle·ment Day *n phr* (Belz) [Hist] A public holiday celebrated on November 19 to commemorate the coming of the first Caribs to Belize. See GARIFUNA SETTLEMENT DAY

set-up² *n* (Jmca) ‖ *setting-up, sitting-up* (Baha) A wake; an all-night vigil with hymn-singing and eating; it is held on the first and ninth nights, or for each of the nine nights after a person's death. [By functional vb > n shift of SET UP¹. See SET¹ Phr 2.8(iii)]

se·ver·al *adj* (CarA) [*X*] Very many; a large number of. **a.** *Mr Deputy Speaker, I think it is true to say that a Barbadian, like his fellow-West Indian, is essentially an immigrant. Not only was he brought here several years ago from parts of Europe, Africa and Asia in many instances against his own will and desire, but through the centuries that he has resided in Barbados like his Caribbean Brother.*—Bdos (Hd, 75.03.19, p.5138) **b.** *I—a man who always found it hard to part with a penny—was now willing, almost eager, to pay this woman several dollars for what a man in my position should have dismissed as ridiculous hocus pocus.*—TRIH:244 [Cp *EDD* several adj and sb Sc, Irel, etc 1. 'a great many; any number of'] □ Cp *OED2* several 4. As a vague numeral: 'of an indefinite (but not large) number exceeding two or three but not very many'. (The chief current sense).

sew·age (sys·tem) *n (phr)* (CarA) [*X*] Sewerage (system). *The Ministry of Health ... has already recommended that the Council start urging Central Government to provide a sewage system for Port Antonio.*—StA(JA) (73.02.13, p.14) [By reduction of consonant cluster /-wr-/ > /-w-/ in pronunc] □ A common error in CE speech and writing. SE *sewage*, 'waste matter' being confused with *sewerage*, 'the system of its disposal'. (This confusion has evid now also spread into IAE).

sé·wé·nal [sewenal] *n* (Dmca) The Christmas-time practice of house-to-house serenading by groups singing ballads in *Dmca* Fr Creole, accompanied by simple musical instruments, the groups expecting to be rewarded with food, drink and small donations; the practice is nowadays often repeated in the pre-CARNIVAL weekend. [Fr Cr < Fr SÉRÉNADE 'serenad(ing)'] Cp PARANG (Tbgo, Trin).

sex¹ *n* PHRASES **1. find/get your sex and size** *vb phr* (Gren) [*AF*] [Usu imper] (To) associate with people of your own age and social class; (to) seek friends among your peers. **2. not be sex (and size) with (sb)** *id phr* (ECar) [*AF—Cr*] Not to be of the same kind, age-group or social class as (sb). *Don[’t] boder tell people you an[d] me is frien[d]—I ain[’t] no sex wid you.*—(Nevs)

sex² *vb* (CarA) [Of a man] To have sexual intercourse with (sb). *She was grabbed by two young men and dragged into a kitchen and there stripped and sexed.*—ToR (76.11.17, p.3) [By functional n > vb shift of SE *sex* in slang sense, 'sexual intercourse'] □ *OED2* notes *sex* as vb intr only.

sha·been *n* (Dmca, StLu, Trin) See CHABEN.

sha(c)k·al [šakal] /1′2/ *adj* (Trin) [*AF—Derog*] Rough, rowdy in appearance and/or behaviour. *The behaviour of these pepper pot people has been, of late, shackal, to say the least; their attitude, more than bite up.*—MN:57 [< Fr *chacal* 'jackal' with anglicized spelling but retaining Francophone pronunc and CE pitch. The association of the jackal with carrion and meanness underlies the sense, with functional n > adj shift perh in early Fr Cr usage]

shack-shack (chac-chac, shak-shak) *n* **1.** (CarA) A child's rattle, sometimes home-made by putting dried seeds in a coconut or other shell. **2.** (Bdos, Guyn) The curved fifteen-inch-long pod of the FLAMBOYANT TREE, wh gets hard and black with rattling seeds when dry and is used as a toy. [Cp *ADMY* Yoruba ṣẹkẹ-ṣẹkẹ, [šɛkɛ-šɛkɛ] 'Flamboyant tree'; also ṣẹkẹrẹ, 'calabash-drum netted with strings of cowries ... shaken to create a resounding noise'. Also *ADHL* Hausa *caki* [čaki] 'a gourd filled with stones for rattling'] **3.** (Bdos, Trin) || WOMAN('S) TONGUE TREE (CarA) **4.** (Trin) || WILD-TAMARIND 1. (Belz, etc) [Senses 3., 4., from resemblance of the sound of a cluster of dry pods to that of a child's rattle] □ The spelling *shack-shack* appears to be most commonly used for these senses, and *chac-chac* preferred for the equivalent as a musical instrument.

shack-shack (shak-shak) tree *n phr* (Antg, BrVi, StLu, StVn) || FLAMBOYANT TREE (CarA) [From the rattling of its dry pods. See SHACK-SHACK 1., 2.]

shad* *n* A silvery fish wh grows up to about 6 ins, sometimes larger in freshwater; it is of good food value; *Pellona spp.* [From its resemblance to the shad (*Alosa spp*) of the northern hemisphere]

shad·dock* *n* (CarA) || *forbidden fruit* (Gren, Guyn, Trin) || *pomelo* (Trin) The largest known variety of citrus fruit (sometimes round and 5 to 6 ins in diameter, sometimes pear-shaped) with a pink or pale yellow flesh that is tougher than that of the grapefruit and a very thick rind that is often candied; *Citrus maxima (Rutaceae).* ['The seed of this was first brought to Barbados by one Captain Shaddock, commander of an East Indian ship, who touched at that island on his passage to England, and left its seed there. They have since carried that name in the W Indies'—*PTT:122*, quoting Sir Hans Sloane, 1707] □ Pl usu *shaddocks*, though sometimes without /-s/. Note Sloane (1707): 'in Barbados their Shaddock surpass those in Jamaica in goodness' (*PTT:122*).

shades *n pl* (CarA) || *sunshades* (Guyn) Dark glasses; sunglasses. *Spend $5 at the Jewelry Counter and get one pair of shades free.*—AdN (Ad, 73.05.31, p.2) □ SE *sunshade* is a hood fixed to keep the sun from the face, or a type of sun-umbrella or sun-hat. However *shades* with CE sense is also IF BrE, AmE—(*pers info, L. Urdang*).

sha·do·be·ni (chado(n)-bé·ni); **sha.dom-vin.ney; shad.ow-ben.ny; shad.ow-vin.nie (bush)** *n* (*phr*) (Gren, StVn, Tbgo, Trin) || FIT-WEED (Bdos, etc) [By folk etym < Fr Cr CHADON BÉNI, prob an early loan < Fr *chardon béni*, 'blessed thistle']

shake¹ *vb* PHRASES **1. shake five** *vb phr* (Guyn) || BREAK FIVES (Bdos, etc) See BREAK Phr 4. **2. shake hands/your hand (at sb)** *vb phr* (Bdos, Guyn) [Esp of children] To wave goodbye (to sb). □ In contrast cp SE idiom *to shake one's fist at sb* 'to threaten violence to sb'. **2.1 (two persons) can shake hands** *id phr* (CarA) [*F*] See HAND¹ Phr 4.3 *You see when it comes to not trusting Russia, Thatcher and Reagan can shake hands, oh yes.*—(Guyn) **3. shake out your mouth** *vb phr* (CarA) [*IF*] To wash or rinse out your mouth. *I went out into the kitchen in my trousers and vest, dipped a calabash of water from the bucket, 'shook out my mouth' and washed my face.*—TRIH:107 **4. shake the/your bodyline** *vb phr* (CarA) To swing the hips merrily in dancing.

shake² *n* (Gren) PHRASE **in a shake** *adv phr* (Gren) [*IF*] || *in two shakes of a duck's tail* (Guyn) In the shortest possible time. *When A hear dey payin[g] today A make to[w]ng and come back in a shake.*—(Gren) [Prob < SE *in two shakes of a lamb's tail* with same meaning]

shake-foot; shake-up *n* (CarA) [*AF—Joc*] A party, dance, or FETE to wh an invitation is not necessary.

shak·er·ism *n* (StVn) The organization and practice of the forms of religious worship observed by the SHAKERS. *St Vincent Legalises Shakerism/Kingstown, St Vincent, March 22— Shakerism is now a legal religion in St Vincent. This morning in the Legislative Council the Chief Minister, Mr Ebenezer Joshua moved the ordinance to repeal the Shakerism Prohibition Ordinance. The object of the Bill was to repeal the Prohibition Ordinance which was enacted over half a century ago and which prohibited the religious practices associated with Shakerism.*—BdN (65.03.23, p.7) [CE SHAKER + SE suff *-ism* 'ideological movement' as in *feminism*, etc] □ Not the same as the *DAE* AmE *shakerism* of the Quakers. See next.

Shak·ers *n pl* (CarA) Any of a number of christian sects, usu comprising Black people, whose forms of worship excite the vigorous shaking of the body in religious ecstasy, spirit-possession, etc. *Certainly if one looks at the type of religion that is being preached in this country, especially by the Anglican Church, we would realise that there is no soul gathering in this country by that particular organisation, and that is why you find that members of what we call 'the shakers' in what we call dilapidated buildings draw more members than the Anglican Church.*—Bdos (Hd, 75.10.09, p.981)

shal·low ben·ay *n phr* (Trin) ‖ FIT-WEED (Bdos, etc) [By folk etym < Fr Cr CHADON BÉNI]

shame[1] *adj* 1. (CarA) [X] Ashamed. **a.** *An[d] everybody know she lie[d]. She was shame so till she couldn['t] look at me straight in my face.*—(Guyn) **b.** *What is the point, what difference does it make what amendment they have, whether it is before Parliament or by the Minister with the discretion. Since when they get shame?*—Gren (Hd, 77.11.18, p.45) [< SE *ashamed* by characteristic loss of initial unstressed vowel and final /-d/] 2. PHRASES **2.1 be/feel (so) shame** *vb phr* (CarA) [X] See FEEL Phrs 6. **2.2 look shame** *vb phr* (CarA) [X] To be embarrassed (by some happening or conduct); to feel disgraced. *I would well and thump some of them when they come back to school the next day or whenever. For making me and the school 'look shame' as the common saying goes. People would believe we don't teach anything in the school.*—EvP (73.02.16, p.6) [< SE *look ashamed*] **2.3 make (sb) shame** *vb phr* (CarA) [AF] To make (sb) ashamed, feel ashamed. *She talk so much stupidness in front the white people she make me shame.*—(StKt)

shame[2] *vb intr* (CarA) [X] To be ashamed. **a.** *The man ain['t] even cold in he grave yet an[d] the two them going out together a[l]ready. They ought to shame.*—(StVn) *She belly big, I does shame for she in the street.*—SCTR:67 (Cso, 'Don't go Joe') [Passing into vbl function from SHAME[1]]

shame-ba·by *n* (Guyn) [AF] ‖ SENSITIVE PLANT (Bdos, etc) [A ref to its shy behaviour in closing up when touched. Cp other ‖ ‖]

shame-bush *n* (Guyn, Trin) ‖ SENSITIVE PLANT (Bdos, etc) [See SHAME-BABY]

shame·face *n* (Bdos, Guyn, Tbgo) [AF—Cr] Shame; embarrassment; shame-facedness. *After she tell such a lie [u]pon you, i[t']s shameface make she won['t] come back.*—(Guyn)

shame-la·dy/-weed *n* (Jmca) ‖ SENSITIVE PLANT (Bdos, etc) *A woody herb, sometimes prostrate but usually partly erect, it has shaggy, prickly stems bearing alternate compound leaves with up to 30 pairs of small leaflets which collapse and close at once when touched. In Jamaica it is given the charming name of Dead-and-awake and that of Shame Lady.*—AdN (79.05.20, p.15, M. Hutt) [See SHAME-BABY]

sham·pa·ta *n* (Jmca) ‖ ALPARGATA (CarA) [< Sp *zapata* 'boot']

sham-sham *n* (StVn) ‖ ASHAM (Antg, etc) [Prob by regressive assimilation < ASHAM. Cp SANSAM (*Trin*)] □ See CHILI(BIBI).

shan·de·lay; shandi.lay *n* (Trin) See CHANDILÉ

Shan·go [šaŋgo] *n* (Gren, Guyn, Tbgo, Trin) 1. [Hist] A Yoruba deity, a god of thunder and thunderbolts, who punishes troublemakers and rewards his worshippers; ritual group-drum beating, animal sacrifice, particular foods, and the colour red are prominent features of worship at his shrines; his priests are immune to fire when possessed; this deity, brought to the Caribbean by slaves, is still worshipped in many parts from Cuba to Brazil. [ADMY Yoruba *Şongo* 'the god of thunder and lightning', etc] 2. [By extension] A cult in wh Yoruba gods or 'powers' are worshipped but whose ritual practices are almost wholly those related to the deity SHANGO, with linkages, in some places with Christian saints; the cult is called on to respond to particular circumstances of a community, family, or person. **a.** *As the islanders got to know more about Shango, they realised that it was not a cult for doing evil, but for doing good unto those who seek for it.*—PGIP:54 **b.** *The ordinary conversation with a Shango follower will never elicit what is the really tangible reasonable traditional base for this custom.*—EMRP:24

shan·to *n* (Guyn) A ballad-like song with a narrative content; it is peculiarly Guyanese. [Prob < SE *shanty*, referring to river boatmen's and pork-knockers' companionship work-songs, with etym infl from CE KAISO/CALYPSO. Note next] □ Pl SHANTOS. Cp CALYPSO(E)S.

shan·to·ni·an *n* (Guyn) An entertainer who specializes in composing and singing SHANTOS. [By analogy with CALYPSONIAN]

shant·well *n* (Trin) See CHANTWÈL

shape *vb* (CarA) [*IF*] **1.** To take shape satisfactorily; to shape up; [by extension] to make progress, get on (with a task). *The canes this season were big and weighed very heavy and with his 'back up' watchman job four days a week, things were shaping pretty alright.*—Com, 1974, p.50 [Cp *EDD shape* vb (Sc, Irel, etc) 6. 'to succeed, get on; to show promise'] **2.** PHRASES **2.1 How you shapin[g]?** *id phr* (CarA) [*AF*] How are things with you?; How are you managing? **2.2 leave/lef[t] (sb) shapin[g]** *vb phr* (Guyn) [*AF—Joc*] See LEAVE Phr 4.

sha·po·tie *n* (Dmca, StLu) ‖ SAPODILLA (CarA) [Fr Cr < Fr *sapotille* with initial affrication]

share (out) *vb tr* (CarA) [*IF*] **1.** To deliver, distribute or give (things one at a time). *You mean you haven't shared out the invitations for the wedding up to now?*—(Guyn) □ Cp SE *share (out)* + mass nouns (food, rice, water, etc). **2.** PHRASES **2.1 share blows/lashes/licks** *vb phr* (Bdos, Guyn, Trin) [*AF*] To whip (a class/group/team, etc) mercilessly; [by extension] to humiliate (an opposing side) publicly. **a.** *When you see he come een in a bad mood, an' he start to share blows, he does run mih een de yard an' on de pavement an' thing.*—MN:42 **b.** *Dey havin' nuff meetings 'bout de place an' the people only sayin' dat de meetin's poor, poor, poor.... and de res' o' parties only waitin' til de election campaign start to share some home-truth licks.*—NaT (90.10.19, p.11, Lickmout' Lou)

shark·ing /2'2/ *adj* (Nevs) [*AF—Derog*] Too greedy; gluttonous. *You too sharking, you always ready to eat anywhere.*—(Nevs)

sharp *adj* **1.** (CarA) [*AF/IF*] [Of a young woman] Fashionably dressed and sexually attractive. *You staying tonight? It have two sharp things does come for coffee here—I think they from Sweden, and you know over there ain't have no inhibition.*—SWOS:141 **2.** (CarA) [*AF/IF*] [Of a man] Slick with women; clever at getting girlfriends. □ Cp SE *sharp* 'clever at everything; astute'. **3.** (Guyn) [Of a person's profile] ‖ CLEAN 2. (CarA) *She didn[t] have no chinee in her, no sir! Perhaps a little Buck-blood but I tell you she had sharp features! If wasn['t] for the eyes she would look like a white woman.*—(Guyn) [Prob a ref to the straight line of the nose] **4.** PHRASE **4.1 look sharp** *vb phr* (CarA) See LOOK Phr 4.10

shave-ice *n* (Guyn, Jmca, StVn, Trin) ‖ S-NO(W)-CONE (CarA) *I did see one fan cooling down with the paper cup and the shave ice.*—WeG (73.07.11, p.13) [In former days the ice was carried as a large block kept covered in a CROCUS-BAG surrounded by saw-dust in the shave-ice-man's BOX-CART, the surface being *shaved* and compressed in a metal, ice-shaver] □ Obsolescent, regularly replaced by SNO-CONE.

shay-shay (shey-shey) *n* (Belz, Jmca, TkCa) A vigorous dance in the earliest form of wh evid

only the lower part of the body was moved in co-ordination with the partner's, and movements accompanied by song; it is prob of African origin. *Cubbenah and Quasheba, Quashie and Beneba, and Cudjoe and Juba were jumping up and down and attempting an improvised shey-shey, while whistling and humming and singing their own subtle, hypnotic tune.*—SD:88 [Cp Yoruba ideoph *ṣeṣe* 'with short steps'. Perh early AmE *sashay* 'to strut, etc' is related. Though OED lists word as '*U.S. Vulgar*', it is 'certainly no longer vulgar'—(*pers info*, L. Urdang)] □ Also used as vb (cp *waltz*, etc).

she [shi ~ shɪ] *pron 3rd pers sg* (CarA) [*AF—Cr*] [Used or occurring frequently in speech in other functions than as subj of a vb or as nominative case] **1.** [*X*] [As obj] Her; it. **a.** *... and the wife say 'Yuh don't have to count out a man when yuh know he can't get up.' But I don't tek on she.*—NaT (91.07.05, p.9, Lowdown) **b.** *And I take note you hop on that donkey quick enough this morning to take she out, tie she up for grass.*—AHR:3 **2.** [*X*] [As possessive] Her. **a.** *... and then Esmeralda had to hold she belly and bawl.*—CISH:111 **b.** *He say the woman shake she waist in the governor face.*—Trin (Cso, 'Mr Prospect', 1960s) [These functions are survivals of CarA Cr basilectal / shi/ wh, except for *Jmca* /(h)im/, functions unchanged for case and gender] □ The stressed form in both functions is [shi], unstressed [shɪ]. See also SHE OWN at OWN 1.1.

shed-roof *n* (Bdos, Mrat ‖ *caboose* (TkCa) ‖ *drop-shed* (Antg, Nevs, StKt A small addition to a CHATTEL-HOUSE, with a flat, sloping roof; it serves esp to add dining and kitchen space at the back end, and sometimes to provide an entrance ensuring the privacy of the BODY-HOUSE. **a.** *The accused added that all of the cops on the raid were on the premises, some in the two bedrooms, some in the shed-roof, and others on the roof.*—AdV (90.06.19, p.5) **b.** *How you mean! And we gon live in style, mahn. No little board and shingle house with a shed roof to cook in. We gon have the best now.*—MBGB:14 [From the shed-like roof, the name being used, by synecdoche, for the whole structure] □ Sometimes referred to as SHED (Bdos).

shell-fish *n phr* (ECar) ‖ COW-FISH 1. (Baha, etc) [From the tough shell-like skin covering the upper part of its body]

she·lote [šɛlo·t ~ šɛlʌt] *n* (Guyn) [*X*] ESCHALOT (Bdos, Guyn) [< (SE) *shallot* or (Fr) *échalote* (cp ESCHALLOT) by aphesis]

shel·ter *vb* PHRASE **shelter (the) rain** (StVn, Trin) [*X*] To seek shelter from the rain. *The woman told the police that she was sheltering rain under a club house in the district around 7 p.m. on Sunday when a man pulled her to the back of the building and assaulted her.*—TrG (79.08.01, p.13) [By loss or deletion of prep extension in vb phr. Cp similarly ModE *arrive (at)/depart (from) a place*]

shen·shay fowl [šɛnše fʊʊl] *n phr* (Nevs) ‖ SEN-SEH-FOWL (CarA) [By affrication of /s/ < SENSEH]

shep·herd *n* (Jmca) The male and dominant leader of an independent revivalist or cultist group; he usu operates a BALM-YARD and determines the requirements for atonement and healing among his followers. *Black cloak spreading like wings of bat. Run, Shepherd John! Do, Shepherd John. Use your staff! Can't speak. Use your staff. Useless. Dust / They screamed in the voice of the unknown tongues. Those that were too possessed were calmed down by the Mothers and armour-bearers and Shepherd John. Those that were slow were held and whirled and lashed with the staff.*—PCOS:152

sher·i·gal-go *n* (ECar) A dark-coloured, flat-backed, oval-shaped crab with a hard shell; it dwells in shallow coastal waters or marshes and is of poor food value; *Callinectes spp* (*Portunidae*).

shey-shey *n* (Belz, Jmca, TkCa) See SHAY-SHAY.

shift [šɪf] *vb* **1.** (Trin) [Of a steelpan] To be/go out of tune. *Awright my ping-pong was de best thing out. Now it spoil ... if you want me play, I go play. I go beat boom. My pan shift so I playing bass.*—HPP:20 [Because some notes have changed or shifted from one key to another] **2.** PHRASE **2.1 shift yourself to suit yourself** *vb phr* (Guyn, Trin) [AF] To look after your own interests; to arrange matters to your own advantage. □ Cp AmE *shift for oneself* with similar sense.

shim·my *n* (Guyn, StKt) [IF] ‖ CHEMISE 3. (Guyn, Trin)

shine *adj* (CarA) [X] Shiny; shining; bright; polished. **a.** *He wore very shine black patent-leather shoes.*—Guyn (Ms) **b.** *She looked at the floor which was incredibly shine. It truly was a marvel to her how these people managed to get and keep their floor so shine*—BM:22

shine (shin·ing/shin·y) bush *n phr* (Bdos, StVn, Tbgo, Trin) A low weed with light-green, semi-translucent stems, shiny heart-shaped leaves, and terminal spikes of tiny greenish-white flowers; it thrives in poor soil and is widely used as a folk-medicine for colds esp in children and as a COOLING; *Peperomia pellucida* (*Piperaceae*).

shirt·jac(k) (shirt-jack) *n* (CarA) A man's loose-fitting, shirt-like garment designed like a bush-jacket without belt, usu with short sleeves and made of light shirting material; it is worn outside the trousers. [Blend of *shirt* + *jack(et)*. The name originated in Guyn in 1969, identified as wear recognized for official occasions] □ The spelling *shirtjac* is common, though *shirtjack* would facilitate the derivative adj *shirtjacked*.

shirt·jac(k)-suit *n* (Bdos, Guyn) ‖ *cariba* (Jmca, Trin) ‖ *kareba* (Jmca) A suit generally consisting of a SHIRTJACK made of suiting material with trousers to match; it is designed for casual wear with short sleeves, and as formal wear with long sleeves.

shit *vb* [AF—Vul] PHRASE **shit in high grass** *vb phr* (Guyn, Jmca, StKt) [AF—Vul] To (try to) reach a place of pride; to get into company or a position well above your social class. [Semantic extension of a folk ref to the field slave who sought, from pride, to defecate in privacy]

shite [šaɪt ~ šdɪt] *n, excl* (Bdos, Guyn) [AF—Vul] [Coarse, emphatic expression of anger, disgust or amazement] **1.** *n* (= Shit) Nonsense. *There is some fellas up here from the islands who talking a lot of shite about Black Power, and I hear that one of them is a Barbadian.*—CWFYS:96 [OED *shite* as alternative of *shit*, going back to 15C *schite*, n and vb, and later *shyt*, *shite*] **2.** *n* [By extension, in intensifying function] *Calvin is the most luckiest one o' we, yuh! Calvin lucky-lucky-lucky as shite!*—CWFYS:92 **3.** *excl* Shit! *O shite! I in a hurry and look the car got a flat.*—(Guyn) [Cp OED2 *shite*, as coarse excl + cits from 1920. The term is much older in CE]

shoes *n sg* (CarA) [X] **1.** A shoe; a pair of shoes. **a.** *Put on your left-side shoes.*—(Guyn) □ Hence also dial pl *shoeses* [X]; *a shoeslace* [X]. **b.** *I have to buy a new shoes.*—(Jmca) **2.** PHRASE **2.1 keep shoes on sb's foot** *vb phr* (Belz) ‖ KEEP CLOTHES ON SB'S BACK (CarA) See CLOTHES Phr. □ See PLURAL FORMS.

sho(o)-shoo *n, vb* (CarA) See SHU-SHU

shoot¹ *vb* PHRASE **shoot balls/bull/shit, etc** *vb phr* (CarA) [AF—Vul] To talk nonsense. *Keep your shirt on Midge. Dat ent nothing to wory bout. You can't stop people shooting a lotta balls.*—HPP:2 [Cp BrE *shoot one's mouth off* 'to talk indiscreetly'; also AmE (pers info, L. Urdang)]

shoot!² *excl* (Bdos, Guyn, StVn) [IF] Good heavens! *O shoot! I came out of the house and forgot to switch off the stove.*—(Guyn) □ A mild exp of surprise, an acceptable euphemism for *shit!*; not considered *Vul*.

shop-la·dy *n* (CarA) See LADY

shop-pa·per *n* (Bdos, Guyn) Sturdy brown wrapping paper. *All I need now is some shop-paper, the khaki-coloured one, to paste up the kite with.*—NaT (80.04.03, p.7, Al's Grapevine) [From its wide use in groceries and food-shops for wrapping goods]

short¹ *adj* PHRASES **1. foot is (too) short** *id phr* (Guyn) [AF—Joc] See FOOT Phr 7. **2. hand is short** *id phr* (Guyn) [IF] See HAND¹ Phr 4.12

short² *adv* **1.** (Trin) [IF] Abruptly; at once. *Helen had never liked jazz and she had stopped dancing short with marriage.*—JJM:75 **2.** PHRASE **2.1 short here** *adv phr* (Bdos) [IF] Not very far away from here; just around the corner; just within sight of where we are. *Slow down. Slow down. My house is short here.*—(Bdos)

short ba·na·na *n phr* (StVn) ‖ CAYENNE BA-NANA (Guyn)

short-knee [ʃɒtni] *n phr* (Crcu, Gren) A tra-ditional CARNIVAL masquerade figure dressed in very colourful costume comprising a starched or towel head-piece, a wire mask with a painted face, a loose-fitting upper garment with long, wide sleeves, and baggy pants reaching to the knees with bells around the bottom, most of the outfit being covered in sequins or mirrors; the traditional custom of reciting passages from his-tory or literature is now replaced by composing topical songs. [A ref to the shortened, knee-length trousers as the essential part of the cos-tume] □ Cp PIERROT GRENADE.

should-a (shoulda, shudda) [ʃuda] *modal aux vb* (CarA) [*AF—Cr*] **1.** [Indicating a past un-fulfilled obligation, but usu followed by infin vb] Should have; ought to have. **a.** *You shoulda buy the costume for her, when you had the chance.*—LDCD:154 **b.** *Jack, yo shoudda see me squeezin' in my small self on da shelf.*—Aaw I.2, p.25 [< SE *should* + enclitic A[8] from EE dial *have*] □ Cp also COULD-A, WOULD-A. Also sometimes re-analysed as *should of* [X]. **2.** PHRASES **2.1 should(-a) did** *vb phr* (Jmca) [*AF—Cr*] Should have been. *Lord Jesus, me should did there. Lord Jesus!*—SNWIC:264 (M. Townshend) **2.2 should(-a) had** *vb phr* (Bdos) [*AF—Cr*] Should have had. *De Dems shunt be scared o' Flies when dey so bold-face to slap down Taitt an' put he below Sandiford in Parliament. Dey should had de same guts to put Flies in he place.*—BeA(BS) (79.11.29, p.43) [In both Phrs 2.1, 2.2. *Should-a* is reduced by apocope]

shout[1] *vb tr* (Bdos, Belz, Guyn) [*IF*] **1.** To greet, hail (sb). *And whenever I feel lazy I could still look through my window and shout Joe or Harold and we can flap we mouth till thy kingdom come.*—AdN (73.04.14, p.11) [Cp *EDD* shout 2. Cum, Yks, Lan, Lin. 'to call, summon; to call for without necessarily raising the voice'] **2.** PHRASE **2.1 shout for murder** *vb phr* (CarA) [*AF*] ‖ HOLLER FOR MURDER (CarA) See HOLLER Phr 2.2

shout[2] *n* **1.** (Belz, Guyn) [*IF*] A greeting; a casual visit. [By functional vb > n shift of SHOUT[1]. See Phr 3.1 below] **2.** (Guyn) A discovery of gold or diamonds in an area being prospected. *Crown allegations are that R— murdered L.H. K—(50) who worked alone at Assai and was leaving there on August 15, 1951, to follow a gold 'shout' at another part of the Cuyuni.*—DaC (52.05.01, p.13) **3.** PHRASES **3.1 give (sb) a shout** *vb phr* (Belz, Guyn) [*IF*] To call on (sb); to pay (a friend) a casual visit. □ Also AmE slang. **3.2 when you hear the shout** *id phr* (CarA) [*IF/AF*] See HEAR Phr 4.12

shout·er(s) *n* (CarA) (A member of) a Baptist sect in wh there is much individual shouting of prayers and praises in a state of religious ecstasy. *African culture survives in many areas of our daily life—in our music, our food, in our indigenous religions, Shango, Obeah, Shouters and other sects in which a synthesis of African and Christian elements is effected.*—ACTT:33

shove (shub) [ʃʌv ~ ʃʊb] *vb tr* (CarA) PHRASE **if push come to shove** *id phr* (CarA) [*AF/IF*] See IF Phr 2.

shov·el *n* **1.** (Guyn) An implement consisting of a narrow metal scoop at the end of a long (shovel-)stick, used for digging and cleaning out mud and slush from drains and canals. □ See SHOVEL-GANG. **2.** (Bdos, Jmca, Mrat, StVn) ‖ **spade[1]** (Guyn) A spade with a flat, rectangular blade fitted with a handle and used for shifting gravel or any loose material. □ See SPADE.

shov·el-gang/-men *n* (Guyn) [Sugar Ind] A group of labourers employed to clean the drains and trenches of a sugar-plantation.

show *vb* **1.** (CarA) To teach or help (sb) to learn; (SE) to show how to (do sth). *He was like a big brother to them, showed them to make kites, showed them to catch crabs ...*—Bdos (Ms) **2.** *vb tr* (Guyn, Jmca, Trin) [*IF*] To give, hand, pass (sth to sb). *Show me the hammer* (= *Pass me the hammer*).—(Guyn) [Prob from IrE. Note: 'All through Ireland you will hear *show* used instead of *give* or *hand* (vb), in such phrases as 'Show me that knife,' i.e. hand it to me.—*JESI*:37] **3.** *vb intr* (CarA) [Of a woman] To begin to be noticeably pregnant; to have an abdomen be-ginning to protrude through pregnancy. *Some fat women don't show until they're nearly ready to give birth.*—(Jmca) □ This usage is added in *OED2* as show vb 28. a. + earliest cit 1936. It is, however, much older in CE. Also sometimes *show belly* [*AF*]. **4.** PHRASES **4.1 show sb a bad face** *vb phr* (Jmca, Tbgo, Trin) [*AF/IF*] See FACE Phr 7. **4.2 show sb a good face** *vb phr* (Jmca, Tbgo, Trin) [*AF/IF*] To show an obvious liking for sb. *I'm separated from my husband because of ill treatment and no love at home. I had found another love. At first he showed me good face and later, bad face. He drank and cursed, he talked loud and had no respect for me.*—PuN (74.12.22, p.19)

shub *vb tr* (CarA) [*AF—Cr*] See SHOVE □ A folk pronunc sometimes so represented in narrative dialogue.

shun·na-foot *adj, n* (Bdos, Guyn) [*AF*] (Hav-ing) feet or toes turned outwards, hence (giving a person) a peculiar gait. [Perh < *DAFL* Twi *sono* '(be) different, peculiar']

shu-shu[1] (shoo-shoo) [ʃu-ʃu] *vb intr* (CarA) To whisper to each other; to gossip. **a.** *Rosie put her finger to her lips and shoo shoo for her to be quiet but made sign for her to come and see.*—PKKK:40

b. *Don't doubt it, he and I. W— are always shoo-shooing in the office every day, and anytime I pop in they always shut up and talk about the goldfish in the aquarium or the air-condition.*—BoM (79.06.01, p.19) **[**Perh < susu² with /s > sh/ shift by palatalization. Cp also Fr *susurrer*, Sp *susurrar* 'to whisper'. Perh also onomatopoeic**]**

shu-shu² (sho(o)-shoo) *n* (Belz, Gren, StKt, Trin) [*AF*] **1.** ‖susu² (Guyn, etc) *The supervisor called the Manager (the issue was too hot for him to handle). / They made their little shu-shu in a corner. A full-scale bank crisis was at hand.*—NeJ (75.05.16, p.1) **2.** ‖ HEAR-SO (Brbu, Jmca)

shut *vb* PHRASES **1. shut your beak/face/mouth/trap (up)** *vb phrs* (CarA) [*AF*] To shut up. □ Various emph, insulting exps in CE to wh many other Vul ones may be added. **2. shut your eye at (sth)** *vb phr* (CarA) [*IF*] To connive at (sth); to refuse to give attention to (some known misconduct); (SE) close one's eyes to (sth). *The police, by shutting their eyes at street-corner gambling, are encouraging the youth in a dangerous habit.*—Jmca (Ms)

shut-pan *n* (Jmca) ‖ FOOD-CARRIER (Guyn) *Naomi has got the shut-pan with our lunch and is walking to the cotton tree under which we will eat.*—RND:100

sick¹ *adj* (CarA) **1.** [Of a person or animal] Ill; sickly; suffering from some bodily ailment. **[**As *OED sick* A. I. 'suffering from illness of any kind; ill, unwell, ailing. Now chiefly literary and US' + cits from earliest (9C) Eng onward**]** □ This is the dominant usage in CE. However, the same usage, labelled 'literary' in *OED*, is tending to supersede the conservative BrE usage 'vomiting or tending to vomit'. **2.** PHRASES **2.1 (as) sick as a dog** *adj phr* (CarA) [*AF/IF*] Very unwell (usu for a few days). □ Also AmE vomiting is not necessarily implied. **2.2 be sick by the foot/hand, etc** *id phr* (CayI) [*IF*] See BY¹ Phr 6.1 **2.3 be sick on your hand** *id phr* (CarA) [*IF*] See HAND¹ Phr 4.2 **2.4 fall/take sick** *vb phr* (CarA) To fall, become ill. **a.** *The events leading up to her death were not recorded by the deceased. But if they had been, it would be recorded that she fell sick last Tuesday and was taken to the casualty of the Queen Elizabeth Hospital around 9 a.m.*—AdN (72.09.30, p.1) **b.** *'Old lady Cojo,' he called out to her, 'what you doing down there this hour of the night? Tomorrow morning somebody in the village will have to come and attend to you when you take sick.'*—Wic (66/3, p.131) □ Also AmE. **2.4.1 take in sick** (Bdos, Guyn, Tbgo) To become suddenly ill; (SE) to be taken ill.

sick² *n* **1.** (Guyn, Tbgo, Trin) [*AF*] Sickness; illness; an ailment. **a.** *Old woman, you makin' dust fly outside there you want to catch sick when that dust fly inside your nose or what?*—KJB:172 **b.** *I ain't an expensive girl, and I ain't have any sick.*—SBB:24 **2.** (Bdos, Guyn) [*IF*] A sick person. **a.** *How is the sick today? (= How is the person today who is sick in your house).*—(Bdos) **b.** *Children don[ʼt] make so much noise. Remember there is a sick in the house.*—(Guyn) **[**A particularization of the collective sense as in Church lang 'Prayers for/Visitation of the sick'**]**

sick³ *vb tr* (Guyn, Jmca, Tbgo) [*AF—Cr*] To cause to be sick; to make ill; to upset the stomach of (sb). *All dat ripe mango and sweetsop you eatin[g] dere go sick you* (i.e. will make you ill).— (Jmca)

sick-bath *n* (Guyn) ‖ BUSH-BATH (CarA)

sick-in *n* (Guyn) [Industrial action] Work-to-rule; a form of workers' protest in wh they work slowly and very cautiously in order to reduce output. *The Cabinet members said sit-ins, sick-ins and strikes are acts of destruction that are not in the interest of the nation as a whole.*—GyN (74/1, p.3) **[**By analogy from ModE *sit-in*. Cp *OED2 sick-in* (US) = *sick-out***]**

sick-out¹ *n* (CarA) **1.** [Industrial action] Deliberate absence from work by many members of a staff on the pretext of being ill, as a form of workers' protest. **a.** *Meanwhile, last Friday workmen at the brewery walked off their jobs after the company refused to back down on its declared intention of not paying unionised members of its staff for two 'sick outs' on Monday and Tuesday last week.*—AdN (72.10.17, p.1) **b.** *Unions have therefore carefully planned their stoppages of labour, open strikes and sickouts to take place at the time when their absence would be most felt.*—ExP (72.12.24, p.4) **[**By analogy from ModE *walk-out*. Listed in *OED2* as = *sick-in*] **2.** PHRASE **2.1 go on/stage a sick-out** *vb phr* (CarA) To be absent from work as a group as a form of protest. *Staff at the Bridgetown Harbour went on a sick-out yesterday, registering disappointment with a delayed salaries revision.*—AdN (76.12.15, p.1)

sick-out² *vb intr* (CarA) ‖ GO ON A SICK-OUT (CarA) □ The forms *to sick-out* and (rarely) *sick-outing* occur but no pa.t. form is recorded.

si·cri [sikri] *n* (Mrat) ‖ APPLE-BANANA (Belz, etc) **[** < Fr *sucre* or adj *sucrier* 'sugar'] □ Cp *sikyé-fig*

side¹ *n* (CarA) [*IF*] **1.** A group with a common interest, such as musicians, sportsmen, pleasure seekers. **a.** *Recalled Belmont old-timer Orville Gladstone: 'After Dimanche Gras fete in town a whole side of us used to go down south for J'Ouvert.'*—ExP (72.05.05, p.15) **b.** *In addition he sees his new-type steelband side as one of the ways of getting around the problem of transportation costs ... / There are things which you can do, musically, with a small side that you cannot do with the larger steelband.*—ExP (73.04.06, p.7) **[**By extension of sense of *side* 'one of two opposing sides or teams'. Cp *EDD side* sb¹ 5. 'a company' + cit from Wor 'A "side" of five or six labourers'**]**

side[2] *n* (CarA) [*IF*] **1.** Region; area; district. **a.** *And this afternoon they had a boy was fishing for welks under La Vierge by Maingot side, and see this thing.*—WSAD:25 **b.** *Go market side and buy six white carrot, big like so.*—KJB:173 **2.** [By extension, identifying a place, position or location] **a.** *When voting time come, Ramroop come village side and make big speech, say he help Indian if we put him government side.*—SABS:203 **b.** *Mistress Joan gone Le Resouvenir side with Meely.*—NR:49 [Cp *EDD* side sb[1] 4. 'a district, region; ... esp used in place-names' + cits from Sc, etc, are 'I'm new come frae Dumbarton side'] **3.** PHRASES **3.1 Go that side! (Go da side!)** [gʌ da said] *imper vb phr* (Guyn, StVn) [*AF*] Away with you!; I won't believe you! **3.2 go/stan[d] one-side** *vb phr* (CarA) [*AF*] Stand aside. **3.3 side and side (with)** *adv, prep* (Jmca, StKt) [*AF*] Side by side; alongside one another; together (with). **a.** *Whenever we go to church, Naomi and me sit side-and-side.*—RND:40 **b.** *She told the Court that she lives at La Guerite and has been 'working land side and side with S— for about four years.'*—DeM(SK) (63.02.16, p.3) **[** < SE *adv phr side by side*] **3.4 side o(f)** *prep phr* (CarA) [*AF*] Beside; at the side of; alongside. *I see G—(the deceased) who lived side of he in she ground forking and C—say he gine kill she...*—AdN (86.11.02, p.2) **3.5 this side (dis side)** *adv phr* (CarA) [*AF—Cr*] Here; in this place. *Go in de city, don't stay dis side.... Every day, same ting dis side.*—SABS:116 **3.6 that side (da side)** *adv phr* (CarA) [*AF—Cr*] Over there; in the place that you have come from. *So you come from Guyana. I hear things bad that side, no!*—(Bdos) **3.7 which side (wisside)** *inter rel adv* (CarA) [*AF*] See WHICH[2] Phr 3.

side·line *n* (Guyn) **1.** Either of two DAMS wh enclose a plantation or estate and so indicate its side boundaries (hence the name); also **sideline dam. 2.** The TRENCH dug to build the boundary DAM, and used for estate drainage; also **sideline trench.** □ *Sideline* is used loosely to refer to the roadway or the waterway, according to context. Cp MIDDLEWALK.

side·way-church *n* (StKt) [*IF*] A small, independent, non-conformist Christian group, usu comprising only Black people; [by extension] the small church-building in wh any such group meets.

sieve *n* PHRASE **have a sieve to carry/tote water** *vb phr* (Baha, TkCa) ‖ HAVE A BASKET TO CARRY WATER (CarA) See BASKET Phr 4.

sif·fleur mon·tagne* **(siflé-montany)** [si flɛ ~ sifle-mɔ̃taŋ] *n* (Dmca) A small bird with an ash-grey body, red and yellow breast, and dull yellow feet that dwells mostly in the mountain valleys; it is renowned for its flute-like whistle; *Myadestes genibarbis (Turdidae).* **[**Fr Cr < Fr *siffleur de montagne* 'mountain whistler'**]**

sight [saɪt] *vb* (CarA) [Rastaf] **1.** See. *You no sight, dread. Sight how dem ballheads make de I*

an' dem walk down to dey office an put a sign to say NO VISITORS. Is pure jesterin, ah tell you! / *The Rastafari brethren share the view that if Mrs Rock had any intentions of helping them she would have made some positive steps towards meeting with them by now.*—CrU (76.10.09, p.5) **2.** [By extension, used as an answer or question] Understand; understood; agreed. *S1: Well you got to make back mo[re] dan what yo[u] pay fo[r] de leather.* / *S2: Sight!*—(Bdos) **3.** [By extension, a greeting] Hail, brother! **4.** PHRASE **4.1 sight up** *vb phr* [Rastaf] To look; to look at (sth); to examine. *Now 'Yoruba' and others like it also run that risk unless they start 'groundsing'—getting out of their niche and making contact outside. Right now they are no more than a small cadre beginning to 'sight up' certain truths.*—MaN (73.11.11, p.8)

sign *n* (Gren, Tbgo) [*AF*] **1.** A surprise. [Cp *OED* sign sb 10. b. 'a marvel or wonder' (Obs)] **2.** PHRASES **2.1 Is a sign** *id phr* (Gren, Tbgo) [*AF*] It is surprising, amazing, a wonder that. *Mary give you mango? Is a sign she give you some, de way she mean.*—(Gren) **2.2 What a sign?** *id phr* (Tbgo) [*AF*] How surprising it is that?, what a wonder it is that? *You mean Ruby hear that her uncle come from America giving away new things? What a sign she ain't reach here yet?* –(Tbgo)

si·kyé-bird (su·crier-bird) [sikie-bə:d] *n* (Trin) ‖ BANANAQUIT (CarA) [From association with SIKYÉ-FIG wh it loves]

si·kyé-fig (su·crier-fig) [sikie-fɪg] *n* (Gren, Trin) ‖ *chiquito banana* (Trin) ‖ *secret-fig* (Gren) A bright yellow, finger-sized and very sweet banana [Fr Cr < Fr *sucrier* adj 'sugar' + CarA Fr *figue* 'banana'] □ Perh also SILK FIG through folk etym.

silk-ba·na·na *n* (Nevs, StKt) ‖ APPLE-BANANA (Belz, etc)

silk-bush *n* (Baha) ‖ AMERICAN SILK-COTTON (BrVi)

silk-cot·ton *n* (CarA) ‖ *kapok* (ViIs) The silky, sometimes brownish, cottonwool-like fibre, surrounding the seeds dispersed by the silk-cotton tree, used for stuffing cushions, etc.

silk-cot·ton tree* *n phr* (CarA) ‖ *ceiba* (CarA) ‖ *cotton-tree* (Baha, Belz, Jmca) ‖ *kapok tree* (ViIs) A massive tree that can rise to well over 100 ft in height, with a spreading crown and thick, 20-ft-high buttresses; the trunk and branches of some varieties are armed with sizeable prickles; the tree bears 4-inch-long pods filled with seeds embedded in a light-brown, silky, cotton-like fibre wh is widely wind-borne; *Ceiba pentandra, C. occidentalis,* or *Eriodendrum anfractuosum (Bombacaceae).* *At Salt Fish Hill, at Cottage and at Banana Gully stand some of the oldest silk-cotton trees in whose shade and among whose branches the ancient African ancestral spirits reside.*—EFOT:15 [From the silky cotton-like fibre dispersed by the tree] □ The tree, wh grows both in Africa and the *CarA*, is widely associated with a number of superstitions both positive and negative. Cp *DAFL* Twi ɔ-bosŏm 'guardian spirit', wh inhabits trees such as *onyãã* 'silk cotton tree'.

silk-fig *n* (Angu, Gren, Nevs, StKt, Tbgo, Trin) **1.** ‖ APPLE-BANANA (Belz, etc) **2.** ‖ SIKYÉ-FIG (Trin) [By a possible shift, through folk etym < SIKYÉ-FIG]

silk-grass ['sɪlkgra·s] *n* (Bdos) ‖ AGAVE (CarA) □ Particularly the variety also called CENTURY-PLANT (*Bdos*)

sil·ver·bal·li *n* (Guyn) [Timber Ind] A tall, tapering forest-tree exceeding 100 ft, the top 20 ft or so bearing its limbs of moderate length, its trunk cylindrical and unbuttressed; it is one of several varieties yielding yellow to dark-brown, straight-grained, aromatic timber wh is highly prized in boat-building for its durability, and in furniture-making for its strength and high polish; *Licaria canella* (*Lauraceae*). [< *BAED* Arawak *shiruabali* 'a collective term for a type of tree']

sil·ver-thatch palm* *n phr* (Baha, Trin) ‖ *b-room-palm* (Trin) ‖ *fan-leaf palm* (Bdos) ‖ *latanyé* (ECar) ‖ *palmetto* (Baha, Berm, TkCa) ‖ *pimento* (Belz) ‖ *silver-top (palm)* (Baha, TkCa) ‖ *thatch (palm)* (CayI, Jmca) A palm with several round, shiny-green, multi-fingered leaves, each standing on a smooth, slender stalk wrapped together at their base with a brown, netted fibre; it often grows wild in sandy places; its dried leaves are much used for straw-work, thatching, and brooms, though it is better known in some territories as a decorative pot-plant or a fully grown (4 to 6 ft) 'landscape' plant; *Thrinax argentea* (*Palmae*). [*Silver* from the shiny surface or bluish-green underside of some varieties + *thatch* from its use for thatch-work]

sil·ver-top (palm) *n* (*phr*) (Baha, TkCa) ‖ S-ILVER-THATCH PALM (Baha, Trin) [See SILVER-THATCH PALM and TOP]

si·ma·ru·pa *n* (Guyn) [Timber Ind] A tall, strongly tapering forest tree that can exceed 120 ft, with a light, loose crown; its trunk is unbuttressed and yields a light, soft-grained, whitish, perishable wood wh is widely used for making rough packing-cases, cheap cupboards, and coffins; *Simaruba amara* (*Simarubaceae*). [< *BAED* Arawak *shimarupa* 'a tree with light, yellow wood']

si·mé-kont·wa [simekontwa] *n* (Dmca, Gren, StLu) ‖ SEMI-CONTRACT (Gren, Jmca) [Fr Cr rendering perh of the original SEMENCONTRA (BUSH)]

si·mi·di·mi¹ (sim·my-dim·my) [sɪmɪdɪmɪ] *n* (Belz, Gren, StVn, Tbgo, Trin) Fuss and confusion; exaggerated behaviour, activity, or display. **a.** *You would think is big wedding the amount*

of simidimi they going on with, when is only a little morning affair with five guests.—(Gren) **b.** *Would you believe a lot of praying, chanting, bell-ringing, candle-burning and sprinkling of water went on. / Would you believe all that simmy-dimmy was to call on the spirits to fix Choko.*—BoM (76.11.12, p.6) **2.** *PHRASE* **2.1 make simidimi²** *vb phr* (CarA) ‖ *simidimi²* (Belz, Gren, StVn, Tbgo, Trin) To make an unnecessary fuss, a song and dance (over sth); [by extension] to provoke by playing the fool; to play tricks. **a.** *Stop turning around making all that simidimi and let's go. It's late.*—(Trin) **b.** *Don[ʔ] make no simidimi! Give me back my purse with my money in it.*—(Guyn)

si·mi·di·mi² [sɪmɪdɪmɪ] *vb* (Gren, Guyn, StVn, Tbgo, Trin) ‖ MAKE SIMIDIMI (CarA) *Before going out she has to simidimi in front of the mirror for an hour or more*—AFSTE:38

sim·pa·wi·rie (sim·per-/sim·pi-/sim·pri-/sim·ple-vi·vy/-wi·vy) [sɪmpəvaɪvi ~ -waɪvi] *n* (BrVi, CayI, StKt, USVI) ‖ ALOES (CarA) [By folk etym < SEMPERVIVE] □ See next

sim·ple-bi·ble (sin·gle-/sin·kle-/sin·tle-bi·ble) *n* (Jmca) ‖ ALOES (CarA) [By folk etym < SEMPERVIVE] □ See prec.

since¹ *conj* (CarA) [*IF*] As soon as; immediately as; from the moment/time that; when. **a.** *Since the boy see the police, if you see him run.*—(Guyn) **b.** *People should demonstrate against a Member since they begin to notice that he is absenting himself from the House and not representing their cause.*—Dmca (Ms, 1970) [By semantic shift of causal to temporal sense, brought about by ambiguous cases such as SE 'Since you said that, I (have) changed my mind'] □ Usu uttered in CE with high pitch /ʒ/ to distinguish meaning from *since* 'because'.

since² *prep* (CarA) **1.** [*X*] For; for as long as; for the (immediate past) period of. **a.** *They have been repairing that road since a year and haven't finished yet.*—StVn (Ms) **b.** *He was hungry. He had not eaten a solid meal since two days before.*—Baj (64/1, p.24) **c.** *Here since the past three days Mr Crewe has been having talks with the corporation's agents.*—DaG (71.05.17, p.1) **2.** *PHRASES* **2.1 (from) since small** *adv phr* (CarA) [*AF/IF*] From early childhood. *I know she was like that since small.*—(Antg) **2.2 since a time; since early/long** *adv phrs* (CarA) [*IF*] For some time now; from an early hour/time.

since³ *adv* (CarA) [*IF*] See separate entries EVER SINCE, EVERY SINCE. *Well, it is obvious the team lacks consistent emotional intensity, and this is from ever since with Plaza teams.*—AmA (80.02.08, p.11)

sin·door (sen·door) ['sɪndu·r] *n* (Guyn, Trin) [Indic] **1.** A vermilion-coloured powder used for ceremonial marking of the face **2.** [By extension] An inch-long mark made with vermilion-coloured powder at the centre front of the parted hair of a married Hindu woman, worn on ceremonial occasions. [Hin *sinduur* 'vermilion']

sing *vb* PHRASE **sing on/[u]pon sb** *vb phr* (Bdos, Guyn, Trin) [*IF*] **1.** To sing a hymn, psalm, or popular song the words of wh are directed at sb with intention to taunt. *When she an[d] de neighbours quarrel she would get in de yard an[d] sing [u]pon dem.*—(Guyn) **2.** [By extension] To enjoy spreading scandal about sb. *'See what I mean?' she had said feeling her sleeve to see if it was still clean, 'every cat, dog, rat and their pal singing on your sister. You can come lower than that?'*—JJM:96

sing·ing an·gel *n phr* (Bdos) ‖ *singing engine* (Guyn) A kite fitted with flaps of thin paper or BULLS around its edges to produce a humming sound as they vibrate in the wind.

sin·gle-bi·ble [sɪŋgl-baɪbl] *n* (Belz, Jmca) ‖ A-LOES (CarA) [By folk etym. See note at SEM-PERVIVE]

sing·let [sɪŋglɪt] *n* (Guyn) ‖ MERINO (CarA) [*COD8* marks this usage as Br only. Linguistic Atlas of Scotland (Map 11) cites the word as current in Cumberland, Edinburgh, and Glasgow areas] □ Used more by older *Guyn* folk. Now often replaced by VEST.

sink *vb* PHRASE **sink a pan** *vb phr* (Trin) To make concave the surface of a STEELPAN, and then the distinctive divisions in it, by hammering the heated surface. *Instead of raising the notes on the pan, he first sunk the pan and then raised the notes. This was not an easy process. Manette had to temper the pan using heat. We thus had a concave pan with raised notes.*—JWSSS:26

sink·a·vi·vy *n* (Jmca); **sink.er-/sin.kle-bi.ble** (Antg, Jmca); **sink-on-bi.ble** (Belz) [sɪŋkʌvaɪ vi ~ sɪŋkʌ-/sɪŋkl-/sɪŋkɒn-baɪbl] ‖ ALOES (CarA) [By folk etym. See note at SEMPERVIVE]

sink·hole *n* (Jmca) **1.** (See cit). *Watch out for Elizabeth, be careful of sinkholes. Sinkholes are deep natural holes in the ground occurring mostly in limestone country.*—RPME:2 **2.** [By extension] The pit of a latrine. *'Now, who would imagine,' Uncle Leonard said calmly, tapping his forehead and shaking his head despondently, 'that they'd buil' the back porch direc'ly over the sink hole of an ol' pit closet, eh?'*—SJS:40 **3.** [By extension] [*AF—Joc*] A large pothole in the road. *Huge 'sinkholes' have deepened creating a hazard to motorists. There is little evidence of any road repairs being undertaken.*—WeS (73.10.26, p.6)

sin·ti-bi·by (Mrat); **sin.tle-bi.ble** (Jmca) [sɪntɪ-baɪbi ~ sɪntl-baɪbl] *n* ‖ ALOES CarA [By folk etym. See note at SEMPERVIVE]

Sint Maar·tian [sɪnt marʃən] *n, adj* (St. Mar-.tin.er) *n* (Neth) (A person or thing) belonging to or characteristic of St Maarten; one of the [Dutch] WINDWARD ISLANDS. **a.** *When Sint Maartians gather for festive occasions, chicken Lokri, that piquant combination of chicken and rice is frequently the pièce de résistance of the menu.*—Neth (Ms) **b.** *Closer cooperation with the University of St. Martin and ... the University of Virgin Islands and the University of the West Indies to promote the integration of young St. Martiners into the international society were also proposed.*—AdV (93.09.14, p.12)

sip *n* (Trin) See CYP.

si·ra·hee (si·ri·hi) *n* (Guyn) A forest trail; [by extension] a narrow path cut through bush to facilitate hunting or exploration. [< *BAED* Arawak *surihi* 'a trail identified by the breaking of twigs far apart']

si·ri·co·te *n* (Belz) See ZIRICOTE.

si·sal ['saɪzʌl] *n* (Baha, CayI, Jmca) ‖ AGAVE (CarA) [Particularly the variety *Agave sisalana*, the leaves of which are stout and armed with a notable terminal spine; (IAE) sisal hemp] □ This IAE name is only used by some speakers, several other folk-names occurring. See AGAVE, CACTUS.

sis·ser·ou (par·rot)* [sɪsəru (parɒt)] *n (phr)* (Dmca) A large mountain-dwelling parrot with greenish-blue feathers on the head, violet on the hind-neck, and purplish under the body and tail; it is indigenous to Dominica and is the country's national bird; *Amazona imperialis (Psittacidae)*.

sit PHRASES **1. sit back down** *vb phr* (CarA) [*IF*] To sit down again; to resume your seat. *And silly Ian, after realising he had made himself look childish in everyone's eyes, smiled sheepishly and then sat back down.*—BoM (80.01.04, p.16) [< *sit down* + BACK⁴ 2(ii)] □ Also AmE. **2. sit down janm-an-kwa** [sɪt dʌŋ žãm-ā-kwa] *vb phr* (Dmca) [*AF—Joc*] ‖ COCK TEN (Guyn) *Since mornin[g] she sittin[g] do[w]ng janm-an-kwa and now she sayin[g] she hungry.*—(Dmca) [Fr Cr < Fr *jambes en croix* 'with legs crossed'] **3. sit down like Miss Priss** *vb phr* (Baha) [*AF—Joc*] ‖ COCK TEN (Guyn) **4. sit down like Miss Queensie** *vb phr* (Dmca) [*AF—Joc*] ‖ COCK TEN (Guyn) **5. sit for an exam; sit for a certificate/licence** *vb phrs* (CarA) [*IF*] To sit or take an examination (for a certificate, etc). **a.** *Mark you, the girls and the boys sat for the same exam. But the girls' father was a professional man; the boys' parents were fishermen.*—AdN (76.01.24, p.4) **b.** *He hasn't sat for his Chemists and Druggists certificate yet.*—(Guyn) □ Also AmE. **6. sit off** *vb phr* (Guyn, Trin) [*AF—Joc*] To sit grandly, idly, flirtatiously. **a.** *She stopped trying to work out which it would be. Whichever would make him a judge at two carnival shows sitting off in a new sharp suit with long slits at the sides of the jacket and a broad polka dotted tie.*—JJM:91 **b.** *You would have picked up with some other little high-tailed ass who would have made you suck salt. Somebody like that Fergus jamette you sitting off with.*—JJM:89

sit·ting chair *n phr* (Guyn) A straight-backed, armless chair . [Perh to distinguish from BERBICE CHAIR, (SE) *rocking chair, lounge chair,* etc]

sit·ting-up *n* (Baha) ‖ SET-UP² (Jmca) *The Bain Town Freedom and Justice Committee, ... announced a memorial service and 'sitting-up' to be held at the Meeting Street Bethel Baptist Church beginning 10 o'clock tonight.*—TrI (76.02.02, p.1)

si·wik (ci·rique) [siwik] *n* (Dmca) An edible freshwater crab with brown, black and yellow claws.

six-o'clock-bee(tle) *n* (Guyn) ‖ ABERDEEN (Tbgo) *The next afternoon as soon as de six o'clock bee whistle, ups come Streiker and put on a big pad-lock on the pipe, and he walk out de yard cool cool, cool.*—Kai.8 (71/12, p.61, D. Jeffrey) [From the fact that the insect makes its high-pitched whistling sound about sunset]

six·pen·ny-nail *n* (Bdos, Jmca) A two-inch nail. *Implanted and baked into one of the loaves and covered with a skin of flour was a rusty six-penny nail.*—NaT (78.02.17, p.1) [Cp *OED* 'a nail originally costing sixpence per hundred' + cits 15C–19C] □ This way of referring to nails is common in *Bdos, Jmca.* Hence also FOURPENNY (1-1/2 in)-, EIGHTPENNY (2-1/2 in)- and TEN-PENNY (3 in)- NAILS. These forms are still used in BrE, but not generally in CE, nails being usu referred to by length.

six-weeks *n* (Antg, Dmca, StKt) ‖ BODI (BEAN) (Gren, etc) [From the length of time from planting to reaping]

si·yé glo [siye glo] *vb phr* (Dmca) To have an impossible-looking task. *How you can expect your father to buy all them things? You expect the man to siyé glo?*—(Dmca) [Fr Cr < Fr *scier de l'eau* 'saw water'] □ Cp GIVE SB A BASKET TO CARRY WATER (*CarA*) (See BASKET Phr 1.)

size down/round/up *vb phr* (Bdos) [*IF*] ‖ D-RESS DOWN² (CarA) (See DRESS² Phr 3.) *Doan min' how tick de crowd is, / Duh will size roun' an gi' yuh a lil' scotch.*—SNWIC:106 (B. St John) [Though this spelling is always used in *Bdos* dial writing, the vb phr is prob < *side* vb + paragogic (-s) as in the CE folk vbs FRIENDS, GROUNDS, KICKS. Note *EDD* side¹ vb 11. 'to stand aside; to move away'; also *OED* side vb 12. intr 'to move or turn sideways']

ska¹ [ska:] *n* (CarA) 1. Jamaican music with a quick, lively 1-2-1-2 drum-beat, accompanied by wind instruments, esp the trombone, and folk lyrics; it originated among poor Jamaican rural folk and was adapted for party-dancing by urban dance-bands; widely popular in the Caribbean in the 1950s/60s, it became the forerunner of ROCK STEADY and REGGAE. *Jamaicans are very nationalistic about their music. That is why over the years we have had from them such big hits as the ska, the blue beat, the rock steady and now*

the ubiquitous reggae.—AdN (73.09.10) 2. [By extension] The dance to such music, involving swinging the arms and feet crosswise, alternating with a pulling action with the fists closed and the body bent forward as if miming hard work. [Prob < Black American *scat* '(1920's) generally attributed to Louis Armstrong who, when he forgot the words of a song would make up syllables, often trying to imitate verbally the sounds of musical instruments, a kind of spontaneous 'sound' poetry ...' (C. Major: *Black Slang*, Routledge 1971). The tunes were (first?) popularized in *Jmca* by a band named 'The Skatalites'. SKA may be a back-formation or the result of *CarA Cr* loss of /-t/ (cp WHA[T] DA[T])]

ska² *vb intr* (CarA) To dance the SKA. *Grand Picnic and Dance—Whit Monday June 7th—Joseph Liburd's Orchestra—These boys will keep you Ska-ing until you're real gone.*—DeM(SK) (Ad, 65.05.29, p.12) □ The phr **to do the ska** is, however, commoner.

skank¹ (scank) [skaŋk] *vb* [*AF*] 1. To loaf, be shifty; [by extension] to use cunning or deceit to outwit sb or to get sth done; to steal and slip or speed away. 2. [By extension] To dance in the particular free style associated with DUB or REGGAE. *'I dub I scrub all the days of my life, in the house of the Lord, Jah Rastafari' goes one line of the song, and whenever Clark goes into that catchy line it is a treat to see how the kids start 'skanking' and stomping to a beat and a song they have made in the last few weeks their own reggae 'anthem'.*—WeS (74.06.07, p.20) [Perh orig an echoic word. Sense 1. is evid older and said by some to be associated with motorbike getaways; sense 2. is derived from the kind of hip-swinging dancing wh is both typical of people of generally low social status and reminiscent of the waist movements of a motor-cyclist speeding in and out of other traffic. Note SKANKER] □ The term in sense 2. has spread beyond *Jmca.*

skank² (scank) *n* (Jmca) A free-style individual dance with a partner, to DUB or REGGAE music. (See cit). *Skank, the new dance / Reggae is on its way out. / As the replacement, local producers are introducing the Skank. / The Skank is boundless, having no limits to what the dancer wishes to do with his body or the scope allowed himself and his partner. / The drums boom, bang and roll, while the heavy bass keeps the rhythm. The dancer, according to his mood, can rock slowly to the bass, or go all out and skank to the drums.*—WeG (73.01.24, p.13) [By functional vb > n shift of SKANK¹ 2.]

skank·er *n* (Jmca) A deceitful, untrustworthy person; a dissolute man. *But please make sure you're not a skanker out to give worries. I don't want you spoiling up my track record and get me in kass-kass.*—WeG (73.07.11, p.13, Partyline) [< vb SKANK¹ 1. + SE agential suff -*er*]

skel·lion (skal·lion) ['skɛliʌn] *n* (CayI, Jmca, Trin) ‖ ESCHALLOT (Bdos, Guyn) [< SE *scallion* pronunc [skælyən]. *Skellion* is, however, Formal *Jmca* spelling and pronunc]

skil·let *n* 1. (Bdos, Belz) ‖ *draw-bucket* (Baha) ‖ *saucepan* 1 (Antg, Brbu, Guyn) An empty gallon-size (paint or other commercial) can, usu with a wire handle, wh is put to domestic use. *The skillet was caught up and canted and the water crashed against my head and down my body in a swishing cataract…. My mother wheeled round, swinging the skillet by its wire handle.*—LICMS: 8 2. (TkCa) ‖ THREE-FOOT POT (Guyn, etc)

skimp·ish *adj* (Guyn) [*IF*] Skimpy. *Why your parcel of bora so skimpish? Put a lil mo[re], nuh?* —(Guyn)

skin[1] *n* (CarA) 1. [Used in specific ref to a person's complexion] See BROWN-SKIN, CLEAR-SKIN, FAIR-SKIN, LIGHT-SKIN, etc. 2. [*AF*] [Used in ref to the whole body] (Your) body, self, person. *Look at how that fool is driving, nuh. Just good for the police to hold him and let the magistrate put a good fine in his skin* (i.e. on him).—(Trin) [A sense and usage most prob drawn from Afr langs. Cp *DAFL* Twi *hõ* 1. (a) 'exterior of things, the outside; (b) the human frame; (c) the whole body; (d) the whole person' 3. 'In a number of expressions wh denote conditions and qualities of the bodily constitution of man' (+ many exs): *Wo hõ te dɛŋ? (Your outside/frame/body is how?)* 'How are you?; etc'] □ See the Phrs at 4. 3. [*AF—Joc*] ‖ *skins* (Gren, StVn) [Perh by extension] A woman (as an object of sexual desire). 4. PHRASES 4.1 a (nice) piece of skin *n phr* (Guyn, Tbgo, Trin) [*AF—Joc/Derog*] A sexually attractive woman. [Cp sense 3.] 4.2 bathe your skin *vb phr* (CarA) [*IF*] ‖ wash your skin (CarA) [*AF*] To shower; to bath. *And quick so. I bathe my skin and put on my good clothes and I gone.*—MTCP:43 4.3 be in sb's skin (to do sth) *vb phr* (Gren) [*AF*] To continually harass, molest sb. *If I don't give this child a computer for Christmas she will drive me crazy. Since August she in me skin to buy her one.*—(Gren) 4.4 beat/ burst/cut/mash/tear sb's skin *vb phrs* (CarA) [*AF/IF*] To flog, beat up, thrash sb severely. **a.** *I have a good mind to tell your father when he comes and let him beat your skin.*—(Guyn) **b.** *Hi Lawd! Manny boy, you lucky oui, I would mash he skin wid de flat of me cutlish.*—RTCS:8 4.5 Fire your skin! *imper vb phr* (Tbgo) [*AF*] ‖ MOVE YOURSELF (Baha, etc) *Look fire your little skin outside and stop plaguing me!*—(Tbgo) 4.6 fly out of your skin (Bdos) *vb phr* [*AF—Joc*] See FLY Phr 3.3 4.7 give me some skin *vb phr* (CarA) [*AF—Joc*] ‖ GIVE ME SOME FLESH (CarA) See FLESH Phr 3.1; also GIVE[1] Phr 11. □ Also (esp Black) AmE slang. 4.8 Haul your skin! *vb phr* (Gren) [*AF*] ‖ HAUL YOURSELF! (Bdos, etc) See HAUL Phr 4.6 4.9 jump from/out of your skin *vb phr* (CarA) [*AF—Joc*] See JUMP Phr 5.2, 5.5 4.10 licks in your skin *n phr* (CarA) [*AF*] A flogging; lashes; blows. *His mother used to shout: 'Gordon come from over by Elizabeth Grant or is licks in your skin?'*—JJM:151 4.11 next skin to nothing *id phr* (Bdos) [*AF—Joc*]

See NEXT Phr 2.2 4.12 pelt/put/throw (some) licks in (sb's) skin *vb phr* (Bdos) [*AF*] See LICKS Phr 3.8 4.13 Pelt your skin! *imper vb phr* (StVn) [*AF*] ‖ MOVE YOURSELF (Baha, etc) 4.14 see your skin *vb phr* (Trin) [*AF—Joc*] See SEE Phr 3.7 4.15 be/stick in sb's skin *vb phr* (Gren, Jmca) [*AF*] ‖ BE BEHIND SB LIKE A SLAVE-DRIVER (CarA) See BEHIND[1] Phr 2. 4.16 (your) skin catch fire (for sth) (Jmca) [*AF—Joc*] ‖ EYE(S) CATCH FIRE (FOR STH) (Gren, etc) 4.17 (your) skin crawls *vb phr* (Guyn) [*IF*] ‖ (YOUR) BLOOD CRAWLS (Gren, Tbgo, Trin) See BLOOD Phr 3.3 *I don't like to see geckos, they make my skin crawl.*—(Guyn) 4.18 your skin is not your own *id phr* (Trin) [*AF*] You are poor and beholden to others; you are so poor that you hardly own yourself. *And she had snapped at the children, 'Allyou stop this car business. Your father's skin not his own and you all letting him fool you with car?*—JJM:30 4.19 wash sb's skin *vb phr* (CarA) [*AF—Joc*] To trounce (sb); to whip, defeat (sb) thoroughly. □ More often metaph, less physical than Phr 4.4 4.19.1 wash your skin *vb phr* (CarA) [*AF*] ‖ BATHE YOUR SKIN (CarA) [*IF*]

skin[2] *vb tr* 1. (Gren, Guyn, StVn) [*AF/IF*] To beat (sb, esp a young person) mercilessly. 2. (Bdos) [*AF*] To rob; to steal from; to pick the pocket of (sb). *Later M— was seen in the Stork Club with the watch and with money and the Police were contacted. P.C. 351 went to the Club and found the watch in M—'s pocket. / He has been jailed for 6 months for skinning a man.*—TrU (64.01.01, p.8) 3. (Bdos) To expose (a pocket, bag, etc) by turning inside out. *The accused's defence was that he went to the gas station and asked to use the telephone and he did not put his hand in the cash box nor did he take any money from it. / He said that he 'skinned' his pockets before leaving the station.*—AdN (75.01.22, p.2) 4. PHRASES 4.1 skin and grin *vb phr* (CarA) [*AF—Derog*] To laugh foolishly or only to give an impression of friendliness; to be superficially friendly; to be untrustworthy. 4.2 skin cuffins *vb phr* (Bdos) [*AF*] ‖ skin-(the)-cat (Baha, USVI) To perform a somersault (esp in swimming). *Girl, over de las' week an' a half, four children get burn-up in fires … dah kin' o' news does mek yuh heart skin cuffins.*—NaT (78.11.10, p.5, Lickmout' Lou) 4.3 skin up *vb phr* (Bdos) (i) [*AF*] To upturn; to expose by overturning. *I hear a noise and hear a table skin up. / I ask the man why he skin up the table, and he ask me who I talking to.*—NaT (90.10.05, p.6) (ii) [*AF—Vul*] [By extension, of a woman] To expose yourself (esp the buttocks) indecently. □ See Phr 4.3.2 below 4.3.1 skin up (with sb) *vb phr* (Bdos, Guyn) [*AF*] To grin ingratiatingly (at/with sb). *When black people come to buy they act like they doin[g] a favour, but as soon as a white face turn up, look how they ready to skin up with them.*—(Bdos) 4.3.2 skin up (your clothes/ dress/yourself) *vb phrs* (Bdos, Guyn) [*AF—Vul*] [Of a woman] To throw the back of the skirt over the head while bending forward and exposing the buttocks as an act of coarse insult to sb. *You and I broke up because you always skinning up your clothes and behaving badly.*—Bdos (CR, 69.09.01) **4.3.3 skin up your face/lip/mouth/nose** *vb phrs* (ECar) [*AF*] [Esp of a young person] To grimace with displeasure, disapproval, scorn, etc. ... *that is why I here feelin' funny at how fellow black people does cock up them eyes and skin up them mout' at a fellow black man posin' as Father Claus ... tryin' to make a few dollars and cents.*—AdV (89.12.24, p.15) □ See also FACE Phr 4., 5., 6. **4.4 skin your teeth** *vb phr* (CarA) [*AF—Derog*] To laugh or grin stupidly; to grin in order to please. **a.** *When people give money, you think they care who get it? Once they open they mouth and skin their teeth for a photo in the papers, they happy, they happy, you hear.*—NTMM:167 **b.** *Calvin start slacking up on the first car wash work, and he humming as he shine the white people car, he skinning his teet in the shine and he smiling.*—CWFYS:98

skin-cat *n* (Baha) A mixture of dough fried in deep oil. [From turning it over. Cp SKIN-(THE)-CAT]

skin-fish *n* (Guyn) Any fish that has no scales esp the CATFISH; such fishes are despised as food by some people for religious or other reasons. *The Lau-Lau is one of the larger Siluroids, or 'scale-less' fishes or, as they are termed locally 'skin-fishes'.*—RFLG:74

skin·(n)ip; **skin.(n)up**, **skin.op** *n* (Gren, StKt) ‖ GUINEP (CarA)

ski·nop (**skin·(n)ip, skin·(n)up**) ['skɪnɪp ~ 'skɪnʌp] *n* (Gren, Guyn, StKt) ‖ GUINEP (CarA) *The skinnup has a pulpy surface covering the seed. It is enclosed in a thin green skin which you crack to get the pulp inside which you may suck, it being the only eatable part of the fruit.*—Gren (Ms, 1978) [Prosthetic /s-/ + kinip, etc (see KENEP) □ *Skinnip* (etc), wh may be regularized as *ski-nop*, is Formal in *StKt* but regarded as *AF* in *Guyn* and possibly elsewhere where GUINEP is preferred.

skins *n sg* (Gren, StVn) [*AF—Joc*] ‖ SKIN¹ 3. (CarA) *He or she becomes the victim of 'give me a bob', 'watch food', 'that is a volkswagen' 'she is carrying her goods in the back', 'look at skins' and lots of other remarks which are degrading.*—WeG (68.07.25, p.4) [SKIN¹ 3. + paragogic /-s/]

skin-teeth [skɪn-ti·t] *n* (CarA) [*AF—Derog*] **1.** The smile or grin of a false friend; a cynical little laugh baring the teeth. *Every skin-teet[h] ain[']t a laugh* (= *Every smile or grin is not to be trusted*).—Guyn (Prov) **2.** PHRASE **2.1 give skin-teet[h]** *id phr* (CarA) See GIVE¹ PHR 2.33., ALSO SKIN² Phr 4.4

skin-(the)-cat [skɪn(dɪ)kyat] **1.** *n* (Baha, USVI) ‖ CUFFUM 2 (Guyn) **2.** *vb phr* (Baha, USVI) See CUFFUM Phr 3.1

skip·per *n* (Bdos, Guyn) [Respectful or in-gratiating form of address to a man] Boss! *Someone will hollo at you, and you stop the car and talk to him, and then somebody else comes up and says 'a word with you skipper, when you done'. Half an hour is gone and you missed your appointment.*—Bdos (Hd, 74.11.26, p.4198) [< IF SE *skipper* 'captain of a ship', a survival of usage from the days when schooners plied regularly between *Bdos* and *Guyn*, the term being transferred to general usage]

skirt *n* (CarA) [Steelband] The vertical rim of a STEELPAN, cut off from the original oil-drum to varying depths that produce the different musical pitches; the shortest cut, or *skirt*, is 6 ins for the TENOR PAN, and the longest *skirt* is the uncut drum used for the BASS.

skulk *vb intr* (Guyn) **1.** ‖ BREAK BICHE (Gren, etc) [Esp in Phrase] ‖ *skulk from school*. See BICHE Phr **2.** [Esp of workmen] To work unwillingly by shirking, hiding, absence, etc. [Cp OED skulk vb 2. 'to hide or conceal oneself, etc; shelter oneself in a cowardly manner; shirk duty, etc'] □ Cp SKULL¹.

skull¹ *vb tr* (Gren, Jmca) [*IF*] **1.** To idle away (time); to skip (a duty) *Instead of going to school we would skull the time and go and play marbles.*—Jmca (Ms) **2.** PHRASE **2.1 skull school** *vb phr* (Gren, Jmca) [*IF*] ‖ *break biche* (Gren, etc) ‖ *scud school* (Antg) To absent yourself from school. [Prob < *skulk* (as for *Guyn*) with characteristic CarA Cr reduction of final /-CC/] □ Cp SKULK.

skull² *n* (Trin) [*AF*] **1.** A trick; an act of deception. [Perh a short form of SE *skulduggery*, or a functional vb > n shift of SKULL¹, also with an extension of sense developing in Trin] **2.** PHRASE **2.1 pull a skull** *vb phr* (Trin) [*AF—Joc*] To try a trick (on sb); to do sth dishonest. *A Pentecostal Pastor who tried to pull a 'skull' on a woman police ended up in court on three charges.*—BoM (80.03.14, p.22)

skunk *vb tr* (Baha) [*AF*] To beat convincingly. □ Usage generally restricted to competitive games. Also *CED* AmE slang.

sky-juice *n* (Jmca) [*AF—Joc*] ‖ SNOW-CONE (CarA) [Fanciful name, since the liquid is sweet and cold. Cp 'snow'. Cp also BALLOON-JUICE]

sky-red *n* (Gren) [*AF/IF*] Arson. *Even Gairy in 1951 was able to terrorise the then establishment more or less out of existence with his frequent preachings of 'sky-red'—whatever he intended that term to mean and incite.*—NeJ (75.02.12, p.8) [From a slogan used ('Let the sky be red' or 'The sky will be red') during the 1951 labour disturbances when buildings were burnt at night in protest against the colonial government's stand] **2.** [By extension] Riotous protest. *In due course we will give labourers their increase and there will be no 'sky-red' because we will take* *the necessary precautions.*—Gren (Hd, 57.10.19, p.23)

slack *adj* (CarA) **1.** [Of persons] Slovenly; irresponsible; sloppy. *You mean she made the man foul up an appointment again? Only a slack secretary would make such a mistake twice.*—(Jmca) [As *OED slack* 1. '... negligent or lax in regard to one's duties'. This sense, one of several related to 'laxness' in SE, is the most frequent one in CE extending to 'looseness' in sense 2., and esp to the frequency of the noun derivative SLACKNESS] **2.** [By extension] [*IF*] Indecent; unprincipled; immoral. *He then explained and apologised that his actions were part of his job and that was the only way to satisfy me. He told me that I must consider him a friend and not as a 'slack' doctor. I would like to know if this doctor was trying to exploit my innocence or if it is really his duty to do what he did to me.*—SuC (76.08.08, p.27)

slack·ness *n* (CarA) **1.** Sloppiness; incompetence; irresponsible behaviour. *Clearly, a lot of slackness is going on at St Ann's and it's a shameless affair for employees to be stealing the food which is supposed to be eaten by patients.*—BoM (79.07.20, p.8) **2.** [*IF*] Vulgarity; indecent behaviour. *All this time the steel band blasting some hot numbers and the old Five, whenever he see Harris watching him, starting to jock waist for so, and fanning with his jacket, and jumping up like if is a real carnival slackness, only to make Harris get vex.*—STLL:99

slam *vb tr* PHRASES **slam a dom; slam dominoes** *vb phrs* (Bdos) [*AF/IF*] To play a game of dominoes. **a.** *... but we do not want to see the young people at 12 o'clock midnight and at 1 and 2 o'clock in the morning slamming dominoes, playing juke boxes and sleeping about.*—Bdos (Hd, 74.03.18, p.3403) **b.** *Wherever Bajans meet to slam a dom and have fun you can be sure that Cockspur Rum will also be there!*—Bdos (B, Ad) [*Dom* is abbr of *domino*. The dominoes are slammed down on the surface being played on with great force throughout the game so that one can hear dominoes being played]

slam-bam *n* (Baha) A sandwich made of plain, sliced sausages between two slices of bread. [Prob an ideophonic ref to the quick, rough-and-ready making]

slang *n* (ECar) [*X*] Any Caribbean creole word or phrase; any item or idiom of Caribbean creolized English. **a.** *Throughout the story ('Mystic Masseur') Naipaul uses down-to-earth words which one will find in current use in Trinidad—a great deal of slangs which add to the humour of the story.*—Trin (Ms) **b.** *Slangs which are used in my country are 'she crabbed him', 'you good day', etc.*—StVn (Ms) □ IAE *slang* refers to a type or level of speech taken as a whole. In CE the term is used to refer to each example of the type as *a slang*, hence the pl in the cits above.

slap *vb tr* PHRASE **slap tar** *vb phr* (Bdos) [*AF—Joc*] ‖BEAT TAR (CayI) *I have been slapping tar for a few days now because my cycle is down with two flat tyres and a knocking in the differential.*—NaT (74.01.13, p.13, Al's Grapevine)

slave-driver *n* [Hist] **1.** ‖*driver* (CarA) The Black foreman of a work-group of slaves, himself a slave, who supervised the group with a bull-whip. **2.** PHRASE **2.1 be behind sb like a slave-driver** *vb phr* (CarA) [*AF—Derog*] See BEHIND[1] Phr 2

slave-liz·ard *n* (Bdos, Trin) ‖WOOD-SLAVE (ECar) [Perh abbr of a redundant compound (CE) WOODSLAVE + (SE) *lizard*]

S.L.C. *abbr* (StLu) Saint Lucia Cross, a national honour awarded for distinguished and outstanding service of national importance to Saint Lucia; the title 'The Honourable' is placed before the recipient's name.

sleep[1] *n* PHRASES **1. kill a sleep** *vb phr* (CarA) [*AF*] See KILL Phr 3.1.1 **2. sleep is killing you** *id phr* (CarA) [*IF/AF*] See KILL Phr 3.1

sleep[2] *vb* **1.** (ECar) [*IF*] [Used of inanimate things] To remain outside during the night. *You let these clothes sleep on the line and look how they are wet from last night's rain.*—(Guyn) **2.** PHRASE **2.1 sleep away/off** *vb phr* (CarA) [*IF*] To fall asleep while in company. *I leavin' ... leavin' for good. Silence. Chan, you sleepin' ... you gone and sleep-away on me, man? No.*—GL:53 (I. Khan) [An extension of *OED sleep* vb 10. with *out* or *away* 'to pass or spend (a certain time) in sleep']

sleeve[1] *n* (CarA) [Banana Ind] An open-ended light-blue, polythene covering for a bunch of bananas used to protect it from insect pests in its maturing. *It must be remembered, however, that sleeves will only protect fruit against rust thrips if the bunch is sleeved early (that is 14–21 days after shooting) and the sleeve covers the complete bunch.*—NeC (76.09.18, p.10)

sleeve[2] *vb tr* (CarA) [Banana Ind] To put a protective polythene covering on (a maturing bunch of bananas). *Bunches are ready for sleeving when the final hand can be seen but before the fingers of the top hand point upwards. Winban strongly recommends growers to sleeve now.*—NeC (76.09.18, p.10) [By functional n > vb shift of SLEEVE[1]]

slice *n* (StLu) ‖FEG (Angu, etc).

slid·ers [slaɪdərz] *n pl* (CarA) Knee-length or longer close-fitting underpants worn by men (esp in former times).

sling *n* (ECar) Very thick, almost jelly-like cane syrup before it begins to crystallize; it was used (esp in former times) to make a sweet drink or for candying pastry, etc. [Cp *OED sling* sb⁵ 2. 'the juice of the sugar-cane, as obtained in the manufacture of sugar'. However the *OED* cits relate better to the *CarA* sense]

sling-mud *n* (Guyn) The massive, shallow silted area wh stretches along the Atlantic coast and estuaries of Guyana; it is an area for shrimp fishing. *What saved us from not being picked up was that we reached the sling-mud fast and their boat could not come any further.*—GyC (78.03.29, p.3) [Perh related to SLING (as prec) because of its consistency. In shallow areas fish are also caught by 'slinging' or 'shying' the mud by hand to confuse them]

slip·per·y back* *n phr* (Angu, ViIs) A shiny, bronze, ground lizard about 6 ins long; *Mabuya mabouia* (*Lacertidae*).

S.L.M.H. *abbr* (StLu) Saint Lucia Medal of Honour, a national honour awarded to a person who has rendered eminent service of national importance or who has performed outstanding brave and humane acts.

S.L.M.M. *abbr* (StLu) Saint Lucia Medal of Merit, a national honour awarded to a person who is considered to have performed long and meritorious service in the Arts, Sciences, Literature, or other such fields.

slop[1] *n* (Baha) The inedible parts of a conch that are dug out and dumped. [< SE *slop* 'unpleasant watery refuse' by extension]

slop[2] *vb* (Baha) To separate the offal of a conch leaving the edible part for use. *Conch—broken, jooked and slopped, offering recipes in every fashion and other sea food delicacies which evade this tiny village.* / *Twenty-five conchs were broken, jooked and slopped in an incredible six minutes and 50 seconds by John Reckley of Rocky Creek.*—NaG (75.10.01, p.7) [By functional n > vb shift of SLOP[1]]

S.L.P.M. *abbr* (StLu) Saint Lucia Les Pitons Medal, a national honour awarded for long and meritorious service tending to promote loyal public service and national welfare or to inculcate and strengthen community spirit.

slut-lamp *n* (Bdos) ‖ BOTTLE-FLAMBEAU (StVn, Trin) [*OED* slut 4. 'a piece of rag dipped in lard or fat and used as a light' + cits from 1609] □ Also sometimes SMUT-LAMP (prob by folk etym).

smack(-boat) *n* **1.** (Belz) A fishing boat built for open-sea fishing; it has a special well in its hull, supplied with fresh sea-water through holes in the bottom of the boat, for keeping the catch alive. **2.** (Baha) (SE) A fishing smack. (See cit) *Sloops (smacks) are larger (25 ft to 35 ft)* [*fishing*] *vessels propelled primarily by sail, although many are fitted with small auxiliary inboard or outboard engines.*—WAAF:35

small *adj* (CarA) **1.** [*IF*] Thin by loss of weight. *You notice how the clothes hangin[g] on me? The sickness make me small.*—(Guyn) **2.** [*IF*] Embarrassed; belittled; humiliated (See Phrs 3.2). **3.** PHRASES **3.1 get small** *vb phr* (Tbgo, Trin) [*IF*] See GET Phr 3.20 **3.2 make (sb) feel/look small** *vb phr* (Guyn) [*IF*] To humiliate or gravely discredit (sb).

Small crop *n phr* (Guyn) [Rice Ind; Sugar Ind] ‖ FIRST CROP, SPRING CROP (Guyn) [So called as being the smaller and earlier of the two crops, in each industry in *Guyn* the later being the BIG CROP]

small gang *n phr* (Antg) See note at GANG.

small-is·land *n, adj* (Trin) [*AF—Joc*] (A person) native of or belonging to any of the economically less developed or geographically smaller islands of the Eastern Caribbean. **a.** *Ah sorry for all dem Grenadians and St Lucians who come over here to make money. If yuh see the small island people in town! All over de place, wayever yuh turn, yuh bouncing up small-island. Dey must be tink Trinidad is ah paradise.*—SABS:136 **b.** *Yet this may be because every Trinidadian black family admits with bemusement that it has small-island origins, generally Barbadian, Grenadian, or 'Vincelonian', as if these were Old World, and Port of Spain as amusedly admits in certain small-island accents of her architecture, so that the small-island, old-world atmosphere of Belmont with its lacy verandahs, packed-tight houses, ferns and rusting roofs is pure Grenada.*—ACTT:22 □ The term (wh usu does not apply to *Tbgo*) has spread in use to *Bdos, Jmca* in ref to other islanders except *Trin*.

smell *vb* PHRASES **1. smell hell (to do sth)** *vb phr* (Bdos, Guyn, USVI) [*AF*] See HELL Phr 2.1, 4. *Ten years went by. Dorothy smelled hell in those ten years ... / Her uncle looked around the house and was shocked almost senseless ... No tables, no rockers. He started asking where's all the furniture?*—PKKK:53 **2. smell high** *vb phr* (Guyn) [*AF/IF*] To have a strong, sharp smell (ref to perfume, cooking or sth rotting). **3. smell stink** *vb phr* (CarA) [*IF*] See STINK[2] Phr 4.2 **4. smell up the place** *vb phr* (ECar) [*IF*] To cause a house, place or area to smell unpleasant or nauseous. *They always puttin[g] a lot o[f] chicken manure on thier plants and smelling up the place*—(Bdos) **5. smell yourself** *vb phr* (Bdos, Guyn, Tbgo) [*AF—Derog*] [Of a young person] To be precocious and disrespectful. *Don'[t] answer me like dat! Hoy!! Well you like yo[u] really smellin[g] yo[ur]self dese days!*—(Bdos) [A ref to the early years of puberty when body odours, esp of the genitals, are more pronounced]

S.M.H. *abbr* (Dmca) The Services Medal of Honour, a national award of the Commonwealth of Dominica for distinguished service in the Disciplined Forces.

smoke *vb* (CarA) *PHRASE* **crapaud smoke your pipe** *id phr* (Dmca, Gren, Guyn, Nevs, Trin) [*AF—Joc*] See CRAPAUD Phr

smoke-her·ring *n* (CarA) Smoke-dried herring; it is widely imported in the Caribbean, formerly a cheap food esp in early post-slavery times. *But Tantie spread some slices of bread alarmingly thickly with butter, heaped some of the smoke'-herring onto a plate with the bread.*—HCCM:18 [< SE *smoked herring* with characteristic CE absence of /-d/ in pa. part]

smouse[1]; **smous·ing** [smɒuz(ɪŋ)] *n* (Guyn) A small dam about 3 or 4 ft high, built of compacted mud, to prevent rising waters from flooding a particular (usu small) area of land. [Of Du origin] □ The term *smousing* is often used for a smaller type of SMOUSE. Cp EMPOLDER *vb* and *n*.

smouse[2] [smɒuz] *vb tr* To protect from flooding by means of a SMOUSE. [By functional *n* > *vb* shift of SMOUSE[1]]

smut(-di·sease) *n* (CarA) [Sugar Ind] A fungal disease wh blackens the stalks of the sugar-cane plant and makes the cane unusable. *Precautions are being taken against an outbreak of smut disease in Barbados. / The disease which is crippling the sugar industry in Jamaica, Martinique and Guyana has not yet reached Barbados, but a spokesman at the Sugar Breeding Station said that there was still a possibility that it could develop.*—NaT (77.08.28, p.35)

smut-lamp [smʌt-lamp] *n* (Bdos) ‖ SLUT-LAMP (Bdos) *Please sir, I ent got no lantern, I did always keep a smut lamp to keep pon de cart at night.*—SBHM:3 [< SLUT-LAMP by folk etym, ref to the soot]

snack·ette [snakɪt ~ snakɛt] *n* (Bdos, Guyn, StKt, Trin) A snack-bar and lunch-counter. **a.** *The Police Service Association will take over the operation of the snackette at the Police Wharf Branch from Monday. / The staff will consist of graduates of the Trinidad and Tobago Catering School.*—ExP (71.02.13, p.28) **b.** *At present the menu at Quik-Eats Snackette is comparable with those found in most of the island's snackettes. Included on the menu are chicken and chips, hamburgers, hot dogs, cheeseburgers, and various types of floats and flavours in milk shakes.*—AdN (73.01.20, p.3) [By analogy < AmE *dinette, launderette*]

snake-bush/-cham·pi·on/-plant *n* (Bdos, Belz, Guyn, USVI) [*IF*] ‖ SANSEVERIA (ViIs) [Both the variegated colouring of the leaves and the belief that the plant attracts or repels snakes may account for this folk-name]

snake-cut *n* (Guyn) A type of herbal vaccination, usu by an incision on the leg, done by Amerindians to prevent or to protect against the bite of any venomous snake.

snake-root *n* (Baha) ‖ BITTER-BUSH 3. (CarA)

snap (schnapp) *n* (Bdos, Guyn) ‖ *billigram* (Belz) ‖ *rum-snap* (Bdos) A small draught of rum, about 1 fluid oz. **a.** *Men stroll casually into shops buying from rum 'snaps' to corned-beef and biscuits to be consumed on the spot.*—AdV (76.02.08, p.11) **b.** *Give some of them a dollar and watch as they make their way to the nearest rumshop for either 'a snap of rum' or a cigarette. But that is more likely to be done by some of the older wanderers.*—AdV (89.02.15, p.3B) [Cp *OED schnapps* 'an ardent spirit resembling Hollands gin', + cits—1818 'Champagne for men and schnapps for Generals'. Perh developed in *Guyn* through dial Du (cp Du *snappen* 'to snatch'). However cp *OED snap* 4. 'a snack' + cit (1818) 'First taste a snap of Hollands'—wh suggests application of the term to drink as well] □ The spelling *schnapp* is regarded as the learned form in Guyn, but is used only by older folk.

snap-glass (schnapp-glass) *n* (Guyn) A small, stemless, colourless glass of about 1 fluid oz in capacity, used esp in serving rum. *Bosie and Stewart poured a shot each in the schnapp glasses and downed it without a flourish.*—CFMG:4 [See SNAP]

snap·per [snapa ~ snapə] *n* (CarA) ‖ *red-fish* (Bdos, Mrat, StVn) Any one of a number of deep-water sea fishes of the family *Lutjanidae* ranging in size from 1 to 7 ft; they feed on small fishes, shrimp, etc, and are of many colours (red, brown, green, yellow, dark grey, etc); they are highly prized for their food value.

snat *n* (CarA) [*X*] Snot; wet mucous from the nose. [By characteristic CarA Cr [ɔ > a] vowel opening, passing into CE]

snat-ap·ple *n* (Gren) [*AF*] ‖ CUSTARD-APPLE (CarA)

snat·ty *adj* (CarA) [*X*] [Esp of children] Snottynosed. [SNAT + SE familiar adj suff '-y']

snob [snɒb] *vb tr* (ECar) [*X*] To snub (sb); to disdain and clearly reject the company of (sb) as being socially inferior. *Cunningham was young, apparently intelligent and, judging by the way he had walked away from me because I snobbed him when he tried to talk with me on the Bay Street pavement that rainy afternoon, he certainly had pride.*—TRIH:91 [By functional shift of SE *snob* *n*, prob reinforced by failure to distinguish SE *snub vb*]

snow-ball *n* (Bdos, Gren, Jmca, Trin) ‖ SNO(W)-CONE (CarA) *A man stands beside his hand-cart dispensing snow-ball which consists of shaved ice covered with scarlet syrup, the cart bearing some such name as Perseverance or In Unity is Strength or Star of Ethiopia.*—SJW:46 [A ref to the compressed, white, shaved ice]

sno(w)-cone (snow-kone) *n* (CarA) ‖ *compress, crush-ice* (Guyn, Trin) ‖ *fresco* (Belz) ‖ *press*[2] (Gren, Trin) ‖ *shave-ice* (Guyn, Jmca) ‖ *sky-juice* (Jmca) ‖ *snow-ball* (Bdos, Gren, Jmca, Trin) Crushed ice packed in a paper-cone or plastic cup with syrup of different flavours poured on it, and sold on the street by the ‖ *snow-cone man*. **a.** *When the snow-kone operators burst upon the dry and thirsty city of Kingston three or four years ago, this man's business was gravely threatened. The snow-kone business was mechanised and motorized and people refreshed themselves to musical accompaniment. A revolution had taken place in the snowball industry.*—DaG (67.05.07, p.5) **b.** *Sno-cone vending provides employment for a large number of mostly young men, who ride their tricycle carts all over the island and sell their refreshing, cooling, sweet ices.*—AdN (78.12.10, p.5)

snow·drop* *n* (Bdos) ‖ AMARYLLIS (CarA) □ This name is usu applied to the white variety. See CROCUS[2].

snow-on-the-moun·tain* *n* (Antg, Bdos, Dmca, Jmca, StVn) ‖ *Christmas-bush* (StKt) ‖ *euphorbia* (Gren) ‖ *snow-poinsettia* (Trin) ‖ *snow-tree* (Dmca, Guyn) ‖ *white poinsettia* (Gren) An erect garden shrub usu about 6 ft tall (but often much taller) plentifully branched, and with an abundance of small, slightly spaced, lanceolate leaves that give way to a massive, luxuriant coverage of white leaf-like flowers throughout the Christmas and New Year season; *Euphorbia articulata (Euphorbiaceae). While Christmas Candles of flaming gold, gracefully adorn the scenery. The gleaming white of 'Snow-on-the-Mountain' the brilliance of red Poinsettia; it's Christmastime–the birth, the life, the blossoming together.*—SuS (79.12.23, p.13) [Name suggested by its dome-like covering of white flowers in December–January]

snow-poin·set·ti·a *n* (Trin) ‖ SNOW-ON-THE-MOUNTAIN (Antg, etc) [*Snow*, from white mass of its flowers, + *poinsettia*, of the same family the red variety of wh blooms at the same time]

snow-tree *n* (Dmca, Gren) ‖ SNOW-ON-THE-MOUNTAIN (Antg, etc)

snuck *vb tr* (ViIs) [*AF/IF*] To grab (sth); to seize (sth) rashly. *I see him go and snuck the money from the li[tt]le boy.*—(BrVi) [Prob an adoption of AmE pa.t. of *sneak.* (Cp similarly CE TO LOSS, TO LEF[T], etc) + semantic shift or extension of sense of *sneak (sth)* 'to take or gain (sth) furtively']

so[1] *adv* (CarA) **1.** [*IF*] [Indicating a place or direction with the hand] Hereabouts; thereabouts; in this/that direction or area. **a.** *My side is hurting me down here so.*—(Guyn) **b.** *Yuh jus go so and den so and den when yuh reach at top, yuh gwine see a road going so dont take dat one,*

go so!—AdN (75.03.09, p.3, Cartoon) [By extension of SE *so* as in *over so* 'over in that direction'] **2.** [*IF*] [Indicating manner with some illustrative gesture] Like that; like this (action); in this manner (that I am showing you). **a.** *'But you can't tell me nothing 'bout Deighton Boyce. Don' forget I raise near that man. My mother and his was like so!'* She held up two fingers twisted around each other.—MBGB:31 **b.** *When Sir Frank leaned into that out-swinger from Bedser, and Sir Frank make a little thing, so! be-Christ, it went to the ... boundary like lightning for four!*—CWFYS:86 **c.** *'Is so I does faint regular. From the time I so high.'* She gestured with her hand.—Cat 1V. 2, p.28) **2.1** [*AF/IF*] As easily as that; so readily. *'And this scent don't pass so,'* said Little, when I going home in a taxi I does be ashamed the way people treat me.'—BoM (75.05.09, p.14) **3.** *adv extension* [*AF*] Suddenly; abruptly; without warning or hesitation. **a.** *I tell you if anybody came and tell me like how I sitting here, that my child get knock down dead, I would go mad straight so.*—(Guyn) **b.** *But you know, somebody oughta take up a gun so and shoot down that man so,'cause he's nothing but the devil-incarnate.*—MBGB:60 **4.** *adv intensifier preverbal* [*IF*] [Often after a neg] Really; very much. **a.** *I do[n't] so like funerals.*—(Trin) **b.** *It is isn't that she so wanted to hurt him but just to get what was her right.*—Bdos (Ms) [Cp EE *so* as in God so loved the world ...', replaced in ModE by 'so much' as complement] **5.** *adv intensifier, post-adj or vb* [*AF*] To such an extent; as much as that; so very much/well. **a.** *Everywhere I go / People want to know / why I happy so.*—Bdos (Folksong) **b.** *Eh! Eh!! How ah sweet so? How ah could wind so? How ah nice so? and she continued winding in front of her.*—ToR (73.03.27, p.5) **6.** *terminal inquiry tag* [*AF/IF*] [For persuasive effect] May I ask? **a.** *Where you been so?* (= *Where did you go, may I ask?*)—(Guyn) **b.** *Which one o[f] you car[ry] it [a]way so?*—(Jmca) **7.** PHRASES **7.1** *do/put sb so vb phr* (CarA) [*AF*] See DO[1] PHR 3.1.1; ALSO PUT Phr 18. **7.2** *for so* /1ˈ3′/ *adv intensifier phr* (ECar) [*AF*—*Joc*] See FOR Phr 17.7 **7.3** *Good so! excl id phr* (CarA) [*AF*] See GOOD[1] Phr 2.4 **7.4** *I[t']s (not) so it go id phr* (Jmca) [*AF*] [Often neg] That is (not) correct; that is (not) the way it is; it is quite otherwise. *Him tell the police one t[h]ing and him moder tell de police dem i[t']s no[t] so it go.*—(Jmca) **7.5** *Is only so ... introductory phr* (Gren, Guyn) See ONLY Phr 2.1 **7.6** *just so adv phr* (CarA) [*IF*] See JUST Phr 4. **7.7** *just for so adv phr* (Bdos, Guyn, Tbgo, Trin) [*IF/AF*] See JUST Phr 2. **7.8** *(like) now so adv phr* (CarA) [*AF*] See NOW Phr 2.3 **7.9** *not so? elliptical tag* (CarA) See NOT Phr 2.14 **7.10** *so till!* (i) *conn phr* (CarA) Until. **a.** *'I laugh so till I cry', said one child.*—WeG (73.11.14, p.13, Partyline) **b.** *Gladys heard her neighbour Muriel 'slandering' her ... 'You thief the people fowl so til dey give you a alias—'Alias Gladys Fowl.'*—DaC (52.07.12, p.5) [Cp KED Krio *sote* = *tete* < Yoruba *ti-ti* 'until'; perh passing elliptically in adv use at (ii)] **(ii)** *adv intensifier phr* (Guyn, Jmca, StKt, Tbgo) [*AF*]

To an unspeakable degree; more than it is possible to say. **a.** *De boy a smoke up nough weed, / An' sey dat it ain't no bad deed. / A friten so till fu me chile, / For when e done smoke im goin wile.*—LMFF:37 **b.** *Everything correct, and Albert shave, and dress so-till; same Albert who scorn soap, and wear pant till they have more patch than pant foot.*—TM:45 (A.L. Hendricks) **7.11 Well i[t']s so!** *id phr* (CarA) Well that's how it is; that's how things stand; I've now told you the story. **7.12 when you see so** *id phr* (Gren, Guyn, Tbgo) [*IF*] See SEE Phr 3.13

so² *post-pron adj* (Bdos, Guyn, Gren, Trin) [*AF*] **1. (i)** [After a pers pron] Of my, their, your, etc kind, class, or sort. **a.** *Them brand o' Trinidadian, Bajan, Jamaican, Grenadian and thing, them so can't understand at-all how Calvin just land and he get rich [already].*—CWFYS:98 **b.** *If you know how glad I am she can handle herself and work for her own money. Not to have to depend on one of all you so.*—JJM:31 [Perh a phonic transfer of Igbo *so* as in *ibem so* 'of my/our kind'] **(ii)** [Focusing a pers pron] For my, their, your, etc part; if it were I, you, etc. *If it wasn't for John and Sheila, me so, even at my age, I would go away and leave you.*—JJM:150 **2.** PHRASES **2.1 nothing/something so** *pron phr* (Bdos, Guyn, Gren, Trin) [*AF/IF*] Nothing/something of the kind. *He told you a lie. It was nothing so.*—(Bdos) **b.** *It smell like some dead cat or something so.*—(Gren)

so³ *pron* (CarA) [*IF*] **1.** [Usu in ref to some unpleasant event or act] This/that (thing, act, happening). **a.** *They didn't have to tell me my husband had died. As I looked at their faces I knew so.*—(StVn) **b.** *Both policemen then began to drag her by her hands, and, when she (M—) exclaimed, 'don't do my mother so' T—'let go my mother's hand.'*—DeM(SK) (63.09.21, p.10) **2.** PHRASE **2.1 (sb) make so** *vb phr* (CarA) [*AF*] To cause sth (unpleasant) to happen. *Yo[u] see mama beat John-John, and i[t']s you make so.*—(Guyn)

so⁴ *conj* [*AF/IF*] **1.** (CarA) So long as; provided that. **a.** *Some people don['t] care if you sink so they swim.*—(Guyn) **b.** *You can go and play yes, so you keep out o[f] de mud.*—(Bdos) **2.** (CayI) [*Connecting two vbs*] So as to; in order to; and. **a.** *Run so bring my shoes.*—KWS:19 **b.** *Go so get some limes.*—FDI:68 [Cp *DAFL* Twi *n'so* adv, conj 'also; besides; but, moreover'. Note phonic closeness to SE (a)*nd so*]

soak·a·way *n* **1.** (Bdos) A hole in the ground about 3 ft deep and 2 ft square, packed with sand and stones to facilitate drainage of water into the soil; (AmE) a dry well (*pers info*, L. Urdang). **2.** (Trin) A pit for sewage disposal. *The manner in which this took place was a result of a wound by a cutlass on his neck in that hole, pit, or soakaway.*—AMGM:149

so·ca *n* (ECar) A dance-tune with accompanying song, the beat of wh combines Black American soul music with Trinidadian calypso; it emerged in Trinidad in the 1978 CARNIVAL. *The association is refusing to accept the CDC's statement that they leave it all up to the judges to decide what is soca and what is calypso and to draw the line between them.*—ExP (78.01.10, p.1) [A blend of so(ul) + ca(lypso). The name is said to have been invented by a Radio Trinidad announcer to identify the creations of Lord Shorty (*G. Blackman*)]

so·cial hang·ing *n phr* (StVn) See HANGING.

so·da *n* (Jmca) ‖ COOL-DRINK (CarA)

so·da-bake(s) *n* [Usu *pl*] (Guyn) ‖ BAKE(S)¹ 2. (Bdos, etc)

soft *adj* (Belz) [Esp of a man] Besotted; infatuated and stupefied. *Beauty looked good and she knew she looked good. She had the Beast soft and she knew she had him soft.*—HF:27

soft-ball (crick·et) *n* (*phr*) (CarA) Cricket played with a rubber or tennis ball. *It must be known that Police had a pavilion for years also in Queen's Park, and there is also a trash house used by people who play soft ball.*—Bdos (Hd, 74.07.09, p.3691)

soft-can·dle *n* (Gren, StKt, StLu, Trin, USVI) ‖ *soft-grease* (Guyn) ‖ *candle-grease* (Bdos) Soft tallow made into a small thin candle-like rod and used as a poultice, in an embrocation, etc. **a.** *A heated leaf, smeared with soft candle, is applied to any swelling and is said to draw boils.*—GNHIG:89 **b.** *The old woman gave Martha a thorough rubbing down with the soft-candle and rum while the others fussed over the leaf-tea*—MBF:88

soft-drink *n* (CarA) ‖ COOL-DRINK (CarA)

soft-grease ['sɒf-gris] *n* (Guyn) ‖ SOFT-CANDLE (Gren, etc)

soft-mash ['sɒf-maš] *n* (StVn) [*AF*] ‖ CREPE-SOLES (Guyn, etc) [Prob orig a humorous name representing the same idea as AmE *sneakers* i.e. 'mash (tread) softly'] □ No pl. Educated usage (*StVn*) is 'a pair of sneakers'.

soft-shoe foot·ball/soc·cer *n* (Gren) ‖ *yachting-shoe football* (Guyn) Football played wearing SOFT-SHOES. *Every year there is a soft-shoe football competition played at Tanteen.*—ToR (76.06.30, p.8)

soft-shoes [sɒf-šuz] *n pl* (Bdos, Gren, StLu) ‖ CREPESOLES (Guyn, etc) *He ... emphasised that despite having brown shoes some children deliberately, and in some cases unknown to their parents, wore to school soft shoes.*—NaT (76.05.02, p.1) [Ref to soft (rubber) soles and soft (canvas) tops of such shoes]

soft-soap vb tr (Guyn, Trin) [AF—Joc] To persuade by flattery; to gain agreement or favour by using encouraging words. *Earline wished she knew what he was thinking; soft soaping somebody's old queen was all right for a few minutes, but this A. Russel was preening herself and taking over the whole damn conversation.*—JPB:115

soft-walk·ers n pl (Angu, Mrat) ‖ CREPESOLES (Guyn, etc) [Cp AmE *sneakers*, the same i.e. shoes in wh you can walk softly. Cp also PUSS-BOOTS (*Jmca*), SOFT-MASH (*StVn*) with same idea]

sol·dier-ant(s) n (Trin) ‖ ARMY-ANT(S) (Trin)

sol·dier-crab n (CarA) A species of hermit-crab that covers itself with the empty shell of a larger mollusc for protection; *Paquarias insignis*, or *Coenobita diogenes*.

sol·dier-rod n (Guyn) ‖ MAN-BETTER-MAN (Dmca, etc) [From the erect spike of spiny bracts wh hurt when pulled against the skin]

sol·id adj (Bdos, Mrat, StVn) [AF] [Of a drinks bar] Fully stocked with liquor. *He added that there was a bar and it was solid, with drinks flowing free and fast.*—AdN (72.10.21, p.1) [Prob an extension of sense from *heavy* drink] □ See BAR¹ Phr 2.1 BAR SOLID

So·lo·mon-Gun·dy n (Jmca) A brown, salty, seasoned paste made mainly of mashed SMOKE-HERRING; it is used on crackers as a snack, some-times as a condiment. [By folk etym (infl by nursery rhyme 'Solomon O'Grundy') < OED *salmagundi* 'a dish composed of chopped meat, anchovies, eggs, onions with oil and condiment' + cits from 1674]

some adv (Guyn, StVn) [IF] Somewhat; [by extension] greatly, considerably, fast, etc. **a.** *Jube sighed heavily. The free leathery flapping of a flock of wild geese ... lightened him some.*—SBB:16 **b.** *Well this motorist could not see the approaching car which was travelling some, and drove out, only to almost run into the other car coming down Bay Street.*—ViN (73.09.07, p.2) [Cp EDD *some* 4. adv 'somewhat, slightly' 5. 'very; rather' + cits from Sc, etc] □ Also occurs in AmE but is not regarded as Standard.

some·bod·y pron 1. (Baha, Belz, Jmca) [AF] Person; a person. *Wen e get da de place de fust somebody e see deh [is] e wife whe e jus done kiss.*—WFSFB:37 □ In AF—Cr usage, pronunc is often /smadi/ in these contexts. **2.** (CarA) [X] [By extension] Anybody. **a.** *I don't know if somebody saw it and picked it up.*—(Jmca) **b.** [After knocking on door] *Somebody at home?* —(Bdos) **3.** (Bdos, StVn) [IF] [In ref to cost in dollars] Something. *In St Vincent you can buy 2 bottles of Scotch for sixteen somebody.*—(StVn)

some per·son /1'22/ pron phr (Bdos) [AF/ IF] Somebody. *There is a St Philip word called 'scrunch', and as I heard some person say, when* the scrunch of the fuel hit us everybody cried out.*—Bdos (Hd, 74.11.26, p.4222) □ See related phrs at PERSON Phr 2.1, 2.2.

some·thing PHRASES 1. **be something else** vb phr (CarA) ‖ BE ANOTHER ONE (CarA) See ANOTHER Phr 2. 2. **be something for yourself** vb phr (CarA) [IF] [Esp of children and young persons] To be given to surprising or amusing answers; to be astonishing in behaviour. **a.** *The little fellow keeps the grandparents laughing heartily. He's something for his little self.*—(Guyn) **b.** *You mean after they were so kind to her, she really brought the police on them? Well she is something for herself, yes!*—(StKt) [Perh via calquing from W Afr langs. Cp Yoruba *nkan ni ẹ* (something it is you) 'You are quite a character' (pers info, A. Banjo). However perh also via or reinforced by IrE . Note 'the pronouns myself, himself, &c., are very often used in Irel in a peculiar way, wh will be understood from the following exs: 'The birds were singing for themselves.' 'I was looking about the fair for myself'*—JESI:33] □ Some speakers use **be good for yourself** also in this sense. See GOOD¹ Phr 2. 3. **something told me (sth/to do sth)** id phr (CarA) [IF] The thought/ idea came to me (that); it occurred to me (to do sth). **a.** *I knew he would come back. Something told me so.*—(Guyn) **b.** *Something just told me to look around and I saw this man staring straight at me.*—(Bdos) □ Not the same as SE *something tells me ... 'I believe that ...'.*

some·time¹ adv (CarA) 1. [X] Sometimes. **a.** *I, for one, refuse to believe that Kingston is ready to lie down and die; ... too many tough people born, ... don't mind that garbage and such things out to choke we sometime.*—StA(JA) (72.11.18, p.10, Partyline) **b.** *Sometime she would send him behind the house to sit under the Taman tree.*— PKKK:91 [By characteristic CarA Cr reduction of final /-CC/] □ SE *sometime* is adj or adv '(being) at one time'. 2. [X] At some time. **a.** *Like any other normal girl, I would like to get married sometime but I think my career is more important at the moment.*—AdN (72.10.09, p.7) **b.** *... respondent lost his job as a casual worker sometime in October 1962.*—StA(JA) (73.02.10, p.5) [By non-standard compounding of two separate words *some time*] □ A common error in written work.

some·time² adj (Belz) [AF] ‖ SOMETIMISH (CarA) *She got sometime ways. She talk to you only when she feel like.*—(Belz)

some·times conj (Bdos, Guyn) [AF] Perhaps; maybe. **a.** *We intend to expand business to Guyana, Trinidad and Jamaica, and sometimes we might be thinking even of the Bahamas and Curaçao.*—Bdos (B, 1/72) **b.** *I search all over the place for my pen. Then I got a feeling that sometimes I must have left it in the drawer and when I look, I find it.*—(Guyn) [By semantic shift brought about by poss double sense in such collocations as 'Sometimes you will/may (do sth)']

some·time·y [sʌmtaimi] *adj* (Baha) ‖ SO-METIMISH (CarA) [A variant of the foll. Cp SE *uppity* < up (adv)] □ *OED2* reports this form as also Black AmE.

some·ti·mish (some·time·ish) [sʌmtaimiš] *adj* (CarA) ‖ *sometime²* (Belz) ‖ *sometimey* (Baha) [Usu of persons] Unstable in friendliness; unpredictable; moody; unreliable; undependable. *He complained bitterly to Tapia about the sometimish policy of the market people. / Last week they put his table right on the angle of the compound across from the big tree. This week, if he only sell a fish there, they would summarily oust him.*—TaP (75.04.27, p.12) [*Sometime(s)* + *ish* in Derog sense. Cp *uppish* also formed from an adv]

son of the soil *n phr* (CarA) A native-born man (who is to be admired for some achievement). *Mr Probyn Ellsworth Inniss, M.B.E., B.A., D.P.A., Barrister-at-law, a native son of the soil, was yesterday sworn in as Governor of this State after Her Majesty Queen Elizabeth II had been graciously pleased so to appoint him.*—LaS (75.08.02, p.1) [The term is also reported to be so used in W Afr]

sook *vb tr* (Gren, Trin) To sick (a dog); to set (a dog) upon (sb). *If you dare come in this yard I will sook the dog on you.*—(Trin) [Perh a false pa.t. of SE *sick (a dog)* developed into a base vb on the pattern of Cr /brok/ 'break', /lef/ 'leave', etc]

soon 1. *adv* (Guyn) [*AF*] Early; as soon as ever. *Soon in the morning she does start to row.*—(Guyn) 2. *conj* (USVI) [*AF—Cr*] As soon as. *All the time me know you, me tink you me fren. Soon me ask you one lil favor you no me fren no mo.*—PKKK:83 3. PHRASES 3.1 **soon as** *conn phr* (CarA) [*AF*] As soon as. *Soon as he find his real clique, we wouldn't see him up here again.*—LDCD:158 [By loss of unstressed first particle 'as'] 3.2 **soon from now** *adv phr* (Bdos) [*IF*] In a short time from now. *The fight is on and it is going to be a serious fight. A lot of you who are laughing over there and smiling from ear to ear, soon from now you are not going to be smiling any more.*—Bdos (Hd, 76.07.27, p.2042) [In order to specify the immediate future, as distinct from *soon after* referring to time in the past]

soor¹ [su·r] *n* (Guyn) [*AF*] A useful or interesting piece of confidential information; [by extension] the same used to flatter or ingratiate. *I did get a soor dat dey kill a calf and did sen[d] roun[d] by Kumar for a sheep or a goat, so I know i[t']s a big t[h]ing they plannin[g] but they ain['t] as[k] me.*—(Guyn) [Mainly Indic, perh with metaph transfer of Hin *surwa* 'gravy']

soor² [su·r] *vb tr* (Guyn) [*AF—Joc*] To ingratiate by flattery (esp in attempting to seduce); to coax (esp a young woman) into intimacy. *I notice Mark soorin[g] Joy real heavy las[t] night, but she won['t] go nowhe[re] with him.*—(Guyn)

so·pra·no pan *n phr* (Trin) An earlier name for the LEAD-PAN. (See note there).

sore *n* PHRASE **(have) a plaster for every sore** *id phr* (CarA) [*AF*] (To have) a ready excuse for every fault, error, or wrongdoing.

sore foot *n phr* (CarA) [*AF—Derog*] Any kind of unsightly, perpetually bandaged sore on the leg; (often) a diabetic sore. *The reader says that everybody knows that a hospital sore foot can be one of the wickedest things around. / He said 'The hospital Sore Foot Award should not be confused with the ordinary sore foot.' / 'For you know how bad the situation is when a sore foot reaches the hospital stage.'*—SuP (80.03.16, p.10) □ Often used attrib as Derog. Cp also LIFE-SORE.

so·ros·se (soros.si) *n* (Baha, Belz) See CERASEE

sor·rel* *n* (CarA) 1. A much branched shrub that can grow to about 6 ft, with numerous, deeply lobed, light-green leaves and many red-centred, rose-like flowers the calyxes of wh develop into deep red, fleshy cups (the fruit), wh cover hairy, green seed-pods; the plant dies after one full bearing; *Hibiscus sabdariffa (Malvaceae)*. *About one third of the cleared land was under cultivation with tomatoes, yams, pigeon peas, dasheen, peppers, chive, passion fruit, sorrel, pawpaw, bananas.*—ExP (73.06.09, p.10) □ Not to be confused with European *sorrel* a wild plant of the genus *Rumex* whose sour-tasting leaves serve culinary purposes or make a drink. 2. The fruit of this plant considered collectively, the red, fleshy calyxes being cut away from the pods; [by extension] the red drink made from a decoction of these fruit, sometimes called *sorrel-drink*. a. *Also available at low prices ... are ... Dry Coconuts, Sorrel, Rounceval peas, Pigeon Peas.*—AdN (72.01.14, p.5) b. *Bring out the mauby, / Ginger and ice. / Pour out the sorrel / Boiled up with spice. / It's Christmas! It's Christmas!*—SUB: 13 [See *OED sorrel* sb¹ and sb² for poss overlapping origins, due to resemblances in taste and colour to CE SORREL] □ There is no pl form in CE. Note cits. The plant, known as *bissap*, is widely used in W Africa.

sor·row-seed *n* (Tbgo) ‖ CERASEE (Baha, etc) [By folk etym. Cp similarly SOROSSE (*Baha, Belz*). The plant is a folk-medicine used for relieving pain and bodily disorders (sorrows ?)]

so-so *adj, adv* 1. *adj* (Belz, Jmca, Tbgo) [*AF*] Just ordinary; only bare; mere. a. *We have no cheese, no jam, no butter. Is so-so bread we have to eat.*—(Tbgo) b. *'It' blackin' up for storm,' Driver said. 'This ain't jus' so-so rain at all.'*—SJS: 119 2. *passing into adv function* (Belz, Jmca, StKt, Tbgo) [*AF*] Only; exclusively. a. *Miss Mary strong sah, she have so-so bwoy pickney.* (= *Miss Mary is strong Sir. She bears only boy children*).—(Jmca) b. *Oman, you mean you mek me bun out me clutch, me brakes an' me geass, jus' ou bring you from dey so so, to ya so so?* (= ... *just to bring you from only there to only here?*)

—LMFF:42 [Also *KED* Krio *so-so* with same sense. Cp Yoruba *ṣoṣo* 'only' (used with 'one')]

sòt¹ (sut¹) [sʌt] *adj* (Dmca, Gren, StLu, Trin, USVI) [*AF*] Stupid; silly; foolish. *An' de little boy smarter dan all of allyu, he gone so long. / Is allyu mash up de meetin' not he; allyu too sut!*—KTT:18 [Fr Cr < Fr *sotte* f. adj, 'foolish'. Perh reinforced by *EDD* sot (Sc, Yks, Suf) 'an idiot; a fool']

sòt² (sut²) [sʌt] *n* (Dmca, Gren, StLu, Trin) [*AF*] Nonsense; foolishness. *Shut up you mouth gal, you talking sut.*—RTCS:4 [By functional adj > n shift of SÒT¹]

sou·a·ri *n* (Guyn) See SAWARI.

sou·cou·yan(t) *n* (ECar) See SOUKOUYAN

sou·flet [suflɛt] *n* (StLu) ‖ TRUMPET-FISH (CarA) [Fr Cr 'a whistle' (< Fr *souffler* 'to blow') a prob ref to the shape of the fish's mouth]

Soufr·i·ere tree* ['sufrɛ(r)tri] *n phr* (StVn) A tree with untidy looking branches, simple pale-green, spear-shaped leaves and pendent clusters of small, pink flowers, wh are the National Flower of St Vincent; the tree is said to be found only in that island; *Spachea perforata* (*Malpighiaceae*). [The tree was first reported, 1804, on the slopes of the Soufrière volcano, hence the name]

sou·kou·yan (sou·cou·yant, su·co·yan, su·ku·ya) [sukuyã] *n* (Dmca, Gren, StLu, Tbgo, Trin) ‖ fire-hag (Bdos) ‖ hag, old-heg (Baha, StVn) ‖ old-higue (Guyn, Jmca) ‖ old-suck (Jmca) A legendary, evil, wrinkled old woman, who hides by day, but by night sheds her skin wh she carefully hides in a jar, then becomes a ball of fire roving in the air to seek out and light upon sleeping victims, esp babies, whose blood she sucks before returning to her skin, wh may have been peppered and salted by those hunting her down to get rid of her by this as their only means. [Fr Cr < Soninke *sukunya* 'man-eating sorcerer', and cognates in Fulfulde [sukunyãdyo], etc (see *MAALV:238, P. Baker*). Cp also *DECG Guad 'soukougnan'* with same sense as *Dmca*, etc. However, certain characteristics—a blood-sucking creature of either gender, a roving ball of fire by night, normal human appearance by day—suggest a wider base of W Afr legendary demons. Cp LOUGAWOU, OLD-HIGUE]

soul *n* 1. (CarA) [*IF*] (Friendly form of address or reference to) an elderly woman. **a.** *'Silla-gal, you still cleaning chicken and night near falling?'* her voice boomed in the quietness. *'How?' | 'I here, soul',* Silla said listlessly.—MBGB:29 **b.** *There was no need to worry about the old woman who talked about the slave. She was doting, poor soul.*—LICMS:63 [Cp *OED* soul III. 13. c. dial. Used in the pl as a form of address: 'friends, fellows' + cit (1874) 'Come in, souls, and have something to eat and drink'] □ Used only by an adult speaker,

esp by a woman to or of another. **2.** (USVI) [*AF*] A girl-friend.

sou·la(rd) (su·la) [sula] *adj* (Dmca, Gren, StLu) [*AF*] ‖ RUM-BIBBER, (ETC) (CarA) *You want Dauphin and the whole coast to say Afa was brave, Afa was pas soulard.*—WSAD:14 [Fr Cr < Fr *soûlard* 'drunkard, boozer']

soul-case *n* (CarA) [*AF—Joc*] **1.** The body; the human frame; a person's 'self', (SE slang) your innards. *Stanley said under his breath, 'Life strange, eh? The musicians play out their soul-case and nobody ain't hugging them up.'*—AFTF:49 [Cp *EDD* soul¹ Var dial uses in Sc, Irel and Eng 1. sb in comb. 2. *soul-case* 'the body'. Perh the Br dial item may be a semantic reflection of OE *ban-cofa (bone-case)* 'the body'] **2.** PHRASES **2.1 burst/bother/rack/wear/work out your soul case** *vb phrs* (CarA) [*AF—Joc*] To overwork yourself; to (have to) work unduly or unreasonably hard. **a.** *She looked gloomy. 'When man don't love you, more you try, more he hate you, man like that. If you love them they treat you bad, if you don't love them they after you night and day bothering your soul case out. I hear about you and your husband,' she said.*—RWSS:91 **b.** *I work out me soul-case for de girl, send she to good school and now she gone away she wouldn[t] even drop a line to say dog how you do.*—(Gren)

soup *n* PHRASES **1. drink soup off/over sb's head** *vb phr* (ECar) [*AF—Joc*] See DRINK Phr 2. **2. hang your mouth where the soup drips** *vb phr* (Guyn) [*AF—Derog*] See MOUTH Phr 4.11

sou·pi(e) (sou·pee) [supi] *n* (Trin) A very light sweet made from egg whites and castor sugar. [Fr Cr < Fr *soupir* 'sigh', metaph ref to its lightness]

sour barge ['sʌwa ba·j] *n phr* (Jmca) ‖ GOOSEBERRY 1. (Baha, etc) [*DJE* baaj…. In Jmca the extremely acid grape-like berries of certain trees were thought to be 'sour like baaj' and the trees bearing them were thence called 'baaj' or *sour baaj*]

sour cher·ry *n phr* **1.** (Trin) ‖ CHILLI-PLUM (Antg, etc) □ This seems to be the commoner rural name, CERISE (*Trin*) being the commoner urban name for this fruit. **2.** (StVn) ‖ BARBADOS-CHERRY (CarA)

sour fig *n phr* (Gren) A small, sour-sweet variety of banana, in wh some tiny, black seeds may be seen. [SE *sour* + CE FIG 'small type of banana']

sour grass *n phr* (Bdos, Tbgo, Trin) One of two varieties of bushy grass growing in abundant bushy tufts about 2 ft high, with silky brown spikelets; it is a forage or pasture grass, sometimes cultivated; (*Bdos*) *Andropogon intermedius, var acidulus*, (*Trin*) *Valota insularis* (*Gramineae*). ['The name Sour Grass applies to its unattractiveness as a fodder, but it is sometimes used for this purpose ... where better grasses will not grow'—*PTT:179*]

sour·ie ['sʌwʌri] *n* (Guyn) ‖ BILIMBI (Guyn, etc) *You must put the souries in pepper-sauce when they are young and green, because the juice tends to ferment and spoil the pepper-sauce when they are too ripe.*—Guyn (Ms) [From its acid juice]

sour or·ange* *n phr* (CarA) ‖ *bitter orange* (Antg, Bdos, BrVi) ‖ *gòspo* (Gren, Trin) ‖ *zowanj-gòspo* (StLu) The Seville orange, a variety with notably rough skin and bitter-acid pulp, said to be very hardy, but rarely eaten; the plant is more often used for grafting and the skin of the fruit for scrubbing floors; *Citrus aurantium* (*Rutaceae*).

sour·sop* [sʌwʌsɒp] *n* (CarA) ‖ *kòwòsòl* (Dmca, StLu) (StLu) A green-skinned, roughly heart-shaped fruit, about 10 ins long, with soft prickles; its thick, white, cotton-like, acid-sweet pulp (embedding many shiny black seeds) is eaten fresh or used for making ice-cream or a drink; *Annona muricata* (*Annonaceae*).

sour·sop-drink *n* (CarA) ‖ BABALÉ (Dmca) A thick and heavy, milky drink made by sugaring the sweet-sour, white pulp of the SOURSOP.

souse [sʊʊs] *n* (CarA) A cold, pickled dish prepared by boiling pork, esp the pig's face, ears and trotters, well seasoned, and served with slices of raw onions, cucumber and red pepper. **a.** *So, standing on the Western Main Road ... we found it difficult to conjure up the image that Raoul remembered ... the line of bake and shark and roti stalls, fish frying in the night, coils of pudding and cuts of souse.*—Peo I.8, p.40 **b.** *Bring your Family to a Brunch at the Masonic Lodge on the Queen's Birthday June 12th, 11.30–1.30 Delicious West Indian dishes such as Saltfish, Souse, ... will be served. / Have a choice of Mauby, Tamarind sizzle, Ginger beer, etc.*—LaS (Ad, 76.06.12, p.5) □ See also PUDDING AND SOUSE. Cp SE *souse* 'a pickling brine'.

sou·sé-glo [suse-glo] *n* (Dmca) ‖ POND-FLY (Bdos, Guyn) [Fr Cr *susé* (< Fr *sucer*) 'suck' + *glo* (< Fr *de l'eau*) 'water' i.e. 'suck-water', from the insect's posture when it alights on still water] □ See also MAKOKÉ-GLO.

sou-sou *n* (ECar) See SUSU.

South·well *n* (CayI) PHRASE **go away with Southwell** *id phr* (CayI) See GO Phr 6.12.1

sow-pig [sɒu-pɪg] *n* (Bdos, Trin) [*AF/IF*] A sow. [A characteristic CarA Cr redundant compound passing into CE. Cp similarly BOAR-PIG, BULL-COW, etc]

space *n* (Bdos, Guyn) [*X*] A place or position (that is to be filled). **a.** *While waiting for a space in a medical school, he worked as Assistant Budget*

Officer in the Treasurer's Office at Howard University.—DaC (52.08.22, p.2) **b.** *Reports state that the DLP candidate to fill Mr Hoppin's space is expected to be a well known medical practitioner who was born in St George North.*—AdN (76.04.02, p.1) [A misascription of sense of *space* 'opening']

spade[1] *n* (CarA) A labourer's implement with a flat rectangular pan-like blade or a gardener's implement with a smaller pointed blade, each fitted with a handle. □ In most places SPADE and SHOVEL are distinctly different implements, but in some places the terms are free variants.

spade[2] *n* (CarA) [*AF—Joc*] A Black person (living in England). [A ref to the 'black' cards, esp the ace of spades, in a pack of playing cards] □ The term is known and used mostly by W Indians living or who have lived in England, esp in London. Also AmE Derog slang.

Span·ish bay·o·net *n phr* (ViIs) ‖ ADAM'S NEEDLE (Angu, Trin)

Span·ish bill/cut·lass/ma·chete[1] *n phr* (Jmca, USVI) ‖ BACK-AND-BELLY 2, 3.

Span·ish Christ·mas-car·ol *n phr* (Trin) ‖ AGUINALDO (Trin) □ This term tends to be more widely used than AGUINALDO with the national popularization of PARANG in Trin.

Span·ish knife *n phr* (TkCa) [*AF*] ‖ PANYA MACHETE (Belz, Jmca) *She's a spanish knife! She told me one thing and on the back she told my friend a different thing altogether.*—(TkCa) [See PANYA MACHETE of wh this is a refinement]

Span·ish ma·chete[2] [-mašɛt] *n phr* (Jmca) ‖ BEAN-TREE (Bdos) [Perh from resemblance of the stamens to a machete]

Span·ish mack·er·el *n phr* (Angu, Antg, Bdos, Gren, Guyn) ‖ CARITE (Trin)

Span·ish nee·dle *n phr* **1.*** (Bdos) ‖ *donkey cactus* (USVI) A variety of AGAVE with firm two-foot long, blade-like, radiating, white-edged leaves each terminating in a painfully sharp spine wh makes the plant impassable to animals; it is popular as a decorative hedge-plant; *Agave angustifolia marginata* (*Agavaceae*). (See also CACTUS). **2.** (Jmca, StKt, StVn, USVI) ‖ DUPPY-NEEDLE (Bdos)

Span·ish net·tle *n phr* (Jmca) ‖ DUPPY-NEEDLE (Bdos) [Prob a false refinement of SPANISH NEEDLE 2. by folk etym]

spar; spar.ring part.ner *n* (*phr*) (Bdos, Guyn, Jmca, Trin) [*AF—Joc*] A chum; a pal; a close friend (of either sex). **a.** *It will mean that many people will have to get used to a way of life which is alien and unfamiliar. They will have to learn to like roast-plantain; ... reggae.... They may even have to get used to being called 'spar' and learn to* use expressions like 'ja-dread', 'iris', 'hail' and so on.—Col I.1, p.19 **b.** *We all, each and everyone, have a sparring partner or partners with whom we move. Some married couples sensibly choose different sections.*—TrG (76.03.21, p.5)

spar·row(-bird) *n* (Angu, Bdos, Dmca, Mrat, USVI) A drab-coloured, greyish-brown or sometimes darker bird about 5 ins long (but often smaller esp in *Bdos*) with a hard, short beak and noticeably thin legs on wh it hops about homes and gardens uttering a shrill, short, repeated call as it seeks crumbs, fruit, insects, etc; *Loxigilla noctis* (*Fringillidae*). **a.** *The study revealed that the sparrow, which many Barbadians believe to be the most harmless of birds, is in fact the most devastating bird pest of vegetables in the island.*—SuS (80.03.23, p.12) **b.** *Boys he know does behave real bad, and throw rock-stones at dogs and cats, and thief people fruits off the trees, and lick-down sparrow-birds and wooddoves with guttapercs.*—AdN (80.12.25, p.10) □ Commonly called SPARROW-BIRD [sparʌ-bərd] in *Bdos, Mrat* it is identified in professional literature as the *Lesser Antillean Bullfinch.*

spar·row-hawk* *n* (CarA) ‖ **gri-gri**[1] **2.** (Gren) ‖ **killi-killi** (Angu, Mrat, USVI) A small, reddish-brown hawk about 10 ins long, with black bars about the eyes and a spotted breast; it makes a shrill cry, feeds on lizards, bats, and sometimes chickens, but it may attack humans during the nesting period; *Falco sparverius* (*Falconidae*).

spawn [spɒn] *n* (Bdos, Guyn, StVn) A handspan, i.e. the distance between the tips of the thumb and the little finger when the hand is fully spread, this being used as a measurement esp in playing marbles and other children's games. [Cp *EDD* spawn sb[2] Bnff 'a span, a term used in the game of 'spawnie']

speak *vb* (CarA) [*IF*] [Often used to mean 'to communicate with sb'] **1.** [Often neg] To be on speaking terms (with sb). *Since the brothers quarrelled over the father's will they don't speak, but their wives still speak.*—(Guyn) **2.** [*AF/IF*] [Esp of a young person] To give a respectful greeting; to say good morning/afternoon. *That child have no manners, when she pass me* [u]*pon a morning she don*['*t*] *speak.*—(Bdos) **3.** PHRASES **3.1 not speaking/talking** *neg adj phr* (CarA) [*AF/ IF*] Not on speaking terms; estranged; silently hostile to each other. *Since they took the husband's side in the divorce she and them not speakin*[g]. —(Bdos) □ SE usu *not talking to each other.* **3.2 speak back** *vb phr* (Bdos, Guyn) [*AF*] To be on speaking terms again; to make up after a quarrel. *I am going crazy after my boyfriend. I love this boy very bad and this is two weeks now that we 'speak back'. Now we have disagreed again. This boy loves me too. Christine, please tell me what to do.*—NaT (75.12.28, p.22, Dear Christine) [SPEAK 1. + BACK[4] 2(ii).] See also TALK[2] Phr 4 **3.3 speak to (a child)** *vb phr* (CarA) [*IF*] ‖ **call to (a child)** (Nevs) To tell (a child) to stop being mischievous, aggressive, etc. *Mother please*

to speak to Sonia how she behaving out here.— (StVn) **3.4 speak up (sb)** *vb phr* (Jmca) [*AF*] To chat up (esp a young woman) with intimacy in view. *'Him! exclaimed Sarah contemptuously; ... Him 'fraid for him aunt, an' yet him want to 'speak up' female.'*—DJC:38

speak-eas·y *n* (CarA) **1.** (Guyn) A small, inferior, back-street night bar. [Cp early AmE *speak-easy* with similar connotation during Prohibition] □ Also used attrib. **2.** (Guyn) [By extension] A small oil-lamp used in such bars. *When it was pointed out that no one could see the writing in the desk, a shiny speakeasy lamp, which had been put under someone's bed against the eventuality of an electricity failure, was lit and hung on the topmost branch.*—HMCH:41 **3.** (ECar) [By extension] A strong white rum illegally made and sold in back-street bars. *Sometimes he does drink he speak easy / And she does ha all de worry.*—LMFF:35

spec·u·la·tor *n* (Bdos) A person who makes a living by buying and selling (formerly) livestock or (in more recent times, by license) fruit. *What is Government's intention towards us speculators? To drag us before the courts, fine and even imprison us through no fault of our own? ... The mere fact that the public is willing to pay 10 cents for a coconut shows that the controlled prices have outlived its time.*—AdV (60.07.23, p.9) [Narrowed sense of *OED speculator* 5. 'one who engages in commercial or financial speculation']

speech *vb* (CarA) [*IF*—*Joc*] **1.** To give a formal address; to make a showy, often admonitory speech. **a.** *Sir Clifford, invited to speech him speech, made the scene in a fancy brown bush jacket while other officials on the platform were similarly shirt-jacked or bush-jacketed, depending on how you look at it.*—WeG (72.10.11, p.13, Partyline) **b.** *She added to our understanding of ourselves, and thus fertilized the self-confidence we are still growing—as a culture. / She did it through hard, practical work, not just by idealistic speeching.*— AdV (88.15.11, p.17) [By Joc n > vb shift of SE *speech* n 'a formal address'] **2.** PHRASE **2.1 speech off** *vb phr* (Trin) [*IF*—*Joc*] To tell off (sb); to dismiss (sb) in choice terms. *They revealed that a delegation went to Mac and asked him to drop these sections from the band, but he speeched them off and refused.*—BoM (75.01.17, p.7)

speech-band *n* (Tbgo, Trin) [Carnival] A group of costumed persons usu with decorated wooden swords, portraying interesting or topical characters and dramatizing situations or events in short rhymes and humorous word-play; the leader, or **'speech-man**/**-maker'**, (accompanied in former times by the music of fiddlers and tambourines) must out-rhyme and/or ridicule his opponent(s) in ex tempore verse ending with a punch-line.

speed PHRASE **under speed** *adv phr* (Belz, Gren) See UNDER Phr 2.4

spell *vb* 1. (Bdos, Guyn) [*AF/IF*] To seek, aim or intend (to do sth or to gain some favour) without openly revealing your desire. *A could see she was spellin[g] to borrow my shoes to go to the weddin[g] but A wouldn['t] take any notice.*— (Guyn) [Perh from early post-slavery days of wider illiteracy when spelling words out was used like a code by the literate] 2. *PHRASE* 2.1 **spell for (sb)** *vb phr* (Guyn) [*AF*] [By extension] To wait to catch out and belittle or beat up (sb). *Let her come home late from school again today. I'm spellin[g] for her good. She goin[g] get such a floggin[g].*—(Guyn)

spence *n* (Guyn) ‖ *spenks* (StKt) Ejaculated semen (esp of a young man). [Cp BrE slang *SSE spend* 2. 'semen; sexual spendings'; also *SSE spendings* 'semen that has been ejaculated'. Perh CE SPENCE is a pl (= *spends*) or a likely paragogic form of *spend*. Cp BRINGS, etc]

spend *vb* (CarA) [*IF*] [In ref to time, usu in a good sense unless indicated by context] *PHRASES* **spend a day/some time (in some place/with sb, etc)** *vb phrs* To enjoy a day or time spent (in/with, etc). *On Christmas day the family would always spend the afternoon together.*—(Jmca) □ Cp SE neutral sense of *spend* 'to pass (time)' AmE slang *spend time* 'to be in jail']

spenks *n* (StKt) ‖ SPENCE (Guyn) [See note at SPENCE. Perh a variant of that]

sper·rit (sper·ret, sper·rid) [spɛrit/id/ɛt] *n* (Baha) [*IF*] ‖ SPIRIT[1] 3. (CarA) **a.** *The disappearance of many people, who had been kidnapped and sold into slavery, was often blamed on ghosts or sperrits.*—TOSR:32 **b.** *The common word in the Bahamas for any form of ghost (or spirit) is 'sperrid'.*—MTTBT:93 [< SE *spirit* 'supernatural being', but distinguished by pronunc and spelling] □ In Baha *spirit* [spirit] refers to SE or religious sense of that word.

sper·rit-um·brel·la *n* (Baha) ‖ DUPPY-PARASOL (Bdos)

spice *n* (Dmca, Gren, Guyn) ‖ CINNAMON (CarA) □ An exclusive sense. Cp the more general sense of the word in SE.

Spice Is·land *n phr* (CarA) Grenada. *In fact, one-third of the world's supply of nutmeg comes from this little island and gives rise to her second name 'Spice Island'.*—Tourist Brochure, 1970

spice-man·go *n* (Guyn) A fist-size, longish mango with sweet, yellow, cheese-smooth flesh of noticeably spicy smell and taste; it is much prized as a delicacy. □ Also known as '*Buxton-spice*', the village of Buxton on the EAST COAST of *Guyn* being specially associated with an abundance of it.

spi·der *n* (Bdos) [Sugar Ind; Hist] A device consisting of a sturdy, iron arc fixed upright between two wheels, so allowing a heavy barrel

of sugar or molasses to be suspended within the arc by a chain and rolled by manpower to the waterside for shipping. [From the rough resemblance to the big house-spider esp when this creature carries its bag of eggs] □ Though still remembered, this device is now out of use in Bdos where it was invented, late 1920s.

spin *vb* *PHRASES* 1. **make sb spin** *vb phr* (Guyn) [*AF*] To cause sb more trouble and anxiety than he/she can cope with; to lead sb a dance maliciously. *The second wife had boyfriends, left him without food, land him in debt—I tell you she make him spin.*—(Guyn) 2. **spin top in mud** *vb phr* (Bdos, Gren, Nevs, Tbgo, Trin) [*AF—Joc*] To waste time over a frustrating task; to fail to make any progress although spending much time and energy. *Can you honestly say that we have progressed? For how much longer will we spin top in mud? Things can't be worse, so for better or for worse we must make a change and the time is now.*—ToR (76.11.14, p.11) [A ref to the frustrating experience of boys trying to spin home-made tops (see for ex BUCK-TOP) on muddy ground]

spin·ach *n* (CarA) ‖ CALALU 1. (CarA) □ *LNFV: 19* lists *spinach* as the term used in more CarA territories (9) than *calaloo* (6) for the same edible *Amaranthus spp.* However IAE *spinach*, though a similar food, is *Spinacia oleracea.*

spin·ners *n pl* (Jmca) Tiny flour dumplings floating in soup or stew (*DJPVP*).

spin·ning *n* *PHRASE* **spinning in the head** *phr* (Jmca, Mrat, Nevs, StKt, StVn) ‖ SWINGING IN THE HEAD (Baha, etc) See HEAD[1] Phr 4.18 *Dis mornin[g] when I get up I get a spinnin[g] in the head and I had to go lie do[w]ng.*—(Mrat) [Cp Mende *nguhu! mbembe* (head-inside spinning) 'spells of dizziness'; also Shona *ndi ne dzungu* (I have spinning-head) 'I am dizzy']

spin·ning-board *n* (Guyn) A horizontal gambling-board consisting of a large painted circle with different coloured segments, sometimes ringed with standing nails; within the circle a clock-hand-like wooden arrow is set spinning, the winners' segment being the one on wh it stops.

spir·it[1] *n* (CarA) 1. [*IF*] The mind; the feelings or emotions; your being or self, natural sensing or inclination. **a.** *'Wait a minute,' she tell Wingrove. 'It have a little stupid man that always annoying my spirit and wouldn't move out from here at all. Looka, help me get this man thing outa we house.'*—CISH:112 **b.** *Under cross-examination by Prosecutor Station Sergeant B. Harding, J— said the only reason he could think of why S— would try to 'frame' him was because 'we raise together and our spirits don't pull at all. We were always in trouble with each other'.*—VoS (76.05.08, p.10) **c.** *The first time I went to the 'doctor' she was sitting in her half-built board church, and according to her the spirit had warned* *her that we were coming.*—WeS (73.12.07, p.18) [Related to SE as *OED spirit* sb 1. 'animating ... principle in man ...; in contrast to the purely material ... etc; but the CE sense is also much influenced from Afr sources. See Phr 4.2 below] **2.** The state of religious ecstasy that takes hold of or 'possesses' a worshipper, esp in some group activity such as singing, dancing, healing, etc. (See POWER 2.); [by extension] the ecstatic dancing associated with this state. □ See Phr 4.2 below. **3.** ‖ *sperrit (sperrid)* (Baha) An unwelcome ghost; a frightening apparition; the unseen soul of a known, dead person whose presence is sensed in some unhappy situation. **a.** *The Big Drum is executed for a number of reasons. The most common of these is the occasion when a 'spirit' appears in a dream and begs for food.*—PGIP:28 **b.** *The East doctor also revealed that these 'spirits pricking her with needles' caused the family to believe that someone in the neighbourhood had put an 'evil spirit' on their daughter.*—SuP (80.03.09, p.3) See Phr 4.2 below. **4.** PHRASES **4.1 call the spirit** *vb phr* (Baha) See CALL[1] Phr 3.8 **4.2 get (into) the spirit** *vb phr* (CarA) See GET Phr 3.22, also sense 2. above. *Trumper said we should move farther away from the worshippers since they had a way of getting into the spirit. When they got into the spirit they danced and shouted in strange language. It was the act of speaking in tongues.... She shook the tambourine and her hips with passionate glee, and Trumper whispered to me that she would soon get the spirit.*—LICMS:176 **4.3 put spirit on (sth)** *vb phr* (Dmca) [AF] ‖ PUT BAD-EYE ON (SB) (Belz, Guyn) See BAD-EYE Phr 2.3 [A ref to sense 3. above. Note cit b.] **4.4 (your) spirit takes/ does not take (to) sb** *id phr* (CarA) ‖ *(your) blood takes/does not take sb* (Gren, Tbgo, Trin) (You) feel/do not feel a ready attraction to sb's general appearance, attitude, mind, personality, etc; take/do not take an immediate liking to sb. *They judged men quickly and without error, by whether 'their spirit take to them' or not, discerning in a moment that the new overseer on the property was 'bad minded', the shopkeeper covetous or 'cubbitch', the new teacher conceited or 'consequential'.*—SWI:153 [Cp Yoruba *okan mi fa si i (heart my draw to him)* 'I took a liking to him'—(pers info, A. Banjo); also Edo *orhiọn mu ... 'spirit catch/take ...'* in similar context—(pers info, A. Amayo]

spir·it(s)[2] *n (pl)* (Gren, Trin) **1.** One of a number of folk-medicinal concoctions made up and offered by an OBEAH-MAN/-WOMAN to relieve the troubles or sufferings of a client. *He said if I wanted the full dose, I would have to take a bath in a mixture of Musk Oil, Otter Rose, Rose Oil, Easy Oil, Seven Spirits of Vinegar, Luck Oil, Asafoetida, Red and White Lavendar, Jasmine Oil, Spirits of Man and Spirits of Spirits.*—SuP (74.10.27, p.24) [An adaptation of SE *OED spirit* sb V. 22. 'an essence, distilled extract or alcoholic solution, of a specified substance' Freq pl esp in later use] **2.** PHRASE **2.1 see spirits** (Guyn) To be disturbed by supposed visions of unknown dead persons. *The old lady would sit* up in bed, staring and muttering like somebody seeing spirits—Guyn (Ms)

spite PHRASE **for spite** (CarA); **for the same spite** (Guyn) *adv phr* [X] See FOR Phr 17.8 **a.** *He stepped on my toe for spite; it was no accident.*—(Tbgo) **b.** *For the same spite I wouldn['t]-a give him none of the guavas, le[t] dem rotten dere.*—(Guyn)

spite-work *n* (Bdos, Guyn, Tbgo, Trin) [AF/ IF] A wilful act of malice done with effect. *A strangled word strained the air. 'Spitework! Spitework,' that's what it is. Because of what I did to yuh father. All these years you been waiting to get at me. Ever since the night you did call me Hitler you been waiting.*—MBGB:250

Splax! *excl ideoph* (CarA) See PRAX!

splif(f) *n* (CarA) A hand-made ganja (cannabis) cigarette; it is usu cone-shaped to facilitate drawing or 'dragging' the smoke. *He was arrested and charged for possession of ganja and cautioned, he said 'Beg yu a chance officer is just a spliff.'*—WeS (75.02.28, p.12) [Perh a blend of CE SPLIT in ref to the ready-made wrap + SE *whiff* 'tobacco-smoke, or its smell, inhaled' (see *OED whiff* sb[1] 2.) The word appears to have originated in *Jmca* and has spread largely with the RASTAFARIAN cult]

split *n* (BrVi) A strip of dried palm leaf used in basket making. *When making a hat or basket, Mrs Malone uses one of two types of palms, white or brown type. Although some of it is locally picked, most of it is bought in St Thomas. / After being put into the sun to dry, these long palm leaves are shredded into lengthwise strips called splits. At this stage the splits can be dyed vivid colours. The splits are then woven into a variety of open or closed patterned plaits.*—Bvi, I. 2, p.29 [Because the dried leaves are easily split along their natural lines]

spoat *n* (Trin) [AF—Derog] See SPORT[2]

spoil *vb tr* (CarA) **1.** [IF] [Esp in ref to sb's name] To damage seriously or ruin (esp a reputation). *Well the youngest one come along and get arrested for t[h]iefin[g] the Government money and spoil the family name.*—(Trin) **2.** [AF] [By extension] To injure gravely. **a.** *Right! The two a' we could ambush him. His face have to spoil the way he spoil mine.*—ViN (76.10.01) **b.** *The obeahman's client is asked to believe that, as Professor Smith puts it, 'To produce death ... the obeahman will ... 'trick' or 'spoil' the soul of his victim, or he may employ a grave-spirit to destroy the person.'*—VoS (73.11.21, p.7)

sport[1] *n* (CarA) **1.** [IF] Fun; anything enjoyable to see or participate in. **a.** *West Indians love Carnival for the sport.*—(StKt) **b.** *He saw some other boys pelting stones at a crapaud and he joined in the sport until the crapaud lay quivering with its legs in the air.*—Guyn (Ms) [As *OED sport* sb¹ 1. 'amusement, entertainment, diversion', etc + cits from 1440] □ Though this is the earliest Eng sense, even before Shak, it is now secondary in ModE to the sense 'organized competitive game' and this causes much misunderstanding in written schoolwork. Observe cits. 2. [By extension] A dance and/or drinking party; merrymaking, esp indoors. **a.** *It turned out to be a wonderful party.... But like all good things the sport came to an end and it was time for home.*—CzN (77.05.24, p.3) **b.** *He would never leave his work or his plans to attend a sport. It was either work or sport, because he had to enjoy himself whenever he went to a sport, and he was a very good dancer too.*—ASG:38 **3.** PHRASES **3.1 for sport** *adv phr* (CarA) [*IF*] For fun. *They hid the old man's hat for sport and laughed to see him looking everywhere for it.*—Bdos (Ms) **3.2 make sport** [mek ~ mɛk spo(r)t] *vb phr* (ECar) [*IF/AF*] **(i)** To make fun; to joke and make others laugh. **a.** *Uncle Joe would come on Saturday afternoon and make a lot of sport with us as children.*—Guyn (Ms) **b.** *A young man of Clevedale, Black Rock, St. Michael, admitted in the District 'A' Court last Monday, that he 'tossed a rock' at a fellow, 'making sport'. He was fined $50.*—AdN (76.04.01, p.2) **(ii)** [By extension, esp in neg] To be ridiculous, absurd (in what you say or do); to put sb or sth at risk by foolish behaviour. **a.** *Mr Chairman, I think the Hon. Senator is really making sport to move that the Schedule stand apart without debate, but this is the appropriate time.*—Bdos (Hd, 75.03.25, p.844) **b.** *Look! Careful how you swingin[g] dat piece o[f] wood near me. Don['t] make sport wit[h] me, yeh.*—(Guyn) □ Cp difference in *OED sport* sb¹ 3. *To make sport* (a) 'to provide entertainment'. (b) 'to find recreation'. Note ModE *make sport of sb/sth* 'to make sb/sth look ridiculous'.

sport² (**spoat**) [spoət] *n* (Trin) [*AF—Derog*] ‖ *sporter* (Jmca) A prostitute. **a.** *I could see the big breasts as she bend to scrub the clothes and I remember the sports in Mucurapo Street and the sun being very hot and everything the first thing I find myself saying is how about a piece.*—SWOS:85 **b.** *'Amy isn't a spoat,' he told Marjorie. / ... 'Isn't a what,' she asked. 'The number of Yankee so-and-so's that woman took and you say she wasn't a wha.a...aat? The woman is a damn garden rat, that is what she is.'*—JPB:60 [Perh an extension of *OED sport* 1. b. 'amorous dalliance or intercourse' (Obs, 18C). Cp the *Jmca* ‖]

sport³ *vb* (Guyn) **1.** To enjoy yourself esp by drinking, dancing and going to parties. *Barrister-at-law Stanley Moore who is representing the accused, explained 'Your Worship, many of them sported through from Friday (Old Year's Day) unto Tuesday and a lot of them hadn't even awaken then.*—CzN (77.01.06, p.3) [By functional n > vb shift of SPORT¹ 2.] **2.** PHRASE **2.1 sport (away/out) money** *vb phr* (Guyn) [*AF—Joc*] To spend money freely in the enjoyments of life. *According to the prosecutor the accused made a confession statement admitting that he did strangle*

the woman because he said she always stole his money and 'sport' it out with friends.—GyC (76.10.28, p.11)

sport·er; sport-girl *n* (Jmca) ‖ SPORT² (Trin) *Father does no' like Adassa, though, for she walks and hoists her backside too much like sport-girls at Port Morant who crowd the promenade when sugar-boats come in.*—RND:17 [Variants of SPORT²]

sport-house *n* (Jmca) [*IF*] A brothel. *A search was made of likely homes, but to no avail. After a fruitless search he was invited to spend the night at a home which turned out to be a 'house of pleasure', but he refused. / When asked to explain what was a 'house of pleasure', Mr Silvera said it is a 'sport-house'.*—StA(JA) (71.07.08, p.1) [Cp SPORT² (*Trin*) < SPORT(-GIRL) + house; cp also AmE *sporting house* 'a brothel']

spot *vb* (Bdos) [*IF*] **1.** *vb intr* [Of a light] To shine. *The witness said that a carlight spotted on the deceased in the road and he saw a gun near the deceased's hand.*—AdN (79.10.29, p.1) **2.** *vb tr* To shine (a light). *The woman said that she spot the light in the accused face after she spoke to him and he threw the stones at her and she ducked.*—AdN (79.01.27, p.2) [Vb by back-formation < SPOTLIGHT]

spot·light *n* (Bdos) ‖ TORCHLIGHT (CarA) *She said that she had a spotlight and she turned it on and spot it on the main road and she didn't see anyone. But when she spot it on the yam ground she saw K. J— with the items in his hands.*—AdN (79.01.27, p.2) [Spec sense of E *spotlight*, a theatrical electric lamp with a focused beam]

spot·ters-and-skinners *n pl* (Bdos) ‖ CRAB-FOOT (Belz, etc) [*CGBD* suggests perh < (SE) *pot-hooks* (i.e. the deep curved stroke in learning to write) + (SE) *skimmers* (perh name for a shallow curve)]

spouge [spu·j] *n* (CarA) **1.** A Barbadian dance rhythm with accompanying lyrics and a quick, bouncy beat wh is felt to combine something of both REGGAE and CALYPSO; the music requires a combo of wind-instruments, bass-guitar and an electronic keyboard, this last being used to produce groups of quick staccato chords; its creation and naming are attributed to the entertainer Jackie Opel in the late 1960s. *Spouge is a good beat and should not be allowed to die. Many Bajans and West Indians love it. So come on Mr Clarke, do like you say and give Spouge the break it deserves. And entertainers, play your part. After all, it's ours.*—AdN (76.02.14, p.16) **2.** [By extension] The dance to this music, usu with a partner, involving the co-ordinated, sharp dropping of the hip to the beat. *We can hope that other enterprising persons will deal with folk forms such as Landship dances, the Xmas time dances, and even go back to the fundamentalist churches therefrom to derive a pop dance even more* *distinctly Bajan than the Spouge.*—AdN (72.10.11, p.4)

spounce (spunks) [spʌŋ(k)s] *n* (Guyn, Trin) [*AF*] **1.** [Often of a young woman] Surprising boldness; brashness; saucy courage. **a.** *She has all that spounce to give rude answers to her old uncle but not enough to tell that damned Casanova to mind his stops with her.*—(Guyn) **b.** *In those days nothing that TTT did was any good, according to Jeremy and he got all the spunks he needed from the Express to harass and ridicule S. Rawlins and his team.*—BoM (77.01.07, p.16) **2.** [By extension] Mettle; raw worth; quality. *Dis jackass gat to show [h]e spounce dis afternoon [Ref: A village donkey race].*—(Guyn) [*Spunks* < IF SE *spunk* 'courage' + paragogic /-s/, developing a pronunc infl by *bounce*]

sprank·sious (spranc·tious) [spraŋ(k)ʃʌs] *adj* (Bdos, Guyn) **1.** [Of a child] Uninhibited and good-looking; precocious. **2.** [Of an old person or an animal] Very lively; not to be restrained; frisky. [Perh < EE *OED sprank*[1] sb 'a show or display' + cits from 16C, the adj being formed on the analogy of such words as *spacious, anxious*, etc]

sprat-net *n* (Angu, Belz, CayI, Jmca, ViIs) ‖ CAST-NET (CarA)

spree[1] *n* (CarA) Anything done extravagantly, excessively, with little restraint. □ The term is not only applied to fun (dancing, drinking, etc) as in IAE, but also, esp in newspaper headlines, to crime (hence *house-breaking spree*, etc) domestic and other activities (hence *hair-dressing spree*, etc).

spree[2] *vb* **1.** (CarA) To enjoy yourself (in any general sense). *Flirtation which may or may not lead to intercourse is 'desporting' or 'spreeing'.*—Pra 74/12, p.845 **2.** PHRASE **2.1 spree away/ out money** *vb phr* (CarA) [*AF/IF*] To spend away money on fun, clothing, etc.

spree-boy/-girl/-man/-woman/-master *n* (CarA) [*AF—Joc*] A person who is more inclined to dress up and have fun than to work; a thoroughgoing fun-seeker.

sprig *n* (Antg) ‖ FEG (Angu, etc) [Perh by extension < *OED sprig* 1. 'a shoot or twig of a plant']

spring-and-rab·bet board *n phr* (Guyn) ‖ LAP-EDGE BOARD (Gren) [Carpentry] [See RABBET-AND-SPRING BOARD (*Bdos*)] □ RABBET is sometimes erron spelled 'rabbit'.

Spring crop *n phr* (Guyn) [Rice Ind; Sugar Ind] ‖ FIRST CROP (Guyn) [Perh now Obs. The name is due to traditional use of European seasonal labels for times of the year, the harvesting of this crop in both industries coinciding with the season of Spring in Britain] □ See also AUTUMN CROP.

spry; spries *n* (Baha, Bdos) A drizzle or a light shower of rain. *Rain coming through an open window, if not too heavy, would be spries of rain.*—Bdos (Ms, 1972) [Prob < dial prununc of SE *spray* as in 'salt sea-spray'. Note *EDD spray* sb with variant *spry*, Ken]

spunks *n* (Guyn, Trin) See SPOUNCE

spur-pep·per *n* (Bdos) ‖ BIRD-PEPPER (CarA) [From the resemblance, in some varieties, to the shape of a cock's spur]

spy-glass *n* (CarA) A boat-captain's telescope; [by extension] a pair of binoculars. □ The sense by extension is commoner at the folk-level, telescopes being unknown in many places.

squash *n* (CarA) ‖ GOURD (BrVi, etc) *She unloaded her big basket of lovely squash and carefully stacked them head and tail on the market pavement.*—Guyn (Ms) [Cp *EDD squash* sb[2] 1. 'a pumpkin' (Glo)] □ The names SQUASH (no pl) or MARROW (pl -s) are the most widely used.

squinge up [skwɪnʤʌp] *vb phr* (Gren, Guyn, Trin) [*IF*] To screw up or contort (esp the face); to wrinkle up; to shrivel up. *When it's a Bill for the Minister of Health, the Minister of Finance doing it. And they sit down there and they feel happy because they are Ministers but they have to keep their tail quiet. Don't squinge up your face; you don't know what tail is?*—Gren (Hd, 76.05.01, p.25) [< *OED squinch* vb (U.S.) 'to screw or distort (the face)', with [č > ʃ] voicing in CE]

squin·gy [skwɪnʤi] *adj* (ECar) [Esp of fruit or sth edible] Shrivelled; wrinkled; undersized and of poor quality. *Well dem sandwich did look tired an' all squingy, squingy / As if somebody sit down on dem.*—KTT:72 [< SQUINGE + SE Derog suff /-y/ as in *messy, watery*, etc]

Sra·nan *n* (Srnm) ‖ *Taki-Taki* (CarA) [*Derog*] A Creole language of Surinam combining grammatical elements of English and W African languages and vocabulary elements mainly of English and Dutch with smaller proportions of Portuguese, African, and Amerindian languages; it is the first or second language of about one-third of the Surinamese population and is a language of national communication, with a literature. [Abbr of *Sranan Tongo* 'Surinam Language' in that language, replacing Du *Neger-Engelsch* 'Negro English'] □ Also called *Surinaams*, SURINAMESE by its speakers, esp outside of Surinam. The older colonial name, TAKI-TAKI, is offensive.

stake out *vb phr* (Bdos) **1.** To tie (livestock) out in a pasture to graze. *I have had goats locked up for three days now because I have nowhere to stake them out.*—AdV (84.03.31, p.1) [From the use of stakes driven into the ground, to wh animals are tied while 'out' to pasture] **2.** [By extension] [*AF—Joc: Cricket*] To keep (an opposing side) fielding a whole day or more without losing many wickets. **3.** (Belz, Trin) [By extension] To ambush; to surround (a place) and lie in wait. *Their arrests followed a police raid on the hotel at Lambie Street, Marabella, after it was staked out for days the court heard. When held, the girls were naked or partly clothed, the police testified.*—ExP (76.04.21, p.17) □ Note closely similar *COD8 stake out* colloq 'place under surveillance'.

staked out *vbl adj phr* (Bdos) [*AF—Joc*] ‖ BUCK-SICK¹ (Guyn)

stamp-and-go *n* (Jmca) A small SALT-FISH fritter. [By transfer from E nautical phr 'Stamp and go' given as an order to sailors (see *OED*); a ref to the promptness of the wayside provision of this 'snack'. Cp the modern terms 'pick-up', 'fast-food', etc in same context]

stand¹ [stan(d)] *vb tr* PHRASES **1. stand your grind** *vb phr* (Tbgo, Trin) [*AF*] See GRIND² Phr 3.1 **2. stand your hand** *id phr* (Guyn, Trin) [*AF*] See HAND¹ Phr 4.27

stand² [sta·n] *vb intr* (CarA) [*AF/IF*] **1.** [Reducing the SE sense of being on your feet; with a foll co-ordinated vb] To be there; to be aware. **a.** *Christine, when I stand and study how men can be, I just feel like destroying myself.*—PeL (79.06.15, p.12) **b.** *You mean to say you stan' dey an' let de chile nasty up de place.*—EFLBB: 19 [Shifted sense of *OED stand* B. I. 5.(c) with cits ... *stand and watch* ..., etc, in wh being on the feet is unconsciously implied] □ In this and foll senses the usu pronunc, with lengthened vowel and reduced /-CC/ as shown, generally distinguishes this usage from STAND¹. **2.** ‖ *stay* 3. (CarA) ‖ *stop* 3. (CarA) [Becoming a copula] To be; to seem to be; to appear as. **a.** *Take my advice. Wha[t]ever you see goin[g] on, you say nothing. Jus[t] stan[d] quiet and go [a]bout yo[ur] business.*—(Guyn) **b.** *How inside a de room stan?* —WFSFB:36 **c.** *Look man, you dat show me where me fowl was. I want you to stand me witness.*—RTCS:20 □ See Phr 4.3. **3.** ‖ *stop* 1. (CarA) To stay; to remain; to reside (with a friend or relative). **a.** *I won[t] invite dem again. Dey can fin[d] somebody else to stan[d] with, or le[t] dem stan[d] right whe[re] dey belong.*—(Guyn) **b.** *When I first entered politics, people, especially in the rural areas were afraid of losing their jobs, and this meant that many stood away from meetings.*—NaT (76.09.05, p.23) **c.** *... and I building a house there at Prospect and anytime you ain't feel like standing here no longer, you know what you kin do.*—CISH:31 □ This usage often leads, in contexts of educated speech as in cit b, to the erron use of SE pa.t. *stood = stayed*. See Phr 4.2. **4.** PHRASES **4.1 Stand good!** *leave-taking phr* (Guyn) [*AF*] See GOOD³ Phr 2.8 **4.2 stand home** *vb phr* (CarA) [*AF*] To remain, stay at home (esp as a matter of practice or habit). *Miss Sealy said, 'Men feel that they are the only ones who should go out and have a good time and we must*

stand home and mind babies.—NaT (76.12.12, p.1) [< sense 3. above] **4.3 stand so** *vb phr* (Baha, Gren, Guyn) [*AF*] ‖ *stay so* (CarA) **a.** *But who goin[g] to pick up money and jus[t] gi[v]e you so? I ain[t] know nobody stand so.*—(Baha) **b.** *But is so dey stan[d], a mean set o[f] people.*— (Guyn) [< Sense 2. above]

stan[d]-home [sta·n-hom] *n* (Guyn) [*AF*] ‖ BAD-FOOD (Bdos, Tbgo) *Another circumstance under which a female client compromises the violation of her privacy is agreeing to the shaving of a part of the pubic hair ... by the obeahman, to be used in the making of love potions or 'stan home' (a concoction to cause a man to reduce his promiscuity ...)*—COYN:13 [A Guyn Cr functional vb > n shift of STAND HOME, as STAND² Phr 4.2]

stand-pipe [sta·npaɪp] *n* (CarA) A source of piped water-supply mounted on a concrete stand and placed at the side of the road for the convenience of the public. (It was for a long time the only access to pipe-borne water esp in rural communities). *Others escape the no water inconvenience by joining the unending queue at the nearest public stand-pipe and more rush to the seaside.*—VoS (73.04.07, p.4) □ Cp SE *stand-pipe* wh is of different structure and purpose.

star-ap·ple* ['starapl ~ 'stʌrapl] *n* (CarA) ‖ *caimite* (Dmca, Gren, StLu, Tbgo, Trin) A round, apple-sized edible fruit, purple when ripe, with a sweet, purplish-white pulp in wh shiny, black seeds are set in a star-shape (seen when the fruit is cut across the middle, and hence the name); its thickish skin carries a sticky latex, and the leaves of the large tree have a glossy green surface and brown underside; *Chrysophyllum cainito* (*Sapotaceae*). □ A green-skinned variety is sometimes called *white star-apple*, the flesh being all white.

starch man·go *n phr* (Gren, StLu, Tbgo) ‖ *mango-mouchach/(-mouchasse)* (Dmca, StLu) A small, very sweet mango with a pink or rosy patch on the skin and pale yellow flesh; *Mangifera spp.* [Prob because of its thick texture like that of a starchy tuber]

star·light *n* (CarA) A hand-held sparkling firework stick. [< *star* + *light*. When lit the sparks from the firework resemble clusters of stars]

starve *n* (Guyn, Trin) [*AF—Joc*] Starvation; nothing to eat. **a.** *Frankly what I think this nation needs is a good dose of starve.*—ExP (73.02.03, p.15) **b.** *They had no father and when the mother dead many days they had a dish o[f] starve.*— (Guyn) [By Joc vb > n shift of SE *starve* vb. Note also *EDD starve* 5. sb 'a fit of abstinence']

stash *vb intr* (Guyn) [*AF—Joc*] [Esp of a woman] To dress very showily.

stash·er [stašər] *n* (Guyn) [*AF—Joc*] A woman who always dresses showily.

sta·shie [steši] *adj* (Gren, StVn) [*AF—Joc*] [Esp of a woman] Smartly dressed. [Prob < SE *ostentatious*, esp in view of pronunc] □ Cp STOCIOUS (*Jmca*).

State *n* (CarA) See ASSOCIATED STATE *Antigua with its dependencies, Barbuda and Redonda, is a 'State in association with the United Kingdom.'—* Cat IV. 1, p.36 □ Hence many derivatives *State-controlled, -owned, -run*, etc, 'controlled, owned, run, etc by the Government of the country'.

State·hood *n* (ECar) The condition of being a recognized STATE or self-determining nation. **a.** *Kittitian leaders in 1966 saw a change in the scene. Statehood was thrust upon the people who knew little of what Statehood meant.—*DeM(SK) (73.04.28, p.2) **b.** *The sixth anniversary of the granting of Antigua's new Statehood constitution was observed yesterday. / But there were no official celebrations. Antigua attained Statehood in association with Britain on February 27, 1967; but the government has set aside November 1 each year as Statehood Day which is celebrated as a Bank holiday.—*AnS (73.02.28, p.1) [STATE + SE suff *-hood* as in *motherhood, fatherhood*, etc] □ Orig chiefly AmE (See *OED*). The use related to CE STATE focuses on nearness to independence.

state·si·der [stetsaɪdər] *n* (USVI) An American citizen belonging to the mainland United States as distinguished from one belonging to the US Virgin Islands.

Sta·tian [stešʌn] *n, adj* (CarA) (A person or thing) native or belonging to St Eustatius, one of the islands of the Netherlands Antilles (WIND-WARD group). *Blue crabs inhabiting the crater of Sint Eustatia's volcanic Quill emerge at night to forage. The enterprising Statians hike up to the crater to hunt the crabs by flashlight, and their catch is frequently used to create this island delicacy.—*FWWC:23 [< Statia, the IF name used for St Eustatius in all the islands of the north eastern *CarA*. The name Stacio is said to be given on a Du. map of 1625 (*ASE:49*), and later Hispanicized as San Eustachio. That would account for the double forms, Statia(n) being the older. Note also the form 'Sint Eustatia' in cit]

sta·tia yam [stešə yam] *n phr* (Baha, Nevs, StKt, StLu) A very large, round, fine-tasting yam with a thick, brown, smooth skin and white flesh. [Named after the island of St Eustatius (called Statia)]

stay *vb* (CarA) **1.** [*AF/IF*] ‖*stop* 2. (ECar) To remain (fixed in one place); to be (here/there without leaving, moving off, etc). **a.** *Compere Czien answered, 'Compere, since ah reach home is here ah stay.—*PSFC:36 **b.** *A done realize a have to get wan man. My husband must di mind somebody else ova da States too, di money stay one amount, no time more, and everything di go up.—*HF:15 [Combining the general senses of

SE *stay* 'remain' (as *OED* stay vb[1] 4. to 9.), but with a sense of 'fixture' wh develops into other usage below] **2.** [*IF*] To survive; to keep existing. **a.** *'How you stay with England, Son?' I asked him, 'Is England friendly with you?'—*RND:334 **b.** *'No state can stay without having emergency powers to deal with situations say like ... a hurricane. There would be need to invoke emergency powers to constitute the ability to establish protection,' he said.—*AdV (87.06.25, p.6, from Gren Hd) [Cp SE *stay* as in *stay the distance* in Sport. See *OED* stay vb[1] 12. 'to last; to keep up (with a competitor)'] **3.** [*AF*] [Becoming a copula] ‖*stand*[2] 2. (CarA) ‖*stop* 3. (ECar) To be; to be like (in appearance, behaviour, character). **a.** *A relative is more important than a friend, but some friends stay closer than a brother.—*RLCF:96 **b.** *This Hanna man should know by now how plenty of these so call professional and qualified Bahamians stay, especially if he say he in the banking business.—*NaG (75.03.06, p.5, Satirically Speaking) See Phrs 4.2, 4.4, 4.5, 4.7 below. **4.** PHRASES **4.1 Is so sb/sth stay** *id phr* (CarA) That is how sb/sth is. **a.** *Is so these Georgetown people stay.—*CBM:115 **b.** *Oh well, friennie, is so life stay. You have wuthless man in every country.—*WeG (73.06.06, Partyline) [A focused form of Phr 4.7] **4.2 leave sb stay** *vb phr* (USVI) To stop interfering with sb; (SE) to let sb be. *Boy, yo don' leave me stay, I chop yo wid dis rockstone.—*RDVI:64 [< IF SE *leave* be 'not interfere with', *be* being replaced by CE STAY 3.] **4.3 stay godfather/godmother for sb** *vb phr* (CarA) [*IF*] (SE) To stand godfather/godmother for sb. *P. Watson stayed for the last child but my dear, he stay for so many people children that I don['t] think he can remember who is and who isn[t] [h]is godchild.—*(Guyn) [An extension of sense 3. above. See SE phr at *OED* stand vb B. I. 15. (b)] □ The sense of sponsoring is further extended in CE to ‘*stay bail, responsible, etc for sb*’. **4.4 Stay good!** *leave-taking phr* (Guyn, Jmca) [*IF*] See GOOD[3] Phr 2.8 [Combining STAY 1. and 2. above + (in) good (health)] **4.5 stay like dog** *vb phr* (StLu) [*AF—Derog*] To be in awful circumstances; to suffer in great poverty. *When the father died the family 'stayed like dog'.—*StLu (Ms) [Combining STAY 2. and 3. above + *like dog(s)*] **4.6 stay like that/stay so and (burst, drop, fall, etc)** *vb phr* (Bdos, Gren, Guyn) [*AF/IF*] To happen (to burst, drop, fall, etc) without warning. **a.** *She say ... that how could a woman just stay like that and drop down dead.—*SNWIC:211 (A.N. Forde) **b.** *I could not use the arm freely. I use the arm now but it have time when I does use it, it does stay so and fall as though a cramp does get me in it.—*Gren (CR, 79/8) [< combining STAY 1. and 2. + co-ordinated vb] **4.7 stay so** *vb phr* (CarA) [*IF—Derog*] ‖*stand so* (Baha, Gren, Guyn) ‖*stop so* (ECar) To be so displeasing, unpleasant (in behaviour, appearance, etc); to look so odd. **a.** *Those people next door are always quick to borrow but think it hard to lend you anything. I don't know why they stay so.—*(Guyn) **b.** *But what makes his face stay so? Could not be gutter-water, for he is a boastie boy who has told me he* has been on Morant Bay streets many times, he one.—RND:50 **c.** You ever see a ripe breadfruit stay so? Da[t] don['t] look good to me.—(Antg) **4.8 stay up** vb phr (Bdos) [AF] To stand up; to be standing. On 28th April 1970 I was staying up talking with Myrtle and Lucille talking. I was backing Emmerton Lane.—Bdos (CR, 71.05.25) **4.9 stay with (an agreement, a decision, etc)** vb phr (CarA) To refuse to change, resist going back on (an agreement, etc). Our Party will stay with the promises made in our manifesto.—(Bdos)

stay-at-home; **stay-home sauce/soup/tea** n (phr) (Bdos, Guyn) [IF] ‖ BAD-FOOD (Bdos, Tbgo) Some said that Charlotte and her godmother worked obeah on him to catch him as a husband. They had put 'stay-at-home' in his food, people said. A concoction of musk and asafoetida and boiled bush.—MLDS:12

steady vb tr PHRASE **steady your head** vb phr (CarA) [AF] To keep your balance; to steady yourself (physically or emotionally). As he had been drinking so much she gave him a strong cup of coffee to steady his head before he got on his bicycle to ride home.—Guyn (Ms) [Cp Yoruba ṣọ ori rẹ (watch your head) 'be careful (i.e. about what you are doing)']

steel n **1.** (CarA) Any piece of iron held suspended and struck by an iron rod or a piece of wood to make a ringing sound as part of a street band in folk festivals. **a.** An unremitting clash is furnished by the 'steel'—a brake drum beaten with an iron rod—and by the shack-shack.—FTT:171 **b.** Sometimes there is another instrument, an iron triangle, known as the 'steel'... An adequate band would have kittle, boom, fife and steel.—AdN (79.12.25, p.10) **2.** (Trin) Any instrument in a STEELBAND or the entire band; [by extension] the sound of STEELPANS. **a.** There were little steelbands mushrooming all over Port of Spain and most of the boys were unemployed and waited for Carnival hoping to make a little money. They stayed in the slums and they beat steel day and night and they were very good.—AKM:66 **b.** And steel rings out on Monday morn / Accompanied betimes by long shrill blast of bugle horn—/ Just at the break of day or 'Jou Ouver'.—HTCLL:4

steel·band n (CarA) **1.** A percussion band consisting of a set of STEELPANS tuned to cover together a complete range of musical notes, keys, and pitches, so allowing for the arrangement and playing of any piece of music. The PANS, ranging in depth of SKIRT from about 6 ins to the whole drum (see DIAGRAM), are usu mounted on stands and struck with rubber-tipped sticks of varying length and size. Such bands, orig created and developed through the Trinidad CARNIVAL, serve widely in the Caribbean for festive open-air music. **2.** [By extension] The playing and/or music of such bands. Steelband is the back-bone of any Carnival celebration. This is the firm view of Mr G. Joseph, temporary Secretary of the Antigua Steelband Association, and he expressed his feelings on this issue at a meeting of steelbandsmen on Saturday afternoon.—AnS (67.05.31, p.2)

steel-don·key n (Bdos) A legendary, supernatural creature whose presence is manifested by unexplained, jangling or metallic sounds and other weird occurrences; it causes panic in neighbourhoods where its presence is reported. □ Cp BALLAHOO[3] 3. (Bdos), ROLLING CALF (Belz, etc).

steel·pan n (CarA) ‖ PAN[2] (CarA) The colonialist attacked the language and music of the Africans, restricted and in some cases, even banned the drum. Under such pressure the African innovated, and we ended up with the Calypso and the wonder of the steelpan—which of course is but the drum in another guise.—TrG (79.09.23, p.2) [< STEEL 1. (CarA) + PAN[2] 1.] □ Orig and still often rendered as **steel pan**.

stell·ing n (Guyn) A long wooden pier extending across the riverside mudflat to deep water to permit embarcation on a steamer or ferry-boat; [by extension] any wharf (usu standing on wooden planks). The 12.45 p.m. ferry left its mooring at 12.45 p.m., which surprised everybody and left a number of people on the stelling waving desperately to attract the captain's attention.—SNWIC:219 (R. Heath) [Du stelling 'scaffolding', in ref to the cross-barred structure of the pier] □ See FERRY-STELLING.

stench [stɛnč] vb (Baha) **1.** To hold open (a window, door) with a stick, stone, or other prop; [by extension] to brace hard against sth/sb with the body or the stiffened arm. **a.** The house had the old-fashioned kind of window you had to stench with a stick.—Baha (Ms) **b.** [Group backing one side in arm-wrestling] Stench him! Stench him!—(Baha) [Cp CSD Sc dial stench[1] 3. vb tr 'to restrain'; also EDD staunch vb[1] var stench, Sc, 3. 'to desist, stay'; also OED stanch, var stenche 6. b. (Obs) 'to restrain' + cits only for 16C] **2.** PHRASES **2.1 stench open/up** vb phr (Baha) To stay, prop open (a door, window). Use this piece of wood to stench up the door, and stench open the window too. It's hot in here.—(Baha) **2.2 stench off** vb phr (Baha) [IF] To stiffen the body in resistance. If I am on the dance floor and somebody holding me too tight I stench off.—(Baha)

step vb intr **1.** (Bdos, Gren, Guyn, Tbgo, Trin) To walk with particular grace and style. On a Sunday afternoon you would see the old man in his three-piece suit, new felt hat and walking-stick, stepping going to see his lady friends, sir.—(Guyn) **2.** PHRASES **2.1 step in** vb phr (CarA) [IF] To come in; to arrive; to visit casually. What would she say to Lias if he should step in now?—PKKK: 28 **2.2 step out** vb phr (Bdos) [IF] To go out temporarily; to leave a place expecting to return shortly. **a.** [Answering a phone call] She has just stepped out. You can call back in a few minutes.—(Bdos) **b.** I thought he had stepped out, but he never came back to work that day.—(Bdos)

step·pish *adj* (Belz) [*AF/IF*] Audacious; ready to take liberties with or advantage of sb. *Mind you keep out o[f] de way o[f] dat boy. You see how he big and you know how he steppish.*—(Belz)

Steups! (Stewps(e)! Stupes! Stupse!) [scŭ·ps] (Bdos, Dmca, Gren, Guyn, Trin) [*AF*] **1.** *ideoph representing* SUCKING THE TEETH **a.** *'Steups' echoed the length and breadth of Federick Street, as they paraded Butler at the head of a drunken, frenzied mob of revellers.*—MoK (72.06.23, p.14) **b.** *I turning back, man! (Stewpse!) I turning back my blasted car,'cause you confusing me.*—PeL (80.08.01, p.2) **c.** *'Conrad, why you muh go a school to-day?' she would scold. 'Stu-ups! Why a can't trust you?'*—FGSOS: 53 **2.** *n, vb* See CHEUPS (Trin) □ Other spellings, *stu-u-ups* are sometimes found, wh attempt to stress the lengthening of the sound on occasions; rarely also others: *stchoops, stroopes, stueeps,* etc. **3.** PHRASE **3.1 steups your teeth** *vb phr* (Tbgo) ‖ SUCK YOUR TEETH (CarA)

stew *vb tr* (Antg, Nevs) [*AF—Derog*] To abort (a pregnancy); to bring about the abortion of (a foetus). *She done stew a chil[d] an[d] she still a-play so neat.*—(Nevs) [Cp *OED* stew vb¹ *Obs* 'to check, restrain' + cits–'1400. Perh this *Obs* form may have survived orally at the folk level]

stew-dump·ling *n* (Bdos, StVn) ‖ DUKUNA (Antg, etc) *The need is for something substantial, for the tasty 'conkies' or 'stew dumplings'.*—AdN (79.04.15, p.10)

St George's *n phr* (Belz) September 10, celebrated annually as a national holiday in Belize to commemorate the defeat by a small armed force of British log-cutters and their Negro slaves of a Spanish attempt at St George's Caye to invade and capture the settlement in 1798.

stick¹ *n* **1.** (ECar) ‖ FIGHTING-STICK (ECar) **2.** ‖ FIRE-STICK (Belz, etc) esp in foll phrs. **3.** PHRASES **3.1 be like a stick of fire** *vb phr* (Gren) To be in a hurry, unable to stay long. *Sit down le[t] we talk nuh, how you rushing so, you like a stick o[f] fire.*—(Gren) **3.2 come for a stick of fire** *vb phr* (Guyn, Trin) To come to ask a quick friendly favour; [by extension] to pay a very brief passing visit. [A ref to borrowing a neighbour's FIRE-STICK, in former times, so as to quickly light your own fire] **3.3 stick of cassava** *n phr* (Guyn) See CASSAVA Phr 2.1

stick² *vb* PHRASES **1. stick in sb's skin** (Gren, Jmca) [*AF*]; **stick on sb like white on rice** (Baha) *vb phrs* ‖ BE BEHIND SB LIKE A SLAVE-DRIVER (CarA) See BEHIND¹ Phr 2. **2. stick the cake** *vb phr* (CarA) [Of a man and woman] To cut a wedding or birthday cake together ceremonially. *At Karen's birthday the mother made four boys draw out of a hat to stick the cake with her.*—Tbgo (Ms) [Because a decorated knife and fork are symbolically stuck into the cake by the two] **2. stick your grind** *vb phr* (Tbgo, Trin) [*AF*] See GRIND² Phr 3.1 *No darling that child aint mine....*

After you mamaguy me and take my money / And still sleeping in Williams bachy / When the baby born stick your grind.—RLCF:219 (Cso)

stick-fight; stick-fighting *n* (ECar) ‖ *bwa* (Dmca, Gren, StLu, Tbgo, Trin) ‖ *kalinda-fighting* (Trin) ‖ *stick-licking* (Bdos, Jmca) A (sometimes fatal) battle between two trained men each using a specially prepared STICK or BWA. □ See also GATKA.

stick-fight·er *n* (ECar) ‖ *bwa-man* (Dmca, Gren, StLu, Tbgo, Trin) ‖ *kalinda-man* (Trin) ‖ *stick-licker* (Bdos, Jmca) ‖ *stick-man* (Bdos, Trin) A man trained to do STICK-FIGHTING.

stick-lick·er *n* (Bdos, Jmca) ‖ STICK-FIGHTER (ECar)

stick-lick·ing *n* (Bdos, Jmca) ‖ STICK-FIGHTING (ECar) [< STICK + LICK¹]

stick-man *n* (Bdos, Trin) ‖ STICK-FIGHTER (ECar)

stick·y ber·ry *n phr* (Antg) ‖ CLAMMY-CHERRY 1. (CarA)

still PHRASES **still and all** (Antg); **still/yet for all** (Guyn, Trin) *adv phr; conj phr* [*IF*] Nevertheless; yet; in spite of which. **a.** *Now the bakkra was always afraid of diseases. Still and all, they took quite a long time before they did anything to clean up the place.*—SSHL:63 **b.** *Sparrow never hit they dog or they cat / Still for all they would not give me a chance / They interfering in my private romance.*—SCTR:21 [Cp *EDD* still adv (Sc, Irel, etc) In phr (1) *still and all* 'nevertheless, notwithstanding, yet']

stilt-man *n* (ECar) ‖ *bwa-bwa¹* **2.** (Dmca) ‖ *bwa-bwa dancer* (StVn) ‖ *moko-jumbie* (Gren, StKt, StLu, Trin, Vils) ‖ *mother-sally* (Guyn) ‖ *Seraphina* (StLu) ‖ *tiltman* (Bdos) A traditional type of masquerade dancer on high stilts, always a man in costume wh, in some territories, is usu a woman's dress.

sting·a·ree (sting·a·ray) *n* (ECar) A stingray; *Dasyatis* spp. [Perh a seaman's variant. *OED2* lists the form as 'US and Austral']

sting·ing-net·tle* /1'122/ *n* (CarA) **1.** ‖ *bath-nettle* (Nevs) ‖ *scratch-bush* (Tbgo) ‖ *zoti* (StLu) ‖ *zouti* 1. (Dmca, Gren, Trin) A shrub growing to about 4 ft 'with a slightly reddish stem, heart-shaped leaves with serrated edges and stinging hairs on both leaves and stems' (*HCWP:86*); *Laportea aestuans* or *Fleurya a.* (*Urticaceae*). **2.** (Trin) ‖ ZOUTI 2. (Trin) □ The plant of the same name and properties in BrE is *Urtica dioica*.

stink¹ *vb* PHRASE **stink up (a place)** *vb phr* (CarA) [*IF*] To cause (a place) to stink; to make (a place) smell bad. *If dogs and cats run over by the traffic are left to stink up our roads, what will* *the tourists think of us?*—Bdos (Ms) □ This phr largely replaces SE *stink* vb, this word functioning in CE mostly as adj. See next and Phr 4.2 there

stink² *adj* 1. (CarA) Stinking; bad-smelling; that stinks. **a.** *It gives off a stink smell which makes us feel to vomit.*—ExP (73.03.29, p.21) **b.** *However, the BMC chairman has refuted these charges and substantiated both Port Health and port workers' statements to the effect that the meat was stink when it arrived in Barbados.*—NaT (80.04.10, p.10) [< SE *stink* by functional vb > adj shift; also by infl of such compounds as *stink-bug, stink-bush* (see *OED*). Note also functional ambiguity resulting from such contexts as 'God be pleased to make their breaths stink and the teeth rot out of them all therefore' (Charles Lamb, 1806)] □ Widely so used by educated persons. Also **stinkest**. 2. [By extension, of a man] Having breath that smells of rum. **a.** *You would believe that nine o'clock in the morning that man talkin[g] to you and you can smell him stink with the rum?*—(Guyn) **b.** *Smell him stink of white rum, he drunk!*—WSAD:16 3. (ECar) [By extension, of behaviour] Crude; angry. □ Used as semi-adv, like a CarA Cr adj; see Phr 4.1 below 4. *PHRASES* 4.1 **get on stink** *vb phr* (ECar) [*AF*] To behave crudely, angrily; to raise a rough, noisy row. *After waiting so long in de bus stand de people get on real stink when de bus come.*—(Gren) 4.2 **smell stink** *vb phr* (CarA) To stink; to give off a bad smell. *Mr Chairman, it is human nature that if I have rubbish to put out, I am going to put it out. I am not going to keep it in my house to smell stink in at me when I can put it outside.*—Bdos (Hd, 73.10.23, p.2694) □ This phr commonly replaces SE *stink* vb in CE. See also STINK¹ Phr.

stink bug *n phr* (Guyn) ‖ **bush-bug** (Gren) ‖ **pea-chink** 1. (Bdos) A green insect about 1 cm in length, with a shield-shaped back; it lives mainly on trees but settles sometimes on indoor drapes; it has a very unpleasant smell when crushed; *Nezara viridula (Pentatomidae)*.

stink·ing-bush/weed *n* (CarA) ‖ WILD COFFEE (Guyn, etc) *Stinking-weed coffee is excellent for kidney and stomach disorders. Rum and lime juice is put into stinking-weed coffee to make a beverage which is used for colds, flu, coughs, and fevers.*—Lal. I. I, p.82 [From the unpleasant smell of the leaves, wh are not eaten by grazing live stock]

stink·ing-toe* *n* 1. (CarA) ‖ **locust** (Bdos, Guyn, Trin) A five-inch long, hard, warty, brown pod, the fruit of a tall timber tree (the LOCUST); the pulp surrounding its seeds has an unpleasant smell (hence the name), though it is sweet and eaten by children; *Hymenea courbaril (Leguminosae)*. 2. (Belz) ‖ **bukut** (Belz) A smooth, brown, fifteen-inch long seed-pod with a sweet-tasting but offensive-smelling pulp, borne on an ornamental flowering tree, *Cassia grandis (Caesalpiniaceae)*. □ Distinguished as **horse cassia** in *Trin*—PTT:108

stink·ness *n* (CarA) A strange or unpleasant odour; stench. *The sea was calm and warm, with a raw luscious stinkness.*—PCOS:110 [STINK² 1. + SE suff *-ness*] □ Cp SE nouns *stink, stench*.

St John·i·an [sɪnt-jo·niən] *n, adj* (ViIs) (A person or thing) belonging to or characteristic of the island of St John, one of the US Virgin Islands. *The majority of St Johnians are either Moravians or Lutherans.*—JNHSJ:1

St John('s) bush* *n phr* (ECar) A low, trailing herb with flowering shoots; it is a common roadside weed wh is widely used as a folk medicine, esp for complaints of the womb; *Blechum brownei (Acanthaceae)*.

St John's *n phr* (CarA) A perfumed liquid used by those who practice OBEAH.

St Lu·cian [sɪnt/sent-lušən] *n, adj* (A person or thing) belonging to or characteristic of St Lucia, an independent State in the (ex-British) WINDWARD ISLANDS.

St Lu·cia par·rot* *n phr* (StLu) ‖ *Jacquot* (StLu) A yellowish-green parrot with a bluish head, red underparts, and a conspicuous red patch on the wing; *Amazona versicolor (Psittacidae)*, found only in St Lucia and the National Bird of that island.

St Maar·tian (**St. Mar·tin·er** *n, adj* (Neth) See SINT MAARTIAN

sto·cious [stošʌs] *adj* (Jmca) [*AF—Joc*] [Of a woman] Attractive; sexy-looking. [Of a man] Stylish; smart; [by extension] snobbish. *Me don't have to tell you that most of us only want a li'l independence and prosperity to lose respect for God and man. They get 'stocious', if you know what me mean.*—BGSB:139 [Cp *OED2* stocious (chiefly Anglo-Irish) slang 'drunk, intoxicated'; but no obvious connection with CE sense. Cp STASHER (*Guyn*), STASHIE (*Gren, StVn*) wh are closer in sense and may be related]

stock *n* 1. (Bdos, StKt, StVn) Livestock (usu excluding horses); animals bred for slaughter (including chickens). *This situation is resulting in serious reduction in some of our best breeding stock, especially the black-belly sheep which is in demand not only in Barbados.*—AdN (72.05.04, p.1) [Cp *OED* stock 54. spec = Livestock] □ No pl (cp sense 2.). This sense was once in much wider currency in *CarA*. Note compounds below. 2. (Bdos) [By extension] [*IF*] An animal or a genus of animals bred for slaughter. *I told him I liked raising a few stocks. He said I had his word that when he became my husband, stocks like black belly sheep, cows, pigs, goats, all the various animals a person could raise in Barbados, he was going to help me become the best small farmer in the Caribbean.* NaT (79.06.01, p.10) 3. *PHRASE* 3.1 **when yo(u) ketch/catch stock** *id phr* (Trin) [*AF—Cr*] ‖ WHEN YOU HEAR THE SHOUT *id phr* (Bdos, etc) See HEAR Phr 4.12 *In them days* coolie beggar-man used to walk around beggin[g] for penny he[re] penny de[re] and when you ketch stock he dead an[d] lef[t] a whole heap o[f] money in a bag.—(Trin) [Variant of SE take stock as OED stock 56. b.]

stock-feed n (Guyn) Animal feed, esp poultry feed. Stockfeed! Stockfeed!! For your next supply of Local and Imported Poultry and Animal Feed—padi, oats, crushed corn (corn crushed at 1/2c per b). Call at Persaud's Stockfeed Factory, Smyth and D'Urban Streets.—DaC (Ad, 52.08.31, p.12)

stock-meat n (Bdos, StKt, StVn) Pasture grass, green leaves and bushes collected as fodder for livestock.

stoke vb tr 1. (Baha) [AF] To spurn or scold (sb) crudely; to treat (sb) humiliatingly. Da's jus[t] good for yo[u]. The girl stoke you.—(Baha) [Perh by semantic shift of SE stoke 'poke (a fire)'. However cp Sc dial CSD stoke vb tr 1. 'pierce' 2. 'thrust'. Cp also sense 2.] 2. (Mrat) To hoe and clear (grass). [Perh a semantic extension of sense 1. However cp Sc dial CSD stook 'to sheave corn, to bundle straw'] 3. PHRASE 3.1 just fit to stoke grass id phr (Mrat) [AF/IF—Derog] (Be) of no worth or quality (as a person).

stom·ach[1] n (CarA) [IF] 1. The chest and abdomen, but often the upper part of the human body (hence Phrs 2.1, 2.3). 2. PHRASES 2.1 a cold on the stomach n phr (CarA) [IF] A chest cold. 2.2 keep your stomach vb phr (Guyn) [IF] ‖ **keep the wind out of your belly/stomach** (CarA) See WIND[1] Phr [Cp Yoruba da ikun duro (cause stomach stop) 'hold off hunger'] 2.3 with your stomach outside adv, adj phr (Bdos, Guyn) [IF] [Esp of a woman] With much of the chest exposed; (dressed) with a very low neckline.

stom·ach[2] vb tr (CarA) [IF] [With person as obj, and usu neg] To tolerate (sb); to accept or put up with (sb's behaviour). I can['t] stomach her at all. Goodness knows how I will manage when she is here the whole day tomorrow.—(Antg) □ SE stomach in this sense is restricted to things, situations, etc. (See COD8 stomach vb tr 2.) However 'a person stomachs (i.e. resents) another' is EE, with opposite sense to CE. (See OED stomach vb 1. c. with cits—'1671)]

stone n (CarA) PHRASE kick stones vb phr (TkCa) [AF—Joc] See KICK Phr 4.

stone-bruise n (Baha, Bdos, Gren, Jmca, Tbgo) A painful, infected area of hardened skin on the heel or sole of the foot caused by walking barefoot.

stone-feast (tomb·stone-feast) n (Crcu) A ritual, day-time feast held at the home of a deceased person, usu a year or two after the burial, to accompany the setting up of a tomb-stone at the person's grave after the earth has settled.

stone-fish n (CarA) ‖SCORPION-FISH (CarA) [Prob from its ability to camouflage itself, looking like a chunk of stone on the sea-bed]

stones n (Gren) ‖ PICK-UPS (CarA)

stoop (down) vb (phr) (CarA) [IF] To crouch; to squat. Counsel: What made you think he was acting suspiciously? / Witness: Well he was stooping down behind the hedge for a long time as if he was waiting to do something.—Guyn (CR) □ Cp SE stoop 'to bend the body forward'. See also HOLD 4. (Bdos), HOLD OVER.

stoop la·bour n phr (Belz) [AF] Unskilled, farm-ground labour that requires working in a crouching or bent posture. We know that millions of Mexicans cross over into the States to work every year, doing 'stoop labour' on the farms.—ReP (80.07.13, p.13)

stop vb intr (CarA) 1. [IF] ‖stand[2] 3. (CarA) To stay; to remain. a. Judge: When the service is done, do the deacons remain by themselves with the parson? / Bristol (slave): Yes sometimes we stop in the chapel / Judge: Do they stop after every other person has gone away? / Bristol: Yes, when we stop, it is for the purpose of going into the house to reckon the money; some of the members stop besides.—LMSPJS:21 b. She was against it, but my life was spoilt already. I couldn't stop a widow all the days of my life, and I went with him.—JMA:124 [Extension of OED stop 36. (a) 'to stay, remain', with implied comp 'in a place, for a purpose'. CE usage is, however, absolute, as in cits] 2. [IF/AF] ‖stay 1. (CarA) [By extension] To lodge; to reside temporarily. a. 'Are you going back to St Vincent de Paul when you get better, Charlie?' / 'Where else ah go stop again?' snapped Charlie.—BoM (74.10.11, p.17) b. 'This yard becoming a real refuge, you know,' she said smiling and shaking her head good-naturedly. 'We got a girl student stopping with us 'til the patrols ease up.—SJT:82 [Cp OED stop 36. (c) 'to sojourn as a visitor, resident or guest' with cits—'1901. The usage is, however, strongly current in CE. Cp also COD8 stop vb 6. intr 'stay for a short time'—a restriction wh does not limit CE usage] 3. (ECar) [AF] [Becoming a copula] ‖STAND 2. (CarA) To be. a. Is so dem Pentecostal people stop, always jealous.—KTT:16 b. You face stop so long; it look like wan giraffe neck.—SGAC:45 [By extension of sense 1. where, for ex, note cit b] 4. PHRASES 4.1 Is so/that's how sb stop id phr (CarA) [AF] ‖Is how/so sb/sth stay (CarA) See STAY Phr 4.1 a. Nough nastiness gine on, don' fool yuhself, an' not a soul en sayin' a t'ing. But dah is how we stop.—NaT (80.11.14, p.7, Lickmout' Lou) b. Dat time she will lie you know. She did well know but is so greedy people stop.—WeN (53.03.09, p.2, Anne & Josephine) [A focused form of Phr 4.5 below] 4.2 stop (away) from vb phr (CarA) [IF] To stay away from. I don't want to stop away from school.—MHJT:17 4.3 stop home vb phr (Bdos, Jmca, Trin) [AF] ‖STAND HOME (CarA) See STAND[2] Phr 4.3 'Boy, where you does go whole evening

instead of stop home here and help your moomah?'
his father asked.—SNWIC:228 (I. Khan) **4.4**
stop in *vb phr* (CarA) **(i)** To visit briefly; to call
in person. *Complete driving comfort and absolute*
control make it the sportiest family car in Cay-
man.... Stop in today and see the full range of
Fiats.—Cay (Ad, 75.06.12, p.5) **(ii)** To live in
(as a housemaid). *Young Woman Seeks Job As*
General help, will work with single person or to
care a baby, will also stop in. Call Joyce, 125
Sundown Cres. off Molynes Road.—StA(JA)
(71.07.03, p.8) [(i) is now also AmE. (ii) derives
from sense 2. above] **4.5 stop so** *vb phr* (ECar)
[*AF*] ‖STAY SO (CarA) See STAY Phr 4.7 *Yuh*
ever hear ting so, Cuz? How some people stop so!?
—BoM (74.09.20, p.19) [STOP 3. + SO[1] 2.] □ A
common folk variant of STAY/STAND SO in some
islands. **4.6 stop there** *id phr, often imper* (BrVi,
Nevs, StKt, StVn) [*IF*] [Usu implying some
contempt] To stay the way you are; not to change
(when change wd be sensible). *She can stop de[re]*
an[d] don['t] study and see how she goin[g] pass de
exam.—(StVn) [Extension of STOP 1. + *there*]

stop-off *n* (Guyn) [Rice Ind, Sugar Ind] A
small earthen dam built for the temporary control of the flow of drainage or irrigation water.
The R.P. request to reduce the height of the water
for them to put in culverts cannot be granted now
as it will adversely affect the rice. It can be granted
in October, but if they do not find it possible to
wait, stop-offs can be put.—DaC (52.08.20, p.7)

storm-surge *n* (CarA) A rise of the sea by 10
to 20 ft above sea-level brought on by the strong
winds of a hurricane, and sweeping inland.

sto·ry[1] *n* **1.** (CarA) [*IF*] An account of a happening; [by extension] a happening, an event.
Story has it, that some of the Lime Stone rocks
from the ruins were broken away to repair the
roadways to the nearby villages of Rock Stone
Pond one, and Rock Stone Pond two.—Bet I, p.15
□ Often without determiners *a, the,* as in cit
and some phrs below. Cp similarly SE *rumour has*
it. **2.** (ECar) [By extension] [*AF*] Trouble; a row;
a brawl. **a.** *He (witness) told them that when the*
boss was away, he was in charge and he did not
want any 'story' to happen in the place.—DaC
(52.09.19, p.3) **b.** *Dat Oval was someting else, is*
den story start. / Tanti Merle try to go through de
people gate / With she parasol open.—KTT:29 **3.**
(Guyn) [By extension] [*IF*] A disturbing, private
matter. *They does spend all their time bothering*
about other people story.—CBM:115 **4.** PHRASES
4.1 have story (with sb) *vb phr* (Guyn) [*AF*]
To have a row, be in bad relationship (with sb).
Some time they had story with the neighbour and
they had to go to court.—(Guyn) **4.2 Look story!**
excl vb phr (Guyn) [*AF*] See LOOK Phr 4.12
[LOOK + STORY 2.] **4.3 mouth open story**
jump out *id phr* (ECar) [*AF—Joc*] All is/will
be revealed. *They had to get the dentist out of*
the country quick because she knew what
happened, you see, so if they let her be questioned,
well! Mouth open story jump out.—(Guyn) [Com-
bining senses 1., 3.] **4.4 pound story** *vb phr*

(Dmca, Mrat, StKt) [*AF*] ‖POUND (SB'S) NAME
See POUND Phr 3.4 **4.5 Story done!** *id phr*
(Guyn, Trin) [*IF/AF*] ‖THE GAME COME (Guyn)
What has amazed me is that in spite of the fact
that Miss Gee, the girl involved, made a statement
about her harassment by men, there does not seem
to have been an inquiry. The poor lady lost her
job—story done.—BoM (79.06.29, p.9) **4.6**
push/put your mouth in sb's story *vb phr*
(CarA) [*AF/IF*] See MOUTH Phr 4.24 *The people*
had their own domestic story and she must go and
put in her mouth because she and the wife were
friends, so that's how she get hit.—(Baha)

sto·ry[2] *adj, vb* (CarA) [*AF—Cr*] **1.** *adj* [Usu
child lang] Untruthful. *Mammy didn['t] give you*
it. Yo[u] too story. You t[h]ief it.—(StVn) [A
functional n > adj shift of SE *stories* in euphemistic phr *telling stories* 'being untruthful'
esp in ref to children] **2.** *vb* [Of a child] To be
untruthful; to tell a lie. *An mih Ma bringing-home*
a t'ousan million. 'Yu story, man', commented
Toddan. / Well come and see nuh. I have twelve
cricket-bal-an forty car an all kinda t'ing—my
Ma buy them for me.—HCCM:50 [By characteristic Cr adj > vb shift]

St Paul; **St Peter** in phr BY ST PETER, etc. See
BY[1] Phr 6.3

straight[1] *adj* (CarA) **1.** [*IF*] Definite; unquestionable; outright; well-established or recognizable. **a.** *But don't be surprised if you can't*
understand the conversations between Thomanians
or Cruzians, because their true speech is a patois
of English. However, when they talk to you they
switch into a delightful variety of 'straight' English,
and you are back in the conversation.—USVI
(Brochure, 1975) **b.** *Mr Richardson said he was*
expecting a report shortly, concerning the real po-
sition at the two companies. / 'Once we catch
anybody it's straight jail,' the AG said.—BoM
(79.07.20, p.7) **c.** *Don['t] bother make no pass at*
she, she got her straight man a[l]ready.—(Gren) **2.**
[Of a Black woman's hair] not naturally crinkly;
STRAIGHTENED. *Of course all the beauty conscious*
girls who do not have straight hair endeavour to
have their hair done in these styles.—TrG
(73.07.07) **3.** [Of a Black person's nose] that is
not flat; pointed and with narrow nostrils. *Mary*
is dark, about six feet tall and thin. Her hair is
liberally streaked with grey. A distinguishing fea-
ture is her 'straight nose'.—ExP (73.01.01, p.21)
4. PHRASE **4.1 have a straight head** *vb phr*
(CarA) [*IF*] To be a clear thinker; to have the
gift of keen concentration or of making sound
decisions. *His wife had a straight head and could*
run the business better than he.—(Tbgo) [Cp IF
SE *get one's head straight*; also cp Yoruba *ori pipẹ*
(*head correct*) 'correct thinking'; also Shona *kuva*
nomusoro wakarurama (*to be with head straight*)
'to be clear thinking']

straight[2] *adv* (CarA) [*IF*] **1.** Directly; immediately; unquestionably; right away. **a.** *An*
moreover, how yer no I ain got no ticket? Where
yer cudda go I goin' straight!—JBJ:81 **b.** *The*

Cross-examination of N. L— ran in part as fol-
lows—Radix: Did G— just walk up the road and
enter the Bamboo Bar straight?—ToR (78.06.25,
p.1) **[**Cp *OED straight* c. adv 1., 2. Also characteristic Cr functional adj > adv shift of
STRAIGHT[1]**] 2.** Bluntly; without compunction;
[by extension] defiantly. **a.** *Ah telling you straight*
de onlyest time you come near minister is de time
you was sweeping the SDA church—period.—ToR
(73.01.31, p.6) **b.** *The next time he dare ask me*
anything so I would watch him and say straight
'Go to Hell!'—(Bdos) **3.** PHRASES **3.1 come/go**
straight (along) and do sth *vb phr* (CarA) *[IF]*
To do sth wilfully and unhesitatingly. *The police*
don't go straight along and arrest people unless they
know something.—(Bdos) **3.2 straight so** *adv*
phr (Bdos, Trin) *[AF]* Without warning; unexpectedly. *... then last night, straight so, no*
provocation, the nigger man walk in an buss up she
mouth.—JPB:100 **[**STRAIGHT[2] 2. + SO[1] 3.**]**

straight·en *vb tr* (CarA) To remove the crinkly
curls of (a Black woman's hair) by one or other
hairdressing process.

straights *n* (CarA) *[AF]* A plain meal of a
single item (rice, plantains, yam, etc) without
gravy, meat, or other accompaniment.

straight·way *adv* (Bdos) Immediately after;
without pause or hesitation; (SE) straightaway.
a. *At a snack bar in a northern parish are about four*
female attendants employed there who, it would
appear, are not trained for the job; they indulge
in talking over the drink and sandwiches when
preparing them; they wipe the counter and straight-
way handle and prepare food.—AdN (72.10.16,
p.4) **b.** *And James straightway gone and start*
taking out marriage licence and thing and next
thing you know they marrid and living in the house
that James build.—CISH:35 [Survival of EE,
through infl of AVB as *Matt IV. 20* 'And they
straightway left their nets, and followed him]
□ Considered archaic in SE.

strain *n* PHRASES **hold strain** *vb phr* (CarA)
[AF] See HOLD Phr 5.11 *... but I will tell my*
members on the committee that I will give it my
support since they have been holding strain, and
whether they have served the country faithfully or
unfaithfully for some period of time, they will be
entitled to some kind of consideration.—Bdos (Hd,
76.06.22, p.6721)

strand out/up (strawn out/up) [stran(d)
~strɒ·n ᴅᴜᴛ/ʌp] *vb phr* (Bdos, Guyn, Jmca,
StVn) To shred, unravel, or reduce to strands
(a rope, cotton, something knitted, woven, etc).
a. *Announcing the price increase from 23 cents to*
28 cents, President of the Cotton Growers As-
sociation Mr Andy Dowding said it indicated that
growers had deemed it necessary since recent heavy
winds have somewhat stranded out the cotton.—
AdN (76.04.02, p.1) **b.** *Me ol[d] straw hat strawn*
up, me stockin[g]s strawn up, A mus[t] [b]e look
like A name Straughn, nuh?—(StVn) **[** < SE *OED*
strand vb[2] 1. 'to break one or more of the strands

(of a rope)'. Also *EDD stranded* (Nhb, Dur) 'of
a rope: having a broken strand or twist'. Cp also
EDD pronunc *strawn* w Sc for *strand* sb[1] (but
with different meaning)**]** □ The CE pronunc,
prob also infl by '*straw*', must be regarded as
AF.

strang·ler fig /1'12/ *n phr* (USVI) See PITCH-
APPLE

straw *n* **1.** (CarA) The strands or fibre from
certain types of dried grasses as used for han-
dicraftwork, hence **straw-basket, straw-mat,**
straw-market, straw-work. 2. (Baha) ‖STRAW-
BED (Baha) **[***OED straw* sb[1] 2. b. *In the straw* 'in
childbed ... so *out of the straw*, recovered after
childbearing' + cits 1661–1832] See also
STRAW-BED **3.** PHRASES **3.1 be out of straw** *vb*
phr (Baha) [Of a woman] To have recovered after
childbirth. **3.2 be right on straw** *vb phr* (Baha)
[Of a woman] To be in confinement. **3.3 cold**
out of straw/right on straw *n phr* (Baha)
‖LYING-IN COLD (Antg, etc) **3.4 not raise a**
straw *neg vb phr* (Gren) *[IF]* See RAISE[1] Phr
6.1

straw-bed *n* (Baha) **1.** A mattress stuffed with
straw, believed by some to be best for a woman's
confinement; [by extension] a woman's confinement in childbirth (see STRAW 2., 3.). [Prob
affected by the special EE sense of STRAW prec.
Note *EDD straw* sb II. Dial uses 1. (I) *straw-bed*
'the yellow bed-straw'] **2.** PHRASE **2.1 go in**
straw-bed *n phr* (TkCa) *[IF]* [Of a woman] To
go into labour, be in confinement.

strawn up/out *vb phr* (Bdos, Guyn, Jmca,
StVn) *[AF]* See STRAND UP/OUT

straw-work *n* (Baha) ‖**string-work** (CayI)
The making of mats, hats, baskets, etc from the
stripped, dried leaves of the fronds of any palm
tree or the coconut-tree.

stray·way *adj* (Gren) *[AF]* Given to roaming
the streets; undisciplined and unsettled. [By
functional vb > adj shift < *stray* [a]*way* vb phr]

stream·er-tail *n* (Jmca) ‖DOCTOR-BIRD 2.
(Jmca) *Most brilliant of all is the long-tailed*
Doctor-Bird, sometimes called Streamer Tail or
Scissors Tail. Swift in flight, it can hover almost
perpendicularly above flower or leaf, brilliant with
its velvet crest, emerald bosom and long tail-
feathers.—SJW:87 [From the long black trailing
tail (about 6 ins) in contrast with its 3-inch long
body] □ One of the names of the National Bird
of *Jmca*.

street-jam *n* (Bdos) A community dance-party
held in the street. *The Brereton Social and Com-*
munity Group regrets the cancellation of their dance
which was advertised for May 27, 1989 at the
Byde Mill Sports Club. / However, one and all
are invited to a street jam on the same date. / It
will be held at Brereton village, No.2 St Philip,

starting at 5 p.m.—AdN (89.04.01, p.5) [< *street* (used attrib) + JAM² 2. (*CarA*)]

stretch-foot *n* (CarA) [*AF/IF*] A stroll; a walking about after sitting for a long time.

strike back *vb phr* (Bdos, Guyn) [*IF*] [Of a child] To differ markedly in appearance, esp in skin-colour, from other members of the immediate family, because of some forgotten or unrecognized hereditary factor; to be a genetic throw-back. *Sometimes in a family one of the children would strike back and people begin to say it's not the father's child.*—(Bdos)

string-band *n* (CarA) **1.** A MASQUERADE-BAND made up of a variety of stringed instruments incl banjo, CUATRO, fife, BAHA, etc. *During Christmas week the country people parade from village to village ... in bright and frilly dresses and headties. They are accompanied by a string band, and are given drinks in return for the songs they sing.*—Caq IV.2, p.110 **2.** A small dance-band composed of stringed instruments. *The music at these functions was usually supplied by a string band, composed of a group of friends of the hosts, among whom might be found D. Toulon on the Mandolin, A. Boyd on the Violin, and R. Toussaint at the piano.*—SDD:49 **3.** PHRASE **3.1 a string-band of children** *n phr* (CarA) [*AF—Joc/Derog*] ‖ *a string of children* (Angu, Guyn, StLu) A large family of children. *When she visits you with her string-band of children they drink up everything you have in the house.*—(Antg)

string-bean* *n* (CarA) ‖ *common bean* (Antg) ‖ *kidney-bean* (Baha, Jmca, Trin) ‖ *red bean* (BrVi, Dmca, TkCa) ‖ *salad-bean* (Trin) ‖ *senebone* (Guyn) A popular kitchen-garden, kidney-shaped bean of many varieties and colours (the commonest being reddish-brown); it is borne in narrow, roundish, green or yellowish pods about 8 ins long on a low bushy plant, sometimes climbing; the pods are boiled as a green vegetable or the beans are cooked green or dried; *Phaseolus vulgaris* (*Leguminosae-Papilionatae*). [From the string-like ribbed edge wh is pulled off a green pod before it is cooked]

string-work *n* (CayI) ‖ STRAW-WORK (Baha) *The 'tops' (thatch palm fronds) are stripped into 'string' which is then 'plaited' into 'string work' ('you get any string work from East End?')*—KWS: 21

strive *vb* (CarA) [*X*] To thrive; to flourish; [by extension] to enjoy life. **a.** *There are certain chemicals that will dry the top of the nut grass when it is sprayed on it and they do not kill the nut. If the nut grass is exposed to sunlight it strives better.*—Bdos (Hd, 73.07.11, p.2495) **b.** *Some people put a silver coin at the bottom of a pot of croton or fern so that 'bad eye' may be cut out and to help the plant to strive.*—COYN:19 **c.** *My father was very amused, but my mother was fuming cross. / 'You know you ain't have no head for rum,' she said. 'When you go out for God sake don't*

drink!' / I remained quiet. / My father said, 'Let the boy strive. This is Christmas.'—AGDR:137 [< SE *thrive* by misascription, or by CE prosthetic /s-/ + CE pronunc of t[h]rive] □ A pa.t. *strived* [*X*] also occurs.

strong¹ *adj* (CarA) [*IF*] **1.** Aggressive in behaviour or character. **2.** PHRASE **2.1 wrong and strong** *adj phr* (Guyn, Trin) Pugnacious; defiant; aggressive although in the wrong.

strong² *adv* (CarA) [*AF/IF*] Strongly; vigorously; excessively; etc. **a.** *Mr Seukeran in passing sentence told R– : 'This is a clear case of tabanca. You should not love so strong. You are an irate jealous lover and although your counsel pointed out that jealousy had no bounds, you should control your emotions.*—ExP (76.02.20, p.3) **b.** *These days the Brother is belching the fire from his guts and once The Voice of St Lucia start attacking him strong, that's cool!*—CrU (76.11.06, p.3) [By characteristic CE adj > adv shift of STRONG¹]

strong³ *n* (Guyn, StVn, Trin) [*IF*] (Usu overproof) rum; WHITE RUM. *... but in the rum-shops of the villages ... you sometimes find that you cannot get anything other than what they call 'strong', which is, as the name implies, a drink which the visitor should approach with care. / This is a white rum which is distilled by some of the major West Indian rum producers.*—Cat IV.2, p.14 [Reduced < strong rum]

strong-back/bark (weed)* *n (phr)* (Baha, Gren, Jmca) Any of a number of plants whose leaves, flowers, or berries are reputed to be effective as folk-medicine to strengthen the body, esp the back, and usu also to stimulate virility. (See *DJE* for different taxonomic names; also *Bourreria spp* (*Gren*)). *While he talked about all the bushes he knew ... and the purposes for which they were used ... I suspected that this prolific Saunders family must have been reared on 'strong back'.*—TrI (72.03.08, p.3)

strong-eye¹ *adj* (Gren, Guyn, Jmca) [*AF—Derog*] Sharp-eyed, covetous, and rather determined to get what you have seen; [by extension] self-willed, domineering. *Don[t't] mind he small so, he's a strong-eye child. Whatever sharin[g] he will fight de big broder fo[r] de best.*—(Guyn) [A prob calque from W Afr langs. Cp *DAFL* Twi *n'ani yɛ deŋ* (he eye be hard) 'he is self-willed, bold, etc']

strong-eye² *n* (Gren, Guyn, Jmca) [*AF—Joc/Derog*] Covetousness; ruthlessness. *Mr Bobo have strong eye too much, he want everybody wife in de vicinity.*—(Gren) [By functional adj > n shift of STRONG-EYE¹]

strong-head·ed *adj* (Bdos, StVn) [*IF*] Stubborn; headstrong. *I tell Johnny not to do law because it too hard; and now he fail everything. He is too strong-headed.*—(StVn) [Perh from an Afr base (Cp structures such as STRONG-EYE,*

HARD-EARS, etc), SE *strong* + *head* 'will' hence 'strong-willed'. Cp also SE 'headstrong']

strong-man weed *n phr* (Jmca) ‖ GULLY-ROOT (CarA) [Prob because of its use 'when steeped in rum, as an aphrodisiac' (*HCWP*:70). □ See also ‖ *kojo-bush*

strong rum *n phr* (CarA) WHITE RUM; overproof rum. *And these same people are now asking you to vote for them and are offering you a plate of food washed down with a strong rum or a beer.*—ToR (76.11.10, p.7)

struck *adj* (Angu) [*AF*] Greedy; gluttonous. *He is too struck—If you let him share anything, the brothers will scarcely get anything.*—(Angu) □ Cp BIG-EYE, STRONG-EYE. Both senses seem to be combined here.

St Tho·mi·an [sɪn(t)-to·mɪən] *n, adj* (ViIs) ‖ *Thomanian* (ViIs) (A person or thing) belonging to or characteristic of St Thomas, one of the US Virgin Islands. **a.** *St Thomas became known as 'the emporium of the West Indies', the place that's on the way to every other place. Bragged St Thomians a century ago, 'St Thomas shakes hands with the universe every day'.*—USVI (Tourist Handbook, 1979, p.146) **b.** *Those who have observed many St Thomian Carnivals could hardly imagine what the parade would be like without the Moco-Jumbie moving along with some good steel band music.*—Aaw.I.2, p.3

stud·i·a·tion (stud·y·a·tion, stud·i·ra·tion) *n* (CarA) [*AF/IF—Joc*] **1.** Studying with books. *It ain[']t no use pushin[g] de chil[d] t[h]rough all dat studiation to get certificate an[d] she steady failin[g] failin[g]. Let her get a wo[r]k.*—(Guyn) **2.** [By extension] Hard, troubled thinking. **a.** *It is the duty of his staff to help every citizen with his tax problems; to look after the 'botheration' and the 'studiation'!*—AdN (74.12.31) **b.** *No easy-come-by freeniss tings, / Nuff labour, some privation, / Not much of diss, an less of dat / An plenty studiration.*—FCV2:159 **3.** [By extension] Shrewdness; (the exercise of) native ingenuity. **a.** *'You was a teacher. You got education,' he grinned. 'I ain't got education, but I got studyation. My gran'mother always use to say studyation beat education.*—TRIH:5 **b.** *'Studyation is better than education,' Bradshaw said, comforting his ageing illiterates from the canefields. It became one of his mots.*—NOB:228 [SE *study* 'consider carefully, investigate' + suff *ation* on analogy of 'botheration, vexation', etc, with a slightly pejorative sense] □ The senses 2., 3. have generally overtaken orig sense 1. in CE.

stud·y *vb* (CarA) [*AF/IF*] **1.** To consider, think about (sb/sth); to give careful thought to (sb/sth). **a.** *Well he's started telling me that he's studying me and what I do, and that he wants me to write him more often. He has even said that some day we may get married.*—AdM (87.06.27, p.8, Dear Wendy) **b.** *'I then made an attempt again to see if I can go to the house and help, but then I study*

and say suppose he do not recover, the Police might not believe my story.—ViN (73.10.19, p.14) **c.** *Jim studied the food-carrier which he was holding in his right hand then looked at Tom. 'O.K. I going with awl you, but I not staying long.'*—SDD:41 **2.** [By extension] To worry about, over (sb/sth). **a.** *Then too, he remembered that the crops he had planted in the mountain needed weeding. 'Lord! so much things a poor man got to study',* he said to himself.—Isl II.1, p.60 **b.** *I got mad and said to myself that you just fixing for one day but you not studying the risk of the lorry drivers that take the crops to St George's.*—ToR (77.11.23, p.8) [Extension of *OED* study vb tr 15. 'to pay practical regard to'; to 'consider' (a person's wishes, feelings or interest)] **3.** PHRASES **3.1 study for (sb)** *vb phr* (Trin) [*AF*] To be of malicious intention towards (sb). **3.2 study on (sb)** *vb phr* (Angu) [*IF*] ‖ STUDY 1. (CarA) *I used to like her but I'm not studying on her any more.*—(Angu) **3.3 study your brain/head** *vb phr* (CarA) [*AF*] To think carefully. **a.** *You better go and study you head good before you talk all that foolishness 'bout you done with school,'cause one o' these days long before you is a old man you going regret it.*—CISH:44 **b.** *And then, you see, I had endorsed a note for her for a hundred and twenty dollars. And she was paying back, but she didn't pay back as much as half yet. So I had to study my head or else I would have had to pay the money.*—JMA:121 [Cp Yoruba *ro ori ṛe daadaa* (stir head-your good-good) 'think carefully']

stuff *n* (Bdos) Garbage; rubbish; waste-heap. *There was once bread in the press along with a leakage of water and by mistake some fell into the water ... so we were all charged for it, then they were thrown into the stuff due to the high scent.*—NaT (77.01.23, p.22) [Cp *OED* stuff sb[1] 8. 'what is worthless; rubbish' as in phr 'stuff and nonsense'. Also *EDD* stuff sb[2] (Obs) Sc 'dust'. Neither sense, however, quite equates to 'garbage']

stuff-bin *n* (Bdos) ‖ *dirt-pan* (Jmca) ‖ *garbage-pan* (StVn) A (usu) metal garbage-can; a large oil-drum kept near the gate for disposing of garbage. □ Cp DIRT-BOX (Belz).

stump PHRASE **stump your foot/toe** *vb phr* (ECar) To strike your foot/toe by accident against sth; (SE) to stub your foot/toe. **a.** *If you stump you big toe, Bad luck for so.*—ToR (78.03.08, p.4) **b.** *If you institute a free medical service, every person with a stumped toe will find himself at the hospital.*—Bdos (Hd, 73.06.19, p.2399) [< SE *stub* vb (your foot/toe) by confusion with *stump* (?). See *OED* stump vb[1] 13. (US colloq) = *stub*, with this sense]

stupe[1] [sčup] *n* (Nevs) [*IF*] ‖ SUCK-TEETH (CarA) [Imitative sound. See next and many other variations of the same at vb phr SUCK YOUR TEETH]

stupe[2] (Trin); **stupe your mouth** (Nevs) *vb (phr)* ‖ SUCK YOUR TEETH (CarA) [As prec]

stupes (stupse) [sču·ps] *n, vb* (Bdos, etc) See
STEUPS

stu·pid [sču̯pɪd] /1'2/ *adj* (CarA) [*AF—Joc/
Derog*] Inconsequential; insignificant; small; [by
extension] contemptible, damned. **a.** *She picked
up some stupid li[tt]le man sayin[g] she in love
with him.*—(Antg) **b.** *I wouldn't ask them for any
lift, they are so fussy with their stupid car.*—(Jmca)
□ Note CE change in pitch pattern /1'2/ for this
sense in contrast with /2'1/ for IAE sense.

stu·pid·ie[1] (**stu·pid·y**[1], **stu·pit·ty**) [sču̯pɪdi/-
ti] *adj* (CarA) [*AF—Derog*] Stupid; idiotic. *Bauy
it look like ah sen' you' to de university to turn
you' head stupidy. Yo' ain' learn a ting mo' but to
call yo' betters liars.*—Vip I.1 **b.** *Mek Sin Kitts
man so stupitty? / Ask dem if dem will married
dem country-woman—/ Who? nat me.*—LMFF:
20 [< SE *stupid* + suff *-ie/-y* in CE *Derog*
function. Similarly MADDY]

stu·pid·ie[2] (**stu·pid·y**[2]) [sču̯pɪdi] (CarA)
[*AF—Derog*] See CHUPIDEE *Any fool, any stupidy,
must tell you that my role on this earth planet is
one that cannot be stopped by the plots and the plans
and the schemes of assassinators, black magicians,
murderers and you call them.*—Gren (Hd,
78.04.07, p.78) [By functional adj > n shift of
STUPIDY[1]]

stu·pid·ness; **chu·pit·ness** (CarA) [*IF/AF*]
‖ **arseness** (Trin) [*Vul*] ‖ **assness** (Trin) ‖ **assishness** (Guyn, Tbgo, Trin) **1.** Nonsense; stupid
thinking; an absurdity. **a.** *We asked Mr James to
attend a Conference, just a few months ago that
was. He said he was not able to go. He is the
President of the Senate and to talk stupidness like
that around this table around such Honourable
Members.*—Gren (Hd, 75.06.22, p.40) **b.** *I think
that the Government should celebrate its seventh
anniversary of independence by the abolition completely of Leave Passages and let Civil Servants
understand that we will give them a better substitute
by way of training to serve the island well and
not Leave Passages. It is stupidness.*—Bdos (Hd,
74.03.05, p.3208) **c.** *Questioned by the judge,
petitioner said that when she told respondent how
his unnatural tendencies were affecting her health
he just said 'that is stupidness.'*—StA(JA)
(73.02.10, p.5) **2.** [By extension] A stupid act;
irritating behaviour; any or several vexatious
incident(s). **a.** *S. W— of Basseterre will have to
shin out $133.60 by next week Monday ... for
what District A Magistrate Mr Clement Arrindell
said ... 'a little stupidness can cause.'*—LaS
(77.04.09, p.11) **b.** *I must be a crass idiot that I
would go and sit down with Happy Bryan and
my friend Asquith Phillips on a Friday night
programme by a message sent by the Secretary. I
am telling the Manager to cut out this stupidness
he is doing.*—Bdos (Hd, 76.02.03, p.5927) **c.** *He
also wanted her to know that he was a man that
didn't stand for any stupidness so she had better
behave herself.*—PKKK:99 [Note *OED* stupidness. Now rare. 'The quality of being stupid
(in various senses of the adj): = stupidity' +

cits mostly from 17C, but notably indicating a
dull bodily feeling, so coinciding with *stupidity*
in Obs senses 1, 2, 3 there given. The CE senses
show a marked shift away. Note that AmE *W1,
W3* treat it as = stupidity] □ This EE word,
superseded in ModE by *stupidity*, covers a much
wider range than the latter in CE. STUPIDNESS
strongly distinguishes external results—'stupid
talk, acts' from 'the intrinsic quality of being
stupid' (= *stupidity*). You may '*talk, do stupidness*' (not 'stupidity') the reason being either
your *stupidity* or some STUPIDNESS 1. As the cits
indicate, the word is accepted at all levels. **3.**
excl Nonsense!; Dammit! *Aw stupidness! Look
how you make the ink mess up my trousers.*—
(Guyn) **4.** PHRASES **4.1 like stupidness** *adv
phr* (Guyn, Trin) [*AF—Joc*] Abundantly; very
much. *It used to have pigeons like stupidness all
about the street—nobody know where they come
from.*—STLL:107

stupse (stupes) [sču·ps] *n, vb* (Bdos, Dmca,
Gren, Guyn, Trin) See STEUPS

St Vin·cent Gren·a·dines *n phr* (CarA) See
GRENADINES

St Vin·cent par·rot* *n phr* (StVn) A brightly
coloured gold, brown, green, and blue parrot
about 16–18 ins long; the National Bird of St
Vincent; *Amazona guildingii (Psittacidae)*. [The
only type of parrot on St Vincent, hence the
name]

style(s)[1] *n (pl)* (ECar) [*IF/AF*] **1.** Manner of
behaviour, esp when either showy or unpleasant;
display; affectation; [by extension, esp in pl]
fastidiousness. **a.** *Who the Ministry think they
fooling? / There was this ad in last Sunday's papers
saying people who wanted temporary jobs with the
CDC ... should apply to the Ministry of Labour,
... / That was only style to fool people / Everybody
knows that these Carnival jobs are given to those
greedy and over-paid civil servants.*—BoM
(77.01.14, p.18) **b.** *If you don't feed him from the
blue bowl and if you don't sing, he won't eat. I never
see a little child with so much styles!*—(Guyn) **2.**
PHRASES **2.1 cut (old) style** *vb phr* (Antg) [*AF*]
‖ MAKE STYLE (ECar) See Phr 2.3 **2.2 like sb's
style** *vb phr* (ECar) [*AF/IF*] To approve of sb.
*I wouldn't expose you. Because, you know what?
I like your style. We is the same sort of people.
You ain't like your stupid, pretensive parents. We
is bacchanal people.*—AKM:23 **2.3 make
style(s)** *vb phr* (ECar) [*AF/IF*] **(i)** To show off
(esp in manner of dress and walking); to swagger;
to brag. **(ii)** To be too fussy; to be fastidious.
*The Chief Returning Officer himself told me that
the only way to stop this sort of thing is to get one
of them locked up. Do not make any style about
this, Mr Speaker.*—Bdos (Hd, 74.08.27, p.3841)

style[2] **(off)** *vb intr (phr)* (CarA) [*AF—Joc*] To
make a stylish, dressy display of yourself; to
walk or act in a way to attract attention. **a.** *She
does only style so 'cause she want people to notice
she.*—EFLBB:20 **b.** *You know as soon as she hear*

'wedding' she ready to spend so much money styling off.—(StVn) [By functional n > vb shift of STYLE¹ + adv OFF²]

suck PHRASES 1. **suck salt** *vb phr* (CarA) [*AF*] To experience hardship over a period of time, to have a hard time of it (esp in domestic need). a. *... and he charged that PNM supporters were being victimised. / 'If you want to suck salt (face hard times) in Tobago, just say you belong to PNM or you are supporters of PNM.' said Chambers.*—AdV (86.12.10, p.13) b. *We take the strain. We pull our belts tight. As tight as we can stand it and more. We suck salt from a wooden spoon. We bear it. And we live through the drought and keep our self-respect.*—SD:13 2. **suck your mouth** *vb phr* (CayI) ‖ SUCK YOUR TEETH (CarA) 3. **suck your teeth (at/on sb)** *vb phr* (CarA) ‖ *cheups* (Tbgo, Trin) ‖ *chip your teeth* (Tbgo) ‖ *chups(e), chupes* (Dmca, Jmca, Tbgo, Trin) ‖ *give a suck-teeth* (CarA) ‖ *hiss/kiss your teeth* (Baha, Jmca) ‖ *steups* (Gren, Trin) ‖ *steups your teeth* (Tbgo, Trin), ‖ *stewpse, stupes* (Bdos, Dmca, Guyn, Trin) ‖ *stupe* (Trin) ‖ *stupe your mouth* (Nevs) ‖ *suck your mouth* (CayI) To suck air in, with a momentary parting of the lips, through the clenched teeth, so producing a short or long unpleasant sound with the saliva, as a sign of disgust, contempt, frustration, vexation or, occasionally, self-pity. a. *The Minister of Agriculture, Forests and Lands, Hon. B.H. Benn, was so irked by the Chairman's ruling that he sucked his teeth and, while the Chairman chided him for appearing, in addition, to have uttered a derogatory statement, Members of the House cried: 'Shame, shame!'*—DaC (63.01.16, p.1) b. *But she only succumbed briefly to the feeling, then her back was stiff again, her face resolute, and she sucked her teeth, dismissing them all.*—MBGB:40 [See SUCK-TEETH] □ This is the Formal phr, nearly all of the ‖ ‖ being *AF/IF*. The sound made (not the phr proper) is strongly disapproved of socially, and esp when made by children.

suck-teeth ['sʌk-ti·t/ti·θ] *n* (CarA) ‖ *cheups, chups(e)* (Jmca, Tbgo, Trin) ‖ *kiss-teeth* (Jmca) ‖ *steups, stupse* (Bdos, Dmca, Gren, Guyn, Trin) ‖ *stupe* (Nevs, Trin) 1. The action or sound of SUCKING YOUR TEETH. a. *'Suck-Teeth Starts Uproar.'*—DaC (H, 63.01.16, p.1) b. *Walter looked at him in surprise and answered with a long-drawn suck-teeth.*—SNWIC:225 (R. Heath) [An ingressive salivary sound similarly made and with similar significance is found throughout W Afr cultures and in other Sub-Saharan cultures as well. There is usu a name for the sound, or a vb (phr) the equivalent of the CE vb phr SUCK YOUR TEETH. Note Mende *i ngi yongɔui vofoin lɔ nya-ma* (he his teeth suck be me-on) 'he sucked his teeth at me' Cp nouns (*ADHL*) Hausa *tsaki* 'the noise *pf* wh one makes contemptuously'; Yoruba *p'ọṣe* 'unhappy sigh made with the saliva'; Efik *asiama* (for the sound); also verbs (*KID*) Ibibio *siɔɔp* 'make a sound of disgust, impatience, etc'; Wolof *čipu* 'to make the rude sound with the lips'; Kikongo *tsiona*

'make an insulting sound with the saliva', etc] 2. PHRASE 2.1 **give a suck-teeth** *vb phr* (CarA) ‖ SUCK YOUR TEETH (AT/ON SB) (CarA)

suck(-well) *n* (Bdos) ‖ DRY WELL (Bdos) [*Suck*, in ref to the layer of sand that sucks the water away] □ Often called a *suck*.

su·cri·er-bird ['sɪkye bɔ:d] *n* (Trin) See SIKYÉ-BIRD and Note at SUCRIER-(FIG).

su·cri·er(-fig) [sukye ~ sɪkye(-fig)] *n* (Trin) See SIKYÉ-FIG □ This commonly used spelling reflects the orig of the name, whereas SIKYÉ reflects the regular Fr Cr pronunc.

sudd·en¹ *adv* (CarA) [*AF*] 1. Suddenly. *It happen sudden so.*—(Bdos, Gren, Trin) 2. PHRASE 2.1 **on a sudden** *adv phr* (CarA) [*IF*] See ON Phr 7.2

sud·den² *pron* (Antg, Brbu, Mrat, StKt) [*AF-Cr*] Something; thing. *Simon: Mary, if a wan sudden me can say bout you, ya very anist. Me no know wa mek nobaddy will marrid to you.* (= *Mary, if there's one thing I can say about you, you're very honest, etc*).—BaV (73/2, p.4) [An epenthetic form /sodn/ > /sobm/ > /sompm/ dial form of 'something'; prob infl also by pronunc of E 'sudden'] □ A representative form much used in narrative dialogue in territories shown.

suf·fer *vb tr* (Tbgo) [*X*] To cause to suffer; to punish (by lack of consideration). *You suffered me, man. You have me here waiting long in the sun.*—(Tbgo) [A semantic misascription, that may be of Afr origin. See PUNISH 2. vb intr (*CarA*) and note re coinciding senses in Igbo]

suf·fer·a·tion *n* (CarA) [*IF—Joc*] Prolonged, intense suffering. a. *Under these conditions of hungryfication and sufferation dat grab de throat of this nation and won't let go, what is de use of music?*—DaN(JA) (79.12.02, p.22) b. *So first he must be patient. Secondly he should be able to handle hardship and sufferation, as there is a lot of this in marriage.*—NaT (90.10.05, p.9, Lowdown) [< SE *suffer* + suff *-ation* on the analogy of *botheration*, etc. Cp STUDIATION]

sug·ar *n* (CarA) [*IF*] 1. The disease diabetes mellitus. [From the association of the use of sugar with diabetes] 2. PHRASES 2.1 **have/suffer from sugar** *vb phr* (CarA) [*IF*] [Of a person] To be diabetic.

sug·ar-ant(s) *n* (*pl*) (Bdos, Gren, Guyn, Jmca, Mrat) ‖ RUNNING-ANT(S) (Bdos, etc) *If you leave those cakes on the table, the sugar ants will soon cover them.*—(Guyn)

sug·ar-ap·ple* *n* (CarA) ‖ *sweet sop* (Antg, Baha, Belz, CayI, Jmca) A green, heart-shaped fruit about 3 to 4 ins in diameter, with an exterior composed of pronounced, rounded tubercles; it has a sweet, white flesh embedding many hard, black seeds; it is borne on a small, leafy tree;

Annona squamosa (Annonaceae). □ In some places (*ViIs*) it is often called '*apple*' and also cooked as a vegetable. In some places in the CarA, both the names SUGAR-APPLE and SWEET SOP are used. See also APPLE-BUSH, KACHIMAN.

sug·ar-bag *n* (CarA) [*IF*] ‖ CROCUS BAG (CarA) *He was all in a recumbent heap on a bed of stripped bois-canot overlaid with dry tapia grass and sugar-bags and flour-sacks.*—NAGOS:39

sug·ar-ba·na·na *n* (Baha, TkCa) ‖ APPLE-BANANA (Belz, etc)

sug·ar-bird *n* (Bdos, USVI) ‖ BANANAQUIT (CarA) *The yellowbreast Sugar-Bird or Bananaquit (Coereba flaveola newtoni) is the official Virgin Island Bird that often builds its shaggy nest near houses as well as in the Dildo cactus whose spines serve as 'nails' for the twigs of the nest.*—JNHSJ:41

sug·ar-boil·er *n* (Bdos) ‖ PAN-BOILER (Bdos, etc)

sug·ar-cake *n* 1. (CarA) ‖ *grater-cake* (Jmca) A confection made by boiling a thick mixture of grated coconut kernel with much brown sugar in some water and dropping spoonfuls of it on to a flat surface to cool. 2. (Guyn) ‖ *chip-chip sugar-cake* (Gren, Trin) ‖ *coconut-cake* (Baha) ‖ *coconut-drop* (Jmca) ‖ *tablèt* (Dmca, StLu) A confection made by boiling hand-chipped slices of dried coconut kernel in a heavy syrup of sugar and water and dropping spoonfuls of it on a flat surface to cool.

sug·ar-cas·sa·va *n* (Guyn) ‖ CASSAVA-CAKE (Belz, Guyn)

sug·ar-fac·tor·y *n* (CarA) A plant where the whole process of making sugar from raw sugar-cane takes place. (Cp SUGAR-MILL).

sug·ar-mill *n* (CarA) [Hist] A cone-shaped, stone windmill for grinding sugar-cane in former times; the juice was channelled off to the separate boiling-house for processing into molasses and sugar. (Cp SUGAR-FACTORY).

sug·ar-plum *n* (Guyn, Jmca) ‖ CHILLI-PLUM (Antg, etc) [Prob as distinguished by its sweet pulp from the sourness of other varieties of 'plum' esp the HOG-PLUM]

sug·ar-punt *n* (Guyn) ‖ PUNT (Guyn)

sug·ar-wa·ter /1'122/ *n* (CarA) A sweet drink of sugar and water, commonly used as early morning TEA or *hot sugar-water* in the slave-plantation era and still so used by poorer rural folk. □ Cp BEVERAGE, SWANK.

suite-couche *n* (Dmca, StLu) See SWIT-KOUCH

su·la *n* (Dmca, etc) [*AF*] See SOULA(RD)

sun-clus·ter *n* (StVn) ‖ CARPET-DAISY (Bdos)

Sun·day *PHRASES* **if/when Sunday fall [u]pon a Monday; if/when Good Friday fall [u]pon a Sunday** *id phrs* (ECar) [*AF—Joc*] **(i)** Never. [Cp *OED Sunday* 1. c. *when two Sundays meet* 'Never'] **(ii)** [Expressing total indifference] *When the wife quarrel he jus[t] go and get drunk and come in singin[g], let not[hi]n[g] bother him even Sunday fall [u]pon a Monday.*—(Guyn)

Sun·day-go-to-meet·ings *n pl* (Bdos) [*IF—Joc*] Clothes considered fit to be worn on Sundays (whether or not to church); (SE) Sunday clothes, Sunday-best. *I have ridden on buses and heard women, dressed in their Sunday-go-to-meetings, criticising other women's dress after church.*—AdN (82.12.05, p.8) [*OED Sunday* 1. c. *Sunday-go-to-meeting clothes,* wh is also said in Bdos, here converted into a n pl, prob infl by pl 'clothes']

sun-fish *n* (Guyn) A round-bodied, river fish about 9 ins long with dark-brown back, pinkish belly, and a large spot on the tail; it is bony and of moderate food value; *Crenicichla saxatilis (Cichlidae).* □ Apparently unrelated to the large, varied family of small, freshwater fishes internationally so named.

sun-hot *n* (Belz, Jmca) [*AF/IF*] The heat of the sun, esp at midday. **a.** *An' you know wha' 'appen to dreamers in this daylight worl'? They get kill off in them sleep, in the middle o' the sun-hot.*—SCAMH:185 **b.** *The youths were working with a will despite some dread sun-hot which was beating down on their tams.*—WeG (73.06.06, Partyline)

sun-shades *n pl* (Guyn) ‖ SHADES (CarA)

sup·per *PHRASE* **cat eat your supper** *id phr* (Gren) [*AF—Joc*] ‖ CRAPAUD SMOKE YOUR PIPE (Dmca, etc)

sup·pose[d] (to be) *vb phr* (Bdos, Guyn) [*AF*] To be actually. *You suppose to be a Queen's College boy and speakin[g] like that?*—(Guyn) [A semantic shift of the IF SE periphrastic form *supposed to* 'expected, understood to']

Sur·i·nam-cher·ry* *n* (CarA) A ribbed, red, cherry-like fruit about 1 inch in diameter, prized for its pleasant taste; it is borne on a flowering tree that can exceed 20 ft in height; *Eugenia uniflora (Myrtaceae). Here we have the Surinam cherry in abundance, and the young leaves are a brownish-red, and make a beautiful bouquet with Garden or Wild flowers.*—DeM(SK) (62.07.28, p.8) [The tree is a native of Brazil (*OGEP:49*) and perh came to the *CarA*) via Surinam] □ Also known as *pitanga* in botanical literature.

Sur·i·nam·ese *n, adj* (CarA) (A person or thing) native of or belonging to Surinam (formerly Dutch Guiana). *Four of NFC's ten seaworthy trawlers are now operating off the*

Surinamese fishing banks while another four boats are expected to shrimp in Cayenne's territorial waters.—TrG (80.04.10, p.1) **[** < Du *Surinamees*. Cp similarly GUYANESE**]** □ The term **Surinamer** is also used, as noun only.

su·su¹ (sou-sou) *n* (ECar) ‖ *asu(e)* (Baha) ‖ *box* (Guyn) ‖ *meeting* (Bdos) ‖ *pardner* (Jmca) ‖ *syndicate* (Belz) A friendly co-operative savings scheme in wh each one of a small group of persons contributes every week or month as agreed an equal portion of money to a trusted 'keeper', who pays the total amount weekly or monthly to each participant in rotation. *For example, the husband and wife from whom I rented a room in Coconut Village each ran his own susu and used his own money to take a hand in the susu.*—RLCF:160 **[**ADMY Yoruba *eesu ~ esusu* 'a fund where several persons pool their money, each paying in a fixed sum weekly, etc' and each participant drawing out the total in rotation**]** □ The spelling **sou-sou** is due to attraction < Fr *sou* 'a coin'. However **susu** is justified by the etym. **2.** PHRASES **2.1 belong to** ...; **hold/keep/run** ...; **throw (a) susu** *vb phrs* (Trin) To participate in ...; to organize a SUSU savings scheme.

su·su² (soo-soo) *n* (Guyn, Jmca, StVn) [*AF*] ‖ *shu-shu* (CarA) **1.** A confidential whispering. *The two of dem get in de corner and had a little susu and decide what to do.*—(Jmca) **2.** ‖ HEAR-SO (Brbu, Jmca) *Is all de susu they get on wit[h] dat bring de trouble.*—(Guyn) **[**Cp *DAFL* Twi *o-susu-kã (the-act-of guess speak)* 'uttering what one thinks; false accusation'**]**

su·su³ (soo-soo) *vb* (Guyn, Jmca, StVn) [*AF*] To gossip, speak ill of or whisper behind sb's back. *Some will eat and drink with you / Then behind them su-su pon you / Only your friend know your secret / So only he could reveal it.*—Rastaman Vibration (Bob Marley) **[**Cp *DAFL* Twi *susuw kã* 'to utter a suspicion'. Cp also SE *sussurate* 'to whisper'**]**

su·su-hand /1′21/ *n* (ECar) ‖ *box-hand* (Guyn) ‖ *hand¹* 3. (Baha, Gren, Guyn, Jmca, Trin) ‖ *meeting-turn* (Bdos) **1.** The weekly or monthly contribution made by each SUSU participant to the savings scheme. **2.** The total sum received by a participant when it is his/her turn to 'draw'. *Mama, I ent t'ink I want to go again, nuh. / You ent what? So what I draw mih sou-sou han' for if wasn't to sen' you way to furder you studies? You want to remain in Trinidad ignorant as you is?*—MN:58 **2.** PHRASES **3.1 draw your (susu-)hand** *vb phr* (ECar) To receive the total sum when it is your turn. **3.2 have/hold one/more than one susu-hand** *vb phr* (ECar) To undertake to make one (or more) contributions.

su·sum·ber [SUSUMBʌ] /1′21/ *n* (Jmca) ‖ BURA-BURA (Guyn) *Susumber is cooked as a vegetable and served with saltfish in Jamaica, and the plant is also used experimentally in grafting tomatoes, to which it is related.*—Jmca (Ms, 1978) **[**Cp *DAFL*

Twi *nsusuaa* 'a species of potherb' (also *susua* 'red') + *amba* (pl) 'seeds, fruits, eggs'**]** □ There are several *CarA* varieties of this plant wh appears to be most recognized in *Jmca*, whereas in some territories it is ignored as a weed.

sut *adj, n* (Dmca, Gren) [*AF*] See SÒT

swale [swel] *n* (Bdos) A shallow dip in the land surface, usu short and narrow, where water passes along or builds up in heavy rain, but wh otherwise remains dry. **[**Cp *OED swale* sb³ (+ Sc variant spellings) 'A hollow, low place, [also] *esp. U.S.* marshy. The word is listed with this sense in current AmE desk dictionaries, but not in *COD7, 8***]**

swal·low-pipe *n* (Bdos) [*AF—Joc*] The windpipe; [by extension] the throat. *Mr Chairman, I do not want you to ask him. I will go and put my hands in his swallow pipe and tell the people of St Peter what I did and get back my seat.*—Bdos (Hd, 73.11.06, p.2760) **[**Cp *OED swallow* sb² 4. 'the throat'. The sense is, however, perh obs**]**

swank *n* (Bdos, Guyn, StKt, StVn) [*AF*] ‖ *beverage* (Antg, CayI, Jmca, StKt) ‖ *switcher* (Baha, TkCa) ‖ *wash²* 2. (Jmca) (Usu a large quantity of) a sweet drink made of brown sugar (formerly molasses) and lime-juice (or other juices) with plenty of water added; (a quantity of) lemonade.

sweat *vb* **1.** (CarA) To cause (fever) to abate by treatment with hot infusions, BUSH-BATHS, etc. **2.** (Gren, Tbgo, Trin) [Cocoa Ind] To extract the wetness from (fresh cocoa-beans) by covering in a specially made box or other device. □ See SWEAT-BOX, SWEATER. **3.** PHRASES **3.1 sweat fever for sb/sweat (for) sb's fever** *vb phrs* (Belz) [*AF*] ‖ TAKE UP SB'S FIRE-RAGE (Antg, etc) *Russia pullin[g] out from Cuba. Dey ain['t] sweatin[g] Cuba's fever no mo[re].*—(Belz)

sweat-box *n* (Gren, Tbgo, Trin) [Cocoa Ind] A large, covered, wooden box built with a bottom that allows drainage of wetness in the process of drying cocoa-beans; it is used by small-scale farmers. See SWEATER. *On arrival the 'wet' cocoa (beans removed from the pod and covered with a glutinous white pulp) is placed in wooden 'sweat boxes' and covered with burlap bags and banana leaves. After 48 hours the contents are shifted to prevent the beans from sticking together to provide enough air circulation in order to discourage the growth of mould.*—IsL-73/6, p.11

sweat·er *n* (Gren) [Cocoa Ind] A small, unventilated, four-sided, wooden house, with a corrugated-iron gable roof, in wh fresh cocoabeans are SWEATED; it is divided into two compartments fitted with large, wooden slats, the cocoa-beans being turned from one compartment into the other periodically for a week to keep them loose.

sweet[1] *adj* (CarA) [*IF*] **1.** [Of food being eaten or any act involving bodily sensation, including sex] Very pleasing to the senses. *This sancoche sweet for so.*—(Trin) **2.** [*AF*] [Of a person who has been drinking] Merry from (alcoholic) drink; tipsy. *The prosecutor said that the driver of the vehicle appeared to be drunk. When he came out of the vehicle he was staggering. | The defendant told the magistrate that he was very sorry as he was a bit 'sweet'.*—GyC (77.12.21, p.4) **3.** [Of a man and woman] In love. *Clifford and Dora sweet for so dese days!*—(Gren) **4.** [*AF*] [Of inanimate things in general] Very satisfying; delightful. **a.** *Margaret Wright ... proclaimed 'Toco was a sweet place' as she spoke of kind and friendly neighbours coupled with the fine times shared with them in the village.*—TrG (80.01.13, p.7) **b.** *His driving on both sides of the wicket was fluent, his timing sweet and if there was an edge or two which brought him valuable runs this is established practice in limited overs cricket.*—AdN (75.06.12, p.14) **c.** *He said he smuggled in cigarettes from Nickerie during the strike and declared 'man ah really mek some sweet dollars.'*—GyC (76.06.29, p.9) **5.** PHRASES **5.1 be sweet with (sb)** *vb phr* (ECar) [*AF/IF*] Be on intimate terms with (sb). *All this time I didn't know the carpenter was sweet with the servant and that she used to pass him some of my husband's drink every day.*—(StVn) **5.2 head is not sweet** *id phr* (ECar) [*AF/IF*] **(i)** [Esp of old people] (Be) suffering from dizzy spells. **(ii)** [Esp of young persons] (Be) mentally unstable.

sweet[2] *adv* (CarA) [*AF*] Well; delightfully; easily. **a.** *But while the Government Ministers living sweet the people are starving. We want our money.*—BeA(BS) (73.11.10, p.3) **b.** *Hear how sweet the Chev running?*—HFGA:57 (D. Joseph) [By characteristic CE functional adj > adv shift of SWEET[1]]

sweet[3] *vb tr* (Antg, Jmca) [*AF*] ‖ **sweeten (sb) up** (CarA) **2.** To amuse; to make happy; to delight. **a.** *He said: 'I only laugh when a joke sweets me. You can give me the world to laugh, but if nothing interests me, I just won't laugh.'*—AnS (62.07.20, p.15) **b.** *A little way along the street Shine started to laugh too. 'What sweet you now?' said Jesmina. | 'That,' he hooked a thumb over his shoulder. 'Well, there's your bad luck. We just left it in the gutter back there.' | Jesmina clung to his arm and started to laugh herself.*—MBM:90

sweet bakes *n phr pl* (StLu) ‖ BAKE(S)[1] *n* 3. (Guyn, StLu) *But for sweet-bakes you have to put sugar with the same mixture for bakes and shape them into balls and fry in oil.*—StLu (Ms, 1980)

sweet bar·zey* *n phr* (Bdos, BrVi, Jmca, StKt, Tbgo, Trin) ‖ ZÈB-A-FANM (Gren, Trin)

sweet boy /1'2/ *n phr* (Bdos, Guyn) [*IF/AF*] A young man whose appearance is much admired by women and is usu reputed to have many love affairs; [by extension] a vain young man.

sweet·bread *n* (CarA) **1.** ‖ *coconut-bread* (Bdos) A sweet pan-loaf of varying heaviness, flavoured with raisins, spices, and often also grated coconut. **2.** PHRASE **2.1 be no sweetbread** *vb phr* (Bdos) [*AF—Joc*] To be prone to get quickly angry and rough. *West Indian cricket fans know CM-J to be no 'sweet-bread' where derogatory remarks about West Indian cricketers are concerned.*—AdV (90.04.23, p.9)

sweet bri·ar *n phr* (Bdos) ‖ ACACIA (TkCa, Trin) [*Sweet* from the mild fragrance of the flowers + *briar* from the thorns]

sweet broom* *n phr* (CarA) ‖ *balyé-dou* (Dmca, Gren) An erect weed with small indented leaves, little, white flowers and tiny, globular capsules; the whole plant (with root) is dried and used to make a pleasant-smelling BUSH-TEA, wh is used for a number of complaints, esp in children; *Scoparia dulcis (Scrophulariaceae)*. *The Italian visitor caught at the airport with marijuana ... claimed unsuccessfully that the stuff was really 'sweet broom' a local weed traditionally brewed for the use as 'tea' and which bears a strong resemblance to the cannabis plant which Jamaicans call ganja.*—Guyn (Ms, 1971)

sweet cas·sa·va *n phr* (CarA) See CASSAVA

sweet cup *n phr* (Jmca) A yellow-skinned variety of PASSION-FRUIT, with a sweet (rather than sourish) pulp; *Passiflora maliformis (Passifloraceae)*. □ See MOUNTAIN SWEET-CUP.

sweet drink *n phr* (CarA) ‖ COOL-DRINK (CarA)

sweet·en·in(g) ['switnɪn] /1'12/ *n* (Bdos, StKt) [*IF*] ‖ CANE-SYRUP (CarA)

sweet·en (up) (sb) *vb tr* (CarA) [*IF—Joc*] **1.** To try to win or succeed in winning (sb's) favour or consent by flattery or minor bribery; [by extension] to persuade. **a.** *'White girls,' Tanty grumble as she put the kettle on the fireplace fire, 'is that what sweeten up so many of you to come to London.'*—STLL:57 **b.** *How you helping me so today? You want to sweeten me up. Ah bet you is somet[h]ing you want.*—(Gren) **2.** ‖ *sweet[3]* (Jmca) [Of an incident] To cause (sb) to be wickedly amused. *Something she was telling them must have sweetened them because they were laughing all the time she was there.*—(Guyn) [Cp *OED sweeten* 7. 'to persuade by flattery; to cajole; to bribe' + cits 16C to 19C]

sweet-eye *n* (CarA) [*AF*] **1.** [Usu of a man] A lustful or sensual wink at sb. [Cp *DAFL* Twi *ani-bere* (*eye-soft, gentle*) 1. 'lust; cupidity'] **2.** PHRASES **2.1 get sweet-eye** *vb phr* (CarA) [*AF*] [Of a woman] To receive affectionate or sexually suggestive glances from a man. *Dey was faithful to duh husban, | Faithful to de en' | Even when duh get sweet-eye | From de husban' bes'-frien'.*—PeL (77.11.11, p.8, J. Layne-Clark) **2.2 give/make**

sweet-eye *vb phr* (CarA) [*AF*] To glance affectionately or wink sensually (at sb of the opposite sex); (SE) to give the glad eye. ... *but I giving dem a little side-look so, you know, under me broad brim hat. I pulling down one side so, and I making me little sweet-eye and I waving me little finger give dem so.*—RTCS:12

sweet grass *n phr* (Antg, Mrat, Trin) ‖ VETIVER (Dmca, etc) *Sweet grass grows in a big clump and the root has a pleasant smell, so you wash it and put it in your clothes closet.*—Mrat (Ms, 1973)

sweet·heart(-bush)* *n* (Dmca, Guyn) ‖ *iron-weed* 1. (Guyn) A straggling weed with small leaves and tiny mauve flowers; it bears short, small, dull green, segmented pods, the sections of wh cling to clothing or skin; an infusion of the entire plant is used as a folk-medicine; *Desmodium spp* (*Fabaceae*).

sweet-lime *n* (ECar) ‖ *myrtle-lime* (Antg, Mrat) A small, shiny red berry with a barely pleasant, sour-sweet pulp; it is sparsely borne on a sturdy, bushy, spiny shrub wh is cultivated as a hedge; [by extension] the hedge so cultivated; *Triphasia trifolia* (*Rutaceae*). *If the aim is a boy-proof, animal-proof, long-lasting, tall-growing hedge, the Sweet-Lime is your baby. This was once very popular in Barbados.*—AdN (72.10.01) □ Listed also as *limeberry* in some botanical literature.

sweet li·quor *n phr* (Bdos) A thin syrup obtained after the boiling of CRACK-LIQUOR, or the second boiling and clarification process of the original raw cane-juice. □ Some recent writers evidently erron use SWEET LIQUOR and BLACK-STRAP as alternative names.

sweet-man *n* (ECar) [*AF—Joc/Derog*] 1. A married woman's lover who receives money and gifts from her. *A man accused of beating up his wife ... told the court that he did so because he was enraged after he found two of his shirts, a pair of trousers and some kitchen utensils belonging to him, in her 'sweet-man's house.' He said that he also found out that she was using his money to 'mind' the man.*—GyC (76.04.06, p.11) 2. [By extension] A man who lives off women who like him sexually. *We in Trinidad don't have the professionals but we have something else—the sweetman—the type who lives off women and in fact have a stable of girls and can take their pick anytime the mood comes on.*—BoM (77.06.17, p.9) 3. A lazy, able-bodied man who lives off friends, including women. *Silky is a sweetman, he getting he clothes wash free, he getting free food from he woman and dem, and he gettin free drinks from he friends. He doesn't raise straw. (Do the lightest type of work).*—Gren (Ms, C.W. Francis)

sweet mar·gar·et* *n phr* (Baha) A large, sturdy shrub with short, tough, slender, jointed limbs, bearing pink flowers and edible, brownish berries; it flourishes near the sea and is used in infusions meant to boost male virility; *Byrsonima lucida* (*Malpighiaceae*).

sweet-mouth[1] *n* (CarA) [*AF*] 1. ‖ *chote*[2], *co-chore*[2] (Guyn) ‖ *sweet-talk*[1] (CarA) Friendly, flattering or easy, deceptive talk intended to persuade sb or pacify people. **a.** *Him was old enough to be me father. I fall for him sweet-mouth and make him take advantage o' me. Him fall me Tom.*—GT:147 (O. Patterson) **b.** *Want to fool everybody and take everything for heself. Full of sweet-mouth. Want to be boss. Boss me eye!*—NAGOS:111 [A calque from W Afr langs. Cp DAFL Twi *n'ano yɛ dɛ papa* (he mouth be sweet too-much) 'He is a flatterer' See also sweet-talk[1] Phr] 2. [Esp of children] A liking for much tasty food; greediness. □ Often in attrib function. 3. PHRASE **3.1 give sb (a lot of) sweet-mouth** *vb phr* (CarA) [*AF*] ‖ SWEET-TALK[2] (CarA) *She only givin[g] them a lot of sweet-mout[h] to make them buy ticket for the church concert.*—(Gren)

sweet-mouth[2] *vb* (CarA) [*AF*] ‖ SWEET-TALK[2] (CarA) *Don't worry sweet-mout[h] me with all dose nice words because I ain['t] coming wid you.*—(StVn)

sweet oil *n phr* (CarA) 1. Almond oil, or olive oil, or any oil used medicinally. *Sometimes, too; the leaves have to be squeezed in a clean piece of cloth and then mixed with an oil—in most cases the commercial olive oil or 'sweet' oil.*—LSFMG: 7 2. Any vegetable oil used in cooking. *A root o' dasheen is a Grenadian meal / A penny sweet-oil and a penny sal'fish / When you pour in di oil / An' you fry it in style.*—EFSLC:40

sweet plum *n phr* (Baha, Jmca) ‖ JAMAICA PLUM (Bdos, etc)

sweet po·ta·to* *n phr* (CarA) ‖ *Anne potato* (TkCa) A sweetish, edible tuber with a purple, pinkish or cream skin and cream or grey flesh wh is used in many Caribbean dishes; it is the swollen root, varying in size, either of a straggling vine or an upright bushy shrub; *Ipomea batatas* (*Convolvulaceae*). □ This vegetable is commonly known as *yam* in parts of the U.S.

sweet-po·ta·to pone *n phr* (Jmca, Tbgo) ‖ *sweet-potato pudding* (Jmca) A pudding made of grated SWEET POTATO mixed with sugar and spices.

sweet-sage *n phr* (Guyn) ‖ SAGE(-BUSH) (CarA)

sweet-skin *adj* (Bdos, Guyn) [*AF—Joc*] [Esp of a young man] Keen to avoid any sweaty labour; [by extension] usu well-dressed and lazy.

sweet-soap *n* (Bdos, CayI, Guyn, Trin) Toilet soap; bath soap. *When asked why he was using this kind of sweet-soap, instead of the usual blue-soap, Bhandat confided to Mr Biswas that that was the soap used by lovely film stars.*—ExP (73.02.13, p.2) [Because of its 'sweet' perfumed smell. Cp SALT-SOAP]

sweet-sop/sap *n* (Antg, Baha, Belz, CayI, Jmca) ‖ SUGAR-APPLE (CarA)

sweet-talk¹ *n* (CarA) [*IF*] **1.** ‖ SWEET-MOUTH¹ (CarA) [*AF*] *Big talk wid nothing behind it / Only fills man bowels wid fear / But sweet-talk can move mountains / Mek friends and drive away care.*—DeM(SK) (62.05.19, p.9) [See SWEET-MOUTH¹] **2.** *PHRASE* **2.1 give sb (a lot of) sweet-talk** *vb phr* (CarA) [*AF/IF*] ‖ SWEET-TALK² (CarA) [Cp Yoruba *sọrọ didun-didun fun ẹ* (say word sweet-sweet give you) 'to flatter you'—(*pers info*, K. Ọmọtọṣọ)]

sweet-talk² *vb tr* (CarA) ‖ *chote¹* (Guyn) ‖ *co-chore¹* (Guyn) ‖ *give sb a basket* (Tbgo) ‖ *give sb (a lot of) sweet-talk* (CarA) ‖ *sweet-mouth²* (CarA) To persuade or pacify (sb) by flattery or by friendly deceptive talk. *No, he continues to import more and more of these commodities. After sweet talking the public into buying them he complains about imports.*—MtM (73.02.16, p.5) [By functional shift of SWEET-TALK¹ *n*]

sweet wa·ter *n phr* (Bdos, Gren, Guyn, Tbgo, Trin) ‖ SUGAR-WATER (Guyn, etc)

sweet-wil·li·am *n* (Dmca, Guyn, Jmca) ‖ AN-TIGUA-HEATH (Bdos, etc)

swell *PHRASE* **swell up your face** *vb phr* (Gren) [*AF*] ‖ MAKE UP YOUR FACE (CarA) [*AF*] See FACE Phr 4.

swell-foot *n* (Guyn) [*AF—Cr*] ‖ BIG-FOOT (Guyn)

swib·bly *adj* (Bdos) [*AF—Cr*] Having a wrinkled skin. *'Swibbly applies only to fruit and to fleshy, flaccid things; a stale mango will become swibbly, and the skin on your fingers turns swibbly after you've been in the sea for a long time, but you would never describe an unironed pair of pants as being swibbly; you'd say they were wrinkled, or 'rumfled'.*—NaT (85.11.19, p.10)

swing *vb* **1.** (Bdos, Guyn) [*IF*] To change direction (by turning left or right); [of a person or vehicle] to come or go around (a corner). **a.** *The track swings inland on occasions behind a thin screen of casuarina trees.*—AdN (77.12.04, p.18) **b.** *As soon as we swung the corner we could see that a house was on fire.*—(Guyn) **2.** (Baha, Belz, Guyn, Mrat, TkCa) To feel dizzy. *Winkie put in his two cents worth, saying 'Yinna feeling tings in ya head; ain nuttin movin'. Yinna head swing', das all!'*—TOSR:28 **2.** *PHRASE* **2.1 swinging in the head** *n phr* (Guyn) See HEAD¹ Phr 4.18

swing·er *n* (Guyn) A child's swing

switch·er *n* (Baha, TkCa) [*IF/AF*] ‖ SWANK (Bdos, etc) [Cp *OED switchel* US 'a drink made of molasses and water, sometimes with vinegar, ginger or rum added'. [Prob the same with /l > r/ shift]

swit-kouch (**suite-couche**) [swit-kuš] *n* (Dmca, StLu) ‖ LYING-IN COLD (Antg, etc) *After she had the baby she went out in the rain and she get swit-kouch.*—(Dmca) [Fr Cr < Fr *suite de couche* 'after-effect of confinement']

swiz·zle *n* (CarA) A drink of Caribbean origin made by adding rum or other alcoholic substance to a milky or sweet liquid base flavoured with grated nutmeg and ANGOSTURA BITTERS and stirring the mixture vigorously with a SWIZZLE-STICK until frothy. [Perh a blend of < *OED switchel* 'a mixed rum drink' (see SWITCHER) + *OED fizz* 3. 'an effervescing drink'. Both these are listed as 19C Eng words, i.e. a period of *CarA* PLANTER-CLASS infl in England that may explain the origin of the type of drink]

swiz·zle-stick *n* (CarA) A sturdy, slender, seasoned stick about 12 ins long (cut from a nutmeg or other suitable tree) with the stumps of shoots remaining at its end to serve to stir a SWIZZLE when rubbed vigorously between the palms of the hand; any stick of similar proportions fitted with wooden spikes or wire twists at the end to provide the stirring effect. *He could hear the boisterous laughter of young men. ... He could distinguish over it all the cherry swish-swash of the swizzle-stick muffled in the lashing foam of gin and bitters and broken ice.*—WTTBB:187 □ In SE, this term is applied to any stirrer supplied with a highball or cocktail (including those made of glass, plastic, paper, etc).

sword *n* (Bdos) [*IF*] ‖ CUTLASS (CarA) *Len[d] me de sword to chop do[w]ng dis bush.*—(Bdos) □ This term remains in use among very old folk.

sword-bean *n* (Bdos) ‖ GRUDGE-PEA (Gren) *The Horse-Bean is also called the Overlook-Bean or Sword-Bean and is eaten as a vegetable, the young pods sliced like Butter Beans.*—AdN (79.05.06, p.14) [Name prob due to the length and stiffness of the pod when fully mature]

sword·fish *n* (Bdos, BrVi) See BILL-FISH

syn·di·cate *n* (Belz) ‖ SUSU (Trin) [Calque < Sp *sindicato*, 'a workers' union']

syve [saɪv] *n* (Gren) See CIVE □ This spelling is prob notional.

T

-t- □ In Creolized E speech /-t-/ often replaces [θ] 'th', requiring spellings in dialogue such as 'ting', 'tink', 'wit'out', 'Cat'olic', 'yout', 'eart', etc for 'thing', 'think', 'without', Catholic', 'youth', 'earth'. This survives from Cr pronunc due to the absence of the sound [θ] in Niger-Congo langs (*WWPAL:79*) and hence from the original speech of the slaves. See -TH- 1(i).

ta·bac-di·able *n* (StLu) See TABAK-DJAB

ta·bac-zom·bie *n* (Dmca) See TABAK-ZONBI

ta·bak-djab (ta·bac-di·able) ['taba·ʃa·b] *n* (StLu) ‖ CATTLE-TONGUE (Antg, etc) [Fr Cr < Fr *tabac-diable* 'devil tobacco', Fr Cr *djab* used here, as commonly in ref to plants, to mean 'wild'. Cp 'zonbi' similarly used]

ta·bak-zon·bi (ta·bac-zom·bie) *n* (Dmca) ‖ CATTLE-TONGUE (Antg, etc) [See *tabak-djab*]

ta·ban·ca¹ (ta·ban·ka) /1ʹ2ʹ1/ [tabaŋka] *n* (Gren, Guyn, Trin) [*AF—Joc*] A state of acute love sickness often leading to irrational behaviour and usu associated with unrequited love or with infidelity. *Had Williams done his research properly he would know that through the ages tabanca makes men do the strangest things, suicide not being uncommon—and Bill Crouch undoubtedly had tabanca.*—BoM (77.12.09, p.16) [Prob of Cariban origin. Cp *FTCC:147* Maçusi *tabangke* 'wonder']

ta·ban·ca² (ta·ban·ka) /1ʹ2ʹ1/ *adj* (Trin) [*AF—Joc*] Very infatuated; passionately in love. *She got you tabanka, boy.*—(Trin) [By functional n > adj shift of TABANCA¹]

tab·by¹ *n* (Baha) A mixture of cement and sand poured into a wooden form with stone to make a wall called a **tabby wall**. [Cp *OED tabby* sb 6. 'a concrete formed of a mixture of lime with shells, gravel ... in equal proportions ...]

tab·by² [tabi] *vb* (Baha) To mix cement and sand together and pour it into a wooden form with stone to make a wall. [By functional n > vb shift of TABBY¹]

tab·lèt (tab·lette) [tablɛt] *n* (Dmca, StLu) ‖ SUGAR-CAKE 2. (Guyn) [Fr Cr < Fr *tablette* 'cake, slab (of chocolate)']

tache (tayche) [teč] *n* (Bdos, Dmca, Gren, Guyn) ‖ *platin(e)* 2. (Gren) [Sugar Ind] One of a series of copper pans used in former times to boil sugar-cane juice before it was transferred to a boiler to be crystallized into sugar. *The planter mixed a solution of this molasses with some inferior cane juice and the froth skimmings from the boiling tayches and left it for about a week to ten days until it started to ferment.*—AdM (76.12.12, p.7) [*OED tache* sb³ '(sugar-boiling) ... pan ...', derived from Obs Fr *tache, tèche* 'plate of iron']

tack·le¹ *vb tr* (Antg, Bdos, Guyn) [*AF/IF*] 1. (Guyn) To steal from (a place). *An e decide dat e gon tackle a certain big store in Regent Street.*—Guyn (Ms, 1976) 2. (Guyn) [Usu of a man] To seek acquaintance with sb with the intention of having a love affair. **a.** *He tacklin[g] June but she won't worry with him because he doesn't have a job.*—(Guyn)

tack·le² *n* (Guyn) [*AF*] The action of getting acquainted with sb with the intention of entering into a love affair.

tack·y *adj* (Jmca) 1. [*AF—Derog*] Tricky; difficult to outsmart; clever. *You can[ʼt] manage him. Him too tacky fi you.*—(Jmca) 2. [*IF*] [Of dress] Smart; [of a performance] good. *She was looking real tacky that night.*—(Jmca) [Perh by semantic shift of SE *tacky* 'sticky and about to dry' (as of fresh paint)]

ta·cou [taku] *adj* (Crcu) [*AF—Derog*] 1. Simple; foolish. 2. PHRASE 2.1 **to be a tacou** *vb phr* (Crcu) [*AF—Derog*] ‖ **to be born with dye-cloth tie you head** (Angu) To be foolish, gullible.

ta·cou·ba (ta·ku·ba) /1ʹ2ʹ2/ [takuba] *n* (Guyn) The trunk of a huge tree wh has fallen across a creek or stream and is used as a means of crossing it. *The Executive Engineer of the Public Works Department following an inspection of the Mongrippo Creek area suggested that instead of attempting to construct a Revetment on the left bank of the Creek, the right bank should be completely cleared of all tacoubas and other obstacles.*—DaC (72.18.10, p.4) [Cp *EILCA:53* Arawak *tak-uukutaahi* (onikan) 'to block + (stream)']

tac·ra (tak·ro) /1ʹ1/ [takrʌ] *adj* (Jmca) [*AF—Derog*] Ugly, unattractive, unrefined (in speech or manner). *What is a pretty girl like you doing* *with that tacra man?*—(Jmca) [Perh of Afr origin. Cp *WSNE* Sran *takroe* 'ugly' + several compounds: takroesiki (= ugly sick) 'leprosy', etc]

tac·tac *n* (Dmca) See TAK-TAK

tac·té *adj* (Dmca, Gren, StLu, Trin) See TAKTÉ

tad·jah (**ta·ja, ta·zia(s)**) [taJa ~ tažia(z)] *n* (*pl*) (Guyn, Trin) [Indic] ‖ *Hosay* 2. (Trin) Replica(s) of the tombs of the Muslim martyrs Hassan and Hosein wh are paraded through the streets in festive celebration during the HOSEIN/ HOSAY festival. **a.** *... the Prime Minister, on his visit to 'Hosay' camps last year, promised to promote the talent shown in the construction of tadjahs and lend help to this 'festivity'.*—ExP (72.02.28, p.17) **b.** *In St James and Tunapuna a big flag is raised at the start of the ceremony and the tazias (replicas of the tombs of the martyrs of seventh-century Arabia, Hasan and Husain, grandchildren of the prophet) are led by specially trained moon dancers to the accompaniment of drum (tassa) beating and 'gatka' (stick or lathi) fighting.*—LCTC: 5 [< Perso-Arabic > Hin *taagiyaa/taaziyaa* 'replica' of the shrines of Hassan and Hosein taken out in procession on the occasion of 'Muharram'. See also HOSEIN 3.] □ The more common form and spelling of this word in CE is *tadjah*.

tag-day *n* (Bdos, Guyn) A special day when paper tags (from a non-profit association) are sold to raise money; the tags are worn by donors during that day. *Tomorrow is Red Cross tag-day, girl.*—(Guyn) [Cp *DAE tag* n b. 'tag day, a day during wh tags are sold to secure money for charitable purposes'] □ Also AmE; BrE is *flag-day* (See *COD8*).

tail *n* (CarA) [*AF—Joc*] A person's buttocks; the arse. *You don't know what tail is. Man we are in a Parliament where all the expressions of the British language are used in a way that express what we feel. If I say people sit down on their tail I mean this because that is the tail end of the anatomy that I refer to.*—Gren (Hd, 76.05.21, p.25) [A euphemism; also BrE slang] **2.** PHRASES **2.1 cut sb's tail** *vb phr* (CarA) See CUT Phr 3.10 **2.2 Fire your tail!** *imper vb phr* (Guyn) [*AF—Vul*] ‖ MOVE YOURSELF! (Baha, etc) See FIRE Phr 4.4 *Ent Ah tell you you mustn't listen when big people talking! Get outside! Fire you' tail out de room!*—MLDS:31 **2.3 haul your tail** *vb phr* (StKt, Trin) [*AF—Vul*] ‖ HAUL YOURSELF (Bdos, etc) See HAUL Phr 4.7 *My mother said, 'Tell that blasted man to haul his tail away from my yard, you hear.'*—HGFA:21 (V.S. Naipaul) **2.4 keep your tail quiet** *vb phr* (CarA) [*AF*] Not to move or stir; to shut up and stay out of trouble. **2.5 pelt/put/throw (some) lashes/ licks in sb's tail** *vb phr* (Bdos) [*AF*] See LICKS Phr 3.8 **2.6 see your tail** *vb phr* (Bdos, Guyn, Tbgo, Trin) [*AF—Joc*] See SEE Phr 3.7

ta·ja [taJa] *n* (Guyn, Trin) See TADJAH

take [tek ~ tɛk] *vb* PHRASES **1. not take sb's height** *vb phr* (CarA) [*IF*] See HEIGHT Phr 2. **2. take a fall** *vb phr* (Dmca, Gren) [*IF*] [Of a person] To fall down; to have a fall; to stumble and fall down. *The men on stilts ... were always reported to have died after Carnival by taking a fall on the way home.*—DoC (65.02.27, p.7) **3. Take a side!** *excl vb phr* (Baha, etc) **4. Take care** *imper vb phr* (i) (CarA) [*IF*] ‖ MIND² 5. (CarA) **a.** *Child, take care you break that glass* (= *be careful not to break that glass*).—(Jmca) **b.** *Mama, it's getting late. Take care we miss the early bus* (= *we must take care not to miss ...*).—(Bdos) [A prob calque from Afr lang structures. Cp Nupe *Tawa bichi yami* (*Be careful my foot*) 'Take care not to tread on my foot'. See more at MIND² 5.] □ The prosodic features that apply in the case of ‖ *mind²* 5. are not significant in this use of TAKE CARE. **(ii)** (Guyn, Tbgo, Trin) [*IF*] [By extension] *in semi-modal function, followed by a finite clause* Isn't it possible that... **a.** *You sure you brought home the umbrella? Take care you left it in the bus.*—(Guyn) **b.** *Take care i[t']s the same man that came in here beggin[g] that carry away the bicycle.*—(Trin) **5. take down low** *vb phr* (StVn) [*IF*] ‖ BE BAD ENOUGH (CarA) See BAD¹ Phr 4.2 **6. take foot** *vb phr* (Belz, CayI, Jmca, Nevs) [*AF*] See FOOT Phr 2.15 **7. take in front** *vb phr* (Gren) [*IF*] To make the first move in your own defence or interest; to anticipate an accusation by first taking offence. *J— may have something to hide or cover up so it is taking in front in an attempt to cloud the issues and thereby sidetrack the bubul.*—GrV (91.12.28, p.8) **8. take licks** *vb phr* (CarA) See LICK² Phr 3.4 **9. take sick** *vb phr* (CarA) [*IF*] See SICK Phr 2.4, 2.4.1 **9.1 take in (sick)** *vb phr* (CarA) [*IF*] To become ill suddenly; to be taken ill unexpectedly. **a.** *She took in while still at home and before they could get her to the hospital she died.*—(Guyn) **b.** *You have to give the telephone number of your mother's or father's workplace in case you take in sick at school.*—(Bdos) □ Also, with intensified sense, *take in bad* (CarA) **10. take sb opposite** *vb phr* (Tbgo, Trin) [*AF/IF*] See OPPOSITE Phr 2.1 **11. take sb's tongue** *vb phr* (Dmca, StLu) [*AF*] ‖ PICK SB'S MOUTH (CarA) See PICK Phr 5.7 **12. take sth good** *vb phr* (CarA) See GOOD³ Phr 2.9 **13. Take that!** (**Tek da!**) *imper vb phr* (Guyn) [*AF*] ‖ *Da fo[r] lick you!* (Bdos) [Expressing cynical delight] And how do you like that!; There's something for you!. **14. Take trick to make luck/trade** *vb phrs* (ECar) See TRICK Phr 15. **take up for (sb)** *vb phr* (CarA) ‖ *pick up for (sb)* (CarA) To speak in defence of or side with (sb) (usu more from affection than with good reason). *Don't bother to complain to the mother, yo[u] know. She always takes up for him no matter what he do.*—(Guyn) [Perh a blend of SE idioms *take sides* + *stand up for*] **15.1 take up (sb's) fire-rage** *vb phr* (Antg, etc) See FIRE-RAGE Phr 2.1 **16. Take up yourself!; Take yourself up!** *excl vb phr* (Jmca, Mrat, StKt) [*AF*] ‖ MOVE YOURSELF! (Baha, etc) **17. take your fastness to sb** *vb phr* (CarA) [*IF*] See FASTNESS Phr 4.1 **18. take (your hand) and

knock sb *vb phr* (Bdos, Guyn) [*X*] To strike or punch sb without due cause; to hit sb deliberately. *Mammy, you see Ronald take and knock me!*—(Guyn) [Prob < *take hand (and) knock/hit*, this being a likely calque of a common pattern in W Afr langs. Cp Igbo *oji aka tiemu (he take hand hit me)* 'he hit me with his fist'] □ The phr in CE is now largely restricted to children's talk. **19. Take yourself!** *excl vb phr* (Belz, Gren, StKt) ‖ MOVE YOURSELF! (Baha, etc) [Cp Yoruba *ba ara ẹ da sọ hun! (take your body turn yonder)* 'Be off with you!'] **20. (your) spirit takes/ does not take sb** *id phr* (Guyn) [*IF*] See SPIRIT¹ Phr 4.4

ta·ke·da [takɪda] *n* (Belz) ‖ AJOUPA (Dmca, etc) [Perh < Sp *taquear* 'to pack tight' in ref to the wattle-and-daub construction. Also poss < SE *stockade* in ref to the fence work] □ Also used Joc in ref to a person's home.

take off *vb phr* (CarA) *PHRASE* **take off (the) obeah (from sb)** *vb phr* (CarA) See OBEAH¹ Phr 3.1

take on *vb phr* (CarA) *PHRASE* **can take on sb** *vb phr* (Gren) ‖ (BE) ABLE WITH SB/STH (CarA) See ABLE Phr 1.

take up *vb phr* *PHRASES* **1. take up sb's fire-rage** *vb phr* (Antg, Bdos, Gren, Guyn) [*AF*] See FIRE-RAGE Phr 2.1 **2. take up your foot and run** *vb phr* (Bdos, Jmca) See FOOT Phr 2.15

Tak·i-Tak·i *n* (CarA) [*Derog*] ‖ SRANAN (Srnm) [< 'talkee-talkee', a Derog label equivalent to 'chatter', orig used by white colonizers and generally copied by others]

tak·ro *adj* (Jmca) See TACRA

tak-tak (tac.tac) *n* (Dmca) **1.** ‖ ACOUSHI ANT (Guyn) **2.** *PHRASE* **2.1 be behind sb like a tak-tak** *vb phr* (Dmca) [*AF—Joc*] ‖ BE BEHIND SB LIKE A SLAVE-DRIVER (CarA) See BEHIND Phr 2. [Prob a ref to this ant as a formidable and persistent pest. See ACOUSHI ANT]

tak·té (tac.té) [takte] *adj* (Dmca, Gren, StLu, Trin) [*IF*] [Of fruit] Having dark spots; being overripe or about to spoil [Fr Cr *takté* 'spotted' perh < Fr *tacheté*]

ta·la·wa [talawa] /2'11/ *adj* (Jmca) [*AF*] [Of a person] Tough-minded; forceful in character; not to be trifled with; [by extension, of a woman] decisive and self-assertive (esp in sexual relationships). *She small but she real talawa, yo[u] se[e], yo[u] can['t] mess wid [h]er.*—(Jmca) [Prob < Sc E *stalwart* as in *CSD stalwart* 4. (Of persons) 'resolute, determined'; 5. 'valiant, courageous'. In Jmca Cr /st- > t-/, intrusive /-a-/ and reduction of final /-CC/ would together produce TALAWA from the Sc pronunc]

talk¹ *n* (Bdos, Gren, Guyn) [*IF*] ‖ *talking* (Bdos, Guyn) **1.** Disagreement, quarrel. **1.1.** *PHRASE*

have talk *vb phr* (Gren) [*IF*] Not to be on speaking terms with sb. *Now this man and she had a little talk and he leave her and gone and now she is broken hearted.*—NaT (77.07.03, p.34) **2.** Gossip, rumour. *It was one talking because the teacher's daughter got pregnant.*—Guyn (Ms) [< SE *talk* in senses 'gossip, rumour', also *talking* 'empty words' with semantic shift in CE]

talk² *vb PHRASES* **1. get and talk** *vb phr* (Bdos, Guyn) [*IF—Derog*] See GET Phr 3.2 **2. not talk in boli** *vb phr* (Gren) [*AF—Joc*] See BOLI Phr 3.1 **3. rum talking** *id phr* (CarA) [*AF—Joc*] See RUM Phr 3.3 **4. talk back** *vb phr* (Bdos, Guyn, Tbgo) [*IF*] ‖ *(a)gree back* (Bdos, Gren) ‖ *make back up* (CarA) ‖ *speak back* (Bdos, Guyn) To become friends again after a serious row; to be on speaking terms again. **a.** *I was surprised to see the two of them walking together. Like they['re] talking back now.*—(Guyn) **b.** *S1: I see you and Lucy are friends again. / S2: Is she who talk back first.*—(Tbgo) **c.** *Christine, she hurted me so badly I couldn't eat nor sleep but I didn't give up hope. I tried talking back to her to see what's the matter but she says nothing to me.*—NaT (77.06.05, p.26, Dear Christine) [< EE TALK 'to speak in conversation' (Samuel Johnson), esp as in neg *not talking* 'not on speaking terms' + CE BACK⁴ adv 2(ii)] □ Note IAE *talk back* 'to answer impudently'. **5. talk flat** *vb phr* (ECar) [*AF/IF*] See FLAT¹ Phr

tam *n* (CarA) ‖ *tamashanta* (Guyn) ‖ *tam-hat* (Gren) A knitted woollen cap, often in rings of red, yellow, black, green, (and sometimes with a peak); it is popular RASTAFARIAN headwear made spacious enough to bag the DREADLOCKS. *Five ringlets of wiry hair stuck out of his red and green tam and above his proud face in all His glory was pinned the image of The Most High Emperor Haile Selassie I*—RHJSS:35 [Shortened form of Sc 'tam-o'-shanter']

ta·ma·le(s) /12'1/ [tama·le(z)] *n* (Belz) ‖ *bollos* (Belz) A dish made of a mixture of Indian corn, chicken, or meat, seasoned with herbs and pepper, wh is then wrapped in roasted plantain leaves and boiled. *A certain establishment which makes tamales for sale has a reputation for the excellent quality of its product.*—AmA (80.03.07, p.7) [Back-formation < Lat Am Sp n pl *tamales* < Nahuatl *tamalli*—'dough made of maize flour mixed with meat and chili pepper wrapped in corn leaves'. Cited as appearing for the first time in Mexico, circa 1532—*Montalban 1986/7, p.56* (M. Arango)] □ The pl form is common, and so often used as sg, hence *a tamales*

ta·ma·rind* (tam·(b)ran, tam·brin) /1'2/ ['tam(ə)rɪn(d) ~ tam(b)rʌn] *n* (CarA) A hard, brown pod about 4 or 5 ins long with several seeds embedded in reddish-brown, acid pulp wh loosens from the shell when ripe; the pulp is eaten raw and also valued for its medicinal use, as well as in cookery, making preserves, etc; the pod is borne abundantly on a large, spreading, densely bushy tree with compound leaves; *Tamarindus indica* (*Leguminosae-Caesalpineae*). *A very pretty sight when the tamarind is in bloom, with the feather-like green leaves and pale yellow flowers. The fruit, which hangs on the stems like brown pea pods, is very acid in flavor. They make a tasty drink, and are also candied.*—PHPVI: 70 □ Many variant spellings reflect CarA dial pronunc, commonly one with homorganic cluster /-mb-/.

ta·ma·rind ball *n phr* (CarA) See BALL 2.

ta·ma·rind bud *n phr* (Guyn, StKt) The young, greenish-pink leaves at the top of the tamarind tree; they are said to be effective in the treatment of fever, esp in young children.

ta·ma·rind drink /1'22/ *n phr* (CarA) ‖ *t-amon bug* [ta·mʌn bʌg] (Angu) ‖ *tamarind juice* (StLu) ‖ *tamarind punch, tamarind sizzle* (StKt) A drink made from the pulp of the TAMARIND.

ta·ma·rind jam *n phr* (CarA) ‖ *tamarind bazan, tamarind preserve* (TkCa) ‖ *tamarind paste* (Baha) ‖ *tamarind stew* (Antg, Gren, Mrat, StVn) A jam or preserve made from the pulp of the TAMARIND and often used as a dessert.

ta·ma·rind lash *n phr* (Bdos) See TAMARIND ROD (Bdos, etc) ... *the pain of waiting for the whip rope tamarind lash, hurled by the thick-necked sweating God who ruled our little school.*—BTA: 73

ta·ma·rind punch/sizzle *n phr* (StKt) ‖ TAMARIND DRINK (CarA)

ta·ma·rind rod/whip /1'22/ [tambrʌn rɒd] *n phr* (CarA) A piece of a young branch of the tamarind tree from wh the leaves are stripped and wh is officially used for administering corporal punishment; hence *tamarind lash*.

ta·ma·rind sea·son *n phr* (Jmca) ‖ HARD-GUAVA DAYS (Guyn)

ta·ma·shan·ta *n* (Guyn) See TAM

tam·bal [tambal] *n* (Dmca) A large tambourine made of goat skin and usu used as part of the accompaniment to the popular 'BÈLÈ' dance. *A brightly dressed group is dancing and singing to the beat of a goat skin or 'la peau cabrit' drum. One of the women, probably the 'chantuelle', claps her hands and sings the 'lavway' while a man provides accompaniment on a 'tambal'. A couple in the centre dance what could be the 'bele'.*—HTDS:44 [Fr Cr < Fr *timbale* 'kettle drum']

tam·boo-bam·boo (tan.bou-ban.bou) ['tambu-'bambu] /1'122/ *n* (Trin) ‖ *bamboo-tamboo* (Trin) Joints of bamboo knocked together to make music, in the streets, esp at CARNIVAL in former times. [Fr Cr < Fr *tambour*

bambou 'bamboo drum'. The variant *bamboo-tamboo* is prob an Anglicized change] □ Sometimes simply BAMBOO, this device preceded the development of the STEELBAND.

tam-hat *n* (Gren) See TAM

ta·mon bug [ta·mʌn bʌg] *n phr* (Angu) ‖ TAMARIND DRINK (CarA)

tam·pi (tam·pee) [tampi] *n* (Gren, Trin) [AF] (Another name for) marijuana. *Since there are many young calypsonians it is evident that there would be some sniffing of 'grass', 'smoke', 'tampi', marijuana, call it what you will at some of the calypso shows.*—Peo.I.8, p.51 [Perh by functional vb > n shift and epenthetic /-i/ from OED *tamp* vb 3. b. 'to pack or consolidate tobacco (in a pipe or a cigarette) by a series of light taps'. Cp also *DAE tamp* vb tr 'to pack by ramming or tapping']

tang *n* (Baha) A surgeon- or lancet-fish with a sharp spine on the tail; it dwells among the reefs and is considered to be of good food value; *Hepatus hepatus*. [Cp OED2 *tang* 1.1 c. 'a sharp point or spike'; also *EDD tang* 1. sb 'any point'] □ Also classified under the scientific name of *Teuthis hepatus* in OED2 where it is referred to as the W Indian variety of surgeon-fish.

tan·ge·rine* [tanʤəri·n] *n* (CarA) ‖ *mandarin* (Dmca, Gren, StLu, Trin) ‖ *portugal* (Trin) ‖ *king-orange* (Jmca, StKt, Trin) A small variety of orange, slightly conical at its top and with a loose skin and segments wh are usu easily removed with the fingers; there are several subtypes varying in size, some remaining green-skinned, but most are yellow when ripe and notably sweet; *Citrus nobilis* or *C. reticulata* (*Rutaceae*). [< *Tanger*, Fr name of Tangier(s), Morocco]

tan·ni·a* (tan·ya) *n* (CarA) ‖ *badoo* (Jmca) ‖ *chou caraibe* (StLu) ‖ *eddo* 3., *(hard)coco, taya* (Jmca) ‖ *tannia-eddoe* (Bdos) A tuber about 4 to 5 ins long, of a rather coarse, pinkish (some varieties yellowish) texture, usu boiled and sliced; the plant is distinguished by its large arrowhead-shaped leaves, with prominent veins, their tall stalks rising straight out of the ground; *Xanthosoma sagittifolium* (*Araceae*). [< DGEG Tupi-Guarani, *taya* 'una planta, malanga ... en las Antillas y otras partes, *Xanthosoma sagittifolium*' with nasalization developing from the semi-vowel /y > ny/] □ In some territories it is considered a type of DASHEEN and loosely so called. In botanical literature the plant is sometimes also referred to as *malanga, tayo,* or *yautia,* sometimes as *a cocoyam.*

tan·nia bush/leaf [tanya buʃ/lif] /1'12/n phr* (CarA) The foliage of the TANNIA plant wh is often used in Caribbean cookery.

tan·ni·a-ed·doe *n* (Bdos) ‖ TANNIA (CarA) [A characteristic CE redundant compound, joining two names for the same vegetable, < *tannia* (of Tupi origin) + *eddoe* (of Fante origin). See these words]

tan·tan *n* 1. (BrVi, Crcu, Gren) [*IF*] ‖ TANTIE (Belz, etc) □ Now often replaced by *tan* sometimes followed by the person's first-name. 2. (USVI) [*IF*] ‖ WILD TAMARIND 1. (Guyn, etc) *The director said to him, 'Now you tell us. What are the chief products of St Thomas?' the boy promptly replied, 'Tantan seed. Jumbee bead and Maran.'*—AHPVI:2 [Prob baby talk from *tamarind* > *taman*, one of the folk variants recorded being **wild taman** < WILD TAMARIND]

tan·ta·ri·a (tan·ta·ri·ah) /12′21/ *n* (Guyn) [*AF—Derog*] A loud, physically aggressive, shrewish woman, given to hurling abuse at others. *I don't want any quarrel with that tantaria because I can't fight.*—(Guyn) [Poss from *OED2 tantara* A. int and sb 'imitative of the sound of the flourish blown on a trumpet, or sometimes of a drum' B. sb 'a fanfare, or flourish of trumpets', hence any similar sound]

tan·tie (tan·ta, tan·ti, tan·ty) [tanti] *n* (ECar) [*IF*] (An affectionate term for) aunt; auntie. *What do people call a mother's sister? Some say auntie, some say tantie.*—RLCF:97 [< Fr Cr from blend of Fr *tante* + Eng 'aunty, auntie']

Tan·to tan·to! /3′322/ *introductory formula* (Dmca, StLu) [*IF*] [Indicating a warning] Your day will come!; Do not be in too much of a hurry to feel secure or to laugh at others!; Watch out! *Tanto Tanto. The day of reckoning will surely come.*—CrU (74.03.09, Cocky & Stocky) [Fr Cr < Fr *Tantôt tantôt!* 'Soon soon!; any time now!']

ta·pa *n* (Trin) Flat object made of any durable material and used to mark the square wh must not be jumped into when the game of hopscotch is being played. [< Sp *tapa* 'a lid, cover, top or cap']

ta·pan·co /11′2/ [ta′paŋko] *n* (Belz) [*IF*] A lean-to made of sticks and palm leaves, used by forestworkers as a temporary shelter. [< *SDGA* Mex Sp *tapanco* 'attic or store-room' < Aztec *tlapantli* 'flat-roofed adobe house']

ta·pi·a ['tapia] *adj* (Trin) A thatched or mud wall or roof; a wattle-and-daub wall or roof. *The typical village house is a tapia (mud) house with a galvanized iron roof, ... the framework for the walls is made by wattling and then filling this in with mud mixed with a grass binder.*—RLCF:36 [< Sp *tapia*, 'mud wall, adobe wall']

ta·pir* ['tapɪr] *n* (Guyn) ‖ **bush-cow, maipuri, wild cow** (Guyn) A heavy, stout and clumsy, hoofed, fruit-eating forest mammal about the size of a donkey but with short legs, a dark-brown body (though its young have white horizontal stripes) a head with a flexible snout and small ears; this animal is regularly hunted for its meat; *Tapirus americanus* (*Tapiridae/Rhinocerotidae*).

[*DGEG* Tupi-Guarani *tapii* 'Tapirus terrestris']

tar *n* (CarA) See TAW

ta·ra (tar·ra) /1′1/ ['tara] *pron, adj* (Belz, Guyn, Jmca) [*AF—Cr*] 1. (SE) The other. *John live tara side the canal.*—(Belz) 2. [Preceded by 'the' in pronominal function] All sorts of things; every conceivable thing. *Dacta fo' de tara.* (= *Doctor for everything*).—(Guyn) [CarA Cr > /tada/ < t'other, contracted form in Eng dial of 'the other' arrived at by folk etym. Cp *DJE tarra*]

ta·ran·tan *n* (Trin) ‖ CHRISTMAS-CANDLE (Bdos, etc) [Prob a surviving Sp loan. Cp Sp ‖ *talantalán* (*PtRi*), also *taratana* (*Mexico*) (*NPHT:176*)]

ta·ran·tu·la* [taran′čʊla] *n* (Guyn, Trin) ‖ **black spider** (Trin) 1. A large black hairy spider of the *Mygale spp* with a venomous bite. *I don't know the scientific name you have given but I do know that generally the name tarantula refers to the large black hairy spider Avicularia, not in fact a true tarantula, other name—bird-eating spider since it is large enough to take small nestlings.*—Trin (Ms, 1984) 2. A large black poisonous, hairy spider of the *Avicularia spp* wh is given the name TARANTULA, but is in fact not of the same genus. [Borrowed name of the European spider, *tarantula*, whose bite is only slightly poisonous]

tar·get ['targɪt] *n* (USVI) A game of marbles played by young children and involving the hitting of a target with the marble from a shooting line drawn on the ground, hence the name.

ta·ri·a (tha·ree, tha·lie) ['tha:ria ~ 'tha:ri ~ 'tha:li] *n* (Guyn, Trin) [Indic] A brass plate now used in Hindu religious ceremonies, but formerly used for eating by old Hindus, esp vegetarians. [Bhoj with /l > r/ shift < Hin *thaalii* 'vessel made of brass']

tar·po·li·an [tar′pɒliən] *n* (Bdos) [*X*] (SE) Tarpaulin. *We'll need to get a tarpolian to spread in case it rains.*—(Bdos) [Cp *OED tarpaulian* sb and adj (Obs) and its several variants including **tarpolian** + cits from 17C]

tar·pon* ['tarpʌn] *n* (Baha, BrVi, Guyn, Trin, USVI) ‖ **bass²** 2 (USVI) A long, silvery-blue fish with big irregular scales; its average weight is 68 lbs, but it can grow to a length of about 8 ft and weigh as much as 350 lbs (*ADF:86*); it is prized as a fighting game fish and is noted for the height to wh it leaps when hooked; *Megalops atlanticus* or *Tarpon a.* (*Clupeidae*).

task [ta·s(k)] *n* (CarA) [*IF*] [Rice/Sugar Ind] ‖ **task-work** (Guyn, Jmca) 1. A specified amount of work that must be completed before the worker is paid. *It appears that the workers on the La Force estate work by task and not by the hour, and therefore, if they are finished by one o'clock, it should be their right to go home.*—Gren (Hd,

78.04.26, p.66) **2.** (Guyn) A portion of a rice field (pre-divided into units measuring 1/8 acre) allotted specially to manual workers. **3.** PHRASE **3.1 work (by) task** *vb phr* (Gren, Guyn, Trin) [*IF*] To work to and be paid for agreed amounts or areas completed. *Man I does usually work task cause it pay better than by the hour.*—(Guyn)

task-gang *n* (Guyn) [Sugar Ind] A group of casual labourers (usu from outside the estate) hired to WORK BY TASK.

task-work *n* (Guyn, Jmca, Mrat) [Sugar Ind] ‖ TASK 1. (CarA) *Joey was a labourer living at Harry Hole; he either worked task-work for the estate which housed his hovel or on his share-cotton plot.*—FGSOS:59

tas·sa *n* 1. (Guyn, Trin) ‖ *tassa drum* (Guyn, Trin) A type of snare-drum beaten at Hindu ceremonies and festivals, particularly weddings. *This is what we thought, anyway, as we moved with the flow of the crowd, responding, in spite of ourselves, to the thump of the tassa and the studied intricacies of the 'hosays'.*—Peo I.8, p.40 [< Perso-Arabic *taasa* 'a kettle drum, a tambour'] **2.** [By extension] (Trin) Cake made from cassava. [By metaph transfer of sense 1. prob from its shape and size]

tas·sa drum·ming /1′222/ *n phr* (Guyn, Trin) (The art of) beating the TASSA at EAST INDIAN festivals. *The other night's presentation was that of the Cedros Village Council, which caused a sensation with their tassa drumming on stage.*—ExP (72.10.19, p.17)

tas·sel *n* (Baha) ‖ ARROW² (CarA)

ta·ta /1′2/ [ta:ta] *n* (Antg, Belz, Jmca, USVI) [*IF*] Father; term of affection or respect for an elderly person. *'Your Tata must know how it is in the mountain, boy', Daddy Sharpe said, using the old African word for father.*—RPME:75 [Cp KID Ibibio *tata, taata* 'address form for father, grandfather'; also CBCD Congo *tata*, Father (used in calling only). See more Afr sources at DJE *taata*. Note also poss reinforcement by Lat Am Sp *tata* 'daddy', wh however may be from similar sources or, in *Jmca*, residual from earlier Sp *taita* 'daddy']

ta·ta·du·hen·de ['tataduɛndɛ] *n* (Belz) ‖ *duhende* (Belz) A legendary creature in the form of a dwarfish, bearded old man clothed in animal skins and a big red hat, carrying machete and pipe and looking human except for his feet wh may be cloven, turned backwards or not touching the ground; he is a forest or pastureland dweller who, in some accounts, is a benevolent guardian of anyone who gets lost, and in others a trickster. [Lat Am Sp *tata* 'daddy' + *duende* 'goblin, ghost'] □ Often abbr to DUHENDE. Cp DOUEN(NE) (*Trin*).

ta·ta·mu·do /112′1/ *adj, n* (Belz) [*IF*] [Of a person] Stuttering; stammering; [by extension]

sb who stammers, stutters. [Sp *tartamudo* adj 'stammering']

ta·ta·ram /1′12/ ['tataram] *n* (Belz) [*AF*—Derog*] [Of a man] Old fool; old reprobate. *Look at that old tataram chasing after young girl.*—(Belz) [< *tata* 'father; daddy' + *ram*, 'a male goat', hence 'daddy goat' 'old goat']

ta·tò·né /1′12/ [tatəne] *vb tr* (Dmca, Gren) [*AF*] To touch, feel, squeeze (sth, usu fruit, or sb). **b.** *'Don't tatòné me tomatoes. If you don't want to buy, leave them alone.'*—(Gren) [Fr Cr < Fr *tâtonner* 'to grope or feel one's way about (in trying to find sth), to feel around']

ta·tu (ta(t)·too) ['tatu] (Gren, Trin) ‖ ARMADILLO (Guyn) [< DGEG Guarani *tatu* 'armadillo'. The name must have reached the *CarA* early from So Amer, since *BDFC* lists a Carib name for 'un tatou, animal']

Tau·li·pangs /1′12/ [taʊlipaŋgz] *n pl* (Guyn) ‖ AREKUNAS (CarA) *Beyond the distant and misty Pakaraimas and the foot-hill region of Roraima and Kukenaam, to the west, where the rugged sandstone mesas and steep upland valleys and forests give way to the rolling plains and savannahs of the Orinoco and the Cotinga lies the territory of the Arekunas or Taulipangs as they are often referred to.*—SuC (76.08.08, p.19)

ta·u·ro·ni·ro (ta·u·ra·ne·ro) /112′1/ [taʊrɒniro ~ taʊranero] *n* (Guyn) A large tree found in the interior of Guyana where it grows to a height of 90 to 120 ft and yields a hard, lustrous, highly durable, dark reddish-brown wood wh is used in the construction industry; an infusion from its bark is used as a folk-medicine to treat stomach ulcers and smallpox, and (mixed with bulletwood) it is also said to be a cure for dysentery; *Humiria balsamifera (Humiriaceae)*. *In a notice sent to all estates, the Committee has given first preference for three woods to be used for framework, floor, external and internal walls and steps, these three being Kakaralli, Wamara and Tauroniro.*—GyC (76.02.02, p.13) [< BAED Arawak *tauarañro* 'a tree with hard wood']

taw (tar) [tɒ ~ ta·] *n* (CarA) **1.** The largest marble shot by children in a game of pitching marbles. **2.** A seed used by boys in place of a marble. **a.** *This is a lucky tar. I will win all your marbles with it.*—(Tbgo) **b.** *'I have a bigger taw than yours,'* said the little boy.—DGF:62 [Cp OED2 *taw* sb² a. 'a large choice or fancy marble, often streaked or variegated, being that with wh the player shoots'. Also similarly EDD *taw* sb¹ in Sc, Irel, Eng and Amer; also *taa* Sc; *tar* Nhb]

ta·wa ['ta·wɒ] *n* (Guyn, Trin) [Indic] ‖ BAKING-IRON (Trin) *'Clean the tawa good' she said 'before you start to make the roti'.*—Trin (Ms, 1975) [Hin *tavaa ~ tawaa* 'an iron plate for baking bread']

tax·i *n* (USVI) Any four-wheeled vehicle, except for heavy duty vehicles like tractors. *He come up here wid a big ole taxi wha[t] could carry [a]bout twenty passenger(s).*—(USVI)

tax·i e·le·ven /ııı2'2/ [taksi i'lεvn] *n phr* (Baha) [*AF—Joc*] 1. A person's two legs. [By *Joc* metaph, the figure 11 being seen as a caricature representation of two legs] 2. PHRASE 2.1 **catch taxi eleven** *vb phr* (Baha) [*AF—Joc*] To go on foot; to walk.

ta·ya *n* (Jmca) ‖ TANNIA (CarA) [The orig Tupi/ Guarani name, now 'chiefly dial' pronunc in *Jmca* (*DJE*)]

tay·bay ['tebe] *n* (Gren) [*AF*] 1. Confusion. 2. PHRASE 2.1 **have/make taybay** *vb phr* (Gren) [*AF*] To cause confusion.

ta·zia *n* (Trin) See TADJAH

T.C. *abbr* (Trin & Tbgo) The Trinity Cross Medal of the Order of the Trinity, a gold medal awarded as a national honour for distinguished and meritorious service to Trin & Tbgo or for gallantry beyond the call of duty; it is the highest national award, and the letters are placed after the recipient's name. [From the Trinity Hill from wh Trinidad received its Sp name]

tea *n* (CarA) 1. [Often among older people, esp in the rural Caribbean] The first meal of the day; breakfast. *Me drink me tea w[h]en me cum back fram de mountin an den cum school.*—(StKt) 2. Any hot drink or beverage. *Speaking of 'roses'; it is true of most of the Bahamas, and not only Bain Town, that any flower was a 'rose', and any hot drink was 'tea'.*—EBT:12 [From the plantation practice of taking a hot drink before sunrise to start the day's work, the first solid meal being delayed until the first break] □ See also BUSH-TEA, CHOCOLATE-TEA, COCOA-TEA, COFFEE-TEA, GREEN-TEA. 3. PHRASE 3.1 **tea, breakfast, and dinner** *n phr* (CarA) The three main meals of the day. □ The phr is used by older folk. See sense 1.

tea-grass *n* (TkCa) ‖ FEVER-GRASS (CarA)

tea-meet·ing *n* (CarA) A lengthy, night-time, social function, esp of former times, consisting of musical and other staged entertainment, prominently featuring competitive items of grandiloquent speech-making, often with artificially invented words and spurious learned references; the entertainment is followed by much eating and drinking, the function being usu held during a festive season to raise funds for a church or a community organization. [Cp *OED tea* 8. c. Special Combs ... *tea-meeting* 'a public social meeting (usu in connexion with a religious organization) at wh tea is taken'; + cit 1897. The CE sense is much extended]

teen (tee·ny) *n* (Nevs, StKt) ‖ MANGO TEEN (Dmca, etc)

teeth [ti:t ~ ti:f ~ tie] *n pl* (CarA) [Used also as *sg* in *AF* CE] PHRASES 1. **hiss your teeth** *vb phr* (Jmca, Tbgo) See HISS Phr 2. **not pick your teeth** *vb phr* (Angu, Bdos, Guyn, Tbgo) [*AF*] See PICK Phr 5.2 3. **pick your teeth to/with (sb)** *vb phr* (Bdos) [*AF*] See PICK Phr 5.11 4. **skin your teeth** *vb phr* (CarA) [*AF—Derog*] See SKIN² Phr 4.4 5. **suck your teeth (at/on sb)** *vb phr* (CarA) See SUCK Phr 3. 6. **unpick your teeth** *vb phr* (Bdos, Trin) [*AF*] See UNPICK Phr 7. **when fowl(-cock) cut/get teeth** *id phr* (Belz, BrVi, Guyn) [*AF—Cr/Joc*] See FOWL Phr 2.3

tek *vb* (CarA) [*AF—Cr*] 1. Take. a. *'But', the man say, 'we going want some money. I tell you what: let us tek up a collection here right now.'*—CISH:15 b. *Me couldn't tek di sore no more for dem used to tease me bout it at school.*—SSLG:9 [A prob survival in CE of E dial pronunc and spelling. Cp *EDD take* 1. Pres. t. (15) *teck* (Cum, Lan, etc) (18) *tek* (Cum, Yks, Lan, Not, etc) 'Tek my word for it', etc 2. Preterite (18) Tek (Yks)] □ A dial spelling much used in narrative dialogue. See TAKE. Cp similarly KETCH, MEK. 2. PHRASE 2.1 **Tek da!** (Guyn) See TAKE Phr 13.

tel·e·phone *n* PHRASE **the telephone wants you** *id phr* (Bdos, Guyn) See WANT Phr 4.2

tell PHRASES 1. **tell sb good morning/hello/ howdy (etc)** *vb phr* (CarA) [*IF*] To say good morning (etc) to sb; to greet or send a greeting to sb. *Now, then, Johnny, you know how our parish people like to tell howdy to one another.*—RND: 24 2. **tell sb say** *vb phr* (CarA) [*AF—Cr*] To tell, say to sb. *Anyway, Sophie talk with the fella and he tell her say that he was ga come to her place the morning dead early.*—NaG (78.06.01, Satirically Speaking) [< SE *tell* + SAY³ by *AF—Cr* infl] 3. **to tell (you the) truth** *disjunctive phr* (CarA) [*IF*] [In downtoning contexts] In fact; (SE) truth to say. a. *I didn't give him all the money because, to tell you the truth, I don't trust him.*—(Guyn) b. *Now the position have Moses uneasy, because to tell truth most of the fellars who coming now are real hustlers, desperate.*—STLL:8 [Perh from IrE infl. See TRUTH Phr 2.] 4. **When I tell you!** *id phr, emphasizer adjunct* (Gren, Guyn, Tbgo, Trin) [*IF*] See WHEN Phr 3.4

ten PHRASES 1. **cock/chop/cut ten** *vb phr* (Belz, Guyn, Jmca) [*AF—Joc*] See COCK² Phr 3.4 2. **One from ten leaves nought!** *catch phr* (CarA) [*IF—Joc*] See ONE¹ Phr 3. 3. **Ten, ten, the Bible ten!** *excl phr* (Baha) [*IF*] See cit. *Individuals repeat 'Ten, Ten, the Bible Ten' usually when passing cemeteries (especially at nights), but it can also be used for protection against being 'hagged' by a 'sperrid' any time. For example, suppose a person is sleeping and suddenly awakens, believing that a 'sperrid' is in the house ... immediately the person would quickly repeat 'Ten, Ten the Bible Ten!'*—MTTBT:6 [By misascription, as 'Ten', of the Christian symbol X representing Christ's cross, and used as abbr for *Christ* as in Xmas]

te·nant·ry /ı'ı2/ n (Bdos) [Hist] A group of CHATTEL HOUSES owned by people who worked on sugar plantations and who were legally allowed tenancy of the land on wh their houses stood; [by extension] such a set of houses owned, on leased land, by the descendants of the original owners. *I happen to be counsel for a tenantry owner. I like to think that it is a well run tenantry. I like to think that the owner is an enlightened landlord, willing to sell spots to his tenants, anxious to put in roads and eager to accommodate and so on.*—Bdos (Hd, 76.08.04, p.7162) □ Socially stigmatized (in *Bdos*) because of its association with conditions existing from the era of slavery.

tend *vb* 1. (CarA) [*AF*] To attend, pay attention to; to visit. *A only 'tend ta show ma face / Fa de family ta see.*—WIE:40 [Aphetic form < SE *attend* found widely in Eng and Amer dial usage. See *EDD* TEND v[1] 1. 'to attend to, look after, take care of; frequently with to' + cits. See also *DAE* TEND vb 1. 'to tend out (on), to attend' 2. 'to tend to business, to pay attention to one's own affairs, or to an immediate task'] 2. *PHRASES* **2.1 tend a/the doctor** *vb phr* (Bdos) [*X*] To visit a/the doctor; to seek the attention, service of a doctor. *When she had she lame foot, she had to tend de doctor a long time.*—(Bdos) [By misascription. Cp 'to attend church'] **2.2 tend to (sb)** *vb phr* (Bdos, Guyn) [*AF*] **(i)** [Of a seller, waiter, etc] To serve, wait on (sb); to attend to the needs of (sb). **(ii)** [By extension] To beat up (sb); to settle accounts with (sb). *He said 'If you only set foot in my yard I going tend to your ass.'*—Bdos (CR, 71.05.10) □ AmE *to take care of sb* similarly used.

ten·e·ment *n* (Guyn) ‖ BARRACK (Trin) *No one who seriously cares for the welfare of those unfortunates who must make their homes in tenements, or rooming-houses ... could agree that the already moderate specifications stipulated by the By-Laws and Regulations should be further narrowed down.*—DaC (53.04.09, p.2) [Cp *OED tenement* 4. b. 'In Scotland, ... a large house constructed or adapted to be let in portions to a number of tenants ... Called also a *tenement of houses*] □ In *Guyn* the word applies to a dwelling of very low social status, unlike the sense in IAE. See also next.

ten·e·ment-house/-room *n* (Guyn) ‖ BARRACK-HOUSE/-ROOM (Trin) *It was a shabby building in a shabby neighbourhood ... / In the back-yard stood a tenement-house of about five or six rooms—a dilapidated-looking place that must teem with vermin. A family of six or eight probably occupied each room.*—MLDS:63

ten·e·ment-yard *n* (Guyn) ‖ BARRACK-YARD (Trin) *If people at the standpipe in the tenement yard are cussed and quarrelsome conditions have made them so.*—SNWIC:254

ten·ga·leh ['tɛŋgalɛ] *n* (Guyn) ‖ BITER (Baha) [Prob of Afr or Amerindian origin]

ten·gre [tɛŋgrɛ] *n, adj* (Jmca) [*AF—Cr*] Stingray. *Then after this I must go in before the Queen's fat Commissioners, cool in their silk suits, and bow and say: Pray Your Honours, in duty bound—and all the while my fingers itch to send a tengre lance clear through their bellies to their behinds?*—RND: 181 [< *sting-ray* with /s-/ loss by aphaeresis]

ten·nis roll /ı12'/ *n phr* (Dmca, Guyn) A small, sweet roll of bread of light texture. [Perh from resemblance to a tennis ball]

ten·or-bass (ten·or-boom) [tɛnə-bes] *n* (ECar) [Steelband] A set of four linked PANS the surface of each of wh is sunk to a less shallow depth than the BASS-PANS and grooved to provide together a range of notes pitched above the bass but lower than the CELLO-PANS; each PAN uses a whole oil-drum.

ten·or-pan *n* (ECar) ‖ LEAD-PAN (Trin) *He was interested in giving the ping pong or tenor pan the leading role in the orchestra, since steelbands had grown to sometimes a hundred or more pans and the lead pan was not heard in some parts of the band.*—JWSSS:29 [From its high pitch]

ten·pen·ny-nail *n* (Bdos, Jmca) See SIX-PENNY-NAIL

ten-pound·er* *n* (Antg, Brbu, Mrat, Nevs) A very bony, silverish-grey fish wh grows to about 6 to 10 lbs in weight and is of moderate food value; *Elopidae spp.*

ten·sil *n* (Antg, StVn, Trin, USVI) [*AF*] ‖ U-TENSIL (Bdos, Guyn) [< *utensil* by aphesis]

tent *n* (CarA) The venue where calypsoes are performed nightly in the period before CAR-NIVAL, CROP-OVER, or equivalent cultural festival. [Because these performances were originally held in bamboo tents]

tent-boat *n* (Guyn) A wooden, keel-bottomed, river boat about 30 ft long, fitted with a raised covering or 'tent'; it is used for long-haul transportation of passengers and goods in the hinterland rivers of Guyana.

test (tess) *n* (Trin) [*AF—Joc*] A person; a fellow or a woman. **a.** *... and don't name me but I think they catch his wife with two tests up the beach.*—FCV2:208 (D. Walcott) **b.** *Them tesses in the offices they does hardly work at all, they does only walk around the streets in tight, tight skirts an' sit at a typewriter an' you should see the salary the people drawing.*—JPB:129 □ Now rare in speech, found mostly in dialogue in literature.

tèt (tête) [tɛt] *n* (Dmca, StLu) (Used in ref to) a particular style of tying the coloured headkerchief as part of a festive costume; hence many types: *tête-calenda, -en-l'air, -fan, -français, -jamette*, etc. *She was neatness itself, and while she wore a simple 'tete marée' during the week, on Sundays her extravagant outfits were* *usually topped by that masterpiece of Creole dress, the 'tete en l'air calendrée', a saffron tinted mouchoir shaped like a turban with a solitary peak on the forehead.*—SDD:26 (M.A. Caudeiron)

tèt-chien (tête-chien) [tɛt-šiɛ̃] *n* (Dmca, StLu, Trin) A black, non-poisonous snake about 6 ft long, with a flat head shaped like a dog's (hence the name); it is of the boa family and swallows rats; *Constrictor orophias (Boidae). The best known is the Tete Chien or boa which may grow up to 2 metres. This snake, contrary to local belief, is not deadly and can be beneficial since it keeps down the rodent population.*—HDNPW:11 [Fr Cr < Fr *tête* + *chien*, 'dog head'] □ This snake is sometimes confused with a larger species *Constrictor constrictor*, the ANACONDA.

te·te (teh-teh) [tɛtɛ] *n* (Guyn, StVn) [AF] A bacterial skin disease (usu of the feet) causing painful, itchy sores; it is said to be caused by walking in dirty water. [Cp *OED tetter* 'a general term for any pustular eruption of the skin'. Also *BAED* Arawak *tete* adj 'itchy']

té·té plum [tete plʌm] *n phr* (Gren) ‖ JAMAICA PLUM (Bdos, etc) [< Fr Cr *tété* 'breast', from the shape of the plum. Cp ‖ *bubby plum*]

te·yer (palm)* /1'12/ [teyə pam] *n (phr)* (ViIs) A slender variety of the SILVER-THATCH; *Coccothrinax argentea (Palmae-Phoenicaceae).*

-th- (CarA) **1.** [θ] (as in SE *with, within, thing*) □ (i) The sound [θ] represented by this SE spelling is widely replaced in CE by [t], hence [tɪŋ] 'thing', [wɪtɪn] 'within', [wɪt] 'with'. Where the contrast is essential to meaning but is lost because of this feature, ex *thin* vs *tin*, *booth* vs *boot*, etc, the meaning has to be recovered by context or physical reference or by an expanded statement, ex *Tin is too tin, A mean too weak—you need a piece o[f] galvanize* 'Tin is too thin, I mean too weak, —you need a piece of galvanized iron'. (ii) The same sound is, though less frequently, also replaced by [f] esp in *Bdos* hence [fɪŋ] 'thing', / Braffit/ 'Brathwaite', [fef, truf] 'faith, truth'; also in Dmca BRAF 'broth'. This occurs more often when [θ] is in final position. **2.** [ð] (as in SE *breathe, brother, that*) □ The sound [ð] represented by this SE spelling is widely replaced in CE by [d], hence [brid] 'breathe', [brʌdə] 'brother', [dat] 'that'. Where the contrast is essential to meaning but is threatened because of this feature, ex *breathe* vs *breed*, *breather* vs *breeder*, *there* vs *dear, dare*, etc the meaning has again to be recovered by the processes stated at 1. above.

than *comparative subordinator* (CarA) [X] [With ellipsis of the prec comparative] Rather than. **a.** *Many Belizeans are prepared to die than continue suffering under them.*—BeA (81.04.25, p.3) **b.** *A Micoud man who prefers to go to prison than pay a fine of $5 and $5 costs, for beating his wife, will serve a sentence of 14 days imprisonment.*—VoS

(65.09.29, p.5) [As *OED2* THAN 3. a. Obs + cits-'1648]

that (dat) (CarA) [IF] **1.** *demonstrative pron* [Sometimes used without implying distance] The one (i.e. thing or person) that is here, there; this. **a.** *Seller: Which you want? / Buyer: That you see I holdin[g] here.*—(Guyn) **b.** *S1: (on telephone): Who is it speaking please? / S2: That's the maid please. I could take a message for the madam.*—(Dmca) **2.** *rel pron* (Replacing SE) who, whom, whose. **a.** *It's the same Haynes that you-all won't vote for that is giving you the answers now.*—(Bdos) **b.** *The one that the husband gone away, well she that said so.*—(Guyn) [By AF—Cr use of da[t]; prob also via IrE. Cp 'He looks like a man that there would be no money in his pocket'; 'there's a man that his wife leaves him whenever she pleases.' / These phrases and the like are heard all through the middle of Ireland, and indeed outside the middle: they are translations from Irish—*JESI:*52] **3.** PHRASES **3.1 Go with that!** *imper vb phr* (Nevs, StKt) See GO Phr 6.34.2 □ Purely emotive, non-demonstrative sense. Also next. **3.2 Take that!** *imper vb phr* (Guyn) See TAKE Phr 13.

thatch* *n* (Baha, CayI, Jmca, StKt) ‖ *cane-lily* (Bdos) ‖ *ping-wing* (Bdos, Jmca) ‖ *screw-pine* (Dmca, Tbgo, Trin) ‖ *wild-pine* (Gren) Name given to more than one type of palm and also to one or two big cane-like shrubs with long, blade-like, coloured leaves wh all have in common the use of their dried leaves for thatching roofs, and also for handcrafted straw-work; *Bromelia pinguin (Bromeliaceae)*, also *Pandanus spp*, also *Thrinax argentea (Palmae)*, etc. □ See ‖ names for some differences. There are also varieties of THATCH: *big-thatch* (StKt), SILVER THATCH (Baha), *white thatch* (StKt), etc.

thatch·ber·ry(-palm)* *n* (Baha) A palm tree of medium height bearing clusters of edible BERRIES and with large fan-like leaves used for thatching roofs; *Thrinax argentea (Palmae)*. (See BERRY 1. (Baha)).

thatch palm* /1'2/ [θač pam] *n phr* (Baha, Guyn) ‖ *troolie* (Guyn) A species of palm wh grows to a height of about 12–14 ft and has low spreading leaves; it is often used in construction to thatch both the roofs and the walls of houses, hence the name; *Thrinax microcarpa, T. parviflora (Palmae)*.

The[1] *determiner* (CarA) [With capital] Part of the official title of several Caribbean states (though often omitted): The Bahamas; The British Virgin Islands; The Commonwealth of Dominica; (The Federation of) The West Indies; The (St Vincent) Grenadines. □ The early historical name of Barbados was The Barbadoes.

the[2] /ði ~ dɪ/ *determiner* **1.** (CarA) [IF] (Replacing possessive pron before a relation) My/ his/your, etc brother/sister/mother/wife, etc. **a.** *S1: ... And how's the wife? / S2: Oh the wife is* *fine thanks.*—(Bdos) **b.** *While the mother was sick they stayed with the aunt* (= ... *their mother ... their aunt*).—(Guyn) [Cp *EDD* the II. 1. dem. adj. Used instead of the possessive pron 'my, his, their' etc, esp in phr *the wife* + cits from Sc, Mun, Nhb, Yks] □ See also DE¹. Note that variant pronunc /di/ occurs commonly in educated speech. **2.** (CarA) [*AF—Derog*] [Before a name, implying contempt] **a.** *He told muh dear-aunt not to worry, the Affie Cumberbatch was as good as dead.*—MBGB:62 **b.** *Whenever the police tried to bring a stop to the madness H— stopped them. The Editor of the 'Workers Voice' was accosted by one 'Pussy' under the eyes of the Donald H— and the police and nothing came of it.*—WoV (72.04.26, p.4) [Poss by infl of W Afr langs. Cp Edo *nene*, 'the said' preceding a name to imply vexation (*pers info, A. Amayo*)] **3.** (Guyn) [*AF—Cr*] [In emphasizing action of a vb] As soon as (sth happened ...). **a.** *The come you come you start trouble* (= *As soon as you come you cause trouble*).—(Guyn) **b.** *Wid de open he open dat door she hit* [*h*]*im one lash wid a stick* (= *As soon as he opened the door* ...).—(Guyn) [Cp Yoruba *Ṣiṣi ti o ṣi ilẹkun* ... *'Opening which he open door* ...' in same context, the vb being front-focused and nominalized (*pers info, A. Banjo*] **4.** PHRASE **4.1 get the rid of sb/sth** *vb phr* (Bdos, Guyn) See GET Phr 3.21

the·a·tre [θieta~tieta)] *n* (Guyn, Jmca, Trin) A cinema. □ This is the most widely understood sense of the word. □ Also known in AmE.

their own /2′1/ *pron phr* (CarA) [*IF*] [In absolute function] Theirs. (See OWN). *The spade belongs to us but the fork is their own.*—(Bdos) □ Distinguished by pitch and stress from *their own* /12′/, possessive adj. Also often rendered as *dey own* /2′1/ [AF—Cr].

their·self; **their.selves** *refl pers pron pl* (CarA) [*IF*] Themselves. **a.** *They tell him that them people wasn't ga tell them nothing what they didn't know before, so they stay on the wall with their plait hair 'rapping' to theirself.*—NaG (75.03.06, p.2, Satirically Speaking) **b.** *And they feel to theirselves I mamaguying she.*—SCTR:39 [Cp *CSD* Sc *theirsel* (late 18C), *theirsels* (late 16C) 'themselves'. Also *EDD theirselves*. In gen dial use in Sc, Irel, and Eng] □ The CE spellings are formalized representations of DEYSELF (See DEMSELF).

them¹ *pers pron pl* (CarA) [*AF*] **1.** [As subj] They. **a.** *Them write say dem coming home for Christmas. I feel there is one or two things I have to tell them before them land.*—WeG (72.12.06, p.12, Partyline) **b.** *How are the yams? I ask an honest trader with whom I have been doing business for 20 years. My old friend refuses to commit herself any further than to say, 'Well, all I can tell you is them cooking white.'*—SuS (87.11.15, p.6) [< *CarA* Cr pron system. See DEM¹ 2. However, note also poss reinforcement from dial Eng, as *OED them* 3.3 'used for the nominative *they* + cits 1901; also *EDD them* 2. + cits from

Yks, etc] **2.** [As possessive] Their. *February, March and April may welcome the bailiff to take them away 'cause like the government, them can't pay them bills.*—AdV (89.12.24, p.15) [Usu a written refinement of CarA Cr DEM¹ 3.] **3.** [Functioning as sg] [*AF—Joc*] [Often of a young person] Him; her. *I see them passin*[g] *he*[*re*] *yesterday* [*u*]*pon a new bicycle*—Guyn [Perh a *Joc* imitation of Cr usage] □ Cp THEY 4(ii)

them² *demonstr adj* (CarA) [*AF*] ∥ **dem**¹ 4. (CarA) **1.** Those. **a.** *You said 'It had Policemen around and if them policemen don't want to say who do it I ent saying too'.*—ToR (78.06.25, p.1) **b.** *I would have put in a call to my daddyo and told him that I was dying to come home and I didn't want to spend any night or two or three in lousy old Jamaica where them Rastas live.*—BoM (74.09.13, p.3) **c.** *'See what I tell you about them bandits!' shouted one of the Beekeepers. 'They seized our letters for two months and seized all our telegrams to Garvin.'*—ReP (80.05.04, p.7) [Prob by Eng dial infl. Cp *EDD them* 7. dem adj 'those' + cits from Sc, Irel, Eng, and Amer] **2.** PHRASE **2.1 them so** *demonstr pron phr* (Bdos, Gren, Guyn, Trin) [*AF*] People of that kind, type. *Yuh mother and them so can do anything they put their mind to.*—MBGB:69 [See SO²]

them³ *post-nominal pl marker* (CarA) [*AF*] **1.** ∥ DEM² (CarA) **a.** *The 'brethers and sisters them' from Fox Hill might have been travelling all the morning, but when they formed for the procession, they were as splendidly bedecked as their Bain Town cousins.*—EBT:32 **b.** *We got a van waiting to take him, and the police-them send for more men.*—SPOC:153 **c.** *'Make you'self useful for a change an' 'elp me clean the knife an' fork them,' she said.*—SJS:47 [A refinement, mostly in written narrative, of CarA Cr DEM²] □ In both this usage and that of the foll phr, the function of THEM as pl marker has become redundant. **2.** PHRASE **2.1. and them** *post-nominal collectivizing phr* (CarA) [*IF/AF*] ∥ AND DEM (Bdos) See DEM² Phr 2.1. *Perhaps if my mother and them could see them they'd stop taking on so about a few old musty brownstones.*—MBGB:177

them·self *refl pers pron* (CarA) [*IF*] ∥ DEMSELF (CarA) **1.** *pl* *You know how them Chinee is, ... how they employ only Chinee like themself in their shop, all you know dat.*—MBF:123 **2.** *sg* *Girl, everybody lookin*[g] *out for themself, and I must look out for myself too*—Guyn). [See etym note at DEMSELF 1]

there¹ *adv* **1.** In that place. **2.** PHRASES **2.1 in there** *n phr* (CarA) [*X*] See IN¹ Phr 5.8 *In there is hot, they shouldn't make in there a waiting room.*—(StVn) **2.2 Look/See her (him/it/them, etc) there!** *id phrs* (CarA) [*IF*] See LOOK Phr 4.5 **2.3 you see her/him/them there** *id phrs* (CarA) [*IF*] That's how she (he/they) is/are although she (etc) may not look it. Cp YOU SEE ME HERE. See HERE¹ Phr 2.

there[2] *n* (CarA) [X] **1.** That place. *There is not a good place to put plants.*—(Antg) [In many Niger-Congo Afr langs the locative adv for 'there' derives from or coincides with n (phr) 'that place'. Cp Twi ɛhɔ, pron 'of place' as well as adv 'there'. See notes at HERE[2] n] **2.** PHRASE **2.1 there so (de-so)** /2'1/ [ðer so ~ de-so] *adv phr* (CarA) [IF] Over there; yonder; thereabouts. *Witness: 'Sir one by the name of 'Precious' L. S—, come out from a corner, the one right down there so (pointing to accused No. 1) after he come from the corner he had his hand behind his back'.*—ToR (77.03.23, p.6) [Cp *ya so* (Guyn Cr) where the addition of 'so' helps to determine the spot. CE *there so* is a refinement of Cr *de-so*]

there[3] PHRASE **there have** *existential introductory phr* (StLu) [X] ‖ THEY HAVE (CarA) See THEY Phr 1. *Montout say to me that there have some things a man must not inquire, and I say okay.*—WMHC:27

they *3rd pers pl pron* (CarA) [IF/AF] PHRASES [In impersonal functions] **1. they have/had** *existential introductory phrs* (CarA) There is/was/were. **a.** *They have many women too who prefer the company of other women but they too are ashamed to come out in the open.*—ExP (72.10.27, p.16) **b.** *They had a lot of rain last night, eh?* —(Guyn) **2. they are/were/can be, will be, etc/have been, etc** *existential introductory phrs* (Bdos) [X] There are/were/can be, will be, etc/ have been, etc. **a.** *But that's just the beginning of the festivities planned for the Independence weekend. So look out now they are gay times ahead.*— AdV (71.11.16, p.7) **b.** *In January 1971 they were 97 acres of cane burnt.*—Bdos (Ms) **c.** *He is the man who the taximen say must go ... or they'll be a total boycott.*—NaT (74.03.03, p.1) **d.** *If they had not been an argument on a simple thing like a title, ... the member for St Michael West would not have been able to come back and tell us that constitutional changes were taking place.*— Bdos (Hd, 74.08.27, p.3905) **e.** *I think the ministers identified, for instance, that they could be new initiatives in the areas of tourism which are not specifically under the CBI arrangements.*—AdV (87.01.16, p.1) [By extension of sense 1. reinforced by confusion of pronunc of *they/there*] □ This is a very common erron structure in *Bdos*. **3. they have it to say** *id phr* (CarA) [IF] It is said. **a.** *They have it to say that he kept his intentions of migrating secret.*—(Guyn) **b.** *Brackley hail from Tobago, which part they have it to say Robinson Crusoe used to hang out with Man Friday.*—RWIN:100 (S. Selvon) **4.** [Functioning as sg] **(i)** [IF] He or she. *Anybody who t[h]ink they could beat me le[t] dem try*—(Bdos) **(ii)** [AF—Joc] [Often of young persons] He; she. *They look like they like you, boy. They dress off in a new dress and lookin[g] in when they passin[g]* —(Trin).

they·self(s) [ðɛsɛlf ~ dɛsɛlf(s)] *refl pron* (CarA) [AF—Cr] Themselves. **a.** *... and the man in the brown suit walking 'round seeing that everybody all right and enjoying theyself.*—CISH:17 **b.** *I*

only givin' them a little rope to hang theyselfs with, but when I move I bet you all this damn foolishness come to a full stop.—JJM:46 [Cp *EDD* they-sel(ves)* refl pron 'themselves' Nrf, Dor, Dev, Amer] □ See also DEMSELF.

thib·bet [θɪbɛt ~ tɪbɛt] *n* (USVI) ‖ WOMAN TONGUE (TREE) (CarA)

thick *adj* (Gren, Guyn, Trin) [AF—Vul] [Of a woman] Buxom; sexually attractive about the bust, hips, and legs. [Cp *EDD* thick 3. Sc 'short, squat, thick-set'. Perh an extension of this]

thick-leaf thyme* /1'21/ *n phr* (Bdos, Guyn) ‖ **broad-leaf thyme** (Bdos, Guyn) ‖ **French thyme, thicky thyme** (StVn) An erect, branching, aromatic herb wh grows to a height of about 1 ft; it has succulent stems and soft, thick, heart-shaped, tooth-edged leaves wh are widely used for seasoning food; *Coleus amboinicus* (Labiatae).

t[h]ief [ti:f] *vb tr* (CarA) [AF—Cr] To steal. **a.** *Thief from thief, child, does make Jehovah laugh. An' I is only a mere mortal. It serve him right. The way he robbing we here with the rent on these nasty little rooms. Every damn night somebody should go in there and carry way something.*— JMRS:32 **b.** *When black man t'ief him t'ief half-a-bit, when backra t'ief him t'ief whole estate.*—SWI:143 (Prov) [By functional n > vb shift of SE *thief* n]

t[h]ief·in[g][1] [tifɪm] /2'1/ *vbl n* (CarA) [AF—Cr] Stealing; thievery. *To use the creolese, there is too much thiefing in this country. No purpose is served in sweeping it under the carpet. Let us proclaim it and then set about to stop it.*—SuC (78.07.23, p.8) [< CarA Cr THIEF vb + *ing*]

t[h]ief·in[g][2] /1'2/ [tifɪm] *adj* (CarA) [AF—Cr] Given to stealing; thievish; thieving. **a.** *Maude, you still there, soul it looks like I got to go at the station house girl, a real tiefin neighbour name Joe Clarke live gainst uh me see, deed fate he hands light like a feather.*—Bdos (Ms Play, 1978) **b.** *Go away you tiefin' dog. You ca'an fool me. Not even a sly mongoose could touch me pear an' me no see.*—FDA:14 □ Note contrasting pitch patterns of adj and prec n; also strong Cr pronunc in adj sense.

thief-man *n* (Bdos, Guyn) [AF] A burglar; a robber who breaks and enters, esp by night. *I been telling you, after them fowl cocks flap the wings in the morning and make me think that thiefman was in the yard I decide to give up the fowls. I invest the money in corn instead.*— HMCH:83 □ A common term at the folk level, used to distinguish such a person from the light-fingered stealer.

t[h]ing *n* (CarA) [AF] **1.** [Used to replace a name momentarily forgotten] What's-his-name. *S1: I saw our friend, t[h]ing, on TV de other night. / S2: Yes, you mean Jackson, Arnold*

Jackson.—(Bdos) **2.** A female sexual friend; a mistress; [by extension] any woman as an object of sexual desire. *Harris feel it was up to him to ask the thing to dance, seeing like they look shy to take the floor, so he ask the girl and she hem a little then she get up.*—STLL:100 **3.** PHRASES **3.1 an[d] t[h]ing** *augmentative phrasal tag* (CarA) [*AF*] And so on; and other things of that sort; etcetera. *De lady dere sellin' her punkin an' ting on de dock an' one wite woman come 'long in er car an' aks 'er ef she get any lime an' lemon or tomater.*—JBJ:80 [Cp *OED2* thing 14. a. *and things* (colloq, unstressed); 'and the like, etcetera'. This may have reinforced W Afr calque. See AND Phr 4.9] **3.2 be in a thing (with sb)** *vb phr* (CarA) [*AF*] ‖ *have a thing going* (CarA) ‖ *keep company (with sb)* (Gren) To be involved in a sexual relationship (with sb). *One time Cap was in a thing with two women. One was a German and the other was English.*—STLL:37 **3.3 one-thing** /1′2∼2′2/ *adv (phr)* (CarA) See ONE-THING[1] *He never talks to you, one thing. He doesn't say two words to you.*—MBGB:77 □ A usu introductory emotive adjunct. **3.4 things (are) brown** *n phr* (CarA) [*AF*] Times are hard; things are difficult. *Things was brown in that island and he make for England and manage to get a work.*—RWIN:100 (S. Selvon)

thing·a·mer·ry *n* (Bdos) [*AF—Joc*] ‖ *thingamerrybob* (Antg) ‖ *thingumsmeribob* (Baha) **1.** (Casual) substitute for sb's name that is either forgotten or unimportant; (SE) thingumabob, etc. **2.** PHRASE **2.1. he, she and thingamerry** *n phr* (Bdos) ‖ HABRA, DABRA AND THE CREW (Bdos) [Cp *EDD* thingamy 'a contemptuous term for a worthless person or thing']

third depth *n phr* (Guyn) [Sugar Ind] An additional area of 250 acres further inland, granted to a plantation for sugar-cane cultivation when most of that granted as SECOND DEPTH has been used.

third gang; third class gang *n phr* (Bdos) ‖ CREOLE GANG (Guyn) *Sir, some of these workers had worked in the third gang from the age of, say, 10, and some of them might have rendered over 50 years' service.*—Bdos (Hd, 75.03.17, p.4965)

this *demonstr adj* PHRASES **1. this time** *adv phr* (CarA) [*IF*] And besides; nevertheless; notwithstanding. *He busy preachin[g] and preachin[g] [a]bout the church debt, this time the people only suckin[g] the[ir] teet[h], they don['t] bother with him.*—(Bdos) □ The phr is used to add focus and dramatic effect to a narrative. **2. this twelve o'clock** *adv phr* (Guyn) At midday today.

this·tle* *n* (StKt, ViIs) ‖ *hollyhock* (Bdos, Gren) ‖ *Mexican poppy* (Jmca, Trin) A herb of average height 2 ft with powdery, light-green, deeply lobed and spiny leaves (resembling holly leaves in shape); it bears yellow, poppy-like flowers and spiny pods and produces a yellow latex; it grows abundantly in sandy soil and the latex and leaf-juice are used as folk-medicines;

Argemone mexicana (Papaveraceae). □ Also named **Mexican thistle, yellow hollyhock, yellow thistle** in botanical literature.

Tho·ma·ni·an [to'menɪən] *n, adj* (ViIs) ‖ ST THOMIAN (ViIs) *But don't be surprised if you can't understand the conversation between Thomanians and Cruzians, because their true speech is a patois of English.*—USVI (Brochure, 1975) □ This is the less used derivative, **St Thomian** being commoner.

thorn-ap·ple* *n* (Bdos, Gren, Guyn, Trin) ‖ *devil's trumpet* (Jmca) ‖ *night shade* (Bdos) A pungent, weedy herb about 3 or 4 ft high with robust stems and coarse, irregularly lobed leaves; it bears erect, white or purplish, funnel-shaped flowers about 4 ins long with claw-like petals that open at night, and ovoid, prickly capsules that split, releasing poisonous seeds; the plant grows wild and has narcotic properties; *Datura stramonium* or *D. fastuosa (Solanaceae).* [From the prickly fruit]

thorn tree *n* (Angu) ‖ MACCA PALM (Belz, etc)

t[h]rash·er* *n* (Baha) A bird about 10 ins long, chiefly grey in colour and darker on the wings and tail; it is noted for its melodious song as well as for its gift of mimicry; *Mimus polyglottos (Mimidae).* [As *OED* thrasher[2] 'a bird of North American genus'] □ Several varieties appear to be common in *Baha.*

thread-bag *n* (Jmca) A small clothbag, tied with a string, in wh a street vendor keeps money. *After we have all exhausted the little we have mustered to knot in our 'thread bags' for 1979, let us approach 1980 with meaning and the will to survive.*—DaG (80.01.15, p.6)

three-cents [tri-sɛns] *adj* (Guyn) [*AF—Joc*] [Often after a neg] Of little account; insignificant. *Yo[u] don['t] buil[d] a house with that kin[d] o[f] finish to rent to t[h]ree-cents people.*—(Guyn) [Cp SE *penny-ha'penny*, an amount of the same value, used attrib with similar connotation]

three-foot pot *n phr* (Bdos, Guyn, Jmca, Tbgo) [*Obs*] ‖ *baking-pot* (Belz) ‖ *Dutch pot* (Baha, CayI) ‖ *Dutchy* (Jmca) ‖ *negro-pot* (Bdos, Belz, Guyn, Jmca) A large, old-fashioned, iron pot without a lid, about 2 ft in diameter at the mouth but bellying out in the middle and equipped with three handles and three legs; a cauldron. *The three-foot pot, a prized possession of old people in Tobago, is still used for ceremonies such as weddings and christenings, steaming away over a wood fire in the backyard.*—Tbgo (Ms, 1981)

throat *n* PHRASE **fly down sb's throat** *vb phr* (Guyn) [*AF*] See FLY[1] Phr 3.1

through *prep* **1.** (Baha) [*X*] [Identifying a location] In, on, at (a street, place). *He has a holiday house through Long Island.*—(Baha) **2.** PHRASE

2.1 (gone) through the eddoes id phr (Bdos) [AF—Joc] See EDDOE Phr 3.1

throw vb tr (CarA) [IF] **1.** [With water or other liquid as obj] [X] To pour (out). **a.** He threw a little soup in a bowl and offered me.—(Angu) **b.** The pot is too full, you have to throw out some of that water.—(Guyn) **2.** PHRASES **2.1 throw a cuff at sb** vb phr (CarA) See CUFF[1] Phr 2.1 **2.2 throw a lash/(the) lashes** vb phr (CarA) [IF] See LASH[2] Phr 2.3 **2.3 throw a tackle** vb phr (Guyn) [AF] See TACKLE[2] **2.4 throw away** vb phr (CarA) [X] [Of a liquid] To spill. Some milk threw away on the floor, now who could have thrown it away?—(Guyn) **2.4.1 throw away belly/a baby/a child** vb phrs (CarA) [AF/IF] To bring about an abortion; to throw away a foetus. His sister-in-law gave his wife something to drink to 'throw away a baby' she was making, and which eventually caused her death.—TrG (73.03.19, p.7) **2.5 throw box** vb phr (Guyn) [IF] ‖ **throw pardner** (Jmca) To participate in a folk savings scheme called a BOX. (See SUSU.) And when it is borne in mind that ... there are friendly societies in existence and what is known locally as the practice of 'throwing box' among the people, no other refutation of what His Excellency was told need be recounted.—DaC (52.07.29, p.2) **2.6 throw cuffum** vb phr (Guyn) See CUFFIN Phr **2.7 throw long-eye on sth** vb phr (Trin) [AF] ‖ PUT YOUR EYE ON STH (Bdos, etc) **2.8 throw remarks** vb phr (CarA) See DROP[1] Phr 3.8 **2.9 throw (some) cuss in sb** vb phr (CarA) [AF] See CUSS[1] Phr 4.1 **2.10 throw (some) licks in sb's skin/tail** vb phr (Bdos) [AF] See LICK[2] Phr 3.8

throw-net n (StLu) ‖ CAST-NET (CarA)

thrush n (Guyn) ‖ RAIN-BIRD[1] (CarA) 1.

ti·bi·si·ri [tɪbɪsiri] n (Guyn) A sturdy fibre made from strands of the young leaves of the ITE PALM wh have been boiled, dried, and twisted into strings; it is used by Amerindians for making hammocks and other domestic items. [Arawak name. See IAIG:283]

tick-bird n phr **1.** (Jmca) ‖ JUMBIE-BIRD 3. (Guyn) In Jamaica ... widely known as the Blackbird and sometimes as the tick-bird. / [Crotophaga ani] is often seen with cattle searching for ticks on their bodies and this is the origin of one of its local names.—TIBJ:11, 12 **2.** (Trin) ‖ CATTLE-EGRET (Bdos, etc) [From this bird's habit of feeding on ticks on the bodies of cattle]

tick·i-tick·i /1'122/ [tɪki-tɪki] n (Jmca) [IF] A tiny fish caught in shoals and fried in bulk. My brother caught crayfish and 'ticki-ticki' and plunged naked in the deeper water with his friends.—GBFBM:10 [Cp Ewe tikitiki, 'crowded, thronging'. See DJE]

tick·ler n (Baha) See BULLY

ticks[1] n pl PHRASE **be behind sb like ticks** vb phr (Jmca, Tbgo) [AF] ‖ BE BEHIND SB LIKE A SLAVE-DRIVER (CarA) See BEHIND[1] Phr 2.

ticks[2] vb tr (Jmca) [AF—Cr] To plague or pester sb like ticks (cp the phr under TICKS[1]). Because him like me off him jus[t] a-ticks me to go out wit[h] [h]im.—(Jmca) [Functional shift n > vb]

tie vb tr (CarA) **1.** [Occultism] To bewitch (esp a man as a husband or lover); to bind (sb) with a spell or love charm (often sth put in food). ... 'cause de singing-crying sound getting stronger an' stronger sinking deeper an' deeper in dem soul an' tie dem lek when woman tie man fo' married an' he can't leave even if she giving he hell.—FGSOS: 37 [Cp ADMY Yoruba di, de, (1) 'to tie' with subsense (o) 'to bewitch, use magic against (sb)'] **2.** (Tbgo) [By extension] To harm the proper functioning of (sb else's farming tool, boat, etc) by casting a magic spell on it. A boat that has been tied by an enemy cannot move fast enough on the water no matter how hard the crew is rowing.—EFOT:41 **3.** PHRASES **3.1 cannot tie bundle** neg vb phr (Guyn) [AF] Be unable to work harmoniously together; [by extension] be unable to settle differences. If the secretary and the President can['t] tie bundle and every meetin[g] is a row, one of them will have to go or the union will suffer.—(Guyn) **3.2 foot is tied** id phr (Guyn, Trin) [AF—Joc] See FOOT Phr 2.5 **3.3 tie a lougawou, ole higue, etc** (ECar) To catch a LOUGAWOU, an OLE HIGUE, etc by some special practice (see cit). There is only one way to tie a lougawou, any 'loupgarou', and that is by putting sand in front of your door; or, if you catch him with his skin off, look under the nearest mortar where the skin ought to be, take it out and season it lavishly with salt, pepper and garlic.—ToR (73.07.08, p.4) **3.4 tie up (sb, esp a male)** vb phr (CarA) [AF/IF—Joc] To infatuate (sb); to catch (sb's) affection; [by extension] to secure (a partner's) sexual loyalty. **a.** She dress off and go out with him a couple o[f] times and it look like she really got him tie up now, he ringin[g] her every day.—(Guyn) **b.** Don't bring that damn nonsense to me. I'm a big man. Not no damn little boy, ready to get myself tie-up the minute some woman tell me she makin' child. So if that is the plan yer hatch to ketch me—This is one big boy that sorry. That plan ent go work at all.—JMRS:54 [A modification of sense 1.] **3.4.1 tie (up) your mouth** vb phr (CarA) [IF] [Of acid, gummy, or unripe fruit] To cause an uncomfortable, astringent feeling in the mouth after eating. Clammy cherry does tie up your mouth if you eat it.—(Bdos) **3.5 tie your belly/guts/waist** vb phr (CarA) [IF] See BELLY Phr 3.26(i)

tie-head n (Bdos) [AF—Joc/Derog] A member of the Spiritual Baptist Church, the female members of wh tie their heads in white scarves, hence the name. Miss Charles is said to be a member of the sons of God Apostolic Spiritual Baptist Church, familiarly known as 'The Tie Heads'.—AdN (76.12.09, p.1)

tie-tongue *n, adj* (CarA) [*AF—Derog*] **1.** A speech impediment; (SE) tongue-tie. **2.** *adj* Having such an impediment. *His act always brought down the house because he had this tie-tongue lisp with a Syrian accent and nothing stopped him.*—BoM (75.01.17, p.11)

tight *adj* PHRASE **hand is tight** *id phr* (CarA) [*IF*] See HAND¹ Phr 4.13

ti·ka *n* (Guyn, Trin) [Indic] **1.** A ceremonial red mark made with the thumb in the middle of the forehead of a Hindu priest, upwards from the cleft of the eyebrows; it is also applied as a blessing to a bridegroom or other person on a devotional occasion. **2.** A red dot, made with SINDOOR or sandalwood paste, placed in the middle of a married Hindu woman's forehead during her husband's life-time. **3.** A black dot placed in the middle of a young child's forehead and meant to ward off evil. [Hin *tiikaa*, name of this mark]

ti·ki·tok (ti·ki-toc) *n* (StLu) ‖ PICK-UPS (CarA)

ti-ko·kom (ti con·combre) *n* (StLu) ‖ WILD CUCUMBER (Bdos, etc) [Fr Cr < Fr *petit concombre* 'little cucumber']

ti·la·pi·a* /1 1′1 1/ [tɪlapia] *n* (Guyn, Trin) ‖ *Atkinson* (StLu) A herbivorous, freshwater fish wh grows to about 6 ozs when mature and is highly prized for its food value; the females breed through the mouth and multiply rapidly; the fish was introduced to the Caribbean in the 1970s for commercial fish-pond farming; *Tilapia nilotica* (*Cichlidae*).

ti·la·ri (til·la·ry) *n* (Guyn) [Indic] An ornate, tiered gold necklace, usu of linked gold discs or coins and filigree work, worn by EAST INDIAN women. [Hin *tilaṛii* 'a necklace of three strings']

till¹ *prep* (CarA) [*IF*] **1.** As far as; up to. **a.** *However the witness was positive: 'He (the Surgeon) tell me to count one, two; and ah count til 50 and me na know wha happen.' / It had to be an operation.*—DaC (52.08.16, p.5) **b.** *Is fete from the dance hall till in the street.*—SCTR:85 [Perh by extension of SE prep usage as in *till nightfall*, etc; but prob reinforced in CE by Irish infl. Note 'In Ulster till is commonly used instead of to > –'I am going till Belfast tomorrow': in the manner until is used for unto'— *JESI:84.* See also foll phrs] **2.** PHRASES **2.1 till away to; till down in; till to; till up (to), etc** *prep phrs* (CarA) [*AF*] All the way to; as far as. **a.** *And now she gone till away to Canada, who the hell he think he foolin[g] [a]bout gettin[g] married?* —(Guyn) **b.** *She come till to me door come trouble me.*—(USVI) **2.2 till over yonder** *adv phr* (ECar) [*AF/IF*] All the way over there.

till² *conj* (CarA) **1.** Until. ▢ In extension of SE conj usage as in *till I return*; as in foll phrs. **2.** PHRASES **2.1 so till** *conj phr, adv phr* (CarA) [*AF*] See SO¹ Phr 7.10 **2.2 till when** *conj phr* (CarA)

[*IF*] Until. *She didn't pay me till when I went back the second time.*—(Bdos) **2.3 till you can't see** *adv phr* (Gren) [*AF*] Mercilessly; as viciously as possible. *Child if I catch you stealin[g] I will beat you till I can't see.*—(Gren)

tilt-man *n* (Bdos) ‖ STILT-MAN (ECar) [< *stilt-man* by aphaeresis]

ti·ma·wi (Ti Ma·rie) *n* (Trin) ‖ SENSITIVE PLANT (Bdos, etc) [Fr Cr < Fr [*pe*]*ti*[*te*] *Marie* 'little Mary', prob a *Joc* ref to the girlish shyness of the plant wh recoils when touched. Cp other ‖ ‖]

tim·ber-grant *n* (Guyn) ‖ GRANT (Guyn)

time¹ *n* PHRASES **1. a-piece-o[f]-time** /1122′/ *adv* (Guyn) [*AF*] At one time in the past; once. *A used to go roun[d] by dem often a-piece-o[f]-time but A don['t] go de[re] no mo[re].*—(Guyn) [Perh orig a variant of SE *once upon a time*] **2. get a/ your time (with a woman)** *vb phr* (Guyn, Trin) [*AF—Vul*] See GET Phr 3.5 **3. not have time with (sb)** *neg vb phr* (CarA) [*AF*] To have no time or use for (sb); to have abandoned a relationship with (sb). [Perh infl by sense 2.] **4. one time** *adv phr* (CarA) [*IF*] See ONE-TIME¹, ONE-TIME² as separate entries. **5. the time** *conj phr* (CarA) [*IF*] When. *The time she called me, the driver was in the car.*—Tbgo (CR, 1977) [A prob calque from W Afr langs. Cp Akan *abere a (the time that)* 'when'. Also *KED* Krio *da-tεm (that time)* 'when, then'. Cp also StLu Fr Cr *lè* (< Fr *l'heure*, time) 'when'] **6. when time** *adv phr* (Bdos, Guyn, Trin) [*AF*] See WHEN Phr 3.7 **7. your time meet/reach** *id phr* (Guyn, Trin) [*AF*] You meet your deserts; this is your comeuppance; [of a pregnant woman] your confinement is upon you. [Cp *KED* Krio *tεm rich (time reach)* 'the appointed time has come']

time² *temporal conj* (Baha, Guyn, Trin) [*AF*] By the time that. **a.** *Why you so dumb? Time yer ole lady reach back frum werk we could reach back ten times a'ready.*—TOSR:11 **b.** *I asked my friend, Kenny / To lend me a penny / But time I reach Tantie it lost.*—TRFSS:15 [By ellipsis. Sometimes expressed as *b'time*] **2.** PHRASE **2.1 time so** *adv phr* (Gren) [*AF/IF*] By that time; by now; by then. *Don['t] bother wid dat rum-bo. Time so he drunk a[l]ready.*—(Gren)

time meet *vb phr* (Guyn, Trin) See TIME Phr 7.

ti·mite [timi·t] *n* (Trin) ‖ TROOLIE-PALM (Guyn)

Tim Tim! *n phr* (Dmca, Gren) Cry by a storyteller announcing to the audience that he/she is about to tell a folktale, the audience being expected to reply BWA CHÈS in acceptance. [Perh via Fr Cr < Fr *Tiens! Tiens!* 'Hello! Look!' etc, calling attention] **2.** [*AF—Joc*] [By extension] A tall tale; an unreliable story. *Eyewitness statements that the fire started in a disused locked lavatory ... cannot at this time be confirmed, nor can some of* *the many tim-tims going on around town, including tales of purposeful destruction of income tax by some outside debtor.*—DoH (65.05.15, p.1) □ Cp NANCY-STORY (*CarA*).

tin; **tin-can** *n* (CarA) [*IF*] A can or container, varying in capacity from a quarter of a pint to several gallons, once commercially used for preserved food or liquid and now turned to domestic use; hence a (small) **condensed-milk tin**, etc or a (large) **kerosene tin**, etc. **a.** *The bags ranged from a one tin to a six tin bag, each tinful costing one dollar. The tin used as the measure was a five-gallon kerosene can.*—Vgi I.3, p.18 **b.** *The tin can, which once contained condensed milk, was Sanyasi's bank.*—NAGOS:195 [Cp *EDD* tin sb and v 1. (3) (a) Var. dial. uses in Sc, Irel and Eng 'a water-can or bucket made of tin'. Also *OED2* tin sb 2. a. 'a vessel made of tin, or more usu of tinned iron, spec a vessel in wh meat, fish, fruit, etc is hermetically sealed for preservation'. See also *DAE* tin-can and cit foll] □ See also TIN-CUP, TINNEN.

tin-cup *n* (ECar) ‖ *can-cup* (Antg) ‖ *pan-cup* (Gren) ‖ *tot* 1. (Bdos) A half-pint or pint-size can (wh once contained a preserved food or liquid) with a handle soldered on to it and used (esp in former times) for domestic purposes. *Over there, nastiness and poverty, a tin cup of weak tea and a johnny cake.*—SABS:98

tin·nen¹ (tin·(n)in¹) [tɪnɪn] /1′1/ *adj* (CarA) [*IF*] Made of tin or of galvanized iron; hence many compounds **tinnen-bucket**, **-cup**, **-fence**, **-pot**, **-spoon**, etc (in diff territories). [From EE as *OED* tinnen 'made or consisting of tin' + cits–1653] □ Although morphologically similar to SE *golden*, *leaden*, etc, this form, wh relates to vessels used in the slave era is stigmatized in CE. See TINNEN², noting pitch change.

tin·nen² (tin·(n)in²) [tɪnɪn] /1′2/ *n* [*AF*] 1. (CarA) A piece or sheet of tinplate or galvanized iron; tin-sheet. **a.** *In the Serrant's plot there is a pigpen surrounded with 'tinin' and the Serrants feed the pigs in this pen twice a day.*—DeM(SK) (63.02.16, p.2) **b.** *... an start bennin up like a vwwww as if it did mek out a tinnin.*—BMP:27 [By functional adj > n shift of TINNEN¹] □ This and the foll extended senses are considered illiterate in CE. 2. (ECar) A TIN-CUP or TIN of any size used for domestic purposes; [by extension] any empty, discarded tin or can. *My mother kept all the cocoa 'tinnens', as we called them, to keep curry powder and other things because they had tight covers, but we had better use for such a tinnen at Christmas time to make carbide bombs.*—Guyn (Ms) 3. (Brbu) An ordinary bucket or a large lard can (of similar capacity and with a handle) used for carrying or storing water.

tir·ed out your·self *vb phr* (CarA) [*X*] SE To tire yourself; to wear yourself out. **a.** *With man, you must give them rope to tired out themself.*—HF:14 **b.** *You only tiredin[g] out yo[ur]self*

for not[h]ing, because when all is said and done you ain[′t] goin[g] get no thanks for it.—(Guyn) [A case of SE pa.t. form in infin function in CE. Cp also MARRIED]

ti·sic [tɪzɪk] *n* (CarA) 1. A chronic sickness in a cat causing it to sneeze frequently and have unhealthy-looking fur; it is said to be harmful to humans. [< SE *phthisic*, adj < *phthisis* 'a wasting pulmonary disease'. Perh the adj was regularly used to describe this condition re cats or humans, in early CE. See sense 2.] 2. [By extension] A sickness in humans esp a chronic cough, said to be caught from a sick domestic cat; or a form of asthma said to be caused by cats' fur.

ti·ti·ri-cake (tri-tri cake) *n* (*phr*) (Gren, StVn) A fritter made of TITIRI mixed into a seasoned batter of flour and eggs.

ti·ti·ri(e) (ti·ti·ree, tri-tri) *n* (Dmca, Gren, StVn) Tiny fish spawned in June, July, August, jamming rivers in thick shoals, and caught and sun-dried in quantity for use as food. [*BDFC: 301* Carib *petit poisson*: 'titiri'. Also *GESV:21* 'trixtixes, the French name for them after the Caribbes']

ti·tle *n* 1. (CarA) [*IF*] Mr, Mrs, or Miss; the formal 'designation' to an ordinary person's name. *'Hey, you can get better cassada dan dat? Woman, be conscionable' says the seller, breaking a stick / 'Look, a ent no woman to you! Bes' min you mannas! A is a lady use to me title.'*—CNH:9 □ Seen as conferring rank, long after the 'post-emancipation' era. 2. (Guyn) [*IF*] A person's proper surname, as opposed to some such familiar substitute as Joe, John, what's-your-name, etc. *But you must stop him callin[g] yo[u] 'Wha-yo-name' like that, yo[u] know, and make him to know you have a title, please.*—(Guyn)

tit·tle-drum *n* (Jmca) ‖ KETTLE-DRUM (ECar) [Perh ideophonic + infl of Sc *kittle-drum*]

tjè-bèf (che-boeuf) [′čɛ-bɛf] *n* (Gren) ‖ CUSTARD-APPLE (CarA) [< Fr Cr *tjè* < Fr *coeur* 'heart' + Fr Cr *bèf* < Fr *boeuf* 'cow'. Cp ‖ *bullock's heart* (Jmca, StVn)]

tjenn·èt (chen·nette) [čɛnɛt] *n* (Dmca, StLu) ‖ GUINEP (CarA) □ Standardized orthography.

tjè-pal·mis (chè-pal.mis) [čɛ-palmis] *n* (Dmca, StLu) ‖ CABBAGE (CarA).

to¹ *prep* [Often overlapping with the functions of other SE preps] 1. (CarA) [*IF*] At. **a.** *Said P:— 'I went down the road into MacLachlan shop to pay a bill that I owed. While in there standing to the western end of the counter waiting for my change L. H— came and stood up side of me ...'*—DeM(SK) (63.07.27, p.4) **b.** *Junior agree with Sophie because he had to put up with the same thing all the time to his work.*—NaG (78.06.01, Satirically Speaking) **c.** *Lias said, 'But you know,*

I didn't see Lijah to the funeral.'—PKKK:32 [Cp
EDD to II. Dial uses Sc, Irel, Eng and Amer.
2. 'at; esp before a place-name' and cits following, ex (Glo) *Young John,'ee wur to the
funer'l to-day;* etc. See also *OED2* TO prep A.
I. 4. 'expressing simple position: at, in (a place,
etc). Now *dial'*] 2. (Jmca, Trin) [*IF*] By (esp in
phr *employed to*). *L. G—, clerk, employed to
the Jamaica Omnibus Service Co., and living at
25 Arnold Road, Kingston 4 gave supporting evidence for the petitioner.*—StA(JA) (73.02.10, p.5)
[Cp *EDD* to prep II. 3. 'by'; esp in phr 'to
trade'] 3. (Bdos, StKt) In. *C. R—, tall, melancholy looking, exclaimed in a grave voice, 'Thank
you, Rose! You put me to jail! All I do for you,
you put me to jail. I thank you!'*—DeM(SK)
(63.01.19, p.8) [Cp *EDD* to II. 6. 'in' + cit
(from w.Som) 'Her's purty well to health'] 4.
(Bdos, Guyn, StVn, Trin) [*IF*] Of. **a.** *If you are
sick and fed up with this man who is ... neglectful
to his children why do you go on living this kind
of life.*—NaT (79.09.12, p.21, Dear Christine)
b. *Once Oswald was dead the truth to the matter
could never be known.*—(Guyn) [Cp *EDD* to II.
7. 'of' + cits, ex (Nhp) 'What became to him']
5. (Baha, Bdos, Guyn, StVn, Trin) [*IF*] On. **a.**
*Makin' tawk an sociable like, I sez to de driver
man, I sez, 'Yinna dus have gale here like we dus
have to de Islun?'*—JBJ:84 **b.** *I can'[t] disturb de
mistress—she speakin[g] to the phone.*—(Bdos) [Cp
EDD to II. 8. 'on, upon + cits, ex (w.Som).
That one is too heavy to carry to your back]
6. (CarA) [*IF*] [Expressing family relationship]
What is he to you?—(Guyn) [Perh a survival
from EE. Cp Shak: 'What's Hecuba to him or
he to Hecuba? / That he should weep for her?']
7. PHRASES **7.1 to besides (too besides)** *adv
phr* (CarA) [*AF*] Besides; moreover. **a.** *'I see
enough trouble,' she said.... 'Too besides the young
master don't like me, and perhaps I don't like him
so much. If I stay here I bring trouble and bone
of contention in your house.'*—RWSS:84 **b.** *To
besides, too many women going in for this pants-suit
business. They don't care about dresses anymore.
Some of them living in jeans and farmer-
browns.*—PuN (76.06.20, p.10 **c.** *... but I sees
sometimes how a thing change, an' when you least
expectin' to besides.*—LICMS:79 [Evid a reduction < (*and*) *too besides*, a redundant adv
phr, with CE pronunc of *too* [tʊ] leading to
development of the phr almost as one word, and
sometimes written *tobesides* (like SE *today,
tomorrow*)] □ Usu sentence-initial and in emotive
contexts. **7.2 To France with sb/sth!** *excl phr*
(CarA) [*IF*] See FRANCE Phrs. **7.3 To my God!**
excl phr (CarA) [*IF*] Well, well!; Of all things!;
Would you believe it!; etc. **7.4 to your face** *adv
phr* (Bdos, Guyn) [*IF*] See FACE Phr 8.

to² *infinitive particle* (CarA) 1. [*IF/AF*] [Used
redundantly as the infinitive marker in cases
where it is omitted in SE] **a.** *St Vincent cannot
afford to let even one single dollar to be left lying
around for another island to pick up.*—ViN
(65.08.14, p.5) **b.** *All Arril did was to hold my
hand and Godding beat me.*—Bdos (CR, 1971)
[Cp *EDD* to II. 18. and cits following. Chs. 'I

saw him to do it'. Oxf. 'I'll let you to know']
□ See also MAKE Phr 5.28 MAKE SB TO KNOW STH.
2. PHRASE **2.1 to tell (you the) truth** *disjunctive
phr* (CarA) [*IF*] See TELL Phr 3.

to·bac·co-dove *n* (Baha) ‖GROUND-DOVE 1.
(CarA)

To·ba·go love *n phr* (Trin) [*IF—Joc*] A restrained or unrefined show of affection; shy love.

To·ba·go·ni·an /112′21/ [tʊbagonɪən ~
tʊbegonɪən] *n, adj* (CarA) (A person or thing)
belonging to or characteristic of Tobago, part of
the State of Trinidad & Tobago.

To·ba·go-pheas·ant *n* (Tbgo, Trin) ‖CO-
CRICO (Tbgo, Trin) [Because so common in *Tbgo*
(though entirely absent from *Trin*) and from
resemblance to European pheasant]

to·bo-foot (**tub·ba-foot**) [tʌbʌ-fʊt] *n* (Guyn,
Tbgo, USVI) [*AF—Derog*] A swollen, infected
foot (usu caused by CHIGO(E) infestation). *'Rockstone, rockstone, clear the way; tobo-foot a come'.*—
Tbgo (Banter song) [Cp *KED* Krio *tobo* 'sore
toe' < Yoruba *tobo* 'gobbet of flesh']

to·day *adv* PHRASES 1. **not today** *neg adv phr*
(Bdos, Guyn) [*IF*] See NOT Phr 2.17 2. **(up) to
today** *adv phr* (CarA) [*IF*] (Right) up to the
present time; up to this day. **a.** *You can see the
remains of those old-time factories up to today.*—
(Antg) **b.** *Not me again. I lent him fifty dollars
some years ago, and to today I haven't seen a penny
of it.*—(Guyn) 3. **(sb/sth) ain't today story** *id
phr* (Guyn, Trin) [*AF—Joc*] (Sb) is much older
than he/she looks; (sth) is an old story. *She might
look like fifty something to you, but da[t] woman got
her years, see. She so ai[n't] today story.*—(Trin) 4.
today self; today today *adv phr* (CarA) [*AF/
IF*] ‖*today-day* (Jmca) ‖*today is today* (Guyn,
Trin) This very day (and no later); right now as
I speak to you. **a.** *Lady I walk he[re] till from
Kitty an[d] you don[']t pay me today today I will
get real ignorant, yeh!*—(Guyn) **b.** *Leela continued
to cry and Ganesh loosened his leather belt and
beat her. She cried out, 'Oh God! Oh God! He
go kill me today self!'*—NTMM:55 **c.** *Up to
today-day when I go to the city with Garth, hard
it is for me to walk side and side with him.*—RND:
30 **d.** *Is me and you boy, today is today.* (= *We
shall have to fight it out now*.)—OT2:25 [Likely
calques from W Afr langs. Cp Igbo *taa taa*
'today today', Yoruba *eni eleni* 'today of today'
with same senses as in CE] □ Cp similarly TO-
MORROW TOMORROW.

to-do-ment [tʊdumɛnt] *n* (Bdos) [*AF—Joc*]
‖KADOOMENT 1. (Bdos) *'In truth,' Virgie Farnum
said, her pale skin flushed from the heat, 'all these
Bajan weddings is nothing but one big to-do-ment.
All this silver 'pon the table. Ice birds kissing.
Candle and caterers and no food!'*—MBGB:118
[< Blend of informal SE *to-do* 'fuss' + *EDD
dooment* 'commotion'. See KADOOMENT]

toe-nail fish /1'12/ *n phr* (Guyn) ‖ CASCADU 1. (Trin) [From resemblance of scales to large toe-nails]

to·ken *n* 1. (Bdos, Guyn) An omen or portent (usu of death). *When my father killed that 'sorrow' snake it was a token, and soon after that my aunt died.*—(Guyn) [Cp *EDD* token sb 6. 'a portent, omen, esp a death-omen; an apparition' and cits following. Cp also *OED* token 'a sign or presage of something to come. (Now Obs)] 2. (Angu) A gaunt, sickly-looking person. [Perh an extension of sense 1, or a Joc metaph 'a mere representation of a human being']

To·li·an [toliən] *n, adj* (ViIs) [*IF*] (A person or thing) belonging to or characteristic of Tortola (*BrVi*).

tom[1] *n* (Guyn) [Gold-mining Ind] A sloping wooden trough about 6 ft x 3 ft x 1-1/2 ft with a piece of perforated iron sheeting or strong mesh at the lower end through wh small stones, that may contain nuggets or diamonds, are washed from the excavated soil dumped into the trough by a PORK-KNOCKER; the perforated iron is called a **tom-iron**.

tom[2] *n* (Bdos) A cheap cigar personally made by rolling cured tobacco leaves (used only by older generation of smokers). *I bumped into a soldierly looking man with a 'tom' in his mouth and the gentlest, courtliest of smiles on his face.*—WWWE:19

tom·a·goff (tom·i·goff, Tom·my Goff) [tɒ magɒf ~ tɒ·migɒf] *n* (Belz) ‖ FER-DE-LANCE [Prob < *SDGA* Lat Am Sp *tamagá(s)* 'very poisonous snake of Honduras and Costa Rica'. The variations may be due to false refinement and folk etymology]

tomb·stone-feast /112'/ *n phr* (Crcu) See STONE-FEAST

To·mi·an /1'12/ [tomiən] *n, adj* (ViIs) [*IF*] (A person or thing) belonging to or characteristic of St Thomas (*USVI*).

tom-i·ron *n* (Guyn) See TOM[1].

to·mor·row *adv* PHRASES **tomorrow self; to-morrow tomorrow** *adv phrs* (CarA) [*AF/IF*] Tomorrow without fail; definitely tomorrow. [A likely calque from W Afr langs. Cp Igbo *echi echi* 'tomorrow tomorrow' (*pers info, C. Azuonye*), Yoruba *ọla ọlola* 'tomorrow of tomorrow' (*pers info, A. Banjo*), phrs with same sense as in CE] □ Cp similarly TODAY Phr 3. TODAY TODAY.

tongue *n* PHRASES 1. **long out your tongue** *vb phr* (Guyn) [*AF*] See LONG[3] Phr 2.2 2. **pull sb's tongue** *vb phr* (Jmca) ‖ PICK SB'S MOUTH (CarA) See PICK Phr 5.7, PULL Phr 2.10 3. **sb's tongue is long** *id phr* (Dmca, Gren, StLu) [*AF—Derog*] Sb is a tale bearer, cannot keep a secret. *Careful what you tell her you know, her tongue is long.*—

(Gren) 4. **take sb's tongue** *vb phr* (Dmca, StLu) [*AF*] ‖ PICK SB'S MOUTH (CarA) See PICK phr 5.7 5. **wash your tongue on sb** *vb phr* (Dmca) [*AF—Derog*] ‖ WASH YOUR MOUTH ON SB (CarA) *... and now everybody washin[g] the[ir] tongue on poor John, and they used to be bowin[g] an[d] scrapin[g] when he was in power.*—(Dmca, 1987)

ton·ka-bean* (ton·ca-bean) [tɒŋka-bi·n] *n* (Guyn, Trin) The black, glossy, two-inch long seed from the pod of a forest-tree; it is almond-shaped and fragrant and is used in food flavouring, perfumery, and as a folk-medicine; [by extension] the canopy tree bearing these pods and exceeding 100 ft in average height, called the **komaro** tree in the interior of Guyana; *Dipteryx odorata (Papilionaceae)*. **a.** *Now purchasing at guaranteed prices—any quantity Tonka Beans—Crawford Mar & Company—We also buy cocoa and coffee.*—EvN (Ad, 80.03.27, p.18) **b.** *Cocoa trees grew in the shade of the immortelles, coffee in the shade of the cocoa, and the hills were covered with tonka bean.*—NHMB:391 □ Note that pl form applies only to the seeds.

ton·ti; ton.to *adj* (Belz) [*AF—Cr*] Silly; foolish; stunned; dizzy; giddy. *I knock mi head. I feel tonti.*—(Belz) [< Sp *tonto* 'foolish, stupid']

ton-wood *n* (Guyn) WALLABA logs split into six-foot lengths to be used as fuel in small industries (such as bakeries, etc), esp in former times. [Because sold by weight, 2-1/2 tons per cord of 128 cu ft]

too *adv* (CarA) [*IF/AF*] 1. [Sometimes sentence initial, unlike SE] Moreover; also. **a.** *Herman, who was also from Jamaica, frequently came to visit her. Too, they were from the same village which strengthened the friendship, also he enjoyed her cooking.*—PKKK:82 **b.** *Some of the injuries suffered might have been very slight. Too one would have to know the extent of head injuries.*—Bdos (Ms, 1964) [Cp *OED* too 1. 'rarely, now never, used at the beginning of a clause'] 2. [With contrastive low pitch after a pron or n phr, qualifying the same with mild rebuke] Shame on (sb); surely (sb) should show more feeling. **a.** *And Miss Murray too! She might-a le[t] de boy tek de two manga an[d] go [a]long [h]e way [in]stead o[f] callin[g] police.*—(Guyn) **b.** *Paster Hall did promise me one but it don't seem to be coming. / Merhue: You know him too, he only makes promises but I sorry to say that they never get fulfil.*—Bdos (Ms, Play, 1976) □ Cp Phr 7.4 below. 3. [Sentence final, after a neg vb] Either. *She didn't give you an exercise book? She didn't give me any too.*—(StVn) 4. [With high contrastive pitch, as empathic intensifier before an adj] Ever so; so very; so charmingly. **a.** *Oh child our French nun is too sweet. I like her best of all.*—MLDS:47 **b.** *'I too glad we make back friend with Rita and Joe,' Urmilla said.*—SABS:209 **c.** *I can feel too proud when I see them around the table on a Sunday afternoon.*—JJM:150 **d.** *She would fling at us, 'Oh, yinna chillun go 'lung, yer too wicked!'*—JBJ:117 [Cp Yoruba *ju*, 'too' similarly used: *o dara ju* (*it good too*) 'It's so very good'—(*pers info, A. Banjo*)] **5.** [X] [As intensifier before a vb] Too much. **a.** *That woman too like walkbout. As you miss her she gone cotch up a somebody else yard. Mark my words, she soon give the old guy the brushoff.*—WeG (73.02.07, p.11, Partyline) **b.** *Last Monday a morning paper … reported that on Sunday gone, we were locked in tense deliberations. They too lie. A complete fabrication. On both counts. Just plain wrong.*—TaP (75.03.30, p.1) [By infl of usage at sense 4. Cp also WAPE *The boy de too spoil somebody name* 'The boy is seriously talking somebody's name'—(*pers info, A. Amayo*)] **6.** [As neg intensifier] (Not) at all. *That others who are not too few in number, by their very behaviour in the streets, do not make us too proud of them.*—BeB (65.06.09, p.3) [Cp SE phr *none too* + adj] □ Also *IF* SE. **7.** PHRASES **7.1 too bad** /ˈ3ˈ1/ *adv phr* (CarA) [*AF*] Very much; excessively; to a great extent. **a.** *He said, 'We could stay here until they strike up the next Castillian. You know what we call Castillian here? Spanish waltz. I like that too bad!'*—AFTF:50 **b.** *Doh play with them Chinee, they smart too bad!*—RSMCD:67 **c.** *But the Premier vibes mek I man larf too bad.*—CrU (76.10.02, p.9) [A prob calque from W Afr langs. Cp Yoruba *O dun buruku* (*it sweet bad*), also WAPE *e sweet bad bad* 'It is very sweet'—(*pers info, A. Banjo*)] □ Note sharp high-falling pitch wh is necessary to this sense. **7.2 too besides** [tʊ-bɪsaɪ(d)z] *adv phr* (CarA) [*AF*] See TO¹ Phr 7.1 TO BESIDES **7.3 too much** [tʊmʌč] *adv intensifier phr* (CarA) [*AF*] [Following an adj or vb] Very much indeed. **a.** *Dese children bad too much.*—(Guyn) **b.** *Oui fout! Make haste nuh, me dear. I want to see you step off too much.*—RTCS:12 **7.4 You (self) too!** [yu sɛlf tu] /ˈ3ˈ21/ *id phr* (CarA) [*AF*] ‖ *Ou-menm too!* (StLu) ‖ *You self!* (CarA) ‖ *You yourself!* (Belz, StVn, Trin) [Expressing restrained rebuke] How unreasonable (thoughtless, silly) can you be? **a.** *'But Meena, you-self too,' he started, 'You think one Englishman go cut another Englishman throat?*—KJB:131 **b.** *You think I can stan[d] all dis business after he done treat me so—you too!*—(Angu) [An extension of sense 2. above]

too·bac *n* (Dmca) See TOUBAK

took *n* (Bdos) See TUK-BAND

toon·sie [ˈtunsi] *n* (Trin) ‖ *jumbie-balsam* (Guyn) Name used by Hindus (*Trin*) for this medicinal and sacred herb wh is often kept indoors; *Ocimum sanctum* (*Labiatae*). [< Hin *tulsi* 'the basil plant'] □ See note at TULSI(E).

too·too *n, vb* (Bdos, etc) See TUTU

too·tool·bay *adj* (Gren, Trin) See TOUTOULBÉ

top¹ *n* **1.** (Baha, CayI) The branches or fronds (i.e. tops) of any kind of palm tree (generally excepting the coconut) wh are used in basketry, mat-making, etc. *One of the occupations of Grand Cayman over the years has been weaving baskets,* hats, and mats. The 'tops' (thatch palm fronds) are stripped into 'string' which is then 'plaited' into 'string work'. ('You get any string work from East End?')—KWS:21 **2.** (Baha) Name applied to any kind of palm tree, except the coconut, whose fronds are used for STRAW-WORK. □ Usu as second element in a compound name, whence *cabbage top* (= CABBAGE PALM), *pond top, silver top, thatch top,* etc.

top² *n* [Child's toy] PHRASE **spinning top in mud** *id phr* (Bdos, Tbgo, Trin) [*AF-Joc*] Spending your energy (or time, money, etc) to no purpose; working hard at a task that is sure to be futile, or frustrated by sth else that you should have been aware of.

top³ *vb tr* (Bdos) [Sugar Ind] To cut off the leafy tops of the sugar-cane during the harvesting process. [Cp *EDD top* v 22. 'to top off the top branches in pruning a hedge' N.I]

top-gal·lant flood *n phr* (Belz) A flood of record height. *We wondered if that city of so-desired dollars / Flowing past like top-gallant floods / Swirling round the glossily labelled food, / … Could be true-true home.*—YFOC:18 [< OED Naut *topgallant* 'at the head of the topmast' … B. *attrib* 'allowing topgallant sails to be used, as *topgallant gale, topgallant weather'.* The Belz usage is an extension of the latter to the related floods experienced in the country's low lying coastland] □ A corruption, *top-gallon flood,* by folk etym, sometimes occurs. The Br naut pronunc [təgælən(t)] does not apply in *Belz* usage.

to·pi-tam·bo(o)* /ˈ1ˈ12ˈ1/ *n* (Dmca, Gren, StLu, Trin) The root tubers of a canna-like plant with 2-ft high leafy shoots *Calathea alluya* (*Maranthaceae*); the tubers resemble small white potatoes and are usu boiled with salt as a delicacy.

top·side¹ (**Top Side**) *n* (*phr*) **1.** (Guyn) The upper reaches of a river or of the interior of Guyana; the mining areas or other outposts far away from the coast. *News from 'topside' hints that Constable Brusche, Mr Guiana, 1949, now residing at Lethem, is trying to come down for the Big Show and is in excellent fettle.*—DaC (52.09.20, p.6) **2.** (Jmca) An upland area, in contrast to a low or 'bottom-side'. **3.** *n phr* (Tbgo) The windward coast or north-eastern end of Tobago. *The North Side Road has historically been the great highway between the 'Top Side' and 'Low Side' (Windward and Leeward) in Tobago.*—EFSLC:12 [Cp *OED topside* a. 'the upperside of anything']

top·side² *adv* (Guyn, Jmca, Tbgo) [*IF*] Towards or in an area indicated by TOPSIDE¹. **a.** *Just as we enter into mango-piece topside, there is heavy bass in front and Father has gone into Bro' Ira D. Sankey's pilgrimage hymn.*—RND:30 **b.**

When last seen he was going topside to his prospecting grant.—Guyn (Ms)

top·side³ *prep* (Jmca) [*AF/IF*] Above; at the upper end or in the upper area of. *He has made a fine house for himself on a hill topside the town o' Morant Bay.*—RND:238 [By semantic shift of Br naut E usage as *OED* topside b. 'the upper part of a ship's side; or by functional adv > prep shift of TOPSIDE²]

top·side⁴ *n* (Guyn) [*AF—Joc*] The head, esp the brain. *His topside isn't good, so don't worry with him.*—(Guyn) [Perh a *Joc* extension of TOPSIDE¹. Also cp IF SE 'not too bright on top'. See also prec re Br naut E]

top·sie (tip·sy) *n* (Bdos, Trin) [*AF*] [Child Talk] ‖ UTENSIL (Bdos, etc)

torch¹ *n* (CayI, Dmca, Gren, Jmca, USVI) **1.** ‖ BOTTLE-FLAMBEAU (StVn, etc) **2.** A flashlight.

torch² *vb* (CayI, Dmca, Gren, Jmca, USVI) To hunt (crabs) in the night with the aid of a torch. *Other times we sat in the moonlight, or we went torchin' for crabs. Yes, we used more arm and leg power in those days before we had electric power.*—JJAIE:68

torch·light *n* (CarA) ‖ *spotlight* (Bdos) (Br E) an electric torch; (AmE) a flashlight. [By characteristic CE reduplicative compounding]

tor·chon [tɒʃɒ̃ ~ tɒʃɒ] *n* (Trin) ‖ LOOFAH (Trin) [Fr Cr pronunc < Fr *torchon* 'duster, cleaning cloth'. The dried fruit so called, or LOOFAH, is used for scrubbing]

to·rec[t]·ly [tʊrɛkli] *adv* (Angu, Baha, Bdos) [*X*] Almost immediately; directly; very soon (now). *Torec[t]ly after you lef[t] I see it and I call de mistress an[d] tell [h]er.*—(Bdos) [Cp *EDD* toreckly adv (I.Ma, Lin, Nrf, etc) (+ variant spellings) 'a corruption of 'directly; presently'. Also found in N. Carolina and other AmE dial]

to·ro¹ ['tʊrʊ ~ 'toro] *n* (Guyn) ‖ CAVALLI (CarA)

to·ro² *n* (Gren) See TURU

Tor·to·li·an (Tor·to·lan) /12'11/ *n, adj* (CarA) (A person or thing) belonging to or characteristic of Tortola, the largest of the Br Virgin Is. □ The form **Tortolian** is preferred in the *BrVi*.

To·shau *n* (Guyn) See TOUCHAU

tot *n* (Bdos) **1.** ‖ TIN-CUP (ECar) **2.** ‖ tinnen (Guyn) A small TIN. *Mr Speaker, the Government is running the country like a poor man who tells his wife to look in the butter tot and see if there is any butter there. If there is any butter in the tot, then he will tell his wife not to buy any butter before the following week. This is exactly how the Government is running this country.*—Bdos (Hd,

73.10.16, p.2673) [Cp *OED* tot sb⁴ 2. 'a very small drinking vessel' + 1845 cit with *Note*: 'Tin pot(s) out of which the European soldiers drink'. Hence the Bdos usage prob derives from the term as used by the Br Regiment garrisoned there 18C and 19C]

tote *vb tr* (CarA) **1.** To carry (a heavy load); to lift and transport. **a.** *As Rosie stumbled and fell under the whiplash, the huge bundle of canes she was toting spread over her body. But the merciless driver overtook her and, flaying her with blows, he urged her to rise and proceed with her work.*—EMRP:14 **b.** *Winkie, Buster, Dinah, and Tara had disappeared so mysteriously that the general opinion in the neighbourhood was that 'sperrit must a tote dem', carried them to some distant place, in another world.*—TOSR:32 [Cp Kikongo, UMbundu, Ci-Luba (and other Bantu langs including Swahili) vb root *-tuta, -tota,* 'to carry, pick up, load'] **2.** PHRASE **2.1 have a sieve to tote water** *vb phr* (Baha, TkCa) ‖ HAVE A BASKET TO CARRY WATER (CarA) See BASKET Phr 4.

to·ta (to·to) *n* (Jmca) A sweet tart made of grated coconut with nutmeg. [Perh < Sp *torta* 'a cake, tart, flan']

tou·bak (too·bac) [tubak] *n* (Dmca) [*AF*] **1.** [School] Truancy. **2.** PHRASE **2.1 make toubak** *vb phr* [*AF*] [School] ‖ BREAK BICHE (Gren, etc) See BICHE Phr *After a while he spoke with decision, 'I not going to school' / 'You not goin'' Jonas enquired timidly / 'No, le's make toobac' / Jonas didn't answer but he knew he would follow Simon.*—LNL:29

tou·blé [tuble] *adj* (Dmca, StLu) ‖ tootoolbay (Gren, Trin) Stupefied; flustered; confused. [Fr Cr < Fr *troublé,* with /r/ loss]

tou·can* /2'1/ [tukan] *n* (Belz, Guyn, Trin) A forest bird of various colorations, from its huge 5-inch-long bill to its big yellow, white, or orange throat, generally black body, crimson rump, and powerful blue legs; it is the national bird of Belize; *Ramphastos toco (Ramphastidae).*

touch PHRASE **touch the flesh** *vb phr* (Guyn) [*AF—Joc*] See FLESH Phr 3.1

Tou·chau (To·shau, Tou·chou, Tu·chaw(a)) ['tuʃaʊ] *n* (Guyn) ‖ AMERINDIAN CAPTAIN (Guyn) Woman Captain / *History was created last Saturday, when Cde. Candida Veras, 29, became the first woman to be elected Touchau in the Rupununi area. / Cde. Veras, a 29-year old housewife, gained a majority 39 votes over her nearest rival to become Touchau of Karasabai village in the South Pakaraimas of the Rupununi Region.*—GyC (76.03.25, p.23) [< *TWD* Wapisiana *toshao* 'chief']

touched *adj* **1.** (Angu, Bdos, Guyn) [Of fruit] Soft or spoiling in certain spots (i.e. where it has been hit or 'touched' by some hard object). *The atmosphere is mixed, with the aroma of fried* *pork, steak fish and chicken, the stench of rotting carrion, 'touched fruit' and human waste in alleyways.*—NaT (76.01.18, p.14) **2.** (Jmca) [Of meat] Tainted; spoiling. *In Jamaica, however, I have only known [touched] applied to meat—especially pork and fish, which, I suppose, are particularly 'touchable'—never to vegetables, for blemishes in which we have our own, apt vocabulary in which fluxy figures prominently.*—DaG (66.11.05, p.3) [Cp *OED touch* vb 7. 'to affect injuriously in some physical way ... esp in a slight degree; ... to infect, taint' (usu in pa. part.) CE usage is perh a specific extension of this] □ Usu **touch** *AF* in folk speech, hence commonly **touch-mango/-banana/-pear**, etc. Cp FLUXY (Jmca)

touch·ous (touch·es) /ı'2/ [tʌčʌs ~ tʌčıs] *adj* (CarA) [*IF*] (SE) Touchy; irritable, too ready to take offence; [by extension] difficult to co-operate with. **a.** *You can't make any joke with her about the child's light colour. She's very touchous about that.*—(StVn) **b.** *Which do most people prefer, a girl or a boy? Indians say boy is most useful, we say love a girl child, she is less touchous with salary, study less for herself and more for the home, more attached to parents.*—RLCF:87 [< *touch* + *ous* also *eous* by analogy with other adjs ending in *-ous*] □ Cp *EDD touchous* adj (Irel, Nhb, etc and Amer) also *touchis* 1. 'irritable, touchy, easily offended'] □ The variant **touches** is commoner in *Antg, Nevs, StKt*.

tou·la·ma (tu·la·ma) ['tulama] /2'21/ *n* (Mrat) See TOULÉMWA

tou·la·ma pap *n phr* (Mrat) A porridge, popular among older folk, made from TOULAMA 'starch'.

tou·lé·mwa (tou-la-ma, tous-les-mois, tou·lo·mon) [tulemwa ~ tulama ~ tulʌmʌn] /ı'12/ *n* (Dmca, Gren, Mrat, StLu, Trin) **1.** A lily-like plant, a small variety of CANNA, growing plentifully and noted for its profuse rhizome roots wh are grated and squeezed to produce a fine white residual 'starch' resembling arrowroot, while the squeezed-out gratings are used for pig-fodder; *Canna edulis (Cannaceae).* **2.** [By extension] The culinary starch produced. [< Fr *tous-les-mois* (= *all months*) 'throughout the year' in ref to the plant as a perennial] □ The form common in *Mrat* is TOULAMA.

tou·lum (too·loom, too·lum, tu·lum) /ı'ı/ [tʊlʊm ~ tʊlum] *n* (Gren, StVn, Trin) A small, round, hard, black cake made of grated coconut, molasses, and sugar; it is much prized as a sweet. [Noted by J.J. Thomas, 1869 (*TTPCG:21*) in two Trin Fr Cr forms *touloume, touroume* 'a coarse kind of sugar cake', without etym, in his list of 'Nouns peculiar to the dialect']

tour·te·relle *n* (Gren, Dmca) See TOUTWEL

tous-les-mois *n* (Dmca, Gren, Mrat, StLu, Trin) See TOULÉMWA

tout·ba·gai (toute ba·gaille) /2'12/ [tut 'ba gaı] *n phr* (Dmca, Gren, StLu, Trin) [*AF—Cr*] The whole lot; everything; everybody. **a.** *Everything. Toute bagaille. You know any patois? / A little bit. I know what toute bagaille is. / He smiled, 'Well that's what we planting today, Shell boy. Everything. Just take a look in those bags.'*—AGDR:116 **b.** *Yet there are none to uphold and support those who are garment workers, bakers and mechanics—tout bagai.*—TrG (73.07.25, p.6) [Fr Cr < Fr *toute (la) pagaille* 'the whole bundle']

tout moune (tout(e) monde, tout moon) /2'ı/ [tut mu·n] *n phr* (Dmca, Gren, StLu, Trin) [*AF—Cr/Joc*] **1.** Everybody you can think of. **a.** *Tout moune was there at the wedding, uncles, aunts and nen-nens.*—AFSTE:44 **b.** *The Banks—there was Denbie DeFreitas—most prominent business houses—Walter St John of Geo. F. Huggins (G'da) Ltd. and wife, Winston Masanto representing ... Masanto & Co. Ltd., Phinsley St Louis of St Louis Services Ltd., ... Bryce Woodroofe and wife of 'Melvill Stores'—toute monde—were there 'living it up' like the local 'Jet Set'.*—ToR (75.10.29, p.10) [Fr Cr < Fr *tout le monde* 'everybody'. The form *moune* developed separately in Fr Cr early as an indefinite pron (*TTPCG:41*) 'people, they, one'] □ The variant spellings are conjectural. **2.** PHRASES **2.1 tout moun an[d] Sam** *n phr* (ECar) [*AF—Cr/Joc*] ‖ **manjack and his brother/and Sally** (Trin) ‖ **marish and the parish** (Bdos, Guyn, Trin) ‖ **tout moon bagai** (Trin) ‖ **tout moon la, Sam Poochey and the duppy** (Bdos) ‖ **tout moon bakaila** (Bdos, StLu) [Intensifying sense 1.] Just about everybody; the world and his wife. **a.** *Politician alone don't get the hard knocks, but Tout, Mun and Sam, longs them have a position and in the public eye.*—LMFF:44 **b.** *He call De Lab name, he call de G.G. name, he call C.J. name, he call Chief Magistrate—'Toute Moon Bagai'—He even call Karl name.*—BoM (77.07.15, p.14) [< Fr Cr TOUT[E] MOUNE 'everybody' + Fr *ensemble* 'together'. The sense of the Fr Cr and Fr elements having been lost in process of time, folk etym effected AND SAM (< *ensemble*) and other elements as illustrated in cits. Cp also prec.]

tou·toul·bé (too·tool·bay) [tutulbe] *adj* (Gren, Trin) ‖ **toublé** (Dmca, StLu) Stupefied; dazed; madly in love (with the implication that this state has been brought about by witchcraft); bewitched. *'Yeah, boy, Indira [Gandhi] gone back. But them fellas really didn't stand a chance against she, you know. That woman send the whole of India tootoolbay,' agreed the driver.*—SuP (80.01.08, p.16) [Fr Cr < Fr *tout troublé* 'all upset' with / r/ loss and metathesis of *troublé*]

tout·wel (tour·te·relle) [tutwɛl] *n* (Dmca, Gren) ‖ GROUND-DOVE 1. (CarA) *Close season for Tourterelle and Mountain Dove begins 1st March.*—Grenada Almanac, 1976 [Fr Cr < Fr *tourterelle* 'turtle-dove']

tow[1] *vb* (Bdos, Gren, Guyn, Trin) [F] || *bar*[2] (Bdos) To give sb a ride on the cross-bar of a bicycle. *So the 'Good Samaritan' generously offered her the bar of his bicycle. He was going to tow her home.*—GyG (56.08.16) [By shift or narrowing of sense of SE *tow* 'to provide carriage of']

tow[2] *n* (Bdos, Gren, Guyn, Trin) A ride on the cross-bar of a bicycle. *Give me a tow down de road.*—(Gren) [By functional vb > n shift of TOW[1]]

to·ward(s) *prep* (CarA) [IF] [Often in looser use than in SE] In regard to; against; about. **a.** *It has been drawn to my attention towards some work which Cable & Wireless is doing in St Andrew's better known as J. Sandy.*—NeJ (75.02.14, p.4) **b.** *Now I am in Kingston working, do you think that madman should come in Kingston where I am working and interfere with me? What actions can I take towards him if he comes to my work place again? Thanks for your advice.*—WeS (74.12.15, p.10) **c.** *He had words of praise for the establishment and said: 'As a lawyer and a citizen, I will not tolerate anyone making any scandalous statements toward the police force.'*—NaT (86.03.12, p.1)

town [tʌŋ ~ toʊn] *n* PHRASE **go to town on sb/sth** *vb phr* (ECar) See GO Phr 6.32

Town Books *n phr pl* (Guyn) The bound registers of title deeds of property within the boundaries of the city. *Seventhly—all that piece or parcel of land known in the Town Books as the west part of the south part of mud lot 'A', Water and Holmes Streets, situate in South Cummingsburg District, in the city of Georgetown, in the county of Demerara, in the Republic of Guyana.*—Guyn (75.05.31, p.1099, Official Gazette) [Cp OED Town book 'a book in wh the records of a town are kept' + cits–'1816]

to·yo (to·ya) [to·yʌ] *n* (Guyn) || GARDEN-BALSAM (Bdos, etc) *Toyo makes a sweet-smelling bush-tea which is especially good for whooping cough and generally for chest colds in children.*—(Guyn)

trace[1] *n* (Gren, Trin) **1.** (Trin) A pathway between a row of houses wh are generally backing on each other. **2.** || *cart-road* (Bdos) || *interval* (Jmca) A side road; a path; unpaved track. [Cp EDD trace n[3] 'a path, trail, or road in a forest or wilderness made by the passage of men or animals'. See also cits there]

trace[2] *vb tr* (Jmca) [AF] || BUSE (ECar) *Dem have some people round here who love to pick argument and trace other people. Me tired of the tracing, and me nuh able fe nobody try haul me into kass-kass.*—JdN (78.06.24, p.13) □ Also *trace off sb.* Cp Phrs at BUSE.

trac·ing *n* (Jmca) [AF] || BUSING (ECar) *Members of the Captive Press whipping up the nerve and flexing the muscle, even sharpening the tongue to prepare for their favourite preoccupation. Tracing.*—DaG (79.12.24, p.6)

trac·ing-match *n* (Jmca) [AF] A loud, nasty, public quarrel between two or more persons (usu women) in wh dirty references and words are freely exchanged.

trade *n* (CarA) **1.** [Often with restricted sense] Any skilled manual craft (usu acquired by apprenticeship). **2.** PHRASE **2.1 take trick to make trade** *id phr* (Bdos) See TRICK Phr

trade-man *n* (Gren) A skilled manual worker, usu one trained by apprenticeship; an artisan. *B.A— had some trade men fixing up downstairs in his new house next door to Mt Royal. Down strolls the neighbour in his cream suit. 'Stop this work right now.' Gairy said that the knocking does not agree with his nerves. So B.A— and the workmen vex.*—NeJ (75.06.13, p.8) [< trade (used largely in restricted sense in CE) 'a skilled craft' + (agential) MAN]

trad·er *n* (Guyn) A TRAFFICKER who trades in domestic items; a person who does business in the PARALLEL MARKET.

traf·fick·er *n* **1.** (Gren, StVn, Tbgo) || *trader* (Guyn) A person who travels back and forth between Caribbean territories trading legally in agricultural produce and needed domestic goods. *This is not to cause undue inconvenience to a trafficker, but is to allow a trafficker to hold a permit which gives him or her the right to travel to Trinidad and other places for the purpose of trafficking without paying what shall be imposed later on as an embarkation tax, or an exit tax.*—Gren (Hd, 68.12.30, p.47) **2.** (Tbgo) || *huckster* (CarA) A person who peddles goods in Tobago using a car or a small boat. □ The connotation of criminal private trade, as in ModE *drug-trafficking*, does not apply. See also TURN-HAND (Nevs, etc.)

trail·er *n* (CarA) [Carnival] A large truck carrying disc jockeys with all necessary electronic equipment, hired for the loud playing of CALYPSO music to accompany a costumed CARNIVAL BAND participating in the PARADE OF THE BANDS. [By shift of sense from 'an open tray in tow' to the whole vehicle + the notion of one or more of these vehicles 'trailing' the main BAND]

train·ing *vbl n* (CarA) PHRASE **have/have no training** *vb phr* (CarA) [IF] [Esp of children] To be well-mannered/ill-mannered. *They don['t] have no trainin' you know. De[ir] mudda ain['t] bring dem up right.* (= *They are quite ill-mannered you know. Their mother didn't bring them up in the right way).*—(Guyn)

tramp *vb intr* PHRASE **go tramping** *vb phr* (CarA) [IF] To stomp in the streets as members of a BAND or in friendly groups to the festive music of a MASQUERADE-BAND or STEELBAND. *When we go tramping, you see a set of St Thomian*

*girls get in with the Island boys and they hook up
together, and set string just as a set of crabs will
string across the street. Dey would make seven lines
an when de bands press forward dos girls and boys
press forward; an when de band press backward,
dey all press backward.*—AawI, 2 □ Cp also BRAM[2]
(Belz), JUMP[1] 4 (CarA), RUSH[1] 2 (Baha)

trans·port[1] *n* (Guyn) [Property Law] Legal
title to the ownership of a piece of landed
property. *And the Managing Director of the
Houston Estate, ... has committed his organization
to pay the fees for the 'Transport' which will
give the membership legal rights to start development works on the land after the final
payment has been made.*—GyC (78.01.12, p.9)
[< Du *transport* 'conveyance', the orig Du
term having originated in early Roman Dutch
Law in *Guyn*] **2.** PHRASES **2.1 get transport**
vb phr (Guyn) [*IF*] To receive legal title to
ownership of land or property. **2.2 pass (the)
transport** *vb phr* (Guyn) To transfer legal
title of a property from one person to another;
to effect a legal conveyance.

trans·port[2] **land/property to (sb)** *vb phr*
(Guyn) To transfer or convey ownership of property to (a purchaser). *The transportee shall not
be at liberty within five years of the passing of
transport to sell, transport or lease any part of the
said lot hereby transported or to sell any building
which he may have erected thereon without the
consent in writing of the Housing Administrator.*—
Guyn (75.05.31, p.1098, Official Gazette) [<
Dutch *transporter* 'to convey'. See TRANS-
PORT[1]]

trash[1] *n* (CarA) **1.** [Sugar Ind/Hist] ‖ BAGASSE
(Bdos, etc) **2.** The dried leaves esp of the sugar-
cane or banana plants used for thatching huts,
or in making carnival costumes, or as agricultural
mulch. *Villages known for their dirt floors and
trash houses and the former slums around St John's
have given way to neat and painted houses.*—AnS
(62.05.11, p.14) □ This is the most widely current sense in CE, hence many compounds *ba-
nana-/cane-trash, trash-hat/-house/-hut*,
etc.

trash[2] *vb* (CarA) [*X*] **1.** To thrash (esp in foll
phrs). [By characteristic CE [ə > t] shift] **2.**
PHRASES **2.1 trash benny** *vb phr* (TkCa) [*AF-
Cr*] ‖ POUND SB'S NAME (CarA) **2.2 trash out** *vb
phr* (CarA) [*X*] To thrash out; (BrE) to thresh
out, over. *Let's trash out our problems together in
'73.*—TrG (H, 73.01.02)

trash-bone *n* (Bdos) The mid-rib of a cane
leaf used to make the frame of a kite. *Those of
us who were less fortunate and consequently more
pennywise, would remember going through the cane-
field selecting trash bone to make kites, sneaking
out of the house with the sewing cotton, and buying
ten cents worth of bread paper to make the kite.*—
SuS (85.04.07, p.7) □ Cp POINTER (*Guyn*) similarly used.

trash-fish *n* (CarA) Any fish considered to be
of low quality and netted in numbers when
fishing for catches of particular value; such fish
are often thrown back into the sea. *Although
shark is regarded as a low status, 'trash' fish
throughout most of the Caribbean, it is widely
accepted as a food in Trinidad and Tobago.*—SuS
(89.10.29, p.6B) □ Also AmE.

tra·vaux [travo] *n* (Gren) **1.** Road repair by
manual labour. **2.** [By extension] The labourer,
usu a woman, who carries and spreads broken
stone in repairing public roads. *From the humble
'travaux' to the well educated 'booge' we are all
prepared to leave the solution of our problems to
something called 'the Government', an organisation
with which we do not identify ourselves.*—ToR
(65.08.13, p.2) □ The term is sometimes in Derog use. **3.** PHRASE **3.1 work (in) travaux** *vb
phr* (Gren) [*IF/AF*] See WORK[2] Phr 5.3

tra·vel *vb* (ECar) [*IF*] [Of a sick person] To be
noticeably (by appearance or by some supernatural manifestation) in the last stages before
death. **a.** *A picture suddenly fell off the wall, you
know, and her lips moved slightly. I said 'Peace!',
but the servant said 'Don't disturb her, Sir. Madam
is travelling'. She just lay still and I don't know
exactly when she died.*—(Guyn) **b.** *'What is it you
want to say, Ma? Tell Indrani. She here beside
you listening'* / *'She spirit travelling already'*,
Urmila murmured. *'It not going to be long
now'.*—NF:145

Treat·y of Cha·gua·ra·mas *n phr* (CarA)
[Hist] An agreement drawn up between thirteen
West Indian territories at the former federal
capital of Chaguaramas in Trinidad, October
1972, to establish the CARIBBEAN COMMUNITY,
with the objectives of economic integration, common services, functional co-operation, and the
co-ordination of foreign policies. □ See CAR-
IBBEAN COMMUNITY.

tree-A (tree·ay) *n* (Trin) See TRIÉ

tree-boa *n* (Gren) ‖ *serpent* **1.** (Gren) A snake
about 6 ft long, with a thin neck, a yellowish-
brown back, and yellow belly; *Boa enadris
(Boidae).*

tree-duck *n* (Trin) ‖ WICISSI-DUCK (Guyn)
[*Tree*, prob to distinguish this swamp-bird from
the ordinary duck, wh is a swimmer. The TREE-
DUCK nests on the ground or in low tree stumps
but is not known to live in trees]

trem·bler* **(trem·bleur)** [trɛmblər] *n* (ECar)
‖ *twanmblè* (Dmca, StLu) A brown and grey
woodland bird about 10 in long, with a long,
slender bill and an upturned tail, distinguished
by its habit of trembling; *Cinclocerthia ruficauda
(Mimidae).*

trench *n* (Guyn) A canal 12 to 20 ft wide and
about 8 ft deep, usu part of an irrigation or
drainage system in low-lying land. *A 13-year*

old schoolboy of Guyhoc Gardens who ignored the advice of his friend by jumping into a trench, died by drowning.—GyC (76.03.22, p.8) [By extension of SE *trench*, 'a dug ditch']

tri·al(s) *n* (*pl*) (CarA) **1.** Any (unexpected or unfair) trouble; tribulation. [Referring to many biblical uses of the word in connection with 'trial of faith'] **2.** PHRASES **2.1 Hear/See/Look (at) my trial(s) (today)!** *id phrs* (CarA) [*AF/IF*] Let everybody bear witness to what is happening to me! *'You see my trial, now?' Mrs Parkinson asked generally, but seeming ... to be addressing the hefty coconut trunks blocking the entrance of the dug-out. 'You see 'ow the sunshine jus' mockin' us an' pourin' out like not a t'ing appen. An' on top o' that we lock up in this 'ole like a bunch o' criminals'.*—SJS:130

trick *n* PHRASE **take trick to make luck** *vb phr* (ECar) [*AF/IF—Derog*] ‖ **take trick to make trade** (Bdos) To take advantage of people's charity for personal gain. *She walks about telling people her husband sick, she have three children and beggin[g] for money, just takin[g] trick to make luck, [in]stead o[f] lookin[g] for work.*—(Guyn) [Cp Yoruba *fi eru gba ibukun* 'with/by trick take blessing' ex: in ref to Jacob's obtaining the blessing due to Esau by trickery]

trick·i·fied (**trick·i·fy**) *adj* (Jmca) [*IF/AF*] Cunning; crafty; full of tricks. *You always callin' him that Anancy-man.... You just don't like Flitters, I guess. / That's right. He's smooth an trickified, that number.*—MHJT:30 [Cp *OED trickify* (Obs) *vb* 'to trick' + cit 1678. However, perh also infl by SAMFIE. Note *vb* form variant]

tri·é (t(h)ree-A, tree·ay) [trie] *n* (Trin) ‖ PICK-UPS (Bdos, etc) [Fr Cr < Fr *trier* 'to hand-pick, select, choose', from the requirement that the player pick up a number of small stones while throwing up a ball] □ The spellings *t'ree-A, three-A* are due to folk etym.

trig·ger·fish *n* (Baha, Dmca, Gren, Jmca) ‖ OLD-WIFE (CarA) *It is a triggerfish, colourful and flat. / Roundish is its mouth, and it has a 'deaf ear'. / Its eyes are independent of each other. / Dry its skin and you have the best floor scrubber.*—TOSR:44

trim·ble [trɪmbl] *adj* (Gren) [*AF—Derog*] Selfish; greedy; afraid of sharing or losing your possessions. *She too trimble, she does never want to share what she have.*—(Gren) [*EDD* tremble sb[1] notes variants *trimble, trimle* (Brks, Sc). The sense is 'a trembling'. Perh this + functional n > adj shift, with extension to 'a fear of sharing', may account for the *Gren* usage]

Trin·ba·go [trɪnbego] *n* (Tbgo, Trin) Trinidad and Tobago. [An experimental blend *Trin(idad)* + (*To)bago*, used esp in the late 1980s to express the single STATEHOOD of the two islands] □ This

succeeded the term '*Trinago*' wh was used in the 1970s.

Trin·ba·go·ni·an [trɪnbagoniən] *n* (Tbgo, Trin) A citizen of the two-island State of Trinidad and Tobago. [Blend of *Tri(nidadian)* + (*To)-bagonian*]

Tri·ni [trɪni] *n, adj* (CarA) [*AF*] ‖ **Trinto** (CarA) Abbr for 'TRINIDADIAN'. **a.** *We'll pay the extra dollars on our grocery bills every week and still be around to jump up for Carnival—we're Trinis, aren't we?*—ExP (73.01.21, p.5) **b.** *These are the individuals who end up leaving Trinidad on Ash Wednesday with thousands of dollars in their pockets. / Why can't it be the other way around Sir, with the dollars staying at home in Trini pockets?*—SuP (77.01.09, p.5)

Tri·ni·dad-ba·na·na *n* (StVn) ‖ CAYENNE BANANA (Guyn)

Tri·ni·dad-fig *n* (Gren) A variety of banana similar to the LACATAN but smaller and sweeter; it is not produced for export; *Musa spp*.

Tri·ni·da·di·an /112′1/ [trɪnɪdadiən] *n, adj* (CarA) (A person or thing) belonging to or characteristic of Trinidad. [< *Trinidad* + SE adj suff -*ian*]

Tri·ni·dad Span·ish *n phr* A rural creolized dialect of Spanish spoken by a remainder of PAYOLS in the northern areas of Trinidad, and preserved mostly in the religious songs of PARANG.

Tri·ni·dad's Pride (**Pride of Tri·ni·dad & To·ba·go**) *n phr* (Tbgo, Trin) ‖ CHACONIA (Tbgo, Trin) [Name promoted since it became the country's National Flower]

Trin·i·dad White *n phr* [*IF*] A person of European descent born in Trinidad; a Trinidadian CREOLE WHITE.

Tri·ni·ty Cross Med·al *n phr* (Trin & Tbgo) See T.C.

Trin·to *n, adj* (CarA) [*AF*] ‖ TRINI (CarA) □ A less common form and more often n.

tri-tri [tritri] *n* (StVn) See TITIRI

troo·lie(-palm) (**tru·li** (**palm**)) *n* (Guyn) ‖ **timite** (Trin) A fruit-bearing palm with immense, broad, undivided leaves wh are much prized by AMERINDIANS for roof-thatching and mat-making; *Manicaria saccifera* (Palmae).

troph·ic *n* (StVn) ‖ TROPIC BIRD (CarA)

trop·ic·al de·press·ion *n phr* (CarA) An area of heavy weather with winds about 35 m.p.h. and much rain; it is the first stage officially noted and signalled in the development of a possible HURRICANE.

trop·ic·al storm *n phr* (CarA) A well-defined area of severe weather with a centre or 'eye' and strong rotary winds that may reach up to 73 m.p.h.; it is the last stage before a HURRICANE is identified as such.

trop·ic·al wave *n phr* (CarA) An area of weak atmospheric pressure bringing cloudy, rainy weather but with no rotary wind circulation; it moves in a north-south wave westerly from the African coast towards and across the Caribbean islands.

trop·ic bird* /112'/ *n phr* (CarA) ‖ *trophic* (StVn) A large, mainly white bird distinguished by two shaft-like tail feathers some 16 ins long or about half the bird's total length; its wing-span much exceeds its full length; it is an ocean bird, feeding on fish and squids or, near the coast, on crabs; *Phaeton aethereus (Phaethontidae)*.

trot *vb intr* PHRASE **(sb/sth) can't ask sb to trot** *id phr* (Bdos, Guyn) Sb is or will be a run-away winner; sb is or will be in a commanding position (in regard to a situation that is referred to.) **a.** *I know he has a son at Queen's there, man! The others can't ask him to trot!—* (Guyn) **b.** *Sir, if you light de fire here so—on dis side, you see? The wind can't ask you to trot!* (i.e. *You, rather than the wind, will control the fire*).—(Bdos)

trou·ble¹ *n* (CarA) [IF] [Note: Often used in more emotive senses than in SE, sometimes almost personified, esp as in Phrs] **1.** (Often pl *troubles*) Worry; disturbed feeling; great personal difficulty. **a.** *Trouble made the monkey eat pepper.*—Guyn (Prov) **b.** *The troubles got my head spinnin[g].*—(Bdos) [Cp Black AmE folksong 'Nobody knows the trouble I see / Nobody knows but Jesus'] **2.** An affliction, ailment or disease of some part of the body; (hence many compounds **back-/heart-/lung-/stomach-**, etc **trouble**). [Cp *SND* Sc *trouble*; also *tribble* I. n 1. 'sickness, a specific ailment or disorder. Also *EDD* Var dial uses in Sc, Irel, Eng *trouble* 7. sb 'an ailment, complaint' 8. 'pain'] **3.** [By extension] [AF] Quarrels with or over one or more sexual partners; (hence compounds **man-/woman-trouble, husband-and-wife trouble**). *I don[']t know wha[t] wrong wid you. Eighteen years ol[d] an[d] you got mo[re] man-trouble than plenty big [w]oman.*—(Guyn) **4.** PHRASES **4.1 be in more trouble than Brown** *vb phr* (Bdos, Gren) [AF—Joc] To be in a lot of trouble or embarrassment; to suffer much annoyance. **4.2 bring trouble on sb's head** *vb phr* (CarA) [IF/AF] To cause sb to be in trouble; to put sb in grave difficulties. *'Girl chile no good, only bring trouble on yuh head...' Ramlal summed up.*—SABS:7 **4.3 catch/get/meet/see trouble** *vb phrs* (CarA) [AF/IF] To land yourself in difficulties; to find yourself in trouble. *In the noon, he explains about the text. About Saul drove David in the bush, because if he went into the house he would get trouble; and about the children of Israel in the Red Sea. David was to get trouble*

himself.—LMSPJS:10 □ Cp also Phr 4.5 below **4.4 Look trouble!** *excl vb phr* (Bdos, Guyn) [AF] See LOOK Phr 4.13 **4.5 Now/Then trouble start!** *id phr* (CarA) [AF—Joc] Prepare for an uproar!; Now/Then the fun begins/began! *Now trouble start. Just as he was getting ready to put the knife to the cock's throat the bird scratched off. See this naked cock up and down with this brother behind him, knife in hand.*—NaT (79.01.26, p.5) **4.6 trouble catch/meet/take sb** *id phr* (CarA) [AF] Sb is in for serious trouble. *If he don[']t pay back the loan by end o[f] the mont[h], trouble take him.*—(Tbgo)

trou·ble² *vb tr* (CarA) **1.** To annoy, molest, bother, interfere with (sb). **a.** *They warned their girl children. Walk straight. If they trouble you, call the police.*—LDCD:166 **b.** *Suppose de police catch you shootin' bird dis time of year. Dem lock you up, you know. / 'Cho,' said Mark, 'they wouldn't trouble me.' / 'Oh yes, sah, dem will arrest you and lock you up.' / 'Not me,' said Mark joking her back. 'They don't trouble white people.'*—HVUW:35 **2.** [With weakened sense] To handle, touch, disturb, interfere with (sth). **a.** *Somebody has been troubling the icing on this cake. Look one of the flowers is broken off.*—(Jmca) **b.** *'Two of my grandchildren were in the bedroom and I heard Jennifer (age five) saying Renaldo was troubling something.' / Gibson said she did not pay any attention to Jennifer because there was a jar of hair grease in the bedroom and she believed it was this he was troubling.*—NaT (87.11.09, p.24) [Evid a survival of EE usage maintained in CE. Cp *OED trouble* vb I. 1. trans. 'to ruffle (water, air, etc)' ... Now rare or arch. 2. trans. 'to disturb, derange, interfere with, interrupt; ... obs. or arch. + cits 1558. 'By her babbling she troubled the hole assembly'; 1607 (Shaks) 'Trouble not the peace'. 4. trans. ... 'to molest, oppress ...' 5. '... to vex, annoy, tease, ... pester, bother. Also Sc *JSDS tribble* vb active. 'to trouble, annoy; handle overmuch, hence, to damage'] □ This usage is Formal in CE, though not in IAE where it is replaced by the vb phr *interfere with*. **3.** PHRASE **3.1 trouble with sb/sth** *vb phr* (CarA) [AF] To interfere with sb/sth (i.e. as in senses 1., 2.) **a.** *Prince, boy. To tell the truth—I sorry fer Mr Adams. I always did like him, yer know. He never trouble with a soul.*—JMRS:70 **b.** *Child don't trouble with that typewriter—you'll damage it.*—(Bdos) [Prob a blend of CE TROUBLE + SE *interfere with*] **3.1.1 trouble with (a disease, etc)** *vb phr* (CarA) [IF] To suffer from (an ailment, etc). *She does trouble with rheumatism.*—(Guyn) [Cp *OED trouble* vb I. 5. 'to distress with sth disagreeable and unwelcome...' (Also *intr* with *with* (Obs)) + cit 1515 If they may find any hole or colour therein, they will trouble with me for the same. Cp also *EDD trouble* vb 6. Phr (1) 'to be troubled, to be frequently subject to (used of an ailment); + cits from Sc, w.Yks, etc: (It has a frequentative force) 'He's a-troubled way the rheumatic (= He suffers from and is subject to it frequently)]

trou·ble[3] *adj* (Jmca) [*AF—Cr*] Troublesome; difficult. **a.** *Dem chil[d]ren too trouble.*—(Jmca) **b.** *Dat look like real trouble work.*—(Jmca) [By functional n > adj shift of TROUBLE[1]]

trou·ble-tree *n* (ECar) [*AF—Joc*] A mischievous little child; [by extension] a troublemaker. *Trouble-tree don't bear no blossom* (= *A trouble-maker brings no good*).—Bdos (Prov)

tru·ba (tu·ber) [ˈtʃʊba ~ ˈtʃʊbʌ] /1′2/ *n* (Nevs, StKt) See CHOBA *Truba is called egg-plant and balongé also. The outside skin is very dark purple and it is either round or long. Some are light purple and white. The inside has many small seeds and it is fleshy. It is commonly used with saltfish or stuffed with meat and baked, or dipped in beaten egg and fried.*—StKt (Ms) [See CHOBA]

truc·tion [ˈtrʌkʃən] *adj* (StVn) ‖ RUCTION (Guyn, StVn) [Perh a blend of *troublesome* + RUCTION]

true *adj* **1.** (Bdos) [*IF*] [With falling or low pitch] That is so; I agree with you. *S1: But they promised to do that road a long time now and they haven't done it up to now. | S2: True.*—(Bdos) **2.** (CarA) [*IF/AF*] [In adverbial function] Truly; really. **a.** *I will tell him so to his face. True!*—(Guyn) **b.** *S1: You know Miss Harris that does sell the toolum? Well I hear she jus[t] dead. | S2: True?*—(Trin) **3.** PHRASES **3.1 for true** *adv phr* (CarA) [*AF*] See FOR Phr 17.10 *He was silent so long that Popo thought he should not have said anything about the harvesting machinery so he said now, 'Not for true. I make up that story.'*—SPOC:60 **3.2 no more than true** *adv adjunct* (Guyn) [*IF*] That is indeed the truth; that seems to be nothing less than the truth. *The boy said his mother told him not to mind if he was late for school, and no more than true, because I used to hear her telling the big sister the same thing myself.*—(Guyn) **3.3 True to God!** *excl phr* (CarA) [*IF*] I swear it!; As sure as ever! *I tell you if you come in here another night after twelve o'clock, you goin[g] to find this door lock! True to God!*—(StVn)

true-true /1′2/ *adj* (CarA) [*AF—Cr*] Real; genuine; actual. **a.** *Then she would shake her head sorrowfully. She couldn't remember her grandmother's true-true name.*—HCCM:32 **b.** *Usually the word 'ambulance' is used in the hospital and outside in a very loose manner, and many of the vehicles referred to as ambulances are in reality buses for the conveyance of patients to and from the hospital, they are not—to use the Barbadian term—'true-true' ambulances.*—Bdos (Hd, 73.11.06, p.2737) **c.** *Now understand me good; | I don't mean the church christening now; | I mean what she would call | The real true-true christening | As you will see as I go on.*—YFOC:24 [From characteristic Cr adj reduplication for emphasis]

trum·pet-bush* *n* (Bdos, BrVi, StKt, StVn, Tbgo, USVI) ‖ *bacano* (Tbgo, Trin) ‖ *bacano(l)e, bwa-kano* (Trin) ‖ *congo pump* (Guyn) ‖ *trumpet-bush tree* (StVn) ‖ *trumpet-tree* (Bdos, Jmca, StVn, USVI) ‖ *trumpet-wood* (USVI) A slender, upright tree growing rapidly to some 50 or 60 ft 'producing one or more hollow greyish coloured trunks' (*PTT:110*) and large, deeply-lobed leaves with a whitish undersurface wh are used as a folk-medicine; *Cecropia peltata* (*Moraceae*). *'At present some scientists are experimenting on bushes for curing of diseases such as 'Trumpet Bush' which is used for curing heart disease,' the Modern High School students said.*—NaT (75.12.21, p.3) [Prob from the trumpet-like shape of its long and hollow leaf-stalks]

trum·pet-fish* /112′/ *n* (CarA) ‖ *souflet* (StLu) A slender, bony, reef fish wh grows to some 30 ins in length; it has a long snout with a trumpet-like mouth, hence the name; *Aulostomus maculatus* (*Aulostomidae*).

trum·pet-flow·er *n* (Bdos) ‖ ANGEL'S TRUMPET (Baha, etc)

trum·pet-tree/-wood *n* (Bdos, Jmca, StVn, USVI) ‖ TRUMPET-BUSH (Bdos, etc)

trust[1] *vb tr* (CarA) [*IF*] [Of a shopkeeper] To sell goods to (sb) on credit; [by extension] to allow (sb) person credit. **a.** *Miss Evvy, uh wants you to trus' me half pung-a flour an' two cake o' soap till Mundee come wid de will o' de Lord.*—BTA:63 **b.** *The old businessman had to trust the porkknocker when he gave him three months rations not knowing whether he will ever strike it rich—or return.*—GyC (76.03.21, p.6) □ Cp SE *to trust* (*a customer*) *for* (*goods given*). **2.** [By extension] To get or take goods on credit. **a.** *Even if you could get credit you could not go too early in the morning to trust. You will have had to wait until the seller had made several cash sales so she could have some luck to take her through the day.*—PKKK:38 **b.** *'I will only give you credit,' the shopkeeper say, to humour Tanty, but before long she spread the ballad all about that anybody could trust if they want, and the fellar get a list of creditors on his hands.*—STLL:63 **c.** *'Don't go yet,' shrieked Charlotte. 'Ah want to tell you dis: you owe me two dollars fo' muffin an' salt fish cake you truss from me long time.'*—TRIH:62 [Cp *EDD trust* 2. 'to buy on credit or 'trust' + cits from Lnk, Oxf, Cor]

trust[2] *n* (CarA) Credit. *As a matter of fact, they get quite suddy when you decide to hold down on how much more trust you're going to give them or cheques that you won't accept.*—WeG (73.08.29, p.127, Partyline) [By extension and vb > n shift of TRUST[1]. Prob also infl by SE *trust* n]

trust[3] *adv* (CarA) [*AF*] On credit. *Give me the bread trust.*—RLCF:236 [By extension and n > adv shift of TRUST[2]]

truth PHRASES **1. for truth** *adv phr* (CarA) [*IF*] See FOR Phr 17.10 **2. to tell (you) the truth; truth to tell** *disjunctive phrs* (CarA) [*IF*] See TELL Phr 3. **a.** *Satisfied with the level of speaking? Well, to tell the truth, I am neither satisfied with what they say, how they say it, nor the amount of work they manage to do after they are given the vote.*—AdV (73.07.25, p.7) **b.** *Truth to tell half the time me don't understanding what them talking bout, but that is not my business, and business so good, me head swell.*—SNWIC:261 [SE has 'if the truth be told', but perh the common CE form is mainly from IrE infl. Note: An assertion or statement introduced by the words 'to tell God's truth' is always understood to be weighty and somewhat unexpected, the introductory words being given as a guarantee of its truth > —'Have you the rest of the money you owe me ready now James?' 'Well to tell God's truth I was not able to make it all up, but I can give you 5 pounds'—*JESI:12*]

try PHRASES **1. Try!** *excl* (Guyn) [*AF*] Have a care, you!; Don't you dare! □ In hostile contexts. **2. try a t[h]ing** *vb phr* (Gren, Guyn, Jmca, Trin) [*AF*] **(i)** To try to succeed by cunning or by taking risks. *I reckon that night cost the lad about $40 (at least), so in these scrunting days, you cannot be against him for 'trying a thing'. | I find he is a fool though, because he should take it as money invested and be looking for interest on a longer term basis.*—PuN (74.09.29, p.16) **(ii)** [By extension, of a man] To try to seduce a woman. *Since neither 'the authorities' nor ordinary men can stop rape—only women can do it. | Man name 'man', he suppose to try a ting. We see our role as a defensive one in the face of male sexuality.*—TaP (76.02.01, p.5) **3. try for me** *vb phr* (Bdos, Guyn) [*IF*] Please help me; please remember me. **4. try (to pull) a fast one** *vb phr* (Guyn) [*AF*] See FAST Phr 5.5 **5. try with sb** *vb phr* (CarA) [*IF*] To try to teach or control sb; to try to remedy sb's weakness or disability. **a.** *Miss Bourne tried with the boy but the boy like he can['t] take in the arithmetic at all.*—(Guyn) **b.** *The wife tries with him and the drinking and he's not such a drunkie nowadays.*—(Trin)

try·sil* [traɪsɪl] *n* (Guyn) A forest-tree whose wood is used for house framing or fuel; an infusion of its bark and leaves is a folk treatment for cuts and sores; *Pentaclethra macroloba* (*Mimosaceae*).

tub·ba-foot /1'12/ [tʌbʌ-fʊt] *n phr* (Guyn) [*AF—Derog*] See TOBO-FOOT

tub·bits *n* (Guyn) [*IF*] See TWO-BITS (Guyn)

tu·ber *n* (StKt) See TRUBA

Tu·chaw(a) *n* (Guyn) See TOUCHAU

tuk [tʊk] *n* (Bdos) The type of folk music characteristic of the TUK-BAND. **a.** *Shilling's box-guitar*

playing made him a household word in Barbadian homes. He played from 'tuk' music to hymns.—AdV (82.04.28, p.1) **b.** *Choirs and 'scrubbers' were significant aspects of the Christmas tradition in Barbados, as were the tuk players who used to take to the streets on Christmas Bank-holiday.*—AdV (87.12.28, p.7) [Cp *EDD* tuck sb² (Sc) 1. 'the beat or sound of a drum or trumpet' + phr 'tuck of drum'. Also *OED* tuck vb², Now *dial*. Chiefly Sc 1. ... 'to beat the drum; also (of a drum) to sound' + cits 1642 ... 'Ordains the drummers to touk throughe the town'. Note also that the term *bumbatuk* was once current in Bdos (*pers info, B. St John*) as an imitative name for the rhythm beaten by the TUK-BAND's drums, < *bum-bam-tuk*, the last syllable representing the dry 'knock' of the KITTLE-DRUM]

tuk-band (**took(-band), tuck-band**) [tʊk-ba·n] *n* (Bdos) ‖MASQUERADE-BAND (CarA) *One Christmas tradition that we still see something of today is the Tuk band. These bands can still be seen on bank holidays and at festivals. The bands comprised three or four men and sometimes one lone woman, 'wukking up.' One variation on the Tuk band was Donkey Belly Dancers, who were so called because the dancer's costume was fashioned like a donkey and tied around his waist. Stiltsmen were sometimes also features of these quartets, which were usually composed of a drummer, flutist, banjo and guitar player.*—AdV (85.12.25, p.8) [< TUK + SE *band*]

tula-ma *n* (Mrat) See TOULAMA

tu·lip-tree /1'21/ *n* (Bdos, BrVi) ‖AFRICAN TULIP-TREE (CarA)

tul·si(e) [ʹtʊlsi] *n* (Guyn) ‖JUMBIE-BALSAM (Guyn) *The tulsi leaves are used for flavouring Indian sweetmeats.*—OGEP:73 [Hin = the basil plant] □ The more accurate alternative to TOONSIE (*Trin*), from the etym evidence.

tune *vb* PHRASES **1. tune a pan** *vb phr* (ECar) [Steelband] To mark out the note sections on the surface of a PAN and determine the right musical pitch of each by a process of hammering and chiseling. *Winston Spree Simon was the recognised inventor of pan. Because of this, he was chosen in 1956 to go to Africa to teach the skill of making and tuning pans.*—JWSSS:29 **2. tune (sb) up** *vb phr* (Antg) [*AF*] To annoy (sb) deliberately. *Because John look so simple don['t] t[h]ink he fooly. If you tune him up you'll regret it.*—(Antg)

Tune-of-the-Crop *n* (Bdos) ‖ROAD-MARCH 2. (ECar) *The National Cultural Foundation (NCF) has also announced that this year's Tune-of-the Crop will be chosen on the basis of which tune is most played during the parade of the bands from the National Stadium to Spring Garden on Grand Kadooment Day, on August 3. | Judges will be positioned at different points along the route where they will tally scores of* *the most popular tunes.*—AdV (87.08.24, p.7) [*Crop* < CROP-OVER 2.(ii)]

tun·er *n* (ECar) [Steelband] A person (usu a man) who creates the musical surface of each PAN of a particular STEELBAND. *The pans themselves are genuine, used, 60-gallon oil drums; and the transformation from industrial waste to musical instrument is the business of the tuner. Each band has at least one, who produces the pans, tunes them, gives them their distinctive sound and blend (Trinidadian enthusiasts can often identify a band just by its tone). The first thing most tuners do is beat one end of the drum into a concave shape, using a five-pound sledgehammer. This creates a concave playing surface, on which the notes will be created. The tuner marks out the individual notes with chalk, then chisels grooves around them and raises each one slightly, hammering from below.*—Cat V.1, 1977, p.20

tun-tun [tʊntʊn] *n* (Tbgo, USVI) [*AF—Vul*] The vagina.

tup; **tup·py** *n* (Jmca) ‖ *tups(e)* (Guyn) A bit, very small amount; [by extension] a small drink of rum or a touch of liquor added to a longer drink. [Abbr of *tuppence*, with extension to 'tuppence worth' hence 'small quantity of sth']

tur·bot *n* (Baha, Jmca, TkCa) ‖ OLD-WIFE (CarA)

tur·key-ber·ry *n* **1.** (Antg, Mrat) ‖ CLAMMY-CHERRY 1. (CarA) **2.** (Jmca) ‖ BURA-BURA (Guyn) [From the use of the fruit to feed turkeys and chickens]

Turk's cap (cactus)*; **Turk's head (cac-.tus)** *n phr* (CarA) ‖ *barrel-cactus* (USVI) ‖ *melon cactus* (Trin) ‖ *pope's head cactus* (USVI) A low, barrel-shaped, or globular growth rising about 12 ins out of sandy dry ground; it is strongly armed with vertical rows of stiff spines and capped with a circular, white, woolly pad with little, pink flowers; *Cactus caesius* or *Melocactus communis* (*Cactaceae*). □ Common on Grand Turk (*TkCa*) and believed by some to account for the island's name.

Turks Is·land *n phr* PHRASE **all the salt in Turks Island couldn't save you** *id phr* See SALT[1] Phr 1.

Turks Islander /2'121/ *n* (CarA) A native of the Turks & Caicos Islands.

turn[1] *vb* **1.** *intr* [Of fruit] To begin to ripen (by showing a change in colour). *Just as a bunch of bananas shows signs of turning on the tree you cut it off and hang it up in the kitchen where the bananas will soon ripen.*—(Jmca) □ Usu of *hair* or *leaves* in SE, but see OED *turn* vb 47. **2.** *intr* (CarA) [*IF*] To become; to grow into (a state or condition of being); hence many phrs **to turn big/a big man/woman; to turn a young lady; to turn old/stupid**, etc. **a.** *Linda ain[']t turn a*

young lady yet (i.e. has not begun to menstruate.)—(Jmca) **b.** *Rheumatism does catch you when you turn ol[d].*—(Bdos) [Cp OED *turn* vb 38. 'to change into; to become', though usu *turn* (*a different) colour*, or *turn into sth*] **3.** *tr* (CarA) To stir (COU-COU, curry, rice) in process of cooking, in order to prevent burning. *You smell the curry burning and you couldn't even turn it for me?*—(Guyn) **4.** PHRASES **4.1 turn and twist** *vb phr* (Gren) ‖ TWIST AND TURN (Guyn) See TWIST Phr 1. **4.2 turn corn coo-coo** *vb phr* (StVn) ‖ SKIN CUFFINS (Bdos) See CUFFIN Phr. *As children we had a great time pillow fighting and 'turning corn coo-coo' on the bed.*—StVn (Ms) **4.3 turn Ole Mas** *vb phr* (ECar) [*AF—Joc*] See OLE-MAS Phr 3.2 *Don't forget, Mr Premier, that in the year 1962, when people were hunting around, trying to save what they could from the wreck of the federation, that they did think this the only choice they had ... By 1965, the senselessness and hopelessness of the exercise were so clear that Barbados decided to seek independence and everything turned 'Ole Mas'.*—Gren (Hd, 68.01.31, p.37) **4.4 turn out** *vb phr* (Baha, Guyn, Trin) To be in attendance (at a funeral); to parade in ceremonial regalia (e.g. as a member of a lodge). *When the N'ongo Yoruba lodge of Bain Town 'turned out' preparations were in progress for weeks.... On that particular Sunday, only the very benighted did not have a new costume in which to 'turn out'.*—EBT: 32 **4.4.1 turn out (bad)** *vb phr* (CarA) [*IF*] [Of a wound, boil, etc] To fester; to become infected and painful. **4.5 turn round and (do sth)** *vb phr* (CarA) [*IF*] **(i)** To do sth furthermore, in addition. *I was baptise, christen, confirm and went to Sunday school at Sin Matthias.... My mother turn round and make me get save at the Church of the Nazarene in Collymore Rock.*—PeL (79.12.07, p.10, A.T. Clarke) **(ii)** [By extension] To do sth bad in return for sth good. *I was the one that lent her money and clothes when he put her out, and then she turn round and steal from me and buse me in the bargain.*—(Trin) **4.5.1 turn round fast** *vb phr* (CarA) [*IF*] To hustle; to move diligently and efficiently; to do what is necessary, essential or required. *This child was so sick, if I didn't turn round fast he would-a dead.*—(Bdos) **4.6 turn (sb) so/like that** *vb phr* (Bdos, Guyn) [*IF*] ‖ PUT (SB) SO (CarA) [*AF/IF*] See PUT Phr 18. *He behaves funny like that out on the street all the time. The people say that somebody turn him like that.*—(Bdos) **4.7 turn your hand** *vb phr* (Gren, Jmca, ViIs) [*AF*] ‖ CATCH YOUR HAND (Bdos, etc) See CATCH Phr 8.11 *She made sugar cakes, jawbones, parched pindars and anything she could get to turn her hands with.*—PKKK:64 **4.8 turn your head** *vb phr* (CarA) [*IF*] To cause you to be temporarily confused. **a.** *De children makin[g] so much noise, enough to turn your head.*—(Antg) **b.** *When we come upstairs at yuh mother step, she took a sudden fright. I ask her what was wrong. And yuh know what—she din know where she was. The head had turn completely from the subway. I had to lead she the way you would lead a child.*—MBGB:99 [Cp Hausa *'kai nai ya juya' (head of him it turn)* 'he lost his direction; he has lost his senses* somewhat'; also Ci-Nyanja *mutu wanga un-azungulira (head of me it turned)* 'I was momentarily disoriented'] □ The further SE sense of this phr 'to affect, influence, sb unduly' is also operative in CE, though perh rarer. **4.9 turn your heart** *vb phr* (Gren) [*IF*] See HEART Phr 5. **4.10 turn your tongue** *vb phr* (StVn) ‖ CHANGE YOUR MOUTH (CarA) See MOUTH Phr 4.4 *You could really turn your tongue. You tell me one thing, and now in front of your husband, you say something else.*—(StVn) **4.11 turn up your face** *vb phr* (Guyn, StLu) [*AF*] ‖ MAKE UP YOUR FACE (CarA) [*IF*] See FACE Phr 4.

turn[2] *n* 1. (Bdos) A shortened form of MEETING-TURN *Turns, boxes and soo-soos are informal arrangements between friends and neighbours whereby each one in turn can make use of the total monthly or weekly savings of the entire group.*—Bdos (Ms, 1959) □ Another shortened form is MEETING 2. PHRASE **2.1 take a turn at/in sb** *vb phr* (Bdos, Belz, Guyn) To tongue-lash sb unexpectedly; to turn upon sb in wrath.

turn-coo·coo *n* (Trin) ‖ COU-COU (Bdos, etc) *Turn-coocoo and fish is a tasty dish.*—Trin (Ms)

turn-corn *n* (Nevs, StKt) ‖ COU-COU (Bdos, etc)

turn-corn·meal (**turn-meal**) *n* (Jmca) ‖ COU-COU (Bdos, etc) *Maas Tom had to remind her say nuff man in this country would glad for a plate of turn cornmeal many a day…. For that matter, Maas Tom say, him personally would not mind a plate of turn Cornmeal like the good old days when Putus did live Downtown and could appreciate fe we kinda food.*—WeG (72.12.06, p.12, Partyline)

turn-hand [tʌn-haˑn] 1. (Nevs, StKt, USVI) [*IF*] A small retailer of goods wh he often buys from neighbouring islands. *Later the government had a brain-wave. People often believe that 'Turn Hands' or the middle men make a lot of money, so government thought it could cut out all the 'Turn Hands' in and around Basseterre by setting up a government Marketing Depot. / So what do we find! The Government Marketing Depot is now the biggest 'Turn Hand' in Basseterre and this it does at a loss it is understood, of some $500.00 a month.*—DeM(SK) (68.02.17, p.2) [By vb phr > n conversion of TURN YOUR HAND (See TURN Phr 4.7)] □ Cp TRADER, TRAFFICKER. 2. (Gren, Trin) [By extension] [*AF*] Money made by small-scale retailing of goods. *Alright, I wouldn't argue with you because although it is the poor people that are suffering and are making the mountain dew and peddling it a little, whatever poor people do to make turn-hand, rich people going to do it better so I'm not arguing with you about getting after shop-keepers and dealers.*—Gren (Hd, 73.08.24, p.49)

turn-out *n* 1. (CarA) Attendance at a funeral, lodge or other organized function, esp when done in procession. **a.** *He was very sorry it had*

had to be a morning funeral. 'The turn-out', he said, 'would have been much better in the afternoon.'*—MLDS:18 **b.** *Next to weddings, the big joint celebrations were the lodge 'turn outs'… The merchants up town placed their orders far in advance for the trappings that supplied these occasions.*—EBT:32 [Cp *OED* turn-out 3. 'an assembling of persons'; reinforced also by vb phr > n conversion of TURN OUT. See TURN[1] Phr 4.4] **2.** (Bdos) An undertaker's presentation of a corpse for burial. *Have you ever thought about the type of 'turn-out' you would like to have when you die? / I have always argued that it is a waste of good money to purchase an expensive casket. Give that money to the poor, I say.*—NaT (74.03.17, p.3) [Cp *OED* turn-out 7. 'get-up, equipment, outfit']

turn·o·ver ['tʌrnovʌ] *n* (Bdos, Guyn, Trin) A small, oblong sweetbread, made by wrapping something sweet (such as grated and sugared coconut) in a thick piece of dough wh is then baked with a coating of sugar.

turn-stick *n* (Antg, Brbu) ‖ COU-COU STICK (Bdos, etc)

turn-tongue *adj* (StVn) [*AF—Derog*] ‖ TWO-MOUTH(ED) *You tell me one t[h]ing an[d] now yo[u] givin[g] a different story. How yo[u] so tu[r] n-tongue.*—(StVn) [By vb phr > n conversion of TURN YOUR TONGUE. See TURN[1] Phr 4.10]

tur·pen·tine-man·go *n* (Belz, Guyn, Jmca, StVn, Trin) Any of a few varieties of mango varying in size but fleshy and smelling noticeably like turpentine.

tur·pen·tine-tree *n* (Angu, Antg, ViIs) ‖ BIRCH-GUM TREE (Bdos, etc) [From the odour of the leaves and bark, and the fact that the juice evaporates into a gum-resin]

tur·tle-grass* 1ˈ12/ *n* (Bdos, USVI) A species of grass wh grows in shallow salt-water, and wh is used as fodder in the rearing of turtles; *Thalassia testudinum (Hydrocharitaceae)*.

tu·ru-palm (to·ro[2]) [turu∼tʊrʊ] A type of palm whose leaves are used by AMERINDIANS for thatching. *In other parts of the country, thatching is done with the young leaves of the … turu palms (Oenocarpus baccaba), which are cut before the leaflets have spread from the midrib.*—IAIG:210 [< *BAED* Arawak *toro* 'a type of palm', *Jessenia batawa*]

tush-teeth *adj, n* (Bdos, Guyn) [*AF—Derog*] Protruding front teeth. *Her tush-teeth really spoil her looks. It's a pity.*—(Guyn) [Cp *EDD* tush sb[1] Sc Eng 1. 'a dial form of 'tusk'; 'a long-shaped tooth; the tooth of an animal' + cit (Rut, Lei) 'applied to any teeth, esp the canines']

tu·tu[1] (too·too) [tutu∼tʊtʊ] *n & vb* (ECar) [*AF*] [Child talk] ‖ JOBBIE (Bdos) **a.** *You see, under a state law which went into effect this week* *in the cities of New York and Buffalo people who have such pets must clean up whatever they put down on any street, sidewalk, gutter or other public area or pay US$100 fines.... So since you cannot tell your dog to hold its too-too until it gets home, pet stores have come to the assistance of the some 400,000 pet owners with large stocks of gadgets.*—NaT (78.08.04, p.6, Al's Grapevine) **b.** *The last time I had my panty was when I tutu my skin ... I tutu my skin and I was messy.*—Tbgo (CR, 1982) [Cp *ADHL* Hausa *tutu* B. 1. 'human excrement'] □ In *Gren, StVn* (note also cit a. from Bdos) the term is generally applied to any excrement.

tu·tu² [tutu] *n* (USVI) A conch shell used as a horn. *By far the hardest lot was that of the field slaves whose working week extended from Monday to Saturday. They were awakened at around four o'clock each morning by the sound of the 'tutu' or conch-shell blown by a 'bomba', or slave driver.*—DHVUS:150 [Perh cp *IMED* Mende *tutu* 'a messenger']

twang *n* (Bdos, Guyn, Tbgo, Trin) [*Derog*] Any speech characterized by a non-native accent; [by extension] a foreign accent put on for effect. [Cp *EDD twang* Sc, Irel, etc 2. sb 'a dialect accent; the vernacular of a district by wh a native is known'] □ The strong implication of nasality in SE *twang* is marginal in CE usage.

twanm·blè (trem·bleur) [twãblɛ] *n* (Dmca) ‖ TREMBLER (ECar)

twen·ty-four hour[s] *n phr* 1. (Trin) A greenish lizard a few inches long, of the chameleon family and related to the iguana; it is harmless though the subject of much superstitious fear; *Polychrus marmoratus* (*Lacertidae*). [From the belief that death will ensue within 24 hours if it jumps on sb] **2.** (Grns, StVn) ‖ SCORPION-FISH (CarA) [A ref to the time within wh the fish's puncture of the skin can be fatal]

twist *vb* PHRASES **1. twist and turn** [twis-antʌ(r)n] /1'1 2/ *vb phr* (Guyn) [*IF/AF*] ‖ *turn and twist* (Gren) To go about business or work indecisively; to fumble and delay instead of setting about work. *He was here since seven o'clock but he twist-and-turn so much that, look, nearly nine and he only nail up one lil board.*—(Guyn) **2. twist up your face** *vb phr* (Gren, Guyn) [*AF*] See FACE Phr 5.

two *adj, n* (CarA) [*IF/AF*] **1.** A few; not many or much. **a.** *If the 'hog' wants a staff-member, he sits at his desk and growls your name. I wouldn't tell you about when he drinks two rums how he gets on.*—NaT (76.08.22, p.26, Dear Christine) **b.** *I'll call you in an hour after I've washed these two pieces of clothes for the family.*—(Antg) **c.** *As soon as two rain start to fall this place does flood.*—(Tbgo) [Replacing *a couple* wh is similarly loosely used] **2.** PHRASES **2.1 not two** *adj phr* (CarA) [*AF—Joc*] **(i)** Very many; very

much. **a.** *I['t]s not two times I tell him so, you know.*—(StVn) **b.** *She ain['t] two mornin[g]s, yeh!* (= *She is quite old.*)—(Bdos) **(ii)** (Trin) [With focus for emphasis] *It ai[n't] two try A try to make back up wid de woman* (= *I tried very hard to mend things with the woman.*)—(Trin) **2.2 in two two's** *adv phr* (CarA) [*IF*] Quickly; swiftly; in short order. **a.** *Ganesh said, 'Don't worry. I giving you something here that will get the boy foot better in two two's. Is a little mixture I make up myself.*—NTMM:12 **b.** *No doubt an ordinary ball thrown with ease would have had him out in two-twos, but as I was saying, it look as if the unusual play of the boys have the Englishers in a quandary.*—SWOS:165 **2.3 (two persons) can shake hands** *id phr* (CarA) [*IF*] See HANDS Phr 4.3

two-bits (tub·bits) ['tʊbɪts] *n* (Guyn) The sum of sixteen cents (in reckoning costs of small items in the market). *Benson may be a St Stanislaus boy, but his [Portuguese] parents viewed life in terms of two-bits and half-a-bit make the world go round.*—MLDS:179 [Two + BITS] □ The spelling *tubbits*, representing the folk pronunc, is sometimes found in narrative dialogue, though the usage is now mostly restricted to older folk.

two-by-two¹/-three/-four [tu-bɪ-tu/-tri/-fo(r)] *n* (CarA) [*AF*] A very small dwelling; a one-room house. *As a child he lived in a little two-by-three in Albuoystown.*—(Guyn) [A *Joc* ref to dimensions, perh 2 yds × 2/3/4 yds]

two-by-two²/-four [tu-bɪ-tu/-fo(r)] *adj* (CarA) [*AF—Joc*] Petty; insignificant; pitifully small. **a.** *We still have the capacity to make a much better life for ourselves. But we can't do it as a set of two-by-two poor-tail 'nations'.*—ToR (76.12.12, p.10) **b.** *All those religious bodies, two-by-four politicians and those countless do-gooders are, as usual, spouting junk to get in the public's eye and skirting the edges of the issue.*—ExP (73.06.18, p.21) [By extension and conversion of TWO-BY-TWO¹/-FOUR] □ Also *IF* AmE usage—(*pers info, L. Urdang*).

two-mouth(ed); two-tongue(d) *adj* (CarA) [*Derog*] ‖ *turn-tongue* (StVn) Deceitful; unreliable; changing or likely to change a statement or assurance given; [by extension] lying. **a.** *If Lloyd lost that match he would have had to seek asylum in South Africa rather than return home to face the wrath of West Indian supporters. But he won the match—and now his two-mouth fans are calling him the most brilliant tactician since Hannibal and Genghis Khan.*—SuC (76.08.22, p.6) **b.** *Would you believe that most of them in fact had previous assignments and instead of saying so, in true two-tongued Trinidad style, they said they were boycotting and gave all sorts of bogus reasons.*—BoM (75.02.07, p.19) [< 'talking with two (different) mouths/tongues.' Cp SE *two-faced*]

ty·pee [taɪpi] *n* (Guyn) [*AF*] **1.** A passionate, almost bewitched infatuation of a man or woman for sb of the other sex. *The fact that stuck in my head, however, that the prettiest thing to one crow is another crow, a male monkey sees a female* *monkey the way Romeo had 'typee' for his Juliet.*— GyC (76.06.27, p.6) **2.** PHRASE **2.1 got/have bad typee (for sb)** *vb phr* (Guyn) [*AF—Joc*] ‖ GOT/HAVE IT BAD (FOR SB) (Guyn) See BAD[2] Phr 5.4

U

UG [yuɹi] *abbr* (Guyn) The University of Guyana. *I left high school last June and I do not yet have a job. I had intended to take a diploma in English at UG.*—GyC (76.05.23, p.27) □ Usu so written rather than 'U.G.' and used without 'The' as in cit. UG was founded in 1963.

ug·li (fruit)* (oog·li, ug·ly¹) [ʌgli~ʊgli] *n (phr)* (CarA) A large, hybrid variety of the tangerine, with a greenish-yellow, thick and misshapen rind that is easily separated from its orange-like inside, the pulp of wh is sourish-sweet; fruit of the hybrid tree *Citrus paradisi X, C. reticulata (Rutaceae)*—*(AFPJ:388)*. [< SE *ugly*. From the discoloration and misshapen nature of the rind compared with other citrus fruit. However, the hybrid is a product of *Jmca*, and UGLI the popularized trade-name] □ Pl *uglies, ooglies,* the latter spelling occurring evid only in *StVn*. The form *uglifruit* also occurs as one word, prob on the analogy of *grapefruit*.

ug·ly¹ *n* (CarA) See UGLI (FRUIT)

ug·ly² *n* (CarA) [*AF—Cr*] Any thing, action, or person that is ugly. **a.** *God don['t] like ugly.*—Bdos, etc (Prov) **b.** *Ugly tell handsome frighten dis fo[r] me (= The evil-doer gets the good man to do his dirty work).*—AGM:19 (Guyn Prov) □ This particular usage seems almost restricted to proverbial sayings. However, in CE, *ugly,* like any adj, may be turned into a personal nickname.

uh [ʌ] *pers pron* **1.** (Bdos) [*AF—Cr*] ‖ A² (CarA) [1st pers sg] I. *But uh cahn laff/it off: uh cahn leff/e: we custom each udder/too much.*—BMP:90 [Cp *WEDG:271* 'The unstressed forms (of the nom of the 1st pers sg) are gen [a] or [ə]. But in the n. Midland dialects [o] is the gen form'. (Note that [o] is a short vowel in Wright's table *WEDG:13*.) Perh the Bdos folk pronunc reflects the latter two of these three unstressed E dial forms] □ This spelling, representing a common Bdos folk pronunc of 'I', is sometimes used in writing narrative dialogue. AH is, however, more often so used. **2.** [Non-native writers of CE may also use *uh* to represent other pers pron forms, ex (*Belz*) *uh* 'him, it' where Belz writers use AM or semi-nasal *a(m)* for these prons]

um [ʌm] *pron, 3rd pers sg* (CarA) [*AF—Cr*] ‖ *am²* (Belz, Guyn) **1.** It. **a.** *From wuh she had to say, um show he dat she know who um is tek*

'Pele' life. But um would appear,'cordin' to Eric, dat she did feel she life was in danger.—NaT (80.02.22, p.7, Lickmout' Lou) **b.** *Howeva, de Dacta rite wan lang lang letta to de Mirror an me a go examine um teday.*—MtM (72.11.17, p.10, Mango Seed Sez) **c.** *He say d' coat don' keep 'im warm—so he gon take um back an' change um.*—DSJS:7 **2.** [*Derog*] Him; her. *Da niega, she na go come! Yo[u] na go see um! (= That nigger, she will not come! You will not see her!)*—(Antg) [Of W Afr origin, and still current in Krio and in WAPE as pronominal /am/. Note *IWAP:191* '/am/ is the substitution for an object. It makes no distinction as to whether the object is 'people' or not' + exs p.188: *Yu nɔ go layk am* 'You will not like it', p.191 *Yu sabi Jon? / A sabi am fayn* 'You know John? / I know him well'. This form is exactly so preserved in *Belz* Cr, but is always sg, whereas in WAPE it may also be pl. However in the *ECar* and *Baha* Crs it has undergone vowel closure > [ʌm], and its application to a person (as in sense 2.) is infrequent] □ This pron form is evid not used in *Jmca,* but occurs widely in other *CarA* Creoles as pron obj. In *Bdos* it is often also used as subj of a sentence (as in cit 1(a)), occasionally also in *Guyn.* The form is accordingly much used to give a comical folk colouring to newspaper columns or narrative dialogue.

um·brel·la-ant(s) *n* (Belz, Guyn) ‖ ACOUSHI ANT(S) (Guyn) [A ref to the ants' habit of carrying pieces of green leaves raised above their bodies as they proceed in columns to store them for food]

un- *negating prefix* (CarA) □ This pref is often called into use as a 'regular' negator of adjs and advs replacing SE 'variants' *in-, non-,* etc, or SE negative phrasing. See separate entries below as some exs; they are not to be taken as restricted to the territories from wh the evidence is cited.

un·bush·ed *adj* (Jmca) Covered in weeds and bush; unweeded. *The sidewalks were unbushed. The Star was told that children and adults had to walk in the middle of the road because of the state of the sidewalks.*—StA(JA) (72.11.18, p.12)

un·but·ton *vb tr* PHRASE **unbutton your teeth** *vb phr* (Bdos) To open your mouth and say something; to speak, ask or answer (by way of politeness). *And that is if you are lucky …. Some of them don't even unbutton their teeth …. They just do as they please.*—Bdos (Ms, 1979)

un·cal·cu·lat·ed *vbl adj* (USVI) [*X*] [Of a person] Unreasoning; irrational; addle-pated. *He was now sure Sarah's head was uncalculated. Here she's accusing him of being ravenous and he hadn't said a word about food.*—PKKK:31 [See note at UN-]

un·call·ful *adj* (Tbgo) [*X*] Unaccounted for; without good cause or reason; unsatisfactory. *He had an uncallful deat[h], so he ca[n't] depart so easy* (= *he cannot be buried so easily*).—(Tbgo) [Perh a blend of *uncall(ed-for)* + *(mourn)ful*]

un·ca·pa·ble *adj* (Bdos) [*X*] Incapable. *He painted a picture of a stony adversary, an unhuman wretch uncapable of pity.*—AdN (72.07.08, p.9, Topic for Today) [See note at UN-]

un·cle *n* 1. (CarA) [*AF/IF*] (A folk term of respect for) any old male person. □ As the term so used as a form of address implies a folk-level relationship, it is, in some cases, resented. 2. (Antg, Guyn, Jmca, Trin) [*IF*] (A term of respect for)a close male friend of your parents. 3. *PHRASES* 3.1 **have to call (sb) uncle** *id phr* (CarA) [*IF*] To be the niece or nephew of (sb). **a.** *What happens is that three persons sit down on someone's gallery, sip a few grogs; one is cousin to the next who is to call the third uncle.*—AdV (86.02.09, p.13) **b.** *You know Sampson the shoemaker in Saffon Street? Well that same Dr Browne has to call him uncle.*—(Guyn) [Prob a phr of Afr origin] □ A roundabout way of expressing a due genetic relationship in contrast with the casual ones in senses 1, 2. See also AUNT phr.

un·cre·du·lous·(ly) *adj* (*adv*) (Bdos) [*X*] Incredulous(ly). *'Leave she, nuh,' Virgie said, 'She taking on 'bout Deighton?' 'Silla taking on 'bout Deighton?' Florrie said uncredulously.*—MBGB: 120 [See note at UN-]

un·cross·ing oil/-pow·der *n phrs* (StKt) An odorous oil or powder that is used by persons practising or using OBEAH to counteract an evil spell or some effect believed to be caused by such a spell. [*Un*, as negator + *crossing* 'putting a cross or curse on (sb)']

un·cus·tom·ed goods *n phr* (Gren, Guyn, StVn) Imported goods landed illegally without due government customs procedure; smuggled goods; contraband. *It is alleged that on December 6 last, B— of Duncan Street, knowingly kept a quantity of uncustomed goods namely ladies' stockings, umbrellas, shoes and a flask, with intent to defraud the revenue.*—GyC (75.12.10, p.3) [*Un*, as negator + *customed* 'passed through customs procedures']

un·del·i·ca·cy *n* (Trin) [*X*] Indelicacy. *But what is definitely reprehensible is the easy relapsing into unabashed undelicacy which unhappily the public appears so much to encourage and the calypsonian with such readiness to pander to.*—ExP (70.02.10, p.8) [See Note at UN-]

un·de·nom·in·a·tion·al school *n phr* (Guyn) [In former times] A non-denominational school; a school whose staffing and control were exclusively the responsibility of the government's Department of Education (as compared with Church or denominationally controlled schools). □ The parallel term *non-denominational* is also found.

un·der *prep* 1. (Guyn) [Of a person, esp a child] Close up to, as if seeking the protection of (sb). *It is not good enough for a big child like that, almost eight, to be still sucking his finger and always under the mother like that.*—(Guyn) [Prob reduced form of metaph *under the wing of*, as chickens are 'under (the wing of) the hen'] 2. *PHRASES* 2.1 **under breeze** *adv phr* (Gren) [*AF—Joc*] Very fast. *He swing the corner under breeze without brakes.*—(Gren) 2.2 **under liquors; under your liquor/rum** *adj phrs* (StKt) [*IF*] Drunk; intoxicated. **a.** *He went home 'under liquors' and awoke next morning to find the door and windows open, the place in disorder, and a box in which he kept documents ransacked.*—DeM(SK) (62.01.13, p.7) **b.** *She told the court that she had been walking home that night with her boyfriend who was 'under his rum' [and so she had to defend herself] when F— attacked them.*—LaS (77.02.12, p.12) [Prob reduced form of SE id *under the influence of liquor*] 2.3 **under manners; under heavy manners** [*IF*] *adj phrs* (Bdos, Gren, Guyn, Jmca) [Esp of children] Under restriction; under (firm) control; [of a person] watched and monitored by his or her spouse. 2.4 **under speed** *adv phr* (Belz, Gren) As fast as possible; at high speed. *Suddenly a truck approached them under a high rate of speed, hitting against the stroller and knocking the baby out of the stroller into the drain.*—BeB (65.06.12, p.1) 2.5 **under the bottom-house** *adv phr* (Guyn) See BOTTOM-HOUSE Phr 4.2.

un·der·hand ball; un.der.hand bowl·ing *n phrs* (Dmca, Guyn) [Cricket, esp in informal children's games] ‖ GROUND-BALL 1. (CarA)

un·dis·put·a·ble; un.dis.put.a.bly *adj, adv* (Bdos) [*X*] Indisputable; indisputably. *Undisputably the top creole in the Southern Caribbean three years ago, his last race was in the 1972 running of the T'dad Governor General's Cup, where he finished limping.*—NaT (75.11.02, p.17) [See Note at UN-]

un·done *vbl adj PHRASE* **leave/lef(t) yourself undone** *refl vb phr* (CarA) [*IF/AF*] See LEAVE Phr 6.

un·doubt·a·bly *adv* (Bdos, Jmca) [*X*] Undoubtedly. *Mr W— was undoubtably exploiting his position as Parliamentary Secretary and from his general conduct and behaviour, his integrity is open to most serious doubt.*—AdN (73.04.07, p.1) [< IAE *undoubtable*. See Note at UN-] □ SE already has *undoubtedly, indubitably.*

un·dress·ed po·lice·man *n phr* (Bdos) [X] A plainclothes policeman; a policeman who is not in uniform though performing a police duty. *Cheryl also claimed that among the men were a St Michael landlord, a uniformed policeman and others whom she believed were undressed police officers carrying guns.*—SuS (82.03.28, p.2) [See Note at UN-]

un·fair *vb tr* (Bdos, Guyn) [X] To treat (sb) unfairly, unjustly; to give an unfair decision (esp in a game or competition) against (sb); to cheat or be dishonest with (sb). **a.** *I go further, Mr Speaker, many a man has been unfaired and sacked at the hands of people with wives. I do not have to quote instances, but the whole world knows that if a wife does not like what is going on, or if she does not like you, you cannot go back to that particular house.*—Bdos (Hd, 73.03.16, p.1908) **b.** *Blackman, 31, national pursuit champion since 1976 told me: 'I think I should finish after 12 years of riding. I feel I got unfaired. Some of the selectors were biased.'*—SuS (83.03.27, p.18) **c.** *I want to say look how all the immigrants unfairing the creoles.*—CTT:11 [By functional adj > vb shift of SE *unfair* adj] □ Though this vb occurs in Formal usage esp in *Bdos*, IAE semantics hardly permits the derivation of vbs from adj opposites in *un-*. Note *to clean, to smooth*, etc, but not '*to unclean, unsmooth*', etc.

un·fix *vb tr* (Baha, Bdos) To remove an evil or controlling spell put on (sb) usu by means of OBEAH. **a.** *Naturally, medical science is often incapable of dealing with the problem of fixing and only the Obeah practitioner who diagnoses and can interpret the reasons for the fix, is capable of unfixing or clearing the individual.*—MTTBT: 117 **b.** *And then she say something that sound very funny to me: she say to wait and see—she going fix he up. And when one o' the womens 'bout this place fix up a man, he don't get unfix, I telling you.*—CISH:116

un·in·hib·it·a·bly *adv* (Bdos) [X] Uninhibitedly. *The rhythms which emanate from our 'Fundamentalist' churches and the gyrations of the devotees as they dance uninhibitably find echoes in the Shango of Trinidad [and] the Pocomania of Jamaica.*—AdN (72.10.11, p.4) [See Note at UN-. Cp also UNDOUBTABLY]

un·less *prep* (Bdos, Guyn) [X] Except. *Another woman, who rents a house in the tenantry, said that she was unable to get in or out of her home unless by wading through the water.*—AdV (66.08.21, p.9 [A prob survival of EE usage. See *OED unless* 3. prep a. 'except' + cits to 1886] □ This usage, duplicating SE *except*, is generally considered faulty in ModE. See also EXCEPT.

un·luck·y blow *n phr* (Guyn) [IF] [Esp among children] A blow causing some unintended injury received while playing or sparring. *You know he had a bad eye from an unlucky blow he got while playing football.*—(Guyn) [Cp *OED2*

unlucky 4. 'causing mishap or harm', among other senses. However, the central sense in *Guyn* E is 'unintended harm']

un·man your·self *vb phr* (Bdos) [IF] [of a man] To belittle yourself; to behave in an unbecoming manner. *I hate to see a big man behaving like a little boy—You think I would unman myself so?*—(Bdos) [Prob a shifted survival of EE. Cp *OED unman* v. 4. 'to divest of the character of a grown man' + cits–'1889; also 7. 'to deprive (oneself) of something' + cit 1694]

un·met·alled road *n phr* (Guyn) [Esp in forest land] A track that is not paved, but is wide enough to take vehicular traffic. *Many prominent Amerindians are of the opinion that an unmetalled road stretching ten to fifteen miles aback from the mill compound is an essential prerequisite to a large scale development of agricultural activity.*—DaC (52.08.03, p.2) [*Un-* 'not' + *metalled* 'covered with *road metal* or crushed stone'] □ Cp CART-ROAD (Bdos, Guyn) wh is much smaller.

un·mount *vb tr* (Gren) To dismantle. *If you lose this bed key you will have trouble to unmount the bed, so put it away carefully.*—(Gren) [*un-* negator + *mount* 'to set up']

un·na *pers pron, 2nd pers (pl)* (Bdos, etc) See UNU.

un·pick *vb tr* PHRASES **unpick your mouth/ teeth** *vb phrs* (Bdos, Trin) [AF] Open your mouth to make the smallest comment. *I listen to everyt'ing she say. But when she done I ain't unpick me teet'; cause I ain't got no one word to say to she.*—ELFBB:10 [See Note at UN-. Perh *un-* is used here as a double negation to stress meaning. See ‖ *(not) pick your mouth/teeth* at PICK Phr 5.2] □ Often used after *ain't, didn't* as in cit. The phrs are commoner (esp in neg contexts) in *Bdos* than in *Trin*.

un·re·lent·less *n* (Trin) [X] Unrelenting; relentless. *Maceo's father had been an unrelentless crusader and fighter in these struggles. Upon his death bed he asked his sons to continue this fight.*—ExP (71.12.09, p.8) [Prob a faulty blend of the two SE forms, but see Note at UN-. Cp also the erron form *irregardless* wh commonly occurs in written E internationally]

un·san·i·ta·ry *adj* (Bdos) [IF] Insanitary. *Health inspectors' discovery of unsanitary conditions in the wooden building had earlier led the Ministry of Health to close it.*—AdV (75.09.20, p.1) □ Though this form is listed in *OED2* + cit–'1871, ModE generally uses *insanitary*.

Un·til[1] *elliptical conj* (Antg, Guyn, StVn, Trin) [AF/IF] [In leave-taking] Until we meet again!, Good-bye for now!; See you later!

un·til[2] *conj* (Baha) PHRASE **so … until** *id phr* (Baha) [X] ‖ so … TILL (CarA) [AF] So (much so) that. *I was so full until I couldn't eat anymore.*—

(Baha) [Prob a false refinement of CarA Cr so TILL]

u·nu (oo·na, oo·noo· oo·nu, un·na, un·nu, u·noo) [unu ~ ʊnʊ ~ ʊnə] *pers pron, 2nd pers (pl)* (Bdos, Belz, CayI, Jmca) [*AF—Cr*] ‖ **wunna** (Bdos) ‖ **yinna** (Baha) ‖ **you-all** (CarA) **1.** You (pl); all of you; you (sg) in particular. **a.** *Davis then spoke up saying: 'Unu think unu bad but we badder dan unu.' And Gillet was taken away to the Training Camp.*—AmA (79.09.21, p.12) **b.** *Man, is wha' unoo tek the money and do? Is stuff you stuff unoo guts wit' it?*—SJT:46 **2.** Your (sg or pl); of all of you. **a.** *The old man replied indignantly 'Yu fe sell it. Yu fadder before yu did sell it retail, an not because yu so establish now ... call oona self pharmacy, yu fe sell it retail. Yu fadder would cry shame at yu!'*—DaG (76.06.24, p.3, Short Story) **b.** *Rachael replied calmly, shifting her walking stick from one hand to the next, 'But lawd, oonoo Rasta seem to 'ave somet'ing up oonoo sleeve like hell. Going on fidgety an' holdin' secret council like mad dem las' few days.'*—PCOS: 85 **3.** PHRASES **3.1 unu all; all o[f] unu** *pron phrs pl* (Bdos, Belz, CayI, Jmca) [*AF—Cr*] All of you. *Yuh ole generation / Oonoo all bawn dung a Bun grung / Oonoo all is Jamaican!*—FCV2: 167 (L. Bennett) [A survival of Igbo *unu* 'you (pl)' wh appears to have been first rooted in *Bdos* and to have spread therefrom in its orig form via slaves transferred to *Jmca, Belz, CayI*; whereas in *Bdos* it underwent an alternative change > WUNNA] □ The form, very often spelled *oonoo*, occurs in *Joc* or *Derog* usage in other *CarA* territories. Note that (a) it is not obligatorily pl and is sometimes used to give a specially *Derog* sense in the sg, (b) it is often deliberately used to give a familiar or aggressive character to a statement in wh SE *you* or Cr /yu/ also freely occurs.

un·wel·comed *adj* (Bdos, Belz) [*X*] Unwelcome; rejected as an unwanted guest. *Some of his visiting team brazenly foisted themselves into homes where they were unwelcomed, and one member of his party provocatively armed himself with a rock, show clearly the real purpose of the visit.*—BeT (79.11.18, p.1) [By functional adj > vb shift of *unwelcome* adj. Cp CE UNFAIR vb]

un-West In·di·an (un·West·in·di·an) *adj* Uncharacteristic or unlike what is considered typical of the West Indies or of its people and their ways. [*Barbados*] *is, first of all, the most un-West Indian of the islands, in appearance and in 'atmosphere'.*—SCE:19 (J. Hearne)

up¹ *adv* (CarA) [*IF*] **1.** [Often, as in SE, as an adv extension in a vb phr indicating completeness, frequency, intensity, vigour; but much more widely used than in SE, and also often with special connotations. Exs *dance up, fix up, jump up, lick up, love up, mash up, much up, work up,* etc] **a.** *'An' what you' moder say, is what I say,' said her father.... 'Don't allow any of those Kingston bwoy to fool you up.'*—DJC:3 **b.** *But [the arm] would never be well enough to*

play no trumpet or work no machine again. So why bother up myself?—MBGB:133 **c.** *Up—A word that has no end of usage, comes in handy front back or in between words to make the feeling felt, to feel humbug-up, sick-up, wex-up, or get your clothes tear up or wet up.*—DaN(ST) (78.04.06, p.11, A. Petersen) **2.** [Loosely used alternatively with *down*, sometimes followed by preps *at, by, in*] Situated away (usu from the city). *For Rent: Furnished apartment at Wanstead Terrace up by the University with a lovely view.*—AdN (Ad, 72.05.05, p.14) **3.** PHRASES **3.1 going up** *vb phr* (CarA) [*IF*] [Said by or to a person about to leave] Leaving; going home. **3.2 Up here/there.** *n phr* (CarA) [*AF*] This/that place (wh is away from another place to wh ref is implied). **a.** *The only qualm she has about leaving Emmerton is that she is now unable to worship at St Mary's Anglican Church 'as I would like to'. 'Up here is nice and windy and I feel good,' she said. Another resited resident, Eurie Stanford, said: 'I like up here very much although I was born in Emmerton Lane. I wish I was up here 10 years ago. I prefer up here to Emmerton.'*—AdV (Mag) (78.01.01, p.1) **b.** *I couldn't live in England. Up there is too cold for me.*—(Guyn) [See HERE² n. This frequent nominalization of the adv phr is a natural functional shift in CE, as may be noticed in cit (a) where the same speaker says 'I wish I was up here 10 years ago'] □ IAE would require impersonal structures such as 'It is nice up here', etc. **3.3 up (in America, Canada, England, etc)** (CarA) [*IF*] Away from and far to the north of the Caribbean. *I have a new doctor now, a Bajan, who studied medicine up in Canada.*—CWFYS: 58 **3.4 up unto now/then, (etc)** *adv phr* (CarA) [*AF/IF*] Up to this/that time, etc; up to now/then, etc. *I lent her some money when she needed it and up unto now I am waiting for her to pay me back.*—(Antg)

up² *adv, adj* (CarA) [*AF*] Above the common and ordinary; proudly; in a conspicuously respectable manner; [slipping into adj senses] full of pride; requiring to be respected. **a.** *As a family they always live up, so now things get hard they can't take poor people work.*—(Guyn) **b.** *Jane, feeling that she occupied a superior and enviable position, said good-naturedly: 'I wish de whole of y'u was going wid me. But I not gwine to have anyt'ing to do wid boys, for I promise me parents to keep meself up.'*—DJC:5 [Developed from the SE adv sense of *up* 'high; highly'] □ Preceded by noticeable open juncture and distinguishing stress.

up³ *prep* (CarA) [*AF*] [Loosely used alternatively with *down*, but without a foll prep. Cp UP¹ adv 2.] **1.** In, at (some place away from town or some central point). **a.** *He ran to his mother's up Plaisance way.*—Tbgo (Ms, 1966) **b.** *Patrick and the boys were having quite a spree up Kitty [village] last Saturday night.*—DyC (53.04.14, p.3) **2.** PHRASES **2.1 up the islands** *adv phr* **(i)** (Guyn) In the Caribbean islands, esp the Eastern Caribbean islands. **(ii)** (USVI) In one of the larger islands to the east or south of the US Virgin Islands. *'Up-the-island-people'* became anathema to the Virgin Islanders and this was aggravated by the belief that their oppression had its roots in Antigua.—HVIS:176 □ May be *Derog.* Cp DOWN THE ISLANDS (See DOWN[2] Phr 2.) **2.2 up top (of); up on top of** *prep phrs* (CarA) Above; on top of. **a.** *She lives up top the grocery.*—(Guyn) **b.** *He had hidden the papers by putting a large book up on top of them.*—Bdos (Ms)

up[4] *vb* [AF/IF] **1.** *vb tr* (CarA) [AF] ‖ UP WITH (CarA) See Phr 5.2 below *I would jus[t] up a stick and hit him one good lash.*—(Gren) [Cp *OED up* vb. 7. b. *colloq.* 'to raise (the arm); to lift or pick up' + cits to 1851] **2.** *PHRASE* **2.1 up hand and hit (sb)** *vb phr* (CarA) [IF] See HAND[1] Phr 4.22 *Said the accused: 'He up his right hand and let it go at me. He struck me on my right cheek and swung away.'*—AdN (76.07.21, p.1) **3.** *vb phr* (CarA) [IF] To raise (a price, level, rank, etc). *In response to popular clamour, the Trinidad Legislative Council upped his grade so that he could get the salary offered him by B.G.*—DaC (52.09.01, p.1) **4.** *vb phr* (Guyn) [AF] [By extension] To take away; to steal. *Somebody up his bicycle from outside the bank.*—(Guyn) **5.** (CarA) [AF/IF] [Indicating sudden, abrupt action] *PHRASES* **5.1 up and (do sth)** *vb phr* (CarA) [AF/IF] ‖ ups and (do sth) (CarA) To do sth rashly, unexpectedly, abruptly. **a.** *'You should have kept them,' Tony said reproachfully 'a mother shouldn't just up and leave her children.'*—JPB:59 **b.** *And now my husband has up and told me that if I don't lose 40 pounds that me and him are done.*—AdV (Mag) (87.08.08, p.8, Dear Wendy) [Cp *OED up* vb. 5. b. *colloq.* or *dial.* + cits–'1898; but *OED2* extends cits to 1979 'we upped and fled'. Also note AmE as in *W3 up*[3] vb intr 1. 'to act abruptly' usu followed by *and*, + cit 'he up and married a showgirl'] □ See also UPS vb. **5.2 up with (sth)** *vb phr* (CarA) [AF/IF] To pick up (sth) aggressively. **a.** *As I passed by her she dashed the water out of the bowl into my shoes...after she up with the bowl to come to me I up with the basin and I strike her with it.*—Bdos (CR, 65.04.12) **b.** *But before she could close the window, the man 'up with the box and forced it through the window'.*—DeM(SK) (62.12.22, p.8) [Cp *EDD up* 16. used verbally with ellipsis; in gen colloq use (in Sc. Irel. and northern counties) + cit from Nhb 'He ups wiv a stone an' hat him']

up·ful(l) *adj* (CarA) [Rastaf] Enlightening; uplifting; educative. *Ghetto poet Oku Onuora is desperately trying to move poetry out of the so-called 'high society bracket' and reach the masses which have been totally deprived of 'upfull and conscious reasoning'.*—DaN(JA) (79.09.07, p.8) [Perh a blend of *up(lifting)* + *(use)ful*]

up·keep *vb tr* (Bdos, Guyn) [X] To maintain; to keep up (a standard, position, etc); to keep (sth) in good order or condition. *Every woman we leave at home employed in our houses every day to look after our children, to upkeep our clothes,* to scrub and wash for us, is making a contribution in money terms that should be properly recognised in the laws of the land.—Bdos (Hd, 75.07.15, p.5237) [By functional n > vb shift of SE *upkeep* n]

up·lift·ment *n* (CarA) Improvement; enlightenment; increase in standing and respect; uplift. **a.** *A part of it in this our tenth year of Independence must be, I think, the general upliftment in the educational standards of the police.*—Bdos (Hd, 76.03.19, p.6338) **b.** *In an effort to play its part in the upliftment of culture, the Catholic Teachers' Association has organised a Calypso Competition for its members.*—ToR (78.06.21, p.8) **c.** *Divali culminates in mental enlightenment, the dispelling of the darkness of ignorance. This is the permanent Divali for the benefit and upliftment of man.*—ExP (72.11.05, p.5) [SE *uplift* vb + *-ment*, by analogy with *improvement*] □ This word is widely used in the best educated CE. Though *OED2* notes it as 'chiefly Black and Indian English', *W3*(1961) lists it as a headword and The Macquarie Dictionary (Australia 1981, rev. 1985) lists it as a derivative, both without comment.

upon *prep* (CarA) [X] [Esp in physical senses] On; (on) to. **a.** *You said that you heard two lashes upon the man outside on the step.*—Dem(SK) (62.11.10, p.9) **b.** *He hold on upon Adelaide, threw her down and give her two kicks.*—Bdos (CR, 71.05.21) [A false refinement of CarA Cr (U)PON 'on']

up·pers *n pl* (Nevs, StKt) ‖ HIGH-CUTS (Bdos)

up·per·side *adv, prep* **1.** (StKt, Tbgo) ‖ ABOVE[1] (CarA) (To the) east (of); (on the) windward (side). **2.** (Guyn) (To the) south (of); above the cataracts of a river. **3.** (Guyn) Away from the river-bank.

up·pish *adj* (CarA) [IF] **1.** Rude (in relation to your social standing); self-assertive in some offensive way (esp as used in the foll phr). **2.** *PHRASE* **2.1 uppish with yourself** *adj phr* (ECar) [IF—*Derog*] Bold; deliberately rude and out of order; precocious. *The young girls nowadays so uppish with themselves; see how some of them pushin[g] deyself up to the men.*—(Bdos) □ IAE *uppish* is a less offensive term. See also BIGGITIVE

ups *vb tr* (Guyn, Trin) [AF—*Joc*] **1.** To pick up promptly; to take up rashly. **a.** *If anybody drop a note or even a tanner by accident, you could be sure it hardly have time settle on the ground before a test ups it.*—SWOS:158 **b.** *Befoe I could digest his statement, Juliet from the next yard ups he, 'Don't worry wid you, every thing for you is a skin-teeth, but I certain dat you aint going get wata dis marnin unless you is a lock-smith.'*—Kai. 8, p.63 (D. Jeffrey) **2.** *PHRASE* **2.1 ups and (do sth)** *vb phr* (CarA) [AF—*Joc*] ‖ UP AND (DO STH) (CarA) [AF/IF] **a.** *Ah say, 'Officer, as how de night so hot we only come to cool orf.' He ups an' tell mih, 'Madam, ah would advise you to go* *home an' drink some coolin'. Doan stop here at all.'*—MN:51 **b.** *When I did ups an' leave home, I did have a wrong picture o' the place, man. We really out o' date bad concernin' the set-up, over 'ere, you know.*—SCHMH:183 **c.** *Because Ah tell you you was wrong to take Penny Farthing money, you ups an' box me.*—TRIH:120 [UP⁴ vb + paragogic /-s/] □ Cp UP AND DO (STH) (See UP⁴ Phr 5.1; UPS AND DO (STH) is less serious and of somewhat lower status]

up·si·ded down *adv phr* (Bdos, Gren, Guyn, Trin) [X] Upside down. **a.** *While taking in the scene at Tuesday's motor racing a car washed out and overturned. This cat standing below me just kept staring with his mouth open. So like I had to ask him if he had a stroke or something to which he replied: 'No, I was just wondering how the driver managed to sit down in there upsided down.'*—AdV (71.12.04, Al's Grapevine) **b.** *The Englishman was so high strung / He buse the Chiney upsided down.*—Trin (Cso, 'China Man', 1971) [< *upside down* by paragoge, or overcorrection infl by *wrong-sided, lop-sided,* etc]

up·side-down ba·na·na *n phr* (Bdos) ‖ J-UMBIE BANANA (StVn) [From the fact that the small bunch of fruit points upwards instead of hanging]

up·stairs¹ *n* 1. (Belz, Bdos, Guyn, Jmca) [AF/ IF] The upper storey of a two-storeyed house. *My dear, they wouldn't want to live under anybody so, poor-ass as they are, they busy looking for an upstairs.*—(Guyn) [Prob abbr < UPSTAIRS HOUSE] **2.** (Dmca, Guyn) [AF—Joc] The head (esp in ref to mental state). **a.** *The brother is a fellow that dresses every day say he going to work, but he ain't got any job, just walks about. Upstairs, not too nice, you know.*—(Guyn) **b.** *A packed Court Room heard V— say that he was 'not feeling too good in the upstairs' when asked by Magistrate J.J. Copeland whether he wanted to ask a witness any questions.*—DoC (65.01.20, p.6) [Joc metaph. Cp IAE 'in the top storey' and AmE 'upstairs' similarly used]

up·stairs² **(of)** *prep* (Baha, Bdos, Guyn, StKt, StVn) [X] Above; on the floor above, or in the storey above (some location). **a.** *Police had one suspect ... in the hold-up of the offices of Theatrical Enterprises Ltd, upstairs the Savoy Theatre in downtown Bay Street.*—NaG (75.10.15) **b.** *As from the 1st February 1973, the Office of Eastern Caribbean Agencies Ltd and St Vincent Import/ Export Company has been moved to new premises upstairs the American Store, opposite Fred J. Dare, Middle Street.*—ViN (Ad, 73.02.10, p.6) **c.** *Visit our Show-Rooms* (Upstairs of our main Store).— SkN (Ad, 63.10.16, p.3) [By functional shift of SE *upstairs* adv]

up·stairs house; up·stairs and down·stairs house *n phrs* (CarA) A two-storeyed house. *For Sale: Sangre Grande. One and a half acres leasehold with large upstairs house, downstairs fully paved.*—TrG (Ad, 70.04.02, p.13)

up·start·ed *adj* (BrVi, Guyn, Trin) [X] ‖ BIG-GITIVE (BrVi, Guyn) *She would turn on them and accuse them of being ungrateful and upstarted, and end by declaring that she alone had the right to criticise her betters.*—CBM:39 [< SE *upstart* adj + *ed* (by paragoge). Cp LATED]

up·wards *adv* (CarA) *PHRASE* **upwards to now/this day** *adv phr* (Bdos) [X] Up to now/ this day. *I think it was las[t] year [a]bout June that the Gov[ern]ment start repairin[g] that road and upwards to now they ain't finish it yet.*—(Bdos) □ The phr is used in emotive contexts.

ur·di *n* (Guyn, Trin) [Indic] A type of hard MUNG-BEAN that is often boiled and ground to be used as an ingredient of PHULOURI; *Papilionaceae spp.* [Bhoj < Hin *urhad,* name of a hard black bean]

ur·ni *n* (Guyn, Trin) See ORHNI

use [yu·z] *vb tr* 1. (Bdos, Guyn, Tbgo) [In ref to food] To eat or drink; to consume (as everyday food). **a.** *Now he says he is a Muslim, so he doesn't use pork or alcohol.*—(Bdos) **b.** *Your hotel offers you half a teaspoonful of last year's coffee grounds in a pint of lukewarm water, since in your folly you said that you 'used' ground coffee—'use', revealingly, being the Guianese word for 'drink' or 'eat'.*—NMP:126 [As OED *use* v. 11. 'to partake of as food, drink, etc' + cits-' 1859. This is the regular sense maintained above in CE, rather than its extension (in OED2) to 'alcoholic drink and narcotic drugs'] **2.** (Gren, Guyn, Trin) [IF] [In ref to a woman] To have sexual intercourse with and then abandon (a woman). *When Lloyd came he went to accused behind the house and said 'Joe a big man like you have Pauline under the house using her.' I did not hear accused reply.*— Gren (CR, 79/8) [Cp OED *use* v. 10. b. 'to have sexual intercourse with'. (Obs.) exc. *dial.* + cits-' 1889] □ See also USES n pl 2. **3.** (CarA) *PHRASES* **3.1 use a word/words (to sb)** *vb phr* (Gren, Guyn, StKt) ‖ CURSE (SB) To use foul language (in addressing sb). **a.** *But Mary said that people interfere with her and on the day in question a woman used a word to her and the 'same word she used to me I return back the same word'.*— DeM(SK) (63.09.28, p.10) **b.** *According to evidence revealed in Court, the defendant and John had some confusion over a mutual 'boyfriend'. On the day in question the defendant was on the bridge and the complainant is alleged to have used 'words' to her.*—ToR (76.05.26, p.3) □ A less emotive term than CURSE (CarA). **3.2 used to (do sth)** [yuzid tʊ]; **uses to (do sth)** [yuziz tʊ] *vb phrs* (Bdos, Guyn, StVn, Trin) [X] Used to (do sth). **a.** *Yes sir, I used to help born all the babies and I used to put up the deads too in Guinea-Corn alley.*—SBHM:5 **b.** *'So—I-could-sleep-in-the-bed—I mean, well, we uses to know one another good in Tobago, and now that you here in London, what you think?'*—RWIN:104 (S. Selvon) [The form USES in this function might have developed from the pronunc of *used* [yuzid] still common in some places, as in cit (b)] □ The phr *uses to* is far the commoner of the two among uneducated speakers. **3.2.1 used was to (do sth); uses was to (do sth)** *vb phrs* (Gren, Guyn, Jmca) [*X*] Used to (do sth). **a.** *Mammy, you forget me used was to cut me own gun outa wood same way?* —SNWIC:264 (M. Townshend) **b.** *In dis country, ah sign dat look like what de late Hitler uses was to do. Mek up lie, talk of war, blowin up, burnin sabotage. Spread hate, recruit chilleren to bring news pon dey parents, put brother against brother.*—ToR (77.01.16, p.5, Contay Si Contay La) [Cp HAD WAS TO. The phrs represent an aspectual CarA Cr attempt, surviving here, to stress the habitual nature of the action in the past] **3.3 use off (sth)** *vb phr* (CarA) [*IF*] To use up or use out (sth) entirely. **a.** *Sylvin use off all of this money, and still making out cheques and know there is no money in the bank on this account.*—Antg (Ms, 73.03.12) **b.** *Yo[u] mean yo[u] use off all de milk and ain['t] leave none for breakfas[t]?*—(StVn) [Cp *OED use* 14. *use off or out* 'use up' + cits–'1849] **3.4 use up (sb)** *vb phr* (Belz) [*AF*] ‖ BUSE (OFF, ETC) (SB) (ECar) *She get outside and use dem up so till dey had to call de police.*—(Belz)

uses [yusɪz] *n pl* **1.** (Bdos) Use. *They ain got no more uses for me and they gone.*—MBGB:251 [Prob a false refinement] **2.** (Trin) [*IF*] Benefits or advantages of sexual intercourse with a woman. *Well, I, of myself, I don' see why a man should really marry, na. I 'fraid that, it does bite, yes. You leave she and have to pay she and you en gettin' the uses of she, somebody else gettin' them, and you still pay.*—RLCF:68 [By functional vb > n shift of USE¹ vb 2.] □ Cp USE vb 2.

u·sing-up *n* (Belz) [*AF*] ‖ BUSING-OFF (ECar) *She gave her neighbours a proper using-up when she heard they talked her name.*—Belz (Ms) □ Cp USE vb Phr 3.4.

u·ten·sil *n* (Bdos, Guyn) ‖ *chimmy* (Jmca) ‖ *night-glass* (Belz, Jmca) ‖ *po, posie* (Guyn, Trin) ‖ *tensil* (Antg, StVn, Trin, USVI) ‖ *topsie* (Bdos) (Euphemism for) a chamber-pot. [Cp *OED utensil* 5. 'a chamber-pot. Spec. *a chamber utensil*' + cits–'1841]

U.W.I. (*abbr*) (CarA) The University of The West Indies. □ Often written UWI and pronounced either as separate letters or, familiarly, as [yuwi].

V

vac·u·um-pan *n* (CarA) [Sugar Ind] A very large, bottle-shaped, copper cylinder, encased in wooden staves, the base section about 10 ft in diameter and about 12 ft tall, the neck-section somewhat smaller; it is used for the last stage of controlled evaporation of thick cane-syrup under low pressure to obtain sugar crystals. [*Vacuum* because the container is enclosed to allow control of pressure + *pan* because the device replaces what used to be, in former times, a large open pan] See PAN¹ 2.

vac·u·um-pan mo·las·ses *n phr* (Bdos) ‖ B-LACK-STRAP (Bdos) □ Commonly referred to also as VP industrially.

va·ga·bond [vagabʌn ~ vaɪgɪbʌn] *n* (Guyn) [*AF/IF—Joc*] **1.** A lazy but inoffensive young man. *I can['t] get that vagabond to come and do the work he promised.*—(Guyn) **2.** An old man who has or seeks young sexual partners temporarily. *You know that old vagabond went and give that poor girl a child?*—(Guyn) □ The term is generally used in friendly mockery. Cp SCAMP *Guyn.*

vage [veɪ] *n* (Trin) ‖ BIRD-VINE I. (Dmca, etc)

vaille-que-vaille *adj, adv* (Dmca, etc) See VAY-KI-VAY

Va·len·ci·a *n* (ECar) A particularly sweet variety of orange; *Citrus sinensis, var Valencia (Rutaceae).*

va·lise [vali·z] *n* (Bdos, Guyn, USVI) ‖ **grip** (Bdos, Guyn) A suitcase; a piece of luggage (usu of medium or large size). □ SE *valise* is usu a small, overnight bag. In AmE a large suitcase also = 'grip'.

val·ue *vb intr* (ECar) [*X*] To be worth. *The land might well value the money asked.*—Nevs (Ms) [A shift in semantic function of SE *value* 'to appraise, to esteem'; or a confusion with the vb phr in 'land *valued* at a certain sum'] □ A common error in written schoolwork.

van·i·ty *n* (Guyn) ‖ DRESSER I (Jmca)

vap¹ *n* (StLu, Trin) [*AF*] **1.** A sudden onset of moodiness; a bad mood. *What you chase the child outside for? You like you have a vap taking you!*—(StLu) [Prob Fr Cr < Fr *vapeur* 'dizziness, light-headedness' (a rarer and earlier

sense)] **2.** [By extension] An impulse; an unaccountable sudden urge. **a.** *Who can tell what was the vap that hit Cap and make him get married? A man like he, who ain't have nothing, no clothes, no work, no house to live in, no place to go?* —STLL:40 **b.** *Discouraging them from continuing to teach by 'vaps', she explicitly and eloquently advises them on the correct approach to educating three to five-year olds.*—TrG (76.03.30, p.4) **3.** *PHRASE* **3.1 catch a vap(se)** *vb phr* (StLu, Trin) [*AF—Joc*] To do (sth) by impulse; to become suddenly active as if on the spur of the moment. *The Students Guild really catch a vapse this year and start publishing magazine and news-sheet and what-not.*—(Trin) [< *Catch a vap* 'be caught by an impulse', often with CE paragogic /-s/, as in *Dads*, etc; often rendered in dial spelling as **ketch a vapse**]

vap!² *ideoph* (Tbgo, Trin) [*AF—Cr*] [Representing the sound of a sudden blow (usu on sb)] *He hit him vap!*—(Tbgo) [Prob carrying over the sense of impulsiveness from VAP¹] □ Cp AmE slang *zap*, vb, interj.

va·ri·e·ty *n* (Bdos) ‖ CAKE-SHOP (Guyn)

vat *n* (Belz, Guyn) A large, wooden, out-of-doors cistern, about 10 ft high, mounted on a low base and shaped like a truncated cone, with a capacity of several thousand gallons; it is made of WALLABA staves secured by stout iron hoops and is used for storing rain-water wh is run into it via the guttering-system of a house and drawn from it by a tap near the bottom. □ Though still found in some areas, the VAT is now obsolete, esp in *Guyn*. In *Belz* the wooden cistern is often replaced nowadays by one made of aluminium.

vay-ki-vay (**vaille-que-vaille, vie-ke-vie, vi·key-vie, vy-ki-vy**) [vaɪkɪvaɪ] *adv, adj* (Dmca, Gren, StLu, Tbgo, Trin) [*AF*] **1.** *adv* In a disorderly way; in an unplanned or haphazard manner; carelessly; shabbily. *But the houses that stick out of the hills, in irregular patterns, like knobs on a draught board lying down vikey-vie have been put up by people working hard with materials that have been scavenged or stolen or bought of the nutten that their labour brings.*—TaP (72.07.30, p.7) [Fr Cr < Fr *vaille que vaille* 'at all costs, come what may', with a shift in sense to 'any old how'] **2.** [By extension] *adj* Shoddy; haphazard; unplanned; unorganized; done on the spur of the moment. *The Honourable Member* must understand that the time has passed when things must be done, to use a colloquial term, in a vaille que vaille fashion. Today things must be done with the proper technological and the proper technical know-how; the proper expertise.—Gren (Hd, 73.02.09, p.51)

ve·ge·ta·ble-brain n (Jmca) ‖ ACKEE (CarA)

ve·ge·ta·ble-mar·row n (Bdos, Jmca) ‖ GOURD (BrVi, etc)

Ve·no [vino] n (Guyn) [AF/IF] A Venezuelan person. [An abbr, prob orig Joc, of Venezuelan] □ Pl **Venoes**.

vèp (vêpres) [vɛp] n (Dmca, StLu) [AF—Joc] A lift; a free ride in a vehicle. [Fr Cr < Fr vêpres 'vespers, evensong', at wh there was no collection—hence a 'free service', in contrast with the morning service when a collection was taken. The shift in meaning to the 'free service' of a friend driving a vehicle is Joc]

ver·y said adj phr (ECar) [X] The very same; the selfsame; definitely the same. You remember they had a case in the papers some years ago about a police corporal rape a young girl? Well he is the very said person.—(Bdos)

vest n (Antg, Bdos, Guyn) ‖ MERINO (CarA).

Ves·try n (Antg, Bdos, Jmca, StKt) [Hist] A body comprising a small number of elected property owners in each PARISH, responsible for managing all aspects of Local Government and Poor Law administration. [OED vestry 2. b. 'the body of parishioners meeting ... and constituting a parochial board or council of management. This body had formerly the administration and management of the whole of the business affairs of the parish ...' + cits to 1882. In the CarA the term was borrowed from, and through the involvement of, the Anglican or State Church, as meaning 'the ruling body of State Church-approved persons'. The system lasted from the 17C to the late 1950s in some islands] □ See CHURCHWARDEN, GUARDIAN.

Ves·try-man n (Antg, Bdos, Jmca, StKt) [Hist] An elected member of a VESTRY.

vest-shirt n (Bdos) 1. ‖ GANSEY (Bdos) 2. A coloured, sleeveless vest (sometimes worn by men out-of-doors as the only upper garment).

ve·ti·ver* (ver·ti·vert grass, vè·ti·vé, ve·ti·vert) ['vɛtivɛ(r)] /1'12/ n (Dmca, Gren, Mrat, StLu, Trin) ‖ **bed-grass** (Nevs, Tbgo) ‖ **cock-roach-grass** 2. (Tbgo). ‖ **cus-cus, khus-khus, kuss-kuss (grass)** (CarA) ‖ **lavender-grass** (Guyn, StVn) ‖ **mat-grass** (Nevs) ‖ **sweet-grass** (Antg, Mrat, Trin) A coarse grass that grows in large clumps about 3 ft high, with tough fibrous roots; it is widely cultivated for soil conservation, for the use of its strong blades in mat-making, and the pleasant smell of its dried roots when

hung in wardrobes; Vetiveria zizanioides or Anatherum z. or Andropogon muricatus (Gramineae). **a.** They make and export very large carpet-size mats of vetiver in Dominica, but in St Lucia we usually make small table-mats and straw hats for the tourists.—StLu (Ms, 1978) **b.** A stimulating tea prepared from vetivert roots is also used for fevers.—PTT:307 [From an abbr of the botanical name vetiveria, the spellings with 'vert' being falsely affected by Fr vert, 'green']

vex¹ adj **1.** (CarA) [IF/AF] ‖ **anwajé** (StLu) Annoyed; very angry; vexed. **a.** These people think too much of race and therefore cannot think straight. They seem to be vex with themselves. There is too much anger.—AdV (90.03.04, p.10) **b.** Dear Sir, I was really vex the other day to hear over the Radio one Miss Shoman telling Belize women how to raise their children.—BeA(BE) (80.05.31, p.4)**c.** Well, you see, the Colonial Office is being advised by Forbes, and he is still damn vex because I used the island's reserve fund to increase the wages of the poor daily paid Government employees.—TRIH:170 [Cp OED vex v 5. intr (Common in the 17C; now rare or Obs) 'to be distressed in mind; to feel dissatisfied; to fret' + cits such as 1663 'It makes us vex if we be crossed ...', also 1804 'I must not vex about it'. This sense of vex was however intensified in CarA Cr becoming the normal emotive word to express 'be angry' and so shifting, with Cr deletion of 'be', into adjectival function. This would have been reinforced by the coincident reduction of the final /-CC/ in SE pa. part. vexed /-kst > ks/, similarly used in EE. Note OED vex v 4. b. with cits such as 1783 '... but I was not vexed', also 1885 'I am always vexed with people who don't care what they eat'] □ In ModE vex vb is much less used, and vexed vb much restricted in use vexed question, (less often) sorely vexed. **2.** PHRASES **2.1** get vex vb phr (CarA) [AF/IF] To be or become (very) angry. So I get vex and tell them a few words, and they get vex and tell me some too, and then I get vexer and had to put my hand 'pon them.—CISH:125 □ See GET Phrs 3.24 and 3.24.1 **2.1.1** get (sb) vex vb phr (CarA) [AF] To make (sb) (very) angry; to irritate (sb). Sahib, you know you getting me vex now. I ain't like other people, you know. I know you is a mystic, but don't provoke me, sahib. When I get vex, I don't know what I could do.—NTMM: 150

vex² vb tr **1.** (CarA) [IF] To make (sb) angry. 'You vex she now', Ada's husband observed, 'She not going stay.'—HMCH:6 □ This sense, though the same (perh less intense) in SE, is rare in conversational ModE, being generally replaced in IAE by annoy, irritate, make angry. Even in CE it occurs more often in the foll phrs. **2.** PHRASES **2.1** vex off vb phr (CarA) [AF] To sulk; to show anger in your looks (but not actively). If he only begin to look at another woman simple, simple so, the wife does start mutterin[g] and vex-in[g] off!—(Trin) **2.2** vex up ¹ vb phr (CarA) [AF] To become fretful and agitated; to be (increasingly) irritated. **a.** Dey could vex-up and

fret-up as dey want, but dey bound to wait.—
RTCS:10 **b.** *That was when he realize that the
policeman get angry, vex up bad and nearly use he
big stick on him.—*LMFF:45 **2.2.1 vex (sb) up;
vex up (sb)** *vb phrs* (CarA) [*AF*] To cause (sb)
to be irritated, agitated. *The comin[g] home late
night after night with boys vex up the mother, so
she stop her goin[g] out.—*(Bdos)

vex·en [vɛksn] *vb tr* (Angu, StLu) [*X*] To vex;
to annoy; to make angry. [Prob by analogy with
SE *madden*, as vb derived from adj *mad*, the CE
form VEX¹ being sensed also as adjectival]

vex-mon·ey *n* (Trin) [*AF—Joc*] Money carried by a girl on a date, as a safeguard in case
she finds she has to get back home on her own
after a vexatious disagreement with her boyfriend. *Of course it may be that in this age of
'no-bra', our chicks have had to find a new place
to keep their vex-money and so they have resorted
to the faithful old handbag.—*SuP (74.12.29, p.5)
[< VEX¹ adj + *money* by ellipsis = 'money (in
case you are) VEX'; cp *OED2 mad-money*, with
same sense]

vex-up² *adj* (CarA) [*AF*] Annoyed; irritated;
agitated; made fretful. *Look I don['t] wan[t] talk!
I too vex-up this mornin[g] after you get on so
las[t] night!—*(Gren) [By functional vb > adj
shift of VEX UP¹. See VEX² Phr 2.2]

vi·cis·si-duck *n* (Guyn) See WICISSI-DUCK

Vic·to·ri·a-palm *n* (Baha) ‖ROYAL PALM
(CarA)

Vic·to·ri·a Re·gi·a* ['vɪktorɪʌ-rigi:ʌ] /
ı′221221/ *n phr* (Guyn) A giant, aquatic plant
with flat circular leaves some 6 ft in diameter,
tough and heavily veined, with upturned rim; it
floats on quiet water, and bears large, fragrant,
pink or white rosette-like lilies, each raised out
of the water on a stout stalk; *Victoria amazonica
(Nymphaeaceae)—(GTWF:30).*

vi(e)-ke-vie *adv, adj* (Dmca, Gren, StLu,
Tbgo, Trin) See VAY-KI-VAY

view *n* PHRASE **with a/the view of** *conn phr*
(Bdos) [*X*] With a view to. *The Union was able
to get the company to admit that its action was not
in keeping with normal industrial relations practice
and both sides then proceeded to discuss the redundancy matter with a view of arriving at a
solution.—*NaT (72.12.15, p.28)

Vil·lage Coun·cil *n phr* (Guyn) A partly elected administrative body, set up as a part of a
system of Local Government and headed by a
Chairman to administer a VILLAGE DISTRICT on
behalf of the central government.

Vil·lage Dis·trict *n phr* (Guyn) A rural, administrative division of several square miles de-
marcated around a village as part of a system of

Local Government and under the control of a
VILLAGE COUNCIL.

vil·lage-head·man *n* (Guyn) ‖CAPTAIN
(Guyn)

vil·lage-ram *n* (CarA) [*AF—Joc/Derog*] A
man, usu one of low social status, who is noted
for his indiscriminate but accepted sexual relationships; a worthless philanderer. [A Joc ref
to the rural practice, in earlier times, of keeping
a specially prized ram on service, the rearing of
goats for milk and meat being habitual in the
post-emancipation era]

Vin·ce·lo·ni·an *n* (ECar) [*IF—Obs ?*] ‖VINCE-
NTIAN (CarA) *The father I knew well. He was
a Vincelonian—you know they liked to recruit
Vincelonians and Barbadians especially in the police force about the 1920s because they made good
policemen in B.G.—*(Guyn) □ A friendly term,
only used as n, and usu by older folk. Cp KIT-
TIFONIAN.

Vin·cen·tian [vɪnsɛnšən] *n, adj* (CarA) ‖ *Vincelonian, Vincie* (ECar) [*IF*] (A person or
thing) of or belonging to the island of St Vincent.

Vin·cen·tian White *n phr* (StVn) A creole
white person, or one so considered, who was
born and lives in St Vincent. *Many West Indians
known to have colored forebears are locally accepted
as white. In St Vincent, for example, even plainly
negro folk by virtue of the mixing with the Whites
in clubs and organisations are counted as pass-for
Whites, or Vincentian Whites.—*FCR:320 (D.
Lowenthal) □ This is often used as an unfriendly
ref to such persons.

Vin·cie *n, adj* (ECar) [*IF—Joc*] ‖VINCENTIAN
(CarA) *It would seem theirs was a real Vincentian
Wedding only in a Grenadian Church. Even the
padre was Vincie.—*ViN (73.12.07, p.2) □ A
friendly term.

Vir·gin Gor·di·an *adj phr, n phr* (CarA) (A
person or thing) of or belonging to the island of
Virgin Gorda, one of the Br Virgin Islands.

Vir·gin Is·land·er *n phr* (CarA) A native or
citizen of one of the Virgin Islands.

vis·yé [visye] *adj* (StLu) [*IF—Derog*] Very untrustworthy; dangerously hypocritical. [Fr Cr <
Fr *vicieux* 'corrupt' (of a person)]

vi·zou (vi·sou) [vizu] *n* (Dmca) ‖CRACK-LIQUOR
(Bdos) *Some farmers crushed cane juice or visou,
which got a good sale locally.—*HTDS:84 [Evid
orig Fr Cr, rendered as Fr *vesou* (Mot Créole:
1667—*LLFL*) 'juice obtained from crushed
sugar-cane']

vo·cal *n* PHRASE **be on vocals** *vb phr* (CarA)
[Entertainment Ind] To have to sing as part of
a dance-band's performance, sometimes while
also playing one of the instruments. *Philip is on*

bass and vocals, Maxi on drums and vocals, Jimmy on rhythm guitar and vocals, Wayne on organ and vocals and Patrick on lead guitar and vocals.—AdN (71.12.24, p.5)

vo·du (vo·doun, voo·doo) [vʊdu~vudu] *n* (CarA) **1.** A system of religious beliefs, basically in the spiritual animation of the natural world by gods and in the presence among men of the spirits of the dead; these are called upon by ritual procedures and performances to effect protection of and vengeance for believers; Christian saints are merged into its rituals. *At the top of the Voodoo hierarchy of authority is the Christian God, Supreme Master of Heaven and Earth, Maker of all the Loas (gods). Whereas the Christian says 'I believe in God' the Voodooist says 'I serve my gods, my loas, my mystere.'*—Int 73/8, p.7 [< Ewe-Fon *vodoun* [vo·dõ] 'a generic name for certain types of (lesser) deities (in) Dahomey'—ARJC:80] □ The Europeanized spelling *voodoo* is the one most commonly found; the cult so named is particularly Haitian, though the term is used loosely as a Derog ref to occult practices, almost the equivalent of OBEAH, throughout the CarA. See also MYAL. **2.** *PHRASE* **2.1 put voodoo on (sth)** *vb phr* (TkCa) [*IF*] ‖ PUT YOUR BAD-MOUTH ON (SB/STH) (CarA) See BAD-MOUTH[1] Phr 3.2 *Like he put voodoo on the mango tree, because nearly everybody who climb it fall do[w]ng.*—(TkCa)

vo·lan·jay (vo·len·jay) ['vʌlʌnje] *n* (Bdos) See BALANJAY [A rare case, in CE, of /b > v/ replacement, the reverse being commoner in CarA Cr. The pronunc occurs among older folk in northern Bdos. Cp *DJE valanghanna*, also noted as Obs] □ EGGPLANT is the widely current name in *Bdos.*

vo·lup·tious [vʌlʌpšʌs] *n* (Guyn) [*AF*] ‖ BIG-AND-PLENTY (Gren) [< SE *voluptuous* by association of sensuality with fatness (esp of the bosom) of a woman, thence a shift of sense to 'big and vulgar' in ref to a woman]

voo·doo [vudu] *n* See VODU

voompse (vumpse) [vʊmps] *vb* (Guyn) [*AF—Joc*] **1.** [Only in neg constructions] To pay attention to (sb). [Perh developed from an ideoph] **2.** *PHRASE* **2.1 not even voompse [u]pon/at (sb)** *vb phr* (Guyn) [*AF—Joc*] To ignore (sb) rudely. *The last time I pass dat vagabon[d] I ain['t] even voompse [u]pon [h]e.*—(Guyn)

voop (vup) [vʊp] *vb* (CarA) [*AF—Joc*] [Cricket] To strike hard and wildly at a ball; to swipe. **a.** *Nex' ting ah know Allen out at ninety-six tryin' to vup / And everybody forget food, tension high in de Oval.*—KTT:31 **b.** *Nearing the end Clive Lloyd sent butterflies into the stomachs of all of us with an astonishing, getting-out voop shot. He's still there. I hope he leaves the bad shots in the pavilion when he resumes today!*—TrG (73.03.28, p.24) [Prob developed from an ideoph. Cp VUP!]

voop·er *n* (CarA) [*AF—Joc*] [Cricket] A swiper; a reckless, unskilled batsman. *One suspects that at the back of their minds was the feeling that the West Indian cricketers were essentially a bunch of 'voopers', quick to crumble in the crunch.*—ExP (80.01.31, p.4) [VOOP *vb* + SE agential suff *-er*]

VP [vi-pi] *abbr* (Bdos) [Sugar Ind] Vacuum-pan molasses. See BLACK-STRAP

Vup! (Voops!) *ideoph* (CarA) [*AF*] [Indicating speed and suddenness, or an unexpected event] *The boy just rushed up to her and voops! Snatch her purse and gone!*—(Guyn)

vy-ki-vy *adv, adj* (Dmca, Gren, StLu, Tbgo, Trin) See VAY-KI-VAY

W

w [-w- □] **1.** (Angu, Baha, CayI, StKt, ViIs) /w/ replaces /v/ in some folk and middle-level speech in these places, and occasionally in the speech of older folk in other Caribbean territories. In some cases also (Angu, BrVi, CayI) /w/ and /v/ may switch places in speech. **a.** *De angry judge ... As if to say de courtroom / Was giwin' orf a stench, too wex to see-dung anymo / He stan' up pon he two foot Rollin' owa he big eye.*—LMFF:18 **b.** *I most get wex an leave, cause I ain' like no foolishiness like dis.*—JBJ:88 **c.** *A voman frum Labar parlement fete em...!dey tell we ... we are free but dey no tell ve ar to pay tax.*—TiM (75.12.19, p.5) [Prob a survival of London Cockney infl. MCPP (pp 280–281) gives exs showing that /w/ ~ /v/ occurred in Cockney pronunc from Elizabethan to Victorian times, waning in the latter period, with /v/ for /w/, as in *voman* (1503), being 'less common', as also mixtures such as *velewet* (1485) 'velvet'] □ See also note at /b/. **2.** (Dmca, StLu) /w/ replaces /r/ in Fr Cr in these places, and the feature appears in loan-words in the Eng of these territories. Hence for ex GIVE MÉPWI, HAVE BOUCH-KABWIT (*Dmca*) LA MAGWIT, LA WOZ FESTIVALS (*StLu*).

wa *adj, pron* (CarA) [*AF—Cr*] See WHA[T]

wa·bine (**wa(h)·been, wha·been**) [wabi·n] *n* (Gren, Trin) [*AF—Derog*] ‖ BAD-WOMAN (Guyn, etc) **a.** *Imagine comin' an ask me to dance, eh? / Ah thought she was ah wabine, / ... / But was grog she had in she head / Is grog dat make she get on so.*—KTT:44 **b.** *The small group of prostitutes and the promiscuous women who might jokingly be referred to as 'susu' or as 'wahbeen' do absorb some of the premarital and extramarital sexual activity of the male.*—RCLF:61 [Metaph extension from the quality and habitat of the fish GUABIN(E), popularly pronounced [wabi·n], wh thrives in dirty waters]

Wac·ca·wa *n* (Guyn) A variant form of AK-AWAIO

Wad·dap! (**Wad·dax!**) *excl ideoph* (CarA) [*AF*] [ECHOIC WORD indicating a sharp, sudden blow] *He was the supreme authority advising where the canes were to be unloaded, and do not forget that there was the 'cow skin' in close proximity, it was a case of 'do as you were told or ... waddax'.*—AdM (79.06.17, p.17, Edward Stoute)

wag·ga-wag·ga *adj* (Jmca) [*AF*] Plentiful; abundant. *We hard to one another, eh? Just because bread not so wagga-wagga like couple weeks ago, ... And is the same gravalicious business why some people start pack up sugar under them mattress and so forth. Which is why some of we can't get any. Cool it, man. Tek some, leave some for the rest of we. Cho.*—StA(JA) (72.11.18, p.10, Partyline) [Cp Twi *wakawaka* 'active, vibrant'; also Yoruba *waga-waga* 'bundled together']

wa·gie (**wag·gi, wa·jy**) [waʤi] *n* (Antg, Mrat) [*AF*] Used clothing; hand-me-downs. [Perh of Afr orig. Cp Igbo *wa* 'to divide', *je* 'to wear']

wag·on; wag.(g)on.ette *n* (Bdos, Guyn) ‖ *sideboard* (Guyn) An old-fashioned piece of dining-room furniture, a stand comprising two or three open ledges about 4 ft x 2 ft each, one above the other (sometimes with a cupboard in the lower section) on wh glassware was kept. [Cp *OED wagon* 9. 'short for *dinner-wagon*'; also listed in 12. *wagon-table* = a moving sideboard. The only *OED* sense of *wag(g)onette* is a four-wheeled carriage] □ Also loosely called DRESSER by some.

wah *adj, pron, excl, etc* (CarA) [*AF—Cr*] See WHA

wa·ha *n* (Belz) ‖ HELICONIA (CarA)

wa·ha leaf *n phr* (Belz) ‖ *heliconia* (CarA) The banana-like leaf of the waha or HELICONIA, used in cooking TAMALES.

wa·hoo* [wahu·] *n* (CarA) A large, speedy, ocean fish that can weigh over 100 lbs, with a dark bluish-green back and silver sides and belly; it is often taken for and sold as KING-FISH wh its lighter meat also resembles; *Acanthocybium solanderi* (*Scombridae*). ['Why he is called 'Wahoo' nobody knows, unless it is because anglers have been known to make this yell when this bruiser strikes'—*ADF:89*]

wah·ree *n* (Antg, etc) See WARRI.

Wai! (**Wae!**) [wa·ŋ] *excl* (Bdos, Belz, Guyn, Jmca) [Exclamation of surprise or shock, usu expressing great grief, but occasionally sudden delight] **a.** *Wai! Wai! Wai! O God! Look de house ketchin[g] afire!! Wa-ai!*—(Guyn) **b.** [At a cricket match] *Wai! Six again!*—(Bdos) [Cp Wolof *Woyy!* 'emphatic exclamation of distress, sympathy or sorrow'—(*pers info, M. Cham*); also

ADHL Hausa *Wayyo* 'My word!'; also *KED* Krio *way* 1. 'excl of pain, fright, sorrow'. 2. 'excl of great amusement'; also *WSNE* Sran *woi* excl of suffering]

Wai·ka [waɪka] *n* **1.** (Belz) [*Derog*] A Miskito Indian or person of mixed Miskito and African blood. [< *DMEI waika* 'brother-in-law, confidant'] □ The term is applied to these people mostly by *Belz* Creoles. **2.** (Guyn) A small ethnic group of Amerindians in the Kamarang and Roraima areas of Guyana (referred to in some accounts as guides). □ See AKAWAIO. Note variant WACCAWA.

wai·ka ba·na·na *n phr* (Belz) ‖ BLUGGO (Belz, etc) [< WAIKA Derog + BANANA 2.] □ For other names in *Belz*, see BLUGGO.

wail *vb intr* **1.** (Jmca) To sing (esp REGGAE songs, soul, etc) with great bodily vigour, with abandon. [A likely back-formation from 'Wailers'. 'The Wailers', originally 'The Wailing Wailers', was the name of a *Jmca* dance-band founded in 1963 by Bunny Livingston, Bob Marley and Peter Tosh, specializing in REGGAE music. The popularization of this name prob expanded the meaning of IAE *wail* to 'give way to self-expression of grief' (related to the ghetto life associated with REGGAE in Kingston) whence, by extension, 'to abandon self-restraint'. Further shifts follow in senses 2, 3.] **2.** (Jmca) [By extension] [*AF*] To behave with aggressive abandon; to be dangerously rough. *Rude Boys cannot fail / Cause dem must get bail / Dem a loot, dem a shoot, dem a wail / A shanty town.*—Jmca (Desmond Dekker's 'Shanty Town', 1968 (?)) **3.** (Trin) [By extension] [*IF*] To dance and make merry with happy abandon; to have a rollicking good time. *Everybody was doing it this weekend—celebrating, sunbathing, and just plain wailing—even the Cubans. / Yes, the Cubans are here, ... and you wouldn't believe they are so friendly.*—SuP (80.04.06, p.9) [The sense of 'release' is prob re-interpreted in *Trin* in the context of FETEING] **4.** PHRASE **4.1 wail down the place** *vb phr* (Trin) [*AF—Joc*] To dance, sing, and shout with complete release. *But when the Vibrations started beating sweet pan, they started dancing and wailing down the place.*—BoM (79.10.19, p.7)

wail·er *n* (Trin) A person who dances with abandon; an uninhibited merry-maker. *Staff are always happy when they hear the boss is coming to their party. / For it's a good chance to see how much of a wailer the boss really is.*—SuP (80.01.06, p.6) [WAIL 3. (*Trin*) + SE suff -*er*. See note at WAIL 1.]

waist PHRASE **tie your waist** *vb phr* (StLu) [*IF*] ‖ TIE YOUR BELLY (Dmca, etc) See TIE Phr 3.5

wait¹ *vb* PHRASES **1. wait on (sb/sth)** *vb phr* (CarA) [*IF*] To wait for (sb/sth). **a.** *We sat in the car waiting on him to join us.*—(StVn) **b.** *'Contrary to a local belief in some circles, Jamaica did not have to wait on England to move for abolition of the jury,' he said.*—AdN (73.03.15, p.11) [Cp EDD *wait* 4. *wait on* 'to wait for' (Lon)] □ Also becoming IF SE—*pers info, L. Urdang.* **2. wait your hand** *imper vb phr* (Guyn) [*IF*] Move your hand out of the way. *Wait yo[ur] han[d] an[d] le[t] me close the door.*—(Guyn) [Perh a survival or shift of EE usage. Cp *OED wait* vb¹ 3. e. (Obs) 'to take precautions, be watchful. In imperative: Take care, see to it that' + cits–'1522]

Wait!² *excl* (Bdos, Guyn) [*IF*] [Expressing surprise or warning] (You) don't say!; What! **a.** *He stated that G—was angry with him ... and she started abusing him. / The accused man said that he asked the woman: 'Wait, you en believe in God?'*—AdV (90.02.05, p.5) **b.** *You hear what that child just said? But wait!*—(Guyn) [Cp EDD *wait* int (nCy, etc) 'Surely!; Indeed!']

wait·er *n* (Bdos, Dmca, Gren, Guyn, USVI) A shallow tray, made of metal or handicraft material, for serving drinks, etc; a salver. *As a token of appreciation, Mr Harrington was presented with a silver waiter and a silver pen.*—DaC (53.04.13, p.2) [Cp EDD *waiter* 4. 'a tea-tray' (Cor); also AmE, see W3 *waiter* 3. Perh infl by sense of SE *server*]

Wai-Wai *n* (Guyn) A pale-skinned, Amerindian ethnic group of Carib stock distinguished by their bright body-paints, the males by ceremonial nose-ornaments and the binding of the hair in a tube down the nape and back; they inhabit the Acarai mountain-range area on the southernmost border of Guyana with Brazil and are said to be the most ancient of aboriginal Guyanese peoples, though their numbers are few now. [Their name 'Wai-Wai' is the Wapisiana for tapioca, and the Brazilians call them 'Indios do Tapioc', and regard them as the 'White Indians'. But their name for themselves is 'Wéwé' or wood, and means people who live in the forest.—*GWW:51*]

wa·jan (wa·jang, wa·jank) ['wajã ~ 'wajaŋ(k)] *n* (Trin) **1.** [*AF—Derog*] ‖ BAD-WOMAN (Guyn, etc) *... the most impeccable, dynamic song that Embryo has recorded thus far, Wajang Woman.*—Kri '78:59 **2.** [*AF—Joc*] An expert at something. *Sollo boy! You feel you is a wajang!*—Trin (Cso—Mighty Conqueror, 1974 ?)

walk¹ *vb intr* **1.** (Antg, Guyn, Jmca, Nevs, StVn) [*AF/IF*] [Of persons or things in wide, general sense] To come, go, travel, etc. **a.** *S1: Which road you-all walk when you went driving yesterday? / S2: De taxi-driver say he prefer to walk de North Road because he had smooth tyres.*—(Nevs) **b.** *It was a easy catch. Dat ball walk right in [h]is hands.*—(StVn) **c.** *Is whe[re] dis road walk go?*—(Jmca) [Perh a calque from a W Afr source; but note *EDD walk* vb¹ 4. 'to take a journey' (Cor)] **2.** PHRASES **2.1 walk a good foot** *vb phr* (Tbgo) [*AF*] To come, arrive at a lucky moment; to come just at the right time.

2.2 walk for conformation/first communion *vb phr* (Gren, USVI) To undergo Christian religious preparation in order to become a communicant member of a church. *A boy walking for confirmation has to know how to conduct himself properly.*—PKKK:72 **2.3 Walk good!** *sending off phr* (Guyn, Jmca, StVn) See GOOD³ Phr 2.10 **a.** *'Walk good' is the Jamaica wish for anyone making a journey, whether it be by foot to the market, or by car to the end of the island or by plane to the end of the world; walk good.*—SJW: 1 **b.** *'I going,' he said and waited for her to protest. 'Goodbye. Walk good,' she told him.*—HMCH: 131 [Cp Twi, sending off phr *Nante yie o* 'Walk well then!'—*pers info, J. Berry*; also Kikongo *Toma diata* 'Good walk'—*pers info, U. Ndoma*] **2.4 walk hand/lashes (on sb)** *vb phr* (StVn, Tbgo, Trin) [*AF*] To beat up (sb); to flog (sb, esp a child). *Ah ain't want to stop in dis house fo' no man to beat me up. An' Ah don't intend to take no blows from no man. Ah'm nat Jerry Mole child fo' him to walk hand 'pon me as he like.*—TRIH: 120 □ In this phr WALK is vb tr. **2.5 walk hip-and-drop/hop-and-(a)-drop** *vb phrs* (ECar) [*AF*] See HIP-AND-DROP, HOP-AND-A-DROP **2.6 walk like you can't mash ants** *vb phr* (Tbgo, Trin) [*AF—Joc*] [Esp of a woman] To have a false air of innocence or chastity; to look incapable of unseemly behaviour or of promiscuity. **2.7 walk on your name** *vb phr* (Guyn) [*IF*] See NAME¹ Phr 6. *Girl yo[u] goin[g] live long. We jus[t] talkin[g] [a]bout you and yo[u] walk on yo[ur] name. You goin[g] live till they sun you.*—(Guyn) **2.8 walk with (sth)** *vb phr* (ECar) [*IF*] To bring, carry, have (sth) with you. **a.** *I didn't walk with any money so I had to run home quick and get some.*—(Tbgo) **b.** *She admitted that he used to keep bad company, but said that he never walked with a knife.*—AdN (76.01.22, p.1) **2.8.1 walk with your two long hands** *vb phr* (Bdos, Gren, Guyn, Tbgo, Trin) [*AF/IF*] To come, go empty-handed; to fail to take with you something that you are expected to. *If you invite people to join in a picnic you don't expect them to walk with their two long hands.*—(Tbgo)

walk² *n* (CarA) A grove or small plantation of cultivated fruit trees (hence many compounds: *banana-, coconut-, mango-, orange-, plantain-walk*, etc). [Cp *EDD walk* sb¹ 13. 'unenclosed lands, esp unenclosed cornfields; also *walk-land*; ... (perh) from the ancient manorial right of sheep-walk over such lands, during a considerable part of the year' + cit from *Annals Agric* (1784–1815). This prob explains the source of the wide use of the word in this sense in the *CarA*, wh *OED walk* sb¹ 10. c. lists as 'West Indian: A plantation']

walk-about (walk-a-leg, walk-a-pick·y) *n* (Angu, Antg, Guyn, Jmca, Nevs) [*AF—Joc/ Derog*] A woman who is a busybody and gossip; a restless news-carrier. □ Often used attrib followed by *Maria, Miss Thomas,* or other women's names. Also sometimes *Walker-leg, Walker-picky*.

Walk·ers & Co *n phr* (Bdos, Gren, Guyn) [*AF—Joc*] **1.** ‖ IDLE HALL (ESTATE) (Bdos, etc) **2.** PHRASE **2.1 work(ing) at Walkers (& Co)** *vb phr* (Bdos, Gren, Guyn) [*AF—Joc*] Be(ing) unemployed.

wall *n* **1.** (Bdos, Gren) [Always used in ref to a concrete or stone wall, as distinct from a wooden wall. See GUARD-WALL, MILL-WALL] **2.1 behind the wall** *adv phr* (StVn) [*IF*] See BEHIND Phr 8. **2.2 wall of the eye** *n phr* (CarA) The ring of savage winds forming a wall around the calm eye of a hurricane; it is the most violent part of the hurricane.

wal·la·ba *n* (Guyn, Trin) [Timber Ind] A flowering, canopy forest-tree that can reach a height of 100 ft with very little tapering of its erect, cylindrical trunk of 16 to 30 ins in diameter; it yields a gummy, reddish-brown, and very tough, straight-grained timber that is widely used in building and esp for utility poles; *Sperua spp (Caesalpiniaceae)*. [*BAED* Arawak, *walaba* 'a tree with lasting wood popular with house-builders']

wal·la·ba-pole *n* (Guyn) ‖ *lantern-post* (Guyn) A utility pole made from the trunk of the WALLABA tree.

wal·la·ba-post *n* (Guyn) A small cylindrical post about 4 ins in diameter and of standard length 8 ft, cut from the limb of the WALLABA tree, widely used as a fence post.

Wal·law! *excl* (Bdos) See WULLAY!

wall-build·ing; wall-house, wall-prop·er.ty *n* (ECar) ‖ *block-house* (Antg) A dwelling-house with walls of coral-stone or concrete blocks (as opposed to wood). □ See also CHATTEL-HOUSE. The distinction is important in that the *wall-house* is immovable property.

wall-robe [wɔl·l(d)ro·b] *n* (Guyn) [*X*] Wardrobe. [By /r > l/ shift in SE *wardrobe* and folk etym, since this item of furniture stands against the wall]

wal·ly *n* PHRASE **call it Wally** *id phr* (Bdos, StVn) See CALL¹ Phr 3.4 *If we can start early and finish all the interviews today we can call that Wally and we won't have to come back tomorrow 'cause the rest is no problem.*—(Bdos)

wa·ma·ra* [wama·ra] *n* (Guyn) [Timber Ind] A forest-tree about 20 ins in diameter rising to about 80 ft in height; it yields an extremely hard and heavy wood whose sharply contrasting dark brown and yellowish colours make it attractive for turned articles and furniture; *Swartzia leiocalycina (Caesalpiniaceae)*. [*BAED* Arawak *wamara* 'a tree with hard, heavy wood'] □ The wood closely resembles ZIRICOTE (*Belz*) in appearance and use.

wan [wan] *determiner (indef art)* (Belz, Brbu, Guyn, Mrat) [*AF—Cr*] A, an. *The first witness called was S—... a fruit vendor and, on June 27, she was selling on a grass parapet opposite the Bourda Market. 'Then wan man come and bring wan $5 note,' the witness continued. 'He call fuh wan shilling banana. Me nah bin want tek de $5; because um look like um din good.'*—DaA (52.09.13, p.4) [< SE *one*. Cp *EDD one* 16. Dev *wan gude lady come i' tha marnin* (1899). The same form occurs in WAPE *wan* 'one'; also Krio, as *KED wan* 6. indef pron ex *wan man* 'a certain man; some man'. Note also poss phonic infl of Hausa *wani* (m) 'a certain; another']

Wan·der·ing Jew *n phr* (Baha, Jmca, USVI) ‖ COCKROACH GRASS (Gren, StKt) *Wandering Jew with its purple stripes is an attractive ground cover ... Wandering Jew tea lowers high blood pressure, according to older St Johnians.*—JNHSJ:67 [Perh from the trailing, shelter-seeking characteristic of this plant]

wan·ga [waŋga] *n* (Tbgo, USVI) ‖ OBEAH (CarA) *He and his wife fell out and she left him, so he decided to work a wanga to get her to come back.*—Tbgo (Ms, 1982) [Cp UMmbundu *wanga* 'witchcraft'; also *VBHUS:115* Tshiluba *buanga* 'charm, fetish; remedy, medicine'; also *HCEF:567* Haiti, *wanga* 'fetish', etc, *wangatè* 'person who uses *wanga* continually']

wan·gla [waŋgla] *n* (Belz, Jmca) The sesame plant; sesame seeds (esp used in flavouring, making sweets, etc). [< *LDKF* Kikongo *waangila* 'sesame']

wan·gler [waŋglər] *n* (Jmca) A SUGAR-CAKE or NUT-CAKE (originally made with sesame seeds). *The duckunoo had got mixed in together with the fufu and the crisply fried sprats and the delicious sugared cakes, wanglers, guava docey, and banana fritters which had been torn loose from their thin grease-oozing brown wrapping paper.*—SD:22 [A refinement of WANGLA 'sesame seeds']

want *vb* 1. (CarA) [In interrog contexts, implying a threat] To be desirous of (sth unpleasant). **a.** *You want a good lash from me?*—(Guyn) **b.** *Ask her if she wants me to come down there to her with the strap.*—(StVn) **2.** (ECar) [*IF*] To be inclined, tend (to resemble sb). *I find that girl wants to look like a cousin of mine in America.*—(Gren) □ Cp also Phr 4.1. **3.** (Bdos) [*IF*] To deserve (some kind of punishment). **a.** *But a boy like that, that would rob his own mother, you don't think he want jailin[g]?*—(Bdos) **b.** *If they rape they want catting. I have no problem with that.*—(Bdos) [Cp *OED want vb* 4. trans 'to stand in need of (something salutary, but often not desired). Hence *colloq* senses ...'] □ Prob shifted from or infl by wider IF SE usage as in *sth needs/wants doing.* **4.** PHRASES **4.1 it wants to rain** *id phr* (CarA) It looks as if it's going to rain; (SE) it looks like rain. [An extension of sense 2, or a personification of 'it' = 'rain' as subj. See note at end of RAIN Phr 7.]

4.2 telephone wants you *id phr* (Bdos, Guyn) There is a (telephone) call for you. □ Cp next Phr. **4.3 want a phone message** *vb phr* (Bdos) [*IF*] To ask permission to make a telephone call. *Yes he came to the back door and said he wanted a phone message, but I didn't like the look of him so I told him the phone was out of order.*—(Bdos) **4.4 want for (sb to do sth/sth to happen, be done)** *vb phr* (CarA) [*AF/IF*] To want (sb to do sth/sth to happen); to have a wish or desire that (sb do sth/sth happen). **a.** *An' you want for me to tell you why I does do what I do?*—KJB:108 **b.** *I know you want for rain to fall and stop the match.*—(Bdos) [Prob infl by SE *wish for*; cp also IF AmE *would like for* similarly used]

want·ing [wa·ntɪn] *adj* (Gren, StVn) [*AF*] Contemptibly greedy; avaricious; covetous. *He always wantin[g]. Me ca[n't] eat me food in peace and he ain['t] beg.*—(StVn)

Wap! *excl ideoph* (CarA) **1.** [Indicating the sound of a sharp lash] *She hit her little sister wap wap with the whip and ordered her to go and do her homework.*—(Tbgo) **2.** [By extension, indicating shock] *Then, wap, Alexander dead and leave me a large sum of money. Me. The man that could not get in Cosmos club.*—Kai '75, p.46

wa·pi·a *n* (Trin) ‖ WHITE-CORNER (Guyn) [Prob a labialized variant of GAPIA(-MOUTH)]

Wa·pi·sha·na (Wa·pi·si·a·na) *n* (Guyn) **1.** An Arawakan ethnic group of people inhabiting the deep south-western savannahs of Guyana. **2.** The language spoken by this people.

wap·(p)ie (wap·(p)ee, whap·pee, whap·pie) [wapi] *n* (Gren, Jmca, Trin) A game of chance played with cards; it is illegal.

wa·ra·hoon *n* (Trin) [*AF/IF—Derog*] A noisy, ill-bred person. *John in his nice short pants, long stockings, hair all wet, brushed down, not like these warahoons they have these days, each one outdoing the next as to who could look the nastiest.*—JJM:25 [Said to be a ref to an (unidentified) set of So Amer coastal Amerindians. Perh confused with WARRAU *(Guyn)* ?]

wa·rap ['warap] *n* **1.** (Trin) The fermented juice of the sugar-cane used as a cheap liquor in former times. *In days gone by the 'payol' drank 'warap'.*—S. Moodie (Ms, 1982) [< So Am Sp *guarapo* 'sugar-cane liquor'] **2(i)** (Gren, Tbgo) [By extension] [*AF—Derog*] A cheap, tasteless meal, esp a soup. **(ii)** (Tbgo) [*AF—Derog*] A cheap meal of GROUND-PROVISIONS and fish or meat boiled together.

wa·ra·shee (wa.ra.shi) *n* (Guyn) See WA-RISHI.

wa·ra-wa·ra[1] *adj* (Guyn) [*AF—Joc*] [Esp of clothing] Of inferior quality; cheap looking. [Cp Yoruba *wara-wara, wara-were* 'in a hurry, in a half-done manner'—(*pers info, A. Onibou-Okuta*)]

wa·ra-wa·ra² *n* (Jmca) [*AF—Joc*] Bits and pieces. [Related to prec? Note also Igbo *warawara* 'a rugged bush-path']

ward *n* (Guyn, Trin) A named and delimited administrative division of a town or county with an elected representative on the town or county council; exs: Kingston, Lacytown, Wortmanville, etc are wards of Georgetown, Guyana; Diego Martin, St Ann's, etc are wards of the county of St George, Trinidad.

wares *n pl* (CarA) Any or all items of kitchenware and tableware used in preparing and serving a meal. **a.** *And tell that worthless scamp that he didn't wash the bowl and spoon properly yesterday. He expect me to wash the wares for him too?*—SPOC:57 **b.** *Ay-ay, shoo! Bonjay! Look me trouble nuh! Me pretty precious wares! Where dis cock come from right on top me table.*—RTCS:18 [The widespread *CarA* use of a pl form to cover 'kichen-and-table vessels and tools' may have been a natural 'decreolizing' overcorrection, wh is now, however, formalized] □ SE *ware* sg 'goods' is literary and exceptional in CE.

wa·ri (wa·(r)·ree) ['wa:ri] *n* (Belz) ‖ PECCARY (Belz, Guyn) [< *DMEI:275, 283* Miskito *wari, wuari* 'peccary'] □ Distinguish from WARRI by spelling.

wa·ri·shi (wa·ra·shee, wa·ra·shi, wa·re·shi, wa·ri·shee) [wariši~waraši] *n* (Guyn) ‖ *macapal* (Belz) An Amerindian basketwork load-carrier wh is borne on the back like a rucksack, suspended by a broad strap usu slung over the head. [Prob of Cariban orig. Cp *GDAA* Akawaio *wariicha*, name of this load-carrier]

wa·ri-tick [wa:ri tık] /1'12/ *n phr* (Belz) **1.** Name loosely applied to any blood-sucking tick that bloats itself and clings to the host animal's skin, esp the cattle-tick and dog-tick. [The reason for the specific ref to the *wari* is not clear, though this bad-smelling wild-pig, hunted for its meat, perh attracts ticks also] **2.** PHRASE **2.1 be behind sb worse than wari-tick** *vb phr* (Belz) [*AF—Joc*] ‖ BE BEHIND SB LIKE A SLAVE-DRIVER (CarA) See BEHIND¹ Phr 2. [The tick cannot be shaken off since it sinks its suckers into the animal's flesh]

warm *adj* (Bdos, Gren, Tbgo, Trin) [*AF—Joc*] A substantial amount of; a lot of. *Babsie did win some warm dollars 'pon de bandits couple weeks aback an' she ax me to come an' g'long wid she, ... so yuh know me! I never busy fuh a freeness!*—NaT (80.03.14, p.7, Lickmout' Lou) [By extension or shift of SE senses of *warm* 'hearty; ardent', etc]

war·man(ts) (war·munce) *n* (Mrat, USVI) [*AF*] Vermin; pest(s); insect(s). etc. *All Patrick know is dat 'e ca'an sit down ina de class wid dem*

six red-ants ... *So all mornin','e rock 'e brains fo' see how 'e could get Obeahman fo' tek dem dangerous warmunce out o' de class.*—FGSOS:44 [< SE *vermin* by /v > w/ shift. Cp *EDD vermin* with variant *warmint* (Nrf). Also *OED varment* with variants *varmunt, warment,* 'vermin'. See -W- I.]

War·rau [warau] *n* (Guyn) **1.** A coastal Amerindian ethnic group of people principally inhabiting the Orinoco Delta and the Northwest Region of Guyana; they are noted for their boat-building skills. ['In fact the word 'Warrau' means 'boat people' '—quoted by W.F. Edwards in a Conference Paper, Society For Caribbean Linguistics, 1978] **2.** The language spoken by this people (belonging neither to the Arawakan nor Cariban group).

war·ree *n* (Belz) See WARI

war·ri (wa·ri, war·rie, wah·ree) [wɒ·ri] *n* (Antg, Bdos, Jmca, USVI) A game played on a board (called a *warri-board*) about 12 ins x 6 ins, with two parallel rows of six bowl-like holes in each of wh four small marbles or NICKERS are placed, two players then competing to capture the most marbles by the rules of the game. *A game, most certainly for those with a head for numbers, warri has failed ... to attract the younger generation.*—AdM (74.03.03, p.12) [< *DAFL* Twi *ware*, Fante ɔware (name of this game, with description given). Perh related to *ware* vb 'to marry'. The game has several other names in other Afr langs] □ Distinguish from WARI by spelling.

was [wʌz~wəz] *vb* **1.** (CarA) [*X*] Have/has been; had been. **a.** *To date, my pension for January 1972 was not increased and further, there has been no information with respect to whether that would reflect itself in the pension for February.*—ExP (70.02.22, p.15) **b.** *He returned on Wednesday morning and discovered that a window was forced open and a drawer containing ceremonial karate uniforms was stolen.*—WeS (76.03.19, p.32) □ The absence of the SE perfect and past-perfect tense structures of *be* is common in such time-situation contexts in the speech and writing of educated persons throughout the *CarA*. Cp HAD. **2.** (CarA) [*X*] Were. **a.** *But they was big books, big big books!*—NTMM:15 **b.** *Immediately, they acted on the suspect and was able to make him talk.*—ToR (76.03.28, p.3) [In the DE-CREOLIZATION process a universal 'past' form WAS developed from a universal 'present' statement-form IS wh itself replaced earliest CarA Cr A, DA. It persists in the speech and writing of many persons. The same applies to senses 3, 4.] **3.** (CarA) [*X*] [In introductory function] It was. **a.** *It wasn't me driving it, man; was my brother.*—HFGA:57 (D.S. Joseph) **b.** *Was about four in the morning when I saw two little girls walking alongside of the road.*—FDI:27 [See prec, but perh this form is also influenced by dial E '*Twas*'] **3.1** (CarA) [*X*] [In introductory function] There was; there were. **a.** *Now because of* *this was a whole heap of people what was hanging round the place the whole time waiting for her and they really get fed up with the situation.*—NaG (78.06.01, Satirically Speaking) **b.** *Was a time when she used four bars of blue soap, and if the dirt and perspiration were still stubborn, bought a bit of washing soda and did her best to get the clothes looking clean again.*—SWOS:74 **4.** (CarA) [X] [In connective function] In order (to); intending (to). **a.** *Now she was looking 'round for another rock-stone was to pelt at he too, but so happen Mr Straker ketch sight o' she.*—CISH:118 **b.** *And this afternoon Debel come back, was to catch crab, and he is not there, only the wood trees and the sand blowing.*—WSAD:25 **4.1** (CarA) [X] [In connective function, often where no connective is needed] Who/which was. **a.** *And this afternoon they had a boy was fishing for welks under La Vierge by Maingot side.*—WSAD:25 **b.** *Suddenly I heard a dog was barking.*—(StVn) **c.** *I gave her the money to buy an alarm clock was twenty-five dollars.*—(Bdos) **5.** (Gren, StLu) [X] Did. **a.** *He stayed on top my belly about half an hour and during that time I was afraid. I did not feel no sweetness because I was not agree.*—Gren (CR, 79/8) **b.** *I was see you.*—(StLu, schoolchild) [Perh by confusion of SE past-marking auxiliaries. Cp DID³ (*Bdos, Gren*)] **6.** PHRASES **6.1 had was to** *modal vb phr* (CarA) [X] See HAD Phr 2.3 *I had was to borro[w] money to buy de book.*—(StVn) **6.2 if wasn['t] for (sb/sth)** *id phr* (CarA) [AF] See IF Phr 3. **6.3 used was to (do sth); uses was to (do sth)** *vb phrs* (Gren, Guyn, Jmca) See USE¹ Phr 3.2.1 **6.4 was ga** *future-in-the-past, aux phr* (Baha) [AF—Cr] Was going to. *And she done tell him that when he come home late he was ga have to find his way in the darkness.*—NaG (78.12.15, Satirically Speaking)

wash¹ *vb* PHRASES **1. wash ashore** *vb phr* (Guyn) [AF] [Esp of fish, fruit] To be available in abundance; to be plentifully in season. □ Mostly in the form WASHING ASHORE, describing abundance. **2. wash off** *vb phr* (CarA) [IF] **(i)** ‖ *clean off* (Tbgo, Trin) To wash or clean parts of your body esp the face, hands, feet and genitals (instead of taking a complete shower). *Boy if you think you going on my new bed and you ain't wash off, you think again.*—(Angu) **3. wash out** *vb phr* (CarA) [AF/IF] [Of the bowels] To purge by using herbal medicines or strong laxatives. ... *But before taking the medicine a good dose of oil or salts should be taken so as to 'wash out' any impurities.*—AdM (74.01.06, p.4, E.A. Stoute) **(ii)** *often in passive* [Of outdoor games] To prevent play because of continuous heavy showers; (SE) to rain off, out. **4. wash your foot and jump in** *vb phr* (Trin) [AF] To rush to join in some public protest, demonstration, etc, without due consideration. *Like when supporters from all walks of life joined the marching cocoa workers that day in Port of Spain, so these industries were keen as mustard to wash their feet and jump in and get a few days or weeks off from work, irregardless, as they say, of who was striking where for what.*—SPOC:129

[By metaph transfer. See WASH-YOUR-FOOT-AND-COME, n] **5. wash your mouth on/[u]pon (sb)** *vb phr* (CarA) [AF] To speak maliciously or abusively about or to (sb); to condemn (sb) in bold, rough language. *Don't bother with what people tell you, you know. I don't believe Bird leave you. Folks does wash their mouth 'pon somebody just because life easy with them. Just because Bird got you and a good life they jealous like, you know.*—HMCH:20 [Cp Yoruba *Maa wẹ ẹnun si mi l'ara* (= *Don't wash mouth to me in-body*) 'Don't use me as an excuse for your faults by speaking ill of me'—(pers info, A.O. Obilade); also Kikongo *Ntomene kunsukula* (= *I thoroughly do him/her wash*) 'I thoroughly abused him'—(pers info, U. Ndoma). Cp also EDD Som, Dev *wash-amouth*, OED *wash-mouth* s.w. dial 'one who blabs out everything'] □ See also AIR² Phr 2.2 *air your mouth*, **6. wash your skin** *vb phr* (CarA) [AF/IF] To bathe; to bath; to take a shower or bath. *When he has done this, then he can go back and get into an aeroplane and have another bird's eye view of the country but not while the people down here are starving and looking for somewhere to live and cannot get water to wash their skins.*—Bdos (Hd, 73.11.13, p.2846) [SKIN commonly occurs as complement (= SE 'self') in lower level CE after *bathe/clean/wash*, etc, where SE requires no 'prop' complement] **6.1 wash (sb)/(sb's skin) in licks/with blows; wash sb's knot/tail** *vb phrs* (CarA) [AF] To flog (sb) severely; to beat, trounce (sb) thoroughly. [Cp SE exs *rain/shower of blows*]

wash² *n* **1.** (CarA) [Rum Ind] A mixture of water and molasses to wh sulphuric acid and ammonium sulphate are added to promote fermentation for a period of time before distillation into rum. *M— after pleading guilty to charges of having in his possession a concealed still, and four barrels of privately made 'wash' for illicit distillation of 'Hammond' frankly admitted to Magistrate Mr A. Redhead that he does no other work, but 'distilling rum to make a living'.*—LaS (77.10.29, p.1) [Cp OED *wash* sb 14. '... malt or other fermentable substance or mixture of substances steeped in water to undergo fermentation preparatory to distillation'] **2.** (Jmca) [By extension] [IF] ‖ SWANK (Bdos, etc) [Cp DJE *black wash* 1. 'sugar-and-water'] □ WASH is now commoner, and of better status. **3.** (Bdos, Guyn, StKt, Trin) [AF—Joc] A large amount, quantity or number (of sth). *Tony felt sorry for her, but he was feeling even sorrier for himself and for poor Doreen and the wash of children that man had given her. The girl was always pregnant.*—JPB:97 [By metaph transfer of notion of quantity in prec senses] **4.** PHRASE **4.1 put a wash of blows on (sb)** *vb phr* (Guyn) [AF] See PUT Phr 4. [See sense 3. above]

wash-a-wom·an (wash·er·wom·an) [wɒ šəwʊmʊn] *n* (Nevs, StKt) ‖ CERASEE (Baha, etc) [Perh from its use in strong amounts as a drastic purgative and an aid to abortion. The form *washer-woman* is prob erron, owing to folk etym]

wash-belly *n* (Jmca) [*AF—Joc*] The last child a woman bears. *It's because Joan is wash-belly why her mother spoils and pets her so much.*—(Jmca) [From the notion that the last child-bearing means a final washing out of the woman's 'belly' i.e. womb]

wash down[1] (sb) *vb phr* (Mrat, StKt, TkCa) ‖ BARK-DOWN (SB) (Antg)

wash-down[2]; **wash.ing-down** *n* (Mrat, StKt, TkCa) ‖ BUSH-BATH (CarA)

wa·shi·cong(s) (wat·che·kong(s)) ['wa šikɒŋz~'wačikɒŋz] *n pl* (Gren, Trin) [*AF/IF*] ‖ CREPESOLES (Guyn, etc) **a.** *... and called things by their proper names, never saying 'washicong' for plimsoll or 'crapaud' when they meant a frog.*—HCCM:89 **b.** *She was proud of Osmond's, proud of Duncan Street, and would at the least opportunity take off her watchekongs and walk in her socks.*—JJM:54 [Prob < dial. Chinese. Cp Mandarin Chinese *Kong hua xie* [kuŋ xwa šiɛ] = 'sandals', literally 'hole flower shoe', since the open hole in sandals often form a flower pattern. The form *hua xie kong kong* = 'flower shoes (wh are) full of holes' (*pers info from S.O.A.S., U/Lond*). This cheap footwear was the most popular among the Chinese indentured labourers in Trin in the late 19C and at the end of their period of indentureship they often became roving street sellers] □ Usu in the pl form. The pronunc is also unstable, hence the spelling variant.

wash·ing a·shore *adj phr* (Guyn) [*AF—Joc*] ‖ KNOCKING DOG (CarA) [Metaph ref to seasonal glut of river-shrimp or fish]

wash·(ing)-out *n* (Bdos, Gren, Guyn, Jmca) [*AF/IF*] A purging of the bowels by the use of a strong laxative.

wash·ing-soap *n* (CarA) Laundry soap; cake(s) of soap for washing clothes. □ To be distinguished from SALT-SOAP and SWEET-SOAP. See also BLUE-SOAP (Bdos)

wash-pan *n* (Bdos, Guyn, Tbgo) A large, oval-shaped, metal wash-tub with a big handle at each end.

wash-(you[r])-foot-and-come *n* (ECar) [*AF—Joc*] ‖ *bashie* (Gren) ‖ *bram*[1] (CarA) An impromptu dance or FETE (sometimes held to raise funds) at wh people may come as they are, i.e. with no particular preparation in the way of dress, even (as in earlier times) barefoot. □ Cp AmE *come-as-you-are party* with similar sense—(*pers info, L. Urdang*).

was·sy [wa·si] *adj* **1.** (Belz) [*AF—Cr*] [Esp of a woman] Sharp-tongued; hot-tempered and aggressive. [< *OED waspy* 'wasp-like' (in shape), but with sense extended in CE to 'waspish'] **2.**

(Trin) [*AF*] [Esp of a young woman] Saucy and flirtatious; wild.

watch *vb* (CarA) **1.** [*IF*] To look at critically; to observe with cynicism or hostility. **a.** *I would like him to know that most people have to go off the Island to the Dutch Islands and the U.S. Virgin Islands to get what they have. So stop watching what people have in their houses and remember this is not England. Why should [he] come from wherever he came from to stick his neck in what does not concern him?*—TiM (75.11.28, p.8) **b.** *Look at her, John, your marvellous highminded sister, the one who wanted to be a Saint or a hero! Watch her!*—JJM:97 **2.** *imper* [By extension] [*X*] See here/there (sth or some happening); Observe (that)!. **a.** *Eh-Eh! Watch ah nice rabbit! and he so fat!*—PSFC:35 **b.** *Teacher, watch Monica brok[e] yo[ur] chalk.*—(Guyn) **3.** *imper* [By extension] [*AF*] Look here!; Listen! *Watch! If yo[u] don['t] behave, I will give you one slap!*—(StVn) **4.** PHRASES **4.1 watch at (sb/sth)** *vb phr* (CarA) [*AF*] To look at. **a.** *They will put you up to it and then watch at you makin[g] yourself a fool, and laugh.*—(Guyn) **b.** *Tiger walked up the hill, where there was a flagpole. He watched down at most of the city—the savannah green and spreading, and all the houses where the white people lived.*—SABS:98 **4.2 Watch me good!** *vb phr* (Guyn) [*AF*] See GOOD[3] Phr 3.7 *And some more of you boys go open the store and see what food we got. And watch me good. Don't break in the rum store.*—NR:130 □ Cp also sense 3. **4.3 watch (sb) cross-eye/cut-eye** *vb phr* (Dmca, Gren) [*AF*] ‖ CUT YOUR EYE AT (SB) (CarA) **4.4 Watch your case!** *imper vb phr* (Guyn, Trin) [*IF*] ‖ *Watch your stitches!* (Baha) [Warning, esp to a child] Beware (of possible punishment)! **4.5 Watch your hip!** *imper vb phr* (Baha) [*AF—Vul*] See HIP Phr 2.2 **4.6 Watch yourself!** *imper vb phr* (CarA) [*IF*] Be careful now! Take care! [Cp *EDD watch* (Sc, Irel, etc) 2. Phr (i) *to watch oneself* 'to take heed to oneself'] □ Also AmE.

wat·che·kong(s) *n pl* (Gren, Trin) See WA-SHICONGS

watch·man [wɒčma·n] *vb* (Gren, Guyn, Trin) [*AF/IF*] To keep watch; [by extension] to act as watchman or overseer (over work or workmen). **a.** *A. G.: 'Now after Precious said that he had to watchman for Collins what did he do?' / WIT: 'He stay in a building. I go down in China Town direction then I went and sleep.'*—ToR (77.03.23, p.7) **b.** *Nowadays yo[u] can['t] watchman people yo[u] employ to do yo[ur] work.*—(Guyn) [By functional n > vb shift of SE *watchman*]

wa·ter *n* **1.** (CarA) [*IF*] Bright's disease or nephritis (wh causes the swelling of the body with fluid). *The mention of older folk gave Ms Maggie another thought: 'Yo know, ain't got nothin more dangerous than if a person reach a certain age an dey start to get stout an dey gather water. Now some people wha past 50 years dey start* *gettin stout an thing. Dey people claim tis cold turn to water, but any way, dey call it water.*—AaW I.1, p.22 **2.** (CarA) [*IF*] Swelling of the knees or ankles (due to different kinds of bodily ailments). **3.** (USVI) [*AF/IF*] (Short for) GOAT-WATER. *So ar'we could nock up a little water tonight / a long time me no taste that / and me dam fed up a de salt-fish, ... / and even the so call pigtail. Ar'we ha ochro, dasheen, yarm, puparys, ...*—Vip I.1 **4.** PHRASES **4.1 blood is thicker than water** *Prov* (CarA) See BLOOD Phr 3.1 □ Note also perh related Phrs 4.2, 4.8 below. **4.2 blood turns (to) water** *vb phr* (Gren, Guyn) [*IF*] See BLOOD Phr 3.2 **4.3 cry long water** *vb phr* (CarA) [*IF*] See CRY Phr 1. **4.4 cry water to boil yams** *vb phr* (Angu) [*AF*] ‖ CRY LONG WATER (CarA) **4.5 drink water off/over (sb's) head** *vb phr* (Belz) See DRINK Phr 2. **4.6 give (sb) a basket to carry/fetch/pitch water** *id phr* (CarA) See BASKET Phrs 1, 2. **4.7 not put water in your mouth to (say sth)** *neg vb phr* (Trin) [*AF—Joc*] See PUT Phr 1. **4.8 run sb's/ your blood to water** *vb phr* (Angu, Gren, Tbgo, Trin) [*AF/IF*] See RUN Phr 6.10 □ Note also Phr 4.2 above. **4.9 water come a/in me eye** *id phr* (Gren, Guyn, Jmca, Trin) [*AF—Cr*] Tears come/came to my eyes. *Boy when A see yo[u] yo[u] mak[e] water come in me eye, yo[u] look so much like yo[ur] fader.*—(Guyn) □ This Cr phr has survived among many older folk in emotive contexts. **4.10 water more than flour** *id phr* (Belz, Gren, Tbgo, Trin) [*AF*] The situation has become impossible; things are getting/have got out of hand; there is more strain/trouble/ shame, etc than you can bear. **a.** *'Go and tell Ramdas that I call him right away,' Gurudeva told Dookhwa. 'Tell him that if he don't come right away, is trouble for him—is water more than flour for him.'*—NAGOS:84 **b.** *Ay ay gal, water more dan flour now, de whole village seh dat Zeela dey wid Bro. Joe, the big church man, she near famaly.*—Tbgo (Ms, Play 1981) [By metaph transfer from bread-making: if too much water has been added to too little flour, the result is a waste that cannot be rescued]

wa·ter-blis·ter *n* (Bdos) ‖ BLADDER 1. (Bdos, Guyn)

wa·ter-boots *n* (ECar) Rubber-boots with tops reaching well up the calves (for use in flood or mud); (BrE) wellingtons. *When the accused came to the shop he was wearing a yellow jersey, long water-boots, dark coloured beret, dark coloured pants.*—Gren (CR, 1972)

wa·ter-ca·la·lu *n* (Guyn) A straggling, flowering vine that thrives in TRENCHES and pools, with a smooth, greenish-brown stem containing a white latex, and erect, smooth, green leaves wh are edible and used as a CALALU; *Ipomea aquatica (Convolvulaceae)*—OGEP:111.

wa·ter-cam·oo·di *n* (Guyn) See CAMOODI

wa·ter-cow *n* (Guyn) ‖ MANATEE (Antg, etc)

wa·ter-co·co·nut /1'1222/ *n* (CarA) The young, green coconut when it is full of the cool liquid or COCONUT-WATER ready to drink. *Anyone who has ridden a long journey in the tropics will realise how refreshing it is to be thus regaled with the gentle sub-acid milk of a young coconut: for such indeed are those known as 'water' coconuts*—WTTBB:116. □ This is the commonly used CE name of the bunches of saleable fruit, (also occasionally *water-nut*) distinguishing it from the industrial DRY-COCONUT and COCONUT in culinary contexts.

wa·ter-dog* *n* (Belz, Guyn) A brownish-black, fish-eating, dog-like, amphibious mammal with webbed feet, a species of otter up to thirty pounds in weight; it is hunted for its skin and is very pugnacious; *Lutra brasiliensis* or *Pteronura sandbachii (Lutrinae).*

wa·ter-glass *n* (Baha) [Fishing Ind] A glass-bottomed bucket or box wh is larger at the bottom; it is used to spot conch, lobsters, or sponges wh are then caught by hooking.

wa·ter-grass* *n* (Bdos, Gren, Jmca, Nevs, StVn, Tbgo, Trin) ‖ **French weed** 2. (Antg) ‖ **zèb-gwa(s)** (Dmca) ‖ **zep-grass** (Guyn) A creeping, succulent, spreading weed, rooting at the nodes, with plentiful two- or three-inch long, lance-shaped leaves on slender, lifting stems; it bears sparse, bright blue, little flowers wh fade or close in bright sunlight; it thrives in damp shady places and is used both as farm food and as a folk-medicinal COOLING; *Commelina diffusa* or *C. elegans (Commelinaceae).*

wa·ter-haas* [wɒtɒ(r)-ha·s] *n* (Guyn) A brownish, coarse-haired, amphibious rodent, looking like a gigantic guinea-pig and weighing up to 100 lbs; it has a flat, snub head and short, stout, hoof-like, webbed feet; it is hunted for its meat; *Hydrochoerus capybara (Hydrochoeridae).* [< SE *water* + Du *haas* 'hare'] □ Listed as *capybara* in standard dictionaries.

wa·ter-hy·a·cinth* *n* (Bdos, Guyn, Jmca, Trin) ‖ **duck-weed** 1., ‖ **water-lily** 2. (Guyn) An aquatic plant with an erect cluster of attractive, lily-like, reddish flowers with blue and yellow blotches standing against a large, separate, upright, purplish, waxy leaf-blade, both about one foot high; it flourishes in still or slow-moving shallow water, often choking drainage; *Eichhornia crassipes (Pontederiaceae).*

wa·ter·ish *adj* (Guyn, StVn, Tbgo, Trin) [Of cooked root vegetables] Lacking taste and firmness of texture; of poor quality or food value. [An EE survival. Cp *OED waterish* 5. a. 'of solids: loose in texture' ... c. 'of a taste: Characteristic of what contains excess of water' + cits (for c.)—1653, other senses marked Obs]

wa·ter-le·mon *n* (ECar) ‖ BELL-APPLE (Guyn, etc) *The food plants are the Passion Flowers of the genus Passiflora, especially the purple-flowered*

Love-in-a-mist, P. foetida, and the pink-and-white petalled Water Lemon, P. laurifolia, often cultivated and found as an escape.—AdN (81.05.20, p.10, M.B. Hutt) [Perh from the acid-sweet taste of the liquid]

wa·ter-li·ly *n* 1. (CarA) Any of a number of varieties of an aquatic plant with flat, circular leaves (of varying sizes) that float on still water, putting up fragrant, wax-like flowers, white or brilliantly coloured, borne on single stalks and opening like rosettes, usu in dull light; *Nymphaea spp.* 2. (Guyn) (Loose name for) the WATER-HYACINTH. 3. (Guyn) (Loose name for) the VICTORIA REGIA.

wa·ter-ma·ma *n* (Guyn) ‖ FAIRMAID (Guyn) a. */Yo na krass wata, na kos wata-mama/* (*Don't curse the water-mama until you have crossed the river*).—Guyn (Prov) b. *Appearing late on moonlight nights near kokers, stellings, rivers or canals, Water Mama is often found combing her hair and singing softly to herself. She is also called Fairmaid. Water Mama has the body of a woman and a fish tail. She has long hair hiding her face which, if seen, appears bestial or to be a skull. Sudden drowning is attributed to her. The drowned person might be the object of her love.*—SCE:92 (R. Heath) [Cp *KED* Krio *mami-wata* 'mermaid'. Also note: 'Canoes frequently capsize on the Calabar River. Efik believe that a supernatural female power called *Udominyaŋ*, also known as *mami wɔta* 'water mother' in pidgin English, seizes the goods wh fall into the river'—*FETOC: 70*] □ Note that MAMA-GLO is the Fr Cr calque of the same name.

wa·ter-nut *n* (CarA) ‖ WATER-COCONUT (CarA) *A few days later, the said Thaddeus told him that if he missed coconuts from his tree it was he (Thaddeus that is) that had taken a couple water-nuts.*—ToR (76.07.25, p.3)

wa·ter-plug *n* (Gren) [*IF*] ‖ BLADDER (Bdos, Guyn) *Dis shoe gi[ve] me a water-plug on me heel oui.*—(Gren)

wa·ter-spout *n* (Bdos, StKt) ‖ AFRICAN TULIP (CarA) [A children's name, from the nature of the central buds wh retain a liquid under pressure; they spout when squeezed]

wa·ter-wash[1] *vb tr* (Bdos, Guyn, Tbgo, Trin) To wash and soap (clothes) without starching or ironing; to rough-dry (clothes). [By extension < wash only with water. Cp similar SE compound structures *hand-pick, spoon-feed,* etc]

wa·ter-wash[2] *adj* (Bdos, Guyn, Tbgo, Trin) [*AF/IF*] [Of clothes] Washed without being starched or ironed; rough dried; [by extension, of dress] wrinkled and lacking in neatness. '*We Guyanese people have bad luck*' wailed a racist militant. '*Queen Victoria was carved in marble and looked like a Queen. Gandhi stands in saintly splendour in the Gardens. But look at Critchlow statue? He looks as if he is wearing water-wash*

clothes.'—GyC (76.06.27, p.6) [By functional vb > adj shift of WATER-WASH[1]]

wa·ter-yam *n* (Belz, etc) ‖ LISBON YAM (Bdos, etc) *Water Yam* (*D. alata*) [*has*] *large tubers, sometimes as long as 1 metre, with dark-brown skin and white or pink flesh.*—OGEP:113

wa·wa *adj* [*AF—Cr*] 1. (Belz) [Usu of a male] Weak; childishly incapable; cowardly; henpecked. 2. (Trin) Sickly (-looking). [Prob < *CSESD* So Am Sp *guagua* 1. adj 'small, little'; 2. n 'a baby; a trifle' + /gu > w/ labialization. Perh also infl by 'Wah! Wah!' as baby talk]

Wax!; **Wax.en!** [waksŋ ~ waksnŋ] *excl ideoph* (Guyn, StKt) [*AF*] [Indicating the sound of a sharp lash or blow with something long and flexible]

wax·y egg *n phr* (Jmca) A medium-boiled egg.

way[1] *n* [*IF*] 1. (CarA) Manner, style or aspect of a happening, situation, etc, (see esp Phrs 4.6, 4.6.1); manner of conduct. a. *And don[']t le[t] me tell yo[u] the way the mother bawl out and carry on when she hear the child foot break. You would think the child dead.*—(Guyn) b. *She go on one way sometimes, especially when she feel like her husband noticing me.*—HF:15 [Perh from IrE infl. Note: The little phrase '*the way*' is used among us in several senses, all peculiar, and all derived from Irish. Sometimes it is a direct translation from *amhlaidh* ('thus,' 'so', 'how', 'in a manner')—*JESI:35*. See also Phr 4.6 below] 2. *also pl* (CarA) [*IF*] (A) good distance. a. *I could see in the sky there was a fire, but some way away.*—(Guyn) b. *Esmeralda and Wingrove used to live just a little ways from me and Vera in St Victoria village.*—CISH:107 [Cp *EDD way* 5. (N.I, Sur, Dev, etc) pl 'way; distance'. Also see *OED2 way sb*, 23. c. dial and US. Also *a ways* (unqualified) + cits '... quite a ways up', etc] 3. (CarA) [*AF/IF*] [After a place or person's name, referring to location] (In the) area or direction (of). a. *Next time yo[u] goin[g] Aunt Effie way you mus[t] carry back her basket.*—(StVn) b. *He alone I always see there. He said he had some lands up by Clozier way.*—Gren (CR, 1972) [Cp *EDD way* 6. 'the direction of; towards; gen immediately preceded by a place-name' + cits from Sc, Yks, etc] □ Also dial AmE. Ex *down Mexico way*, etc. 4. PHRASES 4.1 **go all the way** *id phr* (CarA) See GO Phr 6.6 4.2 **Go your way!** *imper vb phr* (Guyn) [*IF*] See GO Phr 6.35 4.3 **have (your) ways** *vb phr* (CarA) [*IF*] To tend to behave or act in unexpected and peculiar or displeasing ways. *He was a man that had his ways but he was never spiteful, you know, so you could still get along with him.*—(StVn) 4.4 **(in) a certain way** *adj phr* (Bdos) See CERTAIN Phr *You think you's a big woman now, eh? This is why you behaving so? Well, as long as you inside my house you have to conduct yourself in a certain way and right now you going have to explain yourself to me.*—SuS (79.09.16, p.27, T. Callender) 4.5 **see your way** *vb phr* (Bdos, Gren, Guyn) [*IF*] See

SEE Phrs 3.12, 3.12.1 **4.6 that way** *n phr in adv* function (Bdos, Guyn) [*IF*] So; like that. **a.** *A chapped skin with red bumps is unsightly and no one likes to look that way.*—Guyn (Ms, 1966) **b.** *S1: Like the two of them had a quarrel / S2: It looks that way.*—(Bdos) **4.6.1 I know da/that way** *id phr* (Bdos, Guyn) [*AF/IF*] I understand what you mean. *S1: 'I couldn't pay the rent this month because I lost my job.' / S2: I know that way.'*—(Guyn) **4.7 What a way** ... *excl introductory phr* (Jmca) [*AF/IF*] ‖ IS ONLY SO ... (Gren, Guyn). See ONLY Phr 2.1 **a.** *S1: 'What a way de mosquitoes dem plentiful since de rain!' / S2: 'Boy! if me wasn't strong dem no lift me off me bed last night.'*—WeG (73.11.7, p.25, Cartoon) **b.** *What a way this child is growing! When I saw her last she was just waist-high.*—(Jmca) [Perh from IrE infl. Note: Sometimes the word way is a direct translation from the Irish *caoi*, 'a way,' 'a road'; so that the common Irish salutation, *Cad chaoi bh-fuil tu?* is translated with perfect correctness into the equally common IrE salute, 'What way are you?' meaning 'How are you?'—*JESI:36*]

way[2] [we~wɛ] *adv* (CarA) [X] Away (esp as adv extension in vb phrs **go [a]way, run [a]way, throw [a]way**, etc). **a.** *De old lady faint way.*—WFSFB:48 (P. Gillett) **b.** *Praise God I ent have nothing for him to thief. / Come see he must be pra-pra somebody fowl and it get way.*—RTCS:17 **c.** *Calvin mother do a real good job, and when she done pack the things, and she inspect the clothes that Calvin carrying way, she tie-up the two valises with a strong piece o' string.*—CWFYS:93 [< SE *away* by characteristic CarA Cr aphesis. Cp similar development of *IF* IAE *way* 'far away', in such phrs as *way back, way down, way off*, etc] □ Not usu written *'way* as it would be in SE (note cits), this form leads to regularized phrs in schoolwork such as **fall way, take way, throw way**, etc.

way[3] **(we(y), whe(y))** [we~wɛ] *adv* (CarA) [*AF—Cr*] Where. **a.** *I aks one feller 'Way yinna all goin'?*—JBJ:81 **b.** *That's ole talk. Way the hell you go get money to go?*—PGIP:48 **c.** *There are instances where mothers drive their pregnant daughters out.... There are a few cases where they have no way to turn.*—AdN (72.11.13, p.4) [< SE *where* [wɛə(r)] by levelling of diphthong and loss of /-r/. Note *EDD* variant pronunc [wɛə(r)]] □ These variant dial spellings often occur in CE narrative dialogue.

way[4] **(wa, we, wha)** [we~wɛ~wʌ] *rel pron* (CarA) [*AF—Cr*] [In connective function replacing *who, which, that*] **a.** *The witness said that he cautioned the accused, who then said: 'Well, at last all you find out that it is I way kill R—, eh?'*—TrG (73.07.19) **b.** *'He jes' talkin' for talk sake, because all way you see he read dere, is de same t'ing what people know long time.'*—MN:31 **c.** *Dey should pick up all dem wild dog wa go get puppy all over de place.*—(StVn) [Cp *EDD* who (Sc, Irel, Eng) variant pronuncs and spellings:

whae, whay, whe, etc] □ These variant dial spellings often occur in CE narrative.

Wa·ya(h)! [wa:yaŋ] *excl* (Guyn, Jmca) See WOY!

way poo cow *id phr* (Gren) See WÉ POU KO-OU

Wè! [wɛ:ŋ] *excl* (Dmca, StLu) Look!; See!; But I say!; Fancy!, etc *Wè girl, how you get nasty up so?*—(StLu) [Fr Cr loan < *vwè* < Fr *voir* 'to see']

we[1] [wi~wi] *pron 1st pers pl* (CarA) **1.** [Often specially focused or emphasized in folk speech by expansions. See ALL[1] B. 1. ALL-O(F)-WE, etc; 2. A(LL)-WE-SELF; also WE-ALL-SELF as separate entry] **2.** PHRASES **2.1 we go(ing) pick up** [*AF*]; **we go sight** [Rastaf]; **we will catch up** [*IF*] *id phrs* [Leave-taking] Until we meet again. *'Well,' Galahad get up, 'we will pick up. I have to go to school this afternoon to collect the rent.'*—STLL:118 **2.2 we so** *pron phr* (CarA) [*AF*] [Implying self-pity or abnegation] People like ourselves; such (unfortunates) as we. *Dem days, you think we so could go in places like Marine Hotel? Oh no!*—(Bdos) □ WE is frequently used, esp in *AF—Cr* contexts, in other functions than as subj of a vb or in nominative case. See 3., 4., etc. **3.** [X] [As object] Us. **a.** *All of we is Indian together; let we drink and make merry.*—SABS:14 **b.** *Mr Editor I will like to know if the present Government will relax and allow this rich white company to rob we poor Black Vincentians.*—ViN (73.09.14, p.5) [A survival from CarA Cr pron system, as also sense 4., etc. Note the same regularization in *EDD* we pers pron II. Dial uses 1. 'emphatic form of direct and indirect object' + cits, ex 'to git over men like we', etc] **4.** [As possessive] Our. **a.** *He was the hero of the Yorubas and Fox Hill people in general, and they all referred to him as 'we boy'.*—EBT:35 **b.** *We have a society built on the chase of pleasure. We drink we rum and we tumble down. We sing we kaiso an' we play we carnival.*—KTNVS:14 [See note at 2.; and cp *EDD* we II. 2. 'our' + cits ex 'we held we breaths', etc] PHRASES **4.1 we own** /1'2/ *possessive pron phr* (CarA) [X] Our; our own. *If dey can make dey noise in dey house, we can make we own noise in we own house.*—(Trin) □ Note prec.; see also OWN 1, 1.1. **4.1.1 we own t[h]ing** / 12'2/ *id phr* (CarA) [*AF/IF*] What is truly a part of us; our own culture. **a.** *Calypso is Trinidad, reggae is Jamaica but spouge is 'we own thing'.*—Bdos (Ms) **b.** *Many people favour the CXC examinations because they feel 'dat is we own thing' and is more in keeping with nations who have broken free of the old colonial chains.*—BoM (79.06.15, p.4) **4.2 we own** [wi-o·n] /2'1/ *possessive pron phr* (absolute) (CarA) [X] Ours; what belongs to us. *He said D— told him that the jewellery the Police found was P—'s, but 'we own dey safe because whey we bury it I don't think even God can find it.'*—DaC (52.08.23, p.5) □ Note stress and pitch differentiation from 4.1.

we[2]**! (wee!)** [wi] *excl tag* (Dmca, etc) **1.** See OUI **a.** *'Yes Ma', Ram returned. 'I does always behave* *myself, we Ma. I does always behave myself, we Ma.*—Dmca (Ms, 1974) **b.** *Some of these politicians joking, wee! Mr P— say we don't want hospitals and that what we want are sporting complexes and tennis courts, etc.*—ToR (76.12.05, p.10) **2.** PHRASE **2.1 We(e) foot!** *excl* (Dmca, etc) See OUI Phr 2.1

we-all-self [wial'sɛlf] *refl pron (phr)*, 1st pers pl (Crcu) [*AF—Cr*] ‖ A[LL]-WE-SELF (Guyn) *I and Goodwin went into Miss A. J— shop and then we were having drinks among we all self.*—Crcu (CR)

wear PHRASE **wear jacket for (sb)** *vb phr* (Belz, Jmca) [*AF—Derog*] See JACKET² Phr 3.2

weath·er *n* (CarA) [*IF*] **1.** Bad weather; rough weather; storm or hurricane. *The skies were gray and you could feel it in the air that weather was coming in full.*—StKt (Ms) [Cp *EDD* weather 1. (Sc, Cum, etc) 'bad, rough weather'; also *OED* weather sb 1. h (Obs) 'a storm, tempest' + cit 1894 'Don't be late ... there's weather coming'] □ The neutral SE sense of *weather* tends to be secondary in everyday CE usage, and the restricted sense above dominant. The 'Hurricane Preparedness' handbook lists as 'WEATHER SYSTEMS': Tropical Depression, Tropical Storm, Hurricane, Eye [of a storm], Storm Surge. Also, in schoolwork 'weather' is regularly understood as 'storm(s)'. **2.** PHRASE **2.1 weather is building** *id phr* (ECar) [*IF*] Heavy weather is threatening.

weed·ing-gang *n* (Guyn, Jmca) ‖ CREOLE GANG (Guyn) *In the 'weeding gang', a sort of industrial kindergarten in which most of the children from five to eight years old were kept, as much for control as for achievement, there were 20 pickaninnies, all black, under Mirtilla as 'driveress', who had borne and lost seven children of her own. Thirty-nine children were too young for the weeding gang, at least six of whom were quadroons.*—Caq I.1, p.7

weh¹ [wɛ] *adv* (CarA) [*AF—Cr*] See WHERE

weh² [wɛ] *pron* (Belz, Gren, Trin) [*AF—Cr*] See WHEY

weight *n* PHRASE **make (sb) feel the weight of your hand** *vb phr* (ECar) [*AF*] See HAND¹ Phr 4.19 *'You two better watch your step or soon it is you who go be feeling the weight of that on your back'. Mrs Lutchman collared her sons and on each of the two faces ... she delivered a resounding slap.*—NF:80

wel·comed *adj* (CarA) [*X*] Welcome. *'I am open for business and I don't discriminate against anyone, and Mrs M— is quite welcomed,' he added.*—ExP (72.03.14, p.1) [By overcorrection and confusion of the adj *welcome* 'received gladly' with the pa. part. of the vb *to welcome* 'to receive gladly'] □ See also UNWELCOMED.

well¹ *adv* **1.** [As intensifier before adj or vb] (CarA) [*IF*] ‖ *well and* (Baha, Belz, Guyn,

Jmca) Thoroughly; greatly; certainly; quite; very (much). **a.** *De boat turn over, an not a man could swim, / An' partner de water by de jetty well deep yu know.*—KTT:100 **b.** *But when somebody bless they well bless and when somebody stupid they well stupid.*—TaP (76.02.15, p.11) **c.** *'Woman, ge' off this fiel' here today,' he said ponderously, 'or I going well beat you. You hear me.'*—MHBT:59 **d.** *Them Americans well like they curry and roti; I hear they does buy in Port of Spain and eat all about.*—SABS:139 [Cp *OED* well adv IV. As an intensive with adjectives, numerals, adverbs, etc. 16. with adjectives. Formerly in common use, the sense varying from 'fully, completely' to 'fairly, considerably, rather'. Now rare exc as in *... well able, aware, worth, worthy*. Also *EDD* well adv and adj. 5. 'very, quite' + cits (Slg). 'This appeareth to be well hard, Bruce.' *Sermons* (1631); (sNot) 'A'd get well drunk, if a tho't it ud do my head good'] □ Note also **well bad, well low**. See BAD¹ PHR 4.2 BE BAD ENOUGH **2.** PHRASES **2.1 well and** *intensifier phr before adj or vb* (Baha, Belz, Guyn, Jmca) [*IF*] ‖ WELL 1. (CarA) **a.** *The rain came down so suddenly that before I could reach the house I was well and wet, you see.*—(Jmca) **b.** *If the Quibbler was the teacher of some of those school children on the Quiz Programme on Radio Haw Haw on Thursday nights I would well and thump some of them when they come back to school the next day or whenever, for making me and the school 'look shame' as the common saying goes.*—EvP (73.02.16, p.6) [Cp IF E *good and* + adj, with similar sense. Perh a blend of this structure with WELL¹] **2.2 Well done!** /2'1'/ *excl phr* (Gren, Guyn, Jmca, StVn) [*IF*] ‖ **Well me/my done!** (Mrat) [Expressing shock, disbelief] I can hardly believe it! *You mean that boy used those dirty words to his own mother? Well done!*—(StVn) [Cp *EDD* well adv and adj 2. Comb in exclamations (3) *well done* + cit for Dev (On hearing of the death of a friend) 'Well done! Well done!'] (StVn) **2.3 You/ they/he/she do well!** *excl phrs* (CarA) [*AF*] [Expressing vexed rejection or disapproval] How inconsiderate! *Dey t[h]ink dat because yo[u] glad fo[r] de wo[r]k you mus[t] wo[r]k overtime for not[hi]n[g]? Dey do well!*—(StVn)

well² *adj* (CarA) [*X*] Good. **a.** *The holiday had done her well ... the change of environment, as Tiger put it, 'bring back the colour in your face, and learn you to live again.'*—SABS:208 **b.** *The sons put the father out because of his drunkenness, but when they saw the mother crying they didn't feel so well about it.*—(Bdos)

welsh·man (**wench·man**) *n* (Angu, BrVi, Jmca, Mrat, Nevs) A pink or reddish fish with large, black eyes and a prominently bony dorsal fin; it weighs about 2 lbs, and is of good food value; *Holocentrus spp*. [Perh welsh-/wench- pejoratively from its habit of hiding by day, evading esp other fishes that hunt it as food] □ Also known in fishing literature as **squirrelfish**.

went *vb pa.t.* (Bdos) [*X*] [Of persons] Came. **a.** *Look, the postman went already because the box* *got letters.*—(Bdos) **b.** *Sir, the plumber went here this morning to see you. He say to called him at home.*—Bdos (Servant's note) □ Very common usage at the folk level and in written schoolwork. The implication is always that sb came for some purpose and has now gone.

wè pou ko-ou! (way poo cow!) [we pu kɔ-u] *id phr* (Gren) [*AF—Joc*] Watch out for yourself! Look out for the consequences! Beware! *But zootee by any name is still zootee, and if you siddown in it, is way-poo-cow.*—ToR (77.06.19, p.5, Cotay-si Cotay-la) [Fr Cr < *vwè pou ko-ou* < Fr *voir pour corps-vous* (*see for your body*) 'Look out for yourself!']

were [wA(r)] *vb pa. t.* (CarA) [*X*] Was. **a.** *Mr Michel my teacher were a very good sports man. The first match we played were with the Jennings school.*—Antg (Ms, schoolwork) **b.** *Well, well, well, ... the kaisonian of the night, the singer of the night, strangely enough, was a woman. One would have thought, that calypso were dominated by men?*—MoK (73.02.02, p.2) [A common overcorrection due to false refinement in middle-level spoken and written CE]

we·self; **we.selves** *refl pers pron* (ECar) [*AF— Cr*] ‖ *a(ll)-we-self* (Guyn) ‖ *we-all-self* (Crcu) Ourselves. **a.** *Why we weself don't do something about it?*—SABS:189 **b.** *They allow us to run loose until we give we self up so that we could see for weself that all we could do is a dragon dance.*—LDCD:185 **c.** *No place to go. Nowhere to enjoy weselves.*—HFGA:110 (A. Clarke) **d.** *It's sad about we women ... we kill each other for the scarce male and we end up suffering in agony all by weselves.*—Bdos (Ms Play, 1979) [< CarA Cr WE in possessive function + SE emphasizers *self/selves*. Note *EDD we-selves* (Yks, etc) 'ourselves'. Cp also DEMSELF]

West In·di·an; Westin.di.an /1′221/ *n* (*phr*), *adj* (*phr*) (CarA) (A person or thing) of or belonging to any of the English-speaking islands, including the Bahamas archipelago, and the mainland territories that enclose the Caribbean Sea. **a.** *William Demas in everything he has said or written begins with the postulate that West Indians are a people, a nation.*—Unn.80.2, p.4 **b.** *Sociologists say, too, that it is a Westindian tradition to have many children so that they will support you in your old age. But, whatever the reasons, we Westindians do ourselves no good by continuing to produce large families.*—DeM(SK) (76.02.14, p.5) **c.** *Child, there is a kind o' Wessindian man who just loves to live offa women.*—CWFYS:35 [Adj derived from SE *West India*, formerly 'west India', from Columbus's mistake, this form generally replacing 'new Spain' in the late 16C. A ref also to the brown skins of the indigenous peoples who thereby seemed kin to East Indians] □ 1. Though usu written as two words, the one-word form, preferred by some writers (cit b., c.) helps to distinguish the sense

from EAST INDIAN, and also to facilitate derivatives such as WESTINDIANIZE, WESTINDIANIZATION. These are often replaced by *Caribbeanize*, etc. 2. Note also differing connotations of ANTILLEAN, CARIBBEAN.

West-In·di·an al·mond *n phr* (BrVi, Jmca, Trin) ‖ ALMOND (CarA) [Distinguishing the fruit from the European fruit of the same name. See etym note at ALMOND]

West-In·di·an birch *n phr* (Trin) ‖ BIRCH-GUM TREE (Bdos, etc)

West-In·di·an cher·ry *n phr* (CarA) ‖ BARBADOS-CHERRY (CarA)

West-In·di·an e·bo·ny *n phr* (Trin) ‖ WOMAN('S)-TONGUE TREE (CarA) *The heart wood of West Indian ebony makes clarinets and other woodwind instruments.*—Jan (82/9, p.28) [See BARBADOS EBONY]

West·in·di·an·ism; West-In.di.an.ism *n* (CarA) A sense and recognition of a Westindian cultural and historical sameness irrespective of the geographical separation of the territories of the region; an identification of togetherness of Westindian peoples. *We in the West Indies have always been our worst enemies.... We talk about a West Indian nation and about West-Indianism and yet when the nitty-gritty comes, we can never coalesce, cohere or come together.*—Bdos (Hd, 73.06.05, p.2362) □ See note at WEST INDIAN.

West·in·di·an·i·za·tion; West-In.di.an-.i.sa.tion *n* (CarA) The act or process of WESTINDIANIZING. *The policy of West-Indianisation and effective control of foreign enterprise should be honourably and sensibly pursued.*—MtM (73.01.12, p.4) □ See note at WEST INDIAN.

West·in·di·an·ize; West-In.di.an.ise *vb* (CarA) To make sth (such as an institution, a festival, etc) markedly WESTINDIAN in staffing, ownership, composition, or appearance. *Commenting on some of the changes that have taken place in the Methodist Church during the past three decades, the Rev. Lyder said that the Church in the region had become more West-Indianised.* / *'When I entered the ministry most of the ministers were Englishmen, but now there are a few of them,' he said.* / *The Trinidad-born minister said it was a good sign that local men were willing to come into the ministry.*—AdN (78.08.22, p.1)□ See note at WEST INDIAN.

West-In·di·an mi·mo·sa *n phr* (Trin) ‖ WILD TAMARIND 1. (Belz, etc) *The plant West Indian mimosa thrives in dry situations, and in some parts of the Colony covers waste areas.... The foliage, if eaten by horses ... causes shedding of the hair, including the mane and tail.*—PTT:205 [Prob an agriculturist's name since the plant, of the Mimosa family, grows wild throughout the West Indies]

West·in·di·an·ness; West-In.di.an.ness *n*
(CarA) A state, condition, or character that identifies a person, action or thing as being typically
WESTINDIAN. **a.** *Like Cricket, the UWI symbolises
our West Indianness as something really functional.*—Jmca (Ms) **b.** *Try as he may, Naipaul
cannot escape his West Indianness.*—GTTLA:54
□ See note at WEST INDIAN.

West In·di·an sas·pa·ril·la *n phr* (ViIs) See
SASPARILLA.

wet¹ *adj PHRASE* **wet paper could cut you** *id
phr* (Trin) [*AF—Joc*] Things are in a sorry state
with you; you are much distressed, depressed,
troubled by many things. [A Joc hyperbole]

wet² *vb tr* (Gren, StKt) [*AF*] To strike (sb)
hard. **a.** *Da Souza said that he then pulled a rope
from his pocket 'and wet him ... two.'*—DeM(SK)
(62.10.27, p.8) **b.** *I tried to go up a bank at a
neighbour, Nelson wet me a planass in my waist. I
mean he strike me with the cutlass in my waist.*—
Gren (CR, 79/8) [Perh by misascription of SE
whet 'sharpen (sth for attack)'. Note cit b.] **2.**
(Bdos) [By extension] [Cricket] To hit (the bowling) so hard as to upset the bowler.

wet co·coa *n phr* (Gren, Jmca, Trin) Cocoa
beans fresh from the pod, still white, before
being dried or 'cured'; it is retailed to small
buyers in this state. *On arrival the 'wet' cocoa
(beans removed from the pod and covered with a
glutinous white pulp) is placed in wooden 'sweat
boxes' and covered with burlap bags and banana
leaves. After 48 hours the contents are shifted to
prevent the beans from sticking together to provide
enough air circulation in order to discourage the
growth of mould.*—Isl (73/6, p.11) [From their
covering of glutinous substance in this state]

wet sug·ar *n phr* (CarA) Unrefined, dark brown
sugar in the first stage of crystallization; it is
used for confectionery and other purposes in
this state.

wey¹ [we] *adv* (CarA) [*AF—Cr*] See WHERE

wey² [we] *pron* (Belz, Gren, Trin) [*AF—Cr*]
See WHEY

wey-wey *n* (Trin) See WHE-WHE.

wha *interr pron, adj* (CarA) [*AF—Cr*] See
WHA[T]

wha·been *n* (Gren, Trin) See WABINE

whap! *excl ideoph* (CarA) [*AF*] See WAP! *I have
to repeat my name to myself and kick a fence
whap hard so that it hurts.*—JJM:62 □ Functional
extensions of ideophs, as in this cit, are regarded
by many CE speakers as available usage.

whap·peel·pie *n* (Gren, Jmca, Trin) See
WAP(P)EE

wha[t]¹ (wa[h], wat, we[h], whah, whay,
whe[y]) [wa(t)~wɛ~we] *pron* (CarA) [With
widely varying pronunc and dial spellings] **1.**
interr pron (CarA) **a.** *Why you vex? Wha[t] I do?*
—(Guyn) **b.** *Wha sinner like me and you must
do / If the parson and all doing that too.*—StVn
(Ms, 1974) **c.** *The young policeman held back the
hand of a fellow cop as he went to pelt his bottle
and the other cop outside ... said: 'Boy, whey de
Service coming to?'*—ExP (72.09.25, p.17) [<
SE *what* by apocope > /wa/ followed by lip-
spreading in the process of DECREOLIZATION. Cp
also *EDD what* pron (Sc, Irel, etc) (6) *wha*]
2. *PHRASES* **2.1 What about?** *greeting
formula* (Tbgo) [*IF*] How are things with you?; How is
life treating you? *S1: Hi, Mrs Moore! / S2: Hi,
Mrs James. What about?*—(Tbgo) **2.2 what and
what** *non-personal pron phr* (CarA) [*IF*] All the
(likely/necessary, etc) things that; all the facts/
news/details, etc etc. **a.** *In effect Dr Duncan had
said that if Labourites come out on the streets,
what and what they (the PNP) are going to do
with them.*—DaG (79.10.03, p.2) **b.** *She take
him in the kitchen and show him how much food
she had there to cook and she tell him what and what
the other people was cooking.*—NaG (Satirically
Speaking, 1975) **2.3 Wha[t] do?** *id phr* (Gren)
[*AF*] What's happening?; What's up? *A see a lot
o[f] people runnin[g] do[w]ng de road. Wha[t] do?*
—(Gren) [Perh a translation of Fr Cr *Sa ki fè*
(= What is doing?) wh is the normal greeting
among Fr Cr speakers] **2.3.1 Wha[t] do sb/
you?** *id phr* (ECar) [*AF*] **(i)** What's the matter
with you?; Why don't you behave yourself? *Ma:
(As one child tugs at her dress) Wey do dis dam
pickney?*—HF:50 **(ii)** [To a sick person] What
is your trouble? **2.4 Wha[t] fi/fo do?** (CarA)
[*AF—Cr*] [Expressing acceptance of an unfortunate situation] Well so be it, for what can
anybody do about it anyway? *'Parson, don['t] vex
that we late' she said. 'After all i[t']s a funeral.
Wha[t] fo do?'*—StVn (Ms, short story) □ This
exp is often cynically used by educated CE
speakers. **2.5 What happen?** [wa(t)
hapn~wapn~wɒpn] *id phr* (Gren, Guyn, Trin)
[*AF*] **(i)** What's the matter?; What's wrong?;
Why are you behaving like this?; What's your
problem? **a.** *'Wey happen? Yoh go tear dong
mih clothes.' She glared. 'What it is now?'*—ExP
(73.04.29, p.7) **b.** *So a[l]right, it was t[h]ree
mangoes an[d] I eat two, so what happen?*—(Guyn)
□ Also sometimes *What happen for that?.* **(ii)**
(CarA) [*IF*] [Indirect question introducing an
explanation] The fact/position/situation is that
... **a.** *Sorry I couldn['t] come yesterday. What
happen, my grandfather came from St Vincent.*—
(Tbgo) **b.** *What happen I di[d]n['t] have de money
den, see? But I have it now.*—(Bdos) **2.6 What['s]
happenin[g]?; Wha[h]appenin[g]?** *greeting
formula* (CarA) [*IF/AF*] How are (things with)
you? □ Often reduced at folk level to /waapnin/.
2.7 what is to is must is *id phr* (ECar) [*AF*]
What is to be will be. *The people of Grenada have
many vivid expressions to describe rare moments of
life. No Barbadian could find words more suited
to translate an act of God than the Grenadian who
said: 'What is to is, must is.'*—HWII:156 □ The

phr, used often in serious conversation may perh be regarded as proverbial. **2.8 Wha[t] make?** [wa-mɛk] *id phr* (CarA) [*AF—Cr*] [Either introducing a question or in absolute form] Why? **a.** *But tell me nuh Vio, what make some people have to powder dey face so thick and put on all dis rouge and lipstick?*—RTCS:18 **b.** *Wa mek you no carry she Jamaica fo you mudder tell she how fo cook?*—PKKK:83 **c.** *She handed me the fish and bread, shook her head and sadly said, 'No, no Toomatie, Aunt May not tekkin money teeday.' 'Wha mek, Aunt May?'*—Kai VIII 71/6, p.66 [Prob a calque from W Afr langs. Cp Yoruba *kin lo ṣe ... (What it is make ...)* 'Why ...?'] **2.9 What you talkin[g]?** *id phr* (CarA) [*AF—Derog*] What nonsense are you telling me?; You don't really know what you're saying; [by extension] I can't believe what you're saying. **a.** *You get injury on the job, and you don[']t know what to do [a]bout it? What you talking? Man, go an[d] see the Labour Officer, do!*—(Bdos) **b.** *You mean that girl getting a baby for a married man? What you talking? And butter can't melt in her mouth.*—(Gren) □ Cp IF SE equivalent *What the hell are you saying!*. **3.** *rel pron* (CarA) [*X*] [In multi-purpose conn function] Who; which; that. **a.** *Billy Graham? ... Who name so? Billy Graham is the man what save my soul, yes.*—MN: 16 **b.** *Sometimes you get a load a noise if is a case what create interest or what have scandal inside it.*—LMFF:45 **c.** *Anansi shrieked louder while the fiddle wailed like a sick puppy. 'All whay you got give ah we. De burn-burn self give ah we.'*—STTG:72 **d.** *De men whey fix de road / And de wans whey plough de banks / Aal o you Montserrat / Appreciate an' tell you tanks.*—MtM (77.01.14, p.8) **e.** *A talk wid one fella weh di paint di house cross di street from where I work.*—HF:15

wha[t]² *interr adj* (CarA) [*AF*] **1.** [*Derog* expressing rejection of an idea] What kind of?; which? *What doctor? He been away but he ain[']t qualify. He only foolin[g] people, but you ever see he put up a sign?*—(Guyn) **2.** PHRASES **2.1 wha[t] part?** *adv phr* (CarA) [*AF*] Where? **a.** *What part in Tragarete Road you live? (= Where in Tragarete Road, etc).*—(Trin) **b.** *He come in so drunk he can[']t tell you what part he leave the bicycle.*—(CayI) **2.2 wha[t] scene you on?** (Trin, Tbgo) [*AF*] Why are you acting like this?; you don't seem to be aware of the circumstances. *He told M— he was using obscene language and the defendant replied: 'What scene you on? Like you want to dehumanise me.'*—TrG (73.11.04) [Prob infl of IF AmE]

wha[t]³ *excl functions* **1.** *excl tag with falling pitch* (CarA) [*AF—Derog*] ‖*wisside!* (Guyn) [Expressing contempt] In what possible or imaginable way? *Married what? They been living together since in England.*—(Jmca) **2.** PHRASES **2.1 ... or wha[t](?)** *interr expletive* (CarA) [*IF*] [Expressing approximation to some state or action that irritates] (SE) or something (of the kind) (?) **a.** *You goin[g] out to play in the mud wid those clean clothes? You mad or what?*—(Bdos) □ Also AmE slang. **2.2 What a cross(es)!** *excl*

phr (Jmca) [*AF*] [Expressing disgust, anger, shame, etc] Oh Lord!; Oh my God! □ Cp LOOK AT MY CROSSES! See LOOK Phr 4.3 **2.3 What a pistarckle!** *excl phr* (ViIs) [*AF—Joc*] Such a muddle and confusion! [See PISTARCKLE] **2.4 What a way** (+ a statement)! *excl introductory phr* (Jmca) [*IF*] See WAY¹ Phr 4.7

wheel *n* (Baha, Guyn) [*AF*] A bicycle. *I need to get rid of this old bone-shaker and buy myself a new wheel.*—(Guyn) [By synecdoche from ref to the pair of wheels of a bicycle] □ Note *OED wheel* 7. orig and esp U.S. 'a bicycle or tricycle' + cits–'1896; however sense also includes 'cycling']

wheel-lock *n* (Bdos) An iron shoe that can be fitted on the rim of one cart-wheel and held in place by a chain so as to retard and control the downhill descent of an animal-drawn cart; (SE) *drag* (as *OED drag* 3.c.).

whe(h) [wɛ] *adv* (CarA) See WHA[T]¹; WHE(RE)

whelk *n* (Baha, TkCa, USVI) See WILK(S)

whem [wɛm] *n* (Bdos) A swelling (usu on the forehead) caused by a blow. [Cp *EDD wem* sb. Yks, Lan, Lin, eAn, Cor. 1. 'a spot, blemish, flaw', also *wen* sb. nLin¹. 'a blemish, defect'. See also *OED2 wem* sb. Obs. exc. arch. 2 and 4. (By confusion with *wen*¹). 'A raised spot; a protuberance']

when *adv, conj* (CarA) **1.** [As semi-preposition, but really introducing an incomplete clause] [*X*] [At] the time of. **a.** *They did tell me when de wedding [i.e. took place/was to be, etc] but I ain[']t remember.*—(Guyn) **b.** *Honky does go to de communal whenever nature call. He can't even say both of us was dere when de alarm.*—TRIH:198 **2.** [Used as a loose conn] [*X*] That. **a.** *Q— said that it was during a class break when the fight between the two boys took place.*—AdN (74.06.13, p.1) **b.** *It is high time when he should come now.*—(Guyn) **3.** PHRASES **3.1 when come** *adv phr* (Gren, Guyn) [*AF*] When it comes/came to the test; finally. **a.** *He say he payin[g] in time for Christmas, and when come we don[']t get pay.*—(Gren) **b.** *I put a big tin o[f] Bournvita dere, and she use lil bit and lil bit, and when come and I lookin[g] for some, nearly all done.*—(Guyn) **3.1.1 when (it) come(s) to (sth)** *functioning as prep phr* (CarA) [*AF*] In the particular matter of (sth). **a.** *How much I got to tell you, boy, that when it come to cane, it ain't having nothing I don't know?*—SPOC:89 **b.** *He always sick when it come to wo[r]k, but when come to cricket he gone like a engine.*—(Bdos) □ Cp SE *if/when it comes to that*, 'in that particular case'. **3.2 when done** *id phr* (Bdos, Gren, Guyn, Jmca) [*AF—Cr*] When indeed; yet in fact; nevertheless. **a.** *Lord, what a heat! What a crowd a people! When done people say hard time take Jamaica.*—SNWIC (M. Townshend) **b.** *She say she sick and have to stay inside, when done is baby de girl making.*—(Gren) [Cp *EDD when* 2. Phr (3) (Uls, wYks) *when done* 'notwithstanding; after all'**] 3.3 when fowl(-cock) cut/get/make teeth** *id phr* (CarA) [*AF—Cr*] See FOWL Phr 2.3 *He will give up drink when cock get teet*[*h*].—(StVn) **3.4 When I tell you!** *id phr, emphasizer adjunct* (Gren, Guyn, Tbgo, Trin) [*IF*] Believe me when I say (it)!; words cannot adequately describe (it)! *She come in the house these days and she start moving about like some kind of ghost. Quiet, but fast. When I tell you, boy. Those hands of hers just going like that, whish-whish-bam-bam, and that's it.*—NG:125 **3.5 when since?** *interr adv phr* (Jmca) [*AF*] Since when? *Mother looks on me, her arms akimbo, and good it is to hear the laughter that comes deep from her belly. / 'Coo here!' cries Mother. 'When since kling-kling turn into hawk-bird? Heh!'*— RND:147 **3.6 when the day/night come(s)** *adv phr* (Bdos, Guyn, Trin) [*AF/IF*] By day/at night; every day/night. **a.** *Christine, from the time I got married to this man there is no progress in my life. When the night comes I can't sleep. On mornings when I wake up I can't find my panties.*— NaT (Mag) (90.04.27, p.15, Dear Christine) **b.** *As if dis place ent have drama enough wat wid all de rain dat pelting down on people wen de day come and flooding up dey house.*—TrG (79.07.08, p.12) □ An emotive phr focusing on duration rather than on the mere beginning of day/night. **3.7 when time** *adv phr* (Bdos, Guyn, Trin) [*AF*] When the time or opportunity comes. *Don*[*'t*] *bother wid dat married man, you hear? He tell you he goin*[*g*] *to marry you when he get divorce but you will see, when time, he go an*[*d*] *marry somebody else.*—(Guyn) **3.8 when you catch/ketch yourself** *id phr* (CarA) [*IF*] ‖ WHEN YOU HEAR THE CRY/SHOUT (Bdos, etc) See PHR 3.9 **3.9 when you hear the cry/shout** *id phr* (Bdos, Gren, Guyn, Trin) [*IF*] ‖ *when you ketch stock* (Trin) ‖ *when you catch/ketch yourself* (CarA) See HEAR Phr 4.12 *But this white woman keep comin' to the village time an' time again. Then when we hear the shout, it wusn't for no black men,'though she might have had a little time if she feel the itch, an' it wusn't no spirits either. She was encouraging the people who had children to get marry. It wus a hell of a joke.*—LICMS:146 **3.10 when you see so** *id phr* (Gren, Guyn, Tbgo) [*IF*] See SEE Phr 3.13

where[1] **(weh, wey, whe(h), whey)** [wer~weə~we~wɛ] *adv, conj* (CarA) [With variant pronunc and dial spellings] **1.** *interr adv* [*AF—Cr*] [Often dial, without following copula or aux] (SE) Where. **a.** *Please tell me, where daddy gone?*—Guyn (Folksong) **b.** *'Me wife,' e seh, 'wheh de pair a slippers I gi yuh wen we married?'*—WFSFB:36 (S. Scott) **2.** *conn, functioning loosely as rel adv* (CarA) [*X*] In/on/at/by which; of how. **a.** *Rastafarians have a unique way of speaking altogether—a style where only they understand each other.*—SuS (87.09.27, p.26) **b.** *Why is money being paid out for the days where no work was done?*—ExP (72.03.23, p.20) **c.** *A former member of the staff of the circulation department of the then Barbados Advocate, Mr Simmons now works as a seaman on Port and Orient Lines, where he travels all over the world.*—

AdN (74.01.10, p.7) **d.** *This, in itself does not speak well for our society, but it might just be another example where people have grown to believe that patronage is more important than rights.*— AdN (72.04.11, p.4) [A shift of SE function of rel pron *where* as in *place where*. However in such cases the antecedent in SE must be a definitive physical 'location'] □ This usage also occurs in IF SE. **3.** *conn, functioning loosely as causal conj* (CarA) [*X*] Because; since; in (the fact) that. **a.** *But there you cannot say he was telling the truth, where he knew quite well what happened, but kept talking about something else.*—StKt (Ms) **b.** *The general manager also added that agriculture would be particularly beneficial to the Associated States and Guyana where the problem in these countries lies mainly where they are dependent on one crop.*— AdN (74.03.30, p.1) **4.** *conj* (CarA) [*X*] [Esp after *see*, *read*, heading a noun clause] That. **a.** *I see where a motorist is criticising the stopping of the down coming traffic outside the Labour Office. I personally see a lot of that traffic; and I must say that the Traffic Department made a very wise decision.*—ViN (73.02.10, p.2) **b.** *Recently I read where a group of calypsonians stated plans to organise a Calypso Club that would operate throughout the year. / Since then I've heard nothing.*—ExP (72.02.18, p.15) [Cp *OED2 where* 10. b. (b) 'In US use freq equivalent to *that* conj' + cits] □ This usage also occurs in IF SE. **5.** *rel pron* (CarA) [*X*] Which; that. **a.** *When I in a accident is my tail where does have to pay for it.*—HFGA: 59 (D.S. Joseph) **b.** *I really can't bother to pick out any particular bit for discussion, except about their weekly meeting where Mr O. Walker chaired.*—ViN (73.01.27, p.2) [A 'correction' < WHE, *AF—Cr* pronunc of WHAT] **6.** *PHRASES* **6.1 know/find out where barley grow(s)** *id phr* (Guyn, Trin) [*IF*] To have to face up to the consequences of a situation; to pay the penalty for casual, lazy attitudes. *What they want is someone at the helm and a goal around the corner. When I am P.M. they will know where the hell barley growing. Irresponsibility, pushiness and laziness, those are the underlying evils of Trinidad society. Each man feels he is people. Is time to stop all that!*—JJM:91 **6.2 where I am** *id phr* (CarA) [*IF*] As things are with me; in my present circumstances. *Where I am I can't even afford a dress to go to the wedding.*—(Bdos) [A likely calque from W Afr langs. Cp Yoruba *bi mo şe wa yi* (as I be this), also Igbo *ebe a m no* (this place I am in place) 'where I am', wh are adjuncts similarly used. The phr is a refinement of the common CarA Cr phr *whe I deh* 'where I am', used in equivalent contexts] □ Some speakers make the phr **the way I am**. Cp also Phr 6.3 and AmE phrs *where it's at'; 'how things stand'*, etc. **6.3 (where) you see me (here)/him, (etc) there** *id phr* (CarA) [*IF/AF*] *He is smiling but he is really quite sick where you see him there.*—(Gren) See SEE Phr 3.1

where[2] [we(r)~wɛ] *n* (CarA) [*AF*] [Esp in ref to pain] What area or part (of the body). *Where is hurting you, child?*—(Guyn) [Cp *CGAF:61*

Twi *Wo hē yɛ wo yaw?* (*Your where makes you hurt*) 'Where does it hurt?'] □ See also HERE²

whe-whe (wey-wey) /1'2/ [wewe] *n* (Trin) A privately run lottery in wh any of 36 symbols or 'marks' are bought on impulse (often from dreams or superstitions); a 'banker' keeps the secret winning 'mark' upon wh, when revealed, payment is made. [Of Chinese origin]

w(h)ey¹ [wɛ] *adv, conj* (CarA) [*AF—Cr*] See WHERE¹

w(h)ey² [wɛ] *pron* (Gren, Trin) [*AF—Cr*] See WHAT¹

which¹ *rel pron* (CarA) [*X*] **1.** [Ref to persons] Who; whom. **a.** *Maybelle chose box number 13 and when asked why she ... replied that her daughter, which was seated in the audience, was 13 years old.*—WeS (74.11.01, p.24) **b.** *They have asked me to say that these ticket holders ... can have a refund from the person from which they purchased the ticket.*—BoM (75.02.07, p.24) [Noted in *OED which* B. 9. 'used of persons. Now only dial ...' However common usage in the *AVB* and The Book of Common Prayer may have infl the survival of same in CE. Exs: '*Our father which art in heaven ...*'; also Pilate ... *What shall I do then with Jesus, which is called Christ?* Matt. XXVII, 22] **2.** [By extension] Whose. *Glancing at my watch, which ticks competed with my heart for loudness—it read 17 minutes pass 1 a.m.*—ExP (72.03.19, p.22)

which² *rel adj* (CarA) [*AF/IF*] [Used esp in forming interr compound phrs as foll] PHRASES **1. which body** *interr pron phr* (Bdos, Guyn) [*AF*] Who; whom; whose. **a.** *Which body take up my book?*—(Bdos) **b.** *Is so they selfish. They don['t] care [u]pon which body blame fall.*—(Bdos) **c.** *Whosoever it belong to never came back, because the police was watchin[g] to see which body bicycle it was.*—(Guyn) [By disjunctive use of *-body* from SE *somebody, anybody,* etc; prob reinforced by Sc dial use of *body* 'a person' (See *CSD*] **2. which part; which place** *interr adv* (CarA) [*AF*] Where; wherever. **a.** *Which part you are going Monday the Bank Holiday? I would like to take you out.*—NaT (76.10.10, p.7, Al's Grapevine) **b.** *Then I let go the stab at him with my right hand. Then I run off, and look back to see if he coming.... I see him take off the shirt and put it which part he get the cut.*—LaS (75.01.25, p.2) **c.** *... and which part him slip me in the darkness me never know.*—SNWIC:263 (M. Townshend) **d.** *You better go and fin[d] it which place yo[u] lef[t] it.*—(Guyn) [A likely calque from W Afr langs. Cp *CGAF:*60 Akan *ɛhene?* (*which place*) 'where'; also Igbo *olẹẹ ẹbẹ ina ẹjẹ* (*which place you are going?*) 'Where are you going?' (*pers info, B. Oluikpe*); also *KED* Krio *uspat* (*which part*) 'Where?', etc] **3. whi(ch) side** [wɪč saɪd ~ wɪsaɪd] *interr rel adv* (CarA) [*AF*] In what direction?; Where?; (In/to) what place? **a.** *Which side you goin[g] when you leave here?*—(Guyn) **b.** *Wh'side*

you come from?—CGBDS:117 [Of similar origin and function to prec] □ See WISSIDE (*Guyn*).

which³ *conn, as loose co-ordinator* (CarA) [*X*] ‖ **whichin** (Baha, etc) [Linking two statements the second of wh is not a rel clause] And in fact/ indeed; and accordingly. **a.** *I don't live too far but is far enough which I would take a taxi to come.*—(Trin) **b.** *And I have some relatives in St Thomas which I spent some time with them before returning to St Croix.*—(Angu) **c.** *I have to have it cleaned which I am making contact with a man somebody told me would do it good for me.*—(Bdos) [Cp *EDD which* 3. 'Used redundantly in a conjunctive sense' + cits for Not, Glo, Nrf. The usage also occurs in Black AmE]

which·in(g); which.en [wɪčn ~ wɪčɪn ~ wɪčɪŋ] *emphatic conn* (Baha, Bdos, Belz, Guyn, USVI [*X*] **1.** [As anaphoric link] ‖ **which³** (CarA) And in that connection; and indeed; and so; and really. **a.** *Whichin when Jack Smith married me, I mi di breed aready. And I never shame neither.* (= *And indeed when J.S. married me, I was already pregnant. And I was certainly not ashamed.*)—HF:14 **b.** *The morning was a very pleasant one whichin I and my friend decided to go for a walk.*—(Bdos) **c.** *The girl gone to her room because she was a lil bit on the upset side and the phone ring whichen it was the manager.*—NaG (75.10.23, p.2, Satirically Speaking) **2.** [In concessive function] Although; whereas. *She sent me to queue up for sugar, whichin she already had enough.*—(Guyn) **3.** [In causal function] Because; for the reason that. *The neighbours knew he must be dead in there, whichin they could smell how bad the place was smellin[g].*—(Guyn) **4.** [Slipping into simple relative function] Which. **a.** *He almost forget that deep-down he is a christian-minded man and say a bad word, whiching as he did know full-well, God would be vex as hell with him for.*—CWFYS: 94 **b.** *The man check, whichen he didn't have to because he well know that the girl was register there.*—NaG (75.10.23, p.2, Satirically Speaking) [Cp *EDD which* 'var dial uses in Irel and Eng' 1. *which'n* 'which' + cit for Lakel. 'Whichn will thoo hev?' also 3. 'Used redundantly in a conjunctive sense' + cit for Glo 'He told the landlord to bring him some beer which he drawed it and brought it to him' (1839). Also cp *EDD whichens* adv Lan 'How? In what way?' The CE form with shifted functions wh is still strongly current in *Bdos*, may have been spread via Irish/Eng bond-servants by diffusion. The use in sense 4. may be due to overlapping with SE *which* in the DECREOLIZATION process. For a discussion see W.F. Edwards '*Whichin in Guyanese Creole*' Intnl Journal of Lexic III. 2. (1990) pp.103-110]

while¹ *n* (CarA) PHRASES **1. a while ago** *adv phr* (CarA) [*IF*] Some time ago. □ In CE the inference is more often 'a long time ago' than 'a short time ago', this latter usu being expressed as 'a little/short while ago'. **2. a while back** *adv phr* (CarA) [*IF/AF*] A long time ago. *Nowadays a lot o[f] things happenin[g] high day time that* *you would never see a while back.*—(Guyn) □ This phr is, however, less frequent than Phr 1.

while² *conj* (Nevs, StKt) [*IF*] [Introducing a circumstance] Since; seeing that; as. *While you want some tea we will have to make it.*—(StKt) [Perh a shift in one sense and function of SE *while* 'whereas' > *because*]

whilk(s) *n* (Baha, etc) See WILK(S)

whisk/whiss/whist/wis(-bas·ket) *n* (CarA) See WIST(-BASKET)

whis·tling bean /1'12/ *n phr* (Baha) ‖ WOM-AN['S]-TONGUE (CarA)

whis·tling duck *n phr* (Baha, Trin) ‖ WICISSI-DUCK (Guyn) [From its whistling cry as it flies in flocks]

whis·tling frog* /1'12/ *n phr* (CarA) A tiny brown frog with a body about an inch long and padded digits; it is known for the piercing whistle it gives at night esp during the rainy season; *Eleutherodactylus martinicensis* (*Lep-todactylidae*).

whis·tling pine/wil·low *n phr* (Gren, Jmca, StVn, Trin) ‖ CASUARINA (CarA) [From the soughing habit of the full-grown tree, its little cones and general resemblance in shape to a pine, or, by its drooping branches, to a willow]

white¹ *n* **1.** [*IF*] European stock, race, blood. *They are Indians, but they look like they got some white in them*—(Guyn) **2.** PHRASES **2.1 black is white** *adv phr* (ECar) [*AF*] See BLACK² Phr 3.1 **1.2 stick on (sb) like white on rice** *vb phr* (Baha) [*AF*] ‖ BE BEHIND (SB) LIKE A SLAVE-DRIVER (CarA) See BEHIND¹ Phr 2. **2. white(s)** *n* (CarA) Overproof rum (esp when used as a drink without a 'chaser'). *It is the name used in requests at home or in bars or clubs for a drink of rum*—'*An Appleton*'. *The 'Appleton' request only takes second place to the order for a 'whites'*—*an overproof rum produced by the Company.*—Sky Writings 25/1980, p.24 [< *White* (nominalized) + par-agogic /-s/ indicating familiarity. Cp similarly *bruds, dads*]

white² *adj* PHRASE **pass for white** *vb phr* (CarA) See PASS¹ Phr 3.6

white back *n phr* (Jmca) **1.*** A bushy shrub, 5 or 6 ft tall, with elongated, hairy leaves, bearing a kind of yellow pea-flower and silky pods; it is commonly used as a folk-medicine for colds but is said to be harmful; *Crotalaria fulva* (*Pa-pilionaceae*). **2.** An erect, straggling, poisonous shrub about 6 ft tall, with greyish-green leaves with white undersides (hence the name); it bears clusters of pale yellow, sweet-scented flowers and small white fruit; *Senecio discolor* (*Compositae*).

white·bait *n* (Gren, StVn) Any of several spe-cies of small fish wh swarm up the rivers; they

are eaten fried in small quantities. [Cp *OED whitebait* 'a small silvery-white fish, caught in quantity at the estuary of the Thames … es-teemed as a delicacy'; (c) 'applied to other small fishes in different parts of the world resembling this and used as food + cits–'1886]

white bar·ri·ca·der [waɪt barikedʌ] *n phr* (Angu, StKt) ‖ PHYSIC-NUT 1. (Bdos, etc)

white bean *n phr* **1.** (CarA) ‖ LIMA BEAN (Antg, etc) **2.** (Mrat, Trin) ‖ BONAVIST (CarA)

white-belly shrimp(s) *n phr* (Guyn) ‖ FINE SHRIMP(S) (Guyn)

white cap *n phr* (ViIs) ‖ WHITEHEAD BROOM/BUSH (Angu, etc)

white ce·dar* *n phr* (BrVi, Guyn, Nevs, StLu, Trin) [Timber Ind] An evergreen tree wh can grow to a height of 90 ft and wh yields a hard, straight-grained, creamy-coloured wood with dark flecks; it is valued for making paddles, handles, etc; *Tabebuia pallida* or *T. monophylla* (*Bignoniaceae*).

white clair·ie [waɪt-kle·ri] *n phr* (Guyn) ‖ W-ILD-CLARY (Guyn, Jmca) [From the white spike of flowerets, the most common variety in *Guyn*]

white-cor·ner /1'22/ *n* (Guyn) [*AF*—Derog] ‖ *gapia-mouth* (USVI) ‖ *ray-mouth* (Bdos) ‖ *wapia* (Trin) ‖ *white-mouth* (Bdos, Guyn) An unpleasant-looking, white discharge at the corners of the mouth that is caused by vitamin deficiency; *Angular stomatitis*.

white ed·doe *n phr* (Bdos) ‖ EDDOE 1. (Guyn)

white e·gret *n phr* (Angu, Bdos, Jmca) ‖ CAT-TLE-EGRET (Bdos, etc)

white fowl(-cock) *n phr* (CarA) **1.** A white hen or cock (of significant value in survivals of Afr belief systems). **2.** PHRASE **2.1 eat/thief sb('s) white fowl** *vb phr* (Gren, Guyn, Tbgo, Trin) [*AF*] To do (sb) some serious harm or injustice; to endanger sb's well-being. *Look i[t']s not me wha[t] bring police [u]pon yo[u], hear? So don['t] bother look at me like if I eat yo[ur] mother white fowl.*—(Tbgo)

white gaul·in *n phr* (Angu, Dmca, Gren, USVI) (Name loosely applied to) the CATTLE-EGRET and other (sometimes immature) herons; *Ardea spp* (*Ardeidae*).

white grub *n phr* (CarA) ‖ ROOT-BORER (CarA)

white·head broom/bush* *n phr* (CarA) ‖ *white cap* (ViIs) A bushy, aromatic shrub wh grows to a height of about 12 ins and bears loose clusters of tiny, white flowers at the end of long, slender stalks, hence the name; it is widely used as a folk-medicinal treatment for colds, fever, liver conditions, etc; *Parthenium hysterophorus* (*Compositae*).

white man·grove* *n phr* (CarA) A tree wh grows to between 50 and 60 ft in height and yields a reddish, olive-brown wood suitable for fence posts and house-frames; it grows mostly in coastal and estuarine mangrove swamps; *Laguncularia racemosa* (*Combretaceae*).

white mar·lin* *n phr* (Baha, Berm, ViIs) A smaller variety of BILL-FISH weighing less than 100 lbs, with silvery sides (whence the name); *Makaira albida* (*Istiophoridae*) [By contrast with the giant blue marlin, famous in Atlantic game fishing]

white meat *n phr* (CarA) [*AF—Derog*] A white woman (as a man's sexual objective). *What is the ambition of every Trini. It really couldn't be the house in Valsayn, the Jaguar and the brown-skinned wife with dreams of white meat now and then on a Government trip abroad.*—BoM (73.01.12, p.3) [Popularized by a calypso by F. Slinger ('Sparrow')]

white mouth *n phr* (Bdos, Guyn) [*AF—Derog*] ‖ WHITE CORNER (Guyn)

white owl *n phr* (Jmca ‖ JUMBIE-BIRD 1. (Guyn) *The White Owl is nocturnal in habit and when seen flying at dusk the plumage looks almost entirely white, ... is a hunting bird and feeds almost entirely on rats and mice.*—TIBJ:48

white pea *n phr* (Dmca) ‖ LIMA BEAN (CarA)

white peo·ple *n phr* (CarA) [*AF*] [*Obsolescent*] 1. Those (usu Europeans) who are in authority; the white, expatriate, elite class in Caribbean societies. 2. [By extension] The government. *You doan go to school? You carn read de white people sign in big letters up there? Look the sign there, 'Stap'.*—OJS:11 □ Often, as in cit, in attrib use.

white poin·set·ti·a *n phr* (Gren) ‖ SNOW-ON-THE-MOUNTAIN (Antg, etc) [*White*, from its white mass of flowers + *poinsettia*, of the same family as the red variety, wh blooms at the same time]

white po·ta·to *n phr* (Antg, Bdos, Guyn, Mrat, StVn) ‖ ENGLISH POTATO (CarA) [Ref to the colour when peeled in contrast to the pink or purple colour of the SWEET POTATO]

white pud·ding *n phr* (Bdos) A stout, home-made sausage stuffed with the same mixture of SWEET POTATO and herbs used for BLACK PUDDING but without the addition of blood.

white rain *n* (Bdos, Guyn, Jmca, Trin) Almost continuous, light rain that comes and goes throughout the day. [From the greyness of the perpetually overcast skies, in contrast with dark nimbus clouds that produce heavy showers.]

white rice *n phr* (Guyn) [Rice Ind] Rice wh has been fully processed so that all the layers of bran and germ coating have been removed. [By contrast with brown rice, wh has only undergone the first milling process but is sold in that state] □ Note that in SE the contrast is *rice* vs *brown rice*.

white rum *n phr* (Bdos) Colourless rum that has been blended but not aged through a curing process; it is considered 'strong' (lacking mellowness) but is preferred by drinkers for avoiding 'hangovers' and for mixing punches; it is also more widely exported than coloured, wood-cured rums.

white sage* *n phr* (Baha, Bdos, Guyn, StKt) A variety of SAGE-BUSH that bears a larger, white flower-head; it is used as a folk-medicine; *Lantana involucrata* (*Verbenaceae*).

white slave *n phr* (Bdos) ‖ WOOD-SLAVE (ECar) [Perh a variant of WOOD-SLAVE, *white* being due to folk etym, as the *Bdos* variety has an unpleasantly pale skin]

white sug·ar *n phr* (CarA) Sugar that has been refined in Britain, having all molasses content extracted (hence its whiteness). □ Note that in SE the contrast is *sugar* (wh is normally white) vs *brown sugar*.

white wood* *n phr* 1. (Bdos, CayI, Jmca) A tree of average height about 30 ft, with a whitish bark and evenly spreading branches; it bears tubular lilac flowers wh are prominent when it sheds its leaves in the dry season; *Tabebuia heterophylla* or *T. pentaphylla* (*Bignoniaceae*). [From the very hard, white wood under its whitish bark] 2. (Jmca) A small tree with slender trunk and drooping branches, bearing fragrant flowers; its sapwood is yellow; *Drypetes laterifolia* (*Euphorbiaceae*). □ In *Jmca* there are evid other trees to wh this name is also applied. See *DJE*.

whit·ey [waiti] *n* (CarA) [*AF—Derog*] 1. A white person; white people as a race. 2. [By extension] A non-European person, esp one of African descent, who is of light complexion. □ In sense 2. the term is esp abusive. 3. (Jmca) [By extension] [Rastaf] Pork.

white yam* *n phr* 1. (CarA) ‖ *Bajan yam, Barbados-yam* (Gren, Mrat) ‖ *Guinea-yam* (Dmca, Jmca, Tbgo, Trin) ‖ *Lucea-yam* (Jmca) ‖ *negro-yam* (Jmca) A yam prized for its white, mealy texture when boiled; *Dioscorea rotundata* or *D. cayenensis* (*Dioscoreaceae*). [From the whiteness of the flesh esp of the variety *D. rotundata*] □ The name WHITE YAM appears to be used to distinguish more carefully a particular variety in some territories (ex *Gren, StKt, StVn*) than in others (*Jmca, Guyn*). See also AFU YAM and the other ‖ ‖ above. 2. (Dmca) ‖ LISBON YAM (Bdos, etc)

whiz·zy-whiz·zy *vb* (Bdos) See WIZZY-WIZZY

who *rel pron* (CarA) **1.** Whom; whose. **a.** *I don't know with who I am going yet.*—(Jmca) **b.** *She steadily refused to say from who she got it.*—Bdos (Ms, 1978) **c.** *'You see? You see?' she say flouncing round. 'Who excursion you think this is?'*—CISH: 98 **d.** *The Prime Minister who bears overall responsibility for the good government of the country, and the Minister of Home Affairs under who portfolio the issue directly falls, have no defence against the fact that the autocratic methods being applied ... is a blatant breach of the Declaration of Human Rights.*—Jmca (Ms, 1968) □ See *OED2 who* 5. for use of *who* = *whom*. However in ModE the form *whom* is generally retained when the prep immediately precedes, unlike the CE cases cited. SE *whose* occurs only in careful educated CE. **2.** *in interr function, with ellipsis* (Baha, Bdos, Gren, Guyn, Trin) [*AF—Derog*] [Followed by sb's name, usu signalling contempt] Who/which/what (is this person named)? **a.** *Why you comin[g] in here so blasted late? Who Oswald you say bring you home?*—(Guyn) **b.** *'Who Ena Roacheford?' Silla's head snapped up. 'A red woman from Rock Hall ...'*—MBGB:63 □ Usu used in aggressive contexts. **3.** *as a focuser* (CarA) [*AF*] The one who really; the person that. **a.** *Who ain[']t got patience is you.*—(BrVi) **b.** *Who know plenty [a]bout it is that same Eustace, but he ain[']t sayin[g].*—(Guyn) **4.** PHRASES **4.1 Who and you?; He/She/You and who?** *id phr* (CayI, Gren, Guyn, Trin) [Expressing a cynical challenge or a boast] With whose help (is that going to be done? Since obviously you/he/she cannot do it alone); you and who else? **a.** *You? Beat me? You and who?*—(CayI) **b.** *She say the man promise he goin[g] buy a lil house for her. Ha ha! He and who?*—(Guyn) **4.2 Who callin[g]?** *interr phr* (Bdos) [*AF*] ‖ *Who want me?* (Guyn) [*AF*] [Street vendor's cry] Who will buy my goods? (i.e. If you will, call out and stop me as I pass by). □ These phrs are usu preceded by a list of the goods being offered for sale. **4.3 who can[']t hear will feel** *id phr* (CarA) [*IF*] [Expressing a threat, esp to a child] The one who is stubbornly disobedient will be flogged. *A tired tellin[g] you not to do that, but you ain[']t takin[g] me on—who can[']t hear will feel.*—(Guyn) [A likely calque from Afr langs, in some of wh the words for *hear, feel* are identical (exs Hausa *ji*, Fulani *nan*). Hence a proverbial implication: 'if your ears will not hear/feel, your body will hear/feel'] □ See also HEAR Phr 4.11

whole *adj* **1.** (Bdos, Gren, Guyn, Trin) [*AF*] [Esp emphasizing amount of money, time] Entire; no less than; as much as. **a.** *Oh God! Somebody gone wid m[y] purse wid m[y] whole sixty dollars in it.*—(Guyn) **b.** *Boy, I had to wait whole t[h]ree hours to see de doctor, you hear!*—(Trin) [Cp *EDD whole* 4. 'all'; followed by a pl sb + cit for Sc (1798) 'My whole friends are against me'] **2.** PHRASE **2.1 on a whole** *adv phr* (Bdos) [*X*] See ON Phr 7.3 *I think Kerry Packer is opening up the field for cricketers on a whole and West Indian cricketers in particular.*—Bdos (Ms)

whole·sale *adj* (Baha) [*IF*] [Of a house, car, etc] With all furnishing, fittings, accessories, etc; [by extension, of a person] with all your clothes on. *He was so tired that he went to bed wholesale.*—(Baha) [By semantic shift of SE *wholesale* in the sense 'total, all together']

whom; **whom.so.e.ver** *rel prons* (CarA) [Often used as overcorrect forms] Who; whoever. **a.** *The Minister thanked the Canadian Government, teachers and children, the local Ministry of Education, the workmen, Hon. R.M. Cato, whom he said took a special interest in the project.*—ViN (73.01.20, p.8) **b.** *The cascadura, a delicious river fish. Whomsoever eats it, the legend goes, will return to Trinidad.*—Cat III.2, p.46 □ The SE forms *whosoever, whomsoever* are also correctly used in CE writing, surviving through liturgical infl, though they are Obs in IAE, replaced by *whoever, anyone whatever.*

who-you (bird) /1'22/ *n* (*phr*) (Belz, Guyn) A night bird whose cry gives it its name; it is a type of JUMBIE-BIRD associated with some superstitions.

why for? *interr phr* (StLu, Trin) [*X*] Why?; what for? **a.** *Tell me again old man why for you want to work the sea? And you so old?*—WSAD: 15 **b.** *'So why for you wearing this yellow thing, then?' / The man fidgeted with his staff and looked down at his robe. 'It isn't the right thing, you mean?'*—NTMM:37 [Perh by overlap of *why* + *what for*] □ Also dial AmE.

wi! *excl tag* (Dmca, etc) See OUI

wi·chi·chi *n* (Trin) ‖ WICISSI-DUCK (Guyn)

wi·cis·si-duck* (**vi·cis·si-, wis·si-wis·si-duck**) *n* (Guyn) ‖ *tree-duck, whistling duck, wichichi* (Trin) Any of two or three varieties of a swamp-bird with webbed feet, a bright red beak, white face, greyish breast, reddish-brown crown and back, and pink legs; it stands erect varying in height from 10 to 20 ins (the larger varieties being evid migrant in Trinidad); they pass overhead in arrowhead flocks whistling as they go at dawn and dusk, wh makes them easy sport; *Dendrocygna autumnalis, D. viduata, etc* (*Anatidae*). [WICISSI from an imitation of their whistling cry + *duck* from their webbed feet and habitat, though they do not swim] □ The spelling *vicissi* is a *Guyn* variant; *wichichi* is a rarer *Trin* variant.

wick·er *n* (Bdos) A lesbian. [Cp Sc *CSD wick²* 'a wicked person' (ME pronunc *wikke*). Also *EDD wicker* sb³ Obs Sc 'an old, cross-grained woman']

wid *prep* (CarA) [*AF—Cr*] See WITH

-wide *adj or adv suff* (CarA) Relating to or throughout the whole area (to wh it is suff). **a.** *The Islandwide demonstration by Auxiliary*

(Assistant) Nurses which began in the City Hospitals and later spread to the various Government Hospitals ended yesterday.—WeS (74.09.06, p.32) **b.** *Several persons were beaten up at Pearls Airport. At least one was detained at Princess Alice Hospital. One was a Reporter of Caribbean wide repute.*—ToR (73.06.27, p.2) **c.** *We have just heard from a leading member of a West Indian institution that this decline in agriculture is area wide and in the smaller islands it is almost at crisis level.*—AdN (71.05.09) [By analogy < *nationwide*] □ Hence several other forms *countrywide* (esp in *Guyn*), *region-wide, statewide, West Indian-wide*.

wif; wif·out *prep* (Bdos) [*AF—Cr*] See WITH; WITHOUT

wife *n* PHRASES **1. ask (sb) for a piece o[f] wife** *vb phr* (StKt) [*AF*] To ask (a woman) to permit sexual intercourse with her (outside of marriage). **2. give (sb) wife** *vb phr* (Guyn) [*AF*] [Of a woman] To allow a man to have sexual intercourse with her (outside of marriage). *Sack Chul, if me been have shame me wount ah sorry for you an give you wife one-one time.*—SNGD: 28

Wife-No·tice *n* (Antg, Dmca, Guyn, Mrat, StLu) ‖ SEPARATION-NOTICE (Gren, StKt) □ This applies to such a Notice inserted by a husband.

WIGUT [wɪgʌt] *abbr* (CarA) West Indies Group of University Teachers, the trade union of the academic staff of the University of the West Indies with an independent branch on each campus (in Barbados, Jamaica, Trinidad).

wild *adj* PHRASE **be wild behind (sb) to do (sth)** *vb phr* (StKt) [*AF*] ‖ BE BEHIND (SB) ... (CarA) See BEHIND[1] Phr 1.

wild ba·na·na *n phr* **1.** (Dmca, Jmca, StLu, Trin) ‖ JUMBIE BANANA (StVn) [From the inedible banana-like fruit (of the *Musa spp*)] **2.** (Bdos, Jmca, Trin) ‖ BIRD-OF-PARADISE (Bdos, Jmca) *The wild banana was in flower: a solid spray of spear-heads of orange and yellow that never turned to fruit, emerging sticky with mauve gum and slime from the heart of the tree.*—NG: 241 [From the resemblance of the leaves to those of the banana]

wild ba·sil/bass·ley *n phr* (Jmca) ‖ DUPPY-BASIL (Bdos)

wild cane *n phr* (Jmca) ‖ ARROW-CANE (Guyn)

wild cas·sa·va *n phr* (Jmca) ‖ BELLY-ACHE BUSH (Bdos, etc)

wild cher·ry *n phr* (Belz, Guyn) ‖ CLAMMY-CHERRY 2. (Brbu, etc)

wild clam·my-cher·ry *n phr* (Bdos) ‖ CLAMMY-CHERRY 2. (Brbu, etc)

wild cla·ry* [waɪl-kle·ri] *n phr* (Guyn, Jmca) ‖ *scorpion-tail/-weed* (CayI, Jmca) ‖ *white clairie* (Guyn) A weed that can exceed 2 ft in height, with rough-surfaced green leaves and slender stems topped by curved spikes of white or light-mauve flowerets; it thrives in good ground and is widely used as a folk-medicine for treating coughs; *Heliotropium indicum* (*Boraginaceae*).

wild cof·fee* *n phr* (Guyn, Jmca, StKt, Trin) ‖ *creole coffee* (Guyn) ‖ *dandelion* (Jmca) ‖ *jumbie coffee* (StKt, Trin, USVI) ‖ *miamol* (Jmca, Trin) ‖ *negro coffee* (Guyn, Trin) ‖ *piss-a-bed* (Guyn, Jmca) ‖ *pissy-bush* (USVI) ‖ *stinking-bush* (Bdos) ‖ *stinking-weed* (Baha, Jmca, StKt, Trin, USVI) A common shrub with brownish-red young stems, smooth pinnate leaves, and pale yellow flowers; it bears thin four-inch-long pods whose seeds are parched and used as a bitter coffee substitute (hence the name), or as a folk-medicine; an infusion of the leaves is also used as a treatment for sores; *Cassia occidentalis* (*Leguminosae-Caesalpiniaceae*). [Cp *ADMY* Yoruba *rere*, name of the taxonomically identical plant also used medicinally in W Afr and also identified in *TAGD:151* as 'wild coffee ... used for medicinal purposes']

wild co·ril·la [waɪl kʊraɪlʌ] *n phr* (Guyn, Trin) ‖ CERASEE (Baha, etc) [Prob a translation of BANCARILLA, the Indic name for the same plant in *Guyn, Trin*]

wild cow *n phr* (Guyn) ‖ TAPIR (Guyn) [From the hunter's use of its meat and the heavy set of its body]

wild cu·cum·ber *n phr* **1.*** (Bdos, BrVi, Gren, Jmca) ‖ *ti-kokom* (StLu) A pale, greenish-yellow, ovoid, prickly fruit about 2-1/2 ins long, borne on a straggling vine with deeply lobed leaves, and flourishing in damp places; the fruit, wh resembles a small cucumber, is edible but the vine is a weed (hence the name); *Cucumis anguria* (*Cucurbitaceae*). **2.** (Bdos) ‖ BABY-CUCUMBER (Guyn) *I have seen a vine, which is becoming a nuisance to people and that is called 'Wild Cucumber' and ... I find it growing in the hedge around the garden and sometimes endeavouring to take over trees ... and this Wild Cucumber will climb on electric and telephone poles and then along the wires.*—AdM (82.12.05, p.7 Edward Stoute)

wild ed·do(e)* *n phr* (Guyn) A low-growing, stemless plant wh resembles the young EDDOE, though both leaves and tuberous rhizome are inedible; it spreads massively in swampy land and TRENCHES; *Araceae spp*.

wild ge·ra·ni·um *n phr* ‖ BAY-GERANIUM (Baha)

wild hog/-pig *n phr* (Guyn, Trin) ‖ PECCARY (Belz, Guyn)

Wild In·di·an(s) *n phr* (Gren, Tbgo, Trin) (One of a) group of CARNIVAL masqueraders wearing mock AMERINDIAN costumes of bright red-dyed hemp skirts, with painted bodies, neck beads and fanciful head-pieces; they sing set songs and wage mock battles.

wild li·quor·ice *n phr* (Jmca) ‖ BEAD-VINE (BUSH) (Nevs, StKt)

wild me·lon·gene *n phr* (Dmca, StLu) ‖ BURA-BURA (Guyn) *The fruit of the wild melongene, also called 'bata belongene' (from French 'bâtard') and 'melongene jab' (from French 'diable') is still used as a folk medicine for flu in some places.*—Dmca (Ms, 1978)

wild mi·mo·sa *n phr* (Bdos, Berm) ‖ WILD TAMARIND 1. (Belz, etc) *It is said that if horses and mules eat the leaves of this plant, wild mimosa, the hair is affected, the mane and tail dropping, and even the hooves falling off. The seed, on the other hand, is useful as a cattle food.*—GLPFB: 189 [*Wild* 'uncultivated' + *mimosa,* from the plant's botanical classification in the sub-family *Mimosae*]

wild mint* *n phr* 1. (Trin) A creeping perennial herb with long, thin stems and small, purple and white flowers; an infusion of the leaves is used as a folk-medicine; *Hyptis atrorubens (Labiatae).* 2. (Jmca) A variety of SAGE-BUSH wh is used as a folk treatment for chest-colds; *Lantana involucrata (Verbenaceae).*

wild o·kra* *n phr* (Gren, USVI) A hardy shrub wh grows to a height of about 9 ft, has hairy stems and bears yellow flowers; infusions of the leaves, flowers, and seeds are used as folk-medicines; *Malachra alceifolia, M. capitata (Malvaceae).*

(wild) phys·ic-nut *n phr* (Bdos, ViIs) ‖ BELLY-ACHE BUSH (Bdos, etc)

wild pine *n phr* 1.* (Dmca, Gren, Guyn, Jmca, Trin) A common parasite wh is found on the branches of trees; *Tillandsia utriculata (Bromeliaceae).* 2. (Gren) ‖ SCREW-PINE (Dmca, etc) *She made hats and bags from wild-pine, decorated with coloured raffia straw to sell to the Tourist Shop.*—Gren (Ms) 3. (Bdos) ‖ PAIN-KILLER BUSH (BrVi, etc)

wild plan·tain *n phr* (Gren, Guyn, Tbgo, Trin) ‖ HELICONIA (CarA) *The flowers of the wild plantain are borne in large, scarlet boat-shaped sheaths which ... hold water [and] are likely to form breeding grounds for mosquitoes.*—PTT:184 [From the wild habitat of the plant wh is a member of the plantain/banana family]

wild poin·set·tia *n phr* (Tbgo, Trin) ‖ CHACONIA (Tbgo, Trin)

wild po·po·nax *n phr* (Jmca) ‖ ACACIA (TkCa, Trin) [From earlier botanical name *Poponax tortuosa*]

wild sage* *n phr* (Jmca, Trin) One or other variety of SAGE-BUSH wh is used as a folk-medicine; *Lantana spp (Verbenaceae).*

wild sen·na *n phr* (Jmca, Tbgo, Trin) ‖ CHRISTMAS-CANDLE (Bdos, etc)

wild spin·ach* *n phr* (Antg, Bdos, Mrat, StVn) ‖ *bhaji* 1. (Guyn, Trin) ‖ *calalu* 1. (CarA) ‖ *zé-pina* (Dmca) An erect, leafy plant about 2 ft high, with soft, reddish stalk and stems and many spikes of greenish-white flowers; the leaves are eaten stewed (esp by EAST INDIANS) and also used as a folk-medicine; it flourishes in rich, damp, uncultivated ground; *Amaranthus dubius (Amaranthaceae).*

wild ta·ma·rind ['waɪl tam(b)rʌn/-tam(b)rɪn] /1'22/ *n phr* 1.* (Belz, Grns, Trin, ViIs) ‖ *cow-bean, cow-bush* (Baha, TkCa) ‖ *cow-tamarind* (Baha, Gren) ‖ *jumbie-bean* (Baha, Berm) ‖ *lead-tree* (Jmca) ‖ *miamossi, river-tamarind* (Bdos) ‖ *shack-shack* (Trin) ‖ *tantan* (USVI) ‖ *West Indian mimosa* (Trin) ‖ *wild mimosa* (Bdos) A sturdy shrub that grows rapidly to 10 or 12 ft, with compound leaves, small, yellow, mimosa-like flowers, and bunches of thin, dry pods about 6 ins long containing many small, hard, shiny brown seeds wh are widely used in ornamental work; the whole plant is also prized as livestock feed; *Leucaena glauca (Leguminosae-Mimosae).* [Prob from rough resemblance of the dry pod, in shape and colour, to the TAMARIND pod] □ The name is evid applied to a few other sturdy, pod-bearing weeds or bushes in some territories. 2. (CayI) ‖ WOMAN('S)-TONGUE TREE (CarA)

wild tea *n phr* (Guyn) ‖ DITÉ-PÉYI (Dmca, etc)

wild to·bac·co *n phr* (Jmca) ‖ CATTLE-TONGUE (Antg, etc) [From resemblance of the leaf to that of the tobacco plant, though it is not smoked]

wild yam* *n phr* (Jmca) ‖ *yam wawa* (Dmca) A slim, dark-skinned yam with white flesh wh is not very palatable; its reddish vine carries attractive hanging clusters of winged seeds and climbs to the tops of woodland trees; *Dioscorea polygonoides (Dioscoreaceae).*

wilk(s)* (**whelk(s), whilk(s)**) [wɪlk(s)∼ wɛlk(s)] *n* (CarA) 1. ‖ *brigo* (Gren, StLu) An edible sea-snail with a spiral, black and white shell about 3 or 4 ins in diameter; it is a delicacy of much commercial importance; *Cittarium pica (Molluscidae). Many families were busy painting and nailing together plywood booths where they would sell wilks and rice, stew conch, bullfoot soup, chicken leg, johnnycake, and boil fish with hot sauce, red hot sauce!*—JJHAI:128 [See OED *whelk*[1], formerly *wilk* 15C–19C, *whilk* 17C–19C; hence the commoner CE form is prob a survival from EE] □ Often in pl, even if used as sg, esp among fisher-folk. The *wi-* spelling is used in more places than the *wh-* spellings, wh are clearly infl by SE *whelk.* However one authority

(*JNHSJ:19*) states that 'whelks technically are a Florida shell unrelated to our 'wilks'. **2. PHRASES 2.1 pick wilks** *vb phr* (CarA) To collect WILKS from the rocks or sea-bed. □ Cp PICK SEA-EGGS. **2.2 you/he picking wilks** *id phr* (Angu, Antg, BrVi, StKt) [*AF—Joc*] Your/his trousers are noticeably too short. [Ref to rolling up of the trousers in order to PICK WILKS at low tide] □ Cp also FLOOD-PANTS.

will *mod aux* (CarA) [*X*] **1.** Would. **a.** *It was stated at the time that it will be a playground for the use of children over the age of 12 years ... [and] that studs will be placed in the middle of the road.*—DaC (53.04.13, p.2) **b.** *Madam Editor, I would be glad if someone who knows accounting will look through that issue of 'The Antigua Star' and put my understanding right.*—AnT (73.02.24, p.5) □ The use of SE *will* for *would* in past and past conditional contexts is a widespread convenience in CE. The foll phrs are common in both speech and writing. **2. PHRASES 2.1 will able** (CarA) [*X*] Will/would be able. *He is the man who practise the choir, so he will able now to practise the tenor, base, alto, and treble.*—)StVn) **2.2 will like** (CarA) [*X*] Would like. **a.** *I will like the Minister of Works to instruct the county council to repair some of these bad roads for us immediately.*—ExP (71.02.13, p.23) **b.** *Pinpointing his desire for specific developments and improvements, the Chief Minister said, 'I will like to see agriculture production of the maximum possible amount of food and drinks and a substantial saving of money'.*—MtM (73.01.26, p.3)

wil·low *n* (Jmca) ‖ CASUARINA (CarA) [From its resemblance to the European 'weeping willow' *Salix babylonica*]

win *vb tr* (CarA) [*X*] [In a contest] To defeat (sb). **a.** *The West Indies won England by seven wickets in that test.*—(StVn) **b.** *Magistrates don't give police wrong. Police could do you anything and you can't win them in court.*—(Tbgo) [Cp *EDD win* 9. 'to excel, beat' + cit from Not 'A can win yo at cricket'. However the widespread use of *win* in this sense in CE is more likely due to rejection of *beat* (by association with flogging) and absence of *defeat* from popular vocab]

wind¹ [wɪn(d)] *n* (CarA) [*IF*] **1.** Air in the stomach due to hunger. **2. PHRASES 2.1 keep the wind out of your belly/stomach** *vb phr* (CarA) [*AF/IF*] To prevent the pangs of hunger (by drinking water or munching sth).

wind² [waɪn(d)] *vb intr* (ECar) See WINE

wind·ball /1'2/ *n, adj* (Bdos, Gren, Trin) A discarded lawn-tennis ball or any other soft rubber ball of comparable size, esp as used in children's or beach cricket or other games. *If the trend continues more people may stay at home quietly today, and forget all about the beach picnics, the windball cricket, racing and other traditional Easter outdoor sport.*—ExP (76.04.19, p.1)

wind-break *n* (StKt) ‖ GLIRICIDIA (Angu, etc)

wind-flow·er *n* (CarA) ‖ AMARYLLIS (CarA)

Wind·i·ans; Win·dies *n pl* (CarA) [*IF*] [Cricket] The West Indian cricket team. □ Familiar abbr forms used esp in newspaper headlines, occasionally also in IF speech.

win·dow-hood *n* (Bdos) See HOOD

win·dow-stick *n* (CarA) A stick about 3 or 4 ft long used to keep open a shutter or window that is hinged at the top.

wind-pies *n pl* (Bdos, Trin) [*AF—Joc*] ‖ **wind-sandwich** (Belz) **1.** Nothing to eat. **2. PHRASES 2.1 wind-pies and air-sausages** *n phr* (Bdos) [*AF—Joc*] ‖ **wind-pies and nutten-chops** (Trin) ‖ **wind-sandwich and breeze-pie** (Belz) Nothing whatever to eat; no food in the house.

wind-sand·wich *n* (Belz) [*AF—Joc*] ‖ WIND-PIES (Bdos, Trin)

wind·ward *adj, adv, n;* **wind·ward coast** *n phr* (ECar, CayI) ‖ **the East Coast** 1. (ECar) East; the east side or coast of the island. **a.** *Mr Williams ... was brought ashore at Callique, a small town on St Vincent's windward coast about four miles from Kingstown, yesterday morning.*—AdV (72.01.20, p.1) **b.** *So we went to leeward and he went windward. It was two days before we returned to Colliers.*—FDI:57 **c.** *The people living in windward got the full force of the hurricane.*—(Dmca)

Wind·ward Is·lands; Wind·wards, The *n phr pl* (CarA) **1.** [British group] The south-east Caribbean group of islands: Dominica, Grenada, the Grenadines, St Lucia, St Vincent. [So referred to originally by the Spanish (*Islas de Barlovento*) as being to windward of and nearer to the Spanish Main] □ Barbados and Tobago were also once included in this group. See also LEEWARD ISLANDS 1. **2.** [Dutch group] The northeast Caribbean group of islands: Saba, St Eustatius (also familiarly known as Statia), and St Maarten (St Martin). [So referred to by the Dutch (*Bovenwindse eilanden*) as being on the windward curve of the Caribbean archipelago] □ See also LEEWARD ISLANDS 2.

wind·ward sprat *n phr* (StVn) ‖ ANCHOVY (StLu, Trin)

wine (wind) [waɪn ~ waɪŋ] *vb intr* (CarA) [*AF*] ‖ **kawé** (Gren) **1.** [Esp of a woman] To dance erotically by swinging the hips vigorously while thrusting the buttocks back and forth. **a.** *Darling, you put me in trouble / You torture me / The way you wine / I love to see your fat behind / Give me the Bum Bum.*—Trin (Cso, 1978) **b.** *The people went mad with the joy of victory. Everybody—man, woman and child—swarmed into the streets, laughing, singing, shouting, dancing, jumping, chipping, shaking and 'wining'. Aided and abetted by the* *savage rhythm and noise of the modestly improved steelband.*—ACTT:103 **c.** *Take me up foot, up, up over dis stinkin' band' / Past all dese winding backsides, sweaty backs, / Bouncin' buddies, multinational bad-breath.*—KTT:47 [Cp *OED wind* vb[1] 4. *intr Obs, dial* 'to turn this way and that; to writhe, to wriggle'. However the cits refer to pain, restlessness rather than dancing. The characteristic CE pronunc with reduction of final /-nd/ accounts for the more representative and widely adapted spelling 'wine'] **2.** [Of a woman] To walk swinging the hips provocatively. *It was obvious that he regarded this as unjustifiable intrusion on his game, but off June waddled, wiggling and wining, showing off her pretty pretty dress.*— Cav II, p.31 □ This related sense is less common than 1.

win·ing /2'2/ [waɪnɪn ~ waɪŋɪn] *vbl n* (CarA) [*AF*] Erotic or provocative dancing of an individual with vigorous swinging or gyrating of the hips. *Carnival is perhaps best expressed in 'wining'. For some this is rank vulgarity, but for the winer-girl (or man) it is, most times paroxysm, an almost orgiastic experience. She shouts, she sings, she screams and shrieks, she wines against someone ...*—Peo I.8, p.33 [< WIN[D] + ing. See WINE]

wire[1] *n* PHRASE **(and) the wire bend and the story end** *id phr* (CarA) [*AF*] [Conventional formula for ending a folk-tale] (And) that's where my story ends.

wire[2] *n* (Gren, Trin) [*AF*] An informal piece of important news; credible rumour. **a.** *One morning he get a wire that a cigarette factory in the East End was taking fellars, and he hustle and went, but when he get there the fellar say sorry, no vacancies.*—SWOS:126 **b.** *At about ten o'clock it was rumoured by the public 'wire' that the accuseds would in fact attend the Court to plead.*—ToR (76.09.22, p.1) [Joc extension of SE wire(less telegram)]

wire-bend·er *n* (Tbgo, Trin) A person skilled in the craft of creating, in light wire, the supporting outline of an elaborate CARNIVAL costume.

wire-bend·ing; **wire.craft**; **wire-work** *n* (Tbgo, Trin) The craft of the WIRE-BENDER. *Carnival became a tremendous show ... for instance, there was the great copper work of Ken Morris, and the skillful wire-bending. In short, Carnival and its costumes had become a show window of Art.*—ExP (77.08.28, p.33)

wire-mesh *n* (Bdos, Gren, Guyn) ‖ **chicken-wire** (BrVi) ‖ **mesh-wire** (Bdos) ‖ **pot-fish wire** (BrVi) Wire netting, as used for light fencing, making fish-traps, etc. *Possibly an area could be enclosed in fine wire-mesh, in which a number of sea urchins could be placed in the breeding season.*—AdM (76.10.24, p.7) [OED2 lists *wire* 15. a. (attrib) ... -mesh + cits 1932–74. However the term is prob older in *Bdos, Guyn* it being

the standard name used on invoices importing this material for use in fishing and farming]

wi·ri-wi·ri pep·per *n phr* (Guyn) A pea-sized variety of CHERRY-PEPPER borne abundantly on a small bushy plant that is sometimes potted. [Cp *ADMY* Yoruba *wẹẹrẹwẹ* (applied to pl nouns meaning children, grains, fruit); also *wiri-wiri* (of rain) 'drizzle']

wis *n* (CarA) See WIST

wish *vb* (CarA) [*IF*] Want. **a.** *You wish a lash? You wish me to give you a good lash?*—(Bdos) **b.** *Leave me alone.... I don't wish to see and I don' wish to know.... Don't question me and don't force me to ask questions because I don't wish answers.*— JJM:97 [By false refinement re-interpreting SE *want* 'to need', conceived in this sense as a word of lower status inferring 'to be in want/need (of sth)'. However, perh also reinforced by EE. Cp *OED wish* vb 1. (a) 'dial superseded in SE by *wish for* or in certain colloq contexts by *want*' + cits from Shak to Dickens, ex 'Would you wish a little more hot water, ma'am?']

wisk *n* (CarA) See WIST

wis·side *interr adv* (Guyn) [*AF—Cr*] **1.** ‖ **which side** (CarA) (*Wisside you come out?* (= *Where ever do you come from?*)—(Guyn). [< *which* + *side* by fusion] **2.** [*IF*] *excl tag*, with falling pitch ‖ WHAT[3] 1. (CarA) *Nurse wisside? The mother wasn['t] no nurse? I know that family from long, and the mother was a common domestic.*—(Guyn) □ In this usage the Cr form has become fossilized in IF Guyn E.

wist (**whisk, whist, wis(k)**) [wɪs(t)] *n* (CarA) A tough, parasitic vine or any pliant twig or bough, wh is dried and, if necessary, sliced along its length to be used esp in basket-making, but also generally for binding bundles in the field. **a.** *It was discovered by a man who had gone into the gully to cut whisks for making baskets.*—AdN (79.09.20, p.1) **b.** *Native to tropical America, this vine clings to trees and walls with a three-pronged tendril like a cat's paw. The vines are the 'whist' used in basketry.*—JNHSJ:51 [< *OED withe, with* [wɪθ ~ wɪð] 1. b. 'a pliant twig or bough'; 3. b. 'the creeping plant *Heliotropium fruticosum*, of Jamaica, the stems of wh are used for making baskets'. The form *wist* < pl *withs* by metathesis and characteristic Cr [ə > t] shift. Cp EE (1657) 'the roots being far asunder, weeds grew up between, and worse than all weeds, Withs, which are of a stronger growth than the Canes, and ... they wind about them, and pull them down to the ground'—LHOB:87]

wist-bas·ket *n* (CarA) A basket of any shape or size made of WIST, but usu a small one for rough use, such as a DUNG-BASKET.

with [wɪd ~ wɪt ~ wɪθ] *prep* (*also functioning as a general connective focusing on some person, thing, situation, etc*) (CarA) [*IF*] [Note: The following must be regarded as some illustrations, al-phabetically listed, of the convenient use of this particle in CE. It is often spelled WID, WIT in narrative dialogue. Cp similarly FOR] **1.** (CarA) [*IF*] About. **a.** *He said he was very concerned with these students, because they were the ones who would be taking the General Certificate of Education examination.*—DaM (65.11.10, p.3) **b.** *What I like with the shop, it is very clean inside and outside.*—(Guyn) **2.** [*AF—Cr*] As soon as; immediately as. *And wit*[*h*] *he pick up de cutlass, de police shoot him one time* (= *And immediately as he picked up the cutlass, the police shot him instantly*).—(Guyn) **3.** (Jmca) [*IF*] At the same time as (sb else); while also cohabiting with (sb else). *This girl tells me how much she loves me, but one thing bothers me; my girl hardly tells me the truth. She keeps men with me and when I ask her about it, she lies to me.*—WeS (75.02.14, p.8) **4.** (Guyn, Trin) [*AF*] Because of; the blame being on. **a.** *Mother, the glass didn*[*'t*] *break wid me, it happen wid Philip.*—(Guyn) **b.** *Not a woman ever complain yet, with me, ... that I ever left her dissatisfied.*—Trin (Cso, Sparrow) **c.** *With that accident he had, he can*[*'t*] *walk properly.*— (StVn) **5.** (CarA) [*AF/IF*] Between; among. **a.** *I saw an accident with a car and a bicycle.*— (Guyn) **b.** *At the buffet you had to choose with three desserts.*—(Bdos) **6.** (CarA) [*AF/IF*] By a. *'Mind you don't get knock down with car, you know how traffic busy in town!' Urmilla told him.*—SABS:84 **b.** *Before the demonstration the group met ... the Commissioner of Police, Girwood Springer, to pledge its intention to abide with the laws of the land in all its action.*—NaT (74.05.12, p.1) [Cp *EDD with* III. 2. 'by' + cits from Wm, Chs '... get bitten with a dog'] **7.** (CarA) [*AF/ IF*] For. **a.** *They would let you have it with a price.*—(Jmca) **b.** *You have teachers now who would tell a miserable child, 'You could do what you want, I ent have no time with you.'*—ExP (79.07.15, p.27) [Cp *EDD with* III. 4. 'for' + cit from Sc] **8.** (CarA) [*AF—Cr*] Like; the same as; in comparison with. **a.** *Look, you mind how you speak to me. I am not a little boy with you.*— (Tbgo) **b.** *Lada ain*[*'t*] *no car with Toyota, man. What you talkin*[*g*]?—(Bdos) [Cp *EDD with* III. 1. (7) 'to be compared with' + cits from Sc, Yks, Not] **9.** (CarA) [*IF*] [In (the matter of); in (regard to). **a.** *He's good with maths and science but not with his English.*—(Bdos) **b.** *I am sure that if Mr Brown had been my early days teacher and not the later, I would have been more advanced with my education.*—ASOG:28 **10.** (CarA) [*AF/ IF*] Of. **a.** *She don*[*'t*] *take no care with herself at all.*—(Bdos) **b.** *There were two jars full with peas.*—Tbgo (Ms) **c.** *I ain*[*'t*] *goin*[*g*] *to England to die wid de cold.*—(Guyn) [Cp *EDD with* III. 6. 'of' + cits from Sc, Yks] **11.** (CarA) [*IF*] To. **a.** *The scene changes to a sad one: The writer tends to be sympathetic with Tancy due to the task which she had of washing for the family.*—Antg, (Ms) **b.** *For many of you listening to me, these two thoughts may be disappointing ... they seem to have no relation with Christmas.*—ExP (71.12.29, p.10) [Cp *EDD with* III 7. 'to' + cits from Sc] **12.** PHRASES **12.1 be with/deh wid (sb)** *vb phr*

(CarA) [*AF—Derog*] To be living together with (sb). **a.** *The accused then told Miss T—, 'I believe you with him in truth,' and ... her brother said he did not like it.*—DeM(SK) (63.02.09, p.3) **b.** *She been wid him for years, but she deh wid another man now.*—(Guyn) □ The link vb *be* is often omitted in this Phr, reflecting CarA Cr structure. See also DE[3] 2. **12.2 can/cannot see with (sb)** *vb phr* (CarA) [*IF*] To be able/unable to understand sb's point of view (esp a vexed one). *Of course she doesn't want to spend her time and money taking care of him in his old age when he has children and she knows nothing about his will, and I can see with her.*—(Antg) **12.3 trouble with (an internal ailment)** *vb phr* (CarA) [*IF*] To suffer with/from (an internal ailment). *He troubles with arthritis and the heart too.*—(Bdos) **12.4 with regards to (sb/sth)** *prep phr* (CarA) [*X*] See REGARDS Phr 2.3 **a.** *With regards to her staff, she applies the positive method of Teaching ... and believes that everybody loves to work.*—TiM (75.11.28, p.8) **b.** *The laws of Barbados, with regards to employment, are heavily weighed in favour of the employer.*—NaT (81.12.04, p.1) **12.5 with that** *adv phr* (Bdos, Gren, Guyn) [*IF*] Thereupon; as soon as (that) happened. *Chase told me ... 'I came out and just as she reached me she said 'You see you throw water on me' and with that she took up a basin and wounded me on my forehead.'*—Bdos (CR, 65.09.24) [Cp *OED2 with* 16. (b) Followed by a demonstrative pron *with that*, 'when (and often, because) that occurred; thereupon' (Obs). See also *EDD with* III 1. In phr (9)—*that*, 'thereupon; at that moment; because of that' + cits from Sc, Yks, Ir] **12.6 with yourself** *intensifying pers pron phr* (CarA) [*AF*] [Indicating disapproval or mock approval] **a.** *You better pay me for the ticket before you start dressing up all fancy with yourself.*— (Jmca) **b.** *But she had to go dancing up in front the poor minister? You do*[*n't*] *find she is uppish wid herself?*—(Trin) **12.7 with your two long hands** *adj phr* (ECar) [*AF—Joc*] See HAND[1] Phr 4.29 *Whenever I come to Tobago, I don't come with my two long hands; I like to bring something.*— (Tbgo)

with·out *conj* (CarA) [*X*] Unless. **a.** *That is a dog don*[*'t*] *bark without it see somebody strange.*— (Guyn) **b.** *Finally no one run this country without we say so. We must know just how do we fit in.*—Antg (Ms, 1973)

wiz·zy-wiz·zy (**whiz·zy-whiz·zy**) *vb* (Bdos) [*AF—Joc*] To whisper; to speak in huddled secrecy. *It has another meaning when the Big Four get together and 'whizzy-whizzy' at 'So-and-So's' house in Trinidad and Tobago, and that kind of thing.*—Bdos (Hd, 76.06.22, p.6793) [Imitative of the sound of speaking with the lips nearly closed. The spelling with 'wh-' is prob infl by that of 'whisper']

wòb dwi·yèt [wɔb dwiyɛt] *n phr* (Dmca) See DWIYÈT [Fr Cr < Fr *robe douillette* 'dainty dress' in 17C sense of *douillette* (see Cotgrave)]

Woi(i)! *excl* (Gren, StLu) See Woy!

wom·an [wʊmʌn] *n* (CarA) **1.** A female adult (usu of low social status or not respectable); hence such terms as *belly-woman, yard-woman. Foreigners get real fun out of the Grenadian 'lady'. Grenadians go further and object to people being styled 'woman'. Boys at G.B.S.S. objected to a master ... referring to somebody, known to some of them, as 'the woman'... What the teacher said was 'I saw the woman, but I did not know it was Sam's mother.' And he was shocked to hear: 'Sir, how you can call Sam's mother a woman?'*—Gren (Ms, C.W Francis) □ Pl [wʊmɪn] cp SE [wɪmɪn]. The term is widely replaced in neutral contexts in folk-speech by CE LADY. (See note at LADY). **2.** A precocious girl. *If you are a woman I will show you who is the boss in here. I ain[t] the kind of mother to allow that.*—(Bdos) □ Hence the term *big woman* often used to signify an ordinary adult female.

woman·ish [wʊmʌnɪš] *adj* (Bdos, Gren, Guyn, StVn) [Of a girl] Precocious; rude; behaving in an adult manner. *Yesterday dat little girl cuss de teacher. Since when she so womanish.*—(StVn)

wom·an-man /1'1 2/ *n* (Gren) [AF—Derog] A male homosexual who plays the female role in a relationship.

wo·man-pi·a·ba* ['wʊmʌn-piabʌ] *n* (Bdos, Guyn) ‖ *greasy-bush* (Baha, Jmca) A wild, erect herb about a foot high, with a four-sided stalk; it bears small clusters of purplish flowers spaced along its length in the axils of pairs of velvety, lobed leaves, wh are used medicinally; *Leonurus sibiricus (Labiatae-Lamiaceae).* '*Man piaba, woman piaba / Tantan-fall-back and lemon grass / Minnie root, gully root, granny backbone ...*' (opening lines of CarA 'Weed Song', claimed by several territories as an indigenous folk ballad).—(CarA) [From general resemblance to the taller MAN-PIABA of the same family, and also from its medicinal use for women after child-birth. Note also that in *Guad* it is called *Madame Lalie*]

wo·man-rain /1'12/ *n* (Guyn) [AF—Cr/Joc] Light, continuous persistent rain. [From its being likened to the persistent nagging of a woman] □ Cp *DJE old woman rain.*

wo·man('s)-tongue* *n* (*phr*) (CarA) ‖ *Barbados ebony* (Bdos) ‖ *lang-fanm* (StLu) ‖ *monkey-(fiddle)* (TkCa) ‖ *monkey-shack-shack* (Guyn) ‖ *sha(c)k-sha(c)k* (Bdos, Trin) ‖ *West-Indian ebony* (Trin) ‖ *whistling bean* (Baha) ‖ *wild-tamarind* (CayI) A tree that grows to about 30 ft, best known for the great abundance of its dry pods wh are flat, light-brown, an inch broad and some 6 to 12 ins long, chattering incessantly in the wind (hence the folk name); *Albizia lebbeck (Leguminosae-Mimosaceae).*

won·der·ful *adj* (Antg) [IF] [Esp of a girl or woman] Excitable; prone to over-react to a situation. *The needle hasn't touched you yet and you screaming already? Don't be so wonderful.*— (Antg) [A prob calque from W Afr langs. Similar misuse of SE *wonderful* is noted in *BSCEGE:36,* calquing Ewe *ewɔ nuku* 'it is wonderful/remarkable/strange' whence a sentence such as 'The wonderful thing is he was killed at once']

won·der-of-the-world /1'1112/ *n* (Bdos, Gren, Tbgo, Trin) ‖ LEAF-OF-LIFE (Bdos, etc) [Prob from the leaf's remarkable ability to survive and promote growth when detached from the plant and kept indoors]

won·der-world /1'12/ *n* (Bdos) (The commonly reduced folk name of) WONDER-OF-THE-WORLD (*Bdos*).

wood *adj* (ECar) [IF] Wooden. *There's a bungalow ... a large wood building ... to my left, high bush almost surrounding it.*—WBAM:2 [*Wood* used attrib, as nouns often are in CE]

wood-and-block house *n phr* (Antg) ‖ WOOD-AND-WALL HOUSE (Bdos)

wood-and-wall house *n phr* (Bdos) ‖ *wood-and-block house* (Antg) A house a part of wh (the lower storey or the back section) is constructed in stone or concrete blocks, and the rest in wood. □ See WALL-HOUSE.

wood-ant(s) *n* (*pl*) (CarA) ‖ WOOD-LICE (CarA)

wood-dove *n* (Bdos) ‖ GROUND-DOVE 2. (CarA) *You will also see the Wood-Dove which is larger and more common than the Ground Dove. It is a thick-set little bird and its colours are nicely arranged. The upper part of its body is a greyish brown and the rest of it is varied with such colours as black, white and cinnamon.*—HBIH:29

wood-grant *n* (Guyn) ‖ GRANT (Guyn)

wood-lice *n pl* (CarA) ‖ *duck-ants* (CayI, Jmca) ‖ *wood-ants* (CarA) White or black-and-white, soft-bodied, quarter-inch-long termites; they live in the soil and build brittle, covered surface trails along walls or tree-trunks, or eat their way inside as they build a conspicuous black nest on the upper limb of a tree or in the ceiling of a house. [*Wood,* as their habitat + *lice,* as being furtive pests, some types of wh have a bad smell. Cp *OED wood-louse 2 a.* 'a white ant or termite'] □ The sg form is seldom used in CE (cp similarly ANTS). The BrE *wood-louse* is a crustacean, not an insect. See also COMEHEN (Belz)

wood-slave *n* **1.*** (ECar) ‖ *mabouya* (Dmca, StLu) ‖ *night-lizard* (USVI) ‖ *slave-lizard* (Bdos, Trin) ‖ *white-slave* (Bdos) ‖ *zagada* (Trin) A type of gecko or house lizard with a pale, almost translucent skin, prominent eyes that have no lids, and thick padded toes that enable it to cling to walls and ceilings; it has a clicking cry, moves with a fast snake-like wriggle, and is regarded by many with superstitious fear; *Hemidactylus mabouia (Gekkonidae)*. **2.** (Jmca) A small, shiny-skinned lizard that lives mostly out of doors; *Lacertidae spp*.

wool·ly py·rol *n phr* (Trin) ‖ MUNG-BEAN 1. (Belz, etc)

woo-woo band *n phr* (Mrat) A rural folk-band comprising a fife, an iron triangle, a GRAGE and a WOO-WOO DRUM; it is used esp to accompany the JUMBIE-DANCE.

woo-woo drum *n phr* (Mrat) A goat-skin drum about 2 ft in diameter, resembling a large tambourine; it is played by running the index finger around the surface to produce an eerie 'wooing' sound for effect in the JUMBIE-DANCE.

word *n* PHRASES **1. (be) a word and a blow** *id phr* (Guyn) [IF] [Of children] (To be) very pugnacious; (be) given to striking others at the slightest offence. *You can't leave him to play with other children—he's a word and a blow!*—(Guyn) **2. come to words** *vb phr* (Guyn, Tbgo) [IF] ‖ **have words (with sb)** (Gren, Trin, Tbgo) To quarrel; to have a heated argument. *You an[d] me go[i]n[g] come to words if you don['t] stop this foolishness.*—(Guyn) [Prob infl by SE *come to blows*, but note Eng dial sense of *words* 'dispute'. See note at Phr.**5**] **3. drop/throw words** *vb phr* (Gren, Guyn, Tbgo, Trin) [AF—Derog] ‖ **drop/ throw remarks** (Bdos, Guyn) To utter veiled insults; to make offensive or sarcastic remarks indirectly. **4. give words** *vb phr* (Gren, Trin) [IF] [Esp of a junior] To answer rudely or disrespectfully. **5. have words (with sb)** *vb phr* (Tbgo, Trin) [IF] ‖ **come to words** (Guyn) To have a disagreement. *I call you and you ain[']t answer me. What happen? Like we have words or what?*—(Tbgo) [Cp *EDD words* 2. Phr (13) *to have words* 'to have a dispute or quarrel' + cits from Sc, N.I.]

work[1] [wʌ(r)k] *n* **1.** (ECar) [IF] Job. '*You have to get a work now,*' *Mrs Cooper said.* '*Mind you, I not thinking about what you have to pay me, but still you must get a work. Why you don't go and see your headmaster?*'—NTMM:19 □ On use of indef art in such a case see A[4]. **2.** (ECar) [AF] A profession, skill or craft (usu identified by a prec noun); hence **carpenter/doctor/fish-erman/gardener/mason/teacher** (etc) **work**. *How come people have to go to school to learn a trade, or to learn doctor or lawyer or engineer or even office secretary work or cooking, but anybody at all can just get up an' run a country widdout studying a single thing about Gover'ment?*—TRIH:225 □ In senses 1., 2., and in the Phrs, representative spellings **wok, wuk** are often used in narrative dialogue. **3.** (Guyn) A domestic or private rite held either to honour (esp in Indic belief systems) or propitiate (esp in African belief

systems) one or more deities. *It is considered very important by all Hindu East Indians to continue the 'works' of their ancestors, discontinuance of which places all succeeding descendants in danger of divine wrath.*—Guyn (Ms) **4.** PHRASES **4.1 kill (sb) with work** *vb phr* (CarA) [AF] See KILL Phr 3.3.1 **4.2 the work (is) more than (sb)** *id phr* (Guyn) [AF] The task is too difficult for, beyond the capability of (sb). *He and the son buildin[g] the house in the[ir] spare time but the work is more than them. You see how the step cant to one side?*—(Guyn)

work[2] [wʌ(r)k] *vb tr* **1.** (CarA) To till and grow crops on (a piece of land); to cultivate (land) individually for a living. **a.** *When the men are working ground in the hills they don't have time to cook so special, so they make a mixup pot they call Man Soup.*—(BrVi) **b.** *I use[d] to work ground— plant cassava, sweet potato...*—(CayI) [An adaptation of SE *work the land*] **2.** [By extension] To cultivate a particular crop. *The women of Union Island are busy in the field again, working their corn, peas and other vegetable crops.*—ViN (73.19.21, p.11) [Cp *OED work* vb 12. (a) 'to till, cultivate (land); to cultivate (a plant or crop)'. However in CE the usage focuses strongly on individual occupation] □ See GROUND[2] Phrs. **3.** (CarA) [Dressmaking] To work on, make (a dress, etc). *And besides it is too late for me to get somebody to work a dress for me to go to the wedding.*—Guyn (Ms) [Cp *OED work* vb 8. 'to make, form or fashion into something; to make up'] **4.** (CarA) To earn a living by employment on/in (sth); to have (sth) as your particular employment. **a.** *It is alleged that the conductress, who was working an afternoon bus to Silver Sands, found it necessary to reprimand a male passenger for his behaviour en route.*—NaT (76.08.22, p.28) **b.** *Tell me again old man why for you want to work the sea? And you so old?*—WSAD:15 **c.** *On Monday I went by my car. I can't remember seeing U. F., etc. I was working taxi on the Monday.*—Gren (CR, 79/8) [Cp *OED work* vb 12. (j) slang '... (of an itinerant vendor) to hawk, sell'; also 20. 'to operate, manage ... a machine, an institution, etc'] □ In all senses and phrasal occurrences, the spellings **wok, wuk** are used in some narrative dialogues, representing folk pronunc. **5.** PHRASES **5.1 work at Idle Hall** *vb phr* (Bdos, Dmca, Gren) [AF—Joc] See IDLE HALL Phr **5.2 work for the half** *vb phr* (Bdos) To cultivate a piece of land by agreement with the owner to share in half the returns. **5.3 work (in) travaux** [wʌ(r)k (in) travo] *vb phr* (Gren) [IF/AF] To work in a gang of labourers building and repairing roads. [< Fr *travaux* 'works' (re public works)] **5.4 work obeah against/for/on/with (sb)** *vb phr* (CarA) See OBEAH[1] Phr 3.3 **a.** *... and that was exactly what was happening to the lighterman, for he believed that obeah had been worked for him.*—AdM (74.01.06, p.4, E.A. Stoute) **b.** '*I don't want you to feel that it is because obeah has been worked on me that you are being freed. It is only because of a lack of evidence*' *he said in dismissing the charge.*—TrI (75.09.26, p.1) **c.** '*Obeah*', *he thought.* '*Somebody trying to wuk* *obeah wid me, dey no like to see de progress a meking dese days.*—Vip I.1 □ The commonest term is **work obeah on (sb)**, wh is sometimes reduced simply to **work on (sb)**. **5.5 work out yourself** *vb phr* (CarA) [*IF/AF—Cr*] ‖ **work out your soul-case/liver-string** (Bdos, Guyn, Nevs, StLu) ‖ **work your tail off** (CarA) To work very hard (usu for another's benefit); to work to exhaustion. *The poor mother work herself out to mind them and now they all gone to America and leave her.*—(Guyn) **5.6 work by task** *vb phr* (ECar) See TASK Phr 3.1 **5.7 work (the) ground** *vb phr* (CarA) [*AF/IF*] See GROUND[2] Phr 3.1 **5.8 work to your mind** *vb phr* (Guyn) [*AF*] ‖ FOLLOW YOUR MIND (CarA) **5.9 work up** *vb phr* (Bdos, Guyn, USVI) [*AF*] (See separate entry) **5.9.1 work up yourself; work yourself up** *vb phrs* (CarA) [*AF*] **(i)** To get yourself into a temper. *It ain[']t no good workin[g] up yourself over children rudeness dese days.*—(Guyn) □ Also IF BrE. **(ii)** WORK UP YOURSELF only. = WORK UP (as separate entry). **5.10 work you** (Angu, Bdos); **work your belly/bowels** *vb phr* (Guyn, Nevs, Tbgo) To purge; to cause diarrhoea. *If you eat stale pork it will work your belly like castor oil.*—(Guyn) [Cp *EDD* work vb 23. 'to purge' + cits from Sc, Yks, Wm] □ See BELLY[1]. **5.11 work your brain/head** *vb phr* (CarA) [*AF—Cr*] To use your head to solve a problem; to scheme, devise a means. *So Anansi begin to work him head. He pull out his purse. No money in it...*—SWI:148 **5.12 work your tail off** *vb phr* (CarA) [*AF*] ‖ WORK OUT YOURSELF (CarA) See Phr 5.5 *'It wasn't easy at all,' he recalls. 'I was living in the hostel on Upper Henry Street then and I had to work my tail off ... and had to live on $10 a week.'*—SuP (75.05.18, p.9) □ Also IAE slang with variants *work your arse/ass off*.

work·bel·ly /1´2 2/ *n* (Belz, Guyn) [*AF*] ‖ B-ELLY-WORK(ING)S (Antg, etc)

work·er /1´2/ *n* (Bdos, Guyn) ‖ NEEDLE-WORKER (Bdos) *I[t´]s too late now for any worker to make up any wedding dress for Saturday.*—(Guyn) □ To be distinguished from WORKER /2´1/ 'one who works (or belongs to a 'Workers' Union!).

work-per·mit *n* (CarA) A document giving legal permission to a NON-NATIONAL to do specified work in a particular Caribbean State. *Some two hundred and eighty nine non-Montserratians in employment here will seek renewal of their Work Permits within the first two months of this year.*—MtM (73.01.12, p.3)

work up (wuk/wuck up); **wukkin(g) up** [wʌk ʌp] *vb phr* (Bdos, Guyn, USVI) [*AF—Derog*] To dance suggestively or erotically, with vigorous gyrations of the waist and hips. **a.** *There was a time when what is called 'working up' was considered to be a socially unacceptable way of expressing oneself in dance. This form of dancing which calls for mass gyrations of the hips in real Bajan is referred to as 'wucking up', is actually part of our black heritage and followed us all the way across the Atlantic.*—NaT (76.06.27, p.7,

Al's Grapevine) **b.** *I find it rather repulsive to see little girls wukking up, I'm talking about little four year olds and seven year olds gyrating most provocatively much to the amusement of their parents and grown men.*—AdM (89.02.10, p.11) □ In Bdos **wuk up** is increasingly becoming the recognized form of this phr, prompting *Joc* derivatives such as **wukkerupper, wukkupology**, etc.

worm *n* (BrVi, StKt) A coil of metal tubing immersed inside a cistern of cold water to cause the vapour inside to condense; it is still used in making illicit rum. *The Police exhibit room at Dieppe Bay is at present filled with coolers, condensers, boiler drums, worms and overhead pipes.*—DeM(SK) (61.06.10, p.4)

worm-bush/-grass/-weed *n* (CarA) ‖ SEMI-CONTRACT (Gren, Jmca) *GB suddenly complained of a stabbing pain in her head: 'Mi just feel like me hairs turn into pins and needles.' / 'Do you want some worm-grass tea?' Sue asked with solicitude. 'Worm-grass tea is good for rheumatism, flu and 'eadaches as well as worms.'*—BGSB:241 [From its use as a vermifuge]

worm·wood *n* **1.** (Bdos, Trin) ‖ BAY-GERANIUM (Baha) **2.** (Jmca) ‖ ANGELIN (CarA) [From the use of the bark as a vermifuge]

wor·ries *n pl* (CarA) [*IF/AF*] **1.** Distressing difficulties; many problems coming all together. **2.** [By extension] The mental effect of these. *The worries got her starin[g] at people like she mad.*—(Bdos) **3.** PHRASE **be in worries** *vb phr* (Guyn, Tbgo) [*IF*] To have a number of problems; to be in considerable distress. *Boy, A in real worries wit[h] the money situation ah tell you. A ai[n't] even know wha[t] to do.*—(Tbgo)

wor·ry *vb* PHRASES **1. Don't worry to (do sth)** *neg imper vb phr* (CarA) [*IF*] Don't try, attempt to (do sth); Don't even think of (doing sth); [by extension] You must not (do sth). **a.** *Don't worry to ask me for money because the answer already is no.*—(Bdos) **b.** *Don't worry to put on more weight, you know.*—(Trin) **2. (not) worry with (sb/sth)** *neg vb phr* (CarA) [*IF*] ‖ **pay (sb/sth) no mind** (CarA) (Not) to allow yourself to be bothered by (sb/sth); (not) to pay attention to (sb/sth); (not) to concern yourself with (sb/sth). **a.** *Don't worry with what people say or you will never get on.*—(Antg) **b.** *Mr Chairman, I cannot even worry with him when he talks about the broadcast and says we are not talking about C.B.C. Ask him what is the position of C.B.C. now?*—Bdos (Hd, 73.03.20, p.2063) **c.** *The accused then told Miss T, 'I believe you with him in truth', and she D—told him don't worry with the man, he is only provoking you.'*—DeM(SK) (63.02.09, p.3) **3. worry your head** *vb phr* (CarA) [*IF*] To worry; to bother or concern yourself (about sth). *Boychild:* What is that? / *Girlchild:* Don't worry your head to know what it is.—TrU

(67.02.01, p.5) [Cp Hausa: *Kada ka dami kanka* (*Do-not you worry head-of-you*) 'Don't worry yourself! Also Wolof: *Bul getten saboppa* (*Don't worry you-head*) 'Don't worry yourself!'] □ Also BrE slang, more often *bother one's head*.

worse *adj, n* (CarA) [X] Worst. **a.** ... *one suggestion was that they try to let the elevator down to the ground floor by the top pulley and that could have proved fatal, at the worse, or damaging at the very least.*—DaG (68.01.04, p.1) **b.** *What a Time! Well let's hope it won't be quite as bad as that and always remember my adage, when we first started, 'The Worse is yet to come.'*—ViN (74.01.04, p.2) **c.** *Wild Pumpkin has to be seen at its best, or worse, to be believed. The vines reach enormous heights, especially when they cling to tall trees which they sometimes manage to cover almost completely.*—AdN (73.12.23, p.2) [By characteristic CE reduction of final /-CC/, prob reinforced by spelling pronunciation, whence *worst* > *worse*] □ Cp WORSER, WORST.

wors·er [wʌ(r)sʌ] *adj, adv* (CarA) [AF—Cr] Worse. **a.** *Let us recognise that among all categories of man and professionals there are the Good, the Bad and 'Worser'* (as a Minister of Government would say).—CrU (77.01.29, p.2) **b.** *A can' sit down and ley he corrupt me own blood. Joel say he work bad obeah. But dis far worser,'e mek the boy sinful.*—FGSOS:56 [Cp *EDD worser* adj, adv and sb. In gen. dial. and colloq use in Sc, Eng and Amer]

wo(r)s·er·er [wʌsərə] *adj, adv intensifier* (CarA) [AF—Cr/Joc] Extremely bad; even worse than before. [Orig an overcorrection form, now mostly Joc. Cp *EDD worser* with cit from e Yks 'Why that's wahserer and wahserer']

worst *adj, adv* (CarA) [X] Worse. **a.** *Then when I ask that question I'm told 'boy St Vincent is going from bad to worst'.*—ViN (73.11.30, p.4) **b.** *The people want the eighties to be different; not different for the worst, through the advent of Pup-Communism.*—BeA (80.01.19, p.2) **c.** *For Barbados, these are external events over which it has no control and which couldn't have come at a worst time, one in which the island's economy is at its weakest point.*—SuS (90.08.05, p.3) [By overcorrection and confusion (see WORSE) prob in the process of DECREOLIZATION]

worst·est [wʌ(r)sɪs] *adj* (CarA) [AF—Joc] Worst. *But the worstest ting is dat one calling heself Ashford! Toto boy, ah never see a big dotish ass like dat!*—BoM (74.04.13, p.16) [By overcorrection -*est* being felt to be a necessary suffix. Also Cp *EDD worstest* (Yks, etc) similarly used]

wort(h)·less (wot·less, wuf·liss, wuss·less, wut(h)·less, wut·liss) /2'2/~/2'1/ [wʌtlɪs ~ wʌslɪs] (CarA) [AF—Derog] [Specifically of persons] Utterly unworthy; morally depraved; dishonest; loose and lazy; [of a young person]

troublesome; mischievous. **a.** *'Get out me blasted chair!' Rita shouted. 'Get out de house, yuh worthless bitch!*—SABS:143 **b.** *This Affie was running with my wuthless uncle. Now his wife, my dear-aunt Do-Da, was always a thoroughfare, and when she found out she swear she gon kill Affie.*—MBGB: 62 **c.** *The grandmother asked. 'Wait, you bewitched, girl? Is I to be blamed for you wussless behaviour? I know where you went to get yuhself so? I know the dirty place that you does put yuhself in? I know the men you does meet?*—SuS (79.09.16, p.27, T. Callendar) **d.** *I am not going to support the bill, mind you, because the Government too wutliss for that.*—TaP (75.10.19, p.1) [Cp *OED worthless* 2. 'of persons: destitute of moral character; contemptible, despicable' + cits from Shak (1591). From this EE connotation the word, entering 16C CE, has maintained a strongly condemnatory sense, becoming abusive. Its phonetic development, with loss of preconsonantal /r/, [θ > t], etc also reflect early CREOLIZATION, characteristically maintained in *Derog* CE usage]

wort(h)·less·ness (wuf·less·ness, wut·liss·ness) [wʌtlɪsnɪs ~ wʌflɪsnɪs] *n* (CarA) [AF—Derog] Wickedness; vulgarity; moral depravity; irresponsibility. **a.** *Nuff people like Sandi doan stay in politics 'cause dey cahn stan' all de wufless-ness.*—NaT (90.10.19, p.11, Lickmout' Lou) **b.** *Mr B—'s speech was recorded on tape and will remain on the record always as a memorial to his 'wutlessness'.*—ReP (79.11.18, p.2) [< WO(R)T(H)-LESS (see prec) + SE suff -*ness*] □ Strongly emotive with folk pronunc in CE. See etym note at WORTHLESS.

would *modal aux* (CarA) [X] Will. **a.** *Give me one of yours and I would give you one of mine. That's fair.*—(Bdos) **b.** *Surely the Jamaica Olympic Association with its high sense of responsibility and long history of service to local sports would not sit idly by and allow the consuming passions of persons bitten by the power-mania to deny World opportunity to ... the enthusiastic band of young Jamaican athletes at home, who are training assiduously for a ride on the Munich train.*—WeG (72.06.21, p.10) □ A common occurrence in CE usage is the misascription of the modal aux *would*.

would-a (woulda) *past modal aux* (CarA) [AF—Cr] [Usu followed by infin vb] Would have (+ pa. part.); would. **a.** *Ah didn't want to bawl out because dey daag dem woulda start barkin' an ah didn't vant da nosey neighbor hearin' meh mouth so late in dey nite.*—AaW I.2, p.25 **b.** *'If we had a plan,' Roper said, 'things woulda be different. Then they woulda see action.'*—LDCD:185 [Would + enclitic /-a/ < spoken Eng 'would ha', from 17C onwards. See A[8]; cp also COULD-A] □ Also sometimes *would of* [X]. Cp *could of*.

wow·la [wɒula] *n* (Belz) 1. A large crusher snake of the boa family. [< *DMEI* Miskito *waula* 'boa'] □ Cp CAMOODI (*Guyn*). 2. ‖ MATAPEE

(Guyn) [From the resemblance and use of this basketwork device to the crusher snake]

Woy! (Woi(i)!, Wa·yah!) [wɒːɪ! ~ waːya!] *excl* (CarA) [*AF*] [Expression of great surprise, fright or amusement; often reduplicated] **a.** *Woy! Woy! Woy! Looka Miss Applewhaite house ketchin[g] afire!*—(Guyn) **b.** *He said 'Woi, you mean somebody pass and pick up dat rabbit already? Never mind, another one down the road, ah going for it.*—PSFC:36 **c.** *Then one morning when daycloud was peeping, I woke and did no' hear the rain. Creeping out o' my kitty-up, I went to the door and pulled the latch-wood—Wayah!*—RND: 37 [Perh from W Afr coast. Cp Wolof *Wayy!* emphatic expression of distress, etc. Note also *WSNE* Sran *woi* 'exclamation of suffering'. However *DJE waay* also takes etym notice of Sc and N.Eng dial *wae* 'woe']

wo·zo *n* (Dmca, Gren, Tbgo, Trin) See ROSEAU.

wras·tle (wras·(s)le) [rasl] *vb tr/intr* (Bdos, Gren, Guyn, StKt, Trin) [*AF—Cr*] To wrestle. *'He stopped there was wrasling with a man and I walk off', she said.*—DeM(SK) (63.10.26, p.10) [Cp *EDD wrastle* vb¹ (Var dial uses in Sc, Irel, Eng, and Amer... Also written WRASSLE Sc, s.Lan¹, Som, Cor) 1. 'to wrestle; to struggle; to contend with']

wring *vb tr* **1.** (Bdos, Guyn, Jmca) [*IF*] To wrench, twist, sprain (a joint, ankle, wrist, etc). [Cp *EDD wring* v¹ 2. 'to sprain' Ess. 'to wring an ankle'. Also 3. 'to press, pinch; to trouble'. (Cp sense 2. below)] **3.** PHRASE **3.1 to have wring bones/joints** (Bdos) [*IF*] To be doublejointed; to be capable of unusual body contortions. **2.** (Trin) [By extension] To hurt, seriously trouble (sb's feelings). *And for she to be here and know he sufferin' there, it must wring her.*—JMA:238

(w)ring-neck *n* (Guyn) [*AF—Derog*] A rough, brawling type of person, esp a woman; a virago. *'You're an old ring-neck,' the Beak addressed L—, as he told her that she will have to pay $3.00 (costs $1.50), while Kulsum who defended the innocence of her 'lil' girl' paid only $2.50.*—DaC (53.04.09, p.3) [< SE vb phr *wring (a chicken's) neck* by functional shift. The erron spelling **ring-neck**, as in cit, is common]

write back *vb phr* (CarA) [*IF*] To reply (to a letter). *Yes, I received her letter but I haven't written her back yet.*—(StVn) [Write + BACK⁴ 3.]

wrong *n* (CarA) PHRASES **1. (be) wrong and strong** *id phr* (Belz, Gren, Guyn) [*IF*] To behave in a belligerent, aggressive manner towards sb you know you have wronged. *You see Mary, she thief the man mango and when he quarrel she pelt stone at him, she want to be wrong and strong.*—(Gren) **2. come wrong with (sb)** *vb phr* (Guyn) (Guyn) [*AF*] See COME Phr 7.10 **3. give sb wrong** *id phr* (CarA) See GIVE¹ Phr 2.33

wrought·ed [rɒ·tɪd] *adj* (Jmca) [*AF*] Annoyed; roused to anger. *And that is where the article appeared on Friday November 3, which, according to friends in Port of Spain, got Trinidad women most wroughted and upstirrred. It was an interview with 'Jamaican Temptress Carmen Bailey' to quote 'The Bomb', 'seductive bird from Kingston'.*—StA(JA) (72.11.18, p.10) [Prob a (mesolectal) overcorrect form of dial, perh ScE *wrought*. Cp *EDD wrought* 7. 'troubled, annoyed, frightened' + cits from Abd, Ayr; also *CSD* (p.772) *wrought* 'trouble; annoy; also *OED wrought* 9. *wrought-up* 'stirred up'. A more strongly emotive form **raated** may have developed in *Jmca* Cr with characteristic vowel opening and lengthening [ɒ < aː]] □ See note at RAHTID¹.

wuh [wʌ] *pron, etc* (CarA) See WHAT (in all functions) □ A representative dial spelling commonly used in narrative dialogue.

wuk *n, vb* [*AF—Cr*] See WORK¹, WORK²

wuk up; wuk.kin(g) up *vb phr* (Bdos, etc) [*AF—Derog*] See WORK UP *Where did Bajans learn to wuk-up so bad? ... When they hear a sweet calypso or tuk band, [they] lose all control of their waist*—AdV (93.06.25 p.9)

Wul·lay! Wul.loss!; (Wal·law!, Wha-lah!, Wuh·law!) [wʌle·! ~ wala·! ~ wʌlɒ·!] *excl* (Bdos) [*AF*] [Expressing surprise, sudden disappointment, shock and grief, etc, but also sometimes relief] Oh my God! **a.** *Wullay! Look he get knock do[w]ng.*—(Bdos) **b.** *Wulloss! I can[t] wear dis dress—looka it stain!*—(Bdos) **c.** *Wha-lah, is these the children? C'dear, how he could do something like that and get such nice girls.*—MBGB: 117 [Cp *VBHUS:115* Tshiluba *waleulas!* 'Make me cease to feel such anguish!' However, the two excls occur less often in sequence than separately, and the latter may simply be a labialized form of *O Loss!* (euph for *O Lord!*)]

wun·na(h) (wun·no, wun·nuh); un.no [wʊnʌ ~ ʊnə] *pers pron pl* (Bdos) [*AF—Cr*] ∥**allyou; you-all** (CarA) ∥**unu** (Bdos, Belz, CayI, Jmca) ∥**yinna** (Baha) **1.** You (pl); all of you; you (sg) in particular. **a.** *I believe this measure is going to go through the House because as the Deputy Prime Minister used to say when we were both in the Other Place 'Wunno got the numbers'.*—Bdos (Hd, 76.10.12, p.72) **b.** *Dr Cheltenham suggested that she told T— that if he removed the stove she would tell her husband 'wunnuh feel me up'. He also suggested that the witness was blackmailing the accused.*—AdN (74.01.24, p.1) **2.** *possessive* Your; belonging to all of you. **a.** *Wunna come and tek wunna clothes or wha'ever belongin to wunna.*—(Bdos) **b.** *All o[f] wunna mother callin[g] wunna.*—(Bdos) [< Igbo *unu* (pers pron pl) 'you; all of you', with prosthetic /w-/ by labialization. Cp *OE* ān > ModE *one* [wʌn]. The original form *unu* seems, however, to have gone with settlers' slaves to *Jmca*, thence to *Belz, CayI*] □ The form **unno**, older and now rare in *Bdos* is felt by some to be distinctly *Derog*. See UNU.

wuss·less; **wut.liss¹**, **wut.liss.ness** (CarA) [*AF—Derog*] See WO(R)THLESS; WO(R)TH-LESSNESS

wut·liss² /1′2/ *n* (CarA) [*AF—Joc*] [An affectionate form of address to an infant or a mischievously playful child] □ To be distinguished from WUTLISS¹ /2′1/ (see at **wort(h)-less**).

X

X¹ [ɛks] *n* (Bdos) ‖ *nigger-ten* (Bdos) A land-surveyor's mark, cut as the letter X in the coral stone, identifying a boundary. *When the surveyor finds the original X he usually has all the soil and bush cleared and marks the X with red paint.*—(Bdos) [As in 'X marks the spot']

X² [ɛks] *n* (Trin) [*AF—Joc*] The accelerator of a car. *Mahal was a mad Indian fellar who used to go around town playing as if he driving car, putting in gear and stepping on the x and making hand signals and blowing horn.*—STLL:21 [< [aks] abbr of 'accelerator']

x-ing [ɛksɪn ~ ɛksɪŋ] *n* (Bdos, Mrat, Nevs, StKt) [Building Ind] The crossed wooden supports of the handrail of a stairway or verandah, looking like a succession of large X's; they are a common feature of low-cost house-building.

Y

-y [-i] *adj suff* (CarA) [*AF—Cr/Derog*] [A diminutive suffix lessening the force of the adj base. Prob a CE borrowing of SE dim suff of nouns *-y/-ie* as in *doggie, lovey,* etc, and with functional shift applied to SE adjs (like SE -ish)] Slightly; a little bit. Exs *fraidy, reddy, sof[t]y, stupidy, whitey.*

ya [ya] *adv* (CarA) [*AF—Cr*] **1.** Here. **a.** *Man look ya, somebody going still have to cut de wood an' burn de coal fo' you.*—FGSOS:34 **b.** *Nobody pay any mind to him. Nobody and he round ya gree. Man like that, if even he get kill, nobody was going to give evidence for him!*—StA(AG) (63.10.23, p.4) **c.** *Black people mus' learn fe know dem place. Is right here we belong. Right down a' dutty-ground ya.*—PCOS:89 [< SE pronunc [hɪə] with loss of /h-/ and vowel opening; prob reinforced in *Guyn, Trin* by co-incidence of Hin *yahaa* 'here, hither, near'] □ This Cr form, so spelled, is often used in narrative dialogue. Cit. (b) is taken from an account of evidence in court. **2.** PHRASE **2.1 ya so (so)** *adv phr* (Guyn, StKt, StVn) [*AF—Cr*] Right here; right to/on this spot. *'Oman, you mean you mek me bun out me clutch, me brakes an' me geas, jus' ou bring you from dey so so, to ya so so?*—LMFF:42

ya(b)·ba; ya(b).ba-dish/-pot *n* (Antg, Jmca, Mrat, Nevs, USVI) A round, open, earthenware vessel used mostly for cooking; it varies in size from a small shallow bowl to a large, heavy, deep one. [Prob a dial pronunc of *DAFL* Twi *ayawa* 'earthen vessel, dish'] □ The item is known mostly by older, rural folk.

yacht·ing-boots *n* (Guyn) ‖ GYM-BOOTS (Trin) [See next]

yacht·ing (-shoe) *n* (Guyn, Jmca) ‖ CREPE-SOLES (Guyn, etc) *His white yachting shoes flashed along the narrow track that led to the asphalt road. He ran ... feeling the thud, thud of the hard approving earth.*—RHJSS:26 [Cp *OEDS yachting,* vbl sb in attrib use, applied esp to garments designed for use on yachts + cit 1873 'I always wear yachting shoes without heels, made of the white canvas, and with leather toes and straps, as now worn by boating and yachting gentlemen'. (Though there is no early history of yachting as a sport in the *CarA,* these shoes may have first been imported under this name.)] □ A *yachting* (sg), *yachtings* (pl) are common formal usage in *Guyn.*

yacht·ing-shoe foot·ball *n phr* (Guyn) ‖ SOFT-SHOE FOOTBALL (Gren) *A spectators' stand was built on the old Parade Ground opposite the Promenade Gardens in Georgetown to encourage yachting-shoe football competitions.*—Guyn (Ms)

ya(c)k·man *n* **1.** (Guyn) ‖ ARMY-ANT (Trin) *The line of march [of Yackman] was twenty yards broad, and within that space the whole ground was a moving mass of black ants which continued to pass for nearly half an hour. Before them fled cockroaches, beetles, lizards and so on; but they fled in vain, for each was caught ... and was almost immediately devoured.*—IAIG:148 **2.** (Guyn) A snake about 3 to 6 ft long with a shiny, black back, yellow body, and tapering, whip-like tail; it is very fast moving, but non-poisonous, often living in trees and feeding on small birds. [< dial Du *jachtman* 'hunt-man'] □ The name is preserved in rural and interior areas.

Yag *n* (Guyn) [Indic] See BHAGAVAT

yam* *n* (CarA) **1.** A tuberous root of wh there are very many varieties, some of wh are cooked throughout the CarA; *Dioscorea spp.* **a.** *The yam is adapted to the warm tropics and is grown for its tuberous roots or rhizomes. There are over 600 species of this important crop; however, only about ten are of any importance as food. Species are found which are native to both the Old and New World. Great variations in size and shape of tubers exist in the species. Tubers of Dioscorea alata may reach 60 kilograms in weight and be over two meters in length; whereas, the tubers of D. esculenta rarely exceed a few hundred grams.*—Cta.8.4, p.2 **b.** *There are many different types of yams, e.g. moonshine which is reddish in colour, bajan or atuta yam, a yellow yam with a somewhat bitter taste, cush cush, and sweet yams. The yam season usually begins in October and November and ends around May but yams can be grown throughout the year.*— Gren (Ms, 1976) [< /nyam/, an item found in a large number of West and Central Afr langs as n ('meat', food') or vb ('eat'). *KPG:80, 81* lists 55 forms of the n *nnyam, nyiama, ẹnama,* etc 'meat' and also (p.177) a few of the vb ex Pulo (i.e. Fula) *mi nyami nyiri,* Twi *mi ya yoro* 'I eat rice'. The sound would have occurred, with high frequency among Africans in the slave era, with the basic meaning 'food', whence Pg *inhame,* Sp *ñame,* Fr *igname,* E *yam* for the root vegetable wh was the Afr staple food] □ Note that AmE *yam* often = CE SWEET POTATO. **2.** PHRASE **2.1 cry water to boil yams** *vb phr*

(Angu) [*AF*] ‖ CRY LONG WATER (Bdos, etc) [*IF*] *When the husband dead she cry water to boil yams and now only a couple weeks after she stepping out again.*—Angu (Ms)

yam-bank *n* (CarA) ‖ BANK¹ 1. (CarA)

yam-bean *n* (Jmca) ‖ SAEME (Guyn)

yam-head *n* (CarA) The top portion of the yam tuber, wh is cut off to be replanted (the rest of the tuber being used as food).

yam-hill *n* (Jmca) ‖ YAM-BANK (CarA)

yam·pee *n* (Antg, StVn, Trin) See YAMPI(E)²

yam·pi(e)¹ ['yampi] *n* (Belz, CayI, Jmca) ‖ CUSH-CUSH (YAM) (Dmca, etc) a. *In the Caribbean the indigenous Yampi (Cush-cush) Dioscorea trifida, is grown along with D. rotundata and D. cayenensis.*—Cta.8.4, p.2 b. *Some bartered outright, dispensing with ... shillings ..., they exchanged chickens and ducks, cocoa balls and fish from the bay against cockstone and Congo peas, yams and yampies, breadfruit and the unrefined cane sugar that lay caked rich brown and sweet in upright oblong tins.*—RWIN:41 (C. McKay) [Prob from an Afr dialectal variant. Cp Wolof *nyambi* 'yam'] □ Considered, esp in *Jmca*, as a distinctive variety of yam. Note cit b.

yam·pi(e)² (yam·pee) ['yampi] *n* (Antg, Bdos, StVn, Trin, USVI) ‖ *bibby* (Baha) ‖ *bubu* (Guyn) ‖ *kaka-djé* (Gren) ‖ *matter*² (Jmca) ‖ *nampy* (USVI) ‖ *nyampi* (StVn) Mucus exuded in the corner of the eyes, esp after sleeping. *The expletives were directed to the cow, of course (which stood looking at Ramdas with great streaks of yampi running down its eyes).*—NAGOS:79 [Cp *DAFL* Twi *mpe* 'the matter found sometimes, esp after a night's sleep, in the corner of the eye'; also *AFID* Igbo (Ukwaali) *ẹnyampi* 'blind']

yam wa·wa *n phr* (Dmca) ‖ WILD-YAM (Jmca) [Prob W Afr. Cp *DAFL* Twi *wawa* 'large tree', the tree-climbing vine being a distinctive characteristic of this variety]

yan·ga¹ [yaŋga] *n* 1. (Jmca) A dance with hands akimbo, emphasizing the sharp wiggling of the hips; it is mostly rural and perhaps old-fashioned. [Prob of Bantu orig. Cp *SHDNL* Nyanja *nyan'ganyan'ga* 'walking softly on tiptoe'; also *yangala* 'to dance by oneself'; but see note at NYANGA] 2. (Guyn) [*AF—Joc*] ‖ *nyanga* 1. (Guyn, Jmca) Airs; stylish dress and/or way of walking. *The marriage didn['t] last because he come up rough and dat girl had a lot o[f] yanga.*—(Guyn) [See NYANGA of wh it is prob a reduced form]

yan·ga² [yaŋga] *adj* (Guyn) [*AF—Joc*] Putting on airs; making an obvious display of your dress and step. *See him Sunday afternoon with his*

bowtie and sharkskin suit, walking-stick and stepping along with a yanga walk.—(Guyn) [By attrib extension of YANGA¹ 2.]

yan·ga³ [yaŋga] *vb* (Guyn) 1. To dance or [esp of a woman] walk provocatively. 2. To put on airs; to show off. [By functional n > vb shift of YANGA¹] □ So used mostly by older rural folk.

yanm-a·tou·tan (a·tou·ta(n), yam-a-tout-temps) [yam-a-tu-tã] *n* (StLu, Trin) ‖ YELLOW-YAM (Antg, etc) a. *Yam-atoutan, sweet cassada, cent a heap anything.*—(line of old Trin folk-song) b. *Yam-a-tout-temps is usually cheaper than cush-cush.*—Trin (Ms) [< Fr Cr *à tout temps* < Fr *en tout temps* 'at all times' because of the possibility of continual reaping of this species: 'A method practised to some extent in reaping the Guinea and Yellow Yams in the W Indies is ... to allow the lower part being cut, and leaving the top to continue growing .... In good soil this method may be continued with the Yellow Yam up to two years during wh period several crops may be obtained.'—*PTT:150*]

yanm-jònn (yam-jaune) [yăm-žo·n] *n* (Dmca) ‖ YELLOW-YAM (Antg, etc) [Fr Cr < Fr *igname jaune* 'yellow yam']

yanm·pen [yămpẽ] *n* (Dmca) ‖ BREADFRUIT (CarA)

yard *n* 1. (CarA) The enclosed area around or behind a house wh is turned to various domestic uses, including gardening and children's playing. 2. (Jmca) (i) [Hist] ‖ NEGRO-YARD (CarA) *If the collection of huts within the enclosure indeed denoted a Negro Yard, then the notion of yard for the enslaved Jamaican would in addition refer to residence which 'we have designed and built for ourselves'.*—BYCK:6 (ii) (Jmca) [By extension] The home or dwelling-place of a poor urban dweller, esp of Kingston. *She asked the army officer, 'You don't seem to think that this is a decent yard, young man? Why you think it is a yard to search? Is decent people live in here, you know. We don't harbour any form of criminals, here, at all. You can look for yourself, if you want. I can tell you that you won't find no looters or no stolen goods, either. This is a respectable yard.'*—SJT: 86 (iii) (Jmca) [*AF—Joc*] [By extension] Your home. *Look! Bad weather comin[g], you see! Is time I look for my yard! (It is time I get home).*— (Jmca) 3. PHRASE 3.1 **find your yard** (Jmca) [*AF—Derog*] See FIND Phr 2.1. □ See also BALM-YARD.

yard-bean *n* (Gren, Guyn, Trin) ‖ BODI (BEAN) (Gren, etc) [Prob from length of the pod of one variety, wh can grow to 3 ft]

yard-boy *n* (CarA) A man-servant of any age employed to do general outdoor domestic chores.

yard-fowl *n* (Bdos) [*Derog*] A political lackey; a person who makes himself available as a party hack in return for political favours on wh his livelihood depends. *The pulling of strings is interrelated with the possession of friends in the 'right' places, and to keep such friends, one is often required to indulge in such exercises as pimping and toadying, the two main characteristics of a yardfowl.*—NaT (74.07.28, p.14) [YARD 1. + FOWL 'chicken; hen'; such birds live in the enclosed YARD and are fed table and kitchen scraps, hence the analogy]

yard·fowl·ism *n* (Bdos) [*Derog*] The political practice of giving or receiving favours in return for toadying; sycophancy in politics. *It was an attempt to get rid of the system of Party hacks, to eradicate the system of sycophants, and to kill as far as possible the system of yard-fowlism ... which was part of their practice when they were in power.*—Bdos (Hd, 76.10.12, p.68) [*yard-fowl* + SE *-ism* 'system' as in *communism*]

yard·wom·an *n* (Guyn) ‖ *djanmèt*[1] 2. (Trin) ‖ *zamie-tess* (Trin) A woman of rough character, given to vulgar, brawling, shameless fighting, etc. [< woman of the YARD sense 2.(ii), as in IAE *street-woman*]

yar·row [yaraʊ] *n* (Guyn) A bull-nosed fish with a black stripe running along each side; it is a river fish with powerful jaws and sharp teeth, prized for its tasty flesh; *Erythrinus erythrinus* (*Characinidae*)—*RFLG:257*. [*BAED* Arawak *yarau* 'a small fresh-water scale fish']

ya·wa(r)·ri(e) [yawari] *n* (Guyn) ‖ MANICOU (ECar) *When he heard a disturbance in the chicken-pen that night he went down to find a yawarrie attacking them.*—Guyn (Ms) [*BAED* Arawak *yaware* 'a kind of opossum']

yaws *n pl* (CarA) **1.** A disfiguring skin disease; it was common among slaves. **2.** A fatal disease, causing sores about the head, that attacks domestic hens. **3** PHRASES **3.1 bad as yaws** *adj phr* (Tbgo) See BAD[1] Phr 4.1. **3.2 have cocobay on top of yaws** *Prov and id phr* (Guyn, Trin) [*AF—Joc*] See COCOBAY Phr 3.1

yaws(-bush) fruit *n phr* (Guyn) ‖ JUMBIE-SOURSOP (Antg, etc)

y.c. sug·ar *n phr* (Guyn) Abbr See YELLOW-CRYSTAL SUGAR

year-end *n, adj* (ECar) (Taking place at) the end of the year. **a.** *Due to open April 13 in Santiago Chile is a similar follow-up meeting and still another is planned for year end.*—DaC (72.06.08, p.1) **b.** *Mr Meade warned that further increases could force the Jaycees out of year-end entertainment.*—MtM (77.04.15, p.1) [By analogy with SE *weekend* and CE MONTH-END]

yeh? [yɛ] *tag form, (with stressed rising or falling pitch)* (ECar) [*AF*] ‖ *yuh*[2] (Bdos) [Adding warning or advice to preceding statement] I warn you! Let me advise you! **a.** *Yo[u] better don['t] touch dis car, yeh?*—(Bdos) **b.** *Careful wid dat cutlass, it very sharp, yeh?*—(Guyn) [Perh from

dial EE *y[ou] [h]ea[r]*! It is indeed often replaced in informal CE by *yo[u] hear?*]

yel·low-bell *n* (Angu, Antg, Tbgo) ‖ ALLA-MANDA (CarA)

yel·low-boy *n* (Bdos) ‖ DWARF-COCONUT (Belz, etc) [*Yellow*, because of its colour + *boy* because the coconut is a small variety]

yel·low-breast *n* (Antg, Bdos, USVI) ‖ BANA-NAQUIT (CarA)

yel·low-coat plum *n phr* (Jmca) ‖ HOG-PLUM 1. (CarA)

yel·low-crys·tal sug·ar *n phr* (Guyn) [*Obs*'?'] ‖ *y.c. sugar* (Guyn) A golden yellow sugar with relatively coarse, cubical crystals, of a smooth sweetness, popular with children and coffee-drinkers. □ The type once produced mainly in Br Guiana was popularly called DEM-ERARA SUGAR in Britain.

yel·low-dad/-dod *n* (Angu) ‖ LOVE-VINE (CarA) [*Yellow*, from the pervasive colour of the mass of this vine + *dad* < *dod* < DODDER by apocope]

yel·low-dod·der *n* (Nevs) ‖ LOVE-VINE (CarA) (See above)

yel·low-dwarf (co·co·nut) *n (phr)* (Belz, Jmca, StLu) ‖ DWARF-COCONUT (Belz, etc) [*Yellow*, in ref to its colour]

yel·low-love *n* (ViIs) ‖ LOVE-VINE (CarA) [Blend of YELLOW-DODDER *Nevs* + LOVE-VINE]

yel·low-plan·tain /1ʹ122/ *n* (Guyn) ‖ *plantain* (Bdos) The ripe PLANTAIN that has become yellow-skinned and of sweetish texture; it is usu sliced and fried as a special side-dish or menu item.

yel·low-plum *n* (Belz, CayI, Jmca, Trin) ‖ CH-ILLI-PLUM (Antg, etc) [From its tough yellow skin, whence sometimes also called *yellow-coat plum*. However the HOG-PLUM also has a yellow but thin, edible skin]

yel·low pou·i* *n phr* (ECar) A forest-tree that loses all its leaves in the dry season and bursts into a mass of golden yellow, trumpet-shaped flowers wh last for about two to three days; it is prized for its ornamental worth, though its timber is commercially valuable and the tree can exceed 80 ft in height; *Tecoma serratifolia* or *Tabebuia s.* (*Bignoniaceae*). [See POUI]

yel·low·tail[1] *n* (Trin) ‖ BUNYA (Guyn)

yel·low·tail[2] **(-snake)** *n* (Guyn) A snake about 6 ft long with a black back, yellow belly, and brighter yellow tail; it is very fast-moving and can stand on its tail when excited; it eats small animals and chickens. *Snakes, harmless* *ones, horsewhips and yellowtails, slithered, or coiled up secretively in some hole or hollow.*—SBB:7

yel·low·tail[3] **(-snap·per)*** *n* (CarA) A fish wh is a small species of snapper; its back pinkish-blue and yellow-spotted; it has along each side a prominent yellow stripe widening as it reaches a deeply forked, yellow tail; its flesh, though scant, is highly esteemed; *Ocyurus chrysurus* (*Lutjanidae*). *My mom cooked fresh fish, yellowtails and snappers, and—oh boy!—were they ever good! I can't spite nobody by fasting when there's fresh fish for dinner. No, sir! Yellowtails and snappers—oh boy!!*—PCCB:80

yel·low-yam* ['yɛlʌ-ya·m] /1'12/ *n* (CarA) ‖ *afu yam* (Jmca, Tbgo, Trin) ‖ *atouta* (Gren) ‖ *Dominica yam* (StVn) ‖ *dye-yam* (Guyn) ‖ *hard-yam* (Guyn) ‖ *Ibo yam* (Mrat) ‖ *neroo yam* (Guyn) ‖ *prickle yam* (Tbgo, Trin) ‖ *y-anm-atoutan* (StLu, Trin) ‖ *yanm-jònn* (Dmca) A yam that grows to over 2 ft in length and often branches like open legs; it has rough dark-brown skin and light yellow flesh; it is widely cultivated and cooks with a soft texture; *Dioscorea cayennensis* (*Dioscoreaceae*). *The Yellow Yam, known also in Trinidad and Tobago as 'Affou Yam', 'Woman's God', 'Negro Yam', 'Conny Yam', and 'Yam a tout temps', is usually long and cylindrical, often branching from the head so as to form two or more tubers. It has a roughened and bark-like exterior, and pale yellow flesh, which is mealy and dry when boiled.*—PTT:150 [From the light yellow colour of the flesh. See also etym noted at DYE-YAM, YANM JÒNN]

yer·ri-so [yɛrɪsʌ] *n* (Belz) [*AF—Joc*] Hearsay; gossip; rumour. *'In Belize,'* he said, *'one does not go to the market merely to make purchase but to meet friends and to hear the latest 'yerri-so'.*—BsT (81.06.07, p.c) [< abbr and nominalization of /mi yeri so/ 'I hear/heard so'; /yeri/ < SE 'hear' with epenthetic /y-/ as also in *Jmca* Cr]

yes! *tag form* (CarA) [*IF*] ‖ *oui, wi* (StLu, Trin) [Adding emphasis to the preceding statement] **1.** [Esp after an adj] Very. *Time and again people say to her, 'Girl, you lucky yes you can travel and see and do so much abroad, while here we have nothing in the line of entertainment.'*—TrG (76.04.11, p.11) **2.** (i) [Stressing truth, urging attention and belief] I tell you!; Believe me! **a.** *'We got a good chance if we leave now, yes,' Samuel Palmer shouted back.*—SJS:120 **b.** *'Boy I forget everything about that yes,' he replied, 'Is only yesterday I remember.'*—ExP (72.11.05, p.11) **(ii)** [Inviting or persuading, with person-identification following] **a.** *You must go to the wedding, yes man! After all you are still her sister, you know!*—(Guyn) **b.** *But yo[u] have to stop all that playin[g] yes Arthur! The exam is soon!*—(Bdos) **3.** [By extension, without a preceding statement, expressing dismay, surprised approval, etc] *Well everybody know she ai[n't] no super beauty, but when they see this big bride come out the house like a queen, they shout 'Well yes!!'*—(Trin)

ye·si ['yesi] *n* (Guyn) ‖ ARMADILLO (Guyn) [*BAED* Arawak *yeshi* 'the smaller kind of armadillo', presumably the SMALL ARMADILLO, for cp *BAED manoraima* 'the largest kind of armadillo', *yesere* 'the second largest kind of armadillo'] □ This name is used mostly by forest dwellers. (See *RALG:12*).

yes·ter·day *adv* PHRASES **1. not yesterday** *neg adv phr* (Bdos, Guyn) [*IF*] See NOT Phr 2.17 **2. not yesterday story** *n phr* (Guyn) [*AF*] An old story; a vexatious matter of long standing. *What I talkin[g] about isn['t] yesterday story, yo[u] know. Since before you born yo[ur] father and yo[ur] aunt been quarrellin[g] [a]bout yo[ur] grandmother property.*—(Guyn)

yet[1] *adv* PHRASE **yet for all** *conj phr* (Guyn) ‖ STILL FOR ALL (Guyn)

yet[2] *vb tr* (StKt, USVI) [*AF—Cr*] Eat. *Every day A come in he[re] yo[u] yettin somet[h]ing.*—(StKt) [< SE *ate* with prosthetic /y-/. Cp LEF, BROK, etc for Cr use as SE pa.t. as base vb] □ This Cr form/spelling is often used in narrative dialogue.

yeye [yaɪ] *n* (Guyn, Jmca, Mrat, Nevs, StKt) [*AF—Cr*] Eye(s). *When six yeye meet, story done* (= *When six eyes meet, story done i.e. When there are three persons, secrecy is impossible*).—Jmca (Prov) [< SE *eye* with prosthetic /y-/] □ The form is preserved in a number of Cr provs and sayings.

yin·na [yɪna ~ yɪnʌ] *pers pron* (Baha) [*AF—Cr*] ‖ *unu* (Bdos, Belz, CayI, Jmca) **1.** You, all of you [i.e. usu pl, but occasionally sg]. **a.** *Well, Mr Pindling appointed Mr Bowe to the Ministry of Finance and what he seems to be saying is this: 'You tink is dem? Is me. But yinna so fool to put up with the PVC pipe, I could really stick it ter yer.'*—TrI (75.11.01, p.3) **b.** *She continued, 'All I try ter bring yinna up de right way yinna always disgracin' me. I dunno where yinna get dees ways—ya always fightin' like cat an' dog, like y'ain nobody. Errybody [sic] know I is a decent woman. A get up an fall down wid yinna. Tell me. When yinna goin stop disgracin me?'*—TOSR:37 **2.** Your. *Winkie put in his two cents worth, saying 'Yinna feeling tings in ya head; ain nuttin movin'. Yinna head swingin', das all!'*—TOSR:28 [Most likely < Yoruba *yin* [yĩ] 1. 'you people'; 2. 'your'; also 3. used as honorific 2nd pers sg; also Yoruba *ẹyin*, alternative form with similar functions to *yin* 1. and 3. The notable remainders of Yoruba infl in *Baha* would account for the survival of this pronominal form (cp UNU *Bdos*), and /-na/ may have been added by paragoge, or may be due to reinforcement by later Kikongo *yenu* 'you; your' (pl)] □ The form survives in folk speech and is used by educated persons in *Joc* conversational contexts. It is a perh closer parallel to *ECar* ALL-YOU than to YOU-ALL. **3.** PHRASES **3.1 all o[f] yinna** *pron phr pl* (Baha) [*AF—Cr/Joc*] All of you. **3.2 yinna-all** *pron pl* (Baha) [*AF—Cr*] All of you. *I aks one feller 'Way yinna* *all goin?'*—JBJ:81 **3.3 yinna children/fellers/ people**, etc *n phr pl* (Baha) [*AF—Cr*] You children/fellous/people, etc. *He flip open da't li'l suitcase an' he pull out wun paper an' look roun' agen much as t' say, 'Yinna fellers only tink y' bad.'*—DSJS:6

yon·der *adv* (CarA) [Usu while pointing with the arm outstretched] Far away over there. *'Tis a long story,' Miss Foster said. 'Let's go over yonder in the shade.'*—LICMS:17 [As *OED yonder* A. 1. a. 'over there, away there ... at some distance but within sight'] □ *OED* marks this item *literary*, *arch.* or *dial..* In AmE it is adv, but regarded as dial. However, it is still formal CE as adv. It does not occur, however, as adj.

you[1] [yu· ~ yʊ] unstressed *pron 2nd pers* (CarA) [Note: See YOUR, YUH as separate entries] PHRASES **1. It's/Is me and you!** *id phr* (CarA) [*AF/IF*] [Issuing a threat] See AND[3] Phr □ Similarly *It's you and he/she/them!*; *It's the two of you!*. **2. you-all** *pron pl* (CarA) [*IF*] See separate entry below **3. You and all!** ['yu· an a·l] /3'21/ *id phr* (CarA) [*AF*] See ALL[3] Phr 5.14.1 **4. You go [a]long!** ['yu· gʌ lɒ·ŋ] /3'21/ *id phr* (Bdos, Guyn) [*AF*] You are heading for trouble! □ With strong initial stress and falling tone, said as a serious warning to a young person. **5. you have; you had** *id phrs* (CarA) [*IF*] There is/are; there was/were. **a.** *If you have a fire, you can't get out of here so easily.*—(Bdos) **b.** *I did not know you still had people in Jamaica thinking like this. They are stupid, very stupid in these modern times.*—StA(JA) (82.03.24, p.12) □ A freer, looser use of IAE informal *you have* 'there is/ are' as in 'You have shorter working weeks these days'. Cp also THEY HAVE (See HAVE Phr 3.16). CE widely uses a pers pron subj (you/they) in non-personal statements where SE would use statements beginning with *there* or *it*. **6. you one** ['yu· wɒ·n] *pron phr* (CarA) [*AF*] Just you alone. *Is only natural for wind to blow so hard, but you going out you one?*—WSAD:6 □ See also ONE[2] 1. **7. You see you?** [yʊ sɪ 'yu:] *id phr* (ECar) [*AF/IF*] [Introducing a strong rebuke or threat] *George Robinson approached her and said, 'You see you—you from Montserrat but I going to give you a jail before long because I don't like you.'*—DeM(SK) (65.05.08, p.10) **8. You (self) too!** ['yu· sɛlf tʊ] /3'21/ *id phr* (Antg, Gren, Guyn, Mrat, StVn) [*AF*] See TOO Phr **9. You yourself!** ['yu· yʊsɛlf] /3'21/ *id phr* (Belz, Trin) ‖ YOU (SELF) TOO (Antg, etc) *When they got back to the garden he said, 'You yourself, you not have anything to do home? You don't fraid something happen to the child?'*—SABS:134

yo[u][2] [yu· ~ yʊ] unstressed *poss pron* (CarA) [*AF*] Your. *She intoned the words mesmerically: 'I care you pickney. I clean you house. I wash you car. I cook you food. I deliver you mail, you Gleaner. I sell you Star. I fix you car. I cut you lawn. I cut you cane. Then, how come my pickney a get it so hard f'go to school, f'wear clothes, f'find bus fare, f'get lunch money? And I a work like bitch f'get two shilling.'*—SJT:46 [A characteristic Cr

multi-purpose use of one pron form in all functions (cp HE, ME, etc); but perh reinforced by EE dial usage as *OED you* 8. 'your'; *EDD* lists such usage for w.Som]

you-all (you all) *pron (phr)*, *2nd pers pl* (CarA) [*IF*] ‖ **all-you** (CarA) [*AF*] ‖ **among-you** (Crcu, Gren, Guyn) [*IF*] All of you; you (pl). **a.** *This Government has been in power eleven years and this is the first time you all in the Opposition opened you mouths about rice.*—Bdos (Hd, 75.11.06, p.2761) **b.** *Remember how you all treat Carl Francis. Hateful, revengeful, victimization, spiteful. That's the motto of you all.*—TrI (78.04.05, p.5) [Development from CarA Cr need to express a pl *you*; a likely calque from more than one W Afr lang. Cp Twi *mo nyinea mo ŋkɔ* (*You all you go*) 'All of you go!'; also Isoko *wai kpobi* (*you all*) 'all of you', etc. See also UNU, WUNNA (*Bdos*), YINNA (*Baha*)] □ This pron form is rare in *Belz, Jmca*. Some CE speakers also use an overlapping phr **all of you-all** without any clearly indicated emphasis.

you-all's *possessive pron*, *2nd pers pl* (Bdos) [*X*] ‖ **your-all's** (Bdos) [*X*] Your (pl). *And what would you-all's ten percent bring the price down to?* —(Bdos)

you-man *pron* (CarA) [Rastaf] You (who do not belong to my cult). *He had more cause for fear, he said, when one of the Defendants told him 'what you man stand up there for, forward to I man'.*—ToR (77.05.18, p.3) [An intended contrast with I-MAN, used among the brethren of the cult]

Youm·an-Na·bi (Y(a)oum·un-Na·bi) [yʌumʌn-na·bi] *n* (Guyn, Trin) [Indic] The Muslim festival celebrating the birth and death of the Holy Prophet Mohammed on the 12th day of the third month of the Islamic calendar; it is a national holiday in Guyn; the date varies annually within the (western) Gregorian calendar. [< Perso-Arabic *Yaoum-'n-Nabi* 'day of (the) Prophet']

your-all's *possessive pron*, *2nd pers pl* [*X*] ‖ **you-all's** (Bdos) [*X*] Your (pl). *Please move your-all's car from where it is parked.*—(Bdos) [Development of a poss form of YOU-ALL] □ A false refinement almost confined to *Bdos*.

you(r)·self *refl pron* (CarA) [*AF/IF*] **1.** [Used in refl vb phrs in CE more widely than in IAE. See for ex, CARRY YOURSELF! (CARRY Phr 3.5), FIRE YOURSELF! (FIRE[2] Phr 4.4), MOVE YOURSELF (MOVE Phr 2.)] **2.** PHRASE **2.1 You (self/yourself) too!** 3'(2)21/ *id phr* (CarA) [*IF*] See TOO Phr 7.4; also YOU AND ALL!, ALL[3] PHR 5.14.1

Yu·ca·te·can [yuka'tɛkan] *adj*, *n* (Belz) (Of or belonging to) an ethnic and linguistic subgroup of the MAYAN people spreading from Mexico into the northern area of Belize; they are one of three such subgroups. □ See KEKCHI, MOPAN.

yuc·ca [yʌka] *n* (Angu, StLu, USVI) ‖ ADAM'S NEEDLE (ECar) [Of Amerindian orig via Sp *yuca*, name of the plant]

yuck[1] [yʌk] *vb tr* (Baha) [*AF*] To snatch; to pull (sth) away with force; to yank. *Teacher, he yuck the pencil out o[f] my hand.*—(Baha) [A Br dial survival. See *OED yerk, yark, Sc* or *dial.*, v 4. 'to pull, push ... with a sudden movement; to jerk' + cit 1840 'I'd larn him how ... to yawk the reins with both hands']

yuck[2] [yʌk] *n* (Baha) [*AF*] A jerk; a tug; a sharp pull. [By functional vb > n shift of YUCK[1]]

yucks [yʌks] *vb intr* (Baha) [*AF*] [Marbles] To cheat (in a particular way). *I ain't yucks! Is you yucksin[g]!*—(Baha)

yuck up 1. *vb phr* (Baha) [*AF*] To irritate; to provoke to anger. **2.** *vb phr* (Grns) To vomit. □ These two senses may have different origins. Their etym is uncertain.

yuh[1] [yʊ] (CarA) [*AF*] You; your. *Johnny Macco sometimes upbraids Mr Casual. Yuh mean to say you ent know dat! Ketch yuhself, man! Ketch yuhself! Ah, ay! If yuh go on so, Simpson go pass and pick yuh up! Like yuh want to hear 'Abide wid me' singing over yuh head!*—ExP (73.02.25, p.21) □ A dial form/spelling often used in narrative dialogue. Similarly **yuhself**, as in cit.

yuh![2] [yʌ] *tag form, with stressed falling pitch* (Bdos) [*AF*] ‖ YEH (ECar) *He ain't pull out in trute, yuh: he ain't like he pulling out at all, man.*—CWFYS:91 [Prob a variant of YEH < yo[u] hear] □ A dial form/spelling often used in Bdos narrative dialogue.

Z

za·bi·co *n* (Dmca, StLu) See ZABWIKO

za·bò·ka (za·bo·ca) [zaboka] /1ʹ12/ *n* (Dmca, Gren, Mrat, StLu, StVn, Trin) ‖ AVOCADO (-PEAR) (CarA) [Fr Cr < Fr *des—avocats* [de zavoka] by misplaced juncture and characteristic Cr /v > b/ shift] □ ZABOCA is the spelling most commonly found; others, though rare, are *zab-boca, zabooca, zabouka.*

za·bwi·ko (za·bi·ko, z'a·bri·cot) [zab(w)iko] /1ʹ12/ *n* (Dmca, StLu) ‖ MAMMEE-APPLE (CarA) [Fr Cr < Fr *des—abricots* [dezabriko] 'apricots', with misplaced juncture; from the resemblance of the firm yellow flesh to that of the European *apricot*]

za·fè (zaf·faire) [zafɛ] *n* (Dmca, Gren, StLu, Trin) [*AF*] 1. Trouble; problem; concern. *Look, you're invited but if you don't want to come it would be your zaffaire.*—(StLu) 2. PHRASE 2.1 **zafè-ou!; zaffair(e)-you!** [zafɛ-(y)u] /1ʹ21/ *id tag* (Dmca, Gren, StLu) That's your business!; That's your problem, not mine! *Well I done tell yo[u] not to go there, and if you get in any trouble, zaffair you!*—(Gren) 3. (Trin) [By extension] A big, noisy fuss (not necessarily involving trouble). *Naturally, with all that kind of grand zaffaire, little people of Grenada are impressed.*—BoM (77.05.06, p.10) [Fr Cr < Fr *les—affaires* [lezafɛr]] 'business'] □ By misplaced juncture and apocopic loss of /-r/.

za·ga·da (zah-gar·da) *n* 1. (Gren) ‖ GROUND-LIZARD (CarA) 2. (Trin) ‖ WOOD-SLAVE (ECar) [Fr Cr < Fr *lézard gardant* 'watching lizard' by initial misplaced juncture (and analogy with other Fr Cr /z-/ forms)] 3. (Gren) [By extension] An obeahman or obeahwoman. *That's our people, / A calypso people; / This West Indian people. / A people of soucuyant, / Zah-garda and obeah, / Big-drum, Shango / And Kalinda—/ A su-perstitious people.*—ToR (76.05.12, p.7) [De-veloped from the superstitious fear attached to the insidious-looking ZAGADA 2.] 4. (Gren) [By extension] [*AF—Joc*] [Cricket] ‖ GROUND-BALL (CarA) □ Cp ZANDOLI 4.

za·gai [zagaɪ] *n* (Tbgo) A long-handled CUTLASS with a narrow, sometimes curved blade; it is used to cut grass and low-lying bush with a swiping action. [Prob a loan from Fr *zagaie,* SE *assegai, assagai* 'a slender iron-tipped spear' orig from Arabic]

za·ka·cha [zakaš] *n* (Dmca) ‖ ACACIA (TkCa, Trin)

za·mand (zan·mann) [zãman] *n* (Dmca, StLu) ‖ ALMOND (CarA) [Fr Cr < Fr *des—amandes* 'almonds' by misplaced juncture + reduction of final /-CC/]

za·mi(e)[1] [zami] *n* (Crcu, Dmca, Gren, StLu, Trin) [*AF—Derog*] 1. ‖ *zamie-girl* (Trin) A les-bian; a homosexual woman. [Fr Cr < Fr *des—amies* 'friends'. In Fr Cr the phr easily becomes *dé zami* 'two (women-) friends'. A masculine connotation does not seem to apply] 2. PHRASE 2.1 **make zami(e)** *vb phr* (Crcu, Dmca, Gren, StLu, Trin) [*AF—Joc/Derog*] ‖ *zami(e)*[2] (Crcu, Dmca, Gren, StLu, Tbgo, Trin) [Of a woman] To be in sexual relationship with another woman. [A calque from Fr Cr *fè zami* (= Fr 'faire des amies' '?) with same sense]

za·mi(e)[2] [zami] *vb intr* (Crcu, Dmca, Gren, StLu, Tbgo, Trin) [*AF—Joc/Derog*] ‖ MAKE ZA-MI(E) (Crcu, etc) See ZAMI(E)[1] Phr.

za·mi(e)-tess /1ʹ21/ *n* (Trin) [*AF—Derog*] ‖ YARD-WOMAN (Guyn) [ZAMIE[1] + TESS]

za(n)·chwa (zan·chois, za·shwa) [zašwa] *n* (Trin) ‖ ANCHOVY (StLu, Trin) [Fr Cr < Fr *des—anchois* [dezãšwa] 'anchovies' by misplaced juncture]

zan·do·li (zan·do·lee, zann·do·li) /1ʹ12/ *n* (Dmca, Gren, StLu, Trin) ‖ *anole* (Gren, StLu) 1. (Dmca) One of several types of lizard. *Of the lizards, the commonest is the Zandoli which is the only one that changes colour. It may be a moss green or a brown, depending upon its location, and may also change if frightened.... There is another species of lizard, called the Zandoli Clairant be-cause of its shiny skin. Both live off small insects, and the Zandoli Clairant especially frequents houses in search of these.*—HDNPW:12 2. (StLu) A tree-lizard. *In St Lucia most tree-lizards are called 'zandoli'.*—LST:10 3. (Gren, Trin) A fast-moving lizard that lives in holes in the ground. 4. (Trin) [Cricket] ‖ GROUND-BALL 2. (CarA) [BDFC:221 Carib *anaoli* 'a grey lizard almost the length of one's forearm'; hence Fr Cr < Fr *des—anolis* [dezanoli] 'lizards' with misplaced juncture and epenthetic insertion of /-d-/] 5. PHRASE 5.1 **Zandoli find your hole!** *id phr* (Gren, Trin) [*AF—Derog*] See FIND[1] Phr 2.2

There is an 'old time' expression used on the pushy type of person who may have been considered 'out of place', and he was then told 'Zandoli find you hole'.—TrG (73.02.04, p.8)

zan·gi(e) (zan·gé) [zaŋgi ~ zaŋge] *n* (Gren, Trin) An edible fresh-water eel. [Fr Cr < Fr *des—anguilles* [dezãgiy] 'eels' by misplaced juncture]

zan·mann *n* (Jmca, StLu) See ZAMAND.

zan·nan·na (a·na·na) *n* (Dmca, StLu) ‖ PINE-(APPLE) (CarA) [Fr Cr < Fr *des—ananas* [de zanana] 'pineapples', by misplaced juncture. Fr *ananas* < DGEG Guarani *anana* 'pineapple'] □ Pl the same in speech.

zan·té (zan·ter) [zante] *vb intr* (Trin) **1.** [Stick-fighting] To make an aggressive, challenging movement of the body from the hips up, legs bent and apart, meaning to exhibit power and skill. **2.** [By extension] To show off in a grand way. *Everybody is not going to be content with a boundary, some will want to hit a six. You can't expect to give men the basics for the good life and not [expect] there will be many who 'like zante'.*—TaP (75.09.28, p.10)

za·pats *n pl* (Bdos) [*AF*] ‖ ALPARGATAS (CarA) *Jokingly he told the Press: 'I am sorry that I am not wearing zapats or sandals, so you could see for yourself that I have all my toes!'*—SuS (82.04.25, p.1) [< Sp *zapata* 'shoe' with loss of /-a/ by apocope. See ALPARGATAS, SAPATS. Two Sp names *alpargata, zapato* appear to have come into CE, perh from different Latin Amer sources, for the same kind of folk-footwear]

za·shwa *n* (Trin) See ZA(N)CHWA.

za·twap ['zatwap] *n* (Dmca, StLu) ‖ CALABAN (Jmca) [Fr Cr < Fr *les—attrapes* [lez-atrap] by misplaced juncture + regular /r > w/ Fr Cr change]

zèb-a-fanm (z'herbe-à-femme) ['zɛba·fam] /1'12/ *n* **1.** (Gren, Trin) A low bush about one to 2 ft high, with hairy stems and roughly oval-shaped leaves, that bears little clusters of mauve florets; the plant is said to be very effective in treating women's complaints (hence the name); *Ageratum conyzoides* (*Compositae*). **2.** (Dmca) ‖ CARPET-DAISY (Bdos) [Fr Cr < Fr *des—herbe(s)-à-femme* 'woman weed/bush', prob from its reputed use as a folk-medicine 'to clean the womb' after childbirth, or to effect an abortion]

zèb·aj (z'herbage) ['zɛba·ž] *n* (StLu) ‖ CALALU 1. (CarA) [Fr Cr *z'herbage* < Fr *des—herbage(s)* 'green vegetables' by misplaced juncture]

zèb-a-pik (z'herbe-à-pique) ['zɛbapik] /1'12/ *n* (Gren, Trin) ‖ *bitter-bush* 4. (Gren) ‖ *zeb-bapip* (Tbgo, Trin) A shrub about 6 ft high with twelve-inch-long, lance-shaped leaves that make your hand yellow when they are held; it bears clusters of little, tubular, yellow flowers wh, with the leaves, are used to make a bitter 'tea' for the treatment of fevers and menstrual pains; *Neurolaena lobata* (*Compositae-Asteraceae*). [Fr Cr *z'herbe* < Fr *des—herbe(s)*, by misplaced juncture, + *pique* 'lance' (? from shape of leaves), and used as sg]

zeb·ba·pip [zɛbapɪp] /1'12/ *n* (Tbgo, Trin) ‖ ZÈBAPIK (Gren, Trin) [Evid a corruption of the Fr Cr ‖ from *Trin*]

zèb-chat (z'herbe-à-chat) [zɛb(a)šat] /1'12/ *n* (Dmca, Trin) A shrub that can grow 6 ft tall; it has heavily veined, oval-shaped, velvety leaves and bears numerous little clusters of whitish florets on its slender stems; its leaves are used to make a bitter tea wh is said to induce abortion, or ease menstrual pains; *Eupatorium macrophyllum* (*Compositae*). [Fr Cr < Fr *des—herbes à chatte* (? cat-bush) by misplaced juncture and use as sg]

zeb-grass; **zep-grass** [zeb-gra·s] *n* (Dmca, Guyn) ‖ ZÈB-GWA (Dmca) □ In some places this name is applied to three or more varieties of trailing plants of the family *Commelinaceae*. See for ex COCKROACH-GRASS ‖ ‖. This may be due to the co-incidence of Fr Cr *zèb* with the first syllable of the botanical *Zebrina* 'zebra-like' wh refers to the stripes of the ornamental variety.

zèb-gwa (z'herbe grasse) [zɛb gwa ~ zɛb gras] *n* (Dmca) ‖ WATER-GRASS (Bdos, etc) [Fr Cr < Fr *des—herbes grasses* [dezɛbgras] 'fat (i.e. meaty) grass', with misplaced juncture and characteristic Fr Cr /r > w/ shift. Also infl by phonic coincidence of SE 'grass', though the green creeper is not properly a grass. See taxonomy at WATER-GRASS]

zé·pi·na ['zepina·] /1'12/ *n* (Dmca) ‖ CALALU 1. (CarA) [Fr Cr *z'épina(rd)* < Fr *des—épinards* 'spinach' by misplaced juncture]

ze·ri·co·te *n* (Belz) See ZIRICOTE

z'herb·age; **z'herbe-** (compounds) See ZÈBAJ, ZÈB-

z'herbe- See ZÈB-

zi·caque *n* (Dmca, StLu) See ZIKAK

zi·kak (zi·caque, z'i·caque) [zika·k] *n* (Dmca, StLu) ‖ COCO-PLUM 1. (Antg, etc) [Fr Cr < Fr (pl) *des—icaques* [dezika·k] by misplaced juncture and use as sg] □ The name FAT-PORK is also used in *Dmca, StLu.*

zinc (-sheet) *n* (CarA) ‖ GALVANIZE (CarA) □ Similarly **zinc-fence, zinc-roof.**

zi·ri·co·te (si·ri·co·te, zi·ra·co·te, ze·ri·co·te) *n* (Belz) A forest-tree yielding a very hard and heavy wood with sharply contrasting and massive streaks of black, brown, and yellow; it is much favoured for wood-carving; *Cordia dodecandra. She admired the beautiful carving of zericote done by Mr George Gabb.*—AmA (80.03.14, p.11) [< (*SDGA*) Mexican Sp *siricote* 'popular name of a tree of the *anacahuite* family and esp of its fruit'; Aztec *anacahuite* 'fig trees', *Cordia* spp] □ Spellings **siricote, ciricote** also occur

zò·fi (zo(r)·phie) [zɔfi] *n* (Dmca, StLu) ‖ GAR(R) 1. (CarA) [Fr Cr < Fr *des—orphies* [dezɔrfi] 'garfishes' by misplaced juncture]

z'o·range-gros·peau *n* (StLu) See ZOWANJ-GÒSPO

zò·ti (zor·tie) [zɔ·ti] *n* (StLu) ‖ STINGING-NETTLE (Guyn, Trin) [Fr Cr < Fr *des—orties* [dezɔrti] 'nettles' by misplaced juncture]

Zou·ave u·ni·form *n phr* (Bdos) The original ceremonial uniform of the former West India Regiment, consisting of a turban, purple and white coat, velvety blue trousers, and white gaiters; it was retained in some territories and is currently that of the Military Band of the Barbados Regiment. [Fr *Zouave* < *Zwawa*, a Berber people under Fr Colonial rule in 19C, whose bright military uniforms inspired Queen Victoria to command an imperial imitation for wh the British West India Regiment was picked]

zouk[1] [zuk] *n* (ECar) A Caribbean French Creole communal dance and the music for it wh is provided by a band of brasses, drums, electronic guitar and keyboard, with usu two singers and two costumed dancers; the music is vigorously rhythmic, four crotchets to the bar, with bass and singers dominant, and is said to combine features of most other dance music of Caribbean origin. *He describes zouk as the rock of the tropics. Everything that makes people like rock in Europe— the social questioning, the high spirits—all the social aspects of rock can be found in zouk. But rock doesn't make you dance till you fall; zouk, yes.*—Cab, Winter 93/94:10 [Evid a name invented by young people in *Mart* to mean 'an impromptu party', popularized through *Guad*, esp by recordings of the band 'Kassav']

zouk[2] [zuk] *vb intr* (ECar) To dance the ZOUK, esp as a crowd. *The horns take over, full lights on*

the stage; it's time to party, to zouk!—Trin (Ms) [By functional n > vb shift of ZOUK[1]]

zou·ti (zoo·tee, zoo·tie) [zuti] *n* 1. (Dmca, Gren, Trin) The plant also called zòTI in *StLu*. 2. (Trin) A small, twining vine with oblong leaves and inconspicuous flowers; both stems and leaves are covered with stinging hairs; *Tragia volubilis* (*Euphorbiaceae*). *Following recent reports that the cause of the skin rash at Belmont Junior Secondary School has been traced to a nettle locally known as 'Zootie' (botanical name Tragia volubilis), the school yesterday was the scene of beehive activity in preparation for its reopening.*—TrG (81.04.22, p.1) [Fr Cr < zòTI, as in *StLu*, with vowel closure] □ In *Trin* the term STINGING-NETTLE is also used to apply to both senses 1. and 2., the plant and the vine.

zo·wanj-gòs·po (z'o·range-gros·peau, zo·wanj-gòs·po/-bos·ko) [zɔwǎž-gɔspo ~ žɔwǎž-g-] *n* (Dmca, StLu) ‖ SOUR ORANGE (CarA) [Fr Cr < Fr *des-oranges* [dezɔrǎž], 'oranges' with misplaced juncture and characteristic Fr Cr/r > w/shift, + Fr Cr 'gòspo' < Fr *grosse peau* 'coarse skin'; this latter element then > 'bosko' by metathesis among some speakers]

zoy·si·a-grass [zɔɪzia-gra·s] *n* (CarA) A massively thick grass that grows to a carpet-like depth covering the ground entirely; it is used esp for sea-side lawns. [Named after an Austrian botanist. See *OED2*]

Z-pot [zɛd-pɒt] (CarA) [Fishing Ind] A FISH-POT constructed in the shape of a Z, with one funnel at each end.

zug up *vb phr* (Trin) [*AF—Joc*] ‖ **chang-chang** (Gren) To cut (a man's or boy's) hair unevenly (as done by an untrained person).

Z(R)-van [zɛd(ar)-van] *n* (Bdos) A narrow-bodied, ten-foot-long and roughly box-shaped vehicle, used as a passenger PICK-UP, using a flexible route. [Z/ZR from the licence-plate identification for registered (ROUTE-) taxis in *Bdos*]

zwill [zwil] *n* (Gren, Tbgo, Trin) ‖ **raker** (Guyn) A device consisting of one or more razor-blades and/or pieces of sharp-edged tin or glass, fixed on the tail of a kite in order to cut the string of other kites in the air so that they get lost in the wind.

APPENDIX 1

LAYOUT OF STEELBAND

DETAILS OF PAN SURFACES

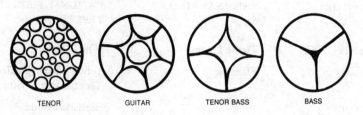

TENOR GUITAR TENOR BASS BASS

TRANSVERSE SECTIONS OF PANS

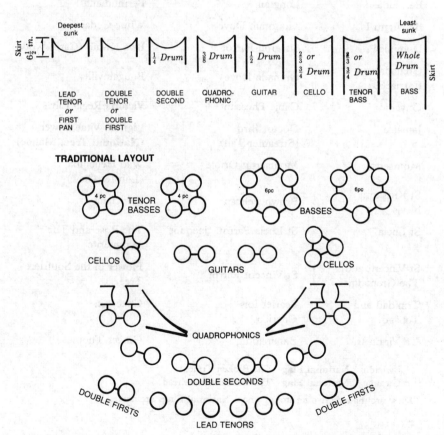

Designed by R. Allsopp ©. Graphics by LRC, UWI, Barbados.

APPENDIX 2

NATIONAL SYMBOLS OF CARIBBEAN STATES

TERRITORY	NATIONAL BIRD	NATIONAL FLOWER/ TREE
Anguilla	Turtle Dove	White Cedar
Bahamas	Flamingo	Yellow Elder (**National Tree**: Lignum Vitae)
Barbados[1]		Barbados Pride
Belize	Keel-billed Toucan	Black Orchid
Bermuda	Longtail	Bermudiana
Br. Virgin Is.	Mountain Dove	White Cedar
Dominica	Sisserou Parrot	Bwa Kwaib (Carib Wood)
Grenada and Carriacou	} Grenada Dove	Bougainvillea
Guyana[2]	Canje Pheasant	Victoria Regia Lily
Jamaica	Doctor Bird (Streamer-Tail)	Lignum Vitae flower (**National Tree**: Mahoe)
Montserrat	Montserrat Oriole	Wild Heliconia (Lobster Claw)
St Kitts and Nevis	} Brown Pelican	Poinciana
St Lucia	St Lucia Parrot, 'Jacquot'	The Rose and The Marguerite
St Vincent and The Grenadines	} St Vincent Parrot	Flower of the Soufriere Tree
Trinidad and Tobago	Scarlet Ibis Cocrico	Chaconia
US Virgin Is.	Bananaquit	Ginger Thomas

[1] Barbados **National Flag**—The Broken Trident
[2] Guyana **National Flag**—The Golden Arrowhead

(These are the only two territories whose **National Flags** are named.)

CITATION CODES FOR BIBLIOGRAPHICAL REFERENCES USED IN THE DICTIONARY

The following is a list of abbreviated codes identifying all sources from which illustrative citations have been taken, and all works of reference cited within glosses, etymological or usage notes. The sources of citation include literary works, newspapers, journals, reports, etc. taken from all the English-speaking West Indian territories covered by this Dictionary. The reader may note, for convenience, that the coding is patterned as follows:

Upper case for books:	ACF	ADAMS, C. Denis
		Caribbean Flora
Upper + lower case for journals:	Aac	*Art & Culture*
Upper + lower + upper for newspapers:	AaT	*Anguilla Times*

Each listing is accompanied by full bibliographical reference as available, and the territory to which the lexicon relates is given in each case, in the last column. Also in the last column, reference works are identified as Ref.

Aac	MITCHELL, Roy (ed.) *Art & Culture*. National Cultural Council.	Trin
AaT	*Anguilla Times*.	Angu
Aaw	*All-ah-wee*. Island Resources Foundation.	USVI
ABB	Prepared by Antigua Teachers. *Antigua and Barbuda Source Book*, 1968.	Antg
ABMOB	ADAMS, C. Denis *The Blue Mahoe & Other Bushes*. Sangsters, 1971.	Jmca
ABSBH	ANDERSON, A. H. *Brief Sketch of British Honduras*. Government Printery, 1958.	Belz
ACF	ADAMS, C. Denis *Caribbean Flora*. London, Thomas Nelson & Sons, 1976.	CarA
ACNT	ANNAMUNTHODO, W., *et al.* (eds) *Calypso '72, with Notes for Tourists*. Unique Services.	Trin
ACPRV	LITTLE, Elbert L., Jr., *et al. Arboles Comunes de Puerto Rico y las Islas Virgenes*. Editorial Universitaria, Univ. de Puerto Rico, 1977.	CarA
ACR	ANTHONY, Michael *Cricket in the Road*. London, Heinemann, 1973.	Trin
ACTT	ANTHONY, Michael and CARR, Andrew *Trinidad & Tobago*. London, André Deutsch, 1975.	Trin
ACWWI	ADAMS, C. D., KASASIAN, L. and SEEYAVE, J. *Common Weeds of the West Indies*. UWI, 1968.	CarA
Ad	Newspaper Advertisement.	
ADF	ALLYN, Rube *Dictionary of Fishes*. 11th edn. Florida, Great Outdoors Pub. Co., 1977.	Ref.

ADFEF	ADZOMADA, Kofi J. *Dictionnaire Français–Ewe, Ewe–Français*, 3rd edn., Togo, 1983.	Ref.
ADHL	ABRAHAM, R. C. *Dictionary of the Hausa Language*. 2nd edn., Univ. of London Pr., 1962.	Ref.
AdM	*Advocate Magazine (Sunday Supplement)*.	Bdos
ADMY	ABRAHAM, R. C. *Dictionary of Modern Yoruba*. Univ. of London Pr., 1958.	Ref.
AdN	*Advocate News*.	Bdos
AdV	*(Barbados) Advocate*.	Bdos
AfF	*Antigua Freedom Fighters*	Antg
AFID	ARMSTRONG, Robert *A comparative Wordlist of Five Igbo Dialects*. Ibadan, Institute of African Studies, 1967.	Ref.
AFPJ	ADAMS, C. Denis *Flowering Plants of Jamaica*. UWI, Mona, 1972.	Jmca
AFSTE	ANTOINE, Judy *French Creole Survivals in Trinidad English*. UWI Caribbean Study Paper, St Augustine.	Trin
AFTF	ANTHONY, Michael *Folk Tales & Fantasies*. Columbus Publishers Ltd., 1976.	Trin
AGDR	ANTHONY, Michael *Green Days by the River*. London, André Deutsch, 1967.	Trin
AGM	ABRAMS, Ovid S. *Guyana Metegee*. Labour Advocate, 1970.	Guyn
AGMCI	ANGOY, Wilton A. *Guyana Man, with Visions of Caribbean Integration*. Barbados, Triumph Pub., 1990.	Guyn
AGTT	ANTHONY, Michael *Glimpses of Trinidad & Tobago*. Columbus Publishers, 1974.	Trin
AGWC	ANTHONY, Michael *The Games Were Coming*. London, Heinemann, 1977.	Trin
AHD	*The American Heritage Dictionary of the English Language*. 2nd edn. New York, American Heritage Pub. Co., 1976.	Ref.
AHFT	ALI, Mehroon *The Hosein Festival in Trinidad*. Caribbean Study Paper, UWI, St Augustine.	Trin
AHID	ATWOOD, Thomas *The History of the Island of Dominica*. London, J. Johnson, 1791, Rep. Frank Cass, 1971.	Dmca
AHR	ABRAHAMS, Robert D. *Humphrey's Ride*. London, Routledge & Kegan Paul, 1964.	Nevs
AKM	ANTHONY, Michael *King of the Masquerade*. London, Thomas Nelson & Sons, 1974.	Trin
ALDC	HORNBY, A. S. *Oxford Advanced Learner's Dictionary of Current English*. New edn., OUP, 1974.	Ref.
AmA	*Amandala*.	Belz
AMAM	ANNAMUNTHODO, W. *Malik Accused—Murder!*. Unique Services, 1972.	Trin
AMEWF	ADAMS, V. *An Introduction to Modern English Word-Formation*. London, Longman, 1973.	Ref.
AMGM	ANNAMUNTHODO, W. *Malik Guilty—Murder*. Unique Services, 1972.	Trin

AMT	ALKINS, M. E. *The Mammals of Trinidad*. Occasional Paper No. 2. Dept. of Zoology, UWI, St Augustine, 1979.	Trin
AMWWI	ABRAHAMS, Roger, D. *The Man-of-Words in the West Indies*. Baltimore, Johns Hopkins, 1983.	CarA
AnS	*Antigua Star*.	Antg
AnT	*Antigua Times*.	Antg
AOAP	ALLADIN, M. P. *3 One-Act Plays*. M. P. Alladin, n.d.	Trin
APOD	JOHNSTON, Grahame (ed.) *The Australian Pocket Oxford Dictionary*. OUP, 1976.	Ref.
APPJ	ADAMS, D., *et al. Poisonous Plants in Jamaica*. No. 2. Extra-Mural Dept., UWI, 1963.	Jmca
APT	ANTHONY, Michael *Profile Trinidad*. London, Macmillan, 1975.	Trin
AQS	AGARD, John *Quetzy as Saviour*. Guyana National Pub. Centre, 1976.	Guyn
ARE	ANNAMUNTHODO, W., *et al. Calypso Revue '71*. Unique Services.	Trin
ARJC	ALLEYNE, M. C. *Roots of Jamaican Culture*. London, Pento Press, 1988.	Jmca
ASBT	ANTHONY, Mavis *Speech Band in Tobago*. Caribbean Study paper, UWI, St Augustine, 1973.	Trin
ASE	ATTEMA, Ypie *St. Eustatius*. De Walburg Pers Zutphen, 1976.	ViIs
ASFC	ADEY, Philip *Sugar from Cane*. London, Longman, 1974.	CarA
ASG	APPLE, Arnold *Son of Guyana*. OUP, 1973.	Guyn
ASOB	ALBURY, Paul *The Story of The Bahamas*. London, Macmillan, 1975.	Baha
ASOC	ANTHONY, Michael *Streets of Conflict*. London, André Deutsch, 1976.	Trin
ATTC	ANNAMUNTHODO, W. *Trinidad & Tobago Carnival '69*. Signs of the Time.	Trin
AVB	*Authorised Version of the Bible* (1611).	Ref.
AYSF	ANTHONY, Michael *The Year in San Fernando*. London, André Deutsch, 1965.	Trin
AZQG	ATTENBOROUGH, David *Zoo Quest to Guiana*. London, Pan Books, 1958.	Guyn
B	Broadcast—radio or television.	
BAED	BENNETT, John P. *An Arawak-English Dictionary*. Georgetown, Walter Roth Museum, 1989.	Guyn
Baj	McKENZIE, C., READER, Gwen, *et al.* (eds.) *The Bajan*. Bridgetown, Carib. Pub. Co. Ltd., and Island Press.	Bdos
Balp	*Bulletin of the Amerindian Languages Project*. Univ. of Guyana.	Guyn
BaV	*The Barbuda Voice*.	Brbu

BaW	*Bajan Woman.* Bridgetown, 1976/1977.	Bdos
BBCWD	BROWNE, Marva and BROWNE, Vernon McD. *A Catta Full of West Indian Dishes.* St John, Caribbean Gifts, 1973.	CarA
BBIP	BROWN, Raymond W. *Bahamas in Poetry.* R. W. Brown.	Baha
BBPP	BROWN, Raymond W. *Bahamas in Poetry & Prose.* R. W. Brown.	Baha
BBR	BROWN, Raymond W. *Bahamas Ramblings.* R. W. Brown.	Baha
BBTT	BARCANT, Malcolm *Butterflies of Trinidad & Tobago.* London, Collins, 1970.	Trin
BBWI	BOND, James *Birds of the West Indies.* 3rd edn., London, Collins, 1974.	CarA
BC	BAPTISTE, Owen *Crisis.* Imprint Caribbean, 1976.	Trin
BCO	BRATHWAITHE, E. Kamau *Contradictory Omens.* (Monograph No. 1) Kingston, Savacou Pub., 1974.	CarA
BCOC	BAIN, Francis J. *A Child of the Carnival.* Unique Services, 1974.	Trin
BCS	BAPTISTE, Owen (ed.) *Caribbean Schooldays.* Imprint Caribbean, 1975.	Trin
BCSJ	BRATHWAITE, E. Kamau *The Development of Creole Society in Jamaica, 1770–1820.* OUP, 1971.	Jmca
BDFC	BRETON, Raymond *Dictionnaire Français-Caraïbe.* Rep. Leipzig, B. G. Teubner, 1900, orig. Auxerre, 1666.	CarA
BdN	*Barbados Daily News.* Bridgetown	Bdos
BDNE 1	BARNHART, C. L., *et al. The Barnhart Dictionary of New English.* Bronxville, NY, Barnhart/Harper & Row, 1973.	Ref.
BDNE 2	BARNHART, C. L., *et al. The Second Dictionary of New English.* Bronxville, NY, Barnhart Books, 1980.	Ref.
BDTM	BURNHAM, Forbes, C. A. NASCIMENTO & R. A. BURROWES (eds.) *A Destiny to Mould.* Longman Caribbean, 1970.	Guyn
BeA(BE)	*The Beacon.* Belize.	Belz
BeA(BS)	*The Beacon.* Bridgetown.	Bdos
BeA(TO)	*The Beacon.* Scarborough.	Tbgo
BeB	*Belize Billboard.* Belize.	Belz
BeS	*The Bermuda Sun.*	Berm
Bes	*Belizean Studies.* Belize Institute of Social Research and Action.	Belz
BeT	*The Belize Times.*	Belz
Bet	*Belize Today.* Eugene Morrison.	Belz
BEW	*Ten Bruggencate Engels Woordenboek,* Vols. 1 and 2. Groningen, Netherlands, 1970.	Ref.
BFAC	BOND, Mary Wickham *Far Afield in the Caribbean.* Wynnewood, P., Livingstone Pub., 1971.	CarA
BFTT	BROOKS, R. L. *Forest Types of Trinidad and their Principal Species.* Government Printing Office 1934.	Trin

BGPS	BRATHWAITE, P. A. *Guyanese Proverbs & Stories*. 1966	Guyn
BGS	BARTEAUX, M. C. *Grandmother's Stories. [From the Sugarcane Island of Barbados]* M. C. Barteaux, 1964/1980.	Bdos
BGSB	BENNETT, Alvin *God, The Stone Breaker*. London, Heinemann, 1974.	Jmca
BGWGJS	BURKE, Eddie and GARSIDE, Anne *Water in the Gourd & Other Jamaican Folk Stories*. OUP, 1975.	Jmca
BHCBG	BRONKHURST, Revd. H. V. P. *Among the Hindus and Creoles of British Guiana*. London, Woolmer, 1888.	Guyn
BHOV	BRATHWAITE, E. Kamau *History of the Voice*. London, New Beacon, 1984.	CarA
Bim	COLLYMORE, F., *et al.* (eds.) *Bim*. Bridgetown.	Bdos
BINSD	BRYANT, Joshua *Account of an Insurrection of Negro Slaves in the Colony of Demerara which broke out 18th August, 1823*. Demerara, 1824.	Guyn
BJL	BENNETT, Louise *Jamaica Labrish*. Sangster, 1966.	Jmca
BL	BROWN, John (ed.) *Leewards*. Extra-Mural Dept., UCWI, Barbados, 1961.	CarA
BMBH	*Bush Medicine—A Story of Belizean Herbs and Barks*. Pub. Government Information Services. 1983.	Belz
BMP	BRATHWAITE, E. Kamau *Mother Poem*. OUP, 1977.	Bdos
BOBB	BROWNE, Katherine J. *Out of the Blue and Blues*. Katherine Browne, 1975.	Belz
BOE	BRATHWAITE, E. Kamau *Other Exiles*. OUP, 1975.	CarA
BoM	*The Bomb*. Port of Spain.	Trin
BPS	BRATHWAITE, E. R. *Paid Servant*. London, New English Library, 1973.	CarA
Bru	*Brukdown*. Brukdown Publications.	Belz
BSCEGE	BROWN, P. P. and SCRAGG, J. *Common Errors in Gold Coast English*. London, Macmillan, 1948.	Ref.
BSCG	BLACKMAN, Marjorie *A Supplement to Frank Collymore's Glossary of Words & Phrases of Barbadian Dialect*. Caribbean Study Paper UWI, Cave Hill, 1966.	Bdos
BSNW	BASCOMBE, William *Shango in the New World*. New York, Holt Rinehart, 1969.	CarA
BsT	*Belize Sunday Times*.	Belz
BTA	BRATHWAITE, E. Kamau *The Arrivants*. OUP, 1973.	CarA
BTCI	BLUME, Helmut *The Caribbean Islands*. London, Longman, 1974.	CarA
BTOJ	BLACK, Clinton V. *Tales of Old Jamaica*. London, Collins, 1966.	Jmca
BTP	BEST, Lloyd *Tapia Pamphlet*. 1970.	Trin
BTR	BARRETT, Leonard E. *The Rastafarians*. Sangsters, 1977/1979.	Jmca
BTTB	BEDDOE, I. B. *Trinidad, Tobago and Beyond. (A Social & Economic Geography)*. Longman Caribbean, 1970/1979.	Trin

BTTTT	BROOKS, R. L. *The More Important Timber Trees of Trinidad & Tobago.* Trinidad Government Printing Office, 1936.	Trin
Bvi	*B.V. Islander.* B. V. I. Publishing Co.	BrVi
BWIP	BAUGH, Edward *West Indian Peotry.* Savacou Pub.	CarA
BWISB	BURGIE, Irving *West Indian Song Book.* Caribe Music Corp.	CarA
BYBB	BREMAN, Paul (ed.) *You Better Believe It.* Penguin, 1973.	CarA
BYCK	BRODBER, Erna *A Study of yards in the City of Kingston*—ISER Working Paper, No. 9, UWI, Mona, 1975.	Jmca
Caa	KOSSACK, Ellie (ed.) *Carib America.* St Croix, Antilles Pub., Inc.	CarA
CaC	*Caribbean Contact.* Bridgetown.	CarA
Cac	ROBERTS, Nathaniel (ed.) *Carnival & Calypso.* Quick Service Printing, 1971.	Trin
Cad	*Caribbean Digest.* Barbados, Horizons Publishing and Publicity House.	CarA
Cai	*Caribbean Issues.* Extra-Mural Studies, UWI, St Augustine.	CarA
Cam	*Camboulay.* Trinidad, Swank Publications.	Trin
Caq	*Caribbean Quarterly.* UWI, Mona, Jamaica.	CarA
Car	*Carib.* West Indies Assoc. of Commonwealth Literature & Language. UWI, Mona, Jamaica.	CarA
CaS	*Catholic Standard.* Georgetown.	Guyn
CAST	CURTIN, P. D. *The Altantic Slave Trade.* Madison, Univ. of Wisconsin, 1969.	CarA
Cat	*Caribbean Tempo.* Trinidad, Key Caribbean Publications.	CarA
Cav	*Cavite.* Guild Press, UWI, Barbados	CarA
Cay	*The Caymanian Compass.*	CayI
CBCD	CRAVEN, H. and BARFIELD, J. *English–Congo & Congo–English Dictionary.* London, 1883.	Ref.
CBGB	CLEARE, L. D. *British Guiana: Birds.* Georgetown, Daily Chronicle, 1962.	Guyn
CBL	CURRY, Robert A. *Bahamian Lore.* Paris, Privately Printed, 1930.	Baha
CBLL	CONINGSBY, F. C. *Bahamian Land Law. Its Development and Divergence from English Law* (Thesis, 1964). UWI Law Library.	Baha
CBM	CAREW, Jan *Black Midas.* Longman Caribbean 1969/1975.	Guyn
CBT	CRUICKSHANK, J. G. *Black Talk.* Demerara, Argosy Co., 1916.	Guyn
CCD	CAYETANO, E. Roy *Chuluha Dan.* Belize, Stencilled MS, 1977.	Belz

Ccn	SHEPPARD, Jill (ed.) *Caribbean Conservation News.* Barbados, Caribbean Conservation Association.	CarA
CCSI	CUMMINS, Willis *Calypsoes, Symphonies and Incest.* Toronto, Arawak Pub. House, 1974.	CarA
CDES	PHYTHIAN, Brian *A Concise Dictionary of English Slang.* London, Hodder & Stoughton, 1976.	Ref.
CDID	COULLS, F. L. *Down In Demerara.* London, 1944.	Guyn
CED	*Collins English Dictionary.* London, Collins, 1979.	Ref.
Ceg	*Carifta Expo '69 in Grenada.* Carifta Expo Office, 1969.	Gren
CEI	CUMMINS, Leslie P. (ed.) *Essequibo Islands.* Dept. of Geography, Univ. of Guyana, 1973.	Guyn
CELW	CORBIN, Cicely *A Study of the English of Local Writers in the Advocate Newspaper.* Caribbean Study Paper, UWI, Cave Hill, 1966.	Bdos
CFMG	CAMPBELL, John *Famous Murder Stories of Guyana.* Labour Advocate, 1980.	Guyn
CGAF	CHRISTALLER, Revd. J. G. *A Grammar of the Asante & Fante Language Called Twi.* Basel, 1875 (Gregg Press rep.)	Ref.
CGBD	COLLYMORE, Frank A. *Notes for a Glossary of Barbadian Dialect.* 4th edn., 1970; 5th edn. 1976. Bridgetown. Barbados National Trust.	Bdos
Chg	*The Cayman Islands Holiday Guide.* Norwester Publication.	CayI
CHMC	CALLENDER, Timothy *How Music Came to the Ainchan People.* Coles Printery, 1979.	Bdos
CHOB	CRATON, Michael *A History of The Bahamas.* London, Collins, 1962/1973.	Baha
CHTUG	CHASE, Ashton *A History of Trade Unionism in Guyana 1900–1961.* New Guyana Co., 1964.	Guyn
CHWP 3	CARTER, E. H., *et al. History of the West Indian People. Book 3.* London, Thomas Nelson & Sons, 1954/1974.	CarA
CHWP 4	CARTER, E. H., *et al. History of the West Indian People. Book 4.* London, Thomas Nelson & Sons, 1954/1974.	CarA
CISH	CALLENDER, Timothy *It so Happen.* Belfast, Christian Journals, 1975.	Bdos
CKAC	CRAHAN, Margaret E. and KNIGHT, Franklin W. *Africa & The Caribbean.* Baltimore, Johns Hopkins, 1979.	Ref.
CKOC	CHEN, Willi *King of the Carnival.* Hertford, Hansib Publishing, 1988.	Trin
CLSFC	COMITAS, Lambros and LOWENTHAL, David *Slaves, Freemen, Citizens.* New York, Anchor Books, 1973.	CarA
CLWFL	COMITAS, Lambros and LOWENTHAL, David *Work and Family Life.* New York, Anchor Books, 1973.	CarA
CNH	CRUICKSHANK, J. G. *Negro Humour.* Demerara, Argosy Co., 1905.	Guyn
COBH	CAMPBELL, P. F. *An Outline of Barbados History.* Caribbean Graphics, 1974.	Bdos

COD 6,7,8	*Concise Oxford Dictionary* 6th, 7th, 8th edns., OUP, 1976, 1982, 1990.	Ref.
Col	MARCH, Michael, *et al.* (eds.) *Caripol.* UWI, Barbados.	CarA
Com	Combermere School *The Combermerian*, Bridgetown.	Bdos
Cotgrave	COTGRAVE, Randle *A Dictionarie of the French and English Tongues.* London, 1611.	Ref.
Cov	*Covicrier.* College of the Virgin Islands.	USVI
COYN	CAMPBELL, John *Obeah. Yes or No.* Labour Advocate, 1976.	Guyn
CPLC	CUTHBERT, Marlene and PIDGEON, M. W. *Language and Communication.* Bridgetown, Cedar Press. 2nd edn. 1979, 3rd edn. 1981.	CarA
CPM	CLARKE, Austin *The Prime Minister.* London, Routledge & Kegan Paul, 1978.	Bdos
CPR	CARTER, Martin *Poems of Resistance.* Univ. of Guyana, 1966. (Lawrence & Wishart, 1954).	Guyn
CPS	CARTER, Martin *Poems of Succession.* London, New Beacon Books, 1977.	Guyn
CR	*(Magistrate's or Supreme) Court Record.*	
CRDOS	CAMPBELL, Hazel D. *The Rag Doll & Other Stories.* Kingston, Savacou Publications, 1978.	Jmca
CRFD	COLLINS and ROBERT *French Dictionary,* 2nd edn. Glasgow/Paris, William Collins Sons & Co. & Dictionnaires le Robert, 1988.	Ref.
CrU	*The Crusader.*	StLu
CSD	ROBINSON, M. (ed.) *The Concise Scots Dictionary.* Aberdeen Univ. Pr., 1985.	Ref.
CSESD	SMITH, Colin, *et al. Spanish–English, English–Spanish Dictionary,* 2nd edn. Glasgow, Ediciones Grijalba & Collins Publishers (William Collins Sons & Co.), 1988.	Ref.
CSFWG	CHAPLIN, C. G. and SCOTT, Peter *Fish Watchers' Guide.* Library of Congress, 1972.	CarA
Cso	*Calypso* (+ Author)	
Csp	*Caribbean Study Paper.* Faculty of Arts & General Studies (UWI) + Author + Date.	CarA
CSP	CARTER, Martin *Selected Poems.* Georgetown, Demerara Publishers, 1989.	Guyn
Cta	NETTLES, Victor F. *Important Root and Tuber Crops of Tropical America.* Vol. 8, No. 4. Center for Tropical Agriculture, 1974.	Ref.
CTCD	MACDONALD, A. M. (ed.) *Chambers Twentieth Century Dictionary.* New edn., 1974.	Ref.
CTOY	COZIER, E. L. *Topics of Yesteryear.* Public Relations Associates (Caribbean) Ltd., 1975.	Bdos
CTT	CAMERON, Norman E. *The Trumpet—A Play in Three Acts.* Demerara, Norma Cameron, 1969.	Guyn
CWFYS	CLARKE, Austin *When He Was Free and Young and Used to Wear Silks.* House of Anansi Press, 1971.	Bdos

CWIC	CLARK, Phyllis E. *West Indian Cookery.* 15th edn., London, Thomas Nelson & Sons, 1945/1972.	CarA
CWSP	CROSS, Malcolm *West Indian School Problems.* Trinidad, Columbus Publishers, 1970.	CarA
CWT	CAMPBELL, Hazel D. *Woman's Tongue.* Kingston, Savacou Pub., 1985.	Jmca
CzN	*The Guyana Citizen.* Georgetown.	Guyn
DaA	*Daily Argosy.* Georgetown.	Guyn
DAAD	DAVIS, A. R. *The Autobiography of Arthur R. Davis, A Patriot of Guyana.* Georgetown, 1980.	Guyn
DAC	WILKES, G. A. *A Dictionary of Australian Colloquialisms.* Routledge & Kegan Paul, 1978.	Ref.
DaC	*Daily Chronicle.* Georgetown.	Guyn
DAE	CRAIGIE, Sir William and HULBERT, James R. *Dictionary of American English.* Chicago, Univ. of Chicago Pr., 1938.	Ref.
DAFG	DeBOER, Bart, *et al. Antillean Fish Guide.* Aruba, National Parks Foundation, 1973.	Neth
DAFL	CHRISTALLER, Revd. J. G. *Dictionary of the Asante & Fante Language called Tshi (Twi).* Basel, 1933.	Ref.
DaG	*The Daily Gleaner; The Sunday Gleaner.* Kingston.	Jmca
DaM	*Daily Mirror.* Port of Spain.	Trin
DaN(Ja)	*The Daily News* (Jamaica). Kingston.	Jmca
DaN(ST)	*The Daily News* (St Thomas).	USVI
DARE	CASSIDY, F. G. (Chief Ed.) *Dictionary of American Regional English.* Harvard, Belknap Press, 1985.	Ref.
DAS	WENTWORTH, H. and FLEXNER, S. B. *Dictionary of American Slang—Second Supplemented Edition.* New York, Thomas Crowell, 1975.	Ref.
DBE	HOLM, J. and SHILLING, A. W. *Dictionary of Bahamian English.* New York, Lexik House, 1982.	Baha
DBGSV	DEVAS, Raymond P. *Birds of Grenada, St. Vincent & The Grenadines.* Carenage Press, 1970.	Gren
DBGT	DANKS, F. S. *Notes on British Guiana Timbers.* Georgetown, Daily Chronicle, 1945.	Guyn
DBH	DUPUCH, Etienne (Jr.) *Bahamas Handbook.* Etienne Dupuch Jr. Pub. 1975–6.	Baha
DBMM	DALRYMPLE, Henderson *Bob Marley, Music, Myth & The Rastas.* Sunbury, Middx., Carib-Arawak Pub., 1976.	Jmca
DBPD	DIEDERICH, Bernard and BURT, Al *Papa Doc.* Penguin Books, 1969/1972.	Hait
DC	DRAYTON, Geoffrey *Christopher.* London, Heinemann, 1972.	Bdos
DCC	DAVID, Christine *Carriacou Culture.* MS, 1972.	Crcu
DCF	POULLET H., *et al. Dictionnaire Créole Français.* Fort-de-France, Hatier-Antilles, 1984.	Guad
DCHP	*A Dictionary of Canadianisms on Historical Principles.* Toronto, W. J. Gage, 1967.	Ref.

DCP	PARTRIDGE, Eric *A Dictionary of Catch Phrases.* London, Routledge, 1977/1978.	Ref.
DECG	POULLET, Hector, *et al. Dictionnaire des Expressions du Créole Guadeloupéen* Fort-de-France, Hatier, 1984.	Ref.
DEIST	DICKSON, Sherill *The Evolution & Subsequent impact of the Steelband on the Society of Trinidad.* Caribbean Study Paper, UWI, St Augustine.	Trin
DELF	DAUZAT, A. *Dictionnaire Etymologique de la langue française.* Paris, Larousse, 1938.	Ref.
DELMP	D'COSTA, Jean *Escape to Last Man Peak.* Longman Caribbean, 1975.	Jmca
DeM(Bs)	*The Democrat.* Bridgetown.	Bdos
DeM(SK)	*The Democrat.* Basseterre.	StKt
DFAF	*Dictionnaire Français-Anglais, Anglais-Français,* 6th edn., Paris, Librairie Larousse, 1968.	Ref.
DFOC	DAVID, Christine *Folklore of Carriacou.* Bridgetown, Coles Printery, 1985.	Crcu
DGEG	PERALTA, A. J. and OSUNA, Thomas *Diccionario Guarani- Espanōl y Espanōl- Guarani.* Buenos Aires, Tupa, 1950.	Ref.
DGF	SEYMOUR, A. J. *Dictionary of Guyanese Folklore.* National Arts Council, 1975.	Guyn
DHBVI	DOOKHAN, Isaac *A History of the BVI.* Caribbean Universities Pr. Epping, Essex, Bowker Pub. Co. 1975.	BrVi
DHGP	DALY, Vere T. *A Short History of the Guyanese People.* London, Macmillan, 1975.	Guyn
DHOB	DOBSON, Narda *A History of Belize.* Longman Caribbean 1973/1977.	Belz
DHVUS	DOOKHAN, Isaac *A History of the Virgin Islands of the United States.* Caribbean Universities Pr. Epping, Essex, Bowker Pub. Co. 1974.	USVI
Did	*Dies Dominica.* Public Relations Office, 1967.	Dmca
DJC	DeLISSER, H. G. *Jane's Career.* London, Heinemann, 1914/1972.	Jmca
DJE	CASSIDY, F. G. and LePAGE, R. B. *Dictionary of Jamaican English.* Cambridge Univ. Pr., 1967, 2nd edn. 1980.	Jmca
DJPVP	D'COSTA, Jean *Jamaican Patois Vocabulary & Phraseology.* J. D'Costa, 1979.	Jmca
DLDLT	De VERTEUIL, Anthony *Sir Louis de Verteuil and his Life & Times.* Columbus Publishers, 1973.	Trin
DLLDA	DAVIS, E. *Language & Literature. (Dic. of Antiguan Words)* MS, 1973.	Antg
DLOG	DAKUBU, M. E. K. *The Languages of Ghana.* London, Kegan Paul, 1988.	Ref.
DLVIE	D'COSTA, J. and LALLA, B. *Voices in Exile.* Univ. of Alabama Press, 1989.	Jmca

DMEI	WARMAN, Adolpho I. V. *Diccionario Trilingue: Miskito-Espanōl-Inglés*. Nicaragua, 1962.	Ref.
DMG	DALY, Vere T. *The Making of Guyana*. London, Macmillan, 1974.	Guyn
DMM	DYER, Patrick *Manie the Manicou*. London, Macmillan, 1975.	Trin
DMMGT	DYER, Patrick *Manie The Manicou Goes Travelling*. London, Macmillan, 1975.	Trin
DMRC	DWARIKI, N. J. *Certificate Level Map Reading for the Caribbean*. Macmillan, 1977.	CarA
DNE	STORY, G. M., KIRWIN, W. J. and WIDDOWSON, J. D. A., (eds.) *Dictionary of Newfoundland English*. University of Toronto Press, 1982.	Ref.
DoC	*The Dominica Chronicle*. Roseau.	Dmca
DoH	*The Dominica Herald*. Roseau.	Dmca
DP	DORANT, St. Clair W. *Panyard*. St. Clair Dorant. 1974.	Trin
DRR	DALY, P. H. *Revolution to Republic*. P. H. Daly, 1970.	Guyn
DSAE 2	BRANFORD, Jean (ed.) *A Dictionary of South African English*. OUP, 1978. 2nd edn. 1980.	Ref.
DSJS	DUPUCH, G. L. *Smoky Joe Says—A Volume in Bahamian Dialect*. Nassau Daily Tribune, 1936.	Baha
DSLHS	DEVAUX, Robert J. *Saint Lucia Historic Sites*. St Lucia National Trust, 1975.	StLu
DSLK	HANCOCK, Ian F. *Dictionary of Sierra Leone Krio*. London, I. Hancock, 1970.	Ref.
DSM	D'COSTA, Jean *Sprat Morrison*. Ministry of Education, 1977.	Jmca
DSUE 1	PARTRIDGE, E. *A Dictionary of Slang and Unconventional English*. Vol. 1. 4th edn., London, Routledge & Kegan Paul, 1951.	Ref.
DSUE 2	PARTRIDGE, E. *A Dictionary of Slang and Unconventional English*. Vol. 2. 6th edn., London, Routledge & Kegan Paul, 1967.	Ref.
DTOC	DaBREO, D. Sinclair *This is our Caribbean*. M.A.P.S., 1976.	StLu
DUDG	DEVAS, Raymond *Uphill and Down Dale in Grenada*. The Grenada Guardian Ltd. & Sands & Co., 1926.	Gren
DWPU	DIJKHOFF, M. *Dikshonario Woordenboek Papiamentu—Ulandes*. Amsterdam, De Walburg Pers, 1980.	Neth
DWSN	DONSELAAR, J. van *Woordenboek van het Surinaams-Nederlands*. Utrecht, 1976.	Srnm
DYP	DELANO, Isaac D. *Yoruba Proverbs—Their Meaning and Usage*. OUP, 1966.	Ref.
EBL	EDGELL, Zee *Beka Lamb*. London, Heineman, 1982.	Belz
EBN	EMANUEL, Lezmore E. *Broo 'Nansi*. General Learning Corp., 1973/74.	USVI

EBT	ENEAS, Cleveland W. *Bain Town*. Timpaul Pub. Co., 1976.	Baha
EDD	WRIGHT, Joseph *The English Dialect Dictionary*. OUP, 1898.	Ref.
EDWLG	EDWARDS, W. F. (ed.) *A Short Dictionary of the Warau Language of Guyana*. Univ. of Guyana, 1980.	Guyn
EFLBB	ELCOCK, Ordene *Folk Labels for Behaviour & Attitudes in Barbados*. Caribbean Study Paper, UWI, Cave Hill, 1973.	Bdos
EFOT	ELDER, J. D. *Folksongs of Tobago*. (unpub. MS), 1977.	Tbgo
EFSLC	ELDER, J. D. *Folk Song & Folk Life in Charlotteville*. Universal Printing Products. Port of Spain, 1971.	Tbgo
EIAA	EDWARDS, W. (ed.) *An Introduction to the Akawaio and Arekuna Peoples of Guyana*. Univ. of Guyana, 1977.	Guyn
EILCA	EDWARDS, W. F. (ed.) *A Brief Introduction to some Aspects of the Language & Culture of Guyana Arawak (Lokono)*. Univ. of Guyana, 1980.	Guyn
ELJF	ELLIS, Phyllis *A list of Jamaican Fruits with Scientific Names*. Jamaica, Min. of Agriculture Information Bulletin No. 1, May 1984.	Jmca
EMG	EDWARDS, Adolph *Marcus Garvey*. London, New Beacon Books, 1967/1972.	Jmca
EMRP	ELDER, J. D. *Ma Rose Point*. National Cultural Council of Trinidad and Tobago, Port of Spain, 1972.	Tbgo
EOCT	EGGLESTON, George T. *Orchids on the Calabash Tree*. London, Frederic Muller, 1963/1970.	StLu
ESGTT	ELDER, J. D. *Song Games of Trinidad & Tobago*. Port of Spain, Community Education Centre, 1961.	Trin
ETC	EVANS, Lancelot O., *et al. The Caribbean*. Sterling Press Co. Inc., 1968/1971.	CarA
EtF	*Ethnic Folkways*. 1956.	USA
EvN	*Evening News*. Port of Spain.	Trin
EvP	*Evening Post*. Georgetown.	Guyn
ExP	*Express*. Port of Spain.	Trin
FAZB	FRASER H., CARRINGTON, S., FORDE, A. and GILMORE, J. *A–Z of Barbadian Heritage*. Kingston, Heinemann Caribbean, 1990.	Bdos
FBGMFP	FANSHAWE, D. B. *Forest Products of British Guiana II: Minor Forest Products*. Br. Guiana Forest Dept., 1950.	Guyn
FBGPT	FANSHAWE, D. B. *Forest Products of British Guiana I: Principal Timbers*. 3rd edn., Br. Guiana Forest Dept., 1961.	Guyn
FCGB	FURLEY, P. A. and CROSBIE, A. J. *Geography of Belize*. London, Collins, 1974.	Belz
FCPMR	FEDON Publishers *Carriacou & Petite Martinique in the Mainstream of the Revolution*. Grenada, Ministry of Education, 1982.	Grns

FCR	FRANKLYN, John Hope *Color & Race*. Boston, Beacon Press, 1969.	CarA
FCV 1	FIGUEROA, John *Caribbean Voices*. Vol. 1. London, Evans Brothers, 1966.	CarA
FCV 2	FIGUEROA, John *Caribbean Voices*. Vol. 2. London, Evans Brothers, 1970.	CarA
FDA	FERGUS, H. A. *Dreams of Alliouagana*. Montserrat, University Centre, 1974.	Mrat
FDI	FULLER, Bob *Duppies Is*. Cayman Authors Ltd., 1967.	CayI
FETOC	FORDE, D. (ed.) *Efik Traders of Old Calabar*. OUP, 1956.	Ref.
FFPG	FANSHAWE, D. B. *Forest Products of Br. Guiana*. Br. Guiana Forest Dept., 1950.	Guyn
FFPRC	FRIEDMAN, Anthony *Flower-Full Puerto Rico & the Caribbean*. Puerto Rico, Caribe Tourist Promotions Inc., n.d.	CarA
FGBTT	ffRENCH, Richard *A Guide to the Birds of Trinidad & Tobago*. Pennsylvania, Asa Wright Nature Centre, 1976.	Trin
FGSN	FONER, Laura and GENOVESE, Eugene D. *Slavery in the New World*. NJ, Prentice Hall, 1969.	CarA
FGSOS	FERGUS, H. A. and GRELL, V. J. *The Seagull & Other Stories*. Montserrat, Alliouagana Commune, 1976.	Mrat
FHA	FERGUS, Howard A. *History of Alliouagana*. Montserrat, University Centre, 1975.	Mrat
FHB	FRANK, Clive A. *History of Begos—The Grenadines*. Bridgetown, Consultant Sales and Marketing, 1976.	StVn
FMEI	FERGUS, Howard A. *Montserrat, Emerald Isle of the Caribbean*. Macmillan Caribbean, 1983.	Mrat
FNEW	FOCKE, Hendrick C. *Neger-Engelsch Woordenboek*. Leiden, Van Den Heuvell, 1855.	Srnm
FNOD	FRANCIS, C. W. *Notes on Dialect*. Grenada, unpub. Ms, n.d.	Gren
FNRD	FRASER, Carmeta *National Recipe Directory*. Bridgetown, Dalton Enterprises, c.1970.	Bdos
Foc	*Focus on Jamaica*. Focus on Jamaica Ltd.	Jmca
FSWLC	FRANKLYN, Francis *A Study of W.I. Language as used in the Calypso*. Caribbean Study Paper, UWI	CarA
FTCC	FARABEE, N. C. *The Central Caribs* Vol. 10, Univ. of Pennsylvania, Anthropological Pub., 1924.	Ref.
FTOT	FORDE, A. N. *Talk of the Tamarinds*. London, Edward Arnold, 1971.	CarA
FTT	FERMOR, Patrick Leigh *The Traveller's Tree*. John Murray, 1950/1968.	CarA
Fwi	*Free West Indian*. St. George's.	Gren
GA 1	GRAY, Cecil *Ambakaila* Book 1. London, Thomas Nelson & Sons, 1976.	CarA
GB	GILL, Pat *Buddhoe*. New York, Wentworth Press, 1976.	USVI

GBB	GONZALES, A. E. *The Black Border—Gullah Stories of the Carolina Coast*. Columbia, SC, 1922.	Gull
GBFBM	GLADWELL, Joyce *Brown Face, Big Master*. London, Inter-Varsity Press, 1969.	Jmca
GBL	GIBSON, Charles *The Black Legend*. New York, Alfred Knopf, 1971.	CarA
GBWISL	GOVEIA, E. V. and BARTLETT, C. J. *The West Indian Slave Laws of the 18th Century*. Caribbean Universities Press, 1970.	CarA
GC	GILKES, Michael *Couvade*. Longman Caribbean, 1974.	Guyn
GCBCD	GRANT, Lowell and CARTWRIGHT, Joe *Bahamas Cook and Drink Book*. Belmont, Ca., Star Publishing Co., 1971.	Baha
GCD	GAMBLE, Alan *Chanté Dominitjen—Folk Songs of Dominica*. The Dominica Institute, 1986.	Dmca
GDAA	EDWARDS, W. F., *et al*. *A Short Grammar & Dictionary of the Akawaio & Arekuna Languages of Guyana*. Univ. of Guyana, 1980.	Guyn
GDEL	GOLDIE, Revd. H. *Dictionary of the Efik Language*. Basel, 1855 (repub. New Jersey, Gregg Press, 1964).	Ref.
GESV	GULLICK, C. M. J. R. *Exiled From St. Vincent. The Black Carib Culture in Central America up to 1945*. Malta, Progress Press, 1976.	Belz
GFBWI	GRISEBACH, A. *Flora of the BWI Islands*. London, Reeve & Co., 1864.	CarA
GGB	GIUSEPPI, N. and U. *Backfire*. London, Macmillan, 1973.	Trin
GGCF	GREENBERG, Idaz *Guide to Corals & Fishes*. Miami, Seehawk Press, 1977.	CarA
GGIT	GREENSILL, T. M. *Gardening in the Tropics*. London, Evans Bros., 1964/1970.	CarA
GGOFS	GIUSEPPI, N. and U. *Out for Stars*. London, Macmillan, 1975.	CarA
GHG	*The Grenada Handbook*, 1918. St George's.	Gren
GI	GRAY, Cecil *Images*. London, Thomas Nelson & Sons, 1973.	CarA
GLLC	GIUSEPPI, Undine *A Look at Learie Constantine*. London, Thomas Nelson & Sons, 1974.	Trin
GLPF	BONNEAU, J. *Grammaire Pounoue et Lexique Pounou-Français*. Brazzaville, 1956.	Ref.
GMAB	GRAHAM, Elizabeth *The Maya and Belize*. Cancun, Mexico, Cubola Productions, 1980.	Belz
GNHIG	GROOME, J. R. *A Natural History of the Island of Grenada*. Trinidad, Caribbean Printers, 1970.	Gren
GP2	GRAY, Cecil *Parang*. Book 2. London, Thomas Nelson & Sons, 1977.	Trin
GPCB	GOODING, E. G. B. *The Plant Communities of Barbados*. Ministry of Education, 1974.	Bdos

GQVT	GILBERT, Tony *The Queen v. Desmond Trotter* (Pamphlet, 16 pp.) Barbados, Yoruba Press, 1976.	Dmca
GR	GRAY, Cecil *Response.* London, Thomas Nelson & Sons, 1969/1973.	CarA
GrV	*The Grenadian Voice.* St George's.	Gren
GSNRC	Guyana Rice Board *Some Notes on Rice Cultivation.* 1976.	Guyn
GST	MULLER, C. A. *Glossary of Sugar Technology.* London, Elsevier, 1970.	Ref.
GTBI	GRANFIELD, Alison *The Bahamas—Island by Island.* Ministry of Tourism.	Baha
GTF	GUY, Rosa *The Friends.* London, Victor Gollancz, 1974.	Trin
Gtg 1	*Official Guide to Grenada.* Vol. 1. Dukare Publication, 1971/72.	Gren
GTMC	GOMES, Albert *Through a Maze of Colour.* Key Caribbean Publications, 1974.	Trin
GTTLA	GONZALEZ, Anson *Trinidad & Tobago Literature On Air.* National Cultural Council, 1974.	Trin
GTWF	GRAHAM, V. E. *Tropical Wild Flowers.* London, Hulton Educational Pub., 1963.	Guyn
GWFW	GRIFFITH, C. C. *Within Four Walls.* 1971.	Guyn
GWIF	GIUSEPPI, U. *Writing Is Fun.* U. Giuseppi, 1972.	Trin
GWTSB	GOODING, Graham *Wayside Trees & Shrubs of Barbados.* London, Macmillan, 1973.	Bdos
GWW	GUPPY, Nicholas *Wai-Wai.* Penguin, 1961.	Guyn
GyC	*The Guyana Chronicle.* Georgetown.	Guyn
GyG	*Guyana Graphic.* Georgetown.	Guyn
GyN	*Guynews.* Georgetown.	Guyn
H	Newspaper Headline.	
HAA	HEWLETT, A. C. *Allo et Au'voir.* Devon, A. H. Stockwell, 1972.	Antg
HAB	HARGREAVES, Dorothy and Bob *African Blossoms.* Hawaii, Hargreaves Co., 1972.	Ref.
Har	Harrison College *The Harrisonian.* Bridgetown, Letchworth Pr.	Bdos
HASH	HARTOG, Dr J. *Aruba—Short History.* Aruba, Van Dorp, 1978.	Neth
HAT	HARGREAVES, Dorothy and Bob *African Trees.* Hawaii, Hargreaves Co., 1972.	Ref.
HB	HUNTE, George *Barbados.* London, Batsford, 1974.	Bdos
HBBVI	HIGHFIELD, Arnold *The Beautiful British Virgin Islands.* Spectra Graphics Inc., 1972.	BrVi
HBCB	HIGGS, Leslie *Bahamian Cook Book.* 11th edn., 1970.	Baha
HBHI	HOYOS, F. A. *Barbados—History—Independence.* London, Macmillan, 1978.	Bdos
HBIH	HOYOS, F. A. *Barbados Our Island Home.* London, Macmillan, 1960/1972.	Bdos

HBM	HARRIS, Wilson *Black Marsden*. London, Faber, 1972.	Guyn
HBMB	HIGGS, Leslie *Bush Medicine in The Bahamas* Leslie Higgs, 1969/1974.	Baha
HBMV	HODGE, Cynthia *Bush Medicine in the Virgin Islands*. Caribbean Study Paper, UWI, 1976.	BrVi
HBND	HUTT, Maurice B. *Barbadian Nature Diary*. Halifax, Layne Co. Printers & Publishers, 1979.	Bdos
HBOB	HOYOS, F. A. *Builders of Barbados*. Macmillan, 1972.	Bdos
HBTT	HERKLOTS, G. A. C. *The Birds of Trinidad & Tobago*. London, Collins, 1961/1969.	Trin
HCCM	HODGE, Merle *Crick Crack, Monkey*. London, André Deutsch, 1970.	Trin
HCCU	HYDE, Evan X. *The Crowd Called UBAD*. Evan X. Hyde, 1970.	Belz
HCEF	VALDMAN, A., *et al.* (eds.) *Haitian-Creole-English-French Dictionary*. Indiana Univ. Creole Institute, 1981.	Ref.
HCF	HEARNE, John *Carifesta Forum*. John Hearne, 1976.	CarA
HCSH	HARTOG, J. *Curaçao—Short History*. Dewit Stores, 1979.	Neth
HCWP	HONYCHURCH, P. N. *Caribbean Wild Plants And Their Uses*. Honychurch, 1980.	CarA
Hd	Parliamentary Hansard.	
HDB	BOXILL, H. D. Word List of Barbadianisms. (Personal MS, 1974)	Bdos
HDNPV	HONYCHURCH, P. N. *Dominica National Park Vegetation*. Dominica National Park Service, 1978.	Dmca
HDNPW	HONYCHURCH, P. N. *Dominica National Park Wildlife*. Dominica National Park Service, 1978.	Dmca
Heh	GLASS, Andrew (ed.) *Here's How*. St Thomas, Here's How Inc., 1976.	USVI
Her	*Hers*. Bridgetown.	Bdos
HF	HYDE, Evan X. *Feelings*. Evan X. Hyde, 1975.	Belz
HFGA	HOWES, Barbara (ed.) *From the Green Antilles*. London, Panther Books, 1971.	CarA
HFGB	HARTWELL, George H. *Fishing Guide to The Bahamas*. Miami, Argos Inc., n.d.	Baha
HFOL	HALL, Douglas *Five of the Leewards 1834–1870*. Caribbean Universities Pr., 1971.	CarA
HGASR	HOYOS, F. A. *Grantley Adams & The Social Revolution*. London, Macmillan, 1974.	Bdos
HGFOC	HANNAU, H. W. and GARRARD, Jeanne *Flowers of the Caribbean*. Miami, Argos Inc., n.d.	CarA
HGTF	HANNAU, H. W. and GARRARD, Jeanne *Tropical Flowers*. London, Robert Hale & Co., 1975.	CarA
HHOS	HARTOG, J. *History of Saba*. Van Guilder, NV, 1975.	Neth
HHSE	HARTOG, J. *History of St. Eustatius*. The Central USA Bicentennial Committee, 1976.	Neth

HHTBC	HARGREAVES, Dorothy and Bob *Tropical Blossoms of the Caribbean*. Hawaii, Hargreaves Co., 1960.	CarA
HHTT	HARGREAVES, Dorothy and Bob *Tropical Trees*. Hawaii, Hargreaves Co., 1960.	CarA
HHTV	HERSKOVITS, M. J. and HERSKOVITS, F. S. *Trinidad Village*. New York, Octagon Books, 1976.	Trin
HICWE	HAYNES, Lilith *A Study of Informal Caribbean Written English*. Caribbean Study Paper, UWI, 1966.	CarA
HIN	HILHOUSE, William *Indian Notices*. National Commission for Research, 1978.	Guyn
HIPJ	HAWKES, Alex D. *Illustrated Plants of Jamaica*. Alex D. Hawkes, 1974.	Jmca
HKS	*Hong Kong Shrubs*. Hong Kong, Urban Services Department, 1971.	Ref.
HLNPG	HAYNES, Lilith M. *Local Names of Plants in Guyana. A Linguistic and Ethnobotanical Study* M. Phil Thesis (unpub.), 1969.	Guyn
HLSSL	HILTON, Anne *Leroy—The Story of a Streak Lizard*. Publishing Associates (WI), 1977.	Trin
HLTB	HUGHES, Rubylette *Local names of trees in Barbados*. Bridgetown., n.d.	Bdos
HLTS	HALLWORTH, Grace *Listen to this Story*. London, Methuen Children's Books, 1977.	CarA
HM	HENDRICKS, A. L. *Muet*. London, Outposts Publications, 1971.	CarA
HMCH	HEATH, Roy A. K. *A Man Come Home*. Longman Caribbean, 1974.	Guyn
HMNP	HERSKOVITS, M. J. *The Myth of the Negro Past*. Boston, Beacon Press, 1958.	Srnm
HMP	HOROWITZ, Michael M. *Morne-Paysan—Peasant Village in Martinique*. New York, Holt, Rinehart & Winston, 1969.	Mart
HNGF	HAYNES, Lilith *Folk Names of Guyanese Flora & Some comparisons with their Barbadian Names*. Caribbean Study Paper, UWI, 1967.	Guyn
HNHB	HUGHES, Griffith *The Natural History of Barbados*. London, Arno Press 1750 (reprint 1972).	Bdos
HPCC	HOROWITZ, Michael M. *Peoples & Cultures of the Caribbean*. New York, Library Of Congress, Natural History Press, 1971.	CarA
HPP	HILL, Errol *The Ping Pong*. UWI, St. Augustine, Trinidad, 1958.	Trin
HPTW	HUNTE, Conrad *Playing to Win*. London, Hodder & Stoughton, 1971.	CarA
HSAG	HEARNE, John *Stranger At The Gate*. London, Faber, 1956.	Jmca

HSMSE	HARTOG, J. *St. Maarten, Saba & St. Eustatius.* Dewit Stores.	Neth
HSOR	HARRIS, Wilson *Sleepers of Roraima.* London, Faber, 1970.	Guyn
HSTCI	HUTCHINGS, C. D. *The Story of The Turks & Caicos Islands.* C. D. Hutchings, 1977.	TkCa
HSTR	HARVEY, Claudia *A Study of the Ramayana.* Caribbean Study Paper, UWI.	Trin
HTAS	HILL, Errol ... *a Time and a Season (8 Caribbean Plays).* Extra-Mural Studies, UWI, Trinidad, 1976.	CarA
HTB	HUNTE, George *The Bahamas.* London, B. T. Batsford, 1975.	Baha
HTCLL	HENRY, Cecil *Trinidad & Tobago Carnival, Landscape & Language (in verse).* C. Henry, 1970.	Trin
HTDS	HONYCHURCH, Lennox *The Dominica Story.* Letchworth Press, Bridgetown, Barbados, 1975.	Dmca
HTOS	HARRIS, Wilson *The Tree of the Sun.* London, Faber, 1978.	Guyn
HTT	HARRIS, Wilson *Tuma-Tumari.* London, Faber, 1968.	Guyn
HTTD	HAYNES, Martin *Trinidad & Tobago Dialect (Plus).* San Fernando, Trinidad, 1987.	Trin
HTUP	HANDLER, Jerome S. *The Unappropriated People.* Baltimore, Johns Hopkins Univ. Pr., 1974.	Bdos
HTWA	HARRIS, Wilson *The Whole Armour.* London, Faber, 1962/1973.	Guyn
HVBVI	HARRIGAN, Norwell and VARLACK, Pearl *The British Virgin Islands.* Research and Consulting Services, 1970.	BrVi
HVUW	HEARNE, John *Voices Under The Window.* London, Faver, 1955/1973.	Jmca
HVVIS	HARRIGAN, Norwell and VARLACK, Pearl *The Virgin Islands Story.* Caribbean Univ. Pr., 1975.	BrVi
HWII	HUNTE, George *The West Indian Islands.* London, B. T. Batsford, 1972.	CarA
HWIIC	HANNAU, Hans W. *The West Indian Islands* (In Full Colour). Miami, Argos Inc., n.d.	CarA
HWTS	HUTT, Maurice B. *Window To The Sea.* Bridgetown, Cedar Press, 1980.	Bdos
Iai	*Journal of the International African Institute,* London.	Ref.
IAIG	Im THURN, Everard F. *Among the Indians of Guiana.* London, Kegan Paul, Trench & Co., 1883.	Guyn
IBEN	NIHALANI, Paroo, *et al. Indian & British English.* OUP, 1979.	Ref.
IFMB	INNISS, Leopatra *Folk Medicines in Barbados.* Caribbean Study Paper, UWI, 1975.	Bdos
IGED	INNES, Gordon *A Grebo-English Dictionary.* CUP, 1967.	Ref.
IHB	INNISS, Sir Probyn *Historic Basseterre.* Sir Probyn Inniss, 1979.	StKt

IIOS	IVES, Charles *The Isles of Summer*. Charles Ives, 1880.	Baha
IMED	INNES, Gordon *A Mende-English Dictionary*. CUP, 1969.	Ref.
InF	*Informer*. St George's.	Gren
Int	*Intouch—The Caribbean Family Magazine*. Antigua, Antillean Services Ltd.	CarA
ISC	(Unidentified author) *Islands of the Sunny Caribbean*. Photoprecision Ltd., 1972.	CarA
Isl	*Islander*. St Vincent, Caribbean Publishing.	CarA
IsS	*The Island Sun*. Tortola.	BrVi
JAA	JONES, S. B. *Annals of Anguilla, 1650–1923*. Christian Journals, 1976.	Angu
Jaj	*Jamaica Journal*. Institute of Jamaica.	Jmca
Jan	*Jamaica News—Newsletter*. Jamaican Embassies, Consulates and High Commissions.	Jmca
Jba	BELISLE, Musa, *et al.* (eds.) *Journal of Belizean Affairs*, Nos. 4 and 6. Belize Institute of Social Research and Action (BISRA). Dec. 1976 and Jan. 1978.	Belz
JBAB	JAMES, C. L. R. *Beyond A Boundary*. London, Hutchinson, 1963.	Trin
JBJ	JOHNSTONE, Wilhelmina Kemp *Bahamian Jottings*. Brice Publishing Co., 1973.	Baha
Jbm	*Journal of Barbados Museum & Historical Society*. Bridgetown.	Bdos
Jbs	EDWARDS, Walter F. 'Speech Acts in Guyana' (from *Journal of Black Studies* Vol. 10 No. 1). Newbury Park, CA, Sage Publications Inc., 1971.	Guyn
JBVK	JACOBS, Richard (ed.) *Butler vs. The King*. Key Caribbean Publications, 1976.	Trin
JBWJ	JEFFREY-SMITH, May *Bird-watching in Jamaica*. Bolivar Pr., 1972.	Jmca
JDBB	JOHNSON, Linton Kwesi *Dread, Beat and Blood*. London, Bogle L'Ouverture Pub., 1975.	Jmca
JdN	*Jamaica Daily News*. Kingston.	Jmca
JEPO	JONES, Daniel *English Pronouncing Dictionary*. 13th edn. (rev. by A. C. Gimson) London, Everyman's Lib., Dent, 1967.	Ref.
JESI	JOYCE, P. W. *English As We Speak It in Ireland*. London, Longman, 1910.	Ref.
Jfa	*Joffa*. Mitcham, Surrey, Jamaica Overseas Families and Friends Association.	Jmca
Jfi	ELDER, J. D. (ed.) *Journal of the Folklore Institute*. Vol. 3 No. 2. Holland, Montor & Co., 1966.	Trin
JJAIE	JADAN, Ivan and Doris *The Adventures of Ivan Environman*. E.S.P. Inc., 1974.	USVI
JJCC	JANE, Cecil (ed.) *The Journal of Christopher Columbus*. New York, Bramball House, 1960.	CarA

JJHAI	JADAN, Ivan and Doris *The Holiday Adventures of Ivan Environman*. E.S.P. Inc., 1975.	USVI
JJM	JONES, Marion Patrick *Jouvert Morning*. Columbus Publishers, 1976.	Trin
JMA	JAMES, C. L. R. *Minty Alley*. London, New Beacon Books, 1971.	Trin
JMRS	JOHN, Errol *Moon on a Rainbow Shawl*. London, Faber, 1958/1971.	Trin
JNBD	JOHN-ROSE, Theodora *Folk Names of Birds in Dominica*. Caribbean Study Paper, UWI, 1973.	Dmca
JNHSJ	JADAN, Doris *A Guide to the National History of St. John*. Virgin Islands Conservation Society, 1971.	USVI
JPB	JONES, Marion Patrick *Pan Beat*. Columbus Publishers, 1973.	Trin
JPOI	JONES, Evan *Protector of the Indians*. Longman Caribbean, 1973.	CarA
JQRB	JOHNSON, Doris L. *The Quiet Revolution in the Bahamas*. The Family Islands Pr., 1972.	Baha
JSD	JAMIESON, John *Jamieson's Scottish Dictionary. An Etymological Dictionary of the Scottish Language*. New edn., New York, AMS Pr. Inc., 1966.	Ref.
JSDS	DONALDSON, David *Supplement to Jamieson's Scottish Dictionary*. (Reprint) AMS Press, 1966.	Ref.
JSMLC	JONES, A. and SEFTON, N. *Marine Life of the Caribbean*. Macmillan Caribbean, 1978.	CarA
JT	JENKINS, C. F. *Tortola*. Ministry of Education, 1972.	BrVi
JTBJ	JAMES, C. L. R. *The Black Jacobins*. New York, Vintage Books, 1963.	Hait
JTR	JOHNSON, Robert Elliot *The Road*. Robert E. Johnson, 1972.	Baha
JWSSS	JONES, Anthony Mark *The Winston 'Spree' Simon Story*. Educo Pr.	Trin
Kai	DOLPHIN, Celeste (ed.) *Kaie*. The National History and Arts Council.	Guyn
KCWT	KASASIAN, L. *Common Weeds of Trinidad*. UWI, 1964.	Trin
KED	FYLE, Clifford N. and JONES, Eldred *A Krio-English Dictionary*. OUP, 1980.	Ref.
Kej	*Key to Jamaica*. City Printery Ltd.	Jmca
KGFT	KING, K. F. S. *A Great Future Together*. Georgetown, Design and Graphics, 1973.	Guyn
KGHD	KNIGHT, E. G. *The Grenada Handbook and Directory*. Bridgetown, Advocate Co., 1946.	Gren
KID	KAUFMAN, Elaine M. *Ibibio Dictionary*. Leiden, African Studies Centre, 1985.	Ref.
KJB	KHAN, Ismith *The Jumbie Bird*. Longman Caribbean, 1974.	Trin

KMRFBC	KIRBY, I. E. and MARTIN, C. I. *The Rise and Fall of the Black Caribs of St. Vincent.* Kirby & Martin, 1972.	StVn
KNB	NOBLE, Ken *Glossary of Colloquial Expressions of Trinidad.* MS, 1977.	Trin
KNED	KALIAI, M. H. I. *Nembe–English Dictionary.* Univ. of Ibadan, 1964.	Ref.
KNWI	KRUYTHOFF, S. J. *The Netherlands Windward Islands.* Aruba, Dewitting, 1964.	Neth
KPG	KOELLE, Sigismund W. *Polyglotta Africana* (1854, Graz) eds. P. E. H. Hair & D. Dalby, 1963.	Ref.
Kri	LAIRD, Christopher and QUESTEL, Victor (eds.) *Kairi—Annual of the Arts.* Port of Spain.	Trin
KSJFC	KOLADIS, Randall S. *St. John on Foot & by Car* Randall S. Koladis, 1974.	USVI
KSWCA	KASASIAN, L. and SEEYAVE, J. *Weedkillers for Caribbean Agriculture.* Trinidad, Regional Research Centre, 1968.	CarA
KTIG	KAY, Frances *This is Grenada.* Caribbean Printers, 1966.	Gren
KTNVS	KING, Cameron G. O. *Towards A New Vincentian Society.* Vini Folk Publication, n.d.	StVn
KTSTFC	KOLADIS, Randall and TODD, Mary Ann *St. Thomas on Foot & by Car.* Randall, Koladis and Mary Ann Todd, 1972.	USVI
KTT	KEENS-DOUGLAS, Paul *Tim Tim.* Paul Keens-Douglas, 1976.	Trin
KTTSTF	KUCK, Loraine E. and TONGG, Richard C. *A Guide to Tropical & Semi-tropical Flora.* Charles E. Tuttle Co., 1977.	CarA
KV	KING, Cameron G. O. *Vision.* Vini Folk Publication, 1973.	StVn
KWMS	KEENS-DOUGLAS, Paul *When Moon Shine.* Paul Keens-Douglas, 1975.	Trin
KWS	KOHLMAN, A. B. *Wotcha Say.* Cayman Free Press, 1979.	CayI
Kyk	SEYMOUR, A. J., McDONALD, I. *et al. Kyk-Over-Al.* Georgetown, *c.* 1945– .	Guyn
LACPV	LITTLE, Elbert L. Jr., *et al. Arboles Comunes de Puerto Rico y las Islas Virgenes.* La Universidad de Puerto Rico, 1977.	PtRi
Lal	LIBURD, Clem Jr. (ed.) *La-Laps. (A Journal)* St Kitts Nat. Pub. House.	StKt
LAS	MATHER, J. Y. and SPEIKEL, H. H. (eds.) *The Linguistic Atlas of Scotland* 1. London, Croom Helm, 1975.	Ref.
LaS	*The Labour Spokesman.* Basseterre.	StKt
LBGIR	LEWIN, Olive *Brown Gal in De Ring—12 Jamaica Folk Songs.* OUP, 1974.	Jmca
LC	LEE WAH, James *Carray!* London, Macmillan, 1977.	CarA

LCAS	LOWENTHAL, David and COMITAS, Lambros *The Aftermath of Sovreignty*. New York, Anchor Books, 1973.	CarA
LCNN	LAUN, Charles *Caribbean Nature Notes*. H. C. Laun, 1974.	CarA
LCSGB	LAMMING, George *Cannon Shot and Glass Beads*. London, Pan Books, 1974.	Bdos
LCTC	LaGUERRE, John *Calcutta to Caroni*. Longman Caribbean, 1974.	Trin
LDCD	LOVELACE, Earl *The Dragon Can't Dance*. London, André Deutsch, 1979.	Trin
LDCE	*Longman Dictionary of Contemporary English*. Avon, Bath, 1978/1986.	Ref.
LDKF	LAMAN, K. E. *Dictionnaire Kikongo Français*. Brussels, 1936.	Ref.
LDSS	LAZARE, Alick, *et al. Dominican Short Stories*. Vol. 1, Arts Council of Dominica Writers Workshop, 1974.	Dmca
LEFSG	LONCKE, Joycelynne *An English–French–Spanish Glossary of Guyanese Fruit, Vegetables and Grain*. Univ. of Guyana, 1973.	Guyn
LFCC	LYNCH, J.W. *Folktale Callaloo for Children*. J. W. Lynch, 1973.	Trin
LGMWI	LEWIS, Gordon *The Growth of the Modern West Indies*. London, Macgibbon & Kee, 1968.	CarA
LHDBC	LUX, William *Historical Dictionary of the British Caribbean*. Methuen, NJ, Scarecrow Press, 1975.	Ref.
LHOB	LIGON, Richard *A True and Exact History of the Island of Barbados*. London, Frank Cass, 1657/1976.	Bdos
LHTBH	LAMB, A. F. A. *Forty-two Secondary Hardwood Timbers of Br. Honduras*. Forest Dept., Bulletin No. 1, 1946.	Belz
LICMS	LAMMING, George *In the castle of My Skin*. New York, Collier Books, 1970. (orig 1953).	Bdos
LISI	LESTER, George *In Sunny Isles*. London, Charles Kelly, 1897.	Baha
LIWIN	LAURENCE, K. O. *Immigration into the West Indies in the 19th Century*. Caribbean Universities Pr., 1971.	CarA
LJFS	LEWIN, Olive *Dandy Shandy—12 Jamaican Folk Songs*. OUP, 1975.	Jmca
LJRB	LINBLAD, Jan *Journey to Red Birds*. London, Collins, 1966.	Trin
LLFL	*Larousse de la langue française—Lexis*. Paris, Larousse, 1979.	Ref.
LMFF	LIBURD, Clem W. *Messages from the Folk*. National Youth Council, 1975.	StKt
LMSPJS	*London Missionary Society's Report of the Proceedings against the late Revd. J. Smith of Demerara (etc. etc.)*. London, 1824.	Guyn
LNBR	LaROSE, John *New Beacon Reviews*. London, New Beacon Books, 1968.	CarA

LNFPB	LIGHT, M. H. S. *Non-Flowering Plants of Barbados.* Ministry of Education, 1976.	Bdos
LNL	LAZARE, A. *Native Laughter.* Roseau, 1985.	Dmca
LNMP	LAMMING, George *Natives of My Person.* London, Pan Books, 1974.	Bdos
LOWI	TAYLOR, Douglas *Languages of the West Indies.* Baltimore, Johns Hopkins Univ. Pr., 1977.	Ref.
LSFMG	LASHLEY, Charles M. *A Study of Folk Medicines of the People of Concord Village in Grenada.* Caribbean Study Paper, UWI, Cave Hill.	Gren
LST	LONG, Earl G. *The Serpent's Tale.* St Lucia, UWI Extra-Mural Department, 1974.	StLu
LTS	LOVELACE, Earl *The Schoolmaster.* London, Heinemann, 1979.	Trin
LTTBV	LEWISOHN, Florence *Tales of Tortola & BVI.* Hollywood, Fla., International Graphics, 1966/1973.	BrVi
LV	LEE, Robert *Vocation.* St Lucia, UWI Extra-Mural Department 1975.	StLu
LVV	LETTSOME, Quincy F. *Virgin Verses.* Quincy F. Lettsome, 1976.	BrVi
LWPWH	LEWISOHN, Florence *What So Proudly We Hail.* St Croix, Prestige Press, 1975.	USVI
MAALV	MUFWENE, S. (ed.) *Africanisms in Afro-American Language Varieties.* Athens, Ga. Bound Conference Papers, Univ. of Georgia, Feb. 1988.	Ref.
Mag	Magazine section of a Sunday Newspaper.	
MAGH	MENEZES, Mary N. *The Amerindians in Guiana, 1803–73. A Documentary History.* London, Cass, 1979.	Guyn
MAHM	MARAJH, Carrington *An Analysis of Hindu Marriages.* Caribbean Study Paper. UWI, Port of Spain.	Trin
MaN	*Manjak.* Bridgetown.	Bdos
MBB	McKAY, Claude *Banana Bottom.* New York, Harper & Row, 1961.	Jmca
MBBA	MAKHANLALL, David P. *The Best of Brer Anansi.* London, Blackie & Son, 1973.	Guyn
MBF	MENDES, Alfred *Black Fauns.* London, New Beacon Books, (1935), 1984.	Trin
MBGB	MARSHALL, Paule *Brown Girl, Brownstones.* New York, Avon Books, 1970/1972.	Bdos
MBL	MAIS, Roger *Black Lightning.* (In: *The 3 Novels of Roger Mais*). London, Jonathan Cape, 1966.	Jmca
MBM	MAIS, Roger *Brother Man.* London, Heinemann, 1974.	Jmca
MBS	McCARTNEY, Tim *Bahamian Sexuality.* Timpaul Publishing Co., 1976.	Baha
MBTV	MURRAY, Dea *Birds of the Virgin Islands.* Hollywood, Fla., International Graphics, 1969.	USVI
MC	*Montserrat Cookbook.* Montserrat Old People's Welfare Association.	Mrat

MCCL	MENDES, John *Cote ce Cote la.* Syncreators, 1985.	Trin
MCE	MAYNARD, Olga Comma *Carib Echoes.* Columbus Publishers, 1972.	Trin
MCFL	MARCHACK, Sandra *Chinese Family Life in Trinidad & Tobago.* Caribbean Study Paper, UWI.	Trin
MCK	MITTELHOLZER, Edgar *Children of Kaywana.* London, New English Library, 1952/1972.	Guyn
MCL	MacPHERSON, John *Caribbean Lands.* Longman Caribbean, 1963/1973.	CarA
MCPP	MATTHEWS, W. *Cockney Past and Present.* London, Routledge, 1938.	Ref.
MCT	MITTELHOLZER, Edgar *Corentyne Thunder.* London, Heinemann, 1941/1970.	Guyn
MFNRV	MURRAY, Dea *Famous Native Recipes of the Virgin Islands.* Hollywood, Fla., Dukane Pr., 1979.	USVI
MFOT	MENTOR, Gertrude *The Folklore of Toco.* Caribbean Study Paper, UWI.	Trin
MFROV	MURRAY, Dea *Famous Rum Drinks of the Virgin Islands.* Dea Murray, 1974.	USVI
MFSB	MARSHALL, Trevor G., *et al. Folk Songs of Barbados.* Bridgetown, Cedar Press, 1981.	Bdos
MFSJ	MURRAY, Tom *Folk Songs of Jamaica.* OUP, 1951.	Jmca
MFTT	MARSHALL, R. C., *et al. Forest Trees of Trinidad & Tobago with special reference to their Timbers.* Government Printing Office, 1931.	Trin
MGWI	MILLS, Therese *Great West Indians.* Longman Caribbean, 1973.	CarA
MHBT	McDONALD, Ian *The Humming Bird Tree.* Heinemann, 1974.	Trin
MHJT	MAIS, Roger *The Hills were Joyful Together.* (In: *The 3 novels of R. Mais.*) London, Jonathan Cape, 1966.	Jmca
MHSJ	MAXWELL, Ken *How To Speak Jamaican.* C. Issa, 1981.	Jmca
MICWM	MacPHERSON, John *Introducing Caribbean Weather Maps.* Longman Caribbean, 1969/1977.	CarA
MIMC	MEOSA, Elaine *East Indian Courtship & Marriage Customs in Trinidad.* Caribbean Study Paper, UWI.	Trin
MIOC	MITCHELL, Carleton *Isles of the Caribbees.* National Geographic Society, 1968.	CarA
MiR	*Mirror—Newspaper of the PPP.* Georgetown.	Guyn
MISG	McINTOSH, Felix, *et al. An Illustrated Story of Grenada.* Key Caribbean Publications, 1974.	Gren
MKB	MITTELHOLZER, Edgar *Kaywana Blood.* London, New English Library, 1954/1972.	Guyn
MKS	MITTELHOLZER, Edgar *Kaywana Stock.* London, New English Library, 1948/1972.	Guyn
MLDS	MITTELHOLZER, Edgar *The Life and Death of Sylvia.* London, Four Square edn., 1953/1963.	Guyn

MLETJ	McCLEAN, Patricia *Comparative Etymology of Terms in Common Usage including Plants, Animals and Kinship Terms in Trinidad & Jamaican English.* Caribbean Study Paper, UWI, St Augustine, 1978.	Trin/ Jmca
Mlr	*Modern Language Review.* Univ. of Guyana.	Guyn
MMAO	MITTELHOLZER, Edgar *A Morning at the Office.* London, Penguin, 1950.	Guyn
MMGHJ	McKAY, Claude *My Green Hill of Jamaica.* Heinemann (Caribbean), 1979.	Jmca
MMIT	MARCELLE, James *The Moravians in Tobago.* Caribbean Study Paper, UWI.	Tbgo
MMNR	MAYNARD, Olga Comma and FITZ, G. *The New Road.* Columbus Publishers, 1969.	Trin
MMRFC	MacPHERSON, John *Map Reading for the Caribbean.* Longman Caribbean, 1976.	CarA
MN	MACAW *Notebook.* Trinidad, 1960.	Trin
MNBSA	MIKES, George *Not By Sun Alone.* London, André Deutsch, 1967.	Jmca
MNT	MARSHALL, R. C., *et al. Native Timbers & Seasonings of Wood.* Government Printer, 1925.	Trin
MOHW	MORRIS, Mervyn *On Holy Week.* Sangster Bookstores, 1976.	Jmca
MoK	*Moko.* Port of Spain.	Trin
MOUC	MISSICK, Rupert *Once Upon a Closeness.* n. pub., n.d.	Baha
MP	MUIRHEAD, Desmond *Palms.* Globe, Ariz., Dale Stuart King, 1961.	CarA
MPPP	MOTTLEY, Elton *People, Parties & Politics.* Yoruba Pr., 1976.	Bdos
MPRT	McBURNIE, Wray *Parang: Its Revival in Trinidad.* Caribbean Study Paper, UWI.	Trin
MRFWB	MADRAMOOTOO, Harry *A Ricefarmer's Word Book.* Guyana Rice Board, 1974.	Guyn
MRSPP	McCARTHY, Cheryl *The Religious Traditions & Superstitions of the 'Payol' People.* Caribbean Study Paper, UWI.	Trin
MRW	MATHURIN, Lucille *The Rebel Woman.* Institute of Jamaica, 1975.	Jmca
MTAL	MENCKEN, H. L. *The American Language.* New York, Knopf, 1967.	Ref.
MTBH	MOSELEY, M. *The Bahamas Handbook.* The Nassau Guardian, 1926.	Baha
MTBL	McKESEY, G. *The Belizean Lingo.* Belize, National Printers Ltd, 1974.	Belz
MTCP	MARSHALL, Paule *The Chosen Place, The Timeless People.* London, Longman, 1969.	Bdos
MtM	*The Montserrat Mirror.* Plymouth.	Mrat
MTOB	MARTINI, Peter C. *A Taste of the Bahamas.* Bahamas Hotel Training Council.	Baha

MTP	MORRIS, Mervyn *The Pond*. London, New Beacon Books, 1973.	Jmca
MTPG	MACMILLAN, H. F. *Tropical Planting and Gardening*. London, Macmillan, 1954.	CarA
MTPS	MARQUEZ, Jennifer *Current Trinidadian English Proverbial Sayings—An Analytical Study*. Caribbean Study Paper, UWI.	Trin
MTTBT	McCARTNEY, Tim *Ten Ten The Bible Ten—Obeah in the Bahamas*. Timpaul Publishing Co., 1976.	Baha
MVIS	MAVROGORDATO, Olga J. *Voices in the Street*. Port of Spain, Imprint Caribbean, 1977.	Trin
MWL	WARNER-LEWIS, Maureen *Manuscript Notes of Trinidad Lexicon*. Personal, n.d.	Trin
MWWT	MARAJH, Carrington *A Study of Whe Whe in Trinidad*. Caribbean Study Paper, UWI.	Trin
NAD	NAIPAUL, V. S. *An Area of Darkness*. London, Penguin Books, 1970.	Trin
NaG	*The Nassau Guardian*. Nassau.	Baha
Nag	*National Geographic*. Washington, National Geographic Society.	Ref.
NAGOS	NAIPAUL, Seepersad *The Adventures of Gurudeva & Other Stories*. London, André Deutsch, 1976.	Trin
Nas	*National Studies*. Belize Institute of Social Research and Action.	Belz
NaT	*The Nation*. Bridgetown.	Bdos
NBA	NICOLE, Christopher *Blood Amyot*. London, Jarrolds Pub., 1964.	Guyn
NC	NICOLE, Christopher *Caribee*. London, Cassell & Co., 1974.	Guyn
NCCG	NAIPAUL, Shiva *The Chip Chip Gatherers*. London, André Deutsch, 1973.	Trin
NEAPR	NAZARIO, M. A. *El Elemento Afronegroide en el Español de Puerto Rico*. San Juan, 1961.	PtRi
NeC	*New Chronicle*. (Formerly *Dominica Chronicle*). Roseau.	Dmca
NeJ	*The New Jewel*. St George's.	Gren
NeN	*New Nation*. Georgetown.	Guyn
NF	NAIPAUL, Shiva *Fireflies*. London, Penguin Books, 1970.	Trin
NFOI	NAIPAUL, V. S. *A Flag on the Island*. London, Penguin Books, 1967.	Trin
NG	NAIPAUL, V. S. *Guerillas*. London, Penguin Books, 1975.	Trin
NHMB	NAIPAUL, V. S. *A House for Mr. Biswas*. London, Penguin Books, 1969.	Trin
NIBE	NIHALANI, P., *et al. Indian and British English*. Delhi, OUP, 1979.	Ref.

NLED	NAIPAUL, V. S. *The Loss of el Dorado.* London, André Deutsch, 1969.	Trin
NMANJ	NETTLEFORD, Rex *Manley and the New Jamaica.* Longman Caribbean, 1971.	Jmca
NMID	*The New Michaelis Illustrated Dictionary. (Brazilian Pg–Eng.)* Wiesbaden, Brockhaus, 1961.	Ref.
NMIM	NAIPAUL, V. S. *The Mimic Men.* London, André Deutsch, 1967.	Jmca
NMM	NETTLEFORD, Rex *Mirror, Mirror.* William Collins & Sangster, 1970/1972.	Jmca
NMP	NAIPAUL, V. S. *The Middle Passage.* London, André Deutsch, 1962.	Trin
NOB	NAIPAUL, V. S. *The Overcrowded Barracoon.* London, André Deutsch, 1972.	Trin
Noj	*News of Jamaica.* Ottawa, Jamaica High Commission, (1981–3).	Jmca
Nor	*The Norwester.* Grand Cayman, Northwestern Co.	CayI
NPHT	PIERRE-NOEL, A. V. *Nomenclature polyglotte des plantes haïtiennes et tropicales.* Presses Nat. d'Haïti, 1971.	Hait
NR	NICOLE, Christopher *Ratoon.* London, Panther Books, 1964.	Guyn
NSOE	NAIPAUL, V. S. *The Suffrage of Elvira.* London, André Deutsch, 1958.	Trin
NTMM	NAIPAUL, V. S. *The Mystic Masseur.* London (Deutsch 1957), Penguin, 1964.	Trin
OCTTT	OTTLEY, C. R. *Creole Talk of Trinidad & Tobago.* Port of Spain, 1971.	Trin/ Tbgo
ODCIE	COWIE, A. P. and MACKIN, R. *Oxford Dictionary of Current Idiomatic English.* OUP, 1975.	Ref.
ODJR	OWENS, Joseph *Dread: The Rastafarians of Jamaica.* Snagster's Bookstores, 1976.	Jmca
OED	*Oxford English Dictionary.* Oxford, Clarendon Press, 1933.	Ref.
OEDS	Supplements to *OED.* Vols. I–IV, 1982–6	Ref.
OED2	*Oxford English Dictionary.* 2nd edn. Vols. I–XX. Oxford, Clarendon Press, 1989.	Ref.
OEWIRT	OTTLEY, C. R. *East & West Indians Rescue Trinidad.* Crusoe Publishing House, 1975.	Trin
OFBCC	OTTLEY, C. R. *Folk Beliefs, Folk Customs & Folk Characters found in Trinidad & Tobago.* C. R. Ottley, 1979.	Trin/ Tbgo
OGA	ORTIZ, F. *Glosario de Afronegrismos.* Havana, 1924.	Ref.
OGEP	OMAWALE *Guyana's Edible Plants.* Univ. of Guyana, 1973.	Guyn
OHMC	OLDENDORP, C. G. A. (ed. J. J. BOSSARD) *History of the Mission on the Caribbean Islands of St Thomas, St Croix & St John (1770).* Eng. trans. Ann Arbor, Karoma Pub., 1987.	USVI

OIAD	OSBOURNE, S. Alex *Introduction to Antiguan Dialect.* Caribbean Study Paper, UWI, 1966.	Antg
OIC	OLSEN, Fred *Indian Creek.* Univ. of Oklahoma Pr., 1974.	Antg
OJS	OTTLEY, C. R. *Jokey Stories.* C. R. Ottley, 1972.	Trin/ Tbgo
OOLSC	OPIE, Iona and Peter *The Lore and Language of School Children.* St Albans, Herts., Granada Publishing, 1977.	Ref.
OSDT	OTTLEY, C. R. *Slavery Days in Trinidad.* C. R. Ottley, 1974.	Trin
OST	OTTLEY, C. R. *Spanish Trinidad.* Longman Caribbean, 1955/1971.	Trin
OSTT	OTTLEY, C. R. *Sayings of Trinidad & Tobago.* (No. 3) 1966.	Trin/ Tbgo
OT1	OTTLEY, C. R. *Trinibagianese* (No. 1) 1966, (orig. Vol. 1, 1965)	Trin/ Tbgo
OT2	OTTLEY, C. R. *Trinibagianese* (No. 2) Vol. 2, 1966.	Trin/ Tbgo
OT3	OTTLEY, C. R. *Trinibagianese* (No. 4) Vol. 3, 1967.	Trin/ Tbgo
OTTTT	OTTLEY, C. R. *Tall Tales of Trinidad & Tobago.* (Orig. '*Legends & True Stories . . .* 1962'). Horsford Printerie, 1972.	Trin/ Tbgo
PAH	PENDERGAST, David M. '*Altun Ha*'. *A Guidebook to the Ancient Maya Ruins.* Government of Belize, 1976.	Belz
PAIB	PALACIO, Joseph O. *Archaeology in Belize.* Cancun, Cubola Productions, 1976.	Belz
PAIJ	PHILLIPS, A. S. *Adolescence in Jamaica.* Jamaica Publishing House, 1976.	Jmca
Pas	*Pastimes.* New York, Pastimes Publications, 1973.	CarA
PBDB	PALMER, C. Everard *Big Doc Bitteroot.* London, André Deutsch, 1968.	Jmca
PBP	PEEK, Basil *Bahamian Proverbs.* Providence Press, 1949.	Baha
PCBC	PRIDMORE, F. *Coins of the British Commonwealth of Nations. Part 3, Bermuda, Br. Guiana, Br. Honduras, Br. West Indies.* London, Spink & Son, 1965.	CarA
PCCB	PALMER, C. Everard *A Cow Called Boy.* London, André Deutsch, 1973.	Jmca
PCOS	PATTERSON, H. Orlando *The Children of Sisyphus.* London, New Authors Ltd., 1964.	Jmca
PDAE	KENYON, J. S. and KNOTT, T. A. *Pronouncing Dictionary of American English.* Springfield, Merriam, 1953.	Ref.
PDLD	PATTERSON, H. Orlando *Die The Long Day.* Granada Publishing, 1972.	Jmca
PDOC	PARTRIDGE, Eric *A Dictionary of Clichés.* Routledge & Kegan Paul, 1941/1978.	Ref.

PED	*The Penguin English Dictionary.* London, Penguin 1969.	Ref.
PEFB	PINDER, E. *Excerpts from The Bus.* (MS play, NIFCA entry) 1977.	Bdos
PeL	*The Pelican.* (Magazine Section of *The Nation.*) Bridgetown.	Bdos
Peo	*People.* Inprint Caribbean Ltd. Port of Spain.	CarA
PEOL	PENN, Verna E. *The Essence of Life.* Verna Penn, 1976.	BrVi
PGIP	PROTAIN, Gertrude, *et al. Grenada Independence 1974—Cultural Pot Pourri.* St George's.	Gren
PHPVI	PETERSEN, Arona *Herbs & Proverbs of the Virgin Islands.* Arona Petersen, 1974/75.	USVI
PHSAV	PAQUIN, Lionel *Historical Sketch of the U.S. Virgin Islands.* Lionel Paquin, 1970.	USVI
Pic	*People in Carnival.* Inprint Caribbean Ltd.	Trin
PJWJ	PARRIS, Terry *Jason Whyte, Jamaican.* OUP, 1973.	Jmca
PKIF	PARMASAD, K. V. *Kheesas—Local Indian Folk Tales.* Caribbean Study Paper, UWI.	Trin
PKKK	PETERSEN, Arona *Kreole, Ketch n' Keep.* Arona Petersen, 1975.	USVI
PMS	PRICE, Richard (ed.) *Maroon Societies.* New York, Anchor Books, 1973.	Jmca
POTS	PUGAGEE PUNGCUSS *Old Time Story: Some Guianese Yarns Re-spun.* Guiana Edn. No. 7. Daily Chronicle, 1943.	Guyn
PPGD	FRANCIS, C. W. *Popular Phrases in Grenada Dialect.* C. W. Francis, 1978.	Gren
Pra	KITZINGER, S. 'Speaking the same Language', in *The Practitioner.* No. 1278, Vol. 213, December 1974.	Ref.
PRCHMW	PASCASCIO, Gilbert and ROCA, Joseph *Can Herbs Make You Well.* Rural Education and Agriculture Project.	Belz
PSAE	PADEN, J. N. and SOJA, E. W. *The African Experience.* Vol. 1. Evanston, Northwestern Univ. Pr., 1970.	Ref.
PSFC	PROTAIN, Gertrude, *et al.* (eds.) *Stories for Children.* Grenada Independence Secretariat, 1974.	Gren
PSHWI	PARRY, J. H. and SHERLOCK, P. M. *A Short History of the West Indies.* London, Macmillan, 1956/1971.	CarA
PSNTB	PATTERSON, Jack and STEVENSON, G. *Native Trees of the Bahamas.* Bahamas, Jack Patterson, 1977.	Baha
PSS	PATTERSON, Orlando *The Sociology of Slavery.* Granada Publishing Ltd., 1967/1973.	CarA
PSUB	PAYNE, Shirleen *A Comparative Study of the Stylistic use of Barbadian Dialect by Four Writers.* Caribbean Study Paper, UWI, 1981.	Bdos
PTCI	PROTHERO, J. H. *The Turks & Caicos Islands.* (Cyclostyled MS, 1974).	TkCa
PTT	WILLIAMS, R. O. and WILLIAMS (Jnr.), R. O. *The Useful & Ornamental Plants of Trinidad & Tobago.* Trinidad, (4th edn.) Government Printer, 1969.	Trin

PuN	*Punch* (Weekly newspaper). Port of Spain.	Trin
PVES	PAYNE, Edward John *Voyages of the Elizabethan Seamen.* (1880) rep. OUP, 1907.	CarA
PVFT	PHILLIPS, Evan *A Voice from the Trees.* E. Phillips.	Guyn
PVPN	POWELL, Dulcie *The Voyage of the Plant Nursery HMS Providence, 1791–1793.* The Institute of Jamaica, 1973.	Jmca
PWOW	PRINGLE, Kenneth *Waters of the West.* London, Allen & Unwin, 1938.	Belz/ CayI
PWTF	PERRERO, Laurie *The World of Tropical Flowers.* Miami, Windward Publishing, 1976.	CarA
PWTWI	PARES, Richard *War & Trade in the West Indies, 1739–1763.* London, Frank Cass & Co., 1936/1963.	CarA
RALG	ROTH, Vincent *Animal Life in British Guiana.* Guiana Edn., No. 3, Georgetown, Daily Chronicle, 1941.	Guyn
RANB	RAHMING, Philip A. *A New Beginning.* Family Island Pr., 1973.	Baha
RCWC	ROHLEHR, F. G. *The Changing World of the Calypso.* (MS) 1969. St Augustine.	Trin
RD	RAHAMAN, Ray *Douglah.* Raylon Enterprises, 1976.	Trin
RDVI	ROY, John D. (ed.) *Description & Dictionary of Language of the Virgin Islands.* 1975.	ViIs
RDVI 2	ROY, J. D. (Compiler) *A Brief Description & Dictionary of the Language used in the Virgin Islands.* Virgin Islands Dept. of Education, 1975.	ViIs
Rel	*Release.* Georgetown, Release Pub.	Guyn
ReP	*The Reporter.* Belize City.	Belz
RFAN	ROSS, Charlesworth *From an Antiguan's Notebook.* Bridgetown, Advocate, 1962.	Antg
RFGW	RICKFORD, John R. (ed.) *A Festival of Guyanese Words.* Univ. of Guyana, 1978.	Guyn
RFLG	ROTH, Vincent *Fish Life in Br. Guiana.* Guiana Edn. No. 8, Georgetown, Daily Chronicle, 1943.	Guyn
RFMB	ROCK, Letnie *Folk Medicines in Barbados.* Caribbean Study Paper, UWI, 1974.	Bdos
RFTG	RIDGEWELL, W. M. *The Forgotten Tribes of Guyana.* Tom Stacey Ltd., 1972.	Guyn
RHBP	REECE, Robert *Hints to Young Barbados Planters.* Bridgetown, 1857.	Bdos
RHCD	STEIN, Jeff (ed.) *The Random House College Dictionary.* Rev. edn. London, Random House, 1975.	Ref.
RHGA	ROGET, J. P. (ed.) *L'Histoire de l'Isle de Grenade en Amérique, 1649–1659.* Presse Universitaire de Montréal.	Gren
RHJSS	ROBINSON, Kim and HEARNE, Leeta *22 Jamaican Short Stories* Kingston, Kingston Publishers 1987.	Jmca
RJH	ROBERTSON, Diane *Jamaican Herbs.* Kingston, Jamaican Herbs Ltd., 1982/86.	Jmca
RLCF	RODMAN, Hyman *Lower Class Families.* OUP, 1971.	Trin

RLIS	REID, Lucille L. *Love in the Sun*. Gibson Pr., 1975.	Bdos
RLLG	RAMSAHOYE, Fenton *The Development of Land Law in British Guiana*. New York, Oceana Publications, 1946.	Guyn
RM	RYAN, Pat *Macafouchette*. Pat Ryan, 1985.	Trin
RND	REID, V. S. *New Day*. London, Heinemann, 1973 (Alfred Knopf, 1947).	Jmca
RPME	REID, Vic *Peter of Mount Ephraim*. Jamaica Publishing House, 1971.	Jmca
RPP	ROTH, Vincent *Roth's Pepper-Pot*. Georgetown, Daily Chronicle, 1958.	Guyn
RR	RAHMING, Pat *Reflections*. House of Sesum, 1973.	Baha
RRC	YANSEN, C. A. *Random Remarks on Creolese*. Georgetown, C. A. Yansen, 1975.	Guyn
RSF	REID, V. S. *Sixty-five*. Longman Caribbean, 1960/1971.	Jmca
RSIG	RICHARDSON, Beryl *Sugar in Guyana*. Beryl Richardson, 1969.	Guyn
RSMCD	RAMKEESON, Peter *Sunday Morning Coming Down*. Scope Publishing Co., 1975.	Trin
RTCS	REDHEAD, Wilfred *Three Comic Sketches*. UWI Extra-Mural Dept., Trinidad, 1966.	Gren
RTYW	REID, V. S. *The Young Warriors*. Longman Caribbean, 1967.	Jmca
RTYY	ROWLANDS, E. C. *Teach Yourself Yoruba*. London, English Universities Pr., 1969.	Ref.
RWIN	RAMCHAND, Kenneth *West Indian Narrative*. London, Nelson & Son, 1966.	CarA
RWSS	RHYS, Jean *Wide Sargasso Sea*. London, Penguin, 1968 (orig. Deutsch 1966).	Dmca
SABS	SELVON, Samuel *A Brighter Sun*. Longman Caribbean, 1952/1971.	Trin
SAGF	SADEEK, Sheik *Across the Green Fields, and Five Other Stories*. S. Sadeek, 1974.	Guyn
SAS	SALKEY, Andrew *Anancy's Score*. London, Bogle L'Ouverture, 1973.	Jmca
SaS	*The Sun on Saturday*. Bridgetown.	Bdos
SASW	SENIOR, Olive *Arrival of the Snake Woman and Other Stories*. Longman Caribbean, 1989.	Jmca
Sav	BRATHWAITE, E. Kamau (ed.) *Savacou*. Kingston, Jamaica.	CarA
SAZJ	SENIOR, Olive *A–Z of Jamaican Heritage*. Kingston, Heinemann & Gleaner, 1983.	Jmca
SB	SALKEY, Andrew (ed.) *Breaklight—An Anthology of Caribbean Poetry*. Hamish Hamilton, 1971.	CarA
SBB	SADEEK, Sheik *Bundarie Boy*. S. Sadeek, 1974.	Guyn
SBBAM	ST. OMER, Garth *J——, Black Bam and the Masqueraders*. London, Faber, 1972.	StLu

SBG	SWAN, Michael *British Guiana, The Land of Six Peoples*. London, HMSO, 1957.	Guyn
SBHM	SPENCER, Flora *The Biggest Half is Mine*. (MS—One Act Play). Bridgetown.	Bdos
SCCD	SCHNEIDER, G. D. *Cameroons Creole Dictionary*. First Draft, Bamenda, Southern Cameroons, 1960.	Ref.
SCCW	SLATER, Mary *Cooking the Caribbean Way*. London, Hamlyn Publishing, 1974.	CarA
SCE	SALKEY, Andrew *Caribbean Essays*. London, Evans Brothers, 1973.	CarA
SCHMH	SALKEY, Andrew *Come Home, Malcolm Heartland*. London, Hutchinson & Co., 1976.	Jmca
SCO	SPENCER, Flora *Crop-Over*. Bridgetown, Commonwealth Caribbean Resource Centre, 1974.	Bdos
SCP	SALKEY, Andrew *Caribbean Prose*. London, Evans Brothers, 1967/1970.	CarA
SCT	SANDERSON, Ivan T. *Caribbean Treasure*. Llanidloes, Wales, Pyramid Pub., 1939.	CarA
SCTR	MIGHTY SPARROW *120 Calypsoes to Remember*. National Recording Co., 1963. Port of Spain.	Trin
SCYT	SANDROCK, Virginia Tate *Caribbean Yesterdays Today*. New York, Vantage Press, 1972.	CarA
SD	SALKEY, Andrew *Drought*. OUP, 1966/1973.	Jmca
SdB	*St. Kitts-Nevis Daily Bulletin*. Basseterre.	StKt
SDCCH	SANKAR, D. P. (ed.) *The Demerara Group of Companies Cultivation Handbook—Glossary of Sugar Industry Terms*. Georgetown, 1973 (MS).	Guyn
SDCE	*Dictionary of Canadian English. Senior Dictionary*. Agincourt, Ont., Gage Education Pub. Co., 1970.	Ref.
SDD	SCOBIE, Edward *Dies Dominica*. Drury Lane, 1965.	Dmca
SDGA	SANTAMARIA, F. J. *Diccionario General de Americanismos*. Mexico, 1942.	Ref.
SDON	SYMONETTE, Michael A. *Discovery of a Nation*. Management Communication Services, 1973.	Baha
SDOP	SHERIDAN, Richard *The Development of the Plantations to 1750*. Caribbean Universities Pr., 1970.	CarA
SDT	SADEEK, Sheik *The Diamond Thieves & Four more Stories*. Georgetown, S. Sadeek, 1974.	Guyn
SEMK	SPEARS, Richard A. *Elementary Maninka-Kan*. Evanston, Northwestern Univ., 1973.	Ref.
Sfu	*Straight From Us*. Student Council, BVI High School.	BrVi
SGAC	SIMON, Veronica *Glossary of Antigua Creole*. Caribbean Study Paper, UWI, 1980.	Antg
SGC	SADEEK, Sheik *Goodbye Corentyne*. S. Sadeek, 1974.	Guyn
SGJ	SALKEY, Andrew *Georgetown Journal*. London, New Beacon Books, 1972.	Guyn

SGWWE	SLATER, L. W. *A Glossary of West Indian Words &* *Expressions.* (MS, n.d.)	CarA
SH	SALKEY, Andrew *Hurricane.* OUP, 1964/1971.	Jmca
SHDNL	SCOTT, D. C. and HETHERWICK, A. *Dictionary of the Nyanja Language.* London, Lutterworth Press, 1929.	Ref.
SIBC	SEIFT, L. B., *et al. Igbo Basic Course.* FSI Washington, 1962.	Ref.
SILIG	SEYMOUR, A. J. *I Live in Georgetown.* Georgetown, Labour Advocate Printery, 1974.	Guyn
SITGW	SEYMOUR, A.J. *Independence 10. Guyanese Writing 1966–76 (Anthology)* Georgetown, National History and Arts Council, 1976.	Guyn
SJEV	ST. JOHN, Bruce *Joyce & Eros & Varia.* Bridgetown. Bruce St. John, 1976.	Bdos
SJJS	STEDMAN, John Gabriel *Journal of John Gabriel Stedman, 1744–97* (ed. S. Thompson). London, Mitre Press, 1962.	Srnm
SJNWI	SEALEY, J. *The Joy of Nature in the West Indies.* Port of Spain, Columbus Publishers, 1976.	Trin
SJS	SALKEY, Andrew *Jonah Simpson.* OUP, 1969.	Jmca
SJT	SALKEY, Andrew *Joey Tyson.* London, Bogle L'Ouverture Pub., 1974.	Jmca
SJW	SHERLOCK, Philip *Jamaica Way.* London, Longman Group, 1962.	Jmca
SKB	SPENCER, Flora and KING, Geoffrey *Bimshire, '73.* Bridgetown. (MS)	Bdos
SkN	*St Kitts-Nevis Bulletin.* Basseterre.	StKt
SLCD	STEWART, John *Last Cool Days.* London, André Deutsch, 1971.	Trin
SM	SEYMOUR, A. J. *Mirror.* Georgetown. A. J. Seymour, 1975.	Guyn
SMGL	SEYMOUR A. J. *The Making of Guyanese Literature.* Georgetown, A. J. Seymour, 1980.	Guyn
SMLNL	SEYMOUR, A. J. and E. *My Lovely Native Land.* London, Longman Group, 1971.	Guyn
SMPTT	SEAFORTH, C. E., ADAMS, C. D. and SYLVESTER, Y. *A Guide to the Medicinal Plants of Trinidad & Tobago.* London, Commonwealth Secretariat, 1983.	Trin/ Tbgo
SND	GRANT, William and MURISTON, David (eds.) *The Scottish National Dictionary.* SND Association (Vol. I 1940–Vol. X 1976).	Ref.
SNGD	SADEEK, Sheik *No Greater Day, & Four More Stories.* Georgetown, S. Sadeek, 1974.	Guyn
SNSCW	SEAMAN, George A. *Not So Cat Walk.* St. Thomas, Enid M. Baa, 1974.	BrVi
SNWIC	SEYMOUR, A. J. (ed.) *New Writing in the Caribbean.* Georgetown, A. J. Seymour, 1972.	CarA

SOED	*Shorter Oxford English Dictionary,* 3rd edn. rev., Oxford, Clarendon Pr., 1973.	Ref.
SPGWK	SCHNEIDER, G. B. *Preliminary Glossary. English-Pidgin English (Wes-Kos).* (Ms, Athens Centre for International Studies, Ohio Univ., 1965).	Ref.
SPM	SEYMOUR, A. J. *Pilgrim Memories.* Georgetown, Labour Advocate Printers, 1978.	Guyn
SPOC	SELVON, Samuel *The Plains of Caroni.* London, MacGibbon & Kee, 1970.	Trin
SQV	SALKEY, Andrew *A Quality of Violence.* London, New Beacon Books, 1978.	Jmca
SR	SALKEY, Andrew *Riot.* OUP, 1973.	Jmca
SRA	SELIGMAN, C. G. *Races of Africa.* 4th edn., London, OUP, 1966.	Ref.
SROB	SHEPPARD, Jill *The Redlegs of Barbados.* New York, KTO Press, 1977.	Bdos
SROH	ST. OMER, Garth *A Room on the Hill.* London, Faber, 1968.	StLu
SSAJ	SANGSTER, Ian *Sugar and Jamaica.* London, Thomas Nelson & Sons, 1973.	Jmca
SSBC	STEVICK, E. W. (ed.) *Shona Basic Course.* Washington, Foreign Service Institute, 1965.	Ref.
SSE	SPEARS, Richard A. *Slang and Euphemism—A Dictionary of Oaths, Curses, etc., etc.* New York, Jonathan David, 1981.	Ref.
SSFF	SHERLOCK, Philip *Shout for Freedom.* Macmillan Education, 1976.	Jmca
SSHL	SMITH, K. B. and SMITH, F. C. *To Shoot Hard Labour.* Scarborough, Ont., Edan, 1986.	Antg
SSHN	SEAMAN, George A. *Sticks from the Hawk's Nest.* George A. Seaman, 1973.	USVI
SSLG	SISTREN, (ed.) Honor F. SMITH *Lionheart Gal.* London, Women's Pr., 1986.	Jmca
SSOS	SADEEK, Sheik *Song of the Sugarcanes.* Georgetown, Sheik Sadeek, 1975.	Guyn
SSRB	ST. HILL, Margaret V. *The Speech Patterns of the Rastafarians of Barbados.* Caribbean Study Paper, UWI, Cave Hill, 1982.	Bdos
StA(DA)	*The Star.* Roseau.	Dmca
StA(JA)	*The Star.* Kingston.	Jmca
StA(SV)	*The Star.* Kingstown.	StVn
STAMG	SINGH, Karna Bahadur *Temples & Mosques—An Illustrated Study of East Indian Places of Worship in Guyana.* Release Publishers, 1980.	Guyn
STAT	SELVON, Samuel *Turn Again Tiger.* London, Heinemann, 1979.	Trin
STFJT	SHERLOCK, Philip *Three Finger Jack's Treasure.* Kingston, Jamaica Publishing House, 1969.	Jmca

STGP	SEYMOUR, A. J. (ed.) *A Treasury of Guyanese Poetry.* Georgetown, Guyana National Lithographic, 1980.	Guyn
STLL	SELVON, Samuel *The Lonely Londoners.* Longman Caribbean, 1956/1972.	Trin
STMM	SADEEK, Sheik *The Malali Makers.* Georgetown, Sheik Sadeek, 1979.	Guyn
STTG	STEELE, B. and ST. JOHN, B. (eds.) *Tim Tim Tales from Grenada.* St George's. UWI Extra-Mural Dept., 1973.	Gren
STWIS	SHERLOCK, Philip *West Indian Story.* Longman Caribbean, 1960/1973.	CarA
SUB	SCOBIE, Carver Milton *Up! Beat!* 1973.	Trin
SuC	*Sunday Chronicle.* Georgetown.	Guyn
SuG	*Sunday Guardian.* Port of Spain.	Trin
Suj	*BWIA Sunjet/Inflight Magazine* Port of Spain.	Trin
SuP	*Sunday Punch.* Port of Spain.	Trin
Sur	*Surinam Adventure* No. 2. Paramaribo, 1973.	Srnm
SuS	*The Sunday Sun.* Bridgetown. The Nation Publishing Co.	Bdos
Svi	*St Vincent & The Grenadines (Independence Souvenir).* Eslee Carberry & Associates.	StVn
SWI	SHERLOCK, Philip *West Indies.* London, Thames & Hudson, 1966.	CarA
SWIFT	SHERLOCK, Philip *West Indian Folk Tales.* OUP, 1966.	CarA
SWIN	SHERLOCK, Philip *West Indian Nations.* Jamaica Publishing House, 1973.	CarA
SWIS	SALKEY, Andrew *West Indian Stories.* London, Faber, 1960/1971.	CarA
SWOS	SELVON, Samuel *Ways of Sunlight.* Longman Caribbean, 1973.	Trin
SXSG	SMITH, Orril Patricia *Xmas Songs of Guyana.* Natural History and Arts Council, 1975.	Guyn
TADH	TAYLOR, D., *et al. Aspects of Dominican History.* Govt. Printing Division, 1972.	Dmca
TaP	*Tapia.* Port of Spain.	Trin
TCAF	TONGE, Gwen *Cooking Antugua's Foods.* 1973.	Antg
TcV	*The Voice.* Grand Turk.	TkCa
TDV	TEJERA, M. J. *Diccionario de Venezolanismos* Caracas, Academia Venezolana de la Lengua, 1983.	Ref.
TF	THOMAS, J. J. *Froudacity.* London, New Beacon Books, (orig. 1889).	CarA
TFED	TAYLOR, F. W. *A Fulani-English Dictionary.* OUP, 1932.	Ref.
TFPAS	THOMPSON, Ivy *Family Patterns of Anguillian Society.* (MS)	Angu
TGSLP	TOYNBER, Mary W. *A Visitor's Guide to St Lucia Patois.* St Lucia Tourist Board, Lithographic Press, 1969.	StLu
The	*Themes, Verse and Prose from U.W.I. St. Augustine* III. Pubs. Literary and Debating Society.	Trin

TIBJ	TAYLOR, Lady R. *Introduction to the Birds of Jamaica.* London, Macmillan, 1955.	Jmca
TiM	*The Times.* Anguilla.	Angu
Tim	*Timehri. Journal of the Royal Agricultural and Commercial Society.* Georgetown.	Guyn
TLDVG	THOMAS, Roy *Little Dix Bay & Virgin Gorda.* Pamphlet, n.d.	BrVi
TLTH	THOMAS, Arundell and LOCKHART, Anthony *Two Heads.* A. Thomas and A. Lockhart.	Dmca
TM	TOCZEK, Nick, *et al. Melanthika—Anthology.* Birmingham, L.W.M. Publications, 1977.	CarA
TOAS	TATEM, Colin *Ordeal at Sea.* Johnson's Publications, 1975.	Baha
ToR	*The Torchlight.* St George's.	Gren
TOSR	TERTULLIEN, Mizpah *Old Stories and Riddles.* Nassau, M. Tertullien, 1977.	Baha
Tou	*Toucan.* Inflight Publications Ltd., 1978.	
TPOT	TAYLOR, D. P. *Parang of Trinidad.* Port of Spain, NCC, 1977.	Trin
Tra	*The Traveller.* Barbados Board of Tourism.	Bdos
Trc	*Trinidad Carnival.* Morvant, Key Caribbean Publications, 1974.	Trin
TRFSS	THOMAS, Odette *Rain Falling Sun Shining.* London, Bogle L'Ouverture Pub., 1975.	Trin
TrG	*The Trinidad Guardian & Sunday Guardian.* Port of Spain.	Trin
TrI	*The Tribune.* Nassau.	Baha
TRIH	THOMAS, G. C. H. *Ruler in Hiroona.* Trinidad, Columbus Publishers, 1972.	StVn
Trn	*Trinidad Naturalist.* S.M. Publications. Port of Spain.	Trin
TrU	*Truth.* Bridgetown.	Bdos
TSA	TEYTAUD, Anton *Sarah & Addie.* Anton Teytaud, 1974.	USVI
TSIS	TOWNSEND, Saida *Sketches in Sepia—(Gullah & Other Poems).* Continental Leasing Co., South Carolina, 1975.	Gull
TSOS	TURNER, Telcine *Song of the Surreys.* London, Macmillan, 1977.	Baha
TtM	*TnT Mirror.* Port of Spain.	Trin
TTPCG	THOMAS, J. J. *The Theory and Practice of Creole Grammar.* 1869. (Reprint London, New Beacon Books, 1969).	Trin
TtR	*Trinidad & Tobago Review.* Port of Spain.	Trin
TVIT	TINDALL, H. R. *Vegetables in the Tropics.* London, Macmillan, 1983.	CarA
TWD	TRACY, Frances V. *Wapishana Dictionary.* Georgetown, Unevangelized Fields Mission, 1972.	Guyn

TWDWE	THOMAS, Gordon and MORGAN, Witts Max *The Day the World Ended.* New York, Stein & Day Publication, 1969.	Mart
TWISM	TROLLOPE, Anthony *The West Indies and the Spanish Main.* London, Chapman & Hall, 1860.	CarA
UHOB	UNSWORTH, Sister Virginia *A History of the Bahamas.* V. Unsworth, 1971.	Baha
Unn	*University Newsletter.* UWI, Mona, Jamaica.	CarA
UWI	*UWI (1949–1974)—(Collection of short stories etc.),* 1974.	StVn
VaN	*Vanguard.* St George's.	Gren
VBHUS	VASS, Winifred K. *The Bantu Speaking Heritage of the United States.* Center for Afro-American Studies. Univ. of California, 1979.	Ref.
VCE	1981 U/E Students Exercise *Examples of Varieties of English spoken in the Caribbean.* Glossary collected by Mary Edwards, 1981.	CarA
VCW	VAN SERTIMA, Ivan *Caribbean Writers.* London, New Beacon Books, 1968.	CarA
VDCSL	VAUGHN, Robert *The Development of a Dictionary of Selected Words and Phrases of the Creole Language as Spoken by the People of St. Lucia.* (Ann Arbor, Univ. Microfilms, 1981.)	StLu
Vgi	*Virgin Islander.* Tortola, Virgin Islands Publishing Co. Ltd.	BrVi
VHTOC	VALDMAN, A. and HIGHFIELD, A. *Theoretical Orientations in Creole Studies.* New York, Academic Press, 1980.	Ref.
VHTV	VARLACK, Pearl and HARRIGAN, Norwell *The Virgins.* St. Thomas, The Caribbean Research Institute, 1977.	BrVi
VID	SEAMAN, George A. *Virgin Islands Dictionary.* St. Croix, G. A. Seaman, 1967/1976.	USVI
ViN	*The Vincentian.* Kingstown.	StVn
Vip	*VIP* Vol. 1, No. 1. St. Thomas College of the Virgin Islands, 1971.	USVI
VISTP	Virgin Islands Soil and Water Conservation District. *Selected Tropical Plants.* St Croix Landmarks Society, n.d.	CarA
VLCD	VOORHOEVE, J. and LICHTVELD, U. M. *Creole Drum.* New Haven, Yale Univ. Pr., 1975.	Srnm
VoS	*The Voice of St. Lucia.* Castries.	StLu
VPIT	VELEZ, Ismael *Plantas Indeseables en los Cultivos Tropicales.* Río Piedras, P.R., Editorial Universitaria, 1950.	PtRi
VSCT	VAN SERTIMA, J. A. *The Creole Tongue.* Georgetown, Argosy, 1905.	Guyn
VWP	VALLS, Lito *What a Pistarckle: A Glossary of Virgin Islands English Creole,* St John, 1981.	USVI

W1	WEBSTER, N. *American Dictionary of the English Language (1828).* Springfield, G. & C. Merriam (1864 revision).	Ref.
W2	*Webster's New International Dictionary of the English Language (1909).* Springfield, G. & C. Merriam (2nd edn. 1934) (1959 revision).	Ref.
W3	*Webster's Third New International Dictionary.* Springfield, G. & C. Merriam, 1961.	Ref.
WAAF	WILLS, J. V. (ed.) *Agriculture and Fisheries.* Public Affairs Dept., Bahamas, 1974.	Baha
WACSS	WARMKE, Germaine L. and ABBOTT, R. Tucker *Caribbean Sea Shells.* Dover Publications Inc., 1962.	CarA
WALS	WELMERS, W. E. *African Language Structures.* Univ. of Berkeley California Pr., 1973.	Ref.
Was	*Washeen.* Roseau, Roots.	Dmca
WASTT	WATSON, Eva *Aspects of Stickfighting in Trinidad & Tobago.* Caribbean Study Paper, UWI.	Trin
WBAM	WAYNE, Rick *It'll be Alright in the Morning.* Star Publishing Co., n.d.	StLu
WBAWI	WILLIAMS, Eric *Britain and the West Indies.* Longmans, Green & Co. Ltd., 1969.	CarA
WBEFS	WHITELEATHER, R. T. and BROWN, H. H. *An Experimental Fishery Survey in Trinidad, Tobago and British Guiana–Anglo-American Caribbean Commission (1945).* [NB. Glossary only pp. 107–9].	CarA
WBH	WALLACE, Susan J. *Back Home—An original Anthology.* London, Collins, 1975.	Baha
WBS	WALLACE, Susan *Bahamian Scene.* Dorrance & Co., 1970.	Baha
WCAF	WATERMAN, Ivan *Chris and Fred.* London, Macmillan, 1977.	Gren
WCAS	WILLIAMS, Eric *Capitalism & Slavery.* London, André Deutsch, 1964/1972.	CarA
WCD9	*Webster's Ninth New Collegiate Dictionary.* Merriam–Webster, 1983.	Ref.
WCFV	WOOD, Beryl *Caribbean Fruits & Vegetables.* Longman Caribbean, 1973.	CarA
WCIB	WATSON, Karl *The Civilized Island Barbados.* Barbados, Karl Watson, 1979.	Bdos
WCR	WICKHAM, John *Casuarina Row.* Belfast, Christian Journals, 1974.	Bdos
WCSL	(Unidentified author) *What's Cooking in St. Lucia.* St Lucia Tourist Board.	StLu
WDAC	WILKES, G. A. *A Dictionary of Australian Colloquialisms.* London, Routledge & Kegan Paul, 1978.	Ref.
WDMM	WALCOTT, Derek *Dream on Monkey Mountain.* London, Jonathan Cape, 1970/1972.	StLu

WEBC	WARBURTON, I., *et al. Ewe Basic Course.* African Studies Program, Indiana Univ., 1968.	Ref.
WEDG	WRIGHT, Joseph *English Dialect Grammar.* Oxford, Frowde, 1905.	Ref.
WeG	*Weekly Gleaner.* Kingston.	Jmca
WeH	*Weekend Heat.* Port of Spain.	Trin
WeI	*The West Indian.* St George's.	Gren
WEIT	WELLER, Judith Ann *The East Indian Indenture in Trinidad.* UWI, 1968.	Trin
WeN	*Weekly Newsletter.* St George's.	Gren
WeS	*Weekend Star.* Kingston.	Jmca
WFCSP	WAFE, Barbara *A Study of French Creole Stories collected at Paramin, Maraval.* Caribbean Study Paper, UWI.	Trin
WFSFB	WARDE, Shirley A. *Folk Stories from Belize—We Jus Catch Um.* Indiana, Pinchpenny Pr., 1974.	Belz
Wic	*West Indies Chronicle.* London, West India Committee.	CarA
Wid	*West Indian Digest.* Royston, Herts., A. Ali.	CarA
WIE	WALLACE, Susan J. *Island Echoes.* London, Macmillan, 1973.	Baha
WIED	WILLIAMS, Kay *Igbo-English Dictionary.* Benin City, Ethiope Pub. Corp. 1972.	Ref.
WIGN	WALCOTT, Derek *In a Green Night.* London, Jonathan Cape, 1962/1972.	StLu
WIT	WILLIAMS, N.D. *Ikael Torass.* Havana, Ediciones Casa de las Américas, 1978.	Guyn
WiW	*West Indian World.* London.	CarA
WJM	WILLIAMS, Lorna W. *Jamaica Mento.* Publishing Associates (WI) 1978.	Jmca
WkI	*Weekend Investigator.* Bridgetown.	Bdos
WLBH	WRIGHT, A. C. S., *et al. Land in British Honduras.* London, HMSO, 1959.	Belz
WMHC	WALCOTT, Roderick *Malfinis or The Heart of a Child.* Trinidad, UWI Extra-Mural Dept., 1967.	StLu
WNNT	WHY, John A. *Nice and Nasty Tales.* Georgetown, J. Why, 1976.	Guyn
WNW	*Webster's New World Dictionary of the American Language.* 2nd College edn., Cleveland, Ohio, Collins & World Pub. Co., 1976.	Ref.
WOB	WALCOTT, Derek *O Babylon.* London, Jonathan Cape, 1979.	Jmca
WoV	*The Worker's Voice.* St John's.	Antg
WSAD	WALCOTT, Derek *The Sea at Dauphin.* Port of Spain, UWI Extra-Mural Dept., 1954.	StLu
WSHEJ	WHYTE, Millicent *A Short History of Education in Jamaica.* London, Hodder & Stoughton, 1977.	Jmca

WSN	DeGROOT, A. *Woordregister Saramakaans–Nederlands.* Paramaribo, 1981.	Srnm
WSNE	*Woordenlijst: Sranan–Nederlands–English.* Paramaribo, Vaco, 1980.	Srnm
WSTC	WAITE-SMITH, Cicely *The Creatures.* Port of Spain, UWI Extra-Mural Dept., 1966.	Trin
WTC	WALCOTT, Derek *The Castaway.* London, Jonathan Cape, 1965/1972.	StLu
WTCB	WILES, Audrey *Tropical Colouring Book with Poems.* Twin Guinep Ltd., 1974.	CarA
WTD	WALROND, Eric *Tropic Death.* New York, Collier, 1926/1972.	Bdos
WTG	WALCOTT, Derek *The Gulf.* London, Jonathan Cape, 1969/1974.	StLu
WTIED	WILLAIMSON, K. and TIMITIMI, A. O. *Short Izon–English Dictionary.* Univ. of Port Harcourt Press, 1983.	Ref.
WTIT	WOOD, Donald *Trinidad in Transition.* OUP, 1968.	Trin
Wts	*The Welcome Tourist Guide.* Island Publishing Service Ltd.	BrVi
WTSE	WALMSLEY, Anne (ed.) *The Sun's Eye.* London, Longmans, 1968.	CarA
WTT	WOODWARD, Marion *Trinidad Tales*, Book II. Port of Spain. Marion Woodward.	Trin
WWPAL	WESTERMAN, D. and WARD, I. C. *Practical Phonetics for Students of African Languages.* OUP, 1933.	Ref.
WWWE	WICKHAM, John *World Without End—Memoirs.* London, New Beacon Books, 1982.	Bdos
Xmt	*Xmas Tide.* Georgetown, Daily Chronicle (1930–45).	Guyn
YCPB	YOUNG, Colville *Creole Proverbs of Belize.* Belize, Colville Young, 1980; 3rd edn., 1988.	Belz
YOCC	YOUNG, Colville *From One Caribbean Corner.* Belize, C. N. Young, 1983.	Belz
ZAGL	ZIMMERMANN, J. *A Grammatical Sketch and Vocabulary of the Akra-Gã Language.* Stuttgart, Basel Missionary Soc., 1858.	Ref.
ZSBP	ZUILL, W. S. *The Story of Bermuda and her People.* Macmillan, 1973.	Berm
ZWD	ZAMORE, Michael *The Wildlife of Dominica.* Roseau, Ministry of Agriculture, 1979.	Dmca

FRENCH AND SPANISH
SUPPLEMENT

INTRODUCTION

The English–French–Spanish Supplement to the Dictionary was compiled with a view to providing foreign-language equivalents for selected everyday items of flora and fauna listed in the main work. The Supplement was approved by the UWI Monitoring Committee in 1986 and systematic work on it was begun in the same year by the editor who is its sole author.

As a foreign-language specialist and teacher-educator, the editor of this Supplement had long perceived the need within the education system for an ordered listing of foreign-language equivalents in a number of areas pertaining to the total Caribbean environment. It is this need which this Supplement has begun to address.

Research for this Supplement was carried out by consulting a number of books, articles, and lists of flora and fauna in all the languages concerned. Those sources are listed in the Bibliography on which the English–French–Spanish Supplement is based. Checking of equivalents was also done in consultation with French and Spanish native speakers in most of the territories identified and by visits to Botanical Gardens and Museums in Martinique and Puerto Rico.

SOURCES OF CARIBBEAN FRENCH AND SPANISH IN THIS SUPPLEMENT

The territories used for the French equivalents are mainly Martinique and Guadeloupe because they are the best-known French islands. Haiti is, however, sometimes included because occasionally the French equivalent required has only been found in Haitian French. For the same reason, though rarely, French Guiana is included.

In the case of Spanish equivalents, the principle is the same. The most representative territories are Puerto Rico and Santo Domingo, the latter being the oldest Spanish-speaking territory in the region. Cuba and Venezuela are, however, also frequently used as being important Hispanophone territories. Venezuela shares many ecological similarities with the English-speaking territories of Trinidad and Guyana. It also qualifies as part of the Caribbean, having a wholly Caribbean sea coast. Spanish loan-words in the English of Trinidad belong historically to the same period of Spanish colonial development of Venezuela. Certain items of fauna are also found only on the South American mainland, so their Spanish equivalents are found largely in Venezuela.

Another area which needs to be considered is that of foreign-language based Creoles. Caribbean English, in the territories which were formerly under French influence—Dominica, St Lucia, Grenada, and Trinidad—has a considerable number of French Creole loan-words. This Supplement, however, is only concerned with giving equivalents to Caribbean English words, and the French equivalents preferred in most cases are those which conform to the morphological norms of Standard French. Accordingly, grammatical gender is identified so that the student can use the correct adjectival agreements. Occasionally, there may be creolized 'noms vernaculaires' in French, but these are very few, occurring only if no other acceptable equivalent is available, e.g. Fr. **herbe-mal-tête** *f.* (Guad, Mart) for English **leaf-of-life**. It is for this reason that there are no items under the letter Z in this Supplement, because all items of flora and fauna occurring under Z in the main Dictionary are French Creole items.

Where certain Caribbean English items have Standard French or Spanish equivalents that show a clear semantic shift from their original meaning, that is indicated in a usage note at the end of the entry. For example, one of the Caribbean Spanish equivalents to English **four-o'clock bush** is **buenas tardes**. At the end of the entry for **four-o'clock bush** there is a note saying, 'The second Sp equivalent is Std. Sp. for "good afternoon"'. Similarly, the Caribbean French and Spanish equivalents for the English item **robin**[1], which is a particular type of fish, both mean 'hen' in Standard French and Standard Spanish. At the end of that entry, there is a note drawing attention to this fact.

There are some general items of flora and fauna which are included in the Supplement, but which are not listed in the main Dictionary. They have been so included because of their everyday importance, e.g. **shrimp, crab, chick-pea, pumpkin**. All such items carry the territorial label (CarA) which means that they are common to the entire region. The label (CarA) occurs after French and Spanish equivalents in this Supplement only when there is no territory-specific name for the item. For example, English **Bombay mango** is in Spanish **mango de Bombay** *m.* (CarA).

It may also be observed that very often the same name is used in French or Spanish for two different items, just as happens quite regularly in Caribbean English. For example, the Caribbean French equivalents for **Christmas-bush** and **jack-in-the-bush** are both **langue à chat**. Similarly, the Spanish equivalents for both **African tulip tree** and **hibiscus** are **amapola**.

Occasionally, only one foreign-language equivalent may be found for an English item in this Supplement. The English item **flat-o'-the-earth** has only a French equivalent, **herbe-au-long-case**; the English item **pac(c)u** has only a Spanish equivalent **cachama**.

In conclusion, since this Supplement is intended to provide users of the main Dictionary with a reliable source of French/Spanish equivalents to items of flora and fauna, the taxonomic names are included to ensure identification.

Since there are many regional varieties of names for the same things in Caribbean French and Caribbean Spanish, complete coverage, especially in a Supplement of this kind, is impractical. However, the Editor would welcome from users constructive suggestions, preferably supported by authentic reference where available, for amendment, advancement, and expansion.

Finally, I express my sincere thanks to Mr Marvel O'Neal, the Consultant Adviser on Computerization for his help with the design, and to Miss Hazelyn Devonish for her continual assistance and her valuable and timely advice in relation to the computerization of this Supplement. The entire work was executed by the Editor on an IBM-compatible Hyundai PC.

J. E. ALLSOPP
Editor

HOW TO USE THE SUPPLEMENT

The Supplement is a selection of items of Caribbean flora and fauna, each a *primary allonym* marked with an asterisk in the main Dictionary. They are listed in alphabetical order in English and accompanied by one (or two) French and Spanish equivalents in Caribbean territories. The Supplement is therefore intended to be used in conjunction with the main body of the Dictionary. Any foreign language student or teacher may use this Supplement in either of two ways.

First, the user may find that the Anglophone item for which he/she is seeking a French or Spanish equivalent is actually listed in the Supplement. In this case, he/she may immediately use the foreign language equivalent given (carefully noting its gender), or make a choice if two equivalents in the same language are offered.

Second, if the desired Anglophone item is not found to be listed in the Supplement, the user may seek it in the main Dictionary where it is more likely to be. The Dictionary's cross-referencing system will identify the *primary allonym* of that territorial item. The user must then seek that *primary allonym* as a listed item in the Supplement, and take the required French or Spanish equivalent from that source. For example, the user seeking a foreign language equivalent for **man-piaba**, and not finding that item in the Supplement, goes to the main Dictionary where it is located, with **ball-bush** given as its *primary allonym*. **Ball-bush** is then found in the Supplement with French **herbe-gros-bouton** *f.* and Spanish **moli-nillo** *m.* as equivalents; those are the same French and Spanish equivalents for **man-piaba**.

It will be noticed that sometimes two equivalents in each foreign language are given for one word or phrase. However, three foreign language equivalents may be given in cases where there is some additional special feature.

It must also be noted that in some cases where a word in the main Dictionary has more than one sense or more than one homonym, only the one sense or one homonym which is marked by an asterisk, is treated in the Supplement. In such cases, the sense number or homonym number is indicated in the Supplement listing.

J. E. ALLSOPP

BIBLIOGRAPHY

ENGLISH REFERENCES CONSULTED

Adams, C. D., *The Flowering Plants of Jamaica*, UWI at Mona, Univ. Press, Glasgow, 1972– .

—— *The Blue Mahoe & Other Bushes—An Introduction to Plant Life in Jamaica*, McGraw-Hill Far Eastern Publishers (S) Ltd., 1971.

Allyn, Rube, *Dictionary of Fishes*, Great Outdoors Publishing Co., Florida, 1977.

Bond, James, *Birds of the West Indies*, 4th edn., Collins, 1974.

Bourne, M. J., Lennox, G. W., and Seddon, S. A., *Fruits and Vegetables of the Caribbean*, Macmillan Caribbean, 1988.

Cleare, L. D., *Birds—British Guiana Nature Study Manuals*, Daily Chronicle Co. Ltd., Guyana, 1962.

FAO Species Identification Sheets—West Central Atlantic, Fishing Area 31, Vols. I–VII.

Flora de Venezuela, Ediciones No. 5 Tricolor, Ministerio de Educaci Direcci General, Caracas, Venezuela, 1969.

Gooding, E. G. B., Loveless, A. R., and Proctor, G. R., *Flora of Barbados*, HMSO, 1965.

Graham, V. E., *Tropical Wild Flowers*, Hulton Educational Publications Ltd., 1963.

Greenberg, Idaz, *Guide to Corals & Fishes of Florida, the Bahamas and the Caribbean*, Seahawk Press, 1977.

Haynes, Lilith M., 'Local Names of Plants in Guyana, South America—A Linguistic & Ethnobotanical Study', MA Thesis, December 1969.

Herklots, G. A. C., *The Birds of Trinidad and Tobago*, Collins, 1969.

Honychurch, P. N., *Caribbean Wild Plants & Their Uses*, Macmillan Caribbean, 1986.

Howard, Richard A., *Flora of the Lesser Antilles—Leeward and Windward Islands*, 6 Vols, Arnold Arboretum, Harvard University, 1989.

Jones, A., and Sefton, N., *Marine Life of the Caribbean*, Macmillan Caribbean, 1978.

Kasasian, L., *Common Weeds of Trinidad*, Regional Research Centre, UWI, 1964.

Liogier, Henri Alain, *Descriptive Flora of Puerto Rico and Adjacent Islands*, Vols. I and II, Editorial de la Universidad de Puerto Rico, Puerto Rico, 1985.

Local Names of Fruits & Vegetables in the English-Speaking Caribbean, Caribbean Food and Nutrition Institute, Supplement to *Cajanus* 1971, Vol. IV, No. 2.

Morton, Julia F., *Atlas of Medicinal Plants of Middle America*, Vols. I and II, Charles C. Thomas Publisher, Illinois, USA, 1981– .

—— *Fruits of Warm Climates*, Creative Resource Systems, Inc., 1987.

Omawale, *Guyana's Edible Plants*, University of Guyana, 1973. Marine Fishery Analysis Unit, Fisheries Division, 1988, *Trinidad and Tobago Gulf-of-Paria Local Names Project*.

Seaforth, C. E., Adams, C. D., and Sylvester, Y., *Medicinal Plants of Trinidad and Tobago*, Commonwealth Secretariat, 1983.

Williams, R. O., *The Useful and Ornamental Plants of Trinidad and Tobago*, Government Printery, Trinidad and Tobago, 1969.

FRENCH REFERENCES CONSULTED

Ebroin, Ary, *Les Succulents Fruits des Antilles*, Editions Caribéennes, Paris, 1989.

Fournet, Jacques, *Flore Illustrée des Phanérogames de Guadeloupe et Martinique*, Institut de la Recherche Agronomique, Paris, 1978.

—— *Fleurs et Plantes des Antilles*, Les Editions du Pacifique, Singapore, 1988.

Le Corre, G., and Exbrayat, A., *Fleurs des Tropiques*, Editions Exbrayat, Fort de France, 1985.

APAG, *Lexique sur la Flore Caraïbe* (Association pour la Promotion de l'Anglais en Guadeloupe), Guadeloupe, n.d.

Magras, Michel, *Fleurs des Antilles*, Les Editions du Latanier, 1989.

Ouensanga, Christian, *Plantes Médicinales et Remèdes Créoles*, Vol. I, Editions Desormeaux, 1983.

Pierre-Noel, Arsène, *Nomenclature Polyglotte des Plantes Haïtiennes et Tropicales*, Presses Nationales d'Haïti, 1971.

—— *Les Plantes et les Légumes d'Haïti qui Guérissent*, Vol. I, Imprimerie Le Natal SA, 1959.

Pinchon, Le Pere R., *Faune des Antilles Françaises*, Fort de France, 1976.

—— *D'Autres Aspects de la Nature aux Antilles*, Fort de France, 1971.

SPANISH REFERENCES CONSULTED

Biaggi, Virgilio, *Las aves de Puerto Rico*, Editorial de la Universidad de Puerto Rico, 3rd edn., 1983.

Cuba en la mano—Enciclopedia popular ilustrada, La Habana, 1940.

Esteva, Francisco Oliva, *Plantas de los jardines de Venezuela*, Ediciones Armitano, C.A., Caracas, Venezuela, 1981.

Gremone, Carlos, Cervigon, Fernando, Gorzula, Stefan, Medina, Glenda, and Novoa, Daniel, *Fauna de Venezuela—Vertebrados*, Editorial Biosfera, n.d.

Liogier, Alain Henri, *La flora de la Española*, Tomos I–V, Ediciones de la UCE, 1982.

Little, Elbert L. Jr, Wadsworth, Frank H., and Marrero, José, *Arboles comunes de Puerto Rico y las Islas Vírgenes*, Editorial Universitaria, Universidad de Puerto Rico, 1977.

Nunez Meléndez, Esteban, *Plantas medicinales de Puerto Rico*, Editorial de la Universidad de Puerto Rico, Puerto Rico, 1989.

Riviero, Juan A., *Los anfibios y reptiles de Puerto Rico*, Editorial Universitaria, Universidad de Puerto Rico, Puerto Rico, 1978.

Rodriguez Martinez, Nelson R., *Plantas alimenticias y medicinales*, Editorial Nani, 1987.

Stockton de Dod, Annabelle, *Guía de campo para las aves de la República Dominicana*, Editora Horizontes de América, 1981.

TERRITORIAL REFERENCES USED IN
THE SUPPLEMENT

FRENCH

FrGy	French Guiana	Guad	Guadeloupe
Hait	Haiti	Mart	Martinique

SPANISH

Cuba	Cuba	PtRi	Puerto Rico
StDo	Santo Domingo	Venz	Venezuela

Note: All territorial codes identifying the English headwords or phrases in the Supplement are the same ones used in the main dictionary.

A

ab·bay *n* (Jmca) *Elaeis guineensis* (*Palmaceae*); FR. *palmier de Guinée m.* (Guad, Mart); SP. *corozo m.* (StDo)

a·ca·cia *n* (TkCa, Trin) *Acacia farnesiana* (*Leguminosae-Mimosae*); FR. *acacia jaune f.* (Guad, Mart); SP. *aromo m.* (PtRi)

ac·kee *n* (CarA) *Blighia sapida* (*Sapindaceae*); FR. *aki m.*, *cervelle végétale f.* (Guad, Mart); SP. *seso vegetal m.* (PtRi)

Adam's nee·dle *n phr* (Angu, Trin) *Yucca aloifolia* (*Liliaceae*); FR. *yucca, salespareille f.* (Guad, Mart); SP. *flor de Jérico f.* (StDo)

A·fri·can tu·lip tree *n phr* (CarA) *Spathodea campanulata* (*Bignoniaceae*); FR. *tulipier du Gabon, immortel étranger m.* (Guad, Mart); SP. amapola *f.* (StDo) *tulipán africano m.* (PtRi, Venz)

afu-yam *n* (Jmca, Tbgo, Trin) *Dioscorea cayennenis* (*Dioscoreaceae*); FR. *igname-guinée f.* (Guad, Mart); SP. *ñame amarillo m.* (Cuba, PtRi, StDo)

a·ga·ve *n* (CarA) *Agave americana* (*Agavaceae*); FR. *langue à boeuf f.* (Guad, Mart); SP. *maguey m.* (PtRi, StDo)

a·gou·ti *n* (Baha, Belz, Gren, Guyn, Trin) *Dasyprocta antillensis, D. albida, D. agouti* (*Dasyproctidae*); FR. *agouti m.* (Mart); SP. *agutí m.* (Venz)

al·ba·core *n* (CarA) *Thunnus alalunga* (*Scombridae*); FR. *germon m.* (Mart); SP. *albacora f.* (Cuba, PtRi, StDo)

al·la·man·da *n* (CarA) *Allamanda cathartica* (*Apocynaceae*); FR. *liane à lait f.* (Guad, Mart); SP. *copa de mantequilla f.* (StDo), *jazmín amarillo m.* (Venz)

al·li·ga·tor *n* (CarA) *Melanosuchus niger* (*Alligatoridae*); FR. *caiman m.* (Guad, Mart); SP. *caimán negro m.* (Venz) □ *Alligator* is also Std. Fr.

al·li·son tu·na *n* (Baha, Berm, USVI) See TUNA

all·spice *n* (CarA) *Pimenta dioica, P. officinalis* (*Myrtaceae*); FR. *piment de la Jamaïque m.* (Guad, Hait); SP. *pimienta f.* (Cuba, PtRi)

al·mond (tree) *n (phr)* (CarA) *Terminalia catappa* (*Combretaceae*); FR. *amandier m.* (Guad, Mart); SP. *almendro m.* (PtRi, StDo) □ *Amande* is Std. Fr. and *almendra* is Std. Sp. for the fruit.

al·oe(s) *n* (CarA) *Aloe vera, A. vulgaris* (*Liliaceae*); FR. *aloës m. pl.* (Guad, Mart); SP. *áloe m., zábila f.* (PtRi, StDo) □ *Aloe* is also Std. Sp. for ALOE(S).

a·ma·ryl·lis *n* (CarA) *Zephyranthes eggersiana, Z. tubispatha, Z. citrina* (*Amaryllidaceae*); FR. *petit lis blanc m.* (Guad, Mart); SP. *duende blanco m.* (StDo)

am·ber·jack *n* (StLu) *Seriola dumerili* (*Scombridae*); FR. *poisson limon m.* (Mart); SP. *medregal m.* (PtRi)

A·mer·i·can silk cot·ton *n phr* (BrVi) *Calotropis procera* (*Asclepiadaceae*); FR. *arbre de soie m.* (Guad, Mart); SP. *algodón de seda m.* (Cuba, PtRi, StDo)

a·na·con·da *n* (Trin) *Eunectes murinus* (*Boidae*); FR. *anaconda m.* (Mart); SP. *anaconda, culebra de agua f.* (Venz)

a·na·to (ar·not·to) *n* (CarA) *Bixa orellana* (*Bixaceae*); FR. *roucou m.* (Guad, Mart); SP. *bija f.* (PtRi, StDo)

an·cho *n* (Trin) *Pomatomus saltatrix* (*Pomatomidae*); FR. *tassergal, poisson bleu m.* (Guad, Mart); SP. *anchova de banco f.* (Cuba)

an·cho·vy *n* (StLu, Trin) *Engraulis eurystole* (*Engraulidae*); FR. *anchois m.* (Guad, Mart); SP. *anchoa, f.* (Cuba), *camiguana f.* (Venz)

an·gel-fish *n* (CarA) *Pomacanthus arcuatus* (*Chaetodontidae*); FR. *scalaire m.* (Guad, Mart); SP. *pez angel m.* (PtRi)

an·gel·i·ca *n* 1. (USVI) *Angelica archangelica* (*Umbelliferae*); FR. *romarin m.* (Guad, Mart); SP. *gallego m.* (PtRi)

an·ge·lin *n* (CarA) *Andira inermis* (*Papilionaceae*); FR. *angelin, bois-olive m.* (Guad, Mart); SP. *palo de burro m.* (StDo)

an·gel's trum·pet *n phr* (Baha, Jmca, Trin) *Datura suaveolens, Brugmansia arborea* (*Solanaceae*); FR. *stramoine odorante f.* (Guad); SP. *campana de París f.* (Cuba, PtRi)

anise *n* (BrVi, Mrat, StKt) *Pimpinella anisum*
(*Umbelliferae*); FR. *anis m.* (Guad); SP. *hinojo*
m. (StDo)

a·no·le (**a·no·lis**) *n* (Gren, StLu) *Anolis aeneus,*
A. richardi (*Iguanidae*); FR. *anoli m.* (Guad,
Mart); SP. *saca banderas m.* (Venz)

ant-bear *n* (Belz, Guyn) *Myrmecophaga jubata*
(*Edentata*); FR. *fourmilier m.* (Guad, Mart); SP.
oso hormiguero m. (Venz)

an·thu·ri·um *n* (CarA) *Anthurium andreanum/*
barbadosense/crystallinum, etc (*Araceae*); FR. *an-*
thurium m. (Guad, Mart); SP. *anturio m.*
(Cuba, StDo)

An·ti·gua heath *n phr* (Angu) *Ruselia equi-*
setiformis (*Scrophulariaceae*); FR. *goutte de*
sang f. (Guad, Mart); SP. *coral de Italia m.*
(PtRi)

ants-bush *n* (Guyn) *Struchium sparganophora*
(*Asteraceae*); FR. *oreille-mouton f.* (Guad); SP.
yerba de faja f. (PtRi)

ap·ple-ba·na·na *n* (Belz, CayI, Guyn, Jmca,
TkCa) *Musa cavendishii* (*Musaceae*); FR. *figue*
naine f., figue banane f. (Hait); SP. *cambur*
pigmeo m. (Venz)

ap·ple-blos·som cas·si·a *n phr* (Bdos, Gren,
Trin) *Cassia javanica* (*Leguminosae-Caesal-*
piniaceae); SP. *acacia rosada f.* (PtRi)

ar·ma·dil·lo *n* (Guyn) *Dasypus novemcinctus*
giganteus (*Dasypodidae*); FR. *tatou m.* (FrGy);
SP. *armadillo, cachicamo montañero m.*
(Venz)

ar·row·root *n* (CarA) *Maranta arundinacea*
(*Marantaceae*); FR. *dictame m.* (Guad, Mart);
SP. *maranta f.* (PtRi)

ars·nick·er *n* (Baha) *Ardea herodias* (*Ardeidae*);
FR. *crabier noir m.* (Guad, Mart); SP. *guard-*
acosta m., garzón cenizo m. (Cuba, PtRi,
StDo)

Au·gust-flow·er *n* (Guyn) *Agati grandiflora,*
Sesbania g. (*Leguminosae-Papilionaceae*); FR.
colibri végétal m., fleur-papillon f. (Guad);
SP. *báculo m.* (PtRi, StDo)

a·vo·ca·do (pear) *n* (*phr*) (CarA) *Persea am-*
ericana (*Lauraceae*); FR. *avocat m.* (Mart); SP.
aguacate m. (StDo)

axe-mas·ter *n* (Belz) *Krugiodendron ferreum*
(*Rhamnaceae*); FR. bois de fer, bois petites feuilles
m. (Guad, Mart); SP. *palo de hierro m.* (PtRi,
StDo), *espejuelo m.* (PtRi)

B

ba·by lime *n phr* (Guyn) *Triphasia trifolia*
(*Rutaceae*); FR. *citronelle f.* (Guad); SP. *li-*
moncillo m. (PtRi)

ba·che·lor's button *n phr* (CarA) *Gomphrena*
globosa (*Amaranthaceae*); FR. *immortelle, mar-*
guerite f. (Guad, Mart); SP. *siempreviva f.*
(PtRi, StDo)

Ba·ha·ma grass *n phr* (CarA) *Cynodon dac-*
tylon (*Gramineae-Poaceae*); FR. *chiendent m.*
(Guad, Mart); SP. *hierba fina f.* (StDo), *pata*
de gallina f. (PtRi, StDo)

ba·la·ta *n* (CarA) *Manilkara bidentata* (*Sa-*
potaceae); FR. *bois-noir m.* (Guad, Hait, Mart);
SP. *balatá m.* (StDo)

ball-bush *n* (Bdos, Jmca) *Leonotis nepetifolia*
(*Labiatae*); FR. *herbe-gros-bouton f.* (Guad,
Mart); SP. *molinillo m.* (PtRi, StDo)

bal·sam *n* (CarA) *Impatiens balsamina* (*Bal-*
saminaceae); FR. *impatience f.* (Guad, Mart);
SP. *espuela de caballeros, espuela de galán*
f. (PtRi, StDo)

bam·boo *n* (CarA) *Bambusa vulgaris* (*Grami-*
neae); FR. *bambou m.* (Guad, Mart); SP. *bambú*
m. (PtRi, StDo)

ba·na·na *n* (CarA) *Musa paradisiaca, M. sapi-*
entum (*Musaceae*); FR. *banane, figue, f., poyo*
m. (Guad, Mart); SP. *plátano guineo m.* (PtRi,
StDo), *cambur m.* (Venz)

ba·na·na·quit *n* (CarA) *Coereba flaveola*
(*Coerebidae*); FR. *sucrier m.* (Guad, Mart); SP.
reinita f. (PtRi), *cigüita f.* (StDo)

ban·ga·ma·ry *n* (Guyn) *Macrodon ancylodon*
(*Sciaenidae*); FR. *acoupa chasseur m.* (Guad,
Mart); SP. *pescadilla real f.* (Cuba, Venz)

Bar·ba·dos-cher·ry *n* (CarA) *Malpighia*
punicifolia (*Malpighiaceae*); FR. *cerise-anti-*
llaise f. (Guad, Mart); SP. *acerola, cereza*
(colorada) f. (PtRi, StDo)

Bar·ba·dos-pride *n* (CarA) *Caesalpinia pul-*
cherrima (*Caesalpiniaceae*); FR. *petit flam-*
boyant (jaune ou rouge) m. (Guad, Mart); SP.
clavellina f. (PtRi, StDo)

bar·ra·cu·da *n* (CarA) *Sphyraena barracuda*
(*Sphyraenidae*); FR. *barracuda f.* (Guad, Mart);
SP. *picuda (barracuda) f.* (PtRi, StDo)

bass[2] *n* 2. (USVI) *Megalops atlanticus* (*Megalopidae*); FR. *tarpon argenté m.* (Guad, Mart); SP. *tarpón m.* (Cuba, PtRi, StDo)

bas·tard ce·dar *n phr* (Belz) 2. *Guazuma ulmifolia* (*Sterculiaceae*); FR. *bois d'orme, m.* (Guad, Hait, Mart); SP. *guácima f.* (PtRi, StDo)

bat[1] *n* 2. (Guyn) *Chiroptera spp*; FR. *chauve-souris m.* (Guad, Mart); SP. *murciélago m.* (Cuba, StDo, Venz)

bay-ge·ra·ni·um (-ge·re·ni·a) *n* (Baha) *Ambrosia hispida* (*Compositae*); FR. *tapis m.* (Guad); SP. *altamisa de playa f.* (PtRi) □ TAPIS is also Std. Fr. for 'carpet'.

bay(-leaf) tree *n phr* (CarA) *Pimenta racemosa* (*Myrtaceae*); FR. *bois d'Inde m.* (Guad, Mart); SP. *malagueta f.* (PtRi, StDo)

bean-tree *n* (Bdos) *Erythrina corallodendrum, E. poeppigiana* (*Leguminosae-Papilionaceae*); FR. *bois immortel m.* (Hait); SP. *piñón espinoso m.* (PtRi)

beard·ed fig-tree *n phr* (Bdos) *Ficus citrifolia* (*Moraceae*); FR. *figuier maudit m.* (Guad, Mart); SP. *cupey m.* (PtRi, StDo)

bed-grass *n* 1. (Baha, CayI) *Andropogon glomeratus* (*Gramineae*); FR. *panache m.* (Hait); SP. *pajón m.* (StDo)

bell-ap·ple *n* (Guyn, Nevs, StVn, Trin, ViIs) *Passiflora laurifolia* (*Passifloraceae*); FR. *pomme-liane f.* (Guad, Mart); SP. *parcha f.* (PtRi, StDo)

bel·ly-ache bush *n phr* (Bdos, Guyn, Jmca, StKt, Trin) *Jatropha gossypifolia* (*Euphorbiaceae*); FR. *médicinier bâtard/rouge m.* (Guad, Mart); SP. *tuatúa/túa-túa f.* (PtRi, StDo, Venz)

ben·ne *n* 1. (Gren, Tbgo, Trin) *Sesamum orientale, S. indicum* (*Pedaliaceae*); FR. *sésame m.* (Guad, Mart); SP. *sésamo m.* (Cuba), *ajonjolí m.* (Cuba, PtRi, StDo)

big·eye[3] *n* 2. (ECar) *Priacanthus arenatus* (*Priacanthidae*); FR. *beauclaire soleil m.* (Mart); SP. *catalufa f.* (PtRi)

big-jack *n* (Dmca, Gren, StVn) *Selar crumenophtalmus* (*Carangidae*); FR. *coulisou m.* (Guad, Mart); SP. *chicharro m.* (Cuba, PtRi)

bi·lim·bi *n* 1. (Guyn, Jmca, Trin) *Averrhoa bilimbi* (*Oxalidaceae*); FR. *cornichon, bilimbi m.* (Guad, Mart); SP. *vinagrillo m.* (StDo)

bill·fish *n* (ECar) *Istiophorus albicans* (*Istiophoridae*); FR. *voilier m.* (Mart); SP. *abanico m.* (PtRi), *pez vela m.* (CarA) □ ABANICO is also Std. Sp. for 'fan'.

birch-gum tree *n phr* (Bdos, Brbu, Trin) *Bursera simaruba* (*Burseraceae*); FR. *gommier blanc m., gommier barrière m.* (Guad, Mart); SP. *almácigo blanco m.* (Cuba, PtRi, StDo)

bird-pep·per *n* (CarA) *Capsicum frutescens* (*Solanaceae*); FR. *piment grive m.* (Guad, Mart); SP. *ají picante m.* (PtRi)

bird·vine *n* 1. (Dmca, Gren, Guyn, Trin) *Phthirusa seitsii/sintenisii* (*Loranthaceae*); FR. *teigne, teigne bord de mer m.* (Guad, Mart); SP. *hicaquillo, muérdago m.* (PtRi)

bit·ter-tal·ly *n* (Bdos, Guyn) *Mikania spp* (*Compositae*); FR. *wappe f.* (Guad, Mart); SP. *guaco m.* (Cuba, PtRi), *matafinca f.* (StDo)

bit·ter-wood *n* 2. (Jmca) *Quassia excelsa* (*Simarubaceae*); FR. *bois amer, quachi m.* (Guad, Mart); SP. *quasia f.* (Cuba)

biz·zi-biz·zi *n* (Guyn) *Cyperus articulatus, C. ligularis, etc* (*Cyperaceae*); FR. *herbe-couteau m.* (Guad, Mart); SP. *junco de agua m.* (Cuba, PtRi), *junco cimarrón m.* (PtRi)

black ant *n phr* (CarA) *Cremastogaster brevispinosa* (*Formicidae*); FR. *fourmi mordant m.* (Guad, Mart); SP. *hormiga f.* (Cuba, PtRi, StDo) □ HORMIGA is Std. Sp. for 'ant'.

black·bird *n* 1. (CarA) (*Holo*)*quiscalus lugubris* (*Passeriformes*); FR. *merle f.* (Hait); SP. *quiebra f.* (Cuba), *pichón prieto m.* (PtRi)

black·eye-peas *n* (CarA) *Vigna unguiculata, V. sinensis* (*Papilionaceae*); FR. *pois yeux-noirs m.* (Guad, Mart); SP. *frijol de carita m.* (Cuba), *frijol de vaca m.* (StDo)

black-sage *n* 1. (CarA) *Cordia curassavica* (*Boraginaceae*); FR. *mahot-bord-de-mer m.* (Guad, Mart); SP. *salvia f.* (PtRi) □ See also SAGE-BUSH.

black-wil·low *n* (Baha, Bdos, Gren, Jmca) *Capparis cynophallophora* (*Capparidaceae*); FR. *bois noir/mabouge m.* (Guad, Mart); SP. *bejuco inglés, burro prieto m.* (PtRi)

bleed·ing-heart *n* 1. (CarA) *Caladium bicolor* (*Araceae*); FR. *palette de peintre f.* (Guad, Mart), *coeur saignant m.* (Hait); SP. *paleta del pintor f.* (PtRi), *pegadora f.* (PtRi, Venz)

blind-eye *n* 1. (Mrat) *Euphorbia tirucalli* (*Euphorbiaceae*); SP. *esqueleto m.* (PtRi)

blue mar·lin *n phr* (Baha, Bdos, ViIs) *Makaira nigricans* (*Istiophoridae*); FR. *varé m.* (Mart); SP. *aguja azul f.* (Cuba, PtRi, StDo)

blue-pea *n* (Baha, Jmca) *Clitoria ternatea* (*Papilionaceae*); FR. *pois-savane, pois sauvage m.* (Guad, Mart); SP. *bejuco de conchitas m.* (PtRi)

blug·go n (Belz, Gren, StLu, Tbgo) *Musa balbisiana* (*Musaceae*); FR. *grand(e) naine* f. (Guad, Mart); SP. *plátano* m. (PtRi) □ It has been explained in *Fournet, Flore Illustrée* and *Liogier, Descriptive Flora of Puerto Rico* that many varieties of the *Musa* species have been combined to produce the different types of bananas that we know and that the precise Fr. and Sp. equivalents may be found in more specialized work on the subject. Here the more generally known equivalents are supplied.

bo·di n (Gren, StLu, StVn, Trin) *Vigna sesquipedalis* (*Papilionaceae*); FR. *pois-ficelle* m. (Guad, Mart); SP. *frijol de bollos* m. (Cuba)

Bom·bay man·go n phr (Gren, Jmca, Mrat) *Mangifera indica* (*Anacardiaceae*); FR. *mango Bombay* m. (Guad, Mart); SP. *mango de Bombay* m. (CarA)

bo·na·vist n (CarA) *Dolichos purpureus, D. lablab* (*Leguminosae-Papilionaceae*); FR. *pois blanc* m. (Guad, Mart); SP. *frijol caballero negro* m. (Cuba), *haba* f. (Venz)

bone-fish n 1. (Baha, CayI, TkCa) *Albula vulpes* (*Albulidae*); FR. *banane de mer* f. (Guad, Mart); SP. *macabí* m. (Cuba, Venz), *ratón* m. (Venz)

bou·gain·vil·lea n (CarA) *Bougainvillea glabra* (*Nyctaginaceae*); FR. *bougainvillée* f. (Guad, Mart); SP. *bougainvillea, trinitaria (roja)* f. (Cuba, PtRi, StDo, Venz)

bread-and-cheese n (CarA) *Pithecellobium unguis-cati* (*Leguminosae*); FR. *griffe-chat* m. (Guad, Mart); SP. *uña de gato* f. (PtRi)

bread·fruit n (CarA) *Artocarpus communis, A. altilis* (*Moraceae*); FR. *fruit à pain* m. (Guad, Mart); SP. *pan de fruta(s)* m. (StDo, Venz)

bread·nut n (CarA) *Artocarpus incisa, A. seminifera* (*Moraceae*); FR. *arbre à pain* m. (Hait), *châtaigne* f. (Guad, Mart); SP. *buen pan* m. (StDo), *castaña* f. (PtRi) □ CHÂTAIGNE is Std. Fr. and CASTAÑA is Std. Sp. both for 'chestnut'.

buck-cot·ton n (Guyn) *Gossypium spp* (*Malvaceae*); FR. *coton-pays* m. (Guad, Mart); SP. *algodón silvestre/del país* m. (PtRi)

bu·ra-bu·ra n (Guyn) *Solanum stramonifolium, S. torvum, S. filicifolium* (*Solanaceae*); FR. *bélangère bâtard* m. (Guad, Mart); SP. *berenjena cimarrona* f. (PtRi)

but·ter·fish n (CarA) *Cephalopholis fulva* or *Nebris microps* (*Sciaenidae*) or *Centropristes striatus* (*Serranidae*); FR. *courbine tiyeux* f. (FrGy), *fanfre noir (d'Amérique)* (CarA); SP. *curvina ojo chico* f. (Venz), *serrano estriado* m. □ This last Sp. name applies more to the last named species and is found in Florida.—*FAO Species Identification Sheets for Fishery Purposes, Vol. V.*

C

cab·bage n (CarA) *Brassica oleracea* (*Cruciferae*); FR. *chou* m. (CarA); SP. *repollo, col* m. (PtRi) □ This refers to the vegetable of European origin, not to the edible heart of the tropical CABBAGE-PALM.

cab·bage palm n phr (CarA) *Oreodoxa oleracea* (*Palmaceae*); FR. *palmiste, palmier* m. (Guad, Mart); SP. *palma* f. (CarA)

ca·ca-bel·ly n 1. (Gren, StLu, StVn) *Labridae spp*; FR. *capitaine* m. (Mart); SP. *capitán* m. (PtRi). □ There is also another species *Scaridae spp*; SP. *judío* m. (PtRi). □ JUDÍO is also Std. Sp. for 'Jew/Jewish'.

cac·tus (hedge) (hedge-cac·tus) n (phr) (CarA) *Euphorbia lactea, E. neviifolia* (*Euphorbiaceae*); FR. *candélabre* m. (Hait); SP. *candelero* m., *raqueta* f. (StDo)

ca·la·bash n (CarA); *Crescentia cujete* (*Bignoniaceae*); FR. *calebasse* f. (Mart); SP. *calabaza* f. (CarA), *güira* f. (Cuba) □ CALABAZA is the Std. Sp. for 'calabash'.

ca·la·lu n (CarA) *Amaranthus spp*; FR. *épinard pays* m. (Guad, Mart); SP. *bledo espinoso* m. (StDo), *blero* m. (PtRi)

cam·pesh n (Dmca, Gren, Trin) *Haematoxylon campechianum* (*Leguminosae-Caesalpiniaceae*); FR. *campêche, bois de campêche* m. (Guad); SP. *campeche* m. (StDo)

can·dle-fly n (Guyn, Trin) *Pyrophorus noctiluca* (*Lampyridae*); FR. *labelle* f. (Mart); SP. *luciérnaga* f. □ No territorial labelling has been attached to the Sp. equivalent because it is a generalized one used in Spanish-speaking countries.

can·dle·wood n 1. (Bdos) *Cupania americana* (*Sapindaceae*); FR. *cupanier* m. (Guad, Mart); SP. *guaraná* m., *guara* f. (StDo)

cane-li·ly n (Bdos) See SCREW-PINE

Can·je pheas·ant n phr (Guyn) *Opisthocomus hoatzin* (*Opisthocomidae*); FR. *hoatzin* m. (FrGy); SP. *chenchena* f. (Venz)

can·ker-ber·ry (kan·ka-ber·ry) n (CarA) *Solanum bahamense* (*Solanaceae*); FR. *boisteurtre* m. (Mart); SP. *ajicón* m. (Cuba)

can·na-li·ly *n* (CarA) *Canna indica* (*Cannaceae*); FR. *balisier rouge, balisier à chapelets m.* (Guad, Mart); SP. *maraca f., platanillo de monte m.* (Venz)

can·non-ball tree *n phr* (CarA) *Couroupita guianensis* (*Lecythidaceae*); FR. *boulet de canon m.* (Guad); SP. *bala de cañón f.* (Cuba), *coco de mona m.* (Venz)

ca·ram·bo·la *n* (CarA) *Averrhoa carambola* (*Oxalidaceae*); FR. *carambole f.* (Guad, Mart); SP. *carambola f.* (StDo)

ca·rite *n* (Trin) *Scomberomorus maculatus* (*Scombridae*); FR. *carite m.* (Guad, Mart); SP. *carite lucio/pintado/chinigua m.* (Venz)

car·pet-dai·sy *n* (Bdos) *Wedelia trilobata* (*Compositae-Asteraceae*); FR. *bouton d'or m.* (Mart), *patte de canard f.* (Guad); SP. *wedelia f.* (PtRi)

car·ri·on-crow *n* (Guyn) *Coragyps atratus* (*Cathartidae*); FR. *corbeau m., corbeau à tête rouge m.* (Guad, Mart); SP. *aura f., aura tiñosa f.* (Cuba). □ This is not quite the same species as the commoner JOHN CROW or TURKEY VULTURE, *Cathartes aura* (*Cathartidae*) wh is found in *Jmca.—BBWI:53.*

cas·ca·du·ra *n* 1. *Hoplosternum littorale, Callichthys littoralis* (*Callichthyidae*); FR. *cascadura f.* (Mart); SP. *cascadura f.* (Venz)

ca·sha 1.(i) *n* (Nevs, StKt, ViIs) *Acacia farnesiana, Vachella farnesiana* (*Leguminosae-Mimosaceae*); FR. *acacia jaune m.* (Guad, Mart); SP. *aromo m.* (PtRi), *cují m.* (StDo) **1.(ii)** *n* (Angu, Jmca) *Prosopis chiliensis, P. juliflora* (*Leguminosae-Mimosaceae*); FR. *bayahonde, bayarone f.* (Hait); SP. *bayahonda f.* (StDo)

ca·shew *n* 1. (CarA) *Anacardium occidentale* (*Anacardiaceae*); FR. *pomme cajou m.* (Guad); SP. *cajuil m.* (PtRi, StDo)

cas·sa·va *n* 1. (CarA) *Manihot esculenta, M. utilissima* (*Euphorbiaceae*); FR. *manioc m., cassave f.* (Guad, Mart); SP. *yuca f.* (PtRi, StDo, Venz)

cas·tor-oil (bush/plant/tree) *n (phr)* (CarA) *Ricinus communis* (*Euphorbiaceae*); FR. *ricin m.* (Guad, Mart); SP. *ricino común m.* (StDo), *tártago m.* (Venz)

cas·ua·ri·na *n* (CarA) *Casuarina equisetifolia* (*Casuarinaceae*); FR. *filao m.* (Guad, Mart); SP. *casuarina f.* (PtRi, StDo)

cat·fish *n* 3. (StLu) *Aelurichthys gronowii, Felichthys marinus* (*Ariidae*); FR. *mâcho:ron coco m.* (Mart); SP. *bagre blanco m.* (Cuba) □ The

other two varieties of CAT·FISH defined in senses 1. and 2. in the main work are both river fish, whereas this variety is a sea fish.

cat-tail *n* (CarA) *Acalypha hispida* (*Euphorbiaceae*); FR. *acalypha f.* (Guad, Mart); SP. *califa f., acalifa japonesa f.* (Cuba), *rabo de gato m.* (PtRi)

cat·tle egret *n phr* (Bdos, Guyn, Trin) *Bubulcus ibis* (*Ardeidae*); FR. *crabier m., garde-boeuf m.* (Guad, Mart); SP. *garza ganadera f.* (PtRi, StDo)

cat·tle-tongue *n* (Antg, Brbu, Mrat, Nevs, StKt) *Pluchea symphytifolia, P. carolinensis, P. odorata* (*Compositae*); FR. *tabac diable m.* (Mart); SP. *salvia f.* (PtRi, StDo)

ca·val·li *n* (CarA) *Caranx hippos* (*Carangidae*); FR. *carangue grasse f., couvalli m.* (Mart); SP. *cojinúa f.* (Cuba, PtRi), *jurel m.* (Venz) □ A number of varieties exist exs *amber cavalli, horse-eye cavalli, roundhead cavalli* as well as *Caranx crysos* (*Carangidae*) or *blue runner*. The Fr. equivalent of the latter is *carangue coubali f.* (Guad, Mart) and the Sp. equivalent of it is *cojinúa negra f.* (PtRi) or *medregal m.* (PtRi, StDo).

ca·yenne ba·na·na *n phr* (Guyn) *Musa spp*; FR. *banane f.* (Guad, Mart); SP. *guineo m.* (PtRi)

ce·ra·see *n* (Baha, Bdos, CayI, Jmca, TkCa) *Momordica charantia, M. balsamina* (*Cucurbitaceae*); FR. *pomme-coolie, pomme-merveille f.* (Guad, Mart); SP. *cundeamor m.* (PtRi, StDo)

cha·co·ni·a *n* (Tbgo, Trin) *Warsziwiczia coccinea* (*Rubiaceae*); FR. *chaconia f.* (Guad, Mart); SP. *chaconia f.* (Venz)

chal·ta *n* (Guyn, Trin) *Dillenia indica* (*Dilleniaceae*); FR. *dillenia f.* (Guad, Mart); SP. *coca f.* (StDo)

chan·na *n* (CarA) *Cicer arietinum* (*Papilionaceae*); FR. *pois-chiche m.* (CarA); SP. *garbanzo m.* (Cuba, PtRi) □ POIS-CHICHE is Std. Fr. for CHICK-PEA.

che·ri·mo·ya *n* (Baha, Jmca) *Annona cherimola* (*Annonaceae*); FR. *cachiman la Chine m.* (Hait, Mart); SP. *chirimoya f.* (Cuba, Venz)

chew·stick *n* (Gren) 2. *Gouania lupuloides, G. domingensis* (*Rhamnaceae*); FR. *liane savon f.* (Guad, Mart); SP. *jaboncillo m.* (Cuba, Venz)

chick·en-hawk *n* (CarA) *Buteo platypteris antillarum, B. latissimus, B. jamaicensis* (*Accipitridae*); FR. *malfini m., manger-poulet m.* (Mart); SP. *gavilán bobo m.* (Cuba)

chick-pea n (CarA) See CHANNA.

chi(l)·li-plum n (Antg, Bdos, Gren, Tbgo, Trin) *Spondias purpurea, S. lutea* (*Anacardiaceae*); Fr. *prune d'Espagne* f., *mombin jaune* m. (Guad, Mart); Sp. *jobo* m., *ciruela morada* f. (StDo) See also JAMAICA-PLUM.

chi·nee ca·la·lu n phr (Guyn) *Amaranthus spp*; Fr. *épinard* m. (Guad, Mart); Sp. *espinaca* f. (Venz)

Chi·nese cab·bage n phr (CarA) *Brassica pekinensis* (*Cruciferae*); Fr. *chou moutarde* m. (Guad, Hait, Mart); Sp. *mostaza* f. (Cuba, PtRi, StDo)

chive(s) n (pl) (Trin) □ See ESCHALLOT.

cho·cho n (Baha, Belz, Jmca, TkCa) See CHRISTOPHENE.

Christ·mas-bush n 1. (CarA) *Eupatorium odoratum* (*Compositae*); Fr. *fleurit Noël* m., *languè a chat* f. (Guad); Sp. *langa chata* f. (StDo), *Santa María* f. (PtRi)

Christ·mas-can·dle n (Bdos, Dmca, Nevs, StLu) *Cassia alata* (*Leguminosae-Caesalpiniaceae*); Fr. *herbe à dartres* f., *casse puante* f. (Guad, Mart); Sp. *dragón* m. (PtRi), *guajabo* m. (StDo)

chris·to·phene n (ECar) *Sechium edule* (*Cucurbitaceae*); Fr. *christophine* f., *chouchoute* f. (Guad); Sp. *chayote* m. (Cuba, PtRi, StDo)

cin·na·mon (tree) n (phr) (CarA) *Cinnamomum zeylanicum* (*Lauraceae*); Fr. *cannelle aromatique* f. (Guad); Sp. *canela de Ceilán* f. (Cuba, StDo)

clam·my-cher·ry n (CarA) 1. *Cordia obliqua* (*Boraginaceae*); Fr. *mahot* m. (Mart); Sp. *ateje* m. (Cuba) 2. (Brbu, Jmca, Mrat, Tbgo) *Cordia collococca* (*Boraginaceae*); Fr. *mapou de rivière* m. (Guad, Mart); Sp. *palo de muñeca* m., *cereza cimarrona* f. (PtRi)

cob·bler n 3. (BrVi, Dmca, StVn) *Trachinotus carolinus* (*Carangidae*); Fr. *pompaneau sole* m. (Mart); Sp. *pómpano amarillo* m. (StDo)

co·chi·neal (cac·tus) n (phr) (Guyn, Jmca, Trin) *Opuntia spp, Nopalea cochenillifera* or *Cereus spp* (*Cactaceae*); Fr. *raquette sans piquant, nopal* m. (Guad, Mart); Sp. *tuna de España, tuna mansa* f. (PtRi)

cock-li·zard n (Bdos) *Anolis aeneus* (*Lacertilia*); Fr. *anolis* m. (Mart); Sp. *lagartija* f., *saca banderas* (Venz)

cock·roach-grass n 1. (Gren, StKt) *Zebrina pendula, Trudescantia tricolor* (*Commelinaceae*);

Fr. *curage-rivière* m., *herbe grasse rivière* f. (Guad, Mart); Sp. *cucaracha* f. (Cuba), *cobitre morado* m. (PtRi) □ CUCARACHA is Std. Sp. for 'cockroach'.

cock·spur n 5. (Jmca) *Pisonia aculeata* (*Nyctaginaceae*); Fr. *croc-chien* m., *amourette* f. (Guad, Mart); Sp. *escambrón* m., *uña de gato* f. (PtRi)

co·coa n 1. (Dmca, Gren, Trin) *Theobroma cacao* (*Sterculiaceae*); Fr. *cacao* m. (Guad, Mart); Sp. *cacao, chocolate* m. (Cuba, PtRi), *cacao criollo/forastero* m. (StDo)

co·co·nut n 1. (CarA) *Cocos nucifera* (*Palmaceae*); Fr. *noix de coco* m. (Guad, Mart); Sp. *coco* m. (PtRi, Venz)

co·co-plum n 1. (Antg, Baha, Belz, Jmca, Trin, USVI) *Chrysobalanus icaco* (*Rosaceae*); Fr. *pomme/prune des icaques* f. (Guad, Mart); Sp. *icaco* m. (Cuba, PtRi, StDo)

co·cri·co n (Tbgo, Trin) *Ortalis ruficauda* (*Cracidae*); Fr. *coquericot* m. (Guad, Mart); Sp. *guacharaca del norte, llanera* f. (Venz)

conch n (CarA) *Strombus gigas* (*Strombidae*); Fr. *lambi* m. (Guad, Mart); Sp. *cobo* m. (Cuba), *lambí* m. (StDo), *carrucho* m. (PtRi) □ Std. Fr. is CONQUE f., Std. Sp. is CONCHA.

co·ra·li·ta n (CarA) *Antigonon leptopus* (*Polygonaceae*); Fr. *belle mexicaine* f. (Guad, Mart); Sp. *coralina* f. (PtRi, StDo)

cor·di·a (red cor·di·a, scar·let cordi·a) n (phr) *Cordia sebestena* (*Boraginaceae*); Fr. *bois-râpe* m. (Guad); Sp. *vomitel colorado* m. (Cuba), *avellana* f. (StDo)

cot·ton n 1. (CarA) *Gossypium hirsutum* (*Malvaceae*) See BUCK-COTTON □ The other variety *G. barbadense maritimum* is the SEA-ISLAND COTTON wh has the following Fr and Sp equivalents—Fr. *coton 'sea-island'* m. (Guad, Mart); Sp. *algodón* m. (PtRi). ALGODÓN is also Std. Sp. for 'cotton'. See also BUCK-COTTON.

cou·ri·da (cou·ri·da-bush, cou·ri·da-tree) n (Guyn) *Avicennia nitida* (*Verbenaceae*); Fr. *palétuvier gris* m. (Guad, Mart); Sp. *mangle prieto/negro* m. (Cuba, Venz)

cow-fish n 1. (Baha, Gren, Mrat, StLu) *Lactophrys quadricornis* (*Ostrăciidae*); Fr. *coffre taureau* m. (Guad, Mart); Sp. *torito azul* m. (Cuba, PtRi, StDo)

cow-foot-bush n (Belz, Guyn) *Lepianthes peltata* or *Piper tuberculum* or *Pothomorphe peltata* (*Piperaceae*); Fr. *bois anisette, herbe à* *mal d'estomac* (Guad, Mart); Sp. *baquiña f.* (PtRi), *broquelejo* (StDo)

cow·itch (cow·hage) *n* 1. (CarA) *Mucuna pruriens (Papilionaceae)*; Fr. *pois gratté m.* (Hait); Sp. *pica-pica* (PtRi) 2. (Trin) *Dalechampia pruriens (Euphorbiaceae)*; Fr. *ortie rouge, daléchampia grimpante f.* (Guad); Sp. *bejuco de grajo m.* (StDo)

crab *n* (CarA) *Cardisoma guanhumi (Gecarcinidae)*; Fr. *crabe (bleu) m.* (Guad, Mart); Sp. *cangrejo (azul) m.* (Cuba), *juey m.* (PtRi) □ CANGREJO is Std. Sp. for 'crab'.

crab-grass *n* 1. (Guyn, Trin) *Digitaria adscendens (Gramineae-Paniceae)*; Fr. *herbe fine femelle f.* (Guad, Mart); Sp. *garranchuelo m.* (Venz) 2. (Bdos, Gren, Jmca, TkCa) *Paspalum distichum* or *Sporobolus virginicus* or *Stenotaphrum secundatum (Poaceae)*; Fr. *herbe-mouton f.* (Guad, Mart); Sp. *cañamazo m.* (StDo)

cra·boo *n* (Belz) *Byrsonima crassifolia (Malpighiaceae)*; Fr. *café d'Ethiopie m.* (Guad); Sp. *nancito m.* (PtRi)

crab·wood *n* (Guyn) *Carapa guianensis (Meliaceae)*; Fr. *bois rouge m.* (Guad, Mart); Sp. *carapo m.* (Venz)

croak·er[1] *n* (Bdos) *Micropogon undulatus, M. furnieri (Sciaenidae)*; Fr. *tambour brésilien m.* (FrGy); Sp. *curvina, curvinata f.* (Venz)

cro·cus[2] *n* (Guyn, Jmca, Trin) □ See AMARYLLIS.

cro·ton *n* (CarA) *Codiaeum variegatum (Euphorbiaceae)*; Fr. *croton m.* (Guad, Hait, Mart); Sp. *crotón de jardín m.* (Cuba, PtRi, Venz), *periquito m.* (PtRi)

cu·cum·ber *n* (CarA) *Cucumis sativus (Cucurbitaceae)*; Fr. *concombre, (gros) concombre m.* (Guad, Hait, Mart); Sp. *pepino (de monte) m.* (PtRi, Venz)

cush-cush (yam)[3] *n* (*phr*) (CarA) *Dioscorea trifida (Dioscoreaceae)*; Fr. *cousse-cousse m.* (Guad, Mart); Sp. *ñame mapuey m.* (Cuba, PtRi)

cus·tard-ap·ple *n* (CarA) *Annona reticulata (Annonaceae)*; Fr. *cachiman m.* (Guad, Mart); Sp. *mamón m.* (Cuba, StDo)

cyp *n* (Dmca, StLu, Trin) *Ocotea caniculata (Lauraceae)* Fr. *laurier m.* (Guad, Mart); Sp. *cigua f.* (Cuba, PtRi) □ There are numerous varieties of this tree throughout the region and in *Trin* this variety is called CYP (*Laurier cypre*).—*Williams, The Useful and Ornamental Plants of Trinidad and Tobago:236*.

D

da·sheen *n* (CarA) *Colocasia globulifera (Araceae)*; Fr. *dachine m.* (Guad, Mart); Sp. *yautía meléndrez m.* (PtRi)

date-palm *n* (CarA) *Phoenix dactylifera (Arecaceae)*; Fr. *dattier m.* (Hait); Sp. *palmera datilera f.* (Cuba, PtRi)

dev·il-fish *n* 1. (Guyn) *Manta birostris, Ceratoptera vampyrus (Mobulidae)*; Fr. *manta f.* (Guad, Mart); Sp. *manta f.* (Cuba)

di·tay-pay·ee *n* (Dmca, Gren, StLu, Tbgo, Trin) *Capraria biflora (Scrophulariaceae)*; Fr. *thé pays m.* (Guad), *thé des Antilles m.* (Mart); Sp. *té criollo m.* (StDo), *té del país m.* (PtRi)

doc·tor-bird *n* 1. (ECar, Guyn) *Trochilidae spp*; Fr. *colibri m.* (Mart); Sp. *colibrí, zunzún m.* (Cuba)

doc·tor-fish *n* (CarA) *Acanthurus chirurgus, A. bahianus, A. coeruleus (Acanthuridae)*; Fr. *bayole f.* (Mart); Sp. *barbero m.* (Cuba) □ BARBERO is Std. Sp. for 'barber'.

dog·wood *n* (Baha, Jmca, USVI) *Piscidia piscipula, P. erythrina, Lonchocarpus latifolius (Papilionaceae)*; Fr. *enivrage m.* (Guad, Mart), *savonnette grand bois f.* (Mart); Sp. *guama de costa f.* (Cuba), *palo hediondo m.* (PtRi). □ There are two very similar types of DOGWOOD, one of the *Piscidia spp* and the other of the *Lonchocarpus spp*. The first in each pair of Fr. and Sp. equivalents represents the first species and the second represents the second species.

duck-weed *n* 2. (Bdos) *Lemna perpusilla (Lemnaceae)*; Fr. *lentille d'eau f.*, *vert de gris m.* (Guad, Mart); Sp. *cola de pato f.* (Cuba) 3. (Bdos) *Pectis humifusa (Compositae)*; Fr. *pectis couché rampant m.* (Guad); Sp. *yerba de San Juan f.* (PtRi) □ In sense 2. the Sp equivalent carries another taxonomic name *Piaropus crassipes (Pontederiaceae)*.

dunk(s) *n* (*pl*) (Bdos, Guyn, StKt, StVn) *Ziziphus mauritania, Z. jujuba (Rhamnaceae)*; Fr. *surette, f.*, *pomme surette f.* (Guad), *jujube f.* (Mart); Sp. *aprín m.* (PtRi), *ponsigué m.* (Venz)

dup·py-ba·sil *n* (Bdos) *Ocimum micranthum, O. sanctum (Labiatae)*; Fr. *basilique grandes feuilles m.* (Hait); Sp. *albahaca cimarrona f.* (Cuba, PtRi, StDo)

dup·py-crab *n* (Bdos) (*Cardisoma guanhumi (Cecarcinidae)*; Fr. *tombourou matoutou m.* (Mart); Sp. *moro de mangle azul m.* (PtRi)

dup·py-nee·dle n (Bdos) Bidens pilosa (Compositae); FR. herbe des aiguilles f. (Guad, Mart); SP. romerillo m. (PtRi, StDo)

dup·py-pa·ra·sol n (Bdos) Agaricus spp; FR. champignon vénéneux m. (Mart); SP. seta venenosa f. (StDo)

dwarf-co·co·nut n (Belz, Dmca, Gren, StKt) Cocos spp; FR. cocotier nain m. (Mart); SP. cocotero m., palma de coco m. (PtRi)

Eng·lish ap·ple n phr (Bdos, BrVi) Pyrus malus (Rosaceae); FR. pomme de France f. (Hait); SP. manzana f. (Cuba, StDo)

Eng·lish po·ta·to n phr (CarA) Solanum tuberosum (Solanaceae); FR. pomme de terre f. (Guad, Mart); SP. papa f. (Cuba, PtRi, Venz) □ Std. Sp. is PATATA.

es·chal·lot n (Bdos, Guyn) Allium ascalonicum, A. fistulosum (Liliaceae); FR. échalotte f. (Guad, Mart); SP. cebollín m. (PtRi)

E

East·er-li·ly n 1. (Berm, Trin) Lilium longiflorum; FR. lis de Pâques m.(Guad, Mart); SP. lirio de Pascua m. (StDo) 2. (Bdos, Dmca, Guyn) Hippeastrum puniceum (Amaryllidaceae); FR. lis rouge/trompette m. (Guad, Mart); SP. taraco m. (Cuba)

e·bo·ny n 1. (CarA) See WOMAN-TONGUE TREE 2. (Baha, CayI, Jmca) Hypelate trifoliata (Sapindaceae); FR. chandelle marron f. (Hait); SP. cocuyo m., cuaba de ingenio f. (Cuba) 3. (Guyn) [Timber Industry] Swartzia bannia (Caesalpiniaceae); FR. bois-olivier m. (Guad); SP. bejuco de peo m. (PtRi) □ These are three different types of wood, the last being used specifically in the Guyana timber industry.

ed·do(e) n (CarA) 1. (Guyn) Colocasia esculenta (Araceae); FR. chou de chine, chou-chine m. (Mart), malanga f. (Guad); SP. malanga (isleña) f. (Cuba, PtRi)

egg·plant (egg-plant) n (CarA) Solanum melongena (Solanaceae); FR. aubergine f., mélongène f. (Guad, Mart); SP. berenjena f. (Cuba, PtRi, Venz)

el·der n (Bdos, Belz, Brbu, Jmca, USVI) Sambucus simpsonii, S. canadensis (Caprifoliaceae); FR. sureau m. (Hait); SP. saúco blanco m. (Cuba, StDo) □ This variety is cultivated unlike the SAUCO AMARILLO wh grows wild—Cuba en la mano:448. See ELDER-BUSH.

el·der-bush n (Bdos, Guyn) Tecoma stans (Bignoniaceae); FR. bois pissenlit m. (Guad); SP. saúco amarillo m. (Cuba, PtRi)

e·le·phant-grass n (CarA) Pennisetum purpureum (Gramineae); FR. herbe éléphant f. (Hait); SP. yerba elefante f. (Cuba)

e·le·phant's ear n phr (Baha, Bdos) Xanthosoma spp (Araceae); FR. malanga bâtard f. (Guad); SP. yautía palma f. (PtRi)

F

fe·ver-grass n (CarA) Cymbopogon citratus (Gramineae); FR. citronelle f. (Guad, Mart); SP. yerba de limón f. (Cuba, PtRi), yerba de calentura f. (Cuba)

fid·dle-wood n (CarA) Citharexylum spp (Verbenaceae); FR. bois carré, bois de fer blanc m. (Guad, Mart); SP. canilla de venado f. (Cuba), café cimarrón m. (StDo)

fit-weed n (Bdos, Gren, Guyn, Jmca, Tbgo, Trin) Eryngium foetidum (Umbelliferae); FR. chardon béni m. (Guad); SP. culantro cimarrón, culantro de monte m. (Cuba, StDo, Venz)

five-fin·ger n 2. (Angu, StKt, USVI) Randia aculeata (Rubiaceae); FR. bois quenouille m., graines noires f. pl. (Guad); SP. agalla de costa f. (Cuba)

flam·boy·ant (tree) n (phr) (CarA) Poinciana regia, Delonix regia (Leguminosae-Caesalpiniaceae); FR. flamboyant m. (Guad, Mart); SP. flamboyant, flamboyán m. (Cuba, PtRi, StDo, Venz)

flat-o'-the-earth n (Guyn) Microtea debilis (Phytolaccaceae); FR. herbe-au-long-case f. (Guad, Mart)

fly·ing fish n phr (CarA) Exocoetidae spp; FR. poisson volant m. (Mart), exocet atlantique m. (Guad, Mart); SP. pez volador m. (Venz)

four-o'clock (bush) n (phr) (CarA) Mirabilis jalapa (Nyctaginaceae); FR. belle de nuit f. (Guad, Hait, Mart); SP. maravilla f. (Cuba, PtRi), buenas tardes f. pl., jazmín m. (StDo) □ The second Sp equivalent is Std. Sp. for 'good afternoon'.

fowl-foot grass n phr (CarA) Eleusine indica (Gramineae); FR. pied-poule m. (Guad, Mart);

Sp. *pata de gallina, yerba dulce* f. (PtRi, StDo)

fran·gi·pa·ni n (CarA) *Plumeria acutifolia, P. rubra, P. alba* (*Apocynaceae*); **Fr**. *frangipanier, frangipanier rouge/rose/blanc* m. (Guad, Mart); **Sp**. *alelí* m., *atabaiba* f. (StDo)

fri·gate-bird n (CarA) *Fregata magnificens* (*Fregatidae/Pelicaniformes*); **Fr**. *frégate* f. (Guad, Mart); **Sp**. *tijereta* f. (PtRi, StDo)

G

gal·ba n (Dmca, Gren, StVn) *Calophyllum antillanum* (*Clusiaceae*); **Fr**. *galba* m. (Guad, Mart); **Sp**. *baría* f., *palo María* m. (Cuba, PtRi, StDo)

gar; **gar-fish** n (CarA) 1. *Strongylura spp, Tylosurus spp*; **Fr**. *aiguillette* f. (Guad, Hait, Mart); **Sp**. *agujón* m. (Cuba), *marao* m. (Venz)

gar·den-bal·sam n (Bdos, Jmca, Trin, USVI) *Justicia pectoralis* (*Acanthaceae*); **Fr**. *herbe à charpentier* f. (Guad, Mart); **Sp**. *curía* f. (PtRi, StDo), *yerba carpintera* f. (StDo)

gil·back·er n (Guyn) *Sciadeichthys flavescens, S. emphysetus* (*Siluridae-Ariidae*); **Fr**. *mâchoiron jaune* m. (Guad, Mart); **Sp**. *bagre amarillo* m. (Cuba, PtRi)

gin·ger-li·ly n 1. (Bdos) *Alpinia purpurata* (*Zingiberaceae*); **Fr**. *lavande rouge* f. (Guad, Mart); **Sp**. *colonia* f. (Cuba), *boca de dragón* f. (Cuba, PtRi, StDo), *pluma de San Juan, pluma rosa* f. (Venz)

gli·ri·ci·di·a n (Angu, Bdos, StLu, StVn) *Gliricidia sepium* (*Leguminosae-Papilionaceae*); **Fr**. *glicéridia, gliricidia* f. (Guad, Mart); **Sp**. *piñón de costa* m. (Cuba), *madre de cacao* f. (PtRi)

goat-fish n (CarA) *Mulloidichthys marinus, Mullus auratus, Pseudupeneus maculatus* (*Mullidae*); **Fr**. *capucin jaune, rouget-barbet doré, rouget-barbé tacheté* m. (Guad, Mart); **Sp**. *salmonete amarillo/colorado/manchado* m. (Cuba) □ The three taxonomic names and the three equivalents in Fr and Sp correspond to the yellow, pink and spotted goat-fish.—*FAO SISFP West Central Atlantic, Vol. III*.

go·bi(e) n 1. (Angu, Nevs, USVI) *Crescentia cujete* (*Bignoniaceae*); **Fr**. *calebassier, pied-calebasse* m. (Guad, Mart); **Sp**. *guïra, totuma*, f. (Cuba) □ The Fr equivalent is the tree, the Sp equivalent is the gourd. See CALABASH.

god-bird n 1. (Gren, Guyn, StVn) *Troglodytes aedon* (*Troglodytidae*); **Fr**. *oiseau bon dieu* m.,

rossignol m. (Guad, Mart); **Sp**. *cucarachero común* m. (Venz) 2. (Baha, TkCa) *Trochilidae spp*; **Fr**. *colibri huppé, colibri falle vert* m. (Guad, Mart); **Sp**. *colibrí, chupaflores* m. (Venz)

god-horse n (CarA) *Phasmidae spp*; **Fr**. *cheval bon dieu* m. (Guad, Mart); **Sp**. *caballo de palo* m. (Venz)

gold·en-ap·ple n 1. (CarA) *Spondias cytherea, S. dulcis* (*Anacardiaceae*); **Fr**. *pomme/prune-cythère* f. (Guad, Mart); **Sp**. *ciruela dulce* f. (Cuba)

gold·en-show·er n (Bdos) *Bignonia unguis, Macfadyena unguis-cati* (*Bignoniaceae*); **Fr**. *griffe à chatte, griffe-chatte* f. (Guad, Mart); **Sp**. *abrazapalo, pegapalo* m. (StDo)

goose·ber·ry n (CarA) *Phyllanthus acidus, P. distichus* (*Euphorbiaceae*); **Fr**. *pomme surelle* f. (Guad, Mart); **Sp**. *grosella* f. (Cuba, StDo)

go·ver·nor-plum n 1. (Baha, Belz, Berm, Gren, Jmca, Mrat, Trin) *Flacourtia indica* (*Flacourtiaceae*); **Fr**. *grosse prune-café* f. (Guad, Mart), *mérise* f. (Mart); **Sp**. *ciruela gobernadora, ciruela de Madagascar* f. (Cuba)

gra·na·dil·la n (CarA) *Passiflora quadrangularis* (*Passifloraceae*); **Fr**. *barbadine* f. (Guad, Mart); **Sp**. *granadilla* f. (Cuba, PtRi, StDo)

grape·fruit n (CarA) *Citrus paridisi, C. reticulata* (*Rutaceae*); **Fr**. *fruit du paradis, grape-fruit* m. (Guad, Mart); **Sp**. *toronja* f. (Cuba, PtRi, StDo, Venz)

grass·quit n (CarA) *Tiaris spp* (*Fringillidae*); **Fr**. *petit des herbes, cici des herbes* m. (Mart); **Sp**. *pechito, tomeguiín* m. (Cuba)

greas·y-bush n 1. (Baha, Jmca) *Hyptis pectinata* (*Menthaceae*); **Fr**. *baume (anglais) camphré, guérit tout* m. (Guad); **Sp**. *alhucema* f. (Cuba) 2. (Tbgo, Trin) *Tournefortia hirsutissima* (*Boraginaceae*); **Fr**. *herbe à malingres* f. (Mart); **Sp**. *nigua* f. (Cuba, PtRi)

green tur·tle (**green sea-tur·tle**) n phr (CarA) *Chelonia mydas* (*Chelonidae*); **Fr**. *tortue verte de l'Atlantique* f. (Guad, Mart); **Sp**. *tortuga verde del Atlántico* f. (Cuba, PtRi, StDo, Venz)

grou-grou n (Gren, StVn, Tbgo, Trin) 1. *Acrocomia aculeata* (*Palmae*); **Fr**. *corosse* f. (Hait); **Sp**. *corojo* m. (Cuba)

ground-dove n 1. (CarA) *Columbigallina passerina* (*Columbidae*); **Fr**. *ortolan* m. (Guad, Mart); **Sp**. *rolita* f. (StDo), 2. *Zenaida aurita, Z.auriculata* (*Columbidae*); **Fr**. *tourterelle* f. (Guad, Mart); **Sp**. *sanjuanera* f. (Cuba), *rolón* m. (StDo)

ground-liz·ard n (CarA) *Ameiva dorsalis, A. exsul* (*Lacertidae*); FR. **anolis-terre** m. (CarA); SP. **lagarto** m. (Cuba), **mato** m. (Venz)

grudge-pea n (Gren) *Canavalia ensiformis* (*Leguminosae-Papilionaceae*); FR. **pois sabre** m. (Guad, Mart); SP. **haba de caballo** f. (Cuba)

grunt n (CarA) *Haemulidae spp, Pomadasyidae spp*; FR. **gorette jaune** f. (Guad, Mart); SP. **ronco amarillo** m. (Cuba)

gua·va n (CarA) *Psidium guajava* (*Myrtaceae*); FR. **goyave** f. (Guad, Mart); SP. **guayaba** f. (Cuba, PtRi, StDo, Venz)

gua·va-ber·ry n (ViIs) *Eugenia floribundia* (*Myrtaceae*); FR. **coco-carette** m. (Guad, Mart); SP. **mije** m. (Cuba), **mijo** m. (StDo)

guin·ea-bird n (Bdos, Guyn, Jmca) *Numida meleagris* (*Numididae*); FR. **pintade** f. (Guad, Mart); SP. **gallina de Guinea** f., **guinea** f. (Cuba, StDo)

guin·ea-corn n (CarA) *Sorghum vulgare, S. durra* (*Gramineae*); FR. **sorgho, gros millet** m. (Guad, Mart); SP. **millo, sorgo,** m. (Cuba)

guin·ea-grass n (CarA) *Panicum maximum* (*Gramineae-Poaceae*); FR. **herbe de Guinée** f. (Guad, Hait, Mart); SP. **yerba de Guinea** f. (Cuba, PtRi, StDo)

guin·ea-shark n (ECar) *Rhincodon typus* (*Rhincodontidae*); FR. **requin baleine** m. (CarA); SP. **tiburón ballena** m. (CarA)

guin·ea-yam n (Dmca, Gren, Jmca, Tbgo, Trin) *Dioscorea cayennensis, D. rotundata* (*Dioscoreaceae*); FR. **igname guinée** f. (Guad, Hait, Mart); SP. **ñame de Guinea** m. (Cuba, PtRi)

gui·nep n (CarA) *Melicoccus bijugatus* (*Sapindaceae*); FR. **quenette** f., **quénèpe** m. (Guad, Hait, Mart); SP. **mamoncillo** m. (Cuba), **mamón** m. (Venz), **quenepa** f. (StDo) □ FR. **quenettier** is the tree.

gul·ly-root n (CarA) *Petiveria alliacea* (*Phytolaccaceae*); FR. **dandail** m., **douvant-nègre** m. (Guad, Mart); SP. **anamú** m. (Cuba)

chasseur m. (FrGy); SP. **pescadilla real** f. (Venz)

hawks·bill (tur·tle) n (phr) (CarA) *Eretmochelys imbricata* (*Chelonidae*); FR. **tortue caret de l'Atlantique** f. (Guad, Mart); SP. **tortuga de carey del Atlántico** m. (Cuba, StDo, Venz)

head·ache-bush n (Angu, Baha, Jmca) *Hedyosum spp* (*Chloranthaceae*); *Acalypha wilkesiana* (*Euphorbiaceae*) and other families; FR. **boissenti, bois de l'eau, bois fragile** m. (Guad, Mart); SP. **acalifa (tropical)** f. (Cuba)

hedge·hog fish n phr (CarA) *Diodon hystrix*(*Diodontidae*); FR. **porc-épique boubou** m. (Guad, Mart); SP. **pejerizo común** m. (Cuba, StDo)

he·li·co·ni·a n (CarA) *Heliconia bihai, H. caribaea* (*Musaceae*); FR. **balisier, balisier rouge/jaune** m. (Guad, Mart); SP. **plátano silvestre** m. (Cuba, StDo)

hi·bis·cus n (CarA) *Hibiscus rosa-sinensis* (*Malvaceae*); FR. **hibiscus** m. (Guad, Mart); SP. **amapola** f. (Cuba, PtRi) □ Cp AFRICAN TULIP.

hind n (CarA) *Epinephelus spp*; FR. **mérou rouge/couronné/géant** m. (Guad, Hait, Mart); SP. **cherna, cherna americana** f., **mero, mero colorado/guasa** m. (Cuba, PtRi, StDo) □ This fish is one of two or three edible species found in the CarA and the Fr. and Sp. equivalents 'mérou' and 'cherna' or 'mero' are qualified by adjectives referring to the different species.

hog-fish n (CarA) *Lachnolaimus maximus* (*Labridae*); FR. **labre capitaine** m. (Guad, Hait, Mart); SP. **doncella de pluma** f. (Cuba, PtRi, StDo)

hog-plum n 1. (CarA) *Spondias mombin* (*Anacardiaceae*); FR. **mombin, prune mombin** f. (Guad, Mart); SP. **jobo** m. (Cuba, PtRi, StDo, Venz)

hum·ming bird n phr (Trin) *Trochilidae spp*; FR. **colibri** m.; SP. **zumbador, zumbadorcito** m. □ These are standard Fr. and Sp. equivalents, each qualified in Eng, Fr and Sp ornithological literature to distinguish the many varieties.

H

ha·i·a·ri n 2. (Guyn) *Lonchocarpus densiflorus, L. ehrenbergii* (*Papilionaceae*); FR. **savonnette** f. (Guad, Mart); SP. **aco** m. (Venz)

ha·i·ma·ra n (Guyn) *Macrodon trahira, Hoplias macropthalmus* (*Sciaenidae*); FR. **acoupa**

I

im·mor·tel n (CarA) *Erythrina micropteryx* (*Papilionaceae*); FR. **immortel vrai** m. (Guad, Mart), **bois immortel vrai, arbre corail** m. (Hait); SP. **búcare espinoso** m. (Cuba, Venz)

In·di·a-rub·ber plant/tree *n phr* (CarA) *Ficus elastica* (*Moraceae*); FR. *caoutchouc m.* (Guad, Hait, Mart); SP. *goma elástica f.* (Cuba), *caucho m.* (StDo) □ CAOUTCHOUC is Std. Fr. for 'rubber', CAUCHO is Std. Sp. for 'rubber'.

In·di·a rub·ber vine *n phr* (CarA) *Cryptostegia grandiflora* (*Asclepiadaceae*); FR. *allamanda pourpre f.* (Guad, Mart); SP. *estrella del norte f.* (Cuba), *vara de cocho f.* (StDo)

in·flam·ma·tion-bush *n* (CarA) *Verbesina alata* (*Compositae*); FR. *camomille rouge f.*, *bouton rouge/jaune m.* (Guad); SP. *botoncillo m.* (Cuba), *capitaneja f.* (PtRi)

i·po·me·a *n* (CarA) *Ipomoea pes-caprae* (*Convolvulaceae*); FR. *patate-bord-de-mer f.* (Guad); SP. *boniata de playa f.* (Cuba), *bejuco m.* (PtRi)

i·ron·wood *n* (CarA) *Exostema caribaeum* (*Rubiaceae*) in *Antg*, *Krugiodendrum ferreum* (*Rhamnaceae*) in *USVI*; FR. *tendre en gomme, quinquina caraïbe f.* (Guad, Mart); *petit bois de fer, bois de fer blanc m.* (Guad, Mart); SP. *carillo m.*, *lirio santana m.* (Cuba); *quina criolla f.* (StDo); *espejuelo m.* (PtRi), *palo de hierro m.* (StDo) □ The first two Fr. and Sp. equivalents match the first taxonomic name *Exostema caribaeum* and the second two Fr. and Sp. equivalents match the second taxonomic name *Krugiodendrum ferreum*.

ix·o·ra *n* (CarA) *Ixora coccinea* (*Rubiaceae*); FR. *corail m.* (Guad, Mart); SP. *amor ardiente m.* (PtRi, Venz), *corona de la reina f.* (StDo)

J

jack[3] (**jack·fish**) *n* (*usu pl*) **1.** (CarA) *Harengula humeralis* (*Clupeidae*); FR. *harengule écailleuse f.* (Guad, Mart); SP. *sardineta escamuda f.* (CarA)

jack·fruit *n* (CarA) *Artocarpus heterophyllus, A. integer* (*Moraceae*); FR. *jacquier m.* (Guad, Mart); SP. *rima f.* (Cuba), *buen pan, albopán m.* (StDo)

jack-in-the-box *n* (Bdos, Guyn) *Hernandia sonora* (*Hernandiaceae*); FR. *mirobolan, mirobolan bâtard m.* (Guad, Mart); SP. *guamiey m.*, *maga f.* (Cuba, PtRi, StDo)

jack-in-the-bush *n* (Jmca) *Eupatorium odoratum* (*Compositae*); FR. *fleurit-Noël m.*, *langue à chat f.*, *guérit-tout m.* (Guad, Mart); SP.

rompezaragüey *m.* (Cuba), *langa chata f.*, *niquibey m.* (StDo)

Jack Span·i·ard *n* (ECar) *Polistes spp*; FR. *marabunta f.* (FrGy); SP. *marabunta f.* (Venz)

jac·quot (par·rot) *n* (*phr*) **1.** (Dmca) *Amazonia arausica* (*Psittacidae*); FR. *jacquot, perroquet m.* (Guad, Mart), *ara de Guadeloupe m.* (Guad, Mart); SP. *periquillo m.*, *cotorra f.* (Cuba)

Ja·mai·ca-plum *n* (Bdos, BrVi, Gren, Tbgo, Trin) *Spondias purpurea* (*Anacardiaceae*); FR. *mombin rouge m.* (Guad, Mart); SP. *ciruela morada f.* (StDo), *ciruela de hueso f.* (Venz)

ja·moon *n* (Guyn) *Syzygium cumini* (*Myrtaceae*); FR. *jamboisie f.*, *tête négresse f.* (Guad, Mart); SP. *jambolán m.* (Cuba), *jambolín m.* (PtRi)

jas·mine *n* **1.** (CarA) *Jasminum spp* (*Oleaceae*); FR. *jasmin blanc/jaune/double m.* (Guad, Mart); SP. *jazmín de Oriza m.* (Cuba), *jazmín de Islas Canarias m.* (PtRi)

Jew-fish (**dew-fish**) *n* **1.** (CarA) *Epinephelus* (*Promicrops*) *itaiara* (*Serranidae*); FR. *mérou géant m.* (Guad, Mart); SP. *mero guasa m.* (Cuba, PtRi, StDo)

jhin·gie *n* (Guyn) *Luffa acutangula* (*Cucurbitaceae*); FR. *liane torchon* (Guad, Mart), *torchon m.* (Hait); SP. *estropajo m.* (Cuba, PtRi), *esponja f.* (StDo)

jip·pi-jap·pa *n* **1.** (Belz, Jmca) *Carludovica palmata, C. jamaicensis* (*Cyclanthaceae*); FR. *ailes à mouche f. pl.* (Guad), *cachibou m.* (Mart); SP. *jipijapa m.* (Cuba) □ A species very similar to *Carludovica* is *Asplundia* and the Fr. equivalent corresponds to the *Asplundia spp*. See *Fournet:411.*

Job's tears *n phr pl* (Bdos, Guyn, Jmca, Trin) *Coix lachryma-jobi* (*Gramineae*); FR. *larmes de Job f.* (Guad, Mart); SP. *Santa Juana f.* (Cuba), *camándulas f. pl.* (PtRi)

Jo·seph's coat *n phr* (Bdos, Brbu, Jmca) *Coleus blumei* (*Labiatae*); FR. *robe-à-l'Evêque f.* (Guad, Mart), *coleus m.* (Guad, Mart); SP. *coleo m.* (PtRi), *Manto de la Virgen m.* (Cuba)

jum·bie-bal·sam *n* (Guyn) *Ocimum canum* (*Labiatae*); FR. *framboisin m.* (Guad, Mart); SP. *albahaca cimarrona f.* (Cuba)

jum·bie-bead *n* **1.** (Brbu, Gren, StKt, Trin, USVI) *Abrus precatorius* (*Leguminosae-Papilionaceae*); FR. *graines d'église f. pl.*, *liane à réglisse f.* (Guad, Mart); SP. *peronías f.*, *ojos de cangrejo m.* (PtRi) **2.** (Guyn) *Erythrina corallodendron, E. pallida* (*Leguminosae-Papilionaceae*); FR. *immortel vrai m.*, *arbre à corail m.* (Guad, Mart); SP. *piñón* *espinoso* m. (PtRi) **3.** (Gren, Trin, USVI) *Adenanthera pavonina* (*Leguminosae-Mimosaceae*); FR. *arbre à réglisse* m. (Guad, Mart); SP. *peonía* f. (StDo), *coralitos* m. (PtRi, StDo) **4.** (Guyn, Trin) *Ormosia coarctata, O. coccinea, O. paraensis* (*Leguminosae-Papilionaceae*); FR. *caconnier rouge* m. (Guad, Mart); SP. *palo de peonía* m. (StDo)

jum·bie-bird n **1.** (Guyn) *Tyto alba hellmayri* (*Tytonidae*); FR. *frezaie* m. (Hait); SP. *lechuza común/blanca* f. (StDo) **3.** (Guyn) *Crotophaga ani* (*Cuculidae*); FR. *gros merle de Sainte Lucie, merle* m. (Hait), *tapé, juif* m. (Guad); SP. *judío* m. (Cuba)

jum·bie-sour·sop n (Antg, Nevs, StVn) *Morinda citrifolia* (*Rubiaceae*); FR. *rhubarbe caraïbe* f. (Guad, Mart); SP. *gardenia hedionda* f. (PtRi)

jump-up-and-kiss-me n (CarA) *Portulaca oleracea, P. pilosa, P. grandiflora* (*Portulacaceae*); FR. *pourprier, pourpre amer* m. (Guad, Mart); SP. *verdolaga* f. (Cuba, StDo)

K

king-fish n (CarA) *Scomberomorus cavalla* (*Cybiidae*); FR. *thazard barré* m. (Guad, Mart); SP. *carite lucio* m. (Cuba, PtRi, StDo)

king-o·range n (StKt, Trin) *Citrus sinensis, C. reticulata* (*Rutaceae*); FR. *orange douce* f. (Guad, Mart); SP. *naranja de China* f. (Cuba, StDo)

kis·ka·dee n (Guyn, Tbgo, Trin) *Pitangus sulphuratus* (*Tyrannidae*); FR. *keskedee* m. (Guad, Mart); SP. *Cristofue* m. (Venz) □ KESKEDEE may be a loan but is used by the *Guad* author Maryse Condé.

kre·ke·teh-hawk n (Guyn) *Rostrhamus sociabilis* (*Accipitridae*); SP. *caracolero* m. (Cuba) □ There is no Fr. equivalent for this bird as it is not found in the Fr islands of the CarA, but only in Cuba and some of the C American countries.

L

leaf-of-life n (Bdos, Dmca, Guyn, Jmca, Trin) *Bryophyllum pinnatum* (*Crassulaceae*); FR.

herbe-mal-tête f. (Guad, Mart); SP. *yerba (de) bruja* f. (PtRi, StDo)

lig·num-vi·tae n (CarA) *Guaiacum officinale* (*Zygophyllacceae*); FR. *gaiac* m. (Guad, Mart); SP. *guayacán, guayaco* m. (PtRi)

Li·ma bean n phr (CarA) *Phaseolus lunatus* (*Leguminosae-Papilionaceae*); FR. *pois savon* m. (Guad, Mart); SP. *haba* f. (PtRi, StDo)

Lis·bon yam n phr (Bdos, Gren, Nevs, StLu, Tbgo, Trin) *Dioscorea alata* (*Dioscoraceae*); FR. *igname blanc* m. (Guad, Mart); SP. *ñame de agua, ñame de mina* m. (PtRi), *yame blanco* m. (StDo)

lob·ster n (CarA) *Metanephrops binghami* (*Nephropidae*); FR. *homard* m. (Guad, Mart) Also *Panulirus argus* (*Palinuridae*); FR. *homard blanc* m. (Mart); SP. *langosta* f. (Cuba, PtRi, StDo) □ LANGOUSTE is the Std. Fr. for 'lobster'.

lo·cust n **2.** (Guyn) See STINKING-TOE

log·ger·head[1] n (CarA) *Caretta caretta* (*Chelonidae*); FR. *tortue caouane* f. (Guad, Mart); SP. *tortuga cahuama* f. (Venz)

log·ger·head[2] n (Angu) *Tyrannus caudifasciatus* (*Tyrannidae*); FR. *pipirite tête-police* m. (Guad); SP. *pitirre cantor, pitirre guatíbere* m. (Cuba, PtRi)

loo·fah n (Gren, Jmca, Trin) *Luffa cylindrica* (*Cucurbitaceae*); FR. *liane torchon* f. (Guad, Mart); SP. *estropajo* m. (Cuba, PtRi), *esponja* f. (PtRi, StDo)

love-vine n (CarA) *Cuscuta americana, C. indecora* (*Convolvulaceae*); FR. *vermicelle* f., *corde à violon* f. (Guad, Mart); SP. *fideo* m. (StDo, Venz)

lu·ka·na·ni n (Guyn) *Cichla ocellaris* (*Cichilidae*); SP. *pavón amarillo* m. (Venz)

M

ma·ca·juel n (Trin) *Constrictor constrictor* (*Boidae*); FR. *anaconda* m. (Guad, Mart); SP. *anaconda* f. (Venz)

ma·caw n **1.** (CarA) *Ara spp* (*Psittacidae*) FR. *ara* f. (Guad, Mart); SP. *cotorra* f. (PtRi, StDo) □ Known generally as *guacamayo* in Std. Sp. The Sp. equivalent does not correspond directly with the taxonomy given. The bird is found largely in *Guyn*, and generally speaking the nearer relation is the *Amazona ventralis* of the same family, found in both *PtRi* and *StDo* and known as *cotorra* in both territories—*Bond:109*. 2. (Antg, Bdos, StKt) *Acromia aculeata* (*Palmaceae*); FR. **glouglou, palmier glouglou** *m.* (Guad, Mart); SP. **corojo** *m.* (Cuba, StDo)

ma·ho·ga·ny *n* (CarA) *Swietenia mahogani, S. macrophylla* (*Meliaceae*); FR. **mahogani petites feuilles** *m.* (Guad, Mart); SP. **caoba** *f.* (Cuba, StDo), **caoba dominicana** *f.* (PtRi) □ In *PtRi* the Sp. equivalent corresponds specifically to the species *Swietenia mahogani*, the other species *Swietenia macrophylla* being known as '*caoba de Honduras/Venezuela*'—*DFPR:303*.

Ma·lac·ca-ap·ple/-pear *n* (Antg, Guyn) *Syzygium malaccense* (*Myrtaceae*); FR. **pomme d'eau/malacca** (Guad, Mart); SP. **pomarrosa de Málaga** *f.* (Cuba)

mam·mee-ap·ple *n* (CarA) *Mammea americana* (*Guttiferae*); FR. **abricot des Antilles, mamey** *m.* (Guad, Mart); SP. **mamey** *m.* (Cuba), **mamey amarillo** *m.* (StDo)

mam·mee-sa·po·te *n* (CarA) *Calocarpum mamosum, Pouteria sapota* (*Sapotaceae*); FR. **sapote** *m.* (Hait); SP. **sapote** *m.* (StDo), **mamey sapote** *m.* (PtRi)

ma·na·tee *n* (Antg, Belz, Guyn, Jmca) *Manatus americanus* (*Trichecludae*); FR. **lamantin** *m.* (Guad, Mart); SP. **manatí** *m.* (Cuba, StDo, Venz)

man-bet·ter-man *n* (Dmca, StLu, Trin) *Achyranthes indica* (*Amaranthaceae*); FR. **grand queue-de-rat, grand collant** *m.* (Guad, Mart); SP. **rabo de gato, rabo de ratón** *m.* (StDo)

man·chi·neel(-tree) *n* (CarA) *Hippomane mancinella* (*Euphorbiaceae*); FR. **mancenillier** *m.* (Guad, Mart); SP. **manzanillo** *m.* (PtRi, StDo), **manzanillo de playa** *m.* (Cuba, Venz) □ Refer to the fruit as **fruit du** Fr. and **fruta del** Sp.

man·dar·in (orange) *n* (*phr*) (Baha, Bdos, Dmca, Gren, StLu, Trin) *Citrus nobilis, C. reticulata* (*Rutaceae*); FR. **mandarine** *f.* (Guad, Mart); SP. **mandarina** *f.* (PtRi, Venz)

man-doc·tor (fish) *n* (*phr*) (Brbu, BrVi) *Acanthus chirurgus* (*Acanthuridae*); FR. **chirurgien docteur** *m.* (Guad, Mart); SP. **navajón cirujano** *m.* (Cuba, PtRi, StDo)

man·ger·ine *n* (Belz, Guyn, Jmca) *Citrus spp* (*Rutaceae*); FR. **mangerine** *f.* (Guad, Mart); SP. **(naranja) tangerina, (naranja) mandarina** *f.* (Cuba, PtRi)

man·go *n* (CarA) *Mangifera spp* (*Anacardiaceae*); FR. **mangue** *f.* (Guad, Mart); SP. **mangó** *m.* (Cuba, PtRi, StDo)

man·go·steen *n* (Bdos, Dmca, Jmca, StLu, StVn, Trin) *Garcinia mangostana* (*Guttiferae*); FR. **abricot bâtard** *m.* (Guad, Mart); SP. **mangostán** *m.* (Cuba, StDo)

man·grove *n* (Belz, CayI, Gren, Guyn, Trin) *Avicennia spp.* (*Verbenaceae*), *Laguncularia racemosa* (*Combretaceae*), *Conocarpus erectus* (*Combretaceae*); FR. **bois de mêche** *m.* (Guad, Mart); SP. **mangle prieto** *m.* (Cuba, StDo, Venz)

man·grove-cuck·oo *n* (BrVi, USVI) See RAIN-BIRD[1] 2.

ma·ni·cou *n* (ECar) *Didelphys marsupialis insularis* (*Didelphyidae*); FR. **manicou** *m.* (Mart); SP. **manicú** *m.* (Venz)

man·ni·ba·li *n* (Guyn) *Moronobea coccinea* (*Guttiferae-Hypericaceae*); FR. **palétuvier jaune, mangle jaune** *m.* (Guad); SP. **mangle amarillo** *m.* (CarA)

man·ta (ray) *n* (*phr*) (Guyn) *Manta birostris* (*Mobulidae*); FR. **manta** (Guad, Mart); SP. **manta** *f.* (Cuba), **diablo del mar** *m.* (Venz)

mar·gate (fish) *n* (*phr*) (Angu, Baha, BrVi, Mrat, TkCa) *Haemulon album* (*Pomadasyidae*); FR. **gorette margate** *f.* (Guad, Mart); SP. **ronco blanco** *m.* (Cuba, PtRi, StDo), **corocoro** *m.* (Venz)

ma·ri·jua·na *n* (CarA) *Cannabis sativa* (*Cannabaceae*); FR. **kaya** *m.* (Guad, Mart); SP. **marijuana** *f.* (CarA) □ MARIJUANA is also Std. Sp.

mar·ried-man pork *n phr* (Guyn) *Ocimum basilicum* (*Labiatae*); FR. **basilic, petit framboisin** *m.* (Guad, Mart); SP. **albahaca de puerco** *f.* (Cuba, PtRi)

mas·tic *n* (Baha, Bdos, Belz, Gren, Trin) *Sideroxylon quadrilocuare* (*Sapotaceae*); FR. **acoma bâtard** *m.* (Guad); SP. **jocuma (amarilla)** *f.* (Cuba)

match·wood *n* (Gren, Guyn, Trin) *Didymopanax morototoni* (*Araliaceae*); FR. **bois flot** *m.*, **aralie grandes-feuilles** *f.* (Guad); SP. **yagrumo macho** *m.* (Cuba, StDo)

min·nie-root *n* (Bdos, Gren, Guyn, Jmca, Trin) *Ruellia tuberosa* (*Acanthaceae*); FR. **chandelier** *m.*, **patate chandelier** *f.* (Guad, Mart); SP. **salta perico** (Cuba), **periquito** *m.* (StDo)

mo·ka-mo·ka *n* (Guyn) *Montrichardia arborescens* (*Araceae*); FR. **malanga-rivière, malanga bâtard** (Guad, Mart); SP. **malanga** *f.* (StDo), **yautía madera** *f.* (PtRi)

mon·goose *n* (CarA) *Herpestes nyula*; FR. **mangouste** *f.* (CarA); SP. **mangosta** *f.* (CarA)

mul·let n (CarA) *Mugil spp*; Fr. *mulet le-branche* m. (Guad, Mart); Sp. *lebrancho* m. (Cuba)

mung(-bean) n (Belz, Guyn, Trin) **1.** (Guyn, Trin) *Phaseolus mungo* (*Leguminosae-Papilionaceae*); Fr. *haricots mungo* m. (Guad, Mart); Sp. *frijolillo* m. (Venz) **2.** (Guyn, Trin) *Phaseolus aureus* (*Leguminosae-Papilionaceae*); Fr. *pois rouge* m. (Guad, Mart); Sp. *frijol mungo* m. (Cuba)

N

na·ked-wood n (Baha) *Myrcianthes fragans* (*Myrtaceae*); Fr. *bois d'Inde bâtard* m., *goya-vier-montagne* m. (Mart); Sp. *arrayán, guay-abillo* m. (StDo) □ Evid more often found in Marie-Galante, Saint-Martin and Saint-Barthelmy—*Fournet:896.*

neem n (Guyn, Jmca, Mrat, Trin) *Azadirachta indica, Melia azedarach* (*Myrtaceae*); Fr. *nime, lilas blanc/mauve* m. (Guad); Sp. *lila* f., *lilayo* m. (StDo)

nick·er n (Angu, BrVi, Jmca) *Caesalpinia bonduc, C. bonducella* (*Caesalpiniaceae*); Fr. *canique grise* f. (Guad, Mart); Sp. *mate de costa* m. (StDo), *mato de playa* m. (PtRi)

nut-grass n (CarA) *Cyperus rotundus* (*Cyperaceae*); Fr. *ti-coco, chien-coq* m. (Guad, Mart); Sp. *cebolleta* f. (Cuba), *coquillo* m. (PtRi, StDo)

O

ocean-gar n (ECar) *Xiphias gladius* (*Xiphiidae*); Fr. *espadon* m. (Guad, Mart); Sp. *pez espada* m. (Cuba, PtRi, StDo)

okra (ochro) n (CarA) *Hibiscus esculentus, H. abelmoschus* (*Malvaceae*); Fr. *gombo, gombo musqué* m.(Guad, Mart); Sp. *quimbombó, quimbombo* m. (Cuba, Venz), *molondrón* m. (StDo)

old-maid (bush) n (*phr*) (CarA) *Vinca rosea* or *Lochnera r.* (*Apocynaceae*); Fr. *pervenche de Madagascar* f., *herbe aux sorciers* f. (Guad, Mart); Sp. *vicaria dominica* f. (Cuba)

old-wife n (Baha, Jmca, TkCa) *Balistes vetula* (*Balistidae*); Fr. *baliste royal* m. (Guad, Mart); Sp. *pejepuerco* m. (Cuba, PtRi, StDo)

o·le·an·der n (CarA) *Nerium oleander* (*Apocynaceae*); Fr. *laurier rose* m. (Guad, Mart); Sp. *rosa francesa* f. (Cuba), *laurel rosado* m. (PtRi, StDo)

oys·ter-plant n (ECar) *Rhoeo discolor, R. spathacea* (*Commelinaceae*); Fr. *gros curage* m. (Guad), *grosse herbe grasse* f. (Mart); Sp. *magueyito* m. (StDo), *sanguinaria* f. (PtRi)

P

pa(c)·cu n (Guyn) **1.** *Pacu myletes, Myletes setiger, Colossoma nigripinnis* (*Characidae*); Sp. *cachama* f. (Venz) □ The taxonomy of the Sp. equivalent is *Colossoma macropomum* (*Characidae*).

pain·kill·er (bush) n (*phr*) (BrVi, Guyn, Mrat, Nevs, USVI) *Morinda citrifolia* (*Rubiaceae*); Fr. *feuille douleur, bois douleur* (Hait), *rhubarbe caraïbe* f. (Guad); Sp. *piña de puerco* f. (StDo), *gardenia hedionda* f. (PtRi)

pan·go·la-grass n (CarA) *Digitaria decumbens* (*Gramineae*); Fr. *pangola* f. (Guad, Mart); Sp. *yerba pangola* f. (PtRi)

pa·paw (pa·pa·ya, paw·paw) n (CarA) *Carica papaya* (*Caricaceae*); Fr. *papaye* f. (Guad, Mart); Sp. *lechoso* m. (Venz), *papaya* f. (Cuba, PtRi, StDo)

pa·ra-grass n (CarA) *Panicum barbinode* or *P. purpurascens* or *Prachiaria mutica* (*Gramineae-Poaceae*); Fr. *herbe para* f. (Hait); Sp. *yerba del pará* f., *yerba pará* f. (PtRi), *ma-lojillo* m. (PtRi)

pas·sion-fruit n (CarA) *Passiflora edulis* (*Passifloraceae*); Fr. *maracudja* f., *fruit de la passion* m. (Guad, Mart); Sp. *parcha*, f. (PtRi)

peach n (Guyn) *Diospyros discolor* (*Ebenaceae*); Fr. *mabolo* m. (Guad, Mart); Sp. *mabolo, sapote de la India* m. (Cuba) □ The more common scientific name is *Diospyros blancoi* but it is also cultivated in *Guad* under the scientific name of *Diospyros discolor.*—*Howard, Flora of the Lesser Antilles* vol. no II:71.

pec·ca·ry n (Belz, Guyn) *Dicotyles torquatus* (*Tayassuidae*); Fr. *pécari* m. (FrGy); Sp. *báquiro de collar, cinchado* m. (Venz) □ Also Sp. *báquiro cachete blanco o careto* m. *Tayassau* *tajacu/pecari (Tayassuidae)—Fauna de Venezuela:62.*

pee-whi(s)t·ler *n* (Bdos) *Elaenia martinica (Tyrannidae)*; FR. *siffleur blanc m.* (Guad, Mart); SP. *juí blanco m.* (PtRi)

phys·ic-nut *n* 1. (CarA) *Jatropha curcas (Euphorbiaceae)*; FR. *médicinier béni m., feuilles médecin f. pl.* (Guad); SP. *piñón m.* (Cuba, PtRi, StDo, Venz)

pi·geon-pea(s) *n (pl)* (CarA) *Cajanus cajan (Papilionaceae)*; FR. *pois d'Angole, pois de bois m.* (Guad, Mart); SP. *gandul m.* (PtRi, StDo), *quinchoncho, chícharo m.* (Venz)

pine·(ap·ple) *n* (CarA) *Ananas comosus (Bromeliaceae)*; FR. *ananas, ananas édule m.* (Guad, Mart); SP. *piña f.* (PtRi, StDo)

ping·wing *n* (Belz, Jmca, USVI) *Bromelia pinguin (Bromeliaceae)*; FR. *ananas sauvage m.* (Guad, Mart); SP. *maya f.* (PtRi, StDo), *pinguín m.* (PtRi)

pitch-ap·ple *n* (ViIs) *Clusia rosea (Guttiferae)*; FR. *figuier marron m.* (Guad, Mart); SP. *copey m.* (Cuba, PtRi, StDo, Venz)

plan·tain *n* (CarA) *Musa paradisiaca (Musaceae)*; FR. *banane f.* (Guad, Mart); SP. *plátano m.* (Cuba, PtRi, StDo)

poin·set·ti·a *n* (CarA) *Euphorbia pulcherrima (Euphorbiaceae)*; FR. *poinsettia rouge, poinsettia f.* (Guad, Mart); SP. *flor de Pascua(s) f.* (Cuba, StDo, Venz), *flor de Navidad f.* (Venz)

pond-fly *n* (Bdos, Guyn) *Ordonata spp, Orthemis ferruginea* or *Brechmorhoga praecox*; FR. *grande libellule verte f.* (Guad, Mart); SP. *libélula f., caballito del diablo m.* (Cuba)

pond-thatch; **pond-top** *n* (Baha) *Sabal palmetto bahamensis (Palmae)*; FR. *amarre, palmier sabal m.* (Guad, Mart); SP. *palma de sombrero f.* (PtRi)

poor-me-one *n* (Gren, Tbgo, Trin) 2. *Nyctibius griseus (Nyctibiidae)*; FR. *chat-huant m.* (Hait); SP. *Don Juan m.* (StDo)

Por·tu·guese man-of-war *n phr* (CarA) *Physalia physalis (Physalidae)*; FR. *galère, méduse argonaute f.* (Guad, Mart); SP. *medusa f.* (Cuba) □ The Fr. and Sp. equivalents are standard forms as there is no special Caribbean Fr. or Sp. equivalent.

po·ta·to *n* (CarA) See ENGLISH POTATO.

pump·kin *n* (CarA) *Cucurbita moschata, Pepo moschata (Cucurbitaceae)*; FR. *giraumont m.* (Guad, Mart); SP. *calabaza f.* (PtRi), *auyama f.* (Venz) □ CITROUILLE is Std. Fr. and CALABAZA Std. Sp. for 'pumpkin'.

Q

queen-of-flow·ers *n* (ECar) *Lagerstroemia flos-regina, L.speciosa (Lythraceae)*; FR. *reine des jardins, reine des fleurs f.* (Guad, Mart); SP. *júpiter m.* (Cuba), *reina de las flores f.* (PtRi)

quer·i·man *n* (Guyn) *Mugil brasiliensis (Mugilidae)*; FR. *mulet lebranche m.* (Guad, Mart); SP. *liza f.* (Venz) □ A larger species of MULLET.

R

rab·bit-meat *n* (Gren, Trin) *Alternanthera ficoidea (Amaranthaceae)*; FR. *herbe à albumine f.* (Guad, Mart); SP. *sanguinaria f.* (PtRi)

rain-bird[1] *n* (CarA) 1. *Tyrannus dominicensis (Tyrannidae)*; FR. *pipiri m.* (Guad, Mart); SP. *pitirre, pitirre abejero m.* (Cuba), *petigre m.* (StDo) 2. *Coccyzus minor (Cuculidae)*; FR. *gangan, coucou manioc m.* (Guad, Mart); SP. *arriero (chico) m.* (Cuba), *primavera f.* (StDo) □ PRIMAVERA is also Std. Sp. for 'spring'.

ram-goat bush *n phr* 1. (StKt) *Turnera ulmifolia (Turneraceae)*; FR. *turnère, thym des savanes m.* (Guad); SP. *marilópez m.* (Cuba, StDo)

ra·zor-grass *n* (CarA) *Scleria spp (Cyperaceae)* or *Paspalum spp (Paniceae)*; FR. *herbe-mouton, herbe à cabrit f.* (Guad, Mart); SP. *pata de conejo f.* (PtRi), *cambute m.* (Cuba)

red-ant *n* (CarA) *Solenopsis spp*; FR. *fourmi rouge m.* (Guad, Mart); SP. *hormiga brava f.* (Cuba)

red ce·dar *n phr* (Bdos, Dmca, Gren, Guyn, Nevs) *Cedrela odorata* or *C. mexicana (Meliaceae)*; FR. *acajou amer/rouge m.* (Guad, Mart); SP. *cedro hembra m.*(StDo), *cedro amargo m.* (Venz)

red-hind *n* (Dmca, Gren, Jmca, USVI) *Epinephelus guttatus (Serranidae)*; FR. *mero couronné m.* (Guad, Mart); SP. *mero colorado m.* (Cuba, PtRi, StDo)

red man·grove *n phr* (Guyn, Trin, USVI) *Rhizophora mangle, R. harrisonii (Rhizophoraceae)*; FR. *palétuvier rouge m.* (Guad,

Mart); Sp. *mangle colorado m.* (Cuba, PtRi, StDo), *mangle rojo m.* (Cuba, Venz)

red·neck·ed pi·geon *n phr* (Jmca) *Columba squamosa* (*Columbidae*); Fr. *ramier cou-rouge m.* (Guad, Mart); Sp. *paloma turca f.* (StDo)

red-sage *n* (Bdos) *Lantana camara* (*Verbenaceae*); Fr. *bois genou m., mille fleurs f. pl.* (Guad, Mart); Sp. *cariaquito blanco/colorado m.* (Venz)

red san·dal·wood *n phr* (Gren, Jmca, Trin) *Adenanthera pavonina* (*Mimosaceae*); Fr. *arbre à réglisse m., graines-réglisse f. pl.* (Guad, Mart); Sp. *peonía f.* (StDo), *coralitos m. pl.* (PtRi)

red-snap·per *n* (CarA) (Bdos, Mrat, Nevs) *Lutjanus campechanus* (*Lutjanidae*); Fr. *vivaneau campèche m.* (Guad, Mart); Sp. *pargo del Golfo m.* (Cuba, PtRi, StDo)

red-yam *n* (Baha, Gren, Jmca, Nevs, StKt) *Dioscorea spp*; Fr. *igname, coussecouche m.* (Guad, Mart); Sp. *ñame peludo m.* (Cuba)

roast-pork (cac·tus) *n* (*phr*) (Jmca) *Opuntia antillana* (*Cactaceae*); Fr. *raquette f., raquette volante f.* (Guad, Mart); Sp. *higuera chumba f.* (StDo)

ro·bin [1] *n* 1. (Angu, Gren, Grns, Nevs, StVn) *Prionotus scutulus* (*Triglidae*); Fr. *poule f.* (Guad, Mart); Sp. *gallina f.* (Venz) □ Fr. and Sp. equivalents are both the standard Fr. and Sp. words for 'hen', prob because of the fish's well developed pectoral fins wh look somewhat like wings.—*Fauna de Venezuela:196.*

rock-bal·sam *n* (Bdos, Guyn, Mrat, USVI) *Clusia plukenetii* (*Guttiferae*), *Peperomia magnoliifolia* (*Piperaceae*) or *Justicia pectoralis* (*Acanthaceae*); Fr. *herbe à charpentiers f.* (Guad, Mart); Sp. *yerba carpintera, curía f.* (PtRi, StDo)

rock-fish *n* (Baha, Berm, CayI) *Mycteroperca venenosa* (*Serranidae*); Fr. *badèche de roche f.* (Guad, Mart); Sp. *cuna de piedra f.* (Cuba, PtRi, StDo)

rock-hind *n* (CarA) *Epinephelus adscensionis* (*Serranidae*); Fr. *mérou oualioua m.* (Guad, Mart); Sp. *mero cabrilla m.* (Cuba, PtRi, StDo)

rose ap·ple *n phr* (CarA) *Syzygium jambos* or *Eugenia j.* (*Myrtaceae*); Fr. *pomme rose f.* (Guad, Mart); Sp. *poma rosa f.* (PtRi, StDo)

ros·eau *n* (Dmca, Gren, Tbgo, Trin) *Gynerium sagittatum, G. saccharoides, Saccharum sagittatum* (*Poaceae*); Fr. *roseau d'Inde m.* (Guad); Sp. *güin m.* (Cuba), *caña brava f.* (PtRi)

rose·ma·ry(-weed) *n* (Bdos, Brbu, CayI, Jmca, USVI) *Rosemarinus officinalis* (*Labiatae*);

Fr. *romarin m.* (Guad, Mart); Sp. *yerba de la niña f.* (Cuba)

round ro·bin *n phr* (Gren, StLu) *Decapterus punctatus* (*Carangidae*); Fr. *comète quiaquia f.* (Guad, Hait, Mart); Sp. *macarela chuparaco f.* (PtRi, StDo)

roy·al palm *n phr* (CarA) *Oreodoxa regia* or *Roystonea princeps* (*Palmaceae*); Fr. *palmier royal m.* (Guad, Mart); Sp. *palma real f.* (Cuba, StDo), *palma real cubana f.* (PtRi)

run·ning ant *n phr* (Bdos, Guyn, Jmca) *Formicidae spp*; Fr. *fourmi folle f.* (Guad, Mart); Sp. *hormiga loca f.* (Cuba, PtRi)

S

saeme *n* 1. (Guyn) *Dolichos erosus, Pachyrrhizus tuberosus* (*Papilionaceae-Fabaceae*); Fr. *poispatate m., patate-cochon f.* (Guad, Mart); Sp. *habilla f.* (PtRi), *yuca de bejuco f.* (Venz)

sage-bush *n* 2. (CarA) *Lantana spp* (*Verbenaceae*); Fr. *herbe à plomb f., sauge f.* (Guad, Mart); Sp. *doña Anita f.* (StDo), *cariaquito m.* (Venz) □ See also BLACK SAGE 1.

sai·jan *n* (Guyn, Trin) *Moringa oleifera* (*Moringaceae*); Fr. *maloko, ben ailé m.* (Guad, Mart); Sp. *paraíso francés m.* (Cuba), *palo de abejas m.* (StDo)

sa·ki·win·ki *n* (Guyn, Trin) *Chrysothrix sciureus* (*Cebidae*); Fr. *sakiwinki m.* (Guad, Mart); Sp. *mono tití m.* (Venz)

sa·li·pen·ta (sa·lem·pen·ter) *n* (Guyn, Tbgo, Trin) *Tupinambis nigropunctatus* (*Tejidae*); Fr. *tupinambis m.* (Guad, Mart); Sp. *mato de agua m.* (Venz)

sa·man *n* (CarA) *Pithecellobium saman* or *Samanea saman* (*Mimosaceae*); Fr. *samana, arbre à la pluie m.* (Guad, Mart); Sp. *guango, samán m.* (PtRi)

sand·box(-tree) *n* (CarA) *Hura crepitans* (*Euphorbiaceae*); Fr. *sablier élastique m.* (Guad, Mart); Sp. *jabillo m.* (StDo)

san·se·vi·e·ri·a *n* (ViIs) *Sansevieria metallica* (*Liliaceae*); Fr. *oreille à bourrique, langue à chat f.* (Guad, Hait); Sp. *lengua de vaca f.* (Cuba, PtRi)

sa·po·dil·la *n* (CarA) *Achras zapota, Manilkara z.* (*Sapotaceae*); Fr. *sapotille f.* (Guad, Mart); Sp. *níspero m.* (PtRi)

sa·van·nah-grass *n* 2. (Bdos, Gren, Jmca, Trin) *Axonopus compressus* (*Gramineae*); FR. *herbe sûre mâle f.*(Guad, Mart); SP. *cañamazo dulce m.* (Cuba), *yerba alfombra f.* (PtRi)

scar·let i·bis *n phr* (Trin) *Eudocimus ruber* (*Thres-Kiornithidae*); FR. *gant rouge m.* (Guad, Mart); SP. *coco (rojo) m.* (Cuba, PtRi, StDo) □ The SCARLET IBIS seems to be indigenous to the S. American continent, and is found in *Trin* wh is ecologically similar to the S. American continent.

scor·pi·on-fish *n* (CarA) *Scorpaena plumieri* (*Scorpaenidae*); FR. *rascasse noir m.* (Guad, Mart); SP. *rascacio negro m.* (Cuba, PtRi, StDo)

screw-pine *n* (Bdos, Dmca, Nevs, Tbgo, Trin) *Pandanus utilis* (*Pandanaceae*); FR. *bacoua f.* (Guad);SP. *palma de tirabuzón f.* (PtRi) □ This species, the *Pandanus utilis*, is also known as the CANE-LILY.

sea-egg *n* (Bdos, Gren) *Tripneustes sphoera* or *Echinus s.* (*Echinoidea*); FR. *hérisson de mer m.* (Guad, Mart); SP. *erizo de mar m.* (Cuba, PtRi), *hueva f.* (Venz)

sea·side-grape *n* (CarA) *Coccoloba uvifera* (*Polygonaceae*); FR. *raisin bord de mer, m.* (Guad, Mart); SP. *uva caleta f.* (Cuba), *uva de playa f.* (PtRi), *uvero de playa m.* (Venz)

sea·side-ma·hoe *n* (Bdos, Guyn, Jmca) *Hibiscus tiliaceus* (*Malvaceae*); FR. *bois flot m.* (Guad, Mart); SP. *majagua f.* (Cuba, PtRi, StDo), *algodoncillo m.* (Venz)

se·mi-con·tract (se·men·con·tra bush) *n* (*phr*) (Gren, Jmca) *Chenopodium ambrosioides* (*Chenopodiaceae*); FR. *semen-contra m.* (Guad, Hait), *thé du Méxique m.* (Guad, Mart); SP. *pasote m., té de México m.* (PtRi)

semp *n* (Trin) *Euphonia violacea, E. musica* (*Thraupidae*); FR. *perruche f., Louis d'Or m.* (Guad, Mart); SP. *jilguerillo m.* (StDo) □ PERRUCHE is also std. Fr. for 'parakeet'.

sen·si·tive plant *n phr* (Bdos, Gren, Guyn, Tbgo, Trin, USVI) *Mimosa pudica* (*Mimosaceae*); FR. *herbe mamzelle, amourette f.* (Guad, Mart); SP. *dormidera f.* (Cuba)

Se·ville orange *n phr* (CarA) *Citrus aurantium* (*Rutaceae*); FR. *orange grosse peau, orange sûre f.* (Guad, Mart); SP. *naranja agria f.* (Cuba, PtRi, StDo, Venz)

shad *n* (Antg, Bdos, BrVi, Gren, Guyn) 1. *Pellona harroweri* (*Clupeidae*); FR. *alose-caille brésilienne f.* (FrGy); SP. *sardina f.* (Venz) □ The Fr. and Sp. equivalents also apply to other species of this family. They are the standard

words for 'shad' and 'sardine' wh are used because of the resemblance of this family of CarA fishes to the N. American and European varieties.

shad·dock *n* (CarA) *Citrus maxima* (*Rutaceae*); FR. *chadèque f.* (Guad, Mart); SP. *toronja f.* (Cuba, PtRi, StDo, Venz)

shark *n* (CarA) *Carcharinus spp*; FR. *requin m.* (Guad, Mart); SP. *tiburón m.* (Cuba, Venz) □ Also *tiburón carite m.* in Venz REQUIN and TIBURÓN are the Std. Fr. and Sp. words for 'shark'.

shark suck·er *n phr* (Baha, Guyn) *Echeneis maucrates* (*Echeneidae*); FR. *rémore f.* (Guad, Mart); SP. *remora f.* (Cuba, PtRi, StDo)

shrimp *n* (CarA) *Penaeus spp*; FR. *crevette f.* (Guad, Mart); SP. *camarón m.* (Cuba, PtRi, StDo, Venz)

sif·fleur mon·tagne *n phr* (Dmca) *Myadestes genibarbis* (*Turdidae*); FR. *siffleur des montagnes m.* (Guad, Mart); SP. *jilguero m.* (StDo)

silk-cot·ton tree *n phr* (CarA) *Ceiba pentandra, C. occidentalis* or *Eriodendrum anfractuosum* (*Bombacaceae*); FR. *fromager, mapou (rouge) m.* (Guad, Mart); SP. *ceiba f.* (Cuba, PtRi, StDo, Venz)

sil·ver-thatch palm *n phr* (Baha, Trin) *Thrinax argentea* (*Palmaceae*); FR. *palme coyau f.* (Hait); SP. *guano de costa m.* (Cuba), *palma de guano f.* (StDo)

sis·ser·ou (par·rot) *n* (*phr*) (Dmca) *Amazonas imperialis* (*Psittacidae*); FR. *ara de Dominique f.* (Guad, Mart) □ Only Fr. equivalent given because this parrot is peculiar to Dmca, the nearest Sp. equivalent being a member of the *Amazona spp* found in Venz, *loro real*.

slip·per·y back *n phr* (Angu, BrVi) *Mabouya mabouia* (*Teiidae*); FR. *chauffé-soleil m.* (Guad, Mart); SP. *lucía f.* (PtRi), *mato m.* (Venz)

snap·per *n* (CarA) □ See RED SNAPPER. There are many kinds of *snapper* of varying size and colour in the the CarA.

snow·drop *n* (Bdos) *Zephyranthes eggersiana, Z. citrina, Z. tubispatha* (*Amaryllidaceae*); FR. *petit lis blanc m.* (Guad, Mart); SP. *duende blanco m.* (StDo)

snow-on-the-moun·tain *n* (Antg, Bdos, Dmca, Jmca, StVn) *Euphorbia articulata* (*Euphorbiaceae*); FR. *bois lait m.* (Guad, Mart); SP. *leche vana f.* (PtRi)

sol·dier-crab *n* (CarA) *Paquarius insignis, Coenobita diogenes;*FR. *bernard l'ermite m.* (CarA); SP. *ermitaño m.* (CarA) □ The Fr. and Sp. equivalents supplied are Std. Fr. and Std. Sp.

which here refer to the species of hermit-crabs in general.

sor·rel *n* (CarA) *Hibiscus sabdariffa (Malvaceae)*; FR. *groseille/oseille de Guinée f.* (Guad, Mart); SP. *agrio de Guinea m.* (PtRi), *aleluya roja de Guinea f.* (Cuba)

Sou·fri·ère tree *n phr* (StVn) *Spachea perforata (Malpighiaceae)*; FR. *spachea f.*, SP. *spachea f.* □ No territories given because this tree is peculiar to *StVn.*

sour orange *n phr* (CarA) *Citrus aurantium (Rutaceae)*; FR. *orange amère, f.* (Guad, Mart); SP. *naranja agria f.* (Cuba, PtRi, StDo, Venz) □ See also SEVILLE ORANGE.

sour·sop *n* (CarA) *Annona muricata (Annonaceae)*; FR. *corossol m.* (Guad, Mart); SP. *guanábana f.* (Cuba, PtRi, StDo, Venz)

spar·row-hawk *n* (CarA) *Falco sparverius (Falconidae)*; FR. *gli-gli, gri-gri m.* (Guad, Mart); SP. *cuyaya f.* (StDo), *cernícalo m.* (PtRi)

star-ap·ple *n* (CarA) *Chrysophyllum caimito (Sapotaceae)*; FR. *caimite m.* (Guad, Mart); SP. *caimito m.* (Cuba, PtRi, StDo, Venz)

sting·ing-net·tle *n* (Guyn, Trin) *Laportea aestuans* or *Fleurya a. (Urticaceae)*; FR. *ortie brûlante f.* (Guad, Mart); SP. *ortiga f.* (Cuba), *picapica f.* (PtRi)

stink·ing-toe *n* **1.** (CarA) *Hymenea courbaril (Leguminosae)*; FR. *courbaril m.* (Guad, Mart); SP. *algarroba f.* (PtRi, StDo) **2.** (Belz) *Cassia grandis (Caesalpiniaceae)*; FR. *casse f.* (Guad, Hait, Mart); SP. *cañafístula cimarrona f.* (PtRi)

St. John('s) bush *n phr* (ECar) *Blechum brownei (Acanthaceae)*; FR. *genou cassé m.*, *herbe-savane f.* (Guad, Mart); SP. *yerba de papagayo f.* (PtRi)

St. Lu·ci·a par·rot *n phr* (StLu) *Amazona versicolor (Psittacidae)*; FR. *jacquot/perroquet de Saint Lucie m.* (Guad, Mart); SP. *periquillo de Santa Lucía m.* □ Only a general Sp. equivalent is given because this parrot is known to be found only in StLu.

string-bean *n* (CarA) *Phaseolus vulgaris (Leguminosae-Papilionaceae)*; FR. *haricot, pois rouge m.* (Guad, Mart); SP. *habichuela f.* (PtRi, StDo)

strong back (weed) *n (phr)* (Baha, Gren, Jmca, TkCa) *Beurreria spp (Boraginaceae)*; FR. *bois-cabrit, bois-cabrit-bâtard m.* (Guad, Mart); SP. *roble de guayo m.* (PtRi)

St. Vin·cent par·rot n phr (StVn) *Amazona guildingii (Psittacidae)*; FR. *jacquot/perroquet de Saint Vincent m.* (CarA); SP. *periquillo de*

San Vicente m. (CarA) □ Only general Fr. and Sp. equivalents are given because the parrot is known only in StVn.

su·gar-ap·ple *n* (CarA) *Annona squamosa (Annonaceae)*; FR. *pomme cannelle f.* (Guad, Mart); SP. *anón m.* (Cuba, PtRi, StDo), *riñón m.* (Venz) □ *Venz* Sp. equivalent is also Std. Sp. for 'kidney'.

Su·ri·nam-cher·ry *n* (CarA) *Eugenia unifloris (Myrtaceae)*; FR. *cerise de Cayenne f., pitanga f.* (Guad, Hait, Mart); SP. *ciruela de Surinam, grosella de México f.* (StDo), *cereza de Cayena, pitanga f.* (PtRi)

sweet bar·zey (sweet ba·sil) *n phr* (Bdos, BrVi, Jmca, StKt, Tbgo, Trin) *Ageratum conyzoides (Compositae)*; FR. *herbe aux sorciers, herbe à femmes f.* (Guad, Mart); SP. *celestina azul f.* (Cuba), *yerba de cabrio f.* (PtRi)

sweet broom *n phr* (Guyn) *Scoparia dulcis (Scrophulariaceae)*; FR. *balai doux, thé-savane m.* (Guad, Mart); SP. *mastuerzo m.* (Cuba, StDo), *escobilla f.* (Cuba)

sweet·heart-(bush) *n* (Dmca, Guyn) *Desmodium spp (Fabaceae)*; FR. *cousin collant m.* (Guad, Mart); SP. *cadillo pegajoso m.* (PtRi)

sweet lime *n phr* (CarA) *Triphasia trifolia (Rutaceae)*; FR. *citronnelle f.* (Guad, Mart); SP. *limoncillo m.* (PtRi, Venz)

sweet mar·ga·ret *n phr* (Baha) *Byrsonima lucida (Malpighiaceae)*; FR. *olivier m.* (Guad); SP. *palo doncella m., sangre de doncella f.* (PtRi)

sweet po·ta·to *n phr* (CarA) *Ipomoea batatas (Convolvulaceae)*; FR. *patate douce f.* (Guad, Mart); SP. *batata f.* (PtRi, StDo, Venz)

Swiss cheese plant *n phr* (Bdos, Trin) *Monstera deliciosa (Araceae)*; FR. *liane percée f.* (Guad, Mart); SP. *monstera f., piñona f.* (PtRi)

swiz·zle-stick tree *n phr* (CarA) *Quararibaea turbinata (Bombacaceae)*; FR. *bois-lélé m.* (Guad); SP. *molinillo m.* (StDo), *palo de garrocha m.* (PtRi)

T

ta·ma·rind *n* (CarA) *Tamarindus indica (Leguminosae-Caesalpiniaceae)*; FR. *tamarin m.* (Guad, Mart); SP. *tamarindo m.* (Cuba, PtRi)

tan·ge·rine *n* (CarA) *Citrus nobilis, C. re-*

ticulata (*Rutaceae*); Fr. **mandarine** *f.* (Guad, Mart); Sp. **naranja mandarina** *f.* (StDo)

tan·nia *n* (CarA) *Xanthosoma spp* (*Araceae*) usu *Xanthosoma sagittifolium* and *Xanthosoma violaceum*; Fr. **chou caraïbe** *m.* (Guad, Mart); Sp. **malanga amarilla** *f.* (Cuba), **yautía amarilla** *f.* (StDo)

ta·pir *n* (Guyn) *Tapirus americanus* (*Tapiridae-Rhinocerotidae*); Fr. **tapir** *m.* (FrGy); Sp. **danta** *f.*, **tapir** *m.* (Venz)

ta·ran·tu·la *n* (Guyn) *Mygale spp* or *Avicularia spp*; Fr. **tarentule** *f.* (Guad, Mart); Sp. **tarántula** *f.* (Cuba, PtRi)

tar·pon *n* (Baha, BrVi, Guyn, Trin) *Megalops atlanticus, Tarpon a.* (*Clupeidae*); Fr. **grande écaille, savalle** *f.* (Guad, Mart); Sp. **sábalo, tarpón** *m.* (Cuba, PtRi)

ten-pound·er *n* (Antg, Brbu, Guyn, Mrat, Nevs) *Elops saurus* (*Elopidae*); Fr. **guinée machète** *f.* (Guad, Mart); Sp. **malacho** *m.* (Cuba, PtRi, StDo, Venz)

te·yer (palm) *n* (*phr*) (USVI) *Coccothrinax argentea* (*Phoenicaceae*); Fr. **latanier à balai** *m.* (Guad, Mart); Sp. **guano de costa, guano blanco** *m.* (Cuba)

thatch *n* (Baha, CayI, Jmca, StKt) *Bromelia pinguin* (*Bromeliaceae*), *Pandanus spp, Thrinax argentea* (*Palmae*); Fr. **karatas, pinguin** *m.* (Guad, Mart); Sp. **maya** *f.* (Cuba), **pinguín** *m.* (PtRi)

thatch·ber·ry(-palm) *n* (Baha) *Thrinax argentea* (*Palmae*); Fr. **palmier à balai** *m.* (Guad, Mart); Sp. **guano de costa** *m.* (Cuba), **guanillo** *m.* (StDo)

thatch palm *n phr* (Baha, Guyn) See TEYER, THATCHBERRY □ The species *Thrinax* and *Coccothrinax* seem to be closely related in general size and appearance and the Fr. and Sp. equivalents are the same with very little variation. Fr. **latanier/palmier à balai** and Sp. **guano de costa, guanillo**.

thick-leaf thyme *n phr* (Bdos, Guyn) *Coleus amboinicus* (*Lamiaceae*); Fr. **gros thym, gros baume** *m.* (Guad, Mart); Sp. **orégano de Cartagena** *m.* (Cuba, PtRi), **orégano francés** *m.* (Cuba)

this·tle *n* 1. (StKt) *Argemone mexicana* (*Papaveraceae*); Fr. **chardon, chardon marbré** *m.* (Guad, Mart); Sp. **cardo santo** *m.* (Cuba, PtRi, StDo)

thorn-ap·ple *n* (Bdos, Gren, Jmca) *Datura fastuosa, D. stramonium* (*Solanaceae*); Fr. **concombre à chien** *m.* (Guad), **concombre diable** *m.* (Mart); Sp. **estramonio** *m.* (PtRi)

thrash·er *n* (Baha) *Mimus polyglottos* (*Mimidae*); Fr. **rossignol** *m.* (Guad, Mart); Sp. **sinsonte** *m.* (Cuba), **ruiseñor** *m.* (StDo) □ Note that both Fr. and Sp. equivalents are Std. Fr. and Sp. for 'nightingale'.

ti·la·pi·a *n* (Guyn, Trin) *Tilapia nilotica, T. mossambica*; Fr. **tilapia** *f.* (Guad, Mart); Sp. **tilapia** *f.* (CarA)

ton·ka bean *n phr* (Guyn, Trin) *Dipteryx odorata* (*Papilionaceae*); Fr. **fève de Tonka** *f.* (Guad, Mart); Sp. **haba Tonka** *f.* (CarA) □ Only a general Sp. equivalent supplied because there is no equivalent specific to any one Spanish-speaking country.

ton ton *n* (*phr*) (Dmca, USVI) 1. (USVI) *Elaeodendron xylocarpum* (*Celastraceae*); Fr. **prune bord-de-mer** *f.* Guad, Mart); Sp. **cocorrón** *m.* (PtRi) □ Also known by the taxonomic name of *Cassine xylocarpa.—Fournet: 121.*

to·pi·tam·boo *n* (CarA) *Calathea allouia* (*Maranthaceae*); Fr. **topinambour** *m.* (Guad, Mart); Sp. **lerenes** *m. pl.* (PtRi, StDo)

torch·wood *n* (Gren) *Cassytha filiformis, Phoebe elongata* (*Lauraceae*); Fr. **corde à violon, liane ficelle** *f.* (Guad, Mart); Sp. **laurel bobo** *m.* (PtRi)

tou·can *n* (Belz, Guyn, Trin) *Rhamphastos toco* (*Rhamphastidae*); Fr. **toucan** *m.* (Guad, Mart); Sp. **tucán** *m.* (Venz)

trem·bler *n* (Dmca) *Cinclocerthia ruficauda* (*Mimidae*); Fr. **grive trembleuse** *f.* (Guad, Mart); Sp. **cocobino** *m.* (PtRi, StDo)

trop·ic bird *n phr* (CarA) *Phaethon aethereus* (*Phaethontidae*); Fr. **paille-en-queue, flèche-en-cul** *f.* (Guad, Mart); Sp. **rabijunco** *m.* (StDo)

trum·pet-bush *n* (CarA) *Cecropia peltata* (*Moraceae*); Fr. **bois trompette** *m.*, **trompette** *f.* (Guad, Mart); Sp. **yagruma** *f.* (Cuba), **yabruma** *f.* (StDo)

trum·pet-fish *n* (CarA) *Aulostomus maculatus* (*Aulostomidae*); Fr. **trompète tachetée** *f.* (Guad, Mart); Sp. **trompeta** *f.* (Cuba, PtRi, StDo)

try·sil *n* (Guyn) *Pentaclethra macroloba* (*Mimosaceae*); Fr. **pentaclethra** *f.* (Guad, Mart); Sp. **carbonero, gavilán** *m.* (Venz)

tu·na *n* (CarA) *Thunnus spp*; Fr. **thon, germon** *m.* (CarA); Sp. **atún, bonito** *m.* (CarA)

Turk's cap (cac·tus); **Turk's head cac.tus** *n phr* (CarA) *Cactus caesius* or *Melocactus communis* (*Cactaceae*); Fr. **tête à l'Anglais** *f.* (Guad); Sp. **melón de costa** *m.* (PtRi), **cardón** *m.* (Cuba)

tur·tle n (CarA) *Chelonia spp*; FR. *tortue f.* (Guad, Mart); SP. *tortuga f.* (Cuba, PtRi, StDo)

tur·tle grass n phr (Bdos, USVI) *Thalassia testudiarum* (*Hydrocharitaceae*); FR. *thalasie, herbe aux tortues f.* (Guad, Mart); SP. *palmas de mar f. pl.* (PtRi), *yerba de manatí f.* (Cuba)

U

ug·li (fruit) n (phr) (CarA) *Citrus paradisi, C. reticulata* (*Rutaceae*); FR. *mandarine de Jamaïque f.* (Guad, Mart); SP. *mandarina de Jamaica f.* (PtRi)

V

ve·ti·ver (grass) n (phr) (Dmca, Gren, Mrat, StLu, Trin) *Vetiveria zizanioides, Anatherum z.* or *Andropogon muricatus* (*Gramineae*); FR. *vétiver m.* (Guad, Mart); SP. *baúl del pobre m.* (PtRi)

Vic·to·ri·a Re·gi·a n phr (Guyn) *Victoria amazonica* (*Nymphaeaceae*); FR. *chapeau d'eau m.* (Guad, Mart); SP. *victoria regia f.* (Venz)

W

wa·hoo n (CarA) *Acanthocybium solanderi* (*Scombridae*); FR. *thazard-bâtard m.* (Guad, Mart); SP. *peto m.* (Cuba, PtRi)

wa·ma·ra n (Guyn) *Swartzia leiocalycina* (*Caesalpiniaceae*); FR. *wamara f.* (CarA); SP. *wamara f.* (CarA)

wa·ter-dog n (Belz, Guyn) *Lutra brasiliensis* or *Pteronura sandbachii* (*Lutrinae*); FR. *chien d'eau m.* (FrGy); SP. *nutria/perro de agua f./m.* (Venz)

wa·ter-grass n (CarA) *Commelina diffusa* or *C. elegans* (*Commelinaceae*); FR. *curage m.* (Mart), *herbe grasse f.* (Guad); SP. *cojitre, cohitre (azul) m.* (PtRi)

wa·ter-haas n (Guyn) *Hydrochaeris capybara* (*Hydrochaeridae*); FR. *capybara f.* (FrGy); SP. *chigüire m.* (Venz)

wa·ter hy·a·cinth n phr (Bdos, Guyn, Jmca, Trin) *Eichhornia crassipes* (*Pontederiaceae*); FR. *jacinthe d'eau f.* (Guad, Mart); SP. *jacinto de agua m.* (Cuba, PtRi)

whis·tling frog n phr (CarA) *Eleutherodactylus martinicensis* (*Leptodactylidae*); FR. *petite grenouille f.* (Guad, Mart); SP. *coquí, coquí de montaña m.* (PtRi)

white back n phr (Jmca) **1.** *Crotalaria fulva* (*Papilionaceae*); FR. *sonnette f., pois-zombi m.* (Guad, Mart); SP. *maraquita f.* (StDo)

white ce·dar n phr (BrVi, Guyn, Nevs, StLu, Trin) *Tabebuia pallida, T. monophylla* (*Bignoniaceae*); FR. *poirier m.* (Guad, Mart); SP. *roble blanco m.* (PtRi)

white·head-broom/bush n (CarA) *Parthenium hysterophorus* (*Compositae*); FR. *matricaire, absinthe bâtard m.* (Guad, Mart); SP. *ajenjo cimarrón m.* (PtRi)

white man·grove n phr (CarA) *Laguncularia racemosa* (*Combretaceae*); FR. *mangle blanc m.* (Guad, Mart); SP. *mangle blanco m.* (Cuba, PtRi, StDo)

white mar·lin n phr (Baha, Berm, ViIs) *Makaira albida* (*Istiophoridae*); FR. *makaire blanc m.* (Guad, Mart); SP. *aguja blanca f.* (Cuba, PtRi, StDo)

white sage n phr (Baha, Bdos, Guyn, StKt) *Lantana spp* (*Verbenaceae*); FR. *baume blanc m., sauge f.* (Guad, Mart); SP. *cariaquillo Santa Maria m.* (PtRi), *Doña Anita f.* (StDo)

white wood n phr **1.** (Bdos, CayI, Jmca) *Tabebuia heterophylla, T. pentaphylla* (*Bignoniaceae*); FR. *poirier blanc m.* (Guad, Mart); SP. *roble de costa m.* (PtRi, StDo) **2.** (Jmca) *Drypetes laterifolia* (*Euphorbiaceae*); FR. *bois côtelette m.* (Hait); SP. *cueriduro m.* (Cuba, PtRi)

white yam n phr **1.** (CarA) *Dioscorea cayennensis, D. rotundata* (*Dioscoreaceae*); FR. *igname guinée f.* (Guad); SP. *ñame Tongo m.* (Cuba, PtRi, StDo)

wi·cis·si duck (wis·si-wis·si duck) n phr (Guyn) *Dendrocygna autumnalis, D. viduata* (*Anatidae*); FR. *dendrocygne f.* (Guad, Mart); SP. *chirirío pinta f.* (PtRi), *guirirí pico rosado m.* (Venz)

wild cla·ry n phr (Guyn, Jmca) *Heliotropium indicum* (*Boraginaceae*); FR. *herbe/verveine à pian, grosse verveine f.* (Guad, Mart); SP. *moco de pavo m.* (StDo), *cotorrera f.* (PtRi)

wild cof·fee *n phr* (Guyn, Jmca, StKt, Trin) *Cassia occidentalis* (*Leguminosae-Caesalpiniaceae*); Fr. *café bâtard m.*, *casse puante f.* (Guad, Mart); Sp. *hedionda f.* (PtRi), *brusca hembra f.* (StDo)

wild cu·cum·ber *n phr* 1. (Bdos, BrVi, Gren, Jmca) *Cucumis anguria* (*Cucurbitaceae*); Fr. *petit concombre, petit cornichon m.* (Guad, Mart); Sp. *cohombro m.* (PtRi, StDo), *pepinillo m.* (PtRi)

wild ed·do(e) *n phr* (Guyn) *Araceae spp* Fr. *malanga cochon f.* (Guad); Sp. *yautía silvestre f.* (PtRi)

wild mint *n phr* 1. (Trin) *Hyptis atrorubens* (*Labiatae*); Fr. *herbe à miel, véronique f.* (Guad, Mart); Sp. *marubio oscuro m.* (PtRi) 2. (Jmca) *Lantana involucrata* (*Verbenaceae*); Fr. *petit baume m.* (Guad); Sp. *filigrana f.* (Cuba)

wild okra *n phr* (Gren, USVI) *Malachra alceifolia, M. capitata* (*Malvaceae*); Fr. *gombo savane m.* (Guad); Sp. *malva, malva de caballo f.* (PtRi)

wild pine *n phr* 1. (Dmca, Gren, Guyn, Jmca, Trin) *Tillandsia utriculata* (*Bromeliaceae*); Fr. *ananas sauvage m.* (Guad, Mart); Sp. *tilandsia encorvada f.* (Venz)

wild sage *n phr* (Jmca, Trin) *Lantana involucrata* (*Verbenaceae*); Fr. *petit baume m.* (Guad, Mart); Sp. *Santa María f.* (PtRi)

wild spin·ach *n phr* (Antg, Bdos, Mrat, StVn) *Amaranthus dubius* (*Amaranthaceae*); Fr. *épinard-pays m.* (Guad); Sp. *blero m.* (PtRi)

wild ta·ma·rind *n phr* 1. (Belz, Grns, Trin, ViIs) *Leucaena glauca* (*Leguminosae*); Fr. *tamarin bâtard m.* (Guad, Mart); Sp. *acacia pálida f.* (PtRi), *granadillo bobo m.* (StDo)

wild yam *n phr* (Jmca) *Dioscorea polygonoides* (*Dioscoreaceae*); Fr. *igname marron f.* (Guad, Mart); Sp. *gunda f.* (PtRi)

wilk(s) **(whelk(s))** *n* (CarA) *Cittarium pica* (*Molluscidae*); Fr. *troque des Antilles f.* (Guad, Mart); Sp. *burgado antillano m.* (Cuba, PtRi, StDo)

wo·man-pi·a·ba *n* (Bdos, Guyn) *Leonurus sibiricus* (*Labiatae-Lamiaceae*); Fr. *herbe à Madame Lalie f.* (Guad, Mart); Sp. *rabo de león m.* (PtRi), *botón de cadete m.* (StDo)

wo·man-tongue **(tree)** *n* (*phr*) (CarA) *Albizzia lebbeck* (*Leguminosae-Mimosaceae*); Fr. *bavardage, vieille fille f.* (Guad, Mart); Sp. *lengua de mujer f.* (PtRi), *chachá f.* (StDo), *barba de caballero f.* (Venz)

wood-slave *n* 1. (ECar) *Hemidactylus mabouia* (*Gekkonidae*); Fr. *mabouya m.* (Guad, Mart); Sp. *largarrabo m.* (Venz)

Y

yam *n* (CarA) *Dioscorea spp*; Fr. *igname f.* (Guad, Mart); Sp. *ñame m.* (Cuba, PtRi, StDo, Venz)

yel·low pou·i *n phr* (ECar) *Tecoma serratifolia, Tabebuia s.* (*Bignoniaceae*); Fr. *fleurs jaunes f. pl.* (Guad, Mart); Sp. *roble amarillo m.* (PtRi)

yel·low tail[3]**(-snap·per)** *n* (CarA) *Ocyurus chrysurus* (*Lutjanidae*); Fr. *vivaneau queue jaune m.* (Guad, Mart); Sp. *rabirubia f.* (Cuba, PtRi, StDo, Venz)

yel·low-yam *n* (CarA) *Dioscorea cayennensis* (*Dioscoreaceae*); Fr. *igname jaune f.* (Guad, Mart); Sp. *ñame amarillo m.* (Cuba, PtRi, StDo)

LOCATION LIST OF SUB-SAHARAN AFRICAN LANGUAGE

referred to in the Dictionary of Caribbean English Usage

AKAN Group	22	Kpelle	19
Asante	.	Krio	18
Ashanti	22	Kru	19
Bini	25	KWA Group	20-25
Ci-Luba		Lingala	31
Tshiluba	31	Mandinka	17
Ci-Nyanja	39-41	Mandingo	
Edo	25	Malinke	
Efik	25-26	Maninka	
Ewe	22-24	Mende	18
Fante		Mfantse = Fante	
Mfantse	22	Mossi	21
Fon	23-24	Nembe	25
Fulani	8, 10, 11	Nupe	25
Fula	14-18	Nyanja =	
Fulbe	20-26	Ci-Nyanja	
Fulfulde		Nzema	22
Gã-Adangme	22	Shona	44
Grebo	19	Soninke	7, 14-16, 21
GUR Group	20, 22	Swahili	31-33, 36, 41
	- 24	Temne	17-18
Hausa	25	Tshiluba = Ci-Luba	
Ibibio	25	Tsonga	41
Idoma	25	Twi	22
Igbo	25	UMbundu	38
Ijọ	25	Wolof	14
Isoko	25	Yoruba	25
Izọn	25		
Kanuri	10		
Ki-Yaka	31		
Kikongo	31		

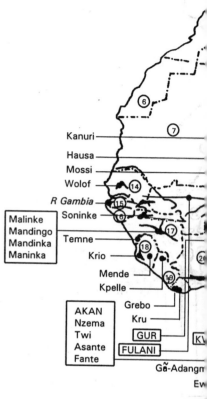

1.	Morocco	17.	Guinea	33.	Kenya
2.	Algeria	18.	Sierra Leone	34.	Rwanda
3.	Tunisia	19.	Liberia	35.	Burundi
4.	Libya	20.	Ivory Coast	36.	Tanzania
5.	Egypt	21.	Burkina Faso	37.	Cabinda
6.	Western Sahara	22.	Ghana	38.	Angola
7.	Mauritania	23.	Togo	39.	Zambia
8.	Mali	24.	Benin	40.	Malawi
9.	Niger	25.	Nigeria	41.	Mozambique
10.	Chad	26.	Cameroun	42.	Namibia
11.	Sudan	27.	Central African Republic	43.	Botswana
12.	Ethiopia	28.	Equitorial Guinea	44.	Zimbabwe
13.	Somalia	29.	Gabon	45.	South Africa
14.	Senegal	30.	Republic of Congo	46.	Swaziland
15.	The Gambia	31.	Zaire	47.	Lesotho
16.	Guinea-Bissau	32.	Uganda		